The Christianity Reader

The Christianity Reader

Edited by Mary Gerhart *&* Fabian E. Udoh

The University of Chicago Press
Chicago & London

Mary Gerhart is professor of religious studies at Hobart and William Smith Colleges.
Fabian E. Udoh is assistant professor of theology at the University of Notre Dame.

The University of Chicago Press, Chicago 60637
The University of Chicago Press, Ltd., London
© 2007 by The University of Chicago
All rights reserved. Published 2007
Printed in the United States of America
16 15 14 13 12 11 10 09 08 07   5 4 3 2 1

ISBN-13 (cloth): 978-0-226-28958-8
ISBN-13 (paper): 978-0-226-28959-5
ISBN-10 (cloth): 0-226-28958-3
ISBN-10 (paper): 0-226-28959-1

Library of Congress Cataloging-in-Publication Data

The Christianity reader / edited by Mary Gerhart & Fabian E. Udoh.
    p. cm.
  Includes index.
  ISBN 0-226-28958-3 (cloth : alk. paper)—ISBN 0-226-28959-1 (pbk. : alk. paper)
  1. Christianity. I. Gerhart, Mary. II. Udoh, Fabian E., 1954–

BR50.C47 2007
270—dc22

                          2006025442

♾ The paper used in this publication meets the minimum requirements of the American
National Standard for Information Sciences—Permanence of Paper for Printed Library
Materials, ANSI Z39.48–1992.

To Aniema, Unyime, and Kufre
To our beloved friends who supported us in this work
And to those who departed before its completion—Robert Jones, Vittorio Falsina,
and Eileen Couch

A labor of love

CONTENTS

ACKNOWLEDGMENTS

We have benefited, in the course of the years needed to finish this project, from the generous help given to us by many individuals and institutions. A National Endowment for the Humanities Fellowship at the W. F. Albright Institute of Archaeological Research, Jerusalem, and travel grants from the Institute for Scholarship in the Liberal Arts, University of Notre Dame, permitted Fabian Udoh to spend the year 2001–2 working in part on the project. From the Institute for Scholarship in the Liberal Arts also came a Seed Grant for Co-operative Research Project (2000) and a Copyright Fees Subvention. Dean's Supplemental Research and Teaching Funds from the College of Arts and Letters, University of Notre Dame (2001–4), have enabled Fabian Udoh to do research and to hire student assistants for this book. The Program of Liberal Studies has been most generous, especially in providing undergraduate assistants. Hobart and William Smith Colleges awarded Summer Faculty Research grants to Mary Gerhart. We are grateful also for the assistance she received from the Provost's Office of the Colleges.

We wish to express our gratitude to the students, from both the University of Notre Dame and Hobart and William Smith Colleges, who have worked over the years on various aspects of this book—in particular, David G. George (Fabian Udoh's graduate research assistant), Adam Weaver, Ellen R. Peters, Arnoldo Brian Casas, Donna Bauters, Peter Tierney (Mary Gerhart's student assistant), Darya Welker, Phil Recchio, Nicole Henderson, Lisa Genovese, Paul D'Andrea, Cooper Harriss, Spencer Dew, John Flack, and Tyler Simons. Susan Reece, departmental secretary at Hobart and William Smith Colleges, worked assiduously on copyright permissions, and Randolph Petilos, assistant editor at the Press, expedited and compiled the final list. Elaine Sinneger and Linda Akins helped organize the texts and files. Copy editor Pam Bruton, Claudia Rex, senior production editor, and Carol Fisher Saller, who assumed editorial responsibility at Claudia's untimely death, polished the entire manuscript, and Martin White prepared the index. We are thankful to Dan Mulvey, Michael Hunter, John Farrance, and Joseph Chmura, librarians, and the circulation desk staff at Hobart and William Smith Colleges for their tireless procurement of texts and information, and to Jeff DeVuyst for his expert computer assistance. Colleagues Renée Schoen-René and Allan Russell were unstinting in their help with penultimate file management and proofreading. Readers of early versions of the book for the Press made discerning observations—as did David Tracy, the measure of whose help is incalculable. Wendy Doniger supported the project from the beginning. Schubert Ogden, Lawrence Cunningham, Michael Signer, Lisa Cahill, Gaspar Martinez, and Gordon Kaufman each made insightful suggestions.

And finally, our special thanks go to Alan Thomas, our editor at the University of Chicago Press, without whose vision, patience, and encouragement this project would have been neither undertaken nor brought to completion.

John Henry Newman described, perhaps better than he knew, one of the important shifts in the history of Christianity when he wrote that each one must rethink for oneself what position one would take in the doctrinal debates that have taken place over the centuries. Of course, Newman, an influential and controversial theologian and historian, was writing about a single controversy in which the issues between English Anglicans and Roman Catholics were relatively well defined. In today's Christianity, the most populous world religion, with some two billion adherents worldwide, such controversies include issues of race, gender, and class. Nevertheless, Newman's statement may be taken today as suggesting that the work of historians and theologians is reconstructive as well as constructive—that their work must both attend to and reconstruct those traces of the past that were decisive for people, in this case people who identified themselves as Christians. Indeed, in light of those reconstructions—and there is no "essence" of Christianity as a whole apart from them—the history of Christianity today can be told as a history of Christianities. Beginning with what we can know of the life and death of the historical Jesus, whoever wishes to understand Christianity as a pluralist adventure will celebrate, for example, the decision by the early eucharistic communities to retain four Gospels rather than either to privilege one text over the other three or to harmonize all four into one text.

In fact, Christianity, a breakaway sect from Judaism, was fragmentary from the beginning: its self-definition is born out of continual bitter struggles, disintegration and reintegration, and translation. This process has resulted in the decline of Eurocentrism and the rise of a global Christianity, one now concentrated (numerically) in the Southern Hemisphere. As a world religion, Christianity has survived, even flourished, because it is capable of taking new forms in new cultures. At its origin Christianity defined itself as a Jewish sect and then as a Greco-Roman religion. The Jesus movement found ways to overcome ethnic particularity and to bring Gentiles into the fold without requiring them to adopt a Jewish covenant identity. By the year 90, it had distinguished itself from its mother religion, Judaism, and membership in the "Body of Christ" was not limited by nationality, ethnic heritage, social class, or gender. This fact is enshrined in the well-known Pauline formula "[In Christ] there is no longer Jew or Greek, there is no longer slave or free, there is no longer male or female" (Gal 3:28). But Paul's Letter to the Galatians is itself ample evidence that early Christian self-definition was achieved through bitter struggles among many competing views. The extant texts of early Christianity are in fact the fragments spared from the blaze of controversy. The present-day Christian faces new challenges that might be different from the self-definition of the past and does so in a context of plurality both within Christianity and in the general world in which one lives one's faith.

The earliest Christian writing is thought by modern scholars to be Paul's First Letter to the Thessalonians, written during the first four decades of the first century. The latest of the twenty-seven books in the New Testament canon was probably the Second Letter of Peter, believed to have been written around 120. Between these two dates other works were produced that, although considered by some to be "Scripture," were left out in the process of canonization. The earliest Christian texts included in this volume are drawn

1

from postcanonical New Testament writings (a number of editions of canonical writings are readily available). We have also attempted to focus on a range of issues. For example, along with multiple Christianities, is there also a plurality of Christs? Works such as Jaroslav Pelikan's *Jesus through the Centuries* (1985) suggest many different Christic ideals—multiple Christologies—all interpretations of Jesus of Nazareth. The central metaphor of incarnation, that God is human, was expressed in doctrinal development and in visionary literature. The Councils of Nicaea and Chalcedon asked questions pressing for their times—"Is Christ divine?" and "Is Christ human?"—and answered them in terms of their contemporary philosophical and cultural traditions. But for many Christians today these questions are no longer burning. For example, in Latin American liberation theology what matters is what the Christic ideal *produces* in the world of human beings. Jesus of Nazareth is still central, but that centrality is determined not only in the celebration of liturgy or a context of debate but in what people think is *happening* in their lives. This source book of texts provides not only texts important to the identification of what has become mainstream Christianity but also texts that represent diversity within Christianity. The selections range, therefore, from early Christian writings that display the diversity of views within earliest Christianity to recent documents on contemporary Church-related issues. We have also included, in chapter 2, texts taken from the various Judaisms of the first century and from the Greco-Roman world, which evoke the contexts in which Christianity developed and defined itself.

However, in all its varieties throughout its twenty centuries, Christianity has been a massive phenomenon, and no selection of texts can do full justice to its entire range. Included here are texts that most Christians and scholars would acknowledge as mainstream, texts by women recently retrieved from oblivion, and texts by people at today's frontiers of Christianity. We are mindful that we have texts by only those who wrote and preserved texts: the silent Church—those who did not produce texts or whose texts were repressed or lost in the course of history, as well as those who have yet to write and publish texts—all these Christians can be only contemplated here. Christians are Christians because they affirm God in the person of Jesus Christ. If the challenge for Christians at the beginning of the tradition was to create a separate and stable identity, the challenge for Christians at the beginning of the third millennium is to reappropriate the best of the tradition and find ways to understand their iden-

tity in relation to the identities of others—Christians as well as people of other religions and humanity as a whole.

Christianity has been many things to many people. The focus of this book, however, is Christianity as a *religion*. Accordingly, we have featured certain elements (baptism, Eucharist, demands on intellect, way of life) and have been parsimonious regarding others (ethics, architecture, music). We ask readers who lament the absence of texts they would have included to look rather for the interplay between the historical and thematic arrangements of the material—the book is designed to be, not a sampler, but a study of Christianity as a religion.

In the November 1998 *Harper's Monthly* Christopher Hitchens wrote, "We dwell in a present-tense culture that somehow, significantly, decided to employ the telling expression 'You're history' as a choice reprobation or insult, and thus elected to speak forgotten volumes about itself" (37). He argued that the conventional way that history is learned—through third-person commentaries on particular times and events—most often fails to promote either an appropriation or a critical appreciation of the past. The study of Christianity is not exceptional in this regard: its students, too, suffer from what Hitchens identifies as the "unmet need, an unanswered yearning, for an intelligible past" (38). Students often take only one course on the subject and therefore have need of a single volume that will address Christianities both early and late. In courses that study Christianity as a world religion, prose summaries are likely to fall short because they often neither present students with nor give them access to the challenges posed by original authors, nor indeed make available original texts written from different points of view. The inspiration for this volume arose out of a felt need for just such "an intelligible past" in a course on the Bible and the Qur'an when one of us searched for but could not find commensurable textbooks on each of three religions, namely, Judaism, Christianity, and Islam.

We begin each chapter with an introduction, which provides a contextual and analytical discussion of the subject matter of the chapter. Our introductions are not in the style of a commentary on commentaries. They aim to elicit the singularity of some voices that have become, or we believe are worthy of becoming, authoritative in the Christian tradition. The emphasis of this volume is, of course, on the texts—the introductions are only a guide.

In addition to these introductions, each text is accompanied by a headnote that provides general information about the text, such as the author (where this is available) and the approximate dates of his or her life, the original date of publication or approximate time of composition, and a brief description of its content. At the end of each text, we provide the bibliographical information for the source from which the text has been taken. The original dates of composition and publication are often earlier than those given in this source information. As a rule, no dates are given for the lives of living authors. All dates are common era (CE) except where otherwise indicated.

Our respective specializations—New Testament and Jewish history (Udoh), philosophy and theology (Gerhart and Udoh), and hermeneutical theory (Gerhart)—inform both our selections of texts and our comments on them. Our own debates and conversations over what to include and to write have resulted in an interdisciplinary volume, unbounded by specializations. All belongs to both authors.

⚘

PECULIARITIES AND TECHNICALITIES

Many of the texts in this book are translations. Wherever there was a choice among different translations, we decided on a translation that seemed to us to be the most accurate and authentic—that is, the translation both earned our admiration for its reliability and caught our imagination. A number of early Christian texts are translations by Fabian Udoh. The ancient texts, even when they have been translated by others, are newly annotated by us. We have signaled our own notes with the sentence "The notes for this selection are by Gerhart and Udoh," placed at the end of the first of such notes on each text. With respect to the texts by modern authors, we have removed or abbreviated many of the notes. We have indicated our own brief inserts to texts with brackets. Ellipses in brackets, *except where otherwise noted,* indicate where text has been cut by Gerhart and Udoh. Some answers to questions raised by or about the texts included in this volume may be sought and found in the source texts (including their introductions, notes, and bibliographies), which are indicated at the ends of the quoted texts. Biblical references are to modern translations of the Bible, except where other versions are specified (Septuagint, Vulgate, etc.). We use the (English) New Revised Standard Version (NRSV).

We have made some terminological decisions in our introductions, headnotes, and footnotes. "Orthodox" with a capital *O* refers to those communities affiliated with the Eastern (Greek or Russian) Orthodox Church. The terms "orthodox" and "orthodoxy" (lowercase *o*), pertaining especially to early Christianity, refer to orthodox faith as different from "heresy" (no value judgment is intended) or even from the diversity that existed in the first few hundred years of Christianity. In texts pertaining to Christianity from the sixteenth century to the present, "orthodox" usually refers to a particular model of theology, again largely without value judgment, that emphasizes the use of analogy in attempting to understand the mysteries of faith. We use the lowercase "catholic" for the "universal" Church in early Christianity, and uppercase "Catholic" to refer to the (Roman) Catholic Church. However, we use the uppercase "Church" to mean the people and the institution (of all Christian denominations and traditions) and the lowercase "church" to refer to a building.

Readers alert to the issues of gender-inclusive language will notice a variety of efforts—at times more and sometimes less graceful—during the last quarter of the twentieth century to compensate for the use of exclusively male language in source texts. Before the 1970s, however, male nouns and pronouns were normative, and we have left this aspect of the texts untouched for no other reason than to preserve the original texts and translations.

Biblical Traditions and Interpretations: Sources of Authority

Christianity, from its beginnings, has been preeminently a "religion of the book." Its earliest traditions go back to those of postexilic Judaism, which themselves were derived to a very large extent from interpretations of a body of texts. Like Judaism, Christianity professes that God's self-revelation is to be known through the words contained in a body of writings: "the Scriptures." The Scriptures of early Christianity were the Greek text of the Jewish Scriptures (commonly called the Septuagint), inherited from the Greek-speaking Diaspora Jews, that is, Jews living outside Palestine. Although a core of accepted Jewish texts had existed for a long time, at the beginning of the Christian movement and perhaps well into the second century CE there was no clearly defined and closed corpus of writings, that is, a "canon," of the Jewish Scriptures. Texts continued to be produced and accepted by various groups within Judaism, as the discoveries at Qumran clearly illustrate. Thus, the Greek Scriptures contained texts that were not in the Hebrew Scriptures. With the Jewish revolt of 66–73 and the consequent destruction, in 70, of Jerusalem and its Temple as the center of Jewish religious life, however, the rabbis reformulated Judaism and centered the religion on "the Book." The problem of establishing the boundaries of the writings that were to be accepted as authoritative then became central, perhaps to some extent concurrently, for both early rabbinic Judaism and early Christianity.

Although the Christian faith was rooted, not in a book, but in the person of Jesus the Christ, considered the (Word) Logos-Savior, almost from the beginning Christians produced writings which they were later to consider "Scripture."

These came in various genres, such as Epistles, Gospels, Acts, Teachings, Revelations, Lives—and in large numbers. For early Christianity the problem of deciding which texts were authoritative was therefore twofold: first, the appropriation of the Greek texts of the Jewish Scriptures, which, by the third century, came to be known as (the writings of) the Old Testament (or Covenant); second, the recognition and acceptance, alongside these others, of its own writings, which now formed an authoritative corpus known as (the writings of) the New Testament (or Covenant).

The texts contained in section 1 of this chapter focus on the question of the recognition, and "canonization," of the texts in the Christian traditions. Later in the history of Christianity attempts were made to settle various questions about the list (that is, canon) of acceptable books by means of decrees issued by Church authorities, for instance in 1546 at the Council of Trent (1545–63). In spite of these efforts, the formation of the Christian canon of the Bible did not come about by the act of an authority. It was, instead, the outcome of a long and complex process that has lasted for much of the history of Christianity—truly a story without a beginning or end.

By the late first century Christians already possessed a central core of texts which they used as authoritative sources of faith. The emergence of explicit lists of acceptable texts was, however, part of the formation of Christian orthodoxy. In the polemics against groups judged to be heretical, especially Gnostics and Montanists (see chapter 3) in the second and third centuries, orthodox faith both reasserted the legitimacy of the received writings and sought to limit the inclusion of "new" authoritative texts. The passages on Marcion by Irenaeus and Tertullian represent these polemics against Christian Gnosticism. Marcion's own writings have not survived. Ironically, Tertullian himself later became the most eminent representative of the Montanist movement. Against Marcion's two Gods and one "gospel," Irenaeus and Tertullian affirm the one Creator-God, who is revealed both in the Jewish Scriptures (rejected by Marcion) and in Jesus Christ. Thus, the normative Christian canon is affirmed to have two parts. The appropriation of the Jewish Scriptures as an "Old Testament" that contains and is completed by a "New Testament," however, had important consequences for both Christian interpretation of the Scriptures and Christian history. As a Christian text, the Jewish Scriptures became a prophetic witness whose hidden meaning is revealed in the reality of Christian faith. Whether as "types," "allegories," "copies," or "shadows," the history, religion, and culture of Israel became witnesses to Christian truths, and with the triumph of Christianity in the fourth century, the Jewish people remained the "people of witness" to God's wrath against obduracy and unbelief.

Apart from Paul's letters, the Gospels and other Christian writings originally circulated anonymously. The traditions attributed to Papias testify to the process of attribution by which Christian writings, accepted as authoritative, were attached to Jesus' apostles and "apostolic men" as their authors. Antiquity and apostolic origin became two of the principal criteria for inclusion in the lists of acceptable texts.

Texts belonged to and were received by specific communities, as were the resulting lists of authoritative texts. The lists of accepted texts differed, therefore, even among the Christian communities that shared orthodox faith. It is not until Athanasius's *Festal Epistle,* written in 367, that we find the first unambiguous use of the word "canon" to designate a fixed list of biblical texts. But even here, Athanasius's list of books "prescribed by the Fathers to be read" (some of which are now part of the Bible as either "deuterocanonical books," for Roman Catholics, or "apocryphal books," for Protestants) shows that the fringes remained open. And in the late fourth and early fifth centuries Augustine and Jerome were still arguing with each other over the respective merits of the shorter canon of the Hebrew Scriptures and the longer canon of the Greek Septuagint. This argument resurfaced in the sixteenth century between the Reformers and the Roman Catholic Church, and although it might be dormant today, it is by no means dead.

Eusebius was bishop of Caesarea, a historian, and the au-

thor, among other works, of *Ecclesiastical History,* a history of the Church up until 324. His approach to the problem of the canon was scholarly, and his summary of the situation, as he knew it, with regard to the New Testament certainly raises questions about the process and criteria by which a text achieved its status as authoritative and its place on the list. A text was thought to be "canonical" because, he says, it was distinguished "according to the tradition of the Church" to be "true, genuine, and recognized from those which are different from these in that they are not canonical but disputed." The decisive criterion, in other words, was traditional acceptable use. But then, if canonical status is conferred by the tradition that recognizes a text as such, is the canon a list of authoritative texts or the authoritative list of texts?

The texts in section 2 deal with the topic of Christian interpretation of the Scriptures. Especially since the section tries to cover the entire history of Christianity, this selection of texts cannot be seen as exhaustive in any sense whatsoever. Instead, these texts are suggestive and seek to indicate some of the principal moments and issues in Christian interpretation.

Read on their own terms (that is, literally), the Jewish Scriptures very quickly manifest their dissonant inconsistency with Christian beliefs. Problems were soon to appear also in the New Testament itself, especially after it had come to be revered (already by the mid–second century) as an ancient source of authority. In other words, central as the Scriptures are to every aspect of Christian life, personal and collective (ritual, doctrine, discipline, and communal structure), they have been and remain, nonetheless, a complex body of writings that is not immediately accessible. Interpretation is needed to show the inner coherence of the Old Testament and its congruency with the Christian faith. Christian interpretation, in the early Church and later, has to do with the development of principles and rules for understanding these texts in ways that are consistent with the Christian faith and relevant to the conflicts, aspirations, needs, and hopes of the various Christian communities. The fact that the Gospels and other writings of the New Testament also are inconsistent internally and with each other, and contain other "difficulties," merely showed that these texts also exhibited the characteristics of "scriptural" texts. They, too, needed the kind of exegetical procedures that would reconcile the differences and reveal their true meaning. Harmonizations and emendations of the texts, to make them fit, still belong to such an exegetical procedure. The early Church, however, rejected the attempt to produce one single Scripture that was internally coherent, either through the expurgations by Marcion or the harmonizations of Tatian's *Diatessaron*.[1]

The principles of interpretation reflect the theological context within which interpretation of the Bible is done by various Christian groups and at various times. The rules pertain to the methodology with which the texts are interpreted in order to render them meaningful for the life of the Christian community. The early Church was unanimous in the conviction that interpretation could not take place outside the matrix of the faith of the Church. Augustine sums up this conviction definitively in *De doctrina Christiana* (3.x.15): Scripture "asserts nothing except the catholic faith, in time past, present, and future. It narrates the past, foretells the future, and demonstrates the present, but all these things serve to nourish and strengthen this love [of God and neighbor], and to overcome and annihilate lust." Principles and rules, faith and method, are therefore interconnected. Thus, "Tradition" and "Scripture" were not considered rival sources of authority in the way they came to be viewed much later in the history of Christianity. The text and its interpretation are inseparable from the Tradition of the Church: Tradition, Text, and Interpretation form what might be called a "hermeneutical circle," since it is Tradition that interprets the text and is itself clarified and nourished by the interpretation.

Allegory, as an interpretive tool, became crucial for Christian appropriation of the Jewish Scriptures and for resolving thorny problems in the New Testament. The greatest Alexandrian allegorists were Clement of Alexandria (ca. 150–215) and his student Origen (ca. 185–254). In his extreme version of the story concerning the translation of the Hebrew Scriptures into Greek, Clement spells out his theory of inspiration. A milder form of this story is told by Greek-speaking Jewish writers (for example, *The Letter of Aristeas,* in chapter 2; see also Jerome, *The Prologue to Genesis,* in this chapter). Clement's theory of inspiration is critical not only for allegorical interpretation but also for other forms of early Christian interpretation: inspiration means that God intervened in the production of both "meaning and wording" of the text. Scripture is the word of God; in it, we see and we hear the voice of the Word, the Logos-Christ. It is in this sense that the text is deemed a "prophecy." Allegorical interpretation, then, uncovers the "prophetic" meaning intentionally hidden by the divine author behind the words of the text.

Allegory was not forced on early Christianity by the evident incompatibility of the Old Testament, in its literal meaning, with the New Testament and Christian beliefs. As Clement and Origen argued, ancient Scriptures were *by definition* considered in the Greco-Roman world to contain "mysteries," the depth of which could never be exhausted: inspired texts said other than what was contained in their "narrative" sense. Sacred texts were thus said to speak "allegorically." Since Christians saw their texts as the inspired texts par excellence, Clement and early Christian writers could argue that this preferred method of interpreting sacred texts and the "philosophy" they yielded had in fact been stolen by Greco-Roman writers from the Christian tradition. In fact, the allegorical method allowed early Christianity to appropriate not only its own Scriptures but also Platonic anthropology and cosmology. While Origen did not always follow, in practice, his threefold sense of Scripture (that is, the body, the soul, and the spirit), his theory that the meaning of Christian Scripture is in the upward ascent of the soul from the body to God (that is, *anagōgē*) gave a definite purpose to Christian exegesis. The Christian exegete had the normative task of uncovering the anagogical—"higher spiritual meaning"—of Scripture, that is, the edifice of the Christian faith and the life of the soul, with the help of the tools of allegorical interpretation: textual criticism, the philological study of words and phrases, etymology, the symbolism of numbers, and natural symbolism.

The Antiochene school of biblical interpretation, generally contrasted with that of Alexandria, had its golden age with Diodore of Tarsus (died ca. 390) and his students: Theodore of Mopsuestia, John Chrysostom, and later Theodoret of Cyrrhus. Earlier, Irenaeus and Tertullian both were opposed to Gnostic allegorical interpretations. They proposed no theoretical justification, however, for the allegorism which they themselves, inevitably, practiced. Instead, they had recourse to the authority of orthodox Christianity as the repository of the authentic Christian tradition. By contrast, the opposition of Diodore of Tarsus and his disciples to Alexandrian allegorization was on exegetical grounds, not least because of the risk that the text will always dissolve into whatever doctrine is in vogue with the interpreter. Yet, although Diodore and his students dismissed *allēgoria* as "foolishness," the Antiochene *theōria* is not antithetically opposed to allegory. *Theōria* is the same search for the "higher spiritual"—anagogical—meaning that characterized allegory. The biblical text is assumed to contain "higher" spiritual and moral truths not immedi-

---

1. Tatian composed his *Diatessaron* ("through [the] four [Gospels]") before 172, probably in Rome. The *Diatessaron,* as the name suggests, is a harmonization of the four Gospel narratives into one coherent and continuous account using the Gospel of John as the general chronological framework.

ately evident to the reader. The texts, especially the Old Testament, still speak prophetically and often figuratively. The difference between the two interpretive methods is the commitment of the Antiochene school to the literal meaning of the text. The fulfillment of the prophecies must first conform to their original historical contexts. The higher meaning uncovered by *theōria,* where there is any to be found, adds to the literal sense without abrogating history. John Chrysostom brings the Antiochene interest in understanding the language of the biblical texts and in reconstructing the history which they narrate to his project of exhortation.

Jerome (ca. 347–420) revised the Old Latin texts of the New Testament on the basis of Greek manuscripts to create the so-called Vulgate; he also translated the Old Testament into Latin directly from the Hebrew text. Both endeavors were controversial, maligned by those he called his "calumniators." His letter to Pope Damasus shows Jerome as the interpreter of the prophetic works, a subject that occupied the later part of his life. Earlier, Jerome had been a devoted disciple of Origen's allegorism. Controversy over Origen forced Jerome to back away somewhat from Origen's interpretive principles and pay attention to those that were being proposed by the Antiochenes. The result was an effort to walk a moderate path between the literalism of Diodore and the allegorism of Origen. Jerome brought a great philological-linguistic rigor, especially his attention to the Hebrew text of the Old Testament, and historical sensitivity to the task of interpretation. This attention to history and to the language of the text is mixed haphazardly, however, with allegorical interpretations.

Augustine's (354–430) masterly treatment of Christian biblical interpretation in his *De doctrina Christiana* draws together the tools and rules needed to undertake the complex and difficult task of interpretation, in view of the principle that the Scriptures everywhere assert the faith of the Church and a correct interpretation is that which nourishes and strengthens the love of God and neighbor. Like Jerome, Augustine tried to ply a middle course between the literal meaning of the text and allegory: "metaphorical" meanings must be sought where the literal meaning of the text cannot conform to the faith of the Church and the purpose of interpretation. To this end, the Bible is conceived of as an open and coherent book, such that the obscurity and ambiguity of one part must be explained by the clarity of another—for everything that requires allegorical interpretation in one part is also said literally in another part. Unlike Jerome, however, Augustine had very limited linguistic competence. He viewed with

great anxiety Jerome's preference of the Hebrew text of the Old Testament to the Greek text, which Augustine held, with much of the Christian tradition, to be specially inspired by God for the needs of the Gentile world.

Augustine's exegetical works were at the service of his pastoral, doctrinal, and polemical preoccupations. So, too, was Pelagius's commentary on Paul's Epistle to the Romans. Unlike Augustine, Pelagius (354–418) was not a bishop, but he was a spiritual counselor and a fervent promoter of the Christian asceticism that was quickly gaining ground in the fourth and fifth centuries. His commentary on Romans 5:12–21 is one of his position statements on the many questions associated with the so-called Pelagian controversy (see chapter 3). Origen casts his long shadow here, not only because of the question of allegory but also because of his commentary on the same Pauline passage and his theories on the origin of sin and the consequences of Adam's fall.

In the last decades of the fourth century, the so-called Cappadocian Fathers—Basil the Great, Gregory of Nyssa, and Gregory of Nazianzus—succeeded the earlier generation led by Athanasius as the defenders of the post-Nicene orthodoxy. With Gregory of Nyssa, however, interpretation moved away from the defense of orthodox faith toward a "mystical" understanding of the text. Gregory's works are among the best later representatives of Origen's *anagōgē*. All of the Scriptures have an allegorical, "mystical" meaning, even the titles of the psalms in the Psalter. In *Treatise on the Inscriptions of the Psalms,* he used these titles to represent the progressive ascent of the soul, from the time it turns away from sin, sense perception, and bodily passions until, by the practice of virtue, it attains blessedness, that is, the likeness of God, the supreme intelligible Good. The historical events narrated in the Scriptures are meant, not to make us knowledgeable, but rather to teach the practice of virtue. Thus, he argues in the Prologue of his *Commentary on the Song of Songs* that, whether by allegory, tropology, *anagōgē,* or even by the acknowledgment of the literal meaning, interpretation has only one purpose: its usefulness for virtuous living.

Medieval theology was *pagina sacra* in the various evolutions of the term and practices of the science. From the rich and long medieval interpretive tradition we present texts from three masters: Gregory the Great from the sixth century and Bonaventure and Thomas Aquinas from the thirteenth. *Morals on the Book of Job* is one of Gregory's greatest exegetical works and influenced all of medieval Western Christianity. With Gregory, that interest in virtuous living to which Gregory of Nyssa's allegorical interpretation was directed took a more psychological turn. The perspectives of the mysticism of monastic life predominate. Gregory proposes a tripartite sense to Scripture. The literal sense is the narrative meaning of the text. In the allegorical sense Gregory sees Tyconius's and Augustine's "Christ and his body": Job is at the same time the figure of Christ (who teaches what we must do) and the figure of his Church. Gregory's interest is above all, however, in the doctrine of Christian morality: the interior privileges and duties of Christian living. Hence, even his literal interpretation of the text has moral considerations well in view. And as his exposition progresses, he abandons any serious attention to the literal meaning of the text, and his allegorical and moral interpretations fuse into one. His treatise, in effect, is much less a commentary on the text than it is an exposition on Christian spiritual and moral theology.

Augustine argued for the multiplicity of meanings in Scripture. Relying on Greek technical rhetorical terms, he recognized four senses in the Old Testament: history, etiology, analogy, and allegory. His interpretive tradition crystallized into the four senses of Scripture that first appeared, in the standard form, in the work of John Cassian (ca. 420): literal, allegorical, tropological, and anagogical. The last three constitute the spiritual or mystical meaning of Scripture. The literal meaning preserved an interest in the language and historical context of the text advocated by the Antiochenes; the allegorical sense, going back to traditional typology, teaches "what must be believed"; the tropological sense focuses on the interest of Christian authors in the moral life and says "what must be done"; and the anagogical, going back to Origen's *anagōgē*, searches for "the end to be attained," that is, the eschatological sense of Scripture. Both Bonaventure and Thomas Aquinas, each in his own context, bring a philosophical and theological rationale to these divisions and expound their significance. Aquinas in particular distilled the essentials of twelve centuries of Christian interpretation and, in so doing, defined the language of the future.

The interpretation of the Bible by the Protestant Reformers must be put in the context of fifteenth- and sixteenth-century Europe, a world profoundly transformed by many intersecting factors: the rediscovery of the classical tradition and the rise of humanism; the discovery of "new worlds"; the emergence of nation-states and national languages; and the invention of the printing press. These developments changed the ways in which what had been the ultimate source of authority, the Bible, was received and interpreted. Here, as ever, the history of the Christian Church was the history of its exposition of Scripture. Martin Luther's consciousness as a Reformer was a product of his exegetical discovery of and struggle with the meaning of the biblical phrase "righteousness of God" (Rom 1:17; 10:3; see also Ps 31:1). He and the other Reformers rediscovered Paul's writings. Luther was a professor of biblical theology at the University of Wittenberg from 1512 until his death in 1546, and he saw his life and work as a Reformer as founded on his oath as a doctor of Holy Scripture. His theological disputes, biblical translations, liturgical prescriptions, views on Church discipline, and political choices were all bound up with his interpretation of the Bible. The same must be said of John Calvin (1509–64), whose *Institutes of the Christian Religion* was meant to be an introduction to the Bible, and John Wesley (1703–91).

The Reformers' revolution consisted principally of the break with the patristic and medieval hermeneutical principle that Scripture and the Church's interpretive Tradition formed one indissoluble whole. Luther, in his *Defense and Explanation of All the Articles,* states this break and maintains that Scripture is self-interpreting and stands alone (*sola scriptura*) as the authority for Christian living. Calvin argues the same position in his *Institutes.* They resituated the authority of Scripture, not in the interpretive tradition of the Church nor in Scripture's formal character as "inspired," but in the content of the text as "gospel," that is, insofar as it "preaches Christ." Scripture, both the Old and the New Testaments, is unique because it is the written witness to the personal Word, Christ, who is preached and believed in for the sake of salvation. Christ is the center and content of the whole Scripture; and Scripture is where the individual believer encounters Christ. Luther is thus able to establish a hierarchy within the canonical texts, even within the New Testament, forming what is now termed "a canon within the canon." For Luther, Calvin, and Wesley the problems encountered in Scripture do not belong to the text but are due to the inadequacy of our human understanding. They are remedied by a more accurate historical and philological knowledge. Luther criticized the traditional four senses of Scripture (literal, allegorical, tropological, and anagogical). Calvin rejected allegory where the text did not constrain it and returned to traditional and ancient typological interpretation. With the dismissal of the Church's interpretive tradition as the control over meaning, however, adjudicating the validity of multiple and competing interpretations of the text became a central problem for the Reformation.

The Enlightenment and the transitions into the modern and "postmodern" worlds have dramatically changed the ways in which the Bible is received and interpreted. No transition is more important than the revolution in consciousness that gave birth in the eighteenth century to the new "science": history. A radical will-to-truth underlies the historian's quest to recover from the past "the facts as they really happened." When one investigates "what really happened," what had previously been accepted as fact is often shown, with shocking consequences, to be fiction. Beginning with Hermann Reimarus (1694–1768), Jesus and the biblical narrative about him became the objects of that radical quest for what actually happened.

Friedrich Schleiermacher (1768–1834) founded the theory of general hermeneutics not only as a philosophical but especially as a theological discipline. Hermeneutics, the art of understanding, becomes a self-conscious art that proceeds by a global system of rules in order to uncover the meaning of a particular discourse. Its object is the discourse or text in its linguistic singularity. According to Schleiermacher, its objective is the comprehension of both the structure of the language of discourse and the particular manifestation of language as individual "thought." Schleiermacher's departures from patristic, medieval, and Reformation understandings of the Bible resulted in the discovery of the Bible as "text," produced by an "author."

By posing the question of the historical distance between the author/text and the interpreting subject, Schleiermacher's hermeneutics both belongs and paves the way to the deepening of historical consciousness. History itself is understood no longer as the permanence of the universal or as ethical model for the present but as the singular, unique, unrepeatable event of the past available to critical investigation. Since the biblical text is the product of an "author" and since gulfs exist between the author and the text, on the one hand, and between the text and the interpreter, on the other hand, the biblical text cannot, for purposes of historical investigation, be accepted at face value as "the proper and true record" (as Reimarus put it) of the events it narrates. It was, however, not until the third decade of the nineteenth century, with David Friedrich Strauss's *The Life of Jesus Critically Examined*, that a rigorous historical analysis, without the limitations of dogmatic presuppositions, was applied to the biblical text. Strauss concluded that the narratives about Jesus, whatever historical events might lie behind them, were to be classified as "myths," that is, the expression in historical form, and embodied in a historical figure, of the religious ideas of their authors.

Paul Ricoeur is one of the contemporary leading theorists

of hermeneutics who has made significant modifications to Schleiermacher's insights. In the text included here, Ricoeur highlights the role of imagination in the construction of a "new possible way of being in the world" through the act of reading the Scriptures.

Issues of biblical interpretation after Reimarus, Schleiermacher, and Strauss may be grouped under four kinds of literary theory of interpretation, all centered on the interpreter's view of the text. First, the biblical texts can be seen as "windows" opening *directly* to (or as "mirrors" *directly* reflecting for) the reader the realities of the world that they describe. Hence, patristic, medieval, and Reformation interpreters accepted as a given that the contents of the Bible were "true" either in the historical events they narrated or in their theological ideas about God, the world, and humanity. This is the view of those Christians today, generally called "Fundamentalists," who (in response to the Enlightenment) see the Bible as a book of facts about such matters as salvation, creation, history, and social ethics.

Second, nineteenth-century and later critical interpretation departs radically from this view. The successive "criticisms"—Literary (Source), Form, and Redaction—all view the Bible as the work of either communal or individual "authors." They seek to unravel the compositional history of the text. William Wrede's *The Messianic Secret* (1901) marked a turning point in this conception. He pointed out, following Strauss's work, that if there is indeed an external (historical) reality beyond the text, that reality is available only to the reader *indirectly* through *historical* investigation. What is directly available in the text are the views of its authors. The Redaction critic, therefore, brackets off the question of the truth of the text's content and studies the text only from the point of view of the author's intention.

The works by Albert Schweitzer, E. P. Sanders, and John P. Meier represent, for the New Testament, pinnacles in traditio-historical criticism, which, using historical-critical methods, seeks to reconstruct the historical events associated with the biblical text. The passage included here from Schweitzer's *Quest of the Historical Jesus* reveals the theological/hermeneutical assumptions with which he worked more than it presents his concrete conclusions about Jesus. With Sanders, especially, Judaism in the first century CE takes center stage as the historical context within which Jesus, the Gospels, and Paul can be understood.

Third, interpretation may be centered on the *text itself* as it is now present to us. Brevard S. Childs was the first to present this shift in perspective in biblical interpretation, to which also belong structuralist and other formalist interpretations of the Scriptures. From this point of view, meaning is found, not in the intention of the authors or by any historical-critical analysis of the text, but in the synchronic analysis of the interrelated parts of the whole as it now stands. This approach is further seen in the excerpt from Amos Wilder's *Early Christian Rhetoric*.

Fourth, some formalist interpreters have shifted attention from the *text itself* to the act of *reading* and *the reader* as the locations of meaning. Here, the meaning of the text is found in the reader's response to the text: "What struck *me* in this passage is . . ." Every reading is always subjective and, in that sense, always valid. The text's significant quality is its ability to persuade, edify, and please the reader. This contemporary view is in continuity with the patristic through Reformation (precritical) view of the Scriptures, which, in Paul's (Rom 1:17) and Luther's expression, were written "from faith to faith." The text testifies to and conducts the hearer or reader to the faith of the Church. It fosters the love of God and neighbor, teaches virtue, leads the soul in its ascent to God, and preaches Christ. It is Scripture, in short, because of the effect/response it produces in the hearer/reader. Correct interpretation, as Augustine emphasized, is one that produces the desired response.

Two other texts presented here, by Elizabeth Cady Stanton and by Elisabeth Schüssler Fiorenza, address another aspect of contemporary biblical exegesis. The acknowledgment and inclusion of "the other" in the very expanded modern Christian world have led to the appropriation of the Bible by groups that previously either did not exist or were marginalized, suppressed, and silenced. The list of groups could be very much enlarged—thematically and territorially—beyond the womanist/feminist interpretations of Stanton and Fiorenza. From the point of view of the principles and rules of interpretation, however, such interpretations fall within the methods or combinations of the methods set out here.

Contemporary critical biblical exegesis is often done, characteristically, apart from (and sometimes against) the faith claims of the Christian Churches. One might see some Christian biblical interpreters' negative reactions to historical-critical methods, and their preference for interpretive methods that focus either on the text itself or on the reader, as the search for methods that serve Christian theological interests (as both Childs and Wilder claim). The texts in this section by the Catholic Church's Second Vatican Council and by the World Council of Churches exemplify the continued search by the Christian Churches for ways of reading their Scriptures so that they remain meaningful for the Churches' faith and life.

1. TEXTS AND CANON

PAPIAS OF HIERAPOLIS

Papias (ca. 60–130) is the first known Christian writer to connect the Gospels to specific authors. Although Papias's writings have not survived, what he wrote about the authorship of the Gospels is found in Eusebius's (on whom, see below) *Ecclesiastical History*, published in about 315.

EUSEBIUS
Ecclesiastical History, III.xxx.ix.3–4, 15–16

3–4. Papias himself, however, according to the preface of his treatises, makes it clear that he was never a hearer or eyewitness of the holy Apostles, but he shows that he received the doctrines of the faith from those who knew them, and

he does so in these words: "I shall not hesitate to set down for you together with my interpretations all that I have ever learned well from the presbyters and recall well, being confident of their truth. For, unlike most, I did not take pleasure in those who say much, but in those who teach the truth, and not in those who relate the commandments of others, but in those who relate the commandments given to the faith by the Lord and derived from the truth itself; but if ever anyone came who had carefully followed the presbyters,[2] I inquired as to the words of the presbyters, what Andrew or what Peter said, or what Philip or what Thomas or James or what John or Matthew or any other of the disciples of the

---

2. See Lk 1:3. (The notes for this selection are by Gerhart and Udoh.)

Lord, and what Aristion[3] and the presbyter John, the Lord's disciples, were saying. For I did not suppose that information from books helped me so much as that from a living and abiding voice."

15–16. In his own writing he [Papias] also passes on interpretations of the Lord's words from Aristion, who has been mentioned before, and traditions from John the presbyter. After referring the studious to these, we shall now of necessity add to his words already quoted a tradition about Mark who wrote the Gospel, which he gives in these words: "This also the Presbyter used to say, 'When Mark became Peter's interpreter, he wrote down accurately, although not in order, all that he [Mark] remembered of what was said or done by the Lord. For he had not heard the Lord nor followed Him, but later, as I have said, he did Peter,[4] who made his teaching fit his needs without, as it were, making any arrangement of the Lord's oracles, so that Mark made no mistake in thus writing some things down as he remembered them. For to one thing he gave careful attention, to omit nothing of what he heard and to falsify nothing in this.'" Now, this has been related by Papias regarding Mark, and regarding Matthew he has spoken as follows: "Now Matthew[5] collected the oracles in the Hebrew language, and each one interpreted them as he was able."

From Eusebius Pamphili, *Ecclesiastical History, Books 1–5,* translated by Roy J. Deferrari, Fathers of the Church, vol. 19 (New York: Fathers of the Church, 1953), 203, 206.

MARCION OF SINOPE

☙ **Marcion** (ca. 80–150), originally from Sinope, in Pontus (in modern-day Turkey), was a Christian Gnostic who founded his own sect (the Marcionites). He taught that the god of the Old Testament was inferior to the god of the New Testament.

Irenaeus (ca. 130–202), bishop of Lyons (about whom, more below), intended to write a special work of refutation against Marcion but never carried out his purpose. In *Against Heresies* (ca. 180), however, Irenaeus polemicizes against the "blasphemy" of Christian Gnosticism as it is found in Marcionite theology.

Tertullian (ca. 155–225) affirms the one Creator-God and (like Irenaeus) renounces Marcion for his rejection of the Jewish Scriptures in *Against Marcion,* written in about 200. Tertullian afterward became an outspoken proponent of Montanism (see chapter 3), against whose claim that the Holy Spirit continued to make revelations the orthodox Church insisted that there were no new revelations and the canon, therefore, was closed.

IRENAEUS OF LYONS
Against Heresies, I.xxvii.2

Succeeding him [Cerdo] was Marcion of Pontus, who developed his doctrine and impudently blasphemed against the God who is proclaimed by the Law and the Prophets. He declared him to be the author of evils, a lover of wars, inconstant of judgment, and self-contradicting. As for Jesus, being from that Father who is above the God that made the world, and coming into Judea in the days of the governor Pontus Pilate, who was the procurator of Tiberius Caesar, he was manifested in the form of a man to the inhabitants of Judea, abolishing the Prophets and the Law and all the works of the God who made the world, whom Marcion also calls Cosmocrator.[6] In addition to this, Marcion mutilates the Gospel according to Luke, removing all that is written in it about the birth of the Lord and eliminating many of the passages of the Lord's teaching in which the Lord most clearly confesses that the Creator of this universe is his Father. In so doing, Marcion persuaded his disciples that he himself was more veracious than the apostles who handed down the Gospel to us, whereas he handed to them, not the Gospel, but a mere fragment of a Gospel. He likewise also dismembered the Epistles of the apostle Paul, eliminating all that is manifestly said by the apostle concerning the God who made the world, namely, that he is the Father of our Lord Jesus Christ, and also those passages where the apostle, by citing the prophetic writings, taught that they announced beforehand the coming of the Lord.

Translated and annotated by Fabian E. Udoh from the Latin text as in Irénée de Lyon, *Contre les hérésies,* Sources chrétiennes, no. 264 (Paris: Éditions du Cerf, 1979), 350.

TERTULLIAN
Against Marcion, I.2; IV.2; V.1, 21

I

2. For, like many even in our day, heretics in particular, Marcion had an unhealthy interest in the problem of evil—

---

3. Nothing is otherwise known of Aristion.

4. On (John) Mark's relationship with Peter, see Acts 12:12; 1 Pet 5:13. He is also, even more closely, related to Paul and Barnabas. See Acts 12:25; 13:5; 15:37–39; Philem 1:24; Col 4:10; 2 Tim 4:11.

5. See Mt 9:9; compare Mk 2:14–15; Lk 5:27–29.

6. Or "World Ruler," "Cosmic Power" (see Eph 6:12).

the origin of it—and his perceptions were numbed by the very excess of his curiosity. So when he found the Creator[7] declaring, *It is I who create evil things,*[8] in that he had, from other arguments which make that impression on the perverse, already assumed him to be the author of evil, he interpreted with reference to the Creator the evil tree that creates evil fruit—namely, evil things in general—and assumed that there had to be another god to correspond with the good tree which [brings] forth good fruits.[9] Discovering then in Christ as it were a different dispensation of sole and unadulterated benevolence, an opposite character to the Creator's, he found it easy to argue for a new and hitherto unknown divinity revealed in its own Christ, and thus with a little leaven has embittered with heretical acidity the whole mass of the faith.[10]

IV

2. [. . .] I lay it down to begin with that the documents of the gospel have the apostles for their authors, and that this task of promulgating the gospel was imposed upon them by our Lord himself. If they also have for their authors apostolic men, yet these stand not alone, but as companions of apostles or followers of apostles: because the preaching of disciples might be made suspect of the desire of vainglory, unless there stood by it the authority of their teachers, or rather the authority of Christ, which made the apostles teachers. In short, from among the apostles the faith is introduced to us by John and by Matthew, while from among apostolic men Luke and Mark give it renewal (all of them) beginning with the same rules (of belief), as far as relates to the one only God, the Creator, and to his Christ, born of a virgin, the fulfilment of the law and the prophets. It matters not that the arrangement of their narratives varies, so long as there is agreement on the essentials of the faith—and on these they show no agreement with Marcion. Marcion, on the other hand, attaches to his gospel no author's name,—as though he to whom it was no crime to overturn the whole body might not assume permission to invent a title for it as well. At this point I might have made a stand, arguing that no recognition is due to a work which cannot lift up its head, which makes no show of courage, which gives no promise of credibility by having a fully descriptive title and the requisite indication of the author's name. But I prefer to join issue on all points, nor am I leaving unmentioned anything that can be taken as being in my favour. For out of those authors whom we possess, Marcion is seen to have chosen Luke as the one to mutilate. [. . .]

V

1. [. . .] Here too our contest shall take place on the same front: my challenge shall be issued from the same stance, of a case already proven: which is, that an apostle whom you deny to be the Creator's, whom in fact you represent as hostile to the Creator, has no right to teach anything, to think anything, to intend anything, which accords with the Creator, but must from the outset proclaim his other god with no less confidence than that with which he has broken loose from the Creator's law. For it is not likely that in diverging from Judaism he did not at the same time make it clear into which god's faith he was diverging: because it would be impossible for anyone to pass over from the Creator, without knowing to whom his transit was expected to lead. Now if Christ had already revealed that other god, the apostle's attestation had to follow: else he would not have been taken for the apostle of the god whom Christ had revealed, and indeed it was not permissible for a god already revealed by Christ to be kept hidden from the apostle. Or if Christ had made no such revelation about that god, there was the greater need for his being revealed by the apostle: for there was now no possibility of his being revealed by any other, and without question there could be no belief in him if not even an apostle revealed him. Such is my preliminary argument. From now on I claim I shall prove that no other god was the subject of the apostle's profession, on the same terms as I have proved this of Christ: and my evidence will be Paul's epistles. That these have suffered mutilation even in number, the precedent of that gospel, which is now the heretic's, must have prepared us to expect.

21. On the Epistle to Philemon. This epistle alone has so profited by its brevity as to escape Marcion's falsifying hands. As however he has accepted this letter to a single person, I do not see why he has rejected two written to Timothy and one to Titus about the church system. I suppose he had a whim to meddle even with the number of the epistles.[11]

From Tertullian, *Adversus Marcionem*, edited and translated by Ernest Evans (Oxford: Oxford University Press, 1972), 7, 61, 513, 641.

---

7. The translator uses "God," "Lord," "Creator" (with initial capital letters) to refer to the God of the Old and New Testaments, and "god," "lord" (with initial lowercase letters) to refer to other gods and to Marcion's superior or "stranger" god. (The notes for this selection are by Gerhart and Udoh.)

8. Isa 45:7.

9. See Mt 7:17; 12:33; Lk 6:43.

10. See 1 Cor 5:6.

11. Tertullian's discussion of Marcion's Pauline corpus (*Apostolicon*) in book V of his *Against Marcion* shows that Marcion accepted ten letters attributed to

IRENAEUS OF LYONS

❦ In his *Against Heresies* (ca. 180), **Irenaeus** offers the first unambiguous correlation in Christian literature between the Gospel texts as we now have them and the authors (Matthew, Mark, Luke, and John) to whom they are attributed.

IRENAEUS OF LYONS

Against Heresies, III.i.1; III.xi.8–9

III

i.1. For we have learnt the "economy" of our salvation through no others than from those through whom the gospel has come down to us. This gospel they at first proclaimed, and afterward, by God's will, handed it to us in the Writings,[12] to be the foundation and pillar of our faith.[13]

For it is not lawful either to allege that they preached before they possessed perfect knowledge, as some dare to say, boasting themselves to be the correctors of the apostles. In fact, after our Lord rose from the dead, and the apostles, when the Holy Spirit came down upon them,[14] were clothed with power from on high,[15] they were filled with all gifts and possessed perfect knowledge.[16] It was then that they departed to the ends of the earth,[17] preaching the good news of the good things[18] which have come to us from God and proclaiming the peace of heaven to all:[19] they indeed possessed, all together and each individually, "the gospel of God."[20]

Thus, Matthew published a written Gospel among the Hebrews in their own tongue, while Peter and Paul were proclaiming the gospel in Rome and were founding the Church. After their death, Mark, the disciple and interpreter of Peter,[21] did also hand down to us in writing what had been preached by Peter. Luke also, the companion of Paul,[22] wrote down in a book the gospel preached by Paul. Afterward, John, the disciple of the Lord, the one who had leaned on his breast,[23] did also publish a Gospel while he resided at Ephesus in Asia.

xi.8. Besides, it is impossible that the Gospels be either more or fewer in number than they are. For, since there are indeed four regions of the world in which we are, and four principal winds, and since the Church is spread throughout all the world, and she has for pillar and ground[24] the gospel and the Spirit of life, it is fitting that she should have four pillars that breathe immortality from every side and give life to human beings. It is evident from this that the Word, the Maker of all things, he who sits upon the cherubim[25] and holds all things together,[26] when he was manifested to human

beings, gave us the gospel in four forms, but held together by one Spirit. It is thus also that David, entreating his coming, says: "You who are enthroned upon the cherubim, manifest yourself."[27] For the cherubim also had four faces,[28] and their faces were images of the activities of the Son of God. For it says, "The first living being was like a lion," symbolizing his effective power, his authority, and royalty; "the second was like an ox," which manifests his sacrificial and priestly office; but "the third had, as it were, a human face," which is evidently a description of his coming as a human being; "the fourth was like a flying eagle," which indicates the gift of the Spirit hovering over the Church.[29] The Gospels are therefore in accord with these beings, on which Christ Jesus is seated. Thus, the Gospel according to John narrates his authoritative, powerful, and glorious generation from the Father, saying: "In the beginning was the Word, and the Word was with God, and the Word was God."[30] Also, "all things were made by him, and without him was nothing made."[31] That is why, also, this Gospel is full of all confidence, for such is its person. The Gospel according to Luke, since it is of priestly character, begins with Zechariah the priest offering sacrifice to God.[32] For already the fatted calf, which was about to be immolated for the finding of the younger son, was made ready.[33] And Matthew narrates his generation as a human being, saying: "The book of the generation of Jesus Christ, the son of David, the son of Abraham";[34] and, again, "The birth of Jesus Christ took place in this way."[35] This Gospel, then, is

---

Paul: Galatians, 1 Corinthians, 2 Corinthians, Romans, 1 Thessalonians, 2 Thessalonians, Laodiceans (= Ephesians), Colossians, Philippians, and Philemon. Besides 1 and 2 Timothy and Titus, Marcion also rejected Hebrews.

12. Or "in the Scriptures." We choose the rendering "in the Writings," primarily to emphasize the transition that Irenaeus makes from oral preaching to the written text. His terminology, moreover, does not seem to have acquired the technical meaning generally associated with the term "Scripture."

13. See "pillar and bulwark of the truth" in 1 Tim 3:15, referring to the Church.

14. See Acts 1:8; 2:1–4.   17. See Acts 1:8; also Rom 10:18; Ps 19:4.

15. See Lk 24:49.   18. See Rom 10:15; Isa 52:7.

16. See Jn 16:13–15.   19. See Lk 2:13–14.

20. See Rom 1:1; 15:16; 2 Cor 11:7; 1 Thess 2:2, 8, 9; 1 Pet 4:17.

21. (John) Mark is connected with Peter in Acts 12:12; 1 Pet 5:13.

22. On Luke as "companion of Paul," see Philem 1:24; Col 4:14; 2 Tim 4:11.

23. See Jn 13:23; 21:20–24.   25. See Isa 37:16; Ezek 10:1–14.

24. See 1 Tim 3:15.   26. See Wis 1:7.

27. Ps 79:2 (Septuagint) = 80:1.

28. See Ezek 1:5–6; 10:14 (the whole of v. 14 is lacking from the Septuagint version of Ezek 10).

29. Rev 4:7; see also Ezek 1:10; 10:14.

30. Jn 1:1.   33. See Lk 15:23–32.

31. Jn 1:3.   34. Mt 1:1.

32. See Lk 1:5–10.   35. Mt 1:18.

of human form.[36] It is also for this reason that, throughout this Gospel, he remains a humble and meek person.[37] Finally, Mark begins with the prophetic spirit coming down from on high to human beings, saying: "The beginning of the Gospel, as it is written in the prophet Isaiah."[38] This shows the winged image of the Gospel, and that is why it has made a brief and cursory proclamation, for such is the prophetic character. Thus, the Word of God himself conversed with the patriarchs who were before Moses, in accordance with his divinity and glory; for those who were under the Law, however, he instituted a priestly and liturgical office.[39] Afterward, being made man for us, he sent the gift of the heavenly Spirit over all the earth, protecting us with his own wings.[40] In sum, therefore, just like the activity of the Son of God, so also is the form of the living creatures; and just like the form of the living creatures, so also is the character of the Gospel: fourfold form of living creatures, fourfold form of gospel, fourfold form of the Lord's activity. This is why four principal covenants were given to the human race: one, before the Flood, under Adam;[41] the second, after the Flood, under Noah;[42] the third, the giving of the Law, under Moses;[43] finally, the fourth, the one that renews humankind and sums up all things in itself and that, by means of the gospel, raises and bears human beings upon its wings into the heavenly kingdom.[44]

xi.9. This being the case, they are vain, ignorant, and, besides, audacious those who reject the form of the gospel, and who introduce aspects of the gospel that are either more in number than already mentioned or fewer. The former do so in order that they may seem to have discovered more than the truth; the latter, that they may reject God's "economies."

Translated and annotated by Fabian E. Udoh from the Greek and Latin texts as in Irénée de Lyon, *Contre les hérésies*, Sources chrétiennes, no. 211 (Paris: Éditions du Cerf, 1974), 20–25, 161–71.

Some Early Lists of the Books of the Bible

☙ **The Muratorian Fragment** is an early example of a list of authoritative texts along with the rationale for inclusion. It is of unknown authorship and dates from the period between the second and fourth centuries. It was probably composed in Rome.

The Muratorian Fragment

1. . . . at which, however, he was present, and so he set it down.[45] 2. The third Gospel is that according to Luke. 3. Luke,

the physician, after the ascension of Christ, 4–5. when Paul had taken him with him as one zealous for the Law,[46] 6. composed it in his own name, according to his belief.[47] Yet he himself had not 7. seen the Lord in the flesh; and thus, as he was able to ascertain it, 8. so indeed he begins to tell the story from the birth of John.[48] 9. The fourth of the Gospels is that of John, [one] of the disciples.[49] 10. To his fellow disciples and bishops, who had been urging him [to write], 11. he said, "Fast with me from today for three days, and what 12. will be revealed to each one 13. let us narrate it to one another." In the same night it was revealed 14. to Andrew, [one] of the apostles, 15–16. that John should write down all things in his own name, while all of them should review them. And therefore, though various 17. elements be taught in the individual books of the Gospels, 18–19. yet this makes no difference to the faith of the believers, since by the one supreme Spirit everything 20. has been declared in all: concerning the 21. Nativity, concerning the Passion, concerning the Resurrection, 22. concerning his dealings with his disciples, 23. and concerning his twofold coming, 24. the first in humility when he was despised, which has come to pass, 25. the second glorious in royal power, 26. which is yet to come. What 27. wonder then if John so consistently 28. mentions particular points also in his Epistles, 29. saying about himself: "What we have seen with our eyes 30. and heard with our ears and our hands 31. have handled, these things we have written to you."[50] 32. For in this manner he professes [himself] to be not only an eyewitness and hearer 33. but also a writer of all the wondrous deeds of the Lord in order. 34. The Acts

---

36. Or "This gospel, then, is anthropomorphic."

37. See Mt 11:29.

38. Mk 1:1–2.

39. Or "a priestly and liturgical order."

40. See Pss 17:8; 61:4.   42. Gen 9:9–17.

41. See Gen 1:26–30; 2:7–17.   43. Ex 19:1–24:11.

44. Alternatively (Greek Fragment 11): "One was that of Noah's flood, under the sign of the rainbow; second, with Abraham, under the sign of circumcision; third, the giving of the Law through Moses; and fourth, that of the gospel, through our Lord Jesus Christ." For Noah's covenant, see Gen 6:11–22; 9:1–19. On the covenant with Abraham, see Gen 17:1–14. For the covenant on Sinai, see Ex 19:1–24:11.

45. The text is broken and begins in the middle of a sentence. The broken sentence may be taken to refer to Matthew and his Gospel. Mark's Gospel would have been the first.

46. Possibly also "as one learned in the Law." On Luke the physician, see Col 4:14, and as Paul's coworker, see also Philem 1:24; 2 Tim 4:11.

47. Possibly also "according to the common belief." "In orderly sequence" has also been conjectured. For these possibilities, see Lk 1:1–3. The author of the Gospel, however, never gives his or her name.

48. See Lk 1:5–25.   49. See Jn 19:35; 21:20–24; 13:23–25.

50. See 1 Jn 1:1–4.

of all the apostles, however, 35. were written in one book. For "most excellent Theophilus"[51] Luke 36. narrated the particular events that took place in his own presence, 37. as he clearly shows by omitting the martyrdom of Peter 38. as well as the departure of Paul from the city [of Rome] 39. when he set out for Spain.[52] The Epistles of 40–41. Paul themselves, however, make clear to those who wish to understand which ones [they are], from what place, and for what reason they were sent. 42. First of all to the Corinthians, prohibiting heretical schisms; 43. next, to the Galatians, against circumcision; 44–46. then to the Romans, however, he wrote at length explaining the plan of the Scriptures and also that Christ is their principal theme. It is necessary 47. for us to discuss these individually, since the blessed 48. apostle Paul himself, following the example of his predecessor 49–50. John, wrote by name to only seven churches[53] in the following order: to the Corinthians 51. first, to the Ephesians second, to the Philippians third, 52. to the Colossians fourth, to the Galatians fifth, 53. to the Thessalonians sixth, to the Romans 54–55. seventh. Although it is true that he wrote once more to the Corinthians and to the Thessalonians for the sake of reproof, 56–57. yet it is evident that there is one Church spread throughout the whole world. For John also in the 58. Apocalypse, although he wrote to seven churches, 59–60. nevertheless speaks to all. Though [Paul wrote] out of affection 61. and love one to Philemon, one to Titus, and two to Timothy, yet in the esteem of the catholic Church 62–63. these are held sacred for the ordering of ecclesiastical discipline. Current also is [an Epistle] to the 64. Laodiceans, another to the Alexandrians, [both of them] forged in Paul's 65. name for the heresy of Marcion, and several others 66. that cannot be accepted in the catholic Church, 67. for it is not fitting that gall be mixed with honey. 68. Of course, the Epistle of Jude and two bearing the name of 69. John are accepted[54] in the catholic [Church], and [the Book of] Wisdom, 70. written by the friends of Solomon in his honor. 71–72. We accept the Apocalypses of John and Peter only, though some 73. of us do not want that the latter be read in church. 74–75. But Hermas wrote the *Shepherd* very recently, in our times, in the city of Rome, while his brother, Bishop Pius, was occupying the [episcopal] chair 76. of the church of the city of Rome. 77. And therefore it ought indeed to be read, but 78. it cannot be read publicly to the people in church either among 79. the prophets, whose number is complete, or among 80. the apostles, for it comes after [their] time. 81–82. We accept nothing whatsoever of Arsinoes or Valentinus or Miltiades, who also composed a new 83. book of psalms for

Marcion, 84–85. together with Basilides, the Asian founder of the Cataphrygians.

Translated and annotated by Fabian E. Udoh from the Latin text reconstructed in Hans Lietzmann, *Das muratorische Fragment und die monarchianischen Prologe zu den Evangelien*, 2nd ed. (Berlin: W. de Gruyter, 1933), 1–16.

❧ In *Ecclesiastical History* (ca. 315), Eusebius (ca. 260–339), bishop of Caesarea, gives witness to the canon as accepted by **Origen** of Alexandria (ca. 185–254).

EUSEBIUS

The Canon of Origen, in *Ecclesiastical History*, VI.xxv.3–14

3–14. But in the first of his [Origen's] *Commentaries on the Gospel according to Matthew*, defending the canon of the Church, he testifies that he knows only four Gospels, writing somewhat as follows: "For I learned by tradition concerning the four Gospels, which alone are indisputable in the Church of God under heaven, that first there was written that according to the one-time tax-collector and later Apostle of Jesus Christ, Matthew,[55] who published it for those who from Judaism came to have the faith, being composed in the Hebrew language; secondly, that according to Mark,[56] which he wrote as Peter guided him, whom also Peter acknowledged as son in his Catholic Epistle, speaking with these words: 'The church that is in Babylon, elected together with you, salutes you: and so does my son Mark';[57] and thirdly, that according to Luke,[58] who composed this Gospel, which was praised by Paul,[59] for Gentile converts; and in addition to them all, that according to John."

And in the fifth Book of his *Expositions on the Gospel according to John* the same writer speaks as follows regarding the Epistles of the Apostles: "But he who was made fit to become a minister of the new testament, not in the letter but in the spirit,[60] Paul, who replenished the Gospel from Jerusalem

---

51. See Acts 1:1; also Lk 1:3.

52. This is Paul's expressed hope in Rom 15:22–24. Acts (28:30–31) ends, however, with Paul's house arrest in Rome.

53. See Rev 1:10–11.

54. Or "used."

55. See Mt 9:9; compare Mk 2:14; Lk 5:27. (The notes for this selection are by Gerhart and Udoh.)

56. See Acts 12:12.

57. 1 Pet 5:13.

58. See Col 4:14.

59. Probably a reference to 2 Cor 8:18.

60. See 2 Cor 3:5–6.

round about as far as unto Illyricum,[61] did by no means write to all the churches which he had taught, but even to those to which he wrote he sent only a few lines. And Peter, on whom the Church of Christ is built, against which the gates of hell shall not prevail,[62] has left behind one acknowledged Epistle, and perhaps also a second, for it is questioned. Why need I speak of him who leaned on the breast of Jesus, John,[63] who has left behind one Gospel, while confessing that he could compose so many that not even the world itself could contain them;[64] who also wrote the Apocalypse, when he had been ordered to keep silence and not to write the words of the seven thunders?[65] He has left behind also an Epistle of very few lines, and perhaps also a second and a third—for not all say that these are genuine—but the two together do not contain a hundred lines."

Besides these he comments as follows on the Epistle to the Hebrews in his *Homilies* upon it; "That the character of the diction of the Epistle entitled 'To the Hebrews' does not possess the Apostle's rudeness of speech, who acknowledged that he was rude in speech,[66] that is, in style, but the Epistle is better Greek in the composition of its diction, as anyone who knows how to distinguish differences of phraseology would admit. And yet again, that the thoughts of the Epistle are admirable, and not inferior to the acknowledged writings of the Apostle, this also anyone would agree to be true who gives attention to reading the text of the Apostles."

Further on he adds to this when he says: "But I would say, if giving my opinion, that the thoughts are those of the Apostle, but the phraseology and the composition are those of someone who recalled to mind the teachings of the Apostle and who, as it were, had made notes on what was said by the teacher. If any church, then, holds this Epistle to be Paul's let it be commended for this, for not without reason have the men of old handed it down as Paul's. Who the author of the Epistle is God truly knows, but the account that has reached us from some is that Clement, who was Bishop of the Romans, wrote the Epistle; from others, that Luke, who wrote the Gospel and the Acts, is the author."

From Eusebius Pamphili, *Ecclesiastical History, Books 6–10,* translated by Roy J. Deferrari, Fathers of the Church, vol. 29 (New York: Fathers of the Church, 1955), 48–50.

The theologian and historian **Eusebius** became bishop of Caesarea in about 313. He offers his list of acceptable texts, along with the reasons for rejecting other circulating books, in his *Ecclesiastical History* (ca. 315).

Ecclesiastical History, III.xxv.1–7

1–7. It seems reasonable, having arrived at this point, to summarize the writings of the New Testament which have been mentioned. First, we must put the holy quaternion of the Gospels, and the writing of the Acts of the Apostles follows these. After this we must reckon the Epistles of Paul. Next to these in order we must recognize the Epistle of John called the first and similarly the Epistle of Peter. After these, if it seem well, we must place the Apocalypse of John, the arguments concerning which we will set forth at the proper time. These are among the recognized books. Among the disputed works, but yet known to most, are extant the so-called Epistle of James, that of Jude, the second Epistle of Peter, and the so-called second and third Epistle of John, whether they really belong to the Evangelist or even to another of the same name. Among the spurious works must be placed the work of the Acts of Paul and the so-called Shepherd, and the Apocalypse of Peter, and in addition to these the extant letter of Barnabas and the so-called Teachings of the Apostles, and again, as I have said, the Apocalypse of John, if it should so appear. Some, as I have said, reject it, but others classify it among the accepted books. Now, among these some have also placed the Gospel according to the Hebrews, in which the Hebrews who have accepted Christ especially delight. All these might be among the disputed books, but we have nevertheless, of necessity, made a list of them, distinguishing those writings which according to the tradition of the Church are true, genuine, and recognized from those which are different from these in that they are not canonical but disputed, although known by most of the writers of the Church, in order that we might be able to know these works themselves and the writings which are published by the heretics under the name of the Apostles, including Gospels such as those of Peter and Thomas and Matthias, and some others besides these, or Acts such as those of Andrew and John and the other Apostles. To none of these has anyone belonging to the succession of the writers of the Church considered it right to refer in his writings. Furthermore, the character of the phraseology is at variance with apostolic style, and both the thought and the purpose of what is related in them is

---

61. See Rom 15:18–19.   64. See Jn 21:24–25.
62. See Mt 16:18.   65. See Rev 10:2–4.
63. See Jn 13:23–25.   66. See 2 Cor 11:6.

especially in discord with true orthodoxy and clearly proves that they really are forgeries by heretics. They ought, therefore, to be placed not even among spurious works, but should be shunned as altogether absurd and impious.

From Eusebius Pamphili, *Ecclesiastical History, Books 1–5,* translated by Roy J. Deferrari, Fathers of the Church, vol. 19 (New York: Fathers of the Church, 1953), 178–80.

☙ The list found in the catalog in the **Codex Claromontanus** is of uncertain date and origin. The codex itself dates from the sixth century.

The Codex Claromontanus

Four Gospels:

    Matthew, 2,600 lines

    John, 2,000 lines

    Mark, 1,600 lines

    Luke, 2,900 lines

Epistles of Paul:

    To the Romans, 1,040 lines

    The First to the Corinthians, 1,060 lines

    The Second to the Corinthians, 70 lines [*sic*]

    To the Galatians, 350 lines

    To the Ephesians, 375 lines

    The First to Timothy, 208 lines

    The Second to Timothy, 289 lines

    To Titus, 140 lines

    To the Colossians, 251 lines

    To Philemon, 50 lines

    —The First to [*sic*] Peter, 200 lines[67]

    The Second to [*sic*] Peter, 140 lines

Of James, 220 lines

The First Epistle of John, 220

The Second Epistle of John, 20

The Third Epistle of John, 20

The Epistle of Jude, 60 lines

—The Epistle of Barnabas, 850 lines

The Apocalypse of John, 1,200

The Acts of the Apostles, 2,600

—The Shepherd, 4,000 lines

—The Acts of Paul, 3,560 lines

—The Apocalypse of Peter, 270

Translated and annotated by Fabian E. Udoh from the Latin text as in F. W. Grosheide, ed., *Some Early Lists of the Books of the New Testament* (Leiden: Brill, 1948), 16–17.

☙ **Athanasius** (ca. 290–373) was patriarch of Alexandria and known as the "Father of Orthodoxy." In his *Festal Epistle,* written in 367, Athanasius gives the lists and categories of the acceptable texts of the Bible.

ATHANASIUS

Festal Epistle, xxxix.4–7

4–7. Of the Old Testament there are, then, in all twenty-two books in number; for, as I have heard, it is handed down that this is also the number of the letters in the Hebrew alphabet. Their respective order and names are as follows: first Genesis, next Exodus, then Leviticus, and after that Numbers, and thereafter Deuteronomy. Following these there are Joshua, the son of Nave, then Judges, and after that Ruth. And again, after these, follow the four books of Kings, the first and second[68] being counted as one book, and so also the third and fourth as one book. After these come the first and second books of Chronicles, both being similarly counted as one book. Next Ezra first and second,[69] likewise counted as one book. After these comes the book of Psalms, then follow Proverbs, next Ecclesiastes, and the Song of Songs. Following these is Job, next the Prophets, the twelve[70] being counted as one book. Then Isaiah, one book, followed by Jeremiah together with Baruch, Lamentations, and the Epistle, one book; afterward, Ezekiel and then Daniel. These constitute the Old Testament.

It is not burdensome to speak again of the [books] of the New Testament. They are, first, the four Gospels: according to Matthew, according to Mark, according to Luke, and according to John. After these come the Acts of the Apostles and the Epistles—called Catholic—by apostles, seven, namely, of James, one; of Peter, two; of John, three; after these, of Jude, one. Besides these, there are fourteen Epistles of the apostle Paul, written in this order: the first, to the Romans; then to the Corinthians, two; after these, to the Galatians; next, to the Ephesians; then to the Philippians; and to the Colossians; after these, to the Thessalonians, two; and

---

67. The dash before 1 Peter (excluded from Grosheide's text) might be a Greek paragraph mark, indicating that 1 Peter and what follows are not to be included among the "Epistles of Paul." The other dashes in the list indicate books that were disputed or doubtful.

68. First and Second Kings are now generally known as First and Second Samuel.

69. Second Ezra is Nehemiah.

70. The twelve so-called minor prophets.

that to the Hebrews; and thereafter, again, two to Timothy; one to Titus; and finally, that to Philemon. And, moreover, the Revelation of John.

These are the founts of salvation, so that they who thirst may be satisfied with the words they contain. In these alone is the doctrine of orthodox faith proclaimed. Let no one add to these; let nothing be taken away from them. For it was about these that the Lord put to shame the Sadducees, when he said: "You err, not knowing the Scriptures."[71] And he reproved the Jews, saying, "Search the Scriptures, for it is these that testify concerning me."[72]

I am obligated, however, for the sake of exactness in writing, to add also that there are other books besides these, not indeed included in the canon but prescribed by the Fathers to be read by those who newly approach us and who wish to be instructed in the knowledge of orthodox faith. The Wisdom of Solomon, also the Wisdom of Sirach, and Esther, and Judith, and Tobit, and the so-called Teaching of the Apostles, and the Shepherd. Whereas the former, beloved, are included in the canon, the latter are being read; nowhere is there any mention of apocryphal writings. They are an invention of heretics, who write them when they wish, bestowing on them their approval and assigning dates to them, so that, invoking them as ancient writings, they may have a way through them to lead astray the simple.

Translated and annotated by Fabian E. Udoh from the Greek and Latin texts as in J. P. Migne, *Patrologiae Cursus Completus, Series Graeca*, vol. 26 (Paris: Librairie Orientaliste Paul Geuthner, 1928–33), 1425–40.

everywhere.[78] Each one grasps the other:[79] like wheels within wheels they roll along[80] and go on to wherever the breath of the Holy Spirit guides them.[81] Paul the apostle writes to seven churches (for the eighth epistle—that to the Hebrews—is placed apart from the others by many people). He instructs Timothy and Titus; he intercedes with Philemon on behalf of his runaway slave. Concerning Paul I think it better to be silent than to write little. The Acts of the Apostles, at first sight, seems to relate a bare narrative describing the infancy of the newborn church. Once we realize, however, that its author is Luke the physician,[82] "whose praise is in the gospel,"[83] we discern that every one of his words is medicine for the sick soul. The apostles James, Peter, John, and Jude published seven epistles at once spiritual and concise, both short and long. Short, that is, in words but long in meaning, so that there are few indeed who are not in the dark when they read them. The Apocalypse of John has as many mysteries as words. What I have said is too little in proportion to the book's merits. All praise of it is inadequate; in its every word lie hidden multiple meanings.

Translated and annotated by Fabian E. Udoh from the Latin text as in A. H. Charteris, *Canonicity: A Collection of Early Testimonies to the Canonical Books of the New Testament* (Edinburgh: W. Blackwood, 1880), 21–22.

☙ One of the so-called Latin Church Fathers, **Jerome** (ca. 347–420) published the Latin version of the Bible known as the Vulgate and translated many of Origen's works into Latin. The canon as accepted by Jerome is found in his Letter 53, written to Paulinus, bishop of Nola, in 394.

JEROME

Letter 53 (to Paulinus), 8

I shall touch briefly on the New Testament. Matthew, Mark, Luke, and John are the Lord's four-horse team and true cherubim,[73] which, interpreted, means a multitude of knowledge. Their whole body is full of eyes,[74] they glisten sparks,[75] they dart to and fro like flashes of lightning,[76] they have straight feet stretched high,[77] and their backs have wings which flutter

71. Mt 22:29; see Mk 12:24.
72. Jn 5:39.
73. See Ezek 1:5; also Ezek 10:1–17; Rev 4:6.
74. See Ezek 1:18 (Vulgate); see Rev 4:8.
75. See Ezek 1:7; see Rev 4:5.
76. See Ezek 1:14.
77. See Ezek 1:7.
78. See Ezek 1:6; Rev 4:8.
79. See Ezek 1:11.
80. See Ezek 1:16.
81. See Ezek 1:20.
82. See Col 4:14.
83. 2 Cor 8:18 (Vulgate).

❧

2. ISSUES OF INTERPRETATION

ALEXANDRIAN INTERPRETATION

❧ **Clement of Alexandria** (ca. 150–215) was best known for his allegorical interpretations of Scripture and his association with the Alexandrian school. In expounding his principles of interpretation in *Strōmateis,* Clement first gives an extreme version of the traditional tale regarding the translation of the Jewish Scriptures from Hebrew into Greek.

CLEMENT OF ALEXANDRIA

Strōmateis, 1.xxii.148.1–150.4; 5.iv.19.1–25.2;
5.ix.56.1–57.2; 1.xxviii.176.1–179.4

1.xxii

148. The Scriptures, both the Law and the Prophets, were translated from the Hebrew tongue into the Greek language, according to some,[84] in the reign of Ptolemy, the son of Lagus,[85] or, according to others, under Ptolemy surnamed Philadelphus; Demetrius Phalereus bringing to this undertaking the greatest zeal and laboring to achieve an accurate translation. For while the Macedonians were still in possession of Asia, the king, aspiring to adorn the library he had founded in Alexandria with all writings, required that the people of Jerusalem translate their prophecies into the Greek tongue. 149. And since they were still subjects of the Macedonians, they chose from those of the highest reputation among them seventy elders versed in the Scriptures and experts in the Greek language and sent them to the king with the divine books. Each one of them translated by himself each prophetic book. When all the translations were compared together, they agreed both in meaning and in wording. For it was by God's will that they exerted themselves for the benefit of Greek ears.

It was not strange that the inspiration of God, who gave the prophecy, should also produce the translation and make it, as it were, Greek prophecy. It so happened also that, when the Scriptures perished in the captivity under Nebuchodonosor, Esdras the Levite, the priest, in the time of Artaxerxes, king of the Persians, was prophetically inspired to restore again the whole of the ancient Scriptures.[86]

150. And Aristobulus,[87] in the first of his books addressed to Philometor, writes: "And Plato himself followed the laws given to us and manifestly had studied with care everything that is said in them. Before Demetrius, previous to the dominion of Alexander and of the Persians, others had translated the account of the departure of our countrymen the Jews from Egypt, all that happened to them, their taking possession of the land, and a detailed account of the whole legislation. It is thus perfectly clear that the above-mentioned philosopher derived much, since he was very learned, just like Pythagoras also, who transferred many things from our teachings to his own doctrines." The Pythagorean philosopher Numenius writes outright: "For what is Plato but Moses speaking in Attic Greek?" This Moses was a theologian and prophet and, according to some, also an interpreter of sacred laws.

5.iv

19. But since they will believe neither in what is good in a just manner nor in knowledge that leads to salvation, we ourselves then—judging that what they claim to be theirs belongs to us, because all things are God's and most especially because what is good proceeded from us to the Greeks—should treat them in the way that they are naturally capable of hearing.[88] For this great crowd approves of what is intelligent or what is right, not by truth, but by what pleases them. Now they are not pleased more by what is different than by what is like themselves. For one who is still blind and deaf, not having understanding or the dauntless and keen vision of the soul that loves contemplation,[89] which only the Savior confers, like the uninitiated at the mysteries[90] or the unmusical at choral dances, not yet being pure and worthy of

---

84. Clement probably depends for this narrative on Irenaeus, *Against Heresies,* 3.xxi.2.

85. After the death of Alexander the Great, Ptolemy I Sōter, the son of Lagus, ruled Egypt from 323 BCE (as king from 305 BCE) to 285 BCE. He was succeeded by his son Ptolemy II Philadelphus, who ruled from 285 to 246 BCE. During this time Palestine was ruled on and off by the kings of Egypt.

86. On Ezra and the Book of the Law, see Neh 7:73–8:12; 1 Esd 8:23; 9:37–48.

87. An Alexandrian Jew of the second century BCE who wrote on Greek philosophy.

88. See Mk 4:33.

89. See Plato, *Republic,* 5.475E: The true philosophers are "the lovers of the sight of the truth."

90. See Plato, *Phaedrus,* 250C.

the pure truth but still discordant, disordered, and material, must be excluded from the divine choir.[91] "For we compare spiritual things with spiritual."[92] This is why, in accordance with the mode of concealment, the truly sacred word,[93] truly divine and most necessary for us, deposited in the innermost sanctuary of truth, was by the Egyptians indicated by what they called sanctuary, and by the Hebrews by the veil.[94] Only those among them who were consecrated—that is, those devoted to God, circumcised in the desire of the passions[95] on account of the love for the divine alone—could approach them. Plato also thought it unlawful for "the impure to touch the pure."[96]

20. It follows that the prophecies and oracles are spoken in enigmas, and the mysteries are not exhibited without restraint to all and sundry, but only after certain purifications and previous instructions:

"For the Muse, in those days, was not yet fond of gain nor yet a hireling; nor did Terpsichorē's sweet, honey-voiced songs pass for sale, songs with silvered faces and soft voices."[97]

Thus, those who received instruction among the Egyptians learned first of all that method of Egyptian writing which is called epistolographic; and second, the hieratic, which the sacred scribes use; lastly, they finish with the hieroglyphic, which is either (by the use of first elements) literal or symbolic. As symbolic, it either expresses literally by means of imitation or writes, as it were, figuratively, or again it is outright allegorical, using certain enigmas.

Thus, wishing to express "sun" in writing, they make a circle, and "moon," a figure of a crescent; this according to the literal shape. In the figurative style, however, they operate by transposing and transferring according to affinity and thus draw characters by changing and by transforming in many ways. 21. They transmit in this manner the praises of their kings in theological myths, writing them in bas-relief. Let the following stand as an example of the third species—the enigmatic. They have figured the rest of the stars, on account of their oblique courses, like the bodies of serpents; but the sun, like that of a beetle, because the beetle makes a round figure of ox dung and rolls it before its face. They say that this animal lives six months underground and the other part of the year aboveground and emits its seed into the ball and so breeds, and that there is no female beetle.

In a word then, all those, both barbarians and Greeks, who have spoken of the divine, have veiled the first principles of things and handed down the truth in enigmas and symbols and allegories and metaphors and similar tropes.[98] Such also

are the oracles among the Greeks; and the Pythian Apollo is called Loxias.

22. The apophtegms also of those among the Greeks called wise men make manifest in a few words the unfolding of matters of considerable importance. Such doubtless is the saying "Spare time": that is to say, either, since life is short, we should not expend this time in vain, or on the contrary, it bids you spare your personal expenses, so that, it says, though you live for many years, necessities may not fail you.

23. In like manner also the saying "Know thyself" points out many things: that you are mortal; that you were born a human being; and also that, in comparison with life's other grandeurs, if you say you are rich or renowned, you are of no account; or, on the other hand, that, being rich and renowned, you honor an ephemeral advantage. And it says also: Know for what you were born and whose image you are, and what is your being and how you were created, and what is your relation with God, and the like.

And the Spirit says by the prophet Isaiah, "I will give you dark and hidden treasures."[99] Now wisdom, hard to acquire, is God's treasure and unfailing riches.[100]

24. But the poets, on their part, taught in theology by those prophets, philosophize much by way of hidden meaning. I mean Orpheus, Linus, Musaeus, Homer, and Hesiod and those who are wise in this way. The poetic persuasion is the veil separating them from the many. Dreams and symbols are all more or less obscure to human beings, not from jealousy (for it is not permissible to conceive of God as subject to passions), but in order that research, penetrating into the understanding of enigmas, may hasten up to the discovery of truth. Thus, Sophocles, the tragic poet, says in a passage:

And God I know to be such a one,
Ever the revealer of enigmas to the wise
But to the perverse bad, although a teacher in a few
    words,

taking "bad" in the sense of "simple."[101]

---

91. On the "divine choir," see Plato, *Phaedrus,* 247A.

92. Or "For we interpret spiritual things for those who are spiritual" (1 Cor 2:13).

93. Or "discourse."

94. See Heb 9:3–5; Ex 26:31–33.

95. See Col 2:11; 3:5.

96. Plato, *Phaedo,* 67B.

97. Pindar, *Isthmian Odes,* II.5–8.

98. See Prov 1:6.

99. Isa 45:3 (Septuagint).

100. See Lk 12:33.

101. Sophocles, *Fragments,* no. 771; see A. C. Pearson, ed., *The Fragments of Sophocles,* vol. 3 (Amsterdam: Adolf M. Hakkert, 1963), 22.

25. In any event, with respect to all our Scripture, it is expressly written in the Psalms that it speaks in parable, "Hear, O my people, my law, incline your ear to the words of my mouth. I will open my mouth in parables, I will utter problems from the beginning."[102] Likewise, the noble apostle says the same thing: "Yet we speak wisdom among those who are perfect, but not the wisdom of this age, nor of the princes of this age, who are doomed to perish. But we speak the wisdom of God hidden in mystery, which God decreed, before the ages, for our glory; wisdom that none of the princes of this age knew. For had they known it, they would not have crucified the Lord of glory."[103]

5.ix

56. But, it appears, in my eagerness to prove my point, I have made a digression and have gone beyond what is appropriate. For my whole life would not suffice to adduce the multitude of those who philosophize in symbolic language. Aiding memory, brevity, and attracting to the truth, such then are the ends sought by the scriptures of barbarian philosophy. For, in fact, they will supply the real philosophy and true theology only to those who approach them assiduously, whose faith and whole life have been tried. Yes, they also wish us to require an interpreter and a guide. For they considered that, if we received them at the hands of those who knew them well, we would be more earnest and less liable to deception, and those who were worthy of them would profit.

Besides, all things that come to light through a veil show the truth more grandly and more majestically, as fruits showing through water and figures through veils, which give added charm to them. For complete lighting is meant to show defects, and moreover, what is evident can be perceived only in one way. 57. It is, however, possible to draw several meanings, as we do, from what is expressed in veiled form. Such being the case, the ignorant and unlearned person fails, whereas the gnostic comprehends.

Now, then, it is not desirable that all things should be exposed indiscriminately to those who just happen to come, or that the benefits of wisdom be communicated to those who have not even in a dream purified their soul; for it is not permissible to hand to every chance comer what has been procured with such laborious struggles, nor are the mysteries of the Logos to be expounded to the profane.

1.xxviii

176. Moses' philosophy is divided into four parts: first, history; second, that which is properly called legislation, both of which belong to a treatise on ethics; third, religious ceremonies, which actually is a part of the theory of nature; and fourth, to crown it all, theology, vision—the *epopteia*[104]—which Plato predicates to the truly great mysteries,[105] whereas Aristotle calls it "metaphysics." Dialectics, according to Plato (as he says in *The Statesman*),[106] is a science devoted to the discovery of the explanation of beings. And the sage must acquire it, not for the sake of saying or doing anything with regard to human affairs (as today the dialecticians do who busy themselves with sophistry), but in order to be able to say and do what is pleasing to God, all according to one's ability. 177. But true dialectic mixed with true philosophy examines things, tests forces and powers, gradually ascends to the sovereign essence of all, and dares to go beyond to the God of the universe. It promises, not the practical experience of mortal things, but the science of things divine and heavenly, from which follows the particular practice of human affairs, in words and deeds. Scripture, therefore, rightly desires to make us such dialecticians and exhorts us "Be approved money changers,"[107] rejecting some things but retaining what is good. For this true dialectic is the science that discerns the objects of thought and that brings to light the principle of each individual thing in its purity; or it is the power of dividing things into genera, descending to their most particular properties, and presents each individual object to be contemplated purely as it is.

178. Therefore, it alone leads to true wisdom, which is the divine faculty to know beings as beings, and has perfection, since it is freed from all passion. This does not happen without the Savior who by the divine Word takes away the gloom of ignorance that has swamped the soul's view as a result of evil training, and who bestows the best faculty, "That we might well distinguish God from man."[108] It is he who has truly shown how we are to know ourselves. It is he who re-

---

102. Ps 77:1–2 (Septuagint) = Ps 78:1–2.

103. 1 Cor 2:6–8.

104. The third and highest stage of initiation into the mysteries of Eleusis (see chapter 2).

105. See, for instance, Plato, *Phaedrus*, 250C.

106. Plato, *The Statesman*, 287A.

107. This saying is not in the Bible we now have, but it was sometimes attributed to Christ or to one of the apostles.

108. Homer, *Iliad*, 5.127.

veals the Father of the universe to whom he wills and insofar as human nature can comprehend. "For no one knows the Son except the Father, and no one knows the Father except the Son and anyone to whom the Son reveals him."[109] 179. Rightly, then, does the apostle say that it was "by revelation" that he knew "the mystery, as I have written above in a few words, such that you are able to perceive my understanding of the mystery of Christ."[110] "Such that you are able," he said, since he knew that some had taken only milk, not yet solid food, and probably not pure milk.[111]

There are four ways of receiving the meaning of Scripture: [It may present a type],[112] it may show a symbol, or it may lay down a precept for right conduct, or it may utter a prophecy. But I know well that to make these distinctions and expound them is the work of a fully grown adult. For the whole Scripture in its meaning is not, as the proverb has it, "a single Myconos."[113] Those who hunt after the sequence of the divine teaching must approach it with utmost dialectics, to the best of their abilities.

Translated and annotated by Fabian E. Udoh from the Greek text as in Clement d'Alexandrie, *Strōmateis*, Sources chrétiennes, no. 30 (Paris: Éditions du Cerf, 1951), 152–53, 173–74; and Clement d'Alexandrie, *Strōmateis*, Sources chrétiennes, no. 278 (Paris: Éditions du Cerf, 1981), 56–64, 114–16.

Origen (ca. 185–254) was a student of Clement of Alexandria and fellow proponent of the allegorical interpretations affiliated with the Alexandrian school. He spells out his methods for the Christian appropriation of the Old Testament through allegory in his *On First Principles,* probably composed between 212 and 215. The work is now extant only in the Latin translation by Rufinus (ca. 345–410).

ORIGEN

On First Principles, IV.ii.2–9

IV.ii

2. Now the reason those we have just mentioned[114] have a false understanding of these matters is quite simply that they understand Scripture not according to the spiritual meaning but according to the sound of the letter. For this reason, as far as our modest perception admits, we shall address those who believe the sacred Scriptures were not composed by any human words but were written by the inspiration of the Holy Spirit and were also delivered and entrusted to us by the will of God the Father through His Only Begotten Son Jesus Christ. And we shall try to make clear to them what seems to us the right way of understanding Scripture, observing that rule and discipline[115] which was delivered by Jesus Christ to the apostles and which they delivered in succession to their followers who teach the heavenly Church.

Now the fact that certain mysterious dispensations are disclosed by the holy Scriptures is something everyone, I think, even the more simple believers, will admit. But what they are or of what sort is something anyone of right mind and who is not plagued with the vice of boasting will confess in the spirit of true religion he does not know. For if someone, for example, points out to us the stories of Lot's daughters and their apparently unlawful intercourse with their father,[116] or of Abraham's two wives,[117] or of the two sisters who married Jacob,[118] or of the two maidservants who increased the number of his sons,[119] what else can we answer than that these are certain mysteries and types of spiritual matters, but that we do not know of what sort they are? Moreover, when we read of the building of the tabernacle,[120] we are, of course, certain that the things that have been described are types of certain obscure matters. But I think it is extremely difficult, I might almost say impossible, to fit them to their own measures and to uncover and describe each one of them. Nevertheless, as I have said, the fact that the description is filled with mysteries does not escape even an ordinary understanding. Indeed, the entire narrative, which seems to be written about weddings or the births of sons or different battles or whatever other stories one wishes, what else must it be believed to be than the forms and types of hidden and sacred matters? But either because people bring too little zeal to the training of their minds or because they think they know before they have learned, it happens that they never begin to learn. On the other hand, if neither zeal nor a teacher is actually lacking and if these matters are sought after as divine and not

---

109. Mt 11:27; Lk 10:22.

110. Eph 3:3–4.

111. See 1 Cor 3:2.

112. This first sense is supplied from the scholia.

113. All the inhabitants of Myconos (Mykonos) were reputed to be bald, hence the proverb: "It is all one." Myconos was one of the islands of the Cylades, next to Delos.

114. That is, Jews, heretics (specifically Marcionites), and "simpler" orthodox Christians, discussed in the previous section (IV.ii.1). (The notes for this selection are by Gerhart and Udoh.)

115. That is, the Rule of Faith.

116. See Gen 19:30–38.   118. See Gen 29:21–30.

117. See Gen 16:1–16.   119. See Gen 30:1–13.

120. See Ex 25:1–27:19.

as though they were human, that is religiously and piously and as matters we hope to be revealed in as many cases as possible through God's revelation, since they are, of course, extremely difficult and obscure for human perception, then perhaps the person who seeks this way will at last find what is right to find.

3. But perhaps this difficulty will be supposed present only in the prophetic words, since it is certainly clear to everyone that the prophetic style is always strewn with types and enigmas.[121] What shall we say when we come to the Gospels? Does not an inner meaning, the Lord's meaning, also lie hidden there that is revealed only by that grace he received who said, "But we have the mind of Christ . . . that we might understand the gifts bestowed upon us by God. And we impart this in words not taught by human wisdom but taught by the Spirit"?[122] And if anyone reads the revelations made to John, how can he fail to be amazed at how great an obscurity of ineffable mysteries is present there? It is evident that even those who cannot understand what lies hidden in them nevertheless understand that something lies hidden. And indeed, the letters of the apostles, which do seem to some clearer, are they not so filled with profound ideas that through them, as through some small opening, the brightness of an immense light seems to be poured forth for those who can understand the meaning of divine wisdom? Since all this is the case and since there are many in error in this life, I do not think that anyone can without danger proclaim that he knows or understands those things that require "the key of knowledge" before they can be opened. This key the Savior said was with those skilled in the Law.[123] At this point, granted it is something of a digression, I think the question should nonetheless be put to those who say that before the coming of the Savior there was no truth with those acquainted with the Law, how it could be said by our Lord Jesus Christ that the "keys of knowledge" are with those who held in their hands the books of the Law and the prophets. For this is what the Lord said, "Woe to you, teachers of the Law, for you have taken away the key of knowledge; you did not enter yourselves, and you hindered those who wanted to enter."[124]

4. Nevertheless, as we began to say, we think that the way that seems to us right for understanding the Scriptures and seeking their meaning is such that we are taught what sort of understanding we should have of it by no less than Scripture itself. We have found in Proverbs some such instruction for the examination of divine Scripture given by Solomon. He says, "For your part describe them to yourself threefold in admonition and knowledge, that you may answer words

of truth to those who question you."[125] Therefore, a person ought to describe threefold in his soul the meaning of divine letters, that is, so that the simple may be edified by, so to speak, the body of the Scriptures; for that is what we call the ordinary and narrative meaning.[126] But if any have begun to make some progress and can contemplate something more fully, they should be edified by the soul of Scripture. And those who are perfect are like those concerning whom the Apostle says, "Yet among the perfect we do impart wisdom, although it is not a wisdom of this world or of the rulers of this world, who are doomed to pass away. But we impart a secret and hidden wisdom of God, which God decreed before the ages for our glorification."[127] Such people should be edified by that spiritual Law[128] which has a shadow of the good things to come,[129] edified as by the spirit of Scripture. Thus, just as a human being is said to be made up of body, soul, and spirit, so also is sacred Scripture, which has been granted by God's gracious dispensation for man's salvation.

We see this also indicated in the book of the Shepherd (which some apparently despise) when Hermas is ordered "to write two books," and afterwards he is himself to "announce to the presbyters of the Church" what he has learned from the Spirit. This is what it says, "And you shall write two books, and give one to Clement and one to Grapte. And Grapte shall admonish the widows and orphans; and Clement shall send the message to all the cities outside; and you shall announce it to the presbyters of the Church."[130] Grapte, then, who is commanded to admonish the orphans and widows, is the plain meaning of the letter itself by which are admonished childlike souls, who have not yet deserved to have God as their Father and for this reason are called "orphans." And the "widows" are those souls that have left that unjust husband to whom they had been joined against the Law, but remain "widows" because they have not yet made sufficient progress to be joined to the heavenly bridegroom.[131] But Clement is ordered to send what has been said to those

---

121. See Prov 1:5–6.

122. 1 Cor 2:16, 12–13.

123. See Lk 11:52.

124. Lk 11:52.

125. Prov 22:20–21 (Septuagint).

126. The Latin is *historia*, reflecting the Greek *historia*, one of whose original meanings is "narrative." The translator translates the term throughout as "narrative meaning." The translations "history" or "historical meaning" would be confusing.

127. 1 Cor 2:6–7.

128. See Rom 7:14.

129. See Heb 10:1.

130. *The Shepherd of Hermas*, Vision II.4.3. Origen considered *The Shepherd of Hermas* to be inspired Scripture.

131. See Mt 25:1–12.

who have already left the letter for those "cities which are outside," just as if it said, to those souls which have been edified by the letter and have begun to be outside concern for the body and outside the desires of the flesh. And Hermas himself is ordered to announce what he had learned from the Holy Spirit not by letters or a book but by his living voice to the presbyters of the churches of Christ, that is, to those who because of their capacity for spiritual teaching support the mature meaning of wisdom.

5. But, of course, we must not ignore the fact that there are certain passages in Scripture in which what we have called the body, that is a logically coherent narrative meaning, is not always to be found, as we shall show in what follows. And there are places where only what we have called the soul and the spirit may be understood. I think this is also indicated in the Gospels, when "six stone jars" are said to be "standing there, for the Jewish rites of purification, each holding two or three measures."[132] As I have said, this verse in the Gospel seems to refer to those whom the Apostle calls "Jews inwardly,"[133] because they are purified by the word of Scripture, sometimes holding "two measures," that is, receiving the meanings of the soul and of the spirit, according to what we have just said, and sometimes holding "three measures," when a reading for edification can keep the bodily meaning, which is the narrative meaning. And "six stone jars" are mentioned because they bear a logical relation to those who are placed in this world to be purified. For we read that in six days (which is a perfect number)[134] this world and everything in it were finished.

6. Now the whole multitude of believers, which believes quite faithfully and simply, is a witness to what great profit lies in the first meaning, which I have called narrative. Nor is much argument needed, since the point is perfectly clear to everyone. And the Apostle Paul has given us a great many examples of that meaning which we have called above the soul, as it were, of Scripture, first, for example, the passage in his letter to the Corinthians, "For it is written, 'You shall not muzzle an ox when it is treading out the grain.'"[135] He goes on to explain how this commandment should be understood and says, "Is it for oxen that God is concerned? Does He not speak entirely for our sake? It was written for our sake, because the ploughman should plow in hope and the thresher thresh in hope of a share in the crop."[136] Moreover, a great many other sayings like this one, which are interpreted from the Law in this way, bestow the greatest instruction upon those who hear them.

Then, the spiritual explanation refers, for example, to

someone who can make clear the heavenly things of which those who are Jews according to the flesh[137] served the copies and shadows[138] and the good things to come of which the Law has a shadow,[139] and any similar things found in the holy Scriptures. And the spiritual meaning is involved when it is asked what is that "secret and hidden wisdom of God, which God decreed before the ages for our glorification, which none of the rulers of this world understand,"[140] or in what the Apostle himself observes when he is using certain examples from Exodus or Numbers and says, "Now these things happened to them in a type, but they were written down for us, upon whom the ends of the ages have come."[141] And he gives us an opportunity of understanding how we can direct our minds to the things of which their experiences were types by saying, "For they drank from the spiritual Rock which followed them, and the Rock was Christ."[142]

Moreover, concerning the tabernacle he makes mention in another letter of the command that had been given to Moses, "You shall make everything according to the pattern which was shown you on the mountain."[143] And when he writes to the Galatians and rebukes those who are apparently reading the Law for themselves but do not understand it, because they are unaware that there are allegories in the Scriptures, he says to them with a certain amount of chiding, "Tell me, you who desire to be under the Law, do you not hear the Law? For it is written that Abraham had two sons, one by a slave and one by a free woman. But the son of the slave was born according to the flesh, the son of the free woman through promise. Now this is an allegory: These women are two covenants, and the rest."[144] In this passage we must also consider how carefully the Apostle said what he did, "You who desire to be under the Law"—and not "you who are under the Law"—"do you not hear the Law?" that is, "do you not understand?" or "do you not know?"

---

132. Jn 2:6.

133. Rom 2:29.

134. In *De opificio mundi*, 3, Philo Judaeus (or Philo of Alexandria) explains why 6 is a perfect number. It is the sum of its factors, $6 = 1 \times 2 \times 3$. It is moreover the product of the first male number, 3, and the first female number, 2. Origen, like Philo before him, clearly did not consider the six days of creation as literal measures of time.

135. 1 Cor 9:9; Deut 25:4.	139. See Heb 10:1.
136. 1 Cor 9:9–10.	140. 1 Cor 2:7–8.
137. See Rom 2:28–29; 9:3–5.	141. 1 Cor 10:11 (see 10:1–11).
138. See Heb 8:5.	142. 1 Cor 10:4.

143. Heb 8:5; Ex 25:40. Origen here assumes that Paul is the author of Hebrews (see his discussion in the *Canon of Origen* above).

144. Gal 4:21–27.

Further, in the letter to the Colossians, embracing and drawing together concisely the meaning of the Law as a whole, he says, "Therefore let no one pass judgment on you in questions of food and drink or with regard to a festival or a new moon or a sabbath. These are a shadow of what is to come."[145] And when he writes, as well, to the Hebrews and discusses those who are from the circumcision, he says, "They serve a copy and shadow of the heavenly things."[146] Now those who accept the Apostle's writings as divinely spoken will probably not doubt this conclusion with respect to the five books of Moses because of the preceding examples. But about the rest of the Old Testament narrative they may ask whether what is included in it may also be said to have happened "in a type"[147] to those about whom it is written. We have noticed that the point is addressed in the letter to the Romans, where Paul uses an example from 1 Kings and says, "I have kept for myself seven thousand men who have not bowed the knee to Baal."[148] Paul takes this as spoken in a type about those who are called Israelites "by election,"[149] in order to show that the coming of Christ brought help not only to the Gentiles but also to a great many of the nation of Israel, who were called to salvation.

7. Since these points have been established, we shall sketch out how we should understand divine Scripture in particular points by using as examples and models what we have been able to find. First, we shall repeat and demonstrate the point that the Holy Spirit, who enlightened the ministers of truth, the prophets, and the apostles, by the providence and will of God through the power of His Only Begotten Word, who was God in the beginning with God,[150] [wished first to teach them how][151] to understand the mysteries of those events or purposes that happen among human beings or from human beings. By human beings I now mean souls placed in bodies. They portrayed those mysteries, known and revealed to them by the Spirit, by narrating them as human deeds or by handing down in a type certain legal observances and rules. They did this so that not anyone who wanted would have these mysteries laid bare and ready, so to speak, to be trodden underfoot, but so that the person who devoted himself to studies of this sort with all purity and continence and careful watching might be able in this way to inquire into the profoundly hidden meaning of God's Spirit that had been woven together with an ordinary narrative looking in another direction. And in this way they thought someone might become an ally of the Spirit's knowledge and a participant in the divine counsel. And this is because no soul can arrive at the perfection of knowledge in any other way than by becom-

ing inspired by the truth of divine wisdom. Therefore, it is chiefly the doctrine of God, that is, the Father, Son, and Holy Spirit, that is described by those men filled with the divine Spirit. And then, as we have said, filled with the divine Spirit, they brought forth the mysteries of the Son of God, how the Word was made flesh[152] and for what purpose He went so far as to take the form of a servant.[153] And then it necessarily followed that they taught the race of mortals with divine words about rational creatures, heavenly as well as earthly, the blessed and the lower, and also about the differences among souls and how these differences arose. And finally, it was necessary for us to learn from the divine words what this world is, why it was made, and why there is so much and such great evil on earth, and whether it is only on earth or also in other places.

8. Therefore, although it is the Holy Spirit's purpose to enlighten holy souls, which have dedicated themselves to the service of truth, concerning such matters and others like them, He has in the second place an aim in regard to those who either cannot or will not give themselves to the effort and diligence by which they might deserve to be taught or to know matters so great and excellent. As we have already said, His aim is to envelop and hide secret mysteries in ordinary words under the pretext of a narrative of some kind and of an account of visible things. Therefore, the account of the visible creation is introduced and the making and fashioning of the first man; then his offspring follow in succession. Also some of the exploits done by certain righteous men are recounted, while along with them certain of their crimes as men are recorded; then some instances of the unchastity or wickedness of the impious are described. Moreover, an account of battles is related in order in a marvelous way; and the different fates, now of those who conquer and now of those who are conquered, are described, by which certain ineffable mysteries are revealed to those who know how to examine accounts of this kind. Moreover, in the legal passages of Scripture the law of truth is sown and prophesied by the amazing teaching of wisdom; each one by some divine art of wisdom is woven into a kind of garment and veil for the spiritual meanings. And this is what we have called the body

---

145. Col 2:16–17.

146. Heb 8:5.

147. See 1 Cor 10:11.

148. Rom 11:4; 1 Kings 19:18.

149. Rom 11:5.

150. See Jn 1:1.

151. These words are missing from the text and are conjectured by the editor of the Greek and Latin texts.

152. See Jn 1:14.

153. See Phil 2:7.

of sacred Scripture—so that even by what we have called the garment of the letter itself, since it has been woven by the art of wisdom, a great many can be edified and make progress who otherwise would be unable to do so.

9. But if in all the parts of this garment, that is, the narrative, the logical coherence of the Law had been kept and its order preserved, because we should have a continuous way of understanding, we should not believe that there was anything shut up within the sacred Scriptures in addition to what is disclosed on the first appearance. For this reason the divine wisdom has arranged for there to be certain stumbling blocks or interruptions of the narrative meaning, by inserting in its midst certain impossibilities and contradictions, so that the very interruption of the narrative might oppose the reader, as it were, with certain obstacles thrown in the way. By them wisdom denies a way and an access to the common understanding; and when we are shut out and hurled back, it calls us back to the beginning of another way, so that by gaining a higher and loftier road through entering a narrow footpath[154] it may open for us the immense breadth of divine knowledge.

Moreover, we should also know that since the chief aim of the Holy Spirit was to keep the logical order of the spiritual meaning either in what is bound to happen or in what has already taken place, if anywhere He found that what happened according to the narrative could be fitted to the spiritual meaning, He composed something woven out of both kinds in a single verbal account, always hiding the secret meaning more deeply. But where the narrative of events could not be coherent with the spiritual logic, He sometimes interspersed either events less likely or absolutely impossible to have happened and sometimes events that could have happened but in fact did not. Sometimes He did this with a few words that seem unable to preserve the truth according to the bodily meaning, sometimes by interspersing many words.

This is found with special frequency in the Law, where there are many commandments that are obviously useful in their bodily form, but where there are a good many in which no straightforward useful purpose is evident; and sometimes impossibilities may even be discerned. All these things, as we have said, the Holy Spirit arranged so that from them, since what first appears cannot be true or useful, we might be called back to examine the truth to be sought more deeply and to be investigated more diligently, and might seek a meaning worthy of God in the Scriptures, which we believe were inspired by God. And not only did the Holy Spirit arrange this for what had been written up to the coming of

Christ, but since He is one and the same Spirit and proceeds from the one God, He likewise did the same thing also in the Gospels and the writings of the apostles. For even those accounts He inspired through them He did not weave together apart from the art of His wisdom, whose character we have already explained. Thus, even in these writings He mingled not a few things by which the order of the narrative account is interrupted or cut up so that by the impossibility He might turn and call back the mind of the reader to the examination of the inner meaning.

From *Origen*, translated by Rowan A. Greer (New York: Paulist Press, 1979), 180–88.

Antiochene Interpretation

In contrast to Clement and Origen, who espoused the allegorical method of interpretation of the Alexandrian school, **Diodore of Tarsus** (died ca. 390), the primary exponent of the Antiochene method, emphasized historical, plain, and literal readings of biblical texts in the Prologue to his *Commentary on the Psalms* and in the Preface to his *Commentary on Psalm 118*.

DIODORE OF TARSUS
Prologue to *Commentary on the Psalms*

We will not shrink from the truth but will expound it according to the historical substance (*historia*) and the plain literal sense (*lexis*). At the same time, we will not disparage anagogy and the higher *theōria*. For history is not opposed to *theōria*. On the contrary, it proves to be the foundation and the basis of the higher senses. One thing is to be watched, however: *theōria* must never be understood as doing away with the underlying sense; it would then be no longer *theōria* but allegory. For whenever anything else is said apart from the foundational sense, we have not *theōria* but allegory. Even the apostle did not discard history at any point although he could introduce *theōria* and call it allegory.[155] He was not ignorant of the term but was teaching us that, if the term "allegory" is judged by its conceptual content, it must be taken in the sense of *theōria*, not violating in any way the nature of the historical substance. But those who pretend to "improve" Scripture and who are wise in their own conceit have

---

154. See Mt 7:13–14.

155. See Gal 4:24. (The notes for this selection are by Gerhart and Udoh.)

introduced allegory because they are careless about the historical substance, or they simply abuse it. They follow not the apostle's intention but their own vain imagination, forcing the reader to take one thing for another. Thus they read "demon" for abyss, "devil" for dragon, and so on. I stop here so that I will not be compelled to talk foolishly myself in order to refute foolishness.

While repudiating this (kind of interpretation) once and for all, we are not prevented from "theorizing" responsibly and from lifting the conceptual content into higher anagogy. We may compare, for example, Cain and Abel to the Jewish synagogue and the church; we may attempt to show that like Cain's sacrifice the Jewish synagogue was rejected, while the offerings of the church are being well received as was Abel's offering at the time;[156] we may interpret the unblemished sacrificial lamb required by the law as the Lord.[157] This method neither sets aside history nor repudiates *theōria*. Rather, as a realistic, middle-of-the road approach which takes into account both history and *theōria,* it frees us, on the one hand, from a Hellenism which says one thing for another and introduces foreign subject matter; on the other hand, it does not yield to Judaism and choke us by forcing us to treat the literal reading of the text as the only one worthy of attention and honor, while not allowing the exploration of a higher sense beyond the letter also. In summary, this is what the person approaching the interpretation of the divine psalms ought to know.

From Karlfried Froehlich, ed. and trans., *Biblical Interpretation in the Early Church* (Philadelphia: Fortress Press, 1984), 85–86.

DIODORE OF TARSUS

Preface to *Commentary on Psalm 118*

In any approach to holy Scripture, the literal reading of the text reveals some truths while the discovery of other truths requires the application of *theōria.* Now, given the vast differences between *historia* and *theōria,* allegory and figuration (*tropologia*) or parable (*parabolē*), the interpreter must classify and determine each figurative expression with care and precision so that the reader can see what is history and what is *theōria,* and draw his conclusions accordingly.

Above all, one must keep in mind one point which I have stated very clearly in my prologue to the psalter: Holy Scripture knows the term "allegory" but not its application. Even the blessed Paul uses the term: "this is said by way of allegory, for they are two covenants."[158] But his use of the word and his application is different from that of the Greeks.

The Greeks speak of allegory when something is understood in one way but said in another. Since one or two examples must be mentioned for the sake of clarity, let me give an example. The Greeks say that Zeus, changing himself into a bull, seized Europa and carried her across the sea to foreign places. This story is not understood as it reads but is taken to mean that Europa was carried across the sea having boarded a ship with a bull as figurehead. A real bull could not possibly swim such a distance across the ocean. This is allegory. Or another example: Zeus called Hera his sister and his wife. The plain text implies that Zeus had intercourse with his sister Hera so that the same person was both his wife and his sister. This is what the letter suggests; but the Greeks allegorize it to mean that, when ether, a fiery element, mingles with air, it produces a certain mixture which influences events on earth. Now, since air adjoins ether, the text calls these elements brother and sister because of their vicinity, but husband and wife because of their mixture. Of such kind are the allegories of the Greeks. The above examples should suffice lest, with all this allegory, I as an interpreter fall into foolishness myself as I mentioned earlier.

Holy Scripture does not speak of allegory in this way. In what way then does it speak? Let me explain briefly. Scripture does not repudiate in any way the underlying prior history but "theorizes," that is, it develops a higher vision (*theōria*) of other but similar events in addition, without abrogating history. As a test case, let us consider the very text of the apostle quoted above. This will be the most effective demonstration of the affirmation that the apostle means this *theōria* when he speaks of allegory. Based on the historical account of Isaac and Ishmael and their mothers, I mean Sarah and Hagar, Paul develops the higher *theōria* in the following way: He understands Hagar as Mount Sinai but Isaac's mother as the free Jerusalem, the future mother of all believers.[159] The fact that the apostle "theorizes" in this way does not mean that he repudiates the historical account. For who could persuade him to say that the story of Hagar and Sarah was untrue? With the account as a firm foundation, he develops his *theōria* on top of it; he understands the underlying facts as events on a higher level. It is this developed *theōria* which the apostle calls allegory. As we said, he is aware of the term "allegory" but does not at all accept its application. I have expressed this

---

156. See Gen 4:3–7.   157. See Ex 12:3–5; Num 28:16–19.
158. Gal 4:24. (The notes for this selection are by Gerhart and Udoh.)
159. See Gal 4:24–28.

conviction in my prologue to the psalter already, but for the sake of clarity it bears repetition here.

Figuration (*tropologia*) is present when, in describing an event, the prophet turns words with an obvious meaning into an expanded illustration of what he is saying. The figurative expression is then clarified by the continuation of the text. For instance, David says of the people: "You (God) removed a vine from Egypt";[160] then having identified the people with the vine and leaving no doubt by adding, "you drove away the nations and transplanted it," he continues describing the people as if he were speaking of a vine. He mentions that the vine grew and unfolded its shoots;[161] he asks: "Why have you broken down its hedge so that all who pass by on their way pick its fruits?"[162] and adds: "A wild boar from the thicket has laid it waste."[163] Now it is quite clear that this is a covert allusion to Antiochus Epiphanes[164] who brought great harm upon the Maccabees, yet at the same time the prophet continues his figure; speaking of the people as a vine, he calls Antiochus a wild boar who tramples down the vine. Isaiah also uses this figure of the people, calling them a vineyard and saying: "My friend had a vineyard on the hillside on fertile ground. I surrounded it with a wall and fenced it in," and so on.[165] At the very end, clarifying the figurative character of the account, or rather of his prophecy, he adds: "For the vineyard of the Lord of hosts is the house of Israel, and the man of Judah is his beloved plantation. I waited for him to execute judgment but he acted lawlessly; instead of righteousness there was an outcry."[166] This is figuration (*tropologia*).

The parabolic expression (*parabolē*) is easy to recognize when it follows upon an introductory "like" or "as." To give some examples: "Like water I am poured out and all my bones are scattered";[167] or "I have become to them like a dead abomination."[168] There are many instances which follow this pattern. Often, however, Scripture speaks parabolically even without this introduction. It says, for instance: "You have made my arm a brazen bow"[169] instead of "like a brazen bow"; or: "And when Abraham looked up with his eyes, he saw three men"[170] instead of "something resembling three men." In these cases, Scripture formulates parables by way of ellipsis, omitting the word "like." Frequently, Scripture also calls a narrative or a teaching "parable," for instance, when we read: "I will open my mouth in a parable, I will utter problems from the beginning."[171] Here the author's teaching, or at least the narrative, is called a parable. Actually, the parable itself may sometimes be called a "problem." Thus, it is even possible to speak of a problem as an "enigma": Samson proposed such a "problem" to the Philistines, or rather to

the Palestinians—the Philistines are in fact the Palestinians—by saying: "Out of the eater came forth food and out of the strong one came forth sweetness."[172] He would have defeated the Palestinians had he not been betrayed, being unable to resist his lust for women, so that his sophisticated problem ended up being foolishness. This is the language of parable and problem, sometimes introduced by "like" or "as," sometimes not.

One would probably classify much of the material in the books of Moses as enigmas (*ainigmata*) rather than allegories. When the author writes: "The serpent said to the woman"; "the woman said to the serpent"; "God said to the serpent,"[173] we have enigmas. Not that there was no serpent; indeed there was a serpent, but the devil acted through it. Moses speaks of the serpent as the visible animal but under this cover hints at the devil in a hidden way. If this was allegory, only the word "serpent" should be there as we explained earlier. The truth is that there was both a reality and an enigma. The reality was the serpent but, since a serpent is by nature irrational and yet was speaking, it is obvious that it spoke empowered by the devil. (Christ), who has the authority to reveal mysteries and enigmas, points this out in the gospels when he says of the devil: "He was a murderer from the beginning and has not stood in the truth . . . , for he is a liar and the father of it."[174] This phrase, "and the father of it," is very apt, for the devil was the first one to lie as well as the one who begot lying. Therefore Christ adds, "and the father of it," instead of saying, "the lie in person." Now the Lord was able to clarify enigmas; the prophets and apostles could only report realities. Therefore, both Moses and the Apostle Paul said "serpent." The latter puts it this way: "I fear lest, as the serpent seduced Eve by its guile, so your minds may be corrupted";[175] here he also hints at the devil by mentioning

---

160. Ps 79:9 (Septuagint) = Ps 80:8.

161. Ps 79:10–12 (Septuagint) = Ps 80:9–11.

162. Ps 79:13 (Septuagint) = Ps 80:12.

163. Ps 79:14 (Septuagint) = Ps 80:13.

164. Antiochus IV Epiphanes (175–164 BCE), the Seleucid king who provoked the Maccabean crisis in 169 BCE.

165. Isa 5:1–2.

166. Isa 5:7.

167. Ps 21:15 (Septuagint) = Ps 22:14.

168. Ps 37:21 (Septuagint, variant reading).

169. Ps 17:35 (Septuagint); see also Ps 18:34.

170. Gen 18:2.

171. Ps 77:2 (Septuagint) = Ps 78:2.

172. Judg 14:14.   174. Jn 8:44.

173. See Gen 3:1–5, 14.   175. 2 Cor 11:3.

the serpent. The serpent is not a rational animal for him but points enigmatically to the devil acting through it. Scheming is not the action of an irrational animal but of a rational being. Our brief remarks here must suffice on the topic of these figurative expressions. We have mentioned only a few points among many, leaving room for industrious scholars to make further points on the basis of similar examples.

In contrast, history (*historia*) is the pure account of the actual event of the past. It is authentic if it is not interwoven with the speaker's reflections, extraneous episodes, characterizations or fictitious speeches as is, for example, the story of Job.[176] A plain, clear, and concise historical account does not weary the reader with reflections of the author and long characterizations.

Let this be enough on this mode of expression. But since, by the grace of God, I intend to interpret the 118th psalm, I had to discuss in detail the above-mentioned modes of expression, as this psalm contains many of them. Therefore, I had to give my readers a clear statement about them in the preface already in order to alert them to the fact that some parts of the psalms are meant to be taken literally while others are figurative expressions, parables, or enigmas. What is emphatically not present is allegory. Of course, some interpreters have fancied that it is. They brush aside any historical understanding, introduce foolish fables of their own making in place of the text, and burden the reader's ears, leaving their minds devoid of pious thoughts. If they said that, being an utterance of God, this psalm accompanies generations of human beings, conforming itself to events both actual and on a higher plane, their interpretation would be quite correct. I am attempting to say something like this: In predicting future events, the prophets adapted their words both to the time in which they were speaking and to later times. Their words sounded hyperbolic in their contemporary setting but were entirely fitting and consistent at the time when the prophecies were fulfilled. For the sake of clarity there is nothing wrong with stressing this point more than once.

From Karlfried Froehlich, ed. and trans., *Biblical Interpretation in the Early Church* (Philadelphia: Fortress Press, 1984), 87–91.

☙ **Theodore of Mopsuestia** (ca. 350–428), a student of Diodore of Tarsus and a member of the Antiochene school of interpretation, expounds upon the meaning of true allegory in his *Commentary on Galatians*, written around the turn of the fifth century.

Commentary on Galatians, 4:24

These things are said allegorically.

There are some people who make it their business to pervert the meaning of the divine Scriptures and to thwart whatever is to be found there. They invent foolish tales of their own and give to their nonsense the name of allegory. By using the apostle's word, they imagine that they have found a way to undermine the meaning of everything in Scripture—they keep on using the apostle's expression "allegorical." They do not realize what a difference there is between their use of the term and the apostle's use of it here. For the apostle does not destroy history; he does not get rid of what has already happened. He sets things out as they happened in the past and uses the history of what happened in support of his own purpose—as when he says, "it corresponds to the Jerusalem that now is"[177] and "as then the one who was born according to the flesh persecuted the one who was born according to the spirit."[178] This shows that he acknowledged the history to be primary. Otherwise he would not have described the things that happened in relation to Hagar as corresponding to "the Jerusalem that now is"—something, that is to say, which he acknowledges to be a present reality. And he would not have said "as" except with reference to something he believed to exist; for the use of the word "as" clearly implies a comparison, and one cannot draw a comparison where the terms of the comparison do not really exist. And by the addition of the word "then" he declares himself uncertain of the length of time involved; but the whole question of time would be irrelevant, if it never happened.

That is how the apostle speaks. But they act in a totally opposite way; their wish is to deny any difference between the whole of the history recorded in divine Scripture and dreams that occur at night. Adam, they say, is not Adam—this being a place where they are especially prone to interpret divine Scripture in a spiritual way (spiritual interpretation is what they like to have their nonsense called)—paradise is not paradise and the serpent is not a serpent. What I would like to say in reply to them is that once they start removing bits of history they will be left without any history at all. In that case, they must tell us how they will be in a position to say

---

176. Thus, the story of Job may not be considered authentic history.
177. Gal 4:25. (The notes for this selection are by Gerhart and Udoh.)
178. Gal 4:29.

who was the first man to be created or how man became disobedient or how the sentence of death was introduced. If it is from the Scriptures that they have learnt their answers to these questions, it follows that their talk of "allegory" is obvious nonsense, because it is clearly irrelevant at all these points. If on the other hand they are right and what is written is not a record of things that happened but is a pointer to some other profound truth in need of interpretation—some spiritual truth it may be, to use the phrase they like, which they have grasped through being such spiritual people themselves—then they must tell us by what means they have acquired these notions. How can they assert these notions, as if they were things they had learnt from the teaching of divine Scripture?

I pass over in silence for the moment the fact that if this were the case, one would be unable to see any reason for the events concerning Christ. The apostle says that he revoked the disobedience of Adam and did away with the sentence of death. What are these things that are said to have happened in the past and where did they happen, if (as they say) the historical account of them does not mean that but means something else? What is to be made of the apostolic saying, "I am afraid that as the serpent seduced Eve,"[179] if there was no serpent, no Eve, and no seduction by him at all? Many other passages too show clearly that the apostle always treated the history of the ancients as something real.

So in this passage he is at pains to prove his point on the basis of things that had happened and which were acknowledged by the Jews. That was his intention all along. And the substance of that intention was to show the superiority of the things of Christ to those of the law and the far greater dignity of the righteousness we have compared to that of the law. So he says there are two testaments, one given through Moses and the other through Christ. What he calls the testament in Christ is the resurrection Christ promised to us all when he was the first to rise from the dead. We have dealt with this point more explicitly in our commentary on the Epistle to the Hebrews.[180] The things that were given by Moses had the intention of enabling those who received the law to live under it and to receive the righteousness that comes from it. (That was why they came out of Egypt and were established in a distant place where they could be free from all intermingling with other nations and could keep the law given to them with appropriate care.) In a similar way the things concerning Christ have the intention and goal of doing away with death, of bringing about the resurrection of all men who have lived at any time, of enabling them to

live the life of an immortal and, greatest of all, of making it impossible for them to sin any more by virtue of that grace of the Spirit which is in them and by which we will be kept safe from every kind of sin. This is true and complete justification. He appropriately gave them both the same name "testament"; for the things taught by the law were the very things put into practice by grace, namely love of God and neighbour. These are the commands that the law told us to keep, clearly teaching that we ought not to sin in any way. Grace brings it to practical fulfillment by means of the resurrection and of that immortality which will then be ours through the Spirit by whom we will then be controlled and so enabled not to sin at all.

So there is justification both in the law and also with Christ. With the law it is achieved by anyone who is able with much effort and sweat to achieve it. It is very hard, or to speak more accurately, impossible—if one chooses to judge the matter with full legal exactitude. For it is impossible for any living man to be wholly free of sin. That can be acquired only by grace; for we shall be enabled not to sin any more at that future time when all effort having been laid aside we will receive the justification that comes from Christ.

He mentions Hagar and Sarah. One of them had a child in the ordinary course of nature while the other was unable to bear a child but had Isaac by grace; and of the two the child born by way of grace turned out to be much the more highly esteemed. He compares them in order to show that now too the justification by Christ is far better than the other, because it is acquired by grace. He relates the one who had a child in the course of nature to the justification which is according to the law and makes the one who had a child against all hope correspond to that justification which is according to grace. This is because a life according to law is appropriate to the present, whereas for those who have once risen again and been made free of corruption, circumcision and the offering of sacrifices, not to mention the observation of special days, are all irrelevant.

There are things that happen in the course of nature—for example the entry into this life by birth—where life according to the law does seem still to have a place. But there is also a birth of grace, by which everyone rises again and is born into a future life in which the justification of Christ is fully implemented. So to represent the justification according to

179. 2 Cor 11:3.
180. Only fragments of which have survived.

the law he has taken the one who bore a child in the order of nature, since the law has a role in controlling those who are born in this life, born according to the order of nature. To represent the justification according to Christ, he has taken the one who bore a child by grace, since this is fulfilled in those who are seen to have risen again at some time and who by grace look forward to that second birth beyond all hope.

This then is why he said: "These things are said allegorically."[181] By allegory he means the comparison which can be made between things which have happened in the past and things which are the case now.

From Maurice Wiles and Mark Santer, eds., *Documents in Early Christian Thought* (Cambridge: Cambridge University Press, 1975), 151–54.

༄ **John Chrysostom** (ca. 354–407) was bishop of Constantinople, a student of Diodore of Tarsus, and a member of the Antiochene school of interpretation. He gives his methods for understanding Scripture in Homily 3 (on Gen 1:1–5).

JOHN CHRYSOSTOM
Homily 3, 1–13

1. Reading the Holy Scriptures is like a treasure. With a treasure, you see, anyone able to find a tiny nugget gains for himself great wealth; likewise in the case of Sacred Scripture, you can get from a small phrase a great wealth of thought and immense riches. The Word of God is not only like a treasure, but is also like a spring gushing with everflowing waters in a mighty flood; this we all perceived from what we did yesterday. We began, remember, at the opening of the book of *Genesis* on the words, "In the beginning God made heaven and earth,"[182] and dealt completely with all its contents, without however being able to grasp it fully. You see, great is the yield of this treasure and the flow of this spiritual fountain. Don't be surprised if we have experienced this: our forebears drank from these waters to the limit of their capacity, and those who come after us will try to do likewise, without risk of exhausting them; instead the flood will increase and the streams will be multiplied.

2. Such, after all, is the nature of spiritual streams: the more earnestly anyone tries to draw the water, the more they abound and the spiritual grace is increased. Hence Christ said, "If anyone thirsts, let him come to me and drink. If anyone believes in me, as Scripture says, rivers of living water will flow from his belly,"[183] indicating to us the abundance

of the waters. So since this is the nature of spiritual waters, come, let us all constantly bring the vessels of our minds to be filled, and thus return home. For whenever the Spirit sees an ardent desire and a watchful mind, he freely grants it abundant grace. So step aside from your daily preoccupations and from things that threaten to suffocate your thinking like weeds, and let us give free rein to spiritual desires so that we may gain great advantage from this consideration and receive much benefit; then we can go home.

3. But in order that the sermon may be clearer to you, let us remind you in your goodness of some details of what was said yesterday so as to fit together, as into one whole, what is to be said today with what was said yesterday. We showed you yesterday, as you will recall, how blessed Moses explained to us the creation of these visible elements in saying that "in the beginning God made heaven and earth; the land was invisible and lacking all shape."[184] And we taught you why he left the land unshaped and unpeopled, and I think you remember it all precisely, so today we must proceed to what follows in the text. You see, when he says, "The land was invisible and lacking all shape," he teaches us precisely how it came to be invisible and lacking all shape, adding, "Darkness was over the deep, and the Spirit of God moved over the water."[185] Notice in this case, I ask you, the economy of the blessed author, how he does not describe all created things individually, but teaches us which items were produced together by mentioning heaven and earth and passing over the rest. I mean, he had made no mention of the creation of the waters, but then said, "Darkness was over the deep, and the Spirit of God moved over the water"; this, you see, was covering the face of the earth, darkness I mean, and the depths of water. From this we learned that all that could be seen was depths of water, covered in darkness and having need of the wise creator to remove all this shapelessness and bring everything to a condition of order.

4. "Darkness," the text says, "was over the deep, and the Spirit of God moved over the water." What is meant by that part of the text, "The Spirit of God moved over the water"? It seems to me to mean this, that some lifegiving force was present in the waters: it wasn't simply water that was stationary and immobile, but moving and possessed of some vital

---

181. Gal 4:24.
182. Gen 1:1. (The notes for this selection are by Gerhart and Udoh.)
183. Jn 7:37–38; see Prov 18:4 (Septuagint); Isa 58:11 (Septuagint).
184. Gen 1:2 (Septuagint).   185. Gen 1:2 (Septuagint).

power. I mean, what doesn't move is quite useless, whereas what moves is capable of many things. So, to teach us that this water, great and cumbersome as it was, had some vital power, he says, "The Spirit of God moved over the water." It is not without reason that Sacred Scripture makes this early comment. Instead, it intends later to describe to us that creatures in these waters were produced by command of the creator of all things, and so at this point it teaches the listener that water was not idly formed, but was moving, and shifting, and flowing over everything.

5. So, when the shapeless mass of all that could be seen lay about on all sides, God the mighty artificer issued his command and the shapeless mass took on form, the surpassing beauty of this blinding light appeared and dissipated the palpable gloom, illuminating everything. "God said," the text reads, "'Let light be created, and light was created.'"[186] He spoke: it was created; he gave his command: darkness was scattered and light produced. See his ineffable power? Yet there are those who ignore the sequence of the text, caught up as they are in their error, and who pay no heed to the words of blessed Moses, "In the beginning God made heaven and earth," and the following verse, "The land was invisible and lacking all shape" on account of its being obscured by the darkness and the waters, the Lord having decided (you see) to create it in the beginning like this. These people say that matter was the basis for creation, and that darkness preexisted. What could be worse than this madness? You heard that "in the beginning God made heaven and earth," and that from nothing things were created, and do you say that matter was the basis for creation? Who in their right minds would come up with such idiocy? Surely the creator is not human, needing some basis for creation so as to reveal his artistry? God it is to whom all things respond as he creates them by word and command. Remember how he merely spoke, and light was created and darkness dissipated.

6. "God separated light from darkness."[187] What is meant by "He separated"? He gave each its own place and defined its appropriate time. And when this had been done, he then gave each its proper name. The text goes on, you see: "God called the light day, and the darkness night."[188] Do you see the excellent distinction and the wonderful craftsmanship, surpassing all comment, happening by a single word and command? Do you see the degree of considerateness employed by the blessed author, or rather the loving God through the tongue of the author, instructing the race of men to know the plan of created things, and who was the creator of all, and how each came into being?

7. I mean, since mankind was yet untutored and could not understand more elaborate matters, the Holy Spirit accordingly explained everything to us by moving the author's tongue in such a way as to take account of the limitations of the listeners. To be convinced that it was on account of the incompleteness of our understanding that he employed such considerateness in his explanation, compare the approach of the Son of Thunder:[189] when humankind had advanced along the path to perfection, no longer did he have them move by this lower way, but led his listeners to a loftier teaching. "In the beginning was the Word," he said, you remember, "the Word was with God, and the Word was God,"[190] and added, "He was the true Light, which enlightened everyone coming into the world."[191] In other words, just as in our text this visible light, produced by command of the Lord, removed the darkness from our vision, in like manner the light coming to our minds dissipated the darkness of error, and led those in error to the truth.

8. So let us receive the teachings of Sacred Scripture with deep gratitude, not resisting the truth nor persisting in darkness, but hastening towards the light and performing actions proper to the light and the day. That is what Paul recommends to us when he says, "Let us walk becomingly as the light of day suggests" and not perform actions proper to the dark.[192]

9. The text goes on: "God called the light day, and he called the darkness night."[193] Now, a detail that almost escaped us we need to pick up again. I mean, when it said, "'Let light be created,' and light was created," it added, "God saw that the light was good."[194] See there, dearly beloved, the extent of the considerateness in the language. What is the point of the remark? Is it that before the light comes into being he does not know it is beautiful, whereas after its appearance the sight of it shows its creator the beauty of what appears? What sort of sense would that make? I mean, if a man works at some piece of craftsmanship, and before he completes the thing he is making and puts final touches to it he sees the use to which he will put the thing he is making, how much more the creator of all, who by his word brings into being everything from non-being, sees that the light is good before he creates it. So why did he use this expression?

186. Gen 1:3.
187. Gen 1:4.
188. Gen 1:5.
189. See Mk 3:17.
194. Gen 1:3–4a.

190. Jn 1:1.
191. Jn 1:9.
192. Rom 13:13.
193. Gen 1:5.

10. This blessed author spoke this way out of considerateness for the way human beings speak. And just as people work on something with great care, and when they bring their efforts to completion they parade what they have made for scrutiny and commendation, so Sacred Scripture speaks in that way, showing considerateness for the limitations of our hearing when it said, "God saw that the light was good,"[195] and added, "God separated light from darkness; he called the light day, and he called the darkness night,"[196] allotting to each its own particular area and establishing limits for each right from the beginning so that they could keep to them permanently without interference. Everyone in his right mind can understand this, how from that time till this the light has not surpassed its limits, nor has darkness exceeded its due order, resulting in confusion and disruption. Really, this fact alone should suffice to oblige people obdurate in their lack of response to come to faith and obedience to the words of Sacred Scripture so as to imitate the order in the elements, respecting as they do their course uninterruptedly, and not overstep their own limitations but rather recognize the extent of their own nature.

11. Then, when he had assigned to each its own name, he linked the two together in the words, "Evening came, and morning came: one day."[197] He made a point of speaking of the end of the day and the end of the night as one, so as to grasp a certain order and sequence in visible things and avoid any impression of confusion.

12. Now, we are in a position to learn from the Holy Spirit, through the tongue of this blessed author, what things were created on the first day and what things on the other days. This itself is a mark of the considerateness of the loving God. I mean, his all-powerful hand and boundless wisdom were not at a loss even to create everything in one day. Why say "one day"? even in a brief moment. Yet it was not because of its utility to him that he produced anything that exists, since being self-sufficient he is in need of nothing. It was rather out of his loving kindness and goodness that he created everything; accordingly he created things in sequence and provided us with a clear instruction about created things through the tongue of the blessed author, so that we might learn about them precisely and not fall into the error of those led by purely human reasoning. You see, if there are still those, despite this manner of creation, who say that things get existence from themselves, what would these people not have been rash enough to invent in their anxiety to say and do everything against their own welfare, had not God employed such considerateness and instruction?

13. After all, what could be more pitiful and more stupid than people coming up with arguments like this, claiming that beings get existence of themselves, and withdrawing all creation from God's providence? How could you have the idea, I ask you, that so many elements and such great arrangement were being guided without anyone to supervise and control it all? Surely no ship ever managed to navigate the waves of the sea without a pilot, or soldier do brave deed with no general in command, or house stand firm with no householder in charge—whereas this immense universe and the design of all these elements could happen simply by chance without anyone present with the power to guide it all, controlling and maintaining all things in existence from his innate wisdom, is this feasible?

From John Chrysostom, *Homilies on Genesis 1–17*, translated by Robert C. Hill, Fathers of the Church, vol. 74 (Washington, DC: Catholic University of America Press, 1986), 39–45.

LATIN INTERPRETATION

The first selection by **Jerome** (ca. 347–420), *Prefaces to the Vulgate Version of the New Testament: The Four Gospels* (addressed to Pope Damasus), was written between 382 and 385 at Rome and presents his views on the controversy generated by his revision of the Old Latin texts of the New Testament on the basis of Greek manuscripts. In the next selection by Jerome, *The Prologue to Genesis*, he addresses the points of contention offered by his detractors when he translated the Old Testament into Latin directly from the Hebrew (398–405). His letter to Pope Damasus, Letter 18A, written from Constantinople in 381, is the earliest of his expository letters and deals with the interpretation of the prophetic works.

JEROME

Prefaces to the Vulgate Version of the New Testament: The Four Gospels

You urge me to revise the old Latin version, and, as it were, to sit in judgment on the copies of the Scriptures which are now scattered throughout the whole world; and, inasmuch as they differ from one another, you would have me decide which of them agree with the Greek original. The labour is

---

195. Gen 1:4a.
196. Gen 1:4b–5a.
197. Gen 1:5b.

one of love, but at the same time both perilous and presumptuous; for in judging others I must be content to be judged by all; and how can I dare to change the language of the world in its hoary old age, and carry it back to the early days of its infancy? Is there a man, learned or unlearned, who will not, when he takes the volume into his hands, and perceives that what he reads does not suit his settled tastes, break out immediately into violent language, and call me a forger and a profane person for having the audacity to add anything to the ancient books, or to make any changes or corrections therein? Now there are two consoling reflections which enable me to bear the odium—in the first place, the command is given by you who are the supreme bishop; and secondly, even on the showing of those who revile us, readings at variance with the early copies cannot be right. For if we are to pin our faith to the Latin texts, it is for our opponents to tell us *which;* for there are almost as many forms of texts as there are copies. If, on the other hand, we are to glean the truth from a comparison of *many,* why not go back to the original Greek and correct the mistakes introduced by inaccurate translators, and the blundering alterations of confident but ignorant critics, and, further, all that has been inserted or changed by copyists more asleep than awake? I am not discussing the Old Testament, which was turned into Greek by the Seventy elders and has reached us by a descent of three steps. I do not ask what Aquila[198] and Symmachus[199] think, or why Theodotion[200] takes a middle course between the ancients and the moderns. I am willing to let that be the true translation which had apostolic approval. I am now speaking of the New Testament. This was undoubtedly composed in Greek, with the exception of the work of Matthew the Apostle, who was the first to commit to writing the Gospel of Christ, and who published his work in Judaea in Hebrew characters. We must confess that as we have it in our language it is marked by discrepancies, and now that the stream is distributed into different channels we must go back to the fountainhead. I pass over those manuscripts which are associated with the names of Lucian and Hesychius,[201] and the authority of which is perversely maintained by a handful of disputatious persons. It is obvious that these writers could not amend anything in the Old Testament after the labours of the Seventy; and it was useless to correct the New, for versions of Scripture which already exist in the languages of many nations show that their additions are false. I therefore promise in this short Preface the four Gospels only, which are to be taken in the following order, Matthew, Mark, Luke, John, as they have been revised by a comparison of the Greek manuscripts. Only early ones

have been used. But to avoid any great divergences from the Latin which we are accustomed to read, I have used my pen with some restraint, and while I have corrected only such passages as seemed to convey a different meaning, I have allowed the rest to remain as they are.

From Saint Jerome, *Letters and Select Works,* translated by W. H. Fremantle, with the assistance of G. Lewis and W. G. Martley, A Select Library of Nicene and Post-Nicene Fathers of the Christian Church, edited by Philip Schaff and Henry Wace, 2nd ser., vol. 6 (1893; Grand Rapids, MI: Eerdmans, 1969), 487–88.

JEROME

The Prologue to Genesis

I have received letters so long and eagerly desired from my dear Desiderius, who, as if the future had been foreseen, shares his name with Daniel,[202] entreating me to put our friends in possession of a translation of the Pentateuch from Hebrew into Latin. The work is certainly hazardous and it is exposed to the attacks of my calumniators, who maintain that it is through contempt of the Seventy that I have set to work to forge a new version to take the place of the old. They thus test ability as they do wine; whereas I have again and again declared that I dutifully offer in the Tabernacle of God what I can, and have pointed out that the great gifts which one man brings are not marred by the inferior gifts of another. But I was stimulated to undertake the task by the zeal of Origen, who blended with the old edition Theodotion's translation and used throughout the work as distinguishing marks the asterisk * and the obelus †, that is the star and the spit, the first of which makes what had previously been defective to beam with light, while the other transfixes and slaughters all that was superfluous. But I was encouraged above all by the authoritative publications of the Evangelists and Apostles, in which we read much taken from

198. Said to have been a Jewish proselyte from Sinope in Pontus, Aquila is credited with having translated the Hebrew Bible into Greek in the second century CE for the use of Greek-speaking Jews, since by this time the Septuagint had become a Christian text. (The notes for this selection are by Gerhart and Udoh.)

199. Probably a Samaritan by birth, Symmachus is said to have produced a third (Theodotion's being the second) translation of the Hebrew Bible. His translation is much less literal than Aquila's.

200. The second translator of the Hebrew Bible after Aquila. Theodotion is said to have been from Ephesus, and his translation, as Jerome goes on to state, is midway between Aquila's literalism and Symmachus's free rendering of the Hebrew text.

201. Both Lucian (in Syria) and Hesychius (in Egypt) produced recensions of biblical manuscripts in the mid–third century.

202. That is, "Man of desires" (*vir desideriorum*), according to the Vulgate text of Dan 9:23. (The notes for this selection are by Gerhart and Udoh.)

the Old Testament which is not found in our manuscripts. For example, "Out of Egypt have I called my Son";[203] "For he shall be called a Nazarene";[204] and "They shall look on him whom they pierced";[205] and "Rivers of living water shall flow out of his belly";[206] and "Things which eye hath not seen, nor ear heard, nor have entered into the heart of man, which God hath prepared for them that love him";[207] and many other passages which lack their proper context. Let us ask our opponents then where these things are written, and when they are unable to tell, let us produce them from the Hebrew. The first passage is in Hosea (11:1), the second in Isaiah (11:1), and the third in Zechariah (12:10), the fourth in Proverbs (18:4), the fifth also in Isaiah (64:4). Being ignorant of all this many follow the ravings of the Apocrypha, and prefer to the inspired books the melancholy trash which comes to us from Spain. It is not for me to explain the causes of the error. The Jews say it was deliberately and wisely done to prevent Ptolemy who was a monotheist from thinking the Hebrews acknowledged two deities. And that which chiefly influenced them in thus acting was the fact that the king appeared to be falling into Platonism. In a word, wherever Scripture evidenced some sacred truth respecting Father, Son, and Holy Spirit, they either translated the passage differently, or passed it over altogether in silence, so that they might both satisfy the king, and not divulge the secrets of the faith. I do not know whose false imagination led him to invent the story of the seventy cells at Alexandria, in which, though separated from each other, the translators were said to have written the same words. Aristeas, the champion of that same Ptolemy, and Josephus, long after, relate nothing of the kind; their account is that the Seventy assembled in one basilica consulted together, and did not prophesy. For it is one thing to be a prophet, another to be a translator. The former, through the Spirit, foretells things to come; the latter must use his learning and facility in speech to translate what he understands. It can hardly be that we must suppose Tully was inspired with oratorical spirit when he translated Xenophon's *Oeconomics,* Plato's *Protagoras,* and the oration of Demosthenes in defence of Ctesiphon. Otherwise the Holy Spirit must have quoted the same books in one sense through the Seventy Translators, in another through the Apostles, so that, whereas they said nothing of a given matter, these falsely affirm that it was so written. What then? Are we condemning our predecessors? By no means; but following the zealous labours of those who have preceded us we contribute such work as lies in our power in the name of the Lord. They translated before the Advent of Christ, and

expressed in ambiguous terms that which they knew not. We after His Passion and Resurrection write not prophecy so much as history. For one style is suitable to what we hear, another to what we see. The better we understand a subject, the better we describe it. Hearken then, my rival; listen, my calumniator; I do not condemn, I do not censure the Seventy, but I am bold enough to prefer the Apostles to them all. It is the apostle through whose mouth I hear the voice of Christ, and I read that in the classification of spiritual gifts they are placed before prophets,[208] while interpreters occupy almost the lowest place.[209] Why are you tormented with jealousy? Why do you inflame the minds of the ignorant against me? Wherever in translation I seem to you to go wrong, ask the Hebrews, consult their teachers in different towns. The words which exist in their Scriptures concerning Christ your copies do not contain. The case is different if they have rejected passages which were afterward used against them by the Apostles, and the Latin texts are more correct than the Greek, the Greek than the Hebrew.

From *Theodoret, Jerome, Gennadius, Rufinus: Historical Writings,* A Select Library of Nicene and Post-Nicene Fathers of the Christian Church, edited by Philip Schaff and Henry Wace, 2nd ser., vol. 3 (1892; Grand Rapids, MI: Eerdmans, 1969), 515–16.

JEROME

Letter 18A (to Pope Damasus), I.1–XII.2 (commentary on Isa 6:1–9)

And it came to pass in the year that King Ozias died: I saw the Lord sitting upon a throne high and elevated, and the house was filled by His glory. 2. And seraphim stood about Him: the one had six wings, and the other had six wings; with two they covered His face, and with two they covered His feet, and with two they flew. 3. And they cried one to the other and said: Holy, holy, holy, the Lord of Sabaoth, all the earth is full of His glory. 4. And the lintel of the door was lifted up at the voice of them that cried, and the house was filled with smoke. 5. And I said: Woe is me (because I felt remorse), because I am a man of unclean lips, and I dwell in the midst of a people that hath unclean lips, and I have seen with my eyes the King the Lord of Sabaoth. 6. And one of the seraphim was sent to

---

203. Mt 2:15 (compare Hos 11:1).
204. Mt 2:23.
205. Jn 19:37 (compare Zech 12:10).
206. Jn 7:38 (compare Prov 18:4 or Isa 58:11).
207. 1 Cor 2:9 (compare Isa 52:15 or Isa 64:4).
208. See 1 Cor 12:28; Eph 4:11.
209. See 1 Cor 12:29–30.

me, and in his hand he had a live coal, which he had taken with the tongs off the altar. 7. And he touched my mouth and said: Behold, this hath touched thy lips, and it shall take away thy iniquities and shall cleanse thy sins. 8. And I heard the voice of the Lord saying: Whom shall I send? and who will go to that people? And I said: Lo, here am I, send me. 9. And He said: Go and say to this people: Ye shall hear with the ear and not understand, and perceiving ye shall behold and shall not see.[210]

I

1. *And it came to pass in the year that King Ozias*[211] *died: I saw the Lord sitting upon a throne high and elevated.* Before we speak of the vision, it seems that we must set forth who this Ozias was, how many years he had reigned, who among the other kings were his contemporaries. 2. And indeed, as regards his character, as we read in the books of Kings and of the Chronicles,[212] he was a just man and *did that which was right in the eyes of the Lord,*[213] building a temple and an aqueduct, providing the instruments of warfare, and deservedly overcoming his adversaries and—what is the greatest indication of his piety—having many prophets in his realm. As long as Zacharias the priest, surnamed the Understanding, was alive, Ozias pleased God and entered His sanctuary with all reverence.[214]

3. But after Zacharias died, desiring to make the religious offerings himself, he infringed upon the priestly office, not so much piously as rashly. And when the Levites and the other priests exclaimed against him: "Are you not Ozias, a king and not a priest?" he would not heed them, and straightway he was smitten with leprosy in his forehead,[215] in accordance with the word of the priest, who said: *Lord, fill their faces with shame.*[216] That is the part of the body which the priest used to cover with a plate of gold,[217] which in Ezechiel the Lord orders to be marked by the imprint of the letter tav.[218] David exults over it, saying: *The light of thy countenance, O Lord, is signed upon us.*[219] It was here also that the insolent alien was smitten by a stone from the sling and died.[220]

4. Now Ozias reigned fifty-two years,[221] at the time when Amulius reigned among the Latins and Agamestor, the eleventh king, among the Athenians. After his death the prophet Isaias saw the vision which we are now endeavoring to explain; that is, in the year in which Romulus, the founder of the Roman empire, was born, as will be evident to those who shall be willing to read the book of the Chronicles which we have translated from the Greek speech into the Latin tongue.[222]

II

1. *And it came to pass in the year that King Ozias died: I saw the Lord sitting upon a throne high and elevated.* After the story has been set forth, there follows the spiritual significance, for the sake of which the story itself has been set forth. While the leprous king lived and, so far as was in his power, was destroying the priesthood, Isaias could not see the vision. 2. As long as he reigned in Judea, the prophet did not lift his eyes to heaven; celestial matters were not revealed to him; the Lord of Sabaoth did not appear, nor was the word "holy" thrice heard in the mystery of the faith. But when he died, all the things which the following discourse will point out made themselves known in clear light. Something analogous to this is written also in Exodus: while Pharaoh lived, the people of Israel did not turn from their work with mud and brick and straws and aspire unto the Lord.[223] While he reigned, no one sought the God of their fathers, Abraham, Isaac, and Jacob.[224]

3. But when he died, the sons of Israel aspired, as the Scripture says: *and their cry went up unto the Lord,*[225] whereas according to history they should then particularly have rejoiced and previously have aspired, while he was alive. Also while Ezechiel was prophesying, Pheltias, the son of Banaias, died, and after the death of that most evil ruler he said: *I fell down upon my face, and cried with a loud voice, and said: Alas, alas, O Lord God: wilt thou make an end of all the remnant of Israel?*[226]

---

210. Isa 6:1–9. (The notes for this selection are by Gerhart and Udoh.)

211. Uzziah, king of Judah, is also known as Azariah. He is called Uzziah in Isa 1:1, here in Isa 6:1, in 2 Kings 15:13, 32, 34, and in 2 Chr 26–27. He is Azariah in the rest of 2 Kings 15. The date of his death is not certain; he died probably between 736 and 732 BCE.

212. See 2 Kings 15:1–7; 2 Chr 26.

213. 2 Kings 15:3; 2 Chr 26:4.

214. See 2 Chr 26:5–15.

215. See 2 Chr 26:16–20.

216. Ps 82:17 (Vulgate); see Ps 83:17.

217. See Ex 28:36–38.

218. See Ezek 9:4. The text, however, does not say what mark Ezekiel was to put on the foreheads. Tav (taw) is the last letter of the Hebrew alphabet, and also means "mark" or "sign." The ancient Hebrew letter tav was a cross.

219. Ps 4:7 (Vulgate); see also Ps 4:7.

220. That is, Goliath; see 1 Sam 17:49–50.

221. 2 Kings 15:2; 2 Chr 26:3.

222. The reference is to the *Chronicles* written (in about 303) by Eusebius of Caesarea. Jerome not only translated it into Latin but added entries to it, updating it to the year 378.

223. See Ex 1:14.

224. For God's titles here, see Ex 3:15.

225. Ex 2:23.

226. Ezek 11:13.

4. If, therefore, you understand in Ozias and Pharaoh and Pheltias and all others of this sort forces opposed to godly living, you will see how none of us can see and aspire and fall repentant while they live. *Let not sin,* says the Apostle, *reign in your mortal body.*[227] While sin reigns, we build cities for the Egyptians, we go about in dust and ashes, we seek chaff instead of grain and structures of mud instead of solid rock.

III

1. Next: *I saw the Lord sitting upon a throne high and elevated.* Daniel, too, saw the Lord seated, but not upon a throne high and elevated.[228] Elsewhere also the divine voice makes a promise, saying: *I will come and will judge the people in the valley of Josaphat,*[229] which is by interpretation the judgment of the Lord.

2. He that is a sinner—like me—sees the Lord sitting in the valley of Josaphat, not on a hill, not on a mountain, but in a valley, and in the valley of judgment. But whosoever is righteous—like Isaias—sees Him sitting upon a throne high and elevated. Again (to make a further suggestion), when I view Him with my mind's eye, reigning over thrones, dominions, angels, and all other virtues,[230] I see His lofty throne. But when I consider how He deals with the human race and is said frequently to descend to earth for our salvation, I see His throne low and very near the earth.

IV

1. Next: *I saw the Lord sitting upon a throne high and elevated: and the house was filled by His glory, and seraphim stood about Him.* Certain ones who have interpreted this passage before me, Greeks as well as Romans, have declared that the Lord sitting upon a throne is God the Father, and the two seraphim which are said to be standing one at each side are our Lord Jesus Christ and the Holy Spirit.

2. I do not agree with their opinion, though they are very learned men. Indeed, it is far better to set forth the truth in uncouth fashion than to declare falsehood in learned style. I dissent especially because John the Evangelist wrote that it was not God the Father but Christ who had been seen in this vision. For when he was speaking of the unbelief of the Jews, straightway he set forth the reasons for their unbelief: *Therefore they could not believe in Him, because Isaias said: "Ye shall hear with the ear and not understand, and perceiving ye shall behold and shall not see." And he said these things when he saw the glory of the Only-begotten and bore witness concerning Him.*[231]

3. In the present roll of Isaias he is bidden by Him who sits on the throne to say: *Ye shall hear with the ear and not understand.*[232] Now He who gives this command, as the Evangelist understands it, is Christ. Whence we comprehend that the seraphim cannot be interpreted as Christ, since Christ is He who is seated.

4. And although in the Acts of the Apostles Paul says to the Jews that agreed not among themselves: *Well did the Holy Ghost speak to our fathers by Isaias the prophet, saying: Go to this people and say: With the ear you shall hear and shall not understand, and seeing you shall see and shall not perceive. For the heart of this people is grown gross, and with their ears have they heard heavily, and their eyes they have shut, lest perhaps they should see with their eyes, and hear with their ears, and understand with their heart, and should be converted, and I should heal them*[233]—for me, however, the diversity of the person does not raise a question, since I know that both Christ and the Holy Spirit are one substance, and that the words of the Spirit are not other than those of the Son,[234] and the Son has not given a command other than the Spirit.

V

1. Next: *And the house was filled by His glory.* The house of God which is above is seen to be full of glory. But I do not know whether this house which is below is full of glory—save perhaps in the sense of the Psalmist when he says: *The earth is the Lord's and the fulness thereof.*[235] Thus we, too, may say that those persons on earth are full of glory who can say: *of His fulness we all have received.*[236]

2. That house wise women build and the foolish pulls it down with her hands;[237] it is that of which Isaias also speaks: *And in the last days the mountain of the Lord shall be manifest, and the house of God on the tops of the mountains, and it shall be exalted above the hills.*[238]

3. This is the house of which the aforesaid Paul elsewhere

---

227. Rom 6:12.   229. Joel 3:12.

228. See Dan 7:9–10.   230. See Eph 1:21; 6:12; Col 1:16.

231. Jn 12:39–41; see Isa 6:10. The Vulgate of Jn 12:41 reads "These things said Isaias, when [*quando*] he saw His glory, and spoke of Him." The reading generally supported in the Greek text is "Isaiah said this because [ὅτι] he saw his glory and spoke about him" (New Revised Standard Version).

232. Isa 6:10.   235. Ps 23:1 (Vulgate) = Ps 24:1.

233. Acts 28:25–27.   236. Jn 1:16.

234. See Jn 16:13–15.   237. See Prov 14:1.

238. Isa 2:2 (Jerome's quotation here contains some variations from the Vulgate).

bears witness with inspired voice: *And Moses indeed was faithful in all his house as a servant, for a testimony of those things which were to be said; but Christ as the Son over His own house, of which house are we, if only we hold fast the first principle of His substance firm unto the end.*[239] Of this he speaks also to Timothy: *These things I write to thee . . . that thou mayest know how thou oughtest to behave thyself in the house of God, which is the church.*[240]

VI

1. Next: *And seraphim stood about Him: the one had six wings and the other had six wings. With two they covered His face and with two they covered His feet, and with two they flew. And they cried one to the other and said: Holy, holy, holy, the Lord of Sabaoth, all the earth is full of His glory.*

2. We wish to know what the seraphim are that are standing about God. What are the six wings of (each) one, and the twelve when they are joined together? How do they cover His face with two and His feet with two and fly with two—since they are said to be standing about God? Or how do they stand about Him when they are but two in number? What is that which they cry, the one to the other, and thrice repeat the word "holy"? How is it that above the house is said to be full of glory, and now the earth is said to be?

3. Since these questions raise no small cloud of dust and at the very outset interpose a difficulty of interpretation, let us pray the Lord together that to me also a coal may be sent from the altar, and that, when all the uncleanness of my sins has been swept away,[241] I may be enabled first to contemplate the mysteries of God and then to tell what I have seen.

4. *Seraphim*, as we have found in the *Translation of Hebrew Words*,[242] may be rendered either "fire" or "the beginning of speech." We ask what this fire may be. The saviour says: *I am come to cast fire on the earth, and how I wish that it may burn!*[243] The two disciples to whom the Lord opened the Scriptures in the way, beginning at Moses and all the prophets, after their eyes were opened knew Him and said: *Did not our heart burn within us in the way while He opened to us the Scriptures?*[244]

5. And in Deuteronomy God Himself is described as a consuming fire.[245] In Ezechiel also His likeness from His loins to His feet is as the appearance of fire.[246] *And the words of the Lord are pure words, as silver of the earth tried by the fire, refined seven times.*[247] And there are many other passages: if I wished to repeat them all from the Scriptures, it would take too long.

6. Therefore, let us inquire, where is this saving fire? No one can doubt that it is in the holy books, by the reading of which all sins of men are washed away. But as to the second rendering, "the beginning of speech," how it can be applied to the Scriptures, I fear that if I begin to explain I shall seem not so much to be interpreting as bringing force to bear upon the Scriptures.

7. The beginning of speech and of general conversation and all that we say is the Hebrew tongue, in which the Old Testament is written. So universal tradition reports. But after diversity of tongues was imposed because of the offense to God in erecting the tower [of Babel], then a variety of speech was spread abroad over all nations.[248] Therefore, both fire and the beginning of speech may be observed in the two Testaments. And it is not surprising that they stand about God, since it is through them that the Lord Himself may be known.

8. *The one had six wings and the other had six wings.* Our Victorinus[249] interprets these as the twelve apostles. We can accept it also as typifying the twelve stones of the altar[250] *which iron hath not touched,*[251] and the twelve precious stones of which the priest's emblem was made,[252] which Ezechiel also mentions[253] and concerning which the Apocalypse is not silent.[254] Which of these interpretations is true, let God judge; which is probable, we shall set forth in what follows.

VII

1. And: *with two they covered His face, and with two they covered His feet, and with two they flew.* They covered not their own but God's face. For who can know His beginning, which was in the eternity of things before He founded this [little]

---

239. Heb 3:5–6. Jerome departs significantly from the Vulgate text of the last two clauses of Heb 3:6, which read: "which house we are, if we hold fast the confidence and glory of hope unto the end."

240. 1 Tim 3:14–15.

241. See Isa 6:6–7.

242. Jerome's *De nominibus Hebraicis* is today recognized as based for the most part on fanciful and popular etymologies of the Hebrew proper names they purport to explain.

243. Lk 12:49 (Jerome's quotation here contains some variations from the Vulgate).

244. Lk 24:32 (quoted by Jerome with omissions).

245. See Deut 4:24.

246. See Ezek 8:2.

247. Ps 11:7 (Jerome's quotation here contains some variations from the Vulgate); see Ps 12:6.

248. See Gen 11:1–9.

249. Victorinus of Pettau died a martyr, probably in 304.

250. See 1 Kings 18:31.

251. Deut 27:5.   253. See Ezek 28:13.

252. See Ex 28:15–21; 39:8–14.   254. See Rev 21:19–21.

world, when He established thrones, dominions, powers, angels, and all the heavenly ministry?

2. *And with two they covered His feet:* not their own but God's. For who can know His bounds? What is to be after the consummation of the age, what after the human race has been judged; what life is to follow: whether there will again be another earth and other elements after the change or if another world and sun must be created. *Tell me the former things and what shall be at the last,* says Isaias, *and I will say that you are gods;*[255] implying that no one can relate what was before the world and what shall be after the world.

3. *And with two they flew:* we know only the intermediate events which are revealed to us by the reading of the Scriptures: when the world was made, when man was fashioned, the time of the flood, when the law was given, how the entire expanse of the lands was populated from one man and how, at the end of the age, the Son of God took flesh for our salvation. But all the other things which we have mentioned these two seraphim have covered in veiling His face and His feet.

4. *And they cried one to the other:* that is well expressed *one to the other.* For whatever we read in the Old Testament, that we find also in the Gospel; and what was gathered together in the Gospel, this is drawn forth from the authority of the Old Testament: nothing is discordant, nothing diverse.

5. *And said: Holy, holy, holy, the Lord of Sabaoth.* In both Testaments the Trinity is made known. But that our saviour, too, is called Sabaoth, take for example the twenty-third Psalm. The powers that served the Lord cried out to the other celestial forces that they should throw open the door to their returning Lord: *Lift up your gates, O ye princes;* or, as Aquila[256] interprets it: *Lift up your heads, O ye gates, and the King of Glory shall enter it.*[257]

6. And then they, because they see Him clad in flesh, amazed at the new mystery, inquire: *Who is this King of Glory?* and receive the reply: *The Lord of Virtues, He is the King of Glory.*[258] In Hebrew this is written Lord of Sabaoth, and we should realize that wherever the seventy translators[259] have used the expression *dominum virtutum* and *dominum omnipotentem,* there is found in the Hebrew "Lord of Sabaoth." Aquila renders this "the Lord of Hosts."[260] The very word "Lord" here consists of the four letters properly used for God: iod, he, iod, he; this is JA repeated. These letters when doubled form the ineffable and glorious name of God.[261]

7. *All the earth is full of His glory.* As yet this is said by the seraphim concerning the advent of our Lord the saviour,

how the preaching of Him is spread abroad into all the world, and the sound of the apostles penetrating the limits of the earth.

VIII

1. Next: *And the lintel of the door was lifted up at the voice of them that cried.* We read in the Old Testament that the Lord always spoke to Moses and Aaron at the door of the Tabernacle, as though before the Gospel He did not yet lead them into the Holy of Holies.[262] Just as the Church was afterwards brought in and said: *The king hath brought me into his room.*[263]

2. So when our Lord descended to the earth, that lintel of the door—that is, an obstacle of some sort—was removed from those desiring to enter, and this whole world was filled with smoke, that is, with the glory of God. But where we read in Latin *elevatum* (i.e., "lifted up"), in the Greek *sublatum* is used.[264] But as the ambiguity of the word makes possible either translation, our [scholars] have interpreted *elevatum* as meaning "removed" (*ablato*).

3. *And the house was filled with smoke.* God, as we have said above, is fire. When He had descended to Moses on Mt. Sinai, at His coming lights were seen flitting about, and the whole mountain was filled with smoke.[265] Whence the saying in the Psalms: *who touchest the mountains, and they will smoke.*[266] From fire, therefore, since we cannot apprehend its entire essence, a certain lighter and, if I may say so, rarer quality, smoke, is spread abroad. Taking this as an example, we may say: *We*

---

255. Isa 41:22–23 (Jerome's quotation here is abbreviated and contains some variations from the Vulgate).

256. See note 198 above.

257. Ps 23:9 (Vulgate); see Ps 24:9.

258. Ps 23:10 (Vulgate, which also has Jerome's "*dominus virtutum*").

259. That is, the translators of the Septuagint; see Jerome's *The Prologue to Genesis* above.

260. That is "*dominus militiarum*" in Jerome's rendering of Aquila's Greek.

261. The Tetragrammaton—"four letters"—became God's personal name among the Jews. The name is written yod he vav he (יהוה), transliterated YHWH, and is today pronounced "Yahweh," although its old pronunciation is not known and the name is rarely spoken among Jews.

262. See Ex 33:9–11.

263. Song 1:3 (Vulgate, which has "his storerooms" [*cellaria sua*] instead of Jerome's "his room" [*cubiculum suum*]); see Song 1:4.

264. The Septuagint of Isa 6:4 has ἐπήρθη, "lifted up." The Vulgate has *commota,* "moved," "shaken." The Latin word *sublatum* with which Jerome translates the Greek is, as he goes on to state, ambiguous. It can mean "taken away," "removed," as well as "lifted up."

265. See Ex 19:16–19.

266. Ps 103:32 (Vulgate) = Ps 104:32.

know in part, and we prophesy in part,[267] and *we see now through a glass in a dark manner.*[268]

IX

1. *And seraphim stood about Him: the one had six wings, and the other had six wings.* One of the Greeks, a man particularly learned in the Scriptures,[269] has explained that the seraphim are certain powers in the heavens which, standing before the tribunal of God, praise Him and are sent on various errands and particularly to those who are in need of cleansing and (by reason of former sins) in some measure need punishment. "Moreover," he says, "that the lintel of the door was lifted up, and the house filled with smoke, is a sign of the destruction of the Jewish temple and the burning of all Jerusalem."

2. Some, however, while agreeing with the preceding, dissent from the latter part [of the interpretation]. For they say that the lintel of the door was lifted up at that time when the veil of the temple was rent[270] and the whole house of Israel was confused by a cloud of error when, as Josephus relates, the priests heard the voice of the heavenly powers from the sanctuary of the temple [saying]: "Let us leave this abode."[271]

X

1. But there is a man from whom I rejoice to have learned a great deal, and who has so refined the Hebrew speech that among their scribes he is regarded as a Chaldean.[272] He approaches the matter by a far different route. For he says that none of the prophets except Isaias has seen seraphim standing about God, and that seraphim are not even to be read about elsewhere; furthermore, that this was a premonitory indication of the end and captivity of Jerusalem which took place under Nabuchodonosor.

2. Now from Ozias,[273] under whom he began to prophesy, to Sedecias, who reigned last and who was blinded and taken to Babylon,[274] there were eleven kings. The twelfth was Godolias, whom the king of Babylon had set up over the land.[275] Him Ismael, the son of Nathanias, slew in the midst of a banquet—that parricide of the remnant of his countrymen.[276] These kings [he says] are the twelve wings, with four of which they veil their faces (as is found in some manuscripts), with four they fly, and with four they cover their feet.

3. As a matter of fact, only four of these twelve kings were righteous kings: Ozias, Joatham, Ezechias, and Josias. These being exalted in various captivities dare to glorify God: *Holy,*

holy, holy, the Lord of Sabaoth. But the rest on account of their sins veil their faces, and others because they were led into captivity hide the tracks of their feet. But the uplifted lintel of the door and the house filled with smoke (as we have said before) he explained as the destruction of Jerusalem and the burning of the temple.

XI

1. Since I have once started to refer to his opinion, I shall touch also on those points not yet alluded to by me: he declared that the tongs by which the live coal was taken from the altar and the mouth cleansed refer to the passion of Isaias himself. He was put to death under Manasses.[277] It was then, when his mouth was truly cleansed, that he said to the Lord: *Lo, here am I, send me,*[278] and he said: *Woe is me (because I felt remorse).*[279]

2. So long as Ozias lives, O Isaias, you do not know that you are wretched, you are not conscience-smitten, you are not moved; but when he is dead, you perceive that you have unclean lips, then you know that you are unworthy of the vision of God. But would that I, too, were more conscience-smitten, and that after my remorse I might be made worthy to preach of God. Because, as I am a man and have unclean lips, I live also in the midst of a people that have unclean lips.

3. Isaias, being a righteous man, had sinned in speech only; therefore he had only unclean lips. But I, who use my eyes for lust and am scandalized hand and foot[280] and transgress with all my members, have all things unclean and, because I have defiled my garment after once being baptized by the Spirit, am in need of the cleansing of a second baptism, that is, by fire.[281]

---

267. 1 Cor 13:9.

268. 1 Cor 13:12.

269. It is not known for certain to whom Jerome is referring; Origen or Gregory of Nazianzus have been suggested.

270. See Mk 15:38; Mt 27:51; Lk 23:45.

271. Josephus, *Jewish War*, vi.300.

272. This person is not known. Some have conjectured him to be the convert from Judaism to Christianity from whom Jerome says he learned Hebrew.

273. See 2 Kings 15:1–7.

274. See 2 Kings 24:17–25:7; Jer 39:1–7.

275. See 2 Kings 25:22; Jer 40:7–12.

276. 2 Kings 25:25; Jer 41:1–2.

277. This reference to Isaiah's death is not in the Bible.

278. Isa 6:8.

279. Isa 6:5.

280. See Mk 9:43–48; Mt 5:29–30; 18:8–9.

281. See Mt 3:11; Lk 3:16.

XII

1. The words of Scripture are not simple, as some suppose; much is concealed in them. The letter indicates one thing, the mystical language another. For example, our Lord in the Gospel is girt with a towel, He prepares a basin to wash the disciples' feet, He performs the service of a slave.[282] Granted, it is to teach humility, that we may minister to each other in turn. I do not deny that. I do not reject it. What is it that He says to Peter upon his refusal? *If I wash not thy feet, thou shalt have no part with me.*[283] And he replied: *Lord, not only my feet, but also my hands and my head.*[284] 2. Because His apostles, as men walking the earth, still had feet stained by the pollution of sin, the Lord, being about to ascend to heaven, desires to free them entirely from their transgressions, that the words of the prophet may be applicable to them: *How beautiful are the feet of those that preach peace!*[285] And that they may have the power to imitate the words of the Church when she says: *I have washed my feet, how shall I defile them?*[286] So that, even if some dust shall cling to them after the resurrection, they may shake it off against the impious city in evidence of their labour,[287] because thus far they have struggled for the salvation of all: for the Jews as Jews, for the Gentiles as Gentiles,[288] so that they have to a certain extent polluted the soles of their own feet.

From *Letters of St. Jerome,* translated by Charles Christopher Mierow, vol. 1, Ancient Christian Writers, no. 33 (Westminster, MD: Newman Press, 1963), 79–91.

✒ **Augustine** (354–430) was bishop of Hippo, in northern Africa. In his treatment of biblical interpretation, *De doctrina Christiana* (begun in ca. 395 and finished in 426 or 427), he places the Scriptures at the center of Christian instruction (*paideia*).

AUGUSTINE

***De doctrina Christiana*, 1.xxxv.39–xl.44; 2.vi.7–8, viii.12, ix.14–xi.16, xiv.21–xvi.23, xvi.25–26, xviii.28, xl.60; 3.i.1–ii.2, ii.5–iii.6, iv.8–vi.10, x.14–xi.17, xii.18–20, xiii.21–xviii.26, xxii.32–xxiii.33, xxiv.34–xxix.40**

1.xxxv

39. The chief purpose of all that we have been saying in our discussion of things[289] is to make it understood that the fulfilment and end of the law and all the divine scriptures is to love[290] the thing which must be enjoyed and the thing which together with us can enjoy that thing (since there is no

need for a commandment to love oneself). To enlighten us and enable us, the whole temporal dispensation was set up by divine providence for our salvation. We must make use of this, not with a permanent love and enjoyment of it, but with a transient love and enjoyment of our journey, or of our conveyances (so to speak) or any other expedients whatsoever (there may be a more appropriate word), so that we love the means of transport only because of our destination.

1.xxxvi

40. So anyone who thinks that he has understood the divine scriptures or any part of them, but cannot by his understanding build up this double love of God and neighbour, has not yet succeeded in understanding them. Anyone who derives from them an idea which is useful for supporting this love but fails to say what the writer demonstrably meant in the passage has not made a fatal error, and is certainly not a liar. In a liar there is a desire to say what is false, and that is why we find many who want to lie but nobody who wants to be misled. [. . .] 41. Anyone with an interpretation of the scriptures that differs from that of the writer is misled, but not because the scriptures are lying. If, as I began by saying, he is misled by an idea of the kind that builds up love, which is the end of the commandment, he is misled in the same way as a walker who leaves his path by mistake but reaches the destination to which the path leads by going through a field. But he must be put right and shown how it is more useful not to leave the path, in case the habit of deviating should force him to go astray or even adrift.

1.xxxvii–xxxviii

It often happens that by thoughtlessly asserting something that the author did not mean an interpreter runs up against

---

282. See Jn 13:2–5.

283. Jn 13:8.

284. Jn 13:9.

285. Isa 52:7 (Jerome's quotation here is abbreviated and contains some variations from the Vulgate).

286. Song 5:3.

287. See Mk 6:11; Mt 10:14; Lk 9:5.

288. See 1 Cor 9:19–20.

289. Augustine's discussion centers on the distinction between "things" and "signs." (The notes for this selection are by Gerhart and Udoh.)

290. See Rom 13:8–10; Gal 5:14; Jas 2:8; 1 Tim 1:5; Mk 12:29–31; Mt 22:37–40; Lk 10:27–28; Deut 6:4; Lev 19:8.

other things which cannot be reconciled with that original idea. If he agrees that these things are true and certain, his original interpretation could not possibly be true, and by cherishing his own idea he comes in some strange way to be more displeased with scripture than with himself. If he encourages this evil to spread it will be his downfall. "For we walk by faith, not by sight,"[291] and faith will falter if the authority of holy scripture is shaken; and if faith falters, love itself decays. For if someone lapses in his faith, he inevitably lapses in his love as well, since he cannot love what he does not believe to be true. If on the other hand he both believes and loves, then by good conduct and by following the rules of good behaviour he gives himself reason to hope that he will attain what he loves. So there are these three things which all knowledge and prophecy serve: faith, hope, and love.[292] But faith will be replaced by the sight of visible reality, and hope by the real happiness which we shall attain, whereas love will actually increase when these things pass away. 42. If, through faith, we love what we cannot yet see, how much greater will our love be when we have begun to see! And if, through hope, we love something that we have not yet attained, how much greater will our love be when we have attained it! There is this important difference between temporal things and eternal things: something temporal is loved more before it is possessed, but will lose its appeal when attained, for it does not satisfy the soul, whose true and certain abode is eternity. The eternal, on the other hand, is loved more passionately when obtained than when desired. No-one who desires it is allowed to think more highly of it than is warranted (it would then disappoint when found to be less impressive); but however high one's expectations on the way one will find it even more impressive on arrival.

1.xxxix

43. Therefore a person strengthened by faith, hope, and love, and who steadfastly holds on to them, has no need of the scriptures except to instruct others. That is why many people, relying on these three things, actually live in solitude without any texts of the scriptures. They are, I think, a fulfilment of the saying "If there are prophecies, they will lose their meaning; if there are tongues, they will cease; if there is knowledge that too will lose its meaning."[293] By these devices (so to speak) such an edifice of faith, hope, and love has been built in them that they do not seek what is imperfect,[294] for they hold what is perfect—perfect, that is, as far as anything can be in this life; for in comparison with the life

to come the life of no righteous or holy man in this world is perfect. This is why scripture says, "there remain faith, hope, and love, these three; the greatest of these is love":[295] when one reaches eternity the other two will pass away and love will remain in an enhanced and a more certain form.

1.xl

44. So when someone has learnt that the aim of the commandment is "love from a pure heart, and good conscience and genuine faith,"[296] he will be ready to relate every interpretation of the holy scriptures to these three things and may approach the task of handling these books with confidence. [. . .]

2.vi

7. But casual readers are misled by problems and ambiguities of many kinds, mistaking one thing for another. In some passages they find no meaning at all that they can grasp at, even falsely, so thick is the fog created by some obscure phrases. I have no doubt that this is all divinely predetermined, so that pride may be subdued by hard work and intellects which tend to despise things that are easily discovered may be rescued from boredom and reinvigorated. Why is it, I wonder, that if someone should say that there exist holy and perfect men by whose lives and conduct the church of Christ tears away those who come to it from their various superstitions, and by inspiring them to imitate their goodness somehow incorporates them into itself; and that there exist servants of the true God, good and faithful men who, putting aside the burdens of this life, have come to the holy font of baptism, arise from it born again with the Holy Spirit, and then produce the fruit of a double love, that is love of God and love of their neighbour—why is it that someone who says this gives less pleasure to an audience than by expounding in the same terms this passage from the Song of Songs, where the church is addressed and praised like a beautiful woman: "Your teeth are like a flock of shorn ewes ascending from the pool, all of which give birth to twins, and there is not a sterile animal among them"?[297] 8. [. . .] It is a wonderful

---

291. 2 Cor 5:7.
292. See 1 Cor 13:8–13.
293. 1 Cor 13:8.
294. See 1 Cor 13:12–13.
295. 1 Cor 13:13.
296. 1 Tim 1:5.
297. Song 4:2 and 6:5 (Augustine's quotation here contains some variations from the Vulgate).

and beneficial thing that the Holy Spirit organized the holy scripture so as to satisfy hunger by means of its plainer passages and remove boredom by means of its obscurer ones. Virtually nothing is unearthed from these obscurities which cannot be found quite plainly expressed somewhere else.

2.viii

12. [. . .] The most expert investigator of the divine scriptures will be the person who, firstly, has read them all and has a good knowledge—a reading knowledge, at least, if not yet a complete understanding—of those pronounced canonical. He will read the others more confidently when equipped with a belief in the truth; they will then be unable to take possession of his unprotected mind and prejudice him in any way against sound interpretations or delude him by their dangerous falsehoods and fantasies. In the matter of canonical scriptures he should follow the authority of as many catholic churches as possible, including of course those that were found worthy to have apostolic seats and receive apostolic letters.[298]

2.ix

14. [. . .] The first rule in this laborious task is, as I have said, to know these books; not necessarily to understand them but to read them so as to commit them to memory or at least make them not totally unfamiliar. Then the matters which are clearly stated in them, whether ethical precepts or articles of belief, should be examined carefully and intelligently. The greater a person's intellectual capacity, the more of these he finds. In clearly expressed passages of scripture one can find all the things that concern faith and the moral life (namely hope and love, treated in my previous book). Then, after gaining a familiarity with the language of the divine scriptures, one should proceed to explore and analyze the obscure passages, by taking examples from the more obvious parts to illuminate obscure expressions and by using the evidence of indisputable passages to remove the uncertainty of ambiguous ones. Here memory is extremely valuable; and it cannot be supplied by these instructions if it is lacking.

2.x

15. There are two reasons why written texts fail to be understood: their meaning may be veiled either by unknown signs or by ambiguous signs. Signs are either literal or meta-phorical. They are called literal when used to signify the things for which they were invented: so, for example, when we say *bovem,* meaning the animal which we and all speakers of Latin call by that name. They are metaphorical when the actual things which we signify by the particular words are used to signify something else: when, for example, we say *bovem* and not only interpret these two syllables to mean the animal normally referred to by that name but also understand, by that animal, "worker in the gospel," which is what scripture, as interpreted by the apostle Paul, means when it says, "You shall not muzzle the ox that treads out the grain."[299]

2.xi

16. An important antidote to the ignorance of literal signs is the knowledge of languages. Users of the Latin language—and it is these that I have now undertaken to instruct—need two others, Hebrew and Greek, for an understanding of the divine scriptures, so that recourse may be had to the original versions if any uncertainty arises from the infinite variety of Latin translators. [. . .]

2.xiv

21. I shall speak later about ambiguous signs; now I am dealing with unfamiliar ones,[300] of which there are two kinds, as far as words are concerned. A reader may be perplexed by either an unfamiliar word or an unfamiliar expression. If they come from other languages the information must be sought from speakers of those languages, or else the languages must be learnt (if time and ability allow), or else a collection of several translations must be consulted. If we are unfamiliar with some words and expressions in our own language, they become known to us by the process of reading and listening. Nothing should be committed to memory more urgently than unfamiliar kinds of words and expressions; so that when we meet a knowledgeable person whom we can ask, or a similar expression which makes clear from the passages which precede and follow it, or both, what is the force or significance of the unfamiliar word, we can easily make a note

---

298. There follows here (2.viii.13) Augustine's list of canonical books (the "Canon of Augustine").

299. 1 Cor 9:9; 1 Tim 5:18; see also Deut 25:4.

300. That is, literal, unfamiliar (unknown) signs.

of it, or find out about it, with the help of our memory. (Yet such is the force of habit, even in learning, that those who are nourished and educated in the holy scriptures are more surprised by expressions from elsewhere, and regard them as worse Latin than the ones which they have learnt in scripture but are not found in Latin literature.) In this area too it is very helpful to collect manuscripts and examine and discuss a number of translations. But inaccuracy must be excluded, for the attention of those who wish to know the divine scripture must first focus on the task of correcting the manuscripts, so that uncorrected ones give place to corrected ones, assuming that they belong to the same class of translation.

2.xv

22. . . . To correct any Latin manuscripts Greek ones should be used: among these, as far as the Old Testament is concerned, the authority of the Septuagint is supreme. Its seventy writers are now claimed in all the more informed churches to have performed their task of translation with such strong guidance from the Holy Spirit that this great number of men spoke with but a single voice. . . .[301] Therefore, even if we find in the Hebrew versions something that differs from what they wrote, I believe that we should defer to the divine dispensation which was made through them so that the books which the Jewish race refused to reveal to other peoples (whether out of religious scruple or envy) might be revealed, through the mediating power of King Ptolemy,[302] well in advance to the peoples that were destined to believe through our Lord. It may indeed be the case that they translated in a way that the Holy Spirit, who was leading them and creating unanimity, judged appropriate to the Gentiles. . . . The Latin manuscripts of the New Testament, if there is any uncertainty in the various Latin versions, should without doubt give place to Greek ones, especially those found in the more learned and diligent churches.

2.xvi

23. As for metaphorical signs, any unfamiliar ones which make the reader puzzled must be examined partly through a knowledge of languages, and partly through a knowledge of things. There is a figurative significance and certainly some hidden meaning conveyed by the episode of the pool of Siloam, where the man who had his eyes anointed by the Lord with mud made from spittle was ordered to wash his face.[303] If the evangelist had not explained this name from an unfamiliar language, this important meaning would have remained hidden. So too many of the Hebrew names not explained by the authors of these books undoubtedly have considerable significance and much help to give in solving the mysteries of the scriptures, if they can be explained at all. Various experts in this language have rendered no small service to posterity by explaining all these individual words from the scriptures and giving the meaning of the names Adam, Eve, Abraham, and Moses, and of place-names such as Jerusalem, Zion, Jericho, Sinai, Lebanon, Jordan, and any other names in that language that are unfamiliar to us. Once these are clarified and explained many figurative expressions in scripture become quite clear. [. . .]

25. An unfamiliarity with numbers makes unintelligible many things that are said figuratively and mystically in scripture. An intelligent intellect (if I may put it thus) cannot fail to be intrigued by the meaning of the fact that Moses and Elijah and the Lord himself fasted for forty days.[304] The knotty problem of the figurative significance of this event cannot be solved except by understanding and considering the number, which comprises four times ten, and signifies the knowledge of all things woven into the temporal order. . . .

26. Many passages are also made inaccessible and opaque by an ignorance of music. It has been elegantly demonstrated that there are some figurative illustrations of things based on the difference between the psaltery and the lyre. [. . .]

2.xviii

28. But whether Varro's story[305] is true or not, we should not avoid music because of the associated pagan superstitions if there is a possibility of gleaning from it something of value for understanding holy scripture. Nor, on the other hand, should we be captivated by the vanities of the theater if we are discussing something to do with lyres or other instruments that may help us appreciate spiritual truths.

---

301. Augustine repeats here the account of the translation of the Septuagint already in Clement of Alexandria. See Clement, *Strōmateis*, above. See also Augustine, *City of God*, 18.42.

302. Ptolemy Philadelphus (285–246 BCE), according to the account in *City of God*.

303. See Jn 9:6–7.

304. See Ex 24:18; 1 Kings 19:8; Mk 1:13; Mt 4:2; Lk 4:1–2.

305. Varro's story explains the origin of the nine Muses and is repeated by Augustine in the previous paragraph (xvii.27).

2.xl

60. Any statements by those who are called philosophers, especially the Platonists,[306] which happen to be true and consistent with our faith should not cause alarm, but be claimed for our own use, as it were from owners who have no right to them. Like the treasures of the ancient Egyptians, who possessed not only idols and heavy burdens which the people of Israel hated and shunned but also vessels and ornaments of silver and gold, and clothes, which on leaving Egypt the people of Israel, in order to make better use of them, surreptitiously claimed for themselves (they did this not on their own authority but at God's command, and the Egyptians in their ignorance actually gave them the things of which they had made poor use)[307]—similarly all the branches of pagan learning contain not only false and superstitious fantasies and burdensome studies that involve unnecessary effort, which each one of us must loathe and avoid as under Christ's guidance we abandon the company of pagans, but also studies for liberated minds which are more appropriate to the service of the truth, and some very useful moral instruction, as well as the various truths about monotheism to be found in their writers. These treasures—like the silver and gold, which they did not create but dug, as it were, from the mines of providence, which is everywhere—which were used wickedly and harmfully in the service of demons must be removed by Christians, as they separate themselves in spirit from the wretched company of pagans, and applied to their true function, that of preaching the gospels. As for their clothing—which corresponds to human institutions, but those appropriate to human society, which in this life we cannot do without—this may be accepted and kept for conversion to Christian purposes.

3.i

1. [. . .] [A]s I began to say, in so far as I can instruct him, the student who is in the proper state of mind to accept my instruction should know that ambiguity[308] in scripture resides either in literal or in metaphorical usages (as the terms were described in Book 2).

3.ii

2. When it is literal usages that make scripture ambiguous, we must first of all make sure that we have not punctuated or articulated the passage incorrectly. Once close consid-

eration has revealed that it is uncertain how a passage should be punctuated and articulated, we must consult the rule of faith, as it is perceived through the plainer passages of the scriptures and the authority of the church. [. . .] 5. Where an ambiguity can be resolved neither by an article of faith nor by the actual context there is no objection to any punctuation which follows one of the meanings that suggest themselves.

3.iii

6. The points that I have just made about problems of punctuation also apply to the problems of reading aloud. These too, unless they are simply mistakes due to a reader's gross carelessness, are resolved by considering either the rules of faith or the surrounding context. If neither of these methods is used to resolve them they will none the less remain in dispute, but in such a way that the reader will not be wrong however the passages are articulated.

3.iv

8. In the field of literal expressions, then, as far as the books of holy scripture are concerned, it is very unusual, and very difficult, to find cases of ambiguity which cannot be resolved either by the particular details of the context—which are a pointer to the writer's intention—or by a comparison of Latin translations or an inspection of the original language.

3.v

9. But the ambiguities of metaphorical words, about which I must now speak, require no ordinary care and attention. To begin with, one must take care not to interpret a figurative expression literally. What the apostle says is relevant here: "the letter kills but the spirit gives life."[309] For when something meant figuratively is interpreted as if it were meant literally, it is understood in a carnal way. No "death of the soul" is more aptly given that name than the situation in which the intelligence, which is what raises the soul above the level

---

306. By "Platonists" Augustine is referring to the philosophers now commonly called "NeoPlatonists," among whom Plotinus was the most prominent from the mid-third century CE onward. See chapter 2 below.

307. Ex 3:21–22; 12:35–36.

308. Augustine now passes from his treatment of "unfamiliar signs (both literal and metaphorical)" to that of "ambiguous signs (both literal and metaphorical)."

309. 2 Cor 3:6.

of animals, is subjected to the flesh by following the letter. A person who follows the letter understands metaphorical words as literal, and does not relate what the literal word signifies to any other meaning. On hearing the word "sabbath," for example, he interprets it simply as one of the seven days which repeat themselves in a continuous cycle; and on hearing the word "sacrifice" his thoughts do not pass beyond the rituals performed with sacrificial beasts and fruits of the earth. It is, then, a miserable kind of spiritual slavery to interpret signs as things, and to be incapable of raising the mind's eye above the physical creation so as to absorb the eternal light.

3.vi

10. But the form this slavery took in the Jewish people was very different from the experience of other nations, since notwithstanding their enslavement to temporal things the idea of monotheism was presented to them in all sorts of ways. And although they observed the signs of spiritual things in place of the things themselves—not knowing what they related to—they nevertheless had an ingrained belief that such slavery made them acceptable to the single God of all, the God whom they were unable to see.

3.x

14. As well as this rule, which warns us not to pursue a figurative (that is, metaphorical) expression as if it were literal, we must add a further one: not to accept a literal one as if it were figurative. We must first explain the way to discover whether an expression is literal or figurative. Generally speaking, it is this: anything in the divine discourse that cannot be related either to good morals or to the true faith should be taken as figurative. Good morals have to do with our love of God and our neighbour, the true faith with our understanding of God and our neighbour. The hope that each person has within his own conscience is directly related to the progress that he feels himself to be making towards the love and understanding of God and his neighbour. All this has been dealt with in Book 1.

15. [. . .] But scripture enjoins nothing but love, and censures nothing but lust, and molds men's minds accordingly. Similarly, if their minds are taken over by a particular prejudice, people consider as figurative anything that scripture asserts to the contrary. But it asserts nothing except the catholic faith, in time past, present, and future. It narrates the past, foretells the future, and demonstrates the present, but all these things serve to nourish and strengthen this love, and to overcome and annihilate lust. 16. By love I mean the impulse of one's mind to enjoy God on his own account and to enjoy oneself and one's neighbour on account of God; and by lust I mean the impulse of one's mind to enjoy oneself and one's neighbour and any corporeal thing not on account of God. What unbridled lust does to corrupt the mind and body is called wickedness; what it does to harm another person is called wrongdoing. All sins can be divided into these two kinds, but wickedness comes first. Once it has depleted the mind and as it were bankrupted it, it rushes on to commit wrongdoing in order to remove the obstacles to wickedness or to find assistance for it. Similarly, what love does to benefit itself is self-interest, and what it does to benefit a neighbour is known as kindness. And here self-interest comes first, because nobody can do good to another out of resources which he does not possess. The more the realm of lust is destroyed, the more the realm of love is increased.

3.xi

17. Any harsh and even cruel word or deed attributed to God or his saints that is found in the holy scriptures applies to the destruction of the realm of lust. If the message is clear, it should not be treated as figurative and related to something else. . . .

3.xii

18. Matters which seem like wickedness to the unenlightened, whether just spoken or actually performed, whether attributed to God or to people whose holiness is commended to us, are entirely figurative. Such mysteries are to be elucidated in terms of the need to nourish love. A person who makes more limited use of transient things than the moral conventions of his own society allow is either self-controlled or superstitious; a person whose use of them exceeds the limits set by the practice of good people in his society is either guilty of wickedness or an indication of some special significance. In all such matters what is reprehensible is not the use made of things but the user's desire. No person in his right mind should ever think that the Lord's feet were anointed by a woman with precious ointment[310] in the same

---

310. See Lk 7:37–38; Jn 12:1–8.

way as the feet of self-indulgent and evil men are anointed at the sort of banquets which we abhor. A good perfume signifies a good reputation: anyone who enjoys this through the deeds of an upright life anoints Christ's feet in a figurative sense with a most precious perfume by following in his footsteps. Again, what is generally speaking wicked in other people is the sign of something great in one who is divine or a prophet. Consorting with a prostitute is one thing in a depraved society, but something quite different in the prophecy of Hosea.[311] . . .

19. We must pay careful attention to the conduct appropriate to different places, times, and persons, in case we make rash imputations of wickedness. It is possible for a wise man to take some kind of costly food without any taint of greed or gluttony, and for an unwise one to yearn for junk food with a most disgusting outburst of greed. [. . .] In all matters of this kind actions are made acceptable or unacceptable not by the particular things we make use of, but by our motives of using them and our methods of seeking them. 20. Righteous men of long ago visualized the kingdom of heaven as an earthly kingdom, and predicted it accordingly. In the interests of creating offspring there was a perfectly blameless practice for one man to have several wives. For the same reason it was not honourable for one woman to have several husbands; that does not make a woman more fertile, and it is indeed a form of immoral prostitution to seek either profit or children through promiscuity. Given such social conventions, things that the saints of those ages could do without any lust—although they were doing something which cannot be done without lust nowadays—are not censured by scripture. Anything of this kind related there is to be understood not only historically and literally but also figuratively and prophetically, and interpreted according to the aim of love, whether it be love of God or love of one's neighbour, or both. [. . .]

3.xiii–xv

21. Whatever accords with the social practices of those with whom we have to live this present life—whether this manner of life is imposed by necessity or undertaken in the course of duty—should be related by good and serious men to the aims of self-interest and kindness, either literally, as we ourselves should do, or also figuratively, as is allowed to the prophets. 22. When those who are unfamiliar with different social practices come up against such actions in their reading, they think them wicked unless restrained by some

explicit authority. They are incapable of realizing that their own sort of behaviour patterns, whether in matters of marriage, or diet, or dress, or any other aspect of human life and culture, would seem wicked to other races or other ages. Some people have been struck by the enormous diversity of social practices and in a state of drowsiness, as I would put it—for they were neither sunk in the deep sleep of stupidity nor capable of staying awake to greet the light of wisdom—have concluded that justice has no absolute existence but that each race views its own practices as just. So since the practices of all races are diverse, whereas justice ought to remain unchangeable, there clearly is no such thing as justice anywhere. To say no more, they have not realized that the injunction "do not do to another what you would not wish to be done to yourself"[312] can in no way be modified by racial differences. When this injunction is related to the love of God, all wickedness dies; and when it is related to the love of one's neighbour, all wrongdoing dies. For nobody wants his own dwelling to be wrecked, and so he should not wish to wreck God's dwelling (which is himself). Nobody wants to be harmed by anybody; so he should not do harm to anybody. 23. So when the tyranny of lust has been overthrown love rules with laws that are utterly just: to love God on his account, and to love oneself and one's neighbour on God's account. Therefore in dealing with figurative expressions we will observe a rule of this kind: the passage being read should be studied with careful consideration until its interpretation can be connected with the realm of love. If this point is made literally, then no kind of figurative expression need be considered.

3.xvi

24. If the expression is a prescriptive one, and either forbids wickedness or wrongdoing, or enjoins self-interest or kindness, it is not figurative. But if it appears to enjoin wickedness or wrongdoing or to forbid self-interest or kindness, it is figurative. Scripture says, "Unless you eat the flesh of the Son of man and drink his blood, you will not have life in you."[313] This appears to enjoin wickedness or wrongdoing, and so it is figurative, a command to participate in the Lord's passion and to store in our memory the pleasurable and use-

---

311. See Hos 1:2–3.
312. Tob 4:16 (Vulgate); see also Tob 4:15; Mt 7:12; Lk 6:31.
313. Jn 6:53.

ful knowledge that his flesh was crucified and wounded for our sake.

3.xvii

25. It often happens that someone who is, or thinks he is, at a higher stage of the spiritual life regards as figurative instructions which are given to those at a lower stage. So, for example, a man who has embraced a life of celibacy and castrated himself for the sake of the kingdom of heaven[314] might maintain that any instructions given in the sacred books about loving or governing one's wife[315] should be taken not literally but figuratively; or someone who has resolved to keep his own daughter unmarried might try to interpret as figurative the saying "Marry off your daughter, and you will have done a great deed."[316] This too, then, will be one of our rules for interpreting scripture: we must understand that some instructions are given to all people alike, but others to particular classes of people, so that the medicine may confront not only the general pathology of the disease but also the particular weakness of each part of the body. What cannot be raised to a higher level must be healed at its own level.

3.xviii

26. Likewise we must take care not to regard something in the Old Testament that is not wickedness or wrongdoing by the standards of its own time—even when understood literally and not figuratively—as capable of being transferred to the present time and applied to our own lives. A person will not do this unless lust is in total control and actively seeking the complicity of the very scriptures by which it must be overthrown. Such a wretch does not realize that these things are written down for a useful purpose, to enable men of good conscience to see, for their own spiritual health, that a practice which they reject can have a good application, and that a practice which they embrace can be damnable, if the love shown by its followers (in the first case) or their greed (in the second) is taken into account.

3.xxii–xxiii

32. So all, or nearly all, of the deeds contained in the books of the Old Testament are to be interpreted not only literally but also figuratively; but (in the case of those which the reader interprets literally) if agents are praised but their actions do not agree with the practices of the good men who

since the Lord's coming in the flesh have been the guardians of the divine precepts, one should take up the figurative meaning into the understanding but not take over the deed itself into one's own behaviour. Many things were done in those times out of duty which cannot be done now except out of lust. 33. But when reading about the sins of great men, even if it is possible to observe or trace a prefiguration of future events in them, one should nevertheless take on board the literal meaning of the act, in this way. Bearing in mind the dangerous storms and miserable shipwrecks suffered by great men one should refrain from boasting of one's own deeds, which would be quite wrong, or despising others as sinners by the standards of one's own justice. Even the sins of these men have been recorded in order to put people everywhere in awe of the apostle's saying "So whoever thinks he stands must take care not to fall."[317] There is hardly a page in the Bible which does not proclaim the message: "God resists the proud, but gives grace to the humble."[318]

3.xxiv

34. The greatest care must therefore be taken to determine whether the expression that we are trying to understand is literal or figurative. When we have worked out that it is figurative, it is easy to study it from various angles, using the rules set out in Book 1, until we reach the true meaning, especially if we have the advantage of experience fortified by the exercise of holiness. We find out if an expression is literal or figurative by considering the criteria mentioned above.

3.xxv

Once this becomes clear, the words in which it is expressed will be found to be taken either from things that are similar or things that are in some way connected. 35. But since there are many ways in which things may resemble other things, we should not imagine that there is a hard and fast rule that a word will always have the meaning that it has in a particular place. The Lord used the word "leaven" in a pejorative sense when he said "Beware of the leaven of the Pharisees,"[319] but

---

314. See Mt 19:12.

315. See Eph 5:22–33; Col 3:18–19; 1 Pet 3:1–7.

316. Sir 7:27 (Vulgate) = Sir 7:25.

317. 1 Cor 10:12.

318. 1 Pet 5:5; Jas 4:6; citing Prov 3:34 (Septuagint).

319. Mk 8:15; Mt 16:6, 11; Lk 12:1.

in a commendatory sense when he said "The kingdom of heaven is like a woman who hid leaven in three measures of wheat until it was all leavened."[320]

36. Examination of these differences reveals two forms. The various meanings of a particular thing may be either contrary or just different. By contrary I mean cases in which a particular thing is used sometimes in a good sense and sometimes in a bad one, like the leaven just discussed. . . .

37. There are other things too which signify not just single ideas but, taken individually, two or often more ideas, depending on the contexts in which they are found. From passages where such things are expressed clearly one should find out how they are to be understood in obscure contexts. . . .

3.xxvii–xvii

38. Sometimes not just one meaning but two or more meanings are perceived in the same words of scripture. Even if the writer's meaning is obscure, there is no danger here, provided that it can be shown from other passages of the holy scriptures that each of these interpretations is consistent with the truth. The person examining the divine utterances must of course do his best to arrive at the intention of the writer through whom the Holy Spirit produced that part of scripture; he may reach that meaning or carve out from the words another meaning which does not run counter to the faith, using the evidence of any other passage of the divine utterances. Perhaps the author too saw that very meaning in the words which we are trying to understand. Certainly the spirit of God who worked through the author foresaw without any doubt that it would present itself to a reader or listener, or rather planned that it should present itself, because it too is based on the truth. Could God have built into the divine eloquence a more generous or bountiful gift than the possibility of understanding the same words in several ways, all of them deriving confirmation from other no less divinely inspired passages? 39. When one unearths an equivocal meaning which cannot be verified by unequivocal support from the holy scriptures it remains for the meaning to be brought into the open by a process of reasoning, even if the writer whose words we are seeking to understand perhaps did not perceive it. But this practice is dangerous; it is much safer to operate within the divine scriptures. When we wish to examine passages obscured by metaphorical expressions, the result should be something which is beyond dispute or which, if not beyond dispute, can be settled by finding and deploying corroboratory evidence from within scripture itself.

3.xxix

40. The literary-minded should be aware that our Christian authors used all the figures of speech which teachers of grammar call by their Greek name of tropes, and that they did so more diversely and profusely than can be judged or imagined by those who are unfamiliar with scripture or who gained their knowledge of figures from other literature. Those who know about these tropes recognize them in sacred literature, and this knowledge to some extent helps them in understanding it. This would not be the proper place to present them to people not familiar with them; I do not wish to look as if I am giving a course on grammar. I recommend that they be learnt independently; as indeed I have recommended already, in Book 2, when discussing the importance of learning languages. (Letters, from which grammar actually takes its name—the Greek word for them is *grammata*—are of course the signs of the sounds involved in the articulation of the words which we use when speaking.) In the divine books we find not only examples of these tropes, as of everything else, but also the names of some of them, like "allegory,"[321] "enigma,"[322] and "parable."[323] Almost all these tropes, which are said to be acquired through one of the "liberal" arts, are also found in the utterances of those who have had no formal teaching in grammar and are content with the style of ordinary people. Don't we all say "so may you flourish?" This is a metaphor. Don't we all refer to a swimming pool by the word *piscina,* which takes its name from fish even though it does not contain fish and was not made for fish? This trope is called catachresis.

From Augustine, *De doctrina Christiana,* edited and translated by R. P. H. Green (Oxford: Clarendon, 1995), 49, 51, 53, 61, 63, 67, 71, 73, 79, 81, 83, 85, 87, 89, 91, 125, 127, 133, 135, 137, 141, 143, 147, 149, 151, 153, 155, 157, 159, 165, 167, 169, 171.

---

320. Mt 13:33; Lk 13:21.
321. See Gal 4:24.
322. See Ezek 17:2; Prov 1:6 (both Vulgate); 1 Cor 13:12.
323. See Ps 77:2 (Vulgate); Prov 1:6 (Vulgate); Mk 3:23; 4:2–20; et passim.

In the fourth and fifth centuries the British monk and theologian **Pelagius** (354–418) was at the center of the so-called Pelagian controversy, which concerned Christian asceticism and the freedom of the will. Pelagius refuted many Augustinian doctrines, such as predestination. In *Commentary on Romans* (ca. 407), he interprets Adam as a "type," in conformity with his theories of the origin and consequences of sin.

PELAGIUS

Commentary on Romans, 5:11–21

11. *What is more, we also glory in God through our Lord Jesus Christ.* Not only shall we be [granted][324] eternal life, but we are promised a certain likeness through Christ to divine glory as well. As the apostle John says: "It has not yet become manifest what we shall be; we know that [when] he appears, we shall be like him."[325] *Through whom we have now received reconciliation.* Thus he means to show that Christ suffered so that we who had forsaken God by following Adam might be reconciled to God through Christ. 12. *Therefore, just as through one person sin came into the world, and through sin death.* By example or by pattern.[326] Just as through Adam sin came at a time when it did not yet exist, so in the same way through Christ righteousness was recovered at a time when it survived in almost no one.[327] And just as through the former's sin death came in, so also through the latter's righteousness life was regained. *And so death passed on to all people, in that all sinned.* As long as they sin the same way, they likewise die.[328] For death did not pass on to Abraham and Isaac [and Jacob], [concerning whom the Lord says: "Truly they are all living"[329]]. But here he says all are dead because in a multitude of sinners no exception is made for a few righteous. So also, elsewhere: "There is not one who does good, not even one,"[330] [and "every" one a liar."[331] Or: Death passed on to all who lived in a human, [and] not a heavenly, fashion. 13. *For before the law sin was in the world.* [The law] came as a punisher of sin. Before its coming sinners enjoyed the length of at least this present life with less restraint. There was indeed sin before the law, but it was not reckoned to be sin because [natural] knowledge had already been almost wiped out.[332] *But sin is not counted against one when the law does not exist.* How did death reign, if sin [was] not counted against one? Unless you understand: it was not counted against one "for the present time." 14. *But death reigned from Adam to Moses, even over those who did not sin after the manner of Adam's transgression.* Either: As long as there was no one who distinguished beforehand

between the righteous and the unrighteous, death imagined that it was lord over all. Or: Death reigned not only over those who, like Adam, transgressed a commandment—such as the sons of Noah, who were ordered not to eat the life in the blood,[333] [and] the sons of Abraham, for whom circumcision was enjoined[334]—but also over those who, lacking the commandment, showed contempt for the law of nature.[335] *Who is a type of the one to come.* Either: He was a type of Christ because, just as Adam was made by God without sexual intercourse,[336] so Christ issued from a virgin by the work of the Holy Spirit.[337] [Or, as] some say: An antithetical type: that is, as Adam is the source of sin, so too Christ is the source of righteousness. 15. *But the gift is not like the trespass.* In case one grants equal value to the type. *For if many died by the trespass of the one, how much more has God's grace and the gift in the grace of the one person Jesus Christ overflowed to more.* Righteousness had more power in bringing to life than sin in putting to death, because Adam killed only himself and his own descendants, but Christ freed both those who at that time were in the body and the following generations. But those who oppose the transmission of sin try to assail it as follows: "If Adam's sin," they say, "harmed even those who were not sinners, then Christ's righteousness helps even those who are not believers. For he says that in like manner, or rather to an even greater degree are people saved through the one than had previously perished through the other." Secondly, they say: "If baptism washes away that ancient sin, those who have been born of two baptized parents should not have this

---

324. Text between brackets [ ] indicates variants omitted by some manuscripts.

325. 1 Jn 3:2. (The notes for this selection are by Gerhart and Udoh.)

326. On the understanding of Adam as a "type," see Rom 5:14–15; 1 Cor 15:21–23, 45–49. This idea by Pelagius, namely, that sin is passed on from Adam to human beings "by example or by pattern" contrasts with the "traducianist" reading, especially by Augustine, of Gen 3 and with Paul's interpretation of this passage.

327. See Rom 3:9–26.

328. Pelagius reads the Latin expression *in quo* in a conditional or causal sense, against the relative sense which Augustine gives to the expression. See our note 583 on Augustine's *Encheiridion* VIII.26 in chapter 3.

329. Lk 20:38. Since these patriarchs are known to have died (see Gen 25:7–11; 35:27–29; 49:28–50:14), Pelagius must mean that they did not suffer *spiritual death*, the result of sinning "as" Adam did.

330. Ps 13:1, 3 (Vulgate) = Ps 14:1, 3; see also Rom 3:12 (Vulgate).

331. Rom 3:4.

332. See Rom 3:10–11; see also Ps 13:1–4 (Vulgate) = Ps 14:1–4.

333. See Gen 9:4.

334. Gen 17:10–14.

335. See Rom 1:18–32.

336. See Gen 1:26–27; 2:7.

337. See Mt 1:18–23; Lk 1:26–35.

sin, for they could not have passed on to their children what they themselves in no wise possessed. Besides, if the soul does not exist by transmission, but the flesh alone, then only the flesh carries the transmission of sin and it alone deserves punishment."[338] [Thus,] declaring it to be unjust that a soul which is born today, not from the lump of Adam, bears so ancient a sin belonging to another, they say that on no account should it be granted that God, who forgives [a person] his own sins, imputes to him another's. 16. *Again, the effect of the gift is not the same as that of the one sinner.* Rather, it is greater. *For the judgement from the one person is to condemnation.* From one [righteous] person who sinned has proceeded a judgement of death. *But grace is from many transgressions to justification.* Because Adam did not come by as much righteousness as he destroyed [by his example],[339] but Christ by his grace discharged the sins of many; and because Adam became only the model for transgression, but Christ [both] forgave sins freely and gave an example of righteousness. 17. *For if by the sin of one person death reigned through one person, how much more shall those who have received an abundance of grace and of the gift and of righteousness reign in life through the one person Jesus Christ.* By which he has forgiven many sins; and an abundance of the gift of the Holy Spirit, because there are many gifts;[340] and also righteousness is given through baptism, and is not gained by merit. 18. *Therefore, just as through one person's transgression in all people to condemnation, so also through one person's righteousness in all people to justification of life.* Death reigned, is understood; "so also grace reigned through justification." 19. *For just as through one person's disobedience many were made sinners, so also through one person's obedience many will be made righteous.* Just as by the example of Adam's disobedience many sinned, so also many are justified by Christ's obedience. Great, therefore, is the crime of disobedience that kills so many. 20. *For the law stole in so that transgression abounded.*[341] In case they say, "But the law forgave us our sins," he says, "It did not come to forgive transgressions, but to point them out, and when it is transgressed knowingly, transgression begins to abound." It is as [if] he were saying, as I see it, that the law did not take away sins, but added to them, and not because of its own fault, but because of theirs. Now it "stole in"—that is, it entered unexpectedly—and so it turned out that transgression abounded. But where transgression abounded, grace abounded all the more. Just as the Saviour says: "One who is forgiven more loves more."[342] For the amount of sin has been revealed so that the greatness of grace might be known and so that we might pay back a corresponding debt of love. 21. *So that, just*

as sin reigned in death, so also grace reigns through righteousness in eternal life, through Jesus Christ our Lord. [So that,] just as the reign of sin was abundantly established through contempt for the law, so also the reign of grace is established through the forgiveness of many sinners and thereafter through the doing of righteousness without cease.

From *Pelagius's Commentary on St. Paul's Epistle to the Romans,* translated by Theodore de Bruyn (Oxford: Clarendon, 1993), 92–96.

CAPPADOCIAN INTERPRETATION

🙐 **Basil the Great** (ca. 330–79) was bishop of Caesarea, in Cappadocia (Turkey), and one of the so-called Cappadocian Fathers, along with Gregory of Nyssa (his brother) and Gregory of Nazianzus (his friend). In *On the Holy Spirit* (written ca. 371) Basil hints at how his understanding of Scripture and its interpretation affects the defense of orthodoxy.

BASIL THE GREAT
On the Holy Spirit, I.1–2; V.7

I.1. My well-beloved and most honorable brother Amphilochios: I applaud your love of learning and your diligence in study. Indeed, I am amazed by the care and sobriety of your thoughts, particularly when you say that none of the words used to describe God should be passed over without exact examination, no matter what their context. You have profited from the Lord's exhortation, "Every one who asks, receives, and he who seeks, finds."[343] It seems to me that your eagerness to learn would move even those who are reluctant to share what they know. But what I admire most about you is that your questions reflect a sincere desire to discover the truth, not like many these days who ask questions only to test others. There is certainly no lack nowadays of people who delight in asking endless questions just to have some-

---

338. For the suggestion that sin is only in "the flesh," understood here as the body, see Rom 6:19; 7:17–18; 8:7–8. The question of the origin of the soul was disputed in the fifth century.

339. The phrase "by his example" may have been a later interpolation.

340. 1 Cor 12:4.

341. By reading the phrase *ut abundaret delictum* (Paul's ἵνα πλεονάσῃ τὸ παράπτωμα) not as a final clause but rather as a result clause, Pelagius avoids making the law the cause of sin.

342. See Lk 7:47.

343. Mt 7:8; Lk 11:10. (The notes for this selection are by Gerhart and Udoh.)

thing to babble about, but it is difficult to find someone who loves truth in his soul, who seeks the truth as medicine for his ignorance. Just as the hunter hides his traps, or an ambush of soldiers camouflages itself, so these questioners spew forth elaborately constructed inquiries, not really hoping to learn anything useful from them, because unless you agree with them and give them the answer they want, they imagine that they are fully entitled to stir up a raging controversy.

I.2. But if "Wisdom shall be given to a fool who seeks after wisdom,"[344] how great is the price at which we should value the "wise hearer," whom the Prophet places in the company of the "honorable counsellor"?[345] He first deserves to be given a hearty welcome, but then he should be urged on in the company of those who share his zeal, who labor with him in all things, as he presses forward to perfection. Those who are idle in the pursuit of righteousness count theological terminology as secondary, together with attempts to search out the hidden meaning in this phrase or that syllable, but those conscious of the goal of our calling realize that we are to become like God, as far as this is possible for human nature. But we cannot become like God unless we have knowledge of Him, and without lessons there will be no knowledge. Instruction begins with the proper use of speech, and syllables and words are the elements of speech. Therefore to scrutinize syllables is not a superfluous task. Just because certain questions seem insignificant is no reason to ignore them. Hunting truth is no easy task; we must look everywhere for its tracks. Learning truth is like learning a trade; apprentices grow in experience little by little, provided they do not despise any opportunity to increase their knowledge. If a man spurns fundamental elements as insignificant trifles, he will never embrace the fullness of wisdom. "Yes" and "No" are only two syllables, yet truth, the best of all good things, as well as falsehood, the worst possible evil, are most often expressed by these two small words. Why do I mention this? Because in former times someone on trial could join the ranks of Christ's martyrs by a single nod of his head, for this one act signified total commitment to true religion. If this is so, what theological term is so insignificant that it will not greatly upset the balance of the scales, unless it is used correctly? We are told that "not one jot nor one title shall pass away from the law;"[346] how then could we safely pass by even the smallest point? The questions that you want us to examine are both small and great: small, because it only takes a moment to utter the words in question—and for this reason they are thought to be negligible—but the force of their meaning is great. They can be compared to the mustard seed, for it is the smallest of

all seeds, but when properly grown its potential is revealed; it is the greatest of shrubs and becomes a tree.[347] Anyone who laughs at the subtlety of our use of syllables, while at the same time craftily devising false subtleties of his own, as the Psalmist says,[348] will end up reaping laughter's barren fruit. But as for us, let us not succumb to the reproaches of men, or be conquered by their contempt, so that we abandon our investigation. Far be it from me to be ashamed of these small matters; indeed, if I ever attain to even a fraction of their dignity, I would congratulate both myself for having won great honor and my brother and fellow-investigator for an achievement far above the mediocre. I am aware that little words express a great controversy, and in hope of winning the prize I will not hesitate to work. I am convinced that this discussion will prove to be useful for me, and fruitful for my hearers. Therefore, I begin this explanation asking the Holy Spirit to enlighten me, and with your approval, in order to point out the direction that the discussion will take, I will return for a moment to the origin of our question.

V.7. Having described our opponents' arguments, we shall now demonstrate our proposal: namely, that the Father does not accept "*from* whom" exclusively, and abandon "*through* whom" to the Son. Furthermore, we reject their arbitrary principle that the Son does not admit the Holy Spirit to share "*from* whom" or "*through* whom." "There is one God, the Father, *from* whom are all things . . . and one Lord Jesus Christ *through* whom are all things."[349] St. Paul does not say this to lay down an arbitrary law of prepositions, but to distinguish between the persons. He writes this not to introduce any division of natures, but to prove that the union of Father and Son is without confusion. It is obvious that the phrases in this passage do not contradict each other, nor do they separate the natures to which they are applied, like army squadrons facing each other in battle. The blessed Paul unites both for the same purpose when he says, "for *from* him and *through* him and *to* him are all things."[350] Even someone not paying much attention to the meaning of the words would admit that this passage clearly refers to the Lord. The Apostle has just quoted the prophecy of Isaiah: "Who has known the

---

344. Prov 17:28 (Septuagint).
345. See Isa 3:3 (Septuagint).
346. Mt 5:18.
347. See Mk 4:31–32; Mt 13:31–32; Lk 13:19.
348. See Ps 118:85 (Septuagint).
349. 1 Cor 8:6.
350. Rom 11:36.

mind of the Lord, or who has been His counsellor?"[351] and then goes on to say that "for from Him and through Him and to Him are all things." The prophet is speaking about God the Word, the Maker of all creation; we learn this from his previous words, "Who has measured the waters in the hollow of His hand and marked off the heavens with a span, enclosed the dust of the earth in a measure, and weighed the mountains in scales and the hills in a balance? Who has known the mind of the Lord or who has been His counsellor?"[352] This passage is not merely a rhetorical question; if it were, "who" could not possibly refer to anyone. Rather, the use of "who" indicates a rare personage. The following passages ask the same: "Who will rise up for me against the evildoers?"[353] or "What man is there who desires life?"[354] or "Who shall ascend the hill of the Lord?"[355] All these questions, including "Who has known the mind of the Lord, or who has been His counsellor?" have the same answer: "For the Father loves the Son, and shows Him all that He Himself is doing."[356] He it is who holds the earth, grasping it with His hands. He has arranged all things in order; He set the mountains in their places and measured the waters. He assigns to each thing in the universe its proper rank. He encompasses the expanse of the heavens with only a small portion of His power, which the prophet in his oracle calls a span. The Apostle's words are well spoken: "For from Him and through Him and to Him are all things." The cause of being comes *from* Him to all things that exist, according to the will of God the Father. *Through* Him structure and preservation are given to all things, for He created everything, and dispenses well-being to all things, according to the need of each. Therefore all things are turned toward Him, looking with irresistible longing and unspeakable love to the creator and sustainer of life as it is written: "The eyes of all look hopefully to Thee,"[357] and "These all look to Thee, to give them their food in due season,"[358] and again, "Thou openest Thy hand, and satisfiest the desire of every living thing."[359]

From Basil the Great, *On the Holy Spirit,* translated and with introduction by David Anderson (Crestwood, NY: St. Vladimir Seminary Press, 1980), 15–17, 22–24.

ory's dominant concern in biblical interpretation is to promote virtuous living.

GREGORY OF NYSSA

Treatise on the Inscriptions of the Psalms, part 1, I.5–8, IV.26–VI.49; part 2, II.11–21, IV.38–48

Part 1, I

5. The goal of the virtuous life is blessedness. For everything that one takes pains in doing is always referable to some goal. Just as the art of the physician looks to health, and the aim of farming is to provide for life, so also the acquisition of virtue looks to the one who lives by it becoming blessed. This is the summation and object of everything conceived in relation to the good. What is truly and properly contemplated and apprehended in this sublime concept, then, would reasonably be called the divine nature. For so the great Paul designated God when he put "blessed" before all the other words about God in one of his letters. He wrote in the following words, *"The blessed and only ruler, the King of kings and Lord of lords, who alone has immortality and who dwells in unapproachable light, whom no human being has seen or can see. To him be honour and rule forever."*[360]

6. All these sublime concepts about the divine would, then, in my opinion, constitute a definition of blessedness. For if someone were asked what beatitude is, he would give a properly pious answer if he followed Paul's statement and said that the nature which transcends everything is first and properly called blessed. Among humans, however, that beatitude, which is the nature of the one participated in, occurs to a certain extent, and is specified, by participation in true being. Likeness to God, therefore, is a definition of human blessedness.

7. Since, then, the truly good, or that which is beyond the good, in which everything that participates becomes blessed, is alone both blessed and desirable by nature, well does the

---

∾ In the first text by **Gregory of Nyssa** (ca. 335–95), *Treatise on the Inscriptions of the Psalms* (written probably between 376 and 378), he expounds on the meanings of the titles of the psalms in the Psalter. His interpretation, relying on Origen's *anagōgē*, is allegorical. Both here and in the second selection, his *Commentary on the Song of Songs* (written probably between 383 and 385), Greg-

351. Rom 11:34; Isa 40:13.

352. Isa 40:12–13.

353. Ps 93:16 (Septuagint) = Ps 94:16.

354. Ps 33:12 (Septuagint); see also Ps 34:12.

355. Ps 23:3 (Septuagint) = Ps 24:3.

356. Jn 5:20.

357. Ps 144:15 (Septuagint) = Ps 145:15.

358. Pss 103:27; 144:15 (Septuagint) = Pss 104:27; 145:15.

359. Ps 144:16 (Septuagint) = Ps 145:16.

360. 1 Tim 6:15–16. (The notes for this selection are by Gerhart and Udoh.)

divine scripture of the Psalter point the way to this for us through a skillful and natural sequence in teaching which is simple in its appearance and lacking in artifice by setting forth systematically in various and diverse forms the method for acquiring the blessing. It is possible, therefore, even in this first hymn[361] to get some idea of what lies ahead of us, and to see how the Word divides virtue into three parts and bears additional witness to beatitude by some suitable analogy for each division.

8. Now, on the one hand, it pronounces separation from evil to be blessed,[362] since this is the beginning of turning to what is better. But after this, it calls the meditation on things that are sublime and more divine blessed,[363] since this actually produces the capacity for what is better. Finally it pronounces blessed the likeness to God which is achieved by those who are being perfected through these stages, and on account of which the blessings previously received are mentioned. This latter is intimated by the evergreen tree, to which the life which has been perfected through virtue is likened.[364]

Part 1, IV

26. It would be appropriate now also to consider the banquet of virtues itself in the treatise according to the systematic theory we proposed earlier.

27. First, one can find virtue separated from evil by obvious indications, so that the difference between the two is distinct. For the distinguishing mark of the specific character of the pursuits is revealed by the joy which occurs in us from them—evil, on the one hand, brings joy to our physical senses, but virtue brings joy to the soul—since the nature of the essence discovered from these indications is fixed and unambiguous.

28. It is possible to discover this also from some other indications, both in the obvious meaning of the text and in the spiritual sense which is embedded in the depth of the thoughts in many psalms. This is especially so in the fourth Psalm, in which he says that they are *dull of heart* who do not distinguish what is *false* and *vain* from the truth, but *love* what is non-existent, and overlook what abides and is worthy of being loved.[365] For he says that *holiness* alone is truly *wonderful*,[366] and that all the other things which men eagerly pursue instead of those things which are good are conceits which have no existence in themselves, but seem to have being in the vain opinion of men.

29. And that he might disclose the teaching on these mat-

ters even more clearly, he goes on to say that the majority define the good in terms of phenomena when they say that that alone is good which one might demonstrate to sense-perception. For *"many,"* he says, *"say, Who will show us the good things?"*[367] He, however, who looks to virtue disregards this abject means of judging the good, and sees the good in the light.

30. And he takes note of the godlike and sublime joy as follows, and says that sense-perception is not of the nature to touch that light which radiates from the face of God. For he says, *"The light of your face has been imprinted on us, Lord."*[368] For the prophet does not seem to me to understand the face of God which is contemplated in certain imprints as anything other than the virtues, for the divine form is imprinted in these.

31. And after he has said this, he mentions the perfect mark of virtue: *"You put joy in my heart,"*[369] referring to the heart in place of the soul and the mind. For the mind cannot be pleased by the allurements of evil. But he opposes this material and physical prosperity to the joy of the heart, by saying that the belly is the criterion of the good for those who look to what is present. For when he says that *grain and wine*[370] are multiplied to such people, he includes all the pleasures of the stomach and food in part by the expression.

32. These pleasures rule every material pursuit, but the zeal for such things achieves no goal, for there is no way, by nature, of preserving the momentary pleasure which people experience, so that the pleasure which they so zealously acquire is stored away for them. On the contrary, it is as though those who love pleasure have grasped some deceptive phantom. Its splendour disappears immediately, and it passes into non-existence.

33. Shame is the one trace of such a phantom which remains after the departure. It stamps a deep and enduring impression of these activities on these people. By means of these traces one might arrive at the point of discerning the nature of the beast, so far as it can exist, by using the skill of hunters who follow tracks. For they, too, recognize the animal by its track when the prey is not seen. If, then, a boar or

---

361. See Ps 1:1–6.

362. See Ps 1:1.

363. See Ps 1:2.

364. See Ps 1:3.

365. See Ps 4:2 (Septuagint).

366. See Ps 4:3 (Septuagint).

367. Ps 4:6a (Septuagint); see also Ps 4:6a.

368. Ps 4:6b (Septuagint); see also Ps 4:6b.

369. Ps 4:7a (Septuagint) = Ps 4:7a.

370. See Ps 4:7b (Septuagint); see also Ps 4:7b.

a lion is made known by its peculiar tracks, it by all means follows that the nature of pleasure too is revealed by the track it leaves behind. Yet truly its track is shame. So it seems then, the pleasure which stamps such an impression on the soul is either, without doubt, shame itself, or is productive of shame.

34. But we considered this earlier in a digression on the topic, for we had to show, in relation to the general instruction which comes through the singing of psalms, what the goal is of each of the two pursuits, namely the pursuit of virtue and the pursuit of evil. Having noted in the aforementioned psalm, therefore, that the goal of virtue is peace, rest, and the abode which is simple and unmingled with the passions, which is attained on the basis of the hope of participating in God, that which is contrary to this was pointed out there by means of silence. Frequently, however, throughout the Psalms one cries out and says, *"The transgressors shall be utterly destroyed,"*[371] and *"The seed of the impious shall utterly perish,"*[372] and *"He who loves injustice hates his own soul,"*[373] and *"He will rain snares upon sinners,"*[374] and countless other words like these.

35. The whole book of Psalms is full of the praises of virtue and the condemnation of those who live in evil. Now the notice differs in the stories in relation to the two aims. On the one hand, it makes the virtue of persons who are honoured something to be envied, but on the other hand, it makes the wickedness of those who are condemned something to be avoided. For whenever it rouses you to virtue by example, it says, *"Moses and Aaron were among his priests, and Samuel among those who call upon him. They called upon the Lord and he heard them. He spoke to them in the pillar of cloud."*[375] But whenever the goal is to point out the wickedness of evil, it relates in detail the sufferings of those condemned in wickedness. *"The earth opened and swallowed Dathan, and covered the congregation of Abiram. The flame consumed the sinful."*[376] And, *"Make them as Madian and Sisara,"*[377] and *"Make their rulers as Oreb, and Zeb, and Zebee, and Salmana, all their rulers,"*[378] and many other such words.

36. From beginning to end the Psalms call out all these individual pieces of advice to you, nowhere neglecting to exhort you to the good, or to point out the means by which one may avoid evil. Everything has been joined together by thoughts which lead to the good. For the acquisition of the good becomes the avoidance and destruction of its opposite. It would be superfluous, however, to set all these things out in detail since the zeal of the treatise for such matters is obvious to those who read this writing.

Part 1, V

37. The entire treatise of the Psalms has been separated into five sections, and there is a systematic arrangement and division in these sections. The circumscription of the sections is obvious, since they conclude in a similar manner with certain ascriptions of praise to God. We must recognize these ascriptions of praise in relation to the division which we show to exist in the Psalms.

38. The number of psalms in each section is as follows: forty in the first section, thirty-one in the second, seventeen in the third, the same number also in the fourth, and forty-five in the fifth. The first part, then, concludes with the fortieth Psalm after the first, and ends with the words, *"Blessed be the Lord God of Israel forever and ever. So be it. So be it."*[379] The second part concludes with the seventy-first Psalm, the ending of which is, *"Blessed be the Lord, the God of Israel, who alone does marvelous things. And blessed be the name of his glory for ever and ever. The whole earth will be filled with his glory. So be it. So be it."*[380] The third part ends with the eighty-eighth Psalm, and this part too concludes in similar fashion, for it ends as follows: *"Blessed be the Lord for ever. So be it. So be it."*[381] The one hundred and fifth Psalm completes the fourth section. Its ending resembles the others. *"Blessed be the Lord the God of Israel from everlasting to everlasting. And all the people shall say, So be it, so be it."*[382] The fifth part extends from this psalm to the last one, whose ending is, *"Let every breathing creature praise the Lord."*[383]

39. It would be appropriate now, therefore, to say a few things about the systematic order we have observed in these sections. He places those who are living in the evil of wicked error in the first division, but he leads them to the choice of what is better. Consequently, they no longer *walk* in the deceits of the *"ungodly,"* nor *stand* deeply in the wicked *path*

---

371. Ps 36:38 (Septuagint) = Ps 37:38.
372. Ps 36:28 (Septuagint); see also Ps 37:28.
373. Ps 10:6 (Septuagint); compare Ps 11:5.
374. Ps 10:7 (Septuagint); see also Ps 11:6.
375. Ps 98:6–7 (Septuagint) = Ps 99:6–7.
376. Ps 105:17–18 (Septuagint) = Ps 106:17–18.
377. Ps 82:9 (Septuagint) = Ps 83:9.
378. Ps 82:11 (Septuagint) = Ps 83:11.
379. Ps 40:13 (Septuagint) = Ps 41:13.
380. Ps 71:18–19 (Septuagint) = Ps 72:18–19.
381. Ps 88:52 (Septuagint) = Ps 89:52.
382. Ps 105:48 (Septuagint) = Ps 106:48.
383. Ps 150:6. Gregory of Nyssa excludes Ps 151, which is found in the Septuagint, from his division and his treatise on the Psalms.

of sin, nor practise for themselves that evil which is *idle* and *seated,* but having attained to the unerring course for themselves, they cling to *"the"* divine *"law"* by *meditation,* so that the habit for what is better, *being watered* by the divine teachings, may become *rooted in* them like a *plant.*[384] The first entrance to the good, therefore, is the departure from those things which are opposite to it. The participation in what is superior occurs by means of this entrance.

40. The person, however, who has once tasted virtue and has come to understand its nature by his own experience of the good is no longer the kind of person who must be dragged away from his passionate attachment to evil by necessity and warning, and compelled to look to virtue. On the contrary, he has an excessive thirst for what is superior. For the Word compares unrestrained and excessive desire to thirst. The most thirsty nature among the beasts was sought out so that the intensity of desire might be shown above all by this beast which has an excessive thirst. And it calls this beast a *"hart,"*[385] whose nature it is to be fattened by the eating of venomous creatures. Now the juices of these creatures are warm, even extremely hot, and when the hart has eaten them it necessarily becomes dryer, having been purged by the juice of the creatures.[386] This is why it has an excessive desire for water, to quench the dryness it experiences from such food.

41. The person, therefore, who has been initiated into the life in virtue in the first part of the Psalter, and has discovered how sweet that which is desired tastes, and has consumed every creeping form of desire in himself, and with the teeth of self-control has devoured the passions in place of creatures, *thirsts* for participation in God more than *"the hart"* longs for *"the fountains of water."*[387] And it follows that the person who finds the fountain after this excessive thirst draws in as much water as the abundance of his desire draws off. But he who has received what he desired in himself is full of what he desired. For that which has become full is not again emptied on the model of physical satiety, nor does that which was drunk remain inactive in itself. In whomever the divine fountain has come into existence, it transforms the one who has embraced it to itself, and imparts to this person a portion of its own power.[388]

Part 1, VI

42. But indeed the capability of contemplating both the potentiality and the actuality of the things which exist is the unique property of deity. He, therefore, who has what he

desired in himself also becomes capable himself of such contemplation, and considers carefully the nature of the things which exist.

43. For this reason the Word has made this beginning of the third section of the Psalter in which it examines especially how the justice of the divine judgement will be preserved in the disparity of life, since good fortune in this life, so far as many things are concerned, does not occur for people in relation to the worth of their choices.[389] For it is frequently possible to observe the two extremes in the same person, namely the depth of evil and the peak of prosperity. Someone seeing this may become slack in his thinking, and think that perhaps what is designated the worse may be better for human nature, and that, on the contrary, which is considered in the portion of the better may be bad.

44. For if righteousness, on the one hand, is praised,[390] but the person who has eagerly pursued it fares badly,[391] and evil, on the other hand, is discredited, yet bestows a sufficient amount of enjoyment of all the things pursued on those who have eagerly pursued it,[392] how can one not think that evil, which is despised, is a preferable choice for life to virtue, which is praised?[393] He, therefore, who was lofty in mind, standing, as it were, on some prominent look-out point and straining his vision to see those things which were far removed, saw wherein the difference between evil and virtue lies.

45. The means of judging these matters is on the basis of their *ends,*[394] not on the basis of what is currently at hand. For by that eye of the soul which is capable of contemplation and discernment he has understood what has been stored up for the good through hope as though it were present, and

384. Summarizing and interpreting the first three verses of Ps 1, Gregory of Nyssa uses them to sum up the content of the first division of the Psalter.

385. In paragraphs 40–41 Gregory is discussing the second division of the Psalter, as is evident from the fact that this discussion is based on the imagery of the soul thirsting for God in Ps 41:1–2 (Septuagint).

386. The stories about deer eating snakes go back to classical authors (see, for example, Pliny, *Natural History,* 8.118; 28.149). They are common among the early Christian writers, beginning with Origen (see, for instance, *Homilies on the Canticle of Canticles,* 2.11).

387. Ps 41:1 (Septuagint) = Ps 42:1.

388. See Jn 4:13–14; 7:37–38.

389. In paragraphs 42–49 Gregory takes up the teaching of the third division of the Psalter. The discussion is based on Ps 72 (Septuagint), the first psalm in this division.

390. See Ps 72:1 (Septuagint) = Ps 73:1.

391. See Ps 72:13–14 (Septuagint) = Ps 73:13–14.

392. See Ps 72:3–12 (Septuagint) = Ps 73:3–12.

393. See Ps 72:2, 13 (Septuagint) = Ps 73:2, 13.

394. See Ps 72:17 (Septuagint) = Ps 73:17.

has passed over in his soul everything which appears to the senses. When he enters the heavenly shrines[395] he upbraids the lack of judgement of those who basely pervert the discernment of what is good to our physical members capable of sense-perception. This is why he says, *"For what do I have in heaven, and what do I desire on earth besides you?"*[396]

46. In the same portion of the Word he marvelously magnifies and exalts what is heavenly in his speech, and contemptuously and mockingly disparages and loathes that which the eyes of fools zealously pursue upon earth.[397] It is as if someone born at night should judge the darkness in which he was nurtured and grew up to be a great good, but later, when he has participated in the beauty of the open air, he despises his former judgement saying, "I used to prefer the darkness to which I was accustomed to such sights as the sun and stars and every beauty in heaven because I was ignorant of that which is superior." For which reason he condemns in advance in the Word his lack of judgement concerning what is good, saying that he was like a *beast*[398] until he saw the good in those things.

47. But, when he came to be *with God,*[399] and *the Word* was *God,*[400] and *was led by the right hand,*[401] and the Word, being on the right hand, became his *leader* by means of *counsel,*[402] and he saw the *glory*[403] in virtue, by means of which the assumption takes place for those who look to heaven, then he makes those statements, one of which considers that which is good in the heavens with wonder, but the other spits on the worthlessness and vanity of that zealousness which is deceived about life. Now the whole text is as follows. *"I became as a beast before you,"*[404] he says, indicating the irrational propensity in such people. Then he adds, *"But I am always with you."*[405]

48. And when he has said this he also adds the manner of union with God, so that we too might learn how the previous beast-like person is united with God after these things. For, he says, *"you grasped my right hand."*[406] He designates the eager desire for understanding in relation to things on the right as God's grasp. And *"by your counsel you have led me,"*[407] for guidance in relation to what is good does not take place without divine counsel. *"And with glory you have received me."*[408] Well does he contrast glory with shame. Glory becomes a chariot and a wing, as it were, of the one who is *received* by the divine hand, whenever one separates himself from the works of shame.

49. And thus he has added to what has been said, *"For what do I have in heaven, and what do I desire on earth besides you?"*[409] In respect to this latter saying, the majority of people

up to the present act as follows. Although such great things are freely theirs in heaven, nevertheless they consider to have come to be with God to be imaginary delusions in the category of a wish in relation to power or honour or wealth or this wretched little glory for which human nature is mad. But he who has come to be in these things consequently adds, *"But it is good for me to adhere to God, to put my hope in the Lord."*[410] He has shown that the one who adheres to God through hope and who has become one with Him is in some way united with him.

Part 2, II

11. In general, then, the subject-matter of the inscription has a twofold aim. For it has been superscribed either to indicate what lies below it, so that we learn the meaning in the words more quickly because we have been taught the aim of the psalm in advance, or, as is often the case, the inscription in and of itself points to something which is achieved in relation to virtue in the meaning in its own words, and instructs our hearing.

12. Or rather, there is one aim in each of the two classes of the scheme of the inscriptions, whether something historical seems to be indicated by what is said, or a mere name is added. This aim is to lead us to some aspect of those things which are good. For the divine scripture has not made use of historical information for the sole purpose of making us knowledgeable of facts through which we learn about certain deeds and experiences of the ancients, but that it might instruct us in teaching related to the virtuous life when the historical consideration is transferred to the more sublime meaning.

---

395. See Ps 72:17 (Septuagint) = Ps 73:17.
396. Ps 72:25 (Septuagint) = Ps 73:25.
397. See Ps 72:18–28 (Septuagint) = Ps 73:18–28.
398. Ps 72:22 (Septuagint) = Ps 73:22.
399. See Ps 72:23 (Septuagint) = Ps 72:23.
400. See Jn 1:1.
401. Ps 72:24, 23 (Septuagint) = Ps 73:23–24.
402. Ps 72:24 (Septuagint) = Ps 73:24.
403. Ps 72:24 (Septuagint); see also Ps 73:24.
404. Ps 72:22 (Septuagint) = Ps 73:22.
405. Ps 72:23 (Septuagint) = Ps 73:23.
406. Ps 72:23 (Septuagint) = Ps 73:23.
407. Ps 72:24 (Septuagint) = Ps 73:24.
408. Ps 72:24 (Septuagint); see Ps 73:24.
409. Ps 72:25 (Septuagint) = Ps 73:25.
410. Ps 72:28 (Septuagint); see also Ps 73:28.

13. If we are in agreement, then, that one must hold such a notion about the inscriptions, our next step, as we have already said, would be to set forth first the more general meaning of those which are similar, and to make an individual examination of those which are presented differently.

14. Since, then, the phrase *"unto the end"* has been inscribed over the greatest number of the psalms,[411] I think we must discern concerning this expression how the understanding of the others who have translated the same scripture clarifies it. For, instead of *"unto the end,"* one says *"for the one who gives victory,"* and another *"song of victory,"* and another *"unto victory."*[412]

15. Since, therefore, victory is the *"end"* of every contest, to which those look who strip down for the games and engage in the struggle, the Word seems to me, by the term *"end"* in this short phrase, to heighten the eagerness in those who are contending by means of virtues in the stadium of life, so that, by looking *"unto the end,"* which is the victory, they might lighten the labour in the contests by the hope of attaining crowns. Indeed we see this happening even now in the games. For when the crown is shown in advance to those wrestling with one another in the stadiums it strengthens their zeal for victory even more, since the labours which they experience in the wrestling are disguised by the honour which is anticipated.

16. Since, then, the stadium for contests lies open to everyone (now the common life of human beings is the stadium), in which there is one adversary, namely evil which contends against the wrestlers with all sorts of deceitful tricks, for this reason the good trainer of souls shows you the *"end"* of your strenuous labours in advance, that is, the adornment with crowns and the public proclamation based on your victory, so that, by looking to that *"end,"* you might entrust yourself to *"the one who gives victory"* and procure the announcement *"of victory"* for yourself.

17. But it would certainly be obvious to those who look to what follows from this starting point how many subsequent concepts of the teaching regarding virtue lurk in these words. For it is clear that the sufferings we experience in our soul are matched by the number of times our enemies grab and throw us. Our mind is frequently dislocated by these events, and wrenched out of place as if it were a limb of the soul, unless one has prepared himself by exercise and, by *struggling in accordance with the rules,* as the apostle says,[413] should attain to a state in which he cannot fall or be thrown in such contests, having acquired the victory for himself, which is *"the end"* of the contests.

18. Now the words which are inscribed along with the phrase *"unto the end"* are suggestions and advice related to victory, by means of which that which is eagerly desired might be attained. For the expression, *"of them that shall be changed,"*[414] enjoins the changing of the soul to the better.

19. And the interpretation of the name *"Maeleth"*[415] stirs the athlete up to greater zeal, since it indicates the choral dance which awaits us when our struggles are over. For the others have clarified this term in this way, translating *"Maeleth"* as *"by means of a choir."*

20. The Word brings together looking *to the hidden things,*[416] and composing *a song for the beloved,*[417] and singing *for the morning protection,*[418] and keeping the *octave*[419] before the eyes, and beholding *her who obtains the inheritance,*[420] and that we might be unrelated to *Core,*[421] and that great word of David, *"destroy not,"*[422] which he addressed to his armour-bearer when he was ready to kill Saul,[423] *to be inscribed as a title*[424] on the soul of each person for an example of patience.

21. Anyone who makes a careful examination would discover, in respect to all such phrases, that they are cheers for the athletes shouted to the combatants by the trainer, that one might attain *to the end* of victory. And likewise, if some historical information is inscribed along with the phrase, *"unto the end,"* it looks to this same goal, namely, that we might be encouraged even more in the contests by means of the historical examples. This is the meaning of the phrase, *"unto the end."*

Part 2, IV

38. The inscription, *"for them that shall be changed,"* seems to me to mean that the divine nature alone is superior to alteration and change.[425] For there is nothing in relation to

---

411. The phrase "unto the end" occurs as the title or as part of the title of fifty-five psalms in the Septuagint beginning with Ps 4 and occurring for the last time in Ps 139, that is, in all of Gregory's five divisions of the Psalter except the fourth. The New Revised Standard Version, following the Hebrew text, renders this phrase as "To the leader."

412. By "others" Gregory means those who had translated the Hebrew Scriptures into Greek, namely, Aquila, Symmachus, and Theodotion. See notes 198–200 above.

413. See 2 Tim 2:5.

414. Pss 59; 79 (Septuagint).

415. See Ps 53 (Septuagint).

416. See Ps 9 (Septuagint).

417. See Ps 44 (Septuagint).

418. See Ps 21 (Septuagint).

419. See Ps 11 (Septuagint).

420. See Ps 5 (Septuagint).

421. See Pss 41; 43–48; 83–84; 86 (Septuagint).

422. See Pss 57; 74 (Septuagint).

423. See 1 Sam 26:9.

424. Ps 59 (Septuagint).

425. See Jas 1:17.

which it might experience alteration, since it is, in general, incapable of experiencing evil, and it cannot be altered to something better. For it is not possible that it admit alteration in relation to anything, since there is nothing better than itself in relation to which it shall change.

39. We humans, however, situated with alteration and change on both sides, become either worse or better by our alternative activity. We become worse whenever we fall away from participation in those things which are good, and we become better again whenever we change to that which is superior. Since, then, we were associated with evil by means of alteration, we stand in need of the good change, so that by this means the transition to what is superior might take place in us. This is obvious from the context of the things recorded with *"them that shall be changed."* For the Word advises not only that it is necessary to be changed, but also suggests in what manner so great a thing may be accomplished by showing the transition to what is superior by means of examples.

40. The text of the inscription is as follows. "Unto the end, for them that shall be changed, for the inscription of a title, to David, for instruction, when he set fire to Mesopotamia of Syria and the Syrian Sobal; and Joab returned and slew the vale of the saltpits, twelve thousand men."[426] For it would be clear through what is said that this passage contains teaching and advice, since it says, "For the inscription of a title, to David, for instruction." For "instruction" would not have been added, if the passage did not have teaching in view.

41. And the expression, *"for the inscription of a title"* (*stēlographia*), shows that it is necessary to keep this word indelibly imprinted on our memory, since the memory is the stela of the soul, and the inscriptions on this stela are instances of good deeds. These were the heroic deeds of the commander-in-chief of David's forces. By these deeds he inflicted a twofold suffering on his enemies, once when they were consumed by fire, and once when they were brought to destruction by a stroke of calamity. For Syria in the middle of the rivers was consumed by fire along with the neighbouring regions of the Syrians, and the *vale of the saltpits* was likewise slaughtered with many thousands.

42. But to set forth the historical sequence accurately would be a long and, at the same time, superfluous task. For what would the advantage be if we were to learn the exposition of what happened in order? But I think it is better to set forth briefly in our treatise that to which the hidden meaning of the historical record leads us, so that so great an *inscription of a title for instruction of our life might occur for us.*

43. What is it, then, that I mean? He designated the en-

tire nation Syria, but divided this into two sections signifying each of them with its own name. For one of them is called *Mesopotamia of Syria,* and the other is designated *Sobal Syria,* and both the first and the second are burned to ashes. And after this, *the vale of the saltpits* is condemned to death with twelve thousand in consequence of the return of the commander-in-chief.

44. Let us think, therefore, that the external form of Syria is twofold. For some of them are encircled by the streams of the rivers. These would be those who are flooded with passions on all sides. Others, however, are opposite to Sobal. The definition indicated by this name is the despotic rule of the hostile power.

45. If, then, this twofold nation of evil should be destroyed by purifying fire, this would be the way of the change to what is superior for us. For just as virtue is characterized by life and thought, so too is evil seen to possess these two. The disorder in life, with which the streams of the passions encircle the soul, is designated the middle of the rivers,[427] and that which is dedicated to the ruler of this world by means of wicked opinions is named *Sobal Syria.*

46. When these have been devoured by the burning and purifying Word, it follows that the unproductive and salty land, which is the camp of the hostile powers, is *slain* by the calamitous stroke of the commander-in-chief. For we would not have experienced victory, had the leader of the hosts not prevailed with his hand. For peace follows the destruction of the enemies as a consequence, and it is to this consequence of victory that the inscription looks when it engraves the instruction to be changed on our memory and shows the deliverance from the passions by means of the historical examples.

47. The teaching about change would become more obvious to us were we to follow the other translators.[428] One of them has added to the statement, *"for the flowers,"*[429] instead of *change,* and the other, *"for the lilies."*[430] For the flower indicates the transition from winter to spring, which signifies the transference from evil to the life of virtue, and the ap-

---

426. Ps 59:1 (Septuagint). In the interpretation that follows, Gregory reads "the vale of the saltpits," instead of "twelve thousand men," as the direct object of the verb "slew."

427. That is, literally, Mesopotamia.

428. That is, the other Greek translations of the title that appears in Ps 79 (Septuagint).

429. Symmachus, according to Origen.

430. Aquila, according to Origen.

pearance of the lily sets forth the end result of the change, for one becomes radiant through change, that is to say, one receives a radiant and snowy expression instead of a black and murky one.

48. I think, therefore, that in every inscription to which the phrase, *"for them that shall be changed,"* has been added one must take the following counsel from the Word. It is always necessary to acquire that change to what is superior by means of prayer and diligence of life.

From *Gregory of Nyssa's Treatise on the Inscriptions of the Psalms,* translated by Ronald E. Heine (Oxford: Clarendon, 1995), 84–85, 92–100, 126–28, 132–35.

GREGORY OF NYSSA

Commentary on the Song of Songs, Prologue, The Song of Songs 1:1–4

Prologue

Greetings in the Lord, to the most worthy Olympias, from Gregory, Bishop of Nyssa.

I have learned as befitting your noble life and pure soul your concern for the Song of Songs which you have expressed to me both in person and by your letters. By an appropriate contemplation of the text, the philosophy hidden in its words become manifest, once the literal meaning has been purified by a correct understanding. Therefore, I have eagerly accepted your solicitude regarding this task. I do not offer you anything that would benefit your conduct, for I am persuaded that your soul's eye is pure from every passionate, unclean thought, and that it looks without hindrance at God's grace by means of these divine words of the Song. However, I hope that my commentary will be a guide for the more fleshly-minded, since the wisdom hidden [in the Song of Songs] leads to a spiritual state of the soul.

Because some members of the Church always think it right to follow the letter of holy scripture and do not take into account the symbolic and allegorical meanings, we must answer those who accuse us of doing so [that is, of using allegory]: there is nothing unusual in searching the divinely inspired scriptures with every means at our disposal. Thus if the literal sense, as it is called, should be of any use, we will readily have the object of our search. But if anything in the hidden, symbolic sense cannot be of use with regard to the literal sense, we will, as the Word teaches and as Proverbs says,[431] understand the passage either as a parable, a dark saying, an utterance of wise men, or as a riddle. With regards to anagogy, it makes no difference what we call it—tropology

or allegory—as long as we grasp the meaning of [scripture's] words.

The great Apostle [Paul] says that the Law is spiritual.[432] He includes under the name of Law the historical narratives, since all the inspired scriptures is Law for those who read them. They teach not only through precepts but through the historical narratives: both lead to knowledge of the mysteries and to a pure way of life for those who have diligent minds. Paul uses exegesis with an eye to what is useful and best for him; he is not concerned about the word necessary to designate the form of his exposition. However, Paul says that the name changes when he is about to transfer the meaning of the historical sense for showing the dispensation of the two Testaments. After mentioning the two children of Abraham—one born of a slave woman and the other from a free woman—Paul calls his consideration of them allegory.[433] In another place, after having related certain details of a story, he says, "These things happened to them as a warning, but they were written down for our instruction."[434] And again, after using the expression "You shall not muzzle an ox when it is treading out the grain,"[435] he added, "God does not care about oxen," but "clearly it has been written for our benefit."[436] Paul calls a mirror and a riddle that which is understood obscurely.[437]

Yet Paul somewhere calls the shift from the corporeal to the spiritual "a turning to the Lord and the removal of a veil."[438] In all these different expressions and names of contemplation Paul is teaching us an important lesson: we must pass to a spiritual and intelligent investigation of scripture so that considerations of the merely human element might be changed into something perceived by the mind once the more fleshly sense of the words has been shaken off like dust. For this reason Paul says, "the letter kills, but the spirit gives life."[439] If we stay only with the mere facts of the text, the historical narratives [of scripture] do not offer us examples of a good life. For what benefit to virtuous living can we obtain from the prophet Osee,[440] or from Isaiah having intercourse with a prophetess,[441] unless something else lies beyond the

431. See Prov 1:6 (Septuagint). (The notes for this selection are by Gerhart and Udoh.)

432. See Rom 7:14.

433. See Gal 4:24.

434. 1 Cor 10:11.

435. 1 Cor 9:9; see also Deut 25:4.

436. 1 Cor 9:9–10.

437. See 1 Cor 13:12.

438. 2 Cor 3:16.

439. 2 Cor 3:6.

440. See Hos 1:2–3.

441. See Isa 8:3.

mere letter? Or how do the stories regarding David, his terrible act of adultery and murder,[442] pertain to virtuous living? If anyone argues that these stories are reprehensible, then the saying of the Apostle will certainly be true:—"the letter kills"—for its examples of evil conduct, and "the spirit gives life." For the apparent, reprehensible sense is changed into something having a divine meaning.

We know that even the Word himself, who is adored by all creation, passed on the divine mysteries when he had assumed the likeness of a man. He reveals to us the meaning of the Law, saying that the two persons whose testimony is true consists of himself and of his Father.[443] The bronze serpent elevated on high which protected the people from the serpent's deadly stings was transformed for us into the dispensation of the Cross.[444] Christ trained his disciples' minds through sayings veiled and hidden in parables, images, obscure words, and terse sayings in riddles. Sometimes he gave an explanation which removed their obscurity.[445] But if the disciples occasionally did not grasp the intent of his words, Christ rebuked their slowness and lack of understanding. For example, he ordered the disciples to stay away from the leaven of the Pharisees, yet they were unhappy because their purses had no bread. Christ then upbraided them for failing to understand that leaven had symbolized their teaching.[446] Again, when his disciples were preparing a table, Christ responded, "I have food to eat of which you do not know." When they supposed he was speaking of bodily food which had been brought to him from elsewhere, Christ explained his own words, that the food proper to him is the fulfilment of the Father's salvific will.[447]

We can present many examples from the Gospel where the literal meaning differs from the text's intention. For example, the water he promised to the thirsty by which those who believe became springs of rivers;[448] the bread that comes down from heaven;[449] the temple which is destroyed and rebuilt after three days;[450] the way;[451] the gate;[452] the stone rejected by the builders and fit as the capstone;[453] the two people in one bed;[454] the mill stone; the woman grinding with one taken and the one left behind;[455] the body;[456] the eagles;[457] and the fig tree which becomes tender and puts forth buds.[458] All these and similar examples should serve to remind us of the necessity of searching the divine words, of reading them, and of tracing in every way possible how something more sublime might be found which leads us to that which is divine and incorporeal instead of the literal sense. Because of this, we believe that the tree from which it was prohibited to eat[459] was not the fig tree as some have maintained, nor any

other fruit trees. If the fig was then deadly, neither would it be edible now. At the same time, we have learned from our Lord, "it is not what goes into the mouth which can defile a man."[460] But we seek another meaning in this statement which is worthy of the lawgiver's majesty. If we hear that paradise was planted by God and that the tree of life is in the center of paradise,[461] we seek to learn from the One who reveals the hidden mysteries of which plants is the Father both the husbandsman and the dresser,[462] and how it is possible that there are two trees in the middle of paradise, one of salvation and the other of destruction. For the exact center as in the drawing of a circle has only one point. However, if another center is somehow placed beside or added to that first one, it is necessary that another circle be added for that center so that the former one is no longer in the middle.

There was only one paradise. How, then, does the text say that each tree is to be considered separately while both are in the middle? And the text, which reveals that all of God's works are exceedingly beautiful,[463] implies that the deadly tree is different from God's. How is this so? Unless a person contemplates the truth through philosophy, what the text says here will be either inconsistent or a fable.

It would take a long time to recount what each of the prophets have uttered. With regard to the last days, Micah says that a mountain will become visible on the peaks of other mountains.[464] He is referring to the mystery of piety which is being revealed for the destruction of the opposing powers. Other examples are as follows: The sublime Isaiah says that a rod will rise up [from Jesse] and a flower from the root,[465] thus revealing the Lord's manifestation in the flesh; the mountain swollen with pride of which David speaks, whose meaning becomes clear in the letter of the text;[466] the ten thousand

---

442. See 2 Sam 11:1–27.

443. See Jn 8:14–18.

444. See Num 21:8–9 and Jn 3:14; 8:28; 12:32–33.

445. See Mk 4:1–34; Mt 13:1–53; Lk 8:4–18.

446. See Mk 8:16–21; Mt 16:5–12.

447. See Jn 4:31–34.   450. See Jn 2:19–22.

448. See Jn 4:13–14; 7:37–39.   451. See Jn 14:4–6.

449. See Jn 6:35, 47–58.   452. See Mt 7:13–14.

453. See Mk 12:10–11; Mt 21:42; Lk 20:17; all citing Ps 117:22–23 (Septuagint).

454. See Lk 17:34.   456. See Mt 24:28; Lk 17:37.

455. See Mt 24:41; Lk 17:35.   457. See Mt 24:28; Lk 17:37.

458. Mk 13:28–29; Mt 24:32–33; Lk 21:29–31.

459. See Gen 2:16–17.   463. See Gen 1:31.

460. Mt 15:11.   464. See Mic 4:1 (Septuagint).

461. See Gen 2:9.   465. See Isa 11:1 (Septuagint).

462. See Jn 15:1–2.   466. Ps 67:16 (Septuagint).

chariots; the gathering of bulls with the heifers of the nations; the foot washed in blood;[467] the dog's tongues;[468] and Lebanon of the cedars jumping like a calf.[469] Many such examples could be gathered from other prophecies to teach us the necessity of contemplating the words according to their deeper meaning. If this contemplation is rejected as some would like to do, it seems to me that it would be like offering wheat for human consumption without having ground the corn; or having divided the seeds from the chaff by winnowing; or having cleaned the grain of husks for flour; or having prepared the bread in the proper way. Therefore, just as food not worked over is fit for beasts and not for man, so one could say that the inspired words, when not worked over by a more subtle contemplation, are food for irrational beasts rather than for rational men. And not only does this apply to the Old Testament, but also to many of the Gospel's teachings: the winnowing fan which cleanses the threshing floor; the chaff which is removed; the grain which remains on the feet of those winnowing it; the unquenchable fire; the good granary;[470] the tree bearing bad fruit;[471] the threat of the axe which shows its terrible edge to the tree;[472] and stones used as metaphors for men.[473]

Let what I have just mentioned stand as my defense against those who advise us to look for nothing more in the divine words than their literal meaning. Although Origen laboriously applied himself to the Song of Songs, we too have desired to publish our efforts.

Song of Songs 1:1–4

The one who establishes this law is Solomon. According to the divine testimony, his wisdom has no measure. It has no comparison with respect to both all who preceded him and all who are to come after him. Nothing escapes his notice.[474] Do not suppose that I mean the same Solomon from Bersabee[475] who offered upon the mountains the sacrifice of a thousand victims,[476] who sinned by following the counsel of a Sidonian woman.[477] No, another Solomon [Christ] is signified here: one who is also descended from the seed of David according to the flesh,[478] one whose name means peace, the true king of Israel and builder of God's temple. This other Solomon comprehends the knowledge of all things. His wisdom is infinite and his very essence is wisdom, truth, as well as every exalted, divine name and thought. [Christ] used Solomon as an instrument and speaks to us through his voice first in Proverbs and then in Ecclesiastes. After these two books he speaks in the philosophy set forth in the Song of

Songs and shows us the ascent to perfection in an orderly fashion.

Not all periods of life according to the flesh are capable of every natural operation; nor do our lives advance in the same way at different periods. (The infant has no share of adult activities, nor is an adult taken up in its nurse's arms, but each time of life has its own proper activity.) So too one can see in the soul an analogy to the body's growth where there is a certain order and sequence leading to a life in accord with virtue.

For this reason, Proverbs teaches in one way and Ecclesiastes in another; the philosophy of the Song of Songs transcends both by its loftier teaching. The instruction in Proverbs provides words fit for the person who is still young, adapting its words of admonition to that period of life. "Hear, my son, your father's instruction and reject not your mother's teachings."[479] You see here that the soul is at a stage of life where it is tender and easily formed. Moreover, it still needs maternal instruction and paternal admonition. In order that the infant may listen more willingly to his parents and be more careful in his lessons, he is promised childish trinkets. Such trinkets are the gold chain shining around his neck and the crown entwined with pretty flowers.[480] It is necessary to understand these things fully if the symbol's intent is to point to something better. Thus Proverbs begins the description of wisdom to the child in several different ways and expounds the ineffable beauty so as not to inspire any fear or constraint; rather, it draws the child by yearning and desire to participate in the good. The description of beauty somehow attracts the desire of the young to what is shown, fanning their desire for a participation in beauty.

In order that our affections may be further intensified after having changed our material inclinations to an immaterial state, Solomon adorns the beauty of wisdom with praise.

---

467. See 3 Kings 20:19 (Septuagint); 1 Kings 22:38.
468. See 1 Kings 21:19.
469. See Ps 28:6 (Septuagint) = Ps 29:6.
470. See Mt 3:12; Lk 3:17.
471. See Mt 7:17–18; 12:33; Lk 6:43–44.
472. See Mt 3:10; Lk 3:9.
473. See 1 Pet 2:5–8.
474. See 3 Kings (Septuagint) = 1 Kings 3:12, 28; 4:29–34.
475. 2 Kings (Septuagint) = 2 Sam 12:24.
476. 3 Kings (Septuagint) = 1 Kings 3:4.
477. 3 Kings (Septuagint) = 1 Kings 11:1–8.
478. See Rom 1:3.
479. Prov 1:8.
480. See Prov 1:9.

Not only does he present its loveliness with words, but he also states the wealth contained in wisdom, whose Lord will surely dwell with us. The wealth is then seen in the showy adornments of wisdom. The adornment of her right hand is all the ages, since the Word says: "Length of existence and years of life are in her right hand."[481] And on her left hand she wears the precious wealth of the virtues together with the splendor of glory: "And on her left hand are wealth and glory."[482] Then Solomon speaks of the fragrance from the bride's mouth which breathes the good odor of righteousness: "From her mouth comes forth righteousness."[483]

In place of the natural redness of the bride's lips, he says, law and mercy blossom.[484] In order that beauty might be fully attributed to such a bride, her gait is also praised: "In the paths of righteousness she walks."[485] In praising her beauty, Solomon also praises her great size which equals that of a flourishing plant shooting up into full bloom. This plant to which her height is compared, he says, is the tree of life which nourishes those who lay hold of her, a firm and stable column to those who lean upon her. I think that both examples refer to the Lord: He is our life and support. Thus the text reads: "She is a tree of life to those who lay hold of her" and for those who lean upon her as upon the Lord she is firm.[486] Strength is included along with the remaining praises, that the praise of wisdom's beauty might be completely filled with all good things. "For God founded the earth by wisdom and prepared the heavens by prudence."[487] All the elements in creation Solomon attributes to the power of wisdom and adorns her with many names, for he means the same thing by wisdom, prudence, sense perception, knowledge, apprehension, and the like.

Solomon next escorts the youth to a special dwelling and exhorts him to gaze at the divine bridal chamber. "Do not let her go, and she will cleave to you. Love her and she will guard you. Secure her and she will exult you. Honor her in order that she may embrace you, that she may give to your head a crown of graces, and may cover you with a crown of delight."[488] The youth now adorned with these nuptial crowns as a bridegroom is exhorted not to depart from wisdom: "Whenever you walk, bring her and let her be with you. Whenever you sleep, let her guard you in order that when you wake she may converse with you."[489] With these and other such exhortations Solomon has inflamed the desire of the one still young according to the inner man, and has shown Wisdom describing herself. In this way Solomon elicits the love of those listening to him. Besides this, Wisdom says: "I love those who love me"[490]—for the hope of

being loved in return disposes the lover to a more intense desire. Along with these words Solomon added other counsels by clear and easily grasped utterances. He leads the youth to a more perfect state in the final verses of Proverbs where he calls "blessed" the union of love in that section pertaining to the praises of the brave woman.[491] Then Solomon adds the philosophy contained in Ecclesiastes for the person who has been sufficiently introduced by proverbial training to desire virtue. After having reproached in that book men's attitudes towards external appearances, and after having said that everything unstable is vain and passing ("everything which passes is vanity").[492] Solomon elevates above everything grasped by sense the loving movement of our soul towards invisible beauty. Having thus cleansed the heart with respect to external matters, Solomon then initiates the soul into the divine sanctuary by means of the Song of Songs. What is described there is a marriage; but what is understood is the union of the human soul with God.

Because of this, the son in Proverbs is named a bride, and Wisdom is changed into the role of a bridegroom so that a person might be espoused to God by becoming a pure virgin instead of a bridegroom. By clinging to the Lord he might become one spirit[493] through a union with what is pure and free from passion and have a pure mind instead of burdened with the flesh's weight. Since it is Wisdom speaking, love as much as you can with your whole heart and strength;[494] desire as much as you can. I boldly add to these words: "Be passionate about it." This affection for incorporeal things is beyond reproach and free from lust as Wisdom states in Proverbs when she prescribes passionate love [ἔρως] for the divine beauty.

But the text now before us gives the same exhortation. It does not merely offer advice regarding love, but through ineffable mysteries it philosophizes and offers an image of the pleasures of life as a preparation for its instruction. The image is one of marriage where the desire for beauty acts as intermediary. The bridegroom does not initiate the desire

---

481. Prov 3:16a.

482. Prov 3:16b.

483. Prov 3:16c (Septuagint).

484. See Prov 3:16c (Septuagint).

485. Prov 8:20.

486. See Prov 3:18a–b (Septuagint).

487. Prov 3:19 (Septuagint).

488. Prov 4:6–9 (Septuagint).

489. Prov 6:22.

490. Prov 8:17.

491. See Prov 31:10–31.

492. Eccl 11:8.

493. See 1 Cor 6:17.

494. See Dt 6:5; Mk 12:30; Mt 22:37; Lk 10:27.

according to normal human custom, but the virgin anticipates the bridegroom without shame, openly makes her passion known, and prays that she may enjoy the bridegroom's
kiss.[495]

Those attending the betrothed virgin are the patriarchs,
prophets, and givers of the Law. They bring divine gifts to the
bride, her wedding gifts, as it were. (Some examples of these
gifts are forgiveness of trespasses, forgetfulness of evil deeds,
the cleansing of sins, transformation of nature, the exchange
of corruptibility for incorruptibility, enjoyment of paradise,
the dignity of God's kingdom, and joy without end.) When
the virgin receives all these divine gifts from the noble bearers who bring them through their prophetic teaching, she
both confesses her desire and hastens to enjoy the favor of
the beauty of the One she so eagerly desires. The virgin's attendants and associates hear her and spur her on to an even
greater desire.[496] The bridegroom then arrives leading a chorus of his friends and well-wishers.[497] These represent either
the ministering spirits by whom men are saved[498] or the holy
prophets. Hearing the bride's voice, they exult and rejoice[499]
at the consummation of the pure union by which the soul
that clings to the Lord becomes one Spirit with Him, as the
Apostle says.[500]

I will take up again what I said at the start of this homily: let no one who is passionate, fleshly and still smelling of
the foul odor of the old man[501] drag down the significance of
the divine thoughts and words to beastly, irrational thoughts.
Rather, let each person go out of himself and out of the material world. Let him ascend into paradise through detachment, having become like God through purity. Then let him
enter into the inner sanctuary of the mysteries revealed in this
book [the Song of Songs]. If the soul is unprepared to hear
this, let it listen to Moses who forbids us to ascend the spiritual mountain before washing the garments of our hearts and
before purifying our souls with the fitting aspersions of our
thoughts. As we apply ourselves to this contemplation, we
must put aside thoughts of marriage as Moses commanded[502]
when he ordered those being initiated to cleanse themselves
from marriage. We must follow his prescriptions when we
are about to approach the spiritual mountain of the knowledge of God: thoughts about women, along with material
goods, are left with the life below. If any irrational notion
should be seen around this mountain, it is destroyed with
firmer thoughts as by stones. Otherwise, we would hardly
be able to hear the sound of that trumpet reverberating with
a great and awesome sound which is beyond the capacity of
those who hear it. This sound comes from the dark obscurity

where God is and who burns with fire every material thing
upon this mountain.[503]

Now let us enter the Holy of Holies, Song of Songs. In the
expression "Holy of Holies" we are taught a certain super-
abundance and exaggeration of holiness. Through the title
Song of Songs the noble text also promises to teach us the
mystery of mysteries. To be sure, there are many songs in
the divinely inspired teaching by which we acquire great
knowledge about God from David, Isaiah, Moses, and many
others. However, we learn from the title Song of Songs that
just as the songs of the saints surpass the wisdom of profane songs, so does the mystery contained here surpass the
songs of the saints. Indeed, human understanding left to its
own resources could neither discover nor absorb the Song's
mystery. The most acute physical pleasure (I mean erotic passion) is used as a symbol in the exposition of this doctrine on
love. It teaches us of the need for the soul to reach out to the
divine nature's invisible beauty and to love it as much as the
body is inclined to love what is akin to itself. The soul must
transform passion into passionlessness so that when every
corporeal affection has been quenched, our mind may seethe
with passion for the spirit alone and be warmed by that fire
which the Lord came to cast upon the earth.[504]

I have said enough about how those who hear these mystical words should have their souls disposed. Now the time
has come to begin our interpretation of the divine words
of the Song of Songs. First let us consider the significance
of the title. It is not accidental, I think, that the book is ascribed to Solomon.[505] This serves as an indication to readers
to expect something great and divine. Solomon's reputation
for wisdom is unexcelled, and everyone is impressed by it.
Therefore, the mention of his name at the outset raises the
reader's expectation to find something great and worthy of
such a reputation.

In the art of painting different colors combine to represent the subject portrayed. However, the person looking at
the image created by the skillful use of colors does not linger
over the colors painted on the tablet; he beholds instead only
the form which the artist has shown. Thus it is with the present scripture: we should not look at the material of the colors

---

495. Song 1:1–2.
496. See Song 1:2–8.
497. See Song 1:9–2:7.
498. See Heb 1:14.
499. See Jn 3:29.
500. See 1 Cor 6:17.
501. See Rom 6:6; Eph 4:22; Col 3:9; 2 Cor 2:16.
502. See Ex 19:14–15.
503. See Ex 19:16–19.
504. See Lk 12:49.
505. Song 1:1.

[i.e. the words]; rather, we should consider the image of the king expressed by them in the chaste concepts. For white, yellow, black, red, blue, or any other color are these words in their obvious meaning—mouth, kiss, myrrh, wire, bodily limbs, bed, maidens, and so forth. The form constituted by these terms is blessedness, detachment, union with God, alienation from evil, and likeness to what is truly beautiful and good. These concepts testify that Solomon's wisdom surpassed the boundaries of human wisdom. What could be more paradoxical than to make nature purify itself of its own passions and teach detachment [ἀπάθεια] in words normally suggesting passion [πάθος]? Solomon does not speak of the necessity of being outside of the flesh's impulses or of mortifying our bodily limbs on earth, or of cleansing our mouths of talk of passion; rather, he disposes the soul to be attentive to purity through words which seem to indicate the complete opposite, and he indicates a pure meaning through the use of sensuous language.

The text should teach us one thing by its introductory words: those introduced into the hidden mysteries of this book are no longer men, but they have been transformed in their nature through the Lord's teaching into something more divine. The Word testified to his disciples that they were more than men. He differentiated them from other men when he said to them: "Who do men say that I am?"[506] The Song's text readily employs words whose obvious meaning indicates the enjoyment of carnal passion. Yet it does not fall into any improper meaning but leads us to the philosophy of divine things by means of chaste concepts. It shows that we are no longer to be men with a nature of flesh and blood;[507] rather, it points to the life we hope for at the resurrection of the saints, an angelic life free from all passion.[508]

After the resurrection, the body, which has been transformed into incorruptibility, will again be joined to the soul. The passions now disturbing us because of the flesh will not be restored with those bodies; rather, we shall become tranquil. No longer will the flesh's prudence dispute with the soul. No longer will there be civil war with the passions set against the mind's law, where the soul is overcome and taken captive by sin.[509] Nature will then be cleansed from all such things, and one spirit will be in both (I mean both in the flesh and in the spirit), and every corporeal disposition will be banished from human nature. Thus the text of the Song exhorts us, even if we now live in the flesh, not to turn to it in our thoughts; rather we should only regard the soul and attribute all manifestations of affection in the text to the surpassing goodness of God as pure, undefiled offerings. For

God alone is truly sweet, desirable and worthy of love. The present enjoyment of God is the starting point for a greater share of his goodness, and it increases our desire for him. Thus, in Moses the bride loved the bridegroom.[510] As the virgin says in the Song: "Let him kiss me with the kisses of his mouth."[511] Moses conversed with God face to face, as scripture testifies,[512] and he thereby acquired a still greater desire for these kisses after the theophanies. He sought God as if he had never seen him. So it is with all others in whom the desire for God is deeply embedded: they never cease to desire, but every enjoyment of God they turn into the kindling of a still more intense desire.

Even now the soul united to God never has its fill of enjoyment. The more it enjoys his beauty, the more its desire for him increases. The words of the bridegroom are spirit and life,[513] and everyone who clings to the Spirit becomes spirit. He who attaches himself to life passes from death into life as the Lord has said.[514] Thus the virginal soul desires to draw near to the fountain of spiritual life. The fountain is the bridegroom's mouth from which the words of eternal life well forth. It fills the mouth drawn to it, just as with the prophet when he drew in the spirit through his mouth.[515] Since it is necessary for the person drawing water from a fountain to apply his mouth to its mouth, and since the Lord himself is a fountain as he says: "If anyone thirsts, let him come to me and drink,"[516] so the thirsting soul wishes to bring its mouth to the mouth that springs up with life and says: "Let him kiss me with the kisses of his mouth."[517] He who wells up with life for all and wishes all to be saved desires every person to share this kiss, for this kiss purges away all filth.

It seems to me that the Lord was reproaching Simon the Leper when he said: "You gave me no kiss."[518] He meant by this: you would have been cleansed of disease if you had drawn purity with your mouth. But in all likelihood Simon was unworthy of love since he had an excess growth of flesh through his illness and remained unmoved in desire for God by reason of his disease. But once the soul has been cleansed and is no longer hindered by the leprosy of the flesh, it looks

---

506. Mk 8:27; Mt 16:13.
507. See Mt 16:17.
508. See Mk 12:25; Mt 22:30; Lk 20:36.
509. See Rom 7:23.   514. See Jn 5:24.
510. See Ex 33:11.   515. See Ps 117:131 (Septuagint).
511. Song 1:2.   516. Jn 7:37–38.
512. See Ex 33:11; Deut 34:10.   517. Song 1:2.
513. See Jn 6:63.   518. Lk 7:45.

to the treasure house of all good things. A name for this treasure house is the heart. From it there comes to the breasts the wealth of divine milk by which the soul is nourished and draws grace in proportion to its faith. Therefore the soul exclaims: "Your breasts are better than wine,"[519] signifying by the breasts the heart. Nobody will err if he understands by the heart the hidden, secret power of God. One would rightly suppose that the breasts are the activities of God's power for us by which he nourishes each one's life and bestows appropriate nourishment.

We are indirectly taught another lesson through the philosophy of this book, namely that perception within us is twofold—bodily and divine. As the Word says in Proverbs, "You will find perception of God."[520] A certain analogy exists between the activities of the soul and the sense organs of the body. This we learn from the present text. Wine and milk are distinguished by taste, while the intellectual and apprehending capacity of the soul grasps spiritual realities. A kiss is effected through the sense of touch; the lips of two persons make contact in a kiss. On the other hand, there is a certain sense of touch in the soul which takes hold of the Word and works in an incorporeal, spiritual way. As John says: "Our hands have handled the word of life."[521] Similarly, the scent of the divine perfumes is not perceived by the nose, but by a certain spiritual and immaterial power drawing in the good odor of Christ[522] by an inhalation of the Spirit. Thus, the next part of the virgin's prayer in the Song's first words says: "Your breasts are better than wine, and the scent of your perfumes is beyond all ointments."[523]

What is signified by these words is, in our opinion, neither trivial nor unimportant. Through the comparison of milk from the divine breasts with the enjoyment obtained from wine we learn, I think, that all human wisdom, science, power of observation and comprehension of imagination cannot match the simple nourishment of the divine teaching. Milk, the food of infants, comes from the breasts. On the other hand, wine, with its strength and warming capacity, is enjoyment for the more perfect. However, the perfection of the wisdom of the world is less than the childlike teaching of the divine world. Hence the divine breasts are better than human wine, and the scent of divine perfumes is lovelier than any fragrance.

The meaning seems to me to be as follows: We understand the perfumes as virtues—wisdom, justice, temperance, fortitude, and so forth. If we anoint ourselves with these aromas, each of us, according to our own capacity and choice, has a good odor. Each of us has his respective odor—one

has wisdom or temperance, another has fortitude or justice, or anything else pertaining to virtue. Another person may have a good odor within himself compounded from all these perfumes. However, all of them together could not compare with that perfect virtue which the heavens contain. As the prophet Habakkuk says: "His virtue covered the heavens."[524] This is God's absolute wisdom, justice, truth, and all the rest. Therefore, the odor of the heavenly ointments, he says, holds a delight which is incomparable to any aroma known by us.

From Saint Gregory of Nyssa, *Commentary on the Song of Songs*, translated by Casimir McCambley (Brookline, MA: Hellenic College Press, 1987), 35–39, 44–56.

MEDIEVAL INTERPRETATION

❧ In his influential exegetical work *Morals on the Book of Job* (begun ca. 579 or 585 and completed ca. 596), **Gregory the Great** (ca. 540–604; Pope Gregory I from 590 to 604) presents his tripartite method of interpreting Scripture: literal, allegorical, and moral.

GREGORY THE GREAT
Morals on the Book of Job,
Preface, 13–21; book I.1–9, 14–29

Preface

13. But amongst these marvelous works of Divine Providence it yields us satisfaction to mark, how, for the enlightening the night of this present life, each star in its turn appears in the face of Heaven, until that towards the end of the night the Redeemer of mankind ariseth like the true Morning Star; for the space of night, being enlightened by the stars as they set and rise in their courses, is passed with the heavens in exceeding beauty. Thus in order that the ray of stars, darting forth at its appointed time, and changed in succession, might reach the darkness of our night, Abel comes to shew us innocence; Enoch, to teach purity of practice; Noah, to win admittance for lessons of endurance in hope and in work; Abraham, to manifest obedience; Isaac, to shew an example of chastity in wedded life; Jacob, to introduce patience in la-

---

519. Song 1:2 (Septuagint).
520. Prov 2:5b.
521. 1 Jn 1:1.
522. See 2 Cor 2:15.
523. Song 1:2–3 (Septuagint).
524. Hab 3:3 (Septuagint).

bour; Joseph, for the repaying evil with the favor of a good turn; Moses, for the shewing forth of mildness; Joshua, to form us to confidence against difficulties; Job, to shew patience amid afflictions. Lo what lustrous stars see we in the sky, that the foot of practice may never stumble as we walk this our night's journey; since for so many Saints as God's Providence set forth to man's cognizance, He, as it were, sent just so many stars into the sky, over the darkness of erring man, till the true Morning Star should rise, Who, being the herald to us of the eternal morning, should outshine the other stars by the radiance of His Divinity.

14. And all the elect, whilst by their holy living serving as His forerunners, gave promise of Him by prophesying both in deeds and words. For there never was any Saint who did not appear as His herald in figure; for it was meet that all should display that goodness in themselves whereby both all became good, and which they knew to be for the good of all, and therefore that blessing ought also to be promised without pause which was vouchsafed both to be received without price and to be kept without end, that all generations might together tell what the end of all should bring to light, in the redemption of which all were partakers. And therefore it behoved that blessed Job also, who uttered those high mysteries of His Incarnation, should by his life be a sign of Him, Whom by voice he proclaimed, and by all that he underwent should shew forth what were to be His sufferings, and should so much the more truly foretell the mysteries of His Passion, as he prophesied then not merely with his lips but also by suffering. But because our Redeemer has shewn Himself to be one with the Holy Church, which He has taken to Himself; for of Him it is said, *Who is the Head of us all;*[525] and of the Church it is written, *the Body of Christ, Which is the Church;*[526] whosoever in his own person betokens Him, at one time designates Him in respect of the Head, at another of the Body, so as to have not only the voice of the Head, but also of the Body; and hence the prophet Isaiah, in giving utterance to the words of the same Lord, says, *He hath put upon me a mitre like unto a Bridegroom, and hath decked me with jewels as a Bride.*[527] Therefore because the same person that in the Head is the Bridegroom, is in the Body the Bride, it follows that when, at times, any thing is spoken from the Head, there must be a turning down by degrees or even at once to the voice of the Body, and again when any thing is said that is of the Body, there must be presently a rising to the voice of the Head. Accordingly the blessed Job conveys a type of the Redeemer, Who is to come together with His own Body: and his wife who bids him curse,[528] marks the life

of the carnal, who having place within the Holy Church with unamended morals, as by their faith they are brought near to the godly, press them the more sorely by their lives, since while they cannot be shunned as being of the faithful, they are endured by the faithful as the greater harm by how much nearer home.

15. But his friends, who, while acting as his counsellors, at the same time inveigh against him, are an express image of heretics, who under shew of giving counsel, are busied in leading astray; and hence they address the blessed Job as though in behalf of the Lord, but yet the Lord does not commend them, that is, because all heretics, while they try to defend, only offend God. Whence they are plainly told, and that by the same holy man; *I desire to reason with God; first shewing that ye are forgers of lies, ye are followers of corrupt doctrines.*[529] According to which it appears that these by their erroneous notions stood a type of heretics, whom the holy man charges with adhering to a creed of corrupt doctrines. But every heretic, in this, that he is seen to defend God, is a gainsayer of His truth, according to the testimony of the Psalmist, who says, *That Thou mightest still the enemy and defender,*[530] for he is an *enemy and defender,* who so preaches God as thereby to be fighting against Him.

16. Now that blessed Job maintains the semblance of the Redeemer to come, his very name is a proof. For Job is, if interpreted, "grieving;" by which same grief we have set forth, either our Mediator's Passion, or the travails of Holy Church, which is harassed by the manifold toils of this present life. Moreover by the word which stands for their name his friends mark out the quality of their conduct. For Eliphas is called in the Latin tongue, "contempt of the Lord," and what else do heretics, than in entertaining false notions of God contemn Him by their proud conceits. Baldad is by interpretation "Oldness alone." And well are all heretics styled, "Oldness alone," in the things which they speak concerning God, forasmuch as it is with no right purpose but with a longing for temporal honour that they desire to appear as preachers. For they are moved to speak not by the zeal of the new man, but by the evil principles of the old life. "Sophar"

---

525. Eph 4:15; Col 2:10. (The notes for this selection are by Gerhart and Udoh.)

526. Col 1:24.

527. Isa 61:10 (Vulgate); see also Isa 61:10.

528. See Job 2:9.

529. Job 13:3–4 (Vulgate).

530. Ps 8:3 (Vulgate); compare Ps 8:2.

too is rendered in the Latin language "dissipation of the prospect," or, "one dissipating the prospect." For the minds of the faithful lift themselves to the contemplation of things above; but as the words of heretics aim to prevent them in their contemplation of right objects, they do their best to "dissipate the prospect." Thus in the three names of Job's friends, we have set forth three cases of the ruin of heretical minds. For unless they held God in contempt, they would never entertain false notions concerning Him; and unless they drew along with them a heart of oldness, they would never err in the understanding of the new life; and unless they marred the contemplations of good things, the Supreme judgements would never condemn them with so strict a scrutiny for the guiltiness of their words. By holding God in contempt, then, they keep themselves in oldness, and by being kept in oldness, they injure the contemplation of right objects by their erring discourses.

17. Now because it sometimes happens that heretics being penetrated with the bountiful streams of Divine grace return to the unity of Holy Church, this is well represented in the very reconcilement of his friends. Yet blessed Job is bidden to intercede for them, because the sacrifices of heretics can never be acceptable to God, unless they be offered in their behalf by the hands of the universal Church, that by her merits they may obtain the recovery of salvation, whom they did strike before by assailing her with the darts of their words; and hence seven sacrifices are recorded to have been offered for them,[531] for whereas in confessing they receive the Spirit of sevenfold grace, they do as it were obtain expiation by seven offerings. It is hence that in the Apocalypse of John the whole Church is represented by the number of seven Churches.[532] Hence it is said of wisdom by Solomon, *Wisdom hath builded her house; she hath hewn out her seven pillars.*[533] And thus by the very number of the sacrifices those reconciled heretics set forth what they were before, in that these are not united to the perfection of sevenfold grace, except by returning.

18. But they are well described as having offered for themselves bulls and rams.[534] For in the bull is figured the neck of pride, and in the ram, the leading of the flocks that follow. What then is it to slaughter bulls and rams in their behalf, but to put an end to their proud leading, so that they may think humbly of themselves, and not seduce the hearts of the innocent to follow after them. For they had started away from the unity of the Church with a swelling neck, and were drawing after them the weak folk like flocks following behind. Therefore let them come to blessed Job; i.e. return to the Church; and present bulls and rams to be slaughtered for

a sevenfold sacrifice, and that they may be united to the universal Church, let them with the interposition of humility kill all the swelling humour wherewith their proud leadership savoured them.

19. Now by Heliu,[535] who speaks indeed with a right sense, yet runs down into foolish words of pride, is set forth a representation of every proud person. For there are many within the pale of Holy Church, that are too proud to put forward in a right manner the right sentiments, which they profess, and hence he is both rebuked with the words of God's upbraiding, and yet no sacrifices offered in his behalf, in that he is a believer indeed, yet high-minded. By the truth of his belief he is within, but by the obstacle which his pride presents he is not acceptable. Him therefore rebuke reproves, but sacrifice does not restore him, because he is indeed in the faith that he ought to be in, yet the Supreme Justice, charging him with things over and above what need to be, keeps him at a distance. Hence Heliu is well rendered in the Latin tongue, "That my God," or, "God, the Lord." For proud men within Holy Church, though they keep away from God by living proudly, yet acknowledge Him by believing truly. For what is it for him to say by his name, "That my God," but to shew forth Him Whom he believed with a public avowal? Or what is it to say, "God the Lord," but to accept Him both as God by virtue of His Divinity, and to hold Him for Man by His Incarnation?

20. It is well that after the losses of his substance, after the death of his children, after the tortures of his wounds, after the strife and conflict of words, he is raised up again with a double reward, clearly, in that Holy Church, even while yet in this present life, receives a double recompense for the toils she undergoes, since having taken in the Gentiles to the full, at the end of the world she converts to herself the souls of the Jews likewise. For it is on this account written, *Until the fulness of the Gentiles be come in. And so all Israel shall be saved.*[536] And she will afterwards receive a double recompense, in that, when the toils of this present time are over, she rises not alone to the joy of souls, but to a blessed estate of bodies. And hence the Prophet rightly says, *therefore in their land they shall possess the double.*[537] For "in the Land of the Living"[538] the Saints possess the double, because we know they are gladdened with

---

531. See Job 42:8.

532. See Rev 1:11–12.

533. Prov 9:1.

534. See Job 42:9.

535. See Job 32:2.

536. Rom 11:25–26.

537. Isa 61:7 (Vulgate).

538. See Ps 142:5.

blessedness both of mind and body. Hence John in the Apocalypse, because it was before the resurrection of bodies that he saw the souls of the Saints crying, beheld how that they had given them a stole to each, saying, *And white robes were given, one to every one of them, and it was said, that they should rest yet for a little season until their fellow-servants also and their brethren, that should be killed as they were, should be fulfilled.*[539] For before the Resurrection they are said to have received a stole to each, for that as yet they are gifted with blessedness of mind alone; and therefore they will receive each one two, whenever, together with the perfect bliss of souls, they shall be clothed also with incorruptibility of bodies.

21. Now it is very properly that the affliction indeed of blessed Job is told, but the length of time that he was under the affliction is kept back, for we see the tribulation of Holy Church in this life, but know nothing for how long she is here to undergo bruising and delay; and hence it is spoken by the mouth of Truth, *It is not for you to know the times or the seasons which the Father hath put in His own power.*[540] Herein then, that the suffering of blessed Job is told us, we are taught what we are made acquainted withal by experience; and herein, that the length of time that he continued in his suffering is withheld, we are taught what it is we must remain ignorant of.

We have drawn out these words of preface to some length, that by briefly running over it we might in a manner give a view of the whole. Now then that by long discoursing we have been brought to the commencement of our discourse, we must first settle the root of the historical meaning, that we may afterwards let our minds take their fill of the fruits of the allegorical senses.

I

1. *There was a man in the land of Uz, whose name was Job.* It is for this reason that we are told where the holy man dwelt, that the meritoriousness of his virtue might be expressed; for who knows not that Uz is a land of the Gentiles? and the Gentile world came under the dominion of wickedness, in the same proportion that its eyes were shut to the knowledge of its Creator. Let us be told then where he dwelt, that this circumstance may be reckoned to his praise, that he was good among bad men; for it is no very great praise to be good in company with the good, but to be good with the bad; for as it is a greater offence not to be good among good men, so it is immeasurably high testimony for any one to have shewn himself good even among the wicked. Hence it is that the same blessed Job bears witness to himself, say-

ing, *I am a brother to dragons, and a companion to owls.*[541] Hence it was that Peter extolled Lot with high commendation, because he found him to be good among a reprobate people; saying, *And delivered just Lot, vexed with the filthy conversation of the wicked; for he was righteous in seeing and hearing, dwelling with them who vexed his righteous soul from day to day with their unlawful deeds.*[542] Now he evidently could not have been vexed unless he had both heard and witnessed the wicked deeds of his neighbours, and yet he is called *righteous both in seeing and in hearing,*[543] because their wicked lives affected the ears and eyes of the Saint not with a pleasant sensation, but with the pain of a blow. Hence it is that Paul says to his disciples, *In the midst of a crooked and perverse nation, among whom ye shine like lights in the world.*[544] Hence it is said to the Angel of the Church of Pergamos, *I know thy works, and where thou dwellest, even where Satan's seat is; and thou holdest fast My name, and hast not denied My faith.*[545] Hence the Holy Church is commended by the voice of the Spouse, where He says to her in the Song of love, *As the lily among the thorns, so is my love among the daughters.*[546] Well then is the blessed Job described, (by the mention of a gentile land), as having dwelt among the wicked, that according to the testimony borne by the Spouse, he might be shewn to have grown up a lily among thorns, for which reason it is well subjoined immediately after, *And that man was simple and upright.*[547]

2. For there are some in such wise simple as not to know what uprightness is, but these walk wide of the innocence of real simplicity, in proportion as they are far from mounting up to the virtue of uprightness; for while they know not how to take heed to their steps by following uprightness, they can never remain innocent by walking in simplicity. Hence it is that Paul warns his disciples, and says, *But yet I would have you wise unto that which is good, and simple concerning evil.*[548] Hence again he says, *Brethren, be not children in understanding, howbeit in malice be ye children.*[549] Hence Truth enjoins Her disciples by Her own lips, saying, *Be ye wise as serpents and harmless as doves.*[550] For in giving them admonition, He needfully joined the two together, so that both the simplicity of the dove might be instructed by the craftiness of the serpent,

---

539. Rev 6:11.
540. Acts 1:7.
541. Job 30:29 (Vulgate).
542. 2 Pet 2:7–8 (Vulgate).
543. This is the Vulgate's rendering of the passage.
544. Phil 2:15.
545. Rev 2:13.
546. Song 2:2.
547. Job 1:1 (Vulgate).
548. Rom 16:19.
549. 1 Cor 14:20.
550. Mt 10:16.

and again the craftiness of the serpent might be attempered by the simplicity of the dove. Hence it is that the Holy Spirit has manifested His presence to mankind, not in the form of a dove only, but also in the form of fire.[551] For by the dove simplicity is indicated, and by fire, zeal. Therefore He is manifested in a dove, and in fire, because all they, who are full of Him, yield themselves to the mildness of simplicity, in such sort as yet to kindle with a zeal of uprightness against the offences of sinners. It follows, *And one that feared God and eschewed evil.*[552]

3. To fear God is never to pass over any good thing, that ought to be done. Whence it is said by Solomon, *Whoso fears God, neglects nothing;*[553] but because there are some, who practise some good actions, yet in such wise that they are by no means withheld from certain evil practices; after he said to have been *one that feared God,* it is still rightly reported of him that he also *eschewed evil;* for it is written, *Depart from evil, and do good;*[554] for indeed those good actions are not acceptable to God, which are stained in His sight by the admixture of evil deeds; and hence it is said by Solomon, *He who offendeth in one point, spoileth many good deeds.*[555] Hence James bears witness, saying, *For whosoever shall keep the whole law, and yet offend in one point, is guilty of all.*[556] Hence Paul saith, *A little leaven leaveneth the whole lump.*[557] So then that it might be shewn us how spotless the blessed Job stood forth in his good actions, it is wisely done that we have it pointed out how far he was removed from evil deeds.

4. But it is the custom of narrators, when a wrestling match is woven into the story, first to describe the limbs of the combatants, how broad and strong the chest, how sound, how full their muscles swelled, how the belly below neither clogged by its weight, nor weakened by its shrunken size, that when they have first shewn the limbs to be fit for the combat, they may then at length describe their bold and mighty strokes. Thus because our athlete was about to combat the devil, the writer of the sacred story, recounting as it were before the exhibition in the arena the spiritual merits in this athlete, describes the members of the soul, saying, *And that man was perfect and upright, and one that feared God, and eschewed evil;*[558] that when the powerful setting of the limbs is known, from this very strength we may already prognosticate also the victory to follow. Next comes,

5. *And there were born unto him seven sons and three daughters.*[559] The heart of the parent is often enticed into avarice by a numerous offspring, for he is the more inflamed with ambition for laying up an inheritance, in proportion as he abounds in the number to inherit it. In order then that it might be

shewn what holiness of mind blessed Job possessed, he is both called righteous, and is said to have been the father of a numerous offspring. And the same man in the beginning of his book is declared devout in offering sacrifices, and besides he afterwards with his own mouth records himself as ready in giving alms. Let us then consider with what resolution he shewed himself to be endowed, whom no feelings of affection for so many heirs could ever dispose to be greedy of an inheritance for them. It proceeds;

6. *His substance also was seven thousand sheep, and three thousand camels, and five hundred yoke of oxen, and five hundred she asses, and a very great household.*[560] We know that the greater the loss, the greater the grief with which it affects the mind; to shew then how great was his virtue, we are told that it was very much, that he lost with patience; for never without pain do we part with aught, saving that which we hold without fondness; therefore while the greatness of his substance is described, yet soon after he is reported as resigned to the loss of it; thus parting with it without regret, it is plain that he had kept it without regard. It is also to be noted that in the first instance the riches of his heart are described, and afterwards the wealth of the body; for an abundant store is wont to make the mind so much the more slack to the fear of God, as it obliges it to be occupied with a diversity of cares; for inasmuch as it is dissipated by a multitude of objects, it is prevented standing fast in that which is within. Which was pointed out by Truth Itself in setting forth the Parable of the sower; He also that received seed among the thorns, is he that heareth the word, and the care of this world, and the deceitfulness of riches, choke the word, and he becometh unfruitful.[561] See how the blessed Job is both said to have great possessions, and a little after is related to be devoutly assiduous in the divine sacrifices.

7. Let us then consider how great was the holiness of that man who though thus busied disengaged himself for such assiduous attendance upon God. Nor had the power of that precept as yet shone out, which bids us leave all things;[562] yet

---

551. See Mk 1:10; Mt 3:16; Lk 3:22; see also Mk 1:8; Mt 3:11; Lk 3:16; Acts 2:2–4.

552. Job 1:1.

553. Eccl 7:19 (Vulgate); compare Eccl 7:18.

554. Ps 36:27 (Vulgate) = Ps 37:27.

555. Eccl 9:18 (Vulgate); compare Eccl 9:18.

556. Jas 2:10.

557. 1 Cor 5:6.

558. Job 1:1.

559. Job 1:2.

560. Job 1:3 (Vulgate).

561. Mt 13:22.

562. See Mk 10:21, 29–30; Mt 10:37–38; 19:21, 29; Lk 12:33; 14:26; 18:22, 29–30.

blessed Job already kept the intent of it in his heart, in that he surely had left his substance in intention, which he kept without taking delight in it.

8. *So that this man was the greatest of all the men of the East.* Who does not know that the men of the East are very wealthy, accordingly "he was the greatest of all the men of the East;" as though it were expressly said that he was even richer than the rich.

9. *And his sons went and feasted in their houses, every one his day; and sent and called for their three sisters to eat and to drink with them.*[563] Greater wealth usually becomes the cause of greater discord between brethren. O, inestimable praise of a father's training! the father is both declared rich, and the sons at peace together, and while the wealth to be divided among them was there, an undivided affection yet filled the hearts of all. . . .

14. . . . These particulars we have gone through cursorily in following out history. Now the order of interpretation requires that beginning afresh we should at this point open the secrets of its allegories.

15. *There was a man in the land of Uz, whose name was Job.*[564] We believe from the history that these things took place, but let us here turn to see in what way they were allegorically fulfilled; for, as we have said, *Job* is interpreted, "a mourner," and *Uz* "a counsellor." Whom else then does the blessed Job express by his name, saving Him, of Whom the Prophet speaks, saying, *Surely he hath borne our griefs?*[565] He dwells in the land of *Uz,* in that He rules the hearts of a people of wise counsels; for Paul saith, that *Christ* is the *Wisdom of God and the Power of God;*[566] and this same Wisdom Herself by the lips of Solomon declareth, *I Wisdom dwell with Prudence, and am in the midst of witty inventions.*[567] So Job is an inhabitant of the land of Uz, because Wisdom, Which underwent the pain of the Passion in our behalf, has made an habitation for Herself in those hearts, which are instinct with the counsels of life.

16. *And that man was perfect and upright.* In uprightness, justice is signified, and in simplicity, mercy. We in following out the straight line of justice, generally leave mercy behind; and in aiming to observe mercy, we deviate from the straight line of justice. Yet the Incarnate Lord maintained simplicity with uprightness; for He neither in shewing mercy parted with the strictness of justice, nor again in the exactitude of justice did He part with the virtue of mercifulness. Hence when certain persons, having brought an adulteress before Him, would have tempted Him, in order that He might step into the fault either of unmercifulness or of injustice, He answered both alternatives by saying, *He that is without sin among you, let him first cast a stone at her.*[568] *He that is without sin among you,* gives us the simplicity of mercy, *let him first cast a stone at her,* gives us the jealous sense of justice. Whence too the Prophet saith to him, *And in Thy Majesty ride prosperously, because of truth, and meekness, and righteousness.*[569] For in executing truth, He kept mercy united with justice, so that He neither lost the jealous sense of rectitude in the preponderance of mercy's scale, nor again unsettled the preponderance of mercy by that jealousy of rectitude.

17. *And one that feared God, and eschewed evil.* It is written of Him, and *the Spirit of the fear of the Lord hath filled Him;*[570] for the Incarnate Lord shewed forth in His own Person whatsoever He hath inspired us withal, that what He delivered by precept, He might recommend by example. So then according to our human nature our Redeemer feared God, for to redeem proud man, He took for man's sake a humble mind.[571] And His acting likewise is fitly designated hereby, in that the blessed Job is said to eschew evil. For He Himself eschewed evil, not evil which He came in contact with in the doing, but which upon meeting with it, He rejected; for He forsook the old life after man's method, which He found at His birth, and He stamped upon the character of His followers that new life, which He brought down with Him.

18. *And there were born to him seven sons and three daughters.*[572] What is conveyed to us in the number of seven, saving the sum of perfection? for to say nothing of the arguments of human reasoning which maintain that it is therefore perfect, because it consists of the first even number, and of the first uneven; of the first that is capable of division, and of the first which is incapable of it; we know most certainly that holy Scripture is wont to put the number seven for perfection, whence also it tells us that on the seventh day the Lord rested from His works; and it is hence too that the seventh day was given to man for a rest; i.e. for a "Sabbath."[573] Hence it is that the year of jubilee, wherein we have a full rest set forth, is accomplished in seven weeks,[574] being completed by the addition of the unit of our uniting together.

---

563. Job 1:4.

564. Job 1:1.

565. Isa 53:4 (Vulgate).

566. 1 Cor 1:24.

567. Prov 8:12 (Vulgate).

568. Jn 8:1–7.

569. Ps 44:5 (Vulgate); see also Ps 45:4.

570. Isa 11:3.

571. See Phil 2:7–8.

572. Job 1:2.

573. See Gen 2:2–3; Ex 20:8–11; 31:12–17.

574. The Jubilee year comes after "seven weeks of years" (Lev 25:8ff.); that is, it is the fiftieth year.

19. Thus *there were born to him seven sons;* namely, the Apostles manfully issuing forth to preach; who in putting in practice the precepts of perfection, as it were maintained in their manner of life the courage of the superior sex. For hence it is that twelve of them were chosen, who should be replenished with the perfection of the sevenfold grace of the Spirit. As from the number seven we rise to twelve; for seven multiplied in its component parts is extended to twelve; for whether four be taken by three or three by four, seven is changed into twelve, and hence, forasmuch as the holy Apostles were sent to proclaim the holy Trinity in the four quarters of the globe, they were chosen twelve in number, that by their very number they might set forth that perfection, which they proclaimed both by their lips and in their lives.

20. *And three daughters.* What do we understand by the daughters but the weaker multitudes of the faithful, who, though they never adhere with a virtuous resolution to perfection of life, yet cleave with constancy to the belief of the Trinity which has been taught them. Thus by "the seven sons" is represented the order of the Preachers, and by "the three daughters" the multitude of the hearers. By "the three daughters" may also be signified the three orders of the faithful, for after mention of the sons the daughters are named, in that succeeding next to the distinguished courage of the Apostles came three divisions of the faithful, in the state of life in the Church; viz. of Pastors, of those following continence, and of the married. And hence the prophet Ezekiel declares that he heard three men named that were set free; viz. Noah, and Daniel, and Job;[575] for what is signified by Noah who guided the Ark in the waters,[576] but the order of rulers, who, while they govern the people for the fashioning of their lives, are the directors of holy Church amidst the waves of temptation? What is represented by Daniel, whose marvelous abstinence we have described to us, but the life of the continent, who, while they give up everything that is of the world, rule with elevated mind over Babylon which lies beneath them? What is signified by Job but the life of the good that are married, who, while they do deeds of mercy by the good things of the world which they possess, do as it were advance to their heavenly country by the paths of earth? Therefore because after the holy Apostles there came these three divisions of the faithful, after the sons rightly follows the mention of the three daughters that were born to him. It proceeds:

His substance also was three thousand sheep and three thousand camels.[577]

21. That believing hearers have been gathered from various manners of life, a truth which is first declared generally by the mention of the daughters, the same is afterwards brought before us in detail by the specification of the animals. For what does he set forth in the seven thousand sheep, but some men's perfect innocency, which comes from the pastures of the Law to the perfect estate of grace? What again is signified by the three thousand camels, but the crooked defectiveness of the Gentiles coming to the fulness of faith. Now in Holy Scripture, sometimes the Lord Himself is expressed by the title of a camel, and sometimes the Gentile people. For the Lord is signified by the name of a camel, as when it is said by that very Lord to the Jews that set themselves against Him, *who strain at a gnat, and swallow a camel.*[578] For a gnat wounds while it whispers, but a camel of free will bends to receive its load. Thus the Jews strained at a gnat, in that they sought that a seditious robber should be let go, but they swallowed a camel, in that Him, Who had come down of His own accord to take upon Him the burthens of our mortal nature, they strove to overwhelm by their clamours.[579] Again, the Gentile state is signified by the naming of a camel; and hence Rebecca on going to Isaac is brought on a camel's back,[580] in that the Church, which hastens from the Gentile state to Christ, is found in the crooked and defective behaviour of the old life; and she, when she saw Isaac, descended,[581] in that when the Gentile world knew the Lord, it abandoned its sins, and descending from the height of self-elation sought the lowly walks of humility; and she too in bashfulness covers herself with a veil,[582] in that she is confounded in His presence for her past life. And hence it is said by the Apostle to these same Gentiles, *What fruit had ye then in those things whereof ye are now ashamed?*[583] Whereas then by the sheep we understand the Hebrews coming to the faith from the pastures of the Law, nothing hinders but that we understand by the camels the Gentile people, crooked in their ways and laden with idolatrous ceremonials. For because they devised them gods of their own selves whom they should worship, there had grown up as it were out of themselves a load upon their back which they should carry.

22. Furthermore in that they are common animals, it is possible that by camels is represented the life of the Samari-

---

575. See Ezek 14:14.
576. See Gen 6:5–9:17.
577. Job 1:3.
578. Mt 23:24.
579. See Mk 15:6–15; Mt 27:15–26; Lk 23:18–25; Jn 18:38–40.
580. See Gen 24:61.
581. See Gen 24:64.
582. See Gen 24:65.
583. Rom 6:21.

tans. For camels chew the cud, but do not divide the hoof.[584] So likewise the Samaritans do as it were *chew the cud,* in that they receive in part the words of the Law, but do not *divide the hoof* as it were, forasmuch as they despise it in part. And they bear a grievous burthen upon the mind's back, in that they weary themselves in whatsoever they do without any hope of eternity.

For they are strangers to faith in the Resurrection, and what can be more grievous or more burthensome than to endure the tribulation of this passing state of existence, and yet never, for relief of mind, to look forward to the joy of our reward; but forasmuch as the Lord, when He appeared in the flesh, both filled the Hebrew people with the grace of perfection, and brought some of the Samaritans to the knowledge of the faith by shewing marvellous works, it might well be said of the shadow which was to express the reality, that he possessed both seven thousand sheep, and three thousand camels. It goes on; *And five hundred yoke of oxen, and five hundred she asses.*

23. We have said above that by the number fifty, which is completed by seven weeks and the addition of an unit, rest is signified, and by the number ten the sum of perfection is set forth. Now forasmuch as the perfection of rest is promised to the faithful, by multiplying fifty ten times, we in this way arrive at five hundred. But in sacred Writ, the title of "oxen" sometimes represents the dulness of the foolish sort, and sometimes the life of well doers. For because the stupidity of the fool is represented by the title of an ox, Solomon says rightly, *he goeth after her straightway, as an ox goeth to the slaughter.*[585] Again, that the life of every labourer is set forth by the title of oxen, the Precepts of the Law are a testimony, which enjoined through Moses; *Thou shalt not muzzle the ox when he treadeth out the corn.*[586] And this again is declared in plain words; *the labourer is worthy of his hire.*[587] By the title of asses, too, we have represented sometimes the inertness of fools, sometimes the unrestrained indulgence of the wanton, sometimes the simplemindedness of the Gentiles; for the inertness of fools is imaged by the designation of asses, as where it is said through Moses, *Thou shalt not plough with an ox and an ass together.*[588] As though he said, "do not associate fools and wise men together in preaching, lest by means of him who has no power to accomplish the work, you hinder him who has abundant power." The unrestrained indulgence of the wanton is likewise set forth by the appellation of asses, as the prophet testifies, where he says, *whose flesh is as the flesh of asses.*[589] Again, by the title of asses is shewn the simplicity of the Gentiles. Hence when the Lord went

up toward Jerusalem, He is related to have sat upon a young ass,[590] for what is it for Him to come to Jerusalem sitting upon an ass, except taking possession of the simple hearts of the Gentiles to conduct them to the vision of peace, by ruling and ordering them? And this is shewn by one passage, and that a very easy one; in that both the workmen of Judaea are represented by oxen, and the Gentile peoples by an ass, when it is said by the Prophet, *The ox knoweth his owner, and the ass his master's crib.*[591] For who appears as the ox, saving the Jewish people, whose neck was worn by the yoke of the Law? and who was the ass but the Gentile world, which was found like a brute animal of every deceiver, and was overlaid with whatever deceit he pleased, without resisting by any exercise of reason? Thus the ox knoweth his owner, and the ass his master's crib, in that both the Hebrews found out the God Whom they worshipped but as yet knew Him not, and the Gentile world received the food of the Law, which it had none of. That therefore which is spoken above in the designation of the sheep and of the camels, is here repeated below in the oxen and the asses.

24. Now even before the coming of the Redeemer Judaea possessed oxen, in that she sent out labourers to preach, to whom it is said by the voice of Truth, *Woe unto you, Scribes and Pharisees, hypocrites! for ye compass sea and land to make one proselyte; and when he is made, ye make him twofold more the child of hell than yourselves.*[592] These were weighed down with the heavy yoke of the Law, because they were burthened with the ordinances of the external letter, to whom it is spoken by the voice of Truth, *Come unto Me, all ye that labour and are heavy laden, and I will refresh you. Take My yoke upon you, and learn of Me, for I am meek and lowly in heart.*[593] That in the Gospel, therefore, rest is promised to those that labour well, is the same thing as that five hundred yoke of oxen are made mention of in this place; for whereunto does their way lead, who submit their necks to the dominion of our Redeemer, excepting to rest? And hence we are told of five hundred she asses, forasmuch as the Gentile folk that are called, so long as

---

584. See Lev 11:4.

585. Prov 7:22.

586. Deut 25:4.

587. Lk 10:7; see also 1 Cor 9:1–4; 1 Tim 5:17–18.

588. Deut 22:10.

589. Ezek 23:19–20.

590. See Mk 11:1–10; Mt 21:1–11; Lk 19:29–40.

591. Isa 1:3.

592. Mt 23:15.

593. Mt 11:28–29.

they desire to attain to rest, gladly bear all the burthens of the commandments; and hence, that this rest should be sought of the Gentiles, Jacob in addressing his sons did mean to signify by the voice of prophecy, saying, *Issachar is a strong ass, crouching down between the boundaries: And he saw that rest was good, and the land that it was pleasant, and bowed the shoulder to bear.*[594] For to crouch down between the boundaries is to rest forestalling the end of the world, and to seek nought of those things, which are now going forward amongst men, but to long after the things that shall be at the last; and the strong ass sees the rest and the pleasant land, when the simple Gentile world lifts itself up to the strong effort of good works, and that because it is on its way to the land of life eternal; and it bows the shoulder to bear, in that having beheld the rest above, it submits itself in doing its work even to severe precepts, and whatever littleness of mind represents as hard to bear, the hope of the reward makes this appear to it light and easy. So because both Judaea and the Gentile world are gathered to eternal rest as a portion of the elect, he is rightly related to have possessed five hundred yoke of oxen, and five hundred she asses. The account goes on;

And a very great household.

25. What means it that the number of the animals is first described, while the household is not mentioned till the end, but that the foolish things of the world are first gathered in to the knowledge of the faith, that afterwards the crafty things of the world may also be called? as Paul bears witness, who says; *For ye see your calling, brethren, how that not many wise men after the flesh, not many noble, not many mighty, are called; But God hath chosen the foolish things of the world to confound the wise.*[595] For the first beginnings of holy Church are reputed to have been without knowledge of letters, plainly for this reason, that in His preachers the Redeemer might manifest to all, that it was not their discourse, but their cause, which had influence with the numbers that believed unto life. It proceeds;

So that this man was the greatest of all the men of the East.

26. That our Redeemer is styled *The East* is declared by the testimony of the Prophet, where he says, *And lo! the Man whose name is The East.*[596] And thus all that live in this Orient by faith, are rightly called *men of the East.* Now because all men are only men, whereas "The East" Himself is both God and Man, it is rightly said, *He was the greatest of all the men of the East.* As though it were said in plain words, He surpassed all those that are born to God in faith. Because it is not by adoption,[597] as others are, but by the Divine Nature that He is exalted, Who though He appeared like to others in His

human Nature, yet in His Divine Nature continued above all men without fellow.

And his sons went and feasted in their houses.[598]

27. The sons went to feast at their houses, when the Apostles as preachers, in the different regions of the world, served the banquet of virtue to hearers as it were to eaters. And hence it is said to those very sons concerning the hungering multitude, *Give ye them to eat.*[599] And again; *And I will not send them away fasting, lest they faint by the way;*[600] that is, let them by your preaching receive the word of consolation, that they may not by continuing to fast to the food of truth, sink under the labours of this life. Hence again it is said to the same sons, *labour not for the meat which perisheth, but for the meat which endureth unto everlasting life.*[601] And how these feasts were set forth is added, whereas it is forthwith subjoined,

Every one in his day.

28. If without any doubt the darkness of ignorance is the night of the soul, the understanding is not improperly styled the day. And hence Paul says, *One man esteemeth one day above another; another esteemeth every day alike.*[602] As if he had said in plain words; "One man understands some things so as that some are left out, and another acquaints himself with all things that are possible to be understood, in such sort as they may be seen." Thus each son sets forth a feast in his day, in that every holy preacher, according to the measure of the enlightening of his understanding, feeds the minds of his hearers with the entertainments of Truth. Paul made a feast in his own day, when he said, *But she is happier if she so abide according to my judgement.*[603] He bade each to take account of his own day; when he said, *Let every man be fully persuaded in his own mind.*[604] It goes on;

And sent and called for their three sisters to eat and to drink with them.

29. The sons call their sisters to the feast, in that the holy Apostles proclaim to hearers that are weak the joys of the refreshment above, and inasmuch as they see their souls to be starved of the food of truth, they feed them with the feast of God's Word. And it is well said, *to eat and to drink with them.* For holy Scripture is sometimes meat to us, and

---

594. Gen 49:14–15 (Vulgate); see also Gen 49:14–15.

595. 1 Cor 1:26–27.

596. Zech 6:12 (Vulgate); compare Zech 6:12.

597. See Rom 8:23; Gal 4:4–7.   601. Jn 6:27.

598. Job 1:4.   602. Rom 14:5.

599. Mk 6:37; Mt 14:16; Lk 9:13.   603. 1 Cor 7:40.

600. Mk 8:3; Mt 15:32.   604. Rom 14:5.

sometimes drink. It is meat in the harder parts, in that it is in a certain sense broken in pieces by being explained, and swallowed after chewing; and it is drink in the plainer parts, in that it is imbibed just as it is found. The Prophet discerned holy Scripture to be meat, which was to be broken in pieces in the explaining, when he said, *The young children ask, and no man breaketh it unto them,*[605] i.e. the weak ones sought that the stronger declarations of holy Scripture might be crumbled for them by explanation, but he could no where be found who should have explained them. The Prophet saw that holy Writ was drink, when he said, *Ho, every one that thirsteth come ye to the waters.*[606] Had not the plain commandments been drink, Truth would never have cried out with His own lips; *If any man thirst, let him come unto Me and drink.*[607] The Prophet saw that there was, as it were, a lack of meat and drink in Judaea, when he declared, *And their honourable men are famished, and their multitude dried up with thirst.*[608] For it belongs to the few to attain a knowledge of the mighty and hidden meanings, but to the multitude it is given to understand the plain sense of the history. And therefore he declares that the honourable men of Judaea had perished not by thirst, but hunger, in that those who seemed to stand first, by giving themselves wholly to the outward sense, had not wherewithal to feed themselves from the inward parts by sifting their meaning, but forasmuch as when loftier minds fall away from the inward sense, the understanding of the little ones even in the outward meaning is dried up; it is rightly added in this place, *And the multitude dried up with thirst.* As if he said in plainer words, "whereas the common sort give over taking pains in their own lives, they now no longer seek even the streams of history." And they bear witness that they understood both the deep and the plain things contained in divine Writ, who in complaining to the Judge that rejects them, say, *We have eaten and drunk in Thy presence;*[609] and this they subjoin in plain terms by explaining it; *And thou hast taught in our streets.*[610] Therefore because the sacred oracles are broken in the more obscure parts, by the explanation thereof, but in the plainer parts are drunk in just as they are found, it may be truly said, *And they sent and called for their three sisters, to eat and to drink with them.* As though it were said in plain terms, they drew every weak one to themselves by the mildness of their persuasions, that both by setting forward great truths contemplatively, they might feed their minds, and by delivering little things historically, they might give them nourishment.

From Gregory the Great, *Morals on the Book of Job,* Library of the Fathers of the Catholic Church, vol. 18 (Oxford: John Henry Parker, 1844), 25–31, 32–36, 38–48.

❦ Like Thomas Aquinas (also writing in the Scholastic period), **Bonaventure** (ca. 1221–74) brings a philosophical sophistication to his theological inquiries. In the Prologue to *Breviloquium* (ca. 1257), he lays out his views on and methodology for interpreting Scripture. In his *Collations on the Ten Commandments,* IV, "On the Third Commandment of the Decalogue" (ca. 1259), Bonaventure applies his literal-spiritual twofold method.

BONAVENTURE

Prologue to *Breviloquium*

1. "For this cause I bow my knees to the Father of our Lord Jesus Christ, of whom all paternity in heaven and earth is named: that He would grant you, according to the riches of His glory, to be strengthened by His Spirit with might unto the inward man: that Christ may dwell by faith in your hearts; that, being rooted and founded in charity, you may be able to comprehend, with all the saints, what is the breadth and length and height and depth; to know also the charity of Christ, which surpasseth all knowledge, that you may be filled unto all the fullness of God."[611]

The great doctor of the nations and preacher of truth, filled with the divine Spirit, the vessel chosen[612] and sanctified, discloses in these words the source, growth, and result of Holy Scripture, which is called theology. He notes that the source of Scripture is discovered in the influence of the Most Blessed Trinity, its growth is in the exigency of one's human capability, and its result or fruit, is in an abundance of the fullest happiness.

2. The source of Scripture is not attributable to human investigation, but to divine revelation which flows "from the Father of lights"[613] from whom all paternity in heaven and earth is named, and from whom through His Son, Jesus Christ, the Holy Ghost flows into us, and through the Holy Ghost, dividing and distributing His gifts to individuals as He pleases, faith is given to us, and through faith Christ dwells in our hearts. This is the knowledge of Jesus Christ from whom the strength and understanding of the whole of Holy Scripture flows as from its source. Hence it is impossible that

---

605. Lam 4:4 (Vulgate).
606. Isa 55:1.
607. Jn 7:37–38.
608. Isa 5:13.
609. Lk 13:26.
610. Lk 13:26.
611. Eph 3:14–19. (The notes for this selection are by Gerhart and Udoh.)
612. See Acts 9:15.
613. Jas 1:17.

anyone should enter into that knowledge unless he first have infused into himself faith in Christ, the light,[614] the door,[615] and the very foundation of all Scripture. This is the faith of all supernatural illuminations as long as we are absent from the Lord[616] and the foundation that stabilizes us, the light that directs us, and the door that lets us in. Further, according to the measure of faith the wisdom given us by God must be determined lest anyone "be more wise than it behooveth to be wise, but to be wise unto sobriety and according as God hath divided to every one the measure of faith."[617] Through the medium of that faith, a knowledge of Sacred Scripture is given to us in accordance with the influence of the Blessed Trinity, as the Apostle expressly states in the first part of the reference cited above.[618]

3. The growth of Holy Scripture is not restricted to the laws of reasoning, defining, and dividing, after the custom of the other sciences, nor is it limited to a part of the universe. Rather, since it proceeds in accord with supernatural light to give to man as wayfarer a sufficient knowledge of things that expedite salvation, it describes partly in common words and partly in mystical words and, as it were, in a kind of summa the contents of the whole universe, in which the breadth is considered; it describes the course, in which the length is considered; it describes the excellence of those who are finally to be saved, and in this the sublimity is considered; it describes the misery of those who are to be damned, and in this consists the depth not only of the universe itself but also of the divine judgment. Thus it describes the whole universe so far as it is expedient to have a knowledge of it for salvation: according to its length and breadth, height and depth. Scripture in its growth has the four qualities that will be declared below. Human capacity plays a part in that it is born to grasp magnificently and in many ways great and numerous ideas. As it were, there is born in man a certain most noble mirror in which the universality of earthly things is reflected naturally and even supernaturally so that the growth of Sacred Scripture is considered according to the exigency of human capacity.

4. The result or fruit of Holy Scripture is not simply any kind, but rather a fullness of eternal happiness. In Scripture are the words of eternal life. It is written not only that we may believe, but also that we may possess eternal life,[619] in which we shall see and love, and our desires will be completely satisfied. When these desires are satisfied, we shall know the overwhelming love of knowledge and thus we shall abound unto all the fullness of God. Divine Scripture tries to

lead us on to this plenitude in accord with the truth of the sentence of the Apostle quoted above.[620] This, then, is the end and this the intention with which Holy Scripture should be studied, taught, and even heard.

5. That we may arrive at that fruit by progress along the true path of the Scriptures, we must make a solemn invocation: that we may ascend with true faith to the Father of lights by bending the knee of our heart and that through His Son in the Holy Ghost, He may grant us true knowledge of Jesus Christ and with this knowledge a love of Him, and that, knowing and loving Him and finally achieving a solid faith and a deep-rooted love, we may be able to know the length and breadth, height and depth, of Holy Scripture, and through this knowledge arrive at the fullness of knowledge and plenitude of love for the Most Blessed Trinity whence the desires of all holy men tend and in whom is found the end and complement of all truth and goodness.

6. Since the end of Sacred Scripture is desired and known, and since its beginning is believed and the invocation made, we may view its course according to its length and breadth, height and depth, following the path and the order of the apostolic document. The breadth of Scripture consists of the multiplicity of its parts, the length in the description of the times and ages, the height in the description of the hierarchies arranged in different levels, and the depth in the multiplicity of the mystical senses and intelligences.

I. The Breadth of Holy Scripture

1. If we wish to behold the breadth of Holy Scripture, the first viewpoint available to us is Scripture divided into two Testaments, namely, the Old and the New. The Old is replete with many books, for it has the books of laws, of history, of wisdom, and of the prophets. Of the first there are five, of the second ten, of the third five, and of the fourth six, and hence in all there is a total of twenty-six books. Similarly, the New Testament has books corresponding to these, and also arranged in a fourfold division. The evangelical books correspond to the books of the laws, the Acts of the Apostles

614. See Jn 1:4–5, 9; 8:12.   616. See 2 Cor 5:6.
615. See Jn 10:7–9.   617. Rom 12:3.
618. See Eph 3:14–17, cited in the first paragraph of the Prologue.
619. See Jn 20:31.
620. See Eph 3:18–19, cited in the first paragraph of the Prologue.

to the historical books, the letters of the Apostles, especially those of Paul, to the books of wisdom, and the Apocalypse to the prophetical books. Thus the remarkable conformity between the Old and the New Testament may be seen not only in consistency of meanings, but also in their fourfold division. In this grouping and arrangement, Ezechiel sees four wheels of faces and a wheel in the midst of the wheel, because the Old is in the New, and the New is in the Old.[621] In the books of the laws and in the evangelical books is the face of a lion because of his powerful authority. In the historical books is the face of a bull because of his convincing strength. In the books of wisdom is the face of a man because of his nice prudence. In the books of the prophets is the face of the eagle because of his perspicacious insight.[622]

2. Holy Scripture is correctly divided into the Old and the New Testament and not into practical and speculative, as in the case of philosophy. The reason for this is that, since Scripture deals properly with what is known by faith which is the strength and foundation of morals, justice and all right living, it follows that there cannot be found in Scripture a knowledge of things as such, or of moral rules based on such a knowledge. This is not, however, the case with philosophy, which treats of the truth of morals and gives consideration to pure speculation. Because Holy Scripture is a knowledge moving toward good and withdrawing from evil, and this is accomplished both by fear and by love, it follows that Scripture is divided into two Testaments, for there is "a narrow margin between fear and love."[623]

3. Because man can be moved in a fourfold manner toward good and away from evil, namely, by precepts of a most powerful authority, by the statements of a most wise truth, by the examples and benefits of a most innocent goodness, or by all of these taken together, it follows that the books handed down to us containing the Holy Scripture should be divided into four groups in the New as well as in the Old Testament to achieve a correspondence with the four methods just outlined. Accordingly, the books of laws move men by the precepts of a most potent authority, the historical books by the examples of a most innocent goodness, the books of wisdom by the statements of a most prudent truth, the prophetical books by a combination of all of these, as clearly appears in their respective contents. Hence these books are, as it were, commemorative of all true wisdom and doctrine.

4. Sacred Scripture is like a very wide river which grows continually in size by the addition of many tributaries as its course lengthens. In the beginning of Scripture are the books of the laws, then is added the stream of wisdom found in

the historical books, and thirdly the doctrine of Solomon the most wise, and after these the doctrine of the holy prophets; and finally the evangelical doctrine is revealed, spread through the mouth of the living Christ, written by the Evangelists, and propagated by the holy apostles together with additional documents which the Holy Ghost, coming down upon them, taught us through them. Thus the apostles, having been taught all truth by the Holy Ghost according to the divine promise,[624] could give the Church of Christ the doctrine of all-saving truth and, by completing Holy Scripture, might enlarge the knowledge of truth.

II. The Length of Holy Scripture

1. Holy Scripture has a length which consists of the description of the times and ages, namely, from the beginning of the world to the day of judgment. It describes the course of the world through three times: the time of the law of nature, the time of the written law, and the time of the law of grace. But in the three times, it distinguishes seven ages. Of these, the first is from Adam to Noe, the second from Noe to Abraham, the third from Abraham to David, the fourth from David to the transmigration of Babylon, the fifth from the transmigration to Christ,[625] the sixth from Christ to the end of the world; the seventh, which runs concurrently with the sixth, begins with the repose of Christ in the sepulcher and runs to the universal resurrection which marks the beginning of the eighth. Thus Scripture is of great length because in its treatment it begins with the commencement of the world and of time, in the beginning of Genesis, and extends to the end of the world and of time, namely, to the end of the Apocalypse.

2. To be correct, universal time, which runs according to a triple law, that is, founded within, given externally, and infused from above, extends through seven ages and ends with the end of the sixth age. Hence the duration of the world follows a plan such that the duration of the greater world corresponds with the duration of the life of the lesser world, namely, man, for whom the greater world was made.

The first age of the world, in which the foundation of the

---

621. See Ezek 1:15–16; 10:9–10.

622. See Ezek 1:10; 10:14.

623. Augustine, *Contra Adimantum*, xvii.2.

624. See Jn 16:13.

625. "From Abraham . . . to Christ"; see Mt 1:17.

world, the fall of the demons, and the strengthening of the angels were completed, corresponds to the first day when light was made distinct from darkness.[626] The second age, in which through the ark and flood the good were saved and the evil destroyed, corresponds to the second day when throughout the firmament a distinction was made of the waters from the waters.[627] The third age, in which Abraham was called and the synagogue begun, which was to bring forth fruit and generate a posterity for the worship of God, corresponds to the third day, when land appeared and brought forth green vegetation.[628] The fourth age, in which the kingdom and the priesthood grew powerful because King David expanded divine worship, corresponds to the fourth day, in which the formation of the suns and stars took place.[629] The fifth age, in which the emigrants were scattered and spread through many nations, corresponds to the fifth day, in which the production of the fishes from the waters was accomplished.[630] The sixth age, in which Christ who is truly the image of God was born in the form of man, corresponds to the sixth day, in which the first man was made.[631] The seventh age, which is the endless rest of souls, corresponds to the seventh day, on which God rested from all His work which He had done.[632]

3. Thus seven ages are distinguished by the signs which are found in their beginning and by reason of which they correspond to the days of the foundation of the world. The first is called the age of infancy because, as our whole infancy is drowned in oblivion, so that first age was drowned by the flood. The second age is childhood because, as in childhood we begin to speak, so in the second age the multiplication of tongues was accomplished. The third age is called adolescence because, as the generative force begins to be actualized at that time, so Abraham was called and circumcision given him and the promise made to him about his seed. The fourth age is called manhood because, as in the period of manhood the age of man flowers, so in the fourth age the synagogue flourished under the kings. The fifth age is called old age because, as man's powers decline in old age and beauty slips away, so in the migration there was a decline in the sacred rites of the Jews. The sixth age is called debility because, as that age is linked with death though possessing the mighty light of wisdom, so the sixth age of the world ends with the day of judgement and in it wisdom grows strong through the doctrine of Christ.

4. Thus the whole world is described in a most orderly sequence by Scripture as proceeding from beginning to end, in accordance with the peculiar beauty of its well-designed song. One can view, following the sequence of time, the va-

riety, multiplicity and symmetry, order, rectitude and beauty of the many judgments proceeding from the wisdom of God governing the world. As no one can see the beauty of a song unless his view extends over the whole verse, so no one sees the beauty of the order and governance of the universe unless he beholds the whole of it. Because no man is so long-lived that he can see the whole of it with the eyes of the flesh and because no man can foresee the future by himself, the Holy Ghost has provided man with Holy Scripture, the length of which is measured by the extent of the universe.

III. The Height of Holy Scripture

1. Holy Scripture in its progress possesses a height which consists of the description of the hierarchies arranged in grades. These hierarchies are: the ecclesiastical, the angelical, and the divine, or in other words, the subcelestial, the celestial, and the supercelestial. Scripture describes the first clearly, the second somewhat more obscurely, and the third more obscurely still. From the description of the ecclesiastical hierarchy, we gather that it is lofty, and from the description of the angelic that it is loftier still, and from the description of the divine that it is the highest loftiness, so that we can quote that saying of the Prophet: "Thy knowledge is become wonderful to me; it is high, and I cannot reach to it."[633]

2. This view has supporting evidence. Since things have existence in matter, they should have existence in spirit through acquired knowledge, have existence in that spirit through grace, have existence in it through glory, and have existence in the eternal art. Philosophy treats of things as they are in nature, or in spirit, according to naturally founded knowledge or even acquired knowledge; but theology, in the last analysis knowledge founded on faith and revealed through the Holy Ghost, deals with those matters which concern grace and glory, and even eternal Wisdom. Whence it is that theology relegates philosophical knowledge to a lower place and assumes about the nature of things whatever is needed for fabricating the mirror through which a representation of things divine takes place. It erects a ladder, as it were, which touches the earth at its base but touches heaven at its top. All this is done through that one hierarch, Jesus Christ, who by

---

626. See Gen 1:3–5.
627. See Gen 1:6–8.
628. See Gen 1:9–13.
629. See Gen 1:14–19.
630. See Gen 1:20–23.
631. See Gen 1:26–31.
632. See Gen 2:1–3.
633. Ps 138:6 (Vulgate) = Ps 139:6.

reason of the human nature He assumed is a hierarch not only in the ecclesiastical hierarchy, but also in the angelic hierarchy, and the middle person in that supercelestial hierarchy of the Most Blessed Trinity. Thus through Him from the very height of God, sanctifying grace descends not only to the beard but also to the skirt of the garment,[634] not only to lofty Jerusalem but to the Church militant.

3. There is a great beauty in the mechanism of the world, but there is far greater beauty in the Church adorned with the beauty of the holy charismata, and the greatest beauty in lofty Jerusalem, and yet the very greatest beauty is to be found in the Trinity, most high and blessed. Hence the Scripture not only possesses the highest matter through which it causes delight and raises aloft the understanding of the mind, but it also is the most elegant matter and in a certain remarkable manner pleases our intellect and thus more and more by such pleasure makes us accustomed to the intuitions and analogies of the divine spectacles.

IV. The Depth of Holy Scripture

1. Lastly, Holy Scripture possesses a depth which consists in the multiplicity of the mystical intelligences. Besides a literal sense, it possesses diverse places capable of triple construction, namely, allegorical, moral, and anagogical. It is allegory when through one fact another fact is indicated, according to what must be believed. We have a tropological or moral sense when, through what took place, we are given to understand something else, which must be done. We have an anagogical sense, a kind of leading upwards, when we are given to understand what should be sought after, namely, the eternal happiness of the saints.

2. Hence this threefold meaning ought to exist in Scripture in addition to the literal meaning, because it satisfies the subject of Scripture, its reader or disciple, its origin, and finally its end. I say that it satisfies the subject because its doctrine deals with God and Christ, with the works of reparation and with what should be believed. The subject of Scripture, so far as it is a substance, is God, so far as it is virtue, is Christ, and so far as it is an operation, is the work of reparation. So far as it is all these things, Scripture is subject to belief. Moreover, God is three and one: one in essence and three in person. Hence Scripture, which is about God, has in the unity of its words a threefold meaning. The same is true of Christ. Since there is one Word, all things are said to have been accomplished through Him and reflect unto Him so that His wisdom is multiform and one. The works of reparation, though

they are many, all have an aspect pointing to the oblation of Christ. What should be believed, as a thing believable, is reflected in many ways in accord with the different station of the believers. Because of its conformity to all that has been pointed out, Holy Scripture produces multiform meaning in one set of words.

3. This qualifies a hearer: namely, that no one is a suitable hearer unless he is humble, clean, faithful, and zealous. Hence under the bark of the evident meaning is hidden a mystical and profound meaning to repress one's pride so that by the profundity lying in the humility of the word, the proud are rebuffed, the unclean are repulsed, the deceitful are turned aside, and the careless are spurred on to the meaning of the mysteries. Because those hearing the doctrine of Scripture are not of one kind but may be of any kind, for it behooves all who want to be saved to know something of this doctrine, it follows that Scripture has a multiform meaning. Thus it may capture every intellect and may equally illumine and inflame every intellect striving diligently to understand it by the multiformity of its resplendence.

4. Scripture satisfies the principle from which it comes because it is from God through Christ and the Holy Ghost speaking by the mouths of the prophets and the others who wrote the document. Because God speaks not only through words but also through deeds, as in Him to say is to do, and to do is to say, and further, because all things created, as effects of God, point to their cause, it follows that in Scripture the truths divinely handed down ought to be signified not only by words but also by deeds. Because Christ is a doctor though He was humble in flesh but mighty in His deity, it is suitable for Him and His doctrine to have a humility in speech with a profundity of meaning, so that, as Christ was wrapped in swaddling clothes,[635] so the wisdom of God in the Scriptures is wrapped in certain humble figures. The Holy Ghost in many ways illuminated and made revelations in the hearts of the prophets. No intellect can lie hidden from Him, and He was sent to teach all truth. Thus it belongs to His teaching that in one speech many meanings are hidden.

5. Yet Scripture is suited to its purpose because it was given so that through it man may be guided in knowing and doing things to enable him finally to obtain what should be desired. Because all creatures were made to serve man in his

---

634. See Ps 132:2 (Vulgate) = Ps 133:2.
635. See Lk 2:7, 12.

effort toward his home above, Scripture considers various species of creatures so that through them it may teach us the wisdom guiding us to things eternal. And because man is not guided to things eternal unless he knows the things to be known as the truth to be believed and performs the good to be performed as the good that ought to be done and directs his desires to seeing, to loving, and to enjoying God, Holy Scripture, given through the Holy Ghost, considers the book of creation by referring to the end with a triple meaning so that through the tropological sense we may have a list of things to be done energetically, through the allegorical sense we may have an indication of the things to be believed truly, and through the anagogical sense a list of things to be sought out for our enjoyment. And all this so that, sanctified through powerful influences, illuminated through resplendent faith, and perfected through a most ardent charity, we may at last obtain the reward of eternal happiness.

V. The Mode of Proceeding in Holy Scripture

1. Hence in such a multiformity of wisdom as is contained in the length, breadth, height, and depth of Holy Scripture, there is one common mode of proceeding, the authentic as it were, and within this is the narrative mode, the instructive, the prohibitive, the hortatory, the commendatory, the threatening, the promising, the deprecative, and the laudatory. All these modes are resolved into one authentic mode and rightly so.

2. Since this doctrine exists that we may become good and be saved and this in turn may not be accomplished merely through intellectual considerations but rather through inclinations of the will, divine Scripture ought to be propounded in such a way that we can be the more strengthened in our inclinations. Because our desire is better stimulated through examples than through arguments, better through promises than through reasonings, better through devotions than through definitions, Scripture ought not to have a mode based on definition, division, and integration, for the stimulation of certain powers of the reader in the manner of the other sciences, but ought to have modes proper to itself, following the various inclinations which propel the soul in diverse ways. And all this, so that if anyone is not moved through precepts and prohibitions, he may at least be moved by the examples narrated; if anyone is not moved by the examples, he may be moved by the benefits which are made plain to him; if anyone is unmoved by either of these, he may be moved by

the wise admonitions, by the truthful promises, and by the terrible threats, so that thus at least he may be aroused to the worship and praise of God in whom he perceives the grace to guide him to virtuous acts.

3. Because these modes of narration cannot follow the path of the certainty of reason since particular acts cannot be tested, it follows that, lest Scripture should vacillate in doubt and consequently convince us less forcefully, God provided Scripture with the certainty of authority in place of the certainty of reason, and this certainty of authority is great enough that it surpasses all the acuteness of human ability. The authority of one who can deceive or be deceived is not a certain authority; and, except God and the Holy Ghost, no one is ignorant that he can deceive and be deceived. Therefore it follows that, inasmuch as Holy Scripture should be perfectly authentic in its own proper way, it has been handed down not through human investigation but through divine revelation.

4. Hence nothing should be despised in Holy Scripture as useless, nothing rejected as false, nothing repudiated as wicked, because the Holy Ghost, its most perfect author, could speak nothing false, nothing superfluous, nothing too insignificant. "Heaven and earth shall pass: but My words (of Holy Scripture) shall not pass"[636] until they are fulfilled. "Till heaven and earth pass, one jot or one tittle shall not pass of the law, till all be fulfilled,"[637] as the Savior has testified. "He therefore that shall break" the teaching of Scripture . . . "and shall so teach men, shall be called the least in the kingdom of heaven. But he that shall do and teach, he shall be called great in the kingdom of heaven."[638]

VI. The Manner of Explaining Holy Scripture

1. As Scripture has a special mode of proceeding, it ought to be understood and explained in a special way according to its mode of proceeding. Since under one word Scripture can shield a multiplicity of meaning, the one who explains Scripture ought to bring the hidden meaning to light and to make manifest what is brought to light through other more evident scriptural passages. Thus, if I should explain that passage of the Psalms: "Take hold of arms and shield; and rise up to help me,"[639] and if I wish to explain what the divine arms are, I should say that they are its truth and good will. That

636. Mt 24:35.
637. Mt 5:18.
638. Mt 5:19.
639. Ps 34:2 (Vulgate) = Ps 35:2.

this is so must be proven through other scriptural evidence, for it is written in another place: "Thou hast crowned us, as with a shield of Thy good will";[640] and again: "His truth shall encompass thee with a shield."[641] No one can develop such a facility except by long practice in reading the text of the Bible and committing it to memory; otherwise he will never be able to be expert in the exposition of the Scriptures. Hence just as he who declines to acquire the first elements out of which speech is constructed will never be able to understand the meaning of spoken things or the right rules of construction, so he who spurns the letter of Holy Scripture will never rise to its spiritual meanings.

2. The one who explains Scripture should recognize that not all the explanations are allegorical and that not all things need to be explained as mystical. For this purpose, we should note that Holy Scripture has four parts. In the first there is a literal treatment of earthly natures. In this manner Scripture handles our reparation as is apparent in the description of the formation of the world. In the second there is a treatment of the doings and wanderings of the people of Israel and in this way Scripture indicates the reparation of mankind. In the third part there is a treatment in plain words which express what is pertinent to our salvation with regard to faith or morals. The fourth part is that in which Scripture treats of the mystery of our salvation, partly in plain words and partly in enigmatic and obscure words. Hence Scripture does not have a uniform exposition in these various places.

3. It behooves the one who is explaining to be guided in the exposition of Holy Scripture by the triple rule which can be drawn from the words of Augustine in the book *De doctrina christiana*.[642] The first rule is this: Wherever in Scripture the immediate meaning of the words points to matters of creation, or individual acts of human intercourse, the very things designated by the words are first implied and then the mysteries of our reparation, and where the primary meaning of the words indicates faith or charity, no allegory should be sought. The second rule is this: Where the words of Scripture designate matters of creation or of the practices of the people of Israel, one should inquire from another source in Scripture what the meaning may be, and finally he may elicit the meaning through words patently indicating a truth of faith or a rule of morals so that if it be said that sheep beget twins,[643] it is clear that sheep there signifies man, and twins signifies a dual charity. The third rule is this: Wherever a part of Scripture has a kind of literal and spiritual meaning, the one who is explaining ought to determine whether the at-

tributed meaning serves a historical or a spiritual purpose, unless perchance it is incapable of serving either. If, however, it fits both, then there ought to be affirmation of its literal and spiritual meaning, but if only a single purpose is indicated, there should be only a spiritual interpretation: just as the statements that the sabbath of the law is perpetual,[644] the priesthood is eternal,[645] the possession of the land is eternal,[646] and the rule of circumcision is eternal,[647] all have reference to a spiritual meaning.

4. In order that a person may invade the forest of Holy Scripture with security in investigation and exposition, it is first necessary that he know the truth of Holy Scripture in explicit words, that is, that he ascertain how Scripture describes the beginning, progress, and consummation of the two groups: of those looking on themselves contrariwise, namely, of the good who humble themselves here that they may be eternally exalted in the future, and of the wicked who exalt themselves here that they may be eternally humbled. Hence Scripture treats of the whole universe as regards height and depth, first and last, and as regards an intermediate course under the form of a certain intelligible cross in terms of which the whole mechanism of the universe has to be described and in a certain way seen by the light of the mind. To understand this we must know the principle of things, God, the creation of those things, their fall, their redemption through the blood of Jesus Christ, their rehabilitation through grace, their cure through the sacraments, and finally their retribution through punishment and eternal glory.

From Bonaventure, *Breviloquium,* translated by Erwin Esser Nemmers (St. Louis, MO: B. Herder Book, 1947), 3–19.

BONAVENTURE

"On the Third Commandment of the Decalogue," in *Collations on the Ten Commandments,* IV

Theme

1. "Remember to keep holy the Sabbath day."[648]

---

640. Ps 5:13 (Vulgate); see Ps 5:12.

641. Ps 90:5 (Vugate); see Ps 91:4.

642. See Augustine, *De doctrina Christiana*, III.33ff.; see above.

643. See Song 4:2; 6:6.

644. See Ex 31:16.　　　　646. See Gen 13:14–15.

645. See Ex 40:14–15.　　　647. See Gen 17:10–14.

648. Ex 20:8. (The notes for this selection are by Gerhart and Udoh.)

Protheme

"The mercy of the Lord is from eternity and to eternity upon those who fear him, and his justice unto children's children, to those who keep his covenant."[649] We stand in need of the divine mercy to pardon our offenses and of the divine justice to reward our merits. The fear of God helps us to find mercy, and the observance of the commandments helps us to find justice. The consideration of the magnificence of God leads to fear of God, and the consideration of divine law leads to the observance of the commandments. And this is shown to us so that we might always reflect on divine law. So the Jews on the Sabbath day were always accustomed to discuss the law of God, because this is the work of God. So at the start let us ask God, etc.

The Third Commandment: Literal Interpretation

2. "Remember," etc. I said to you that on the first table are contained three commandments which order us to God according to three attributes appropriated to the three divine persons. In the first commandment a humble adoration of the divine majesty is prescribed;[650] in the second, the faithful confession of the highest truth;[651] in the third, a sincere love of the highest good.[652] And now we come to the third commandment and the summation of it is the phrase: "Remember to keep holy the Sabbath day."[653] And this is what follows: "Six days will you labor and do all your work. But the seventh day is the Sabbath of the Lord your God. You will not do any work on it, you or your son or your daughter, your manservant or your maidservant, your beast or the stranger who is within your gates. For in six days the Lord made the heavens and the earth, the sea, and all the things that are in them. And the Lord rested on the seventh day. Therefore the Lord blessed the Sabbath day and sanctified it."[654]

3. Note that it is the Holy Spirit who has written the tables of the commandments in these words because the Holy Spirit is understood as the Finger of God, who wrote all the commandments with the greatest diligence,[655] giving the commandments their purity and fullness.

In this commandment the Lawgiver commands something, allows something, and forbids something. The Lawgiver commands that we keep holy the Sabbath day by saying: "remember to keep holy the Sabbath day." For keeping holy is a turning of the spirit to the holy God, to the true God and to the God who is to be loved above all. The Lawgiver

allows something with that commandment by saying: "Six days will you labor and do all your work." The Lawgiver forbids something—that is, servile work—by saying: "You will not do any work on it," etc. This is a perfect rest which has good works added to it and servile works prohibited from it.

4. The reason for the commandment is added, where it says: "In six days the Lord made the heaven and the earth, the sea, and all the things that are in them, and rested on the seventh day. Therefore the Lord blessed and sanctified it." But why does the Lord command us to be at rest [on that day]? Certainly because: "The Lord has blessed and sanctified it." And so you, who are a creature of God and an imitator of Christ, must also do this.

5. But the Jews ridicule us and say: You keep the Decalogue and the Decalogue has only moral precepts. A moral precept deals with what is necessary for all times. The seventh day is the Sabbath day, which is called Saturday. The first day of the week it is lawful to work and the seventh day it is not lawful to work. But you rest on Sunday in place of the Sabbath day. Further, it is said: "You will not do any work on it," but you do much work on it and thus you lose the entire point of it.

6. See, beloved ones, it must be understood that the commandment has something that is purely moral, something that is purely ceremonial and something that is a mixture of the moral and the ceremonial. When the Lord commands this sanctification—that is, a rest for the purpose of loving—this is a purely moral commandment. So blessed Peter says: "But sanctify the Lord Christ in your hearts,"[656] that is, love [Him]! For the one who loves God above all things, for the sake of God and not for the sake of anything else, is the one who sanctifies or makes holy the Sabbath day.

7. Likewise, there is something figurative in the commandment—the meaning of the seventh day. For the seventh day signifies the rest of the spirits, and the rest of the Lord in the tomb and an abstention from all servile work together with rest and with the contemplation of God. For God created everything in six days, but not because it would have been impossible to have done it all in one. What must be understood

649. Ps 102:17–18 (Vulgate) = Ps 103:17–18.
650. See Ex 20:1–6.
651. See Ex 20:7.   654. Ex 20:9–11.
652. See Ex 20:6.   655. See Ex 31:18.
653. Ex 20:8.   656. 1 Pet 3:15.

here is that the world has one standing in the eternal art.[657] This is eternal being, which is an eternity of life and a single possession of life[658] in which there is no before or after. And this[659] God has imprinted on the angelic intellects. The world has another standing once it is in a created intelligence, namely as something which has a before and an after by nature, even though it is simultaneous[660] in terms of duration. The world has yet another standing according to duration (not according to nature) so far as it is in matter. This is not because of a defect in the maker, but rather because of God's condescension. He chose all things and specified them in his first works. And just as he produced the roots of all operations in those first works, so also he produced fully the seeds of all works and of rest.

Therefore, on the seventh day the Lord rested and re-called the spirits existing in limbo to the rest of paradise.[661] So the meaning of the seventh day is figurative with respect to the rest of the spirits. And therefore in this commandment there is contained something purely moral—that God is to be loved above all; and something purely ceremonial—the meaning of the seventh day.

8. Also something that is partly moral and partly ceremonial is contained here, namely the abstention from labors. And in regard to this, some things should be understood in general and some in particular. If we understand this in a general sense, like the Jews who say that there should be a total abstention from all servile work, then what is said to Christians is that they should abstain from all sin. If, however, we understand this in a particular sense—that we should abstain from some things and not from others—this is moral; not, however, for the sake of commanding us, but rather for the sake of our well-being. And in this way it continues to exist as the command of the Church.

9. I say that servile works are the mechanical works, of which there are seven. These are agriculture, which includes all the ways of cultivating the earth; weaving, that consists in every work and kind of clothing; fabricating, whether it is in iron or metal or stone or wood; hunting, which includes all the work of bakers and of cooks and all the ways of preparing foods; medicine, which consists in the art of making ointments or syrups and things of this kind; navigation, which includes all the work of sailors at sea and all the work of merchants; and theatrics, which involves all the ways of acting and of pleasure.

10. In all these works there are some which are completely servile, some which are always needed and some which are purely for pleasure. Those which are completely servile are prohibited by the Church. Those which are always needed, such as those which are for the preservation of life or health, are allowed inasmuch as they are necessary and are prohibited inasmuch as they are servile. Those which are purely for pleasure are permitted and not prohibited. They are permitted by the Church because of our weaknesses. And so in this way we are able to answer the Jews.

11. But you say: Why does God confuse and mix together the moral and the ceremonial? I say that this commandment: "Remember to keep holy the Sabbath day," is one of love. And whatever is revealed or concealed in the other commandments is brought to completion in this commandment. And so God mixes together the ceremonial and the moral so that we can better commit it to memory. If the commandment had been given in great detail it would have weighed down our memory.

The Third Commandment: Spiritual Interpretation

12. There are three things which are required for perfect love. The first is the divine rest which directs the soul to God. The second is the imitation of Christ in good works. The third is the abstention from all servile work, which renders the heart pure and clean.

The turning of a soul back to God is accomplished by means of seven works. Without these works the soul is not turned towards perfect rest in God. Three of these are interior and are done by meditating, by praying and by praising. And from these three comes contemplation. The other four are exterior and are accomplished by reading, by singing the psalms, by offering sacrifice and by fulfilling the divine law. And this is done either by hearing, or by teaching, or by conferring with others. And this is why it says: "Remember to keep holy the Sabbath day." Therefore the Lord first commands a rest in which the soul can turn towards God.

---

657. This is a statement of Bonaventure's doctrine of exemplarism, that is, that all creation (sensible reality) is a reflection of their perfect forms, which are found in God. All creation, therefore, mirrors God.

658. See Boethius's definition of eternity: *"Interminabilis vitae tota simul et perfecta possessio"* (The total and perfect possession of endless life all at once) (*On the Consolation of Philosophy*, 5.6).

659. That is, the eternal exemplar of the world.

660. See the *simul* in Boethius's definition (n. 658 above).

661. On the idea that Christ, after his death, descended into the underworld to bring up from there the saints of the Old Testament, see Eph 4:8–10; 1 Pet 3:18–20.

13. Secondly, God commands the imitation of himself by saying: "Six days will you labor." Of that imitation the Apostle says: "Be imitators of God as dearest children,"[662] and in Luke it says: "Be merciful even as your Father is merciful."[663]

There are six works of mercy: to feed the hungry, to give drink to the thirsty, to clothe the naked, to care for the stranger, to visit the sick and to ransom the captive. A work of perfect virtue is not possible unless a creature is conformed to Christ in these things.

14. Six things are required to do a work of virtue, corresponding to the works of the six days of creation. These are: provident consideration, right intention, pure affection, just or correct choice, a vigorous carrying out and a putting on of love. The first is understood in the work of the first day, when God said: "Let there be light," and there was light.[664] This is provident consideration. Secondly, one should direct oneself to the right end in God. This is noted when it says: "Let there be a firmament in the midst of the waters, and God called the firmament heaven,"[665] because one should be directed heavenwards, so as to have a right intention with respect to God. Thirdly, pure affection is required. This is what is understood in the third work when God divided the land from the water, thus separating worldly affections from divine affections.[666] Fourthly, a just or correct choice is required, so that all our works might be done in an orderly way, as they should be. This is noted in the fourth work, when it says: "Let there be lights in the firmament of the heaven,"[667] that is, let our works be ordered.

Fifthly, a vigorous carrying out is required. This is noted in the fifth work, when God produced living beings in the water, such as fish, and in the air, such as birds.[668] Sixthly, a putting on the form of love is required, so that the works might be complete, prepared for all circumstances according to the demands of the law of divine love. For love is the perfect form of all things, and the one who has love has all six requirements. So the sixth work is the putting on of love. This is noted when it says: "God made man in the image and likeness of himself."[669] When the work of a human person brings together these six elements, then it is said the person lives rightly.

15. But it is not sufficient to do a work of virtue unless one guards oneself against evil work. This is touched on when it says: "You shall do no work on it," that is, no sin.

There are five ways in which a person can sin: first, by sinning against a commandment; second, by inciting another to sin; third, by defending the sinner; fourth, by accepting the sinner; fifth, by ignoring the sinner, neither arguing with nor punishing him. And this is the greatest peril, when anyone neglects to reprove another.

16. The first sin is touched on when it says: "You shall do no work on it," that is, you shall not commit any sin. The second sin is touched on when it says: "Neither son or daughter," that is, you shall not be the father of sin by instigating another to sinning either by word or by deed or by example. The third sin is touched on when it says: "Neither your manservant or your maidservant." The one "who does sin is the servant of sin,"[670] but the one who defends sin is the lord of sin by shewing patronage to those sinning. The fourth sin is when someone accepts the sinner. That is touched on when it says: "Neither your beast of burden." The beast of burden, while it is tied, cannot be led to work unless the master accepts the fact that this be done,[671] and that acceptance is a retying. The fifth sin is when someone neglects to reprove another. That is touched on when it says: "Not the stranger who is within your gates." One considers a person to be a stranger when one sees him sinning and says: What is your sin to me? And so when one does not reprove the sin of another, one is made a partner in that person's sin. A person can become a partner in the sin of another in many other ways. For this reason the *Psalm* says: "From my secret sins cleanse me O Lord, and from those of others spare your servant."[672]

From *St. Bonaventure's Collations on the Ten Commandments,* translated by Paul J. Spaeth (St. Bonaventure, NY: Franciscan Institute, 1995), 61–69.

☙ **Thomas Aquinas** (ca. 1225–74) is often called the "Christian Aristotle" for his knowledge and integration of Aristotelian philosophy into Christian theology. His approach to the biblical texts is informed by the Christian biblical interpretation of the previous twelve centuries, as seen in his *Summa theologiae* (written between 1266 and 1273), 1a.1, 10, "Can One Passage of Holy Scripture Bear Several Senses?"

---

662. Eph 5:1.

663. Lk 6:36.

664. Gen 1:3.

665. Gen 1:6.

666. Gen 1:9–10.

667. Gen 1:14–15.

668. Gen 1:20–21.

669. Gen 1:27.

670. Jn 8:34.

671. See Mk 11:1–6; Mt 21:1–3; Lk 19:29–34.

672. Ps 18:13–14 (Vulgate); see also Ps 19:12–13.

THOMAS AQUINAS

"Can One Passage of Holy Scripture Bear Several Senses?" in *Summa theologiae,* 1a.1, 10

THE TENTH POINT: 1. It would seem that the same text of holy Scripture does not bear several senses, namely the historical or literal, the allegorical, the tropological or moral, and the anagogical. Allow a variety of readings to one passage, and you produce confusion and deception, and sap the foundations of argument; examples of the stock fallacies, not reasoned discourse, follow from the medley of meanings. Holy Scripture, however, should effectively display the truth without fallacy of any sort. One text, therefore, should not offer various meanings.

2. Besides, St. Augustine holds that Scripture which is entitled the Old Testament has a fourfold meaning, namely according to history, to etiology, to analogy, and to allegory.[673] Now these four appear inconsistent with the four mentioned above; which therefore appear awkward headings for interpreting a passage of Scripture.

3. Further, there is also a parabolic sense, not included among them.

ON THE OTHER HAND, St. Gregory declares that holy Scripture transcends all other sciences by its very style of expression, in that one and the same discourse, while narrating an event, transmits a mystery as well.[674]

REPLY: That God is the author of holy Scripture should be acknowledged, and he has the power, not only of adapting words to convey meanings (which men also can do), but also of adapting things themselves. In every branch of knowledge words have meaning, but what is special here is that the things meant by the words also themselves mean something. That first meaning whereby the words signify things belongs to the sense first-mentioned, namely the historical or literal. That meaning, however, whereby the things signified by the words in their turn also signify other things is called the spiritual sense; it is based on and presupposes the literal sense. Now this spiritual sense is divided into three. For, as St. Paul says, *The Old Law is the figure of the New,*[675] and the New Law itself, as Dionysius says, *is the figure of the glory to come.*[676] Then again, under the New Law the deeds wrought by our Head are signs also of what we ourselves ought to do. Well then, the allegorical sense is brought into play when the things of the Old Law signify the things of the New Law; the moral sense when the things done in Christ and in those who prefigured him are signs of what we should carry out; and the anagogical sense when the things that lie ahead in

eternal glory are signified. Now because the literal sense is that which the author intends, and the author of holy Scripture is God who comprehends everything all at once in his understanding, it comes not amiss, as St. Augustine observes, if many meanings are present even in the literal sense of one passage of Scripture.[677]

Hence: 1. These various readings do not set up ambiguity or any other kind of mixture of meanings, because, as we have explained, they are many, not because one term may signify many things, but because the things signified by the terms can themselves be the signs of other things. Consequently holy Scripture sets up no confusion, since all meanings are based on one, namely the literal sense. From this alone can arguments be drawn, and not, as St. Augustine remarks in his letter to Vincent the Donatist, from the things said by allegory.[678] Nor does this undo the effect of holy Scripture, for nothing necessary for faith is contained under the spiritual sense that is not openly conveyed through the literal sense elsewhere.

2. These three, history, etiology, and analogy, are grouped under the one general heading of the literal sense. For as St. Augustine explains in the same place, you have history when any matter is straightforwardly recorded; etiology when its cause is indicated, as when our Lord pointed to men's hardness of heart as the reason why Moses allowed them to set aside their wives;[679] analogy when the truth of one Scriptural passage is shown not to clash with the truth of another. Of the four senses enumerated in the argument, allegory stands alone for the three spiritual senses of our exposition. For instance Hugh of St. Victor included the anagogical sense under the allegorical, and enumerated just three senses, namely the historical, the allegorical, and the tropological.[680]

3. The parabolical sense is contained in the literal sense, for words can signify something properly and something figuratively; in the last case the literal sense is not the figure of speech itself, but the object it figures. When Scripture speaks of the arm of God, the literal sense is not that he has a physi-

---

673. Augustine, *On the Profit of Believing,* III.5. (The notes for this selection are by Gerhart and Udoh.)

674. Gregory the Great, *Morals on the Book of Job,* xx.3.

675. Heb 10:1.

676. Pseudo-Dionysius, *Ecclesiastical Hierarchy,* v. 2.

677. Augustine, *Confessions,* xii.31.

678. Augustine, Letter 93 (to Vincentius), 8.

679. See Mk 10:5; Mt 19:8.

680. Hugh of St. Victor, *De sacramentis,* I, Prologue, 4.

cal limb, but that he has what it signifies, namely the power of doing and making. This example brings out how nothing false can underlie the literal sense of Scripture.

From Thomas Aquinas, *Summa theologiae*, vol. 1 (London: Blackfriars, 1963), 37, 39, 41.

REFORMATION INTERPRETATION

By posting the Ninety-five Theses in 1517, **Martin Luther** (1483–1546) started the Protestant Reformation. He describes his "evangelical discovery" (or "tower experience," which occurred in ca. 1519), whereby he came to believe in salvation by faith rather than works, in *Preface to Latin Writings*, written in Wittenberg in 1545. In the next selection, *Defense and Explanation of All the Articles,* Luther responds to the papal Bull *Exsurge Domine*, issued by Pope Leo X on June 15, 1520, which condemned forty-one of Luther's theses. In *Defense and Explanation,* written in March 1521, Luther sets out his most important theological principle, namely, that Scripture alone (*sola scriptura*) is the authority for the Church. *Against Latomus* is Luther's reply to a book that Latomus (ca. 1475–1544) wrote against Luther (both works were published in 1521). Luther discusses the four senses (literal, allegorical, tropological, and anagogical) of Scripture as he comments on the Psalms in his *First Lectures on the Psalms,* given at the University of Wittenberg from 1513 to 1515. In *Lectures on Galatians* (1519), Luther's interpretive principles are applied to Paul's letter.

MARTIN LUTHER

Preface to Latin Writings

Meanwhile, I had already during that year[681] returned to interpret the Psalter anew. I had confidence in the fact that I was more skilful, after I had lectured in the university on St. Paul's epistles to the Romans, to the Galatians, and the one to the Hebrews. I had indeed been captivated with an extraordinary ardor for understanding Paul in the Epistle to the Romans. But up till then it was not the cold blood about the heart,[682] but a single word in Chapter 1 [:17], "In it the righteousness of God is revealed," that had stood in my way. For I hated that word "righteousness of God," which, according to the use and custom of all the teachers, I had been taught to understand philosophically regarding the formal or active righteousness, as they called it, with which God is righteous and punishes the unrighteous sinner.

Though I lived as a monk without reproach, I felt that I was a sinner before God with an extremely disturbed conscience. I could not believe that he was placated by my satisfaction. I did not love, yes, I hated the righteous God who punishes sinners, and secretly, if not blasphemously, certainly murmuring greatly, I was angry with God, and said, "As if, indeed, it is not enough, that miserable sinners, eternally lost through original sin, are crushed by every kind of calamity by the law of the decalogue, without having God add pain to pain by the gospel and also by the gospel threatening us with his righteousness and wrath!" Thus I raged with a fierce and troubled conscience. Nevertheless, I beat importunately upon Paul at that place, most ardently desiring to know what St. Paul wanted.

At last, by the mercy of God, meditating day and night, I gave heed to the context of the words, namely, "In it the righteousness of God is revealed, as it is written, 'He who through faith is righteous shall live.'"[683] There I began to understand that the righteousness of God is that by which the righteous lives by a gift of God, namely by faith. And this is the meaning: the righteousness of God is revealed by the gospel, namely, the passive righteousness with which merciful God justifies us by faith, as it is written, "He who through faith is righteous shall live." Here I felt that I was altogether born again and had entered paradise itself through open gates. There a totally other face of the entire Scripture showed itself to me. Thereupon I ran through the Scriptures from memory. I also found in other terms an analogy, as, the work of God, that is, what God does in us, the power of God, with which he makes us strong, the wisdom of God, with which he makes us wise, the strength of God, the salvation of God, the glory of God.

And I extolled my sweetest word with a love as great as the hatred with which I had before hated the word "righteousness of God." Thus that place in Paul was for me truly the gate to paradise. Later I read Augustine's *The Spirit and the Letter,* where contrary to hope I found that he, too, interpreted God's righteousness in a similar way, as the righteousness with which God clothes us when he justifies us.[684] Although this was heretofore said imperfectly and he did not explain all things concerning imputation clearly, it nevertheless was pleasing that God's righteousness with which we are

---

681. That is, in 1519. (The notes for this selection are by Gerhart and Udoh.)
682. See Virgil, *Georgics*, 2.484.
683. See Rom 1:17; see also Hab 2:4.
684. See Augustine, *On the Spirit and the Letter*, 15–16.

justified was taught. Armed more fully with these thoughts, I began a second time to interpret the Psalter. And the work would have grown into a large commentary, if I had not again been compelled to leave the work begun, because Emperor Charles V in the following year convened the diet at Worms.[685]

I relate these things, good reader, so that, if you are a reader of my puny works, you may keep in mind that, as I said above, I was all alone and one of those who, as Augustine says of himself, have become proficient by writing and teaching. I was not one of those who from nothing suddenly become the topmost, though they are nothing, neither have labored, nor been tempted, nor become experienced, but have with one look at the Scriptures exhausted their entire spirit.

To this point, to the year 1520 and 21, the indulgence matter proceeded. Upon that followed the sacramentarian and the Anabaptist affairs. Regarding these a preface shall be written to other tomes, if I live.

Farewell in the Lord, reader, and pray for the growth of the Word against Satan. Strong and evil, now also very furious and savage, he knows his time is short and the kingdom of his pope is in danger. But may God confirm in us what he has accomplished and perfect his work which he began in us, to his glory, Amen. March 5, in the year 1545.

Translated by Lewis W. Spitz Sr., in *Luther's Works,* edited by Jaroslav Pelikan, vol. 34 (Philadelphia: Muhlenberg, 1960), 336–38.

MARTIN LUTHER

Defense and Explanation of All the Articles

They say also that I propose new ideas and it is not to be expected that everybody else should have been so long in error. That, too, the ancient prophets had to hear. If length of time were sufficient proof, the Jews would have had the strongest kind of case against Christ on that ground. His doctrine was different from any they had heard for a thousand years. The Gentiles, too, would have been justified in regarding the apostles with contempt, since their ancestors for more than three thousand years held to a different faith. There have been murderers, adulterers, and thieves since the beginning of the world, and will be to its end. Does that make their actions right? I preach nothing new, but I say that all Christian things have perished among the very people who ought to have preserved them, namely, the bishops and scholars. But I have no doubt that the truth has been retained in some hearts to this day, if only in the hearts of infants in their cradles. In Old

Testament times also, the spiritual understanding of the law was retained among some of the common people, though it was lost by the high priests and the learned who ought to have preserved it. Thus Jeremiah says that he has found less understanding and justice among the leaders than among the laity and the common folk.[686] Likewise today, poor peasants and children understand Christ better than pope, bishops, and doctors. Everything is topsy-turvy.

Now, if that is the way they want it, well and good. Let them make me out a heathen. But what would their answer be, or how should we present our case, if a Turk were to ask us to give reasons for our faith? He doesn't care how long we have believed a certain way or how many or how eminent the people are who have believed this or that. We would have to be silent about all these things and direct him to the holy Scriptures as the basis for our faith. It would be absurd and ridiculous if we were to say: look here, so many priests, bishops, kings, princes, lands, and peoples have believed this and that ever so long.

Let them now treat me the same way. Let us see what our reasons and resources are. Let us examine them, if only for our own reassurance and attention. Shall we have such good reasons and not know them? Shall we keep them hidden when it is the will of Christ that they shall be generally known to all men? He says in Matt. 5 [:15], "Nor do men light a lamp and put it under a bushel, but on a stand, and it gives light to all in the house." Christ allowed his hands, his feet, his sides to be touched so that the disciples might be sure that it was he, himself.[687] Why, then, should we not touch and examine the Scriptures—which are in truth the spiritual body of Christ—to make sure whether we believe in them or not? For all other writings are treacherous; they may be spirits in the air[688] which have no flesh or bone, as Christ had.

This is my answer to those also who accuse me of rejecting all the holy teachers of the church. I do not reject them. But everyone, indeed, knows that at times they have erred, as men will; therefore, I am ready to trust them only when they give me evidence for their opinions from Scripture, which has never erred. This St. Paul bids me to do in I Thess. 5:21, where he says, "Test everything; hold fast what is good." St. Augustine writes to St. Jerome to the same effect, "I have

---

685. Luther interrupted his commentary at Ps 21, having received the summons to the diet in March 1521.

686. See Jer 5:1–31. (The notes for this selection are by Gerhart and Udoh.)

687. See Jn 20:27.

688. See Eph 2:2.

learned to do only those books that are called the holy Scriptures the honor of believing firmly that none of their writers has ever erred. All others I so read as not to hold what they say to be the truth unless they prove it to me by holy Scripture or clear reason."[689]

Holy Scripture must necessarily be clearer, simpler, and more reliable than any other writings. Especially since all teachers verify their own statements through the Scriptures as clearer and more reliable writings, and desire their own writings to be confirmed and explained by them. But nobody can ever substantiate an obscure saying by one that is more obscure; therefore, necessity forces us to run to the Bible with the writings of all teachers, and to obtain there a verdict and judgment upon them. Scripture alone is the true lord and master of all writings and doctrine on earth. If that is not granted, what is Scripture good for? The more we reject it, the more we become satisfied with men's books and human teachers.

Translated by Charles M. Jacobs, revised by George W. Forell, in *Luther's Works*, edited by Jaroslav Pelikan, vol. 32 (Philadelphia: Muhlenberg, 1958), 10–12.

MARTIN LUTHER

Against Latomus

Does this mean, you ask, that I do not believe what the fathers say? To this I reply: Should I believe? Who has commanded that I believe them? Where is the precept of God regarding such belief? And why don't they believe these fathers of theirs—especially Augustine who wished to be free and commanded everyone to be free in regard to all human writings?[690] The sophists have imposed tyranny and bondage upon our freedom to such a point that we must not resist that twice accursed Aristotle, but are compelled to submit. Shall we therefore be perpetually enslaved and never breathe in Christian liberty, nor sigh from out of this Babylon for our Scriptures and our home? Yet you say they were saints and illuminated the Scripture. Who has shown that they made the Scriptures clearer—what if they obscured them? By whose pronouncement do you prove that they threw light on Holy Writ? Will you say in the fashion of Louvain and Cologne that, "it seems so to me," and, "so they say"? To be sure, they may say so and it may seem so, but let them prove the thing to me, or else stop urging me with their empty words. I am commanded to believe the Word of God, not their fancies. There is one teacher,[691] even Christ, and the fathers are to be tested by the judgment of the divine Scriptures so that it may be known who has clarified and who has obscured them.

Thus Paul orders us to "test everything; hold fast to what is good."[692] In I Cor. 14 [:29] he says, "Let two or three prophets speak, and let the others weigh what is said." He commands that all be tested and that there be no exceptions—neither Augustine, nor Origen, nor any man, not even the Antichrist, the pope. But doesn't obscure Scripture require explanation? Set aside the obscure and cling to the clear. Further, who has proved that the fathers are not obscure? Are we once again going to have your, "it seems," and their, "they say"? What did the fathers do except seek and present the clear and open testimonies of Scripture? Miserable Christians, whose words and faith still depend on the interpretations of men and who expect clarification from them! This is frivolous and ungodly. The Scriptures are common to all, and are clear enough in respect to what is necessary for salvation, and are also obscure enough for inquiring minds. Let everyone search for his portion in the most abundant and universal Word of God, and let us reject the word of man, or else read it with discrimination. This is enough regarding this matter, and much more than enough.

Translated by George Lindbeck, in *Luther's Works*, edited by Jaroslav Pelikan, vol. 32 (Philadelphia: Muhlenberg, 1958), 216–17.

MARTIN LUTHER

First Lectures on the Psalms, I, Preface to the Glosses, Preface of Jesus Christ, Psalm 4:1, Psalm 64:6–9

Preface to the Glosses

"I will sing with the spirit and I will sing with the mind also."[693] To sing with the spirit is to sing with spiritual devotion and emotion. This is said in opposition to those who sing only with the flesh. And these appear in a twofold sense: The first are those who with an unsettled and weary heart sing only with the tongue and the mouth. The second are those who indeed sing with a cheerful and devout heart but are still enjoying it more in a carnal way, as, for example, taking pleasure in the voice, the sound, the staging, and the harmony. They act as boys usually do, not concerned about the meaning or the fruit of the spirit that is to be raised up to

---

689. Augustine, Letter 82 (to Jerome).

690. See Augustine, Letter 93 (to Vincentius). (The notes for this selection are by Gerhart and Udoh.)

691. See Mt 23:8.

692. 1 Thess 5:21.

693. 1 Cor 14:15. (The notes for this selection are by Gerhart and Udoh.)

		The killing letter	The life-giving spirit concerning the Babylonian ecclesiastical body
Mount Zion	historically:	the land of Canaan	The people living in Zion
	allegorically:	the synagog or a prominent person in it	the church or any teacher, bishop, or prominent man
	tropologically:	the righteousness of the Pharisees and of the Law	the righteousness of faith or some other prominent matter
	anagogically:	the future glory after the flesh	the eternal glory in the heavens
On the contrary, Kidron Valley from the opposite point of view			

God. In the same way, to sing with the mind is to sing with spiritual understanding. And there are likewise two opposites of these: The first are those who understand nothing of what they sing, as nuns are said to read the Psalter. The others are those who have a carnal understanding of the Psalms, like the Jews, who always apply the Psalms to ancient history apart from Christ. But Christ has opened the mind of those who are His so that they might understand the Scriptures.[694]

More often, however, the spirit enlightens the mind, the emotions, the intellect, yes, also vice versa, because the spirit lifts up to the place where the illuminating light is, whereas the mind assigns a place to the emotions. Therefore both are required, but the elevating spirit is better, etc.

Jerusalem: allegorically: the good people
                      tropologically: virtues
                      anagogically: rewards

Babylon: allegorically: the bad people
                      tropologically: vices
                      anagogically: punishments

In the Scriptures, therefore, no allegory, tropology, or anagogy is valid, unless the same truth is expressly stated historically elsewhere. Otherwise Scripture would become a mockery. But one must indeed take in an allegorical sense only what is elsewhere stated historically as mountain in the sense of righteousness in Ps. 36:6:[695] "Thy righteousness is like the mountains of God." For that reason it is best to distinguish the spirit from the letter in the Sacred Scriptures, for this is what makes one a theologian indeed. And the church has this only from the Holy Spirit, not from human understanding. Thus Ps. 72:8[696] says: "May He have dominion from sea to sea." Before the Spirit's revelation no one could know that this dominion means a spiritual dominion, especially because

he adds "from sea to sea" according to the historical sense. Therefore those who interpret this dominion as referring to the flesh and to earthly majesty have the killing letter, but others have the life-giving spirit.[697]

For that reason I often understand the Psalms as referring to the Jews, because we know that what the Law says it speaks to those who are under the Law. Rom. 3:19.

Preface of Jesus Christ, Son of God and Our Lord, to the Psalter of David

"I am the door; if anyone enters by Me, he will be saved, and will go in and out and find pasture." John 10:9. "The words of the Holy One, the True One, who has the key of David, who opens and no one shall shut, who shuts and no one opens." Rev. 3:7. "In the roll of the book it is written of Me." Ps. 40:7. "Even what I have told you from the beginning." John 8:25. "Therefore My people shall know My name; therefore in that day they shall know that it is I who speak; here am I"[698] (Is. 52:6).

THE FIRST WITNESS: MOSES

"If Thy presence will not go with me, do not carry us up from here." "And the Lord said, 'My presence will go with you, and I will give you rest.'" Ex. 33:15, 14.

---

694. See Lk 24:45.

695. The translator notes that Luther's original manuscript has "Ps. 57." Since Luther commonly cited the Scriptures from memory, his references are often inaccurate.

696. The translator notes that Luther's manuscript has "Ps. 7." See previous note.

697. See 2 Cor 3:6.

698. The translator observes that Luther adds here the following gloss: "If the Old Testament can be interpreted by human wisdom without the New Testament, I should say that the New Testament has been given to no purpose. So Paul concluded that 'Christ died to no purpose' if the Law were sufficient (Gal. 2:21)."

THE SECOND WITNESS: ZECHARIAH THE PROPHET

"The Lord [Jesus Christ] is the eye, [the light and the vision] of man and all the tribes of Israel."[699]

THE THIRD WITNESS: PETER THE APOSTLE

"And all the prophets who have spoken, from Samuel and those who came afterwards, also proclaimed these days." Acts 3:24.

THE FOURTH WITNESS: PAUL THE APOSTLE

"For I decided to know nothing among you except Jesus Christ and Him crucified." 1 Cor. 2:2.

From these we draw the following guideline for this dark, yet holy labyrinth: Every prophecy and every prophet must be understood as referring to Christ the Lord, except where it is clear from plain words that someone else is spoken of. For thus He Himself says: "Search the Scriptures, . . . and it is they that bear witness to Me."[700] Otherwise it is most certain that the searchers will not find what they are searching for. For that reason some explain very many psalms not prophetically but historically, following certain Hebrew rabbis who are falsifiers and inventors of Jewish vanities. No wonder, because they are far away from Christ (that is, from the truth). "But we have the mind of Christ," says the apostle.[701]

Whatever is said literally concerning the Lord Jesus Christ as to His person must be understood allegorically of a help that is like Him and of the church conformed to Him in all things. And at the same time this must be understood tropologically of any spiritual and inner man against his flesh and the outer man. Let this be made plain by means of examples. "Blessed is the man who walks not, etc."[702] Literally this means that the Lord Jesus made no concessions to the designs of the Jews and of the evil and adulterous age that existed in His time. Allegorically it means that the holy church did not agree to the evil designs of persecutors, heretics, and ungodly Christians. Tropologically this means that the spirit of man did not accede to the persuasions and suggestions of the inimical flesh and of the ungodly stirrings of the body of sin. Thus also Ps. 2:1 says: "Why do the nations conspire, etc." Literally this refers to the raging of the Jews and Gentiles against Christ during His suffering. Allegorically it is directed against tyrants, heretics, and ungodly leaders of the church. Tropologically it has to do with the tyranny, temptation, and tempest of the carnal and outer man who provokes and torments the spirit as the dwelling place of Christ. Thus, Ps. 3:1 reads: "O Lord, how many are my foes." This is literally Christ's complaint concerning the Jews, His enemies. Allegorically it is a complaint and accusation of the church regarding tyrants, heretics, etc. But tropologically it is a complaint, or prayer, of the devout and afflicted spirit placed into trials. In their own way we must also judge in other places, lest we become burdened with a closed book and receive no food.

Lecture on Psalm 4:1

When I called, Thou didst answer me, O God of my righteousness. In tribulation Thou didst make room for me.

The third enlargement[703] is that of comfort and joy in the Holy Spirit. So the apostle says in 2 Cor. 1:3–4: "Blessed be the God and Father of our Lord Jesus Christ, the Father of mercies and God of all comfort, who comforts us in all our affliction." And this belongs to the Holy Spirit, who is the Paraclete, that is, the Comforter. Thus a psalm says: "Out of my distress I called on the Lord; the Lord answered me in a large space."[704] And Hannah, the mother of Samuel, in I Sam. 2:1 says: "My mouth is opened wide." Thus it is clear that the blessed Trinity offers a threefold enlargement to His living image, which is man. The mind is enlarged through education and understanding, the memory, or substance or nature of the soul, is enlarged through the strength and vigor of grace, and the will is enlarged through joy and comfort. On the contrary, all of these are diminished by sin and error and sadness. So Is. 54:2 exhorts: "Enlarge the place of your tent, and let the curtains of your habitations lie stretched out, etc." Similarly, in an allegorical sense, the church received a threefold enlargement. For they were exceedingly multiplied by Pharaoh's oppression,[705] and the truth of the faith was made illustrious, and their joy in the spirit was increased. Note lastly, that he adds for me. This is the remarkable grace of God, that He does not cause these enlargements to be repayment and reward in this life. But he says, "for me," for my

---

699. See Zech 9:1. And Luther adds the following gloss: "Ps. 34:5: 'Look to Him and be radiant; and your faces will never be ashamed.' But others make a detour and purposely, as it were, avoid Christ, so do they put off approaching Him with the text. As for me, when I have a text that is like a nut with a hard shell, I immediately dash it against the Rock and find the sweet kernel." See previous note.

700. Jn 5:39.

701. 1 Cor 2:16.

702. Ps 1:1.

703. Luther is commenting on the second part of the verse. He already has noted two of the "threefold enlargements which God provides in tribulation": (1) education—"for in tribulation one learns many things which he did not know before"; (2) strength—"Thus love, faith, hope, and all others grow larger in persecution . . ." (p. 49).

704. Ps 118:5.

705. See Ex 1:7, 12.

good, for my salvation, for my benefit. God indeed enlarges and exalts many to their destruction, their ruin and judgment. But this is not the case with those who "are enlarged in tribulation."

But the question arises why he does not say: "In tribulation you have lengthened or deepened for me." Perhaps because of change and imperfection. For in this life these enlargements experience constant change, and nothing is long and settled, but it will be so in the future, where it will be forever. But it is not yet perfect. For what is partial here will then be made perfect, and it will then be both deep and bottomless.

These things compel us, finally, to observe that it is customary with Scripture frequently to put the words in an absolute and unqualified way. He does not say here what He enlarged—the heart, the spirit, or the soul. So it is also in that Psalm: "Thou hast done for those who trust in Thee;"[706] and again: "Truly, Thou hast placed for them because of deceptions":[707] and elsewhere: "I will place him in safety, I will confidently deal with him."[708] Here you see that he does not say what, but has only the meaning of the verb without qualification. So also the Lord in the Gospel says: "My Word does not take hold in you."[709] Therefore in all of these places the vocable should be drawn out as broadly as possible, as a genus is divided into all its species, and the whole into its parts. For such a way of speaking is always very rich and fertile, and therefore it is put in this unqualified way. This is what I just did with the verb "Thou didst make room." I applied it not only to the will but to everything that is capable of enlargement in tribulation.

Before we move on to the second verse, there are two noteworthy things which he was pleased to insert here by the way, lest they be forgotten. The first is, that this verse and many others are beautifully woven like a cord, the following one always from the preceding one, and the expression, or utterance, always seems to be the reason for what follows, and what precedes is, as it were, the fountain and source of what follows. It is as if you were fashioning a chain or necklaces or a garland. For example, the first statement is "When I called," which is the reason for what follows, as if you were asking, "Why did You hear me?" There follows beautifully "Because I called." The third statement is "God of my righteousness." Why did you call Him that? Because He answered me, and if He had not answered me, He would be the God not of my righteousness but of my punishment. Then the fourth statement, "in tribulation." Why does this follow the third? Answer: Because He is the God of my righ-

teousness. "Those who desire to lead a godly life will suffer persecution,"[710] and whom the Lord justifies He soon puts to the test. Finally, why did the Lord enlarge you? From what does this follow? Or by what manner of reasoning does this follow and not something else? Answer: Because I am afflicted. For God is with them in tribulation, etc. From this it is clear that there is a wonderful value in the sequence of the words and fitness in their order. You are enlarged because you are afflicted. And this because you are righteous in God's view. And this because He answered you in His mercy. And this because you called on Him. Therefore the prayer leads to answer, the answer to righteousness, the righteousness to tribulation, the tribulation to consolation. In a similar manner you could busy yourself also with other verses. This device, which is called climax, the apostle also makes use of in Rom. 5 and 10, saying: "Suffering produces endurance, and endurance produces character, and character produces hope, and hope produces glory, because it does not disappoint us."[711] And chapter 10: "How are men to call upon Him in whom they have not believed? And how are they to believe in Him of whom they have never heard? And how are they to hear without a preacher? And how can men preach unless they are sent?"[712] But you notice that in these three climaxes there are neither less nor more than five steps, so that you may understand that these things are for the sole benefit of the fivefold one, that is, man, who is represented by the five virgins.[713]

The second [thing inserted here] is that Christ is the Head of all saints, the Fountain of all, the Source of all rivers, of whom all partake, and "from His fullness all have received."[714] From this it follows that "in the roll" (that is, in the chief sense) "of the book," that is, of the entire Scripture and especially of the Psalms, "it is written concerning Him."[715] And as all His saints flow from Him like rivers, so Scripture, being similarly constituted and thus representing Him with His saints, speaks of Him in the sense of the first source. Then it distributes the same sense to the rivers (that is, individual explanations), speaking the same words concerning the saints by way of participation. For if they participate with Him in grace and inherit all things from Him, then also the words

---

706. Ps 31:19.
707. Ps 73:18.
708. Ps 12:5.
709. Jn 8:37.
710. 2 Tim 3:12.

711. Rom 5:3–5.
712. Rom 10:14–15.
713. See Mt 25:2.
714. Jn 1:16.
715. Ps 40:7.

of Scripture which speak of Christ participate with Him in a similar way and inherit the same words of praise and description from Him and with Him and in Him, "who is blessed."[716] In this way all four senses of Scripture flow together into one very large stream. So, for example, the present psalm is understood first of all concerning Christ, who calls and is heard; then, allegorically, concerning the church, His body; and finally, in a tropological sense, concerning any holy soul. It can also be understood thus with reference to the person of David and anyone at all. The reason for all is that God makes all His saints to be "conformed to the image of His Son";[717] for that reason the same words are suitable for all of them.

Lecture on Psalm 64:6–9

6. *A man will come to a deep heart.* According to St. Augustine, this is said first concerning Christ, as I indicated in the gloss.[718] Second, in the view of Cassiodorus, a man, any believer, will come to a deep heart through a contemplation of divine things and through faith, and in this way God [Christ][719] is exalted not in Himself, but in such a heart. [For the divinity of Christ is not recognized unless the mind is lifted up through faith.][720] Third, a man will come to a deep, that is, a lowly or humble, heart, for the more we humble ourselves, the more we exalt God, so that the person who considers himself nothing truly regards God as the highest and best, and vice versa. Fourth, since the Greek[721] has "and a deep heart" where we[722] have simply "heart," some have explained this to mean a man will come, that is, Christ will come, who is man and of a deep mind, and God will be glorified throughout the world. Or: Christ will come, namely, to us through faith and to God through Himself. [Another possibility: The deep heart is a heart that is spiritually aware. For a spiritual man is judged by no one and is hidden in the depth of God, and in such a heart God is exalted. But a carnal heart is deep, yet empty without the Spirit, that is, in it God is not exalted, but rather the person himself. Job 11:12: "A vain man is lifted up into pride."][723] But it seems to me rather that it is a Hebrew idiom, like Song of Sol. 3:8: "A man and his sword upon his thigh," which we would translate "every man's sword upon his thigh." Therefore here, too, the word "human being" or "man" is used of individuals or of each one, as Jerome has it here. And Micah 7:2: "A man (that is, each man) hunts his brother to death." And Micah 2:2: "They have oppressed a man and his house (that is, each man together with his house), a man and his inheritance." Is. 9:19: "A man (that is, every man or each individual) spares not his brother." Is. 3:5–6: "The people will op-

press one another, man against man, and each one against his neighbor. And a man shall take hold of his brother." And Ps. 49:7: "A brother shall not redeem, a man shall not redeem," that is, man, as individuals or each one. For that word אִישׁ denotes a man, a human being, a prince, and each person individually. Hence so much variety has arisen. As in this psalm and in Ps. 49 the word is put in the sense of human being, so it could be put everywhere in the cited passages. Or, as it was used there in the sense of man and "each one," so it could also be used here, as St. Jerome did it, as will become clear. Therefore in line with this manner of speaking, the meaning seems to me to be: Let a man, or each one, come with a deep heart, as above (Song of Sol. 3:8), a man and his sword, that is, a man with his sword. Thus whether we read "and the heart" or "to the heart," it clearly has the same meaning. Or, if it is said concerning Christ, it means: Christ, true Man and Hero, will come with a profound heart, not like the sons of men, with a heavy heart, and thus He will be exalted.

Fifth, the Hebrew reads as follows: "They have failed, searching with a search in the thoughts of the individuals," or of each one, or of man and man, human being and human being, or individually. The meaning is: They have failed, each one individually, in their search and in their thoughts, that is, their counsels, and in a deep heart. For anyone at all brought his own counsel and his own thoughts to this search, as is clear in the Gospel in the house of Caiaphas,[724] and yet they failed and did not find, though they were deep of heart, yet here the deep heart did not prevail, nor did each one's counsel. [There was no one who would find, as "He has scattered the proud in the mind of their heart,"[725] so they failed in their thoughts. And Ps. 5:10: "Let them fall by their own counsels."][726]

7. *God will shoot His arrows at them.* Those arrows were the Romans, sent against them by the Lord. *Their wounds will be*

---

716. See Paul's doxology in Rom 1:25 and 2 Cor 11:31.

717. Rom 8:29.

718. The translator observes that Luther writes in the gloss: *"There will come, they will fail, but there will approach, a man, I, Christ, true Man, to the deep heart, of God the Father, from whom He was born from eternity, that is, to equality with the Father."*

719. This, according to the translator, is a marginal addition.

720. This, according to the translator, is a marginal addition.

721. The Septuagint (Ps 63:6).

722. The Vulgate (Ps 63:7).

723. This, according to the translator, is a marginal addition.

724. See Mk 14:53, 55–60; Mt 26:57, 59–61.

725. Lk 1:51.

726. This, according to the translator, is a marginal addition.

inflicted suddenly with a javelin, that is, they were unexpectedly destroyed by the Romans.

8. *They will rush in against themselves with their tongues,* that is, they will kill themselves with regard to the soul by doctrines of treachery against Christ. Hence Lyra translates: "And their tongues will cause them to stumble." For they will be ashamed because of pride to confess again Him whom they have once denied. And thus, by the words of defense and justification by which they killed Him before Pilate, they rush headlong and are offended, so that they do not believe in Christ. This happens to all who proudly arrive at affirming and denying anything, as people who have been convicted are ashamed to take back or change their word. So also the heretics act. Therefore they all come to ruin with their tongues. But if they would renounce them and speak with the tongues of Christ and confession, they would certainly not fall to ruin but rise up. *All who see them will flee,* namely, to Christ, away from them.

9. *And all men will be afraid* (that is, they are able to fear and flee, because the spectacle is frightening enough). *And they will declare the work of God,* that is, they will say that this is the vengeance of God and the rain of arrows from heaven, *and they will understand His work,* that is, they will understand that it is the work of God, but they will not be wretched themselves. But our translation[727] can be made to agree with this in this way: *A man will come to a deep heart* (v. 6), that is, men will be searching out iniquities. Each one of them ponders within himself and is earnestly concerned to find false witness against Jesus. Therefore Matt. 26:59–60 says: "Though many false witnesses had come forward" and "They sought false witness, but they found none." Behold, how they failed and yet came forward. And thus they failed in the thoughts of each one and with a deep heart. *And God will be exalted* (v. 7), namely, Christ. Then, when He will shoot His arrows at them, by that very fact He will be shown to be exalted over them. *The arrows of children were made their* (that is, the Romans') *wounds,* the swift javelin of God. And in this way their wounds were brought to bear, for here he calls the Romans children. Or, *the arrows of children,* by which the children themselves, the Jews, were suddenly killed. Other interpretations as above. *Their tongues were weak against them* (v. 8), that is, their tongues do not save but rather destroy them, because by these they lead themselves astray. But because this is too much violence, the harmonization must be abandoned and attempted in another way. Thus:

The statement *the Lord will shoot sudden arrows at them or strike them with a swift javelin* can also be taken to refer to the preaching of the apostles, for suddenly, while they were hoping that Christ was destroyed, the apostles rose up against them and hurled the words of the Holy Spirit against them. And this agrees with our translation and explanation: *the arrows of children,* namely, of apostles and disciples. Then *their wounds are inflicted, or their blows are struck,* that is, because the Lord shot arrows at them. This was the source of their troubles, because they did not accept His Word, but rather became worse. And thus were struck their blows, that is, they came or had their beginning. For *they rushed in on themselves with their tongues, or their tongues caused them to stumble* (v. 8), namely, because they preferred not to call back their tongues rather than to defend them. Or these things may also be understood in a good sense; for by this means they came to recognize their wounds and they slipped into salvation. But this does not seem correct. Therefore *all who have seen them will flee,* as explained above.

And they will declare the work of God and understand His work (v. 9), that is, the work of redemption accomplished by Christ and the work of the entire life of Christ, and they will understand that the work of God is judgment and truth and equity, but not shadow and vanity, as is shown in Ps. 111:7 below and Ps. 28:5 above. For the earthly-minded Jews look to the Lord only for visible works and such as are helpful to this shadowy life. But the works of God are spiritual and productive of eternal life. Consequently they cannot be understood by those people, but by the apostles and believers. Therefore His works are called truth. The works of God are intelligible, that is, perceptible only by the understanding and by faith, in hope, not in reality. For he who only follows the sense is necessarily offended by the cross of Christ and by the way of His church, since he sees in it nothing but the penalties and privations of this life. And so the cross of Christ becomes a scandal to him.[728] For that reason we must have understanding, so that the wisdom of God is not folly to us.[729] Similarly the works of God in the wicked who live positively in this life only are intellectual, for those to whom God grants physical life are condemned before God spiritually. And so the works of the Lord are truth for the saints and judgment for the ungodly. [Indeed, for both, since they are truth because of the saved spirit and judgment because of the despised and rejected flesh. In the wicked, on the contrary, . . .][730] Therefore also in this a person

---

727. That is, the Vulgate.

728. See 1 Cor 1:23.

729. See 1 Cor 1:23.

730. This, according to the translator, is a partially preserved marginal addition.

will be offended unless he understands it, as the psalmist complains in Ps. 37:7f. and in Ps. 73:2: "My feet almost stumbled." Then he says: "I thought that I would understand, but this is a wearisome task to me."[731] That is to say, "I would not grasp it on the basis of my own investigation, if through faith it were not revealed to me from elsewhere, namely, from God." For that reason he continues, "until I went," namely, by turning the eye through faith away from visible things toward the invisible, "into the sanctuary of God,"[732] that is, into the mystery and the church and the holy place, not secular but spiritual. "And thus I understand," I became a person of understanding, "with regard to their end."

The works can also be understood differently, in accordance with the way I explained it in connection with Ps. 28:4. Accordingly, the works of God are deeds in Christ and the church. But the deeds are Christ Himself and the church, second causes, so to say, of the works of God.

Third, as explained below in the margin in connection with Ps. 92:3f. See it there.

Fourth, in this way: Because all the works of creation and of the old law are signs of the works of God, which He does and will do in Christ and His saints, therefore all those already in the past are as signs which are fulfilled in Christ. For all of them are transitory, symbolizing those things that are eternal and enduring. The latter are works of truth, while all the former are shadows and works of foreshadowing. Therefore Christ is the end and center of them all. To Him they all look and point, as if they were saying: "Look, He is the One who is in reality, but we are not; we are only signs." Therefore the Jews are rebuked, Ps. 28:4, because they did not understand the works and did not view the works of the old law intellectually, but only in a physical way, not as signs and tokens of reality, but as the reality itself. Because what is understood is invisible, it is something far different from what is seen. Therefore the apostles proclaimed the works of God (as done in Christ), and then they understood His deeds, that is, the things of the past in acts also of creation. That is, they understood that those works of Christ were of old prefigured and signified in them. For the sign is then perfectly understood when the reality itself of the sign is seen. Therefore all of us, too, understand the deeds of God only in the church (that is, we receive them intellectually and spiritually), namely, the deeds done anciently in the Law and in nature. The Jews, however, do not understand the same deeds, but only feel them to the present day.

Thus these things can be briefly brought down to the fourfold sense with regard to the works of God:

All of these are Christ at the same time {

Literally, the work of God is the creation of the world and the deeds of the old law.

Tropologically, the work of God is the righteousness of faith, not the righteousness that belongs to the Law, signified by the righteousness of the Law and nature.

Allegorically, the work of God is the church, signified by the synagog and other nations.

Anagogically, the work of God is the church triumphing in glory.

In these three understanding is necessary. The Jews go astray in two, the second and third. . . . [733]

Translated by Herbert J. A. Bouman, in *Luther's Works*, edited by Jaroslav Pelikan, vol. 10 (St. Louis, MO: Concordia, 1974), 3–7, 50–52, 307–12.

MARTIN LUTHER

Lectures on Galatians, 2:15–16

15. *We ourselves, who are Jews by birth and not Gentile sinners,*

Paul compares the Jews and the Gentiles. "It is true," he says, "that we, who are Jews by nature, excel the Gentiles, who are sinners if they are compared with us, in the righteousness of the Law, since they have neither the Law nor the works of the Law. But this does not make us righteous before God. This righteousness of ours is external." In Rom. 1:18ff. and 2:17ff. Paul discusses this thought in detail. Here he declares first that the Gentiles were very great sinners; but in the second chapter he turns to the Jews and asserts that even though they are not such sinners as he had described the Gentiles to be, they are sinners nevertheless, because they have kept the Law outwardly but not inwardly, and while glorying in the Law have dishonored God by transgressing the Law.

16. *Yet who know that a man is not justified by works of the Law but through faith in Jesus Christ, even we have believed in Christ Jesus, in order to be justified by faith in Christ, and not by works of the Law.*

---

731. Ps 73:16.

732. Ps 73:17.

733. A line is left untranslated because of severe damage to the text.

"We are righteous," says Paul, "inasmuch as we are by nature Jews, not sinners, like the Gentiles; but it is a righteousness of the works of Law, and by this righteousness no one is justified before God." For this reason we, too, like the Gentiles, consider our own righteousness as dung[734] and seek to be Justified through faith in Christ—we who are now sinners along with the Gentiles and are Justified along with the Gentiles, since God "made no distinction between us and them," as Peter says in Acts 15:9, "but cleansed their hearts by faith." But because this passage seems absurd to those who have not yet become accustomed to Paul's theology, and because even Saint Jerome wearies himself no end trying to understand this, we shall expand the comments we began to make above about the traditions of the fathers. Among the extant authors I fail to find anyone except Augustine alone who treats this thought in a satisfactory manner; and even he is not satisfactory everywhere. But where he opposes the Pelagians, the enemies of God's grace, he will make Paul easy and clear for you.[735]

Above all, therefore, it is necessary to know that there are two ways in which man is justified, and that these two ways are altogether contrary to each other.

In the first place, there is the external way, by works, on the basis of one's own strength. Of such a nature are human righteousnesses which are acquired by practice (as it is said) and by habit. This is the kind of righteousness Aristotle and other philosophers describe—the kind produced by laws of the state and of the church in ceremonies, the kind produced at the behest of reason and by prudence. For they think that one becomes righteous by doing righteous things, temperate by doing temperate things, and the like. This is the kind of righteousness the Law of Moses, even the Decalog itself, also brings about, namely, when one serves God out of fear of punishment or because of the promise of a reward, does not swear by God's name, honors one's parents, does not kill, does not steal, does not commit adultery, etc. This is a servile righteousness; it is mercenary, feigned, specious, external, temporal, worldly, human. It profits nothing for the glory to come but receives in this life its reward, glory, riches, honor, power, friendship, well-being, or at least peace and quiet, and fewer evils than do those who act otherwise. This is how Christ describes the Pharisees[736] and how St. Augustine describes the Romans in the eighth chapter of the first book of *The City of God*.[737] Strangely enough, this righteousness deceives even men who are wise and great, unless they have been well instructed in Holy Writ.

Jeremiah calls this kind of righteousness "a broken cistern that holds no water";[738] yet, as he says in the same chapter,[739] it causes people to take for granted that they are without sin. It is completely like the actions which we see done by a monkey when it imitates human beings, or like those displayed by actors on stages and in plays. It is entirely characteristic of hypocrites and idols. Consequently, in the Scriptures it is called a lie and an iniquity. Hence the name *Bethaven*, "house of iniquity."[740] To their kind belong also those who deceive souls today, who in reliance on their free will make a good resolution (as they say) and, after eliciting from their natural powers the act of loving God above all things, at once take for granted in the most shameful manner that they have obtained the grace of God. These are the people who strive to cure the woman with an issue of blood (that is, a guilty conscience) by means of works and, after exhausting her resources, make her worse.[741]

In the second place, there is the inward way, on the basis of faith and of grace, when a man utterly despairs of his former righteousness, as though it were the uncleanness of a woman in menstruation,[742] and casts himself down before God, sobs humbly, and, confessing that he is a sinner, says with the publican: "God, be merciful to me a sinner!"[743] "This man," says Christ, "went down to his house justified."[744] For this righteousness is nothing else than a calling upon the name of God. Now the name of God is mercy, truth, righteousness, strength, wisdom, and the accusation of one's own name. On the other hand, our name is sin, falsehood, vanity, and folly, as is written: "All men are liars"[745] and "Every man walks in a vain show."[746]

But calling upon the name of God, if it is in the heart and truly from the heart, shows that the heart and the name of the Lord are one and cling to each other. For this reason it is impossible for the heart not to share in the virtues in which the name of the Lord abounds. But it is through faith that the heart and the name of the Lord cling together.[747] Faith,

---

734. See Phil 3:8–9. (The notes for this selection are by Gerhart and Udoh.)

735. See Augustine, *On the Spirit and the Letter*, 4–52.

736. See, for instance, Mt 6:1–6, 16–18; 15:1–20; 16:6, 11–12; 23:1–36.

737. Augustine, *City of God*, I.8.

738. Jer 2:13.

739. Jer 2:23.

740. See, for instance, Josh 7:2; 1 Sam 13:5–6; Hos 4:15; 5:8; 10:5.

741. See Mk 5:25–26.

742. See Lev 15:19–24.   744. Lk 18:14.

743. Lk 18:13.   745. Ps 116:11.

746. Ps 38:6 (Vulgate); see also Ps 39:6.

747. See Rom 10:9–13.

however, comes through the Word of Christ, by which the name of the Lord is preached, as is written: "I will tell of Thy name to my brethren,"[748] and again: "That men may declare in Zion the name of the Lord."[749] Therefore just as the name of the Lord is pure, holy, righteous, true, good, etc., so, if it touches, or is touched by, the heart (which happens through faith), it makes the heart entirely like itself. Thus it comes about that for those who trust in the name of the Lord all sins are forgiven, and righteousness is imputed to them "for Thy name's sake, O Lord,"[750] because this name is good. This does not come about because of their own merit, since they have not deserved even to hear of it. But when the heart has thus been justified through the faith that is in His name, God gives them the power to become children of God[751] by immediately pouring into their hearts His Holy Spirit,[752] who fills them with His love and makes them peaceful, glad, active in all good works, victorious over all evils, contemptuous even of death and hell. Here all laws and all works of laws soon cease; all things are now free and permissible, and the Law is fulfilled through faith and love.[753]

Behold, this is what Christ has gained for us, namely, that the name of the Lord (that is, the mercy and truth of God) is preached to us and that whoever believes in this name will be saved. Therefore if your conscience troubles you and you are a sinner and are seeking to become righteous, what will you do? Will you look around to see what works you may do or where you may go? No. On the contrary, see to it that you hear or recall the name of the Lord, that is, that God is righteous, good, and holy; and then cling to this, firmly believing that He is such a One for you. Now you are at once such a one, like Him. But you will never see the name of the Lord more clearly than you do in Christ. There you will see how good, pleasant, faithful, righteous, and true God is, since He did not spare His own Son.[754] Through Christ He will draw you to Himself. Without this righteousness it is impossible for the heart to be pure. That is why it is impossible for the righteousness of men to be true. For here the name of the Lord is used for the truth; there it is used for an empty show. For here man gives glory to God and confusion to himself; there he gives glory to himself and insult to God. This is the real cabala of the name of the Lord, not of the Tetragrammaton, about which the Jews speak in the most superstitious manner. Faith in the name of the Lord, I say, is the understanding of the Law, the end of the Law, and absolutely all in all. But God has placed this name of His on Christ, as He foretold through Moses.[755]

This is a righteousness that is bountiful, given without cost, firm, inward, eternal, true, heavenly, divine; it does not earn, receive, or seek anything in this life. Indeed, since it is directed toward Christ and His name, which is righteousness, the result is that the righteousness of Christ and of the Christian are one and the same, united with each other in an inexpressible way. For it flows and gushes forth from Christ, as He says in John 4:14: "The water that I shall give will become in him a spring of living water welling up to eternal life." Thus it comes about that just as all became sinners because of another's sin, so by Another's righteousness all become righteous, as Rom. 5:19 says: "As by one man's disobedience many were made sinners, so by the righteousness of one Man, Christ, many are made righteous." This is the mercy foretold by all the prophets; this is the blessing promised to Abraham and to his seed,[756] as we shall see later.

Coming back now to the text, we see how right the apostle is when he says: "Knowing that a man is not justified on the basis of the works of the Law but [as is obvious] only on the basis of faith in Jesus Christ, we, too, believe in Christ Jesus, in order that we may be justified, on the basis of faith in Jesus Christ, not on the basis of the works of the Law." In these words he describes both kinds of righteousness. He rejects the former and embraces the latter. May you do likewise, dearest brother. First hear that Jesus means "salvation" and that Christ means "the anointing of mercy"; then firmly believe this unheard-of salvation and mercy, and you will be justified. That is, believe that He will be your salvation and mercy, and beyond all doubt He will be. Therefore it is altogether godless and exceedingly heathenish to teach that remission of sins takes place through trifling little works of satisfaction and through compulsory acts of contrition, while—as the great mass of sententiarists[757] peddle their theology today—the doctrine of faith in Christ is completely neglected.

Nevertheless, it should be noted here that the apostle does not reject the works of the Law as Jerome also points out in this connection. He rejects reliance on the works of the Law.

---

748. Ps 22:22.
749. Ps 102:21.
750. Ps 25:11.
751. See Jn 1:12.
752. See Gal 4:6; Rom 5:5.
753. See Rom 8:3–4; 13:8–10; Gal 5:14.
754. See Rom 8:32.
755. Luther is possibly thinking here of Ex 23:20–22.
756. See Gal 3:16; Gen 12:7; 13:15.
757. This was the name of opprobrium for the commentators on the *Sentences*, a work by the medieval theologian Peter Lombard.

That is, he does not deny that there are works, but he does deny that anyone can be justified through them. Therefore one must read the apostle's statement with emphasis and close attention when he says: "A man is not justified on the basis of the works of the Law"; as if he were saying: "I grant that works of the Law are done; but I say that a man is not justified because of them—except in his own sight and before men, and as a reward in this life. Let there be works of the Law, provided that one knows that in the sight of God they are sins and no longer true works of the Law." In this way he totally demolishes reliance on our own righteousness, because there is need of a far different righteousness—a righteousness beyond all works of the Law, namely, a righteousness of the works of God and His grace.

Furthermore, you must also observe that Paul speaks of "works of the Law" in general not merely of those that relate to the Ceremonial Law but certainly also of all the works of the Decalog. For these, too, when done apart from faith and the true righteousness of God, are not only insufficient; but in their outward appearance they even give hypocrites false confidence. Therefore he who wants to be saved must despair altogether of all strength, works, and laws.

Furthermore, you must note for yourself a manner of speaking that is characteristic of this apostle, namely, that he does not, as others are accustomed to do, call the works by which the Law itself is fulfilled "works of the Law." For the apostle's way of putting it accounts for the fact that very many fail to understand him. They cannot understand works of the Law as being anything but righteous and good, since the Law itself is good and righteous.[758] Hence they are driven to understand the Law as meaning ceremonial requirements, because, as they say, these were evil and dead at that time. But they are mistaken. Just as the Ceremonial Law was good and holy at that time, so it is good and holy now; for it was instituted by God Himself.

The apostle consistently declares that the Law is fulfilled only through faith, not through works. Because the fulfilling of the Law is righteousness and this is surely a matter of faith, not of works, one cannot understand the works of the Law to mean those works by which the Law is satisfied. What then? The apostle's rule is this: It is not works that fulfill the Law, but the fulfilment of the Law produces works. One does not become righteous by doing righteous deeds. No, one does righteous deeds after becoming righteous. Righteousness and fulfilment of the Law come first, before the works are done, because the latter flow out of the former. That is why Paul calls them "works of the Law" in distinction from works

of grace or works of God; for works of the Law are really the Law's, not ours, since they are done, not by the operation of our will, but because the Law extorts them through threats or elicits them through promises. But whatever is not done freely of our own will but is done under the compulsion of another is no longer our work. No, it is the work of him who requires it. For works belong to him at whose command they are done. But they are done at the command of the Law, not at the pleasure of one's own will. It is clear enough that if a person were free to live without the Law, he would never do the works of the Law of his own accord. Hence the Law is called an enforcer when in Is. 9:4 it is spoken of as "the staff for his shoulder, the yoke of his burden, the rod of his oppressor, as on the day of Midian." For through the Child who was given to us (Is. 9:6) and in whom we believe we become free and take pleasure in the Law; and we no longer belong to the Law, but the Law belongs to us. And our works are not works of the Law; they are works of grace, from which there spring up freely and pleasantly those deeds which formerly the Law used to squeeze out with harshness and power.

You will understand this if you arrange works in four categories: (1) Works of sin, which are done under the domination of lust, with no resistance on the part of grace; (2) works of the Law, which are done when lust is held in check outwardly but glows all the more inwardly and hates the Law, that is, works that are good in appearance but evil in the heart; (3) works of grace, which are done when lust resists, but the spirit of grace is nevertheless victorious; (4) works of peace and perfect well-being, which are done with the fullest ease and pleasantness after lust has been extinguished—as will be the case in the life to come. Here there is only a beginning.

because by works of the Law shall no one be justified.

Paul draws the same conclusion in Rom. 3:9ff. And there he proves it extensively on the basis of Ps. 14:3: "There is no one who is righteous, who does good." Therefore the works of the Law must be sins; otherwise they would certainly justify. Thus it is clear that Christian righteousness and human righteousness are not only altogether different but are even opposed to each other, because the latter comes from works, while works come from the former. No wonder, therefore, that Paul's theology vanished entirely and could not be understood after Christians began to be instructed by men who declared falsely that Aristotle's ethics are entirely in accord

---

758. See Rom 7:12.

with the doctrine of Christ and of Paul, by men who failed completely to understand either Aristotle or Christ. For our righteousness looks down from heaven and descends to us. But those godless men have presumed to ascend into heaven by means of their righteousness and from there to bring the truth which has arisen among us from the earth.

Therefore Paul stands resolute: "No flesh is justified on the basis of works of the Law," as Ps. 143:2 also says: "No man living will be justified before Thee." The only thing left is that the works of the Law are not works of righteousness—except of the righteousness that is of our own making.

Translated by Jaroslav Pelikan, in *Luther's Works*, edited by Jaroslav Pelikan, vol. 27 (St. Louis, MO: Concordia, 1964), 218–25.

ॐ *Institutes of the Christian Religion*, by **John Calvin** (1509–64), is one of the most influential Protestant systematic theological works ever written. Calvin published five editions of the *Institutes* (1536, 1539, 1543, 1550, 1559) in both Latin and French. Many translations soon followed, including Spanish (1540), Italian (1557), Dutch (1560), and German (1572). In *Institutes of the Christian Religion* (1559), book 1, Calvin lays out his doctrine of and principles for interpreting Scripture. In his *Commentary on Galatians* (written in Geneva in 1548) and his *Commentary on 1 Corinthians* (Geneva, 1546), his interpretive methods are put in practice.

JOHN CALVIN

Institutes of the Christian Religion, book 1, chapter VI.3; chapter VII.1–2, 5

1.VI

3. *Without Scripture we fall into error*

Suppose we ponder how slippery is the fall of the human mind into forgetfulness of God, how great the tendency to every kind of error, how great the lust to fashion constantly new and artificial religions. Then we may perceive how necessary was such written proof of the heavenly doctrine, that it should neither perish through forgetfulness nor vanish through error nor be corrupted by the audacity of men. It is therefore clear that God has provided the assistance of the Word for the sake of all those to whom he has been pleased to give useful instruction because he foresaw that his likeness imprinted upon the most beautiful form of the universe would be insufficiently effective. Hence, we must strive onward by this straight path if we seriously aspire to the pure contem-

plation of God. We must come, I say, to the Word, where God is truly and vividly described to us from his works, while these very works are appraised not by our depraved judgment but by the rule of eternal truth. If we turn aside from the Word, as I have just now said, though we may strive with strenuous haste, yet, since we have got off the track, we shall never reach the goal. For we should so reason that the splendor of the divine countenance, which even the apostle calls "unapproachable,"[759] is for us like an inexplicable labyrinth unless we are conducted into it by the thread of the Word; so that it is better to limp along this path than to dash with all speed outside it. David very often, therefore, teaching that we ought to banish superstitions from the earth so that pure religion may flourish, represented God as regnant.[760] Now he means by the word "regnant" not the power with which he is endowed, and which he exercises in governing the whole of nature, but the doctrine by which he asserts his lawful sovereignty. For errors can never be uprooted from human hearts until true knowledge of God is planted therein.

VII. Scripture Must Be Confirmed by the Witness of the Spirit. Thus May Its Authority Be Established as Certain; and It Is a Wicked Falsehood That Its Credibility Depends on the Judgment of the Church

1. *Scripture has its authority from God, not from the church*

Before I go any farther, it is worthwhile to say something about the authority of Scripture, not only to prepare our hearts to reverence it, but to banish all doubt. When that which is set forth is acknowledged to be the Word of God, there is no one so deplorably insolent—unless devoid also both of common sense and of humanity itself—as to dare impugn the credibility of Him who speaks. Now daily oracles are not sent from heaven, for it pleased the Lord to hallow his truth to everlasting remembrance in the Scriptures alone.[761] Hence the Scriptures obtain full authority among believers only when men regard them as having sprung from heaven, as if there the living words of God were heard. This matter is very well worth treating more fully and weighing more carefully. But my readers will pardon me if I regard more what the plan of the present work demands than what the greatness of this matter requires.

---

759. See 1 Tim 6:16. (The notes for this selection are by Gerhart and Udoh.)
760. See, for instance, Pss 47:2, 7; 93:1; 96:10; 97:1; 99:1.
761. See Jn 5:39.

But a most pernicious error widely prevails that Scripture has only so much weight as is conceded to it by the consent of the church. As if the eternal and inviolable truth of God depended upon the decision of men! For they mock the Holy Spirit when they ask: Who can convince us that these writings came from God? Who can assure us that Scripture has come down whole and intact even to our very day? Who can persuade us to receive one book in reverence but to exclude another, unless the church prescribe a sure rule for all these matters? What reverence is due Scripture and what books ought to be reckoned within its canon depend, they say, upon the determination of the church. Thus these sacrilegious men, wishing to impose an unbridled tyranny under the cover of the church, do not care with what absurdities they ensnare themselves and others, provided they can force this one idea upon the simple-minded: that the church has authority in all things. Yet, if this is so, what will happen to miserable consciences seeking firm assurance of eternal life if all promises of it consist in and depend solely upon the judgment of men? Will they cease to vacillate and tremble when they receive such an answer? Again, to what mockeries of the impious is our faith subjected, into what suspicion has it fallen among all men, if we believe that it has a precarious authority dependent solely upon the good pleasure of men!

2. The church is itself grounded upon Scripture

But such wranglers are neatly refuted by just one word of the apostle. He testifies that the church is "built upon the foundation of the prophets and apostles."[762] If the teaching of the prophets and apostles is the foundation, this must have had authority before the church began to exist. Groundless, too, is their subtle objection that, although the church took its beginning here, the writings to be attributed to the prophets and apostles nevertheless remain in doubt until decided by the church. For if the Christian church was from the beginning founded upon the writings of the prophets and the preaching of the apostles, wherever this doctrine is found, the acceptance of it—without which the church itself would never have existed—must certainly have preceded the church. It is utterly vain, then, to pretend that the power of judging Scripture so lies with the church that its certainty depends upon churchly assent. Thus, while the church receives and gives its seal of approval to the Scriptures, it does not thereby render authentic what is otherwise doubtful or controversial. But because the church recognizes Scripture to be the truth of its own God, as a pious duty it unhesitatingly venerates Scripture. As to their question—How can we be assured that this has sprung from God unless we have recourse to the decree of the church?—it is as if someone asked: Whence will we learn to distinguish light from darkness, white from black, sweet from bitter? Indeed, Scripture exhibits fully as clear evidence of its own truth as white and black things do of their color, or sweet and bitter things do of their taste.

5. Scripture bears its own authentication

Let this point therefore stand: that those whom the Holy Spirit has inwardly taught truly rest upon Scripture, and that Scripture indeed is self-authenticated; hence, it is not right to subject it to proof and reasoning. And the certainty it deserves with us, it attains by the testimony of the Spirit. For even if it wins reverence for itself by its own majesty, it seriously affects us only when it is sealed upon our hearts through the Spirit. Therefore, illumined by his power, we believe neither by our own nor by anyone else's judgment that Scripture is from God; but above human judgment we affirm with utter certainty (just as if we were gazing upon the majesty of God himself) that it has flowed to us from the very mouth of God by the ministry of men. We seek no proofs, no marks of genuineness upon which our judgment may lean; but we subject our judgment and wit to it as to a thing far beyond any guesswork! This we do, not as persons accustomed to seize upon some unknown thing, which, under closer scrutiny, displeases them, but fully conscious that we hold the unassailable truth! Nor do we do this as those miserable men who habitually bind over their minds to the thralldom of superstition; but we feel that the undoubted power of his divine majesty lives and breathes there. By this power we are drawn and inflamed, knowingly and willingly, to obey him, yet also more vitally and more effectively than by mere human willing or knowing!

God, therefore, very rightly proclaims through Isaiah that the prophets together with the whole people are witnesses to him;[763] for they, instructed by prophecies, unhesitatingly held that God has spoken without deceit or ambiguity. Such, then, is a conviction that requires no reasons; such, a knowledge with which the best reason agrees—in which the mind truly reposes more securely and constantly than in any reasons; such, finally, a feeling that can be born only of heavenly revelation. I speak of nothing other than what each believer experiences within himself—though my words fall far beneath a just explanation of the matter.

---

762. Eph 2:19–20.
763. Isa 43:10.

I now refrain from saying more, since I shall have opportunity to discuss this matter elsewhere. Let us, then, know that the only true faith is that which the Spirit of God seals in our hearts. Indeed, the modest and teachable reader will be content with this one reason: Isaiah promised all the children of the renewed church that "they would be God's disciples."[764] God deems worthy of singular privilege only his elect, whom he distinguishes from the human race as a whole. Indeed, what is the beginning of true doctrine but a prompt eagerness to hearken to God's voice? But God asks to be heard through the mouth of Moses, as it is written: "Say not in your heart, who will ascend into heaven, or who will descend into the abyss: behold, the word is in your mouth."[765] If God has willed this treasure of understanding to be hidden from his children, it is no wonder or absurdity that the multitude of men are so ignorant and stupid! Among the "multitude" I include even certain distinguished folk, until they become engrafted into the body of the church. Besides, Isaiah, warning that the prophetic teaching would be beyond belief, not only to foreigners but also to the Jews who wanted to be reckoned as members of the Lord's household, at the same time adds the reason: "The arm of God will not be revealed" to all.[766] Whenever, then, the fewness of believers disturbs us, let the converse come to mind, that only those to whom it is given can comprehend the mysteries of God.[767]

From John Calvin, *Institutes of the Christian Religion*, edited by John T. McNeill, translated by Ford Lewis Battles, Library of Christian Classics, vol. 20 (London: SCM, 1961), 72–73, 74–76, 80–81.

JOHN CALVIN

Commentary on Galatians, 4:21–26

Tell me, ye that desire to be under the law, do ye not hear the law? For it is written, that Abraham had two sons, one by the handmaid, and one by a free-woman. But he who was of the handmaid was born after the flesh; but he of the free-woman was through promise. Which things are an allegory: for these women are the two covenants: one from mount Sinai, bearing children unto bondage, which is Hagar. For this Hagar is mount Sinai in Arabia, and correspondeth to the Jerusalem that now is; for she is in bondage with her children. But the Jerusalem that is above is free, which is the mother of us all.[768]

21. *Tell me.* After these exhortations to touch their feelings, he follows up his former teaching with a fine illustration. As an argument it is not very strong, but as confirmation of his earlier vigorous reasoning, it is not to be despised.

To be under the law here signifies to come under the yoke of the law, with the condition that God will deal with you according to the covenant of the law and that you in return bind yourself to keep the law. In another sense, all believers are under the law, but here, as we have said, he treats of the law with its appendages.

22. *For it is written.* No man with a choice will be so mad as to despise freedom and choose slavery. But here the apostle teaches us that they who are under the law are slaves. Unhappy men who voluntarily choose this state when God wills to free them! He gives an image of this in the two sons of Abraham, one of whom, born a slave, kept his mother's condition, whereas the other, the child of a free-woman, obtained the inheritance.[769] He afterwards applies the whole story to his purpose and illustrates it gracefully.

In the first place, because their adversaries armed themselves with the authority of the law, he quotes the law on the other side. "The law" was the name usually given to the five books of Moses. Again, as the story which he cites seems to have nothing to do with the question, he gives it an allegorical interpretation. But he writes that these things are ἀλληγορού-μενα. Origen, and many others along with him, have seized this occasion of twisting Scripture this way and that, away from the genuine sense (*a genuino sensu*). For they inferred that the literal sense is too meager and poor and that beneath the bark of the letter there lie deeper mysteries which cannot be extracted but by hammering out allegories. And this they did without difficulty, for the world always has and always will prefer speculations which seem ingenious, to solid doctrine. With such approbation the licence increased more and more, so that he who played this game of allegorizing Scripture not only was suffered to pass unpunished but even obtained the highest applause. For many centuries no man was thought clever who lacked the cunning and daring to transfigure with subtlety the sacred Word of God. This was undoubtedly a trick of Satan to impair the authority of Scripture and remove any true advantage out of the reading of it. God avenged this profanation with a just judgment when He suffered the pure meaning to be buried under false glosses.

Scripture, they say, is fertile and thus bears multiple mean-

---

764. Isa 54:13.

765. Deut 30:12, 14; the phrase "descend into the abyss" is from Ps 107:26 = 106:26 (Vulgate).

766. Isa 53:1.

767. See Mat 13:11.

768. Gal 4:21–26. (The notes for this selection are by Gerhart and Udoh.)

769. See Gen 16:1–16; 21:1–21.

ings. I acknowledge that Scripture is the most rich and inexhaustible fount of all wisdom. But I deny that its fertility consists in the various meanings which anyone may fasten to it at his pleasure. Let us know, then, that the true meaning of Scripture is the natural and simple one (*verum sensum scripturae, qui germanus est et simplex*), and let us embrace and hold it resolutely. Let us not merely neglect as doubtful, but boldly set aside as deadly corruptions, those pretended expositions which lead us away from the literal sense (*a literali sensu*).

But what shall we reply to Paul's assertion? He certainly does not mean that Moses deliberately wrote the story so that it might be turned into an allegory, but is pointing out in what way the story relates to the present case. That is, when we see there the image of the Church figuratively delineated. And an *anagoge* of this sort is not foreign to the genuine and literal meaning, when a comparison was drawn between the Church and the family of Abraham. For as the house of Abraham was then the true Church, so it is beyond doubt that the principal and most memorable events that happened in it are types for us. Therefore, as in circumcision, in sacrifices, in the whole Levitical priesthood there was an allegory, as there is today in our sacraments, so was there likewise in the house of Abraham. But this does not involve a departure from the literal meaning (*a literali sensu*). In a word, it is as if Paul says that there is depicted in the two wives of Abraham a figure of the two covenants, and in the two sons a figure of the two peoples. And Chrysostom indeed acknowledges that in the word allegory is κατάχρησις;[770] which is quite true.

23. *But he who was of the handmaid.* Both were begotten by Abraham according to the flesh. But Isaac was different in that he had the promise of grace. In Ishmael there was nothing beyond nature; in Isaac was the election of God. And this is suggested by his very birth, which was not ordinary but miraculous. Yet he hints at the calling of the Gentiles and the rejection of the Jews. For the latter boast of their ancestry, whereas the former have become the spiritual offspring of Abraham by faith and without human advantages.

24. *These women are the two covenants.* I have preferred to translate it like this so as not to destroy the beauty of the comparison. Paul compares the two διαθῆκαι to the two mothers; but to use *testamentum,* which is neuter, for denoting a mother would be awkward. The word *pactio* is therefore more appropriate. But I have aimed at clarity rather than elegance.

The comparison is now formally introduced. As in the house of Abraham there were two mothers, so are there also in the Church of God. Doctrine is the mother by whom God begets us. It is twofold, legal and evangelical. The legal bears children to bondage; hence the simile of it is Hagar. But Sarah represents the second, which bears children to freedom. In fact, however, Paul begins higher and makes our first mother Sinai and our second Jerusalem. So that if anyone wants to work out the details more finely, he will make the law into the seed from whence are begotten the children of Sinai and from the Gospel the children of Jerusalem. But this has nothing to do with the argument in itself. The two covenants are like mothers from whom it is sufficient to hold that dissimilar children are born. For the legal covenant makes slaves and the evangelical covenant free-men.

But all this may seem absurd at first sight; for there is none of God's children who is not born to freedom; therefore the comparison does not apply. I answer that what Paul says is true in two respects. The law formerly brought forth its disciples (that is, the holy prophets and the other believers) to slavery, yet not to permanent slavery, but because God had placed them for a time under a schoolmaster.[771] Their freedom was concealed under the veil of ceremonies and of the whole economy by which they were governed. To the outward eye appeared nothing but slavery. Paul says the same thing to the Romans, "Ye have not received the spirit of bondage again to fear."[772] Those holy fathers, though inwardly they were free in the sight of God, yet in outward appearance were no different from slaves and so are related to their mother's condition. But the doctrine of the Gospel bestows perfect freedom on its children as soon as they are born and brings them up in freedom.

I admit that Paul does not speak of that kind of children, as the context will show. By the children of Sinai, it will afterwards be explained, are meant hypocrites, who are at last expelled from the Church of God and deprived of the inheritance. What then is the bearing of children to bondage, which he is now discussing? It denotes those who wickedly abuse the law by conceiving nothing but slavery from it. Not so the godly fathers who lived under the old testament; for their slavish birth by the law did not prevent them having Jerusalem for their mother in spirit. But those who cleave to the bare law and do not know it as a schoolmaster to bring them to Christ, but rather make it a barrier against coming to Him, are the Ishmaelites born to slavery.

---

770. That is, an imprecise use, or misuse, of a word.
771. See Gal 3:24.
772. Rom 8:15.

It will again be objected, why does the apostle say that such are born of God's covenant and are regarded as in the Church? I reply, they are not strictly God's children but are degenerate and spurious, and are disclaimed by God whom they falsely call their Father. They are regarded as in the Church, not because they are members of it in reality but because for a time they usurp a place and deceive men by the mask they wear. The apostle here considers the Church as it is seen in this world. But we shall speak of this later.

25. *Hagar is mount Sinai.* I shall not waste time in refuting other expositions. For Jerome's conjecture that Mount Sinai had two names is trifling. And the philosophizing of Chrysostom about the agreement of the names is no less childish. Sinai is called Hagar, because it is a type or figure; just as the Passover was Christ. The position of the mountain is expressed in contempt. It lies in Arabia, he says, beyond the borders of the Holy Land, which is the symbol of the eternal inheritance. The wonder is that in so straightforward an application they should go so far astray.

And corresponds on the other hand. The old translator renders it "is joined" (*coniunctus est*); and Erasmus, "borders on" (*confinis*). I have translated it as above to avoid obscurity. For the apostle certainly does not refer to propinquity or situation but to the comparison, which he treats figuratively. Σύστοιχα denotes things that are so arranged as to have a mutual relation to each other; and συστοιχία, when applied to trees and so on, means that they are set in a regular order. In the same way Mount Sinai is said συστοιχεῖν to that which is now Jerusalem, just as Aristotle writes that rhetoric is the ἀντίστροφος or counterpart to dialectic, by a metaphor borrowed from the lyric, which was usually arranged in two parts, adapted to one another in harmony. In short, συστοιχεῖν means simply to be, so to say, coordinated.

But why does he compare the present Jerusalem with Mount Sinai? Although I once held the opposite opinion, I now agree with Chrysostom and Ambrose, who expound it of the earthly Jerusalem, and indeed that it had then degenerated into a slavish doctrine and worship. This is why he says, *which now is.* It ought to have been a lively image of the heavenly Jerusalem and an expression of its character. But such as it now is, he says, it is related to Mount Sinai. Although the two places are far apart, they are completely and perfectly accordant. This is a severe reproach to the Jews, who had fallen from grace and whose real mother was not Sarah but the spurious Jerusalem, twin sister of Hagar. They were therefore slaves born of a slave, though they haughtily claimed to be the sons of Abraham.

26. *But Jerusalem which is above.* What he calls heavenly is not shut up in heaven, nor are we to seek for it outside the world. For the Church is spread over the whole world and is a pilgrim on the earth. Why then is it said to be from heaven? Because it originates in heavenly grace. For the sons of God are born, not of flesh and blood, but by the power of the Holy Spirit. The heavenly Jerusalem, which derives its origin from heaven and dwells above by faith, is the mother of believers. For she has the incorruptible seed of life deposited in her by which she forms us, cherishes us in her womb and brings us to light. She has the milk and the food by which she continually nourishes her offspring.

This is why the Church is called the mother of believers. And certainly, he who refuses to be a son of the Church desires in vain to have God as his Father. For it is only through the ministry of the Church that God begets sons for Himself and brings them up until they pass through adolescence and reach manhood. This is a title of wonderful and highest honour. But the Papists are foolish and worse than puerile when they plead this to annoy us. For their mother is an adulteress, who brings forth into death the children of the devil. How foolish is the demand that the children of God should surrender themselves to her to be cruelly slain! Could not the synagogue of Satan at that time have boasted with far more honest claim than Rome today? And yet we see how Paul strips her of every honourable distinction and assigns to her the lot of Hagar.

From John Calvin, *Calvin's Commentaries*, vol. 11, *The Epistles of Paul the Apostle to the Galatians, Ephesians, Philippians, and Colossians*, translated by T. H. L. Parker and John W. Fraser (Grand Rapids, MI: Eerdmans, 1972), 83–88.

JOHN CALVIN

Commentary on 1 Corinthians, 10:1–4, 11

For I would not, brethren, have you ignorant, how that our fathers were all under the cloud, and all passed through the sea; and were all baptized unto Moses in the cloud and in the sea; and did all eat the same spiritual meat; and did all drink the same spiritual drink: for they drank of a spiritual rock that followed them: and the rock was Christ.[773]

Paul now uses examples in support of what he had been teaching by his twofold comparison. The Corinthians were doing just as they liked, and were boasting, as if they were veterans already, or at least had completed their course,

---

773. 1 Cor 10:1–4. (The notes for this selection are by Gerhart and Udoh.)

when in fact they had hardly left the start-line. Paul describes this groundless exultation and confidence in this way: since I see that you are quite content to mark time on the very starting-point and not move on, I would not have you ignorant about what happened to the Israelites for doing the same thing, so that their example may make you wake up. When examples are used, any difference tends to destroy the force of the comparison; therefore Paul says, first of all, that there is no point of difference between the Israelites and us, which would put our whole situation in a different category from theirs. Therefore, because he intended to threaten the Corinthians with the same vengeance which befell the Israelites, he begins like this: do not take pride in some special privilege, as if your standing with God is better than theirs was. For they had the same benefits which we enjoy today. The Church of God was in their midst, as in ours today. They had the same sacraments, to be testimonies to them of the grace of God. But when they abused their gifts, they did not escape the judgement of God. Therefore, you should be afraid, because the same thing threatens you. Jude uses the same argument in his letter.[774]

1. *They were all under the cloud.* The apostle intends to show that the Israelites were the people of God, just as much as we are, so that we may realize that we will not escape with impunity from the hand of God, which punished them so severely. For the point is this: if God did not spare them, He will not spare us, for our situation is the same as theirs. Paul proves this similarity from the fact that they had been furnished with the same signs of the grace of God. For the sacraments are tokens by which the Church of God is discerned. Paul deals first with baptism, and he teaches that the cloud, which protected the Israelites from the heat of the sun in the desert, and directed them on their line of march, as well as their crossing of the sea, was indeed like baptism in their case. He says that in the manna and the water flowing out of the rock, there was a sacrament, which corresponded to the Holy Supper.

He says: *they were baptized into Moses,* in other words, under the ministry or leadership of Moses. For I take the preposition εἰς to have been adopted here in place of ἐν, because without a doubt we are baptized "in the name of Christ," and not of any man at all, as Paul said in chapter 1.13. There are two reasons for that. The first reason is that in baptism we are initiated into the teaching of Christ alone, and the other is that only His name is invoked, since baptism rests solely upon His power. Therefore they were baptized "in Moses," i.e. under his guidance and ministry, as I have already said. How? "In the cloud and in the sea." "Therefore," someone will say, "they were baptized twice." To that I reply that two signs are referred to, but they effect one baptism, corresponding to ours.

But a more difficult question arises. For there is no doubt that these gifts, about which Paul tells us, produced temporal benefits. For the cloud sheltered them from the heat of the sun, and showed them their way, and these are physical benefits, concerned with this present life. In the same way the crossing of the sea meant their escape from the cruelty of Pharaoh and their deliverance from the immediate danger of death. But the benefit of our baptism is spiritual. Why then does Paul make sacraments out of earthly benefits, and seek some spiritual mystery in them? I answer that Paul had good cause for seeking something more than physical advantages in miracles of that sort. For even if God was willing to give help to His people relating to life in this world, His main purpose however was to bear witness to Himself, and reveal Himself, as their God, and eternal salvation is included under that.

Throughout the Scriptures the cloud is called the sign of His presence.[775] Therefore when He declared, by the cloud, that He was present with them, as His own chosen people, there is no doubt that they had, in the cloud, not only an earthly blessing, but also a token of spiritual life. Thus the cloud had a double purpose; and it was the same with the crossing of the sea. For the way was opened up for them through the middle of the sea, so that they escaped from the hand of Pharaoh; but the only reason for that was the fact that the Lord, having once taken them under His care and protection, was determined to guard them in every way. Therefore they concluded from this that they were the objects of God's care, and that He was concerned about their salvation. That is also why the Passover, which was instituted to keep the remembrance of their deliverance,[776] was, nevertheless, at the same time, a sacrament of Christ. How is that so? Because God had shown Himself as their saviour in something that was a benefit for them in this world. Anyone who will give proper attention to these things will find nothing absurd in what Paul says. More than that, he will see, both in spiritual substance and visible form, the closest agreement between the baptism of the Jews and ours.

---

774. See Jude 1:5–16.

775. See, for instance, Ex 13:21–22; 14:19–20; 16:10; 19:9, 16; 20:21; 24:15–18; 40:34–38; 1 Kings 8:10–11; Mk 9:7; Mt 17:5; Lk 9:34–35; Rev 14:14–16.

776. See Ex 12:14–28, 43–51; 13:3–10.

Somebody makes the further objection, however, that not a word is said about all this in the Scriptures. I admit as much, but there is no doubt that, acting by His Spirit, God made good the lack of explicit reference. For example, we find that in the case of the brazen serpent,[777] Christ Himself bears witness to the fact that it was a spiritual sacrament.[778] Yet we do not find any mention of that aspect of it. But, in His own way, the Lord revealed the secret, which would otherwise have been unknown, to the believers of that time.

3. *The same spiritual meat.* Paul now mentions the other sacrament, which corresponds to the most Holy Supper of the Lord. He says: "The manna and the water which flowed out of the rock were not only of value as food for the body, but also as spiritual nourishment for the soul." It is certainly true that both provided sustenance for the body, but that did not prevent them from serving another purpose as well. Therefore when the Lord met the needs of the body in this world, He provided for the eternal welfare of souls at the same time. These two aspects are easily reconciled, were it not for the difficulty raised by the words of Christ in John 6.31ff., where he treats manna as corruptible food for our stomachs, and contrasts it with the true food of the soul. His words seem to differ a good deal from what Paul says here. This problem can be easily solved. When the writers of Scripture are dealing with the sacraments, or other things for that matter, sometimes their method is to be guided in what they say by the capacity of the people with whom they are dealing. For example, Paul does not always speak about circumcision in the same way. When he examines it from the point of view of its being an institution of God, he says that it was "a seal of the righteousness of faith."[779] On the other hand when he is contending with those who were boasting in the mere outward sign, and were wrongly putting their trust in it for salvation, he says that it is the sign of being under a curse, because by it men put themselves under obligation to keep the whole law.[780] He is dealing only with what the false apostles[781] thought about it, for he is not concerned to argue against the unadulterated institution of God, but against their perversion of the truth. Thus, when the carnal crowd preferred Moses to Christ, because he had fed the people in the desert for forty years, and they thought of the manna only as food for the stomach, not looking for anything else indeed, Christ, in His reply to them, does not explain the significance of manna, but, ignoring everything else, makes what He has to say suit the minds of His listeners. He might have put it this way: "You think very highly of Moses, to the point of wonder indeed, as a most outstanding prophet, be-cause he filled the stomachs of your fathers in the desert. For you have this one objection against me, I count for nothing in your eyes because I do not supply you with an abundance of food for your stomachs. But if you consider corruptible food so valuable, what are you to think about bread which gives life, and nourishes our souls unto eternal life?" We see, therefore, that in that passage the Lord is not influenced in what He says by the nature of the manna, but rather by the understanding of His hearers. On the other hand Paul is dealing here with the ordinance of God, and not with the way unbelievers abuse it.

Further, when Paul says that the *fathers ate the same spiritual meat,* he first of all gives a hint of what the power and efficacy of the sacrament is; and secondly he shows that the old sacraments of the law had the same power as ours have today. For if manna was spiritual food, it follows that bare forms (*figuras nudas*) are not exhibited to us in the sacraments, but the reality figured is truly given at the same time (*rem figuratam simul vere dari*). For God is not so deceitful as to nourish us on empty appearances (*figmentis*). A sign (*signum*) is indeed a sign, and retains its own substance (*substantiam*). But just as the Papists, on the one hand, are ridiculously dreaming of some sort of transformations, so, on the other hand, we have no right to separate the reality and the figure (*veritatem et figuram*) which God has joined together. The Papists confound the reality and the sign (*rem et signum*); unbelievers such as Schwenkfeld and men like him separate the signs from the realities (*signa a rebus*). Let us preserve a middle position, that is, let us keep the union made by the Lord, but at the same time the distinction between them, so that we do not, in error, transfer what belongs to one to the other.

We have still to deal with the second point about the resemblance between the old signs and ours. It is a well-known dogma of the Schoolmen[782] that "the sacraments of the old Law merely figured (*figurasse*) grace, but that ours confer it (*conferre*)." This passage is most suitable for refuting that error. For it proves that the reality of the sacrament (*rem sacramenti exhibitam*) was conveyed to the people of old just as much as to us. It is therefore wicked of the men of the Sorbonne to suppose that the holy fathers had the signs without

---

777. See Num 21:8–9.

778. See Jn 3:14–15.

781. See Gal 2:4; 2 Cor 11:13.

782. That is, medieval Scholastic theologians.

779. See Rom 4:11.

780. See Gal 3:10; 5:3.

the reality under the Law. I am quite ready to agree that the efficacy of the signs is at once richer and more abundant for us since the incarnation of Christ than it was for the fathers under the Law. So the difference between us and them is only one of degree, or, as the common saying goes, one of "more or less," because what they had in small measure, we have more fully (*plenius*). But it is not the case that they had mere figures while we obtain the reality.

Some people explain these words as if the Israelites together ate the same bread among themselves, and they do not mean that they are to be compared with us. But these people do not pay attention to Paul's intention. For what he is driving at here is just this, that the ancient people were provided with the same benefits as we are, and shared in the same sacraments, so that we may not imagine that, by trusting in some special privilege, we will be exempt from the punishment which they had to undergo. However, I do not want to quarrel with anyone about this; I am simply stating my own point of view. Nevertheless I am well aware of the attractive case presented by those who take the opposite explanation, viz. that it agrees very well with the simile which had just been used; that the same race-track was laid out for all the Israelites; they all set out from the same starting-point; they all proceeded along the same course; they all shared in the same hope, but many of them were debarred from the prize. Yet when I examine everything closely, I am not induced by these reasons to give up my point of view, for the apostle has good reason for mentioning two sacraments only, and baptism in particular. Why did he do this but to contrast them with us? Certainly if he had kept his comparison within the limits of the body of the Israelites, he would have cited circumcision and other better known and more important sacraments instead. But he preferred to take those which were not so well-known, because they were more effective for bringing out the contrast between us and them. Otherwise the lesson which he adds would not be very apposite, viz. "all these things happened to them to be an example (*in figuram*) to us, because we see the judgements of God that fell on them, and also threaten us, if we get involved in similar sins."

4. *And the rock was Christ.* Some people are stupid enough to distort these words of Paul, as if he said that Christ was the spiritual rock, and as if he had nothing to say about that rock which was a visible symbol; for we know quite well that Paul is dealing with outward signs. Their objection, that the rock is actually described as spiritual, is a trifling one, because this epithet is only applied to it so that we may know that it

was the symbol of a spiritual mystery. All the same, there is no doubt that Paul compares our sacraments with those of the Israelites.

Their second objection is more foolish and childish. They ask: "How could a rock, which remained fixed in one spot, *follow* the Israelites?" They ask that, as if it were not as clear as can be, that the word rock denotes the stream of water, which never failed the people. For Paul is praising the grace of God, because He commanded the water, which was brought out of the rock, to flow along wherever the people journeyed, as if the rock itself accompanied them. Now, if Paul meant that Christ is the spiritual foundation of the Church, why did he use the past tense of the verb *was?* It is quite clear that he is referring to something which only affected the fathers. Let us hear no more, then, about this silly fiction, which gives a chance to quarrelsome men to show how impudent they are, rather than allow sacramental forms of speaking.

I have already said that in the old sacraments the reality was united with the signs and conveyed to the people. Therefore, since they were figures (*figurae*) of Christ, it follows that Christ was tied to them, not locally indeed, and not in a union of nature or substance, but sacramentally. That is why the apostle says that the rock was Christ, for metonymy is very commonly used when speaking about the sacraments. Therefore the name of the reality is transferred to the sign here, because it applies to it, not properly, but figuratively, because of that union about which I have already spoken. But since this will be dealt with more fully in chapter eleven, I am making only a slight reference to it here.

There is still another question. Since we now eat the body and drink the blood of Christ, how were the Jews partakers of the same spiritual meat and drink, when the flesh of Christ was not yet in existence for them to eat? To that I reply that although the flesh did not yet exist, it was food for them all the same. And that is not a piece of useless sophistry; for their salvation depended on the benefit of the death and resurrection, and for that reason on the flesh and blood, of Christ. Therefore it was necessary for them to receive the flesh and blood of Christ, so that they might share in the blessing of redemption. The receiving of it was the secret work of the Holy Spirit, who was active in such a way that the flesh of Christ, even if it was not yet created, might be efficacious in them. He means, however, that they ate in their own way, which was different from ours, and, as I have said already, that Christ is now conveyed to us more fully, because of the greater degree of revelation. For in our day the eating is substantial (*substantialis est manducatio*), something which was not yet possible in their time. In other words, Christ feeds us with His flesh, which was sacrificed for us, and which was appointed to be our food, and from this we draw our life.

11. *Now all these things happened as types.* He again repeats that all these things happened to the Israelites so that they may be "types" to us, in other words examples by which God sets His judgements before our eyes. I know very well that others make more ingenious theories about these words, but I think that I have grasped what was in the apostle's mind when I say that these examples bring home to us, as if they were pictures painted by an artist, what sort of judgement threatens idolaters, fornicators, and others who despise God; for these are living pictures revealing God to us in His anger with sins like those. This explanation, as well as being simple and realistic, also has the advantage of silencing certain madmen, who distort this passage in order to prove that the only things ever done among that ancient people were things which foreshadowed what was to come. They first of all take it for granted that that people prefigure (*esse figuram*) the Church. From that they conclude that all that God promised them or gave them, whether benefits or punishments, only prefigured what had to be brought to full reality with the coming of Christ. This is a most damaging piece of nonsense, because it does serious injury to the holy fathers, and still more serious injury to God. For those people foreshadowed the Christian Church in such a way that they were at the same time a genuine Church. Their circumstances so delineated ours that the essential features of a Church were nonetheless already present in those days. The promises given to it adumbrated the Gospel in such a way that it was included in them. Their sacraments served to prefigure ours but in such a way that they were still true sacraments with an efficacy applying to their day as well. To sum up, those who made a proper use of the Word (*doctrina*) and sacraments (*signis*) in those days were endowed with the same Spirit of faith as we are. These words of Paul, then, give no support to those fools, for these words do not mean that the events of that age were "types" in the sense that they had no real significance for that time, but were a kind of empty show. But on the contrary, as I have explained, they plainly teach us that there, as in pictures, plain for us to see, are things which should be a warning to us.

And they were written for our admonition. This second clause draws out the first. For the fact that these things were committed to writing was no advantage to the Israelites, but only to us. However it does not follow from that that those retributions were not real punishments of God, which effec-

tively disciplined them at that time; but God not only put His judgements into effect at that time, but also intended that there should be a perpetual record of them for our admonition. For what use would the account of them be to the dead? And what use would it be to the living, if they did not take warning from the examples of the other people, and come to their senses? But Paul takes for granted the principle, about which all believers should be in agreement, that nothing is recorded in the Scriptures which is not to our advantage to know.

From John Calvin, *Calvin's Commentaries*, vol. 19, *The First Epistle of Paul the Apostle to the Corinthians*, translated by John W. Fraser (Grand Rapids, MI: Eerdmans, 1960), 200–205, 210–11.

☙ After publishing *Explanatory Notes upon the New Testament* (1755), **John Wesley** (1703–91), founder of the Methodist denomination, was importuned to write *Explanatory Notes upon the Old Testament* (1766). In his Preface to the latter, written in Edinburgh on April 25, 1765, Wesley provides a condensed version of his methodology for interpreting the Bible. In "An Address to the Clergy," written in London on February 6, 1756, Wesley notes what a minister needs, both in knowledge and in method, to interpret Scripture adequately.

JOHN WESLEY

Explanatory Notes upon the Old Testament, Preface, 1.15–18

15. Every thinking man will now easily discern my design in the following sheets. It is not to write sermons, essays, or set discourses, upon any part of Scripture. It is not to draw inferences from the text, or to show what doctrines may be proved thereby. It is this: To give the direct, literal meaning of every verse, of every sentence, and, as far as I am able, of every word, in the oracles of God. I design only, like the hand of a dial, to point every man to this; not to take up his mind with something else, how excellent soever; but to keep his eye fixed upon the naked Bible, that he may read and hear it with understanding. I say again, and I desire it may be well observed, that none may expect what they will not find, it is not my design to write a book which a man may read separate from the Bible, but barely to assist those who fear God in hearing and reading the Bible itself, by showing the natural sense of every part in as few and plain words as I can.

16. And I am not without hopes, that the following Notes

may in some measure answer this end, not barely to unlettered and ignorant men, but also to men of education and learning; although it is true, neither these nor the Notes on the New Testament were principally designed for them. Sure I am, that tracts written in the most plain and simple manner are of infinitely more service to me than those which are elaborated with the utmost skill, and set off with the greatest pomp of erudition.

17. But it is no part of my design to save either learned or unlearned men from the trouble of thinking. If so, I might perhaps write folios too, which usually overlay rather than help the thought. On the contrary, my intention is to make them think, and assist them in thinking. This is the way to understand the things of God: "Meditate thereon day and night";[783] so shall you attain the best knowledge, even to "know the only true God, and Jesus Christ whom he hath sent."[784] And this knowledge will lead you "to love Him, because He hath first loved us";[785] yea, "to love the Lord your God with all your heart, and with all your soul, and with all your mind, and with all your strength."[786] Will there not then be all "that mind in you which was also in Christ Jesus?"[787] And in consequence of this, while you joyfully experience all the holy tempers described in this book, you will likewise be outwardly "holy as He that hath called you is holy, in all manner of conversation."[788]

18. If you desire to read the Scriptures in such a manner as may most effectually answer this end, would it not be advisable, (1) To set apart a little time, if you can, every morning and evening for that purpose? (2) At each time, if you have leisure, to read a chapter out of the Old, and one out of the New, Testament; if you cannot do this, to take a single chapter, or a part of one? (3) To read this with a single eye, to know the whole will of God, and a fixed resolution to do it? In order to know his will, you should, (4) Have a constant eye to the analogy of faith, the connexion and harmony there is between those grand, fundamental doctrines, original sin, justification by faith, the new birth, inward and outward holiness. (5) Serious and earnest prayer should be constantly used before we consult the oracles of God; seeing "Scripture can only be understood through the same Spirit whereby it was given." Our reading should likewise be closed with prayer, that what we read may be written on our hearts. (6) It might also be of use, if, while we read, we were frequently to pause and examine ourselves by what we read, both with regard to our hearts and lives. This would furnish us with matter of praise, where we found God had enabled us to conform to his blessed will; and matter of humiliation and prayer, where

we were conscious of having fallen short. And whatever light you then receive should be used to the uttermost, and that immediately. Let there be no delay. Whatever you resolve, begin to execute the first moment you can. So shall you find this word to be indeed the power of God unto present and eternal salvation.

From *The Works of John Wesley*, 3rd ed., vol. 14 (Grand Rapids, MI: Baker Books, 1978), 251–53.

JOHN WESLEY

"An Address to the Clergy," I.2

2. And as to acquired endowments, can he take one step aright, without first a competent share of knowledge? a knowledge, First, of his own office; of the high trust in which he stands, the important work to which he is called? Is there any hope that a man should discharge his office well, if he knows not what it is? that he should acquit himself faithfully of a trust, the very nature whereof he does not understand? Nay, if he knows not the work God has given him to do, he cannot finish it.

Secondly. No less necessary is a knowledge of the Scriptures, which teach us how to teach others; yea, a knowledge of all the Scriptures; seeing scripture interprets scripture; one part fixing the sense of another. So that, whether it be true or not, that every good textuary is a good Divine, it is certain none can be a good Divine who is not a good textuary. None else can be mighty in the Scriptures; able both to instruct and to stop the mouths of gainsayers.

In order to do this accurately, ought he not to know the literal meaning of every word, verse, and chapter; without which there can be no firm foundation on which the spiritual meaning can be built? Should he not likewise be able to deduce the proper corollaries, speculative and practical, from each text; to solve the difficulties which arise, and answer the objections which are or may be raised against it; and to make a suitable application of all to the consciences of his hearers?

Thirdly. But can he do this, in the most effectual manner, without a knowledge of the original tongues? Without this,

---

783. Ps 1:2. (The notes for this selection are by Gerhart and Udoh.)
784. Jn 17:3.
785. 1 Jn 4:19.
786. Mk 12:30; see Mt 22:37; Lk 10:27; Deut 6:5.
787. Phil 2:5.
788. 1 Pet 15–16; see also Lev 11:44–45.

will he not frequently be at a stand, even as to texts which regard practice only? But he will be under still greater difficulties, with respect to controverted scriptures. He will be ill able to rescue these out of the hands of any man of learning that would pervert them: For whenever an appeal is made to the original, his mouth is stopped at once.

Fourthly. Is not a knowledge of profane history, likewise, of ancient customs, of chronology and geography, though not absolutely necessary, yet highly expedient, for him that would throughly understand the Scriptures? since the want even of this knowledge is but poorly supplied by reading the comments of other men.

Fifthly. Some knowledge of the sciences also, is, to say the least, equally expedient. Nay, may we not say, that the knowledge of one, (whether art or science,) although now quite unfashionable, is even necessary next, and in order to, the knowledge of the Scripture itself? I mean logic. For what is this, if rightly understood, but the art of good sense? of apprehending things clearly, judging truly, and reasoning conclusively? What is it, viewed in another light, but the art of learning and teaching; whether by convincing or persuading? What is there, then, in the whole compass of science, to be desired in comparison of it?

Is not some acquaintance with what has been termed the second part of logic, (metaphysics,) if not so necessary as this, yet highly expedient, (1) In order to clear our apprehension, (without which it is impossible either to judge correctly, or to reason closely or conclusively,) by ranging our ideas under general heads? And, (2) In order to understand many useful writers, who can very hardly be understood without it?

Should not a Minister be acquainted too with at least the general grounds of natural philosophy? Is not this a great help to the accurate understanding several passages of Scripture? Assisted by this, he may himself comprehend, and on proper occasions explain to others, how the invisible things of God are seen from the creation of the world; how "the heavens declare the glory of God, and the firmament showeth his handiwork";[789] till they cry out, "O Lord, how manifold are thy works! In wisdom hast thou made them all."[790]

But how far can he go in this, without some knowledge of geometry? which is likewise useful, not barely on this account, but to give clearness of apprehension, and an habit of thinking closely and connectedly.

It must be allowed, indeed, that some of these branches of knowledge are not so indispensably necessary as the rest; and therefore no thinking man will condemn the Fathers of the Church, for having, in all ages and nations, appointed some

to the ministry, who, suppose they had the capacity, yet had not had the opportunity of attaining them. But what excuse is this for one who has the opportunity, and makes no use of it? What can be urged for a person who has had an University education, if he does not understand them all? Certainly, supposing him to have any capacity, to have common understanding, he is inexcusable before God and man.

Sixthly. Can any who spend several years in those seats of learning, be excused, if they do not add to that of the languages and sciences, the knowledge of the Fathers? the most authentic commentators on Scripture, as being both nearest the fountain, and eminently endued with that Spirit by whom all Scripture was given. It will be easily perceived, I speak chiefly of those who wrote before the Council of Nice. But who would not likewise desire to have some acquaintance with those that followed them? with St. Chrysostom, Basil, Jerome, Austin; and, above all, the man of a broken heart, Ephraim Syrus?

Seventhly. There is yet another branch of knowledge highly necessary for a Clergyman, and that is, knowledge of the world; a knowledge of men, of their maxims, tempers, and manners, such as they occur in real life. Without this he will be liable to receive much hurt, and capable of doing little good; as he will not know, either how to deal with men according to the vast variety of their characters, or to preserve himself from those who almost in every place lie in wait to deceive.

From *The Works of John Wesley*, 3rd ed., vol. 10 (Grand Rapids, MI: Baker Books, 1978), 482–84.

POST-ENLIGHTENMENT INTERPRETATION: HISTORY AND HERMENEUTICS

☙ The German theologian and philosopher **Hermann Reimarus** (1694–1768), who initiated the so-called quest for the historical Jesus, laid out his interpretive philosophy in his controversial work *Apology* [*Apologie oder Schutzschrift für die vernünftigen Verehrer Gottes*]. Several fragments of these essays were published posthumously (and for a time, anonymously, because of the challenges they presented) by Gotthold Ephraim Lessing from 1774 to 1778 in a series known as the Wolfenbüttel Fragments.

---

789. Ps 19:1. (The notes for this selection are by Gerhart and Udoh.)
790. Ps 104:24.

HERMANN REIMARUS

"Concerning the Intention of Jesus and His Teaching,"
§§1–4, 6–7

§1

It can be seen from the foregoing book [concerning the Old Testament] that the doctrine of the salvation and immortality of the soul, which must be the essential element of a religion, especially a revealed religion, had not yet been expounded by the writers of the Old Testament and thus had been unknown to the Jews during the days of their own prophets. Rather, later Jews had learned and accepted this important tenet through contacts with rational heathens and their philosophers. The Pharisees maintained and advanced the doctrine principally in opposition to the Sadducees, and since they were unable to prove it in the true, literal sense by Moses and the prophets they employed an artificial, allegorical, and cabalistic explanation.[791] Accordingly, even before Jesus' time, the Pharisees had sought to relate to the proper intention of religion the matters of the law found in the writings of their fathers. Indeed, they would not have been reproached too greatly if, in attempting to avoid the appearance of creating an innovation among the people, they had applied Moses and the prophets to this grand purpose, even when to do so contradicted truth. But to the extent that they seemed to base the reason for religion on this one thing they ruined very nearly everything by prescribing almost no other duties than those involving external ceremonies of the law. Indeed, they so refined and increased the latter by their additions that genuine godliness and virtue were almost obscured and smothered, and it all came to sheer hypocrisy and sanctimoniousness.[792]

§2

Now when Jesus began to teach he undertook primarily to castigate and reform the trifling matters and the misuse committed by the Pharisees and to preach a better righteousness than theirs. From a reading of the New Testament it can be obvious to everyone that a great portion of Jesus' sayings is directed against the distorted sanctimoniousness of the scribes and Pharisees in outward ceremonies. Nevertheless, he admitted the correctness of their view concerning immortality and salvation, and not only defended this opinion against the Sadducees, but impressed it diligently upon the people. He introduces Abraham and Lazarus into his

parables, representing them as living in abundant joy in the realm of glory;[793] he urges the people not to fear those who can merely destroy the body and not the soul. Rather, they should fear God, who can plunge both body and soul into hell; he speaks urgently of the kingdom of heaven and the last judgment that God shall preside over, etc. Consequently, his teaching had a considerable advantage not only over that of the Pharisees, but also over that of the Old Testament, where such essential principles of religion were not even considered and where there is mention only of earthly promises and rewards, all hope for man ending abruptly with his death. Thus Paul correctly says of him that he did away with death and in its place brought to light life and immortality through the gospel.[794] For it was not the law that made perfect, but the introduction of a better hope, by means of which we approach God. Augustine says, *jam Christi beneficio etiam idiotis notam creditamque animae immortalitatem vitamque post mortem futuram.* ["It is Christ's merit that he also taught the ignorant about the immortality of the soul and life after death so that they believed in it."] Thus it seems to be chiefly to the Christian doctrine that we must ascribe the fact that the Sadducees and their followers from that time on almost completely lost ground among the Jews. I shall add to this advantage of Jesus' teaching the further fact that Jesus also invites the heathen into the kingdom of God and, unlike Moses, does not command that they be despised and eradicated with fire and sword. "Go," he says, "and teach all heathen, preach the Gospel to all creatures."[795] Indeed, he does not entirely exclude from this hope even those heathen who remain firmly rooted in their imperfect understanding; he says that it shall go easier with Tyre and Sidon at the last judgment than with many of the Jews.[796]

---

791. Cabala refers to the esoteric or mystic lore concerning God and the universe, originally oral, which by the geonic period was connected with a Mishna-type book, the Sefer-Yezirah, and which from the thirteenth century branched into an extensive literature alongside and opposed to the Talmud. Cabalistic here is a reference to the more fanciful types of interpretation characteristic of the Cabala.

792. Reimarus, like many Christians, takes the portrait of the Pharisees in the Gospels, especially Mt 23, at face value. It is now generally accepted that the harsh tone and distorted portrait is the result of Jewish-Christian tensions in the closing decades of the first century and that the Pharisaism known to Jesus cannot merely be equated with that known to the first evangelist because, for example, the Revolt of 66–70 brought fundamental changes in first-century Judaism in Palestine. The recovery of the historical Pharisees is no less difficult than the recovery of the historical Jesus.

793. Abraham: Mt 8:11; Lk 13:28. Lazarus: Lk 16:23, 25.

794. 2 Tim 1:10.

795. Mt 28:19 combined with Mk 16:15.

796. Mt 11:22; Lk 10:14.

§3

Hence, just as there can be no doubt that Jesus in his teaching referred man to the true great goal of religion, namely, eternal salvation, we are concerned now with just this one question: What sort of purpose did Jesus himself see in his teaching and deeds? Jesus left us nothing in writing; everything that we know of his teaching and deeds is contained in the writings of his disciples. Especially where his teaching is concerned, not only the evangelists among his disciples, but the apostles as well undertook to present their master's teaching. However, I find great cause to separate completely what the apostles say in their own writings from that which Jesus himself actually said and taught, for the apostles were themselves teachers and consequently present their own views; indeed, they never claim that Jesus himself said and taught in his lifetime all the things that they have written. On the other hand, the four evangelists represent themselves only as historians who have reported the most important things that Jesus said as well as did. If now we wish to know what Jesus' teaching actually was, what he said and preached, that is a *res facti*—a matter of something that actually occurred; hence this is to be derived from the reports of the historians. Now since there are four of them and since they all agree on the sum total of Jesus' teaching, the integrity of their reports is not to be doubted, nor should it be thought that they might have forgotten or suppressed any important point or essential portion of Jesus' teaching. Thus it is not to be assumed that Jesus intended or strove for anything in his teaching other than what may be taken from his own words as they are found in the four evangelists. Everyone will grant, then, that in my investigation of the intention of Jesus' teaching I have sufficient reason to limit myself exclusively to the reports of the four evangelists who offer the proper and true record. I shall not bring in those things that the apostles taught or intended on their own, since the latter are not historians of their master's teaching but present themselves as teachers. Later, when once we have discovered the actual teaching and intention of Jesus from the four documents of the historians, we shall be able to judge reliably whether the apostles expressed the same teaching and intention as their master.

§4

Jesus' discourses in the four evangelists can not only be read through quickly, but we also immediately find the entire content and intention of his teaching expressed and summa-

rized in his own words: "Repent, and believe in the gospel."[797] Or, in another place, "Repent, for the kingdom of heaven is at hand."[798] And in another place he says, "I have come to call sinners to repentance."[799] Further, "I must preach the good news of the kingdom of God . . . for I was sent for this purpose."[800] And it is this very thing that impelled John, Jesus' forerunner, to prepare the way for him, "Repent, for the kingdom of heaven is at hand."[801] Both these things, the kingdom of heaven and repentance, are so connected that the kingdom is the goal, while repentance is the means or preparation for this kingdom. By the kingdom that was at hand, announced to the Jews by the gospel or "joyful news," we understand (to use the Jewish expression) the kingdom of the Christ or Messiah for which the Jews had so long waited and hoped. The matter is self-evident: Since Jesus had come as the Messiah and since John specifically proclaimed this, it is expressed in the figure of speech actually used among the Jews of that day so that, when they heard of the kingdom of heaven that was to come, they understood nothing other than the kingdom of the Messiah. Since Jesus and John do not explain this term in any other way they wanted to have it understood in the familiar and customary meaning. Thus when it is said that the kingdom of heaven is near at hand, that means the Messiah will soon reveal himself and establish his kingdom. When it says believe in the gospel, that is another way of saying, believe in the joyful news of the imminent coming of the Messiah and his kingdom. The people were thus to prepare and make themselves ready through repentance for this now imminent kingdom of the Messiah, that is, by a change in thinking and spirit, in that they leave off wickedness and the tendency to commit it and with all their hearts turn to good and godliness. This demand was not only reasonable in all ages, but also was considered necessary among the Jews for the advent of the Messiah, just as they indeed believe to this present day that it is particularly the lack of repentance and betterment that delays the Messiah's advent, so that if they once were to do the proper penance the Messiah would come immediately. The person who reads and reflects upon all Jesus' words will find that their content applies collectively to these two things: either he describes the kingdom of heaven and commands his disciples to proclaim it, or he shows how men must undergo a

---

797. Mk 1:15.   800. Lk 4:43.
798. Mt 4:17.   801. Mt 3:2.
799. Mk 2:17; Mt 9:13; Lk 5:32.

sincere repentance and not cling to the sanctimonious nature of the Pharisees.

§6

Thus the goal of Jesus' sermons and teachings was a proper, active character, a changing of the mind, a sincere love of God and of one's neighbor, humility, gentleness, denial of the self, and the suppression of all evil desires. These are not great mysteries or tenets of the faith that he explains, proves, and preaches; they are nothing other than moral teachings and duties intended to improve man inwardly and with all his heart, whereby Jesus naturally takes for granted a general knowledge of man's soul, of God and his perfections, salvation after this life, etc. But he does not explain these things anew, much less present them in a learned and extravagant way. To the same extent that he wished to see the law fulfilled and not done away with in respect to his own person, he shows others how the whole law and the prophets hang on these two commandments:[802] that one love God with all his heart, and his neighbor as himself, and that consequently the repentance and improvement of man is contained in this essence of the whole Old Testament. Jesus calls this to the attention of the people when they come to him and ask what they must do to be saved: "Do that, and you shall live." He says that salvation depends simply upon one's doing the will of his heavenly father, and he recognizes as brothers all who do such. Even if on that day men would say, "Lord, Lord! did we not prophesy in your name . . . and do many mighty works in your name?" Jesus will still say, "Depart from me, you evildoers."[803] Unlike these are the sheep that he will place on his right hand and the blessed who shall inherit the kingdom, those who have fed the hungry, given drink to the thirsty, lodging to the stranger, clothing to the naked, and who have visited those in prison.[804] When now he sends his disciples out into all the world to teach he immediately explains what this teaching is to consist of: "Teach them to observe all that I have commanded you."[805] The criterion that he also applies to false prophets is not whether they entertain this or that mistaken opinion, or have a false system, or are heterodox and heretical or cause others to be so, but "by their works you shall know them." In his view the false prophets are those who go about in sheep's clothing but who are like ravenous wolves beneath; that is, their sole intent, beneath the guise of love and innocence, is nothing more than to cause harm to other men; further, those who

produce such fruits as does a rotten tree, or who fail to do the will of the heavenly father, are evildoers.[806]

§7

I cannot avoid revealing a common error of Christians who imagine because of the confusion of the teaching of the apostles with Jesus' teaching that the latter's purpose in his role of teacher was to reveal certain articles of faith and mysteries that were in part new and unknown, thus establishing a new system of religion, while on the other hand doing away with the Jewish religion in regard to its special customs, such as sacrifices, circumcision, purification, the Sabbath, and other Levitical ceremonies. I am aware, of course, that the apostles, especially Paul, worked at this and that later teachers in part forged more and more mysteries and articles of faith and in part also abandoned the Jewish ceremonies more and more, until eventually Moses' laws were completely done away with and an entirely different religion had been introduced. But I cannot find the least trace of either of these things in all the teachings, sermons, and conversations of Jesus. He urged nothing more than purely moral duties, a true love of God and of one's neighbor; on these points he based the whole content of the law and the prophets and commanded that the hope of gaining his kingdom and salvation be constructed on them. Moreover, he was born a Jew and intended to remain one; he testifies that he has not come to abolish the law, but to fulfill it. He simply points out that the most essential thing in the law does not depend upon external things. The further remarks that he makes about the immortality and salvation of the soul, the resurrection of the body to face judgment, the kingdom of heaven and the Christ or Messiah who was promised in Moses and the prophets were both familiar to the Jews and in accord with the Jewish religion of that day, and were especially aimed at his intention of establishing such a kingdom of heaven among them as their Messiah, thus bringing about the blessed condition, both in religion and in external things, for which they had long since been given cause to hope. In order that this may be more clearly understood I shall show in more detail two aspects of Jesus' teaching: (1) that he pro-

---

802. Mt 22:37–40; Mk 12:29–31; Lk 10:27.

803. Mt 7:22, 23.   805. Mt 28:20.

804. Mt 25:32ff.   806. Mt 7:15–23.

posed no new mysteries or articles of faith, and (2) that he had no intention of doing away with the Levitical ceremonial law.

From Hermann Reimarus, *Fragments,* edited by Charles Talbert, translated by Ralph S. Fraser (Chico, CA: Scholars Press, 1985), 61–67, 69–72.

   ❧ **Friedrich Schleiermacher** (1768–1834) was a German theologian and philosopher. In "On the Concept of Hermeneutics,"[807] an academy address given in 1829 at the University of Berlin, he founds his general theory of interpretation as a philosophical and as a theological discipline. [Ellipses in original.]

FRIEDRICH SCHLEIERMACHER

"On the Concept of Hermeneutics"

The First Address, August 12

Many, perhaps most, of the activities which make up human life may be carried out at one of three levels. One level is almost spiritless and entirely mechanical; the second is based on a wealth of experiences and observations; and the third is artistic in the true sense of the term. It seems to me that interpretation, too, is marked by these three levels, at least insofar as the word "interpretation" refers to understanding all foreign or strange speech. The first and lowest level we encounter daily, in the market place and in the streets as well as in many circles of society, wherever people converse about common topics in such a way that the speaker always knows almost immediately and with certainty what the other will respond, and language is tossed back and forth as a ball. Most of the time we seem to operate at the second level. This sort of interpretation is practiced in our schools and universities and in the commentaries of philologians and theologians, the two groups who have worked this field most extensively. The treasure of instructive observations and references found in their works adequately attests that many of them are true artists of interpretation. Even so, juxtaposed to this wealth of information we often find instances where difficult passages are given wild and arbitrary explanations and where some of the most beautiful passages are carelessly overlooked or foolishly distorted because of the interpreter's pedantic lack of sensitivity. But when a person who is not himself proficient in such matters is called upon to interpret, he needs, in addition to these treasures, a primer with a solid methodology that not

only presents the fruits of masterful studies but also presents in reputable scientific forms the total range and foundations of the method. This is all the more necessary when that person is supposed to introduce inquisitive youth to the art of interpretation and to direct them in it. Consequently, for my own sake as well as for that of my audience, when I began to lecture on hermeneutics I searched for the best treatment of the method. But my search was in vain. Neither the numerous theological compendia—though many of them, such as [Johann] Ernesti's book, are considered products of sound philological study—nor even the few purely philological essays on interpretation offered more than compilations of individual rules extracted from the researches of the masters.[808] Moreover, although these rules were sometimes clear, frequently they were quite ambiguous; and although they were now and again arranged in a helpful fashion, at other times the arrangement was unsatisfactory. I had high expectations when [G. G.] Fülleborn's philological encyclopedia, based on [Friedrich August] Wolf's lectures, was published.[809] But the few references to hermeneutics in it did not amount even to a sketch of a general hermeneutical theory. And since this work was directed specifically to the literature of classical antiquity, just as most handbooks are designed specifically for the study of the Holy Scriptures, I found myself no more content than before.

The essays mentioned in the title of this address are the most significant ones to appear since that time. Because Wolf is one of the best minds among us, and one of our most independent and creative philologians, and because [Friedrich] Ast is trying to develop a philosophically-oriented philology, it would seem all the more instructive and useful to combine the strengths of both. Thus I thought it appropriate to follow their lead and to relate my own ideas about the task of interpretation to theirs.

Wolf intentionally avoids structuring his essay in a systematic form. This may be because he always takes care to avoid even the slightest hint of pedantry, preferring to leave to others the laborious and rather banal task of putting together the remarks he strews about so gracefully and elegantly, or

---

807. On the different datings from Schleiermacher and Jonas, see Kimmerle's introduction to *Hermeneutics: The Handwritten Manuscripts* (Missoula, MT: Scholars Press, 1977), 24–25.

808. In the history of Protestant theology since Flacius, *Clavis scripturae sacrae,* hermeneutical texts were republished many times.

809. G. G. Fülleborn, *Encyclopaedia philologica* (Bratislava, 1798). Schleiermacher refers here to the second edition, edited by D. J. Kaulfuss (Bratislava, 1805).

it may be because he does not consider such a structure suitable for a lead article in a general journal that advances no systematic position of its own.[810] Ast, in contrast, considers a systematic form essential, and at the outset he asserts that no theory can be communicated scientifically without philosophical support.[811] Nonetheless, since Wolf assures us that he intended the contents of his essay to serve as an introduction for a philological encyclopedia, we may assume that he had thought through his statements with this purpose in mind, and we are justified in believing that his own theory is contained in this essay.[812]

Wolf puts together grammar, hermeneutics, and criticism as preparatory studies that provide entry to the philological disciplines per se, as the organon of the science of antiquity. Ast, however, attempts to treat these same three disciplines as an appendix to his as yet unpublished outline of philology. The two men are not so far apart. Even Ast's view, although he is not very clear about how the appendix is related to the main work, certainly means that his exposition of philology has led him to see the necessity of treating all three disciplines scientifically. No one would dare to deny that grammar, criticism, and hermeneutics are closely related, as these men maintain. But I would like to focus on hermeneutics, leaving the other two aside for the moment.

Certainly the works of classical antiquity, as masterpieces of human language, are the most excellent and worthy subject with which the art of interpretation normally has to deal. But it is undeniable, too, that many scholars have worked on other texts with great success, especially on the Christian Bible, which is not such a rich source for philologians. Were an encyclopedia for the study of these texts to be constructed, then without question hermeneutics, along with several other preparatory studies, would constitute an organon for Christian theology.[813] If, then, hermeneutics is important for Christian theology in the same way as it is for classical studies, then neither theological nor classical hermeneutics represents the essence of the matter. Rather, hermeneutics itself is something greater out of which these two types flow. To be sure, only these two, classical philologians and philological theologians, have contributed to our discipline. Juristic hermeneutics is a different matter. In the main it is concerned only with determining the extent of the law, that is, with applying general principles to particular cases which had not been foreseen at the time the principles were formulated.

Ast could almost induce me to assert that hermeneutics should be restricted to these two areas of study. For at the very beginning of his outline, where he describes the task of understanding, he leads us up to the very height of the unity of spirit and concludes that all our cultural activities are directed toward the unification of the Greek and Christian life. Thus hermeneutics, too, is directed to these two alone.[814] And if hermeneutics introduces, on the one hand, the science of antiquity and, on the other hand, Christian theology, then both studies would be carried out in the spirit of their unity. Moreover, there would be justification for hermeneutics to deal both with oriental texts, which represent the common point of origin for classical and Christian studies, and with romantic literature, which is clearly close to the unity of the two. Were oriental and romantic literature regarded as self-contained spheres in the way classical philosophy and Biblical studies are, we would require four hermeneutics, each constructed in a distinctive manner to serve as the organon for its particular discipline. Then, however, there would have to be a still higher organon common to all four.

Now although I want to ascend to this higher sphere, I am afraid of Wolf's shadow. In the few sentences he devotes to hermeneutics Wolf laments that this theory is by no means complete, and he notes that several investigations remain to be undertaken before it can be established. These investigations do not lie on such dizzy heights, but in quite moderate zones. They deal with the meanings of words, the senses of sentences, and the coherence of statements. Yet at the same time he states, as a consolation, that this incompleteness is not too damaging, since the results of these investigations would contribute but little to awaken the talent of the interpreter or to enhance his intellectual ability. Then, as a warning, he refers to the distinction he makes between the type of theories advanced by the ancients, which actually facilitated a task (in this case, the task of interpretation), and those theories to which we moderns are inclined, which become engrossed in abstruse accounts of the nature and bases of

---

810. The essay by Wolf opened the journal *Museum der Altertumswissenschaft*, edited by F. A. Wolf and Philip Buttmann, 79, n. 1.

811. See Friedrich Ast, *Grundlinien der Grammatik, Hermeneutik und Kritik* (Landshut, 1808), iii–viii.

812. See Friedrich August Wolf, "Darstellung der Altertumswissenschaft nach Begriff, Umfang, Zweck und Wert," *Museum der Altertumswissenschaft* (Berlin, 1809), 3–6.

813. In his *Brief Outline of Theology* (1811, 1830), Schleiermacher drafted a theological encyclopedia. In addition to hermeneutics, Schleiermacher presents higher and lower criticism, knowledge of language, and mastery of the historical milieu as the organon of "exegetical theology," which is itself of fundamental importance for theology as a whole. (See second edition, nos. 110–46).

814. Ast, 167–71.

the art and so fail to be of any practical value.[815] I fear he was referring to the distinction with which I began. In that case the purely scientific theory is one that will be of no use; the only useful theory is the one that offers an orderly collection of philological observations. Yet, on the one hand, it seems to me that this collection of observations requires something more in order that we may determine the extent to which the rules should be applied. The "modern" kind of theory certainly supplies that. On the other hand, I think that this "modern" kind, even though it deals only with the nature and bases of an art, will always exercise some influence on the practice of that art. But since I do not want to endanger the applicability of the theory, I prefer to leave the speculative guides to their soaring and follow the practical one.

These leaders explain above all (although only parenthetically and without much emphasis) that hermeneutics is the art of discovering with necessary insight the thoughts contained in the work of an author.[816] And this next assertion salvages much of what I had hoped to gain by following the more speculative guides: Hermeneutics does not apply exclusively to classical studies, nor is it merely a part of this restricted philological organon; rather, it is to be applied to the works of every author. Therefore, its principles must be sufficiently general, and they are not to be derived solely from the nature of classical literature. Ast makes me uncomfortable with such a well-formulated statement, but even so I must try to draw its component parts together.

He begins with the concept of something foreign which is to be understood. Now, to be sure, he does not state this concept in its sharpest form. If what is to be understood were so completely foreign to the one trying to understand it that there was nothing in common between the two, then there would be no point of contact for understanding at all.[817] But I conclude that the concept holds in a relative sense. It then follows that, just as hermeneutics would be unable to begin its work if what is to be understood were completely foreign, so there would be no reason for hermeneutics to begin if nothing were strange between the speaker and hearer. That is, understanding would always occur immediately upon reading or hearing, or it would be already given in a divinatory manner, and understanding would take place by itself.

I am quite content to restrict the application of hermeneutics to the area between these two extremes. But I must also admit that I want to claim this entire area for it, meaning that wherever one encounters something strange in the way thoughts are being expressed in speech, one is faced with a task which can be solved only with the help of a theory,

presupposing of course some common point between the speaker and the one who is to understand.

My two guides, however, restrict me at several points. The one states he is interested only in understanding authors, as though the same problems do not arise in conversation and direct speech. The other wants to restrict what is "foreign" to something written in a foreign language, and, more specifically, to works marked by genius [*Werke des Geistes*], a sphere even narrower than that of authors in general.[818] But we can come to learn a great deal from works which have no outstanding intellectual content, for example, from stories narrated in a style similar to that normally used in ordinary conversation to tell about minor occurrences, a long way from artistic historical writing, or from letters composed in a highly intimate and casual style. Even such cases as these present equally difficult tasks for the work of hermeneutics. Moreover, I submit that Wolf's view is really not much different than Ast's, and were I to ask him whether such authors as newspaper reporters or those who write newspaper advertisements are to be treated by the science of interpretation, he would not give me a very friendly response. Although many of these materials are such that there can be nothing foreign between the author and the reader, there are exceptions, and I cannot understand why these strange elements can or must be made intelligible in some way other than more artistic writings. Further, there are other cases (epigrams, for example, that are not significantly different from newspaper articles) which are impossible to differentiate into two classes, or two different methods or theories. Indeed, I must reiterate that hermeneutics is not to be limited to written texts. I often make use of hermeneutics in personal conversation when, discontented with the ordinary level of understanding, I wish to explore how my friend has moved from one thought to another or try to trace out the views, judgments, and aspirations which led him to speak about a given subject in just this way and no other. No doubt everyone has such experiences, and I think they make it clear that the task for which we seek a theory is not limited to what is fixed in writing but arises whenever we have to understand a thought or series of thoughts expressed in words.

Nor is the hermeneutical task restricted to a foreign language. Even in our native language, and without considering the various dialects of the language or the peculiarities

---

815. Wolf, 37.
816. Ibid.

817. Ast, 167–68.
818. See Wolf, 34–35; Ast, 173–74.

of a person's speech, the thoughts and expressions of another person, whether written or spoken, contain strange elements. Indeed, I readily acknowledge that I consider the practice of hermeneutics occurring in immediate communication in one's native language very essential for our cultured life, apart from all philological or theological studies. Who could move in the company of exceptionally gifted persons without endeavoring to hear "between" their words, just as we read between the lines of original and tightly written books? Who does not try in a meaningful conversation, which may in certain respects be an important act, to lift out its main points, to try to grasp its internal coherence, to pursue all its subtle intimations further? Wolf—especially Wolf, who was such an artist in conversations, but who said more by intimation than by explicit statement, and even more by innuendo—would not deny that these were being understood by his listeners in an artistic way, so that he could count on the audience always knowing what he meant. Should the way we observe and interpret experienced, worldly-wise and politically shrewd persons really differ from the procedure we use with books? Should it be so different that it would depend on entirely different principles and be incapable of a comparably developed and orderly presentation? That I do not believe. On the contrary, I see two different applications of the same art. In the one application certain motives are more prominent, while others remain in the background; and in the others the relationship is just the reverse. In fact, I would go even further and assert that the two applications are so closely related that neither can be practiced without the other. To be specific, however, and to deal with matters which are most similar to the interpretation of written works, I would strongly recommend diligence in interpreting significant conversations. The immediate presence of the speaker, the living expression that proclaims that his whole being is involved, the way the thoughts in a conversation develop from our shared life, such factors stimulate us, far more than some solitary observation of an isolated text, to understand a series of thoughts as a moment of life which is breaking forth, as one moment set in the context of many others. And this dimension of understanding is often slighted, in fact, almost completely neglected, in interpreting authors. When we compare the two, it would be better to say that we see two parts rather than two forms of the same task. To be sure, when something strange in a language blocks our understanding, we must try to overcome the difficulty. But even if we do come to understand this strange element, we may still find ourselves blocked because we cannot grasp the co-

herence of what someone is saying. And if neither approach is able to overcome the difficulty, the problem may well go unsolved.

To return then to the explanations we mentioned above, I must first lodge a protest against Wolf's claim that hermeneutics should ascertain the thoughts of an author with a necessary insight.[819] I do not mean to suggest that I consider this demand too stringent. To the contrary, for many cases it is not too stringent at all. Yet I am afraid that by stating the task in these terms, many cases for which this formulation of the problem is simply not appropriate would be passed over, and I do not want them to be overlooked. There are, of course, many instances in which one can prove that a given word in its context must mean "this" and nothing else, although such proof is difficult to find without recourse to those investigations into the nature of word meanings which Wolf, perhaps too summarily, has rejected. And, taking up a position somewhere outside of this circle, one may put together a number of these elementary proofs in order to arrive at a satisfactory proof of the sense of a sentence. But how many other cases there are—and they are crucial for interpreting the New Testament, especially—where a necessary insight is impossible, and interpreters come to equally probable meanings according to their points of view. Even in the field of criticism it often happens that some know no other way to oppose the result of a thorough investigation than to claim that some other meaning is still "possible." Of course, in the long run such remonstrances do not accomplish very much, but until each and every such possibility has been definitively eliminated, there can be no talk of a necessary insight. And if we go further and remember how advisable it is to undertake the difficult task of establishing the coherence of thoughts in the larger sections of the text, and to ascertain the hidden supplements of, as it were, lost intimations, then understanding is not only, as Wolf portrays it, a matter of collating and summarizing minute historical moments. Rather it becomes sensitive to the particular way an author combines the thoughts, for had those thoughts been formulated differently, even in the same historical situation and the same kind of presentation, the result would have been different. In such cases we may be fully convinced of our view, and it may even be convincing to our contemporaries who are engaged in similar studies. Nonetheless, it would be futile to try to pass this account off as a demonstration. This is not said to dis-

_____

819. Wolf, 37.

parage such studies, but in this area, especially, we may cite the otherwise rather paradoxical words of a distinguished scholar who has only recently been taken from us: an assertion is much more than a proof.[820] Moreover, there exists a completely different sort of certainty than the critical one for which Wolf is praised, namely, a divinatory certainty which arises when an interpreter delves as deeply as possible into an author's state of mind [*Verfassung*].[821] Thus it is often the case, as the Platonic rhapsodist admits, though quite naively, that he is able to offer an outstanding interpretation of Homer, but frequently cannot shed light on other writers, whether poets or prosaists.[822] For, provided the knowledge is available to him, an interpreter can and should show himself to be equally competent in every area related to language and to the historical situation of a people and of an age. Yet, just as in life we are most successful in understanding our friends, so a skillful interpreter is most successful in correctly interpreting an author's process of drafting and composing a work, the product of his personal distinctiveness in language and in all his relationships, when the author is among those favorites with whom he is best acquainted. For works of other authors, however, an interpreter will content himself with knowing less about these things; he will not feel ashamed to seek help from colleagues who are closer to them. In fact, it might be maintained that the entire practice of interpretation is to be divided as follows. One class of interpreters deals more with the language and with history than with personalities, granting equal consideration to all of the authors who write in a given language, regardless of the fact that the authors excel in different areas. A second class of interpreters, however, deals primarily with the observation of persons, regarding the language merely as the medium by which persons express their history and as the modality within which they exist. Thus each interpreter limits himself to that writer who is most readily understandable to him. This description may well be accurate except that writers of the latter group come less frequently to public attention because their work is less susceptible to polemical discussions, and they enjoy the fruits of each other's labors in quiet contentment. Still, several passages indicate that Wolf has by no means completely overlooked this side of interpretation, but, at least in part, has taken into account that certainty which we have described as more divinatory than demonstrable. It is worthwhile for us to investigate one of these places more closely.

In his *Compendium* Ast presents grammar, hermeneutics and criticism together as correlated disciplines without adding anything else as related knowledge. But we have no way of comprehending how they are interrelated because he relegates them to an appendix. Wolf, however, does not consider these three alone sufficient for an organon of the science of antiquity, but adds to them fluency in style and the art of composition, which, because it includes poetry, involves classical meter.[823] At first glance this is very surprising. For my own part I would have been content to have understood the fluency in ancient styles of writing—and in the case of the languages of antiquity this is the only aspect of composition we are discussing—as the mature fruit of long-term studies in the science of antiquity. For one must have lived just as fully and vigorously in the ancient world as in the present, and one must be keenly aware of all the forms of human existence and of the special nature of the surrounding objects at that time, in order to excel in weaving such graceful patterns based on set formulae and to form in Roman and Hellenistic ideas works which can affect us deeply even today, and to reproduce these in the most ancient way possible. How then can Wolf demand such art from us as the admission fee, so to speak, to the shrine of the science of antiquity? And by what honest means are we supposed to obtain it? Assuming there is no magical way, I see no other than that of tradition and that of adopting a procedure that is, fortunately, not merely imitative, but also divinatory—methods that would ultimately lead to fluency as the fruits of study. This path leads us in a kind of circle for we cannot gain a style of writing Latin—for which we must know Greek as well—in the same immediate way as those who, by virtue of having Latin and Greek as their native languages, developed their stylistic fluency from their immediate existence and not from such studies as these. Nor had I expected Wolf to demand a knowledge of meter. It seemed to me that this was one of the more specialized aspects of the science of antiquity rather than an essential part of the ancient theory of art. It had as much to do with the science of orchestration as with the science of poetry, and the theory of prose rhythm and declamation which was drawn from it represents the whole development of the national temper as shown in the character of artistic movements.

But let us put meter aside, for regardless of what is in-

820. According to Patsch, "Zur Frühgeschichte der romantischen Hermeneutik," Schleiermacher is referring to Friedrich Schlegel, who died January 12, 1829.

821. Wolf, 240–41.

822. See Plato, *Ion*, 530c–531d.

823. Wolf, 42–44.

volved in one's fluency in ancient composition, the true key to this Wolfian research is the following: Wolf does not require this fluency directly for the specialized disciplines of the science of antiquity, but for hermeneutics, that is, for gaining a correct and complete understanding in the higher sense of the term. And although he does not especially emphasize it, it is obvious, with respect to both criticism and meter, that his entry to the shrine of the science of antiquity is founded on two steps. The lower step is grammar, in his view the foundation of hermeneutics and criticism, and the fluency of style. The higher step is hermeneutics and criticism. Now just as Wolf sets forth his grammar in great detail and not in the elementary way which we could use with beginning students, so, too, we may be certain that by fluency of style he is not referring to the Latin exercises done in our high schools, which are skilled imitations and applications of grammatical knowledge. But since it is also certain that only a person who had worked through the entire literature of antiquity could perform the actual operation which the ancients did in the two languages in a free and individual fashion, is it perhaps possible that this great scholar is referring to something other than a knowledge of the various forms of presentation, their limits and possibilities, which is acquired by actual practice?[824] And this other element is of great influence on that less demonstrable aspect of the art of interpretation which is oriented toward the internal intellectual activity of an author. Herewith a new understanding of this side of interpretation is opened to us, and surely Wolf had it in mind, even though he did not give it much emphasis at the beginning of his exposition.[825]

In essence, then, the matter is as follows. When we view, on the one hand, the different forms of outstanding oratorical art and, on the other hand, the different types of style used for scientific and commercial activities which have developed in a language, it is evident that the entire history of literature is divided into two contrasting periods, the characteristics of which may later reappear simultaneously, but only in a subordinate fashion. The first period is that in which these forms are gradually developed; the second is that in which they predominate. And if the task of hermeneutics is to reproduce the whole internal process of an author's way of combining thoughts, then it is necessary to know with as much certainty as possible to which of these two periods he belongs. For if an author belongs to the first period, he was creating purely from his own resources, and from the intensity of his production and his linguistic power we may conclude not only that he produced a distinctive work, but that to a certain ex-

tent he originated a new type of work, which persists in the language. The same thing may be said, although not in such strong terms, about every author who especially modified these forms, introduced new elements in them, or founded a new style in them. However, the more a writer belongs in the second period and so does not produce the form but composes work in forms which are already established, the more we must know these forms in order to understand his activity. Even in the initial conception of a work, an author is guided by the established form. Its power affects the arrangement and organization of the works, and its particular laws close off certain areas of language and certain modifications of ideas, and opens up others. Thus the power of the form modifies not only the expression, but also—and the two can never be fully separated—the content. Consequently, an interpreter who does not see correctly how the stream of thinking and composing at once crash against and recoil from the walls of its bed and is diverted into a course other than it would have taken by itself cannot correctly understand the internal movement of the composition. Even less can he ascertain the author's true relation to the language and to its forms. He will not become aware of how an author may have more fully and forcefully expressed the images and thought which inspired him had he not been restricted by a form which in many respects conflicted with his personal individuality. He will not know how to assess correctly an author who would not have ventured very far into a genre had he not stood within the protective and guiding power of a form, for a form may aid as well as limit an author. And of the two kinds of authors he will not sufficiently appreciate the one who, rather than struggle with a form, is stimulated just as freely by an existing form as if he had just produced it himself. This insight into an author's relationship to the forms imbedded in his literature is such an essential aspect of interpretation that without it neither the whole nor the parts can be correctly understood. There is no doubt, of course, that Wolf is right to maintain that an interpreter cannot "divine" correctly unless he himself has experienced how an author can work within the given limits and rules which exist in a language and how he may struggle against them. And though here as elsewhere the comparative operation is set over against the divinatory, it cannot replace it completely. For how are we to find a point for beginning the compara-

---

824. Ibid., 36–37.

825. Ibid., 42–44.

tive operation if it is not given by a proper search? And it is for this reason that meter is to be considered, since the emphasis on the syllables of a poetical composition is essentially a matter of choosing expressions and since the position of the thoughts is conditioned by the form. And it is in the influence which this exercises on their work that the different relations to the clearest passages are to be found. Yet in all the languages with which we are dealing here the relationship between the content and the form during the process of composition is essentially and in the main the same. And so I would not insist as strongly as Wolf that the training necessary for interpretation must be acquired solely from practice in the ancient languages. Were that necessary, I would not be able to understand why the Roman language was able to supplant the Greek.

I want to underscore here a consideration about the character which these exercises will always display when we apply ourselves to the thoughts in the literature of a given language, because several significant conclusions are to be developed from what has been written above. We must always remember that whenever we practice this art, we must remain conscious of both methods, the divinatory and the comparative. This rule is so universal that, on the one hand, we can regard an immediate understanding, in which no particular mediating activities can be detected, as a temporarily indistinguishable combination and interaction of the two methods and, on the other hand, we can see that even the most complex applications of the art of interpretation involve nothing other than a constant shifting from the one method to the other. In this interaction the results of the one method must approximate more and more those of the other. Otherwise, very few satisfactory conclusions can be gained. This distinction between the more grammatical aspect, which aims at understanding the discourse in terms of the totality of language, and the more psychological aspect, which aims at understanding the discourse in terms of a continuous production of thoughts, is based on the following premise. Just as both methods are necessary to obtain complete understanding, so every combination of the one method will be supplemented by further applications of the other.

We must ask, then, whether these two methods apply to both the grammatical and technical aspects of interpretation, or whether each method is appropriate for only one aspect. For example, when Wolf, on the basis of the role he assigns to meter and fluency in composition, tries to argue that only a comparative procedure can be used for the more psycho-

logical aspect of interpretation, is he implying that the other, more grammatical aspect must be furthered by the divinatory method? His essay does not provide us with a direct and definitive answer to this question. But his investigations into the meanings of words and the senses of sentences, although not organized in a very helpful fashion, evidently have to do only with the grammatical aspect of interpretation and require a comparative method.[826]

An examination of the task itself leads to the same conclusion. All grammatical difficulties are overcome by a comparative operation alone, by repeatedly comparing what is already understood with what is not yet understood, so that what is not understood is confined within even narrower bounds. And, on the other side, the finest fruit of all esthetic criticism of artistic works is a heightened understanding of the intimate operations of poets and other artists of language by means of grasping their entire process of composition, from its conception up to the final execution. Indeed, if there is any truth to the dictum that the height of understanding is to understand an author better than he understood himself, this must be it. And in our literature we possess a considerable number of critical works which have performed this task with good success.[827] But how is such success possible except by a comparative procedure which helps us gain a thorough understanding about where and how an author has gone beyond or lagged behind others, and in what respects his kind of work is related to or different from theirs? Nonetheless, it is certain that the grammatical side of interpretation cannot dispense with the divinatory method. For whenever we come upon a gifted author [*genialer Autor*] who has for the first time in the history of the language expressed a given phrase or combination of terms, what do we want to do? In such instances only a divinatory method enables us rightly to reconstruct the creative act that begins with the generation of thoughts which captivate the author and to understand how the requirement of the moment could draw upon the living treasure of words in the author's mind in order to produce just this way of putting it and no other. But here, too, our conclusions will be uncertain unless the comparative operation is applied to the psychological aspect.

Therefore, we must answer the question before us as follows. If our first reading of a text does not immediately

---

826. Ibid., 37.

827. Here the basic hermeneutical principle of the "psychological" interpretation of "composition" is interpreted as an inner "process."

give us a certain and complete understanding, then we must employ both methods in both aspects—though naturally in varying degrees according to the difference of their objects—until the result approximates as nearly as possible that of immediate understanding. We surely must accept what I have said about one class of interpreters inclining more to the psychological and another to the grammatical aspect. We know that many a virtuoso in grammatical interpretation gives scant attention to the internal process of combining thoughts in one's mind and feeling. And, vice versa, there are fine interpreters who reflect about the special relationship of a text to its language only minimally and then only in those rare cases when they are forced to consult a dictionary. If we take this into account and apply it equally to the two methods, we must conclude that just as we can regard immediate and instantaneous understanding as having arisen in either way, thus directing our attention to the author's creativity or to the objective totality of the language, so we can regard the successful completion of a more artful method in interpretation in these same terms. We can now say that all of the points of comparison, for the psychological as well as for the grammatical aspects, have been brought together so perfectly that we no longer need to consider the divinatory method and its results. We can then add that the divinatory operation has been conducted with such thoroughness and precision that the comparative method is rendered superfluous. Likewise, the internal process has been made so transparent by the divinatory and the comparative methods that, since what has been intuited is a thought, and there is no thought without words, the entire relationship between the production of the thoughts and its formation in language is now fully and immediately evident. But the reverse would also be true.

Yet, even as I am dealing here with the completion of the operation, I am driven back almost involuntarily to the very beginning in order to encompass the whole within these two points. This very beginning, however, is the same as when children begin to understand language. How, then, do our formulae apply to these beginnings? Children do not yet have language but are seeking it. Nor do they know the activity of thinking, because there is no thinking without words. With what aspect, then, do they begin? They do not yet have any points of comparison, but they acquire them gradually as a foundation for a comparative operation that, to be sure, develops remarkably fast. Are we not tempted to say that each child produces both thinking and language originally, and that either each child out of himself by virtue of an inner

necessity engenders them in a way that coincides with the way it had happened in others or gradually as he becomes capable of a comparative procedure he approximates others? But in fact this inner movement toward producing thoughts on one's own, although initially stimulated by others, is the same as that which we have called "the divinatory." This divinatory operation, therefore, is original, and the soul [*die Seele*] shows itself to be wholly and inherently a prescient being [*ein ahndendes Wesen*]. But with what an enormous, almost infinite, power of expression does the child begin! It cannot be likened to later developments, nor to anything else. The two ways must be grasped simultaneously as essentially one, since each supports the other, and only gradually are the two distinguished, as the language objectifies itself by fixing particular words to objects and to images which themselves become increasingly clear and certain. But at the same time the act of thinking is able—how should I say—to use these in order to reproduce them, or to reproduce them in order to grasp them. These first activities of thinking and knowing are so astonishing that it seems to me that when we smile at the false applications which children make of the elements of language they have acquired—and to be sure often with all too great consistency—we do so only in order to find consolation or even to take revenge for this excess of energy which we are no longer able to expend.

Viewed in this light, whenever we do not understand we find ourselves in the same situation as the children although not to the same degree. Even in what is familiar we encounter something that is unusual in the language, when a combination of words does not become evident to us, when a train of thought strikes us as odd, even though it is analogous to our own, [or] when the connection between the various parts of a train of thought or its extension remains uncertain and hovers unsteadily before us. On such occasions, we can always begin with the same divinatory boldness. Therefore, we ought not simply contrast our present situation to those immense beginnings in childhood, for the process of understanding and interpretation is a whole which develops constantly and gradually, and in its later stages we must aid each other more and more, since each offers to others points of comparison and similarities which themselves begin in this same divinatory way. This is the gradual self-discovery of the thinking self. But, just as the circulation of blood and the rhythm of breathing gradually diminish, so the soul, too, the more it possesses, becomes more sluggish, in inverse proportion to its receptivity. This is true of even the most active people. Since each person, as an individual, is the not-being of the other, it is never possible to eliminate non-understanding completely. But although the speed of the hermeneutical operation diminishes after its early stages, a more deliberate movement and a longer duration of each aspect enhance this process.

Finally there comes that period when hermeneutical experiences are collected and become guidelines—for I prefer to call them this rather than rules. A technical theory, however, cannot develop, as should be obvious from what I have said, until we have penetrated the language of an author in its objectivity and the process of producing thoughts, as a function of the life of the individual mind, in relationship to the nature of thinking. For only in these terms can the way thoughts are combined and communicated and the way understanding takes place be explicated in a fully coherent fashion.

Yet in order to clarify fully the relationship between these two operations, we must give due attention first to a notion which seems to give Ast the advantage over Wolf, although until we fully determine the form of hermeneutics from it, it seems to be more a discovery than an invention. This is the notion that any part of a text can be understood only by means of an understanding of the whole, and that for this reason every explanation of a given element already presupposes that the whole has been understood.

From Friedrich Schleiermacher, "The Academy Addresses of 1829: On the Concept of Hermeneutics, with Reference to F. A. Wolf's Instructions and Ast's Textbook," in *Hermeneutical Inquiry,* vol. 1, *The Interpretation of Texts,* edited by David E. Klemm (Atlanta, GA: Scholars Press, 1986), 61–75.

❧ The German theologian and philosopher **David Friedrich Strauss** (1808–74) applies his methods of biblical interpretation in "Annunciation and Birth of the Baptist: Mythical View of the Narrative in Its Different Stages," in his *The Life of Jesus Critically Examined* (originally published in four editions from 1835 to 1904).

DAVID FRIEDRICH STRAUSS

"Annunciation and Birth of the Baptist: Mythical View of the Narrative in Its Different Stages," in *The Life of Jesus Critically Examined,* §19

The above exposition of the necessity, and lastly, of the possibility of doubting the historical fidelity of the gospel narrative, has led many theologians to explain the account of the birth of the Baptist as a poetical composition; suggested by the importance attributed by the Christians to the fore-runner of Jesus, and by the recollection of some of the Old Testament histories, in which the births of Ishmael, Isaac, Samuel, and especially of Samson, are related to have been similarly announced. Still the matter was not allowed to be altogether invented. It may have been historically true that Zacharias and Elizabeth lived long without offspring; that, on one occasion whilst in the temple, the old man's tongue was suddenly paralyzed; but that soon afterwards his aged wife bore him a son, and he, in his joy at the event, recovered the power of speech. At that time, but still more when John became a remarkable man, the history excited attention, and out of it the existing legend grew.

It is surprising to find an explanation almost identical with the natural one we have criticised above, again brought forward under a new title; so that the admission of the possibility of an admixture of subsequent legends in the narrative has little influence on the view of the matter itself. As the mode of explanation we are now advocating denies all confidence in the historical authenticity of the record, all the details must be in themselves equally problematic; and whether historical validity can be retained for this or that particular incident can be determined only by its being either less improbable than the rest, or else less in harmony with the spirit, interest, and design of the poetic legend, so as to make it probable that it had a distinct origin. The barrenness of Elizabeth and the sudden dumbness of Zacharias are here retained as incidents of this character: so that only the appearing and prediction of the angel are given up. But by taking away the angelic apparition, the sudden infliction and as sudden removal of the dumbness loses its only adequate supernatural cause, so that all difficulties which beset the natural interpretation remain in full force: a dilemma into which these theologians are, most unnecessarily, brought by their own inconsequence; for the moment we enter upon mythical ground, all obligation to hold fast the assumed historical fidelity of the account ceases to exist. Besides, that which they propose to retain as historical fact, namely, the long barrenness of the parents of the Baptist, is so strictly in harmony with the spirit and character of Hebrew legendary poetry, that of this incident the mythical origin is least to be mistaken. How confused has this misapprehension made, for example, the reasoning of Bauer! It was a prevailing opinion, says he, consonant with Jewish ideas, that all children born of aged parents, who had previously been childless, became distinguished personages. John was the child of aged parents, and became a notable preacher of repentance; consequently it was thought justifiable to infer that his birth was predicted by an angel. What an illogical conclusion! for which he has no other ground than the assumption that John was the son of aged parents. Let this be made a settled point, and the conclusion follows without difficulty. It was readily believed, he proceeds, of remarkable men that they were born of aged parents, and that their birth, no longer in the ordinary course of nature to be expected, was announced by a heavenly messenger; John was a great man and a prophet; consequently, the legend represented him to have been born of an aged couple, and his birth to have been proclaimed by an angel.

Seeing that this explanation of the narrative before us, as a half (so called historical) mythus, is encumbered with all the difficulties of a half measure, Gabler has treated it as a pure philosophical, or dogmatical, mythus. Horst likewise considers it, and indeed the entire two first chapters of Luke, of which it forms a part, as an ingenious fiction, in which the birth of the Messiah, together with that of his precursor, and the predictions concerning the character and ministry of the latter, framed after the event, are set forth; it being precisely the loquacious circumstantiality of the narration which betrays the poet. Schleiermacher likewise explains the first chapter as a little poem, similar in character to many of the Jewish poems which we meet with in their apocrypha. He does not however consider it altogether a fabrication. It might have had a foundation in fact, and in a widespread tradition; but the poet has allowed himself so full a license in arranging, and combining, in moulding and embodying the vague and fluctuating representations of tradition that the attempt to detect the purely historical in such narratives must prove a fruitless and useless effort. Horst goes so far as to suppose the author of the piece to have been a Judaising Christian; whilst Schleiermacher imagines it to have been composed by a Christian of the famed Jewish school, at a period when it comprised some who still continued strict disciples of John; and whom it was the object of the narrative to bring over to Christianity, by exhibiting the relationship of John to the Christ as his peculiar and highest destiny; and also by holding out the expectation of a state of temporal greatness for the Jewish people at the reappearance of Christ.

An attentive consideration of the Old Testament histories, to which, as most interpreters admit, the narrative of the annunciation and birth of the Baptist bears a striking affinity, will render it abundantly evident that this is the only just view of the passage in question. But it must not here be imagined, as is now so readily affirmed in the confutation of the mythical view of this passage, that the author of our narrative first

made a collection from the Old Testament of its individual traits; much rather had the scattered traits respecting the late birth of different distinguished men, as recorded in the Old Testament, blended themselves into a compound image in the mind of their reader, whence he selected the features most appropriate to his present subject. Of the children born of aged parents, Isaac is the most ancient prototype. As it is said of Zacharias and Elizabeth, "they both were advanced in their days"[828] προβεβηκότες ἐν ταῖς ἡμέραις αὐτῶν, so Abraham and Sarah "were advanced in their days" בָּאִים בַּיָּמִים,[829] when they were promised a son. It is likewise from this history that the incredulity of the father, on account of the advanced age of both parents, and the demand of a sign, are borrowed in our narrative. As Abraham, when Jehovah promises him he shall have a son and a numerous posterity who shall inherit the land of Canaan, doubtingly inquires, "Whereby shall I know that I shall inherit it?" κατὰ τί γνώσομαι αὐτήν ὅτι κληρονομήσω,[830] so Zacharias—"Whereby shall I know this?" κατὰ τί γνώσομαι τοῦτο. The incredulity of Sarah is not made use of for Elizabeth; but she is said to be of the daughters of Aaron, and the name Elizabeth may perhaps have been suggested by that of Aaron's wife.[831] The incident of the angel announcing the birth of the Baptist is taken from the history of another late-born child, Samson. In our narrative indeed, the angel appears first to the father in the temple, whereas in the history of Samson he shows himself first to the mother, and afterwards to the father in the field. This, however, is an alteration arising naturally out of the different situations of the respective parents.[832] According to popular Jewish notions, it was no unusual occurrence for the priest to be visited by angels and divine apparitions whilst offering incense in the temple. The command which before his birth predestined the Baptist—whose later ascetic mode of life was known—to be a Nazarite, is taken from the same source. As, to Samson's mother during her pregnancy, wine, strong drink, and unclean food were forbidden, so a similar diet is prescribed for her son, adding, as in the case of John, that the child shall be consecrated to God from the womb. The blessings which it is predicted that these two men shall realize for the people of Israel are similar,[833] and

---

828. [Gen 15:]7.

829. Gen 18:11; Septuagint: προβεβηκότες ἡμερῶν.

830. sc. τὴν γῆν. Gen 15:8, 18. Septuagint.

831. Ex 6:23. Septuagint.

832. Judg 13.

833. Cf. Lk 1:16, 17, with Judg 13:5.

each narrative concludes with the same expression respecting the hopeful growth of the child. It may be too bold to derive the Levitical descent of the Baptist from a third Old Testament history of a late-born son—from the history of Samuel;[834] but the lyric effusions in the first chapter of Luke are imitations of this history. As Samuel's mother, when consigning him to the care of the high priest, breaks forth into a hymn,[835] so the father of John does the same at the circumcision; though the particular expressions in the Canticle uttered by Mary—of which we shall have to speak hereafter—have a closer resemblance to Hannah's song of praise than that of Zacharias. The significant appellation *John* (יְתוֹתָנָן = Θεόχαρις), predetermined by the angel, had its precedent in the announcements of the names of Ishmael and Isaac;[836] but the ground of its selection was the apparently providential coincidence between the signification of the name and the historical destination of the man. The remark, that the name of John was not in the family,[837] only brought its celestial origin more fully into view. The tablet (πινακίδιον) upon which the father wrote the name,[838] was necessary on account of his incapacity to speak; but it also had its type in the Old Testament. Isaiah was commanded to write the significant names of the child Maher-shalal-hash-baz upon a tablet.[839] The only supernatural incident of the narrative, of which the Old Testament may seem to offer no precise analogy, is the dumbness; and this is the point fixed upon by those who contest the mythical view. But if it be borne in mind that the asking and receiving a sign from heaven in confirmation of a promise or prophecy was usual among the Hebrews;[840] that the temporary loss of one of the senses was the peculiar punishment inflicted after a heavenly vision;[841] that Daniel became dumb whilst the angel was talking with him, and did not recover his speech till the angel had touched his lips and opened his mouth:[842] the origin of this incident also will be found in the legend, and not in historical fact. Of two ordinary and subordinate features of the narrative, the one, the righteousness of the parents of the Baptist,[843] is merely a conclusion founded upon the belief that to a pious couple alone would the blessing of such a son be vouchsafed, and consequently is void of all historical worth; the other, the statement that John was born in the reign of Herod (the Great),[844] is without doubt a correct calculation.

So that we stand here upon purely mythical-poetical ground; the only historical reality which we can hold fast as positive matter of fact being this:—the impression made by John the Baptist, by virtue of his ministry and his relation to Jesus, was so powerful as to lead to the subsequent glorifica-

tion of his birth in connection with the birth of the Messiah in the Christian legend.

From David Friedrich Strauss, *The Life of Jesus Critically Examined*, edited by Peter C. Hodgson, translated by George Eliot (Philadelphia: Fortress Press, 1972), 104–7.

✎ **Elizabeth Cady Stanton** (1815–1902), an American leader in the women's rights movement, published *The Woman's Bible* in 1895. In the Preface, she lays out her objectives in editing *The Woman's Bible*. "Comments on Genesis" (introduced by Lillie Devereux Blake, a member of the Revising Committee) puts into practice the methodology Stanton advocates.

ELIZABETH CADY STANTON

The Woman's Bible

Preface

So many letters are daily received asking questions about the Woman's Bible—as to the extent of the revision, and the standpoint from which it will be conducted—that it seems best, though every detail is not as yet matured, to state the plan, as concisely as possible, upon which those who have been in consultation during the summer, propose to do the work.

I. The object is to revise only those texts and chapters directly referring to women, and those also in which women are made prominent by exclusion. As all such passages combined form but one-tenth of the Scriptures, the undertaking will not be so laborious as, at the first thought, one would imagine. These texts, with the commentaries, can easily be compressed into a duodecimo volume of about four hundred pages.

II. The commentaries will be of a threefold character, the writers in the different branches being selected according to their special aptitude for the work:

1. Two or three Greek and Hebrew scholars will devote themselves to the translation and the meaning of particular words and texts in the original.

---

834. Cf. I Sam 1:1; I Chr 7:27.   840. Cf. Isa 7:2ff.
835. I Sam 2:1.   841. Acts 9:8, 17ff.
836. Gen. 16:11 (Septuagint).   842. Dan 10:15f.
837. [Lk 1:]61.   843. [Lk 1:]6.
838. [Lk 1:]63.   844. [Lk 1:]5.
839. Isa 8:1ff.

2. Others will devote themselves to Biblical history, old manuscripts, to the new version, and to the latest theories as to the occult meaning of certain texts and parables.

3. For the commentaries on the plain English version a committee of some thirty members has been formed. These are women of earnestness and liberal ideas, quick to see the real purport of the Bible as regards their sex. Among them the various books of the Old and New Testament will be distributed for comment.

III. There will be two or more editors to bring the work of the various committees into one consistent whole.

IV. The completed work will be submitted to an advisory committee assembled at some central point, as London, New York, or Chicago, to sit in final judgment on "The Woman's Bible."

As to the manner of doing the practical work:

Those who have been engaged this summer have adopted the following plan, which may be suggestive to new members of the committee. Each person purchased two Bibles, ran through them from Genesis to Revelations, marking all the texts that concerned women. The passages were cut out, and pasted in a blank book, and the commentaries then written underneath.

Those not having time to read all the books can confine their labors to the particular ones they propose to review.

It is thought best to publish the different parts as soon as prepared so that the Committee may have all in print in a compact form before the final revision.

August 1st, 1895.   E[lizabeth]. C[ady]. S[tanton].

Introduction

From the inauguration of the movement for woman's emancipation the Bible has been used to hold her in the "divinely ordained sphere," prescribed in the Old and New Testaments.

The canon and civil law; church and state; priests and legislators; all political parties and religious denominations have alike taught that woman was made after man, of man, and for man, an inferior being, subject to man. Creeds, codes, Scriptures and statutes, are all based on this idea. The fashions, forms, ceremonies and customs of society, church ordinances and discipline all grow out of this idea.

Of the old English common law, responsible for woman's civil and political status, Lord Brougham said, "it is a disgrace to the civilization and Christianity of the Nineteenth Century." Of the canon law, which is responsible for woman's status in the church, Charles Kingsley said, "this will never be

a good world for women until the last remnant of the canon law is swept from the face of the earth."

The Bible teaches that woman brought sin and death into the world, that she precipitated the fall of the race, that she was arraigned before the judgment seat of Heaven, tried, condemned and sentenced. Marriage for her was to be a condition of bondage, maternity a period of suffering and anguish, and in silence and subjection, she was to play the role of a dependent on man's bounty for all her material wants, and for all the information she might desire on the vital questions of the hour, she was commanded to ask her husband at home. Here is the Bible position of woman briefly summed up. . . .

E[lizabeth]. C[ady]. S[tanton].

Comments on Genesis 3

Note the significant fact that we always hear of the "fall of man," not the fall of woman, showing that the consensus of human thought has been more unerring than masculine interpretation. Reading this narrative carefully, it is amazing that any set of men ever claimed that the dogma of the inferiority of woman is here set forth. The conduct of Eve from the beginning to the end is so superior to that of Adam. The command not to eat of the fruit of the tree of knowledge was given to the man alone before woman was formed.[845] Therefore the injunction was not brought to Eve with the impressive solemnity of a Divine Voice, but whispered to her by her husband and equal. It was a serpent supernaturally endowed, a seraphim as Scott and other commentators have claimed, who talked with Eve, and whose words might reasonably seem superior to the second-hand story of her companion—nor does the woman yield at once. She quotes the command not to eat of the fruit, to which the serpent replies "Dying ye shall not die,"[846] literal translation. In other words telling her that if the mortal body does perish, the immortal part shall live forever, and offering as the reward of her act the attainment of Knowledge.

Then the woman fearless of death if she can gain wisdom takes of the fruit; and all this time Adam standing beside her interposes no word of objection. "Her husband with her" are the words of verse 6. Had he been the representative of the divinely appointed head in married life, he assuredly would have taken upon himself the burden of the discussion with

---

845. Gen 2:17.
846. Gen 3:4.

the serpent, but no, he is silent in this crisis of their fate. Having had the command from God himself he interposes no word of warning or remonstrance, but takes the fruit from the hand of his wife without a protest. It takes six verses to describe the "fall" of woman, the fall of man is contemptuously dismissed in a line and a half.

The subsequent conduct of Adam was to the last degree dastardly. When the awful time of reckoning comes, and the Jehovah God appears to demand why his command has been disobeyed, Adam endeavors to shield himself behind the gentle being he has declared to be so dear. "The woman thou gavest to be with me, she gave me and I did eat," he whines—trying to shield himself at his wife's expense! Again we are amazed that upon such a story men have built up a theory of their superiority!

Then follows what has been called the curse. Is it not rather a prediction? First is the future fate of the serpent described, the enmity of the whole human race—"it shall lie in wait for thee as to the head."[847] Next the subjection of the woman is foretold, thy husband "shall rule over thee."[848] Lastly the long struggle of man with the forces of nature is portrayed. "In the sweat of thy face thou shalt eat food until thy turning back to the earth."[849] With the evolution of humanity an ever increasing number of men have ceased to toil for their bread with their hands, and with the introduction of improved machinery, and the uplifting of the race there will come a time when there shall be no severities of labor, and when women shall be freed from all oppressions.

"And Adam called his wife's name Life for she was the mother of all living."[850]

It is a pity that all versions of the Bible do not give this word instead of the Hebrew Eve. She was Life, the eternal mother, the first representative of the more valuable and important half of the human race.

L[illie]. D[evereux]. B[lake].

From Elizabeth Cady Stanton et al., eds., *The Woman's Bible*, part 1, *Comments on Genesis, Exodus, Leviticus, Numbers and Deuteronomy* (New York: European Publishing Co., 1895), 5–7, 26–27.

William Wrede (1859–1906) was a German Evangelical Lutheran. His critique of naïve historicism opened the way not only to traditio-historical study of the New Testament but also to literary (Form and Redaction) criticisms. Wrede discusses the problems of methodology in the introduction to his *Messianic Secret*, published in 1901.

Introduction to *The Messianic Secret*

Requisites for Research on Jesus' Life

Historical criticism has carried out painstaking work on the literary sources of Jesus' history. Assuredly it has not lacked its reward. Little may have been settled, but progress say since Strauss's *Leben Jesu* (1835) has been extensive and unmistakable.

There seems to be a less substantial gain to record in the primary task of making use of the sources for historical purposes.

In individual particulars these last decades are, of course, the period which, with its variety of fresh stimuli, has richly augmented our scholarly resources. Many are the transmitted sayings of Jesus that have come closer to being understood, and many the standpoints dominating the Gospels that have been more clearly opened up for us through our knowledge of the historical background.

But the two decisive questions are still these: What do we know of Jesus' life? and—a question with its own independent importance—What do we know of the history of the oldest views and representations of Jesus' life? The two questions can also be subsumed in one: How do we manage to dissect the Gospel tradition in these two directions: how do we separate what belongs properly to Jesus from what is the material of the primitive community?

Coming to the recent literature on Jesus' life (in the widest sense) with these questions in mind, one feels the onset of a sense of disappointment. Looked at more closely, this impression is seen to be in part the consequence of the unusual difficulties that inevitably attach to the subject itself; and in part to be attributable to the predominance of literary work on the sources, with its frequent obscuring of our awareness about the latest and chiefest undertakings of research. But in substantial measure it also stems from a defective critical method. This seems to become obvious specifically at three points.

First of all, it is indeed an axiom of historical criticism in general that what we have before us is actually just a later narrator's conception of Jesus' life and that this conception

---

847. [Gen 3:]15, literal translation.
848. [Gen 3:]16.
849. [Gen 3:]19, literal translation.
850. [Gen 3:]20, literal translation.

is not identical with the thing itself. But *the axiom exercises much too little influence.* As a rule it is remembered only when certain things shock us; which means essentially (1) where we find strictly miraculous features, (2) where there are manifest contradictions in the same source, and (3) where one report clashes with another. Where such shocks do not occur we feel, without going very deeply into it, that we are on firm ground in the life of Jesus itself, that we are through with criticism when by dint of work on the sources and reflections on the subject we have arrived at the oldest account.

There is no clarity of principle in this. I should never for an instant lose sight of my awareness that I have before me descriptions, the authors of which are later Christians, be they never so early—Christians who could only look at the life of Jesus with the eyes of their own time and who described it on the basis of the belief of the community, with all the viewpoints of the community, and with the needs of the community in mind. For there is no sure means of *straightforwardly* determining the part played in the accounts by the later view—sometimes a view with a variety of layers.

A second point is very closely bound up with this one. *We are in too great a hurry to leave the terrain of the evangelists' accounts.* We urgently want to utilise it for the history of Jesus itself. In order to do so features that cannot be credited are cut out and the meaning is worked out in such a way as to become historically serviceable; that is to say, *something which was not in the writer's mind is substituted for the account and represented as its historical content.* There is extremely little sensitivity to the tremendous precariousness of this procedure; but above all no questions are asked about whether the characteristic life which belongs to the account itself is eliminated by it. Our first task must always be only that of thoroughly illuminating the accounts on the basis of their own spirit and of asking what the narrator in his own time intended to say to his readers; and this work must be carried out to its conclusion and made the basis of criticism.

Thirdly, psychology is to be taken into account. By no means do I wish to speak here only of researchers—of whom there are many in different camps—who exhibit for every Gospel story such a precise knowledge of the historical circumstances and, specifically, such an intimacy with the inner life of Jesus that one might well doubt whether one is listening to a confidant of Jesus or reading a novel. I am also thinking about the fortunately numerous scholars who demonstrate more tact and reserve in this.

Psychology is all very well if it is a question of produc-

ing the necessary connection between fixed points or if its service is exploratory, where there is a strict check on the possibilities and necessities deriving from established facts or even, for the matter of that, from supposed facts. But scientifically psychology fails to carry conviction if the crucial points are not themselves determined or if there is a facile proffering of what may well be in itself conceivable as if it were already the real thing.

And this is the malady to which we must here allude—let us not dignify it with the euphemism "historical imagination." *The scientific study of the life of Jesus is suffering from psychological "suppositionitis"* which amounts to a sort of historical guesswork. For this reason interpretations to suit every taste proliferate. The number of arbitrary psychological interpretations in literature of facts, words and contexts in the Gospels is legion. Nor is it simply a matter of harmless superfluities. These interpretations at the same time form the basis for important structures of thought; and how often do people think that the task of criticism has already been discharged by playing tuneful psychological variations on a given factual theme!

I am by no means asserting that all work in this direction has been entirely useless, but it seems to me to be an urgent necessity that we should have done with subjective judgments. The psychological treatment of facts is permissible only when we know that they are indeed facts and even then we must still call a supposition a supposition. Otherwise there is a blunting of our awareness that scholarship finds value not in emotive descriptions which afford the reader pleasure but only in strict accuracy and certainty of knowledge; otherwise we will forget that we must at least always be *striving* for these things and that it is better to have a little real knowledge, whether positive or "negative," than a great assortment of spurious knowledge.

These reflections will appear somewhat presumptuous to the well-disposed, and even more to the ill-disposed, reader as I have done nothing to exemplify these maladies of criticism; and they will seem pointless so long as I do not say what observational basis I have for making these pronouncements. Let my readers then consider my remarks to be a sort of motto which I should like to prefix to the investigations which follow. To be sure those who read them will not find here by a long way everything I think I can offer by way of proof, but I hope that from a series of examples they will be able to see what my meaning is and that those in essential agreement with the investigation will lend the seal of their approval to the motto.

The Subject and the Sources, with Special Reference to Mark

The question of the messianic self-consciousness of Jesus which is exercising modern scholarship is far from the thoughts of the Gospel narrators; indeed for them it simply does not exist at all. From the beginning of his life or of his work, from his birth or his baptism, Jesus for them *is* objectively the Messiah. This naturally implies a corresponding consciousness, but the idea of this consciousness and of its genesis is not present. It would be a complete misunderstanding of the mind of these writers to presuppose that they had any ideas about the development of this consciousness.

On the other hand, the evangelists do offer us certain data relevant to the other question of *when Jesus was acknowledged as Messiah or when he made himself known as such.* If scholarship can reach the stage of making any certain pronouncements about Jesus' messianic consciousness from this starting-point, then it must manifestly be by way of inferences.

My intention in the following investigation is to subject these allegations, together with whatever else is relevant to them, to an examination. This, of course, is only a very provisional and inexact paraphrase of my intentions.

In this undertaking we must refer to all four Gospels. I would add to them the older extra-canonical Gospels of which we have some fragments, were it not possible to say at once that for the problem under consideration these have nothing worth mentioning to offer. The canonical Gospels must be considered separately. This is important.

With the great majority of modern critics I share the opinion that our Gospel of Mark, or something extremely like it, lies behind the two other synoptics. I naturally do not venture in making this assumption to solve *every* individual literary problem posed by the parallel portions of the three Gospels; but despite continued contradiction of it, the main point seems to me to be so well established that we may use it as the basis for new ventures.

If this thesis is correct and if the fourth Gospel must remain out of account as a completely secondary picture, then the whole burden of responsibility falls almost entirely on Mark in regard to all questions touching the authentic story of Jesus and in particular *the course and development of his life.* The reliability or unreliability of Mark's tradition in this connection is essentially decisive for the reliability or otherwise of the Gospel tradition as a whole. Mark must therefore stand in the forefront of our investigation.

Matthew and Luke, however, are not on this account valueless even when they themselves depend on Mark, nor of course is John. To hold them valueless can be the approach only of those for whom the question of the most primitive development of the *interpretation* of the life of Jesus gets lost to view behind the question of the real life of Jesus.

I am making no presupposition about the antiquity of Mark. There can be no talk as yet of a *proof* that it was written before AD 70. On the other hand, the usual arguments are also hardly sufficient really to guarantee a later date. Indeed researchers with essentially the same presuppositions now champion this view and now the other.

In the same way, however, I am also leaving completely open the question of the relationship of the Gospel to Peter. In an investigation of the kind we are undertaking the intrusion of such problems could only have a harmful effect. Everything to do with the internal circumstances of the Gospel must first be explored on its own account. Only afterwards can we ask whether the result favours the tradition of a Petrine basis for the Gospel or not.

As against this another presupposition must indeed be made: namely that the Markan narratives are something essentially other than records of Jesus' life taken down on the spot. This is to be sure a platitude, yet, on the other hand, there is nothing platitudinous about it when one sees that in practice criticism again mostly makes meagre use of this theoretically uncontested thesis.

At best Mark wrote something like thirty years after the events, and at best gave a free reproduction in part of his book of what an eyewitness had reported to him of his reminiscences, long enough before they were written down. It will suffice to refer to the doublet in the feeding stories (ch. 6 and ch. 8) to prove that he does not everywhere follow this eyewitness, if indeed he follows him at all. Everyone who knows anything about human tradition must admit that even when we make these favourable assumptions the faithfulness and exactness of individual reports becomes somewhat uncertain. If, on the other hand, one looks at how the critics go on drawing quite assured conclusions from the most inconsiderable and characterless details and from the position of sentences and phrases in the narrative, or from the appearance or absence of individual words or concepts, one should by rights believe in a miraculous process of transmission.

Yet another consideration is more to the point here and must be compelling at least for all those who recognise only historical standards in Gospel research. Mark actually has a large share of unhistorical narratives in his Gospel. No critical theologian believes his report on the baptism of Jesus, the raising of Jairus's daughter, the miraculous feedings, the walking of Jesus on the water, the transfiguration, or the conversation of the angel with the women at the tomb, in the sense in which he records them. If the theologian sees facts behind such information he is nevertheless compelled to grant that they have undergone a very substantial transformation and distortion, whether in the mind of Mark or otherwise.

Can this knowledge have no consequences for the rest of the Gospel's contents? A real distrust of concrete portions of the record naturally cannot have its basis here, nor should this lead to its being expressed. But we are certainly warned forcefully by the Gospel itself against a too ready confidence and from the start are challenged to check its contents rigorously. It is not a matter of indifference whether this is or is not clearly grasped by those coming to the Gospel. To bring a pinch of vigilance and skepticism to it is not to indulge a prejudice but to follow a clear hint from the Gospel itself.

From William Wrede, *The Messianic Secret,* translated by J. C. G. Greig (Greenwood, SC: Attic Press, 1971), 4–10.

✑ In the section entitled "Results" of his influential *Quest of the Historical Jesus* (published in 1913), **Albert Schweitzer** (1875–1965) provides the theological and hermeneutical framework that undergirds his critical study of the life of Jesus.

ALBERT SCHWEITZER

"Results," in *The Quest of the Historical Jesus*

Those who are fond of talking about negative theology can find their account here. There is nothing more negative than the result of the critical study of the Life of Jesus.

The Jesus of Nazareth who came forward publicly as the Messiah, who preached the ethic of the Kingdom of God, who founded the Kingdom of Heaven upon earth, and died to give His work its final consecration, never had any existence. He is a figure designed by rationalism, endowed with life by liberalism, and clothed by modern theology in an historical garb.

This image has not been destroyed from without, it has fallen to pieces, cleft and disintegrated by the concrete historical problems which came to the surface one after another, and in spite of all the artifice, art, artificiality, and violence which was applied to them, refused to be planed down to fit the design on which the Jesus of the theology of the last hundred and thirty years had been constructed, and were no sooner covered over than they appeared again in a new form.

The thoroughgoing skeptical and the thoroughgoing eschatological school have only completed the work of destruction by linking the problems into a system and so making an end of the *Divide et impera* of modern theology, which undertook to solve each of them separately, that is, in a less difficult form. Henceforth it is no longer permissible to take one problem out of the series and dispose of it by itself, since the weight of the whole hangs upon each.

Whatever the ultimate solution may be, the historical Jesus of whom the criticism of the future, taking as its starting-point the problems which have been recognised and admitted, will draw the portrait, can never render modern theology the services which it claimed from its own half-historical, half-modern, Jesus. He will be a Jesus, who was Messiah, and lived as such, either on the ground of a literary fiction of the earliest Evangelist, or on the ground of a purely eschatological Messianic conception.

In either case, He will not be a Jesus Christ to whom the religion of the present can ascribe, according to its long-cherished custom, its own thoughts and ideas, as it did with the Jesus of its own making. Nor will He be a figure which can be made by a popular historical treatment so sympathetic and universally intelligible to the multitude. The historical Jesus will be to our time a stranger and an enigma.

The study of the Life of Jesus has had a curious history. It set out in quest of the historical Jesus, believing that when it had found Him it could bring Him straight into our time as a Teacher and Saviour. It loosed the bands by which He had been riveted for centuries to the stony rocks of ecclesiastical doctrine, and rejoiced to see life and movement coming into the figure once more, and the historical Jesus advancing, as it seemed, to meet it. But He does not stay; He passes by our time and returns to His own. What surprised and dismayed the theology of the last forty years was that, despite all forced and arbitrary interpretations, it could not keep Him in our time, but had to let Him go. He returned to His own time, not owing to the application of any historical ingenuity, but by the same inevitable necessity by which the liberated pendulum returns to its original position.

The historical foundation of Christianity as built up by rationalistic, by liberal, and by modern theology no longer exists; but that does not mean that Christianity has lost its historical foundation. The work which historical theology thought itself bound to carry out, and which fell to pieces just as it was nearing completion, was only the brick facing of the real immovable historical foundation which is independent of any historical confirmation or justification.

Jesus means something to our world because a mighty spiritual force streams forth from Him and flows through our time also. This fact can neither be shaken nor confirmed by any historical discovery. It is the solid foundation of Christianity.

The mistake was to suppose that Jesus could come to mean more to our time by entering into it as a man like ourselves. That is not possible. First because such a Jesus never existed. Secondly because, although historical knowledge can no doubt introduce greater clearness into an existing spiritual life, it cannot call spiritual life into existence. History can destroy the present; it can reconcile the present with the past; can even to a certain extent transport the present into the past; but to contribute to the making of the present is not given unto it.

But it is impossible to over-estimate the value of what German research upon the Life of Jesus has accomplished. It is a uniquely great expression of sincerity, one of the most significant events in the whole mental and spiritual life of humanity. What has been done for the religious life of the present and the immediate future by scholars such as P. W. Schmidt, Bousset, Jülicher, Weinel, Wernle—and their pupil Frenssen—and the others who have been called to the task of bringing to the knowledge of wider circles, in a form which is popular without being superficial, the results of religious-historical study only becomes evident when one examines the literature and social culture of the Latin nations, who have been scarcely if at all touched by the influence of these thinkers.

And yet the time of doubt was bound to come. We modern theologians are too proud of our historical method, too proud of our historical Jesus, too confident in our belief in the spiritual gains which our historical theology can bring to the world. The thought that we could build up by the increase of historical knowledge a new and vigorous Christianity and set free new spiritual forces rules us like a fixed idea, and prevents us from seeing that the task which we have grappled with and in some measure discharged is only one of the intellectual preliminaries of the great religious task. We thought that it was for us to lead our time by a roundabout way through the historical Jesus, as we understood Him, in order to bring it to the Jesus who is a spiritual power in the present. This roundabout way has now been closed by genuine history.

There was a danger of our thrusting ourselves between men and the Gospels, and refusing to leave the individual man alone with the sayings of Jesus.

There was a danger that we should offer them a Jesus who was too small, because we had forced Him into conformity with our human standards and human psychology. To see that, one need only read the Lives of Jesus written since the sixties, and notice what they have made of the great imperious sayings of the Lord, how they have weakened down His imperative world-contemning demands upon individuals, that He might not come into conflict with our ethical ideals, and might tune His denial of the world to our acceptance of it. Many of the greatest sayings are found lying in a corner like explosive shells from which the charges have been removed. No small portion of elemental religious power needed to be drawn off from His sayings to prevent them from conflicting with our system of religious world-acceptance. We have made Jesus hold another language with our time from that which He really held.

In the process we ourselves have been enfeebled, and have robbed our own thoughts of their vigour in order to project them back into history and make them speak to us out of the past. It is nothing less than a misfortune for modern theology that it mixes history with everything and ends by being proud of the skill with which it finds its own thoughts—even to its beggarly pseudo-metaphysic with which it has banished genuine speculative metaphysic from the sphere of religion—in Jesus, and represents Him as expressing them. It had almost deserved the reproach: "he who putteth his hand to the plough, and looketh back, is not fit for the Kingdom of God."[851]

It was no small matter, therefore, that in the course of the critical study of the Life of Jesus, after a resistance lasting for two generations, during which first one expedient was tried and then another, theology was forced by genuine history to begin to doubt the artificial history with which it had thought to give new life to our Christianity, and to yield to the facts, which, as Wrede strikingly said, are sometimes the most radical critics of all. History will force it to find a way to transcend history, and to fight for the lordship and rule of Jesus over this world with weapons tempered in a different forge.

We are experiencing what Paul experienced. In the very moment when we were coming nearer to the historical Jesus than men had ever come before, and were already stretching out our hands to draw Him into our own time, we have been obliged to give up the attempt and acknowledge our failure

---

851. Lk 9:62. (The notes for this selection are by Gerhart and Udoh.)

in that paradoxical saying: "If we have known Christ after the flesh yet henceforth know we Him no more."[852] And further we must be prepared to find that the historical knowledge of the personality and life of Jesus will not be a help, but perhaps even an offence to religion.

But the truth is, it is not Jesus as historically known, but Jesus as spiritually arisen within men, who is significant for our time and can help it. Not the historical Jesus, but the spirit which goes forth from Him and in the spirits of men strives for new influence and rule, is that which overcomes the world.

It is not given to history to disengage that which is abiding and eternal in the being of Jesus from the historical forms in which it worked itself out, and to introduce it into our world as a living influence. It has toiled in vain at this undertaking. As a water-plant is beautiful so long as it is growing in the water, but once torn from its roots, withers and becomes unrecognisable, so it is with the historical Jesus when He is wrenched loose from the soil of eschatology, and the attempt is made to conceive Him "historically" as a Being not subject to temporal conditions. The abiding and eternal in Jesus is absolutely independent of historical knowledge and can only be understood by contact with His spirit which is still at work in the world. In proportion as we have the Spirit of Jesus we have the true knowledge of Jesus.

Jesus as a concrete historical personality remains a stranger to our time, but His spirit, which lies hidden in His words, is known in simplicity, and its influence is direct. Every saying contains in its own way the whole Jesus. The very strangeness and unconditionedness in which He stands before us makes it easier for individuals to find their own personal standpoint in regard to Him.

Men feared that to admit the claims of eschatology would abolish the significance of His words for our time; and hence there was a feverish eagerness to discover in them any elements that might be considered not eschatologically conditioned. When any sayings were found of which the wording did not absolutely imply an eschatological connexion there was a great jubilation—these at least had been saved uninjured from the coming *débâcle*.

But in reality that which is eternal in the words of Jesus is due to the very fact that they are based on an eschatological worldview, and contain the expression of a mind for which the contemporary world with its historical and social circumstances no longer had any existence. They are appropriate, therefore, to any world, for in every world they raise the man who dares to meet their challenge, and does not turn and twist them into meaninglessness, above his world and his time, making him inwardly free, so that he is fitted to be, in his own world and in his own time, a simple channel of the power of Jesus.

Modern Lives of Jesus are too general in their scope. They aim at influencing, by giving a complete impression of the life of Jesus, a whole community. But the historical Jesus, as He is depicted in the Gospels, influenced individuals by the individual word. They understood Him so far as it was necessary for them to understand, without forming any conception of His life as a whole, since this in its ultimate aims remained a mystery even for the disciples.

Because it is thus preoccupied with the general, the universal, modern theology is determined to find its world-accepting ethic in the teaching of Jesus. Therein lies its weakness. The world affirms itself automatically; the modern spirit cannot but affirm it. But why on that account abolish the conflict between modern life, with the world-affirming spirit which inspires it as a whole, and the world-negating spirit of Jesus? Why spare the spirit of the individual man its appointed task of fighting its way through the world-negation of Jesus, of contending with Him at every step over the value of material and intellectual goods—a conflict in which it may never rest? For the general, for the institutions of society, the rule is: affirmation of the world, in conscious opposition to the view of Jesus, on the ground that the world has affirmed itself! This general affirmation of the world, however, if it is to be Christian, must in the individual spirit be Christianised and transfigured by the personal rejection of the world which is preached in the sayings of Jesus. It is only by means of the tension thus set up that religious energy can be communicated to our time. There was a danger that modern theology, for the sake of peace, would deny the world-negation in the sayings of Jesus, with which Protestantism was out of sympathy, and thus unstring the bow and make Protestantism a mere sociological instead of a religious force. There was perhaps also a danger of inward insincerity, in the fact that it refused to admit to itself and others that it maintained its affirmation of the world in opposition to the sayings of Jesus, simply because it could not do otherwise.

For that reason it is a good thing that the true historical Jesus should overthrow the modern Jesus, should rise up against the modern spirit and send upon earth, not peace, but a sword. He was not teacher, not a casuist; He was an im-

---

852. 2 Cor 5:16.

perious ruler. It was because He was so in His inmost being that He could think of Himself as the Son of Man. That was only the temporally conditioned expression of the fact that He was an authoritative ruler. The names in which men expressed their recognition of Him as such, Messiah, Son of Man, Son of God, have become for us historical parables. We can find no designation which expresses what He is for us.

He comes to us as One unknown, without a name, as of old, by the lake-side, He came to those men who knew Him not. He speaks to us the same word: "Follow thou me!" and sets us to the tasks which He has to fulfil for our time. He commands. And to those who obey Him, whether they be wise or simple, He will reveal Himself in the toils, the conflicts, the sufferings which they shall pass through in His fellowship, and, as an ineffable mystery, they shall learn in their own experience Who He is.

From Albert Schweitzer, *The Quest of the Historical Jesus: A Critical Study of Its Progress from Reimarus to Wrede,* translated by W. Montgomery (New York: Macmillan, 1968), 398–403.

✎ In *Dogmatic Constitution on Divine Revelation* (*Dei verbum,* November 18, 1965), the Roman Catholic Church's **Second Vatican Council** (1962–65) sets out the Church's official position regarding the inspiration and interpretation of the Bible.

THE SECOND VATICAN COUNCIL

"Sacred Scripture: Its Divine Inspiration and Its Interpretation," in *Dogmatic Constitution on Divine Revelation*, paragraphs 11–13

11. The divinely revealed realities, which are contained and presented in the text of sacred Scripture, have been written down under the inspiration of the Holy Spirit. For Holy Mother Church, relying on the faith of the apostolic age, accepts as sacred and canonical the books of the Old and the New Testaments, whole and entire, with all their parts, on the grounds that, written under the inspiration of the Holy Spirit,[853] they have God as their author, and have been handed on as such to the Church herself.[854] To compose the sacred books, God chose certain men who, all the while he employed them in this task, made full use of their powers and faculties[855] so that, though he acted in them and by them,[856] it was as true authors that they consigned to writing whatever he wanted written, and no more.[857]

Since, therefore, all that the inspired authors, or sacred

writers, affirm should be regarded as affirmed by the Holy Spirit, we must acknowledge that the books of Scripture, firmly, faithfully and without error, teach that truth which God, for the sake of our salvation, wished to see confided to the sacred Scriptures.[858] Thus "all Scripture is inspired by God, and profitable for teaching, for reproof, for correction and for training in righteousness, so that the man of God may be complete, equipped for every good work."[859]

12. Seeing that, in sacred Scripture, God speaks through men in human fashion,[860] it follows that the interpreter of sacred Scriptures, if he is to ascertain what God has wished to communicate to us, should carefully search out the meaning which the sacred writers really had in mind, that meaning which God had thought well to manifest through the medium of their words.

In determining the intention of the sacred writers, attention must be paid, *inter alia,* to "literary forms for the fact is that truth is differently presented and expressed in the various types of historical writing, in prophetical and poetical texts," and in other forms of literary expression. Hence the exegete must look for that meaning which the sacred writer, in a determined situation and given the circumstances of his time and culture, intended to express and did in fact express, through the medium of a contemporary literary form.[861] Rightly to understand what the sacred author wanted to affirm in his work, due attention must be paid both to the customary and characteristic patterns of perception, speech and narrative which prevailed at the age of the sacred writer, and to the conventions which the people of his time followed in their dealings with one another.[862]

---

853. Cf. Jn 20:31; 2 Tim 3:16; 2 Pet 1:19–21; 3:15–16.

854. Cf. Vatican Council I, Constitution *dogm. de fide catholica,* c. 2 (de revelatione): H. Denzinger, *Enchiridion symbolorum* [hereafter *Denz.*], 32nd edition 1787 (3006). *Bibl. Commission,* Decr. 18 June 1915: *Denz.* 2180 (3629); EB 420; Holy Office, *Letter,* 22 Dec. 1923: EB 499.

855. Cf. Pius XII, Encycl. *Divino afflante spiritu,* 30 Sept. 1943: *Acta apostolicae sedis* 35 (1943); 314; EB 556.

856. *In* and *by* man: cf. Heb 1:1; 4:7 (in); 2 Sam 23:2; Mt 1:22 and *passim* (by); Vatican Council I, *Schema de doctr. cath.,* note 9; Coll. Lac., VII, 522.

857. Leo XIII, Encycl. *Providentissimus Deus,* 18 Nov. 1893: *Denz.* 1952 (3293); EB 125.

858. Cf. St. Augustine, *Gen. ad litt.,* 2, 9, 20: Migne, *Patrologia Latina* [hereafter *PL*] 34, 270–71; *Epist,* 82, 3: *PL* 33, 277; *Corpus scriptorum ecclesiasticorum Latinorum* [hereafter *CSEL*] 34, 2, 354.—St. Thomas, *De ver.* q. 12, a. 2, C.—Council of Trent, Session IV, *de canonicis scripturis: Denz.* 783 (1501).—Leo XIII, Encycl. *Providentissimus:* EB 121, 124, 126–27.—Pius XII, Encycl. *Divino afflante:* EB 539.

859. 2 Tim 3:16–17, Gk. text.

860. St. Augustine, *De civ. Dei,* XVII, 6, 2: *PL* 41, 537; *CSEL* 40, 2, 228.

861. St. Augustine, *De doctr. Christ.,* III, 18, 26; *PL* 34, 75–76.

862. Pius XII, *loc. cit.: Denz.* 2294 (3829–3830); EB 557–562.

But since sacred Scripture must be read and interpreted with its divine authorship in mind,[863] no less attention must be devoted to the content and unity of the whole of Scripture, taking into account the Tradition of the entire Church and the analogy of faith, if we are to derive their true meaning from the sacred texts. It is the task of exegetes to work, according to these rules, towards a better understanding and explanation of the meaning of sacred Scripture in order that their research may help the Church to form a firmer judgment. For, of course, all that has been said about the manner of interpreting Scripture is ultimately subject to the judgment of the Church which exercises the divinely conferred commission and ministry of watching over and interpreting the Word of God.[864]

13. Hence, in sacred Scripture, without prejudice to God's truth and holiness, the marvellous "condescension" of eternal wisdom is plain to be seen "that we may come to know the ineffable loving-kindness of God and see for ourselves how far he has gone in adapting his language with thoughtful concern for our nature."[865] Indeed the words of God, expressed in the words of men, are in every way like human language, just as the Word of the eternal Father, when he took on himself the flesh of human weakness, became like men.

Translated by Wilfred Harrington, in *Vatican Council II: The Conciliar and Post Conciliar Documents,* edited by Austin Flannery (Collegeville, MN: Liturgical Press, 1975), 756–58.

✒ **The World Council of Churches** is an organization of various Christian denominations that was established in 1948 to promote ecumenism. Its document "Scripture, Tradition and Traditions," composed at the organization's assembly in Montreal in 1963, addresses the relationship of the biblical texts to the Christian "Tradition" and "traditions."

THE WORLD COUNCIL OF CHURCHES

"Scripture, Tradition and Traditions"

Introduction

38. We find ourselves together in Montreal, delegates of churches with many different backgrounds and many different histories. And yet despite these differences we find that we are able to meet one another in faith and hope in the one Father, who by his Son Jesus Christ has sent the Holy Spirit to draw all men into unity with one another and with him. It is on the basis of this faith and hope and in the context of a common prayer to the one God, Father, Son and Holy Spirit,

that we have studied together anew the problem of the one Tradition and the many traditions, and despite the fact of our separations, have found that we can talk with one another and grow in mutual understanding. The Section warmly commends for study by the churches the Report of the Theological Commission on "Tradition and Traditions,"[866] which was the main documentary foundation of its work.

39. In our report we have distinguished between a number of different meanings of the word *tradition*. We speak of the *Tradition* (with a capital T), *tradition* (with a small t) and *traditions*. By *the Tradition* is meant the Gospel itself, transmitted from generation to generation in and by the Church, Christ himself present in the life of the Church. By *tradition* is meant the traditionary process. The term *traditions* is used in two senses, to indicate both the diversity of forms of expression and also what we call confessional traditions, for instance the Lutheran tradition or the Reformed tradition. In the latter part of our report the word appears in a further sense, when we speak of cultural traditions.

40. Our report contains the substance of the work of three subsections. The first considered the subject of the relation of Tradition to Scripture, regarded as the written prophetic and apostolic testimony to God's act in Christ, whose authority we all accept. The concern of the second was with the problem of the one Tradition and the many traditions of Christendom as they unfold in the course of the Church's history. The third discussed the urgent problems raised both in the life of the younger churches and in the churches of the West, concerning the translation of Christian Tradition into new cultures and languages.

41. Part I received a full discussion and the complete approval of the Section. Owing to the lack of time it was not possible to give the same detailed attention to Parts II and III. The Section in general recommends them for study.

I. Scripture, Tradition and traditions

42. As Christians we all acknowledge with thankfulness that God has revealed himself in the history of the people of

863. Cf. Benedict XV, Encycl. *Spiritus Paraclitus,* 15 Sept. 1920: EB 469. St. Jerome, *In Gal* 5, 19–21: *PL* 26, 417 A.

864. Cf. Vatican Council I, *Const. dogm. de fide catholica,* c. 2 (de revelatione): *Denz.* 1788.

865. St. John Chrysostom, *In Gen* 3, 8 (hom. 17, 1): J. P. Migne, *Patrologia Graeca* [hereafter *PG*] 53, 134. *Attemperatio* corresponds to the Greek *synkatábasis.*

866. Faith and Order Findings, part IV, 3–63.

God in the Old Testament and in Christ Jesus, his Son, the mediator between God and man. God's mercy and God's glory are the beginning and end of our own history. The testimony of prophets and apostles inaugurated the Tradition of his revelation. The once-for-all disclosure of God in Jesus Christ inspired the apostles and disciples to give witness to the revelation given in the person and work of Christ. No one could, and no one can, "say that Jesus is Lord, save by the Holy Spirit."[867] The oral and written tradition of the prophets and apostles under the guidance of the Holy Spirit led to the formation of Scriptures and to the canonization of the Old and New Testaments as the Bible of the Church. The very fact that Tradition precedes the Scriptures points to the significance of tradition, but also to the Bible as the treasure of the Word of God.

43. The Bible poses the problem of Tradition and Scripture in a more or less implicit manner; the history of Christian theology points to it explicitly. While in the Early Church the relation was not understood as problematical, ever since the Reformation "Scripture and Tradition" has been a matter of controversy in the dialogue between Roman Catholic and Protestant theology. On the Roman Catholic side, tradition has generally been understood as divine truth not expressed in Holy Scripture alone, but orally transmitted. The Protestant position has been an appeal to Holy Scripture alone, as the infallible and sufficient authority in all matters pertaining to salvation, to which all human traditions should be subjected. The voice of the Orthodox Church has hardly been heard in these Western discussions until quite recently.

44. For a variety of reasons, it has now become necessary to reconsider these positions. We are more aware of our living in various confessional traditions, e.g., that stated paradoxically in the saying "It has been the tradition of my church not to attribute any weight to tradition." Historical study and not least the encounter of the churches in the ecumenical movement have led us to realize that the proclamation of the Gospel is always inevitably historically conditioned. We are also aware that in Roman Catholic theology the concept of tradition is undergoing serious reconsideration.

45. In our present situation, we wish to reconsider the problem of Scripture and Tradition, or rather that of Tradition and Scripture. And therefore we wish to propose the following statement as a fruitful way of reformulating the question. Our starting point is that we are all living in a tradition which goes back to our Lord and has its roots in the Old Testament, and are all indebted to that tradition inasmuch as we have received the revealed truth, the Gospel, through

its being transmitted from one generation to another. Thus we can say that we exist as Christians by the Tradition of the Gospel (the *paradosis* of the *kerygma*) testified in Scripture, transmitted in and by the Church through the power of the Holy Spirit. Tradition taken in this sense is actualized in the preaching of the Word, in the administration of the Sacraments and worship, in Christian teaching and theology, and in mission and witness to Christ by the lives of the members of the Church.

46. What is transmitted in the process of tradition is the Christian faith, not only as a sum of tenets, but as a living reality transmitted through the operation of the Holy Spirit. We can speak of the Christian Tradition (with a capital T), whose content is God's revelation and self-giving in Christ, present in the life of the Church.

47. But this Tradition which is the work of the Holy Spirit is embodied in traditions (in the two senses of the word, both as referring to diversity in forms of expression, and in the sense of separate communions). The traditions in Christian history are distinct from, and yet connected with, the Tradition. They are the expressions and manifestations in diverse historical forms of the one truth and reality which is Christ.

48. This evaluation of the traditions poses serious problems. For some, questions such as these are raised. Is it possible to determine more precisely what the content of the one Tradition is, and by what means? Do all traditions which claim to be Christian contain the Tradition? How can we distinguish between traditions embodying the true Tradition and merely human traditions? Where do we find the genuine Tradition, and where impoverished tradition or even distortion of tradition? Tradition can be a faithful transmission of the Gospel, but also a distortion of it. In this ambiguity the seriousness of the problem of tradition is indicated.

49. These questions imply the search for a criterion. This has been a main concern for the Church since its beginning. In the New Testament we find warnings against false teaching and deviations from the truth of the Gospel. For the post-apostolic Church the appeal to the Tradition received from the apostles became the criterion. As this Tradition was embodied in the apostolic writings, it became natural to use those writings as an authority for determining where the true Tradition was to be found. In the midst of all tradition, these early records of divine revelation have a special basic value, because of their apostolic character. But the Gnostic

---

867. 1 Cor 12:3.

crisis in the second century shows that the mere existence of apostolic writings did not solve the problem. The question of interpretation arose as soon as the appeal to written documents made its appearance. When the canon of the New Testament had been finally defined and recognized by the Church, it was still more natural to use this body of writings as an indispensable criterion.

50. The Tradition in its written form, as Holy Scripture (comprising both the Old and the New Testament), has to be interpreted by the Church in ever new situations. Such interpretation of the Tradition is to be found in the crystallization of tradition in the creeds, the liturgical forms of the sacraments and other forms of worship, and also in the preaching of the Word and in theological expositions of the Church's doctrine. A mere reiteration of the words of Holy Scripture would be a betrayal of the Gospel which has to be made understandable and has to convey a challenge to the world.

51. The necessity of interpretation raises again the question of the criterion for the genuine Tradition. Throughout the history of the Church the criterion has been sought in the Holy Scriptures rightly interpreted. But what is "right interpretation"?

52. The Scriptures as documents can be letter only. It is the Spirit who is the Lord and Giver of life. Accordingly we may say that the right interpretation (taking the words in the widest possible sense) is that interpretation which is guided by the Holy Spirit. But this does not solve the problem of criterion. We arrive at the quest for a hermeneutical principle.

53. This problem has been dealt with in different ways by the various churches. In some confessional traditions the accepted hermeneutical principle has been that any portion of Scripture is to be interpreted in the light of Scripture as a whole. In others the key has been sought in what is considered to be the centre of Holy Scripture, and the emphasis has been primarily on the Incarnation, or on the Atonement and Redemption, or on justification by faith, or again on the message of the nearness of the Kingdom of God, or on the ethical teachings of Jesus. In yet others, all emphasis is laid upon what Scripture says to the individual conscience, under the guidance of the Holy Spirit. In the Orthodox Church the hermeneutical key is found in the mind of the Church, especially as expressed in the Fathers of the Church and in the Ecumenical Councils. In the Roman Catholic Church the key is found in the deposit of faith, of which the Church's *magisterium* is the guardian. In other traditions again the creeds, complemented by confessional documents or by the definitions of Ecumenical Councils and the witness of the Fathers,

are considered to give the right key to the understanding of Scripture. In none of these cases where the principle of interpretation is found elsewhere than in Scripture is the authority thought to be alien to the central concept of Holy Scripture. On the contrary, it is considered as providing just a key to the understanding of what is said in Scripture.

54. Loyalty to our confessional understanding of Holy Scripture produces both convergence and divergence in the interpretation of Scripture. For example, an Anglican and a Baptist will certainly agree on many points when they interpret Holy Scripture (in the wide sense of interpretation), but they will disagree on others. As another example, there may be mentioned the divergent interpretations given to Matt 16:18 in Roman Catholic theology on the one hand, and in Orthodox or Protestant theology on the other. How can we overcome the situation in which we all read Scripture in the light of our own traditions?

55. Modern biblical scholarship has already done much to bring the different churches together by conducting them towards the Tradition. It is along this line that the necessity for further thinking about the hermeneutical problem arises: i.e., how we can reach an adequate interpretation of the Scriptures, so that the Word of God addresses us and Scripture is safeguarded from subjective or arbitrary exegesis. Should not the very fact that God has blessed the Church with the Scriptures demand that we emphasize more than in the past a common study of Scripture whenever representatives of the various churches meet? Should we not study more the Fathers of all periods of the Church and their interpretations of the Scriptures in the light of our ecumenical task? Does not the ecumenical situation demand that we search for the Tradition by re-examining sincerely our own particular traditions?

II. The Unity of Tradition and the Diversity of Traditions

56. Church and tradition are inseparable. By tradition we do not mean traditionalism. The Tradition of the Church is not an object which we possess, but a reality by which we are possessed. The Church's life has its source in God's act of revelation in Jesus Christ, and in the gift of the Holy Spirit to his people and his work in their history. Through the action of the Holy Spirit, a new community, the Church, is constituted and commissioned, so that the revelation and the life which are in Jesus Christ may be transmitted to the ends of the earth and to the end of time. The Tradition in its content not only looks backward to its origin in the past but also forward to

the fulness which shall be revealed. The life of the Church is lived in the continuous recalling, appropriation and transmission of the once-for-all event of Christ's coming in the flesh, and in the eager expectation of his coming in glory. All this finds expression in the Word and in the Sacraments in which "we proclaim the Lord's death till he come."[868]

57. There are at least two distinctive types of understanding of the Tradition. Of these, the first is affirmed most clearly by the Orthodox. For them, the Tradition is not only the act of God in Christ, who comes by the work of the Holy Spirit to save all men who believe in him; it is also the Christian faith itself, transmitted in wholeness and purity, and made explicit in unbroken continuity through definite events in the life of the catholic and apostolic Church from generation to generation. For some others, the Tradition is substantially the same as the revelation in Christ and the preaching of the Word entrusted to the Church which is sustained in being by it, and expressed with different degrees of fidelity in various historically conditioned forms, namely the traditions. There are others whose understanding of the Tradition and the traditions contains elements of both these points of view. Current developments in biblical and historical study, and the experience of ecumenical encounter, are leading many to see new values in positions which they had previously ignored. The subject remains open.

58. In the two distinctive positions mentioned above, the Tradition and the traditions are clearly distinguished. But while in the one case it is held that it is to be found in the organic and concrete unity of the one Church, in the other it is assumed that the one Tradition can express itself in a variety of forms, not necessarily all equally complete. The problem of the many churches and the one Tradition appears very differently from each of those points of view. But though on the one side it is possible to maintain that the Church cannot be, and has not been, divided, and on the other to envisage the existence of many churches sharing in the one Tradition even though not in communion with each other, none would wish to acquiesce in the present state of separation.

59. Many of our misunderstandings and disagreements on this subject arise out of the fact of our long history of estrangement and division. During the centuries the different Christian communions have developed their own traditions of historical study and their own particular ways of viewing the past. The rise of the idea of a strictly scientific study of history, with its spirit of accuracy and objectivity, in some ways ameliorated this situation. But the resultant work so frequently failed to take note of the deeper theological issues involved in church history that its value was severely limited. More recently, a study of history which is ecumenical in its scope and spirit has appeared.

60. We believe that if such a line of study is pursued, it can be of great relevance to the present life and problems of the Church: "those who fail to comprehend their histories are doomed to re-enact them" (Santayana). We believe, too, that it would have great value in offering possibilities of a new understanding of some of the most contested areas of our common past. We therefore specifically recommend that Faith and Order should seek to promote such studies, ensuring the collaboration of scholars of different confessions, in an attempt to gain a new view of crucial epochs and events in church history, especially those in which discontinuity is evident.

61. But at this point another problem arises. At a moment when mankind is becoming ever more aware of itself as a unity, and we are faced with the development of a global civilization, Christians are called to a new awareness of the universality of the Church, and of its history in relation to the history of mankind. This means that, both at the level of theological study and of pastoral teaching, an attempt has to be made to overcome the parochialism of most studies in church history, and to convey some idea of the history of God's people as a whole. But how is this to be done? Does it not demand the work of historians with more than human capabilities? Is it possible for the scholar, limited as he is by his own cultural, historical and ecclesiastical background, to achieve this vision? Clearly it is not, though we believe that by working in collaboration something could be accomplished. For specialized but limited insights and points of view can be checked and supplemented by those of others; for example, a group may command a larger number of languages and literatures than is possible for an individual. Questions are being raised in the philosophy and theology of history, pointing both to the danger of mere traditionalism and the permanent value of authentic traditionalism. These demand our constant consideration.

62. Still a third kind of historical concern has been with us. We are aware that during the period of this Conference we have been passing through a new and unprecedented experience in the ecumenical movement. For the first time in the Faith and Order dialogue, the Eastern Orthodox and the other Eastern Churches have been strongly represented

---

868. 1 Cor 11:26.

in our meetings. A new dimension of Faith and Order has opened up, and we only begin to see its future possibilities. It is clear that many of our problems of communication have arisen from the inadequate understanding of the life and history of the Eastern Churches to be found even among scholars in the West, and vice versa. Here again is an area in which we would recommend further study, e.g., of the problem of the filioque,[869] its origin and consequences. There are two other studies which we recommend to the Faith and Order Commission. We believe it important to undertake together a study of the Councils of the Early Church, and we recommend an examination of the catechetical material at present in use by the churches, and of the methods whereby it could be revised in the light of the ecumenical movement.

63. In all this we are not blind to the nature of the world in which we live, nor to the cultural and intellectual problems of our day. To many of our contemporaries a concern with the past will immediately appear suspect, as revealing a desire for the mere resuscitation of old customs and ideas, which have no relevance for the urgent questions of our time. We recognize that in many places human traditions—national, social, and indeed religious—are being shaken; and that in this age of scientific and technological achievement many tend to regard the heritage of the past as unimportant. We recognize the positive elements in the present situation. It is for this reason that we have placed the contrast of tradition and traditionalism at the beginning of this part. The past of which we speak is not only a subject which we study from afar. It is a past which has value for us, in so far as we make it our own in an act of personal decision. In the Church it becomes a past by which we live by sharing in the one Tradition, for in it we are united with him who is the Lord of history, who was and is and is to come; and he is God not of the dead but of the living.

From Günther Gassmann, ed., *Documentary History of Faith and Order* (Geneva: World Council of Churches, 1993), 10–15.

∾ **Amos Wilder** (1898–1993) was one of the first New Testament scholars to focus on the literary imagination at work in biblical language. A poet, literary critic, and scholar, he considers the relationship between literary forms and content in the New Testament in his *Early Christian Rhetoric* (originally published in 1964).

AMOS WILDER

"The New Utterance," in *Early Christian Rhetoric*

I

Those who are acquainted with New Testament studies know the importance of what is called form-criticism and form-history in the analysis of the Gospels. We are fortunate in having survivals in the Gospels of what Jesus said and did, or of early reports of what he said and did. Most of such carry-overs and vestiges reach us now in the connected narratives of our Gospels. But these writings break down transparently into a large number of short separate episodes or anecdotes and sayings that came down for a considerable period by oral transmission. These units can again be sorted out according to style and character in the light of comparable oral tradition. There are laws of form in social tradition as there are in geology. As Henry J. Cadbury has observed, to look beneath the surface in one of our Gospels is like digging into an ancient mound: one finds successive strata, and in each of them distinctive and tell-tale objects and artifacts.

In the Old Testament scholars have uncovered various formal patterns of language in the poetry and history and codes, reaching far back into a long pre-literary, that is, oral period. Comparative studies of world-wide saga, epic, folklore and ritual-texts have thrown a great deal of light upon the ancient oral elements which are embedded in our written Old Testament library. Similarly with the New Testament. What we find, moreover, is not only a question of the forms themselves, say a parable or a doxology or a poem; it is also a question of their matrix—the workshop, as it were, of the earliest Church in which these forms were transmitted and reshaped. All such findings of technical form-criticism we shall keep in mind.

But we would like to go behind this kind of observation to the question of language itself. How does the whole phenomenon of language, speech, communication, rhetoric present itself in the rise of Christianity? What modes of discourse are specially congenial to the Gospel? What is the special role of oral as against written discourse? What is the theological significance of particular rhetorical patterns used

---

869. "And the Son": the Western Church added this phrase to the Creed of the Council of Constantinople. Thus, the Holy Spirit proceeds from the Father and the Son. (This note is by Gerhart and Udoh.)

or neglected in the Early Church? What comparisons can be drawn in this area between the language of the Gospels and that of contemporary Judaism or Hellenism, or between earlier and later phases of the New Testament Church itself?

To suggest the promise of these lines of inquiry let us cite an analogy: that of the arts. This is relevant, since we are, indeed, concerned here with the arts of language in the Early Church. Different cultures favour different arts. In one culture the drama will be the most representative art-form and reach a high level of perfection. In another culture it may be painting or music. Even in the same culture, changed circumstances will bring about changed priorities in the arts or in their styles. Similarly with religions; one will favour one art-form and may even proscribe another, as Israel restricted the use of the graphic arts, and as certain modern sects have banned the use of the organ. Of course, all faiths avail themselves of language and the arts of language. But there are immense differences here. And it is not only in *what* they say that religions differ, that is, in their doctrines and myths, but also in *how* they speak, in the particular oral and literary vehicles which they prefer. In one religion, or in one religion at one stage, the oracular mode or incantation may be typical; in another the prose-code, in another the philosophical-mystical hymn. In some modern types of Christianity, the rational proposition has been prominent, in others the pure language of Zion. In any given cult or sect, of course, we usually find a variety of rhetorics, but one or other will predominate.

Certain modes of utterance, moreover, are more primitive or naive than others; the oracle and the cult-story or myth stand nearer the birth of religion than the code. Yet even at a sophisticated level the believer may return to the fountain-head. So in modern painting the artist returns for revitalization to the a-b-c's of sensibility and perception of the primitives.

To return to the particular arts of language of particular periods. These no doubt are conditioned by the cultural heritage and expectation of the setting. Jesus used the parable partly because it was a current and meaningful genre. Paul used the diatribe style for the same reason, and thus could communicate all the more effectively. But the greater speakers and writers, as in these cases also, create new forms and styles or at least renew the old forms, still in relation to their audience. F. O. Matthiessen has shown how Walt Whitman spoke with a new tongue in his declamatory verse, yet found precedents for it in current speech-forms.

Whitman saw himself as contributing to "the growth of an American English enjoying a distinct identity," and wrote, "I sometimes think the *Leaves* [i.e. *Leaves of Grass*] is only a language experiment."[870] But the peculiar form of his verse was shaped by contemporary rhetorics, especially as Matthiessen shows, by the cadences of public oratory and of operatic recitative and aria, both reinforcing his belief that poetry was not something written but uttered.[871] In the case of Emerson, the distinctive essay form was shaped from local cultural roots in the New England sermon and the Lyceum lecture tradition. "I look," said he, "upon the lecture-room as the true church of today, and as the home of a richer eloquence than Faneuil Hall or the Capitol ever knew."[872] Herman Melville, for his part, found his media and style in dependence on patterns familiar to his public, the English Bible and Shakespeare.

We cite these analogies only to suggest, arguing from the lesser to the greater, that the new speech-modes of Jesus and his followers had deep conditioning-factors in the rhetorics of their time, but also in the cultural crisis that demanded new styles. Therefore any study of the rhetorical forms of the New Testament is not a superficial matter. Form and content cannot long be held apart.

We should stress here one implication of our topic to be kept in mind throughout even when we may seem to have forgotten it. The character of the early Christian speech-forms should have much to say to us with regard to our understanding of Christianity and its communication today. We may well go back to the fountain-head of the Gospel in this respect also. This is not to be taken in a trite sense; for example, that because Jesus used parables we also should use illustrations from life, or because the New Testament has a place for poetry we also should use it. All this is true. But there is rather the question of what kind of story and what kind of poetry. Nor should we feel ourselves enslaved to biblical models whether in statement, image or form. But we can learn much from our observations as to the appropriate strategies and vehicles of Christian speech and then adapt these to our own situation. It is significant, for example, how large a place the dramatic mode has in the faith of the Bible and in

---

870. *American Renaissance* (New York: [Oxford University Press], 1941), 517. "He wanted to devise a wholly new speaking style, far more direct and compelling than any hitherto . . ." (557; ellipsis in original).

871. Ibid., 559.

872. Cited by Matthiessen, ibid., 23.

its forms of expression, even though we find no theatre-art as we know it in the Bible or among the early believers. The important role of religious drama in our churches today has, nevertheless, very specific justification in biblical theology and in New Testament rhetorical forms.

III

Jesus of Nazareth and his first followers broke into the world of speech and writing of their time, and, indeed, into its silence, with a novel and powerful utterance, that is, with a "word," and the word of a layman. Ignatius of Antioch states the matter in his own surrealist style:

> Jesus Christ, his son, who is his word proceeding from silence, (*Ad Magn.* 8.2.)
> He is the mouth which cannot lie, by which the Father has spoken truly. (*Ad Rom.* 8.2)

Just on the secular level note how significant this was and has been. At least there was here a new dynamics in human speech. One thinks of what John Keats said about "the indescribable gusto of the Elizabethan voice." But one searches for more significant analogies. It is a question of a word from the depths, with power. One analogy would be that of the man who stands up when a panic is spreading in a theatre or a riot in the streets and recalls men to their true selves by a compelling word of authority. But this new word in Israel initiated a new world of meaning that went on spreading through ancient society. Here an analogy would be that of the impact of Dante's use of his vernacular dialect rather than Latin upon the spiritual culture of Europe. One can think also of the train of consequences that ensued upon the writing by the teenager Arthur Rimbaud of his *Bateau ivre*. This new spring of symbolist incantation determined much of the history of modern poetic utterance.

Thus we can understand the sense in which Ernst Fuchs has called the rise of the Gospel a "speech-event" (*Sprachereignis*). By this he means a new departure, not just in the sense of a new religious teaching, but rather the opening up of a new dimension of man's awareness, a new breakthrough in language and symbolization. He can also say that the Gospel represented a renewal of myth in Israel and the ancient world. The new enlargement of language took on ever new articulation in the course of the Apostolic Age.

To quote Professor Fuchs further:

Primitive Christianity is itself a speech-phenomenon. It is for that very reason that it established a monument in the new style-form which we call a "gospel." The Johannine apocalypse and, indeed, in the first instance the apostolic epistle-literature, these are creations of a new utterance which changes everything that it touches.[873]

He adds that it is only on the margin of the New Testament that one can observe direct assimilation of pagan rhetoric, as for example in the Pastoral Epistles and in post-canonical writings; at a time, that is, when ecclesiastical patterns had begun to solidify.

Early Christianity, of course, brought forth new forms not only in language but in life itself, not only in writing but in ritual. One could say the same thing about other religions. But the spoken and written word have a basic role in the Christian faith. We note the background for this in the Old Testament. The religion of Israel is very much a matter of hearing rather than of seeing.[874] Even God's actions are spoken of by the prophets as his word. No man can see God and live, but he is known in his speaking. By contrast it is the gods of the nations that are mute, and their visible images are dumb.[875] As we read in Ps 115:7, "They do not make a sound in their throat." Throughout Scripture, revelation is identified above all with speaking and hearing, with writing and reading, with colloquies and recitals, with tablets and scrolls and parchments, rather than with the imagery of the visual arts. Even visions are converted into writing: "Write the vision," we read in Hab 2:2; and, "write what you see in a book," in Rev 1:11. The seer, indeed, seems to confuse the senses when he speaks of seeing the voice or of the "little scroll" which he was bidden to eat which was "as sweet as honey" in his mouth.[876] Of course, like all religions Christianity has its sacred actions and spectacles, sacred places and times, sacred arts and objects, but it is in connection with God speaking that they are sacred.

It is intriguing to classify religions or even Christian groups according as they assign priority to auditory or visual images. On the one hand we have religion identified with

---

873. "Die Sprache im Neuen Testament," *Zur Frage nach dem historischen Jesus* (Tübingen: [JCB Mohr (Siebeck)], 1960), 261.

874. [See] Thorleif Boman, *Hebrew Thought Compared with Greek* (London: [Westminster Press], 1960) 206–7.

875. Hab 2:18–19; Ps 115:5, 7; Isa 46:7; Jer. 10:5.

876. Rev 10:10.

word and answer; on the other with vision and ecstasy or metamorphosis. The New Testament speaks of the divine apprehension in terms of all the senses, not only hearing and sight but touch and smell (this last in the form of incense and fragrant odours). Yet the hearing mode is primary. The spirit may be rapt in vision, but it is with the heart that man hears the word of faith and with his mouth that he confesses and is saved (Rom 10.8–10). Language, then, is more fundamental than graphic representation, except where the latter is itself a transcript in some sense of the word of God. In this connection it is interesting to note what a psychologist writes about the determination of human consciousness by language.

> "Reality" becomes a meaningful part of consciousness only through the interpretation of reality-contacts by language. The importance of auditory experiences for the interpretation of reality is proven through observation of deaf children. . . . A world without sound is a dead world: when sound is eliminated from our experience, it becomes clear how inadequate and ambiguous is the visual experience if not accompanied by auditory interpretation. . . . Vision alone without acoustic perceptions does not provide understanding. Deaf persons are prone to paranoid interpretations of outside events.[877]

In this light it is significant that the emotional dynamics of the Gospel were always controlled by the meaningfulness of speech. To this, visionary and psychic phenomena were subordinated. And the language in question was not only the spoken word but personal address; it was not only in the indicative mode but in the imperative; it was not only in the third person but in the second and the first; it was not only a matter of declaration but of dialogue.

We can, therefore, appreciate the special incentives to the literary arts that Christianity has always provided, just as other faiths have provided special incentives to the visual arts or to music and dancing. Christianity is a religion of the Book and this has had its corollaries for its total cultural thrust. It is true that when the Church took over the heritage of classical culture—ancient rhetoric, architecture, painting and sculpture—it related itself to all the arts and has exploited them all ever since in changing situations. But the thesis still holds that the faith identifies itself fundamentally with the arts of hearing as against those of sight and touch. Even when the Christian paints or carves or dances or sings he does so to a

text, and identifies himself with an archetypal dialogue between God and man.

Even so far as the literary arts themselves are in view—arts which have, of course, come to consummate expression in many religious traditions—one could argue that particular genres are at home both in the Church and in particular Christian cultures of different periods. . . . One can also say that the novel as it has evolved in the modern period is a form which is only possible in a world whose view of man and society has been shaped by Christian presupposition.

From Amos Wilder, *Early Christian Rhetoric: The Language of the Gospel* (Cambridge, MA: Harvard University Press, 1971), 2–5, 9–12.

✎ **Brevard S. Childs,** a biblical theologian influenced by Barth, provides the process and methods of his "canonical," theological interpretation in his *Book of Exodus: A Critical, Theological Commentary.* Childs interprets both the Old and the New Testament as pointing to a "single reality"—Jesus Christ. The study of how they do so is the focus of his work.

BREVARD S. CHILDS

The Book of Exodus: A Critical, Theological Commentary

Preface

The purpose of this commentary is unabashedly theological. Its concern is to understand Exodus as scripture of the church. The exegesis arises as a theological discipline within the context of the canon and is directed toward the community of faith which lives by its confession of Jesus Christ.

Yet the author is also aware that serious theological understanding of the text is dependent on a rigorous and careful study of the whole range of problems within the Bible which includes text and source criticism, syntax and grammar, history and geography. Nor can the hearing of the text by the Christian church be divorced from that other community of faith which lives from the same Bible, and from the countless other stances outside of any commitment to faith or tradition.

---

877. Clemens E. Benda, "Language, Consciousness and Problems of Existential Analysis (*Daseinsanalyse*)," *American Journal of Psychotherapy* 14/2 (April 1960), 262.

It will be immediately clear from this perspective that a different understanding of the role of biblical interpretation is being offered from that currently held by the majority of scholars within the field. Even the format of the exegesis offers an implicit criticism of the usual concept of a commentary. The issue at stake does not lie in the degree of technicality of the exegesis—whether or not a knowledge of Hebrew and Greek is assumed—but in the concept of the task. The rash of recent popularizations offers nothing qualitatively different from the technical volumes.

I am fully aware of the risks involved when one cuts oneself away from the safe and well-charted boundaries which the canons of historical critical scholarship have come to regard as self-evident, and perhaps even sacrosanct. Nevertheless, it seems to me imperative for the health of the discipline and certainly of the church that the generally accepted areas in which the exegete works be greatly broadened. I have tried to show why an adequate interpretation of the Bible for the church must involve a continuous wrestling with the history of interpretation and theology. Yet who can control equally well the fields of Semitic philology, ancient Near Eastern history, text and form criticism, rabbinics, New Testament, patristics, medieval and Reformation studies, philosophy and dogmatics? Still the effort has to be made to sketch the true parameters of the discipline of biblical interpretation, even if there are gaps and deficiencies in one man's attempt.[. . .]

Introduction

1. The Goal of Exegesis

The aim of this commentary is to seek to interpret the book of Exodus as canonical scripture within the theological discipline of the Christian church. As scripture its authoritative role within the life of the community is assumed, but how this authority functions must be continually explored. Therefore, although the book in its canonical form belongs to the sacred inheritance of the church, it is incumbent upon each new generation to study its meaning afresh, to have the contemporary situation of the church addressed by its word, and to anticipate a fresh appropriation of its message through the work of God's Spirit.

The author does not share the hermeneutical position of those who suggest that biblical exegesis is an objective, descriptive enterprise, controlled solely by scientific criticism, to which the Christian theologian can at best add a few homiletical reflections for piety's sake. In my judgment, the

rigid separation between the descriptive and constructive elements of exegesis strikes at the roots of the theological task of understanding the Bible. Nevertheless, it does belong to the task of the scholar in the church to deal seriously with the Old Testament text in its original setting within the history of Israel and to make use of research done by many whose understanding of the exegetical task differs widely from the one being suggested. Conversely, it is to be hoped that the actual exegesis of this commentary can prove useful and illuminating to those who do not share the author's general concept of the discipline.

It seems inappropriate in a commentary to launch into an essay on hermeneutics. Whether or not the exegesis is successful cannot be judged on its theory of interpretation, but on the actual interpretation itself. However, perhaps it is in order to explain briefly the rationale for the format of the commentary and to offer suggestions as to how the various sections within a chapter can be used by the reader.

2. The Format of the Commentary

1. Each section begins with a new translation of the Hebrew text. The ancient versions have been constantly checked, with the goal not only of restoring the best text, but of seeking to understand how the text was heard and interpreted by later communities. Although the most significant textual variants are discussed in detail, the emphasis of the section falls on syntactical problems which most often affect the actual exegesis. Alternative renderings by modern translators have frequently been noted and evaluated as an aid to the non-specialist.

2. The historical development which lay behind the final form of the biblical text is treated in considerable detail with regard to both the oral and literary levels. In this section a form-critical, traditio-historical analysis is offered which seeks to explore the early forces at work in the shaping of the oral tradition. Again, a fresh source analysis has been attempted which treats the various literary strands which comprise the present narrative. Finally, observations on the history of redaction discuss the final ordering of the passage. At times the results of the prehistory of the text have direct bearing on the interpretation of the canonical text; at other times the prehistory is quite irrelevant to understanding the synchronistic dimension of the biblical text. In the exegetical section which follows the prehistory, an evaluation of the role of the various earlier stages of the text is usually attempted, but by design no general theory of a relationship which obtains in

every case within Exodus is proposed. The section is printed in smaller type to indicate its subsidiary role within the commentary.

3. The first major section, entitled Old Testament context, forms the heart of the commentary. This section attempts to deal seriously with the text in its final form, which is its canonical shape, while at the same time recognizing and profiting by the variety of historical forces which were at work in producing it. In my judgment, the failure of most critical commentaries to deal with the final shape of the text without falling into modern midrash is a major deficiency. From a literary point of view there is a great need to understand the present composition as a piece of literature with its own integrity. The concentration of critical scholars on form-critical and source analysis has tended to fragment the text and leave the reader with only bits and pieces. But an even more important reason for interpreting the final text is a theological one. It is the final text, the composite narrative, in its present shape which the church, following the lead of the synagogue, accepted as canonical and thus the vehicle of revelation and instruction. Much of the frustration which the preacher experiences in using commentaries stems from the failure of the interpreter to deal with the text in its canonical shape. Rather, the interest of the commentator centers on various problems of its prehistory. In my judgment, the study of the prehistory has its proper function within exegesis only in illuminating the final text.

4. The section on the New Testament's treatment of the Old Testament is a conscious attempt to take seriously the church's confession that her sacred scripture consists of an Old and a New Testament. The New Testament's reading of the Old is therefore not just included within the section on history of interpretation, but functions as the voice of the apostles which the church hears along with that of the prophets. The New Testament uses the Old Testament in a variety of ways. Its exegesis shares a Hellenistic environment both in form and content, and often reflects the ongoing exegetical traditions of Judaism which had developed beyond the Old Testament. This section attempts to describe how the early church understood the Old Testament scripture in the light of the new confession of Jesus Christ.

5. The section on history of exegesis offers an analogy to the section on the prehistory of the text. The one deals with the period before the text's complete formation, the other with its interpretation after its formation. Both have a significant, albeit indirect, relationship to the major exegetical task of interpreting the canonical text. The history of exegesis is

of special interest in illuminating the text by showing how the questions which are brought to bear by subsequent generations of interpreters influenced the answers which they received. No one comes to the text *de novo,* but consciously or unconsciously shares a tradition with his predecessors. This section therefore tries to bring some historical controls to the issue of how the present generation is influenced by the exegetical traditions in which we now stand.

The concern of this commentary with the history of exegesis is also an attempt to broaden the increasingly narrow focus of the field on a few names within recent Old Testament scholarship. This tendency has not only ignored the impressive scholarship of many earlier generations, but finds itself unable to comprehend many of the major issues which the biblical text has evoked. Because this section must be highly selective, I have tried to deal with the major Jewish and Christian expositors throughout the commentary, and in addition bring in those special studies which were influential for each particular passage at crucial periods.

6. The last section offers a theological reflection on the text within the context of the Christian canon. It seeks to relate the various Old Testament and New Testament witnesses in the light of the history of exegesis to the theological issues which evoked the witness. It is an attempt to move from witness to substance. This reflection is not intended to be timeless or offer biblical truths for all ages, but to present a model of how the Christian seeks to understand the testimony of the prophets and apostles in his own time and situation. The section is not simply random homiletical ruminations; it attempts to build on the previous exegetical and historical work of the commentary, and to develop a more rigorous method of actualizing the text for the church's present task. . . . It is my deep concern that the task of relating biblical exegesis and theology can be thus aided, and the systematic and moral theologian will recognize issues which directly affect his discipline and which will evoke his joint participation in a common enterprise.

From Brevard S. Childs, *The Book of Exodus: A Critical, Theological Commentary* (Philadelphia: Westminster, 1974), ix–x, xiii–xvi.

☙ The French phenomenologist, humanist, and philosopher **Paul Ricoeur** elaborates on the poetic dimension of language as it relates to revelation and interpretation in "Toward a Hermeneutic of the Idea of Revelation" (first published in 1977), from his *Essays on Biblical Interpretation.* He uses a nonreligious sense of revelation to show what is manifested through biblical writing, the work as a whole, and the world of the text.

PAUL RICOEUR

"Toward a Hermeneutic of the Idea of Revelation," in *Essays on Biblical Interpretation*

The World of the Text and the New Being

My first investigation, into what I will call the space of the manifestation of things, takes place within precise limits. I will not speak of our experience of being-in-the-world, beginning from a phenomenology of perception as may be found in the works of Husserl and Merleau-Ponty, nor in terms of a phenomenology of care or preoccupation as may be found in Heidegger's *Being and Time*—although I believe that they may be connected by means of the detour I propose. Instead I will begin directly from the manifestation of the world by the text and by scripture.

This approach may seem overly limited due to the fact that it proceeds through the narrow defile of one cultural fact, the existence of written documents, and thus because it is limited to cultures which possess books, but it will seem less limited if we comprehend what enlargement of our experience of the world results from the existence of such documents. Moreover, by choosing this angle of attack, we immediately establish a correspondence with the fact that the claim of revealed speech reaches us today through writings to be interpreted. Those religions which refer back to Abraham—Judaism, Christianity, and Islam—are in their different ways, and they are often very different ways, religions of the book. So it is therefore appropriate, I believe, to inquire into the particular revelatory function attached to certain modalities of scripture which I will place under the title *Poetics,* in a sense I will explain in a moment. In effect, under the category of poetics, philosophical analysis encounters those traits of revelation which may correspond with or respond to the nonviolent appeal of biblical revelation.

To introduce this idea of a revelatory function of poetic discourse, I will draw upon three preparatory concepts. . . .

The first one is the very concept of writing itself. We underestimate the phenomenon of writing if we reduce it to the simple material fixation of living speech. Writing stands in a specific relation to what is said. It produces a form of discourse that is immediately autonomous with regard to its author's intention. And in this autonomy is already contained everything that I will call in a moment, following Hans

Georg Gadamer, the *issue* of the text which is removed from the finite intentional horizon of the author. In other words, thanks to writing, the world of the text can burst the world of the author. This emancipation with regard to the author has its parallel on the side of whoever receives the text. The autonomy of the text also removes this reader from the finite horizon of its original audience.

The second preparatory concept is that of the work. By this I mean the shaping of discourse through the operation of literary genres such as narration, fiction, the essay, etc. By producing discourse as such and such a work taking up such and such a genre, the composition codes assign to works of discourse that unique configuration we call a style. This shaping of the work concurs with the phenomenon of writing in externalizing and objectifying the text into what one literary critic has called a "verbal icon."

The third preparatory concept continues in the same direction and goes a bit further. It is what I call the world of the text. By this I mean that what is finally to be understood in a text is not the author or his presumed intention, nor is it the immanent structure or structures of the text, but rather the sort of world intended beyond the text as its reference. In this regard, the alternative "either the intention or the structure" is vain. For the reference of the text is what I call the issue of the text or the world of the text. The world of the text designates the reference of the work of discourse, not what is said, but about what it is said. Hence the issue of the text is the object of hermeneutics. And the issue of the text is the world the text unfolds before itself.

On this triple basis—autonomy through writing, externalization by means of the work, and the reference to a world—I will construct the analysis central to our discussion of the revelatory function of poetic discourse.

I have not introduced the category of poetics heretofore. It does not designate one of the literary genres discussed in the first part of my presentation, but rather the totality of these genres inasmuch as they exercise a referential function that differs from the descriptive referential function of ordinary language and above all of scientific discourse. Hence I will speak of the poetic function of discourse and not of a poetic genre or a mode of poetic discourse. This function, in turn, is defined precisely in terms of its referential function. What is this referential function?

As a first approximation, we may say that the poetic function points to the obliterating of the ordinary referential function, at least if we identify it with the capacity to describe familiar objects of perception or the objects which science alone determines by means of its standards of measurement. Poetic discourse suspends this descriptive function. It does not directly augment our knowledge of objects.

From here it is only a short step to saying that in poetry language turns back on itself to celebrate itself. But if we say this we accede too quickly to the positivist presupposition that empirical knowledge is objective knowledge because it is verifiable. Too often, we do not notice that we uncritically accept a certain concept of truth defined as adequation to real objects and as submitted to a criterion of empirical verification. That language in its poetic function abolishes the type of reference characteristic of such descriptive discourse, and along with it the reign of truth as adequation and the very definition of truth in terms of verification, is not to be doubted. The question is whether this suspension or abolition of a referential function of the first degree is not the negative condition for the liberating of a more primitive, more originary referential function, which may be called a second order reference only because discourse whose function is descriptive has usurped the first rank in daily life and has been supported in this regard by modern science.

My deepest conviction is that poetic language alone restores to us that participation-in or belonging-to an order of things which precedes our capacity to oppose ourselves to things taken as objects opposed to a subject. Hence the function of poetic discourse is to bring about this emergence of a depth-structure of belonging-to amid the ruins of descriptive discourse. Once again, this function is in no way to be identified with poetry understood as something opposed to prose and defined by a certain affinity of sense, rhythm, image, and sound. I am first defining the poetic function in a negative manner, following Roman Jakobson, as the inverse of the referential function understood in a narrow descriptive sense, then in a positive way as what . . . I call the metaphorical reference. And in this regard, the most extreme paradox is that when language most enters into fiction—e.g., when a poet forges the plot of a tragedy—it most speaks truth because it redescribes reality so well known that it is taken for granted in terms of the new features of this plot. Fiction and redescription, then, go hand in hand. Or, to speak like Aristotle in his *Poetics,* the *mythos* is the way to true *mimesis,* which is not slavish imitation, or a copy, or mirror-image, but a transposition or metamorphosis—or, as I suggest, a redescription.

This conjunction of fiction and redescription, of *mythos* and *mimesis,* constitutes the referential function by means of which I would define the poetic dimension of language.

In turn, this poetic function conceals a dimension of reve-

lation where revelation is to be understood in a nonreligious, nontheistic, and nonbiblical sense of the word—but one capable of entering into resonance with one or the other of the aspects of biblical revelation. How is this so?

In the following manner. First the poetic function recapitulates in itself the three preparatory concepts of the autonomy of the text, the externality of the work, and the transcendence of the world of the text. Already by means of these three traits an order of things is revealed that does not belong to either the author or the original audience. But to these three traits the poetic function adds a split reference by means of which emerges the Atlantis submerged in the network of objects submitted to the domination of our preoccupations. It is this primordial ground of our existence, of the originary horizon of our being-there, that is the revelatory function which is coextensive with the poetic function.

But why call it revelatory? Because through all the traits that it recapitulates and by what it adds, the poetic function incarnates a concept of truth that escapes the definition by adequation as well as the criteria of falsification and verification. Here truth no longer means verification, but manifestation, i.e., letting what shows itself be. What shows itself is in each instance a proposed world, a world I may inhabit and wherein I can project my ownmost possibilities. It is in this sense of manifestation that language in its poetic function is a vehicle of revelation.

By using the word revelation in such a nonbiblical and even non-religious way, do we abuse the word? I do not think so. Our analysis of the biblical concept of revelation has prepared for us a first degree analogical use of the term and here we are led to a second degree analogy. The first degree analogy was assured by the role of the first analogue, prophetic discourse, with its implication of another voice behind the prophet's voice. This meaning of the first analogue was communicated to all the other modes of discourse to the extent that they could be said to be inspired. But we also saw that this analogy with reference to the *princeps* discourse, that of prophecy, did not do justice to the specific character of each of the other modes of discourse, above all narrative discourse where what is said or recounted, the generative historical event, came to language through the narration. And the philosophical concept of revelation leads us back to this primacy of what is said over the inspiration of the narrator by means of a second analogy that is no longer that of inspiration, but that of manifestation.

This new analogy invites us to place the originary expressions of biblical faith under the sign of the poetic function of language; not to deprive them of any referent, but to put them under the law of split reference that characterizes the poetic function. Religious discourse is poetic in all the senses we have named. Being written down as scripture removes it from the finite horizon of its authors and its first audience. The style of its literary genres gives it the externality of a work. And the intended implicit reference of each text opens onto a world, the biblical world, or rather the multiple worlds unfolded before the book by its narration, prophecy, prescriptions, wisdom, and hymns. The proposed world that in biblical language is called a new creation, a new Covenant, the Kingdom of God, is the "issue" of the biblical text unfolded in front of this text.

Finally, and above all, this "issue" of the biblical text is indirectly intended beyond the suspension of descriptive, didactic, and informative discourse. This abolition of the reference to objects that we can manipulate allows the world of our originary rootedness to appear. Just as the world of poetic texts opens its way across the ruins of the intraworldly objects of everyday existence and of science, so too the new being projected by the biblical text opens its way across the world of ordinary experience and in spite of the closed nature of that experience. The power to project this new world is the power of breaking through and of an opening.

Thus this areligious sense of revelation helps us to restore the concept of biblical revelation to its full dignity. It delivers us from psychologizing interpretations of the inspiration of the scriptures in the sense of an insufflation of their words into the writers' ears. If the Bible may be said to be revealed this must refer to what it says, to the new being it unfolds before us. Revelation, in short, is a feature of the biblical world proposed by the text.

Yet if this areligious sense of revelation has such a corrective value, it does not for all that include the religious meaning of revelation. There is a homology between them, but nothing allows us to derive the specific feature of religious language—i.e., that its referent moves among prophecy, narration, prescription, wisdom, and psalms, coordinating these diverse and partial forms of discourse by giving them a vanishing point and an index of incompleteness—nothing, I say, allows us to derive this from the general characteristics of the poetic function. The biblical hermeneutic is in turn one regional hermeneutic within a general hermeneutic and a unique hermeneutic that is joined to the philosophical hermeneutic as its *organon*. It is one particular case insofar as the Bible is one of the great poems of existence. It is a unique case because all its partial forms of discourse are referred to

that Name which is the point of intersection and the vanishing point of all our discourse about God, the name of the unnameable. This is the paradoxical homology that the category of the world of the text establishes between revelation in the broad sense of poetic discourse and in the specifically biblical sense.

From Paul Ricoeur, *Essays on Biblical Interpretation* (Philadelphia: Fortress Press, 1980), 98–104.

∽ **Elisabeth Schüssler Fiorenza,** biblical scholar and theologian, in "Introduction: In Search of Women's Heritage," explains some of her methods for reconstructing Christian origins in the light of feminist theology. The excerpt from "The Early Christian Missionary Movement" exemplifies one result of this reading.

ELISABETH SCHÜSSLER FIORENZA

In Memory of Her: A Feminist Theological Reconstruction of Christian Origins

Introduction: In Search of Women's Heritage

In the passion account of Mark's Gospel three disciples figure prominently: on the one hand, two of the twelve—Judas who betrays Jesus and Peter who denies him—and on the other, the unnamed woman who anoints Jesus. But while the stories of Judas and Peter are engraved in the memory of Christians, the story of the woman is virtually forgotten. Although Jesus pronounces in Mark: "And truly I say to you, wherever the gospel is preached in the whole world, what she has done will be told in memory of her,"[878] the woman's prophetic sign-action did not become a part of the gospel knowledge of Christians. Even her name is lost to us. Wherever the gospel is proclaimed and the eucharist celebrated another story is told: the story of the apostle who betrayed Jesus. The name of the betrayer is remembered, but the name of the faithful disciple is forgotten because she was a woman.

Although the story of the anointing is told in all four Gospels,[879] it is obvious that the redactional retelling of the story seeks to make the story more palatable to a patriarchal

---

878. Mk 14:9.

879. For an extensive discussion of the exegetical literature, see Robert Holst, "The Anointing of Jesus: Another Application of the Form-Critical Method," *JBL* [*Journal of Biblical Literature*] 95 (1976) 435–46.

Greco-Roman audience. Whereas the Fourth Gospel identifies the woman as Mary of Bethany who as faithful friend of Jesus shows her love by anointing him, Luke shifts the focus of the story from woman as disciple to woman as sinner. Whether Luke used Mark's text or transmits a different tradition is disputed. But this exegetical dispute does not matter much since we are used to reading the Markan story in the light of Luke. In the process the woman becomes a great sinner who is forgiven by Jesus.

Despite their differences, all four Gospels reflect the same basic story: a woman anoints Jesus. This incident causes objections which Jesus rejects by approving of the woman's action. If the original story had been just a story about the anointing of a guest's feet, it is unlikely that such a commonplace gesture would have been remembered and retold as the proclamation of the gospel. Therefore, it is much more likely that in the original story the woman anointed Jesus' head. Since the prophet in the Old Testament anointed the head of the Jewish king, the anointing of Jesus' head must have been understood immediately as the prophetic recognition of Jesus, the Anointed, the Messiah, the Christ. According to the tradition it was a woman who named Jesus by and through her prophetic sign-action. It was a politically dangerous story.[880]

In Mark's Gospel the story is sandwiched between the statement that the leaders of Jesus' people wanted to arrest him and the announcement of Jesus' betrayal by Judas for money. Mark thus depoliticizes the story of Jesus' passion: first, by shifting the blame for his death from the Romans to the Jewish establishment; and second, by theologically defining Jesus' messiahship as one of suffering and death. Whereas according to Mark the leading male disciples do not understand this suffering messiahship of Jesus, reject it, and finally abandon him, the women disciples who have followed Jesus from Galilee to Jerusalem suddenly emerge as the true disciples in the passion narrative. They are Jesus' true followers (*akolouthein*) who have understood that his ministry was not rule and kingly glory but diakonia, "service."[881] Thus the women emerge as the true Christian ministers and witnesses. The unnamed woman who names Jesus with a prophetic sign-action in Mark's Gospel is the paradigm for the true disciple. While Peter had confessed, without truly understanding it, "you are the anointed one," the woman anointing Jesus recognizes clearly that Jesus' messiahship means suffering and death.

Both Christian feminist theology and biblical interpretation are in the process of rediscovering that the Christian gospel cannot be proclaimed if the women disciples and what they have done are not remembered. They are in the process of reclaiming the supper at Bethany as women's Christian heritage in order to correct symbols and ritualizations of an all-male Last Supper that is a betrayal of true Christian discipleship and ministry.[882] Or, in the words of the artist Judy Chicago: "All the institutions of our culture tell us through words, deeds, and even worse silence that we are insignificant. But our heritage is our power."[883]

The explorations of this book have two goals: they attempt to reconstruct early Christian history as women's history in order not only to restore women's stories to early history but also to reclaim this history as the history of women and men. I do this not only as a feminist historian but also as a feminist theologian. The Bible is not just a historical collection of writings but also Holy Scripture, gospel, for Christians today. As such it informs not only theology but also the commitment of many women today. Yet as long as the stories and history of women in the beginnings of early Christianity are not theologically conceptualized as an integral part of the proclamation of the gospel, biblical texts and traditions formulated and codified by men will remain oppressive to women.

Such a reconstruction of early Christian history as women's history and of biblical-historical theology as feminist theology presupposes historical and theological critical analysis as well as the development of a feminist biblical-historical hermeneutics. Since I am trained in New Testament exegesis, I will limit my explorations to the beginnings of Christianity but not include all of biblical history. Methodologically, however, it will be necessary to go beyond the limits of the New Testament canon since it is a product of the patristic church, that is, a theological document of the "historical winners." To forego such an undertaking because historical critical scholarship and hermeneutics are "male" but not feminist does an intellectual disservice to women. Since it reinforces male-female role stereotypes, such an assumption is not capable of naming the particular oppressive assumptions and androcentric components of such scholarship.

Reconstruction of early Christian history in a feminist

---

880. Cf. J. K. Elliott, "The Anointing of Jesus," *Exp Tim* [*Expository Times*] 85 (1974) 105–7.

881. Mk 15:41.

882. Cf. also Elizabeth E. Pratt, "The Ministry of Mary of Bethany," *Theology Today* 34 (1977) 29–39.

883. Judy Chicago, *The Dinner Party: A Symbol of Our Heritage* (New York: Doubleday, Anchor Books, 1979), 246–49.

perspective raises difficult hermeneutical, textual, and historical problems. Since feminism has developed different theoretical perspectives and models, this reconstruction must also include the formulation of a feminist heuristic framework or model that allows for the oppression as well as for the historical agency of women in early Christianity.

[. . .] A fundamental methodological insight of historical criticism of the Bible was the realization that the *Sitz im Leben* or life setting of a text is as important for its understanding as its actual formulation. Biblical texts are not verbally inspired revelation nor doctrinal principles but historical formulations within the context of a religious community. Although this insight is challenged today by literary formalism as well as textual biblicism, it nevertheless remains basic to any historical reconstruction. Studies of the social world of Israel and early Christianity are in the process of developing heuristic models that comprehend more fully the social-historical context of the biblical texts.

Similarly, feminist theory insists that all texts are products of an androcentric patriarchal culture and history. The current feminist movement has therefore engendered an explosion of scholarly works in all areas of scientific inquiry and research.[884] Historians, philosophers and anthropologists have emphasized that current scholarly theory and research are deficient because they neglect women's lives and contributions and construe humanity and human history as male. Feminist scholarship in all areas, therefore, seeks to construct heuristic models and concepts that allow us to perceive the human reality articulated insufficiently in androcentric texts and research.

The explorations of this book begin therefore with the hope of moving away from the pervasive apologetic that characterizes most treatments of women in the Bible, to a historical-critical reconstruction of women's history and women's contributions to early Christian beginnings. Moreover, I have assumed that the new questions raised by feminist scholarship will enhance our understanding of early Christian history. The attempt to "write women back into early Christian history" should not only restore early Christian history to women but also lead to a richer and more accurate perception of early Christian beginnings. If scholars employ philosophical, sociological, or psychological analyses for constructing new interpretive models of early Christian development, nothing should prevent us from utilizing feminist heuristic concepts as well, in order to reconstruct an early Christian history in which women are not hidden and invisible. While an androcentric model cannot do justice to those texts that

positively mention women's leadership in early Christianity, a feminist model can positively integrate them. [. . .]

The Early Christian Missionary Movement: Equality in the Life of the Spirit

[. . . Women's] impact and importance must not be seen as exceptional, but must be understood within the structures of the early Christian missionary movement that allowed for the full participation and leadership of women.

This chapter, therefore, proceeds by reconstructing a model of that movement whose constitutive institutional elements were the missionary agents, on the one hand, and the house church and local associations on the other. The forms of religious propaganda and the reciprocal patronage system of Greco-Roman society, not the patriarchal structures of the Greco-Roman household, were constitutive organizational elements of this movement. Such a reconstruction of the Christian missionary movement in terms of organizational structures provides the social framework that makes women's leadership not only plausible but also intelligible. Traveling missionaries and house churches were central to the early Christian mission, which depended on special mobility and patronage, and women were leaders in both areas.

Missionaries

The remarkable expansion of oriental mystery religions in the western Mediterranean has not lacked scholarly attention. Many preceded the Christian missionaries to Greece and Rome, thereby creating the climate in which a new Eastern cult such as Christianity could be propagated. The wandering preachers of that day manifest a whole range of missionary propagandists,[885] from philosophers, prophets, itinerant preachers, mendicants, and sorcerers to the traveling merchants, state officials, immigrants, slaves, and soldiers. Common to all were mobility and dedication to their philosophy

---

884. *Signs: Journal of Women in Culture and Society,* which was founded in 1975, has regular reviews of scholarship in various areas. Of equal importance are the *Women's Studies International Quarterly* and *Feminist Studies.* See also Dale Spender, ed., *Men's Studies Modified: The Impact of Feminism on the Academic Disciplines* (Oxford: Pergamon Press, 1981).

885. Cf. A. D. Nock, *Conversion: The Old and the New in Religion from Alexander the Great to Augustine of Hippo* (London: Oxford University Press, 1961); and the literature in E. Schüssler Fiorenza, ed., *Aspects of Religious Propaganda in Judaism and Early Christianity* (Notre Dame: University of Notre Dame Press, 1976).

or religion. Jewish proselytism of the first century must be seen in this context of Eastern cults. In Rome and throughout the Mediterranean, large numbers—many of whom were women—were attracted to the monotheism and high moral standards of Judaism. Among Godfearers and proselytes many women, often of high social status, are mentioned.[886]

Like Judaism the Christian gospel was spread by traveling missionaries, trade and business people, who depended on the hospitality and support provided by house churches.[887] Thus, the charismatic missionaries were not necessarily itinerant beggars. Barnabas seems to have been wealthy enough to support the community of Jerusalem by selling land. Paul was one of the distinguished circle of foreign Jews, who belonged to the privileged Hellenistic families in Tarsus and who had received Roman citizenship in turn for services rendered. E. A. Judge's conclusion, therefore, seems appropriate: "Christianity in its canonical form, then, is not so much the work of Galileans, as of a very cultivated section of internationalized Jewry; they were at any rate its principal sponsors."[888] The exceptional contribution of prominent women of wealth and social status to the Jewish as well as Christian missionary movements is more and more acknowledged in scholarship.[889]

The practice of missionary partners in the Jesus movement seems to have been followed by the Christian missionary movement as well.[890] This allowed for the equality of women and men in missionary work. It is likely that these missionary partners were at first couples. By the time of Paul, however, sexual ascesis and celibacy were being urged as preferred preconditions for missionary work. Whether or not some form of "spiritual marriage," in which two ascetics lived together as a couple, has its roots in this missionary practice of partnership is unclear, but possible. Pauline references to women missionaries, however, do not reflect on their sexual status and gender roles, or classify them as widows or virgins.

The Pauline letters mention women as Paul's coworkers, but these women were not the "helpers" of Paul or his "assistants." Only five of Paul's coworkers, all of whom are male (Erastus, Mark, Timothy, Titus, and Tychicus), "stand in explicit subordination to Paul serving him or being subject to his instructions."[891] The genuine Pauline letters apply missionary titles and such characterizations as coworker (Prisca), brother/sister (Apphia), *diakonos* (Phoebe), and apostle (Junia) to women also. They usually equate coworkers and "those who toil." In 1 Cor 16:16ff. Paul admonishes the

Corinthians to be "subject to every coworker and laborer'" and to give recognition to such persons. 1 Thes 5:12 exhorts the Thessalonians to "respect those who labor among you, and are over you in the Lord, and admonish you." It is significant, therefore, that Paul uses the same Greek verb *kopian,* "to labor" or "to toil"[892] not only to characterize his own evangelizing and teaching but also that of women. In Rom 16:6, 12, he commends Mary, Typhaena, Tryphosa, and Persis for having "labored hard" in the Lord.

Paul also affirms that women worked with him on an equal basis. Phil 4:2–3 explicitly states that Euodia and Syntyche have "contended" side by side with him. As in an athletic race these women have competed alongside Paul, Clement, and the rest of Paul's co-missionaries in the cause of the gospel.[893] Paul considers the authority of both women in the community at Philippi so great that he fears that their dissension could do serious damage to the Christian mission. The Philippians had entered with Paul into an equal partnership, a partnership endangered by the disagreement of these two outstanding women missionaries. J. P. Sampley has pointed out that, according to Roman legal traditions, consensual legal partnership "is operative as long as the partners in *eodem sensu* [of the same mind], as long as they are 'of the same mind' about the centrality of the purpose around which the partnership was formed in the first place."[894] When, therefore, Paul admonishes the two women "to be of the same mind" he reminds them of their original shared partnership

886. Cf. M. Radin, *The Jews among the Greeks and Romans* (Philadelphia: Jewish Publication Society, 1915), 149–62; K. G. Kuhn and H. Stegemann, "Proselyten," Supplement to Pauly-Wissowa 9 (1962) 1248–83; F. Siegert, "Gottesfürchtige und Sympathisanten," *Journal for the Study of Judaism* 4 (1973) 109–64.

887. Cf. D. W. Riddle, "Early Christian Hospitality: A Factor in the Gospel Transmission," *JBL* [*Journal of Biblical Literature*] 57 (1938) 141–54; Helga Rusche, *Gastfreundschaft in der Verkündigung de Neuer Testaments und ihr Verhältnis zur Mission* (Münster: Missionswissenschaftliches Intitut, 1958)

888. E. A. Judge, *The Social Patterns of Christian Groups in the First Century* (London: Tyndale Press, 1960), 57.

889. See especially H. Gülzow, "Soziale Gegebenheiten der altkirchlichen Mission," in H. Frohnes and U. W. Knorr, eds., *Kirchengeschichte als Missionsgeschichte* (Munich: Kaiser, 1974), 1.189–226: esp. 200–206; and already A. von Harnack, *The Mission and Expansion of Christianity in the First Three Centuries* (New York: Putnam, 1908), 2.64–84.

890. Cf. G. Schille, *Die urchristliche Kollegialmission* (Zürich: Zwingli Verlag, 1967), 89ff., for mission by pairs; he does not mention couples, however.

891. E. E. Ellis, "Paul and His Co-workers," *NTS* [*New Testament Studies*] 17 (1970/71): 439.

892. A. von Harnack ("'Kopos' [. . .] im frühchristlichen Sprachgebrauch," ZNW 27 [1928] 1–10) argues against von Dobschütz that "those who labor" constituted an official circle of ministers, most of whom were probably presbyters.

893. Cf. W. D. Thomas, "The Place of Women in the Church at Philippi," *Exp Tim* 83 (1972): 117–20.

894. J. P. Sampley, *Pauline Partnership in Christ* (Philadelphia: Fortress, 1980), 62.

and commitment to the same gospel. At stake here, then, are not personal disagreements or quarrels but the shared ground and the purpose of their equal partnership in the "race" for the gospel.

Elisabeth Schüssler Fiorenza, *In Memory of Her: A Feminist Theological Reconstruction of Christian Origins* (New York: Crossroad, 1983), xiii–xvi, 168–70.

☙ **E. P. Sanders** is well known for his work on Judaism in Palestine in the first century CE and on early Christianity. His groundbreaking contributions to the "New Quest" for the historical Jesus and to the study of Paul place early Christianity within the context of first-century Judaism. In *Paul, the Law, and the Jewish People,* he revisits the problems of Paul's theology in this historical context.

E. P. SANDERS

From *Paul, the Law, and the Jewish People*

Introduction: Different Questions, Different Answers

It is with more than a little hesitation that one picks up again the question of Paul and the law. It is a topic that has been discussed by numerous scholars in great detail, with the result that one pauses before thinking that fresh light can be shed on it. This consideration points to others: the subject is difficult,[895] and all the scholarly labor that has been spent on it has resulted in no consensus. The difficulty of the topic, however, is matched by its importance, and it merits the effort that has been expended. It is a subject which must be penetrated if one is to understand Paul's thought, and it is no less crucial for understanding an important moment in the divorce of Christianity from Judaism. If despite the difficulty and the scope of the problem I venture to address it in relatively short compass, it is in the hope that a few clarifying proposals can be made, even if every exegetical problem cannot be solved.

There is a tantalizing quality to the study of Paul's view of the law. He says a lot about it, and one should be able, by using the normal tools of exegesis, to determine precisely what he thought. The subject is not like the study of the historical Jesus, where one has to distinguish redaction from tradition, probe to find the earliest traditions, and try to establish criteria for determining authentic material. Nor is it like the study of "wisdom" in 1 Corinthians, where there is too little material at hand to allow us to be sure just which "wisdom" Paul was replying to. In the study of "Paul and

the law" we have before us a lot of unquestionably authentic statements by Paul on the subject; and, further, we know what law Paul was talking about. With a few exceptions, he meant the *Tanak,* the Jewish Torah. Yet the search for what he "really meant" goes on. One may ask, of course, whether or not he did have a single and well-thought-out position on the law, and that question will be posed here. But a priori one would expect him to have had a clear position on the law. The law, it would appear from his own testimony, had been his life before God revealed his son to him.[896] His break with it was self-conscious.[897] His reaction to the possibility that his Galatian converts might accept the law was so forceful that one expects him to have had a clear and decisive reason for responding as he did. And yet, to repeat, there is no agreement among scholars as to what that reason was, and still less is there agreement as to how to understand the relationship of his numerous other statements about the law to the position which he took in the Galatian controversy.

One of the factors which makes Paul's statements about the law hard to unravel is the general difficulty of distinguishing between the reason for which he held a view and the arguments which he adduces in favor of it. To take an example: It is clear in 1 Corinthians 11 that Paul thinks that men should pray with heads uncovered and that women should pray with heads covered. In favor of this view he says that for a woman to pray with head uncovered is the same as if her head were shaved.[898] He also says that she should pray with her head covered "because of the angels."[899] He then asserts that nature itself teaches that men should have short hair and women long hair (although how this supports his main point is not quite clear).[900] Finally he says to those still unconvinced that "we recognize no other practice," nor do the other churches.[901] In this particular case he may never state the real

---

895. H. J. Schoeps (*Paul: The Theology of the Apostle in the Light of Jewish Religious History* [Philadelphia: Westminster Press, 1961], 168) commented that the law is the most difficult aspect of Paul's thought. Cf. Peter Stuhlmacher, "Das Ende des Gesetzes," *ZTK* [*Zeitschrift für Theologie und Kircke*] 67 (1970): 35; "Das Gesetz als Thema biblischer Theologie," *ZTK* 75 (1978): 272.

896. Phil 3:4–6; Gal 1:13–15.

897. Already the problems begin: is it correct to say he broke with it; and, if so, in what way and to what extent did he do so? For the self-consciousness of some sort of break, however, one may point to Phil 3:7.

898. 1 Cor 11:5.

899. It is not necessary for the present purpose to discuss the reason for which he uses *exousia* in 11:10. The general point is clear enough.

900. 11:14f; perhaps the reasoning is this: a woman should have long hair; uncovered hair is the same as a shaved head; therefore she must pray with her head covered.

901. 11:16.

reason for his position: he was Jewish.[902] Nevertheless, we see how he can mingle all sorts of arguments. This fact, as we shall see, helps to explain why scholars disagree about why he said what he said about the law: reason and argument are not always easy to distinguish.

The proposal of the present monograph is that the different things which Paul said about the law depend on the question asked or the problem posed. Each answer has its own logic and springs from one of his central concerns; but the diverse answers, when set alongside one another, do not form a logical whole, as might have been expected had he set out to discuss the problem of law as such. The primary aim is to show that this is the case and to sketch the principal questions and answers. Each category is not treated in equal exegetical detail, and the first category—why Paul said that no one is justified by works of law—receives more attention than the others. Before launching into the first category, however, it will be helpful to describe the general understanding of Paul's thought which governs much of the following discussion. [. . .]

Chapter One: The Law Is Not an Entrance Requirement

Our first category is the one which has attracted the most extensive exegetical work and which is usually taken as being the most characteristic thing which Paul says about the law: one is righteoused by faith, not by works of law. Three principal problems have arisen in the course of scholarly debates. (1) Against whom is the statement directed? (2) Why does Paul hold that righteousness cannot come by law? (3) What is the relationship between saying that righteousness is not by law and the statement that judgment is on the basis of deeds or that, at the judgment, those who have done the law will be righteoused?[903] We shall now consider the [first] two.

There is a narrow range of answers possible to the first question. The statement "no one is righteoused by works of law" can be understood as directed against the Jewish understanding of salvation, against Paul's Christian opponents (whether Jewish or Gentile), or both. The second question produces more debate and a wider range of answers. Paul holds the view which he so often asserts because it is impossible to do the entire law (the "quantitative" answer); because doing the law itself estranges—doing it is worse than not doing it, as Heikki Räisänen has remarked[904] (the "qualitative" answer); because of his exclusivist soteriology (only by faith in Christ, therefore not by law); because of the exigencies of the Gentile mission.[905] It is naturally possible to com-

bine some of these explanations of Paul's view, and Hans Hübner has recently proposed that the quantitative answer appears in Galatians, the qualitative in Romans.[906]

I do not plan to take up and assess each problem and the various answers to it one by one, but rather to discuss the principal passages and to draw conclusions at the end.

Galatians 2–3

We first meet the formulation "not by works of law" in Galatians, which is in many ways fortunate, for both the setting and the main thrust of Galatians are relatively easy to determine, and they tell us rather a lot about Paul's treatment of the law in the letter. To understand the statements about the law in Galatians, it is important to be clear about two points: (1) The subject of Galatians is not whether or not humans, abstractly conceived, can by good deeds earn enough merit to be declared righteous at the judgment; it is the condition on which Gentiles enter the people of God. (2) Paul's arguments about the requirement for admission are largely taken from Scripture, and he is in all probability replying to topics introduced by the rival missionaries. While both these points are important for understanding Paul's treatment of the law, the first is absolutely vital. Nevertheless, I do not propose to prove either in advance. The evidence will appear as the argument proceeds. We begin with a sketch of the situation in Galatia; the burden of discussion with other scholars will be borne by the notes.

Missionaries were attempting, apparently with some success, to convince Paul's Gentile[907] converts that to be heirs of the biblical promises they had to accept the biblical law. To

---

902. Cf. *Sifre Num.* 11 (on 5:18).

903. Rom 2:13.

904. In reading Rudolf Bultmann "one gets the impression that zeal for the law is more damaging than transgression": Heikki Räisänen, "Legalism and Salvation by the Law," in *Die Paulinische Literatur und Theologie* (Aarhus: Forlaget Aros, 1980), 68.

905. Three positions on why Paul said "not by law" will receive little or no attention here: (1) It was a standard Jewish view that the law ceases with the messianic era (Schweitzer, Schoeps); (2) Romans 7 shows that Paul had become frustrated in his attempt to find righteousness under the law and therefore denounced it (many scholars, especially of an earlier period); (3) Paul had an apocalyptic view of the law as a monolithic totality and could thus dismiss it *in toto* (Wilckens). On these see E. P. Sanders, *Paul and Palestinian Judaism* (Philadelphia: Fortress Press, 1977), 478–80 and notes (hereafter cited as *PPJ*).

906. Hans Hübner, *Das Gesetz bei Paulus,* 2d ed. (Göttingen: Vandenhoeck and Ruprecht, 1980).

907. In reviewing Betz's commentary on Galatians, Davies challenges the view that the converts were pagan Gentiles (W. D. Davies's review of *Galatians* by Hans Dieter Betz, *RSR* [*Religious Studies Review*] 7 [1981]: 312–14).

put it in the terms used earlier: the Gentile converts could enter the people of God only on condition that they were circumcised and accepted the law. In their own terms, the missionaries held the position that those who wanted to be true sons of Abraham and heirs of the promises must do as Abraham did and be circumcised.[908] Precisely who these missionaries were remains uncertain, but their position seems to be materially the same as that of the people whom Paul calls "false brethren" in Gal 2:4. It thus seems likely that they were "right wing" Jewish Christians.[909]

Theirs was an entirely reasonable position, and its great strength was almost certainly the support which reading the Bible would give it. The most forceful passage is Gen 17:9–14, where God tells Abraham that he and his seed (to sperma)[910] must be circumcised and that any male who is not circumcised will be destroyed (cf. Paul's reply, Gal 5:4). The oppos-

ing missionaries could also have read to the Galatians Isa 56:6–8, where the "foreigners" who join the people of God are expected to hold fast to the covenant (circumcision) and especially to keep the Sabbath. Thus most of Paul's arguments against the opposing position are based on the Bible (Gal 3:1–5 is a notable exception), as he apparently wished to counter his opponents on their own ground and to show, *by Scripture*, that the biblical commandments were not a necessary or sufficient condition for admission to "the Israel of God."[911]

It is easy to imagine how the disagreement arose. Many Jews, and all the Jewish Christians whose views are known to us, expected Gentiles to be brought into the people of God in the messianic period.[912] There was, however, no accepted *halakah* governing the conditions of their admission. The prophetic and poetic passages (e.g., *Sib. Or.* III. 72–75) which envisage the entry or submission of the Gentiles in the last days generally do not give legal detail.[913] The Jewish Christians, who considered the end to be near, however, had to make practical decisions. The normal requirement for entering the people of God was to make full prosely-

---

908. Gen 17:9–14, 26f. Most scholars agree that the opposing missionaries introduced such biblical themes as sonship to Abraham. See, for example, Jose Eckert, *Die urchristliche Verkündigung im Streit zwischen Paulus und seinen Gegnern nach dem Galaterbrief* (Regensburg: F. Pustet, 1971), 76, 105; Hübner, *Gesetz*, 17f. A few have doubts: Brendan Byrne, *"Sons of God"—"Seed of Abraham"* (Rome: Biblical Institute Press, 1979), 148f.

909. Most scholars agree that the opposing missionaries were Christian. Note Paul's description of their message as "a different gospel" (Gal 1:6) and his accusation that his opponents wish to escape being persecuted for the cross of Christ (6:12). In addition, his appeals to the defeat of the "false brethren" in Jerusalem and to the agreement with Peter and James have point only if the dispute is an inner-Christian one. For the history of research see Heinrich Schlier, *Der Brief an die Galater*, 5th ed. (Göttingen: Vandenhoeck & Ruprecht, 1971), 19–24; Franz Mussner, *Der Galaterbrief* (Freiburg: Herder, 1974), 11–29 (with a detailed summary of positions); Hans Dieter Betz, *Galatians* (Philadelphia: Fortress Press, 1979), 4–9; Eckert, *Verkündigung*, 1–18.

Munck made it a main thesis in his attack on the Tübingen school that "the Judaizing opponents in Galatians are Gentile Christians"; Johannes Munck, *Paul and the Salvation of Mankind* (Atlanta: John Knox Press, 1977), 87f. The principal evidence is the present participle *hoi peritemnomenoi* in 6:13. Cf. Pierre Bonnard, *L'Epitre de Saint Paul aux Galâtes*, 2d ed. (Neuchâtel and Paris: Delachaux & Niestlé, 1972), 2–5, 13: the opponents were certainly Christians, probably of Hellenistic Jewish origin or former pagans who had proselytized before embracing Christianity. George Howard (*Crisis in Galatia* [New York: Cambridge University Press, 1979], 17–19) takes full account of the present participle but nevertheless concludes that the opponents were probably Jewish Christians; see generally his chapter 1. He proposes that they may not have known that Paul had reached agreement with the "pillars."

Some have attempted to describe the situation of the opposing missionaries more precisely. Thus, for example, Robert Jewett ("The Agitators and the Galatian Congregation," *NTS* 17 [1970/71]: 198–212) proposed that they were acting under "zealotic" pressure from non-Christian Jews. This view seems to be accepted by W. D. Davies in "Paul: From the Semitic Point of View," *Cambridge History of Judaism II*.

For the present purpose, it is the position of the opponents, not their precise identity, which is important. Here only one other scholarly proposal need be mentioned. Some have argued that Paul faced a "second front" in Galatia and that chapter 5 is his response to libertines. I follow the majority as seeing the paraenesis in chap. 5 against the background of Paul's own denial of the law in chaps. 3 and 4. The last two chapters of Galatians presuppose the same polemical situation as the first four. Note the references to the law in 5:14, 18, 23; 6:2. On all this see Eckert, *Verkündigung*, 15–18 (literature, 64–71 (reply), 149f.).

910. Cf. Gal 3:16, 19.

911. I am grateful to J. Louis Martyn for several discussions on the occasion and purpose of Galatians and on the position of the opposing missionaries.

912. "Jewish Christians" here include Paul. On the Jewish expectation see J. Jeremias, *Jesus, Promise to the Nations* (Philadelphia: Fortress Press; London: SCM Press, 1982), 61. It should be added that another Jewish view is attested: that the Gentiles would be destroyed. So 1QM; Jub. 22:20f. and elsewhere.

Many scholars have emphasized the eschatological setting of Paul's work and his view of the mission to the Gentiles. Thus Schoeps (*Paul*, 219): "Throughout his life the same prophetic promises were the impelling force behind this activity, the promise that in the Messianic age the nations would join Israel in the worship of its God. . . ." (citing Zeph 3:9). Munck especially emphasized the eschatological setting of the mission to the Gentiles, as well as Paul's reversal of the traditional scheme in Romans 9–11. See his *Christ and Israel* (Philadelphia: Fortress Press, 1967), 11f. (citing Isa 2:2–4 and Mic 4:1–4); *Paul*, 123, 255–58, 276f., 303–5. See also Ernst Käsemann, *Commentary on Romans* ET (Grand Rapids: Wm. B. Eerdmans, 1980), 307, 312. The principal evidence is supplied by Romans 9–11, especially Paul's struggling with the reversal of the traditional scheme (so that the inclusion of the Gentiles precedes the full salvation of Israel) in 11:13–26.

Drane does not agree with the statement that all Jewish Christians whose views are known favored the mission to the Gentiles, disagreeing only as to the conditions on which Gentiles should be admitted. "On any account of the history of the earliest church, one of the most difficult questions for the Christians of the first generation was to decide whether the Christian faith was to be just a sect of Judaism, and whether therefore their preaching should be restricted to Jews, or whether the message was intended for Gentiles also" (J. W. Drane, *Paul: Libertine or Legalist?* [London: SPCK, 1975], 24). He has in view Matt 10:5ff., which does indeed raise the question. The difficulty is in finding the *Sitz im Leben* of that passage. In any case, as far as the evidence of Galatians goes, the alternative is not "either a sect of Judaism" or "the Gentile mission," but "the Gentile mission without requiring the law" or "the mission to the Gentiles while requiring full proselytization."

913. Isa 56:6–8 does give *halakah* (circumcision and Sabbath), but the passage is not cited in Paul's letters, and we cannot know whether or not it was used against him.

tization,[914] and some Jewish Christians obviously thought that the same condition should be maintained even in the last days.[915] It is this view which the "false brethren" of Gal 2:4 held and this view which Paul attacks in the body of Galatians. Paul's view was at the other extreme: Gentiles were to be brought into the people of God without being required to accept the law of Moses, but by faith in Christ alone, and it was his mission to bring them in. We shall later have to consider whether or not, or the degree to which, Paul applied to native Jews the admission requirement of faith to the *exclusion* of circumcision and the law, but the problem as it meets us in Galatians is that of the admission of the Gentiles. Peter and James appear basically to have agreed with Paul on the question of the Gentiles. It was not their mission to bring them in, but it was correct for Paul to do so without requiring proselytization. It was probably Peter's responsibility to the circumcised, which might be hindered if he himself were not Torah-observant, not disagreement with Paul's mission as such, which led him to withdraw from the Gentiles in Antioch.[916]

If we assume that all the parties named or referred to in Galatians were Christians, we should also assume that the rival missionaries did not argue against "faith in Christ." The latter is a common Christian formulation,[917] though doubtless it meant different things to different people.[918]

If this description of the situation is at all correct, then we can readily grasp the broad outline of Paul's argument. The argument of Galatians 3 is against Christian missionaries, not against Judaism, and it is against the view that Gentiles must accept the law *as a condition* of or as a basic requirement for membership.[919] Paul's argument is not in favor of faith per se, nor is it against works per se. It is much more particular: it is against requiring the Gentiles to keep the law of Moses in order to be true "sons of Abraham."[920]

We have become so sensitive to the theological issue of grace and merit that we often lose sight of the actual subject of the dispute. Many scholars who view the opposing missionaries as Jewish Christians nevertheless see Galatians 3 as Paul's rebuttal of Judaism.[921] But the quality and character of

---

914. We need not here discuss the question of whether some Jews in the first century allowed proselytization without circumcision. On this see Neil J. McEleney, "Conversion, Circumcision and the Law," *NTS* 20 (1974): 319–41, esp. 328–33; Peder Borgen, "Observations on the Theme 'Paul and Philo': Paul's Preaching of Circumcision in Galatia (Gal 5:11) and Debates on Circumcision in Philo," in *Die Paulinische Literatur und Theologie* (Aarhus: Forlaget Aros, 1980), 88; Larry Schiffman, "At the Crossroads: Tannaitic Perspectives on the Jewish Christian Schism," in *Jewish and Christian Self-Definition*, vol. 2, *Aspects of Judaism in the Graeco-Roman Period* (Philadelphia: Fortress Press; London: SCM Press, 1981), 127 and the note on 342; Eckert, *Verkündigung*, 53–58. The rival missionaries in Galatia obviously took the view that circumcision was required.

915. Munck argued otherwise: the Jewish Christians (other than Paul) did not oppose the mission to the Gentiles (*Paul*, 119), but rather they "neither thought about nor laid down regulations for the admission of Gentiles into the Church." They presumed "that Israel's conversion would result in the saving of Gentiles" (130; cf. 255–58). It is clear in Gal 2:3f., however, that the coming of Titus to Jerusalem forced the matter to the attention of the Jerusalem Christians (even if nothing else did); and the fact that emissaries came from James (Gal 2:12) shows that some in Jerusalem were thinking about the consequences of the Gentile mission, even if for their own part they were prepared to leave it to others.

916. See, for example, F. F. Bruce, *Paul: Apostle of the Heart Set Free* (Grand Rapids: Wm. B. Eerdmans, 1977), 176f.; Peter Richardson, "Pauline Inconsistency: I Corinthians 9:19–23 and Galatians 2:11–14," *NTS* 26 (1980): 347–62, esp. 348, 360.

917. This point is well made by Bultmann in *TDNT* [*Theological Dictionary of the New Testament*] 6: 203–19. Cf. *PPJ*, 441 n. 54, 445.

918. The formula quoted in Rom 10:9 (*pisteuein hoti*), for example, is to be distinguished from Paul's characteristic usage.

919. H. Räisänen, in an article with which the present essay is in close agreement ("Legalism and Salvation by the Law"), poses the very interesting question of why Paul set up the law as a means of salvation only in order to knock it down (77). His answer gives a convincing account of part of Paul's history (78–82). I would, however, pose the problem differently. Neither side sees the law as a possible means of salvation in the sense of producing sufficient merit. Paul's opponents take the standard Jewish view that to enter into the biblical promises one has to accept the biblical condition: the law of Moses. On doing the law as the *condition* of salvation, but not as earning it, see *PPJ*, index, s.v. obedience.

920. Cf. Lloyd Gaston, "Paul and the Torah," in *Anti-Semitism and the Foundations of Christianity* (New York: Paulist Press, 1979), 56: "It is remarkable that in the endless discussions of Paul's understanding of the law, few would have asked what a first century Jew would have thought of the law *as it related to Gentiles*." He then, however, discusses the rabbinic concepts of "the righteous among the nations of the world," the Noachian Commandments, etc. One must be still more precise. In Rom 2:14 the question of "righteous Gentiles" comes up, but the question of how much of the law Gentiles must do in order to be righteous *by the law's own standards* is not the principal question in Galatians. The question is a Gentile one, but it is the question of circumcision and admission.

921. Or of "Pharisaic soteriology." See, for example, Betz, *Galatians*, 116 (on 2:16); modified on 146 (on 3:12): "not only against Judaism in general but also against the Galatians' expectation, introduced by the anti-Pauline opposition." Hübner holds that the argument is against Judaism as Paul understood it, leaving open the possibility that he misunderstood it. (See, e.g., "Identitätsverlust und paulinische Theologie," *KuD* [*Kerygma und Dogma*] 24: 183). The distinction is irrelevant if the argument is not against Judaism. On Galatians 3 as against Jews as such see also G. Wagner, "Pour comprendre l'apôtre Paul," *Lumière et Vie* 27 (1978): 5–20; Ferdinand Hahn, "Das Gesetzesverständnis im Römer und Galaterbrief," *ZNW* [*Zeitschrift für die neutestamentliche Wissenschaft*] 67 (1976–77): 51f. (following an excellent discussion of aspects of the law in Romans, Hahn curiously says that Galatians deals almost exclusively with Judaism); Ulrich Luz, *Das Geschichtsverständnis des Paulus* (Munich: Chr. Kaiser, 1968), 219 (Galatians is the earliest letter to confront Judaism). Among relatively recent treatments, that of Herman Ridderbos is remarkable for its lack of attention to occasion and context (*Paul: An Outline of His Theology* [Grand Rapids: Wm. B. Eerdmans, 1975]). He maintains with absolute consistency that Paul's discussions of the law are directed against Judaism. See 131–43, 151, 170, 178. There is no treatment of the position of Paul's opponents in Galatia, and Paul is depicted as attacking Jewish legalistic works—righteousness, salvation by meritorious deeds, etc. (esp. 131–53).

That the opponents in Galatia are Jewish Christians, not Jews, has been especially emphasized by Franz Mussner, who also sees the theological implications of the distinction. See *Der Galaterbrief*, 11–29; "Theologische 'Wiedergutmachung' am Beispiel der Auslegung des Galaterbriefes," *Freiburger Rundbrief* 26 (1974): 7–11. Richardson (*Israel* [Peter Richardson, *Israel in the Apostolic Church* (Cambridge: Cambridge University Press, 1969)], 91) points out that the discussion of the law in Galatians, though offensive to Jews, is against opponents

Judaism are not in view; it is only the question of how one becomes a true son of Abraham, that is, enters the people of God. I believe that the reason for which Galatians 3 is seen as Paul's argument against Judaism is this: Paul's argument about righteousness by faith or by works of law in Galatians 2 and 3 is viewed as if he were arguing that an individual cannot merit salvation by achieving enough good deeds to present a favorable balance before God.[922] It is believed to be characteristic of Judaism to hold such a position, so that Paul's argument is perceived to be against Judaism. A study of Jewish material does not reveal such a position. More to the point, that is not Paul's argument in any case. The question is not about how many good deeds an individual must present before God to be declared righteous at the judgment, but, to repeat, whether or not Paul's Gentile converts must accept the Jewish law in order to enter the people of God or to be counted truly members.

In focusing on the controversy as one regarding "entry," I do not mean to imply that the requirement of faith alone for entry (to be a descendant of Abraham; to be righteoused) is a fleeting one which has no significance for continuing life in the people of God. The debate in Galatians is a debate about "entry" in the sense of what is essential in order to be considered a member *at all*.[923] Paul holds that faith is the sole membership requirement; his opponents would require also circumcision and acceptance of the Mosaic law. [. . .] It is not doing the law in and of itself which, in Paul's view, is wrong. Circumcision is, from one perspective, a matter of indifference.[924] It is completely wrong, however, when it is made an essential requirement for membership.

The controversy centers on the admission rite, circumcision, but includes other aspects of the law as well, such as food and "days."[925] It thus appears that Paul's opponents took the position—which is, to repeat, entirely understandable—that Gentile converts to the people of God had to be circumcised and accept the rest of the law. [. . .] Paul's view is equally straightforward, although the reason for which he held it is not immediately evident. Gentiles do not need to accept the Mosaic law in order to be members of the people of God. Thus we have a debate which is both understandable and of obvious importance.

From E. P. Sanders, *Paul, the Law, and the Jewish People* (Minneapolis, MN: Fortress Press, 1983), 3–4, 17–20.

☙ **John P. Meier** lays out his methodology for research into the historical Jesus in the first volume of *A Marginal Jew: Rethinking the Historical Jesus*. Meier, a Catholic New Testament scholar, is known for his contributions to the "Third Quest" for the historical Jesus.

JOHN P. MEIER

"Criteria: How Do We Decide What Comes from Jesus?" in *A Marginal Jew: Rethinking the Historical Jesus*

In the previous chapters we have seen that, in our quest for the historical Jesus, we are dependent, for the most part, on the four canonical Gospels. Since these Gospels are suffused with the Easter faith of the early Church and were written from forty to seventy years after the events narrated, we are left asking: How can we distinguish what comes from Jesus (Stage I, roughly AD 28–30) from what was created by the oral tradition of the early Church (Stage II, roughly AD 30–70) and what was produced by the editorial work (redaction) of the evangelists (Stage III, roughly AD 70–100)?[926] All too often, popular books on Jesus pick and choose among the

---

within Christianity (Richardson views the opponents as Gentile Christians): "it is not a polemic directed against those who by birth are under that mantle."

922. Cf. Betz, *Galatians*, 117; Ridderbos in the preceding note.

923. So also Ulrich Wilckens, "Über Abfassungszweck und Aufbau des Römerbriefs," in *Rechtfertigung als Freiheit: Paulusstudien* (Neukirchen-Vluyn: Neukirchener Verlag, 1974), 132: the argument of the opponents in Galatians is that "the Gentiles must first of all accomplish the fundamental presupposition of full membership in the Church of God, namely, belonging to Israel."

Cf. W. D. Davies, "Paul and the People of Israel," *NTS* 24 (1977): 10: "Even when [in Galatians] he most forcefully presents the doctrine of justification by faith, Paul . . . was essentially concerned with establishing who constitute the true people of God"; so also Davies, in his review of Betz's *Galatians*, 317; "Paul: From the Semitic Point of View": the struggle over the law, as well as the doctrine of justification by faith, has to do with "the central question as to who constituted 'Israel,' the people of God."

In a paper presented at the meeting of the Society of Biblical Literature in December 1981, Robert Gundry argued that, from Paul's point of view, the question in Galatians is how one *stays* in, not how one gets in. There is a sense in which that is entirely correct. Those who accept the law will be cut off from Christ (Gal 5:4). But that does not change the fact that the argument is about a membership requirement: how to be righteoused or how to be a true descendant of Abraham. Paul argues that the Galatian Christians already have that status and must not accept the law, represented by circumcision, in order truly to be "in." Accepting another membership requirement besides faith in Christ means rejecting the one which, in Paul's view, really counts.

924. Gal 6:15.

925. Gal 2:11–14; 4:10.

926. This is a schematic statement of the problem. The actual situation was naturally much more complex: e.g., some disciples of Jesus may have begun to collect and arrange sayings of Jesus even before his death (Stage I), and the oral tradition continued to develop during the period of the redaction of the Gospels (Stage III).

Gospel stories in a haphazard way, the authors deciding at any given moment that what strikes them as reasonable or plausible is therefore historical. More technical books usually enunciate rules for judging the Gospel material ("criteria of historicity"), but the rules sometimes seem to be forgotten when the Gospel pericopes are treated in detail. In this chapter, I will spell out which rules of judgment (i.e., "criteria") are helpful in reaching a decision about what material comes from the historical Jesus.[927]

Granted the nature of ancient history in general and the nature of the Gospels in particular, the criteria of historicity will usually produce judgments that are only more or less probable; certainty is rarely to be had.[928] Indeed, since in the quest for the historical Jesus almost anything is possible, the function of the criteria is to pass from the merely possible to the really probable, to inspect various probabilities, and to decide which candidate is most probable. Ordinarily, the criteria cannot hope to do more.[929]

Scholars seem to vie with one another to see who can compile the longest list of criteria. Sometimes a subtle apologetic motive may be at work: so many criteria surely guarantee the results of our quest! More sober scholars, instead, are no doubt seeking as many controls as possible over the difficult material. Often, however, what is naturally a single criterion is "chopped up" to create a number of criteria; and what are at best secondary, if not dubious, criteria are mixed in with truly useful ones. I agree with Occam that categories are not to be multiplied without necessity. Hence I prefer to distill five "primary" criteria from the many suggested. After we have looked at these five, we will consider five "secondary" (some would say "dubious") criteria; some of these secondary criteria may at times offer post-factum confirmation of decisions we have already reached on the basis of the five primary criteria.

Primary Criteria

1. The Criterion of Embarrassment

The criterion of "embarrassment" (so Schillebeeckx) or "contradiction" (so Meyer) focuses on actions or sayings[930] of Jesus that would have embarrassed or created difficulty for the early Church. The point of the criterion is that the early Church would hardly have gone out of its way to create material that only embarrassed its creator or weakened its position in arguments with opponents. Rather, embarrassing material coming from Jesus would naturally be either sup-

pressed or softened in later stages of the Gospel tradition, and often such progressive suppression or softening can be traced through the Four Gospels.[931]

A prime example is the baptism of the supposedly superior and sinless Jesus by his supposed inferior, John the Baptist, who proclaimed "a baptism of repentance for the forgiveness of sins." Mysterious, laconic, stark Mark recounts the event with no theological explanation as to why the superior sinless one submits to a baptism meant for sinners (Mk 1:4–11). Matthew introduces a dialogue between the Baptist and Jesus prior to the baptism; the Baptist openly confesses his unworthiness to baptize his superior and gives way only when Jesus commands him to do so in order that God's saving plan may be fulfilled (Matt 3:13–17, a passage marked by language typical of the evangelist). Luke finds a striking solution to the problem by narrating the Baptist's imprisonment by Herod

---

927. René Latourelle ("Critères d'authenticité historique des Evangiles," *Greg* [*Gregorianum*] 55 [1974]: 609–37, esp. 618) rightly warns against confusing criteria with proof. Criteria are rules or norms that are applied to the Gospel material to arrive at a judgment.

928. In the quest for the historical Jesus, sometimes certainty is more easily had about "secondary" circumstances than about the words and deeds of Jesus himself. For example, the converging evidence of the Four Gospels and the Acts of the Apostles, Josephus, Philo, Tacitus, and the Caesarea Maritima inscription (found in 1961) makes it at least morally, if not physically, certain that Pontius Pilate was the Roman governor of Judea in AD 28–30. Even here, though, moral certitude is really just a very high degree of probability. The fact of Pilate's governorship is not absolutely or metaphysically certain, for it is not theoretically or metaphysically impossible that Josephus is mistaken or that the references to Pilate in Philo are Christian interpolations or that the Caesarea Maritima inscription is a fraud. But since any of these possibilities (not to mention all of them together) is so extremely unlikely, we are justified in considering our conclusion morally certain, especially since, in daily life, we constantly make firm theoretical judgments and practical decisions on the basis of high probability. Any talk about "proof" of authentic Jesus material must be understood within this context of a range of probabilities.

929. Sometimes scholars seek to distinguish between "criteria" and "indices" or even to substitute the word "index" for "criterion." [. . .] However, scholars favoring some sort of distinction do not always agree among themselves as to what constitutes the distinction. Sometimes "criterion" indicates what allows a fairly certain judgment, while "index" suggests a lower level of probability. [. . .] Others use indices for individual observations relevant to the question of authenticity, while criteria refer to more general rules. [. . .] Meyer prefers to drop the language of "criteria" in favor of "indices." Personally, I see no great value in the various distinctions or changes in terminology. My own view is that our judgments about authenticity deal for the most part with a range of probabilities; I do not claim that the use of the criteria I propose will generate absolute certitude. Hence, I see no need to distinguish "criteria" from "indices"; the former term will be used throughout what follows.

930. While the criteria are usually aimed at the sayings of Jesus in particular, it must be remembered that they can also be applied to the actions of Jesus. In some forms of the quest, the actions of Jesus and their relation to his sayings are almost ignored.

931. This phenomenon is sometimes listed as the separate criterion of either "modification" or "tendencies of the developing Synoptic tradition." What I think valid in these two suggested criteria I have subsumed under the criterion of embarrassment.

before relating the baptism of Jesus; Luke's version never tells us who baptized Jesus (Lk 3:19–22). The radical Fourth Evangelist, John, locked as he is in a struggle with latter-day disciples of the Baptist who refuse to recognize Jesus as the Messiah, takes the radical expedient of suppressing the baptism of Jesus by the Baptist altogether; the event simply never occurs in John's Gospel. We still hear of the Father's witness to Jesus and the Spirit's descent upon Jesus, but we are never told when this theophany occurs (Jn 1:29–34). Quite plainly, the early Church was "stuck with" an event in Jesus' life that it found increasingly embarrassing, that it tried to explain away by various means, and that John the Evangelist finally erased from his Gospel. It is highly unlikely that the Church went out of its way to create the cause of its own embarrassment.

A similar case is the affirmation by Jesus that, despite the Gospels' claim that he is the Son who can predict the events at the end of time, including his own coming on the clouds of heaven, he does not know the exact day or hour of the end. Almost at the conclusion of the eschatological discourse in Mark 13, Jesus says: "But concerning that day or hour no one knows, neither the angels in heaven, nor the Son, but only the Father" (Mk 13:32). It is not surprising that a few later Greek manuscripts simply dropped the words "nor the Son" from the saying in Mark. A significantly larger number of manuscripts omit "nor the Son" in the parallel verse in Matthew (Mt 24:36),[932] which was more widely used in the patristic Church than Mark—hence the desire to suppress the embarrassing phrase especially in Matthew.[933] The saying is simply not taken over by Luke. In John, not only is there nothing similar, but the Fourth Evangelist goes out of his way to stress that Jesus knows all things present and future and is never taken by surprise (see, e.g., 5:6; 6:6; 8:14; 9:3; 11:11–15; 13:1–3, 11). Once again, it is highly unlikely that the Church would have taken pains to invent a saying that emphasized the ignorance of its risen Lord, only to turn around and seek to suppress it.

An intriguing corollary arises from these cases of "embarrassment." All too often the oral tradition of the early Church is depicted as a game of "anything goes," with charismatic prophets uttering anything or everything as the words of the Lord Jesus and storytellers creating accounts of miracles and exorcisms according to Jewish and pagan models. The evangelists would simply have crowned this wildly creative process by molding the oral tradition according to their own redactional theology. One would get the impression that throughout the first Christian generation there were no eyewitnesses to act as a check on fertile imaginations, no

original-disciples-now-become-leaders who might exercise some control over the developing tradition, and no striking deeds and sayings of Jesus that stuck willy-nilly in people's memories. The fact that embarrassing material is found as late as the redaction of the Gospels reminds us that beside a creative thrust there was also a conservative force in the Gospel tradition.[934] Indeed, so conservative was this force that a string of embarrassing events (e.g., baptism by John, betrayal by Judas, denial by Peter, crucifixion by the Romans) called forth agonized and varied theological reflection, but not, in most cases, convenient amnesia.[935] In this sense, the criterion of embarrassment has an importance for the historian far beyond the individual data it may help verify.

Like all the criteria we will examine, however, the criterion of embarrassment has its limitations and must always be used in concert with the other criteria. One built-in limitation to the criterion of embarrassment is that clear-cut cases of such embarrassment are not numerous in the Gospel tradition; and a full portrait of Jesus could never be drawn with so few strokes. Another limitation stems from the fact that what we today might consider an embarrassment to the early Church was not necessarily an embarrassment in its own eyes. A prime example is Jesus' "cry of dereliction" from the cross: "My God, my God, why have you forsaken me?" (Mk 15:34; Mt 27:46; the words are a citation of Ps 22:1). At first glance, this seems a clear case of embarrassment; the unedifying groan is replaced in Luke by Christ's trustful commendation of his spirit to the Father (Lk 23:46) and in John by a cry of triumph, "It is accomplished!" (Jn 19:30).

But the matter is not so simple. True, the cry of dereliction does not fit the later theological agendas of Luke or John. But form-critical studies of the Passion Narrative show

---

932. The few manuscripts that omit "nor the Son" in Mark include codex X (10th century).

933. The manuscripts that drop "nor the Son" in the Matthean version of the saying include the codices K, L, W, and the vast majority of later texts; the first scribe who sought to correct this text in codex Sinaiticus also omitted the phrase.

934. As Stein ("The 'Criteria' for Authenticity," *Gospel Perspectives*, vol. 1, ed. R. France and D. Wenam [Sheffield: *JSOT* (*Journal for the Study of the Old Testament*), 1980], 227) notes, another indication of the conservative force of the Jesus tradition is that several of the major problems that the early Church encountered never show up in the sayings of Jesus; a glaring case is the absence of any explicit pronouncement of Jesus on the question of circumcision for Gentiles. In a letter to me dated Oct. 13, 1990, David Noel Freedman points out an OT analogy. From the viewpoint of the Deuteronomistic Historian(s), Hezekiah and Josiah were the two best kings of Judah after David. Their military defeats, which raise questions about Yahweh's rewarding of the just, are not denied but rather explained theologically in somewhat contorted fashion.

935. My proviso "in most cases" takes cognizance of the Fourth Gospel's suppression of the baptism of Jesus.

that the earliest stages of the passion tradition used the OT psalms of lamentation, especially the psalms of the suffering just man, as a primary tool for theological interpretation of the narrative. By telling the story of Jesus' passion in the words of these psalms, the narrative presented Jesus as the one who fulfilled the OT pattern of the just man afflicted and put to death by evildoers, but vindicated and raised up by God. Allusions to, rather than direct quotations of, these psalms are woven throughout the Passion Narrative. A good example is the dividing of Jesus' garments. The words of Psalm 22:19 are made part of the narrative in Mark 15:24, Matt 27:35, and Luke 23:34; only John marks off the words as a citation of Scripture (Jn 19:24).

Therefore, it is not very surprising, from a form-critical point of view, that the dramatic first words of Psalm 22 supply the climax of the crucifixion and Jesus' last words in Mark's Gospel. The cry is by no means so unedifying or even scandalous as moderns might think. The OT psalms of lamentation regularly direct forceful complaints to God; their strong—to our ears, irreverent—address to God expresses neither doubt nor despair, but the pain of one who fully trusts that a strangely silent God can act to save if he so chooses. The very bitterness of the complaint paradoxically reaffirms the closeness the petitioner feels to this God he dares confront with such boldness. From the Babylonian exile to Auschwitz, pious Jews have used the words of Psalm 22 and other laments without being accused by their fellow religionists of impiety or despair.

Granted the roots of the Passion Narrative in the psalms of lamentation, as well as the bold address to God in those psalms—well understood by early Christian Jews but often misunderstood since—there is no reason for thinking that the earliest Christians (Jews who knew their Scriptures well) would have found the "cry of derelection" at all embarrassing. Whether or not Jesus actually spoke Ps 22:1 on the cross, the criterion of embarrassment, taken in isolation, cannot establish the historicity of those words. It is not impossible that all of the "seven last words"—including the "cry of derelection"—represent the theological interpretation of the early Church and the evangelists. But that is a question we will have to face later. The point here is that the criterion of embarrassment—like any other criterion—must not be invoked facilely or in isolation.

2. The Criterion of Discontinuity

Closely allied to the criterion of embarrassment,[936] the criterion of discontinuity (also labeled dissimilarity, original-ity, or dual irreducibility) focuses on words or deeds of Jesus that cannot be derived either from Judaism at the time of Jesus or from the early Church after him.[937] Examples often given are his sweeping prohibition of all oaths (Mt 5:34, 37; but cf. Jas 5:12), his rejection of voluntary fasting for his disciples (Mk 2:18–22 par. [and parallel passages]), and possibly his total prohibition of divorce (Mk 10:2–12 par.; Lk 16:18 par.).

This criterion is at once the most promising and the most troublesome. Norman Perrin hails it as the fundamental criterion, the basis of all reconstructions, since it gives us an assured minimum of material to work with.[938] But the criterion is not without its detractors. Morna Hooker complains that the criterion presupposes what we do not possess: a sure and full knowledge of what Judaism at the time of Jesus and Christianity right after him were like, and what they could or would not say.[939]

Her objection does remind us of the healthy modesty required of any historian delving into the religious scene of 1st-century Palestine. Yet historical-critical work of the last two centuries has made notable advances in our understanding of 1st-century Judaism and Christianity. Moreover, one cannot overlook the glaring difference between knowledge about Jesus on the one hand and knowledge about 1st-century Judaism and Christianity on the other. We do have 1st-century documents coming directly from the latter movements—Qumran, Josephus, and Philo for Judaism, most of the NT for Christianity—to say nothing of important archaeological finds. We have no such documents coming directly from Jesus. Indeed, Professor Hooker's own work on the Son of Man title presupposes that we know something about early Judaism and Christianity and can apply such knowledge to outstanding problems. No doubt our present-day judgments will need correction by future generations of scholars. But if we were to wait until we possessed a fullness of knowledge

---

936. Allied, but not reducible to discontinuity; in this I disagree with Polkow, "Method and Criteria for Historical Jesus Research," *Society of Biblical Literature Seminar Papers* 26 (1987): 336–56, 341.

937. In his masterful essay ("The Historical-Critical Method's 'Criteria of Authenticity': The Beatitudes in Q and Thomas as a Test Case," *The Historical Jesus and the Rejected Gospels*, [*Semeia* 44, ed. Charles W. Hedrick (Atlanta: Scholars, 1988], 17–21), Boring highlights the methodological problem of whether we should speak of material that *can* be derived from Judaism or Christianity or material that *must* be so derived. I think it is preferable to speak in terms of "can."

938. Perrin, *Rediscovering the Teaching of Jesus* (New York and Evanston: Harper and Row, 1969), 39–43.

939. Hooker, "Christology and Methodology," *NTS* [*New Testament Studies*] 17 (1970): 480–87.

that excluded later revision, we would postpone all NT scholarship until the parousia.

A more serious objection is that the criterion of discontinuity, instead of giving us an assured minimum about Jesus, winds up giving us a caricature by divorcing Jesus from the Judaism that influenced him and from the Church that he influenced. Jesus was a 1st-century Jew whose deeds and sayings the early Church revered and handed on.[940] A complete rupture with religious history just before or just after him is a priori unlikely. Indeed, if he had been so "discontinuous," unique, cut off from the flow of history before and after him, he would have been unintelligible to practically everyone. To be an effective teacher (which Jesus seems to have been by almost every scholar's admission) means adapting oneself to the concepts and positions of one's audience, even if one's purpose is to change those concepts and positions. No matter how original Jesus was, to be a successful teacher and communicator he would have had to submit himself to the constraints of communication, the constraints of his historical situation. To paint a portrait of Jesus completely divorced from or opposed to 1st-century Judaism and Christianity is simply to place him outside of history.

Imagine, for the sake of argument, that in the 16th century Martin Luther had delivered all his teachings orally and that they had been written down only later on by his disciples. If we excluded from the record of Luther's words and deeds everything that could be paralleled in late medieval Catholic authors before him or in 17th-century Lutheran theologians after him, how much would remain—and would it give anything like a representative portrait of Luther?

Hence, while the criterion of discontinuity is useful, we must guard against the presupposition that it will automatically give us what was central to or at least fairly representative of Jesus' teaching. By focusing narrowly upon what may have been Jesus' "idiosyncrasies," it is always in danger of highlighting what was striking but possibly peripheral in his message.[941] Especially with this criterion, complementary and balancing insights from other criteria are vital.

Of course, the same need for balance and correction holds true for the emphasis on Jesus' historical continuity with Judaism and early Christianity. In the case of Judaism in particular, we always have to pose the question: With what sort or branch or tendency of Judaism was Jesus "continuous" in a given saying or action? Moreover, just as we are not to decide that Jesus *must* have been discontinuous with the Judaism of his day in this or that matter, so we cannot decide a priori that he *must* have been in agreement with Judaism in all things.

History does have its Luthers and Spinozas. One is surprised, for instance, to read E. P. Sanders's summary judgment on the historicity of Jesus' statement that all foods are clean (Mk 7:15). Without going into detailed arguments, Sanders simply declares: "In this case the saying attributed to Jesus . . . appears to me to be too revolutionary to have been said by Jesus himself."[942] In a sense, Sanders simply takes Perrin's view of the primacy of the criterion of discontinuity and stands it on its head. Instead of "if it is discontinuous, it must be from Jesus," we now have "if it is discontinuous, it cannot be from Jesus." Obviously, dogmatism in either direction must give way to a careful testing of claims in each case.

A further problem that often bedevils the criterion of discontinuity is a terminological one. Scholars will claim that this criterion isolates what is "unique" to Jesus. "Uniqueness" is a slippery concept in historical investigation. In some sense, Beethoven may be hailed as a "unique genius" in music, but that hardly means that individual aspects of his music cannot be found in composers like Bach before him or Mahler after him. Indeed, while it is hard enough for an individual like Beethoven to be "uniquely" different from anyone who has preceded him, it is asking far too much to require as well that he be "uniquely" different from all who follow. The gifted individual could hardly control that, and the more outstanding he was, the more likely he would be to have imitators.[943] Perhaps Beethoven's uniqueness is to be located instead in the special configuration of his personality, talent, production, and career, seen as a whole in a par-

---

940. The emphasis on Jesus' connections with the Judaism of his time is common in scholarship today and is well documented by Daniel J. Harrington, "The Jewishness of Jesus: Facing Some Problems," *CBQ* [*Catholic Biblical Quarterly*] 49 (1987): 1–13. It is curious that even skeptical scholars use the language of "handing on the Jesus tradition" and engage in tradition criticism. Yet if there really was a complete rupture in history between Jesus and the earliest Christians, there can be no talk of handing on tradition. However one defines the exact relationship between Jesus and the early Church, it is a fact of history, disputed by almost no scholar, that shortly after the death of Jesus some Jews, including people who had been his closest followers during his public ministry, gathered together to revere and celebrate him as Messiah and Lord, to recall and hand on his teachings, and to spread his teachings among other Jews.

941. So rightly William O. Walker, "The Quest for the Historical Jesus: A Discussion of Methodology," *ATR* [*Anglican Theological Review*] 51 (1969): 48: "Unique features are not necessarily the most characteristic features . . ."; cf. Boring, "The Historical-Critical Method's 'Criteria of Authenticity,'" 21. We might add that even what was strikingly characteristic about Jesus' message may not have been at the very heart of his message.

942. E. P. Sanders, *Jewish Law from Jesus to the Mishnah: Five Studies* (London: SCM; Philadelphia: Trinity, 1990), 28.

943. This problem was pointed out to me in a letter by David Noel Freedman, dated Oct. 15, 1990. For Freedman, to be unique, "it would be enough to be markedly different from those who preceded. What happened afterwards would not affect that status."

ticular historical context, rather than in any one aspect of his work, seen in isolation.

Something similar might be said of the uniqueness of Jesus. When dealing with an individual saying or deed of Jesus, perhaps it is better to speak of what is "strikingly characteristic" or "unusual" in Jesus' style of speaking or acting, instead of claiming uniqueness at every turn. This distinction is especially important when we treat such characteristic phrases as "Amen, I say to you" or "Abba" addressed to God in prayer. Since we are not terribly well informed about popular Jewish-Aramaic religious practices and vocabulary in early 1st-century Galilee, modesty in advancing claims is advisable. Similarly, when we deal with the public actions of Jesus, it may be wiser to speak of "the sort of things Jesus did" (e.g., exorcisms, faith healings) instead of asserting that a particular story tells us precisely what Jesus did on one particular occasion. The same distinction can be applied to the sayings tradition taken as a whole. We can have some hope of learning the basic message of Jesus, the "kind of thing" he usually or typically said (the *ipsissima vox*).[944] Rarely if ever can we claim to recover his exact words (the *ipsissima verba*).

3. The Criterion of Multiple Attestation

The criterion of multiple attestation (or "the cross section") focuses on those sayings or deeds of Jesus that are attested in more than one independent literary source (e.g., Mark, Q, Paul, John) and/or in more than one literary form or genre (e.g., parable, dispute story, miracle story, prophecy, aphorism).[945] The force of this criterion is increased if a given motif or theme is found in both different literary sources and different literary forms.[946] One reason that critics so readily affirm that Jesus did speak in some sense of the kingdom of God (or kingdom of heaven) is that the phrase is found in Mark, Q, special Matthean tradition, special Lucan tradition, and John,[947] with echoes in Paul, despite the fact that "kingdom of God" is not Paul's preferred way of speaking.[948] At the same time, the phrase is found in various literary genres (e.g., parable, beatitude, prayer, aphorism, miracle story). Granted this wide sweep of witnesses in different sources and genres, coming largely from the first Christian generation, it becomes extremely difficult to claim that such material is simply the creation of the Church.[949]

When one moves from general motifs and phrases to precise sayings and deeds, one cannot usually expect such a broad range of attestation. Still, such key sayings as Jesus' words over the bread and wine at the Last Supper (Mk 14:22–

25; 1 Cor 11:23–26; cf. Jn 6:51–58) and his prohibition of divorce (Mk 10:11–12; Lk 16:18 [= Q]; 1 Cor 7:10–11) are found in two or three independent sources.[950] Then, too, we may find "cross-referencing" between sayings dealing with a particular topic and actions of Jesus that also touch on that topic—e.g., sayings about the destruction of the Jerusalem temple and Jesus' prophetic "cleansing" of the temple. The example of the destruction of the temple is all the more forceful when we notice that both sayings and dramatic action are witnessed in more than one source and context (e.g., Mk 13:2; 14:58; Jn 2:14–22, esp. v 19).

Harvey K. McArthur was so taken with the force of the criterion of multiple attestation that he asserted that it was "the most objective" criterion and should be given first place.[951] Yet even McArthur admitted that multiple attestation was not an infallible indicator of historicity. In an individual case

---

944. See Robert H. Stein, "The 'Criteria' for Authenticity," 228–29.

945. The qualification "independent" is important. The mere fact that Peter's confession that Jesus is the Messiah is recorded in Mark, Matthew, and Luke does not satisfy the criterion of multiple attestation, since both Matthew and Luke are dependent on Mark for the basic narrative (though Matthew may be relying on a separate tradition for Jesus' praise and commission of Peter in 16:17–19). There is only one *independent* source for the core of the story. If the focus were broadened to "some sort of confession that Peter addresses to Jesus at a critical moment in the public ministry," then John 6:66–71 could be used; but we could no longer speak of Peter's confession of faith in Jesus precisely as the Messiah; both the location and the content of the confession in John's Gospel are different.

946. Some count multiple attestation in sources and multiple attestation in forms as two different criteria. Like Polkow ("Method and Criteria," 341), I think that they are better dealt with together under one criterion.

947. Once again I must stress that I do not accept the a priori exclusion of John from consideration as a possible source for knowledge of the historical Jesus.

948. Those who accept the Coptic *Gospel of Thomas* as another independent source would naturally add it to this list. So Boring, "The Historical-Critical Method's 'Criteria of Authenticity,'" 13, 25–28.

949. Harvey K. McArthur ("The Burden of Proof in Historical Jesus Research," *ExpTim* [*The Expository Times*] 82 [1970–71]: 118) claims that the following motifs are witnessed to by all four strands of the Synoptic tradition (i.e., Mark, Q, M, and L): Jesus' proclamation of the kingdom of God, the presence of disciples around Jesus, healing miracles, a link with John the Baptist, use of parables, concern for outcasts, especially tax collectors and sinners, a radical ethic, emphasis on the love commandment, a demand that the disciples practice forgiveness, clashes with his contemporaries over Sabbath observance, sayings about the Son of Man, and the Hebrew word "Amen" used to introduce Jesus' sayings.

950. I do not bother to list the "peeling away" of additions and modifications made by the oral tradition and the final redactor, since I consider such judgments a necessary part of the use of the criterion of multiple attestation. One would like to say that such judgments are simply "preliminary criteria" that precede the use of the "primary criteria" (so Polkow, "Method and Criteria," 342–45). But actual practice of the historical-critical method shows that all the way through the process one is constantly testing and revising one's judgments about modifications made by the oral tradition and the redactor.

951. McArthur, "A Survey of Recent Gospel Research," *Int* [*Interpretation*] 18 (1964): 48; idem, "The Burden of Proof," 118.

it is not a priori impossible that a saying invented early on by a Christian community or prophet met the needs of the Church so perfectly that it rapidly entered into a number of different strands of tradition. Then, too, the mere fact that a saying occurs only in one source is no proof that it was not spoken by Jesus. For example, the Aramaic invocation *Abba* ("my own dear Father") occurs on the lips of Jesus only once in all four Gospels (Mk 14:36), yet many critics ascribe it on other grounds to the historical Jesus. Once again, we are reminded that no criterion can be used mechanically and in isolation; a convergence of different criteria is the best indicator of historicity.

4. The Criterion of Coherence

The criterion of coherence (or consistency or conformity) can be brought into play only after a certain amount of historical material has been isolated by the previous criteria. The criterion of coherence holds that other sayings and deeds of Jesus that fit in well with the preliminary "data base" established by using our first three criteria have a good chance of being historical (e.g., sayings concerning the coming of the kingdom of God or disputes with adversaries over legal observance). As can be readily seen, this criterion, by its very nature, is less probative than the three on which it depends.[952] Since we should not conceive of the earliest Christians as totally cut off or different from Jesus himself, there is no reason why they could not have created sayings that echoed faithfully his own "authentic" words. In a loose sense such derived sayings could be considered "authentic" insofar as they convey the message of the historical Jesus; but they cannot be considered "authentic" in the technical sense, i.e., actually coming from Jesus himself.[953]

Despite this limitation, the criterion of coherence has a certain positive use, namely, broadening an already established data base. One must, however, be wary of using it negatively, i.e., declaring a saying or action inauthentic because it does not seem to be consistent with words or deeds of Jesus already declared authentic on other grounds. Jesus would hardly be unique among the great thinkers or leaders of world history if his sayings and actions did not always seem totally consistent to us. Moreover, we must remember that ancient Semitic thought, much more than our Western tradition of Aristotelian logic, delighted in paradoxical statements that held opposites in tension. (Even in our own day, American and European professors are often befuddled when they find out that students from Asia, while fiercely intelligent,

may not subscribe to the Western philosophical principle of noncontradiction.) Then, too, Jesus was a popular preacher addressing a wide range of audiences on particular occasions with great oral skill; we should hardly seek in the various expressions of his teaching the type of systematic presentation expected of a written treatise.[954] Hence the debate between those scholars who stress the eschatological nature of Jesus' core message and those who portray Jesus teaching a wisdom tradition bereft of any eschatological slant may be misplaced. There is no reason why the preaching of Jesus may not have contained elements of both apocalyptic eschatology and traditional Israelite wisdom. Both Jesus and his contemporaries might have been surprised by the charge (a very modern academic one) that such a message would be inconsistent or incoherent. In short, the criterion of coherence has a certain positive value; but its negative use, to exclude material as inauthentic, must be approached very cautiously.

5. The Criterion of Rejection and Execution

The criterion of Jesus' rejection and execution is notably different from the first four criteria. It does not directly indicate whether an individual saying or deed of Jesus is authentic. Rather, it directs our attention to the historical fact that Jesus met a violent end at the hands of Jewish and Roman officials and then asks us what historical words and deeds of Jesus can explain his trial and crucifixion as "King of the Jews." While I do not agree with those who turn Jesus into a violent revolutionary or political agitator, scholars who favor a revolutionary Jesus do have a point. A tweedy poetaster who spent his time spinning out parables and Japanese koans, a literary aesthete who toyed with 1st-century deconstructionism, or a bland Jesus who simply told people to look at the lilies of the field—such a Jesus would threaten no one, just as the university professors who create him threaten no

---

952. Obviously, the conclusions drawn by the criterion of coherence are as good as the data base on which they depend.

953. I should make clear that it is in this technical and restricted sense that I use the word "authentic" when discussing criteria of historicity; cf. Stein, "The 'Criteria' for Authenticity," 228. The word must not be taken to mean that, from the viewpoint of faith, what the oral tradition or final redaction contributed to our Gospels is any less inspired, normative, or true.

954. These considerations should make one wary about declaring a priori that Jesus could not possibly have spoken of the kingdom of God as both present and future or that he could not possibly have prophesied both a coming kingdom and a coming Son of Man. It is a matter of fact that the evangelists, and probably the gospel traditions before them, did just that. Nor are Paul's authentic letters totally devoid of paradoxes that strike some as blatant contradictions.

one. The historical Jesus did threaten, disturb, and infuriate people—from interpreters of the Law through the Jerusalem priestly aristocracy to the Roman prefect who finally tried and crucified him. This emphasis on Jesus' violent end is not simply a focus imposed on the data by Christian theology. To outsiders like Josephus, Tacitus, and Lucian of Samosata, one of the most striking things about Jesus was his crucifixion or execution by Rome. A Jesus whose words and deeds would not alienate people, especially powerful people, is not the historical Jesus.

From John P. Meier, *A Marginal Jew: Rethinking the Historical Jesus,* vol. 1, *The Roots of the Problem and the Person* (New York: Doubleday, 1991), 167–77.

CHAPTER 2

Early Influences on Emerging Christianity

Jesus was a Palestinian Jew whose language was Aramaic. However, the Christian writings about him, the texts that later on formed the New Testament, were written in Greek and were directed toward the non-Palestinian world. Christianity began in the first century CE and later flourished in the Roman Empire, whose culture owed much to the Greeks. Christianity was a Greco-Roman religion. The early Christian communities, therefore, defined themselves in reference to at least two realities in the Greco-Roman world: Judaism and the "pagan," that is, non-Jewish, culture and religions of the Roman Empire. In the first century CE Judaism was a very complex phenomenon, so complex that one might more safely speak of Judaisms. Judaism of the Greek-speaking Diaspora ("Hellenistic Judaism") was influenced by the intellectual traditions of the Greek world and differed from Judaism in the land of Israel ("Palestinian Judaism"). Judaism in Israel was not, however, completely free from Greek influence. In Israel a wide variety of groups, practices, and beliefs existed side by side. Following the destruction of Jerusalem and the Jewish Temple in 70 CE, Judaism, both in the Diaspora and in Palestine, was gradually transformed into rabbinic Judaism. The Christian movement began as one of the groups within Judaism. For centuries after it broke from Judaism, Christianity maintained the dual polemics that, on the one hand, sought to represent the Christian movement as the "New Israel" and, on the other hand, stressed Christianity's distinctiveness from Judaism.

Non-Jewish religion and culture in the Roman Empire can be classified under three headings: (1) philosophy, (2) civic and imperial religion, and (3) personal religion, especially Greek and "Eastern" mystery religions. Philosophy in the Roman Empire was multiform. It was represented by competing "schools," principal among which were the Platonists, going back to Plato (ca. 429–347 BCE) and Socrates (469–399 BCE); the Peripatetics, with Aristotle (384–322 BCE) as the founder; the Pythagoreans, following the traditions of Pythagoras, son of Mnesarchus (ca. 582–500 BCE); the Cynics, linked to Diogenes of Sinope (ca. 400–325 BCE); the Stoics, founded by Zenon of Cyprus (335–263 BCE); and the Epicureans, named after Epicurus of Samos (341–270 BCE). In spite of being divided into schools and the existence of an "Academy," philosophy in the Roman Empire was not just one of many academic subjects one studied in a university. Philosophy was the sum total of the intellectual culture; it was, as its Greek name says, the love of wisdom, a way of life. To be a philosopher was to be engaged in an ethical endeavor. Despite the sometimes bitter disputes among the schools, therefore, philosophy had a common goal, namely, the search for self-sufficiency (*autarkeia*) through freedom from passion (*apatheia*). By the middle of the second century CE, Christianity considered itself a philosophy, the true philosophy. Thus, while it argued for its distinctive character here as well, Christianity defined itself within the Greco-Roman philosophical tradition, appropriating its language, themes, and overriding objectives.

Jews and Christians joined philosophers, like the Platonists, in criticizing Greco-Roman polytheistic civic religion and in rejecting Rome's imperial religion of state and emperor. Viewed from the outside, Christianity was one of several mystery cults from the eastern Roman Empire. Viewed from within, Christianity saw itself as competing with these other cults, which, with their secret initiations, mysteries, renunciations, and rites, promised to their members the same benefits that Christianity offered: deliverance from the "evils" of this present world and a blessed immortality in the afterlife.

The texts in this chapter supply some perspective on the general context in which early Christianity was formed. The influence which this historical context exerted on different aspects of formative Christianity varied, of course, and it is thus to be expected that the relationship between Christianity and other thought patterns, practices, and beliefs in the Greco-Roman world was often complex.

The Jewish historian Flavius Josephus (ca. 37–100) is the best extant source for the history, religion, and culture of Palestine in the early Roman Empire. He provides a picture of the complex Palestinian society in which Christianity was born. He describes the principal groups within Judaism as "Jewish philosophies" and depicts them and their "doctrines" in terms that make them comparable to Greco-Roman philosophical schools. The occasion for his description is the census in the year 6 CE by Quirinius (of which we have echoes in Lk 2:1–7 and Acts 5:37), which was conducted when Archelaus was deposed as ethnarch of Judea. According to Josephus, at this time a certain Judas, called "the Galilean," founded the "fourth philosophy." This is the group Josephus tried to blame for the insurrection that led to the war with Rome from 66 to 73. Otherwise, Jewish society comprised three main "parties," namely, the Sadducees, the Pharisees, and the Essenes. One notes that Josephus does not speak of the priests and Levites. This is partly because priests and Levites could belong to any of the three named groups, but also because there were many Jews—priests and Levites among them—who did not belong to any of these "parties." If Josephus's Essenes are indeed responsible for the settlements and documents discovered at Qumran (see below), then we have more information on them than on the other two groups. No Saducean writings have been found. Thus, apart from what is said of them by Josephus and the New Testament, very little is known of this group, to which belonged Israel's priestly aristocracy. The rabbis who reformulated Judaism after the fall of Jerusalem are generally thought to have been Pharisees. Pharisaism in the first century CE, however, has remained elusive in spite of what can be learned about the Pharisees from Josephus's works and from the New Testament.

The authenticity of Josephus's passage about Jesus, the so-called Testimonium Flavianum, in his *Jewish Antiquities* is disputed. Many scholars reject it as a Christian forgery. The most significant arguments against its authenticity are, first,

that Josephus, a self-declared Pharisee, did not believe that Jesus was the Messiah—as Origen acknowledged (*Comment. in Matthew,* xiii.55; *Contra Celsum,* i.47)—and would not, therefore, have stated that Jesus "was the Messiah." Second, although the text contains some phrases that belong to Josephus's style, it also has some stylistic peculiarities. Josephus's works were preserved and extensively cited by early Christian writers. Even those scholars who accept that the Testimonium Flavianum is substantially what Josephus wrote acknowledge that a Christian interpolator had made some changes. The authenticity of Josephus's account of the death of James, the brother of Jesus, like that of his account of the death of John the Baptist (see *Jewish Antiquities,* xviii.116–19), is generally accepted.

The discoveries, starting in 1947, of numerous scrolls in the caves near the Dead Sea marked a turning point in the study of ancient Judaism. A coherent picture is emerging that links the Dead Sea Scrolls, the subsequently discovered settlements at neighboring Qumran, and the descriptions of the Essenes in Josephus and other sources. When this picture is combined with what was already available from *The Damascus Document,* a text first discovered in 1896 in the Cairo Genizah (a Jewish repository for used sacred scrolls) and afterward also among the Dead Sea Scrolls, we see a widespread Essene movement, with a variety of forms, within Judaism. Some scholars think that John the Baptist might, at some point, have been an Essene.

The Dead Sea document entitled *The Community Rule* is the first such writing in ancient Judaism. In form and content it is an earlier example of the genre of Church Orders (*Didache, Didascalia, Apostolic Constitution*) and, later, of the monastic Rules produced by early Christianity. The significance for early Christianity of the Essene movement and the documents it produced, however, might lie not so much in the possibility of direct contact and dependence as in their common context, beliefs, and practices. The Essenes, after all, belonged to a sectarian movement produced by competing views about the interpretation of the Law and the shape of Jewish life. They arrogated to themselves the name "Israel," traced their origins to the singular personality of the Teacher of Righteousness, and lived in expectation of two Messiahs for the eschatological fulfillment of their hopes.

There is perhaps nothing of greater significance for Hellenistic Judaism and for early Christianity—apart from Jesus himself—than the translation of the Jewish Scriptures into Greek. The Greek Scriptures (the Septuagint) were produced to meet the needs of the Jews of Alexandria, Egypt. The text might have begun to take shape in the third century BCE, but it was not completed until the first century BCE. This Greek Bible, which early Christians inherited from Greek-speaking Jews, was not, properly speaking, a translation. In many respects it was a rewriting. Its canon, as we noted in chapter 1, was wider than that of the Hebrew Bible; the translators sometimes worked from Hebrew texts that differed from those in use in Palestine; they changed the meaning of the texts by choosing particular terms from Hellenistic Greek and introduced Greek concepts into the texts. For early Christians, Jerome excepted, the legend about the translation of the Greek Bible, of which a version is found in *The Letter of Aristeas,* was evidence that the Greek Bible had been specially inspired by God for the sake of the Greeks.

Philo Judaeus (also known as Philo of Alexandria), an older contemporary of John the Baptist, Jesus, and Paul, was a prominent Jewish citizen of Alexandria, which was the intellectual center of the Hellenistic world, the principal home of Hellenistic Jewry, and later the intellectual epicenter of early Christianity. Perhaps by virtue of his philosophical eclecticism, Philo is the earliest extant representative of the "Middle Platonism" of the first century BCE to the second century CE, influenced in the main by Stoicism, Aristotelianism, and Neopythagoreanism. With Philo, Aristotle's Prime Mover became Plato's Supreme Good, and the Supreme God of Judaism. Plato's subsistent ideas and forms became thoughts in the divine mind. The God of biblical revelation was, thus, no other than the object of thought in the Greek philosophical traditions. Philo turned the Logos into the biblical God's creative Word, the Divine Reason, and the Mediator between creatures and the transcendent and incomprehensible God.

Whatever Philo's merits as a philosophical thinker might be, the importance of his vast works also resides in the fact that they forged the link between Judaism and Hellenism by his use of allegory to interpret biblical narrative and Law in terms of Greek philosophy. This link between Judaism and Hellenistic thought was crucial for formative Christianity. Philo's direct influence on the New Testament authors, especially the author of the Prologue of the Gospel according to John, might be debated. By the end of the first century, however, Philo's exegetical method and philosophical concepts had become mainstays of Christian thought, implicitly in Justin Martyr but explicitly in the Alexandrians Clement and Origen. The enthusiasm with which Philo's writings were received by Christians preserved his works for posterity.

Jewish teachers (rabbis) fled from Jerusalem after its de-

struction in 70 and settled at Javneh. Here they began to develop and codify the oral "traditions of the elders" that, for about two hundred years before the destruction of the Temple, had guided—at least for the Pharisees—the interpretation of God's revelation in the Bible and Jewish beliefs and practices in the land of Israel. The resulting Oral Torah ("Law"; "Revelation"), the Mishnah, was finally compiled by Rabbi Judah the Patriarch at the end of the second century CE and stood alongside the Written Torah (that is, the Bible) as the two pillars on which the rabbis built the Judaism that eventually became normative. The Mishnah ("Repetition," that is, the teaching or study of the Law) has attained canonical status in Judaism, much like the New Testament in Christianity. The Mishnah was followed by the Tosefta, the Jerusalem Talmud, and the Babylonian Talmud in the corpus of Jewish religious texts now known as "Talmudic literature." In this corpus Jewish Law is systematically codified either in the form of direct scholarly discussions of legal points (*halakhah,* "walking") or in the form of the scholarly interpretation of the historical and religious-doctrinal sections of the Bible (*haggadah,* "teaching"). Both *halakhah* and, especially, *haggadah* may take the form of an interpretive commentary on the Bible. Such a commentary is called a *midrash* ("inquiry"). The work of interpreting the Written Torah was continued by another category of rabbinic writings, the Midrashim, which commented on the books of the Bible passage by passage. The Targums were the traditional and popular translations of the Scriptures into Aramaic.

It is certainly debatable to what extent the rabbinic view of such celebrations as the Passover meal and the Day of Atonement corresponds to actual practice in the Temple before its destruction. It may also be doubted whether the rabbinic legal and interpretive constructs substantially affected actual Jewish belief and practice in the first centuries CE. In the first century and after, however, both Judaism and Christianity were faced with the task of reformulating the significance and practice of their central rituals. And while Christianity erected its edifice of "apostolic authority" by reference to the apostolic succession in the episcopate, the rabbis constructed a competing line of succession of *aboth,* "fathers," which went back to God's self-revelation at Sinai. Both the rabbis and early Christian writers undertook the interpretive rewriting of biblical history and religion. Such Christian authors as Origen and Jerome are known to have been in contact with Jewish teachers and were influenced by them. Many more Christian writers polemicized against the rabbis. Whatever the points of contact, the parallels, and actual dependence between the two religions, rabbinic Judaism provided an alternative way of receiving and understanding God's self-revelation in the Bible, an alternative that Christianity never ignored.

Among the texts representing Greco-Roman philosophical traditions, we first provide Plato's (ca. 429–347 BCE) critique of Greek civic religion in *The Republic* and his dialogue on love in *The Symposium*. Then we present selections from Epictetus's *Handbook* (*Encheiridion*). Epictetus (ca. 55–135 CE) was born to a slave woman in Hierapolis in Phrygia and grew up a slave in the house of Emperor Nero's powerful freedman and secretary Epaphroditus. At an early age he attended the lectures of the Stoic Musonius Rufus and, granted freedom by his master, taught philosophy on Rome's street corners and in the marketplace. He was banished with other philosophers by Domitian (in 89 or 92) and settled in Nicopolis, Greece, where he founded a school. Stoicism, which Epictetus taught in his *Discourses* and *Handbook,* was the "soul" of the Roman Empire, and early Christianity's debt to it is far-reaching, beginning with the apostle Paul. Later Christian writers found in Epictetus a kindred spirit; Origen, Gregory of Nazianzus, and Augustine (among others) ranked him higher than Plato in some respects. To Stoicism are traced such early Christian conceptions as the Divine (Holy) Spirit, Logos, God as one and yet many, conscience, individual moral responsibility, self-sufficiency, freedom, freedom of speech, and virtue. With some minor changes, Epictetus's *Handbook* was adopted by some Christian ascetics (see chapters 3 and 5 in this volume) as the rule of life.

Plotinus (ca. 204–70 CE) studied in Alexandria under Ammonius Saccas, with whom Origen was at least familiar. His essays and discussions were gathered by his pupil Porphyry, who edited and published them, dividing them into six sections, each containing nine books (that is, "enneads"). The *Enneads* is the most authoritative exposition of Neoplatonism, which was also much influenced by Aristotelian, Stoic, and Neopythagorean elements. Plotinus's philosophy is first an account of the procession of reality from the absolutely transcendent First Principle (the One or Good) as it descends in a succession of stages from the Divine Intellect, in which are the Forms, through the soul and finally to the last and the lowest realities, that is, the objects of sense perception. In the reverse, it is also an account of the way the human soul, by intellectual activity and ethical self-purification, can return to union with the Good (in which alone is the soul's happiness). This union of souls with the One, through the Intellect, is the final end of Plotinus's philosophy.

The general intellectual atmosphere in the third and fourth centuries, especially in Alexandria, was such that one would look in vain for any difference between Porphyry and his Christian contemporaries. It was through Augustine that a major flow of Neoplatonism came into Christian thought. Augustine, by his own admission, was first converted to Neoplatonism, and even after he abandoned philosophy, his thinking remained imbued with the system. He and early Christianity had to overcome metaphysical materialism and learn from Platonism that God was a timeless incorporeal existence and that evil existed in relation to the Good, as its absence. With the work of Pseudo-Dionysius (who lived sometime in the third to fifth centuries; see chapter 6 in this volume), Neoplatonism made another entry into Christianity, this time as a major source of Christian mysticism.

The study of Greco-Roman mystery religions has played a very important role in the understanding of early Christianity on account of their shared cosmology and perspectives on life and, especially, on death and the afterlife. In the mystery religions, as in Christianity, the union with the divine and final return of the soul, which philosophers like Plotinus sought, was achieved and assured by means of cultic rites. Very few literary sources on the cults have survived. It is difficult, therefore, to make many statements about the beliefs of the participants in mystery cults and indeed about the religions of the Greco-Roman world generally. Much has to be reconstructed from archaeological remains, reliefs, and inscriptions.

The mystery religions had two main characteristics. First, they all had a secret rite, a "mystery," the details of which could not be revealed by participants to noninitiates. Second, they promised salvation to initiates. The rites of initiation were a onetime objective experience that transformed the individual participant and put him or her in a state to receive salvation. Initiation was preceded by various purification rituals, including fasting and abstinence from certain foods and from sexual intercourse. The benefits of salvation reflected the whole range of human yearnings: protection from Fate (the vicissitudes of this life, including misfortune and sickness) and above all the promise of the final salvation of the soul after death. Salvation was attained by the imitation of the experience and deeds of the god or goddess of the cult, identification with the godhead, a vision of the deity, and finally union with the deity and divinization of the initiate. Initiates received a religious message in the form of secret phrases, symbols, emblems, and signs of recognition, and they took part in sacred meals. Although only the initiates possessed the secret of salvation, the name of the god or goddess granting salvation and the cult legend were matters of common knowledge. Mystery cults were not exclusive; that is, a participant in one was not thereby barred from other cults. And all who met the necessary qualifications could participate in them.

The major mystery cults of the Greco-Roman world included the Greek mysteries of Dionysus and the Eleusinian mysteries, and the eastern cults of Isis and of Mithras. *The Homeric Hymn to Demeter* is the official cult legend of the mysteries of Eleusis. The statement by Clement of Alexandria in his *Exhortation to the Greeks* (2.21.2; ca. 190) probably constitutes a revelation of the two secrets of the cult. Initiands traveled to Eleusis, in Greece, for initiation into the three stages of the mystery, which were the Lesser Mysteries, the Greater Mysteries, and (a year later) the Apopteia. The ancient Egyptian deities Isis and her brother-consort, Osiris, were the first of the eastern gods to become important in the Greco-Roman world. Osiris was later combined with Apis in the Greek world to produce the god Sarapis, or Serapis in Latin. Isis was identified with the most important goddess of the Hellenistic world, Demeter (afterward with Aphrodite), the goddess of agriculture and mysteries. Isis is generally depicted with the "Isis knot" on her dress, a disk, two ears of grain, and two feathers in her headdress. She frequently is portrayed suckling her infant son, Horus, a depiction thought to be a precedent for the Christian Madonna and Child. The most significant extant account of initiation into Isis's mystery cult is found in Apuleius's (ca. 123–80 CE) novel *Metamorphoses*.

The citations in Porphyry's (ca. 233–310 CE) *De antro nympharum* and *De abstinentia* are two of the otherwise-rare literary sources on the cult of Mithras. Mithra was the Persian god of oaths, good faith, loyalty, and light and was identified with the Sun. Transferred to Rome and Italy probably in the late first century CE as Mithras, he was associated and identified with the deity Sol (Sun) and worshiped as Sol Invictus, the Invincible Sun. The god was consistently represented with a Phrygian cap and slaying a bull. The Mithraic cult narrative included the birth of Mithras from a rock, his bringing forth of water from a rock with an arrow, and his victory over and slaying of the bull out of which all creation

and life arose. At his birth he carried a torch and a dagger. With the torch he brought light, which he himself was, and with the dagger he killed the bull and thereby created life. The Mithraic place of worship, the Mithraeum, was a cave or a cavelike structure where the initiations and the cultic meals were held. Apart from the ordinary initiates to the cult, there appear to have been seven grades of priests: Raven, Bridegroom, Soldier, Lion, Persian, Runner of the Sun, and Father, the highest grade. However, the cult lacked an internal administrative organization.

Mithraism did not admit women. At first, its membership included soldiers, minor administrative officials of the Roman Empire, slaves, freedmen, and ordinary Roman citizens. Later, however, the cult was patronized by emperors and high imperial officials. Of all the eastern cults, Mithraism was the most similar to Christianity. Justin Martyr (see *The First Apology* in chapter 3) reports that the devil had introduced a ritual meal similar to the Christian Eucharist into the Mithras cult, celebrated with bread and wine and possibly with the same spoken words and signification. Tertullian confirms that, like Christians, Mithraists believed that consumption of the bread and wine brought about rebirth. Christ was a deity of light. He was the Light of the world, much like Mithras was the Invincible Sun. Most of the parallels between the two religions seem, however, to have come from their common cultural contexts. Christianity appears initially to have tried either to minimize the parallels or to incorporate them. Thus, the "Day of the Lord" became "Sunday" and Jesus' birth was celebrated on the festival of Mithras's birth: December 25. Mithraism, like the other Greco-Roman cults, was not exclusive (as long as you were male) and had no missionary spirit, unlike early Christianity, which was exclusive and embraced a proselytizing mission. At the decisive battle (in 323) between Emperor Licinius (308–24) and Emperor Constantine (306–37), Licinius's troops fought under the banner of the Sun god Mithras and were defeated by Constantine, whose Sun god was Christ. Mithraism and the other mystery cults disappeared soon after (except for a brief revival under Julian in 361–63), leaving behind archaeological evidence of the violence that accompanied Christianity's triumph over "paganism."

1. CONTEMPORARY PALESTINIAN AND HELLENISTIC JUDAISMS

The Jewish historian **Flavius Josephus** (ca. 37–100) provides insight into the beliefs, practices, and configurations of first-century Judaism in his *Jewish Antiquities* (published ca. 95). In the section entitled "On Jewish Philosophies," Josephus describes the three main "philosophies," or groups, that composed Jewish society: the Sadducees, the Pharisees, and the Essenes. Our next selection from *Jewish Antiquities,* the so-called Testimonium Flavianum, is one of the earliest references to Jesus, though its authenticity is disputed. Our last selection is the report (generally accepted as authentic) of the death, in 62, of Jesus' brother, James, the leader of the Christian movement in Jerusalem.

FLAVIUS JOSEPHUS

"On Jewish Philosophies," *Jewish Antiquities,* xviii.2–25

Coponius, a man of equestrian rank, was sent along with him [Quirinius] to rule over the Jews with full authority. Quirinius also visited Judaea, which had been annexed to Syria, in order to make an assessment of the property of the Jews and to liquidate the estate of Archelaus. Although the Jews were at first shocked to hear of the registration of property, they gradually condescended, yielding to the arguments of the high priest Joazar, the son of Boethus, to go no further in opposition. So those who were convinced by him declared, without shilly-shallying, the value of their property. But a certain Judas, a Gaulanite from a city named Gamala, who had enlisted the aid of Saddok, a Pharisee, threw himself into the cause of rebellion. They said that the assessment carried with it a status amounting to downright slavery, no less, and appealed to the nation to make a bid for independence. They urged that in case of success the Jews would have laid the foundation of prosperity, while if they failed to obtain any such boon, they would win honour and renown for their lofty aim; and that Heaven would be their zealous helper to no lesser end than the furthering of their enterprise until it succeeded—all the more if with high devotion in their hearts they stood firm and did not shrink from the bloodshed that might be necessary. Since the populace, when they heard their appeals, responded gladly, the plot to strike boldly made serious progress; and so these men sowed the seed of every kind of misery, which so afflicted the nation that words are inadequate. When wars are set afoot that are bound to rage beyond control, and when friends are done away with who

might have alleviated the suffering, when raids are made by great hordes of brigands and men of the highest standing are assassinated, it is supposed to be the common welfare that is upheld, but the truth is that in such cases the motive is private gain. They sowed the seed from which sprang strife between factions and the slaughter of fellow citizens. Some were slain in civil strife, for these men madly had recourse to butchery of each other and of themselves from a longing not to be outdone by their opponents; others were slain by the enemy in war. Then came famine, reserved to exhibit the last degree of shamelessness, followed by the storming and razing of cities until at last the very temple of God was ravaged by the enemy's fire through this revolt. Here is a lesson that an innovation and reform in ancestral traditions weighs heavily in the scale in leading to the destruction of the congregation of the people. In this case certainly, Judas and Saddok started among us an intrusive fourth school of philosophy; and when they had won an abundance of devotees, they filled the body politic immediately with tumult, also planting the seeds of those troubles which subsequently overtook it, all because of the novelty of this hitherto unknown philosophy that I shall now describe. My reason for giving this brief account of it is chiefly that the zeal which Judas and Saddok inspired in the younger element meant the ruin of our cause.

The Jews, from the most ancient times, had three philosophies pertaining to their traditions, that of the Essenes, that of the Sadducees, and, thirdly, that of the group called the Pharisees. To be sure, I have spoken about them in the second book of the *Jewish War,*[1] but nevertheless I shall here too dwell on them for a moment.

The Pharisees simplify their standard of living, making no concession to luxury. They follow the guidance of that which their doctrine has selected and transmitted as good, attaching the chief importance to the observance of those commandments which it has seen fit to dictate to them. They show respect and deference to their elders, nor do they rashly presume to contradict their proposals. Though they postulate that everything is brought about by fate, still they do not deprive the human will of the pursuit of what is in man's power, since it was God's good pleasure that there should

---

1. See *Jewish War,* ii.119–66. (This note is by Gerhart and Udoh.)

be a fusion and that the will of man with his virtue and vice should be admitted to the council-chamber of fate. They believe that souls have power to survive death and that there are rewards and punishments under the earth for those who have led lives of virtue or vice: eternal imprisonment is the lot of evil souls, while the good souls receive an easy passage to a new life. Because of these views they are, as a matter of fact, extremely influential among the townsfolk; and all prayers and sacred rites of divine worship are performed according to their exposition. This is the great tribute that the inhabitants of the cities, by practising the highest ideals both in their way of living and in their discourse, have paid to the excellence of the Pharisees.

The Sadducees hold that the soul perishes along with the body. They own no observance of any sort apart from the laws; in fact, they reckon it a virtue to dispute with the teachers of the path of wisdom that they pursue. There are but few men to whom this doctrine has been made known, but these are men of the highest standing. They accomplish practically nothing, however. For whenever they assume some office, though they submit unwillingly and perforce, yet submit they do to the formulas of the Pharisees, since otherwise the masses would not tolerate them.

The doctrine of the Essenes is wont to leave everything in the hands of God. They regard the soul as immortal and believe that they ought to strive especially to draw near to righteousness. They send votive offerings to the temple, but perform their sacrifices employing a different ritual of purification. For this reason they are barred from those precincts of the temple that are frequented by all the people and perform their rites by themselves. Otherwise they are of the highest character, devoting themselves solely to agricultural labour. They deserve admiration in contrast to all others who claim their share of virtue because such qualities as theirs were never found before among any Greek or barbarian people, nay, not even briefly, but have been among them in constant practice and never interrupted since they adopted them from of old. Moreover, they hold their possessions in common, and the wealthy man receives no more enjoyment from his property than the man who possesses nothing. The men who practise this way of life number more than four thousand. They neither bring wives into the community nor do they own slaves, since they believe that the latter practice contributes to injustice and that the former opens the way to a source of dissension. Instead they live by themselves and perform menial tasks for one another. They elect by show of hands good men to receive their revenues and the produce of

the earth and priests to prepare bread and other food. Their manner of life does not differ at all from that of the so-called Ctistae among the Dacians, but is as close to it as could be.

As for the fourth of the philosophies, Judas the Galilaean set himself up as leader of it. This school agrees in all other respects with the opinions of the Pharisees, except that they have a passion for liberty that is almost unconquerable, since they are convinced that God alone is their leader and master. They think little of submitting to death in unusual forms and permitting vengeance to fall on kinsmen and friends if only they may avoid calling any man master. Inasmuch as most people have seen the steadfastness of their resolution amid such circumstances, I may forgo any further account. For I have no fear that anything reported of them will be considered incredible. The danger is, rather, that report may minimize the indifference with which they accept the grinding misery of pain. The folly that ensued began to afflict the nation after Gessius Florus, who was governor, had by his overbearing and lawless actions provoked a desperate rebellion against the Romans. Such is the number of the schools of philosophy among the Jews.

From *Josephus IX: Jewish Antiquities, Books xviii–xix,* translated by Louis H. Feldman, Loeb Classical Library (Cambridge, MA: Harvard University Press, 1981), 5, 7, 9, 11, 13, 15, 17, 19, 21, 23.

FLAVIUS JOSEPHUS

Testimonium Flavianum, *Jewish Antiquities,* xviii.63–64

About this time there lived Jesus, a wise man, if indeed one ought to call him a man. For he was one who wrought surprising feats and was a teacher of such people as accept the truth gladly. He won over many Jews and many of the Greeks. He was the Messiah. When Pilate, upon hearing him accused by men of the highest standing amongst us, had condemned him to be crucified, those who had in the first place come to love him did not give up their affection for him. On the third day he appeared to them restored to life, for the prophets of God had prophesied these and countless other marvelous things about him. And the tribe of the Christians, so called after him, has still to this day not disappeared.

From *Josephus IX: Jewish Antiquities, Books xviii–xix,* translated by Louis H. Feldman, Loeb Classical Library (Cambridge, MA: Harvard University Press, 1981), 49, 51.

FLAVIUS JOSEPHUS

"The Death of James the Brother of Jesus," *Jewish Antiquities,* xx.200–203

Possessed of such a character, Ananus thought that he had a favourable opportunity because Festus was dead and Albinus[2] was still on the way. And so he convened the judges of the Sanhedrin and brought before them a man named James, the brother of Jesus who was called the Christ, and certain others. He accused them of having transgressed the law and delivered them up to be stoned. Those of the inhabitants of the city who were considered the most fair-minded and who were strict in observance of the law were offended at this. They therefore secretly sent to King Agrippa urging him, for Ananus had not even been correct in his first step, to order him to desist from any further such actions. Certain of them even went to meet Albinus, who was on his way from Alexandria, and informed him that Ananus had no authority to convene the Sanhedrin without his consent. Convinced by these words, Albinus angrily wrote to Ananus threatening to take vengeance upon him. King Agrippa, because of Ananus' action, deposed him from the high priesthood which he had held for three months and replaced him with Jesus the son of Damnaeus.

From *Josephus X: Jewish Antiquities, Book xx,* translated by Louis H. Feldman, Loeb Classical Library (Cambridge, MA: Harvard University Press, 1981), 107, 109.

⟡ The **Dead Sea Scrolls** are so named because of their discovery in 1947 near the Dead Sea. They provide a picture of a sectarian form of Judaism (usually associated with the Essenes) whose followers lived at Qumran during the last few centuries BCE and the first century CE. *The Community Rule,* one of the oldest of the Qumran documents (ca. 100 BCE), legislates for a kind of monastic community. *The Damascus Document* (probably written later than *The Community Rule*) concerns the communities living in the cities of Palestine. *The Messianic Rule* (ca. 50 BCE) provides insight into the sect's strong eschatological (they thought they were living in the last days) and messianic (they expected two Messiahs) expectations.

The Community Rule, I–IV

I. [The Master shall teach the sai]nts to live(?) {according to the Book}[3] of the Community [Rul]e, that they may seek God with a whole heart and soul, and do what is good and

right before Him as He commanded by the hand of Moses and all His servants the Prophets; that they may love all that He has chosen and hate all that He has rejected; that they may abstain from all evil and hold fast to all good; that they may practise truth, righteousness, and justice upon earth and no longer stubbornly follow a sinful heart and lustful eyes, committing all manner of evil. He shall admit into the Covenant of Grace all those who have freely devoted themselves to the observance of God's precepts, that they may be joined to the counsel of God and may live perfectly before Him in accordance with all that has been revealed concerning their appointed times, and that they may love all the sons of light, each according to his lot in God's design, and hate all the sons of darkness, each according to his guilt in God's vengeance.

All those who freely devote themselves to His truth shall bring all their knowledge, powers, and possessions into the Community of God, that they may purify their knowledge in the truth of God's precepts and order their powers according to His ways of perfection and all their possessions according to His righteous counsel. They shall not depart from any command of God concerning their times; they shall be neither early nor late for any of their appointed times, they shall stray neither to the right nor to the left of any of His true precepts. All those who embrace the Community Rule shall enter into the Covenant before God to obey all His commandments so that they may not abandon Him during the dominion of Belial because of fear or terror or affliction.

On entering the Covenant, the Priests and Levites shall bless the God of salvation and all His faithfulness, and all those entering the Covenant shall say after them, "Amen, Amen!"

Then the Priests shall recite the favours of God manifested in His mighty deeds and shall declare all His merciful grace to Israel, and the Levites shall recite the iniquities of the children of Israel, all their guilty rebellions and sins during the dominion of Belial. And after them, all those entering the Covenant shall confess and say: "We have strayed! We have [disobeyed!] We and our fathers before us have sinned and done wickedly in walking [counter to the precepts] of truth and righteousness. [And God has] judged us and our fathers also; II. but He has bestowed His bountiful mercy on

---

2. Lucceius Albinus was appointed procurator of Judea in 62 CE. (This note is by Gerhart and Udoh.)

3. The translator places hypothetical reconstructions of the text between [square brackets]. Text supplied from other manuscripts of the same document appear between {braces}, and glosses needed for better fluency are between (parentheses). (This note is by Gerhart and Udoh.)

us from everlasting to everlasting." And the Priests shall bless all the men of the lot of God who walk perfectly in all His ways, saying: "May He bless you with all good and preserve you from all evil! May He lighten your heart with life-giving wisdom and grant you eternal knowledge! May He raise His merciful face towards you for everlasting bliss!"

And the Levites shall curse all the men of the lot of Belial, saying: "Be cursed because of all your guilty wickedness! May He deliver you up for torture at the hands of the vengeful Avengers! May He visit you with destruction by the hand of all the Wreakers of Revenge! Be cursed without mercy because of the darkness of your deeds! Be damned in the shadowy place of everlasting fire! May God not heed when you call on Him, nor pardon you by blotting out your sin! May He raise His angry face towards you for vengeance! May there be no 'Peace' for you in the mouth of those who hold fast to the Fathers!" And after the blessing and the cursing, all those entering the Covenant shall say, "Amen, Amen!"

And the Priests and Levites shall continue, saying: "Cursed be the man who enters this Covenant while walking among the idols of his heart, who sets up before himself his stumbling-block of sin so that he may backslide! Hearing the words of this Covenant, he blesses himself in his heart and says, 'Peace be with me, even though I walk in the stubbornness of my heart' (Deut 29:18–19), whereas his spirit, parched (for lack of truth) and watered (with lies), shall be destroyed without pardon. God's wrath and His zeal for His precepts shall consume him in everlasting destruction. All the curses of the Covenant shall cling to him and God will set him apart for evil. He shall be cut off from the midst of all the sons of light, and because he has turned aside from God on account of his idols and his stumbling-block of sin, his lot shall be among those who are cursed for ever." And after them, all those entering the Covenant shall answer and say, "Amen, Amen!"

Thus shall they do, year by year, for as long as the dominion of Belial endures. The Priests shall enter first, ranked one after another according to the perfection of their spirit; then the Levites; and thirdly, all the people one after another in their Thousands, Hundreds, Fifties, and Tens, that every Israelite may know his place in the Community of God according to the everlasting design. No man shall move down from his place nor move up from his allotted position. For according to the holy design, they shall all of them be in a Community of truth and virtuous humility, of loving-kindness and good intent one towards the other, and (they shall all of them be) sons of the everlasting Company.

No man [shall be in the] Community of His truth who refuses to enter [the Covenant of] God so that he may walk in the stubbornness of his heart, for III. his soul detests the wise teaching of just laws. He shall not be counted among the upright for he has not persisted in the conversion of his life. His knowledge, powers, and possessions shall not enter the Council of the Community, for whoever ploughs the mud of wickedness returns defiled (?). He shall not be justified by that which his stubborn heart declares lawful, for seeking the ways of light he looks towards darkness. He shall not be reckoned among the perfect; he shall neither be purified by atonement, nor cleansed by purifying waters, nor sanctified by seas and rivers, nor washed clean with any ablution. Unclean, unclean shall he be. For as long as he despises the precepts of God he shall receive no instruction in the Community of His counsel.

For it is through the spirit of true counsel concerning the ways of man that all his sins shall be expiated, that he may contemplate the light of life. He shall be cleansed from all his sins by the spirit of holiness uniting him to His truth, and his iniquity shall be expiated by the spirit of uprightness and humility. And when his flesh is sprinkled with purifying water and sanctified by cleansing water, it shall be made clean by the humble submission of his soul to all the precepts of God. Let him then order his steps {to walk} perfectly in all the ways commanded by God concerning the times appointed for him, straying neither to the right nor to the left and transgressing none of His words, and he shall be accepted by virtue of a pleasing atonement before God and it shall be to him a Covenant of the everlasting Community.

The Master shall instruct all the sons of light and shall teach them the nature of all the children of men according to the kind of spirit which they possess, the signs identifying their works during their lifetime, their visitation for chastisement, and the time of their reward.

From the God of Knowledge comes all that is and shall be. Before ever they existed He established their whole design, and when, as ordained for them, they come into being, it is in accord with His glorious design that they accomplish their task without change. The laws of all things are in His hand and He provides them with all their needs.

He has created man to govern the world, and has appointed for him two spirits in which to walk until the time of His visitation: the spirits of truth and injustice. Those born of truth spring from a fountain of light, but those born of injustice spring from a source of darkness. All the children of righteousness are ruled by the Prince of Light and walk in the ways of light, but all the children of injustice are ruled by the Angel of Darkness and walk in the ways of darkness. The Angel of Darkness leads all the children of righteousness astray, and until his end, all their sin, iniquities, wickedness, and all their unlawful deeds are caused by his dominion in accordance with the mysteries of God. Every one of their chastisements, and every one of the seasons of their distress, shall be brought about by the rule of his persecution; for all his allotted spirits seek the overthrow of the sons of light.

But the God of Israel and His Angel of Truth will succour all the sons of light. For it is He who created the spirits of Light and Darkness and founded every action upon them and established every deed [upon] their [ways]. And He loves the one IV. everlastingly and delights in its works for ever; but the counsel of the other He loathes and for ever hates its ways.

These are their ways in the world for the enlightenment of the heart of man, and so that all the paths of true righteousness may be made straight before him, and so that the fear of the laws of God may be instilled in his heart: a spirit of humility, patience, abundant charity, unending goodness, understanding, and intelligence; (a spirit of) mighty wisdom which trusts in all the deeds of God and leans on His great loving-kindness; a spirit of discernment in every purpose, of zeal for just laws, of holy intent with steadfastness of heart, of great charity towards all the sons of truth, of admirable purity which detests all unclean idols, of humble conduct sprung from an understanding of all things, and of faithful concealment of the mysteries of truth. These are the counsels of the spirit to the sons of truth in this world.

And as for the visitation of all who walk in this spirit, it shall be healing, great peace in a long life, and fruitfulness, together with every everlasting blessing and eternal joy in life without end, a crown of glory and a garment of majesty in unending light.

But the ways of the spirit of falsehood are these: greed, and slackness in the search for righteousness, wickedness and lies, haughtiness and pride, falseness and deceit, cruelty and abundant evil, ill-temper and much folly and brazen insolence, abominable deeds (committed) in a spirit of lust, and ways of lewdness in the service of uncleanness, a blaspheming tongue, blindness of eye and dullness of ear, stiffness of neck and heaviness of heart, so that man walks in all the ways of darkness and guile.

And the visitation of all who walk in this spirit shall be a multitude of plagues by the hand of all the destroying angels, everlasting damnation by the avenging wrath of the fury of God, eternal torment and endless disgrace together with shameful extinction in the fire of the dark regions. The times of all their generations shall be spent in sorrowful mourning and in bitter misery and in calamities of darkness until they are destroyed without remnant or survivor.

The nature of all the children of men is ruled by these (two spirits), and during their life all the hosts of men have a portion of their divisions and walk in (both) their ways. And the whole reward for their deeds shall be, for everlasting ages, according to whether each man's portion in their two divisions is great or small. For God has established the spirits in equal measure until the final age, and has set everlasting hatred between their divisions. Truth abhors the works of injustice, and injustice hates all the ways of truth. And their struggle is fierce in all their arguments for they do not walk together. But in the mysteries of His understanding, and in His glorious wisdom, God has ordained an end for injustice, and at the time of the visitation He will destroy it for ever. Then truth, which has wallowed in the ways of wickedness during the dominion of injustice until the appointed time of judgement, shall arise in the world for ever. God will then purify every deed of man with His truth; He will refine for Himself the human frame by rooting out all spirit of injustice from the bounds of his flesh. He will cleanse him of all wicked deeds with the spirit of holiness; like purifying waters He will shed upon him the spirit of truth (to cleanse him) of all abomination and injustice. And he shall be plunged into the spirit of purification, that he may instruct the upright in the knowledge of the Most High and teach the wisdom of the sons of heaven to the perfect of way. For God has chosen them for an everlasting Covenant and all the glory of Adam shall be theirs. There shall be no more lies and all the works of injustice shall be put to shame.

Until now the spirits of truth and injustice struggle in the hearts of men and they walk in both wisdom and folly. According to his portion of truth so does a man hate injustice, and according to his inheritance in the realm of injustice so is he wicked and so hates truth. For God has established the two spirits in equal measure until the determined end, and until the Renewal, and He knows the reward of their deeds from all eternity. He has allotted them to the children of men that they may know good [and evil, and] that the destiny of all the living may be according to the spirit within [them at the time] of the visitation.

From Geza Vermes, *The Complete Dead Sea Scrolls in English* (New York: Penguin, 1997), 98–103.

The Damascus Document, II.1–VI.10

II. Hear now, all you who enter the Covenant, and I will unstop your ears concerning the ways of the wicked.

God loves knowledge. Wisdom and understanding He has set before Him, and prudence and knowledge serve Him. Patience and much forgiveness are with Him towards those who turn from transgression; but power, might, and great flaming wrath by the hand of all the Angels of Destruction towards those who depart from the way and abhor the Precept. They shall have no remnant or survivor. For from the beginning God chose them not; He knew their deeds before ever they were created and He hated their generations, and He hid His face from the Land until they were consumed. For He knew the years of their coming and the length and exact duration of their times for all ages to come and throughout eternity. He knew the happenings of their times throughout all the everlasting years. And in all of them He raised for Himself men called by name that a remnant might be left to the Land, and that the face of the earth might be filled with their seed. And He made known His Holy Spirit to them by the hand of His anointed ones, and He proclaimed the truth (to them). But those whom He hated He led astray.

Hear now, my sons, and I will uncover your eyes that you may see and understand the works of God, that you may choose that which pleases Him and reject that which He hates, that you may walk perfectly in all His ways and not follow after thoughts of the guilty inclination and after eyes of lust. For through them, great men have gone astray and mighty heroes have stumbled from former times till now. Because they walked in the stubbornness of their heart the Heavenly Watchers fell; they were caught because they did not keep the commandments of God. And their sons also fell who were tall as cedar trees and whose bodies were like mountains. All flesh on dry land perished; they were as though they had never been because they did their own will and did not keep the commandment of their Maker so that His wrath was kindled against them. III. Through it, the children of Noah went astray, together with their kin, and were cut off. Abraham did not walk in it, and he was accounted a friend of God because he kept the commandments of God and did not choose his own will. And he handed them down to Isaac and Jacob, who kept them, and were recorded as friends of God and party to the Covenant for ever. The children of Jacob strayed through them and were punished in accordance with their error. And their

sons in Egypt walked in the stubbornness of their hearts, conspiring against the commandments of God and each of them doing that which seemed right in his own eyes. They ate blood, and He cut off their males in the wilderness. And at Kadesh He said to them, *Go up and possess the land* (Deut 9:23). But they chose their own will and did not heed the voice of their Maker, the commands of their Teacher, but murmured in their tents; and the anger of God was kindled against their congregation. Through it their sons perished, and through it their kings were cut off; through it their mighty heroes perished and through it their land was ravaged. Through it the first members of the Covenant sinned and were delivered up to the sword, because they forsook the Covenant of God and chose their own will and walked in the stubbornness of their hearts, each of them doing his own will.

But with the remnant which held fast to the commandments of God He made His Covenant with Israel for ever, revealing to them the hidden things in which all Israel had gone astray. He unfolded before them His holy Sabbaths and his glorious feasts, the testimonies of His righteousness and the ways of His truth, and the desires of His will which a man must do in order to live. And they dug a well rich in water; and he who despises it shall not live. Yet they wallowed in the sin of man and in ways of uncleanness, and they said, "This is our (way)." But God, in His wonderful mysteries, forgave them their sin and pardoned their wickedness; and He built them a sure house in Israel whose like has never existed from former times till now. Those who hold fast to it are destined to live for ever and all the glory of Adam shall be theirs. As God ordained for them by the hand of the Prophet Ezekiel, saying, *The Priests, the Levites, and the sons IV. of Zadok who kept the charge of my sanctuary when the children of Israel strayed from me, they shall offer me fat and blood* (Ezek 44:15).

The *Priests* are the converts of Israel who departed from the land of Judah, and (the *Levites* are) those who joined them. The *sons of Zadok* are the elect of Israel, the men called by name who shall stand at the end of days. Behold the exact list of their names according to their generations, and the time when they lived, and the number of their trials, and the years of their sojourn, and the exact list of their deeds . . .

(They were the first men) of holiness whom God forgave, and who justified the righteous and condemned the wicked. And until the age is completed, according to the number of those years, all who enter after them shall do according to that interpretation of the Law in which the first (men) were instructed. According to the Covenant which God made with the forefathers, forgiving their sins, so shall He forgive their sins also. But when the age is completed, according to the number of those years, there shall be no more joining the house of Judah, but each man shall stand on his watch-tower: *The wall is built, the boundary far removed* (Mic 7:11).

During all those years Belial shall be unleashed against Israel, as He spoke by the hand of Isaiah, son of Amoz, saying, *Terror and the pit and the snare are upon you, O inhabitant of the land* (Isa 24:17). Interpreted, these are the three nets of Belial with which Levi son of Jacob said that he catches Israel by setting them up as three kinds of righteousness. The first is fornication, the second is riches, and the third is profanation of the Temple. Whoever escapes the first is caught in the second, and whoever saves himself from the second is caught in the third (Isa 24:18).

The "builders of the wall" (Ezek 13:10) who have followed after "Precept"—"Precept" was a spouter of whom it is written, *They shall surely spout* (Mic 2:6)—shall be caught in fornication twice by taking a second wife while the first is alive, whereas the principle of creation is, *Male and female created He them* (Gen 1:27). V. Also, those who entered the Ark went in two by two. And concerning the prince it is written, *He shall not multiply wives to himself* (Deut 17:17); but David had not read the sealed book of the Law which was in the ark (of the Covenant), for it was not opened in Israel from the death of Eleazar and Joshua, and the elders who worshipped Ashtoreth. It was hidden and (was not) revealed until the coming of Zadok. And the deeds of David rose up, except for the murder of Uriah, and God left them to him.

Moreover, they profane the Temple because they do not observe the distinction (between clean and unclean) in accordance with the Law, but lie with a woman who sees her bloody discharge.

And each man marries the daughter of his brother or sister, whereas Moses said, *You shall not approach your mother's sister; she is your mother's near kin* (Lev 18:13). But although the laws against incest are written for men, they also apply to women. When, therefore, a brother's daughter uncovers the nakedness of her father's brother, she is (also his) near kin.

Furthermore, they defile their holy spirit and open their mouth with a blaspheming tongue against the laws of the Covenant of God saying, "They are not sure." They speak abominations concerning them; *they are all kindlers of fire and lighters of brands* (Isa 50:11), *their webs are spiders' webs and their eggs are vipers' eggs* (Isa 59:5). No man that approaches them

shall be free from guilt; the more he does so, the guiltier shall he be, unless he is pressed. For (already) in ancient times God visited their deeds and His anger was kindled against their works; *for it is a people of no discernment* (Isa 27:11), *it is a nation void of counsel inasmuch as there is no discernment in them* (Deut 32:28). For in ancient times, Moses and Aaron arose by the hand of the Prince of Lights and Belial in his cunning raised up Jannes and his brother when Israel was first delivered.

And at the time of the desolation of the land there arose removers of the bound who led Israel astray. And the land was ravaged because they preached rebellion against the commandments of God given by the hand of Moses and VI. of His holy anointed ones, and because they prophesied lies to turn Israel away from following God. But God remembered the Covenant with the forefathers, and he raised from Aaron men of discernment and from Israel men of wisdom, and He caused them to hear. And they dug the Well: *the well which the princes dug, which the nobles of the people delved with the stave* (Num 21:18).

The *Well* is the Law, and those who dug it were the converts of Israel who went out of the land of Judah to sojourn in the land of Damascus. God called them all *princes* because they sought Him, and their renown was disputed by no man. The *Stave* is the Interpreter of the Law of whom Isaiah said, *He makes a tool for His work* (Isa 54:16); and the *nobles of the people* are those who come to dig the *Well* with the staves with which the *Stave* ordained that they should walk in all the age of wickedness—and without them they shall find nothing—until he comes who shall teach righteousness at the end of days.

From Geza Vermes, *The Complete Dead Sea Scrolls in English* (New York: Penguin, 1997), 128–32.

The Messianic Rule, I.26–II

These are the men who shall be called to the Council of the Community . . .

All the wi[se men] of the congregation, the learned and the intelligent, men whose way is perfect and men of ability, together with the tribal chiefs and all the Judges and officers, and the chiefs of the Thousands, [Hundreds,] II. Fifties, and Tens, and the Levites, each man in the [cla]ss of his duty; these are the men of renown, the members of the assembly summoned to the Council of the Community in Israel before the sons of Zadok the Priests.

And no man smitten with any human uncleanness shall

enter the assembly of God; no man smitten with any of them shall be confirmed in his office in the congregation. No man smitten in his flesh, or paralyzed in his feet or hands, or lame, or blind, or deaf, or dumb, or smitten in his flesh with a visible blemish; no old and tottery man unable to stay still in the midst of the congregation; none of these shall come to hold office among the congregation of the men of renown, for the Angels of Holiness are [with] their [congregation]. Should [one] of them have something to say to the Council of Holiness, let [him] be questioned privately; but let him not enter among [the congregation] for he is smitten.

[*This shall be the ass*]*embly of the men of renown* [*called*] *to the meeting of the Council of the Community*

When God engenders (the Priest-) Messiah, he shall come with them [at] the head of the whole congregation of Israel with all [his brethren, the sons] of Aaron the Priests, [those called] to the assembly, the men of renown; and they shall sit [before him, each man] in the order of his dignity. And then [the Mess]iah of Israel shall [come], and the chiefs of the [clans of Israel] shall sit before him, [each] in the order of his dignity, according to [his place] in their camps and marches. And before them shall sit all the heads of [family of the congreg]ation, and the wise men of [the holy congregation,] each in the order of his dignity.

And [when] they shall gather for the common [tab]le, to eat and [to drink] new wine, when the common table shall be set for eating and the new wine [poured] for drinking, let no man extend his hand over the firstfruits of bread and wine before the Priest; for [it is he] who shall bless the firstfruits of bread and wine, and shall be the first [to extend] his hand over the bread. Thereafter, the Messiah of Israel shall extend his hand over the bread, [and] all the congregation of the Community [shall utter a] blessing, [each man in the order] of his dignity.

It is according to this statute that they shall proceed at every me[al at which] at least ten men are gathered together.

From Geza Vermes, *The Complete Dead Sea Scrolls in English* (New York: Penguin, 1997), 159–60. [Ellipsis in original.]

꙾ *The Letter of Aristeas* (ca. 170 BCE) narrates one version of the legend about the translation of the Jewish Scriptures into Greek. It is from this story that the name "Septuagint" is derived (abbreviated LXX, "seventy") for the Greek version of the Old Testament.

The Letter of Aristeas, 9–11, 28–51, 172–81, 301–21

9. On his appointment as keeper of the king's[4] library, Demetrius of Phalerum undertook many different negotiations aimed at collecting, if possible, all the books in the world. By purchase and translation he brought to a successful conclusion, as far as lay in his power, the king's plan. 10. We were present when the question was put to him, "How many thousand books are there (in the royal library)?" His reply was, "Over two hundred thousand, O King. I shall take urgent steps to increase in a short time the total to five hundred thousand. Information has reached me that the lawbooks of the Jews are worth translation and inclusion in your royal library."

11. "What is there to prevent you from doing this?" he said. "Everything for your needs has been put at your disposal."

Demetrius replied, "Translation is needed. They use letters characteristic of the language of the Jews, just as Egyptians use the formation of their letters in accordance with their own language. The Jews are supposed to use Syrian language, but this is not so, for it is another form (of language)."

The king, in answer to each point, gave orders that a letter be written to the high priest of the Jews that the aforementioned project might be carried out. . . .

28. [. . .] All measures were taken by these kings[5] by means of edicts and in complete safety, with no trace of negligence or carelessness. For this reason I have set down the copies of the report and of the letters, as well as the number of those returned and the state of each, because each of them was outstanding in magnificence and skill. 29. The copy of the memorandum is as follows: "To the great king from Demetrius. Your command, O King, concerned the collection of missing volumes needed to complete the library, and of items which accidentally fell short of the requisite condition. I gave highest priority and attention to these matters, and now make the following further report: 30. Scrolls of the Law of the Jews, together with a few others, are missing (from the library), for these (works) are written in Hebrew characters and language. But they have been transcribed somewhat carelessly and not as they should be, according to the report of

---

4. Ptolemy II Philadelphus (285–246 BCE). (The notes for this selection are by Gerhart and Udoh.)

5. That is, Ptolemaic kings.

the experts, because they have not received royal patronage. 31. These (books) also must be in your library in an accurate version, because this legislation, as could be expected from its divine nature, is very philosophical and genuine. Writers therefore and poets and the whole army of historians have been reluctant to refer to the aforementioned books, and to the men past (and present) who featured largely in them, because the consideration of them is sacred and hallowed, as Hecataeus of Abdera says. 32. If you approve, O King, a letter shall be written to the high priest at Jerusalem, asking him to dispatch men of the most exemplary lives and mature experience, skilled in matters pertaining to their Law, six in number from each tribe, in order that after the examination of the text agreed by the majority, and the achievement of accuracy in the translation, we may produce an outstanding version in a manner worthy both of the contents and of your purpose. Farewell always." 33. On receiving this report, the king ordered a letter to be written to Eleazar regarding these matters, announcing also the actual release of the prisoners. He made them a gift also for the provision of cups and goblets and a table and libation vessels weighing fifty talents of gold, seventy talents of silver, and a goodly number of (precious) stones—he commanded the treasurers to allow the craftsmen to select whatever they might prefer—and of currency for sacrifices and other requirements one hundred talents. 34. We will show you details of the provisions after we have given the copies of the letters. The letter of the king was of the following pattern. 35. "King Ptolemy to Eleazar the high priest, hearty greetings. It is a fact that a large number of the Jews settled in our country after being uprooted from Jerusalem by the Persians during the time of their ascendancy, and also came with our father into Egypt as prisoners. 36. He put many of them into the military forces on generous pay, and in the same way, having judged the veterans to be trustworthy, he set up establishments which he handed over to them, to prevent the Egyptian people feeling any apprehension on their account.

Having now inherited the throne, we adopt a more liberal attitude to all our subjects, and more especially to your citizens. 37. We have freed more than a hundred thousand prisoners, paying to their captors the price in silver proportionate to their rank. We also make amends for any damage caused by mob violence. We decided to do this as a religious obligation, making of it a thank offering to the Most High God, who has preserved the kingdom for us in peace and highest renown throughout the whole world. Those at the peak of their youth we have appointed to the army, and those

who are able to be at our court, being worthy of confidence in our household, we have put in charge of (some) ministries. 38. It is our wish to grant favors to them and to all the Jews throughout the world, including future generations. We have accordingly decided that your Law shall be translated into Greek letters from what you call the Hebrew letters, in order that they too should take their place with us in our library with the other royal books. 39. You will therefore act well, and in a manner worthy of our zeal, by selecting elders of exemplary lives, with experience of the Law and ability to translate it, six from each tribe, so that an agreed version may be found from the large majority, in view of the great importance of the matters under consideration. We believe that the completion of this project will win (us) high reputation. 40. We have dispatched on this business Andreas of the chief bodyguards and Aristeas, men held in high esteem by you, to confer with you; they bring with them firstfruits of offerings for the Temple and one hundred talents of silver for sacrifices and the other requirements. Write to us on any matters you wish, and your requests will be gratified; you will be performing also an act worthy of friendship for what you choose will be carried out with all dispatch. Farewell." 41. In reply to this letter Eleazar wrote in acceptance as follows: "Eleazar the high priest to King Ptolemy, dear friend, greeting. Good health to you and to Queen Arsinoe, your sister, and to your children; if that is so, it would be well, and as we wish. We too are in good health. 42. On receipt of your letter we rejoiced greatly because of your purpose and noble plan; we therefore collected together the whole multitude and read it to them, that they might know your piety toward our God. We also showed them the vessels which you sent, twenty of silver and thirty of gold, five cups, and a table for offering, and for the performance of the sacrifices and the furnishing of the Temple requirements one hundred talents of silver, 43. brought by two men highly esteemed by you, Andreas and Aristeas, gentlemen of integrity, outstanding in education, worthy in every respect of your conduct and justice. They also communicated to us your messages, in reply to which they have heard from us also sentiments consistent with what you wrote. 44. Everything which is to your advantage, even if it is unnatural, we will carry out; this is a sign of friendship and love. You have also bestowed great unexpected benefits upon our citizens in many ways. 45. We therefore offered sacrifices without delay for you, your sister, your children, and your friends. The whole multitude made supplication that it should come to pass for you entirely as you desire, and that God the ruler of all should preserve your kingdom in peace and glory, and that the translation of the sacred Law should come to pass in a manner expedient to you and in safety. 46. In the presence of the whole assembly we selected elders, honorable men and true, six from each tribe, whom we have sent with the Law in their possession. It will be a noble deed, O righteous King, if you command that once the translation of the books is complete these men be restored to us again in safety. Farewell." 47. The names of the men are as follows: First tribe: Joseph, Ezekiah, Zachariah, John, Ezekiah, and Elissaeus; second tribe: Judas, Simon, Somoel, Adaeus, Mattathias, and Esclemias; third tribe: Neemiah, Joseph, Theodosius, Baseas, Ornias, and Dakis; 48. fourth tribe: Jonathan, Abraeus, Elissaeus, Ananias, Chabrias;[6] fifth tribe: Isaac, Jacob, Jesus, Sabbataeus, Simon, Levi; sixth tribe: Judas, Joseph, Simon, Zachariah, Somoel, and Selemiah; 49. seventh tribe: Sabbataeus, Sedekiah, Jacob, Isaac, Jesias, Natthaeus; eighth tribe: Theodosius, Jason, Jesus, Theodotus, John, and Jonathan; ninth tribe: Theophilus, Abram, Arsam, Jason, Endemias, and Daniel; 50. tenth tribe: Jeremiah, Eleazar, Zachariah, Baneas, Elissaeus, and Dathaeus; eleventh tribe: Samuel, Joseph, Judas, Jonathan, Chabeu, and Dositheus; twelfth tribe: Isael, John, Theodosius, Arsamus, Abietes, and Ezekiel. Seventy-two in all. 51. The matters relating to the king's letter received the aforementioned reply from Eleazar and his advisers. [. . .]

172. Eleazar offered sacrifice, selected the men, and made ready an abundance of gifts for the king. He then sent us forth on our journey with a large escort. 173. When we reached Alexandria, news of our arrival was given to the king. Andreas and I were introduced to the court, we paid our warm respects to the king, and presented the letters from Eleazar. 174. The king was anxious to meet the members of the deputation, so he gave orders to dismiss all the other court officials, and to summon these delegates. 175. The unprecedented nature of this step was very clear to all, because it was an established procedure that important bona fide visitors should be granted an audience with the king only four days after arrival, while representatives of kings or important cities are rarely admitted to the court within thirty days. However, he deemed the present arrivals to be deserving of greater honor, having regard to the preeminence of him who had sent them. So he dismissed all the officials whom he considered superfluous and remained walking among the delegates until he had greeted the whole delegation. 176. So they arrived with the gifts which had been sent at their hands and with the fine skins on which the Law had been written in letters of gold in Jewish characters; the parchment had been

excellently worked, and the joining together of the letters was imperceptible. When the king saw the delegates, he proceeded to ask questions about the books, 177. and when they had shown what had been covered and unrolled the parchments, he paused for a long time, did obeisance about seven times, and said, "I offer to you my thanks, gentlemen, and to him who sent you even more, and most of all to the God whose oracles these are." 178. They all, visitors and the court present alike, said together and with one voice, "It is well, O King." At this the king was moved to tears, so deeply was he filled with joy. Intensity of feeling coupled with the greatness of the honor received do force men to tears in the moment of success. 179. The king commanded the parcels to be returned in order, and then immediately greeted the delegates with these words: "It is (meet and) right, O men of God, first to render homage to the documents for the sake of which I have sent for you, and after that to extend to you the right hand of greeting. This explains my first action. 180. I regard this day of your arrival as of great importance, and it shall be specially marked year by year throughout the time of our life, for by a happy chance it coincides with our victory at sea against Antigonus. It will therefore be my wish to dine with you this day. 181. Everything of which you partake," he said, "will be served in compliance with your habits; it will be served to me as well as to you." They expressed their pleasure and the king ordered the finest apartments to be given them near the citadel, and the preparations for the banquet to be made. [. . .]

301. Three days afterward, Demetrius took the men with him, traversed the mile-long jetty into the sea toward the island, crossed the bridge, and went in the direction of the north. There he assembled them in a house which had been duly furnished near the shore—a magnificent building in a very quiet situation—and invited the men to carry out the work of translation, all that they would require being handsomely provided. 302. They set to completing their several tasks, reaching agreement among themselves on each by comparing versions. The result of their agreement thus was made into a fair copy by Demetrius. 303. The business of their meeting occupied them until the ninth hour, after which they were free for bodily rest and relaxation, everything which they desired being furnished on a lavish scale. 304. Apart from all this, Dorotheus also provided for them all that was prepared for the king—this was the order which

---

6. The name of the sixth member is missing from the text.

he had received from the king. At the first hour of the day they attended the court daily, and after offering salutations to the king, retired to their own quarters. 305. Following the custom of all the Jews, they washed their hands in the sea in the course of their prayers to God, and then proceeded to the reading and explication of each point. 306. I asked this question: "What is their purpose in washing their hands while saying their prayers?" They explained that it is evidence that they have done no evil, for all activity takes place by means of the hands. Thus they nobly and piously refer everything to righteousness and truth. 307. In this way, as we said previously, each day they assembled in their quarters, which were pleasantly situated for quiet and light, and proceeded to fulfill their prescribed task. The outcome was such that in seventy-two days the business of translation was completed, just as if such a result was achieved by some deliberate design. 308. When it was completed, Demetrius assembled the company of the Jews in the place where the task of the translation had been finished, and read it to all, in the presence of the translators, who received a great ovation from the crowded audience for being responsible for great blessings. 309. Likewise also they gave an ovation to Demetrius and asked him, now that he had transcribed the whole Law, to give a copy to their leaders. 310. As the books were read, the priests stood up, with the elders from among the translators and from the representatives of the "Community," and with the leaders of the people, and said, "Since this version has been made rightly and reverently, and in every respect accurately, it is good that this should remain exactly so, and that there should be no revision." 311. There was general approval of what they said, and they commanded that a curse should be laid, as was their custom, on anyone who should alter the version by any addition or change to any part of the written text, or any deletion either. This was a good step taken, to ensure that the words were preserved completely and permanently in perpetuity.

312. When the king received messages about these events, he rejoiced greatly, because it seemed that the purpose which he shared had been safely accomplished. All of the version was read by him, and he marveled profoundly at the genius of the lawgiver. He said to Demetrius, "How is it that after such great works were (originally) completed, none of the historians or poets took it upon himself to refer to them?" 313. He said, "Because the legislation was holy and had come from God, and indeed, some of those who made the attempt were smitten by God, and refrained from their design." 314. Moreover, he said that he had heard Theopompus declare that, just when he was about to quote in a misleading way

some of the previously translated passages from the Law, he had a mental upset for more than thirty days; at its abatement, he besought God to make clear to him the cause of this occurrence. 315. It was revealed to him in a dream that it was due to his meddlesome desire to disclose the things of God to common man, and then—he said—he ceased and so recovered. 316. I have also received from Theodectus the tragic poet (the report) that when he was about to include in a play a passage from what is written in the Bible,[7] he was afflicted with cataract of the eyes. He suspected that this was why the affliction had befallen him, so he besought God for many days and recovered. 317. When the king had received, as I previously mentioned, Demetrius' account on these matters, he bowed and gave orders for great care to be taken of the books and for their hallowed preservation. 318. He invited the translators to visit him often after their return to Judea. It was, he said, only fair for their departure to take place, but when they returned he would, as was right, treat them as friends, and they would receive the most liberal hospitality at his hands. 319. He ordered preparations to be made for their departure, and treated the men magnificently, presenting to each one three robes of the finest materials, two talents of gold, a cup worth a talent, and complete furnishing for a dining room. 320. He also sent to Eleazar, along with their luggage, ten silver-footed couches, with all accessories to go with them, a cup worth thirty talents, ten robes, purple cloth, a magnificent crown, one hundred lengths of finest linen, vessels, bowls, and two golden goblets for a dedication. 321. He also wrote with an invitation that if any of the men desired to return to him, there would be no impediment, because he attached great importance to the company of men of culture, and invested his wealth liberally in such men, and not in useless expenditure.

Translated by R. J. H. Shutt, in *The Old Testament Pseudepigrapha*, edited by James H. Charlesworth, vol. 2 (London: Darton, Longman, and Todd, 1985), 12, 14–16, 24, 32–34.

➚ **Philo Judaeus** (ca. 20 BCE–50 CE), a Hellenistic Jewish philosopher from Alexandria (and thus sometimes referred to as Philo of Alexandria), bridged the gap between Judaism and Hellenism by allegorically interpreting the Jewish Scriptures in Greek philosophical, "Middle Platonic" terms. *On the Account of the World's*

---

7. This appears to be the first time the term "Bible" is used to refer to what is now called the "Old Testament."

Creation Given by Moses is Philo's rewriting of the creation story in Genesis. Our next selection, a brief passage in Philo's *Who Is the Heir?* is central to Philo's understanding of God's creative Word (Logos) as mediator between God and creation. In our last selection, *On the Posterity of Cain and His Exile,* Philo offers not only an interpretation of the Cain story but also insights into the problems of the biblical texts and into his allegorical methodology itself.

PHILO JUDAEUS

On the Account of the World's Creation Given by Moses, I.1–VII.28

I. While among other lawgivers some have nakedly and without embellishment drawn up a code of the things held to be right among their people, and others, dressing up their ideas in much irrelevant and cumbersome matter, have befogged the masses and hidden the truth under their fictions, Moses, disdaining either course, the one as devoid of the philosopher's painstaking effort to explore his subject thoroughly, the other as full of falsehood and imposture, introduced his Laws with an admirable and most impressive exordium. He refrained, on the one hand, from stating abruptly what should be practised or avoided, and on the other hand, in face of the necessity of preparing the minds of those who were to live under the Laws for their reception, he refrained from inventing myths himself or acquiescing in those composed by others. His exordium, as I have said, is one that excites our admiration in the highest degree. It consists of an account of the creation of the world, implying that the world is in harmony with the Law, and the Law with the world, and that the man who observes the Law is constituted thereby a loyal citizen of the world, regulating his doings by the purpose and will of Nature, in accordance with which the entire world itself also is administered.

Now it is true that no writer in verse or prose could possibly do justice to the beauty of the ideas embodied in this account of the creation of the kosmos. For they transcend our capacity of speech and of hearing, being too great and august to be adjusted to the tongue or ear of any mortal. Nevertheless they must not on this account be passed over in silence. Nay, for the sake of the God-beloved author we must be venturesome even beyond our power. We shall fetch nothing from our own store, but, with a great array of points before us, we shall mention only a few, such as we may believe to be within reach of the human mind when possessed by love and longing for wisdom. The minutest seal takes in

under the graver's hand the contours of colossal figures. So perchance shall the beauties of the world's creation recorded in the Laws, transcendent as they are and dazzling as they do by their bright gleams the souls of readers, be indicated by delineations minute and slight. But first we must draw attention to a matter which ought not to be passed over in silence.

II. There are some people who, having the world in admiration rather than the Maker of the world, pronounce it to be without beginning and everlasting, while with impious falsehood they postulate in God a vast inactivity; whereas we ought on the contrary to be astonished at His powers as Maker and Father, and not to assign to the world a disproportionate majesty. Moses, both because he had attained the very summit of philosophy, and because he had been divinely instructed in the greater and most essential part of Nature's lore, could not fail to recognize that the universal must consist of two parts, one part active Cause and the other passive object; and that the active Cause is the perfectly pure and unsullied Mind of the universe, transcending virtue, transcending knowledge, transcending the good itself and the beautiful itself; while the passive part is in itself incapable of life and motion, but, when set in motion and shaped and quickened by Mind, changes into the most perfect masterpiece, namely this world. Those who assert that this world is unoriginate unconsciously eliminate that which of all incentives to piety is the most beneficial and the most indispensable, namely providence. For it stands to reason that what has been brought into existence should be cared for by its Father and Maker. For, as we know, it is a father's aim in regard of his offspring and an artificer's in regard of his handiwork to preserve them, and by every means to fend off from them aught that may entail loss or harm. He keenly desires to provide for them in every way all that is beneficial and to their advantage: but between that which has never been brought into being and one who is not its Maker no such tie is formed. It is a worthless and baleful doctrine, setting up anarchy in the well-ordered realm of the world, leaving it without protector, arbitrator, or judge, without anyone whose office it is to administer and direct all its affairs. Not so Moses. That great master, holding the unoriginate to be of a different order from that which is visible, since everything that is an object of sensible perception is subject to becoming and to constant change, never abiding in the same state, assigned to that which is invisible and an object of intellectual apprehension the infinite and undefinable as united with it by closest tie; but on that which is an object of the senses he bestowed "genesis," "becoming," as its appropriate name. Seeing then that this world is both visible and perceived by the senses, it follows that it must also have had an origin. Whence it was entirely to the point that he put on record that origin, setting forth in its true grandeur the work of God.

III. He says that in six days the world was created, not that its Maker required a length of time for His work, for we must think of God as doing all things simultaneously, remembering that "all" includes with the commands which He issues the thought behind them. Six days are mentioned because for the things coming into existence there was need of order. Order involves number, and among numbers by the laws of nature the most suitable to productivity is 6, for if we start with 1 it is the first perfect number, being equal to the product of its factors (i.e. 1 × 2 × 3), as well as made up of the sum of them (i.e. 1 + 2 + 3), its half being 3, its third part 2, its sixth part 1. We may say that it is in its nature both male and female, and is a result of the distinctive power of either. For among things that are it is the odd that is male, and the even female. Now of odd numbers 3 is the starting-point, and of even numbers 2, and the product of these two is 6. For it was requisite that the world, being most perfect of all things that have come into existence, should be constituted in accordance with a perfect number, namely six; and, inasmuch as it was to have in itself beings that sprang from a coupling together, should receive the impress of a mixed number, namely the first in which odd and even were combined, one that should contain the essential principle both of the male that sows and of the female that receives the seed.

Now to each of the days He assigned some of the portions of the whole, not including, however, the first day, which He does not even call "first," lest it should be reckoned with the others, but naming it "one" He designates it by a name which precisely hits the mark, for He discerned in it and expressed by the title which He gives it the nature and appellation of the unit, or the "one."

IV. We must recount as many as we can of the elements embraced in it. To recount them all would be impossible. Its pre-eminent element is the intelligible world, as is shown in the treatise dealing with the "One." For God, being God, assumed that a beautiful copy would never be produced apart from a beautiful pattern, and that no object of perception would be faultless which was not made in the likeness of an original discerned only by the intellect. So when He willed to create this visible world He first fully formed the intelligible world, in order that He might have the use of a pattern

wholly God-like and incorporeal in producing the material world, as a later creation, the very image of an earlier, to embrace in itself objects of perception of as many kinds as the other contained objects of intelligence.

To speak of or conceive that world which consists of ideas as being in some place is illegitimate; how it consists (of them) we shall know if we carefully attend to some image supplied by the things of our world. When a city is being founded to satisfy the soaring ambition of some king or governor, who lays claim to despotic power and being magnificent in his ideas would fain add a fresh luster to his good fortune, there comes forward now and again some trained architect who, observing the favourable climate and convenient position of the site, first sketches in his own mind wellnigh all the parts of the city that is to be wrought out, temples, gymnasia, town-halls, marketplaces, harbours, docks, streets, walls to be built, dwelling-houses as well as public buildings to be set up. Thus after having received in his own soul, as it were in wax, the figures of these objects severally, he carries about the image of a city which is the creation of his mind. Then by his innate power of memory, he recalls the images of the various parts of this city, and imprints their types yet more distinctly in it: and like a good craftsman he begins to build the city of stones and timber, keeping his eye upon his pattern and making the visible and tangible objects correspond in each case to the incorporeal ideas.

Just such must be our thoughts about God. We must suppose that, when He was minded to found the one great city, He conceived beforehand the models of its parts, and that out of these He constituted and brought to completion a world discernible only by the mind, and then, with that for a pattern, the world which our senses can perceive.

V. As, then, the city which was fashioned beforehand within the mind of the architect held no place in the outer world, but had been engraved in the soul of the artificer as by a seal; even so the universe that consisted of ideas would have no other location than the Divine Reason, which was the Author of this ordered frame. For what other place could there be for His powers sufficient to receive and contain, I say not all but, any one of them whatever uncompounded and untempered? Now just such a power is that by which the universe was made, one that has as its source nothing less than true goodness. For should one conceive a wish to search for the cause, for the sake of which this whole was created, it seems to me that he would not be wrong in saying, what indeed one of the men of old did say, that the Father and

Maker of all is good; and because of this He grudged not a share in his own excellent nature to an existence which has of itself nothing fair and lovely, while it is capable of becoming all things. For of itself it was without order, without quality, without soul, (without likeness); it was full of inconsistency, ill-adjustment, disharmony: but it was capable of turning and undergoing a complete change to the best, the very contrary of all these, to order, quality, life, correspondence, identity, likeness, perfect adjustment, to harmony, to all that is characteristic of the more excellent model.[8]

VI. Now God, with no counselor to help Him (who was there beside Him?), determined that it was meet to confer rich and unrestricted benefits upon that nature which apart from Divine bounty could obtain of itself no good thing. But not in proportion to the greatest of His own bounties does He confer benefits—for these are without end or limit—but in proportion to the capacities of the recipients. For it is not the nature of creation to receive good treatment in like manner as it is the nature of God to bestow it, seeing that the powers of God are overwhelmingly vast, whereas creation, being too feeble to entertain their abundance, would have broken down under the effort to do so, had not God with appropriate adjustment dealt out to each his due portion. Should a man desire to use words in a more simple and direct way, he would say that the world discerned only by the intellect is nothing else than the Word of God when He was already engaged in the act of creation. For (to revert to our illustration) the city discernible by the intellect alone is nothing else than the reasoning faculty of the architect in the act of planning to found the city. It is Moses who lays down this, not I. Witness his express acknowledgement in the sequel, when setting on record the creation of man, that he was moulded after the image of God (Gen 1:27). Now if the part is an image of an image, it is manifest that the whole is so too, and if the whole creation, this entire world perceived by our senses (seeing that it is greater than any human image), is a copy of the Divine image, it is manifest that the archetypal seal also, which we aver to be the world descried by the mind, would be the very Word of God.

VII. Then he says that "in the beginning God made the heaven and the earth," taking "beginning" not, as some think, in a chronological sense, for time there was not before there was a world. Time began either simultaneously with the world or after it. For since time is a measured space determined by the world's movement, and since movement could not be prior to the object moving, but must of neces-

sity arise either after it or simultaneously with it, it follows of necessity that time also is either coeval with or later born than the world. To venture to affirm that it is elder born would be to do violence to philosophic sense. And since the word "beginning" is not here taken as the chronological beginning, it would seem likely that the numerical order is indicated, so that "in the beginning He made" is equivalent to "He made the heaven first": for it is indeed reasonable that it should come into existence first, being both best of created things and made from the purest of all that is, seeing that it was destined to be the most holy dwelling-place of manifest and visible gods. For, even if the Maker made all things simultaneously, order was none the less an attribute of all that came into existence in fair beauty, for beauty is absent where there is disorder. Now order is a series of things going on before and following after, in due sequence, a sequence which, though not seen in the finished productions, yet exists in the designs of the contrivers; for only so could these things be fashioned with perfect accuracy, and work without leaving their path or clashing with each other.

From *Philo*, translated by F. H. Colson and G. H. Whitaker, vol. 1, Loeb Classical Library (repr., Cambridge, MA: Harvard University Press, 1962), 7, 9, 11, 13, 15, 17, 19, 21, 23.

PHILO JUDAEUS

Who Is the Heir? 205–6

205. To His Word, His chief messenger, highest in age and honour, the Father of all has given the special prerogative, to stand on the border and separate the creature from the Creator. This same Word both pleads with the immortal as suppliant for afflicted mortality and acts as ambassador of the ruler to the subject. 206. He glories in this prerogative and proudly describes it in these words "'and I stood between the Lord and you' (Deut 5:5), that is, neither uncreated as God, nor created as you, but midway between the two extremes, a surety to both sides; to the parent, pledging the creature that it should never altogether rebel against the rein and choose disorder rather than order; to the child, warranting his hopes that the merciful God will never forget His own work. For I am the harbinger of peace to creation from that God whose will is to bring wars to an end, who is ever the guardian of peace."

From *Philo*, translated by F. H. Colson and G. H. Whitaker, vol. 4, Loeb Classical Library (repr., Cambridge, MA: Harvard University Press, 1958), 385, 387.

---

8. See Plato, *Timaeus*, 29e. (This note is by Gerhart and Udoh.)

PHILO JUDAEUS

On the Posterity of Cain and His Exile, I.1–III.11

I. "And Cain went out from the face of God, and dwelt in the land of Naid, over against Eden" (Gen 6:16). Let us here raise the question whether in the books in which Moses acts as God's interpreter we ought to take his statements figuratively, since the impression made by the words in their literal sense is greatly at variance with truth. For if the Existent Being has a face, and he that wishes to quit its sight can with perfect ease remove elsewhere, what ground have we for rejecting the impious doctrines of Epicurus, or the atheism of the Egyptians, or the mythical plots of play and poem of which the world is full? For a face is a piece of a living creature, and God is a whole not a part, so that we shall have to assign to Him the other parts of the body as well, neck, breasts, hands, feet, to say nothing of the belly and genital organs, together with the innumerable inner and outer organs. And if God has human forms and parts, He must needs also have human passions and experiences. For in the case of these organs, as in all other cases, Nature has not made idle superfluities, but aids to the weakness of those furnished with them. And she adjusts to them, according to their several needs, all that enables them to render their own special services and ministries. But the Existent Being is in need of nothing, and so, not needing the benefit that parts bestow, can have no parts at all.

II. And whence does Cain "go out"? From the palace of the Lord of all? But what dwelling apparent to the senses could God have, save this world, for the quitting of which no power or device avails? For all created things are enclosed and kept within itself by the circle of the sky. Indeed the particles of the deceased break up into their original elements and are again distributed to the various forces of the universe out of which they were constituted, and the loan which was lent to each man is repaid, after longer or shorter terms, to Nature his creditor, at such time as she may choose to recover what she herself had lent.

Again he that goes out from someone is in a different place from him whom he leaves behind. (If, then, Cain goes out from God), it follows that some portions of the universe are bereft of God. Yet God has left nothing empty or destitute of Himself, but has completely filled all things.

Well, if God has not a face, transcending as He does the peculiarities that mark all created things; if He is to be found not in some particular part only, seeing that He contains all

and is not Himself contained by anything; if it is impossible for some part of this world to remove from it as from a city, seeing that nothing has been left over outside it; the only thing left for us to do is to make up our minds that none of the propositions put forward is literally intended and to take the path of figurative interpretation so dear to philosophical souls. Our argument must start in this way. If it is a difficult thing to remove out of sight of a mortal monarch, must it not be a thousandfold more difficult to quit the vision of God and be gone, resolved henceforth to shun the sight of Him; in other words to become incapable of receiving a mental picture of Him through having lost the sight of the soul's eye? Men who have suffered this loss under compulsion, overwhelmed by the force of an inexorable power, deserve pity rather than hatred. But those who have of their own free choice turned away and departed from the Existent Being, transcending the utmost limit of wickedness itself—for no evil could be found equivalent to it—these must pay no ordinary penalties, but such as are specially devised and far beyond the ordinary. Now no effort of thought could hit upon a penalty greater and more unheard of than to go forth into banishment from the Ruler of the Universe.

III. Adam, then, is driven out by God; Cain goes out voluntarily. Moses is showing us each form of moral failure, one of free choice, the other not so. The involuntary act, not owing its existence to our deliberate judgement, is to obtain later on such healing as the case admits of, "for God shall raise up another seed in place of Abel whom Cain slew" (Gen 6:25). This seed is a male offspring, Seth or "Watering," raised up to the soul whose fall did not originate in itself. The voluntary act, inasmuch as it was committed with forethought and of set purpose, must incur woes for ever beyond healing. For even as right actions that spring from previous intention are of greater worth than those that are involuntary, so, too, among sins those which are involuntary are less weighty than those which are voluntary.

From *Philo*, translated by F. H. Colson and G. H. Whitaker, vol. 2, Loeb Classical Library (repr., Cambridge, MA: Harvard University Press, 1958), 329, 331, 333.

☙ The **Mishnah** is a compilation of Jewish (especially Pharisaic) oral traditions, known as the Oral Torah, that had been passed on for about two hundred years and served as a guide in interpreting the Written Torah (Hebrew Bible). The Mishnah was compiled by Rabbi Judah the Patriarch around the end of the second century

CE. After the destruction of Jerusalem in 70 CE, the Jews were forced to reformulate the observance and central meanings of their primary religious ceremonies, including the Passover meal and the Day of Atonement. The rabbinic provisions for these festivals are found in *Pesachim* (Feast of Passover) and *Yoma* (Day of Atonement), respectively. In *Aboth,* the rabbis established a line of succession of "fathers" (*aboth*), similar to the early Christian notion of apostolic succession, as a way of imparting authority to interpretations.

Pesachim, 10.1–9: The Passover Meal

10.1. On the eve of Passover, from about the time of the Evening Offering,[9] a man must eat naught until nightfall. Even the poorest in Israel must not eat unless he sits down to table, and they must not give them less than four cups of wine to drink, even if it is from the [Paupers'] Dish.

10.2. After they have mixed him his first cup, the School of Shammai say: He says the Benediction first over the day and then the Benediction over the wine. And the School of Hillel say: He says the Benediction first over the wine and then the Benediction over the day.

10.3. When [food] is brought before him he eats it seasoned with lettuce, until he is come to the breaking of bread; they bring before him unleavened bread and lettuce and the *haroseth,*[10] although *haroseth* is not a religious obligation. R. Eliezer b. R. Zadok says: It is a religious obligation. And in the Holy City they used to bring before him the body of the Passover-offering.

10.4. They then mix him the second cup. And here the son asks his father (and if the son has not enough understanding his father instructs him [how to ask]), "Why is this night different from other nights? For on other nights we eat seasoned food once, but this night twice; on other nights we eat leavened or unleavened bread, but this night all is unleavened; on other nights we eat flesh roast, stewed, or cooked, but this night all is roast." And according to the understanding of the son his father instructs him. He begins with the disgrace and ends with the glory; and he expounds from *A wandering Aramean was my father . . .* until he finishes the whole section.[11]

10.5. Rabban Gamaliel used to say: Whosoever has not said [the verses concerning] these three things at Passover has not fulfilled his obligation. And these are they: Passover,[12] unleavened bread,[13] and bitter herbs:[14] "Passover"—because God passed over the houses of our fathers in Egypt; "unleavened bread"—because our fathers were redeemed from Egypt; "bitter herbs"—because the Egyptians embittered the lives of our fathers in Egypt. In every generation a man must so regard himself as if he came forth himself out of Egypt, for it is written, *And thou shalt tell thy son in that day saying, It is because of that which the Lord did for me when I came forth out of Egypt.*[15] Therefore are we bound to give thanks, to praise, to glorify, to honour, to exalt, to extol, and to bless him who wrought all these wonders for our fathers and for us. He brought us out from bondage to freedom, from sorrow to gladness, and from mourning to a Festival-day, and from darkness to great light, and from servitude to redemption; so let us say before him the *Hallelujah.*

10.6. How far do they recite [the *Hallel*]? The School of Shammai say: To *A joyful mother of children.*[16] And the School of Hillel say: To *A flintstone into a springing well.*[17] And this is concluded with the *Ge'ullah.*[18] R. Tarfon says: "He that redeemed us and redeemed our fathers from Egypt and brought us to this night to eat therein unleavened bread and bitter herbs." But there is no concluding Benediction. R. Akiba adds: "Therefore, O Lord our God and the God of our fathers, bring us in peace to the other set feasts and festivals which are coming to meet us, while we rejoice in the building-up of thy city and are joyful in thy worship; and may we eat there of the sacrifices and of the Passover-offerings whose blood has reached with acceptance the wall of thy Altar, and let us praise thee for our redemption and for the ransoming of our soul. Blessed art thou, O Lord, who hast redeemed Israel!"

10.7. After they have mixed for him the third cup he says the Benediction over his meal. [Over] a fourth [cup] he completes the *Hallel*[19] and says after it the Benediction over song. If he is minded to drink [more] between these cups he may drink; only between the third and the fourth cups he may not drink.

10.8. After the Passover meal they should not disperse to join in revelry.[20] If some fell asleep [during the meal] they

---

9. See Num 28:8. (The notes for this selection are by Gerhart and Udoh.)

10. A dish made from fruit, nuts, and spices finely ground together and mixed with vinegar, used as a sauce to mitigate the bitterness of the bitter herbs.

11. Deut 26:5b–19.

12. Ex 12:27. 15. Ex 13:8.

13. Ex 12:39. 16. End of Ps 113.

14. Ex 1:14. 17. End of Ps 114.

18. The "Blessing of Redemption." Since the Mishnah does not say what the prayer should be, both Rabbi Tarfon and Rabbi Akiba propose their versions.

19. Pss 115–18.

20. The passage is traditionally interpreted to mean that the participant may not at the end of the Passover meal say, "Let us have the dessert now."

may eat [again]; but if all fell asleep they may not eat [again]. R. Jose says: If they but dozed they may eat [again]; but if they fell into deep sleep they may not eat [again].

10.9. After midnight the Passover-offering renders the hands unclean. The Refuse[21] and Remnant[22] make the hands unclean. If a man has said the Benediction over the Passover-offering it renders needless a Benediction over [any other] animal-offering [that he eats]; but if he said the Benediction over [any other] animal-offering it does not render needless the Benediction over the Passover-offering. So R. Ishmael. R. Akiba says: Neither of them renders the other needless.

From *The Mishnah,* translated by Herbert Danby (Oxford: Oxford University Press, 1987), 150–51. [Ellipsis in original.]

Yoma, 3.7–9; 4.1–5.7; 6.2–7.4; 8.1–9:
The Day of Atonement

3.7. In the morning he was clothed in Pelusium linen worth twelve *minas,* and in the afternoon in Indian linen worth eight hundred *zuz.* So R. Meir. But the Sages say: In the morning he wore [vestments] worth eighteen *minas* and in the afternoon [vestments] worth twelve *minas,* thirty *minas* in all. These were at the charges of the congregation, and if he was minded to spend more he could do so at his own charges.

3.8. He came to his bullock[23] and his bullock was standing between the Porch and the Altar, its head to the south and its face to the west;[24] and he set both his hands upon it and made confession. And thus used he to say: "O God, I have committed iniquity, transgressed, and sinned before thee, I and my house. O God, forgive the iniquities and transgressions and sins which I have committed and transgressed and sinned before thee, I and my house, as it is written in the Law of thy servant Moses, *For on this day shall atonement be made for you to cleanse you; from all your sins shall ye be clean before the Lord."*[25] And they answered after him, "Blessed be the name of the glory of his kingdom for ever and ever!"

3.9. He came to the east, to the north of the Altar, with the Prefect[26] on his right and the chief of the father's house on his left. And two he-goats[27] were there and there also was a casket in which were two lots. They were of box-wood, but Ben Gamla made some of gold, and his memory was kept in honour.

4.1. He shook the casket and took up the two lots. On one was written "For the Lord," and on the other was written "For Azazel." The Prefect was on his right and the chief of the father's house on his left. If the lot bearing the Name came up in his right hand the Prefect would say to him, "My

lord High Priest, raise thy right hand"; and if it came up in his left hand the chief of the father's house would say to him, "My lord High Priest, raise thy left hand." He put them on the two he-goats and said, "A Sin-offering to the Lord!"[28] R. Ishmael says: He needed not to say "A Sin-offering," but only "To the Lord." And they answered after him, "Blessed be the name of the glory of his kingdom for ever and ever!"

4.2. He bound a thread of crimson wool on the head of the scapegoat and he turned it towards the way by which it was to be sent out; and on the he-goat that was to be slaughtered [he bound a thread] about its throat. He came to his bullock the second time, laid his two hands upon it, and made confession. And thus used he to say: "O God, I have committed iniquity and transgressed and sinned before thee, I and my house and the children of Aaron, thy holy people. O God, forgive, I pray, the iniquities and transgressions and sins which I have committed and transgressed and sinned before thee, I and my house and the children of Aaron, thy holy people, as it is written in the law of thy servant Moses, *For on this day shall atonement be made for you to cleanse you: from all your sins shall ye be clean before the Lord."*[29] And they answered after him, "Blessed be the name of the glory of his kingdom for ever and ever!"

4.3. He slaughtered [the bullock] and received its blood in a bason; and he gave it to the one that should stir it up on the fourth terrace of the Sanctuary so that it should not congeal. He took the fire-pan and went up to the top of the Altar; and he cleared the coals to this side and to that, and scooped out glowing cinders from below, and came down and set the fire-pan on the fourth terrace in the Temple Court.

4.4. Other days he used to scoop out [the cinders] with a [fire-pan] of silver and empty it into one of gold, but this day he scoops them out with the one of gold in which also he brings in [the cinders]. Other days he used to scoop them out with one holding four *kabs* and empty it into one holding three *kabs;* but this day he scoops them out with one hold-

---

21. Lev 7:18; 19:5–7.

22. Lev 7:15.

23. Lev 16:3, 6.

24. That is, facing the sanctuary.

25. Lev 16:30. Instead of the customary circumlocution, "Lord" (Adonai), for the last word, the high priest pronounces God's name as it is written: Yahweh.

26. Chief officer of the Temple, next in rank to the high priest.

27. Lev 16:5, 7.

28. Again the high priest pronounces the divine name.

29. Lev 16:30.

ing three *kabs* in which also he brings in [the cinders]. R. Jose says: Other days he used to scoop them out with one holding a *seah* and empty it into one holding three *kabs;* but this day he scoops them out with one holding three *kabs* in which also he brings in [the cinders]. Other days it was a heavy one, but this day a light one. Other days its handle was short, but this day long. Other days it was of yellow gold, but this day of red gold. So R. Menahem. Other days he used to offer half a *mina* [of incense] in the morning and half a *mina* in the afternoon; but this day he adds also his two hands full. Other days it was of fine quality, but this day it is the finest of the fine.

4.5. Other days the priests went up on the east side of the [Altar-]Ramp and came down on the west side, but this day the High Priest goes up in the middle and comes down in the middle. R. Judah says: The High Priest always goes up in the middle and comes down in the middle. Other days the High Priest sanctified his hands and his feet [in water] from the laver; but this day from a golden jug. R. Judah says: The High Priest always sanctified his hands and his feet from a golden jug.

4.6. Other days there were four wood-stacks there,[30] but this day five. So R. Meir. R. Jose says: Other days three, but this day four. R. Judah says: Other days two, but this day three.

5.1. They brought out to him the ladle and the fire-pan and he took his two hands full [of incense] and put it in the ladle, which was large according to his largeness [of hand], or small according to his smallness [of hand]; and such [alone] was the prescribed measure of the ladle. He took the fire-pan in his right hand and the ladle in his left. He went through the Sanctuary until he came to the space between the two curtains separating the Sanctuary from the Holy of Holies. And there was a cubit's space between them. R. Jose says: Only one curtain was there, for it is written, *And the veil shall divide for you between the holy place and the most holy.*[31] The outer curtain was looped up on the south side and the inner one on the north side. He went along between them until he reached the north side; when he reached the north he turned round to the south and went on with the curtain on his left hand until he reached the Ark. When he reached the Ark[32] he put the fire-pan between the two bars.[33] He heaped up the incense on the coals and the whole place became filled with smoke. He came out by the way he went in, and in the outer space he prayed a short prayer. But he did not prolong his prayer lest he put Israel in terror.

5.2. After the Ark was taken away[34] a stone remained there from the time of the early Prophets, and it was called "Sheti-

yah."[35] It was higher than the ground by three fingerbreadths. On this he used to put [the fire-pan].

5.3. He took the blood from him that was stirring it and entered [again] into the place where he had entered and stood [again] on the place whereon he had stood, and sprinkled the [blood] once upwards and seven times downwards, not as though he had intended to sprinkle upwards or downwards but as though he were wielding a whip. And thus used he to count: One, one and one, one and two, one and three, one and four, one and five, one and six, one and seven. He came out and put it on the golden stand in the Sanctuary.

5.4. They brought him the he-goat. He slaughtered it and received its blood in a bason. He then entered [again] into the place wherein he had entered and stood [again] on the place whereon he had stood, and sprinkled [the blood] once upwards and seven times downwards, not as though he had intended to sprinkle upwards or downwards, but as though he were wielding a whip. And thus used he to count: One, one and one, one and two, one and three, one and four, one and five, one and six, one and seven. He came out and put it on the second stand in the Sanctuary. R. Judah says: Only one stand was there. He took the blood of the bullock and set down [in its place] the blood of the he-goat, and [then] sprinkled [the blood of the bullock] on the curtain outside, opposite the Ark, once upwards and seven times downwards, not as though he had intended to sprinkle upwards or downwards, but as though he were wielding a whip. And thus used he to count: One, one and one, one and two, one and three, one and four, one and five, one and six, one and seven. Then he took the blood of the he-goat and set down [in its place] the blood of the bullock, and [then] sprinkled [the blood of the he-goat] on the curtain outside, opposite the Ark, once upwards and seven times downwards, not as though he had intended to sprinkle upwards or downwards, but as though he were wielding a whip; and thus used he to count: One, one and one, one and two, one and three, one and four, one and five, one and six, one and seven. He emptied out the blood of the bullock into the blood of the he-goat and poured [the contents of] the full [vessel] into the empty one.

---

30. That is, on the altar.

31. Ex 26:33.

32. Or, in the Second (Herod's) Temple, where the Ark used to be.

33. Ex 25:13–22.

34. When the First (Solomon's) Temple was destroyed.

35. The "Foundation Stone."

5.5. Then he went to the Altar which is before the Lord[36]—that is the Golden Altar.[37] When he begins to sprinkle[38] downwards, where does he begin? From the north-east horn, then the north-west, then the south-west, then the north-east. Where he begins the sprinkling of the outer Altar, there he completes the sprinkling of the inner Altar. R. Eliezer says: He used to stand in the one place and sprinkle, and he sprinkled every horn from below upwards, excepting the horn before which he was standing, which he used to sprinkle from above downwards.

5.6. He then sprinkled the cleansed surface[39] of the Altar seven times and poured out the residue of the blood at the western base of the outer Altar; and [the residue] of [the blood sprinkled on] the outer Altar he poured out at the southern base. Both mingled together in the channel and flowed away into the brook Kidron. And it was sold to gardeners as manure, and the law of Sacrilege[40] applied to it.

5.7. Every act [of the High Priest] on the Day of Atonement here enumerated according to the prescribed order—if one act was done [out of order] before another act, it is as if it was not done at all. If he [sprinkled] the blood of the he-goat before the blood of the bullock, he must start anew and sprinkle the blood of the he-goat after the blood of the bullock. And if the blood was poured away before [the High Priest] had finished the sprinklings within [the Holy of Holies], he must bring other blood and start anew and sprinkle afresh within [the Holy of Holies]. So, too, in what concerns the Sanctuary and the Golden Altar, since they are each a separate act of atonement. R. Eleazar and R. Simeon say: At the place where he broke off there he begins again.

6.2. He then came to the scapegoat and laid his two hands upon it and made confession. And thus used he to say: "O God, thy people, the House of Israel, have committed iniquity, transgressed, and sinned before thee. O God, forgive, I pray, the iniquities and transgressions and sins which thy people, the House of Israel, have committed and transgressed and sinned before thee; as it is written in the law of thy servant Moses, *For on this day shall atonement be made for you to cleanse you: from all your sins shall ye be clean before the Lord.*"[41] And when the priests and the people which stood in the Temple Court heard the Expressed Name come forth from the mouth of the High Priest, they used to kneel and bow themselves and fall down on their faces and say, "Blessed be the name of the glory of his kingdom for ever and ever!"

6.3. They delivered it to him that should lead it away. All were eligible to lead it away, but the priests had established the custom not to suffer an Israelite[42] to lead it away. R. Jose

said: It once happened that Arsela of Sepphoris led it away and he was an Israelite.

6.4. And they made a causeway for it because of the Babylonians who used to pull its hair, crying to it, "Bear [our sins] and be gone! Bear [our sins] and be gone!" Certain of the eminent folk of Jerusalem used to go with him to the first booth. There were ten booths from Jerusalem to the ravine [which was at a distance of] ninety *ris* (which measure seven and a half to the mile).

6.5. At every booth they used to say to him, "Here is food, here is water," and they went with him from that booth to the next booth, but not from the last booth; for none used to go with him to the ravine; but they stood at a distance and beheld what he did.

6.6. What did he do? He divided the thread of crimson wool and tied one half to the rock and the other half between its horns, and he pushed it from behind; and it went rolling down, and before it had reached half the way down the hill it was broken in pieces. He returned and sat down beneath the last booth until nightfall. And from what time does it render his garments unclean? After he has gone outside the wall of Jerusalem. R. Simeon says: From the moment that he pushes it into the ravine.

6.7. [The High Priest] came to the bullock and the he-goat which were to be burnt.[43] He cut them open and took away the sacrificial portions[44] and put them on a dish and burnt them upon the Altar. He twisted [the limbs of the beasts] around carrying-poles, and brought them out to the place of burning. And from what time do they render garments unclean?[45] After they have gone outside the wall of the Temple Court. R. Simeon says: When the fire has caught a hold on the greater part of them.

6.8. They said to the High Priest, "The he-goat has reached the wilderness." And whence did they know that the he-goat had reached the wilderness? They used to set up sentinel-posts and [from these] towels were waved and [so] they would know that the he-goat had reached the wilderness. R.

---

36. Lev 16:18.
37. Ex 30:1–10.
38. "Cleanse from sin" (Ex 29:36).
39. Lev 16:19.
40. Lev 5:15.
41. Lev 16:30.
42. That is, one who is not a priest.
43. Lev 16:27.
44. Lev 4:8–10.
45. Lev 16:28.

Judah said: And had they not a most manifest sign? From Jerusalem to Beth Haroro was three miles; they could walk a mile, return a mile, wait time enough to go a mile, and then they would know that the he-goat had reached the wilderness. R. Ishmael says: Had they not another sign also?—a thread of crimson wool was tied to the door of the Sanctuary and when the he-goat reached the wilderness the thread turned white; for it is written, *Though your sins be as scarlet they shall be as white as snow.*[46]

7.1. Then the High Priest came to read. If he was minded to read in the linen garments he could do so; otherwise he would read in his own white vestment. The minister of the synagogue used to take a scroll of the Law and give it to the chief of the synagogue, and the chief of the synagogue gave it to the Prefect, and the Prefect gave it to the High Priest, and the High Priest received it standing and read it standing. And he read *After the death . . .*[47] and *Howbeit on the tenth day . . .*[48] Then he used to roll up the scroll of the Law and put it in his bosom and say, "More is written here than I have read out before you." *And on the tenth . . .*[49] which is in the Book of Numbers, he recited by heart. Thereupon he pronounced eight Benedictions: for the Law, for the Temple-Service, for the Thanksgiving, for the Forgiveness of Sin, and for the Temple separately, and for the Israelites separately, and for the priests separately; and for the rest a [general] prayer.

7.2. He that can see the High Priest when he reads cannot see the bullock and the he-goat that are being burnt; and he that can see the bullock and the he-goat that are being burnt cannot see the High Priest when he reads: not that it was not permitted, but because the distance apart was great and both acts were performed at the same time.

7.3. If he read in the linen vestments, he [afterward] sanctified his hands and his feet, stripped off his clothes, went down and immersed himself, and came up and dried himself. They brought to him the vestments of gold, and he put them on and sanctified his hands and his feet and went out and offered his ram[50] and the ram of the people and the seven unblemished lambs of a year old.[51] So R. Eliezer. R. Akiba says: They offered these with the morning Daily Whole-offering, and the bullock for the Whole-offering and the he-goat that is offered outside[52] were offered with the afternoon Daily Whole-offering.

7.4. He then sanctified his hands and his feet, stripped off his clothes, went down and immersed himself, and came up and dried himself. They brought to him the white vestments, and he put them on and sanctified his hands and his feet. He then went in to bring out the ladle and the fire-pan. He sanc-

tified his hands and his feet, stripped off his clothes, went down and immersed himself, came up and dried himself; and they brought to him the golden vestments; and he put them on and sanctified his hands and his feet, and went in to burn the afternoon incense[53] and trim the lamps.[54] He sanctified his hands and his feet and stripped off his clothes. Then they brought to him his own raiment and he put it on. And they went with him to his house. And he made a feast for his friends for that he was come forth safely from the Sanctuary.

8.1. On the Day of Atonement, eating, drinking, washing, anointing, putting on sandals, and marital intercourse are forbidden. A king or a bride may wash their faces and a woman after childbirth may put on sandals. So R. Eliezer. But the Sages forbid it.

8.2. If a man ate a large date's bulk, the like of it together with its stone, or if he drank a mouthful, he is culpable.[55] Any foods may be included together to make up the date's bulk, and any liquids may be included together to make up the mouthful. What a man eats and what he drinks may not be included together.

8.3. If he both ate and drank in a single act of forgetfulness[56] he is liable to one Sin-offering only. If he ate and also performed an act of work, he is liable to two Sin-offerings. If he ate foods which are not fit for eating or drank liquids which are not fit for drinking, or even if he drank brine or fish-brine, he is not culpable.

8.4. They do not cause children to fast on the Day of Atonement, but they should exercise them therein one year or two years before [they are of age], that they may become versed in the commandments.

8.5. If a pregnant woman smelled [food and craved after it], they may give her food until she recovers herself. He that is sick may be given food at the word of skilled persons; and if no skilled persons are there, he may be given food at his own wish, until he says, "Enough!"

8.6. If ravenous hunger seized a man he may be given even unclean things to eat until his eyes are enlightened. If a mad dog bit him he may not be given the lobe of its liver

---

46. Isa 1:18.

47. Lev 16:1–34.

48. Lev 23:26–32.

49. Num 29:7–11.

54. Ex 27:20–21.

50. Lev 16:3.

51. Num 29:8.

52. Num 29:11.

53. Ex 30:8.

55. Sin offering is made by one who mistakenly transgresses the law (Lev 4:27–35, see 8.3 below); one who transgresses purposefully is punished by "Extirpation" (Lev 23:29).

56. He forgot that it was the Day of Atonement.

to eat; but R. Mattithiah b. Heresh permits it. Moreover R. Mattithiah b. Heresh said: If a man has a pain in his throat they may drop medicine into his mouth on the Sabbath, since there is doubt whether life is in danger, and whenever there is doubt whether life is in danger this overrides the Sabbath.

8.7. If a building fell down upon a man and there is doubt whether he is there or not, or whether he is alive or dead, or whether he is a gentile or an Israelite, they may clear away the ruin from above him. If they find him alive they may clear it away [still more] from above him; but if dead, they leave him.

8.8. The Sin-offering[57] and the unconditional Guilt-offering[58] effect atonement; death and the Day of Atonement effect atonement if there is repentance. Repentance effects atonement for lesser transgressions against both positive and negative commands in the Law; while for graver transgressions it suspends punishment until the Day of Atonement comes and effects atonement.

8.9. If a man said, "I will sin and repent, and sin again and repent," he will be given no chance to repent. [If he said,] "I will sin and the Day of Atonement will effect atonement," then the Day of Atonement effects no atonement. For transgressions that are between man and God the Day of Atonement effects atonement, but for transgressions that are between a man and his fellow the Day of Atonement effects atonement only if he has appeased his fellow. This did R. Eleazar b. Azariah expound: *From all your sins shall ye be clean before the Lord*[59]—for transgressions that are between man and God the Day of Atonement effects atonement; but for transgressions that are between a man and his fellow the Day of Atonement effects atonement only if he has appeased his fellow. R. Akiba said: Blessed are ye, O Israel. Before whom are ye made clean and who makes you clean? Your Father in heaven; as it is written, *And I will sprinkle clean water upon you and ye shall be clean.*[60] And again it says, *O Lord the hope (mikweh) of Israel;*[61]—as the *Mikweh* cleanses the unclean so does the Holy One, blessed be he, cleanse Israel.

From *The Mishnah*, translated by Herbert Danby (Oxford: Oxford University Press, 1987), 165–72. [Brackets in original.]

Aboth, 1.1–2.16; 3.6, 10–11, 14–18; 4.1–3: The Fathers

1.1. Moses received the Law from Sinai and committed it to Joshua, and Joshua to the elders,[62] and the elders to the Prophets;[63] and the Prophets committed it to the men of the Great Synagogue. They said three things: Be deliberate in judgement, raise up many disciples, and make a fence around the Law.

1.2. Simeon the Just was of the remnants of the Great Synagogue. He used to say: By three things is the world sustained: by the Law, by the [Temple-]service, and by deeds of loving-kindness.

1.3. Antigonus of Soko received [the Law] from Simeon the Just. He used to say: Be not like slaves that minister to the master for the sake of receiving a bounty, but be like slaves that minister to the master not for the sake of receiving a bounty; and let the fear of Heaven be upon you.

1.4. Jose b. Joezer of Zeredah and Jose b. Johanan of Jerusalem received [the Law] from them. Jose b. Joezer of Zeredah said: Let thy house be a meeting-house for the Sages and sit amid the dust of their feet and drink in their words with thirst.

1.5. Jose b. Johanan of Jerusalem said: Let thy house be opened wide and let the needy be members of thy household; and talk not much with womankind. They said this of a man's own wife: how much more of his fellow's wife! Hence the Sages have said: He that talks much with womankind brings evil upon himself and neglects the study of the Law and at the last will inherit Gehenna.

1.6. Joshua b. Perahyah and Nittai the Arbelite received [the Law] from them. Joshua b. Perahyah said: Provide thyself with a teacher and get thee a fellow[-disciple]; and when thou judgest any man incline the balance in his favour.

1.7. Nittai the Arbelite said: Keep thee far from an evil neighbour and consort not with the wicked and lose not belief in retribution.

1.8. Judah b. Tabbai and Simeon b. Shetah received [the Law] from them. Judah b. Tabbai said: Make not thyself like them that would influence the judges; and when the suitors stand before thee let them be in thine eyes as wicked men, and when they have departed from before thee let them be in thine eyes as innocent, so soon as they have accepted the judgement.

1.9. Simeon b. Shetah said: Examine the witnesses diligently and be cautious in thy words lest from them they learn to swear falsely.

---

57. Lev 4:27–35.
58. See Lev 5:15; 6:6. Lev 5:17ff.
59. Lev 16:30.
60. Ezek 36:25.
61. Jer 17:13.
62. See Josh 24:31.
63. See Jer 7:25.

1.10. Shemaiah and Abtalion received [the Law] from them. Shemaiah said: Love labour and hate mastery and seek not acquaintance with the ruling power.

1.11. Abtalion said: Ye Sages, give heed to your words lest ye incur the penalty of exile and ye be exiled to a place of evil waters, and the disciples that come after you drink [of them] and die, and the name of Heaven be profaned.

1.12. Hillel and Shammai received [the Law] from them. Hillel said: Be of the disciples of Aaron, loving peace and pursuing peace, loving mankind and bringing them nigh to the Law.

1.13. He used to say: A name made great is a name destroyed, and he that increases not decreases, and he that learns not is worthy of death, and he that makes worldly use of the crown shall perish.

1.14. He used to say: If I am not for myself who is for me? and being for mine own self what am I? and if not now, when?

1.15. Shammai said: Make thy [study of the] Law a fixed habit; say little and do much, and receive all men with a cheerful countenance.

1.16. Rabban Gamaliel said: Provide thyself with a teacher and remove thyself from doubt, and tithe not overmuch by guesswork.

1.17. Simeon his son said: All my days have I grown up among the Sages and I have found naught better for a man than silence; and not the expounding [of the Law] is the chief thing but the doing [of it]; and he that multiplies words occasions sin.

1.18. Rabban Simeon b. Gamaliel said: By three things is the world sustained: by truth, by judgement, and by peace, as it is written, *Execute the judgement of truth and peace.*[64]

2.1. Rabbi[65] said: Which is the straight way that a man should choose? That which is an honour to him and gets him honour from men. And be heedful of a light precept as of a weighty one, for thou knowest not the recompense of reward of each precept; and reckon the loss through [the fulfilling of] a precept against its reward, and the reward [that comes] from transgression against its loss. Consider three things and thou wilt not fall into the hands of transgression: know what is above thee—a seeing eye and a hearing ear and all thy deeds written in a book.

2.2. Rabban Gamaliel the son of R. Judah the Patriarch said: Excellent is study of the Law together with worldly occupation, for toil in them both puts sin out of mind. But all study of the Law without [worldly] labour comes to naught

at the last and brings sin in its train. And let all them that labour with the congregation labour with them for the sake of Heaven, for the merit of their fathers supports them and their righteousness endures for ever. And as for you, [will God say,] I count you worthy of great reward as though ye [yourselves] had wrought.

2.3. Be heedful of the ruling power for they bring no man nigh to them save for their own need: they seem to be friends such time as it is to their gain, but they stand not with a man in his time of stress.

2.4. He used to say: Do his will as if it was thy will that he may do thy will as if it was his will. Make thy will of none effect before his will that he may make the will of others of none effect before thy will.

2.5. Hillel said: Keep not aloof from the congregation and trust not in thyself until the day of thy death, and judge not thy fellow until thou art come to his place, and say not of a thing which cannot be understood that it will be understood in the end; and say not, When I have leisure I will study: perchance thou wilt never have leisure.

2.6. He used to say: A brutish man dreads not sin, and an ignorant man cannot be saintly, and the shamefast man cannot learn, and the impatient man cannot teach, and he that engages overmuch in trade cannot become wise; and where there are no men strive to be a man.

2.7. Moreover he saw a skull floating on the face of the water and he said unto it, Because thou drownedst they drowned thee and at the last they that drowned thee shall be drowned. He used to say: The more flesh the more worms; the more possessions the more care; the more women the more witchcrafts; the more bondwomen the more lewdness; the more bondmen the more thieving; the more study of the Law the more life; the more schooling the more wisdom; the more counsel the more understanding; the more righteousness the more peace. If a man has gained a good name he has gained [somewhat] for himself; if he has gained for himself words of the Law he has gained for himself life in the world to come.

2.8. Rabban Johanan b. Zakkai received [the Law] from Hillel and from Shammai. He used to say: If thou hast wrought much in the Law claim not merit for thyself, for to this end wast thou created. Five disciples had Rabban Johanan b. Zak-

---

64. Zech 8:16.

65. Rabbi Judah the Patriarch, who compiled the Mishnah.

kai, and these are they: R. Eliezer b. Hyrcanus, and R. Joshua b. Hananiah, and R. Jose the Priest, and R. Simeon b. Nathaniel, and R. Eleazar b. Arak. Thus used he to recount their praise: Eliezer b. Hyrcanus is a plastered cistern which loses not a drop; Joshua b. Hananiah—happy is she that bare him; Jose the Priest is a saintly man; Simeon b. Nathaniel is fearful of sin; Eleazar b. Arak is an ever-flowing spring. He used to say: If all the Sages of Israel were in the one scale of the balance and Eliezer b. Hyrcanus in the other, he would outweigh them all. Abba Saul said in his name: If all the Sages of Israel were in the one scale of the balance and with them Eliezer b. Hyrcanus, and Eleazar b. Arak was in the other, he would outweigh them all.

2.9. He said to them: Go forth and see which is the good way to which a man should cleave. R. Eliezer said, A good eye. R. Joshua said, A good companion. R. Jose said, A good neighbour. R. Simeon said, One that sees what will be. R. Eleazar said, A good heart. He said to them: I approve the words of Eleazar b. Arak more than your words, for in his words are your words included. He said to them: Go forth and see which is the evil way which a man should shun. R. Eliezer said, An evil eye. R. Joshua said, An evil companion. R. Jose said, An evil neighbour. R. Simeon said, He that borrows and does not repay. He that borrows from man is as one that borrows from God, for it is written, *The wicked borroweth and payeth not again but the righteous dealeth graciously and giveth.*[66] R. Eleazar said, An evil heart. He said to them: I approve the words of Eleazar b. Arak more than your words for in his words are your words included.

2.10. They [each] said three things. R. Eliezer said: Let the honour of thy fellow be dear to thee as thine own, and be not easily provoked, and repent one day before thy death; and warm thyself before the fire of the Sages, but be heedful of their glowing coals lest thou be burned, for their bite is the bite of a jackal and their sting the sting of a scorpion and their hiss the hiss of a serpent, and all their words are like coals of fire.

2.11. R. Joshua said: The evil eye and the evil nature and hatred of mankind put a man out of the world.

2.12. R. Jose said: Let the property of thy fellow be dear to thee as thine own; and fit thyself for the study of the Law, for [the knowledge of] it is not thine by inheritance; and let all thy deeds be done for the sake of Heaven.

2.13. R. Simeon said: Be heedful in the reciting of the *Shemaʿ* and in the *Tefillah;* and when thou prayest make not thy prayer a fixed form, but [a plea for] mercies and supplications before God, for it is written, *For he is gracious and full of*

compassion, slow to anger, and plenteous in mercy, and repenteth him of the evil;[67] *and be not wicked in thine own sight.*

2.14. R. Eleazar said: Be alert to study the Law and know how to make answer to an unbeliever;[68] and know before whom thou toilest and who is thy taskmaster who shall pay thee the reward of thy labour.

2.15. R. Tarfon said: The day is short and the task is great and the labourers are idle and the wage is abundant and the master of the house is urgent.

2.16. He used to say: It is not thy part to finish the task, yet thou art not free to desist from it. If thou hast studied much in the Law much reward will be given thee, and faithful is thy taskmaster who shall pay thee the reward of thy labour. And know that the recompense of the reward of the righteous is for the time to come.

3.6. R. Halafta b. Dosa of Kefar Hanania said: If ten men sit together and occupy themselves in the Law, the Divine Presence rests among them, for it is written, *God standeth in the congregation of God.*[69] And whence [do we learn this] even of five? Because it is written, *And hath founded his group upon the earth.*[70] And whence even of three? Because it is written, *He judgeth among the judges.*[71] And whence even of two? Because it is written, *Then they that feared the Lord spake one with another: and the Lord hearkened, and heard.*[72] And whence even of one? Because it is written, *In every place where I record my name I will come unto thee and I will bless thee.*[73]

3.10. R. Hanina b. Dosa said: He whose fear of sin comes before his wisdom, his wisdom endures; but he whose wisdom comes before his fear of sin, his wisdom does not endure. He used to say: He whose works exceed his wisdom, his wisdom endures; but he whose wisdom exceeds his works, his wisdom does not endure.

3.11. He used to say: He in whom the spirit of mankind finds pleasure, in him the spirit of God finds pleasure; but he in whom the spirit of mankind finds no pleasure, in him the spirit of God finds no pleasure. R. Dosa b. Harkinas said: Morning sleep and midday wine and children's talk and sitting in the meeting-houses of the ignorant people put a man out of the world.

3.14. R. Akiba said: Jesting and levity accustom a man to lewdness. The tradition is a fence around the Law; Tithes are

---

66. Ps 37:21.
67. Joel 2:13.
68. Literally, "Epicurean."
69. Ps 82:1.
70. Am 9:6.
71. Ps 82:1.
72. Mal 3:16.
73. Ex 20:24.

a fence around riches; vows are a fence around abstinence; a fence around wisdom is silence.

3.15. He used to say: Beloved is man for he was created in the image [of God]; still greater was the love in that it was made known to him that he was created in the image of God, as it is written, *For in the image of God made he man.*[74] Beloved are Israel for they were called children of God; still greater was the love in that it was made known to them that they were called children of God, as it is written, *Ye are the children of the Lord your God.*[75] Beloved are Israel, for to them was given the precious instrument; still greater was the love, in that it was made known to them that to them was given the precious instrument by which the world was created, as it is written, *For I give you good doctrine; forsake ye not my Law.*[76]

3.16. All is foreseen, but freedom of choice is given; and the world is judged by grace, yet all is according to the excess of works [that be good or evil].

3.17. He used to say: All is given against a pledge, and the net is cast over all living; the shop stands open and the shop-keeper gives credit and the account-book lies open and the hand writes and every one that wishes to borrow let him come and borrow; but the collectors go their round continually every day and exact payment of men with their consent or without their consent, for they have that on which they can rely; and the judgement is a judgement of truth; and all is made ready for the banquet.

3.18. R. Eleazar b. Azariah said: If there is no study of the Law there is no seemly behaviour, if there is no seemly behaviour there is no study of the Law; if there is no wisdom there is no fear [of God], if there is no fear [of God] there is no wisdom; if there is no knowledge there is no discernment, if there is no discernment there is no knowledge; if there is no meal there is no study of the Law, if there is no study of the Law there is no meal. He used to say: He whose wisdom is more abundant than his works, to what is he like? To a tree whose branches are abundant but whose roots are few; and the wind comes and uproots it and overturns it, as it is written, *He shall be like a tamerisk in the desert and shall not see when good cometh; but shall inhabit the parched places in the wilderness.*[77] But he whose works are more abundant than his wisdom, to what is he like? To a tree whose branches are few but whose roots are many; so that even if all the winds in the world come and blow against it, it cannot be stirred from its place, as it is written, *He shall be as a tree planted by the waters, and that spreadeth out his roots by the river, and shall not fear when heat cometh, and his leaf shall be green; and shall not be careful in the year of drought, neither shall cease from yielding fruit.*[78]

4.1. Ben Zoma said: Who is wise? He that learns from all men, as it is written, *From all my teachers have I got understanding.*[79] Who is mighty? He that subdues his [evil] nature, as it is written, *He that is slow to anger is better than the mighty, and he that ruleth his spirit than he that taketh a city.*[80] Who is rich? He that rejoices in his portion, as it is written, *When thou eatest the labour of thy hands happy shalt thou be, and it shall be well with thee.*[81] *Happy shalt thou be*—in this world; *and it shall be well with thee*—in the world to come. Who is honoured? He that honours mankind, as it is written, *For them that honour me I will honour, and they that despise me shall be lightly esteemed.*[82]

4.2. Ben Azzai said: Run to fulfil the lightest duty even as the weightiest, and flee from transgression; for one duty draws another duty in its train, and one transgression draws another transgression in its train; for the reward of a duty [done] is a duty [to be done], and the reward of one transgression is [another] transgression.

4.3. He used to say: Despise no man and deem nothing impossible, for there is not a man that has not his hour and there is not a thing that has not its place.

From *The Mishnah*, translated by Herbert Danby (Oxford: Oxford University Press, 1987), 446–53. [Brackets in original.]

☙ The **Midrashim** is a collection of rabbinic writings that comment on the books of the Bible passage by passage. The rabbinic commentary concerning Abraham's sacrifice of Isaac in Genesis 22:1–19 is found in *Genesis Rabbah*.

Genesis Rabbah, 56.1–11: "The Binding of Isaac"

1. ON THE THIRD DAY, etc. (22:4). It is written, *After two days He will revive us, on the third day He will raise us up, that we may live in His presence* (Hos 6:2). E.g. on the third day of the tribal ancestors: *And Joseph said unto them the third day: This do, and live* (Gen 42:18); on the third day of Revelation: *And it came to pass on the third day, when it was morning* (Ex 19:16); on the third day of the spies: *And hide yourselves there three days* (Josh 2:16); on the third day of Jonah: *And Jonah was in*

---

74. Gen 9:6.

75. Deut 14:1.

76. Prov 4:2.

77. Jer 17:6.

78. Jer 17:8.

79. Ps 119:99.

80. Prov 16:32.

81. Ps 128:2.

82. 1 Sam 2:30.

the belly of the fish three days and three nights (Jon 2:1); on the third day of those returning from the Exile: *And we abode there three days* (Ezra 8:32); on the third day of resurrection: *"After two days He will revive us, on the third day He will raise us up"*; on the third day of Esther: *Now it came to pass on the third day, that Esther put on her royal apparel* (Esth 5:1)—i.e. she put on the royal apparel of her ancestor. For whose sake? The Rabbis say: For the sake of the third day, when Revelation took place. R. Levi maintained: In the merit of what Abraham did on the third day, as it says, ON THE THIRD DAY, etc.

AND SAW THE PLACE AFAR OFF (*ib.*). What did he see? He saw a cloud enveloping the mountain, and said: "It appears that that is the place where the Holy One, blessed be He, told me to sacrifice my son."

2. He then said to him [Isaac]: "Isaac, my son, seest thou what I see?" "Yes," he replied. Said he to his two servants: "See ye what I see?" "No," they answered. "Since ye do not see it, ABIDE YE HERE WITH THE ASS," (22:5), he bade them, for ye are like the ass, whence it follows that slaves are like an ass. The Rabbis proved [it from this verse spoken at] the Revelation: *Six days shalt thou labour, and do all thy work . . . thou, nor thy daughter, nor thy man-servant, nor thy maid-servant, nor thy cattle* (Ex 20:10).

R. Isaac said: This place shall one day be alienated from its Owner. For ever? [No], for it is stated, *This is My resting-place for ever; here will I dwell for I have desired it;* (Ps 132:14)—when he comes of whom it is written, *Lowly, and riding upon an ass* (Zech 1:9).[83]

AND I AND THE LAD WILL GO YONDER—ʿad koh. Said R. Joshua b. Levi: We will go and see what is to be the eventual outcome of *koh*.[84]

AND WE WILL WORSHIP, AND *WE* WILL COME BACK TO YOU. He thus informed him that he [Isaac] would return safely from Mount Moriah. R. Isaac said: Everything happened as a reward for worshipping. Abraham returned in peace from Mount Moriah only as a reward for worshipping: AND WE WILL WORSHIP, AND WE WILL COME BACK TO YOU. Israel were redeemed only as a reward for worshipping: *And the people believed . . . then they bowed their heads and worshipped* (Ex 4:31). The Torah was given only as a reward for worshipping: *And worship ye afar off* (ib. 24.1). Hannah was remembered only as a reward for worshipping: *And they worshipped before the Lord* (1 Sam 1:19). The exiles will be reassembled only as a reward for worshipping: *And it shall come to pass in that day, that a great horn shall be blown; and they shall come that were lost . . . and that were dispersed . . . and they shall worship the Lord in the*

holy mountain at Jerusalem (Isa 27:13). The Temple was built only as a reward for worshipping: *Exalt ye the Lord our God, and worship at His holy hill* (Ps 99:9). The dead will come to life again only as a reward for worshipping: *O come, let us worship and bend the knee; let us kneel before the Lord our Maker* (Ps 95:6).

3. AND ABRAHAM TOOK THE WOOD OF THE BURNT-OFFERING (22:6)—like one who carries his stake on his shoulder. AND HE TOOK IN HIS HAND THE FIRE AND THE KNIFE (MAʾAKELETH). R. Hanina said: Why is a knife called *maʾakeleth*? Because it makes food (*oklim*) fit to be eaten. While the Rabbis said: All eating (*akiloth*) which Israel enjoy in this world, they enjoy only in the merit of that MAʾAKELETH (KNIFE).

AND THEY WENT BOTH OF THEM TOGETHER (*ib.*): one to bind and the other to be bound, one to slaughter and the other to be slaughtered.

4. AND ISAAC SPOKE UNTO ABRAHAM HIS FATHER, AND SAID: MY FATHER (22:7). Samael[85] went to the Patriarch Abraham and upbraided him saying: "What means this, old man! Hast thou lost thy wits? thou goest to slay a son granted to thee at the age of a hundred!" "Even this I do," replied he. "And if He sets thee an even greater test, canst thou stand it?" said he, as it is written, *If a thing be put to thee as a trial, wilt thou be wearied* (Job 4:2)? "Even more than this," he replied. "To-morrow He will say to thee, 'Thou art a murderer, and art guilty.'" "Still am I content," he rejoined. Seeing that he could achieve nought with him, he approached Isaac and said: "Son of an unhappy mother! He goes to slay thee." "I accept my fate," he replied. "If so," said he, "shall all those fine tunics which thy mother made be a legacy for Ishmael, the hated of her house?" If a word is not wholly effective, it may yet avail in part; hence it is written, AND ISAAC SPOKE UNTO ABRAHAM HIS FATHER, AND SAID: MY FATHER: why HIS FATHER . . . MY FATHER? So that he should be filled with compassion for him. AND HE SAID: BEHOLD, THE FIRE AND THE WOOD. "May that man be drowned who has thus incited him," exclaimed he. "At all events, GOD WILL PROVIDE HIMSELF THE LAMB, O my son; and if not, THOU ART FOR A BURNT-OFFERING, MY SON." SO THEY WENT BOTH OF THEM TOGETHER—one to slaughter and the other to be slaughtered.

5. AND THEY CAME TO THE PLACE WHICH GOD HAD TOLD HIM

---

83. That is, the Messiah. (The notes for this selection are by Gerhart and Udoh.)

84. That is, the outcome of God's promise: "So [*koh*] shall your descendants be" (Gen 15:5).

85. This is the name of a wicked angel.

OF; AND ABRAHAM BUILT THE ALTAR THERE (22:9). And where was Isaac? Said R. Levi: He had taken and hidden him, saying, "Lest he who sought to seduce him throw a stone at him and disqualify him from serving as a sacrifice." AND BOUND ISAAC HIS SON. R. Ḥanina b. Isaac said: Even as Abraham bound his son Isaac below, so the Holy One, blessed be He, bound the Princes of the heathens above. Yet they did not remain [thus bound]. For when Israel alienated themselves [from God] in the days of Jeremiah, the Holy One, blessed be He, said to them: "What think ye: that those fetters still exist?" as it says, *For shall they be like tangled thorns (sirim) for ever* (Nah 1:10), which means: For are the Princes (*sarim*) to be entangled [i.e. bound] for ever? No; for *When they* [the Israelites] *are drunken according to their drink* (ib.), their fetters are broken, for it is written, *They shall be devoured as stubble fully dry* (ib.).

When the Patriarch Abraham stretched forth his hand to take the knife to slay his son, the angels wept, as it says, *Behold, their valiant ones* [the angels] *cry without—ḥuẓah* (Isa 33:7). What does "*ḥuẓah*" mean? R. Azariah said: It is unnatural. It is unnatural that he should slay his son with his own hand. And what did they say? *The highways lie waste?* (ib. 8)—does not Abraham show hospitality to travellers? *The wayfaring man ceaseth—shabath* (ib.)—as in the verse, *It had ceased* (ḥadal) *to be with Sarah* (Gen 18:11). *He hath broken the covenant* (Isa *loc. cit.*), viz. *But My covenant will I establish with Isaac* (Gen 17:21). *He hath despised the cities* (Isa *loc. cit.*), viz. *And* [Abraham] *dwelt between Kadesh and Shur* (Gen 20:1). *He regardeth not man* (Isa *loc. cit.*)—has Abraham no merit in his favour? And who says that this verse refers to the angels?—Here it says, UPON (MI-MAʿAL) THE WOOD, while in another passage it says, *Above* (mi-maʿal) *Him stood the seraphim* (Isa 6:2).

6. AND ABRAHAM STRETCHED FORTH HIS HAND, AND TOOK THE KNIFE. Rab asked R. Ḥiyya the Elder: Regarding Rabbi's teaching, in which he said: How do we know that ritual slaughtering must be with a movable object? From this verse: AND ABRAHAM STRETCHED FORTH HIS HAND, AND TOOK THE KNIFE—did he tell you this as *haggadah,* in which case he might retract; or did he state it as a tradition, in which case he would not retract from it? For R. Levi taught: If they [e.g. sharp flints] were fast [to the ground or rocks] from the very beginning, they are unfit; but if they had been originally detached but subsequently fixed in the ground, they are fit. For we learned: If one slaughters with a hand-sickle, a flint, or a reed, the slaughtering is fit. R. Jose b. Abin said: Five things were said of a reed stalk: You may not slaughter, circumcise, cut meat, wipe your hands, nor pick your teeth with it, because an evil spirit rests upon it.

7. AND THE ANGEL OF THE LORD CALLED UNTO HIM OUT OF HEAVEN, AND SAID: ABRAHAM, ABRAHAM (22:11). R. Ḥiyya taught: This is an expression of love and encouragement. R. Liezer said: [The repetition indicates that He spake] to him and to future generations: There is no generation which does not contain men like Abraham, and there is no generation which does not contain men like Jacob, Moses, and Samuel.

AND HE SAID: LAY NOT THY HAND UPON THE LAD, etc. (22:12). Where was the knife? Tears had fallen from the angels upon it and dissolved it. "Then I will strangle him," said he [Abraham] to Him. "LAY NOT THY HAND UPON THE LAD," was the reply. "Let us bring forth a drop of blood from him," he pleaded. "NEITHER DO THOU ANY THING TO HIM," He answered—"inflict no blemish upon him.[86] FOR NOW I KNOW—I have made it known to all—that thou lovest Me, AND THOU HAST NOT WITHHELD, etc. And do not say, 'All ills that do not affect one's own person are not ills,' for indeed I ascribe merit to thee as though I had bidden thee sacrifice thyself and thou hadst not refused."

8. Another comment: R. Issac said: When Abraham wished to sacrifice his son Isaac, he said to him: "Father, I am a young man and am afraid that my body may tremble through fear of the knife and I will grieve thee, whereby the slaughter may be rendered unfit and this will not count as a real sacrifice; therefore bind me very firmly. Forthwith, HE BOUND ISAAC: can one bind a man thirty-seven years old? (another version: twenty-six years old) without his consent? Presently, AND ABRAHAM STRETCHED FORTH HIS HAND—he stretched forth his hand to take the knife while the tears streamed from his eyes, and these tears, prompted by a father's compassion, dropped into Isaac's eyes. Yet even so, his heart rejoiced to obey the will of his Creator. The angels assembled in groups above. What did they cry? *The highways lie waste, the wayfaring man ceaseth; He hath broken the covenant, He hath despised the cities* (Isa 33:8)—has He no pleasure in Jerusalem and the Temple, which He had intended giving as a possession to the descendants of Isaac? *He regardeth not man* (ib.): if no merit has stood in Abraham's favour, then no creature has any value before him.

R. Aḥa said: [Abraham wondered]: Surely Thou too indulgest in prevarication! Yesterday Thou saidest, *For in Isaac shall seed be called to thee* (Gen 21:12); Thou didst then retract and say, *Take now thy son* (ib. 22:2); while now Thou biddest me, LAY NOT THY HAND UPON THE LAD! Said the Holy One,

---

86. A word play, *meʾumah* (anything) being read as *mumah* (blemish).

blessed be He, to him: "O Abraham, *My covenant will I not profane* (Ps 89:35), *And I will establish My covenant with Isaac* (Gen 17:21). When I bade thee, '*Take now thy son,*' etc., *I will not alter that which is gone out of My lips* (Ps *loc. cit.*). Did I tell thee, Slaughter him? No! but, '*Take him up.*' Thou hast taken him up. Now take him down."

9. AND ABRAHAM LIFTED UP HIS EYES, AND LOOKED, AND BEHOLD BEHIND HIM (AḤAR) A RAM (22:13). What does AḤAR mean? Said R. Judan: After all that happened, Israel still fall into the clutches of sin and [in consequence] become the victims of persecution; yet they will be ultimately redeemed by the ram's horn, as it says, *And the Lord God will blow the horn,* etc. (Zech 9:14). R. Judah b. R. Simon interpreted: At the end of [after] all generations Israel will fall into the clutches of sin and be the victims of persecution; yet eventually they will be redeemed by the ram's horn, as it says, "*And the Lord God will blow the horn,*" etc. R. Ḥanina b. R. Isaac said: Throughout the year Israel are in sin's clutches and led astray by their troubles, but on New Year they take the *shofar* and blow on it, and eventually they will be redeemed by the ram's horn, as it says, "*And the Lord God will blow the horn.*" R. Abba b. R. Pappi and R. Joshua of Siknin in R. Levi's name said: Because the Patriarch Abraham saw the ram extricate himself from one thicket and go and become entangled in another, the Holy One, blessed be He, said to him: "So will thy children be entangled in countries, changing from Babylon to Media, from Media to Greece, and from Greece to Edom; yet they will eventually be redeemed by the ram's horn," as it is written, *And the Lord God will blow the horn . . . the Lord of hosts will defend them* (ib. 14f.).

AND ABRAHAM WENT AND TOOK THE RAM, AND OFFERED HIM UP FOR A BURNT-OFFERING IN THE STEAD OF HIS SON (ib.). R. Judan said in R. Banai's name: He prayed to him: "Sovereign of the Universe! Look upon the blood of this ram as though it were the blood of my son Isaac; its *emurim* as though they were my son's *emurim,*" even as we learned: When a man declares: This animal be instead of this one, in exchange for that, or a substitute for this, it is a valid exchange. R. Phinehas said in R. Banai's name: He prayed: "Sovereign of the Universe! Regard it as though I had sacrificed my son Isaac first and then this ram instead of him," [IN THE STEAD being understood] as in the verse, *And Jotham his son reigned in his stead* (2 Kings 15:7).

It is even as we learned: [When one declares: I vow a sacrifice] like the lamb or like the animals of the Temple stalls, R. Joḥanan said: He meant, like the lamb of the daily burnt-offering: Resh Laḳish said: He meant, like Isaac's ram. There

[in Babylon] they say: Like the offspring of a sin-offering. Bar Ḳappara taught: He meant, like the lamb which has never given suck.

10. AND ABRAHAM CALLED THE NAME OF THE PLACE ADONAI JIREH—THE LORD SEETH (22:14). R. Bibi Rabbah said in R. Joḥanan's name: He said to Him: "Sovereign of the Universe! When Thou didst order me, '*Take now thy son, thine only son*' (ib. 2), I could have answered, 'Yesterday Thou didst promise me, *For in Isaac shall seed be called to thee* (ib. 21:12), and now Thou sayest, "*Take now thy son,*" etc.' Yet Heaven forfend! I did not do this, but suppressed my feelings of compassion in order to do Thy will. Even so it may be Thy will, O Lord our God, that when Isaac's children are in trouble, Thou wilt remember that binding in their favour and be filled with compassion for them."

Abraham called it "Jireh": AND ABRAHAM CALLED THE NAME OF THAT PLACE ADONAI—JIREH. Shem called it Salem [Shalem]: *And Melchizedek king of Salem* (Gen 14:18). Said the Holy One, blessed be He: "If I call it Jireh as did Abraham, then Shem, a righteous man, will resent it; while if I call it Salem as did Shem, Abraham, the righteous man, will resent it. Hence I will call it Jerusalem, including both names, Jireh Salem." R. Berekiah said in R. Ḥelbo's name: While it was yet Salem the Holy One, blessed be He, made Himself a tabernacle and prayed in it, as it says, *In Salem also is set His tabernacle, and His dwelling-place in Zion* (Ps 76:3). And what did He say: "O that I may see the building of the Temple!"

Another interpretation: This verse teaches that the Holy One, blessed be He, showed him the Temple built, destroyed and rebuilt. For it says, AND ABRAHAM CALLED THE NAME OF THAT PLACE ADONAI—JIREH (THE LORD SEETH): this alludes to the Temple built, as in the verse, *Three times in a year shall all thy males be seen . . . in the place where He shall choose* (Deut 16:16); AS IT IS SAID TO THIS DAY: IN THE MOUNT refers to it destroyed, as in the verse, *For the mountain of Zion, which is desolate* (Lam 5:18); WHERE THE LORD IS SEEN refers to it rebuilt and firmly established in the Messianic era, as in the verse, *When the Lord hath built up Zion, when He hath been seen in His glory* (Ps 102:17).

11. AND THE ANGEL OF THE LORD CALLED UNTO ABRAHAM A SECOND TIME OUT OF HEAVEN, AND SAID: BY MYSELF HAVE I SWORN (22:15f.). What was the need of this oath? He had begged Him: "Swear to me not to try me again henceforth, nor my son Isaac." R. Levi in the name of R. Ḥama b. R. Ḥanina gave another reason for this oath: He had begged: "Swear to me not to test me again henceforth." This may be likened to a king who was married to a noble lady. She gave

birth to her first son by him, and he divorced her; a second, and he divorced her; a third, and he divorced her. When she had given birth to a tenth son by him, they all assembled and demanded of him: "Swear to us not to divorce our mother again." Similarly, when Abraham had been tried for the tenth time, he said to Him: "Swear to me not to test me again." R. Ḥanan commented: BECAUSE THOU HAST DONE THIS THING (*ib.*)—it was the tenth trial, yet you say, BECAUSE THOU HAST DONE *THIS THING*! The fact, however, is that this was the last trial, which was as weighty as all the rest together, and had he not submitted to it, all would have been lost.

THAT IN BLESSING I WILL BLESS THEE, etc. (22:17): a blessing for the father and a blessing for the son; AND IN MULTIPLYING WILL I MULTIPLY: an increase for the father and an increase for the son.[87] AND THY SEED SHALL POSSESS THE GATE OF HIS ENEMIES (*ib.*). Rabbi said: This alludes to Tadmor. Happy is he who will see the downfall of Tadmor which took part in both destructions. R. Judan and R. Ḥanina—one of them said: At the destruction of the first Temple she supplied eighty thousand archers, and at the destruction of the second, eight thousand archers.

SO ABRAHAM RETURNED UNTO HIS YOUNG MEN (22:19). And where was Isaac? R. Berekiah said in the name of the Rabbis

of the other place:[88] He sent him to Shem to study Torah. This may be compared to a woman who became wealthy through her distaff. Said she: "Since I have become wealthy through this distaff, it will never leave my hand." Thus said Abraham: "All that has come to me is only because I engaged in Torah and good deeds; therefore I am unwilling that it should ever depart from my seed." R. Jose b. R. Ḥanina said: He sent him [home] at night, for fear of the [evil] eye. For from the moment that Hananiah, Mishael, and Azariah ascended unscathed from the fiery furnace they are no more mentioned. Whither then had they gone? R. Leazar said: They died through the spittle; R. Jose b. R. Ḥanina said: They died through an [evil] eye. R. Joshua b. Levi said: They changed their locality and went to Joshua, the son of Jehozadak, to study Torah; that is meant by the verse, *Hear now, O Joshua the high priest, thou, and thy fellows that sit before thee; for they are men that are a sign* (Zech 3:8). R. Tanḥuma b. Abina commented in R. Ḥanina's name: For this very purpose did Hananiah, Mishael, and Azariah descend into the fiery furnace, that a sign should be wrought through them.

From *Midrash Rabbah: Genesis*, 3rd ed., vol. 1, translated by H. Freedman (New York: Soncino Press, 1983), 491–503. [Brackets in original.]

2. GRECO-ROMAN PHILOSOPHY

Plato (ca. 429–347 BCE), one of the most influential philosophers of antiquity, was the founder of the Academy (ca. 387 BCE–529 CE) in Athens after the death of Socrates (ca. 469–399 BCE), whom he interprets. In *The Republic* (usually dated during the middle segment of Plato's writing career, ca. 380–360), Plato gives his criticism of Greek civic religion in his investigation into the nature of the deity. In *The Symposium* (also usually dated during the middle segment of Plato's writing career), Plato contemplates absolute beauty using the dialectical method with Socrates as the literary dialogist.

PLATO

The Republic, 377b–383c

"Don't you know that the beginning is the most important part of every work and that this is especially so with anything

young and tender? For at that stage it's most plastic, and each thing assimilates itself to the model whose stamp anyone wishes to give to it."[89]

"Quite so."

"Then shall we so easily let the children hear just any tales fashioned by just anyone and take into their souls opinions for the most part opposite to those we'll suppose they must have when they are grown up?"

"In no event will we permit it."

---

87. It is the repetition of the verb (in the original Hebrew) that gives rise to both comments.

88. That is, Babylon.

89. This conversation is between Socrates and Adeimantus, brother to Glaucon, Socrates' other interlocutor. Both were Plato's brothers. Socrates speaks first. (The notes for this selection are by Gerhart and Udoh.)

"First, as it seems, we must supervise the makers[90] of tales; and if they make a fine tale, it must be approved, but if it's not, it must be rejected. We'll persuade nurses and mothers to tell the approved tales to their children and to shape their souls with tales more than their bodies with hands. Most of those they now tell must be thrown out."

"Which sort?" he said.

"In the greater tales we'll also see the smaller ones," I said. "For both the greater and the smaller must be taken from the same model and have the same power. Don't you suppose so?"

"I do," he said. "But I don't grasp what you mean by the greater ones."

"The ones Hesiod and Homer told us, and the other poets too. They surely composed false tales for human beings and used to tell them and still do tell them."

"But what sort," he said, "and what do you mean to blame in them?"

"What ought to be blamed first and foremost," I said, "especially if the lie a man tells isn't a fine one."

"What's that?"

"When a man in speech makes a bad representation of what gods and heroes are like, just as a painter who paints something that doesn't resemble the things whose likeness he wished to paint."

"Yes, it's right to blame such things," he said. "But how do we mean this and what sort of thing is it?"

"First," I said, "the man who told the biggest lie about the biggest things didn't tell a fine lie—how Uranus did what Hesiod says he did, and how Cronos in his turn took revenge on him. And Cronos' deeds and his sufferings at the hands of his son, not even if they were true would I suppose they should so easily be told to thoughtless young things; best would be to keep quiet, but if there were some necessity to tell, as few as possible ought to hear them as unspeakable secrets, after making a sacrifice, not of a pig but of some great offering that's hard to come by, so that it will come to the ears of the smallest possible number."

"These speeches are indeed harsh," he said.

"And they mustn't be spoken in our city, Adeimantus," I said. "Nor must it be said within the hearing of a young person that in doing the extremes of injustice, or that in punishing the unjust deeds of his father in every way, he would do nothing to be wondered at, but would be doing only what the first and the greatest of the gods did."

"No, by Zeus," he said. "To say this doesn't seem fitting to me either."

"Above all," I said, "it mustn't be said that gods make war on gods, and plot against them and have battles with them—for it isn't even true—provided that those who are going to guard the city for us must consider it most shameful to be easily angry with one another. They are far from needing to have tales told and embroideries woven about battles of giants and the many diverse disputes of gods and heroes with their families and kin. But if we are somehow going to persuade them that no citizen ever was angry with another and that to be so is not holy, it's just such things that must be told the children right away by old men and women; and as they get older, the poets must be compelled to make up speeches for them which are close to these. But Hera's bindings by her son, and Hephaestus' being cast out by his father when he was about to help out his mother who was being beaten, and all the battles of the gods Homer made, must not be accepted in the city, whether they are made with a hidden sense or without a hidden sense. A young thing can't judge what is hidden sense and what is not; but what he takes into his opinions at that age has a tendency to become hard to eradicate and unchangeable. Perhaps it's for this reason that we must do everything to insure that what they hear first, with respect to virtue, be the finest told tales for them to hear."

"That's reasonable," he said. "But if someone should at this point ask us what they are and which tales we mean, what would we say?"

And I said, "Adeimantus, you and I aren't poets right now but founders of a city. It's appropriate for founders to know the models according to which the poets must tell their tales. If what the poets produce goes counter to these models, founders must not give way; however, they must not themselves make up tales."

"That's correct," he said. "But, that is just it; what would the models for speech about the gods[91] be?"

"Doubtless something like this," I said. "The god must surely always be described such as he is, whether one presents him in epics, lyrics, or tragedies."

"Yes, he must be."

"Then, is the god really good, and, hence, must he be said to be so?"

"Of course."

---

90. The Greek word from which the English words "poet" and "poetry" are derived is *poiein*, "to make." Thus, poetry is an instance, and for Plato the most revealing kind, of making. The poet is thus *the* maker.

91. "Speech about the gods" translates the Greek word *theologia*.

"Well, but none of the good things is harmful, is it?"

"Not in my opinion."

"Does that which isn't harmful do harm?"

"In no way."

"Does that which does not harm do any evil?"

"Not that, either."

"That which does no evil would not be the cause of any evil?"

"How could it be?"

"What about this? Is the good beneficial?"

"Yes."

"Then it's the cause of doing well?"

"Yes."

"Then the good is not the cause of everything; rather it is the cause of the things that are in a good way, while it is not responsible for the bad things."

"Yes," he said, "that's entirely so."

"Then," I said, "the god, since he's good, wouldn't be the cause of everything, as the many say, but the cause of a few things for human beings and not responsible for most. For the things that are good for us are far fewer than those that are bad; and of the good things, no one else must be said to be the cause; of the bad things, some other causes must be sought and not the god."

"What you say," he said, "is in my opinion very true."

"Then," I said, "we mustn't accept Homer's—or any other poet's—foolishly making this mistake about the gods and saying that

> Two jars stand on Zeus's threshold
> Full of dooms—the one of good,
>   the other of wretched;

and the man to whom Zeus gives a mixture of both,

> At one time he happens on evil,
>   at another good;

but the man to whom he doesn't give a mixture, but the second pure,

> Evil misery, drives him over the divine
>   earth;[92]

nor that Zeus is the dispenser to us

> Of good and evil alike.[93]

And, as to the violation of the oaths and truces that Pandarus committed, if someone says Athena and Zeus were responsible for its happening, we'll not praise him; nor must the young be allowed to hear that Themis and Zeus were responsible for strife and contention among the gods,[94] nor again, as Aeschylus says, that

> God plants the cause in mortals
> When he wants to destroy a house utterly.

And if someone produces a 'Sorrows of Niobe,'[95] the work where these iambics are, or a 'Sorrows of the Pelopidae,' or the 'Trojan Sorrows,' or anything else of the sort, either he mustn't be allowed to say that they are the deeds of a god, or, if of a god, he must find a speech for them pretty much like the one we're now seeking; and he must say the god's works were just and good, and that these people profited by being punished. But the poet mustn't be allowed to say that those who pay the penalty are wretched and that the one who did it was a god. If, however, he should say that the bad men were wretched because they needed punishment and that in paying the penalty they were benefited by the god, it must be allowed. As for the assertion that a god, who is good, is the cause of evil to anyone, great exertions must be made against anyone's saying these things in his own city, if its laws are going to be well observed, or anyone's hearing them, whether he is younger or older, whether the tale is told in meter or without meter. For these are to be taken as sayings that, if said, are neither holy, nor advantageous for us, nor in harmony with one another."

"I give my vote to you in support of this law," he said, "and it pleases me."

"Now, then," I said, "this would be one of the laws and models concerning the gods, according to which those who produce speeches will have to do their speaking and those who produce poems will have to do their making: the god is not the cause of all things, but of the good."

"And it's very satisfactory," he said.

---

92. See Homer, *Iliad*, XXIV.527–32.

93. The passage is not found in Homer. However, *Iliad*, IV.84 reads:

> What is to come? Bad days again
> in the bloody lines? Or can both sides be friends?
> Which will it be from Zeus, who holds the keys
> and rationing of war?

94. See Homer, *Iliad*, XX.1–74.

95. This work by Aeschylus is now lost.

"Now, what about this second one? Do you suppose the god is a wizard, able treacherously to reveal himself at different times in different *ideas,* at one time actually himself changing and passing from his own form into many shapes, at another time deceiving us and making us think such things about him? Or is he simple and does he least of all things depart from his own *idea?*"

"On the spur of the moment, I can't say," he said.

"What about this? Isn't it necessary that, if something steps out of its own *idea,* it be changed either by itself or something else?"

"Yes, it is necessary."

"Are things that are in the best condition least altered and moved by something else—for example, a body by food, drink, and labor, and all plants by the sun's heat, winds, and other affections of the sort; aren't the healthiest and strongest least altered?"

"Of course."

"And a soul that is most courageous and most prudent, wouldn't an external affection least trouble and alter it?"

"Yes."

"And, again, the same argument surely also holds for all composites, implements, houses, and clothing; those that are well made and in good condition are least altered by time and the other affections."

"That's so."

"Hence everything that's in fine condition, whether by nature or art or both, admits least transformation by anything else."

"It seems so."

"Now, the god and what belongs to the god are in every way in the best condition."

"Of course."

"So, in this way, the god would least of all have many shapes."

"Least of all, surely."

"But would he be the one to transform and alter himself?"

"It's plain," he said, "if he's altered at all."

"Does he transform himself into what's better and fairer, or what's worse and uglier than himself?"

"Necessarily into what's worse," he said, "if he's altered at all. For surely we won't say that the god is wanting in beauty or virtue."

"What you say is very right," I said. "And, if this is so, in your opinion, Adeimantus, does anyone, either god or human being, willingly make himself worse in any way at all?"

"It's impossible," he said.

"Then it's impossible," I said, "for a god to want to alter himself, but since, as it seems, each of them is as fair and as good as possible, he remains forever simply in his own shape."

"That's entirely necessary, in my opinion at least," he said.

"Then, you best of men," I said, "let none of the poets tell us that

> The gods, like wandering strangers,
> Take on every sort of shape and visit
>   the cities[96]

and let none tell lies about Proteus and Thetis[97] or bring on an altered Hera, either in tragedies or the other kinds of poetry, as a priestess

> Making a collection for the life-giving children
>   of Inachus, Argos' river[98]

and let them not lie to us in many other such ways. Nor should the mothers, in their turn, be convinced by these things and frighten the children with tales badly told—that certain gods go around nights looking like all sorts of strangers—lest they slander the gods while at the same time making the children more cowardly."

"No, they shouldn't," he said.

"But," I said, "while the gods themselves can't be transformed, do they make us think they appear in all sorts of ways, deceiving and bewitching us?"

"Perhaps," he said.

"What?" I said. "Would a god want to lie, either in speech or deed by presenting an illusion?"

"I don't know," he said.

"Don't you know," I said, "that all gods and human beings hate the true lie, if that expression can be used?"

"What do you mean?" he said.

"That surely no one," I said, "voluntarily wishes to lie about the most sovereign things to what is most sovereign in himself. Rather, he fears holding a lie there more than anything."

---

96. Homer, *Odyssey,* XVII.485.

97. See, for instance, Homer, *Odyssey,* IV.456–58; Pindar, *Nemean Odes,* IV.60ff.

98. Aeschylus, *The Xantriai.* The play is not extant.

"I still don't understand," he said.

"That's because you suppose I mean something exalted," I said. "But I mean that to lie and to have lied to the soul about the things that are, and to be unlearned, and to have and to hold a lie there is what everyone would least accept; and that everyone hates a lie in that place most of all."

"Quite so," he said.

"Now what I was just talking about would most correctly be called truly a lie—the ignorance in the soul of the man who has been lied to. For the lie in speeches is a kind of imitation of the affection in the soul, a phantom of it that comes into being after it, and not quite an unadulterated lie. Isn't that so?"

"Most certainly."

"So the real lie is hated not only by gods, but also by human beings."

"Yes, in my opinion."

"Now, what about the one in speeches? When and for whom is it also useful, so as not to deserve hatred? Isn't it useful against enemies, and, as a preventive, like a drug, for so-called friends when from madness or some folly they attempt to do something bad? And, in the telling of the tales we were just now speaking about—those told because we don't know where the truth about ancient things lies—likening the lie to the truth as best we can, don't we also make it useful?"

"It is very useful in such cases," he said.

"Then in which of these cases is a lie useful to the god? Would he lie in making likenesses because he doesn't know ancient things?"

"That," he said, "would be ridiculous."

"Then there is no lying poet in a god?"

"Not in my opinion."

"Would he lie because he's frightened of enemies?"

"Far from it."

"Because of the folly or madness of his intimates?"

"None of the foolish or the mad is a friend of the gods," he said.

"Then, there's nothing for the sake of which a god would lie?"

"There is nothing."

"Then the demonic and the divine are wholly free from lie."

"That's completely certain," he said.

"Then the god is altogether simple and true in deed and speech, and he doesn't himself change or deceive others by illusions, speeches, or the sending of signs either in waking or dreaming."

"That's how it looks to me too when you say it," he said.

"Do you then agree," I said, "that this is the second model according to which speeches and poems about gods must be made: they are neither wizards who transform themselves, nor do they mislead us by lies in speech or in deed?"

"I do agree."

"So, although we praise much in Homer, we'll not praise Zeus' sending the dream to Agamemnon,[99] nor Thetis' saying in Aeschylus[100] that Apollo sang at her wedding, foretelling good things for her offspring,

> Free from sickness and living long lives,
> Telling all that the friendship of the gods
>   would do for my fortunes,
> He sang the paean, gladdening my spirit.
> And I expected Phoebus' divine mouth
> To be free of lie, full with the diviner's art.
> And he, he who sang, who was at this feast, who
>   said this, he is the one who slew my son.

When someone says such things about gods, we'll be harsh and not provide a chorus; and we'll not let the teachers use them for the education of the young, if our guardians are going to be god-revering and divine insofar as a human being can possibly be."

"I am in complete agreement with these models," he said, "and would use them as laws."

From Plato, *The Republic*, 2nd ed., translated by Allan Bloom (New York: Basic Books, 1991), 55–61.

PLATO

The Symposium, 204c–206a, 210a–212c

204c–206a

"Tell me then, my friend," I said, "for your words carry conviction, what function Love performs among men, if this is his nature." "That is precisely what I am going to try to teach you, Socrates. The nature and parentage of Love are as I have described, and he is also, according to you, love of beauty. But suppose we were to be asked: 'In what does love of beauty consist, Socrates and Diotima?'[101] or, to put it

---

99. Homer, *Iliad*, II.1–34.

100. It is not known for certain which works of Aeschylus Plato is citing.

101. Socrates converses with his fictive "teacher," Diotima.

more plainly, 'What is the aim of the love which is felt by the lover of beauty?'" "His aim is to attain possession of beautiful things," I answered. "But that merely raises a further question. What will have been gained by the man who is in possession of beauty?" I said that I could supply no ready answer to this question. "Well," she said, "let us change our terms and substitute good for beautiful. Suppose someone asked you: 'Now, Socrates, what is the aim of the love felt by the lover of the good?'" "Possession of the good," I replied. "And what will have been gained by the man who is in possession of the good?" "I find that an easier question to answer; he will be happy." "Presumably because happiness consists in the possession of the good, and once one has given that answer, the inquiry is at an end; there is no need to ask the further question 'Why does a man desire to be happy?'" "Quite so."

"Now do you suppose that this desire and this love are characteristics common to all men, and that all perpetually desire to be in possession of the good, or what?" "That is exactly what I mean; they are common to all men." "Why is it then, Socrates, if all men are always in love with the same thing, that we do not speak of all men as being in love, but say that some men are in love and others not?" "I wonder what the reason can be." "There's no need to wonder; the truth is that we isolate a particular kind of love and appropriate for it the name of love, which really belongs to a wider whole, while we employ different names for the other kinds of love." "Can you give me another example of such a usage?" "Yes, here is one. By its original meaning poetry means simply creation, and creation, as you know, can take very various forms. Any action which is the cause of a thing emerging from non-existence into existence might be called poetry, and all the processes in all the crafts are kinds of poetry, and all those who are engaged in them poets." "Yes." "But yet they are not called poets, but have other names, and out of the whole field of poetry or creation one part, which deals with music and metre, is isolated and called by the name of the whole. This part alone is called poetry, and those whose province is this part of poetry are called poets." "Quite true." "It is just the same with love. The generic concept embraces every desire for good and for happiness; that is precisely what almighty and all-ensnaring love is. But this desire expresses itself in many ways, and those with whom it takes the form of love of money or of physical prowess or of wisdom are not said to be in love or called lovers, whereas those whose passion runs in one particular channel usurp the name of lover, which belongs to them all, and are said to be

lovers and in love." "There seems to be truth in what you say," I remarked. "There is indeed a theory," she continued, "that lovers are people who are in search of the other half of themselves, but according to my view of the matter, my friend, love is not desire either of the half or of the whole, unless that half or whole happens to be good. Men are quite willing to have their feet or their hands amputated if they believe those parts of themselves to be diseased. The truth is, I think, that people are not attached to what particularly belongs to them, except in so far as they can identify what is good with what is their own, and what is bad with what is not their own. The only object of men's love is what is good. Don't you agree?" "Certainly I do." "May we then say without qualification that men are in love with what is good?" "Yes." "But we must add, mustn't we, that the aim of their love is the possession of the good for themselves?" "Yes." "And not only its possession but its perpetual possession?" "Certainly." "To sum up, then, love is desire for the perpetual possession of the good." "Very true."

210a–212c

"The man who would pursue the right way to this goal must begin, when he is young, by applying himself to the contemplation of physical beauty, and, if he is properly directed by his guide, he will first fall in love with one particular beautiful person and beget noble sentiments in partnership with him. Later he will observe that physical beauty in any person is closely akin to physical beauty in any other, and that, if he is to make beauty of outward form the object of his quest, it is great folly not to acknowledge that the beauty exhibited in all bodies is one and the same; when he has reached this conclusion he will become a lover of all physical beauty, and will relax the intensity of his passion for one particular person, because he will realize that such a passion is beneath him and of small account. The next stage is for him to reckon beauty of soul more valuable than beauty of body; the result will be that, when he encounters a virtuous soul in a body which has little of the bloom of beauty, he will be content to love and cherish it and to bring forth such notions as may serve to make young people better; in this way he will be compelled to contemplate beauty as it exists in activities and institutions, and to recognize that here too all beauty is akin, so that he will be led to consider physical beauty taken as a whole a poor thing in comparison. From morals he must be directed to the sciences and contemplate their beauty also, so that, having his eyes fixed upon beauty in the widest sense, he may no longer be the slave of a base and mean-spirited devotion to an individual example of beauty, whether the object of his love be a boy or a man or an activity, but, by gazing upon the vast ocean of beauty to which his attention is now turned, may bring forth in the abundance of his love of wisdom many beautiful and magnificent sentiments and ideas, until at last, strengthened and increased in stature by this experience, he catches sight of one unique science whose object is the beauty of which I am about to speak. And here I must ask you to pay the closest possible attention."

"The man who has been guided thus far in the mysteries of love, and who has directed his thoughts towards examples of beauty in due and orderly succession, will suddenly have revealed to him as he approaches the end of his initiation a beauty whose nature is marvellous indeed, the final goal, Socrates, of all his previous efforts. This beauty is first of all eternal; it neither comes into being nor passes away, neither waxes nor wanes; next, it is not beautiful in part and ugly in part, nor beautiful at one time and ugly at another, nor beautiful in this relation and ugly in that, nor beautiful here and ugly there, as varying according to its beholders; nor again will this beauty appear to him like the beauty of a face or hands or anything else corporeal, or like the beauty of a thought or a science, or like beauty which has its seat in something other than itself, be it a living thing or the earth or the sky or anything else whatever; he will see it as absolute, existing alone with itself, unique, eternal, and all other beautiful things as partaking of it, yet in such a manner that, while they come into being and pass away, it neither undergoes any increase or diminution nor suffers any change."

"When a man, starting from this sensible world and making his way upward by a right use of his feeling of love for boys, begins to catch sight of that beauty, he is very near his goal. This is the right way of approaching or being initiated into the mysteries of love, to begin with examples of beauty in this world, and using them as steps to ascend continually with that absolute beauty as one's aim, from one instance of physical beauty to two and from two to all, then from physical beauty to moral beauty, and from moral beauty to the beauty of knowledge, until from knowledge of various kinds one arrives at the supreme knowledge whose sole object is that absolute beauty, and knows at last what absolute beauty is."

"This above all others, my dear Socrates," the woman from Mantinea continued, "is the region where a man's life should be spent, in the contemplation of absolute beauty. Once you have seen that, you will not value it in terms of

gold or rich clothing or of the beauty of boys and young men, the sight of whom at present throws you and many people like you into such an ecstasy that, provided that you could always enjoy the sight and company of your darlings, you would be content to go without food and drink, if that were possible, and to pass your whole time with them in the contemplation of their beauty. What may we suppose to be the felicity of the man who sees absolute beauty in its essence, pure and unalloyed, who, instead of a beauty tainted by human flesh and colour and a mass of perishable rubbish, is able to apprehend divine beauty where it exists apart and alone? Do you think that it will be a poor life that a man leads who has his gaze fixed in that direction, who contemplates absolute beauty with the appropriate faculty and is in constant union with it? Do you not see that in that region alone where he sees beauty with the faculty capable of seeing it, will he be able to bring forth not mere reflected images of goodness but true goodness, because he will be in contact not with a reflection but with the truth? And having brought forth and nurtured true goodness he will have the privilege of being beloved of God, and becoming, if ever a man can, immortal himself."

From Plato, *The Symposium*, translated by Walter Hamilton (London: Penguin, 1951), 83–86, 92–95.

☙ **Epictetus** (ca. 55–135 CE), although born a slave, eventually founded a school in Nicopolis in Epirus (in northwestern Greece) and was, according to Origen, more popular in his day than Plato was in his. Herodes Atticus (ca. 101–77) called Epictetus the greatest of Stoics, though Epictetus wrote nothing for publication. Flavius Arrian (ca. 86–160), Epictetus's student, published his notes of Epictetus's teaching in *The Discourses* and *The Handbook* (*Encheiridion*), both of which greatly influenced early Christianity, especially Christian asceticism. In the following selections from *The Handbook*, Epictetus gives his philosophy on virtuous living.

EPICTETUS

The Handbook, 1–5, 8–9, 13–14, 17, 27, 31, 41, 53

1. Some things are up to us and some are not up to us. Our opinions are up to us, and our impulses, desires, aversions—in short, whatever is our own doing. Our bodies are not up to us, nor are our possessions, our reputations, or our public offices, or, that is, whatever is not our own doing. The things that are up to us are by nature free, unhindered, and unim-

peded; the things that are not up to us are weak, enslaved, hindered, not our own. So remember, if you think that things naturally enslaved are free or that things not your own are your own, you will be thwarted, miserable, and upset, and will blame both gods and men. But if you think that only what is yours is yours, and that what is not your own is, just as it is, not your own, then no one will ever coerce you, no one will hinder you, you will blame no one, you will not accuse anyone, you will not do a single thing unwillingly, you will have no enemies, and no one will harm you, because you will not be harmed at all.

As you aim for such great goals, remember that you must not undertake them by acting moderately, but must let some things go completely and postpone others for the time being. But if you want both those great goals and also to hold public office and to be rich, then you may perhaps not get even the latter just because you aim at the former too; and you certainly will fail to get the former, which are the only things that yield freedom and happiness.

From the start, then, work on saying to each harsh appearance,[102] "You are an appearance, and not at all the thing that has the appearance." Then examine it and assess it by these yardsticks that you have, and first and foremost by whether it concerns the things that are up to us or the things that are not up to us. And if it is about one of the things that is not up to us, be ready to say, "You are nothing in relation to me."

2. Remember, what a desire proposes is that you gain what you desire, and what an aversion proposes is that you not fall into what you are averse to. Someone who fails to get what he desires is *un*fortunate, while someone who falls into what he is averse to has met *mis*fortune. So if you are averse only to what is against nature among the things that are up to you, then you will never fall into anything that you are averse to; but if you are averse to illness or death or poverty, you will meet misfortune. So detach your aversion from everything not up to us, and transfer it to what is against nature among the things that are up to us. And for the time being eliminate desire completely, since if you desire something that is not up to us, you are bound to be unfortunate, and at the same time none of the things that are up to us, which it would be good to desire, will be available to you. Make use only of impulse and its contrary, rejection, though with reservation, lightly, and without straining.

3. In the case of everything attractive or useful or that you are fond of, remember to say just what sort of thing it is, beginning with the least little things. If you are fond of a jug,

say, "I am fond of a jug!" For then when it is broken you will not be upset. If you kiss your child or your wife, say that you are kissing a human being; for when it dies you will not be upset.

4. When you are about to undertake some action, remind yourself what sort of action it is. If you are going out for a bath, put before your mind what happens at baths—there are people who splash, people who jostle, people who are insulting, people who steal. And you will undertake the action more securely if from the start you say of it, "I want to take a bath and to keep my choices in accord with nature"; and likewise for each action. For that way if something happens to interfere with your bathing you will be ready to say, "Oh, well, I wanted not only this but also to keep my choices in accord with nature, and I cannot do that if I am annoyed with things that happen."

5. What upsets people is not things themselves but their judgments about the things. For example, death is nothing dreadful (or else it would have appeared dreadful to Socrates), but instead the judgment about death that it is dreadful—*that* is what is dreadful. So when we are thwarted or upset or distressed, let us never blame someone else but rather ourselves, that is, our own judgments. An uneducated person accuses others when he is doing badly; a partly educated person accuses himself; an educated person accuses neither someone else nor himself.

8. Do not seek to have events happen as you want them to, but instead want them to happen as they do happen, and your life will go well.

9. Illness interferes with the body, not with one's faculty of choice, unless that faculty of choice wishes it to. Lameness interferes with the limb, not with one's faculty of choice.[103] Say this at each thing that happens to you, since you will find that it interferes with something else, not with you.

13. If you want to make progress,[104] let people think you are a mindless fool about externals, and do not desire a reputation for knowing about them. If people think you amount to something, distrust yourself. Certainly it is not easy to be on guard both for one's choices to be in accord with nature

---

102. The Greek word *phantasia* rendered here by "appearance" can also be translated as "presentation" or "impression." *Phantasia* is the immediate sense experience, which may or may not represent actual external reality.

103. The "faculty of choice" (*proairesis*) is a rational faculty of the soul.

104. That is, the movement toward the ideal human condition represented by the Stoic "sage."

and also for externals, and a person who concerns himself with the one will be bound to neglect the other.

14. You are foolish if you want your children and your wife and your friends to live forever, since you are wanting things to be up to you that are not up to you, and things to be yours that are not yours. You are stupid in the same way if you want your slave boy to be faultless, since you are wanting badness not to be badness but something else. But wanting not to fail to get what you desire—*this* you are capable of. A person's master is someone who has power over what he wants or does not want, either to obtain it or take it away. Whoever wants to be free, therefore, let him not want or avoid anything that is up to others. Otherwise he will necessarily be a slave.

17. Remember that you are an actor in a play, which is as the playwright wants it to be: short if he wants it short, long if he wants it long. If he wants you to play a beggar, play even this part skillfully, or a cripple, or a public official, or a private citizen. What is yours is to play the assigned part well. But to choose it belongs to someone else.

27. Just as a target is not set up to be missed, in the same way nothing bad by nature happens in the world.

31. The most important aspect of piety toward the gods is certainly both to have correct beliefs about them, as beings that arrange the universe well and justly, and to set yourself to obey them and acquiesce in everything that happens and to follow it willingly, as something brought to completion by the best judgment. For in this way you will never blame the gods or accuse them of neglecting you. And this piety is impossible unless you detach the good and the bad from what is not up to us and attach it exclusively to what is up to us, because if you think that any of what is not up to us is good or bad, then when you fail to get what you want and fall into what you do not want, you will be bound to blame and hate those who cause this. For every animal by nature flees and turns away from things that are harmful and from what causes them, and pursues and admires things that are beneficial and what causes them. There is therefore no way for a person who thinks he is being harmed to enjoy what he thinks is harming him, just as it is impossible to enjoy the harm itself. Hence a son even abuses his father when the father does not give him a share of things that he thinks are good; and thinking that being a tyrant was a good thing is what made enemies of Polyneices and Eteocles.[105] This is why the farmer too abuses the gods, and the sailor, and the merchant, and those who have lost their wives and children.

For wherever someone's advantage lies, there he also shows piety. So whoever takes care to have desires and aversions as one should also in the same instance takes care about being pious. And it is always appropriate to make libations and sacrifices and give firstfruits according to the custom of one's forefathers, in a manner that is pure and neither slovenly nor careless, nor indeed cheaply nor beyond one's means.

41. It shows lack of natural talent to spend time on what concerns the body, as in exercising a great deal, eating a great deal, drinking a great deal, moving one's bowels or copulating a great deal. Instead you must do these things in passing, but turn your whole attention toward your faculty of judgment.

53. On every occasion you must have these thoughts ready:

> Lead me, Zeus, and you too, Destiny,
> Wherever I am assigned by you;
> I'll follow and not hesitate,
> But even if I do not wish to,
> Because I'm bad, I'll follow anyway.[106]

> Whoever has complied well with necessity
> Is counted wise by us, and understands divine affairs.[107]

> Well, Crito, if it is pleasing to the gods this way, then let it happen this way.[108]

> Anytus and Meletus can kill me, but they can't harm me.[109]

From Epictetus, *The Handbook,* translated by Nicholas P. White (Indianapolis: Hackett, 1983), 11–14, 15, 16, 19, 21, 25, 29.

🙰 **Plotinus** (ca. 204–70 CE), considered the founder of Neoplatonism, was born in Egypt and studied in Alexandria under Ammonius Saccas (ca. 175–242). He later set up a school in Rome, where his writings and lectures were collected and edited by his

---

105. See Sophocles' tragedy *Antigone.*
106. Taken from the Stoic Cleanthes.
107. A fragment of Euripides' work.
108. Plato, *Crito,* 43d.
109. Plato, *Apology,* 30c–d. This text is slightly modified and, together with the piece from *Crito,* is assumed to be by Socrates.

student Porphyry (ca. 233–310) and then published in 300 CE under the title *Enneads*. In the selection given here, Plotinus discusses the nature and source of evil.

PLOTINUS

"The Nature and Source of Evil," in *Enneads*, I.8.1–5

1. Those inquiring whence Evil enters into beings, or rather into a certain order of beings, would be making the best beginning if they established, first of all, what precisely Evil is, what constitutes its Nature. At once we should know whence it comes, where it has its native seat, and where it is present merely as an accident; and there would be no further question as to whether it has Authentic-Existence.

But a difficulty arises. By what faculty in us could we possibly know Evil?

All knowing comes by likeness. The Intellectual-Principle and the Soul, being Ideal-Forms, would know Ideal-Forms and would have a natural tendency towards them; but who could imagine Evil to be an Ideal-Form, seeing that it manifests itself as the very absence of Good?

If the solution is that the one act of knowing covers contraries, and that as Evil is the contrary to Good the one act would grasp Good and Evil together, then to know Evil there must be first a clear perception and understanding of Good, since the nobler existences precede the baser and are Ideal-Forms while the less good hold no such standing, are nearer to Non-Being.

No doubt there is a question in what precise way Good is contrary to Evil—whether it is as First-Principle to last of things or as Ideal-Form to utter Lack (to Non-entity): but this subject we postpone.

2. For the moment let us define the Nature of the Good as far as the immediate purpose demands.

The Good is that on which all else depends, towards which all Existences aspire as to their source and their need, while Itself is without need, sufficient to Itself, aspiring to no other, the measure and Term of all, giving out from itself the Intellectual-Principle and Existence and Soul and Life and all Intellective-Act.

All until The Good is reached is beautiful; The Good is beyond-beautiful, beyond the Highest, holding kingly state in the Intellectual-Cosmos, that sphere constituted by a Principle wholly unlike what is known as Intelligence in us. Our intelligence is nourished on the propositions of logic, is skilled in following discussions, works by reasonings, examines links of demonstration, and comes to know the world of Being also by the steps of logical process, having no prior grasp of Reality but remaining empty, all Intelligence though it be, until it has put itself to school.

The Intellectual-Principle we are discussing is not of such a kind: It possesses all: It is all: It is present to all by Its self-presence: It has all by other means than having, for what It possesses is still Itself, nor does any particular of all within It stand apart; for every such particular is the whole and in all respects all, while yet not confused in the mass but still distinct, apart to the extent that any participant in the Intellectual-Principle participates not in the entire as one thing but in whatsoever lies within its own reach.

The Intellectual-Principle is the first Act of The Good and the first Existence; The Good remains stationary within itself, but the Intellectual-Principle acts in relation to It and, as it were, lives about It.

And the Soul, outside, circles around the Intellectual-Principle, and by gazing upon It, seeing into the depths of It, through It sees God.

Such is the untroubled, the blissful, life of divine beings, and Evil has no place in it; if this were all, there would be no Evil but Good only, the first, the second, and the third Good. "All," thus far, "is with the King of All, unfailing Cause of Good and Beauty and controller of all; and what is Good in the second degree depends upon the Second-Principle and tertiary Good upon the Third."

3. If such be the Nature of Beings and of That which transcends all the realm of Being, Evil cannot have place among Beings or in the Beyond-Being; these are good.

There remains, only, if Evil exist at all, that it be situate in the realm of Non-Being, that it be some form or mode, as it were, of the Non-Being, that it have its seat in something in touch with Non-Being or to a certain degree communicate in Non-Being.

By this Non-Being, of course, we are not to understand something that simply does not exist, but only something of an utterly different order from Authentic-Being: there is no question here of movement or rest with regard to Being; the Non-Being we are thinking of is, rather, an image of Being or perhaps something still further removed than even an image.

Now this (the required faint image of Being) might be the sensible universe with all the properties it possesses, or it might be something of even later derivation, accidental to the realm of sense, or again, it might be the source of the sense-world or something entering into it to complete its character.

Some conception of it would be reached by thinking of measurelessness as opposed to measure, of the unbounded against bound, the unshaped against a principle of shape, the ever-needy against the self-sufficing: think of the ever-undefined, the never at rest, the all-accepting but never sated, utter poverty (Penia); and make all this character not mere accident in it but its equivalent for essential-being, so that, whatsoever fragment of it be taken, that part is all lawless void, while whatever participates in it and resembles it becomes evil, though not of course to the point of being, as itself is, Evil-Absolute.

In what substantial-form (hypostasis) then is all this to be found—not as accident but as the very substance itself?

For if Evil can enter into other things, it must have in a certain sense a prior existence, even though it may not be an essence. As there is Good, the Absolute, as well as Good, the quality, so, together with the derived evil entering into something not itself, there must be the Absolute Evil.

But how? Can there be Unmeasure apart from an unmeasured object?

Yes: precisely as there is Measure apart from anything measured, so there is Unmeasure apart from the unmeasured. If Unmeasure could not exist independently, it must exist either in an unmeasured object or in something measured; but the unmeasured could not need Unmeasure and the measured could not contain it.

There must, then, be some Undetermination-Absolute, some Absolute Formlessness; all the qualities cited as characterizing the Nature of Evil must be summed under an Absolute Evil; and every evil thing outside of this must either contain this Absolute by saturation or have taken the character of evil and become a cause of evil by consecration to this Absolute.

What will this be?

That Kind (Matter) whose place is below all the patterns, forms, shapes, measurements, and limits, that which has no trace of good by any title of its own, but (at best) takes order and grace from some Principle outside itself, a mere image as regards Absolute-Being but the Authentic Essence of Evil—in so far as Evil can have Authentic Being. In such a Kind Reason recognizes the Primal Evil, Evil Absolute.

4. The bodily Kind, in that it partakes of Matter, is an evil thing. What form is in bodies is an untrue form: they are without life: by their own natural disorderly movement they make away with each other; they are hindrances to the Soul in its proper Act; in their ceaseless flux they are always slipping away from Being.

Soul, on the contrary, since not every soul is evil, is not an evil Kind.

What, then, is the evil Soul?

It is, we read, the Soul that has entered into the service of that in which soul-evil is implanted by nature, in whose service the unreasoning phase of the Soul accepts evil—unmeasure, excess, and shortcoming, which bring forth licentiousness, cowardice, and all other flaws of the Soul, all the states, foreign to the true nature, which set up false judgements, so that the Soul comes to name things good or evil not by their true value but by the mere test of like and dislike.

But what is the root of this evil state? how can it be brought under the causing principle indicated?

Firstly, such a Soul is not apart from Matter, is not purely itself. That is to say, it is touched with Unmeasure, it is shut out from the Forming-Idea that orders and brings to measure, and this because it is merged into a body made of Matter.

Then if the Reasoning-Faculty too has taken hurt, the Soul's seeing is baulked by the passions and by the darkening that Matter brings to it, by its decline into Matter, by its very attention no longer to Essence but to Process—whose principle or source is, again, Matter, the Kind so evil as to saturate with its own pravity even that which is not in it but merely looks towards it.

For, wholly without part in Good, the negation of Good, unmingled Lack, this Matter-Kind makes over to its own likeness whatsoever comes in touch with it.

The Soul wrought to perfection, addressed towards the Intellectual-Principle is steadfastly pure: it has turned away from Matter; all that is undetermined, that is outside of measure, that is evil, it neither sees nor draws near; it endures in its purity, only, and wholly, determined by the Intellectual-Principle.

The Soul that breaks away from this source of its reality, in so far as it is not perfect or primal, is, as it were, a secondary, an image, to the loyal Soul. By its falling-away—and to the extent of the fall—it is stripped of Determination, becomes wholly indeterminate, sees darkness. Looking to what repels vision, as we look when we are said to see darkness, it has taken Matter into itself.

5. But, it will be objected, if this seeing and frequenting of the darkness is due to the lack of good, the Soul's evil has its source in that very lack; the darkness will be merely a secondary cause—and at once the Principle of Evil is removed from Matter, is made anterior to Matter.

No: Evil is not in any and every lack; it is in absolute lack.

What falls in some degree short of the Good is not Evil; considered in its own kind it might even be perfect, but where there is utter dearth, there we have Essential Evil, void of all share in Good; this is the meaning of Matter.

Matter has not even existence whereby to have some part in Good: Being is attributed to it by an accident of words: the truth would be that it has Non-Being.

Mere lack brings merely Not-Goodness: Evil demands the absolute lack—though, of course, any very considerable shortcoming makes the ultimate fall possible and is already, in itself, an evil.

In fine, we are not to think of Evil as some particular bad thing—injustice, for example, or any other ugly trait—but as a principle distinct from any of the particular forms in which, by the addition of certain elements, it becomes manifest. Thus there may be wickedness in the Soul; the forms this general wickedness is to take will be determined by the environing Matter, by the faculties of the Soul that operate, and by the nature of their operation, whether seeing, acting, or merely admitting impression.

But supposing things external to the Soul are to be counted Evil—sickness, poverty, and so forth—how can they be referred to the principle we have described?

Well, sickness is excess or defect in the body, which as a material organism rebels against order and measure; ugliness is but matter not mastered by Ideal-Form; poverty consists in our need and lack of goods made necessary to us by our association with Matter, whose very nature is to be one long want.

If all this be true, we cannot be, ourselves, the source of Evil, we are not evil in ourselves; Evil was before we came to be; the Evil which holds men down binds them against their will; and for those that have the strength—not found in all men, it is true—there is a deliverance from the evils that have found lodgement in the Soul.

The gods of heaven (the star-souls) have Matter, but are free from Evil, free from the vice in men. Not all men are vicious; some overcome vice, some, the better sort, are never attacked by it; and those who master it win by means of that in them which is not material.

From Plotinus, *The Enneads,* translated by Stephen MacKenna, Paul Brunton Philosophic Foundation (Burdett, NY: Larson, 1992), 76–80.

❧

3. OTHER CONTEMPORARY RELIGIONS: PAGANISM AND ORIENTAL CULTS

THE ELEUSINIAN MYSTERIES

🕶 *The Homeric Hymn to Demeter* was composed around the seventh century BCE. Although in antiquity it was commonly attributed to Homer, Alexandrian scholars (third and fourth centuries BCE) denied Homeric authorship. The hymn tells the story of Persephone's abduction by Hades and Demeter's desperate search for her daughter, and thus it served as the etiological hymn of the Eleusinian mysteries.

The Homeric Hymn to Demeter, 33–50, 92–97, 188–211, 239–98, 359–69, 458–89

So long as the goddess gazed on earth and starry
    heaven,
on the sea flowing strong and full of fish,
and on the beams of the sun, she still hoped   35
to see her dear mother and the race of immortal gods.

For so long hope charmed her strong mind despite her
    distress.
The mountain peaks and the depths of the sea echoed
in response to her divine voice, and her goddess mother
    heard.
Sharp grief seized her heart, and she tore the veil   40
on her ambrosial hair with her own hands.
She cast a dark cloak on her shoulders
and sped like a bird over dry land and sea,
searching. No one was willing to tell her the truth,
not one of the gods or mortals;   45
no bird of omen came to her as truthful messenger.
Then for nine days divine Deo[110] roamed over the earth,
holding torches ablaze in her hands;

---

110. Deo is another name for Demeter. (The notes for this selection are by Gerhart and Udoh.)

in her grief she did not once taste ambrosia
or nectar sweet-to-drink, nor bathed her skin.   50

Withdrawing from the assembly of the gods and high
    Olympus,
she went among the cities and fertile fields of men,
disguising her beauty for a long time. No one of men
nor deep-girt women recognized her when they
    looked,   95
until she came to the house of skillful Keleos,
the man then ruler of fragrant Eleusis.

But the goddess stepped on the threshold. Her head
reached the roof and she filled the doorway with
    divine light.
Reverence, awe, and pale fear seized Metaneira.   190
She gave up her chair and bade the goddess sit down.
But Demeter, bringer of seasons and giver of rich gifts,
did not wish to be seated on the shining seat.
She waited resistant, her lovely eyes cast down,
until knowing Iambe set out a well-built stool   195
for her and cast over it a silvery fleece.
Seated there, the goddess drew the veil before her face.
For a long time she sat voiceless with grief on the stool
and responded to no one with word or gesture.
Unsmiling, tasting neither food nor drink,   200
she sat wasting with desire for her deep-girt daughter,
until knowing Iambe jested with her and
mocking with many a joke moved the holy goddess
to smile and laugh and keep a gracious heart—
Iambe, who later pleased her moods as well.   205
Metaneira offered a cup filled with honey-sweet wine,
but Demeter refused it. It was not right, she said,
for her to drink red wine; then she bid them mix barley
and water with soft mint and give her to drink.
Metaneira made and gave the drink to the goddess as
    she bid.   210
Almighty Deo received it for the sake of the rite.

At night, she[111] would bury him[112] like a brand in the fire's
    might,
unknown to his own parents. And great was their
    wonder
as he grew miraculously fast; he was like the gods.   240
She would have made him ageless and immortal,
if well-girt Metaneira had not in her folly
kept watch at night from her fragrant chamber

and spied. But she shrieked and struck both thighs   245
in fear for her child, much misled in her mind,
and in her grief she spoke winged words.
"Demophoön, my child, the stranger buries you
deep in the fire, causing me woe and bitter cares."
Thus she spoke lamenting. The great goddess
    heard her.   250
In anger at her, bright-crowned Demeter snatched
from the flames with immortal hands the dear child
Metaneira had borne beyond hope in the halls and,
raging terribly at heart, cast him away from herself
    to the ground.
At the same time she addressed well-girt Metaneira: 255
"Mortals are ignorant and foolish, unable to foresee
destiny, the good and the bad coming on them.
You are incurably misled by your folly.
Let the god's oath, the implacable water of Styx, be
    witness,
I would have made your child immortal and ageless   260
forever; I would have given him unfailing honor.
But now he cannot escape death and the death spirits.
Yet unfailing honor will forever be his, because
he lay on my knees and slept in my arms.
In due time as the years come round for him,   265
the sons of Eleusis will continue year after year
to wage war and dread combat against each other.
For I am honored Demeter, the greatest
source of help and joy to mortals and immortals.
But now let all the people build me a great temple   270
with an altar beneath, under the sheer wall
of the city on the rising hill above Kallichoron.
I myself will lay down the rites so that hereafter
performing due rites you may propitiate my spirit."
Thus speaking, the goddess changed her size and
    appearance,   275
thrusting off old age. Beauty breathed about her and
from her sweet robes a delicious fragrance spread;
a light beamed far out from the goddess's immortal skin,
and her golden hair flowed over her shoulders.
The well-built house flooded with radiance like
    lightning.   280
She left the halls. At once Metaneira's knees buckled.

---

111. Demeter.

112. Demophoön, the son of Keleos and Metaneira, whom Metaneira gave
to Demeter to raise.

For a long time she remained voiceless, forgetting
to pick up her dear only son from the floor.
But his sisters heard his pitiful voice and
leapt from their well-spread beds. Then one took   285
the child in her arms and laid him to her breast.
Another lit the fire; a third rushed on delicate feet
to rouse her mother from her fragrant chamber.
Gathering about the gasping child, they bathed and
embraced him lovingly. Yet his heart was not
    comforted,   290
for lesser nurses and handmaids held him now.
All night they tried to appease the dread goddess,
shaking with fear. But when dawn appeared,
they explained to wide-ruling Keleos exactly
what the bright-crowned goddess Demeter
    commanded.   295
Then he called to assembly his innumerable people
and bid them build for fair-tressed Demeter
a rich temple and an altar on the rising hill.

At once he[113] urged thoughtful Persephone:
"Go, Persephone, to the side of your dark-robed
    mother,   360
keeping the spirit and temper in your breast benign.
Do not be so sad and angry beyond the rest;
in no way among immortals will I be an unsuitable
    spouse,
myself a brother of father Zeus. And when you are
    there,
you will have power over all that lives and moves,   365
and you will possess the greatest honors among the gods.
There will be punishment forevermore for those
    wrongdoers
who fail to appease your power with sacrifices,
performing proper rites and making due offerings."

Mother and daughter were glad to see each other
and rejoiced at heart. Rheia of the delicate veil then said:
"Come, child, Zeus, heavy-thundering and
    mighty-voiced,   460
summons you to rejoin the tribes of the gods;
he has offered to give what honors you choose among
    them.
He agreed that his daughter would spend one-third
of the revolving year in the misty dark, and two-thirds
with her mother and the other immortals.   465
He guaranteed it would be so with a nod of his head.

So come, my child, obey me; do not rage overmuch
and forever at the dark-clouded son of Kronos.
Now make the grain grow fertile for humankind."
So Rheia spoke, and rich-crowned Demeter did not
    disobey.   470
At once she sent forth fruit from the fertile fields
and the whole wide earth burgeoned with leaves
and flowers. She went to the kings who administer law,
Triptolemos and Diokles, driver of horses, mighty
Eumolpos and Keleos, leader of the people, and
    revealed   475
the conduct of her rites and taught her Mysteries to
    all of them,
holy rites that are not to be transgressed, nor pried into,
nor divulged. For a great awe of the gods stops the voice.
Blessed is the mortal on earth who has seen these rites,
but the uninitiate who has no share in them never   480
has the same lot once dead in the dreary darkness.
When the great goddess had founded all her rites,
the goddesses left for Olympus and the assembly of the
    other gods.
There they dwell by Zeus delighting-in-thunder,
    inspiring
awe and reverence. Highly blessed is the mortal   485
on earth whom they graciously favor with love.
For soon they will send to the hearth of his great house
Ploutos, the god giving abundance to mortals.

From Helen P. Foley, ed. and trans., *The Homeric Hymn to Demeter* (Princeton: Princeton University Press, 1994), 4, 6, 12, 14, 16, 20, 24, 26.

☙ The following statement by **Clement of Alexandria** (ca. 150–215 CE) in his *Exhortation to the Greeks* (ca. 190) is a rare report of the "sign" of the Eleusinian mysteries and is a possible description of the initiation rite, both of which were well-guarded secrets.

CLEMENT OF ALEXANDRIA
Exhortation to the Greeks, 2.21.2

This is the sign [*synthēma*] of the Eleusian mysteries:

> I fasted;
> I drank the mixed potion [*kykeōn*];

---

113. Aidoneus, Hades, "lord of the dead."

I took from the chest;

Having performed,

I put it into the basket

and then out of the basket into the chest.

Translated by Fabian E. Udoh. For a critical Greek text, see *Clement of Alexandria*, edited by G. W. Butterworth, Loeb Classical Library (New York: G. P. Putman's Sons, 1919), 42.

The Cult of Isis

❧ *Metamorphoses* (written ca. 170), by **Apuleius** (ca. 123–80 CE), is a romance novel that includes stories about Cupid and Psyche and is the only Latin novel that survives in its entirety. The last portion of the book, referred to as "The Isis Book," describes the initiation of the hero (Lucius) into the mysteries of Isis and Osiris. It is the most informative surviving account of initiation into a Greco-Roman mystery cult and testifies to a profound personal religious faith.

APULEIUS
Metamorphoses, XI.1–6, 23–25

XI

1. [. . .] Then with a tear-stained face I prayed to the all-powerful goddess thus:

2. "O Queen of Heaven—whether thou art Ceres, the primal and bountiful mother of crops, who, glad in the return of her daughter, removed the brutish acorn provender of old, and showed to men gentler nourishment, after which thou now honourest the soil of Eleusis; or whether thou art heavenly Venus, who didst unite the difference of the sexes in the first beginnings of nature by creating Love, and after bringing forth mankind with its unceasing offspring, art worshipped in the island shrine of Paphos; or the sister of Phoebus, who didst relieve the delivery of young ones by soothing remedies, thus rearing such teeming masses, and art now adored in the celebrated temples of Ephesus; or whether as Proserpine, dreaded in cries that pierce the night, repelling attacks of ghosts with thy threefold countenance, and keeping barred the bolts of the earth, wandering the while in groves here and there, thou art propitiated with differing rites—whoever thou art, illumining all city walls with that womanly light, nourishing with bright fires the joyous seeds, and bestowing uncertain illumination only during digressions from thy path, by whatever name or ceremony or visage it is

right to address thee, help me now in the depth of my trouble, strengthen my crushed fortune, grant respite and peace after the endurance of dire ills; regard this as enough of toil, enough of danger. Remove the cruel four-footed form, restore me to the sight of my loved ones, restore me to my own self as Lucius. And if some deity is angered so as to pursue me with implacable cruelty, at least allow me to die, if I am not allowed really to live."

3. When I had thus poured out my prayers, adding pitiable wailings, sleep again spread over my wilting spirit and overpowered me on that same sandy bed. I had scarcely settled down when lo! from the middle of the sea a face divine arose, showing above the waves a countenance which even gods must admire; and then gradually the radiant image of the whole body, when the brine had been shaken off, seemed to stand before me. I will try to communicate to you her wonderful appearance if the poverty of human speech affords me the means of description or if the deity herself lends me her rich store of rhetorical eloquence.

First, her abundant, long hair, gently curled over her divine neck or loosely spread, streamed down softly. A crown of many designs with all kinds of flowers had girt her lofty head; in its centre a flat disk above the forehead shone with a clear light in the manner of a mirror or indeed like the moon, while on its right and left it was embraced by coils of uprising snakes; from above it was adorned also with outstretched ears of corn. Her tunic too was of many colours, woven entirely of fine linen, now bright with a white gleam, now yellow with saffron hue, now fiery with roseate ruddiness. But what most of all overwhelmed my sight further was the cloak of deepest black, resplendent with dark sheen; it went round about her, returning under the right side to the left shoulder, a part of the garment being dropped in the manner of a knot; and hanging down with many folds, the whole robe undulated gracefully with tasselled fringes to its lowest edges.

4. Along the embroidered border and in the very body of the material there gleamed stars here and there, and in their midst a half-moon breathed a flame of fire. But wherever the sweep of that magnificent mantle moved, a wreath garlanded of all manner of flowers and fruits was indivisibly joined to it. The things she carried were of quite varied kind. For in her right hand she bore a bronze rattle in which a few rods in the middle, thrust across a thin sheet of metal that was curved like a belt, emitted a tinkling sound when the arm made three quivering jolts. From the left hand then there hung a golden vessel on whose handle, where it was

conspicuous, there rose a serpent which reared its head high and puffed its neck thickly. Her ambrosian feet were covered by sandals woven with leaves of victorious palm. Such was the great goddess who, breathing the blessed fragrance of Arabia, deigned to address me with divine voice.

5. "Lo, I am with you, Lucius, moved by your prayers, I who am the mother of the universe, the mistress of all the elements, the first offspring of time, the highest of deities, the queen of the dead, foremost of heavenly beings, the single form that fuses all gods and goddesses; I who order by my will the starry heights of heaven, the health-giving breezes of the sea, and the awful silences of those in the underworld: my single godhead is adored by the whole world in varied forms, in differing rites and with many diverse names.

"Thus the Phrygians, earliest of races, call me Pessinuntia, Mother of the Gods; thus the Athenians, sprung from their own soil, call me Cecropeian Minerva; and the sea-tossed Cyprians call me Paphian Venus, the archer Cretans Diana Dictynna, and the trilingual Sicilians Ortygian Proserpine; to the Eleusinians I am Ceres, the ancient goddess, to others Juno, to others Bellona and Hecate and Rhamnusia. But the Ethiopians, who are illumined by the first rays of the sun-god as he is born every day, together with the Africans and the Egyptians who excel through having the original doctrine, honour me with my distinctive rites and give me my true name of Queen Isis.

"I am here taking pity on your ills; I am here to give aid and solace. Cease then from tears and wailings, set aside your sadness; there is now dawning for you, through my providence, the day of salvation. For this reason pay careful heed to these commands of mine. The day which will follow the coming night has been dedicated to me by eternal religious sanction. Then, when the storms of winter have been calmed, and the wild waves of the sea have been stilled, my priests are wont to vow a new barque to the now navigable sea and offer it as first-fruits of a new year's navigation. You should await that sacred rite with a mind neither anxious nor profane.

6. "For at my suggestion a priest in the very midst of the moving procession will carry a crown of roses attached to the sistrum in his right hand. Without delay, therefore, push through the crowds and eagerly join the procession, relying on my favour; then get close to the priest and gently, as if you meant to kiss his hand, pluck off the roses with your mouth and forthwith cast off the hide of that vile beast that has long since been hateful to me. Nor need you fear any of my instructions as being difficult. For at this very moment when I

come to you, I am there also with my priest, instructing him in his sleep as to what he must do next. At my command the dense crowds of people will make way for you, nor will anyone amid the joyous rites and festive revelries shudder at that ungainly guise you bear, or explain amiss your sudden change of form and attack you spitefully for it. But especially remember, and ever hold enshrined deep in your heart, that the remaining course of your life, even to the limit of your last breath, is dedicated to me. Nor is it wrong that you should devote to her, by whose favour you shall return to men, the rest of your life. You shall live indeed a happy man, you shall live full of glory in my protection, and when you have completed the span of your lifetime, you will pass down to the nether world, but there also, in the very midst of the subterranean hemisphere, you shall often worship me, whom you now see, as one who favours you, shining in the darkness of Acheron and ruling in the Stygian depths, when you the while shall dwell in the Elysian fields. But if with diligent service, religious tendance and constant chastity you will be worthy of my godhead, know that I alone have power to prolong your life also beyond the span determined by your destiny."

23. [. . .] Since the occasion, as the priest said, now demanded it, he led me with an escort of the faithful to the baths at hand and first submitted me to the customary ablution. Then he prayed for the forgiveness of the gods and besprinkling me cleansed me most purely. When he had taken me back again to the temple, two thirds of the day having now passed, he set me before the feet of the goddess herself and gave me certain secret instructions too holy to be uttered. One command, however, he announced clearly for all present to hear, that for the ten following days I should curb my desire for food, abstaining from all animal flesh and from wine. After I had kept these rules with reverent restrain, now came the destined day of the divine pledge. The veering sun was bringing on the evening, when lo! from all sides surged out crowds of devotees paying tribute to me after the ancient rite with their several different gifts. Next, when all the uninitiated had been far removed, I was dressed in a hitherto unworn linen garment and the priest, taking my hand, led me to the very heart of the holy shrine.

You would perchance enquire quite eagerly, attentive reader, what was then said and done. I would tell you, if it were lawful; you would get to know all, were it lawful for you to hear. But both ear and tongue would incur equal guilt through such daring curiosity. Yet you are perchance racked by religious longing, so I shall not torture you with prolonged anguish. Listen then, but believe, for my account is true. I approached the boundary of death and treading on Proserpine's threshold, I was carried through all the elements, after which I returned. At dead of night I saw the sun flashing with bright effulgence. I approached close to the gods above and the gods below and worshipped them face to face. Behold, I have related things about which you must remain in ignorance, though you have heard them.

Therefore I shall recount only what can be communicated without guilt to the understanding of the uninitiated.

24. By morning all was over and the rites being completed I went forth after receiving the initiate's twelve robes, a mode that was indeed most exalted, but no restraint prevented my speaking of it since from that moment many bystanders saw me. For at the priest's behest I ascended a wooden dais set in the very heart of the sanctuary before the statue of the goddess, and I attracted attention by reason of my tunic; it was only of linen, but bore sumptuous decorations. Further, from my shoulders, behind my back down to my heels, there hung a precious cloak. Wherever you looked, I was adorned by beasts embroidered round about my garments in varied colours. Here were Indian dragons, there were griffons from the far north, animals created in the form of a winged bird by a world other than ours. The initiates call this the Olympian robe. But in my right hand I carried a torch with rearing flames and my head was garlanded gracefully by a crown of gleaming palm whose leaves stood out like rays. When I had thus been adorned like the sun and set up in the manner of a divine statue, suddenly the curtains were drawn and the people crowded to behold me. Then I celebrated the most happy birthday of my initiation, and there were welcome feasts and merry banquets.

The third day was celebrated with an equal show of rites; there was a sacred meal and my initiation was duly consummated. Having tarried there for a few days longer, I enjoyed the ineffable pleasure of the image of the goddess, to whom I was now pledged by a favour that could not be repaid.

But at length, instructed by the goddess, when I had rendered humble thanks, admittedly not in full, but according to my lowly ability, I prepared my journey home, though tardily in all conscience, for the bonds of my fervent longing had scarcely yet been broken. I laid myself down at last in obeisance before the goddess and for a long time wiped her feet with my face. Then with welling tears, breaking my speech with frequent sobs and swallowing my words, I addressed her thus:

25. "Thou in truth art the holy and eternal saviour of the human race, ever beneficent in helping mortal men, and thou bringest the sweet love of a mother to the trials of the unfortunate. No day nor any restful night, nor even the slightest moment passes by untouched by thy blessings, but ever on sea and land thou art guarding men, and when thou hast stilled the storms of life thou dost stretch out thy saving hand, with which thou unravelest even those threads of fate which are inextricably woven together; thou dost pacify the gales of Fortune and keep in check the baleful movements of the stars. Thee do the gods above honour, and thou art worshipped by those below; thou dost revolve the sphere of heaven, and illumine the sun, thou dost guide the earth, and trample Hell under thy feet. For thee the constellations move, for thee the seasons return; the divine beings rejoice for thee, and the elements are thy slaves. By thy command breezes blow and rain-clouds nourish, seeds sprout and buds grow. Awe of thy majesty imbues the birds that move in the sky, the wild beasts that roam the mountains, the serpents that glide in the earth, and the monsters that swim in the sea. But I am bereft of talent in singing thy praises, and have scarce means to offer thee fit sacrifices. Nor have I the rich power of speech to express what I feel about thy majesty; indeed a thousand mouths and tongues are not enough for the task, nor an everlasting sequence of tireless talk. Therefore I shall try to do the only thing possible for one who is devoted but indigent; I shall keep for ever, stored in my inmost heart, the memory of thy divine countenance and most holy godhead."

When I had prayed thus humbly to the supreme deity, I embraced Mithras the priest, who was now as my father, and clinging to his neck with many kisses I begged him to pardon me because I was unable to recompense him justly for so great favours.

From Apuleius of Madauros, *The Isis-Book (Metamorphoses, Book XI)*, edited and translated by J. Gwyn Griffiths (Leiden: Brill, 1975), 71, 73, 75, 77, 99, 101, 103.

THE MYSTERIES OF MITHRAS

☙ Although inscriptions and reliefs have been discovered in various Mithraic places of worship (called Mithraeums), two of the very few literary sources on the cult of Mithras (Mithra) are *De antro nympharum* and *De abstinentia* by **Porphyry** (ca. 233–310 CE).

De antro nympharum, 5–6, 15–16, 18, 20, 24

5. Our ancestors appear to have adorned and consecrated grottos and caves. . . . 6. so the Persians also initiate the novice into the mysteries by an allegorical descent of the souls to the lower world and a return, and they use the name cave. In the first instance, according to the report of Eubulus, Zoroaster consecrated a natural cave in the adjacent mountains of Persis, carpeted with grass and with fresh springs, to the honour of Mithra creator and father of all, in imitation of the world-cave which Mithra fashioned, and of the natural elements and regions which bore within at regular intervals symbolic representations. And after Zoroaster the custom was observed amongst others also of celebrating their rites in grottos and caves either natural or artificial.

15. The votaries use honey for many and diverse symbolic purposes, because of its variety of properties, since it possesses both purgative and preserving virtue. For by honey many things are preserved from corruption and wounds of long standing are cleansed. It is also sweet to the taste and is gathered from flowers by bees which are regarded as born of cattle. When therefore into the hands of those initiated into the lion grade honey is poured for washing instead of water, they are charged to keep their hands clean from all wrong and injury and defilement; the offering of actual water to the initiate is avoided as being hostile to the fire with its purifying qualities. The tongue also is purified from all sin by honey.

16. And when honey is offered to the Persian[114] as the guardian of the fruits, its preservative virtue is symbolically expressed.

18. The bowls symbolize the springs, as in the ritual of Mithra the bowl is set for the spring. . . . Our ancestors used to call the priestesses of Demeter, as being an earth goddess, mystic bees, and the maiden herself honied; to the moon also as presiding over birth they gave the name of bee, especially since the moon is a bull and the moon culminates in the Bull, and bees are bull-begotten. And souls when they come to birth are bull-begotten, and the god who secretly promotes birth is a stealer of bulls.

20. Our earliest ancestors therefore, before temples were invented, used to consecrate to the gods recesses and caves in Crete to the Zeus of the Curetes, in Arcadia to Selene and the Lycaean Pan, and in Naxos to Dionysus. And wherever Mithra is known, the sanctuary where he is worshipped is a cave.

24. He (i.e. Homer) has not described the entrances therefore by east or west or by the equinoxes, i.e. by the ram and the scales, but by north and south (gates opening to the south being most exposed to wet, those to the north to cold), because the cave is sacred to souls and the water-nymphs, and the regions of birth and death appertain to souls. Mithra's own seat however is determined by the equinoxes. He bears therefore the sword of the ram, the Aries of the zodiac, and rides on Aphrodite's bull, since the bull is generator and he (Mithra) is lord of creation. Moreover according to the equinoctial cycle he is represented with the north on his right and the south on his left, his southern hemisphere being so assigned because of its warmth, his northern because of the cold of the wind. And to souls that come to the birth and depart from life it was natural to assign winds, because they also bring with them breath, as some have supposed, and are of similar nature. But the north is appropriate to those that come to the birth.

From A. S. Geden, ed. and trans., *Mithraic Sources in English* (Hastings, East Sussex, UK: Chthonios Books, 1990), 47–49.

De abstinentia, II.56, IV.16

II.56. Pallas[115] declares that under the emperor Hadrian human sacrifices were almost entirely abolished; and he is the best exponent of the mysteries of Mithra.

IV.16. Among the Persians those who are learned in the doctrines of the gods and minister in their service bear the name of magi. For this is the meaning of magian in their native tongue. And this class has been regarded among the Persians as so great and honourable that Darius Hystaspes had inscribed upon his tomb in addition to his other titles that he had been a teacher of Magian lore. The magi were divided into three grades, according to the assertion of Eubulus who wrote the history of Mithraism in many books. Of these the highest and most learned neither kill nor eat any living thing, but practise the long-established abstinence from animal food. The second use such food, but do not kill any tame beasts. And following their example not even the third permit themselves the use of all. For in all the highest grades the doctrine of metempsychosis is held, which also is apparently signified in the mysteries of Mithra; for these through the living creatures reveal to us symbolically our community of nature with them. So the mystics who take

---

114. "The Persian" is the fifth grade of Mithraic initiation.

115. Pallas is otherwise unknown.

part in the actual rites are called lions, the women hyaenas, the servants crows, and of the fathers . . . for these bear the names of eagles and hawks. He who is invested with the character of the lion adopts various forms of living creatures, the reason of which is said by Pallas in his work on Mithra to be the belief in their common life-history, which extends over the course of the zodiacal cycle; and a true and precise conception of human souls is set forth in symbol, for these they say pass through various bodies.

From A. S. Geden, ed. and trans., *Mithraic Sources in English* (Hastings, East Sussex, UK: Chthonios Books, 1990), 49–50.

CHAPTER 3

Early Forms of Christianity

If one were to accept the fourth-century Church historian Eusebius's view of Christian history, orthodox Christian tradition would have no history at all. Tradition, by definition, is stable and invariable through time, whereas history speaks of movement and change. According to this view, the Christian faith is, to use Vincent of Lérins's (d. ca. 450) well-known definition, "what is believed everywhere, at all times, and by everyone" (*quod ubique, quod semper, quod ab omnibus creditum est*). It was taught once and for all, and is believed eternally. According to Eusebius, heresy has a history because its various versions were introduced as innovations by particular founders and teachers. Eusebius's view, however, cannot be sustained, for, in fact, Christianity is several movements that are linked to specific times and to specific places in human history. From its beginnings it has existed as a variety of teachings. The crystallization of those teachings into an orthodox Tradition is itself part of a historical process of growth, change, continuity, and diversity. The discernible unity within this Tradition—by virtue of which there is a "Christian faith"—continues to exist in the context of a variety of traditions of theological conceptions, practices of worship, and community organizations.

In the first few centuries of Christian history, all around the Mediterranean world within the limits of the Roman Empire, and even more so beyond the limits of the empire, Christian orthodoxy was generally a late phenomenon. Everywhere, forms of early Christianity existed which varied significantly from, and often were at odds with, that form which later was to define itself as normative. The emergence of that normative self-definition, however one may account for it, was without doubt mediated by a series of religious

and cultural conditions (language, history, and community), of which polemics and syncretism were essential elements.

The first few centuries of the history of Christianity were crucial in shaping the subsequent development of the Christian faith. From the beginning of the second to the end of the sixth century (100–600) Christianity defined the language of its theological discourse, formulated its basic ideas about God, the person of Christ, the world, and the human condition, and established its patterns of worship and the structures of its communal organization. Therefore, all those who share the Christian faith and all who are interested in it either as a religion or as a historical phenomenon must pay particular attention to this vital period of its history.

The texts in this section present some of the moments in this crucial period, from the early post–New Testament era to the Council of Chalcedon, in 451. History is usually dictated by the victors, and this applies also to the history of Christianity. The result is that the views of the losing parties often have survived only in fragmentary citations in the works of those who opposed them, their original works having been destroyed. Where the original works exist, they must be preferred to the representations by antagonists, if grave distortions are to be avoided. It must be noted also that in the controversies of the first centuries of Christian history there was no way of determining in advance who the heroes and the vanquished villains, the "orthodox" and the "heretics," were to be. All the parties agreed with the assumption that there was one faith, one true doctrine, and each party claimed to possess it. Therefore, what the opposition taught was not a different form of the same doctrine but a false doctrine.

Jesus was a Jew. The earliest Christians, including Paul,

were Jews, and the earliest Christian traditions arose from and in conflict with Jewish traditions. Hence, the writings which now constitute the canonical Gospels were the products of Jewish Christianity. Conflicts about the continuing validity of Jewish traditions and the distinctiveness of the Christian faith, fueled by the gradual preponderance of non-Jews in the Christian movement, led to the cleavage between Christianity and the mother religion. There continued to exist, however, even after the destruction of Jerusalem in 70 CE, Jewish-Christian communities. These Christians continued to combine their practice of the Law, given to Moses by God, and their faith in Jesus the Christ. Such harmony between the Law and faith in Christ, and Jewish-Christian interpretations of the person of Jesus, were later judged heretical by other Christians, and the Jewish-Christian communities eventually disappeared. The two Gospels that are attributed to these communities exist only as fragments cited by early Christian writers. The first is the Gospel of the Ebionites. The name "Ebionites," that is, "the Poor," is derived apparently from Galatians 2:10 (see also Rom 15:26), which says that Paul collected money from the Gentile Churches that he founded for the sake of "the poor" in the Church in Jerusalem. The second is the Gospel of the Nazarenes (also called the Gospel according to the Hebrews). Early Christian writers thought this Gospel was the original Aramaic or Hebrew version of the Gospel according to Matthew.

The literary genre of religious apologetics (Latin *apologia*, "defense") emerged in the Greco-Roman world as the attempt to defend a religion against its opponents, real or perceived. Essentially, apologetics was the effort by religions to create and maintain boundaries. It was at the same time a self-defense and a self-definition, by rejection and appropriation. Christianity defended and defined itself against two competitors: Judaism and Greco-Roman religious and intellectual culture. With respect to the latter, some Christian writers such as Clement of Alexandria (see chapter 1) assumed that there was a natural theology, that is, the possibility of the knowledge (or at least an awareness) of God prior to the revelation of God through the Bible, in Jesus Christ, and through the Church. Christians could, therefore, adopt and build on the insights of non-Christians. Other Christian authors, like Tertullian, stressed the radical difference of the Christian revelation and rejected all three categories of Roman natural theology: philosophy, mythology, and civic practice (see the introduction to chapter 2). With regard to Judaism, early Christian apologists entered into a love-hate relationship with the older religion. Their principal concern

was to demonstrate the continuity between the Christian faith and the history of God's self-revelation in the Old Testament. And yet they needed to show in what ways the new religion was not only different from but also had replaced Judaism as the legitimate heir of that self-revelation. And thus, against the extreme views that emphasized the radical distinctiveness of Jesus and the Christian gospel, most early Christian apologists sought above all to show that the Christian faith was the legitimate continuation of the ancient Jewish religious traditions and consonant with what was best in Greek thought.

The letter was an important literary form during this period and was appropriated as a vehicle for Christian apologetics. Given that Christian apologetic literature was an attempt by a minority group to come to terms with the larger culture in which it lived, however, it is very doubtful that Christian apologetic material was read outside the Church, even by their purported addressees. Its significance lay in Christian self-definition and intra-Church polemics. Hence, in general, the most astute and eloquent Christian apologist was also the most prolific writer. And every major writer of the first five centuries of Christian history was also an apologist, carrying out the work of defense and of positive exposition at the same time.

The purpose of *The Epistle to Diognetus*, as the unknown author sets it out in the first paragraph, is to expose the follies of paganism and the "superstition" of Judaism and to expound "the religion of the Christians," who constitute "a new race" and "resident aliens" in the world.

Justin Martyr was a convert to the Christian faith. He says of himself that he pursued his search for the Truth by studying the philosophies of the schools of the Stoics, Peripatetics, Pythagoreans, and finally the Platonists. It was while he was contemplating God through Platonic philosophy that he came (in about 130) to know the "only sure and useful philosophy," that is, the Christian religion. He later opened a philosophical school in Rome. Justin's *First Apology* is not only a defense of Christianity against explicit accusations but also a positive statement of his Logos theology.

To Scapula was possibly Tertullian's last work. It relates in substance to his earlier treatise *Apology*, since the argument is the same in the two works: it is the non-Christians who are guilty of sacrilege and treason. In *To Scapula* Tertullian concentrates on the issue of God's anger at the shedding of Christian blood.

The first hostile contacts between Roman imperial authorities and the Christian movement might have been purely accidental. As Justin's *First Apology* indicates, there were explicit charges against Christians, the popular ones being incest and cannibalism. However, the charges were not the reason for the first persecution of Christians, by Emperor Nero (54–68). Nero blamed and killed the Christians of Rome for the fire that engulfed the city in 64. The persecution by Nero created a precedent by which Christians could be executed by Roman magistrates for being Christians. Matters were different under Emperor Domitian (81–96), who declared himself "Master and God" and made the oath "by the genius of the emperor" an official and compulsory act. Domitian thus created a situation in which those who (like Jews and Christians) refused to comply with the demands of the imperial cult were accused of atheism and treason. In 112 Pliny the Younger (governor of Bithynia in Asia Minor) wrote to Emperor Trajan (98–117) asking for guidance because he was puzzled about the nature of the crime with which Christians could be charged: was the name "Christian" sufficient to merit an execution, even if the accused was not guilty of any of the vices associated with the name? Could circumstances—youth and infirmity, for instance—mitigate the punishment? And could the accused recant by cursing Christ and making the appropriate sacrifices before the statue of the emperor? Pliny had also discovered, by interrogating Christians, that they were virtuous and not dangerous—though they were obstinate in their refusal to participate in the religious traditions of the empire. Trajan did not answer the main questions put by Pliny but asked the governor to pay no attention to anonymous accusations and to pardon anyone who recanted. Subsequent persecutions of Christians were sporadic and locally limited. They were neither continuous nor systematic.

From the Christian point of view, martyrdom was, like apologetics, an aspect of the Christian response to the world. This response was constituted not only by the "acts" of suffering and death recounted, whatever their veracity, but especially by the literary genres in which these acts were narrated. The narratives of the circumstances and actions of the martyrs leading up to their deaths were called Acts. When the accounts included the martyrdom itself, they were called Passions. Thus, whereas *The Acts of the Abitinian Martyrs* (see the section on Donatism below) belongs to the genre of Acts, *The Martyrdom of Saint Polycarp* and *The Martyrdom of Saints Perpetua and Felicitas* are both Acts and Passions. Martyrs were, literally, the primary "witnesses" to Christianity, testifying to its superiority both to the outside world, which persecuted them, and, especially, to the Christian community, which was in this fashion reaffirmed. Martyrdom, and

the Acts and Passions which narrate them, are therefore intimately related to apologetic literature. The martyr bore the fullest possible witness to his or her faith in Christ and received the unalloyed crown of perfection. The Church received maximum confirmation and publicity. In the words of Tertullian (*Apology*, 50.13): "We multiply whenever we are mown down by you; the blood of Christians is seed [*semen est sanguis Christianorum*]."

Polycarp is said to have been one of the last who had been directly in contact with Jesus' apostles. The narrative of his martyrdom, stylized to mirror the Gospels, is designed to show the martyr's imitation of Jesus. *The Martyrdom of Saints Perpetua and Felicitas*, by virtue of the dreams and revelations it contains, is also an Apocalypse and became, for this reason, the archetype for later Acts of Christian martyrs. The visions of Perpetua and Saturus provide insight into the beliefs of the African Christian community, particularly the belief in the power of the Spirit, new prophecies, and new visions. The account, part of which is written as notes from Perpetua's diary, stresses a woman's point of view. On the whole, the youth and vitality of the growing African Church of the late second century is everywhere in evidence here.

The ascetic ideal of living a celibate life without private property was expressed and valued from very early in the history of the Christian movement (see Mk 10:17–31; Mt 19:10–12, 16–30; Lk 18:18–30; Acts 2:44–47; 4:32–37; 1 Cor 7:1–40). Christianity was influenced in this by the ascetic ideal of the Greco-Roman philosopher: *apatheia*. The philosopher achieved freedom from "passions" in the Pythagorean and Platonic schools by disciplining and subjugating the body, so that the soul could escape the body in which it was imprisoned. (The Stoics sought, instead, to accept the will of God and to be content with whatever Nature sent their way.) Moreover, in the Greco-Roman mystery religions, to which early Christianity had close affinities, abstinence from sexual intercourse and from certain foods was required in order that the body be freed for union with the deity.

The monastic life is a manifestation of asceticism, that is, the "practice" or "training" for holiness. The roots of Christian monasticism are found in Jewish monasticism: in the communities of the Essenes and of the Therapeutae and in the Old Testament communities of "the sons of prophets" before them. There seem to have been communities of men and women living celibate lives without private property, as "a more perfect" way of serving God, from early in the history of Christianity. The third and fourth centuries saw the beginning of solitary asceticism, the Anchorites, who lived in the desert of Upper Egypt and confronted the devil there. Antony the Great was one of the first of these solitary ascetics. Pachomius is credited with having written the first Rule for a life in common, thus founding the community of monks who lived a common life in organized communities, the Cenobites (see chapter 5). *The Letters of Saint Antony the Great* and *The Sayings of the Desert Fathers* present us with the experiences, practices, attitudes, and theological insights of the desert ascetics.

As asceticism took center stage in the life of the Church in the fourth century, Christian writers went to great lengths to justify ascetic practices and exhort Christians to undertake them. Christian asceticism had some defining characteristics: withdrawal from "the world"; conflict with the devil in the desert; virginity (and celibacy), with denunciations of marriage as inferior and sometimes as evil; renunciation of wealth and possessions; self-inflicted mortifications (fasting, lack of sleep, lack of bodily comforts in dress and lodging); the desire to imitate the martyrs of times past; and continual prayer—all in the effort to subdue "the body," transcend oneself, and dispose "the soul" for union with God. Jerome's letter to Eustochium lays out at great length the exegetical and theological arguments with which he and other Christian writers constructed their views of Christian asceticism. Since women were often the primary objects of the exhortations by such writers, and were in dialogue with them, it is interesting to see how the women actually responded (and with what consequences) to the call to the life of virginity and renunciation. *The Life of Melania the Younger* is a prime illustration.

Christian writers used the name "gnostic" (one who possesses knowledge) to refer to the Christian, who was said to have earned the knowledge (*gnosis*) revealed in Christ. The term "Gnosticism," referring to a heresy, is to a large extent a creation of modern scholarship. The term groups together various Christian movements which were known by the names of their founders, such as Simon Magnus, Valentinus, Cerdo, Marcion, Basilides, and Cerinthus. Early Gnosticism represented the first attempts by Christians to comprehend the contents of the Christian faith in categories taken from Greek philosophical systems. Gnostic systems taught the cosmic redemption of the spirit through knowledge. They consisted of syncretistic combinations of speculative philosophical thought, mythology, magic, and teachings about Jesus. They were based on a distinctive doctrine about God and God's relation to the world that enabled Gnostic thinkers to account for the problems of creation, fall, and redemption

within the philosophical dualisms of "matter" and "spirit" and of "good" and "evil." Until the discovery in 1945 of the Nag Hammadi library, Gnostic thought was by and large reconstructed from the writings of its opponents, such as Tertullian's treatise *Against Marcion* and Irenaeus's *Against Heresies* (see chapter 1). The Valentinian *Gospel of Truth* is one of the original works of Christian Gnosticism now available to us. The importance of Gnostic thinking in early Christianity is evident from the fact that virtually every early Christian writer undertook to combat it. Considerable affinity exists, however, between some of the Gnostic teachings and the orthodox doctrines of such writers as Justin Martyr, Clement of Alexandria, and Origen.

Manichaeism may be considered a form of Gnosticism. Mani, a Persian by birth, seems to have settled in Babylon in the middle of the third century. Here he received the mission from "the Paraclete" to preach the gospel as an apostle of Christ. The movement that he founded mixed Persian Zoroastrian dualism and Christian elements, including those of the Gnostic thinkers Marcion and Basilides. By the fourth century, when Augustine came in contact with it, Manichaeism had become a major competitor in the West against the emerging orthodox Christianity. The doctrinal roots of Manichaeism are the same as those of other Gnostic systems. Tertullian observed with regard to Marcion (see chapter 1): "For, like many even in our day, heretics in particular, Marcion had an unhealthy interest in the problem of evil—the origin of it—and his perceptions were numbed by the very excess of his curiosity." One must recognize, however, that the problem of evil not only is a Gnostic problem but lies at the very heart of Christianity. "Salvation" is what Christianity offers to believers: "Christ came to save"—and one is saved from an "evil." The concrete reality of the world—snakes, crocodiles, locusts, and sex—raised for Marcion and other Gnostic thinkers the question of evil. The Christian faith assumes that evil *is*. But what is it? How did it come about? More importantly, how is it related to a providential, benevolent, Creator-God? And, therefore, in what consists "salvation"?

Manichaeism proposed two antagonistic principles of light and of darkness and two opposing human wills. "Salvation" is contingent upon the relationship between these principles. Mani's doctrine circulated through his work *Kephalaia of the Teacher*, which now exists only in fragments. Augustine was a Manichaeist for about eleven years (from ca. 373 to 384). After he became a catholic Christian, he contended against the doctrine in numerous writings. His letter to Deuterius (written ca. 395–96) describes Manichaean practices, and in his *Confessions,* Augustine takes a retrospective look at the problem of the will as proposed by Manichaeism. There are not two wills, he concludes, but one "sick" will that causes the conflict whereby one wills without willing. In *The Way of Life of the Manichaeans,* Augustine turns the concrete problem of evil into a philosophical question and puts forward what is now the accepted catholic Christian doctrine: evil is not a substance but a privation of good. Thus, there can be no absolute Evil, since that would be absolute Nothing. God, the absolute Good and source of all things (goods), therefore, cannot be the source of evil.

Little is known of the actual teachings of the second-century Phrygian presbyter Montanus, since they survive only in fragmentary citations in the later works of catholic opponents of the Montanist movement, such as Epiphanius's (ca. 315–403) *Panarion,* with the customary and expected distortions. Tertullian (ca. 155–225), after he had become a Montanist, is the best source for the doctrines of the movement as a whole, though even these works must be treated with some caution, since Tertullian must have put his own stamp on the doctrine he conveyed.

From a later historical perspective, Montanism appears as a move to preserve in the Church a pristine anticipation of the imminent return of Christ and to oppose the emerging structures by which the Church was acquiring a permanent form in expectation of a longer historical development. The origins of the movement lie in the apocalyptic visions of both Judaism and Christianity. These visions had been eclipsed by the gradual organizational rigidity of the second-century Church. With the rise of the episcopacy, the Church had adjusted institutionally to the prospect of a very long delay in the Lord's Second Coming. In consequence, eschatological hope had further declined. This decline was accompanied by the decline in the *charismata,* the spiritual gifts, which had characterized the early Christian Church as a prophetic movement. As Irenaeus noted, the early Church had been full of men and women "who possess prophetic gifts, and who through the Spirit speak all kinds of language and bring to light for the general benefit the hidden things of men, and declare the mysteries of God" (*Adversus haereses,* V.vi.13–17). The manifestation of these spiritual gifts had enabled early Christianity to argue that prophecy was dead among the Jews and was reborn in the Church.

Montanus claimed that the Spirit, the Paraclete promised by Christ, was in him and his followers as the sign of the end. He was a passive instrument, "a lyre," in the hands of the divine musician, a mouthpiece of the divine. The point

is not so much ecstatic speech as the claim of inspiration. *The Martyrdom of Saints Perpetua and Felicitas,* particularly its introduction, evidences a strong Montanist influence. It was contemporary with Tertullian and, some scholars think, perhaps by him. Tertullian's *On the Veiling of Virgins* affirms that, whereas "the rule of faith, indeed, is completely one, alone unalterable and irreformable," the "articles, indeed, of discipline and life admit new revisions." The content of Montanist visions and prophecies was not doctrinal but ethical; they brought a new discipline, not a new teaching. They were a call to the Church to repent, for the kingdom of God was at hand. The Spirit was absent from the Church because of moral laxity: remarriage of widows, laxity in the observance of fasting, flight from martyrdom and penitential discipline.

If, as the so-called Anonymous Anti-Montanist Author contends, "the Apostle held that the gift of prophecy must exist in all the Church until the final coming," then the prophetic spirit was supposed to be present in the Church, in principle, as a guarantee of the continual presence and work of the Spirit in the life of the Church. The Church in the second century was embarrassed and put to the test, however, when this principle was put into practice by the Montanists. Since the early opponents of the Montanist movement could not deny the continued presence and activity of the Spirit in the Church, they instead attacked Montanist ecstatic experiences (which were quite out of character with "respectable" behavior) and claimed that the experiences were from demonic spirits. The Roman presbyter Hippolytus rejected the Montanist apocalyptic thesis that the Church was living at the end of time and defended the Church's adjustment to the delay in Christ's coming. Prophecy, he contended, was indeed a thing of the past. It ended with the apostle John. Between John and Montanus, however, lay at least fifty years of Christian history. Hippolytus's rejection of the Montanist movement was a repudiation of that history as well. Nevertheless, in the context of the Church in the late second century, Montanus's "apocalyptic spontaneity" was an anachronism. The Church had altered its conception of the activity of the Spirit and had begun to find the guarantees of the presence of the Spirit in the threefold apostolic authority articulated by Irenaeus: the emerging apostolic canon of Scripture, the apostolic creed, and the apostolic succession in the episcopate.

The early-fourth-century Donatist controversy brought thorny theological issues sharply into view. According to the Donatists, one who had relapsed in faith could not validly perform the sacraments, and anyone baptized by such a cleric needed to be rebaptized. *The Acts of the Abitinian Martyrs* tells the story of the origins of and the issues concerning Donatism from the Donatist point of view. Augustine's *Letter* 105, addressed to the Donatists, presents the catholic view of the issues. The actions of Mensurius, the bishop of Carthage, and of his archdeacon Caecilian in opposing the supporters of the Abitinian martyrs, the appeals to Emperor Constantine, and the subsequent imperial laws against the Donatists all marked the beginning of a new era in Christian history: Christians now opposed and persecuted each other with the power of the Roman Empire, which shortly before had persecuted them. Donatism owed its rise and persistence in part to the resistance of the native African Church to Romanization. That resistance only hardened with the violent attempts to suppress the Donatist movement.

At his death in 311, Mensurius was replaced by his archdeacon, Caecilian, who was consecrated by Felix, bishop of Aptunga. Felix was accused by some members of the Church in Carthage of having handed over sacred books for destruction during the persecution of the Donatists under Diocletian. He was a *traditor,* and the sacraments performed by him, as one who had relapsed in his faith, were thus invalid. Caecilian was, therefore, not validly consecrated a bishop and, in his place, his opponents consecrated Majorinus as bishop of Carthage. He was succeeded by Donatus the Great, after whom the Donatist movement was named.

Christianity was forced to think about the makeup of the Church. Do "sinners" have a place in it? Is the Church a congregation of the pure, or is it rather a "spotted actuality" where purity is pursued? What are the nature and effects of the sacraments? If one who had been baptized sinned again, does such a person need a new baptism? And what if the person who baptizes is a "heretic" or a sinner? In other words, what is the connection between God's grace conferred through the Church in the sacraments and the perfection of the clergy who perform the act? Do the sacraments have an objective efficacy all of their own in conferring grace, or is their efficacy produced by the one who performs the act? Cyprian, the great bishop of Carthage, had insisted that those who had apostatized during the persecution under Emperor Decius in 250–51 needed to be rebaptized if they were to be readmitted into the Church. He also rejected the validity of baptism performed by the Christian groups he judged heretical. Donatists could lean on his authority and claim, against the counterclaims of others, such as Augustine, that the catholic Church in its purity subsisted in their Church.

Another issue that needed to be worked out was the Christian conception of the deity. From the religion of Israel, Christianity inherited a faith in the one and only God. Christianity quickly came to understand this monotheistic faith in terms borrowed from Platonic and Stoic philosophical traditions. But, in its own Scriptures, liturgy, and piety, Christianity spoke of the deity as having a Son and giving a Spirit to believers. Hence, the baptismal formula of Matthew 28:19 gives the deity a triadic structure: Father, Son, and Holy Spirit. Such a pattern is also found in other New Testament passages, such as John 16:13–15; Romans 1:1–4; 1 Corinthians 6:11; 12:3–6; Hebrews 10:29; and 1 Peter 1:2. In some other passages of the New Testament a twofold pattern is found, for instance, John 3:16–17, 35–36; 14:10–13; Romans 8:11; 2 Corinthians 4:14; Philippians 1:2; 1 Timothy 1:2; and 1 John 1:22–23.

Neither in the New Testament nor in the apostolic Fathers, however, is there any effort to go beyond the formulas and the functions of the Father, Son, and Spirit in creation and redemption into a discussion of the internal structure of the deity. Jesus was sometimes thought to be a supreme angel or a preexistent spirit. The most significant development in the move toward the explicit formulation of the relationship among Father, Son, and Spirit in the Christian conception of God comes with the identification of the Son with the Platonic and Stoic *logos,* the "word" or "reason" of the universe. Philo Judaeus had already identified the personified Wisdom (Prov 3:19–20; 8:22–36) of the Jewish Scriptures with the personified Logos (see chapter 2). It was the early Christian apologists (see above) who, depending on Philo's work, first thought out the relationship between Christ and the Logos, God's preexistent Word.

The apologists thought of the Logos-Christ especially as mediator in God's work of creation. He was the Word by which God created the cosmos. He existed before all creatures. For some of the Christian writers this meant that the Logos was divine and eternal. But such assertions of divinity had to be balanced against Christian belief in the one God. The affirmation of the divinity of the Logos alongside the one God gave rise to pressing questions: was the Logos the Son, God's creative expression, at the moment when God created the world? Is there a distinction to be made between God's immanent self-expression and God's creative Word? How is the Word related to the Father? To answer this last question, early Christian writers had recourse to a variety of images. The Logos was "generated" and is thus related to God as a Son to his Father. He is like light and its source, or the sun and its beams. He is like thought and its expression.

The reaction against this Logos theology came in the

early third century by Christian thinkers who thought that the unity of God in Christian monotheism was being jeopardized. Characteristic of this reaction is the position attributed to Sabellius, who thought that God was a monad (hence the name "Monarchianism") with three different operations. Thus, the Son and the Spirit are none other than different expressions of the one God.

Origen's discussion of the Trinity in his *On First Principles* marks a watershed in the Logos theology and provides the main link between what preceded and the controversy of the early fourth century. For Origen, the Logos was the mediation between the plurality of created intelligences and the transcendent God. Origen conceived of the universe as hierarchical. The Father, uncreated and ungenerated, was the Creator, whose action extended to the entire universe. The Logos-Son was generated and was Mediator in God's work of creation. The Spirit was the first of the beings generated by God through the Logos and was the Sanctifier. But Father, Logos-Son, and Spirit were modes of existence. The Father and the Logos-Son were two different "hypostases." It was only the Father who was God in the absolute sense. The Logos-Son was God by generation and thus by derivation and was an archetype because he was always with the Father. The Logos-Son was eternal and it could not be said that "there was once when he was not." The Son was generated from the Father, not by a corporeal birth, but like the will is generated from the mind, by a continuous act of the Father's will. And the Logos-Son was united with the Father, like the wife to her husband, by a union of love and action.

The Trinitarian controversy itself might originally have been about the competing interpretation of Proverbs 8:22–31 by Alexander, bishop of Alexandria, and by his presbyter Arius (ca. 250–336). Arius's views are certainly best appraised from his own writings, that is, his *Letter to Eusebius of Nicomedia* and the letter of confession of faith addressed to his bishop, Alexander of Alexandria. His *Thalia* is extensively cited by Athanasius in his *Orations*. But Athanasius's representation of Arius's views are polemical and should be treated with due caution. Alexander of Alexandria's views are found in his *Letter to Alexander of Thessalonica*.

Arius emphasized Origen's view that the Logos was created by and different from the Father and had to be viewed in his relationship to creation. Alexander, on his part, underlined Origen's idea that the Logos-Son was eternally united with the Father and was divine. Although Alexander considered the Logos-Son to be coeternal with the Father, he thought that he was a distinct hypostasis. God therefore had

two hypostases that shared the same nature. The issue clearly was the Logos-Son's coeternity with the Father, and not so much the unity of the Godhead.

Since the dispute quickly spread outside Alexandria, Emperor Constantine, who had become the first "Christian emperor" and was anxious to safeguard the unity of the empire, summoned a universal (ecumenical) council and convened it at Nicaea in June 325. The council produced something new in the history of Christianity, a *creed,* a formulary by which all Christian doctrine would be measured. But it is far from clear what the council meant to teach by the central statements that the Son was "from the *ousia* [substance] of the Father" and was therefore *"homoousios* [consubstantial] with the Father,"* a phrase placed in the creed by Emperor Constantine.

Athanasius was the leading defender of the Nicene doctrine of *homoousios.* His *Orations against the Arians* provides the formula by which the Nicene Creed was thenceforth to be understood: "And so, since they are one, and the Godhead itself one, the same things are said of the Son, which are said of the Father, except His being said to be Father."

The Nicene Creed did not silence all disputes. The search for more satisfactory formulas and expressions continued. The divinity of the Holy Spirit, barely mentioned by the Nicene Creed, was not defined until 381 at the Council of Constantinople, whose creed is generally mistaken for the Nicene Creed.

Pelagius arrived in Rome in the early 380s and stayed until 410. He wrote his *Commentary on Romans* (see chapter 1 in this volume) there. The context of the Pelagian controversy is the ascetic life of the fourth-century Church, especially among the devout Christian aristocracy of Roman society, including Marcella, Paula, Eustochium, Melania the Elder (grandmother of Melania the Younger, see above), Melania the Younger, and many others. Pelagius, as well as Jerome, was one of the mentors and father confessors of these women and men in their pursuit of Christian perfection. Asceticism was controversial, however. There was considerable uneasiness about the severity of the practices advocated, and, theologically, the line that distinguished catholic Christian asceticism from Manichaean practices was very thin. De facto, each group disparaged marriage and practiced self-denial with respect to food, wine, and bodily necessities. Against Manichaeists, catholic Christians argued that their ascetic practices were undertaken, not with a view toward the end of material/bodily existence, but for the extirpation of passion, which obscured the vision of God. Nonetheless, there was the problem of the actual source and merit of these practices: is the human will free to choose between good and evil? In other words, are ascetic practices moral acts meriting divine reward, and their opposite (self-indulgence and sin) deserving of punishment? Manichaeism, with its doctrine that sin is a necessary part of the will, was in fact a continuation of the ancient Greek and Roman determinism expressed in the concepts of "destiny" and "fate." To this ancient notion of fatalistic necessity in human action, early Christianity had responded by emphasizing human responsibility and the ability to choose, without which there can be neither sin nor moral action. But Christianity also taught that God was all-powerful, creator of both the world and human beings, and providential. Moreover, salvation was by God's free gift: "grace." Salvation was redemption from (in Cyprian's words) "the contagion of the ancient death," which resulted from Adam's fall.

The initial phase of the controversy provoked by Pelagius's defense of the freedom of the will to choose either to do good or to sin was from 394 to 420. Pelagius's own teachings must carefully be distinguished from later developments by his followers, and especially from the distortions of his teachings in the writings of Augustine, his principal antagonist. The *Letter to Demetrias* was Pelagius's manifesto. *On the Possibility of Not Sinning* was a later treatise by a Pelagian. The issues of the Pelagian controversy exercised Augustine for a long time, and he articulated his positions on them in a wide range of writings, in particular his *Encheiridion* and *On Nature and Grace.*

There is hardly any controversy more central to the history of the Latin Church than the Pelagian controversy. The controversy was continued by the Reformers in the fifteenth and sixteenth centuries. The issues involved are as complex and divisive as they are critical and decisive. There are questions that concern Christian anthropology: Is the human person endowed with the natural freedom to choose to do good or to do evil? That is, are human beings creatures of fate, acting out of some intrinsic necessity? In ethical terms, can we perform a truly ethical, that is, free, action? And is sin a culpable fault? If, as Augustine contended against Manichaeists, evil is the absence of good, for which the providential God cannot be held responsible, how did evil (both moral and physical) come about? Christianity received from the Jewish Scriptures the story of Adam's "fall." How is this fall to be understood? In what ways was it a fall? And, most importantly, what were the consequences of the fall for the world, and particularly for humanity, such that it accounts for the origin of evil? How is present humanity related to

Adam and his fall? Do we inherit his sin, as a genetic disease, or did he merely establish a precedent that later generations have imitated? Is the human "soul" preexistent, created at the moment of conception when the "body" is being formed, or transmitted along with the body (from father to child) by the human seed through the sexual act? Are humans mortal by nature? And what is "nature"?

Related to these questions, and others like them, are questions about the nature of salvation: From what, precisely, did Christ save humanity and how was this accomplished? What is it in human beings that needs to be saved? Can human freedom either contribute to or impede salvation, or is salvation entirely an act of God's election ("by grace")? There are also problems that touch on the conceptions of God: Is an omnipotent and providential Creator-God reconcilable with any notion of human freedom? Would such a God not be accountable for evil and for the suffering of the innocent? Is God just to condemn? Augustine's views on many of these questions, as on other questions, have been central to the doctrinal developments within Western Christianity.

Early on, the Christian movement shifted from emphasizing Jesus' proclamation of the coming of "the kingdom of God" to proclaiming Jesus himself and worshiping him in liturgy as "Lord" and "Son of God." The anticipated salvation that he had proclaimed in a restored kingdom of God was thought already to have become, in some way, real in the lives of those who had joined the Christian movement. Jesus himself became the bearer of this salvation, the mediator through whom one entered into the kingdom that he had proclaimed in his lifetime. The Hebrew word "messiah," meaning "the anointed one," was rendered as "Christ" in Greek and became Jesus' personal name and received a new meaning: the crucified Son of God, the risen Lord, initiator and mediator of salvation. This conjunction between "Christ" (Messiah) and "Son of God," it must be noted, constitutes a specific Christian innovation.

Christology, the discourse on the Christ, concerns the relationship between the man Jesus of Nazareth and the one who now is worshiped as the "Son of God." It is the attempt to understand Jesus' *messianic character*, that is, his identity and relationship to God as the one through whom God had acted to effect salvation for humanity. The problem of Christology concerns (as Athanasius put it) "the genuine and true generation of the Son from the Father" (*Orations against the Arians,* I.8). The Trinitarian controversy, we pointed out, began with the question of the relationship of the Logos-Christ to God. Having formally, and in very specific language, defined the Logos-Christ as being "from the *ousia* of the Father" and "*homoousios* with the Father," Christianity quickly shifted the question from that of the relationship of God (Logos-Christ) to God (Father) to that of the relationship of God (Logos-Christ) to human beings in the earthly person of Jesus of Nazareth. What does it mean to say that "the Logos was made flesh"?

As was the case with the Trinitarian controversy, the question of Christology was not one with which earliest Christianity was occupied in the New Testament period and in the times of the apostolic Fathers. Several models exist from these periods, therefore, for understanding Jesus as the Christ. Earliest Christianity likely would have proclaimed Jesus as "a man attested . . . by God with deeds of power, wonders, and signs that God did through him" (Acts 2:22), the Messiah through whom God was to bring about the kingdom. God would have been thought to have made him "both Lord and Messiah" and "Son" either at his baptism (Mk 1:9–11; Mt 3:13–17; Lk 3:21–22), at his crucifixion (Mk 15:39), or when God raised him from the dead (Rom 1:3–4; Acts 2:32–36). The title "Son of God" in this sense would be closer to the Jewish understanding of the term and would designate, not an intrinsic quality of divinity, but the fact that Jesus had been specially chosen by God to fulfill a specific function in God's plan of salvation.

As Christianity spread in the Mediterranean world among people of non-Jewish origin, however, Jesus came to be seen (already in the New Testament period) as a heavenly being who embodied God's eternal purposes and who was "sent" and was "born" (Gal 4:4–5) in order to accomplish these purposes for humanity. In him God was at work on earth (2 Cor 5:18–19). He was the human presence of "God with us" (Mt 1:23). The early Christian "Christological Hymn" in Philippians 2:6–11 brings together the vital elements of this line of thought. Here Jesus is seen as a heavenly being "who, though he was in the form of God, did not regard equality with God something to be exploited, but emptied himself, taking the form of a slave, being born in the human likeness. . . . became obedient to the point of death" (Phil 2:6–8).

We observed in relation to the Trinitarian controversy that a crucial phase in the development of the Christian notion of Christ as God occurred when Christians identified Christ with the Stoic and Platonic *logos,* and this *logos* with the biblical Wisdom of Proverbs 3:19–20 and 8:22–36. Before this dual identification, Paul had spoken of Jesus as "Christ the power of God and the wisdom of God" and of "Christ Jesus, who became for us wisdom from God, and righteous-ness and sanctification and redemption" (1 Cor 1:24, 30). This Jesus is "God's wisdom, secret and hidden, which God decreed before the ages for our glory" (1 Cor 2:7). The author of Colossians (1:15–17) could, therefore, think of Jesus as God's Son who "is the image of the invisible God, the first-born of all creation; for in him all things in heaven and on earth were created, things visible and invisible. . . . He himself is before all things, and in him all things hold together." And equally in Hebrews (1:2–3), the Son is the one whom God "appointed heir of all things, through whom he also created the worlds. He is the reflection of God's glory and the exact imprint of God's very being [hypostasis]." It is this "wisdom theology" already in contact with the speculations about the preexistent Logos, especially of Hellenistic Judaism, that received its classical expression in the prologue of the Gospel of John (1:1–14) with its startling assertion: "And the Word [Logos] became flesh and lived among us, and we have seen his glory, the glory as of the Father's only Son, full of grace and truth."

Early Christian writers appealed to the Logos tradition to counter the doctrine of those Christians—"Docetists"—who, rejecting material existence, thought Jesus' "flesh" was only an appearance. Thus, Marcion considered Jesus' body a phantasm, and other Gnostics thought of a duality of Christs, the earthly Jesus being accompanied or shadowed by the true Christ. Against these, writers like Justin Martyr, Irenaeus, and Tertullian insisted that Jesus was the Logos and *mediator* between God and humanity. They did not, however, clarify in what way the Logos-Jesus could be said to be a mediator. Was he a mediator because, as Origen seems to suggest, he stood "midway between all these creatures and God," that is, halfway between divinity and humanity? Or does being a mediator imply that in Jesus God and humanity existed *together*? Moreover, early Christian theology assumed, as a self-evident axiom, the Platonic idea of God as absolute, transcendent, and impassible. The absoluteness and impassibility of the divine nature were predicated also of the Logos-Christ.

Book 2 of Origen's *On First Principles* brings these ideas together. Origen's theory is set within the Platonic hierarchical universe: God-Logos-Soul-Body. The Logos mediates God to created intelligences, as does the soul to the body. Origen believed in the preexistence of souls. In Jesus, the Logos was united to his soul in a union of loving contemplation, which Origen explains by recourse to classical philosophical illustrations of the mixture of substances. It is this mixture that took on a body at birth. Jesus then is a human person, that is, a soul inside a body, but his soul is perfectly united with the Logos. The soul of Jesus acts "as a medium between God and the flesh (for it was not possible for the nature of God to mingle with a body apart from some medium)."

The Logos theology of the early Church culminated with the definitions of the Nicene Creed. But these definitions, while they settled for a moment the question of the relationship between the Christ-Logos and the one God, merely opened up new divisive questions, since the Council of Nicaea and the later development of its doctrine did not specify in what manner the God (Christ-Logos) was present in the man (Jesus of Nazareth).

Athanasius's *Orations against the Arians* deals with the question of the Incarnation of the Logos in a post-Nicene context. Athanasius (ca. 296–373) seeks to answer the problems that the Nicene Creed and his own earlier work, *On the Incarnation,* raised. If, as Athanasius contends, against Origen's understanding, the Logos-God was Jesus' *self* and was thus *directly* united with his body, the questions that Origen (and the Arians afterward) raised now loom large. According to the universal axiom accepted by early Christianity, God's mode of being is antithetical to and, in terms of classical logic, irreconcilable with that of human persons: immutable/contingent, immortal/mortal, omniscient/ignorant, impassible/passible. Scripture attests that Jesus was born, grew, and died; he was ignorant; he suffered and was anguished, angry, hungry, thirsty. Athanasius's distinction between the Logos *in himself* and the Logos *with his flesh* accounts, again in a Platonic universe, for such bodily conditions as hunger, thirst, and physical death. Athanasius is, however, unable to account satisfactorily for conditions that arise from human self-consciousness, for instance, ignorance, fear of death, and anguish.

Athanasius neither directly raised nor answered the questions concerning Jesus' human rational soul and, therefore, whether or not he possessed a human center of consciousness. That Jesus had no human rational soul is assumed, however, by his theory of the direct union of the Logos with the body of Jesus. Apollinaris of Laodicea (ca. 315–92), Athanasius's friend, subsequently denied explicitly that Jesus had a human soul and consciousness, for instance, in his *On the Union in Christ of the Body with the Godhead.* The Logos in Jesus shared the attributes of his body just as his body shared the attributes of the Logos, forming "one composite nature" and one subsistent reality (hypostasis).

The Christological controversy became a cause célèbre in 428 with the publication of *The First Sermon against the*

Theotokos, delivered by Nestorius, bishop of Constantinople (d. 451). The ensuing debate was the result of the collision between two competing theological traditions, Alexandrian and Antiochene, and was first carried out by the exchange of acrimonious correspondence between the fanatical and political schemer Cyril (ca. 376–444), bishop of Alexandria, who reacted swiftly to Nestorius's sermon, and the no-less-dogmatic Nestorius. The controversy was fueled by the ongoing political rivalry between the two Churches and episcopal sees in Alexandria and Antioch and by the intrigues at the imperial court in Constantinople. Accounts of the political maneuvers (in particular by Cyril and his supporters), the involvement of the bishops of Rome (first Celestine and later Leo), the various synods and counter-synods, and the opposition of the "Oriental" bishops are all readily available.

Nestorius's sermon was a direct challenge to the Alexandrian (Athanasian-Apollinarian) understanding of the person and redemptive work of Christ. The term *theotokos* ("God bearer," or "mother of God"), probably first used by Alexander of Alexandria in 324 in the debate against Arius, arose out of Alexandrian piety and speculation about the life of the Virgin Mary. Since the issue in the Alexandrian devotion to Mary was the nature of the birth of Christ, the term *theotokos* summed up the Alexandrian tradition about the person of Christ: Mary gave birth to the God-Logos. In the sermon, Nestorius proposes the term *theodochos* (recipient of God).

The term *theodochos* and Nestorius's discussion both reflect the Antiochene tradition, especially as it was worked out by Theodore of Mopsuestia (ca. 350–428), whose disciple Nestorius was. The Alexandrian-Apollinarian tradition spoke of "one hypostasis" and "one nature." And Cyril's doctrine is summed up in his formula "hypostatic union" or "union in hypostasis." The Antiochenes rejected the view that the Logos was the subject of Christ. Cyril's formulation, in Nestorius's view, suggested a kind of "confusion" or "mixture" of substances in which the divine nature and the human nature would necessarily be modified. The Antiochenes spoke, instead, of a union of "two hypostases" and "two natures." In Antiochene theology, there was in Christ a union of *prosōpon* (of "person") between the Logos and the human being, a union that was fulfilled at the Resurrection, when God conferred on the human being the dignity that had belonged to the Logos. In Christ there were two subjects in one *prosōpon*, produced by the "indwelling" of the Logos (divine nature) in the human being, whose human nature remained fully intact and willed and acted with the divine Logos. Mary, properly speaking, conceived and gave birth to the human being in whom the divine Logos was received.

Also included in this section are Nestorius's *Second Letter to Cyril of Alexandria* and Cyril's *Third Letter to Nestorius,* with its famous twelve "anathemas." Special mention must be made of three other documents as well. The first of these is Cyril's *Second Letter to Nestorius.* Next is the *Formular of Reunion,* which was the peace agreement reached in 433 (after Nestorius's condemnation and exile by Cyril's Council of Ephesus in 431) between Cyril and the supporters of Nestorius in Antioch and among the other bishops of the East. In this agreement the Antiochenes conceded that Mary could be called *theotokos,* while Cyril conceded that it was proper to speak of "two natures" in Christ (the Logos-made-flesh), to distinguish between his human attributes and his divine attributes. And finally there is Pope Leo's *Tome.* The *Tome* had been rejected by Dioscorus, Cyril's nephew and successor in Alexandria, who in 449 presided over another Council at Ephesus to restore Eutyches and his "Monophysite" doctrine of "one nature after the union." In the *Tome,* Pope Leo sets out the tradition of the West: in Christ was one "person," with two "natures" that each constituted a principle of a distinct mode of activity.

The two Christological models show two interpretations of the same received traditions and sources of faith. First, the differing Christological constructions in Alexandria and Antioch were in part the product of divergent views about the validity of allegorical interpretations of Scripture, especially the Old Testament (see chapter 1). There were also two dif-ferent conceptions of the salvific work of Christ. In Alexandria, salvation was "divinization," wherein the divine Logos communicated to the human "flesh" the qualities of divinity: impassibility and immortality. It was essential in this conception, for instance, that in the Eucharist the bread received by the faithful be truly "the body of Christ" transformed by the divine and divinizing Logos. In this way the eucharistic bread was a "vivifying seed," an antidote against corruption. Cyril's Christology owed much to this eucharistic piety and doctrine. Both the Alexandrians and the Antiochenes insisted that divine impassibility in the Logos could not be compromised. Both sides also agreed that impassibility and immortality were the results of salvation. In Antioch, however, this salvation was achieved, not by the deifying transformation of human nature, but by the restoration of human beings to authentic humanity accomplished by one who was himself fully human. The Logos-God could not be said to have suffered, but his humanity was an active agent in the work of redemption. The human being, Jesus, having suffered and triumphed over death—thanks to the indwelling of the Logos-God—will confer to his brothers and sisters the gifts of salvation at the resurrection of the dead.

The Council of Chalcedon's *Definition of Faith* (which adopted Cyril's *Second Letter to Nestorius,* Cyril's letter to John of Antioch accepting the *Formular of Reunion* of 433, and Leo's *Tome*) was born from these many views and pressures. It set limits to the Christian language about Christ and his work of redemption.

1. JEWISH CHRISTIANITY

THE GOSPEL OF THE EBIONITES

☙ The Gospel of the Ebionites, probably composed in the first half of the second century, is the name modern scholars have given to a Gospel that was supposedly used by a group of Jewish-Christians called the Ebionites. Since the Gospel of the Ebionites is no longer extant, our knowledge of the Ebionites comes by way of **Epiphanius** (ca. 315–403), bishop of Salamis, who wrote a treatise (in ca. 374–77) against more than fifty heresies—beginning from the time of Jesus—entitled *Against Heresies.*

EPIPHANIUS
Against Heresies, 30.3, 13–14, 16, 22

30.3

And they only accept the Gospel of Matthew. This alone they use, as do also the followers of Cerinthus and Merinthus. They call it the Gospel of the Hebrews. To tell the truth, Matthew wrote only in Hebrew and in Hebrew letters the narrative and preaching of the Gospel in the New Testament. Others again have asserted that the Gospel of John is kept in a Hebrew translation in the treasuries of the Jews—namely at Tiberias—and that it is hidden there as some converts from Judaism have told us accurately. Even the book of the Acts of the Apostles translated from the Greek into the Hebrew is said to be kept there in the treasuries, so that the Jews, who told us this and read it, came in this way to belief in Christ.

30.13

In the Gospel of Matthew used by them—not in a perfect but in a mutilated and castrated form—called the Gospel of the Hebrews it is recorded: "And there was a man named Jesus, and he was about thirty years old; he has chosen us and he came into Capernaum and entered into the house of Simon, surnamed Peter, and he opened his mouth and said, 'As I walked by the sea of Tiberias, I chose John and James, the sons of Zebedee, and Simon and Andrew and Thaddaeus and Simon Zelotes, and Judas Iscariot; you also, Matthew, when you were sitting at the receipt of custom, did I call and you followed me. According to my intention you shall be twelve apostles for a testimony to Israel.'"[1]

And it came to pass when John baptized, that the Pharisees came to him and were baptized, and all Jerusalem also. He had a garment of camels' hair, and a leathern girdle about his loins. And his meat was wild honey, which tasted like manna, formed like cakes of oil.[2]

The beginning of their Gospel reads thus: "It came to pass in the days of Herod, King of Judaea, that John came and baptized with the baptism of repentance in the river Jordan; he is said to be from the tribe of Aaron and a son of Zacharias the priest and of Elizabeth, and all went out to him."[3]

And after many other words it goes on: "After the people had been baptized, Jesus came also, and was baptized by John. And as he came out of the water, the heavens opened, and he saw the Holy Spirit descending in the form of a dove and entering into him. And a voice was heard from heaven, 'You are my beloved Son, and in you am I well pleased.' And again, 'This day have I begotten you.' And suddenly a great light shone in that place. And John, seeing him, said, 'Who are you, Lord?' Then a voice was heard from heaven, 'This is my beloved Son, in whom I am well pleased.' Thereat John fell at his feet and said, 'I pray you, Lord, baptize me.' But he would not, saying, 'Suffer it, for thus it is fitting that all should be accomplished.'"[4]

30.14

They also deny that he is a man, basing their assertion on the word which he said when he was told: "Behold your mother and your brethren stand outside." "Who is my mother and who are my brethren?" And he stretched forth his hand toward his disciples and said, "My brethren and my mother and sisters are those who do the will of my Father."[5]

30.16

They say that he is not begotten by God the Father but created like one of the archangels, being greater than they. He rules over the angels and the beings created by God and he came and declared, as the gospel used by them records: "I have come to abolish the sacrifices: if you do not cease from sacrificing, the wrath [of God] will not cease from weighing upon you."[6]

30.22

Those who reject meat have inconsiderately fallen into error and said, "I have no desire to eat the flesh of this Paschal Lamb with you." They leave the true order of words and distort the word which is clear to all from the connection of the words and make the disciples say: "Where do you want us to prepare for you to eat the Passover?" To which he replied, "I have no desire to eat the flesh of this Paschal Lamb with you."[7]

From J. K. Elliott, ed. and trans., *The Apocryphal New Testament* (Oxford: Clarendon, 1993), 14–16.

THE GOSPEL OF THE NAZARENES

The Gospel of the Nazarenes (also called the Gospel according to the Hebrews) is a Jewish-Christian Gospel used by Chris-

---

1. See Mt 4:18–22; 9:9; 10:1–4; and parallels. (The notes for this selection are by Gerhart and Udoh.)

2. See Mt 3:1–10 and parallels. Locusts are lacking here from John's diet.

3. See Lk 3:1–3 and parallels. According to Lk 3:1, however, John preached, not in the days of Herod (the Great), king of Judea, but under his son Herod Antipas, tetrarch of Galilee.

4. See Mt 3:13–17 and parallels.

5. See Mk 3:31–35 and parallels.

6. Compare Mt 5:17.

7. See Mk 14:12–16 and parallels.

tians in Palestine. It was probably written in the first half of the second century. Like the Gospel of the Ebionites, it has not survived. Information regarding the Nazarenes is found in **Pseudo-Origen,** *On Matthew* (a text of unknown authorship and date but attributed to Origen in antiquity); in **Eusebius** of Caesarea (ca. 260–339), *Theophania* (written near the end of the third century or early in the fourth); and in three works by **Jerome** (ca. 347–420): *De viro illustro* (ca. 392–93), *On Matthew* (ca. 405), and *Dialogi contra Pelagianos* (ca. 415).

PSEUDO-ORIGEN

On Matthew, 15:14

It is written in a certain Gospel, which is styled "according to the Hebrews," if any one pleases to receive it, not as an authority, but as an illustration of the subject before us: Another rich man said to him, "Master, what good thing shall I do to live?" He said to him, "O man, fulfill the law and the prophets." He replied, "I have done that." He said to him, "Go, sell all that you possess, distribute it to the poor, and come, follow me." But the rich man began to scratch his head and it did not please him. And the Lord said to him, "How can you say, 'I have fulfilled the law and the prophets,' since it is written in the law: You shall love your neighbour as yourself, and lo! many of your brethren, sons of Abraham, are clothed in filth, dying of hunger, and your house is full of many goods, and nothing at all goes out of it to them." And returning to Simon, his disciple, who was sitting by him, he said, "Simon, son of Jonas, it is easier for a camel to enter the eye of a needle than for a rich man (to enter) into the kingdom of heaven."[8]

From J. K. Elliott, ed. and trans., *The Apocryphal New Testament* (Oxford: Clarendon, 1993), 10–11.

EUSEBIUS

Theophania, 4.12, 22

The cause therefore of the divisions of souls that take place in houses Christ himself taught, as we have found in a place in the Gospel existing among the Jews in the Hebrew language, in which it is said: "I will choose for myself the best which my Father in heaven has given me."[9]

Since the Gospel which has come down to us in the Hebrew language pronounces the threat not against the man who hid the money, but against him who spent it in riotous living. . . . (The master) had three servants; one spent the substance of the master with harlots and with flute girls; the

second multiplied it; the third hid the talent; then the first was received, the second was blamed, and the third was cast into prison. I imagine that according to Matthew the threat which was spoken after the word addressed to the idle one does not concern him, but, by way of epanalepsis, the one mentioned before who had eaten and drunk with the drunkard.[10]

From J. K. Elliott, ed. and trans., *The Apocryphal New Testament* (Oxford: Clarendon, 1993), 11.

JEROME

De viro illustro, 3.3

Now this Hebrew (viz. Matthew) is preserved to this day in the library at Caesarea, which Pamphilus the Martyr so diligently collated. I also obtained permission from the Nazarenes of Beroea in Syria, who use this volume, to make a copy of it. In this it is to be observed that, throughout, the evangelist, when quoting the witness of the Old Testament, either in his own person or in that of the Lord and Saviour, does not follow the authority of the Seventy translators, but the Hebrew Scriptures, from which he quotes these two sayings: "Out of Egypt have I called my Son"[11] and "hence he shall be called a Nazarene."[12]

From J. K. Elliott, ed. and trans., *The Apocryphal New Testament* (Oxford: Clarendon, 1993), 11–12.

JEROME

On Matthew, 6:11; 12:13; 27:16, 51

In the Gospel of the Hebrews for the "supersubstantial bread" I found "Mahar" which signifies "tomorrow's," so that the meaning would be: "give us this day the bread for the morrow."[13]

In the Gospel that the Nazarenes and Ebionites use, which

---

8. See Mk 10:17–31 and parallels. (The notes for this selection are by Gerhart and Udoh.)

9. Compare Jn 6:37–39.

10. See Mt 25:14–30.

11. Mt 2:15. The Hebrew text of Hos 11:1 has "Out of Egypt I called my son," as in Matthew. Compare, however, (Septuagint) Hos 11:1 ("Out Egypt I recalled his son"); Num 23:22 ("God led them out of Egypt"); Num 24:8 ("God guided him out of Egypt").

12. Mt 2:23. The text as Matthew cites it does not exist in the Old Testament. The title, "Nazōraios," that Matthew uses might be related to the Hebrew word for a Nazarite, *nāzîr* (see, for example, Judg 13:5–7), or for "shoot," *nezēr* (Isa 11:1). Compare (Septuagint) Judg 3:5 (*naziraios*), Isa 11:1 (*rabdos*).

13. See Mt 6:11; Lk 11:3.

I recently translated from the Hebrew into Greek and which most people designate as the authentic text of Matthew, we read that the man with the withered hand was a mason, who asked for help with these words: "I was a mason, working for my bread with my hands. I pray to you, Jesus, restore me to health so that I do not eat my bread in disgrace."[14]

In the so-called Gospel of the Hebrews, Barabbas who was condemned for sedition and murder[15] is interpreted by "son of their teacher."

In the Gospel often mentioned we read that "the very great lintel of the Temple broke and fell into pieces."[16]

From J. K. Elliott, ed. and trans., *The Apocryphal New Testament* (Oxford: Clarendon, 1993), 12.

JEROME
Dialogi contra Pelagianos, 3.2

In the Gospel of the Hebrews which is written in the Syro-Chaldaic tongue but in Hebrew characters, which the Naza-renes make use of at this day, and which is also called the "Gospel of the Apostles," or as many think, "that of Matthew," and which is in the library of Caesarea, the following narrative is given: "Behold, the mother of the Lord and his brothers said to him, 'John the Baptist baptizes for the remission of sins; let us go and be baptized by him.'" But he said, "What have I committed, that I should be baptized of him, unless it be that in saying this I am in ignorance?"[17] In the same volume (i.e. in the Gospel of the Hebrews) we read, "If your brother has sinned in word against you and has made satisfaction, forgive him up to seven times a day." Simon, his disciple, said to him, "Seven times?" The Lord answered saying, "Verily I say to you: until seventy times seven! For even in the prophets the word of sin is found after they have been anointed with the Holy Spirit."[18]

From J. K. Elliott, ed. and trans., *The Apocryphal New Testament* (Oxford: Clarendon, 1993), 13.

2. CHRISTIAN APOLOGETICS AND PROSELYTIZING

  The Epistle to Diognetus was probably composed during the second century and is never quoted by an ancient writer in any extant source. The author is anonymous (he gives himself the title "Mathētēs" [Disciple], which is sometimes given as his name by scholars). The addressee, Diognetus, cannot be identified with certainty. Despite these unknowns, *The Epistle to Diognetus* is considered one of the first Christian apologies.

The Epistle to Diognetus, I–II, IV–IX

I

Since I perceive, most excellent Diognetus, that you are exceedingly zealous to learn the religion of the Christians and are making very clear and careful inquiry about them— both who is the God in whom they trust and how they worship Him, so that all disdain the world and despise death, and neither account those to be gods who are esteemed such by the Greeks, nor observe the superstition of the Jews; and what is the affection which they have for one another; and why it is that this new race of men or mode of living has entered into our world now and not formerly—I welcome this eager desire in you, and I ask of God, who bestows on us *the power*[19] both of speech and of hearing, that it may be given to me so to speak that you may be edified as much as possible by your hearing, and to you so to hear that I by my speaking may suffer no regret.

II

1. Come then, clear yourself of all the bias that occupies your mind, and get rid of the habit that deceives you, and become as it were from the beginning a new man, as one

---

14. See Mt 12:9–13 and parallels.   15. Mt 27:16.

16. See Mt 27:51.   17. Compare Mt 3:13–15.

18. Compare Mt 18:21–22.

19. Words in italics are added by the translator for the sake of clarity. The translator sometimes encloses such additions in parentheses. (The notes for this selection are by Gerhart and Udoh.)

too who is to hear a new story, even as you yourself also ac- knowledged. See not only with your eyes, but also with your understanding, what substance or form they chance *to have* whom you declare and esteem to be gods. 2. Is not one a stone, like that which we tread on, another bronze, no bet- ter than the implements which have been forged for our use, another wood already decayed, another silver, which needs a man to guard it lest it be stolen, another iron eaten through by rust, another earthenware, not a bit more pleasing than that made for the meanest service? 3. Are not all these of perishable matter? Have they not been forged by iron and fire? Did not the sculptor fashion one of them, the brass- worker another, the silversmith another, the potter another? Before they were modelled by these men's arts into the form of these *gods,* was not each of them subjected to transforma- tion—and still *is so* even now—at the hands of each artificer? Might not the vessels now formed out of the same material, if they met with the same workmen, be made similar to such *images* as these? 4. Again, could not these things which are now worshipped by you become at the hands of men vessels like the rest? Are they not all dumb? Are they not blind? Are they not without souls? Are they not destitute of feeling? Are they not without motion? Are they not all rotting away? Are they not all in course of decay? 5. These things you call gods! These are what you serve! These you worship and in the end you become like them! 6. For this reason you hate (the) Christians—because they do not think that these are gods. 7. For is it not you, who, although you consider and think that you are praising *the gods,* are much more despising them? Are you not much rather mocking and insulting them, when you worship those of stone and earthenware, which you leave unguarded, and yet those of silver and gold you lock up at night and in the day-time set guards by them, lest they be stolen? 8. And by the honours that you think to offer them you are punishing them rather, if indeed they are en- dued with sense; but, if they lack sensibility, you are refuting them by the very fact of worshipping them with blood and steaming fat. 9. Let anyone of you endure this treatment, let him bear with these things being done to him! Nay, there is not a single man who will, if he can help it, suffer this inflic- tion, for he has sense and reason. But the stone suffers *it,* for it has no feeling. You do not then (by your offerings) show up its sensibility! 10. Well, I could say many other things about the fact that Christians are not in bondage to such gods. But if to anyone even these arguments should not seem suffi- cient, I think it needless to say more.

IV

1. But, in truth, I do not think that you need to learn from me that, after all, their (the Jews') qualms concerning food and their superstition about the Sabbath, and the vaunting of circumcision and the cant of fasting and new moon, are utterly absurd and unworthy of any argument. 2. For how can it be other than unlawful to receive some of the things created by God for man's use as created "good" and to refuse others as useless and superfluous? 3. And is it not impious to slander God as though He forbids the doing of a good deed on the Sabbath day? 4. And to glory in the mutilation of the flesh as evidence of their election, as if they were on this ac- count especially beloved by God—does this not call for de- rision? 5. And their star-gazing and watching of the moon, so as to observe months and days and to distribute at their own inclinations the orderings of God and the changes of the seasons, *making* some into feasts and others into times of mourning—who would consider this an example of piety and not much more of folly? 6. Well then, I think that you have learned sufficiently that Christians are right in keeping aloof from the general fatuity and deceit and from the med- dlesomeness and pride of the Jews; but as for the mystery of the Christians' own religion, do not expect to be able to learn this from man.

V

1. For Christians are distinguished from the rest of men neither by country nor by language nor by customs. 2. For nowhere do they dwell in cities of their own; they do not use any strange form of speech or practise a singular mode of life. 3. This lore of theirs has not been discovered by any design and thought of prying men, nor do they champion a mere human doctrine, as some men do. 4. But while they dwell in both Greek and barbarian cities, each as his lot was cast, and follow the customs of the land in dress and food and other matters of living, they show forth the remarkable and admittedly strange order of their own citizenship. 5. They live in fatherlands of their own, but as aliens.[20] They share all things as citizens and suffer all things as strangers. Every foreign land is their fatherland, and every fatherland a foreign land. 6. They marry, like all others; they breed children, but

---

20. See 1 Pet 2:11.

they do not cast out their offspring. 7. Free board they provide, but no carnal bed. 8. They are "in the flesh," but they do not live "after the flesh." 9. They pass their days on earth, but they have their citizenship in heaven. 10. They obey the appointed laws, yet in their own lives they excel the laws. 11. They love all men, and are persecuted by all. 12. They are unknown, yet they are condemned; they are put to death, yet they are made alive. 13. "They are poor, yet they make many rich."[21] They suffer the lack of all things, yet they abound in all things. 14. They are dishonoured, and yet are glorified in their dishonour. They are evil spoken of, yet are vindicated. 15. "They are reviled, and they bless";[22] insulted, they repay with honour. 16. When doing good they are punished as evildoers; suffering punishment, they rejoice as if quickened into life. 17. By the Jews they are warred against as foreigners, and are hunted down by the Greeks. Yet those who hate them cannot state the cause of their hostility.

VI

1. Broadly speaking, what the soul is in the body, that Christians are in the world. 2. The soul is dispersed through all the members of the body, and Christians throughout the cities of the world. 3. The soul dwells in the body, but is not of the body; and Christians dwell in the world, but "are not of the world."[23] 4. The soul, itself invisible, is guarded in the body which is visible; so Christians are known as being in the world, but their religion remains unseen. 5. The flesh hates the soul, and, though it suffers no wrong, wars *against it,* because the flesh is hindered from indulging its pleasures;[24] so too the world, though in no wise wronged, hates Christians, because they set themselves against its pleasures. 6. The soul loves the flesh that hates it, and the limbs; so Christians love them that hate them. 7. The soul is enclosed within the body, but itself curbs the body; and Christians are detained in the world as in a prison, but themselves restrain the world. 8. The soul, though immortal, dwells in a mortal tabernacle; and Christians sojourn among corruptible things, awaiting the incorruptibility which is in heaven. 9. When faring ill in food and drink the soul becomes better; so Christians when buffeted day by day flourish the more. 10. To so high a rank has God appointed them, and it is not right for them to refuse it.

VII

1. For this is not, as I said, an earthly discovery which was committed to them, and no mortal idea which they think it

their duty to guard with such care, nor have they been entrusted with the stewardship of mere human mysteries. 2. But in truth God Himself, the all-sovereign and all-creating and invisible God, Himself from heaven established among men the truth and the holy and incomprehensible word and fixed it firmly in their hearts, not, as one might surmise, by sending to men some servant, or an angel, or ruler, or one of those who administer the affairs of earth, or one of those entrusted with the ordering of things in heaven, but the very Artificer and Maker of the universe himself, by whom He created the heavens, by whom He confined the sea in its own bounds; whose mysteries all the elements faithfully guard, from whom the sun has received the measure of its daily rounds to keep, whom the moon obeys as he bids her shine by night, whom the stars obey as they follow the course of the moon, by whom all things have been ordered and determined and placed in subjection, the heavens and the things in the heavens, the earth and the things therein, the sea and what is in the sea, fire, air, abyss, the things in the heights, the things in the depths, the things in the realm between—him He sent unto them. 3. Did He send him, as a man might conclude, to rule in tyranny and terror and awe? 4. Not so, but in gentleness and meekness He sent him, as a king sending a son who is a king, He sent him as God, He sent him as Man unto men. He was as it were saving when He sent him, (as) persuading, not compelling (for force is no attribute of God). 5. When He sent him God was calling, not pursuing; He sent him as in love, not in judgement. 6. For He will send him to be our judge, and who shall stand at his coming? 7. *Do you not see*[25] *them* thrown to wild beasts that they may deny the Lord, and *yet* unconquered? 8. Do you not see that as more of them are punished, so much do others abound? These things do not seem to be the works of man; they are a mighty deed of God; they are proofs of His presence.

VIII

1. For what man had any knowledge at all of what God is, before he came? 2. Or do you accept the vain and trumpery statements of those specious philosophers of whom some

---

21. See 2 Cor 6:10.
22. See Mt 5:44–45; Lk 6:27–28; Rom 12:14.
23. See Jn 15:19.
24. See Gal 5:17.
25. There is a lacuna at this point in the text.

said that God was fire (what they themselves are destined to go to, that they call God!), and others water, and others some other of the elements created by God? 3. And yet, if any of these arguments is admissible, each one of the other created things could in like manner be declared God. 4. But these things are mere miracle-mongering and deceit of the magicians. 5. No man has either seen or known *Him,* but God manifested Himself. 6. And He manifested Himself through faith, by which alone it is given to see God. 7. For God, Master and Maker of the universe, who made all things and disposed *them* in their *due* order, proved Himself not only a lover of man but also long-suffering. 8. Nay, such He ever was and is and will be, kind and good and free from anger and true, and He alone is good. 9. And having conceived a great and unutterable design He communicated it to His Child alone. 10. And so long as He held it in a mystery and guarded His wise counsel He seemed to have no concern or care for us. 11. But when He revealed it through His beloved Child, and manifested the things prepared from the beginning, He bestowed upon us all things at once, both to share in His blessings and to see and understand. Who of us would ever have expected these things?

IX

1. Having therefore planned everything already in His own mind with His Child, He suffered us up to the former time to be borne along by unruly impulses, as we willed, in the clutches of pleasures and lusts. Not at all because He took pleasure in our sins, but out of His forbearance; not in approval of the season of iniquity which was then, but creating the season of righteousness which is now, so that we who in past time were from our own deeds convicted as unworthy of life might now by the goodness of God be deemed worthy, and when we had shown clearly that of ourselves it was impossible "to enter into the kingdom of God," might be made able by the power of God. 2. But when our iniquity was fulfilled and it had been made fully manifest that its reward of punishment and death was awaited, and the season came which God had appointed to manifest henceforth[26] His own goodness and power (O the exceeding kindness and love of God!), He did not hate us or repel us or remember our misdeeds, but was long-suffering, bore with us, Himself in mercy took on Him our sins, Himself gave up His own Son as a ransom for us, the holy One for the wicked, the innocent for the guilty, "the just for the unjust,"[27] the incorruptible for the corruptible, the immortal for mortals. 3. For what

else could cover our sins but his righteousness? 4. In whom was it possible for us, wicked and impious as we were, to be justified, except in the Son of God alone? 5. O the sweet exchange, O work of God beyond all searching out, O blessings past our expectation, that the wickedness of many should be hidden in one righteous Man and the righteousness of the One should justify many wicked! 6. Having then convinced us in the former time of the powerlessness of our nature to gain life, and having now shown the Saviour in his power to save even powerless creatures, in both these ways His will was that we should believe His goodness, and regard Him as guardian, father, teacher, counsellor, healer, mind, light, honour, glory, strength, life, and have no anxiety about clothing and food.[28]

From Henry G. Meecham, trans., *The Epistle to Diognetus* (Manchester, UK: Manchester University Press, 1949), 75, 77, 79, 81, 83, 85, 87.

❧ **Justin Martyr** (who was martyred in ca. 165) addressed *The First Apology* to Emperor Antoninus Pius (138–61), his son Verissimus (Marcus Aurelius, 121–80), and the Roman Senate and people. Justin was the first Christian writer to combine Platonism with biblical religion to produce the Christian Logos theology, and he was also the first to address his work to non-Christians and opponents of the Church.

JUSTIN MARTYR

The First Apology, 4–12, 14–17, 19

Refutation of Anti-Christian Slanders

4. By the mere statement of a name,[29] nothing is decided, either good or evil, apart from the actions associated with the name; indeed, as far as the name with which we are accused goes, we are most gentle[30] people. But we do not think it just to ask to be acquitted on account of the name, if we are convicted as evildoers, so, on the other hand, if we are

---

26. Or "at last."

27. See Rom 5:6–8; 2 Cor 5:21.

28. See Mt 6:25–34; Lk 12:22–31.

29. That is, the name "Christian." It is uncertain whether there was a specific Roman law against being a Christian. (The notes for this selection are by Gerhart and Udoh.)

30. "Gentle" (*chrēstos*) is Justin's play on the name "Christ" (Christos). See Lk 6:35; Mt 11:30.

found to have committed no wrong, either in the appellation of the name, or in our citizenship, you must be exceedingly anxious[31] against incurring righteous judgment by unjustly punishing those who are not convicted. For from a name neither approval nor punishment could fairly come, unless something excellent or evil in action could be shown about it. For you do not punish the accused among yourselves before they are convicted; but in our case you take the name as proof against us, and this although, as far as the name goes, you ought rather to punish our accusers. For we are accused of being Christians, and to hate what is favorable is unjust. Again if one of the accused deny the name, saying that he is not [a Christian],[32] you acquit him, as having no proof that he is an evildoer; but if any one acknowledges that he is one, you punish him on account of this acknowledgement. You ought also to enquire into the life both of the confessor and the denier, that by his deeds it would appear what kind of person each is. For as some who have been taught by the Teacher, Christ, not to deny him[33] encourage others when they are put to the test, so similarly do those who lead evil lives give some excuse to those who, without consideration, like to accuse all the Christians of impiety and wickedness. And this also is improper. For in philosophy, too, some assume the name and the dress who do nothing worthy of their profession; and as you are aware those among the ancients whose opinions and teachings were quite different are yet called by the one name of philosopher. And some of these taught atheism;[34] and those who became poets get a laugh out of the impurity of Zeus with his own children. And those who follow such teaching are unrestrained by you; but, on the contrary, you offer prizes and honors to those who euphoniously insult them.

5. Why, then, should this be? In our case, who pledge ourselves to do nothing wicked, nor to hold these godless opinions, you do not investigate the charges made against us; but, giving in to unreasoning passion, and the instigation of evil demons,[35] you punish us without trial or consideration. For the truth shall be told; since of old these evil demons manifested themselves, both defiled women and corrupted boys, and showed terrifying sights to people, that those who did not use their reason in judging the acts that were done, were filled with terror; and being taken captive by fear, and not knowing that these were demons, they called them gods, and gave to each the name which each of the demons had chosen for himself. And when Socrates[36] tried, by true reasoning and definite evidence, to bring these things to light, and deliver people from the demons, then the demons themselves, by

means of people who rejoiced in wickedness, compassed his death, as an atheist and impious person, on the charge of introducing new divinities;[37] and in our case they show a similar activity. For not only among the Greeks through Socrates were these things revealed by reason [logos], but also among the Barbarians[38] were they revealed by logos personally, when He had taken shape, and become man, and was called Jesus Christ; and in obedience to Him, we not only deny that they who did such things as these are gods, but state that they are wicked and impious demons, whose actions will not bear comparison with those even of people who long after virtue.

The Principal Charges—Atheism, Immorality, and Disloyalty

6. Hence we are called atheists. And we confess that we are atheists with reference to gods such as these, but not with reference to the most true God, the Father of righteousness and temperance and the other virtues, who is unmixed with evil. But we worship and adore both Him and the Son who came from Him, and taught us these things, and the army of the other good angels, who follow Him and are made like Him, and the prophetic Spirit, giving honor [to Him] in reason and truth;[39] and to everyone who wishes to learn handing over,[40] without grudging, what we have been taught.

7. But someone will say, "Already some have been arrested and convicted as evildoers." For you often condemn many, when at any time you inquire into the lives of those who are being accused, but you do not do so because of those convicted before. And this we acknowledge, that just as among the Greeks those who teach what pleases them are all listed under the name philosophy, though their doctrines are opposed, so also among the Barbarians the name which is now

---

31. Latin *laborare.*

32. Words in brackets have been added by the translator for clarity.

33. See Mt 10:33; see also Mk 8:38; Lk 9:26.

34. For example, Cynicism and Epicureanism, which were influential in the second century.

35. On the reality of demons, see 1 Cor 10:19–22. Justin shared the widespread belief in their existence.

36. Socrates' work, for Justin, was a preparation for the work of Christ. Socrates had, in part, knowledge of the *logos* that was incarnate in Christ (see *First Apology,* 46). And Justin's apologies for Christians are parallel to the *Apology* of Socrates.

37. See especially Plato, *Apology,* 24B; Xenophon, *Memorabilia,* 1.1.

38. That is, non-Greeks.

39. See Jn 4:24–25; 5:23.

40. Technically: "Tradition." See 1 Cor 11:23; 15:3.

made against them is the common property of those who are and those who appear to be wise. For all are called Christians. So we ask that the deeds of those who are denounced to you be judged, in order that each one who is convicted may be punished as an evildoer, but not as a Christian; and if it should appear that anyone is blameless, that he may be acquitted as a Christian who has done no wrong. For we will not ask that you punish our accusers, for they are sufficiently punished by their present wickedness and their ignorance of the good.

8. Consider that we have said these things for your sakes, for it is in our power when we are examined to deny [our Christianity]; but we would not live by telling a lie. For, impelled by the desire for the eternal and pure life, we seek to dwell with God, the Father and Demiurge[41] of all things, and hasten to confess [our faith], being persuaded and convinced that those who have shown to God by their works that they follow Him, and long to dwell with Him where there is no evil to cause disturbance, are able to obtain these things. This, then, to speak briefly, is what we look for and have learned from Christ, and teach. Likewise Plato said that Rhadamanthus and Minos would punish the wicked who came before them;[42] and we say that this is what will happen, but at the hand of Christ, and to the same bodies, reunited with their souls and destined for eternal punishment, and not for a thousand-year period only, as he said. And if anyone says that this is incredible or impossible, this mistake of ours is one which concerns us only, and no one else, as long as we are not convicted of doing any evil.

9. But neither do we honor with many sacrifices and garlands of flowers the objects that people have formed and set in temples and named gods; since we know that they are lifeless and dead and have not the form of God [for we do not think that God has such a form as some say is fashioned to His honor], but have the names and shapes of those evil demons which have appeared.[43] For why must we tell you who already know, what the craftsmen fashion their material into, by planing and cutting, casting and hammering? And often out of vessels used for dishonorable purposes,[44] by merely changing the form, and making an image of the appropriate shape, they make what they call gods. We consider this not only irrational, but to be even insulting to God, who, though of ineffable glory and form, yet has His name set upon things which are corruptible and need to be cared for. And that the craftsmen of these are impure and, not to enter into details, are given to all kinds of vice, you very well know; they even corrupt their own slave girls who work alongside them. What

stupidity, that dissolute people should be said to fashion and make gods for public worship, and that you should appoint such people the guardians of temples where they are set up, not recognizing that it is unlawful even to think or say that people are the guardians of gods.

10. But we have received [from tradition][45] that God does not need material offerings from people, seeing that He Himself is the provider of all things. And we have been taught, and are persuaded, and believe that He accepts only those who imitate the good things which are in Him, temperance and righteousness and well-doing, and whatsoever else truly belongs to God who is called by no given name. And we have been taught that in the beginning He of His goodness, for people's sakes, formed all things out of unformed matter;[46] and if they, by their actions, show themselves worthy of His design, they are accounted worthy, so we have received, of reigning with Him,[47] being delivered from corruption and suffering. For as in the beginning He created us when we were not, so we consider that those who likewise choose what is pleasing to Him are, on account of their choice, counted worthy of incorruption and of fellowship with Him. For the coming into being was not our choice; but in order that we may follow those things that please Him, choosing them by means of the rational powers He has given us, He both persuades us and leads us to faith. And we think it for the good of all people that they are not prevented from learning these things, but are even urged to consider them. For the restraint which human laws could not bring about, the logos, being divine, would have brought about, save that the evil demons, with the help of the evil desire[48] which is in every person and which expresses itself in various ways, had scattered abroad many false and godless accusations,[49] none of which apply to us.

11. And when you hear that we look for a kingdom, you uncritically suppose that we speak of a human one; whereas

41. See Plato, *Republic*, 530A.

42. See Plato, *Apology*, 41A; *Republic*, 615A; *Phaedrus*, 249A–B; *Gorgias*, 523E–524A.

43. According to Justin, demons are at the origin of the worship of idols, which are their shapes (*schēmata*).

44. See Rom 9:21.

45. See 1 Cor 11:23; 15:1, 3.

46. See Justin Martyr, *First Apology*, 59, 67; Wis 11:17.

47. See 2 Tim 2:12.

48. This is possibly a reference to the Jewish notion of "evil inclination" (see Gen 8:21; 4 Ezr [= 2 Esd] 3:21; 4:30–32; Sir 15:11–14).

49. Christians were charged with atheism, cannibalism, and promiscuity. See Suetonius, *Nero*, 16; Tacitus, *Annals*, 15.44.

we speak of that with God,[50] as appears also from the confession of their faith made by those who are charged with being Christians, although they know that death is the penalty meted out to him who so confesses. For if we looked for a human kingdom, we would deny it, that we might not be slain; and we would try to escape detection, that we might obtain the things we look for. But since we do not have our hope on the present, we do not heed our executioners since death is in any case the debt of nature.

12. And more than all other people we are your helpers and allies in the cause of peace, convinced as we are that it is alike impossible for the wicked, the covetous, the conspirator, and the virtuous to escape the notice of God, and that everyone goes to eternal punishment or salvation in accordance with the character of his acts. If all people knew this, no one would choose wickedness even for a little while, knowing that he goes to eternal punishment by fire; but would by all means restrain himself, and order his path with virtue, that he might receive the good gifts of God, and avoid the punishments. There are some people who endeavor to conceal their wrongdoing because of the laws and punishments you impose, knowing that since you are only men and women it is possible for wrongdoers to escape you; if they were to learn and were convinced that our thoughts as well as our acts cannot be hidden from God, they would by all means live decently, at least because of the impending penalties, as even you yourselves will admit. But you seem to fear lest all people become righteous, and you no longer have any to punish. This would be the concern of public executioners, not of good rulers. But, as we said before, we are convinced that these things are brought about by evil spirits, who demand sacrifices and service from people who live irrationally; but as for you, we assume that you who aim at piety and philosophy will do nothing unreasonable. But if you also, like thoughtless people, prefer the custom to truth, do what you have power to do. But just so much power have rulers who respect reputation rather than truth, as brigands have in a desert. And that you will not succeed is shown by the Word, and after God who begat Him we know of no ruler more kingly or more just than He. For as all people shrink from inheriting the poverty or sufferings or obscurity of their fathers, so whatever the Word forbids to be chosen, the sensible person will not choose. That all these things would come to pass, I say, our Teacher foretold, who is both Son and Apostle[51] of God the Father and Master of all, that is Jesus Christ; from whom also we have received the name of Christians. We are more assured that all the things taught by Him are so, since

whatever He predicted before is seen in fact coming to pass; and this is the work of God, to announce something before it happens, and as it was predicted so to show it happening. We could pause here and add no more, having made clear that we demand what is just and true; but because we know that it is not easy suddenly to change a mind enchained by ignorance, we are encouraged to add a few things for the sake of persuading those who love the truth, knowing that ignorance may be escaped from, if the truth is set over against it.

The Moral Power of Christianity

14. For we warn you in advance to be on your guard, lest the demons whom we have previously accused should deceive you and divert you from reading and understanding what we say. For they strive to have you as their slaves and servants, and sometimes by appearances in dreams, sometimes by magical tricks, they subdue all who do not struggle to the utmost for their own salvation, as we do also who, after being persuaded by the Word, renounced them,[52] and follow the only unbegotten God through His Son. Those who formerly delighted in fornication now embrace chastity alone; those who formerly made use of magical arts have dedicated themselves to the good and unbegotten God; we who once valued above everything the gaining of wealth and possessions now bring what we have into a common stock, and share with everyone in need; we who hated and destroyed one another, and would not share the same hearth with people of a different tribe on account of their different customs, now since the coming of Christ live familiarly with them, and pray for our enemies, and try to persuade those who unjustly hate us to live according to the good advice of Christ, to the end that they may share with us the same joyful hope of a reward from God the Master of all. But lest we should seem to deceive, we consider it right, before embarking on our promised demonstration, to cite a few of the precepts given by Christ Himself. It is for you then, as powerful rulers, to find out whether we have been taught and do teach these things truly. Short and concise utterances come from Him, for He was no sophist, but His word was the power of God.

15. Concerning chastity he said this: "Whosoever looks

---

50. Compare Jn 18:36.

51. See Justin Martyr, *First Apology*, 63, in chapter 4 of this volume.

52. Possibly the renunciation of the devil at baptism. See Justin Martyr, *First Apology*, 61 and 65, in chapter 4 of this volume.

upon a woman to lust after her has already committed adultery with her in his heart before God."[53] And: "If your right eye offends you, cut it out; for it is better for you to enter into the Kingdom of Heaven with one eye, than with two eyes to be cast into eternal fire."[54] And: "Whosoever shall marry her that is divorced from another husband commits adultery."[55] And: "There are some who have been made eunuchs by men, and some who were born eunuchs, and some who have made themselves eunuchs for the Kingdom of Heaven's sake; but not all can receive this saying."[56] So that all who according to human law make second marriages[57] are sinners in the sight of our Master, as are those who look on a woman to lust after her. For not only the man who in act commits adultery is condemned by Him, but also the man who desires to commit adultery; since not only our deeds but also our thoughts are open before God. And many, both men and women, who have been Christ's disciples from childhood, have preserved their purity at the age of sixty or seventy years; and I am proud that I could produce such from every race of men and women. For what shall we say then of the countless multitude of those who have turned away from intemperance and learned these things? For Christ did not call the righteous and temperate to repentance, but the ungodly and licentious and unrighteous. So He said, "I came not to call the righteous, but sinners to repentance."[58] For the Heavenly Father desires the repentance of a sinner, rather than his punishment.[59] And concerning our affection for all people He taught so: "If you love those who love you, what new thing do you do? For even the fornicators do this. But I say to you, Pray for your enemies, and love those who hate you, and bless those who curse you, and pray for those who despitefully use you."[60] And that we should share with the needy, and do nothing for glory, He said these things: "Give to everyone who asks and turn not away from him who wishes to borrow. For if you lend to those from whom you hope to receive, what new thing do you do? Even the publicans do this.[61] Lay not up for yourselves treasure upon earth, where moth and rust corrupt and thieves break in; but lay up for yourselves treasure in heaven, where neither moth nor rust corrupts.[62] For what will it profit a man, if he should gain the whole world, but lose his own soul? or what will he give in exchange for it?[63] Lay up treasure therefore in heaven, where neither moth nor rust corrupts."[64] And: "Be kind and merciful, as your Father also is kind and merciful, and makes His sun to rise on sinners and the righteous and the wicked.[65] Take no thought what you will eat, or what you will put on: are you not better than the birds and the beasts? And God feeds them. Take no

thought, therefore, what you will eat or what you will wear; for your Heavenly Father knows that you need these things. But seek the Kingdom of Heaven, and all these things will be added to you.[66] For where his treasure is, there is also the mind of man."[67] And: "Do not do these things to be seen of men; otherwise you have no reward from your Father who is in heaven."[68]

16. And concerning our being long-suffering and servants to all and free from anger, this is what He said: "To him that smites you on the one cheek, offer also the other; and to him that takes away your shirt do not forbid your cloak also.[69] And whosoever shall be angry is in danger of the fire.[70] And whosoever compels you to go one mile, follow him for two.[71] And let your good works shine before men, that they, seeing them, may wonder at your Father who is in heaven."[72] For we ought not to quarrel; neither has He desired us to imitate wicked people, but He has exhorted us to lead all people, by patience and gentleness, from shame and evil desires. And this indeed we can show in the case of many who were once of your way of thinking, but have turned from the way of violence and tyranny, being conquered, either by the constancy of life which they have traced in [Christian] neighbors, or by the strange endurance which they have noticed in defrauded fellow travelers or have experienced in those with whom they had dealings. And concerning our not swearing

---

53. The following material is composed of free quotations from the Sermon on the Mount (on the Plain; see Lk 6:17ff). See Mt 5:28.

54. Mt 5:29; 18:9; Mk 9:47.

55. Lk 16:18 (notably without the exceptive clause that occurs in Mt 5:32b).

56. Mt 19:11–12.

57. There are three possible interpretations of "second marriages": (1) bigamy, (2) divorce and remarriage, and (3) remarriage after the death of a spouse. Bigamy was not permitted by "human law" (that is, Roman law). Remarriage was permitted by law after the death of a spouse but was condemned by Stoic philosophy. The Stoic view was adopted by early Christian asceticism (see the readings in section 4, Asceticism and Hermitism, in this chapter). This extreme view is not, however, the teaching of Jesus in the Gospel passages. Paul also did not consider those who remarried after the death of their spouses to be "sinners" (see 1 Cor 7:8–9; 39–40; Rom 7:2–3). Justin is most likely speaking of divorce and remarriage.

58. Lk 5:32; see also Mt 9:13; Mk 2:17.

59. See Ezek 18:23; 1 Tim 2:3–4; 2 Pet 3:9.

60. Mt 5:44–47; Lk 6:27–32.

61. Lk 6:30–35; Mt 5:42, 46–47.

62. Mt 6:19–20; see also Lk 12:33.

63. Mt 16:26; Mk 8:36–37; Lk 9:25.

64. Mt 6:20.

65. Lk 6:35–36; Mt 5:45, 48.

66. Lk 12:22–24, 31; Mt 6:25–26, 33.

67. Mt 6:21; Lk 12:34.   70. Mt 5:22.

68. Mt 6:1.   71. Mt 5:41.

69. Lk 6:29; see also Mt 5:39–40.   72. Mt 5:16.

at all, but always speaking the truth, He commanded thus: "Swear not at all, but let your yes be yes and your no, no. For what is more than these is from the evil one."[73] And that we ought to worship God alone He showed us when he said: "The greatest commandment is, You shall worship the Lord your God and Him only shall you serve with all your heart and all your strength, the Lord who made you."[74] And, when a certain man came to Him and said, "Good Master," He answered and said, "There is none good, except God only who made all things."[75] Those who are found not living as He taught should understand that they are not really Christians, even if they profess with the lip the teachings of Christ; for not those who profess, but those who do the works will be saved. For He said this: "Not everyone who says to me, Lord, Lord, will enter into the Kingdom of Heaven, but he who does the will of my Father who is in heaven.[76] For whosoever hears me, and does what I say, hears Him who sent me.[77] But many will say to me, Lord, Lord, have we not eaten and drunk in your name, and done wonders? And then I will say to them, Depart from me, you workers of iniquity.[78] Then there will be weeping and gnashing of teeth, when the righteous will shine as the sun, but the wicked shall be sent into eternal fire.[79] For many will come in my name, clothed outwardly in sheep's clothing, but inwardly being ravening wolves.[80] By their works you will know them. And every tree that does not bring good fruit is hewn down and thrown into the fire."[81] And as to those who are not living in accordance with His teachings, but are Christians only in name, we demand that all such shall be punished by you.

17. And everywhere we try to pay to those appointed by you, more readily than all people, the taxes and assessments,[82] as we have been taught by Him. For at that time some came and asked Him if it was necessary to pay tribute to Caesar. And He answered, "Tell me, whose image does this coin bear?" And they said, "Caesar's." And again He answered them, "Give therefore to Caesar the things that are Caesar's, and to God the things that are God's."[83] So we worship God only, but in other things we gladly serve you, acknowledging you as emperors and rulers of men and women, and praying that with your imperial power you may also be found to possess sound judgment.[84] But if you pay no regard to our prayers and frank statements, we shall suffer no injury, since we believe, or rather are indeed persuaded, that every person will suffer punishment in eternal fire according to the merit of his actions, and will give account according to the ability[85] he has received from God, as Christ reminded us when He said, "To whom God has given more, from him more will be required."[86]

19. And to any thoughtful person what would seem more incredible, than if we were not in the body, and someone should say it was possible that from a small drop of human seed, bones and sinews and flesh were formed into a shape such as we see? For let this now be said by way of supposition: If you were not such as you now are, born of such parents, and one were to show you the human seed and a picture of a man or woman, and were to say confidently that from such a substance such a being could grow, would you believe before you saw it happening? No one would dare to contradict [and say that you would disbelieve].[87] In the same way, then, you are now incredulous because you have never seen a dead man rise again. But as at first you would not have believed it possible that from a small drop such persons could be produced, yet now you see them thus produced, so also consider that it is not impossible for the bodies of men and women, dissolved and like seeds resolved into earth,[88] to rise again in God's appointed time and put on incorruption.[89] For we are unable to conceive what power worthy of God can be held by those who say that each thing returns into that from which it came, and that not even God Himself can do anything beyond this;[90] but this we see clearly, that they would not have believed it possible for such creatures as they are to have come into being, and produced from such materials, as they now see both themselves and the whole world to be.

---

73. Mt 5:34, 37; Jas 5:12.

74. Mt 22:38 and Mt 4:10; Lk 4:8; Mk 12:30; Lk 10:27.

75. Mk 10:17–18; Lk 18:18–19; Mt 19:16–17.

76. Mt 7:21.

77. Lk 10:16; Mt 10:40; Jn 12:44.

78. Mt 7:22–23; Lk 13:26–27.

79. Mt 8:11–12; 13:41–43; Lk 13:28.

80. Mt 24:5; 7:15; see also Mk 13:6; Lk 21:8.

81. Mt 7:16, 19–20; 3:10; Lk 6:43–44; 3:9.

82. See Rom 13:7.

83. Mk 12:13–17; Mt 22:15–22; Lk 20:20–26.

84. See Rom 13:1–7; 1 Tim 2:1–2.

85. See Mt 25:15.

86. See Lk 12:48.

87. Justin's elliptical phrase creates some confusion. The overall meaning of the passage is that, if we did not know for a fact that it does happen, it would have seemed incredible that a human person would evolve from a drop of semen. Similarly, the Resurrection seems incredible; but it is no more incredible than this case. However, Justin's question ("would you believe before you saw it happening?") implies a negative assertion ("no, you would not believe"). Nobody, says Justin, would "contradict" his negative assertion.

88. See 1 Cor 15:37–38.

89. See 1 Cor 15:53.

90. Justin objects, first, to Stoic materialism and pantheism, according to which the soul, after purgation, resolves into the *anima mundi*, which permeates the universe. Second, he rejects the Stoic doctrine of fate.

And we have learned that it is better to believe things impossible to our own nature and to men and women, than to disbelieve like the rest of the world; since we know that our Master Jesus Christ said, "the things that are impossible with men are possible with God,"[91] and, "Fear not those who kill you and after that can do no more; but fear Him who after death is able to cast both body and soul into Gehenna."[92] And Gehenna is a place where those who have lived unrighteously will be punished,[93] and those who do not believe that these things which God has taught us through Christ will come to pass.

From Saint Justin Martyr, *The First and Second Apologies,* translated by Leslie William Barnard, Ancient Christian Writers, no. 56 (New York: Paulist Press, 1997), 24–30, 31–35, 36–37.

Tertullian (ca. 155–225), writing from Carthage, addressed *To Scapula* to the Roman proconsul of Africa in 212. As in his earlier treatise *Apology,* Tertullian defends Christianity against charges of sacrilege and treason against Rome. He also warns of God's anger at the killing of Christians.

TERTULLIAN

To Scapula, I–III, V

I

We are, indeed, neither dismayed nor greatly disturbed at the persecutions which we suffer from ignorant men, since we joined this way of life with the understanding that we pledged ourselves to enter into the present conflicts at the risk even of our lives, wishing to obtain those things which God promises in return, and fearing to suffer those things which He threatens for any contrary course of life. Accordingly, we battle against all your cruelty, even rushing voluntarily to the contest, and we rejoice more when condemned than when acquitted. We have therefore presented this petition to you, not fearing for ourselves, and by no means for our friends, but for you and for all our enemies. For, we are commanded by the teachings of our religion to love even our enemies and to pray for those who persecute us: so that our goodness may be perfect[94] and peculiar to us, and not that of the run of the world. To love friends is the custom for all men, but to love enemies is customary only for Christians. We, then, who are saddened by your ignorance, have compassion on human error, and look ahead into the future, seeing signs of

it threatening daily—we, I say, must proceed to set before you in this way what you do not wish to hear openly.

II

We worship one God, whom you all know, since nature is your teacher, at whose lightning and thunder you tremble, at whose benefits you rejoice. The rest you yourselves think to be gods, but we know to be demons. It is the law of mankind and the natural right of each individual to worship what he thinks proper, nor does the religion of one man either harm or help another. But, it is not proper for religion to compel men to religion, which should be accepted of one's own accord, not by force, since sacrifices also are required of a willing mind. So, even if you compel us to sacrifice, you will render no service to your gods. They will not desire sacrifices from the unwilling unless they are quarrelsome—but a god is not quarrelsome. Finally, He who is the true God bestows all His gifts equally—on the unholy as well as on His own. This is why He also appointed an eternal judgment for those who are thankful and for those who are not. You have never caught us, whom you consider sacrilegious, in theft; much less, in committing sacrilege. But, all those who rob the temples both swear by the gods and worship the same; they are not Christians, yet they are caught in committing sacrilege. It would be tedious to relate in what other ways all the gods are ridiculed and despised, even by their own worshippers.

So, too, we are defamed regarding the majesty of the emperor, yet never could the followers of Albinus, or of Niger, or of Cassius be found among the Christians;[95] but, those same men who, up to the very day before, had sworn by the

---

91. Lk 18:27; see also Mk 10:27; Mt 19:26.

92. Lk 12:4–5; Mt 10:28.

93. "Gehennah," or "the Valley of Hinnom," which lies outside Jerusalem, was infamous as the place of Israel's "abominations" (see Jer 7:31–32; 32:35). In the New Testament it is the place of punishment after the Last Judgment (see Mk 9:45; Mt 5:22; 18:9).

94. See Mt 5:44–48; Lk 6:27–36; Rom 12:14–21. (The notes for this selection are by Gerhart and Udoh.)

95. Avidius Cassius, who was a general under Emperor Marcus Aurelius (161–80), revolted in 175, after he had been falsely informed that the emperor was dead. Although he was proscribed by the Senate, he had many followers in the eastern parts of the empire. He was assassinated in August 175, but Aurelius was clement toward his followers. After Emperor Commodus (180–93) died without leaving a successor, L. Septimius Severus was proclaimed emperor by the Danubian legions. Likewise, C. Pescennius Niger was proclaimed emperor by the Syrian legions, and D. Clodius Albinus by the legions in Britain and on the Rhine. In the civil war that ensued, Severus defeated and killed Niger in 194, and Albinus in 197. Thereafter, Severus, unlike Aurelius, cruelly persecuted the supporters of both Albinus and Niger.

genii of the emperors, who had both offered up and vowed sacrifices for their health, who had often condemned the Christians, were found to be enemies of the emperors. A Christian is an enemy of no one, much less of the emperor. Since he knows him to be appointed by his own God, he must love, reverence, honor, and wish him well, together with the whole Roman Empire, as long as the world shall last. For, so long the Roman Empire will last. In this way, then, do we honor the emperor, as is both lawful for us and expedient for him, as a man next to God: who has received whatever he is from God; who is inferior to God alone. This, too, he himself will desire. For, in this way he is greater than all, since he is inferior only to the true God. Thus, he is even greater than gods themselves, since they, too, are also in his power. This is why we also offer sacrifice for the welfare of the emperor, but to God, who is our God and his—and in the way God commanded us, with pure prayer. God, the Maker of the universe, does not need any odor or blood. These are the food of demons. And the demons we not only reject, but convict; we daily expose them, and cast them out of men, as is well known to many. Therefore, we pray in a better way for the welfare of the emperor, asking it from Him who is able to give it. Surely, it can be sufficiently clear to you that we act according to the teachings of godly patience, when, as such a great multitude of men—almost the majority in every city—we live in silence and loyalty, known, perhaps, more as individuals than as a group, and knowable in no other way than by the reformation of our former vices. For far be it from us to take it ill that we suffer things for which we long, or to plot of ourselves any vengeance which we await from God.

III

Nevertheless (as we have said before), we must grieve, because no city will go unpunished for the shedding of our blood, as was the situation under the governorship of Hilarian,[96] when they had cried out concerning our burial grounds: "Let them have no *areae*—no burial grounds!" But, the result was that they themselves had no *areae*—no threshing-floors: they did not gather their harvest. Moreover, with regard to the rains of the past year, it has become clear of what they have reminded mankind, namely, that there was a deluge in ancient times because of the unbelief and wickedness of men. What the fires which lately hung all night over the walls of Carthage threatened is known to those men who were eye witnesses. Of what message the sounds of the preceding thunders were portents is known to those men who hardened themselves against them. All these are signs of the impending wrath of God, which we must, in whatever way we can, both announce and proclaim, and in the meanwhile pray that it may be only local. The universal and final wrath will be felt in due time by those who interpret these samples of it in another fashion. The well-known strange appearance of the sun, when its light was almost extinguished,[97] during the meeting of the court at Utica, also was an omen, inasmuch as the sun could not have suffered this from an ordinary eclipse, since it was situated in its own height and abode in the heavens. You have astrologers; consult them about it.

We can likewise call to your attention deaths of certain governors who at the close of their lives realized that they had sinned by tormenting the Christians. Vigellius Saturninus, who was the first to draw his sword against us in this province,[98] lost his eyesight. In Cappadocia, Claudius Lucius Herminianus,[99] taking it ill that his wife had become a convert to our mode of life, had treated the Christians cruelly. Left alone in his palace, and wasted by the plague, even to the point of breaking out with worms, he said while still alive: "Let no one know it, lest the Christians rejoice and Christian wives conceive new hopes." Afterwards, he recognized his error in having caused some to fall away from their resolution because of torture, and died, almost a Christian. Caecilius Capella, during the well-known doom which overtook Byzantium, cried out: "Christians, rejoice."[100] But, even those persecutors who believe that they have gone unpunished will come to the day of divine judgment. To yourself, also, we wish it may have been only as a warning that, after you condemned Mavilus of Hadrumetum to the beasts, this recent calamity immediately followed.[101] And, now, this hemorrhage of yours is for the same reason. But, think of the future.

---

96. Procurator of the Roman province of Africa, under whom Perpetua and Felicitas suffered martyrdom at Carthage in ca. 203. See *The Martyrdom of Saints Perpetua and Felicitas* below.

97. An eclipse of the sun that modern astronomers think took place on August 14, 212.

98. According to the Acts of the first African martyrs now extant, this martyrdom took place in Numidia on July 17, 180.

99. He cannot be identified with any certainty.

100. He was the provincial governor of Byzantium and one of the generals of Niger. In 196, during Emperor Septimius Severus's campaign against his rivals Albinus and Niger, Septimius Severus destroyed Byzantium and killed its principal inhabitants.

101. It is likely that "this recent calamity" was the rains which Tertullian speaks of above as a "deluge" which brought about a crop failure.

V

Your cruelty is our glory. Only, see to it whether, just because we endure such things, we do not appear to burst out for this one purpose alone, namely, to prove that we do not fear these things, but willingly call them down upon ourselves. When Arrius Antoninus[102] was carrying out a vehement persecution in Asia, all the Christians of the city appeared in a body before his tribunal. After ordering a few to be led away to execution, he said to the rest: "Wretched men, if you wish to die, you have precipices and ropes to hang yourselves." If it should come into our mind to do the same thing here, also, what will you do with so many thousands of human beings, so many of both sexes—men and women—of every age, of every station, giving themselves up to you? How many stakes, how many swords, will you need? What will Carthage itself endure, which you will have to decimate, when every man will recognize his own relatives and companions among them, when, perhaps, he will see even men of your own rank among them, noble ladies, and all the outstanding persons of the city, and the relatives or friends of your own friends? Spare yourself, then, if not us. Spare Carthage, if not yourself. Spare the province which, when your intention became manifest, fell victim to the vexatious accusations both of the soldiers and each man's private enemies.

We have no master but God alone. He, to whom you can do nothing, is before you and cannot be hidden. But, those whom you regard as masters over you are men, and they themselves one day will die. Our religion, however, which you know is growing stronger at the very moment when it seems to be cut down, will never perish. For, whoever beholds such noble endurance will first, as though struck by some kind of uneasiness, be driven to inquire what is the matter in question, and, then, when he knows the truth, immediately follow the same way.

From Tertullian, *Apologetical Works and Minucius Felix Octavius*, translated by Rudolph Arbesmann et al., Fathers of the Church, vol. 10 (New York: Fathers of the Church, 1950), 151–56, 160–61.

3. MARTYRDOM

Polycarp, bishop of Smyrna (according to Tertullian, he was appointed by John the Evangelist), was said to have been martyred at the age of eighty-six. This would place his death in the second half of the second century (proposed dates vary from 155 to 177). *The Martyrdom of Saint Polycarp*, written in the form of a letter from the Church of Smyrna to the Church of Philomelium, is the earliest known account of a Christian martyrdom, or Passion.

The Martyrdom of Saint Polycarp, 4–19

4. There was a Phrygian named Quintus who had only recently come from Phrygia, and when he saw the wild animals he turned cowardly. Now he was the one who had given himself up and had forced some others to give themselves up voluntarily. With him the governor used many arguments and persuaded him to swear by the gods and offer sacrifice. This is the reason, brothers, that we do not approve of those who come forward of themselves: this is not the teaching of the Gospel.

5. Now at first when the most admirable Polycarp heard of this, he was not disturbed and even decided to stay in Smyrna; but most people advised him to slip out quietly. And so he left secretly for a small estate on the outskirts, staying there with a few friends. Day and night he did little else but pray for everyone and for all the churches scattered throughout the world, as he was indeed accustomed to do.

Three days before he was captured he fell into a trance while at prayer: he saw his pillow being consumed by fire. He turned and said to his companions: "I am to be burnt alive."

6. The pursuivants persisted on his trail, and so he moved to a different estate. Shortly thereafter they arrived. Not finding Polycarp they seized two slaves, and one of them told everything under torture. Indeed, it was impossible for Polycarp to remain in hiding when he had betrayers in his own household. The police captain, who was called Herod, was eager to bring him to the amphitheatre: destiny had given him the same name, that Polycarp might fulfil the lot that was appointed to him, becoming a sharer with Christ, and those who betrayed him might receive the punishment of Judas.

---

102. Governor of the province of Asia, ca. 184–85.

7. With the slave then, the police and cavalry set out on Friday at the dinner hour with the usual arms *as though against a brigand*.[103] It was late in the evening when they closed in: they found him reclining in a small room upstairs. He could have left and gone elsewhere but he refused, saying: *"May the will of God be done."*[104] And so, hearing that they had arrived he went downstairs to talk with them, while all those present were surprised at his composure and his old age, and why there should have been such concern to capture so elderly a man.

At any rate Polycarp immediately ordered food and drink to be set before them, as much as they wished, even at this hour, and only requested that they might grant him an hour to pray undisturbed. When they consented, he stood up and began to pray facing the east, and so full was he of God's grace that he was unable to stop for two hours, to the amazement of those who heard him, and many were sorry that they had come out to arrest such a godlike old man.

8. Finally he finished his prayer, after calling to mind all those who had ever come into contact with him, both important and insignificant, famous and obscure, and the entire Catholic Church scattered throughout the world. It was now time to go, and so they put him on a donkey and thus conducted him into the city. It was now a great Sabbath day.[105]

The police captain Herod with his father Nicetes came up to meet Polycarp; they shifted him into their own carriage, and after sitting down beside him they tried to persuade him, saying: "Now what harm is there for you to say 'Caesar is lord,' to perform the sacrifices and so forth, and thus save your life?"

At first Polycarp would not answer them; but when they persisted, he said: "I do not intend to do what you advise."

They then gave up their attempt to move him and spoke threateningly to him, and took him down from the carriage so hastily that he scraped his shin. But taking no notice, as though nothing had happened, he walked on eagerly and quickly; and as he was brought into the amphitheatre there was such an uproar there that no one could even be heard.

9. As Polycarp entered the amphitheatre, a voice from heaven said: *"Be strong, Polycarp, and have courage."*[106] No one saw who was speaking, but those of our people who were present heard the voice.

Then, as he was brought in, a great shout arose when the people heard that it was Polycarp who had been arrested. As he was brought before him, the governor asked him: "Are you Polycarp?" And when he admitted he was, the governor tried to persuade him to recant, saying: "Have respect for your age" (and other similar things that they are accustomed to say); "swear by the Genius of the emperor. Recant. Say, 'Away with the atheists!'"

Polycarp, with a sober countenance, looked at all the mob of lawless pagans who were in the arena, and shaking his fist at them, groaned, looked up to heaven, and said: "Away with the atheists!"

The governor persisted and said: "Swear and I will let you go. Curse Christ!"

But Polycarp answered: "For eighty-six years I have been his servant and he has done me no wrong. How can I blaspheme against my king and saviour?"

10. But the other insisted once again, saying: "Swear by the emperor's Genius!"

He answered: "If you delude yourself into thinking that I will swear by the emperor's Genius, as you say, and if you pretend not to know who I am, listen and I will tell you plainly: I am a Christian. And if you would like to learn the doctrine of Christianity, set aside a day and listen."

The governor said: "Try to move the people."

And Polycarp said: "I should have thought you worthy of such a discussion. For we have been taught to pay respect to the authorities and powers that God has assigned us (for this does not harm our cause). But as for the mob, I do not think they deserve to listen to a speech of defence from me."

11. The governor said: "I have wild animals, and I shall expose you to them if you do not change your mind."

And he answered: "Go and call for them! Repentance from a better state to one that is worse is impossible for us. But it is good to change from what is wicked to righteousness."

And he said again to him: "Since you are not afraid of the animals, then I shall have you consumed by fire—unless you change your mind."

But Polycarp answered: "The fire you threaten me with burns merely for a time and is soon extinguished. It is clear you are ignorant of the fire of everlasting punishment and of the judgement that is to come, which awaits the impious. Why then do you hesitate? Come, do what you will."

12. As he said these and many other words he was filled with a joyful courage; his countenance was filled with grace,

---

103. See Mt 26:55. (The notes for this selection are by Gerhart and Udoh.)
104. See Mt 26:39; Mk 14:36; Lk 22:42; Acts 21:14.
105. Compare Jn 19:31.
106. Compare Acts 18:9–10; see also Deut 31:6–7, 23; Josh 1:6–7.

and not only did he not collapse in terror at what was said to him, but rather it was the governor that was amazed. He sent his herald into the centre of the arena to announce three times: "Polycarp has confessed that he is a Christian."

After the herald had spoken, the entire mob of pagans and Jews from Smyrna shouted out aloud in uncontrollable rage: "Here is the schoolmaster of Asia—the father of the Christians—the destroyer of our gods—the one that teaches the multitude not to sacrifice or do reverence!"

And while they were saying all this they shouted and asked Philip the Asiarch to have a lion loosed on Polycarp. But he said that he was not allowed to do this since the days of the animal games were past. Next they decided to shout out all together that Polycarp should be burnt alive. For the vision he had seen regarding his pillow had to be fulfilled, when he saw it burning while he was at prayer and turned and said to his faithful companions: "I am to be burnt alive."

13. All of this happened with great speed, more quickly than it takes to tell the story: the mob swiftly collected logs and brushwood from workshops and baths, and the Jews (as is their custom) zealously helped them with this. When the fire was prepared, Polycarp took off all his clothing, loosed his belt and even tried to take off his own sandals, although he had never had to do this before: for all the Christians were always eager to be the first to touch his flesh. Even before his martyrdom he had been adorned in every way by reason of the goodness of his life. Straightway then he was attached to the equipment that had been prepared for the fire. When they were on the point of nailing him to it, he said: "Leave me thus. For he who has given me the strength to endure the flames will grant me to remain without flinching in the fire even without the firmness you will give me by using nails."

14. They did not nail him down then, but simply bound him; and as he put his hands behind his back, he was bound like a noble ram chosen for an oblation from a great flock,[107] a holocaust prepared and made acceptable to God. Looking up to heaven, he said: "O Lord, omnipotent God[108] and Father of your beloved and blessed child Christ Jesus, through whom we have received our knowledge of you, the God of the angels, the powers, and of all creation, and of all the family of the good who live in your sight: I bless you because you have thought me worthy of this day and this hour, to have a share among the number of the martyrs in the cup of your Christ, *for the resurrection unto* eternal *life*[109] of both the soul and the body in the immortality of the Holy Spirit. May I be received this day among them before your face as a rich and acceptable sacrifice, as you, the God of truth who cannot deceive, have

prepared, revealed, and fulfilled beforehand. Hence I praise you, I bless you, and I glorify you above all things, through that eternal and celestial high priest, Jesus Christ, your beloved child, through whom is glory to you with him and the Holy Spirit now and for all ages to come. Amen."

15. He had uttered his Amen and finished his prayer, and the men in charge of the fire started to light it. A great flame blazed up and those of us to whom it was given to see beheld a miracle. And we have been preserved to recount the story to others. For the flames, bellying out like a ship's sail in the wind, formed into the shape of a vault and thus surrounded the martyr's body as with a wall. And he was within it not as burning flesh but rather as bread being baked, or like gold and silver being purified in a smelting furnace.[110] And from it we perceived such a delightful fragrance as though it were smoking incense or some other costly perfume.

16. At last when these vicious men realized that his body could not be consumed by the fire they ordered a *confector* to go up and plunge a dagger into the body. When he did this there came out such a quantity of blood that the flames were extinguished, and even the crowd marvelled that there should be such a difference between the unbelievers and the elect. And one of the elect indeed was the most venerable martyr Polycarp, who was in our day a teacher in the apostolic and prophetic tradition and a bishop of the Catholic Church in Smyrna. Every word that he uttered from his mouth was indeed fulfilled and shall be fulfilled.

17. The jealous and envious Evil One,[111] who is the adversary of the race of the just, realizing the greatness of his testimony, his unblemished career from the beginning, and seeing him now crowned with the garland of immortality and the winner of an incontestable prize, prevented us even from taking up the poor body, though so many were eager to do so and to have a share in his holy flesh. Hence he got Nicetes, Herod's father and Alce's brother, to petition the governor not to give up his body. "Otherwise," he said, "they may abandon the Crucified and begin to worship this man."

And all of this was at the suggestion and insistence of the Jewish people, who even kept watch as we were on the point of removing his body from the fire. Little did they know that

---

107. See Lev 5:15.

108. Rev 4:8; 11:17; 15:3; 16:7; 21:22.

109. Jn 5:29.

110. See Wis 3:6; Prov 17:3; Rev 1:13–15.

111. See, for instance, Mt 5:37; 6:13; 13:19, 38; Jn 17:15; Eph 6:16; 1 Jn 2:13–14; 5:18–19.

we could never abandon Christ, for it was he who suffered for the redemption of those who are saved in the entire world, the innocent one dying on behalf of sinners.[112] Nor could we worship anyone else. For him we reverence as the Son of God, whereas we love the martyrs as the disciples and imitators of the Lord, and rightly so because of their unsurpassed loyalty towards their king and master. May we too share with them as fellow disciples!

18. And so, when the centurion noticed the conflict caused by the Jews, he put the body out before everyone and had it cremated, as is their custom. Thus at last, collecting the remains that were dearer to us than precious stones and finer than gold, we buried them in a fitting spot. Gathering here, so far as we can, in joy and gladness, we will be allowed by the Lord to celebrate the anniversary day of his martyrdom, both as a memorial for those who have already fought the contest and for the training and preparation of those who will do so one day.

19. This then was the story of the blessed Polycarp, who, counting those from Philadelphia, was the twelfth to be martyred in Smyrna; yet he alone is especially remembered by everyone and is everywhere mentioned even by the pagans. He was not only a great teacher but also a conspicuous martyr, whose testimony, following the Gospel of Christ, everyone desires to imitate. By his perseverance he overcame the unjust governor and so won the crown of immortality; and rejoicing with the apostles and all the blessed he gives glory to God the almighty Father and praise to our Lord Jesus Christ, the saviour of our souls, the pilot of our bodies, and the shepherd of the Catholic Church throughout the world.

From Herbert Musurillo, ed. and trans., *The Acts of the Christian Martyrs* (Oxford: Clarendon, 1972), 5, 7, 9, 11, 13, 15, 17.

☙ *The Martyrdom of Saints Perpetua and Felicitas* is the account of the martyrdom of six Christians arrested for their faith. The events take place near Carthage, probably on March 7, 202 or 203, during the reign of Emperor Septimius Severus. The group consisted of two slaves, Revocatus and Felicitas, two free men, Saturninus and Secundulus, and, perhaps most significantly, Vivia Perpetua, who was of noble birth, and Saturus. Saturus seems to have been their instructor in the faith, and he chose to share their punishment. The introductory portion of the text shows evidence of strong Montanist influence, and since sections 3–10 were written apparently by Perpetua herself in prison before her death,

The Martyrdom of Saints Perpetua and Felicitas is one of the earliest pieces of writing by a Christian woman.

The Martyrdom of Saints Perpetua and Felicitas, 2–4, 6, 9–12, 14–21

2. A number of young catechumens were arrested, Revocatus and his fellow slave Felicitas, Saturninus and Secundulus, and with them Vibia Perpetua, a newly married woman of good family and upbringing. Her mother and father were still alive and one of her two brothers was a catechumen like herself. She was about twenty-two years old and had an infant son at the breast. (Now from this point on the entire account of her ordeal is her own, according to her own ideas and in the way that she herself wrote it down.)

3. While we were still under arrest (she said) my father out of love for me was trying to persuade me and shake my resolution. "Father," said I, "do you see this vase here, for example, or waterpot or whatever?"

"Yes, I do," said he.

And I told him: "Could it be called by any other name than what it is?"

And he said: "No."

"Well, so too I cannot be called anything other than what I am, a Christian."

At this my father was so angered by the word "Christian" that he moved towards me as though he would pluck my eyes out. But he left it at that and departed, vanquished along with his diabolical arguments.

For a few days afterwards I gave thanks to the Lord that I was separated from my father, and I was comforted by his absence. During these few days I was baptized, and I was inspired by the Spirit not to ask for any other favour after the water but simply the perseverance of the flesh. A few days later we were lodged in the prison; and I was terrified, as I had never before been in such a dark hole. What a difficult time it was! With the crowd the heat was stifling; then there was the extortion of the soldiers; and to crown all, I was tortured with worry for my baby there.

Then Tertius and Pomponius, those blessed deacons who tried to take care of us, bribed the soldiers to allow us to go to a better part of the prison to refresh ourselves for a few hours. Everyone then left that dungeon and shifted for himself. I nursed my baby, who was faint from hunger. In my

---

112. See Rom 5:6–8; Heb 7:26.

anxiety I spoke to my mother about the child, I tried to comfort my brother, and I gave the child in their charge. I was in pain because I saw them suffering out of pity for me. These were the trials I had to endure for many days. Then I got permission for my baby to stay with me in prison. At once I recovered my health, relieved as I was of my worry and anxiety over the child. My prison had suddenly become a palace, so that I wanted to be there rather than anywhere else.

4. Then my brother said to me: "Dear sister, you are greatly privileged; surely you might ask for a vision to discover whether you are to be condemned or freed."

Faithfully I promised that I would, for I knew that I could speak with the Lord, whose great blessings I had come to experience. And so I said: "I shall tell you tomorrow." Then I made my request and this was the vision I had.

I saw a ladder of tremendous height made of bronze, reaching all the way to the heavens,[113] but it was so narrow that only one person could climb up at a time. To the sides of the ladder were attached all sorts of metal weapons: there were swords, spears, hooks, daggers, and spikes; so that if anyone tried to climb up carelessly or without paying attention, he would be mangled and his flesh would adhere to the weapons.

At the foot of the ladder lay a dragon[114] of enormous size, and it would attack those who tried to climb up and try to terrify them from doing so. And Saturus was the first to go up, he who was later to give himself up of his own accord. He had been the builder of our strength, although he was not present when we were arrested. And he arrived at the top of the staircase and he looked back and said to me: "Perpetua, I am waiting for you. But take care; do not let the dragon bite you."

"He will not harm me," I said, "in the name of Christ Jesus."

Slowly, as though he were afraid of me, the dragon stuck his head out from underneath the ladder. Then, using it as my first step, I trod on his head[115] and went up.

Then I saw an immense garden, and in it a grey-haired man sat in shepherd's garb; tall he was, and milking sheep. And standing around him were many thousands of people clad in white garments. He raised his head, looked at me, and said: "I am glad you have come, my child."

He called me over to him and gave me, as it were, a mouthful of the milk he was drawing; and I took it into my cupped hands and consumed it. And all those who stood around said, "Amen!" At the sound of this word I came to, with the taste of something sweet still in my mouth. I at once told this to my brother, and we realized that we would have to suffer, and that from now on we would no longer have any hope in this life.

6. One day while we were eating breakfast we were suddenly hurried off for a hearing. We arrived at the forum, and straight away the story went about the neighbourhood near the forum and a huge crowd gathered. We walked up to the prisoner's dock. All the others when questioned admitted their guilt. Then, when it came my turn, my father appeared with my son, dragged me from the step, and said: "Perform the sacrifice—have pity on your baby!"

Hilarianus the governor, who had received his judicial powers as the successor of the late proconsul Minucius Timinianus, said to me: "Have pity on your father's grey head; have pity on your infant son. Offer the sacrifice for the welfare of the emperors."

"I will not," I retorted.

"Are you a Christian?" said Hilarianus.

And I said: "Yes, I am."

When my father persisted in trying to dissuade me, Hilarianus ordered him to be thrown to the ground and beaten with a rod. I felt sorry for father, just as if I myself had been beaten. I felt sorry for his pathetic old age.

Then Hilarianus passed sentence on all of us: we were condemned to the beasts, and we returned to prison in high spirits. But my baby had got used to being nursed at the breast and to staying with me in prison. So I sent the deacon Pomponius straight away to my father to ask for the baby. But father refused to give him over. But as God willed, the baby had no further desire for the breast, nor did I suffer any inflammation; and so I was relieved of any anxiety for my child and of any discomfort in my breasts.

9. Some days later, an adjutant named Pudens, who was in charge of the prison, began to show us great honour, realizing that we possessed some great power within us. And he began to allow many visitors to see us for our mutual comfort.

Now the day of the contest was approaching, and my father came to see me overwhelmed with sorrow. He started tearing the hairs from his beard and threw them on the ground; he then threw himself on the ground and began to curse his old age and to say such words as would move all creation. I felt sorry for his unhappy old age.

---

113. See Gen 28:12. (The notes for this selection are by Gerhart and Udoh.)
114. See Rev 12:3.
115. See Gen 3:15.

10. The day before we were to fight with the beasts I saw the following vision. Pomponius the deacon came to the prison gates and began to knock violently. I went out and opened the gate for him. He was dressed in an unbelted white tunic, wearing elaborate sandals. And he said to me: "Perpetua, come; we are waiting for you."

Then he took my hand and we began to walk through rough and broken country. At last we came to the amphitheatre out of breath, and he led me into the centre of the arena.

Then he told me: "Do not be afraid. I am here, struggling with you." Then he left.

I looked at the enormous crowd who watched in astonishment. I was surprised that no beasts were let loose on me; for I knew that I was condemned to die by the beasts. Then out came an Egyptian against me, of vicious appearance, together with his seconds, to fight with me. There also came up to me some handsome young men to be my seconds and assistants.

My clothes were stripped off, and suddenly I was a man. My seconds began to rub me down with oil (as they are wont to do before a contest). Then I saw the Egyptian on the other side rolling in the dust. Next there came forth a man of marvellous stature, such that he rose above the top of the amphitheatre. He was clad in a beltless purple tunic with two stripes (one on either side) running down the middle of his chest. He wore sandals that were wondrously made of gold and silver, and he carried a wand like an athletic trainer and a green branch on which there were golden apples.

And he asked for silence and said: "If this Egyptian defeats her he will slay her with the sword. But if she defeats him, she will receive this branch." Then he withdrew.

We drew close to one another and began to let our fists fly. My opponent tried to get hold of my feet, but I kept striking him in the face with the heels of my feet. Then I was raised up into the air and I began to pummel him without as it were touching the ground. Then when I noticed there was a lull, I put my two hands together linking the fingers of one hand with those of the other and thus I got hold of his head. He fell flat on his face and I stepped on his head.

The crowd began to shout and my assistants started to sing psalms. Then I walked up to the trainer and took the branch. He kissed me and said to me: "Peace be with you, my daughter!" I began to walk in triumph towards the Gate of Life.[116] Then I awoke. I realized that it was not with wild animals that I would fight but with the Devil, but I knew that I would win the victory. So much for what I did up until the eve of the contest. About what happened at the contest itself, let him write of it who will.

11. But the blessed Saturus has also made known his own vision and he has written it out with his own hand. We had died, he said, and had put off the flesh, and we began to be carried towards the east by four angels who did not touch us with their hands. But we moved along not on our backs facing upwards but as though we were climbing up a gentle hill. And when we were free of the world, we first saw an intense light. And I said to Perpetua (for she was at my side): "This is what the Lord promised us. We have received his promise."

While we were being carried by these four angels, a great open space appeared, which seemed to be a garden, with rose bushes and all manner of flowers. The trees were as tall as cypresses, and their leaves were constantly falling. In the garden there were four other angels more splendid than the others. When they saw us they paid us homage and said to the other angels in admiration: "Why, they are here! They are here!"

Then the four angels that were carrying us grew fearful and set us down. Then we walked across to an open area by way of a broad road, and there we met Jucundus, Saturninus, and Artaxius, who were burnt alive in the same persecution, together with Quintus who had actually died as a martyr in prison. We asked them where they had been. And the other angels said to us: "First come and enter and greet the Lord."

12. Then we came to a place whose walls seemed to be constructed of light. And in front of the gate stood four angels, who entered in and put on white robes. We also entered and we heard the sound of voices in unison chanting endlessly: "Holy, holy, holy!"[117] In the same place we seemed to see an aged man with white hair and a youthful face, though we did not see his feet. On his right and left were four elders, and behind them stood other aged men. Surprised, we entered and stood before a throne: four angels lifted us up and we kissed the aged man and he touched our faces with his hand. And the elders said to us: "Let us rise." And we rose and gave the kiss of peace. Then the elders said to us: "Go and play."

To Perpetua I said: "Your wish is granted."

She said to me: "Thanks be to God that I am happier here now than I was in the flesh."

---

116. The "Gate of Life" (Porta Sanavivaria) was the gate by which victorious gladiators, or those whose lives had been spared by the people, made their exit. Those who were vanquished and died were transported through the "Gate of Libitina" (Porta Libitinensis; Libitina was the goddess of the dead).

117. Rev 4:8; see Isa 6:3.

14. Such were the remarkable visions of these martyrs, Saturus and Perpetua, written by themselves. As for Secundulus, God called him from this world earlier than the others while he was still in prison, by a special grace that he might not have to face the animals. Yet his flesh, if not his spirit, knew the sword.

15. As for Felicitas, she too enjoyed the Lord's favour in this wise. She had been pregnant when she was arrested, and was now in her eighth month. As the day of the spectacle drew near she was very distressed that her martyrdom would be postponed because of her pregnancy; for it is against the law for women with child to be executed. Thus she might have to shed her holy, innocent blood afterwards along with others who were common criminals. Her comrades in martyrdom were also saddened; for they were afraid that they would have to leave behind so fine a companion to travel alone on the same road to hope. And so, two days before the contest, they poured forth a prayer to the Lord in one torrent of common grief. And immediately after their prayer the birth pains came upon her. She suffered a good deal in her labour because of the natural difficulty of an eight months' delivery.

Hence one of the assistants of the prison guards said to her: "You suffer so much now—what will you do when you are tossed to the beasts? Little did you think of them when you refused to sacrifice."

"What I am suffering now," she replied, "I suffer by myself. But then another will be inside me who will suffer for me, just as I shall be suffering for him."

And she gave birth to a girl; and one of the sisters brought her up as her own daughter.

16. Therefore, since the Holy Spirit has permitted the story of this contest to be written down and by so permitting has willed it, we shall carry out the command or, indeed, the commission of the most saintly Perpetua, however unworthy I might be to add anything to this glorious story. At the same time I shall add one example of her perseverance and nobility of soul. The military tribune had treated them with extraordinary severity because on the information of certain very foolish people he became afraid that they would be spirited out of the prison by magical spells.

Perpetua spoke to him directly. "Why can you not even allow us to refresh ourselves properly? For we are the most distinguished of the condemned prisoners, seeing that we belong to the emperor; we are to fight on his very birthday.[118] Would it not be to your credit if we were brought forth on the day in a healthier condition?"

The officer became disturbed and grew red. So it was

that he gave the order that they were to be more humanely treated; and he allowed her brothers and other persons to visit, so that the prisoners could dine in their company. By this time the adjutant who was head of the gaol was himself a Christian.

17. On the day before, when they had their last meal, which is called the free banquet, they celebrated not a banquet but rather a love feast. They spoke to the mob with the same steadfastness, warned them of God's judgement, stressing the joy they would have in their suffering, and ridiculing the curiosity of those that came to see them. Saturus said: "Will not tomorrow be enough for you? Why are you so eager to see something that you dislike? Our friends today will be our enemies on the morrow. But take careful note of what we look like so that you will recognize us on the day." Thus everyone would depart from the prison in amazement, and many of them began to believe.

18. The day of their victory dawned, and they marched from the prison to the amphitheatre joyfully as though they were going to heaven, with calm faces, trembling, if at all, with joy rather than fear. Perpetua went along with shining countenance and calm step, as the beloved of God, as a wife of Christ, putting down everyone's stare by her own intense gaze. With them also was Felicitas, glad that she had safely given birth so that now she could fight the beasts, going from one blood bath to another, from the midwife to the gladiator, ready to wash after childbirth in a second baptism.

They were then led up to the gates and the men were forced to put on the robes of priests of Saturn, the women the dress of the priestesses of Ceres. But the noble Perpetua strenuously resisted this to the end.

"We came to this of our own free will, that our freedom should not be violated. We agreed to pledge our lives provided that we would do no such thing. You agreed with us to do this."

Even injustice recognized justice. The military tribune agreed. They were to be brought into the arena just as they were. Perpetua then began to sing a psalm: she was already treading on the head of the Egyptian. Revocatus, Saturninus, and Saturus began to warn the onlooking mob. Then when they came within sight of Hilarianus, they suggested by their motions and gestures: "You have condemned us, but God will condemn you" was what they were saying.

---

118. Probably Geta's birthday. Geta was the son and successor of Emperor Septimius Severus.

At this the crowds became enraged and demanded that they be scourged before a line of gladiators. And they rejoiced at this that they had obtained a share in the Lord's sufferings.

19. But he who said, *Ask and you shall receive*,[119] answered their prayer by giving each one the death he had asked for. For whenever they would discuss among themselves their desire for martyrdom, Saturninus indeed insisted that he wanted to be exposed to all the different beasts, that his crown might be all the more glorious. And so at the outset of the contest he and Revocatus were matched with a leopard, and then while in the stocks they were attacked by a bear. As for Saturus, he dreaded nothing more than a bear, and he counted on being killed by one bite of a leopard. Then he was matched with a wild boar; but the gladiator who had tied him to the animal was gored by the boar and died a few days after the contest, whereas Saturus was only dragged along. Then when he was bound in the stocks awaiting the bear, the animal refused to come out of the cages, so that Saturus was called back once more unhurt.

20. For the young women, however, the Devil had prepared a mad heifer. This was an unusual animal, but it was chosen that their sex might be matched with that of the beast. So they were stripped naked, placed in nets and thus brought out into the arena. Even the crowd was horrified when they saw that one was a delicate young girl and the other was a woman fresh from childbirth with the milk still dripping from her breasts. And so they were brought back again and dressed in unbelted tunics.

First the heifer tossed Perpetua and she fell on her back. Then sitting up she pulled down the tunic that was ripped along the side so that it covered her thighs, thinking more of her modesty than of her pain. Next she asked for a pin to fasten her untidy hair: for it was not right that a martyr should die with her hair in disorder, lest she might seem to be mourning in her hour of triumph.

Then she got up. And seeing that Felicitas had been crushed to the ground, she went over to her, gave her her hand, and lifted her up. Then the two stood side by side. But the cruelty of the mob was by now appeased, and so they were called back through the Gate of Life.

There Perpetua was held up by a man named Rusticus who was at the time a catechumen and kept close to her. She awoke from a kind of sleep (so absorbed had she been in ecstasy in the Spirit) and she began to look about her. Then to the amazement of all she said: "When are we going to be thrown to that heifer or whatever it is?"

When told that this had already happened, she refused to believe it until she noticed the marks of her rough experience on her person and her dress. Then she called for her brother and spoke to him together with the catechumens and said: "You must all *stand fast in the faith*[120] and love one another, and do not be weakened by what we have gone through."

21. At another gate Saturus was earnestly addressing the soldier Pudens. "It is exactly," he said, "as I foretold and predicted. So far not one animal has touched me. So now you may believe me with all your heart: I am going in there and I shall be finished off with one bite of the leopard." And immediately as the contest was coming to a close a leopard was let loose, and after one bite Saturus was so drenched with blood that as he came away the mob roared in witness to his second baptism: "Well washed! Well washed!" For well washed indeed was one who had been bathed in this manner.

Then he said to the soldier Pudens: "Good-bye. Remember me, and remember the faith. These things should not disturb you but rather strengthen you."

And with this he asked Pudens for a ring from his finger, and dipping it into his wound he gave it back to him again as a pledge and as a record of his bloodshed.

Shortly after he was thrown unconscious with the rest in the usual spot to have his throat cut. But the mob asked that their bodies be brought out into the open that their eyes might be the guilty witnesses of the sword that pierced their flesh. And so the martyrs got up and went to the spot of their own accord as the people wanted them to, and kissing one another they sealed their martyrdom with the ritual kiss of peace. The others took the sword in silence and without moving, especially Saturus, who being the first to climb the stairway was the first to die. For once again he was waiting for Perpetua. Perpetua, however, had yet to taste more pain. She screamed as she was struck on the bone; then she took the trembling hand of the young gladiator and guided it to her throat. It was as though so great a woman, feared as she was by the unclean spirit, could not be dispatched unless she herself were willing.

Ah, most valiant and blessed martyrs! Truly are you called and chosen for the glory of Christ Jesus our Lord! And any man who exalts, honours, and worships his glory should read for the consolation of the Church these new deeds of heroism which are no less significant than the tales of old. For

---

119. Mt 7:7; Lk 11:9; Jn 16:24.
120. 1 Cor 16:13; see also Acts 14:22.

these new manifestations of virtue will bear witness to one and the same Spirit who still operates, and to God the Father almighty, to his Son Jesus Christ our Lord, to whom is splendour and immeasurable power for all ages. Amen.

From Herbert Musurillo, ed. and trans., *The Acts of the Christian Martyrs* (Oxford: Clarendon, 1972), 109, 111, 113, 115, 117, 119, 121, 123, 125, 127, 129, 131.

◈ **Tertullian** (ca. 155–225), like Perpetua, lived in Carthage. He probably wrote *To the Martyrs* in 197, before he became an outspoken proponent of Montanism.

TERTULLIAN

To the Martyrs, I–IV

I

1. Blessed martyrs elect, along with the nourishment for the body which our Lady Mother the Church[121] from her breast, as well as individual brethren from their private resources, furnish you in prison, accept also from me some offering that will contribute to the sustenance of the spirit. For it is not good that the flesh be feasted while the spirit goes hungry. Indeed, if care is bestowed on that which is weak, there is all the more reason not to neglect that which is still weaker.[122] 2. Not that I am specially entitled to exhort you. Yet, even the most accomplished gladiators are spurred on not only by their trainers and managers but also from afar by people inexperienced in this art and by all who choose, without the slightest need for it, with the result that hints issuing from the crowd have often proved profitable for them.

3. In the first place, then, O blessed, "do not grieve the Holy Spirit"[123] who has entered prison with you. For, if He had not accompanied you there in your present trial, you would not be there today. See to it, therefore, that He remain with you there and so lead you out of that place to the Lord. 4. Indeed, the prison is the Devil's house, too, where he keeps his household. But you have come to the prison for the very purpose of trampling upon him right in his own house. For you have engaged him in battle already outside the prison and trampled him underfoot. 5. Let him, therefore, not say: "Now that they are in my domain, I will tempt them with base hatreds, with defections or dissensions among themselves." Let him flee from your presence, and let him, coiled and numb, like a snake that is driven out by charms or smoke, hide away in the depths of his den. Do not allow him

the good fortune in his own kingdom of setting you against one another, but let him find you fortified by the arms of peace among yourselves, because peace among yourselves means war with him. 6. Some, not able to find this peace in the Church, are accustomed to seek it from the martyrs in prison. For this reason, too, then, you ought to possess, cherish and preserve it among yourselves that you may perhaps be able to bestow it upon others also.[124]

II

1. Other attachments, equally burdensome to the spirit, may have accompanied you to the prison gate; so far your relatives, too, may have escorted you. From that very moment on you have been separated from the very world. How much more, then, from its spirit and its ways and doings? Nor let this separation from the world trouble you. For, if we reflect that it is the very world that is more truly a prison, we shall realize that you have left a prison rather than entered one. 2. The world holds the greater darkness, blinding men's hearts. The world puts on the heavier chains, fettering the very souls of men. The world breathes forth the fouler impurities—human lusts. 3. Finally, the world contains the larger number of criminals, namely, the entire human race. In fact, it awaits sentence not from the proconsul but from God. 4. Wherefore, O blessed, consider yourselves as having been transferred from prison to what we may call a place of safety. Darkness is there, but you are light;[125] fetters are there, but you are free before God. It breathes forth a foul smell, but you are an odor of sweetness.[126] There the judge is expected at every moment, but you are going to pass sentence upon the judges themselves.[127] 5. There sadness may come upon the man who sighs for the pleasures of the world. The Christian, however, even when he is outside the prison, has renounced the world, and, when in prison, even prison itself. It does not matter what part of the world you are in, you who are apart

---

121. This is the first reference in Latin Christian writings to the Church as "mother." (The notes for this selection are by Gerhart and Udoh.)

122. See Mk 14:38; Mt 26:41.

123. Eph 4:30.

124. This "peace" would come especially in the form of letters of recommendation written by the soon-to-be martyr ("confessor") to the bishop on behalf of a lapsed Christian. Such a letter usually would have the effect of shortening the length of the penitent's canonical penance and, therefore, hastening his or her readmission to the communion of the Church.

125. See Mt 5:14; 1 Thess 5:5; Eph 5:8.

126. See 2 Cor 2:14–16; Eph 5:2; Ezek 20:41.

127. See 1 Cor 6:2; Wis 3:8.

from the world. 6. And if you have missed some of the enjoyments of life, remember that it is the way of business to suffer some losses in order to make larger profits.

I say nothing yet about the reward to which God invites the martyrs. Meanwhile, let us compare the life in the world with that in prison to see if the spirit does not gain more in prison than the flesh loses there. 7. In fact, owing to the solicitude of the Church and the charity of the brethren, the flesh does not miss there what it ought to have, while, in addition, the spirit obtains what is always beneficial to the faith: you do not look at strange gods; you do not chance upon their images; you do not, even by mere physical contact, participate in heathen holidays; you are not plagued by the foul fumes of the sacrificial banquets, not tormented by the noise of the spectacles, nor by the atrocity or frenzy or shamelessness of those taking part in the celebrations; your eyes do not fall on houses of lewdness; you are free from inducements to sin, from temptations, from unholy reminiscences, free, indeed, even from persecution.

8. The prison now offers to the Christian what the desert once gave to the Prophets.[128] Our Lord Himself quite often spent time in solitude to pray there more freely,[129] to be there away from the world. In fact, it was in a secluded place that He manifested His glory to His disciples.[130] Let us drop the name 'prison' and call it a place of seclusion. 9. Though the body is confined, though the flesh is detained, there is nothing that is not open to the spirit. In spirit wander about, in spirit take a walk, setting before yourselves not shady promenades and long porticoes but that path which leads to God. As often as you walk that path, you will not be in prison. 10. The leg does not feel the fetter when the spirit is in heaven. The spirit carries about the whole man and brings him wherever he wishes. And where your heart is, there will your treasure be also.[131] There, then, let our heart be where we would have our treasure.

III

1. Granted now, O blessed, that even to Christians the prison is unpleasant—yet, we were called to the service in the army of the living God in the very moment when we gave response to the words of the sacramental oath.[132] No soldier goes out to war encumbered with luxuries, nor does he march to the line of battle from the sleeping chamber, but from light and cramped tents where every kind of austerity, discomfort, and inconvenience is experienced. 2. Even

in time of peace soldiers are toughened to warfare by toils and hardships: by marching in arms, by practising swift maneuvers in the field, by digging a trench, by joining closely together to form a tortoise-shield. Everything is set in sweating toil, lest bodies and minds be frightened at having to pass from shade to sunshine, from sunshine to icy cold, from the tunic to the breastplate, from hushed silence to the warcry, from rest to the din of battle.

3. In like manner, O blessed, consider whatever is hard in your present situation as an exercise of your powers of mind and body. You are about to enter a noble contest[133] in which the living God acts the part of superintendent and the Holy Spirit is your trainer, a contest whose crown is eternity, whose prize is angelic nature, citizenship in heaven and glory for ever and ever. 4. And so your Master, Jesus Christ, who has anointed you with His Spirit[134] and has brought you to this training ground, has resolved, before the day of the contest, to take you from a softer way of life to a harsher treatment that your strength may be increased. For athletes, too, are set apart for more rigid training that they may apply themselves to the building up of their physical strength. They are kept from lavish living, from more tempting dishes, from more pleasurable drinks. They are urged on, they are subjected to torturing toils, they are worn out: the more strenuously they have exerted themselves, the greater is their hope of victory. 5. And they do this, says the Apostle,[135] to win a perishable crown. We who are about to win an eternal one recognize in the prison our training ground, that we may be led forth to the actual contest before the seat of the presiding judge well practised in all hardships, because strength is built up by austerity, but destroyed by softness.

IV

1. We know from our Lord's teaching that, while the spirit is willing, the flesh is weak.[136] Let us, however, not derive de-

---

128. See 1 Kings 19:4.

129. See Mk 1:12, 35; Mt 4:1–2; Lk 4:1–2, 42.

130. Mk 9:2–3; Mt 17:1–2; Lk 9:28–29; 2 Pet 1:16–18.

131. See Mt 6:21; Lk 12:34.

132. *Sacramentum*, referring here to the Christian baptismal vows, is a military term for the military oath of allegiance.

133. See 1 Tim 6:12.

134. See 1 Jn 2:20, 27; an anointing that, according to Tertullian, is comparable to the anointing of the body of athletes in the palaestra.

135. 1 Cor 9:24–27.

136. Mk 14:38; Mt 26:41.

lusive gratification from the Lord's acknowledgment of the weakness of the flesh. For it was on purpose that He first declared the spirit willing: He wanted to show which of the two ought to be subject to the other, that is to say, that the flesh should be submissive to the spirit, the weaker to the stronger, so that the former may draw strength from the latter. 2. Let the spirit converse with the flesh on their common salvation, no longer thinking about the hardships of prison but, rather, about the struggle of the actual contest. The flesh will perhaps fear the heavy sword and the lofty cross and the wild beasts mad with rage and the most terrible punishment of all—death by fire—and, finally, all the executioner's cunning during the torture. 3. But let the spirit present to both itself and the flesh the other side of the picture: granted, these sufferings are grievous, yet many have borne them patiently, nay, have even sought them on their own accord for the sake of fame and glory; and this is true not only of men but also of women so that you, too, O blessed women, may be worthy of your sex.

4. It would lead me too far were I to enumerate each one of those who, led by the impulse of their own mind, put an end to their lives by the sword. Among women there is the well-known instance of Lucretia. A victim of violence, she stabbed herself in the presence of her kinsfolk to gain glory for her chastity. Mucius burnt his right hand on the altar that his fair fame might include this deed. 5. Nor did the philosophers act less courageously: Heraclitus, for instance, who put an end to his life by smearing himself with cow dung; Empedocles, too, who leaped down into the fires of Mt. Etna; and Peregrinus who not long ago threw himself upon a funeral pile. Why, even women have despised the flames: Dido did so in order not to be forced to marry after the departure of the man she had loved most dearly; the wife of Hasdrubal, too, with Carthage in flames, cast herself along with her children into the fire that was destroying her native city, that she might not see her husband a suppliant at Scipio's feet. 6. Regulus, a Roman general, was taken prisoner by the Carthaginians, but refused to be the only Roman exchanged for a large number of Carthaginian captives. He preferred to be returned to the enemy, and, crammed into a kind of chest, suffered as many crucifixions as nails were driven in from the outside in all directions to pierce him. A woman voluntarily sought out wild beasts, namely, vipers, serpents more horrible than either bull or bear, which Cleopatra let loose upon herself as not to fall into the hands of the enemy.

7. You may object: "But the fear of death is not so great as the fear of torture." Did the Athenian courtesan yield on that account to the executioner? For, being privy to a conspiracy, she was subjected to torture by the tyrant. But she did not betray her fellow conspirators, and at last bit off her own tongue and spat it into the tyrant's face to let him know that torments, however prolonged, could achieve nothing against her. 8. Everybody knows that to this day the most important festival of the Lacedaemonians is the διαμαστίγωσις, that is, The Whipping. In this sacred rite all the noble youth are scourged with whips before the altar, while their parents and kinsfolk stand by and exhort them to perseverance. For they regard it as a mark of greater distinction and glory if the soul rather than the body has submitted to the stripes.

9. Therefore, if earthly glory accruing from strength of body and soul is valued so highly that one despises sword, fire, piercing with nails, wild beasts and tortures for the reward of human praise, then I may say the sufferings you endure are but trifling in comparison with the heavenly glory and divine reward. If the bead made of glass is rated so highly, how much must the true pearl be worth? Who, therefore, does not most gladly spend as much for the true as others spend for the false?

From Tertullian, *Disciplinary, Moral and Ascetical Works,* translated by Rudolph Arbesmann et al., Fathers of the Church, vol. 40 (New York: Fathers of the Church, 1959), 17–28.

4. ASCETICISM AND HERMITISM

Ascetic ideals and practices have always been a part of Christianity, but it was with **Antony the Great** (ca. 251–356) that asceticism took the form of a mass movement of men and women into the desert of Upper Egypt. He is thus considered the father of the solitary ascetics, the Anchorites. In his *Letter* 1, Antony provides firsthand testimony to the ascetic life in the desert.

ANTONY THE GREAT

Letter 1

A Letter of Antony the Solitary and Chief of Solitaries to the brethren dwelling in every place.

First of all—peace to your love in the Lord!

I think, brethren, that the souls which draw near to the love of God are of three sorts, be they male or female.

There are those who are called by the law of love which is in their nature, and which original good implanted in them at their first creation. The word of God came to them, and they doubted not at all but followed it readily, like Abraham the Patriarch: for when God saw that it was not from the teaching of men that he had learnt to love God, but from the law implanted in the nature of his first compacting, God appeared to him and said, "Get thee out from thy country and from thy kindred and from thy father's house, unto a land that I will show thee."[137] And he went nothing doubting, but was ready for his calling. He is the pattern of this approach, which still persists in those who follow in his footsteps. Toiling and seeking the fear of God in patience and quiet, they achieve the true manner of life, because their souls are ready to follow the love of God. This is the first kind of calling.

The second calling is this. There are men who hear the written Law testifying of pains and torments prepared for the wicked, and of the promises prepared for those who walk worthily in the fear of God; and by the testimony of the written Law their thoughts are roused up to seek to enter into the calling, as David testifies when he says: "The law of the Lord is undefiled, converting the soul: the testimony of the Lord is sure, and giveth wisdom unto the simple."[138] And in another place he says, "The opening of thy words giveth light and understanding unto the simple";[139] and much else, all of which we cannot mention now.

The third calling is this. There are souls which at first were hard of heart and persisted in the works of sin; and somehow the good God in his mercy sends upon such souls the chastisement of affliction, till they grow weary, and come to their senses, and are converted, and draw near, and enter into knowledge, and repent with all their heart, and they also attain the true manner of life, like those others of whom we have already spoken. These are the three approaches by which souls come to repentance, till they attain to the grace and calling of the Son of God.

Now, as regards those who have entered with all their heart, and have made themselves despise all afflictions of the flesh, valiantly resisting all the warfare that rises against them, until they conquer—I think that first of all, the Spirit calls them, and makes the warfare light for them, and sweetens for them the works of repentance, showing them how they ought to repent in body and soul, until He has taught them how to be converted to God who created them. And He delivers to them works whereby they may constrain their soul and their body, that both may be purified and enter together into their inheritance.

First the body is purified by much fasting, by many vigils and prayers, and by the service which makes a man to be straitened in body, cutting off from himself all the lusts of the flesh. And the Spirit of Repentance is made his guide in these things, and tests him by means of them, lest the enemy should turn him back again.

Then the Spirit that is his guide begins to open the eyes of his soul, to give to it also repentance, that it may be purified. The mind also starts to discriminate between the body and the soul, as it begins to learn from the Spirit how to purify both by repentance. And, taught by the Spirit, the mind becomes our guide to the labours of body and soul, showing us how to purify them. And it separates us from all the fruits of the flesh which have been mingled with all the members of the body since the first transgression, and brings back each of the members of the body to its original condition, having nothing in it from the spirit of satan. And the body is brought under the authority of the mind, being taught by

---

137. Gen 12:1. (The notes for this selection are by Gerhart and Udoh.)
138. Ps 19:7.
139. Ps 119:130.

the Spirit, as St. Paul says: "I keep under my body, and bring it into subjection."[140] For the mind purifies it from food and from drink and from sleep, and in a word from all its motions, until through its own purity it frees the body even from the natural emission of seed.

And, as I think, there are three types of motion of the body. There is that which is implanted in the body by nature, compacted with it in its first creation; but this is not operative if the soul does not will it, save only that it signifies its presence through a passionless movement in the body. And there is another motion, when a man stuffs his body with food and drink, and the heat of the blood from the abundance of nourishment rouses up warfare in the body, because of our greed. For this cause the Apostle said, "Be not drunk with wine, wherein is excess."[141] And again the Lord enjoined His disciples, "Take heed lest at any time your hearts be overcharged with surfeiting and drunkenness"[142] or pleasure. Especially those who seek the measure of purity ought to be saying, "I keep under my body, and bring it into subjection."[143] And there is a third motion, from the evil spirits which tempt us out of envy, and seek to defile those who are setting out on the way of purity.

And now, my beloved children, in these three types of motion, if the soul exerts itself and perseveres in the testimony which the Spirit bears within the mind, both soul and body are purified from this kind of sickness. But if in regard to these three motions the mind spurns the testimony which the Spirit bears within it, evil spirits take authority over it, and sow in the body all the passions, and stir up and quicken strong war against it; till the soul grows weary and sick, and cries out and seeks from whence help may come to it, and repents, and obeys the commandments of the Spirit, and is healed. Then it is persuaded to make its rest in God, and that He is its peace.

These things I have said to you, beloved, that you may know how it is required of a man to repent in body and soul, and to purify them both. And if the mind conquers in this contest, then it prays in the Spirit, and begins to expel from the body the passions of the soul which come to it from its own will. Then the Spirit has a loving partnership with the mind, because the mind keeps the commandments which the Spirit has delivered to it. And the Spirit teaches the mind how to heal all the wounds of the soul, and to rid itself of every one, those which are mingled in the members of the body, and other passions which are altogether outside the body, being mingled in the will. And for the eyes it sets a rule, that they may see rightly and purely, and that in them there

may be no guile. After that it sets a rule also for the ears, how they may hear in peace, and no more thirst or desire to hear ill speaking, nor about the falls and humiliations of men; but how they may rejoice to hear about good things, and about the way every man stands firm and about the mercy shown to the whole creation, which in these members once was sick.

Then again the Spirit teaches the tongue its own purity, since the tongue was sick with a great sickness; for the sickness which afflicted the soul was expressed in speech through the tongue, which the soul used as its organ, and in this way a great sickness and wound was inflicted upon it, and especially through this member—the tongue—was the soul stricken. The Apostle James testifies to us and says, "If any man thinketh himself to be religious, and bridleth not his tongue, but deceiveth his own heart, this man's religion is vain."[144] And in another place he says, "The tongue is a little member, and defileth the whole body"[145]—and much besides, which I cannot all quote now. But if the mind is strengthened with the strength that it receives from the Spirit, first it is purified and sanctified, and learns discrimination in the words that it delivers to the tongue, that they may be without partiality and without self-will, and so the saying of Solomon is fulfilled, "My words are spoken from God, there is nothing froward nor perverse in them."[146] And in another place he says, "The tongue of the wise is healing";[147] and much besides.

After this again the Spirit heals the motions of the hands, which once were moved in a disorderly way, following the will of the mind. But now the Spirit instructs the mind in their purification, that it may labour with them in almsgiving and in prayer; and the word is fulfilled concerning them which says, "Let the lifting up of my hands be an evening sacrifice";[148] and in another place, "The hands of the diligent make rich."[149]

After this again the Spirit purifies the belly in its eating and drinking; for, so long as the desires of the soul were active within it, it was never satisfied in its greedy longing for food and drink, and in this way demons made their onslaught on the soul. About this the Spirit speaks by David, "With him that hath a high look and a proud heart I would

---

140. 1 Cor 9:27.

141. Eph 5:18.

142. Lk 21:34.

143. 1 Cor 9:27.

144. Jas 1:26.

145. Jas 3:5.

146. Prov 8:8.

147. Prov 12:18.

148. Ps 141:2.

149. Prov 10:4.

not eat."[150] And to those who seek purity in this, the Spirit assigns rules of purification, to eat in moderation sufficient for the strength of the body, but in so doing not to have the taste of concupiscence: and in this way the saying of Paul is fulfilled, "Whether ye eat or drink, or whatever ye do, do all to the glory of God."[151]

Then in regard to the sexual thoughts which are moved from below the belly, again the mind is taught by the Spirit, and makes discrimination between the three types of motion of which we spoke above, and perseveres in their purification, as the Spirit helps and strengthens it; and all the motions are quenched by the power of the Spirit, which makes peace in the whole body, and cuts off from it all passions. This is what St Paul says: "Mortify your members which are upon the earth, fornication, uncleanness, passion, evil concupiscence,"[152] and so on.

After all this, it gives to the feet also their purification. At one time they were not making their steps aright according to God; but now the mind, being unified under the authority of the Spirit, effects their purification, that they should walk according to its will, going and ministering in good works, so that the whole body may be changed and renewed and be under the authority of the Spirit. And I think that when the whole body is purified, and has received the fulness of the Spirit, it has received some portion of that spiritual body which it is to assume in the resurrection of the just.

This I have said concerning the sicknesses of the soul which are mingled with the members of the bodily nature in which the soul moves and works; and so the soul becomes guide to the evil spirits which by it have been working in the limbs of the body. But I have said that the soul has also other passions apart from the body; and this we will now demonstrate. Pride is a sickness of the soul apart from the body; so also are boastfulness, envy, hatred, impatience, sloth and the rest. But if the soul gives itself to God wholeheartedly, God has mercy upon it and gives it the Spirit of Repentance, which testifies to it about each sin, that it may not again draw near to them; and shows it those who rise up against it and seek to prevent it separating itself from them, contending with it greatly that it may not abide in repentance. But if it endures and obeys the Spirit which counsels it to repentance, suddenly the Creator has mercy on the weariness of its repentance, and seeing its bodily toils, in much prayer and fasting and supplication and learning of the words of God, in renunciation of the world, in humility and tears and perseverance in contrition, then the merciful God, seeing its toil and submission, has pity upon it and delivers it.

The end of the letter which the holy Antony sent to the brethren.

From *The Letters of St. Antony the Great,* translated by Derwas J. Chitty, Fairacres Publication, no. 50 (Oxford: SLG Press, 1975), 1–5.

✎ **Amma (Mother) Theodora** was one of the hermits or nuns presumed to have lived in the Egyptian desert during the fourth to fifth century. We know of her only through "The Sayings of Amma Theodora," which were preserved by her disciples and eventually became part of the collections of sayings by the desert ascetics.

AMMA THEODORA
"The Sayings of Amma Theodora"

1. Amma Theodora asked Archbishop Theophilus about some words of the apostle saying, "What does this mean, 'Knowing how to profit by circumstances'?"[153] He said to her, "This saying shows us how to profit at all times. For example, is it a time of excess for you? By humility and patience buy up the time of excess, and draw profit from it. Is it the time of shame? Buy it up by means of resignation and win it. So everything that goes against us can, if we wish, become profitable to us."

2. Amma Theodora said, "Let us strive to enter by the narrow gate.[154] Just as the trees, if they have not stood before the winter's storms, cannot bear fruit, so it is with us; this present age is a storm and it is only through many trials and temptations that we can obtain an inheritance in the kingdom of heaven."

3. She also said, "It is good to live in peace, for the wise man practises perpetual prayer. It is truly a great thing for a virgin or a monk to live in peace, especially for the younger ones. However, you should realize that as soon as you intend to live in peace, at once evil comes and weighs down your soul through *accidie,* faintheartedness, and evil thoughts. It also attacks your body through sickness, debility, weakening of the knees, and all the members. It dissipates the strength

---

150. Ps 101:5.
151. 1 Cor 10:31.
152. Col 3:5.
153. See Col 4:5. (The notes for this selection are by Gerhart and Udoh.)
154. See Mt 7:13–14; Lk 13:24.

of soul and body, so that one believes one is ill and no longer able to pray. But if we are vigilant, all these temptations fall away. There was, in fact, a monk who was seized by cold and fever every time he began to pray, and he suffered from headaches, too. In this condition, he said to himself, 'I am ill, and near to death; so now I will get up before I die and pray.' By reasoning in this way, he did violence to himself and prayed. When he had finished, the fever abated also. So, by reasoning in this way, the brother resisted, and prayed and was able to conquer his thoughts."

4. The same Amma Theodora said, "A devout man happened to be insulted by someone, and he said to him, 'I could say as much to you, but the commandment of God keeps my mouth shut.'" Again she said this, "A Christian discussing the body with a Manichean expressed himself in these words, 'Give the body discipline and you will see that the body is for him who made it.'"

5. The same Amma said that a teacher ought to be a stranger to the desire for domination, vain-glory, and pride; one should not be able to fool him by flattery, nor blind him by gifts, nor conquer him by the stomach, nor dominate him by anger; but he should be patient, gentle and humble as far as possible; he must be tested and without partisanship, full of concern, and a lover of souls.

6. She also said that neither asceticism nor vigils nor any kind of suffering are able to save, only true humility can do that. There was an anchorite who was able to banish the demons; and he asked them, "What makes you go away? Is it fasting?" They replied, "We do not eat or drink." "Is it vigils?" They replied, "We do not sleep." "Is it separation from the world?" "We live in the deserts." "What power sends you away then?" They said, "Nothing can overcome us, but only humility." "Do you see how humility is victorious over the demons?"

7. Amma Theodora also said, "There was a monk, who, because of the great number of his temptations said, 'I will go away from here.' As he was putting on his sandals, he saw another man who was also putting on his sandals and this other monk said to him, 'Is it on my account that you are going away? Because I go before you wherever you are going.'"

8. The same Amma was asked about the conversations one hears; "If one is habitually listening to secular speech, how can one yet live for God alone, as you suggest?" She said, "Just as when you are sitting at table and there are many courses, you take some but without pleasure, so when secular conversations come your way, have your heart turned to-wards God, and thanks to this disposition, you will hear them without pleasure, and they will not do you any harm."

9. Another monk suffered bodily irritation and was infested with vermin. Now originally he had been rich. So the demons said to him, "How can you bear to live like this, covered with vermin?" But this monk, because of the greatness of his soul, was victorious over them.

10. Another of the old men questioned Amma Theodora saying, "At the resurrection of the dead, how shall we rise?" She said, "As pledge, example, and as prototype we have him who died for us and is risen, Christ our God."

From *The Sayings of the Desert Fathers*, rev. ed., translated by Benedicta Ward (Kalamazoo, MI: Cistercian, 1984), 82–84.

✎ **Abba Moses** (ca. 332–400) was from Ethiopia and was sometimes referred to as "Moses the Black." Once a slave and a well-known thief, he became devoted to asceticism at Scetis, in the western desert of Egypt, under the guidance of Isidore of Pelusium. Literary evidence of his life and thought is found in the work of **Palladius** (ca. 368–430), in "The Sayings of Abba Moses," and in "Seven Instructions."

ABBA MOSES
"The Sayings of Abba Moses," 1–6

1. It happened that Abba Moses was struggling with the temptation of fornication. Unable to stay any longer in the cell, he went and told Abba Isidore. The old man exhorted him to return to his cell. But he refused, saying, "Abba, I cannot." Then Abba Isidore took Moses out onto the terrace and said to him, "Look towards the west." He looked and saw hordes of demons flying about and making a noise before launching an attack. Then Abba Isidore said to him, "Look towards the east." He turned and saw an innumerable multitude of holy angels shining with glory. Abba Isidore said, "See, these are sent by the Lord to the saints to bring them help, while those in the west fight against them. Those who are with us are more in number than they are." Then Abba Moses gave thanks to God, plucked up courage and returned to his cell.

2. A brother at Scetis committed a fault. A council was called to which Abba Moses was invited, but he refused to go to it. Then the priest sent someone to say to him, "Come, for everyone is waiting for you." So he got up and went. He took a leaking jug, filled it with water and carried it with him. The others came out to meet him and said to him, "What is this,

Father?" The old man said to them, "My sins run out behind me, and I do not see them, and today I am coming to judge the errors of another." When they heard that they said no more to the brother but forgave him.

3. Another day when a council was being held in Scetis, the Fathers treated Moses with contempt in order to test him, saying, "Why does this black man come among us?" When he heard this he kept silence. When the council was dismissed, they said to him, "Abba, did that not grieve you at all?" He said to them, "I was grieved, but I kept silence."

4. It was said of Abba Moses that he was ordained and the ephod was placed upon him. The archbishop said to him, "See, Abba Moses, now you are entirely white." The old man said to him, "It is true of the outside, lord and father, but what about Him who sees the inside?" Wishing to test him the archbishop said to the priests, "When Abba Moses comes into the sanctuary, drive him out, and go with him to hear what he says." So the old man came in and they covered him with abuse, and drove him out, saying, "Outside, black man!" Going out, he said to himself, "They have acted rightly concerning you, for your skin is as black as ashes. You are not a man, so why should you be allowed to meet men?"

5. Once the order was given at Scetis, "Fast this week." Now it happened that some brothers came from Egypt to visit Abba Moses and he cooked something for them. Seeing some smoke, the neighbours said to the ministers, "Look, Moses has broken the commandment and has cooked something in his cell." The ministers said, "When he comes, we will speak to him ourselves." When the Saturday came, since they knew Abba Moses' remarkable way of life, the ministers said to him in front of everyone, "O Abba Moses, you did not keep the commandment of men, but it was so that you might keep the commandment of God."

6. A brother came to Scetis to visit Abba Moses and asked him for a word. The old man said to him, "Go, sit in your cell, and your cell will teach you everything."

From *The Sayings of the Desert Fathers*, rev. ed., translated by Benedicta Ward (Kalamazoo, MI: Cistercian, 1984), 138–39.

ABBA MOSES

"Seven Instructions"

1. The monk must die to his neighbour and never judge him at all, in any way whatever.

2. The monk must die to everything before leaving the body, in order not to harm anyone.

3. If the monk does not think in his heart that he is a sin-

ner, God will not hear him. The brother said, "What does that mean, to think in his heart that he is a sinner?" Then the old man said, "When someone is occupied with his own faults, he does not see those of his neighbour."

4. If a man's deeds are not in harmony with his prayer, he labours in vain. The brother said, "What is this harmony between practice and prayer?" The old man said, "We should no longer do those things against which we pray. For when a man gives up his own will, then God is reconciled with him and accepts his prayers." The brother asked, "In all the affliction which the monk gives himself, what helps him?" The old man said, "It is written, 'God is our refuge and strength, a very present help in trouble.'"[155]

5. The old man was asked, "What is the good of the fasts and watchings which a man imposes on himself?" and he replied, "They make the soul humble. For it is written, 'Consider my affliction and my trouble, and forgive all my sins.'[156] So if the soul gives itself all this hardship, God will have mercy on it."

6. The old man was asked, "What should a man do in all the temptations and evil thoughts that come upon him?" The old man said to him, "He should weep and implore the goodness of God to come to his aid, and he will obtain peace if he prays with discernment. For it is written, 'With the Lord on my side I do not fear. What can man do to me?'"[157]

7. A brother asked the old man, "Here is a man who beats his servant because of a fault he has committed; what will the servant say?" The old man said, "If the servant is good, he should say, 'Forgive me, I have sinned.'" The brother said to him, "Nothing else?" The old man said, "No, for from the moment he takes upon himself responsibility for the affair and says, 'I have sinned,' immediately the Lord will have mercy on him. The aim in all these things is not to judge one's neighbour. For truly, when the hand of the Lord caused all the first-born in the land of Egypt to die, no house was without its dead."[158] The brother said, "What does that mean?" The old man said, "If we are on the watch to see our own faults, we shall not see those of our neighbour. It is folly for a man who has a dead person in his house to leave him there and go to weep over his neighbour's dead. To die to one's neighbour is this: To bear your own faults and not

---

155. Ps 46:1. (The notes for this selection are by Gerhart and Udoh.)
156. Ps 25:18.
157. Ps 118:6.
158. See Ex 12:29–30.

to pay attention to anyone else wondering whether they are good or bad. Do no harm to anyone, do not think anything bad in your heart towards anyone, do not scorn the man who does evil, do not put confidence in him who does wrong to his neighbour, do not rejoice with him who injures his neighbour. This is what dying to one's neighbour means. Do not rail against anyone, but rather say, 'God knows each one.' Do not agree with him who slanders, do not rejoice at his slander and do not hate him who slanders his neighbour. This is what it means not to judge. Do not have hostile feelings towards anyone and do not let dislike dominate your heart; do not hate him who hates his neighbour. This is what peace is: Encourage yourself with this thought, 'Affliction lasts but a short time, while peace is for ever, by the grace of God the Word. Amen.'"

From *The Sayings of the Desert Fathers*, rev. ed., translated by Benedicta Ward (Kalamazoo, MI: Cistercian, 1984), 141–43.

❧ In response to the tensions and controversies concerning the severity and the theological implications of ascetic practices, **Ambrose,** bishop of Milan (ca. 340–97) sets forth his views concerning the theological rationale for the ascetic life in *On Virginity* (written in 377).

AMBROSE

On Virginity, V.25–26; VI.27–29, 31–33; XII.70–74; XIII.79–83; XIV.88–89; 91–92

V

25. One says, "You advocate virginity, and successfully." I wish this were so; I wish the effects of this "crime" could be demonstrated. I would not fear your grudge if I could see some signs of this success. In fact, I wish you who criticise my words could accuse me of particular instances instead. But, alas, my detractors err when they blame me for accomplishments that others would praise.

26. Another says, "You forbid maidens to marry who have solemnly consecrated their virginity to God." I only wish I could appeal to those who are going to be married, that I could change their bridal veils for the holy veils that symbolise the unmarried state. To some it seems almost shameful that virgins who have consecrated their lives to God were not snatched back from the very altar and forced to marry. Why can a maiden, who may choose a husband, not be allowed to

choose God instead? In fact, it has always been the privilege of bishops to sow the seeds of celibacy, to encourage a desire for virginity. Why should I be ashamed of doing so? Why should my case be any different?

VI

27. Let me ask, then, whether my actions are criticised because they are reprehensible, because they are unprecedented, or because they are useless. If they are reprehensible, then everyone's vows are equally so. The angels themselves become reprehensible for their heavenly existence is the model for those who will one day rise again: "They neither marry nor are given in marriage, but are like the angels in heaven."[159] Hence, whoever condemns virginity condemns the promise of the resurrection. What has been established for us as a reward can hardly be called reprehensible. There can be nothing offensive in a way of life which actually anticipates our final state.

28. Whatever it may be, it is not reprehensible. Is it, then, unprecedented? If so, we shall be first to condemn it, along with every other novelty not taught by Christ, our unchanging Way. If Christ did not teach what we are teaching, it is, we readily admit, detestable. Therefore let us ask what Christ taught about the unmarried state, one way or the other. "There are," he said, "eunuchs who have made themselves eunuchs for the sake of the kingdom of heaven."[160] Consecrated virginity, then, may be described as a brilliant militia waging war for the kingdom of heaven. And so the Lord has taught us that a zeal for chastity ought to be uncontaminated.

29. Even the Apostles recognised its pre-eminence when they said, "If this is the case of a man with his wife, it is not expedient to marry."[161] In these words they were admitting that the grace of true celibacy is to be preferred to the heavy bond of marriage. The Lord knew that all may be invited to remain unmarried, but few do so: "Not all can receive this saying, but only those to whom it is given."[162] Here we have a form of celibacy which is uncommon, even extraordinary, for it is not the result of a weakness, but the reward of strength. Christ said, "There are eunuchs who have made themselves

---

159. Mk 12:25; Mt 22:30; see also Lk 20:35–36. (The notes for this selection are by Gerhart and Udoh.)

160. Mt 19:12.

161. Mt 19:10.

162. Mt 19:11.

eunuchs for the sake of the kingdom of heaven," to demonstrate that no half-hearted effort could succeed: "He who is able to receive this, let him receive it."[163]

31. At this place we may invoke the authority of God's word. The general context is the indissolubility of marriage (except in the case of fornication), which leads up to the idea that celibacy can be a gift and a grace. Christ teaches that no one may condemn marriage although an earnest desire for celibacy is preferable. Who could be so false, so perverse, as to condemn marriage? But who could be so unreasonable as not to perceive the bonds of marriage? For "the unmarried woman or virgin is anxious about the affairs of the Lord, how to be holy in body and spirit; but the married woman is anxious about worldly affairs, how to please her husband."[164]

32. There are other drawbacks, too, although there is no sin in marrying.[165] A wife has many burdens to bear; the grievous labours of childbirth, the heavy task of forming and educating children. St. Paul referred to these earlier to make sure that no one would be led astray by these difficulties. For many, after experiencing the hardships of childbirth, decide to renounce marriage; and many men, who do not have these burdens to bear, are cast aside by wives who prefer others. This is why the Apostle began by saying, "Are you bound to a wife? Do not seek to be free."[166] He put it well: "Are you bound?" Man and wife are joined to each other by a sort of loving bond, tied together by cords of affection.

33. The bond of marriage is a good thing, but it is a bond nonetheless; marriage is a good thing, but it is borne as a yoke nonetheless, and sometimes a worldly yoke as when a wife would rather please her husband than please God. But the wounds of love are good too, better than kisses. For "useful are the wounds of a friend; profuse are the kisses of an enemy."[167] Peter betrayed the Lord, and Judas kissed him.[168] But the kiss condemned Judas because it carried a traitorous venom; the wound inflicted by Peter also cured him because he washed away his fault with his tears. Thus the beneficial wounds of love are prophetically ascribed to the Church in the *Canticle of Canticles:* "For I am wounded by love."[169]

XII

70. You hear the voice of the one knocking at the gate saying "Open to me, my sister, rise my beloved, my dove, my perfect one."[170] Beloved for his charity, a dove in his simplicity, and perfect in his virtue. "For my head is wet with dew."[171] As the dew from the heavens removes the dryness

of the night, so the dew of our Lord Jesus Christ descends as the moisture of eternal life into the nocturnal shadows of the world. This is the head which knows nothing of the dryness caused by the heat of this world. Wherefore he says, "If they do this when the wood is green, what will happen when it is dry?"[172] For this head is full of dew for others, just as it abounds in dew for itself. And it is a good thing that Christ's head abounds, for your head is Christ, who is always plentiful. His liberalities are not completely spent, his daily largesse does not fail; nor shall a sword be raised against this head, no instruments of war, no sign of discord.

71. Now look and see what sort of dew is here. It is not the common liquid. It is a matter of curly hair in these drops of the night. My friend, do not think of curling real hair, for that is more fault than ornament, allurements of form rather than precepts of virtue. Far different are the locks of a Nazarite which no razor has touched, now have they been trimmed. Their arrangement is not produced by the curling iron, their design by no artifice; here the curlers shine forth by the grace of their bright virtues. Learn from the past what sort of curls a Nazarite has, for as long as Samson kept them intact, he could never be conquered. In losing his curly hair he cast aside the reward of his virtue.[173]

72. Once you have listened to the voice of the Word and have put off your tunic at night, do not seek how you may again put it on, for he is offended and frequently exposed by wickedness of spirit. I hope that you will forget altogether how to put it on. May you rise troubled but free from bodily bonds as if the Lord were now beside you. May you prepare your inner mind by prayers when you arise, so that moving away from lowly things you may strain after the highest, eager to open the gates of your heart. And as you extend your hands to Christ, your actions will breathe out the perfume of faithfulness.

73. Therefore present your hands to your nostrils and explore with unwearied and ever-watchful alacrity of mind the perfume of your deeds. The smell of your right hand will be musty to you, and your limbs will be redolent with the ar-

163. Mt 19:12.

164. 1 Cor 7:34.

165. See 1 Cor 7:28.

166. 1 Cor 7:27.

167. Prov 27:6 (Vulgate).

168. See Mk 14:43–50, 66–72, and parallels.

169. Song 2:5 (Vulgate).

170. Song 5:2 (Vulgate).

171. Song 5:2 (Vulgate).

172. Lk 23:31.

173. See Judg 13–16.

dour of the resurrection; your fingers will exude myrrh, spiritual actions that glow with the grace of true faith. As then, from within your body, O virgin, do you grasp pleasure, and you are sweet to yourself and agreeable, with no hint of the displeasure sinners often feel; for utter simplicity will be the more pleasing to you once you have stripped away the coatings of misleading corporeality.

74. This is how Christ has desired you, Christ has chosen you. The door being open, he enters, and one who has promised to be himself the door cannot deceive. So embrace whom you have sought; approach him to be filled with light; hold him and ask him not to depart quickly, pleading with him not to go away. For the Word of God moves, and fastidiousness will not seize it nor neglect to hold it. Your soul should go to meet his Word and you should place yourself on the path of heavenly wisdom, for it quickly passes on.

XIII

79. In this way Christ is found and held; he who puts his hand through your window is found. What is our window if not that through which we see the actions of Christ—namely, the eye of the soul and the gaze of the mind? And so, O virgin, let Christ come in through your window, let Christ put his hand in through the window, let the love, not of the body, but of the Word come to you. And if the Word puts his hand through your window, note how you should prepare your window, note how you should wipe them clean from all the grime of your sins. Let the window of a virgin have nothing foul about it, nothing adulterous. Off with eye cosmetics and other follies of artificial beauty. Off with the allurements of an adulterous affection. And regarding your ears: they were not made to carry heavy loads or to suffer wounds. Their only suitable decoration is to listen to what is profitable.

80. Learn also to bolt your door during the hours of the night; may no one discover it to be opened readily. Your Bridegroom himself desires that it be closed when he knocks. This door of ours is our mouth, which should open to Christ alone. Let it not open unless the Word of God has already knocked, as it is written, "A garden locked is my sister, my bride, a garden locked, a fountain sealed."[174] Your mouth should neither open easily nor respond to every commonplace address. In fact, this should be your rule, even in spiritual matters, unless you are responding to an address by the Word of God. Why do you concern yourself with anything else? Speak to Christ, alone, converse with Christ alone. For

if "women should keep silence in church,"[175] how much more unfitting it is for a virgin to open her door, for a widow to open her courtyard. How quickly the waylayer of modesty creeps up, how quickly he elicits the word you would have wanted to recall.

81. If Eve's door had been closed, Adam would not have been deceived and she, under question, would not have responded to the serpent.[176] Death entered through the window, i.e., through the door of Eve. And death will come in through your door if you speak falsely, lasciviously, or impudently especially when there is no call upon you to speak. Therefore, let the gates of your lips be closed and the vestibule of your voice remain bolted; then, perhaps they will be unbolted when you hear the voice of God, when you hear the Word of God.

82. Then you will be drenched with myrrh, then you will be infused with the grace of baptism so that by the elements of the world, you may die and with Christ may rise. "Why do you live," it says, "as if you still belonged to the world? Do not handle, do not taste, do not touch. Which perish as they are used."[177] For corruptible things ought to be far from those who are chaste. Therefore bury the cares of the flesh and of the world. "If, then, you have been raised with Christ, seek the things that are above, where Christ is."[178] When you are seeking Christ you will see God, the Father, for Christ is seated at the right hand of God.

83. But she who seeks Christ ought not to be well known; she should not be in the square or in the streets with tremulous voice, an easy stride, a ready ear, and a vulgar appearance. The Apostle denies earthly society to you, instructing you to fly to heaven on spiritual wings, almost beyond the limits of nature. "Set your minds on things that are above," he says, "not on things that are on earth."[179] But this was impossible to those encased, as it were, in the narrow confines of the body. While we live the soul is bound by a certain law of nature, but after we die it is said to fly back to higher places. Therefore he added, "For you have died, and your life is hidden with Christ in God."[180] If it is hidden with Christ in God it should not be apparent to the world. For Christ is dead to the world, but he lives to God.

---

174. Song 4:12 (Vulgate).
175. 1 Cor 14:34.
176. See Gen 3:1–6.
180. Col 3:3.

177. See Col 2:20–22.
178. Col 3:1.
179. Col 3:2.

XIV

88. But how are these watchmen angels, who raise up the cloak of a chaste soul? A virgin's cloak is one thing, that of young women of the market place another. One, seeking Christ in the market place, has put off the cloak she had; for prudence is to be had not in a market place nor in a square, but in the church. And perhaps—that we too may come with them into favour and learn that the Lord is tender-hearted towards everyone, they too find Christ at one time or another, that is, if they continually seek him—the cloak is the garment of the body.

89. Therefore she who on her couch sought Christ—but sought as he did who said, "Thus I remembered you upon my couch";[181] sought him during the nights, as it is written, "By night lift up your hands to the holy place";[182] sought him in the city, in the market place and the squares out of which are gathered those who come together at the Lord's banquet—she can meet angels, the watchmen of God's city, in her seeking howsoever long.

91. But if it is a matter of reaching angels by good merits, why does one arrive wounded? but it is such a good sword and such a good wound from his sword! The Word of God inflicts a wound, but it does not produce a sore. There is a wound of righteous love, there are wounds of charity, as she has said, "I am wounded with love."[183] Who is perfect is wounded with love. Therefore the wounds of the Word are good, and good are the wounds of the lover: "More useful are the wounds of a friend than the profuse kisses of an enemy."[184] Rebecca was wounded with love when she left her parents and journeyed to her husband.[185] Rachel was wounded with love when she envied her sister and loved her husband. (For Rachel was barren at that time, and so she envied her sister who had many children.)[186] In this Rachel is seen to be a type of the Church, to whom it is said, "Sing, O barren one, who did not bear; break forth into singing and cry aloud, you who have not been in travail!"[187]

92. Thus the watchmen found her and wounded her and took her cloak from her; that is, they removed the coverings of bodily behaviour, so that in utter simplicity the mind could seek Christ. For no one can see Christ who has assumed the garment of philosophy or, specifically, the dress of secular wisdom. It is a good thing that the garment of philosophy was taken from her, so that no one might prey upon her by philosophy. Well and good, that this cloak is taken from her who is approaching Christ. Thus may she enter with a pure heart, as one who will see God. For "Blessed are the pure in heart, for they shall see God."[188] And having cleansed her heart, she then finds the Word, she then sees God.

From *On Virginity*, by Ambrose, Bishop of Milan, translated by Daniel Callam (Toronto: Peregrina Publishing, 1989), 17–21, 36–38, 40–42, 44–46.

☙ **Jerome** (ca. 347–420) wrote *Letter 22* in Rome in 384 and addressed it to Eustochium, a woman who had adopted chastity. In it he gives the theological basis for his stance on the practices of Christian asceticism. This letter became one of Jerome's most famous and controversial works.

JEROME

Letter 22 (to Eustochium),
I.1–III.1; IV.1–2; V.1–3; VI.6–VIII.4; X–XII; XIII.4–XVII.1–2; XVIII.1–XXI.7; XXI.9–XXII.2; XXIII

I

1. *Hearken, O daughter, and see, and incline thy ear, and forget thy people and thy father's house; and the king shall greatly desire thy beauty.*[189] In Psalm 44, God is speaking to the human soul: that, following the example of Abraham,[190] it should go out from its own country and its kindred and forsake the Chaldeans (that is, by interpretation, the demons) and dwell in the land of the living, which elsewhere the prophet sighs for, saying: *I believe to see the good things of the Lord in the land of the living.*[191]

2. But it is not enough for you to go out from your native country, unless you forget your people and your father's house and, despising the flesh, are united in your bridegroom's embraces. *Look not back,* it says, *neither stay thou in all the country about; save thyself in the mountain, lest perchance thou be taken captive.*[192] It is not profitable, after putting one's

---

181. Ps 62:7 (Vulgate) = Ps 63:6.

182. Ps 133:2 (Vulgate) = Ps 134:2.

183. Song 2:5 (Vulgate).   185. See Gen 24.

184. Prov 27:6 (Vulgate).   186. See Gen 29:31–30:5.

187. Isa 54:1 (Vulgate); see also Isa 54:1.

188. Mt 5:8.

189. Ps 44:11–12 (Vulgate) = Ps 45:10–11. (The notes for this selection are by Gerhart and Udoh.)

190. See Gen 12:1–4.

191. Ps 26:13 (Vulgate) = Ps 27:13.

192. Gen 19:17 (Jerome's quotation here contains some variations from the Vulgate).

hand to the plow, to look back,[193] nor to return home from the field, nor after accepting Christ's tunic to descend from the roof to put on any other garb.[194]

3. A great marvel: a father exhorts his daughter: "Do not remember your father." *You are of your father the devil, and the desires of your father you will do.*[195] This is said to the Jews. And elsewhere: *He that committeth sin is of the devil.*[196] In the first place, being born of such a parent we are black; after repentance (having not yet ascended to the pinnacle of virtue) we say: *I am black and beautiful, a daughter of Jerusalem.*[197]

4. I went out from the home of my infancy, I forgot my father, I am reborn in Christ. What do I receive as a reward for this? The Bible says: *And the king shall greatly desire thy beauty.*[198] This, accordingly, is the great sacrament:[199] *Wherefore a man shall leave father and mother, and shall cleave to his wife, and they shall be two—in one flesh?*[200] Now not, as in that text, in one flesh, but in one spirit.[201]

5. Your bridegroom is not arrogant. He is not proud. He has married an Ethiopian woman.[202] As soon as you desire to hear the wisdom of the true Solomon[203] and come to Him, He will divulge to you all that He knows. And the King will conduct you into His chamber,[204] and when your color has been changed in marvelous fashion that passage will be applicable to you: *Who is this that cometh up, being made white?*[205]

II

1. I write this to you, my lady Eustochium—I must call you lady, as the bride of my Lord—for this reason, that from the very beginning of my dissertation you may learn that I am not now about to speak the praises of virginity (which you have so excellently demonstrated by adopting it), nor to enumerate the disadvantages of wives: pregnancy, a wailing infant, the torment of a husband's unfaithfulness, household cares, and how death at last cuts off all fancied blessings. For married women have their place: honorable wedlock and an undefiled bed.[206] But I would have you understand that as you go out from Sodom, you must be warned by the fate of Lot's wife.[207] 2. There is no flattery in this book; for the flatterer is a persuasive enemy. There will be no display of rhetorical speech to set you now among the angels and put the world beneath your feet through the beauty of virginity.

III

1. I do not wish pride to come upon you by reason of your decision, but fear. If you walk laden with gold, you must beware

of a robber. This mortal life is a race. Here we struggle, that elsewhere we may be crowned.[208] No one walks without anxiety amid serpents and scorpions. *My sword is inebriated,* saith the Lord, *in heaven,*[209] and do you think of peace on earth,[210] which brings forth thorns and thistle which the serpent eats?[211]

IV

1. As long as we are imprisoned within this frail little body, as long as *we have this treasure in earthen vessels,*[212] and the spirit lusteth against the flesh and the flesh against the spirit,[213] there is no sure victory. Our adversary the devil, as a roaring lion, goes about seeking what he may devour.[214] *Thou hast appointed darkness,* says David, *and it is night. In it shall all the beasts of the woods go about, the young lions roaring after their prey and seeking their meat from God.*[215]

2. The devil seeks not unbelievers, not those that are without[216] and whose flesh the Assyrian king boils in a pot:[217] he makes haste to drag victims from the Church of Christ. The elect, according to Habacuc,[218] are his food. He seeks to pervert Job,[219] and after he has devoured Judas seeks authority to sift the apostles.[220] The Saviour came not to send peace on earth but the sword.[221]

V

1. If the Apostle Paul, a vessel of election[222] and prepared for the gospel of Christ,[223] because of the stings of the flesh

---

193. See Lk 9:62.

194. See Mt 24:17–18.

195. Jn 8:44.

196. 1 Jn 3:8.

197. Song 1:4 (Jerome's quotation here contains some variations from the Vulgate) = Song 1:5.

198. Ps 44:12 (Vulgate) = Ps 45:11.

199. See Eph 5:32.

200. Gen 2:24 (Vulgate); see Mk 10:7–8; Mt 19:5; Eph 5:31.

201. See 1 Cor 6:16–19.

202. See Num 12:1–3.

203. See Mt 12:42; Lk 11:31.

204. Song 1:3 (Vulgate) = Song 1:4.

205. See Song 8:5; 6:9 (Vulgate) = 6:10. Neither passage in the Vulgate has Jerome's "being made white?"

206. See Heb 13:4.

207. See Gen 19:26.

208. See 1 Cor 9:24–27.

209. Isa 34:5.

210. See Mt 10:34.

211. See Gen 3:18, 14.

212. 2 Cor 4:7.

213. See Gal 5:17.

214. See 1 Pet 5:8.

215. Ps 103:20–21 (Vulgate) = Ps 104:20–21.

216. See Mk 4:11; 1 Cor 5:12–13.

217. See Am 4:2 (Vulgate).

218. See Hab 1:4, 16.

219. See Job 2:1–7.

220. See Lk 22:31.

221. See Mt 10:34.

222. See Acts 9:15.

223. See Gal 1:15–16; Rom 1:1–6.

and the enticements of the vices,[224] chastises his body and brings it into subjection, lest while preaching to others he himself should be rejected[225]—but in spite of everything he sees another law in his members, contending against the law of his mind and subjugating him to the law of sin;[226] if after nakedness, fasting, hunger, imprisonment, stripes, punishments,[227] he exclaims to himself: *Unhappy man that I am, who shall deliver me from the body of this death?*[228] do you think you should consider yourself safe?

2. Take care, I pray, lest sometime God may say of you: *The virgin of Israel has fallen; there is none to raise her up.*[229] I speak audaciously: although God can do all things, He cannot raise up a virgin after she has fallen. He has power, indeed, to free her from the penalty, but He has no power to crown one who has been corrupted.

3. Let us fear that prophecy, lest it be fulfilled in us: *and good virgins shall faint.*[230] Note what he says: *good virgins shall faint*—because there are also bad virgins. *Whosoever shall look on a woman to lust after her,* He says, *hath already committed adultery with her in his heart.*[231] Virginity, therefore, may be lost even by thinking. Those are the bad virgins, virgins in the flesh, not in the spirit: foolish virgins who, having no oil, are shut out by the bridegroom.[232]

VI

6. Hear the Psalmist who says: O daughter of Babylon, miserable: blessed shall he be who shall repay thee thy payment; blessed be he that shall take and dash thy little ones against the rock.[233] Because, therefore, it is impossible for a man's senses to escape being assailed by the well-known inner passion,[234] that man is praised, he is called blessed, who as soon as he begins to cherish such thoughts, stifles his imaginings and dashes them against the rock. And the rock is Christ.[235]

VII

1. How often, when I was established in the desert[236] and in that vast solitude which is scorched by the sun's heat and affords a savage habitation for monks, did I think myself amid the delights of Rome! I would sit alone because I was filled with bitterness.[237] My limbs were roughly clad in sackcloth—an unlovely sight. My neglected skin had taken on the appearance of an Ethiopian's body. Daily I wept, daily I groaned, and whenever insistent slumber overcame my resistance, I bruised my awkward bones upon the bare earth. 2. Of food and drink I say nothing, since even the sick drink

only cold water, and to get any cooked food is a luxury. There was I, therefore, who from fear of hell had condemned myself to such a prison, with only scorpions and wild beasts as companions. Yet I was often surrounded by dancing girls. My face was pale from fasting, and my mind was hot with desire in a body cold as ice. Though my flesh, before its tenant, was already as good as dead, the fires of the passions kept boiling within me.

3. And so, destitute of all help, I used to lie at Jesus' feet. I bathed them with my tears, I wiped them with my hair.[238] When my flesh rebelled, I subdued it by weeks of fasting. I do not blush at my hapless state; nay rather, I lament that I am not now what I was then. I remember that I often joined day to night with my lamentation and did not cease beating my breast until peace of mind returned with the Lord's rebuke. I was afraid even of my little cell—as though it were conscious of my thoughts. Angry at myself and tense, I used to go out alone into the desert. 4. Whenever I saw some deep valley, some rugged mountain, some precipitous crags, it was this I made my place of prayer, my place of punishment for the wretched flesh. And—as my Lord Himself is witness—after many tears, after fixing my eyes on the heavens, I sometimes seemed to myself to be surrounded by companies of angels and rejoiced, singing happily: *We run after thee to the odor of thy ointments.*[239]

VIII

1. But if those who with emaciated frame are assailed by their thoughts alone, endure such trials, what must a girl endure who is thrilled by luxuries? Of course, the Apostle has said it: *She is dead while she is living.*[240] Therefore, if there can

---

224. See 2 Cor 12:7. In this passage Paul does not specify what the "thorn in the flesh" is that God gave to him.

225. See 1 Cor 9:27.   227. See 2 Cor 11:23–27.

226. See Rom 7:22–23.   228. Rom 7:24.

229. Am 5:2 (Vulgate, which reads "is cast down upon the ground" instead of Jerome's "has fallen").

230. Am 8:13 (Vulgate, which reads "the beautiful virgins" instead of Jerome's "good virgins").

231. Mt 5:28.

232. See Mt 25:1–12.

233. Ps 136:8–9 (Vulgate) = Ps 137:8–9.

234. See Virgil, *Aeneid*, 8.389.

235. 1 Cor 10:4.

236. Jerome lived as a hermit in the desert of Chalcis (in Syria, southwest of Antioch) for a few years.

237. See Ruth 1:20.   239. Song 1:3 (Vulgate).

238. See Lk 7:38.   240. 1 Tim 5:6.

be any good counsel in me, if credence may be placed in one who has had experience, in the first place I advise you—I entreat you as the bride of Christ—avoid wine like poison. 2. This is the first weapon used by demons against youth. Less effective are the shattering of greed, the inflation of pride, the delight of ambition. We readily rid ourselves of the other vices. This foe is shut up within. Wherever we go, we carry the enemy with us. Wine and youth doubly inflame the fires of pleasure. Why do we add fuel to a poor body that is ablaze? 3. Paul writes to Timothy: *Do not still drink water, but use a little wine for thy stomach's sake and thy frequent infirmities.*[241] Note for what reasons a drink of wine is condoned: scarcely does this pain in the stomach and a chronic ailment merit it. And lest perhaps we should become indulgent because of sickness, he recommends that only a little should be taken, rather upon prescription by a physician than by an apostle—though an apostle too is a spiritual physician—and to avert the danger of Timothy's being unable to go about and preach the gospel because of being overcome by weakness. Besides, he remembered that he had said: *wine, wherein is luxury,*[242] and: *It is good for a man not to drink wine and not to eat flesh.*[243]

4. Noe drank wine and became drunk when the world was still uncivilized, and then for the first time planted the vine. Perhaps he did not know that wine was intoxicating. And that you may understand the mystery of the Scripture at all points—for the word of God is a pearl and can be pierced from side to side—after his drunkenness followed the uncovering of his thighs:[244] lust is close to wantonness. First the belly and then the rest; *for the people ate and drank, and they rose up to play.*[245] Lot, the friend of God, after he was saved upon the mountain as the one man out of so many thousands found to be righteous,[246] was made drunk by his daughters. And although they thought that the race of men had come to an end and did this rather because of a desire for children than out of lust, nevertheless they knew that a righteous man would not act thus unless he was drunk. Finally, he did not know what he had done.[247] And—although this wrongdoing was not deliberate—the penalty of the fault followed: there were born of these unions the Moabites and the Ammonites,[248] enemies of Israel, who unto the fourteenth generation—and even forever—shall not enter into the church of God.[249]

X

1. Countless are the passages dispersed through Holy Writ which condemn gluttony and approve of simple food. But because it is not now my purpose to discuss fasting, and to list all the references would require a separate treatise and a whole book, let these few examples out of many[250] suffice.

2. Besides, you may learn for yourself from these examples how the first man was cast out of Paradise into this vale of tears[251] for obeying his belly rather than God.[252] It was with hunger that Satan tempted the Lord Himself in the desert.[253] The Apostle exclaims: *Meat for the belly, and the belly for meats, but God shall destroy both it and them,*[254] and of the wanton he says: *whose God is their belly.*[255] Actually, each one worships what he loves. Wherefore we must take anxious care that abstinence may bring back those whom repletion expelled from Paradise.

XI

1. But if you wish to make reply that you—a girl born of noble family always reared on delicacies, always surrounded by down pillows—cannot abstain from wine and luxurious foods, and that you cannot live more austerely under these regulations, I shall reply: "Live then by your law, since you cannot live by the law of God." Not because God, the Creator of the universe and its Lord, takes delight in the rumbling of the intestines, the emptiness of our stomach, or the inflammation of our lungs, but because chastity cannot be preserved otherwise.

2. Job was dear to God and by his own testimony was pure and a man of integrity.[256] Hear his estimate of the devil: *His strength is in his loins, and his power in his navel.*[257] For the sake of propriety, the male and female organs of generation are called by other names. 3. Hence the promise that one from the loins of David is to sit upon his throne;[258] and the seventy-

---

241. 1 Tim 5:23.
242. Eph 5:18.
243. Rom 14:21 (Jerome has left out the second part of the passage).
244. See Gen 9:20–21.
245. Ex 32:6.
246. See Gen 19:1–23; also Gen 18:23–33.
247. See Gen 19:30–36.
248. See Gen 19:37–38.
249. See Deut 23:3 (which has "tenth generation"); Neh 13:1.
250. The examples are in section IX.1–4, which we have excluded.
251. See Ps 83:7 (Vulgate).   254. 1 Cor 6:13.
252. See Gen 3:1–24.   255. Phil 3:19.
253. See Mt 4:1–4; Lk 4:1–4.   256. See Job 29:1–31:40.
257. Job 40:11 (Jerome's quotation here contains some variations from the Vulgate) = Job 40:16.
258. See Ps 131:11 (Vulgate) = Ps 132:11; 2 Sam 7:12; 1 Kings 8:19; Acts 2:30.

five souls that entered Egypt are said to have issued from Jacob's thigh.[259] And after the breadth of his thigh shrunk as he wrestled with the angel, Jacob ceased to beget children.[260]

One who is about to celebrate the Passover is bidden to do so with loins girt up[261] and mortified. And God says to Job: *Gird up thy loins like a man.*[262] John too wears a leather girdle.[263] The apostles are ordered to gird their loins and hold in their hands the lamps[264] of the gospel. 4. To Jerusalem, moreover, when found in the plain of error all sprinkled with blood, Ezechiel says: *Thy navel was not cut.*[265] Accordingly, all the strength of the devil against men is in the loins, all his force against women is in the navel.

XII

1. Do you wish to be reassured that it is as we say? Samson was stronger than a lion and harder than rock. Alone and without armor he put to flight a thousand men. In the embraces of Delilah he became weak.[266] David was chosen as a man after the Lord's heart,[267] and with his holy lips he had often prophesied the coming of Christ, yet after he was ensnared by the naked beauty of Bethsabee while walking on the roof of his house, he added murder to adultery.[268] 2. Wherein take brief note of this fact also, that even in one's own home it is never safe to look. Wherefore David in penitence says to God: *To thee only have I sinned, and have done evil before thee.*[269] For he was a king and feared no one else but God. Solomon, through whom wisdom herself spoke, *who treated* [about trees] *from the cedar of Libanus, unto the hyssop that cometh out through the wall,*[270] went back from the Lord because he was a lover of women.[271] And lest anyone put confidence in blood relationship, Amnon, her brother, was inflamed by an unlawful passion for Thamar, his sister.[272]

XIII

4. There are women who make themselves conspicuous in public by their walk and draw a throng of young men after them by furtive winks. It is they to whom the words of the prophet inevitably apply: *Thou hadst a harlot's face, thou wouldst not blush.*[273] Let them have but a little purple in their dress and a head loosely bound, so that the hair may fall, tawdry sandals, and over their shoulders a fluttering little cloak, tight sleeves clinging to their arms, and a loose-kneed manner of walking: this is all such a person's virginity amounts to. Let women of that sort have their admirers and let them

exact more pay for their ruin because of their reputation for virginity. With such I rejoice to be unpopular.

XIV

1. I am ashamed to speak of so scandalous a thing; it's sad but true. How has this disgrace of "dearly beloved sisters" come into the Church? Whence this other use of the name "wives" for the unwed? Nay, whence this new kind of concubines? I will go even farther: whence these one-man harlots? They are sheltered by the same house, by a single bedroom, often by one bed—and they call us suspicious if we think anything about it.

2. A brother deserts his unmarried sister, a virgin despises her bachelor brother, and (although they pretend to be devoted to the same aim) they seek spiritual solace among strangers—to have carnal intercourse at home. In the Proverbs of Solomon God makes accusation, saying: *Can a man hide fire in his bosom and his garments not burn? Or can he walk upon hot coals and his feet not be burnt?*[274]

XV

1. Let us, therefore, drive off and banish those who wish not to be but to seem virgins. Now all I have to say is directed to you. Since you are the first woman of high rank in the city of Rome who has undertaken to be a nun,[275] you will have to strive the more earnestly not to lose both present and future advantages. You have, to be sure, learned from an example in your own family the sorrows of wedlock and the uncertainties of marriage. For your sister Blesilla, older in years but weaker in strength of will, after taking a husband became a widow in

---

259. See Gen 46:27; Ex 1:5 (both passages have the number seventy, not seventy-five).

260. Gen 32:25 (Vulgate). Benjamin, Jacob's last child, was born, however, after Jacob had wrestled with the angel (Gen 35:16–18).

261. See Ex 12:11.

262. Job 38:3.

263. See Mk 1:6; Mt 3:4.

264. See Lk 12:35; see also Eph 6:14; 1 Pet 1:13.

265. Ezek 16:4.

266. See Judg 14:1–16:21.

267. See 1 Sam 13:14.

268. See 2 Sam 11:2–27.

269. Ps 50:6 (Vulgate) = Ps 51:4.

270. 1 Kings 4:29–33.

271. See 1 Kings 11:1–8.

272. See 2 Sam 13:1–19.

273. Jer 3:3.

274. Prov 6:27–28 (see also v. 29).

275. An alternative translation is "who has undertaken to be a virgin." The high-ranking Roman women who had earlier on taken up the life of asceticism were widows.

the seventh month. 2. O unhappy mortal lot, so ignorant of the future! She has lost both the crown of virginity and the joy of marriage, and although she may keep the second degree of chastity, yet what torment do you suppose she endures every moment, seeing daily in her sister what she herself has lost? While it is harder for her to do without the pleasure she has experienced, she receives less credit for continence.[276] Still she may be at peace, she may rejoice: the hundredfold and the sixtyfold harvest come from the same seed of chastity.[277]

XVI

1. I would not have you consort with married women. I would not have you visit houses of the distinguished. I would not have you see frequently what you disdained in your desire to be a virgin. If ordinary women pride themselves because their husbands are judges and dignified by some high rank, if an emperor's wife is thronged by self-seeking flatterers, why do you insult your Husband? Why do you, the bride of God, make haste to call on the wife of a mortal man? Attain a holy pride in this relationship. 2. Know that you are better than they. Nor do I desire only that you avoid association with those women who are puffed up by their husbands' honors, whom crowds of eunuchs surround, and in whose garments are woven metallic threads. Avoid those also whom necessity has made widows. Not that they ought to wish for the death of their husbands, but that they should gladly seize an opportunity for chastity. But as it is, they change merely their dress; their former ruling passion is unchanged. A row of eunuchs precedes their spacious sedan chairs. Their red lips and their sleek, plump skin would make you think not that they had lost a husband but that they were seeking one. 3. Their houses are full of guests—full of flatterers. Even the clergy, who should have afforded guidance and merited respect, kiss the brows of their patronesses. They extend a hand, so that you might suppose they wished to bestow a blessing upon them—did you not know that they are accepting a fee for their visit! Meanwhile the women, when they see that the priests are in need of their help, are puffed up with pride and, because they prefer the liberty of widowhood after having experienced a husband's domination, are called chaste nuns, and after a luxurious repast they dream about apostles!

XVII

1. Let your companions be those whom you may see to be thin from fasting, of pallid countenance, approved years

and manner of life, who daily sing in their hearts: *Where is it thou feedest, where is it thou liest in the midday?*[278] who lovingly say: *I desire to be dissolved and to be with Christ.*[279] Be subject to your parents:[280] imitate your Spouse. Appear in public infrequently. Let the martyrs be sought by you in your own bedroom. Never will the occasion for going out be lacking if you intend always to go out—when it is necessary and when it is not. 2. Take food in moderation and never to repletion. There are very many women who, although they are sober as regards wine, are intoxicated by overindulgence in food. When you arise at night for prayer, let not indigestion but hunger affect your breathing. Read much and learn as much as possible. Let sleep creep upon you with a book in your hand, and let the sacred page catch your head as you nod. Fast daily, and let refreshment fall short of satiety. There is no advantage in carrying an empty stomach for two or three days, if it is correspondingly overwhelmed with food, if the fast is compensated by gorging. The mind when sated grows sluggish, and watered ground puts forth thorns of lust.

XVIII

1. Be the grasshopper of the night. Wash your bed and water your couch every night with your tears.[281] Keep awake and become like a lonely sparrow.[282] Sing with your spirit, sing also with your understanding, the Psalm: *Bless the Lord, O my soul, and never forget all He hath done for thee, who forgiveth all thy iniquities, who healeth all thy diseases and redeemeth thy life from corruption.*[283]

2. Who of us can say from the heart: *For I did eat ashes like bread and mingled my drink with weeping?*[284] Should I not weep, should I not groan, when the serpent invites me again to the forbidden food,[285] when, in having driven me

---

276. Blesilla died in 384, the same year that Jerome wrote this letter to Eustochium. Jerome was criticized and blamed by those who thought that her death was due to the austerities she undertook following her conversion to (ascetic) Christianity.

277. See Mk 4:20; Mt 13:8.

278. Song 1:6 (an indirect question in the Vulgate) = Song 1:7.

279. Phil 1:23.

280. See Lk 2:51 (compare Eph 5:22).

281. See Ps 6:7 (Vulgate) = Ps 6:6.

282. See Ps 101:8 (Vulgate) = Ps 102:7.

283. Ps 102:2–4 (Jerome's quotation here contains some variations from the Vulgate) = Ps 103:2–4.

284. Ps 101:10 (Vulgate) = Ps 102:9.

285. See Gen 3:1–5.

from the paradise of virginity, he wishes to clothe me in skins[286] such as Elias cast upon the earth as he was returning to paradise?[287] What have I to do with pleasure which is so soon at an end? What have I to do with this sweet and death-dealing song of the sirens?[288] 3. I would not come under the sentence which was passed upon man upon his condemnation: *In sorrow and anxieties shalt thou bring forth children, O woman* (that law does not apply to me), *and thy turning shall be to thy husband.*[289] She who has not Christ for her husband, let her turning be to her husband, and at the last *thou shalt die the death,*[290] that is, the end of marriage. My undertaking is one independent of sex. Let married women have their own status and title. My virginity is dedicated in the person of Mary and of Christ.

XIX

1. Someone may say: "And do you dare disparage marriage, which was blessed by the Lord?" It is not disparaging marriage when virginity is preferred to it. No one compares evil with good. Let married women glory too, since they come second to virgins. *Increase,* He says, *and multiply, and fill the earth.*[291] Let him who is to fill the earth increase and multiply. Your company is in heaven. 2. This command is fulfilled after Paradise, and nakedness, and the fig leaves that betoken the lasciviousness of marriage.[292] Let him marry and be given in marriage who eats his bread in the sweat of his face, for whom the earth brings forth thorns and thistles,[293] whose crops are choked with brambles.[294] My seed produces fruit a hundredfold.[295] *All men take not God's word, but these to whom it is given.*[296] It is necessity that makes another a eunuch, my own choice makes me so.[297] 3. There is a time to embrace and a time to withhold the hands from embracing, *a time to scatter stones and a time to gather.*[298] After sons of Abraham have been begotten from the hardness of the heathen, sacred stones began to roll upon the earth.[299] And they pass through the storms of this world and are whirled in God's car with the speed of its wheels. Let them sew themselves coats who have lost the raiment that was without seam, woven from the top throughout,[300] those whom the wailing of infants delights—a cry at the very outset of life, lamenting that they have been born. 4. Eve was a virgin in Paradise. After the garments of skins her married life began. Paradise is where you belong. Continue as you were born and say: *Turn, O my soul, into thy rest.*[301] And that you may know that virginity is natural and that marriage came after the offense: it is virgin flesh that is born of wedlock, restoring in the fruit what it

had lost in the root. *There shall come forth a rod out of the root of Jesse, and a flower shall rise up out of the root.*[302] 5. That rod is the mother of the Lord—simple, pure—having no origin of life from without clinging to its untouched body and, like God Himself, fruitful in unity. The flower of the rod is Christ, who says: *I am the flower of the field and the lily of the valleys.*[303] In another passage He is foretold to be a stone cut out of a mountain without hands:[304] a prophecy signifying that He would be born a virgin of a virgin. "Hands" is, of course, to be understood of the marital act, as in the verse: *His left hand is under my head, and his right hand shall embrace me.*[305] That this is the intention of the meaning is shown by the fact that the animals which were led into the ark in pairs are unclean: an unequal number of the clean animals was taken;[306] also from the fact that Moses and Josue, the son of Nave, are bidden to walk with bare feet upon the holy ground,[307] and the disciples are despatched to preach the gospel without the weight of shoes and fastenings of leather;[308] that the soldiers who divided the garments of Jesus had no shoes to carry off.[309] For the Lord could not have what He had forbidden His servants.

XX

1. I praise marriage, I praise wedlock, but I do so because they produce virgins for me. I gather roses from thorns, gold from the earth, the pearl from the shell. And tell me, is the plowman to plow all day long? Shall he not rejoice in the fruit of his labor? Marriage is honored the more when the fruit of the union is more loved. Why, mother, begrudge your daughter her virginity? She was nourished by your milk,

---

286. See Gen 3:21.

287. See 2 Kings 2:13.

288. See Homer, *Odyssey,* XII.35–54, 154–200.

289. Gen 3:16.				292. See Gen 3:7.

290. Gen 2:17.				293. See Gen 3:17–19.

291. Gen 1:28.				294. See Mk 4:7; Mt 13:7; Lk 8:7.

295. See Lk 8:8.

296. Mt 19:11 (Jerome's quotation here contains some variations from the Vulgate).

297. See Mt 19:12.				299. See Zech 9:16.

298. Eccl 3:5.				300. See Jn 19:23.

301. Ps 114:7 (Vulgate) = Ps 116:7.

302. Isa 11:1.				304. See Dan 2:34.

303. Song 2:1.				305. Song 2:6.

306. See Gen 7:2–3 (Vulgate).

307. See Ex 3:5; Josh 5:16 (Vulgate) = Josh 5:15.

308. See Lk 9:3; 10:4; Mt 10:10; compare Mk 6:8–9.

309. See Mk 15:24; Mt 27:35; Lk 23:34; Jn 19:23–25.

taken from your body; she grew in your embrace. You kept her safe by your protecting love. Are you angry because she was unwilling to be a soldier's bride, but would be the bride of the King? She has bestowed a great honor upon you: you have become a mother-in-law of God.

2. *Concerning virgins,* says the Apostle, *I have no commandment of the Lord.*[310] And why? Because he too was a virgin—not by compulsion but of his own free will. Nor should we pay any attention to those who pretend that Paul had a wife. When he discusses continence and recommends perpetual chastity, he says: *For I would that all men were even as myself;*[311] and later: *But I say to the unmarried and to the widows: It is good for them if they so continue, even as I.*[312] And in another passage: *Have we not power to carry about wives as well as the rest of the apostles?*[313] 3. Why, therefore, does he not have a commandment of the Lord concerning virginity?[314] Because that has more value which is not taken by force but is voluntary. Because if virginity had been commanded, marriage would seem to have been forbidden. And it would have been very hard to impose what is against nature and to require of mankind the life of angels, and in a certain manner to condemn the plan of creation.

XXI

1. Under the Old Law there was a different conception of happiness. Blessed is he who has seed in Sion and a family in Jerusalem, and cursed is the barren who did not bear children.[315] And: Thy children shall be as olive plants, round about thy table.[316] And there is a promise of riches in the statement: There shall not be one that is feeble in thy tribes.[317] 2. But now the saying is: Do not think that you are a dry tree; you have a place for sons and daughters, eternal in the heavens.[318] Now the poor are blessed,[319] and Lazarus is preferred to the rich in his purple.[320] Now he that is weak is the stronger.[321] The world used to be empty and—to say nothing of those who were types—the only blessing was that of children. 3. That is why Abraham, when already an old man, married Cetura,[322] and Jacob was hired with mandrakes,[323] and why Rachel the beautiful (who is a symbol of the Church) complains of the closing of her womb.[324] But as the crop gradually increased, a reaper was sent in. Elias was a virgin, Eliseus was a virgin, many sons of the prophets were virgins. To Jeremias it is said: Thou shalt not take a wife.[325] Having been sanctified in the womb, he was forbidden to take a wife as the time of the captivity drew near.

4. The Apostle says the same thing in other words: *I think,*

therefore, that this is good for the present necessity, that it is good for a man so to be.[326] What necessity is this that takes away the joys of marriage? It is the shortening of the time: *It remaineth that they also who have wives be as if they had none.*[327] 5. Nabuchodonosor is near: *The lion is come up out of his den.*[328] What end is to be served by my marrying a wife who will become the slave of a most haughty king? Or children, of whom the prophet says, bewailing them: *The tongue of the sucking child hath stuck to the roof of his mouth for thirst; the little ones have asked for bread, and there was none to break it unto them.*[329] 6. So then, as we have said, this virtue of continence used to be found solely in men, and Eve continuously bore children in sorrow.[330] 7. But after a virgin conceived in the womb and bore for us a Son upon whose shoulders is the government, God the mighty, the Father of the world to come,[331] the curse has been abrogated. Death came through Eve, life through Mary. And therefore a richer gift of virginity has flowed upon women, because it began with a woman. Immediately after the Son of God set foot on earth, He established a new household for Himself, so that He who was adored by angels in heaven might have angels also on earth.

9. For no soldier goes to battle with a wife.[332] The disciple who desires to go and bury his father is not permitted to do so.[333] *The foxes have holes, and the birds of the air nests, but the Son of Man hath not where to lay his head*[334]—that you might not be sorrowful when in straitened circumstances. *He that is without a wife is solicitous for the things that belong to the Lord, how he may please God. But he that is with a wife is solicitous for the things of this world, how he may please his wife. There is a difference between a married woman and a virgin. The unmarried woman thinketh on the things of the Lord, that she may be holy*

---

310. 1 Cor 7:25.
311. 1 Cor 7:7.
312. 1 Cor 7:8.
313. 1 Cor 9:5.
314. See 1 Cor 7:25.
315. See Isa 31:9; 54:1; 1 Sam 1:6–11.
316. Ps 127:3 (Vulgate) = Ps 128:3.
317. Ps 104:37 (Vulgate, where the verb is in the past tense) = Ps 105:37.
318. See Isa 56:3–5.
319. See Lk 6:20; Mt 5:3.
320. See Lk 16:19–31.
321. See 2 Cor 11:10.
322. See Gen 25:1.
323. See Gen 30:14–18.
324. See Gen 30:1–2.
325. Jer 16:2.
326. 1 Cor 7:26.
327. 1 Cor 7:29.
328. Jer 4:7.
329. Lam 4:4.
330. See Gen 3:16.
331. See Isa 9:6–7; Lk 1:31–33.
332. Jerome in XXI.8 cites Mk 1:19–20; Mt 4:21–22; Lk 5:9–11; Mk 8:34; Mt 16:24; Lk 9:23.
333. See Mt 8:21–22; Lk 9:59–60.
334. Mt 8:20; Lk 9:58.

both in body and in spirit. For she that is married thinketh on the things of the world, how she may please her husband.[335]

XXII

1. How many annoyances marriage involves, and by how many anxieties it is entangled, I believe I have briefly set forth in the book I wrote against Helvidius on the perpetual virginity of Mary. To repeat the same arguments now would take too long, and anyone who pleases may drink from that little spring. 2. But lest I should appear to have omitted it entirely, I will say now that the Apostle bids us pray without ceasing,[336] and that one who lives up to his obligations in the married state cannot so pray; we either pray continually and are virgins, or we cease to pray in order to be obedient to our marriage vows. *And if a virgin marry,* he says, *she does not sin; nevertheless, such shall have tribulation of the flesh.*[337]

XXIII

1. I'm starting on a new path. I'm not extolling virginity but preserving it. Nor is it enough to know what is good unless what has been chosen is zealously guarded. The former is a matter of judgment, the latter of effort. The former we have in common with many, the latter with few. *He that shall persevere unto the end,* He says, *he shall be saved.*[338] And: *Many are called, but few chosen.*[339]

2. Therefore, I adjure you before God and Christ Jesus and His chosen angels not lightly to expose to the public the vessels of the temple, which priests alone are permitted to behold. Let no profane person look within the shrine of God. Ozias, who touched the ark—which was forbidden—was smitten by sudden death.[340] For no gold or silver vessel has ever been so dear to God as the temple of a virgin's body.[341]

3. The semblance preceded, now the reality is at hand. You indeed speak with simplicity and in your kindness do not belittle strangers, but unchaste eyes see differently. They know nothing of beauty of soul but consider only the beauty of bodies. Ezechias showed God's treasure to the Assyrians, but the Assyrians beheld in it merely something to covet.[342] Consequently Judea was torn by frequent wars, and first of all the vessels of the Lord were seized and carried off.[343] Baltasar used them as drinking cups at the feast and amid throngs of concubines, because it is the culmination of vice to pollute what is noble.[344]

From *The Letters of St. Jerome,* translated by Charles Christopher Mierow, vol. 1, Ancient Christian Writers, no. 33 (Westminster, MD: Newman Press, 1963), 134–38, 139–42, 143–48, 149–56.

☙ **Melania the Younger** (ca. 385–439) was born into a wealthy Roman political family, married a patrician (Pinian), and gave birth to two children, who died young. After their deaths, she bargained with Pinian so that she could live a chaste, monastic life. She founded monasteries in Jerusalem and other places. Her travels included visits to Augustine, Alypius, and Jerome. The monk **Gerontius,** a contemporary, wrote her biography in 452 or 453.

GERONTIUS

The Life of Melania the Younger,
1–9, 19, 20–27, 29, 31–32, 49, 60–61

1. This blessed Melania, then, was foremost among the Romans of senatorial rank. Wounded by the divine love, she had from her earliest youth yearned for Christ, had longed for bodily chastity. Her parents, because they were illustrious members of the Roman Senate and expected that through her they would have a succession of the family line, very forcibly united her in marriage with her blessed husband Pinian, who was from a consular family, when she was fourteen years old and her spouse was about seventeen. After she had had the experience of marriage and totally despised the world, she begged her husband with much piteous wailing, uttering these words: "If, my lord, you consent to practice chastity along with me and live with me according to the law of continence, I contract with you as the lord and master of my life. If, however, this seems burdensome to you, and if you do not have the strength to bear the burning passion of youth, just look: I place before you all my possessions; hereafter you are master of them and may use them as you wish, if only you will leave my body free so that I may present it spotless, with my soul, to Christ on that fearsome day. For it is in this way that I shall fulfill my desire for God."

At first, however, he neither accepted her proposal nor did he, on the other hand, completely rule out her plan. Rather,

---

335. 1 Cor 7:32 (Jerome's quotation here contains some variations from the Vulgate).

336. 1 Thess 5:17; Eph 6:18.

337. 1 Cor 7:28.

338. Mt 10:22; 24:13.

339. Mt 22:14; see also 20:16 (Vulgate).

340. See 2 Sam 6:6–7; 1 Chr 13:9–10.

341. See 1 Cor 6:19–20.

342. See 2 Kings 20:13–18 (Babylonians, not Assyrians).

343. See 2 Kings 24:10–13; 25:13–17; 2 Chr 36:10, 18.

344. See Dan 5:2–4.

he replied to her in these words: "If and when by the ordinance of God we have two children to inherit our possessions, then both us together shall renounce the world." Indeed, by the will of the Almighty, a daughter was born to them, whom they promptly dedicated to God for the virginal estate.

2. But Melania's heart burned even more strongly with the divine fire. If, as was the custom, she sometimes was sent to the baths by her parents, she went even though she did not want to. When she entered the hot air room, in order to show her obedience, she washed her eyes with warm water, and wiping them with her clothes, she bribed with gifts those who accompanied her so that they would not tell anybody what she had done. Thus the blessed woman constantly had the fear of God before her eyes.

3. The young man, however, was still desirous of worldly glory. Although she frequently asked him to keep bodily chastity, he would not agree, saying that he wanted to have another child.

4. Therefore the saint kept trying to flee and to leave him all her possessions. When this matter was brought to the attention of the holy men, they advised her to wait a short while longer, so that through her patience she might fulfill the apostolic saying, "Wife, how do you know if you will save your husband?"[345] Under her silken clothing she began to wear a coarse woolen garment. Her aunt noticed this and pleaded with her not to be so rash as to clothe herself in such a garment. Melania, however, was exceedingly distressed that she had not escaped notice and begged her not to reveal to her parents what she had done.

5. Later on, when the prayers of the saint had taken effect and she was about to give birth to her second child, the feast of Saint Lawrence arrived. Without taking any rest and having spent the whole night kneeling in her chapel, keeping vigil, at dawn the next day she rose early and went with her mother to the Church of the martyr. With many tears she prayed to God that she might be freed from the world and spend the rest of her days in the solitary life, for this is what she had yearned for from the beginning. And when she returned from the martyr's shrine, she commenced a difficult labor and gave birth prematurely to a child. It was a boy, and after he was baptized, he departed for the Lord.

6. After this, when her blessed husband saw that she was exceedingly troubled and was giving up on life, he lost courage and was himself endangered. Running to the altar, he cried aloud with tears to the Lord for her life. And while he was sitting next to the altar, the saint declared to him: "If you

want me to continue living, give your word before God that we will spend the rest of our lives in chastity, and then you will see the power of Christ." And since he was very fearful that he might never see her again alive in the flesh, he promised this joyfully. Because of grace from on high and the young man's promise, she was cheered; she got better and completely regained her health. She took the occasion of her child's death to renounce all her silk clothing.

At this time, their daughter who was devoted to virginity also died. Then both Melania and Pinian hastened to fulfill their promises to God. They would not consent to their parents' desires, and were so unhappy that they refused to eat unless their parents would agree with them and consent to release them so that they could abandon their frivolous and worldly mode of life and experience an angelic, heavenly purpose.

But their parents, whom we mentioned before, were wary of peoples' reproaches and would not agree to their children's wishes. Melania and Pinian suffered much pain since they were unable to take up the yoke of Christ freely because of their parents' compulsion. They planned with each other to go into seclusion and flee the city. As the blessed woman told us for our edification, while they were plotting these things, as evening was coming on, immediately and suddenly a heavenly perfume descended on them and changed the sadness of their grief to inexpressible joy. Thanking God, they were emboldened against the schemes of the Enemy.[346]

7. After the passage of some time, her father's last illness finally came upon him. As he loved Christ greatly, he called the blessed ones and said, "Forgive me, my children. I have fallen into a great sin because of my enormous folly. Because I feared the abuses of blasphemous men, I have pained you, by keeping you from your heavenly calling. But now see that I am going to the Lord, and from now on you have the power to gratify your desire for God as you please. May you only intercede on my behalf with God, the ruler of all." They heard these words with much joy. Right away they felt free from fear; they left the great city of Rome and went to her suburban property where they devoted themselves to training in the practice of the virtues. They clearly recognized that it was impossible for them to offer pure worship to God unless they made themselves enemies to the confusions of secular life, just as it is written, "Hear, daughter, and see; turn your

---

345. 1 Cor 7:16. (The notes for this selection are by Gerhart and Udoh.)
346. Here and elsewhere in the text "the Enemy" is the devil.

ear and forget your people and your father's house, and the king will desire your beauty."[347]

8. When they began the angelic way of life, the blessed Melania was twenty years old and Pinian, who was henceforth her brother in the Lord, was twenty-four years old. Although at the time they were not able to practice rigorous asceticism because of their pampered youth, they clothed themselves in cheap garb. Thus the blessed woman wore a garment that was exceedingly cheap in value and very old, trying in this way to extinguish the beauty of youth. As for Pinian, he then once and for all rejected the magnificent clothes and luxury of his recent life, and garbed himself in Cilician clothes.[348] The blessed woman was immeasurably saddened to see that he had not yet completely scorned the embellishments of dress. She feared to censure him openly, however, because he was yet unproven in years and experienced the ardor of youth; she saw that he was still vigorous in body. She therefore changed her approach with him and said to him, "From the time when we began to carry out our promise to God, has your heart not been receptive to the thought of desiring me?" And the blessed man, who knew well the rectitude of his thoughts, affirmed in the Lord's presence, "From the time when we gave our word to God and entered the chaste life, I have looked on you in the same way as your holy mother Albina." Melania then exhorted him, saying, "Then be persuaded by me as your spiritual mother and sister, and give up the Cilician clothes; it is not fitting for a man who has left behind worldly frivolities for the sake of God to wear such things." And he saw that her exhortation was for his own good. Straightway he obeyed her excellent advice, judging this to be advantageous for the salvation of them both. And changing his Cilician garments, he clothed himself in those of the Antiochene style that were natural-colored and were worth one coin.

9. Thus by God's grace having successfully accomplished this virtue, they turned anew to another one. Together they wisely considered the matter and said, "If we take upon ourselves an ascetic discipline that is beyond our strength, we will not be able to bear it because of the softness of our way of life. Our body will not be able to bear it, will weaken completely, and later we will be likely to surrender ourselves to sensuality." For this reason they chose this righteous practice for themselves. They went around to simply all who were sick, visiting them in order to attend to them. They lodged strangers who were passing through, and cheering them with abundant supplies for their journey, sent them on their way. They lavishly assisted all the poor and needy. They went

about to all the prisons, places of exile, and mines, setting free those who were held because of debt and providing them with money. Like Job, the blessed servant of the Lord, their door stood open to any of the helpless.[349] Henceforth they began to sell their goods, remembering the saying of the Lord that he uttered to the rich man: "If you would be perfect, sell your goods and give them to the poor, and you will have treasure in heaven.[350] Take your cross and follow me."[351]

19. Furthermore, they fearlessly gave away the remainder of their possessions in Rome, as we have said before—possessions that were, so to speak, enough for the whole world. For what city or country did not have a share in their enormously good deeds? If we say Mesopotamia and the rest of Syria, all of Palestine, the regions of Egypt and the Pentapolis, would we say enough? But lest we continue on too long, all the West and all the East shared in their numerous good deeds. I myself, of course, when I traveled the road to Constantinople, heard many old men, especially lord Tigrius, the priest of Constantinople, give thanks to the holy ones. When they acquired several islands, they gave them to holy men. Likewise, they purchased monasteries of monks and virgins and gave them as a gift to those who lived there, furnishing each place with a sufficient amount of gold. They presented their numerous and expensive silk clothes at the altars of churches and monasteries. They broke up their silver, of which they had a great deal, and made altars and ecclesiastical treasures from it, and many other offerings to God.

When they had sold their properties around Rome, Italy, Spain, and Campania, they set sail for Africa. Just then Alaric set foot on the property the blessed ones had just sold. Everybody praised the Lord of all things, saying, "Lucky are the ones who anticipated what was to come and sold their possessions before the arrival of the barbarians!" And when they left Rome, the prefect of the city, who was a very ardent pagan, decided along with the entire Senate to have their property confiscated to the public treasury. He was eager to have this accomplished by the next morning. By God's providence, it happened that the people rebelled against him because of a bread shortage. Consequently he was dragged off

---

347. Ps 45:10–11.

348. This and what follows suggest that Cicilian linen was considered to be of good, but not the best, quality. The translator cites Clement of Alexandria (*Paedagogus*, 2.10.115.2) in support of this view.

349. See Job 29:11–17; 31:32.

350. Mk 10:21; Mt 19:21; Lk 18:22.

351. See Mk 8:34; Mt 16:24; Lk 9:23.

and killed in the middle of the city. All the others were then afraid and held their peace.

They set sail from Sicily to the most holy bishop Paulinus, to whom even at the beginning they also bade farewell. By the dispensation of God, adverse winds prevented their ship from sailing; a great and sudden storm came upon them. Since there were many people on the boat, a water shortage developed, and for a brief while they were all in danger. When the sailors claimed that this had come about by the wrath of God, the blessed woman said to them, "It is certainly not God's will for us to go to the place we had intended. Therefore give the boat over to what carries it and do not struggle against the winds." They took the saint's advice, stretched the sail, and came to a certain island that the barbarians had blockaded after having carried off the most important men of the city with their wives and children. The barbarians had demanded from them a certain sum of gold which, if they gave it, they would be freed, but if they did not, they themselves would be murdered and the city would be burned by the barbarians. As the saints were disembarking from the ship, the bishop heard of their arrival. He came to them with others, fell on his knees, and said, "We have as much gold as the barbarians want except for 2500 coins." Melania and Pinian willingly presented them with this amount, freeing the whole city from the barbarians. They also gave them an extra 500 coins, and the bread and other provisions they were carrying with them, thus rescuing the suffering people from both famine and distress. And not only did they do this; they provided 500 coins to ransom one distinguished woman in their midst who had been captured by the barbarians.

20. Then they departed from the island and sailed toward Africa, as we mentioned before. When they arrived there, they immediately sold their property in Numidia, Mauretania, and in Africa itself.[352] Some of the money they sent for the service of the poor and some for ransoming captives. Thus they distributed the money freely and rejoiced in the Lord and were gladdened, for they were fulfilling in action what had been written, "He has given funds; he gave to the poor; his righteousness remains from age to age."[353]

When the blessed ones decided to sell all their property, the most saintly and important bishops of Africa (I mean the blessed Augustine, his brother Alypius, and Aurelius of Carthage) advised them, saying, "The money that you now furnish to monasteries will be used up in a short time. If you wish to have memorial forever in heaven and on earth, give both a house and an income to each monastery." Melania and Pinian eagerly accepted the excellent counsel of the holy

men and did just as they had been advised by them. Henceforth, advancing toward perfection, they tried to accustom themselves to complete poverty in their living arrangements and in the food they ate.

21. The town of the very blessed bishop Alypius, named Thagaste, was small and exceedingly poor. The blessed ones chose this as their place to live, especially because this aforesaid holy man Alypius was present, for he was most skilled in the interpretation of the Holy Scriptures. Our blessed mother held him dear, for she was a friend of learning. Indeed, she herself was so trained in Scriptural interpretation that the Bible never left her holy hands. She adorned the church of this holy man with revenue as well as offerings of both gold and silver treasures, and valuable veils, so that this church which formerly had been so very poor now stirred up envy of Alypius on the part of the other bishops in that province.

22. They also constructed two large monasteries there, providing them with an independent income. One was inhabited by eighty holy men, and the other by 130 virgins. The holy woman made progress in the virtues. She saw herself become a little lighter from the burden of possessions. Fulfilling the work of Martha, she began henceforth to imitate Mary, who was extolled in the Gospel as having chosen the good part.[354] Indeed, in the beginning, Melania would just taste a little oil and take a bit of something to drink in the evening (she had never used wine during her worldly life, because the children of the Roman senatorial class were raised in this way). Then after that she began to mortify her body with strenuous fasting. At first she took food without oil every two days, then every three days, and then every five, so that it was only on Saturday and Sunday that she ate some moldy bread. She was zealous to surpass everyone in asceticism.

23. She was by nature gifted as a writer and wrote without mistakes in notebooks. She decided for herself how much she ought to write every day, and how much she should read in the canonical books, how much in the collections of homilies. And after she was satisfied with this activity, she would go through the *Lives* of the fathers as if she were eating dessert. Then she slept for a period of about two hours. Straightway after having gotten up, she roused the virgins who were leading the ascetic life with her, and said, "Just as the blessed

---

352. "Africa" here means the Roman province of Africa (Proconsularis).
353. Ps 111:9 (Vulgate) = Ps 112:9.
354. See Lk 10:38–42.

Abel and each of the holy ones offered first-fruits to God, so we as well in this way should spend the first-fruits of the night for God's glory. We ought to keep awake and pray at every hour, for, just as it is written, we do not know at what hour the thief comes."[355] She gave strict rules to the sisters with her that no idle word or reckless laughter should come forth from their mouths. She also patiently inquired about their thoughts and refused to allow filthy imaginations to dwell in them in any way.

24. As we said earlier, she fasted from the week of holy Pentecost until Easter, not taking oil at all. Many who knew her well testified that she never slept outside her sackcloth nor ate on Saturday before she finished the entire divine office.

25. After she had lived in this ascetic routine for many years, Melania began to fast on the holy day of Christ's resurrection as well. Her blessed mother, who imitated the holy women of old (her virtuous life requires another person to write about it), was greatly grieved. It is enough for me to say this about Albina, that from the fruit the tree is known, and a glorious fruit comes from a good root. Albina used to make such comments as these to Melania: "It is not right for a Christian to fast on the day of our Lord Jesus Christ's resurrection; rather, we should refresh our body just as we also refresh our spirit." By saying these things, she scarcely persuaded her blessed daughter to take oil for the three days of the holiday and then return once more to her usual ascetic discipline, just as the excellent farmer who owns a fertile field hastens to his own happy task.

26. The blessed woman read the Old and New Testaments three or four times a year. She copied them herself and furnished copies to the saints by her own hands. She performed the divine office in company with the virgins with her, reciting by heart on her own the remaining Psalms. So eagerly did she read the treatises of the saints that whatever book she could locate did not escape her. To the contrary, she read through the books that were bought, as well as those she chanced upon, with such diligence that no word or thought remained unknown to her. So overwhelming was her love of learning that when she read in Latin, it seemed to everyone that she did not know Greek, and, on the other hand, when she read in Greek, it was thought that she did not know Latin.

27. She showed an inexpressible sweetness to those who trained themselves in philosophy.[356] She had such zeal for the name of our Lord Jesus Christ and the orthodox faith that if she heard that someone was a heretic, even in name,

and advised him to make a change for the better, he was persuaded. . . . But if he was not persuaded, she would in no way accept anything from him to give for the service of the poor.

29. Melania yearned so exceedingly for chastity that by money and admonitions she persuaded many young men and women to stay clear of licentiousness and an impure manner of life. Those whom she encountered, she taught with these words: "The present life is brief, like a dream in every way. Why then do we corrupt our bodies that are temples of the Lord, as the apostle of God states?[357] Why do we exchange the purity in which Christ teaches us to live for momentary corruption and filthy pleasures? Truly, the value of virginity is so great that our Lord Jesus Christ deemed it worthy to be born of a virgin." Many who heard these things were zealous for purity and leaped into the arena of virtue. Only the Lord himself knows how many saints' feet she washed, how many servants of God she served, some through money and some through the exhortation of the word, how many Samaritans, pagans, and heretics she persuaded through money and exhortations to come back to God! Through him she accomplished such great and numerous feats.

31. Melania made for herself a garment, a veil, and a hood of haircloth, and did not abandon these clothes from the time of holy Pentecost until the fifth day of the festival of holy Easter, not by day or by night. Such was her burning love for God, even though she had been delicately raised as a member of such an important senatorial family. Those who knew well how she had been reared as a child said that when she still was wearing worldly clothes, it once happened that the embroidery of the expensive dress she was wearing touched her skin and an inflammation developed from it, because of her extreme delicacy. But the Lord who says, "Ask and it shall be given to you, seek and you shall find it, knock and it shall be opened unto you,"[358] gave her the strength from on high for which she asked.

32. Since she had been wounded by the divine love, she could not bear to live the same life any longer, but prepared herself to contend in even greater contests. She decided to shut herself up in a tiny cell and to see no one at all, spending her time uninterruptedly in prayer and fasting. This was

---

355. See Lk 12:39; Mt 24:42–44; 1 Thess 5:2; see also Mk 13:32–37.

356. The term "philosophy" is used here, as it is by other early Christian writers, to denote Christian truth.

357. See 1 Cor 6:15–19.

358. Mt 7:7; Lk 11:9.

impossible to carry out because many profited from her inspired teaching and for this reason everyone bothered her. Thus she did not carry out her plan, but rather set specific hours for herself when she would help those who had come to her for good conversation. For the remaining hours, in contrast, she spoke to God in prayer and accomplished her spiritual work. She had a wooden chest built for herself of such dimensions that when she was lying in it, she could turn neither to the right nor to the left, nor was she free to extend her body. Although she possessed such great and numerous virtues, she never became proud about her own righteous deeds, but always made herself lowly, called herself a useless servant.

49. While our holy mother Melania was waging her contests, her most blessed brother completed the measure of his life in the flesh. Having fought the good fight, he was crowned with a wreath[359] because of his voluntary poverty and obedience to the divine precepts, and joyfully departed to the God of all things, eight years before Melania's own death. It was God who arranged matters thus to be in accord with Melania's good purpose, so that the blessed woman, contesting even more, might more illustriously carry out her way of life in the Lord.

After her brother, whom we have mentioned, fell asleep in the Lord, Melania remained in the Aposteleion that she had constructed a short time before and in which she had also deposited the remains of the blessed man. She remained here for about four years, very much wearing herself out in fasting, vigils, and constant sorrow. After these things occurred, aroused by divine zeal, she wished to build a monastery for holy men that they might carry out their nightly and daily psalmody without interruption at the place of the Ascension of the Lord and in the grotto where the Savior talked with his holy disciples about the end of time. Some people balked at her good proposal, however, alleging that she would not be able to complete such a great undertaking because of her extreme poverty. But the Lord, who is rich in everything, fulfilled the wishes of that holy soul by arranging for a certain man who loved Christ to offer her two hundred coins. Receiving them with great joy, she called the priest with her, whom she had taken from the world and presented to God as an offering—and that man was my own pitiable self—and said to him, "Since you believe that you will receive the compensation for this labor from the Lord in the ages to come, take these few coins and buy stones for us, so that we may begin construction of the men's monastery, in the name of our Lord Jesus Christ. Thus while I am still in the flesh I

may see both the divine service being offered without interruption in the church and the bones of my mother and my master find rest through their chanting."

And when, under God, she began this project, the Lord who worked with her in all things completed the vast undertaking in one year, so that everyone was astounded to learn that truly it was by a heavenly influence that the work had been accomplished. She lodged there holy men, lovers of God, who cheerfully performed the divine service in the Church of Christ's Ascension and in that of the Apostles, where the blessed ones were also buried.

60. I shall try to recall a few of the many miracles that the Lord performed through her, for I am not capable of relating all of them, both because of their great number and because of my personal incapacity. Now one day a certain young woman was seized by a very evil demon. Her mouth and her lips were shut for many days. It was completely impossible for her either to talk or to take nourishment, so that quite soon she was in danger of starvation. Many doctors had lavished a number of drugs on her but were not able to make her move her lips even a bit. When medical skill had proven to be incapable of driving out the demon, then at last they carried her with an escort to the saint, with her parents following along. The blessed woman, who shunned the glory of men, said to them, "Since I am a sinner, I am incapable of doing this. Let us bring her to the holy martyrs and by their direct intercession, the God who loves humankind will cure her." As they arrived there, the saint earnestly called upon the Master of all things. She took the oil consecrated from the relics of the holy martyrs and with this she touched the mouth of the sick woman three times, saying in a clear voice, "In the name of our Lord Jesus Christ, open your mouth." And straightway at the calling on the Lord, the demon, who was disgraced or rather frightened, fled, and the woman opened her mouth. The saint gave her something to eat and all who saw this glorified God. The woman who had been cured returned home with great joy, praising the Lord. Likewise another woman who had suffered from the same sickness was cured by Melania.

61. Once again, a woman had a very difficult labor and the fetus died in the mother's womb. The wretched woman could neither live nor die. When the true servant of the Lord heard about this, she was very sympathetically grieved. Pitying the woman, she said to the virgins with her, "Let us go to

---

359. See 2 Tim 2:7–8.

visit the sick woman, so that by seeing the suffering of those who live in the world, we can also thus understand from how many difficulties God has relieved us." When they arrived at the house where the woman was who was dangerously ill, they said a prayer. Immediately the suffering woman, scarcely able to whisper in a weak voice, said to the saint, "Have pity on me." Melania stood there a long time supplicating God earnestly on the woman's behalf. She loosened her own belt which bound her around and placed it on the woman, an-nouncing, "I have received this blessing from a great man, and I believe that his prayers will cure her speedily." Immediately the dead fetus emerged. Having fed the woman, Melania straightway returned home. And God was glorified, as usual. Melania said in humility, "The belt belongs to a saint, whose prayers cured the endangered woman." Thus she always attributed her virtuous deeds to the saints.

From *The Life of Melania, the Younger,* translated by Elizabeth A. Clark (Lewiston, NY: Edwin Mellen, 1984), 27–33, 41–49, 61–62, 72–73.

5. "SECTS" AND FORMATIVE CONTROVERSIES

GNOSTICISM

☙ *The Gospel of Truth* is a Christian Gnostic text probably composed between 140 and 180. Copies have survived in Coptic, though they are believed to have been translations of a Greek original. Its style and its teachings on the work and person of Jesus show similarities to the Valentinian school of Gnostic Christianity, named after Valentinus (a Valentinian work called *The Gospel of Truth* is mentioned in Irenaeus's *Against Heresies,* III.xi.9).

The Gospel of Truth, 17.4–19.27; 24.9–27.34; 30.31–31.35; 33.33–36.39

17 . . . When the totality went about searching for the one from whom they had come forth—and the totality was inside of him, the incomprehensible, inconceivable one who is superior to every thought—ignorance of the Father brought about anguish and terror; and the anguish grew solid like a fog, so that no one was able to see. For this reason error became powerful; it worked on its own matter foolishly, not having known the truth. It set about with a creation, preparing with power and beauty the substitute for the truth.

This was not, then, a humiliation for him, the incomprehensible, inconceivable one, for they were nothing, the anguish and the oblivion and the creature of deceit, while the established truth is immutable, imperturbable, perfect in beauty. For this reason, despise error.

Thus it had no root; it fell into a fog regarding the Father, while it was involved in preparing works and oblivions and terrors, in order that by means of these it might entice those of the middle and capture them.

The oblivion of error was not revealed. It is not a 18 [. . .][360] from the Father. Oblivion did not come into existence from the Father, although it did indeed come into existence because of him. But what comes into existence in him is knowledge, which appeared in order that oblivion might vanish and the Father might be known. Since oblivion came into existence because the Father was not known, then if the Father comes to be known, oblivion will not exist from that moment on.

Through this, the gospel of the one who is searched for, which <was>[361] revealed to those who are perfect through the mercies of the Father, the hidden mystery, Jesus, the Christ, enlightened those who were in darkness through oblivion. He enlightened them; he showed (them)[362] a way; and the way is the truth which he taught them.

For this reason error grew angry at him, persecuted him, was distressed at him (and) was brought to naught. He was nailed to a tree (and) he became a fruit of the knowledge of the Father. It did not, however, cause destruction because it was eaten, but to those who ate it it gave (cause) to become glad in the discovery, and he discovered them in himself, and they discovered him in themselves.

As for the incomprehensible, inconceivable one, the Father, the perfect one, the one who made the totality, within him is the totality and of him the totality has need. Although

---

360. Square brackets around ellipsis dots indicate a lacuna in the manuscript. Square brackets around a word or part of a word indicate where the text has been reconstructed by the translators. (The notes for this selection are by Gerhart and Udoh.)

361. Angle brackets indicate correction of a scribal omission or error.

362. Parentheses enclose word(s) inserted by the translators.

he retained their perfection within himself which he did not give to the totality, the Father was not jealous. What jealousy indeed (could there be) between himself and his members? 19 For, if this aeon had thus [received] their [perfection], they could not have come [. . .] the Father. He retains within himself their perfection, granting it to them as a return to him and a perfectly unitary knowledge. It is he who fashioned the totality, and within him is the totality and the totality was in need of him.

As in the case of a person of whom some are ignorant, he wishes to have them know him and love him, so—for what did the totality have need of if not knowledge regarding the Father?—he became a guide, restful and leisurely. In schools he appeared (and) he spoke the word as a teacher. There came the men wise in their own estimation, putting him to the test. But he confounded them because they were foolish. They hated him because they were not really wise.

24 . . . The Father reveals his bosom.—Now his bosom is the Holy Spirit.—He reveals what is hidden of him—what is hidden of him is his Son—so that through the mercies of the Father the aeons may know him and cease laboring in search of the Father, resting there in him, knowing that this is the rest. Having filled the deficiency, he abolished the form—the form of it is the world, that in which he served.—For the place where there is envy and strife is deficient, but the place where (there is) Unity is perfect. Since the deficiency came into being because the Father was not known, therefore, when the Father is known, from that moment on the deficiency will no longer exist. As in the case of the ignorance of a person, when he comes to have knowledge, his ignorance vanishes of itself, as the darkness vanishes when light appears, 25 so also the deficiency vanishes in the perfection. So from that moment on the form is not apparent, but it will vanish in the fusion of Unity, for now their works lie scattered. In time Unity will perfect the spaces. It is within Unity that each one will attain himself; within knowledge he will purify himself from multiplicity into Unity, consuming matter within himself like fire, and darkness by light, death by life.

If indeed these things have happened to each one of us, then we must see to it above all that the house will be holy and silent for the Unity. (It is) as in the case of some people who moved out of dwellings having jars that in spots were not good. They would break them, and the master of the house would not suffer loss. Rather <he> is glad because in place of the bad jars (there are) full ones which are made perfect. For such is the judgment which has come from 26 above.

It has passed judgment on everyone; it is a drawn sword, with two edges, cutting on either side. When the Word appeared, the one that is within the heart of those who utter it—it is not a sound alone but it became a body—a great disturbance took place among the jars because some had been emptied, others filled; that is, some had been supplied, others poured out, some had been purified, still others broken up. All the spaces were shaken and disturbed because they had no order nor stability. Error was upset, not knowing what to do; it was grieved, in mourning, afflicting itself because it knew nothing. When knowledge drew near it—this is the downfall of (error) and all its emanations—error is empty, having nothing inside.

Truth appeared; all its emanations knew it. They greeted the Father in truth with a perfect power that joins them with the Father. For, as for everyone who loves the truth—because the truth is the mouth of the Father; his tongue is the Holy Spirit—he who is joined 27 to the truth is joined to the Father's mouth by his tongue, whenever he is to receive the Holy Spirit, since this is the manifestation of the Father and his revelation to his aeons.

He manifested what was hidden of him; he explained it. For who contains, if not the Father alone? All the spaces are his emanations. They have known that they came forth from him like children who are from a grown man. They knew that they had not yet received form nor yet received a name, each one of which the Father begets. Then, when they receive form by his knowledge, though truly within him, they do not know him. But the Father is perfect, knowing every space within him. If he wishes, he manifests whomever he wishes by giving him form and giving him a name, and he gives a name to him and brings it about that those come into existence who, before they come into existence, are ignorant of him who fashioned them.

30 . . . When he had appeared instructing them about the Father, the incomprehensible one, when he had breathed into them what is in the thought, doing his will, when many had received the light, they turned 31 to him. For the material ones were strangers and did not see his likeness and had not known him. For he came by means of fleshly form, while nothing blocked his course because incorruptibility is irresistible, since he, again, spoke new things, still speaking about what is in the heart of the Father, having brought forth the flawless word.

When light had spoken through his mouth, as well as his voice which gave birth to life, he gave them thought and understanding and mercy and salvation and the powerful spirit from the infiniteness and the sweetness of the Father. Having made punishments and tortures cease—for it was they which were leading astray from his face some who were in need of mercy, in error and in bonds—he both destroyed them with power and confounded them with knowledge. He became a way for those who were gone astray and knowledge for those who were ignorant, a discovery for those who were searching, and a support for those who were wavering, immaculateness for those who were defiled.

33 . . . For the Father is sweet and in his will is what is good. He has taken cognizance of the things that are yours that you might find rest in them. For by the fruits does one take cognizance of the things that are yours because the children of the Father 34 are his fragrance, for they are from the grace of his countenance. For this reason the Father loves his fragrance and manifests it in every place, and if it mixes with matter he gives his fragrance to the light and in his repose he causes it to surpass every form (and) every sound. For it is not the ears that smell the fragrance, but (it is) the breath that has the sense of smell and attracts the fragrance to itself and is submerged in the fragrance of the Father, so that he thus shelters it and takes it to the place where it came from, from the first fragrance which is grown cold. It is something in a psychic form, being like cold water which has frozen (?), which is on earth that is not solid, of which those who see it think it is earth; afterwards it dissolves again. If a breath draws it, it gets hot. The fragrances, therefore, that are cold are from the division. For this reason faith came; it dissolved the division, and it brought the warm pleroma of love in order that the cold should not come again but there should be the unity of perfect thought.

This <is> the word of the gospel of the discovery of the pleroma, for those who await 35 the salvation which is coming from on high. While their hope, for which they are waiting, is in waiting—they whose image is light with no shadow in it—then, at that time, the pleroma is proceeding to come. The <deficiency> of matter came to be not through the limitlessness of the Father, who is coming to give time for the deficiency, although no one could say that the incorruptible one would come in this way. But the depth of the Father was multiplied and the thought of error did not exist with him. It is a thing that falls, it is a thing that easily stands upright (again) in the discovery of him who has come to him whom he shall bring back. For the bringing back is called repentance.

For this reason incorruptibility breathed forth; it pursued the one who had sinned in order that he might rest. For for-

giveness is what remains for the light in the deficiency, the word of the pleroma. For the physician runs to the place where sickness is, because that is the will that is in him. He who has a deficiency, then, does not hide it, because one has what the other lacks. So the pleroma, which has no deficiency, but fills up the deficiency, is what he 36 provided from himself for filling up what he lacks, in order that therefore he might receive the grace. For when he was deficient, he did not have the grace. That is why there was diminution existing in the place where there is no grace. When that which was diminished was received, he revealed what he lacked, being (now) a pleroma; that is the discovery of the light of truth which rose upon him because it is immutable.

That is why Christ was spoken of in their midst, so that those who were disturbed might receive a bringing back, and he might anoint them with the ointment. The ointment is the mercy of the Father who will have mercy on them. But those whom he has anointed are the ones who have become perfect. For full jars are the ones that are usually anointed. But when the anointing of one (jar) is dissolved, it is emptied, and the reason for there being a deficiency is the thing by which its ointment goes. For at that time a breath draws it, a thing in the power of that which is with it. But from him who has no deficiency, no seal is removed nor is anything emptied, but what he lacks the perfect Father fills again. He is good. He knows his plantings, because it is he who planted them in his paradise. Now his paradise is his place of rest.

Translated by Harold W. Attridge and George W. MacRae, in *The Nag Hammadi Library in English,* 3rd ed., edited by James M. Robinson (Leiden: Brill, 1988), 40–41, 43–45, 46, 47–48.

MANICHAEISM

Mani (ca. 216–76) was the founder of a Christian sect now called Manichaeism, which contained Zoroastrian, Elkhasittic, Gnostic, and even Buddhist elements. *The Kephalaia of the Teacher* (also referred to as just *The Kephalaia*) was composed around 240 and is extant in Coptic fragments dating from about 400. It gives detailed teachings of Mani and Manichaeism. In the Introduction, Mani describes his revelations from the living "Paraclete."

MANI

Introduction to *The Kephalaia of the Teacher*

The living Paraclete came down and spoke to me. It was he who revealed to me the secret Mystery that was hidden from the worlds and the generations: the Mystery of the Depth and the Height. He revealed to me the Mystery of the Light and the Darkness, the Mystery of their conflict and the great war which the Darkness stirred up . . . by their intermixture and . . . was set up this world-order. . . . It was he who enlightened me on the Mystery of the forming of Adam, the first man. He instructed me on the Mystery of the Tree of Knowledge of which Adam ate and his eyes were opened; and the Mystery of the Apostles who were sent out into the world to choose out the Churches. . . . Thus was revealed to me by the Paraclete all that has been and that shall be, all that the eye sees and the ear hears and the thought thinks.

From Andrew Welburn, ed., *Mani, the Angel and the Column of Glory: An Anthology of Manichaean Texts* (Edinburgh: Floris Books, 1998), 160.

MANI

The Kephalaia of the Teacher,
VI.30–VII.36, LXIV.157–58, LXXI.175–76

VI

30. *Concerning the Five Storehouses that have po[ured f]orth[363] from the Land of Darkness since the [Beginning]; the Five Rulers, the Five Spiri[ts], the Five Bodies, the Five Tastes.*

Once again the enlightener speaks to his disciples: Five s[to]rehouses have arisen since the beginning in the land of darkn[ess! The] fiv[e] elements poured out of them. Also, from the five e[le]ments were fashioned the five trees! Again, from the five tre[es] were fashioned the five genera of creatures in each world, male and female. And the five worlds thems[el]ves [ha]ve five kings therein, and five spiri[ts, five] bodies, five [tastes]; in each world, they n[ot] resembling [one another]!

The King of the world of Smoke [. . .][364] who came up from the depth of [darkness; this is he who is] the head of all wickedness, and [all] mal[ignity]. The beginning of the spread of the war occurred [thr]ough him; all the battl[es], fights, quarrelling, dan[ger]s, destructions, f[i]ghts, wrestling-contests! That is the o[ne who fir]st [made] arise [dan]ger and war, with his worl[ds and his] powers. Af[te]rwards, also, he waged war with the light. H[e pitched] a battle wi[th] the exalted kingdom.

Now, regarding the King] of Darkness, there are five shapes on him! His head [is lion-faced; his] hands and feet are demo[n and devil]-faced; [his] shoulders are eagle-faced; while h[is] belly [is dragon-faced; 31. his tail is fish-faced.

These five shapes, the marks of his [fi]v[e] worlds, exist on the King of the realms of Darkness!

Now, [th]ere are five other properties in him. The first is his [dark]ness. The second is his putridity. The third is h[i]s ugliness. The fourth is his bitterness, his own soul. The fifth is his burning, which burns like an iron as if poured out from fire.

[There are] also th[r]ee oth[ers] in him! The first, that hi[s body is ha]rd and very tough, even as she has formed him [. . .] cru[el-hear]ted; namely Matter, who is the though[t] of death, [the o]ne w[ho] sculpted him from the nature of the land of darkness. T[his] is the manner [of] the body of the ruler of Sm[oke]. He is h[ar]der than every [ir]on, copper and steel and [lea]d; as there is no cleaver at all, nor any iron implement, can [. . .] him and cut him. For Matter, his fashioner, has formed him [. . .] strong and hard.

The second, that he wounds [an]d kills by the word of his magic arts. His recitation and hearing, all his foolish instruction, make magic and invocations for him. When it pleases him, he can make an invocation [o]ver himself, and by his magic arts be hidden from his compan[ions]. Again, when it [plea]ses him, he can be manifested over his powers [and] appear to [them]; so that these enchantments nowadays, which peo[ple] utilise (?) [. . .] this world, are the mysteries [of] the King of Da[rkness]. Concerning this, I command you (pl.) all the [ti]me: K[ee]p away from the magic arts and enchantments [of] darkness! For any person who will be taught them, and who [d]oes and accompl[ishes them]; at the last, in the place wh[ere] will be bound the King [of] the realms of Darkness with his powers, there will bind t[ha]t one also, [the s]oul of whoever has lived freely among them and [wal]ked in the [magic ar]ts of error. Whether it is a man or a [woman, this is] the sentence given, cut [. . . f]rom God's judgement, that whoever will [. . .] with their King.

32. The third, that the King of the realms of Darkness knows the [co]nverse and language of his five worlds. He understands every thing he hears from their mouths, as they address one another; each one of them in his language. [Every] design they will consider against him, every snare they debate with one another to bring upon him, he knows them! He can also understand the gesturing they signal between

---

363. The brackets indicate where the text has been reconstructed and/or expanded in the translation for the sake of the English reader. (The notes for this selection are by Gerhart and Udoh unless marked otherwise.)

364. [. . .] indicates a lacuna of unspecified length in the text.

one another. Yet, his powers and his rulers, who are s[ub]ject to him, can not understand his wordy converse. While all these things are unveiled to him; still, their heart is not manifested to him. He k[n]ows not their mind nor their thought; he can not ponder their beginning and their end. Rather, he only knows and apprehends what is before his eyes.

Also, another different thing is found in the King of [the] realms of Darkness! For when it pleases him to move, he spreads all his limbs out and walks. When it comes to mind, he with[draws] his limbs and takes them in, and is rolled (?) to his companions; and he falls to the ground like a grape and a great iron ball! He terrifies by his cry, he is frightful. He frightens his powers with his [s]ound; bec[a]use when he speaks, being like thunder in the clouds, he resembles the [. . .] of the rocks [. . .] When he cries out and [. . .] and calls [. . .] over his powers, they shall tremble and to[tter a]nd fall under f[oot]; even as some birds would be [. . .] the bird [. . .] and they fall down to the earth. Still, [thi]s thing only: he knows not what is far from him, he sees not w[ho is at] a distance, nor does he hear him. Rat[her], whoever is befo[re] his face he sees, hea[ri]ng him and knowing him.

These sign[s a]nd these evil marks are found in the chief of the d[e]mons and fiends, the King of all the mountains of Darkne[ss . . . the one] to [whom] the land of darkness has given birth, be[gotten in its cru]elty, in its wickedness and its wrath [. . .] 33. more than all his fellow rulers, who are in all his worlds.

Gold is the body of the King of the realms of Darkness. The body of all the powers who belong to the world of Smoke is gold. And also, the taste of its fruits is salty. The spirit of the King, of the realms of Darkness, is this one who reigns today in the principalities and authorities of the earth and the entire universe. I mean these who reign over the entire creation, humiliating mankind with tyranny, according to their heart's desire.

In contrast, the King of the worlds of Fire is lion-faced, the foremost of all the beasts. Copper is his bo[dy]. Again, [the bo]dy of all the rulers who belong to Fire is copper. Their taste is the sour taste that is in every form. Also, the spirit of the King, of they that belong to the world of Fire, is this one who reigns i[n the] greater ones and the leaders; who are under the command of the principalities and authorities and the kings of the world. Also a spirit of his is found in these sects that worship [fi]re, as their sacrifices are offered to Fire.

Again, the King of the wor[l]d[s] of Wind is eagle-face. His body is iron. Also, the body of all they who belong to the Wind is iron. Their taste is the sharp taste that is in every form. His spirit is the one of idolatry to the spirits of error who are in every temple, the sit[es] of ido[l]s, the sites of statue- and image-worship, the shrines o[f the] error of the world.

For his part, [the K]ing of the w[o]rld of Water is fish-face. His body is silv[er]. All the other rulers who belong to Water, silver is their body. Also, the taste of their fruit is [the] sweetness of water, the sweet taste that is in every (form).[365] Again, the spirit of the King, of the rulers of Water, is this one who reigns today in the sects of error; these that [d]ip the baptism of the waters, (setting) their hope [and] their tru[st] in the baptism of the waters.

Again, [the Kin]g of the [wor]ld of Darkness is a dragon. His [body is lead] and tin. All the other rulers [who belong to the world of] Darkness, their body is lead and 34. tin. And also, the taste of their fruits is bitterness. Again, the spirit who reigns in them is the spirit who speaks till today in the soothsayers, giving oracl[es]; in the givers of portents, every typ[e]; in they who are possessed; and the other spirits that give oracles, every type.

Concerning this I tell you, my [bret]hren and my limbs, the perfect faithful, the holy elect: Hold your heart close to you, and you stay away from the five enslavements of the five dark spirits. Put behind you the service of their five bodies. Live not in them, that you may break loose their chain and their chastening for ever!

VII

34. *The Seventh, concerning the Five Fathers.*

Once again the enlightener, our father [the] apostle of truth, is sitting in the midst of his disciples and preaching to them of the greatnesses of God. Again, he speaks to them like this, in his revelation: Five fathers exist, they were summoned forth one of one. [Also], one did come out of another!

The first Father is the Father of Greatness, the blessed one of glory, the [on]e who has no measure to his gr[ea]tness; who also is the first o[n]ly begotten, the f[i]rst eternal; who exists with fiv[e fa]thers for ever; the one who exists before every thing that has existed, and that will exist.

---

365. Parentheses enclose the translator's explanatory material.

Now he, the glorious Father, summon[ed] from him three emanations. The [fi]rst is the Gre[at] Spirit, the first Mother, who came out of the Father. She appeared first.

The seco[nd i]s the Belo[ved of] the Lights, the great glori[ous] Beloved, [the one w]ho is honour[ed; w]ho came out of the Father. [He ma]nifested ou[t of h]im.

The third father[366] is the Thir[d Ambassador], the eldest of [al]l the counsell[ors; who came out of] 35. the first Father. He appeared.

This is the first Father, the first power, the one from whom the three great powers came out. This is the first Father, the first eternal, the root of all the lights; from whom the three emanations came out. They have humiliated the darkness. They have brought its heart's desire to naught. They have given themselves the victory. They have also given the victory to their aeons.

The second father, who came out of the first Father, is the Third Ambassador, the model of the King of lights. And again, he too summoned and sent out of him three powers.

One is the Pillar of Glory, the Perfect Man; the one who bears up under all things; the great Pillar of blessing; the great porter, who is greater than all the porters.

The second is glorious Jesus the Splendour; [the] one through whom shall be given life eternal.

The third is the Virgin of Light, the glorious wisd[o]m; the one who takes away the heart of the [rul]ers and the powers by her image, as she fulfills the pleas[u]re of the greatness.

The third father, who came out of the second father; he is glorious Jesus the Splendour. And, again, he too summoned three evocations after the pattern of the second father.

The first power whom he summoned is the Light Min[d], the father of all the apostles, the eldest of [a]ll the [ch]urches; the one whom Jesus has appointed corresponding to our pattern in the holy church.

The second power whom Jesus summo[n]ed is the gre[at Jud]ge, who gives judgement on all the souls [of] mankind, [his] dwelling being established in the atmosphere under [. . .] wheel [. . .] stars.

The third power is [the Y]outh, the gre[at . . .] light in his two persons, in [. . .], I am speaking about that which has been established [i]n the summons [and] the obedience. [He] too [stood] with his fa[ther the] king [. . .] the savio[ur . . .] seen, as he tells [. . .] I, what I have seen with my Father, [I tell to] you. For yourselves, what you have seen [with your fath]er, do that.[367]

36. The fourth father is the Light Mind, the one who chooses all the churches. And, again, he too summoned three powers after the pattern of Jesus.

The first power is the Apostle of Light; the one who shall on occasion come and assume the church of the flesh, of humanity; and he becomes inner leader of righteousness.

The second is the counterpart, who shall come to the apostle and appear to him, becoming companion to him, sticking close to him everywhere; and providing help to him all the time, from all afflictions and dangers.

The third is the Light Form; the one whom the elect and the catechumens shall receive, should they renounce the world.

And also the fifth father is this Light Form; the one who shall appear to everyone who will g[o] out from his body, corresponding to the pattern of the image to the apostle; and the thr[ee] great glorious angels who are come with her.

One (angel) ho[ld]s the prize in his hand. The second bears the light garment. The third is the one who possesses the diadem and the wreath and the crown of light. These are the three angels of light, the ones who shall come with this Light Form; and they appear with her to the elect and the catechumens.

These are the five fathers who have come out of one another. They have appeared and man[ifes]ted through one another!

Blessed is he who will know and understand th[em]! For he may find life eternal; and receive these light garments that shall be given to the righteous, [the faithful], the givers of peace, and the doers of good things.

LXIV

157. *[Concerning] Adam.*

Once again he speaks to his disciples, who listen to his words: Three great things that are distinct were revealed in Ad[am] the first human. Indeed, due to this, he was found to be better and more outstanding than the conjoined powers that are in heaven and on earth.

The first: The image of the exalted one was placed upon him.[368] The creators and moulders of his body sealed him

---

366. The translator observes that there is a textual error here. The "Ambassador" is the second father but the third emanation of the first Father.

367. Jn 8:18, 38.

368. See Gen 1:26–27.

after the shining form of the image that had been displayed to them above. Indeed, due to this, the image of Adam was found to be surpassingly beautiful beyond any conjoined power above and below.

The second thing: Adam was shaped in his structure throug[h the li]ght of the first-born of heaven and [earth . . .] the five sons. Indeed, due to this, his struct[ure] was found to differ from the structure of even the other creations; [sin]ce the form of all creations is different. As for Adam, the formation of his soul fits over the correct distribution of the elements. Therefore, he has intelligence surpassing that of the other creations and beasts.

The third are the teachings and counsels and the seal of all the powers above and below. The creators, who set him in order, gathered them and sealed them in him. (Adam) and his consort Eve became a dwelling and home for the signs of the zodiac and the stars; and the months, the days and the years. For the seal of the entire universe is stamped upon Adam. Indeed, due to this, heaven and earth moved because of him; trouble and disorder arose on his account between they that are good and they that are evil. So, the good induce him to life because of their image and shape placed upon him; while the [wi]cked were drawing him to death, so that they would have po[w]er through him and they would conceive the kingdom, and through him humiliate the entire universe.

Furthermore, understand that [the ru]lers determined and formed Adam so that they would be masters t[hrough him a]nd c[onceiv]e the kingdom because of seven things.

158. The first: He became the enlightener in their creati[o]n; instead of the light of the image of the Ambassador wh[o] had displayed himself to them above. For they all desi[re]d the likeness of the image of the Ambassador. Their heart was drawn after it.

The second: So that they would scoop up the light through him and restrain and obstruct it from its ascent to the heights.

The third: So that because of the image of the Ambassador that is placed upon him the entirety of the divine that is above and below would be humiliated; on account of the likeness of the splendour, of the beauty of his superiority. For he is superior in his appearance to all creatures.

The fourth: [He] is a seal-ring and a new impression, so [that] all births who will be begotten might be brought forth after his s[eal].

The fifth: That might be displayed through him all the

skil[ls] of the powers, they above and below, secret and manifest; and that they might determine through him the totality, and every thing be revealed in him.

The sixth: That there would come to be a great protection for them through the image of the exalted one that was placed upon him; for as the heavenly would [. . .] even rulers; and no evil thing would be done to them on account of Adam.

The seventh: That he might become chief and king and master over all creatures; and they might conceive the kingdom through him.

LXXI

175. Concerning the Gathering in of the [E]lements.

[Onc]e more the enlightener speaks: In what way shall [the] elements be gathered in, from one to another?

The l[igh]t shall be gathered in [to] the fire, and the fire itself gathered [in to the water, and the wa]ter gathered in to the wind, and the 176. [win]d gathered to the air, and the air gathered to the answer, [an]d the answer gathered to the summons. Also, the summons [to the] purified Mind, which is the intellectual. The intellectual to [the P]illar of Glory, [the P]illar of Glory to the First [M]an, the Man to the Ambassador, the Ambassador [to] the aeons of greatness.

They are gathered in like this; but, [they] will be gathered on one occasion only, and go up a[b]ove to the place of rest for ever and ever.

From *The Kephalaia of the Teacher*, edited and translated by Iain Gardner (Leiden: Brill, 1995), 34–41, 165–67, 185.

Augustine (354–430) was a follower of Manichaeism from around 373 to 384. After he converted to catholic Christianity (ca. 384), he became a leading adversary of Manichaeism and polemicized against it in numerous writings. In *Letter 236* (to Deuterius, a bishop of Mauretania), written around 395–96 after he became bishop of Hippo, Augustine provides insight into the practices of Manichaeism. He examines the Manichaean notions regarding the will in *Confessions* (written between 397 and 401), book 8. In *The Way of Life of the Manichaeans* (written in 388), Augustine borrows from his philosophical training, especially from Plato and Plotinus, and proposes what has become the standard catholic Christian doctrine concerning the nature of evil.

AUGUSTINE
Letter 236 (to Deuterius)

. . . Those who are called hearers among them (the Manichaeans) eat flesh meat, till the soil, and, if they wish, have wives, but those called elect do none of these things. The hearers kneel before the elect that these may lay a hand on the supplicant, and this is done not only toward their priests or bishops or deacons, but toward any of the elect. Like these, they adore and pray to the sun and moon. Like them, they fast on Sunday; like them, they believe all the blasphemies for which the heresy of the Manichaeans is to be abominated; denying, for example, that Christ was born of a virgin, claiming that His Body was not real but apparent, and for this reason insisting that His passion was apparent, too, and that there was no resurrection. They revile the patriarchs and prophets. They say that the Law given through Moses, the servant of God, did not come from the true God, but from the Prince of darkness. They think that the souls of men as well as of beasts are of the substance of God and are, in fact, pieces of God. Finally, they say that the good and true God fought with the tribe of darkness and left a part of himself mingled with the Prince of darkness, and they assert that this part, spread over the world, defiled and bound, is purified by the food of the elect and by the sun and moon; and whatever is left of that part of God which cannot be purified is bound with an everlasting and penal bond at the end of the world. As a consequence, they believe that God is not only subject to violation, corruption, and contamination, since it was possible for a part of Him to be brought to such an evil pass, but the whole God cannot even be purified from such foulness and filthiness and misery even at the end of the world.

That subdeacon, posing as a Catholic, not only believed those intolerable blasphemies as the Manichaeans do, but he taught them as vigorously as he could. He was discovered by his teaching when he trusted himself, so to speak, to his pupils. Indeed, he asked me, after he had confessed that he was a Manichaean hearer, to lead him back to the way of truth of Catholic doctrine, but I confess I was horrified at his duplicity under his clerical guise and I took steps to have him confined and driven from the city. And I was not satisfied with that until I had notified your Holiness by letter that he should be known to all as a person to be shunned, having been degraded from his clerical rank with fitting ecclesiastical severity. If he seeks an opportunity for repentance, let him be believed if he will make known to us the other Manichaeans whom he knows, not only at Malliana but in the whole province.

From Saint Augustine, *Letters*, translated by Sister Wilfrid Parsons, Fathers of the Church, vol. 32 (New York: Fathers of the Church, 1953), 180–81.

AUGUSTINE
Confessions, Book 8.IX–X

IX

Why this monstrousness? And what is the root of it? Let Your mercy enlighten me, that I may put the question: whether perhaps the answer lies in the mysterious punishment that has come upon men and some deeply hidden damage in the sons of Adam. Why this monstrousness? And what is the root of it? The mind gives the body an order, and is obeyed at once: the mind gives itself an order and is resisted. The mind commands the hand to move and there is such readiness that you can hardly distinguish the command from its execution. Yet the mind is mind, whereas the hand is body. The mind commands the mind to will, the mind is itself, but it does not do it. Why this monstrousness? And what is the root of it? The mind I say commands itself to will: it would not give the command unless it willed: yet it does not do what it commands. The trouble is that it does not totally will: therefore it does not totally command. It commands insofar as it wills; and it disobeys the command insofar as it does not will. The will is commanding itself to be a will—commanding itself, not some other. But it does not in its fullness give the command, so that what it commands is not done. For if the will were so in its fullness, it would not command itself to will, for it would already will. It is therefore no monstrousness, partly to will, partly not to will, but a sickness of the soul to be so weighted down by custom that it cannot wholly rise even with the support of truth. Thus there are two wills in us, because neither of them is entire: and what is lacking to the one is present in the other.

X

Let them perish from thy presence, O God, as perish vain talkers and seducers of the soul, who observing that there are two wills at issue in our coming to a decision proceed to assert [as the Manichees do] that there are two minds in us of different natures, one good, one evil. For they are evil themselves in holding such evil opinions; and they will become good only if they perceive truth and come to it as your Apostle says to them: *You were heretofore darkness but now light in the Lord.*[369] But these men thought they want to be light, want to be light in themselves and not in the Lord, imagining the nature of the soul to be the same as God. Thus they become not light but deeper darkness, since in their abominable arrogance they have gone further from You, *the true Light that enlightens every man that comes into this world.*[370] Take heed what you say and blush for shame: *draw near unto Him and be enlightened, and your faces shall not be ashamed.*[371] When I was deliberating about serving the Lord my God, as I had long meant to do, it was I who willed to do it, I who was unwilling. It was I. I did not wholly will, I was not wholly unwilling. Therefore I strove with myself and was distracted by myself. This distraction happened to me though I did not want it, and it showed me not the presence of some second mind, but the punishment of my own mind. Thus it was not I who caused it but *the sin that dwells in me,*[372] the punishment of a sin freely committed by Adam,[373] whose son I am.

For if there be as many contrary natures in man as there are wills in conflict with one another, then there are not two natures in us but several. Take the case of a man trying to make up his mind whether he would go to the Manichees' meeting-house or to the theatre. The Manichees would say: "Here you have two natures, one good, bringing him to the meeting-house, the other evil, taking him away. How else could you have this wavering between the two wills pulling against each other?" Now I say that both are bad, the will that would take him to the Manichees and the will that would take him to the theatre. But they hold that the will by which one comes to them is good. Very well! Supposing one of us is trying to decide and wavering between two wills in conflict, whether to go to the theatre or to *our* church, will not the Manichees be in some trouble about an answer? For either they must admit, which they do not want to, that a good will would take a man to our church as they think it is a good will that brings those who are receivers of their sacrament and belong to them to their church; or they must hold that there are two evil natures and two evil wills at conflict in one man, and what they are always saying will not be true—namely that there is one good will and one evil will. Otherwise, they must be converted to the truth and not deny that when a man is taking a decision there is one soul drawn this way and that by diverse wills.

Therefore, when they perceive that there are two wills in conflict in man, they must not say that there are two opposing minds in conflict, one good, one bad, from two opposing substances and two opposing principles. For You, O God of truth, refute them and disprove them and convict them of error: as in the case where both wills are bad, when, for instance, a man is deliberating whether he shall kill another man by poison or by dagger; whether he should seize this or that part of another man's property, when he cannot seize both; whether he should spend his money on lust or hoard his money through avarice; whether he should go to the games or the theatre if they happen both to come on the same day. Let us add a third possibility to this last man, whether he should go and commit a theft from someone else's house, if the occasion should arise: and indeed a fourth, whether he should go and commit adultery, if the chance occurs at the same time. If all four things come together at the same point of time, and all are equally desired, yet all cannot be done, then they tear the mind by the conflicting pull of four wills—or even more, given the great mass of things which can be desired. Yet the Manichees do not hold such a multitude of different substances.

The same reasoning applies to wills that are good. For I ask them whether it is good to find delight in the reading of the Apostle, and good to find delight in the serenity of a Psalm, and good to discuss the Gospel. To each of these they answer that it is good: but, if all these things attract us at the same moment, are not different wills tugging at the heart of man while we deliberate which we should choose? Thus they are all good, yet they are all in conflict until one is chosen, and then the whole will is at rest and at one, whereas it had been divided into many. Or again, when eternity attracts the higher faculties and the pleasure of some temporal good holds the lower, it is one same soul that wills both, but not either with its whole will; and it is therefore torn both ways and deeply troubled while truth shows the one way as better but habit keeps it to the other.

From Augustine, *Confessions,* rev. ed., translated by F. J. Sheed (Indianapolis: Hackett, 1993), 141–44.

---

369. Eph 5:8. (The notes for this selection are by Gerhart and Udoh.)

370. Jn 1:9.   372. Rom 7:20.

371. Ps 33:6 (Vulgate) = Ps 34:5.   373. See Gen 3:1–24.

AUGUSTINE

The Way of Life of the Manichaeans,
II.2–3; III.5–VII.9; X.19; XI.21–XII.26; XVIII.65

II

2. You Manichaeans often, if not always, ask those whom you endeavor to win over to your heresy where evil comes from. Suppose that I had just met you for the first time. And here, if you do not mind, I request a favor—that you lay aside for the time being the impression that you already know the answer, and approach this great question as an untrained mind would approach it. You ask me where evil comes from, and I, in turn, ask you what evil is. Who is asking the right question, those who ask where evil comes from although they know not what it is, or he who thinks he must first ask what it is, so as not to perpetrate the greatest of all absurdities—seeking out the origin of an unknown thing?

You are quite correct in asking who is so blind mentally as not to see that the evil for any kind of thing is that which is contrary to its nature. But once this is established, your heresy is overthrown. For evil is not a nature if it is that which is contrary to nature. Yet you claim that evil is a certain nature and substance. Moreover, whatever is contrary to nature opposes nature and attempts to destroy it, seeking to make what is cease to be. For a nature is nothing else than that which a thing is understood to be in its species. And just as we call what a being is by the new word *essence* or, more often, *substance,* so the ancients who did not have these terms used the word *nature.* And, therefore, if you are willing to put aside all obstinacy, you will see that evil is that which falls away from essence and tends to non-being.

3. When the Catholic Church declares that God is the author of all natures and substances, those who understand what this means understand at the same time that God is not the author of evil. For how can He who is the cause of the being of all things be at the same time the cause of their not being—that is, of their falling away from being and tending to non-being, which is precisely what sound reason declares evil to be. And how can that species of evil of yours, which you like to call the supreme evil, be contrary to nature, that is, to substance, when you claim that it is a nature and a substance? For if it acts against itself, it destroys its own being, and if it were even to succeed completely in this, it would then have reached the supreme evil. But this will not happen, inasmuch as you choose, not only to have it be, but to be

eternal. Therefore, what is considered to be a substance cannot be the supreme evil.

III

5. Let us, therefore, pursue this question more carefully and, if possible, more precisely. I ask you once again, "What is evil?" If you say it is that which is harmful, you will not be speaking falsely. But I beg of you to apply yourself earnestly, put aside all party spirit, and seek the truth in order to find it, not to fight it. Whatever is harmful deprives that to which it is harmful of some good, for if no good is taken away, no harm whatever is done. What, may I ask, could be more obvious than this? What could be plainer or more easy to understand by a person of even ordinary intelligence, provided he were not stubborn? However, once this is granted, it seems to me that the consequences become apparent. Surely, no harm can come to anything in that order which you look upon as the supreme evil since nothing there is good.

But if you affirm that there are two natures, the realm of light and the realm of darkness, and you admit that the realm of light is God, to whom you concede a simple nature in which no part is inferior to any other, then you must grant something that is irreconcilably opposed to your position yet unavoidable, namely, that this nature, which you do not deny to be the supreme good and even vehemently proclaim to be so, is immutable, impenetrable, incorruptible, and inviolable. Otherwise, it would not be the supreme good, for the supreme good is that than which there is nothing better. Now, to such a nature no harm can come in any way. Therefore, if to harm is to deprive of good, no harm can be done to the realm of light because it is inviolable. To what, then, can the evil you speak of do harm?

IV

6. Since you are unable to extricate yourself from this difficulty, observe how easily the problem is solved according to Catholic doctrine. There is one good in itself and in the highest sense, that is, by its own nature and essence and not by participation in some other good. And there is another good that is good by participation, deriving its good from the supreme good which, however, continues to be itself and loses nothing. This good, as we have said before, is a creature to whom harm can come through defect, but God is not the

author of such defect, since He is the author of existence and, as I say, of being.

It becomes clear, then, how the term evil is to be employed, for it is properly applied, not to essence, but to privation. And it is apparent what nature it is to which harm can come. For this nature cannot be the supreme evil, since good is taken away from it when it suffers harm. Nor is it the supreme good, since it can fall away from good and is called good, not because it is good in its own being, but because it has goodness. And no thing which is spoken of as being made can be good by nature, since to be made means to receive goodness from another. Thus God is the supreme good, and the things which He has made are all good, although they are not as good as He who made them. For it would be madness to demand that the works be equal to the workman, the creatures equal to the Creator. What more do you Manichaeans want? Do you wish something even plainer than this?

V

7. Then let me ask you for the third time, "What is evil?" You will perhaps reply, "Corruption." And who would deny that this pertains to evil in general, for corruption does not exist in itself; it exists in some substance which it corrupts, for corruption itself is not a substance. Therefore, the thing which it corrupts is not corruption, is not evil, for what is corrupted is deprived of integrity and purity. That which has no purity of which it can be deprived cannot be corrupted, while that which has purity is good by participation in purity.

Furthermore, what is corrupted is perverted, and what is perverted is deprived of order. But order is good. Therefore, what is corrupted is not devoid of good, and it is for this very reason that it can be deprived of good in being corrupted. Thus, if the realm of darkness were devoid of all goodness, as you say it is, it could not be corrupted, for it would not have anything that corruption could take away, and if corruption takes nothing away, it does not corrupt. Now try to say, if you can, that God and the kingdom of God can be corrupted, when you have not even found a way in which the kingdom of the devil, as you describe it, can be corrupted.

VI

8. What is the Catholic view on this subject? What do you suppose it is but the truth—that what is able to be corrupted is a created substance, for that which is not created (which is the supreme good) is incorruptible; and that corruption itself, which is the supreme evil, cannot be corrupted, since it is not a substance. If, however, you wish to know what corruption is, notice the state to which it tends to bring what it corrupts, for it affects these things in accordance with its own nature. By corruption all things cease to be what they were and are brought to non-permanence, to non-being, for being implies permanence. Hence, what is called the Supreme and Perfect Being is so called because it endures in itself. Anything that changes for the better changes, not on account of its permanence, but because it had been altered for the worse, that is, it had suffered a loss of essence, a loss which cannot be attributed to the being who produced the essence.

Some things, therefore, change for the better and in so doing tend toward being. They are not said to be perverted by the change, but rather reverted or converted, for perversion is the opposite of a setting in order. But those things which tend toward being tend toward order, and, in attaining order, they attain being, so far as it can be attained by creatures. Order reduces whatever it orders to a certain harmony. To be, however, is nothing but to be one. And so, to the extent that a thing acquires unity, to that extent it has being, for unity brings about the harmony and uniformity by which composite things have their measure of being. Simple things exist in themselves because they are one, but those which are not simple imitate unity through the harmony of their parts, and, in the measure that they achieve this harmony, they exist.

From all of this, we can conclude that order produces being, and disorder, which is also called perversion or corruption, produces non-being. And, therefore, whatever is corrupted tends by that very fact not to be. All you need do now in order that you may discover the supreme evil is to consider what corruption brings about, for it is the supreme evil that corruption seeks to achieve.

VII

9. But the goodness of God does not permit a thing to be brought to this point. It disposes all things that fall away so that they occupy the place most suited to them until, by an ordered movement, they return to that from which they fell away. And even the rational souls that fall away from Him, although they possess that immense power of free choice, are placed in the lower ranks of creatures where such souls ought to be. And thus, by the divine judgment, they are made to suffer since they are ranked in accordance with their merits.

From this we see the excellence of those words which you are always railing away at so vehemently: "I make good things and create evil things."[374] For to create means to order and arrange. And so in most manuscripts it is written: "I make good things and order evil things." To make is to give being to something that did not exist at all, but to order is to arrange something that already exists in such a way that it becomes greater and better. Thus, when God says: "I order evil things," He means those things which fall away, which tend to non-being, and not those which have attained their end. For it has been said that, owing to the Divine Providence, nothing is permitted to reach a state of non-being.

X

19. Now that I have shown how much darkness and error surround your views concerning good and evil things in general, let us turn our attention to the three symbols which you esteem so highly among your moral practices and boast so much about. What are these symbols? The mouth, the hands, and the breast. And what do they signify? That man should be pure and innocent in mouth, hands, and breast, we are told. But what if he sins with his eyes, or ears, or nose? What if he injures or even kills someone with his foot? How can we hold him responsible when he has not sinned with his mouth, his hands, or his breast?

You answer that the mouth should be understood as referring to all the senses located in the head, while by the hand is meant every action, and by the breast every movement of the passions. Where, then, does blasphemy belong? To the mouth or to the hand? For it is an action of the tongue. If all actions come under one class, why do you include the action of the feet with that of the hands, but exclude the action of the tongue? Is it because the tongue signifies something in words that you wish to separate it from those actions which are not for this purpose, thus allowing the hands to symbolize abstinence from all evil actions which are not meant to express something? But then, what if a person sins by expressing something with his hands as we do when we write or when we indicate something by a gesture? This cannot be attributed to the mouth or tongue since it is done with the hands. Is it not rather absurd when you say there are three symbols—the mouth, the hands, and the breast—that some sins committed by the hands be attributed to the mouth? And if action in general is represented by the hands, what reason can there be for including the action of the feet, but not that of the tongue? Do you not see all the difficulties your love of

novelty and its companion error have created for you? For you can find no way of including under these three symbols, which you advertise as a kind of new classification, the purification of all the various sins.

XI

21. But when you commence to relate your fables, in your extraordinary blindness, you try to make others believe, and some are blind enough to be persuaded, that God is corruptible, changeable, subject to injury, want, and weakness, and capable of suffering affliction. And this is the least of it, for you also say that God is not only corruptible but corrupted, not only changeable but changed, not only subject to injury but injured, not only able to suffer want but in want, not only capable of but already given over to weakness, not only able to suffer affliction but actually suffering it. You say that the soul is God or part of God. But I do not see how it can be, that what is part of God is not God, for a part of gold is gold, a part of silver is silver, and a part of stone is stone. And to come to greater things, a part of earth is earth, a part of water is water, and a part of air is air. If you take a part away from fire, you will not deny that it is fire, and any part whatever of light cannot be other than light. Why, then, should part of God not be God? Or is God a being made up of joints like man and the other animals? For a part of man is not man.

22. Let us take up each of these notions and consider it separately. If you wish to claim that God's nature is like that of light, then you cannot refuse to acknowledge that any part of God must be God. Accordingly, when you say that the soul is part of God, yet do not deny that it must be corrupted inasmuch as it is foolish, and changed inasmuch as it was once wise, that it is injured inasmuch as it lacks its proper perfection, in want since it needs help, weak since it requires medicine, and suffering affliction inasmuch as it seeks after happiness—when you do not deny these things, yet say that the soul is part of God, you sacrilegiously attribute all of them to Him.

If, on the other hand, you deny that these imperfections pertain to the soul, then it will not be necessary for the Holy Spirit to lead it to truth,[375] since it is not lacking in understanding. Nor will the soul be renewed by the true religion,

---

374. Isa 45:7 (see Vulgate: *Ego Dominus . . . faciens pacem et creans malum . . .*). (The notes for this selection are by Gerhart and Udoh.)

375. See Jn 16:13.

since it has not grown old in sin. It will not have to be made perfect by your symbols, since it is already perfect, and God will not offer it help, inasmuch as it will need none. Nor will Christ be its Physician,[376] since it already possesses health, and the promise of a happy life will mean nothing to it. Why, then, is Jesus called the Liberator, as He Himself proclaims in the Gospel: "If, therefore, the Son makes you free, you will be free indeed"?[377] And the Apostle Paul says: "You have been called to liberty."[378] The soul, as not yet having attained this liberty, must then still be in servitude. Therefore, if you say that part of God is God, you must maintain that God is corrupted by foolishness, changed by having fallen, and injured by a loss of perfection, that he is in need of help, weakened by disease, weighed down by affliction, and debased by servitude.

23. Even if part of God is not God, still He cannot be incorrupt if there is corruption in one of His parts. Nor can He be unchanged when some part of Him is changed, nor inviolate when He is not perfect in every part. He cannot be free from want when He is busily attempting to recover part of Himself, nor altogether sound when some part of Him is weak. Nor can He be perfectly happy when He suffers affliction in one of His parts, nor altogether free when a part of Him has been reduced to servitude. All of these things you are forced to say when you maintain that the soul, which you perceive to be overwhelmed by misfortunes such as these, is a part of God. If you could eliminate these and many similar errors from the doctrines of your sect, then only would you be able to say that your mouth was free from blasphemy. Or, better still, abandon the sect altogether, for if you cease to believe and to affirm what Manichaeus has written, you are Manichaeans no longer.

24. If we wish to avoid blasphemy, we must either understand or hold it on faith that God is the supreme good, the being than which nothing better can be or be conceived. There is a certain law of numbers which can in no way be violated or changed, and no nature can, by any amount of force, bring it about that the number coming after one be other than the double of one. It is altogether impossible to change this, yet you speak of God as changeable. The integrity of this law is inviolable, yet, you do not wish to admit as much of God Himself. Let the race of darkness take the intelligible number of three, which is so unified that it lacks all parts, and cause it to be divided into two equal parts. Doubtless, your mind perceives that no amount of hostility could bring this about. Then, can what is incapable of violating the law of numbers violate God? If not, why, may I ask, was it

necessary that part of Him be mixed with evil and forced to suffer such misery?

XII

25. This gives rise to the perplexing question that plagued us even when we were your devoted Hearers, and which we were unable to resolve, namely, what the race of darkness would have done to God had He refused to fight with it because of the great damage it would bring to part of Himself. For, we complained, if by remaining at peace He would have suffered no harm, it was cruel to have made us endure such hardship. If, however, He would have suffered harm, then His nature is not incorruptible, as the nature of God ought to be.

In answer to this question, some said that God did not seek to escape evil or to spare Himself from harm, but that, on account of His natural goodness, He wished to bring order to the perverse and restless nature (of the race of darkness). The books of the Manichaeans do not say this; what they both state and indicate repeatedly is that God took precautions against an invasion by His enemies. But assuming that this view, proffered by those who could find nothing else to say, was actually held by the Manichaeans—would God, then, be defended against the charge of cruelty or weakness? For this goodness of His to a hostile race brought great calamity upon His own. And furthermore, if His nature could not be corrupted or changed, then neither could any evil corrupt or change us; and that order to be established in an alien nature could have been brought about without deprivation to us.

26. At that time, they did not give the answer that I heard recently at Carthage. There, a certain person, whom I would very much like to see liberated from his error, when faced with the same perplexing question, ventured to say that the kingdom of God had some territory which could be invaded by a hostile race, but that God Himself could not be violated in any way. But nothing could have induced your founder to make such a reply, for he would have seen in this opinion more than any other the resultant ruin of his sect. And, actually, even an individual of ordinary intelligence, were he to hear that this nature is violable in part and inviolable in part,

---

376. See Mk 2:17; Mt 9:12; Lk 5:31.
377. Jn 8:36.
378. Gal 5:13.

would immediately conclude that there are not merely two natures involved but three—one inviolable, another violable, and a third violating.

XVIII

65. There remains the symbol of the breast to which your very questionable chastity pertains. For you do not forbid sexual intercourse, but, as the Apostle long ago predicted, you forbid marriage in the true sense, which is the only worthy justification for it.[379] No doubt, you will loudly protest against this and hurl reproaches at me, saying that you highly esteem perfect chastity and recommend it, but do not prohibit marriage since your Hearers, who are in the second rank among you, are not forbidden to have wives. When you have done shouting in great indignation, let me quietly ask you this question: Is it not you who regard the begetting of children, by which souls are bound up in flesh, to be a more serious sin than sexual union? Is it not you who used to urge us to observe, to the extent that it was possible, the time when a woman after her menstruation is likely to conceive, and to abstain from intercourse at that time for fear that a soul might become entangled in flesh?

It follows, then, that it is not for the procreation of children that you allow one to have a wife, but for the satisfying of lust. Yet the marriage law itself declares that man and woman are united together in marriage for the procreation of children. Therefore, anyone who calls the procreation of children a worse sin than sexual union actually prohibits marriage and makes of a woman, not a wife, but a harlot who, in return for certain benefits, is joined to the man for the purpose of gratifying his lust. Where there is a wife, there must be marriage. But there is no marriage where action is taken to prevent motherhood, and, hence, there is no wife. In this way, you prohibit marriage, and it is impossible to defend yourself against this charge which the Holy Spirit long ago prophesied concerning you.

From Saint Augustine, *The Catholic and the Manichaean Ways of Life,* translated by Donald A. Gallagher and Idella J. Gallagher, Fathers of the Church, vol. 56 (Washington, DC: Catholic University Press of America, 1966), 66–72, 78–79, 80–83, 109–10.

MONTANISM

☙ The Montanists were first called "Cataphrygians," which derives from the Greek *hoi kata Phrygos,* "those among the Phry-

gians." They later became known by the name of one of the founders of their sect, **Montanus,** a Phrygian presbyter. Montanus, along with cofounders Maximilla and Priscilla (Prisca), lived between 135 and 175. Since none of the voluminous Montanist writings are extant, information about the Montanist movement survives primarily in works by their catholic adversaries. **Epiphanius** (ca. 315–403), bishop of Salamis, wrote the *Panarion* sometime between 374 and 377 (*panarion,* "medicine chest," that is, a stock of remedies to offset the poisons of heresy).

EPIPHANIUS

Panarion, 48.4.1

Behold, a human being is like a lyre, and I flitter like a plectrum; a human being sleeps, and I watch; behold, it is the Lord who deranges the human heart and gives human beings a heart.

Translated by Fabian E. Udoh. For a critical Greek text, see Epiphanius, *Works,* edited by Karl Holl, vol. 2 (Leipzig: J. C. Hinrichs'sche Buchhandlung, 1922), 224–225.

☙ In *The Martyrdom of Saints Perpetua and Felicitas* (see also section 3 above), the author defends the Montanist notion that prophesies and visions, considered to be works of the Spirit, were not restricted to the past.

The Martyrdom of Saints Perpetua and Felicitas, 1

1. The deeds recounted about the faith in ancient times were a proof of God's favour and achieved the spiritual strengthening of men as well; and they were set forth in writing precisely that honour might be rendered to God and comfort to men by the recollection of the past through the written word. Should not then more recent examples be set down that contribute equally to both ends? For indeed these too will one day become ancient and needful for the ages to come, even though in our own day they may enjoy less prestige because of the prior claim of antiquity.

Let those then who would restrict the power of the one Spirit to times and seasons look to this: the more recent events should be considered the greater, being later than those of old, and this is a consequence of the extraordinary graces promised for the last stage of time. *For in the last days, God*

---

379. See 1 Tim 4:3.

declares, I will pour out my Spirit upon all flesh and their sons and daughters shall prophesy and on my manservants and my maidservants I will pour my Spirit, and the young men shall see visions and the old men shall dream dreams.[380] So too we hold in honour and acknowledge not only new prophecies but new visions as well, according to the promise. And we consider all the other functions of the Holy Spirit as intended for the good of the Church; for the same Spirit has been sent to distribute all his gifts to all, as the Lord apportions to everyone.[381] For this reason we deem it imperative to set them forth and to make them known through the word for the glory of God. Thus no one of weak or despairing faith may think that supernatural grace was present only among men of ancient times, either in the grace of martyrdom or of visions, for God always achieves what he promises, as a witness to the non-believer and a blessing to the faithful.

And so, my brethren and little children, *that which we have heard and have touched with our hands we proclaim also to you, so that* those of *you* that were witnesses may recall the glory of the Lord and those that now learn of it through hearing *may have fellowship* with the holy martyrs and, through them, *with* the Lord *Christ Jesus,*[382] to whom belong splendour and honour for all ages. Amen.

From Herbert Musurillo, ed. and trans., *The Acts of the Christian Martyrs* (Oxford: Clarendon, 1972), 107, 109.

☙ **Tertullian** (ca. 155–225) wrote *On the Veiling of Virgins* in 206, after he had joined the Montanist movement. He argues that the purpose of the Paraclete is to provide new guidance for the Church, especially in matters of ethical concern.

TERTULLIAN

On the Veiling of Virgins, 1.3–11

3. It is not so much novelty as truth which refutes heresies. Whatever smacks of opposition to the truth will be heresy, even if it is an ancient custom. On the other hand, he who is ignorant of something has himself to blame. For what is not known was to be inquired after in the same way as what is well known was to be received.

4. The rule of faith, indeed, is completely one, alone unalterable and irreformable, that is, of believing in one God alone, omnipotent, creator of the world, and in his son Jesus Christ, born of the virgin Mary, crucified under Pontius Pilate, resurrected from the dead on the third day, received into

heaven, now seated at the Father's right hand, who will come to judge the living and the dead by the resurrection of their flesh also.

5. While this law of faith is permanent, the other articles, indeed, of discipline and life admit new revisions, since the grace of God continues to operate, of course, and advance until the end. For how is it that while the devil is always operating and adds daily to the inventions of iniquity, the work of God has either ceased or desisted from advancing? 6. It was indeed for this reason that the Lord sent the Paraclete, that, since human mediocrity could not grasp everything at once, discipline could, little by little, be directed and regulated, and brought to perfection by that vicar of the Lord, the Holy Spirit. 7. "I still have many things to say to you," he said, "but you cannot yet bear them; when that Spirit of truth has come, he will lead you into all truth, and will announce to you things to come."[383] But he also made a declaration about this work of his above.[384] 8. What then is the Paraclete's assistance if not this: to direct discipline, to reveal the Scriptures, to reform the understanding, to advance the understanding to better things? There is nothing without its time; all things await their moment. For the Preacher says: "There is a time for everything."[385] 9. Behold, creation itself is advanced to fruit gradually. First there is the grain, and from the grain the sprout appears, and from the sprout the bush grows up, then branches and leaves increase, and the whole, called a tree, expands, then the bud swells and blossoms, and from the blossom the fruit is revealed. The fruit too, rough and shapeless for a while, gradually, in the course of its season, ripens into a mellow taste. 10. So also righteousness (for the God of righteousness and the God of the creation is the same) was first in a crude state, fearing God by nature; hence it progressed through the law and the prophets to a state of infancy; from there through the gospel it knew the vigor of youth; now, through the Paraclete it is being brought to maturity. 11. He alone will be the teacher after Christ;[386] he is to be both so designated and honored. For he does not speak from himself, but speaks what he is

---

380. Acts 2:17–18; see also Joel 2:28–29. (The notes for this selection are by Gerhart and Udoh.)

381. See 1 Cor 12:4–11; Rom 12:4–8.

382. See 1 Jn 1:1–3.

383. Jn 16:12–13. (The notes for this selection are by Gerhart and Udoh.)

384. See Jn 14:26.

385. Eccl 3:1.

386. See Jn 14:26.

commanded by Christ.[387] He alone is our forerunner, for he alone comes after Christ. Those who have received him have preferred truth to custom. Those who have heard him prophesying even to the present veil virgins. [. . .]

From Ronald E. Heine, ed. and trans., *The Montanist Oracles and Testimonia* (Macon, GA: Mercer University Press, 1989), 63, 65.

An attack on the Montanist movement (here called the "Cataphrygian heresy") by the **Anonymous Anti-Montanist Author** (as he is known in scholarship) was excerpted in Eusebius's *Ecclesiastical History* (ca. 315).

EUSEBIUS
Ecclesiastical History, V.xvi.1–xvii.5

xvi.1. Now, against the so-called Cataphrygian heresy, the power which is the defender of the truth raised up a powerful and invincible weapon at Hierapolis, namely, Apolinarius, of whom our work has made mention before, and many others with him of the learned men of that day, by whom a great groundwork for history has been left behind to us. 2. Now, one of the aforesaid, when he began his work against them, first indicates that he had also entered an oral controversy against them. He makes his introduction in the following manner: 3. "For a very long and sufficient time, my dear Abercius Marcellus, I have been urged by you to compose a treatise against the heresy of those called after Miltiades[388] but somehow I have continued in a state of reluctance until now, not because of any lack of ability to refute the falsehood and to bear testimony to the truth, but because of my fear and scruples lest in some way I appear to some to be adding to or extending the word of the new covenant of the Gospel, to which one who has chosen to live according to the Gospel cannot add and from which he cannot take away.[389] 4. But, when I was at Ancyra in Galatia recently, and perceived that the local church was disturbed by this new, not prophecy, as they say, but much rather, as will be shown, false prophecy, in so far as it was possible and opportunity permitted, we disputed for many days in the church about these people themselves and matters brought up individually by them, so that the Church rejoiced and was strengthened in the truth, and those of the opposition were crushed for the moment, and our adversaries grieved. 5. Therefore, the local presbyters asked us to leave behind some record of what had been said against the opponents of the Word of the truth, when Zoticus of Otrous, our

fellow presbyter, was also present. We did not do this, but we promised to write from home, when the Lord granted, and to send it to them speedily."

6. After having said these and then other similar things in the beginning of his treatise, he proceeds with the narration of the cause of the above-mentioned heresy in the following manner: "So their opposition and renowned heretical schism from the Church had the following cause. 7. There is said to be in Mysia near Phrygia a certain village called Ardabav. There, they say, first, that a certain one of the recent converts, Montanus by name, when Gratus was proconsul of Asia,[390] in an unrestrained desire of soul for primacy gave to the Adversary access to himself, and became obsessed, and, falling suddenly into a kind of frenzy and distraction, raved and began to babble and utter strange things, prophesying contrary to the custom of the Church according to the tradition and the succession of the Church from the beginning. 8. Some of those who at that time were within hearing of the bastard utterances were angry at him as being possessed and being controlled by a devil and in a spirit of error and as disturbing the populace; they censured him, and forbade him to talk, remembering the distinction made by the Lord and his warning to be on guard against the coming of false prophets;[391] and others, elevated by a holy spirit and a prophetic grace and not a little puffed up, forgot the Lord's distinction and encouraged the maddening and seducing and people-misleading spirit, being cheated and deceived by it until it no longer was kept in check so as to keep silence. 9. And by some device, rather, by a scheme of evil planning, the Devil devised destruction for the disobedient and, being honored by them unworthily, excited and inflamed their understanding which had been lulled to sleep away from the faith according to truth, so that he even roused two more women and filled them with the bastard spirit, with the result that they babbled insanely and improperly and strangely, like the aforesaid Montanus. And the spirit pronounced them blessed as they rejoiced and were conceited over him, and puffed them up by the magnitude of its promises. Sometimes it condemned them openly, wisely, and faithfully, that it might appear also

---

387. See Jn 16:13–15.

388. He was probably one of the leaders of the Montanist movement. (The notes for this selection are by Gerhart and Udoh.)

389. See Rev 22:18–19.

390. Since the date of this proconsulship cannot be fixed, it is impossible to determine exactly when Montanism began.

391. See Mt 7:15.

to be critical, but few were those of the Phrygians who were deceived. But, when the arrogant spirit taught to blaspheme the entire Catholic Church in the whole world, 10. because the spirit of false prophecy received neither honor from it nor entrance into it, and when the faithful in Asia had gathered together for this purpose and had examined the recent utterances and pronounced them profane and rejected the heresy, then at last they [the Montanists] were expelled from the Church and were excommunicated."[392]

11. These things he related in the beginning, and throughout the whole work he brings in proof of the error among them, and in Book 2 he speaks as follows about the end of the aforesaid: 12. "Since, then, they even called us slayers of the prophets, because we did not accept their unrestrained prophets (for they say that these are the ones whom the Lord announced that He would send to the people),[393] let them give answer to us before God. Is there anyone, finest of men, who began to babble after Montanus and the women, who was persecuted by Jews or killed by the wicked?[394] No one. Was there not at least someone who was overpowered and crucified for the name? No, there was not.[395] But, was not some one of the women ever flogged in the synagogues of the Jews or stoned? No, never anywhere. 13. But Montanus and Maximilla are said to have died by a different death. For there is a report that they each at the instigation of a maddening spirit hung themselves at different times, and at the time of the death of each there was much gossip that they had died thus and that they had destroyed their lives like the traitor Judas. 14. Thus, too, a widespread report holds that that remarkable man, the first steward, as it were, of their so-called prophecy, a certain Theodotus, was sometimes taken up and received into heaven, and fell into trances, and entrusted himself to the spirit of deceit, and was hurled down and died miserably. At least they say that this happened so. 15. But let us not think that we know any of these things when we did not see them, my friend. Perhaps Montanus and Theodotus and the above-mentioned women died in this manner, and perhaps they did not."

16. Again, in the same treatise, he says that the holy bishops of that time tried to refute the spirit that was in Maximilla, but were prevented by others who evidently co-operated with the spirit, and he writes as follows: 17. "And let not the spirit that speaks through Maximilla say in the same book according to Asterius Orbanus,[396] 'I am driven away from the sheep, like a wolf. I am not a wolf. I am word and spirit and power.' But let him show clearly and prove the power in the spirit, and let him through the spirit force those to confess who were then present for the purpose of testing and conversing

with the spirit as it spoke—eminent men and bishops, Zoticus from the village of Cumane, and Julian from Apamea, whose mouths the followers of Themiso[397] muzzled, and did not permit the false and people-seducing spirit to be refuted by them."

18. Again, in the same work, meanwhile having said other things to refute the false prophecies of Maximilla, he both indicates the time when he wrote this and quotes her predictions, in which she prophesied that there would be wars and revolutions. He corrects the falsehood of these in the following words: 19. "How has this falsehood also not already been made evident? For to this day it is more than thirteen years since the woman died, and neither partial nor complete war has broken out in the world; rather, even for Christians, a continuous peace by the mercy of God."

20. This is from Book 2. And from Book 3 I shall present short passages in which he says the following against those who boast that more of them had been martyrs: "When, then, they are at a loss because refuted in all the discussion, they try to take refuge with the martyrs, saying that they have many martyrs and that this is a trustworthy proof of the power of the so-called prophetic spirit among them. But this, indeed, as it appears, is more untrue than anything. 21. For, some of the other heresies have a very large number of martyrs, and surely we shall not agree with them on this account, nor admit that they possess the truth. First of all, the so-called Marcionists of the heresy of Marcion say that they have a very large number of martyrs, yet they do not confess Christ himself according to truth."

22. And after a few remarks, he adds to this, saying: "Wherefore whenever those of the Church who have been called to martyrdom for the faith according to truth meet with some of the so-called martyrs of the Phrygian heresy, they separate from them and achieve perfection without associating with them, because of their unwillingness to agree with the spirit in Montanus and the women. And that this is true and really

---

392. Synods of bishops might have been held to discuss the movement, but there is little evidence when and where they took place.

393. See Jn 14:26.

394. See Mt 23:34.

395. As Tertullian testifies (see, for example, above) and the present author, contradicting this statement, acknowleges below, numerous Montanists were martyrs.

396. He was a Montanist and wrote a book in defense of the movement.

397. Possibly a leader of the movement after the death of Montanus. The present author elsewhere calls him a "confessor" and says he was the author of a catholic epistle (5.28).

happened in our time in Apamea on the Meander is clear from the case of those followers of Gaius and Alexander of Eumeneia who suffered martyrdom."

xvii.1. In this work he also quotes Miltiades as a writer, inasmuch as he himself wrote a treatise against the above-mentioned heresy. After quoting some of their phrases, he continues, saying: "I discovered this in a work of theirs written in opposition to a work of Alcibiades[398] the brother, in which he gives proof on the fact that a prophet need not speak in ecstasy, and I made a summary of it." 2. Going on in the same work, he makes a list of those who have prophesied in the New Testament, and among these he numbers a certain Ammia and Quadratus, speaking thus: "But the false prophet speaks in ecstasy, which is accompanied by ease and freedom from fear, beginning with voluntary ignorance, but turning into involuntary madness already been said. 3. But they will not be able to show that any prophet of those in the Old Testament or of these in the New was inspired in this manner; they will boast neither of Agabus,[399] nor of Judas, nor of Silas,[400] nor of the daughters of Philip,[401] nor of Ammia in Philadelphia, nor of Quadratus, nor of any others who do not belong to them." And again, after brief remarks, he speaks as follows: 4. "For, if the Montanist woman received the prophetic gift after Quadratus and Ammia in Philadelphia, let them show who among them succeeded the followers of Montanus and the women; for the Apostle held that the gift of prophecy must exist in all the Church until the final coming.[402] But they would not be able to show this anywhere today, the fourteenth year after the death of Maximilla."

5. So much, then, does he write. The Miltiades he mentioned has left us other records also of his own zeal for the oracles of God in the treatises which he composed against the Greeks and against the Jews, replying separately to each charge in two books; besides, he composed an *Apology* against the secular rulers in defense of the philosophy which he held.

From Eusebius Pamphili, *Ecclesiastical History, Books 1–5,* translated by Roy J. Deferrari, Fathers of the Church, vol. 19 (New York: Fathers of the Church, 1953), 311–21.

DONATISM

⌘ Donatism, considered a "schism" rather than a "heresy," arose in the North African Church at the beginning of the fourth century during the persecution by Emperor Diocletian (284–305) in 303. Donatism owes its name to Donatus, known as Donatus the Great (d. 355), who succeeded Majorinus as bishop of Car-

thage in 315. An anonymous fourth-century text, *The Acts of the Abitinian Martyrs,* reveals the origins of and issues related to Donatism from the Donatist point of view.

The Acts of the Abitinian Martyrs, 1–11, 17–21

1. Everyone endowed with reverence for the most holy faith exalts and glories in Christ.[403] Once error has been condemned, let whoever rejoices in the Lord's truth read the records of the martyrs so as to hold fast to the Catholic Church and distinguish the holy communion from the unholy. These [records][404] were inscribed in the indispensable archives of memory lest both the glory of the martyrs and the condemnation of the traitors[405] fade with the passing of the ages. Therefore, I begin an account of celestial battles and struggles undertaken anew by the bravest soldiers of Christ,[406] the unconquered warriors, the glorious martyrs. I want to emphasize that I begin to write [my account] using public records. I am endowed not so much with any talent as I am joined to them by the respect of a fellow-citizen. I write with a specific two-fold resolve: that we might prepare our very selves for martyrdom by imitating them and that, when we have committed to writing the battles and victories of their confessions, we may entrust to everlasting memory those whom we believe to live forever and reign with Christ.[407] But, most beloved brothers and sisters, I have difficulty with where to start or how to undertake the delightful confession of the most holy martyrs, i.e., with finding a beginning for my praise, because I am captivated by great events and by great virtues. Whatever I see in them, I admire it all as divine and heavenly: faith in their devotion, sanctity in their lives, constancy in their confessions, and victory in their sufferings. As much as these all shine forth like the sun in their [collec-

398. The translator points out that the manuscript evidence supports the reading "Alcibiades." This is possibly a mistake, going back to Eusebius, for Miltiades, whose work is presently being discussed.

399. See Acts 11:28; 21:10.

400. For both Judas and Silas, see Acts 15:22.

401. See Acts 21:8–9.

402. See 1 Cor 1:7; Eph 4:11–16.

403. See Gal 6:14. (The notes for this selection are by Gerhart and Udoh.)

404. Words in brackets have been added by the translator for clarity.

405. The word "traitor" (*traditor* in Latin) is central in the Donatist controversy. It is etymologically related to the Latin verb *tradere*, "to hand over," which is used of the person who cooperated with the Roman authorities by handing over Christian books, particularly the Scriptures, to them during the time of persecution.

406. See Eph 6:13–17.

407. See 2 Tim 2:11–12.

tive] virtues, so much are they all the more brilliant in the individual martyrs.

Now it seems good here at the beginning to treat the background of this war and to discuss the turning point which was decisive for the whole world. Of necessity, I must be brief and proceed with all speed so that, once the truth is recognized, one may know the rewards of the martyrs and the punishments of the traitors.

2. In the times of Diocletian and Maximian, the devil waged war against the Christians in this manner: he sought to burn the most holy testaments of the Lord, the divine scriptures, to destroy the basilicas of the Lord, and to prohibit the sacred rites and the most holy assemblies from celebrating in the Lord. But the army of the Lord did not accept such a monstrous order and it bristled at the sacrilegious command. Quickly it seized the arms of faith and descended into battle. This battle was to be fought not so much against human beings as against the devil. Some fell from faith at the critical moment by handing over to unbelievers the scriptures of the Lord and the divine testaments so they could be burned in unholy fires. But how many more in preserving them bravely resisted by freely shedding their blood for them! When the devil had been completely defeated and ruined and all the martyrs were filled with God's presence, bearing the palm of victory over suffering,[408] they sealed with their own blood the verdict against the traitors and their associates, rejecting them from the communion of the Church. For it was not right that there should be martyrs and traitors in the Church of God at the same time. Therefore, these enormous battle lines of confessors flew onto the field of combat from all sides, and where any of them found the enemy, there they pitched the camp of the Lord.

Now when the war trumpet sounded in the city of Abitina, the glorious martyrs set up the standards of the Lord in the home of Octavius Felix. While they were celebrating the sacraments of the Lord, as was their custom, they were taken into custody by the magistrates of the town and by the soldier stationed there. Those arrested were Saturninus and his four children, i.e., Saturninus Jr. and Felix, the lectors; Maria, the consecrated virgin; and the child Hilarianus. Also arrested were: Dativus, the one who was a senator, Felix, another Felix, Emeritus, Ampelius, Rogatianus, Quintus, Maximus, Telica, Rogatianus, Rogatus, Januarius, Cassianus, Victorianus, Vincentius, Cecelianus, Restituta, Prima, Eva, Rogatianus, Giualius, Rogatus, Pomponia, Secunda, Januaria, Saturnina, Martinus, Clautus, Felix, the elder Margarita, Honorata, Regiola, Victorinus, Pelusius, Faustus, Datianus,

Matrona, Cecilia, Victoria, Hecretina, and another married woman named Januaria. These detainees were led briskly to the forum, now the first field of battle.

3. Dativus went first, the one whom his holy parents bore, an upright senator in the heavenly senate house.[409] Then came the presbyter Saturninus surrounded by his numerous children. He chose some of them as his companions in martyrdom; he left the others to the Church as a memorial to his name. Following them came the army of the Lord. In it shone the splendor of heavenly armor: the shield of faith, the breastplate of justice, the helmet of salvation, and the sword which is the word of God.[410] Relying on this armor, they promised hope of victory to the brothers and sisters.

They came to the forum of the above-named city. Having been brought together there, they first bore the palm of confession to their arraignment before the magistrate. In this very same forum heaven had already battled on behalf of the scriptures of the Lord when Fundanus, formerly the bishop of the city, handed over the scriptures of the Lord to be burned. When the officials kindled the unholy fires under them, rain suddenly poured out of a clear sky. Just as the fire approached the holy scriptures, it was extinguished. Hail stones fell and the whole area was devastated by raging weather on behalf of the scriptures of the Lord.

4. Here the martyrs of Christ first received the chains they had longed for, and formed into a line, happy and cheerful, they sang hymns and songs to the Lord[411] all along the road from this city to Carthage. When they arrived at the office of Anulinus who was then the proconsul, they stood in battle formation, steadfast and brave. Their steadfastness in the Lord beat back the blows of the raging devil. But when the fury of the devil could not prevail over all the soldiers of Christ together, he demanded them in combat one by one.

When it comes to the struggles of their battles I shall not proceed so much in my own words as in those of the martyrs so that the boldness of the raging enemy may be known in the torments and the sacrilegious invective, and the power of their leader Christ the Lord may be praised in the endurance of the martyrs and by their confession itself.

5. Therefore, since they were handed over by the local of-

---

408. The palm carried by the martyr is the iconographic representation of the *palma*, the trophy or symbol of victory in, for instance, athletic contests.

409. By analogy to his rank in the civil hierarchy and honor, Dativus is also a senator in the Christian (heavenly) hierarchy.

410. See Eph 6:14–17.

411. See Eph 5:19.

ficials to the proconsul and since it had been proposed that the Christians be sent by the officials of Abitina—for they celebrated the Lord's Supper against the prohibition of the emperors and the caesars—the proconsul first asked Dativus what his station in life was and whether he had come to the assembly. When he declared that he was a Christian and that he had come to the assembly, the proconsul demanded the name of the leader of this most holy assembly. Immediately he ordered the official on duty to put Dativus on the rack and, once he was stretched out, to prepare the claws. The executioners carried out their cruel orders with dreadful speed, and standing there filled with rage down to their fingertips, with the claws raised, they threatened the wounded sides of the martyr which were already stripped and exposed.

Next Tazelita, the bravest martyr, in front of everyone submitted himself to torments and exclaimed, "We are Christians." He said, "We do assemble." Then the anger of the proconsul blazed hot. Groaning and severely wounded by a spiritual sword, the executioner struck the martyr of Christ with heavy blows as he hung there on the rack. He stretched him out and tore at him with the horrible grating claws. But in response, in the midst of the fury of the executioners, Tazelita, the most glorious martyr, poured out his prayer of thanksgiving to the Lord in this manner: "Thanks be to God. In your name, O Christ, son of God, free your servants."

6. In response to such a prayer the proconsul asked, "Who is the leader of your congregation?" To the executioner now attacking more fiercely he responded loudly, "Saturninus the presbyter and all of us." O martyr, giving primacy to all! He does not give the presbyter priority over the sisters and brothers but he joins them to the presbyter in the fellowship of their confession. That is why he pointed to Saturninus when the proconsul asked. He did not do it to single out the person whom he saw fighting equally with him against the devil, but to explain fully that he celebrated in the assembly with them as their presbyter.

Blood flowed out along with his voice as he prayed to the Lord, and, mindful of the precepts of the gospel, he asked for forgiveness for his enemies even as his body was being torn apart.[412] Then in the midst of the most severe tortures of the blows he reproached his torturers and the proconsul equally with these words: "You act unjustly, you wretches, you struggle against God. O God most high, do not hold these sins against them.[413] You are sinning, you wretches, you struggle against God. We keep the precepts of God most high. You act unjustly, you wretches. You tear apart the innocent. We are not murderers. We are not criminals. O God,

have mercy. To you be thanks. For your name's sake, give me endurance. Free your servants from the captivity of this world. To you be thanks. I cannot thank you enough."

His sides shook violently as claws bit into them like a plow. A wave of gore flowed out from the blood-red furrows. He heard the proconsul saying to him, "You are only beginning to feel what you ought to suffer." But Tazelita continued, "To glory. I thank you, God of all kingdoms. May the eternal kingdom come, an incorruptible kingdom. Lord Jesus, we are Christians; we serve you. You are our hope. You are the hope of Christians. God most holy, God most high, God omnipotent, we praise you for your name."

He prayed this way while the devil, through the judge, said, "You ought to obey the law of the emperors and the caesars." From a body now tormented, a victorious spirit answered with a strong and persistent voice, "I respect only the Law of God which I have learned. That is what I obey. I die for it. I am consumed by it, by the Law of God. There is no other."[414] By saying such things, it was the most glorious martyr himself who tormented Anulinus even worse than his own great torments. Finally, his anger fattened with ferocity, Anulinus said, "Stop," and he bound over to a well-deserved passion the martyr confined in his prison.

7. Next Dativus was strengthened for battle by the Lord. He had been closely associated with Tazelita. While he was tortured, he observed Tazelita hanging on the rack. Repeatedly Dativus bravely proclaimed that he was a Christian and had taken part in the assembly. The brother of the most holy martyr Victoria arrived on the scene. He was quite a distinguished Roman citizen, but at that time he was hostile to the practice of the most holy religion. Now he was reproving the martyr hung on the rack with unholy words, "Sir," he said, "this is the man who in the absence of our father kept trying to seduce our sister Victoria while we were studying here. He lured her from this most splendid city of Carthage all the way out to the town of Abitina along with Secunda and Restituta. He never came into our house except to lead their young hearts astray with his proselytizing."

But Victoria, the most distinguished martyr, did not endure her associate and fellow martyr being assailed by the lying senator. With Christian candor she immediately said, "No one persuaded me to leave and it was not with him that

---

412. See Mt 6:14; Lk 23:34.
413. See Acts 7:60.
414. See Deut 4:35.

I went to Abitina. By the testimony of [free] citizens I can prove this: I did everything on my own initiative and by my own free will. Certainly I have been a member of the assembly; I have celebrated the Lord's Supper with my brothers and sisters because I am a Christian."

Then her shameless legal counsellor flung even more foul-mouthed abuse against the martyr [Dativus]. But from his place on the rack, the glorious martyr refuted all the charges with his truthful rebuttal.

8. Meanwhile Anulinus grew more angry and ordered the claws to be applied to the martyr. Immediately the executioners attacked his sides which had been stripped and prepared for their blows by his bloody wounds. Their savage hands flew, more swift than their speedy orders. His skin was cut and his viscera torn. They laid open the recesses of his chest to the cruel gaze of the impious. In the midst of these events, the mind of the martyr stands firm and even if his limbs were broken, his viscera torn to pieces and his sides ripped apart, nevertheless, the soul of the martyr endures whole and unshaken. Finally, mindful of his dignity,[415] Dativus the senator poured out his prayer to the Lord as follows in the presence of the mad executioner: "O Christ, Lord, let me not be put to shame."[416] With these words the most blessed martyr merited so easily what he had so succinctly requested from the Lord.

Finally now, the mind of the proconsul was deeply disturbed. In spite of himself he burst forth: "Stop!" The executioners stopped, for it was not right that the martyr of Christ should be tortured for the sake of Victoria his co-martyr.

9. Although Pompeianus the savage prosecutor attacked him with unjustified suspicion and initiated a slanderous suit [against him], the martyr fixed a look on him and deeply affected him saying: "What are you doing in this place, you devil? What are you trying to do to the martyrs of Christ?" The senator of the Lord and martyr overcame both the power and rage of this lawyer. But how the most famous martyr had to be racked for Christ! Questioned whether he had been in the assembly, he firmly confessed and said that when there was an assembly, he had come; along with his sisters and brothers he had celebrated the Lord's Supper with a devotion befitting his religion; and that there was one single organizer of this most holy assembly. This again so readily incited the proconsul against him and his savagery broke out again. The dignity of the martyr is redoubled as he is flogged with the furrowing claws. But the martyr tormented in the midst of his most cruel wounds repeated his original prayer:

"I beseech you, O Christ, let me not be put to shame.[417] What have I done? Saturninus is our presbyter."

10. While the harsh and grim executioners scraped Dativus' sides with crooked claws, as if their teacher were Cruelty itself showing them the way, Saturninus the presbyter is summoned to the battle. In his contemplation of the heavenly kingdom, he considers these things truly small and of no consequence. He began to support his fellow martyrs and to fight alongside them. The proconsul said, "You acted against the order of the emperors and the caesars when you gathered all of these people together." Saturninus the presbyter, with the prompting of the Spirit of the Lord, fearlessly responded, "We celebrated the Lord's Supper."

The proconsul said, "Why?" He responded, "Because it was not possible to neglect the Lord's Supper." When Saturninus had said these things, the proconsul immediately ordered Dativus to be prepared for torture. Dativus meanwhile watched the tearing of his body rather than grieve. His mind and spirit depended on the Lord. He thought nothing of the pain in his body but only prayed to the Lord saying, "Come to my aid, I pray. O Christ, have pity on my soul. Care for my spirit. Let me not be put to shame, I pray, O Christ."

The proconsul said to him, "It would have been better if you had called others from this most splendid city to a right disposition and if you had not acted against the order of the emperors and the caesars." But steadfastly and constantly he cried out, "I am a Christian." Overcome by this reply, this devil said, "Stop!" Throwing him also into prison, the proconsul set this martyr aside for a worthy passion.

11. But while the presbyter Saturninus hung on the rack anointed by the newly shed blood of the martyrs, he was incited to persist in the faith of those in whose blood he stood fast. While he was being interrogated whether he had been the organizer and whether he had gathered everyone together, he said, "I was there in the assembly." Contending alongside the presbyter, Emeritus the lector springing up for battle said, "I am the organizer in whose home the assemblies were held." But by now the proconsul had so often been gotten the better of that he shook with horror at the attack of Emeritus. Nevertheless, turning toward the presbyter, he said, "Why did you act against the order? What do you get

---

415. See 2 Macc 6:23.
416. See Ps 31:17.
417. See Ps 31:17.

out of confessing?" Saturninus said to him, "The Lord's Supper could not be neglected; so the Law orders."[418] Then the proconsul said, "Nonetheless, you should not have made light of what was forbidden but rather you should have observed the order of the emperors and not acted against them." And with a voice well practiced against the martyrs, he admonished the torturers to begin to torment him.

He is obeyed with willing compliance. The executioners fall on the elderly body of the presbyter and, with their anger raging, they tear the broken bonds of his sinews. You should have seen the lamentable tortures and the exquisite torments of a new kind inflicted on the priest of God. You should have seen the executioners vent their anger as if they had a rabid hunger for wounds as food and for the entrails now open to the horror of those watching. Amidst the red of the blood, the bones gleamed white. Lest his soul being pressed out from his body desert it in the delays between rackings, the presbyter prayed to the Lord in this way: "I beseech you, O Christ, hear me. I give you thanks, O God. Order me to be beheaded. I beseech you, O Christ, have mercy. Son of God, come to my aid."

The proconsul said to him, "Why do you act against the order?"

The presbyter said, "Thus does the Law order. Thus does the Law teach." O divine reply of the learned presbyter, truly wondrous enough to be proclaimed! Even under torture the presbyter preaches the most holy Law for which he freely withstood torture. At last, frightened by the mention of the Law, Anulinus said, "Stop!" Throwing him back into the confinement of prison he destined him for the suffering for which he hoped.

17. And lest the most devoted sex of women and the brightest band of holy virgins be deprived of the glory of such a battle, all of the women, with the help of Christ the Lord, were brought in and crowned in victory. Now Victoria, the holiest of the women, the flower of virgins, the glory and grandeur of confessors, came from a respectable family. She was most devoted to her religion and temperate in her morals. In her the goodness of nature shone forth in brilliant modesty. To the beauty of her body there corresponded in her mind an even more beautiful faith and integrity of holiness. She rejoiced in the second pledge of victory granted to her in martyrdom for the Lord.

Clear signs of her virtue had been shining forth from her very infancy. Even in her tender years, a most chaste firmness of mind and a sure worthiness for her future suffering

appeared. Finally, after total virginity complemented the mature part of her life, and when the young woman unwillingly and reluctantly was forced into a marriage and her parents gave her a bridegroom against her will, the young woman secretly threw herself off a cliff so that she might flee the man who would carry her off like booty. Supported by compliant breezes, she was received unharmed on the lap of the earth. She should not have had to suffer for Christ since she had already died for the sake of her singular modesty.

Therefore, freed from marriage and at the same time from both an abusive bridegroom and her parents, leaping forth almost from the very midst of the crowd at the wedding, the unconquered virgin took refuge at the house of modesty and the harbor of chastity, the Church. There with unblemished honor she reserved the most holy hair of her head, consecrated and dedicated to God in perpetual virginity. Then, hurrying on to martyrdom, she held before her in her right hand the flowering palm of triumphant modesty.

When the proconsul asked her what she professed, she responded with a clear voice, "I am a Christian." When Fortunatianus, her distinguished brother and counselor, said that her mind had been captivated by inane arguments, Victoria responded: "My mind is made up," she said, "I've never changed."

In response the proconsul said, "Do you want to go with Fortunatianus your brother?" She answered, "I do not want to because I am a Christian and my brothers are those who keep the commands of God."[419] O young woman, strengthened by the authority of divine Law! O glorious virgin rightly consecrated to the eternal king! O most blessed martyr, most famous for her evangelical profession! With a dominical saying she responded: "My brothers are those who keep the commands of God."

When he heard these words, Anulinus, laying aside the authority of his office, stepped down to reason with the young woman. "Have some regard for your situation," he said. "You see that your brother is concerned with providing for your welfare." The martyr of Christ said to him, "My mind is made up. I've never changed. I was in the assembly and I celebrated the Lord's Supper with the sisters and brothers because I am a Christian."

---

418. In the writings of North African Christian authors, in particular those by Donatists, the Bible is often spoken of as "the Law."

419. See Mk 3:33–35; Mt 12:48–50; Lk 8:21.

As soon as he heard these things, Anulinus, raging, agitated, and burning with anger, chained the most holy young woman, the martyr of Christ, in prison, along with the others. He reserved them all for suffering like the Lord's."

18. But Hilarianus, one of the children of the presbyter-martyr Saturninus, still remained. He overcame his diminutive age with his great devotion. Rushing to be united to the triumph of his father and brothers, he scarcely feared the dire threats of the tyrant because he reckoned them as nothing. When it was said to him, "Are you imitating your father or your brothers?" suddenly a youthful voice is heard from his tiny body and the little heart of the boy is opened to a full confession of the Lord in his response: "I am a Christian, and of my own will and volition I attended the assembly with my father and brothers."

Have you not been listening to the voice of his father Saturninus the martyr coming from the sweet lips of his son! Have you not been listening to the tongue confessing Christ as Lord, secure in the example of his brother! But the stupid proconsul did not realize that he was not fighting against human beings but against God[420] because he did not notice the great spirit in his youthful years. He thought the boy could be terrified with infantile torments. At last he said, "I'll cut off your hair and nose and ears and I'll release you that way."[421]

The child Hilarianus, glorious in the virtues of his father and brothers, had already learned from his elders to disdain torments; to these remarks he responded with a clear voice: "Do whatever you wish to do, for I am a Christian." Soon he too is ordered to be taken back into the prison and the voice of Hilarianus is heard saying with great joy: "Thanks be to God."

Here one battle in the great war is brought to an end; here the devil is overcome and conquered; here the martyrs of Christ rejoice with eternal joy concerning the eternal glory of their future suffering.[422]

19. For truly, as we have already said, the time of schism admonishes us by so many and such great confessions to collect the pronouncements of the martyrs and to link the most holy injunctions of the friends of God to the preceding deeds. By necessity I shall review only briefly all those things which the martyrs in prison did ordain on the basis of divine Law and which they leave reserved for those who succeed them. In my haste I shall omit neither the arrogance of the lapsed nor the impudence of the traitors because faith, love of the Law, the condition of the Church, public welfare and the common life force me to omit nothing that happened.

Based on this account, one will be able to recognize which church is the Catholic Church, if the pestiferous defect of the traitors is revealed for all ages by their impious deeds as well as by the judgment of the martyrs.

Therefore, after the long-desired prison received the above mentioned martyrs of Christ, the confessors there, whose cases had already been postponed, joined their triumphant right hands to the hands of the victors as they entered. Moreover, many other confessors came to that same place from diverse parts of the province. Among them were bishops, presbyters, deacons and others of clerical rank. They all upheld the Law of the Lord and steadfastly and bravely celebrated the assembly of the Lord. They saved the scriptures of the Lord and the divine testaments from flames and burning. For the sake of the divine Law, they offered their very selves to menacing fires and diverse tortures in the manner of the Maccabees.[423]

20. Even though in this calamity the terrible prison and thick darkness held the most faithful witnesses of God closed up within them and subdued their faithful members with the heavy weight of chains, even though hunger weakened them, thirst exhausted them, and cold battered them, and the crowd pressed the very sides broken at last by a recent mangling with claws, nevertheless, gathering together as a council, amidst chains of iron and all the instruments of torture, on the authority of divine Law, they established a heavenly decree which the martyrs preserved for themselves and their descendants.

Truly the living Spirit, the Holy Spirit, directed the minds of the confessors by infusing them with eternal and divine discourse. Then after the cruel calamity and the horrible threats of persecution, when by these threats tyrannical rage had attacked the Christian religion, so that the eternal peace of the Christian Name might shine ever more pure and more serene, there was lacking neither intense deception on the part of all those traitors nor the conspiracy of the noxious remainder of those whose faith had been shipwrecked. These were brought together by diabolical art which, under the guise of religion, attacked faith, overturned law and disturbed divine authority. When Mensurius, so-called bishop of Carthage, polluted by the recent handing over of scripture,

---

420. See Acts 5:38–39.

421. See 2 Macc 7:3–4.

422. Their executions, which took place at various times and places, are excluded from the narrative.

423. See 2 Macc 6:1–7:42.

repented of the malice of his misdeeds and then began to reveal greater crimes, he who had had to beg and implore from the martyrs pardon for burning the books, raged against the martyrs with the same resolve with which he had handed over the divine laws, thus adding to his transgressions even more shameful acts. More ruthless than the tyrant, more bloody than the executioner, he chose Caecilian his deacon as a suitable minister of his misdeeds and he stationed him before the doors of the prison, armed with whips and lashes so he might turn away from the entrance and exit all those who brought food and drink to the martyrs in prison, further harming those already wronged by grave injustice. People who came to nourish the martyrs were struck down right and left by Caecilian. The cups for the thirsty inside in chains were broken. At the entrance to the prison food was scattered only to be torn apart by the dogs. Before the doors of the prison the fathers of the martyrs fell and the most holy mothers. Shut out from the sight of their children, they kept their vigil day and night at the entrance of the prison. There was the dreadful weeping and the bitter lamentation by all who were there. To keep the pious from the embrace of the martyrs and to keep Christians from a duty of piety, Caecilian was more ruthless than the tyrant, more bloody than the executioner.

21. Meanwhile neither the squalor of prison nor the pain of the flesh nor, finally, the lack of anything disturbed the martyrs of Christ. But already near to the Lord by their merits and their confession, they directed those who succeeded them, the renewed progeny of the Christian name, to be separated from all filth and communion with traitors by this warning: "If anyone communicates with the traitors, that person will have no part with us in the heavenly kingdom." And they endorsed this verdict of theirs by the authority of the Holy Spirit written in such evidence: "It is written," they said, "in the Apocalypse, 'Whoever adds to this book one part of a letter or one letter, to him will the Lord add innumerable afflictions. And whoever blots them out, so will the Lord blot out his share from the Book of Life.'[424] If, therefore, a part of a letter added or a letter omitted cuts off a person at the roots from the Book of Life and if such constitutes a sacrilege, it is necessary that all those who handed over the divine testaments and the honored laws of the omnipotent God and of the Lord Jesus Christ to be burned in profane fires should be tormented in the eternal flames of Gehenna and inextinguishable fire. And, therefore, as we have already said, 'If anyone communicates with the traitors, that person will not have a share with us in the heavenly kingdom.'"

Sharing in these judgments, one by one, they hurried off to the glory of suffering and to the ultimate testimony. Each one of the martyrs signed the judgment with their own blood. Accordingly, the Holy Church follows the martyrs and curses the treachery of the traitor Mensurius.

From Maureen A. Tilley, trans., *Donatist Martyr Stories: The Church in Conflict in Roman North Africa* (Liverpool: Liverpool University Press, 1996), 27–36, 41–46.

❧ **Augustine** (354–430) polemicizes about the story concerning the Abitinian martyrs and the issues surrounding the Donatist controversy, including the question of priests who relapsed in faith, from the catholic point of view in *Letter* 105 (to the Donatists), written in 404.

AUGUSTINE

Letter 105 (to the Donatists)

. . . You say that we are betrayers, a charge which your ancestors could not prove against our ancestors, nor will you ever be able to prove it against us. What do you want us to do to you? We tell you to listen to us patiently while we plead your cause and ours, and you do nothing but rant and rage. We could certainly show you that the real betrayers were those who condemned Caecilian and his coworkers on a fictitious charge of betrayal. And you say: "Keep away from our flocks," whom you teach to believe in you and not to believe in Christ. You tell them that because of betrayers—whom you do not produce—the Church of Christ exists only in Africa, in the sect of Donatus; and you do not give any authority for your statement, either from the Law, or from a Prophet, or a psalm, or an Apostle, or the Gospel, but only from your own feeling, and the false reports of your parents. But Christ says: "And that penance and remission of sins should be preached in his name unto all nations, beginning at Jerusalem."[425] Yet, you are not in communion with that Church which was announced by the word of Christ, and you do not want others, whom you drag down into your own ruin, to be set free.

If you are angry with us because you are forced by the decrees of the emperors[426] to rejoin us, you brought this on

---

424. Rev 22:18–19.
425. Lk 24:47. (The notes for this selection are by Gerhart and Udoh.)
426. Reference here is to the decrees of 405, which reaffirmed earlier laws.

yourselves by stirring up violence and threats whenever we wished to preach the truth, and you tried to prevent anyone from listening to it in safety or choosing it voluntarily. Do not hiss and stir up your minds; think tolerantly, if you can, over what we say; call to memory the deeds of your Circumcellions[427] and the clerics who have always been their leaders, and you will see what brought this on you. Your complaints are baseless because you forced the enactment of all these decrees. Not to go back over numerous past instances, consider, at least, your recent conduct. Mark, a priest of Casphaliana became a Catholic of his own free will, without compulsion from anybody; thereupon your people pursued him and would almost have killed him, if the hand of God had not restrained their violence by means of some passers-by. Restitutus of Victoriana came over to the Catholic faith without any compulsion, and was dragged from his house, beaten, rolled in the water, clothed in reeds, kept in custody I don't know how long, and would probably not have been restored to liberty if Proculeianus[428] had not seen himself threatened with a show-down, largely on his account. Marcian of Urga chose Catholic unity of his own free will, and, when he went into hiding, your clerics took his subdeacon, beat him almost to death, and stoned him. For this crime their houses were destroyed.

What is the use of saying more? Lately, you sent a herald to proclaim at Sinitus: "If anyone remains in communion with Maximinus,[429] his house will be burned down." Why? Before he had been converted to the Catholic faith, when he had not yet returned from overseas, why else did we send there a priest of Sinitus, except to visit our people without troubling anyone, and, from his lawful dwelling, to preach Catholic unity to those who were willing to hear him? But your people expelled him, and did him a great wrong. What other purpose did we have when one of ours, Possidius, Bishop of Calama, was traveling to the estate of Figulina, to visit our flock, few as they were, and to give an opportunity to any who wished it to hear the word of God and return to the unity of Christ? But, while he was on his way, they lay in wait for him like a band of brigands and, failing to catch him in their toils, they attacked him violently at the farm of Oliveta, left him half-dead and tried to burn down the house from which he had escaped. They would have done it, too, if the tenants of that same farm had not three times put out the flames which endangered their own safety. Yet, when Crispinus[430] was convicted in the proconsular court as a heretic of this very deed, he was let off the fine of ten pounds of gold, at the request of this same Bishop Possidius. He not

only showed no gratitude for this kindly indulgence, but he even went so far as to appeal to the Catholic emperors.[431] This is what has brought down on you the wrath of God with greater force, and persistence, and you complain of it!

You see, you are suffering for your own evil deeds, not for Christ, when you stir up violence against the peace of Christ. What kind of madness is it to claim the glory of martyrdom when you are being justly punished for your evil life and your deeds of brigandage? If you, private citizens, so boldly and violently force men either to accept error or to remain in it, how much greater right and duty have we to resist your outrages by means of the lawfully constituted authority, which God has made subject to Christ, according to His prophecy, and so to rescue unfortunate souls from your tyranny, to free them from long-continued false teaching and let them breathe the clear air of truth! As for those who, according to you, are compelled to join us against their will, many of them wish to be compelled, as they admit to us both before and after conversion, for only thus can they escape your oppressive treatment.

Which, then, is the better course: to publish the decrees of the emperors in behalf of unity, or to proclaim a mistaken amnesty in behalf of heresy, as you have done, when you have suddenly filled the whole of Africa with your lies?[432] By this conduct you have proved nothing else except that the sect of Donatus, relying on falsehood, is tossed and tumbled about by all the winds, as it is written "He that trusteth to lies, feedeth the winds."[433] Thus, that amnesty was as true as the crimes of Caecilian and the betrayal of Felix of Aptunga, by whom he was consecrated, and all the other charges which you commonly make against the Catholics, in order to separate unhappy souls from the peace of the Church of Christ and be yourselves unhappily separated from it. But, we on our side do not rely on any power of man, although,

---

427. Circumcellions (from the Latin, *circum cellas euntes,* that is, "those who go among the cells") were ascetics, with roots in the Donatist movement, who flourished especially in the fourth century. They either wandered around the countryside (*circum cellas*) or they stayed by the farmhouses (*cellae rusticanae*) in North Africa. They combined social rebellion with the veneration of the martyrs. They actively sought their own martyrdom.

428. Donatist bishop of Hippo.

429. Donatist bishop of Sinitus. He became a Catholic and remained in the same see.

430. Donatist bishop of Calama.

431. Honorius and Arcadius.

432. The report by Donatists that the imperial decrees against them had been abrogated.

433. Prov 10:4 (Vulgate).

no doubt, it would be much more honorable to rely on the emperors than to rely on Circumcellions, and to rely on laws than to rely on rioting, but we recall what is written: "Cursed be everyone who putteth his hope in man."[434] So, then, if you want to know on whom we rely, think of Him whom the Prophet foretold, saying: "All the kings of the earth shall adore him; all nations shall serve him."[435] That is why we make use of this power of the Church which the Lord both promised and gave to it.

If the emperors were in error—perish the thought!—in accordance with their error they would issue laws against the truth, and through these the just would be both tried and crowned by not doing what was commanded because it was forbidden by God. Thus Nabuchodonosor had commanded his golden statue to be adored,[436] and they who refused to do it pleased God who forbade such acts. But, when the emperors hold to the truth, in accordance with that truth they give commands against error, and whoever despises them brings down judgment on himself. He pays the penalty exacted by men and he has no standing before God, because he refused to do what truth itself commanded him by the "heart of the king."[437] Thus Nabuchodonosor himself was afterward moved by the miracle of the preservation of the three children, and, turning against error and toward truth, he published an edict that "Whoever should speak blasphemy against the God of Sidrach, Misach and Abdenago should be destroyed and their houses laid waste."[438] And do you refuse to admit that Christian emperors should give like commands against you, when they know that Christ is mocked by you in those whom you rebaptize? If the commands of a king do not extend to the preaching of religion and the prevention of sacrilege, why do you single out the edict of a king giving such commands? Do you not know that the words of a king are "signs and wonders [which] the most high God hath wrought toward me. It hath seemed good in my sight to publish how great and mighty is his kingdom, an everlasting kingdom, and his power to all generations."[439] When you hear this, do you not answer "Amen,"[440] and, making your reply in a loud voice, do you not enroll yourselves under the king's edict with sacred ceremony? But, because you have no influence with the emperors, you want to make trouble for us in that quarter; if you had influence, what would you not do, when, having none, you stop at nothing?

Know this, that your earliest predecessors appealed the case of Caecilian to Emperor Constantine. Challenge us on this; let us prove it to you, and, if we do not prove it, treat us according to your power. But, because Constantine did

not dare to judge the case of a bishop, he assigned it to bishops to be discussed and settled. This was done at Rome with Melchiades presiding as bishop of that Church, together with many of his colleagues. They declared Caecilian innocent, and gave a verdict against Donatus for having caused a schism at Carthage, whereupon yours went a second time to the emperor to denounce the verdict of the bishops, which had gone against them. But, can a guilty plaintiff ever praise the verdict of those by whom he is convicted? A second time our most clement emperor gave them a court of bishops, at Arles, a city of Gaul, and yours appealed from them to the emperor in person, and he personally examined the case and pronounced Caecilian innocent, and themselves guilty of false witness. Yet, they did not subside after this series of rebuffs, but wearied the emperor by daily appeals about Felix of Aptunga, by whom Caecilian had been consecrated, saying that he had been a betrayer and Caecilian therefore could not be a bishop because he had been consecrated by a betrayer. Finally, by the emperor's orders, the case of Felix was examined by Aelianus, the proconsul, and he was proved innocent.

Thus, Constantine was the first to issue an extremely rigorous law against the sect of Donatus. His sons imitated him with similar edicts. They were succeeded by Julian,[441] a deserter and enemy of Christ, who yielded to the petition of your sectaries, Rogatian and Pontius, by giving freedom to the sect of Donatus, to their own peril, and by giving back their basilicas to the heretics, while he was also restoring the temples to the demons. He thought that in this way the name of Christian could be blotted out from the earth, if he should attack the unity of the Church from which he had apostatized, and should allow the accursed forces of dissension to be free of restriction. This was his famous justice, which was praised by his petitioners, Rogatian and Pontius, who said—to an apostate!—that justice had found refuge in him alone. He was succeeded by Jovian, who died soon after his accession and gave no orders about such things. Then came Valentinian; read what he decreed against you. After

---

434. Jer 17:5.   436. See Dan 3:1–18.

435. Ps 71:11 (Vulgate) = Ps 72:11.   437. Prov 21:1.

438. Dan 3:95–96 (Vulgate) = 3:28–29.

439. Dan 3:99–100 (Vulgate).

440. That is, in the office of Holy Saturday, when these words were chanted and the congregation responded "Amen."

441. Emperor Julian (361–63 CE), called "the Apostate," tried to revive pagan culture and religion in the Roman Empire.

him, Gratian and Theodosius; read when you will what they enacted against you. Why, then, are you surprised at the sons of Theodosius, as if they ought to have followed a different course in this matter than that prescribed by the verdict of Constantine, which was enforced so strictly by so many Christian emperors?

However, as we have said, and as we will show you whenever you wish, if you still do not know it, your ancestors took the case of Caecilian to Constantine of their own accord. Constantine died, but Constantine's decree remained in force against you. Your people had sent their case to him; they denounced the bishops' court to him; they appealed from the bishops' court to him; they wearied him with constant demands about Felix of Aptunga; however often they came away defeated and put to shame, they never gave up their desperate fury and hatred, but left it as a legacy to you, their posterity. The result is that you shamelessly display hatred for the commands of Christian emperors, and, if it were allowed, you would not now appeal to Constantine the Christian against us, but you would raise the apostate Julian from the dead, and, if any such thing really happened, it would bring great misfortune to nobody but you. Nothing can cause more complete death to the soul than freedom to disseminate error.

But, let us now put all that out of the way; let us love peace, which everyone, learned and unlearned, recognizes as preferable to discord; let us cherish and maintain unity. The emperors command this, and it is what Christ also commands, because, when they command what is good, Christ gives the command through them. The Apostle also begs us all to say the same thing, and that there be no schisms among us; not to say: "I indeed am of Paul, and I am of Apollo, and I am of Cephas, and I of Christ."[442] But, at the same time, let us all be for none but Christ, for Christ is not divided; neither was Paul crucified for you, much less Donatus! We were not baptized in the name of Paul, much less of Donatus.[443] The emperors say this because they are called Catholic Christians, not servers of idols like your Julian; not heretics, as certain ones have been and have persecuted the Church, when true Christians have suffered the most glorious martyrdom for Catholic truth, not justly deserved penalties for heretical error.

Note with what perfectly clear truth God himself speaks through the "heart of the king which is in the hand of God,"[444] by means of that very law which you say was promulgated against you. If you could understand, it was promulgated for

your benefit. Note what the emperor's words say: "If the rite of baptism, in the case of those who were first received into the Church, is considered invalid because those from whom it was received were deemed sinners, it will be necessary for the sacrament thus received to be renewed as often as the minister of the rite of baptism is found to be unworthy; and our faith will not be founded on the choice of our own will and the gift of divine grace but on the merits of priests and the character of clerics."[445] Let your bishops hold a thousand councils, but let them give an answer to this one sentence, and we will agree to anything you wish. See now how wrong and wicked is that customary saying of yours that if a man is good he sanctifies the one whom he baptizes; if he is bad and the one baptized does not know it, then God sanctifies him. If this is true, men ought to pray to be baptized by bad men whose wickedness is unknown to them rather than by good men, known to be such, so as to be sanctified by God rather than by men. God forbid that we should accept such foolish beliefs! Why not speak truly and recognize that the grace is always God's and the sacrament is God's, but the ministry is man's? If the minister is a good man, he keeps close to God and works with God; if he is a bad man, God performs the visible action of the sacrament through him, but Himself gives the invisible grace. Let us all acknowledge this, and let us not have schism between us.

Be at peace with us, brothers. We love you; we wish the same for you as we do for ourselves. If you hate us so deeply because we do not allow you to go astray and be lost, say so to God, whose threats to the faithless shepherds we fear, when He says: "That which was driven away you have not brought again, neither have you sought that which was lost."[446] This is what God Himself does for you through us, either by beseeching or threatening or chastising; by loss or trouble; by His secret warnings or trials; or by the laws of secular powers. Understand what is being done to you: God does not wish you to be lost, cut off from your mother, the Catholic Church, in the midst of a sacrilegious dissension. You have not at any time been able to prove anything against us. When your bishops were called together by us, would they confer peaceably with us, or did they avoid converse with us as if we were sinners? Could anyone endure such pride? As if Paul the

---

442. 1 Cor 1:10–12.
443. See 1 Cor 1:13.
444. Prov 21:1

445. See *Codex Theodosianus* 16.6.
446. Ezek 34:4.

Apostle did not converse with sinners, and with quite abandoned ones! Read the Acts of the Apostles and see. As if the Lord Himself did not hold speech with the Jews by whom He was crucified, and answer them courteously! Finally, the Devil is the chief of all sinners, since it will never be possible for him to be converted to goodness, yet the Lord Himself did not disdain to answer him about the Law,[447] by which you may know that the Donatists refuse to confer with us because they know that their case is lost.

We do not know why men make threats against themselves by rejoicing in lying dissensions. In the Scriptures we have learned Christ; in the Scriptures we have learned the Church. We both possess the Scriptures; why do we not both hold to Christ and the Church in them? Where we recognize Him of whom the Apostle said: "To Abraham were the promises made and to his seed. He saith not: and to his seeds, as of many, but of one: and to thy seed, which is Christ,"[448] there we also recognize the Church of which God said to Abraham: "In thy seed shall all nations be blessed."[449] Where we recognize Christ prophesying of Himself in the psalm: "The Lord hath said to me: Thou art my son, this day have I begotten thee," there we recognize the Church in the words which follow: "Ask of me and I will give thee the Gentiles for thy inheritance and the utmost parts of the earth for thy possession."[450] . . .

We do not know why you speak of betrayers when you have never been able to prove your charge, never even been able to point them out. I do not say this because it was rather your people who were found out, and who admitted their crime openly—what have we to do with the burdens of others, except those whom we are able to amend by chastisement or by some discipline applied in the spirit of mildness and the anxious care of love? As to those whom we are not able to amend, even if necessity requires, for the salvation of others, that they share the sacraments of God with us, it does not require us to share in their sins, which we should do by consenting to or condoning them. We tolerate them in this world, in which the Catholic Church is spread abroad among all nations, which the Lord called His field,[451] like the cockle among the wheat;[452] or on this threshing floor of unity, like chaff mingled with the good grain;[453] or in the nets of the word and the sacrament, like the bad fishes enclosed with the good.[454] We leave them until the time of the harvest, or of the winnowing, or of the arrival on shore, so as not, on their account, to root up the wheat; or to winnow the good grain away from the threshing floor, before the time, not to

store it in the granary but to throw it out, to be gathered by the birds; or, with our nets broken by schism, to swim out into the sea of dangerous freedom, in trying to avoid the bad fishes. For this reason the Lord strengthened the patience of His servants by these and other parables, to prevent them from thinking that their virtue would be defiled by contact with wicked men, and thus, through human and vain dissensions, they should lose the little ones, or these should perish. The heavenly Master went so far in forewarning them that He even warned His people against bad rulers, lest, on their account, the saving chair of doctrine should be forsaken, in which even the wicked are forced to utter truth; for the words they speak come not from themselves but from God, and He has placed the teaching of truth upon the chair of unity. Therefore, He, being truthful and the very truth itself, says of rulers, doing their own evil deeds but speaking the good things of God: "What they say, do ye, but according to their works do ye not, for they say and do not."[455] Doubtless He would not have said: "according to their works do ye not," if their works had not been manifestly evil.

Let us not destroy ourselves in evil dissension, because of evil men, although we can prove to you, if you will let us, that your ancestors were not denouncers of bad men, but accusers of innocent ones. But, whoever and whatever they may have been, let them bear their own burdens. Here are the Scriptures which we share; here we know Christ; here we know the Church. If you hold to Christ, why do you not hold to the Church? If, because of the truth of the Scriptures, you believe in Christ, whom you read of, but do not see, why do you deny the Church which you both read of and see? By saying these things to you, and by forcing you to receive this good of peace and unity and charity, we have become enemies to you and to the laws, because you will kill us for speaking the truth to you and for preventing you, to the utmost of our power, from perishing in error. May God protect us from you; may he destroy your error, and may you rejoice with us in the truth. Amen.

From Saint Augustine, *Letters*, translated by Sister Wilfrid Parsons, Fathers of the Church, vol. 32 (New York: Fathers of the Church, 1953), 196–206, 209–11.

447. See Mt 4:1–10; Lk 4:1–12.
448. Gal 3:16.
449. Gen 22:18.
450. Ps 2:7–8.
451. See Mt 13:38.
452. See Mt 13:24–30.
453. See Mt 3:12; Lk 3:17.
454. See Mt 13:47–48.
455. Mt 23:1–3.

THE TRINITARIAN CONTROVERSY

❧ The so-called Trinitarian controversy began, probably in 318, as a dispute between Alexander (d. 326), the patriarch of Alexandria, and the presbyter **Arius** (ca. 250–336) over the interpretation of Proverbs 8:22–31. The central disagreement was whether the Logos-Son was eternal or was created, albeit before the rest of creation. Arius's letter of confession of faith to his bishop, *Letter to Alexander of Alexandria* (written in 320), shows that Arius did not consider his beliefs to be out of line with what his teacher Lucian of Antioch (d. 312) and Alexander himself taught. Arius's teachings, which later became known as the heresy of Arianism, are elucidated in his *Letter to Eusebius of Nicomedia,* written around 319. Eusebius of Nicomedia, also a pupil of Lucian, died in 341.

ARIUS

Letter to Alexander of Alexandria

1. The presbyters and deacons send greetings in the Lord to our blessed pope and bishop, Alexander.

2. Our faith, from our ancestors, which we have learned also from you, is this. We know one God—alone unbegotten, alone everlasting, alone without beginning, alone true, alone possessing immortality, alone wise, alone good, alone master, judge of all, manager, director, immutable and unchangeable, just and good, God of Law, Prophets, and New Testament—who begot an only-begotten Son before eternal times, through whom he made the ages and everything. But he begot him not in appearance but in truth, having submitted him to his own will, an immutable and unchangeable perfect creature of God, 3. but not as one of the creatures—an offspring, but not as one of those born—nor as Valentinus decreed that the offspring of the Father is an emanation, nor as Manes propounded that the offspring of the Father is part of the same substance, nor as Sabellius, who divides the monad, says "Father-and-Son," nor as Hieracas believes a light from a light as a lamp divided into two; nor is he the one who was before, later begotten or created into a Son as you yourself also, Blessed Pope, very often have forbidden throughout the midst of the church and in council those who teach these things. But, as we say, he was created by the will of God before times and ages, and he received life, being, and glories from the Father as the Father has shared them with him. 4. For the Father, having given to him the inheritance of all, did not deprive himself of those things which he has in himself without generation, for he is the source of all.

Thus there are three *hypostases.* God being the cause of all is without beginning, most alone; but the Son, begotten by the Father, created and founded before the ages, was not before he was begotten. Rather, the Son begotten timelessly before everything, alone was caused to subsist by the Father.[456] For he is not everlasting or co-everlasting or unbegotten with the Father. Nor does he have being with the Father, as certain individuals mention things relatively and bring into the discussion two unbegotten causes. But God is thus before all as a monad and cause. Therefore he is also before the Son, as we have learned from you when you preached throughout the midst of the church.

5. Therefore, insofar as he has from God being, glories, and life, and all things have been handed over to him, thus God is his cause. For he, as his God and being before him, rules him. But if "from him"[457] and "from the womb"[458] and "I came from the Father and I come"[459] are thought by some to signify that he is a part of him and an emanation, the Father will be according to them compounded, divided, mutable and a body, and, as far as they are concerned, the incorporeal God suffers things suitable to the body.

I pray that you are well in the Lord, Blessed Pope.

Arius, Aeithales, Achillas, Carpones, Sarmates, and Arius—presbyters.

Euzoius, Lucius, Julius, Menas, Helladius, Gaius—deacons.

Bishops Secundus of Pentapolis, Theonas of Libya, and Pistus.

From William G. Rusch, ed. and trans., *The Trinitarian Controversy: Sources of Early Christian Thought* (Philadelphia: Fortress, 1980), 31–32.

ARIUS

Letter to Eusebius of Nicomedia

1. To a most longed-for lord, a faithful man of God, orthodox Eusebius; Arius, who is unjustly persecuted by Pope Alexander on account of the all-prevailing truth which you also protect, sends greetings in the Lord.

2. Since my father Ammonius was coming into Nicomedia, it appeared to me reasonable and fitting to address you through him and in like manner to remind your innate love and disposition, which you have toward the brothers because of God and his Christ, that the bishop greatly pil-

---

456. See Prov 8:22–23. (The notes for this selection are by Gerhart and Udoh.)

457. Rom 11:36.

458. Ps 110:3.

459. Jn 16:28.

lages us and persecutes us, and invoking all things moves against us, so that he might drive us as godless men from the city. All this is because we do not agree with him when he states in public, "Always God always Son," "At the same time Father, at the same time Son," "The Son ingenerably co-exists with God," "Ever-begotten, ungenerated-created, neither in thought nor in some moment of time does God proceed the Son," "Always God always Son," "The Son is from God himself."

3. And since Eusebius, your brother in Caesarea, and Theodotus, Paulinus, Athanasius, Gregory, Aetius, and all the bishops throughout the East, say that God without beginning exists before the Son, an anathema was pronounced against them—except Philogonius, Hellanicus, and Macareius—heretical and ignorant men, who speak about the Son. Some of them say that he is a belching, others an emanation, and still others alike-ingenerate.

4. If the heretics should threaten us with myriads of deaths, we are not able even to hear these impieties.

But what do we say and think? What have we taught and what do we teach? That the Son is not unbegotten or a portion of the unbegotten in any manner or from any substratum, but that by the will and counsel of the Father he subsisted before times and ages, full of grace and truth, God, only-begotten, unchangeable.

5. And before he was begotten or created or defined or established, he was not.[460] For he was not unbegotten. But we are persecuted because we say, "The Son has a beginning, but God is without beginning." Because of this we are persecuted because we say, "The Son has a beginning, but God is without beginning." We are persecuted because we say, "He is from nothing." But we speak thus inasmuch as he is neither part of God nor from any substratum. On account of this we are persecuted. You know the rest. I pray that you are strong in the Lord, recalling our afflictions, fellow pupil of Lucian, truly "Eusebius."[461]

From William G. Rusch, ed. and trans., *The Trinitarian Controversy: Sources of Early Christian Thought* (Philadelphia: Fortress, 1980), 29–30.

☙ Although **Alexander,** patriarch of Alexandria, and the presbyter Arius were both Origenists, they disagreed as to the Logos-Son's coeternity with the Father. Alexander expresses his views, including his emphasis on the Logos-Son's divinity and coeternity, in his *Letter to Alexander of Thessalonica,* written in 324.

ALEXANDER OF ALEXANDRIA
Letter to Alexander of Thessalonica, 1–36

1. The ambitious and covetous calculation of rascally men has produced plots against the apparently greater dioceses. Through intricate pretenses such individuals are attacking the orthodox faith of the church. Driven wild by the devil at work in them for pleasures at hand, they skipped away from every piety and trampled on the fear of God's judgment. 2. It was necessary for me who is suffering to make clear to Your Reverence these matters so that you might be on guard against such persons, lest some of them dare to come even into your dioceses, either through themselves (for cheats are equal to dissemble for deceit) or through basely refined rescripts, which are able to snatch away a person intent on a simple and pure faith.

3. At any rate, Arius and Achillas have just now entered into a conspiracy, and they have revealed the covetousness of Colluthus, to a much worse degree than even he himself. For Colluthus in bringing charges against them found an excuse for his own ambitious course of action. But they, when they saw him making Christ a source of gain, were not patient to remain as subjects of the church; after constructing for themselves robbers' caves, they held in them incessant assemblies, slandering Christ and us by night and day. 4. They denounced every pious apostolic doctrine; they organized in a Jewish manner a work group contending against Christ. They deny the divinity of our Savior, and proclaim him equal to all. Singling out every expression of his economy for salvation and of his humiliation for our sake, they attempt from them to bring together the proclamation of their own impiety, and from the beginning they turn away from expressions of his divinity and from words of his indescribable glory with the Father. 5. Confirming the impious doctrine of the Greeks and Jews about Christ, as much as possible they pursue praise for themselves. They undertake all those things for which others laugh at us, arousing daily strife and persecutions. They organize this court action through an accusation of disorderly women, whom they have led into error. They are tearing Christianity into pieces by the indecent running

---

460. See Prov 8:22–23. (The notes for this selection are by Gerhart and Udoh.)

461. The Greek *eusebēs* means "pious," "religious," or "dutiful," particularly in the discharge of one's sacred duties.

around of their young women on every street. The seam-less robe of Christ which the executioners resolved not to di-vide,[462] they dared to split. 6. Therefore, after we understood what was befitting their life and unholy attempt—and we did this slowly because it was concealed—we expelled them alto-gether from the church that worships Christ's divinity.

7. And by running to fellow ministers of one mind with us, they attempted to turn them against us. They dissembled a reputation under the show of peace and unity, but in truth they were eager to carry certain of the ministers away into their disease by fair words, and they requested from them re-scripts that were too wordy, so that by reading them, in addi-tion to those deceived by them, they would make them both unrepentant in those things in which they were mistaken and destroyed in impiety. This they did on the grounds that they have bishops who agree and are of one mind with them. 8. They do not confess to them those things which they wick-edly taught and effected, on account of which they were ex-pelled by us, but they either hand them on in silence or de-ceive, obscuring them with fabricated words and writings.

9. Concealing their ruinous teaching with sermons that are too persuasive and of low quality, they seize the person involved in deceit. They do not even desist from slandering our orthodox faith in the presence of everyone. So it happens that certain persons subscribing to their writings admit them into the church. I think that the great slander belongs to our fellow ministers who allow this—for the apostolic rule does not assent to this—who thereby inflame slanderous action against Christ by those who oppose us.

10. For this reason, with no delay, I aroused myself, be-loved, to make clear to you the unbelief of those who say, "There was once when the Son of God was not" and "He who before was not, later came into existence; and when he came into existence, he became as every human being is by nature." 11. They say, "For God made all things from nothing," including even the Son of God with the creation of all rational and irrational creatures. In accord with this, they even say that he is of a mutable nature, capable of both virtue and evil, and with their supposition "from nothing" they destroy the divine Scriptures' witness that he always is, which Scriptures indicate the immutability of the Word and the divinity of the Wisdom of the Word, which is Christ. The wretches state, "Then we too are able to become sons of God, just as he." For it was written, "I have begotten and raised up sons."[463] 12. And when they add the statement from the text "But they rejected me,"[464] which does not belong to the nature of the Savior, who is of an immutable nature, they

abandon every reverence. They say that God, knowing about him by foreknowledge and prevision, would not reject him and chose him from all. 13. For he does not have by nature something special from other sons (for they say that no one is by nature Son of God), nor does he have some distinctive property in relation to God, but he, being of a mutable na-ture, because of the diligence of his manners and not reject-ing his training for the inferior status—he was chosen. 14. As if both a Paul and a Peter would persist at improvement, then their sonship would differ in no way from his. To explain this crazy teaching, they act insultingly toward Scripture and propose the passage in the Psalms about Christ which reads, "You have loved righteousness and hated injustice; on ac-count of this, God, your God, anointed you with the oil of great joy beyond your partners."[465]

15. Therefore, concerning the fact that the Son of God came into existence from nothing and that there was not once when he was not, John the evangelist instructed suf-ficiently, writing about him, "the only-begotten Son who is in the bosom of the Father."[466] For the divine teacher in fore-sight shows that the two things, the Father and the Son, are inseparable from one another. There he specified that he is in the bosom of the Father. 16. And in regard to the fact that the Word of God is not numbered with those who come into existence from nothing, the same John declares that all things came into existence through him.[467] For John makes clear the Word's distinctive *hypostasis,* saying, "In the beginning was the Word and the Word was with God and the Word was God. All things came into existence through him, and with-out him nothing came into existence."[468] 17. If all things came into existence through him, how is it that he who gave being to the ones who came into existence once was not? For the Word, that which makes, is not defined so as to be of the same nature as those who came into existence, if he was in the beginning and all things came into existence through him and he made them from nothing. 18. For that which is and is exceedingly aloof seems opposite to those who came into existence from nothing. 19. This shows that no distance ex-ists between the Father and Son, and that the soul is not able, as far as any thought is concerned, to form an image of this relationship of Father and Son. But the fact that the universe

---

462. See Jn 19:23–24. (The notes for this selection are by Gerhart and Udoh.)

463. Isa 1:2.   466. Jn 1:18.

464. 1 Sam 8:7.   467. See Jn 1:3.

465. Ps 45:7.   468. Jn 1:1, 3.

was fashioned from nothing has a newer *hypostasis* and a fresh origin, since all things received such origination by the Father through the Son. Since the most orthodox John saw that "was"[469] is far from the Word of God and raised high beyond the thought of originated things, he would not speak of the Word's origin and creation, and he did not dare to specify in equivalent syllables the maker with those who came into existence—and not because the Son is unbegotten, for the Father is the one unbegotten, but because the indescribable *hypostasis* of the only-begotten God is beyond the sharpened apprehension of the evangelists, and perhaps of the angels. I do not think that those persons who dare to inquire as far as these matters give thought for the orthodox faith, because they are not willing to hear "Seek not that which is too difficult for you, and do not inquire about that which is too high for you."[470] 20. For if the knowledge of many things incomparably more imperfect than this is hidden with regard to human apprehension—such thoughts are in Paul, "which things God has prepared for those who love him, eye knew not and ear heard not, and have not entered into the heart of man,"[471] and God said to Abraham that the stars are not able to be counted,[472] and still he says, "The sands of the sea and drops of rains, who will count them?"[473]—how does anyone meddle with the *hypostasis* of the Word of God unless he happens to be seized with a melancholic disposition? 21. Concerning this, the prophetic Spirit says, "Who will describe his generation?"[474] Thus even our Savior himself, in showing kindness to those who were the pillars of the whole world, was eager to rid them of the knowledge of this knowledge. Therefore he said to all of them that it was beyond nature for them to apprehend this, and that the knowledge of this most divine mystery is the Father's alone. He said, "No one knows who the Son is except the Father, and no one knows the Father except the Son."[475] I think that concerning this the Father said, "My mystery is for me."[476] 22. But the phrase "from nothing" shows at once that it is crazy to think that the Son came into existence from nothing with the temporal purpose. This is true even if silly individuals are ignorant of the madness of their own voice. The expression "he was not" is necessarily in reference either to time or to some interval of the age. 23. Therefore it is true that all things came into existence through him; it is clear that every age, time, interval, and "when," in which the expression "he was not" is found, came into existence through him. How is it not incredible to say that once he was not, he who made times, ages, and seasons, with which the expression "he was not" is united? It is incomprehensible and totally ignorant to state that the cause

of anything having come into existence is itself later than its generation.

24. For according to them, that interval preceded the Wisdom of God which fashioned all things—an interval in which they say that the Son was not begotten by the Father. Thus, according to them, Scripture played false in proclaiming that he is the firstborn of every creature.[477] 25. Then in harmony with this teaching Paul shouts in his loudest voice, saying about him, "Whom he placed as heir of all through whom he also made the ages"[478] but also, "In him all things were created, those in heaven and those on earth, and seen and unseen, whether principalities or powers or dominions or thrones, all things were created through him and for him, and he himself is before all things."[479] 26. Therefore, since the argument "from nothing" seems most impious, it is necessary that the Father is always the Father. But he is Father of the always present Son, on account of whom he is called Father; and with the Son always present with him, the Father is always perfect, unfailing in goodness, who begot the only-begotten Son not temporally or in an interval or from nothing. 27. Why is it not unjust to say that once the Wisdom of God was not—the Wisdom who says, "I was with him as one united to him, I was the one in whom he rejoiced"[480]—or that once the power of God was not, or once his Word was mutilated, or any other things from which the Son is known and the Father is designated? To say that the brightness of the glory is not, destroys completely the archetypal light of which it is the brightness. And if the image of God was not always,[481] it is clear that he whose image it is, is not always. 28. But also with the nonexistence of the express image of the *hypostasis* of God, he who is imaged by him is destroyed. Thus it is possible to see that the Sonship of the Savior has nothing in common with the sonship of the others. 29. Just as his inexpressible *hypostasis* has been shown in incomparable excess to excel all with whom he himself has been granted being, so that his sonship, possessing by nature his paternal divinity, differs by an unmentionable excess from those who have been adopted as sons through him by adoption. He possesses an immutable nature, being perfect and

---

469. See Jn 1:1–4.
470. Sir 3:21.
471. 1 Cor 2:9; see Isa 64:4; 52:15.
472. See Gen 15:5.
473. Sir 1:2.
474. Isa 53:8 (Septuagint).
475. Mt 11:27.

476. Isa 24:16 (Septuagint).
477. See Col 1:15.
478. Heb 1:2.
479. Col 1:16–17.
480. Prov 8:30 (Septuagint).
481. See Col 1:15.

in want of nothing, but they who are subject to change in either of two ways need assistance from him. 30. Why might the Wisdom of God be able to advance, or what might absolute truth be able to add? Or how might God the Word be able to be improved, or life or the true light?[482] But if this is so, by how much does a great occurrence beyond nature happen, namely, that wisdom at some time becomes capable of folly, or that the power of God is connected with weakness, or that reason is dimmed by the absence of reason, or that darkness is mingled with true light? The apostle states of his own accord, "What is there in common between light and darkness, or what is there between Christ and Belial?"[483] Solomon declares that as far as any thought, it would be impossible that the ways of a snake be found on a rock,[484] which according to Paul is Christ.[485] But they, men and angels, being his creatures, also received blessings to advance in virtues, disciplined by his customary commands so as not to sin. 31. Therefore our Lord, being Son of the Father by nature, is worshiped. And those who have put off the spirit of slavery, from acts of virtue and progress, and who received the spirit of adoption as sons,[486] become sons by adoption being shown a kindness by the Son,[487] who is Son by nature.

32. Therefore Paul made known his legitimate, distinctive, essential, and special sonship, saying about God, ". . . Who did not spare his own son but delivered him for us"[488] (who are clearly not sons by nature). 33. For to make a distinction between those who are not his own, Paul said that he was his own Son. And in the Gospel, "This is my beloved son in whom I am well pleased."[489] In the Psalms the Savior says, "The Lord said to me, 'You are my son.'"[490] Explaining the true Sonship, he indicates that there are not some other legitimate sons besides himself. 34. What does the phrase "from the womb before morning I begot you"[491] indicate? Is it not plainly the essential sonship of the paternal birth, which obtains this not by attention to manners and practice of progress but by the characteristic property of nature? But that the adoption of the rational ones as sons is not according to nature but by aptitude of manners and God's gift, and liable to change, the Word knows, "for the sons of God having seen the daughters of men took them to themselves as wives" etc.,[492] and we were taught that God spoke through Isaiah, "I have begotten sons and exalted them, but they rejected me."[493]

35. Although I am able to say many things, beloved, I pass them by, thinking that it is burdensome to remind teachers of one mind of more items. For you yourselves, taught by God, are not ignorant that the teaching, which has just now risen

up against the church's piety, is of Ebion and Artemas and is an emulation of Paul of Samosata's teaching at Antioch. He was excommunicated from the church by a synod and judgment of all the bishops. 36. Lucian, who succeeded him, remained excommunicated from three bishops during many years. Now among us have grown up those "from nothing" who drained the dregs of the impiety of Ebion, Artemas, and Paul: their hidden offsets, I mean Arius, Achillas, and the assembly of rogues with them.

From William G. Rusch, ed. and trans., *The Trinitarian Controversy: Sources of Early Christian Thought* (Philadelphia: Fortress, 1980), 33–40.

Emperor Constantine (306–37) called an ecumenical (universal) council at Nicaea (in northwestern Turkey) in June 325 to settle the issues raised by Arius and his followers. The **Council of Nicaea** produced a creed, *The Profession of Faith of the 318 Fathers* (also known as the Nicene Creed), by which Christian orthodoxy was to be judged.

THE COUNCIL OF NICAEA

The Profession of Faith of the 318 Fathers

We believe in one God the Father all powerful, maker of all things both seen and unseen. And in one Lord Jesus Christ, the Son of God, the only-begotten begotten from the Father, that is from the substance of the Father, God from God, light from light, true God from true God, begotten not made, consubstantial with the Father, through whom all things came to be, both those in heaven and those in earth; for us humans and for our salvation he came down and became incarnate, became human, suffered and rose up on the third day, went up into the heavens, is coming to judge the living and the dead. And in the holy Spirit.

And those who say "there once was when he was not," and "before he was begotten he was not," and that he came to be from things that were not, or from another hyposta-

---

482. See Jn 14:6; 8:12.

483. 2 Cor 6:14–15.

484. See Prov 30:19.

485. See 1 Cor 10:4.

486. See Rom 8:15.

487. See Eph 2:7; Titus 3:4.

488. Rom 8:32.

489. Mt 3:17.

490. Ps 2:7.

491. Ps 109:3 (Septuagint); see also Ps 110:3.

492. Gen 6:2.

493. Isa 1:2.

sis or substance, affirming that the Son of God is subject to change or alteration—these the catholic and apostolic church anathematises.

From Norman P. Tanner, ed., *Decrees of the Ecumenical Councils*, vol. 1 (Washington, DC: Georgetown University Press, 1990), 5.

☙ **Athanasius** (ca. 296–373) was Alexander's secretary at Nicaea and replaced him as bishop of Alexandria (328–73). He was the foremost defender of the Nicene Creed and became known as the Father of Orthodoxy. Athanasius polemicizes against Arius and the Arians (through his prolific citations of Arius's *Thalia*) in his *Orations against the Arians*, probably written in 356 or 358. In so doing, he provides the classical formula by which Nicaea's controversial *homoousios* was to be understood.

ATHANASIUS

Orations against the Arians, I.5–6; III.1–4

I

5. Now the commencement of Arius's Thalia and flippancy, effeminate in tune and nature, runs thus:—

> "According to faith of God's elect, God's prudent ones,
> Holy children, rightly dividing, God's Holy Spirit
>   receiving,
> Have I learned this from the partakers of wisdom,
> Accomplished, divinely taught, and wise in all things.
> Along their track, have I been walking, with like opinions,
> I the very famous, the much suffering for God's glory;
> And taught of God, I have acquired wisdom and
>   knowledge."

And the mockeries which he utters in it, repulsive and most irreligious, are such as these:—"God was not always a Father"; but "once God was alone, and not yet a Father, but afterwards He became a Father." "The Son was not always"; for, whereas all things were made out of nothing, and all existing creatures and works were made, so the Word of God Himself was "made out of nothing," and "once He was not," and "He was not before His origination," but He as others "had an origin of creation." "For God," he says, "was alone, and the Word as yet was not, nor the Wisdom. Then, wishing to form us, thereupon he made a certain one, and named Him Word and Wisdom and Son, that he might form us by

means of Him." Accordingly, he says that there are two wisdoms, first, the attribute coexistent with God, and next, that in this wisdom the Son was originated, and was only named Wisdom and Word as partaking of it. "For Wisdom," saith he, "by the will of the wise God, had its existence in Wisdom." In like manner, he says, that there is another Word in God besides the Son, and that the Son again, as partaking of it, is named Word and Son according to grace. And this too is an idea proper to their heresy, as shewn in other works of theirs, that there are many powers; one of which is God's own by nature and eternal; but that Christ, on the other hand, is not the true power of God; but, as others, one of the so-called powers, one of which, namely, the locust and the caterpillar, is called in Scripture, not merely the power, but the "great power."[494] The others are many and are like the Son, and of them David speaks in the Psalms, when he says, "The Lord of hosts" or "powers."[495] And by nature, as all others, so the Word Himself is alterable, and remains good by His own free will, while He chooseth; when, however, He wills, He can alter as we can, as being of an alterable nature. For "therefore," saith he, "as foreknowing that He would be good, did God by anticipation bestow on Him this glory, which afterwards, as man, He attained from virtue. Thus in consequence of His works fore-known, did God bring it to pass that He, being such, should come to be."

6. Moreover he has dared to say, that "the Word is not the very God"; "though He is called God, yet He is not very God," but "by participation of grace, He, as others, is God only in name." And, whereas all beings are foreign and different from God in essence, so too is "the Word alien and unlike in all things to the Father's essence and propriety," but belongs to things originated and created, and is one of these. Afterwards, as though he had succeeded to the devil's recklessness, he has stated in his Thalia, that "even to the Son the Father is invisible," and "the Word cannot perfectly and exactly either see or know His own Father"; but even what He knows and what He sees, He knows and sees "in proportion to His own measure," as we also know according to our own power. For the Son, too, he says, not only knows not the Father exactly, for He fails in comprehension, but "He knows not even His own essence";—and that "the essences of the Father and the Son and the Holy Ghost are separate in nature, and estranged, and disconnected, and alien, and

---

494. See Joel 2:25. (The notes for this selection are by Gerhart and Udoh.)
495. See Ps 24:10.

without participation of each other"; and, in his own words, "utterly unlike from each other in essence and glory, unto infinity." Thus as to "likeness of glory and essence," he says that the Word is entirely diverse from both the Father and the Holy Ghost. With such words hath the irreligious spoken; maintaining that the Son is distinct by Himself, and in no respect partaker of the Father. These are portions of Arius's fables as they occur in that jocose composition.

III

1. The Ario-maniacs, as it appears, having once made up their minds to transgress and revolt from the Truth, are strenuous in appropriating the words of Scripture, "When the impious cometh into a depth of evils, he despiseth";[496] for refutation does not stop them, nor perplexity abash them; but, as having "a whore's forehead," they "refuse to be ashamed"[497] before all men in their irreligion. For whereas the passages which they alleged, "The Lord created me,"[498] and "Made better than the Angels,"[499] and "First-born,"[500] and "Faithful to Him that made Him,"[501] have a right sense, and inculcate religiousness towards Christ, so it is that these men still, as if bedewed with the serpent's poison, not seeing what they ought to see, nor understanding what they read, as if in vomit from the depth of their irreligious heart, have next proceeded to disparage our Lord's words, "I in the Father and the Father in Me";[502] saying, "How can the One be contained in the Other and the Other in the One?" or "How at all can the Father who is the greater be contained in the Son who is the less?" or "What wonder, if the Son is in the Father, considering it is written even of us, 'In Him we live and move and have our being'?"[503] And this state of mind is consistent with their perverseness, who think God to be material, and understand not what is "True Father" and "True Son," nor "Light Invisible" and "Eternal," and Its "Radiance Invisible," nor "Invisible Subsistence," and "Immaterial Expression" and "Immaterial Image." For did they know, they would not dishonour and ridicule the Lord of glory, nor interpreting things immaterial after a material manner, pervert good words. It were sufficient indeed, on hearing only words which are the Lord's, at once to believe, since the faith of simplicity is better than an elaborate process of persuasion; but since they have endeavoured to profane even this passage to their own heresy, it becomes necessary to expose their perverseness and to shew the mind of the truth, at least for the security of the faithful. For when it is said, "I in the Father and the Father in Me,"[504] They are not therefore, as these suppose, discharged into Each Other, fill-

ing the One the Other, as in the case of empty vessels, so that the Son fills the emptiness of the Father and the Father that of the Son, and Each of Them by Himself is not complete and perfect (for this is proper to bodies, and therefore the mere assertion of it is full of irreligion), for the Father is full and perfect, and the Son is the Fulness of Godhead. Nor again, as God, by coming into the Saints, strengthens them, thus is He also in the Son. For He is Himself the Father's Power and Wisdom,[505] and by partaking of Him things originate are sanctified in the Spirit; but the Son Himself is not Son by participation, but is the Father's own Offspring.[506] Nor again is the Son in the Father, in the sense of the passage, "In Him we live and move and have our being";[507] for, He as being from the Fount of the Father is the Life,[508] in which all things are both quickened and consist; for the Life does not live in life, else it would not be Life, but rather He gives life to all things.[509]

2. But now let us see what Asterius the Sophist says, the retained pleader for the heresy. In imitation then of the Jews so far, he writes as follows; "It is very plain that He has said, that He is in the Father and the Father again in Him, for this reason, that neither the word on which He was discoursing is, as He says, His own, but the Father's, nor the works belong to Him, but to the Father who gave Him the power."[510] Now this, if uttered at random by a little child, had been excused from his age; but when one who bears the title of Sophist, and professes universal knowledge, is the writer, what a serious condemnation does he deserve! And does he not shew himself a stranger to the Apostle, as being puffed up with persuasive words of wisdom,[511] and thinking thereby to succeed in deceiving, not understanding himself what he says nor whereof he affirms?[512] For what the Son has said as proper and suitable to a Son only, who is Word and Wisdom and Image of the Father's Essence,[513] that he levels to all the creatures, and makes common to the Son and to them; and he says, lawless man,[514] that from the power of the Father receives power, that from this his irreligion it may follow to say that in a son the Son was made a son, and the Word received a

---

496. Prov 18:3 (Septuagint).

497. Jer 3:3.

498. Prov 8:22.

499. Heb 1:4.

500. Col 1:15.

501. Heb 3:2.

502. Jn 14:10, 11.

503. Acts 17:28.

504. Jn 14:10, 11.

505. See 1 Cor 1:24.

506. See Gal 3:16.

507. Acts 17:28.

508. See Jn 4:14.

509. See Jn 1:3–4.

510. See Jn 4:34; 9:4; 17:4; 14:10.

511. See 1 Cor 2:4.

512. See 1 Tim 1:7.

513. See Col 1:15; Heb 1:3.

514. See 2 Cor 2:8.

word's authority; and far from granting that He spoke this as a Son, He ranks Him with all things made as having learned it as they have. For if the Son said, "I am in the Father and the Father in Me," because His discourses were not His own words but the Father's, and so of His works, then,—since David says, "I will hear what the Lord God shall say in me,"[515] and again Solomon, "My words are spoken by God,"[516] and since Moses was minister of words which were from God, and each of the Prophets spoke not what was his own but what was from God, "Thus saith the Lord," and since the works of the Saints, as they professed, were not their own but God's who gave the power, Elijah for instance and Elisha invoking God that He Himself would raise the dead,[517] and Elisha saying to Naaman, on cleansing him from the leprosy, "that thou mayest know that there is a God in Israel,"[518] and Samuel too in the days of the harvest praying to God to grant rain,[519] and the Apostles saying that not in their own power they did miracles but in the Lord's grace[520]—it is plain that, according to Asterius, such a statement must be common to all, so that each of them is able to say, "I in the Father and the Father in me"; and as a consequence that He is no longer one Son of God and Word and Wisdom, but, as others, is only one out of many.

3. But if the Lord said this, His words would not rightly have been, "I in the Father and the Father in Me," but rather, "I too am in the Father, and the Father is in Me too," that He may have nothing of His own and by prerogative, relatively to the Father, as a Son, but the same grace in common with all. But it is not so, as they think; for not understanding that He is genuine Son from the Father, they belie Him who is such, whom alone it befits to say, "I in the Father and the Father in Me." For the Son is in the Father, as it is allowed us to know, because the whole Being of the Son is proper to the Father's essence, as radiance from light, and stream from fountain; so that whoso sees the Son, sees what is proper to the Father, and knows that the Son's Being, because from the Father, is therefore in the Father. For the Father is in the Son, since the Son is what is from the Father and proper to Him, as in the radiance the sun, and in the word the thought, and in the stream the fountain: for whoso thus contemplates the Son, contemplates what is proper to the Father's Essence, and knows that the Father is in the Son. For whereas the Form and Godhead of the Father is the Being of the Son, it follows that the Son is in the Father and the Father in the Son.

4. On this account and reasonably, having said before, "I and the Father are One,"[521] He added, "I in the Father and the Father in Me," by way of shewing the identity of Godhead and the unity of Essence. For they are one, not as one thing divided into two parts, and these nothing but one, nor as one thing twice named, so that the Same becomes at one time Father, at another His own Son, for this Sabellius holding was judged an heretic. But They are two, because the Father is Father and is not also Son, and the Son is Son and not also Father; but the nature is one; (for the offspring is not unlike its parent, for it is his image), and all that is the Father's, is the Son's. Wherefore neither is the Son another God, for He was not procured from without, else were there many, if a godhead be procured foreign from the Father's; for if the Son be other, as an Offspring, still He is the Same as God; and He and the Father are one in propriety and peculiarity of nature, and in the identity of the one Godhead, as has been said. For the radiance also is light, not second to the sun, nor a different light, nor from participation of it, but a whole and proper offspring of it. And such an offspring is necessarily one light; and no one would say that they are two lights, but sun and radiance two, yet one the light from the sun enlightening in its radiance all things. So also the Godhead of the Son is the Father's; whence also it is indivisible; and thus there is one God and none other but He.[522] And so, since they are one, and the Godhead itself one, the same things are said of the Son, which are said of the Father, except His being said to be Father:[523] for instance, that He is God, "And the Word was God";[524] Almighty, "Thus saith He which was and is and is to come, the Almighty";[525] Lord, "One Lord Jesus Christ";[526] that He is Light, "I am the Light";[527] that He wipes out sins, "that ye may know," He says, "that the Son of man hath power upon earth to forgive sins";[528] and so with other attributes. For "all things," says the Son Himself, "whatsoever the Father hath, are Mine";[529] and again, "And Mine are Thine."[530]

From Saint Athanasius, *Select Writings and Letters,* A Select Library of Nicene and Post-Nicene Fathers of the Christian Church, edited by Philip Schaff and Henry Wace, 2nd series, vol. 4 (1892; Grand Rapids, MI: Eerdmans, 1978), 308–9, 393–95.

---

515. Ps 84:8 (Septuagint); see also Ps 85:8.

516. 1 Kings 10:24.

517. See 1 Kings 17:20–21; 2 Kings 4:33–35.

518. See 2 Kings 5:8, 15. 520. See Acts 3:12–16.

519. See 1 Sam 12:16–18. 521. Jn 10:30.

522. See Deut 6:4; Isa 46:9.

523. This is the "rule of Athanasius," which states the proper understanding of the Nicene Creed, namely, that the Son is "consubstantial [*homoousion*] with the Father."

524. Jn 1:1. 528. Mk 2:10; Mt 9:6; Lk 5:24.

525. Rev 1:8. 529. Jn 16:15.

526. 1 Cor 8:6. 530. Jn 17:10.

527. Jn 8:12.

PELAGIANISM

☙ Being wary of Manichaeist determinism, **Pelagius** (ca. 354–418) defended Christian asceticism as both achievable and meritorious. Pelagius wrote *Letter to Demetrias* in 413, at the petition of his exiled friend Juliana and her daughter, Demetrias. Pelagius defends the freedom of the will to choose either to do good or to sin.

PELAGIUS

Letter to Demetrias, I.1; II.1–VIII.4

I

1. Even if I could claim to possess natural talent of a high quality and an equally high degree of artistic skill and believed myself for that reason to be capable of fulfilling with ease the obligation of writing, I would still not be able to enter upon this arduous task without considerable fear of the difficulties involved. It is to Demetrias that I have to write, that virgin of Christ who is both noble and rich and, which is more important, spurns both nobility and riches; assuredly it is as difficult for me to instruct her as it is easy for all to praise her out of admiration for her outstanding virtue. Who could possibly lack words to sing the praises of one who, though born in the highest station, brought up in the height of wealth and luxury, held fast by the strength and variety of this life's delights as if in the grip of the most tenacious of fetters, suddenly broke free and exchanged all her bodily goods simultaneously for goodness of the soul? Of one who cut off with the sword of faith, that is, her own free will, the very flower of a life still only just beginning and, by crucifying her flesh with Christ, dedicated it as a living and holy sacrifice to God and for love of virginity renounced the prospect of providing posterity for a very noble stock? An easy, simple way to make a speech is to let the very richness of the subject-matter speed it along its course; but we have to proceed along a very different road, since our purpose is to write a manual of instruction for the virgin, not an encomium, to portray not so much the virtues which she has already acquired as those which she has still to acquire, and to order the remainder of her life rather than to honour that part of it which is now in the past.

II

1. Whenever I have to speak on the subject of moral instruction and the conduct of a holy life, it is my practice first to demonstrate the power and quality of human nature and to show what it is capable of achieving, and then to go on to encourage the mind of my listener to consider the idea of different kinds of virtues, in case it may be of little or no profit to him to be summoned to pursue ends which he has perhaps assumed hitherto to be beyond his reach; for we can never enter upon the path of virtue unless we have hope as our guide and companion and if every effort expended in seeking something is nullified in effect by despair of ever finding it. I also think that on this occasion, when the good in our nature calls for a fuller exposition commensurate with the greater perfection of life which has to be inculcated in the listener's mind, I have special grounds for adhering to the same sequence of exhortation as I have followed in my other minor works, in order that the mind may not become more negligent and sluggish in its pursuit of virtue as it comes to believe less in its ability to achieve it, supposing itself not to possess something simply because it is unaware that it is present within. When it is desirable for a man to put a certain capacity to use, it always has to be brought to his attention, and any good of which human nature is capable has to be revealed, since what is shown to be practicable must be put into practice. Let us then lay this down as the first basis for a holy and spiritual life: the virgin must recognize her own strengths, which she will be able to employ to the full only when she has learned that she possesses them. The best incentive for the mind consists in teaching it that it is possible to do anything which one really wants to do: in war, for example, the kind of exhortation which is most effective and carries most authority is the one which reminds the combatant of his own strengths.

2. First, then, you ought to measure the good of human nature by reference to its creator, I mean God, of course: if it is he who, as report goes, has made all the works of and within the world good, exceeding good,[531] how much more excellent do you suppose that he has made man himself, on whose account he has clearly made everything else? And before actually making man, he determines to fashion him in his own image and likeness[532] and shows what kind of creature he intends to make him. Next, since he has made all animals subject to man and set him as lord over creatures[533]

---

531. See Gen 1:4, 10, 12, 18, 21, 25, 31. (The notes for this selection are by Gerhart and Udoh.)

532. See Gen 1:26–27.

533. See Gen 1:28–29.

which have been made more powerful than men either by their bodily size and greater strength or by the weapons which they have in their teeth, he makes it abundantly clear how much more gloriously man himself has been fashioned and wants him to appreciate the dignity of his own nature by marvelling that strong animals have been made subject to him. For he did not leave man naked and defenceless nor did he expose him in his weakness to a variety of dangers; but, having made him seem unarmed outwardly, he provided him with a better armament inside, that is, with reason and wisdom, so that by means of his intelligence and mental vigour, in which he surpassed the other animals, man alone was able to recognize the maker of all things and to serve God by using those same faculties which enabled him to hold sway over the rest. Moreover, the Lord of Justice wished man to be free to act and not under compulsion; it was for this reason that "he left him free to make his own decisions"[534] and set before him life and death, good and evil, and he shall be given whatever pleases him.[535] Hence we read in the Book Deuteronomy also: I have set before you life and death, blessing and curse; therefore choose life, that you may live.[536]

III

1. That is why we must now take precautions to prevent you from being embarrassed by something in which the ignorant majority is at fault for lack of proper consideration, and so from supposing, with them, that man has not been created truly good simply because he is able to do evil and is not obliged by the overpowering inclination of his own nature to do good on compulsion and without any possibility of variation. If you reconsider this matter carefully and force your mind to apply a more acute understanding to it, it will be revealed to you that man's status is better and higher for the very reason for which it is thought to be inferior: it is on this choice between two ways, on this freedom to choose either alternative, that the glory of the rational mind is based, it is in this that the whole honour of our nature consists, it is from this that its dignity is derived and all good men win others' praise and their own reward. Nor would there be any virtue at all in the good done by the man who perseveres, if he could not at any time cross over to the path of evil.

2. It was because God wished to bestow on the rational creature the gift of doing good of his own free will and the capacity to exercise free choice, by implanting in man the possibility of choosing either alternative, that he made it his peculiar right to be what he wanted to be, so that with his

capacity for good and evil he could do either quite naturally and then bend his will in the other direction too. He could not claim to possess the good of his own volition, unless he were the kind of creature that could also have possessed evil. Our most excellent creator wished us to be able to do either but actually to do only one, that is, good, which he also commanded, giving us the capacity to do evil only so that we might do his will by exercising our own. That being so, this very capacity to do evil is also good—good, I say, because it makes the good part better by making it voluntary and independent, not bound by necessity but free to decide for itself. We are certainly permitted to choose, oppose, approve, reject, and there is no ground for preferring the rational creature to the others except that, while all the others possess only the good derived from their own circumstances and necessity, it alone possesses the good of free will also.

3. But most of those who, from lack of faith as much as of knowledge, deplore the status of man are—I am ashamed to admit it—criticising the Lord's work and asserting that man ought to have been so made that he could do no evil at all, and we are then in a position where what is moulded says to its moulder: Why have you made me thus?[537] And these most shameless of men, while hiding the fact that they are managing quite well with what they have been made, would prefer to have been made otherwise; and so those who are unwilling to correct their own way of life appear to want to correct nature itself instead, the good of which has been so universally established in all that it sometimes reveals itself and brings itself to notice even in pagans who do not worship God. For how many of the pagan philosophers have we heard and read and even seen for ourselves to be chaste, tolerant, temperate, generous, abstinent and kindly, rejecters of the world's honours as well as its delights, lovers of justice no less than knowledge? Whence, I ask you, do these good qualities pleasing to God come to men who are strangers to him? Whence can these good qualities come to them, unless it be from the good of nature? And since we see the qualities of which I have spoken contained either all in one person or severally in several persons and since the nature of all is one and the same, by their example they show each other that all qualities which are found either all together in all or severally in each one are able to exist in all alike. But if even men without God can show what kind of creatures they were made by

---

534. Sir 15:14.
535. See Sir 15:17.

536. Deut 30:19.
537. See Rom 9:20.

God, consider what Christians are able to do whose nature and life have been instructed for the better by Christ and who are assisted by the aid of divine grace as well.

IV

1. Come now, let us approach the secret places of our soul, let everyone examine himself more attentively, let us ask what opinion our own personal thoughts have of this matter, let our conscience itself deliver its judgement on the good of nature, let us be instructed by the inner teaching of the mind, and let us learn about each of the good qualities of the mind from no other source but the mind itself. Why is it, I ask you, that we either blush or fear at every sin we commit, displaying our guilt for what we have done at one moment by the blush on our countenance, at another by its pallor, anxiously trying to avoid any witness even of our smallest offences and suffering pangs of conscience all the while? And why, on the other hand, are we happy, resolute, bold after every good deed we have done and, if this fact is hidden from sight, desire and wish it to be seen in broad daylight? Why else unless it is because nature itself is its own witness and discloses its own good by the very fact of its disapproval of evil and, by putting its trust only in a good deed, shows what alone benefits it? Hence it comes about that frequently, though a murderer's identity remains concealed, torments of conscience make furious attacks on the author of the crime, and the secret punishment of the mind takes vengeance on the guilty man in hiding; nor is there any room for escape from punishment after the crime has been committed, since guilt is itself the penalty. That is why the innocent man, contrariwise, enjoys the peace of mind that comes from a good conscience even while undergoing torture and, though he fears punishment, still glories in his innocence.

2. There is, I maintain, a sort of natural sanctity in our minds which, presiding as it were in the mind's citadel, administers judgement equally on the evil and the good and, just as it favours honourable and upright actions, so too condemns wrong deeds and, on the evidence of conscience, distinguishes the one side from the other by a kind of inner law; nor, in fine, does it seek to deceive by any display of cleverness or of counterfeit brilliance in argument but either denounces or defends us by our thoughts themselves, surely the most reliable and incorruptible of witnesses. This is the law which the apostle recalls when he writes to the Romans, testifying that it is implanted in all men and written as it were on the tablets of the heart: For when gentiles who have not the law do by nature what the law requires, they are a law to themselves, even though they do not have the law. They show that what the law requires is written in their hearts, while their conscience also bears them witness and their conflicting thoughts accuse or perhaps excuse them.[538] It is this law that all have used whom scripture records as having lived in sanctity and having pleased God between the time of Adam and that of Moses: some of these must be set before you as examples, so that you may not find it difficult to understand how great is the good of nature, when once you have satisfied yourself that it has replaced the law in the task of teaching righteousness.

V

1. Abel was the first to follow this mistress and so served the Lord that, when he offered him a victim, his sacrifice was so gratefully received by God that it aroused the jealousy of his brother,[539] and the Lord himself, recalling this righteous man in the Gospel, briefly set forth the grounds of his perfection.[540] For every form of virtue is contained under the name of righteousness: we read that the blessed Enoch so pleased God that he snatched him away from the midst of mortals and translated him from his earthly habitation, after reaching perfection in this world.[541] Noah is said to have been "a righteous man, blameless in his generation,"[542] and his holiness is all the more to be admired in that he alone was found to be righteous, when literally the whole world was declining from righteousness, nor did he seek a model of holiness from another but supplied it himself. And for that reason, when the destruction of the whole world was imminent, he alone of all men was found worthy to hear the words: Go into the ark, you and all your household, for I have seen that you are righteous before me in this generation.[543]

2. Before God, moreover, that man is esteemed righteous who is holy both in body and heart: Melchizedek is said to have been "a priest of god,"[544] and his merit can be easily understood from this fact, that he signified in advance the Lord's sacrament which was to come later and expressed the mystery of the body and the blood by the sacrifice of bread and wine and by the manner of this sacrifice of his prefigured the

---

538. See Rom 2:14–15.
539. See Gen 4:2–10.
540. See Mt 23:35.
541. See Gen 5:22–24.
542. Gen 6:9.
543. Gen 7:1.
544. Gen 14:18.

priesthood of Christ, to whom it is said by the Father: Thou art a priest for ever, after the order of Melchizedek.[545] Also, because he blesses Abraham, the first of the patriarchs, who is father of the Jews through the covenant of circumcision and father of the nations by his faith,[546] he highlights most distinctly the example of him who by his faith has bestowed a blessing both on Jews and gentiles. Lot too, following the holy Noah in virtue, did not forsake righteousness, though living among examples of so many sinners, but, as the example of the whole world could not overcome the latter, so he too maintained his holiness against the vices of the multitude, when all the region in which he lived was sinning; and he, as the blessed Peter says, "was righteous in his seeing and hearing"[547] and, set as he was among most evil men, shunned their evil deeds both with his eyes and with his ears and for that reason was snatched away from the fire,[548] as Noah had been snatched away from the Flood.

3. What shall I say of Abraham, friend of God, what of Isaac and Jacob? How completely they fulfilled the will of the Lord we are able to determine even from this, that he wanted himself to be named their God as an intimate and special mark of distinction; I am, he said, the God of Abraham, the God of Isaac, and the God of Jacob; this is my name for ever, and thus I am to be remembered throughout all generations.[549] Joseph, a faithful servant of the Lord from boyhood, is shown to be even more righteous and perfect through his tribulations: first he was sold into slavery to the Ishmaelites by his brothers and then sold again by those by whom he had seen himself worshipped in a dream; next, though handed over to an Egyptian master, yet he always retained the freeborn dignity of his soul[550] and by his example taught slaves and free men alike that it is not a man's personal situation that tells against him when he sins but his mental attitude.

4. At this point, I beg you, virgin, pause for a moment or two and carefully consider the chaste attitude of Joseph's mind: as a young man he is desired by his master's wife but resists her attempts to make him desire her; she solicits, he rebuffs, and so the one who is accustomed to give the orders in all other matters is reduced to coaxing and begging in this one alone, since the lover of God cannot be vanquished by the love of a woman nor can his chaste mind be swayed by his adolescence or his lover's authority. Having been rebuffed several times, his mistress now sets her ambushes closer to his lines of defence: in secret and with no witnesses she lays hand upon him shamelessly and in even more wanton language urges him to commit the crime; yet not even thus is he overcome but returns deeds for deeds, as he has previously

returned words for words and, having refused when asked, he now escapes when trapped and, before that word in the gospel was spoken: Every one who looks at a woman lustfully has already committed adultery with her in his heart;[551] he, after having been seduced not only by the sight of her but almost by her very embrace, still does not lust after the woman.

5. You have marvelled at the strength of this man's chastity; now regard his benevolence. Before the prophet said: Let no man remember in his heart the ill will of his neighbour,[552] *he* repaid hatred with love and, when he saw his brothers—nay rather, the enemies who were once his brothers—and wanted to be recognized by them, he bore witness that it was love, not resentment, that he felt for them; *he* kissed each of them in turn and with the water of his tears, which he poured over the necks of his frightened brothers, washed away their hatred with tears of love and loved them always with true brotherly love both during his father's lifetime and after his death.[553] Nor did he recall to mind the pit into which he was cast down to die or give a thought to the way in which his brotherhood had been sold for a price but, "repaying good for evil,"[554] he fulfilled the apostle's instruction when he was still subject only to the law of nature.

VI

1. What shall I say of the blessed Job, that most renowned athlete of God, whose wealth was snatched from him, whose estate was utterly destroyed, whose sons and daughters died all together, and who, after all this, yet fought against the devil to the very end with his body? Everything that he possessed on the outside was taken from him, and his external possessions suddenly fell away, so that those more truly his own stood out clearly; he was as if stripped of absolutely all his outer garments and yet was able to stand triumphant in his nakedness, stronger and less encumbered, and, by bearing his own punishment, to overcome again the same enemy whom he had previously defeated by bearing his own losses.[555] This is the testimony of the Lord himself upon him: Have you considered my servant Job? For there is none like him on

---

545. Heb 5:6; see also Ps 110:4.   547. See 2 Pet 2:7–8.

546. See Rom 4:9–12.   548. See Gen 19:1–26.

549. Ex 3:15; see also Mk 12:26; Mt 22:32; Lk 20:37.

550. See Gen 37:5–36; 39:1–23.   553. See Gen 45:1–15; 50:15–21.

551. Mt 5:28.   554. Rom 12:17.

552. Lev 19:18 (Vulgate).   555. See Job 1:1–2:12.

the earth, a man against whom there is no complaint, a true worshipper of God, keeping himself away from all evil.[556] Nor was this testimony undeserved, for, as he himself says, he always feared the Lord as the waves raging over him and was unable to bear the weight of his presence; at no time did he dare to scorn one whom he believed to be ever present with him but said: I am safe, for my heart does not reproach me for any of my days.[557]

2. Even before the time when the Lord enjoined that enemies should be loved, Job could say: If I have rejoiced at the troubles of my enemy, if I have said in my heart, "It has been well done."[558] When the Lord had not yet commanded in his gospel: Give to every one who begs from you,[559] Job could already say: If I suffered a poor man to go out of my door with his purse empty.[560] When he had not been able to read that word of the apostle: Masters, treat your servants justly and fairly,[561] Job could call confidently to the Lord: If I have harmed a manservant, if I have injured a maidservant, Lord, you know all.[562] Before the same apostle enjoined the rich "not to be haughty, nor to set their hopes on uncertain riches,"[563] he could possess his riches in such a way as to show himself to be rich in other respects: I put no trust in riches or in precious stones.[564]

3. And he proved this not in words only but by deeds, since he did not grieve when he lost everything but could still say through it all: The Lord gave, and the Lord has taken away; as it pleased the Lord, so it has been done; blessed be the name of the Lord for ever. Naked I came from my mother's womb, and naked shall I return there.[565] When we lose something, we show with what affection we possess it, and the desire for enjoyment is betrayed by our grief at our loss; for how could a man experience desire for something when lost, if he had no desire for it when he possessed it? What a man Job was! A man of the gospel before the gospel was known, a man of the apostles before their commands were uttered! A disciple of the apostles who, by opening up the hidden wealth of nature and bringing it out into the open, revealed by his own behaviour what all of us are capable of and has taught us how great is that treasure in the soul which we possess but fail to use and, because we refuse to display it, believe that we do not possess it either.

VII

1. After the many things which we have said about nature we have also shown its good by the examples of holy men and have proved it. And lest, on the other hand, it should be thought to be nature's fault that some have been unrighteous, I shall use the evidence of the scriptures, which everywhere lay upon sinners the heavy weight of the charge of having used their own will and do not excuse them for having acted only under constraint of nature. In Genesis we read: The brothers Simeon and Levi have carried out their wickedness of their own free will.[566] To Jerusalem the Lord said: Because they themselves have forsaken my way which I set before them, and have not obeyed my voice, but have followed the will of their own evil hearts.[567] And again the same prophet: And you sinned against the Lord and did not obey his voice and refused to walk in his commands and in his laws and in his testimonies.[568] He spoke also through the prophet Isaiah: If you are willing and obedient, you shall eat the good of the land; but if you refuse and rebel, you shall be devoured by the sword.[569] And again: All of you shall bow down in the slaughter; because, when I called, you did not obey, when I spoke, you did not listen, but you did evil before my eyes and chose what I did not delight in.[570] The Lord also says in the gospel: O Jerusalem, Jerusalem, killing the prophets and stoning those who are sent to you! How often would I have gathered your children together as a hen gathers her brood under her wings, and you would not![571] When we see "willing" and "not willing," "choosing" and "rejecting," it is not the force of nature but the freedom of the will that is then understood to be at work. The books of both Testaments are full of evidence of this kind, wherein all good, as well as all evil, is described as voluntary, and we omit it now only for the sake of brevity, especially when we know that, dedicated as you are to sacred reading, you can drink more copious draughts direct from the fountain itself.

VIII

1. Yet we do not defend the good of nature to such an extent that we claim that it cannot do evil, since we undoubtedly declare also that it is capable of good and evil; we merely try to protect it from an unjust charge, so that we may not

556. Job 1:8; 2:3.
557. Job 27:6.
558. Job 31:29.
559. Mt 5:42; Lk 6:30.
560. See Job 31:16, 32.
561. Col 4:1.
562. See Job 31:13.
563. 1 Tim 6:17.
564. See Job 31:24.
565. Job 1:21.
566. See Gen 49:5–6.
567. See Jer 9:13–14.
568. Jer 44:23.
569. Isa 1:19–20.
570. Isa 65:12.
571. Mt 23:37; Lk 13:34.

seem to be forced to do evil through a fault in our nature, when, in fact, we do neither good nor evil without the exercise of our will and always have the freedom to do one of the two, being always able to do either. For on what grounds are some to be judges, others to be judged, unless it is because the will works in different ways in one and the same nature and because, though all of us are able to do the same, we actually do different things? And so, in order that this essential fact may stand out more clearly, we must cite some examples. Adam is cast out of paradise,[572] Enoch is snatched away from the world;[573] in both the Lord shows freedom of choice at work, for, just as the one who sinned could have pleased the Lord, so the other, who did please him, could have sinned instead. Neither would the former have deserved to be punished nor the latter to be chosen by a just God, unless both had been able to choose either course of action. This is how we are to understand the matter of Cain and Abel[574] and also of Jacob and Esau,[575] the twin brothers, and we have to realize that, when merits differ in the same nature, it is will that is the sole cause of an action.

2. Noah in his righteousness rejected the world when it was destroyed by flood because of its sins, Lot in his holiness passed judgement on the crimes of the Sodomites; and the fact that those first men were without the rebukes of the law for the space of so many years gives us no small grounds for acknowledging the good of nature, not, assuredly, because God at any time did not care for his creatures but because he knew that he had made human nature such that it would suffice them in place of the law for the practice of righteousness. In a word, as long as a nature which was still comparatively fresh was in vigorous use and long habituation to sinning did not draw a dark veil, as it were, over human reason, nature was set free and left without law; but when it had now become buried beneath an excess of vices and as if tainted with the rust of ignorance, the Lord applied the file of the law to it, and so, thoroughly polished by its frequent admonishments, it was enabled to recover its former brilliance.

3. Nor is there any reason why it is made difficult for us to do good other than that long habit of doing wrong which has infected us from childhood and corrupted us little by little over many years and ever after holds us in bondage and slavery to itself, so that it seems somehow to have acquired the force of nature. We now find ourselves being resisted and opposed by all that long period in which we were carelessly instructed, that is, educated in evil, in which we even strove to be evil, since, to add to the other incentives to evil, innocence itself was held to be folly. That old habit now attacks our new-found freedom of will, and, as we languish in ignorance through our sloth and idleness, unaccustomed to doing good after having for so long learned to do only evil, we wonder why sanctity is also conferred on us as if from an outside source.

4. So much then by way of a cursory explanation of the good of nature, as it is also stated in another of my works: it was something which we had to provide in order to pave your way to perfect righteousness and make it more level and easier for you to run along in the knowledge that there is nothing uneven or unapproachable confronting you. Even before the law was given to us, as we have said, and long before the arrival of our Lord and Saviour some are reported to have lived holy and righteous lives; how much more possible must we believe that to be after the light of his coming, now that we have been instructed by the grace of Christ and reborn as better men: purified and cleansed by his blood, encouraged by his example to pursue perfect righteousness, we ought surely to be better than those who lived before the time of the law, better even than those who lived under the law, since the apostle says: For sins will have no dominion over you, since you are not under law but grace.[576]

From *The Letters of Pelagius and His Followers*, edited and translated by B. R. Rees (Rochester, NY: Boydell Press, 1991), 35–36, 36–45.

In the treatise *On the Possibility of Not Sinning*, written after Pelagius's *Letter to Demetrias*, an anonymous author defends the Pelagian notion of the will to choose freely not to sin.

On the Possibility of Not Sinning, II.1–IV.3

II

1. It has also reached my humble ears that you are heaping such praises on my insignificant person that you appear to think that there is nothing to be criticised in it except what is beyond criticism. That you should suppose this is typical of your inborn sense of kindness and your conscientiousness, and you can find no other or better way of praising one whom you love than by claiming that he is so faultless that

---

572. See Gen 3:22–24.

573. See Gen 5:24.

574. See Gen 4:1–7.

575. See Gen 25:21–34; 27:1–45.

576. Rom 6:14.

the only fault which can be found in him is something with which no one can rightly find fault. But because I do know my own conscience, I realise that there are many things in me which merit criticism. So there is no call to hold me blameworthy in matters which are free from blame, since I can see for myself that I am open to criticism in matters for which I ought to be blamed.

2. It is quite different if, as often happens, actions which we know to have been done purposely and conscientiously are either censured in ignorance or misunderstood through lack of charity. For what can we believe to be so worthy of understanding, so consistent with godliness, as that God, the founder of righteousness and equity, cannot be seen to have done anything which ought even to be suspected of being unfair and unrighteous? Consider how far removed from any suspicion of unrighteousness he should be who has no love for a man when there is any wickedness in him, but deprives him of his kingdom and delivers him up to the fires of hell if some mark of wickedness still remains in him. If then the one who has been created must be wholly righteous, what are we to expect of the one who created him? And if the one who is to be judged has to be wholly righteous, what are we to think of the one who judges? Surely it would be fitting for God to have given a command which it is impossible to fulfil, if such a thing is fitting for even a man to do; but if even human nature thinks it unfair to order anyone to do something impossible, how perverse it is to believe God to be capable of something which not even the nature of mortals would respect!

3. Is there anyone so thoughtless, so unrighteous, so totally ignorant of equity, as to dare to order a servant or any of his subjects to do what he knows to be beyond his capability? For instance, will any man instruct his servant to complete in one day a journey which takes four days or despatch him to swim across the waves of the wide sea rather than to sail over them or to climb impassable and inaccessible mountains with slippery peaks or to do anything else beyond his natural capabilities? If he presumed to give such an instruction, who would not think him not only unfair but mad as well, seeing him impose upon a man instructions which his own natural powers could by no means carry out? And if such a judgement can justifiably be made of a man of this kind, I leave it to your common sense to decide what men would think of a God whom they suppose to have given them an order which is beyond their natural capabilities.

4. So I beg you to set aside for a while any opinion which is based on a deep-rooted conviction, to rid yourself of any spirit of contention, to listen to my humble words with an open mind free from prejudice and to give your attention not to the opinions that are expressed in everyday intercourse but to the truth that is based on righteousness and reason. For I know that you are a man of understanding and that I am therefore able to proceed without undue concern, because I am defending a reasonable case before a reasonable judge.

III

1. But someone will say, "Is it then possible for a man not to sin?" Such a claim is indeed a hard one and a bitter pill for sinners to swallow; it pains the ears of all who desire to live unrighteously. Who will find it easy now to fulfil the demands of righteousness, when there are some who find it hard even to listen to them? Or how is a man to undertake with equanimity the works which are required, when the teaching underlying them sounds so unpleasant? Why do we any longer ask whether a thing is possible, when it is considered to be so unusual and contrary to nature that men cannot even listen to it? When will the bloodthirsty and cruel gladly accept such a claim? When will the greedy and lustful cease to be terrified by it? When will the extravagant and the mean bear it with equanimity? To sum all this up briefly: When will a man guilty of any crime or sin accept with a tranquil mind that his wickedness is a product of his own will, not of necessity, and allow what he now strives to attribute to nature to be ascribed to his own free choice? It affords endless comfort to transgressors of the divine law if they are able to believe that their failure to do something is due to inability rather than disinclination, since they understand from their natural wisdom that no one can be judged for failing to do the impossible and that what is justifiable on grounds of impossibility is either a small sin or none at all. So the unhappy wretches rush headlong into various sins without any reflection and therefore maintain afterwards that they have not done things from which they claim that they were unable to abstain; and so it comes about that, under the plea that it is impossible not to sin, they are given a false sense of security in sinning.

2. Even if this were so, it should never be spoken of, since it would destroy those who hear it instead of edifying them. Anyone who hears that it is not possible for him to be without sin will not even try to be what he judges to be impossible, and the man who does not try to be without sin must perforce sin all the time, and all the more boldly because he enjoys the false security of believing that it is impossible for him not to sin. Such a man will never do penance appropriate to his misdeeds but will believe that God will lightly remit what rightly

he ought not even to impute. But if he were to hear that he is able not to sin, then he would have to exert himself to fulfil what he now knows to be possible and when he is striving to fulfil it, to achieve his purpose for the most part, even if not entirely. Also, if he is prevented by some offence resulting from human frailty, at least his sins will undoubtedly be less frequent and more trivial. The man who labours and strives to be without any sin will humbly and submissively express his regret for the error of his ways, when he realizes that he has done what he could have avoided if he had but wanted to. Just as the former appreciation of the situation is prejudicial to those who listen to it in two ways, by giving them a false feeling of security when they sin and by leading them to conclude that penitence is not really a necessary means of redress, so the latter perception is understood to help in two ways, by encouraging them not to sin, because they have the capacity to avoid it, and by urging them more forcefully to repent and admit their voluntary transgression, if, as often happens, they have fallen into the error of committing a sin.

IV

1. If you object to this, saying, "A man cannot by any means be without sin," then consider first whether that which is such that a man cannot be without it ought to be described as "sin" at all; for everything which cannot be avoided is now put down to nature but it is impious to say that sin is inherent in nature, because in this way the author of nature is being judged at fault. To say that a man cannot be without sin is like saying that a man cannot live without food or drink or sleep or other such things without which our human state cannot exist. But if that is what we must hold, how can it be proper to call sin by that name if, like other natural things, it cannot be avoided, since all sin is to be attributed to the free choice of the will, not the defects of nature?

2. But first we ought to understand the definition of sin itself, so that we may then be able to argue with greater cogency about the propositions that it is possible or impossible to avoid it. We have to find a definition of sin which covers two eventualities—failure to avoid things which are forbidden, and failure to do things which are commanded. Now I want to ask the conscience of anyone with normal human feelings what are his views on the things which God has forbidden us to do—can they be avoided or not? If the former, he has rightly forbidden them; if the latter, I ask, first, on what reasonable grounds have they been forbidden, and, secondly, what is the justice in reckoning as a sin the commission of an

act which cannot by any means be avoided; I also ask if the commands that have been given can be obeyed or not. If they can, then they have been reasonably and justly given; if they cannot, then they must be regarded as pointless, nor can I see the justice of holding disobedience of orders which cannot possibly be implemented to be a sin. Again, if only things which could have been avoided have been forbidden and only things which could have been done have been commanded, how can we possibly refuse to accept that a man can be without sin, when we are ready to admit that nothing impossible has either been forbidden or been commanded—that is, if, as we have stated, all sin is included under the headings above?

3. But, to make the point still more plainly, you say that a man cannot be without sin. I ask first whether he was commanded to be without sin or was not so commanded. "I believe that he was," you reply. Why then was he so commanded, if it was quite impossible for him to carry out the command? You have to accept one of these alternatives, either that the command was not given, seeing that it cannot be carried out, or that it *can* be carried out, because it *was* commanded, since, as we have said earlier, God would never have commanded the impossible. But, to make it absolutely clear that the command *was* given, let us make use of examples from the holy law. It is written: You shall be holy, for I, the Lord your God, am holy.[577] And in the gospel our Saviour says: You must be perfect, as your heavenly Father is perfect.[578] And the blessed apostle Paul says: Do all things without grumbling or questioning, that you may be blameless and innocent, as the children of God are without blemish.[579] And elsewhere: And you, who once were estranged and hostile to his mind, doing evil deeds, but have now been reconciled to him in the body of his flesh by his death, present yourselves as holy and blameless and irreproachable before him.[580]

From *The Letters of Pelagius and His Followers*, edited and translated by B. R. Rees (Rochester, NY: Boydell Press, 1991), 166–70.

Pelagius's emphasis on free will drew the ire of prominent theologians, including **Augustine** (354–430) and Jerome (ca. 347–420), and led to the so-called Pelagian controversy. Augustine

---

577. Lev 19:2. (The notes for this selection are by Gerhart and Udoh.)

578. Mt 5:48.

579. Phil 2:14–15.

580. Col 1:21–22. The rest of this letter, which must have been substantial, is lost.

composed the *Encheiridion (Handbook)* in 421, at the request of the Roman Laurentius. In the *Encheiridion,* Augustine defends the primacy of grace over free will and elaborates on his anthropological and theological concepts concerning the doctrine of original sin. Augustine's *On Nature and Grace,* written in 415, is a refutation of Pelagius's *On Nature,* also written in 415 but no longer extant.

AUGUSTINE

Encheiridion, VIII.23–27; IX.30–31; XIII.41–47; XIV.48–50

VIII

23. Having discussed these problems with the brevity that the present treatise requires, we must now look into the causes of good and evil, to the extent at least that is sufficient for the way leading to the kingdom where there will be life without death, truth without error, bliss without fear. And here we cannot doubt at all that the cause of the good things which are ours is God's goodness alone, and that the cause of evil is the defection of the will in a being mutably good—first it was the will of an angel, then that of man—from the immutable good.

24. Here we have the first evil to befall rational creation, that is to say, its first privation of good. After that there crept in even against man's will ignorance of things to be done and a craving for things that are harmful. And as companions to these came error and pain. Again, when these two latter evils are felt to be imminent, the state of the soul seeking to escape them is called fear. Furthermore, when the mind realizes the objects of its desires and because of error fails to perceive how harmful or empty they are, it is either fascinated by a morbid delectation or even transported with silly joy. From these diseased fountains—fountains, not of abundance, but of want—flows all the woe that is the portion of rational beings. 25. Yet, in the midst of such evils these beings could not lose their desire for happiness.

Now, these are evils common to both men and angels whom God in His justice condemned because of their wickedness. But in addition man has received a penalty peculiar to himself, in that he is also punished with death of the body. For God had threatened man with the penalty of death, should he sin.[581] He gave him free will, so as still to guide him by His command and to deter him by the menace of death; and He placed him in the happiness of Paradise, in a life of security, as it were, whence, provided he preserved his innocence, he was to rise to better things.

26. Having sinned, he was banished from that place,[582] and by his sin he laid upon all his descendants, whom he had vitiated in himself as their source, the penalty of death and condemnation. As a result all the children born of him and his spouse who had led him into sin and was condemned together with him—children born through carnal lust as a retribution in kind for the act of disobedience—contracted original sin. Because of this sin they were drawn through a variety of aberrations and sufferings to that final unending punishment together with the rebel angels, their corrupters and masters and companions. Thus, *by one man sin entered into the world, and by sin death; and so death passed upon all men, in whom all have sinned.*[583] By the "world" the Apostle in that passage of course means the whole human race.

27. And so the matter stood. The whole mass of condemned[584] human nature lay prone in evil, indeed, wallowed in it, and precipitated itself from one evil into another; and having aligned itself with the group of angels that had sinned, it was, like them, paying the well-deserved penalties for an impious rebellion. For certainly the just anger of God is reflected in whatever the wicked freely do through blind and uncontrolled lust, and in whatever punishments they are made to suffer against their will—known and unknown to others. But the goodness of the Creator does not indeed cease to administer even to the bad angels life and vitality, without which they would cease to exist. Nor does He cease to create and endow with life the seed of men, though born of a vitiated and condemned stock, to harmonize their mem-

581. See Gen 2:16–17. (The notes for this selection are by Gerhart and Udoh.)

582. See Gen 3:1–24.

583. Rom 5:12. The rendering of the last phrase of Rom 5:12 in the Vulgate as *"in quo omnes peccaverunt"* (in whom all have sinned) is critical for Augustine's understanding of the passage and for his doctrine of original sin. He found both the Latin text and the understanding, which he adopted, also in the so-called *Ambrosiaster* (Pseudo-Ambrosius), the name given to the author of a commentary on Saint Paul's letters, long attributed to Saint Ambrose (d. 397), bishop of Milan. The Greek text of the passage reads ἐφ᾽ ᾧ πάντες ἥμαρτον, which is correctly translated "because [inasmuch as] all have sinned." It is possible that the translator of the *uetus latina* (Old Latin) text of Romans (from where the Latin expression originated) also understood the Latin construction in this causal or conditional sense. This is certainly the case in Rom 8:3, 2 Cor 5:4, and Phil 3:12, where the Vulgate renders, respectively, ἐν ᾧ by *in quo,* ἐφ᾽ ᾧ by *eo quod,* and ἐφ᾽ ᾧ again by *in quo.* In Augustine's text, and reading, on the contrary, *in quo* is understood in a relative sense, and Adam is the "one man . . . *in whom* all have sinned." He therefore "vitiates" his descendants by passing down to them his one ("original") sin, as an inheritance.

584. *Massa damnati* is a term that Augustine also took from the *Ambrosiasta* and used often in his anti-Pelagian writings. Human beings are, as it were, "lumped" together in their solidarity in sin, the one sin of Adam. Augustine also often uses the expressions *massa peccati* and *massa perditionis.* The term *massa* is derived from Rom 9:21: "Has the potter no right over the clay, to make out of the same lump [*massa*] one object for special use and another for ordinary use?"

bers, to quicken their senses throughout the periods of time and the reaches of places, and to provide them with nourishment. For He deemed it better to bring good out of evil than not to permit any evil to exist at all.

And assuming it to have been God's will that there should be absolutely no rehabilitation in the case of men, as there was none on the part of the wicked angels: would it not have been just if the being that had deserted God, that abusing its endowment had trampled under foot and transgressed the law of its Creator when it could so very easily have kept it, that had obstinately turned away from His light, defiling the image of the Maker which it bore, and had maliciously and deliberately broken with the wholesome subjection of legislation—would it not have been just if such a being had been abandoned by God in its entirety and unto eternity and made to undergo everlasting punishment, as it deserved? Certainly God would have done this, were He only just and not also merciful and had He not chosen to give proof far more striking of His unmerited mercy by setting free those who were undeserving of it.

IX

30. But can these members of the human race to whom God promised deliverance and a place in the eternal kingdom, be saved by the merits of their works? That is out of the question. For what good work can one do who is ruined, except so far as he has been delivered from his ruin? Can he do so by the free determination of his will? That, too, is out of the question. For it was by the evil use of his free will that man destroyed both himself and his free will. When, for instance, a man kills himself, he is of course alive in the act; but once he has killed himself, he no longer lives, nor is he able to restore himself to life. So, too, when by free will sin was committed, sin being the conqueror, free will was lost; *for by whom a man is overcome, to the same also is he bound as slave.*[585]

This is certainly the mind of the Apostle Peter. And since this is true, what sort of liberty, I ask you, can the bondslave possess except the liberty to sin? For he serves freely who freely does the will of his master. Hence, he who is the servant of sin is free to sin. And therefore he will not be free to do what is right until, freed from sin, he begins to be the servant of justice.[586]

This is what constitutes true liberty—the joy experienced in doing what is right. At the same time it is a holy servitude arising from obedience to precept. But whence is man, sold and held in bondage, to have that liberty to do good, unless

He buy him back who said: *If therefore the Son shall make you free, then you shall be free indeed?*[587] But before man begins to be in this state, how could anyone take glory in a good work as though proceeding from his free will, when he is not yet free to do what is right? Puffed up with silly pride, he would only be boasting. But this the Apostle reproves, saying: *By grace you are saved through faith.*[588] 31. And lest they (the Ephesians) should arrogate to themselves their own faith at least, and not understand that it was given to them by God, the same Apostle, who says in another place that he had *obtained mercy of the Lord to be faithful,*[589] here also added, saying: *and that not of yourselves, but it is the gift of God; not of works, that no man may glory.*[590] And lest good works be thought to be wanting in the faithful, he added again: *For we are His fashioning, created in Christ Jesus in good works, which God hath prepared that we should walk in them.*[591]

Consequently, we shall then be made truly free when God fashions us, that is, forms and creates us, not as men, which He has already done, but as good men, which He now does by His grace, in order that we may be *a new creature in Christ*[592] according to the words: *Create a clean heart in me, O God.*[593] Of course, as regards the physical, human heart, God had already created this.

XIII

41. Christ was therefore begotten and conceived of no lust of carnal concupiscence. For this reason He brought with Him no original sin. Again, by the grace of God He was most intimately united in a wonderful and ineffable way in one Person of the Word, the Only-Begotten of the Father, His Son not by grace but by nature; and for this reason He was also free from personal sin. Yet, because of the *likeness of sinful flesh* in which He came,[594] He was Himself called sin,[595] destined as He was to be sacrificed in order to wash away sin. In fact, under the Old Law sacrifices for sins were called sins.[596] And He, of whom those sacrifices were but shadows, was Himself truly made sin. Hence, when the Apostle said,

---

585. 2 Pet 2:19.
586. See Rom 6:16–19.
587. Jn 8:36.
588. Eph 2:8.
589. 1 Tim 1:13–14.
590. Eph 2:8–9.
591. Eph 2:10.
592. See Gal 6:15; 2 Cor 5:17.
593. Ps 50:12 (Vulgate) = Ps 51:10.
594. See Rom 8:3.
595. See 2 Cor 5:21.
596. See Lev 4:1–5:13; 6:24–30; 14:19.

For Christ we beseech you to be reconciled with God, he immediately added: *Him, who knew no sin. He hath made sin for us, that we might be the justice of God in Him.*[597] He does not say, as some faulty copies read: "He who knew no sin did sin for us," as though Christ Himself sinned for us; but he said: *Him, who knew no sin,* Christ, that is to say, God—to whom we are to be reconciled—*hath made sin for us,* that is, a sacrifice for sin by which we might be reconciled to God.

He, then, was sin, as we are justification; but this justification is not our own but God's, not in ourselves but in Him, just as He was sin, not His own but ours; and that it was enrooted not in Himself but in us, He demonstrated in *the likeness of sinful flesh* in which He was crucified. Thus, since sin was not in Him, He wishes to die, so to speak, to sin while dying in the flesh in which was the likeness of sin; and He who Himself had never lived the old life of sin wished by His Resurrection to seal our new life, rising up again from the old death by which we had been dead in sin.

42. This is precisely what is meant by the great sacrament of baptism which is solemnized among us: all who attain to this grace should die to sin, just as He is said to have died to sin because He died in the flesh, that is, in the likeness of sin; and they should live by being born again from the font, as did Christ by rising again from the sepulchre. The age of a person makes no difference. 43. For, as no one, from the infant newly born to the old man bent with age, is to be barred from baptism, so there is no one who in baptism does not die to sin. But infants die to original sin only, while adults die also to all those other sins which by their evil lives they have added to the sin they contracted at birth.

44. But even these latter are often said to die to sin, although without doubt they do not die to one sin but to all the many sins which they committed personally in thought, word, and deed. The evident reason is that the plural number is often indicated by the singular, as in the words of the poet:

They fill its belly with the armed soldier—[598]

whereas they did this with many soldiers. And we read in our own Scriptures: *Pray therefore to the Lord that He may take from us the serpent.*[599] The writer does not say "serpents," as he should, since the people were being plagued by them. And there are countless other instances of the same kind. When, on the other hand, that single original sin is spoken of in the plural number, as when we say that infants are baptized "unto the remission of *sins*" instead of saying "unto the

remission of *sin,*" then we have the converse figure of speech in which the singular is expressed by means of the plural. Thus, when Herod was dead, the Gospel says: *For they are dead that sought the life of the child,*[600] and not, "he is dead." And in Exodus we read: *They made to themselves gods of gold,*[601] although the people had made but one calf, of which they said: *These are thy gods, O Israel, that have brought thee out of the land of Egypt*[602]—thus also putting the plural for the singular.

45. However, even in that one sin which *by one man entered into the world*[603] and passed on to all men, and because of which even infants are baptized, a plurality of sins can be discovered if we break it down, so to speak, into its component parts. For in it there is pride, since man chose to be under his own dominion rather than under God's; also blasphemy, since man refused to believe God; and murder, for he rushed headlong into death; and spiritual fornication, since the innocence of the human soul was corrupted by the seduction of the serpent; and theft, since man appropriated to himself forbidden food; and avarice, since he craved for more than sufficed for his needs; and whatever else may be found by diligent reflection to have been involved in the commission of this one sin.

46. It is said with a real basis of probability that children are involved not only in the sin of our first parents but also in the sins of their own parents of whom they are born. For that divine sentence, *I shall visit the iniquities of the fathers upon their children,*[604] certainly applies to them before they come under the New Testament through regeneration. And it was this Testament that was foretold when Ezechiel said that the sons should not in the future bear the sins of their fathers and that no longer should that byword apply to Israel: *Our fathers have eaten sour grapes, and the teeth of the children are set on edge.*[605]

Every one, therefore, who is born again, is born again in order that whatever sin was in him at the time of birth should be absolved. For the sins which are committed later on through evil actions can be washed clean by penance, as we see done after baptism. And for this reason alone was the rebirth instituted, because our birth is sinful and sinful to

---

597. 2 Cor 5:21.

598. Virgil, *Aeneid,* II.20: *"Ingentes uterumque armato milite complent."*

599. Num 21:7 (the Vulgate, however, has the plural *serpentes*).

600. Mt 2:20.   602. Ex 32:4, 8.

601. See Ex 32:8.   603. See Rom 5:12.

604. Ex 20:5; 34:7; see also Num 14:18; Jer 32:18.

605. Ezek 18:2; see also Jer 31:29–30.

such a degree that even one who had been born in lawful wedlock said: *I was conceived in iniquities; and in sins did my mother nourish me in her womb.*[606] Nor did he say, as he might have done correctly, "in iniquity" and "in sin"; but he chose to say "iniquities" and "sins," because in that one sin which passed on to all men and which was so great that by it human nature was changed and subjected to the necessity of dying, many more sins, as I explained above, are found; and because there are other sins—those of our parents—which cannot, it is true, change our nature in the same manner, but which nevertheless involve the children in guilt, unless the gratuitous grace and mercy of God intervenes.

47. But concerning the sins of a different group of parents, the ancestors through whom a man traces his lineage from Adam to his own father, a debate might well be raised. Is that man at his birth involved by their evil doings and multiplied transgressions, so that the later he is born the worse off he is? Or does God threaten to visit the sins of the parents upon their posterity only unto the third and fourth generations, because with merciful restraint He does not permit His wrath to encompass the guilt of more distant forebears? He does not want those who do not receive the grace of regeneration, eternally condemned as they are, to be crushed under too heavy a load, as they would be if they were forced to contract as their own the sins of all those who from the beginning of the human race preceded their own parents, and to pay the penalty due to them. Whether or not a more painstaking study and interpretation of Holy Scripture might yield some other solution of so momentous a problem, is a question which I dare not answer offhand.

XIV

48. Still, that one sin, committed in a place and a state of such great happiness, a sin of such enormity that through one man the whole human race was originally and, I might say, radically, condemned, is absolved and blotted out only through *the one Mediator of God and man, the man Christ Jesus,*[607] who alone could be so born as not to need to be reborn.

49. Those who were baptized by the baptism of John, by whom He also was baptized, were not regenerated. But through the ministry of this precursor who kept saying, *Prepare ye the way for the Lord,*[608] they were made ready for Him in whom alone they could be born again. For His baptism is not by water alone, as was John's, but also by the Holy Spirit.[609] Thus, whosoever believes in Christ is born again of that Spirit, of whom Christ also was born, though He needed

not to be born again. Hence, too, those words of the Father spoken over Him at His baptism: *This day have I begotten thee,*[610] pointed not to that one day in time on which He was baptized, but to that of changeless eternity, to show us that this man was identical with the Person of the Only-Begotten. For, where a day neither begins with the close of yesterday, nor ends with the beginning of tomorrow, there it is eternal today.

He, therefore, chose to be baptized in water by John, not in order that any sin of His might be washed away but that His great humility be made manifest. For baptism certainly found nothing in Him that needed to be washed away, just as death found nothing in Him that needed to be punished. Hence, it was by strict justice and not by a mere imposition of force that the devil was crushed and conquered, for, as he had most unjustly caused Him to be slain who was free from all guilt of sin, most justly should he lose through Him those whom he held in subjection because of the guilt of sin. To both, then, that is, to baptism and death, did Christ submit Himself, following a special plan—not because of a pitiable necessity but by His own free act of taking pity on us—by which one Man was to take away the sin of the world, as one man had brought sin into the world, that is, upon the whole human race.

50. But there is this difference: whereas the one man brought one sin into the world, this Man took away not only that one sin, but also all the others which He found added to it. The Apostle therefore says: *Not as it was by one sin, so also the gift. For judgment, indeed, was by one unto condemnation, but grace is of many offences, unto justification.*[611] Evidently, that one sin which man contracts at birth would, even if it were his only one, make him liable to condemnation; but grace justifies from many transgressions man who has committed, besides the one sin which at birth he drew upon himself in common with all others, many sins wholly his own.

From Saint Augustine, *Faith, Hope, and Charity,* translated by Louis A. Arand (Westminster, MD: Newman Bookshop, 1947), 33–36, 37–39, 49–55.

---

606. Ps 50:7 (Vulgate) = Ps 51:5.

607. 1 Tim 2:5.

608. Mk 1:3; Mt 3:3; Lk 3:4; Jn 1:23; see also Isa 40:3.

609. See Mk 1:8; Mt 3:11; Lk 3:16.

610. Heb 5:5; see also Lk 3:22 (in some manuscript traditions); Ps 2:7.

611. Rom 5:16.

AUGUSTINE

On Nature and Grace, I.1–IX.10; XIX.21–XXI.23; XXX.34–XXXII.36; XXXIV.39

I.1. The book which you have sent to me,[612] dearly beloved sons Timasius and James, I have read through somewhat rapidly—having set aside for a little while the books which I was reading—but with considerable attention. I saw [in this book] a man inflamed with a very ardent zeal against those who, although they ought, when they sin, to censure the human will, try instead to accuse the nature of human beings and thus to excuse themselves. He has flared up excessively against this plague, which even writers of secular literature have strongly reproved, exclaiming: "The human race wrongly brings a complaint against its own nature."[613] With all the strength of his intellectual talents, your author also has piled up support for precisely this judgment. I fear, nevertheless, that he will instead give support to those "who have a zeal for God, but not according to knowledge; for they, not knowing the justice of God, and seeking to establish their own, have not submitted themselves to the justice of God."[614] The Apostle makes clear the meaning of "the justice of God" in this passage by adding immediately, "For the end of the law is Christ, to justice for everyone who believes."[615] Therefore, whoever understands that the justice of God lies not in the precept of the law, which incites fear, but in the help given by the grace of Christ—and it is to this grace alone that the fear of the law, as of a pedagogue,[616] leads—he understands why he is a Christian. "For if justice is through the law, then Christ died in vain."[617] However, if he did not die in vain, then only in him is the ungodly man justified, and to him who "believes in him who justifies the ungodly, his faith is attributed for his justification."[618] "For all have sinned and are deprived of the glory of God and are justified freely through his blood."[619] But those who do not believe that they belong to the "all" who "have sinned and are deprived of the glory of God" do not, of course, have any necessity to become Christians, for those who are healthy do not need a physician, but rather those who are ill. For this reason Christ came to call, not the just, but sinners.[620]

II.2. And thus the nature of the human race, born from the flesh of the one transgressor, ought, if it could be sufficient to itself to fulfill the law and to achieve justice, to be sure of its reward, that is, of eternal life, even[621] *if in some nation or in some past time faith in the blood of Christ was not known to it. For God is not unjust and would not deprive the just of their reward for justice, if the mystery of Christ's nature as* both human and divine, which was manifest in the flesh, had not been proclaimed to them. For how could they believe what they had not heard? Or how could they hear without a preacher?[622] For "Faith is from hearing," as Scripture says, "and hearing by the word of Christ. But I say," says St. Paul, "Have they not heard? 'Their sound has gone forth into all the earth, and their words unto the ends of the whole world.'"[623] However, before all this has begun to be accomplished, before that preaching itself finally reaches the ends of the whole earth—for there still exist some people in remote places, although it is said that they are few in number, to whom the gospel has not yet been preached—what should human nature do or what has it done, either before when it had not yet heard that salvation was to come to pass, or now if it has not learned that it was accomplished? What should it do except fulfill God's will by believing in him who made heaven and earth, and who created human nature itself (as it naturally perceives), and by living rightly, even though it has not been tinged with any faith in the passion and resurrection of Christ? If this could have been done or can be done, I also say what the Apostle said about the law: "Christ died in vain."[624]* For if he declared this regarding the law accepted by the one Jewish people, how much more truly may it be said concerning the law of nature which all mankind has received, "If justice is derived from [human] nature, then Christ died in vain." But if he did not die in vain, then human nature can in no way be justified and redeemed from the most righteous wrath of God, that is from punishment, unless through faith and the sacrament of the blood of Christ.

III.3. In the beginning man's nature was created without any fault and without any sin: however, this human nature in which we are all born from Adam now requires a physician, because it is not healthy.[625] Indeed, all the good qualities which it has in its organization, life, senses, and understanding, it possesses from the most high God, its creator and shaper.

---

612. The book was Pelagius's *De natura.* (The notes for this selection are by Gerhart and Udoh.)

613. See Sallust, *Bellum Iugurthinum,* 1.1.

614. Rom 10:2–3.   616. See Gal 3:24.

615. Rom 10:4.   617. Gal 2:21.

618. Rom 4:5.

619. Rom 3:23–24 (both the Greek text and the Vulgate read "grace" in lieu of Augustine's "blood").

620. See Mk 2:17; Mt 9:12–13; Lk 5:31–32.

621. Augustine's quotations from Pelagius's works are printed in italics.

622. See Rom 10:14.

623. Rom 10:17–18.

624. Gal 2:21.

625. See Mk 2:17; Mt 9:12–13; Lk 5:31–32.

On the other hand, the defect which darkens and weakens all those natural goods, so that there is a need for illumination and healing, is not derived from its blameless maker but from that original sin that was committed through free will. Consequently, that criminal nature draws upon itself the most righteous punishment. For, if we are now a new creation in Christ,[626] "we were," nevertheless, "children of wrath, even as the rest. But God, who is rich in mercy, because of the great love with which he loved us, even when we were dead through our offenses, has given us life together with Christ, by whose grace you have been saved."[627]

IV.4. This grace of Christ, then, without which neither children nor adults can be saved, is given gratuitously and not for our merits, and for this reason it is called "grace." "[They are] justified," says the Apostle, "freely by his blood."[628] Consequently, those who are not liberated through grace, either because they have not yet been able to hear, or because they have not wished to obey, or also because, when on account of their age they were not capable of hearing, they did not receive the bath of regeneration,[629] which they could have received and by means of which they would have been saved, are justly condemned. For they are not without sin, either that which they contracted originally or that which they added through their own misconduct. "For all have sinned," either in Adam or in themselves, "and are deprived of the glory of God."[630]

V.5. Consequently, the whole human mass ought to be punished, and if the deserved punishment of damnation were rendered to all, beyond all doubt it would be justly rendered. This is why those who are liberated from it by grace are not called vessels of their own merits but "vessels of mercy."[631] But whose mercy was it but his who sent Jesus Christ into this world to save sinners,[632] whom he foreknew, predestined, called, justified, and glorified?[633] Hence, who could be so advanced in foolish insanity as not to render ineffable thanks to the mercy of this God who liberates those whom he has wished, considering that one could not in any way reproach the justice of God in condemning all entirely?

VI.6. If we understand this according to Scripture, we are not obliged to dispute against the grace of Christ nor to try to show that human nature, in infancy, needs no physician because it is sound and, in adults, can be sufficient, if it wishes, to obtain justice for itself. These opinions indeed seem here to be expressed incisively, but in a "wisdom of speech," which makes void the cross of Christ.[634] "For this is not wisdom descending from above."[635] I do not wish to quote the words that follow, that we may not be thought to do injustice to our

friends, whose most strong and quick minds we wish to see run in a straight, rather than a perverse, course.

VII.7. Therefore, however great is the zeal with which the author of this book which you have sent is inflamed against those who base a defense plea for their sins on the infirmity of human nature, with equal and more ardent zeal must we be inflamed, so that the cross of Christ may not be made void.[636] But it is made void if it is said that one can arrive at justice and eternal life in any way besides its sacrament. And that is what is done in this book—I do not wish to say by someone who knows what he is doing, so that I may not judge that he who wrote it should not even be considered a Christian, but, as I tend to believe, by someone who writes in ignorance, though admittedly with great power. I only wish his powers were sound, and not the sort which madmen are accustomed to display.

8. First of all Pelagius[637] makes this distinction: *It is one thing to ask whether something can be (which has to do only with its possibility) and another to ask whether it is.* No one doubts this distinction to be true, for if something is, it follows that it could have been, but it does not follow that what can be also is. For, given the fact that the Lord raised Lazarus,[638] it is evident that he was able to do so. But since he did not, in fact, raise Judas, are we to say, "He was not able to"? Certainly, he was able—but he was not willing. For if he had been willing, he could have done this too by the same power. For the Son gives life to whomever he wills.[639] Observe, however, where he is going with this obvious and evident distinction and what he endeavors to establish from it. *We are treating,* he says, *only of possibility, from which, unless something certain has been established, we would regard it as very serious and out of proper order to pass on to something else.* He considers this idea from many different aspects and at great length, so that no one would think that he was investigating anything else than the possibility of not committing sin. The following is one of the many arguments which Pelagius uses in treating this subject: *Once more I repeat: I say that it is possible for a man*

---

626. See 2 Cor 5:17; Gal 6:15.
627. Eph 2:3–5.
628. Rom 3:24.
629. See Titus 3:5.
630. Rom 3:23.
631. Rom 9:23.
632. See 1 Tim 1:15.
633. See Rom 8:29–30.
634. See 1 Cor 1:17.
635. Jas 3:15.
636. See 1 Cor 1:17.

637. Augustine does not mention Pelagius by name in the entire treatise; the name is introduced here by the translator for the sake of clarity.
638. See Jn 11:43–44.
639. See Jn 5:21.

to be without sin. And what do you say? That it is impossible for a man to be without sin? But I do not say, he adds, *that there is a man without sin, nor do you say that there is not a man without sin. We are disputing about what is possible and impossible, not about what is and is not.* Next he notes that a number of the passages of Scripture which are usually invoked against them do not bear upon the question in dispute, namely, whether or not a man can be without sin: "For there is no man free from pollution,"[640] and, "There is no man that does not sin,"[641] and, "There is no just man on the earth,"[642] and, "There is no one that does good."[643] *These and other similar texts,* he says, *apply to non-existence, not to impossibility. By examples of this kind it is shown how some men were at a given time, not that they could not have been something else. For this reason they are justly found to be guilty. For if they were as they were because they could not have been otherwise, then they are free from blame.*

VIII.9. Notice what he has said. I, however, for my part, say that an infant born where it was not possible for him to be rescued through the baptism of Christ, having been overtaken by death, was thereby in such a state—that is, of having departed without the "bath of regeneration"[644]—because he could not have been otherwise. Therefore, our author would absolve him and, contrary to the statement of the Lord, would open to him the kingdom of heaven. But the Apostle does not absolve him when he says, "By one man sin entered into this world, and by sin, death, and so death passed upon all men, in whom all have sinned."[645] Justly, therefore, because of the condemnation which runs through the whole mass of humanity, he is not admitted into the kingdom of heaven, even though he not only was not a Christian but could not have been one.

IX.10. *But they say, He is not damned, because "All have sinned in Adam" is said, not because of sin contracted in the origin of one's birth, but rather because of imitation of him.* If, therefore, it may be said that Adam is the author of all the sins which followed his own, since he was the first sinner among men, how then does it happen that Abel is not placed at the head of the just, rather than Christ, because Abel was the first just man? But I do not speak of an infant. Consider instead the case of a young man, or of an old man, who died in a place where he could not have heard the name of Christ. Could he, or could he not, have become just by his own nature and free will? If they say he could have, then see what amounts to rendering the cross of Christ void:[646] to contend that without it anyone can be justified by the law of nature and the choice of his will. Let us also say here: "Then Christ died in vain."[647] For this is something which everyone

could do, even if Christ had not died. And if they were unjust, it would be because they wished to be, and not because they could not be just. If, however, one could not be justified in any way without the grace of Christ, let Pelagius absolve him, if he dares, in accordance with his statement that, *If he was as he was because he could not have been otherwise, then he was free from blame.*

XIX.21. Now consider—which is most central to our subject—how Pelagius tries to present human nature as if it were entirely without fault and how, against the clearest evidence of God's Scriptures, he prefers that "wisdom of speech" by which the cross of Christ is made void.[648] But certainly it will not be made void, rather this "wisdom" will be overturned. When we have shown this, perhaps the mercy of God will intervene, so that Pelagius may regret that he ever said these things. *First,* he says, *we must dispute the view which maintains that our nature has been weakened and changed through sin. I think, therefore, that before all else we must inquire what sin is. Is it some substance, or is it a name wholly lacking substance, by which is expressed neither a thing, nor an existence, nor some kind of body, but the action of doing something evil?* Then he adds, *I believe it is the latter, and if it is,* he says, *how could that which lacks substance have weakened or changed human nature?* Observe, I beseech you, how he endeavors in his ignorance to distort the most salutary words of our health-giving Scriptures: "I said, O Lord, be merciful to me; heal my soul, for I have sinned against thee."[649] But what is healed if nothing is wounded, nothing injured, nothing weakened and corrupted? But if there is something to be healed, whence came the injury? You hear the Psalmist confessing—what need is there for discussion? "Heal my soul," he says. Ask him how the soul, which he prays to be healed, became injured, and listen to what follows: "For I have sinned against thee." Let our author question him, let him ask of him what he thinks ought to be asked and say, "Oh you who cry, 'Heal my soul, for I have sinned against thee,' tell me, what is sin? Is it some substance, or is it a name lacking all substance, by which is expressed neither a thing nor an existence nor some kind of

---

640. Job 14:4 (Septuagint).

641. 1 Kings 8:46.

642. Eccl 7:21 (Vulgate) = Eccl 7:20.

643. Ps 13:1, 3 (Vulgate) = Ps 14:3; see also Rom 3:10–11.

644. See Titus 3:5.

645. Rom 5:12. See our note on *Encheiridion*, 8.26.

646. See 1 Cor 1:17.   648. See 1 Cor 1:17.

647. Gal 2:21.   649. Ps 40:5 (Vulgate) = Ps 41:4.

body, but merely the action of doing something evil?" The Psalmist replies, "It is just as you say: sin is not some substance, but only the act of doing something evil is expressed by this name." Then Pelagius objects, "Then why do you cry out, 'Heal my soul, for I have sinned against thee'? How could that which lacks substance have injured your soul?" Then would not his respondent, exhausted by the anguish of his wound, briefly, so that he may not be diverted from prayer by the discussion, answer, "Leave me, I beg of you! Instead discuss the issue, if you can, with him who said, 'They that are in health need not a physician, but they that are ill. . . . I am not come to call the just, but sinners,'[650] where clearly he calls the just 'healthy,' while he calls sinners 'ill.'"

XX.22. Do you not perceive where this discussion is leading and what outcome it is reaching toward? It is that it will be thought to be said completely in vain, "And you will call his name Jesus. For he shall save his people from their sins."[651] For how can he bring about salvation where there is no sickness? For the sins from which the gospel says the people of Christ have to be saved are not substances and hence, according to our author, are not capable of injuring. O my brother, it is good for you to remember that you are a Christian! Perhaps it would be sufficient to believe these words, but, since you wish to continue the discussion, there is no reason not to do so, indeed it may do some good, provided the strongest faith precede, and we do not suppose that human nature cannot be corrupted by sin, but rather, believing with the divine Scriptures that it is corrupted by sin, we inquire how this could have come about. Since we have already learned that sin is not a substance, let us consider (omitting other things) whether abstinence from food is also not a substance. One indeed abstains *from* a substance, since food is a substance. But to abstain from food is not a substance—yet nevertheless if we abstain entirely from food, the substance of our body languishes and is so impaired by frailty of health, so exhausted of strength, and so weakened and broken with weariness, that even if it were able in some way to continue to live, it would barely be capable of being restored to the use of that food, by abstaining from which it became corrupted. Likewise, sin is not a substance, but God is a substance, the supreme substance, the only true nourishment of the rational creature. Listen to how the Psalmist expresses what it is to withdraw from him by disobedience and to be unable through weakness even to receive that in which one truly ought to rejoice: "My heart is withered and beaten like grass, because I forgot to eat my bread."[652]

XXI.23. But observe how Pelagius with superficially plausible arguments continues to oppose the truth of Holy Scripture. The Lord Jesus, who is called Jesus because "He shall save his people from their sins"[653]—the Lord Jesus therefore declares, "They that are in health need not a physician, but they that are ill. . . . For I am come not to call the just but sinners."[654] In accordance with this, the Apostle also says, "A faithful saying and worthy of all acceptance, that Christ Jesus came into the world to save sinners."[655] However, Pelagius, contrary to this "faithful saying and worthy of all acceptance," says, *This sickness should not have been contracted by sins, lest the punishment of sin should come to this: that more sins are committed.* So great a physician is sought as a help even for infants, and yet Pelagius asks, *What do you seek? Those for whom you seek a physician are in good health. And not even the first man was condemned to death for such a reason, for he did not sin afterwards.* It is as though he had heard something of his perfection in justice afterwards, aside from what the Church commends: that Adam himself had been liberated by the mercy of Christ our Lord. *His descendants also,* he says, *not only are not weaker than he, but have actually fulfilled more commandments, since he neglected to obey even the one.* He who saves his people from their sins[656] sees these descendants to be born in such a state (in which Adam certainly was not created) that they not only are not capable of obeying precepts of which they are altogether unaware, but are scarcely capable of taking the breast when they are hungry, yet nevertheless, he wishes to save by his grace even these, in the bosom of Mother Church. But men oppose him and, as if they had a deeper insight into the creature than does God, who made it, declare, with a statement that is not sound, that such infants are sound.

XXX.34 What does Pelagius mean in the following passage? *Next, how can a man be answerable to God for the guilt of a sin which he knows is not his own? For if it is necessary, it is not his own. Or if it is his own, it is voluntary; and if it is voluntary, it can be avoided.* We answer, Beyond all doubt it is his own, but the fault through which it was committed has not yet been completely healed. And the fact that it grows in us happens because we did not correctly use the

---

650. Mk 2:17; Mt 9:12–13; Lk 5:31–32.

651. Mt 1:21.

652. Ps 101:5 (Vulgate) = Ps 102:4.

653. Mt 1:21.

654. Mk 2:17; Mt 9:12–13; Lk 5:31–32.

655. 1 Tim 1:15.

656. That is, Jesus (see Mt 1:21).

good health with which we were endowed. From this fault man, who is now becoming increasingly ill, through weakness or blindness commits more sins. He ought to pray that he may be healed and that from then on he may enjoy a life of perpetual good health, not becoming proud, as if a man could be healed by the very same power by which he became corrupted.

XXXI.35. And indeed I would have said these things in such a way as to confess my ignorance of the profound judgment of God—why he does not cure at once this pride which, in good actions, easily insinuates itself into the human soul. It is for this cure that pious souls supplicate him with tears and great sighs, imploring him to extend a hand to them in their efforts, in order to conquer this pride and in some way beat it down and crush it. For when a man has rejoiced that he has overcome pride in some good work, from this very joy he raises his head and says, "Behold I live, why do you triumph? Indeed, I live because you triumph." Perhaps he delights prematurely in that triumph over pride, as if it were already conquered, when in fact its last shadow will be absorbed in the light of noon, the noon that is promised by Scripture in the verse, "And he will bring forth your justice as the light, and your judgment as the noonday,"[657] if it is done as written in the preceding words, "Commit your way to the Lord, and trust in him, and he will do it"[658]—not, as some think, because they do it themselves. For when he said, "and he will do it," evidently he had no one else in mind than those who declare, "We do it," that is, we ourselves justify ourselves. We do in fact work, but when we work, we cooperate with God who works, for his mercy comes before us.[659] It comes before us, however, that we may be healed, as it also will follow, so that being healed we may gain strength. It comes before us so that we may be called, and it will follow, so that we may be glorified. It comes before us so that we may lead pious lives; it will follow so that we may always live with him, for without him we can do nothing.[660] For Scripture says both, "He is my God, his mercy shall come before me,"[661] and, "Your mercy will follow me all the days of my life."[662] Therefore, let us reveal to him our way through confession, rather than praise it by defending it. For if it is not his way but ours, then surely it is not the right way. Let us reveal it to him by our confession, for it is not hidden from him, even if we try to conceal it. For "it is good to confess to the Lord."[663]

XXXII.36. Thus, he will give us what pleases him, if whatever in us displeases him also displeases us. As Scripture says, "he will turn aside our ways from his way,"[664] and make his way our own, for he extends this favor to those who believe in him and trust in him that he will do it.[665] For this is the way of justice, ignored by those who "have a zeal for God, but not according to knowledge, and who, seeking to establish their own justice, have not submitted themselves to the justice of God. For the end of the law is Christ, unto justice for everyone that believes,"[666] Christ who said, "I am the way."[667] Yet even those who have already begun to walk in his way are fearful of the voice of God, fearful that they may praise themselves for walking in his way by their own strength. This is why the Apostle has said to them, "With fear and trembling work out your salvation. For it is God who works in you, both to will and to accomplish, according to his good will."[668] For the same reason the psalm says to them, "Serve the Lord in fear, and rejoice unto him with trembling. Embrace discipline, so that at some time the Lord may not be angry, and you perish from the just way, when his wrath shall be enkindled in a short time upon you."[669] He does not say, "So that at some time the Lord may not be angry and not show you the way of justice," or, "not lead you into the way of justice," but even when they are walking in that way, he could instill fear into them in saying, "that you may not perish from the just way." How could this be if not from pride, which, as I have said so many times and must keep saying often, has to be guarded against even in things which are rightly done, that is, in the way of justice itself, so that a man, regarding what is of God as his own, may not lose what is of God and be reduced to what is his own? Therefore, let us follow the concluding words of that psalm, "Blessed are all they that trust in him,"[670] so that he himself acts and shows us his own way, he to whom it is said, "Show us, O Lord, your mercy";[671] may he himself grant salvation, so that we can walk in his way, he to whom it is said, "And grant us your salvation";[672] may he him-

---

657. Ps 36:6 (Vulgate) = Ps 37:6.
658. Ps 36:5 (Vulgate) = Ps 37:5.
659. See Ps 58:11 (Vulgate); see also Ps 59:10.
660. See Jn 15:5.
661. Ps 58:11 (Vulgate).
662. Ps 22:6 (Vulgate) = Ps 23:6.
663. Ps 91:2 (Vulgate); see also Ps 92:1.
664. See Ps 43:19 (Vulgate); see also Ps 44:18.
665. See Ps 36:5 (Vulgate) = Ps 37:5.
666. Rom 10:2–4.
667. Jn 14:6.
668. Phil 2:12–13.
669. Ps 2:11–13 (Vulgate); see also Ps 2:11–12.
670. Ps 2:13 (Vulgate).
671. Ps 84:8 (Vulgate) = Ps 85:7.
672. Ps 84:8 (Vulgate) = Ps 85:7.

self guide us in this way, he to whom it is said, "Guide me, O Lord, in your way, and I will walk in your truth";[673] may he himself direct us to that promised happiness, wheresoever his way leads, he to whom it is said, "There also shall your hand lead me, and your right hand shall guide me";[674] may he himself there feed those who sit down with Abraham, Isaac, and Jacob, he of whom it is said, "He will make them sit down to eat and will pass by and minister to them."[675] In recalling these words we do not take away the freedom of the will, but rather we preach the grace of God. For to whom are these words helpful, except to the one who uses his own will, but uses it humbly, not priding himself in the strength of his will, as if it alone were sufficient to achieve justice?

XXXIV.39. Beyond this, however, when he thinks that he is serving the cause of God by defending nature, he forgets that in declaring this nature to be sound he rejects the mercy of the physician. But the same person who created him is also his savior. Therefore, we should not so praise the creator that we are compelled to say, or rather convicted of saying, that there is no need for the savior. Therefore let us honor man's nature with fitting praises, and let us attribute these praises to the glory of the creator; but let us not be grateful to him for having created us in such a way that we are ungrateful to him for having healed us. Let us not attribute our defects of which we are healed to the action of God, but rather to the will of man and to his just punishment. Nevertheless, we must admit that it was in our power that they should not have come about, just as we confess that their cure depends upon his mercy more than upon our own power. However, Pelagius reduces this mercy and healing aid of the savior to the fact that he forgives the transgressions of the past, not that he will help us to avoid sins in the future. Here he is most dangerously mistaken, for, however unknowingly, he hinders us from being careful, and from praying that we "enter not into temptation,"[676] since he maintains that it is entirely within our power that it should not happen to us.

From Saint Augustine, *Four Anti-Pelagian Writings,* translated by John A. Mourant and William J. Collinge, Fathers of the Church, vol. 86 (Washington, DC: Catholic University of America Press, 1992), 22–29, 35–38, 47–50, 51. [Ellipsis in original.]

THE CHRISTOLOGICAL CONTROVERSY

Origen (ca. 185–254) probably composed *On First Principles* between 212 and 215; the text is extant only in the translation by Rufinus (ca. 345–410). It is the first significant attempt to elucidate

the Logos's (which Christians identified with Christ) mediation between God and humanity.

ORIGEN

On First Principles, II.VI.1–6

1. Now that these points have been discussed, it is time to resume our inquiry into the incarnation of our Lord and Saviour, how he became man and dwelt among men. We have considered, to the best of our small ability, the divine nature, from a contemplation of his own works rather than from our feelings, and while beholding his visible creatures we have also by faith contemplated those that are invisible. For human frailty can neither see everything with the eyes nor comprehend everything by reason, since we men are beings weaker and frailer than all other rational creatures, those that dwell in heaven or above the heavens surpassing us in excellence. Our next task is to inquire about him who stands midway between all these creatures and God, that is, the Mediator,[677] whom the apostle Paul declares to be the "firstborn of all creation."[678] And when we see what is related in the Holy Scriptures of his majesty, and perceive that he is called the "image of the invisible God" and the "firstborn of all creation," and that "in him were created all things visible and invisible, whether thrones or dominions or principalities or powers, all were created through him and in him, and he is before all, and in him all things consist,"[679] who is the "head of all," having as his head only God the Father, as it is written, "the head of Christ is God";[680] and when we see too that it is written, "No man knoweth the Father save the Son, nor doth any know the Son save the Father"[681]—for who can know what "wisdom" is, except him who brought it into being; or who knows for certain what "truth" is, except the Father of truth; who indeed could trace out the universal nature of his "Word" and of that God who is from God except God alone "with whom the Word was"?[682]—we ought to hold it as certain that none else save the Father alone knows this Word (or reason, if he should be so called), this wisdom, this truth, of

---

673. Ps 85:11 (Vulgate) = Ps 86:11.

674. Ps 138:10 (Vulgate) = Ps 139:10.

675. Lk 12:37.

676. Mk 14:38; Mt 26:41; Lk 22:46; see also Mt 6:13; Lk 11:4.

677. See 1 Tim 2:5. (The notes for this selection are by Gerhart and Udoh.)

678. Col 1:15.   680. 1 Cor 11:3.

679. Col 1:15–17.   681. Mt 11:27.

682. Jn 1:1.

whom it is written, "I suppose that not even the world itself could contain the books which should be written,"[683] about the glory, that is, and about the majesty of the Son of God. For it is impossible to put into writing all that belongs to the Saviour's glory.

When, therefore, we consider these great and marvellous truths about the nature of the Son of God, we are lost in the deepest amazement that such a being, towering high above all, should have "emptied himself"[684] of his majestic condition and become man and dwelt among men,[685] a fact which is evidenced by the "grace poured upon his lips"[686] and by the witness which the heavenly Father bore him,[687] and confirmed by the signs and wonders and mighty deeds which he did.[688] And before that personal appearance which he manifested in the body, he sent the prophets as heralds and messengers of his coming; while after his ascension into the heavens he caused the holy apostles, unlearned and ignorant men from the ranks of tax-gatherers or fishermen but filled with his divine power, to travel throughout the world, in order to gather together out of every nation and all races a people composed of devout believers in him.

2. But of all the marvellous and splendid things about him there is one that utterly transcends the limits of human wonder and is beyond the capacity of our weak mortal intelligence to think of or understand, namely, how this mighty power of the divine majesty, the very word of the Father, and the very wisdom of God, in which were created "all things visible and invisible,"[689] can be believed to have existed within the compass of that man who appeared in Judaea; yes, and how the wisdom of God can have entered into a woman's womb and been born as a little child and uttered noises like those of crying children; and further, how it was that he was troubled, as we are told, in the hour of death, as he himself confesses when he says, "My soul is sorrowful even unto death";[690] and how at the last he was led to that death which is considered by men to be the most shameful of all,—even though on the third day he rose again.

When, therefore, we see in him some things so human that they appear in no way to differ from the common frailty of mortals, and some things so divine that they are appropriate to nothing else but the primal and ineffable nature of deity, the human understanding with its narrow limits is baffled, and struck with amazement at so mighty a wonder knows not which way to turn, what to hold to, or whither to betake itself. If it thinks of God, it sees a man; if it thinks of a man, it beholds one returning from the dead with spoils after vanquishing the kingdom of death. For this reason we must pursue our contemplation with all fear and reverence, as we seek to prove how the reality of each nature exists in one and the same person, in such a way that nothing unworthy or unfitting may be thought to reside in that divine and ineffable existence, nor on the other hand may the events of his life be supposed to be the illusions caused by deceptive fantasies.[691] But to utter these things in human ears and to explain them by words far exceeds the powers we possess either in our moral worth or in mind and speech. I think indeed that it transcends the capacity even of the holy apostles; nay more, perhaps the explanation of this mystery lies beyond the reach of the whole creation of heavenly beings. It is then in no spirit of rashness, but solely in response to the demands of our inquiry at this stage, that we shall state in the fewest possible words what we may term the content of our faith concerning him rather than anything which needs to be proved by arguments of human reason, bringing before you our suppositions rather than any clear affirmations.

3. The only-begotten Son of God, therefore, through whom, as the course of our discussion in the previous chapters has shown, "all things visible and invisible were made,"[692] according to the teaching of Scripture both made all things and "loves what he made."[693] For since he is the invisible "image" of the "invisible God,"[694] he granted invisibly to all rational creatures whatsoever a participation in himself, in such a way that each obtained a degree of participation proportionate to the loving affection with which he had clung to him. But whereas, by reason of the faculty of free-will, variety and diversity had taken hold of individual souls, so that one was attached to its author with a warmer and another with a feebler and weaker love, that soul of which Jesus said, "No man taketh from me my soul,"[695] clinging to God from the beginning of the creation and ever after in a union inseparable and indissoluble, as being the soul of the wisdom and word of God and of the truth and the true light, and receiving him wholly, and itself entering into his light and splendour, was made with him in a pre-eminent degree one spirit, just as the apostle promises to them whose duty it is

---

683. Jn 21:25.

684. Phil 2:7.

685. See Jn 1:14.

686. Ps 44:2 (Septuagint) = Ps 45:2.

687. See Mk 1:11; Mt 3:17; Lk 3:22.

688. See Acts 2:22.

689. Col 1:16; see also Prov 3:19; 8:27–31.

690. Mk 14:34; Mt 26:38.

691. Such was the belief of the Docetist sects.

692. Col 1:16.

693. Wis 11:24.

694. Col 1:15.

695. Jn 10:18.

to imitate Jesus, that "he who is joined to the Lord is one spirit."[696] This soul, then, acting as a medium between God and the flesh (for it was not possible for the nature of God to mingle with a body apart from some medium), there is born, as we said, the God-man, the medium being that existence to whose nature it was not contrary to assume a body. Yet neither, on the other hand, was it contrary to nature for that soul, being as it was a rational existence, to receive God, into whom, as we said above, it had already completely entered by entering into the word and wisdom and truth.

It is therefore right that this soul, either because it was wholly in the Son of God, or because it received the Son of God wholly into itself, should itself be called, along with that flesh which it has taken, the Son of God and the power of God, Christ and the wisdom of God; and on the other hand that the Son of God, "through whom all things were created,"[697] should be termed Jesus and the Son of man. Moreover the Son of God is said to have died, in virtue of that nature which could certainly admit of death, while he of whom it is proclaimed that "he shall come in the glory of God the Father with the holy angels" is called the Son of man.[698] And for this reason, throughout the whole of Scripture, while the divine nature is spoken of in human terms the human nature is in its turn adorned with marks that belong to the divine prerogative. For to this more than to anything else can the passage of Scripture be applied, "They shall both be in one flesh, and they are no longer two, but one flesh."[699] For the Word of God is to be thought of as being more "in one flesh" with his soul than a man is with his wife. Moreover what could more appropriately be "one spirit"[700] with God than this soul, which joined itself so firmly in love to God as to be worthy of being called "one spirit" with him?

4. To prove that it was the perfection of his love and the sincerity of his true affection which gained for him this inseparable unity with God, so that the taking up of his soul was neither accidental nor the result of personal preference, but was a privilege conferred upon it as a reward for its virtues, listen to the prophet speaking to it thus; "Thou hast loved righteousness and hated iniquity; wherefore God hath anointed thee, thy God, with the oil of gladness above thy fellows."[701]

As a reward for its love, therefore, it is anointed with the "oil of gladness," that is the soul with the word of God is made Christ; for to be anointed with the oil of gladness means nothing else but to be filled with the Holy Spirit. And when he says, "above thy fellows," he indicates that the grace of

the Spirit was not given to it as to the prophets, but that the essential "fulness" of the Word of God himself was within it, as the apostle said, "In him dwelleth all the fulness of the godhead bodily."[702] Finally, this is the reason why he not only said, "Thou hast loved righteousness," but added, "and hated iniquity." For to hate iniquity is the same thing which the Scripture says of him: "He did no sin, neither was guile found in his mouth";[703] and again, "He was tempted in all points like as we are, yet without sin."[704] Further, the Lord himself says, "which of you convicteth me of sin?"[705] And again he says of himself, "Lo, the prince of this world cometh and findeth nothing in me."[706] All of which shows that no consciousness of sin existed in him. And the prophet, in order the more clearly to point out this fact, that the consciousness of iniquity had never entered his mind, says, "Before the boy could know how to call for his father or mother, he turned himself from iniquity."[707]

5. But if the above argument, that there exists in Christ a rational soul, should seem to anyone to constitute a difficulty, on the ground that in the course of our discussion we have often shown that souls are by their nature capable of good and evil, we shall resolve the difficulty in the following manner. It cannot be doubted that the nature of his soul was the same as that of all souls; otherwise it could not be called a soul, if it were not truly one. But since the ability to choose good or evil is within the immediate reach of all, this soul which belongs to Christ so chose to love righteousness as to cling to it unchangeably and inseparably in accordance with the immensity of its love; the result being that by firmness of purpose, immensity of affection and an inextinguishable warmth of love all susceptibility to change or alteration was destroyed, and what formerly depended upon the will was by the influence of long custom changed into nature. Thus we must believe that there did exist in Christ a human and rational soul, and yet not suppose that it had any susceptibility to or possibility of sin.

6. To explain the matter more fully it will not appear ab-

---

696. 1 Cor 6:17.
697. Jn 1:3; Col 1:16; Heb 1:2.
698. Mk 8:38; Mt 16:27; Lk 9:26.
699. Mt 19:5, 6; see also Gen 2:24; Mk 10:8; 1 Cor 7:16.
700. 1 Cor 6:17.
701. Ps 44:7 (Septuagint) = Ps 45:7.
702. Col 2:9.   705. Jn 8:46.
703. 1 Pet 2:22.   706. Jn 14:30.
704. Heb 4:15.   707. See Isa 7:16; 8:4.

surd if we use an illustration, although on so high and difficult a subject there is but a small supply of suitable examples.
However, if we may use this one without offence, the metal
iron is susceptible of both cold and heat. Suppose then a lump
of iron be placed for some time in a fire. It receives the fire in
all its pores and all its veins, and becomes completely changed
into fire, provided the fire is never removed from it and itself
is not separated from the fire. Are we then to say that this,
which is by nature a lump of iron, when placed in the fire
and ceaselessly burning can ever admit cold? Certainly not; it
is far truer to say of it, what indeed we often detect happening in furnaces, that it has been completely changed into fire,
because we can discern nothing else in it except fire. Further,
if anyone were to try to touch or handle it, he would feel the
power of the fire, not of the iron. In this manner, then, that
soul which, like a piece of iron in the fire, was for ever placed
in the word, for ever in the wisdom, for ever in God, is God in
all its acts and feelings and thoughts; and therefore it cannot
be called changeable or alterable, since by being ceaselessly
kindled it came to possess unchangeability through its unity
with the word of God. And while, indeed, some warmth
of the Word of God must be thought to have reached all the
saints, in this soul we must believe that the divine fire itself
essentially rested, and that it is from this that some warmth
has come to all others.

From Origen, *On First Principles*, translated by G. W. Butterworth (Gloucester, MA: Peter
Smith, 1973), 108–13.

❧ In his polemical *Orations against the Arians* (probably written
in 356 or 358), **Athanasius** (ca. 296–373) examines, with a Platonic
predilection, Christological issues, including the Incarnation of
the Logos, in the context of his defense of the Nicene Creed.

ATHANASIUS

Orations against the Arians, III.26–27, 29–35, 37–38

26. For behold, as if not wearied in their words of irreligion,
but hardened with Pharaoh, while they hear and see the
Saviour's human attributes in the Gospels, they have utterly
forgotten, like the Samosatene, the Son's paternal Godhead,
and with arrogant and audacious tongue they say, "How can
the Son be from the Father by nature, and be like Him in essence, who says, 'All power is given unto Me';[708] and 'The Father judgeth no man, but hath committed all judgment unto
the Son';[709] and 'The Father loveth the Son, and hath given all

things into His hand; he that believeth in the Son hath everlasting life';[710] and again, 'All things were delivered unto Me
of My Father, and no one knoweth the Father save the Son,
and he to whomsoever the Son will reveal Him';[711] and again,
'All that the Father hath given unto Me, shall come to Me'?"[712]
On this they observe, "If He was, as ye say, Son by nature,
He had no need to receive, but He had by nature as a Son."
"Or how can He be the natural and true Power of the Father,
who near upon the season of the passion says, 'Now is My
soul troubled, and what shall I say? Father, save Me from this
hour; but for this came I unto this hour. Father, glorify Thy
Name. Then came there a voice from heaven, saying, I have
both glorified it, and will glorify it again.'[713] And He said the
same another time; 'Father, if it be possible, let this cup pass
from Me';[714] and 'When Jesus had thus said, He was troubled
in spirit and testified and said, Verily, verily, I say unto you,
that one of you shall betray Me.'"[715] Then these perverse men
argue; "If He were Power, He had not feared, but rather He
had supplied power to others." Further they say; "If He were
by nature the true and own Wisdom of the Father, how is it
written, 'And Jesus increased in wisdom and stature, and in
favour with God and man'?[716] In like manner, when He had
come into the parts of Caesarea Philippi, He asked the disciples whom men said that He was;[717] and when He was at
Bethany He asked where Lazarus lay;[718] and He said besides
to His disciples, 'How many loaves have ye?'"[719] "How then,"
say they, "is He Wisdom, who increased in wisdom, and was
ignorant of what He asked of others?" This too they urge;
"How can He be the own Word of the Father, without whom
the Father never was, through whom He makes all things, as
ye think, who said upon the Cross, 'My God, My God, why
hast Thou forsaken Me?'[720] and before that had prayed, 'Glorify Thy Name,'[721] and, 'O Father, glorify Thou Me with the
glory which I had with Thee before the world was.'[722] And
He used to pray in the deserts[723] and charge His disciples to

---

708. Mt 28:18. (The notes for this selection are by Gerhart and Udoh.)

709. Jn 5:22.

710. Jn 3:35–36.

711. Mt 11:27.

712. Jn 6:37.

713. Jn 12:27–28.

714. Mt 26:39; see Mk 14:36; Lk 22:42.

715. Jn 13:21.

716. Lk 2:52.

717. See Mk 8:27; Mt 16:13; Lk 9:18.

718. See Jn 11:34.

719. Mk 6:38; 8:5; Mt 15:34.

720. Mk 15:34; Mt 27:46.

721. Jn 12:28.

722. Jn 17:5.

723. See Mk 1:12–13, 35; Mt 4:1–2; Lk 4:1–2, 42; 5:16; 6:12.

pray lest they should enter into temptation;[724] and, 'The spirit indeed is willing,' He said, 'but the flesh is weak.'[725] And, 'Of that day and that hour knoweth no man, no, nor the Angels, neither the Son.'"[726] Upon this again say the miserable men, "If the Son were, according to your interpretation, eternally existent with God, He had not been ignorant of the Day, but had known as Word; nor had been forsaken as being co-existent; nor had asked to receive glory, as having it in the Father; nor would have prayed at all; for, being the Word, He had needed nothing; but since He is a creature and one of things originate, therefore He thus spoke, and needed what He had not; for it is proper to creatures to require and to need what they have not."

27. This then is what the irreligious men allege in their discourses; and if they thus argue, they might consistently speak yet more daringly; "Why did the Word become flesh at all?" and they might add; "For how could He, being God, become man?" or, "How could the Immaterial bear a body?" or they might speak with Caiaphas still more Judaically, "Wherefore at all did Christ, being a man, make Himself God?"[727] for this and the like the Jews then muttered when they saw, and now the Ario-maniacs disbelieve when they read, and have fallen away into blasphemies. If then a man should carefully parallel the words of these and those, he will of a certainty find them both arriving at the same unbelief, and the daring of their irreligion equal, and their dispute with us a common one. For the Jews said; "How, being a man, can He be God?"[728] And the Arians, "If He were very God from God, how could He become man?" And the Jews were offended then and mocked, saying, "Had He been Son of God, He had not endured the Cross";[729] and the Arians, standing over against them, urge upon us, "How dare ye say that He is the Word proper to the Father's Essence, who had a body, so as to endure all this?" Next, while the Jews sought to kill the Lord, because He said that God was His own Father and made Himself equal to Him, as working what the Father works,[730] the Arians also, not only have learned to deny, both that He is equal to God and that God is the own and natural Father of the Word, but those who hold this they seek to kill. Again, whereas the Jews said, "Is not this the Son of Joseph, whose father and mother we know? how then is it that He saith, 'Before Abraham was, I am, and I came down from heaven?'"[731] the Arians on the other hand make response and say conformably, "How can He be Word or God who slept as man, and wept, and inquired?" Thus both parties deny the Eternity and Godhead of the Word in consequence of those human attributes which the Saviour took on Him by reason of that flesh which He bore.

29. Now the scope and character of Holy Scripture, as we have often said, is this,—it contains a double account of the Saviour; that He was ever God, and is the Son, being the Father's Word and Radiance and Wisdom; and that afterwards for us He took flesh of a Virgin, Mary Bearer of God, and was made man. And this scope is to be found throughout inspired Scripture, as the Lord Himself has said, "search the Scriptures, for they are they which testify of Me."[732] But lest I should exceed in writing, by bringing together all the passages on the subject, let it suffice to mention as a specimen, first John saying, "In the beginning was the Word, and the Word was with God, and the Word was God. The same was in the beginning with God. All things were made by Him, and without Him was made not one thing";[733] next, "And the Word was made flesh and dwelt among us, and we beheld His glory, the glory as of one Only-begotten from the Father";[734] and next Paul writing, "Who being in the form of God, thought it not a prize to be equal with God, but emptied Himself, taking the form of a servant, being made in the likeness of men, and being found in fashion like a man, He humbled Himself, becoming obedient unto death, even the death of the Cross."[735] Any one, beginning with these passages and going through the whole of the Scripture upon the interpretation which they suggest, will perceive how in the beginning the Father said to Him, "Let there be light," and "Let there be a firmament," and "Let us make man";[736] but in fulness of the ages, He sent Him into the world, not that He might judge the world, but that the world by Him might be saved,[737] and how it is written, "Behold, the Virgin shall be with child, and shall bring forth a Son, and they shall call his Name Emmanuel, which, being interpreted, is God with us."[738]

30. The reader then of divine Scripture may acquaint himself with these passages from the ancient books; and from

---

724. See Mk 14:38; Mt 6:13; 26:41; Lk 11:4; 22:40, 46.

725. Mk 14:38; Mt 26:41.

726. Mk 13:32.

727. See Mk 15:60–64; Mt 26:62–66; Lk 22:66–71.

728. See Jn 5:18.

729. See Mt 27:40–44; Mk 15:29–32; Lk 23:35–39.

730. See Jn 5:17–18.

731. Jn 6:42; 8:58; see also Lk 4:22; Mk 6:3; Mt 13:55.

732. Jn 5:39.

733. Jn 1:1–3.

734. Jn 1:14.

735. Phil 2:6–8.

736. Gen 1:1, 6, 26.

737. See Jn 12:47.

738. Mt 1:23; see also Isa 7:14 (Athanasius's quotation here contains some variations from the Septuagint).

the Gospels on the other hand he will perceive that the Lord became man; for "the Word," he says, "became flesh, and dwelt among us."[739] And He became man, and did not come into man; for this it is necessary to know, lest perchance these irreligious men fall into this notion also, and beguile any into thinking, that, as in former times the Word was used to come into each of the Saints, so now He sojourned in a man, hallowing him also, and manifesting Himself as in the others. For if it were so, and He only appeared in a man, it were nothing strange, nor had those who saw Him been startled, saying, Whence is He? and wherefore dost Thou, being a man, make Thyself God? for they were familiar with the idea, from the words, "And the Word of the Lord came" to this or that of the Prophets.[740] But now, since the Word of God, by whom all things came to be, endured to become also Son of man, and humbled Himself, taking a servant's form, therefore to the Jews the Cross of Christ is a scandal, but to us Christ is "God's power" and "God's wisdom";[741] for "the Word," as John says, "became flesh"[742] (it being the custom of Scripture to call man by the name of "flesh," as it says by Joel the Prophet, "I will pour out My Spirit upon all flesh";[743] and as Daniel said to Astyages, "I do not worship idols made with hands, but the Living God, who hath created the heaven and the earth, and hath sovereignty over all flesh";[744] for both he and Joel call mankind flesh).

31. Of old time He was wont to come to the Saints individually, and to hallow those who rightly received Him; but neither, when they were begotten, was it said that He had become man, nor, when they suffered, was it said that He Himself suffered. But when He came among us from Mary once at the end of the ages for the abolition of sin (for so it was pleasing to the Father, to send His own Son "made of a woman, made under the Law"[745]), then it is said, that He took flesh and became man, and in that flesh He suffered for us (as Peter says, "Christ therefore having suffered for us in the flesh"[746]), that it might be shewn, and that all might believe, that whereas He was ever God, and hallowed those to whom He came, and ordered all things according to the Father's will,[747] afterwards for our sakes He became man, and "bodily,"[748] as the Apostle says, the Godhead dwelt in the flesh; as much as to say, "Being God, He had His own body, and using this as an instrument, He became man for our sakes." And on account of this, the properties of the flesh are said to be His, since He was in it, such as to hunger, to thirst, to suffer, to weary, and the like, of which the flesh is capable; while on the other hand the works proper to the Word Himself, such as to raise the dead, to restore sight to the blind, and to

cure the woman with an issue of blood, He did through His own body. And the Word bore the infirmities of the flesh, as His own, for His was the flesh; and the flesh ministered to the works of the Godhead, because the Godhead was in it, for the body was God's. And well has the Prophet said "carried";[749] and has not said, "He remedied our infirmities," lest, as being external to the body, and only healing it, as He has always done, He should leave men subject still to death; but He carries our infirmities, and He Himself bears our sins, that it might be shewn that He has become man for us, and that the body which in Him bore them, was His own body; and, while He received no hurt Himself by "bearing our sins in His body on the tree,"[750] as Peter speaks, we men were redeemed from our own affections, and were filled with the righteousness of the Word.

32. Whence it was that, when the flesh suffered, the Word was not external to it; and therefore is the passion said to be His: and when He did divinely His Father's works, the flesh was not external to Him, but in the body itself did the Lord do them. Hence, when made man, He said, "If I do not the works of the Father, believe Me not; but if I do, though ye believe not Me, believe the works, that ye may know that the Father is in Me and I in Him."[751] And thus when there was need to raise Peter's wife's mother, who was sick of a fever, He stretched forth His hand humanly, but He stopped the illness divinely.[752] And in the case of the man blind from the birth, human was the spittle which He gave forth from the flesh, but divinely did He open the eyes through the clay.[753] And in the case of Lazarus, He gave forth a human voice, as man; but divinely, as God, did He raise Lazarus from the dead.[754] These things were so done, were so manifested, because He had a body, not in appearance, but in truth; and it became the Lord, in putting on human flesh, to put it on whole with the affections proper to it; that, as we say that the body was His own, so also we may say that the affections of the body were proper to Him alone, though they did not touch Him according to His Godhead. If then the body had

739. Jn 1:14.
740. See Jer 1:4, 11, 13; 2:1; Ezek 1:3; 3:16; 6:01, et passim.
741. 1 Cor 1:23–24. 744. Dan 14:5 (Septuagint) = Bel 5.
742. Jn 1:14. 745. Gal 4:4.
743. Joel 2:28; see also Acts 2:17. 746. 1 Pet 4:1.
747. Ps 32:9–11 (Septuagint); see also Ps 33:9–11.
748. Col 2:9. 752. See Mk 1:29–31; Mt 8:14–15.
749. Isa 53:4; see also Mt 8:17. 753. See Jn 9:1–7.
750. 1 Pet 2:24. 754. See Jn 11:41–44.
751. Jn 10:37–38.

been another's, to him too had been the affections attributed; but if the flesh is the Word's (for "the Word became flesh"),[755] of necessity then the affections also of the flesh are ascribed to Him, whose the flesh is. And to whom the affections are ascribed, such namely as to be condemned, to be scourged, to thirst, and the cross, and death, and the other infirmities of the body, of Him too is the triumph and the grace. For this cause then, consistently and fittingly such affections are ascribed not to another, but to the Lord; that the grace also may be from Him, and that we may become, not worshippers of any other, but truly devout towards God, because we invoke no originate thing, no ordinary man, but the natural and true Son from God, who has become man, yet is not the less Lord and God and Saviour.

33. Who will not admire this? or who will not agree that such a thing is truly divine? for if the works of the Word's Godhead had not taken place through the body, man had not been deified; and again, had not the properties of the flesh been ascribed to the Word, man had not been thoroughly delivered from them; but though they had ceased for a little while, as I said before, still sin had remained in him and corruption, as was the case with mankind before Him; and for this reason: —Many for instance have been made holy and clean from all sin; nay, Jeremiah was hallowed even from the womb,[756] and John, while yet in the womb, leapt for joy at the voice of Mary Bearer of God;[757] nevertheless "death reigned from Adam to Moses, even over those that had not sinned after the similitude of Adam's transgression";[758] and thus man remained mortal and corruptible as before, liable to the affections proper to their nature. But now the Word having become man and having appropriated what pertains to the flesh, no longer do these things touch the body, because of the Word who has come in it, but they are destroyed by Him, and henceforth men no longer remain sinners and dead according to their proper affections, but having risen according to the Word's power, they abide ever immortal and incorruptible. Whence also, whereas the flesh is born of Mary Bearer of God, He Himself is said to have been born, who furnishes to others an origin of being; in order that He may transfer our origin into Himself, and we may no longer, as mere earth, return to earth, but as being knit into the Word from heaven, may be carried to heaven by Him. Therefore in like manner not without reason has He transferred to Himself the other affections of the body also; that we, no longer as being men, but as proper to the Word, may have share in eternal life. . . .

34. And that one may attain to a more exact knowledge of the impassibility of the Word's nature and of the infirmities ascribed to Him because of the flesh, it will be well to listen to the blessed Peter; for he will be a trustworthy witness concerning the Saviour. He writes then in his Epistle thus; "Christ then having suffered for us in the flesh."[759] Therefore also when He is said to hunger and thirst and to toil and not to know, and to sleep, and to weep, and to ask, and to flee, and to be born, and to deprecate the cup, and in a word to undergo all that belongs to the flesh, let it be said, as is congruous, in each case, "Christ then hungering and thirsting 'for us in the flesh'"; and "saying He did not know, and being buffeted, and toiling 'for us in the flesh'"; and "being exalted too, and born, and growing 'in the flesh'"; and "fearing and hiding 'in the flesh'"; and "saying, 'If it be possible let this cup pass from Me,' and being beaten, and receiving, 'for us in the flesh'"; and in a word all such things "for us in the flesh." For on this account has the Apostle himself said, "Christ then having suffered," not in His Godhead, but "for us in the flesh," that these affections may be acknowledged as, not proper to the very Word by nature, but proper by nature to the very flesh.

Let no one then stumble at what belongs to man, but rather let a man know that in nature the Word Himself is impassible, and yet because of that flesh which He put on, these things are ascribed to Him, since they are proper to the flesh, and the body itself is proper to the Saviour. And while He Himself, being impassible in nature, remains as He is, not harmed by these affections, but rather obliterating and destroying them, men, their passions as if changed and abolished in the Impassible, henceforth become themselves also impassible and free from them for ever, as John taught, saying, "And ye know that He was manifested to take away our sins, and in Him is no sin."[760] . . .

35. These points we have found it necessary first to examine, that, when we see Him doing or saying aught divinely through the instrument of His own body, we may know that He so works, being God, and also, if we see Him speaking or suffering humanly, we may not be ignorant that He bore flesh and became man, and hence He so acts and so speaks. For if

---

755. Jn 1:14.

756. See Jer 1:5.

757. See Lk 1:43. The term "bearer of God" (*theotokos*) will become central in the controversy between Nestorius and Cyril.

758. Rom 5:14.

759. 1 Pet 4:1.

760. 1 Jn 3:5.

we recognise what is proper to each, and see and understand that both these things and those are done by One, we are right in our faith, and shall never stray. But if a man looking at what is done divinely by the Word, deny the body, or looking at what is proper to the body, deny the Word's presence in the flesh, or from what is human entertain low thoughts concerning the Word, such a one, as a Jewish vintner mixing water with the wine,[761] shall account the Cross an offence, or as a Gentile, will deem the preaching folly.[762] This then is what happens to God's enemies the Arians; for looking at what is human in the Saviour, they have judged Him a creature. Therefore they ought, looking also at the divine works of the Word, to deny the origination of His body, and henceforth to rank themselves with Manichees. But for them, learn they, however tardily, that "the Word became flesh";[763] and let us, retaining the general scope of the faith, acknowledge that what they interpret ill, has a right interpretation.

37. And while such is the sense of expressions like these, those which speak humanly concerning the Saviour admit of a religious meaning also. For with this end have we examined them beforehand, that, if we should hear Him asking where Lazarus is laid,[764] or when He asks on coming into the parts of Caesarea, "Whom do men say that I am?"[765] or, "How many loaves have ye?"[766] and, "What will ye that I shall do unto you?"[767] we may know, from what has been already said, the right sense of the passages, and may not stumble as Christ's enemies the Arians. First then we must put this question to the irreligious, why they consider Him ignorant? for one who asks, does not for certain ask from ignorance; but it is possible for one who knows, still to ask concerning what He knows. Thus John was aware that Christ, when asking, "How many loaves have ye?" was not ignorant, for he says, "And this He said to prove him, for He Himself knew what He would do."[768] But if He knew what He was doing, therefore not in ignorance, but with knowledge did He ask. From this instance we may understand similar ones; that, when the Lord asks, He does not ask in ignorance, where Lazarus lies, nor again, whom men do say that He is; but knowing the thing which He was asking, aware what He was about to do. And thus with ease is their clever point exploded; but if they still persist on account of His asking, then they must be told that in the Godhead indeed ignorance is not, but to the flesh ignorance is proper, as has been said. And that this is really so, observe how the Lord who inquired where Lazarus lay, Himself said, when He was not on the spot but a great way off, "Lazarus is dead,"[769] and where he was dead; and how

that He who is considered by them as ignorant, is He Himself who foreknew the reasonings of the disciples, and was aware of what was in the heart of each, and of "what was in man,"[770] and, what is greater, alone knows the Father and says, "I in the Father and the Father in Me."[771]

38. Therefore this is plain to every one, that the flesh indeed is ignorant, but the Word Himself, considered as the Word, knows all things even before they come to be. For He did not, when He became man, cease to be God; nor, whereas He is God does He shrink from what is man's; perish the thought; but rather, being God, He has taken to Him the flesh, and being in the flesh deifies the flesh. For as He asked questions in it, so also in it did He raise the dead; and He shewed to all that He who quickens the dead and recalls the soul, much more discerns the secret of all. And He knew where Lazarus lay, and yet He asked; for the All-holy Word of God, who endured all things for our sakes, did this, that so carrying our ignorance, He might vouchsafe to us the knowledge of His own only and true Father, and of Himself, sent because of us for the salvation of all, than which no grace could be greater.

From Saint Athanasius, *Select Writings and Letters,* A Select Library of Nicene and Post-Nicene Fathers of the Christian Church, edited by Philip Schaff and Henry Wace, 2nd series, vol. 4 (1892; Grand Rapids, MI: Eerdmans, 1978), 407–8, 409–14.

☙ **Apollinaris of Laodicea** (ca. 315–92), Athanasius's ally in the crusade against Arianism, made explicit the assumptions of Athanasius's conception of the Incarnation and drew the logical conclusions. Apollinaris, a well-respected supporter of the Nicene Creed who taught without opposition for thirty years, was condemned as a heretic first by Damasus, bishop of Rome (366–84), then by a local synod at Antioch, and finally by the Council of Constantinople in 381. His surviving work, *On the Union in Christ of the Body with the Godhead,* written around 361, was transmitted under pseudonyms.

---

761. See Isa 1:22 (Septuagint).
762. See 1 Cor 1:23.
763. Jn 1:14.
764. See Jn 11:34.
765. Mk 8:27; Mt 16:13; Lk 9:18.
766. Mk 6:38; 8:5; Mt 15:34.
767. Mk 10:51; Mt 20:32; Lk 18:41.
768. Jn 6:6.
769. Jn 11:14.
770. Jn 2:24–25; see also Mk 2:6–8; Mt 9:3–4; Lk 5:21–22; 6:7–8.
771. Jn 14:11.

On the Union in Christ of the Body with the Godhead

1. Rightly is the Lord confessed to have been a child who was holy from the beginning, even in what concerns his body. And in this regard he differs from every other body, for he was conceived in his mother not in separation from the Godhead but in union with it, just as the angel says, "The holy Spirit shall come upon you, and the power of the Most High shall overshadow you, so that your holy offspring will be called Son of God."[772] Moreover, there was a heavenly descent, not merely a birth from a woman; it is said not only "Born of a woman, born under the Law"[773] but also "No one shall ascend into heaven, save he who came down from heaven, the Son of man."[774] 2. And it is not possible to take the body separately and call it a creature, since it is altogether inseparable from him whose body it is. Rather, it shares in the title of the uncreated and in the name of God, because it is conjoined into unity with God, just as it is said that "the Word became flesh"[775] and, by the apostle, "The last Adam became a life-giving Spirit."[776]

3. Just as we attribute glory to the body by reason of the divine conjunction and its unity with God, so we ought not to deny the inglorious attributes that stem from the body. These are, in the words of the apostle, "to be born of a woman"[777] and, in the words of the prophet, "to have been formed from the womb as a slave to God,"[778] really to be named "human being" and "Son of man" and to be reckoned later than Abraham by the many generations after which he became man. 4. Indeed, it is necessary to speak and to hear [of him][779] in human terms, even as, when he is called truly a human being, no one will deny the divine essence which, together with the body, that title signifies; and when he is called a slave by reason of his body,[780] no one will deny the royal nature which, together with the body, is signified by name of slavery; and again, when a heavenly man is said to have descended from heaven, no one will deny that the earthly body is knit together with the Godhead. He is not divided either in fact or in name when, by reason of his conjunction with the form of a slave and with the created body, the Lord is called a slave, and the uncreated is styled "made."

5. The confession is that in him the creature is in unity with the uncreated, while the uncreated is commingled with the creature, so that one nature is constituted out of the parts severally, and the Word contributes a special energy to the whole together with the divine perfection. The same thing happens in the case of the ordinary man, made up as he is of two incomplete parts which together fill out one nature and are signified by one name; for at the same time the whole is called "flesh" without the soul's being thereby stripped away, and the whole is styled "soul" without the body's being stripped away (if, indeed, it is something else alongside the soul). 6. So the God who became human, the Lord and ruler of all that comes to be, may have come to be of a woman, yet he is Lord. He may have been formed after the fashion of slaves, yet he is Spirit. He may be proclaimed as flesh because of his union with the flesh, yet according to the apostle he is not a human being; and though he is preached as human by the same apostle, yet he calls the whole Christ invisible God transformed by a visible body, uncreated God made manifest in a created garment. He emptied himself after the fashion of a slave, but in his divine essence he is unemptied and unaltered and undiminished (for no alteration can affect the divine nature), neither is he decreased or increased.

7. When he says, "Glorify me," this utterance stems from the body, and the glorification touches the body, but the reference is to Christ as a whole, because the whole is one. He adds, ". . . with the glory which I possessed with you before the existence of the world"[781] and manifests the eternally glorious Godhead, but though this expression peculiarly befits the Godhead, it was spoken inclusively with reference to the whole. 8. Thus he is both coessential with God in the invisible Spirit (the flesh being comprehended in the title because it has been united to that which is coessential with God), and again coessential with men (the Godhead being comprehended with the body because it has been united to what is coessential with us). And the nature of the flesh is not altered by its union with what is coessential with God and by its participation in the title of *homoousios*, even as the nature of the Godhead is not changed by its participation of a human body and by bearing the name of a flesh coessential with us.

9. When Paul said, ". . . who was begotten of the seed of David according to the flesh,"[782] he meant that the Son of

---

772. Lk l:35. (The notes for this selection are by Gerhart and Udoh.)
773. Gal 4:4.   776. 1 Cor 15:45.
774. Jn 3:13.   777. Gal 4:4.
775. Jn 1:14.   778. Isa 49:5.
779. Words in brackets have been added by the translator.
780. See Phil 2:7.
781. Jn 17:5.
782. Rom 1:3.

God was so born, and he did not name the flesh as something separate and say, "The flesh was born of the seed of David." When he says, "Let this mind be in you which was also in Christ Jesus, who, being in the form of God, did not judge equality with God a thing to be grasped at,"[783] he did not make a division and say, "Whose Godhead, [being] in the form of God the Logos, did not judge equality with God a thing to be snatched at." And yet the Godhead was not named "Jesus" before his birth from a virgin;[784] neither did it receive the chrism of the holy Spirit, because the Word of God is the giver of the Spirit, not the one who is sanctified by the Spirit.

10. Furthermore, he says, "On their account I sanctify myself, in order that they themselves may be sanctified in truth."[785] He does not make a division and say, "I sanctify the flesh." Rather, he makes a conjunction and says, "I sanctify myself," even though, for anyone who considers the matter with care, it is not possible for him to be the agent of his own sanctification, for if the whole sanctifies, what is sanctified? And if the whole is sanctified, what is the sanctifying agent? Nevertheless, he preserves the one person and the indivisible manifestation of one life, and attributes both the act of sanctifying and the sanctification which results to the whole Christ. This he does in order that it may be clear and certain to us that one agent does not sanctify another in the prophetic or apostolic fashion—as the Spirit sanctifies the prophets and apostles just as Paul says, concerning the whole church, "called to be saints and sanctified in Christ Jesus,"[786] and the Savior himself says concerning the apostles, "Sanctify them in truth."[787] 11. For humankind as a whole is involved in being sanctified, not in sanctifying. And the angelic order, like the whole creation, is being sanctified and illuminated, while the Spirit sanctifies and illuminates. But the Logos sanctifies and illuminates through the Spirit, being in no wise sanctified, for the Logos is Creator and not creature. Here, however, there is sanctification, and embodiment as well, and though the two things are distinct, they are one by reason of the union of the flesh with the Godhead, so that there is no separation of one which sanctifies and another which is sanctified, and the incarnation itself is in every way a sanctification.

12. To those who said, "You, being a man, make yourself God,"[788] the Savior gave, by way of reply, the rationale of his own manhood. He said, "Do you say, 'You blaspheme,' to him whom the Father sanctified and sent into the world, because I said, 'I am the Son of God'?"[789] What sanctification is this of which he speaks, save the sanctification of the flesh by the Godhead? For in these circumstances the body lives by the sanctification of the Godhead and not by the provision of a human soul, and the whole is completely joined in one. Moreover, his saying "whom the Father sanctified and sent" means that the sanctifier is sanctified together with that which is sanctified; he attaches the sanctifier to that which is sanctified. 13. Elsewhere he explains this sanctification [by saying] that it was the birth from a virgin. "For to this end was I born and to this end did I come into the world, that I might bear witness to the truth."[790] The ordinary man is ensouled and lives by the will of the flesh and the will of the husband; the spermatic substance which is emitted carries the life-giving power into the receptive womb. But the holy child born of the Virgin was constituted by the coming of Spirit and the overshadowing of power.[791] A spermatic substance did not bring about the divine life; rather, a spiritual and divine power afforded a divine conception to the Virgin and gave the gift of the divine offspring. 14. Thus, both the exaltation of Christ and his being accorded the name above every name[792] [took place] in accordance with the manner of the union, even though the exaltation is proper to the flesh which ascended from below. But because the flesh does not ascend by itself, the whole [Christ] is inclusively termed "exalted," and the reception of grace is connected with him in virtue of the flesh which was brought from humiliation to glory, for grace does not add glory to the ever-glorious Word; what was existing and abiding existed in the form of God and was equal to God.

15. Even in the flesh the Lord says that he is equal to God, since according to John he says that God is his own Father and he makes himself equal to God.[793] What he possesses he cannot receive, even as, because the flesh receives what it does not possess (impassibility instead of affliction with passions, a heavenly instead of an earthly way of life, royal authority instead of slavery in subjection to men, being worshipped by the whole creation instead of giving worship to another), his being graced with the Name above every name is ascribed to the whole [Christ]. 16. Furthermore, if anyone dares to separate mention of grace from the Name above every name, neither of the two will be properly spoken, for if the gift is to the Word as to one who does not possess it,

---

783. Phil 2:5–6.

784. See Lk 1:30–31.

785. Jn 17:19.

786. 1 Cor 1:2.

787. Jn 17:17.

788. Jn 10:33.

789. Jn 10:36.

790. Jn 18:37.

791. See Lk 1:35.

792. See Phil 2:9–10.

793. See Jn 5:18.

the Name above every name is no longer given by grace. And if he possesses this not by gift but by nature (as he does possess it in his Godhead), then it is not possible that this be given him. 17. Of necessity, therefore, both that which is corporeal and that which is divine are predicated of the whole Christ. And the man who cannot, in different things which are united, recognize what is characteristic of each shall fall clumsily into contradictions, but he who both acknowledges the distinctive characteristics and preserves the union shall neither falsify the nature nor be ignorant of the union.

From Richard A. Norris Jr., ed. and trans., *The Christological Controversy* (Philadelphia: Fortress, 1980), 103–7. [Ellipsis in original.]

⮞ The Christological controversy, in its classical form, erupted in 428 due to the publication of *The First Sermon against the Theotokos* by **Nestorius** (d. 451), a monk from Antioch, who in that year had become the bishop of Constantinople. Nestorius argued against the Alexandrian use of the title *theotokos,* meaning "God bearer" (that is, "mother of God"), for the Virgin Mary, proposing instead the term *theodochos,* "recipient of God." Cyril of Alexandria, Nestorius's political and theological rival, responded quickly, and a heated theological correspondence between Nestorius and Cyril ensued that escalated the ongoing strife between the Antiochene and Alexandrian traditions. In *The Second Letter to Cyril of Alexandria,* Nestorius responds to Cyril's criticisms by maintaining his belief in the union of "two hypostases" and "two natures."

NESTORIUS

The First Sermon against the Theotokos

The human race was adorned with ten thousand gifts when it was dignified by a gift which was furthest away and nearest to hand—the Lord's incarnation. Because humanity is the image of the divine nature, but the devil overthrew this image and cast it down into corruption, God grieved over his image as a king might grieve over his statue, and renewed the ruined likeness. Without male seed, he fashioned from the Virgin a nature like Adam's (who was himself formed without male seed) and through a human being brought about the revival of the human race. "Since," Paul says, "death came through a human being, through a human being also came the resurrection of the dead."[794]

Let those people pay attention to these words who, blinded with regard to the dispensation of the Lord's incarnation, "do not understand either the words they employ or the things they are talking about."[795] I mean those who, as we have now learned, are always inquiring among us now this way and now that: "Is Mary *theotokos,*" they say (that is, the bearer or mother of God), "or is she on the contrary *anthropotokos*" (that is, the bearer or mother of a human being)?

Does God have a mother? A Greek without reproach introducing mothers for the gods! Is Paul then a liar when he says of the deity of Christ, "without father, without mother, without genealogy"?[796] Mary, my friend, did not give birth to the Godhead (for "what is born of the flesh is flesh"[797]). A creature did not produce him who is uncreatable. The Father has not just recently generated God the Logos from the Virgin (for "in the beginning was the Logos," as John says[798]). A creature did not produce the Creator, rather she gave birth to the human being, the instrument of the Godhead. The Holy Spirit did not create God the Logos (for "what is born of her is of the Holy Spirit"[799]). Rather, he formed out of the Virgin a temple for God the Logos, a temple in which he dwelt.

Moreover, the incarnate God did not die; he raised up the one in whom he was incarnate. He stooped down to raise up what had collapsed, but he did not fall ("The Lord looked down from heaven over the sons of men"[800]). Nor, because he stooped to lift up the guilty who had fallen, may he be disparaged as if he himself had sunk to the ground. God saw the ruined nature, and the power of the Godhead took hold of it in its shattered state. God held on to it while himself remaining what he had been, and lifted it up high.

For the sake of an illustration of what is meant, note this: If you want to lift up someone who is lying down, do you not touch body with body and, by joining yourself to the other person, lift up the hurt one while you, joined to him in this fashion, remain what you were? This is the way to think of the mystery of the incarnation. [. . .]

That is why Paul also says, "who *is* the radiance of his glory,"[801] lest, namely, someone who had heard the words "He *was* in the form of God"[802] should conjecture that his nature is transitory and has been altered. John, it is true, when describing the shared and mutual eternity of the Logos and the Father, uses these words: "In the beginning was the Logos."[803] He does not use the word *is,* he did not say, "In the beginning

---

794. 1 Cor 15:21. (The notes for this selection are by Gerhart and Udoh.)

795. 1 Tim 1:7.

796. Heb 7:3.

797. Jn 3:6.

798. Jn 1:1.

799. Mt 1:20.

800. Ps 13:2 (Septuagint) = Ps 14:2.

801. Heb 1:3.

802. Phil 2:6.

803. Jn 1:1.

is the Logos, and the Logos *is* with God." No. He said, "In the beginning *was* the Logos, and the Logos *was* with God, and the Logos *was* God." For the question concerned the original subsistence of the being which carried the humanity. Paul, however, recounts all at once everything which happened, that the [divine] being has become incarnate and that the immutability of the incarnate deity is always maintained after the union. That is why, as he writes, he cries out, "Let this mind be in you which was also in Christ Jesus, who being in the form of God . . . emptied himself, taking the form of a slave."[804] He did not say, "Let this mind be in you which was in God the Logos, who being in the form of God, took the form of a slave." Rather, he takes the term *Christ* to be an expression which signifies the two natures, and without risk he applies to him both the style "form of a slave," which he took, and that of God. The descriptions are different from each other by reason of the mysterious fact that the natures are two in number.

Furthermore, it is not only this—that Christ as God is unaffected by change—which must be proclaimed to Christians but also that he is benevolent, that he takes "the form of a slave" while existing as he was, in order that you may know not only that he was not altered after the union but that he has been revealed as both benevolent and just.

For the sinless death for sinners belongs to his flesh, and it is a gift of inestimable benevolence that he did not spurn a death on behalf of his enemies, for according to Paul, "one will scarcely die for a righteous person."[805] Furthermore, to accept the human race by the agency of a human being and to reconcile Adam represents a vast policy of justice. It was just to set free this nature which had offended, now again made pleasing to God, and it is just to absolve the nature, formerly liable to punishment, which had incurred the debt. Humanity owed God an unblamable life lived without complaint, but it fell short in carrying out its duty. Since the soul was stripped of virtues, the passions resulting from its heedlessness drove it hither and thither, and rare were the possessors of piety and virtue—just consider the people who, in the deprived circumstances of that time, seemed or were thought to possess it! Through the whole earth debt was in power ("For all," says Paul, "have sinned, and fall short of the glory of God"[806]), and the consequences of sin were growing.

What, then, of the Lord Christ? Perceiving that the human race was tied up in its sins and unworthy of restoration, he did not dissolve the debt by an order, lest mercy violate justice. And the apostle Paul is a witness of this when he exclaims, "Christ, whom God set forth as an expiation through faith in his blood to demonstrate his justice"[807]—that mercy, he means, may be shown to be just and not something bestowed without judgment here and there and how you please.

Consequently, Christ assumed the person of the debt-ridden nature and by its mediation paid the debt back as a son of Adam, for it was obligatory that the one who dissolved the debt come from the same race as he who had once contracted it. The debt had its start from a woman,[808] and the remission had its start from a woman.[809]

But learn what the nature of the debt was, in order that you may learn what the repayment was. Adam became liable to punishment because of food. Christ releases him from this punishment by fasting in the desert, by spurning the devil's counsel about the refreshment that food brings.[810] Adam fell into the guilt of seeking divinity for himself in opposition to God, since he had heard the devil say, "You will be as gods,"[811] and had quickly snatched the bait. But Christ releases him by his answer to the devil when the latter made a promise of power (for he said to him, "I will give you everything if you will fall down and worship me").[812] Christ himself rejected the devil's words: "Depart, Satan; you shall worship the Lord God and you shall serve him alone."[813] Because of his disobedience in the case of a tree, Adam was under sentence of punishment; Christ made up for this debt, too, "having become obedient"[814] on a tree. That is why Paul said, "He took away the handwritten bond of our sins, which stood against us, nailing it to the cross."[815] Moreover, the one who made restoration on our behalf is Christ, for in him our nature discharges its debt. He had assumed a person of the same nature [as ours], whose passions were removed by his passion, since, as Paul put it, "We have redemption in his blood."[816]

Now see our nature, in God's company in Christ, pleading its case against the devil and employing the following valid arguments. "I am oppressed by wrong, O most just judge. The wicked devil attacks me; he uses my powerlessness against me in a manifest assertion of unjust power. Be it so that he handed the former Adam over to death because he was the occasion of [Adam's] sinning; and now the Second Adam,

---

804. Phil 2:5–7.
805. Rom 5:7.
806. Rom 3:23.
807. Rom 3:24–25.
808. See Gen 3:1–16.
809. See Gal 4:4–5.
810. See Mt 4:1–4; Lk 4:1–4.

811. Gen 3:5.
812. Mt 4:9; see also Lk 4:7.
813. Mt 4:10; see also Lk 4:8.
814. Phil 2:8.
815. Col 2:14.
816. Eph 1:7.

whom you have formed out of a virgin—for what offense, O King, has he crucified him? What is the reason that he has hanged thieves together with him? Why is it that he who did no sin, neither was guile found in his mouth, is reckoned with the transgressors?[817] Or is it possible that his execrable intent is not obvious? He is openly envious of me, Lord, in my role as your image. Without any occasion, he attacks me and attempts to overthrow me. But show yourself a just judge on my behalf. You have been angry at me by reason of Adam's transgression. I beseech you, on his behalf, to be favorable, if it be the case that you have joined to you an Adam who is without sin. Be it so that on account of the former Adam you have handed me over to corruption; on this one's account, make me partake of incorruption. Both of them have my nature. As I shared in the death of the former, so I shall become a participant in the immortal life of the second. . . . "

Just as the devil held the protoplast's sin against his whole posterity and sustained the original charge, so too, when our nature had in Christ come into possession of the guiltless firstfruits of its total body, it struggled against the devil and conquered, by means of the very weapons which the adversary had used previously. If the devil urges the earlier causes of our condemnation on the basis of what Adam did, it pleads against him with complete justification the blameless origin of its firstfruits in Christ. Paul says, "It is Christ, who died for our sins, and more, who rose from the dead and is at the right hand of God, who also intervenes on our behalf."[818] Our nature, having been put on by Christ like a garment, intervenes on our behalf, being entirely free from all sin and contending by appeal to its blameless origin, just as the Adam who was formed earlier brought punishment upon his race by reason of his sin. This was the opportunity which belonged to the assumed man, as a human being to dissolve, by means of the flesh, that corruption which arose by means of the flesh. The third-day burial belonged to this man, not to the deity. His feet were fastened down by nails; he is the one whom the Holy Spirit formed in the womb. It was about this flesh that the Lord said to the Jews, "Destroy this temple and in three days I will raise it up."[819]

Am I the only one who calls Christ "twofold"? Does he not call himself both a destroyable temple and God who raises it up? And if it was God who was destroyed—and let that blasphemy be shifted to the head of Arius!—the Lord would have said, "Destroy this God and in three days I will raise him up." If God died when consigned to the grave, the Gospel saying "Why do you seek to kill me, a man, who have spoken truth to you?"[820] is meaningless.

But Christ is not a mere man, O slanderer! No, he is at once God and man. If he were God alone, he would have needed, O Apollinaris, to say, "Why do you seek to destroy me, who am God, who have spoken the truth to you?" What, in fact, he says is, "Why do you seek to kill me, a man?" This is he who is crowned with the crown of thorns.[821] This is he who says, "My God, my God, why have you forsaken me?"[822] This is he who suffered a death of three days' duration. But I worship this one together with the Godhead because he is a sharer in the divine authority; "for let it be apparent, men and brothers," says the Scripture, "that the remission of sins is preached to us through Christ."[823]

I adore him as the instrument of the Lord's goodness, for he says, "Be kind and merciful to one another, even as God has given to us in Christ."[824] I honor him as the meeting place of God's counsels, for "I want you to have knowledge of the mystery of God the Father and Christ, in whom all the treasures of wisdom and knowledge are hidden."[825] I receive him as the "form"[826] which makes promise on God's behalf for us. "He who sent me," he says, "is true, and I speak the things which I have heard from him."[827] I bless him as the pledge of peace; "for he," it says, "is our peace, who made the two one, and destroyed the wall of division in between, enmities in his flesh."[828] I worship him as the expiation of divine wrath: "Christ," he says, "God set forth as an expiation for faith through faith in his blood."[829] I love and revere him as the beginning of immortality for mortals; "for he," it says, "is the head of his body, the church, who is the beginning, the firstborn from the dead."[830] I embrace him as the mirror of the resplendent deity: for "God," it says, "was in Christ reconciling the world to himself."[831] I adore him as the living glory of the King; for "constituted in the form of God, he emptied himself, taking the form of a slave, and was found in the condition of a human being."[832] I praise him as the hand of God which snatches me out of the hand of death for life; for "when I have been lifted up," he says, "from the earth, then I will draw all to myself."[833] And who it is who is exalted

817. See 1 Pet 2:22; Isa 53:12.

818. Rom 8:34.

819. Jn 2:19, 21.

820. Jn 8:40.

821. See Mk 15:17; Mt 27:29; Jn 19:2.

822. Mk 15:34; Mt 27:46.

823. Acts 13:38.

824. Eph 4:32.

825. Col 2:1–3.

826. See Phil 2:6–7.

827. Jn 8:26.

828. Eph 2:14.

829. Rom 3:24–25.

830. Col 1:18.

831. 2 Cor 5:19.

832. Phil 2:6–7.

833. Jn 12:32.

the faithful scribe tells us when he says, "For this he said to show by what death he would die."[834] I marvel at him as the door through which one enters upon divine things; for "I am the door," he says; "anyone who enters through me will be set free and will go in and go out and will find a dwelling."[835] I worship him as the image of the all-sovereign deity; for "God exalted him and gave him the name above every name, so that at the name of Jesus every knee shall bow, of things in heaven and things on earth and things under the earth, and every tongue confess that Jesus Christ is Lord."[836] I revere the one who is borne because of the one who carries him, and I worship the one I see because of the one who is hidden. God is undivided from the one who appears, and therefore I do not divide the honor of that which is not divided. I divide the natures, but I unite the worship.

Attend to what is said here. That which was formed in the womb is not in itself God. That which was created by the Spirit was not in itself God. That which was buried in the tomb was not in itself God. If that were the case, we should manifestly be worshipers of a human being and worshipers of the dead. But since God is within the one who was assumed, the one who was assumed is styled God because of the one who assumed him. That is why the demons shudder at the mention of the crucified flesh; they know that God has been joined to the crucified flesh, even though he has not shared its suffering.

Therefore also this one who appeared to people's sight will come as judge, because he is joined to omnipotent deity. "For at that time," it says, "the sign of the Son of man will appear in the sky, and they will see the Son of man coming on the clouds of the sky with power and great glory."[837] Just as a king whose victory has been won appears in his cities with the arms with which he conquered the enemy in war and wants himself to be seen in their company, so the King who is Lord of all things will come to his creatures with a cross and with flesh, to be seen with these arms by which he overcame impiety. And with almighty power he will judge the earth in the form of a human being, in accordance with Paul's proclamation: "The times of ignorance God overlooked, but now he commands all persons everywhere to repent, since he has determined a day on which he will judge the world through a man, in whom he determined to give an assurance to all by raising him from the dead."[838] [. . .]

[. . .] so let us begin to tremble at the Lord's incarnation, speaking in divine terms of the "form" which received God (*theodochos*) together with the divine Logos, as the inseparable image of the divine authority, as the image of the hid-

den Judge. We confess both and adore them as one, for the duality of the natures is one on account of the unity. Hear Paul proclaiming both the eternity of the Only Begotten's deity and the recent birth of the humanity, and the fact that the dignity of the association or conjunction has been made one. "Jesus Christ," he says, "is the same yesterday and today and forever."[839] Amen.

From Richard A. Norris Jr., ed. and trans., *The Christological Controversy* (Philadelphia: Fortress, 1980), 124–31.

NESTORIUS

The Second Letter to Cyril of Alexandria

To his most reverend and God-fearing fellow minister Cyril Nestorius sends greeting in the Lord.

The rebukes which your astonishing letter brings against us I forgive. What it deserves is a healing generosity of spirit and the reply which comes to it at the proper time by way of actual deeds. This, though, does not permit silence, for if silence be kept, great danger is involved. On this account, standing against your prolixity as far as may be possible, I will attempt to make my exposition brief and maintain my distaste for obscure and indigestible haranguing.

I shall begin from Your Charity's all-wise utterances, having first quoted them expressly. Here, then, are some statements from the astonishing teaching of your letter.

"The great and holy synod[840] stated that the unique Son himself—naturally begotten out of God the Father, true God out of true God, light out of light, through whom the Father made everything that exists—descended, was enfleshed, became human, suffered, rose." These are Your Piety's words, and you doubtless acknowledge them as yours.

Now hear our brotherly exhortation on behalf of true religion, in accordance with the testimony which that great one, Paul, gave to Timothy his friend. "Give heed to reading, to exhortation, to teaching . . . , for by doing this you will save both yourself and your hearers."[841]

What does this phrase "give heed" mean to me? That in reading the doctrine of those holy men superficially, you did not recognize the excusable want of perception in your judg-

---

834. Jn 12:33.
835. Jn 10:9.
836. Phil 2:9–11.
837. Mt 24:30.
838. Acts 17:30–31.
839. Heb 13:8.
840. That is, of Nicaea. (The notes for this selection are by Gerhart and Udoh.)
841. 1 Tim 4:13–16.

ment that they assert the possibility of the Logos who is coeternal with God. So if it seems right, examine what was said more closely, and you will discover that the divine chorus of the Fathers did not say that the coessential Godhead is passible or that the Godhead which is coeternal with the Father has only just been born, or that he who has raised up the temple which was destroyed[842] has [himself] risen. And if you will give me your attention for the sake of brotherly correction, I will explain to you the utterances of those holy men and deliver you from calumnies against them and, through them, against the Holy Scriptures.

"We also believe," they said, "in our Lord Jesus Christ, his only-begotten Son." Observe how they first of all establish, as foundations, the titles which are common to the deity and the humanity—"Lord" and "Jesus" and "Christ" and "Only Begotten" and "Son"—and then build on them the teaching about his becoming human and his passion and resurrection, in order that, since the titles which signify and are common to both natures are set in the foreground, the things which pertain to the sonship and lordship are not divided and the things peculiar to the natures within the unitary sonship do not get endangered by the suggestion of a confusion.

Paul himself was their instructor in this matter. He refers to the divine act of becoming human, and since he is about to add mention of the passion, he first posits the title "Christ," the title which, as I said earlier, is common to the two natures, and then introduces words that are appropriate to the two natures. What does he say? "Let this mind be in you which was also in Christ Jesus, who being in the form of God, did not think equality with God something to be snatched at, but"—to shorten the quotation—"became obedient to death, even the death of the Cross."[843] Since he was about to recall the death, lest anyone for that reason suppose that God the Logos is passible, he inserts the word "Christ," because it is the term which signifies the impassible and the passible essence in one unitary person, with the result that Christ is without risk called both impassible and passible—impassible in the Godhead but passible in the nature of the body.

I could say many things about this—first that those holy fathers spoke not of birth when they were thinking of God's saving dispensation but of coming to be in a human being—but I realize that my opening promise of brevity constrains my speech and turns me to Your Charity's second head. In this connection I commended the distinction of natures in accordance with the special character of humanity and deity, the conjunction of these natures in one person, the denial that the Logos has need of a second birth from a woman,

and the confession that the Godhead is not susceptible to passion. Certainly such beliefs are most truly orthodox and contrary to the evil teachings of all the heresies about the Lord's natures. If, however, the remainder conveys some hidden wisdom, incapable of being grasped by the hearing of its readers, that is for your acuteness to understand. To me it seemed right to center interest on the primary issues, for I do not see how he reintroduced as passible and newly created one who had first been proclaimed as impassible and incapable of a second birth—as if the qualities which attach naturally to God the Logos are corrupted by his conjunction with his temple; or as if people consider it a small thing that the sinless temple, which is also inseparable from the divine nature, underwent birth and death on behalf of sinners; or as if the Lord's saying, cried out to the Jews, is not worthy of belief: "Destroy this temple and in three days I will raise it."[844] He did not say, "Destroy my divinity and in three days I will raise it."

Wishing again to expand on this theme too, I am brought to a halt by the recollection of my promise. Nevertheless, I must speak, while using brevity.

Everywhere in Holy Scripture, whenever mention is made of the saving dispensation of the Lord, what is conveyed to us is the birth and suffering not of the deity but of the humanity of Christ, so that by a more exact manner of speech the holy Virgin is called Mother of Christ, not Mother of God. Listen to these words of the Gospels: "The book of the birth of Jesus Christ, son of David, son of Abraham."[845] It is obvious that the son of David was not the divine Logos. And hear another witness, if it seems right: "Jacob begat Joseph, the husband of Mary, of whom was born Jesus who is called Christ."[846] Consider another voice bearing witness for us: "The birth of Jesus Christ was on this wise, for when his mother Mary was betrothed to Joseph, she was discovered to have conceived in her womb by the Holy Spirit."[847] Shall I suppose that the deity of the Only Begotten is a creature of the Spirit? And what shall it mean that "the mother of Jesus was there"?[848] And again, "with Mary the mother of Jesus";[849] and "that which is born in her is of the Holy Spirit";[850] and "Take the child and his mother and flee into Egypt";[851] and "con-

842. See Jn 2:19–22.
843. Phil 2:5–8.
844. Jn 2:19.
845. Mt 1:1.
846. Mt 1:16.
847. Mt 1:18.
848. Jn 2:1.
849. Acts 1:14.
850. Mt 1:20.
851. Mt 2:13.

cerning his Son, who was born of the seed of David according to the flesh";[852] and again this, concerning the passion: "God sent his Son in the likeness of sinful flesh, and because of sin, and condemned sin in the flesh";[853] and again, "Christ died for our sins";[854] and "Christ suffered in the flesh";[855] and "This is," not my deity, but "my body which is broken for you"[856]—and thousands of other statements warning the human race not to think that the deity of the Son is a new thing, or susceptible to bodily passion, but rather the flesh which is united to the nature of the Godhead.

That is why Christ calls himself both Lord and son of David. He says, "'What do you think about the Christ? Whose son is he?' They say to him, 'David's.' Jesus answered and said to them, 'How then does David, speaking in the Spirit, call him Lord, saying, "The Lord said to my Lord, 'Sit on my right hand'"'?"[857] because he is entirely the son of David according to the flesh but Lord according to the deity. The body therefore is the temple of the Son's deity, and a temple united to it by a complete and divine conjunction, so that the nature of the deity associates itself with the things belonging to the body, and the body is acknowledged to be noble and worthy of the wonders related in the Gospels.

To attribute also to him, in the name of this association, the characteristics of the flesh that has been conjoined with him—I mean birth and suffering and death—is, my brother, either the work of a mind which truly errs in the fashion of the Greeks or that of a mind diseased with the insane heresy of Arius and Apollinaris and the others. Those who are thus carried away with the idea of this association are bound, because of it, to make the divine Logos have a part in being fed with milk and participate to some degree in growth and stand in need of angelic assistance because of his tearfulness at the time of the passion.[858] I say nothing about circumcision and sacrifice and tears and hunger, which, being joined with him, belong properly to the flesh as things which happened for our sake. These things are taken falsely when they are put off on the deity, and they become the occasion of just condemnation for us who perpetrate the falsehood.

These are the teachings of the holy fathers. This is the message of the divine Scriptures. This is the way in which one speaks theologically both of the things which belong to God's love for the human race and of the things which belong to his majesty. "Be diligent in these things, concern yourself with them, that your progress may be evident to all,"[859] says Paul to everyone.

It is right for you, since you are withstood, to give thought to those who are scandalized. And thanks be to your soul, mindful as it is of divine things, giving thought to people here as well. Know, however, that you have been misled by the clergy of your own persuasion, by those deposed here by the holy synod because they thought like Manichaeans. The affairs of the church make progress in every quarter, and the laity are increasing at such a rate, through the grace of God, that those who see the multitudes cry out the words of the prophet, "The earth shall be filled with the knowledge of the Lord as a great water covers the sea."[860] Also, the affairs of the emperors are in a state of overflowing joy because the teaching has been illumined. And—in order that I may bring my letter to an end—may people discover that amongst us, where all heresies hateful to God and the correct teaching of the church are concerned, this word has been fulfilled: "The house of Saul went on and became weaker and the house of David went on and became stronger."[861]

This is our counsel, given as from brother to brother. "But if anyone seems contentious," as Paul cried out for our sakes to such a person, "we have no such custom, neither the churches of God."[862] I and all who are with me send many greetings to the whole brotherhood of your company. May you continue in good health and praying for us, O most entirely honored and beloved of God!

From Richard A. Norris Jr., ed. and trans., *The Christological Controversy* (Philadelphia: Fortress, 1980), 135–40.

❧ In the ongoing Christological controversy of the fifth century, **Cyril of Alexandria** (ca. 376–444), bishop of Alexandria, responds to Nestorius with his famous "twelve anathemas" in *The Third Letter to Nestorius,* written around 430, before the Council of Ephesus in 431. He defends his Christological position of one person–one "hypostasis" and therefore argues that Mary should rightly be called *theotokos.*

---

852. Rom 1:3.

853. Rom 8:3.

854. 1 Cor 15:3.

855. 1 Pet 4:1.

856. 1 Cor 11:24; see also Lk 22:19.

857. Mt 22:42–44; see also Ps 110:1.

858. See Lk 22:43–44.

859. 1 Tim 4:15.

860. Isa 11:9 (Septuagint).

861. 2 Sam 3:1.

862. 1 Cor 11:16.

CYRIL OF ALEXANDRIA

The Third Letter to Nestorius

. . . Following in every respect the confessions of the holy Fathers,[863] which they drew up as the Holy Spirit spoke in them, and pursuing the track of their thoughts, and taking as it were the royal road, we say that the unique Word of God himself, who was begotten of the very substance of the Father, who is true God of true God, the Light of Light, through whom all things came into being, both things in heaven and things in earth, coming down for the sake of our salvation, and humbling himself even to emptying,[864] was made flesh and became man. That is, taking flesh of the holy Virgin, and making it his own from the womb, he underwent a birth like ours, and came forth a man of woman, not throwing off what he was, but even though he became [man] by the assumption of flesh and blood, yet still remaining what he was, that is, God indeed in nature and truth. We do not say that the flesh was changed into the nature of Godhead, nor that the ineffable nature of the Word of God was transformed into the nature of flesh, for he is unchangeable and unalterable, always remaining the same according to the Scriptures. But when seen as a babe and wrapped in swaddling clothes, even when still in the bosom of the Virgin who bore him, he filled all creation as God, and was enthroned with him who begot him. For the Divine cannot be numbered or measured, and does not admit of circumscription.

So confessing the Word united hypostatically to flesh, we worship one Son and Lord Jesus Christ, neither putting apart and dividing man and God, as joined with each other by a union of dignity and authority—for this would be an empty phrase and no more—nor speaking of the Word of God separately as Christ, and then separately of him who was of a woman as another Christ, but knowing only one Christ, the Word of God the Father with his own flesh. For then he was anointed[865] in human wise like us, though he himself gives the Spirit to those who are worthy to receive it, and not by measure, as says the blessed Evangelist John.[866] Neither do we say that the Word of God tabernacled in him who was begotten of the holy Virgin as in an ordinary man—lest Christ should be thought of as a God-bearing man. For though the Word did tabernacle among us,[867] and it is said that in Christ dwelt all the fullness of the Godhead bodily,[868] yet we so conceive [of this] that when he was made flesh, we do not define the indwelling in him in precisely the same manner as that in which one speaks of an indwelling in the saints; but being

united by nature and not changed into flesh, he effected such an indwelling as the soul of man might be said to have in its own body.

[There is] therefore one Christ and Son and Lord, not as if man were conjoined with God by a union of dignity or authority. For equality of honor does not unite the natures, and Peter and John, for instance, are of equal honor with each other, as both apostles and holy disciples, but the two are not [made] into one. Nor do we think of the mode of conjunction as by association, for this is not enough for a natural union;[869] nor as by an acquired relation, as we, being joined to the Lord, as it is written, are one spirit with him.[870] Indeed we reject the term "conjunction," as not sufficiently indicating the union . . . [nor is the Word the God or Lord of Christ, since God the Word and his flesh are united in one *hypostasis* though as man he was under God and under the law].[871]

We refuse to say of Christ, "I adore him who was born for the sake of him who bore him, I worship him who was seen for the sake of the invisible," and it is horrible to say in addition to this, "He who was assumed is styled as God with him who assumed." He who says this divides him again into two Christs, and puts a man apart separately and God similarly. For he confessedly denies the union, according to which he is not worshiped as one [person] along with another, nor does he [merely] share the style of God. But one Christ Jesus is thought of, the unique Son, honored by one worship with his own flesh. And we confess that he who was begotten from God the Father as Son and God only-begotten,[872] though being by his own nature impassible, suffered in the flesh for us, according to the Scriptures,[873] and he was in the crucified flesh impassibly making his own the sufferings of his own flesh. So by the grace of God he tasted death for everyone,[874]

---

863. That is, in the Nicene Creed just quoted by Cyril. (The notes for this selection are by Gerhart and Udoh.)

864. See Phil 2:7.

865. So interpreting the descent of the Spirit at Jesus' baptism. See Mk 1:10; Mt 3:16; Lk 3:21–22; Jn 1:32–34. Jesus is thus Christos (Anointed).

866. See Jn 3:34.

867. See Jn 1:14.

868. See Col 2:9.

869. That is, *henōsis physike*, "union of natures" or "union in nature."

870. See 1 Cor 6:17.

871. See Gal 4:4. The translator here selectively paraphrases the rest of Cyril's paragraph.

872. See Jn 1:18 (reading *monogenēs theos* instead of *monogenēs huios*).

873. See 1 Cor 15:3.

874. See Heb 2:9.

giving up his own body to it, although by nature he was life, and was himself the resurrection.[875] [. . .]

We must necessarily add this: proclaiming the death in the flesh of the unique Son of God, that is, Jesus Christ, and confessing his return to life from the dead, and his reception into heaven, we celebrate the unbloody service in the churches.[876] So we approach to the mystical gifts[877] and are sanctified, becoming partakers of the holy flesh and the honorable blood of Christ the Saviour of us all, not receiving it as ordinary flesh—God forbid—nor as that of a man sanctified and conjoined with the Word by a unity of honor, or as one who had received a divine indwelling, but as truly life-giving and the Word's own flesh. For being by nature, as God, life, when he had become one with his own flesh, he made it life-giving.[878] [. . .]

We do not divide the terms used in the Gospels of the Saviour as God or man between two *hypostases,* or Persons, for the one and only Christ is not twofold, though he is thought of as out of two, and as uniting different entities into the indivisible unity—as man is thought of as of body and soul, and yet not as twofold, but one out of both. . . . For if it is necessary to believe that being God by nature, he became flesh, that is, man ensouled with a rational soul, for what reason should some be embarrassed by some of his sayings that may be such as befit humanity? . . . All the terms used in the Gospels are to be referred to one Person, the one incarnate *hypostasis* of the Word. There is one Lord Jesus Christ, according to the Scriptures. [. . .]

Since the holy Virgin gave birth after the flesh to God who was united by *hypostasis*[879] with flesh, therefore we say that she is *theotokos,* not as though the nature of the Word had the beginning of its existence from flesh . . . [nor that the Word needed human birth, but that by accepting it he blessed the beginning of our existence, and removed the curse from it]. . . . For this cause we say that he also in his [earthly] dispensation blessed marriage itself, and went when he had been invited to Cana of Galilee with the holy apostles.[880]

We have learned to hold these things from the holy apostles and Evangelists and all the God-inspired Scripture, and by the true confession of the blessed Fathers. All these it is necessary for Your Reverence to accept and support without deceit; and what Your Reverence must anathematize is subjoined to this our letter:

1. If anyone does not confess that Emmanuel is God[881] in truth, and therefore the holy Virgin is *theotokos*—for she bore in the flesh the Word of God become flesh—let him be anathema.

2. If anyone does not confess that the Word of God the Father was united by *hypostasis* to flesh and is one Christ with his own flesh, that is, the same both God and man together, let him be anathema.

3. If anyone divides the *hypostases* in the one Christ after the union, joining them only by a conjunction in dignity, or authority or power, and not rather by a coming together in a union by nature, let him be anathema.

4. If anyone distributes between two persons or *hypostases* the terms used in the evangelical and apostolic writings, whether spoken of Christ by the saints or by him about himself, and attaches some to a man thought of separately from the Word of God, and others as befitting God to the Word of God the Father alone, let him be anathema.

5. If anyone dares to say that Christ was a God-bearing man, and not rather God in truth, being by nature one Son, inasmuch as the Word became flesh, and is made partaker of blood and flesh precisely like us,[882] let him be anathema.

6. If anyone says that the Word of God the Father was the God or Master of Christ, and does not rather confess the same both God and man, the Word having become flesh according to the Scriptures, let him be anathema.

7. If anyone says that Jesus was energized as a man by the Word from God, and clothed with the glory of the Only-begotten, as being another besides him, let him be anathema.

8. If anyone dares to say that the man who was assumed ought to be worshiped with God the Word and glorified with him, and with him styled God, as being one [being] in a different one—for the constantly added "with" forces one to think this—and does not rather honor Emmanuel with one veneration, and send up to him one doxology, inasmuch as the Word has become flesh, let him be anathema.

9. If anyone says that the one Lord Jesus Christ was glorified by the Spirit, as making use of an alien power that worked through him, and received from him the power to prevail over unclean spirits and to accomplish divine won-

---

875. See Jn 11:25.

876. The phrases are taken from the Eucharistic Prayer.

877. That is, the sacramental "gifts" of the body and blood of Christ.

878. See Jn 6:33, 35, 48–51.

879. Cyril's "union of natures" is also a "union by hypostasis" (*kath' hypostasin*). Since he recognizes a duality neither of "nature" (*physis*) nor of "hypostasis" in Christ, his concept of "one incarnate hypostasis of the Word" (which is Apollinarian in origin) will lend support to the Monophysite view of the Person of Christ.

880. See Jn 2:1–2.

881. See Mt 1:23.

882. See Jn 1:14; Heb 2:14.

ders among men, and does not rather say that it was his own Spirit, through whom also he worked the divine wonders, let him be anathema.

10. The divine Scripture speaks of Christ as the High Priest and Apostle of our confession,[883] and [says that] he offered himself for us for an odor of sweet savor to his God and Father.[884] If anyone says that the Word of God himself did not become our High Priest and Apostle, when he became flesh and man for us, but as it were another [who was] separately from him man of woman—or if anyone says that he offered the offering for himself, and not rather for us alone, for he who knew no sin had no need of offering,[885] let him be anathema.

11. If anyone does not confess that the flesh of the Lord is life-giving, and the own [flesh] of the Word of God the Father, but as of another besides him, associated with him in dignity, or having received merely a divine indwelling—and not rather life-giving, as we said, because it became the own [flesh] of the Word who is able to give life to all things, let him be anathema.

12. If anyone does not confess that the Word of God suffered in the flesh and was crucified in the flesh and tasted death in the flesh, and became the first-born of the dead,[886] although he is as God Life and life-giving, let him be anathema.

From Edward Rochie Hardy, ed., *Christology of the Later Fathers,* Library of Christian Classics, vol. 3 (Philadelphia: Westminster Press, 1954), 349–54.

᪥   After the Council of Ephesus (431) had condemned and exiled Nestorius, Eutyches (ca. 378–452) mounted a vigorous attack on Nestorius's teaching. His emphasis on the unity of the person of Christ led Eusebius, bishop of Dorylaeum, to charge him (in 448) with the ("Monophysite") heresy of denying that Jesus of Nazareth was truly human. The **Council of Chalcedon,** convened by Emperor Marcian (450–57) in 451, condemned both Nestorius and Eutyches and, in its *Definition of Faith,* reconciled the contending Alexandrian (represented by Cyril) and Antiochene (represented by Nestorius) positions.

THE COUNCIL OF CHALCEDON

Definition of Faith

[. . . This sacred and great and universal synod] is opposed to those who attempt to tear apart the mystery of the economy into a duality of sons; and it expels from the assembly of the priests those who dare to say that the divinity of the Only-begotten is passible; and it stands opposed to those who imagine a mixture or confusion between the two natures of Christ; and it expels those who have the mad idea that the servant-form he took from us[887] is of a heavenly or some other kind of being; and it anathematises those who concoct two natures of the Lord before the union but imagine a single one after the union.

So, following the saintly fathers, we all with one voice teach the confession of one and the same Son, our Lord Jesus Christ: the same perfect in divinity and perfect in humanity, the same truly God and truly man, of a rational soul and a body; consubstantial with the Father as regards his divinity, and the same consubstantial with us as regards his humanity; like us in all respects except for sin;[888] begotten before the ages from the Father as regards his divinity, and in the last days the same for us and for our salvation from Mary, the virgin God-bearer, as regards his humanity; one and the same Christ, Son, Lord, only-begotten, acknowledged in two natures which undergo no confusion, no change, no division, no separation; at no point was the difference between the natures taken away through the union, but rather the property of both natures is preserved and comes together into a single person and a single subsistent being; he is not parted or divided into two persons, but is one and the same only-begotten Son, God, Word, Lord Jesus Christ, just as the prophets taught from the beginning about him, and as the Lord Jesus Christ himself instructed us, and as the creed of the fathers handed it down to us.

Since we have formulated these things with all possible accuracy and attention, the sacred and universal synod decreed that no one is permitted to produce, or even to write down or compose, any other creed or to think or teach otherwise. As for those who dare either to compose another creed or even to promulgate or teach or hand down another creed for those who wish to convert to a recognition of the truth from Hellenism or from Judaism, or from any kind of heresy at all: if they be bishops or clerics, the bishops are to be deposed from the episcopacy and the clerics from the clergy; if they be monks or layfolk, they are to be anathematised.

From Norman P. Tanner, ed., *Decrees of the Ecumenical Councils,* vol. 1 (Washington, DC: Georgetown University Press, 1990), 85–87.

---

883. See Heb 3:1.
884. See Eph 5:2.
885. See 2 Cor 5:21; Heb 7:26–28.
886. See Col 1:18.
887. See Phil 2:7. (The notes for this selection are by Gerhart and Udoh.)
888. See Heb 4:15.

CHAPTER 4

Rituals and Patterns of Worship

Ritual observance was one of the earlier ways Christians came to be identified as Christians. Baptism is the ritual initiation into Christianity. Baptism was already practiced among first-century Jews. But the Christian formula—baptism "in the name of the Father and of the Son and of the Holy Spirit" (as stated in *The Didache*) or "in the name [of Christ]" and "into Christ"—brought something new to the older practice of baptism. Paul's Letter to the Galatians explicitly states that "there is no longer Jew or Greek, there is no longer slave or free, there is no longer male and female; for all of you are one in Christ Jesus" (3:28).

The ritual celebration of the Eucharist—daily to annually—continues what was begun in the baptismal conversion: a turning away from preoccupation with things of the body and toward things of the spirit manifest in Christ Jesus. The Christian community was distinguished as a "eucharistic community"; Jews among the first Christians met to "break bread" in addition to attending synagogue. The word "Eucharist" has two meanings: translated as "thanksgiving" or "gratitude," the Eucharist commemorates those who attended Jesus' Last Supper and their knowing him in the "breaking of the bread" and the appearances after his death. The early Christians also used "Eucharist" to refer to the Lord's table (1 Cor 10:21), recalling the sacrificial death of Jesus. This designation distinguished the Lord's table from the altars of other religions. Among the variety of readings and liturgical forms, worship is recognizable as Christian if it is governed explicitly or implicitly by the event of Jesus Christ, here Jesus' Last Supper with the apostles.

This chapter focuses on baptism and the Eucharist because they have been central and constant—with differing emphases and interpretation—throughout the tradition. The number of sacraments has varied among Christian denominations, being reduced both in the thirteenth century and (by Protestants) at the time of the Reformation. Some sacraments denote rites of passage at particular life junctures. Only Roman, Orthodox, and Anglican Catholic Churches today recognize five sacraments in addition to baptism and the Eucharist—reconciliation (or penance), confirmation (or chrismation), matrimony, ordination, and healing (or last rites and extreme unction)—although many of these continue to be practiced in Protestant Churches as rites (ceremonial acts) rather than sacraments (enactment of a spiritual reality). The texts on rituals and patterns of worship in this chapter span the first century through the twentieth.

In section 1, The Rise of Sacraments as the Central Focus of Community, texts by early Christian writers—*The Didache*, Justin Martyr's *First Apology,* and Hippolytus's *Apostolic Tradition*—enable us to compare and contrast the different liturgical practices among Christian communities, as well as their different self-understandings. *The Didache* (meaning "teaching"; also called *Teaching of the Twelve Apostles*), for example, is an early collection of instructions used by itinerant missionaries—male and female prophets and apostles—in ministering to the earliest communities. Justin Martyr, a member of a second-century Greek philosophical school in Rome, identifies the hierophany of the "nameless" God who spoke to Moses in the burning bush as the same God who was manifest in the flesh of Jesus, whom he calls Angel, Prophet, and Logos of God. Justin bases his own identity in his memory of "being made new in Christ." His description of the "eucharistization" of the bread and wine reflects what he saw as the results of rebirth in the community: the washing away of the effects of past sins, the ability to say "Amen" to the act of giving thanks to God, and the well-off coming to the aid of the poor. Justin contrasts baptism and the rite of sprinkling oneself before entering a pagan temple, the Logos-Christ (in creation and incarnation) and the divinity attributed to the daughters and sons of Zeus, and the Eucharist and Mithraic liturgies. Writing in the early third century, Hippolytus believes that the washing in baptism signifies an inner enlightenment, an awakening to divine inspiration and immortality. For both Justin and Hippolytus, God is hidden (in Justin, "ineffable" and ultimately unnamable), and the essential Christian disposition is love of neighbor (in Hippolytus, "when everything is over, let each hasten to do good work").

By the fourth century, differences among the communities led to dissension over the meaning and ritual of baptism, with each community prescribing only what was important to them in the entrance rite. Later these differences would be understood in terms of heresy versus orthodoxy (Arians versus Gnostics, for example) or as local variants (between Alexandria and Hippo, Hippo and Carthage, or Carthage and Rome, for example). Cyprian, bishop of Carthage, forcefully advocated the rebaptism of the *lapsi* (those who had apostasized). The Donatists maintained Cyprian's position, but Augustine declared that he recognized only one baptism. Earlier, Tertullian had denounced infant baptism; Augustine promoted it and argued theologically as if it were a given. If there is anything that we do not have in earliest Christian liturgy, it is uniformity.

The liturgy of the Middle Ages is distinctive for its pageantry. Sunday and high-holiday Masses frequently included processions that dramatized the particular feast being commemorated. Before the fourteenth century or so, as stated by Gregory Dix in his study of the liturgy, diverse rites and several dialects of plainsong (or chant) were in circulation. Men's and women's religious orders and even some military orders commonly developed their own rites and composed distinctive psalmody. In section 2, Medieval Liturgies and Pageantry, the nun Egeria's account of her pilgrimage to the Holy Land in the late fourth century reveals the extent to which the Holy Week liturgy enveloped daily life. "The Quem-Quaeritis Trope" is a ninth-century or earlier dramatic embellishment of a phrase in the sung liturgy of the Mass; such dramatizations of biblical events would lead to full-fledged mystery plays (plays based on biblical

events). We also present some surprising twelfth-century letters that show Hildegard of Bingen's serious regard for liturgical practices. One need not agree with all of Gregory Dix's assessments to appreciate his retrieval of the diverse forms of Christian liturgies that developed during the first millennium of the Christian Church and that still existed in the Middle Ages. Most of the distinctive variations introduced by religious orders have been discontinued, and celebration of the Mozarabic rite is today permitted only in a cathedral chapel in Toledo, Spain. Eamon Duffy's *Stripping of the Altars* provides a "thick interpretation" (to use Clifford Geertz's happy phrase) of liturgy in late-medieval England. Using quotations from contemporaries who participated in Holy Week ceremonies, Duffy evokes the dramatic effect that the Holy Week liturgical events must have had in that culture.

In 1215, the Fourth Lateran Council (the last to be convened in the Middle Ages) formalized the eucharistic doctrine of transubstantiation and several sacramental obligations. The Council of Trent (1545–63) emphasized the "real presence" of Jesus in the Eucharist in reaction to the Reformation emphasis on justification and reduced the number of sacraments to seven. Four centuries later, the Second Vatican Council's *Constitution on Sacred Liturgy* (excerpted in section 3, Tridentine and Vatican Reforms) would take a significantly different focus. Vatican II (1962–65) sought to reform and explain the existing liturgical rites so that people can understand and participate in them "fully, actively, and as a community." This document, rooted in thirty years of historical research and worldwide liturgical movements, was the first to be completed by the council and had effects outside, as well as within, the Catholic Church.

In the Eastern Orthodox liturgy (see section 4) the Byzantine rite, with local variations, had supplanted all others by the thirteenth century and was adapted into several languages besides the original Greek. Timothy Ware argues that the Church at large is foremost a eucharistic society but the eucharistic liturgy can take place only locally. For this reason, the local community is the Church in its fullness whenever it receives the body and blood of the Lord in the sacrament. In the Eastern Church, baptism, confirmation, and first communion are united and performed together as acts of initiation. Form is emphasized by Robert Taft as he describes the etymology of "sacrament" and the history of the Eastern Orthodox liturgical custom of communion by intinction (immersing the bread in the wine and consuming them at the same time).

In "Commonly Called Sacraments," James White shows that in Protestant Churches a pluralism of beliefs regarding baptism and the Eucharist developed after the Reformation. These beliefs are represented in section 5, Liturgical Issues in Sixteenth- and Twentieth-Century Protestantism. Eucharistic reform began with Luther's *Babylonian Captivity of the Church* (1520), a treatise that affected most early Protestant understandings of the sacraments and their legacy in Protestant Churches today. Luther's and Huldrych (Ulrich) Zwingli's differences regarding the meaning of the Eucharist led to debates, such as the Marburg Colloquy, among the Reformers. The report by Rudolph Collin presented here is one of several made by individuals who attended and took notes on the Marburg debate. *The Book of Common Prayer* (1549) achieved classic status among Anglican and Independent liturgies and reflects several views of the Eucharist. The World Council of Churches, organized in 1948 by Protestant and Eastern Orthodox leadership, has published several documents showing the results of ongoing ecumenical liturgical discussions, two of which, "Baptism, Confirmation, and Eucharist" (1971) and "Beyond the Lima Liturgy" (1982), we present here.

Many diverse Christian communities—traditionally categorized as sects, denominations, and churches, depending on their size and kinds of organization—originated in the twentieth century (see section 6, "Independent" and Holiness Christian Liturgies). However, in addition to the phenomenal spread of Mormonism, the major areas of growth in contemporary Christianity have been in Pentecostal and evangelical groups, many of which continue affiliation with other communities and may be non- or interdenominational. Evangelical groups tend to be conservative and less united than the media suggest. They are strongly represented in British and some American Protestant Churches. Pentecostals see the experiential dimension of religion as central to Christian life. Pentecostal movements have sprung up here and there throughout the history of Christianity, and charismatic leaders have frequently led reform movements within their Church or denomination to restore the desire for perfection. These groups tend not to be schismatic and to care most about the experience and practice of the gifts of the Holy Spirit such as speaking in tongues. Neo-Pentecostal movements in the 1960s began to include Roman Catholic and Eastern Orthodox groups. Independent Churches grew out of mission Churches or began as black Churches. These have strong ecumenical relationships and combine elements of the founding denominations with indigenous elements. They resist the effects of colonialism and emphasize commitments that are univocal and intense and lead to religious transformation. Many Holiness Churches trace their roots to Acts 2, which says that, after Jesus' death, the Holy Spirit was "poured out" upon the disciples, empowering them generally and enabling them to speak in tongues, prophesy, and dream dreams. These Churches are conservative and radical in their expressions of perfection: emotionalism, prophetic utterances, avowals of faith, and ecstasy are characteristic in Holiness church meetings.

Section 7, Contemporary and Popular Ritual, begins with Edward Foley's discussion of the theological importance of ritual or liturgical music and is followed by selections from hymnbooks, including a Mexican Marian hymn, a Christmas carol, an African American spiritual, a polyphonic anthem, an evangelical song of praise, and a Methodist revivalist hymn. These selections, as well as several modes of formal chant, illustrate some of the different forms of Christian musical inspiration throughout two millennia.

Contemporary feminist theology provides grounds for reforming liturgy so that it is gender inclusive and reflects women's, as well as men's, experience. Janet Walton offers suggestions for meeting these goals and for creating new liturgies. In Juan Diego's story of Our Lady of Tepeyac, which records events that took place in the sixteenth century, we catch sight of the immense devotion that Catholics have for the Virgin Mary, who hears the prayers of God's people. Karen McCarthy Brown reports on the syncretist features of Vodou (Voodoo), which combines Haitian faith traditions and Roman Catholicism, as personified in the character and actions of the Brooklyn priestess Mama Lola.

Section 8, Art and Architecture, examines architectural and artistic expressions of faith and liturgy. Richard Krautheimer documents the variety of meeting places in first- through third-century Christian communities. When Christianity became a newly approved religion within the Roman Empire under Constantine, it needed larger spaces than private homes and burial chambers for worship and administrative needs—for example, for the organization of bodily works of mercy (feeding the hungry and caring for orphans and the elderly). By the fourth century, eucharistic celebrations were taking place in buildings considerably larger than the original sites.

The early Christians shared the Jewish repudiation of idolatry (worship of false gods and of objects as a god). In principle and in practice, however, the Christian tradition has been iconic, as evidenced throughout its history from ancient catacomb frescoes to modern sculpture. Moreover, the discovery of Jewish frescoes adorning a synagogue in the third-century Syrian city of Dura Europos in the 1930s has called into question the strict aniconicity of the Jewish tradition. Gregory I (pope from 590 to 604) argued for the instructional and edificatory value of representational religious art, and John of Damascus (ca. 645–ca. 750) made the theological connection between iconic art and the Incarnation of Christ in 726, when he wrote: "Of old God the incorporeal and uncircumscribed was not depicted at all. But now that God has appeared in the flesh and lived among men I make an image of God who can be seen. I do not worship matter but I worship the creator of matter who for my sake became material and deigned to dwell in matter, who through matter effected my salvation" ("Concerning the Icons"). Despite its defenders, the iconicity of the tradition was severely tested in the Eastern Church in the eighth

and ninth centuries and in the Western Church by the Swiss Reformation leader Zwingli and the English general and statesman Oliver Cromwell in the sixteenth century. The Second Council of Nicaea (787) records the defeat of the first iconoclastic movement in the Eastern Church—a defeat negotiated successively by two women of royalty, first Empress Irene and then Empress Theodora. Finally, Abbot Suger reveals the sacramental impulse to see all creation in the service of the holy in the materials he gathers for the building of the church of Saint-Denis in Paris in the twelfth century, and Edward Foley reflects on the reciprocal influence brought to bear by liturgical needs and contemporary architectural design.

By whatever name—whether "worship," "liturgy," "sacrament," or "rite of passage"—ritual in the Christian tradition is both particular in being centered in the Eucharist and baptism and general in its reach to all who seek and celebrate a living God.

---

1. THE RISE OF SACRAMENTS AS THE CENTRAL FOCUS OF COMMUNITY

☙ This excerpt from *The Didache,* which dates from the late first or early second century, provides some of the earliest descriptions of specifically Christian formulas for baptism, Eucharist, prayer, and fasting.

The Didache, VII.1–X.7

VII

1. Now concerning baptism, baptize as follows: after you have reviewed[1] all these things, baptize "in the name of the Father and of the Son and of the Holy Spirit"[2] in running water. 2. But if you have no running water, then baptize in some other water; and if you are not able to baptize in cold water, then do so in warm. 3. But if you have neither, then pour water on the head three times "in the name of Father and Son and Holy Spirit." 4. And before the baptism, let the one baptizing and the one who is to be baptized fast, as well as any others who are able. Also, you must instruct the one who is to be baptized to fast for one or two days beforehand.

VIII

1. But do not let your fasts coincide with those of the hypocrites. They fast on Monday and Thursday, so you must fast on Wednesday and Friday.

2. Nor should you pray like the hypocrites. Instead, "pray like this," just as the Lord commanded in his Gospel:

> Our Father in heaven
> hallowed be your name,
> your kingdom come,
> your will be done
>   on earth as it is in heaven.
> Give us today our daily bread,

---

1. "Review," that is, with those about to be baptized. This locution indicates that there was a period of prebaptismal instruction, or catechumenate. (The notes for this selection are by Gerhart and Udoh.)

2. Mt 28:19.

and forgive us our debt,
    as we also forgive our debtors;
and do not lead us into temptation,
but deliver us from the evil one;[3]
for yours is the power and the glory forever.

3. Pray like this three times a day.

IX

1. Now concerning the Eucharist,[4] give thanks as follows.
2. First, concerning the cup:

We give you thanks, our Father,
for the holy vine of David your servant,
which you have made known to us
through Jesus, your servant;
to you be the glory forever.

3. And concerning the broken bread:

We give you thanks, our Father,
for the life and knowledge
which you have made known to us
through Jesus, your servant;
to you be the glory forever.

4. Just as this broken bread was scattered
        upon the mountains and then was
    gathered together and became one,
so may your church be gathered together
    from the ends of the earth into your kingdom;
for yours is the glory and the power
    through Jesus Christ forever.

5. But let no one eat or drink of your Eucharist except those who have been baptized into the name of the Lord, for the Lord has also spoken concerning this: "Do not give what is holy to dogs."[5]

X

1. And after you have had enough, give thanks as follows:

2. We give you thanks, Holy Father,
for your holy name which you
    have caused to dwell in our hearts,
and for the knowledge and faith and immortality
    which you have made known to us
    through Jesus your servant;
to you be the glory forever.

3. You, almighty Master, created all things for your name's
        sake,
and gave food and drink to men to enjoy,
    that they might give you thanks;
but to us you have graciously given
    spiritual food and drink,
    and eternal life though your servant.

4. Above all we give thanks because you are mighty;
to you be the glory forever.

5. Remember your church, Lord,
to deliver it from all evil
and to make it perfect in your love;
and gather it, the one that has been sanctified,
from the four winds into your kingdom,
which you have prepared for it;
for yours is the power and the glory forever.

6. May grace come, and may this world pass away.
Hosanna to the God of David.
If anyone is holy, let him come;
if anyone is not, let him repent.
Maranatha![6] Amen.

7. But permit the prophets to give thanks however they wish.

Translated by J. B. Lightfoot and J. R. Harmer, in *The Apostolic Fathers,* 2nd rev. ed., edited by J. B. Lightfoot (Grand Rapids, MI: Baker Book House, 1992), 259–63.

---

3. See Mt 6:5–15.

4. The Greek work *eucharistia* means "thanksgiving" or "thankfulness" in the New Testament, as in Acts 24:3; 1 Cor 14:16; Phil 4:6. The word quickly became a technical term for the "Lord's Supper."

5. Mt 7:6.

6. That is, Hebrew for "Our Lord, come!" See 1 Cor 16:22.

☙ In *The First Apology*, written ca. 150, **Justin Martyr** (ca. 100–ca. 165), a Roman philosopher who became a Christian, discusses the centrality and significance of both baptism and the eucharistic meal for Christian living. He also contrasts Christian liturgical rites with parallel practices found in other Greco-Roman religions.

JUSTIN MARTYR

The First Apology, 61–67

61. I will also explain the manner in which we dedicated ourselves to God when we were made new through Christ, since if we left this out in our exposition we would seem to falsify something. As many as are persuaded and believe that the things we teach and say are true, and undertake to live accordingly, are instructed to pray and ask God with fasting for the remission of their past sins, while we pray and fast with them.[7] Then they are brought by us where there is water, and are born again in the same manner of rebirth by which we ourselves were born again,[8] for they then receive washing in water in the name of God the Father and Master of all, and of our Savior, Jesus Christ, and of the Holy Spirit.[9] For Christ also said, "Except you are born again, you will not enter into the Kingdom of heaven."[10] Now it is clear to all that it is impossible for those who have once come into being to enter into their mothers' wombs.[11] And it is said through Isaiah the prophet, as we wrote before, in what manner those who have sinned and repent shall escape from their sins. He thus spoke: "Wash, become clean, put away evil doings from your souls, learn to do good, judge the orphan and plead for the widow, and come and let us reason together, says the Lord. And though your sins be as scarlet, I will make them white as wool, and though they be as crimson, I will make them white as snow. But if you will not listen to me, a sword will devour you; for the mouth of the Lord has spoken these things."[12] And we have learned from the Apostles this reason for this [rite].[13] Since at our first birth we were born of necessity without our knowledge, from moist seed[14] by the intercourse of our parents with each other, and were brought up in bad habits and wicked behavior; in order that we should not remain children of necessity and ignorance, but of free choice and knowledge, and obtain remission of the sins formerly committed,[15] there is named at the water over him who has chosen to be born again, and has repented of his sinful acts, the name of God the Father and Master of all; they who lead to the washing the one who is to be washed call on this [name] alone. For no one can give a name to the ineffable God; and if anyone should dare say there is one, he raves with a hopeless insanity. And this washing is called illumination, as those who learn these things are illuminated in the mind.[16] And he who is illuminated is washed in the name of Jesus Christ, who was crucified under Pontius Pilate, and in the name of the Holy Spirit, who through the prophets foretold all the things about Jesus.

62. And the demons, indeed, having heard this washing proclaimed through the prophet, arranged that those who enter their temples and are about to approach them to offer libations and burnt offerings should also sprinkle themselves;[17] and they cause them also to wash themselves completely as they approach, before they enter into the sanctuaries where their images are. And the order, too, given by the priests to those who enter into the temples and to those who serve them [i.e., the demons], to remove their shoes,[18] the devils imitated when they learned what happened to Moses, the prophet mentioned before. For at that time when Moses was ordered to go down into Egypt and to lead out the people of the Israelites who were there, as he was tending the sheep of his maternal uncle in the land of Arabia,[19] our Christ conversed with him in the form of fire out of a bush, and said, "Unloose your sandals and come near and hear."[20] But when he had unloosed them and drawn near he heard that he was

---

7. See *Didache* VII.4 above. The period of catechumenate ends with prayer and fasting. (The notes for this selection are by Gerhart and Udoh.)

8. On baptism as a "new birth," see Jn 3:3–8; 1 Pet 1:3.

9. See also *Didache* VII above, and Mt 28:19.

10. Jn 3:3–5; Mt 18:3.

11. See Jn 3:4.

12. Isa 1:16–18, 20.

13. Words in brackets have been added by the translator for clarification. The apostolic tradition to which Justin appeals can be found, for instance, in Mk 1:8; Mt 3:11; Lk 3:16; Jn 1:26–27, 33; 3:3–10; Acts 1:4–5; 19:1–7; Rom 6:3–11; 1 Cor 12:12–13; Gal 3:27–29; Col 2:11–15; 1 Pet 3:18–22.

14. Even the "new birth" is associated with moisture. On the contrast between baptism and natural birth, see 1 Pet 1:23.

15. See Acts 2:38; 22:16; Rom 3:23–25; 6:4; Gal 4:22–26; 5:1; 1 Pet 1:14.

16. Justin is the first Christian writer to use the noun *phōtismos*, "illumination," specifically to refer to baptism. The verbal form of the word is used in Heb 6:4 (see also 10:32) with reference to the enlightenment received at baptism. The verb is otherwise used in the New Testament to refer to Christian faith (see 2 Cor 4:4; Eph 1:18; 2 Tim 1:9–10). "Illumination," for Justin, is the presence of the whole Logos in the soul of the baptized Christian.

17. See also Tertullian, *On Baptism*, 5. Sprinkling oneself was a common part of the rites of purification practiced in pagan temples.

18. See also Tertullian, *Apology*, 40.14.

19. See Ex 3:1. Justin's statement that Moses "was tending the sheep of his maternal uncle" probably indicates a confusion with Jacob's tending the sheep of Laban (see Gen 29:9–30; 31:10–13), since Jethro was Moses' father-in-law, not uncle.

20. See Ex 3:5.

to go down into Egypt and lead out the people of the Isra-elites there; and he received mighty power from Christ, who spoke to him in the form of fire, and went down and led out the people having done great and marvelous things; which if you want to learn about, you will learn accurately from his writings.

63. And even now all the Jews teach that the nameless God spoke to Moses. Wherefore the prophetic Spirit, accusing them through Isaiah the prophet mentioned before, as we wrote before, said: "The ox knows his owner and the ass his master's crib, but Israel does not know me and my people do not understand."[21] And Jesus the Christ, because the Jews did not know the nature of the Father and the Son, in like manner upbraided them and himself said: "No one knows the Father except the Son, nor the Son except the Father and those to whom the Son will reveal Him."[22] Now the Word of God is His Son, as we have said before. But he is also called "Angel" and "Apostle";[23] for He announces whatever we ought to know, and is sent forth to testify to what is announced, as Our Lord Himself also said: "He that hears me hears Him who sent me."[24] This also will be made clear from the writings of Moses. For so it is written in them: "And the Angel of God spoke to Moses in a flame of fire out of the bush and said, I am He who is, God of Abraham, God of Isaac, God of Jacob, the God of your fathers. Go down into Egypt and bring out my people."[25] Those who wish to can learn what followed from this; for it is impossible to write down everything in these [pages]. But these words were spoken to prove that Jesus the Christ is Son of God and Apostle, being of old the logos, and appeared now in the form of fire, now in the image of bodiless creatures;[26] but now having become man by the will of God for the human race He endured whatever sufferings the demons managed to have brought upon Him by the senseless Jews. Who though they have it clearly stated in the writings of Moses, "And the Angel of God spoke to Moses in a flame of fire in a bush and said, I am He who is, the God of Abraham, and the God of Isaac, and the God of Jacob," yet say that he who said these things was the Father and Demiurge of the Universe. Whence also the prophetic Spirit reproves them saying, "Israel does not know me, and the people has not understood me."[27] And Jesus again, as we have already shown, while he was with them said, "No one knows the Father except the Son, nor the Son except the Father and those to whom the Son will reveal Him." Therefore the Jews being throughout of the opinion that the Father of the Universe had spoken to Moses, though He who spoke to Him was the Son of God, who is called both Angel and Apostle, are rightly censured both by the prophetic Spirit and by Christ Himself, since they knew neither the Father nor the Son. For those who affirm that the Son is the Father are shown neither to have known the Father, nor to know that the Father of the Universe has a Son; who being the logos and First-begotten is also God.[28] And formerly He appeared in the form of fire and in the image of a bodiless being to Moses and to the other prophets; but now in the times of your rule,[29] as we said before, He became man of a virgin according to the will of the Father for the salvation of those who believe in Him and endured both contempt and suffering, that by dying and rising again He might conquer death.[30] And what was said out of the bush to Moses, "I am He who is, the God of Abraham and the God of Isaac and the God of Jacob and the God of your fathers," signified that they though dead are yet in existence and are men and women belonging to Christ Himself.[31] For they were the first of all people who busied themselves with the search after God, Abraham being the Father of Isaac, and Isaac of Jacob, as Moses also wrote.

64. From what has been said you can understand how the demons, in imitation of what was said through Moses, contrived also to raise up the image of the so-called Kore over the springs of the waters saying that she was a daughter of Zeus. For Moses said, as we wrote before:[32] "In the beginning God made the heaven and the earth. And the earth was invisible and unfurnished, and the Spirit of God moved over the waters."[33] In imitation, then, of what is said of the Spirit of God moving on the water they spoke of Kore, daughter of Zeus.[34] And likewise behaving with trickery they spoke of

---

21. Isa 1:3.

22. See Mt 11:27; Lk 10:22. Justin's passage varies considerably from the biblical passages.

23. See Ex 3:2. In the Greek, the words are synonyms. For Christ as "Apostle," see Heb 3:1. Justin is mistaken, however, because the New Testament does not call Christ an "angel." Nevertheless, in *Dialogue*, 60, Justin argues, against Trypho, that "angel" and "God" are identical, since the Logos (Christ) is both God and Angel.

24. See Lk 10:16; Mt 10:40; also Jn 12:44; 14:24.

25. See Ex 3:2, 6, 10, 14, 15.

26. "Bodiless creatures," that is, angels; see Ex 3:2.

27. Isa 1:3.

28. See Jn 1:1; Phil 2:6.

29. Justin's *First Apology* is addressed to Emperor Antoninus Pius, his son, and the Roman Senate and people.

30. This statement and paragraph 61 above might contain an early baptismal creed.

31. Ex 3:14; see also Mk 12:26–27; Mt 22:31–32; Lk 20:37–38.

32. See *First Apology*, 59.2.

33. Gen 1:1–2.

34. See possibly Diodorus Siculus, 5.4, on the mysteries of Andania.

Athena as a daughter of Zeus, not by sexual union, but, since they knew that God conceived and made the world through the logos, they spoke of Athena as the first thought;[35] which we consider to be very absurd, to bring forward the female form of an intellectual image. And likewise their actions condemn the others who are called sons of Zeus.

65. But we, after thus washing the one who has been convinced and has assented[36] [to our instruction], lead him to those who are called brethren,[37] where they are assembled; and we offer prayers in common for ourselves and for the one who has been illuminated and for all others everywhere, that we may be accounted worthy, having learned the truth, by our deeds also to be found good citizens and guardians of what is commanded, so that we may be saved with eternal salvation. Having ended the prayers we greet one another with a kiss.[38] Then there is brought to the Ruler of the Brethren[39] bread and a cup of water and [a cup] of wine mixed with water, and he taking them sends up praise and glory to the Father of the Universe through the name of the Son and of the Holy Spirit, and offers thanksgiving[40] at some length for our being accounted worthy to receive these things from Him. When he has concluded the prayers and the thanksgiving, all the people present assent by saying, Amen. Amen in the Hebrew language signifies "so be it."[41] And when the Ruler has given thanks and all the people have assented, those who are called by us deacons give to each of those present a portion of the eucharistized bread and wine and water, and they carry it away to those who are absent.[42]

66. And this food is called among us eucharist, of which no one is allowed to partake except one who believes that the things which we teach are true, and has received the washing that is for the remission of sins and for rebirth, and who so lives as Christ handed down. For we do not receive these things as common bread nor common drink; but in like manner as Jesus Christ our Savior having been incarnate by God's logos took both flesh and blood for our salvation, so also we have been taught that the food eucharistized through the word of prayer that is from Him, from which our blood and flesh are nourished by transformation, is the flesh and blood of that Jesus who became incarnate.[43] For the Apostles in the memoirs composed by them, which are called Gospels,[44] thus handed down what was commanded them: that Jesus took bread and having given thanks said: "Do this for my memorial, this is my body"; and likewise He took the chalice and having given thanks said: "This is my blood"; and gave it to them alone.[45] Which also the wicked demons have imitated in the mysteries of Mithra and handed down to be

done; for that bread and a cup of water are placed with certain words said over them in the secret rites of initiation, you either know or can learn.[46]

67. And afterward we constantly remind each other of these things. And the wealthy come to the aid of the poor, and we are always together. Over all that we receive we bless the Maker of all through His Son Jesus Christ and through the Holy Spirit. And on the day called Sunday[47] all who live in cities or in the country gather together in one place, and the memoirs of the Apostles or the writings of the prophets are read, as long as time permits.[48] Then when the reader has finished, the Ruler in a discourse instructs and exhorts to the imitation of these good things. Then we all stand up together and offer prayers; and, as we said before, when we have finished the prayer, bread is brought and wine and water, and the Ruler likewise offers up prayers and thanksgivings to the best of his ability,[49] and the people assent, saying the Amen; and the distribution and the partaking of the eucharistized elements is to each, and to those who are absent a portion is sent by the deacons. And those who prosper, and so wish, contribute what each thinks fit; and what is collected is deposited with the Ruler, who takes care of the orphans and widows, and those who, on account of sickness or any other cause, are in want, and those who are in bonds, and the strangers who are sojourners among us, and in a word [He] is the guardian of all those in need. But we

---

35. Athena was considered to have been born full-grown from Zeus's brain.

36. That is, by confessing the faith, possibly in the form of a credal interrogation.

37. See Mt 23:8.

38. This is the liturgical kiss of peace which evolved from the kiss of love and fellowship (see 1 Thess 5:26; 1 Cor 16:20; 2 Cor 13:12; 1 Pet 5:14).

39. That is, the head of the Christian community, probably the bishop, though Justin does not use the technical term.

40. That is, in Greek, "eucharistia."

41. The original thanksgiving of the Last Supper is expanded with elements borrowed from Judaism, including the response "Amen," which was left untranslated (because it was untranslatable) in the liturgy after 100 CE.

42. This is the earliest mention of this custom.

43. See Mk 14:22–24; Mt 26:26–28; Lk 22:17–20; Jn 6:35–58; 1 Cor 11:23–26.

44. The term "memoir" is probably an imitation of Xenophon's *Memoirs of Socrates*. Justin's "Gospels" seem to have corresponded in substance to our synoptic Gospels (Matthew, Mark, and Luke).

45. Mk 14:22–24; Mt 26:26–28.

46. See the section on Mithraism in chapter 2 of this volume and Tertullian, *On Prescription against Heretics,* 40.4.

47. In Christian literature "Sunday" is usually called "the Lord's Day." The Sabbath (Saturday) remained for Christians the day of rest until the fourth century.

48. This is the first reference to the reading of the Gospels as part of the liturgy.

49. See *Didache,* X.7, above.

all hold this common gathering on Sunday, since it is the first day, on which God transforming darkness and matter made the Universe, and Jesus Christ our Savior on the same day rose from the dead. For they crucified Him on the day before Saturday, and on the day after Saturday, He appeared[50] to His Apostles and disciples and taught them these things which we have passed on to you also for your consideration.

From Saint Justin Martyr, *The First and Second Apologies,* translated by Leslie William Barnard, Ancient Christian Writers, no. 56 (New York: Paulist Press, 1997), 66–72.

⮞ In *The Apostolic Tradition,* written ca. 215, **Hippolytus** (ca. 170–ca. 236) describes the interrogations—a questioning of candidates prior to baptism. He also lists the occupations and actions that would prevent conversion.

HIPPOLYTUS

The Apostolic Tradition, 15–21

15. On Newcomers to the Faith

Those who present themselves for the first time for instruction [lit., to hear the word][51] shall first of all be brought to the teachers before the congregation arrives. They shall be asked about the reason for coming to the faith, and those who have brought them [i.e., their sponsors] will testify about whether they are ready for instruction [lit., capable of hearing the word]. They shall be asked about the kind of life they lead: whether he [*sic*] has a wife or whether he is a slave. And if any is the slave of one of the faithful, whether he has his master's approval for taking instruction. If his master does not testify that he is a good man, let him be rejected. If his master is a pagan, teach him to please his master lest scandal arise. If, however, one [of the candidates] have a wife, or a wife, a husband, let them be taught to be content, husband with wife and wife with husband. If, however, someone does not have a wife, let him be taught not to fornicate but to take a wife according to the law, or to remain single [lit., as he is].[52] Should someone be possessed of a demon, he is not to be instructed in the teaching until he is pure.

16. On Jobs and Professions

Moreover, inquiry shall be made about the jobs and occupations of those who seek to be instructed. If anyone runs a house of prostitution, let him cease or be sent away. If anyone

is a sculptor or paints, let him be taught not to make idols: let him either cease or repent. If anyone is an actor or is engaged in theatrical presentations, let him cease or be rejected. As for him who teaches children, it is best that he cease; if he has no [other] craft, let him be allowed to continue. Likewise, the charioteer who competes in the games and those who take part in them, let them cease or be rejected. The gladiator, or one who trains gladiators to fight, or one who engages in the arena hunt, or an official in the gladiatorial enterprise, let him cease or be rejected. He who is a priest of idols, or an idol attendant, let him cease or be rejected.

An enlisted man [lit., a soldier under orders] shall not kill anyone. If he is ordered to, he shall not carry out the order, nor shall he take the [military oath]. He who has the power to execute [lit., of the sword] or the city magistrate who wears the purple, let him cease or be rejected. A catechumen, or one of the faithful who wants to become a soldier, let them be rejected, because they have shown contempt for God.

The prostitute, or the profligate, or the eunuch, or one who does unspeakable things, let them be rejected; they are impure.

A magician is not to be brought to the inquiry. The maker of charms, or the astrologer, or the diviner, or the interpreter of dreams, or the charlatan, or the fringe-cutter, or the phylactery-maker, let them either cease or be rejected.

Someone who is a concubine, if she is a slave and if she brings up her children and remains faithfully attached to one man, let her hear the word; otherwise let her be sent away. The man who has a concubine, let him cease and take a wife according to the law; if, however, he refuses, let him be rejected.

If we have omitted anything, the occupations [in question] will instruct you; for all of us have the Spirit of God.[53]

17. Concerning the Period of Instruction

Catechumens will be under instruction for a period of three years. If someone is zealous and applies himself well to the work of the catechumenate [lit., to the thing], not the period of time but [evidence of] conversion alone shall be judged.

---

50. Jesus was crucified on the eve of the Sabbath, that is, on Friday evening (a "day" being understood as beginning after sunset rather than after midnight), and was raised on the day after the Sabbath. See Mk 15:42–43; 16:1–6; Mt 27:57–28:7; Lk 23:50–24:7; 19:31–20:25.

51. Words in brackets have been added by the translator for clarification. (The notes for this selection are by Gerhart and Udoh.)

52. See 1 Thess 4:3–8; 1 Cor 7:1–9.

53. See 1 Cor 7:40.

18. Concerning the Prayer of Those under Instruction

When the teacher has finished his instruction, the catechumens will pray among themselves, apart from the faithful; the women, whether catechumens or faithful, will stand and pray together in a specially designated place [lit., some place] in the church. When [the catechumens] have finished praying, however, they will not give the kiss of peace, because their mouths are not holy. The faithful, nonetheless, greet each other, men, the men, women, the women; the men, however, will not greet the women; moreover, let the women cover their heads with a mantle, and not just with a kind of linen, for [such] is not a veil.[54]

19. Concerning the Imposition of the Hand

After a prayer, when the teacher has imposed his hand over the catechumens, let him pray and dismiss them. Whether he is a cleric or layman, let him do so. If a catechumen is arrested on account of the name of the Lord [i.e., because he is a Christian], let him not be of divided heart [lit., of double heart] about the testimony; should violence come to him and he is killed, although his sins are not yet forgiven [i.e., he is not yet baptized], he will [nonetheless] be justified. For he has received baptism in his own blood.

20. Concerning Those to Be Baptized

When those to be baptized are chosen, let the life of each be examined: whether they have lived with integrity while they were catechumens, whether they visited the sick, whether they did every [sort of] good work. When those who accompanied them testify about him [sic], "He has thus acted," let them hear the gospel. From the moment when they are set apart, let the hand be imposed over them daily, while they are exorcised. When the day of their baptism approaches, the bishop will exorcise each one of them to learn whether he is pure. If someone is not good or not pure, he will set them aside, because [such a one] has not heard the instructions with faith. For it is not possible that the alien [i.e., Satan] hide himself forever.

Immediate Preparations

Let those to be baptized be instructed to bathe on Thursday [lit., the fifth day of the week]. If a woman, however, is in her period, let her be put aside and baptized another day. Let those to receive baptism fast on the eve of the Sabbath [Friday] and on the Sabbath [as well]; and on the Sabbath let them be assembled in a place the bishop designates. Let him command them all to pray and kneel. And, imposing his hand over them, let him command every alien spirit to flee from them and not to return again to them. When he has finished exorcising them, let him exhale on their faces, and when he has signed their forehead, ears and noses [with the cross], let him raise them to a standing position. They will [then] pass the entire night in vigil, hearing [Scripture] reading and instruction [thereon].

Let those about to be baptized bring nothing with them except what each brings for the Eucharist. For it is fitting from that very hour that he who has been made worthy offer the oblation.

21. Concerning the Giving of Holy Baptism

At cockcrow, first let prayer be offered over the water; let the water flow or be poured into the font. Let it be done this way, unless there be some necessity. If, however, the necessity is permanent and urgent, use such water as you find.

Renunciation of Satan

[Those about to be baptized] shall take off [their] clothes. First baptize the children. Let those who can, speak for themselves. But those unable to speak for themselves, let their parents or someone from their family speak for them. Then, baptize the men and finally the women, after they have let down their hair and put away [any] gold jewelry they are wearing. And let none take any alien object [amulet] down into the water [with him].

At the appointed time for baptism, let the bishop give thanks over the oil, which he puts in a vial and calls the oil of thanksgiving. He then takes some other oil, which he exorcises and calls the oil of exorcism. A deacon then carries the oil of exorcism and stations himself at the left hand of the presbyter; another deacon takes the oil of thanksgiving and stands at the presbyter's right. Taking each candidate for baptism, let the presbyter command him to renounce saying, "I renounce you, Satan, and all your service and all your

---

54. See 1 Cor 11:2–16.

works." And when each one has renounced [Satan], let [the presbyter] anoint him with the oil of exorcism, saying to him: "May every spirit depart from you." And in this way let him [the anointing presbyter] hand the naked candidate to the bishop or to the presbyter who stands close to the water, in order to baptize him.

Immersion

Let the deacon descend with the candidate this way. When he who is to be baptized descends into the water, the one who baptizes imposes his hand on him and asks: "Do you believe in the Father Almighty?" [In the Sahidic, Ethiopic, and Arabic versions there follows a post-Nicene baptismal creed.]

And for his part, let him who is being baptized say: "I believe." And again he who is doing the baptizing, let him impose his hand on his head. Then, let him say: "Do you believe in Christ Jesus the Son of God, who was born from the Holy Spirit and from the Virgin Mary, was crucified under Pontius Pilate, died, [was buried], rose on the third day from the dead, ascended into the heavens, and sits at the right hand of the Father; and who will come to judge the living and the dead?" When he has said, "I believe," let him [the one baptizing] say, "Do you believe in the Holy Spirit and in the holy church and in the resurrection of the flesh?" Let him who is being baptized say: "I believe"; so a third time let him be baptized.

Chrismation, Prayer, the Kiss of Peace

Afterwards, when [the newly baptized] has emerged [from the font], let him be anointed with oil which has been consecrated [i.e., the oil of thanksgiving] by a presbyter saying: "I anoint you with holy oil in the name of Jesus Christ." When each [newly baptized] has dried, let them dress and then enter the church.

With his hand imposed [over] them, let the bishop say the following prayer, "Lord God, you who have made them worthy to receive the remission of sins through the bath of regeneration by the Holy Spirit, send into them your grace that they may serve you according to your will; for to you is glory, to the Father and the Son with the Holy Spirit, both now and for the ages of the ages. Amen."

Then, as he pours consecrated oil from his hand and imposes his hand on [the newly baptized's] head, let [the bishop] say: "I anoint you with holy oil in the Lord Father almighty and Christ Jesus and the Holy Spirit." And as he signs him on the forehead, let him offer the kiss and say: "The Lord be with you." Then let him who is signed say: "And with your spirit." The bishop will do thus to each. Then [the newly baptized] shall pray together with the congregation, for they do not pray with the faithful unless all these [rites] have been completed. And when they have prayed, they shall offer the kiss of peace.

The Eucharist

Next let the offering be presented to the bishop by the deacons and he will give thanks over the bread as a representation—which the Greeks call "antitype"—of the body of Christ; and over the cup mixed with wine as an antitype—which the Greeks call "likeness"—of the blood which was poured out for all those who believe in him; and over the mixture of milk and honey in fulfillment of the promise made to the fathers when [God] spoke about a land flowing [with] milk and honey,[55] and for which Christ also gave his flesh through which those who believe are nourished, making the bitterness of the heart sweet by the sweetness of his word; and over water presented in the offering as a sign of the [baptismal] bath, that the inner man, that is, the soul, may obtain the same effects as the body. The bishop will explain all these things to those who receive them.

When [the bishop] has broken the bread and as he offers each the kiss of peace, he will say: "The bread of heaven in Christ Jesus." Each one who receives will respond: "Amen." If there are not enough presbyters, let deacons take the cups and stand with deference in the proper order: the first is to be he who holds the water, the second, the milk, and the third, the wine.

Those who receive will taste of each of the three cups, as he who offers says, "In God the Father Almighty." He who receives then says: "And in the Lord Jesus Christ" [and the recipient will say, "Amen."] "And in the Holy Spirit and the holy church." And he will say: "Amen." This is to be done for each recipient. Moreover, when everything is over, let each hasten to do good work[s].

From Thomas M. Finn, ed., *Early Christian Baptism and the Catechumenate: Italy, North Africa, and Egypt,* Message of the Fathers of the Church, vol. 6 (Collegeville, MN: Liturgical Press, 1992), 46–51.

---

55. See Ex 3:8, 17, et passim.

2. MEDIEVAL LITURGIES AND PAGEANTRY

Egeria, a nun who made a pilgrimage to Jerusalem sometime in the late fourth or early fifth century, kept a detailed journal of her travels. Since the beginning and end of the manuscript are missing, all we know about Egeria must be inferred from the text: for example, that she traveled with companions, was respected and welcomed by her hosts, and stayed in the Holy Land for more than a year. We do not know where she traveled from. In these excerpts from *Account of Her Pilgrimage,* she describes the liturgical rites practiced by the Christian community during Holy Week in Jerusalem. The processions through Jerusalem that she describes appear to have been characteristic of Holy Week observances in other cities of the period.

EGERIA

Account of Her Pilgrimage, 29–42

29. [. . .] From the Sabbath[56] to Thursday, when after supper the Lord was arrested in the night, is six days. Everyone returns directly to the city and in the Anastasis the Lucernare is celebrated according to custom.

30. The next day, the Lord's Day, begins the Paschal week, which they call the Great Week. When the rites have been celebrated from cock crow until morning, according to custom in the Anastasis and the Cross, on the Lord's Day the people proceed according to custom to the great church which is called the Martyrium[57] because it is behind the Cross, where the Lord suffered, and therefore is a martyr's shrine. When all things are celebrated according to custom in the great church, before the dismissal, the archdeacon calls out and first says: "During the whole week which begins tomorrow, let us come together to the Martyrium, the great church." Then he speaks again and says: "Today at one let us all be prepared to go to the Eleona." When the dismissal is given in the great church, the Martyrium, the bishop is led with hymns to the Anastasis, and there are done all the things which it is the custom to do on the Lord's Day at the Anastasis after the dismissal at the Martyrium. Then each one goes home to eat a quick meal, so that by one o'clock[58] all will be ready to go to the church which is in Eleona, which is on Mount Olivet, where is the cave in which the Lord taught.

31. At one o'clock all of the people go up to Mount Olivet, that is, the Eleona, into the church: the bishop is seated, they sing hymns and antiphons appropriate to the day and place, as are the readings. And when it is about three o'clock, they go down singing hymns to the Imbomon which is in the place from which the Lord ascended into heaven, and everyone sits down there, for in the bishop's presence all the people are ordered to sit down, so that only the deacons remain standing. There hymns and antiphons appropriate to the day and place are sung; similarly readings and prayers are interspersed. When it is about one o'clock, that place in the Gospel is read where infants with palms and branches ran to the Lord, saying, "Blessed is he who comes in the name of the Lord."[59] Immediately the bishop rises with all of the people and then they all walk from there to the summit of Mount Olivet. For all the people walk before the bishop singing hymns and antiphons, always responding: "Blessed is he who comes in the name of the Lord." And whatever children in this place, even those not able to walk, are carried on their parent's shoulders, all holding branches, some of palm, some of olive; thus the bishop is led in the same way that the Lord once was. And from the height of the mountain all the way to the city, and from there to the Anastasis through the whole city, all go on foot, the matrons as well as the noble men thus lead the bishop, singing responses, going slowly so that the people may not tire. Then by evening they arrive at the Anastasis. When they have arrived there, although it is evening, they nonetheless say the Lucernare, and another prayer is said at the Cross and the people are dismissed.

32. The next day, Monday, all which is customary from cock crow until dawn is done at the Anastasis, and at nine o'clock and at noon as during the whole of Lent. But at three o'clock everyone gathers in the Great Church, the Martyrium, and there they sing hymns and antiphons until seven in the evening; Scripture passages appropriate to the day and place are read; prayers are interspersed. The Lucernare is held there, when the time comes. Thus finally by night they give the dismissal at the Martyrium. When the dismissal is

---

56. Egeria habitually calls Saturday the Sabbath, and Sunday the Lord's Day.

57. A *martyrium* is a shrine with relics of a saint, originally the shrine of a martyr.

58. Romans measured 12 hours after sunrise; thus the length of the hour varied from season to season. In general, one should add or subtract six to the Roman hour, depending on the relationship to noon.

59. Mt 21:9.

given they lead the bishop from there to the Anastasis with hymns. But when he has entered into the Anastasis, a hymn is sung, a prayer offered, the catechumens blessed, then the faithful, and the dismissal given.

33. On Tuesday all things are done as they were on Monday. One thing alone is added on Monday, that [is added] in the late evening, after the dismissal has been given at the Martyrium, and they have gone to the Anastasis and to the church which is on Mount Eleona. When they have arrived at that church, the bishop goes into the cave where the Lord was accustomed to teach the disciples, and he takes the codex of the Gospels, and the bishop stands and reads the words of the Lord which are written in the Gospel according to Matthew, where he says: "Watch that no one seduce you."[60] Then the bishop reads the whole discourse. When he has finished he prays, blesses the catechumens, as well as the faithful, dismissal is given, and each one returns home for it is quite late at night.

34. On Wednesday everything is done during the whole day from the first cock crow on as on Monday and Tuesday, except that after the dismissal at night from the Martyrium the bishop is led with hymns to the Anastasis. The bishop immediately enters the cave which is in the Anastasis and stands within the railing; but a presbyter stands before the railing and takes the Gospel and reads the passage where Judas Iscariot went to the Jews that they might say exactly what they would give him if he would hand over the Lord.[61] While the passage is being read, there is great moaning and groaning among the people, so that there is no one who is not moved to tears at that hour. Afterwards, a prayer is offered, the catechumens are blessed, and finally the faithful are dismissed.

35. On Thursday that which is customary is done from cock crow until the morning at the Anastasis, as well as at nine and twelve o'clock. At two o'clock according to custom, all the people gather together at the Martyrium, but before the appointed time on other days, because the dismissal must be given more quickly. When all the people have gathered, everything which is appointed is done. The Oblation is offered at the Martyrium and the dismissal is made at about four. But before the dismissal, the archdeacon calls out and says: "At the first hour of the night let us all gather at the church which is on the Eleona because great labor awaits us tonight." The dismissal having been given at the Martyrium the people go behind the Cross, and there a hymn is sung, prayer is made, and the bishop offers the Oblation and communicates everyone. Except on this one day out of the whole year the Oblation is never offered behind the Cross. This

dismissal having been given there, they go to the Anastasis, pray, and the catechumens are blessed [because] they have come into Gethsemani. First a suitable prayer is offered, then a hymn is sung, and the place in the Gospel is read where the Lord was arrested. While this passage is being read, there is such moaning and groaning with weeping among the people that they can be heard by all the people of the city.

36. At that hour they go back to the city on foot, singing hymns; they come to the gate at the hour when people can begin to tell one person from another; from there all the way through the middle of the city each and everyone, old and young, rich, poor, all are ready, for particularly on this day no one leaves the vigil until daybreak. Thus the bishop is led from Gethsemani up to the gate and from there through the whole city up to the Cross. But when they have come there before the Cross, it is beginning to be clear daylight. Then they read the place in the Gospel where the Lord is led up to Pilate, and everything is written which Pilate spoke to the Lord or to the Jews.[62] Afterwards the bishop addresses the people, comforting them, because they have labored the whole night long and they are to work this whole day, encouraging them not to weaken, but to have hope in God, who will for this labor bestow on them an even greater reward. So comforting them as he is able, he addresses them: "Now go again, each one of you to your homes, sit there for a while, and be ready to be back here about eight o'clock, so that from that hour until about noon you may be able to see the holy wood of the Cross, which we believe to be profitable to the salvation of each of us. And from noon on we must again assemble here, that is, before the Cross, that we may devote ourselves to readings and prayers until the night."

37. After this, the dismissal is given from the Cross before sunrise, and everyone who is full of energy goes to Sion to pray at the column where the Lord was whipped. From there they go back to rest in their homes for a short while, and then are ready. Then the bishop's chair is set up on Golgotha behind the Cross, which now stands there; the bishop is seated on the chair, and before is placed a table covered with a linen cloth. The deacons stand in a circle around the table and the silver casket decorated with gold is brought in, in which is the holy wood of the Cross. It is opened and taken out, and both the wood of the Cross and the title are placed on

---

60. Mt 24:41.

61. Mt 26:3–16.

62. Jn 18:28–19:16; Mt 27.

the table. While it is on the table, the bishop sits and grasps the ends of the holy wood with his hands, and the deacons, who are standing around him, keep watch. Here is why they guard it so. It is the custom that all of the people here come one by one, the faithful and the catechumens, bowing before the table, kissing the holy Cross and moving on. I was told that because someone (I do not know who) bit off and stole some of the holy Cross, now it is guarded by the deacons so that it dare not be done by someone again.

So all of the people pass through one by one, bowing, first with their foreheads and then with their eyes touching the Cross and the title, and so kissing the Cross they pass through, but no one is permitted to put a hand on the Cross. But when they have kissed the Cross, they go on, and a deacon stands holding a ring of Solomon and the horn from which kings are anointed. They kiss the horn and venerate the ring from about eight o'clock, and even until noon all the people pass by, going in through one door and exiting through another. This takes place where the day before, Thursday, the Oblation was offered.

When noon comes, they go before the Cross, rain or shine, because the place is outdoors and like a large and very beautiful atrium, between the Cross and the Anastasis. All the people are so crowded there that one cannot even open a door. The bishop's chair is placed before the Cross, and from noon to three nothing is done except that Biblical passages are read. First there are readings from the Psalms, whatever speaks of the Passion, then there are readings from the Acts of the Apostles or from the Epistle, whatever speaks of the Passion of the Lord, then places from the Gospels where the Lord suffers, then readings from the prophets where they speak of the Passion; then they read the Gospels where he foretells the Passion. And so from noon to three either there are readings or hymns so that all the people may be shown that whatever the prophets foretold of the Passion of the Lord is done either in the Gospels or the Apostolic writings. And thus during this three hours the people are taught that nothing happened which was not first foretold, and nothing was foretold which was not completed. Prayers are always interspersed, and those prayers are always fitting to the day. At each reading and prayer there is such emotion and weeping by all the people that it is a wonder; for there is no one, old or young, who does not on this day weep for these three hours more than can be imagined because the Lord has suffered for us. After this, when it is about the ninth hour, the passage in the Gospel of John is read, where he delivers up his

spirit; after that reading a prayer is offered and the dismissal.[63] When the dismissal is given before the Cross, immediately everyone gathers in the great church of the Martyrium and they do there those things they have been doing weekly between three o'clock and evening, when they gather at the Martyrium according to custom.

The dismissal having been given, they go from the Martyrium to the Anastasis. And when they have come there, the passage in the Gospel is read where Joseph asks Pilate for the body of the Lord, that he might place it in a new tomb. After the reading a prayer is offered, the catechumens are blessed and the dismissal is given. On this day no voice is raised to say that there will be a vigil at the Anastasis because everyone knows that the people are tired, but it is the custom that the vigil be there. And so, those among the people who wish, or who can, keep vigil: those who cannot, however, do not keep vigil until dawn. Those of the clerics who are stronger or younger keep vigil until dawn, and the whole night hymns and antiphons are sung there until morning. A great crowd keep vigil, some from evening, others from midnight, but all doing what they can.

38. On the Sabbath, the next day, all is done according to custom at nine o'clock and again at noon; but three is not observed as usually on the Sabbath; rather, the Paschal vigil is prepared in the great church, the Martyrium. The Paschal vigil is observed just as with us, but one thing is done more elaborately: the infants,[64] when they have been baptized and clothed, as soon as they come from the font are first led with the bishop to the Anastasis. The bishop goes within the enclosure of the Anastasis, sings a hymn, and thus he returns with them to the great church, where according to custom all the people are keeping watch. Everything is done there which is customary with us, and having offered the Oblation the dismissal is given. After the dismissal of the vigil service they come with hymns to the Anastasis and there again the passage of the resurrection gospel is read, and again the bishop makes the offering. But all is done quickly for the sake of the people, that they may not be delayed too long, and so the people are dismissed. On this day the hour of their dismissal is the same as with us.

39. These Paschal days are observed until late evening just as with us, and the services are performed in due order

---

63. Jn 19:30.

64. "Infants" refers to the newly baptized, regardless of chronological age.

during the eight Paschal days as it is done everywhere during the Pasch. One finds the same decoration and arrangements through the eight Paschal days as at Epiphany, both in the major church and the Anastasis and the Cross as well as Eleona, and in Bethlehem and the Lazarium, for these are the Paschal days. All proceed on the Lord's Day first to the great church, the Martyrium, and on Monday and Tuesday; when after the dismissal from the Martyrium they all come with hymns to the Anastasis. But on Wednesday all proceed to the Eleona, Thursday to the Anastasis, Friday to Sion, on the Sabbath before the Cross, but on the Lord's Day, the octave, again to the great church, the Martyrium. Every one of the eight days of the Pasch after lunch the bishop with all the clergy and all the new born, those who have just been baptized, and all of the *aputactitae,* male and female, and all the other people who wish to, go up to the Eleona. They sing hymns, and pray both in the church which is Eleona, where is the cave where Jesus taught the disciples, as well as in the Imbomon, which is that place where the Lord ascended into heaven. After they have sung psalms and prayed they go back down to the Anastasis for the Lucernare. This is done on all eight days. On the Lord's Day during the Pasch after the dismissal of the Lucernare from the Anastasis, the people conduct the bishops with hymns to Sion. When they have arrived there they sing hymns appropriate to the time and place, pray and read that place in the Gospel where the Lord, on the same day and in the same place where now the church of Sion is located, came into the midst of the disciples, even though the doors were shut. That was when Thomas, one of the disciples, was not present, and returning and being told by the disciples that they had seen the Lord, he said: "I will not believe, unless I see."[65] After this reading, a prayer is offered, the catechumens are blessed, then the faithful, and each one returns home late, about eight o'clock at night.

40. Then on the Lord's Day, the octave of the Pasch, immediately after noon all the people go up with the bishop to the Eleona; first everyone sits for a while in the church which is there, then they sing hymns and antiphons which are appropriate to the day and place, and pray suitably for the day and place. Then they go from there with hymns up to the Imbomon, and they observe things as at the Eleona. When the hour approaches all the people and the *aputactitae* lead the bishop with hymns to the Anastasis. They arrive at the Anastasis at the hour when the Lucernare is observed. The Lucernare is observed at the Anastasis as well as the Cross, and from there all of the people without exception lead the bishop with hymns to Sion. When they have arrived there, they as usual sing hymns appropriate to the time and place, then they read the place in the Gospel where on the Paschal octave the Lord entered into where the disciples were, and reproached Thomas because he had been unbelieving.[66] Then the whole reading is completed. When it is finished a prayer is offered; the catechumens are blessed, then the faithful according to custom, and each one returns home as on the Pasch, at about eight o'clock at night.

41. From the Pasch until the fortieth day, which is Pentecost, absolutely no one fasts here, not even those who are *aputactitae.* For on those days all things are done according to custom at the Anastasis from cock crow to morning; likewise at the sixth hour and at the Lucernare. On the Lord's Day everyone proceeds as usual to the Martyrium, the great church, according to custom, and from there they go to the Anastasis with hymns. But on Wednesdays and Fridays, because absolutely no one fasts here on these days, they proceed to Sion, but in the morning the service is performed according to the appointed order.

42. On the fortieth day after the Pasch, which is Thursday, the day before noon on Wednesday everyone goes to Bethlehem to celebrate the vigil. They keep the vigil in the church in Bethlehem, in the church where is the cave where the Lord was born. On the next day, Thursday, the fortieth day, the service is celebrated according to its usual order, so that presbyters and the bishop preach, saying words appropriate to the day and place. Afterwards in the evening everyone returns to Jerusalem.

Translated by Patricia Wilson-Kastner, in Patricia Wilson-Kastner et al., *A Lost Tradition: Women Writers of the Early Church* (Lanham, MD: University Press of America, 1981), 118–25.

❧ **"The Quem-Quaeritis Trope,"** a text that first appears in sources from the ninth century, is one of the earliest examples of "dialogued song" in the liturgy. The trope, sung during the Easter Mass service, is taken from Mark 16:1–8, where the three Marys speak with the angel at the empty sepulcher. In the medieval English Church, this trope developed into the literary genre "mystery play" (a play based on a biblical event), which, along

---

65. Jn 20:19–25.
66. Jn 20:26–29.

with "miracle" and "morality" plays, is regarded as the origin of secular drama in the West.

"The Quem-Quaeritis Trope"

De Resurrectione Domini	Of the Lord's Resurrection
Int[errogatio]:	Question [of the angels]:
Quem quaeritis in sepulchro,	*Whom seek ye in the sepulchre,*
[o] Christicolae?	*O followers of Christ?*
R[esponsio]:	Answer [of the Marys]:
Jesum Nazarenum	*Jesus of Nazareth, which was*
crucifixum, o caelicolae.	*crucified, O celestial ones.*
[Angeli:]	[The angels:]
Non est hic; surrexit	*He is not here; he is risen,*
sicut praedixerat.	*just as he foretold.*
Ite, nuntiate quia surrexit	*Go, announce that he is risen*
de sepulchro.	*from the sepulchre.*

From St. Gall MS 484, in *Chief Pre-Shakespearean Dramas: A Selection of Plays Illustrating the History of the English Drama from Its Origin down to Shakespeare,* edited by Joseph Quincy Adams (Boston: Houghton Mifflin, 1924), 3.

✍ "The Easter Sepulchre," an account of Good Friday and Easter liturgies practiced at the monastic church of Durham, England, is taken from a source originally published in 1593.

"The Easter Sepulchre"[67]

I. Depositio Crucis [*Good Friday.*]

Within the Abbey Church of Durham, upon Good Friday, theire was marvelous solemne service, in the which service time, after the Passion was sung, two of the eldest Monkes did take a goodly large CRUCIFIX, all of gold, of the picture of our Saviour Christ nailed upon the crosse, lyinge upon a velvett cushion, havinge St. Cuthbert's armes upon it all imbroydered with gold, bringinge that betwixt them upon the said cushion to the lowest greeces in the Quire; and there betwixt them did hold the said picture of our Saviour, sitting of every side, on ther knees, of that, and then one of the said Monkes did rise and went a pretty way from it, sitting downe upon his knees, with his shooes put of, and verye reverently did creepe away upon his knees unto the said Crosse, and most reverently did kisse it. And after him the other Monke did so likewise; and then they did sitt them downe on every side of the Crosse, and holdinge it betwixt them; and after that the Prior came forth of his stall, and did sitt him downe

of his knees, with his shooes off, and in like sort did creepe also unto the said Crosse; and all the Monkes after him, one after another, in the same order; and in the mean time all the whole quire singing an himne. The service being ended, the two Monkes did carrye it to the SEPULCHRE with great reverence, which Sepulchre was sett upp in the morninge on the north side of the Quire, nigh to the High Altar, before the service time; and there lay it within the said SEPULCHRE with great devotion, with another picture of our Saviour Christ, in whose breast they did enclose, with great reverence, the most holy and blessed Sacrament of the Altar, senceinge it, and prayinge unto it upon theire knees, a great space, settinge two tapers lighted before it, which tapers did burne unto Easter day in the morninge, that it was taken forth.

II. Elevatio Crucis [*Easter Day.*]

There was in the Abbye Church of Duresme[68] verye solemne service upon Easter Day, betweene three and four of the clocke in the morninge, in honour of the RESURRECTION, where two of the oldest Monkes of the Quire came to the Sepulchre, being sett upp uppon Good Friday, after the Passion, all covered with red velvett and embrodered with gold, and then did sence it, either Monke with a pair of silver sencers sitting on theire knees before the Sepulchre. Then they both rising came to the Sepulchre, out of which, with great devotion and reverence, they tooke a marvelous beautifull IMAGE OF OUR SAVIOUR, representing the resurrection, with a crosse in his hand, in the breast wherof was enclosed in bright christall the holy Sacrament of the Altar, throughe the which christall the Blessed Host was conspicuous to the behoulders. Then, after the elevation of the said picture, carryed by the said two Monkes upon a faire velvett cushion, all embrodered, singinge the anthem of *Christus resurgens,* they brought it to the High Altar, settinge that on the midst therof, whereon it stood, the two Monkes kneelinge on theire knees before the Altar, and senceing it all the time that the rest of the whole quire was in singinge the foresaid anthem of *Christus resurgens.* The which anthem beinge ended, the two Monkes tooke up the cushions and the picture from the Altar, supporting it betwixt them, proceed-

---

67. For a more primitive form of the *Despositio Crucis* and the *Elevatio Crucis,* see the Latin text from the *Regularis Concordia* of St. Ethelwold, printed by E. K. Chambers, *The Medieval Stage,* ii, 306.

68. Durham.

ing, in procession, from the High Altar to the south Quire dore, where there was four ancient Gentlemen, belonginge to the Prior, appointed to attend theire cominge, holdinge upp a most rich CANNOPYE of purple velvett, tached round about with redd silke and gold fringe; and at everye corner did stand one of theise ancient Gentlemen, to beare it over the said image, with the Holy Sacrament, carried by two Monkes round about the church, the whole quire waitinge uppon it with goodly torches and great store of other lights, all singinge, rejoyceinge, and praising God most devoutly, till they came to the High Altar againe, whereon they did place the said image, there to remaine untill the Ascension day.

From J. Raine, ed., "A Description or Brief Declaration of all the Ancient Monuments, Rites and Customes belonginge or beinge within the Monastical Church of Durham before the Suppresion" (Surtees Society, xv), in *Chief Pre-Shakespearean Dramas: A Selection of Plays Illustrating the History of the English Drama from Its Origin down to Shakespeare*, edited by Joseph Quincy Adams (Boston: Houghton Mifflin, 1924), 4–5.

☙ The letters of **Hildegard of Bingen** (1098–1179)—composer, theologian, visionary, and Benedictine founder—provide a glimpse into medieval liturgical practices. The first letter presented here, addressed to the prelates at Mainz and written in 1178–79 (Letter 23), describes her dismay at the prelates' injunction against the use of liturgical music imposed upon her community because she allowed a former excommunicate to be buried in the monastic cemetery. The second letter, written to Hildegard by Mistress Tengswich in 1148–50 (Letter 52), inquires about irregular liturgical practices endorsed by Hildegard. In the third letter, written to "the congregation of nuns" in 1148–50 (Letter 52r), Hildegard justifies the practices that Tengswich impugns.

HILDEGARD OF BINGEN
Letter 23 (Hildegard to the prelates at Mainz)

By a vision, which was implanted in my soul by God the Great Artisan before I was born, I have been compelled to write these things because of the interdict by which our superiors have bound us, on account of a certain dead man buried at our monastery, a man buried without any objection, with his own priest officiating. Yet only a few days after his burial, these men ordered us to remove him from our cemetery. Seized by no small terror, as a result, I looked as usual to the True Light, and, with wakeful eyes, I saw in my spirit that if this man were disinterred in accordance with their commands, a terrible and lamentable danger would come upon us like a dark cloud before a threatening thunderstorm.

Therefore, we have not presumed to remove the body of the deceased inasmuch as he had confessed his sins, had received extreme unction and communion, and had been buried without objection. Furthermore, we have not yielded to those who advised or even commanded this course of action. Not, certainly, that we take the counsel of upright men or the orders of our superiors lightly, but we would not have it appear that, out of feminine harshness we did injustice to the sacraments of Christ, with which this man had been fortified while he was still alive. But so that we may not be totally disobedient we have, in accordance with their injunction, ceased from singing the divine praises and from participation in Mass, as had been our regular monthly custom.

As a result, my sisters and I have been greatly distressed and saddened. Weighed down by this burden, therefore, I heard these words in a vision: It is improper for you to obey human words ordering you to abandon the sacraments of the Garment of the Word of God, Who, born virginally of the Virgin Mary, is your salvation. Still, it is incumbent upon you to seek permission to participate in the sacraments from those prelates who laid the obligation of obedience upon you. For ever since Adam was driven from the bright region of paradise into the exile of this world on account of his disobedience, the conception of all people is justly tainted by that first transgression. Therefore, in accordance with God's inscrutable plan, it was necessary for a man free from all pollution to be born in human flesh, through whom all who are predestined to life might be cleansed from corruption and might be sanctified by the communion of his body so that he might remain in them and they in him for their fortification. That person, however, who is disobedient to the commands of God, as Adam was, and is completely forgetful of Him must be completely cut off from participation in the sacrament of His body, just as he himself has turned away from Him in disobedience. And he must remain so until, purged through penitence, he is permitted by the authorities to receive the communion of the Lord's body again. In contrast, however, a person who is aware that he has incurred such a restriction not as a result of anything that he has done, either consciously or deliberately, may be present at the service of the life-giving sacrament, to be cleansed by the Lamb without sin, Who, in obedience to the Father, allowed Himself to be sacrificed on the altar of the cross that he might restore salvation to all.

In that same vision I also heard that I had erred in not going humbly and devoutly to my superiors for permission to participate in the communion, especially since we were not at fault in receiving that dead man into our cemetery. For, after all, he had been fortified by his own priest with proper Christian procedure, and, without objection from anyone, was buried in our cemetery, with all Bingen joining in the funeral procession. And so God has commanded me to report these things to you, our lords and prelates. Further, I saw in my vision also that by obeying you we have been celebrating the divine office incorrectly, for from the time of your restriction up to the present, we have ceased to sing the divine office, merely reading it instead. And I heard a voice coming from the Living Light concerning the various kinds of praises, about which David speaks in the psalm: "Praise Him with sound of trumpet: praise Him with psaltery and harp," and so forth up to this point: "Let every spirit praise the Lord."[69] These words use outward, visible things to teach us about inward things. Thus the material composition and the quality of these instruments instruct us how we ought to give form to the praise of the Creator and turn all the convictions of our inner being to the same. When we consider these things carefully, we recall that man needed the voice of the living Spirit, but Adam lost this divine voice through disobedience. For while he was still innocent, before his transgression, his voice blended fully with the voices of the angels in their praise of God. Angels are called spirits from that Spirit which is God, and thus they have such voices by virtue of their spiritual nature. But Adam lost that angelic voice which he had in paradise, for he fell asleep to that knowledge which he possessed before his sin, just as a person on waking up only dimly remembers what he had seen in his dreams. And so when he was deceived by the trick of the devil and rejected the will of his Creator, he became wrapped up in the darkness of inward ignorance as the just result of his iniquity.

God, however, restores the souls of the elect to that pristine blessedness by infusing them with the light of truth. And in accordance with His eternal plan, He so devised it that whenever He renews the hearts of many with the pouring out of the prophetic spirit, they might, by means of His interior illumination, regain some of the knowledge which Adam had before he was punished for his sin.

And so the holy prophets, inspired by the Spirit which they had received, were called for this purpose: not only to compose psalms and canticles (by which the hearts of listeners would be inflamed) but also to construct various kinds of musical instruments to enhance these songs of praise with melodic strains. Thereby, both through the form and quality of the instruments, as well as through the meaning of the words which accompany them, those who hear might be taught, as we said above, about inward things, since they have been admonished and aroused by outward things. In such a way, these holy prophets get beyond the music of this exile and recall to mind that divine melody of praise which Adam, in company with the angels, enjoyed in God before his fall.

Men of zeal and wisdom have imitated the holy prophets and have themselves, with human skill, invented several kinds of musical instruments, so that they might be able to sing for the delight of their souls, and they accompanied their singing with instruments played with the flexing of the fingers, recalling, in this way, Adam, who was formed by God's finger, which is the Holy Spirit. For, before he sinned, his voice had the sweetness of all musical harmony. Indeed, if he had remained in his original state, the weakness of mortal man would not have been able to endure the power and the resonance of his voice.

But when the devil, man's great deceiver, learned that man had begun to sing through God's inspiration and, therefore, was being transformed to bring back the sweetness of the songs of heaven, mankind's homeland, he was so terrified at seeing his clever machinations go to ruin that he was greatly tormented. Therefore, he devotes himself continually to thinking up and working out all kinds of wicked contrivances. Thus he never ceases from confounding confession and the sweet beauty of both divine praise and spiritual hymns, eradicating them through wicked suggestions, impure thoughts, or various distractions from the heart of man and even from the mouth of the Church itself, wherever he can, through dissension, scandal, or unjust oppression.

Therefore, you and all prelates must exercise the greatest vigilance to clear the air by full and thorough discussion of the justification for such actions before your verdict closes the mouth of any church singing praises to God or suspends it from handling or receiving the divine sacraments. And you must be especially certain that you are drawn to this action out of zeal for God's justice, rather than out of indignation, unjust emotions, or a desire for revenge, and you must always be on your guard not to be circumvented in your decisions by Satan, who drove man from celestial harmony and the delights of paradise.

Consider, too, that just as the body of Jesus Christ was born of the purity of the Virgin Mary through the operation of the Holy Spirit so, too, the canticle of praise, reflecting celestial harmony, is rooted in the Church through the Holy

---

69. Ps 150.3, 6.

Spirit. The body is the vestment of the spirit, which has a living voice, and so it is proper for the body, in harmony with the soul, to use its voice to sing praises to God. Whence, in metaphor, the prophetic spirit commands us to praise God with clashing cymbals and cymbals of jubilation,[70] as well as other musical instruments which men of wisdom and zeal have invented, because all arts pertaining to things useful and necessary for mankind have been created by the breath that God sent into man's body. For this reason it is proper that God be praised in all things.

And because sometimes a person sighs and groans at the sound of singing, remembering, as it were, the nature of celestial harmony, the prophet, aware that the soul is symphonic and thoughtfully reflecting on the profound nature of the spirit, urges us in the psalm[71] to confess to the Lord with the harp and to sing a psalm to Him with the ten-stringed psaltery. His meaning is that the harp, which is plucked from below, relates to the discipline of the body; the psaltery, which is plucked from above, pertains to the exertion of the spirit; the ten chords, to the fulfillment of the law.

Therefore, those who, without just cause, impose silence on a church and prohibit the singing of God's praises and those who have on earth unjustly despoiled God of His honor and glory will lose their place among the chorus of angels, unless they have amended their lives through true penitence and humble restitution. Moreover, let those who hold the keys of heaven beware not to open those things which are to be kept closed nor to close those things which are to be kept open, for harsh judgment will fall upon those who rule, unless, as the apostle says,[72] they rule with good judgment.

And I heard a voice saying thus: Who created heaven? God. Who opens heaven to the faithful? God. Who is like Him? No one. And so, O men of faith, let none of you resist Him or oppose Him, lest He fall on you in His might and you have no helper to protect you from His judgment. This time is a womanish time, because the dispensation of God's justice is weak. But the strength of God's justice is exerting itself, a female warrior battling against injustice, so that it might fall defeated.

From *The Letters of Hildegard of Bingen*, vol. 1, translated and edited by Joseph L. Baird and Radd K. Ehrman (New York: Oxford University Press, 1994), 76–80.

HILDEGARD OF BINGEN

Letter 52 (Mistress Tengswich to Hildegard)

To Hildegard, mistress of the brides of Christ, Tengswich, unworthy superior of the sisters at Andernach, with a prayer that she eventually be joined to the highest order of spirits in heaven.

The report of your saintliness has flown far and wide and has brought to our attention things wondrous and remarkable. And, insignificant as we are, these reports have highly commended the loftiness of your outstanding and extraordinary mode of religious life to us. We have learned from a number of people that an angel from above reveals many secrets of heaven for you to record, difficult as they are for mortal minds to grasp, as well as some things that you are to do, not in accordance with human wisdom, but as God himself instructs them to be done.

We have, however, also heard about certain strange and irregular practices that you countenance. They say that on feast days your virgins stand in the church with unbound hair when singing the psalms and that as part of their dress they wear white, silk veils, so long that they touch the floor. Moreover, it is said that they wear crowns of gold filigree, into which are inserted crosses on both sides and the back, with a figure of the Lamb on the front, and that they adorn their fingers with golden rings. And all this despite the express prohibition of the great shepherd of the Church, who writes in admonition: Let women comport themselves with modesty "not with plaited hair, or gold, or pearls, or costly attire."[73] Moreover, that which seems no less strange to us is the fact that you admit into your community only those women from noble, well-established families and absolutely reject others who are of lower birth and of less wealth. Thus we are struck with wonder and are reeling in confusion when we ponder quietly in our heart that the Lord himself brought into the primitive Church humble fishermen and poor people, and that, later, at the conversion of the gentiles, the blessed Peter said: "In truth, I perceive that God is no respecter of persons."[74] Nor should you be unmindful of the words of the Apostle in Corinthians: "Not many mighty, not many noble, but God hath chosen the contemptible and the ignoble things of this world."[75] We have examined as accurately as possible all the precedents laid down by the fathers of the Church, to which all spiritual people must conform, and we have found nothing in them comparable to your actions.

O worthy bride of Christ, such unheard-of practices far exceed the capacity of our weak understanding, and strike us

---

70. Cf. Ps 150.5.
71. Cf. Ps 32.2, 91.4.
72. Cf. Rom 12.8.

73. 1 Tim 2.9.
74. Acts 10.34; cf. Rom 2.11.
75. 1 Cor 1.26–28.

with no little wonder. And although we feeble little women wholeheartedly rejoice with all the esteem due your spiritual success, we still wish you to inform us on some points relative to this matter. Therefore, we have decided to send this humble little letter to you, saintly lady, asking by whose authority you can defend such practices, and we devoutly and meekly beseech, worthy lady, that you not disdain to write back to us as soon as possible. Farewell, and remember us in your prayers.

From *The Letters of Hildegard of Bingen*, vol. 1, translated and edited by Joseph L. Baird and Radd K. Ehrman (New York: Oxford University Press, 1994), 127–28.

HILDEGARD OF BINGEN

Letter 52r (Hildegard to the congregation of nuns)

The Living Fountain says: Let a woman remain within her chamber so that she may preserve her modesty, for the serpent breathed the fiery danger of horrible lust into her. Why should she do this? Because the beauty of woman radiated and blazed forth in the primordial root, and in her was formed that chamber in which every creature lies hidden. Why is she so resplendent? For two reasons: on the one hand, because she was created by the finger of God and, on the other, because she was endowed with wondrous beauty. O, woman, what a splendid being you are! For you have set your foundation in the sun, and have conquered the world.

Paul the apostle, who flew to the heights but kept silent on earth so as not to reveal that which was hidden,[76] observed that a woman who is subject to the power of her husband,[77] joined to him through the first rib, ought to preserve great modesty, by no means giving or displaying her vessel to another man who has no business with her, for that vessel belongs to her husband.[78] And let her do this in accordance with the word spoken by the master of the earth in scorn of the devil: "What God hath joined together, let no man put asunder."[79]

Listen: The earth keeps the grass green and vital, until winter conquers it. Then winter takes away the beauty of that flower, and the earth covers over its vital force so that it is unable to manifest itself as if it had never withered up, because winter has ravaged it. In a similar manner, a woman, once married, ought not to indulge herself in prideful adornment of hair or person, nor ought she to lift herself up to vanity, wearing a crown and other golden ornaments, except at her husband's pleasure, and even then with moderation.

But these strictures do not apply to a virgin, for she stands in the unsullied purity of paradise, lovely and unwithering,

and she always remains in the full vitality of the budding rod. A virgin is not commanded to cover up her hair, but she willingly does so out of her great humility, for a person will naturally hide the beauty of her soul, lest, on account of her pride, the hawk carry it off.

Virgins are married with holiness in the Holy Spirit and in the bright dawn of virginity, and so it is proper that they come before the great High Priest as an oblation presented to God. Thus through the permission granted her and the revelation of the mystic inspiration of the finger of God, it is appropriate for a virgin to wear a white vestment, the lucent symbol of her betrothal to Christ, considering that her mind is made one with the interwoven whole, and keeping in mind the One to whom she is joined, as it is written: "Having his name, and the name of his Father, written on their foreheads"[80] and also "These follow the Lamb whithersoever he goeth."[81]

God also keeps a watchful eye on every person, so that a lower order will not gain ascendancy over a higher one, as Satan and the first man did, who wanted to fly higher than they had been placed. And who would gather all his livestock indiscriminately into one barn—the cattle, the asses, the sheep, the kids? Thus it is clear that differentiation must be maintained in these matters, lest people of varying status, herded all together, be dispersed through the pride of their elevation, on the one hand, or the disgrace of their decline, on the other, and especially lest the nobility of their character be torn asunder when they slaughter one another out of hatred. Such destruction naturally results when the higher order falls upon the lower, and the lower rises above the higher. For God establishes ranks on earth, just as in heaven with angels, archangels, thrones, dominions, cherubim, and seraphim. And they are all loved by God, although they are not equal in rank. Pride loves princes and nobles because of their illusions of grandeur, but hates them when they destroy that illusion. And it is written that "God does not cast off the mighty, since He himself is mighty."[82] He does not love people for their rank but for their works, which derive their savor from Him, just as the Son of God says: "My food is to do the will" of my Father.[83] Where humility is found, there Christ always prepares a banquet. Thus when individu-

---

76. Cf. 2 Cor 12.2ff.
77. Cf. Eph 5.22ff.; Col 3.18.
78. Cf. 1 Thess 4.4.
79. Mt 19.6.
80. Apoc 14.1.
81. Apoc 14.4.
82. Job 36.5.
83. Jn 4.34.

als seek after empty honor rather than humility, because they believe that one is preferable to the other, it is necessary that they be assigned to their proper place. Let the sick sheep be cast out of the fold, lest it infect the entire flock.

God has infused human beings with good understanding so that their name will not be destroyed. It is not good for people to grab hold of a mountain which they cannot possibly move. Rather, they should stand in the valley, gradually learning what they are capable of.

These words do not come from a human being but from the Living Light. Let the one who hears see and believe where these words come from.

From *The Letters of Hildegard of Bingen*, vol. 1, translated and edited by Joseph L. Baird and Radd K. Ehrman (New York: Oxford University Press, 1994), 128–30.

≈ *The Shape of the Liturgy* (first published in 1944), by **Dom Gregory Dix** (1901–52), is an early contribution in the field of liturgical scholarship. In it Dix provides a broad overview of the development of eucharistic rites in the Western tradition of Christianity.

DOM GREGORY DIX

"The Development of the Western Rites," in *The Shape of the Liturgy*

The Western development is more complicated and diverse [than the Eastern] and continued for much longer. It will occupy the remainder of this chapter, and can most conveniently be set out by following up separately the various regional developments which come to their synthesis in the tenth century, and then continuing from that. But there are certain essential general observations which must be borne in mind all through, if we are to understand the matter.

The importance and interest of the special developments of the Gallican and Mozarabic rites have been much obscured in modern study. This is due partly to the fact that they have been for so many centuries virtually museum pieces, and it is correspondingly difficult to enter into their particular spirit. Partly also it is due to less excusable mistakings of their history and significance, the most serious of which is the persistent attempt to find for them a non-Western origin. These rites certainly contain Eastern elements (like the *Aios* and the *Kyries* and the *Sanctus*), just as the Roman rite contains Eastern elements (like the *Kyries* and the *Sanctus* and the *Agnus Dei*), and for the same reason—the deliberate piecemeal bor-

rowing, now of one item, now of another, from Eastern and especially from Syrian sources. The Gallican and Mozarabic rites contain rather more of these items than the Roman only because Rome rather less readily admitted innovations from any source. But in all the Western rites these Eastern borrowings are relatively late and of superficial importance, matters of decoration rather than of substance. Structurally and in their fundamental spirit and origin these French and Spanish rites are as Western as any in Italy. Such structural differences as they exhibit from the Roman rite are due to slightly different arrangements of those lesser prayers of the "second *stratum*," which only began to be introduced one by one into any of the Western rites about or after AD 400.

The question has often been debated as to the relation of these rites with those of Rome and Africa. Attempts have been made to shew that Africa used the "Gallican" rite, or alternatively that it used the Roman. It has been held that the so-called "Gallican" rite is really the original form of the Roman, faithfully preserved in the provinces when the mother-church (secretly and without record) turned its own rite upside down; or alternatively, that the churches of France and Spain originally used the pure Roman rite and that the whole of the Gallican and Mozarabic liturgical development is a novel and rootless local experiment of the dark ages. I can only say that this whole way of regarding the matter has come to seem to me not only mistaken but perversely unhistorical. And I suspect that it is not unconnected (however unconsciously) with partisan positions, for and against, on the modern problem of "Rome." In reality it is wholly unwarrantable to read back into the fifth and sixth centuries—or for the matter of that with any rigour into the seventh or even the eighth centuries, though the conception was developing about then—anything like the modern conception of "rites" as defined and separate entities, ranged alongside one another in conscious difference and even in rivalry. Who is going to tell us whether the compilers of the *Bobbio Missal* or the *Missale Francorum* on the one hand, or the various Frankish "Gelasian" missals on the other, supposed their books with their heterogeneous contents to be books of the "Gallican" or the "Roman" rites? Even with modern scientific methods of classification it is difficult, sometimes impossible, to decide; and what is quite clear is that the compilers themselves never even asked themselves the question. In the fifth and even sixth century, as in the fourth, there were still no "rites" in our modern sense, but only "the liturgy," which everyone knew to be the same thing everywhere. Every local church had its own traditional way of doing it, which it was free to revise or augment or improve as it saw fit, from its own inventions or by borrowings from elsewhere. There were tentative efforts after local uniformity, like those of the Councils of Milevis and Vaison; but they were still occasioned by local circumstances, and limited and temporary in their real effect on what went on in practice at the altars in the churches. In every church contemporary fashions and novelties had their own attractions in each generation. Local tradition still played a preponderating part. In the long run *racial* temperament and characteristics (rather than geographical distinctions) made their different and immensely powerful influences felt on the wording of prayers and above all on the character of devotion and rites. In the circumstances this was inevitable; there were as yet no artificial national unities in the West, and Europe was in the melting pot. We know little enough about the African rites. But to an impartial view even the scanty evidence available indicates that they were neither "Roman" nor "Gallican" but *African*—the local development of the pre-Nicene African tradition, enriched by borrowings from other churches, not only Western but Eastern, but the whole moulded by the mind and spirit of the African local churches. The passage from the African sixth century prayer cited by Fulgentius (297) indicates that it was *not* variable like the contemporary French and Spanish prayers. But it certainly is not "Roman" any more than it is "Gallican," though it is quite easily recognisable as "Western."

And it was the same elsewhere. All the Western rites have their roots in the old pre-Nicene tradition, which as regards the Shape of the Liturgy was oecumenically the same. As regards the contents of the prayer the Western rites as a group have preserved the old conceptions of the eucharist more faithfully in some things than those of the East, which underwent more radical changes during the fourth century. Certain peculiarities common to the whole of the West (e.g. the "naming" in connection with the offertory) make their appearance in the fourth century, and grow into real distinctions from the Eastern rites during the fifth and sixth centuries. (This is partly the result of *different* innovations being made simultaneously in the East.) All this is a consequence of the need for adapting the eucharist to a public worship. Most important of all for the future, the new Western principle of varying the prayers according to the calendar makes its appearance in the fifth century and is applied by the various Western churches in rather different ways, or perhaps it is truer to say, to a varying extent. In the course of the sixth–seventh century, when political confusion is great and intercourse between the Western churches much inter-

rupted, these local Western differences in the application of a common principle harden into real distinctions, obvious to all and disconcerting to some minds, e.g. to that of S. Augustine of Canterbury. The Roman "rite," the Milanese and Beneventan "rites," the Gallican "rite," the Mozarabic "rite," in our modern sense, are all substantially products of this period—it might even be said of the single sixth century. But in AD 600 men were not yet conscious of them as separate things, but still thought of them rather as different ways of doing the same thing. Each is the outcome of a local tradition and a local *population* living a local history; each is subject to particular influences from outside, as well as to local developments, working diversely upon the roughly similar basis all had inherited from the fixed rites of the fourth century, under the new influence of the ecclesiastical year and the calendar. [. . .]

Mediaeval and Post-mediaeval Developments

The Western rite never shewed any signs of reaching that immobility which finally sets in in the Byzantine rite in this very period. But the wisdom of Alcuin is shewn by this, that there are no more changes of shape or principle in the Western liturgy, but only a continual and vivacious development within the principles he had fixed. Even the most remarkable of the "derived rites" of the Middle Ages—Paris, Carthusian, Trier, Sarum, Autun, Dominican, Rouen, Hereford, Carmelite and the forty or fifty others—are none of them new "rites" in the technical sense, still less different rites from the Western rite, as e.g. the old Alexandrian, Antiochene and Roman rites had really been different rites from one another. They are only local dialects, some of them hardly more than "accents," of the one universal "Western" rite which the work of Alcuin had created. Their variants lie in details of ceremonial, which are sometimes quite striking, and in the texts of the propers and the priest's private prayers.

The old freedom to compose and use local propers was hardly affected by Charlemagne's reform. In practice the freedom to replace the texts of the propers of seasons by new compositions was not much used, but for the saints' days the formation of local propers continued unabated throughout the middle ages. It gave rise to "sub-dialects," as it were, within the derived rites themselves, so that the prayers for the saints' days in a Norwich-Sarum book are not entirely the same as those of a Salisbury-Sarum one. Even within the centrally controlled rite of the modern post-Tridentine church, liberty is still found for a supplement of propers for each diocese and abbey of the Latin rite—some 1,500 in all—thus continuing the old freedom of the propers, which the Popes had naturally always respected as an inheritance from the second and third century, and which Alcuin had wisely retained. The old practice of borrowing feasts and texts between different local churches, too, continued unaffected, so that e.g. the English feast of the Conception of our Lady appears at Lyons, carried thither by an English canon of Lyons, Gilbert, later bishop of London, even before it had been officially authorised by the Norman bishops of England; and the new Belgian feast of the Holy Trinity invented by Stephen of Liege was providing the dedication of new English cathedrals like Norwich and Chichester before it was accepted (or apparently heard of) at Rome. The writing of new "votives" for all sorts of devotional *attraits* and necessities of secular life also continued throughout the middle ages and beyond. It was a form of piety which Alcuin himself had found attractive—the mass in the present missal "in time of war," amongst others, seems to be his compilation from older materials—and some of the mediaeval votives (e.g. "the Five Wounds of our Lord Jesus Christ" and "against the pagans") are fine compositions.

The insertion of new feasts not only of modern saints but of our Lord (e.g. "the Precious Blood of our Lord Jesus Christ" by Pius IX and "Christ the King" by Pius XI) has slowly been centralised in the hands of the curial Congregation of Rites in the post-Tridentine church. The French dioceses continued to do this for themselves (in the old Frankish way) down to the French revolution; and the system of curial control as a whole never became fully effective until the nineteenth century. Yet even thus limited, the freedom of the propers and the special influence of the calendar on the Western rites (which had brought in the variable prayers not only of the propers but the votives) have continued to prevent that fossilisation of the liturgy which inevitably beset the Byzantine rite once it had perfected its two alternative sets of celebrant's prayers. No doubt when unwisely exercised these qualities can degenerate into the fostering of cults which are mere devotional side-issues at the best, distracting popular interest from the grand facts of redemption to some aspect of them which happens to have become a pious fashion at the moment. But christian good sense has a way of reasserting itself in the end over all sacristy pieties. The history of Western catholicism is littered with discarded devotions of all kinds, most of which found their representation in the missal for a while until popular interest waned and that mass was removed. These are the inevitable effects of a living contact of the liturgy with the prayers of the christian people

in each age. The people have a certain right to be vulgar; and the liturgy, even while it must teach them, has never a right to be academic, because it is their prayer. The ease with which the Western system of variable prayers can enable it to respond to the people's special interests and devotions at any time may have its dangers. But it has given the Western rite a closer and more intimate grasp of human life than any other.

From Dom Gregory Dix, *The Shape of the Liturgy* (1944; New York: Seabury Press, 1982), 549–51, 585–86.

In "The Ceremonies of Holy Week," in his *Stripping of the Altars,* **Eamon Duffy,** a professor of the history of Christianity, describes the pageantry in liturgical celebrations of Holy Week typical of English Churches during the fifteenth and sixteenth centuries.

EAMON DUFFY

"The Ceremonies of Holy Week," in *The Stripping of the Altars*

Holy Week, the period from Palm Sunday to Easter Day, constituted the heart of the late medieval Church's year, just as the Passion of Christ, solemnly commemorated then, lay at the heart of late medieval Christianity. The ceremonies of Holy Week were extremely elaborate, especially from the Wednesday onwards, when each day had its distinctive ritual observances. But much of the ceremonial prescribed in the Sarum rite had by the fifteenth century long since lost its imaginative power for lay people. The Easter Vigil, for example, with its elaborate ceremony of light, even now one of the most striking and moving parts of Catholic liturgy, was not held in darkness but on the morning of Holy Saturday, in broad daylight, and appears to have attracted no lay interest whatever. Lay people did attend the Tenebrae services on Wednesday, Thursday, and Friday. These were celebrations of the divine Office during which candles were snuffed out one by one to symbolize the abandonment of Jesus by his disciples: the standard sermon collections include explanations of this striking ceremony. But to judge by lay sources of the fifteenth and sixteenth centuries, the aspects of Holy Week which consistently seemed to matter to parishioners were the Palm Sunday procession, the veneration or "creeping to the cross" on Good Friday, the observances associated with the Easter sepulchre, and of course the annual reception of communion—"taking one's rights"—on Easter Sunday, an action which was necessarily preceded by going to confession. Confession and communion will be dealt with elsewhere, but an exploration of the other components of Holy Week observance will do much to flesh out our sense of the ways in which the laity appropriated and used the liturgy.

The Palm Sunday procession was by the end of the Middle Ages the most elaborate and eloquent of the processions of the Sarum rite, with the possible exception of the special case of Corpus Christi. The parish Mass began as usual with the blessing and sprinkling of holy water. Immediately that had been done the story of Christ's entry into Jerusalem and greeting by the crowds with palms was read from St John's Gospel. The priest then blessed flowers and green branches, which were called palms but were usually yew, box, or willow.[84] The palms were distributed and clergy and people processed out of the church, led by a painted wooden cross without a figure. The procession moved to a large cross erected in the churchyard, normally on the north side of the building at its east end, the choir singing a series of anthems recapitulating the biblical story of Palm Sunday.

While the palms were being distributed a special shrine supported on two poles was prepared, into which the church's principal relics were placed, along with the Blessed Sacrament to represent Christ. According to the rubrics, this shrine, carried by two clerks and sheltered by a silken canopy, was now brought in procession to join the parishioners and clergy at the churchyard Palm cross. By the end of the Middle Ages this aspect of the rite had been simplified in many places, the Host being carried instead in a monstrance by single priest. In the meantime the story of Christ's triumphal entry into Jerusalem from Matthew's Gospel was read to the parishioners in the churchyard. The procession with the Blessed Sacrament now approached the parochial procession gathered at the Cross, and, according to the ritual, three clerks wearing surplices and plain choir copes sang an anthem, "Behold, O Sion, thy king cometh," after which clergy and choir venerated the Sacrament by kneeling and kissing the ground before it. In popular English practice this part of the ritual was elaborated, the singers of the anthem being costumed as Old Testament prophets with flowing wigs and false beards: payments "for hyering of the heres for the p[ro]fetys upon Palme Sundaye" are a regular item of expense in many surviving sets of churchwardens' accounts.[85] At Long Melford in Suffolk the part of the prophet was played by "a boy with a thing in his hand," a wand or staff of some sort or possibly a

scroll, who stood on the turret over the Rood-loft stairs, on the outside of the Clopton aisle on the north side of Melford church, and pointed to the Sacrament while the "Ecce Rex Tuus" was sung. The two processions then merged, and a series of invocations to the Host were sung:

> Hail, thou whom the people of the Hebrews bear witness
>   to as Jesus . . .
> Hail, light of the world, king of kings, glory of heaven
> Hail, our salvation, our true peace, our redemption, our
>   strength . . .

During the singing the procession moved round the east end of the church to the south side, where a high scaffold had been erected. Seven boys stood on this scaffold and greeted the Host with the hymn "Gloria, Laus et honor" ("All glory, laud and honour to Thee, Redeemer King"). In a further elaboration of the prescribed ritual, flowers and unconsecrated Mass-wafers ("obols" or "singing-cakes") were usually strewn before the Sacrament from this scaffolding, to be scrambled for by the children. At Long Melford they were "cast over among the boys." There is no doubting the attraction of this picturesque feature of the Palm Sunday ceremonies to lay people, or its dramatic potential, and the singing of the hymn "Gloria, Laus" and scattering of flowers before the procession were adopted wholesale in the "N-Town" play of the Entry into Jerusalem.

The procession then moved to the west door, where the clerks carrying the Sacrament in its shrine stood on either side of the door and raised the poles above their heads. In many parishes the priest elaborated the prescribed ceremony at this point by taking the processional cross and striking the door with its foot, symbolically demanding entry for Christ, a gesture interpreted as representing Christ's harrowing of Hell, after bursting the gates of death. For some reason this gesture was expressly forbidden by the rubricists, but it was clearly widespread and evidently spoke to many parishioners: Margery Kempe comments specifically on its devotional effect on her. The clergy and people entered the church, pass-

---

84. *Missale [ad Usum Insignis et Praeclarae Ecclesiae Sarum*, ed. F. H. Dickinson, Burntisland, 1861–83], cols 253–7. The palms were intended, of course, for use in the procession, but were certainly to be taken back to people's homes [. . .]; one of the benedictions prayed for the banishment of "adverse powers" wherever the palms were brought and blessings for the inhabitants of any such home.

85. J. C. Cox, *Churchwardens' Accounts*, London, 1913, 254–55.

ing under the shrine with the Sacrament, and then the whole procession moved to its culminating point before the Rood-screen. All through Lent a great painted veil had been suspended in front of the Crucifix on the Rood-screen. This veil was now drawn up on pulleys, the whole parish knelt, and the anthem "Ave Rex Noster" was sung, while the clergy venerated the cross by kissing the ground:

> Hail, our King, Son of David, Redeemer of the World, whom the prophets proclaimed the saviour of the house of Israel who is to come. You indeed are the saving victim whom the Father has sent into the world, for whom the saints have waited from the beginning of the world. Blessed is he who comes in the name of the Lord, Hosanna in the highest.

Mass then began, but at the Gospel there was a final, striking deviation from the normal Sunday liturgy. The whole of the Passion story from St Matthew's Gospel was sung, by three clerks in churches which had the resources, the words of Jesus in a bass register, the narrator in a tenor one, and the words of the crowd in an alto. It was widely believed that crosses made during this reading of the Passion narrative had apotropaic powers, and many people brought sticks and string to church on Palm Sunday to be made up into crosses, a dimension of popular participation in the ritual which became a particular target of reformed criticism. Less controversially, in many parishes the reading of the Gospel was elaborated in the interests of dramatic effect and it was often sung by clerks standing in the Rood-loft itself, at the foot of the Crucifix which the whole parish had just venerated. With regional variations, this highly dramatic ritual was enacted all over late medieval Europe, but the English versions had a number of distinctive features, of which the most important was the use of the Blessed Sacrament to represent Christ. In many parts of Europe the presence of Christ was symbolized by a cross or a Gospel book, in Germany usually by a life-sized wooden carving of Christ on a donkey, which ran on wheels, the *Palmesel*.

The *Palmesel* was an obvious manifestation of a feature of late medieval worship we have already noticed in connection with the Candlemas rituals, the tendency to turn liturgy into "sacred performance." The use of the Sacrament in English Palm Sunday ceremonies was at once more and less dramatic than the representational realism evident in the *Palmesel,* which looked like Jesus and directly represented the ride into Jerusalem. The Blessed Sacrament did not look

like Jesus, but, far more vividly, *was* Jesus, body, blood, soul, and divinity, taking part in the communal re-enactment of his entry into the city not by a wooden proxy, but with all the overwhelming reality which late medieval believers attributed to the Host.

The Host was rarely carried in procession outside the church: the other festival on which this was done, Corpus Christi, was conceived and presented in late medieval communities as a celebration of the corporate life of the body social, created and ordered by the presence of the Body of Christ among them. The Palm Sunday procession, from which much of the Corpus Christi ritual was derived, was also a celebration of the redeeming presence of the divine within the community, made visible and concrete as the Host was carried around the churchyard, surrounded by the entire parish. The York play of the entry into Jerusalem catches this dimension of the Palm Sunday celebrations particularly clearly, when eight citizens of Jerusalem greet Christ in a series of invocations which are highly reminiscent of, and probably modelled on, the "Ave" invocations of the Palm Sunday procession:

> Hayll conqueror, hayll most of myght,
> Hayle rawnsoner of synfull all,
> Hayll pytefull, hayll lovely light,
> Hayll to us welcome be schall,
> Hayll kyng of Jues.
> Hayll comely corse that we the call
> With mirthe that newes.
> Hayll domysman dredful, that all schall deme,
> Hayll that all quyk and dede schall lowte,
> Hayll whom our worscippe most will seme
> Hayll whom all thyng schall drede and dowte.
> We welcome the,
> Hayll and welcome of all abowte
> To owre cete.[86]

The similarity of these invocations to the prayers used by the laity at the elevation at Mass is very striking. The dramatic Christ of the play has been subsumed into the Eucharistic Christ. The play's "Burghers of Jerusalem" are patently citizens of York, welcoming the presence of Christ among them, like the four yeomen who carried the canopy over the Sacrament on Palm Sunday at Long Melford, instead of

---

86. R. Beadle (ed.), *The York Plays,* London, 1982, 219.

the solitary clerk stipulated in the rubrics. It was precisely this entry into "owre cete" of Christ, ransomer and doomsman, in the form of the "comely corse," Corpus Christi, surrounded by "al the pepil," that the parish liturgy of Palm Sunday celebrated. As the *Ludus Coventriae* play of the entry has it, "Neyborys gret joye in our herte we may make that this hefly kyng wole vycyte this cyte."[87]

Palm Sunday was emphatically a celebration of the saving work of Christ: the cross and the miracle of the Mass which perpetuated the effects of the cross within the community lay at its centre. But the last days of Holy Week, from Maundy Thursday to Easter Day, formed a distinctive unit by themselves. They were packed with striking ceremonial and charged with intense religious emotion, for the ceremonies and texts of these days gathered up and gave eloquent expression to all the major themes of late medieval piety. There can be no question of the importance of these ceremonies for lay people, an importance reflected in the extended Holy Week meditation which forms chapters 78–81 of *The Book of Margery Kempe*. It is not perhaps surprising to find an aspirant to sanctity like Margery interested in these solemn ceremonies, but their wider appeal was grudgingly acknowledged by John Mirk, in his *Festial*. In addition to the model sermons for each of the major days of Holy Week, Mirk provided a compendium of ritual notes for unlearned clergy unable to make "a graythe answer" to the eager questions put to them by parishioners anxious to make sense of the unusually rich ceremonial of the season. Mirk, writing at a time of anxiety about the spread of Lollardy, chose to interpret such questioning as springing from a desire to expose the ignorance of the clergy, but there was no denying the phenomenon. "Lewde men," he complained, "wheche buthe of many wordys and proude in hor wit" will insist on asking priests questions "of thynges that towchen to servyce of holy chyrche, and namly of thys tyme."[88]

The Easter Triduum began with Maundy Thursday, when Mass was celebrated with extra solemnity, the priest consecrating three Hosts, one for his communion at the Mass, one for his communion at the Good Friday liturgy, and the third to be used in the sepulchre ceremonies. After Mass the altars of the church were ritually stripped of all their coverings and ornaments, while a series of responsories from the Passion narratives and the prophets were sung. As each altar was stripped the priest intoned a collect of the saint to whom it was dedicated. Each of the altars then had water and wine poured on it and was washed, using a broom of sharp twigs. Every detail of this vivid ceremony was allegorized in popu-

lar preaching—the stripping of the altars was the stripping of Jesus for death, the water and wine were the water and blood from his side, the broom of twigs the scourges or the crown of thorns. In cathedrals, religious houses, and great churches this ceremony was followed immediately by the Maundy, or solemn washing of feet, in imitation of Christ in the account of the last supper in St John's Gospel. To judge by the silence on this subject of surviving Holy Week parish sermons explaining the ritual, this foot washing was omitted in many parish churches. In Mirk's compendium of information on the ceremonies of Holy Week the scriptural foot washing is mentioned, but he is more directly concerned to explain a feature of the ceremonies of the day which would have impinged directly on lay liturgy, the absence of the pax from the Maundy Mass, "for Iudas betrayd Crist thys nyght wyth a cosse."[89]

Good Friday in the late Middle Ages was a day of deepest mourning. No Mass was celebrated, and the main liturgical celebration of the day was a solemn and penitential commemoration of the Passion. The whole of the narrative from St John's Gospel was read, with a small dramatic embellishment: at the words "They parted my garments among them" the clerks parted and removed two linen cloths which had been specially placed for the purpose on the otherwise bare altar. After the Gospel there was a series of solemn prayers for the world and the Church. A veiled Crucifix was then brought into the church, while the "Improperia" or "Reproaches" were sung, a series of scriptural verses contrasting the goodness of God and the ingratitude of his people. The cross was then unveiled in three stages, the priest singing, each time on a higher tone, "Behold the wood of the cross, on which hung the saviour of the world. Come, let us worship."

Clergy and people then crept barefoot and on their knees to kiss the foot of the cross, held by two ministers. After the adoration of the cross, a Host consecrated at the previous day's Mass was brought, and the priest, having recited the Lord's Prayer, communicated as if at Mass. The service concluded with the recitation of vespers without any music.

From Eamon Duffy, *The Stripping of the Altars: Traditional Religion in England, c. 1400–c. 1580* (New Haven: Yale University Press, 1992), 22–29.

---

87. *Ludus Coventriae or the Plaie called Corpus Christi*, ed. K. S. Block, EETS [Early English Text Society], 1922, 240.

88. John Mirk, *Mirk's Festial: A Collection of Homilies by Johannes Mirkus*, ed. T. Erbe, EETS, 1905, 126.

89. Mirk, *Festial*, 126.

3. TRIDENTINE AND VATICAN REFORMS

The following decrees concerning justification, sacraments, and Holy Eucharist from the **Council of Trent** (1545–63) explicate the Eucharist in terms of the real presence of God, gift, and sanctification in relation to gratuitous justification by faith.

THE COUNCIL OF TRENT

Sixth Session, Celebrated on the Thirteenth Day of January, 1547

"Decree concerning Justification"

Chapter VII — In What the Justification of the Sinner Consists, and What Are Its Causes

This disposition or preparation [that is, faith by hearing, doing penance, and being baptized] is followed by justification itself, which is not only a remission of sins but also the sanctification and renewal of the inward man through the voluntary reception of the grace and gifts whereby an unjust man becomes just and from being an enemy becomes a friend, that he may be an heir according to hope of life everlasting.[90] The causes of this justification are: the final cause is the glory of God and of Christ and life everlasting; the efficient cause is the merciful God who washes and sanctifies[91] gratuitously, signing and anointing with the holy Spirit of promise, who is the pledge of our inheritance;[92] the meritorious cause is His most beloved only begotten, our Lord Jesus Christ, who, when we were enemies,[93] for the exceeding charity wherewith he loved us,[94] merited for us justification by His most holy passion on the wood of the cross and made satisfaction for us to God the Father; the instrumental cause is the sacrament of baptism, which is the sacrament of faith, without which no man was ever justified; finally, the single formal cause is the justice of God, not that by which He Himself is just, but that by which He makes us just, that, namely, with which we, being endowed by Him, are renewed in the spirit of our mind,[95] and not only are we reputed but we are truly called and are just, receiving justice within us, each one according to his own measure, which the Holy Ghost distributes to everyone as He wills,[96] and according to each one's disposition and cooperation. For though no one can be just except he to whom the merits of the passion of our Lord Jesus Christ are communicated, yet this takes place in that justification of the sinner, when by the merit of the most holy passion, the charity of God is poured forth by the Holy Ghost in the hearts[97] of those who are justified and inheres in them; whence man through Jesus Christ, in whom he is ingrafted, receives in that justification, together with the remission of sins, all these infused at the same time, namely, faith, hope and charity. For faith, unless hope and charity be added to it, neither unites man perfectly with Christ nor makes him a living member of His body. For which reason it is most truly said that faith without works is dead[98] and of no profit, and in Christ Jesus neither circumcision availeth anything nor uncircumcision, but faith that worketh by charity.[99] This faith, conformably to Apostolic tradition, catechumens ask of the Church before the sacrament of baptism, when they ask for the faith that gives eternal life, which without hope and charity faith cannot give. Whence also they hear immediately the word of Christ: If thou wilt enter into life, keep the commandments.[100] Wherefore when receiving true and Christian justice, they are commanded, immediately on being born again, to preserve it pure and spotless, as the first robe[101] given them through Christ Jesus in place of that which Adam by his disobedience lost for himself and for us, so that they may bear it before the tribunal of our Lord Jesus Christ and may have life eternal. . . .

Seventh Session, Celebrated on the Third Day of March, 1547

"Decree concerning the Sacraments: Foreword"

For the completion of the salutary doctrine on justification, which was promulgated with the unanimous consent of the Fathers in the last session, it has seemed proper to deal with the most holy sacraments of the Church, through which all true justice either begins, or being begun is increased, or being lost is restored. Wherefore, in order to destroy the errors and extirpate the heresies that in our stormy times are directed against the most holy sacraments, some of

---

90. Titus 3:7.
91. See 1 Cor 6:11.
92. Eph 1:13f.
93. Rom 5:10.
94. Eph 2:4.
95. Eph 4:23.
96. See 1 Cor 12:11.
97. Rom 5:5.
98. James 2:17, 20.
99. Gal 5:6, 6:15.
100. Mt 19:17.
101. Lk 15:22.

which are a revival of heresies long ago condemned by our Fathers, while others are of recent origin, all of which are exceedingly detrimental to the purity of the Catholic Church and the salvation of souls, the holy, ecumenical and general Council of Trent, lawfully assembled in the Holy Ghost, the same legates of the Apostolic See presiding, adhering to the teaching of the Holy Scriptures, to the Apostolic traditions, and to the unanimous teaching of other councils and of the Fathers, has thought it proper to establish and enact these present canons; hoping, with the help of the Holy Spirit, to publish later those that are wanting for the completion of the work begun.

Canons on the Sacraments in General

Canon 1. If anyone says that the sacraments of the New Law were not all instituted by our Lord Jesus Christ, or that there are more or less than seven, namely, baptism, confirmation, Eucharist, penance, extreme unction, order and matrimony, or that any one of these seven is not truly and intrinsically a sacrament, let him be anathema. [. . .]

Thirteenth Session, Which is the Third under the Supreme Pontiff Julius III, Celebrated on the Eleventh day of October 1551

"Decree concerning the Most Holy Sacrament of the Eucharist"

Chapter I — The Real Presence of Our Lord Jesus Christ in the Most Holy Sacrament of the Eucharist

First of all, the holy council teaches and openly and plainly professes that after the consecration of bread and wine, our Lord Jesus Christ, true God and true man, is truly, really and substantially contained in the august sacrament of the Holy Eucharist under the appearance of those sensible things. For there is no repugnance in this that our Savior sits always at the right hand of the Father in heaven according to the natural mode of existing, and yet is in many other places sacramentally present to us in His own substance by a manner of existence which, though we can scarcely express in words, yet with our understanding illumined by faith, we can conceive and ought most firmly to believe is possible to God.[102] For thus all our forefathers, as many as were in the true Church of Christ and who treated of this most holy sacrament, have most openly professed that our Redeemer instituted this wonderful sacrament at the last supper, when, after blessing the bread and wine, He testified in clear and definite words that He gives them His own body and His own blood. Since these words, recorded by the holy Evangelists[103] and afterwards repeated by St. Paul,[104] embody that proper and clearest meaning in which they were understood by the Fathers, it is a most contemptible action on the part of some contentious and wicked men to twist them into fictitious and imaginary tropes by which the truth of the flesh and blood of Christ is denied, contrary to the universal sense of the Church, which, as the pillar and ground of truth[105] recognizing with a mind ever grateful and unforgetting this most excellent favor of Christ, has detested as satanical these untruths devised by impious men.

Chapter II — The Reason for the Institution of This Most Holy Sacrament

Therefore, our Savior, when about to depart from this world to the Father, instituted this sacrament, in which He poured forth, as it were, the riches of His divine love towards men, making a remembrance of His wonderful works,[106] and commanded us in the participation of it to reverence His memory and to show forth His death until He comes[107] to judge the world. But He wished that this sacrament should be received as the spiritual food of souls,[108] whereby they may be nourished and strengthened, living by the life of Him who said: He that eateth me, the same also shall live by me,[109] and as an antidote whereby we may be freed from daily faults and be preserved from mortal sins. He wished it furthermore to be a pledge of our future glory and everlasting happiness, and thus be a symbol of that one body of which He is the head[110] and to which He wished us to be united as members by the closest bond of faith, hope and charity, that we might all speak the same thing and there might be no schisms among us.[111]

Chapter III — The Excellence of the Most Holy Eucharist over the Other Sacraments

The most Holy Eucharist has indeed this in common with the other sacraments, that it is a symbol of a sacred thing and

102. Mt 19:26; Lk 18:27.
103. Mt 26:26–28; Mk 14:22–24; Lk 22:19f.
104. See 1 Cor 11:24f.   108. Matt 26:26f.
105. See 1 Tim 3:15.   109. Jn 6:58.
106. Ps 110:4.   110. See 1 Cor 11:3; Eph. 5:23.
107. Lk 22:19; 1 Cor 11:24–26.   111. See 1 Cor 1:10.

a visible form of an invisible grace; but there is found in it this excellent and peculiar characteristic, that the other sacraments then first have the power of sanctifying when one uses them, while in the Eucharist there is the Author Himself of sanctity before it is used. For the Apostles had not yet received the Eucharist from the hands of the Lord, when He Himself told them that what He was giving them is His own body.[112] This has always been the belief of the Church of God, that immediately after the consecration the true body and the true blood of our Lord, together with His soul and divinity exist under the form of bread and wine, the body under the form of bread and the blood under the form of wine *ex vi verborum;* but the same body also under the form of wine and the same blood under the form of bread and the soul under both, in virtue of that natural connection and concomitance whereby the parts of Christ the Lord, who hath now risen from the dead, to die no more,[113] are mutually united; also the divinity on account of its admirable hypostatic union with His body and soul. Wherefore, it is very true that as much is contained under either form as under both. For Christ is whole and entire under the form of bread[114] and under any part of that form; likewise the whole Christ is present under the form of wine and under all its parts.

Transubstantiation

But since Christ our Redeemer declared that to be truly His own body which He offered under the form of bread, it has, therefore, always been a firm belief in the Church of God, and this holy council now declares it anew, that by the consecration of the bread and wine a change is brought about of the whole substance of the bread into the substance of the body of Christ our Lord, and of the whole substance of the wine into the substance of His blood. This change the holy Catholic Church properly and appropriately calls transubstantiation.

From H. J. Schroeder, ed. and trans., *Canons and Decrees of the Council of Trent* (Rockford, IL: TAN Books, 1978), 33–34, 51, 74–75.

֍ In *The Constitution on Sacred Liturgy (Sacrosanctum concilium,* December 4, 1963), the **Second Vatican Council** (1962–65) explains and reforms existing liturgical rites in accordance with the contemporary needs of the Church. This document reveals the changes that had taken place in Roman liturgical theology since the Council of Trent.

THE SECOND VATICAN COUNCIL

The Constitution on Sacred Liturgy, 1–4, 19–26, 47–54, 59–77

Introduction

1. The sacred Council has set out to impart an ever increasing vigor to the Christian life of the faithful; to adapt more closely to the needs of our age those institutions which are subject to change; to foster whatever can promote union among all who believe in Christ; to strengthen whatever can help to call all mankind into the Church's fold. Accordingly it sees particularly cogent reasons for undertaking the reform and promotion of the liturgy.

2. For it is the liturgy through which, especially in the divine sacrifice of the Eucharist, "the work of our redemption is accomplished,"[115] and it is through the liturgy, especially, that the faithful are enabled to express in their lives and manifest to others the mystery of Christ and the real nature of the true Church. The Church is essentially both human and divine, visible but endowed with invisible realities, zealous in action and dedicated to contemplation, present in the world, but as a pilgrim, so constituted that in her the human is directed toward and subordinated to the divine, the visible to the invisible, action to contemplation, and this present world to that city yet to come, the object of our quest.[116] The liturgy daily builds up those who are in the Church, making of them a holy temple of the Lord, a dwelling-place for God in the Spirit,[117] to the mature measure of the fullness of Christ.[118] At the same time it marvelously increases their power to preach Christ and thus show forth the Church, a sign lifted up among the nations,[119] to those who are outside, a sign under which the scattered children of God may be gathered together[120] until there is one fold and one shepherd.

112. Mt 26:26; Mk 14:22.

113. Rom 6:9.

114. Lk 22:19; Jn 6:48ff.; 1 Cor 11:24.

115. Secret Prayer of 9th Sunday after Pentecost. [The Secret Prayer was a part of the pre-Vatican Mass propers (that is, the parts of the Mass that varied according to the liturgical calendar), said inaudibly by the celebrant just before the Preface.]

116. Cf. Heb 13:14.

117. Cf. Eph 2:21–22.

118. Cf. Jn 11:12.

119. Cf. Jn 11:52.

120. Cf. Jn 10:16.

3. That is why the sacred Council judges that the following principles concerning the promotion and reform of the liturgy should be called to mind, and that practical norms should be established.

Among these principles and norms there are some which can and should be applied both to the Roman rite and also to all the other rites. The practical norms which follow, however, should be taken as applying only to the Roman rite except for those which, in the very nature of things, affect other rites as well.

4. Finally, in faithful obedience to tradition, the sacred Council declares that Holy Mother Church holds all lawfully recognized rites to be of equal right and dignity; that she wishes to preserve them in the future and to foster them in every way. The Council also desires that, where necessary, the rites be revised carefully in the light of sound tradition, and that they be given new vigor to meet present-day circumstances and needs.

Chapter I. Part II. [. . .] Instruction and Participation

19. With zeal and patience pastors of souls must promote the liturgical instruction of the faithful and also their active participation, both internal and external, taking into account their age condition, way of life, and standard of religious culture. By so doing pastors will be fulfilling one of the chief duties of a faithful dispenser of the mysteries of God, and in this matter they must lead their flock not only by word but also by example.

20. Transmission of the sacred rites by radio and television, especially in the case of Mass, shall be done with delicacy and dignity. A suitable person, appointed by the bishops, should direct it and have the responsibility for it.

Chapter I. Part III. The Reform of the Sacred Liturgy

21. In order that the Christian people may more certainly derive an abundance of graces from the sacred liturgy, holy Mother Church desires to undertake with great care a general restoration of the liturgy itself. For the liturgy is made up of unchangeable elements divinely instituted, and of elements subject to change. These latter not only may be changed but ought to be changed with the passage of time, if they have suffered from the intrusion of anything out of harmony with the inner nature of the liturgy or have become less suitable. In this restoration both texts and rites should be drawn up so as to express more clearly the holy things which they signify. The Christian people, as far as is possible, should be able to understand them with ease and take part in them fully, actively, and as a community.

Therefore, the sacred Council establishes the following general norms:

A. General Norms

22. (1) Regulation of the sacred liturgy depends solely on the authority of the Church, that is, on the Apostolic See, and, as laws may determine, on the bishop. (2) In virtue of power conceded by law, the regulation of the liturgy within certain defined limits belongs also to various kinds of bishops' conferences, legitimately established, with competence in given territories. (3) Therefore no other person, not even a priest, may add, remove, or change anything in the liturgy on his own authority.

23. In order that sound tradition be retained, and yet the way remain open to legitimate progress, a careful investigation—theological, historical, and pastoral—should always be made into each part of the liturgy which is to be revised. Furthermore the general laws governing the structure and meaning of the liturgy must be studied in conjunction with the experience derived from recent liturgical reforms and from the indults granted to various places.

Finally, there must be no innovations unless the good of the Church genuinely and certainly requires them, and care must be taken that any new forms adopted should in some way grow organically from forms already existing.

As far as possible, notable differences between the rites used in adjacent regions should be avoided.

24. Sacred scripture is of the greatest importance in the celebration of the liturgy. For it is from it that lessons are read and explained in the homily, and psalms are sung. It is from the scriptures that the prayers, collects, and hymns draw their inspiration and their force, and that actions and signs derive their meaning. Hence in order to achieve the restoration, progress, and adaptation of the sacred liturgy it is essential to promote that sweet and living love for sacred scripture to which the venerable tradition of Eastern and Western rites gives testimony.

25. The liturgical books are to be revised as soon as possible. Experts are to be employed on this task, and bishops from various parts of the world are to be consulted.

B. Norms Drawn from the Hierarchic and Communal Nature of the Liturgy

26. Liturgical services are not private functions but are celebrations of the Church which is "the sacrament of

unity," namely, "the holy people united and arranged under their bishops."[121] Therefore, liturgical services pertain to the whole Body of the Church. They manifest it, and have effects upon it. But they also touch individual members of the Church in different ways, depending on their orders, their role in the liturgical services, and their actual participation in them.

Chapter II. The Most Sacred Mystery of the Eucharist

47. At the Last Supper, on the night he was betrayed, our Savior instituted the eucharistic sacrifice of his Body and Blood. This he did in order to perpetuate the sacrifice of the Cross throughout the ages until he should come again and so to entrust to his beloved Spouse, the Church, a memorial of his death and resurrection: a sacrament of love, a sign of unity, a bond of charity,[122] a paschal banquet in which Christ is consumed, the mind is filled with grace, and a pledge of future glory is given to us.[123]

48. The Church, therefore, earnestly desires that Christ's faithful, when present at this mystery of faith, should not be there as strangers or silent spectators. On the contrary, through a good understanding of the rites and prayers they should take part in the sacred action, conscious of what they are doing, with devotion and full collaboration. They should be instructed by God's word, and be nourished at the table of the Lord's Body. They should give thanks to God. Offering the immaculate victim, not only through the hands of the priest but also together with him, they should learn to offer themselves. Through Christ, the Mediator,[124] they should be drawn day by day into ever more perfect union with God and each other, so that finally God may be all in all.

49. For this reason the sacred Council having in mind those Masses which are celebrated with the faithful assisting, especially on Sundays and holidays of obligation, has made the following decrees so that the sacrifice of the Mass, even in the ritual forms (of its celebration), may have full pastoral efficacy.

Decrees

50. The rite of the Mass is to be revised in such a way that the intrinsic nature and purpose of its several parts, as well as the connection between them, may be more clearly manifested, and that devout and active participation by the faithful may be more easily achieved.

For this purpose the rites are to be simplified, due care being taken to preserve their substance. Parts which with the passage of time came to be duplicated, or were added with little advantage, are to be omitted. Other parts which suffered loss through accidents of history are to be restored to the vigor they had in the days of the holy Fathers, as may seem useful or necessary.

51. The treasures of the Bible are to be opened up more lavishly so that a richer fare may be provided for the faithful at the table of God's word. In this way a more representative part of the sacred scriptures will be read to the people in the course of a prescribed number of years.

52. By means of the homily the mysteries of the faith and the guiding principles of the Christian life are expounded from the sacred text during the course of the liturgical year. The homily, therefore, is to be highly esteemed as part of the liturgy itself. In fact at those Masses which are celebrated on Sundays and holidays of obligation, with the people assisting, it should not be omitted except for a serious reason.

53. The "common prayer" or "prayer of the faithful" is to be restored after the gospel and homily, especially on Sundays and holidays of obligation. By this prayer in which the people are to take part, intercession will be made for holy Church, for the civil authorities, for those oppressed by various needs, for all mankind, and for the salvation of the entire world.[125]

54. A suitable place may be allotted to the vernacular in Masses which are celebrated with the people, especially in the readings and "the common prayer," and also, as local conditions may warrant, in those parts which pertain to the people, according to the rules laid down in Article 36 of this Constitution.

Nevertheless care must be taken to ensure that the faithful may also be able to say or sing together in Latin those parts of the Ordinary of the Mass which pertain to them.

Wherever a more extended use of the vernacular in the Mass seems desirable, the regulation laid down in Article 40 of this Constitution is to be observed.

121. St. Cyprian, "On the Unity of the Catholic Church," 7; ed. G. Hartel, in CSEL [*Corpus scriptorum ecclesiasticorum Latinorum*], III, 1, Vienna, 1868; cf. Letter 66, n. 8, 3.

122. Cf. St. Augustine, *Tractatus in Ioannis Evangelium*, ch. 6, n. 13.

123. Roman Breviary: Feast of Corpus Christi, Second Vespers, Antiphon to Magnificat.

124. Cf. St. Cyril of Alexandria: "Commentary on the Gospel of St. John," Book 11, ch. 11–12.

125. Cf. 1 Tim 2:1–2.

Chapter III. The Other Sacraments and the Sacramentals

59. The purpose of the sacraments is to sanctify men, to build up the Body of Christ, and, finally, to give worship to God. Because they are signs they also instruct. They not only presuppose faith, but by words and objects they also nourish, strengthen, and express it. That is why they are called "sacraments of faith." They do, indeed, confer grace, but, in addition, the very act of celebrating them most effectively disposes the faithful to receive this grace to their profit, to worship God duly, and to practise charity.

It is, therefore, of the greatest importance that the faithful should easily understand the sacramental signs, and should eagerly frequent those sacraments which were instituted to nourish the Christian life.

60. Holy Mother Church has, moreover, instituted sacramentals. These are sacred signs which bear a resemblance to the sacraments. They signify effects, particularly of a spiritual nature, which are obtained through the Church's intercession. By them men are disposed to receive the chief effect of the sacraments, and various occasions in life are rendered holy.

61. Thus, for well-disposed members of the faithful the liturgy of the sacraments and sacramentals sanctifies almost every event of their lives with the divine grace which flows from the paschal mystery of the Passion, Death, and Resurrection of Christ. From this source all sacraments and sacramentals draw their power. There is scarcely any proper use of material things which cannot thus be directed toward the sanctification of men and the praise of God.

62. With the passage of time, however, there have crept into the rites of the sacraments and sacramentals certain features which have rendered their nature and purpose far from clear to the people of today. Hence some changes are necessary to adapt them to present-day needs. For that reason the sacred Council decrees as follows concerning their revision:

63. Because the use of the vernacular in the administration of the sacraments and sacramentals can often be of very great help to the people, this use is to be extended according to the following norms:

(a) In the administration of the sacraments and sacramentals the vernacular may be used according to the norm of Article 36.

(b) The competent territorial ecclesiastical authority designated in Article 22:2 of this Constitution shall forthwith prepare, in accordance with the new edition of the Roman Ritual, local rituals adapted linguistically and otherwise to the needs of the different regions. These rituals, on authentication by the Apostolic See, are to be followed in the regions in question. But in drawing up those rituals or particular collections of rites, the instructions prefixed to the individual rites in the Roman Ritual, whether they be pastoral and rubrical or whether they have a special social import, shall not be omitted.

64. The catechumenate for adults, comprising several distinct steps, is to be restored and brought into use at the discretion of the local ordinary. By this means the time of the catechumenate, which is intended as a period of suitable instruction, may be sanctified by sacred rites to be celebrated at successive intervals of time.

65. In mission countries, in addition to what is furnished by the Christian tradition, those elements of initiation rites may be admitted which are already in use among some peoples insofar as they can be adapted to the Christian ritual in accordance with Articles 37–40 of this Constitution.

66. Both rites for the baptism of adults are to be revised, not only the simpler rite but also, taking into consideration the restored catechumenate, the more solemn rite. A special Mass "For the conferring of Baptism" is to be inserted into the Roman Missal.

67. The rite for the baptism of infants is to be revised, its revision taking into account the fact that those to be baptized are infants. The roles of parents and godparents, and also their duties, should be brought out more clearly in the rite itself.

68. The baptismal rite should contain variants, to be used at the discretion of the local ordinary when a large number are to be baptized. Likewise a shorter rite is to be drawn up, especially for mission countries, which catechists, and also the faithful in general, may use when there is danger of death and neither priest nor deacon is available.

69. In place of the rite called "Rite for supplying what was omitted in the baptism of an infant" a new rite is to be drawn up. This rite should indicate more fittingly and clearly that the infant baptized by the short rite has already been received into the Church.

So also a new rite is to be drawn up for converts who have already been validly baptized. It should indicate that they are now admitted to communion with the Church.

70. Baptismal water, outside of paschal time, may be blessed within the rite of Baptism itself by an approved shorter formula.

71. The rite of Confirmation is to be revised also so that the intimate connection of this sacrament with the whole of

the Christian initiation may more clearly appear. For this reason the renewal of baptismal promises should fittingly precede the reception of this sacrament.

Confirmation may be conferred within Mass when convenient. For conferring outside Mass, a formula introducing the rite should be drawn up.

72. The rite and formulae of Penance are to be revised so that they more clearly express both the nature and effect of the sacrament.

73. "Extreme Unction," which may also and more fittingly be called "Anointing of the Sick," is not a sacrament for those only who are at the point of death. Hence, as soon as anyone of the faithful begins to be in danger of death from sickness or old age, the fitting time for him to receive this sacrament has certainly already arrived.

74. In addition to the separate rites for Anointing of the Sick and for Viaticum, a continuous rite shall be prepared in which a sick man is anointed after he has made his confession and before he receives Viaticum.

75. The number of the anointings is to be adapted to the occasion, and the prayers which belong to the rite of Anointing are to be revised so as to correspond to the varying conditions of the sick who receive the sacrament.

76. Both the ceremonies and texts of the Ordination rites are to be revised. The addresses given by the bishop at the beginning of each ordination or consecration may be in the vernacular.

In the consecration of a bishop the laying on of hands may be done by all the bishops present.

77. The Marriage rite now found in the Roman Ritual is to be revised and enriched so that it will more clearly signify the grace of the sacrament and will emphasize the spouses' duties.

If any regions use other praiseworthy customs and ceremonies when celebrating the sacrament of Matrimony the sacred Synod earnestly desires that these by all means be retained.[126]

Translated by Joseph Rodgers, in *Vatican Council II: The Conciliar and Post Conciliar Documents,* edited by Austin Flannery (Collegeville, MN: Liturgical Press, 1975), 1–2, 9–10, 16–18, 21–23.

꧁

4. EASTERN ORTHODOX LITURGY

☙ In his "Doctrine and Worship in the Orthodox Church: The Earthly Heaven," **Timothy Ware** elicits particular features of Eastern Orthodox liturgy from historical narratives and letters: its splendor and beauty, its embrace of two worlds (heaven and earth) at once, and its fusion of right belief and right worship. Since 1982, Ware has served as assisting bishop in the Orthodox Archdiocese of Thyatira (Turkey) and Great Britain.

TIMOTHY WARE

"Doctrine and Worship in the Orthodox Church: The Earthly Heaven," in *The Orthodox Church*

The church is the earthly heaven in which the heavenly God dwells and moves.

Germanus, Patriarch of Constantinople (died 733)

There is a story in the *Russian Primary Chronicle* of how Vladimir, Prince of Kiev, while still a pagan, desired to know which was the true religion, and therefore sent his followers to visit the various countries of the world in turn. They went first to the Moslem Bulgars of the Volga, but observing that these when they prayed gazed around them like men possessed, the Russians continued on their way dissatisfied. "There is no joy among them," they reported to Vladimir, "but mournfulness and a great smell; and there is nothing good about their system." Travelling next to Germany and Rome, they found the worship more satisfactory, but complained that here too it was without beauty. Finally they journeyed to Constantinople, and here at last, as they attended the Divine Liturgy in the great Church of the Holy Wisdom, they discovered what they desired. "We knew not whether we were in heaven or on earth, for surely there is no such splendour or beauty anywhere upon earth. We cannot describe it to you: only this we know, that God dwells there among men, and that their service surpasses the worship of all other places. For we cannot forget that beauty."

---

126. Council of Trent, Session 24: On Reform, ch. 1. Cf. Roman Ritual, Title 8, ch. 2, n. 6.

In this story can be seen several features characteristic of Orthodox Christianity. There is first the emphasis upon divine beauty: *we cannot forget that beauty.* It has seemed to many that the peculiar gift of Orthodox peoples—and especially of Byzantium and Russia—is this power of perceiving the beauty of the spiritual world, and expressing this celestial beauty in their worship.

In the second place it is characteristic that the Russians should have said, *we knew not whether we were in heaven or on earth.* Worship, for the Orthodox Church, is nothing else than "heaven on earth." The Holy Liturgy is something that embraces two worlds at once, for both in heaven and on earth the Liturgy is one and the same—one altar, one sacrifice, one presence. In every place of worship, however humble its outward appearance, as the faithful gather to perform the Eucharist, they are taken up into the "heavenly places"; in every place of worship when the Holy Sacrifice is offered, not merely the local congregation are present, but the Church universal—the saints, the angels, the Mother of God, and Christ himself. "Now the celestial powers are present with us, and worship invisibly."[127] *This we know, that God dwells there among men.*

Orthodox, inspired by this vision of "heaven on earth," have striven to make their worship in outward splendour and beauty an icon of the great Liturgy in heaven. In the year 612, on the staff of the Church of the Holy Wisdom, there were 80 priests, 150 deacons, 40 deaconesses, 70 subdeacons, 160 readers, 25 cantors, and 100 doorkeepers: this gives some faint idea of the magnificence of the service which Vladimir's envoys attended. But many who have experienced Orthodox worship under very different outward surroundings have felt, no less than those Russians from Kiev, a sense of God's presence among men. Turn, for example, from the *Russian Primary Chronicle* to the letter of an Englishwoman, written in 1935:

> This morning was so queer. A very grimy and sordid Presbyterian mission hall in a mews over a garage, where the Russians are allowed once a fortnight to have the Liturgy. A very stage property iconostasis and a few modern icons. A dirty floor to kneel on and a form along the wall. And in this two superb old priests and a deacon, clouds of incense and, at the Anaphora, an overwhelming supernatural impression.[128]

There is yet a third characteristic of Orthodoxy which the story of Vladimir's envoys illustrates. When they wanted to discover the true faith, the Russians did not ask about moral rules, nor demand a reasoned statement of doctrine, but watched the different nations at prayer. The Orthodox approach to religion is fundamentally a liturgical approach, which understands doctrine in the context of divine worship: it is no coincidence that the word "Orthodoxy" should signify alike right belief and right worship, for the two things are inseparable. It has been truly said of the Byzantines: "Dogma with them is not only an intellectual system apprehended by the clergy and expounded to the laity, but a field of vision wherein all things on earth are seen in their relation to things in heaven, first and foremost through liturgical celebration."[129] In the words of Georges Florovsky: "Christianity is a liturgical religion. The Church is first of all a worshipping community. Worship comes first, doctrine and discipline second."[130] Those who wish to know about Orthodoxy should not so much read books as follow the example of Vladimir's retinue and attend the Liturgy. As Philip said to Nathanael: "Come and see."[131]

Because they approach religion in this liturgical way, Orthodox often attribute to minute points of ritual an importance which astonishes western Christians. But once we have understood the central place of worship in the life of Orthodoxy, an incident such as the schism of the Old Believers will no longer appear entirely unintelligible: if worship is the faith in action, then liturgical changes cannot be lightly regarded. It is typical that a Russian writer of the fifteenth century, when attacking the Council of Florence, should find fault with the Latins, not for any errors in doctrine, but for their behaviour in worship:

> What have you seen of worth among the Latins? They do not even know how to venerate the church of God. They raise their voices as the fools, and their singing is a discordant wail. They have no idea of beauty and reverence in worship, for they strike trombones, blow horns, use organs, wave their hands, trample with their feet, and do many other irreverent and disorderly things which bring joy to the devil.[132]

---

127. Words sung at the Great Entrance in the Liturgy of the Presanctified.

128. *The Letters of Evelyn Underhill,* 248.

129. G. Every, *The Byzantine Patriarchate,* first edition, ix.

130. "The Elements of Liturgy in the Orthodox Catholic Church," in the periodical *One Church,* vol. XIII (New York, 1959), nos. 1–2, 24.

131. Jn 1:46.

132. Quoted in N. Zernov, *Moscow the Third Rome,* 37; I cite this passage simply as an example of the liturgical approach of Orthodoxy, without necessarily endorsing the strictures on western worship which it contains!

Orthodoxy sees man above all else as a liturgical creature who is most truly himself when he glorifies God, and who finds his perfection and self-fulfilment in worship. Into the Holy Liturgy which expresses their faith, the Orthodox peoples have poured their whole religious experience. It is the Liturgy which has inspired their best poetry, art, and music. Among Orthodox, the Liturgy has never become the preserve of the learned and the clergy, as it tended to be in the medieval west, but it has remained *popular*—the common possession of the whole Christian people:

> The normal Orthodox lay worshipper, through familiarity from earliest childhood, is entirely at home in church, thoroughly conversant with the audible parts of the Holy Liturgy, and takes part with unconscious and unstudied ease in the action of the rite, to an extent only shared in by the hyper-devout and ecclesiastically minded in the west.[133]

In the dark days of their history—under the Mongols, the Turks, or the communists—it is to the Holy Liturgy that the Orthodox peoples have always turned for inspiration and new hope; nor have they turned in vain.

The Outward Setting of the Services: Priest and People

The basic pattern of services is the same in the Orthodox as in the Roman Catholic Church: there is, first, the *Holy Liturgy* (the Eucharist or Mass); secondly, the *Divine Office* (i.e. the two chief offices of Matins and Vespers, together with the six "Lesser Hours" of Nocturns, Prime, Terce, Sext, None, and Compline);[134] and thirdly, the *Occasional Offices*— i.e. services intended for special occasions, such as Baptism, Marriage, Monastic Profession, Royal Coronation, Consecration of a Church, Burial of the Dead. (In addition to these, the Orthodox Church makes use of a great variety of lesser blessings.)

While in many Anglican and almost all Roman Catholic parish churches, the Eucharist is celebrated daily, in the Orthodox Church today a daily Liturgy is not usual except in cathedrals and large monasteries; in a normal parish church it is celebrated only on Sundays and feasts. But in contemporary Russia, where places of worship are few and many Christians are obliged to work on Sundays, a daily Liturgy has become the practice in many town parishes.

The Divine Office is recited daily in monasteries, large and small, and in some cathedrals; also in a number of town parishes in Russia. But in an ordinary Orthodox parish church it is sung only at week-ends and on feasts. Greek churches hold Vespers on Saturday night, and Matins on Sunday morning before the Liturgy; in Russian parishes Matins is usually "anticipated" and sung immediately after Vespers on Saturday night, so that Vespers and Matins, followed by Prime, together constitute what is termed the "Vigil Service" or the "All-Night Vigil." Thus while western Christians, if they worship in the evening, tend to do so on Sundays, Orthodox Christians worship on the evening of Saturdays.

In its services the Orthodox Church uses the language of the people: Arabic at Antioch, Finnish at Helsinki, Japanese at Tokyo, English (when required) at New York. One of the first tasks of Orthodox missionaries—from Cyril and Methodius in the ninth century, to Innocent Veniaminov and Nicholas Kassatkin in the nineteenth—has always been to translate the service books into native tongues. In practice, however, there are partial exceptions to this general principle of using the vernacular: the Greek-speaking Churches employ, not modern Greek, but the Greek of New Testament and Byzantine times, while the Russian Church still uses the ninth-century translations in Church Slavonic. Yet in both cases the difference between the liturgical language and the contemporary vernacular is not so great as to make the service unintelligible to the congregation. In 1906 many Russian bishops in fact recommended that Church Slavonic be replaced more or less generally by modern Russian, but the Bolshevik Revolution occurred before this scheme could be carried into effect.

In the Orthodox Church today, as in the early Church, all services are sung or chanted. There is no Orthodox equivalent to the Roman "Low Mass" or to the Anglican "Said Celebration." At every Liturgy, as at every Matins and Vespers, incense is used and the service is sung, even though there may be no choir or congregation, but the priest and a single reader alone. In their Church music the Greek-speaking Orthodox continue to use the ancient Byzantine plain-chant, with its eight "tones." This plain-chant the Byzantine missionaries took with them into the Slavonic lands, but over the centuries it has become extensively modified, and the various Slavonic Churches have each developed their own style and tradition of ecclesiastical music. Of these traditions the Rus-

---

133. Austin Oakley, *The Orthodox Liturgy* (London, 1958), 12.

134. In the Roman rite Nocturns is a part of Matins, but in the Byzantine rite Nocturns is a separate service. Byzantine Matins is equivalent to Matins and Lauds in the Roman rite.

sian is the best known and the most immediately attractive to western ears; many consider Russian Church music the finest in all Christendom, and alike in the Soviet Union and in the emigration there are justly celebrated Russian choirs. Until very recent times all singing in Orthodox churches was usually done by the choir; today, a small but increasing number of parishes in Greece, Russia, Romania, and the diaspora are beginning to revive congregational singing—if not throughout the service, then at any rate at special moments such as the Creed and the Lord's Prayer.

In the Orthodox Church today, as in the early Church, singing is unaccompanied and instrumental music is not found, except among certain Orthodox in America—particularly the Greeks—who are now showing a *penchant* for the organ or the harmonium. Most Orthodox do not use hand or sanctuary bells inside the church; but they have outside belfries, and take great delight in ringing the bells not only before but at various moments during the service itself. Russian bell-ringing used to be particularly famous. "Nothing," wrote Paul of Aleppo during his visit to Moscow in 1655, "nothing affected me so much as the united clang of all the bells on the eves of Sundays and great festivals, and at midnight before the festivals. The earth shook with their vibrations, and like thunder the drone of their voices went up to the skies."[135] "They rang the brazen bells after their custom. May God not be startled at the noisy pleasantness of their sounds!"[136]

An Orthodox Church is usually more or less square in plan, with a wide central space covered by a dome. (In Russia the church dome has assumed that striking onion shape which forms so characteristic a feature of every Russian landscape.) The elongated naves and chancels, common in cathedrals and larger parish churches of the Gothic style, are not found in eastern church architecture. There are as a rule no chairs or pews in the central part of the church, although there may be benches or stalls along the walls. An Orthodox normally stands during Church services (non-Orthodox visitors are often astonished to see old women remaining on their feet for several hours without apparent signs of fatigue); but there are moments when the congregation can sit or kneel. Canon xx of the first Ecumenical Council forbids all kneeling on Sundays or on any of the fifty days between Easter and Pentecost; but today this rule is unfortunately not always strictly observed.

It is a remarkable thing how great a difference the presence or absence of pews can make to the whole spirit of Christian worship. There is in Orthodox worship a flexibility,

an unselfconscious informality, not found among western congregations, at any rate north of the Alps. Western worshippers, ranged in their neat rows, each in his proper place, cannot move about during the service without causing a disturbance; a western congregation is generally expected to arrive at the beginning and to stay to the end. But in Orthodox worship people can come and go far more freely, and nobody is greatly surprised if one moves about during the service. The same informality and freedom also characterizes the behaviour of the clergy: ceremonial movements are not so minutely prescribed as in the west, priestly gestures are less stylized and more natural. This informality, while it can lead at times to irreverence, is in the end a precious quality which Orthodox would be most sorry to lose. They are at home in their church—not troops on a parade ground, but children in their Father's house. Orthodox worship is often termed "otherworldly," but could more truly be described as "homely": it is a *family* affair. Yet behind this homeliness and informality there lies a deep sense of mystery.

In every Orthodox Church the sanctuary is divided from the rest of the interior by the *iconostasis,* a solid screen, usually of wood, covered with panel icons. In early days the chancel was separated merely by a low screen three or four feet high. Sometimes this screen was surmounted by an open series of columns supporting a horizontal beam or architrave: a screen of this kind can still be seen at Saint Mark's, Venice. Only in comparatively recent times—in many places not until the fifteenth or sixteenth century—was the space between these columns filled up, and the iconostasis given its present solid form. Many Orthodox liturgists today would be glad to follow Father John of Kronstadt's example and revert to a more open type of iconostasis; in a few places this has actually been done.

The iconostasis is pierced by three doors. The large door in the centre—the *Holy Door*—when opened affords a view through to the altar. This doorway is closed by double gates, behind which hangs a curtain. Outside service time, except during Easter week, the gates are kept closed and the curtain drawn. During services, at particular moments the gates are sometimes open, sometimes closed, while occasionally when the gates are closed the curtain is drawn across as well. Many Greek parishes, however, now no longer close the gates or

---

135. Paul of Aleppo, *The Travels of Macarius 1652–1660,* edited Lady Laura Ridding (New York: Arno Press, 1971), 27.
136. Ibid., 6.

draw the curtain at any point in the Liturgy; in a number of churches the gates have been removed altogether, while other churches have followed a course which is liturgically far more correct—keeping the gates, but removing the curtain. Of the two other doors, that on the left leads into the "chapel" of the *Prothesis* or Preparation (here the sacred vessels are kept, and here the priest prepares the bread and the wine at the beginning of the Liturgy); that on the right leads into the *Diakonikon* (now generally used as a vestry, but originally the place where the sacred books, particularly the Book of the Gospels, were kept together with the relics). Laymen are not allowed to go behind the iconostasis, except for a special reason such as serving at the Liturgy. The altar in an Orthodox Church—the Holy Table or Throne, as it is called—stands free of the east wall, in the centre of the sanctuary; behind the altar and against the wall is set the bishop's throne.

Orthodox Churches are full of icons—on the screen, on the walls, in special shrines, or on a kind of desk where they can be venerated by the faithful. When an Orthodox enters church, his first action will be to buy a candle, go up to an icon, cross himself, kiss the icon, and light the candle in front of it. "They be great offerers of candles," commented the English merchant Richard Chancellor, visiting Russia in the reign of Elizabeth I. In the decoration of the church, the various iconographical scenes and figures are not arranged fortuitously, but according to a definite theological scheme, so that the whole edifice forms one great icon or image of the Kingdom of God. In Orthodox religious art, as in the religious art of the medieval west, there is an elaborate system of symbols, involving every part of the church building and its decoration. Icons, frescoes, and mosaics are not mere ornaments, designed to make the church "look nice," but have a theological and liturgical function to fulfil.

The icons which fill the church serve as a point of meeting between heaven and earth. As each local congregation prays Sunday by Sunday, surrounded by the figures of Christ, the angels, and the saints, these visible images remind the faithful unceasingly of the invisible presence of the whole company of heaven at the Liturgy. The faithful can feel that the walls of the church open out upon eternity, and they are helped to realize that their Liturgy on earth is one and the same with the great Liturgy of heaven. The multitudinous icons express visibly the sense of "heaven on earth."

The worship of the Orthodox Church is communal and popular. Any non-Orthodox who attends Orthodox services with some frequency will quickly realize how closely the whole worshipping community, priest and people alike, are bound together into one; among other things, the absence of pews helps to create a sense of unity. Although most Orthodox congregations do not join in the singing, it should not therefore be imagined that they are taking no real part in the service; nor does the iconostasis—even in its present solid form—make the people feel cut off from the priest in the sanctuary. In any case, many of the ceremonies take place in front of the screen, in full view of the congregation.

Orthodox laity do not use the phrase "to *hear* Mass," for in the Orthodox Church the Mass has never become something done by the clergy for the laity, but is something which clergy and laity perform *together*. In the medieval west, where the Eucharist was performed in a learned language not understood by the people, men came to church to adore the Host at the Elevation, but otherwise treated the Mass mainly as a convenient occasion for saying their private prayers.[137] In the Orthodox Church, where the Liturgy has never ceased to be a common action performed by priest and people together, the congregation do not come to church to say their private prayers, but to pray the public prayers of the Liturgy and to take part in the action of the rite itself. Orthodoxy has never undergone that separation between liturgy and personal devotion from which the medieval and post-medieval west has suffered so much.

Certainly the Orthodox Church, as well as the west, stands in need of a Liturgical Movement; indeed, some such movement has already begun in a small way in several parts of the Orthodox world (revival of congregational singing; gates of the Holy Door left open in the Liturgy; more open form of iconostasis, and so on). Yet in Orthodoxy the scope of this Liturgical Movement will be far more restricted, since the changes required are very much less drastic. That sense of corporate worship which it is the primary aim of liturgical reform in the west to restore has never ceased to be a living reality in the Orthodox Church.

There is in most Orthodox worship an unhurried and timeless quality, an effect produced in part by the constant repetition of *Litanies*. Either in a longer or a shorter form, the Litany recurs several times in every service of the Byzantine rite. In these Litanies, the deacon (if there is no dea-

---

137. All this, of course, has now been changed in the west by the Liturgical Movement.

con, the priest) calls the people to pray for the various needs of the Church and the world, and to each petition the choir or the people replies *Lord, have mercy*—*Kyrie eleison* in Greek, *Gospodi pomilui* in Russian—probably the first words in an Orthodox service which the visitor grasps. (In some Litanies the response is changed to *Grant this, O Lord*.) The congregation associate themselves with the different intercessions by making the sign of the Cross and bowing. In general the sign of the Cross is employed far more frequently by Orthodox than by western worshippers, and there is a far greater freedom about the times when it is used: different worshippers cross themselves at different moments, each as he wishes, although there are of course occasions in the service when almost all sign themselves at the same time.

From Timothy Ware, *The Orthodox Church* (Hammondsworth, NY: Ringwood, 1963), 269–79.

► In "Communion via Intinction," first published in 1966, **Robert F. Taft,** professor of Eastern liturgies, discusses the historical development of the Eastern Orthodox liturgical practice of administering the Eucharist. Intinction is the practice of immersing the bread in the wine and consuming them at the same time.

ROBERT F. TAFT

"Communion via Intinction"

With the widespread restoration of the ancient (and in my view sole liturgically justifiable) tradition of communion under both species in Roman Catholic worship in the aftermath of the liturgical renewal resulting from Vatican II, communion via intinction—i.e., by dipping the consecrated host into the chalice and receiving both species together—has become common. The AIDS scare has given new impetus to this practice even in churches where communion in the cup continues to be served separately to those who wish to drink from it.

Communion via intinction has long been practiced in the Christian East.[138] Indeed, the only ones to maintain intact the ancient usage of adult lay communion under both species separately, and in the hand, are the Coptic and Ethiopian Orthodox Churches, and the East-Syrian (Assyrian) Church of the East. Though why the other churches shifted to distributing both species together via intinction is by no means clear, this usage had become widespread by the end of the first millennium.

I. The Beginnings of Intinction in the East

Much earlier, however, sporadic evidence for communion by intinction at least in some circumstances begins to emerge in the East at the dawn of the Middle Ages. St. Sophronius, born in Damascus c. 560, later (c. 619) a monk in Palestine, and Patriarch of Jerusalem from 634–38, is, as far as I have been able to determine, the first explicit eastern witness to this innovation of communion by intinction. In miracle 12 of his *Narratio miraculorum SS. Cyri et Iohannis,* a writing judged to be authentic, Sophronius describes the miraculous appearance of the martyrs Cyrus and John to the young Julian, a sick follower of the Monophysite bishop Julian of Halicarnassus. The invalid was paralyzed after being poisoned by his paramour, whom he had abandoned along with his dissolute life. When medical remedies proved useless, Julian's parents appealed to the intercession of the two holy martyrs, who heard their prayers and gave the paralytic some relief from his agony. The two saints also appeared to the invalid frequently during the night, exhorting him to abandon his heresy and embrace the Catholic communion. During these visitations, "they also frequently used to bring him the holy chalice filled with the holy body of the Lord and the blood, and invited him to approach, appearing themselves to communicate, and calling upon Julian to communicate with them too."[139] From the context it would seem that the one chalice contained the consecrated bread and wine together—i.e., the bread immersed or intincted in the wine. Note, however, that here as in the earliest instances in the West, it is a case of communion outside the liturgy: communion brought to the sick or to those otherwise impeded from attending the eucharistic service.

Another Syro-Palestinian Greek text, the *Narrationes* 43 of St. Anastasius, a monk of the Monastery of St. Catherine on Sinai in the latter part of the seventh century, tells of a saintly stylite-presbyter receiving communion on his pillar under both species together, by intinction, by means of a spoon. Whether this was by then common practice or an exigency of the peculiar situation is not clear from the text, though the

---

138. The Assyrians give the children communion by intinction, the Ethiopians give infants communion in this way, and the Copts will sometimes give the laity communion via intinction if there are many communicants.

139. N. Fernandez Marcos, ed., *Los "Thaumata" de Sofronio. Contribución al estudio de la "incubatio" cristiana,* Consejo superior de investigaciones cientificas, Manuales y anejos de emerita 31 (Madrid: 1975) 266 = *PG* [Migne, *Patrologia Graeca*] 87.3:3457C. All translations here and below are by Robert Taft.

latter seems more likely for several reasons: the early date of this witness, the general acceptance of communion via intinction only later, and, in most witnesses, its restriction to communion of the laity.

From the ninth century on, the evidence for communion via intinction becomes more consistent. And by the turn of the millennium, the usage is well in place. [. . .] But the shift to intinction from the ancient usage of the laity communicating under both species separately did not occur without polemic or controversy.

From Robert F. Taft, "Communion via Intinction," *Studia Liturgica* 26 (1996): 225–27.

✌

5. LITURGICAL ISSUES IN SIXTEENTH- AND TWENTIETH-CENTURY PROTESTANTISM

☙ In his chapter "Commonly Called Sacraments," **James F. White** examines the history and impact of liturgical changes that have arisen in various Protestant Churches in response to debate regarding the sacraments, with special attention to the sacrament of penance.

JAMES F. WHITE

"Commonly Called Sacraments,"
in *The Sacraments in Protestant Practice and Faith*

The Reformation narrowed the number of sign-acts that could be called sacraments, just as the thirteenth century also had in selecting seven instead of an undetermined number. But in neither case did that mean that the rites and ceremonies not designated as sacraments disappeared. The rite of religious profession still survived even if the latter scholastics no longer considered it a sacrament. Such rites as penance, the healing of the sick, Christian marriage, ordination, and Christian burial obviously served important functions within the life of Protestant communities, just as they had before the Reformation. But they were not considered as instituted by Christ in scripture and hence no longer were called sacraments.

One can question whether this distinction made much difference to the average worshiper. It did in the sense that baptism and the Lord's Supper were regarded as obligatory on the basis of divine command, whereas extreme unction or penance could quietly fade away or become transmuted in various ways. And marriage and Christian burial could be secularized and pushed outside the church doors at different times and places. Defining only two actions as sacraments also meant that their form and matter were fixed with more certainty whereas other acts could be more fluid and evolve on their own.

It is also instructive what new rites did not develop. With the Reformers' emphasis on the sanctity of any useful vocation, it is strange that no rites for entering a vocation evolved. The stress on reading the Scriptures pushed education into new prominence and shaped confirmation or public profession of faith into something resembling graduation exercises. Much of this has already been discussed under baptismal practices. We shall not repeat our consideration of confirmation here, although the Anglican Articles of Religion list confirmation as one of the five "commonly called Sacraments."

Several actions, such as marriage and caring for the dead, are common to all humanity, whether Christian or not. We can refer to them as "natural sacraments." Others, such as penance and healing, are referred to in the Acts of the Apostles[140] and elsewhere in the epistles.[141] So we may speak of them as "apostolic sacraments." Confirmation we shall regard as part of baptism, misplaced by a series of historical accidents. The Lord's Supper and baptism we can refer to as "gospel sacraments," beginning with the Last Supper and the baptism of Jesus.

Not all of these natural or apostolic sacraments have been pursued with equal vigor in the nearly five centuries of Protestantism. But there are strong indications that today each of them is receiving fresh attention. We shall make a quick survey of how Protestants at various times and places have prioritized or neglected penance, the healing of the sick, Christian marriage, ordination, and Christian burial. In each case, changing practices, controversies, and meanings have surfaced over the past five centuries. This should suggest the

---

140. Acts 2:38; 16:18, etc.
141. Jas 5:14–16; Heb. 6:4, etc.

basically sacramental nature of each and help raise the question of whether either the thirteenth or the sixteenth century was justified in limiting the number of actions called sacraments. Perhaps the first twelve Christian centuries were right in keeping the number open.

Penance, Confession, or Reconciliation

By definition, all Christians are sinners, falling far short of the perfection the Gospels urge. So the Christian life is a recurring process of reconciliation with God and neighbor, usually through some acts of confession and pardon. The church has had to deal with these realities ever since its beginnings.[142] By a long process, moving from public penance before the whole community for notorious sinners only, penance became a private act expected of everyone of the age of reason. The Fourth Lateran Council of 1215 mandated annual confession, and the minimum often became the norm. "Late medieval penance, then, stressed the therapeutic element, purification, to remove sin and eliminate the debt of eternal punishment incurred by mortal sin. . . . Other means, indulgences in particular, were necessary to deal with the temporal punishment due to sin."[143] The priest alone possessed the power of the keys to retain or to remit sin, for the community no longer functioned in penance.

Luther's initial outburst of anger was directed to the sale of indulgences as vitiating the orderly care of souls through penance. He was concerned to reform penance, not abolish it. In 1519 he could say, "There is no greater sin than not to believe this article of 'the forgiveness of sins' which we pray daily in the Creed."[144] God's word acts in absolution to comfort and strengthen sinners. Luther is willing at first to call penance a sacrament in his *Babylonian Captivity* because of its "word of divine promise."[145] Despite abuses, Luther wished to retain penance: "As to the current practice of private confession, I am heartily in favor of it, . . . and I would not have it abolished."[146] Luther's most radical statement is that "Christ has given to every one of his believers the power to absolve even open sins,"[147] thereby breaking every clerical monopoly of the sacrament.

Penance plays an important role in Luther's catechisms. One may confess one's sins to "God alone or to our neighbor." But Luther also provided "A Short Order of Confession before the Priest for the Common Man" in the 1529 edition of the Small Catechism and later revised it in 1531. It takes the form of a general confession of sin with particular details confessed, if necessary. In 1531, the "father confessor" pro-

nounces that "I, by the command of Jesus Christ our Lord, forgive thee all thy sin."[148] Absent is a cataloging by species and number of sinful acts. But it is a definite act of confession and absolution of a penitent before a priest. It was certainly Luther's intention that penance be continued as an important act of reassuring the sinner of God's forgiveness.

Much less of this survived than Luther wished. There was a revival of this practice in nineteenth-century Germany under Pastor Wilhelm Loehe, with a visit to the pastor necessary before each communion. A remnant has survived today in the Lutheran practice of notifying the pastor before receiving communion. But Luther's expectation that penance would play a major role in pastoral life had a rather short history.

In a way that Luther did not expect, and probably did not relish, the Anabaptists developed a strong force for the discipline of their communities by the use of the ban. According to the Schleitheim Confession of 1527, the ban is employed for those who "somehow slip and fall into error and sin, being inadvertently overtaken. The same [shall] be warned twice privately and the third time be publicly admonished before the entire congregation according to the command of Christ."[149] Matthew 18:15–17 was their source, as well as 1 Corinthians 5:11–13. The whole purpose was that a pure gathering could share in communion together.

But the power of the keys, which all the baptized exercised, was meant to heal. As Menno Simons wrote, "we do not want to expel any, but rather to receive; not to amputate, but rather to heal; not to discard, but rather to win back; not to grieve, but rather to comfort; not to condemn, but rather to save."[150] But he was also aware that "one scabby sheep mars the whole flock."[151] Debates raged over how se-

142. Heb 6:4.

143. James Dallen, *The Reconciling Community: The Rite of Penance* (New York: Pueblo Publishing Company, 1986), 158.

144. *The Sacrament of Penance*, trans. Theodore E. Bachmann, in *Luther's Works*, vol. 35 (Philadelphia: Muhlenburg Press, 1960), 14.

145. *The Babylonian Captivity of the Church*, trans. A. T. W. Steinhäuser and Frederick C. Ahrens and Abdel Ross Wentz, in *Luther's Works*, vol. 36 (Philadelphia: Muhlenburg Press, 1959), 81–82.

146. Ibid., 86.

147. Ibid., 88.

148. *How One Should Teach Common Folk to Shrive Themselves*, trans. Joseph Stump and Ulrich S. Leopold, in *Luther's Works*, vol. 53 (Philadelphia: Fortress Press, 1965), 121.

149. The Schleitheim Confession, in *Legacy of Michael Sattler*, ed. and trans. John Howard Yoder (Scottdale, Pa.: Herald Press, 1973), 36–37.

150. "Admonition on Church Discipline," ed. John C. Wenger, trans. Leonard Verduin, in *The Complete Writings of Menno Simons* (Scottdale, Pa.: Herald Press, 1973), 36–37.

151. Simons, "Account of Excommunication," in *Complete Writings*, 471.

vere the shunning of the person banned should be, whether it could even divide husband and wife, and whether "the commandment regarding marriage" was stronger than that about shunning.

Some Anabaptists developed a sign-act of reconciliation or readmission. This was not unlike the reconciliation of penitents in the early church and in effect was a renewal of baptism. "So also after he fell," Peter Riedeman counseled, when one "was separated from the church he must likewise be received by a sign, that is through the laying on of hands, which must be done by a servant of the gospel. This indicates that he once more has part and is rooted in the grace of God."[152] The minister by a tangible sign-act effected reconciliation with the community.

These forms of penance endure partly because of the small, disciplined, sectarian nature of Mennonite, Amish, and Hutterite communities. Whether this discipline could have succeeded in larger church-type communities is a good question, although the New England Puritan community made the experiment. *The Scarlet Letter* is not all fiction.

For most of the Reformed Tradition, another course opened up. The Fourth Lateran Council of 1215 had linked confession to the eucharist, a fateful move. The late medieval eucharist had become increasingly penitential, laden with apologies for one's unworthiness. The Reformed Tradition took this even further, making each eucharist a fresh occasion for examination of conscience and a dose of introspection. The prevailing eucharistic piety of the late Middle Ages was enshrined in Reformed liturgies down to the present. It is significant that the Presbyterian eucharist still mandates general confession and pardon as part of the Gathering rite. The eucharist is always prefaced by confession.

More than anyone else, Martin Bucer led the way. His eucharistic rite published in Strasbourg in 1539 begins with three possible confessions. The most impressive of these is based on a paraphrase of the Ten Commandments. One confesses that "I have sinned in manifold ways against thee and thy commandments" and then examines all kinds of possibilities.[153] Calvin's rite begins with the confession that "we are . . . born in iniquity and corruption, prone to do evil, incapable of any good, and that in our depravity we transgress thy holy commandments without end or ceasing."[154] As if that were not enough, the congregation then sings the first table of the Commandments.

The Decalogue was to have an even more lasting incarnation as part of the eucharist. It began with the Anglican prayer book of 1552 and lasted to the present in the English prayer book and until 1965 in the American Methodist eucharist, although in 1935 the Beatitudes became an option instead. The same instinct reached its culmination in the Scottish sacramental seasons of the late seventeenth century, in which once each year the eucharist provided a several-day occasion of self-examination and preparation.

The consequence was that for most Protestants, penance became subsumed in a penitential eucharist. The eucharist became, as the Methodist rite of 1939 said, a time to "ask God's mercy for their transgressions in times past and grace to keep the law in time to come."[155] In such a fashion, the eucharist remained a somber reminder of Good Friday. In Dutch churches, the eucharist was always celebrated on Good Friday, and people wore their funeral clothes. Penance did not disappear, it simply attached itself to the eucharist.

In the hands of John Wesley, a new form of penance appeared in the group discipline of class meetings. Here spiritual direction was performed in a corporate fashion, based on James 5:16: "Confess your sins to one another, and pray for one another, so that you may be healed." This involved weekly meetings for those who had affirmed such questions as "Do you desire to be told of all your faults, and that plain and home?" Each week they would be asked: "What known sins have you committed since our last meeting?"[156] It was a stringent discipline, and it worked well for over a century until Methodism expanded into a church. This form of "Christian conference" made penance a group process.

In the Catholic Revival in the Church of England in the nineteenth century, a major effort was made to revive private confession to a priest, or "auricular confession," as it was known. This aroused stubborn opposition as a betrayal of the Reformation and led to salacious imaginations about priests hearing the confessions of women. The title of a tract tells it all: "The House of Lords on Ritualism in the Church, Confession & Absolution: Shocking Disclosures."[157]

152. Peter Riedeman, *Account of Our Religion, Doctrine, and Faith,* in *Anabaptism in Outline,* ed. Walter Klaasen (Scottdale, Pa.: Herald Press, 1956), 413.

153. Martin Bucer, Strasbourg Liturgy, in *Liturgies of the Western Church,* ed. Bard Thompson (1961; reprint, Minneapolis: Fortress Press, 1980), 168–69.

154. John Calvin, "The Form of Church Prayers," in *Liturgies of the Western Church,* 197.

155. *The Methodist Hymnal* (Nashville: Methodist Publishing House, 1939), 524.

156. "The Rules of the United Societies," in *John Wesley,* ed. Albert C. Outler (New York: Oxford University Press, 1964), 181.

157. *The House of Lords on Ritualism in the Church, Confession & Absolution: Shocking Disclosures* (Manchester: John Heywood, n.d.).

One of the reasons given for advancing confession to a priest was that both of Cranmer's rites for the Visitation of the Sick had invited confession by the sick person. But to many Victorians, it appeared a strange and dangerous practice.

What took its place, instead, for most Protestants was a ministry of counseling. That had a long precedent, such as the advice in Richard Baxter's *The Reformed Pastor,* which advocated visiting from house to house to examine the state of parishioners' souls.[158] In the twentieth century, new psychological insights made counseling both a spiritual discipline and a form of therapy. It was meant to heal more than to chasten. At times, a view of psychological professionalism tended to dominate; at others counseling took the form of spiritual direction.

In recent years, the possibilities of corporate services of confession have been discussed but rarely acted on. As Reinhold Niebuhr pointed out, we are often willing to sin as a group by doing acts we would abhor as individuals, as in war. United Methodists so far have not published official services of corporate repentance which could serve in times of national turmoil over racism, sexism, war, and other forms of corporate guilt. The Episcopal Church has an individual office for "Reconciliation of a Penitent" but not yet a corporate office of reconciliation.[159] Lutherans have a "Brief Order for Confession and Forgiveness" often used as a preface to the eucharist, but its emphasis is almost entirely on individual sin.[160] Presbyterians have produced "A Service of Repentance and Forgiveness for Use with a Penitent Individual," meant to be used in private.[161]

Certainly sin is alive and well, and various forms of relieving the soul of its burden are practiced in private. But relatively little has been done so far in providing corporate forms for confessing corporate sins. Maybe these will come in the next stage of liturgical revision.

From James F. White, *The Sacraments in Protestant Practice and Faith* (Nashville: Abingdon, 1999), 119–25. [Ellipses in original.]

❧ **Rudolph Collin** (n.d.) was a friend of Zwingli's (1484–1531) and accompanied him to Marburg as part of the delegation from Zurich. Collin's "Report of *The Marburg Colloquy* between Martin Luther and Ulrich Zwingli" (1529) focuses on the participants' different beliefs regarding the presence of Christ's body in the sacramental bread of the Eucharist.

RUDOLPH COLLIN

"Report of *The Marburg Colloquy* between Martin Luther and Ulrich Zwingli"

Before the colloquy began, and as he was about to debate with Zwingli and Oecolampadius, *Luther* had written on his table, "This is my body," in order that he might not allow himself to be diverted from these words. Then in a long speech he testified in advance that he disagreed with the persons of the opposing party and that he would continue to do so, since Christ has said most clearly: "Take, eat, this is my body." Here, he said, it must be shown that the body is not the body. He cited the opinion of his opponents, but would allow no questioning on such a clear text. He excluded all rational understanding and common opinion. He rejected carnal or mathematical arguments, saying that God is above and beyond mathematics and that the words of God are to be honored and spoken of with awe. God, however, commands: "Take, eat; this is my body."

Oecolampadius replies to Luther's arguments and proposes that the sixth chapter of John be dealt with because in it the other passages of Scripture are explained. To the saying, "This is my body," he relates, "I am the true vine."[162] He does not deny the divine possibility here. He proceeds from the bodily to the spiritual eating. He says his own opinion is neither meaningless nor godless, for it is based on faith and Scripture.

Luther acknowledges that there are metaphors. "This is my body" is taken to be a demonstrative sentence: for [only] a general sentence permits a metaphor. Then he asks in what way spiritual eating excludes bodily eating. He concedes that the fathers would be partly on his [Oecolampadius's] side if his interpretation of them were admitted.

Oecolampadius: "I am the true vine" is also a demonstrative sentence. It is possible. How is it possible?

Luther does not deny that there are figures of speech, but he wants him [Oecolampadius] to prove that here [in the

---

158. Richard Baxter, *The Reformed Pastor* (NY: American Tract Society, n.d.), 156–59.

159. *The Book of Common Prayer* (New York: Church Hymnal Corporation, 1979), 147–52.

160. *Lutheran Book of Worship* (Minneapolis: Augsburg Publishing House, 1978), 56.

161. *Book of Common Worship* (Louisville: Westminster/John Knox Press, 1993), 1023–24.

162. Jn 15:1.

Lord's Supper] it [the argument] results from begging the question: When Christ said, "This is," the close connection is required.

Oecolampadius reads from the sixth chapter of John and afterwards proves that Christ is dealing there with spiritual eating and is directing attention away from the bodily eating. Therefore, it is not a bodily eating.

Luther repeats the quotation from the sixth chapter of John and says: You think that the spiritual eating is to be separated from the bodily eating. The Jews held that Christ was to be eaten as bread and meat are eaten in a dish, or like roast pork.

Oecolampadius replied: This is a base understanding, on which there has been a lengthy dispute and contention on both sides.

Oecolampadius [added]: To believe that Christ is in the bread is an opinion, not faith. It is dangerous to attribute too much to the elements.

Luther: To pick up a piece of straw at the command of the Lord is a spiritual act. He explains the example of the horseshoe at length. One must look not so much upon what is said but, rather, upon who says it. When God says something, we poor, weak humans should listen. When he commands something, the world must obey, and all of us should honor his word; for there is nothing to which we should be more attentive.

After this argument *Oecolampadius* said: Since we have the spiritual eating, what need is there for bodily eating?

Luther: I care not what is necessary, but since it is written, "Take, eat," etc., it is to be done and to be believed altogether. One must do it. Luther urged this again and again. If he should command me, he said, to eat dung, I should do so, knowing full well that this is salutary for me.

Oecolampadius quotes the passage from the sixth chapter of John: "The flesh is of no avail" [v. 63]. If the flesh, when eaten, is of no avail, but the Spirit is, then we must look to that which is of avail, and pay close attention to the will of God.

Finally both men [Oecolampadius and Luther] testified that they would persevere in their opinion, since neither of the two had convinced the other.

Zwingli begins to accuse Luther of prejudice because he [Luther] testifies that he is unwilling to abandon his view. In the same way Helvidius, with reference to the word "brother," could prove [that Jesus had brothers], since it is clearly written "his brothers."[163] We should compare one pas-

sage of Scripture with another. Therefore, if we do not have a passage which says, "This is the figure of my body," we nevertheless have a passage which leads us away from bodily eating. For that reason [it follows] he did not give his body physically in the Supper.

They were of one mind on the cardinal point, namely, the spiritual eating.

Then he [Zwingli] treats the sixth chapter of John, especially these words: "The spirit gives life, the flesh is of no avail."[164] He deals with Christ's humanity which suffered; for that was a salutary act. By the logic of his words he proves in a most powerful manner that the flesh which is eaten does not avail in any way. He accuses Luther of trickery in the use of the words "tearing apart" and "lacerating," since the word "to eat" [*esthiein*] is the same as to eat, to eat up, or to manducate. "When I shall have ascended into heaven," then you shall see that I am not to be eaten bodily, essentially, etc. Spirit and flesh are opposed to one another. He renews the argument about a base understanding and says: Some things were excellently spoken by you, others were childish, namely: "If God would command us to eat dung," etc. For what God does command, he commands for our good and our salvation. God gives light and he does not spread darkness. Therefore, he does not say, "This is my body," essentially, really, and in a carnal way, since Scripture opposes this. The oracles of the demons are obscure, not the words of Christ. The soul "eats" spirit; therefore [it does] not [eat] flesh.

Luther proves from Scripture against Helvidius that the word "brother" can be used for "cousin." But it cannot be proved that "This is my body" is a trope. If God told me to eat a crabapple, I would eat spiritually. For wherever the word of God is, there is spiritual eating. Therefore, since he added the bodily eating by saying, "This is my body," it is to be believed. By faith we eat this body which is given for us. The mouth receives the body of Christ, the soul believes the words that it is eating the body.

Zwingli: From Scripture it can be proved that the thing signified is often used for the sign; in Ezekiel,[165] in the "passover."[166] Since in passages of Scripture which are uncertain a comparison is demanded, passages similar to them are to be believed.

He accuses Luther of rhetoric and fictitious arguments

---

163. Jn 7:3.
164. Jn 6:63.

165. 5:1ff.
166. Ex 12:27.

when the latter says: "If God would command those things or such matters"; for we know that God does not command those things or such matters. The word, he said, is made ambiguous by you.

Words only signify to us the will of God. God does not set before us incomprehensible matters. That Christ is true God and man is not unknown to the believer. We have the example of Mary who asked: "How can this be?"[167] When she had become more certain through inquiry she then believed. But here in chapter 6 the disciples expressed doubt about the carnal eating because he himself [Christ] taught a spiritual eating. —As to your words, "The word of God is the eating," I do not deny this; but the word is to be believed.

Luther: The passages from Ezekiel and the "passover"[168] are allegories. But allegory or signification has no meaning in this case. As to the efficacy of the word, we do not say that the body is produced by our words, but rather, we are speaking of the institution of Christ. These are not our words but the words of the Lord.

"Do this," etc.[169]—this word causes the hand of the priest to be the hand of Christ. It is not my mouth, it is not my tongue, but both are Christ's. [This is true] even though I were a knave or rascal. The same applies to baptism. Let us take the example of a prince who defeats the enemy and puts him to flight. In that case the hands of all [the soldiers] are said to be the hands of the prince. "If you will say to this mountain, ['Move hence to yonder place,'] it will move" [Matt 17:20]. I am not debating whether the "is" may be "signifies," but I am satisfied that Christ says: "This is my body." Even the devil is powerless over against these words. This is what I want: The words are not to be dependent on my power but on the power and command of the Lord. The soul eats the body [of Christ]. The body is also present bodily in the word. If I question it, I would fall from faith and would become a fool on account of it. Why do you not also make a trope out of, "He ascended into heaven?"[170] Therefore, believe the plain words and give glory to God.

Zwingli: We, too, ask you to give glory to God and to stop begging the question. Where do you prove your thesis? I am not going to abandon this passage [from John], which is unassailable and which you treat so lightly. You will have to change your tune.

Luther: You are speaking spitefully.

Zwingli asks whether be believes that Christ in the sixth chapter of John wanted to help the ignorant.

Luther: You want to win your case with bold words. "This is a hard saying," etc. [Jn 6:60]; the Jews are speaking about

something which is impossible and absurd. But we will pass over that text because it does not deal with the matter at hand.

Zwingli: No, no, this passage (meaning John 6) is going to break your neck.

Luther: Don't boast too much. You are in Hesse and not in Switzerland. Necks do not break so easily here. On account of this statement other accusations were made and there was much shouting. Yet Luther used a similar phrase in his book *Against the Heavenly Prophets,* where he says: "Let us take the rogue," meaning Karlstadt, "by the throat." . . .

Zwingli apologized for having used an expression common among his people. Recognizing that there were diverse manners of expression, the prince [Philip Melanchthon, who sponsored the debate] with a nod of his head and an oral statement accepted the excuse.

Zwingli cited Luther's postil in which he had written that Christ had said of himself: "The flesh is of no avail."[171] Then he introduced Melanchthon's remarks about the same passage. That the body is eaten in a bodily way is not established in his statement. When the fathers said that the body of Christ feeds the soul, I understand this to mean the resurrection.

Luther: I do not care what we have written. Prove that "This is my body" is not his body. The body [of Christ] nourishes man's body for eternity. When the mouth receives the body, a person acquires a kind of immortality. For the word on the basis of God's command supplies strength. God says, "Take, do," and so it comes to pass. He speaks and it is done. There is a difference between our speaking and God's command. If St. Peter were present, we would not know whether he believes. Consequently, God does not establish the sacrament upon our sanctity but upon his word. The worst priest can celebrate the sacrament.

Zwingli: It would be an absurdity if the impious could perform this sacred act.

Luther: It is not in the least absurd, for a bad person may baptize. The ungodly minister on the basis of the word of God. "For they [the scribes and the Pharisees] sit on Moses' seat."[172] Augustine says against the Donatists that the ministry must not be entrusted solely to the virtuous and godly because our accomplishment is dependent on the word of God.

---

167. Lk 1:34.

168. In Ex 12.

169. Lk 22:19.

170. Mk 16:19.

171. Jn 6:63.

172. Mt 23:2ff.

Zwingli: It makes a difference whether the Pharisees teach or whether a person does what Christ says. The ministry of preaching is greater than the ministry of baptizing. The words, "This is my body," belong to the ministry of preaching.

Oecolampadius again takes up John 6. He also brings up the passage about Nicodemus and explains it.[173]

Luther: Faith looks upon the body [of Christ] as present [in the sacrament] and upon the body which is in heaven.

Oecolampadius: Luther always impresses upon us the same thing, as if we had the bread without the word of God. The church is founded on the word, "You are the Son of God,"[174] and not on the word, "This is my body."

Luther: I am not adhering to this passage without a reason. "This is my body" is enough for me. I confess that the body is in heaven, I also confess that it is in the sacrament. I am not concerned about what is contrary to nature but only about what is contrary to faith.

Oecolampadius: In all these things Christ has been made like us. As he is like the Father in his divinity in every respect, so he is like us in his humanity in every respect.

Luther: We are to partake of the Supper "until he comes," etc.[175] You are distinguishing between his humanity and his divinity; I am not concerned about this. "For you always have the poor with you, not me," etc.[176] This is the best argument you have presented today. Christ is thus in the sacrament substantially, as he was born of the Virgin. Here the analogy of faith is demanded according to the definition of faith in Hebrews 11[:1].

Oecolampadius: We do not know Christ according to the flesh.

Philip [Melanchthon]: That is according to our flesh.

Oecolampadius: You do not admit a trope in the words of institution, and yet you understand them as synecdoche. This is contrary to the understanding of the teachers of the church universal.

Luther: May God decide that question! We have synecdoche in sayings like the sword with the sheath, a mug with beer; it is therefore an inclusive way of speaking. "This is my body"; here the body is in the bread, even as the sword is in the sheath. The text demands this figurative form of speech; but the metaphor does away with the content altogether, as when one says "body," that is, "figure of the body." Here is an example: "On whom you see the Spirit descend";[177] the Holy Spirit was in the dove.

Oecolampadius laid hold of this example[178] and related it to his view in a most excellent way.

Zwingli: Romans 8[:3]: "God . . . sent his Son in the likeness of sinful flesh." Philippians [2:7–8]: "He emptied himself . . . . [And being found] in human form. . . ." Hebrews 2[:17]: "Therefore he had to be made like his brethren in every respect." Consequently, he had a finite humanity. If Christ's body is above, it must be in one place as Augustine, Fulgentius, and others state. The conclusion of the matter is: The body of Christ is in one place; therefore, it cannot be in many places.

Luther, repeating [the passage, that is, Phil 2:7], said "powers" [*hexeis*], "form" [*schemati*]. To be like us in all things would mean that he had a wife, dark eyes, etc. As to the body being there locally, I have told you before and I make it known now that I do not care about mathematics. I have often repeated this. How he is in the Supper and how he is in a place, we do not care.

Zwingli quoted Paul in Philippians 2[:7–8]: "Who, though he was in the form of God" [*Hos en morphē theou huparchōn*] and "taking the form of a servant" [*morphēn doulou labōn*].

Luther: Read Latin or German, not Greek.

Zwingli: He excuses himself in Latin [and explains] that he has used nothing but the Greek New Testament for twelve years. Continuing, he said: Christ therefore is finite, as we are finite.

Luther: I admit that. We have the illustration of the kernel and the shell. So it is with the body of Christ. God can cause the body of Christ either not to be in a place or to be in a place. There followed a considerable controversy concerning "place."

When *Luther* had conceded that the body of Christ was finite, *Zwingli* wanted to conclude that it was therefore in a place. If it was also in a certain place and in heaven, it could not be in the bread. Then *Luther,* not wanting to hear anything more about place or locality, said: I do not want this matter discussed. I do not want these expressions used. —*Zwingli:* Must everything then be done according to your wishes?

Supper was ready and the debate was interrupted.

Zwingli: The body of Christ is finite, therefore it is in a certain place.

Luther: The body is not in one place when it is in the sacrament. It can either be in a place or not be in a place. God

---

173. Jn 3:1ff.

174. Mt 16:16.

175. 1 Cor 11:26.

176. Mt 26:11.

177. Jn 1:33.

178. From Jn 1:33.

can arrange my body so that it is not in one place. For the sophists also say that one body can be in various places; I do not reject this argument. For example, the universe is a body; nevertheless, it is not in one place.

Zwingli: You are arguing from what may be to what exists. Prove that the body of Christ can simultaneously be in various places.

Luther: "This is my body."

Zwingli reads a passage from Fulgentius, stating that Christ is in one place. He objects that Luther has written: "Everything is filled with the body of Christ," and "If the divinity had not suffered in Christ, then it would not be my Christ."

Luther: Fulgentius is not speaking about the Lord's Supper but against the Manichaeans. Luther brought up a passage in Fulgentius concerning the Lord's Supper in which mention of the sacrifice is made.

Zwingli: "It is offered" means "the remembrance of the sacrifice is celebrated."

At this point *Luther* called into question [this interpretation of] "sacrifice" so that he would not have to abandon his point of view. But when *Zwingli* opposed him he again allowed the use of the expression. *Luther* again sought to prove that the body of Christ is in many places by the words: "This is my body." Here *Zwingli* caught him [in a contradiction]. *Luther* repeated his words: I leave it to God whether the body of Christ is in a place or not. For me this is enough: "This is my body." *Zwingli* said repeatedly: You are begging the question. In the same way a quarrelsome person could say: John was the son of Mary, for Christ said, "Behold your son!" and he would keep on repeating, "Christ said, 'Behold your son, behold your son!'"[179]

Luther: We are not begging the question, for one article of faith is not proved by another.

Zwingli: Scripture passages ought to be compared with one another and to be explained by themselves. Tell me, is the body of Christ in a place? *Brenz:* It is not in a place. *Zwingli:* Augustine says it must be in one place.

Luther: Augustine is not talking of the Lord's Supper.

Luther at length admitted that the body is not in the sacrament as in a place.

Oecolampadius drew this conclusion: Therefore, it is not here corporeally, with a real body.

Oecolampadius repeated: They had conceded that the body of Christ is not in the sacrament as in a place and so he inquired in all sincerity: In what way then is the body there? He reads from Augustine and Fulgentius.

Luther: You have Augustine and Fulgentius on your side, but the remaining fathers are on our side.

Oecolampadius asks them to bring up the fathers who are on their side; but they refuse.

Luther admits that the sacrament is a sign of a sacred thing; he further concedes that the symbols are sacred and as such they signify something which is beyond them and represent something that transcends the mind. They agree concerning the differences between natural signs and signs instituted by God.

Luther, among other things, rejected Augustine because he had written his work against the Manichaeans as a young man and because as an author he was obscure and out of date. He concludes.

Oecolampadius says that they quote the fathers for this reason, lest theirs appear to be a new and unheard-of opinion. So he, too, concludes.

Zwingli did the same. *Bucer* gave his testimony along with Zwingli.

Translated by Martin E. Lehmann, in *Luther's Works,* edited by Jaroslav Pelikan, vol. 38 (Philadelphia: Fortress Press, 1971), 52–62. [Ellipses and brackets in original.]

᪄ Churches in the Anglican tradition draw their liturgical foundations from the original *Book of Common Prayer.* The Preface to *The First Book of Common Prayer* (1549) outlines the rationale for its adoption by the Church of England.

Preface to *The First Book of Common Prayer*

There was never any thing by the wit of man so well devised, or so sure established, which in continuance of time hath not been corrupted: as, among other things, it may plainly appear by the common prayers in the Church, commonly called Divine Service: the first original and ground whereof, if a man would search out by the ancient fathers, he shall find, that the same was not ordained, but of a good purpose, and for a great advancement of godliness: For they so ordered the matter, that all the whole Bible (or the greatest part thereof) should be read over once in the year, intending thereby, that the Clergy, and especially such as were Ministers of the congregation, should (by often reading, and medi-

---

179. Jn 19:26.

tation of God's word) be stirred up to godliness themselves, and be more able to exhort others by wholesome doctrine, and to confute them that were adversaries to the truth. And further, that the people (by daily hearing of holy Scripture read in the Church) should continually profit more and more in the knowledge of God, and be the more inflamed with the love of his true religion.

But these many years passed, this godly and decent order of the ancient fathers hath been so altered, broken, and neglected, by planting in uncertain stories, Legends, Responds, Verses, vain repetitions, Commemorations, and Synodals, that commonly when any book of the Bible was begun, before three or four Chapters were read out, all the rest were unread. And in this sort the book of Isaiah was begun in Advent, and the book of Genesis in Septuagesima; but they were only begun, and never read through. After a like sort were other books of holy Scripture used. And moreover, whereas St. Paul would have such language spoken to the people in the Church, as they might understand, and have profit by hearing the same, the Service in the Church of England (these many years) hath been read in Latin to the people, which they understood not; so that they have heard with their ears only; and their hearts, spirit, and mind, have not been edified thereby. And furthermore, notwithstanding that the ancient fathers had divided the Psalms into seven portions, whereof every one was called a nocturn, now of late time a few of them have been daily said (and oft repeated), and the rest utterly omitted. Moreover, the number and hardness of the Rules called the Pie, and the manifold changings of the service, was the cause, that to turn the Book only, was so hard and intricate a matter, that many times, there was more business to find out what should be read, than to read it when it was found out.

These inconveniences therefore considered, here is set forth such an order, whereby the same shall be redressed. And for a readiness in this matter, here is drawn out a Kalendar for that purpose, which is plain and easy to be understood, wherein (so much as may be) the reading of holy Scripture is so set forth, that all things shall be done in order, without breaking one piece thereof from another. For this cause be cut off Anthems, Responds, Invitatories, and such like things, as did break the continual course of the reading of the Scripture.

Yet because there is no remedy, but that of necessity there must be some rules: therefore certain rules are here set forth, which, as they be few in number; so they be plain and easy

to be understood. So that here you have an order for prayer (as touching the reading of the holy Scripture), much agreeable to the mind and purpose of the old fathers, and a great deal more profitable and commodious, than that which of late was used. It is more profitable, because here are left out many things, whereof some be untrue, some uncertain, some vain and superstitious: and is ordained nothing to be read, but the very pure word of God, the holy Scriptures, or that which is evidently grounded upon the same; and that in such a language and order as is most easy and plain for the understanding, both of the readers and hearers. It is also more commodious, both for the shortness thereof, and for the plainness of the order, and for that the rules be few and easy. Furthermore, by this order the curates shall need none other books for their public service, but this book and the Bible: by the means whereof, the people shall not be at so great charge for books, as in time past they have been.

And where heretofore, there hath been great diversity in saying and singing in churches within this realm: some following Salisbury use, some Hereford use, some the use of Bangor, some of York, and some of Lincoln: now from henceforth, all the whole realm shall have but one use. And if any would judge this way more painful, because that all things must be read upon the book, whereas before, by reason of so often repetition, they could say many things by heart: if those men will weigh their labor with the profit in knowledge, which daily they shall obtain by reading upon the book, they will not refuse the pain, in consideration of the great profit that shall ensue thereof.

And forasmuch as nothing can, almost, be so plainly set forth, but doubts may arise in the use and practicing of the same: to appease all such diversity (if any arise), and for the resolution of all doubts, concerning the manner how to understand, do, and execute, the things contained in this book: the parties that so doubt, or diversely take any thing, shall always resort to the Bishop of the Diocese, who by his discretion shall take order for the quieting and appeasing of the same; so that the same order be not contrary to any thing contained in this book.

Though it be appointed in the afore written preface, that all things shall be read and sung in the church in the English tongue, to the end that the congregation may be thereby edified: yet it is not meant, but when men say Matins and Evensong privately, they may say the same in any language that they themselves do understand. Neither that any man shall be bound to the saying of them, but such as from time to time, in Cathedral and Collegiate Churches, parish Churches, and Chapels to the same annexed, shall serve the congregation.

From Episcopal Church, *Book of Common Prayer and Administration of the Sacraments and Other Rites and Ceremonies of the Church* (New York: Church Hymnal Corp., 1976), 866–67.

⚜ "Baptism, Confirmation, and Eucharist" is a statement issued by the **World Council of Churches** in 1971. The statement begins by acknowledging the consensus among the Churches that the central meaning of baptism is participation in Christ and then, given the diversity of liturgical practices in the member churches, asks what the consequences are of this agreement for the rites of baptism, confirmation, and Eucharist.

THE WORLD COUNCIL OF CHURCHES
"Baptism, Confirmation, and Eucharist"

Introduction

Baptism and eucharist have always been topics of theological discussion in the ecumenical movement. The present document reports on a study which was initiated in 1967. The Faith and Order Commission had already dealt with the theme of baptism in the period between the Third World Conference on Faith and Order in Lund (1952) and the Fourth in Montreal (1963). The results of that discussion were presented in the report *One Lord, One Baptism*[180] and favourably received by the Fourth World Conference in Montreal.[181] A few years later the Faith and Order Commission decided that the subject should be studied afresh. The report *One Lord, One Baptism* had been concerned primarily with establishing a common understanding of baptism without as yet drawing concrete conclusions for the churches' liturgy and practice. The new study on "Baptism, Confirmation and the Eucharist" was to include these aspects and to explore whether agreement could be reached on them.

Various meetings were held. A first consultation was organized in spring 1968. It produced a brief analysis of the theme[182] which was subsequently discussed and commented on by a large number of regional groups. A second international consultation was held two years later (September 1970 in Revnice, Czechoslovakia) to discuss some problems in more detail. The findings of the whole study were summarized, reconsidered and revised by a working group which met in Geneva in December 1970.

The Churches are agreed that the central meaning of baptism is participation in Christ. Through his baptism in the Jordan Jesus accepted solidarity with sinners; he continued this solidarity as he followed the path of the Suffering Servant through passion, death and resurrection. The Spirit which came upon Jesus when he was baptized comes also on the Church and unites Christ's people with him in death and resurrection, in and through the baptismal action. Baptism is a gift of God's redeeming love to the Church. Those who receive baptism are baptized by the one Spirit into one body; baptism is the sign and seal of their discipleship in obedience to the Lord.

Since there is wide agreement on the meaning of baptism one might expect that the Churches would be able to recognize one another's baptism without restrictions. This is, however, not the case. Baptism has certainly been seen as a unifying bond. But the Churches have not yet succeeded in achieving full mutual recognition. A number of issues have remained unsolved, and as the Churches face the contemporary situation new ones have emerged which require attention. Can the old controversy on believers' and infant baptism be overcome? What is the relation between baptism and chrismation or confirmation? Does one not have to take into account all the stages of Christian initiation if the mutual recognition is to be fully real? Does mutual recognition of baptism not call for the mutual recognition of the eucharist? Above all, can the Churches maintain their inherited practices without modification? For instance, can they any longer defend, in a secularized society, the practice of indiscriminate baptism?

The present paper makes an attempt to carry the discussion further in the direction of answering these questions. It starts from the assumption that the process of Christian initiation must be looked at as a whole. Baptism, confirmation and the eucharist are inseparable. The paper gives first a brief review of present baptismal practices in the Churches (I). After a few methodological considerations (II) it examines the interdependence of ecclesiology and baptismal practice (III) and then lists a number of ethical implications (IV) which are of particular importance for any reform of baptism and confirmation. The following section deals with li-

---

180. *One Lord, One Baptism*, SCM Press, London 1960.

181. *The Fourth World Conference on Faith and Order*, The Report from Montreal 1963, edited by P. C. Rodger and L. Vischer (New York: Association Press, 1964).

182. See *Study Encounter*, IV/4, 1968, 194ff.

turgical aspects (V) and the final chapter deals with the question of mutual recognition of baptism as it presents itself in the life of the Churches today (VI).

I. The Present Practice of the Churches

A brief survey of the practice of the different Churches shows at once the variation in the forms of initiation into the Body of Christ. It is impossible to mention all the differences here; only the most important are given. Clearly too, each tradition leaves certain questions unanswered and must therefore submit to questioning in the light of the practice of the other traditions.

1. In the Eastern tradition baptism and confirmation (chrismation) are administered in immediate succession even when the recipient is an infant. The initiation is then complete. The person baptized is at once admitted to the eucharist without further ceremony. Here the question must be asked whether children are given sufficient opportunity of making for themselves the confession of faith made on their behalf at baptism.

2. In the Western tradition, baptism and the laying on of hands (confirmation) were separated at quite an early date. Whereas baptism could be performed by the priest, the laying on of hands was reserved to the bishop. This meant that usually some time elapsed between baptism and confirmation. Where the person baptized was an infant, the time interval could be of some years. Confirmation thus gradually became independent of baptism although the close connection between the two was never completely forgotten. Confirmation came to mean strengthening by the gift of the Holy Spirit. Admission to eucharistic fellowship could take place either before or after confirmation. All Western Churches face the problem of refusing to admit children to the eucharist even though they have been baptized.

The Western practice of initiation is to be found particularly in the Roman Catholic Church. Recently this Church has been more willing to admit confirmation by a priest in certain special cases, and to emphasize, especially in the case of adults, the unity of the process of initiation.

Western practice prompts the question whether the division of initiation into two related yet distinct sacramental acts does not prejudice the unique once-for-all character of baptism. The Churches of the Reformation sought to reassert the sufficiency of baptism. Since they found no basis in Scripture for confirmation as a sacramental act, it was abandoned. Other reasons, however, led the Churches of the Reforma-

tion to adopt an act similar to the sacramental act of confirmation. Baptized children are not admitted to the eucharist until they are able to make for themselves the profession of faith made for them at baptism. Confirmation furnishes the occasion for this act: a service of worship is held in which baptism is recalled and the persons previously baptized make a public profession of faith and are consecrated for their service. From then on they are admitted to the eucharist. This tradition shares the difficulty common to all the Western traditions. But the practice of this kind of confirmation presents a special problem. Confirmation normally takes place when children reach a given age. This frequently makes confirmation into a social formality in practice. Many Protestant Churches have consequently begun to change their practice in this matter, some even going so far as to drop insistence on confirmation as an essential condition for admission to the eucharist.

In Anglicanism the practice of episcopal confirmation was retained. It has always involved both the personal ratification by the candidate of the promises made on his behalf at baptism, and the laying on of hands with prayer for his strengthening by the gift of the Holy Spirit. It is regarded as the way of entrance into communicant status.

The Churches of the Baptist tradition administer baptism only to those who make profession of faith. They have no rite of chrismation or confirmation, but in some Churches there is a laying on of hands upon those who have been baptized. In all cases those who have been baptized are admitted at once to the eucharist. Often the children of baptized parents are dedicated at a special service of worship.

In the 17th century the Society of Friends so stressed the inward life that they were led to reject the outward sacramental signs of both baptism and eucharist. Emphasis on the inward spiritual event has led other Churches to attach no real importance to the external sign of baptism. What really matters is that the Gospel is heard, conversion takes place and a new life begins. Churches born from 18th and 19th century revival movements, therefore, show relatively little interest in the external sign of baptism (e.g. Salvation Army).[183] The question is how rejection of the outward signs can be consistent with the New Testament witness.

3. In almost all Churches baptism is normally performed

---

183. Not all Churches which do not practise water baptism give this as their reason. In certain cases the decision has been determined by historical factors (Kimbanguist Churches, for example).

by the *ordained minister.* On the other hand, almost all the Churches agree that baptism does not have to be administered exclusively by an ordained minister. Thus in certain circumstances it may be performed by lay people.[184] In the episcopal Churches, however, confirmation may only be administered by the bishop or by an ordained minister nominated by him. But since confirmation is usually performed in the presence of the worshipping congregation, even in other Churches it is *de facto* the ordained minister who administers confirmation.

Historical factors have played a large part in determining the role of ordained ministers in baptism and confirmation. For instance, the fact that lay people administer baptism is partly explained by the high infant mortality rate of earlier centuries; it was felt essential to administer baptism immediately after birth; at first the lay people involved were usually the midwives.

4. The different practices of the Churches cannot be described without at the same time drawing attention to the fact that many Churches today are seriously concerned about their practice and liturgy of baptism and confirmation. In recent years, a number of Churches including in particular the Roman Catholic Church have introduced far-reaching reforms and revised their liturgical texts. Other Churches are still engaged in such revision and it is probable that this process will continue in the years ahead. Union negotiations provided occasions to review baptismal practices and to relate different approaches to one another. The need for reforms arises, however, also in other contexts. In traditionally Christian countries the question is increasingly being asked: Can the inherited practice continue unchanged? Does the present practice take baptism seriously enough, judged by the light of the New Testament witness? Has not baptism often become more a badge of membership in Christian society than a sign of God's gracious gift in Christ and of the call to serve him? At a time when the Church's relationship to society is clearly undergoing considerable changes, it is not surprising that the question of the nature of baptism should arise simultaneously with fresh urgency in so many Churches. Many Churches have been led to question the indiscriminate baptism of infants and, quite independently of church union negotiations, the view that believers' baptism and infant baptism should be practised side by side in the same Church has been gaining ground.

II. Questions of Approach

How are the Churches to reach agreement in this situation? How are they to advance beyond their differences in doctrine and practice to a common mind? The following methodological reflections may be important for determining the right approach.

1. Clearly the New Testament assumes the practice of baptism though it does not anywhere speak of it systematically nor does it provide us with incontestable historical evidence as to its origin and practice. What is said about baptism occurs in many different contexts and throws light therefore only on certain aspects of baptism in widely varied first century settings. Many questions we should like to have answered today receive no direct answer from the witness of the New Testament. No Church can therefore base its practice on the New Testament evidence alone; tradition and history play a significant role in shaping the Churches' practice and provide the way in which the New Testament is interpreted and understood. The recognition of this fact is important. Churches must exercise caution in their judgements of each other's practice and expose their own practice to the critical questions of others: How far is this practice really governed by the revelation in Christ? The recognition of this fact is also important since it makes it clear that the Church today, like the Church in earlier times, can exercise a certain freedom in determining its practice.

2. The variety of practice in the Ancient Church is also evident. For example, in the Syrian Church chrismation seems to have preceded baptism by water. This variety is significant. Clearly the evidence of the New Testament and of the early centuries does not require a uniform baptismal practice throughout the whole Church. One and the same baptism may be administered in different ways within certain limits in one and the same Church. This point is important not only for the ecumenical movement but also for new expressions appropriate to baptism in Churches living in other cultural settings (e.g. Africa).

3. Historical events and controversies have greatly influenced the practice of the various Churches. For instance, the christianisation of the Roman Empire and the disappearance of the catechumenate and adult baptism had a profound ef-

---

184. There are exceptions to this rule. The older Reformed tradition, which is tending to disappear, constitutes one of them. The Reformed attitude has two primary reasons; first that the ministry of the sacraments is closely connected with the ministry of the word in the Reformed tradition; and second that baptism is understood primarily as incorporation into the Body of Christ rather than in terms of individual salvation. Most Churches of the Reformation do not regard water baptism as a condition for salvation, either of infants or adults. Hence the need for lay-administered baptism in cases where death seems imminent is lessened.

fect on East and West alike. The Donatist controversy deeply affected the Western tradition. The 16th century controversies between the Reformers and the Anabaptists have influenced and continue to influence the practice of Protestant Churches. The missionary experience outside Europe, which has involved multitudes of adults, has given new insights into the meaning of baptism. It is important to bear such historical factors in mind if we are to arrive at a mature judgement. This is especially important because each Christian has personally undergone one particular form of initiation and instruction and his spiritual life has been influenced by this particular form. He will therefore be inclined to judge all baptismal practices from this standpoint.

4. The history of baptism makes it clear that the rite existed in a developed form from the very earliest times. Particular aspects of baptism had been expressed and stressed by particular actions and gestures. Such adaptations are not merely still possible in principle today, but are actually required. Baptism needs translation and explanation not merely in words but also at the level of signs.

III. Ecclesiology and the Reform of Baptismal and Confirmation Practice

Obviously, there is a close connection between christology, ecclesiology and the understanding and the practice of baptism. Since baptism is the sign of incorporation into the Body of Christ which is the Church, any shift in the understanding of the nature of the Church almost inevitably affects the approach to baptism. In the ecclesiological debate of recent years there is a noticeable convergence on a number of new emphases. It may be useful to list some of them which are particularly relevant for a fresh approach to baptism.

1. *The Church as a Eucharistic Community.* In many Churches there has been a rediscovery of the meaning and the practice of the eucharist. Faith in Christ can be alive only within the fellowship of the Church. Faith requires corporate life. The eucharist is the visible sign giving expression to this communion of Christians with Christ and with one another. This emphasis on the communal aspect of Christian life also has consequences for the understanding of baptism. Baptism is the sign and seal of salvation but it is equally incorporation into the messianic people. It leads into the eucharistic community. This dimension has often been neglected in baptismal and confirmation practice.

2. *The Church as a Genuine Fellowship in the Holy Spirit.* The Church is to be a genuine fellowship in the Spirit. Such fellowship can exist only on the basis of the spontaneous adherence of its members. It cannot be secured by external structures and rules which have to be taken for granted and accepted without too many questions. The Church must be a charismatic fellowship leaving room for new and unexpected charismata. There is an increasing emphasis in contemporary ecclesiological discussions on the work of the Holy Spirit who both gives gifts to each one and at the same time unites all into one, thus reconciling freedom and fellowship. The development of Pentecostal movements reminds the historic Churches how much they have neglected the life in the Spirit. This has consequences for baptism and confirmation. Baptism is the anointing with the Spirit. Through the Messiah, the Anointed One, the baptized participates in the royal and priestly dignity for which man was created by God. How far does this understanding inform the present practice of baptism and confirmation? How far is it designed to facilitate and promote genuine spontaneous fellowship? Today, baptism and confirmation are felt by many to be no more than external rites which are imposed on people but not really appropriated by them. Should the presence and the demands of Christ not be given fuller expression? Questions like these provide a strong impetus for the reform of both baptism and confirmation.

3. *The Church as a Missionary Fellowship.* The Church is the people which is called to declare the wonderful deeds of Him who called it out of darkness into His marvellous light. It praises its Lord in adoration and gratitude and stands before Him in intercession for the whole world. It can praise Him only if it is a real sign to men of God's presence and love. In each generation this missionary task has to be perceived afresh and it is quite clear today that the Churches are in a new situation. Societies once considered "Christian" can no longer be considered so. Whatever may have been the advantages or disadvantages of the "Christian" society of previous generations, today the Churches have to learn again to be a minority missionary fellowship. More than ever before, such a fellowship calls for Christians who are aware of their fellowship with Christ and recognize the commission this implies. Does this not also mean a shift in the understanding and practice of baptism? Does it not call for a greater emphasis on the note of commission? It is significant that in the Churches which especially associate confirmation with the gift of the Spirit this rite is being given an increasingly missionary perspective.

4. *The Church as a Universal Fellowship.* By its very nature the Church is a fellowship which is intended to include all men. As such it transcends all national, racial, class and other barriers. Almost no ecclesiology has neglected to express this

truth, but the course of history has created a new situation. The Church must demonstrate its essential catholicity in a new way. It needs to be freed from the restrictions placed on its catholicity. The principle of catholicity needs to become a reality which is lived and experienced. Baptismal practice must make it clear that Christians, while belonging to a local fellowship, are at the same time members of a fellowship which is universal.

5. *The Church as an Open Fellowship.* For various reasons, ecclesiological discussion today is concerned with the problem of the Church's boundaries. For one thing, the problem arises in connection with the ecumenical movement. Even more urgently it arises in connection with the relationship between Church and world. How can the Church at one and the same time preserve its identity and also be a sign to men of Christ's presence? The Church should not cut itself off from the world. It must identify with the world in ministering to the world's needs but not with the world's estrangement and alienation from God. At present, however, is not its identity too often determined by identification with certain sociological entities, a nation, a particular section of the people, etc.? Are not the present boundaries between Church and world therefore unreal and inadequate? It is not that there will no longer be any boundaries. The problem is rather how to express the real identity of the Church in a convincing way. This raises important questions about baptism and confirmation. The sign of baptism establishes and confirms a boundary. Baptized persons are distinguished from non-baptized persons. But is this really the distinguishing line of the Gospel? Many feel that baptism creates an identification with a particular sociological community and for this reason hides rather than expresses its real meaning. How can baptism place the boundary in the right place?

IV. Baptismal Life

Baptism has always been understood as the entrance upon a new life. This means that one has died to a previous life and been raised to life with Christ. It means too that he has received the Spirit and been made a sharer in the mystery of Pentecost. This has happened once-and-for-all, but since sin persists, this death and resurrection with Christ is in constant need of renewal. Life under the Lordship of Christ calls us again and again for new acts of repentance and obedience. Life created by baptism can best be described as living in communion with Christ in anticipation of the coming of God's

kingdom. The reform of baptism and confirmation requires in the first place a spiritual renewal. It cannot be achieved simply by changing the order or the liturgy. Baptismal life needs to be renewed. In this respect, the following emphases are of particular importance today:

1. When a person is baptized, his whole life is placed under the sign of God's invitation and gift. All that he is now and will be and do in the future is placed at the service of Christ. The future, however, is less predictable today than ever. An awareness that the conditions in which we live are subject to constant change is a feature of our times. Problems need to be faced which could not have been anticipated even a short while before. Ideas, assumptions and aims which even a short while ago seemed assured are being called in question. Faith has to prove itself in constantly changing situations. The commitment which baptism implies cannot, therefore, be defined once and for all by specific ethical claims. The Christian has been given an identity which in communion with Christ he needs to rediscover again and again. Baptism is to be seen, rather, as the beginning—*initium*—a new way to be travelled with Christ.

2. When a person is baptized, he becomes a member of the Body of Christ. In other words, he is accepted into a fellowship of baptized persons. Baptism normally takes place in the presence of the local congregation which receives the newly baptized and accepts a certain responsibility for him. Baptism, however, is at the same time incorporation into the universal Church. The baptized person is not only a member of the local congregation which has received him, but at the same time of the universal fellowship which transcends all boundaries and barriers and is characterized by a wide variety. This latter aspect needs to be given particular stress today because it must be realized that the life of the baptized person will be lived in many different contexts and constantly new forms of Christian fellowship. Baptism must direct him towards the whole people of God.

3. When today a person is baptized, he normally becomes a member of a particular Church belonging to a particular confessional tradition. Generally speaking, there is no other way for him to become a member either of a particular fellowship or of the universal fellowship. But the Churches today live in hope of the ending of their divisions. They live today between division and unity. In fact, baptism is one of the grounds for this hope. Baptism may not, therefore, be administered in a way which implies that confessional divisions will continue to the end of time. On the contrary, baptism

must be the occasion of giving expression to the hope and the expectation that unity can be achieved.

V. Liturgical Aspects

Baptism should be a congregational act, included in worship, in which God's invitation and gift in Christ are proclaimed and accepted. When the candidate has confessed his faith, he is baptized with water in the name of the Father, the Son and the Holy Spirit.

Adult baptism has to be regarded as the primary form of baptism. The liturgy for infant baptism has therefore been an adaptation of that primary form. It includes the same elements even if in a modified form. The two liturgies should not differ fundamentally. Otherwise they give the impression that adult and infant baptism are two different baptisms.

The liturgy of baptism should provide for the following elements though they need not appear in the order given here:

1. An acknowledgement of God's initiative in salvation, of His continuing faithfulness, and of our total dependence upon His grace.
2. An explanation of the meaning of baptism as it appears from Scripture (reference to participation in the dying and rising of Christ, to the new birth of water and of the Spirit, to the incorporation into his Body, to the forgiveness of sins in and through Christ . . .).
3. An invocation of the Holy Spirit.
4. A renunciation of evil (possibly accompanied by exorcism).
5. A profession of faith in Christ and the affirmation of allegiance to God: Father, Son and Holy Spirit.
6. A declaration that the person baptized has become a child of God, and witness to the Gospel.

Through baptism the gift of the Spirit is imparted to the baptized. Therefore, it seems appropriate that the baptism in water should be followed by the laying on of hands or a chrismation. For some Churches the strengthening by the gift of the Spirit is the central meaning of confirmation which is conceived of as a separate act, usually not performed at the same time as baptism by water. When confirmation is separated from baptism by an interval of time, should not the imparting of the Spirit be expressed also in the liturgy of baptism itself in order to avoid the impression that the only meaning of baptism is the remission of sins? This is even more

important in traditions where confirmation has simply the meaning of recalling baptism and providing the opportunity of making an act of personal commitment. The liturgical action should always enable the candidate and the congregation to participate fully in it. Frequent opportunities should be provided for Christians to recall the meaning of their baptism. It might be helpful to celebrate baptism at Easter or Pentecost, thereby stressing the connection between baptism and Christ's death and resurrection or the outpouring of the Holy Spirit. Other occasions, such as confirmations and eucharists, can be appropriate for administering baptism. In the early centuries baptism was frequently performed by immersion. A recovery of this early form by those who have abandoned it would enhance the symbolism of the liturgy.

Baptismal practice and liturgies should avoid the impression that one can be baptized only as an infant or only as an adult. Older children too may be brought for baptism, in which case the confession of faith should be made both by the parents and the child.[185]

Where baptism is deferred until adulthood, children of Christian parents may be brought for a service of dedication. Of course, this is not a substitute for baptism but an act in preparation of it. It might then be appropriate for the children to be enrolled as catechumens with a view to baptism.

VI. The Unity of Baptismal Initiation

Both the New Testament and the Creeds speak of "one baptism." Baptism is meant to be a sign which in Christ unites people into one fellowship with each other. It is a sign of unity.

Is it really recognized as such? It is often stated that all Churches recognize baptism as God's gift and invitation no matter which Church has administered it. Baptism is therefore regarded by many as the clearest expression of unity which already exists or rather still exists between the Churches. But is this assumption really true? Do all Churches really recognize all other Churches' baptisms?

It can be said that all Churches are convinced that the "one baptism" referred to in the Creeds is a unique and non-repeatable act.[186] If they "repeat" baptism they do so because

---

185. The Roman Catholic Church is engaged in preparing such a liturgy.

186. Some African Independent Churches practise repeated baptism of their own members.

they believe that the ceremony performed by the other Church has not really been baptism as willed by the Lord. Such difference in interpretation seriously reduces the full mutual recognition of baptism. The difficulty arises particularly between Churches which exclusively practise believers' baptism and those which practise infant baptism as well.

There are, however, other restrictions on the mutual recognition of baptism which need to be taken into account. Recognition of baptism does not usually include recognition of chrismation and confirmation. Many Churches which recognize the baptism administered by other Churches are in the habit of "repeating" confirmation. But baptism and confirmation are inseparably inter-related and baptism is not yet fully recognized if confirmation is not.

This study has been led increasingly to the conviction that this unsatisfactory situation is largely due to the fact that baptismal initiation is not sufficiently recognized as one single coherent process which must always be looked upon as a whole. Baptism is a unique event, and even where the various elements of the rite have been separated in time the basic unity of the baptismal initiation must be retained. Most of the difficulties which today complicate the question of mutual recognition arise from undue separation in this respect. For instance, when the close connection between baptism and confirmation is lost sight of, it is much more difficult to recognize believers' and infant baptism as one and the same baptism. Furthermore, the different concepts of confirmation arising from the separation of the baptismal initiation into two rites constitute a hindrance to full mutual recognition. One may argue that this separation made possible the Western practice of recognizing baptism administered by another Church or outside the Church. Since confirmation was to be performed later by the bishop, baptism could be recognized without compromising the role of the Church and the ministry in administering the sacraments. The fact remains that, in this case, recognition is not complete and that the different concepts of confirmation make it difficult to extend this recognition. Also the uncertainty of the Churches as to the conditions and the time of admission to the eucharist finds its explanation here.

Therefore, the confession of the Church that there is and can be only "one baptism" must be developed afresh in the baptismal practices of the Churches. Their practice must be examined as to whether they obscure this basic affirmation. A new insistence on the unity of the baptismal initiation might open the way to an agreed approach in both the understand-ing and the practice of baptism. It might also make possible the drastic changes in practice which many call for today.

The General Problem of Mutual Recognition

Conditions for recognizing that baptism administered by another Church has been true baptism are not the same in all Churches. If mutual recognition is to become a full reality it is essential to agree upon certain common criteria.

The following statement is offered here for consideration: Baptism is to be recognized by all Churches when Jesus Christ has been confessed as Lord by the candidate, or, in the case of infant baptism, by the Church on his behalf and when baptism has been performed with water in the name of the Father and the Son and the Holy Spirit.

Of course, this statement is not to be misunderstood as an attempt to reduce the baptismal liturgies to the bare minimum. It simply lists the elements which are of primary importance for the mutual recognition of baptism. The Churches could greatly facilitate mutual recognition if they were to take them into account in their baptismal practice. Generally speaking, the principle of the non-repeatability of baptism needs to be respected even more consistently than it is today if the unique character of baptism is to become manifest among the Churches. Any "repetition" of baptism, even if it is done for valid doctrinal reasons, creates the impression of relativizing the unity of baptismal initiation.

Obviously the above statement leaves many questions open. In particular, it does not yet take the problem of believers' and infant baptism fully into account, nor does it deal with the problem of mutual recognition of confirmation. These questions require special attention.

Believers' and Infant Baptism

Some Churches only baptize adults who are able personally to confess Christ. Other Churches also baptize infants and children. The significance of baptism is often presented so differently in each case that it is difficult to tell whether it is really one and the same baptism. The same often applies to Churches which baptize both adults and infants. The significance given to the act and the liturgies used for it differ so widely that its identity is by no means obvious. In the case of believing adults the baptized person can make his own personal confession of faith and commitment. The baptism of infants looks forward to this personal confession of faith and commitment. Thus the identity of adult believers' baptism and infant baptism can only be evident if the Churches insist on the necessity of the vicarious faith of the congregation as well as of the parents and sponsors. The act of faith also involves the belief that participation in the corporate life of the Body of Christ is an essential element in the salvation of each member and that the baptized infant is initiated into this corporate life. Indiscriminate infant baptism is irresponsible and turns infant baptism into an act which can hardly be understood to be essentially the same as adult believers' baptism.

The problem of the relationship between adult baptism and infant baptism has come into sharper focus through church union negotiations. It is a hopeful sign that in some cases agreement has been possible between Churches which practise only believers' baptism and Churches which have mainly practised infant baptism. United Churches of this kind have been inaugurated in North India and Pakistan. In Ceylon, Ghana, New Zealand and the United States union proposals in which this question figures prominently are before the Churches. In all these schemes it is recognized that in order to hold together the two traditions in one Church there is a need for mutual charity, patience and respect for differing convictions, but in all cases it is confidently expected that this will be possible. Although in these situations the great majority of Christians concerned come from traditions practising infant baptism, most schemes explicitly recognize that the baptism of adults reveals most clearly the nature of the baptismal act. Great stress is laid on the seriousness of the faith of those bringing children for baptism and on the necessity of ensuring that the child shall grow into the maturity of responsible faith. On the other hand, Churches of the Baptist tradition have found it possible to accept the co-existence of the two practices in view of the fact that the process of Christian initiation—baptism / confirmation / first communion—is understood as one whole.

The importance of the solution favoured in these cases is not confined to the sphere of church union. Even Churches which have not been facing the problem of church union have arrived independently at similar conclusions.

The different understandings of chrismation and confirmation constitute a particular problem for the mutual recognition of both baptism and confirmation. Here again, much could be gained by stressing the unity of the baptismal initiation. Though initiation may be effected in two stages, the once-for-all character of baptism should not be diminished nor destroyed. Confirmation, whether given sacramental

significance or not, tends to give the impression of qualifying the uniqueness of baptism or even of repeating it. But the once-for-all character of baptism must be preserved. Confirmation must not be allowed to take over certain elements which belong properly to baptism alone. For example, though in all traditions in which confirmation (chrismation) is thought of as a sacrament it is associated with the gift of the Spirit, it would be wrong to understand baptism exclusively as the sign of the forgiveness of sins, while the gift of the Spirit is exclusively connected with confirmation. As long as baptism and confirmation are administered simultaneously, there is little danger of such separation. But once baptism and confirmation are separated in time, the once-for-all character of baptism may be lost. Confirmation cannot do more than underline or for some traditions complete what has already been achieved in baptism. If this once-for-all character of baptism is fully recognized the mutual recognition of baptism becomes much more meaningful. The fact that certain Churches confirm baptized persons coming from other Churches is less significant if this confirmation is not to be understood as an essential part of baptism but simply as its recalling or completion.

The baptismal event needs to be recalled, and provision needs to be made so that baptism can be an ever present reality. This is especially important for those who have been baptized as infants. The opportunity must be given for appropriating baptism by personal confession and engagement. In many churches confirmation provides this opportunity. But can this recalling and re-affirmation of baptismal vows take place on one given occasion? Is there not need for several occasions? Does not this "once-for-all" confirmation again rather blur than underline the once-for-all character of baptism? In any case, confirmation should not take place exclusively at a fixed age, but should rather be performed when the candidate is ready for it on his own initiative.

The once-for-all character of baptism calls for immediate admission to the eucharist. If the admission is deferred the impression is created that the incorporation into the Body of Christ has not yet fully taken place. Should baptism not be the gateway to eucharistic fellowship? Several Churches have been led to admit children to the eucharist at a much earlier age than they used to do in the past. They do not regard confirmation or the personal confession as the condition for admission to the eucharist but dissociate admission from confirmation and let it take place at an earlier age. Though this is in the logic of emphasizing the unity of the baptismal initiation, it is recognized that this reform may lead to a greater polarization of the Churches practising infant baptism and those practising believers' baptism. In any case, the insistence on the provision for opportunities of genuine personal commitment (confirmation, confession, etc.) becomes all the more important.

From Günther Gassmann, ed., *Documentary History of Faith and Order* (Geneva: World Council of Churches, 1993), 104–15. [Ellipsis in original.]

☙ "Beyond the Lima Liturgy," by **Thomas F. Best, Dagmar Heller, and others,** acknowledges the need for the creation of a eucharistic liturgy specifically for celebrations in ecumenical contexts and offers guidelines for those planning such celebrations. The Lima liturgy itself was an ecumenical order for worship used to close the 1982 World Council of Churches Faith and Order plenary commission meeting in Lima, Peru.

THOMAS F. BEST, DAGMAR HELLER, ET AL.

"Beyond the Lima Liturgy: A Proposal" in *Eucharistic Worship in Ecumenical Contexts*

Meeting at the Ecumenical Institute at Bossey, Switzerland, 12–21 May 1995, Christians from different churches and confessions throughout the world have considered the growing phenomenon of celebrations of the eucharist in ecumenical contexts.

Those gathered together have given thanks to God for the wide influence of the Lima liturgy in many churches and for the tentative further steps which these churches have sometimes taken in the spirit of the Lima liturgy and of the *Baptism, Eucharist and Ministry* document.[187] They have noted that celebrations of the eucharist have taken place at international ecumenical gatherings, at regional and local ecumenical events and in small ecumenical communities. They have noted that these celebrations have, in the spirit of the Lima liturgy, often moved beyond one liturgical tradition simply showing its historic or current forms to the assembled Christians, many of whom are from other traditions. Rather, there has emerged a challenging new form of ecumenical prayer arising from a concern to enable the present actual community to pray together, from a theological convergence emerging from many sources, from a continued and shared scholarly exploration of the liturgical heritage of Christians, and from an eagerness to see that heritage celebrated in ways ap-

propriate to the dignity and gifts of specific human cultural contexts throughout the world.

A substantial number of us, liturgists, theologians and pastors, have considered this phenomenon in more detail. Under discipline from the larger group, and in continuing discussion with it, we have felt moved to propose, on our own initiative and responsibility, the following pattern and guidelines to anyone engaged in planning eucharistic worship in an ecumenical context. In making this proposal, we have been helped especially by three classic texts important to the eucharist:

(1) the account in Luke 24:13–35 of the risen Christ transforming two despairing disciples and sending them on mission by means of his living interpretation of the scriptures and his presence in the breaking of bread;

(2) the 2nd-century account of Justin Martyr[188] of the shape of the ancient eucharist on Sunday as including gathering, scripture reading, preaching, interceding, setting out the food, giving thanks, eating and drinking, sending to the absent and collecting for the poor;

(3) the late 2nd-century report of Irenaeus of Lyon concerning the time when, in order to show unity, Anicetus, bishop of Rome, "yielded the thanksgiving" at the eucharistic table in the Roman church to Polycarp, the bishop of Smyrna.[189]

We have also been helped significantly by two of the widespread and growing fruits of the ecumenical movement: the *liturgical* convergence on a common pattern of eucharistic celebration reflected in the worship life of many churches, and the *theological* convergence on the meaning and grace of the eucharist represented by the Eucharist section of *BEM*.

What follows are suggestions, offered in a spirit of love and prayer, which we present for consideration by those contemplating the celebration of a eucharist in an ecumenical context. None of these are intended to criticize the liturgies of participating churches or the liturgical traditions of denominations, confessions or communions. They come, rather, as a strong, descriptive proposal in order to urge planners not to forget the spirit of the Lima liturgy: a liturgical celebration recognizable to all, which nonetheless calls us all beyond our own experience to a wider unity.

---

187. Faith and Order paper no. 111, Geneva, WCC, 1982, abbreviated here as *BEM*.

188. 1 *Apology*, 67.

189. Eusebius, *Ecclesiastical History,* 5:24:11–18.

We have found in the pattern of eucharistic worship we here present, and in our varied celebrations of this pattern, a witness to the historic catholic faith. We have also encountered therein a simple form of celebration which may be carried out in a rich variety of ways, which responds to the needs of the world in the present time, and which is capable of inculturation in many places. This basic pattern (*ordo*) is found . . . below. It is consistent with the listing given in *BEM;* but our presentation seeks to show the inherent simplicity and clarity of the eucharistic service, to reveal its underlying structure, to make plain which parts are essential (and which optional), and to suggest both the movement and flow of the service as a whole, and the dynamic relationships among its parts.

We have also found that these discoveries lead us to important conclusions regarding Christian unity. For example, we are well aware that it is often primarily questions of ministry and authority which prevent Christians from coming together at the table of the Lord. We are well aware of the complexity and sensitivity of the issues involved. And we yet continue to wonder whether the churches, on the basis of the acceptance of this pattern by all participating communions, might be prepared to extend to each other an "interim eucharistic hospitality" (that is, the giving of an invitation for all present at an event to receive communion), at least for major ecumenical gatherings.

But whatever answer might be given to this question, we would ask any group of Christians planning eucharistic worship in an ecumenical context to consider these questions with us:

1. Do you recognize this liturgical pattern as bearing the historic catholic faith which unites your church to the other Christian churches?
2. Do you recognize this liturgical pattern as bearing the world in which we live, as showing forth its conditions plainly, and proclaiming its transformation in Christ?
3. If so, what implications flow from these recognitions?

In order to aid your planning and to give a basis for these questions we share with you the following convictions. They are intended to be read in conjunction with the pattern (*ordo*) for eucharistic worship given [. . .] below.

1. A celebration of the eucharist in an ecumenical context includes a clear service of the word and a clear service of the table.

This event of word and table should be preceded by a holy gathering of the assembly into the grace, love and koinonia of the triune God and followed by an appropriate sending of the assembly in witness and service. In regard to this gathering and sending, see paragraphs 7 and 8 below.

2. The service of the word in such a eucharist includes two clear components: scripture reading *from the Old and the New Testaments, and* proclamation *of the crucified and risen Jesus Christ as the source and ground of our life in God's grace. Readings and preaching together should then lead the assembly to a response to the word in intercessions for the need of the world and for the unity of the church, confession of the faith, and song.*

The confession of the faith should occur, either here, after the sermon, or in preparation for the service of the table, in the original text of the Nicene Creed (Constantinople 381 CE), as that text which expresses the widest measure of doctrinal consensus amongst the churches.

A collection for people in need or in support of an agreed cause may also be an appropriate response at this point, associated with the intercessions, or it may occur at the end of the service of the table.

Biblical texts should be carefully chosen with respect to the occasion and with attention to the various lectionaries represented in the participating churches.

The proclamation of Christ will ordinarily take the form of a prepared sermon. In smaller groups, it may also involve the preacher engaging the assembly in active reflection on the word.

The service of the word may also include other elements which respond to and support these components, for example, meditating on the word in silence, the singing of hymns and contemporary songs, the singing of psalms; the singing of the classic short hymns appropriate to a feast day (*kontakia*) and the hymns or antiphons made up of psalm verses which may accompany a scripture reading (*prokeimena*), and other such liturgical elements of the Eastern traditions; or alleluia verses and sequences and other such liturgical elements of the Western tradition. The exchange of the peace may conclude and seal the intercessions and prepare for the service of the table.

3. The service of the table in such a eucharist includes two clear components: a thanksgiving *at table, and the* communal eating *and drinking of the bread and cup of the thanksgiving, the holy gifts of Jesus Christ's living and active presence. Thanksgiving and communion together should then lead the assembly to mission.*

The thanksgiving should include the historic dialogue (*sursum corda*), praise to God for creation and redemption, the words of Christ at the institution of the supper, the explicit memorial (anamnesis) of the passion, death and resurrection of Jesus Christ, the explicit prayer for the coming day of God, expressed in invocation of the Holy Spirit (epiclesis) and commemorations, the "amen" of the entire assembly, and the Lord's prayer. This thanksgiving is best proclaimed with frequent responses from the entire assembly.

The use of a single loaf of bread and a large single cup should be seriously considered. The collection for those in need may also occur at the end of the service of the table, but it ought not to be omitted nor should it be used for ecclesiastical expenses nor for the costs of the event. It may consist of gifts of food for the hungry.

The service of the table may also include a ceremonial presentation of gifts, an invitation to communion, and the singing of classic or modern communion songs.

4. *The entire event of such a eucharist should be musical, with the great structure of the assembly's action unfolded in the culturally diverse song and movement of the churches of the world.*

That music—and the space of the liturgy together with its visual arts—should serve the essential flow of the structure of the rite, not obscure it. It should engage the assembly in that flow. For example, great care needs to be exercised in the choice of such words in hymnody and song as most clearly express the shared catholic faith, the scripture readings of the celebration, their place in the order, the sense of the Sunday or festival, and the unity of the church.

The sharing of our different heritages of music, our creativity, and the exploration of our cultures have made a vital contribution to ecumenical worship over recent years. We have learned that every culture has a rich gift to bring to worship, and that worship may be enhanced by many musical styles and rhythms, chosen with care and sensitivity to their liturgical function.

5. *The celebration of such a eucharist involves a participating assembly and many liturgical ministries. Its unity is best served by one person presiding, in order to serve the unity and flow of the whole liturgy and to draw forth the gifts present in the assembly.*

A celebration of the eucharist in an ecumenical context should, as far as possible, while respecting ecclesial disciplines, involve the active participation of all the assembly. The planning should involve members, both ordained and lay, of all the traditions represented. It should also involve the liturgical ministry of both lay and ordained Christians in reading, singing and leading song, praying, dancing, serving and gathering.

A single ordained pastor, presbyter or bishop, whose ministry is recognized in a participant church, should preside. "In

order to fulfil its mission, the church needs persons who are publicly and continually responsible for pointing to its fundamental dependence on Jesus Christ, and thereby provide, within a multiplicity of gifts, a focus of its unity."[190] Careful reflection should be given to this leadership. The presider may come from the leadership of a local host church. Ordinarily the presider will greet the assembly, preach, proclaim the thanksgiving and bless the assembly as they are sent. Presiding may sometimes take the form of the presider yielding place to another preacher or to another leader of the eucharistic prayer. "Concelebration," understood as group presidency by ordained ministers from different confessions, raises more ecumenical problems than it solves.

The ministers, lay and ordained, who lead this service could each be clothed in a garment which may be recognized as proclaiming our common baptism into Christ and as representing the entire assembly. Other signs of festivity or service, drawn from the historic Christian vestments or the current cultures of the churches, may mark the principal ministers, especially the presider.

6. *In planning such a celebration of the eucharist, consideration should be given to holding the celebration on a Sunday or other Christian festival as a sign of the mystery of the resurrection that unites us.*

In many places in the world, the special sense of Sunday needs to be recovered. The Lord's supper belongs first of all to the Lord's day. Furthermore, ecumenism is central, not peripheral, to the life of the churches. This is not intended to preclude the choice of other days when Sunday or festivals are not practicable for a particular ecumenical event.

7. *The gathering may include various actions, but it should draw the assembly, bearing in itself the need and longings of the world and the reality of each local place, into the grace and mercy of God.*

Such a gathering is based upon our common baptism into the mystery of the triune God and so into the church. This gathering may include singing the praise of God, confession and forgiveness or some other baptismal remembrance, a call to worship or biblical greeting, a kyrie or litany of entrance, gloria in excelsis or other doxology, and a traditional collect or prayer of entrance. It is not suggested that all of these ways of gathering should be used, nor that more possibilities should be planned for a large event or fewer for a small: but

---

190. Ibid., *Ministry,* 21.

people in each place need to ask how gathering in the grace and mercy of God can take place appropriately *here,* reflecting local cultural customs.

8. *The dismissal may include various actions, but it should send the assembly to serve in love and to bear witness to the freedom of life in Christ, and to the justice, peace and integrity of creation willed by God.*

The dismissal will receive and enact all the ways in which the liturgy has stirred the assembly to action. It may be marked by a post-communion prayer committing the communicants to the mission of Christ, by singing, a blessing on departure, a word of dismissal, the possible sending of the holy communion or other gifts to those who are absent, or the sending of food to the poor.

9. *Participation in the proclaimed word and the prayers of the assembly is participation in Christ. It is also Christ who, in the power of the Spirit, invites all to eat and drink his holy gift.*

Nonetheless, participants in the liturgy who are not able to receive communion at all, or not able to receive one or the other of the holy gifts, should not be shamed or made to feel unwelcome. They should be encouraged to participate as far as they are able, to behold in love and adoration Christ who gives himself to these others of his people, to understand themselves as belonging through baptism to Christ as well, and to pray for the day of fuller Christian unity.

10. *The extensive options listed here ought not obscure the simple order proposed: this liturgy could be celebrated with great simplicity or with extensive local experiment toward an emerging pattern of the future.* The pattern is quite simple (see the ordo [below]), and, granted a clear word and table structure, local ecumenical groups are encouraged to discover how this great gift of God might be newly and faithfully unfolded. A simple service, however, should not omit the central elements of Christ's gift nor should an elaborate or experimental service obscure them.

11. *As a liturgy is prepared according to these proposals, texts for the principal parts of the eucharist may best be chosen from prayers which have been accorded a wide ecumenical reception.*

In the selection of texts for the liturgy, including the scripture version to be used, careful attention should be given to the use of inclusive language. Different cultures will call for different solutions, but the goal is always to find language which will include as many as possible in full participation in the prayer.

Following the interim guidelines for the Canberra assembly of the World Council of Churches, biblical language and significant traditional formulas should be preserved.

The Fundamental Pattern (*Ordo*) of the Eucharistic Service

GATHERING of the assembly into the grace, love and koinonia of the triune God

WORD SERVICE

   Reading of the scriptures of the Old and New Testaments
   Proclaiming Jesus Christ crucified and risen as the ground
      of our hope
   (and confessing and singing our faith)
   and so *interceding* for all in need and for unity
   (sharing the peace to seal our prayers and prepare for the
      table)

TABLE SERVICE

   Giving thanks over bread and cup
   Eating and drinking the holy gifts of Christ's presence
   (collecting for all in need)
   and so

BEING SENT (DISMISSAL) in mission in the world.

From Thomas F. Best and Dagmar Heller, eds., *Eucharistic Worship in Ecumenical Contexts* (Geneva: World Council of Churches, 1998), 29–35.

6. "INDEPENDENT" AND HOLINESS CHRISTIAN LITURGIES

As understood by the Church of Jesus Christ of Latter-day Saints, *The Book of Mormon* is the historical record (from 600 BCE to 421 CE) of the aboriginal ancestors of the American Indians. Mormon and his son, Moroni, compiled and continued the ancient record, which in 1827 was revealed by Moroni in a vision to **Joseph Smith** (1805–1844) in Manchester, New York. For the benefit of the Lamanites who were then persecuting him, Moroni in the book named after him, describes rituals practiced after the appearance of the resurrected Christ to the Nephites, who had emigrated from Jerusalem to America.

JOSEPH SMITH, TRANSLATOR

The Book of Mormon

Book of Moroni

Chapter 1

4. . . . I write a few more things, contrary to that which I had supposed; for I had supposed not to have written any more; but I write a few more things, that perhaps they may be of worth[191] unto my brethren, the Lamanites, in some future day, according to the will of the Lord.

Chapter 6

1. And now I speak concerning baptism. Behold, Elders,[192] Priests,[193] and Teachers were baptized;[194] and they were not baptized save they brought forth fruit meet that they were worthy of it.

2. Neither did they receive any unto baptism save they came forth with a broken heart and a contrite spirit, and witnessed unto the church that they truly repented of all their sins.

3. And none were received unto baptism save they took upon them the name[195] of Christ, having a determination to serve him to the end.

4. And after they had been received unto baptism, and were wrought upon and cleansed by the power[196] of the Holy Ghost, they were numbered among the people of the church of Christ; and their names were taken, that they might be remembered and nourished by the good word of God, to keep them in the right way, to keep them continually watchful unto prayer,[197] relying alone upon the merits of Christ, who was the author and the finisher of their faith.

5. And the Church did meet together oft, to fast[198] and to pray, and to speak one with another concerning the welfare of their souls.

6. And they did meet together oft to partake[199] of bread and wine, in remembrance of the Lord Jesus.

7. And they were strict to observe that there should be no iniquity among them, and whoso was found to commit iniquity, and three[200] witnesses of the church did condemn them before the elders, and if they repented not, and confessed not, their names were blotted out, and they were not numbered among the people of Christ.

8. But as oft[201] as they repented and sought forgiveness, with real intent, they were forgiven.

9. And their meetings were conducted by the Church after the manner of the workings of the Spirit, and by the power of the Holy Ghost; for as the power[202] of the Holy Ghost led them whether to preach, or to exhort, or to pray, or to supplicate, or to sing, even so it was done.

The Book of Mormon: An Account Written by The Hand of Mormon upon Plates Taken from the Plates of Nephi, translated by Joseph Smith Jr.; division into chapters and verses, with references, by Orson Pratt Sr. (Kansas City, MO: The Southwestern States Mission Publishers, 1902).

∾ In his "Church Activities" anthropologist and sociologist **J. D. Y. Peel** describes the church services of various Christian groups in the Aladura movement. Aladura (meaning "people of prayer") is an indigenous independent church movement among Yoruba-speaking Nigerians that began in the 1920s in reaction to Anglican mission oversight. Among the practices of these prophetic groups are spiritual healing, divine inspiration, charismatic leadership, and self-reliance.

J. D. Y. PEEL

"Church Activities"
in *Aladura: A Religious Movement among the Yoruba*

Church Services

A building of their own is something every congregation, and every prophet starting out by himself, aspires to. The early churches, and churches to this day in villages on the farmland, were simple rectangular buildings of the typical mud brick, plastered and whitewashed outside and in, with a corrugated iron roof and perhaps a false ceiling of boards or matting below this, to keep the interior cool and to lessen the noise of falling rain. There is no glass in the windows, but shutters; the interior is very barely furnished with wooden benches or pews, and the sanctuary, containing a table and chairs for the pastor and laypreachers, is set off by wooden

---

191. Second Book of Nephi 3:7, 11, 12, 19-21. See c, Second Book of Nephi 27.
192. Book of Moroni 3:1.
193. See c, Book of Mosiah 6.
194. See u, Second Book of Nephi 9.
195. See e, Book of Mosiah 5.
196. See y, Third Book of Nephi 9.
197. See e, Second Book of Nephi 32.
198. See t, Book of Mosiah 27.
199. See b, Third Book of Nephi 18.
200. Doctrine and Covenants 42:80, 81.
201. Book of Mosiah 26:31.
202. See c, Book of Moroni 3.

railings. There is a wooden box pulpit to one side, and to the other a lectern, probably a stiff wooden eagle imitated by the local craftsmen from a bronze one imported from England in one of the Lagos churches. There will be a vestry, perhaps two, and near the church a house for the pastor.

If this is a common denominator there is today much variation and development. Although indigenous Yoruba buildings are not architecturally very impressive (the obas' palaces are remarkable more for the extent of ground they cover and the sculpture they contain), the possibility of collective display through building was very soon realized by the Yoruba. The style is eclectic—colonial Brazilian introduced by the repatriated slaves and widely used for houses, tropical English Perpendicular from England through Sierra Leone (much used by the Anglican Church), and today, various local expedients adopted by the local contractors, who do the building and often make the designs too. The parallel with medieval English village church building is not superficial— the churches are symbols of communal pride, and in a small town or village are easily the most impressive building; the work of building is carried on for years in a piecemeal way as the funds are slowly raised; the local contractors design and build, and copy larger and admired churches in an *ad hoc* way; designs spread from town to town and church to church as congregations emulate one another; the big churches, Christ Church Cathedral in Lagos in 1880 or St. John's, Ilesha, today, are the fountains of stylistic innovation. The Anglican church at Gbongan (a small town between Ibadan and Ile Ife), built between the wars, with a large tower, decorated with cement sculptural motifs, and Perpendicular windows, was, I am told, an object of jealous emulation in those parts; in Ondo today the Central Mosque, nearing completion, has a handsome sturdy hexagonal tower; a Christ Apostolic church has copied this, thinner but taller; and the Cherubim and Seraphim have erected the walls of a new church which also will have a hexagonal tower. In Ibadan the cathedral of St. James is the model for a number of churches, especially the two largest Christ Apostolic churches, and the central building of the Cherubim and Seraphim.

These large town churches have a vast expanse of solid pews, choir-stalls behind which the elders sit, and a large sanctuary with many chairs and praying-stools. The pulpit will often be an impressive affair, presented by one of the church societies, based on Gothic English pulpits, or with the classical Brazilian forms; but this architectural detail will become plastic and sculptural at the hands of the local carpenter. As the C.M.S. [Church Mission Society] is evangelical and Low-Church, its churches in Nigeria are not very much ornamented, but there may be nicely painted Biblical mottoes, or boards painted with *Ofin Mẹwa* (Ten Commandments), sometimes in decorated letters. And if the decoration cannot be liturgical there may be elaborate balustrades of cement fret-work, and well-shaped architectural fancies and mouldings. Today these historical styles are giving way to a new contractors' style, similar to that employed on secular buildings; but there are still very many buildings of an older type, whose whitewashed or pastel-colour painted towers relieve the monotony of red laterite walls and rusting corrugated iron roofs. And many churches of the simplest type survive, reminding one of how Christianity looked in its formative years in Yorubaland. The newer Aladura churches, with congregations of under a hundred members, look like this too.

Christ Apostolic churches look like Anglican or Methodist churches, outside and inside, except that the sanctuary is barer. There is no cross on the altar table; the eye is drawn to the pastor or prophet sitting in the sanctuary, to the lectern and the pulpit. The Bible, containing God's Word as the pastor expounds it, and the bell, calling attention to God's Word as the prophet reveals it, are the most prominent religious symbols of the Christ Apostolic Church. At Oniyanrin (Ibadan), a large church with a big western tower, situated on bare rising ground with a commanding view over an important tarred road within the city, the Sunday morning service begins at 9 a. m. The large church is full, perhaps 600 adults. There are two aisles, so that the seats are in three blocks. The north aisle is occupied by men, who tend to sit in clusters based on the church societies; to the front are the keenest of the youth. The south aisle is all women, the front seats being occupied by wives of the elders; the central aisle is mostly women, with teenage girls sitting at the front with their Bibles and handbags, and towards the back are some men. On rush matting in front of the people sprawl a few infants. In this space stand the lectern to one side and the pulpit to the other. Then come the choir-stalls facing inwards, at the back of which on one side is a small organ, and on the other, the elders' bench. Finally, comes the sanctuary, occupied by the pastor and a guest preacher if there is one.

The service starts at 9 a.m. sharp, though people have been arriving since 8:30 a.m., and they are occupied in singing choruses, led by young men dressed in white European suits, who pace up and down the space at the front of the seats, beating or stamping time, singing the words to which the congregation will respond with the choruses, and generally exhorting them to be enthusiastic and to sing louder.

These chants are often made up spontaneously, or are copied from church to church; sometimes they are collected in a book by a pastor, but typically they are ephemeral, something like popular songs. The tunes are sometimes Yoruba, but more often have an evangelical European flavour, even when locally composed.[203] Here are three popular ones, with very typical words:

Jesu yio joba, Jesu yio joba
    b' araiye fe, b' araiye ko,
 	
Jesu yio joba.
	Jesus will reign, Jesus will reign,
	if the world wants it, if the
	    world doesn't,
	Jesus will reign.

Awa dupe Baba, Awa dupe
    Omo
Emi Mimo o se, Tire
    ni Ogo.
	We thank the Father, we thank
	    the Son,
	Holy Spirit thank-you, Thine
	    is the Glory.

Agbara mbe, Agbara mbe *Agbara mbe, ninu eje Jesu.*	There is Power, there is Power, There is Power in the Blood of Jesus.

The singing of these choruses stops just before 9 a.m., and the choir, clad in cassocks and surplices in the Anglican manner, file in singing the first hymn. They are followed by the elders, wearing *agbadas,* voluminous gowns of cotton or wool. The pastor may be wearing a European suit or an *agbada;* prophets usually wear a long garment, reaching to well below the knees, and in cut something between a cassock and a top-coat. There are variations in the cut and colour of this, and it is not obligatory.

After the Lord's Prayer, said by the pastor, there are numerous other prayers extemporized by the elders, then some led by members of the congregation. Some of the prayers are topical: may God help the quarterly revival, or bless the tithe-payers, or bring peace to Nigeria. All are followed by thunderous *Amins.* The praying is virtuoso, lyrical, and earnest, phrases and petitions strung rhapsodically together, with frequent invocation, not at all restrained or stereotyped, sometimes so earnest, with shakings and expressive gestures of the hands, that it becomes incoherent. It is from this praying that Christ Apostolic members are sometimes disparagingly referred to by outsiders as *elekun,* "weepers and wailers." Prayers are concluded with the words *l'oruko Jesu Kristi, Oluwa wa, Amin,* "in the name of Jesus Christ, Our Lord, Amen!" Hymns alternate with the prayers, the Lesson and church notices, read out by the leader, assistant to the pas-

tor. The hymns, in the special Christ Apostolic hymn-book, are mostly from evangelical collections, such as Moody and Sankey, or from the mission hymn-books, and are sung to English tunes.

After about an hour, the pastor mounts the pulpit for the sermon. On this occasion he takes a favourite text, Acts 2, the story of the first pentecostal baptism. He notes the church's name *Ijo Aposteli ti Kristi,* and demands that all the members should consider themselves as apostles, here, at Oniyanrin; they must set themselves to do *ise awon Aposteli,* "acts of the Apostles." Who are the true apostles? he asks. *Awa mbe,* "we are," comes the enthusiastic response of the congregation. The pastor says that they are all apostles, even the sinners, for all are sinners; he attacks the view of God as an easy way, and reminds them of the dramatic change in their lives which the Holy Spirit can work.

This sermon is perhaps more doctrinal than usual. The preacher is usually very active in the pulpit, with emphatic gestures as he illustrates his points, until he is wet with sweat. He addresses many questions to the congregation, who vie between one another to be the first to read out the texts the preacher announces. The references are carefully followed in the Bibles open on the laps of the congregation. Most often the sermon is practical rather than theoretical, with many exemplary stories and illustrative anecdotes, but addressed to two aims, to promulgate the church's doctrine, especially on divine healing, and to justify, help, encourage, or console people in their day-to-day affairs. Usually these aims are combined; I once heard a whole sermon devoted to the danger of eating poisoned food (something Yorubas have a cultural dread of, like witchcraft), and the wisdom of praying to God before eating; this was illustrated with some gruesome stories, and many Bible quotations.

After the sermon, which has probably lasted an hour (and sometimes much longer) there is a hymn, the pastor says the Blessing, and before the choir recesses out, the whole congregation gives three hearty Hallelujahs, and shouts *Ogo!,* "Glory," and shakes their arms in the air with clenched fists, a traditional sign of honour and respect. The elders, and the various church societies, collect in various parts of the church to hold their meetings, and some stand outside on

---

203. Since Yoruba is a tonal language, English tunes almost never fit the words, and indeed Yoruba music stands in a much closer dependence on the particular words. It is curious that so much of the free tune composition is English in type, distorting the tones.

the wide flight of steps which leads up to the porch from the road, chatting in little groups in the hot sunshine before they go home.

This is the main service of the week, attended by the largest number, but there are services every morning for prayers before work at 6 a.m. and every evening at 5 p.m., mainly attended by women, who come with their babies to collect bottles of *omi iye*. "Tarrying meetings" to pray for the Baptism of the Holy Ghost, are less frequent, perhaps once a month. The structure of these other services is more informal, with hymns, prayer, choruses with clapping, Bible reading, and a sermon or short address. The general aura of a Christ Apostolic service is like that of a revivalist European sect; there is no mystification, adoration of sacred objects, use of incense, or, indeed, much sense of passive adoration of the Divine.

Cherubim and Seraphim services are rather different. Although the church buildings resemble other churches externally, the interior is often quite dissimilar, as befits an *Ile Adura*, or "House of Prayer." This is a descendant of the private or shared houses of prayer, usually rooms in a house, which were used in the early days (and are still to be found in some pious non-Aladura houses, like private oratories) for prayer and spiritual concentration. The *Ile Adura* will be free of chairs, the floor covered in linoleum or carpets, all bright and clean. There will be religious mottoes painted on the walls, and over the chancel arch, the words MIMỌ MIMỌ MIMỌ OLUWA ỌLỌRUN OLODUMARE, as the Seraphim sing in praise to God in heaven. Beyond the altar, on which may be a sevenfold candlestick, will perhaps be a triptych, showing Christ with two angels. There may also be, perhaps, banners of Holy Michael or pictures of Orimolade. In most cases there will be movable chairs and benches for congregational services, though it is never forgotten that the church is primarily *Ile Adura*. At Oke Seni, the Ibadan headquarters, the ordinary services are held in a large but inelegant schoolroom set in the compound besides the handsome *Ile Adura*, spoken of as the temple. The consistent theme of the architectural setting is the interrelated prayer-with-worship. [. . .]

At Oke Seni, Ibadan, besides the temple and schoolroom meeting house, there are lodgings for the *wolis*, more schoolrooms, the baptismal pool, a well, and a small house where the *Baba Olomiye* lives (the old man who looks after the *omi iye*). The service with the biggest attendance starts at 10 a.m. on Sunday morning, and takes place in the large schoolroom. The congregation, about 200, sit as in the Christ Apostolic Church, the sexes segregated. Most of them wear white prayer-gowns, and those without them sit at the back. In front of the congregation is a single lectern (though most Seraphim churches have a pulpit also), placed in a large open space, at one side of which sit the choir and at the other the lady leader and other leading women members, then a small table, covered with a white cloth, on which are collection bowls and a sevenfold candlestick. Behind this is a dais, upon which, behind another table, sits whoever is conducting the service—a duty taken in turn by the apostles and other leading members. To either side of the dais sit elders. The various social divisions, men and women, youth and elders, are emphasized by these seating arrangements.

Preceded by a cross-bearer, the choir process in, followed by a long line of elders wearing their distinctive robes. The service follows an Anglican pattern, with a Creed, and is ritualistic, but there are free prayers as in the Christ Apostolic Church, though not said in quite such a fervent way. The most distinctive features are a section where people who have received blessings come forward to testify, followed by *Idupẹ* (thanksgiving), when to the hymn *A f'ọpẹ f'Ọlọrun* (C.M.S. "Now thank we all our God"), the congregation file up, dancing, to offer thanksgivings at the small table. Often there are several collections, marked apart for different purposes, building fund or school fund, or just thanksgiving. Most of the hymns come from the Seraphim's own collection (there are at least three of these in circulation), and are notable for their resounding choruses, sung with great gusto to the accompaniment of a harmonium and drums.[204] Singing and dancing are much enjoyed, and they are a main feature of the worship.

The sermon is usually similar to those in the Christ Apostolic Church, discursive, anecdotal, punctuated with Biblical quotations. A rather typical one started off with a detailed exposition of the relation between God and the Seraphim. The apostle quoted Isaiah 6:1–8, dramatically illustrating the Seraphim worshipping God before His throne. This led to an exaltation of God, and the congregation broke into the hymn:[205]

---

204. These drums have only one pitch, being rectangular frames with a skin stretched over one side. The "talking drum," whose pitch can be varied, which is beaten with a curved stick, is not used because of its association with Egungun drummers.

205. *Oba Alaiyeluwa* is the standard description of an *oba; Kabiyesi* is the special greeting; *Awamaridi* is one of the traditional Yoruba epithets of the High God.

Kabiyesi Ọba Alaiyeluwa	Hail King, Majesty,
Metalọkan Alagbara	Powerful Trinity,
Awamaridi Olodumare	Incomprehensible, Almighty
To nṣe iṣe iyanu	Who does wondrous works.
Ọba mi de! Aṣegun mi de!	My King comes, My Victor comes,
Ogo, Ọla at'Agbara at'Ipa	Glory, Honour, Power and Might
F'Ọdagutan to gunwa	To the Lamb who sits in Majesty.

The latter part of the sermon took up the theme of God's majesty, and said that since He was so powerful we must obey His words and rely on Him, not going secretly to *babalawos*. At the end of the service there are shouts of Hallelujah, and the choir recesses, to be finally dismissed with a prayer and a blessing by the apostle. After the service the church societies meet and some people may be seen going into the temple for special prayer.

Apart from morning prayers, and evening prayers in the temple three days a week, there is the Saturday-Sunday vigil, lasting from midnight till 2 or 3 in the morning. This is the oldest and most important service of the week. After washing their feet the members process in to a psalm (there is no instrumental accompaniment), and at the door, as they cross themselves, they are purified with incense. The interior, lit with not very strong electric lights, is cloudy and mysterious with incense, and the members file in singing, the men to one side and the women to the other. The service is solemn and liturgical, hymns and long stretches of prayer alternating with one another. There are no chairs, and people bow right down to pray, in the Muslim fashion. In corners of the *Ile Adura* stand visioners, who have been fasting. Occasionally (by vision) an unusual ceremony is performed, called *Gbigba Ọwọ Ida* ("raising the hand of the sword"), at which the whole congregation, led by the apostle, hold up in the air in their right hands a Bible ("the sword of the spirit"), and recite a solemn curse on witches, sorcerers, *irunmọle* (the pagan *orisa*), and workers of iniquity in general; this is repeated four times, to each point of the compass.

After about an hour the singing, which has hitherto been most restrained, becomes louder and more rhythmic with clapping, and one or two small circles are formed, especially of young men, who clap energetically till the sweat runs down their faces. Then the hymns give way to choruses asking for the Holy Spirit to descend. At this point somebody (most likely a woman) may become possessed and speak in-

coherently with tongues, shaking uncontrollably, while the lady leader tries to calm her. When the singing stops and the congregation is seated on the floor, the possessed woman, now more in control of herself, speaks with tongues. The words do not pour out in an uninterrupted stream, but she pauses after every few sentences while *Woli Ẹlẹmi* ("prophetess with the spirit"), a young woman with the gift of interpretation, tries to interpret the tongues, walking up and down with an air of cool concentration, nodding her head occasionally and saying *"Ehe!"*, as the Yoruba do, as if to say, "So that's it!" Sometimes she cannot interpret; but usually she delivers the message, whose content is like that of the visions (which are also revealed at this service) quoted [in source text]. The vision-recorder puts all down carefully in a book. In fact at any time in any service a person may stand up and reveal a vision, "before God and man," as they say. The glossolalic aspect of the vigil was not an original element of it. The vigil may go on till 3 a.m., after which the members of the society, now looking rather tired, hurry back to their houses with their lanterns along the uneven dusty paths and alleys of Ibadan.

These are the regular services. There are numerous other periodical revivals, festivals like Holy Michael's Day for the Seraphim (for which there is a five-hour service in the evening with many visions and pentecostal revelations), special Lenten services (the Oke Seni Seraphim had printed programmes of sermons, given by the leading elders in turn, on a planned sequence of moral and doctrinal subjects), anniversaries, and revivals.

A singularly impressive ceremony is the ordination of spiritual workers in the Seraphim, which takes place on All Souls' Day on Olorunkole Hill, the grey granite inselberg where Egunjobi saw the angel in 1912. This falls on the afternoon of the middle day of a three-day retreat for prayer and fasting. On the top of the hill are piles of preachers' rods (vehicles for spiritual power), bottles of water, bells, and Bibles, within a circle which marks the hallowed ground. Around this are clustered a good many members, all robed in white. The ordinands are robed, kiss the Bible, swear an oath and are anointed with olive oil; finally they all ring their bells as a sign of victory. It is an emotional occasion, and with the incense, the white robes, and the sense of holy separation on the Hill of the Lord, everyone feels the spiritual presence; the sun shines down, and below the forest stretches away for miles; there is no sound but the rustling trees, the intonation of prayer, and the singing of the Seraphim. A far cry, this, from the clamorous urgency of a Christ Apostolic revival, or the measured stiffness of evensong at St. James's Cathedral.

Praying Bands

The praying band is the essence of Aladura churches—an association of people of like mind who meet together to pray, to sing hymns, and to read and discuss the Bible, their religious handbook. There is a scale of formality, from a few friends who meet quite informally to sustain one another in their religious activities, to a praying band which is organized with branches in different churches under a central direction, like the Praying Battalion of the Christ Apostolic Church. A praying band today will give a good idea of what the Faith Tabernacle or early Seraphim congregations were like. First, a historical record of such a meeting in 1935 at Akinyele's house at Alafara, Ibadan; this meeting lasted twelve hours, and concerned the nucleus of members.[206]

7 a.m.	Thanksgiving.
8 a.m.	Tarrying for the Holy Spirit.
9 a.m.	Thanks for the Spirit given us.
10 a.m.	Prayer for the reformation of adulterers.
11 a.m.	Prayer for shelter and safety for the lambs and little children from sin, for Adetayo and his wife.
12 Noon	For Revival, which we expect through the ministry of Pastor Vaughan (a European pastor of the Apostolic Church) . . . for all the pastors, black and white, and for all the churches of Nigeria.
1 p.m.	For the households of the sons of God, for the life of Holiness in His house; Love and amity of husband and wife; for the children of the house to learn the Love and Fear of the Lord of Peace; for Healing and Relief; Provision for the wants of the house.
2 p.m.	For the church at Abeokuta; for Fatope, Adeosun, Abeke, and for unity in all the churches there.
3 p.m.	For the Senior Pastor . . . for the cure of Onabanjo's leg, and Lawoyin's eyes: Blessing of the Lord on the work of Pastor Odusanya in Iyagba.
4 p.m.	For Great Revival.
5 p.m.	For the Seraphim societies, for harmony amongst them.
6 p.m.	For the Protection and Victory of all churches.
7 p.m.	Prayer Requests.

There follow what Akinyele described as "*Ifihan ti o ba jade l'akoko adura wonyi*" or "Impressions"; this means visions which follow from the fasting and prayer. Praying bands today do not usually have such long meetings or are so concerned with the general welfare of the church, but their *raison d'être* and assumptions are the same. The *Egbẹ Aladura*, or Praying Band, which is the central organ of the Seraphim Society, still retains these functions, but has changed through having acquired in addition many of the central administrative tasks of a church, so I will consider two praying bands in the Christ Apostolic Church.

Egbẹ Alago Meje ("Seven O'Clock Band") was founded at Oniyanrin in 1954 by A. O. Komolafe, a young Ijebu, and others, who helped in the establishment of C. A. C. Agbokojo, a daughter church, in that year. Komolafe was then twenty-two, a trader, and was stimulated by the greater zealousness, he says, of the Ibadan people, compared to those at home in Ijebu Ode, and also by the Apostolic Faith, an American revivalist mission in Ibadan. Its aim is to "revive the church and win more souls for Christ." There are branches of Alago Meje at five different Christ Apostolic churches in Ibadan now, and from its ranks have sprung several catechists and evangelists. Its organization is minimal, Komolafe being informally recognized as leader, and has no business meetings, committees, social gatherings, or accounts; one man is deputed to keep and distribute any occasional donations. Thus it is exclusively concerned with prayer and revival. It meets every week-day evening except Thursday, at 7 p.m., hence its name, and sometimes holds open-air preaching in the neighbourhood.

The dusk is deepening as the members gather in one of the Oniyanrin church schoolrooms, a building which, many years ago, served as the church. Inside it is plain and dingy, poorly lit, with the children's desks, and charts on the walls. The members do not gossip to one another but kneel down to pray at the desks, singly. These private prayers, noisy and

---

206. Record of an *Ipade Afaduraṣona* ("Prayer-watch Meeting") on 30 August 1935, *Akinyele Papers;* I have altered the Yoruba personal names. Akinyele kept many notebooks in which he recorded, in Yoruba, these prayer-meetings, as well as special prayers and sermon notes.

fervent, invocations of God interspersed with thanksgiving and petition, especially for spiritual power, last for about thirty minutes, the room full of the hubbub of prayer. Then three hymns are sung in succession, informally announced by Mr. Komolafe, ending with *Wa, Ẹmi Mimọ, wa* ("Come, Holy Spirit, come"), an Anglican hymn which acquires full meaning in this pentecostal context. There are now nearly fifty people, all men, present. Komolafe gives a short address on the Holy Spirit, and introduces the preacher, a freelance Apostolic pastor, attached to no particular church. His subject is prayer: he advises two hours of prayer a day; "we must pray through to victory"; prayer is necessary to understand scripture, for "certain veils cover our eyes." This coherent exhortation, delivered in a mixture of English and Yoruba, lasts about half an hour, and after more prayers and a blessing, the meeting breaks up. Sometimes the members are inspired to lead a revival somewhere, and may go out in a bunch about the neighbourhood, singing and ringing bells, urging religious activity.

Occasionally upwards of 150 people attend, but 30 or 40 is more usual. An analysis of the characteristics of 16 people, whom Komolafe considers to be the core, is revealing. Their ages range from 20 to 32, and the average is 25. [. . .]

The society appeals in particular to literate young men, engaged in modern occupations, and particularly those living away from home. It is notable that Ibadan indigenes, who form upwards of a quarter of the congregation, are less prominent in this kind of supererogatory religious activity; the social type is similar to what was found in the early congregations before the revivals of the 1930s. When Komolafe spoke of "Ibadan people" he meant people at Ibadan, rather than Ibadan indigenes.

Similar young men are the regulars of the Praying Battalion (*Egbẹ Afadurajagun*). This is a much wider organization, with branches all over Yorubaland in the large urban centres, and a central committee under a chairman, Mr. S. I. Fagbo, in Ibadan. Mr. Fagbo is in his forties, a prosperous tailor; he comes from Imesi Ile (an Ijesha town), and joined the Christ Apostolic Church as a young man. In 1949 when Evangelist Babajide (now the successor to Babalola) came to conduct a revival in Ibadan, Fagbo was one of a number of youths who helped him. During the revival they accompanied him and prayed that he might be given power, and afterwards they fasted and prayed "to help find where our enemy the Devil is hiding." After six months this informal band was made a spiritual society, following the inspiration of the Holy Ghost through Babajide. The intention was to meet at night for

prayer; its fortunes fluctuated, numbers dropped, and several times Fagbo slept lonely in the church; but today there are numerous branches, and Fagbo travels about to see how they are progressing. The aim is to make the youths "active in spirit," and to make them surpass their fathers in the work of the church.

Mr. Fagbo is an elder of Oke Anu Church, and the following meeting took place there. It starts at 10 p.m. and there are about twenty-five people present, nearly all young men. The meeting is in the temporary wooden church, now being replaced by a fine ferro-concrete one. There is a table for Mr. Fagbo, and the members draw their benches into a semicircle about it. The proceedings are similar to those of *Alago Meje*, prayer, hymns, Bible reading, a short sermon. At midnight Fagbo rings a little bell, and from behind a matting partition in the hall come the women who are sleeping in the church. They have come to Oke Anu ("Mercy Hill") because of the divine healing of the prophet who has established the church, and every three hours someone says prayers for them. Any Aladura church, especially if it has a powerful prophet, will attract such women, either to stay (there are rough facilities for this), or just to attend revivals. Everyone says a prayer for these women, and after a hymn they go back, and the Battalion members spread out mats, roll up their *agbada*s or wrap some clothes round their Bibles for pillows, and go to sleep.

Some of us stay talking for a while. One member says the purpose of joining the Praying Battalion is, as he puts it, "to become a spiritualist";[207] everyone has the potentiality, and it needs training and discipline, prayer and fasting, to bring it out. "It is like training and tempering the body's spiritual activities." Two hours later Mr. Fagbo rings a bell, and the members, still heavy with sleep, rouse themselves with a hearty hymn. The meeting continues much as before, but instead of a sermon the chairman asks if any members have had any dreams or visions; the meanings of these are interpreted by Mr. Fagbo.[208] One man saw himself being led by two legs, and falling into a dirty pit (signifying falling into sin); then he saw a burnt hand (signifying hell); then a high building like Cocoa House with some clerks, who knocked him down (signifying people who opposed God); then he

---

207. "Spiritualist" does not mean someone who communicates with the dead, but someone who is strong in spiritual power.

208. Dream interpretation is a widespread Yoruba interest, and one can buy manuals to help one, stemming from Muslim or esoteric Western sources. Some people have the spiritual gift of interpretation, but in this case the symbols have mostly fairly obvious meanings.

saw himself washing from a calabash (the mercy of Oke Anu), and finally angels in white gowns singing a Christ Apostolic hymn (signifying the virtuous). The general lesson of this, says Mr. Fagbo, is a warning against spiritual laziness. Another man says he saw a bowl of peeled oranges (blessings) and an electric cable (strength). Besides these dreams which promise blessings to the virtuous, and in general support the church's values, there are some testimonies of blessings received or of disasters averted by revelation—for which prayers of thanksgiving are said. It is after 4 a.m., and still dark, when the members disperse to their homes. The Praying Battalion meets two nights a week in this way. The general tenor of its meetings is similar to that of *Alago Meje;* its active members are almost identical in type.

These young men are in many ways the most characteristic of the Aladura members, the keenest at specifically Aladura activities, the type who created the doctrines in the 1920s and 1930s and still the sort of people to whom the doctrines and the practices they entail have the most attraction. One is impressed by the associational character of the praying bands; their members, in their twenties mostly, have most likely come to Ibadan from Ijebu or Ekiti, and live in the tenement houses, probably with some of their fellow-townsmen, of the newer suburbs like Ekotedo. Probably the members of a praying band, becoming prosperous in their forties, will eventually come to be the elders of a church.

For the clearly marked categories of youth and elders have different functions in the religious sphere. The former, like the young warriors of nineteenth-century Ibadan, are to be active against the enemy—fighting in prayer, the shock troops of the church, resolved not to be less valiant than their fathers, who were like this before them. Their fathers, the elders, lead the whole congregation, and take wise counsels; they lead the prayers on Sundays, but recognize that all-night prayer-meetings and revivalistic bands are things for the youth. As in other Yoruba situations, this division of function is fully in line with the traditional way of organizing activities, and feasible in the modern urban setting.

The members' outlook on religion is rationalistic. Its most prominent features are Bible interpretation and exposition, the reading, digesting, discussion, and application of various tracts and pamphlets, and the relation of their spiritual activities to their day-to-day concerns. It is felt that the Bible, revelations, and their religious content can and should be systematically employed. So one member of the Praying Battalion (a schoolteacher) keeps four notebooks in which he records dreams and visions, notes on what to pray for, proph-

ecies, and "activities" (i.e., various secular plans and projects, such as whether to take up driving or stamp-collecting). These praying activities, and the enthusiasm for revival, are part of the same plan for religious action as the Biblical fundamentalism.

From J. D. Y. Peel, *Aladura: A Religious Movement among the Yoruba* (London: Oxford University Press, 1968), 157–71.

❦ "Shamans and Entrepreneurs: Primal Spirituality on the Asian Rim" examines Pentecostal spirituality in South Korea. Drawing from his research on Pentecostal communities, **Harvey Cox,** Harvard professor of religion, here pays particular attention to the interaction between Christian cultures developed in the West and local traditions indigenous to Korea.

HARVEY COX

"Shamans and Entrepreneurs: Primal Spirituality on the Asian Rim,"
in *Fire from Heaven: The Rise of Pentecostal Spirituality and the Reshaping of Religion in the Twenty-first Century*

Late on the afternoon of February 8, 1991 the house lights in the Royal Theatre of Canberra, Australia, dimmed dramatically, and a petite Korean woman named Hyun Kyung Chung entered from the rear of the hall. She was accompanied by nineteen Korean dancers with bells, candles, drums, gongs, and clap sticks. As a vast crowd of nearly 4,000 people craned to watch, the retinue advanced toward the stage led by two Australian Aboriginal dancers dressed only in loincloths and body paint. Both were playing a traditional wind instrument known as the didgeridoo. When they had all reached the stage, Chung and her companions stepped through a synchronized pattern which combined Aboriginal movement with traditional Korean folk dance.

If this had been a traveling Asian folklore troupe the scene might not have been noteworthy. But the audience was not the usual matinee crowd. It consisted of Anglican priests, Lutheran bishops, Baptist and Methodist lay leaders, Presbyterian ministers, journalists, and theologians from 100 different countries who had gathered in Canberra for the Seventh General Assembly of the World Council of Churches. And the dancer was not an international entertainment celebrity, but a professor of Christian Studies at the Ewha Women's University in Seoul, Korea. Dr. Chung had been invited to give one of the two keynote addresses at this, the opening session of the gathering. The topic she had been asked to address was the overall theme of the assembly: "Come Holy Spirit, Renew Thy Whole Creation." The other keynote, scheduled just before Dr. Chung's, was entrusted to a venerable Eastern Orthodox theologian, His Beatitude Parthenios III, Patriarch of Alexandria and All Africa. In inviting both a Korean woman and an Orthodox patriarch to address the assembly's theme at the same session, the planners were no doubt making an important symbolic gesture. They were publicly signaling the importance of women, third world churches, and Christians from the long-repressed Orthodox realm in the ecumenical movement. They were also acknowledging that both the Eastern Orthodox tradition and the lively new nonwestern churches focus more attention on the Holy Spirit than most western churches, either Catholic or Protestant, do.

What the leaders did not anticipate was that Dr. Chung's keynote would come to overshadow almost everything else that took place at the assembly and would stir up a dispute within the council's membership that eventually came perilously close to splitting it apart. Both the address itself and the controversy it sparked constitute a kind of epiphany. Taken together, they reveal much, both about the rapid spread of the Spirit-oriented forms of Christianity in Asia, and about the unsettling feeling this expansion stirs up in many people, including Christians.

The World Council was founded just after World War II as a largely pan-Protestant network, but by the time of the Canberra meeting the council included the major Eastern Orthodox churches based in Russia, Romania, and Greece. It also included many of the so-called new churches of Africa and Asia. Since only two of the many hundreds of pentecostal denominations in the world belong to the World Council of Churches, this movement was dramatically underrepresented. But, even though pentecostals had not selected the theme of the meeting, it was one that was obviously influenced by their burgeoning presence in the world. "Come Holy Spirit, Renew Thy Whole Creation" is a topic dear to their hearts.

In fact, as the weary delegates climbed off their planes after the long flight there was every indication that some acknowledgment of the reemergence of suppressed and neglected spiritualities, and some recognition of the growing strength of the pentecostal wave, would have to be part of the assembly's agenda. A self-conscious openness to indigenous practices has become a hallmark of the new generation of Asian Christians who had come to Canberra. But just *how*

much these issues would dominate the meeting was probably not foreseen by the leaders of the World Council when they invited the slight, soft-spoken Korean woman to deliver the second keynote. The World Council has never been quite the same since.

Hyun Kyung Chung is one of an emerging group of theologians from the fast-growth area of Christianity who like to refer to themselves as the "second generation." They are the young scholars and intellectuals from areas such as Asia, Africa, and Latin America which were once looked upon as "mission fields" but now contain the majority of the world's Christian population. The term "second generation" cannot be taken literally, of course, since various forms of Christianity have been present in some of these areas for centuries. But these theologians have gone beyond either slavishly embracing or mechanically rejecting the versions of the faith the missionaries brought to them. Instead they are crafting theologies and liturgies that draw on their own indigenous cultures. A prominent European Roman Catholic thinker once remarked that Catholicism would never be securely grounded in Africa "until the Mass is drummed and danced." An equivalent observation could be made about Christianity in other parts of the nonwestern world. Dr. Chung and her colleagues in the "second generation" are—quite literally—the drummers and dancers of this new theology, as the thousands of delegates gathered in Canberra were soon to find out.

The established rubric for keynote speeches in such assemblies as the Canberra meeting is clear . . . a straightforward address usually read from a prepared text. The contribution of the Orthodox theologian was read by another representative since the patriarch was unable to attend. Though Parthenios is himself a lively and engaging person, the fact that his scholarly address had to be delivered by someone else gave it a more than usual stodgy and arid character. His Beatitude argued that the kind of unity Christians seek already exists in the Holy Trinity, but needs to be made visible, and this was the task of the Seventh General Assembly. People applauded politely. But when the house lights went down and Dr. Chung with her troupe filed to the podium something new in the annals of World Council of Churches presentations took place.

True to her "second generation" vision, Chung not only spoke about the importance of the Spirit in a faith which, while claiming to honor the Trinity, has lavished nearly all its attention on God and Jesus Christ, she also provided a living demonstration of what she was talking about. When the dance procession had reached the stage, Chung stepped to the microphone and invited all those present in the audience to take off their shoes. She explained that this followed the custom of many Asian and Aboriginal peoples and was meant to honor the holy ground on which they were meeting. She also reminded them that God had asked Moses to remove his shoes at the burning bush. The gesture, she said, would help everyone to assume an attitude of humility before the Spirit of God.

As she began her talk, Chung invoked "the spirits of the women, children and men killed by oppression." She specifically mentioned the victims of the Gulf War which had just broken out when the meeting started. She also invoked the spirits of the rain-forest, the earth, the air, the water, all the sea creatures and—finally—"the spirit of the Liberator, Jesus Christ." Next she set fire to long strips of rice paper on which she had written the names of the spirits she had summoned. Then, with considerable panache and dignity she held the flaming papers high in her hands until they disappeared in smoke.

When she addressed the audience directly Chung explained that in Korean folk tradition, *han* spirits are the wandering souls of those who are filled with anger, bitterness, and resentment because they were killed or died unjustly or for many other reasons. It is because of these *han* spirits, she said, that "we can feel, touch and taste the concrete, bodily historical presence of the Holy Spirit in our midst." Turning to the theme-prayer of the assembly, "Come Holy Spirit, Renew Thy Whole Creation," she insisted that it should not be used as an excuse for passivity, merely waiting for the Spirit. Rather it required active solidarity with all forms of life. "I no longer believe in an omnipotent God," she declared. "I rely on the compassionate God who weeps with us in the midst of the cruel destruction of life." She ended her address by describing her personal image of the Holy Spirit. The Spirit, she said, is like a bodhisattva, an enlightened being, a goddess of compassion and wisdom. Indeed the Holy Spirit "might also be a feminine image of the Christ . . . who goes before and brings others with her." She closed with a ringing appeal which, though delivered in a very different tone from that of Parthenios, actually echoed the same sentiment: "Let us tear down the walls of division which separate us." When the verbal part of her address ended, she concluded the session with a dance meant to dramatize the recent coming to awareness of Korean women and to contrast with the overly verbal idiom of many western liturgies.

The presentation was greeted, as one delegate later observed, with both "thunderous applause and thunderous silence." Some hailed it as a long-needed step toward the recognition of an authentically Asian Christianity. They called it electrifying, powerful, evocative, haunting. Others termed it pantheistic and outrageous and dismissed it as syncretism of the worst order, the abject surrender of Christianity to a pagan environment. Some thought Dr. Chung's performance was merely an example of youthful excess, understandable if not wholly excusable. After all she was only a woman. Several of the Eastern Orthodox delegates, who had for a long time nursed other complaints about the World Council, threatened to withdraw their churches from the organization completely. Their millennia-old devotion to the Holy Spirit plainly did not encompass the invoking of the spirits of the land.

For the next days the thousands of delegates and visitors sang and prayed and discussed the other papers and reports. But what continued to buzz at the coffee breaks and dinner conversations were the questions Dr. Chung's keynote had raised about the future direction not only of the World Council of Churches but of Christianity itself. In fact what had happened at Canberra was the dramatic eruption of the primal spirituality that we have charted in several other areas. Only this time the geyser of underground energy spouted before the very eyes of the stolid old World Council of Churches itself.

Spirit and fire, cleansing rituals, shamanic invocations, Aboriginal blessings, all under the auspices of the oft-neglected third person of the Christian Trinity: what Hyun Kyung Chung did might have seemed unfamiliar, even menacing, to many of the delegates at the World Council of Churches. But those familiar with the varieties of pentecostalism would recognize this cluster of elements immediately. That is why Dr. Chung's keynote performance and the anxious response it generated can rightly be referred to as an epiphany. Her performance and the reaction to it point beyond Christianity itself. They reveal something both about the other fast growing religious movements in this decidedly post-death-of-God era and also about the unease their appearance evokes. Finally, the fact that this event happened under the direction of a Korean, whose homeland is itself a paradigm of many of the economic, cultural, and religious changes that are occurring in the nonwestern world today, is highly significant.

Hyun Kyung Chung is not a member of a pentecostal church. But that makes the controversy surrounding her keynote address even more significant because it demonstrates that the energies pentecostalism draws upon transcend its own borders. My worldwide exploration of the expansion of pentecostal types of Christianity has convinced me that for any religion to grow in today's world, it must possess two capabilities: it must be able to include and transform at least certain elements of preexisting religions which still retain a strong grip on the cultural subconscious. It must also equip people to live in rapidly changing societies where personal responsibility and inventiveness, skills associated with a democratic polity and an entrepreneurial economy, are indispensable.

Both of these key ingredients are present in Korean pentecostalism, which helps explain its dramatic success. Despite its own protestations to the contrary, pentecostalism in Korea seems able to incorporate many of the characteristics of shamanism and also to prepare people remarkably well for modern political and economical survival. South Korea is a kind of litmus test. Its religious culture—Buddhism and Confucianism overlaying folk shamanism—is similar to many other Asian countries. Its emerging democratic polity and guided market economy are also similar. Consequently, if we can understand the pentecostal phenomenon in Korea, we may get some important hints about its prospects in China and the rest of Asia, and possibly its global prospects as well. Let us ask first about the issue which—depending on one's point of view—can be labeled either negatively as the "syncretism" question, or positively as the power of the Spirit to transform preexistent faiths.

There may be no better way to grasp the astonishing scope and baffling complexity of Korean pentecostalism than by paying a visit to the Yoido Full Gospel (Pentecostal) Church in Seoul, South Korea. This church, whose pastor, the Reverend David Yonggi Cho, has become something of a religious celebrity in Korea, is only a few decades old but has already become the largest single Christian congregation on earth. Such megachurches are not unusual in Korea. On the list of the "top ten" largest churches in the world, three are in Seoul and one is in Inchon.

The Yoido Full Gospel Church is also located in what is a prototypical area for such pell-mell expansion: a pullulating megacity in a rapidly changing third world country. Clearly, in order to appeal to so many people, this church and the wider movement it represents must have satisfied, at least in some measure, the two basic conditions I have just mentioned. First, it must help people hold on to at least some elements of the traditional culture and religion that seem to be falling to pieces before their eyes. In South Korea, as in the rest of Asia, this is a particularly challenging condition for

pentecostalism since the culture's historic religious traditions are not Christian. And second, Korean pentecostalism must also help people cope with both the rampant urbanization and the wrenching demands of new economic and political realities, which have completely transformed the once isolated peninsula known as the Hermit Kingdom. Korea has left its sequestered past far behind and has become one of the most energetic of the newly industrializing east Asian countries. But the pace of change in Korea has taken a toll. Its prodigious economic derring-do and its constant political uncertainties perch uneasily on an underlying cultural edifice that is heaving and straining as people try to embrace modernity while still clinging to whatever bits of tradition they can salvage. Religion is the arena within which much of this wrestling match between old values and new life-style is fought. And pentecostal Christianity is both the principal vehicle and the main battleground of this confrontation.

Protestant Christianity in Korea is only about 100 years old. At the end of World War II, Christians still accounted for only about 8 percent of the populace. But by 1994 the churches had recruited over one-third of the population of South Korea. If current trends continue it will become the majority faith by the year 2000. In Korea Christianity is anything *but* otherworldly. After the Korean War ended in 1951, South Korean churches inspired a courageous opposition to the authoritarian regimes of Syngman Rhee and Chung Hee Park, during which many Christian pastors and students were beaten and jailed. Korean Christians invented their own form of "liberation theology" called "minjung theology," using the Korean term for the ordinary, nonelite people among whom Christianity first spread. More recently, Christianity in South Korea has helped ignite an Asian Rim version of the Protestant ethic, a zest for hard work that has fueled the country's dazzling entrepreneurial take-off and made it one of the most formidable of the so-called seven dragons.

It is true that statistically at least South Korea is quickly becoming a Christian nation. But, as in many third world countries, the traditional western denominational labels mean very little (what does it mean, for example, to be a South Korean Dutch Reformed?). Besides, it is the pentecostals, not the Catholics or the Presbyterians, who are bringing in the most converts. Therefore, to understand the phenomenal growth of Christianity in Korea (and elsewhere on the Asian Rim) we must put to the pentecostal movement the two questions we asked earlier. Does it amalgamate previous, pre-Christian religious practices, which in Korea are a mixture of shamanism, Buddhism, and Confucianism? And how does it assist in providing the essential *Geist* that lubricates the country's rough-and-tumble market economy?

The best way to answer the first question may be to look at the example of the Yoido Full Gospel (Pentecostal) Church. As we have noted, the Yoido congregation is a megachurch. Its 800,000 membership makes it the largest congregation in the world. With an initial membership of 5 in 1958, its rapid growth is a parable of pentecostal expansion both in Asia and in similar areas elsewhere. In some ways its story reminds me of one of those time-lapse films that chart the blooming of a rose from bud to petals, except that this sudden spurt of increase took place in real time. It compresses into a few decades the whole pentecostal story.

There are many ways to try to explain the eruption of Christianity and pentecostalism in South Korea. Many of these explanations credit the painful aftermath of the Korean War and the rapid economic and social changes that have taken place since then, including the extraordinary concentration of more and more people in the cities of South Korea, especially Seoul itself. But there are other factors as well. The sprouting of giant cities is a common factor in the spread of pentecostalism elsewhere in the world, but there are several factors peculiar to Korea, or at least east Asia. Some characteristics of Korean pentecostalism in particular are deeply embarrassing and upsetting to western pentecostals.

Few pentecostals anywhere in the world would be uncomfortable with the fact that a principal reason for the Yoido church's growth is its reputation as a center for spiritual healing. Healing, after all, is an integral part of the pentecostal message everywhere. But what disquiets them is that one of the key reasons for Korean pentecostalism's extraordinary growth is its unerring ability to absorb huge chunks of indigenous Korean shamanism and demon possession into its worship. This capacity for absorption, as we have seen, is not unusual for pentecostalism. In fact it is surely one of the primary reasons for its spread. What troubles pentecostals elsewhere about the Korean case is that the *degree* of importation is so extensive that some wonder out loud what has absorbed what. Is this a particularly successful, non-Catholic example of "drumming the mass," of the so-called indigenization of Christianity in an Asian culture? Or is it merely the continuation of the most salient forms of previous Korean folk religion wearing a Christian mask? The debate goes on, and the Yoido Full Gospel Church is an especially vivid case in point.

In 1963, within five years of its founding, the church had 2,000 members. Each became a dedicated messenger and recruiter, bringing others into the ever enlarging fold. By 1971 there were 15,000 members; by 1981 there were 200,000. The congregation now lists over 800,000, most of whom take part in small face-to-face prayer and study groups in addition to the plenary gatherings in the church's massive temple. The Yoido Full Gospel Church is still growing and its enthusiastic members insist they will top a million by the year 2000. They probably will. This church's story is singular but not unique. While it was growing, pentecostalism was expanding all over South Korea. A reliable recent estimate says there are now more than 5,000 Christian church buildings in Seoul alone. That number, as Koreans wryly remark, even exceeds the count of coffee shops and drugstores. Not all of those churches bear the pentecostal label, of course, but pentecostal congregations, and others with similar modes of worship, are multiplying faster than all the others put together.

As one steps out of the street and into the Yoido Full Gospel Church, even the most practiced observer of pentecostal worship elsewhere is in for a shock. Take what is called "Hallelujah-robics" for example. It is a form of dancing to hymns played to an ear-piercing rock beat by an ensemble of electric organ, drums, accordion, and other instruments. The dancing is led by enthusiastic teams from the church's youth division. When the music stops temporarily the congregation takes up what sounds like the religious equivalent of the cheers used at an Ohio State football game. At full volume they shout "Aboji Hananim" (Our Father, who art in Heaven) and then with hands raised many begin praying in words and phrases of no known language. Then more singing begins, with the songs arranged to the tune of pop melodies. The worshippers rock back and forth and wave their arms. Sometimes the band increases the tempo of the song, the way the Israeli tune "Havah Nagila" is often rendered, and the people move faster and faster until, no longer able to keep it up, they stop in happy exhaustion.

While the shouting and singing goes on, the ministers walk through the congregation sometimes striking the palms of their hands against someone's head or back. The gesture is strongly reminiscent of the practice in some Zen Buddhist monasteries where one of the monks walks up and down among the seated meditators and, to stave off dozing, strikes this or that one on the shoulder with a bamboo rod. Finally, when the singing, shouting, and dancing are over the minister begins leading a prayer which sounds more like an incantation than an invocation. He repeats over and over again, sometimes a hundred times or more, such phrases as "Hallelujah!" or "O Lord!" or "the Spirit fills!" while the congregation joins him. During these incantatory prayers, many of the women and a few of the men begin to weep and cry and flail their arms. Meanwhile, the ministers keep assuring everyone that, whatever their illnesses or infirmities might be, they will certainly be healed.

When the minister returns to the podium people file by to receive both the "laying on of hands" from the ministers and possibly another clap on some part of the back or shoulders. Often a minister will address the "demons of ill health" directly with commands like "Get out!" or the Korean equivalent of "Scat, shoo!" As the service ends, the people who believe they have been healed shout out short prayers of gratitude and stream out of the church, leaving behind those who are still caught up in the fervor and continue to sway and pray until evening comes, the lights are extinguished, and the building is closed. Now everyone leaves. But those who have clearly not been healed do not appear discouraged. They will be back another day.

To a visitor schooled in comparative religion, the worship at the Yoido Full Gospel Church bears a striking resemblance to what is ordinarily known as "shamanism," but when one points this out to Korean pentecostal ministers they firmly deny that there is any similarity. They open well-thumbed Bibles to the passage in 2 Corinthians in which Paul describes his ecstatic experience of being "caught up into the third heaven," and of hearing "words so secret that human lips can not repeat them." If the Apostle himself could have such visions in a trancelike state, they argue, why shouldn't we? They also point out that the New Testament is full of demon possession and exorcisms. They recall the Garasene demoniac and the description of Mary Magdalene as one from whom Jesus expelled seven demons.

It is hard to refute these biblical arguments. But something sounds out of focus, and as their explanations continue, the Koreans do not always reassure their western brethren that they are operating within the usual parameters of pentecostal practice. The sources of these illnesses, some pastors explain, are dead relatives and ancestors who never accepted Christ and are therefore angry and troubled. They return to afflict the living, so they have to be sent packing. Hence the commands to "get out, shoo!"

The underlying issue is not unfamiliar to students of the history of religion. The living are frequently anxious about the condition of the dead. The Catholic Church, over many centuries, evolved the doctrine of Purgatory to respond to precisely this anxiety. Praying for the souls in Purgatory enables those who are still in this world to assuage their own

worries and to do something they believe will help those who have already passed on to the next. But making the departed ones the agents of disease represents a twist on this theology that is virtually unknown among Christians in the west.

From Harvey Cox, *Fire from Heaven: The Rise of Pentecostal Spirituality and the Reshaping of Religion in the Twenty-first Century* (Reading, MA: Addison-Wesley, 1995), 213–24.

In *Taking Up Serpents* **David L. Kimbrough** recounts how the Holiness serpent handlers of eastern Kentucky test their faith by handling venomous snakes. This practice follows the Gospel teaching laid out in Mark 16:17–18, which lists taking up serpents among the signs that will announce those who believe.

DAVID L. KIMBROUGH

Taking Up Serpents: Snake Handlers of Eastern Kentucky

The Holiness serpent handlers, who originated in 1910 among the Church of God Holiness, are one of the most controversial religious groups in American history.[209] For the most part, all the general public knows about this religious group

209. Most scholars have given George Went Hensley credit for founding the snake-handling movement; however, these scholars offer little or no evidence for their claim, and the scholarship itself reflects much confusion over the movement's origin. Most earlier studies claim that Hensley instituted serpent handling in 1909. (See La Barre, *They Shall Take Up Serpents*; Sims, "Snake Handlers"; Stekert, "Snake-Handling Sect of Harlan County, Kentucky"; and J. B. Collins, *Tennessee Snake Handlers*.) Hensley himself gave different dates of origin. In a March 9, 1956 interview with the *Tampa Morning Tribune* ("Preacher Juggles Snake Again, Says It Bit Him"), Hensley claimed that he had been handling snakes for twenty-three years. That would make the date of origin 1919. Probably the most reliable interview with George Hensley that included questions on when snake handling began was conducted by Keith Kerman of the *St. Louis Post-Dispatch* in the summer of 1938 at Harlan County, Ky. Hensley informed Kerman that he "had introduced the practice twenty-eight years before in Sale Creek, Tennessee" (Kerman, "Rattlesnake Religion," 101). This would make the date of origin 1910. Another interview that supports 1910 as the date of origin was an article by Charles Crane of the *Chattanooga News Free Press* for July 20, 1945 ("Demonstrations of Faith with Gyrations Held in Dolly Pond Church"). The column stated that George Hensley was credited with founding the cult in the area "about 35 years ago."

Other evidence, however, suggests that Hensley was not the first person to handle snakes in Appalachia. Homer A. Tomlinson states that the ritual of taking up serpents in religious services began in 1908 (*Shout of a King*, 39). Also, I have received isolated reports of serpent handling before Hensley, although I have been unable to satisfactorily document them. In an interview at Cleveland, Tenn. on February 19, 1988, George Hensley's son, James Roscoe Hensley, stated that his father had seen a man handle poisonous snakes at a religious service. He claimed that this experience is what caused his father to become a snake handler. If Hensley was not the first to handle serpents, he was responsible for the spread of the snake-handling movement. Once he started preaching snake handling, the movement boomed throughout Appalachia.

are the highly sensationalized events reported by magazines, television, or newspapers. Generally, the media makes little effort to explore the heritage of the snake handlers' beliefs, instead leaving the public to conclude that they are freaks or weirdos. In fact, the snake handlers are not weird or strange. They have a strong fundamentalist base firmly grounded in a religious heritage that can easily be traced to the revivals conducted at Cambuslang, Scotland, in the seventeenth century.

The snake handlers have also been persecuted by the authorities, and this persecution has given the general public a bad impression of their religion. Throughout the history of the movement, law officials have badgered church members by ridiculing them, jailing them, and using other means to break up snake-handling religious gatherings. However, the religion has endured the attacks, and meetings continue to be conducted—every night, in some locations.

Adopting a form of old-line fundamentalist Appalachian religion, snake handlers believe that the Holy Ghost grants them the power to heal the sick; perform exorcisms; speak in new tongues; drink poisons like strychnine, battery acid, or lye; and handle deadly serpents. They base their beliefs primarily upon a passage from Mark that reports the words of Christ before his ascension into the heavens: "And these signs shall follow them that believe; in my name shall they cast out devils; they shall speak with new tongues; they shall take up serpents; and if they drink any deadly thing, it shall not hurt them; they shall lay hands on the sick and they shall recover" (Mark 16:17–18; all biblical quotations are from the King James version).

They also cite several other passages to sanction their beliefs and practices, including Luke 10:19 ("Behold, I give unto you power to tread on serpents and scorpions, and over the power of the enemy: and nothing by any means shall hurt you"); Acts 28:3–6, which says that Paul shook off a viper that was "fastened on his hand" without suffering any ill effects; and Exodus 4:2–4, which tells how Moses, at God's command, transformed his rod into a serpent and picked it up by its tail.

Some believers argue that Jesus was a serpent handler, citing 2 Timothy 2:6 as evidence: "The husbandman that laboureth must be first partaker of the fruits." Anthropologist Steven M. Kane, who spent many years doing research among the snake handlers, states that he was given an additional text—John 20:30, "And many other signs truly did Jesus in the presence of his disciples, which are not written in this book."[210] After quoting these passages, the snake handlers

add, "He wouldn't tell you to do something he didn't do himself." From the pulpits of eastern Kentucky the signs are preached on nightly, along with reports of other miracles, such as levitations and raising the dead.

Sunday morning service is conducted at 11 a.m. In one service that I witnessed, members began to gather around 10 a.m. in order to socialize and to discuss events that had transpired in the mountains during the past week. On many occasions the congregations have visitors from Alabama, Michigan, and Indiana. As more of the faithful arrived, members of the same sex shook hands, hugged, and occasionally kissed each other on the lips, as dictated in Romans 16:16 ("Salute one another with a Holy kiss"). Men and women exchanged only handshakes. Some younger male members affectionately hugged older women who were special to them.

Many people arrived with a variety of musical instruments, including acoustic and electric guitars, fiddles, steel guitars, bass guitars, pianos, harmonicas, drums, banjos, and cymbals. Generally, the musicians in the churches play with great skill. As more people entered the church, the musicians began to tune their instruments. When the preacher entered the building, he hugged people and welcomed the gathering. Some members of the congregation greeted him with statements such as "Bless him, Lord," or "Be with him, Jesus." The pastor displayed considerable fondness toward the young children in the gathering. He asked one young boy, "Are you married yet, son?" The young man blushed and replied, "No, I'm not even out of school yet." The congregation laughed, and the preacher moved to the next child to pick on. All of the children appeared to love the pastor and joked back with him.

Around 10:30 the church began to fill, and members began to get serious. As in most snake-handling churches in eastern Kentucky, men sat on one side of the building and women on the other. A few male members brought in wooden boxes covered with wire mesh; these boxes contained rattlesnakes, copperheads, and cottonmouths. Some boxes housed a single snake, while others held up to five. The boxes were placed under the deacon's bench.[211]

---

210. Kane, "Snake Handlers of Southern Appalachia," 94.

211. In 1947, Joe Creason of the *Louisville Courier-Journal* reported that he saw some snake boxes that were made from wood scraps taken from the coal mines, which were appropriately stenciled "Dynamite." See Joe Creason, "The Grapevine," *Louisville Courier-Journal,* October 26, 1947, magazine sec., 4.

As the church filled, some musicians began to play hymns, and a few female members started singing and clapping their hands. They were soon joined by the whole congregation. The sound was deafening. Cymbals clashed, tambourines jingled, feet stomped, hands clapped, as the worshipers sang a song called "Feel Like Traveling On":

> My heavenly home is bright and fair,
> I feel like traveling on,
> Nor pain, nor death, can enter there,
> I feel like traveling on.
>
> Yes, I feel like traveling on,
> I feel like traveling on,
> My heavenly home is bright and fair,
> I feel like traveling on.
>
> Its glittering towers the sun outshine,
> I feel like traveling on.
> That heavenly mansion shall be mine,
> I feel like traveling on.
>
> Let others seek a home below,
> I feel like traveling on,
> Which flames devour, or waves o'erflow,
> I feel like traveling on.
>
> The Lord has been so good to me,
> I feel like traveling on,
> Until that blessed home I see,
> I feel like traveling on.

Some members raised their hands in the air during the music and began shouting and talking in unknown tongues, as described in Mark 16. A few jumped up and down, screaming phrases like "Praise the Lord" and "Hallelujah, precious Jesus." One young man jumped up from his seat and ran to the front of the church. He reached into one of the snake boxes, removed a large rattlesnake, and shouted, "Glory, thank you, Lord." An elderly gentleman clad in bib overalls opened a box and handled five rattlesnakes simultaneously. The music continued, and some of the congregation danced and shook uncontrollably. Many communicants focused their attention on the snake handling, while others were involved in their own spiritual experience.

The young man who first handled the snake passed it to another man. This member began to cry and jump up and down, screaming, "Thank you, Jesus!" The minister took a rattlesnake and placed it on an open Bible that sat on the lectern. The snake immediately coiled, as if it was ready to strike the pastor. The preacher then laid his head on the reptile without being bitten. Church members shouted, "Bless him, Lord." The preacher started talking in tongues: "Oh-shana-dee, oh shana-dee-la-inter-dee-cors." He picked up the snake and rubbed it in his face, again escaping injury. A man in his mid-forties placed his bare feet in a box of copperheads, while a thirty-five-year-old man opened a box of snakes and placed it over his head and danced ecstatically. Neither man was bitten.

A young woman shouted, "Sweet Jesus," and grabbed a snake from a fellow member. She jumped up and down several times and also spoke in tongues. A young child started walking toward the front of the church, where the snakes were being handled, and was stopped immediately. (Snake handling is usually performed in the front of the building in order to protect those who do not participate in the ritual.)

After forty-five minutes of singing and snake handling, the excitement began to subside. Then an elderly woman jumped up and testified to the congregation, "I love the Lord today. He is so good to me. He has healed my body many times. I praise him for it. Lots of times I got down and out but the Lord has always come to my rescue. He healed my body many times and I love him so. Hallelujah to God! Pray for me that I will never get out of the Lord. Hallelujah!" Other members shouted, "Bless her, Glory to God." The woman returned to her seat, and the minister cheered, "Hallelujah! If you people have something to say say it! I said, say it! Praise the Lord!"

The preacher then asked the congregation if any prayer requests were needed. A gentleman from Alabama stood and said, "Brother, a woman from Fort Payne lost her son in a terrible automobile accident. She is so hurt. Please remember her in your prayers." A woman stood and stated, "My father is getting weaker every day. I beg you all to pray for him." Other members made special prayer requests in regard to catastrophic events, illness, and hope for "sinners who have done wrong." When the prayer began, many worshippers went to the front of the church, to a clear area between the pulpit and the first row of seats. Other members, stayed at their benches. They turned to the back of their seat and knelt, resting their arms on the seat and bowing their heads. Some members of the congregation knelt on the floor. All of the congregation prayed aloud in unison. Again, some members spoke in unknown tongues. This ritual lasted for approximately fifteen minutes. The minister then asked for someone to rise and "sing us a song." A woman rose and sang,

Can't nobody hide, can't nobody hide,
Can't nobody hide from God.
You may hide it from the preacher,
But you shore can't hide it from God.

Can't nobody hide, Well can't nobody hide,
Can't nobody hide from God.
You may hide it from the deacon,
But you shore can't hide it from God.

Can't nobody hide, Well can't nobody hide.
Can't nobody hide from God.

The instrumentalists joined in, and the hymn lasted for about ten minutes. One man opened a snake box and handled a copperhead. After the song, the preacher walked to the front of the church and began to deliver his message. "I'm glad to see you all here today. We have people from Florida, Alabama, Georgia, and Indiana with us Kentuckians today. Isn't that wonderful, praise God. I wish we could be in church all of the time. Praise God. There will be a day that we can, if we continue to live right. I tell you, Brother Bob, it has got to be Holiness. Peter didn't say, I build these churches on these rocks. He said, On this rock I build this church." Many members shouted, "Amen." The preacher continued,

You can't live like other people and make it to heaven. The other day, I was in a woman's house and she had a television playing. Her children was watching that thing, Ah. No good can come from that. Ah. When I questioned her about it, Ah, she said she only had it on for the news, Ah. Brother Jim, you must keep away from evil such as television, Ah. They contain every kind of filth known to man, Ah. You should never let your children watch television, Ah. I tell you, many of you care more about your dogs than you do your children, Ah. You chain up your dogs to keep them from getting hurt, Ah. You turn your babies out on the street to get hurt, Ah. When they are watching television or on the street, they see prostitution, homosexuality, drugs, and every kind of evil there is.[212]

The preacher began to shake and cry frantically. He screamed, "You've got to keep your babies in church, Brother Ben. Some of these preachers say they have a vision. The only vision they have is television. My own son came home from school one day with an earring in his ear. When I saw

that, I threw him clear out of the house. Now many of you say that little earring can't hurt anything. Let me tell you this. That little earring will only lead to worse things. Before long the spirit of the homosexual will be on you. I want to live clean and not look like some sissy."

The crowd shouted, "Amen," and the preacher continued with a fiery message that lasted an hour. After he completed his sermon, he pulled out a handkerchief and wiped the perspiration from his face. He then said, "Thank God. Now let's hear one of you brothers testify. Come on, Brother Bob." Brother Bob walked to the lectern and preached for fifteen minutes on the evils of the federal government. He concluded, "I tell you brothers something. They may be in power now, but they will have to answer for the evils for all eternity, and eternity is forever."

Everyone was given a chance to testify, and ten people did so, on various topics. Some declared that they have been blessed with miraculous cures. One woman stood and asked the congregation to pray for her. Many members walked to the front of the church and placed their hands on the woman. They formed a circle around her and rubbed olive oil on her forehead. All of the members prayed aloud and in their own words. Three other people then walked to the front of the church and asked to be "prayed over."

The preacher proclaimed, "The Lord will heal you if you believe. The Bible says, These signs will follow those who believe. They shall lay their hands on the sick and they shall recover."[213] As the service draws to an end, the pastor said, "Come on, boys. Do your job. Let's hear a song." The ser-

212. When Holiness preachers reach an emotional height, they frequently punctuate each sentence with an "Ah" or a deep breath. In this excited state they stride back and forth and their voices rise and fall, fluctuating between a roar and a whisper. Deborah Vansau McCauley refers to this type of preaching as the "holy tone."

213. Generally, snake-handling preachers such as Park Saylor do not claim credit for healing if a miracle occurs; they give full honor to God. It is also necessary for the sick to have faith that they will be healed by the "laying on of hands." Holiness beliefs hold that if the anointing is strong enough in the minister, and if it is God's desire, the sick will be healed. I have viewed two means of healing: the laying on of hands, as described in Mark 16:17, and the use of prayer cloths, as described in Acts 19:11–12.
A prayer cloth was passed around the church at Crockett, Ky., in an attempt to heal the daughter of Kale Saylor. His daughter had been injured in a terrible automobile accident in December 1987. She was taken to Knoxville, Tenn., for medical attention, and there was a consensus among the doctors that she would die. On March 6, 1988, the prayer cloth was passed among Crockett's congregation of 350 people. Each person prayed over the fabric, and serpents were actually passed over it in some instances. As Brother Asher passed the prayer cloth from aisle to aisle, in the same way that offering plates are conveyed in other churches, he held a giant rattlesnake in his hands. It was a very moving event. On that day Kale Saylor's daughter's condition improved. She is now out of the hospital living in the Straight Creek area.

vice had lasted for four hours. A young man rose and began a hymn, and the instrumentalists joined in.

> I wanna live so God can use me,
> Oh, anywhere Lord anytime.
> I wanna live so God can use me,
> Well, anywhere Lord anytime.
>
> I wanna sing so God can use me,
> Oh, anywhere Lord anytime.
> I wanna sing so God can use me,
> Well, anywhere Lord anytime.
>
> I wanna pray so God can use me,
> Oh, anywhere Lord anytime.

> I wanna pray so God can use me,
> Well, anywhere Lord anytime.

The congregation then began to handle snakes again. One man rolled over coiled rattlesnakes that he had placed on the floor; he escaped unharmed. Another man grabbed a fire bottle, lit it, and held it to his face for sixty seconds. He received no burns; various parts of his body were smoke-blackened, but he showed no other signs of having been in the fire. One by one the worshipers started to leave the building, as the musicians continued playing various songs. Later in the evening, the congregation would return for Sunday night service.

From David L. Kimbrough, *Taking Up Serpents: Snake Handlers of Eastern Kentucky* (Chapel Hill: University of North Carolina Press, 1995), 13–22.

7. CONTEMPORARY AND POPULAR RITUAL

In "Toward a Theology of Christian Ritual Music" **Edward Foley** considers the theological implications of the use of sound and music in liturgical rites. Foley, a professor of liturgical history and theory, compares the nature of sound to the nature of God and explores the notion of liturgical music as sacrament.

EDWARD FOLEY

"Toward a Theology of Christian Ritual Music," in *Ritual Music*

The Properties of Sound and Judaeo-Christian Revelation

Constructing a theology of ritual music[214] requires, first of all, that we recall the properties of sound discussed above and note how the sound phenomenon, by its very nature, serves the revelation of God as understood in the Judaeo-Christian tradition.

The Judaeo-Christian God as Historical. One of the most celebrated and distinctive aspects of the God of the Hebrew and Christian Scriptures is that this God intervenes in history. Not merely remembered as acting "once upon a time" or in some other mythic moment,[215] the God of Moses and Jesus intervened in specific times and places, liberating the Hebrews from Pharaoh and Jesus from death.

We have already noted that one of the most frequently cited characteristics of sound events like music [is] their transitory nature. Sound events are time-bound, history-bound events. Because of this existential quality music is able to image a God who, in the Judaeo-Christian tradition, intervenes in time and reveals Self in human history. Furthermore, this time-bound art has the ability to engage the community in the present reality of worship and signal that union with God is an existential possibility, here and now.

The Judaeo-Christian God as an Elusive Presence. Whereas the God of Judaeo-Christian revelation is perceived as One who intervenes in history, it is also clear that this is an elusive presence. The God of Abraham and Jesus is One who is both present and hidden.[216] The paradox of Judaeo-Christian revelation is that the Divine Self is both recognizable while remaining the unnameable "I am who I am" (Ex 3:14). Even

---

214. "Christian Ritual Music is the term employed in *The Music of Christian Ritual: Universa Laus Guidelines 1980* to describe "the vocal and instrumental practices integral to Christian Liturgy," n.1.3 as cited in *The Bulletin of Universa Laus* 30 (1980): 5. In order to establish continuity more clearly between the phenomenon of ritual music and that of Christian ritual music, the latter term will be employed [. . .] instead of its [. . .] synonym, "liturgical music."

215. Mircea Eliade, *The Sacred and the Profane,* trans. Willard R. Trask (New York: Harper & Row, 1961), 110–11.

216. Samuel Terrien, *The Elusive Presence* (London: Wipf and Stock, 2000), 470.

Christianity, which claims for itself the incarnate revelation of God in Jesus Christ, must reckon with a savior who came once in time and who will come again at the end of time. In the interim, however, while we long for and sometimes succeed in experiencing "real presence," we also struggle with God's "real absence."[217]

The paradox of all sound phenomena including music is that sound is perceivable but elusive, recognizable but uncontainable. The apparently insubstantial nature of music is one of the reasons why it has symbolized the mysterious and wholly other since the dawn of creation. Music, as a nondiscursive symbol, as we have noted, is especially distinguished by its ambivalence of content. This elusiveness in form and content is part of the reason why music is so often used for communicating with the spirit world. In the Judaeo-Christian tradition music is an effective means for communicating with a God who is both present and hidden. Furthermore, music offers itself as a powerful symbol for the divine Self who is recognizable while remaining the unnameable. Music thus enables us to encounter and know God without presuming to capture or contain the divine Self.

The Judaeo-Christian God as Dynamic. Besides being a God who is remembered as having intervened in human history, the God of Jews and Christians is also perceived as a dynamic and responsive God. This characteristic not only emphasizes God's historical intervention but further expresses the belief that God has been and continues to be engaged in the individual and corporate lives of humankind. The "call-response" dynamic of the Scriptures presents a God who continuously initiates encounters and, with astounding regularity, calls upon unsuspecting prophets (Jer 1:48) and unwilling disciples (Jn 1:46–49). Moreover, it is the promised continuation of this divine dialogue that gives these religions life.

Sound in general and music in specific have the ability not only to announce presence but also to engage another in dialogue and communion. Because of sound's ability to resonate inside two individuals at the same time, it has the capacity to strike a common chord and elicit sympathetic vibrations from those who hear. It is dynamic in its ability to enter the world of the other and elicit a response. Thus music effectively reflects the dialogic impulse of God in the Judaeo-Christian tradition who continuously initiates dialogue with believers. This characteristic emphasizes not only God's historical intervention or personal nature but further embodies the belief that God has been and continues to be engaged in the individual and corporate life of humankind.

The Judaeo-Christian God as Relational. Closely related to the dynamic character of the Judaeo-Christian God is the relational basis of this revelation. The God of Jews and Christians not only reveals Self in time—in a dynamic way that calls forth an individual response from believers—but is a God who also calls us into relationship with Godself and each other. The appropriate response to this revelation is not simply personal belief and activity, but the forging of a common identity and way of life as a people (Ex 6:6), as a community (Acts 2:42). Ultimately, the God of Judaeo-Christian revelation is one who calls forth a network of relationships, sealed in a covenant.

As we have noted, sound events like music are fundamentally unitive: uniting singer with the song, listener with the song, singer with the listener, the listener with other listeners, and even in a new way the listener with herself or himself. To be in the presence of a sound event is to be engaged in that sound event and to be engaged with those who produce the sound, as well as with the others who hear it. Sound events such as music, therefore, are strong metaphors for the God who calls us and for the network of relationships demanded by such a call.

The Judaeo-Christian God as Personal. Not only is the God of Judaeo-Christian revelation recognized as a power intervening in history and calling us into relationship, but more so is this God imaged as a person who intervenes on behalf of a beloved. Time and time again the Scriptures present to us a God imaged as mother (Is 66:13), lover (Wis 2:8), friend (Ti 3:4) and father (Lk 11:2). Not an impersonal natural power or some arbitrary force of fate, this is a personal God who loves.

Sound encounters, as noted above, are not simply experiences of something other, but of *another*. Sound encounters are keyed to personal encounters. They occur in the realm of acoustic space which is translated by the human imagination as an arena of personal presence. Thus the sound event by its very nature supports the revelation of a God who is perceived as a person. Music, in particular, is an infallible indicator of human presence since music, properly speaking, is a human creation that does not otherwise occur in nature.[218] Consequently music serves as a special sound metaphor for the unnameable God who chooses to reveal Self in personal terms.

---

217. Donald Grey, "A real Absence: A note on the Eucharist," *Living Bread, Saving Cup,* ed. R. Kevin Seasoltz (Collegeville: The Liturgical Press, 1982), 190–96.

218. Victor Zuckerkandl, *Man the Musician: Sound and Symbol,* 2 vols., trans. Norbert Guterman, Bollingen Series 44–2 (Princeton: Princeton University Press, 1973), 2:15.

Music as Revelatory in the Liturgical Event

We have indicated how sound, by its very nature, serves the revelation of God in the Judaeo-Christian tradition. Its temporality, seemingly insubstantial nature, dynamism, unitive properties, and evocation of the personal enable it to serve as a unique medium for communicating the presence of God. Sound phenomena are thus able to suggest presence without confinement, elicit wonder without distance, and enable union in a particular and unparalleled way.

Music as the most refined of all sound phenomena—especially as it unites to ritual—does even more in serving the revelation of the Judaeo-Christian God. We have noted above how music easily and consistently weds itself to the ritual moment. True in so many other religions, this is well attested throughout the history of Christianity. It is also true that in Christianity the liturgy is considered the church's first theology and the primary expression of the church's belief.[219] This concept was reaffirmed by the *Constitution on the Sacred Liturgy*, which called the church's worship, especially the eucharist, the fount and summit of the church's life (n. 10). Music wed to ritual so conceived thus places music's revelatory power at the very center of belief.

If sound, by its very nature, resonates with essential characteristics of the God of Judaeo-Christianity, and if liturgy, more than any other event, is the locus for encounter with and revelation of such a God, then it is eminently understandable why music, as the most refined of sound phenomena, weds itself so intimately to Christian liturgy. The combination of the two enables the possibility of encounter and revelation as no other combination of human artifacts and events.

The unparalleled power resulting from the wedding of lyricism and rite becomes even clearer when one reckons with the word-centered nature of Judaeo-Christian revelation and liturgy. The God of Abraham and of Jesus is not only perceived as a personal God, but a God who speaks and whose word is law and promise. Ultimately God's word is at the core of Judaeo-Christian revelation and is central to the worship in this tradition.

Like the word, music is a sound event. Unlike the word, however, music is a presentational and not a discursive symbol. Music is not capable of a fixed meaning and is celebrated for its "ambivalence of content." Consequently there is no inherent clash or contradiction of meanings when presentational symbol weds to discursive symbol, that is, when music

weds to texts. Rather, there is the possibility for new levels of meaning as the music heightens and interprets the text.

This natural alliance between text and tune is a further reason why one can speak of the integral relationship between music and Christian liturgy for, like no other art form, music has a special capacity to heighten and serve the word which occupies a central place in worship. Such an awareness was reflected in the *Constitution on the Sacred Liturgy*, which, when noting the integral relationship between music and liturgy, pointed in particular to the binding of sacred song and text as the main reason for this integrality (n. 112).

In summary, therefore, music can be considered as a necessary or integral element in the liturgy because it has the capacity to reveal central images of God and the community as well as to realize the implications of those images at the very heart of the church's liturgy. Thus music has rightly been called "a sounding image of the Wisdom of God." Furthermore, music has an unparalleled capacity to wed itself to that central element of the church's worship, the word. As it bonds with the word, music fulfills its proper ministerial function. Thus, as we noted earlier, Martin Luther could claim that "next to the Word of God, music deserves the highest praise."

The Sacramental Nature of Christian Ritual Music

Part of the confusion about how or why music is integral to Christian worship may, in part, be a result of the language of integrality. Although "integral" is a useful term, there is yet much ambiguity about the exact meaning of the phrase "music forms an integral part of the solemn liturgy." The *Constitution on the Sacred Liturgy offers* "necessary" [*necessariam*] as a synonym to "integral" [*integralem*]. This is probably an unfortunate interpolation into the document, because it gives the impression that music is indispensable in Christian worship. Many people's experience and significant scholarly opinion, however, disagree with that stance.[220] Rather than speaking of the integral nature of Christian ritual music, or

---

219. The *locus classicus* of this notion is the maxim of Prosper of Aquitaine, *legem credendi lex statuat suplicandi* (*Patrologia Latina* 51:209); for a further discussion of this concept see Paul De Clerck, "'Lex Orandi, Lex Credendi,' Sens originel et avatars historiques d'un adage èquivoque," *Questions liturgiques* 59 (1978) 193–212.

220. "In Christian liturgy, music is not indispensable, but its contribution is irreplaceable." *The Music of Christian Ritual: Universa Laus Guidelines 1980*, Conviction 21, as cited in *The Bulletin of Universa Laus* 30 (1980): 14.

its "holiness,"[221] it seems more appropriate to employ more traditional language, and speak about the sacramental nature of Christian ritual music.

Although the church limited the designation "sacrament" to seven particular rituals, under the influence of theologians such as Peter Lombard (+ 1160), originally the term sacrament was not so narrowly defined. Prior to developments in the twelfth and thirteenth centuries, sacrament was a rather elusive concept, easily predicated of a wide range of ecclesial arts and artifacts. Augustine, for example, listed over three hundred actions and/or objects as "sacraments."[222] By the high Middle Ages, however, the term sacrament was being restricted to those seven rites of the church thought to convey sanctifying grace *ex opere operato*. All other rites, not thought to convey sanctifying grace, were called "sacramentals"—a term coined by Peter Lombard.[223]

In some respects the current situation in sacramental theology is akin to that which prevailed before the work of Lombard when the church did not limit itself to a vocabulary of seven sacraments. Today scholars such as Otto Semmelroth, Edward Schillebeeckx, and Karl Rahner have helped to expand our sacramental horizons. They and others have assisted us in understanding that Christ is the primordial sacrament, and that the church is the abiding presence of that primordial sacrament in the world, and remains the source of all other sacraments. Such formulations are now part of mainstream Roman Catholic thought, embedded in the documents of the Second Vatican Council, which teaches that the church is the sacrament of Christ, who, in turn, is the source of every other sacrament.[224]

It is in this broadening theological context that it is possible and appropriate to assert the sacramental character of Christian ritual music. Schillebeeckx, for example, asserts that sacraments are

> . . . ecclesial acts of worship, in which the church in communion of grace with its heavenly head (i.e. together with Christ) pleads with the Father for the bestowal of grace on the recipient of the sacrament, and in which at the same time the church itself, as saving community in holy union with Christ, performs a saving act.[225]

As noted previously, music not only has the ability to wed itself to our ritual—to ecclesial acts of worship—but in some situations (i.e., our category "music alone") becomes itself the ecclesial act of worship. This is but the clearest example of Christian ritual music as sacrament, as ecclesial act of

worship in which the community is "graced" by the presence of Christ[226] and in which the church, in union with Christ, performs a saving act.

According to Rahner, sacrament in the strict sense occurs

> . . . when the church in her official, organized, public capacity precisely as the source of redemptive grace meets the individual in the actual ultimate accomplishment of her nature . . . [which] bring[s] into activity the very essence of the church herself.[227]

What more powerful means for the church in its "public capacity" to meet the individual than in ritual song? As previously noted, music by its very nature is a unitive event, uniting the singer with the song, and singers with each other. In Christian ritual song the unitive event weds assembly with the source and the content of the song, who is Christ.[228] The song of the assembly is so rich that, according to the *Constitution on the Sacred Liturgy*, it is an event of the presence of Christ. What fuller assertion could there be of the sacramental nature of Christian ritual music, especially the song of the assembly?

To assert the sacramentality of Christian ritual music is not to allege its superiority over other liturgical art forms, nor even to separate it from the other arts. Contrarily, to claim the sacramentality of Christian ritual music is to broaden the sacramental embrace beyond that allowed by the scholastic mind, so that it precisely might include the other liturgical arts. Ultimately, however, sacramental language should be employed for Christian ritual music because, more than any other language available to us, it effectively underscores and communicates music's power in worship.

---

221. In *Tra le sollecitudini* Pius X delineated three criteria for "sacred music," the first of which was that it must be holy (n. 2). Although the *Constitution on the Sacred Liturgy* reinterpreted holiness in terms of the function of the music in the ritual and not simply the music in and of itself, it continues to use the term: "sacred music will be the more holy the more closely it is joined to the liturgical rite" (n. 112).

222. For a discussion of the flexible meaning of sacrament in Augustine, . . . see C. Couturier, "'Sacramentum' et 'Mysterium' dans l'oeuvre de Saint Augustine," *Etudes augustiniennes* (Paris: Aubier, 1953), 161–301.

223. Lombard, *Sententiae* 4.6.8 (PL 192:855).

224. See the *Dogmatic Constitution on the Church*, nn. 1, 9, and 48.

225. Edward Schillebeeckx, *Christ the Sacrament of the Encounter with God* (New York: Sheed and Ward, 1963), 66.

226. The *Constitution on the Sacred Liturgy* unequivocally teaches that Christ is present when the Church sings (n. 7).

227. Karl Rahner, *The Church and the Sacraments,* Quaestiones Disputatae 9, trans. W. J. O'Hara (Freiburg im Br.: Herder, 1963), 22.

228. Clement of Alexandria, *Protreptikos*, I.6.5.

The term sacrament does not occur in the New Testament. Rather, *sacramentum* is the Latin translation for the New Testament term *musterion* or secret. St. Paul teaches that *musterion* is not simply an impenetrable divine secret, but a divine secret in the process of being revealed (1 Cor 2:10ff.). Music at the service of Christian ritual is one of the agents of that revelation. Not only does music assist in this revelatory process, but it contributes something to the revelation of God and the engagement of the community that no other human artifacts or art form achieves. Thus can we assert music's integral or sacramental role in Christian worship, and note in a new way its unique contribution to the liturgical event.

From Edward Foley, *Ritual Music* (Beltsville, MD: Pastoral Press, 1995), 117–23. [Ellipses and brackets in original.]

✎ The following hymns illustrate some of the varieties of style and subject matter that exist in Christian liturgical music. "Las Apariciones Guadalupanas" is a traditional Mexican song that embraces both religious devotion and ethnic identity. The German hymn "Silent Night" is a meditation on the nativity of Jesus that has been translated into over one hundred languages. "Go Down, Moses" is a traditional African American spiritual on the theme of the Israelites' enslavement in Egypt. "Jesu, Joy of Man's Desiring" and "O for a Thousand Tongues to Sing" are both hymns of praise. Finally, "Trusting Jesus" is a hymn of trust in the person of Jesus, who is at the center of Christian life.

"Las Apariciones Guadalupanas"

1. From heaven a beautiful morning, (*repeat*)
   the Guadalupana,
   the Guadalupana,
   the Guadalupana
   came down to the Tepeyac.[229] (*repeat*)

2. Imploring, with the hands together, (*repeat*)
   and they were Mexican,
   and they were Mexican,
   and they were Mexican
   her appearance and her face. (*repeat*)

3. Her arrival filled with happiness, (*repeat*)
   peace and harmony,
   peace and harmony,
   peace and harmony
   to all the Anáhuac.[230] (*repeat*)

4. Near the mountain Juan Diego was passing by, (*repeat*)
   he then got closer,
   and he then got closer,
   and he then got closer
   to hear the singing. (*repeat*)

5. "Dear Juan Diego," Our Lady told him, (*repeat*)
   "this hill I select,
   this hill I select,
   this hill I select
   to erect my altar." (*repeat*)

6. And on the poncho in between painted roses, (*repeat*)
   her beloved image,
   her beloved image,
   her beloved image
   she deigned to leave. (*repeat*)

7. It is since then that for the Mexican, (*repeat*)
   to be Guadalupano,
   to be Guadalupano,
   to be Guadalupano
   it is something essential. (*repeat*)

8. Beloved mother[231] of the Mexicans, (*repeat*)
   that you are in heaven,
   that you are in heaven,
   that you are in heaven
   pray for us to God. (*repeat*)

9. In his sorrows he [the Mexican] kneels down, (*repeat*)
   and raises his eyes,
   and raises his eyes,
   and raises his eyes
   toward the Tepeyac. (*repeat*)

Translated by Rosario Vivado-Millington from the Spanish text as in *Flor y Canto* (Portland, OR: OCP Publications, 2001), no. 453.

---

229. Tepeyac is a mountain in Mexico where legend places the Lady of Guadalupe's appearance to Juan Diego.

230. Anáhuac is a place inhabited by a group of natives known as the Anáhuac Indians that speak the Anáhuac language, one of the many different languages of Mexico.

231. The Spanish word *madrecita*, translated here as "mother," is used when directing one's prayers to the Virgin, Mother of God, regardless of what other name is given, e.g. Virgin del Carmen, Virgin del Perpetuo Socorro, etc.

WORDS BY JOSEF MOHR, MUSIC ASCRIBED TO FRANZ GRÜBER
"Silent Night"

Silent night, holy night,
All is calm, all is bright
Round yon virgin mother and child.
Holy infant, so tender and mild,
Sleep in heavenly peace.
Sleep in heavenly peace.

Silent night, holy night,
Shepards quake at the sight,
Glories stream from heaven afar,
Heavenly hosts sing Alleluia;
Christ, the Savior, is born!
Christ, the Savior is born!

Silent night, holy night,
Son of God, love's pure light
Radiant beams from thy holy face,
With the dawn of redeeming grace,
Jesus, Lord, at thy birth.
Jesus, Lord, at thy birth.

From *The Hymnal 1982* (New York: Church Hymnal Corp., 1985), no. 111.

"Go Down, Moses"

Go down, Moses,
Way down in Egypt Land,
Tell ole Pharaoh,
Let my people go.

When Israel was in Egypt Land,
Oppressed so hard they could not stand;
"Thus saith the Lord," bold Moses said,
If not I'll smite your first born dead;

"No more shall they in bondage toil,
Let them come out with Egypt's spoil."
When Israel out of Egypt came,
And left the proud oppressive land;
O, 'twas a dark and dismal night,
When Moses led the Israelites;
'Twas good old Moses and Aaron, too,
'Twas they that led the armies through;
The Lord told Moses what to do,

To lead the children of Israel through;
O come along Moses, you'll not get lost,
Stretch out your rod and come across;
As Israel stood by the water side,
At the command of God it did divide.
When they had reached the other shore,
They sang a song of triumph o'er;
Pharaoh said he would go across,
But Pharaoh and his host were lost;
O, Moses, the cloud shall cleave the way,
A fire by night, a shade by day;
You'll not get lost in the wilderness,
With a lighted candle in your breast;
Jordan shall stand up like a wall,
And the walls of Jericho shall fall,
Your foes shall not before you stand,
And you'll possess fair Canaan's land;
'Twas just about in harvest time,
When Joshua led his host divine.

O let us all from bondage flee,
And let us all in Christ be free;
We need not always weep and moan,
And wear these slavery chains forlorn;
This world's a wilderness of woe,
O, let us on to Canaan go;
What a beautiful morning that will be,
When time breaks up in eternity;
O bretheren, bretheren, you'd better be engaged,
For the Devil he's out on a big rampage;
The Devil he thought he had me fast,
But I thought I'd break his chains at last;
O take your shoes from off your feet,
And walk into the golden street;
I'll tell you what I likes the best,
It is the shouting Methodist;
I do believe without a doubt,
That a Christian has the right to shout.

Go down, Moses,
Way down in Egypt Land,
Tell ole Pharaoh,
Let my people go.

From Erskine Peters, ed., *Lyrics of the Afro-American Spiritual: A Documentary Collection* (Westport, CT: Greenwood Press, 1993), 166–67.

WORDS BY MARTIN JANUS, MUSIC BY JOHANN SCHOP, ARRANGED BY J. S. BACH

"Jesu, Joy of Man's Desiring"

Jesu, joy of man's desiring,
Holy wisdom, love most bright,
Drawn by Thee, our souls aspiring
Soar to uncreated light.

Word of God, our flesh that fashioned
With the fire of life impassioned,
Striving still to truth unknown
Soaring, dying round Thy throne.

Through the way where hope is guiding,
Hark, what peaceful music rings
Where the flock, in Thee confiding,
Drink of joy from deathless springs.

Theirs is beauty's fairest pleasure,
Theirs is wisdom's holiest treasure,
Thou dost ever lead Thine own
In the love of joys unknown.

From Carl F. Mueller, *Three-Part Anthem Book* (New York: Carl Fischer, 1951), 55–60.

CHARLES WESLEY

"O for a Thousand Tongues to Sing"

O for a thousand tongues to sing
My dear Redeemer's praise!
The glories of my God and King,
The triumphs of his grace!

My gracious Master, and my God,
Assist me to proclaim,
To spread through all the earth abroad
The honours of thy name.

Jesus, the name that charms our fears,
That bids our sorrows cease—
'Tis music in the sinner's ears,
'Tis life, and health, and peace.

He breaks the power of cancelled sin,
He sets the prisoner free;
His blood can make the foulest clean—
His blood availed for me.

Hear him, ye deaf; his praise, ye dumb,
Your loosened tongues employ;
Ye blind, behold your Saviour come,
And leap, ye lame, for joy!

Look unto him, ye nations, own
Your God, ye fallen race;
Look, and be saved through faith alone,
Be justified by grace!

See all your sins on Jesus laid:
The Lamb of God was slain,
His soul was once an offering made
For every soul of man.

Awake from guilty nature's sleep,
And Christ shall give you light,
Cast all your sins into the deep,
And wash the Ethiop white.

With me, your chief, ye then shall know,
Shall feel your sins forgiven;
Anticipate your heaven below,
And own that love is heaven.

From Franz Hildebrandt, ed., *The Works of John Wesley*, vol. 7, *A Collection of Hymns for the Use of the People Called Methodists* (Nashville, TN: Abingdon, 1983), 79–81.

WORDS BY EDGAR P. STITES, MUSIC BY IRA D. SANKEY

"Trusting Jesus"

1. Simply trusting every day,
   trusting through a stormy way,
   even when my faith is small,
   trusting Jesus—that is all.

2. Brightly doth his Spirit shine
   into this poor heart of mine;
   while he leads I cannot fall,
   trusting Jesus—that is all.

3. Singing if my way is clear,
   praying if the path be drear,
   if in danger, for him call,
   trusting Jesus—that is all.

4. Trusting him while life shall last,
   trusting him till earth be past,

till within the jasper wall,

trusting Jesus—that is all.

Refrain

Trusting as the moments fly,

trusting as the days go by,

trusting him whate'er befall,

trusting Jesus—that is all.

From Donald P. Hustad et al., eds., *The Worshiping Church: A Hymnal* (Carol Stream, IL: Hope Publishing Co., 1990), no. 526.

෧ In "Feminist Liturgy: Its Tasks and Principles," liturgical scholar **Janet Walton** explores the need for new Christian liturgies that celebrate women's rites of passage. She offers principles for creating and revising such liturgies.

JANET WALTON

"Feminist Liturgy: Its Tasks and Principles," in *Feminist Liturgy: A Matter of Justice*

The tasks and principles of feminist liturgy developed in this matrix of historical and social change. They are rooted in a dialogue between history and liturgy, that is, between the realities of history and the expectations and potential of liturgy. They express the webbing of awareness and hope.

Feminist liturgy seeks to engage imagination, resist discrimination, summon wonder, receive blessing, and strengthen hope. It intends to enact redeemed, free, and empowered relationships. Feminist liturgy builds on basic assumptions:

We come together to name what is "true" for us;

We invite one another to listen, speak, and act;

We know God as constant surprise, more than what we've been taught, more than we can imagine;

We use a variety of forms and resources, traditional and emerging;

We anticipate new awarenesses and change;

We resist whatever demeans or hurts;

We account to each other for what we do;

We struggle with differences;

We play as we pray;

We expect to embody justice for ourselves, our world, and God.

Our goal, as liturgical scholar Mary Collins states, is to "ritualize relationships that emancipate and empower women,"[232] and subsequently all those marginalized by class, race, differing abilities, sexual orientations, and age.

Because feminist liturgy began in the wake of the second phase of the women's movement, with an explicit scrutinizing of ways in which women fared in all aspects of society, we use the word "feminist" to describe it. Women's experiences are focal. They provide a critical lens to understand all kinds of exclusion and harm. Though a patriarchal perspective limited the participation of most people, it actually excluded *all* women. [. . .]

During the almost thirty years of the development of feminist liturgies women have learned that the changes we have incorporated into our ritualizing have radically altered what we expect from liturgical experiences. In the beginning we knew only that what we inherited was not true, that is, to know the revelation of God only through male experiences was not credible any longer. But we had no sense of what would emerge when we tried to broaden the spectrum of expression, that is, to do liturgy differently. Now we understand that when we listen to one another we can shape liturgical experiences that honor rather than demean, that correct what hurts, and that make consistent efforts to embody justice.

Our liturgies are not perfect; our learning continually evolves. A description of what we say about feminist liturgies will inevitably be incomplete because what we enact is shaped by changing lives. We are always practicing, a practicing Ronald Grimes defines as "the action of attending . . . . to what presents itself."[233] [. . .]

A. Honoring One Another and God

Fundamental to the understanding of feminist liturgy is a simple fact: since people are different, the naming and cherishing of our differences is essential in our liturgical experiences. For many centuries following dominant cultural norms, the language of liturgies did not take distinctions into account. Feminist liturgies seek to change this habit. Honoring various experiences recognizes more fully what each person knows about being human and about relating to God. When anyone is invisible, aspects of God, too, are also rendered invisible.

232. Mary Collins, "Principles of Feminist Liturgy," in *Women at Worship: Interpretations of North American Diversity*, ed. Marjorie Procter-Smith and Janet Roland Walton (Louisville: Westminster/John Knox Press, 1993), 9.

233. Ronald L. Grimes, *Marrying and Burying: Rites of Passage in a Man's Life* (Boulder, CO: Westview Press, 1995), 220.

Our liturgies rely on various languages: words, space, gestures, and sounds. What we say and read, whom and what we look at, and the ways in which we use our bodies; all of these factors communicate what we believe and influence how we act. Verbal language, especially the predominance of male imagery, offered one of the first clues to many of us that something was wrong with our institutional liturgies. Many resources have become available that offer informed, detailed discussions about the languages of liturgies, their problems and their possibilities. Because changing long-established traditions of language requires care, respect, and in the end, movement into uncharted paths, study and conversation are essential to our attempts to right this wrong. Listed below are some examples of what we discovered when we began to shape feminist liturgies. These samples will inevitably suggest others.

1. Words

When we name ourselves precisely as women, girls, sisters, and daughters, several experiences happen at the same time. We think about what these particular relationships mean to us. We are not sons, brothers, men, or boys, though for many years, by reason of male power and preference, we've heard ourselves described as such. We are daughters, sisters, girls, females with quite distinctive experiences socially, physically, and relationally. These differences matter. As we talk about these experiences, we begin not only to claim our distinctions as females, but also to respect and enjoy them. With respect comes power, both personal and collective. We have the strength to act from what we know: to seek what energizes us and to say no to anything that diminishes or hurts us. This kind of authority is what we expect to provide one another in feminist liturgies.

No longer can we accept words about our identity as females that are subsumed in male terms such as mankind, man, sons, or brothers. Males and females share humanness. Together we constitute the human species. Male terms for males and females are confusing and demeaning. Lexicographer Alma Graham puts it this way:

> If a woman is swept into the water, the cry is "man overboard." If she is killed by a hit-and-run driver, the charge is "manslaughter." If she is injured on the job, the coverage is "workmen's compensation." But if she arrives at a threshold marked "Men Only," she knows the admonition is not intended to bar animals or plants or inanimate objects. It is meant for her.[234]

Feminist liturgies expect accuracy. They reject words that support deception and distortion and violence. "Man" is no less partial than "woman," just as clearly as "white" is no less partial than "black" or "brown," "red" or "yellow." Naming females precisely is critical to reversing dishonesty. It is just one step toward honoring females, no doubt, but it also protects all of us from recurring harm. No one can presume power over women; nor are females required to give it. Precision in naming speeds a process of truth telling and faithful relationships. It is an act of justice.

Another example of inaccuracy that leads to discrimination is color-coded language. The common use of the color "black" to describe or refer to what is bad or evil supports fear and suspiciousness of black people. In a racist society, color-coded language promotes a bias that black people are evil, more prone to violence and sin than whites. We honor one another when we stop using any words that vilify one another.

In a similar way, language that connects able-bodied people to goodness and disabled people to sin (I am blind, but now I see) dishonors. As Valerie Stiteler points out, "As long as images of body disability [blindness, deafness, lameness] are used negatively . . . few of the disabled . . . can participate fully in worship or receive the salvation offered to all humans."[235]

Words that categorize people dehumanize them as well. One such example is references to people by adjectives without nouns. I refer to expressions like "the poor," "the homeless," "the blind." We are speaking about *people in our midst* for whom we are all accountable. They are poor people, homeless people, people who are blind. They are women, men, and children—not a lump of unknown, general convenient groupings of marginalized beings. No one is less human for being sense-impaired or out of luck.

Age is also a stereotypical cause of discrimination in our culture. The young and the old are the primary victims. Teenagers are seen as rude and cynical and old or retired people are perceived to be out of step. Institutional liturgies rarely use emerging or ancient metaphors that express the wisdom of varying ages, e.g., "crone" to evoke the wisdom of aging women. Feminist liturgies seek to counter cultural presuppositions about age.

234. Alma Graham as cited in Casey Miller and Kate Swift, *Words and Women: New Language in New Times* (Garden City: Anchor Books, 1977), 25.

235. Valerie C. Jones Stiteler, "Singing without a Voice: Using Disability Images in the Language of Public Worship," in *The Anna Howard Shaw Center Newsletter* 8:1 (Fall 1991).

Finally, feminist liturgies challenge words and practices that dishonor God. There is always a danger of making God what we want rather than accepting what God is. We know God as ever more than we can conceive. Feminist liturgies attempt to guard against limiting God to what we want, whether it be part of a long-accepted tradition or what we desire to be "right." We hope to avoid measuring ourselves against an image of our own making. "All images are necessarily partial," writes Marcia Falk, "the authentic expression of a monotheism is not a singularity of image but an embracing unity of a multiplicity of images, as many as are needed to express and reflect the diversity of our individual lives."[236] Not even names we have used for thousands of years can possibly convey the total reality of God. To believe otherwise is idolatrous. A continual process of naming God seems more consistent with an ever-revealing God than a tendency to employ only a few traditional names of the divine. Feminist liturgies aspire to act on this premise.

Naming what we know or are coming to know about God is a critical part of the process of feminist liturgy. As Marjorie Procter-Smith points out, naming God is "urgent and primary because liturgy is not reflection but address; an encounter is presumed."[237] Feminist liturgy is more than talk; it is enacting relationships that promote justice among us and beyond us. When we meet we call out to each other and to God; we expect to show God to each other. Liturgy is a "showing of a doing,"[238] an action in which we try to "be" what we do. As such it requires constant examination and experimentation.

2. Space: Objects and Arrangements

Not only our words but also what we see matters in the performance of feminist liturgies. Because women regularly gather in each other's homes, in places that women often have some part in designing, we noticed immediately that we enjoyed this new (but, in reality, ancient) environment for our liturgies. In a place decorated with things we cherish, objects that encourage our memories, pictures of families and friends who are our forebears, symbols that evoke all kinds of stories, we knew quickly how important the physical space was in our gatherings.

This recognition leads to wondrous care about the environment of liturgy. As in our homes, in our feminist liturgies we want our space to be evocative, honest, connected to our everyday lives, all its heartaches, terrors, and accomplishments; as well as what we yearn to know and be. In planning our liturgies we intentionally gather whatever we need to meet this goal, whether it be pictures, objects, or traditional liturgical symbols such as water, candles, oil, or food.

Some things are used once; others reappear regularly. Each time we expect the symbols to disclose layer upon layer of meanings, e.g., a wreath of unadorned boughs may remind us primarily about the dying of life at one liturgy, and, at another time, the same wreath, decorated differently with bright colors or unfolding buds, may accent the living of life. We explore multiple aspects of the objects we use with the intention of knowing, and sometimes being surprised by, their fresh connections.

Because we know that part of any dynamic relationship is to uncover more and more about the "other" we experiment with images of God, too. We learn from trying: making new pictures or shapes, using found objects in original arrangements, uncovering nuances in traditional visualizations, and most of all, from listening to each other, hearing about images that make connections with what is ultimately holy. Though we certainly know we cannot contain the essence of God with any real accuracy, we do know we can deepen our own relationships through a never-ending process of imagining.

Objects are one aspect of the environment, while another is the arrangement of ourselves in the space. Most often we try to arrange the furniture so that we can be near each other. All of us are primary visible agents of each other's freedom and development. We are all images of God. We do not want to look away from each other nor establish great distances from each other. Though there are leaders who volunteer to prepare and guide each liturgy, the arrangement of the space does not privilege any person over another as if any person has an edge on holiness, God, or special knowing. The arrangement of space is the first invitation in liturgies. Too often it separates us rather than unites us. We recognize its power to transform our work together.

---

236. Marcia Falk, "Notes on Composing New Blessings: Toward a Feminist Jewish Reconstruction of Prayer," in *The Journal of Feminist Studies in Religion* 3:1 (Spring 1987): 41.

237. Marjorie Procter-Smith, *In Her Own Rite: Constructing Feminist Liturgical Tradition* (Nashville: Abingdon, 1990), 88.

238. Tom F. Driver develops this concept amply and compellingly in his book, *Liberating Rites: Understanding the Transformative Power of Ritual* (Boulder, CO: Westview Press, 1998).

3. Gestures[239]

Horizontal gestures prevail in feminist liturgies; they suggest equality and interdependence; they affirm God known among us. Generally we do not look up to find God. We connect with each other to give and receive blessings.

We pray with our eyes open and without bowing our heads. Not that we do not acknowledge God's authority, but we know God does not require bowing our heads and closing our eyes. Bowing our heads for a blessing, as Marjorie Procter-Smith points out, is a "non-reciprocal action"[240] related to experiences that remind us of male domination. It signals an inferior social status that has not promoted women's well-being. Closing one's eyes is dangerous in an unjust society. Though we presume we are safe in our gatherings, we do not repeat actions that have historically limited, demeaned, or hurt us.

Kneeling poses problems, too. We recognize its value to remind us of reverence for God and one another, but when women kneel to receive Communion or a blessing from men, rather than promoting an experience of reverence, it can be a reminder of sexual violation or subservience. Since women are frequently victims of violence at the hands of men, we practice standing and sitting rather than kneeling. We want to remind ourselves every time we can that sexual violence is rooted in misplaced power, that is, when anyone presumes power over another. Feminist liturgies intend to provide occasions to practice gestures of resistance and expressions of shared power.

4. Sounds

No particular sounds characterize feminist liturgies, but some guidelines frame our choices. We search for music that has been forgotten, composers or performers made invisible throughout history because of their marginalization. We consciously include music of many styles, such as drumming, chanting, wailing, rapping, as well as a variety of instruments, especially percussion. We reject songs with texts or tunes that limit or demean anyone; we rewrite words to familiar, well-known, or well-loved melodies; and sometimes, we commission new songs to meet particular needs.

5. Movement

Whereas in many institutional liturgies we limit our movements to processions or changing our postures, in feminist liturgies we make conscious efforts to engage the resources of our bodies more fully. Though we may be self-conscious and awkward, we dance, we move together, we touch each other in actions of solidarity, play, and blessing. We value the revelations of our bodies along a wide spectrum of abilities and disabilities.

The first phase of the tasks and principles of feminist liturgies, honoring God, ourselves, one another, and other-kind, involved naming what was inaccurate, distinguishing what was true, believing what we learned, and resisting naysayers. The next phase required correction. Honoring and correcting are inextricably intertwined. [. . .]

C. Doing Liturgy Differently

Since we come together to invite each other to listen, to speak, and to act, feminist liturgies require participation that is reciprocal, accountable, and relational. Every person contributes to the action, though in different proportions at different times, but each shares some responsibility for what happens. No one embodies God's invitation to us more than any other. Every person counts.

1. Feminist Participation Is Reciprocal

Whereas in a patriarchal ritual one or a few men traditionally mediate power to and from God and to and from the people, feminist ritualizing eliminates the impression that there is an elite group on whom divine power and presence depends. Not that feminist liturgies exclude ordained leaders, but they do presume that each person is needed, ordained or not. The whole community draws out the interaction with each other and with God. Leadership is reordered as collective authority, and power is imaged in new ways.

The primary task of leaders in feminist liturgies is to set a context in which everyone can participate, to provide opportunities for a variety of kinds of participation. The goal is a spirit of celebration in which each person knows that she or he depends on another, learns from another, and evokes the other. All kinds of expertise are needed and welcome.

---

239. Much of what is included here is from an important article by Marjorie Procter-Smith, "Reorganizing Victimization: The Intersection between Liturgy and Domestic Violence," in *The Perkins Journal* (October 1987): 17–27.

240. Procter-Smith (1987), 25.

2. Feminist Participation Is Accountable

Closely related to reciprocity is accountability. It is not enough to participate actively when it feels good or is convenient. At the heart of feminist liturgies is *collective* work. They require being there for each other, in good times and bad. They presume that we listen, speak, and act. But, they do not presume we will always "get it right." In order to avoid the mistake of continuing what has always been done because it is familiar and comfortable, at the center of our commitment to feminist liturgies is both experimentation and regular critique. What does not work is not repeated.

3. Feminist Participation Is Relational

Feminist liturgy seeks to summarize the discoveries reported in this section. It intends "to actualize redeemed and redeeming relationships that allow women [and all marginalized people] to claim their full power as human persons."[241] To ensure empowered relationships in a culture that resists change, Mary Collins suggests four moments in a process:

> *suspicion* in approaching all cultural materials, especially those considered to be a particular culture's highest achievements, *retrieval* of aspects of women's cultural experience of all kinds of significant relationships, *affirmation* of what has been retrieved both of women's achievements and stories of women's suffering exacted as the price of maintaining patriarchal relationships, and *introducing a future* that affirms the full humanity of women and the value and truth of their achievements.[242]

Ultimately, feminist liturgy is about making available for one another an embodied vision of relationships rooted in valuing each person, drawing collective strength from each other and from the presence and promises of the Holy One. This vision expands regularly because feminist liturgy is organic, that is, it continually evolves around data from our lives. As our lives change so, too, do the content and form of our liturgies. Texts are not read because they are assigned or because an authority outside our own requires it. Likewise nothing is eliminated merely because it is part of a long tradition. Something is read because it is assumed there will be a connection with the ways we live and die. Something is heard with the hope that it will evoke a fresh insight or a powerful memory. Something is done as fuel for an act of resistance for what we do beyond the ritual space. Every component

of the liturgy is evaluated from this perspective. The way we live and die is inextricably connected to an understanding of an unpredictable transcendent being, one who is known intimately and expected to be revealed in our midst.

Feminist liturgies and perspectives span a wide spectrum of expressions, but they are all about inviting and receiving one another as images of God. In these interactions a new vision emerges, not a perfect one, not a whole one, but rather one that we can use for a while as an alternative to an outmoded vision that has excluded marginalized persons, especially all women.

From Janet Walton, *Feminist Liturgy: A Matter of Justice* (Collegeville, MN: Liturgical Press, 2000), 31–39, 45–47. [Ellipses and brackets, except bracketed ellipses, in original.]

☙ "The Drama of Guadalupe" is the account of the appearances of Our Lady of Tepeyac to Juan Diego. Mary, the mother of Jesus, charges Juan Diego, an Amerindian, to go to the local bishop to demand that he build a church in her honor so that she can show her compassion and mercy by helping the Mexican people. This account by **Juan Diego** and **Antonio Valeriano** is drawn from the earliest documents recording these appearances, which were removed from Mexico and brought to the United States in 1847, during the Mexican War.

JUAN DIEGO AND ANTONIO VALERIANO
"The Drama of Guadalupe"

On Saturday, December 9, 1531, early in the morning, Juan Diego, a Christian Indian of middle age, was on his way to participate in early Mass at Tlatelolco. Juan heard very beautiful music. He believed that he was either dreaming or in paradise.

He stopped, looked around, and tried to discover where the music came from. He heard a soft voice saying: "Juanito, Juan Dieguito." Without even noticing what he was doing, he began walking towards the direction of the call.

When he came to the top of the hill, he saw a lady of glowing beauty. Her dress radiated like the sun and her face had an expression of love and compassion. She said to him:

---

241. Mary Collins, in Procter-Smith and Walton, eds., *Women at Worship: Interpretations of North American Diversity* (Louisville: Westminster/John Knox Press, 1993), 11.

242. Collins, in Procter-Smith and Walton, 12.

"Juanito, the smallest of my children, where are you going?" He responded, "My dear child, I have to go to your house of Mexico, Tlatelolco, to hear about the divine things which are given and taught to us by our priests, the delegates of Our Lord."

She then spoke to him and made known her will: "Know and understand, you the dearest of my children, that I am the ever holy Virgin Mary, Mother of the true God through whom one lives, of the Creator of heaven and of earth.

"I have a living desire that there be built a temple, so that in it I can show and give forth all my love, compassion, help, and defense, because I am your loving mother: to you, to all who are with you, to all the inhabitants of this land, and to all who love me, call upon me, and trust in me. I will hear their lamentations and will remedy all their miseries, pains, and sufferings.

"In order to bring about what my mercy intends, *go to the palace of the bishop and tell him how I have sent* you to manifest to him what I very much desire, that here on this site below the hill, a temple be built to me." Immediately, he made an inclination, and said to her: "My Lady, I am already on the way to fulfill your mandate."

Juan Diego went quickly to the palace of the bishop. After a long wait, he was able to see the bishop and gave him the message of the Lady. The bishop was kind to him, but told him to return on another day when he could slowly hear his entire story from beginning to end. Juan Diego left in great sadness because he had failed in his mission.

He went directly on to the top of the hill where he had spoken with the Lady, and seeing her, said: "My dear child, I went where you sent me to fulfill your mandate. It was with great difficulty that I entered the room of the bishop. I gave him your message, just as you had told me to do. He received me kindly and he heard me attentively, but he did not believe as true what I told him. He told me to come again and he would hear me out slowly. My dear Lady, I understood perfectly well in the way in which he responded that he believes that perhaps it is an invention of mine that you want them to build you a temple here. Thus, I beg you entrust your mission to one of the important persons who is well known, respected, and esteemed so that they may believe him. You know that I am a nobody, a nothing, a coward, a pile of old sticks, just like a bunch of leaves. I am nothing. You have sent me to walk in places where I do not belong. Forgive me and please do not be angry with me, my lady and mistress."

The Lady answered him: "Listen, my son, the smallest of my children, I want you to understand that I have many ser-vants and messengers to whom I can entrust this message, but in every aspect it is precisely my desire that you seek help so that with your mediation, my wish will be fulfilled. I beg you with great insistence, my son, the smallest of my children, and I sternly command you, once again, to go tomorrow to see the bishop. Greet him in my name and make known my will to him, that he has to begin work on the temple which I am asking for. And once again tell him that I personally, the ever holy Virgin Mary, Mother of God, sends you."

Juan Diego responded: "My dear Lady, I will gladly go to fulfill your mandate. I will go to do your will. They probably won't listen to me, or if they listen, they will probably not believe me. But in any case, I will return tomorrow afternoon to report to you."

The next day he went from his home to Tlatelolco to the palace of the bishop. Once again it was with great difficulty that he was able to gain an audience with the bishop. This time the bishop asked him many questions—where he saw her, what did she look like, etc., but he answered the bishop perfectly. He explained with the greatest precision about her figure and everything which he had admired; nevertheless, the bishop did not believe him and told him that his word was not sufficient evidence, that he needed some sign to believe that it was truly the heavenly Lady who was sending him.

Without hesitation, Juan Diego responded: "Tell me what is the sign that you are asking for so that I may go and ask the Lady for it."

The bishop, seeing that he was not disturbed in the slightest, and that he did not change his story in any way, dismissed him, but he immediately sent some of his household to follow him to see where he was going and whom he was speaking with. They started out after him. He went directly to the hill of Tepeyac but when he arrived, they lost track of him. They tried to find him, but they could not and returned to the bishop tired and angered. They begged the bishop not to believe him because he was obviously just inventing the stories.

In the meantime, Juan Diego was already with the Virgin telling her the response of the bishop. Having heard the response, the Lady said to him, "Very well, my son, you will return here tomorrow so that you may take to the bishop the sign which he has asked for. With that, he will believe you and will have no further doubts; and know well, my beloved son, that I will repay you for your care, work, and fatigue which you have done on my account. Go and I will await you here tomorrow."

The next day, when Juan Diego was supposed to take the sign so that he might be believed, he did not return. When he had arrived home the previous day, he had discovered his uncle, Juan Bernardino, gravely ill. Juan Diego spent the day searching for a medical person to assist his uncle. Having failed to do so, he promised his uncle that early in the morning he would go to Tlatelolco to call one of the priests to confess him and prepare him for death, because it was evident that it was time for him to die and that he would not get up from his bed to regain his health.

Very early on the morning of Tuesday, December 12, 1531, Juan Diego rushed to Tlatelolco to get the priest. When he came near the hill of Tepeyac, he thought to himself that it was better not to stop because the Lady might see him and stop him. He did not want to displease her, but he did have to rush to get the priest for his dying uncle. As he was going by the other side of the hill, in order to avoid her, he saw the Lady coming down from the top of the hill, and coming to him, said: "What's happening, my son, the smallest of my children? Where are you going?"

He became very embarrassed and, greeting her, said: "My dear Lady, I hope you are happy; I am going to cause you some affliction. I want you to know that my uncle is ready to die. Now I am rushing to your house in Mexico to call one of the beloved priests of our Lord to go and confess him and prepare him for death. As soon as I have taken care of this, I will return here so that I may take your message. Forgive me, I am not lying to you. I will come first thing tomorrow."

The Virgin answered him, "Hear me, my son, that which scares you and causes you anguish is nothing; do not let your heart be troubled, do not be afraid of that sickness. Am I not here who am your Mother? Your uncle will not die of this sickness; be assured that he is healthy." Juan was greatly consoled and was very happy. Then the Virgin told him to go to the top of the hill where he would find various flowers. She told him to cut and gather the flowers and bring them to her. He obeyed immediately and when he arrived at the top, he was astounded to discover numerous exquisite roses from Castile, especially since it was long before their normal time. They had a beautiful aroma and were covered with the morning dew. He immediately began to cut them and returned to the Lady with the roses. She took them into her hands and rearranged them in his tilma. She then said, "My son, the smallest of my children, this diversity of roses is the proof and sign that you will take to the bishop. You will tell him in my name that he is to see my will in this and he must fulfill it. You are my ambassador and most worthy of trust. I rigorously command you to unfold your mantle only in the presence of the bishop and to show him what you have with you. You are to tell everything. You will say that I told you to go to the top of the hill to cut the flowers, and tell everything that you saw and admired, so that you may convince the prelate to give his help in building the temple that I have asked for."

Immediately after receiving his instructions from the Lady, he set out without haste to the house of the bishop. He was happy and had no doubt that this time he would be believed.

When he arrived at the palace of the bishop, the servants of the bishop came out to see him. He begged them to please tell the bishop that he had to see him, but none of them wanted to listen to him. They acted as if he were not around. But seeing that he would not go away, that he simply stayed patiently in his place, the servants decided that they had better inform the bishop. Soon the strong aroma of the roses began to spread and the servants also were able to get a few glimpses of what he had with him. They were surprised to see roses of various kinds and of great beauty, and at first tried to take them from him, but he held on all the more. They finally went to tell the bishop what they had seen and that it would be good to see the Indian.

The bishop became very excited, for he sensed that this was the sign that he had been asking for. He immediately asked for Juan Diego to be shown into his study. As soon as Juan Diego came in, he made his reverence to the bishop and began to tell him once again everything that he had seen and admired and also the message of the Lady. He said: "Sir, I did what you ordered me to do, to go and tell my Lady, the Lady of Heaven, Holy Mary, precious mother of God, that you asked for a sign in order to believe me, that you are to build a temple on the site that she is asking for. Furthermore, I told her that I had given you my word that I would bring you a sign and proof of her will. She accepted your request and kindly produced what you asked for, a sign and proof so that her will may be fulfilled."

"Today, very early in the morning, she once again ordered me to come and see you. I asked her for the sign so that you might believe me, as she had told me that she would do. And at that moment she produced the sign. She sent me to the top of the hill, where I had seen her before, to cut the roses from Castile. After I had cut them, I came back down to the bottom of the hill where she took them into her hands, rearranged them, and put them into my mantle so that I might personally bring them to you."

"Even though I was well aware that the top of the hill was no place for flowers, because there are only cactus, mesquites, and other kinds of wild brush, I did not doubt. When I went to the top of the hill, I saw that I was in paradise with all the varieties of roses of Castile, shining with the morning dew. She told me why I was to give them to you. That is what I am doing now so that in them you may see the sign which you have asked for and thus you will fulfill her will; also that the truthfulness of my word may be evident. Here they are, accept them."

As he unfolded his tilma, all the roses dropped to the floor and as they did the precious image of the always holy Virgin Mary, Mother of God, appeared on the tilma in the presence of the bishop and his household, the image, which has defied time and scientists, and appears just as beautiful today as on December 12, 1531. The same tilma is in the temple built in her honor on Tepeyac, called Guadalupe. As she appeared in their presence on the tilma, they were amazed and fell to their knees. They greatly admired the image and showed by their actions that they truly saw her in their minds and in their hearts.

From Virgil Elizondo, *La Morenita: Evangelizer of the Americas* (San Antonio, TX: Mexican American Cultural Center, 1980), 75–81.

✎ Vodou, a Haitian religion, is a blend of Roman Catholicism and several African faith traditions. Sociologist of religion **Karen McCarthy Brown** explores some of the characteristics of Vodou in *Mama Lola: A Vodou Priestess in Brooklyn*.

KAREN MCCARTHY BROWN

Introduction to *Mama Lola: A Vodou Priestess in Brooklyn*

Moments later, standing in the makeshift living room outside the door of her altar room (a door which remained resolutely closed on that initial visit), I got my first good look at a person who was to be central in my life for years to come. Alourdes, who also responds to the nickname Lola or Mama Lola, is a big woman—not tall, but round and solid. That day she wore a loose, sleeveless cotton housecoat. Her hair was covered by a scarf knotted tightly around her head. Floppy bedroom slippers revealed swollen feet and ankles. Even though Alourdes was then in her mid-forties, her skin looked as fresh and smooth as a child's. Yet she seemed like anything but a child to me; in fact, she made me quite uncomfortable. The fluorescent light in the basement accentuated the

broad fleshy planes of her face and exaggerated the expression she wore, one I interpreted as either anger or fatigue. I quickly decided we were intruding. "Perhaps we could come back another time," I said, smiling politely at Alourdes while nudging Theodore back toward the stairs.

Alourdes looked confused. "You don't want no coffee? Theodore is my friend. Long time I don't see him. Long time. You going make him go before we even got a chance to talk? Ehhh? Theodore like my child! Even I don't see him, I know he thinking about me. Right, Theodore?" Breaking into a dazzling smile, she enfolded Theodore in her enormous arms, and the two of them did a little dance round and round to the music of their mutual laughter. The thick body was suddenly light and graceful; the sullen face warm, even beautiful. I have come to accept these mercurial changes in Alourdes, and sometimes I enjoy them. But I never know what I will find when I visit her, and I still feel vaguely guilty when she is in one of her dour moods. The observation of an anthropologist friend helped: "That look," she remarked after a joint visit some months later, "is the psychic's torpor."

I went back to see Alourdes several times before the project for the Brooklyn Museum was completed. She finally let me photograph her amazing altars: crowded tabletops with tiny flickering flames; stones sitting in oil baths; a crucifix; murky bottles of roots and herbs steeped in alcohol; shiny new bottles of rum, scotch, gin, perfume, and almond-sugar syrup. On one side was an altar arranged in three steps and covered in gold and black contact paper. On the top step an open pack of filterless Pall Malls lay next to a cracked and dusty candle in the shape of a skull. A walking stick with its head carved to depict a huge erect penis leaned against the wall beside it. On the opposite side of the room was a small cabinet, its top littered with vials of powders and herbs. On the ceiling and walls of the room were baskets, bunches of leaves hung to dry, and smoke-darkened color lithographs of the saints.

The lithographs included several different images of the Virgin Mary and one each of Saint Patrick with snakes at his feet; Saint Gerard contemplating a skull; Saint James, the crusader on his rearing horse; and Saint Isidore, the pilgrim kneeling to pray by a freshly plowed field. These I recognized as images of the Vodou spirits. Each of these spirits has both a Catholic and an African name: Mary is Ezili, the Vodou love spirit; Saint Patrick is the serpent spirit, Danbala; Saint Gerard is Gede, master of the cemetery; Saint James is the warrior Ogou; and Isidore is the peasant farmer Azaka. Vodou, the new religion that emerged from the social chaos and agony of Haiti's eighteenth-century slave plantations, blended several distinct African religions with French colonial Catholicism. Dozens of the resulting Vodou-Catholic spirits continue to thrive in the twentieth century, where they reign over one or another troublesome area of human endeavor and act as mediators between God (Bondye) and "the living."

In this altar room, Alourdes practices a healing craft that has been passed down through at least three generations of her family. She is a priestess (manbo) in the Haitian Vodou tradition. As such, she is not unique or even rare. Rather, she is one of hundreds of similar professionals who minister to the approximately 450,000 Haitian immigrants living in New York City.

Many other Vodou leaders—mostly men—operate on a much grander scale. For example, I know a priest (oungan) who rents the basement of a large apartment house on one of the main arteries in Brooklyn, where he stages dancing and drumming events attended by two to three hundred people. In contrast, Alourdes, like the great majority of Haitian healers in New York, works in her home. Much of her time is spent consulting with clients, one or two at a time, and the spirit feasts she holds several times a year rarely draw more than thirty people. She does not usually have drummers; they are expensive, and, more to the point, she does not want to attract the attention of her neighbors. Given the negative image Vodou has in the United States, many devotees prefer that their Vodou "families" operate on a small scale.

Alourdes does have an enviable reputation, however. She has a group of steady followers who appreciate her for being trustworthy and discreet as well as effective. It is also widely known that she adheres to a tradition that discourages making large profits from healing work. Her reputation, spread by word of mouth, has led to invitations to perform "treatments" throughout the eastern United States and Canada and in several places in the Caribbean and Central America. In these respects, there are not many like Mama Lola.

Healing is at the heart of the religions that African slaves bequeathed to their descendants, and Alourdes's Vodou practice is no exception. She deals both with health problems and with a full range of love, work, and family difficulties. Like healers in related traditions found throughout the Caribbean and South America, Alourdes combines the skills of a medical doctor, a psychotherapist, a social worker, and a priest.

It can be argued that Haitians are more religious than people from many of the other former slave colonies and also that Haitian Vodou is closer to its African roots than most other forms of New World African religion. Vodou's closer ties to its African origins are primarily a result of Haiti's virtual isolation from the rest of the world for nearly a century following its successful slave revolution (1791–1804). The strength of religious belief in Haiti can be accounted for, in part, by the poverty and political oppression that have characterized life for most Haitians from independence to the present. Haiti is currently the poorest country in the Western Hemisphere, a country whose inhabitants are beset by disease and malnutrition. The wonder of Haiti is that its people seem to have responded to suffering throughout history by augmenting their stores of aesthetic and spiritual riches.

A well-worn joke claims, with some truth, that of Haiti's six million people 85 percent are Catholic, 15 percent are Protestant, and 100 percent serve the Vodou spirits. Among Haitians living in the United States, the few who have made a place for themselves in the middle class have tended to leave Vodou behind—except in times of crisis. But the vast majority of Haitian immigrants are poor, and these people maintain the habit of turning to healers like Alourdes for help with their stressful lives.

Half a dozen times a year, on or around the saints' days set by the Catholic calendar, Alourdes holds "birthday parties" for her favored spirits, or lwa, as they are also called. Clients, friends, and relatives gather around a decorated "niche," whose center-piece is a table laden with food. Here they pray, clap, and sing until the crowd is sufficiently "heated up" to entice a Vodou spirit to join the party, to "ride" Alourdes. In a trance state from which she will later emerge with little or no memory of what has transpired, her body becomes the "horse" of the spirit, her voice the spirit's voice, her words and behavior those of the spirit.

These possession-performances, which blend pro forma actions and attitudes with those responsive to the immediate situation, are the heart of a Vodou ceremony.[243] The spirits talk with the faithful. They hug them, hold them, feed them, chastise them. Group and individual problems are aired through interaction with the spirits. Strife is healed and misunderstanding rectified. At these ceremonies, crucial community bonds are reinforced through the process of giving gifts of food and entertainment to the Vodou spirits.

Haitians, like their African forebears, operate from understandings of the divine and the virtuous that are markedly

---

243. I use the term "possession-performance" not to indicate that possession is playacting but to emphasize the theatrical quality of visits from the Vodou spirits.

different from those of mainstream Catholicism. Bondye does not get involved in the personal, day-to-day affairs of human beings. "He is too busy," Alourdes told me. Instead, it is the spirits and the ancestors—neither properly referred to as gods—who handle day-to-day problems and who, if necessary, mediate between the living and God.

Although the *lwa* who possess Alourdes are often called *sen-yo* (saints), they are not saintly types in the traditional Christian sense. For example, in stories about the soldier spirit Ogou/Saint James, he not only liberates his people but also betrays them. Ezili Dantò/Mater Salvatoris, the mother, cradles and cares for her children but also sometimes lashes out at them in rage. The Vodou spirits are not models of the well-lived life; rather, they mirror the full range of possibilities inherent in the particular slice of life over which they preside. Failure to understand this has led observers to portray the Vodou spirits as demonic or even to conclude that Vodou is a religion without morality—a serious misconception.

Vodou spirits are larger than life but not other than life. Virtue for both the *lwa* and those who serve them is less an inherent character trait than a dynamic state of being that demands ongoing attention and care. Virtue is achieved by maintaining responsible relationships, relationships characterized by appropriate gifts of tangibles (food, shelter, money) and intangibles (respect, deference, love). When things go as they should, these gifts flow in continuous, interconnected circles among the living and between the living and the spirits or ancestors. In the ongoing cycle of prestation and counter-prestation, each gives and receives in ways appropriate to his or her place in the social hierarchy—an overarching, relentless hierarchy that exempts neither the young child nor the most aged and austere spirit. Moral persons are thus those who give what they should, as defined by who they are.

From Karen McCarthy Brown, *Mama Lola: A Vodou Priestess in Brooklyn* (Berkeley and Los Angeles: University of California Press, 1991), 2–7.

※

8. ART AND ARCHITECTURE

❧ In "Christian Building prior to Constantine" and in "Constantinian Church Building," **Richard Krautheimer** (1897–1994) describes the meeting places of Christian communities in the first three centuries CE. He charts the progression from house churches and underground oratories to public basilicas.

RICHARD KRAUTHEIMER

Early Christian and Byzantine Architecture

Christian Building prior to Constantine

AD 50–150

During the first three centuries of the Christian era, two elements determine the position of Christianity: that it evolved a new faith, and that it did so primarily within the social, cultural, and religious framework of the Late Roman Empire. Christianity's organization, its needs, and even its conflicts with Rome were largely determined by conformity with or by opposition to this framework; and its architecture, as far as we know it, must be seen within the context of the Roman-Hellenistic world.[244]

Religion in Imperial Rome had split into two spheres.

Public worship of the gods that guaranteed the welfare of the Empire—Jupiter, the Invincible Sun, or the Emperor's Divine Majesty—was a civic duty performed according to state ritual; worship was required only of those in the sphere or under the scrutiny of officialdom. Spiritual needs were satisfied by divinities of one's personal choice: either native tribal gods or saviour gods, frequently of oriental origin. All these cults, whether centred on Mithras, on the Great Mother, or on Isis, guaranteed salvation after death to the initiated—small, select, and segregated groups in which the brethren might forget social distinctions. No conflict need arise as long as the cult of the Emperor and the cults of personal salvation were not mutually exclusive, or as long as the mandatory worship of officialdom could be avoided. And for the poor, the latter was not difficult.

Within the sphere of Late Antique saviour religions, Christianity grew almost unnoticed for at least a generation

---

244. The early establishment of Christian congregations in Mesopotamia, Iran, and elsewhere beyond the pale of the Empire, while important for the development of Eastern Christianity, had no impact on the rise and spread of a Christian architecture.

after Christ's death. Indeed, were it not for St Paul, the first Christian congregations might well have remained insignificant heretical groups within the Jewish communities of Palestine—that obstreperous Aramaic-speaking backwater. Paul planted the seeds of a world religion in Christianity. He spread the gospel to both Jews and heathens living in the hellenized cities of Greece, along the coast of Asia Minor, and in Rome. He severed Christianity's ties to Judaism and to Jewish nationalism. And he laid down a policy of evading the social and political demands of Roman society. Converts were recruited largely from the metropolitan proletariat, with an occasional member of the middle classes—a retired non-commissioned officer, a freedman, or the like. By AD 100, the new faith, while largely centred in the big cities, had spread all over the East to small towns and even to villages.[245] Within the congregations a loose organization gradually developed. Business and other practical matters were taken care of by a group of volunteer administrators, the overseers (*episkopoi*, bishops), and stewards (*diakonoi*, deacons). Religious inspiration came from migrating preachers, first from the Disciples, later from "apostles" and "prophets." Ritual was also loosely organized, even at the beginning of the second century. The congregation would assemble at sunrise on Sunday for prayer, and towards evening for a meal (*agape*)—recalling the Jewish meal on the Eve of the Sabbath. This evening ritual opened with a blessing over the breaking of the bread and ended with a second blessing over a cup of wine. Prayers were offered either during the meal or after, hymns were sung, and at times a spiritual discourse evolved. A "prophet," if present, would deliver a sermon or would speak ecstatically in tongues.[246]

These early believers had neither the means, the organization, nor the slightest interest in evolving an ecclesiastical architecture. They met in whatever place suited the occasion. To win proselytes, a group might assemble in a Jewish place of worship—in Jerusalem the Temple precinct, elsewhere a synagogue. But with the widening gap between old and new believers, such mission meetings became increasingly difficult.[247] Christians might assemble at a street corner, as did St Paul and his listeners in the market place at Athens. Rarely would they be able to hire a public hall, as did the congregation at Ephesus at the time of St Paul's visit.[248]

In contrast to such mission meetings—which ceased with the death of the Disciples—regular gatherings would of necessity be held in private, in the house of one or the other of the brethren, "breaking the bread from house to house."[249] Since the core of the service was a meal, the given place of

the meeting would be the dining-room. And as the congregations were recruited by and large from the lower and middle classes, their houses would have been typical cheap houses. Such houses are known to us, if not from the first and second centuries, at least from the fourth and fifth. In the Eastern provinces, they were apparently one-family buildings up to four storeys high. The dining-room on top was the only large room, and often opened on a terrace. This is the upper floor, the *anageion* or *hyperôon* frequently mentioned in the Acts,[250] the room "high up, open to the light," of which Tertullian still speaks after AD 200.[251] The furnishings would simply consist of a table and three surrounding couches, from which the dining-room takes its name in Latinized Greek—the *triclinium*. The main couch opposite the entrance was presumably reserved for the elder, the host, and the speaker as honoured guest. The congregation might crowd the room, including the window sills, so that at Troas—from the heat of the many lamps and the length of the sermon—a young man fell from the fourth floor (the *tristegon*), only to be resurrected by the preacher St Paul.[252] In Rome, where tenement houses with horizontal apartments were the rule, not necessarily including a dining-room, any large chamber may have served for these gatherings. No other rooms would have been required by the congregations. *Postulants,* desiring to be converted, and *catechumens,* converts not yet baptized, were not admitted to "breaking the bread," and may have left the room before that climax of the meeting. Baptism, originally administered only in flowing water, was performed in standing water, either warm or cold, as early as the beginning of the second century; it took place presumably at a fountain or well in the courtyard of the house, in a bathroom, or in a small, privately owned public bath.

Until AD 200, then, a Christian architecture did not and could not exist. Only the state religion erected temples in

---

245. Pliny the Younger, *Letters*, x, 96 (L.C.L. [Loeb Classical Library], II, 400ff.); A. von Harnack, *The Expansion of Christianity* [in the First Three Centuries, trans. James Moffatt, *Die Mission und Ausbreitung des Christentums* (Leipzig, 1902).]

246. Clement of Rome, I Corinthians 13:8; 19:4. The service in an Eastern congregation around AD 100 is reflected in the Didache, chapters 9ff. (*Ante-Nicene Fathers*, ed. P. Schaff, New York, 1889, 1). [. . .]

247. Acts 13:15, 17; 17:2ff.; 18:4, 19, 26; 19:8.

248. Acts 16:13; 17:7; 19:9.

249. Acts 2:46.

250. Acts 1:17; 20:8; and passim.

251. Tertullian, *Adversus Valentinianos*, cap. 3 (*P.L.* [Migne, *Patrologiae cursus, series Latina*], II, 580).

252. Acts 20:5–10.

the tradition of Greek and Roman architecture. The saviour religions, depending on the specific form of their ritual and the finances of their congregation, built oratories above or below ground, from the simplest to the most lavish but always on a small scale. Christian congregations prior to 200 were limited to the realm of domestic architecture, and further, to inconspicuous dwellings of the lower classes. This limitation, and particularly the evasion of the architecture of official worship, is something that becomes decisive for the early development of Christian architecture.

AD 150–250

The position and outlook of Christianity changed radically after the middle of the second century. By 250, Asia Minor was sixty per cent Christian. The congregation in Rome numbered thirty to fifty thousand. North Africa counted hundreds of small-town congregations.[253] Through the continuous controversies with pagans and Jews as well as among its own members, dogma became more clearly defined. The last years of the second and the first half of the third century saw the first great Church fathers: Tertullian and Cyprian in Africa, Hippolytus in Rome, Clemens and Origen in Alexandria. Men of wealth and rank rose to leadership: Calixtus, a freedman and wealthy banker, held the office of deacon in Rome, then that of bishop from 217 to 222. By 230, the congregations counted among their members high civil servants and courtiers; Christians, so says Tertullian, have penetrated town councils, the palace, the senate, the forum; and bishops, so says another Church father, had become stewards of the Emperors.[254] The congregations had become increasingly organized and expanded their activities of divine worship and care of souls to include charity, the tending of cemeteries, the administration of property, and instruction classes for proselytes. Bishops, elders (presbyters), and deacons grew into the hierarchy of a professional ordained clergy, each degree entrusted with different spiritual and administrative functions. In Rome, Bishop Dionysius (259–68) established a parochial organization and a similar set-up prevailed throughout the Empire, one bishop presiding over the Christians in each town. As early as 220, the bishops of the metropolitan centres—Rome, Carthage, Alexandria, Ephesus, and possibly Antioch—had gained actual leadership in their respective provinces.

The new strength of Christianity was bound to lead to conflicts with the State. Christianity found it increasingly impossible to evade the demands and avoid the challenges of of-

ficialdom. As early as the second century, the self-segregation of the Christians and their voluntary exclusion from official worship and government service had led to suspicion and to sporadic pogroms. By and large, however, the authorities were inclined to consider the Christians harmless sectarians. Persecutions remained localized and far apart: in Rome in 64, at Smyrna in 117, at Lyons in 177. But by 250 the situation had changed. The Christian segment of the population had grown large and influential. Their refusal to participate in sacrifice, prayer, and public rejoicing for the welfare and success of the Emperor's Divine Majesty forced government into action. Millions of citizens were obviously subversive, refused to take oath on the Emperor's godhead, could not be called up for military and civil service, and, indeed, began to claim future secular and political power. Closing both eyes would not do. Two bloody general persecutions, in 250 and 257–60, led to the arrest and execution of Christian leaders in Carthage, Alexandria, and Rome, and to the enforcement of sacrifice, the prohibition of assembly by Christian congregations, and confiscation of Christian property. But organization of the Church was too strongly built, and the trust of the faithful in ultimate salvation too strong. The Emperor Gallienus ended the persecution in 260 and restored to Churches their property, their buildings of worship and cemeteries, and their right of assembly.[255]

The holding of property by Christian communities both before and after the persecutions, then, is assured. The legal basis for such holdings remains a moot question. Possibly the congregations were incorporated as funeral associations and held property under that title. More likely, they purchased and held property by proxy, through a member of the congregation or the bishop. All in all, except for short times of persecution, Christianity was tolerated by Roman practice, if not by law. The large Christian congregations of the Empire, by 250, certainly did not live in hiding. They held services, proselytized, baptized, buried their dead, assisted their needy—and to these ends owned property, either legally or by sufferance.[256]

---

253. Harnack, op. cit., passim.

254. Cyprian, *De Lapsis*, cap. 6, in J. Martin, ed., *Florilegium Patristicum*, XXI (Bonn, 1930), 14.

255. Eusebius, *Ecclesiastical History*, VII, xiii, I (*L.C.L.*, 11, 168f.), gives the text of the Imperial rescript.

256. The Edict of Milan as quoted by Lactantius, *De mortibus persecutorum*, cap. 48 (*P.L.* VII, 267), returns to the Christians both the "houses where they are used to meet and others belonging to their corporation" (*ad jus corporis corum*), that is, to their Churches not to individuals.

The structures wanted by the congregation were to serve two purposes: the spiritual needs and social welfare of the living and the cult of the dead. Outside the cities, cemeteries had to be established and maintained where the dead could rest undefiled by neighbouring pagans, where tombs of martyrs were marked by monuments, and where the living could assemble in appropriate structures for memorial services and funeral banquets. Within the cities, congregations needed buildings suitable for assembly of the faithful, administration of the community, and distribution of charities. Poor congregations might well continue to meet in private houses; leaders of large communities too would revert to this practice in times of persecution, or else assemble in the less conspicuous buildings in cemeteries. This latter apparently occurred in 250 when the Roman bishop and his deacons were arrested "on the cemetery of Callixtus." But as a rule, from the early third century, congregations must have held structures of their own for their manifold needs—structures within the local tradition of domestic building in the Roman-Hellenistic world, yet adapted to the new needs of the Christian congregations.

These needs, both religious and social, had expanded rapidly. A rich and clear liturgy had evolved by AD 200. The common meal had been relegated to rare occasions: meals offered to the poor (agapai), or funeral and memorial banquets (refrigeria) held in cemeteries near sites hallowed by martyrs. The regular service consisted of two parts. The first was attended by both the faithful and catechumens and comprised scriptural readings, sermon, and common prayer (Mass of the Catechumens). The second part (Mass of the Faithful) was reserved for fully-fledged members in good standing. It consisted of three parts: the procession of the faithful bringing offerings, for the Sacrifice and contributions for the maintenance of the poor and the church; the Sacrifice proper—the Eucharist; and the communion. The assembly room, no longer a dining-room, had to be large, easily accessible, and divided between clergy and laymen.[257] The bishop, flanked by his presbyters, would preside over the assembly from a platform (tribunal, solium), seated in an armchair like a Roman magistrate. The congregation was seated outside this presbytery, supervised by the deacons and arranged in a set order. A Syrian church order of c. 250 places children in front, then men, and finally women. In Rome, men apparently occupied one side of the room, women the other, as continued to be the custom in later times. The furniture was simple, presumably wooden and movable: the bishop's chair, a table (mensa) for the Eucharist, and a second table for the offerings (the first table within or in front of the presbytery, the second to one side). A low wooden railing might separate the clergy from the laymen, and this railing, or another, was used to enclose the altar. An anteroom (vestibulum) was needed for catechumens and penitents who, dismissed after the first part of the Mass, were to hear, but not see, the Mass of the Faithful. Baptism had also evolved an elaborate liturgy, preceded by anointment and followed by confirmation, requiring both a baptistery and a confirmation room (consignatorium). All these rooms, varying in size, had to communicate and allow for a smooth sequence of baptism, confirmation, and regular assembly. Moreover, auxiliary chambers had to be provided: classrooms for instruction of neophytes; a dining-room for celebration of agapai; a vestry in which to store altar vessels; and, at times, a library as well. The charities of the Church required the storage, distribution, and administration of food and clothing. Offices and living quarters were needed for the clergy, their families, and the clerical staff. These manifold ends could not be met either by a private house, taken over unchanged, or by an apartment temporarily at the disposal of the congregation. They could be met only by a regular meeting house, owned by the congregation in practice, if not in fact. Such a structure would be called a domus ecclesiae, an oikos ekklisias, or, in the local parlance of Rome, a titulus;[258] community centre or meeting house best renders the meaning of the various terms. Once purchased, the structure would as a rule have to be altered to fit the congregation's needs. Occasionally community houses may even have been built ex novo. But all known community houses remain bound in plan and design to the tradition of utilitarian domestic architecture, as well as subject to the regional variations of third-century building within the Roman Empire. Christianity thought of its practical needs along purely utilitarian and private lines. It shied away from the official sphere and from official and religious architecture, which was nearly all loaded with pagan connotations in third-century Rome. Temples were dedicated to the gods of the State; sanctuaries were sacred to pagan saviour gods; and public assembly halls were linked to the worship of the Emperor or the Welfare of the State. "We have no temples, we have no altars," says Minucius Felix.[259] Inconspicuousness was both prudent

---

257. The arrangement and furniture of the assembly rooms in the early centuries can be gathered from scattered references in the early Fathers and from Church orders such as the Syrian Didascalia, chapter 12 (ed. H. Conolly, Oxford, 1929, 120).

258. J. P. Kirsch, Die röminschen Titelkirchen im Altertum (Bonn, 1918). [. . .]

259. Minucius Felix, Octavius, chap. xxxii (P.L., III, 353).

and ideologically desirable for Christianity, and could be best achieved behind the facade of domestic middle-class architecture.

Christian community houses of this description, formerly known only dimly from literary evidence, have come to light during the last forty years. None among those known dates from after 400, none from prior to 230. The oldest known building stood at Dura-Europos (Qalat es Sālihïye), near the eastern border of the Empire, and is representative of the position and requirements of a small-town congregation in hellenized-Mesopotamian surroundings. The community houses found in Rome, tenements remodeled in the third and fourth centuries for use by Christian congregations, are typical of the needs and position of the large Christian community in the capital of the Empire.

The meeting house at Dura-Europos is securely dated. It was destroyed with the neighbouring Jewish synagogue and other houses when the town wall was reinforced in 257.[260] When built on the edge of the town, it was an ordinary town dwelling of the customary peristyle type: a courtyard, entered from an alley through a narrow passage, was surrounded on three sides by rooms of varying sizes, and on the fourth side by a portico; into the fresh plaster of one of the rooms a bored workman scratched the year: AD 231/2. Whether or not this house was used as such by the Christian congregation for its assemblies is uncertain. But the structure was certainly in the hands of the congregation between 240 and 250. At that time it underwent alterations designed to adapt it better to its functions as a community house. The *divan* in the south wing—the reception room, surrounded on three sides by benches—was merged with the adjoining south-west room. The enlarged room—5 by 13 m. (16½ by 43 ft) would have seated a congregation of fifty or sixty. A dais for the bishop occupied the short east wall. Nearby, a door led into a small room with wall niches which was apparently a vestry. Large doors, taken over from the older building, opened into the courtyard and into a good-sized room— 4 by 7 m. (13 by 23 ft)—in the west wing. This room, offering space for roughly thirty, would have been an ideal place for the catechumens to hear but not see the Mass of the Faithful, to receive instruction, and to prepare themselves for baptism. Its three doors open into the courtyard, the meeting hall, and into a smaller rectangular baptistery to the north. A tub surmounted by a canopy leans against the west wall of the baptistery; and the murals centre on the ideas of original sin, salvation, resurrection—ideas closely linked in Early Christian thought to the symbolism of baptism.

Presumably community houses were similarly adapted from private residences in small towns all over the Empire. The minutes of a confiscation of Christian property in a North African country town in 303 vividly reflect the plan of such a *domus ecclesiae* and the function of its several rooms. Moving through the house, the police impound chalices, lamps, and chandeliers in the meeting room; wearing-apparel for the poor in a storeroom; bookcases and chests in the library chests and large jugs in a dining-room.[261] Nor were private residences only assimilated to Christian meeting houses. In Dura itself, but a few blocks from the Christian building, the remnants of a Jewish community centre prove that around 200 the Jews also housed their meeting room and needed annexes in a structure much like an ordinary Dura house: a small courtyard enclosed by smaller and larger rooms, among the larger the synagogue, among the smaller a sacristy and two divans, of which one possibly served as a dining-room and the other as a court room. This building was replaced in 245 by a new community centre in which the rooms were larger, the synagogue preceded by a regular forecourt and lavishly decorated with wall paintings—the oldest surviving Old Testament cycle. But all this remained hidden behind windowless walls. Seen from the street, both the Jewish community centres of about 200 and 245 and the Christian *domus ecclesiae* were indistinguishable from any other house in the neighbourhood. This was only natural. Both congregations were small minorities, and although the environment was not necessarily hostile, there was no reason to call attention to an alien element through a conspicuously different structure. Nor is it surprising that both congregations installed their community centres in the district near the city wall, traditionally the quarter of the poor. Financial limitations, the social background of their membership, and the natural desire to be inconspicuous would have made them prefer such a location.

Community houses in the large cities of the Empire— whether Jewish or Christian—would differ from those in country towns for a number of reasons: the greater wealth and larger size of the congregations, the metropolitan surroundings, and the tradition of large-city domestic architecture. But like their country cousins, the *domus ecclesiae* in the

260. C. H. Kraeling, *The Christian Building (The Excavations at Dura Europos . . . Final Report,* VIII, 2) (New Haven, 1967).

261. See the anti-Donatist documents, collected in Migne, (P.L. [*Patrologia Latina*], VIII, 673ff. as *Monumenta Vetera ad Donatistarum historiam pertimentia,* esp. col. 231).

metropolitan centres of the Empire were rooted in domestic architecture and would preserve their unobtrusive presence among the ordinary houses of a large city. Metropolitan architecture, by the early third century, had indeed developed two distinct types, each with a number of variations. The private residences of the wealthy, the *domus*, followed the plan of the old hellenistic or Italo-hellenistic peristyle house. Far more numerous were the buildings designed for the teeming masses of the urban population: tenement houses of up to five or more storeys—either tower-like, as in Alexandria, the apartments heaped on top of each other, or forming large blocks (*insulae*), as in Rome and Ostia, with shops, small thermae, or warehouses at street level and numerous apartments on each of the upper floors. Crowded along narrow, shady, smelly streets bustling with life and noise, these tenements must have looked very much like their late descendants in present-day Rome or Naples.

The Christian communities of Rome installed their *domus ecclesiae* in just such tenements. Their resemblance to ordinary tenements would have made these *tituli* as hard to identify as the meeting rooms of contemporary sects installed in the tenements of New York's Harlem or London's East End. The term *titulus* is a legal one, derived from the marble slab which bore the owner's name and established his title to a property. By the early fourth century the parish organization of Rome rested on twenty-five *tituli,* known under such names as *titulus Clementis, titulus Praxedis, titulus Byzantis,* and the like. These *tituli* exist to this day in name and law, with "saint" prefixed to the owner's name, or with the original *titulus* name replaced by that of a saint; and each *titulus* is assigned to one of the cardinals of the Roman Church as his title church. Most of these *tituli* are now regular church buildings, laid out from the fourth to the ninth centuries, and often remodeled later. However, incorporated into their walls or preserved below their floors are, almost without exception, the remnants of large tenement houses or private thermae dating from the second or third centuries, or at least from the period before Constantine. Hence it becomes very likely that the pre-Constantinian structures were used as *domus ecclesiae* until replaced much later by regular church buildings which retained the original names of *titulus Clementis,* and so forth.

It is tempting to assume that a large number of these pre-Constantinian structures incorporated into present-day title churches were Christian community centres as early as the third century. But such generalization is hazardous, since no *titulus* can yet be traced beyond the early fourth century by documentary evidence. Concomitantly, the mere presence of a pre-Constantinian tenement incorporated into a fourth-century or later title church constitutes no proof that the structure was a *domus ecclesiae* prior to Constantine. Such proof exists only where the building was remodeled for Christian use in pre-Constantinian times, either structurally or in decoration. Even where a *titulus* was installed in a pre-Constantinian structure as late as the fourth century, however, this use of a tenement or a thermae building is presumably a survival of earlier times when Christian architecture was still fully rooted in domestic architecture. [. . .]

Constantinian Church Building

[. . .]Church building under these new conditions could no longer remain in the realm of domestic architecture, where it had been rooted for the last two hundred and fifty years. Community centres had no future once the Church had become the Establishment of the Empire. They were too small to accommodate the thousands of new converts. Too many functions were crowded into them, religious, administrative, social, utilitarian. Situated in the slums and hidden indiscriminately behind the plain facade of an ordinary house, they were incompatible with the dignity of the Church and of its Imperial patron. For want of other facilities, the old *domus* continued to be used and occasionally even new ones were purchased. But Christianity under Constantine had to find a new architecture of a higher order, public in character, resplendent in material, and spacious in layout.

For both practical and ideological reasons it was impossible that this new Christian architecture should evolve from the religious architecture of pagan antiquity. Christianity obviously saw in paganism and all its works the very opposite of its own intentions. It shied away from pagan temples to such a degree that neither they nor even their sites were occupied by the Church before the late fourth century in the East or before the sixth century in the West.[262] Just as important, no pagan religious building was adaptable to the needs of Christian worship. The temples of the old gods, an obsolete type by 320 in any event, had been designed to shelter an image, not to accommodate a congregation of both laymen and clergy. To be sure, the sanctuaries of the Neo-Pythagoreans, of Baal, Mithras, the Great Mother, and Attys,

---

262. F. W. Deichmann, *J.D.A.I.* [*Jahrbuch des Deutschen archäologischen Instituts*] LIV (1939), 105ff.

all oriental cults, were designed to hold small congregations numbering twenty or thirty, assembled along a central passageway and subordinate to a priest officiating at an altar. The Christian communities of Constantine's time, however, comprised hundreds or thousands of members, and had to evolve their churches within a different framework.

Given her new official standing under Constantine and her new concept of Christ the King, the Christian Church in search of an architecture was bound to turn to the realm of public, official architecture.[263] Within it, she would inevitably single out a building type which combined religious connotations with the criteria of official building. Such a building type existed: the basilica. Since the second and first centuries BC, basilicas had been built all through the Roman world. In modern architectural parlance, a basilica is a building divided into a nave and two or more aisles, the former higher and wider than the latter, and lit by the windows of a clerestory. But Roman basilicas were rarely, if ever, of this type. In their simplest form they were aisleless halls, occasionally subdivided by supports. In more elaborate form, the nave was enveloped by aisles or by aisles and galleries; or aisles and galleries were doubled; or they ran parallel to the nave instead of enveloping it. The clerestory might be high or low, the entrance could be either on the long or short side, or on both. The tribunal, the seat of the magistrate, rose on a plain dais either inside the nave or in the aisles, or in an apse of rectangular or semicircular plan. Again, this apse might project either from one of the short sides or from the long side, or the number of apses might be doubled or tripled. Open timber roofs or flat ceilings were the rule.

By AD 300 this variety had increased even further. Much in contrast to temple architecture the basilica remained immensely alive and prone to change in plan under the impact of other building types. The Basilica of Maxentius was designed as a huge vaulted nave flanked by niches, resembling a thermae hall. Throne basilicas in Imperial palaces occasionally seem to have adopted central plans. Sometimes, though rarely, an open area surrounded by porticoes may have served as a basilica. The most common type, however, at the turn of the fourth century was apparently a longitudinal, timber-roofed hall without aisles, terminated and thus dominated by a raised apse. Huge windows in single or double rows along the flanks lit the interior. The palace basilica at Piazza Armerina, the basilica at Trier, two forum basilicas at Sétif in Algeria, and the hall, now SS. Cosma e Damiano, on the forum in Rome are examples. In conformity with general contemporary practice, the exterior was dominated by plain stretches of wall, the interior was resplendent with marble revetments and gilded capitals and ceilings.

However, in Roman parlance, the term basilica applies to the function rather than to the design of the building, and despite variation the function of Roman basilicas is easily described: a basilica was but a large meeting hall. The forum basilica, found in any Roman town, was but a covered extension of the adjoining marketplace—a hall to transact business and to exchange town gossip and news from the Empire, a *souk* to display wares, much like the *galleria* in any modern Italian town. On a dais, the tribunal, the magistrate, and his assessors would sit in court; surmounting it, a shrine sheltered the effigy of the Emperor, in whose presence alone law could be dispensed and business contracts validly concluded. In large cities a number of basilicas might be assigned different functions: stock and money exchanges, clothing bazaars, florists' arcades, special law courts, each designated by an explanatory epithet. Army camps had their riding and drill basilicas, opening on to a sanctuary where the eagles of the legion and the Emperor's effigy were kept. Large thermae might boast a basilica, where clients could disport themselves. Beginning in the second century AD, basilicas adapted to the demands of the specific ritual had come to be used by religious sects: the large hall in the sanctuary of Isis and Osiris at Pergamon; the basilica of the Tree Bearers in Rome; a group of synagogues in Galilee. Or again, a funerary college might gather in a tiny funerary basilica. Large reception rooms in wealthy houses were likewise termed basilicas. Outstanding among these were the audience halls, within or near the Imperial palaces, where the Emperor's divine Majesty, enthroned in the apse, would solemnly appear to his subjects.

At the same time, the direction Christian architecture was to take was determined by the religious connotations which all such basilicas had carried for centuries. These sacred overtones grew stronger with the growing import of the cult of the Emperor's divinity. The palace basilica in which he sat enthroned was *ipso facto* a religious building. The drill basilica of a barracks became religious ground as the garrison paraded and swore loyalty before the Emperor's bust. In forum

---

263. Numberless theories, beginning in the fifteenth century, have been propounded regarding the origin of the Christian basilica. The building type has been variously derived from the secular forum basilica; the palace basilica, religious pagan basilicas, synagogues; funerary pagan basilicas; the Italic atrium house; the peristyle of the hellenistic house; the plan of Imperial palaces; hellenistic heroa; the layout of Roman Imperial fora; or from the colonnaded streets of Roman cities. Or else it has been evolved entirely from the requirements of the Christian liturgy, or from a combination of some or of all of these factors.

basilicas, his divine effigy consecrated official and private business. Even in thermae basilicas, the image of the godhead received the homage of those gathered. The borderline between the secular and religious functions of the basilica is fluid throughout Late Antiquity, and the wide variety of purposes for which the buildings served fluctuated between these two poles.

It was almost inevitable that the Church under Constantine would develop, within the framework set by the genus basilica, the buildings she specifically required for the solemn celebration of Mass amidst an assembled congregation presided over by her high dignitaries, bishop and clergy. Clearly, however, the newly-built Christian basilicas were not derived from any specific type of Roman basilica—be it the forum basilica, the Imperial audience hall, or a funerary or a religious basilica. On the contrary, the Christian basilica both in function and design was a new creation within an accustomed framework. In the eyes of contemporaries this was nothing extraordinary. The Christian assembly halls simply represented one more type of basilica created by a new demand. In Constantine's time, the Christian basilica was viewed as just another monumental public meeting hall with religious overtones. Its function had to be explained by a distinctive epithet, such as *"basilica id est dominicum,"* an assembly hall that is a house of the Lord, or, "a basilica for the Apostolic and Catholic congregation." Or else, Constantine himself refers to the church on Golgotha as "a basilica more beautiful than all others anywhere," and thus places it on a level with any other assembly hall built for whatever purpose.[264]

Modest basilicas may already have been built by Christian congregations in the years preceding the Peace of the Church: S. Crisogono in Rome is an example. But only under Constantine did architects meet the requirements of the Christian ritual by creating new variations on the ever variable type of the genus basilica. From this background, the Christian basilica drew three or four features which by AD 300 had become essential characteristics common to the majority of basilicas whatever their function: the oblong plan; the longitudinal axis; the timber roof, either open or concealed by a flat ceiling—vaulting, as in the Basilica of Maxentius, having remained exceptional in Roman basilicas; finally, the terminating tribunal, whether rectangular or in the form of an apse. Division into nave and aisles and a high clerestory with large windows became preponderant, but they remained optional; galleries remained rare. Within this framework, the Christian basilica had to be brought in line with the demands for greater dignity and monumentality newly created by the

Constantinian spirit of Christianity and had to be adapted to specific liturgical requirements, to the financial means and the social standing of the patron, and to local building practice—all widely diverging. The patron might be a poor country congregation, a wealthy bishop, or the Emperor himself. Local building practices might prescribe stone, brick, or concrete construction. The liturgy, while uniform in its general lines, varied locally in implementation. As a result, the clergy might be seated in the apse or in front of it; the altar might be in the apse or in the nave; the offering tables near the altar or in adjoining rooms; the catechumens might withdraw to a forechurch, to the atrium, to the aisles, or to a separate building. Conditions varied further where a building was intended not for the regular services of a congregation, but for the sporadic meetings of local congregations and pilgrims at the tombs of their dead or at the graves of a martyr or at a holy site. Indeed, prior to 350 there was no such thing as *the* Christian basilica; there were only a large number of variants on the theme basilica, adapted to liturgical requirements, building practice, and the wishes of patrons.

From Richard Krautheimer, *Early Christian and Byzantine Architecture,* Pelican History of Art (Harmondsworth, UK: Penguin, 1965), 23–29, 41–43.

☙ The **Second Council of Nicaea** (787), called by the Byzantine empress Irene (ca. 750–802), dealt with the question of iconic representation in Eastern Christianity. These "Extracts from the Acts of the Council of Nicaea" record the defeat of the first iconoclastic movement in the Eastern Church. They deal with the problem of the distinction to be made between the worship given to God alone and the appropriate veneration of icons.

THE SECOND COUNCIL OF NICAEA

"Extracts[265] from the Acts of the Council of Nicaea, Session I"

[Certain bishops who had been led astray by the Iconoclasts came, asking to be received back. The first of these was Basil of Ancyra.]

The bishop Basil of Ancyra read as follows from a book:

---

264. Eusebius, *Life of Constantine* (trans. by S. Bagster and E.C. Richardson), (New York, 1890).

265. See also Labbe and Cossart, *Concilia,* Tom. VII, col. 53. This note is by Gerhart and Udoh from information in the source text: "If anyone shall not

Inasmuch as ecclesiastical legislation has canonically been handed down from past time, even from the beginning from the holy Apostles, and from their successors, who were our holy fathers and teachers, and also from the six holy and ecumenical synods, and from the local synods which were gathered in the interests of orthodoxy, that those returning from any heresy whatever to the orthodox faith and to the tradition of the Catholic Church, might deny their own heresy, and confess the orthodox faith,

Wherefore I, Basil, bishop of the city of Ancyra, proposing to be united to the Catholic Church, and to Hadrian the most holy Pope of Old Rome, and to Tarasius the most blessed Patriarch, and to the most holy apostolic sees, to wit, Alexandria, Antioch, and the Holy City, as well as to all orthodox high-priests and priests, make this written confession of my faith, and I offer it to you as to those who have received power by apostolic authority. And in this also I beg pardon from your divinely gathered holiness for my tardiness in this matter. For it was not right that I should have fallen behind in the confession of orthodoxy, but it arose from my entire lack of knowledge, and slothful and negligent mind in the matter. Wherefore the rather I ask your blessedness to grant me indulgence in God's sight.

I believe, therefore, and make my confession in one God, the Father Almighty, and in one Lord Jesus Christ, his only begotten Son, and in the Holy Ghost, the Lord and Giver of Life. The Trinity, one in essence and one in majesty, must be worshipped and glorified in one godhead, power, and authority. I confess all things pertaining to the incarnation of one of the Holy Trinity, our Lord and God, Jesus Christ, as the Saints and the six Ecumenical Synods have handed down. And I reject and anathematize every heretical babbling, as they also have rejected them. I ask for the intercessions (πρεσβείας) of our spotless Lady the Holy Mother of God, and those of the holy and heavenly powers, and those of all the Saints.[266]

And receiving their holy and honourable reliques with all honour (τιμῆς), I salute and venerate these with honour (τιμητικῶς προσκυνέω), hoping to have a share in their holiness. Likewise also the venerable images (εἰκόνας) of the incarnation of our Lord Jesus Christ, in the humanity he assumed for our salvation; and of our spotless Lady, the holy Mother of God; and of the angels like unto God; and of the holy Apostles, Prophets, Martyrs, and of all the Saints—the sacred images of all these, I salute and venerate—rejecting and anathematizing with my whole soul and mind the synod which was gathered together out of stubbornness and madness, and which styled itself the Seventh Synod, but which

by those who think accurately was called lawfully and canonically a pseudo-synod, as being contrary to all truth and piety, and audaciously and temerariously against the divinely handed down ecclesiastical legislation, yea, even impiously having yelped at and scoffed at the holy and venerable images, and having ordered these to be taken away out of the holy churches of God; over which assembly presided Theodosius with the pseudonym of Ephesius, Sisinnius of Perga, with the surname Pastillas, Basilius of Pisidia, falsely called "tricaccabus"; with whom the wretched Constantine, the then Patriarch, was led (ἐματαιώθη) astray.

These things thus I confess and to these I assent, and therefore in simplicity of heart and in uprightness of mind, in the presence of God, I have made the subjoined anathematisms.

Anathema to the calumniators of the Christians, that is to the image breakers.

Anathema to those who apply the words of Holy Scripture which were spoken against idols, to the venerable images.

Anathema to those who do not salute the holy and venerable images.

Anathema to those who say that Christians have recourse to the images as to the gods.

Anathema to those who call the sacred images idols.

Anathema to those who knowingly communicate with those who revile and dishonour the venerable images.

Anathema to those who say that another than Christ our Lord hath delivered us from idols.

Anathema to those who spurn the teachings of the holy Father and the tradition of the Catholic Church, taking as a pretext and making their own the arguments of Arius, Nestorius, Eutyches, and Dioscorus, that unless we were evidently taught by the Old and New Testaments, we should not follow the teachings of the holy Fathers and of the holy Ecumenical Synods, and the tradition of the Catholic Church.

---

confess that the Ever-virgin Mary is properly and truly the Mother of God, and more exalted than every creature, whether visible or invisible, and does not seek her intercessions with sincere faith, because she has confidence in approaching our God, who was born of her, let him be anathema" (L[abbe] and C[ossart], *Conc.* Tom. VII., col. 524). "If anyone does not confess that all the Saints from the beginning down to now, who whether before the Law, or under the Law, or in grace pleased God, should be honoured in his presence both with soul and body; and does not seek their prayers, according to the tradition of the Church as of those having confidence to plead for the world, let him be anathema" (Ibid., col. 528).

266. Thus far there was no expression of opinion from which the Iconoclasts would have dissented, for in all that regarded the Blessed Virgin and the Saints and their invocation and patronage, the heretics agreed with the orthodox.

Anathema to those who dare to say that the Catholic Church hath at any time sanctioned idols.

Anathema to those who say that the making of images is a diabolical invention and not a tradition of our holy Fathers.

This is my confession [of faith] and to these propositions I give my assent. And I pronounce this with my whole heart, and soul and mind.

And if at any time by the fraud of the devil (which may God forbid!) I voluntarily or involuntarily shall be opposed to what I have now professed, may I be anathema from the Father, the Son and the Holy Ghost, and from the Catholic Church and every hierarchical order a stranger.

I will keep myself from every acceptance of a bribe and from filthy lucre in accordance with the divine canons of the holy Apostles and of the approved Fathers.

Tarasius, the most holy Patriarch, said: This whole sacred gathering yields glory and thanks to God for this confession of yours, which you have made to the Catholic Church.

The Holy Synod said: Glory to God which maketh one that which was severed.

[Theodore, bishop of Myra, then read the same confession, and was received. The next bishop who asked to be received read as follows (col. 60):]

Theodosius, the humble Christian, to the holy and Ecumenical Synod: I confess and I agree to (συντίθεμαι) and I receive and I salute and I venerate in the first place the spotless image of our Lord Jesus Christ, our true God, and the holy image of her who bore him without seed, the holy Mother of God, and her help and protection and intercessions each day and night as a sinner to my aid I call for, since she has confidence with Christ our God, as he was born of her. Likewise also I receive and venerate the images of the holy and most laudable Apostles, prophets, and martyrs and the fathers and cultivators of the desert. Not indeed as gods (God forbid!) do I ask all these with my whole heart to pray for me to God, that he may grant me through their intercessions to find mercy at his hands at the day of judgment, for in this I am but showing forth more clearly the affection and love of my soul which I have borne them from the first. Likewise also I venerate and honour and salute the reliques of the Saints as of those who fought for Christ and who have received grace from him for the healing of diseases and the curing of sicknesses and the casting out of devils, as the Christian Church has received from the holy Apostles and Fathers even down to us today.

Moreover, I am well pleased that there should be images in the churches of the faithful, especially the image of our Lord Jesus Christ and of the holy Mother of God, of every kind of material, both gold and silver and of every colour, so that his incarnation may be set forth to all men. Likewise there may be painted the lives of the Saints and Prophets and Martyrs, so that their struggles and agonies may be set forth in brief, for the stirring up and teaching of the people, especially of the unlearned.

For if the people go forth with lights and incense to meet the "laurata" and images of the Emperors when they are sent to cities or rural districts, they honour surely not the tablet covered over with wax, but the Emperor himself. How much more is it necessary that in the churches of Christ our God, the image of God our Saviour and of his spotless Mother and of all the holy and blessed fathers and ascetics should be painted? Even as also St. Basil says: "Writers and painters set forth the great deeds of war; the one by word, the other by their pencils; and each stirs many to courage." And again the same author, "How much pains have you ever taken that you might find one of the Saints who was willing to be your importunate intercessor to the Lord?" And Chrysostom says, "The charity of the Saints is not diminished by their death, nor does it come to an end with their exit from life, but after their death they are still more powerful than when they were alive," and many other things without measure. Therefore I ask you, O ye Saints! I call out to you. I have sinned against heaven and in your sight. Receive me as God received the luxurious man, and the harlot, and the thief. Seek me out, as Christ sought out the sheep that was lost, which he carried on his shoulders; so there may be joy in the presence of God and of his angels over my salvation and repentance, through your intervention, O all-holy lords! Let them who do not venerate the holy and venerable images be anathema! Anathema to those who blaspheme against the honourable and venerable images! To those who dare to attack and blaspheme the venerable images and call them idols, anathema! To those who do not diligently teach all the Christ-loving people to venerate and salute the venerable and sacred and honourable images of all the Saints who pleased God in their several generations, anathema! To those who have a doubtful mind and do not confess with their whole hearts that they venerate the sacred images, anathema!

Sabbas, the most reverend hegumenus of the monastery of the Studium, said: According to the Apostolic precepts and the Ecumenical Synods he is worthy to be received back.

Tarasius, the most holy Patriarch, said: Those who formerly were the calumniators of orthodoxy, now are become the advocates of the truth.

[Near the end of this session (col. 77):]

John, the most reverend bishop and legate of the Eastern high priests said: This heresy is the worst of all heresies. Woe to the iconoclasts! It is the worst of heresies, as it subverts the incarnation (οἰκονομίαν) of our Saviour.

From Henry R. Percival, ed., *The Seven Ecumenical Councils of the Undivided Church: Their Canons and Dogmatic Decrees*, 2nd series, vol. 14 (New York: Charles Scribner's Sons, 1900), 533–35.

❧ "On What Was Done under His Administration" is the personal account of **Suger** (1081–1151), abbot of Saint-Denis in Paris. He reveals the aesthetic, liturgical, and theological principles he employed in building one of the earliest Gothic churches.

ABBOT SUGER
"On What Was Done under His Administration"

I

In the twenty-third year of our administration, when we sat on a certain day in the general chapter, conferring with our brethren about matters both common and private, these very beloved brethren and sons began strenuously to beseech me *in charity*[267] that I might not allow the fruits of our so great labors to be passed over in silence; and rather to save for the memory of posterity, in pen and ink, those increments which the generous munificence of Almighty God had bestowed upon this church, in the time of our prelacy, in the acquisition of new assets as well as in the recovery of lost ones, in the multiplication of improved possessions, in the construction of buildings, and in the accumulation of gold, silver, most precious gems and very good textiles. For this one thing they promised us two [things] in return: by such a record we would deserve the continual fervor of all succeeding brethren in their prayers for the salvation of our soul; and we would rouse, through this example, their zealous solicitude for the good care of the church of God. We thus devoutly complied with their devoted and reasonable requests, not with any desire for empty glory nor with any claim to the reward of human praise and transitory compensation; and lest, after our demise, the church be diminished in its revenue by any or anyone's roguery and the ample increments which the generous munificence of God has bestowed in the time of our administration be tacitly lost under bad successors, we have deemed it worthy and useful, just as we thought fitting to begin, in its proper place, our tale about the construction of the buildings and the increase of the trea-

sures with the body of the church of the most blessed Martyrs Denis, Rusticus, and Eleutherius (which [church] has most tenderly fostered us from mother's milk to old age), so to inform present and future readers about the increase of the revenue [by starting] from his own little town, that is to say, his first resting-place, and its vicinity on all sides.

XXIV Of the Church's Decoration

Having assigned the increase of the revenue in this manner, we turned our hand to the memorable construction of buildings, so that by this thanks might be given to Almighty God by us as well as by our successors; and that by good example their ardor might be roused to the continuation and, if necessary, to the completion of this [work]. For neither any want nor any hindrance by any power will have to be feared if, for the love of the Holy Martyrs, one takes safely care of oneself by one's own resources. The first work on this church which we began under the inspiration of God [was this]: because of the age of the old walls and their impending ruin in some places, we summoned the best painters I could find from different regions, and reverently caused these [walls] to be repaired and becomingly painted with gold and precious colors. I completed this all the more gladly because I had wished to do it, if ever I should have an opportunity, even while I was a pupil in school.

XXV Of the First Addition to the Church

However, even while this was being completed at great expense, I found myself, under the inspiration of the Divine Will and because of that inadequacy which we often saw and felt on feast days, namely the Feast of the blessed Denis, the Fair, and very many others (for the narrowness of the place forced the women to run toward the altar upon the heads of the men as upon a pavement with much anguish and noisy confusion), encouraged by the counsel of wise men and by the prayers of many monks (lest it displease God and the Holy Martyrs) to enlarge and amplify the noble church consecrated by the Hand Divine; and I set out at once to begin this very thing. In our chapter as well as in church I implored Divine mercy that He Who is the One, *the beginning and the ending, Alpha and Omega,*[268] might join a good end to a good beginning by a safe

---

267. 1 Cor 4:21; 16:14; Eph 1:4; 3:17; 4:2, 16; Col 2:2; 1 Thes 5:13; 2 Thes 3:5.
268. Rev 21:6; cf. ibid. 1:8 and 22:13.

middle; that He might not repel from the building of the temple a *bloody man*[269] who desired this very thing, with his whole heart, more than to obtain the treasures of Constantinople. Thus we began work at the former entrance with the doors. We tore down a certain addition asserted to have been made by Charlemagne on a very honorable occasion (for his father, the Emperor Pepin, had commanded that he be buried, for the sins of his father Charles Martel, outside at the entrance with the doors, face downward and not recumbent); and we set our hand to this part. As is evident we exerted ourselves incessantly with the enlargement of the body of the church as well as with the trebling of the entrance and the doors, and with the erection of high and noble towers.

XXVIII Of the Enlargement of the Upper Choir

In the same year, cheered by so holy and so auspicious a work, we hurried to begin the chamber of divine atonement in the upper choir where the continual and frequent Victim of our redemption should be sacrificed in secret without disturbance by the crowds. And, as is found in [our] treatise about the consecration of this upper structure, we were mercifully deemed worthy—God helping and prospering us and our concerns—to bring so holy, so glorious, and so famous a structure to a good end, together with our brethren and fellow servants; we felt all the more indebted to God and the Holy Martyrs as He, by so long a postponement, had reserved what had to be done for our lifetime and labors. *For who am I, or what is my father's house,*[270] that I should have presumed to begin so noble and pleasing an edifice, or should have hoped to finish it, had I not, relying upon the help of Divine mercy and the Holy Martyrs, devoted my whole self, both with mind and body, to this very task? But He Who gave the will also gave the power; because the good work was in the will therefore it stood in perfection by the help of God. How much the Hand Divine Which operates in such matters has protected this glorious work is also surely proven by the fact that It allowed that whole magnificent building [to be completed] in three years and three months, from the crypt below to the summit of the vaults above, elaborated with the variety of so many arches and columns, including even the consummation of the roof. Therefore the inscription of the earlier consecration also defines, with only one word eliminated, the year of completion of this one, thus:

"The year was the One Thousand, One Hundred, Forty and Fourth of the Word when [this structure] was consecrated."

To these verses of the inscription we choose the following one to be added:

> Once the new rear part is joined to the part in front,
> The Church shines with its middle part brightened.
> For Bright is that which is brightly coupled with the bright,
> And bright is the noble edifice which is pervaded by the new light;
> Which stands enlarged in our time,
> I, who was Suger, being the leader while it was being accomplished.

Eager to press on my success, since I wished nothing more under heaven than to seek the honor of my mother church which with maternal affection had suckled me as a child, had held me upright as a stumbling youth, had mightily strengthened me as a mature man, and had solemnly *set me among the princes* of the Church and the realm, we devoted ourselves to the completion of the work and strove to raise and to enlarge the transept wings of the church [so as to correspond] to the form of the earlier and later work that had to be joined [by them].

XXXIII

[. . .] Much of what had been acquired and more of such ornaments of the church as we were afraid of losing—for instance, a golden chalice that was curtailed of its foot and several other things—we ordered to be fastened there. And because the diversity of the materials [such as] gold, gems and pearls is not easily understood by the mute perception of sight without a description, we have seen to it that this work, which is intelligible only to the literate, which shines with the radiance of delightful allegories, be set down in writing. Also we have affixed verses expounding the matter so that the [allegories] might be more clearly understood:

> Crying out with a loud voice, the mob acclaims Christ: "Osanna."
> The true Victim offered at the Lord's Supper has carried all men.
> He Who saves all men on the Cross hastens to carry the cross.

269. 2 Kings 16:7; cf. also ibid., 8. Further Ps 25:9; 54:24; 58:3; 138:19.
270. Freely quoted from 1 Kings 18:18.

> The promise which Abraham obtains for his seed is sealed
> by the flesh of Christ.
> Melchizedek offers a libation because Abraham triumphs
> over the enemy.
> They who seek Christ with the Cross bear the cluster of
> grapes upon a staff.

Often we contemplate, out of sheer affection for the church our mother, these different ornaments both new and old; and when we behold how that wonderful cross of St. Eloy—together with the smaller ones—and that incomparable ornament commonly called "the Crest" are placed upon the golden altar, then I say, sighing deeply in my heart: *Every precious stone was thy covering, the sardius, the topaz, and the jasper, the chrysolite, and the onyx, and the beryl, the sapphire, and the carbuncle, and the emerald.*[271] To those who know the properties of precious stones it becomes evident, to their utter astonishment, that none is absent from the number of these (with the only exception of the carbuncle), but that they abound most copiously. Thus, when—out of my delight in the beauty of the house of God—the loveliness of the many-colored gems has called me away from external cares, and worthy meditation has induced me to reflect, transferring that which is material to that which is immaterial, on the diversity of the sacred virtues: then it seems to me that I see myself dwelling, as it were, in some strange region of the universe which neither exists entirely in the slime of the earth nor entirely in the purity of Heaven; and that, by the grace of God, I can be transported from this inferior to that higher world in an anagogical manner. I used to converse with travelers from Jerusalem and, to my great delight, to learn from those to whom the treasures of Constantinople and the ornaments of Hagia Sophia had been accessible, whether the things here could claim some value in comparison with those there. When they acknowledged that these here were the more important ones, it occurred to us that those marvels of which we had heard before might have been put away, as a matter of precaution, for fear of the Franks, lest through the rash rapacity of a stupid few the partisans of the Greeks and Latins, called upon the scene, might suddenly be moved to sedition and warlike hostilities; for wariness is preeminently characteristic of the Greeks. Thus it could happen that the treasures which are visible here, deposited in safety, amount to more than those which had been visible there, left [on view] under conditions unsafe on account of disorders. From very many truthful men, even from Bishop Hugues of Laon, we had heard wonderful and almost incredible reports about the superiority of Hagia Sophia's and other churches' ornaments for the celebration of Mass. If this is so—or rather because we believe it to be so, by their testimony—then such inestimable and incomparable treasures should be exposed to the judgment of the many. *Let every man abound in his own sense.*[272] To me, I confess, one thing has always seemed preeminently fitting: that every costlier or costliest thing should serve, first and foremost, for the administration of the Holy Eucharist. If golden pouring vessels, golden vials, golden little mortars used to serve, by the word of God or the command of the Prophet, to collect the *blood of goats or calves or the red heifer: how much more* must golden vessels, precious stones, and whatever is most valued among all created things, be laid out, with continual reverence and full devotion, for the reception of the *blood of Christ.*[273] Surely neither we nor our possessions suffice for this service. [. . .]

XXXIV

We also changed to its present form, sympathizing with their discomfort, the choir of the brethren, which had been detrimental to health for a long time on account of the coldness of the marble and the copper and had caused great hardship to those who constantly attended service in church; and because of the increase in our community (with the help of God), we endeavored to enlarge it.

We also caused the ancient pulpit, which—admirable for the most delicate and nowadays irreplaceable sculpture of its ivory tablets—surpassed human evaluation also by the depiction of antique subjects, to be repaired after we had reassembled those tablets which were moldering all too long in, and even under, the repository of the money chests; on the right side we restored to their places the animals of copper lest so much and admirable material perish, and had [the whole] set up so that the reading of Holy Gospels might be performed in a more elevated place. In the beginning of our abbacy we had already put out of the way a certain obstruction which cut as a dark wall through the central nave of the church, lest the beauty of the church's magnitude be obscured by such barriers.

Further, we saw to it, both on account of its so exalted function and of the value of the work itself, that the famous

---

271. Ez 28:13.
272. Rom 14:5.
273. Heb 9:13–14.

throne of the glorious King Dagobert, worn with age and dilapidated, was restored. On it, as ancient tradition relates, the kings of the Franks, after having taken the reins of government, used to sit in order to receive, for the first time, the homage of their nobles.

Also we had regilded the Eagle in the middle of the choir which had become rubbed bare through the frequent touch of admirers.

Moreover, we caused to be painted, by the exquisite hands of many masters from different regions, a splendid variety of new windows, both below and above; from that first one which begins [the series] with the *Tree of Jesse* in the chevet of the church to that which is installed above the principal door in the church's entrance. One of these, urging us onward from the material to the immaterial, represents the Apostle Paul turning a mill, and the Prophets carrying sacks to the mill. The verses of this subject are these:

> By working the mill, thou, Paul, takest the flour out of
> the bran.
> Thou makest known the inmost meaning of the Law of
> Moses.
> From so many grains is made the true bread without bran,
> Our and the angels' perpetual food.

From Edwin Panofsky, *Abbot Suger on the Abbey Church of St.-Denis and Its Art Treasures* (Princeton: Princeton University Press, 1946), 41, 43, 45, 49, 51, 63, 65, 73, 75. [Brackets in original.]

☙ In his "Ecclesiastical Architecture," **Edward Foley** reflects on nineteenth- and twentieth-century innovations in the construction of worship spaces. Foley also discusses the impact that liturgical considerations have on the architectural design of worship spaces.

EDWARD FOLEY

"Ecclesiastical Architecture," in *From Age to Age: How Christians Have Celebrated the Eucharist*

Although the nineteenth century was a revolutionary time for Western architecture, this was not true for church architecture. The most notable development in church architecture during this period was the Gothic Revival. Augustus Pugin (d. 1852) was the revival's most outspoken proponent. Pugin's argument that Gothic was the only appropriate ecclesiastical style was accepted not only by the Catholic church, but also by other religious traditions in his native England.

This revival, however, had little impact outside of England, the United States and, to a lesser degree, France.

Some innovations did occur in church buildings in the early twentieth century, but these essentially were structural. St. Eugene (1854–1855) in Paris, designed by Louis-Auguste Boileau (d. 1896), for example, was the first ironframed church. Northwest of Paris in Le Raincy, Auguste Perret (d. 1954) constructed the church of Notre-Dame (1922–1923) completely out of reinforced concrete, a design that had much in common with the hall churches of the thirteenth century. A few years later, Otto Bartning (d. 1959) created the steel and copper *Stahlkirche* in Cologne that, again, offered technological innovation within a traditional configuration.

It was not until Le Corbusier designed Notre-Dame-du-Haut in Ronchamps (1950–1955) that a breakthrough occurred in church architecture. Beyond new technology, this church offers a fresh vision of sacred space, but without a fully renewed vision of the liturgy. For example, although innumerable barriers traditionally found between the assembly and the sanctuary were omitted, the space does not assert the primacy of the assembly. Rather, the interior of Notre-Dame-du-Haut appears as a collection of devotional spaces under a single roof—a perspective that Le Corbusier's own words seem to confirm.[274] However, the processional path to the church and the exterior choir, which faces east—calling the eucharistic community to stand in the light of day—are compelling liturgical elements. Overall, Notre-Dame-du-Haut exists more as a triumph of sacred architecture than as a model of liturgical space.

Ultimately, it was not the accumulation of technological advances, nor even the new vision of the sacred offered by Le Corbusier, that changed the face of twentieth-century Christian architecture in the West. Rather, it was the success of the liturgical movement, which reasserted the corporate nature of worship and the centrality of the community in that worship. Although this perspective was held by many reformers, who often opted for central-plan churches, many Protestant churches lost this vision. Under the influence of the nineteenth-century Cambridge Movement, many English-speaking churches returned to more traditional forms in the

---

274. "In building this chapel I wished to create a place of silence, prayer, of peace and spiritual joy. Our efforts were inspired by their sacred aim. . . . The Virgin is extolled by various symbols and some written words. The cross—the real cross of suffering—is erected in this ark; henceforth the Christian drama is in possession of the place. . . . What all of us have recorded here will, I hope, find an echo in you and in those who climb this hill." Le Corbusier's address to the bishop (June 25, 1955).

various architectural revivals (Gothic, classical and Roman-esque) that marked that century. James White has noted a similar return to traditional forms resulting from nineteenth-century revivalism, where emphasis on pulpit personalities and massed choirs developed the concert-stage arrangement.

Although a few visionaries, including Otto Bartning, ex-perimented with central-plan spaces as a way to affirm the unity and centrality of the assembly, these remained isolated experiments. Eventually, however, the liturgical movement, reflecting the movement in society toward freedom and equality, brought a greater emphasis to the communal aspect of worship. At first this emphasis took place mainly through scholarship, but it eventually had an impact on the worship space. In some sense, this meant an adoption of "functional-ism" in liturgy,[275] 'more commonly expressed in terms of the "ritual requirements" of the space. Thus, a space must serve not only as a place for individual encounter with the Holy, but also, and primarily, as a place for the enactment of public ritual. Christian liturgical space is rendered sacred first of all by the action of the community.

In many respects, functionalism in the liturgy is grounded in the architectural principles that dominated Europe and the United States earlier in the twentieth century: respect for individuals and their freedom; a preference for open, free-flowing, flexible spaces suited to their environment; the achievement of a sense of volume rather than of mass; a concern for the authenticity of materials; the exposure of the essential elements of the construction and the nature of the materials; and the rejection of ornamentation. Whereas Frank Lloyd Wright shaped his domestic spaces around a huge open hearth, an increasing number of liturgical churches are shaping their space around the ambo and the altar.

This renewed awareness that the liturgy must shape the space has resulted in numerous church renovations remi-niscent of those that followed the Reformation. In some churches, the interior has been completely reoriented, giv-ing a building designed as a longitudinal arch the feeling of a central plan. Newer constructions also reflect a preference for central-plan interiors. These buildings attempt to place the assembly concretely, and not simply theoretically, at the center of the church's prayer.

Summary

Although twentieth-century architecture in the West was not by nature ecclesial, it did express certain principles that were well accepted in ecclesial circles. Most important were the functionalists' attention to the purpose of the building and the need for integrity in materials, construction and design in fulfilling that purpose. This has resulted in a revolution in ecclesiastical architecture since the 1950s. No longer is the repetition of a particular "sacred" design acceptable merely because it is traditional. Rather, each building's design must respect and support the reformed liturgy and the commu-nity responsible for its enactment. Only then will communi-ties again understand that it is not any structure, whatever its style, but the assembly that is the church of living stones.

From Edward Foley, *From Age to Age: How Christians Have Celebrated the Eucharist* (Chi-cago: Liturgy Training, 1991), 146–50.

---

275. "A space acquires a sacredness from the sacred action of the faith com-munity which uses it." U.S. Bishops' Committee on the Liturgy, *Environment and Art in Catholic Worship* (1978), 41.

CHAPTER 5

Structures of Community: Ways of Living, Decision-Making

The early Christians who gathered once a week for the Lord's Supper considered their gathering a "eucharistic community." They soon considered themselves an "Ecclesia," a "Church," that is, an assembly, a congregation of a "people" with a common faith, in the same way that Israel was God's people. The separation of the early Christian movement from Judaism, the numerical growth of the movement, and the need to demonstrate that Christians were not a rabble, among other factors, made it necessary for early Christians to find modes of organizing their communities. We observed in chapter 3, in connection with the Montanist movement, that the Church of the second century, abandoning the expectation of the imminent return of Christ, had begun to evolve organizational structures with a view to long-term survival. The Christian community, then, that interpreted its Scriptures (chapter 1), that worshiped (chapter 4), that developed, experienced, and thought its faith (chapters 3 and 6), became also an organized and structured community. What had been individual and personal charisms—prophesy, teaching, and liturgical ministry—were gradually formalized into overall and socialized structures within which the individual experienced God and received salvation.

On the whole, therefore, the organizational structures of Christian communities are intimately connected with the communities' conceptions of their teaching authority and life of worship, in particular the Eucharist. The texts in this chapter focus on those structures and the demands they make on Christian living. Two aspects are discernible in the selections: first, the evolution of the structures themselves and their relationship to questions of authority and ministry; and, second, the demands that Christianity, as structured

communities, places on the believers in their search for Christian perfection and salvation.

The first set of texts, from the period of the apostolic Fathers, belongs to the time of the emergence in early Christianity of what might be called "the catholic consciousness." From the point of view of the organization of the Christian movement, we see here the gradual transition from an earlier situation of a diversity of powers—prophet, apostle, and teacher—originally exercised by individuals who usually were itinerant missionaries. Later, these powers became vested in local bodies of presbyters (*presbuteros,* "elders") and finally in a single bishop (*episkopos,* "overseer," "supervisor") set at the head of the presbyters and aided by deacons. The terminology and the beginning of this process are present in the New Testament itself, especially in the pastoral Epistles, where Timothy and Titus are represented as Paul's delegates to whom he entrusted the supervision of the presbyters of the Churches in Ephesus and Crete. The evolution of this hierarchical structure of the Church's organization goes hand in hand with the recourse to the criterion of apostolicity as the guarantee of authority. Whether the bishop's authority is thought to derive from an unbroken chain of authorized teachers beginning with the apostles (as Irenaeus argues) or from an unbroken chain of ordinations (as Clement of Rome seems to suggest), the bishop is seen as the successor of the apostles. He is the local embodiment of the prophetic, teaching, and liturgical functions exercised by the apostles of former times. As such, he is the living witness and guarantee of authentic faith.

In the *Didache,* as in Ephesians 4:11, the diverse charisms of apostles, teachers, and prophets coexist in the same community with resident bishops and deacons. The bishop is the same official as the presbyter and, with the deacon, is said to carry out also "the ministry of the prophets and teachers." Itinerant prophets and teachers are not yet replaced by permanent resident ministers.

The First and Second Letters of the Romans to the Corinthians are attributed to Clement, bishop of Rome, and were sent from the Christian community in Rome to the community in Corinth. These late-first-century letters reveal the connectedness of and mutual care among the early Christian communities, which were crucial factors for the emergence of a sense of catholicity, that is, "universality" among the Churches. Clement's Church was organized on the analogy of biblical Jewish society, with high priests, priests, Levites, and laypersons. In his actual terminology, however, those who minister in the Church are the "bishops and deacons." Moreover, he uses the terms "bishops" and "presbyters" as synonyms referring to the same group of people. The presbyter-bishops are the legitimately appointed priests who, like the priests of Israel, offer the sacrifice of the Eucharist. Acting on Christ's instructions, he says, the apostles appointed their "firstfruits" as presbyter-bishops and in this way provided for the future ministry. What Clement says about the process of appointing the successive generations of presbyter-bishops, and the implications of that process for the theory of apostolic succession, are all issues that need to be worked out.

Other than what can be learned from his seven letters, not much is known about Ignatius (ca. 30–107), bishop of Antioch. We see from his letters that the bishop has taken over in his single person the functions of teacher, prophet, and apostle. He is at the center of the community, and without his consent no decision may be taken and no liturgical services may be performed. For the first time, we encounter one bishop presiding over a body of presbyters and deacons. Ignatius, however, seems to lack a theory of apostolic succession, and one might wonder how widespread was the image he paints of the Church.

In chapter 3 we noted how, in the fourth century, the ordering of Christian life took another turn with the creation of Christian ascetic communities. Complex factors led the Christians of the fourth century to choose a life of retirement from the world (*anchōrēsis*). Among such factors, certainly, were the radical social changes that attended upon the triumphal Church as it became the religion of the state under Emperor Constantine and his successors. The Church and "the world" began to be coextensive, and Christians ceased to be a minority, or "resident aliens," in a world thought to

be ruled by demons. At the heart of the monastic movement, then, lay the desire to return to the pristine radicality of the Christian message. Christians could no longer attain the heroic perfection of martyrdom. Christian perfection would now be found in virginity. The prison cells, deprivations, torture, and combat with the devil by which Christian martyrs had lived their faith in Christ to the full would now be sought in the conditions of the desert. Although the relationship between the anchorite (eremitic) and the cenobitic (communal) movements is a matter of dispute, it can be said that Christian asceticism becomes Christian monasticism only with the organization of structured communities. With the communities organized by Pachomius came a new category of Christian literature: Rules.

Pachomius (ca. 290–346) was born in the Thebaid in Upper Egypt. His parents were not Christians and he knew neither Greek nor Latin. Drafted into the army during the civil war between Licinius and Maximin, he was moved by the charity of the Christians who came out to bring supplies to a convoy of young recruits to which he belonged. At the end of the civil war he was baptized and lived as an anchorite under the direction of Palamon. From about 320, thousands of men and women gathered in numerous communities (*koinōnia*) to pray, work, and share all goods, with absolute equality. They all submitted themselves completely to a Rule and a hierarchical structure of governance instituted by Pachomius. By establishing a *koinōnia,* that is, a "communion," "fellowship," or "sharing" (Acts 2:42; 1 Cor 10:16), Pachomius shifted the emphasis away from himself, the master, to the community. It was in this "fellowship of brothers" that the Spirit was to be found. The common Rule of life and the hierarchy it set up established a life in common, a society that possessed the structures of the Church. In this new society Pachomius reestablished the perfect fellowship of the apostolic age, that is, the Church of the apostles. It is in the *Lives* that one gets an insight into the principles which guided Pachomian monasticism.

In its fully developed form, the Pachomian monastery was an elaborate structure capable of accommodating hundreds of monks and nuns. It was divided into "houses," each with its own house master and a deputy, and was surrounded by a wall. Besides the living quarters for the monks and nuns, the monastery had a gatehouse, a guesthouse, a kitchen, a dining room, an infirmary, and an assembly room for common prayers. The whole establishment was overseen by a "superior" or "steward."

At the end of his studies in Athens in 355 and a brief stint as teacher of rhetoric in Neo-Caesarea (in Asia Minor), Basil (ca. 330–79) and his friend Gregory of Nazianzus decided in about 358 to take up a "philosophic," that is, ascetic way of life. Following his baptism, Basil undertook a tour in search of a guide to monastic life. He came in contact with Antony's anchorite system and the Pachomian cenobitism in Syria, Palestine, and Upper Egypt. On his return to Cappadocia, he retired from public life and undertook an intense study of Scripture, possibly in an effort to find a solid theological basis for Christian ascetic life. *The Moral Rules* (written ca. 360) contains his statement of the principles of Christian living. For Basil, the only Rule of Christian living was the Scriptures. His collections are, thus, somewhat improperly termed *Short Rule* and *Long Rule,* since they are not collections of regulations analogous to those of Pachomius, Benedict, and others.

For Basil, as for Pachomius, the ideal of Christian life was the fellowship of the apostolic Christian community of Acts 4:32–37. Christian living had as its end the twofold love of God and of neighbor. He considerably modified the Pachomian system: he created monasteries of moderate size, outlawed rivalries in ascetic rigor, and made bodily austerity subject to obedience to the superior. Obedience itself became a kind of asceticism, characterized by the renunciation of family relations and submission to a common life under the direction of a superior. Basil was very critical of the solitary life. Such a life was self-centered, in his view, and did not offer the opportunity for the practice of humility and the exercise of obedience and charity. He insisted on the necessity of prayer and work for Christian living. Work, undertaken for the sake of discipline and in order to provide for one's livelihood and that of one's neighbor, must not interfere, however, with the community's ordered tranquility. Prayer was to be so continuous that it became a spontaneous habit of the mind. Basil provided the systematic formulation of the guiding principles of monastic life, which were later to be found in the Rules of Benedict and his successors. Basil's influence is most notable, however, on monasticism in the Eastern Church, which considers all its monastic life to derive from him.

The ascetic ideal was an essential theme in Augustine's (354–430) conversion. His conversion in 386 was linked to his reading of Athanasius's life of Saint Antony. In 386–87, following his conversion, he withdrew with his friends to the country estate of Cassiciacum and lived in a kind of society of Christian philosophers. He then moved to Thagaste, where he founded a community in 388. Later, after he was

ordained a priest in 391, he established and lived in a community for laypeople in Hippo. Consecrated bishop of Hippo in 395 or 396, he turned his episcopal residence into a community for his own priests and other clergy and insisted that all his clergy live there.

Augustine's community was not so much along the lines of the Egyptian model, which was a gathering of disciples around a spiritual father. Rather, it was an association of friends in the common search for the ideal of wisdom. Much emphasis is laid on fraternal relationship and humaneness. Augustine's Rule existed in both a masculine and a feminine version and is the first legislative text in the history of early Western monasticism to be appropriate for both men and women. From the fifth century, his Rule was considered one of the great Rules of monastic life. Its influence on other Rules, including Benedict's, was extensive, and Augustine's model contributed to the development in the Church of the canons regular.

Since Benedict (ca. 480–ca. 543) is not mentioned in contemporary literature and left no other writing apart from his Rule, where he does not identify himself, all that is known about him is derived from the *Dialogues,* written in 593–94 by Pope Gregory the Great. Benedict was converted to Christianity in Rome, where he went to school; he lived as one of the ascetics in Enfide (identified with modern Affile) and then for five years in complete solitude in Subiaco. He was later joined by numerous disciples, for whom he established twelve monasteries and appointed deans over them. Afterward he left these communities and established a fully cenobitic community in Cassino, some eight miles south of Rome.

The overall context of Benedict's monasticism is the collapse in the West of political, civil, and religious life and authority in the fifth and sixth centuries. Civil society was ravaged by "barbarian" invasions and the decay of ancient Roman culture. Benedict's community in Cassino was destroyed during the invasion of the Lombards, though the monks escaped. Religious society was being torn apart by controversies and schisms, in particular Arianism, the Christological controversy, and Pelagianism (see chapter 3). Although solitary ascetics continued to exist in large numbers, the tendency in the West, because of the general breakdown of order in society and the need to preserve orthodoxy, was toward cenobitic communities and greater regimentation. Various other Rules preceded Benedict's. They grew out of the life of specific communities, which they were designed to regulate, and they drew what was needed from the earlier ascetic and monastic traditions from Antony to Jerome. A Rule typically had two parts. It began with a theoretical statement of spirituality, followed by rules and regulations to govern the practicalities of the community's daily life by specifying such matters as the nature of authority, the time and length of common prayer, food, sleep, and work, and relationships with outsiders. The wide influence that Benedict exerted on monastic life in the West was a measure of the extent to which his Rule had succeeded in crystallizing the entire tradition on which he depended.

The world in which the next set of religious orders, congregations, and their Rules came into existence was that of Europe after the collapse of the Carolingian Empire (eighth to tenth centuries), followed by fresh invasions. By the beginning of the eleventh century, the invading barbarian Northmen and Hungarians had become settled populations and embraced Christianity. The stage was set for the resurgence of Western European civilization leading up to the High Middle Ages. An essential element in that resurgence was the political, social, and religious revolution generally called the "Gregorian Reform," which reached its climax under Pope Gregory VII (1073–85) and was continued by his successors. An important part of the Reform was the reform of monasticism, not so much because of moral decline and laxity in monastic discipline but because of a new religious perception and sensitivity. Characteristic of the new religious reality was the reemergence of the love of poverty—radical and absolute poverty—which, bypassing the moderation enjoined by *The Rule of Saint Benedict,* strove for the poverty of Christ on the Cross. Critics of the traditional Benedictine monasteries, especially the "empire" at Cluny and its affiliates, could point to these monasteries' abandonment of manual labor and solitude, their riches, comfort, and pomp, their entanglement with feudal society, and their political activities.

The renewal of poverty as a desired way of life was seen as the return to the simplicity and innocence of the primitive Church, the ancient apostolic Church. In practice, the return to the apostolic life meant the return to pre-Benedictine eremitism. The hermit not only withdrew from society but lived in complete renunciation, in absolute internal and external poverty. The apostles, it was claimed, were monks, and the monk, as in the fourth century, was a solitary "poor man of Christ." Life in the monastery was seen only as training for the solitary life in a hermitage. The fascination with absolute poverty and the apostolic life was not limited, however, only to those among the clergy who sought the solitude of a hermitage. Canons regular and laypeople were inspired as well.

The result was a grassroots religious movement, a spontaneous monasticism that not only could not be fitted into the existing Rules but rejected outright the notion of rules in favor of the simple rule of Christ in the Gospels. Consequently, from the eleventh century onward there was a proliferation of eccentric itinerant preachers of poverty, some beyond the pale of orthodoxy, and of new religious movements and foundations which sought new institutional combinations of the ideals of absolute poverty, solitude, and apostolic life.

To curb the resulting "excessive diversity," which would have appeared dangerously anarchic to Church authorities, the Fourth Lateran Council (1215) decreed that neither new communities nor new Rules nor even new forms of religious life might be founded. All intending to lead a religious life must enter an already-existing and approved community; and any who founded a new religious house must adopt an already-existing Rule. Before that decision, however, several successful foundations had already come into existence, among which must be counted the Carthusians of Chartreuse, founded by Bruno in 1084; the Prémontré, founded by Norbert of Xanten in 1120; and the Abbey of Cîteaux (Cistercians), founded by Robert of Abrissel in 1098. The Cistercians, whose reforms transformed Western monasticism, became the first religious "order" in the medieval Church, that is, a cohesive body of interconnected communities under the same constitution and dependent on one central organization, as distinct from the many autonomous foundations and the loose affiliations of the Benedictine communities. The Cistercians also instituted the "General Chapter" as an administrative tool for religious foundations and the inclusion of "lay-brothers" to perform the secular and physical work of the foundations.

Pope Urban II preached the First Crusade in 1097. The Second Crusade was launched by Bernard, the prodigious Cistercian abbot of Clairvaux, in 1147, by order of the Cistercian pope Eugenius III (1145–53). Apparently, during this period pilgrims and crusaders in Palestine gathered in a community at the traditional fountain of Elijah on Mount Carmel. The foundation was very much in line with eleventh-century reforms, involving strict eremitism and poverty; the monks lived in complete seclusion in separate huts or cells, meeting only in the oratory for liturgical prayers. They devoted their lives of silence to manual labor and prayer. *The Rule of Carmel* was given by Albert, the Latin patriarch of Jerusalem. Unable to remain in Palestine because of the defeats suffered by the crusader armies, in 1240 the Carmelite hermits dispersed to England, France, Sicily, and Cyprus.

Francis (1182–1226), the "Little Poor Man of Assisi," was impelled by his vision in the church of Saint Damiano to the love of Christ crucified and to be wedded to what he called "Lady Poverty." This involved the absolute renunciation not only of property but of self and also the requirement to share the indigence and suffering of the poor. His inspiration to "repair" the Church was consonant with that of those reformers who understood the apostolic life as a call to mendicant, itinerant preaching, just as Jesus required of the apostles in Matthew 10:5–15. Moreover, also in tune with the spirit of the times, Saint Francis saw no need for a formal Rule other than the rule to follow the teachings and the footsteps of Christ in the Gospels, which he sought to read and obey without addition, modification, or interpretation. The growth of the community that gathered around him, however, obligated him to compose a primitive Rule of life. He was later persuaded by the more learned members of his order to rewrite an expanded version of this Rule to meet the legal precision needed for papal approval.

Although Clare of Assisi (1194–1253) has been generally regarded from the point of view of her association with Francis and his spirituality, she is in her own right distinguished as the first woman to have written a Rule of life meant for women. She founded the order known as the Poor Clares and was canonized in 1255.

Dominic de Guzmán understood the literal living out of the apostolic life as a call to preach the gospel. He was born (according to tradition, in ca. 1170) in Caleruega, a town of Old Castile, which, like the rest of the Iberian Peninsula, was returning to the Christian faith after the Moslem invasion. Following his education, he became a canon regular in the cathedral chapter of Osma, which accepted *The Rule of Saint Augustine* in 1199. Here he forged a friendship with Diego d'Acebes, whose assistant he became when Diego succeeded to the bishopric of Osma. Diego's and Dominic's offer, in 1205, to preach the gospel to the tribes of Eastern Europe was refused by Pope Innocent III. Their opportunity came, however, the next year when the Cistercian papal legates in Languedoc, France, asked for their advice on how to win back the territory from the dualistic doctrine of Cathar. Diego and Dominic embarked together on the apostolic "preaching of Jesus Christ," begging their bread from door to door. They settled the women converts from Catharism as nuns in the church of St. Mary at Prouille, probably in 1206. Bishop Diego died in 1207.

By 1215, Dominic had gathered a small band of companions and moved into a house given to them in Toulouse. The Fourth Lateran Council, which Dominic attended, helped crystallize his conception of the new order that he was to found. Along with the prohibition of new religious communities, the council called for the apostolic ministry of preaching and the education of the clergy. Obedient to this call, Dominic's founding charter for what later came to be called the Dominican Order combined preaching and learning with mendicant poverty.

Those men and women who chose individual solitary existence lived either as hermits, mostly in remote places begging their way or growing their own food, or as anchorites in permanent enclosures attached to a church in the midst of a town or village. Women leading the enclosed anchoritic life were known as anchoresses. The cloister into which they fled the evil world and God's anger was their prison or desert where they fought with self and demons. The thirteenth-century *Ancrene Wisse* (*Guide for Anchoresses*) was meant to give such anchoresses a program of spiritual guidance.

Iosif Volotsky (1439–1515) was born in Ivan Sasin, Russia, and became abbot of the monastery in Borovsk in 1477. His search for strict communal life led him first to an unsuccessful reform of his own monastery, then to residence in various other monasteries, and finally to the foundation of his own monastery in Volok (also known as Volokolamsk) in 1479. Like some of his counterparts in the West, Volotsky was politically involved and active. And like them he fought heretics, in his case the so-called Judaizers, whose violent suppression he achieved at the hand of the state in 1504. Although Volotsky emphasized austerity for the individual monk, it was necessary for the community as a whole to prosper so that it could render the service of charity to society. As the greatest champion of the right of monasteries to own property, Volotsky insisted on, and obtained, the right of monasteries to own landed property. He was instrumental in developing, in the Eastern Church, the practice of choosing bishops from among monks. By his death, his monastery had become the largest center for social services in the state and the most fertile nursery for prelates.

Ignatius of Loyola was born, most likely in 1491, in his family castle of Loyola, which lay in the northern Basque region of Guipúzcoa. The Europe into which Ignatius was born was complex and tumultuous. Feudal states were gradually giving way to nation-states. Spain was spearheading the discovery of new worlds and was consequently acquiring a far-flung empire, which it ruled through a hierarchical administrative structure with the king at the top. The acquisition of new territories led to a missionary drive to convert their inhabitants to Christianity. At home, Christianity stood in dire need of administrative and moral reforms, as Ignatius said, "in head and members." The Protestant Reformation was already under way; Luther was excommunicated in 1521, and in 1534 Henry VIII became the head of the Church of England.

Ignatius was destined to a military career, though he never became a professional soldier, and a life at court. In 1521, while he was leading a brave but ill-advised action in Pamplona against the besieging French forces, a cannonball shattered a bone in one of his legs and wounded the flesh of the other. While he recovered from the surgeries to repair his injuries, he was converted through his reading of the Dominican Jacobus de Voragine's (d. 1298) lives of the saints, *Golden Legend*. Once he recovered, Ignatius thought of himself as a pilgrim and resolved to enlist in Christ's "militia." Having failed to find a place to live in Palestine, he returned to Europe to begin the painful process of earning an education beyond the basics of reading and writing. By 1523 he had already completed the first draft of his influential *Spiritual Exercises,* a powerful tool for spiritual experience and reform. While a student at the University of Paris, he gathered around him a small group of companions who vowed to live an ascetic life and to put themselves at the service of the pope, should they not manage to go to Jerusalem to preach the Christian faith. After having become masters of theology and having failed to go to Jerusalem, the companions put themselves at the service of Pope Paul III in November 1538. The risk of missionary dispersion obliged them to formalize their relationship into a religious order, called the Society of Jesus. This was achieved when Ignatius's "First Sketch of the Institute of the Society of Jesus" was approved by Pope Paul III in the papal Bull *Regimini militantis ecclesiae* of September 27, 1540. *The Jesuit Constitution* was drafted by Ignatius and adopted in 1558 by the Jesuits (as the members of the order were called).

The Society of Jesus was in many ways a new phenomenon in the history of Christian religious life. It was a body of clerics regular, but without the formal obligation to live communally. Its administrative structure was a chain of command with the pope at its head and a general as his vicar who presided over a number of subordinate "superiors." Ignatius's spiritual vision was centered on the "greater glory of God," to which every creature had to be subordinated as a tool. "Glory" meant at the same time "praise" and "service." Members of the new order had, therefore, to be "contemplatives in action." The God who is worshiped in contemplative

prayer is served also in whatever mission the pope and the superior might assign the individual Jesuit.

Although the Protestant Reformation on the whole rejected traditional Christian monastic life, in 1940 Roger Schutz founded a monastery in Taizé, near the ancient Benedictine monastery in Cluny. Brother (Frère) Roger, as he has come to be known, was born in 1915 in Switzerland. While writing his doctoral dissertation, on early Christian monasticism, in the University of Lausanne Theology Faculty, he became leader of a small group of Protestant students. In 1940 he bought a mansion in Taizé, which he used also as a shelter for Jews and refugees from the Second World War until 1942, when the German occupation of France forced him to move his community to Geneva. They resettled in Taizé in 1944. *The Rule of Taizé* was written in 1952 and revised in 2000. The Taizé community is both international and interdenominational. It has been outstanding for its work on, among other things, Christian reconciliation and unity: ecumenism (see chapter 7 of this volume).

In the next section of this chapter, we return to the topic of the continuing evolution of the larger structures of Christian communities, apart from monasticism. That evolution cannot be understood solely as the growth of papal authority and the primacy of the Church of Rome, nor can the later structures that came to characterize the Western Church be retrojected into the early Church. The primacy of the Church of Rome and papal authority have been, nonetheless, critical elements in Western Christianity until the Protestant Reformation, in the Roman Catholic Church thereafter, and in the continuing search for Christian reconciliation and unity.

The first five texts in the section are some of the primary sources for understanding the interrelationship among the early Christian Churches, especially the major centers, namely, Alexandria, Antioch, Constantinople, and Rome. Included in this interrelationship are the ways in which the Church of Rome and its bishop were received, and the bases for that reception, by the other Churches within the communion of regional Churches. The texts have been, for obvious reasons, the source of much interpretation and controversy. Clement of Rome's *First Letter of the Romans to the Corinthians* (see above) is significant for the initiative taken by the Church in Rome to deal with problems in the Church in Corinth and also for its statements about the Church of Rome itself. In *Against Heresies,* Irenaeus offers the clearest formulation of the theory of apostolic succession. In *Ecclesiastical History,* Eusebius's account of the controversy between the Church of Rome and the Churches in Asia about the date of Easter exemplifies the extent and limits of communion among the Churches. The Decree of the Council of Chalcedon in 451 is significant for what it says in its *Definition of Faith* about the status of Pope Leo's *Tome* (see chapter 3 of this volume) and for its statements in *Canon 28* about Rome and Constantinople.

The histories of the diverging developments of Christianity in the East and the West after the fifth century are readily available. The next four documents point to the greater and greater centralization of power in the Western Church (especially after it broke with the East), in the Church of Rome, and in the person of its bishop. The document known as *The Donation of Constantine* became part of Gratian's *Decretum* by the twelfth century, even though Leo of Vercelli had called it a forgery at the end of the tenth century. Throughout the Middle Ages, it was considered genuine by both friends and foes of papal claims. Two men who dared to doubt its genuineness were burnt in Strassburg in 1229. In 1440, Lorenzo Valla definitively demonstrated that the document was a forgery, although at the time he only sparked off a long controversy.

It was in the midst of the Gregorian renaissance that the breach between the East and the West took place, with the mutual excommunication in 1054 between Pope Leo IX and Patriarch Michael Cerularius of Constantinople. The schism was aggravated by Pope Innocent III's decision to appoint bishops for the Churches in the East, including Constantinople, after this city had been sacked in the Fourth Crusade (1204). Innocent III's decision was prepared by Gregory VII's Reform, which sought to free the papacy from the princes and bring about the moral reform of the Church by linking the Churches in the West more closely to Rome. Gregory's *Dictatus papae* paved the way for the papal theocracy, which finds its clearest expression in the Bull by Pope Boniface VIII, *Unam sanctam.*

Pope Boniface's *Unam sanctam* was published in the midst of widespread debate and conflicts about the claims of papal authority. Boniface himself died in 1303, a captive of Philip the Fair, king of France. With respect to the structure of the Church itself, the debate centered on the conciliar theory, that is, the authority of councils as opposed to the monarchical power of the pope. The First Vatican Council's Constitution, *Pastor aeternus,* gave dogmatic expression to the theory of the pope's absolute authority. The story of the document is fascinating, as are indeed the time and person of Pope Pius IX (1846–78), who summoned the council. It is certainly the case also that a "mild" reading of the Constitution is possible.

The document was, however, conceived and written in the atmosphere of ultramontanism (that is, the tendency—as seen from the Churches "beyond the mountains," namely, the Alps—to consider Rome "the center of the Church" and to concentrate all Church authority there). Ultramontanist views tended to guide the Constitution's subsequent interpretation. The consequences are evident in the faith that was taught to believers in the nineteenth-century *Baltimore Catechism.*

The centerpiece document of the Second Vatican Council is the *Dogmatic Constitution on the Church (Lumen gentium).* While explicitly affirming to continue the teachings of the First Vatican Council, the *Constitution* lays out a new understanding of the Church and its structure. Chapter 3 (opening with paragraph 18) of the document contains its most central dogmatic affirmations about the nature of the Church. The Church is now seen as the "People of God," constituted essentially by the local Church headed by its bishop. The unity of the Church comprises the communion of all the local Churches and their bishops, "successors of the apostles," with each other and with the bishop of Rome. On November 21, 1964, the council also passed the *Decree on Ecumenism.* This decree, the openness of the council itself, the numerous gestures and declarations by the popes and other officials of the Catholic Church during and after the council, opened a new era of dialogue and mutual understanding between the Catholic Church and the other Christian Churches, and of these among themselves. The meeting of Patriarch Dimitrios I with Pope John Paul II and their declarations in 1979 were some of the high points of this new search for understanding and unity.

The texts in the rest of section 3 focus on various issues and structures of the Eastern Orthodox Church, the Churches of the Protestant Reformation, and "grassroots" Churches. Timothy Ware's *Orthodox Church* lays out the theological framework and the structures that underpin the self-definition of the complex reality known as the Orthodox Church. In the Eastern Churches, the pristine notion of the unity of the Church as a communion among "equals" is preserved. Chrysostomos Konstantinidis, in his "The Significance of the Eastern and Western Traditions within Christendom," revisits the thorny, but crucial, problem of Tradition. The road to Christian self-understanding and unity meanders through the attempts to revalue the Christian Tradition and the many traditions of the Christian Churches.

"Retraditioning" is the term that Konstantinidis gives to the Protestant Reformation's rejection of much of the

Church's accumulated tradition and its structures of authority (see chapter 6 below, particularly Luther's *To the Christian Nobility of the German Nation*). Conrad Grebel's *Letters to Thomas Müntzer* in 1524 lay out some of the essential theological tenets of the Anabaptist movement, which, with its teaching of "separation," made the Reformation rejection of the traditional structures of authority more radical. Following the massacre of members of the Anabaptist movement in Münster, Menno Simons became the leader of a radical pacifist branch of the movement in the Netherlands. Anabaptists ("those who baptize again"), as they were called by their opponents, seem initially to have been a radical apocalyptic faction of Ulrich Zwingli's reform movement in Zurich. They rejected Zwingli's link to, and dependence on, Zurich's city council as well as the general principle of a Christian state. In their view, the name "Christian" applied, not to any baptized person, but only to those who truly followed Jesus. Menno Simons's *On the Ban* legislates for the movement he led. *The Brotherly Union of a Number of Children of God concerning Seven Articles* (also known as *The Schleitheim Confession*) was the first and most widely circulated collective Anabaptist statement from the sixteenth century. The widely influential *Book of Discipline*, revised by Walter Travers, prescribes the Church structure considered by Elizabethan Puritan Reformers to have been given by Christ in the Scriptures.

The outcome of Christian mission in the past seven hundred years has not been the formation of Christian communities forever tied to the theological visions and community structures of the traditional European Churches. On the contrary, Christianity everywhere has seen an explosion, and in many cases veritable revolutions, in theological conceptions and community organizations (see chapter 8). The rise and rapid growth of the numerous African, so-called Independent, Churches are an example (see Peel, *Aladura: A Religious Movement among the Yoruba,* in chapter 4). Leonardo Boff's "A New Experience of Church" traces the origins, the theological significance, and structure of "Christian base-communities," the ecclesiological component of Latin America's liberation theology (see chapter 6 below). Robert Anthony Orsi, in his *Madonna of 115th Street,* presents the history, theology, and organization of the devotion to "la Madonna del Carmine" among the Italian immigrants of Harlem, New York.

The formation of new Christian structures of faith can take place within the organizational structures of the traditional Christian Churches. This is the case with the devotion to la Madonna del Carmine. In other instances, older structures are renewed, such as with Latin America's Christian base-communities. Other movements reach out for something they consider to be entirely new. Paul Heelas describes one of these efforts in his *New Age Movement.*

In the Catholic Church, the life of Christian perfection came to be recognized within the structures of a religious order or a religious congregation where the vows of poverty, chastity, and obedience were publicly made in the context of a life lived in common. A new category of the "state of perfection" came into existence, however, with the formation of the Societies of Common Life, which were communities of men or women living together for the sake of pastoral ministry but without the profession of public vows. The Catholic Foreign Mission Society of America (Maryknoll), the White Fathers, and the Oratorians are examples of such communities. The destruction of traditional monasticism during the French Revolution, in the late eighteenth century, and Christianity's battle with secularism brought to the fore a development in the forms of Christian living which had long been neglected, especially in the Roman Catholic tradition, namely, the call in the Gospels to all Christians to strive for perfection in every station of life. This call was given official recognition when Pope Pius XII, in his Bull *Provida mater ecclesia* of February 2, 1947, gave approval to those organizations of men and women (mostly lay) who, while they labored "in the world," sought to live the call to Christian perfection. Thus were born the Secular Institutes, whose members were bound neither by public vows nor by the obligations of communal life. The Work of Mary, popularly known as the Focolare movement, is one of these institutes.

The final section of this chapter focuses more precisely on the question of ethics. The problems of Christian morality and ethics are already both implied and explicitly raised by the different aspects of Christianity covered in this volume. The decision to withdraw from "the world" is itself an act of moral judgment. More generally, no Christian can escape from the human imperative to decide, choose, and put into operation an activity that produces real consequences—good or evil—in the world. From this point of view, Christianity appears as a vision of and foundation for a moral life. Richard A. McCormick's essay "Does Religious Faith Add to Ethical Perception?" examines the seemingly obvious relationship between Christian faith and moral decision. H. Richard Niebuhr's "Responsibility and Christ" brings the Christological question of the dual nature of Christ to bear on Christian ethics.

"Racism and the Elections: The American Dilemma, 1966" raises the moral questions which Christians face as members of an "idolatrous" American racist body politic. "Justice," one of the sixteen final Medellín Documents issued by the Second General Conference of Latin American Bishops provides a theological basis for liberation theology's critique of socioeconomic institutions. Lisa Sowle Cahill's essay "Sex, Gender, and the Problem of Moral Argument" takes up the problem of sex and gender from feminist and Christian perspectives. Finally, from Augustine's almost passing remarks in his *Letter* 138 and *Letter* 189, through Aquinas's systematic discussion of war in his *Summa theologiae,* to John Howard Yoder's "Criteria of the Just-War Tradition," the Christian "just-war" theory is considered.

1. EARLY COMMUNITY STRUCTURES

The Didache, written near the end of the first century or the beginning of the second by an unknown author, is one of the earliest witnesses to the changing structure of the early Church, evidenced by the gradual shift from diverse itinerant individuals (such as apostles and prophets) to a localized hierarchy of bishops overseeing presbyters and deacons.

The Didache, XI.1–XV.3

XI

1. So, if anyone should come and teach you all these things that have just been mentioned above, welcome him. 2. But if the teacher himself goes astray and teaches a different teaching that undermines all this, do not listen to him. However, if his teaching contributes to righteousness and knowledge of the Lord, welcome him as you would the Lord.

3. Now concerning the apostles and prophets, deal with them as follows in accordance with the rule of the gospel. 4. Let every apostle who comes to you be welcomed as if he were the Lord. 5. But he is not to stay for more than one day, unless there is need, in which case he may stay another. But if he stays three days, he is a false prophet. 6. And when the apostle leaves, he is to take nothing except bread until he finds his next night's lodging. But if he asks for money, he is a false prophet.

7. Also, do not test or evaluate any prophet who speaks in the spirit, for every sin will be forgiven, but this sin will not be forgiven.[1] 8. However, not everyone who speaks in the spirit is a prophet, but only if he exhibits the Lord's ways. By his conduct, therefore, will the false prophet and the prophet be recognized. 9. Furthermore, any prophet who orders a meal in the spirit shall not partake of it; if he does, he is a false prophet. 10. If any prophet teaches the truth, yet does not practice what he teaches, he is a false prophet. 11. But any prophet proven to be genuine who does something with a view to portraying in a worldly manner the symbolic meaning of the church[2] (provided that he does not teach you to do all that he himself does) is not to be judged by you, for his judgment is with God. Besides, the ancient prophets also acted in a similar manner. 12. But if anyone should say in the spirit, "Give me money," or anything else, do not listen to him. But if he tells you to give on behalf of others who are in need, let no one judge him.

XII

1. Everyone "who comes in the name of the Lord" is to be welcomed. But then examine him, and you will find out—for you will have insight—what is true and what is false. 2. If the one who comes is merely passing through, assist him as much as you can. But he must not stay with you for more than two or, if necessary, three days. 3. However, if he wishes to settle among you and is a craftsman, let him work for his living. 4. But if he is not a craftsman, decide according to your own judgment how he shall live among you as a Christian, yet without being idle. 5. But if he does not wish to cooperate in this way, then he is trading on Christ. Beware of such people.

XIII

1. But every genuine prophet who wishes to settle among you "is worthy of his food." 2. Likewise, every genuine

---

1. See Mk 3:28–29; Mt 12:31; Lk 12:10. (The notes for this selection are by Gerhart and Udoh.)

2. Literally: "who acts with a view to the earthly mystery of the church." The meaning of the phrase is not at all clear.

teacher is, like "the worker, worthy of his food."[3] 3. Take, therefore, all the firstfruits of the produce of the wine press and threshing floor, and of the cattle and sheep, and give these firstfruits to the prophets, for they are your high priests.[4] 4. But if you have no prophet, give them to the poor. **5.** If you make bread, take the firstfruit and give in accordance with the commandment. 6. Similarly, when you open a jar of wine or oil, take the firstfruit and give it to the prophets.[5] 7. As for money and clothes and any other possessions, take the "firstfruit" that seems right to you and give in accordance with the commandment.

XIV

1. On the Lord's own day gather together and break bread and give thanks, having first confessed your sins so that your sacrifice may be pure. 2. But let no one who has a quarrel with a companion join you until they have been reconciled, so that your sacrifice may not be defiled.[6] 3. For this is the sacrifice concerning which the Lord said, "In every place and time offer me a pure sacrifice, for I am a great king, says the Lord, and my name is marvelous among the nations."[7]

XV

1. Therefore appoint for yourselves bishops and deacons worthy of the Lord, men who are humble and not avaricious and true and approved, for they too carry out for you the ministry of the prophets and teachers. 2. You must not, therefore, despise them, for they are your honored men, along with the prophets and teachers.

3. Furthermore, correct one another, not in anger but in peace, as you find in the Gospel;[8] and if anyone wrongs his neighbor, let no one speak to him, nor let him hear a word from you, until he repents.

Translated by J. B. Lightfoot and J. R. Harmer, in *The Apostolic Fathers,* 2nd rev. ed., edited by J. B. Lightfoot (Grand Rapids, MI: Baker Book House, 1992), 263, 265, 267.

♋ *The First Letter of the Romans to the Corinthians,* also known as *1 Clement* (written ca. 96), is the earliest extant Christian document outside the New Testament. The letter was written by **Clement of Rome** (ca. 30–100), who, according to tradition (as reported by Irenaeus and Tertullian, among others), was the third bishop of Rome after Peter. The letter was addressed to the Church in

Corinth, where, it would seem, the leaders of the community had been deposed for unknown reasons.

CLEMENT OF ROME

The First Letter of the Romans to the Corinthians, XL.1–XLIV.6

XL

1. Since, therefore, these things are now clear to us and we have searched into the depths of the divine knowledge, we ought to do, in order, everything that the Master has commanded us to perform at the appointed times. 2. Now he commanded the offerings and services to be performed diligently, and not to be done carelessly or in disorder, but at designated times and seasons. 3. Both where and by whom he wants them to be performed, he himself has determined by his supreme will, so that all things, being done devoutly according to his good pleasure, might be acceptable to his will. 4. Those, therefore, who make their offerings at the appointed times are acceptable and blessed: for those who follow the instructions of the Master cannot go wrong. 5. For to the high priest the proper services have been given, and to the priests the proper office has been assigned, and upon the Levites the proper ministries have been imposed. The layman is bound by the layman's rules.

XLI

1. Let each of you, brothers, in his proper order give thanks to God, maintaining a good conscience, not overstepping the designated rule of his ministry, but acting with reverence. 2. Not just anywhere, brothers, are the continual daily sacrifices offered, or the freewill offerings, or the offerings for sin and trespasses, but only in Jerusalem. And even there the offering is not made in every place, but in front of the sanctuary at the altar, the offering having been first inspected for blemishes by the high priest and the previously mentioned ministers. 3. Those, therefore, who do anything contrary to the

---

3. See Mt 10:10; Lk 10:7; 1 Tim 5:18; also 1 Cor 9:6–14.

4. See Num 18:12–18.

5. See Deut 18:4–5; Lev. 23:17; Num 15:20–21.

6. See Mt 5:23–24.

7. Mal 1:11.

8. See Mt 18:15–18.

duty imposed by his will receive death as the penalty. 4. You see, brothers, as we have been considered worthy of greater knowledge, so much the more are we exposed to danger.

XLII

1. The apostles received the gospel for us from the Lord Jesus Christ; Jesus the Christ was sent forth from God. 2. So then Christ is from God, and the apostles are from Christ. Both, therefore, came of the will of God in good order. 3. Having therefore received their orders and being fully assured by the resurrection of our Lord Jesus Christ and full of faith in the Word of God, they went forth with the firm assurance that the Holy Spirit gives, preaching the good news that the kingdom of God was about to come. 4. So, preaching both in the country and in the towns, they appointed their firstfruits, when they had tested them by the Spirit, to be bishops and deacons for the future believers. 5. And this was no new thing they did, for indeed something had been written about bishops and deacons many years ago; for somewhere thus says the Scripture: "I will appoint their bishops in righteousness and their deacons in faith."[9]

XLIII

1. And is it any wonder that those who in Christ were entrusted by God with such a work appointed the officials just mentioned? After all, the blessed Moses, "who was a faithful servant in all his house,"[10] recorded in the sacred books all the injunctions given to him, and the rest of the prophets followed him, bearing witness with him to the laws that he enacted. 2. For when jealousy arose concerning the priesthood, and the tribes were quarreling about which of them was to be decorated with the glorious title, he commanded the leaders of the twelve tribes to bring him rods inscribed with the name of each tribe. And taking them he tied and sealed them with the signet rings of the leaders of the tribes, and deposited them on the table of God in the tent of the testimony. 3. Then, having shut the tent, he sealed the keys as well as the doors 4. and said to them, "Brothers, the tribe whose rod blossoms is the one God has chosen to be priests and to minister to him." 5. Now when morning came, he called all Israel together, all six hundred thousand men, showed the seals to the leaders of the tribes, opened the tent of testimony, and brought out the rods. And the rod of Aaron was found not only to have blossomed, but also to be bearing fruit.[11] 6. What

do you think, dear friends? Did not Moses know beforehand that this would happen? Of course he knew. But in order that disorder might not arise in Israel, he did it anyway, so that the name of the true and only God might be glorified, to whom be the glory for ever and ever. Amen.

XLIV

1. Our apostles likewise knew, through our Lord Jesus Christ, that there would be strife over the bishop's office. 2. For this reason, therefore, having received complete foreknowledge, they appointed the officials mentioned earlier and afterwards they gave the offices a permanent character; that is, if they should die, other approved men should succeed to their ministry.[12] 3. Those, therefore, who were appointed by them or, later on, by other reputable men with the consent of the whole church, and who have ministered to the flock of Christ blamelessly, humbly, peaceably, and unselfishly, and for a long time have been well spoken of by all—these men we consider to be unjustly removed from their ministry. 4. For it will be no small sin for us, if we depose from the bishop's office those who have offered the gifts blamelessly and in holiness. 5. Blessed are those presbyters who have gone on ahead, who took their departure at a mature and fruitful age, for they need no longer fear that someone might remove them from their established place. 6. For we see that you have removed certain people, their good conduct notwithstanding, from the ministry which had been held in honor by them blamelessly.

Translated by J. B. Lightfoot and J. R. Harmer, in *The Apostolic Fathers,* 2nd rev. ed., edited by J. B. Lightfoot (Grand Rapids, MI: Baker Book House, 1992), 73, 75, 77, 79.

On his way to Rome, where he died a martyr under Emperor Trajan (98–117), **Ignatius of Antioch** (ca. 30–107) wrote seven letters, three of which are excerpted here. According to Eusebius, Ignatius was the third bishop of Syrian Antioch, succeeding Evodius, who had succeeded Peter. In Ignatius's letters, we first see

---

9. Isa 60:17 (Septuagint); compare Isa 60:17. (The notes for this selection are by Gerhart and Udoh.)

10. Num 12:7; Heb 3:5.

11. See Num 17:1–8.

12. The translators observe that this translation attempts to maintain the notorious ambiguity of both this and the following sentences.

the Church organized in local communities led by a single bishop at the head of a body of presbyters and assisted by deacons.

IGNATIUS OF ANTIOCH
Letter to the Ephesians, III.1–VI.1

III

1. I am not commanding you, as though I were somebody important. For even though I am in chains for the sake of the Name,[13] I have not yet been perfected in Jesus Christ. For now I am only beginning to be a disciple, and I speak to you as my fellow students. For I need to be trained by you in faith, instruction, endurance, and patience. 2. But since love does not allow me to be silent concerning you, I have therefore taken the initiative to encourage you, so that you may run together in harmony with the mind of God. For Jesus Christ, our inseparable life, is the mind of the Father, just as the bishops appointed throughout the world are in the mind of Christ.

IV

1. Thus it is proper for you to act together in harmony with the mind of the bishop, as you are in fact doing. For your presbytery, which is worthy of its name and worthy of God, is attuned to the bishop as strings to a lyre. Therefore in your unanimity and harmonious love Jesus Christ is sung. 2. You must join this chorus, every one of you, so that by being harmonious in unanimity and taking your pitch from God you may sing in unison with one voice through Jesus Christ to the Father, in order that he may both hear you and, on the basis of what you do well, acknowledge that you are members of his Son. It is, therefore, advantageous for you to be in perfect unity, in order that you may always have a share in God.

V

1. For if I in a short time experienced such fellowship with your bishop, which was not merely human but spiritual, how much more do I congratulate you who are united with him, as the church is with Jesus Christ and as Jesus Christ is with the Father, that all things might be harmonious in unity. 2. Let no one be misled: if anyone is not within the sanctuary, he lacks the bread of God.[14] For if the prayer of one or two has such power, how much more that of the bishop together with the whole church! 3. Therefore whoever does not meet with the congregation thereby demonstrates his arrogance

and has separated himself, for it is written: "God opposes the arrogant."[15] Let us, therefore, be careful not to oppose the bishop, in order that we may be obedient to God.

VI

1. Furthermore, the more anyone observes that the bishop is silent, the more one should fear him. For everyone whom the Master of the house sends to manage his own house we must welcome as we would the one who sent him. It is obvious, therefore, that we must regard the bishop as the Lord himself.

Translated by J. B. Lightfoot and J. R. Harmer, in *The Apostolic Fathers*, 2nd rev. ed., edited by J. B. Lightfoot (Grand Rapids, MI: Baker Book House, 1992), 139, 141.

IGNATIUS OF ANTIOCH
Letter to the Trallians, I.1–III.1

I

1. I know that you have a disposition that is blameless and unwavering in patient endurance, not from habit but by nature, inasmuch as Polybius your bishop informed me when, by the will of God and Jesus Christ, he visited me in Smyrna; so heartily did he rejoice with me, a prisoner in Christ Jesus, that in him I saw your entire congregation. 2. Having received, therefore, your godly good will through him, I praised God when I found out that you were, as I had learned, imitators of God.

II

1. For when you are subject to the bishop as to Jesus Christ it is evident to me that you are living not in accordance with human standards but in accordance with Jesus Christ, who died for us in order that by believing in his death you might escape death. 2. It is essential, therefore, that you continue your current practice and do nothing without the bishop, but be subject also to the presbytery as to the apostles of Jesus Christ, our hope, in whom we shall be found, if we so live. 3. Furthermore, it is necessary that those who are deacons of the "mysteries"[16] of Jesus Christ please everyone in every re-

---

13. "The Name" of Christ. See Acts 5:41. (The notes for this selection are by Gerhart and Udoh.)

14. See Jn 6:33.

15. Prov 3:34; Jas 4:6; 1 Pet 5:5.

16. See 1 Cor 4:1. (The notes for this selection are by Gerhart and Udoh.)

spect. For they are not merely "deacons" of food and drink,[17] but ministers of God's church. Therefore they must avoid criticism as though it were fire.

III

1. Similarly, let everyone respect the deacons as Jesus Christ, just as they should respect the bishop, who is a model of the Father, and the presbyters as God's council and as the band of the apostles. Without these no group can be called a church.

Translated by J. B. Lightfoot and J. R. Harmer, in *The Apostolic Fathers*, 2nd rev. ed., edited by J. B. Lightfoot (Grand Rapids, MI: Baker Book House, 1992), 159, 161.

IGNATIUS OF ANTIOCH

Letter to the Smyrneans, VIII.1–IX.1

VIII

1. Flee from divisions, as the beginning of evils. You must all follow the bishop, as Jesus Christ followed the Father, and follow the presbytery as you would the apostles; respect the deacons as the commandment of God. Let no one do anything that has to do with the church without the bishop. Only that Eucharist which is under the authority of the bishop (or whomever he himself designates) is to be considered valid. 2. Wherever the bishop appears, there let the congregation be, just as wherever Jesus Christ is, there is the catholic[18] church. It is not permissible either to baptize or to hold a love feast[19] without the bishop. But whatever he approves is also pleasing to God, in order that everything you do may be trustworthy and valid.

IX

1. Finally, it is reasonable for us to come to our senses while we still have time to repent and turn to God. It is good to acknowledge God and the bishop. The one who honors the bishop has been honored by God; the one who does anything without the bishop's knowledge serves the devil.

Translated by J. B. Lightfoot and J. R. Harmer, in *The Apostolic Fathers*, 2nd rev. ed., edited by J. B. Lightfoot (Grand Rapids, MI: Baker Book House, 1992), 189, 191.

2. MONASTIC LIFE AND RULES, EAST AND WEST

Before **Pachomius** (ca. 290–346) there had been ascetic Christian hermits, and sometimes groups of hermits living near one another, but Pachomius was the first to organize a religious community that shared all goods and prayed together. In about 320 he established the first of these communities, known as a *koinōnia,* that is, a "communion," a "fellowship," or "sharing" (Acts 2:42; 1 Cor 10:16), based on the ideal as stated in Acts 4:32–37. The Rule for Pachomian communities has survived through a Latin translation by Jerome and in Coptic and Greek fragments. The Rule is a collection of regulations dealing with practical matters of order and structure that were written as the need and occasion arose. The Paralipomena, a series of anecdotes repeated variously in the *Lives* of Pachomius, is an important source of what we know about early Pachomanian monastic life.

Paralipomena, in *Pachomian Chronicles and Rules*

Prologue

In my opinion, what has been written about the Holy Man can be of great profit. And to continue on the same subject does not cause any harm, for to hark back to these things leads the hearer more firmly toward the contemplation of what was said. On the other hand, to decline through negligence to write these things brings danger upon him who so declines. Therefore, let us hark back on what was said and recount a few things akin to what was written before.

Chapter 1. About Holy Theodore

1. It was a custom with the brothers of our God-loving and holy father Pachomius, to assemble every evening in an

---

17. Taking "deacons" literally as "servers"; see Acts 6:1–6.

18. Appearing here for the first time in Christian literature, the term "catholic" (*katholikē*) must be taken in its generic senses: "universal," "general," or probably "whole." Later in the history of Christianity the term acquired a technical sense and, hence, "the catholic Church" stood in opposition to those Christian groups that were considered "heretical" by this Church. (The notes for this selection are by Gerhart and Udoh.)

19. On "love feast" (*agapē*), see Jude 12. The community meal would have included the "Lord's Supper"; see 1 Cor 11:20–34.

appointed place in the monastery to hear his teaching. Once, as they were assembled as usual to hear the Great Man, he commanded a certain Theodore, who had been in the monastery twenty years, to speak to the brothers. Straightaway, without any disobedience, he spoke to them about things profitable to them. Some of the eldest [brothers], when they saw what was happening, did not want to listen to him. They said within themselves, "He is a beginner and he is teaching us! We will not hear him." They left the *synaxis* [gathering] of the brothers and withdrew to their cells.

When the brothers were dismissed from the instruction, the Great Man sent for and called those who had withdrawn. They came to the Holy Man and he asked them, "Why did you leave us and withdraw to your cells?" They said, "Because you have made a boy teacher of us, a large group of old men and of other brothers." When the Great Man heard this, he groaned and said, "Do you know where the beginning of evil came into the world from?" As they said, "From where?," he replied and told them, "From pride, for which *the bright star dawning in the morning was dashed in pieces upon the ground* [Isa 14:12], and for which also Nebuchadnezzar, the king of Babylon, *dwelt among the wild beasts* [Deut 5:21]. Or, have you not heard what is written, *The man with an arrogant heart is abhorrent to the Lord?* [Prov 15:9; 16:5] *For everyone who exalts himself will be humbled* [Lk 14:11]. Now you have been despoiled by the devil of all your virtue, not knowing that pride is the mother of all evils. For it was not Theodore whom you left when you went away, but you fled from the word of God and you fell away from the Holy Spirit. Truly wretched are you, and worthy of all pity. How is it that you did not understand that it was Satan who was causing this in you, and because of this you have been separated from God? O what a great wonder! *God humbled Himself and became obedient even unto death* [Phil 2:8] for our sake; and yet we, who are by nature lowly, puff ourselves up. The order is overthrown by us: He who is above all things and exceedingly great brought the world to himself through his humility, when he could have burned it up by a mere glance! And we who are nothing make ourselves proud, not knowing that by this we are pushing ourselves into the depths of the earth. Did you not see that I was standing and listening to his teaching? In truth I tell you, I profited greatly from listening to him. For it was not to test him that I enjoined him to speak to you, but because I expected to draw profit for myself. How much more then ought you to have heard his word with great eagerness and humility? Verily I, your father in the Lord, was listening to him with all my soul as one who *does not know his right hand from his left*

[Jn 4:11]. Therefore, before God, I tell you that if you do not show great repentance for this error, and if you do not weep and mourn for yourselves so that what happened may be forgiven you, *you will go to perdition* [Dan 2:5]."

Chapter 2. About Silvanos

2. Once there was a brother called Silvanos, who had been wearing the monastic habit for twenty years. He was originally an actor. In the beginning of his [life of] renunciation he was extremely vigilant about his soul, spending all his time in fasting and frequent prayers and in all humility. But after a long time had elapsed, he began so to disregard his own salvation that he wanted to live softly and enjoy himself, and even fearlessly declaimed among the brothers improper quips from the theater.

Our holy father Pachomius called him in and in the presence of the brothers ordered him to be stripped of the monastic habit, to be given secular clothes, and to be expelled from the monastery by the brothers. He fell at [Pachomius's] feet and entreated him saying, "Father, if you forgive me this once, and do not expel me, you will cause me to do penance for the things in which I have showed negligence, so that you shall rejoice at the change of my soul." The Holy Man answered him, "You know how much I have borne with you, and how much I have admonished you, even beating you many times. I am a man who does not want to stretch out his hand with this intent, and when I was obliged to do this in your case, I suffered more in my soul through sympathy than did [you] who were being beaten. I thought to beat you for the sake of your salvation in God, so that by this means we might be able to correct you from your error. Now if you did not change when I admonished you, and did not improve when I exhorted you, and did not fear when I beat you, how is it possible for me to forgive you any more?"

Silvanos multiplied his entreaties and promised to amend in the future. Then the Great Man asked sureties from him, that after he was forgiven he would no more continue the same behavior. And when a certain Petronios made himself a surety for him for the things he had promised, the Great Man forgave him. Silvanos, having received remission, so struggled with all his soul that he became a pattern of every virtue of religion to all the brothers, small and great.

3. The outstanding achievement among his virtues was his absolute humility and the tears that flowed from his eyes unceasingly. When he was eating with the brothers he was unable to control his weeping, and *his tears were mingled with*

his food [cf. Ps 102(101):9]. And when the brothers told him that he should not behave like that in the sight of strangers, he would affirm strongly, "I have often wanted to control my tears for this reason, and I was not able." Then the brothers said, "It is possible for him who is pricked by compunction to weep by himself and to do likewise when he is at prayer with the brothers. But when someone eats at table with the brothers, it is possible for his soul to weep continually without those visible tears. Therefore we want to know what thought keeps you so ceaselessly soaked with tears that many of us seeing you are turned from eating to satiety."

He answered those who were questioning him, "Do you not want me to weep when I see holy men waiting upon me, the very dust of whose feet I am not worthy? Ought I not then to mourn for myself, when I, a man from the theatre, am being waited on by such holy men? I weep therefore, brothers, fearing to be swallowed up like Dathan and Abiram, especially because when I had come from ignorance to knowledge I did not care for my soul's salvation, so that I fell into the danger of being expelled by the brothers and I had to give sureties with awful oaths that I would not longer disregard my life. For this reason I am not ashamed to continue this behavior. *I know my sins, indeed* [Ps 51(50):3], for which, even if I could give my soul, there is no grace for me."

4. As he was struggling in this manner, the Great Man bore testimony about him before all the brothers, saying, "Behold, brothers, *I bear testimony before God* [1 Tim 5:21] that from the time this Community came into existence, among all the brothers who have been with me, there has been no one who has completely copied my example, save only one." When the brothers heard this, some of them thought that the one man of whom he spoke was Theodore, others Petronios or Horsiesios. And when Theodore asked the Holy Man about whom he had said this, the Great Man did not want to say. But as he persisted, along with the other great brothers, entreating him to let them know who it was, the Great Man answered, "If I knew that he about whom I am going to speak would become vainglorious for being praised, I would not have commended such a man. But since I know that when he is praised he rather humbles himself and thinks scorn of himself all the more, I will, before you all, call him blessed, so that you may imitate his example. You, Theodore, and all those like you who are striving in the monastery, have bound the devil *like a sparrow* [Job 40:29] placing him under your feet, and daily you trample him down like dust. But if you neglect yourselves, the devil under your feet will rise up and flee, and he will again make war against you. As for the

young Silvanos, who but a short time ago was about to be expelled by me from the monastery for his negligence, he has so completely subjugated the devil and slain him that the devil will never be able to approach him, for he has utterly vanquished him by his very great humility. When you humble yourselves, you do so as men who have [to their credit] works of righteousness and are augmenting their virtue, relying on what you have already done. As for this man, the more he struggles, the more he declares that he is unworthy, thinking from his whole soul and mind that he is useless and contemptible. This indeed is why he is always on the verge of tears, belittling himself utterly and saying that he is unworthy even of the visible things. You outdo him in your knowledge and your endurance and in your contests against Satan that are beyond measure; but he has surpassed you in humility. And nothing so weakens the demon as humility coming with active power from the whole soul."

When he had struggled in this manner for eight whole years, he completed his contest, laying down his life. The servant of God testified of his departure that an endless throng of holy angels took his soul with great rejoicing and psalmody, and brought it to God as a choice sacrifice, and as a marvellous incense offering to God found among men.

From *Pachomian koinonia*, vol. 2, *Pachomian Chronicles and Rules*, translated by Armand Veilleux (Kalamazoo, MI: Cistercian Publishers, 1981), 19–25. [Brackets in original.]

◈ **Basil the Great** (ca. 330–79), one of the Cappadocian Fathers (along with his brother Gregory of Nyssa and his friend Gregory of Nazianzus), is considered the founder of Eastern monasticism. After he became bishop of Caesarea in 370, he composed answers to various queries on the ascetic life. These were translated into Latin by Rufinus and entitled the *Little Asceticon* (Rule). There later came into existence an expanded collection, known as *The Long Rule*.

BASIL THE GREAT
Preface to *The Long Rule*

Since by God's grace, we have gathered together in the Name of our Lord Jesus Christ—we who have set before ourselves one and the same goal, the devout life—and since you have plainly manifested your eagerness to hear something of the matters pertaining to Salvation, I, for my part, am under obligation to proclaim the justifications of God, mindful as I am night and day of the Apostle's words, "for three years I ceased not with tears to admonish every one of you night and day."[20] Since, moreover, the present is the most opportune time and this place provides quiet and complete freedom from external disturbances, let us pray together that we may provide for our fellow servants their measure of wheat in due season,[21] and that you, on your part, may, like fertile soil, receive the word and produce in turn the fruit of justice, perfect and manifold, as it is written.[22] I implore you, then, by the charity of our Lord Jesus Christ who gave Himself for our sins,[23] let us at length apply our minds to the affairs of our souls and grieve for the vanity of our past life. Let us, on behalf of the rewards which are to come, take up the combat for the glory of God and of Christ and of the adorable Holy Spirit. Let us not remain in our present state of negligence and passivity and, by ever postponing to the morrow and the future the beginning of the work, fritter away the time at hand by our continued sloth. Then, being taken unprepared, with our hands empty of good works, by Him who demands our souls from us, we shall not be admitted to the joy of the nuptial chamber and we shall then bewail and lament the time of our life wasted in evil doing, when penance is no longer possible. "Now is the acceptable time," says the Apostle, "now is the day of salvation."[24] This is the time for repentance; the next life, for recompense. Now is the time to endure; then will be the day of consolation. Now, God is the Helper of such as turn aside from the evil way; then, He will be the dread and unerring Inquisitor of the thoughts and words and deeds of men. Now, we enjoy His longanimity; then, we shall know His just judgment, when we have risen, some unto never-ending punishment, others unto life everlasting, and everyone shall receive according to his works.[25] How long shall we defer our obedience to Christ, who has called us to His heavenly Kingdom? Shall we not rouse ourselves unto sobriety? Why will we not recall ourselves from our accustomed way of life to the strict observance of the Gospel? Why will we not place before our eyes that fearsome and manifest day of the Lord, when the kingdom of heaven will receive those who, because of their works, take their place on the right hand of the Lord, but the gehenna of fire and eternal darkness will envelop those who, because of their lack of good works, have been rejected and placed at the left hand. "There," He says, "shall be weeping and gnashing of teeth."[26]

We say, indeed, that we desire the kingdom of heaven, yet we are not solicitous for the means whereby it is attained. Although we suffer no hardship on behalf of the Lord's command, we, in the vanity of our minds, expect to achieve equal honor with those who have resisted sin even unto death. What man who sits at home or slumbers during the sowing ever filled the fold of his garment with sheaves at the harvest? Who has gathered grapes from a vine which he has not planted and tended? They who labor possess the fruits. Rewards and crowns belong to the victors. Who would ever crown one who did not even strip himself for the combat with his adversary? According to the Apostle, indeed, it is necessary not only to conquer but to strive lawfully;[27] that is, not to neglect a small part even of what has been enjoined, but to carry out each detail as we have been commanded; for "blessed is that servant whom when his lord shall come, he shall find"—not doing anything whatever, but "so doing"[28]—and again, "If thou didst make thy offering well but didst not rightly divide it, thou didst sin."[29] But, if we think that we fulfilled some one of the commandments (I should not presume to say we actually had done so; for all the commandments form an interconnected whole, according to the valid sense of the Scripture, so that in breaking one commandment we necessarily violate the others also), we do not expect to be visited with wrath on the score of the commandments which we have transgressed, but we anticipate rewards for our alleged observance. The man who withholds one or two, perhaps, of the ten talents entrusted to him, but restores the rest, is not looked upon as generous for paying back the major part of the sum; by his withholding the lesser part he is shown to be unjust and avaricious. Withholding, do I say? When he who was entrusted with one talent subsequently gave back this same talent whole and entire as he had received it, he was condemned for not having added to what had been given him.[30] He who has honored his father for ten years, and later on strikes him once only, is not esteemed as dutiful but is condemned as a parricide. "Going," says the Lord, "teach ye all nations, teaching them" not to observe some things and neglect others, but "to observe all things whatsoever I have commanded you."[31] And the Apostle writes in a similar vein: "Giving no offence to any man, that our ministry be not blamed; but in all things let us exhibit ourselves as ministers of God."[32] Unless all were necessary to attain the goal of salvation, all the commandments

---

20. Acts 20:31.
21. Lk 2:42.
22. Mt 13:23.
23. Titus 2:14.
24. 2 Cor 6:2.
25. Rom 2:6.
26. Mt 25:30.

27. 2 Tim 2:5.
28. Lk 12:43.
29. Gen 4:7 (Septuagint).
30. Mt 25:24ff.
31. Mt 28:19, 20.
32. 2 Cor 6:3, 4.

would not have been written down, nor would it have been declared that all must be kept. What do all other righteous actions avail me if I am to be liable to hell-fire because I called my brother "fool"?[33] What profit is there in being free from many masters if I am held in bondage by one? "Whosoever committeth sin, is the servant of sin," says the Scripture.[34] And what gain is there in not being afflicted with many maladies, if my body is being wasted by one?

Well, then, someone will say, will the large number of Christians who do not keep all the commandments practice the observance of some of them in vain? In this connection, it is well to recall blessed Peter, who, after he had performed so many good actions and had been the recipient of such great blessings, was told, upon his being guilty of one lapse only: "If I wash thee not, thou shalt have no part with me."[35] I shall not point out that his act bore no signs of indifference or contempt but was a demonstration of honor and reverence. But, someone might say, it is written: "Everyone that shall call upon the name of the Lord shall be saved,"[36] and, therefore, the very invocation of the Name of the Lord is sufficient to save him who invokes it. But let the objector hear also the words of the Apostle: "How then shall they call on him in whom they have not believed?"[37] And, if you believe, hearken to the Lord saying: "Not everyone that saith to me, Lord, Lord, shall enter into the kingdom of heaven; but he that doth the will of my Father who is in heaven."[38] Certainly, whenever anyone does the will of the Lord, but not as God wills nor with dispositions of love for God, his zeal is to no purpose, according to the words of our Lord Jesus Christ Himself, who says: "They act to be seen by men. Amen I say to you, they have received their reward."[39] Wherefore, Paul the Apostle was taught to say: "And if I should distribute all my goods to feed the poor and if I should deliver my body to be burned and have not charity, it profiteth me nothing."[40] To sum up, I note the following three kinds of disposition which necessarily compel our obedience: we avoid evil through fear of punishment and take the attitude of a slave; or, seeking to obtain the reward, we observe the commandments for our own advantage and in this we are like hirelings; or else, for the sake of the virtuous act itself and out of love for Him who gave us the law, we rejoice to be deemed worthy to serve a God so good and so glorious and we are thus in the dispositions of sons. Nor will he who observes the commandments in fear and who is ever wary of incurring the penalty for sloth keep some of the commandments laid upon him and neglect others, but he will regard the punishment of every act of disobedience as equally to be dreaded. For

this reason he who is in all things fearful out of pious timidity is called blessed,[41] and he stands firm in the truth who is able to say: "I set the Lord always in my sight; for he is at my right hand that I be not moved"[42]—meaning that he would overlook none of the things that he is obliged to do. Again: "Blessed is the man that feareth the Lord." Why? Because "he shall delight exceedingly in his commandments."[43] It is not likely, then, that they who fear will overlook any command or execute it carelessly. Yet, neither does the hireling will to disobey orders; how would he receive the pay for his tending of the vine if he did not do all that had been agreed? If by failing to provide one necessary attention he renders the vine profitless to the owner, who would pay a reward, so long as the damage remains, to him who wrought the mischief? The third form of service is that prompted by love. Now, what son, having in view his father's good pleasure and giving joy to his heart in the more important matters, will wish to cause him pain as regards even the most insignificant ones? And this filial devotion he will render even more earnestly when he recalls the words of the Apostle: "And grieve not the Holy Spirit of God whereby you are sealed."[44]

How, therefore, would they who break the greater number of the commandments be classified—they who do not serve God as their Father nor believe that He has promised great rewards, nor submit to Him as Lord? "If, then, I be a father," says the Prophet, "where is my honor? And if I be a master, where is my fear?"[45]—for he that feareth the Lord "shall delight exceedingly in his commandments."[46] "By transgression of the law," says the Apostle, "thou dishonourest God."[47] How, then, if we prefer a life of pleasure to the life of obedience to the commandments, can we expect for ourselves a life of blessedness, fellowship with the saints, and the delights of the angelic company in the presence of Christ? Such expectations are truly the fantasies of a foolish mind. How shall I be worthy of the company of Job—I who do not accept even an ordinary mishap with thanksgiving? How shall I who am lacking in magnanimity toward my enemy stand in the presence of David? Or of Daniel, if I do not seek

---

33. Mt 5:22.
34. Jn 8:34.
35. Jn 13:8.
36. Joel 2:32.
37. Rom 10:14.
38. Mt 7:21.
39. Mt 6:5.
40. 1 Cor 13:3.

41. Prov 28:14.
42. Ps 15:8.
43. Ps 111:1.
44. Eph 4:30.
45. Mal 1:6.
46. Ps 111:1.
47. Rom 2:23.

for God in continual continency and earnest supplication? Or of any of the saints, if I have not walked in their footsteps? What judge of a contest is so uninformed as to think that the victor and he who has not taken part in the contest should receive crowns of equal merit? What general ever summoned to an equal share in the spoils with the conquerors those who were not even present at the battle?

God is good, but He is also just, and it is the nature of the just to reward in proportion to merit, as it is written: "Do good O Lord, to those that are good and to the upright of heart. But such as turn aside into bonds, the Lord shall lead out with the workers of iniquity."[48] He is merciful, but He is also a judge, for "the Lord loveth mercy and judgment," says the psalmist.[49] And he therefore also says: "Mercy and judgment I will sing to thee, O Lord."[50] We have been taught who they are upon whom He has mercy: "Blessed are the merciful," says the Lord, "for they shall obtain mercy."[51] You see with what discernment He bestows mercy, neither being merciful without judgment nor judging without mercy; for, "the Lord is merciful and just."[52] Let us not, therefore, know God by halves nor make His loving kindness an excuse for our indolence; for this, His thunders, for this, His lightnings—that His goodness may not be held in despite. He who causes the sun to rise[53] also strikes men with blindness.[54] He who sends the rain[55] also causes the rain of fire.[56] By the one He manifests His goodness; by the other, His severity. For the one let us love Him, for the other let us fear, that it may not be said also to us: "Or despisest thou the riches of his goodness and patience and longsuffering? Knowest thou not that the benignity of God leadeth thee to penance? But according to thy hardness and impenitent heart, thou treasurest up to thyself wrath against the day of wrath."[57]

Since, then, they cannot be saved who do not their works according to the command of God and since no precept may safely be overlooked (for it is great presumption to set ourselves up as critics of the Lawgiver by approving some of His laws and rejecting others), let us who are striving to live the devout life, who value the life of retirement and freedom from worldly distractions as an aid to the observance of evangelical doctrine, let us make it our common concern and resolve not to allow any precept whatsoever to elude our vigilance. If the man of God must be perfect (as it is written[58] and as our words have already shown), it is all-important that he be made perfect through the observance of every commandment "unto the measure of the age of the fullness of Christ,"[59] for, according to divine law, an offering which is mutilated, even if it be pure, is unacceptable as a sacrifice

to God. Whatever each one regards as wanting in himself, therefore, he should refer to the common consideration. That which is obscure can be more easily discerned by the earnest scrutiny of several persons, since, to be sure, God grants issue to the quest under the guidance and counsel of the Holy Spirit, according to the promise of our Lord Jesus Christ.[60] Consequently, as "a necessity lieth upon me; for woe is unto me if I preach not the gospel,"[61] so upon you also rests a similar danger if you are remiss in discovering or languid and half-hearted in observing and fulfilling the precepts which have been handed down to us. The Lord says, therefore: "The word that I have spoken, the same shall judge him in the last day."[62] Again: "And the servant who knew not the will of his lord and did things worthy of stripes, shall be beaten with few stripes; but he who knew and did not do nor prepared himself, according to his will, shall be beaten with many stripes."[63]

Let us pray, therefore, that I may exercise the ministry of the Word blamelessly, and that my teaching may be fruitful in you. Knowing as we do that at the tribunal of Christ the words of the Holy Scripture will confront us (for He says: "I will reprove thee and set thy sins before thy face"[64]), let us in all sobriety attend to the words of the divine teaching and hasten to put them into practice, for we know not the day nor the hour when our Lord will come.[65]

From Saint Basil, *Ascetical Works,* translated by Sister M. Monica Wagner, Fathers of the Church, vol. 9 (Washington, DC: Catholic University of America Press, 1962), 223–31.

🙟 **Augustine** (354–430) composed *The Rule of Saint Augustine* around 397, after he was consecrated bishop of Hippo in 395 or 396. Probably first intended for his community of laypeople in Hippo, Augustine's Rule exerted considerable influence on subsequent Rules, including Benedict's. There are two versions of Augustine's *Rule,* the "Feminine Version" being a modification, for gender and situation, of the male version.

48. Ps 124:4, 5.
49. Ps 32:5.
50. Ps 100:1.
51. Mt 5:7.
52. Ps 116:5.
53. Mt 5:45.
54. 2 Kings 6:18.
55. Zech 10:1.
56. Gen 19:24.
57. Rom 2:4, 5.
58. 2 Tim 3:17.
59. Eph 4:13.
60. Jn 14:26.
61. 1 Cor 9:16.
62. Jn 12:48.
63. Lk 12:47.
64. Ps 49:21.
65. Mt 24:42.

AUGUSTINE

The Rule of Saint Augustine (Feminine Version)

This text is identical with the masculine text, but transposed as to gender, so that it is appropriate for communities of women

I. The Basic Ideal: Mutual Love Expressed in the Community of Goods and in Humility

1. We urge you who form a religious community to put the following precepts into practice.

2. Before all else, *live together in harmony* (Ps 67[68]:7), *being of one mind and one heart* (Acts 4:32) on the way to God. For is it not precisely for this reason that you have come to live together?

3. Among you there can be no question of personal property. Rather, take care that you share everything in common. Your superior should see to it that each person is provided with food and clothing. She does not have to give exactly the same to everyone, for you are not all equally strong, but each person should be given what she personally needs. For this is what you read in the Acts of the Apostles: *"Everything they owned was held in common, and each one received whatever he or she had need of"* (Acts 4:32; 4:35).

4. Those who owned possessions in the world should readily agree that, from the moment they enter the religious life, these things become the property of the community.

5. But those who did not have possessions ought not to strive in the religious community for what they could not obtain outside it. One must indeed have regard for their frailty by providing them with whatever they need, even if they were formerly so poor that they could not even afford the very necessities of life. They may not, however, consider themselves fortunate because they now receive food and clothing which were beyond their means in their earlier lives.

6. Nor should they give themselves airs because they now find themselves in the company of people whom they would not have ventured to approach before. Their hearts should seek the nobler things, not vain earthly appearances. If, in the religious life, rich people were to become humble and poor people haughty, then this style of life would seem to be of value only to the rich and not to the poor.

7. On the other hand, let those who appear to have had some standing in the world not look down upon their sisters who have entered the religious life from a condition of poverty. They ought to be more mindful of their life together with poor sisters than of the social status of their wealthy parents. And the fact that they have made some of their possessions available to the community gives them no reason to have a high opinion of themselves. Otherwise people would more easily fall prey to pride in sharing their riches with the community than they would have done if they had enjoyed them in the world. For while all vices manifest themselves in wrongdoing, pride lurks also in our good works, seeking to destroy even them. What good does it do to distribute one's possessions to the poor and to become poor oneself, if giving up riches makes a person prouder than she was when she had a fortune?

8. You are all to live together, therefore, one in mind and one in heart (cf. Acts 4:32), and honour God in one another, because *each of you has become his temple* (2 Cor 6:16).

II. Community Prayer

1. *Persevere faithfully in prayer* (Col 4:2) at the hours and times appointed.

2. The place of prayer should not be used for any purpose other than that for which it is intended and from which it takes its name. Thus if someone wants to pray there even outside the appointed hours, in her own free time, she should be able to do so without being hindered by others who have no business being there.

3. When you pray to God in psalms and songs, the words spoken by your lips should also be alive in your hearts.

4. When you sing, keep to the text you have, and do not sing what is not intended to be sung.

III. Community and Care of the Body

1. As far as your health allows, keep your bodily appetites in check by fasting and abstinence from food and drink. Those who are unable to fast the whole day may have something to eat before the main meal which takes place in the late afternoon. They may do this, however, only around midday. But the sick may have something to eat at any time of the day.

2. From the beginning of the meal to the end listen to the customary reading without noise or protest against the Scriptures, for you have not only to satisfy your physical hunger, *but also to hunger for the word of God* (cf. Am 8:11).

3. There are some who are weaker because of their former manner of life. If an exception is made for them at table, those who are stronger because they have come from a different way of life ought not to take this amiss or to consider

it unfair. They should not think that the others are more fortunate because they receive better food. Let them rather be glad that they are capable of something which is beyond the strength of the others.

4. There are some who, before entering the religious life, were accustomed to living comfortably, and therefore they receive something more in the way of food and clothing: better bedding, perhaps, or more blankets. The others who are stronger, and therefore happier, do not receive these things. But, taking into account the former habits of life of the rich, keep in mind how much they now have to do without, even though they cannot live as simply as those who are physically stronger. Not everyone should want to have the extra she sees another receive, for this is done not to show favour but only out of concern for the person. Otherwise a deplorable disorder would creep into the religious life, whereby the poor begin to drift easily along while the rich put themselves out in every possible way.

5. The sick should obviously receive suitable food; otherwise their illness would only get worse. Once they are over the worst of their sickness, they ought to be well cared for so that they may be fully restored to health as quickly as possible. And this holds good even if they formerly belonged to the very poorest class in society. During their convalescence they should receive the same that the rich are entitled to because of their former manner of life. But once they have made a complete recovery they are to go back to living as they did earlier on, when they were happier because their needs were fewer. The simpler a way of life, the better it is suited to servants of God.

When a sick person has been restored to health, she will have to be careful not to become the slave of her own desires. She will have to part with the privileges granted because of her illness. Those who have the strength to lead simple lives should consider themselves the richest of people. For it is better to be able to make do with a little than to have plenty.

IV. Mutual Responsibility in Good and Evil

1. Do not attract attention by the way you dress. Endeavour to impress by your manner of life, not by the clothes you wear.

2. When you go out, go with somebody else, and stay together when you have reached your destination.

From *The Rule of Saint Augustine: Masculine and Feminine Versions,* translated by Raymond Canning (London: Darton, Longman, and Todd, 1984), 25–29.

Benedict, who was born in Nursia (or Norcia, in Italy) around 480 and died around 543, became known as the Father of Western Monasticism. The influence of *The Rule of Saint Benedict* lies mainly in its successful synthesis of the whole tradition on which it relied. The Prologue presents Benedict's basic principles for the monastic life.

BENEDICT

Prologue to *The Rule of Saint Benedict*

Listen carefully, my son,[66] to the master's instructions, and attend to them with the ear of your heart. This is advice from a father who loves you; welcome it, and faithfully put it into practice. The labor of obedience will bring you back to him from whom you had drifted through the sloth of disobedience. This message of mine is for you, then, if you are ready to give up your own will,[67] once and for all, and armed with the strong and noble weapons of obedience to do battle for the true King, Christ the Lord.

First of all, every time you begin a good work,[68] you must pray to him most earnestly to bring it to perfection. In his goodness, he has already counted us as his sons, and therefore we should never grieve him by our evil actions. With his good gifts which are in us, we must obey him at all times that he may never become the angry father who disinherits his sons, nor the dread lord, enraged by our sins, who punishes us forever as worthless servants for refusing to follow him to glory.

Let us get up then, at long last, for the Scriptures rouse us when they say: *It is high time for us to arise from sleep* (Rom 13:11). Let us open our eyes to the light that comes from God,[69] and our ears to the voice from heaven that every day calls out[70] this charge: *If you hear his voice today, do not harden your hearts* (Ps 94[95]:8). And again: *You that have ears to hear, listen to what the Spirit says to the churches* (Rev 2:7). And what does he say? *Come and listen to me, sons; I will teach you the fear*

---

66. The mode of address represented by the opening words [. . .] , "Listen carefully, my son," [. . .] echoes that to be found in the wisdom tradition of the Old Testament (cf. Prov 1:8; 4:1, 10, 20; 6:20).

67. "own will" (*propriis voluntatibus*): When used in the plural, as here, this phrase refers to the particular promptings or suggestions of will. The human will is not considered evil in itself, but the renunciation of one's own particular desires is undertaken in imitation of Jesus.

68. "you begin a good work"[. . .] : The semi-Pelagians of the fifth and sixth centuries [. . .] overstressed personal initiative in the economy of salvation. St. Benedict carefully joins work and prayer at the beginning of monastic life.

69. The light is Sacred Scripture.

70. There is reference here to the daily use of Ps 94 (95) as the Invitatory.

of the Lord (Ps 33[34]:12). *Run while you have the light of life, that the darkness of death may not overtake you* (Jn 12:35).

Seeking his workman in a multitude of people, the Lord calls out to him and lifts his voice again: *Is there anyone here who yearns for life and desires to see good days?* (Ps 33[34]:13) If you[71] hear this and your answer is "I do," God then directs these words to you: If you desire true and eternal life, *keep your tongue free from vicious talk and your lips from all deceit; turn away from evil and do good; let peace be your quest and aim* (Ps 33[34]:14–15). Once you have done this, my *eyes will be upon you and my ears will listen for your prayers; and even before you ask me, I will say to you: Here I am* (Isa 58:9). What, dear brothers, is more delightful than this voice of the Lord calling to us? See how the Lord in his love shows us the way of life. Clothed then with the faith and the performance of good works, let us set out on this way, with the Gospel for our guide, that we may deserve to see him *who has called us to his kingdom* (1 Thess 2:12).

If we wish to dwell in the tent of this kingdom, we will never arrive unless we run there by doing good deeds. But let us ask the Lord with the Prophet: *Who will dwell in your tent, O Lord; who will find rest upon your holy mountain?* (Ps 14[15]:1) After this question, brothers, let us listen well to what the Lord says in reply, for he shows us the way to his tent. *One who walks without blemish*, he says, *and is just in all his dealings; who speaks the truth from his heart and has not practiced deceit with his tongue; who has not wronged a fellowman in any way, nor listened to slanders against his neighbor* (Ps 14[15]:2–3). He has *foiled the evil one*, the devil, at every turn, flinging both him and his promptings far *from the sight* of his heart. While these temptations were still *young, he caught hold of them and dashed them against Christ.* (Ps 14[15]:4; 136[137]:9). These people *fear the Lord,* and do not become elated over their own good deeds; they judge it is the Lord's power, not their own, that brings about the good in them. *They praise* (Ps 14[15]:4) the Lord working in them, and say with the Prophet: *Not to us, Lord, not to us give the glory, but to your name alone* (Ps 113[115:1]:9). In just this way Paul the Apostle refused to take credit for the power of his preachings. He declared: *By God's grace I am what I am* (1 Cor 15:10). And again he said: *He who boasts should make his boast in the Lord* (2 Cor 10:17). That is why the Lord says in the Gospel: *Whoever hears these words of mine and does them is like a wise man who built his house upon rock; the floods came and the winds blew and beat against the house, but it did not fall: it was founded on rock* (Mt 7:24–25).

With this conclusion, the Lord waits for us daily to translate into action, as we should, his holy teachings. Therefore our life span has been lengthened by way of a truce, that we may amend our misdeeds. As the Apostle says: *Do you not know that the patience of God is leading you to repent?* (Rom 2:4) And indeed the Lord assures us in his love: *I do not wish the death of the sinner, but that he turn back to me and live* (Ezek 33:11).

Brothers, now that we have asked the Lord who will dwell in his tent, we have heard the instruction for dwelling in it, but only if we fulfill the obligations of those who live there. We must, then, prepare our hearts and bodies for the battle of holy obedience[72] to his instructions. What is not possible to us by nature, let us ask the Lord to supply by the help of his grace. If we wish to reach eternal life, even as we avoid the torments of hell, then—while there is still time, while we are in this body and have time to accomplish all these things by the light of life—we must run and do now what will profit us forever.

Therefore we intend to establish a school[73] for the Lord's service. In drawing up its regulations, we hope to set down nothing harsh, nothing burdensome. The good of all concerned, however, may prompt us to a little strictness in order to amend faults and to safeguard love. Do not be daunted immediately by fear and run away from the road that leads to salvation. It is bound to be narrow at the outset. But as we progress in this way of life and in faith, we shall run on the path of God's commandments, our hearts overflowing with the inexpressible delight of love.

From *The Rule of St. Benedict*, edited by Timothy Fry et al. (Collegeville, MN: Liturgical Press, 1981), 157, 159, 161, 163, 165. [Brackets in original.]

❧ Pilgrims and crusaders (those who settled after the First Crusade, in 1097, and the Second Crusade, in 1145–53) formed an eremitic community of strict poverty, seclusion, manual labor, silence, and prayer in Palestine at the traditional fountain of Elijah on Mount Carmel. *The Rule of Carmel* was given between 1206

---

71. "you" (*tu*): English conceals that the pronoun is singular here but plural in v. 18. Though no doubt the shift is partly due to the quotation, it may also suggest that to God's individual call each must first make an individual response, and then our individual responses bind us together as a community of those seeking God.

72. [T]he image of military and civil service refers to the labor of obedience. [. . .] The "battle of holy obedience" means the "battle for holy obedience," i.e., the struggle to achieve obedience. One might compare this with the phrase "civil rights struggle," which means, of course, "struggle for civil rights."

73. [A] place where the monks both learn how to serve the Lord and actually do so.

and 1214 by **Albert,** the Latin patriarch of Jerusalem, who was prevented by his death in 1214 from attending the Fourth Lateran Council (which forbade new religious communities and Rules, 1215). Albert's *Rule* was approved by Pope Honorius III (1216–27) in 1226.

ALBERT OF JERUSALEM

The Rule of Carmel

Introduction

Albert, called by God's favor to be Patriarch of the church of Jerusalem, bids health in the Lord and the blessing of the Holy Spirit to his beloved sons in Christ, B. and the other hermits under obedience to him who live near the spring on Mount Carmel.

Many and varied are the ways in which our saintly forefathers laid down how everyone, whatever his station or the kind of religious observance he has chosen, should live a life of allegiance to Jesus Christ—how, pure in heart and stout in conscience, he must be unswerving in the service of his Master. It is to me, however, that you have come for a rule of life in keeping with your avowed purpose, a rule you may hold fast to henceforward; and therefore:

Chapter One

The first thing I require is for you to have a prior, one of yourselves, who is to be chosen for the office by common consent, or that of the greater or maturer part of you. Each of the others must promise him obedience—of which, once promised, he must try to make his deeds the true reflection—(Inn.)[74] and also chastity and the renunciation of ownership.

Chapter Two

(Inn.) If the prior and the brothers see fit, you may have foundations in solitary places or where you are given a site that is suitable and convenient for the observance proper to your Order.

Chapter Three

Next, each one of you is to have a separate cell, situated as the lie of the land you propose to occupy may dictate, and allotted by disposition of the prior with agreement of the other brothers, or the more mature among them.

Chapter Four

(Inn.) However, you are to eat whatever may have been given you in a common refectory, listening together meanwhile to a reading from Holy Scripture where that can be done without difficulty.

Chapter Five

None of the brothers is to occupy a cell other than that allotted to him or to exchange cells with another, without leave of whoever is prior at the time.

Chapter Six

The prior's cell should stand near the entrance to your property, so that he may be the first to meet those who approach, and whatever has to be done in consequence may all be carried out as he may decide and order.

Chapter Seven

Each one of you is to stay in his cell or nearby, pondering the Lord's law day and night and keeping watch at his prayers unless attending to some other duty.

Chapter Eight

(Alb.) Those who know their letters, and how to read the psalms, should, for each of the hours, say those our holy forefathers laid down and the approved custom of the Church appoints for that hour. Those who do not know their letters must say 25 Our Fathers for the night office, except on Sundays and solemnities when that number is to be doubled so that the Our Father is said 50 times; the same prayer must be said seven times in the morning in the place of Lauds, and seven times too for each of the other hours, except for Vespers when it must be said 15 times.

(Inn.) Those who know how to say the canonical hours with those in Orders should do so, in the way those holy forefathers of ours laid down, and according to the Church's approved custom. Those who do not know the hours must say

---

74. For the purpose of comparison, changes in St. Albert's original rule made by Pope Innocent IV in 1247 are indicated by (Inn.). Where this occurred, Albert's original rule is indicated by (Alb.).

25 Our Fathers for the night office, except on Sundays and solemnities when that number is to be doubled so that the Our Father is said 50 times; the same prayer must be said seven times in the morning in the place of Lauds, and seven times too for each of the other hours except for Vespers when it must be said 15 times.

Chapter Nine

(Alb.) None of the brothers must lay claim to anything as his own, but your property is to be held in common; and of such things as the Lord may have given you each is to receive from the prior—that is the man he appoints for the purpose—whatever befits his age and needs. However, as I have said, each one of you is to stay in his own allotted cell, and live, by himself, on what is given out to him.

(Inn.) None of the brothers is to lay claim to anything as his own, but you are to possess everything in common; and each is to receive from the prior—that is the brother he appoints for the purpose—whatever befits his age and needs. (Inn.) You may have as many asses and mules as you need, however, and may keep a certain amount of livestock or poultry.

Chapter Ten

An oratory should be built as conveniently as possible among the cells, where, if it can be done without difficulty, you are to gather each morning to hear Mass.

Chapter Eleven

On Sundays too, or other days if necessary, you should discuss matters of discipline and your spiritual welfare; and on this occasion indiscretions and failings of the brothers, if any be found at fault, should be lovingly corrected.

Chapter Twelve

You are to fast every day, except Sundays, from the feast of the Exaltation of the Holy Cross until Easter Day, unless bodily sickness or feebleness, or some other good reason, demand a dispensation from the fast; for necessity overrides every law.

Chapter Thirteen

(Alb.) You are always to abstain from meat, unless it has to be eaten as a remedy for sickness or great feebleness.

(Inn.) You are to abstain from meat, except as a remedy for sickness or feebleness. But as, when you are on a journey, you more often than not have to beg your way; outside your own houses you may eat foodstuffs that have been cooked with meat, so as to avoid giving trouble to your hosts. At sea, however, meat may be eaten.

Chapter Fourteen

Since man's life on earth is a time of trial, and all who live devotedly in Christ must undergo persecution, and the devil your foe is on the prowl like a roaring lion looking for prey to devour, you must use every care to clothe yourselves in God's armor so that you may be ready to withstand the enemy's ambush. Your loins are to be girt with chastity, your breast fortified by holy meditations, for, as Scripture has it, holy meditation will save you. Put on holiness as your breastplate, and it will enable you to love the Lord your God with all your heart and soul and strength, and your neighbor as yourself. Faith must be your shield on all occasions, and with it you will be able to quench all the flaming missiles of the wicked one; there can be no pleasing God without faith; (and the victory lies in your faith). On your head set the helmet of salvation and so be sure of deliverance by our only Savior, who sets his own free from their sins. The sword of the spirit, the word of God, must abound in your mouths and hearts. Let all you do have the Lord's word for accompaniment.

Chapter Fifteen

You must give yourselves to work of some kind, so that the devil may always find you busy; no idleness on your part must give him a chance to pierce the defenses of your souls. In this respect you have both the teaching and the example of St. Paul the Apostle, into whose mouth Christ put his own words. God made him preacher and teacher of faith and truth to the nations; with him as your leader you cannot go astray. We live among you, he said, laboring and weary, toiling night and day so as not to be a burden to any of you; not because we have no power to do otherwise but so as to give you, in our own selves, an example you might imitate. For the charge we gave you when we were with you was this: that whoever is not willing to work should not be allowed to eat either. For we have heard that there are certain restless idlers among you. We charge people of this kind, and implore them in the name of our Lord Jesus Christ, that they earn their own bread by silent toil. This is the way of holiness and goodness; see that you follow it.

Chapter Sixteen

The Apostle would have us keep silence, for in silence he tells us to work. As the prophet also makes known to us: Silence is the way to foster holiness. Elsewhere he says: Your strength will lie in silence and hope. (Alb.) For this reason I lay down that you are to keep silence from Vespers until Terce the next day, unless some necessary or some good reason, or the prior's permission, should break the silence. (Inn.) For this reason I lay down that you are to keep silence from after Compline until after Prime the next day. At other times, although you need not keep silence so strictly, be careful not to indulge in a great deal of talk, for, as Scripture has it—and experience teaches us no less—sin will not be wanting where there is much talk, and he who is careless in speech will come to harm; and elsewhere: The use of many words brings harm to the speaker's soul. And Our Lord says in the Gospel: Every rash word uttered will have to be accounted for on Judgment Day. Make a balance then, each of you, to weigh his words in; keep a tight rein on your mouths, lest you should stumble and fall in speech, and your fall be irreparable and prove mortal. Like the Prophet, watch your step lest your tongue give offense, and employ every care in keeping silent, which is the way to foster holiness.

Chapter Seventeen

You, brother B., and whoever may succeed you as prior, must always keep in mind and put into practice what our Lord said in the Gospel: Whoever has a mind to become a leader among you must make himself servant to the rest, and whichever of you would be first must become your bondsman.

Chapter Eighteen

You other brothers too, hold your prior in humble reverence, your minds not on him but on Christ who has placed him over you, and who, to those who rule the churches, addressed the words: Whoever pays you heed pays heed to me, and whoever treats you with dishonor dishonors me; if you remain so minded you will not be found guilty of contempt, but will merit life eternal as fit reward for your obedience.

Here then are a few points I have written down to provide you with a standard of conduct to live up to; but our Lord, at his Second Coming, will reward anyone who does more than he is obliged to do. See that the bond of common sense is the guide of the virtues.

Translated by Bede Edwards, in John Welch, *The Carmelite Way: An Ancient Path for Today's Pilgrim* (New York: Paulist Press, 1996), 175–81.

❧ **Francis of Assisi** (1182–1226), known as the "Little Poor Man of Assisi," had a vision in 1206 at the church of Saint Damiano which compelled him to renounce property and to share in the suffering of the poor. As his followers increased, he reluctantly composed a Rule of life, which was orally approved in 1209 by Pope Innocent III. This Rule, no longer extant, was expanded into the Rule of 1221, which was not submitted for approval. Francis rewrote the 1221 Rule—aided by his companions Bonizo and Leo of Bologna and by Cardinal Hugolino (later Pope Gregory IX)—and submitted it for papal approval. The resulting *First Rule of Saint Francis,* known as the *Regula bullata,* was approved by Pope Honorius III (1216–27) in the Bull *Solet annuere* of November 29, 1223.

FRANCIS OF ASSISI
The First Rule of Saint Francis

Chapter One. The Rule and Life of the Friars Minor Is This:

"In the Name of the Lord! Here begins the manner of the Friars Minor. The Rule and Life of the Friars Minor is this: to observe the Holy Gospel of our Lord Jesus Christ through a life in obedience, without anything of their own, and in chastity. Brother Francis promises obedience and reverence to the Lord Pope Honorius and to his lawful successors, and to the Roman Church. And let the other friars be bound to give obedience to Brother Francis and to his successors."

Chapter Two. Of Those Who Would Embrace This Life and How They Should Be Received

1. Acceptance into the Order

"Should any persons come to the friars with the desire to adopt this way of life, they are to be directed to the ministers provincial. Only to the latter and to none other may the power be granted to receive new brethren. On their part, let the ministers subject such persons to a most careful examination on the Catholic faith and the Sacraments of the Church. They must be found to have true belief in all these matters, and the firm intention to profess loyally what they believe and steadfastly to conform their whole life long to such beliefs. Furthermore, they must not be married; or, if they are married, then their wives must either already have entered a monastery or with the authority of the bishop of the diocese have given their consent and themselves taken a vow of continence; moreover, in this latter instance, the wives must be of such an age as to place them above suspicion.

"If these requirements are fulfilled, then the ministers are to tell them, in the words of the Holy Gospel, to go and sell all that belongs to them and arrange to distribute them to the poor. Should they be unable to do this, it shall suffice if they have the good will. But let the friar and their ministers keep themselves from any interest in the temporal affairs of the candidates, so that the latter are left free to do with their goods whatever the Lord may inspire them. Yet if they stand in need of counsel, the ministers may have leave to refer them to some godfearing persons who might advise them how to give what they have to the poor."

2. The Novitiate

"When all this has been done, they are to give them the clothing worn during the year of probation, that is, two tunics without a hood, a cord, knee-breeches and a little cape which reaches to the cord. In this matter, however, the ministers may make other provisions if at some time it seems right to them according to the will of God."

3. The Profession

"When the year of probation is ended, they are to be received to obedience, whereby they will promise always to live according to this way and rule of life. And by no manner or means shall they be allowed to leave this Order, both because the Pope forbids them and because according to the Holy Gospel, 'No one, having put his hand to the plow and looking back, is fit for the kingdom of God.'"

4. The Clothing of the Professed

"And those who have already promised obedience are to have one tunic with a hood; and, if they wish, a second without a hood. And those who are in need thereof may wear shoes. And all the friars are to wear clothing inferior in quality and appearance; and with the blessing of God they can quilt them with pieces of sack or other material."

5. The Friars and Other Christians

"I caution the friars and beg them not to look down upon or pass judgment on those people whom they see wearing soft and colorful garments and enjoying the choicest food and drink. Instead, each must criticize and despise himself."[75]

Edited and translated by Ignatius Brady, in *The Marrow of the Gospel: A Study of the Rule of Saint Francis of Assisi* (Chicago: Franciscan Herald Press, 1958), 107, 117–18, 123, 124, 126, 127.

☙ **Clare of Assisi** (1194–1253) was the first woman to compose a Rule of life for women. *The Rule of Saint Clare,* the product of forty years of experience in various communities, was influenced by *The Rule of Saint Benedict,* Francis's Rule of 1221, *The Rule of Cardinal Hugolino,* and *The Rule of Pope Innocent IV.* Clare's *Rule* is, however, notably distinct in its conceptions of the role of authority, co-responsibility, and charity. Through a long and difficult process, Clare's *Rule* was finally approved by Innocent IV on August 9, 1253, two days before her death.

CLARE OF ASSISI
The Rule of Saint Clare, chapters I–II, VII–VIII

Chapter I. In the Name of the Lord Begins the Form of Life of the Poor Sisters

The form of life of the Order of the Poor Sisters which the blessed Francis founded is this: to observe the holy Gospel of our Lord Jesus Christ by living in obedience, without anything of one's own, and in chastity.

Clare, unworthy handmaid of Christ and little plant of the most blessed Father Francis, promises obedience and reverence to the Lord Pope Innocent and to his successors canonically elected and to the Roman Church. And just as in the beginning of her own conversion she together with her Sisters promised obedience to the blessed Francis, even so does she promise to preserve the same inviolably to his successors. And the other Sisters shall always be bound to

---

75. Gospel poverty is loved, nourished and perfected only in the truly humble man who knows that what he is and what he has is due to the grace of God and not to himself, who is fully conscious that if God had given as much grace to a robber, the latter would likely soon be more pleasing to God. Therefore, he does not look down upon or judge others, but despises himself, for all that is his are his "sins and defects."

obey the successors of the blessed Francis, and so, too, Sister Clare and the other Abbesses canonically elected who shall succeed her.

Chapter II. Those Who Desire to Embrace This Life and How They Are to Be Received

If, by divine inspiration, anyone should come to us desiring to embrace this life, the Abbess is bound to seek the consent of all the Sisters; and if the greater part shall have been in agreement she may receive her, having had the permission of our Lord Cardinal Protector.

And if she judges her acceptable, let the Abbess carefully examine her or have her examined concerning the Catholic faith and the sacraments of the Church. And if she believe all these things and is willing to confess them faithfully and to observe them steadfastly to the end and if she has no husband (or, if she does have, he has already entered religious life with the authority of the Bishop of the diocese and already made a vow of continence), and if there is no impediment to the observance of this life such as advanced age or ill-health or mental weakness let the tenor of our life be thoroughly explained to her.

And if she be suitable, let the words of the holy Gospel be addressed to her: that she should go and sell all that she has and take care to distribute the proceeds to the poor. But if she cannot do this her good will suffices. And let the Abbess and her Sisters be on their guard not to be anxious about her temporal affairs, so that she may freely do with her possessions whatsoever the Lord may inspire her. If, however, some advice would be needed, let them send her to some discerning and God-fearing men by whose counsel let her goods be distributed to the poor.

Afterwards, her hair having been cut off round and her secular dress laid aside, she is to be allowed three tunics and a mantle.

From then on it shall not be permitted her to go outside the monastery except for a useful, reasonable, clear and approved cause.

When the year of probation is ended, she may be received to obedience, promising to observe perpetually our life and form of poverty.

No one may be veiled during the time of probation. The Sisters may also have little mantles for the convenience and propriety of their service and labor. Indeed the Abbess should with good judgment provide them with garments according to the differences of persons and according to

places and seasons and cold climates as she may deem it of necessity right to do.

Young girls received into the monastery before the age required by law shall have their hair cut off round and, their secular dress being laid aside, shall be clothed in religious garb as it shall seem fitting to the Abbess. But when they have reached the age required by law, they shall make their profession clothed after the manner of the others.

And for these as well as for the other novices, the Abbess must solicitously provide a Mistress from among all the more discerning of the monastery who shall devotedly form them in holy living and becoming behavior according to the form of our profession.

The same form as above shall be observed in the examination and reception of the Sisters serving outside the monastery; they may wear shoes.

No one may live with us in the monastery unless she has been received according to the form of our profession.

And for the love of the most holy and most beloved Child wrapped in such poor little swaddling clothes and laid in a manger, and of his most holy Mother, I direct, pray and exhort my Sisters that they be always clothed in the garments of the lowly.

And as I, together with my Sisters, have always been solicitous to safeguard the holy poverty which we promised to the Lord God and to the blessed Francis, so shall the Abbesses who succeed me in office and all the Sisters be bound to observe it inviolably to the end: namely, by not receiving or having possession or ownership either of themselves or through an intermediary person, or even anything which could reasonably be called ownership, except so much land as necessity requires for the integrity and seclusion of the monastery; and that land may not be cultivated except as a garden for their own needs.

Chapter VII. The Manner of Working

The Sisters to whom the Lord has given the grace of working should labor faithfully and devotedly after the hour of Terce at work which contributes to integrity and the common good: and this in such a way that idleness, the enemy of the soul, being banished they do not extinguish the spirit of holy prayer and dedication whose purpose all other temporal things ought to serve.

And the Abbess or her Vicaress is bound to assign to each one at Chapter in the presence of all, those things to be done by the work of her hands. The same thing should be done if some alms are sent by any persons for the needs of the Sisters, so that recommendation may be made for them in common. And all these things should be given out for the common good by the Abbess or her Vicaress with the advice of the Discreets.

Chapter VIII. Non-appropriation; Begging Alms; the Sick Sisters

The Sisters shall not claim anything as their own, neither a house nor a place nor anything whatsoever; and as pilgrims and strangers in this world, serving the Lord in poverty and humility, let them confidently send for alms. Nor should they feel hesitant since the Lord made himself poor in this world for us. This is that height of most high poverty who has appointed you, my most dear Sisters, heiresses and queens of the kingdom of heaven, made you poor in things, exalted you in virtues. Let her who leads you into the land of the living be your portion. Totally clinging to her, most beloved Sisters desire for the name of our Lord Jesus Christ and his most holy Mother to have nothing else forever under heaven.

From *Rule and Testament of St. Clare: Constitutions for Poor Clare Nuns,* translated by Mother Mary Francis (Chicago: Franciscan Herald Press, 1987), 5, 7–9, 18–19, 21.

◆ **Dominic de Guzmán** (ca. 1170–1221), a contemporary of Francis of Assisi, founded a new order in 1216 that was influenced by the Fourth Lateran Council (1215), which he had attended. Dominic's Order of Preachers combined mendicant poverty, preaching, and learning. They adopted *The Rule of Saint Augustine* and, adding thereto the "Consuetudines" regarding monastic practices and mendicant poverty, produced their "Fundamental Constitution." The order was certified by Pope Honorius III (1216–27) in 1216.

THE DOMINICAN ORDER

"The Fundamental Constitution"

I. The purpose of the Order was expressed by Pope Honorius III writing to St. Dominic and his brothers in these words: "He who ever makes His Church fruitful with new offspring,[76] wanting to make these modern times measure up to former times, and to propagate the Catholic faith, inspired you with a holy desire by which, having embraced poverty and made profession of regular life, you have given yourselves to the proclamation of the Word of God, preaching the name of our Lord Jesus Christ throughout the world."[77]

II. For the Order of Friars Preachers founded by St. Dominic "is known from the beginning to have been instituted especially for preaching and the salvation of souls."[78] Our brethren, therefore, according to the command of the founder "must conduct themselves honorably and religiously as men who want to obtain their salvation and the salvation of others, following in the footsteps of the Savior as evangelical men speaking among themselves or their neighbors either with God or about God."[79]

III. In order that we many be perfected in the love of God and neighbor through this following of Christ, we are incorporated into our Order by profession and consecrated totally to God, and in particular we are dedicated in a new way to the universal Church, "being appointed entirely for the complete evangelization of the Word of God."[80]

IV. We also undertake as sharers of the apostolic mission the life of the Apostles in the form conceived by St. Dominic, living with one mind the common life, faithful in the profession of the evangelical counsels, fervent in the common celebration of the liturgy, especially of the Eucharist and the divine office as well as other prayer, assiduous in study, and persevering in regular observance. All these practices contribute not only to the glory of God and our sanctification, but serve directly the salvation of mankind, since they prepare harmoniously for preaching, furnish its incentive, form its character, and in turn are influenced by it. These elements are closely interconnected and carefully balanced, mutually enriching one another, so that in their synthesis the proper life of the Order is established: a life in the fullest sense apostolic, in which preaching and teaching must proceed from an abundance of contemplation.

V. Made cooperators of the episcopal order by priestly ordination, we have as our special function the prophetic office by which the Gospel of Jesus Christ is proclaimed everywhere both by word and example, with due consideration for the conditions of persons, times, and places so that faith is awakened or penetrates more deeply all life in the building up of the body of Christ, which is perfected by the sacraments of faith.

---

76. From the Good Friday prayer for catechumens.

77. Honorius III: Letter to St. Dominic and his companions, 18 January 1221 (*MOPH* [*Monumenta ordinis fratrum praedicatorum historica*] XXV, 144).

78. Prologue of the *Primitive Constitutions.*

79. *Primitive Const.* Dist II, c. 31.

80. Honorius III: Letter to all Prelates of the Church, 4 February 1221 (*MOPH* XXV, 145).

VI. The structure of the Order as a religious society arises from its mission and fraternal communion. Since the ministry of the word and of the sacraments of faith is a priestly office, ours is a clerical Order, whose mission the cooperator brothers, exercising in a special way the common priesthood, also share in many ways. Moreover, the total commission of the Preachers to the proclamation of the Gospel by word and work is revealed in the fact that by solemn profession they are entirely and perpetually united with the life and mission of Christ.

Since our Order in union with the entire Church has been sent to all nations, it has a universal character. In order that its mission may be fulfilled more suitably, it enjoys exemption, and is strengthened by a sound unity in its head, the Master of the Order, to whom all the brethren are bound immediately by profession since study and evangelization require mobility of everyone.

From that same mission of the Order the personal responsibility and gifts of the brethren are affirmed and promoted in a special way. On the completion of his formation every brother is regarded as a mature adult, since he can instruct others and undertake various works in the Order. For this reason the Order maintains that its own laws do not bind under sin, so that the brethren may wisely embrace them "not like slaves under the law, but like freemen established under grace."[81]

Finally, by reason of the purpose of the Order, a superior has the faculty of dispensation "when it seems to him to be expedient, especially in those matters which seem to impede study, preaching, or the good of souls."[82]

VII. The communion and universality of our religious life shape its government as well. Its government is noted for an organic and balanced participation of all its members for pursuing the special end of the Order. For the Order is not restricted to a conventual fraternity even though this is its fundamental unit, but extends to the communion of convents which constitutes a province, and to the communion of provinces which constitutes it as a whole. For this reason its authority which is universal in its head, namely a general chapter and the Master of the Order, is shared proportionately and with corresponding autonomy by the provinces and convents. Consequently our government is communitarian in a special way, for superiors ordinarily take office through election by the brethren and confirmation by a higher superior. Furthermore, through chapter and council, communities in many ways have a role in exercising their own government and in settling important matters.

This communitarian form of government is particularly suitable for the Order's development and frequent renewal. Superiors and the brethren, through their delegates with equal right and freedom in general chapters of provincials and of diffinitors, provide in common so that the Order's mission may be advanced and the Order itself be suitably renewed. This continual revision of the Order is necessary, not only on account of a spirit of perennial Christian conversion, but also on account of the special vocation of the Order which impels it to accommodate its presence in the world for each generation.

VIII. The fundamental purpose of the Order and the form of life flowing from it retain their value in every age of the Church. Nevertheless in times of greater change and evolution, as we are taught by our tradition, understanding and evaluation of these matters become particularly urgent. In these circumstances, it is characteristic of the Order to renew itself courageously and to adjust itself to these circumstances by discerning and testing what is good and useful in mankind's aspirations and by introducing the results into the unchangeable harmony of the fundamental elements of its life.

These elements, indeed, cannot be changed substantially among us, and they must continue to inspire forms of living and of preaching suited to the needs of the Church and of mankind.

IX. The Dominican family is composed of clerical and cooperator brothers, nuns, sisters, members of secular institutes, and fraternities of priests and laity. The Constitutions and Ordinations which follow concern only the brethren, unless it is expressly stated otherwise; by these regulations the necessary unity of the Order is protected without excluding a necessary diversity according to those same laws.

From Brother Damian Byrne, ed., *Book of Constitutions and Ordinations of the Order of Friars Preachers* (Rome, Italy: General Curia, 1984), 3, 5, 7, 9.

꙳ The **anchoresses** were women who lived in permanent enclosures attached to a church in the midst of a town or village. The *Ancrene Wisse* (*Guide for Anchoresses*)—of which we present here part III, "The Inner Feelings"—was not written by the anchoresses themselves but by their spiritual counselors, who prob-

---

81. *Rule of St. Augustine*, final paragraph.
82. *Primitive Constitutions*, Prologue.

ably belonged to the Augustinian Order. It was meant to provide them with a coherent program of spiritual readings. The text comes from England, written in the thirteenth century and in fine English prose at a time when the principal languages of England were Latin and Anglo-Norman French.

"The Inner Feelings," in *Ancrene Wisse*

My dear sisters, just as you guard well your senses outwardly, so, above all else, see to it that you are gentle and mild and humble within—sweet and tender-hearted, and patient in the face of evil words said of you and deeds done to you—lest you lose everything.

David says this verse against bitter anchoresses: *Similis factus sum pelicano solitudinis, et cetera* (Ps 101:7)—"I am," he says, "like a pelican who lives by itself." The pelican is a bird so ill-humored and so angry that it often kills its own chicks in fury when they anger it; and then soon after it becomes very sorry, and makes a very great lamentation, and strikes itself with the bill it has just killed its chicks with, and draws blood from its breast; and with that blood it brings back to life its slain chicks. This bird, the pelican, is the ill-humored anchoress; her chicks are her good works, which she often kills with the bill of acute anger. But when she has done so she does as the pelican does: repents very soon, and with her own bill rends her breast—that is, with confession of her mouth, with which she sinned and killed her good works, she draws the blood of sin out of her breast, that is, out of the heart, in which is the life of the soul. And in this way her slain chicks, which are her good works, will be brought back to life.

Blood symbolizes sin, for just as a person covered with blood is grim and horrible to the human eye, so is the sinner before the eye of God. Yet no one can test blood properly before it has cooled. So it is with sin. While the heart boils with anger inwardly, it lacks right judgment; again, while the desire is hot for any sin, you cannot at the time judge well what it is, or what will come of it. But let desire pass over, and you will be glad; let the heat cool, as someone does who wants to test blood, and you will rightly judge the sin, that you thought fair, foul and loathsome, and productive of so much evil if you had done it while the heat lasted, that you will judge you were made when you were inclined to it. This is true of every sin, which is why blood symbolizes it, and especially of anger. *Impedit ira animum ne possit cernere verum*—"Anger, while it lasts," it says, "so blinds the heart that she cannot know the truth."[83] *Maga quedam est transformans naturam humanum*—"Anger is an enchanter, like one

hears of in stories, for she deprives a person of their wits and changes their whole appearance, and transforms them from a human into the likeness of a beast."[84] An angry woman is a wolf; a man is a wolf or lion or unicorn; for as long as anger is in a woman's heart, though she say her versicles, *Hail Marys, Our Fathers,* she does nothing but howl. In God's eyes she looks just like someone who has turned into a wolf; in his keen ears she has a wolf's voice. *Ira furor brevis est*—"Anger is a madness."[85] Is not someone who is angry mad? How do they look, how do they speak, how are their hearts within? What is their outward behavior like? They do not know other people—how then are they human? *Est enim homo animal mansuetum natura*—"By nature humans are mild";[86] as soon as they lose their mildheartedness they lose their human nature, and anger, the enchanter, transforms them into beasts, as I said before. And what if any anchoress, Jesus Christ's spouse, is transformed into a wolf: is this not a sorry thing? All she can do is to shed that rough pelt from about her heart at once, and make herself smooth and soft with soft reconciliation, as a woman's skin is by nature. For with that wolf's pelt nothing that she does is pleasing to God.

See! Here are many remedies against anger, a great flock of comforts[87] and a variety of helps. If people insult you, think that you are earth. Does one not tread on earth, and spit on earth? Even if they did this to you, they treated the earth properly. If you bark back, you have a dog's nature; if you sting back, you have an adder's nature, and not that of Christ's spouse. Think if he did so, *Qui tanquam ovis ad occisionem ductus est et non aperuit os suum* (Isa 53:7); after all the shameful tortures that he suffered on the long night of Good Friday, they led him out in the morning to hang him on a criminal's gallows, and to drive iron nails through his four

---

83. *Distichs of Cato* II.4, edited by J. W. and A. M. Duff (Loeb Classical Library, 1934): a collection much used throughout the Middle Ages.

84. Untraced.

85. Horace, *Epistolae* I.ii.62.

86. Alexander Neckham, *De Naturis Rerum* 156.

87. The way these "comforts" are intended to work is perhaps most easily appreciated in this [and the next] paragraph on insulting words as wind. The process of self-comfort involves the anchoress first seeing such words as a physical, rather than emotional, phenomenon—as wind—and thinking of herself as another physical object in danger of being blown over; then transforming the anger generated by the words, by imagining herself deflecting them, so that they pass underneath her and blow her up toward heaven; and only then, after insistently focusing on these somewhat comic images, allowing herself to dwell on her situation as a minor martyrdom and to confront it in some of its real human complexity. Spiritual struggle is transformed into a simpler physical struggle, and the transformation of anger into charity is dealt with in separable stages. *Ancrene Wisse* is the finest of all guides in English to the tactics of the spiritual life.

limbs—but "No more than a sheep," as the Holy Writ says, "did he struggle or speak."

Think also, on the other hand, what is a word but wind? She is too weakly buttressed whom a puff of wind, a word, can fell and cast into sin. And who would not find it extraordinary that an anchoress should be felled by wind? Yet again, does she not show that she is dust and an unstable thing, if she is immediately blown over by a little word's wind? The same puff out of someone's mouth, if you cast it beneath you, would bear you up toward the joy of heaven—but indeed, our great folly is to be wondered at! Understand this saying: St. Andrew could endure that the hard cross should hoist him up toward heaven, and lovingly embraced it; St. Lawrence also endured that the griddle should hoist him upward with the burning coals; St. Stephen endured the stones they threw at him, and took them gladly, and prayed on bended knees for those who threw them at him—and we cannot endure that the wind of a word may bear us toward heaven! But we are angry at them, whom we ought to thank as those who perform us a great service, though it be unwillingly. *Impius vivit pio velit nolit:* "All that the wicked and the evil do for evil, all of it is good for the good, all is to their advantage and builds them up toward joy." Let them braid your crown, and that gladly. Think how the holy man in *The Lives of the Fathers* kissed and blessed the hand of the other one who had harmed him, and said most earnestly, while kissing it eagerly, "Blessed be this hand for ever, for it has built me the joys of heaven."[88] And you should say this too about the hand that harms you, and also about the mouth which insults you in any way: "Blessed be your mouth," say, "for you make of it a tool to build my crown. I am glad for my good, but sorry for your evil, for you benefit me and harm yourself." If any man or woman has said or done you harm, dear sisters, so should you say. But it is very strange, if we consider it well, how God's saints suffered wounds on their bodies, and we are angry if a wind blows a little at us—and the wind wounds nothing but only the air. For the wind—that is, a word someone says—can neither wound you in your flesh nor befoul your soul, even if it blows on you, unless you cause it to happen yourself. Bernard: *Qui irritavit, quid inflammaris ad verbi flatum, qui nec carnem vulnerat nec inquinat mentem?* (*Why are you irritated, why inflamed, at a word's breath, which can neither wound your flesh nor soil your mind?*).[89] You can easily perceive that little of the fire of charity that is kindled entirely from our Lord's love was there; there was not much fire if a puff blew it out. For where there is a great fire it grows with the wind.

See here finally the best remedy against harmful deeds or words—and know it through this illustration. A man who lay in prison and had to pay an enormous ransom, and could in no way come out except to be hanged unless he had paid his ransom in full—would he not greatly thank someone who threw a bag of coins at him to redeem himself with and release himself from suffering—even if it was thrown very hard at his heart? All the pain would be forgotten in his gladness. In the same way we are all in prison here, and owe God great debts of sin, so that we cry to him in the *Our Father, Et dimitte nobis debita nostra*—"Lord," we say, "forgive us our debts, as we forgive our debtors." Any wrong that is done us, either by word or by deed, that is our ransom with which we should redeem ourselves and settle our debts, which are our sins, toward our Lord. For without payment no one is taken out of this prison who is not hanged at once, either in purgatory or in the torment of hell. And our Lord himself said, *Dimittite et dimittetur vobis* (Luke 6:37)—"Forgive, and I will forgive you": as though he said, "You are heavily in debt toward me with your sins, but would you like to make a good deal? All that anyone ever says or does against you I will reckon against the debt that you owe me." Now, even if a word should hit you very hard on the breast, so that you think at first that it hurt your heart, think of it as the prisoner would whom the other person hurt badly with the bag of coins, and take it gladly to free yourself with, and thank the one who sent it to you—even though God can never thank him for sending it. He harms himself and benefits you, if you can endure it. For as David said, and very well, "God puts the wicked and the evil in his treasury, so that with them he may pay, as one does with money, people who fight well"—*Ponens in thesauris abyssos: Glossa: crudeles quibus donat milites suos* (Psalm 32:7).

Also, on the other hand, this bird the pelican has another feature, that it is always lean. Thus as I said, David compares himself to one in the person of an anchorite, speaking in an anchorite's voice: *Similis factus sum pelican solitudinis* (Ps 101:7)—"I am like a pelican which dwells by itself." And the anchoress should say this, and be like a pelican in its leanness. *Judith clausa in cubiculo ieiunabat omnibus diebus vite sue, et cetera* (Jdt 8:5–6)—"Judith, enclosed," as it tells in her book, "led a very hard life; she fasted and wore haircloth." "Judith

---

88. *Vitae Patrum* VII.3 (*PL* [*Patrologia Latina*] 73, col. 1029).

89. See Geoffrey of Auxerre, *Declamationes de colloquio Simonis cum Iesu ex S. Bernardi sermonibus collectae* XXXVI.43 (*PL* 184, col. 461).

enclosed" figures the enclosed anchoress who ought to lead a hard life as the lady Judith did, according to her capacity, not as a pig shut up in a sty to grow fat and large waiting for the axe's blow.

There are two kinds of anchoress whom our Lord speaks about. And he says in the gospel, about the false and the true: *Vulpes foveas habent et volucres celi nidos* (Mt 8:20)—that is, "Foxes have their holes and birds of heaven have their nests." The foxes are false anchoresses, for the fox is the falsest of beasts. These "have holes," he says, which they burrow into the earth with earthly vices. And they draw into their hole all that they can grab and run with. So hoarding anchoresses are compared by God in the gospel to foxes. The fox is also an insolent beast, and voracious with it; and the false anchoress draws into her hole and eats both geese and hens, as a fox does. Like the fox, they have an innocent look some of the time, and yet they are full of guile. They pretend to be other than they are, like the fox, who is a hypocrite. They expect to beguile God, as they fool simple men—and they beguile themselves most. They boast, as the fox does, and brag of their goodness whenever they dare and can. They chatter about idle things, and become so very worldly that in the end their name stinks, like the fox whenever he goes out. For if they do evil, what people say of them is even worse.

From *Anchoritic Spirituality: Ancrene Wisse and Associated Works,* translated by Anne Savage and Nicholas Watson (New York: Paulist Press, 1991), 93–96.

☙ *The Monastic Rule,* by **Iosif Volotsky** (1439–1515), testifies to the rich monastic tradition that continued to flourish in the Orthodox East into the late Middle Ages. *The Monastic Rule* was written after the foundation of Volotsky's monastery in Volok in 1479. Volotsky's monasticism was a cenobitic system that stressed austerity for the individual monk, service to society, and the right of monasteries to own property.

IOSIF VOLOTSKY

The Monastic Rule, Discourse III

How it is proper to have garments and footwear and other things, and how it is not proper for anyone to take anything anywhere, neither an object belonging to the monastery nor that of any brother, without the superior's or the cellarer's blessing.

Discourse III

[1] Just as we have said concerning foods and beverages that it is good to select the simple and unexcessive and to do everything in keeping with the counsel of the spiritual superior; [so too] have the clothing that is necessary, simple, very mean, and appropriate for the place and climate, and do not by means of demonic cunning seek out the very expensive and excessive.

[2] The Canons of the Seventh Ecumenical Council say: *Bishops,* monks,[90] *or clergymen who have adorned themselves with colorful and bright clothing should on this account be reprimanded. If they persist, they shall be given a penance. If someone starts to laugh at those who are wearing worthless garments, they shall be corrected with a penance. Indeed from the first years, every monastic and priestly man passed his life in humble and worthless garments.*[91]

[3] The most supreme Peter said to his disciple Clement: *Clement, you have not understood my life, that I eat only bread, olives and the most worthless vegetables, and that my coat is old. This is my garment, and I do not need another, for my mind always beholds the eternal and the good out there and does not regard anything here.*[92]

[4] It is said in the *Life* of Chrysostom that after his elevation to the archbishopric of Constantinople, his food was strained ground barley, which was placed in water for a day, and he took a correctly measured quantity. His garment was a tattered hairshirt, and he did not have a third one for changing.[93]

[5] Saint Gregory the Theologian says of Basil the Great: *Basil the Great said to the prefect: "I am not afraid of pillage, for I have nothing, unless you need one of my hair-shirts."*[94]

[6] And again, Father Isaiah says: *Do not seek vainglory in clothing, but remember the sheepskin of Elijah and the sackcloth of Isaiah, and do not forget the Baptist's garment, which was of camel's hair.*[95]

[7] It is written of Arsenius the Great that when he was in the world he wore the brightest of all clothing, and when he was a monk, he wore the most worthless.[96]

---

90. "Monks" was added by Iosif.

91. Nicea 2.16; *Councils,* 566 (Mansi 13:754AC), as found in Nikon, *Pandekty* 37:283ᵛ–284.

92. Pseudo-Clement *Homilies* 12.6:293; PG 2:305BC, as found in Nikon, *Pandekty* 37:282ᵛ–283.

93. Cf. Nikon, *Pandekty* 37:283ᵛ.

94. *Funeral Oration* 411; PG 36:560C, as found in Nikon, *Pandekty* 37:283 ob.

95. Nikon, *Pandekty* 37:281ᵛ, . . . before a citation attributed to Isaiah.

96. Arsenius 4; *Sayings,* 8 . . . , probably as in Nikon, *Pandekty* 37:281ᵛ.

[8] When Sabas the Great went to the emperor, they drove him from the place as a beggar, for he was wearing an old and tattered shirt.

[9] The holy Fathers say that all luxury and adornment is alien to the priestly and monastic habit.[97] Therefore from the earliest years all the saints went about deprived, grieving, and maltreated in sheepskins and goatskins, *and the whole world was not worthy of them.*[98] "He who is adorned with clothing in the worldly life obtains glory from man; he who has humble and very worthless clothing in the monastic life prepares glory for himself in the heavens."[99]

[10] Father Isaac said: *Our fathers wore old rags. Now you wear the most expensive clothing. Go away from here, for you have devastated this place.*[100]

[11] Saint Ephraim said concerning this: *He who loves bright garments is stripped of divine clothing, and our robe spoils love of goodness in that it has nothing in common with the heavenly kingdom; the beauty of our garment signifies that we are stripped of that glory.* Again he says: *For you the Lord accepted abuses on the cross, and you, wretched one, adorn yourself with garments! Does your heart not tremble? Is your mind not horrified when you hear this? The Passionless One suffered passion, that you might adorn yourself not with the rotten garments, foods, or meals of common people, but with those proper to monks. The crucified Lord will seek out an answer for all of your indifference, for you, who are listening, are now indolent, eating luxuriously, adorning yourself with vestments, and laughing. When that great and terrible day comes, you will cry incessantly in the fire and will wail from the weakness of your soul!*[101]

[12] Saint Symeon the New Theologian says about this: *We, the passionate and the wretched who have abandoned the great and the admirable and have entered a monastery, now love shiny garments, belts, cutlery, sandals, and drapery, sweet foods, and drink, and apples, and beautiful fruits. In loving them, we fall away completely from Christ the King and become his enemies.*[102]

[13] The holy Fathers say that a debauched demon observes the monk's vestments to see if he has the best one for the sake of conversation. This is a *typicon* for debauchery, and we shall therefore be condemned with the publicans and sinners and with the rich, who have lived in debauchery.

[14] Let us, then, exert ourselves with all our strength to abstain from avarice, adornment of garments, and passion for things, and not only not have possessions, but also not even desire them.

[15] Basil the Great says, in writing the rules of the common life: "*Do not acquire any personal possessions, nor do anything in secret to the detriment of the brotherhood, or become a bad model for those who are predisposed to salvation. When someone has scorned*

fear of God and the laws of the Holy Spirit and wants to have some personal possessions, he has become enslaved to materialism and possessions. Similarly, he produces evidence of disbelief against himself; he does not trust that God spiritually and physically comforts those gathered in his name for 'if two or three are gathered in Christ's name, he is among them.'[103] *Indeed no needed thing will be wanting when Christ is our superior; if it is wanting for the sake of testing us, then it is better to be wanting and to be with Christ than to become rich in all worldly goods and to be without communion with him.*"[104]

[16] Indeed it was to laymen that the Apostle said: "Having food and clothing, let us be content; but they who desire to be rich will fall into temptations and the snares"[105] of demons. Then how much more proper is it for monks not to desire riches but to love non-possession and Christ-like poverty. It is not easy for those who are not in a coenobium, where we have security regarding our most basic needs, to exercise this virtue.

[17] The unknown incursion of death, moreover, must always be before our eyes, lest Our Lord come at an unexpected hour and find our conscience polluted by avarice and materialism and say to us what is said to the rich man in the Gospel: "Fool, this night your soul shall be required of you and these things which you have prepared, whose will they be?"[106] On this account, our holy Fathers, all having the same understanding, handed down to us as a tradition that one cannot lay any firm foundation for the perfection of virtues if one does not exercise perfected non-possession, from which are born humility and compunction.

[18] He who desires to be worthy of divine grace in the present age and in the future must have perfected non-possession and Christ-like poverty, just as the Lord Christ himself says: "The Son of Man has nowhere to lay his head,"[107] and "I came down from heaven, not to be served but to serve;[108] I am among you as one who serves."[109] And again it is said: "He took a towel and washed the disciples' feet and

---

97. Nicaea 2.16; *Councils* 566 (Mansi 13:754B).

98. Heb 11:38.

99. Nikon, *Pandekty* 37:281, attributed to Ephraim.

100. Isa 7; *Sayings* 85; PG [*Patrologia Graeca*] 65:225B, as in Nikon, *Pandekty* 37:281.

101. Source unknown.

102. Pseudo-Symeon, *O ezhe kako podobaet* 10–10ᵛ.

103. Mt 18:20.

104. Nikon, *Pandekty* 3:28–29, quoting Basil *Constitutiones* 34; PG 31:1425BC.

105. Cf. 1 Tim 6:8–9.

106. Lk 12:20.

107. Mt 8:20; Lk 9:58.

108. Jn 6:38; Mk 10:45.

109. Mt 20:28; Mk 20:27.

said, 'Just as I, your Lord and teacher, have washed your feet, you ought also to wash one another's feet. For I have given you an example that you should do as I have done.'"[110]

[19] Therefore it is proper for all of us to imitate that humility and poverty, especially those of us who have renounced the world and vowed to endure every affliction for the sake of the heavenly kingdom. Saint Poemen says: *If you desire to live in a coenobium, renounce everything, and do not have dominion over even a cup, and thus shall you be saved in a coenobium.*[111]

[20] In like manner the Lord Christ says: "I have a commandment, what I should say and what I should speak,"[112] and "I do not do my own will, but the will of the Father who sent me."[113] He who created the land and the sea and everything visible and invisible by his Word, displayed such humility to give us a model; so it is even more proper for us not to have our own wills, but to do everything in keeping with the superior's blessing.

[21] Consult the superior about what, when, and how it is proper to eat and drink foods and drinks, and also about what quantity and value to have of clothing and footwear, holy icons, books, and all things, and silver coins, and for working handicrafts, buying and selling, and writing and sending letters, or if anyone is sent a letter or anything else.

[22] In like manner, the officials are not to buy for themselves anything special with the monastery's money without the superior's or the cellarer's blessing. And they shall distribute and take back and do everything in keeping with the superior's blessing and not have or consider anything their own. Rather, everything belongs to the monastery. For all the Divine Writings and coenobitic traditions dictate to those living in coenobia to act in such a manner.

[23] We have more to say concerning garments and footwear, and we shall also place these in three orders.

[24] The first order. If someone wants to have perfected non-possession according to the words spoken by Christ: "Do not acquire a second coat,"[114] then he shall have one mantle, one cassock, one skin coat, two or three tunics, one of each type of clothing—everything being mean and ragged—and one of each cell object—everything being mean and unlovely. Such a person is a perfect disciple of Christ and an imitator and emulator of the saints, who suffered winter, coldness, nakedness, calamities, labors, and coercion for the sake of Christ, and on his account walked "the narrow way, that leads to life."[115] This person can say to Christ with boldness: "We have forsaken all and followed you."[116] To him the Lord says: "If anyone serves me, he must follow me; wherever I am, there shall my servant be also."[117]

[25] The second order. One shall have one big untattered mantle and one cowl, cassock, and skin coat—not vaingloriously or cravingly. This person walks along a blessed way, follows the first, and knows not if he has reached the end.

[26] The third order. We are not legislating details but rather setting limits on account of those who are greedy for things, possess in excess, and know no measure. *Therefore, if someone wants to have more than this, the superior and the brothers shall not allow this to be, but let them have these: one new mantle and a second old one; one new cowl and a second old one; one new cassock and a second old one; three tunics—one new and two old; one new pair of boots and a second dilapidated pair; several undershoes; two winter caps and two summer caps, one new and the other old.*[118]

[27] It is proper to have "simple and inexpensive" garments in the storeroom just as the Divine Writings dictate.

[28] It is proper for the treasurer, while issuing garments and footwear, to make an inquiry. If someone has two garments and he wants a third, do not give it to him. When someone takes a new garment from the storeroom, he is to give back the old one, and if he does not surrender it, then do not issue him a new one. If someone wants to exchange apparel, and he really needs three skin coats, then he should surrender a cassock or a mantle and take the skin coat. Likewise if he wants another garment, he is to surrender something which he does not need of similar value. Everyone shall have the equivalent of two of each garment, one in good condition and one old, except in cases of debility and the offices which take place outside the monastery.

[29] And it is according to the witness of the Divine Writings that I have established three orders for food and drink and garments and footwear. *For all are not equal, because of lack of zeal and exhaustion of strength.*[119] Indeed our Lord Jesus Christ has said in the holy Gospel in the parable of the seeds: "Others," he said, "fell on good ground and brought forth fruit, some an hundred-fold, some sixty-fold, and some thirty-fold."[120] Notice that they fell into the same ground and yielded unequal fruits. And it is not the case that anyone who

---

110. Jn 13:4–5, 14–15.
111. Poemen 152; *Sayings* 158; PG 65:360B, cited in Nikon, *Pandekty* 4:30.
112. Jn 12:49.
113. Jn 6:30.
114. Lk 3:11.
115. Mt 7:14.
116. Mt 19:27.
117. Jn 12:26.
118. Cf. Nikon, *Taktikon* 1:13ᵛ.
119. Cf. *Prosvetitel'* 4:160. . . . Also Gregory of Sinai. *Praecepta;* PG 150:1336A, possibly as in Nil Sorsky, *Ustav* 2:26.
120. Mt 13:8, 23.

did not create an hundred-fold fell down; rather sixty-fold is welcomed, and thirty-fold is not rejected.

From Iosif Volotsky, *The Monastic Rule of Iosif Volotsky,* edited and translated by David M. Goldfrank (Kalamazoo, MI: Cistercian Publishers, 1983), 93–98.

❧ **Ignatius of Loyola** (1491–1556) and a small group of followers put themselves at the service of Pope Paul III (1534–49) in November 1538. Ignatius's initial document, *The First Sketch of the Institute of the Society of Jesus* presented to Pope Paul III in 1539, was incorporated into the pope's Bull of approval *Regimini militantis ecclesiae* of September 27, 1540. *The Jesuit Constitution,* parts of which are excerpted here, was drafted by Ignatius and finally adopted by the first General Congregation of the Society of Jesus, also known as the "Jesuits," in 1558.

IGNATIUS OF LOYOLA

The Jesuit Constitution

I. Formulas of the Institute of the Society of Jesus, Approved and Confirmed by Julius III

Taken from the apostolic letter Exposcit debitum, *July 21, 1550:* ". . . *A petition has been humbly submitted to us, begging us to confirm the formula which now contains the aforementioned Society's Institute, expressed more accurately and clearly than before, because of the lessons learned through experience and usage, but in the same spirit. The content of the formula follows, and it is this*":

1. Whoever desires to serve as a soldier of God beneath the banner of the cross in our Society, which we desire to be designated by the name of Jesus, and to serve the Lord alone and the Church, his spouse, under the Roman pontiff, the vicar of Christ on earth, should, after a solemn vow of perpetual chastity, poverty, and obedience, keep what follows in mind. He is a member of a Society founded chiefly for this purpose: to strive especially for the defense and propagation of the faith and for the progress of souls in Christian life and doctrine, by means of public preaching, lectures, and any other ministration whatsoever of the word of God, and further by means of the Spiritual Exercises, the education of children and unlettered persons in Christianity, and the spiritual consolation of Christ's faithful through hearing confessions and administering the other sacraments. Moreover, he should show himself ready to reconcile the estranged, compassionately assist and serve those who are in prisons or hospitals, and indeed to perform any other works of charity, ac-

cording to what will seem expedient for the glory of God and the common good. Furthermore, he should carry out all these works *altogether free of charge and without accepting any salary for the labor expended in all the aforementioned activities.* Still further, let any such person take care, as long as he lives, first of all to keep before his eyes God and then the nature of this Institute which is, so to speak, a pathway to God; and then let him strive with all his effort to achieve this end set before him by God—each one, however, according to the grace which the Holy Spirit has given to him and according to the particular grade of his own vocation.

2. Consequently, lest anyone should perhaps show zeal, but a zeal which is not according to knowledge, the decision about each one's grade and the selection and entire distribution of employments will be in the power of the superior general or prelate who at any future time is to be elected by us, or in the power of those whom this superior general may appoint under himself with that authority, in order that the proper order necessary in every well-organized community may be preserved. This superior general, with the advice of his associates, shall possess the authority to establish constitutions leading to the achievement of this end which has been proposed to us, with the majority of votes always having the right to prevail. He shall also have the authority to explain officially doubts which may arise in connection with our Institute as comprised within this Formula. The council, which must necessarily be convoked to establish or change the Constitutions and for other matters of more than ordinary importance, **such as the alienation or dissolution of houses and colleges once erected,**[121] should be understood (**according to the explanation in our Constitutions**) **to be the greater part of the entire professed Society**[122] which can be summoned without grave inconvenience by the superior general. In other matters of lesser importance, the same general, aided by counsel from his brethren to the extent that he will deem fitting, will have the full right personally to order and command whatever he judges in the Lord to pertain to the glory of God and the common good, as will be explained in the Constitutions.

3. All who make the profession in this Society should bear in mind, not only when they first make their profession but

---

121. Abrogated by CN 390, §3, with the approval of Pope John Paul II in a letter of June 10, 1995.

122. Abrogated by GC 34, d. 23 A, no. 2, 1°–2° (approved by Pope John Paul II in a letter dated June 10, 1995).

as long as they live, that this entire Society and the individual members who make their profession in it are campaigning for God under faithful obedience to His Holiness Pope Paul III and his successors in the Roman pontificate. And although we are taught by the Gospel, and we know from the orthodox faith, and we firmly profess that all of Christ's faithful are subject to the Roman pontiff as their head and as the vicar of Jesus Christ, for the sake of greater devotion in obedience to the Apostolic See, of greater abnegation of our own wills, and of surer direction from the Holy Spirit, we have nevertheless judged it to be supremely profitable that each of us and any others who will make the same profession in the future should, in addition to that ordinary bond of the three vows, be bound by this special vow to carry out whatever the present and future Roman pontiffs may order which pertains to the progress of souls and the propagation of the faith; and to go at once, without subterfuge or excuse, as far as in us lies, to whatsoever provinces they may choose to send us—whether they decide to send us among the Turks or any other infidels, even those who live in the regions called the Indies, or among any heretics whatever, or schismatics, or any of the faithful.

4. Therefore those who will come to us should, before they take this burden upon their shoulders, ponder long and seriously, as the Lord has counseled [Luke 14:30], whether they possess among their resources enough spiritual capital to complete this tower; that is, whether the Holy Spirit who moves them is offering them so much grace that with his aid they have hope of bearing the weight of this vocation. Then, after they have enlisted through the inspiration of the Lord in this militia of Christ, they ought to be prompt in carrying out this obligation which is so great, being clad for battle day and night [Eph. 6:14; 1 Peter 1:13].

5. However, to forestall among us any ambition of such missions or provinces, or any refusal of them, all our members should have this understanding: They should not either by themselves or through someone else carry on negotiations with the Roman pontiff about such missions, but leave all this care to God, and to the pope himself as his vicar, and to the superior general of the Society. Indeed, this general too, just like the rest, should not treat with the said pontiff about his being sent or not, unless after advice from the Society.

6. All should likewise vow that in all matters which pertain to the observance of this Rule they will be obedient to the one put in charge of the Society. (He should be the one best qualified for this office and will be elected by a majority of votes, as will be explained in the Constitutions.) Moreover, he should possess all the authority and power over the Society which are useful for its good administration, correction, and government. He should issue the commands which he knows to be opportune for achieving the end set before him by God and the Society. In his superiorship he should be ever mindful of the kindness, meekness, and charity of Christ and of the pattern set by Peter and Paul, a norm which both he and the aforementioned council should keep constantly in view. Assuredly, too, because of the immense value of good order and for the sake of the constant practice of humility, never sufficiently praised, the individual subjects should not only be obliged to obey the general in all matters pertaining to the Society's Institute but also to recognize and properly venerate Christ as present in him.

7. From experience we have learned that a life removed as far as possible from all infection of avarice and as like as possible to evangelical poverty is more gratifying, more undefiled, and more suitable for the edification of our neighbors. We likewise know that our Lord Jesus Christ will supply to his servants who are seeking only the kingdom of God what is necessary for food and clothing. Therefore our members, one and all, should vow perpetual poverty in such a manner that *neither the professed, either as individuals or in common, nor any house or church of theirs can acquire any civil right to any annually recurring produce, fixed revenues, or possessions or to the retention of any stable goods* (except those which are proper for their own use and habitation); but they should instead be content with whatever is given them out of charity for the necessities of life.

8. However, since the houses which the Lord will provide are to be dedicated to labor in his vineyard and not to the pursuit of scholastic studies; and since, on the other hand, it appears altogether proper that workers should be provided for that same vineyard from among the young men who are inclined to piety and capable of applying themselves to learning, in order that they may be a kind of seminary for the Society, including the professed Society; consequently, to provide facilities for studies, the professed Society should be capable of having colleges of scholastics wherever benefactors will be moved by their devotion to build and endow them. We now petition that as soon as these colleges will have been built and endowed (but not from resources which it pertains to the Holy See to apply), they may be established through authorization from the Holy See or considered to be so established. These colleges should be capable of having fixed revenues, annuities, or possessions which are to be applied

to the uses and needs of the students. The general or the Society retains the full government or superintendency over the aforementioned colleges and students; and this pertains to the choice of the rectors or governors and of the scholastics; the admission, dismissal, reception, and exclusion of the same; the enactment of statutes; the arrangement, instruction, edification, and correction of the scholastics; the manner of supplying them with food, clothing, and all the other necessary materials; and every other kind of government, control, and care. All this should be managed in such a way that neither may the students be able to abuse the aforementioned goods nor may the professed Society be able to convert them to its own uses, but may use them to provide for the needs of the scholastics. These students, moreover, should have such intellectual ability and moral character as to give solid hope that they will be suitable for the Society's functions after their studies are completed, and that thus at length, after their progress in spirit and learning has become manifest and after sufficient testing, they can be admitted into our Society. Since all the members should be priests, they should be obliged to recite the Divine Office according to the ordinary rite of the Church, but privately and not in common or in choir. Also, in what pertains to food, clothing, and other external things, they will follow the common and approved usage of reputable priests, so that if anything is subtracted in this regard in accordance with each one's need or desire of spiritual progress, it may be offered, as will be fitting, out of devotion and not obligation, as a reasonable service of the body to God.

9. These are the matters which we were able to explain about our profession in a kind of sketch, through the good pleasure of our previously mentioned sovereign pontiff Paul and of the Apostolic See. We have now done this, that we may give succinct information, both to those who ask us about our plan of life and also to those who will later follow us if, God willing, we shall ever have imitators along this path. By experience we have learned that the path has many and great difficulties connected with it. Consequently we have judged it opportune to decree that no one should be permitted to pronounce his profession in this Society unless his life and doctrine have been probed by long and exacting tests (as will be explained in the Constitutions). For in all truth this Institute requires men who are thoroughly humble and prudent in Christ as well as conspicuous in the integrity of Christian life and learning. Moreover, some persons will be admitted to become coadjutors either for spiritual or temporal concerns or to become scholastics. After sufficient

probations and the time specified in the Constitutions, these too should, for their greater devotion and merit, pronounce their vows. But their vows will not be solemn (except in the case of some who with permission from the superior general will be able to make three solemn vows of this kind because of their devotion and personal worth). Instead, they will be vows by which these persons are bound as long as the superior general thinks that they should be retained in the Society, as will be explained more fully in the Constitutions. But these coadjutors and scholastics too should be admitted into this militia of Jesus Christ only after they have been diligently examined and found suitable for that same end of the Society. And may Christ deign to be favorable to these our tender beginnings, to the glory of God the Father, to whom alone be glory and honor forever. Amen.

The First and General Examen Which Should Be Proposed to All Who Ask for Admission into the Society of Jesus

Chapter 1: The Institute of the Society of Jesus and the Diversity of Its Members

1. This least congregation, which at its earliest foundation was named the Society of Jesus by the Holy See, was first approved by Pope Paul III, of happy memory, in the year 1540. Later it was confirmed by the same Holy Father in 1543 and by his successor Julius III in 1550. On other occasions too it is mentioned in different briefs and apostolic letters granting it various favors, after highly approving and confirming it.

2. *This Examen is usually proposed to all after they enter the house of the first probation. Nevertheless, if in a particular case discretion should suggest that another and more summary examen be proposed, or that the present text be handed out to be read without asking for replies about its contents, or if the knowledge possessed about some candidate is already sufficient, it would not be necessary to examine him by means of this present text. The examiner, however, ought to discuss this with the superior and follow his opinion. In most instances, it is before the candidates enter the house that they will be examined about certain essential matters, especially those which bar admission.*

3. The end of this Society is to devote itself with God's grace not only to the salvation and perfection of the members' own souls, but also with that same grace to labor strenuously in giving aid toward the salvation and perfection of the souls of their neighbors.

4. To achieve this end more effectively, the three vows of obedience, poverty, and chastity are taken in the Society. Pov-

erty is understood to mean that the Society neither wishes nor is able to possess any fixed revenues for its living expenses or for any other purpose. This holds true not only for the individual members but also for the churches or houses of the professed Society. Neither may the members accept any stipend or alms for Masses, sermons, lectures, the administration of any of the sacraments, or for any other pious function among those which the Society may exercise in accordance with its institute (even though such acceptance would be permissible for others). Such stipends or alms are customarily given in recompense for the ministries mentioned; but the Society's members may not accept them from anyone other than God our Lord; and it is purely for his service that they ought to do all things.

5. Furthermore, although the Society owns colleges and houses of probation which have fixed revenues for the living expenses of the scholastics before they enter into the professed Society or its houses, nevertheless, in conformity with the bull which is explained in the Constitutions, these revenues may not be used for another purpose. Neither the houses of the professed nor anyone of the professed or their coadjutors may use these revenues for themselves.

6. *These houses of probation are like branches of the colleges where those who will later be placed in the colleges are received and tested for a time.*

7. In addition to the three vows mentioned, the professed Society also makes an explicit vow to the present or future sovereign pontiff as the vicar of Christ our Lord. This is a vow to go anywhere His Holiness will order, whether among the faithful or the infidels, without pleading an excuse and without requesting any expenses for the journey, for the sake of matters pertaining to the worship of God and the good of the Christian religion.

8. In other respects, for sound reasons and with attention always paid to the greater service of God, in regard to what is exterior the manner of living is ordinary. It does not have any regular penances or austerities which are to be practiced through obligation. But those may be taken up which each one, with the superior's approval, thinks likely to be more helpful for his spiritual progress, as well as those which the superiors have authority to impose upon the members for the same purpose.

9. *This decision will be left within the superior's power; and he may delegate his authority to the confessor or other persons when he thinks this expedient.*

10. The persons who are received into this Society of Jesus, considered as a whole, are of four classes, in view of the end which the Society pursues. But on the side of those who enter, all ought to be men of the fourth class which will be described below.

11. *In addition to these four classes of members, some are accepted for solemn profession of three vows, in conformity with the bull of Julius III.*

12. First, some are received to make the profession in the Society with four solemn vows [. . .], after they have undergone the required experiences and probations. These members should possess sufficient learning, as is explained later on in the Constitutions [. . .], and they should be tested at length in their life and habits, in conformity with what such a vocation requires. Also, all of them must be priests before their profession.

13. The second class consists of those who are received to become coadjutors in the service of God and to aid the Society in either spiritual or temporal matters. After their experiments and probations these are to take three simple vows of obedience, poverty, and chastity, without taking the fourth vow of obedience to the pope or any other solemn vow. They should be content with their grade, knowing that in the eyes of our Creator and Lord those gain greater merit who with greater charity give help and service to all persons through love of his Divine Majesty, whether they serve in matters of greater moment or in others more lowly and humble.

14. The third class consists of those who are received to become scholastics, since they seem to have the ability and other qualifications suitable for studies. They are received so that after being educated they may be able to enter the Society either as professed or as coadjutors, as will be judged expedient. To become approved as scholastics of the Society, these too must undergo their experiments and probations and then pronounce the same three simple vows of poverty, chastity, and obedience, along with a promise that they will enter the Society in one of the two manners just mentioned [. . .], for the greater glory of God.

15. The fourth class consists of those who are received indeterminately for whatever they will in time be found fit. The Society does not yet determine for which of the aforementioned grades their talent is best suited. They in turn should enter as still indifferent with respect to whichever of the previously mentioned grades the superior will think best. In fact all, as far as they themselves are concerned, ought to enter with a disposition of this kind, as has been said.

16. Furthermore, before anyone is admitted to profession

or is required according to our Institute to take the previously mentioned simple vows of a coadjutor or of a scholastic, he will have two complete years of probation. Further still, to be admitted into either of the first two grades, the professed or the formed coadjutors, the scholastics will have an additional year after the completion of their studies. This time may be prolonged when the superior thinks it advisable.

17. *Although they have an appointed period of two years, those who desire to take their vows before the two years expire are not deprived of the freedom, devotion, spiritual profit, and merit which are found in binding oneself to Christ our Lord. However, it is good that they not take these vows without the superior's permission. Nor will they through taking them be admitted before the ordinary time either as professed, or as formed coadjutors, or as approved scholastics.*

18. During this two-year period (in which no special habit of the Society is received), and before the time when they ought to bind themselves by vows in the Society, each one ought on several occasions to see and ponder the bulls of the Institute of the Society, and the Constitutions and rules which he must observe in it. The first time is when he is in the house of the first probation, where those desiring to enter the Society are customarily received as guests for twelve or fifteen days so that they may reflect more carefully upon their whole situation, before they enter a house or college of the Society to live and associate with the others. The second time is upon completing their six months of experiments and probations. The third is after another six months, . . . and the one who is to be an approved scholastic pronounces his three vows with his promise. This is done so that both sides may proceed with greater clarity and knowledge in our Lord, and also that the more the subjects' constancy has been tested, the more stable and firm they may be in the divine service and in their original vocation, for the glory and honor of his Divine Majesty.

19. *Although there is no specified habit, it will be left to the discretion of the one in charge of the house to decide whether he will allow the novices to go about in the same clothes which they brought from the world or have them wear others; or again, when the garments become worn, whether he will give to the novices others more suitable for their own needs and for their service of the house.*

20. *It will not be necessary for the novices to see all of the Constitutions, but only an extract showing what they need to observe, unless for special reasons the superior may think that some person should be shown all of them.*

21. *The phrase "to live and associate with the others" is used because at their first entrance the candidates are kept apart from*

the rest for twelve or fifteen days, or even as long as twenty, in the house of the first probation.

From *The Constitutions of the Society of Jesus and Their Complementary Norms: A Complete English Translation of the Official Latin Texts,* translated by George E. Ganss (Saint Louis: Institute of Jesuit Sources, 1996), 3–14, 23–28.

❧ In an effort to bring back traditional monastic practice to Protestantism, **Roger Schutz,** known as Brother (Frère) Roger, began a monastic foundation in Taizé, France, in 1940. The Taizé community is cenobitic and includes members from various countries and Christian denominations. Its community life stresses common prayer and work, including that of farmers, artists, editors, printers, doctors, and theologians. *The "Little Source" of Taizé* (2000) is a revision of *The Rule of Taizé,* which was written in 1952.

ROGER SCHUTZ
The "Little Source" of Taizé

You are no longer alone

Desiring as you do to give your life because of Christ and the Gospel,[123] always keep in mind that you are advancing with him towards the light, even in the midst of your own darkness.

So, no longer looking back,[124] run forward in the footsteps of Jesus the Christ. He is leading you along a path of light: I am, but also, you are the light of the world.[125]

You wish to prepare the ways of the Lord Christ for many others,[126] kindling a fire even in the world's darkest nights.[127]

You know that Jesus the Christ came for all,[128] not just for a few. Risen, he is united with every human being without exception. Such is the catholicity of heart God has set within you.

Will you let an inner life grow within you, one which has neither beginning nor end? There, you stand at the threshold of the Gospel's joy, where human solidarities plunge their roots.

Making the earth a place where all can live, be they nearby or far away, is one of the beautiful pages of the Gospel for you to write by your life.

123. Mk 10:29 and Mt 16:25.   126. Mk 1:3.
124. Lev 9:62.   127. Lk 12:49.
125. Jn 8:12 and Mt 5:14.   128. Tit 2:11.

By forgetting yourself, by not seeking your own advantage, you are enabled to stand firm in the midst of the human family's situations with all their constant ebb and flow. Will you seek to understand, without letting yourself be carried away by the successive waves?

By sharing, are you among those who, with very little, generate a fine human hope?

With almost nothing, are you a creator of reconciliation in that communion of love which is the Body of Christ, his Church?

Sustained by a shared momentum, rejoice. You are no longer alone; in all things you are advancing together with your brothers. With them, you are called to live the parable of community.

From Brother Roger of Taizé, *The Sources of Taizé* (Chicago: GIA, 2000), 48–49.

---

3. EVOLVING STRUCTURES OF MINISTRY AND POWER

The Catholic Church

The First Letter of the Romans to the Corinthians, also known as *1 Clement* (written ca. 96), is the earliest extant Christian document outside the New Testament. The letter was written by **Clement of Rome** (ca. 30–100), who, according to tradition (as reported by Irenaeus and Tertullian, among others), was the third bishop of Rome after Peter. The letter was addressed to the Church in Corinth, where, it would seem, the leaders of the community had been deposed for unknown reasons.

CLEMENT OF ROME

The First Letter of the Romans to the Corinthians, V.1

V

1. But to pass from the examples of ancient times, let us come to those champions who lived nearest to our time. Let us set before us the noble examples which belong to our own generation. 2. Because of jealousy and envy the greatest and most righteous pillars[129] were persecuted, and fought to the death. 3. Let us set before our eyes the good apostles. 4. There was Peter, who, because of unrighteous jealousy, endured not one or two but many trials, and thus having given his testimony went to his appointed place of glory. 5. Because of jealousy and strife Paul by his example pointed out the way to the prize for patient endurance. 6. After he had been seven times in chains, had been driven into exile, had been stoned,[130] and had preached in the East and in the West, he won the genuine glory for his faith, 7. having taught righteousness to the whole world and having reached the farthest limits of the West.[131] Finally, when he had given his testimony before the rulers, he thus departed from the world and went to the holy place, having become an outstanding example of patient endurance.

Translated by J. B. Lightfoot and J. R. Harmer, in *The Apostolic Fathers,* 2nd rev. ed., edited by J. B. Lightfoot (Grand Rapids, MI: Baker Book House, 1992), 35.

Irenaeus (ca. 130–202), bishop of Lyons, sets forth his classic formulation of the theory of apostolic succession in *Against Heresies,* written around 180.

IRENAEUS

Against Heresies, III.iii.1–3

III.iii

1. It is within the power of all, therefore, in every Church, who may wish to see the truth, to contemplate clearly the tradition of the apostles manifested throughout the whole world; and we are in a position to reckon up those who were by the apostles instituted bishops in the Churches, and [to demonstrate] the succession of these men to our own times; those who neither taught nor knew of anything like what these [heretics] rave about. For if the apostles had known hidden mysteries, which they were in the habit of imparting

---

129. That is "pillars" of the Church. See Gal 2:9. (The notes for this selection are by Gerhart and Udoh.)

130. See 2 Cor 11:23–28.

131. See Rom 15:18–29.

to "the perfect" apart and privily from the rest, they would have delivered them especially to those to whom they were also committing the Churches themselves. For they were desirous that these men should be very perfect and blameless in all things, whom also they were leaving behind as their successors, delivering up their own place of government to these men; which men, if they discharged their functions honestly, would be a great boon [to the Church], but if they should fall away, the direst calamity.

2. Since, however, it would be very tedious, in such a volume as this, to reckon up the successions of all the Churches, we do put to confusion all those who, in whatever manner, whether by an evil self-pleasing, by vainglory, or by blindness and perverse opinion, assemble in unauthorized meetings; [we do this, I say,] by indicating that tradition derived from the apostles, of the very great, the very ancient, and universally known Church founded and organized at Rome by the two most glorious apostles, Peter and Paul; as also [by pointing out] the faith preached to men, which comes down to our time by means of the successions of the bishops. For it is a matter of necessity that every Church should agree with this Church, on account of its preeminent authority,[132] that is, the faithful everywhere, inasmuch as the apostolical tradition has been preserved continuously by those [faithful men] who exist everywhere.

3. The blessed apostles, then, having founded and built up the Church, committed into the hands of Linus the office of the episcopate. Of this Linus, Paul makes mention in the Epistles to Timothy.[133] To him succeeded Anacletus; and after him, in the third place from the apostles, Clement was allotted the bishopric. This man, as he had seen the blessed apostles, and had been conversant with them, might be said to have the preaching of the apostles still echoing [in his ears], and their traditions before his eyes. Nor was he alone [in this], for there were many still remaining who had received instructions from the apostles. In the time of this Clement, no small dissension having occurred among the brethren at Corinth, the Church in Rome dispatched a most powerful letter to the Corinthians, exhorting them to peace, renewing their faith, and declaring the tradition which it had lately received from the apostles, proclaiming the one God, omnipotent, the Maker of heaven and earth, the Creator of man, who brought on the deluge, and called Abraham, who led the people from the land of Egypt, spake with Moses, set forth the law, sent the prophets, and who has prepared fire for the devil and his angels. From this document, whosoever chooses to do so, may learn that He, the Father of

our Lord Jesus Christ, was preached by the Churches, and may also understand the apostolical tradition of the Church, since this Epistle is of older date than these men who are now propagating falsehood, and who conjure into existence another god beyond the Creator and the Maker of all existing things. To this Clement there succeeded Evaristus. Alexander followed Evaristus; then, sixth from the apostles, Sixtus was appointed; after him, Telephorus, who was gloriously martyred; then Hyginus; after him, Pius; then after him, Anicetus. Soter having succeeded Anicetus, Eleutherius does now, in the twelfth place from the apostles, hold the inheritance of the episcopate. In this order, and by this succession, the ecclesiastical tradition from the apostles, and the preaching of the truth, have come down to us. And this is most abundant proof that there is one and the same vivifying faith, which has been preserved in the Church from the apostles until now, and handed down in truth.

From Alexander Roberts and James Donaldson, eds., *The Ante-Nicene Fathers*, vol. 1 (Edinburgh: T. and T. Clark, 1867–72; repr., Grand Rapids, MI: Eerdmans, 1989), 415–16.

🕮 In his *Ecclesiastical History*, written around 315, **Eusebius** (ca. 260–339), bishop of Caesarea, reports on the controversy between the Church of Rome under Victor (bishop ca. 189–99) and the Churches in Asia concerning the date of the celebration of Easter.

EUSEBIUS

Ecclesiastical History, V.xxii.1–xxv.1

V.xxii.1

1. In the tenth year of the reign of Commodus,[134] Victor succeeded Eleutherus, who had administered the episcopacy for thirteen years.[135] In this year, also, when Julian had com-

---

132. This statement is central and much controverted. The Latin text reads: *"Ad hanc enim ecclesiam propter potiorem principalitatem necesse est omnem convenire ecclesiam."* Since we do not know what (original) Greek words were translated into the Latin phrase *"potiorem principalitatem,"* it is impossible to decide with any certainty what should be the meaning and import of Irenaeus's statement. (The notes for this selection are by Gerhart and Udoh.)

133. See 2 Tim 4:21.

134. That is, in 189. (The notes for this selection are by Gerhart and Udoh.)

135. From the testimony of other sources, Eleutherus apparently was bishop for fifteen years. Thirteen years given here by Eusebius for the length of Eleutherus's episcopate is wrong.

pleted his tenth year, Demetrius was entrusted with the administration of the dioceses at Alexandria, and again at this time Serapion, whom we have already mentioned above and the eighth from the Apostles, was still known at that time as Bishop of the Church at Antioch. Theophilus was in charge of Caesarea in Palestine, and Narcissus likewise, of whom our work has made mention before, still at that time had the administration of the Church in Jerusalem, and at the same time Bacchyllus was Bishop of Corinth in Greece and Polycrates of the diocese at Ephesus. And there were in these times, of course, countless other prominent men, but we have naturally given a list of those whose orthodoxy of faith has come down to us in writing.

V.xxiii.1–4   *Quartodecima*

1. Now, at this time, no small controversy was stirred up because the dioceses of all Asia, as according to an older tradition, thought that they should observe the fourteenth day of the moon, on which the Jews had been ordered to sacrifice the lamb, as the feast of the Saviour's Passover, so that it became absolutely necessary to bring the days of fasting to an end on whatever day of the week this fell.[136] But it was not the custom for the churches throughout all the rest of the world to end it in this way, since they preserved a custom which from apostolic tradition has prevailed to our own day, according to which it is not right to end the fasting on any other day than that of the Resurrection of our Saviour. 2. Then, synods and conferences of bishops on the same question took place, and they unanimously formulated in their letters a doctrine of the Church for people everywhere, that the mystery of the Lord's Resurrection from the dead be celebrated on no other day than the Lord's Day,[137] and that on this day alone we should observe the close of the Paschal fast. 3. There is still in circulation today a writing of those who then assembled in Palestine, over whom Theophilus, Bishop of the diocese of Caesarea, presided and Narcissus, Bishop of the diocese of Jerusalem; and, similarly, another of those assembled at Rome on the same problem, which indicates Victor as bishop; and of the bishops in the Pontus over whom Palmas presided as the oldest; 4. and of the dioceses of Gaul of which Irenaeus was bishop; and still others of those in Osrhoene and the cities there; and particularly a writing of Bacchyllus, Bishop of the Church at Corinth; and of numerous others who expressed one and the same opinion and judgment, and cast the same vote.

V.xxiv.1–18

1. To these belonged the one definition which has just been indicated, but Polycrates led the bishops of Asia in confidently proclaiming that they must preserve the custom handed down to them from of old. Polycrates himself, in a writing which he composed to Victor and the Church of Rome, describes the tradition which had come down to him, in these words: 2. "We, therefore, keep the precise day, neither adding nor taking away, for even in Asia great luminaries[138] have fallen asleep, which shall rise on the day of the coming of the Lord, when he comes with glory from heaven and shall seek out all the saints, Philip of the twelve Apostles,[139] who have been sleeping in Hieropolis, and two of his daughters who had grown old as virgins, and another daughter of his who lived in the Holy Spirit and rests at Ephesus. 3. Furthermore, there is also John, who leaned on the breast of the Lord,[140] and was a priest wearing the breastplate, and a martyr, and teacher. This one rests at Ephesus. 4. Then there is also Polycarp in Smyrna, both bishop and martyr; and there is Thraseas, both bishop and martyr, from Eumenaea, 5. who rests at Smyrna. And why need I mention Sagaris, bishop and martyr, who rests in Smyrna, and also Papirius the blessed and Melito the eunuch, who lived entirely in the Holy Spirit and lies in Sardis awaiting the visitation from heaven when he will rise from the dead? 6. All these observed the fourteenth day of the Passover according to the Gospel, never deviating, but following according to the rule of the faith. And I also, Polycrates, do so, the least of you all, according to the tradition of my kinsmen, some of whom I have followed. Seven of my kinsmen were bishops, and I am the eighth. And my kinsmen always observed the day when the people put away the leaven. 7. So, my brethren, having lived sixty-five years in the Lord and having associated with the brethren from the entire world and having read all holy Scripture, I am not frightened at

---

136. That is, instead of celebrating the anniversary of Jesus' death on Good Friday, the Churches of Asia celebrated it on the Jewish Passover, on the fourteenth day after the new moon in the month of Nisan (on whatever day it fell). They came to be called Quartodecimans.

137. That is, the first day of the week, Sunday. Thus, the Crucifixion must be celebrated on a Friday.

138. In late Greek, *stoicheia* (see, for instance, Gal 4:3) often referred to the planets.

139. See Mk 3:18; Mt 10:3; Lk 6:14.

140. See Jn 13:23; 21:20.

what is threatened us,[141] for those greater than I have said, 'We ought to obey God rather than men.'"[142]

8. To this he adds about the bishops who were with him as he wrote and were of one opinion with him, speaking as follows: "I could mention the bishops who were present with me, whom you requested to be summoned by me and I summoned them, and their names, if I record them, are most numerous. They, having seen my feeble humanity, gave their consent to the letter, knowing that I did not bear my grey hairs in vain, but have always lived in Christ Jesus."

9. Thereupon, Victor, who was in charge of the Church at Rome, immediately tried to cut off the dioceses of all Asia, together with the adjacent churches, as being heterodox, from the common unity, and he inveighed against them by letters and proclaimed all the brethren there as absolutely excommunicated, but this did not please all the bishops. 10. Then they issued counter requests to him to consider the matters of peace and of unity and of love toward one's neighbors, and the words of these as they sharply rebuked Victor are in circulation. 11. Among these, Irenaeus, too, writing in the name of the brethren whom he guided in Gaul, defends the necessity of celebrating the mystery of the Lord's Resurrection on the Lord's Day only, but he properly and at length exhorts Victor not to cut off entire churches of God because they kept a tradition of ancient custom, and he continues with the following words: 12. "For the controversy is not only concerning the day, but also about the very manner of the fast. Some think that they ought to fast one day; others, two; others, even more; some measure their day as forty hours day and night.[143] 13. And such a variation on the part of those observing the feast did not originate now in our time, but much earlier in the days of our predecessors, who, as is likely, without maintaining it strictly, established a practice for the future which is simple and permits personal preference, and all these nevertheless lived in peace, and we also lived in peace with one another, and the disagreement respecting the fast confirms our unanimity in the faith."

14. To this he also adds a story which I shall with propriety present, and it goes like this: "Among those, too, were the presbyters before Soter, who presided over the Church which you now rule: we mean Anicetus and Pius and Telesphorus and Xystus. Neither did they themselves observe, nor did they enjoin it upon their followers; nevertheless, although not observing it themselves, they were at peace with those who came to them from dioceses in which it was observed,[144] although to observe it was more objectionable to those who did not do so. 15. Yet, never were any cast out because of this

form, and the presbyters themselves before you sent the Eucharist to those from other dioceses who did; 16. and when the blessed Polycarp sojourned in Rome in the time of Anicetus, although they had small difficulties about certain other matters, they immediately made peace, having no desire for strife among themselves on this outstanding question. Neither was Anicetus able to persuade Polycarp not to observe it, inasmuch as Polycarp had always observed it, together with John the disciple of our Lord and the other Apostles with whom he had lived; nor, on the other hand, did Polycarp persuade Anicetus to observe it, for Anicetus said that he was obliged to cling to the practice of those who were presbyters before him. 17. And under these conditions they communicated with each other, and in the church Anicetus conceded the celebration of the Eucharist to Polycarp, obviously out of respect for him, and they departed from each other peacefully, for they maintained the peace of the entire Church, both those who observed and those who did not."

18. And Irenaeus, being a person well named, a peacemaker both by name[145] and by very character, made exhortations of this kind for the peace of the churches and acted as the Church's ambassador; and the same Irenaeus discussed by letter, not only with Victor but also with a great many others who governed churches, the various aspects of the problem which had been raised.

V.xxv.1

1. Those in Palestine, whom we have recently mentioned, Narcissus and Theophilus, and with them Cassius, Bishop of the Church at Tyre, and Clarus, Bishop of the Church at Ptolemais, and those who had come together with them, discussed at great length the tradition concerning the Passover which had come down to them from the succession of the Apostles, and at the end of the writing they added the following in these very words: "Try to send copies of our letter

---

141. See Phil 1:27–28.

142. Acts 5:29.

143. Important for the discussions on the origin of Lent, this passage shows that the Greek name for Lent, "fortieth" ($\tau\epsilon\sigma\sigma\alpha\rho\alpha\kappa\omega\sigma\tau\dot{\eta}$), is older than the practice of a forty-day fast before Easter. Irenaeus here knows only of a forty-hour fast, by some; the practice of a forty-day fast developed gradually later in the fifth century.

144. Victor's predecessors even allowed those who came to Rome from the dioceses of Asia to observe the fourteenth of Nisan, even though the Quartodeciman practice would sometimes result in those from Asia celebrating as Easter Day what the Romans observed as Good Friday.

145. His Greek name, Eirenaios, derives from the word *eirene*, "peace."

into every diocese, that we may not be culpable before those who easily deceive their own souls. And we point out to you that in Alexandria, also, they keep the feast on the same day as do we, for letters are conveyed from us to them and from them to us, so that we keep the holy day harmoniously and at the same time."

From Eusebius Pamphili, *Ecclesiastical History, Books 1–5*, translated by Roy J. Deferrari, Fathers of the Church, vol. 19 (New York: Fathers of the Church, 1953), 332–39.

❧ The **Council of Chalcedon** in 451 provided a theological response to the Christological controversies of the fourth and fifth centuries. The council is also significant for its affirmation of Pope Leo's (d. 461) *Tome* of 449 against Eutyches (ca. 378–452; see chapter 3 above) in the *Definition of Faith* and for its statements in *Canon 28: Resolution concerning the Prerogatives of the See of Constantinople,* regarding the interrelationship of Constantinople and Rome.

THE COUNCIL OF CHALCEDON
Definition of Faith

The sacred and great and universal synod by God's grace and by decree of your most religious and Christ-loving emperors Valentinian Augustus and Marcian Augustus assembled in Chalcedon, metropolis of the province of Bithynia, in the shrine of the saintly and triumphant martyr Euphemia, issues the following decrees.

In establishing his disciples in the knowledge of the faith, our lord and saviour Christ said: "My peace I give you, my peace I leave to you,"[146] so that no one should disagree with his neighbour regarding religious doctrines but that the proclamation of the truth would be uniformly presented. But the evil one never stops trying to smother the seeds of religion with his own tares[147] and is for ever inventing some novelty or other against the truth; so the Master, exercising his usual care for the human race, roused this religious and most faithful emperor to zealous action, and summoned to himself the leaders of the priesthood from everywhere, so that through the working of the grace of Christ, the master of all of us, every injurious falsehood might be stayed off from the sheep of Christ, and they might be fattened on fresh growths of the truth.

This is in fact what we have done. We have driven off erroneous doctrines by our collective resolution, and we have renewed the unerring creed of the fathers. We have proclaimed to all the creed of the 318;[148] and we have made our own those fathers who accepted this agreed statement of religion—the 150 who later met in great Constantinople[149] and themselves set their seal to the same creed.

Therefore, whilst we also stand by the decisions and all the formulas relating to the creed from the sacred synod which took place formerly at Ephesus,[150] whose leaders of most holy memory were Celestine of Rome and Cyril of Alexandria, we decree that pre-eminence belongs to the exposition of the right and spotless creed of the 318 saintly and blessed fathers who were assembled at Nicaea when Constantine of pious memory was emperor: and that those decrees also remain in force which were issued in Constantinople by the 150 holy fathers in order to destroy the heresies then rife and to confirm this same catholic and apostolic creed.

The creed of the 318 fathers at Nicaea.

And the same of the 150 saintly fathers assembled in Constantinople.

This wise and saving creed, the gift of divine grace, was sufficient for a perfect understanding and establishment of religion. For its teaching about the Father and the Son and the holy Spirit is complete, and it sets out the Lord's becoming human to those who faithfully accept it.

But there are those who are trying to ruin the proclamation of the truth, and through their private heresies they have spawned novel formulas: some by daring to corrupt the mystery of the Lord's economy on our behalf, and refusing to apply the word "God-bearer" to the Virgin; and others by introducing a confusion and mixture, and mindlessly imagining that there is a single nature of the flesh and the divinity, and fantastically supposing that in the confusion the divine nature of the Only-begotten is passible.

Therefore this sacred and great and universal synod, now in session, in its desire to exclude all their tricks against the truth, and teaching what has been unshakeable in the proclamation from the beginning, decrees that the creed of the 318 fathers is, above all else, to remain inviolate. And because of those who oppose the holy Spirit, it ratifies the teaching about the being of the holy Spirit handed down by the 150 saintly fathers who met some time later in the imperial city—the

---

146. Jn 14:27. (The notes for this selection are by Gerhart and Udoh.)
147. See Mt 13:24–30.
148. That is, the creed of the Council of Nicaea (325).
149. That is, in 381.
150. The council met in 431.

teaching they made known to all, not introducing anything left out by their predecessors, but clarifying their ideas about the holy Spirit by the use of scriptural testimonies against those who were trying to do away with his sovereignty.

And because of those who are attempting to corrupt the mystery of the economy and are shamelessly and foolishly asserting that he who was born of the holy virgin Mary was a mere man, it has accepted the synodical letters of the blessed Cyril, pastor of the church in Alexandria, to Nestorius and to the Orientals, as being well-suited to refuting Nestorius's mad folly and to providing an interpretation for those who in their religious zeal might desire understanding of the saving creed.

To these it has suitably added, against false believers and for the establishment of orthodox doctrines, the letter of the primate of greatest and older Rome, the most blessed and most saintly Archbishop Leo, written to the sainted Archbishop Flavian to put down Eutyches's evil-mindedness, because it is in agreement with great Peter's confession and represents a support we have in common.

From Norman P. Tanner, ed., *Decrees of the Ecumenical Councils,* vol. 1 (Washington, DC: Georgetown University Press, 1990), 83–85.

Canon 28: Resolution concerning the Prerogatives of the See of Constantinople

Following in every way the decrees of the holy fathers and recognising the canon which has recently been read out—the canon of the 150 most devout bishops who assembled in the time of the great Theodosius of pious memory, then emperor, in imperial Constantinople, new Rome—we issue the same decree and resolution concerning the prerogatives of the most holy church of the same Constantinople, new Rome. The fathers rightly accorded prerogatives to the see of older Rome, since that is an imperial city; and moved by the same purpose the 150 most devout bishops apportioned equal prerogatives to the most holy see of new Rome, reasonably judging that the city which is honoured by the imperial power and senate and enjoying privileges equalling older imperial Rome should also be elevated to her level in ecclesiastical affairs and take second place after her.[151] The metropolitans of the dioceses of Pontus, Asia and Thrace, but only these, as well as the bishops of these dioceses who work among non-Greeks, are to be ordained by the aforesaid most holy see of the most holy church in Constantinople.

That is, each metropolitan of the aforesaid dioceses along with the bishops of the province ordain the bishops of the province, as has been declared in the divine canons; but the metropolitans of the aforesaid dioceses, as has been said, are to be ordained by the archbishop of Constantinople, once agreement has been reached by vote in the usual way and has been reported to him.

From Norman P. Tanner, ed., *Decrees of the Ecumenical Councils,* vol. 1 (Washington, DC: Georgetown University Press, 1990), 99–100.

☙ *The Donation of Constantine* details the purported grants made by Emperor Constantine (306–37) to Pope Silvester (314–35) and his successors. It was first used in support of papal prerogatives by Pope Leo IX (1049–54) in his letter of 1054 to Michael Caerularius, the patriarch of Constantinople (1043–58), and from then on, it was increasingly used for this purpose by both popes and canon lawyers. The humanist Lorenzo Valla (1405–57) definitively demonstrated its inauthenticity in 1440 (it dates from the eighth century). But as late as 1533, it was considered a heresy in the Catholic Church to dispute its authenticity.

The Donation of Constantine

In the name of the holy and undivided Trinity, the Father, the Son and the Holy Spirit. The Emperor Caesar Flavius Constantinus in Christ Jesus (one of the same Holy Trinity, our Saviour, Lord and God), faithful, merciful, mighty, beneficent, Alamannicus, Gothicus, Sarmaticus, Germanicus, Brittanicus, Hunicus, pious, fortunate, victorious triumphant, ever August; to the most holy and blessed father of fathers, Silvester, Bishop of the Roman city and Pope; and to all his successors, the pontiffs, who shall sit in the chair of blessed Peter to the end of time; as also to all the most reverend and God-beloved Catholic bishops, by this our imperial constitution subjected throughout the world to this same Roman church, whether they be appointed now or at any future time—Grace, peace, love, joy, long-suffering, mercy from God the Father almighty and Jesus Christ His Son and the Holy Spirit be with you all. . . .

For when a horrible and filthy leprosy invaded all the flesh

---

151. See Canon 3 of the Council of Constantinople.

of my body and I was treated by many assembled doctors but could not thereby attain to health, there came to me the priests of the Capitol, who said I ought to erect a font on the Capitol and fill it with the blood of innocent children and that by bathing in it while it was warm I could be healed. According to their advice many innocent children were assembled; but, when the sacrilegious priests of the pagans wished them to be slaughtered and the font filled with their blood, our serenity perceived the tears of their mothers and I thereupon abhorred the project; and, pitying them, we ordered their sons to be restored to them, gave them vehicles and gifts and sent them back rejoicing to their homes. And when the day had passed, and the silence of night had descended upon us and the time of sleep had come, the apostles SS. Peter and Paul appeared to me saying, "Since thou hast put an end to thy sins and hast shrunk from shedding the blood of the innocent, we are sent by Christ, our Lord God, to impart to thee a plan for the recovery of thy health. Hear therefore our advice and do whatever we bid thee. Silvester, bishop of the city of Rome, flying from thy persecutions, is in hiding with his clergy in the caverns of the rocks on Mount Serapte. When thou hast called him to thee, he will show thee the pool of piety; and, when he has thrice immersed thee therein, all the strength of this leprosy will leave thee. When that is done, make this return to thy Saviour, that by thy command all the churches throughout the world be restored; and purify thyself in this way, by abandoning all the superstition of idols and adoring and worshipping the living and true God, who alone is true, and devote thyself to His will. . . ."

And so the first day after my reception of the mystery of Holy Baptism and the cure of my body from the squalor of leprosy I understood that there is no other God than the Father, the Son and the Holy Spirit, whom most blessed Silvester, the Pope, preaches, a Trinity in unity and Unity in trinity. For all the gods of the nations, whom I have hitherto worshipped, are shown to be demons, the works of men's hands. And the same venerable father told us clearly how great power in heaven and earth our Saviour gave to His Apostle, blessed Peter, when in answer to questioning He found him faithful and said: "Thou art Peter, and upon this rock I will build My Church; and the gates of hell shall not prevail against it."[152] Attend, ye mighty, and incline the ear of your heart to what the good Lord and Master gave in addition to His disciple when He said: "I will give unto thee the keys of the kingdom of heaven, and whatsoever thou shalt bind on earth shall be bound in heaven, and whatsoever thou shalt loose on earth shall be loosed in heaven."[153] And when I learned these things at the mouth of the blessed Silvester, and found that I was wholly restored to health by the beneficence of blessed Peter himself, we—together with all our satraps and the whole senate, and the magnates and all the Roman people, which is subject to the glory of our rule—considered that, since he is seen to have been set up as the vicar of God's Son on earth, the pontiffs who act on behalf of that prince of the apostles should receive from us and our empire a greater power of government than the earthly clemency of our imperial serenity is seen to have conceded to them; for we choose the same prince of the apostles and his vicars to be our constant witnesses before God. And inasmuch as our imperial power is earthly, we have decreed that it shall venerate and honour his most holy Roman Church and that the sacred see of blessed Peter shall be gloriously exalted above our empire and earthly throne. We attribute to him the power and glorious dignity and strength and honour of the Empire, and we ordain and decree that he shall have rule as well over the four principal sees, Antioch, Alexandria, Constantinople, and Jerusalem, as also over all the churches of God in all the world. And the pontiff who for the time being presides over that most holy Roman Church shall be the highest and chief of all priests in the whole world, and according to his decision shall all matters be settled which shall be taken in hand for the service of God or the confirmation of the faith of Christians. For it is right that the sacred law should have the centre of its power there where the Founder of the sacred laws, our Saviour, commanded blessed Peter to have the chair of his apostolate, and where, bearing the suffering of the cross, he accepted the cup of a blessed death and showed himself an imitator of his Lord and Master; and that there the nations should bow their necks in confession of Christ's name, where their teacher, blessed Paul, the apostle, offered his neck for Christ and was crowned with martyrdom. There for ever let them seek a teacher, where lies the holy body of that teacher; and there, prone in humility, let them perform the service of the heavenly King, God, our Saviour, Jesus Christ, where proudly they used to serve the empire of an earthly king. . . .

---

152. Mt 16:18. (The notes for this selection are by Gerhart and Udoh.)
153. Mt 16:19.

To the holy apostles, my lords the most blessed Peter and Paul, and through them also to blessed Silvester, our father, supreme pontiff and universal pope of the city of Rome, and to the pontiffs, his successors, who to the end of the world shall sit in the seat of blessed Peter, we grant and by this present we convey our imperial Lateran palace, which is superior to and excels all palaces in the whole world; and further the diadem, which is the crown of our head; and the mitre; as also the super-humeral, that is, the stole which usually surrounds our imperial neck; and the purple cloak and the scarlet tunic and all the imperial robes; also the rank of commanders of the imperial cavalry. . . .

And we decree that those most reverend men, the clergy of various orders serving the same most holy Roman Church, shall have that eminence, distinction, power and precedence, with which our illustrious senate is gloriously adorned; that is, they shall be made patricians and consuls. And we ordain that they shall also be adorned with other imperial dignities. Also we decree that the clergy of the sacred Roman Church shall be adorned as are the imperial officers. . . .

Wherefore that the pontifical crown should not be made of less repute, but rather that the dignity of a more than earthly office and the might of its glory should be yet further adorned—lo, we convey to the oft-mentioned and most blessed Silvester, universal pope, both our palace, as preferment, and likewise all provinces, palaces and districts of the city of Rome and Italy and of the regions of the West; and, bequeathing them to the power and sway of him and the pontiffs, his successors, we do (by means of fixed imperial decision through this our divine, sacred and authoritative sanction) determine and decree that the same be placed at his disposal, and do lawfully grant it as a permanent possession to the holy Roman Church.

Wherefore we have perceived that our empire and the power of our government should be transferred and removed to the regions of the East and that a city should be built in our name in the best place in the province of Byzantium and our empire there established; for it is not right that an earthly emperor should have authority there, where the rule of priests and the head of the Christian religion have been established by the Emperor of heaven. . . .

Given at Rome, March 30th, when our lord Flavius Constantinus Augustus, for the fourth time, and Galliganus, most illustrious men, were consuls.

From R. G. D. Laffan, *Select Documents of European History: 800–1492* (London: Methuen, 1930), 1–6. [Ellipses in source text.]

℞ *Unam sanctam,* the Bull by Pope **Boniface VIII** (1294–1303) published on November 18, 1302, provides the clearest expression of papal theocracy. The Bull follows in the tradition of Pope Gregory VII's (1073–85) *Dictatus papae* (a collection of twenty-seven short statements about the primacy of Rome, including the use of the title "Pope" exclusively for the bishop of Rome, made in 1073).

BONIFACE VIII

Unam sanctam

We are obliged by the faith and hold—and we do firmly believe and sincerely confess—that there is one Holy Catholic and Apostolic Church, and that outside this Church there is neither salvation nor remission of sins, as the spouse proclaims in the Song, "One is my dove, one is my perfect one, the only one from her mother, preferred before her that bore her.[154]

She represents the one mystical Body of which Christ is the head, God being the head of Christ.[155] In this Church there is "one Lord, one faith, one baptism."[156] At the time of the flood there was one ark of Noah, symbolizing the one Church; this was completed in one cubit,[157] and had one, namely Noah, as helmsman and captain; outside which all things on earth, we read, were destroyed.[158] We venerate her, the only one, as the Lord said through his prophet: "Deliver, O God, my soul from the sword, and my only one from the foot of the dog!"[159] For he prayed at the same time for the soul, that is to say, for himself, the head, and for the body, since he called the body his only one, that is, the Church, because of the unity between the Church and her spouse, in the faith, in the sacraments and in love. She is the seamless robe of the Saviour, not torn but taken by lot.[160] This is why this Church, the one and only, has only one body and one head—not two heads, like a monster—namely Christ, and Christ's vicar is Peter, and Peter's successor, for the Lord said to Peter himself, "Feed my sheep."[161] "My sheep" he said in general, not these or those sheep; wherefore he is understood to have committed them all to him. Therefore if the

---

154. Song 6:9. (The notes for this selection are by Gerhart and Udoh.)
155. See Eph 4:15; 5:23; Col 1:18; 1 Cor 11:3.
156. Eph 4:5.
157. See Gen 6:16.
158. See Gen 6:11–7:23.
159. Ps 21:21 (Vulgate) = Ps 22:20.
160. See Jn 19:23.
161. Jn 21:17.

Greeks or others say that they were not committed to Peter and his successors, they necessarily confess that they are not of Christ's sheep, for the Lord says in John, "There is one fold and one shepherd."[162]

And we learn from the words of the gospel that in this Church and in her power are two swords, the spiritual and the temporal. For when the apostles said "Behold, here" (that is, in the Church, since it was the apostles who spoke) "are two swords"—the Lord did not reply, "It is too much," but "It is enough."[163] Truly he who denies that the temporal sword is in the power of Peter misunderstands the words of the Lord, "Put up thy sword into the sheath."[164] Both are in the power of the Church, the spiritual sword and the material. But the latter is to be used for the Church, the former by her; the former by the priest, the latter by kings and captains but at the will and by the permission of the priest. The one sword, then, should be under the other, and temporal authority subject to spiritual. . . . The Truth attests that the spiritual power can establish the earthly power and can judge it if it is not good. . . . If, therefore, the earthly power err, it shall be judged by the spiritual power; and if a lesser power err, it shall be judged by a greater. But if the supreme power err, it can be judged only by God, not by man; for the testimony of the apostle is: "The spiritual man judgeth all things, yet he himself is judged of no man."[165] For this authority, although given to a man and exercised by a man, is not human, but rather divine, given at God's mouth to Peter and established on a rock for him and his successors in him whom he confessed, the Lord saying to Peter himself, "Whatsoever thou shall bind. . . ."[166] Whoever therefore resists this power thus ordained of God, "resists the ordinance of God,"[167] unless like Manes[168] he imagines that there are two beginnings (*principia*); an opinion which we judge false and heretical for, according to Moses, it was not in the beginnings (*in principiis*) but "in the beginning (*in principio*) God created the heaven and the earth."[169]

Furthermore we declare, state, define and pronounce that it is altogether necessary to salvation for every human creature to be subject to the Roman pontiff.

Translated by John de Satgé, in J.-M.-R. Tillard, *The Bishop of Rome* (Wilmington, DE: Michael Glazier, 1983), 56–57. [Ellipses in original.]

꧁ The further development of the notion of the pope's absolute *plenitudo potestatis* (fullness of power) found its dogmatic ex-

pression in *Pastor aeternus: First Dogmatic Constitution on the Church of Christ,* which defines the doctrine of papal infallibility. The decree was promulgated on July 18, 1870, by the **First Vatican Council,** which was summoned by Pope Pius IX (1846–78).

THE FIRST VATICAN COUNCIL

Pastor aeternus: First Dogmatic Constitution on the Church of Christ

First dogmatic constitution on the church of Christ

Pius, bishop, servant of the servants of God, with the approval of the sacred council, for an everlasting record. The eternal shepherd and guardian of our souls,[170] in order to render permanent the saving work of redemption, determined to build a church in which, as in the house of the living God, all the faithful should be linked by the bond of one faith and charity. Therefore, before he was glorified, he besought his Father, not for the apostles only, but also *for those who were to believe in him through their word, that they all might be one as the Son himself and the Father are one.*[171] So then, just as he sent apostles, whom he chose out of the world,[172] even as he had been sent by the Father,[173] in like manner it was his will that in his church there should be shepherds and teachers until the end of time. In order, then, that the episcopal office should be one and undivided and that, by the union of the clergy, the whole multitude of believers should be held together in the unity of faith and communion, he set blessed Peter over the rest of the apostles and instituted in him the permanent principle of both unities and their visible foundation. Upon the strength of this foundation was to be built the eternal temple, and the church whose topmost part reaches heaven was to rise upon the firmness of this foundation.[174] And since the gates of hell trying, if they can, to overthrow the church, make their assault with a hatred that increases day by day against its divinely laid foundation, we judge it necessary, with the approbation of the sacred council, and for the protection,

---

162. Jn 10:16.
163. Lk 22:38.
164. Jn 18:11.
165. 1 Cor 2:15.
166. Mt 16:19.
167. Rom 13:2.
168. The founder of Manichaeism. See chapter 3 of this volume.
169. Gen 1:1.
170. See 1 Pet 2:25.
171. Jn 17:20–21.
172. See Jn 15:19.
173. See Jn 20–21.
174. Leo I, *Serm.* (Sermons), 4 (elsewhere 3), ch. 2 for the day of his birth (54, 150).

defence and growth of the catholic flock, to propound the doctrine concerning the institution, permanence and nature of the sacred and apostolic primacy, upon which the strength and coherence of the whole church depends. This doctrine is to be believed and held by all the faithful in accordance with the ancient and unchanging faith of the whole church. Furthermore, we shall proscribe and condemn the contrary errors which are so harmful to the Lord's flock.

Chapter 1. On the Institution of the Apostolic Primacy in Blessed Peter

We teach and declare that, according to the gospel evidence, a primacy of jurisdiction over the whole church of God was immediately and directly promised to the blessed apostle Peter and conferred on him by Christ the lord. It was to Simon alone, to whom he had already said *You shall be called Cephas*,[175] that the Lord, after his confession, *You are the Christ, the son of the living God*, spoke these words: *Blessed are you, Simon Bar-Jona. For flesh and blood has not revealed this to you, but my Father who is in heaven. And I tell you, you are Peter, and on this rock I will build my church, and the gates of the underworld shall not prevail against it. I will give you the keys of the kingdom of heaven, and whatever you bind on earth shall be bound in heaven, and whatever you loose on earth shall be loosed in heaven.*[176] And it was to Peter alone that Jesus, after his resurrection, confided the jurisdiction of supreme pastor and ruler of his whole fold, saying: *Feed my lambs, feed my sheep.*[177] To this absolutely manifest teaching of the sacred scriptures, as it has always been understood by the catholic church, are clearly opposed the distorted opinions of those who misrepresent the form of government which Christ the lord established in his church, and deny that Peter, in preference to the rest of the apostles, taken singly or collectively, was endowed by Christ with a true and proper primacy of jurisdiction. The same may be said of those who assert that this primacy was not conferred immediately and directly on blessed Peter himself, but rather on the church, and that it was through the church that it was transmitted to him in his capacity as her minister.

Therefore, if anyone says that blessed Peter the apostle was not appointed by Christ the lord as prince of all the apostles and visible head of the whole church militant; or that it was a primacy of honour only and not one of true and proper jurisdiction that he directly and immediately received from our lord Jesus Christ himself: let him be anathema.

Chapter 2. On the Permanence of the Primacy of Blessed Peter in the Roman Pontiffs

That which our lord Jesus Christ, the prince of shepherds and great shepherd of the sheep, established in the blessed apostle Peter, for the continual salvation and permanent benefit of the church, must of necessity remain for ever, by Christ's authority, in the church which, founded as it is upon a rock, will stand firm until the end of time.[178] For no one can be in doubt, indeed it was known in every age, that the holy and most blessed Peter, prince and head of the apostles, the pillar of faith and the foundation of the catholic church, received the keys of the kingdom from our lord Jesus Christ, the saviour and redeemer of the human race; and that to this day and for ever he lives and presides and exercises judgment in his successors the bishops of the holy Roman see, which he founded and consecrated with his blood.[179] Therefore whoever succeeds to the chair of Peter obtains, by the institution of Christ himself, the primacy of Peter over the whole church. So what the truth has ordained stands firm, and blessed Peter perseveres in the rock-like strength he was granted, and does not abandon that guidance of the church which he once received.[180] For this reason it has always been necessary for every church—that is to say the faithful throughout the world—to be in agreement with the Roman church because of its more effective leadership. In consequence of being joined, as members to head, with that see, from which the rights of sacred communion flow to all, they will grow together into the structure of a single body.[181]

Therefore, if anyone says that it is not by the institution of Christ the lord himself (that is to say, by divine law) that blessed Peter should have perpetual successors in the primacy over the whole church; or that the Roman pontiff is not the successor of blessed Peter in this primacy: let him be anathema.

---

175. Jn 1:42.

176. Mt 16:16–19.

177. Jn 21:15–17.

178. See Mt 7:25; Lk 6:48.

179. From the speech of Philip, the Roman legate, at the 3rd session of the council of Ephesus (D no. 112).

180. Leo I, *Serm.* (*Sermons*), 3 (elsewhere 2), ch. 3 (PL [Migne, *Patrologiae cursus, series Latina*] 54, 146).

181. Irenaeus, *Adv. haeres.* (*Against Heresies*), III 3 (PG [Migne, *Patrologiae cursus, series Graeca*] 7, 849); Council of Aquilea (381), to be found among: Ambrose, *Epistolae* (*Letters*), 11 (16, 946).

Chapter 3. On the Power and Character of the Primacy of the Roman Pontiff

And so, supported by the clear witness of holy scripture, and adhering to the manifest and explicit decrees both of our predecessors the Roman pontiffs and of general councils, we promulgate anew the definition of the ecumenical council of Florence,[182] which must be believed by all faithful Christians, namely, that the apostolic see and the Roman pontiff hold a world-wide primacy, and that the Roman pontiff is the successor of blessed Peter, the prince of the apostles, true vicar of Christ, head of the whole church and father and teacher of all Christian people. To him, in blessed Peter, full power has been given by our lord Jesus Christ to tend, rule and govern the universal church. All this is to be found in the acts of the ecumenical councils and the sacred canons.

Wherefore we teach and declare that, by divine ordinance, the Roman church possesses a pre-eminence of ordinary power over every other church, and that this jurisdictional power of the Roman pontiff is both episcopal and immediate. Both clergy and faithful, of whatever rite and dignity, both singly and collectively, are bound to submit to this power by the duty of hierarchical subordination and true obedience, and this not only in matters concerning faith and morals, but also in those which regard the discipline and government of the church throughout the world. In this way, by unity with the Roman pontiff in communion and in profession of the same faith, the church of Christ becomes one flock under one supreme shepherd.[183] This is the teaching of the catholic truth, and no one can depart from it without endangering his faith and salvation.

This power of the supreme pontiff by no means detracts from that ordinary and immediate power of episcopal jurisdiction, by which bishops, who have succeeded to the place of the apostles by appointment of the holy Spirit, tend and govern individually the particular flocks which have been assigned to them. On the contrary, this power of theirs is asserted, supported and defended by the supreme and universal pastor; for St Gregory the Great says: "My honour is the honour of the whole church. My honour is the steadfast strength of my brethren. Then do I receive true honour, when it is denied to none of those to whom honour is due."[184]

Furthermore, it follows from that supreme power which the Roman pontiff has in governing the whole church, that he has the right, in the performance of this office of his, to communicate freely with the pastors and flocks of the entire church, so that they may be taught and guided by him in the way of salvation. And therefore we condemn and reject the opinions of those who hold that this communication of the supreme head with pastors and flocks may be lawfully obstructed; or that it should be dependent on the civil power, which leads them to maintain that what is determined by the apostolic see or by its authority concerning the government of the church has no force or effect unless it is confirmed by the agreement of the civil authority.

Since the Roman pontiff, by the divine right of the apostolic primacy, governs the whole church, we likewise teach and declare that he is the supreme judge of the faithful,[185] and that in all cases which fall under ecclesiastical jurisdiction recourse may be had to his judgment.[186] The sentence of the apostolic see (than which there is no higher authority) is not subject to revision by anyone, nor may anyone lawfully pass judgment thereupon.[187] And so they stray from the genuine path of truth who maintain that it is lawful to appeal from the judgments of the Roman pontiffs to an ecumenical council as if this were an authority superior to the Roman pontiff.

So, then, if anyone says that the Roman pontiff has merely an office of supervision and guidance, and not the full and supreme power of jurisdiction over the whole church, and this not only in matters of faith and morals, but also in those which concern the discipline and government of the church dispersed throughout the whole world; or that he has only the principal part, but not the absolute fullness, of this supreme power; or that this power of his is not ordinary and immediate both over all and each of the churches and over all and each of the pastors and faithful: let him be anathema.

Chapter 4. On the Infallible Teaching Authority of the Roman Pontiff

That apostolic primacy which the Roman pontiff possesses as successor of Peter, the prince of the apostles, includes also the supreme power of teaching. This holy see has always

---

182. Council of Florence, session 6.

183. See Jn 10:16.

184. *Ep. ad Eulog. Alexandrin.* (*Letter to Eulogius of Alexandria*), VIII 29 (30) (MGH [*Monumenta Germaniae historica*], *Ep.* 2, 31 28–30; *PL* 77, 933).

185. Pius VI, Letter *Super soliditate* dated 28 Nov. 1786.

186. From Michael Palaeologus's profession of faith which was read out at the second council of Lyons (D no. 466).

187. Nicholas I, *Ep. ad Michaelem imp.* (*Letter to the emperor Michael*) (119, 954).

maintained this, the constant custom of the church demonstrates it, and the ecumenical councils, particularly those in which East and West met in the union of faith and charity, have declared it. So the fathers of the fourth council of Constantinople, following the footsteps of their predecessors, published this solemn profession of faith: The first condition of salvation is to maintain the rule of the true faith. And since that saying of our lord Jesus Christ, *You are Peter, and upon this rock I will build my church,*[188] cannot fail of its effect, the words spoken are confirmed by their consequences. For in the apostolic see the catholic religion has always been preserved unblemished, and sacred doctrine been held in honour. Since it is our earnest desire to be in no way separated from this faith and doctrine, we hope that we may deserve to remain in that one communion which the apostolic see preaches, for in it is the whole and true strength of the Christian religion.[189] What is more, with the approval of the second council of Lyons, the Greeks made the following profession: "The holy Roman church possesses the supreme and full primacy and principality over the whole catholic church. She truly and humbly acknowledges that she received this from the Lord himself in blessed Peter, the prince and chief of the apostles, whose successor the Roman pontiff is, together with the fullness of power. And since before all others she has the duty of defending the truth of the faith, so if any questions arise concerning the faith, it is by her judgment that they must be settled."[190] Then there is the definition of the council of Florence: "The Roman pontiff is the true vicar of Christ, the head of the whole church and the father and teacher of all Christians; and to him was committed in blessed Peter, by our lord Jesus Christ, the full power of tending, ruling and governing the whole church."[191]

To satisfy this pastoral office, our predecessors strove unwearyingly that the saving teaching of Christ should be spread among all the peoples of the world; and with equal care they made sure that it should be kept pure and uncontaminated wherever it was received. It was for this reason that the bishops of the whole world, sometimes individually, sometimes gathered in synods, according to the long established custom of the churches and the pattern of ancient usage, referred to this apostolic see those dangers especially which arose in matters concerning the faith. This was to ensure that any damage suffered by the faith should be repaired in that place above all where the faith can know no failing.[192] The Roman pontiffs, too, as the circumstances of the time or the state of affairs suggested, sometimes by summoning ecumenical councils or consulting the opinion of the churches scattered throughout the world, sometimes by special synods, sometimes by taking advantage of other useful means afforded by divine providence, defined as doctrines to be held those things which, by God's help, they knew to be in keeping with sacred scripture and the apostolic traditions. For the holy Spirit was promised to the successors of Peter not so that they might, by his revelation, make known some new doctrine, but that, by his assistance, they might religiously guard and faithfully expound the revelation or deposit of faith transmitted by the apostles. Indeed, their apostolic teaching was embraced by all the venerable fathers and reverenced and followed by all the holy orthodox doctors, for they knew very well that this see of St Peter always remains unblemished by any error, in accordance with the divine promise of our Lord and Saviour to the prince of his disciples: *I have prayed for you that your faith may not fail; and when you have turned again, strengthen your brethren.*[193]

This gift of truth and never-failing faith was therefore divinely conferred on Peter and his successors in this see so that they might discharge their exalted office for the salvation of all, and so that the whole flock of Christ might be kept away by them from the poisonous food of error and be nourished with the sustenance of heavenly doctrine. Thus the tendency to schism is removed and the whole church is preserved in unity, and, resting on its foundation, can stand firm against the gates of hell.

But since in this very age when the salutary effectiveness of the apostolic office is most especially needed, not a few are to be found who disparage its authority, we judge it absolutely necessary to affirm solemnly the prerogative which the only-begotten Son of God was pleased to attach to the supreme pastoral office.

Therefore, faithfully adhering to the tradition received from the beginning of the christian faith, to the glory of God our saviour, for the exaltation of the catholic religion and for the salvation of the christian people, with the approval of the sacred council, we teach and define as a divinely revealed dogma that when the Roman pontiff speaks *ex cathedra,* that is, when, in the exercise of his office as shepherd and teacher

---

188. Mt 16:18.

189. From Pope Hormisdas's formula of the year 517 (D no. 171).

190. From Michael Palaeologus's profession of faith which was read out at the second council of Lyons (D no. 466).

191. Council of Florence, session 6.

192. Bernard, *Ep.* (*Letters*) 190 (182, 1053).

193. Lk 22:32.

of all Christians, in virtue of his supreme apostolic authority, he defines a doctrine concerning faith or morals to be held by the whole church, he possesses, by the divine assistance promised to him in blessed Peter, that infallibility which the divine Redeemer willed his church to enjoy in defining doctrine concerning faith or morals. Therefore, such definitions of the Roman pontiff are of themselves, and not by the consent of the church, irreformable.

So then, should anyone, which God forbid, have the temerity to reject this definition of ours: let him be anathema.

From Norman P. Tanner, ed., *Decrees of the Ecumenical Councils,* vol. 2 (Washington, DC: Georgetown University Press, 1990), 811–16.

❧ *The Baltimore Catechism* can trace its roots to the Council of Trent (1545–63). To counter the Protestant Reformation, the council published a manual of Catholic teaching called the *Catechismus Romanus* in Latin (*catechismus* means "instruction"), as a guide for the clergy in matters of doctrine and instruction. In 1884 the bishops of the United States gathered in Baltimore and decided to publish an English version of the *Roman Catechism* for use by American schoolchildren, which was issued in 1885. The first *Baltimore Catechism,* published in 1891, contained 100 questions and answers. A larger edition, no. 2, had 421 questions and answers, and a still larger version, no. 3, had 1,274 questions and answers plus prayers. *The Baltimore Catechism,* no. 4, lesson 11, questions 116–21; lesson 12, questions 122–25, 127–29, also known as *An Explanation of the Baltimore Catechism of Christian Doctrine: For the Use of Sunday-School Teachers and Advanced Classes* (originally published in 1921), gives witness to the consequences of *Pastor aeternus: First Dogmatic Constitution on the Church of Christ.*

The Baltimore Catechism

Lesson 11

116   Q. Who is the invisible head of the Church?
       A. Jesus Christ is the invisible head of the Church.

"Invisible head." If, for example, a merchant of one country wishes to establish a branch of his business in another, he remains in the new country long enough to establish the branch business, and then appointing someone to take his place, returns to his own country. He is still the head of the new establishment, but its invisible head for the people of that country, while its visible head is the agent or representative he has placed in charge to carry on the business in his name and interest. When Our Lord wished to establish His Church He came from Heaven; and when about to return to Heaven appointed St. Peter to take His place upon earth and rule the Church as directed. You see, therefore, that Our Lord, though not on earth, is still the real head and owner of the Church, and whatever His agent or vicar—that is, our Holy Father, the Pope—does in the Church, he does it with the authority of Our Lord Himself.

117   Q. Who is the visible head of the Church?
       A. Our Holy Father the Pope, the Bishop of Rome, is the vicar of Christ on earth and the visible head of the Church.

The **"Bishop of Rome"** is always Pope. If the Bishop of New York, or of Baltimore, or of Boston, became Pope, he would become the Bishop of Rome and cease to be the Bishop of New York, Baltimore, or Boston, because St. Peter, the first Pope, was Bishop of Rome; and therefore only the bishops of Rome are his lawful successors—the true Popes—the true visible heads of the Church. The bishops of the other dioceses of the world are the lawful successors of the other Apostles who taught and established churches throughout the world. The bishops of the world are subject to the Pope, just as the other Apostles were subject to St. Peter, who was appointed their chief, by Our Lord Himself.

"Vicar"—that is, one who holds another's place and acts in his name.

118   Q. Why is the Pope, the Bishop of Rome, the visible head of the Church?
       A. The Pope, the Bishop of Rome, is the visible head of the Church because he is the successor of St. Peter, whom Christ made the chief of the Apostles and the visible head of the Church.

"Of Rome." That is why we are called Roman Catholics; to show that we are united to the real successor of St. Peter, and are therefore members of the true apostolic Church.

119   Q. Who are the successors of the other APOSTLES?
       A. The successors of the other Apostles are the bishops of the holy Catholic Church.

We know the Apostles were bishops, because they could make laws for the Church, consecrate other bishops, ordain priests, and give Confirmation—powers that belong only to bishops, and are still exercised by them.

120   Q. Why did Christ found the Church?
       A. Christ founded the Church to teach, govern, sanctify, and save all men.

"**Teach**" religion. "**Govern**" in things that regard salvation. "**Sanctify,**" make good. "**Save**" all who wish to be saved.

121   Q. Are all bound to belong to the Church?
       A. All are bound to belong to the Church, and he who knows the Church to be the true Church and remains out of it, cannot be saved.

Lesson 12. On the Attributes and Marks of the Church

122   Q. Which are the attributes of the Church?
       A. The attributes of the Church are three: authority, infallibility, and indefectibility.

123   Q. What do you mean by the authority of the Church?
       A. By the authority of the Church I mean the right and power which the Pope and the bishops, as the successors of the Apostles, have to teach and govern the faithful.

Authority is the power which one person has over another, so as to be able to exact obedience. A teacher has authority over his scholars, because they must obey him; but the teacher need not obey the scholars, because they have no authority over him. God alone has authority of Himself and from Himself. All others who have authority receive it from God, either directly or through someone else. The Pope has authority from God Himself, and the priests get theirs through their bishops. Therefore, to resist or disobey lawful authority is to resist and disobey God Himself. If one of you were placed in charge of the class in my absence, he would have lawful authority, and the rest of you should obey him—not on account of himself, but on account of the authority he has. Thus the President of the United States, the governor, the mayor, etc., are only ordinary citizens before their election; but after they have been elected and placed in office they exercise lawful authority over us, and we are bound as good citizens and as good Catholics to respect and obey them.

124   Q. What do you mean by the infallibility of the Church?
       A. By the infallibility of the Church I mean that the Church cannot err when it teaches a doctrine of faith or morals.

"**Infallibility.**" When we say the Church is infallible, we mean that it cannot make a mistake or err in what it teaches; that the Pope, the head of the Church, is infallible when he teaches *ex cathedra*—that is, as the successor of St. Peter, the vicar of Christ. *Cathedra* signifies a seat, *ex* stands for "out of"; therefore, *ex cathedra* means out of the chair or office of St. Peter, because chair is sometimes used for office. Thus we say the presidential chair is opposed to this or that, when we intend to say the president, or the one in that office, is opposed to it. The cathedral is the church in which the bishop usually officiates, so called on account of the bishop's cathedra, or throne, being in it.

125   Q. When does the Church teach infallibly?
       A. The Church teaches infallibly when it speaks through the Pope and bishops united in general council, or through the Pope alone when he proclaims to all the faithful a doctrine of faith or morals.

But how will we know when the Pope speaks *ex cathedra,* when he is speaking daily to people from all parts of the world? To speak *ex cathedra* or infallibly, three things are required:

(1) He must speak as the head of the whole Church, not as a private person; and in certain forms of words by which we know he is speaking *ex cathedra.*

(2) What he says must hold good for the whole Church—that is, for all the faithful, and not merely for this or that particular person or country.

(3) He must speak on matters of faith or morals—that is, when the Holy Father tells all the faithful that they are to believe a certain thing as a part of their faith; or when he tells them that certain things are sins, they must believe him and avoid what he declares to be sin. He could not make a mistake in such things. He could not say that Our Lord taught us to believe and do such and such, if Our Lord did not so teach, because Our Lord promised to be with His Church for all time, and to send the Holy Ghost, who would teach it all truth and abide with it forever. If then the Church could make mistakes in teaching faith and morals, the Holy Ghost could not be with it, and Our Lord did not tell the truth—to say which would be blasphemy. But remember, the Pope

is not infallible unless he is teaching faith or morals; that is, what we believe or do in order to save our souls. If the Holy Father wrote a book on astronomy, mathematics, grammar, or even theology, he could make mistakes as other men do, because the Holy Ghost has not promised to guide him in such things. Nevertheless, whatever the Pope teaches on anything you may be pretty sure is right. The Pope is nearly always a very learned man of many years' experience. He has with him at Rome learned men from every part of the world, so that we may say he has the experience of the whole world. Other rulers cannot and need not know as much as the Holy Father, because they have not to govern the world, but only their own country. Moreover, there is no government in the whole world as old as the Church, no nation that can show as many rulers without change; so we may say the Pope has also the experience of all the Popes who preceded him, from St. Peter down to our present Holy Father, Pius XI—two hundred and sixty-one popes. Therefore, considering all this, we should have the very greatest respect for the opinions and advice of the Holy Father on any subject. We should not set up our limited knowledge and experience against his, even if we think that we know better than he does about certain political events taking place in our country, for we are not sure that we do. The Holy Father knows the past history of nations; he knows the nature of mankind; he knows that what takes place in one nation may, and sometimes does, take place in another under the same circumstances. Thus the Holy Father has greater foresight than we have, and we should be thankful when he warns us against certain dangers in politics or other things. He does not teach politics; but as everything we do is either good or bad, every statesman or politician must consider whether what he is about to do be right or wrong, just or unjust. It is the business and duty of the Holy Father to declare against the evil or unjust actions of either individuals or nations, and for that reason he seems at times to interfere in politics when he is really teaching morals. At times, too, governments try to deprive the Church or the Holy Father of their rights; and when he defends himself against such injustice and protests against it, his enemies cry out that he is interfering with the government.

You understand now what the infallibility of the Pope implies, and that it does not mean, as the enemies of the Church say, that the Pope cannot sin, cannot be mistaken in anything. The Pope can sin just the same as anyone else; he could be a very bad man if he wanted to be so, and take the punishment God would inflict for his sins. Could he not be very angry, entirely neglect prayer, or pray with willful distraction; could

he not be proud, covetous, etc.? And these are sins. Therefore he could sin; and hence he has to go to confession and seek forgiveness just as we do. Therefore remember this: whether the Pope be a bad man or a good man in his private life, he must always tell the truth when he speaks *ex cathedra,* because the Holy Ghost is guiding him and will not permit him to err or teach falsehood in faith or morals.

We have examples in the Bible (Numbers 22, 23) where God sometimes makes even bad men foretell the truth. Once He gave an ass the power to speak, that it might protest against the wrongdoing of its wicked and cruel rider.

We have seen how governments interfere with the rights of the Holy Father, and thus he has need of his temporal power that he may be altogether independent of any government. Now let me explain to you what is meant by the Temporal Power of the Pope. Well, then, the Holy Father should have some city or states, not belonging to any government, in which he would be the chief and only ruler. Up to the year 1870 the Holy Father did have such states: they were called the Papal States, and the power he had over them—just like that of any other ruler—was called the temporal power. Now how did he get those states and how did he lose them? He got them in the most just manner, and held possession of them for about a thousand years.

Hundreds of years ago the people of Rome and the surrounding countries elected the Pope their sole ruler. He was already their spiritual ruler, and they made him also their temporal ruler. Then the Pope protected and governed them as other rulers do. Later, kings and princes added other lands, and thus by degrees the possessions of the Pope became quite extended.

How did he lose these possessions? The Italian government took them from him in the most unjust manner. Besides the lands, they deprived the Church of other property donated to it by its faithful children. No ruler in the world had a more just claim or better right to his possessions than the Holy Father, and a government robbed him of them as a thief might take forcibly from you whatever had been justly given to you, when he found you were unable to defend yourself against him.

But has the Holy Father need of his temporal power? Yes, the Holy Father has need of some temporal power. He must be free and independent in governing the Church. He must be free to say what he wishes to all Catholics throughout the world, and free to hear whatever they have to say to him. But if the Pope is under another ruler he cannot be free. That ruler may cast him into prison, and not allow him to communicate with the bishops of the world. At least, he can say nothing about the injustice of the ruler who is over him. Therefore the Pope must have some possessions of his own, that he may not be afraid of the injustice of any ruler, and may speak out the truth boldly to the whole world, denouncing bad rulers and praising good ones as they deserve.

Mind, I do not say what possessions the Holy Father should have but simply that he should have some, in which he would be altogether independent. In justice he should have all that was taken from him. We have a good example here in the United States to illustrate the need of the independence of the Pope. You know every State in the United States is a little government in itself, with its own governor, legislature, laws, etc. Now over all these little governments or States we have the government of the United States, with the President at its head. In the beginning the members of the United States Government assembled to transact the business of the nation sometimes in one State and sometimes in another—sometimes in New York and sometimes in Pennsylvania, etc. But they soon found that in order to be independent of every State and just to all, they must have some territory or possessions of their own not under the power of any State. So some of the States granted them Washington and the country about it for ten miles square—now called the District of Columbia—in which the United States government could freely perform its duties. In a similar manner the Holy Father is over all the governments of the world in matters of religion—in matters of justice and right; and just as the United States government has to decide between the rights of one State and the rights of another, so the Holy Father has sometimes to decide between the rights of one government and the rights of another, and must, in order to be just with all, be free and independent of all.

Again, the temporal power of the Pope is very useful to the Church; for with the money and goods received from his possessions the Holy Father can educate priests and teachers, print books, etc., for the foreign missions. He can also support churches, schools, and institutions in poor countries, and especially where the missionaries are laboring for the conversion of the native heathens.

When the Holy Father had his own possessions he could do much that he cannot now do for the conversion of pagan nations. At present he must depend entirely upon the charitable offerings of the faithful for all good works, even for his own support. The offering we make once a year for the support of the Holy Father is called "Peter's pence," because it began by everyone sending yearly a penny to the Pope, the successor of St. Peter.

127   Q. In whom are these attributes found in their fullness?
      A. These attributes are found in their fullness in the Pope, the visible head of the Church, whose infallible authority to teach bishops, priests, and people in matters of faith or morals will last to the end of the world.

128   Q. Has the Church any marks by which it may be known?
      A. The Church has four marks by which it may be known: it is one; it is holy; it is catholic; it is apostolic.

129   Q. How is the Church one?
      A. The Church is one because all its members agree in one faith, are all in one communion, and are all under one head.

The Catholic Church is **"one,"** first in government and second in doctrine. In *government* every pastor has a certain parish or territory in which all the people belong to his congregation—they form his flock. He has to take care only of these, to teach them, give them the Sacraments, etc. He has not to be responsible for those outside his parish. Then over the pastor we have the bishop, who looks after a certain number of pastors; then comes the archbishop over a certain number of bishops; next comes the primate, who is head of all the archbishops in the country; and over all the primates of the world we have the Holy Father. Thus, when the Holy Father speaks to the bishops, the bishops speak to the priests, and the priests to the people. The Church is therefore one in government, like a great army spread over the world. We can go up step by step from the lowest member of the Church to the highest—the Holy Father; and from him to Our Lord Himself, who is the invisible head of all. This regular body of priests, bishops, archbishops, etc., so arranged, one superior to the other, is called the hierarchy of the Church.

The Church is one also in *doctrine*—that is, every one of the three hundred million of Catholics in the world believes exactly the same truths. If any Catholic denies only one article of faith, though he believes all the rest, he ceases to be a Catholic, and is cut off from the Church. If, for example, you would not believe Matrimony or Holy Orders a Sacrament, or that Our Lord is present in the Holy Eucharist, you would not be a Catholic, though you believed all the other teachings of the Church.

Therefore the Church is one both in government and teaching or doctrine. Now, has any other Church claiming to be Christ's Church that mark? No. The Protestant religions are not one either in government or belief. The Protestants of England have no authority over the Protestants of America, and those of America have nothing to say over those of Germany or France. So every country is independent, and they have no chief head. Neither are they one in belief. In the same country there are many kinds of Protestants—Episcopalians, Presbyterians, Methodists, etc., who do not believe the same thing. Even those who attend the same church and profess the same religion do not all believe the same. Everyone, they say, has a right to interpret the Holy Scriptures according to his own views, so they take many different meanings out of the very same words. There must be some chief person to tell the true meaning of the Holy Scriptures when there is a dispute about it; but they have no such chief, and the result is they are never done disputing.

The United States has a constitution and laws. Now, suppose every citizen was allowed to construe the laws to suit himself, without any regard for the rights of others, what a fine state of affairs we should soon have. But the wise makers of the constitution and laws of the United States did not leave us in such danger. They appointed judges to interpret or explain the laws and give the correct meaning when disputes arise. Then in Washington there is a chief judge for the whole United States; and when he says the words of the law mean this or that, every citizen must abide by his decision, and there is no appeal from it. Just in the same way Our Lord made laws for all men, and while He was upon earth He explained them Himself. He never left all men free to take their own meaning out of them. He appointed judges—the bishops; and a chief judge for the whole world—the Pope. The Holy Ghost guides him, as we have seen above, so that he cannot make mistakes in the meaning of Christ's laws; and when he says, this is what the words of Our Lord in His law signify, no one who is a true Christian can refuse to believe, or can appeal from his decision.

From Thomas L. Kinkead, *An Explanation of the Baltimore Catechism of Christian Doctrine* (Rockford, IL: TAN Books, 1988), 114–26.

left off, Vatican II defined a new vision of the nature of the Church in chapter 3, "The Church Is Hierarchical," of its decree *Dogmatic Constitution on the Church* (*Lumen gentium,* November 21, 1964).

THE SECOND VATICAN COUNCIL

"The Church Is Hierarchical," 18–25, in *Dogmatic Constitution on the Church*

The Hierarchical Structure of the Church, with Special Reference to the Episcopate

18. For the nurturing and constant growth of the People of God, Christ the Lord instituted in His Church a variety of ministries, which work for the good of the whole body. For those ministers who are endowed with sacred power are servants of their brethren, so that all who are of the People of God, and therefore enjoy a true Christian dignity, can work toward a common goal freely and in an orderly way, and arrive at salvation.

This most sacred Synod, following in the footsteps of the First Vatican Council, teaches and declares with that Council that Jesus Christ, the eternal Shepherd, established His holy Church by sending forth the apostles as He Himself had been sent by the Father (cf. Jn. 20:21). He willed that their successors, namely the bishops, should be shepherds in His Church even to the consummation of the world.

In order that the episcopate itself might be one and undivided, He placed blessed Peter over the other apostles, and instituted in him a permanent and visible source and foundation of unity of faith and fellowship.[194] And all this teaching about the institution, the perpetuity, the force and reason for the sacred primacy of the Roman Pontiff and of his infallible teaching authority, this sacred Synod again proposes to be firmly believed by all the faithful.

Continuing in the same task of clarification begun by Vatican I, this Council has decided to declare and proclaim before all men its teaching concerning bishops, the successors of the apostles, who together with the successor of Peter, the Vicar of Christ[195] and the visible Head of the whole Church, govern the house of the living God.

☙ **The Second Vatican Council,** or Vatican II, opened under Pope John XXIII in 1962 and closed under Pope Paul VI in 1965. While professing to pick up where the First Vatican Council had

194. Cf. Vatican Council I, Session 4, the dogmatic constitution "Pastor aeternus": *Denz.* [H. Denzinger, *Enchiridion symbolorum*] 1821 (3050f.).

195. Cf. the Council of Florence, "Decretum pro Graecis": *Denz.* 694 (1307); and Vatican Council I as cited in the preceding footnote: *Denz.* 1826 (3059).

19. The Lord Jesus, after praying to the Father and calling to Himself those whom He desired, appointed twelve men who would stay in His company, and whom He would send to preach the kingdom of God (cf. Mk. 3:13–19; Mt. 10:1–42). These apostles (cf. Lk. 6:13) He formed after the manner of a college or a fixed group, over which He placed Peter, chosen from among them (cf. Jn. 21:15–17). He sent them first to the children of Israel and then to all nations (cf. Rom. 1:16), so that as sharers in His power they might make all peoples His disciples, sanctifying and governing them (cf. Mt. 28:16–20; Mk. 16:15; Lk. 24:45–48; Jn. 20:21–23). Thus they would spread His Church, and by ministering to it under the guidance of the Lord, would shepherd it all days even to the consummation of the world (cf. Mt. 28:20).

They were fully confirmed in this mission on the day of Pentecost (cf. Acts 2:1–26) in accordance with the Lord's promise: "You shall receive power when the Holy Spirit comes upon you, and you shall be witnesses for me in Jerusalem and in all Judea and in Samaria and even to the very ends of the earth" (Acts 1:8). By everywhere preaching the gospel (cf. Mk. 16:20), which was accepted by their hearers under the influence of the Holy Spirit, the apostles gathered together the universal Church, which the Lord established on the apostles and built upon blessed Peter, their chief, Christ Jesus Himself remaining the supreme cornerstone (cf. Apoc. 21:14; Mt. 16:18; Eph. 2:20).[196]

20. That divine mission, entrusted by Christ to the apostles, will last until the end of the world (Mt. 28:20), since the gospel which was to be handed down by them is for all time the source of all life for the Church. For this reason the apostles took care to appoint successors in this hierarchically structured society.

For they not only had helpers in their ministry,[197] but also, in order that the mission assigned to them might continue after their death, they passed on to their immediate cooperators, as a kind of testament, the duty of perfecting and consolidating the work begun by themselves,[198] charging them to attend to the whole flock in which the Holy Spirit placed them to shepherd the Church of God (cf. Acts 20:28). They therefore appointed such men, and authorized the arrangement that, when these men should have died, other approved men would take up their ministry.[199]

Among those various ministries which, as tradition witnesses, were exercised in the Church from the earliest times, the chief place belongs to the office of those who, appointed to the episcopate in a sequence running back to the beginning,[200] are the ones who pass on the apostolic seed.[201] Thus,

as St. Irenaeus testifies, through those who were appointed bishops by the apostles, and through their successors down to our own time, the apostolic tradition is manifested[202] and preserved[203] throughout the world.

With their helpers, the priests and deacons, bishops have therefore taken up the service of the community,[204] presiding in place of God over the flock[205] whose shepherds they are, as teachers of doctrine, priests of sacred worship, and officers of good order.[206] Just as the role that the Lord gave individually to Peter, the first among the apostles, is permanent and was meant to be transmitted to his successors, so also the apostles' office of nurturing the Church is permanent, and was meant to be exercised without interruption by the sacred order of bishops.[207] Therefore, this sacred Synod teaches that by divine institution bishops have succeeded to the place of the apostles[208] as shepherds of the Church, and that he who hears them, hears Christ, while he who rejects them, rejects Christ and Him who sent Christ (cf. Lk. 10:16).[209]

---

196. Cf. St. Gregory, "Liber sacramentorum," Praef. in natali S. Matthiae et S. Thomae: *PL* 78, 51 and 152—compare *Cod. Vat. lat.* 3548, f. 18; St. Hilary, "In Ps.," 67, 10: *PL* 9, 450 (*CSEL* [*Corpus scriptorum ecclesiasticorum Latinorum*], 22, p. 286); St. Jerome, "Adv. Iovin.," 1, 26: *PL* 23, 247 A; St. Augustine, "In Ps.," 86, 4: *PL* 37, 1103; St. Gregory the Great, "Mor. in Iob," XXVIII, V: *PL* 76, 455–6; Primasius, "Comm. in Apoc.," V: *PL* 68, 924 BC; and Paschasius Radbertus, "In Matth.," Bk. VIII. c. 16: *PL* 120, 561 C. Also, Leo XIII, epistle "Et sane," Dec. 17, 1888: *Acta Sanctae Sedis* 21 (1888), p. 321.

197. Cf. Acts 6:2–6; 11:30; 13:1; 14:23; 20:17; 1 Thes. 5:12; Phil. 1:1; Col. 4:11 and passim.

198. Cf. Acts 20:25–27; 2 Tim. 4:6f., taken together with 1 Tim. 5:22; 2 Tim. 2:2; Tit. 1:5; and St. Clement of Rome, "Ad Cor.," 44, 3: ed. Funk, 1, p. 156.

199. St. Clement of Rome, "Ad Cor.," 44, 2: ed. Funk, 1, pp. 154f.

200. Tertullian, "Praescr. haer.," 32: *PL* 2, 52f.; and St. Ignatius of Antioch, passim.

201. Cf. Tertullian, "Praescr. haer.," 32: *PL* 2, 53.

202. Cf. St. Irenaeus, "Adv. haer.," III, 3, 1: *PG* 7, 848 A (Harvey, 2, 8; Sagnard, pp. 100f.): "manifestatam" ["having been made manifest"].

203. Cf. Irenaeus, "Adv. haer.," III, 2, 2: *PG* 7, 847 (Harvey, 2, 7; Sagnard, p. 100): "custoditur" ["is guarded"]. And see also St. Irenaeus, "Adv. haer.," IV, 26, 2: *PG* 7, 1053 (Harvey, 2, 236); IV, 33, 8: *PG* 7, 1077 (Harvey, 2, 262).

204. St. Ignatius of Antioch, "Ad Philad.," Praef.: ed. Funk, I, p. 264.

205. St. Ignatius of Antioch, "Ad Philad.," 1, 1; "Ad Magn.," 6, 1: ed. Funk, I, pp. 264 and 234.

206. St. Clement of Rome, "Ad Cor.," 42, 3–4; 57, 1–2: ed. Funk, I, 152, 156, 171f.; St. Ignatius of Antioch, "Ad Philad.," 2; "Ad Smyrn.," 8; "Ad Magn.," 3; "Ad Trall.," 7: ed. Funk, I, pp. 265f., 282, 232, 246f. etc.; St. Justin, "Apol.," 1, 65: *PG* 6, 428; and St. Cyprian, "Epist.," passim.

207. Cf. Leo XIII, encyclical "Satis Cognitum," June 29, 1896: *Acta Sanctae Sedis* 28 (1895–96), p. 732.

208. Cf. the Council of Trent, Session 23, the decree "De sacr. Ordinis," c. 4: *Denz.* 960 (1768); Vatican Council I, Session 4, the first dogmatic constitution "De Ecclesia Christi," c. 3: *Denz.* 1828 (3061); Pius XII, encyclical "Mystici Corporis," June 29, 1943: *AAS* [*Acta apostolicae sedis*] 35 (1943), pp. 209 and 212; and the Code of Canon Law, c. 329, 1.

209. Cf. Leo XIII, epistle "Et sane," Dec. 17, 1888: *Acta Sanctae Sedis* 21 (1888), pp. 321f.

21. In the bishops, therefore, for whom priests are assistants, our Lord Jesus Christ, the supreme High Priest, is present in the midst of those who believe. For sitting at the right hand of God the Father, He is not absent from the gathering of His high priests,[210] but above all through their excellent service He is preaching the Word of God to all nations, and constantly administering the sacraments of faith to those who believe. By their paternal role (cf. 1 Cor. 4:15), He incorporates new members into His body by a heavenly regeneration, and finally by their wisdom and prudence He directs and guides the people of the New Testament in its pilgrimage toward eternal happiness.

These pastors, selected to shepherd the Lord's flock, are servants of Christ and stewards of the mysteries of God (cf. 1 Cor. 4:1). To them has been assigned the bearing of witness to the gospel of God's grace (cf. Rom. 15:16; Acts 20:24), and to the ministration of the Spirit and of God's glorious power to make men just (cf. 2 Cor. 3:8–9).

For the discharging of such great duties, the apostles were enriched by Christ with a special outpouring of the Holy Spirit, who came upon them (cf. Acts 1:8; 2:4; Jn. 20:22–23). This spiritual gift they passed on to their helpers by the imposition of hands (cf. 1 Tim. 4:14; 2 Tim. 1:6–7), and it has been transmitted down to us in episcopal consecration.[211] This sacred Synod teaches that by episcopal consecration is conferred the fullness of the sacrament of orders, that fullness which in the Church's liturgical practice and in the language of the holy Fathers of the Church is undoubtedly called the high priesthood, the apex of the sacred ministry.[212]

But episcopal consecration, together with the office of sanctifying, also confers the offices of teaching and of governing. (These, however, of their very nature, can be exercised only in hierarchical communion with the head and members of the college.) For from tradition, which is expressed especially in liturgical rites and in the practice of the Church both of the East and of the West, it is clear that, by means of the imposition of hands and the words of consecration, the grace of the Holy Spirit is so conferred,[213] and the sacred character so impressed,[214] that bishops in an eminent and visible way undertake Christ's own role as Teacher, Shepherd, and High Priest, and that they act in His person.[215] Therefore it devolves on the bishops to admit newly elected members into the episcopal body by means of the sacrament of orders.

22. Just as, by the Lord's will, St. Peter and the other apostles constituted one apostolic college, so in a similar way the Roman Pontiff as the successor of Peter, and the bishops as the successors of the apostles, are joined together. The collegial nature and meaning of the episcopal order found expression in the very ancient practice by which bishops appointed the world over were linked with one another and with the Bishop of Rome by the bonds of unity, charity, and peace;[216] also, in the conciliar assemblies[217] which made common judgments about more profound matters[218] in decisions reflecting the views of many.[219] The ecumenical councils held through the centuries clearly attest this collegial aspect. And it is suggested also in the practice, introduced in ancient times, of summoning several bishops to take part in the elevation of someone newly elected to the ministry of the high priesthood. Hence, one is constituted a member of the episcopal body by virtue of sacramental consecration and by hierarchical communion with the head and members of the body.

But the college or body of bishops has no authority unless it is simultaneously conceived of in terms of its head, the Roman Pontiff, Peter's successor, and without any lessening of his power of primacy over all, pastors as well as the general faithful. For in virtue of his office, that is, as Vicar of Christ and pastor of the whole Church, the Roman Pontiff

---

210. St. Leo the Great, "Serm.," 5, 3: *PL* 54, 154.

211. The Council of Trent, Session 23, c. 3, cites the words of 2 Tim. 1:6–7 to show that order is a true sacrament: *Denz.*, 959 (1766).

212. In the "Apostolic Tradition," 3, ed. Botte, "Sources Chr.," pp. 27–30, there is attributed to the bishop "primatus sacerdotii" ["primacy of priesthood"]. See the "Sacramentarium Leonianum," ed. C. Mohlberg, "Sacramentarium Vernonense" (Rome, 1955), p. 119: ". . . ad summi sacerdotii ministerium. . . . Comple in sacerdotibus tuis mysterii tui summam . . ." [". . . to the ministry of the high priest. . . . Fill up in Your priests the highest point of Your mystery . . ."]; and the same editor's "Liber-Sacramentorum Romanae Ecclesiae" (Rome, 1960), pp. 121–2: "Tribuas eis, Domine, cathedram episcopalem ad regendam Ecclesiam tuam et plebem universam" ["Give them, Lord, the episcopal see to rule Your Church and Your entire people"]. See *PL* 78, 224.

213. "Apostolic Tradition," 2: ed. Botte, p. 27.

214. The Council of Trent, Session 23, c. 4, teaches that the sacrament of order imprints an indelible character: *Denz.* 960 (1767). See the allocution of John XXIII, "Jubilate Deo," May 8, 1960: *AAS* 52 (1960), p. 466; and the homily of Paul VI in St. Peter's Basilica, Oct. 20, 1963: *AAS* 55 (1963), p. 1014.

215. St. Cyprian, "Epist.," 63, 14: *PL* 4, 386 (Hartel, IIIB, p. 713): "Sacerdos vice Christi vere fungitur" ["The priest truly acts in the place of Christ"]; St. John Chrysostom, "In 2 Tim.," Hom. 2, 4: *PG* 62, 612: The priest is the "symbolon" of Christ; St. Ambrose, "In Ps.," 38, 25–6: *PL* 14, 1051–2 (*CSEL*, 64, 203–4); Ambrosiaster, "In 1 Tim.," 5, 19: *PL* 17, 479 C and "In Eph.," 4, 11–12: *PL* 17, 387C; Theodore of Mopsuestia, "Hom. Catech.," XV, 21 and 24: ed. Tonneau, pp. 497 and 503; and Hesychius of Jerusalem, "In Lev.," 2, 9, 23: *PG* 93, 894 B.

216. Cf. Eusebius of Caesarea, "Hist. Eccl.," V, 24, 10: *GCS* [*Die griechischen christlichen Schriftsteller der ersten drei Jahrhunderte*] II, 1, p. 495 (ed. Bardy, "Sources chr.," II, p. 69); and Dionysius as given in Eusebius of Caesarea, "Hist. Eccl.," VII, 5, 2: *GCS* II, pp. 638f. (ed. Bardy, II, pp. 168f.).

217. For the ancient Councils, cf. Eusebius of Caesarea, "Hist. Eccl.," V, 23–4: *GCS* II, 1, pp. 488ff. (ed. Bardy, II, pp. 66ff.) and passim. Council of Nicaea, can. 5: "Conc. Oec. Decr.," p. 7.

218. Tertullian, "De ieiunio," 13: *PL* 2, 972 B (*CSEL*, 20, p. 292, lines 13–6).

219. St. Cyprian, "Epist.," 56, 3: Hartel, III B, p. 650 (ed. Bayard, p. 154).

has full, supreme, and universal power over the Church. And he can always exercise this power freely.

The order of bishops is the successor to the college of the apostles in teaching authority and pastoral rule; or, rather, in the episcopal order the apostolic body continues without a break. Together with its head, the Roman Pontiff, and never without this head, the episcopal order is the subject of supreme and full power over the universal Church.[220] But this power can be exercised only with the consent of the Roman Pontiff. For our Lord made Simon Peter alone the rock and keybearer of the Church (cf. Mt. 16:18–19), and appointed him shepherd of the whole flock (cf. Jn. 21:15ff.).

It is definite, however, that the power of binding and loosing, which was given to Peter (Mt. 16:19), was granted also to the college of apostles, joined with their head (Mt. 18:18; 28:16–20).[221] This college, insofar as it is composed of many, expresses the variety and universality of the People of God, but insofar as it is assembled under one head, it expresses the unity of the flock of Christ. In it, the bishops, faithfully recognizing the primacy and pre-eminence of their head, exercise their own authority for the good of their own faithful, and indeed of the whole Church, with the Holy Spirit constantly strengthening its organic structure and inner harmony.

The supreme authority with which this college is empowered over the whole Church is exercised in a solemn way through an ecumenical council. A council is never ecumenical unless it is confirmed or at least accepted as such by the successor of Peter. It is the prerogative of the Roman Pontiff to convoke these councils, to preside over them, and to confirm them.[222] The same collegiate power can be exercised in union with the Pope by the bishops living in all parts of the world, provided that the head of the college calls them to collegiate action, or at least so approves or freely accepts the united action of the dispersed bishops that it is made a true collegiate act.

23. This collegial union is apparent also in the mutual relations of the individual bishops with particular churches and with the universal Church. The Roman Pontiff, as the successor of Peter, is the perpetual and visible source and foundation of the unity of the bishops and of the multitude of the faithful.[223] The individual bishop, however, is the visible principle and foundation of unity in his particular church,[224] fashioned after the model of the universal Church. In and from such individual churches there comes into being the one and only Catholic Church.[225] For this reason each individual bishop represents his own church, but all of them together

in union with the Pope represent the entire Church joined in the bond of peace, love, and unity.

The individual bishops, who are placed in charge of particular churches, exercise their pastoral government over the portion of the People of God committed to their care, and not over other churches nor over the universal Church. But each of them, as a member of the episcopal college and a legitimate successor of the apostles, is obliged by Christ's decree and command[226] to be solicitous for the whole Church.

This solicitude, though it is not exercised by an act of jurisdiction, contributes immensely to the welfare of the universal Church. For it is the duty of all bishops to promote and to safeguard the unity of faith and the discipline common to the whole Church, to instruct the faithful in love for the whole Mystical Body of Christ, especially for its poor and sorrowing members and for those who are suffering persecution for justice' sake (cf. Mt. 5:10), and, finally, to foster every activity which is common to the whole Church, especially efforts to spread the faith and make the light of full truth dawn on all men. For the rest, it is a sacred reality that by governing well their own church as a portion of the universal Church, they themselves are effectively contributing to the welfare of the whole Mystical Body, which is also the body of the churches.[227]

The task of proclaiming the gospel everywhere on earth devolves on the body of pastors, to all of whom in common Christ gave His command, thereby imposing upon them a common duty, as Pope Celestine in his time reminded the Fathers of the Council of Ephesus.[228] From this it follows

---

220. Cf. official "Relatio" of Zinelli during Vatican Council I: Mansi, 52, 1109 C.

221. Cf. Vatican Council I, schema for the second dogmatic constitution "De Ecclesia Christi," c. 4: Mansi, 53, 310. See also the "Relatio" of Kleutgen on the revised schema: Mansi, 53, 321 B–322 B; and the statement by Zinelli: Mansi, 52, 1110 A. And see, too, St. Leo the Great, "Serm.," 4, 3: PL 54, 151 A.

222. Cf. Code of Canon Law, c. 227.

223. Cf. Vatican Council I, the dogmatic constitution "Pastor aeternus": Denz. 1821 (3050f.).

224. Cf. St. Cyprian, "Epist.," 66, 8: Hartel, III B, p. 733: "Episcopus in Ecclesia et Ecclesia in episcopo" ["The bishop is in the Church and the Church in the bishop"].

225. Cf. St. Cyprian, "Epist.," 55:24: Hartel, III B, p. 642, line 13: "Una Ecclesia per totum mundum in multa membra divisa" ["The one Church divided throughout the entire world into many members"]; and "Epist.," 36, 4: Hartel, III B, p. 575, lines 20–21.

226. Cf. Pius XII, encyclical "Fidei donum," Apr. 21, 1957: AAS 49 (1957), p. 237.

227. Cf. St. Hilary of Poitiers, "In Ps.," 14, 3: PL 9, 206 (CSEL 22, p. 86); St. Gregory the Great, "Moral," IV, 7, 12: PL 75, 643; and pseudo-Basil, "In Is.," 15, 296: PG 30, 637 C.

228. St. Celestine, "Epist.," 18, 1–2 to the Council of Ephesus: PL 50, 505 AB (Schwartz, "Acta Conc. Oec.," I, 1, 1, p. 22). Cf. Benedict XV, apostolic epistle

that the individual bishops, insofar as the discharge of their duty permits, are obliged to enter into a community of effort among themselves and with the successor of Peter, upon whom was imposed in a special way the great duty of spreading the Christian name.[229] With all their energy, therefore, they must supply to the missions both workers for the harvest and also spiritual and material aid, both directly and on their own account, as well as by arousing the ardent cooperation of the faithful. And finally, in a universal fellowship of charity, bishops should gladly extend their fraternal aid to other churches, especially to neighboring and more needy dioceses, in accordance with the venerable example of antiquity.

By divine Providence it has come about that various churches established in diverse places by the apostles and their successors have in the course of time coalesced into several groups, organically united, which, preserving the unity of faith and the unique divine constitution of the universal Church, enjoy their own discipline, their own liturgical usage, and their own theological and spiritual heritage. Some of these churches, notably the ancient patriarchal churches, as parent-stocks of the faith, so to speak, have begotten others as daughter churches. With these they are connected down to our own time by a close bond of charity in their sacramental life and in their mutual respect for rights and duties.[230]

This variety of local churches with one common aspiration is particularly splendid evidence of the catholicity of the undivided Church. In like manner the episcopal bodies of today are in a position to render a manifold and fruitful assistance, so that this collegiate sense may be put into practical application.

24. To the Lord was given all power in heaven and on earth. As successors of the apostles, bishops receive from Him the mission to teach all nations and to preach the gospel to every creature, so that all men may attain to salvation by faith, baptism, and the fulfillment of the commandments (cf. Mt. 28:18; Mk. 16:15–16; Acts 26:17f.). To fulfill this mission, Christ the Lord promised the Holy Spirit to the apostles, and on Pentecost day sent the Spirit from heaven. By His power they were to be witnesses to Christ before the nations and peoples and kings, even to the ends of the earth (cf. Acts 1:8; 2:1ff.; 9:15). Now, that duty, which the Lord committed to the shepherds of His people, is a true service, and in sacred literature is significantly called "diakonia" or ministry (cf. Acts 1:17, 25; 21:19; Rom. 11:13; 1 Tim. 1:12).

The canonical mission of bishops can come about by legitimate customs which have not been revoked by the supreme and universal authority of the Church, or by laws made or recognized by that same authority, or directly through the successor of Peter himself. If the latter refuses or denies apostolic communion, a bishop cannot assume office.[231]

25. Among the principal duties of bishops, the preaching of the gospel occupies an eminent place.[232] For bishops are preachers of the faith who lead new disciples to Christ. They are authentic teachers, that is, teachers endowed with the authority of Christ, who preach to the people committed to them the faith they must believe and put into practice. By the light of the Holy Spirit, they make that faith clear, bringing forth from the treasury of revelation new things and old (cf. Mt. 13:52), making faith bear fruit and vigilantly warding off any errors which threaten their flock (cf. 2 Tim. 4:1–4).

Bishops, teaching in communion with the Roman Pontiff, are to be respected by all as witnesses to divine and Catholic truth. In matters of faith and morals, the bishops speak in the name of Christ and the faithful are to accept their teaching and adhere to it with a religious assent of soul. This religious submission of will and of mind must be shown in a special way to the authentic teaching authority of the Roman Pontiff, even when he is not speaking ex cathedra. That is, it must be shown in such a way that his supreme magisterium is acknowledged with reverence, the judgments made by him are sincerely adhered to, according to his manifest mind and will. His mind and will in the matter may be known chiefly either from the character of the documents, from his frequent repetition of the same doctrine, or from his manner of speaking.

Although the individual bishops do not enjoy the prerogative of infallibility, they can nevertheless proclaim Christ's doctrine infallibly. This is so, even when they are dispersed around the world, provided that while maintaining the bond of unity among themselves and with Peter's successor, and while teaching authentically on a matter of faith or morals,

---

"Maximum illud": *AAS* 11 (1919), p. 440; Pius IX, encyclical "Rerum Ecclesiae," Feb. 28, 1926: *AAS* 18 (1926), p. 69; Pius XII, encyclical "Fidei Donum," April 21, 1957: *AAS* 49 (1957), p. 237.

229. Cf. Leo XIII, encyclical "Grande Munus," Sept. 30, 1880: *AAS* 13 (1880), p. 145. Cf. Code of Canon Law, c. 1327; c. 1350, §2.

230. On the rights of patriarchical sees, see the Council of Nicaea, canon 6 on Alexandria and Antioch, canon 7 on Jerusalem: "Conc. Oec. Decr.," p. 8; Lateran Council IV in the year 1215, Constitution V: "De dignitate Patriarcharum"; "Conc. Oec. Decr.," p. 212; and the Council of Ferrara-Florence: "Conc. Oec. Decr.," p. 504.

231. Cf. Code of Law for Eastern Churches cc. 216–314: on Patriarchs; cc. 324–39: on major archbishops; cc. 362–91: on other dignitaries; and in particular, cc. 238, §3; 216; 240; 251; 255: on the naming of bishops by a Patriarch.

232. Cf. Council of Trent, Decree on reform, Session 5, c. 2, n. 9; and Session 24, c. 4: "Conc. Oec. Decr.," pp. 645 and 739.

they concur in a single viewpoint as the one which must be held conclusively.[233] This authority is even more clearly verified when, gathered together in an ecumenical council, they are teachers and judges of faith and morals for the universal Church. Their definitions must then be adhered to with the submission of faith.[234]

This infallibility with which the divine Redeemer willed His Church to be endowed in defining a doctrine of faith and morals extends as far as extends the deposit of divine revelation, which must be religiously guarded and faithfully expounded. This is the infallibility which the Roman Pontiff, the head of the college of bishops, enjoys in virtue of his office, when, as the supreme shepherd and teacher of all the faithful, who confirms his brethren in their faith (cf. Lk. 22:32), he proclaims by a definitive act some doctrine of faith or morals.[235] Therefore his definitions, of themselves, and not from the consent of the Church, are justly styled irreformable, for they are pronounced with the assistance of the Holy Spirit, an assistance promised to him in blessed Peter. Therefore they need no approval of others, nor do they allow an appeal to any other judgment. For then the Roman Pontiff is not pronouncing judgment as a private person. Rather, as the supreme teacher of the universal Church, as one in whom the charism of the infallibility of the Church herself is individually present, he is expounding or defending a doctrine of Catholic faith.[236]

The infallibility promised to the Church resides also in the body of bishops when that body exercises supreme teaching authority with the successor of Peter. To the resultant definitions the assent of the Church can never be wanting, on account of the activity of that same Holy Spirit, whereby the whole flock of Christ is preserved and progresses in unity of faith.[237]

But when either the Roman Pontiff or the body of bishops together with him formulates a definition, they do so in accord with revelation itself. All are obliged to maintain and be ruled by this revelation, which, as written or preserved by tradition, is transmitted in its entirety through the legitimate succession of bishops and especially through the care of the Roman Pontiff himself.

Under the guiding light of the Spirit of truth, revelation is thus religiously preserved and faithfully expounded in the Church.[238] The Roman Pontiff and the bishops, in conformity with their duty and as befits the gravity of the matter, strive painstakingly and by appropriate means to inquire properly into that revelation and to give apt expression to its

contents.[239] But they do not accept any new public revelation as part of the divine deposit of faith.[240]

Translated by Cornelius Williams, in *Vatican Council II: The Conciliar and Post Conciliar Documents*, edited by Austin Flannery (Collegeville, MN: Liturgical Press, 1975), 369–81.

☙ In addition to *Dogmatic Constitution on the Church* (*Lumen gentium*), of November 21, 1964, the Second Vatican Council also passed the *Decree on Ecumenism*. This decree began a new era of understanding and dialogue between the Catholic Church and the other Christian Churches, including the Orthodox Church. This new era is evidenced by the "Address by Pope John Paul II in the Patriarchal Church of St. George at the Phanar at the Conclusion of the Patriarchal and Synodal Liturgy (30 November 1979)" and the "Address in Reply by Patriarch Dimitrios I to Pope John Paul II (30 November 1979)."

JOHN PAUL II

"Address by Pope John Paul II in the Patriarchal Church of St. George at the Phanar at the Conclusion of the Patriarchal and Synodal Liturgy (30 November 1979)"

Your Holiness, my very dear brother: "Behold, how good and pleasant it is when brothers dwell in unity" (Ps 133:1). [These opening words were spoken in Greek.]

These words of the Psalmist spring from my heart on this day when I am in your company. Yes, how good it is, how pleasant, to be all brothers together.

We are gathered to celebrate St. Andrew, the First-Called among the Apostles, and brother of Peter, the leader of their group. This fact emphasizes the ecclesial meaning of our meeting today. Andrew was an Apostle, that is to say one of

---

233. Cf. Vatican Council I, the dogmatic constitution "Dei Filius," 3: *Denz.* 1712 (3011). Cf. note (taken from St. Robert Bellarmine) adjoined to Schema I "De Ecclesia": Mansi, 51, 579 C; as well as the revised Schema for the second constitution "De Ecclesia Christi" with the commentary of Kleutgen: Mansi, 53, 313 AB. Cf. Pius IX, epistle, "Tuas libenter": *Denz.* 1683 (2879).

234. Cf. Code of Canon Law, cc. 1322–3.

235. Cf. Vatican Council I, the dogmatic constitution "Pastor aeternus": *Denz.* 1839 (3074).

236. Cf. explanation of Gasser at Vatican Council I: Mansi, 52, 1213 AC.

237. Gasser, Vatican Council I: Mansi, 52, 1214 A.

238. Gasser, Vatican Council I: Mansi, 52, 1215 CD, 1216–7 A.

239. Gasser, Vatican Council I: Mansi, 52, 1213.

240. Vatican Council I, the dogmatic constitution "Pastor aeternus," 4: *Denz.* 1836 (3070).

those men chosen by Christ to be transformed by his Spirit and sent into the world, as he himself had been sent into the world by his Father (cf. Jn 17:18). They were sent to announce the good news of the reconciliation given in Christ (cf. 2 Cor 2:18–20), to call men and women to enter by Christ into communion with the Father in the Holy Spirit (cf. 1 Jn 1:1–3), and thus to gather them, now become children of God, into a great people in which all are brothers and sisters. To gather all things together in Christ in praise of God's glory (cf. Eph 1:10–12): this is the mission of the Apostles, this is the mission of those who, in their wake, were also chosen and sent, and this is the vocation of the Church.

This Apostle, patron of the renowned Church of Constantinople, is Peter's brother. It is true that all the Apostles are bound together by the new brotherhood which unites those whose hearts have been renewed by the spirit of the Son (cf. Rom 8:15), and to whom the ministry of reconciliation has been confided (cf. 2 Cor 5:18); but this does not cancel out—far from it—the special ties created by birth and upbringing in the same family. Andrew and Peter were brothers, and within the Apostolic circle they must have been bound by a greater intimacy and united in a closer collaboration in the Apostolic task.

Here again today's celebration reminds us that special bonds of brotherhood and intimacy exist between the Church of Rome and that of Constantinople, and that a closer collaboration is natural between these Churches.

Peter, Andrew's brother, is the leader of the Apostles. Thanks to the inspiration of the Father, he fully recognized in Jesus Christ the Son of the living God (cf. Mt 16:16); owing to this faith, he received the name of Peter, so that the Church might rest on this Rock (cf. Mt 16:18). He had the task of seeing to the apostolic preaching. A brother among brothers, he received the mission of strengthening them in the faith (cf. Lk 22:32); he in the first place has the responsibility of watching over the union of all, of seeing that there is a symphony of the holy Churches of God in fidelity to "the faith which was once for all delivered to the saints" (Jude 3).

It is in this spirit, urged on by these feelings, that Peter's successor wanted on this day to visit the Church whose patron saint is Andrew, to visit its venerated pastor, its hierarchy and all its faithful. He wanted to come and take part in its prayer. This visit to the first see of the Orthodox Church shows clearly the will of the whole Catholic Church to go forward in the march towards the unity of all. It also shows its conviction that the reestablishment of full communion

with the Orthodox Church is a fundamental stage in the decisive progress of the whole ecumenical movement. The division between us may not, perhaps, have been without an influence on the other and later divisions.

The new step I have taken fits in with the gesture of openness by John XXIII. It takes up and continues the memorable initiatives of my predecessor Paul VI. To begin with, that which took him in the first place to Jerusalem, where for the first time there was a moving embrace with the Ecumenical Patriarch of Constantinople, and the first exchanges by word of mouth were made in the very place where the mystery of Redemption to unite the dispersed children of God was enacted. Then there was the meeting which took place here, just over twelve years ago, anticipating the visit of Patriarch Athenagoras who came in his turn to visit Paul VI in the Roman see. These two great figures have left us to join God: they have completed their ministry, in which they were both straining towards full communion and almost impatient to bring it about in their lifetime. As for me, I did not want to delay any longer in coming to pray with you, in your country. Among my apostolic journeys, already carried out or planned, this one had special importance and urgency in my eyes. I venture to hope that Patriarch Dimitrios and I will be able to pray together again, and this time on the tomb of the Apostle Peter. Such actions express our impatience for unity before God and before the whole people of God.

For nearly a whole millennium, the two sister Churches grew side by side, as two great vital and complementary traditions of the same Church of Christ, keeping not only peaceful and fruitful relations, but also concern for the indispensable communion in faith, prayer and charity, which they did not at any cost want to imperil, despite their different kinds of sensibility. The second millennium, on the contrary, was darkened, apart from some fleeting bright intervals, by the sense of estrangement which the two Churches felt toward each other, with all the fatal consequences of this. The wound is not yet healed. But the Lord can cure it and he bids us do our best to help the process. Here we are now at the end of the second millennium. Surely it is time to quicken our pace towards perfect brotherly reconciliation, so that the dawn of the third millennium may find us standing side by side, in full communion, witnessing together to salvation before the world, which needs this sign of unity if it is to be evangelized.

On the practical plain, today's visit also shows the importance that the Catholic Church attaches to the Theological

Dialogue which is about to begin with the Orthodox Church. With realism and wisdom, in conformity with the wish of the Apostolic See of Rome and also with the desire of the Pan-Orthodox Conferences, it had been decided to renew relations and contacts between the Catholic Church and the Orthodox Churches which would enable them to recognize one another and create the atmosphere required for a fruitful theological dialogue. It was necessary to create the context again before trying together to rewrite the texts.

This period has rightly been called the dialogue of charity. This dialogue has allowed us to become aware again of the deep communion that already unites us, and enables us to consider and treat each other as sister Churches. A great deal has already been done, but this effort must be continued. It is necessary to draw the consequences of this mutual theological rediscovery, wherever Catholics and Orthodox live together. Habits of isolation must be overcome so that we may collaborate in all fields of pastoral action in which this collaboration is possible, given the almost complete communion that already exists between us.

We must not be afraid to reconsider, on both sides, and in consultation with one another, canonical rules established when awareness of our communion—now close even if it is still incomplete—was still dimmed. These rules perhaps no longer correspond to the results of the dialogue of charity and to the new and promising openings which have been thus created. It is important that the faithful on both sides should realize the progress that has been made, and it would be desirable that those who are to be responsible for the dialogue should keep in mind the consequences for the life of the faithful of the kinds of progress still to come.

This Theological Dialogue which is about to begin now will have the task of overcoming the misunderstandings and disagreements which still exist between us, if not at the level of faith, at least at the level of theological formulation. It should take place not only in the atmosphere of the dialogue of charity, which must be developed and intensified, but also in an atmosphere of worship and openness of mind and will.

It is only in worship, with a keen sense of the transcendence of the inexpressible mystery "which surpasses knowledge" (Eph 3:19), that we will be able to see our divergences in their proper setting and "to lay . . . no greater burden than these necessary things" (Acts 15:28), so as to reestablish communion (cf. *Unitatis Redintegratio,* 18). It seems to me, in fact, that the question we must ask ourselves is not so much whether we can reestablish full communion, but rather whether we still have the right to remain separated. We must ask ourselves this question in the very name of our faithfulness to Christ's will for his Church, for which constant prayer must make us both increasingly open and ready in the course of the Theological Dialogue.

If the Church is called to gather men in praise of God, St. Irenaeus, the great Doctor of the East and of the West, reminds us that "the glory of God is living man" (*Adv. Haer.* IV, 20, 7). Everything in the Church is ordered to allowing man to live really in this full freedom which comes from his communion with the Father through the Son in the Spirit. St. Irenaeus indeed immediately continues: "and man's life is the vision of God"—the vision of the Father manifested in the Word.

The Church can respond fully to this vocation only by bearing witness through her unity to the newness of this life given in Christ: "I in them and you in me, that they may become perfectly one, so that the world may know that you have sent me and have loved them even as you have loved me" (Jn 17:23).

In the certainty that our hope cannot be disappointed (cf. Rom 5:5), I repeat, beloved brothers, how glad I am to be among you, and with you I give thanks to the Father from whom every perfect gift comes (cf. Jas 1:17).

From E. J. Stormon, ed. and trans., *Towards the Healing of Schism: The Sees of Rome and Constantinople* (New York: Paulist Press, 1987), 359–63.

DIMITRIOS I

"Address in Reply by Patriarch Dimitrios I to Pope John Paul II (30 November 1979)"

"How beautiful are the feet of those who
proclaim peace, who announce good news." (Rom 10:15)

Most Holy Brother,

With these words, which are those both of the Prophet and the Apostle, we greet Your venerable Holiness as you make your historic visit to the holy Church of Constantinople, which serves the Orthodox East, and we hail your presence, which is full of significance, at this feast commemorating the glorious Apostle Andrew the First-Called, and at the Eucharistic Liturgy celebrated upon his altar.

Your journey to us from Rome is indeed that of a messenger of peace and good things, and of one who comes, we are convinced, not only to us and our Holy Orthodox Church, but to this great country of ours, and much further still afield. It is the expression of a new journey of Your Holiness to man made in the image of God, whose worth as a person is so sorely tried today. This journey has been undertaken because of those threatened values and good things which are intrinsic to the very being of humanity, and determine the deepest reason for our existence on earth.

Looking at your visit and giving it its true worth in this wide and extended setting, seeing it as one made to this country, which is a bridge between East and West, and to this city, which is the cradle of great civilizations, of important religious developments and Christian forms of culture, we remain convinced that we are formulating the outlook of the Church of Christ about the world and man. At the same time, we acknowledge the fact that, from the time of your accession to the Roman see, all the measures you have adopted and the journeys you have made—and these also concern causes and peoples external to your see—have the same meaning as what we express. Thus you are putting to use, in accordance with the inscrutable decrees of the Lord, the talent of liberty which was given you, and make your way forth out of walls of every sort to bring glad tidings of peace and good things to all men without distinction.

So, "how beautiful are the feet of those who publish peace, who preach good news."

Most holy brother,

From yesterday we have welcomed you to our humble see as one who brings glad tidings of peace, of the peace of Christ and of the good things that go with it, and as one who was moved to do this by sheer goodness.

We, too, long for and seek out peace for both the Church and the world. It is in the pursuit of this common aim that we come together. It was with this same holy purpose that our two great and renowned predecessors met in Jerusalem, here at Constantinople, and at Rome. It was with this aim in mind that our two Churches issued forth from their state of isolation and mutual alienation, not to say their hostility, and took the road towards fresh encounter and reconciliation. For this purpose the anathemas between us were lifted. With faith in the will of the Lord, the Ruler and Father of peace, who would have us be one (Jn 17:21), but also drawing upon courage, patience, wisdom, and hope, and holding exchanges with one another in charity, we have both covered a long road in a relatively short time, and have reached the position where we stand today. Throughout this journey the Risen Christ was with us, accompanying us on our way, indeed guiding us along it, leading us to the breaking of the Bread.

So it was with our gaze fixed on this full communion in the breaking of the Bread that we made our way together up till today. As from today we are inaugurating a new and most important stage through your presence, symbolic and significant in so many ways as it is, at the liturgical assembly of the Church of Constantinople.

Most holy brother,

The two Churches which we represent at this moment, the Roman Catholic and the Orthodox, and the other Christian Churches and Confessions, the other religions, and the world in general, are waiting to learn what particular stage in our journey towards Christian unity has been reached by our meeting today, which was brought about at the cost of so much effort on your part.

Thanks be to God, we are both able to answer today by saying that we are entering on a new phase of the attainment of brotherhood, indeed a serious and important phase, of which the issue will be decisive for the goal to which we look, namely unity.

We are entering on the phase of the official Theological Dialogue between the two Churches, Roman Catholic and Orthodox.

We prepared the ground through the "dialogue of charity" by means of mutual endeavors, not to mention ecclesiastical declarations and acts, and we made the prior arrangements for the Theological Dialogue through the work done on either side by the commissions appointed for this purpose. Given these facts, we the Roman Catholic and Orthodox Churches are happy to announce that we have officially set up two Theological Commissions, which, under the form of a single Joint Theological Commission will soon engage in the first phase of the Dialogue following the daily program arranged and approved by the two Churches acting together.

Our meeting here today makes it possible then to announce this definite practical fact.

Perhaps Christians of other Churches and Confessions will be wondering whether this dialogue between the Roman Catholic and the Orthodox Churches whose beginnings we applaud today is as far as we aim to go.

To this question we are both able to answer No. And we would both go on immediately to say that our ultimate and crowning aim is not merely the union of our two Churches, but total Christian unity in the same Lord and a common sharing of the one holy Chalice.

And to those non-Christians who might be wondering

what Christian unity really means—whether it represents an alliance or common front against non-Christians—our reply would be this. The Christian unity which we are trying to achieve is not aimed against anyone. It represents rather a positive contribution and service to all, regardless of sex, or race, or religion, or social class, in keeping with the fundamental Christian principle: "there is neither Jew nor Greek, there is neither slave nor free, there is neither male nor female" (Gal 3:28).

Most holy brother,

It is in such a divine-human embrace of humankind by the Church of Christ that we embrace you and the Roman Catholic Church today in this holy center of Orthodoxy.

Doubtless various obstacles loom up before us. In the first place we have to reckon with serious theological problems which concern essential points of the Christian faith; it is to solve these that we are arranging the Theological Dialogue. At the same time there are the obstacles arising from distrust, from irresponsibility, from the non-theological factors in the differences between Christians, from intolerance and fanaticism, whether between Christians or members of different religions—in short all those pointed weapons that belong to Lucifer's armory. From Lucifer, for that matter, come all the heresies and divisions and the various forms of opposition of man to God and man to his fellow man.

We live and endeavor to fulfil the will of God and to spread the Gospel of love, unity, and peace at a critical hour for the human race, when Lucifer, the one who in his person is opposed to God and is the spirit of evil, is tempting humankind beyond its strength.

Indeed, Your Holiness, we find ourselves before a heightened state of temptation and of the action of the evil one in the world, in every sphere, the religious, social, cultural, political, to such a degree that before us we see the single victim of all of this: man who was made in the image of God. We are in the presence of a phenomenon, a sign of the times, which could be described as a return to the age of religious fanaticism, of "holy wars," of the mutual shattering of men and faiths, and all this constantly done in the name of God. Before this picture of humanity stretching out before us in all its naked and tragic reality, and with the thread of Satanic anarchy on every side, Your Holiness comes to us, so that we may together proclaim the Gospel of peace and goodness, looking to every quarter of the globe.

According to a very ancient and pious tradition of the Church, the Apostle Andrew the First-Called, brother of

Peter, the leader of the Apostolic group, was crucified upon a cross having the shape of the Greek letter X, which means that he was crucified upon the monogram of Christ. From that time onwards that cross is his throne and the throne of his successors. From it we greet you, and together with you bear testimony to love, peace, and salvation, before the whole world.

From E. J. Stormon, ed. and trans., *Towards the Healing of Schism: The Sees of Rome and Constantinople* (New York: Paulist Press, 1987), 363–67.

THE EASTERN ORTHODOX CHURCH

In "The Church of God," from his *The Orthodox Church,* **Timothy Ware** sketches the theological foundations of the Orthodox Church, which grew out of the ancient Eastern Churches, especially after the break with the Church in Rome in 1054.

TIMOTHY WARE

"The Church of God," in *The Orthodox Church*

Christ loved the Church, and gave himself up for it.

Ephesians v. 25

The Church is one and the same with the Lord—His Body, of His flesh and of His bones. The Church is the living vine, nourished by Him and growing in Him. Never think of the Church apart from the Lord Jesus Christ, from the Father and the Holy Spirit.

Father John of Kronstadt

God and His Church

An Orthodox Christian is vividly conscious of belonging to a community. "We know that when any one of us falls," wrote [Alexei] Khomiakov, "he falls alone; but no one is saved alone. He is saved in the Church, as a member of it and in union with all its other members."[241] [. . .]

[. . .] All Orthodox thinking about the Church starts with the special relationship which exists between the Church and God. Three phrases can be used to describe this relation: the Church is (1) the Image of the Holy Trinity, (2) the Body of Christ, (3) a continued Pentecost. The Orthodox doctrine of the Church is Trinitarian, Christological, and "pneumatological."

241. *The Church Is One,* [Seattle: St. Nectarias Press, 1979], section 9.

(1) *The Image of the Holy Trinity.* Just as each man is made according to the image of the Trinitarian God, so the Church as a whole is an icon of God the Trinity, reproducing on earth the mystery of unity in diversity. In the Trinity the three are one God, yet each is fully personal; in the Church a multitude of human persons are united in one, yet each preserves his personal diversity unimpaired. The mutual indwelling of the persons of the Trinity is paralleled by the coinherence of the members of the Church. In the Church there is no conflict between freedom and authority; in the Church there is unity, but no totalitarianism. When Orthodox apply the word "Catholic" to the Church, they have in mind (among other things) this living miracle of the unity of many persons in one.

This conception of the Church as an icon of the Trinity has many further applications. "Unity in diversity"—just as each person of the Trinity is autonomous, so the Church is made up of a number of independent Autocephalous Churches; and just as in the Trinity the three persons are equal, so in the Church no one bishop can claim to wield an absolute power over all the rest.

This idea of the Church as an icon of the Trinity also helps us to understand the Orthodox emphasis upon Councils. A council is an expression of the Trinitarian nature of the Church. The mystery of unity in diversity according to the image of the Trinity can be seen in action, as the many bishops assembled in council freely reach a common mind under the guidance of the Spirit.

The unity of the Church is linked more particularly with the person of Christ, its diversity with the person of the Holy Spirit.

(2) *The Body of Christ:* "We, who are many, are one body in Christ" (Rom 12:5). Between Christ and the Church there is the closest possible bond: in the famous phrase of Ignatius, "where Christ is, there is the Catholic Church."[242] The Church is the extension of the Incarnation, the place where the Incarnation perpetuates itself. The Church, the Greek theologian Chrestos Androutsos has written, is "the centre and organ of Christ's redeeming work; . . . it is nothing else than the continuation and extension of His prophetic, priestly, and kingly power. . . . The Church and its Founder are inextricably bound together. . . . The Church is Christ with us."[243] Christ did not leave the Church when He ascended into heaven: "Lo! I am with you always, even to the end of the world," He promised (Matt 28:20), "for where two or three are gathered together in my name, there am I in the midst of them" (Matt 18:20). It is only too easy to fall into the mistake of speaking of Christ as absent:

And still the Holy Church is here,
Although her Lord is gone.[244]

But how can we say that Christ "is gone," when He has promised us His perpetual presence?

The unity between Christ and His Church is effected above all through the sacraments. At Baptism, the new Christian is buried and raised with Christ; at the Eucharist the members of Christ's Body the Church receive His Body in the sacraments. The Eucharist, by uniting the members of the Church to Christ, at the same time unites them to one another: "We, who are many, are one bread, one body; for we all partake of the one bread" (I Cor 10:17). The Eucharist creates the unity of the Church. The Church (as Ignatius saw) is a Eucharistic society, a sacramental organism which exists—and exists in its fullness—wherever the Eucharist is celebrated. It is no coincidence that the term "Body of Christ" should mean both the Church and the sacrament; and that the phrase *communio sanctorum* in the Apostles' Creed should mean both "the communion of the holy people" (communion of saints) and "the communion of the holy things" (communion in the sacraments).

The Church must be thought of primarily in sacramental terms. Its outward organization, however important, is secondary to its sacramental life.

(3) *A continued Pentecost.* It is easy to lay such emphasis on the Church as the Body of Christ that the rôle of the Holy Spirit is forgotten. But, as we have said, in their work among men Son and Spirit are complementary to one another, and this is as true in the doctrine of the Church as it is elsewhere. While Ignatius said "where Christ is, there is the Catholic Church," Irenaeus wrote with equal truth "where the Church is, there is the Spirit, and where the Spirit is, there is the Church."[245] The Church, precisely because it is the Body of Christ, is also the temple and dwelling place of the Spirit.

The Holy Spirit is a Spirit of freedom. While Christ unites us, the Holy Spirit ensures our infinite diversity in the Church: at Pentecost the tongues of fire were "cloven" or divided, descending *separately* upon each one of those present. The gift of the Spirit is a gift to the Church, but it is at the same time a personal gift, appropriated by each in his own way. There are

---

242. *To the Smyrnaeans*, viii, 2.
243. *Dogmatic Theology*, Athens, 1907, 262–5 (in Greek).
244. From a hymn by J. M. Neale.
245. *Against the Heresies*, III, xxiv, 1.

diversities of gifts, but the same Spirit" (I Cor 12:4). Life in the Church does not mean the ironing out of human variety, nor the imposition of a rigid and uniform pattern upon all alike, but the exact opposite. The saints, so far from displaying a drab monotony, have developed the most vivid and distinctive personalities. It is not holiness but evil which is dull.

Such in brief is the relation between the Church and God. This Church—the icon of the Trinity, the Body of Christ, the fullness of the Spirit—is both *visible* and *invisible,* both *divine* and *human.* It is visible, for it is composed of concrete congregations, worshipping here on earth; it is invisible, for it also includes the saints and the angels. It is human, for its earthly members are sinners; it is divine, for it is the Body of Christ. There is no separation between the visible and the invisible, between (to use western terminology) the Church militant and the Church triumphant, for the two make up a single and continuous reality. "The Church visible, or upon earth, lives in complete communion and unity with the whole body of the Church, of which Christ is the Head."[246] It stands at a point of intersection between the Present Age and the Age to Come, and it lives in both Ages at once.

Orthodoxy, therefore, while using the phrase "the Church visible and invisible," insists always that there are not two Churches, but one. As Khomiakov said:

> It is only in relation to man that it is possible to recognize a division of the Church into visible and invisible; its unity is, in reality, true and absolute. Those who are alive on earth, those who have finished their earthly course, those who, like the angels, were not created for a life on earth, those in future generations who have not yet begun their earthly course, are all united together in one Church, in one and the same grace of God. . . . The Church, the Body of Christ, manifests forth and fulfils itself in time, without changing its essential unity or inward life of grace. And therefore, when we speak of "the Church visible and invisible," we so speak only in relation to man.[247]

The Church, according to Khomiakov, *is accomplished on earth without losing its essential characteristics;* it is, in Georges Florovsky's words, "the living image of eternity within time."[248] This is a cardinal point in Orthodox teaching. Orthodoxy does not believe merely in an ideal Church, invisible and heavenly. This "ideal Church" exists visibly on earth as a concrete reality.

Yet Orthodoxy does not forget that there is a human element in the Church as well as a divine. The dogma of Chal-

cedon must be applied to the Church as well as to Christ. Just as Christ the God-Man has two natures, divine and human, so in the Church there is a synergy or cooperation between the divine and the human. Yet between Christ's humanity and that of the Church there is this obvious difference, that the one is perfect and sinless, while the other is not yet fully so. Only a part of the humanity of the Church—the saints in heaven—has attained perfection, while here on earth the Church's members often misuse their human freedom. The Church on earth exists in a state of tension: it is already the Body of Christ, and thus perfect and sinless, and yet, since its members are imperfect and sinful, it must continually become what it is.

But the sin of man cannot affect the essential nature of the Church. We must not say that because Christians on earth sin and are imperfect, therefore the Church sins and is imperfect; for the Church, even on earth, is a thing of heaven, and cannot sin.[249] Saint Ephraim of Syria rightly spoke of "the Church of the penitents, the Church of those who perish," but this Church is at the same time the icon of the Trinity. How is it that the members of the Church are sinners, and yet they belong to the communion of saints? "The mystery of the Church consists in the very fact that *together* sinners become *something different* from what they are as individuals; this 'something different' is the Body of Christ."[250]

Such is the way in which Orthodoxy approaches the mystery of the Church. The Church is integrally linked with God. It is a new life according to the image of the Holy Trinity, a life in Christ and in the Holy Spirit, a life realized by participation in the sacraments. The Church is a single reality, earthly and heavenly, visible and invisible, human and divine.

The Unity and Infallibility of the Church

"The Church is one. Its unity follows of necessity from the unity of God."[251] So wrote Khomiakov in the opening words of his famous essay. If we take seriously the bond between God and His Church, then we must inevitably think of the

---

246. Khomiakov, *The Church is One,* section 9.

247. Ibid., section 1.

248. "Sobornost: The Catholicity of the Church," in *The Church of God,* edited by E. L. Mascall, 63.

249. See the *Declaration on Faith and Order* by the Orthodox Delegates at Evanston in 1954, where this point is put very clearly.

250. J. Meyendorff, "What Holds the Church Together?" in the *Ecumenical Review,* vol. XII (1960), 298.

251. *The Church Is One,* section 1.

Church as one, even as God is one: there is only one Christ, and so there can be only one Body of Christ. Nor is this unity merely ideal and invisible; Orthodox theology refuses to separate the "invisible" and the "visible Church," and therefore it refuses to say that the Church is invisibly one but visibly divided. No: the Church is one, in the sense that here on earth there is a single, visible community which alone can claim to be the one true Church. The "undivided Church" is not merely something that existed in the past, and which we hope will exist again in the future: it is something that exists here and now. Unity is one of the essential characteristics of the Church, and since the Church on earth, despite the sinfulness of its members, retains its essential characteristics, it remains and always will remain visibly one. There can be schisms *from* the Church, but no schisms *within* the Church. And while it is undeniably true that, on a purely human level, the Church's life is grievously impoverished as a result of schisms, yet such schisms cannot affect the essential nature of the Church.

In its teaching upon the visible unity of the Church, Orthodoxy stands far closer to Roman Catholicism than to the Protestant world. But if we ask how this visible unity is maintained, Rome and the east give somewhat different answers. For Rome the unifying principle in the Church is the Pope whose jurisdiction extends over the whole body, whereas Orthodox do not believe any bishop to be endowed with universal jurisdiction. What then holds the Church together? Orthodox answer, the act of communion in the sacraments. The Orthodox theology of the Church is above all else a *theology of communion*. Each local Church is constituted, as Ignatius saw, by the congregation of the faithful, gathered round their bishop and celebrating the Eucharist; the Church universal is constituted by the communion of the heads of the local Churches, the bishops, with one another. Unity is not maintained from without by the authority of a Supreme Pontiff, but created from within by the celebration of the Eucharist. The Church is not monarchical in structure, centered round a single hierarch; it is collegial, formed by the communion of many hierarchs with one another, and of each hierarch with the members of his flock. The act of communion therefore forms the criterion for membership of the Church. An individual ceases to be a member of the Church if he severs communion with his bishop; a bishop ceases to be a member of the Church if he severs communion with his fellow bishops.

Orthodoxy, believing that the Church on earth has remained and must remain visibly one, naturally also believes itself to be that one visible Church. This is a bold claim, and to many it will seem an arrogant one; but this is to misunderstand the spirit in which it is made. Orthodox believe that they are the true Church, not on account of any personal merit, but by the grace of God. They say with Saint Paul: "We are no better than pots of earthenware to contain this treasure; the sovereign power comes from God and not from us" (II Cor 4:7). But while claiming no credit for themselves, Orthodox are in all humility convinced that they have received a precious and unique gift from God; and if they pretended to men that they did not possess this gift, they would be guilty of an act of betrayal in the sight of heaven. [. . .]

[. . .] Does it therefore follow that anyone who is not visibly within the Church is necessarily damned? Of course not; still less does it follow that everyone who is visibly within the Church is necessarily saved. As Augustine wisely remarked: "How many sheep there are without, how many wolves within?"[252] While there is no division between a "visible" and an "invisible Church," yet there may be members of the Church who are not visibly such, but whose membership is known to God alone. If anyone is saved, he must *in some sense* be a member of the Church; *in what sense,* we cannot always say.

From Timothy Ware, *The Orthodox Church* (Hammondsworth, NY: Ringwood, 1963), 243–52.

  Chrysostomos Konstantinidis examines the complicated issue of tradition in "The Significance of the Eastern and Western Traditions within Christendom." In analyzing the many traditions of the Christian Churches and the Churches' self-understanding of tradition, Konstantinidis sheds light on the structures and practices of Christian Churches in the East and in the West.

CHRYSOSTOMOS KONSTANTINIDIS

"The Significance of the Eastern and Western Traditions within Christendom"

1. The importance and the difficulties of the subject

There is no doubt that the subject "The significance of the Eastern and Western Traditions within Christendom"

---

252. *Homilies on John*, XIV, 12.

has as great an interest from the Orthodox point of view as from the Protestant and ecumenical. Certainly, in the extensive interconfessional dialogues of the last decades within the ecumenical movement, the discussion of the subject of "Tradition" has acquired great importance, especially in the examination of the relation of this fundamental conception with our particular "traditions."

Of course, the study of this subject presents many difficulties. They mainly spring from the historical and theological background of the term "tradition," from the diversity in meaning and interpretation which has been or can be given to this term, and from Orthodox and Protestant reactions, which put the Orthodox Church on guard lest its fundamental teaching about Tradition should be endangered, and which require the Protestant world not to abandon any of the old "theses" of Protestantism, which wishes to continue faithful to its biblical foundation.

Therefore, the subject of Tradition is pre-eminently delicate for the Orthodox speaker as well as for his Protestant colleague.

I shall try, however, to analyse this subject from the broadest possible perspective. I know it is not possible to use the word "Tradition" properly as far as Protestantism is concerned. In the meantime, it is known that our Protestant brothers have sufficiently progressed in the discovery and adoption of some of the basic elements of "Tradition." We should not forget that a special Commission within the Faith and Order Commission under the name "Tradition and traditions" brought Orthodox and Protestant theologians together for a free discussion on this subject, a subject which had never been brought up before.

2. The historical misunderstanding and the common theological ground of understanding of Tradition

I sincerely believe that a broader study and inquiry into the notion of Tradition will be precious for the contact and mutual understanding of our two worlds. It only needs an unprejudiced understanding on both sides about this subject; it is necessary for the Protestants to understand what is meant by Tradition in Orthodoxy, and for us Orthodox to know what the term "tradition" would mean in Protestantism.

Before any study or inquiry is made of the subject, I think we should recognize that there certainly is a historical misunderstanding about tradition, but that, at the same time, there also exists a minimum theological ground of common

understanding and acceptance of the meaning and reality of what we call Tradition in our Church.

In fact, in the way the subject is to be treated, I shall confine myself to these two main points: the historical misunderstanding, and the common theological ground of understanding, of Tradition.

I. Tradition and Its Significance in the Early Church

3. Revelation and Tradition

I shall not discuss the well-known points of our Theology concerning the ways of transmission of the revelation to the primitive Church. We know that Scripture was not the only and exclusive way of this transmission. The "unbound" word of God was free to be transmitted, and in fact inevitably was transmitted from the very first through the spoken word and oral teaching. The Christian message was not "written." It was oral, it was a preaching by word of mouth delivered to the Church.

The testimonies of Our Lord (Mt 28:9; Mk 16:15; Acts 1:8), of the Apostles (Jn 20:30; 21:35; II Jn 12; I Cor 11:34; 15:11) and of Saint Paul (I Tim 6:20; II Tim 1:13 and 2:2; Rom 16:17) are clear on this point. The Apostles never accepted anything written from the Lord; they received by His own word in their hearts the Revelation made by the Holy Spirit; and the believers, similarly, received the word of God from the mouth of the Apostles "ἐξ ἀκοῆς" [what is heard] (Rom 10:17) and preserved in their hearts the delivered Truth by the Grace of the Paraclete, who co-operates in the preaching of the word of God. Thus was created by tradition the *depositum*, the "παρακαταθήκη" [deposit] of the revealed Truth.

4. The "written" and "unwritten" transmission of the Revelation

We are, therefore, face to face with a very early "oral tradition," which was anterior to Scripture, and from which the contents of the New Testament have been compiled. Certainly the whole "oral tradition" was not exhausted, and besides, it did not cease to remain what it formerly was, that is to say Scripture has never replaced tradition.

In this parallel manifestation of the Holy Revelation we only have the "written" and the "unwritten" tradition of the word of God. The written tradition, being completed by the last of the inspired Apostles, formed the Canon of the New Testament. The unwritten tradition of the Apostles, on the other hand, which was formed under the action of the Paraclete, has been preserved in the Church, first orally and then in the form of literary monuments, as the great Tradition of the Church, i.e. the "apostolic," or the "ecclesiastical," or simply the "holy" Tradition, according to our conceptions.

5. Apostolic and Ecclesiastical Tradition

Certainly, from all that we are saying now, it is evident that Tradition, when considered in temporal perspective, can be distinguished, from the quantitative as well as the qualitative point of view, in two different forms: as apostolic tradition and as ecclesiastical tradition. These two terms are not mutually exclusive. The Apostolic Tradition is also ecclesiastical, but the ecclesiastical is large enough to contain some other forms of tradition, which are "forms of tradition *in the Church*," but not directly apostolic. The others do not interest us here.

When we say Apostolic and ecclesiastical Tradition we mean only those elements which concern the faith and the salvation of mankind, and which come from the Lord and the Apostles. These elements have been preserved, interpreted and formulated in the Church without losing any element of their apostolicity and have been still further enriched from the treasure of the ecclesiastical *"depositum"* of the faith.

The historical misunderstanding between us and our Protestant brothers appears at this point. And here is the reason.

6. Points of transition from the Apostolic to the Ecclesiastical Tradition

Though we Orthodox consider it quite normal to have some sort of transition from the unwritten to the written word and vice versa, since these are the only two ways of transmission and preservation of the revelation by man, Protestants find this difficult to understand.

The revelation and its preservation and interpretation have known, in the inevitable perspective of time, some quite normal points of transition. There was first a relatively long period of "oral transmission" of the revelation (which we can name "tradition," with a small "t"); this period was followed by a second one, a period of "written transmission" of the revelation (which we can name "Scripture," with a capital "S"); this second period was followed by a third one, which produced more and more varied forms of written expression, interpretation and formulation of the formerly

delivered Truth (which we can name "scripture," with a small "s"); and finally the fourth state has been derived from the previous one, and this we may name "Tradition" in the proper sense of the word.

7. The contents of the Holy Tradition

This conception can be represented graphically as follows:

t-radition — S-cripture — s-cripture — T-radition
/ t- S- s- T- /

I do not think there is any natural evolution of these ideas besides those which can thus be represented. Only in a perspective such as this can one understand why we, Orthodox, consider Holy Scripture and Holy Tradition as two sources of the revelation of equal weight and authority, as two equivalent sources of the dogma and of supernatural faith. It is only through this prism that one can understand how Holy Tradition can be divided into Tradition concerning the faith and consequently of equal authority to the Holy Scripture, and traditions of a more ecclesiastical character, that is to say, historical, liturgical, canonical, and other traditions, changeable, and with only relative authority; because they do not affect, of course, the faith and dogmas of the Orthodox Church.

In the fourth period of this transition, which we named "Tradition" with a capital "T," we find that the teaching of the Church, which the Lord and the Apostles transmitted and which had been preserved in the Church, has already been incorporated in concrete literary monuments, which are the principal forms of Holy Tradition. They are (1) the valid and authentic interpretation of Scripture in the Church; (2) the official formulations and confessions of faith; (3) the formulations, definitions and creeds of the Ecumenical Councils; (4) the larger accords of the teaching of the Fathers and ecclesiastical authors, in other words, the *"Consensum Patrum"*; (5) the forms, acts and institutions of worship and liturgies of the Early Church, which form the living expression of the apostolic spirit in the ways of worship in the Church. Everything which remains outside these forms of the *"depositum"* of faith of the Church can be a tradition in the Church, but it cannot be Tradition of dogma and saving faith; it is not the Holy Tradition.

This Tradition—static in its divine origin, like Scripture, but dynamic in its external forms—remained integral and undivided in the Church, as a living and continuous expression of the revelation.

8. The ecclesiological meaning of This Tradition

It is not necessary to say what is the significance of this integral and undivided Tradition of Christendom. Primarily it is of ecclesiological importance, because tradition, stable and undivided, not only projects the divine and continually living substance of the Church, but becomes also the most secure criterion of its unity. Here is how Saint Athanasius the Great expresses this truth: "There is" he says "a primary tradition and teaching and faith of the Catholic Church, which the Lord Jesus gave, the apostles preached and the Fathers preserved: on it the whole Church has been founded."[253]

This Tradition, described by Saint Athanasius, is the ecclesiological element of our Christian unity, and the uniting element of the undivided Church. The refusal of this Tradition is equivalent to having no faith. "One who does not believe according to the tradition of the catholic Church," says Saint John of Damascus, "is without faith."[254]

II. The Dichotomy of Tradition in the Schism: Eastern and Western Traditions

9. Tradition and the Schism between East and West

The second aspect of Tradition within the Church is that which begins with the manifestations of the historical division of the Church into the Eastern and Western Churches, as we are accustomed to say.

Two different types of tradition have been formed under different local and temporary limits. These are the "differentiated Traditions of the East and the West." And so the subject of Tradition appears, once more, as a clear ecclesiological theme; the divided Church appears in divided Tradition, and this dichotomized Tradition corresponds to a Church divided in itself.

10. The Continuity of Tradition

Certainly, at this point it is necessary to say that Tradition, in spite of this historical dichotomy, has not ceased to exist as the one, integral and undivided Tradition of the Church. In its basic and supernatural meaning it cannot but continue to be an unbroken whole within the "One, Holy, Apostolic and Catholic Church." But in its external form and its historical conception, as a different way of cultivation of the revealed Truth by the different Christian communities, Tradition can be considered as cultivated in any other Christian community or confession while being in error.

This means that Tradition is "One," in principle, and "Undivided," as the revealed Truth; but it does not prevent us from speaking about some "traditions," which are met within the differentiated forms of the Church. This is the case of the multiple examples of all heresies; but it became more evident in the case of the great Schism of the 11th century and has been multiplied in later centuries.

The existence of one or more parallel traditions beside the one Tradition of the Church does not obscure or destroy the sacred character of the one Tradition; in the same way erroneous interpretations of the one revealed Truth do not destroy the Truth itself, but only damage the man who is misled by them.

If therefore we speak about the Eastern and Western Traditions separately, or about Tradition and the "traditions" within other Churches, we must not forget that above these two, the former or the latter, and even above the different "traditions" or forms of tradition, stands the One Undivided Unbroken Tradition of the Church. And according to our teaching, the Eastern Tradition is not one of the regular forms of Tradition, but it is the Holy Tradition of the Church of Christ itself.

11. The significance of dichotomized Tradition

In spite of the continuing and unbroken Tradition of the Church, the existence of other forms of "traditions" within divided Christendom raises the question of the significance of this differentiated or dichotomized Tradition in the Church.

We can, I think, summarize our thoughts about this problem in the following points:

(1) The differentiated forms of Tradition emphasize the significance of Tradition itself, one and undivided in its base and substance.

(2) The measure to which they depart from the one and undivided Tradition of the Lord and the Apostles determines the ecclesiological depth of the Church to which they belong. The *vestigia Ecclesiae* and the *"vestigia Traditionis"* are directly proportional.

---

253. Athanasius, *Epist. ad. Serapionem*, 28, PG 26, 593.

254. John of Damascus, *Expositio Fidei Orthodoxae*, IV, 10, PG 94, 1128.

(3) No matter how far these differentiated forms of Tradition depart from each other, yet often they still co-exist in such a way that the question of unity becomes the occasion of their meeting.

(4) The longer these differentiated forms of Tradition follow and get to know each other, the more their points are in contact, the more positive and beneficent is the influence of true Tradition upon them, and the greater is the possibility of their re-integration into the One Tradition.

III. Tradition and Traditions

12. The Protestant Schism and the Polytomy of Tradition

When the second great Schism in Christendom took place, i.e., the Reformation, the theme of the tradition became broader. The already separated Western Tradition developed into the newly appeared Reformation under a quite different theological but also historical conception.

13. The theological conception of Tradition in Protestantism

Theologically the subject of Tradition became a point of dissension between Protestantism and the one Tradition of the Eastern Church on one hand, and on the other between Protestantism and the differentiated form of tradition in the Latin West.

An anti-traditional system, depending onesidedly on the Bible as Protestantism did, ignored Tradition. I will not examine the well-known thesis of Protestant theology on this subject. I think it is enough to say that Tradition is rejected as a source of revelation equivalent to Scripture. A first and common period of Tradition for the Early Church is accepted, as a historical reality, but without any ecclesiastical authority.

14. The historical reality of the "traditions" in Protestantism

Though this is the theological conception of the Tradition in Protestantism, our subject, from the historical point of view, can be presented as follows:

All forms of Protestantism, even the most liberal ones, have their own "traditions," some of which spring from their historical background, and some others have been created in their own bodies. I say "they have their own 'traditions,'" because no Church can be conceived to be without traditions.

15. "New churches—old traditions"

Do not let us consider this an exaggeration! Take the example of the young churches that arose from missionary work. It is not possible in the long history of missionary work, for one newly founded church or community not to be the outcome of one of the traditions, of one of the old forms of Christianity. No one of these churches is a "new church" in the proper sense of the word, i.e., as new a church as the Church of Pentecost, because the Church is not a continuously repeated foundation *ex nihilo,* exactly as the created world is not a repetition of the six-day creation *ex nihilo.* The multiplication of the number of churches is a continuation for ever of the Church, which has been founded by the Lord's sacrifice. Therefore, new forms of Christianity, or new churches and traditions, are things that presuppose each other.

16. What Do the "traditions" represent in Protestantism?

Needless to say these "traditions" present some common points with the One Tradition of the Church, but they have also their different character which renders them "Protestant traditions" in the proper sense of the word.

These "traditions" are the most positive reflection of the world from which the Protestant communities arose. They are in general "western traditions." They include many historical, racial, national, rational and linguistic elements, and many other elements of mentality, psychology, civilization and culture, but also elements which are clearly theological and ecclesiological, which are common to the whole of Christianity.

The same "traditions" are at the same time realities which Protestantism has lived and still lives, or has created and still creates in its body in every moment of history. In personal terms, these "traditions" contain all the figures of the active Reformation, from Luther and Calvin, Zwingli and Melanchthon up to the last missionary of today. The same "traditions" find their reflection in all the realities which make up the Protestantism of yesterday and today. This Protestantism with its varieties and ramifications, with its historical confessions and statements of faith, with its contemporary tendencies and currents, with its interconfessional and unionist dispositions and desires, with its mutual "repulsions" as well as its rivalries, with its missionary experiences, with its special way of thinking and living the commandments of the Holy Gospel, and finally with its proper "Theology" is the most inclusive conception of what we define as "western traditions." And we Orthodox are called to know and to evaluate exactly these "traditions."

17. These "traditions" and the teaching of the Lord and the Apostles

What are these "traditions" for our Protestant brothers? The answer is given in an antinomy: their "traditions" are not the One Tradition, but the teaching of their communities, their message to the world. This teaching is biblical, and reflects the teaching of the Lord and the Apostles.

Of course, from the Orthodox point of view, such a conception can be disputed. On the other hand, it is not possible to forget that this teaching of Protestantism claims for itself a true "churchly" or "ecclesial" character. Therefore, automatically, this teaching acquires a notion of Tradition. What kind of Tradition? Here, as the Orthodox see it, is the most essential "crisis" of contemporary Protestantism. It is not the Tradition of the "One, Holy, Apostolic and Catholic Church" which safeguards the integrity of revealed Truth. But it appears to us to be a kind of *"consensus,"* a kind of symphony of the individuals under the Grace of Christ, a kind of accord which is itself quite subjective and elastic. In other words, it is an accord of each Christian member of the Church, illuminated by the Holy Spirit in the reading, understanding and interpretation of the Bible. This accord presupposes the presence of the Paraclete, but there is no criterion to render this presence more tangible to the Christian.

18. The "traditions" and the "consensus" of Individuals

In fact, such a conception of the *"consensus"* renders the *"crisis"* within Protestantism more evident. It is constrained to find some "non-biblical criteria" for the correct interpretation and understanding of revealed Truth. We may, I think, ask at this point:

Would it not be of great utility for our Protestant brothers to emphasize here that these criteria lie in what we call "Tradition"? We said: In Tradition we have the whole teaching of the Church; it is the teaching of the Lord and the Apostles; it is a *depositum fidei,* parallel to Holy Scripture.

And something else: Would not this *"consensus"* of individuals be more positive and theologically more concentrated if accepted as a *"consensus Traditionis"*? And the Grace of Christ which assists and illuminates the individuals, can it not be considered as the Grace which acts upon individuals as fathers of the Church, and upon the Church itself, when it interprets and formulates its dogmas and its saving truth? Does not this accord of individuals have a greater value when it has the character of catholicity, antiquity and of larger numerical agreement? On this point we need to bear in mind the definition of Tradition given by Saint Vincent of Lerins: *Quod semper, quod ubique, quod ab omnibus creditum est, hoc est vere proprieque catholicum.*[255]

19. The "traditions" in Protestantism and their relations with Orthodoxy

Let us now look at the "traditions" within Protestantism from the above perspective and emphasize the points in which these "traditions" present some points of contact with our Orthodox world, and not the points in which, theologically, Protestantism diverges from us on the subject of Tradition.

In fact, if we examine the "western traditions" through this prism, we see that in the vicissitudes of history, while the Roman Catholic tradition continuously goes further away from the Eastern Tradition, the Protestant form of the Western tradition followed another course, as Orthodoxy also followed a course which led towards Protestant "traditions."

In the presence of the extreme developments of the conception of Tradition within the Papacy, the Protestant world showed greater sympathy for the Orthodox Tradition, even though Protestantism rejected the notion of the Holy Tradition.

On the other hand, Eastern Orthodoxy tried to present its Tradition in a way which would be comprehensible for Protestant minds. This is the significance, I think, of most of the relations between Orthodoxy and the churches of the Reformation in these last four centuries. The Orthodox confessions of faith of the 17th and 18th centuries, the long exchange of letters, the published "Tomoi," the mutual contacts and visits between Schools and individuals, and also the political and diplomatic relations between the Protestant authorities of the West and Greek (and Slavonic) speaking Orthodoxy, were the most natural ways for Orthodoxy to make its Tradition comprehensible in this sympathetic world of Protestantism. And all these ways were neither the refusal of, or treachery towards, Orthodox teaching; nor were they suspicious means by which proselytism to Orthodoxy threatened any member of the communities of the western traditions. If we are ac-

---

255. Vincent of Lerins, *Commonitorium,* 2, PL 50, 640.

customed to speak about some influences of Protestantism upon Orthodoxy, I think, we must remember that beyond any question of influence, the biggest preoccupation of Orthodox writers was to render the Orthodox Tradition more and more comprehensible to the Protestant world.

It is another question whether the critical antinomy in Protestantism, which refused to accept any Tradition above its own "traditions," could permit our Protestant brothers to come to a real restoration of the conception of Tradition, to a real "re-traditioning."

Conclusion

20. "Retraditioning," ecclesiological restoration and reunion

"Retraditioning"! Let us finish this paper by this term. Please do not consider it either too bold or too unusual.

My Protestant brothers will agree with me that the period from the beginning of the Reformation until now was a period of "detraditioning" in spite of some notions of "traditions" which they have cultivated from time to time. They will also agree that this period of detraditioning was negative for ecclesiological restoration. We have already said: Church and Tradition are bound together.

If we now take into consideration that with the delay of ecclesiological restoration, any desire and attempt for reunion must remain unfruitful, we can understand, I think, what is meant by "retraditioning."

We cannot consider ecclesiological restoration and reunion except as a sincere effort for "retraditioning."

From Constantin Patelos, ed., *The Orthodox Church in the Ecumenical Movement* (Geneva: World Council of Churches, 1978), 222–30.

THE RADICAL REFORMATION CHURCH

Many of the Reformers rejected the authority of the Roman Church, along with its traditions. This rejection became radicalized in the Anabaptist movement and its doctrine of "separation." **Conrad Grebel** was born in 1498 and died in 1526 from complications associated with the plague, which he caught while in prison for disrupting religious unity in Zurich. His 1524 *Letters to Thomas Müntzer* (who was born in 1489 and executed on May 27, 1525, for his leading role in the Peasants' Revolt in Thuringia in 1524–25) provides a theological blueprint for what would become known as the Anabaptist ("those who baptize again") movement.

CONRAD GREBEL

Letters to Thomas Müntzer by Conrad Grebel and Friends

Zurich, September 5, 1524[256]

To the sincere and true proclaimer of the gospel, Thomas Müntzer at Allstedt in the Hartz, our true and beloved brother with us in Christ: May peace, grace, and mercy from God, our Father, and Jesus Christ, our Lord, be with us all. Amen.[257]

Dear Brother Thomas:

For God's sake do not marvel that we address thee without title, and request thee like a brother to communicate with us by writing, and that we have ventured, unasked and unknown to thee, to open communications between us. God's Son, Jesus Christ, who offers himself as the one master and head of all who would be saved, and bids us be brethren by the one common word given to all brethren and believers, has moved us and compelled us to make friendship and brotherhood and to bring the following points to thy attention. Thy writing of two tracts on fictitious faiths[258] has further prompted us. Therefore we ask that thou wilt take it kindly for the sake of Christ our Saviour. If God wills, it shall serve and work to our good. Amen.

Just as our forebears fell away from the true God and from the one true, common, divine Word, from the divine institutions, from Christian love and life, and lived without God's law and gospel in human, useless, unchristian customs and ceremonies, and expected to attain salvation therein, yet fell far short of it, as the evangelical preachers have declared, and to some extent are still declaring, so today too every man wants to be saved by superficial faith, without fruits of faith, without baptism of trial and probation, without love and hope, without right Christian practices, and wants to persist in all the old manner of personal vices, and in the common ritualistic and anti-Christian customs of baptism and of the Lord's Supper, in disrespect for the divine Word and in re-

256. The Letters are not only a documentation of Evangelical Anabaptism. They also constitute a *pièce justificative* on both sides of the contemporary scholarly controversy as to whether Anabaptism took its rise in Saxony in opposition to Luther and was hence *primitively* revolutionary (Müntzer and Münster), as the Leipzig Luther scholars Heinrich Böhmer and Karl Holl and their schools have held, or whether it rose in Switzerland in opposition to Zwingli and was hence consistently pacifistic as the American Mennonite scholar Harold Bender and his associates maintain.

257. The phrasing evokes the memory of the introductory verses of the Epistle to Titus and the two to Timothy.

258. *Von dem getichten glawben* (1524) and *Protestation odder Empietung vnnd tzum anfang von dem rechten Christenglawben vnnd der tawffe* (1524).

spect for the word of the pope and of the antipapal preachers, which yet is not equal to the divine Word nor in harmony
with it. In respecting persons and in manifold seduction there
is grosser and more pernicious error now than ever has been
since the beginning of the world. In the same error we too
lingered as long as we heard and read only the evangelical
preachers who are to blame for all this, in punishment for our
sins. But after we took Scripture in hand too, and consulted it
on many points, we have been instructed somewhat and have
discovered the great and harmful error of the shepherds, of
ours too, namely, that we do not daily beseech God earnestly
with constant groaning to be brought out of this destruction
of all godly life and out of human abominations, to attain to
the true faith and divine practice. The cause of all this is false
forbearance, the hiding of the divine Word, and the mixing
of it with the human. Aye, we say it harms all and frustrates
all things divine. There is no need of specifying and reciting.

While we were marking and deploring these facts, thy
book against false faith and baptism[259] was brought to us, and
we were more fully informed and confirmed, and it rejoiced
us wonderfully that we found one who was of the same
Christian mind with us and dared to show the evangelical
preachers their lack, how that in all the chief points they
falsely forbear and act and set their own opinions, and even
those of Antichrist, above God and against God, as befits not
the ambassadors of God to act and preach. Therefore we
beg and admonish thee as a brother by the name, the power,
the word, the spirit, and the salvation, which has come to
all Christians through Jesus Christ our Master and Saviour
(*seligmacher*), that thou wilt take earnest heed to preach only
the divine Word without fear, to set up and guard only divine
institutions, to esteem as good and right only what may be
found in pure and clear Scripture, to reject, hate, and curse
all devices, words, customs, and opinions of men, including
thy own.

(1) We understand and have seen that thou hast translated
the Mass into German and hast introduced new German
hymns.[260] That cannot be for the good, since we find nothing taught in the New Testament about singing, no example
of it. Paul scolds the learned among the Corinthians more
than he praises them, because they mumbled in meeting as if
they sang,[261] just as the Jews and the Italians chant their words
song-fashion. (2) Since singing in Latin grew up without divine instruction and apostolic example and custom, without
producing good or edifying, it will still less edify in German
and will create a faith of outward appearance only. (3) Paul
very clearly forbids singing in Eph 5:19 and Col 3:16 since he
says and teaches that they are to speak to one another and
teach one another with psalms and spiritual songs, and if anyone would sing, he should sing and give thanks in his heart.
(4) Whatever we are not taught by clear passages or examples must be regarded as forbidden, just as if it were written:
"This do not; sing not." (5) Christ in the Old and especially in
the New Testament bids his messengers (*botten*) simply proclaim the word. Paul too says that the word of Christ profits
us, not the song. Whoever sings poorly gets vexation by it;
whoever can sing well gets conceit. (6) We must not follow
our notions; we must add nothing to the word and take nothing from it. (7) If thou wilt abolish the Mass, it cannot be
accomplished with German chants, which is thy suggestion
perhaps, or comes from Luther. (8) It must be rooted up by
the word and command of Christ. (9) For it is not planted
by God. (10) The Supper of fellowship Christ did institute
and plant. (11) The words found in Matt, ch. 26, Mark, ch.
14, Luke, ch. 22, and 1 Cor, ch. 11, alone are to be used, no
more, no less. (12) The server from out of the congregation
should pronounce them from one of the Evangelists or from
Paul. (13) They are the words of the instituted meal of fellowship, not words of consecration. (14) Ordinary bread ought
to be used, without idols and additions. (15) For [the latter]
creates an external reverence and veneration of the bread,
and a turning away from the inward. An ordinary drinking
vessel too ought to be used. (16) This would do away with the
adoration and bring true understanding and appreciation of
the Supper, since the bread is nought but bread. In faith, it is
the body of Christ and the incorporation with Christ and the
brethren. But one must eat and drink in the Spirit and love, as
John shows in ch. 6 and the other passages, Paul in 1 Cor, chs.
10 and 11, and as is clearly learned in Acts, ch. 2. (17) Although
it is simply bread, yet if faith and brotherly love precede it, it
is to be received with joy, since, when it is used in the church,
it is to show us that we are truly one bread and one body, and
that we are and wish to be true brethren with one another,
etc. (18) But if one is found who will not live the brotherly
life, he eats unto condemnation, since he eats it without discerning, like any other meal, and dishonors love, which is the
inner bond, and the bread, which is the outer bond. (19) For
also it does not call to his mind Christ's body and blood, the
covenant of the cross, nor that he should be willing to live

---

259. *Protestation.*
260. Grebel may have seen Müntzer's three liturgical works.
261. Cf. 1 Cor 14:9, 16.

and suffer for the sake of Christ and the brethren, of the head and the members. (20) Also it ought not to be administered by thee.[262] That was the beginning of the Mass that only a few would partake, for the Supper is an expression of fellowship, not a Mass and sacrament. Therefore none is to receive it alone, neither on his deathbed nor otherwise. Neither is the bread to be locked away, etc., for the use of a single person, since no one should take for himself alone the bread of those in unity, unless he is not one with himself—which no one is, etc. (21) Neither is it to be used in "temples" according to all Scripture and example, since that creates a false reverence. (22) It should be used much and often. (23) It should not be used without the rule of Christ in Matt 18:15–18, otherwise it is not the Lord's Supper, for without that rule every man will run after the externals. The inner matter, love, is passed by, if brethren and false brethren approach or eat it [together]. (24) If ever thou desirest to serve it, we should wish that it would be done without priestly garment and vestment of the Mass, without singing, without addition. (25) As for the time, we know that Christ gave it to the apostles at supper and that the Corinthians had the same usage. We fix no definite time with us, etc.

Let this suffice, since thou art much better instructed about the Lord's Supper, and we only state things as we understand them. If we are not in the right, teach us better. And do thou drop singing and the Mass, and act in all things only according to the Word, and bring forth and establish by the Word the usages of the apostles. If that cannot be done, it would be better to leave all things in Latin and unaltered and mediated [by a priest]. If the right cannot be established, do not then administer according to thy *own* or the priestly usage of Antichrist. And at least teach how it ought to be, as Christ does in John, ch. 6, and teaches how we must eat and drink his flesh and blood, and takes no heed of backsliding and anti-Christian caution,[263] of which the most learned and foremost evangelical preachers have made a veritable idol and propagated it in all the world. It is much better that a few be rightly taught through the Word of God, believing and walking aright in virtues and practices, than that many believe falsely and deceitfully through adulterated doctrine. Though we admonish and beseech thee, we hope that thou wilt do it of thy own accord; and we admonish the more willingly, because thou hast so kindly listened to our brother[264] and confessed that thou too hast yielded too much, and because thou and Carlstadt[265] are esteemed by us the purest proclaimers and preachers of the purest Word of God. And if ye two rebuke, and justly, those who mingle the words and

customs of men with those of God, ye must by rights cut yourselves loose and be completely purged of popery, benefices, and all new and ancient customs, and of your own and ancient notions. If your benefices, as with us,[266] are supported by interest and tithes, which are both true usury, and it is not the whole congregation which supports you, we beg that ye free yourselves of your benefices. Ye know well how a shepherd should be sustained.

We have good hopes of Jacob Strauss[267] and a few others, who are little esteemed by the slothful scholars and doctors at Wittenberg. We too are thus rejected by our learned shepherds. All men follow them, because they preach a sinful sweet Christ,[268] and they lack clear discernment, as thou hast set forth in thy tracts, which have taught and strengthened beyond measure us who are poor in spirit. And so we are in harmony in all points, except that we have learned with sorrow that thou hast set up tablets,[269] for which we find no text or example in the New Testament. In the Old it [the law] was to be written outwardly, but now in the New it is to be written on the fleshly tablets of the heart, as the comparison of both Testaments proves, as we are taught by Paul, 2 Cor 3:3; Jer 31:33; Heb 8:10; Ezek 36:26. Unless we are mistaken, which we do not think and believe, do thou abolish the tablets again. The matter has grown out of thy own notions, a futile expense, which will increase and become quite idolatrous, and spread into all the world, just as happened with the idolatrous images. It would also create the idea that something external always had to stand and be set up in place of the idols, whereby the unlearned might learn—even if it be only the external word which is so used, as is declared to us, according to all example and commandment of Scripture, especially 1 Cor 14:16 and Col 3:16. This kind of learning from

---

262. The objection here appears to be against the perpetration of the priestly conception of administering the elements. To avoid any suggestion of a sacerdotal act, Müntzer, ordained to the old priesthood, should relinquish to a server from out of the congregation the distribution of the elements.

263. False forbearance.

264. This is undoubtedly Hans Hujuff[. . . .]

265. Andreas Bodenstein von Carlstadt, originally an ally of Luther in Wittenberg, subsequently an opponent on the issues of the Supper and Scripture.

266. That is, in Zwingli's Zurich.

267. Dr. Jacob Strauss, born in Basel, was active as a Lutheran preacher in Tyrol, then in Wertheim and Eisenach. He was conspicuously opposed to usury in his espousal of the cause of the peasants who listed him third (next to Luther and Melanchthon) in the South German Peasant Constitution of Memmingen, February, 1524.

268. The "bitter" as opposed to the "sweet" Christ is pointed up by Müntzer in *Von dem getichten glawben*.

269. Two tablets bearing the Ten Commandments.

this word only might in time become insidious, and even if it would never do any harm, yet I would never want to invent and set up anything new and to follow and imitate the slothful and misleading scholars with their false forbearance, and from my own opinion invent, teach, and establish a single thing.

Go forward with the Word and establish a Christian church with the help of Christ and his rule, as we find it instituted in Matt 18:15–18 and applied in the Epistles. Use determination and common prayer and decision according to faith and love, without command or compulsion. Then God will help thee and thy little sheep to all sincerity, and the singing and the tablets will cease. There is more than enough of wisdom and counsel in the Scripture, how all classes and all men may be taught, governed, instructed, and turned to piety. Whoever will not amend and believe, but resists the Word and action of God and thus persists, such a man, after Christ and his Word and rule have been declared to him and he has been admonished in the presence of the three witnesses and the church,[270] such a man, we say, taught by God's Word, shall not be killed,[271] but regarded as a heathen and publican and let alone.

Moreover, the gospel and its adherents are not to be protected by the sword, nor are they thus to protect themselves, which, as we learn from our brother, is thy opinion and practice. True Christian believers are sheep among wolves, sheep for the slaughter; they must be baptized in anguish and affliction, tribulation, persecution, suffering, and death; they must be tried with fire, and must reach the fatherland of eternal rest, not by killing their bodily, but by mortifying their spiritual, enemies. Neither do they use worldly sword or war, since all killing has ceased with them—unless, indeed, we would still be of the old law. And even there [in the Old Testament], so far as we recall, war was a misfortune after they had once conquered the Promised Land. No more of this.

On the matter of baptism thy book pleases us well, and we desire to be further instructed by thee. We understand that even an adult is not to be baptized without Christ's rule[272] of binding and loosing. The Scripture describes baptism for us thus, that it signifies that, by faith and the blood of Christ, sins have been washed away for him who is baptized, changes his mind, and believes before and after; that it signifies that a man is dead and ought to be dead to sin and walks in newness of life and spirit, and that he shall certainly be saved if, according to this meaning, by inner baptism he lives his faith; so that the water does not confirm or increase faith, as the scholars at Wittenberg say, and [does not] give very great

comfort [nor] is it the final refuge on the deathbed. Also baptism does not save, as Augustine, Tertullian, Theophylact,[273] and Cyprian have taught, dishonoring faith and the suffering of Christ in the case of the old and adult, and dishonoring the suffering of Christ in the case of the unbaptized infants. We hold (according to the following passages: Gen 8:21; Deut 1:39; 30:6; 31:13; and 1 Cor 14:20; Wisdom of Solomon 12:19; 1 Peter 2:2; Rom, chs. 1; 2; 7; 10 [allusions uncertain]; Matt 18:1–6; 19:13–15; Mark 9:33–47; 10:13–16; Luke 18:15–17; etc.) that all children who have not yet come to the discernment of the knowledge of good and evil, and have not yet eaten of the tree of knowledge, that they are surely saved by the suffering of Christ, the new Adam, who has restored their vitiated life, because they would have been subject to death and condemnation only if Christ had not suffered; but they're not yet grown up to the infirmity of our broken nature—unless, indeed, it can be proved that Christ did not suffer for children. But as to the objection that faith is demanded of all who are to be saved, we exclude children from this and hold that they are saved without faith, and we do not believe from the above passages [that children must be baptized], and we conclude from the description of baptism and from the accounts of it (according to which no child was baptized), also from the above passages (which alone apply to the question of children, and all other scriptures do not refer to children), that infant baptism is a senseless, blasphemous abomination, contrary to all Scripture, contrary even to the papacy; since we find, from Cyprian and Augustine, that for many years after apostolic times believers and unbelievers[274] were baptized together for six hundred years, etc. Since thou knowest this ten times better and hast published thy protests against infant baptism, we hope that thou art not acting against the eternal word, wisdom, and commandment of God, according to which only believers are to be baptized, and art not baptizing children. If thou or Carlstadt will not write sufficiently against infant baptism with all that applies, as to how and why we should baptize, etc., I (Conrad Grebel) will try

---

270. Mt 18:15–17.

271. Grebel is thinking here of the Inquisitorial punishment of heretics and Paul's excommunication of the Corinthian sinner in 1 Cor 5:5. . . . [T]here is an interesting parallel [of 1 Cor 5:5] in the Dead Sea Manual of Discipline.

272. That is, without submitting to the rule of Mt 18:15–17.

273. Theophylact (c. 1038–c. 1118), archbishop of Achreda, wrote commentaries on the New Testament widely esteemed.

274. Grebel means that adults from believing homes, like Augustine, and converts from among the unbelieving pagans were alike baptized on confession of faith.

my hand, and I have already begun to reply to all who have hitherto (excepting thyself) misleadingly, and knowingly, written on baptism and have deceived concerning the senseless, blasphemous form of baptism, as for instance Luther, Leo,[275] Osiander,[276] and the men at Strassburg,[277] and some have done even more shamefully. Unless God avert it, I and we all are and shall be surer of persecution on the part of the scholars, etc., than of other people. We pray thee not to use nor to receive the old customs of the Antichrists, such as sacrament, Mass, signs, etc., but to hold to and rule by the word alone, as becomes all ambassadors (*gesanten*), and especially thee and Carlstadt, and ye do more than all the preachers of all nations.

Regard us as thy brethren and take this letter as an expression of great joy and hope toward you through God, and admonish, comfort, and strengthen us as thou art well able. Pray to God the Lord for us that he may come to the aid of our faith, since we desire to believe. And if God will grant us also to pray, we too will pray for thee and all, that we all may walk according to our calling and estate. May God grant it through Jesus Christ our Saviour. Amen. Greet all brethren, the shepherds and the sheep, who receive the word of faith and salvation with desire and hunger, etc.

One point more. We desire an answer, and if thou dost publish anything, that thou wilt send it to us by this messenger and others. We also desire to be informed if thou and Carlstadt are of one mind. We hope and believe it. We commend this messenger to thee, who has also carried letters from us to our brother Carlstadt. And if thou couldst visit Carlstadt, so that ye could reply jointly, it would be a sincere joy to us. The messenger is to return to us; what is lacking in his pay shall be made up when he returns.

God be with us.

Whatever we have not understood correctly, inform and instruct us.

Given at Zurich on the fifth day of September in the year 1524. Conrad Grebel [et al.]

From George Williams and Angel M. Mergal, eds., *Spiritual and Anabaptist Writers: Documents Illustrative of the Radical Reformation and Evangelical Catholicism* (Philadelphia: Westminster, 1957), 73–82.

bishop of Münster in June 1535. *On the Ban: Questions and Answers by Menno Simons* (1550) legislates on matters of practice within the movement. By 1542, Dutch authorities in Leeuwarden had publicized a reward of 500 guilders for Menno's capture, though, remarkably, he eluded arrest for the next two decades.

MENNO SIMONS

On the Ban: Questions and Answers by Menno Simons

QUESTION 1.[278] Is separation a command or is it a counsel of God? *Answer.* Let everyone weigh the words of Christ and of Paul [1 Cor 5:11] . . . and he will discover whether it is a divine commandment or whether it is a counsel. Everything which Paul says in regard to separation he generally speaks in the imperative mode, that is, in a commanding manner. *Expurgate,* that is, purge, 1 Cor 5:7. *Profligate,* that is, drive out. *Sejungere,* that is, withdraw from, 1 Tim 6:5. *Fuge,* that is, flee, Titus 3:9. Again (2 Thess 3:6): We command you, brethren, in the name of our Lord Jesus Christ. I think, brethren, these Scriptures show that it is a command; and even if it were not a command but an advice of God, should we not diligently follow such advice? If my spirit despise the counsel of the Holy Spirit, then I truly acknowledge that my spirit is not of God. And to what end many have come who did not follow God's Spirit, but their own, may be read in many passages of sacred history and may be seen in many instances, at the present time.

QUESTION 2. If any person should not observe this ban and yet be pious otherwise, should such a one be banned on that account? *Answer.* Whoever is pious will show his piety in obedience, and not knowingly or willfully despise and disregard the word, commandment, will, counsel, admonition, and doctrine of God. For if anyone willfully keeps *commercium* with such whose company is forbidden in Scripture, then we must come to the conclusion that he despises the Word of God, yea, is in open rebellion and refractoriness (I speak of those who well know and acknowledge, and yet do not do). For rebellion is as the sin of witchcraft and stubbornness is as iniquity and idolatry (1 Sam 15:23).

⮞ **Menno Simons** (1496–1561), after whom the Mennonite movement was later named, was the pacifist Anabaptist leader in the Netherlands who consolidated, organized, and guided the movement after their members were massacred by the prince-

275. Leo Judae (d. 1541), Zwingli's close associate in Zurich.

276. Andreas Osiander (d. 1552), Lutheran reformer of Nuremberg, who developed special views on justification which led to the Osiander controversy.

277. Particularly Martin Bucer and Capito.

278. This is part of a larger series of questions and answers (*Sommige Vragen*) printed in the Amsterdam edition of 1681 (473–474) and translated into English at Elkhart, Indiana, in 1871.

Since the Scripture admonishes and commands that we shall not associate with such, nor eat with them, nor greet them, nor receive them into our houses, etc.; and then if somebody should say, I will associate with them, I will eat with them, I will greet them in the Lord, and receive them into my house—he would plainly prove that he did not fear the commandment and admonition of the Lord, but that he despised it, rejected the Holy Spirit, and that he trusted, honored, and followed his own opinion rather than the Word of God. Now judge for yourself what kind of sin it is not to be willing to hear and obey God's Word. Paul says (II Thess 3:6, 14): Now we command you, brethren, in the name of our Lord Jesus Christ, that ye withdraw yourselves from every brother that walketh disorderly, and not after the tradition which ye received of us; again: And if any man obey not our word by this epistle, note that man, and have no company with him, that he may be ashamed. Inasmuch as the ban was so strictly commanded by the Lord, and practiced by the apostles (Matt 18:17), therefore we must also use it and obey it, since we are thus taught and enlightened by God, or else we should be shunned and avoided by the congregation of God. This must be acknowledged and confessed.

QUESTION 3. Should husband and wife shun each other on account of the ban—as also parents and children? *Answer.* First, that the rule of the ban is a general rule, and excepts none: neither husband nor wife, neither parent nor child. For God's word judges all flesh with the same judgment and knows no respect of persons. Inasmuch as the rule of the ban is general, excepts none, and is no respecter of persons—therefore it is reasonable and necessary to hear and obey the Word of the Lord in this respect; no matter whether it be husband or wife, parents or children.

Secondly, we say that separation must be made in the congregation; and therefore the husband must consent and vote with the church in the separation of his wife; and the wife in the separation of her husband. If the pious consort must give his consent, then it is also becoming that he also shun her, with the church; for what use is there in the ban when the shunning and avoiding are not connected with it?

Thirdly, we say that the ban was instituted to make ashamed unto reformation. Do not understand this shame as the world is ashamed; but understand as in the conscience, and therefore let it be done with all discretion, reasonableness, and love. If then my husband or wife, parent or child is judged in the church, in the name of and by the power of Christ, to be banned, it becomes us (inasmuch as the evan-

gelical ban is unto reformation), according to the counsel of the Holy Spirit, to seek the reformation of my own body, namely, of my spouse, and also of our nearest kinsfolk as parent or child; for spiritual love must be preferred to anything else. Aside from this I would care for them and provide the temporal necessaries of life, so far as it would be in my power.

Fourthly, we say that the ban was given that we should not be sullied by the leaven of false doctrine or unclean-living flesh, by apostates. And as it is plain that none can corrupt and leaven us more than our own spouses, parents, etc., therefore the Holy Spirit counsels us to shun them, lest they leaven our faith and thus make us ashamed before God. If we love husband or wife, parent or child more than Christ Jesus, we cannot possibly be the disciples of Christ.

Some object to this, saying that there is no divorce but by reason of adultery. This is just what we say; and therefore we do not speak of divorce, but of shunning, and that for the aforementioned reasons. To shunning, Paul (I Cor 7:10) has decidedly consented, although this is not always coupled with adultery; but not to divorce. For divorce is not allowed by the Scripture except by reason of adultery (Matt 5:32; Luke 16:18); therefore we shall never consent to it for other reasons.

Therefore we understand it that the husband should shun his wife, the wife her husband, parents their children and the children their parents when they apostatize. For the rule of the ban is general. They [the godly] must consent, with the church, to the sentence; they must aim at Scriptural shame unto reformation and diligently watch, lest they [themselves] be leavened by them, as said above.

My beloved in the Lord, I would here sincerely pray you that you would make a difference between commandment and commandment and not consider all commandments as equally weighty. For adultery, idolatry, shedding blood, and the like shameful and abominable works of the flesh will be punished more severely than a misunderstanding in regard to the ban, and particularly when not committed willfully and perversely. Therefore beware that in this matter of matrimony you press no one farther than he is taught of God in his heart and that he in his conscience can bear, lest you boil the kid while it is still sucking its mother's milk [cf. Deut 14:21]. On every hand the Scriptures teach that we should bear with the weak. Brethren, it is a delicate matter. I know too well what has been the result of pressing this matter too far by some in my time. Therefore I advise you to point all to the sure and certain ground. And those consciences that are, through the Scripture and the Holy Spirit, free and unencumbered will freely, without the interference of anyone, by the unction of the Holy Spirit and not by human encouragement, do that which he advises, teaches, and commands in the Holy Scripture, if it should be that one's spouse should be banned. For verily I know that whoever obeys the Holy Spirit, with faithful heart will never be made ashamed.

QUESTION 4. Should we greet one that is banned, with the common, everyday greeting, or return our respects at his greeting? For John says (2 John 10f.): If there come any unto you, and bring not this doctrine, receive him not into your house, neither bid him God speed; for he that biddeth him God speed is partaker of his evil deeds. *Answer.* Mildness, politeness, respectfulness, and friendliness to all mankind becomes all Christians. If, then, an apostate should greet me with the common greeting of Good Morning or Good Day and I should be silent; if he should be respectful to me and I should turn my face from him, and bear myself austerely and unfriendly toward him, I might well be ashamed of myself, as Sirach says. For how can such a one be convinced, led to repentance, and be moved to do better by such austerity? The ban is not given to destroy but to build up.

If should be said that John has forbidden such greeting, I for myself would answer that, before my God, I cannot understand that John said this in regard to the everyday greeting, but that he says, if some deceiver should come to us who has left the doctrine of Christ, that we should not receive such a one into our houses, lest he mislead us; and that we should not greet him as a brother lest we have communion with him. But not so with the worldly greeting. For if the worldly greeting have such power in itself that it causes the communion of the vain works of those whom I greet, then it must follow that I would have communion with the fornication, adultery, drunkenness, avarice, idolatry, and bloodshed of the world, whenever I should greet a worldly man with the common greeting or return his compliment. Oh no! But the greeting or kiss of peace does signify communion. Yet if one should have conscientious scruples in this matter, with such a one I do not dispute about it. For it is not worth contending about. But I would much rather see all scruples in regard to this matter removed and have Christian discretion, love, politeness, and respectfulness practiced for [our] improvement rather than stubbornness, unfriendliness, malice, and unmercifulness unto disruption. Brethren, beware of discord and controversy. The Lord grant every

God-fearing person a wholesome understanding of his holy Word. Amen.

QUESTION 5. Are we allowed to show the banned any charity, love, and mercy? *Answer.* Everyone should consider, (1) the exact meaning of the word *commercium;* (2) for what reason and purpose the ban was ordained by the Holy Spirit in the Scriptures; (3) how a real true Christian is reborn, bred, and endowed; (4) how the merciful Father himself acts with those who are already worthy of his judgment and wrath.

All those who can rightly see into these will doubtlessly not deny necessary services, love, and mercy to the banned. For the word *commercium* does not forbid these, but it forbids daily company, conversation, society, and business, as was explained above. The ban is also a work of divine love and not of perverse, unmerciful, heathenish cruelty. A true Christian will serve, aid, and commiserate with everybody; yea, even with his most bitter enemies. Austerity, cruelty, and unmercifulness he hates with all his heart. He has a nature like his Father of whom he is born: for he maketh his sun to rise on the evil and on the good, and sendeth rain on the just and on the unjust. If I, then, be of a different nature than he, I show that I am not his child.

Therefore I say with our faithful brother Dietrich Philips that we should not practice the ban to the destruction of mankind (as the Pharisees did their Sabbath) but to its improvement; and thus we desire to serve the bodies of the fallen, in love, reasonableness, and humility, with our temporal goods when necessary, and their souls with the spiritual goods of the holy Word. And we should rather, with the Samaritan, show mercy to the wounded than to pass by him with the priest and Levite. James says (ch. 2:13): For he shall have judgment without mercy, that hath showed no mercy, and mercy rejoiceth against judgment. Be ye therefore merciful as your Father also is merciful. Blessed are the merciful; for they shall obtain mercy. In short, if we understand the true meaning and nature of the word *commercium,* we understand for what reason and purpose the ban was instituted, how a true Christian is and should be minded; and if we conform ourselves to the example of Christ and of God, then the matter is all helped along. And if we have not this grace, we will shamefully err in this ban and be cruel, unmerciful Christians; from which error and abomination may the gracious Father eternally save all his beloved children.

My brethren, I tell the truth and lie not when I say that I hate with all my heart such unmercifulness and cruel-mindedness. Nor do I wish to be considered a brother of such unmerciful, cruel brethren, if there should be such, unless they desist from such abomination and discreetly follow, in love and mercy, the example of God and Christ. For my heart cannot consent to such unmerciful action which exceeds the cruelty of the heathen and Turks; and by the grace of God I will fight against it with my Lord's sword unto death. For it is against the doctrine of the New Testament, and contrary to the Spirit, mind, and nature of God and Christ, according to which all the Scriptures of the New Testament should be judged and understood. All those who do not understand it thus are already in great error.

But in case my necessary service, charity, love, and mercy should become a *commercium,* or that my soul should thereby be led into corruption, then we confess (the Lord must be praised) that our daily intercourse is forbidden in the Scripture, and that it is better to leave off our charity, love, and mercy than to ensnare our souls thereby and lead them into error. The unction of the Holy Spirit will teach us what we should best do in these matters.

QUESTION 6. Are we allowed to sell to, and buy of, the apostates inasmuch as Paul says (1 Cor 5:11) that we should not have intercourse with them? And yet the disciples bought victuals in Sychar, and the Jews dealt with the Gentiles (John 4:5). *Answer.* That the apostles bought victuals in Sychar proves nothing at all; for many of the Samaritans were a remnant of the ten tribes, as we have sufficiently shown above, from the Holy Scripture. But we do not deny that the Jews dealt with the Gentiles, yet they shunned their *commercium,* that is, their daily association, company, and conversation, and did not eat or drink with them, as the writings of the Evangelist sufficiently and plainly show in many Scriptural passages.

And inasmuch as Christ points us to the Jewish ban or shunning, namely, that as they shunned the Gentiles and sinners, so we should likewise shun an apostate Christian; and as the Jews had dealings with them, although they shunned their daily intercourse in company, association, and conversation; therefore we say that we cannot maintain, either by the Jewish example to which Christ points or by any explicit Scripture, that we should not in any manner deal with the apostate, if no such daily intercourse arises therefrom. For such intercourse with the apostate is strictly prohibited by Scripture; and since it is prohibited, it is manifest that a pious, God-fearing Christian could have no apostate as a regular buyer or seller. For as I have daily to get my cloth, bread, corn, salt, etc., and exchange for it my grain, butter, etc., it cannot fail but that intercourse will arise therefrom. But with a trading which is conducted without such intercourse this is not the case.

And because such business which is carried on without intercourse cannot be shown to be disallowed by virtue of the Scripture, as was said, therefore we would pray all God-fearing brethren and sisters in the Lord, for the sake of God and of love, to act in this matter, as in all others, as reasonable, good, discreet, wise, and prudent Christians and not as vain, reckless, self-conceited, proud, obdurate, and offensive boasters; for a true Christian should always strive after that which is the best and the surest, and follow the pure, unfeigned love, lest he abuse the freedom which he seems to have, to the injury and hindrance of his own soul, to the affliction and destruction of his beloved brethren, to the scornful boasting of the perverse, and to the shameful defamation of the holy Word and the afflicted church of Christ. Besides, I pray and desire in like manner that none will thus in the least be offended at his brother and mistake and judge him by an unscriptural judgment; as he has in this case no reproving example among the Jews nor forbidding word.

O my sincerely beloved brethren, let us sincerely pray for understanding and wisdom that all misunderstanding, error, jealousy, offense, division, and untimely reports may be utterly exterminated, root and branch; that a wholesome understanding, doctrine, friendship, love, edification, and a sound judgment may get under way and prevail. Let everyone look with pure eyes and impartial hearts to the example to which Christ points, and to the wholesome, natural meaning of the holy apostles, and let true, Christian love take precedence; and everyone will know, by the grace of God, how he should act and proceed concerning this matter.

QUESTION 7. Are we allowed to be seated with an apostate in a ship or wagon, or to eat with him at the table of a tavern? *Answer.* The first part of this question . . . we deem childish and useless, since this so often happens without intercourse and must needs happen. As to the second part, namely, [whether] to eat at the table with an apostate, while traveling, we can point the questioner to no surer ground and answer than this, namely, we advise, pray, and admonish every pious Christian, as he loves Christ and his Word, to fear God sincerely, and follow the most certain way, that is, not to eat by or with him; for thereby none can be deceived; and if perchance some God-fearing brother might do so, then let everyone beware, lest he sin against his brother by an unscriptural judgment; for none may judge unless he have the judging word on his side.

Whosoever fears God, whosoever desires to follow after his holy Word, with all his strength loves his brother, seeks to avoid all offense, and desires to walk in the house of God in all peace and unity, will act justly in all things and will not offend or afflict his brethren.

QUESTION 8. Who, according to Scripture, should be banned or excommunicated? *Answer.* Christ says (Matt 18:15–17): If thy brother trespass against thee, etc., and will not hear thee or the witnesses, nor the church, let him be unto thee as a heathen man and a publican. And Paul (1 Cor 5:11): If any man that is called a brother be a fornicator, or covetous, or an idolater, or a railer, or a drunkard, or an extortioner; with such a one do not eat. To this class also belong perjurers, thieves, violent persons, haters, fighters, and all those who walk in open, well-known, damnable works of the flesh, of which Paul enumerates a great many (Rom 1:29; Gal 5:19; 1 Cor 6:9; Eph 5:5). Again, disorderly persons, working not at all, but who are busybodies; such as do not abide in the doctrine of Christ and his apostles and do not walk therein, but are disobedient (2 Thess 3:11, 14). Again, masters of sects. Again, those who give offense, cause dispute and discord concerning the doctrine of Christ and of his apostles. In short, all those who openly lead a shameful, carnal life, and those who are corrupted by a heretical, unclean doctrine (Titus 3:10), and who will not be overcome by the wine and oil of the Holy Spirit, but remain, after they have been admonished and sought to be regained in all love and reasonableness, obdurate in their corrupted walk and opinion. They should, at last, in the name of our Lord Jesus Christ, by the power of the Holy Spirit, that is, by the binding Word of God, be reluctantly but unanimously separated from the church of Christ and thereupon, according to the Scriptures, be shunned in all divine obedience, until they repent.

From George Williams and Angel M. Mergal, eds., *Spiritual and Anabaptist Writers: Documents Illustrative of the Radical Reformation and Evangelical Catholicism* (Philadelphia: Westminster Press, 1957), 263–71. [Ellipsis in original.]

↪ *The Brotherly Union of a Number of Children of God concerning Seven Articles,* or *The Schleitheim Confession* as it is commonly known, was ratified on February 24, 1527, during an assembly of Anabaptists in the northern Swiss village of Schleitheim. The author of the widely circulated *Seven Articles* is believed to be **Michael Sattler,** of Stauffen, Germany, who was born around 1495 and martyred on May 21, 1527, by the Catholic authorities. In

1527, Ulrich Zwingli translated the *Seven Articles* into Latin and attempted to refute it. It was in print in its original German form as early as 1533. John Calvin used a now-lost French translation in his refutation of Anabaptism published in 1544.

MICHAEL SATTLER

The Brotherly Union of a Number of Children of God concerning Seven Articles

The Cover Letter

May joy, peace, mercy from our Father, through the atonement[279] of the blood of Christ Jesus, together with the gift of the Spirit—who is sent by the Father to all believers to [give] strength and consolation and constance in all tribulation until the end, Amen, be with all who love God and all children of light, who are scattered everywhere, wherever they might have been placed by God our Father, wherever they might be gathered in unity of spirit in one God and Father of us all; grace and peace of heart be with you all. Amen.

Beloved brothers and sisters in the Lord; first and primordially we are always concerned for your consolation and the assurance of your conscience (which was sometimes confused), so that you might not always be separated from us as aliens and by right almost completely excluded, but that you might turn to the true implanted members of Christ, who have been armed through patience and the knowledge of self, and thus be again united with us in the power of a godly Christian spirit and zeal for God.

It is manifest with what manifold cunning the devil has turned us aside, so that he might destroy and cast down the work of God, which in us mercifully and graciously has been partially begun. But the true Shepherd of our souls, Christ, who has begun such in us, will direct and teach the same unto the end, to His glory and our salvation, Amen.

Dear brothers and sisters, we who have been assembled in the Lord at Schleitheim on the Randen[280] make known, in points and articles, unto all that love God, that as far as we are concerned, we have been united to stand fast in the Lord as obedient children of God, sons and daughters, who

---

279. See the source text for excellent notes on the translation of "atonement" and other theological terms. (This note is by Gerhart and Udoh.)

280. The "Langer Randen" and the "Hoher Randen" are hills overlooking Schleitheim.

have been and shall be separated from the world in all that we do and leave undone, and (the praise and glory be to God alone) uncontradicted by all the brothers, completely at peace. Herein we have sensed the unity of the Father and of our common Christ as present with us in their Spirit. For the Lord is a Lord of peace and not of quarreling, as Paul indicates.[281] So that you understand at what points this occurred, you should observe and understand [what follows]:

A very great offense has been introduced by some false brothers among us, whereby several have turned away from the faith, thinking to practice and observe the freedom of the Spirit and of Christ. But such have fallen short of the truth and (to their own condemnation) are given over to the lasciviousness and license of the flesh. They have esteemed that faith and love may do and permit everything and that nothing can harm nor condemn them, since they are "believers."

Note well, you members of God in Christ Jesus, that faith in the heavenly Father through Jesus Christ is not thus formed; it produces and brings forth no such things as these false brothers and sisters practice and teach. Guard yourselves and be warned of such people, for they do not serve our Father, but their father, the devil.

But for you it is not so; for they who are Christ's have crucified their flesh with all its lusts and desires.[282] You understand me well, and [know] the brothers whom we mean. Separate yourselves from them, for they are perverted. Pray the Lord that they may have knowledge unto repentance, and for us that we may have constance to persevere along the path we have entered upon, unto the glory of God and of Christ His Son. Amen.[283]

The Seven Articles

The articles we have dealt with, and in which we have been united, are these: baptism, ban, the breaking of bread, separation from abomination, shepherds in the congregation, the sword, the oath.

I. Notice concerning baptism. Baptism shall be given to all those who have been taught repentance and the amendment of life and [who] believe truly that their sins are taken away through Christ, and to all those who desire to walk in the resurrection of Jesus Christ and be buried with Him in death, so that they might rise with Him; to all those who with such an understanding themselves desire and request it from us; hereby is excluded all infant baptism, the greatest and first abomination of the pope. For this you have the reasons and the testimony of the writings and the practice of

the apostles.[284] We wish simply yet resolutely and with assurance to hold to the same.

II. We have been united as follows concerning the ban. The ban shall be employed with all those who have given themselves over to the Lord, to walk after [Him][285] in His commandments; those who have been baptized into the one body of Christ, and let themselves be called brothers or sisters, and still somehow slip and fall into error and sin, being inadvertently overtaken. The same [shall] be warned twice privately and the third time be publicly admonished before the entire congregation according to the command of Christ (Matt. 18). But this shall be done according to the ordering of the Spirit of God before the breaking of bread so that we may all in one spirit and in one love break and eat from one bread and drink from one cup.

III. Concerning the breaking of bread, we have become one and agree thus: all those who desire to break the one bread in remembrance of the broken body of Christ and all those who wish to drink of one drink in remembrance of the shed blood of Christ, they must beforehand be united in the one body of Christ, that is the congregation of God, whose head is Christ, and that by baptism. For as Paul indicates,[286] we cannot be partakers at the same time of the table of the Lord and the table of devils. Nor can we at the same time partake and drink of the cup of the Lord and the cup of devils. That is: all those who have fellowship with the dead works of darkness have no part in the light. Thus all who follow the devil and the world have no part with those who have been called out of the world unto God. All those who lie in evil have no part in the good.

So it shall and must be, that whoever does not share the calling of the one God to one faith, to one baptism, to one spirit, to one body together with all the children of God, may not be made one loaf together with them, as must be true if one wishes truly to break bread according to the command of Christ.[287]

---

281. 1 Cor 14:33.

282. Gal 5:24.

283. This is the conclusion of the introductory letter and of the epistolary style. The "cover letter" is not in the Bern manuscript, and the *Seven Articles* probably circulated most often without it.

284. Mt 28:19; Mk 16:6; Acts 2:38; 8:36; 16:31–33; 19:4.

285. *Nachwandeln*, to walk after, is the nearest approximation in the Schleitheim text to the concept of discipleship (*Nachfolge*) which was later to become especially current among Anabaptists.

286. 1 Cor 10:21.

287. The Anabaptist understanding of close communion refers not to the sacrament but to the participants. It is invalidated not by an unauthorized

IV. We have been united concerning the separation that shall take place from the evil and the wickedness which the devil has planted in the world, simply in this; that we have no fellowship with them, and do not run with them in the confusion of their abominations. So it is; since all who have not entered into the obedience of faith and have not united themselves with God so that they will to do His will are a great abomination before God, therefore nothing else can or really will grow or spring forth from them than abominable things. Now there is nothing else in the world and all creation than good or evil, believing and unbelieving, darkness and light, the world and those who are [come] out of the world, God's temple and idols, Christ and Belial, and none will have part with the other.

To us, then, the commandment of the Lord is also obvious, whereby He orders us to be and to become separated from the evil one, and thus He will be our God and we shall be His sons and daughters.[288]

Further, He admonishes us therefore to go out from Babylon and from the earthly Egypt, that we may not be partakers in their torment and suffering, which the Lord will bring upon them.[289]

From all this we should learn that everything which has not been united with our God in Christ is nothing but an abomination which we should shun. By this are meant all popish and repopish[290] works and idolatry,[291] gatherings, church attendance,[292] winehouses, guarantees and commitments of unbelief, and other things of the kind, which the world regards highly, and yet which are carnal or flatly counter to the command of God, after the pattern of all the iniquity which is in the world. From all this we shall be separated and have no part with such, for they are nothing but abominations, which cause us to be hated before our Christ Jesus, who has freed us from the servitude of the flesh and fitted us for the service of God and the Spirit whom He has given us.

Thereby shall also fall away from us the diabolical weapons of violence—such as sword, armor, and the like, and all of their use to protect friends or against enemies—by virtue of the word of Christ: "you shall not resist evil."[293]

V. We have been united as follows concerning shepherds in the church of God. The shepherd in the church shall be a person according to the rule of Paul,[294] fully and completely, who has a good report of those who are outside the faith. The office of such a person shall be to read and exhort and teach, warn, admonish, or ban in the congregation, and properly to preside among the sisters and brothers in prayer, and in the breaking of bread, and in all things to take care of the body of Christ, that it may be built up and developed, so that the name of God might be praised and honored through us, and the mouth of the mocker be stopped.

He shall be supported, wherein he has need, by the congregation which has chosen him, so that he who serves the gospel can also live there-from, as the Lord has ordered.[295] But should a shepherd do something worthy of reprimand, nothing shall be done with him without the voice of two or three witnesses. If they sin they shall be publicly reprimanded, so that others might fear.

But if the shepherd should be driven away or led to the Lord by the cross,[296] at the same hour another shall be ordained[297] to his place, so that the little folk and the little flock of God may not be destroyed, but be preserved by warning and be consoled.

VI. We have been united as follows concerning the sword. The sword is an ordering of God outside the perfection of Christ. It punishes and kills the wicked, and guards and protects the good. In the law the sword is established[298] over the wicked for punishment and for death, and the secular rulers are established to wield the same.

But within the perfection of Christ only the ban is used for the admonition and exclusion of the one who has sinned, without the death of the flesh,[299] simply the warning and the command to sin no more.

Now many, who do not understand Christ's will for us, will ask: whether a Christian may or should use the sword

---

officiant or an insufficient concept of sacrament, but by the absence of real community among those present.

288. 2 Cor 6:17.

289. Rev 18:4ff.

290. ["Repopish" refers to] having retained or reinstated certain characteristics of Catholicism.

291. "Idolatry" was a current designation in the whole Zwinglian movement for the place of statues and pictures in Catholic worship.

292. *Kilchgang,* literally meaning church attendance, . . . refers to the conformity to established patterns of those who, while perhaps sympathizing with the Anabaptists, still avoided any public reproach by regularly being seen at the state church functions.

293. Mt 5:39.

294. 1 Tim 3:7.

295. 1 Cor 9:14.

296. "Cross" is already by this time a "technical term" designating martyrdom.

297. Perhaps "installed" would be less open to the sacramental misunderstanding. *Verordnet* has no sacramental meaning.

298. "Law" here is a specific reference to the Old Testament. "[S]word" refers to the judicial and police powers of the state.

299. A possible allusion to 1 Cor 5.

against the wicked for the protection and defense of the good, or for the sake of love.

The answer is unanimously revealed: Christ teaches and commands us to learn from Him, for He is meek and lowly of heart and thus we shall find rest for our souls.[300] Now Christ says to the woman who was taken in adultery,[301] not that she should be stoned according to the law of His Father (and yet He says, "what the Father commanded me, that I do")[302] but with mercy and forgiveness and the warning to sin no more, says: "Go, sin no more." Exactly thus should we also proceed, according to the rule of the ban.

Second, is asked concerning the sword: whether a Christian shall pass sentence in disputes and strife about worldly matters, such as the unbelievers have with one another. The answer: Christ did not wish to decide or pass judgment between brother and brother concerning inheritance, but refused to do so.[303] So should we also do.

Third, is asked concerning the sword: whether the Christian should be a magistrate if he is chosen thereto. This is answered thus: Christ was to be made king, but He fled and did not discern the ordinance of His Father. Thus we should also do as He did and follow after Him, and we shall not walk in darkness. For He Himself says: "Whoever would come after me, let him deny himself and take up his cross and follow me."[304] He Himself further forbids the violence of the sword when He says: "the princes of this world lord it over them etc., but among you it shall not be so."[305] Further Paul says, "Whom God has foreknown, the same he has also predestined to be conformed to the image of his Son," etc.[306] Peter also says: "Christ has suffered (not ruled) and has left us an example, that you should follow after in his steps."[307]

Lastly one can see in the following points that it does not befit a Christian to be a magistrate: the rule of the government is according to the flesh, that of the Christians according to the Spirit. Their houses and dwelling remain in this world, that of the Christians is in heaven. Their citizenship is in this world, that of the Christians is in heaven.[308] The weapons of their battle and warfare are carnal and only against the flesh, but the weapons of Christians are spiritual, against the fortification of the devil. The worldly are armed with steel and iron, but Christians are armed with the armor of God, with truth, righteousness, peace, faith, salvation, and with the Word of God. In sum: as Christ our Head is minded, so also must be minded the members of the body of Christ through Him, so that there be no division in the body, through which it would be destroyed. Since then Christ is as is written of Him, so must His members also be the same, so that His body may remain whole and unified for its own advancement and upbuilding. For any kingdom which is divided within itself will be destroyed.[309]

VII. We have been united as follows concerning the oath. The oath is a confirmation among those who are quarreling or making promises. In the law it is commanded that it should be done only in the name of God, truthfully and not falsely. Christ, who teaches the perfection of the law, forbids His [followers] all swearing, whether true nor false; neither by heaven nor by earth, neither by Jerusalem nor by our head; and that for the reason which He goes on to give: "For you cannot make one hair white or black." You see, thereby all swearing is forbidden. We cannot perform what is promised in swearing, for we are not able to change the smallest part of ourselves.[310]

Now there are some who do not believe the simple commandment of God and who say, "But God swore by Himself to Abraham, because He was God (as He promised him that He would do good to him and would be his God if he kept His commandments). Why then should I not swear if I promise something to someone? The answer: hear what Scripture says: "God, since he wished to prove overabundantly to the heirs of His promise that His will did not change, inserted an oath so that by two immutable things we might have a stronger consolation (for it is impossible that God should lie)."[311] Notice the meaning of the passage: God has the power to do what He forbids you, for everything is possible to Him. God swore an oath to Abraham, Scripture says, in order to prove that His counsel is immutable. That means: no one can withstand and thwart His will; thus He can keep His oath. But we cannot, as Christ said above, hold or perform our oath, therefore we should not swear.

Others say that swearing cannot be forbidden by God in the New Testament when it was commanded in the Old, but that it is forbidden only to swear by heaven, earth, Jerusalem, and our head. Answer: hear the Scripture. He who swears by heaven, swears by God's throne and by Him who sits thereon.[312] Observe: swearing by heaven is forbidden, which is only God's throne; how much more is it forbidden to swear

---

300. Mt 11:29.
301. Jn 8:11.
302. Jn 8:22.
303. Lk 12:13.
304. Mt 16:24.
305. Mt 20:25.
306. Rom 8:30.
307. 1 Pet 2:21.
308. Phil 3:20.
309. Mt 12:25.
310. Mt 5:34–37.
311. Heb 6:7ff.
312. Matt 5:35.

by God Himself. You blind fools, what is greater, the throne or He who sits upon it?

Others say, if it is then wrong to use God for truth, then the apostles Peter and Paul also swore.[313] Answer: Peter and Paul only testify to that which God promised Abraham, whom we long after have received. But when one testifies, one testifies concerning that which is present, whether it be good or evil. Thus Simeon spoke of Christ to Mary and testified: "Behold: this one is ordained for the falling and rising of many in Israel and to be a sign which will be spoken against."[314]

Christ taught us similarly when He says: Your speech shall be yea, yea; and nay, nay; for what is more than that comes of evil. He says, your speech or your word shall be yes and no, so that no one might understand that He had permitted it. Christ is simply yea and nay, and all those who seek Him simply will understand His Word. Amen.

The Cover Letter

Dear Brothers and Sisters in the Lord; these are the articles which some brothers previously had understood wrongly and in a way not conformed to the true meaning. Thereby many weak consciences were confused, whereby the name of God has been grossly slandered, for which reason it was needful that we should be brought to agreement in the Lord, which has come to pass. To God be praise and glory!

Now that you have abundantly understood the will of God as revealed through us at this time, you must fulfill this will, now known, persistently and unswervingly. For you know well what is the reward of the servant who knowingly sins.

Everything which you have done unknowingly and now confess to have done wrongly is forgiven you, through that believing prayer, which is offered among us in our meeting for all our shortcomings and guilt, through the gracious forgiveness of God and through the blood of Jesus Christ. Amen.

Watch out for all who do not walk in simplicity of divine truth, which has been stated by us in this letter in our meeting, so that everyone might be governed among us by the rule of the ban, and that henceforth the entry of false brothers and sisters among us might be prevented.

Put away from you that which is evil, and the Lord will be your God, and you will be His sons and daughters.[315]

Dear brothers, keep in mind what Paul admonished Titus.[316] He says: "The saving grace of God has appeared to all, and disciplines us, that we should deny ungodliness and worldly lusts, and live circumspect righteous and godly lives

in this world; awaiting the same hope and the appearing of the glory of the great God and of our Savior Jesus Christ, who gave himself for us, to redeem us from all unrighteousness and to purify unto himself a people of his own, that would be zealous of good works." Think on this, and exercise yourselves therein, and the Lord of peace will be with you.

May the name of God be forever blessed and greatly praised, Amen. May the Lord give you His peace, Amen.

Done at Schleitheim, St. Matthew's Day,[317] Anno MDXXVII.

From John H. Yoder, ed. and trans., *The Schleitheim Confession* (Scottdale, PA: Herald Press, 1977), 7–19.

◆ In 1570, **Walter Travers** (1548–1635) was forced to leave Cambridge because of his nonconformist views and went to Geneva, where he befriended Theodore Beza, Calvin's successor. In Geneva Travers wrote his principal work, *Ecclesiasticae disciplinae et Anglicanae Ecclesiae ab illa aberrationis plena e verbo Dei et dilucida explicatio* (with the English title *Full and plaine declaration of Ecclesiasticall Discipline owt off the word off God, and off the declininge off the churche off England from the same*), which defended the Presbyterian form of Church government and strongly influenced the policy of the Puritan Reformers. It was published in 1574 and translated into English by Thomas Cartwright, another leader of Elizabethan Puritanism. Toward the end of 1584, a Puritan conference held in London submitted a short book of discipline (original author unknown) to Walter Travers for correction. Travers's revision, *The Book of Discipline,* as it was known in the Elizabethan period, had a broad and enduring influence, though not published until 1644.

WALTER TRAVERS
The Book of Discipline

The Sacred Discipline of the Church, Described in the Word of God

The discipline of Christ's church that is necessary for all times is delivered by Christ, and set down in the holy Scrip-

---

313. The argument here [is], "if it is bad to swear, or even to use the Lord's name to confirm the truth, then the apostles Peter and Paul sinned: for they swore."

314. Lk 2:34.

315. 2 Cor 6:17.

316. Titus 2:11–14.

317. February 24.

tures. Therefore the true and lawful discipline is to be fetched from thence, and from thence alone. And that which resteth upon any other foundation ought to be esteemed unlawful and counterfeit.

Of all particular churches there is one and the same right order and form: therefore also no one may challenge to itself any power over others; nor any right which doth not alike agree to others.

The ministers of public charges in every particular church ought to be called and appointed to their charges by a lawful ecclesiastical calling, such as hereafter is set down.

All these for the divers regard of their several kinds are of equal power amongst themselves.

No man can be lawfully called to public charge in any church, but he that is fit to discharge the same. And none is to be accounted fit, but he that is endued with the common gifts of all the godly; that is, with faith, and a blameless life: and further also, with those that are proper to that ministry wherein he is to be used, and necessary for the executing of the same; whereupon for trial of those gifts some convenient way and examination is to be used.

The party to be called must first be elected, then he is to be ordained to that charge whereunto he is chosen, by the prayers of that church whereunto he is to be admitted; the mutual duties of him and of the church, being before laid open.

The ministers of the church are, first they that are ministers of the Word. In their examination it is specially to be taken heed unto, that they be apt to teach, and tried men, not utterly unlearned, nor newly planted and converted to the faith.

Now these ministers of the word are, first pastors, which do administer the Word and Sacraments, then teachers, which are occupied in wholesome doctrine.

Besides there are also elders, which watch over the life and behavior of every man, and deacons, which have care over the poor.

Further, in every particular church there ought to be a presbytery, which is a consistory, and as it were a senate of elders. Under the name of elders here are contained they who in the church minister doctrine, and they who are properly called elders.

By the common counsel of the eldership all things are directed that belong to the state of their church. First, such as belong to the guidance of the whole body of it in the holy and common assembly gathered together in the name of the Lord, that all things may be done in them duly, orderly,

and to edification. 2. Then also such as pertain to particular persons. First, to all the members of that church, that the good may enjoy all the privileges that belong unto them, that the wicked may be corrected with ecclesiastical censures according to the quality of the fault, private and public, by admonishing or by removing either from the Lord's Supper by suspension (as it is commonly called) or out of the church by excommunication. The [*sic*] which belong specially to the ministers of public charge in the church to their calling either to be begun or ended, and ended either by relieving or punishing them, and that for a time by suspension or altogether by deposition.

For directing of the eldership let the pastors be set over it, or if there be more pastors than one in the same church, let the pastors do it in their turns.

But yet in all the greater affairs of the church, as in excommunicating of any, and in choosing and deposing of church ministers, nothing may be concluded without the knowledge and consent of the church.

Particular churches ought to yield mutual help one to another, for which cause they are to communicate amongst themselves.

The end of this communicating together is, that all things in them may be so directed both in regard of doctrine and also of discipline, as by the Word of God they ought to be.

Therefore the things that belong hereunto are determined by the common opinion of those who meet so to communicate together, and whatsoever is to be amended, furthered or procured in any of those several churches that belong to that assembly. Wherein, albeit no particular church hath power over another, yet every particular church of the same resort, meeting and counsel ought to obey the opinion of more churches with whom they communicate.

For holding of these meetings and assemblies there are to be chosen by every church belonging to that assembly, principal men from among the elders, who are to have their instructions from them, and so to be sent to the assembly. There must be also a care had, that the things they shall return to have been godly agreed on by the meetings, be diligently observed by the churches.

Further in such assemblies there is also to be chosen one that may be set over the assemblies, who may moderate and direct them. His duty is to see that the assemblies be held godly, quiet and comely. Therefore it belongeth unto him to begin and end the conference with prayer, to know every man's instructions, to propound in order the things that are to be handled, to gather their opinions, and to propound what is the opinion of the greater part. It is also the part of the rest of the assembly to speak their opinions of the things propounded godly and quietly.

The Synodical Discipline Gathered Out of the Synods and Use of the Churches Which Have Restored It according to the Word of God, and Out of Sundry Books That Are Written of the Same, and Referred unto Certain Heads

Of the Necessity of a Calling

Let no man thrust himself into the executing of any part of public charge in the administration of the Word, sacraments, discipline or care over the poor. Neither let any such sue or seek for any public charge of the church, but let every one tarry until he be lawfully called.

The Manner of Entering and Determining of a Calling and against a Ministry of No Certain Place; and the Desertion of a Church

Let none be called but unto some certain charge ordained of God, and to the exercising of the same in some particular congregation. And he that is so called let him be so bound to that church that he may not after be of any other, or depart from it without the consent thereof. Let none be called, but they that have first subscribed the confession of doctrine and discipline. Whereof let them be admonished to have copies with themselves.

In the examination of ministers the testimony of the place from whence they come is to be demanded, whereby it may be understood what life and conversation he hath been of, and whether he hath been addicted to any heresy, or to the reading of any heretical books, or to curious and strange questions and idle speculations; or rather whether he be accounted sound and consenting in all things to the doctrine received in the church. Whereunto if he agree, he is also to expound some part of the holy Scriptures twice or oftener, as it shall seem meet to the examiners, and that before the conference, and that church which is interested. Let him also be demanded of the principal heads of divinity. And whether he will diligently execute and discharge his ministry, and in the execution thereof propound unto himself not his own desires and commodities, but the glory of God and edification of the church. Lastly, whether he will be studious and careful to maintain and preserve wholesome doctrine, and ecclesiastical discipline. Thus let the minister be examined not only by one eldership, but also by some greater meeting and assembly.

Of Election

Before the election of a minister and the deliberation of the conference concerning the same, let there be a day of fast kept in the church interested.

Of the Place of Exercising This Calling

Albeit it be lawful for a minister upon just occasion to preach in another church than that whereof he is minister, yet none may exercise any ordinary ministry elsewhere, but for a certain time upon great occasion, and by the consent of his church and conference.

Of the Office of the Ministers of the Word, and First of the Order of Liturgy, or Common Prayer

Let the minister that is to preach name a psalm or a part of a psalm (beginning with the first, and so proceeding) that may be sung by the church, noting to them the end of their singing (to wit) the glory of God and their own edification. After the psalm let a short admonition to the people follow of preparing themselves to pray duly unto God. Then let there be made a prayer containing a general confession. First of the guilt of sin both original and actual, and of the punishment which is due by the Law for them both. Then also of the promise of the Gospel, and in respect of it supplication of pardon for the said guilt and punishment, and petition of grace promised, as for the duties of the whole life, so especially for the godly expounding and receiving of the Word. Let this petition be concluded with the Lord's Prayer. After the sermon, let prayer be made again, First for grace to profit by the doctrine delivered, the principal heads thereof being remembered; then for all men, but chiefly for the universal Church and for all estates and degrees of the people; which is likewise to be ended with the Lord's Prayer and the singing of a psalm as before. Last of all let the congregation be dismissed, with some convenient form of blessing taken out of the Scripture, such as is Numb. 6:24; 2 Cor. 13:13.

Of Preaching

Let him that shall preach choose some part of the Canonical Scripture to expound, and not of the *Apocrypha*. Further in his ordinary ministry, let him not take postils (as they are called) but some whole book of the holy Scripture, especially of the New Testament, to expound in order. In choice whereof regard is to be had both of the minister's ability, and of the edification of the church.

He that preacheth must perform two things, the first that his speech be uncorrupt, which is to be considered both in regard of the doctrine, that it be holy, sound, wholesome and profitable to edification, not devilish, heretical, leavened, corrupt, fabulous, curious, or contentious; and also in respect of the manner of it, that it be proper to the place which is handled, that is, which either is contained plainly in the very words; or if it be gathered by consequent, that the same be fit and clear and such as may rise upon the property of the word, grace of speech and suit of the matter, and not be allegorical, strange, wrested or far-fetched. Now let that which is such, and chiefly which is fittest for the times and occasions of the church, be delivered. Further let the explication, confirmation, enlargement and application, and the whole treatise and handling of it be in the vulgar tongue, and let the whole confirmation and proof be made by arguments, testimonies and examples taken only out of the holy Scriptures, applied fitly and according to the natural meaning of the places that are alleged.

The second thing to be performed by him that preacheth is a reverend gravity; this is considered first in the style, phrase and manner of speech, that it be spiritual, pure, proper, simple and applied to the capacity of the people, not such as human wisdom teacheth, nor favoring of new fangledness, nor either so affected as it may serve for pomp and ostentation, or so careless, and base, as becometh not ministers of the Word of God. Secondly, it is also to be regarded as well in ordering the voice, in which a care must be had that (avoiding the keeping always of one tune) it may be equal, and both rise and fall by degrees; as also in ordering the gesture, wherein (the body being upright) the guiding and ordering the whole body is to follow the voice, there being avoided in it all unseemly gestures of the head or other parts and often turning of the body to divers sides. Finally let the gesture be grave, modest and seemly, not utterly none, nor too much neither like the gestures of players or fencers.

These things are to be performed by him that preacheth, whereby when need requireth they may be examined who are trained and exercised to be made fit to preach: Let there be, if it may be, every Sabbath day two sermons, and let them that preach always endeavor to keep themselves within one hour, especially on the weekdays. The use of preaching at burials is to be left as it may be done conveniently, because there is danger that they may nourish the superstition of some, or be abused to pomp and vanity.

Of the Catechism

Let the Catechism be taught in every church. Let there be two sorts. One more large applied to the delivering of the sum of religion by a suit and order of certain places of the Scriptures, according to which some point of the holy doctrine may be expounded every week. Another of the same sort but shorter, fit for the examination of the rude and ignorant before they be admitted to the Lord's Supper.

Of the Other Parts of Liturgy or Divine Service

All the rest of the liturgy or divine service consisteth in the administration of the sacraments and by the custom of the church in the blessing of marriage. The most commodious form thereof is that which is used by the churches that have reformed their discipline according to the Word of God.

Of Sacraments

Let only a minister of the Word that is a preacher minister the sacraments, and that after the preaching of the Word, and not in any other place than in the public assemblies of the church.

Of Baptism

Women only may not offer unto baptism those that are to be baptized, but the father if it may be, or in his name some other. They which present unto baptism ought to be persuaded not to give those that are baptized the names of God or of Christ, or of angels or of holy offices, as of Baptist, Evangelist, etc., nor such as savor of paganism or popery; but chiefly such whereof there are examples in the holy Scriptures in the names of those who are reported in them to have been godly and virtuous.

Of the Communion

Let the time of celebrating the Communion be made known eight days before, that the congregation may prepare themselves, and that the elders may do their duty in going to and visiting whom they ought.

Of Signifying Their Names That Are to Communicate

Let them which before have not been received to the Lord's Table, when they first desire to come to it, give their names to the minister seven days before the Communion that care of enquiring of them may be committed to the elders, that if there be any cause of hindrance there may be stay made betime; but if there be no such thing let them proceed (where need may be) to the examining of their faith before some of the elders and ministers every month before the Communion. Let this whole treatise of discipline be read in the consistory, and let the ministers, elders and deacons be censured one after another; yet so that the minister concerning doctrine be censured of ministers only.

Let them only be admitted to the Communion that have made confession of their faith, and submitted themselves to the discipline; unless they shall bring letters testimonial of good credit from some other place, or shall approve themselves by some other sufficient testimony.

Children are not to be admitted to the Communion before they be of the age of 14 years except the consistory shall otherwise determine.

On the Sabbath-day next before the Communion, let mention be made in the sermon of the examination, whereunto the Apostle exhorteth, and of the peace that is by faith. On the day of the Communion, let there be speech of the doctrine of the sacraments, and especially of the Lord's Supper.

Of Fasting

Let the day of fasting be published by the pastor according to the advice of the Consistory, either for supplication, for turning away of calamities present or threatened, or for petition of some special grace. Let the sermons upon the same day before and after noon (as on the Lord's day) be such as may be fit for the present occasion.

Of Holydays

Holydays are conveniently to be abolished.

Of Marriage

Let espousing go before marriage. Let the words of espousing be of the present time, and without condition, and before sufficient witnesses on both sides. It is to be wished that the minister or an elder be present at the espousals, who having called upon God may admonish both parties of their duties. First, may have care of avoiding the degrees forbidden both by the law of God and man: and then they may demand of them, whether they be free from any bond of marriage, which if they profess and be strangers, he may also require sufficient testimony. Further also they are to be demanded, whether they have been married before, and of the death of the party with whom they were married, which if they acknowledge and be strangers he may demand convenient testimony of the death of the other party. Finally, let them be asked if they be under the government of any; whether they whom it concerneth have consented.

The espousals being done in due order, let them not be dissolved, though both parties should consent. Let the marriage be solemnized within two months after. Before the marriage let the promise be published three several Sabbath days; but first, let the parties espoused, with their parents or governors, desire the publishing thereof of the minister and two elders at the least, that they may be demanded of those things that are needful, and let them require to see the instrument of the covenant of the marriage, or at least sufficient testimony of the espousals. Marriage may be solemnized and blessed upon any ordinary day of public prayer, saving upon a day of fast.

Of Schools

Let children be instructed in Schools, both in other learning, and especially in the catechism, that they may repeat it by heart, and understand it; when they are so instructed, let them be brought to the Lord's Supper, after they have been examined by the minister, and allowed by him.

Of Students of Divinity, and Their Exercises

In every church where it may conveniently be done, care is to be had that some poor scholars studious of divinity being fit for theological exercises, and especially for expounding of holy Scripture, may by the liberality of the godly rich be taught and trained up to preach.

Let that exposition as often as it shall be convenient to be had be in the presence at least of one minister, by whose presence they may be kept in order, and in the same sort, (as touching the manner of preaching) that public sermons are made. Which being ended, let the other students (he being put apart that was speaker) note wherein he hath failed in any of those things that are to be performed by him that preacheth publicly, as is set down before. Of whose opinion let the minister that is present and is moderator of their exercise judge and admonish the speaker, as he shall think meet.

Of Elders

Let the elders know every particular house and person of the church, that they may inform the minister of the condition of every one, and the deacons of the sick, and poor, that they may take care to provide for them: they are not to be perpetual, neither yet easily to be changed.

From Iain H. Murray, ed., *The Reformation of the Church*, rev. ed. (Carlisle, PA: Banner of Truth, 1987), 178–86.

GRASSROOTS MOVEMENTS

Leonardo Boff, a former Catholic priest from Brazil, traces the origins, the theological consequences, and structures of "base-communities" (*comunidades de base*) in "A New Experience of Church," from his book *Ecclesiogenesis*. There are more than 100,000 of these grassroots Christian groups in Brazil. They are important ecclesiological components of Latin America's liberation theology.

LEONARDO BOFF

"A New Experience of Church," in *Ecclesiogenesis: The Base-Communities Reinvent the Church*

Modern society has produced a wild atomization of existence and a general anonymity of persons lost in the cogs of the mechanisms of the macro-organizations and bureaucracies. These massive structures produce uniformity—uniformity of behavior, of societal framework, of schedules and timetables, and so on. But there has been a reaction. Slowly, but with ever-increasing intensity, we have witnessed the creation of communities in which persons actually know and recognize one another, where they can be themselves in their individuality, where they can "have their say," where they can be welcomed by name. And so, we see, groups and little communities have sprung up everywhere. This phenomenon exists in the church, as well: grassroots Christian communities, as they are known, or basic church communities.

The Basic Church Community

Through the latter centuries, the church has acquired an organizational form with a heavily hierarchical framework and a juridical understanding of relationships among Christians, thus producing mechanical reified inequalities and inequities. As Yves Congar has written: "Think of the church as a huge organization, controlled by a hierarchy, with subordinates whose only task it is to keep the rules and follow the practices. Would this be a caricature? Scarcely!"[318]

In reaction, the basic church communities have sprung up. They represent a new experience of church, of community, of communion of persons within the more legitimate (in the strict sense of the word) ancient tradition. It would be simplistic and would betray the lack of a sense of history to conceive of the basic church communities as a purely contingent, transitory phenomenon. They represent "a specific response to a prevailing historical conjuncture."[319] Theologically they signify a new ecclesiological experience, a renaissance of very church, and hence an action of the Spirit on the horizon of the matters urgent for our time.[320] Seen in this way, the basic church communities deserve to be contemplated, welcomed, and respected as salvific events. Not that we are thereby dispensed from a diligent quest for lucidity and for better ways. Our every effort at comprehension is called for, as we undertake a theological contemplation of the eminent ecclesial value of these communities.

Within this more general frame of reference, however, we are also moved by more specific considerations of the actual situation of the church and its new awareness. The rise of the basic communities is also due to the crisis in the church institution. The scarcity of ordained ministers to attend to the needs of these communities has aroused the creative imagination of the pastors themselves, and they have come to entrust the laity with more and more responsibility. Although the great majority of basic church communities owe their origin to a priest or a member of a religious order, they nevertheless basically constitute a lay movement. The laity carry forward the cause of the gospel here, and are the vessels, the vehicles of ecclesial reality even on the level of direction and decision-making. This shift of the ecclesial axis contains, in seed, a new principle for "birthing the church," for "starting the church again."[321] It is a transposition that bids fair to form the prin-

---

318. Yves M.-J. Congar, "Os grupos informais na Igreja," in Alfonso Gregory, ed., *Comunidades eclesiais de base: utopia ou realidade?* (Petrópolis, Brazil: Vozes, 1973), 144–45.

319. Pedro Demo, *Relatório da pesquisa sobre as comunidades eclesiais de base*, 18–19.

320. Pope Paul VI, in statement appearing in *Revista Eclesiástica Brasileira* 34 (1974): 945.

321. Congar, "Grupos informais," 129–30.

ciple of a genuine "ecclesiogenesis"—to use a word that was employed on several occasions in the Vitória dialogue of January 1975. We are not dealing with the expansion of an existing ecclesiastical system, rotating on a sacramental, clerical axis, but with the emergence of another form of being church, rotating on the axis of the word and the laity. We may well anticipate that, from this movement, of which the universal church is becoming aware, a new type of institutional presence of Christianity in the world may now come into being.

A new phenomenon creates its own language and establishes its own categories for coming to self-expression. The phenomenon of the basic communities constitutes no exception to this rule. The basic communities are generating a new ecclesiology, formulating new concepts in theology. This is still just beginning, still in process. It is not accomplished reality. Pastors and theologians, take warning! Respect the new way that is appearing on the horizon. Do not seek at once to box this phenomenon within theological-pastoral categories distilled from other contexts and other ecclesial experiences. Instead, assume the attitude of those who would see, understand, and learn. Maintain a critical watchfulness, and help us to discern true paths from false. The history of the church is not merely the history of the actualization of ancient forms or of a return to the pristine experiences of the historical past. The history of the church is genuine history: the creation of never-before-experienced novelty. Even the New Testament, like the history of the church, presents a pluriform institutional incarnation of the faith. The church's path from Christ's first coming to the Parousia is not rectilinear. It moves through historical variations, carrying the world through different ages, and offers it to God. Perhaps we are now in a phase of the emergence of a new institutional type of church. Our situation will have to be understood in the light of the Holy Spirit. We must conquer our mental resistance, modify our church habits, and stay open. Otherwise we may smother the Spirit.

A vast spectrum of questions is tied up with the subject of the basic communities. We can hope to list only the most pressing ones, and so we shall select those that seem to be the most significant: the ecclesiality of these communities, their contribution to a transcendence of the church's current structure and, as *quaestiones disputatae,* the historical Jesus and the institutional forms of the church, the possibility of a lay person celebrating the Lord's Supper, and women's priesthood and its possibilities. Before moving on to these questions, however, let us briefly survey the emergence and inherent possibilities of basic church communities.

"Building a Living Church"

The emergence of the basic church communities in Brazil began with a community evangelization movement in Barra do Pirai, R.J. (Rio de Janeiro district) and the efforts of lay catechists there. Specific concerns were with a movement for grassroots community catechetics and general education via radio, from Natal, R.J., and various lay apostolate experiments and parish renewal within the framework of a renewal movement projected in the national pastoral plans (1962–65). One of the plans recounts these beginnings:

In 1956 Dom Agnelo Rossi initiated an evangelization movement, using lay catechists, for regions of Brazil not being reached by pastors. It all began with the lament of one humble old woman: "Christmas Eve, all three Protestant churches were lit up and full of people. We could hear them singing. . . . And the Catholic church, closed and dark! . . . Because we can't get a priest." A question hung in the air. If there are no priests, must everything grind to a halt? At this juncture, Dom Agnelo, in Barra do Pirai, decided to train community coordinators "to do everything a lay person can do in God's church in current ecclesiastical discipline. At the least, these catechists will gather the people once a week for religious instruction. Normally they will also celebrate daily prayer with the people. On Sundays and Holy Days they will gather the people from all over the district for a 'Massless Sunday,' or 'priestless Mass,' or 'Catholic worship,' and lead them spiritually and collectively in the same Mass as is being celebrated by the pastor in the distant mother church. They will recite morning and evening prayers with the people, as well as novenas, litanies, May and June celebrations, and so on" (*Revista Eclesiástica Brasileira* 17 [1957]:731–37). Thus catechesis became the center of a community, and someone was responsible for religious life. Instead of chapels, meeting halls were built and then used for school, religious instruction, sewing lessons, and meetings for solving community problems, even economic ones.

To deal with grave human problems of illiteracy, epidemic, and so on, "radio schools" were created, along with the MEB (Movement for Basic Education), in Natal, for the archdiocese. Reading and writing, along with other school subjects and, of course, religion, were taught by radio. On Sundays, communities without a priest would gather around the radio and pray aloud the people's parts of the Mass being celebrated by the bishop, and hear his homily.

By 1963 there were 1,410 radio schools in the country (*REB* 23 [1963]:781). By then the movement had spread all over the northeast and centerwest.

The Better World Movement created an atmosphere of renewal throughout the country. A team of fifteen persons traveled about the country for five years, giving 1,800 courses and stimulating all areas of church life. Priests, bishops, religious, laity, and movements all experienced this renewal. This program resulted in the Brazilian Bishops' Conference's Emergency Plan, and the First Nationwide Pastoral Plan (1965–70), which said, in part: "Our present parishes are or ought to be composed of various local communities and 'basic communities,' in view of their great extent, population density, and percentage of persons baptized and hence juridically belonging to them. It will be of great importance, then, to launch a parish renewal in each place, for the creation and ongoing dynamics of these 'basic communities': The mother church will itself gradually become one of these communities, and the pastor will preside in all of them, because all are to be found in the portion of the Lord's flock with which he has been entrusted."[322]

Ever since the Medellín conference (1968) this new ecclesial reality has been winning its citizenship, and today it constitutes, without a doubt, one of the great principles of church renewal worldwide. The basic communities mean "building a living church rather than multiplying material structures."[323] The communities are built on a more vital, lively, intimate participation in a more or less homogeneous entity, as their members seek to live the essence of the Christian message: the universal parenthood of God, communion with all human beings, the following of Jesus Christ who died and rose again, the celebration of the resurrection and the Eucharist, and the upbuilding of the kingdom of God, already under way in history as the liberation of the whole human being and all human beings.

Christian life in the basic communities is characterized by the absence of alienating structures, by direct relationships, by reciprocity, by a deep communion, by mutual assistance, by communality of gospel ideals, by equality among members. The specific characteristics of society are absent here: rigid rules; hierarchies; prescribed relationships in a framework of a distinction of functions, qualities, and titles. The enthusiasm generated by a community life of interpersonal ties, and the experience of breathing the fulfilling atmo-

sphere of the gospel frequently lead to a problem that is not without its gravity. Pastors should be attentive here, and not succumb to illusions. The question is: May the basic church communities be seen as an alternative to the church as such? Or less audaciously: May one arouse and nourish the expectation that the whole church may one day be transformed into a community? What degree of probability may we ascribe to this expectation? Can the entire church in its globalism be transformed into authentic community?

In order to develop a response to this question, theology must listen to what the "social sciences"—or better, the sciences of the social—have to say from their meditation on the relation between communitarian and societal aspects of human life. Here we have help in sociologist Pedro Demo's most competent study on the "sociological problems of community."[324] Sociology today has gone beyond F. Tönnies's classic contrast between society and community. For Tönnies, *a community is a social formation in which human beings are oriented by a sense of reciprocity and "belonging"; a society, by contrast, is a social formation in which anonymity and indirect relationships prevail.* This is not to deny that there are social formations whose relationships are based on a communitarian spirit—on intimate, direct, trusting, informal, reciprocal, egalitarian contact, with a maximum of exchange, interchange, and equivalency. Still, in concrete history, no social formation, not even in the presence of these values, has ever succeeded in extinguishing all traces of conflict, selfishness, individualism, individual and group interest, the pressure to have order and rules, and the establishment of goals with a rigid process for their attainment.

Community does not constitute a typical phase of human-group formation. Nor is it possible for community to exist in a pure state. Concretely, there is always a power structure, in either the dominative or the solidarity version. There are always inequalities and stratified roles, in function of some particular scale of values. There are conflicts and particular interests. Historically, social formations are mixed: they have some societal and some communitarian characteristics. Thus in a certain sense, it is unrealistic to struggle for a "classless society"—a society that would be simply and totally a com-

322. Brazilian Bishops' Conference, *Plano pastoral de conjunto* (1962–1965), 58.

323. José Marins, "Comunidades eclesiais de base na América Latina," in *Concilium* 104 (Portuguese edition, 1975), 27.

324. Demo, article in *Comunidades: Igreja na base,* Estudos da CNBB no. 3 (São Paulo: Paulinas, 1975), 67–110.

munity of brothers and sisters, without any conflict at all. Realistically, one can only struggle for a type of sociability in which love will be less difficult, and where power and participation will have better distribution. Community must be understood as a spirit to be created, as an inspiration to bend one's constant efforts to overcome barriers between persons and to generate a relationship of solidarity and reciprocity.

As Demo well says: "In terms of the relationship of community to society, community can be said to be society's utopia."[325] Human togetherness will always be charged with tension between the "organizational impersonal" and the "intimate personal": A struggle for the supremacy of the communitarian dimension implies a struggle to prevent structures and grades from becoming substantive, a struggle to see that they assist the humanization of the human being, and thus bring human beings ever nearer to one another and to the values of the gospel. The supremacy of the communitarian over the societal comes more easily in small groups. Hence the importance of the basic church communities. They are communities within church society.

In order to maintain its vitality as a force for renewal, the communitarian spirit stands in constant need of nourishment and stimulation. Simply for the faithful to be together in the execution of certain tasks is not enough. Clubs and other associations do this, but are not considered communities for it. What constitutes a human group as a community is the effort to create and maintain community involvement as an ideal, as a spirit ever to be re-created and renewed by overcoming routine and refusing to yield to the spirit of institutionalization and "rut." Demo writes:

> The relative attainment of the communitarian spirit normally supposes some preparation, since, after all, not all the members of society at large have the personal detachment required for shared intimacy—for a mutual experience of the reciprocal gift of self, for the acceptance of one's colleagues without selfish restraint.[326]

Christianity, with its values rooted in love, forgiveness, solidarity, the renunciation of oppressive power, the acceptance of others, and so on, is essentially oriented to the creation, within societal structures, of the communitarian spirit.

Meanwhile there is a warning to be heeded. Institutionalization is inevitable in any group that means to last, to be established. With institutionalization comes the codification of successful experiments, and here there can be a threat

to community. For its self-preservation, the communitarian spirit has constant need of revitalization. This task will be facilitated if the groups keep relatively small and refuse to allow themselves to be absorbed by institutionality. Here Demo draws an important conclusion for our consideration. *A large organization can be renewed by a community, but it cannot be transformed into a community.* Demo goes even further:

> Therefore all hope vanishes of organizing an entire church along lines of a communitarian network. This would be tantamount to institutionalizing the de-institutionalizing aspect of community. This is not to say that [a community's] formation cannot be organized by well-prepared teams. But its internal experience seems to renew its vitality daily, drinking at its own wells. Indeed, here is its source of strength for protest, here is where it draws its utopian attraction.[327]

In other words the basic church communities, while signifying the communitarian aspect of Christianity, and signifying it within the church, cannot pretend to constitute a global alternative to the church as institution. They can only be its ferment for renewal.

Institutional and Communitarian Elements of the Church in Coexistence

When we say that the basic communities cannot hope to constitute a global alternative to the institutional church, we are not underestimating their genuine value for a renewal of the fabric of the church. We are merely seeking to situate their significance and meaning within the church globally. Without a doubt these communities can be a stimulus for mobilizing new strength in the institutional church, and they represent a call for a more thorough living of the authentically communitarian values of the Christian message. Jesus' whole preaching may be seen as an effort to awaken the strength of these community aspects. In the horizontal dimension Jesus called human beings to mutual respect, generosity, a communion of sisters and brothers, and simplicity in relationships. Vertically he sought to open the human

---

325. Ibid., 110.
326. Ibid., 79.
327. Ibid., 92.

being to a sincere filial relationship with God, to the artlessness of simple prayer, and to generous love for God. Jesus was not much concerned with the institution, apart from demanding that it live in the spirit in which all expressions of human togetherness ought to be lived.

The church in its globalism is the concrete, vital coexistence of the societal, institutional dimension with the communitarian dimension. In the church is an organizing element that transcends particular communities and procures the communion of them all. There is an authority here that symbolizes oneness in love and hope. There is a creed that expresses a basic oneness in faith. There are global goals common to all local communities. Sociological reflection within this church acquires relevance for theology by dispelling illusions, and so helping to keep the correlatives of institution and charism on realistic foundations. Old historical and ecclesiological errors can infiltrate under new names—like too much insistence on a polarization of "traditional church" and "evangelical church," church of the foundation and church of the steeple, ecclesiogenesis and ecclesiology. There can be a genuine renewal of the institutional framework of the church, springing from the impulses of the grassroots communities, without the church losing its identity or being distorted in its historical essence. *The church sprung from the people is the same as the church sprung from the apostles.* What is different is its sociological physiognomy in the world, its forms of liturgical, canonical, and organizational expression. There is no change in the ongoing coexistence of one aspect that is more static, institutional, and permanent with another that is more dynamic, charismatic, and vital. The will to impregnate the institutional organizational aspect of the church with the spirit of community will never die in the church, and this is the wellspring of its vitality.

After all, the problem of church does not reside in the counterpoint of institution and community. These poles abide forever. *The real problem resides in the manner in which both are lived, the one as well as the other:* whether one pole seeks to absorb the other, cripple it, liquidate it, or each respects the other and opens itself to the other in constant willingness to be put to the question. The latter attitude will not permit the institutional to become necrophiliac and predominate. Nor will it permit the communitarian to degenerate into pure utopianism, which seeks to transform the global church into community. In the church the institutional may not be allowed to predominate over the communitarian. The latter must ever preserve its primacy. The former lives in

function of the latter. The communitarian, for its part, must always seek adequate institutional expression.

In the dynamic wave of postconciliar renewal and post-Medellín liberation, two ecclesiological models have emerged in neat distinction. One is oriented to the church as grand institution, with all its services institutionally organized and oriented to the needs of the church universal, the dioceses, and the parishes. This model of the church generally finds its sociological and cultural center in society's affluent sectors, where it enjoys social power and constitutes the church's exclusive interlocutor with the powers of society. The other is centered in the network of the basic communities, deep within the popular sectors and the poor masses, on the margin of power and influence over the media, living the horizontal relationships of coresponsibility and a communion of brothers and sisters more deeply.

Developments in recent years have shown that the church as great institution can no more exist in and for itself, refusing to lend universality to the basic communities and providing them with a linkage with the past, than the network of communities can prescind from the church as great institution. More and more the institution is discovering its meaning and responsibility in the creation, support, and nurture of the communities. To be sure, this has led to a weakening in institutional commitment to the influential sectors of society and state, coupled with a strengthening of evangelical purity and prophecy. For their part, the communities have come more and more to understand their need of the church as great institution, for the maintenance of their continuity, for their Catholic identity, and for their oneness with one another. The convergence of these two ecclesiological models, and their dialectical interaction, has contributed to a profound conscientization of the church as a whole with regard to its missionary activity, especially among the poor of this world, in whose passion it assists and shares. For the church as great institution, the crucial option is becoming daily more difficult to escape: either continue good relations with the state and the wealthy classes represented by the state or take the network of basic communities seriously, with the call for justice and social transformation that this will imply. With the first option, the church as great institution will have its personal and institutional security guaranteed, and will have reliable support for its assisting aid. But it will have to renounce the possibility of efficaciously evangelizing the great masses of the poor. With the second option, the church will recover its prophetic mission, and will carry to the throne of God the cries for justice that rise up from the bowels of the earth.

With this option comes also insecurity, official displeasure, and the fate of disciples of Jesus.

What lies in store for the basic community? This, we recall, is the question we asked above. In view of the data we have assembled, we believe we can answer: the basic community has a permanent future, provided it can understand itself in counterpoint to the church as institution. It dare not seek the utopian impossible, and delude itself into believing that it can exhaust the concept of community in its own being, in such wise that no other group or formation could exist. It dare not present itself as the only way of being church today. As we shall see, the basic community constitutes instead a bountiful wellspring of renewal for the tissues of the body ecclesial, and a call and a demand for the evangelical authenticity of ecclesial institutions, so that they may come more closely to approximate the utopian community ideal.

The church never lost this authenticity. It may have lain hidden, like live coals covered with ashes, but today it is emerging in a way never before seen: a rejuvenating leaven of the gospel ideals of communion, in a community of sisters and brothers simply living one and the same faith in the spontaneous worship of Christ in the midst of humanity, and in disinterested service of and concern for the needs of each member. The utopia of the kingdom anticipated in the community of the faithful, a community of more humanities, more lively faith, and more profound communion of members, never died in the church. The basic church community, if it hopes to keep the communitarian spirit alive, may not allow itself to replace the parish. It will have to remain small in order to avoid bureaucratization and to maintain a direct personal relationship among all its members. Although it will have to open up to the communion of the church universal, with all the latter's societal institutions and forms, yet it will have to maintain a dialectical tension with this global church in order not to be absorbed by it. In this way it will deteriorate neither into a fanatical group of futurists nor into a reactionary group in love with the past. Instead it will continue as the abiding leaven of the whole church.

From Leonardo Boff, *Ecclesiogenesis: The Base-Communities Reinvent the Church,* translated by Robert R. Barr (Maryknoll, NY: Orbis Books, 1986), 1–9. [Ellipses in original.]

❧ In "The Origins of the Devotion to Mount Carmel in Italian Harlem," in his *Madonna of 115th Street,* **Robert Anthony Orsi** presents the historical origins, theological framework, and structural organization of the devotion to "la Madonna del Carmine"

among the Italian immigrants of Harlem, New York, in the late nineteenth and early twentieth centuries.

ROBERT ANTHONY ORSI

"The Origins of the Devotion to Mount Carmel in Italian Harlem," in *The Madonna of 115th Street: Faith and Community in Italian Harlem, 1880–1950*

The Madonna of 115th Street shared the history of the people of Italian Harlem. She journeyed to the new world with the immigrants and lived among them in their neighborhood. She shared the poverty and ostracism of their early days. When Italians were relegated to the basements of churches in East Harlem, so was she; like the immigrants, she was an embarrassment to the Catholic church in New York City. The Madonna left the basement of the church on 115th Street at the same time that Italians and their children were beginning to take control of political and social life in Italian Harlem: just at the time when the Italian language was accepted by the Board of Education for study in New York's public high schools, when LaGuardia took his seat in Congress and Corsi began his long career at Harlem House, and just at the time of Italian Harlem's first successful rent strike, the Madonna took her place on the main altar of the church.

She heard the changing needs of the community. First she heard prayers for families left behind in Italy and then she began to hear prayers for families sinking roots in the new world. She was asked for help in finding jobs during the Depression. Her protection was sought for the men of Italian Harlem who went off to fight in the Second World War, and she was taken out of the church to greet them when they returned. In the years after the war, she heard younger voices pleading for assistance in school and in finding homes and success outside of Harlem; and she heard the voices of older men and women pleading with her to keep their children from forgetting them and the ways of life of Italian Harlem. Like these older men and women, she waited in her home in Harlem for those who had left to come back and visit, which they did at least once a year. Images of the Madonna were taken away by those who left and set up on bureaus in the Bronx and Westchester next to pictures of the folks still in Harlem and of themselves when they had lived there too.

The story of the devotion to la Madonna del Carmine in East Harlem begins in the summer of 1881, when immigrants from the town of Polla, in the province of Salerno, formed a mutual aid society named after the Madonna, who was the protectress of Polla.[328] Mutual aid societies, which were quite popular in Italian American colonies, were regional organizations composed of immigrants from the same Italian town who gathered together to provide some unemployment and burial benefits and to socialize. They allowed paesani to get together and enjoy each other's company; they also encouraged and enabled the immigrants to remember and preserve traditional customs in the new world. One of Covello's informants described the meaning of mutual aid societies in these terms: "the Italian feels safer when he pays homage to the patron saint of his hometown or village who in the past was considerate to the people. . . . Our Italians, and I mean the old folks, feel that without guardianship of their former patron saint, life would be next to impossible." These interwoven themes of protection, mutual support, and faithfulness to the values and history of the paese are expressed in the most important function of the societies, according to the immigrants—the assurance of support for burial in accordance with southern Italian customs. Covello's informant emphasized this function of the mutual aid societies:

> The older Italians, even while in good health, are never overlooking the event of death. Preservation of funeral rituals is sacred to the old folks. Prospects of a "potter's field" fills them with terror. . . . To bury one without proper customs is hurtful to the pride of every Italian. And so the Mutual Aid Societies are fulfilling their probably most important role in assuring a member of a dignified funeral.

But the deep need for this assurance was also indicative of a profound mistrust of the effect the United States might have on Italian faithfulness and tradition: "I personally also think that the main motive of joining a society for burial reasons is the man's constant suspicion that here in America his relatives may skip on their traditional duties and be negligent towards him when he dies." So the formation of the mutual aid society by Pollese in East Harlem in 1881 expressed the immigrants' commitment to their past but also their uncertainty and unease in the present.

The members of the new society determined to organize a festa in honor of their patroness. The first celebration took place in 1882 in the courtyard of a house on 110th Street near the East River; in the following year, the festa was held on the first floor of a house on 111th Street and the East River in a rented room that measured eight by thirty feet. The other rooms in the building were let out to poor Italian workers, and in the back courtyard, right behind the altar of the little cha-

pel to the Madonna, there was a rag-sorting yard where local rag pickers brought their daily hauls to be sorted, washed, and packed. Such celebrations were common among Italian immigrants. One Catholic observer noted in 1900 that when immigrants from the same town managed to take over an entire tenement, they would transform the building's backyard into the setting of their religious celebrations. Another Catholic commentator remarked in 1899 that Italians seemed to prefer outdoor devotions to entering a church.

During these earliest years, the festa was intimate and intense and intensely Neapolitan, and there is no indication of any ecclesiastical supervision; it was a popular, lay-organized celebration—as these feste usually were, to the consternation of both the American and Italian Catholic clergy. The first celebrations were quite simple. The immigrants knelt in someone's apartment or behind a tenement, in a courtyard—though this euphemism undoubtedly obscures the real conditions of the setting—especially decorated for the occasion, before a small printed picture of the Madonna that had been sent for from Polla. They said the rosary, prayed the Magnificat, and then sat down to a huge meal together. In 1883, for the first time, an Italian priest, Domenico Vento, was present at the festa. He said mass, joined in the procession, and delivered, as was the custom, a moving panegyric on the life of the Virgin and on the wonders she had performed for the people of Polla. Father Vento remained in the community throughout 1883, saying mass and administering the sacraments on the first floor of a house on 111th Street and the East River. Then he disappears from the story.

By 1884, the official history tells us, the devotion to the Madonna del Carmine in northern Manhattan had already become a great popular celebration. By this time, the Confraternity had sent for and received a statue of the Madonna from Polla, a transaction which, together with the acquisition of benches for the chapel and rent, put the group in serious debt. In a historical sketch on the devotion prepared for the church in the mid-1920s, it is noted that thousands gathered for the celebration in 1884, coming from far and wide, both immigrants and their children. This proved to be an important year in the history of the devotion to Mount Carmel in East Harlem for a number of reasons. It was, first of all, the year that the Pallotine fathers arrived in the community. Slowly awak-

---

328. Note by Gerhart and Udoh: This account of how the devotion to La Madonna del Carmine began in Italian Harlem is taken from several sources as listed in the notes to the source text.

ening to the "problem"—as it would be called for the next thirty years—of the religious life of Italian immigrants, the New York Archdiocese, at this time under the actual direction of Bishop Michael Corrigan ruling on behalf of the dying John Cardinal McCloskey, invited the Pallotine order to New York to work with the growing Italian population. The Pallotines had been conducting a ministry among Italian immigrants in London, where Cardinal McCloskey had met them and been impressed. The first Pallotine priest, Father Emiliano Kirner, arrived in New York in May 1884 and was soon given care of the little chapel on 111th Street in East Harlem.

The ecclesiastical history of the devotion to Mount Carmel also begins in 1884 with the completion of the church on 115th Street and the formation of the official "Congregazione del Monte Carmelo della 115ma strada." The latter, which was a church society more or less under the authority of the parish clergy, replaced the regional society of Pollese as the official sponsor of the church celebration. Both the erection of the church and the formation of the society mark an official change in the public life of the devotion, which was now officially associated with a church. The members of the society were all male, as was customary with such organizations. For the entire history of the devotion, this celebration of a woman, in which women were the central participants, was presided over by a public male authority.

Finally, two events took place in 1884 that served as the background against which the devotion to Mount Carmel developed in the Italian colonies in New York City. First, Bishop Corrigan fought to prevent the confiscation of the North American Seminary in Rome by the Italian government. Corrigan's participation in this struggle proved important in shaping his attitude toward Italians. The Third Plenary Council of the American hierarchy also met in 1884; it was at this council, as we will see, that American prelates managed to offend the Vatican by their high-handed treatment of the Italian "problem."

Father Kirner encountered on 111th Street the powerful devotion of the people for la Madonna and discovered that they were eager to build a suitably beautiful and dignified residence for their patroness. Soon the plans were ready for a church on 115th Street near the river, a church, in the words of the official history, "built by Italians, the first church which would be called, 'the church of the Italians in New York.'" So committed were the immigrants to this project that many of them came home after terrible and exhausting days of work and with their own hands dug the foundation of the new church and laid its bricks. Junkmen and icemen lent their carts and horses to carry building materials and people in the community prepared refreshments for the workers. When organizers from the masons' union objected to the free work being done by Italian men on the church, Italian women from the neighborhood tied back their hair and took over the job. Kirner's expenses were considerably reduced by this labor.

Despite this participation of Italian immigrants, the Church of Our Lady of Mount Carmel was built just outside, although close by, the Italian neighborhood, which ended at the time at about 113th Street. After this, the blocks became a mixture of German and Irish, and it was mainly from these groups that funds for the building came. Kirner's original intention was to name the church after Saint Vincent Pallotti, the founder of the order he belonged to, but the Italians in the community begged him to put the church under the protection of their patroness, and he agreed. When the work was completed, in the same year it was begun—the first mass was celebrated at the church on December 8, 1884—Italians were sent into the lower church to worship. They remained there until Gaspare Dalia became pastor in 1919. They remained in *la chiesa inferiore* despite the fact that, in 1884, 86 out of 90 children baptized at Mount Carmel were Italian; in 1885, 229 out of 302; in 1886, 345 out of 511. By 1898, although they were still worshiping in the basement, Italian baptisms numbered about 1,600. The Italian community resented this basement exile and remembers Dalia as the man who rescued their devotion from indignity.

From Robert Anthony Orsi, *The Madonna of 115th Street: Faith and Community in Italian Harlem, 1880–1950* (New Haven, CT: Yale University Press, 1985), 50–54.

❧ In "Manifestations," in his *New Age Movement*, **Paul Heelas** provides insight into the varied and complex belief system commonly termed "New Age" in contemporary Britain, along with comments on North America and other places where New Age beliefs are popular.

PAUL HEELAS

"Manifestations," in *The New Age Movement: The Celebration of Self and the Sacralization of Modernity*

The Term "New Age"

It all starts with self.   Shirley MacLaine, 1988, 5

My intention for your experience of religion is that it becomes a religion of the self.   Ron Smothermon, 1980, 157

How are we to characterize the New Age Movement? The term "new age"—together with similar formulations such as "new times," "new era," or "new world"—is typically used to convey the idea that a significantly better way of life is dawning. Terms of this variety are used in a number of more specific ways, change sometimes being thought of in political fashion, sometimes in economic, in religious, and so on.

During the 1980s, for example, contributors to *Marxism Today* wrote of "new times." Also during the 1980s, Mikhail Gorbachev announced, "I feel that all mankind is entering a new age, and that the world is beginning to obey new laws and logic, to which we have yet to adjust ourselves."[329] In 1951, the Festival of Britain was designed to convey Labour's "brave new world." Somewhat earlier, Arnold Toynbee supposed that social crisis could be the birth pangs of a new, more humane global culture. Earlier still, the Great Seal of the United States—its Latin phrase *novus ordo seclorum* proclaiming a "new order of ages"—was designed in 1782. (The Seal can be found on the reverse side of the current dollar bill.)

Coming back to contemporary times, the media are fond of using the term to refer to various aspects of the "information revolution"; Eugene Rabinowitch's *The Dawn of a New Age* (1963) reflects on political change; and posters of the Communist Party of India proclaim a "New Age" for that country. Despite such variegated usage, however, the term (especially as in "the New Age *Movement*") has come to acquire a relatively distinctive currency. It has come to be used to designate those who maintain that inner spirituality—embedded within the self and the natural order as a whole—serves as *the* key to moving from all that is wrong with life to all that is right.

Several clarifications are immediately in order. First, the word "new" should not be taken to imply that there is anything novel about the spiritual teaching under consideration. It might be new for many in the west in that increased numbers have adopted this form of spirituality during the last thirty or so years, the term gaining some of its currency from this fact. Nevertheless, the spirituality is found in many religions both east and west, including, to give a western example, millenarian movements such as the Brethren of the Free Spirit of the time of Cromwell (Cohn, 1970, 172–6).

Second, the word "movement," should not be taken to imply that the New Age is in any sense an organized entity. Far from being centrally administered, it is comprised of diverse modes of operation: well-organized NRMs [New Religious Movements] and communities (for example, est/The Forum and Findhorn), networks (for example, the Wrekin Trust), one-to-one paths within (for example, the New Age healer working with his or her client), centres (for example, the Open Centre), the individual running events at home or in the office, camps (for example, tepee camps in Wales), the week-end training seminar, holiday homes and centres, festivals (for example, Glastonbury), gatherings (for instance, as when "Cloud Nine" gathers for a couple of weeks or so during the late summer to pick magic mushrooms growing in the Yorkshire Dales), shops (for example, those in Neal's Yard, London), businesses (for example, the communications group, Programmes), clubs (for example, Megatripolis), schools (for instance, the couple run by the School of Economic Science), New Age relationships and families, banks (such as the Bank of Credit and Commerce International), and—last but by no means least—the individual pursuing a relatively solitary spiritual quest. Furthermore, there is also the consideration that adherents of particular paths not infrequently think of themselves as better than those engaging in other (possibly very similar) activities. There is in fact considerable rivalry between various camps. In short, the term "movement" simply refers to the assumption that humanity is progressing into a new era.[330]

Third, use of the term "New Age" should not be taken to imply that all those discussed under the rubric are themselves happy with the expression. Many dislike the term, feeling that it has come to be associated with (supposedly) corrupted versions, such as those addressing materialistic prosperity. Others scorn the term simply because they do not like being labelled. Such attitudes, though, do not mean that we are not entitled to employ the term to characterise what those concerned have in common, essentially questing within to effect change.[331]

And fourth, Britains today tend to associate the term with travellers. The expression "New Age travellers" has been extensively propagated by the media. There might well be a sense in which these travellers are "New Age"—namely that they are seeking an alternative way of life—but few would appear to be committed to the spiritual quest within. In terms of the point of view adopted in this volume, it follows, travellers are of marginal concern.

---

329. Michael Ray and Alan Rinzler, eds., *The New Paradigm in Business* (New York: Jeremy P. Tarcher, 1993), 12.

330. Perhaps only as few as 5 or 10 percent of New Agers belong to and are faithful members of particular New Age organizations.

331. It should also be noted that the term has also been used to refer to theistic forms of new religiosity, such as the Unification Church: forms which stand in some contrast to those under discussion here.

As for the history of the term—used, that is, to refer to what flows from inner spirituality—we are initially led back to the beginning of this century. Alfred Orage (1873–1934)—an occult Nietzschean influenced by Theosophy and later a Gurdjieffian—and Holbrook Jackson took over the editorship of the weekly paper, the *New Age,* in 1907. (Orage was to remain editor until 1934.) In their first editorial they stated:

> Believing that the darling object and purpose of the universal will of life is the creation of a race of supremely and progressively intelligent beings, the *New Age* will devote itself to the serious endeavour to cooperate with the purposes of life and to enlist in that noble service the help of serious students of the new contemplative and imaginative order. (cited in Webb, 1980, 206)

Prior to this century, American Warren Felt Evans published *The New Age and Its Message* in 1864. (The "message" had previously been transmitted by Swedenborg [1688–1772], Swedenborg himself using the term "New Jerusalem.") Samson Mackay (1765–1843), influenced by India, liked the term "golden age," and Godfrey Higgens (1772–1833), influenced by the "Celtic Druids," wrote of the "new aera." (See Godwin, 1994, 70, 85, for the last two usages.) Although the research does not appear to have been done, it is virtually inconceivable that the term has not been used much earlier: by those involved in some of the millenarian movements discussed by Cohn (1970), for example, or in eastern settings.

The Essential *Lingua Franca:* Self-spirituality

Looking more closely at what lies at the heart of the matter, the basic teaching has three main elements. It explains why life—as conventionally experienced—is not what it should be; it provides an account of what it is to find perfection; and it provides the means for obtaining salvation. The elements are introduced by expressions which—with equivalents—are used throughout the New Age as we are portraying it.

"Your lives do not work"

Describing the beginning of an est (Erhard Seminars Training) "transformational" event, Mark Brewer (1975) reports:

> They [the trainees] were present, he [the trainer] roared in command voice, because their lives did not work. Their lives were shit. Hopeless. They did not know what they were doing, did not know how to experience life, were struggling, desperate, confused. They were ASSHOLES! (39)

Those participating in New Age activities—workshops, retreats, seminars, lectures, rituals, or healing sessions—are given the opportunity to appreciate that all is far from well with their lives. In the case of est, "beliefs" are held to be a major spanner in the works, the trainer continuing, "the reason why your lives don't work is that you're all living mechanically in your belief systems instead of freshly in the world of actual experience." Or consider the words of Gurdjieff (who almost certainly has been a strong influence on est): ". . . all the people you see, all the people you know, all the people you may get to know, are machines, actual machines working solely under the power of external influences" (cited by Bancroft, 1978, 63).

The great refrain, running throughout the New Age, is that we malfunction because we have been indoctrinated—or, in the New Age sense of the term, been "brainwashed"—by mainstream society and culture. The mores of the established order—its materialism, competitiveness, together with the importance it attaches to playing roles—are held to disrupt what it is to be authentically human. To live in terms of such mores, inculcated by parents, the educational system and other institutions, is to remain the victim of unnatural, deterministic and misguided routines; to be enslaved by unfulfillable desires and deep-seated insecurities; to be dominated by anxiety-generating imperatives such as creating a good impression; to be locked into the conflictual demands of the ideal relationship. Thus New Ager Arianna Stassinopoulos refers to "the melodrama which goes on in many of our heads most of the time, the fear, anxiety, guilt and recrimination; the burden of the past which continues to dominate our present responses, and produces exaggerated or inappropriate reactions to current circumstances," continuing to speak of "self-limiting images and beliefs which make us feel we are not terribly worthwhile" and of "the sense of oneself as victim, as the passive recipient of life's circumstances" (cited by Wallis, 1984, 32). Or as a brochure of Andrew Ferguson's London-based The Breakthrough Centre puts it, "When you feel angry or depressed, in a self-defeating way, this is the result of negative or irrational inner-speech that you may not even be aware of. . . . These evaluations are linked to earlier times, when they were instilled by force of painful experience." Danish-derived isa (the Institute for Self-Actualization) simply refers to the "baggage" that you have accumulated (brochure).

"You are Gods and Goddesses in exile"

Perfection, it is maintained, cannot be found by tinkering with what we are by virtue of socialization. Neither can it be found by conventional (political, etc.) attempts at social engineering. Perfection can be found only by moving beyond the socialized self—widely known as the "ego" but also as the "lower self," "intellect" or the "mind"—thereby encountering a new realm of being. It is what we are *by nature*. Indeed, the most pervasive and significant aspect of the *lingua franca* of the New Age is that the person is, in essence, spiritual. To experience the "Self" itself is to experience "God," the "Goddess," the "Source," "Christ Consciousness," the "inner child," the "way of the heart," or, most simply and, I think, most frequently, "inner spirituality." And experiences of the "Higher Self," to use another favoured term, stand in stark contrast to those afforded by the ego. The inner realm, and the inner realm alone, is held to serve as the source of authentic vitality, creativity, love, tranquility, wisdom, power, authority and all those other qualities which are held to comprise the perfect life.

As will become increasingly apparent, New Agers differ in how they portray the inner life. Virtually anything can be found in the depths of the person, including things like tennis (Tim Gallwey stating, "Perfect tennis is in us all" [cited by Adam Smith, 1976, 191]) or "the writer within" (*Skyros* magazine). But whatever the case with regard to specific qualities, New Agers invariably conceive their essence in spiritual terms. As a member of the Programmes business community told me, "I believe in a God but through me. I am my own God." Or consider fashion and beauty image expert, Jane Hundley. Based in the United States, she writes, "Beauty in the New Age is a reality of self-love emanating harmony, grace, and light in the world. . . . You are an eternal essence of God. You have chosen a body as the vehicle of expression between your spirit and the world around you" (in Ray, 1990, 207). And then there are those formulations of a non-individuated variety, William Bloom, for example, writing that "All life—all existence—is the manifestation of spirit" (cited by Perry, 1992, 33).

"Let go/drop it"

Given that people are not who they think they are, how are they to move out of exile into authentic experience? The third great theme of Self-spirituality is that what lies within quite naturally comes *into* experience once that great barrier or stumbling-block, the ego, has been dealt with. The ego, that internalized mode of the traditions, parenting routines and all those other inputs which have constructed it, must lose authority. To this end, the New Age provides a great range of spiritual disciplines, variously known as "processes," "rituals" or "psychotechnologies," for example. Whether they take the form of meditation, activities similar to those found in psychotherapies, physical labour, dance, shamanic

practices, magic, or, for that matter, fire-walking, sex, tennis, taking drugs or using virtual reality equipment, the aim (in the words of a well-known song by the Doors) is to "break on through to the other side." Practices provide paths within, from being "at cause" to being "at effect." And this they do by working on the ego to exorcize the tyrannical hold of the socialized mode of being. The Self must be liberated; "de-identification" must be effected; the person must drop "ego-attachments" or "games." The past, for the ego is constructed from the time of birth (if not from previous lives), loses its hold—thereby enabling a new future.

From Paul Heelas, *The New Age Movement: The Celebration of Self and the Sacralization of Modernity* (London: Blackwell, 1996), 15–20.

Chiara Lubich, winner of numerous international peace awards, founded the Work of Mary, also called the Focolare movement (the Italian word *focolare* means "hearth," "the family fireside," or "home"), in Trent, Italy, in 1943. She describes the structure and theological framework of her ecumenical Christian movement in "General Statutes of the Work of Mary."

CHIARA LUBICH

"General Statutes of the Work of Mary"

The Premise to Every Other Rule
Mutual and constant charity,
which makes unity possible
and brings the presence
of Jesus among all,
is, for the members of the Work of Mary,
the basis of every single aspect
of their lives:
it is the norm of norms,
the premise to every other rule.

Part One. Nature, Aim, Spirit

Chapter 1. The Nature of the Work of Mary

Art. 1. The Work of Mary is a private, universal association of the faithful, of Pontifical right, with juridical status as per canons 298–311 and 321–329. It is constituted in accordance with the norms of the Catholic Church and of these General Statutes which are approved by the Holy See. These Statutes contain the norms of life and of government for all those who are part of the Work of Mary, without detriment to the norms stated in the Regulations of its Sections, Branches and Movements.[332]

Art. 2. The name "Work of Mary" indicates a special bond with Our Blessed Lady, mother of Christ and of every human being. This bond is expressed through the marian spirituality of the Work of Mary, through its ecclesial characteristics, through the diversity of its composition, through its universal extension, through its relationships of collaboration and friendship with Christians of different denominations and ecclesial communities, with people of different faiths, and with people of no religious affiliation, and finally, through the fact that its President is a lay woman. The Work of Mary desires to be—insofar as this is possible—a presence of Mary, a continuation of her presence on earth.

Art. 3. Just as a child resembles its mother, so too does the Work of Mary reflect, in a certain sense, the characteristics of the Church.[333] Its orientation towards the renewal of individuals, of the Church and of society, the diversity and universality of its composition, and its goals, aspects, and works, all to some extent reflect this likeness to the Church.

Art. 4. The Work of Mary, because of its special bond with Our Blessed Lady and its likeness to the Church, aims to contribute to the re-establishment of unity among all Christians and to help guide the whole of humanity to Christ.

Its specific characteristic is unity which imbues its spirit, goals, structure and government.

Chapter 2. The Aims of the Work of Mary

General Aim

Art. 5. The general aim of the Work of Mary is to guide its members towards the perfection of charity, by means of the key points and aspects of the Gospel-based spirituality of the Work of Mary as they are expressed in these Statutes and in the Regulations of the Sections, Branches and Movements.

Specific Aim

Art. 6. The Work of Mary, faithful to its experience of the Holy Spirit who has guided its foundation and development, seeks constantly to merit, in its internal life, the gift of unity, according to the prayer of Jesus to the Father: "that they may all be one" (Jn 17:21).

On this foundation the Work of Mary is committed:

—to working, first and foremost, for an ever deeper unity among the faithful of the Catholic Church;

—to establishing, in all possible ways, relationships of fraternal communion and of common witness with other Christian sisters and brothers, as a contribution to the restoration of full unity.

Furthermore the Work of Mary aims:

—to achieve, through dialogue with persons of other religions, and through activities of common interest, the deepest possible union in God among all believers as a way of making Christ known to them;

—to establish a dialogue with persons of no religious affiliation and work together with them towards common goals in order to strengthen universal brotherhood throughout the world and to open up their hearts to Christ.

Chapter 3. The Spirit of the Work of Mary

Art. 7. The Work of Mary places itself under the special protection of Our Blessed Lady, honouring her under all her splendid titles. The members of the Work of Mary imitate her as their model, love her as their mother and as mother of the Church and of every person. She is invoked in the Work of Mary as the Mother of Unity.

Art. 8. The members of the Work of Mary desire to follow the way of Christian love, in accordance with their Gospel-based spirituality and in unity with the magisterium of the Church, imitating the saints by fulfilling, as they did, God's will for them.

They strive therefore to love God who is Love with all their heart, mind and strength. They choose him as the ideal of their life (cf. Mt 22:37 and 1 Jn 4:8, 16–18).

—In order to love God who is Love they seek to conform their will to his (cf. Mt 7:21).

---

332. These Statutes, which apply to those who are part of the Work of Mary, take into account their different levels of participation (cf. Art. 15–20). These articles concerning the spirituality . . . are fully relevant only to those who are *members* or *adherents* of the Work of Mary. Brothers and sisters of other Christian denominations and ecclesial communities live the spirituality in accordance with their faith. The faithful of other Religions adhere to the Work of Mary as *associates*. Their religious view of life forms the common bond which allows them to live, to some degree, the spirit of the Work of Mary. People of good will with no religious convictions, who highly respect the spiritual and moral dimensions of the Work of Mary, may adhere to it as *associates,* collaborating in its objectives according to their conscience.

[Note by Gerhart and Udoh: Subsequent articles not included in our excerpt address each of the foregoing items.]

333. Cf. John Paul II, Discourse Mariapolis Centre, Rocca di Papa, 19/8/1994.

—In order to carry out God's will they strive to love every neighbour (cf. Mt 22:36–40; Mk 12:28–31).

—While seeking to love every neighbour, they make a particular commitment to live as perfectly as possible Jesus' New Commandment among themselves: "This is my commandment, that you love one another as I have loved you" (Jn 15:12) and to establish this relationship with others as well.

—Through the practice of mutual love they aim at attaining, as perfectly as possible, the unity asked of the Father in the testament of Jesus: "that they may all be one, as you, Father, are in me and I am in you" (Jn 17:21).

—As they strive for this unity, they seek to maintain the constant presence of Jesus in their midst, in accordance with his promise: "Where two or three are gathered in my name, I am there among them" (Mt 18:20).

For the members of the Work of Mary, mutual and constant love, which makes unity possible and brings about Jesus' presence among all, is the basis of their life in all its aspects: it is the norm of norms, the premise to every other rule.

—In their commitment to live out unity, the members of the Work of Mary have a special love for, and seek to re-live in themselves, Jesus Crucified, who at the height of his passion cried out: "My God, my God, why have you forsaken me?" (Mk 15:34; Mt 27:46). In this moment of Jesus' abandonment, he generated unity between God and the human race and unity among all people.

—Jesus Crucified and Forsaken is the divine model of those who desire to co-operate in bringing about the unity of human beings with God and with one another. Love for him leads the members of the Work of Mary to be detached from everything around them and, above all, to inner detachment. This is necessary in order to attain unity on a supernatural level.

Furthermore, love for Jesus Crucified and Forsaken urges them to work generously on behalf of those whose lives reflect the anguish of Jesus' abandonment—people who are desperate, without hope, abandoned, in error, sinful, alienated from God, orphaned, etc.

Love for Jesus Forsaken spurs members of the Work of Mary on to overcome every possible disunity within the Work of Mary and the Catholic Church, and to work toward the healing of every separation among Christians. Love for Jesus Forsaken leads them to give to believers of other religions the knowledge of the God of Jesus Christ which they lack. This love leads them to dedicate themselves in a special way to those sectors of humanity most alienated from God because of secularism, atheism, etc.

—To foster an ever greater unity with Jesus and with one another, the members of the Work of Mary are committed to becoming ever more similar to him: to acquiring his way of thinking, of willing, of loving, by evangelizing themselves, that is, by nourishing themselves daily with the Word of God, by putting it into practice and sharing with one another the resulting experiences, for the edification of all.

—In order to live their ideal of unity they nourish themselves as frequently as possible with Jesus in the Eucharist. The Eucharist, bond of unity, unites them to God and to one another, by transforming them into Christ and making them his body.

—They imitate Mary, having discovered in the significant moments of the life of the Mother of God the very stages of their spiritual itinerary towards him. The way of love they follow is therefore known as "The way of Mary."

—They try to imitate Mary, the mother of Jesus, particularly in their commitment to generate and constantly renew the mystical presence of Christ in every community, large or small.

—They seek to re-live Mary Desolate who experienced the anguish of separation from her son, Jesus, in order to embrace, in John, all people of the earth as their mother. They recognize her as the one who most fully re-lived Jesus Crucified and Forsaken. They find inspiration in the perfect way she lived charity and all the other virtues of which love is mother and queen.

—They try to live as perfectly as possible the reality of the Mystical Body. They try to be, everywhere and at all times, the living Church, by means of their mutual love, constantly renewed, and by being ever more deeply rooted in the Church through the most deeply-felt, sincere, filial unity with the Pope and the Bishops, successors of the Apostles.

—They have a special devotion to the Holy Spirit, Spirit of Love, Soul of the Church, divine Atmosphere[334] in which the Work of Mary desires to live.

—They strive to merit the fullness of the gifts of the Holy Spirit. They resolve to always heed the inner voice of the Holy Spirit so that the Work of Mary may grow and develop in accordance with his plans.

Translated by Margaret Linard in an unpublished document, included here with the permission of Chiara Lubich.

---

334. "In him we live and move and have our being" (Acts 17:28).

༄

4. QUESTIONS OF ETHICS

❧ In "Does Religious Faith Add to Ethical Perception?" American Catholic ethicist **Richard A. McCormick** (1922–2000) analyzes the distinctiveness of Christian morality.

RICHARD A. MCCORMICK

"Does Religious Faith Add to Ethical Perception?"

The particular question I want to raise can be posed in a number of ways. Let me try just a few. How does religious faith affect decision-making in government—or in any other area for that matter (e.g., the practice of medicine, the profession of law)? Does one's faith add to one's ethical perceptions, and if it does, what does it add? Is not a morally wrong judgment morally wrong independent of religious belief? Is not a right decision right whether one is a believer or not?

Theologians have been deeply concerned with this question in recent years. They formulate the question variously. For example is there a specifically Christian ethics? Does Christian faith add material content to what is in principle knowable by reason? Is Christian morality autonomous? Is Christ the norm for the morally good and right, and in what sense? These questions may appear academic, at the margin of real life. Actually, the proper answer to them is of great importance.

For instance, if Christian faith, rooted in God's revelation, tells us things about right and wrong in human affairs that we would not otherwise know, then it is clear that decision-making in government risks integrity unless it is Christianly informed and inspired. Furthermore, the answer to the question raised affects public policy. Public policy, while not identical with sound morality, draws upon and builds upon moral conviction. If Christian faith adds new material (concrete, behavioral) content to morality, then public policy is even more complex than it seems. For example, if Christians precisely as Christians know something about abortion that others cannot know unless they believe it as Christians, then in a pluralistic society there will be problems with discussion and decision in the public forum.

Moreover, the answer to these questions affects the churches' competence to teach morality authoritatively, and how this is to be conceived and implemented. Thus, if Christian faith and revelation add material content to what is knowable in principle by reason, then the churches conceivably

could teach moral positions and conclusions independently of the reasons and analyses that recommend these conclusions. This could lend great support to a highly juridical and obediential notion of Christian morality. The very processes we use or do not use to judge the moral rightness or wrongness of many concrete projects (e.g., donor insemination, in vitro fertilization, warfare, poverty programs, apartheid) would be profoundly affected. The question, then, is of enormous importance.

I. Faith and Ethics

Before entering the discussion of this question, some precision must be given to the terms "faith" and "ethics." By faith, I refer to *explicit,* Christian faith, not a faith that remains implicit or nonthematic. I say this because there is a sense in which even explicit nonbelievers can be said to encounter the grace of Christ, be touched by it and therefore be living the life of faith even though it remains unrecognized as such.

Next a word on the term "ethics" (as it is used in the question: does faith add to one's ethical perceptions?). There are four levels at which the term can be understood where rightness or wrongness of conduct is concerned. Only one level is of special concern, at least in terms of the discussion as we find it in recent theological literature.

(1) First, there is what we might call an *essential* ethic.[335] By this term we mean those norms that are regarded as applicable to all persons, where one's behavior is but an instance of a general, essential moral norm. Here we could use as examples the rightness or wrongness of killing actions, of contracts, of promises and all those actions whose demands are rooted in the dignity of the person.

(2) Second, there is an *existential* ethic. This refers to the choice of a good that the individual as individual should realize, the experience of an absolute ethical demand addressed to the individual. Obviously, at this level not all persons of good will can and do arrive at the same ethical decisions in concrete matters. For instance, an individual might conclude that his/her own moral-spiritual life cannot grow and thrive

---

335. [McCormick borrows] this usage from Norbert Rigali, S.J., "On Christian Ethics," *Chicago Studies* 10 (1971), 227–47.

in government work, hence that this work ought to be abandoned. Or, because of background, inclination, talent (etc.) an individual might choose to concentrate time and energy on a particular issue rather than on others.

(3) Third, there is *essential Christian* ethics. By this we refer to those ethical decisions a Christian must make precisely because he/she belongs to a community to which the non-Christian does not belong. These are moral demands made upon the Christian *as Christian*. For instance, to regard fellow workers as brothers and sisters in Christ (not just as autonomous, to-be-respected persons), to provide a Christian education for one's children, to belong to a particular worshipping community. These are important ethical decisions that emerge only within the context of a Christian community's understanding of itself in relation to other people. Thus, to the extent that Christianity is a Church in the above sense and has preordained structures and symbols, to this extent there can be and must be a distinctively Christian ethic, an essential ethics of Christianity which adds to the ordinary essential ethics of persons as members of the universal human community the ethics of persons as members of the Church-community.

(4) Fourth, there is *existential Christian* ethics—those ethical decisions that the Christian *as individual* must make, e.g., the choice to concentrate on certain political issues not only because these seem best suited to one's talent, but above all because they seem more in accord with the gospel perspectives.

II. Christian Faith and Essential Ethics

The problem that has above all concerned theologians involves ethics in the first sense only, i.e., *essential* ethics. In light of the foregoing precisions, the question could be worded as follows: does explicit Christian faith add to one's ethical (*essential* ethics) perceptions of obligation new content at the material or concrete level? This is the more precise form of the question now agitating theologians under a different formulation: [that is to say], is there a specifically Christian ethics? But this latter formulation I judge to be too vague and sprawling, and one that allows discussants to seem to disagree with each other, when in reality they are not addressing the same question. More concretely, it should be readily granted that revelation and our personal faith do influence ethical decisions at the latter three levels (existential, essential Christian, existential Christian). One's choice of issues, and the dispositions and motivations he/she brings to these issues, can be profoundly affected by one's personal appro-

priation of revealed truth, by one's prayer life, and by the community in which these develop. It is this level and these modalities that are highlighted in most literature when it refers (cf. below) to a "style of life" and "intentionality," a "new dynamism and power," "special context."

A few statements of opinion on this question will help give the flavor of the discussion. John Macquarrie, the well known Anglican theologian, states that the Christian ethic is not distinctive in its ultimate goals or its fundamental principles. These are shared with all serious minded people of all traditions. Therefore the distinctiveness is not to be found in the concrete moral obligations derived from an authentic humanity but in the degree of explicitness surrounding the notion of authentic humanity. "The distinctive element is the special context within which the moral life is perceived. This special context includes the normative place assigned to Jesus Christ and his teaching—not, indeed, as a paradigm for external imitation, but rather as the criterion and inspiration for a style of life."[336]

J. M. Aubert prepares the way for his own answer by studying the question in St. Thomas.[337] Thomas' point of view is gathered from his treatment of the relation of human virtues to Christian virtues, and from his discussion of the relation between the law of Christ and human morality. With regard to the virtues, Aubert maintains that Thomas clarified a long patristic heritage by explaining the autonomy and value of human virtue. An earlier Augustinian concern to avoid Pelagianism tended to smother the human with the overwhelming gratuity and supremacy of the theological virtues. Thomas recovered this human aspect with no compromise on the supremacy of the theological order. For him charity was the form of the virtues, suffusing and dynamizing them, but leaving them intact as the genuinely human expressions or ways of charity.

With regard to law, Thomas taught that the law of Christ should animate and transfigure all of human life. This implies that human life already has a moral content to which charity will give a new sense. But Thomas insisted that the law of Christ adds of itself no new particular moral prescriptions. It introduces a new dynamism and power. The resultant new life is essentially a more total and divinized way of

---

336. John Macquarrie, *Three Issues in Ethics* (New York: Harper and Row, 1970), 89.

337. J. M. Aubert, "La Spécificité de la morale Chrétienne selon Saint Thomas," *Supplément* 92 (1970), 55–73.

leading a human life, a human life having its own proper demands which man perceives by reason and conscience.

On the basis of his study Aubert concludes that it is faith which is the truly distinguishing (or formal) cause of the specificity of Christian morality. But this must be properly understood. Since there is only one destiny possible to all men, there is existentially only one morality common to Christians and non-Christians. That means that there is a material identity between Christian moral demands and those perceivable by reason. However, faith operates [with] a distinctiveness in the manner and intentionality of living these common moral demands. That is, it renders explicit the presence of charity. The Christian builds a life style on this explicitness. Therefore the specificity of Christian morality is found essentially in the very style of life, the manner of comporting oneself and of accomplishing the moral tasks which the Christian has in common with other men—a manner more dynamic, more assured, more joyous, more capable of following the example of Christ dying for other men. For it is ultimately the law of the cross which remains the essentially Christian model of the manner of practicing the moral law. . . .

In several valuable studies Joseph Fuchs, S.J., pursues in depth the notion of "Christian intentionality" mentioned by Aubert.[338] It is Fuchs' thesis that prescinding from this intentionality Christian morality is, in its materiality and concreteness, human morality. Therefore both Christians and non-Christians must seek the answers to moral questions by determining what is genuinely human. It is the intentionality brought to the authentically human which specifies Christian morality.

How are we to understand this intentionality? To explain it, Fuchs recalls that in the moral act there are two aspects: the specific act itself and through it one's self-realization with reference to an Absolute. This self-realization in relation to an Absolute is the decisive element in morality, even though we are not reflexly conscious of it. Thus there is "a certain intentionality which transcends and fulfills the individual moral act." Now the Christian does not relate himself to God only as the Absolute, but to God as Father, to God who gave us His love in the person of Christ, and who is in His Christ our salvation. It is this deep-seated stamp on our consciousness which is distinctive of Christian morality. [. . .]

III. Faith and Its Influence on Morality

[. . .] This tradition must be carefully understood. It refers above all to the intelligibility of moral norms and asserts that while there can be mysteries of faith, there can be no mysterious ethical norms which are simply closed off to human insight. Thus "human insight and reasoning" must be understood in its broadest sense. That broad sense would include two clarifications. First, it does not exclude the fact that the individual values that generate a norm can experience a special grounding and ratification in revelation. Quite the contrary. Thus our faith that God loves each individual and calls each to salvation deepens our insight into the worth of the individual.

Secondly this broad sense of "human insight and reasoning" suggests that there are factors at work in moral convictions that are reasonable but not always reducible to the clear and distinct ideas that the term "human reason" can mistakenly suggest. When all these factors are combined, they suggest that the term "moral reasoning" is defined most aptly by negation: "reasonable" means not ultimately mysterious.

This portion is found in Suarez, Vermeersch, H. Küng, A. Auer, B. Schüller, and a host of other Catholic theologians. It is also broadly shared by Protestant authors like Bultmann, Cullmann, E. Troeltsch.[339] [. . .]

[. . .] I should now like to develop a possible understanding of the matter in the hope that it may provide a structure within which the relation of religious belief to decision-making in government can be enlightened. I shall proceed in two steps: the origin of moral judgments and the relation of Christian perspectives to these judgments.

Origins of Moral Judgments

The first thing to be said is that moral convictions do not originate from rational analyses and arguments. Let me take slavery as an example. We do not hold that slavery is humanly demeaning and immoral chiefly because we have argued to this rationally. Rather, first our sensitivities are sharpened to the meaning and value of human persons and certainly religious faith can play an important part in the sharpening. As Böckle notes, it can influence our insights. We then *experience* the out-of-jointness, inequality, and injustice of slavery. We then *judge* it to be wrong. At this point we develop "arguments" to criticize, modify, and above all communicate this

---

338. Joseph Fuchs, S.J., "Gibt es eine specifisch Christliche Moral?" *Stimmen der Zeit* 185 (1970), 99–112; "Human, Humanist and Christian Morality," in *Human Values and Christian Morality* (Dublin: Gill and Macmillan, 1970), 112–47.

339. Cf. Bruno Schüller, S.J., "Zur Diskussion über das Proprium einer Christlichen Ethik," *Theologie und Philosophie* 51 (1976), 331.

judgment. Reflective analysis is an attempt to reinforce rationally, communicably, and from other sources what we grasp at a different level. Discursive reflection *does not discover* the right and good, but only *analyzes* it. The good that reason seems to discover is the good that was already hidden in the original intuition.

This needs more explanation. How do we arrive at definite moral obligations, prescriptions, and proscriptions? How does the general thrust of our persons toward good and away from evil become concrete, even as concrete as a code of do's and don't's, and caveats? It happens somewhat as follows—and in this I am following closely the school of J. de Finance, G. de Broglie, G. Grisez, John Finnis, and others who are heavily reliant on the Thomistic notion of "natural inclinations" in explaining the origin of basic moral obligation. We proceed by asking what are the goods or values man can seek, the values that define his human opportunity, his flourishing? We can answer this by examining man's basic tendencies. For it is impossible to act without having an interest in the object, and it is impossible to be attracted by, to have interest in something, without some inclination already present. What then are the basic inclinations?

With no pretense at being exhaustive, we could list some of the following as basic inclinations present prior to acculturation: the tendency to preserve life; the tendency to mate and raise children; the tendency to explore and question; the tendency to seek out other men and obtain their approval—friendship; the tendency to establish good relations with unknown higher powers; the tendency to use intelligence in guiding action; the tendency to develop skills and exercise them in play and the fine arts. In these inclinations our intelligence spontaneously and without reflection grasps the possibilities to which they point, and prescribes them. Thus we form naturally and without reflection the basic principles of practical or moral reasoning. Or as philosopher John Finnis renders it:

> What is spontaneously understood when one turns from contemplation to action is not a set of Kantian or neo-scholastic "moral principles" identifying this as right and that as wrong, but a set of values which can be expressed in the form of principles as "life is a good-to-be-pursued and realized and what threatens it is to be avoided."[340]

We have not yet arrived at a determination of what concrete actions are morally right or wrong; but we have laid the basis. Since these basic values are equally basic and irreducibly attractive, the morality of our conduct is determined by the adequacy of our openness to these values. For each of these values has its self-evident appeal as a participation in the unconditioned Good we call God. The realization of these values in intersubjective life is the only adequate way to love and attain God.

Further reflection by practical reason tells us what it means to remain open and to pursue these basic human values. First we must take them into account in our conduct. Simple disregard of one or other shows we have set our mind against this good. Second, when we can do so as easily as not, we should avoid acting in ways that inhibit these values, and prefer ways that realize them. Third, we must make an effort on their behalf when their realization in another is in extreme peril. If we fail to do so, we show that the value in question is not the object of our efficacious love and concern. Finally, we must never choose against a basic good in the sense of spurning it. What is to count as "turning against a basic good" is, of course, the crucial moral question. Certainly it does not mean that there are never situations of conflicted values where it is necessary to cause harm as we go about doing good. Thus there are times when it is necessary to take life in the very defense of life, in our very adhering to this basic value. That means that taking life need not always involve one in a "turning against a basic good." Somewhat similarly, one does not necessarily turn against the basic good of procreation (what Pius XII called a "sin against the very meaning of conjugal life") by avoiding child-bearing. Such avoidance is only reproachable when *unjustified*. And the many conflicts (medical, economic, social, eugenic) that justify such avoidance were acknowledged by Pius XII. Suppressing a value, or preferring one to another in one's choice, cannot be simply identified with turning against a basic good. My only point here is that particular moral judgments are incarnations of these more basic normative positions, which have their roots in spontaneous, prereflective inclinations.

Even though these inclinations can be identified as prior to acculturation, still they exist as culturally conditioned. We tend toward values as perceived. And the culture in which we live shades our perception of values. Philip Rieff in *The Triumph of the Therapeutic* notes that a culture survives by the power of institutions to influence conduct with "reasons"

340. John M. Finnis, "Natural Law and Unnatural Acts," *Heythrop Journal* 11 (1970), 365–87.

that have sunk so deeply into the self that they are implicitly understood.[341] In other words, decisions are made, policies set not chiefly by articulated norms, codes, regulations, and philosophies, but by "reasons" that lie below the surface. This is the dynamic aspect of a culture, and in this sense many of our major moral problems are cultural. Our way of perceiving the basic human values and relating to them is shaped by our whole way of looking at the world.

Let me take an example from another area of concern, that of bioethics; in relating to the basic human values several images of man are possible, as Callahan has observed.[342] First there is a power-plasticity model. In this model, nature is alien, independent of man, possessing no inherent value. It is capable of being used, dominated, and shaped by man. Man sees himself as possessing an unrestricted right to manipulate in the service of his goals. Death is something to be overcome, outwitted. Second, there is the sacral-symbiotic model. In its religious forms, nature is seen as God's creation, to be respected and heeded. Man is not the master; he is the steward and nature is a trust. In secular forms, man is seen as a part of nature. If man is to be respected, so is nature. We should live in harmony and balance with nature. Nature is a teacher, showing us how to live with it. Death is one of the rhythms of nature, to be gracefully accepted.

The model which seems to have "sunk deep" and shaped our moral imagination and feelings—shaped our perception of basic values—is the power-plasticity model. We are, corporately, *homo technologicus.* The best solution to the dilemmas created by technology is more technology. We tend to eliminate the maladapted condition (defectives, retardates, and so on) rather than adjust the environment to it. Even our language is sanitized and shades from view our relationship to basic human values. We speak of "surgical air strikes" and "terminating a pregnancy," ways of blunting the moral imagination from the shape of our conduct. My only point here is that certain cultural reasons qualify or shape our perception of and our grasp on the basic human values. Thus these reasons are the cultural soil of our moral convictions and have a good deal to say about where we come out on particular moral judgments.

Once the basic values are identified along with their cultural tints and trappings, theologians and philosophers attempt to develop "middle axioms" or mediating principles. These relate the basic values to concrete choice. The major problem any professional ethic faces is to reinterpret the concrete demands of the basic values in new circumstances without forfeiting its grasp on these values.

IV. The Christian Perspective and Moral Judgments

There may be many ways to explain the influences of Christian faith on the moral norms that guide decision-making. For instance, the very notion one entertains of the Supreme Being can influence normative statements. If one thinks of God above all as the creator and conserver of order, then this yields a certain attitude toward human interventions into the givenness of the world. If, however, one also believes God is the enabler of our potentialities, then a quite different normative stance becomes feasible, as James Gustafson has pointed out.[343] (Cf. Haughey.)

My own view on the relation of Christian belief to *essential* ethics would be developed as follows. Since there is only one destiny possible to all men, there is existentially only one *essential* morality common to all men, Christians and non-Christians alike. Whatever is distinctive about Christian morality is found essentially in the style of life, the manner of accomplishing the moral tasks common to all persons, not in the tasks themselves. Christian morality is, in its concreteness and materiality, *human* morality. The theological study of morality accepts the human in all its fullness as its starting point. It is the *human* which is then illumined by the person, teaching, and achievement of Jesus Christ. The experience of Jesus is regarded as normative because he is believed to have experienced what is to be human in the fullest way and at the deepest level.

The Second Vatican Council stated something similar to this when it asserted that "faith throws a new light on everything, manifests God's design for man's total vocation, and thus directs the mind to solutions which are *fully human.*"[344] It further stated "But only God, who created man to His own image and ransoms him from sin, provides a fully adequate answer to these questions. This he does through what he has revealed in Christ His Son, who became man. Whoever follows after Christ, the perfect man, *becomes himself more of a man.*"[345]

Traditionally, theologians referred to moral knowledge as

---

341. Philip Rieff, *The Triumph of the Therapeutic* (New York: Harper and Row, 1966).

342. Daniel Callahan, "Living with the New Biology," *Center Magazine 5* (July–Aug. 1972), 4–12.

343. James Gustafson, *The Contributions of Theology to Medical Ethics* (Milwaukee: Marquette University, 1975).

344. *The Documents of Vatican II* (New York: America Press, 1966), 209.

345. Ibid., 240.

originating in "reason *informed* by faith." The word "inform" is important. It does not mean *replaced* by faith. It is in explaining the term "inform" that we may hope to see more precisely how faith influences moral judgments at the *essential* level.

I have noted that our concrete moral judgments are applications originating in insights into our inclinations toward basic human values or goods. I have also suggested that our reasoning processes about these basic values can be distorted by cultural biases.

Let us take an example. It can be persuasively argued that the peculiar temptation of a technologically advanced culture such as ours is to view and treat persons functionally. Our treatment of the aged is perhaps the sorriest symptom of this. The elderly are probably the most alienated members of our society. More and more of them spend their declining years in homes for senior citizens, in chronic hospitals, in nursing homes. We have shunted them aside. Their protest is eloquent because it is helplessly muted and silent. But it is a protest against a basically functional assessment of their persons. "Maladaptation" is the term used to describe *them* rather than the environment. This represents a terribly distorted judgment of the human person.

Love of and loyalty to Jesus Christ, the perfect man, sensitizes us to the meaning of persons. The Christian tradition is anchored in faith in the meaning and decisive significance of God's covenant with men, especially as manifested in the saving incarnation of Jesus Christ, his eschatological kingdom which is here aborning but will finally only be given. Faith in these events, love of and loyalty to this central figure, yields a decisive way of viewing and intending the world, of interpreting its meaning, of hierarchizing its values. In this sense the Christian tradition only illumines human values, supports them, provides a context for their reading at given points in history. It aids us in staying human by underlining the truly human against all cultural attempts to distort the human. It is by steadying our gaze on the basic human values that are the parents of more concrete norms and rules that faith influences moral judgment and decision-making. That is how I understand "reason informed by faith."

In summary, then, Christian emphases do not immediately yield moral norms and rules for decision-making. But they affect them. The stories and symbols that relate the origin of Christianity and nourish the faith of the individual affect one's perspectives. They sharpen and intensify our focus on the human goods definitive of our flourishing. It is persons so informed, persons with such "reasons" sunk deep in their being, who face new situations, new dilemmas, and reason together as to what is the best policy, the best protocol for the service of all the values. They do not find concrete answers in their tradition, but they bring a world-view that informs their reasoning—especially by allowing the basic human goods to retain their attractiveness and not be tainted by cultural distortions. This world-view is a continuing check on and challenge to our tendency to make choices in light of cultural enthusiasms which sink into and take possession of our unwitting, pre-ethical selves. Such enthusiasms can reduce the good life to mere adjustment in a triumph of the therapeutic; collapse an individual into his functionability; exalt his uniqueness into a lonely individualism or crush it into a suffocating collectivism. In this sense I believe it is true to say that the Christian tradition is much more a value-raiser than an answer-giver. And it affects our values at the spontaneous, prethematic level. One of the values inherent in its incarnational ethos is an affirmation of the goodness of man and all about him—including his reasoning and thought processes. The Christian tradition refuses to bypass or supplant human deliberation and hard work in developing ethical protocols within a profession. For that would be blasphemous of the Word of God become human. On the contrary, it asserts their need, but constantly reminds men that what God did and intends for man is an affirmation of the human and therefore must remain the measure of what man may reasonably decide to do to and for himself.

V. The Influence of Faith

If this is a satisfactory account of the relation of Christian faith to decision-making (at the *essential* level), it means that faith informs reason because the reasoner has been transformed. This transformation means practically: (1) a *view* of persons and their meaning; (2) a *motivation* in the following of Christ; (3) a *style* of performing the moral tasks common to persons (communitarian, sacramental, cross of Christ, Holy Spirit). I think it quite possible that persons with such a view, motivation, style, might come to some different practical conclusions on moral matters, as indeed the historical Christian churches have. But these conclusions will not be in principle unavailable to human insight and reasoning in the broadest sense. [. . .]

In sum, one need not be a Christian to be concerned with the poor, with health, with the food problem, with justice and rights. But if one is a Christian and is not so concerned, something is wrong with that Christianity. It has ceased to be

Christian because it has ceased to be what its founder was—human.

From Charles E. Curran and Richard A. McCormick, eds., *Readings in Moral Theology*, no. 2, *The Distinctiveness of Christian Ethics* (New York: Paulist Press, 1980), 156–61, 163–70, 172–73.

H. Richard Niebuhr (1894–1962), the younger brother of theologian Reinhold Niebuhr (1892–1971) and a leading twentieth-century American Protestant theologian, addresses the topic of Christian ethics in light of the dual nature of Christ in "Responsibility and Christ."

H. RICHARD NIEBUHR

"Responsibility and Christ," in *The Responsible Self: An Essay in Christian Moral Philosophy*

Christ as Paradigm of Responsibility

There are doubtless as many ways of associating Jesus Christ with the responsible life as there have been ways of associating him with the ideal life or the obedient or dutiful one. And it is only an old, though deeply established, prejudice which will lead us to believe that there is only one fitting answer to the question, one ideal solution of the problem, one right relationship. "God fulfills himself in many ways lest one good custom should corrupt the earth." A theory of ethics must not be confused with a life decision or with an absolute imperative. Decisions have a kind of exclusive validity; once we have decided that a certain act is right or good or fitting we must proceed and accept the consequences for ourselves. A theory, however, is not such a personal decision. We commit ourselves to a theory only tentatively. The imperative in it is only hypothetical. With this warning to ourselves not to take ourselves too seriously we can decide to proceed nevertheless and make a resolute effort to understand Christian life in terms of responsibility.

In the older theories of Christian idealism and of Christian obedience Jesus Christ usually functions in a double way, as prophet and as priest, or as king and as priest. On the one hand he appears as the perfect illustration or the incarnate pattern, as the first and only Christian. On the other hand his personal, historical action is understood as God's way of making what is impossible for men possible. Christ makes it possible for men to participate in his kind of life, to become somewhat like Christ despite the vast disparity between a

unique son of God and all the prodigal children of the Almighty. Thus he is understood as man, perfectly directed toward God as his end, or perfectly obedient to the Father; and he is acknowledged as divine, as the power of God or as act or Word of God that redirects men who had lost their relation to their end, become enslaved to false goals or had fallen into disobedience. In whatever form we interpret Christian ethics, in it Christ always has something of this double character. In him man is directed toward God; in him also God is directed toward men. Hence the Christian ethos is that of a community which knows through reason and through Jesus Christ what it and man in general should make out of life, or what law ought to be obeyed, and how; or what goal chosen; it also knows man's lack of power to undertake such a construction, pursue such a pilgrimage, or be obedient to such a will and law; finally, it is a community that finds itself driven to attempt what lies beyond man's strength and to persist hopefully in a hopeless journey toward the unattainable goal that Christ attained, to attempt an obedience that is ever in need of forgiveness; yet forgiven it attempts again to obey. That is the empowerment it receives from Christ.

(This duality of the function of Christ in the Christian life seems largely responsible for the difficulties Christians encounter in relating their ethics to the ethics of the philosophers—a problem which we cannot pursue at this time.)

When we look at the Jesus Christ of the New Testament story and as he exists symbolically in the Christian consciousness, from the point of view of responsibility, we note a similar duality of function. First of all, he is the responsible man who in all his responses to alterations did what fitted into the divine action. He interpreted every alteration that he encountered as a sign of the action of God, of the universal, omnificent One, whom he called Father. He responded to all action upon him as one who anticipated the divine answer to his answers. Will of God meant for him not only or primarily divine imperative but the divine action, carried out through many agencies besides those of men obedient to commandment. To pray, "Thy will be done in earth as it is in heaven," did not evidently mean "Make us obedient," though that petition may be implied. The Gethsemane prayer, "Not my will but thine be done," did not refer to commandments but to acts of God that were to be carried out by men who did not inquire about the will of God. The statement, "It is not the will of the Father that one of these little ones should perish," seems to refer to what God does as much as to what he requires human agents to do. The will of God is what God does in all that nature and men do. It is the universal that contains and transforms, includes and fashions, every partic-ular. Will of God is present for Jesus in every event from the death of sparrows, the shining of sun and descent of rain, through the exercise of authority by ecclesiastical and polit-ical powers that abuse their authority, through treachery and desertion by disciples, to the impending beleaguerment of Jerusalem and the end of the aeon. All this interpretation of every alteration as included in, or as taken up by, the ac-tion of God was neither fatalistic nor mechanical. The idea that all acts of finite agents had been predesigned, as though God were the author of a play in which each actor played a predestined role, is remote from Jesus' way of thinking. The Universal One whom he calls Father is Lord of heaven and earth. His action is more like that of the great wise leader who uses even the meannesses of his subjects to promote the public welfare.

Let us take a few examples of Jesus' interpretation of al-teraction, that is to say, of the kinds of finite events to which all men respond in one way or another in accordance with their interpretations of what these events mean. Consider how he interprets natural happenings, those acts occurring in the natural environment which are important elements in every human ethos, since we are always reacting to them in accordance with our interpretations. We see them as parts of a large pattern; we read them as words in a sentence which get their meaning from the whole sentence. What is the large pattern, what the inclusive action to which Jesus responds with his evaluations and other actions, when he encounters a natural event? He sees as others do that the sun shines on criminals, delinquents, hypocrites, honest men, good Samari-tans, and VIP's without discrimination, that rains come down in equal proportions on the fields of the diligent and of the lazy. These phenomena have been for unbelief, from the beginning of time, signs of the operation of a univer-sal order that is without justice, unconcerned with right and wrong conduct among men. But Jesus interprets the com-mon phenomena in another way: here are the signs of cos-mic generosity. The response to the weather so interpreted leads then also to a response to criminals and outcasts, who have not been cast out by the infinite Lord. So it is also with carefree birds who deserve no pay for useful work, and with flowers that have done no heroic deeds to merit their colorful ribbons and brilliant medals. Are these appearances to be in-terpreted as signs that the power of life expressed in natural things is unconcerned with the quality of what issues from it? Or are they to be understood as signs of the presence of an overflowing creativity, of an infinite artistry, that rejoices

in its creations, that rejects, because it is all grace, the censor-ships of human laws, not because it falls below the common human standard, but rises far above it? There is a righteous-ness of God for Jesus; there is a universal ordering for good; but it is different in all its working from the provincial, even planetary righteousness that men have discovered or devised. Thus he understands and reacts to natural events as expres-sive of an omnificent intention that is wholly affirmative of what it brings into being.

What is true of the extrahuman, natural world is true of the human. To children, whose angels behold the face of the Father who is in heaven, to sinners who are also the children of Abraham, to the sick and lost whose salvation is to be to the glory of God—to all these he responds as having a mean-ing derived from their place in that divine action, which hates nothing that it has made but wills it to be and to be whole.

In his responses also to the limiting and destructive ac-tions to which he is subject, Jesus acts as one who interprets them in the context of divine, of universal, action. He reads these signs also as words in a divine sentence. He responds to the infinite intention, behind or inclusive of all the finite intentions. He understands that Pilate would have no power over him had it not been granted to the procurator from above. He pronounces woes on his betrayer, yet the son of man goes as it has been determined, not by betrayer but by the will beyond all finite wills. So it is also with those words and actions of Jesus that relate to the coming end of his time or of the aeon, which occasion much difficulty to those inter-preters of his ethical sayings who use idealistic or legal pat-terns of interpretation. The significance of eschatology in the gospels lies for them in the fact that the time is short before the consummation of all things. Hence the telos is confused by an eschaton, the normal law by a law for the interim. But the evident weight in these sayings about the future does not lie on the time-factor so much as on the God-factor. The di-vine rule, the divine action in all things, which now men only dimly perceive and understand in their encounter with cre-ative and destructive events, will be clearly revealed at last, in the end. What is to become clear in the end, however, is not something new. It is now an emergency that is coming. The actuality of the present is to become emergent. God whose rule is hidden and whose rule will become manifest is ruling now, despite all hiddenness. Realized eschatology is realized theology.

If then we try to summarize the ethos of Jesus in a for-mula we may do so by saying that he interprets all actions upon him as signs of the divine action of creation, government, and salvation and so responds to them as to respond to divine action. He does that act which fits into the divine action and looks forward to the infinite response to his response.

The Christian ethos so uniquely exemplified in Christ himself is an ethics of universal responsibility. It interprets every particular event as included in universal action. It is the ethos of citizenship in a universal society, in which no being that exists and no action that takes place is interpretable outside the universal context. It is also the ethos of eternal life, in the sense that no act of man in response to action upon him does not involve repercussions, reactions, extending onward toward infinity in time as well as in social space.

As ethos of universal responsibility the ethos exemplified in Jesus Christ is not unique. It has affinities to other forms of universal ethics. Insistence on the absolute uniqueness of the Christian ethos has never been able to meet either the theoretical or the practical test. In practice, Christians undertaking to act in some fashion in conformity with Christ find themselves doing something like what some others, conforming to other images, are doing. Identity of action there has not been; likeness, however, has often been present. (Christians have had no monopoly on humanitarianism or concern for those suffering deprivation; in reverence for life they have often been excelled by others.) On the theoretic side, when Christians have undertaken to set forth the pattern present in the action of Christ they have found kinship between it and certain patterns of moral conduct set forth by universalist philosophers, that is, by thinkers who saw man first of all as a citizen of the universe, as endowed with a reason that seeks universal truth, as subject to laws that are universal. For the most part these affinities of the Christian ethos with other types of universal ethics have been stated in terms of idealism or of legalism, as when Platonic or Aristotelian ethics on the one hand, Kantian thought or universal utilitarianism on the other, have been associated with Christian ethics. [. . .]

To many a Christian it is a far cry from Epictetus and Spinoza to the gospels and epistles of the New Testament. But let them remember how much greater is the distance to the latter from all those styles of life that are developed by men who live in a world in which all events outside the limited sphere of man's domain are the results of the collisions of blindly running atoms, or of the acts of little gods that rule in partiality over small areas. Instead of distinguishing between styles of life by contrasting the search for happiness with the search for virtue, or by contrasting obedience to natural, ra-

tional law with obedience to revealed law, we shall do well, I think, to mark the lines of division that run between egoisms of every kind, social, closed-society ethics of every sort, and the universalisms, whether these be presented to us as ethics of aspiration after universal good, or of obedience to universal law, or of responsibility in universal society, [or][346] to universal power.

There is an egoistic style of life, even one which calls itself Christian, but has nothing in common with what we see in Jesus Christ, since it seeks only its own happiness and interprets whatever happens to it as action of a God whose only concern is just with this lonely self, a God who is the counterpart of individuality, not the Lord of being. There is also a social style which lives in an enclave in the universe; when this appears in Christian form the enclave is a Christian church, which participates in a special history—and which finds divine action really only in the creation, government, and salvation of that special society of the elect. Such ethics indeed has little in common with Stoic or Spinozistic universalism. It has much in common with every kind of closed-society ethics. But the ethics of Jesus Christ, as the way of life of one who responds to the action of the universal God in all action, in whatever happens, is an ethics of universal responsibility and not wholly alien to all those styles of life that men have developed when they lifted up their eyes beyond the particularities of their situation and looked for the universal good beyond all special goods, the universal law beyond all local law, the universal action beyond all particular action.

Before we now proceed to ask how Jesus Christ works in the Christian consciousness in a second way, we need to answer one evident objection to the foregoing sketch of his ethics. Does not this way of understanding him, and so of understanding the model Christian life, make of this life an affair of pure resignation to the will of God? Is not this interpretation one of fatalism? One answer to this objection is that submission to determination in the form in which it is represented, for instance, by Islam may be less foreign to the Christianity of Jesus Christ than is all the ethics of absolute human freedom, the ethics of man the conqueror of the conditions in which he lives, the ethics of human mastery. More important, however, is the question how the determining power, the One who acts in all the many, is understood. When this One is understood, with the use of the symbols of making and of design, as the predesigner, the foreordainer of

---

346. Insertion by Gerhart and Udoh.

all that happens, then indeed nothing but fatalism could result from an ethics of response to God. Then Judas' treachery is predesigned, and then Russia's attack on the West is fore-ordained, and you and I play out the roles which have been written down for us in the script. But such a Determiner of Destiny is not the One to whom Jesus Christ made his responses; nor is he the God of Isaiah; nor would he be One to whom we have access. The God and Father of our Lord Jesus Christ is the loving dynamic One, who does new things, whose relation to his world is more like that of father to his children than like that of the maker to his manufactures; it is more like that of the ruler to his realm than like that of the designer to his machines. The symbols fatalism uses to interpret what is happening do not fit the situation. The [images] of the kingdom and of the family are, to be sure, symbols also, but they do greater justice to our actual experience of life. They fit this dialogue in which our free acts take place in response to actions over which we have no power, in which our free acts are not truly *ours,* and free, unless they are the consequences of interpretation. They fit the dialogue also in which our free actions can never be freed from the responses that will be made to them. Our freedom presupposes and anticipates action not subject to our control. To think of the determination to which we are so subject as in itself invariant after the manner of a machine is to become enslaved by an erroneous myth. Since we shall in any case use myths, let us use our myths critically and with discrimination.

From H. Richard Niebuhr, *The Responsible Self: An Essay in Christian Moral Philosophy* (New York: Harper and Row, 1963), 162–68, 171–73.

❧ On November 3, 1966, the **National Committee of Negro Churchmen** (which would soon change its name to the National Committee of Black Churchmen) gathered at the steps of the Statue of Liberty to highlight the issues the country would face in the upcoming elections, giving rise to "Racism and the Elections: The American Dilemma, 1966."

NATIONAL COMMITTEE OF NEGRO CHURCHMEN
"Racism and the Elections: The American Dilemma, 1966"

A few days ago the 80th anniversary of the Statue of Liberty was celebrated here on Liberty Island. On November 8, a so-called "white backlash" will confront the American people with a fateful choice in the elections across the country. We, an informal group of Negro churchmen, assembled from the four corners of this land, gather here today in order to highlight the critical moral issues which confront the American people in those elections—issues symbolized here in the Statue of Liberty.

Our purpose here is neither to beg nor to borrow, but to state the determination of black men in America to exact from this nation not one whit less than our full manhood rights. We will not be cowed nor intimidated in the land of our birth. We intend that the truth of this country, as experienced by black men, will be heard. We shall state this truth from the perspective of the Christian faith and in the light of our experience with the Lord of us all, in the bleakness of this racially idolatrous land.

The inscription inside the Statue of Liberty, entitled "The New Colossus," refers to America as the "Mother of Exiles." It concludes with these moving words:

> "Keep ancient land, your storied pomp" cries she
> With silent lips. "Give me your tired, your poor,
> Your huddled masses yearning to breathe free.
> The wretched refuse of your teeming shore.
> Send these, the homeless, tempest-tost to me.
> I lift my lamp beside the Golden Door!"

This poem focuses on the linked problems of identity and power which have been so tragically played out on the stage of this nation's history. "Mother of Exiles" and "The New Colossus"—these symbols capture both the variety of groups and experience out of which this nation has been hammered and the fervent hope of many early Americans that in this land the world would see a new and more human use of power, dedicated to the proposition that all men are created equal.

We remind Americans that in our beginnings we were all exiles, strangers sojourning in an unfamiliar land. Even the first black men who set foot on these shores came, as did most white men, in the role of pilgrims, not as slaves. Sharing common aspirations and hopes for a land where freedom could take root and live, for the briefest of moments black men and white men found each other in a community of trust and mutual acceptance.

However, if America became a "Mother of Exiles" for white men she became at the same time a cruel system of bondage and inhumanity to black men. Far from finding here a maternal acceptance, her black sons were thrust into the depth of despair, at times so hopeless that it wrung from their lips the sorrow song: "Sometimes I feel like a motherless child." What anguish is keener, what rejection more complete, or what alienation more poignant than this experience which called forth the metaphor, "motherless child"?

But that is only part of our story. For somewhere in the depth of their experience within this great land, those same black men and women found a ground of faith and hope on which to stand. Never accepting on the inside the identity forced upon them by a brutalizing white power, they also sang—even prior to emancipation—"Before I'll be a slave, I'll be buried in my grave and go home to my Lord and be free." A faith of this quality and integrity remains alive today.

There is, to be sure, a continuing dilemma of "crisis and commitment" in our country. But it is not the quarrels among the civil rights leaders, nor is it the debate about Black Power, nor is it the controversy surrounding the riots in our cities. The crisis is what it has always been since shortly after the first black Americans set foot upon these shores. It is not a crisis rooted in the Negro community. It is a "crisis of commitment" among white Americans who have consistently taken two steps forward toward becoming mature men on race and one and a half steps backward at the same time. The power of "The New Colossus" has never been fully committed to eliminating this monstrous racism from the life of the American People.

Look at the record of fitful and mincing steps forward and of cowardly steps away from the goal of racial justice. The slaves were freed in 1863, but the nation refused to give them land to make that emancipation meaningful. . . . Simultaneously, the nation was giving away millions of acres in the midwest and west—a gift marked "for whites only." Thus an economic floor was placed under the new peasants from Europe but America's oldest peasantry was provided only an abstract freedom. In the words of Frederick Douglass, emancipation made the slaves "free to hunger; free to the winter and rains of heaven . . . free without roofs to cover them or bread to eat or land to cultivate. . . . We gave them freedom and famine at the same time. The marvel is that they still live."

We should, therefore, be neither shocked nor surprised that our slums today confront us with the bitter fruits of that ancient theft. Is it conceivable that the shrill cry "Burn, Baby, Burn" in Watts, Los Angeles, and across this country, could ever be invented by men with reasonable chances to make a living, to live in a decent neighborhood, to get an adequate education for their children? Is it conceivable that men with reasonable prospects for life, liberty and the pursuit of happiness for themselves and for their children could ever put the torch to their own main streets? The answer is obvious. These are the anguished, desperate acts of men, women and children who have been taught to hate themselves and who have been herded and confined like cattle in rat-infested slums.

Frederick Douglass is indeed correct when he suggests that "the marvel is that Negroes are still alive" not to mention sane. Look at the record. We submit that to pass a Civil Rights Bill as this nation did in 1875 and then refuse to enforce it; to pass another Civil Rights Bill (weaker this time) in 1964 and then refuse to enforce it; to begin an anti-poverty program with insufficient funds in the first place and then to put the lion's share of this miniscule budget into Head Start programs when unemployment among Negro men continues to skyrocket; to declare segregation in our schools unconstitutional as the Supreme Court did in 1954, and refuse to end it forthwith; to set up guidelines for desegregating hospitals and then refuse to appropriate moneys for the enforcement of these guidelines; to insist on civil rights legislation aimed at the south and then to defeat the first piece of such legislation relevant to areas outside the south; to preach "law and order" into the anguish of Negro slums in full view of the contributions of policemen to that anguish and then to insist that policemen be their own judges; to hear suburban politicians declaim against open occupancy in one breath and in the very next breath insist that they are not racists: these are the ironies which stare us in the face and make it all but impossible to talk about how much "progress" has been made. The fact of the matter is if black Americans are not accorded basic human and constitutional rights which white Americans gain immediately upon their entry into citizenship, then there really are no substantive gains of which to speak.

Therefore, we will not be intimidated by the so-called "white backlash," for white America has been "backlashing" on the fundamental human and constitutional rights of Negro Americans since the 18th century. The election of racists in November will merely be a continuation of this pattern.

But: Let us try to be very clear about one thing, America. Black Americans are determined to have all of their full human and constitutional rights. We will not cease to agitate this issue with every means available to men of faith and dignity until justice is done.

We are dealing at bottom with a question of relationship between black and white, between rich and poor, ultimately between believers in different gods. We support all of our civil rights leaders for we believe that they all have important insights to share with us on this critical question. For our part, we submit that our basic goal in this struggle is to make it possible for all persons and groups to participate with power at all levels of our society. Integration is not an aesthetic goal designed to add token bits of color to institutions controlled entirely by whites. Integration is a political goal with the objective of making it possible for Negroes and other Americans to express the vitality of their personal and group life in institutions which fundamentally belong to all Americans.

If the tremendous power of this nation—this "New Colossus"—begins to move "with conquering limbs astride from land to land," then we are bound to forget the tired, the poor, the "huddled masses yearning to be free." America is rich and powerful. But America is neither infinitely rich nor omnipotent. Even America must make choices.

We submit that the resolution of the crisis which is upon us requires a change in the nation's priorities. The welfare and dignity of all Americans is more important than the priorities being given to military expansion, space exploration or the production of supersonic jet airliners.

To this end, we of the Negro church call for a massive mobilization of the resources in the Negro community in order to give leadership in the fulfillment not only of our own destiny but in order to help produce a more sane white America.

We further call upon white churchmen to join us by endeavoring to mobilize the resources of the white community in completing with us the task at hand.

Finally, we say to the American people, white and black, there is no turning back of the clock of time. America cannot be America by electing "white backlash" candidates in the November elections.

Again we say: America is at the crossroad. Either we become the democracy we can become, or we tread the path to self-destruction.

From James H. Cone and Gayraud S. Wilmore, eds., *Black Theology: A Documentary History, 1966–1979* (Maryknoll, NY: Orbis Books, 1979), 31–34. [Ellipses in original.]

⁓ In August 1968, Pope Paul VI convoked the **Medellín Conference**, which was the Second General Conference of Latin American Bishops (CELAM). The sixteen final Medellín Documents issued by CELAM, including "Justice," provide a theological basis for a critique of social institutions, both national and international.

THE SECOND GENERAL CONFERENCE OF LATIN AMERICAN BISHOPS

"Justice"

I. Pertinent Facts

1. There are in existence many studies of the Latin American People. The misery that besets large masses of human beings in all of our countries is described in all of these studies. That misery, as a collective fact, expresses itself as injustice which cries to the heavens.[347]

But what perhaps has not been sufficiently said is that in general the efforts which have been made have not been capable of assuring that justice be honored and realized in every sector of the respective national communities. Often families do not find concrete possibilities for the education of their children. The young demand their right to enter universities or centers of higher learning for both intellectual and technical training; the women, their right to a legitimate equality with men; the peasants, better conditions of life; or if they are workers, better prices and security in buying and selling; the growing middle class feels frustrated by the lack of expectations. There has begun an exodus of professionals and technicians to more developed countries; the small businessmen and industrialists are pressed by greater interests and not a few large Latin American industrialists are gradually coming to be dependent on the international business enterprises. We cannot ignore the phenomenon of this almost universal frustration of legitimate aspirations which creates the climate of collective anguish in which we are already living.

2. The lack of socio-cultural integration, in the majority of our countries, has given rise to the superimposition of cultures. In the economic sphere systems flourished which consider solely the potential of groups with great earning power. This lack of adaptation to the characteristics and to the potentials of all our people, in turn, gives rise to frequent political instability and the consolidation of purely formal institutions. To all of this must be added the lack of solidarity which, on the individual and social levels, leads to the committing of serious sins, evident in the unjust structures which characterize the Latin American situation.

II. Doctrinal Bases

3. The Latin American Church has a message for all men on this continent who "hunger and thirst after justice." The very God who creates men in his image and likeness creates the "earth and all that is in it for the use of all men and all nations, in such a way that created goods can reach all in a more just manner,"[348] and gives them power to transform and per-

---

347. Cf. Song 2:3; Lk 1:46–55.
348. Cf. Mt 5:3.

fect the world in solidarity.[349] It is the same God who, in the fullness of time, sends his Son in the flesh, so that He might come to liberate all men from the slavery to which sin has subjected them:[350] hunger, misery, oppression and ignorance, in a word, that injustice and hatred which have their origin in human selfishness.

Thus, for our authentic liberation, all of us need a profound conversion so that "the kingdom of justice, love and peace," might come to us. The origin of all disdain for mankind, of all injustice, should be sought in the internal imbalance of human liberty, which will always need to be rectified in history. The uniqueness of the Christian message does not so much consist in the affirmation of the necessity for structural change, as it does in the insistence on the conversion of men which will in turn bring about this change. We will not have a new continent without new and reformed structures, but, above all, there will be no new continent without new men, who know how to be truly free and responsible according to the light of the Gospel.

4. Only by the light of Christ is the mystery of man made clear. In the economy of salvation the divine work is an action of integral human development and liberation, which has love for its sole motive. Man is "created in Christ Jesus,"[351] fashioned in Him as a "new creature."[352] By faith and baptism he is transformed, filled with the gift of the Spirit, with a new dynamism, not of selfishness, but of love which compels him to seek out a new, more profound relationship with God, his fellow man, and created things.

Love, "the fundamental law of human perfection, and therefore of the transformation of the world,"[353] is not only the greatest commandment of the Lord; it is also the dynamism which ought to motivate Christians to realize justice in the world, having truth as a foundation and liberty as their sign.

5. This is how the Church desires to serve the world, radiating over it a light and life which heals and elevates the dignity of the human person, which consolidates the unity of society and gives a more profound reason and meaning to all human activity.

Doubtless, for the Church, the fullness and perfection of the human vocation will be accomplished with the definitive inclusion of each man in the Passover or Triumph of Christ, but the hope of such a definitive realization, rather than lull, ought to "vivify the concern to perfect this earth. For here grows the body of the new human family, a body which even now is able to give some kind of foreshadowing of the new age."[354] We do not confuse temporal progress and the King-

dom of Christ; nevertheless, the former, "to the extent that it can contribute to the better ordering of human society, is of vital concern to the Kingdom of God."[355]

The Christian quest for justice is a demand arising from biblical teaching. All men are merely humble stewards of material goods. In the search for salvation we must avoid the dualism which separates temporal tasks from the work of sanctification. Although we are encompassed with imperfections, we are men of hope. We have faith that our love for Christ and our brethren will not only be the great force liberating us from injustice and oppression, but also the inspiration for social justice, understood as a whole of life and as an impulse toward the integral growth of our countries.

From Joseph Gremillion, ed., *The Gospel of Peace and Justice* (Maryknoll, NY: Orbis Books, 1976), 445–47.

In her essay "Sex, Gender, and the Problem of Moral Argument," Catholic theologian **Lisa Sowle Cahill** seeks common ground among traditional Christian teachings and feminist and postmodernist perspectives regarding sex, parenthood, family, and related areas.

LISA SOWLE CAHILL

"Sex, Gender, and the Problem of Moral Argument," in *Sex, Gender, and Christian Ethics*

Sexual identity and behavior and gender roles are intimate components of the ordinary life of every human being. Thus, normative interpretations of sex and gender have a potentially enormous significance for all of us. This is particularly the case when they are backed by heavy social or psychological sanctions, as they have been in traditional Christian teaching about the proper hierarchy of gender, and about sexual sin. Sex and gender are so controverted today because the rigidity and stringency of their traditional moral presentation has collided head-on with historicized or "post-

---

349. Cf. Am 2:6–7.

350. Cf. Philem 2:5–8.

351. Cf. 2 Cor 8:9.

352. Cf. Paul VI, Enc. *Ecclesiam suam*, No. 50.

353. Cf. Paul VI, *Homily of the Mass on Development Day*, Bogotá, 23 August 1968.

354. Cf. Vatican Council II, decree *Presbyterorum ordinis*, No. 21.

355. Cf. ibid., No. 8.

modern" interpretations of moral systems. The latter select sexual norms as an example *par excellence* of culturally relative assumptions parading as timeless absolutes. In particular, feminist critiques have suggested provocatively that the social control of women is a major motivation underlying a high proportion of traditional Christian sexual morality.

This project is sympathetic to these critiques. Yet, as I will also argue, Christian morality can fund strong criticism of sexual and reproductive behavior, gender expectations, and family forms which dominate women. But the fundamentally egalitarian inspiration of Christianity is perennially liable to perversion by powerful authorities interested in maintaining their status. This book is thus written from a feminist perspective, by which is meant simply a commitment to equal personal respect and equal social power for women and men. This does not necessarily mean that the sexes have no innate differences; it does mean such differences—whatever they may be—will not be accepted as warrants for social systems which grant men in general authority and power over women in general.

In addition to a feminist perspective in Christian ethics, I propose critical realism as an approach to moral knowledge. Radical deconstruction of moral foundations simply leads to a cultural relativism which enervates real moral communication, intercultural critique, and cooperation in defining and building just conditions of life for men and women. I will draw primarily on the Aristotelian—Thomistic ethical tradition to argue that it is possible to establish shared moral values, at least at a fundamental and general level. Distinguishing my project from neo-Kantian approaches to moral universality, I will make a case that it is possible to come to agreement about values which are substantive and not merely formal. The foundations of morality are not best understood as innate structures of consciousness or rationality which are self-evident at an abstract level, but as broad areas of agreement about human needs, goods, and fulfillments which can be reached inductively and dialogically through human experience. All humans—as embodied, self-conscious, intersubjective, and social—share common ground for moral obligation, insight, communication, and action. This is true without prejudice to the fact that immense personal and cultural differences create an equally immense variety of human ways of being.

One aim of the present study will be to show that many feminist deconstructions of moral foundations create a normative vacuum which cripples their political critique. At the same time, they allow values like autonomy and freedom,

tracing to Enlightenment roots, to slide in as tacit universals, operative without intercultural nuancing or explicit defense. These modern values are important, and, I believe, implied by the basic human experience of being a self whose identity is developed dialectically among other selves who are all finally irreducible to one another. The signature Enlightenment appreciation of the interiority and inviolability of the self accounts for the high profile that self-determination and freedom have achieved in subsequent moral thought. This includes modern Christian thought about sex and gender.

However, these are neither the only, nor without question the paramount, experiences and values defining moral agency. Human embodiedness, as to some extent structuring our social relations, needs to be reintegrated with freedom. All must be elements in a Christian ethics of sex and gender which is committed to equality, to intercultural discernment of real goods and evils, and to the human and moral interdependence of sexual desire and pleasure, sexual commitment, and responsible parenthood.

The State of the Current Discussion

The moral authorities traditionally most decisive for Christian self-understanding have been the Bible and some conception of human nature or a natural moral law. *Scripture* reveals God's will for human behavior, and maintains continuity with Jesus' life and ministry and with the first discipleship communities. Christian interpretations of *human "nature,"* as divinely created and as directed to certain goods recognizable by reason, have provided a realist approach to morality and promised common ground with other religious and philosophical traditions. Natural-law ethics presupposes natural and intelligible goods which orient virtuous activity in the practical realms of life that all cultures share (for example, care for physical life and well-being, marriage and family, education, politics, and religion). While Scriptural sources have been most central in Protestant theological ethics, an ethics of the natural law has been formative for Roman Catholic moral theology.

Incrementally, since the middle of this century, critical hermeneutics has shaken both these traditional moral foundations. Proliferating "postmodern" philosophies question whether objective moral assessments are possible at all; reason has lost its footing, they claim, and traditions their right to claim transcendence of history. Resounding with the energetic iconoclasm of Foucault and his followers, Jean-François Lyotard warns, in the final lines of *The Postmodern Condition,* against "the fantasy to seize reality" and charges, "Let us wage a war on totality"![356]

It was precisely the premises of stability, consistency, rationality, and the intelligibility of beings in themselves that had provided the anchor for Roman Catholic natural-law thinking about sex in terms of natural capacities and purposes. The new emphasis on the historical production of knowledge has challenged both natural law and the assumption that biblical traditions and the teachings of a historical community can be reliable indicators of the will of God. It has raised the question whether biblical writings and Christian teachings favoring monogamy, prohibiting divorce, and abominating homosexuality are anything more than artifacts of cultural bias.

Among these philosophical influences, the writings of Michel Foucault have had perhaps the most drastic and disturbing effect on Christian sexual morality, and they will be addressed in more depth [elsewhere]. Although few Christian ethicists adopt Foucault's program entirely, many have imbibed his resistance to traditional sexual norms along with his refusal to endorse any new authority for sexual behaviors. Many feminist authors have developed Foucault's deconstruction of sexual identity and value, applying it more explicitly both to sexual orientation and to gender. To take just one example, Judith Butler maintains that gender identities are intelligible only within the binary oppositions of "compulsory heterosexuality." This socially constructed system links and regulates sex, gender, and desire, in stipulated constellations of "male" and "female," "masculine" and "feminine," for purposes of reproduction.[357] Butler is interested not only in achieving "the denaturalization of gender as such," but even in "confounding the very binarism of sex, and exposing its fundamental unnaturalness."[358]

Few if any theologians have gone so far as to premise their sexual ethics on the erasure of a two-sexed humanity. But many have asked whether gender is a dominative cultural elaboration of biological sex, not a natural category. Many are skeptical about the moral virtue supposedly inherent in some forms of sexual expression, and about the natural viciousness of others. John Boswell has questioned whether heterosexuality has functioned historically with the "natural" and normative status which anti-homosexual polemic now claims for it.[359] Mary Daly, a post-Christian feminist originally indebted to Aquinas, has rejected all patriarchal interpretations of female identity, and imaginatively reconstructed separate female worlds, words, and roles.[360] William Countryman finds that biblical teachings about sexual conduct, many of them directed toward control of women's activity, have their origin in social concerns about "purity" (i.e., as markers of social cohesion) or about property rights (including rights over women and children).[361]

Postmodern ideas have taken increasing theological hold in the last three decades. Various Christian authors have adopted a quasi-deconstructionist stance toward nature and biblical authority; yet few have given up the idea that there are some human values which sex ought to express. Most still insist on the essentially sexual nature of the person, and the liberation of sexuality from imposed constraints. Ironically, this is the very project Foucault dismissed as cooptation by a sex-focused discourse of control. Yet a newly positive Christian view of sex is put forth as a necessary and normative corrective to Stoic, gnostic, and Augustinian elements in the tradition which denigrated the body, condemned sexual desire, urged sexual abstinence, and tolerated sexual activity only in view of procreative intentions. Sexuality and sexual pleasure are now affirmed as good and as essential routes to personal fulfillment.

This balancing move may, as Foucault warned, endow sex with a disproportionate centrality among human experiences and goods, unduly marking sexual orientation as a constituent of personal identity. But it is *de facto* the case that contemporary Western Christian ethics has tended to focus on the personal and intersubjective meanings of sex, both as communicative and as pleasurable; has downplayed procreation; has highlighted equality and freedom in establishing sexual relationships; and has prized sexuality as foundational for personality, for social interactions, and even for religious experience.

In a widely cited book, even a landmark for the recent revisionist Christian appreciation of sex, the Protestant (United Church of Christ) theologian James Nelson claimed two decades ago that "our bodies are always sexual bodies, and

---

356. *The Postmodern Condition: A Report on Knowledge*, trans. Geoff Bennington and Brian Massumi (England: Manchester University Press, 1984), 82.

357. Judith Butler, *Gender Trouble: Feminism and the Subversion of Identity* (New York and London: Routledge, 1990), 17–18.

358. Ibid., 149.

359. John Boswell, *Christianity, Social Tolerance, and Homosexuality: Gay People in Western Europe from the Beginning of the Christian Era to the Fourteenth Century* (Chicago and London: University of Chicago Press, 1980).

360. Among her many works, see *Beyond God the Father: Toward a Philosophy of Women's Liberation* (Boston: Beacon Press, 1973); and *Gyn-ecology: The Metaethics of Radical Feminism* (Boston: Beacon Press, 1978).

361. L. William Countryman, *Dirt, Greed, and Sex: Sexual Ethics in the New Testament and Their Implications for Today* (Philadelphia: Fortress Press, 1988).

our sexuality is basic to our capacity to know and to experience God."[362] He endorsed the emergent norm of fulfillment of one's own sexuality (sexual desire and pleasure) through freely chosen and affectively intimate relationships with other adults. Almost simultaneously, a Roman Catholic study group defined sex as "a force that permeates, influences, and affects every act of a person's being at every moment of existence," and drew the conclusion that it "is in the genital union that the intertwining of subjectivities, of human existences, has the potential for fullest realization."[363] The moral standard to guide such union is "creative growth toward integration—intrapersonally and interpersonally."[364] Robin Scroggs, writing of homosexuality, refers to a general sexual "ideal" of "a caring and mutual relationship between consenting adults."[365] Countryman develops six principles for Christian sexual ethics today which focus on ownership of one's own sexuality as "sexual property," individual freedom, equality, mutual respect, and permanency of commitment in marriage.[366] Disclaiming as "procreationist" the "assumption that sex is naturally oriented toward creation of human life," Christine Gudorf has recently said that "the general direction in which humanity needs to move is toward more pleasurable, spiritually fulfilling, frequent sex, coupled with a reduction in world population."[367]

Even the Roman Catholic teaching authority, as committed as ever to absolute norms, has come to see sex as essentially constitutive of personal identity, has adopted the language of the couple's intersubjectivity to express sex's moral meaning, and has dimmed the limelights once beamed on procreation. According to John Paul II, "sexuality, by means of which man and woman give themselves to one another through the acts which are proper and exclusive to spouses, is by no means something purely biological, but concerns the innermost being of the human person as such," and is a sign of "a total personal self-giving."[368]

All these authors, to an extent even the pope, write in reaction to restrictive traditions which inhibit the recognition, liberation, and enjoyments of the sexual self. All see these traditions as products of historical forces whose bias can be revealed by exposing their origins in attitudes or practices which run counter to what is regarded as the central gospel message: the dignity, freedom, and acceptance of all individuals, and of the goodness of God's creation.

Such revisions of traditional Christian sexual morality have raised challenges on several fronts, theological, pastoral, and disciplinary. Standard teachings and practices of the churches have been disrupted, often with divisive effects. The

concrete shape of these consequences varies denominationally. In Roman Catholicism, the issue is largely one of the authority which continues to be invested in traditional norms, despite the shift, even in official documents, to more personalist foundations. The magisterium confronts the prospect of widespread noncompliance among church members, aided and abetted by "dissenting" theological voices (such as the authors of the Catholic Theological Society of America report cited). The reaction from Rome is usually to draw the lines more tightly around orthodox positions, and to promulgate them more loudly.

For example, Pius XI reacted to the acceptance of artificial birth control by Anglicans, at the 1930 Lambeth conference, with the encyclical *Casti Connubii*, reasserting the Catholic prohibition. A furor over artificial contraception erupted in the 1960s, first with the Second Vatican Council, then with the papal commission on birth control (whose majority recommended acceptance of artificial contraception on the grounds of the interpersonal meaning of the marital relationship), and finally with the 1968 publication of *Humanae Vitae*, which overturned the commission's recommendation and insisted that the prohibitive tradition be maintained. At the twenty-fifth anniversary of the encyclical, the furor continued, barely abated, and a new papal encyclical (*Veritatis Splendor*, 1993) defending the moral authority of the church in all matters was shortly thereafter produced. The church has also taken strong positions in Vatican-originated documents against reproductive technologies, homosexual practice, abortion, and women's ordination. But, as the Catholic laity inhabit increasingly secularized cultures in Europe and move from immigrant to mainstream status in North America, they are less persuaded to live by countercultural and, to most, counterexperiential ideals.

It should be noted, at the same time, that the debates in Catholicism do not concern so much the traditional ideal of

---

362. James B. Nelson, *Embodiment: An Approach to Sexuality and Christian Theology* (Minneapolis: Augsburg, 1978), 126.

363. Anthony Kosnick, William Carroll, Agnes Cunningham, Ronald Modras, and James Schulte, *Human Sexuality: New Directions in American Catholic Thought*, A Study Commissioned by The Catholic Theological Society of America (New York/Paramus/Toronto: Paulist Press, 1977), 81, 85.

364. Ibid., 86.

365. *The New Testament and Homosexuality* (Philadelphia: Fortress Press, 1983), 126.

366. *Dirt, Greed, and Sex*, 240–53, 263.

367. Christine Gudorf, *Reconstructing Christian Sexual Ethics: Body, Sex and Pleasure as Grace and Gift* (Cleveland: The Pilgrim Press, 1994), 29, 33.

368. John Paul II, *Familiaris Consortio*, no. 11.

heterosexual, procreative monogamy, which most Catholics support, but the nature and extent of permissible exceptions to that norm. The area of agreement on traditional sexual values is much broader among Roman Catholics than the band of disagreement, however polarized the debates between Catholic "liberals" and "conservatives" may appear. Due partly to the influence of a monolithic teaching authority, even narrow issues, like whether contraception is permissible in marriage, have become "tests" of Catholic orthodoxy.

Many mainstream Protestant denominations have in this century maintained the Reformation's decentralization of authority, and assimilated liberal social and political values to their interpretation of Christian living, at least in the industrialized nations. Indeed, the membership of the Protestant churches has been a primary contributor to Western cultural ideals of tolerance, individual freedom, the responsibility of conscience, and personal fulfillment over against constraining "medieval" traditions. Not only Reformation faith, but also Enlightenment reason and existentialist decision-making, have been formative of modern Christian attitudes toward sexual morality, especially in liberal Protestant theology. Divorce and even premarital sex are becoming more or less accepted by laity and theologians. The front-line issue for these churches is now homosexuality, especially the ordination of men or women openly in homosexual relationships.

According to the sub-dean of Westminster Abbey, the Church of England is suffering from a conflict between a formal traditional sexual ethic which forbids divorce and all sex outside marriage, while civil law, popular expectations, and their own pastoral sense lead many clergy to perform weddings for divorced persons whose former spouse is still alive. As for a couple's right to express physically a deep homosexual love, "it is difficult to see why they should not."[369] Yet the bishops have concluded that relations approved tacitly for laity are not appropriate for the clergy, primarily because of potentially alienating and divisive effects on their parishes.

In the last decade, the United Methodist Church, the Presbyterian Church (USA) and the Episcopal Church have established progressive study committees, whose recommended changes in traditional sexual teachings, among which those on homosexuality were the most provocative, were eventually turned down by the membership as a whole. The Evangelical Lutheran Church in America produced a draft statement in late 1994, and circulated it for comment in preparation for a June 1995 second draft. The document, controversial in the church immediately upon publication, defined marriage as a "loving binding commitment between two people," with or without ceremony, and not limited to heterosexuals.

Tensions in Protestant sexual ethics often arise from a combination of liberal leadership, an unfocused mediation of theological and moral traditions, and a membership both committed to liberal democratic values and invested in the middle-class "nuclear" family. An unresolved issue in Protestant sex and gender ethics is whether traditional Christian moral teachings, modified by Luther and Calvin in favor of the importance of spousal companionship beside procreation, can and should reshape the sexual ethos of a liberal Christianity gone too far toward individualism and subjectivism.

Sexual ethics debates in both Protestantism and Catholicism generally arise in relation to contested practical *norms* about activities which once were condemned and now are gaining acceptance. This is symptomatic of a forest-and-trees problem, which, as Michel Foucault once observed,[370] has been better overcome in relation to gender critique than to sexual ethics *per se*. Feminists have long refused to accept that sexual activity can be assessed morally without re-examining the wider social significance of sex within male and female gender assignment. They have also refused to concede that sex should be central in defining women's roles or identity. But both the revisers and defenders of traditional sexual morality tend to agree that sex and sexual identity are of central moral importance. In the contemporary setting, they also agree that the primary test which approved behaviors or choices should meet is interpersonal relationship and fulfillment. These assumptions should be subjected to more careful scrutiny. I will argue that they have considerable validity (especially the second), but that they need to be placed in a deeper and more nuanced social context, with better attention both to the familial ramifications of sexual partnerships, and to differences and similarities in cross-cultural experiences of sex, gender, and family.

---

369. A. E. Harvey, *Promise or Pretence? A Christian's Guide to Sexual Morals* (London: SCM Press, Ltd., 1994), 115.

370. Foucault contrasted the women's movement and "American homosexual movements" on this point. "[. . .]The real strength of the women's liberation movements is not that of having laid claim to the specificity of their sexuality and the rights pertaining to it, but that they have actually departed from the discourse conducted within the apparatuses of sexuality." There has resulted "a veritable movement of desexualization, a displacement effected in relation to the sexual centering of the problem, formulating the demand for forms of culture, discourse, language, and so on, which are no longer part of that rigid assignation and pinning-down to their sex" (Colin Gordon, ed., *Michel Foucault, Power/Knowledge: Selected Interviews and Other Writings* [New York: Pantheon Books, 1980], 219–20).

Christian sexual ethics today, in its characteristic themes and emphases (the sexual body as pleasure-giving, the interpersonal meanings of sex, the priority of equality and freedom in defining sexual morality), has been quite effective in addressing the human suffering caused by legacies of negativity and even oppression concerning sex. Yet I am concerned these themes will not be adequate to the task of shaping a positive ethic of sex and gender for the future. I perceive two major problems. *First,* this renewed and more person-centered sexual ethics tends to focus on sex as a pleasurable and intimate activity of individuals and couples, and to neglect the social meanings of the body realized through parenthood and kinship. But it is the reproductive, economic, and kin-oriented contributions of sexual partnerships, as well as social control over them, which are the major practical dimensions of the human sexual experience cross-culturally and historically. Christian sexual ethics needs an analysis of the social ramifications of sex which is both critical and constructive.

Second, Western Christian sexual ethics today engages its own procreation-focused past with a hermeneutic of suspicion, but fails to deal with the fact that cultural attitudes may be at the opposite end of the spectrum from any procreative ethos, or any requirement that sex be limited to lifelong marriage. The traditional Christian assumption that sex belongs with procreation and in marriage has given Christians a tacit fund of shared values, even while it has also given them a highly visible target. But a new generation of sexual attitudes and practices in liberal democratic societies presents mutual consent as practically the sole behavior-guiding norm, and hardly encourages ongoing responsibility either for one's sexual partner, or for the procreative potentials of sex. And when an autonomous and decontextualized freedom is the only sexual guide, control of sexual "choice" by unexamined gender and reproductive roles can still be operative. "Freedom from" traditional repressions needs to be translated into an ethic of meaning, purpose, and even discipline which can meet cultural trivializations and distortions of sex. For Christian sexual ethics to have a future as more than a sectarian relic, it must ground sexual freedom and fulfillment in some account of the human goods at stake in sex and in the relationships built upon it.

Contemporary Christian ethicists debating sex and gender rightly hold up equality, intimacy, and fulfillment as moral criteria. But they often fail to ask whether these values are any less relative or more objective than the sexual systems they are eager to dismantle. The practical *meanings* of equality and inclusion may be debated by adversaries in the sex wars, but their acceptability as moral concepts is usually taken for granted. When we place these typically Western, even liberal, criteria in the moral perspective of cultures, subcultures, and continents in which hierarchy and inequality are quite explicitly invoked as moral norms, the vulnerability of "our" own presuppositions becomes evident. Even seemingly obvious values like equal respect and personal fulfillment require a self-conscious defense carried out within a serious and appreciative intercultural dialogue. Any ethical perspective which simply interprets cultures foreign to it in terms of "difference," or which can bring to them only the fruits of its own particular cultural struggle, without showing how and why that struggle and theirs may be relevant and revelatory for one another, will not have the right to describe itself as "seeking justice."

An ability to speak in a meaningful way about sex as a shared human reality, and not merely the product either of individual choice or of cultural shaping, is an especially important precondition of social and cultural criticism. Although Western Christian sexual ethics needs to finish cleaning its own house, it also needs to develop a discourse of sex and gender justice which can speak to and hear multiple moral traditions in its own culture and in other cultures. This will require meeting the postmodern critiques of rationality and of moral value, and reconstructing some recognizable foundations for sex and gender ethics.

From Lisa Sowle Cahill, *Sex, Gender, and Christian Ethics* (Cambridge: Cambridge University Press, 1996), 1–12.

THE JUST-WAR TRADITION

▶ **Augustine** (354–430) examines the welfare and safety of the state in light of biblical teaching, including concepts of war and military service, in his Letter 138, to Marcellinus (written in 412).

AUGUSTINE

Letter 138 (to Marcellinus)

Now let us see what is the nature of the next point in your letter. You added that they say that Christ's preaching and doctrine are not adaptable in any way to the customs of the state, and they give as an example the precept that we are not to return evil for evil to anyone; that we should turn the other cheek when anyone strikes us; that we should let go our cloak when anyone takes our coat; and when anyone forces us to go with him we should go twice as far: all of which things are contrary to the customs of the state. "For who," they say, "could allow anything to be taken from him by an enemy, or who would not wish to return evil, as the law of war allows, to the ravager of a Roman province?" I might find it a laborious task to refute these and other such words of critics, or of men who say things by way of inquiry rather than of criticism, if it were not that this discussion is directed to men of culture and education. So, what use is it for me to labor the point; rather, why not ask them how those early patriots were able to govern and enlarge the state which they had changed from a small, poor one to a great, rich one, when "they preferred to pardon the wrongs they had suffered rather than avenge them?"[371] How could Cicero, praising the conduct of Caesar as ruler of the state, say that he never forgot anything but wrongs?[372] He said this either as high praise or as high flattery: if it was praise, he knew that Caesar was like that; if it was flattery, he was showing that the ruler of a state ought to be such as he falsely described him. But, what is the meaning of not returning evil for evil, if it is not abhorrence of the passion of revenge; and what is the meaning of preferring to pardon wrongs suffered rather than avenge them, if it is not forgetfulness of wrongs?

When men read of these traits in their authors, they publish and applaud them; such conduct as is described and praised seems to them worthy of the beginning of a state which was to rule over so many nations, as when they say that "they preferred to pardon wrongs suffered rather than avenge them." But, when they read the command of divine authority that evil is not to be returned for evil, when this advice is preached from the pulpit to congregations of people, in these universal schools of both sexes and of every age and rank, religion is charged with being an enemy of the state. If this teaching had been heard as it deserved to be, it would have founded, sanctified, strengthened, and enlarged the state very much more successfully than Romulus, Numa, Brutus and those other famous men of Roman birth did.[373] For, what is the commonwealth if not the common property? Therefore, the common property is the property of the state. And what is the state but the generality of men united by the bond of common agreement? In their authors we read: "In a short time a scattered and wandering mob became a state by mutual agreement."[374] But, indeed, what precept of agreement did they ever decree to be read in their temples, when they were unhappily obliged to find out how they could worship gods without offense to any of them, when these disagreed among themselves? For, if they chose to imitate them in their discord, their state was likely to fall apart, by the breaking of the bond of agreement, so that, as their morals declined and lost their purity, they began to be involved in civil war.

But, who is so ill-versed in our religion, or so deaf, as not to know the great precepts of agreement, not worked out by human arguments but written by divine authority, which are read in the Churches of Christ? To this teaching those precepts belong which look rather to action than to learning: to turn the other cheek to the striker; to give the coat to him who tries to take away the cloak; to make a double journey when forced to go with anyone.[375] Thus it happens that the evil man is overcome by the good one, or, rather, evil is overcome by good[376] in the evil man, and the man is set free, not from an exterior foreign evil, but from an interior, personal one, by which he is more grievously and ruinously laid waste than he would be by the inhumanity of any enemy from without. Therefore, he overcomes evil by good who suffers the loss of temporal goods with patience, in order to show how far these goods are to be despised for the sake of faith and justice. And the one who becomes evil by loving these goods to excess, and who does the wrong, is to learn from the very one to whom he did the wrong what kinds of goods these are that made him do the wrong, and so he is to be brought to repentance and to agreement—than which nothing is more useful to the state—overcome by the goodness of his victim rather than by the strength of an avenger. The right time for this to be done is when it seems likely to benefit the one for whose sake it is done, in order to bring about correction and a return to agreement. And this certainly is the intention one must have when this remedy is applied to correct and win over the offender, and, in a sense, to cure and restore him to sanity, and it must be done even if the outcome is otherwise and he refuses to accept either correction or peace-making.

Otherwise, if we notice the words and imagine that they are to be kept literally, we might suppose the right cheek is not to be offered if the left is struck, since it says: "If one strike thee on thy right cheek, turn to him also the left."[377]

371. Sallust, *Bellum Catilinae*, 52.19, 9.5.

372. Cicero, *Pro ligario*, 12.35

373. Romulus, founder and first king of Rome; Numa Pompilius, second king of Rome, who gave the Romans their religious institutions; Brutus, founder of the Roman republic.

374. Cicero, *De re publica*, frag. 1.1.25.39.40.

375. Mt 5:39–41.

376. Rom 12:21.

377. Cf. Mt 5:39.

The left is much more likely to be struck, because it is easier to strike a blow with the right hand. But it is usually understood as if it were said: If anyone makes an attempt on your best possessions, give him your less precious ones, too; otherwise, you might show vengeance rather than patience, and thereby despise eternal goods in favor of temporal ones, whereas temporal goods are to be despised in favor of eternal ones, as things on the left are to be despised in favor of those on the right. This has always been the aim of the holy martyrs. A final just vengeance is looked for, that is, the last supreme judgment, only when no chance of correction remains. But, now, we must be on our guard, more than anything else, not to lose patience in our eagerness to be justified, for patience is to be more highly prized than anything an enemy can take from us against our will. Another Evangelist, expressing the same thought, makes no mention of right cheek, but says, "the other cheek,"[378] and in order to make this expression "other" more intelligible, he simply recommends the same patience. Therefore, an upright and devout man ought to bear with patience the malice of those whom he seeks to make good, in order to increase the number of the good rather than add himself to the number of the bad.

Finally, those precepts refer rather to the interior disposition of the heart than to the act which appears exteriorly, and they enjoin on us to preserve patience and kindly feeling in the hidden places of the soul, revealing them openly when it seems likely to be beneficial to those whose welfare we seek. This is clearly shown in the case of the Lord Christ Himself, a unique model of patience, who was struck on the face and answered: "If I have spoken evil, give testimony of the evil, but if well, why strikest thou me?"[379] If we look at the words literally, He obviously did not fulfill His own precept, for He did not offer His other cheek to the striker; on the contrary, He forbade the one who did it to augment the wrong, yet He came prepared not only to be struck on the face, but even to die on the cross for those from whom He suffered these wrongs, and when He hung on the cross He prayed for them: "Father, forgive them, for they know not what they do."[380] The Apostle Paul apparently did not keep the command of his Lord and Master either, when he was also struck on the face, and said to the chief priest: "God shall strike thee, thou whited wall. Thou sittest to judge me according to the law, and contrary to the law, thou commandest me to be struck."[381] And when the bystanders said: "Dost thou revile the high priest?"[382] he chose to give them a warning by speaking in mockery, so that those who were wise might understand that the whited wall, that is, the hypocrisy of the Jewish

priesthood, had been destroyed at the coming of Christ; for he said: "I knew not, brethren, that he is the high priest, for it is written: Thou shalt not speak evil of the prince of thy people."[383] Now, undoubtedly, since he had grown up among those same people and had there been instructed in the Law, he could not but know that that person was the high priest, nor could he, in any wise, deceive those to whom he was known into believing that he did not know.

Therefore, those precepts of patience are always to be preserved in the heart, to keep it in readiness, and those kindly feelings which keep us from returning evil for evil are always to be developed in the will. But, we often have to act with a sort of kindly harshness, when we are trying to make unwilling souls yield, because we have to consider their welfare rather than their inclination, and this sort of thing has been lavishly praised in their literature describing the beginnings of the state. For, in punishing a son, however harshly, a father's love is certainly not cast aside, yet what he does not want, and what makes him suffer, happens because it appears that he can be cured only by unwilling suffering. Thus, if the earthly state observes those Christian teachings, even war will not be waged without kindness, and it will be easier for a society whose peace is based on piety and justice to take thought for the conquered. He whose freedom to do wrong is taken away suffers a useful form of restraint, since nothing is more unfortunate than the good fortune of sinners, who grow bold by not being punished—a penalty in itself—and whose evil will is strengthened by the enemy within. But the depraved and distorted hearts of men esteem human fortunes happy when the splendor of buildings is in evidence, and the collapse of souls is not noticed; when magnificent theatres are erected, and the foundations of virtue are undermined; when the madness of extravagance is glorified, and the works of mercy are scoffed at; when actors live in luxury at the expense of the excessively wealthy, and the poor scarcely have the necessaries of life; when God, who thunders against this public evil through the public voices of His doctrine, is blasphemed by impious nations, and the kind of gods sought after are those whose worship is attended by that theatrical degradation of body and soul. If God permits these abuses to flourish, it is a sign of His greater wrath; if He lets them go unpunished, that is a very deadly punish-

---

378. Lk 6:29.
379. Jn 18:23.
380. Lk 23:34.
381. Acts 23:3.
382. Acts 23:4.
383. Acts 23:5; Exod 22:28.

ment. But, when He withdraws the sustenance of vice and impoverishes the riches of lust, He opposes them in mercy, for it would be a sign of mercy—if that were possible—that even wars should be waged by the good, in order to curb licentious passions by destroying those vices which should have been rooted out and suppressed by the rightful government.

If Christian practice condemned war in general, then the soldiers in the Gospel who asked how they were to be saved should have been given the advice to throw down their arms and give up military service entirely. But what was told them was: "Do violence to no man, neither calumniate any man; and be content with your pay."[384] When He told them they ought to be content with their pay, He obviously did not forbid them to serve in the army. Therefore, let those who say that the teaching of Christ is opposed to the welfare of the state produce such provincial administrators, such husbands, such wives, such parents, such sons, such masters, such slaves, such kings, such judges, and finally such tax-payers and collectors of public revenue as Christian teaching requires them to be, and then let them dare to say that this teaching is opposed to the welfare of the state, or, rather, let them even hesitate to admit that it is the greatest safety of the state, if it is observed.

From Saint Augustine, *Letters*, translated by Sister Wilfrid Parsons, Fathers of the Church, vol. 20 (New York: Fathers of the Church, 1953), 41–48.

☙ In his Letter 189, to Boniface[385] (written in ca. 418), **Augustine** briefly sets forth an early Christian notion of just war, along with prescriptions for peace and mercy.

AUGUSTINE

Letter 189 (to Boniface)

Do not imagine that no one can please God while he is engaged in military service. Among such was holy David to whom the Lord gave such high testimony. Among such were many just men of that time. Among such, also, was that centurion who said to the Lord: "I am not worthy that thou shouldst enter under my roof, but only say the word and my servant shall be healed. For I also am a man, subject to authority, having under me soldiers, and I say to this one: Go, and he goeth; and to another: Come, and he cometh; and to my servant: Do this, and he doth it"; of him the Lord said: "Amen I say to you I have not found so great faith in Israel."[386]

Among such, also, was that Cornelius to whom the angel was sent, who said: "Cornelius, thy prayer is heard and thy alms are accepted," when he advised him to send to the blessed Apostle Peter, to hear from him what he ought to do. And to summon the Apostle to him he sent a religious soldier.[387] Among such, also, were those who came for baptism to John, the holy precursor of the Lord and friend of the bridegroom, of whom the Lord said: "There hath not arisen among them that are born of women a greater one than John the Baptist."[388] When they asked him what they ought to do, he answered them: "Do violence to no man, neither calumniate any man, and be content with your pay."[389] Obviously, he did not forbid them to serve in the army when he commanded them to be satisfied with their pay.

Those who serve God with the highest self-discipline of chastity, by renouncing all these worldly activities, have a more prominent place before Him: "But everyone hath his proper gift from God, one after this manner and another after that."[390] Thus, some fight for you against invisible enemies by prayer, while you strive for them against visible barbarians by fighting. Would that one faith were found in all, for there would be less striving and the Devil and his angels would be overcome more easily! But as it must needs be in this world that citizens of the kingdom of heaven are troubled by temptations in the midst of the erring and the godless, so that they may be tested and tried as gold in the furnace,[391] so we should not wish to live before the time with the holy and upright only, that we may deserve to receive this reward in its own time.

Think first of this, then, when you are arming for battle, that your strength, even of body, is a gift of God, for so you will not think of using the gift of God against God. When your word is pledged, it must be kept even with the enemy against whom you wage war, how much more with the friend for whom you are fighting! Your will ought to hold fast to peace, with war as the result of necessity, that God may free you from the necessity and preserve you in peace.

---

384. Lk 3:14.

385. Boniface was count or governor of Africa under Honorius and Placidia. Unjustly disgraced through the treachery of his rival Aetius, he allied himself with Genseric and the Vandals, whom he invited into Africa in 429. Later, vindicated and restored to favor, he fought the invaders. Saint Augustine died during the siege of Hippo, one of the results of the invasion. Boniface died in Italy in battle in 432.

386. Mt 8:8–10; Lk 7:6–9.	389. Lk 3:12–14.
387. Acts 10:1–8; 30–33.	390. 1 Cor 7:7.
388. Mt 11:11.	391. Wis 3:5, 6.

Peace is not sought for the purpose of stirring up war, but war is waged for the purpose of securing peace. Be, then, a peacemaker even while you make war, that by your victory you may lead those whom you defeat to know the desirability of peace, for the Lord says: "Blessed are the peacemakers for they shall be called the children of God."[392] Yet, if human peace is so sweet as a means of assuring the temporal welfare of mortals, how much sweeter is divine peace as a means for assuring the eternal welfare of angels! Therefore, let it be necessity, not choice, that kills your warring enemy. Just as violence is meted out to him who rebels and resists, so mercy is due him who is defeated or captured, especially where no disturbance of peace is to be feared.

From Saint Augustine, *Letters*, translated by Sister Wilfrid Parsons, Fathers of the Church, vol. 20 (New York: Fathers of the Church, 1953), 268–70.

≈ **Thomas Aquinas** (ca. 1225–74) provides a lengthy and theologically in-depth analysis of warfare. He asks the questions "Are some wars permissible?" and "May belligerents use subterfuge?" in *Summa theologiae* (written between 1266 and 1273 and published posthumously).

THOMAS AQUINAS

Summa theologiae, 2a2ae.40.1 and 3

Question 40. War

We must now consider war, and here there are four points of inquiry:

1. are some wars permissible?
2. may clerics engage in warfare?
3. may belligerents use subterfuge?
4. may war be waged on feast days?

Article 1. Is it always a sin to wage war?

THE FIRST POINT: 1. It would seem that it is always a sin to wage war. Punishments are meted out only for sin. But our Lord named the punishment for people who wage war when he said, *All who draw the sword will die by the sword.*[393] Every kind of war then is unlawful.

2. Moreover, whatever goes against a divine command is a sin. But war does that. Scripture says, *I say this to you, offer the wicked man no resistance.*[394] Also, *Not revenging yourselves,*

my dearly beloved, but give place unto wrath.[395] War is always a sin then.

3. Besides the only thing that stands as a contrary to the act of virtue is a sin. Now war is the contrary of peace. Therefore it is always a sin.

4. Besides, if an action is lawful, practising for it would be lawful, as is obvious in the practise involved in the sciences. But warlike exercises which go on in tournaments are forbidden by the Church, since those killed in such trials are denied ecclesiastical burial. Consequently war appears to be plainly wrong.

ON THE OTHER HAND, Augustine says,[396] in a sermon on the centurion's son, If Christian teaching forbade war altogether, those looking for the salutary advice of the Gospel would have been told to get rid of their arms and give up soldiering. But instead they were told, Do violence to no man, be content with your pay.[397] If it ordered them to be satisfied with their pay, then it did not forbid a military career.

REPLY: Three things are required for any war to be just. The first is the authority of the sovereign on whose command war is waged. Now a private person has no business declaring war; he can seek redress by appealing to the judgment of his superiors. Nor can he summon together whole people, which has to be done to fight a war. Since the care of the commonweal is committed to those in authority they are the ones to watch over the public affairs of the city, kingdom or province in their jurisdiction. And just as they use the sword in lawful defence against domestic disturbance when they punish criminals, as Paul says, *He beareth not the sword in vain for he is God's minister, an avenger to execute wrath upon him that doth evil,*[398] so they lawfully use the sword of war to protect the commonweal from foreign attacks. Thus it is said to those in authority, *Rescue the weak and the needy, save them from the clutches of the wicked.*[399] Hence Augustine writes, *The natural order conducive to human peace demands that the power to counsel and declare war belongs to those who hold the supreme authority.*[400]

Secondly, a just cause is required, namely that those who

392. Mt 5:9.
393. Mt 26:52.
394. Mt 5:32.
395. Rom 12:19. *Never try to get revenge; leave that, my friends, to God's anger.*
396. Augustine, *Epist. 138 ad Marcell.* 2. PL 33, 531.
397. Lk 3:14.
398. Rom 13:4.
399. Ps 81:4.
400. Augustine, *Contra Faustum* XXII, 74. PL 42, 448.

are attacked are attacked because they deserve it on account of some wrong they have done. So Augustine, *We usually describe a just war as one that avenges wrongs, that is, when a nation or state has to be punished either for refusing to make amends for outrages done by its subjects, or to restore what it has seized injuriously.*[401]

Thirdly, the right intention of those waging war is required, that is, they must intend to promote the good and to avoid evil. Hence Augustine writes, *Among true worshippers of God those wars are looked on as peacemaking which are waged neither from aggrandisement nor cruelty, but with the object of securing peace, of repressing the evil and supporting the good.*[402] Now it can happen that even given a legitimate authority and a just cause for declaring war, it may yet be wrong because of a perverse intention. So again Augustine says, *The craving to hurt people, the cruel thirst for revenge, the unappeased and unrelenting spirit, the savageness of fighting on, the lust to dominate, and suchlike—all these are rightly condemned in wars.*[403]

Hence: 1. Augustine writes, *"To draw the sword" is to arm oneself and to spill blood without command or permission of superior or lawful authority.*[404] But if a private person uses the sword by the authority of the sovereign or judge, or a public person uses it through zeal for justice, and by the authority, so to speak, of God, then he himself does not "draw the sword," but is commissioned by another to use it, and does not deserve punishment. Still even those who do use it sinfully are not always slain with the sword. Yet they will always "die by the sword" since they will be punished eternally for their sinful use of it unless they repent.

2. These words, as Augustine says,[405] must always be borne in readiness of mind, so that a man must always be prepared to refrain from resistance or self-defence if the situation calls for it. Sometimes, however, he must act otherwise for the common good or even for the good of his opponents. Thus Augustine writes, *One must do many things with a kind of benign severity with those who must be punished against their will. Now whoever is stripped of the lawlessness of sin is overcome for his own good, since nothing is unhappier than the happiness of sinners. It encourages guilty impunity, and strengthens bad will, the enemy inside us.*[406]

3. Even those who wage a just war intend peace. They are not then hostile to peace, except that evil peace which our Lord *did not come to send on the earth.*[407] So Augustine again says, *We do not seek peace in order to wage war, but we go to war to gain peace. Therefore be peaceful even while you are at war, that you may overcome your enemy and bring him to the prosperity of peace.*[408]

4. Warlike exercises are not completely forbidden; only those which are excessive and dangerous and end in killing and looting. In olden times they presented no such danger. So, as Jerome writes, they were called *practices of arms* or *wars without blood.*[409]

Article 3. Is it lawful to use subterfuge in war?

THE THIRD POINT: 1. It would seem that it is not lawful to use subterfuge in war. Scripture says, *Strict justice must be your ideal.*[410] But since subterfuge is a kind of deception it would seem to be an injustice. Therefore subterfuge should not be used even in a just war.

2. Moreover, subterfuge and deception, like lies, seem to stand against honesty. But since we must be honest with all men we cannot lie to anyone, as Augustine says.[411] Since, then, *one is bound to be honest with one's enemy,*[412] it would seem wrong to use subterfuge against him.

3. Again, Scripture has it, *So always treat others as you would have them treat you,*[413] a dictum which must be observed with all neighbours. But our enemy is our neighbour. Since no one wants subterfuge or deception worked on him, how then can anyone carry on war through subterfuge?

ON THE OTHER HAND, Augustine writes, *Open or concealed tactics do not affect the justice of the war, provided, of course, it is a just war.*[414] He proves this on the authority of the Lord who ordered Joshua to lay an ambush for the people of Ai.

REPLY: Subterfuge is used to fool the enemy. Now a man may be deceived by another's actions or words in two ways. He may be told a falsehood or given a promise which is not kept. This is always unlawful, and no one should fool an enemy like that. As Ambrose says,[415] rights of war and agreements even with the enemy do exist and should be kept.

401. Augustine, *Quaest. in Heptateuch.; in Josue 10, super Josue 8,* 2. PL 34, 781.
402. Gratian, *Decretum* 11, 23, 1, can. 6, ed. Richter-Friedberg 1, 893.
403. *Contra Faustum* XXII, 74. PL 42, 447.
404. Ibid. 70. PL 42, 444.
405. Augustine, *De Sermo Domini in Monte* 1, 19. PL 34, 1260.
406. *Epist.* 138 *ad Marcell.* 2. PL 33, 531.
407. Mt 31:34.
408. Augustine, *Epist.* 189 *ad Bonifacium,* 6. PL 33, 856.
409. Not Jerome, but Vegetius in *Instit. rei milit.* I, 9–28; II, 23.
410. Deut 16:20.
411. Augustine, *Contra Mendacium* XV, 31. PL 40, 539.
412. *Epist. ad Bonifacium* 189. PL 33, 856.
413. Mt 7:12.
414. *Quaest. in Heptateuch.* On Joshua 8, 2. PL 34, 781.
415. Ambrose, *De Officiis* I, 29. PL 16, 63.

But a man may be fooled by our words or actions in another way, namely, when we do not display our intention or meaning to him. We are not always bound to do this, since even in the sacred teaching many things must be concealed, particularly from the disbelieving lest they ridicule them: *Do not give dogs what is holy*.[416] All the more then should we hide from the enemy our plans against him. Indeed special insistence is laid on concealing operational orders against the enemy's attempts to obtain them. Frontinus *On Strategy*[417] makes that clear. Now this sort of concealment is the idea behind the subterfuge one may lawfully use in just wars. Properly speaking this is not deception, nor does it go against justice, nor against a well-regulated will. A man's will would be undisciplined if he always wanted others to keep back nothing from him.

From this the answers to the objections will be clear.

From Thomas Aquinas, *Summa theologiae*, vol. 35, edited and translated by Thomas R. Heath (London: Blackfriars, 1972), 81, 83, 85, 89, 91.

⌘ **John Howard Yoder** (1927–97), an influential Mennonite theologian, examines the history of the just-war tradition in Christian theology in "Criteria of the Just-War Tradition."

JOHN HOWARD YODER

"Criteria of the Just-War Tradition,"
in *When War Is Unjust: Being Honest in Just-War Thinking*

Everyone agrees that the just-war tradition consists of a set of criteria to be used to test whether a war (or a particular activity within a war) is justified. The criteria are commonsensical. Yet as we have already observed, there is not a single, standard, normative list. We need, therefore, to make our own listing of the main concerns of the tradition.

The criteria here gathered in a logical order are telescoped chronologically over the centuries. For many items in the list sources are cited. The intent of the citation is not proof but illustration, in order to provide the reader with a sense of the texture of the centuries-long conversation and also of the contextual and dated quality of many of the statements. Some were at home in medieval times and are considered inappropriate now. Nonetheless, their place in history may teach us something about the logic of the tradition. Occasionally in this list, therefore, a provision most clearly at home in medieval times and not taken seriously now is labeled (MA). Other statements have been elaborated only re-

cently. No attempt is here made to clarify the logically important internal questions which must arise in the application of these criteria, such as:

- how the varied criteria interlock,
- whether they ever contradict one another,
- whether any have priority over others, or
- how completely they must be met.

The reader is undoubtedly aware from the rest of the book that all of these questions are also crucial as to whether the system can work to give shape to firm decisions.

I. War may be waged only by a *legitimate authority*.
   A. Criteria for a legitimate ruler:
      1. dynastic descent from a previous ruler;
      2. election according to custom or constitution;
      3. legitimacy may be forfeited by being a bad ruler or "tyrant"; thus "justice" or "good government" or de facto ability to govern may be indirectly a criterion: "The kingdom is forfeited if a king sets out with a truly hostile intent to destroy a whole people" (Grotius, *On the Law of War and Peace*, I.IV.11);
      4. religious heresy may be held to disqualify a ruler; thus religious orthodoxy may become a part of legitimacy (this arises c. 1600).
   B. This criterion of legitimacy excludes:
      1. war by private citizens (except in emergency defense) (see Thomas, ST II-II, Q. 40, art. 1);
      2. war by bandits or privateers;
      3. war between political units not on the same level;
      4. war against one's own sovereign (see Grotius, *On the Law of War and Peace*, I.IV.7, 15). For much of the history of the just-war tradition rebellion is not admitted. Later it comes to be admitted under conditions:
         a. that an evil ruler has forfeited the right to rule (cf. Grotius, *On the Law of War and Peace*, I.IV.8);
         b. that "lesser magistrates" with a clearly just cause act to resist the ruler (e.g., Magna Carta) or to depose the tyrant;
         c. (hypothetically) that the entire people rises up "as one";

---

416. Mt 7:6.

417. Frontinus, *Strategematum* I, 1. Sextus Julius Frontinus, governor of Britain (75–78).

d. that the ruler becomes illegitimate by persecuting true religion.

C. Only a soldier under oath and under the control of the sovereign may fight.

1. Clergy, religious, and penitents are excluded or dispensed: "But the thought of warlike matters seems to be foreign to the duty of our office, for we have our thoughts fixed more on the duty of the soul than on that of the body; nor is it our business to look to arms, but rather to the affairs of peace" (Ambrose, *On the Duties of the Clergy*, I.35).

   a. military orders (Knights Templar, Knights of Malta) in a crusade are exceptions, with a special episcopal mandate, to the exclusion of clergy;

   b. since the inception of conscription, the churches have tended to consider clergy exemption as a right that Western governments theoretically ought to grant, but most churches have not usually made it an issue. Clergy have generally not refused to serve if drafted, although in canon law they should have that right. A man who has killed in even a just war is disqualified from becoming a priest (MA).

2. A mercenary may only hire on to fight for a cause he knows is just (MA).[418]

D. Sometimes the question of authority to wage war is confused with that of authority to decide when a war is just.

1. Since the criteria of the just war are objective, and since the facts they measure are verifiable, any moralist, lawyer, journalist, or counsellor to a king can make the judgment on a particular war or weapon, though there is room for honest difference on some details. Especially a bishop would have that authority. This can be tested in international tribunals or by third-party mediation or arbitration: "Senators and petty rulers and in general all who are admitted on summons or voluntarily to the public council or the prince's council ought, and are bound, to examine into the cause of an unjust war. . . . Again, a king is not by himself capable of examining into the causes of a war and the possibility of a mistake on his part is not unlikely and such a mistake would bring great evil and ruin to multitudes. Therefore, war ought not to be made on the sole judgment of the king, nor, indeed, on the judgment of a few, but

on that of many, and they wise and upright men" (Vitoria, *On the Law of War*, para. 24).

In modern democratic thought, citizens can and should test a decision made by their government.

2. The facts on the basis of which a decision is made may however not always be publicly accessible or seen in the same light by all concerned. This makes it possible for both sides (or the public, the subjects on both sides of a conflict) to think they are in the right.

3. A crusade in the canonical sense, which entitles the soldiers to indulgences, can be declared only by an episcopal council, pope, or prophet (MA).

II. A war may be fought only for a *just cause*.

A. The offense must be:

1. actual, not only possible;

2. intentional, not inadvertent or unintended or an honest error;

3. of substantial importance;

   a. it is wrong to go to war for a trifle: "It is not lawful for slight wrongs to pursue the authors of the wrongs of war" (Vitoria, *On the Law of War*, para. 14);

   b. the selfish interests of the princely house do not suffice; the whole community's interests and rights must be at stake: "Neither the personal glory of the prince nor any other advantage to him is a just cause of war" (ibid., para. 12).

4. objective, verifiable, as to fact;

5. unilateral, not provoked. If there is doubt as to the provocation, the recourse is to arbitrate. However, a just cause might arise if in a process of escalation the side responsible for a provocation sought to make amends, and the other party attacked anyway.

B. The offense may be:

1. an aggression demanding defense or a threat demanding deterrence;

2. an injustice demanding reparation, such as:

   a. seizure of property;

   b. denial of free passage on land or sea;

   c. breach of treaty obligations;

---

418. Geneva 1977 condemns mercenaries. During the first millennium of the just-war tradition, however, it was not assumed that soldiers needed to be citizens of the nation they fought for.

d. insult to the honor of nation or sovereign (MA) (see Vitoria, *On the Law of War,* para. 19);

e. failure of a government to punish or make reparation for its subjects' crimes, or to make them pay their debts;

f. interference with the passage of pilgrims, with the freedom of missionaries, or with the worship of a subject Christian population (MA) (see Thomas, ST II-II, Q. 10, art. 8).

C. The offense may be committed against a third nation:

1. against one's ally: "Next to subjects, and indeed on an equal footing with them in this respect, that they ought to be defended, are allies, in whose treaty of alliance this obligation is embraced" (Grotius, *On the Law of War and Peace,* II.XXV.4). This was the U.S. claim in Vietnam and in Kuwait.

2. against some innocent subjects on whose behalf a third party intervenes "on humanitarian grounds." This was recently done by India in Bangladesh and by Tanzania in Uganda, considered by the United Nations for Somalia and by the European Union for Bosnia.

D. The *cause* may be moral guilt demanding punishment:

1. heresy, blasphemy, other offenses against God's honor (MA);

2. violations of the laws of nature and the rights of peoples. In colonial times it was held, for example, that European intervention in South America, Africa, and Asia was justified by the practices of cannibalism, human sacrifice, or sexual immorality by natives, or by their natural inferiority, or by their inability by themselves to govern themselves or build a civilization;

3. violations of the laws of nations needing to be punished in the interest of world order.

III. A war may be fought only with a *right intention.*

Intention in the objective sense (*finis operis*) is the goal or end of the entire military/political enterprise, which must be justified in terms of the global common good.

A. The only valid objective intention is the restoration of peace; that is, the creation of a total world state of affairs better than what would obtain without the intervention: "Peace should be the object of your desire; war should be waged only as a necessity and waged only that God may by it deliver men from the necessity and preserve them in peace. For peace is not sought in order to the kindling of war, but war is waged in order that peace may be obtained" (Augustine, "Letter to Boniface," para. 16).

This universal commonweal includes the enemy's real best interests. It may contradict the notion of punishment.

B. National honor, territorial or commercial aggrandizement, and the weakening or destruction of enemy regimes are not in themselves valid ends, although they may be served by activities justified on other grounds.

C. This is one reason unconditional surrender is an inappropriate demand. The right intention should always be present in the form of the publicly stated terms of peace always offered to the enemy.

IV. A war may be fought only with *right intention.*

Intention in the subjective sense (*finis operantis*) is motivation, or attitude.

A. Inadmissible intentions are:

1. hatred, vengefulness, enmity;

2. cruelty, love of violence;

3. desire for power or fame;

4. material gain (booty, slaves, or territory) (Thomas, ST II-II, Q. 40, art. 1).

The cause may be justified, but participation may still be sinful if the intention is wrong in one of these ways.

B. Valid components of subjective intention:

1. love for the victims of the aggression: "Now it is in the love of innocent men that both capital punishment and just wars have their origin" (Grotius, *On the Law of War and Peace,* I.II.8 and 10);

2. trust in God;

3. willingness to face risk or sacrifice;

4. love for the enemy, desire to restore him to righteousness (see Augustine, "Letter to Marcellinus," chap. II, para. 14);

5. humility and regret at the needfulness of the evil of war: "Wars and conquests may rejoice unprincipled men, but are a sad necessity in the eyes of men of principle" (Augustine, *City of God,* IV.15). [. . .]

C. Showing mercy after winning is frequently listed as a criterion. It cannot be measured, except as a stated intention, before the war. If sincerely intended, it will make a difference in the choice of means.

1. Do not use means which will interfere with the reestablishment of peace after the war: "Military

necessity does not include any act of hostility which makes the return to peace unnecessarily difficult."[419]

2. When the war is over it will not be marked by triumphal self-congratulation, but by somber regret for the victims.

D. *The Challenge of Peace* (1983) added to the classical list a new term—*comparative justice*. This term seems at first to denote a call to modesty about the imperfections of one's own society, and thereby to make it more difficult to meet the criteria of cause or authority.

1. In actual usage (as *The Challenge of Peace* was concerned primarily with the USSR as adversary), the notion that "nobody's perfect" tends to work in the opposite direction. It tends to undercut concrete discrimination, as long as our cause is (in our minds) "relatively" better than the enemy's. The worse the enemy, the less hard we need to be on ourselves. This view was accentuated by certain critics who held that if the evils of Soviet imperialism provide the "just cause," concern for legitimate means could be set aside.

2. The intent of the author who added this term (Bryan Hehir) was something else again, namely, to recognize the fact that both sides may *think* they have the just cause, and the obligation to respect the entire set of just-war criteria should not depend on all the wrong being on one side (see V/F below).

3. [. . .] It is in fact not a criterion (a criterion is something to measure by) but rather one additional consideration (or two) to keep in mind when thinking about just cause.

The above categories (I–IV) are generally grouped under the heading *jus ad bellum;* that is, the law having to do with going to war or "the right to fight." Until these criteria have been met, there is no need to discuss proper means.

V. Due Process: A war is illegitimate unless the criteria apply with procedural integrity.

The phrases "due process" and "procedural integrity" are modern. They do not appear in the standard documents. They do, however, enable a helpful clarification. The items grouped here appear on all the standard lists as qualifying phrases, whether under cause, intention, authority or means. Because of their procedural quality, and because they apply both *ad bellum* and *in bello,* it is fitting that we should group them here under a separate heading.

A. War must be a last resort, only after everything else has been tried. Refusal of other resources for redress invalidates an otherwise just complaint. Such other resources are:

1. negotiation, mediation, arbitration: in the Middle Ages episcopal mediation or arbitration could be effective (cf. recent mediation by the pope between Argentina and Chile);

2. recourse to international tribunals and good offices;

3. "cooling off" time, time for the enemy to back down;

4. the formality of a declaration of war, preceded by a warning, followed by time to sue for peace (see Cicero, *De Officiis,* I.11).

5. The war goals must be stated:

a. as an act of accountability to the world community (see Grotius, *On the Law of War and Peace,* II.XXVI.4, 7);

b. so that the enemy may at any time sue for peace on those terms.

B. The enemy must always be able to sue for peace:

1. the war goal may not be unconditional surrender;

2. pursuing hostilities beyond reasonable redress makes a previously valid cause unjust;

3. pursuing hostilities when the enemy has offered to negotiate makes the cause unjust;

4. this is the other side of the notion of last resort.

C. There must be respect for international law, customs, treaties, and international agencies.

D. The entire war must promise to be proportionately prudent, that is, to cause less harm than the harm it seeks to prevent: "To have recourse to violent warfare it is not enough to have to defend overall against any kind of injustice. If the injury caused by warfare exceeds the injury suffered by tolerating the injustice done, one may be obliged to suffer that particular injustice."[420] [. . .]

E. The war must be winnable, otherwise one suffers both evils (the evil to be prevented and the evil of war).

---

419. Francis Lieber, "General Orders No. 100: Instructions for the Government of Armies of the United States in the Field" (approved by President Lincoln in 1863), art. XVI.

420. Pope Pius XII, Address to the XVIth Congress of the International Bureau of Documentation on Military Medicine (October 19, 1953), *Discorsi e Radiomessaggi* XV, 422.

1. This follows obviously from proportionality and is a safeguard against crusading enthusiasms.

2. However, some versions of the just-war tradition make an exception for heroic self-defense, even if hopeless.

F. Objectively a war can be just only on one side. Subjectively, however, both parties may believe in good faith that they are in the right.

   1. This is the reason for third-party involvement.

   2. This is why subjects or citizens or soldiers should not accept their ruler's word unquestioningly.

   3. In individual battles citizens even on the erring side have a right to defend themselves. Thus the fact that they do so cannot be considered a war crime.

   4. This is why enemy combatants who fight fairly (*in bello*) deserve respectful and legal treatment, however wrong we think their cause.

      A war may be fought only by the use of legitimate means, *jus in bello,* "fighting right." This is the second major traditional category.

VI. Means must be indispensable, the only way, "necessary."

A. Unnecessary combat is to be avoided even in a just cause.

B. During combat no unnecessary death or wanton destruction may be inflicted (see Cicero, *De Officiis,* I.11, I.24).

C. What commanders consider necessary has different meanings:

   1. Legal texts name necessity as a requisite *within* what the rest of the rules allow.

   2. Much argument in popular and political settings, however, appeals to necessity as grounds for *breaking* the rules. Then necessity is not a criterion but an argument for indulgence.

VII. Means must be proportional.

A. The damage must not be greater than the damage prevented or the offense being avenged.

B. The damage or punishment inflicted must not be disproportionate to the guilt of the offender (this cannot apply to particular battles).

C. Proportion must be tested on every level—a given weapon, a tactic, a strategy, a given battle. A measure that appears disproportionate on one level may appear proportionate on a higher one; for example, the disproportionate cost of one battle may be held to be outweighed if it wins the war. The modest cost of a

battle, on the other hand, may be wrong if the war is already lost.

VIII. The means used must respect the immunity of the innocent.

"The deliberate slaughter of the innocent is never lawful in itself. . . . Wrong is not done by an innocent person. Therefore war may not be employed against him. . . . Hence it follows that even in war with the Turks it is not allowable to kill children. This is clear, because they are innocent. Aye, and the same holds with regard to the women of unbelievers" (Vitoria, *On the Law of War,* paras. 35f.).

A. *Innocent* means those who are no threat:

   1. women, children, the aged, infirm;

   2. clergy, religious, foreigners;

   3. unarmed persons going about their ordinary vocations;

   4. even soldiers on leave or who have become prisoners.

B. *Innocent* does not mean that persons are not patriotic, do not morally support the war effort, or do not participate in the wartime economy, but only that they are no threat, are not combatant: "A quite obstinate devotion to one's own party, provided only that the cause is not altogether dishonorable, does not deserve punishment. . . . Or, if such devotion is punished in any way, the penalty should not be carried so far as death, for no just judge would so decide" (Grotius, *On the Law of War and Peace,* III.XI.16). The clarity of this criterion has recently been compromised, though not logically set aside, by the notion of a quasi-combatant work force.

C. Obviously the innocent include neutral third parties.

D. Special offenses against the innocent are:

   1. reprisals and the taking or killing of hostages;

   2. terrorism.

E. But noncombatants may come into jeopardy indirectly

   1. by staying in a besieged city;

   2. by being close to a military target.

F. Even combatants may be killed only when they are a threat:

   1. a surrendered soldier may not be killed;

   2. a soldier returned to civilian life may not be killed;

   3. after the war, those guilty of war crimes may be punished only by due process:

      a. as vengeance / correction (MA);

      b. as deterrence / prevention;

c. as part of the rule of law needing no other justification;

d. but there should be mercy if possible.

G. Slaves may be taken (MA), but not if the defeated soldiers or the subjugated population is Christian.

IX. The means used must be discriminating, that is, subjected to measured control.

This is prerequisite if proportionality and noncombatant immunity are to be respected. If any weapon, any strategy, any military unit becomes uncontrollable, then that abandonment of discrimination infringes in principle upon the discipline of necessary and legitimate means, *even if* the illicit actions have not yet been taken. If any government or command center *says* it intends to strike indiscriminately, that is already immoral as intention even though it has not been carried out.[421]

X. The means used must respect the dignity of humankind as rational and social.

A. No slander.

B. No unnatural cruelty (mutilation, torture).

C. Keeping faith with the enemy (truces, safe conducts, no treason, perfidy, perjury).

D. Lying is always wrong (although one may use ambush and subterfuge or permit the enemy to gather false impressions) (see Thomas, ST II-II, Q. 40, art. 3).[422]

E. There is to be no pillage and no destruction of property unless the enemy might use it. Even when sacking a city can be justified to deprive the enemy of its resources, the women should not be raped, or the temples plundered, or the fruit trees cut.

F. Do not poison wells or rivers.

G. Do not fight on holy days (MA) or during times of proclaimed truce.

H. Do not profane churches or cemeteries; respect sanctuary (MA).

I. Give quarter; that is, do not kill even in combat an enemy who surrenders.

XI. Means used must not be forbidden by positive law or treaties.

In medieval times such prohibitions were part of canon law, but since all the rulers of Europe claimed to be Christian and Catholic, they were valid civil law as well. They included the Third Lateran Council (1139) prohibition against the crossbow and the Fourth Lateran Council (1215) prohibition against the catapult.

A. For example, the following precisely defined prohibitions figure in articles XXII and XXIII of Convention IV of The Hague (1907):[423]

1. to employ poison or poisoned weapons;

2. to kill or wound treacherously individuals belonging to the hostile nation or army;

3. to kill or wound an enemy who, having laid down his arms, or having no longer means of defense, has surrendered;

4. to declare that no quarter will be given;

5. to employ arms, projectiles, or material calculated to cause unnecessary suffering;

6. to make improper use of a flag of truce, of the national flag, or of the military insignia and uniform of the enemy, as well as the distinctive badges of the Geneva Convention (e.g., Red Cross);

7. to destroy or seize the enemy's property, unless such destruction or seizure be imperatively demanded by the necessities of war;

8. to declare abolished, suspended, or inadmissible in a court of law the rights and actions of the nationals of the hostile party.

B. A belligerent is forbidden to compel the nationals of the hostile party to take part in the operations of war directed against their own country, even if they were in the belligerent's service before the commencement of the war.

C. Respect for the Peace of God or the Truce of God when declared by the competent episcopal authority (MA).

D. Respect for cease-fire agreements.

E. Occupied populations should be governed justly. Soldiers who surrender must not be killed. Spies and terrorists, however, forfeit these rights.

F. For many of these matters there are extensive international agreements that define and defend the pertinent rights and obligations. The degree of bindingness of specific treaty rules varies

---

421. This logic becomes especially important in the nuclear case, but it would also apply to "scorched earth," "ethnic cleansing," and other intrinsically indiscriminate acts.

422. Aquinas's argument in this article is not that a particular kind of lying is not wrong, but that a particular kind of subterfuge is not deception or lying. All lying remains wrong, as it did for Augustine.

423. Article XXII of the Regulations Annexed to The Hague Convention of 1907 states that "the right of belligerents to adopt means of injuring the enemy is not unlimited."

1. depending on whether one nation has signed the convention;
2. depending on whether the other party has signed; the declarations of Paris (1856) and St. Petersburg (1868) specify that they are not binding when fighting a non-signatory;
3. depending on whether the other party has belligerent status.

Yet morally, the bindingness of the rights at stake does not depend on whether texts were signed by all parties. The particular formulations were defined in particular texts, but the rules based in moral and customary law apply to all.

From John Howard Yoder, *When War Is Unjust: Being Honest in Just-War Thinking,* 2nd ed. (Maryknoll, NY: Orbis Books, 1996), 147–60.

Mysticism, Philosophy, Theology:
Demands on the Intellect

Mysticism, philosophy, and theology are frequently understood as oppositional or contradictory. Nevertheless, all three have been important in the Christian traditions and manifested as different kinds of demands on the intellect and in varying degrees of intensity. These demands are most generally expressed as a need for understanding and a need for faith. Just how those demands are experienced is described perhaps most exquisitely by mystics. Yet mystics sometimes think like philosophers and theologians, and occasionally philosophers and theologians write like mystics.

It is sometimes said that, of all the world religions, Christianity has been most attentive to issues of belief and right thinking. Whether or not that claim is justified, the writings of theologians and mystics in diverse Christian traditions provide ample evidence of a thirst for ways of knowing God and world, together with an acute sense of the ambiguity of such knowing. Attempting to be faithful to the God revealed in Jesus Christ as revealed in the Scriptures, Christians generation after generation have responded to theological questions and demands arising from both within and outside the traditions. However much the questions and contexts of understanding have changed since the time of their writing, the texts retain their original intellectual acuity and passion.

The first section of this chapter, Mystics, Mysticism, and Visionaries, contains selections best understood as mystical theology. Mysticism has been defined in a spiritual sense as union with God. In a cognitive sense, mystical theology has to do with breaking the boundaries of thought and language about the sacred—of finding ways to express that which is glimpsed beyond the bounds of ordinary experience and expression.

The history of Christian mysticism can be traced to Saint John's Gospel—the last Gospel to be written—with its emphasis on the faithful being already a part of Christ's body. In the Middle Ages, this "membering" of Christ was doctrinally formulated as the "mystical Body." The *Dictionnaire de spiritualité* defines mystical experience as "the transcendent, the mystery that invades/floods/overcomes human existence." Although some take mysticism to be "world denying," others see it as world affirming and opening up possibilities.

Mysticism has played a large role in both the Eastern Orthodox and the Western Catholic traditions. Mystical theology originally concerned the stages of spiritual growth that culminated in the Beatific Vision—the expected outcome of any Christian life. The noun "mysticism," created in the sixteenth century, refers to spiritual life, which, since the Middle Ages, has become increasingly thought of as interior and private.

How mysticism has been understood varies within and across denominations. In Catholicism, spiritual life was strongly communal and liturgical until the Middle Ages. Mystical accounts written as "confessions" or "testimonies" to personal experience can be traced to the High Middle Ages. Mystical writings frequently supplement reason and logic when they struggle to contain excessive claims about God. Five of the texts in the first section—by Bernard of Clairvaux, Mechthild of Magdeburg, Bonaventure, and Saint Catherine of Siena and the anonymous *Cloud of Unknowing*—span the twelfth through fourteenth centuries. Their genres range from testimony to treatise, sometimes within the same text. The anonymous *Pilgrim's Tale* is a medieval Russian Orthodox text (even though the version extracted here is probably from the nineteenth century) and typifies the mystic as a pilgrim on a literal journey to Siberia and a spiritual journey to Jerusalem. The other two texts in this section are from the sixteenth century and are by John of the Cross and Teresa of Avila.

Mysticism is not restricted to earlier centuries nor is it exclusively Catholic. Mysticism has been cited as an influence on the Reformation in its preoccupation with the interior life. In his "The Meaning of Mysticism as Seen through Its Psychology," the idealist philosopher and theologian William Hocking (1873–1966) made a persuasive case for the prominence of mysticism in the Protestant tradition since the Reformation. He argued that this experience is primarily non-conceptual and it is had by individuals who properly open themselves to it. William James (1842–1910), the well-known philosopher and psychologist, took mystical experience to be paradigmatic for religious experience at large in his well-known *Varieties of Religious Experience*. According to his view, mystical experience is a heightened form of religious experience and it illuminates other forms that are obscure or subsumed under other names.

The writers included in the second section of this chapter, Philosophy and Theology, often focus more on the cognitive than the experiential. They provide arguments for Christian facts and beliefs as they pertain to the experience of God. With new access to Greek texts through ninth-century Arab translations, theology became concentrated in the university schools, and medieval theologians used Aristotelian logic to classify and to deliberate over the—by then—large collection of theological opinions. Although exegesis had been the major mode of reflection, philosophical theology assumed primacy over exegesis in the academy. This was a precarious moment in the history of Christianity in the sense that the growth or demise of philosophical theology was at stake. And while the medieval debates introduced methodological issues, only later do methods become issues by themselves. By the seventeenth century philosophical reflection both on claims and on methods of making claims often superseded attention to the description and progress of religious experience.

Because he so explicitly articulates the two types of classical theology—apophatic, or negative, theology (knowing God by what God is not) and cataphatic, or positive, theology (knowing God through relatively adequate analogies)—a text by Pseudo-Dionysius (third to fifth century) initiates each of the two main sections in this chapter. Pseudo-Dionysius's distinction between affirmative theologies (by way of analo-gies, for example, in *The Divine Names*) and negative theologies (by way of a dialectic of negations in *The Mystical Theology*) demonstrates the fruitful reciprocity between the two theological types. His *Mystical Theology*, written as though it were a first-century letter, shows the continuing Platonic influences on philosophical theology and is a strong but different invocation of Scripture as authority.

Disagreements among earlier theologians centered primarily on the meanings of Scripture and of the Christ event. Many of the questions of definition had been answered in earlier debates—often using philosophical terms familiar to the ancient world. Questions of method began to emerge as explicit in the Middle Ages. Works by Anselm of Canterbury (ca. 1033–1109) and Hildegard of Bingen (1098–1179) give attention to question *as question* and are among the earliest acknowledgments that questions for understanding traditional resources are a crucial part of theological work. In his *Proslogion*, Anselm of Canterbury's meditation results in what came to be known as the ontological argument for the existence of God. His famous phrase *"fides quaerens intellectum"* (faith seeking understanding), a variation of Augustine's *"Intellige ut credas. Crede ut intelligas"* (Understand in order to believe. Believe in order to understand), proceeds from his desire to understand what he believes. Although both Augustine and Anselm presuppose that faith is a basis for understanding, in Anselm's formulation the emphasis is on the capacity of reason to make coherent the things we affirm by faith. Peter Abelard's (1079–1144) *Christian Theology*, exemplifying dialectical logic, earned the denunciation of the mystical theologian Bernard of Clairvaux at the Council of Sens in 1140.

Hildegard of Bingen is an exceptional theologian for the diversity of her interests and voluminous writing—even though, as she says, she lacked formal training in grammar. Until the rise of universities, women were educated within monasteries—although still not as broadly or as formally as men. Double monasteries—houses and centers of learning for both women and men, some headed by an abbess—were common until the Counter-Reformation. The twentieth century saw the retrieval of many medieval texts, including Hildegard's major works, of which *Scivias* is best known. Although this text is sometimes referred to as a *summa*, a comprehensive treatise on doctrine, it is not commonly included in the canon of medieval theology.

Bonaventure's essay *On the Reduction of the Arts to Theology* is an example of Augustinian deductionist theology, in the manner of Platonic thinking. Bonaventure (1217–74) is not sanguine about the capacity of reason: the whole point of knowing God is to love God. Of all theologians in the Middle Ages, Thomas Aquinas (1224/25–1274) was the most eminent and his *Summa Theologica* unrivaled. His synthesis of the roles of reason and faith in human understanding is a lasting achievement. For him, theology is a matter of proportion between the finite created order and infinity; truth is thought and thing coming together in an affirmation, and goodness is the fulfillment of desire. His use of Aristotelian metaphysics was controversial at the time, however, and of 219 propositions condemned at Paris and Oxford in 1277, 19 reflected his thinking. He was canonized in 1323, and his work became the dominant text in the teaching of Catholic theology through Vatican II.

As with any institution, there is continuing need for reform—for renewal of purpose and practice. By the time of the Middle Ages, most of the questions regarding definitions had been settled. New questions focused on regulatory issues (indulgences, celibacy, papal authority, and issues of emphasis in doctrine, for example) and on faith, grace, and good works. The relative unity that had prevailed through the thirteenth century broke apart, and theological debate became intensely adversarial as some of the reform movements that sprang up between the thirteenth and fifteenth centuries rejected the authority of the Roman Catholic Church. The Protestant Reformation originated in the sixteenth century as one such reform movement within the Church and resulted in the formation of separate Churches.

The Protestant Reformation began with a single letter from Martin Luther (1483–1546) to his archbishop objecting to one especially blatant abuse of the granting of indulgences and asking for disciplinary action. However, when Luther made his objections public, they ignited and set in motion forces that resulted in his break with the papacy, his excommunication, and the founding of the Lutheran Church. His *Disputation against Scholastic Theology,* included here, is from the same year as the Ninety-five Theses he proclaimed in Wittenberg in October 1517 and is believed to have grown out of a commentary on the first book of Aristotle's *Physics* that Luther was writing at the time. His *Freedom of a Christian* (1520) states his position on the faith–versus–good works controversy that rent Christianity into Protestant versus Catholic. His *To the Christian Nobility of the German Nation* (1520) is a polemical treatment of the sacraments.

John Calvin (1509–64) created one of the most influential systematic theologies with his *Institutes of the Christian Religion* (1536). Whereas Luther's vision was to retrieve an originating Christianity, Calvin's was to initiate an ideal Christian life disciplined by a government subordinate to religious leadership. Richard Hooker (ca. 1554–1600), an Anglican theologian, wrote eight books on Church governance. Some understand Hooker's ideas as being close to advocating a secular state. In the selection from *Of the Laws of Ecclesiastical Polity* (1593), Hooker's adversaries are Anabaptists, who reject the present (English) state as being inconsistent with what the Bible wants. They would prefer a "religious polity," such as that constructed by Calvin in Geneva, Switzerland.

Seventeenth- and eighteenth-century Enlightenment thinkers in the main had opposed reliance on religious authority and Scripture and had exalted reason as the sole basis for faith. Two writers, better known as philosophers than theologians, challenged the Enlightenment overconfidence in reason: Immanuel Kant (1724–1804) and Georg Wilhelm Friedrich Hegel (1770–1831). Kant critiqued the claims of both science and classical metaphysics. Hegel clarified the dialectical character of understanding and found in the Christian religion an intensification of Spirit's consciousness of itself. Along with Kant's and Hegel's philosophical attempts to shore up the cleavage between reason and religious faith, other now-familiar theological "isms" appeared: deism, pantheism, theism, panentheism, atheism. John Henry Newman (1801–90) examines historical claims regarding Christianity in order to distinguish those that are extreme from those that are more reasonable.

Twentieth-century approaches in Christian theology are difficult to categorize since the work of some theologians can be classified in more than one way. David Tracy, in *Blessed Rage for Order* (1975), distinguishes among major contemporary approaches in two ways: how theologians understand themselves and what they take to be the referent of theological understanding.

The nineteenth- and early-twentieth-century *liberal* Protestant theologians, represented here by Friedrich Schleiermacher and Paul Tillich, and *modernist* Catholic theologians, here, Maurice Blondel, understand themselves as embracing many basic values of modernity—especially those of uninhibited inquiry, judgments rooted in individual autonomy, and fair investigations of all claims to meaning and truth. They embrace the claims and values of the Christian vision: belief in God made human in Jesus Christ and in Jesus' continued presence in the Spirit's gifts and transformative power. For them, critical inquiry reveals a continuity between religious faith and secular faith. For Tillich, faith is ecstatic freedom manifest in the ontological structure of the human being.

Orthodox theologians (represented here by Hans Urs Von Balthasar, and in chapters 4 and 5 by Timothy Ware) generally understand themselves as believers according to a specific Church tradition and understand the object of belief to be analogical. Traditionally, orthodox theologians generally have an appreciation for a systematic understanding of the doctrines of their tradition. In contrast, *neo-orthodox* theologians writing between or shortly after the twentieth-century world wars are likely to understand themselves less as Christian believers than as human beings living by basic Christian attributes of faith, hope, and agapic love. The writings of Karl Barth and Reinhold Niebuhr exemplify neo-orthodox theology in its emphasis on God's transcendence. Barth is a dialectical thinker by virtue of his strong resistance to philosophical attempts to reconcile Christianity and culture.

Although their distinctiveness is unquestioned, some characteristics of the foregoing theological models can be found in the work of Søren Kierkegaard, Rudolf Bultmann, Karl Rahner, and Bernard Lonergan. Kierkegaard, like Barth, was a dialectical thinker. He located authentic subjectivity in inward commitment to Christ's way of life rather than in knowledge. Bultmann was preoccupied with the existential estrangement of the contemporary human being and recommended demythologizing the Gospels in order to sort out their essential meanings. Rahner's work, informed by early-twentieth-century liturgical reform and phenomenology, is now classic. In his multivolume *Theological Investigations* he employs philosophical reflection to ask new and old questions in the context of what it means for human beings to be open to God conceived of as the most incomprehensible of all that human beings do not know. A contemporary of Bultmann and Rahner, Bernard Lonergan is best known for bridging Continental philosophy and Anglo-American empiricism with his *Insight: A Study of Human Understanding.* In *Method in Theology* he applies this earlier work to all the tasks that compose the field of theology.

Fundamentalist and evangelical theologians are often not differentiated because both tend toward a historicist and literalist interpretation of Scripture and traditions. However, fundamentalists tend to be antisecular and to literalize the transformative dimension of religious experience as supernatural, whereas evangelicals emphasize salvation through personal conversion and prioritize preaching over ritual. One strength of both fundamentalists and evangelicals is their extensive knowledge of biblical texts. One weakness is that they, like most "technological" thinkers, according to George Marsden, tend not to wrestle with theoretical principles: "Truth [in technological thinking] is a matter of true and precise propositions that, when properly classified and orga-

nized, will work. Fundamentalism fits this mentality because it is a form of Christianity with no loose ends, ambiguities, or historical developments." Marsden's nuanced account of fundamentalist and evangelical thought is helpful in understanding many American-born religions, such as Mormonism and Christian Science. J. Gresham Machen provides an example of a fundamentalist critique of religious liberalism.

For *radical* theologians—Thomas Altizer (see below), William Hamilton, and Gabriel Vahanian—God is dead and therefore humanity may live "authentically." They see most contemporary theological work other than their own as impeding rather than assisting the struggle for liberation from oppression. This postmodern position affirms secular values and calls for a Christocentric, rather than a theocentric, formulation of the Christian tradition. Some radical theology echoes mystical themes of classical negative theology, such as Meister Eckhart's radical prayer to God to "save" him from God.

Liberation theologians Gustavo Gutiérrez, James Cone, Delores Williams, and Elizabeth Johnson are perhaps best understood in terms of a revised neo-orthodox model. They bring new resources to heighten awareness of exploitation and evil masked by euphemism. Gutiérrez, for example, holds to the principle that whatever is optimal for the poor should inform all work on issues of institutional justice and political structures. Cone asserts in his *Black Theology of Liberation* (1970), "We must become black with God!" Williams uses "wilderness experience" to broaden the concept of experience to include the secular, the negative, and the prophetic dimensions of black women's lives. Johnson extracts from Scripture and theology feminist resources that have been overlooked in a theology dominated by masculinist language and perspective.

Revisionary theologians see something new in the contemporary beliefs, values, and faith of both authentic secularity and authentic Christianity. The two main sources of theological reflection are generally referred to as experience and Scripture. In the revisionary model, these sources are reformulated as interpretations of what is known through human experience in general and of what is known through the Christian tradition. Tracy's description of the revisionary theologian's major task in *Blessed Rage for Order*—"the dramatic confrontation, the mutual illuminations and corrections, the possible basic reconciliation between the principal values, cognitive claims, and existential faiths of both a reinterpreted post-modern consciousness and a reinterpreted Christianity" (32)—is an apt description of his own work as well, from his early work on the limit-character of human experience and language to his later work on naming God. Gordon Kaufman argues that theological language originates as a work of constructive imagination. He understands God to be perceivable only indirectly, nonempirically, and primarily in symbol and image. He develops the idea of an "attachment" to God that can be intensified, deepened, or weakened through other experiences. Religious diversity and the possibility of nuclear warfare are two explicit contexts for his theological reflection.

This chapter embraces many different forms of theological reflection. The work of these mystics and theologians discloses that people experience God in different ways and differently at different times in their own lives: as gracious, as just, as hidden (even obstructive), as calling into account, as merciful and caring. All attempts by either mystics or theologians to understand human beings' relations with God make positive and negative demands on the intellect—demands sometimes to think more and sometimes to think less, in any case differently. Some would even see a self-correcting process at work within the tradition—a process at times too human and perhaps also divine.

1. MYSTICS, MYSTICISM, AND VISIONARIES: APOPHATIC AND CATAPHATIC TENSIONS

In this selection from *The Divine Names,* **Pseudo-Dionysius** (ca. third to fifth century) reflects on the paradox of there being many names for God and, at the same time, strictly speaking, no name for God in the sense that God's name is above all naming.

PSEUDO-DIONYSIUS
The Divine Names

Marvelously, our minds will be like those in the heavens above. We shall be "equal to angels and sons of God, being sons of the resurrection."[1] That is what the truth of scripture affirms.

But as for now, what happens is this. We use whatever appropriate symbols we can for the things of God. With these analogies we are raised upward toward the truth of the mind's vision, a truth which is simple and one. We leave behind us all our own notions of the divine. We call a halt to the activities of our minds and, to the extent that is proper, we approach the ray which transcends being. Here, in a manner no words can describe, preexisted all the goals of all knowledge and it is of a kind that neither intelligence nor speech can lay hold of it nor can it at all be contemplated since it surpasses everything and is wholly beyond our capacity to know it. Transcendently it contains within itself the boundaries of every natural knowledge and energy. At the same time it is established by an unlimited power beyond all the celestial minds. And if all knowledge is of that which is and is limited to the realm of the existent, then whatever transcends being must also transcend knowledge.

How then can we speak of the divine names? How can we do this if the Transcendent surpasses all discourse and all knowledge, if it abides beyond the reach of mind and of being, if it encompasses and circumscribes, embraces and anticipates all things while itself eluding their grasp and escaping from any perception, imagination, opinion, name, discourse, apprehension, or understanding? How can we enter upon this undertaking if the Godhead is superior to being and is unspeakable and unnameable?

I said in my *Theological Representations* that one can neither discuss nor understand the One, the Superunknowable, the Transcendent, Goodness itself, that is, the Triadic Unity possessing the same divinity and the same goodness. Nor can one speak about and have knowledge of the fitting way in which the holy angels can commune with the comings or with the effects of the transcendently overwhelming Goodness. Such things can neither be talked about nor grasped except by the angels who in some mysterious fashion have been deemed worthy. Since the union of divinized minds with the Light beyond all deity occurs in the cessation of all intelligent activity, the godlike unified minds who imitate these angels as far as possible praise it most appropriately through the denial of all beings. Truly and supernaturally enlightened after this blessed union, they discover that although it is the cause of everything, it is not a thing since it transcends all things in a manner beyond being. Hence, with regard to the

---

1. Lk 20:36.

supra-essential being of God—transcendent Goodness transcendently there—no lover of the truth which is above all truth will seek to praise it as word or power or mind or life or being. No. It is at a total remove from every condition, movement, life, imagination, conjecture, name, discourse, thought, conception, being, rest, dwelling, unity, limit, infinity, the totality of existence. And yet, since it is the underpinning of goodness, and by merely being there is the cause of everything, to praise this divinely beneficent Providence you must turn to all of creation. It is there at the center of everything and everything has it for a destiny. It is there "before all things and in it all things hold together."[2] Because it is there the world has come to be and exists. All things long for it. The intelligent and rational long for it by way of knowledge, the lower strata by way of perception, the remainder by way of the stirrings of being alive and in whatever fashion befits their condition.

Realizing all this, the theologians praise it by every name—and as the Nameless One. For they call it nameless when they speak of how the supreme Deity, during a mysterious revelation of the symbolical appearance of God, rebuked the man who asked, "What is your name?" and led him away from any knowledge of the divine name by countering, "Why do you ask my name, seeing it is wonderful?"[3] This surely is the wonderful "name which is above every name"[4] and is therefore without a name. It is surely the name established "above every name that is named either in this age or in that which is to come."[5]

And yet on the other hand they give it many names, such as "I am being,"[6] "life,"[7] "light,"[8] "God,"[9] the "truth."[10] These same wise writers, when praising the Cause of everything that is, use names drawn from all the things caused: good,[11] beautiful,[12] wise,[13] beloved,[14] God of gods,[15] Lord of Lords,[16] Holy of Holies,[17] eternal,[18] existent,[19] Cause of the ages.[20] They call him source of life,[21] wisdom,[22] mind,[23] word,[24] knower,[25] possessor beforehand of all the treasures of knowledge,[26] power,[27] powerful, and King of Kings,[28] ancient of days,[29] the unaging and unchanging,[30] salvation,[31] righteousness[32] and sanctification,[33] redemption,[34] greatest of all and yet the one in the still breeze.[35] They say he is in our minds, in our souls,[36] and in our bodies,[37] in heaven and on earth,[38] that while remaining ever within himself[39] he is also in[40] and around and above the world, that he is above heaven[41] and above all being, that he is sun,[42] star,[43] and fire,[44] water,[45] wind,[46] and dew,[47] cloud,[48] archetypal stone,[49] and rock,[50] that he is all, that he is no thing.

And so it is that as Cause of all and as transcending all,

he is rightly nameless and yet has the names of everything that is. Truly he has dominion over all and all things revolve around him, for he is their cause, their source, and their destiny. He is "all in all,"[51] as scripture affirms, and certainly he is to be praised as being for all things the creator and originator, the One who brings them to completion, their preserver, their protector, and their home, the power which returns them to itself, and all this in the one single, irrepressible, and supreme act. For the unnamed goodness is not just the cause of cohesion or life or perfection so that it is from this or that providential gesture that it earns a name, but it actually contains everything beforehand within itself—and this in an uncomplicated and boundless manner—and it is thus by virtue of the unlimited goodness of its single all-creative Providence. Hence the songs of praise and the names for it are fittingly derived from the sum total of creation.

These are not the only names for God favored by the scripture writers, these drawn from universal or individual acts of Providence or from those provided for. Some too have their origin in spiritual visions which enlightened initiates or prophets in the holy places or elsewhere. For all sorts of reasons and because of all sorts of dynamic energies they have applied to the divine Goodness, which surpasses every name and every splendor, descriptions of every sort—human,[52] fiery, or amber

2. Col 1:17.	28. 1 Tim 6:15.
3. Judg 13:17f.	29. Dan 7:9, 13, 22.
4. Phil 2:9.	30. Mal 3:6.
5. Eph 1:21.	31. Rev 19:1.
6. Ex 3:14.	32. 1 Cor 1:30.
7. Jn 11:25.	33. Ibid.
8. Jn 8:12.	34. Ibid.
9. Gen 28:13.	35. 1 Kings 19:12.
10. Jn 14:6.	36. Wis 7:27.
11. Mt 19:17.	37. 1 Cor 6:19.
12. Song 1:16.	38. Ps 115:3.
13. Job 9:4.	39. Ps 102:27.
14. Isa 5:1.	40. Jn 1:10.
15. Deut 10:17.	41. Ps 113:4.
16. Deut 10:17.	42. Mal 4:2.
17. Dan 9:24 (Septuagint).	43. 2 Pet 1:19.
18. Isa 40:28, Bar 4:8.	44. Ex 3:2.
19. Ex 3:14.	45. Jn 7:38.
20. Heb 1:2.	46. Jn 3:5–8, 4:24.
21. 2 Macc 1:25.	47. Isa 18:4.
22. Prov 8:22–31.	48. Ex 13:21f., 24:16, 33:9.
23. Isa 40:13.	49. Ps 118:22.
24. Jn 1:1.	50. Ex 17:6.
25. Sus 42.	51. 1 Cor 15:28.
26. Col 2:3.	52. Gen 3:8, 18:2.
27. Rev 19:1; 1 Cor 1:18; Ps 24:8.	

shapes and forms;[53] they praise its eyes,[54] ears,[55] hair,[56] face,[57] and hands,[58] back,[59] wings,[60] and arms,[61] a posterior,[62] and feet.[63] They have placed around it such things as crowns,[64] chairs, cups,[65] mixing bowls,[66] and similar mysterious items of which I will do my best to speak in *The Symbolic Theology.*[67] However let us for the moment proceed to an explication of the conceptual names of God, collecting, for this purpose, what scripture has to say and being guided in the manner I have already mentioned. And as hierarchical law leads us whenever we study the entire Word of God, let us behold these acts of heavenly contemplation—which is indeed what they are—ready for a sight of God and our hearing made holy as we listen to the explication of the divine names. As the divine tradition so commands us, let the holy be there only for the holy, and let such things be kept away from the mockery and the laughter of the uninitiated. Or, rather, let us try to rescue such men and turn them from their hostility to God.

So, my good Timothy, you must guard these things in accordance with divine command and you must never speak nor divulge divine things to the uninitiated. As for me, I pray that God should allow me to praise in a divine way the beneficent and divine names of the unutterable and unnameable Deity, and that he "take not the word of truth from out of my mouth."[68]

Chapter Two. Concerning the Unified and Differentiated Word of God, and What the Divine Unity and Differentiation Is

It is the entire divine subsistence—whatever absolute goodness defines and reveals that to be—which is praised by the scriptures. How else are we to understand the sacred Word of God when it declares that the Deity, speaking of itself, had this to say: "Why do you ask me about what is good? No one is good but God alone."[69]

I have discussed all this elsewhere and I have shown how in scripture all the names appropriate to God are praised regarding the whole, entire, full, and complete divinity rather than any part of it, and that they all refer indivisibly, absolutely, unreservedly, and totally to God in his entirety. Indeed, as I pointed out in my *Theological Representations,* anyone denying that such terminology refers to God in all that he is may be said to have blasphemed. He is profanely daring to sunder absolute unity.

So all this terminology has to be employed in respect to the entire divinity.

From Pseudo-Dionysius, *The Complete Works,* translated by Colm Luibhéid in collaboration with Paul Rorem (New York: Paulist Press, 1987), 53–58.

   The sermon "On the Kiss" is the second in a series of eighty-six sermons on the Song of Songs written between 1135 and 1153 by **Bernard of Clairvaux** (1091–1153). Bernard interprets the verse "Let him kiss me with the kiss of his mouth" (Song 1:1) as the incarnation of God in the person of Jesus.

BERNARD OF CLAIRVAUX

"On the Kiss," I.1–2; II.2–4; III.4–7

I

1. When I reflect, as I often do, on the ardor with which the patriarchs longed for the incarnation of Christ, I am pierced with sorrow and shame. And now I can scarcely contain my tears, so ashamed am I of the lukewarmness and lethargy of the present times. For which of us is filled with joy at the realization of this grace as the holy men of old were moved to desire by the promise of it?

Soon now we shall be rejoicing at the celebration of his birth (Lk 1:14). But would that it were really for his birth! How I pray that that burning desire and longing in the hearts of these holy men of old may be aroused in me by these words: "Let him kiss me with the kiss of his mouth" (Sg 1:1). In those days a spiritual man could sense in the Spirit how great would be the grace released by the touch of those lips (Ps 44:3). For that reason, speaking in the desire prompted by the Spirit (Isa 26:8), he said, "Let him kiss me with the kiss of his mouth," desiring with all his heart that he would not be deprived of a share in that sweetness.

2. The good men of those days could say, "Of what use to me are the words the prophets have uttered? Rather, let him who is beautiful beyond the children of men (Ps 44:3) kiss me with the kiss of his mouth. I am no longer content with what Moses says, for he sounds to me like someone who cannot speak well" (Ex 4:10). Isaiah is "a man of unclean lips" (Isa 6:5).

---

53. Ezek 1:26f.
54. Pss 11:4, 17:2, 33:18, 34:15.
55. Pss 17:6, 34:15, 102:2.
56. Dan 7:9.
57. Ex 33:23.
58. Ex 33:22.
59. Deut 32:11 (Septuagint).
60. Deut 32:11.
61. Deut 33:27.
62. Ex 33:23.
63. Ex 24:10.
64. Rev 14:14.
65. Ps 75:8.
66. Prov 9:2.
67. The lost or fictitious *Symbolical Theology* concerned those biblical symbols for God taken from the realm of sense perception. As such, it follows the presentation of names taken from the realm of concepts (*The Divine Names*) as part of the descent or procession from lofty simplicity to lowly plurality.
68. Ps 119:43.
69. The question is from Mt 19:17; the answer is from Mk 10:18.

Jeremiah is a child who does not know how to speak (Jn 1:6). All the prophets are empty to me.

But he, he of whom they speak, let *him* speak to me. Let him kiss me with the kiss of his mouth. Let him not speak to me in them or through them, for they are "a watery darkness, a dense cloud" (Ps 17:12). But let him kiss me with the kiss of his mouth, whose gracious presence and eloquence of wonderful teaching cause a "spring of living water" to well up in me to eternal life (Jn 4:14). Shall I not find that a richer grace is poured out upon me from him whom the Father has anointed with the oil of gladness more than all his companions, if he will deign to kiss me with the kiss of his mouth (Ps 44:8)? His living and effective word (Heb 4:12) is a kiss; not a meeting of lips, which can sometimes be deceptive about the state of the heart, but a full infusion of joys, a revelation of secrets, a wonderful and inseparable mingling of the light from above and the mind on which it is shed, which, when it is joined with God, is one spirit with him (1 Cor 6:17).

It is with good reason, then, that I have nothing to do with dreams and visions, reject figures and mysteries, and even the beauty of angels seems tedious to me. For my Jesus outshines them so far in his beauty and loveliness (Ps 44:5). That is why I ask him, not any other, angel or man, to kiss me with the kiss of his mouth.

II

2. I do not presume to think that I shall be kissed by his mouth. That is the unique felicity and singular prerogative of the humanity he assumed. But, more humbly, I ask to be kissed by the kiss of his mouth, which is shared by many, those who can say, "Indeed from his fullness we have all received" (Jn 1:16).

3. Listen carefully here. The mouth which kisses signifies the Word who assumes human nature; the flesh which is assumed is the recipient of the kiss; the kiss, which is of both giver and receiver, is the Person which is of both, the Mediator between God and man, the Man Christ Jesus (1 Tm 2:5). For this reason, none of the saints presumed to say, "Let him kiss me with his mouth," but, "with the kiss of his mouth," thus acknowledging that prerogative of him on whom uniquely once and for all the Mouth of the Word was pressed, when the whole fullness of the divinity gave itself to him in the body (Col 2:9).

O happy kiss, and wonder of amazing self-humbling which is not a mere meeting of lips, but the union of God with man. The touch of lips signifies the bringing together of souls. But this conjoining of natures unites the human with the divine and makes peace between earth and heaven (Col 1:20). "For he himself is our peace, who made the two one" (Eph 2:14). This was the kiss for which the holy men of old longed, the more so because they foresaw the joy and exultation (Sir 15:6) of finding their treasure in him, and discovering all the treasures of wisdom and knowledge in him (Col 2:3), and they longed to receive of his fullness (Jn 1:16).

4. I think that what I have said pleases you. But listen to another meaning.

III

4. The holy men who lived before the coming of the Savior understood that God had in mind a plan to bring peace to the race of mortal men (Jer 29:11). For the Word would do nothing on earth which he did not reveal to his servants the prophets (Am 3:7). But this Word was hidden from many (Lk 18:34), for at that time faith was rare upon the earth and hope was very faint even in the hearts of many of those who were waiting for the redemption of Israel (Lk 2:38). Those who foreknew also proclaimed that Christ would come in the flesh and that with him would come peace. That is why one of them says, "There will be peace when he comes to our earth" (cf. Mic 5:5). By divine inspiration they preached faithfully that men were to be saved through the grace of God. John, the forerunner of the Lord, recognized that this was to be fulfilled in his own time, and he declared, "Grace and truth have come through Jesus Christ" (Jn 1:17), and all Christian peoples now experience the truth of what he said.

5. In those days, although the prophets foretold peace, the faith of the people continually wavered because there was no one to redeem or save them (Ps 7:3), for the Author of peace delayed his coming (Mt 25:5). So men complained at the delay, because the Prince of Peace (Isa 9:6), who had been so often proclaimed, had not yet come, as had been promised by the holy men who were his prophets from of old (Lk 1:70). They began to lose faith in the promises and they demanded the kiss, the sign of the promise of reconciliation. It was as if one of the people were to answer the messengers of peace, "How much longer are you going to keep us waiting?" (Jn 10:24). You foretell a peace which does not come. You promise good things and there is still confusion (Jer 14:19). See, many times and in many ways (Heb 1:1) angels announced to the patriarchs and our fathers proclaimed to us (Ps 43:2), saying, "Peace. And there is no peace" (Jer 6:14). If God wants me to believe in his benevolent will which he has so often spoken of through the

prophets but not yet shown in action, "Let him kiss me with the kiss of his mouth," and so by this sign of peace make peace secure. For how am I to go on believing in mere words? They need to be confirmed by deeds. Let him confirm that his messengers spoke the truth, if they were his messengers, and let him follow them in person, as they have so often promised; for they can do nothing without him. He sent a boy bearing a staff (Jn 15:5) but no voice or life (2 Kings 4:26–31).

I do not rise up or awaken; I am not shaken free of the dust (Isa 52:2); I do not breathe in hope, if the prophet himself does not come down and kiss me with the kiss of his mouth.

6. Here we must add that he who makes himself our Mediator with God is the Son of God and he is himself God. What is man that he should take notice of him, or the son of man, that he should think of him (Ps 143:3)? Where am I to find the faith to dare to trust in such majesty? How, I say, shall I, who am dust and ashes, presume to think that God cares about me (Sir 10:9)? He loves his Father. He does not need me, nor my possessions (Ps 15:2). How then shall I be sure that he will never fail me?

If it is true, as you prophets say, that God has the intention of showing mercy, and thinks to make himself manifest for our reassurance (Ps 76:8), let him make a covenant of peace (Sir 45:30), an everlasting covenant with me (Isa 61:8) by the kiss of his mouth.

If he is not going to go back on what he has said (Ps 88:35), let him empty himself, humble himself (Phil 2:7), bend low and "kiss me with the kiss of his mouth." If the Mediator is to be acceptable to both sides, let God the Son of God become man; let him become the son of man, and make me sure of him with the kiss of his mouth. When I know that the Mediator who is the Son of God is mine, then I shall accept him trustingly. Then there can be no mistrust. For he is brother to my flesh (Gen 37:27). For I think that bone of my bone and flesh of my flesh cannot spurn me (Gen 2:23).

7. So, therefore, the old complaint went on about this most sacred kiss, that is, the mystery of the incarnation of the Word, while faith faints with weariness because of its long and troubled waiting, and the faithless people murmured against the promises of God because they were worn out by waiting. Am I making this up? Do you not recognize that this is what Scripture says, "Here are complaints and the loud murmur of voices, order on order, waiting on waiting, a little here, a little there" (Isa 28:10)? Here are anxious prayers full of piety, "Give their reward, Lord, to those who wait on you, so that your prophets may be found faithful" (Sir 36:18). Again, "Bring about what the prophets of old prophesied in

your name" (Sir 36:17). Here are sweet promises full of consolation, "Behold the Lord will appear; and he will not lie. If he seems slow, wait for him, for he will come, and that soon" (Heb 2:3). Again, "The time of his coming is near and his days will not be prolonged" (Isa 14:1), and, from the Person of him who was promised, "Behold," he says, "I am running toward you like a river of peace, and like a stream in flood with the glory of the nations" (Isa 66:12).

In these words, both the urgency of the preachers and the lack of faith of the people is clear enough. And so the people murmured and faith wavered and, as Isaiah puts it, "The messengers of peace weep bitterly" (Isa 33:7). Therefore, because Christ delayed his coming lest the whole human race should perish in desperation while they thought their weak mortality condemned them and they did not trust that God would bring them the so-often promised reconciliation with him, those holy men who were made sure by the Spirit looked for the certainty that his presence could bring, and urgently demanded a sign that the covenant was about to be renewed for the sake of the weak in the faith.

From *Bernard of Clairvaux: Selected Works,* translated by G. R. Evans (New York: Paulist Press, 1987), 215–19.

☙ **Mechthild of Magdeburg** (ca. 1210–85) wrote *Flowing Light of the Godhead* between 1250 and 1264. A section, "How Love and the Queen Spoke to Each Other," is a mystical dialogue between the soul (characterized as an exalted queen) and divine love (seen as being even more exalted). Mechthild was one of the first Beguines—women who led religious lives of devotion, poverty, and chastity without belonging to a formally approved religious order.

MECHTHILD OF MAGDEBURG

"How Love and the Queen Spoke to Each Other," in *Flowing Light of the Godhead*

One Should Receive This Book Eagerly, for It Is God Himself Who Speaks the Words[70]

This book I hereby send as a messenger to all religious people, both the bad and the good; for if the pillars fall, the building

---

70. The first paragraph of this prologue, which is best understood as an introduction to *Flowing Light* as a whole, has been pieced together [probably by the compiler or early editor] from sentences coming later in the text[. . . .] The words are spoken by Our Lord or God, in their original context.

cannot remain standing; and it signifies me alone and proclaims in praiseworthy fashion my intimacy. All who wish to understand this book should read it nine times.

This Book Is Called a *Flowing Light of the Godhead*

"Ah, Lord God, who made this book?"

"I made it in my powerlessness, for I cannot restrain myself as to my gifts."[71]

"Well then, Lord, what shall the title of the book be, which is to your glory alone?"

"It shall be called a flowing light of my Godhead into all hearts that live free of hypocrisy."

1. How Love and the Queen Spoke to Each Other[72]

The soul came to Love, greeted her with great deference, and said:

"God greet you, Lady Love."

"May God reward you, Mistress and Queen."

"Lady Love, you are indeed perfect."

"Mistress and Queen, that is why I am above all things."

"Lady Love, you struggled many a year before you forced the exalted Trinity to pour itself utterly into the humble virginal womb of Mary."

"Mistress and Queen, that was to your honor and benefit."

"Lady Love, you have now come here to me and have taken from me everything I ever gained on earth."

"Mistress and Queen, you have made a happy exchange."

"Lady Love, you have taken from me my childhood."

"Mistress and Queen, in its place I have given you heavenly freedom."

"Lady Love, you have taken from me all my youth."

"Mistress and Queen, in its place I have given you many a holy virtue."

"Lady Love, you have taken from me possessions, friends, and relatives."

"Come now, Mistress and Queen, that is a petty complaint."

"Lady Love, you have taken from me the world, worldly honor, and all earthly riches."

"Mistress and Queen, I shall make that up to you in one hour with the Holy Spirit on earth, just as you wish it."

"Lady Love, you have brought me to such a pass that my body is racked by a strange weakness."

"Mistress and Queen, in exchange I have given you much sublime knowledge."

"Lady Love, you have devoured my flesh and my blood."

"Mistress and Queen, you have thereby been purified and drawn into God."

"Lady Love, you are a robber; for this as well shall you make reparation."

"Mistress and Queen, then take me."

"Lady Love, now you have recompensed me a hundredfold on earth."

"Mistress and Queen, in addition you may demand God and all his kingdom."

2. Concerning Three Persons and Three Gifts[73]

God's true greeting, coming from the heavenly flood out of the spring of the flowing Trinity, has such force that it takes away all the body's strength and reveals the soul to herself, so that she sees herself resembling the saints, and she takes on a divine radiance. Then the soul leaves the body, taking all her power, wisdom, love, and longing. Just the tiniest bit of her life force remains with the body as in a sweet sleep. Then she sees one complete God in three Persons and knows the three Persons in one God undivided.

He greets her in courtly language that one does not hear in this kitchen, clothes her in the garments that one fittingly wears in a palace, and surrenders himself into her power. Then she can wish for and ask whatever she wants. It is granted her and she is enlightened. What she is not enlightened about is the first cause of the Three Persons. Then he draws her further to a secret place. There she is not permitted to beg on anyone's behalf or ask, because all alone with her he wants to play a game that the body does not know, nor the peasants at their plows, nor knights at their tournaments, nor his lovely mother, Mary—not even she may play it there. Then she soars further to a blissful place of which I neither will nor can speak. It is too difficult; I do not dare, for I am a very sinful person. Yet when infinite God brings the unfathomable soul to the heights, she loses sight of the earth in her astonishment and is not aware of ever having

---

71. An example of clever wordplay gets lost in the translation: *gemachet* and *unmaht*. The word *gemachet* (made) recalls God's *maht* (might or power). Thus his *unmaht* (un-might) is his powerlessness to withhold the gift of *making* the book.

72. The *dialogue* was a popular device in courtly-love poetry. Here it is combined with allegory: in courtly fashion the soul (queen) converses with the allegorical figure Lady Love.

73. In this chapter Mechthild offers us a poetic description of mystical union or the experience of ecstasy, which she calls God's *greeting*.

been on earth. Just when the game is at its best, one has to leave it.

From Mechthild of Magdeburg, *The Flowing Light of the Godhead,* translated by Frank Tobin, Classics of Western Spirituality (New York: Paulist Press, 1998), 39–41.

In "On Contemplating God through His Image Stamped upon Our Natural Powers" (1259), **Bonaventure** (1217–74) describes the third of six stages of the soul's spiritual journey. Bonaventure shows how the trinity of the soul's powers—memory, understanding, and choice—brings the soul close to God.

BONAVENTURE

"On Contemplating God through His Image Stamped upon Our Natural Powers"

1. The two previous stages, by leading us
into God
through his vestiges,
through which he shines forth
in all creatures,
have led us to the point
of reentering into ourselves, that is,
into our mind,
where the divine image shines forth.
Here it is that, now in the third stage,
we enter into our very selves;
and, as it were, leaving the outer court,
we should strive to see God
through a mirror
in the sanctuary, that is, in the forward area of the tabernacle.
Here the light of truth,
as from a candelabrum,
glows upon the face of our mind,
in which the image of the most blessed Trinity
shines in splendor.[74]
Enter into yourself, then, and see
that your soul loves itself most fervently;
that it could not love itself
unless it knew itself,
nor know itself
unless it remembered itself,
because our intellects grasp only what is present to our memory.
From this you can observe,
not with the bodily eye, but with the eye of reason,
that your soul has a threefold power.

Consider, therefore,
the operations and relationships of these three powers,
and you will be able to see God
through yourself as through an image,
which is to see *through a mirror in an obscure manner.*[75]

2. The function of memory is to retain and represent not only present, corporeal and temporal things but also successive, simple and eternal things. For the memory retains the past by remembrance, the present by reception and the future by foresight. It retains also simple things, such as the principles of continuous and discrete quantities like the point, the instant and the unit. Without these it is impossible to remember or to think of things which originate from them. The memory also retains the principles and axioms of the sciences, as everlasting truths held everlastingly. For while using reason, one can never so completely forget these principles that he would fail to approve and assent to them once they are heard, not as if he perceives them anew, but rather as if he recognizes them as innate and familiar. This is clearly shown when we propose to someone the following: "On any matter, one must either affirm or deny," or "Every whole is greater than its part," or any other axiom which cannot be contradicted "by our inner reason."[76]

In its first activity, therefore—the actual retention of all temporal things, past, present and future—the memory is an image of eternity, whose indivisible presence extends to all times. From its second activity, it is evident that memory is informed not only from outside by sensible images, but also from above by receiving and holding within itself simple forms which cannot enter through the doors of the senses by means of sensible images. From the third activity, we hold that the memory has an unchangeable light present to itself in which it remembers immutable truths. And so from the activities of the memory, we see that the soul itself is an image of God and a likeness so present to itself and having God so present that the soul actually grasps him and potentially "is capable of possessing him and of being a partaker in him."[77]

---

74. Cf. Ps 4:7.

75. 1 Cor 13:12.

76. Aristotle, *Anal. Post.,* I, t. 77, c. 10 (76b 24–27); the first quotation is a formulation of the principle of contradiction and is derived from Aristotle, *Metaph.,* IV, t. 15, c. 4. (1006a 1–29); the second is derived also from Aristotle, ibid., V, t. 30f., c. 25f. (1023b 12–36).

77. Augustine, *De Trinitate,* XIV, c. 8, no 11.

3. The function of the intellective faculty consists in understanding the meaning of terms, propositions and inferences. Now, the intellect grasps the meaning of terms when it comprehends in a definition what a thing is. But definitions are constructed by using more universal terms; and these are defined by more universal terms until we come to the highest and most universal. Consequently, unless these latter are known, the less universal cannot be grasped in a definition. Unless we know what being per se is, we cannot fully know the definition of any particular substance. We cannot know being per se unless we also know its properties, which are: one, true, good. Now, being can be considered as incomplete or complete, as imperfect or perfect, as being in potency or being in act, qualified being or unqualified being, partial being or total being, transient being or permanent being, being through another or being through itself, being mixed with nonbeing or pure being, dependent being or absolute being, posterior being or prior being, changeable being or unchangeable being, simple being or composite being. Since privations and defects can in no way be known except through something positive, our intellect does not come to the point of understanding any created being by a full analysis[78] unless it is aided by a knowledge of the Being which is most pure, most actual, most complete and absolute, which is unqualified and Eternal Being, in which are the principles of all things in their purity. How could the intellect know that a particular being is defective and incomplete if it had no knowledge of the Being which is free from all defect? The same holds true for the other properties previously mentioned.

The intellect can be said truly to comprehend the meaning of propositions when it knows with certitude that they are true. To know this is really to know because the intellect cannot be deceived in this kind of comprehension. For it knows that this truth cannot be otherwise; therefore, it knows that this truth is unchangeable. But since our mind itself is changeable, it can see such a truth shining forth unchangingly only by means of some light which shines in an absolutely unchangeable way; and it is impossible for this light to be a changeable creature. Therefore our intellect knows in that Light *which enlightens every man coming into this world,* which is *the true Light* and the *Word* who *was in the beginning with God* (John 1:9, 1).

Our intellect truly grasps the meaning of an inference when it sees that the conclusion follows necessarily from the premises. It sees this not only in necessary but also in contingent terms such as the following: If a man is running, the man is moving. Our intellect perceives this necessary relationship not only in existing things, but also in nonexisting things. For if a man actually exists, it follows that if he is running, he is moving; the same conclusion follows even if he does not exist. The necessity, therefore, of this inference does not come from the existence of the thing in matter since it is contingent; nor from the existence of the thing in the soul because that would be a fiction if the thing did not exist in reality. Therefore the necessity of such an inference comes from its exemplarity in the Eternal Art, according to which things are mutually oriented and related to one another because they are represented in the Eternal Art. As Augustine says in *On the True Religion:* The light of everyone who reasons truly is enkindled by that Truth which he also strives to reach.[79] From this it is obvious that our intellect is joined to Eternal Truth itself since it can grasp no truth with certitude if it is not taught by this Truth. You can see, therefore, through yourself the Truth which teaches you, if your desires and sensory images do not hinder you and interpose themselves like clouds between you and the rays of Truth.

4. The function of the power of choice is found in deliberation, judgment and desire. Deliberation consists in inquiring which is better, this or that. But *better* has meaning only in terms of its proximity to *best;* and this proximity is in terms of greater resemblance. No one, therefore, knows whether this is better than that unless he knows that it bears a greater resemblance to the best. No one knows that something bears a greater resemblance to another unless he knows the other. For I do not know that a certain man resembles Peter unless I know Peter or have some acquaintance with him. Therefore, the notion of the highest good is necessarily imprinted in everyone who deliberates.

A judgment of certitude on matters of deliberation is made according to some law. But no one judges with certitude according to law unless he is certain that the law is right and that he should not judge the law itself. But our mind judges about itself. Since, then, it cannot judge about the law through which it judges, that law is higher than our mind; and our mind judges by means of that law insofar as it is imprinted on our mind. But nothing is higher than the human mind except him alone who made it. Therefore in judging, our deliberative power touches the divine laws if it reaches a solution by a full analysis.

---

78. Bonaventure's technical term *plene resolvens,* which means a movement of the mind back to the absolute Being, whereby what is understood is known in relation to the absolute Being.

79. Augustine, *De vera religione,* XXXIX, 72.

Now desire tends principally toward what moves it most; but what moves it most is what is loved most, and what is loved most is happiness. But happiness is had only in terms of the best and ultimate end. Therefore human desire seeks nothing except the highest good or what leads to or has some likeness to it. So great is the power of the highest good that nothing can be loved by a creature except out of a desire for it. Creatures, when they take the image and copy for the Truth, are deceived and in error.

See, therefore, how close the soul is to God, and how, in their operations, the memory leads to eternity, the understanding to truth and the power of choice to the highest good.

5. These powers lead us to the most blessed Trinity itself in view of their order, origin and interrelatedness. From memory, intelligence comes forth as its offspring, since we understand when a likeness which is in the memory leaps into the eye of the intellect in the form of a word. From memory and intelligence love is breathed forth as their mutual bond. These three—the generating mind, the word and love—are in the soul as memory, understanding and will, which are consubstantial, coequal and coeval, and interpenetrate each other. If, then, God is a perfect spirit, he has memory, understanding and will; and he has the Word generated and Love breathed forth, which are necessarily distinct since one is produced by the other—not in the order of essence, not in the order of accident, therefore in the order of persons.

When, therefore, the soul considers itself, it rises through itself as through a mirror to behold the blessed Trinity of the Father, the Word and Love: three persons, coeternal, coequal and consubstantial. Thus each one dwells in each of the others; nevertheless one is not the other but the three are one God.

6. When the soul considers its Triune Principle through the trinity of its powers, by which it is an image of God, it is aided by the lights of the sciences which perfect and inform it and represent the most blessed Trinity in a threefold way. For all philosophy is either natural or rational or moral. The first deals with the cause of being and therefore leads to the power of the Father; the second deals with the basis of understanding and therefore leads to the wisdom of the Word; the third deals with the order of living and therefore leads to the goodness of the Holy Spirit.

Again, the first, natural philosophy, is divided into metaphysics, mathematics and physics. The first deals with the essences of things; the second with numbers and figures; and the third with natures, powers and diffusive operations. Therefore the first leads to the First Principle, the Father; the second to his Image, the Son; and the third to the gift of the Holy Spirit.

The second, rational philosophy, is divided into grammar, which makes men able to express themselves; logic, which makes them skillful in arguing; and rhetoric, which makes them capable of persuading and moving others. This likewise suggests the mystery of the most blessed Trinity.

The third, moral philosophy, is divided into individual, domestic and political. The first suggests the unbegottenness of the First Principle; the second, the relatedness of the Son; and the third, the liberality of the Holy Spirit.

7. All these sciences have certain and infallible rules,
    like rays of light shining down upon our mind
        from the eternal law.
    And thus our mind, illumined and flooded
        by such brilliance,
            unless it is blind,
        can be led through itself
    to contemplate that Eternal Light.
    The radiation and contemplation
        of this Light
    lifts up the wise in wonder;
        and on the contrary
    it leads to confusion the fools
who do not believe so that they may understand.
    Thus this prophecy is fulfilled:
    You enlighten wonderfully
    from the eternal hills;
    all the foolish of heart
    were troubled.[80]

From Bonaventure, *The Soul's Journey into God,* translated by Ewert Cousins (New York: Paulist Press, 1978), 79–86.

ᴥ **Catherine of Siena** (1347–80) is the first of three women "doctors" of the Roman Catholic Church, a title given to the most eminent theologians. In her Prologue to *The Dialogue,* "In the Name of Christ Crucified and of Gentle Mary" (1378), she gives theological insights underlying her life of prayer, study, love of neighbor, and political activism in Siena and Florence.

80. Ps 75:5–6.

CATHERINE OF SIENA

Prologue to *The Dialogue:*
"In the Name of Christ Crucified and of Gentle Mary"

A soul rises up, restless with tremendous desire for God's honor and the salvation of souls. She has for some time exercised herself in virtue and has become accustomed to dwelling in the cell of self-knowledge in order to know better God's goodness toward her, since upon knowledge follows love. And loving, she seeks to pursue truth and clothe herself in it.

But there is no way she can so savor and be enlightened by this truth as in continual humble prayer, grounded in the knowledge of herself and of God. For by such prayer the soul is united with God, following in the footsteps of Christ crucified, and through desire and affection and the union of love he makes of her another himself. So Christ seems to have meant when he said, "If you will love me and keep my word, I will show myself to you, and you will be one thing with me and I with you."[81] And we find similar words in other places from which we can see it is the truth that by love's affection the soul becomes another himself.

To make this clearer still, I remember having heard from a certain servant of God[82] that, when she was at prayer, lifted high in spirit, God would not hide from her mind's eye his love for his servants. No, he would reveal it, saying among other things, "Open your mind's eye and look within me, and you will see the dignity and beauty of my reasoning creature.[83] But beyond the beauty I have given the soul by creating her in my image and likeness, look at those who are clothed in the wedding garment of charity,[84] adorned with many true virtues: They are united with me through love. So I say, if you should ask me who they are, I would answer," said the gentle loving Word, "that they are another me; for they have lost and drowned their own will and have clothed themselves and united themselves and conformed themselves with mine."

It is true, then, that the soul is united to God through love's affection.

Now this soul's will was to know and follow truth more courageously. So she addressed four petitions to the most high and eternal Father, holding up her desire for herself first of all—for she knew that she could be of no service to her neighbors in teaching or example or prayer without first doing herself the service of attaining and possessing virtue.

Her first petition, therefore, was for herself. The second was for the reform of holy Church. The third was for the whole world in general, and in particular for the peace of Christians who are rebelling against holy Church with great disrespect and persecution.[85] In her fourth petition she asked divine providence to supply in general and in particular for a certain case which had arisen.[86]

From Catherine of Siena, *The Dialogue,* edited by Giuliana Cavallini, translated by Suzanne Noffke (New York: Paulist Press, 1980), 25–26.

☙ This excerpt from the spiritual treatise *The Cloud of Unknowing,* written in late-fourteenth-century England, explains why one should put certain thoughts under the "cloud of forgetting." The anonymous author combines monastic spirituality with early Scholastic theology and emphasizes the need to discern, rather than to learn, especially in the unitive stage of the mystical life.

FOURTEENTH-CENTURY ENGLISH

The Cloud of Unknowing

An accurate treatment, by question and answer, of certain doubts that may arise during this exercise; the suppression of rational investigation, knowledge and intellectual acumen; distinguishing the various levels and divisions of the active and contemplative lives.

But now you will ask, "What is this thought that presses upon me in this work, and is it a good or an evil thing?" "If it is an evil thing," you say, "then I am very much surprised, because it serves so well to increase a man's devotion; and at times I believe that it is a great comfort to listen to what it has to say. For I believe that sometimes it can make me weep very bitterly out of compassion for Christ in his passion, and sometimes for my own wretched state, and for many other reasons. All these, it seems to me, are very holy and do me

---

81. Cf. Jn 14:21–23.

82. Catherine refers to herself in the third person throughout the *Dialogue.* (Cf. 2 Cor 12:2.) Almost imperceptibly at this point she changes from present to past tense, a perspective she maintains in the narrative passages throughout the rest of the work.

83. *La mia creatura che à in sé ragione* is one of Catherine's favorite expressions for the human person.

84. In Catherine's writings *carità* and *amore* are often used quite interchangeably.

85. The conflicts, often bloody, between the Italian city-states and the papacy.

86. There is no clear evidence as to what this "certain case" was. Some have thought that the reference is to Niccolò di Tuldo, the youth Catherine accompanied to execution. [. . .] Others have seen a possible reference to Frate Simone da Cortona, whose despair figures in a number of letters. [. . .]

much good. And therefore I believe that these thoughts can in no way be evil; and if it is good, and their sweet tales do me so much good, then I am very surprised why you bid me put them deep down under the cloud of forgetting!"

This strikes me as being a very good question. And so I must reflect in order to answer it as well as my feebleness permits. First, when you ask me what this thought is that presses so hard upon you in this exercise, offering to help you in this work, I answer that it is a well-defined and clear sight of your natural intelligence imprinted upon your reason within your soul. And when you ask me whether it is good or evil, I say that it must of necessity be always good in its nature, because it is a ray of God's likeness.[87] But the use of it can be both good and evil. It is good when it is illumined by grace, so that you may see your wretched state, the passion, the kindness and the wonderful works of God in his creatures, bodily and spiritual. And so it is no wonder that it increases your devotion as much as you say. But the use of it is evil when it is swollen with pride, and with the curiosity which comes from the subtle speculation and learning, such as theologians have, which makes them want to be known not as humble clerics and masters of divinity or of devotion, but proud scholars of the devil and masters of vanity and falsehood.[88] And in other men and women, whether they be religious or seculars, the use and exercise of this natural understanding is evil when it is swollen with proud and clever learning of worldly things and earthly ideas, for the coveting of worldly honours and rich possessions, and the pleasure and vain-glory which comes from men's flatterings.

Next, you ask me why you should put down such thoughts under the cloud of forgetting, since it is true that they are good of their kind, and when well used they do you so much good and greatly increase your devotion. My answer is that you must clearly understand that there are two kinds of lives in holy Church.[89] One is the active life, and the other is the contemplative life. The active life is the lower and the contemplative life is the higher. Active life has two degrees, a higher and a lower; and the contemplative life also has two degrees, a lower and a higher. Further, these two lives are so joined together that though in part they are different, neither of them can be lived fully without having some part in the other. For the higher part of the active life is the same as the lower part of the contemplative life. Hence, a man cannot be fully active unless he is partly a contemplative, nor can he be fully contemplative here below unless he is in some way active. It is the nature of the active life both to be begun and ended in this life. Not so, however, of the contemplative life,

which is begun in this life and shall last without end. That is why the part that Mary chose shall never be taken away. The active life is troubled and anxious about many things; but the contemplative sits in peace, intent only on one thing.[90]

The lower part of the active life consists in good and honest corporal works of mercy and of charity. The higher part of the active life, and the lower part of the contemplative, consists in good spiritual meditations and earnest consideration of a man's own wretched state with sorrow and contrition, of the passion of Christ and of his servants with pity and compassion, and of the wonderful gifts, kindness, and works of God in all his creatures, corporeal and spiritual, with thanksgiving and praise. But the higher part of contemplation, insofar as it is possible to possess it here below, consists entirely in this darkness and in this cloud of unknowing, with a loving impulse and a dark gazing into the simple being of God himself alone.

In the lower part of the active life, a man is outside himself and beneath himself. In the higher part of the active life, and the lower part of the contemplative life, a man is within himself and on a par with himself. But in the higher part of the contemplative life, a man is above himself and under his God. He is above himself, because he makes it his purpose to arrive by grace whither he cannot come by nature: that is to say, to be knit to God in spirit, in oneness of love and union of wills.

One can understand that it is impossible for a man to come to the higher part of the active life unless he leaves, for a time, the lower part. In the same way, a man cannot come to the higher part of the contemplative life unless he leaves for a time the lower part. It would be a wrong thing for a man engaged on meditation, and a hindrance to him, to turn his mind to the outward corporal works which he had done or should do, even though in themselves they are very holy works. In the same way, it would be very inappropriate

---

87. The author is speaking of the "divine immissions," the *theoriae* that in Dionysian language are the graces proper to the purgative and illuminative lives. As Julian of Norwich teaches, in her own clear and simple language, the Christian is assimilated to the God revealed in Christ by contemplating him: ". . . the soul who thus contemplates him is made like to him who is contemplated. . ." *(Showings,* 164).

88. The author is here reflecting on the dangers that can accrue from attributing the "lights" granted in meditative prayer to one's own theological erudition.

89. The medieval Dionysians teach that the twofold knowledge of God—speculative and unitive—is at the basis of the distinction between the "two lives": and that the first will precede and ordinarily lead to the second.

90. In this contemplative exercise, the affection as well as the intellect must be purified, so that the soul in its love might tend to God alone [Lk 10:41–].

and a great hindrance to a man who ought to be working in this darkness and in this cloud of unknowing, with an affective impulse of love to God for himself alone, to permit any thought or any meditation on God's wonderful gifts, kindness or his work in any of his creatures, bodily or spiritual, to rise up in his mind so as to press between him and his God, even if they should be very holy thoughts, and give him great happiness and consolation.

This is the reason why I bid you put down any such clear and insinuating thought, and cover it up with a thick cloud of forgetting, no matter how holy it might be, and no matter how well it might promise to help you in your endeavour. Because it is love alone that can reach God in this life, and not knowing. For as long as the soul dwells in this mortal body, the clarity of our understanding in the contemplation of all spiritual things, and especially of God, is always mixed up with some sort of imagination; and because of it this exercise of ours would be tainted, and it would be very surprising if it did not lead us into great error.

From *The Cloud of Unknowing*, edited by James Walsh (New York: Paulist Press, 1981), 135–39.

⌘ **Teresa of Avila** (1515–82) was the second woman to be named "doctor" of the Roman Catholic Church. Teresa wrote *The Interior Castle* between June and November of 1577. In the last chapter, "The Seventh Dwelling Place," she describes how mystical union with God in prayer gives birth to good works. Teresa argues that the different tasks of hospitality shown by Mary and Martha to Jesus in the New Testament story (Lk 10:38–42) are to be joined together in the soul's work of bringing souls to God.

TERESA OF AVILA

The Interior Castle

"The Seventh Dwelling Place"

You must not think, Sisters, that the effects I mentioned are always present in these souls. Hence, where I remember, I say "ordinarily." For sometimes our Lord leaves these individuals in their natural state, and then it seems all the poisonous creatures from the outskirts and other dwelling places of this castle band together to take revenge for the time they were unable to have these souls under their control.

2. True, this natural state lasts only a short while, a day at most or a little more. And in this great disturbance, usually occasioned by some event, the soul's gain through the good company it is in becomes manifest. For the Lord gives the soul great stability and good resolutions not to deviate from His service in anything. But it seems this determination increases, and these souls do not deviate through even a very slight first movement. As I say this disturbance is rare, but our Lord does not want the soul to forget its being, so that, for one thing, it might always be humble; for another, that it might better understand the tremendous favor it receives, what it owes His Majesty, and that it might praise Him.

3. Nor should it pass through your minds that, since these souls have such determination and strong desires not to commit any imperfection for anything on earth, they fail to commit many imperfections, and even sins. Advertently, no; for the Lord must give souls such as these very particular help against such a thing. I mean venial sins, for from what these souls can understand they are free from mortal sins, although not immune. That they might have some sins they don't know about is no small torment to them. They also suffer torment in seeing souls go astray. Even though in some way they have great hope that they themselves will not be among these souls, they cannot help but fear when they recall some of those persons Scripture mentions who, it seems, were favored by the Lord, like Solomon, who communed so much with His Majesty, as I have said.[91] The one among you who feels safest should fear more, for *blessed is the man who fears the Lord*,[92] says David. May His Majesty protect us always. To beseech Him that we not offend Him is the greatest security we can have. May He be praised forever, amen.

4. It will be good, Sisters, to tell you the reason the Lord grants so many favors in this world. Although, if you have paid attention, you will have understood this in learning of their effects, I want to tell you again here lest someone think that the reason is solely for the sake of giving delight to these souls; that thought would be a serious error. His Majesty couldn't grant us a greater favor than to give us a life that would be an imitation of the life His beloved Son lived. Thus I hold for certain that these favors are meant to fortify our weakness, as I have said here at times, that we may be able to imitate Him in His great sufferings.

5. We have always seen that those who were closest to Christ our Lord were those with the greatest trials. Let us look at what His glorious Mother suffered and the glorious

---

91. 1 Kings 11.
92. Ps 112:1.

apostles. How do you think St. Paul could have suffered such very great trials? Through him we can see the effects visions and contemplation produce when from our Lord, and not from the imagination or the devil's deceit. Did St. Paul by chance hide himself in the enjoyment of these delights and not engage in anything else? You already see that he didn't have a day of rest, from what we can understand, and neither did he have any rest at night since it was then that he earned his livelihood.[93] I like very much the account about St. Peter fleeing from prison and how our Lord appeared to him and told him "I am on my way to Rome to be crucified again." We never recite the office of this feast, where this account is, that I don't find particular consolation.[94] How did this favor from the Lord impress St. Peter or what did he do! He went straight to his death. And it was no small mercy from the Lord that Peter found someone to provide him with death.

6. O my Sisters! How forgetful this soul, in which the Lord dwells in so particular a way, should be of its own rest, how little it should care for its honor, and how far it should be from wanting esteem in anything! For if it is with Him very much, as is right, it should think little about itself. All its concern is taken up with how to please Him more and how or where it will show Him the love it bears Him. This is the reason for prayer, my daughters, the purpose of this spiritual marriage: the birth always of good works, good works.

7. This is the true sign of a thing, or favor, being from God, as I have already told you. It benefits me little to be alone making acts of devotion to our Lord, proposing and promising to do wonders in His service, if I then go away and when the occasion offers itself do everything the opposite. I was wrong in saying it profits little, for everything having to do with God profits a great deal. And even though we are weak and do not carry out these resolutions afterward, sometimes His Majesty will give us the power to do so, even though, perhaps, doing so is burdensome to us, as is often true. Since He sees that a soul is very faint-hearted He gives it a severe trial, truly against its will, and brings this soul out of the trial with profit. Afterward, since the soul understands this, the fear lessens and one can offer oneself more willingly to Him. I meant "it benefits me little" in comparison with how much greater the benefit is when our deeds conform with what we say in prayer; what cannot be done all at once can be done little by little. Let the soul bend its will if it wishes that prayer be beneficial to it, for within the corners of these little monasteries there will not be lacking many occasions for you to do so.[95]

8. Keep in mind that I could not exaggerate the impor-

tance of this. Fix your eyes on the Crucified and everything will become small for you. If His Majesty showed us His love by means of such works and frightful torments, how is it you want to please Him only with words! Do you know what it means to be truly spiritual! It means becoming the slaves of God. Marked with His brand, which is that of the cross, spiritual persons, because now they have given Him their liberty, can be sold by Him as slaves of everyone, as He was. He doesn't thereby do them any harm or grant them a small favor. And if souls aren't determined about becoming His slaves, let them be convinced that they are not making much progress, for this whole building, as I have said, has humility as its foundation. If humility is not genuinely present, for your own sake the Lord will not construct a high building lest that building fall to the ground. Thus, Sisters, that you might build on good foundations, strive to be the least and the slaves of all, looking at how or where you can please and serve them. What you do in this matter you do more for yourself than for them and lay stones so firmly that the castle will not fall.

9. I repeat, it is necessary that your foundation consist of more than prayer and contemplation. If you do not strive for the virtues and practice them, you will always be dwarfs. And, please God, it will be only a matter of not growing, for you already know that whoever does not increase decreases. I hold that love, where present, cannot possibly be content with remaining always the same.

10. It will seem to you that I am speaking with those who are beginning and that after this beginner's stage souls can rest. I have already told you that the calm these souls have interiorly is for the sake of their having much less calm exteriorly and much less desire to have exterior calm. What, do you think, is the reason for those inspirations (or to put it better, aspirations) I mentioned, and those messages the soul sends from the interior center to the people at the top of the castle and to the dwelling places outside the center where it is! Is it so that those outside might fall asleep! No, absolutely not! That the faculties, senses, and all the corporeal will not be idle, the soul wages more war from the center than it did when it was outside suffering with them, for

---

93. Allusion to 1 Thess 2:9.

94. This *quo vadis* legend appeared in the Carmelite breviary, used in the time of St. Teresa, on the feast of St. Peter (June 29).

95. There is a Teresian proverb that [. . .] might go like this in English: "Look for virtue not in corners away from the din but right amidst the occasions of sin."

then it didn't understand the tremendous gain trials bring. Perhaps they were the means by which God brought it to the center, and the company it has gives it much greater strength than ever. For if here below, as David says, in the company of the saints we will become saints,[96] there is no reason to doubt that, being united with the Strong One through so sovereign a union of spirit with spirit, fortitude will cling to such a soul; and so we shall understand what fortitude the saints had for suffering and dying.

11. It is very certain that from that fortitude which clings to it there the soul assists all those who are in the castle, and even the body itself which often, seemingly, does not feel the strength. But the soul is fortified by the strength it has from drinking wine in this wine cellar, where its Spouse has brought it[97] and from where He doesn't allow it to leave; and strength flows back to the weak body, just as food placed in the stomach strengthens the head and the whole body. Thus the soul has its share of misfortune while it lives. However much it does, the interior strength increases and thus, too, the war that is waged; for everything seems like a trifle to it. The great penances that many saints—especially the glorious Magdalene, who had always been surrounded by so much luxury—performed must have come from this center. Also that hunger which our Father Elijah had for the honor of his God[98] and which St. Dominic and St. Francis had so as to draw souls to praise God. I tell you, though they were forgetful of themselves, their suffering must have been great.

12. This is what I want us to strive for, my Sisters; and let us desire and be occupied in prayer not for the sake of our enjoyment but so as to have this strength to serve. Let's refuse to take an unfamiliar path, for we shall get lost at the most opportune time. It would indeed be novel to think of having these favors from God through a path other than the one He took and the one followed by all His saints. May the thought never enter our minds. Believe me, Martha and Mary must join together in order to show hospitality to the Lord and have Him always present and not host Him badly by failing to give Him something to eat. How would Mary, always seated at His feet, provide Him with food if her sister did not help her! His food is that in every way possible we draw souls that they may be saved and praise Him always.[99]

13. You will make two objections: one, that He said that Mary had chosen the better part. The answer is that she had already performed the task of Martha, pleasing the Lord by washing His feet and drying them with her hair.[100] Do you think it would be a small mortification for a woman of nobility like her to wander through these streets (and perhaps

alone because her fervent love made her unaware of what she was doing) and enter a house she had never entered before and afterward suffer the criticism of the Pharisee and the very many other things she must have suffered? The people saw a woman like her change so much—and, as we know, she was among such malicious people—and they saw her friendship with the Lord whom they vehemently abhorred, and that she wanted to become a saint since obviously she would have changed her manner of dress and everything else. All of that was enough to cause them to comment on the life she had formerly lived. If nowadays there is so much gossip against persons who are not so notorious, what would have been said then? I tell you, Sisters, the better part came after many trials and much mortification, for even if there were no other trial than to see His Majesty abhorred, that would be an intolerable one. Moreover, the many trials that afterward she suffered at the death of the Lord and in the years that she subsequently lived in His absence must have been a terrible torment. You see she wasn't always in the delight of contemplation at the feet of the Lord.

14. The other objection you will make is that you are unable to bring souls to God, that you do not have the means; that you would do it willingly but that not being teachers or preachers, as were the apostles, you do not know how. This objection I have answered at times in writing, but I don't know if I did so in this *Castle*. Yet since the matter is something I believe is passing through your minds on account of the desires God gives you I will not fail to respond here. I already told you elsewhere that sometimes the devil gives us great desires so that we will avoid setting ourselves to the task at hand, serving our Lord in possible things, and instead be content with having desired the impossible. Apart from the fact that by prayer you will be helping greatly, you need not be desiring to benefit the whole world but must concentrate on those who are in your company, and thus your deed will be greater since you are more obliged toward them. Do you think such deep humility, your mortification, service of all and great charity toward them, and love of the Lord is of little benefit? This fire of love in you enkindles their souls, and with every other virtue you will be always awakening

---

96. Ps 18:26.

97. Allusion to Song 2:4.

98. Allusion to 1 Kings 19:10. The shield of the Carmelite order takes as its motto the prophet Elijah's words: *Zelo zelatus sum pro Domino Deo Exercituum*.

99. Lk 10:38–42.

100. Allusion to Lk 7:37–38.

them. Such service will not be small but very great and very pleasing to the Lord. By what you do in deed—that which you can—His Majesty will understand that you would do much more. Thus He will give you the reward He would if you had gained many souls for Him.

15. You will say that such service does not convert souls because all the Sisters you deal with are already good. Who has appointed you judge in this matter? The better they are the more pleasing their praises will be to our Lord and the more their prayer will profit their neighbor.

In sum, my Sisters, what I conclude with is that we shouldn't build castles in the air. The Lord doesn't look so much at the greatness of our works as at the love with which they are done. And if we do what we can, His Majesty will enable us each day to do more and more, provided that we do not quickly tire. But during the little while this life lasts—and perhaps it will last a shorter time than each one thinks—let us offer the Lord interiorly and exteriorly the sacrifice we can. His Majesty will join it with that which He offered on the cross to the Father for us. Thus even though our works are small they will have the value our love for Him would have merited had they been great.

16. May it please His Majesty, my Sisters and daughters, that we all reach that place where we may ever praise Him. Through the merits of His Son who lives and reigns forever and ever, may He give me the grace to carry out something of what I tell you, amen. For I tell you that my confusion is great, and thus I ask you through the same Lord that in your prayers you do not forget this poor wretch.

[Epilogue][101]

JHS[102]

Although when I began writing this book I am sending you I did so with the aversion I mentioned in the beginning, now that I am finished I admit the work has brought me much happiness, and I consider the labor, though I confess it was small, well spent. Considering the strict enclosure and the few things you have for your entertainment, my Sisters, and that your buildings are not always as large as would be fitting for your monasteries, I think it will be a consolation for you to delight in this interior castle since without permission from the prioress you can enter and take a walk through it at any time.

2. True, you will not be able to enter all the dwelling places through your own efforts, even though these efforts

may seem to you great, unless the Lord of the castle Himself brings you there. Hence I advise you to use no force if you meet with any resistance, for you will thereby anger Him in such a way that He will never allow you to enter them. He is very fond of humility. By considering that you do not deserve even to enter the third you will more quickly win the favor to reach the fifth. And you will be able to serve Him from there in such a way, continuing to walk through them often, that He will bring you into the very dwelling place He has for Himself. You need never leave this latter dwelling place unless called by the prioress, whose will this great Lord desires that you comply with as much as if it were His own. Even though you are frequently outside through her command, you will always find the door open when you return. Once you get used to enjoying this castle, you will find rest in all things, even those involving much labor, for you will have the hope of returning to the castle which no one can take from you.

3. Although no more than seven dwelling places were discussed, in each of these there are many others, below and above and to the sides, with lovely gardens and fountains and labyrinths, such delightful things that you would want to be dissolved in praises of the great God who created the soul in His own image and likeness.[103] If you find something good in the way I have explained this to you, believe that indeed His Majesty said it so as to make you happy; the bad that you might find is said by me.

4. Through the strong desire I have to play some part in helping you serve my God and Lord, I ask that each time you read this work you, in my name, praise His Majesty fervently and ask for the increase of His Church and for light for the Lutherans. As for me, ask Him to pardon my sins and deliver me from purgatory, for perhaps by the mercy of God I will be there when this is given you to read—if it may be seen by you after having been examined by learned men. If anything is erroneous it is so because I didn't know otherwise; and I submit in everything to what the holy Roman Catholic Church holds, for in this Church I live, declare my faith, and promise to live and die.

---

101. This epilogue was sent in the form of a letter along with the original manuscript to the Discalced Carmelite nuns in Seville.

102. This is the anglicized form of the Latin letters IHS (the letter "J" does not exist in the Latin alphabet). IHS are the first three letters of Jesus' name in Greek (ΙΗΣΟΥΣ): iota, eta, and sigma. The form of the letter sigma when it occurs at the end of a word (ς) is similar to our letter s. Teresa uses JHS as a prayerful ejaculation.(This note is by Gerhart and Udoh.)

103. Allusion to Gen 1:26.

May God our Lord be forever praised and blessed, amen, amen.

5. This writing was finished in the monastery of St. Joseph of Avila in the year 1577, the eve before the feast of St. Andrew,[104] for the glory of God who lives and reigns forever and ever, amen.

From *The Collected Works of St. Teresa of Avila*, translated by Kieran Kavanaugh and Otilio Rodriguez, vol. 2 (Washington, DC: Institute of Carmelite Studies, 1980), 444–52.

❧ In the Prologue to his *Spiritual Canticle* (1584–86), **John of the Cross** (1549–91), Teresa of Avila's spiritual adviser and confrère in the Carmelite reform, provides some "general light" for understanding this now classic mystical text. John maintains that the utterances of his canticle cannot be bound to any single explanation because "the abundant meanings of the Holy Spirit cannot be caught in words."

JOHN OF THE CROSS

Prologue to *The Spiritual Canticle*

Prologue[105]

1. These stanzas, Reverend Mother, were obviously composed with a certain burning love of God. The wisdom and charity of God is so vast, as the Book of Wisdom states, that it reaches from end to end (Wis 8:1), and a person informed and moved by it bears in some way this very abundance and impulsiveness in his words. As a result I do not plan to expound these stanzas in all the breadth and fullness that the fruitful spirit of love conveys to them. It would be foolish to think that expressions of love arising from mystical understanding, like these stanzas, are fully explainable. The Spirit of the Lord, who abides in us and aids our weakness, as St. Paul says (Rom 8:26), pleads for us with unspeakable groanings in order to manifest what we can neither fully understand nor comprehend.

Who can describe the understanding He gives to loving souls in whom He dwells? And who can express the experience He imparts to them? Who, finally, can explain the desires He gives them? Certainly, no one can! Not even they who receive these communications. As a result these persons let something of their experiences overflow in figures and similes, and from the abundance of their spirit pour out secrets and mysteries rather than rational explanations.

If these similitudes are not read with the simplicity of the

spirit of knowledge and love they contain, they will seem to be absurdities rather than reasonable utterances, as will those comparisons of the divine Canticle of Solomon and other books of Sacred Scripture where the Holy Spirit, unable to express the fullness of His meaning in ordinary words, utters mysteries in strange figures and likenesses. The saintly doctors, no matter how much they have said or will say, can never furnish an exhaustive explanation of these figures and comparisons, since the abundant meanings of the Holy Spirit cannot be caught in words. Thus the explanation of these expressions usually contains less than what they in themselves embody.

2. Since these stanzas, then, were composed in a love flowing from abundant mystical understanding, I cannot explain them adequately, nor is it my intention to do so. I only wish to shed some general light on them, since Your Reverence has desired this of me. I believe such an explanation will be more suitable. It is better to explain the utterances of love in their broadest sense so that each one may derive profit from them according to the mode and capacity of his spirit, rather than narrow them down to a meaning unadaptable to every palate. As a result, though we give some explanation of these stanzas, there is no reason to be bound to this explanation. For mystical wisdom, which comes through love and is the subject of these stanzas, need not be understood distinctly in order to cause love and affection in the soul, for it is given according to the mode of faith, through which we love God without understanding Him.

3. I shall then be very brief, although I do intend to give a lengthier explanation when necessary and where the occasion arises for a discussion of some matters concerning prayer and its effects. Since these stanzas refer to many of the effects of prayer, I ought to treat of at least some of these effects.

Yet, passing over the more common effects, I will briefly deal with the more extraordinary ones, which take place in those who with God's help have passed beyond the state of beginners. I do this for two reasons: first, because there are many writings for beginners; second, because I am addressing Your Reverence, at your request. And our Lord has fa-

---

104. That is, Nov. 29, 1577, close to six months after she had begun writing on June 2 of that same year.

105. This commentary on the stanzas which deal with the exchange of love between the soul and Christ, its Bridegroom, explains certain matters about prayer and its effects. It was written at the request of Mother Ann of Jesús, prioress of the Discalced Carmelite nuns of St. Joseph's in Granada, 1584.

vored you and led you beyond the state of beginners into the depths of His divine love.

I hope that, although some scholastic theology is used here in reference to the soul's interior converse with God, it will not prove vain to speak in such a manner to the pure of spirit. Even though Your Reverence lacks training in scholastic theology by which the divine truths are understood, you are not wanting in mystical theology which is known through love and by which one not only knows but at the same time experiences.

4. And that my explanations—which I desire to submit to anyone with better judgment than mine and entirely to Holy Mother the Church—may be worthy of belief, I do not intend to affirm anything of myself nor trust in any of my own experiences nor in those of other spiritual persons whom I have known or heard of. Although I plan to make use of these experiences, I want to explain and confirm at least the more difficult matters through passages from Sacred Scripture. In using these passages, I will quote the words in Latin, and then interpret them in regard to the matter being discussed.

From *The Collected Works of St. John of the Cross*, translated by Kieran Kavanaugh and Otilio Rodriguez (Washington, DC: Institute of Carmelite Studies, 1979), 408–10.

☙ *The Pilgrim's Tale—On the Occasion of His Second Meeting, 13 December 1859* (1881) cautions against substituting the love of a text—in this case, the *Philokalia* (an Eastern Orthodox collection of ascetic and mystical writings from the fourth through the fifteenth centuries, published in 1783)—for love of the Spirit. It celebrates the Pilgrim's joy at discovering the truth of the text in the events of his life.

The Pilgrim's Tale—On the Occasion of His Second Meeting, 13 December 1859

All who fear the Lord, come, and I will tell you how much he has done for my soul.[106]

For a long time I wandered through various places with the Jesus prayer as my traveling companion. It encouraged and consoled me on all my paths, in all my encounters and in every situation. I began to feel at last that it would be better if I stopped in one place somewhere so as to be alone more conveniently and to study the *Philokalia*. Although I read a little from it when I took shelter for the night or rested during the day, still I strongly desired to apply myself to it more

seriously and, with faith, to draw from it true instruction for the salvation of my soul by means of the prayer of the heart. In spite of this desire of mine, however, I was unable to hire myself out anywhere for heavy labor because I have suffered a total lack of control over my left arm since my childhood. Being thus unable to have a permanent shelter, I went to Siberia to visit the relics of Bishop Innokenty of Irkutsk.[107] My intention was that walking the woods and steppes of Siberia would be quieter and consequently more conducive to prayer and reading.

So off I went and I continually repeated the prayer aloud. In no great length of time I felt that the prayer somehow was beginning to move into my heart by itself. That is, it seemed that as it beat normally my heart began to form the words of the prayer inside itself with every heartbeat; for example, at the first beat, Lord; at the second, Jesus; at the third, Christ; and so on. I stopped saying the prayer vocally and began to listen carefully to my heart speaking. So too I seemed to be looking into my heart with my eyes, and I remembered how my late elder used to explain this to me. Then I began to sense such agreeable pain in my heart and such love for Jesus Christ in my thoughts that it seemed that if I were to catch sight of him somewhere I would throw myself at his feet and not let him out of my arms, sweetly kissing and tearfully thanking him because on account of his Name he bestows such consolation on his unworthy and sinful creature in accordance with his mercy and love. Furthermore, a kind of blessed warming arose in my heart, and this warmth spread throughout my breast. This experience in particular led me to an assiduous reading of the *Philokalia* in order to verify my feelings, but equally to study a further lesson on the interior prayer of the heart. Without such verification I was afraid of succumbing to its charm, or of taking natural movements for ones of grace and becoming puffed up because I had acquired this prayer so rapidly. I had heard such a warning from my late elder. For this reason I walked more by night and I spent the days for the most part sitting under trees in the forest and reading the *Philokalia*. . . .

Oh, how many new things, how many wise and hitherto unknown things did my reading reveal! In practicing them I tasted such sweetness the likes of which until then I had not

---

106. Ps 65:16.

107. The Relics of Bishop Innokenty (d. 1731) were preserved in the Ascension monastery, located approximately 5 km from Irkutsk on the Angara River. Innokenty was canonized for general veneration in the Russian Orthodox Church in 1804. Feast day, 26 November.

even been able to imagine. It is true that when I was reading, certain passages were beyond the grasp of my dull mind, but they were made clear to me by the effects of the prayer of the heart. In addition, I now and then saw my late elder in my dreams and he explained many things to me and above all inclined my witless soul toward humility.

For almost two summer months I was blissfully happy, traveling mostly through the woods and along country roads. If I came into a village, I would ask for a bag of dried crusts and a handful of salt; I would fill my bark flask with water and then go on walking about one hundred kilometers.

Whether on account of the sins of my accursed soul, or because trials are necessary in the spiritual life, or for the sake of better instruction and experience, temptations were in the offing for me at the end of the forest. Indeed, I walked out onto the main road and was overtaken at twilight by two men whose heads gave them away as soldiers. They began demanding money from me. When I answered that I did not have even a kopeck, they did not believe me and shouted insolently: "You're lying! Pilgrims collect lots of money!" Why bother talking with him," one of them said and he struck me on the head with a cudgel so that I lost consciousness. I don't know how long I lay there unconscious, but when I came to, I realized that I was lying at the edge of the forest near the road, all rumpled. I no longer had my pouch, only the cut cords from which it used to hang. Glory be to God that they did not take my passport, which I kept in my old rag of a cap in case I needed to show it quickly upon request. When I stood up I began to weep bitterly not so much because of my aching head as for my missing books: the Bible and the *Philokalia* were in the stolen bag. I did not stop grieving and crying day or night. Where is it now, the Bible which I read since childhood and which I always had with me? Where is my *Philokalia,* from which I drew both instruction and consolation? Unhappy me, I had lost the first and last treasure of my life without having had my fill of it. It were better had they killed me outright than for me to live without my spiritual nourishment. I can never get them back again!

For two days I could barely drag my feet, exhausted from this misfortune, and on the third day, strained to the breaking point, I dropped under a bush and fell asleep. I dreamt that I was in the hermitage, and in my elder's cell I bemoaned my misfortune. The elder comforted me and said:

"This is a lesson for you on indifference toward earthly things, so that you may more easily advance toward heaven. It has been allowed to happen to you so that you do not fall into spiritual voluptuousness. God wants Christians to re-

nounce their own will, desire, and every predilection completely and to surrender themselves entirely to his divine will. He arranges every event for the benefit and salvation of the individual, *for he wills that all men and women be saved.*[108] Thus, take courage and believe that *with the testing the Lord will also provide the way out.*[109] And soon you will be consoled much more than you now are grieving."

At these words I woke up and I felt increased vitality and my soul seemed full of light and peace. "Let the Lord's will be done," I said and making the sign of the cross I stood up and went on my way. The prayer once again began to function in my heart as before and for three days I traveled in peace.

Suddenly on the road I came upon a convoy of convicts being led under escort. As I came up alongside of them I saw the two men who had robbed me, and since they were walking in the outside file, I fell at their feet and earnestly begged them to tell me where my books were. At first they paid no attention to me but then one of them said:

"If you give us something, we'll tell you where they are. Give us a ruble."

I assured them that I would give it to them even if I had to beg the ruble from someone for the sake of Christ. "Here, if you wish, take my passport as a pledge."

They said that my books were being transported in a wagon following the prisoners with the rest of the booty they were found with.

"How can I get them back?"

"Ask the captain who is escorting them." I rushed to the captain and explained everything to him in detail. He asked me:

"Can you really read the Bible?"

"Not only can I read it all," I answered, "but I can even write. You will see an inscription in the Bible that this book is mine. And in my passport the same name is given."

The captain said: "These men are swindlers and runaway soldiers who have been living in an earthen hut and plundering many people. Yesterday they were caught by a clever coachman whose carriage and three [horses] they wanted to steal. I'll return your books to you if they are there. Why don't you come with us to the night camp? It's not far, about four kilometers, and then we won't have to stop the convoy for your sake."

I gladly walked beside the captain's riding horse and struck up a conversation with him. I noticed that he was a good and

---

108. 1 Tim 2:4.
109. 1 Cor 10:13.

honest fellow and no longer young. He asked me who I was, where I came from, and where I was going. I answered all his questions with complete honesty. And so we went, right on to the night-camp station house. Finding my books, he returned them to me and said: "Where will you go, now that it is nightfall? Spend the night here in my anteroom." And so I did. When I got the books, I was so happy that I did not know how to thank God; I pressed the books to my breast and held them there until my hands grew stiff. Tears poured from my eyes out of joy and my heart beat sweetly with delight. The captain watched me and said: "It is clear that you love reading the Bible." I was so overjoyed that I could not give him any answer; I just wept. He continued: "I too, brother, read the Gospel carefully," at which point he unbuttoned his full-dress uniform and took out a small Gospel printed in Kiev and bound in silver. "Sit down there; I will tell you how this came about and serve me supper!"

We sat at table and the captain began his tale. "Ever since I was a young man I have served in the army, not in a garrison but in the field. The superior officers liked me for being a conscientious second lieutenant. But I was young then and so were my friends. Unfortunately, I took up drinking, and toward the end it developed into a sickness. When I don't drink, I'm a conscientious officer; but once I start up, I'm six weeks flat on my back. My fellow officers put up with me for a long time. Finally, on account of the rudeness and quarreling committed when I was drunk, they reduced me to the ranks for three years and transferred me to a garrison. If I didn't improve myself and stop drinking they threatened me with an even harsher punishment. In this hapless state, try as I might to control myself and no matter how often I submitted myself to a cure, I still was entirely unable to throw off my passion. For this reason they planned to transfer me to a convict labor gang. When I learned about this, I didn't know what to do with myself. One day I was sitting in the barracks lost in reverie. Suddenly some monk came in with a book to collect alms for the church. Anyone who could give did so. Approaching me he asked:

"Why are you so sad?'

"Striking up a conversation with him, I recounted my troubles to him. The monk sympathized with my situation and said:

"Exactly the same thing happened to my brother, and here is what helped him. His spiritual father gave him a copy of the Gospels with strict orders to read a chapter of the Gospels without delay should he feel the desire for wine; if he desired it again, he should read the next chapter. My brother began to do this and in a short period of time his desire for

wine disappeared and now it has been fifteen years since he has taken a single drop of alcohol to his mouth. If you do the same thing, you'll see how it helps. I have a copy of the Gospels. Do let me bring it to you.'

"After hearing him out I said to him: 'How can your Gospel help me when none of my efforts and no medicinal means were able to control me?' I said this because I had never read the Gospel.

"Don't say that,' objected the monk. 'I assure you that it will be of use.'

"The next day the monk actually brought me this very copy of the Gospels. I opened it, looked it over, began to read and said: 'I can't take it. I don't understand anything in it. And I'm not accustomed to reading church script.' The monk continued to assure me, arguing that in the very words of the Gospel there was a gracious power, for what was written in it was what God himself had said. 'There is no need to understand, only read it diligently. One of the saints said: "If you do not understand the Word of God, the demons do understand what you are reading and they tremble." Your passion for drinking is certainly the result of the demons' provocation. I'll tell you another saying. Saint John Chrysostom writes that even the very chamber in which a copy of the Gospels is kept terrifies the spirits of darkness and is an unsuitable point of assault for their crafty schemes.'

"I gave the monk something, though what it was escapes me, took the copy of the Gospels from him and placed it in my little trunk with my other things. And then I forgot about it. A little while later, the time came for me to begin drinking again. I was dying for a drink and I quickly unlocked the little trunk to get some money and run to the tavern. But as soon as I opened the lid the first thing that struck my eyes was the Gospel book, and I vividly recalled everything that the monk had told me. I unwrapped the copy and began reading the first chapter of Matthew. Although I read it through to the end I understood precisely nothing and I wondered: the monk said that the book contained God's exact words, but there were only names in the chapter. Okay, I said, let's read another chapter. I did so and it was more understandable. Let's read the third chapter. As soon as I started it, a bell sounded in the barracks—everyone had to go to their bunk. As a result it was impossible to get beyond the gates, and so I stayed put. When I got up the next morning, set on going for a drink, I thought: What if I read a chapter from the Gospel! I read one and did not understand it. Again I began craving a drink. I started reading again and it became easier. This encouraged me, so that every time I felt the urge for a drink I began reading a chapter from the Gospel. The further I read, the easier everything was; finally when I had finished all four evangelists the desire for drinking completely went away and I developed a loathing for it. And so, for exactly twenty years I have not had a drop of alcohol. Everyone was amazed at how much I had changed. After three years passed I was once again inducted into the officers' rank and then into the following ranks, and finally I was made a commanding officer. I married; I lucked out on a good wife. We have made a fortune and, glory be to God, we go on living life. We help the poor as we are able and welcome pilgrims. My son is already an officer and a good fellow to boot.

"Listen! Since the day I was cured of alcoholism I swore an oath that I would read the Gospels every day for the rest of my life, one entire Evangelist in twenty-four hours without letting any obstacle stand in the way. And even now this is what I do. If a lot of work arises from my duties and I am extremely worn out, I have my wife or my son read the whole Gospel to me in the evening after I have gone to bed. And so I fulfill my rule without omission. In gratitude and to the glory of God I bound this copy of the Gospels in pure silver and carry it in my breast pocket always."

I listened with delight to the captain's words and then said to him:

"I too have seen a similar case. At the factory in our village there was a certain craftsman who was very skilled at his job, a good and dear fellow; unfortunately he too used to indulge in drinking bouts, and rather often for that matter. A certain God-fearing individual advised him whenever he desired to drink wine to say thirty-three Jesus prayers in honor of the Most Holy Trinity and in keeping with the thirty-three years

of Jesus Christ's earthly life. The craftsman obeyed. He began to carry this out and soon quit drinking altogether. And what is more! Three years later he entered a monastery."

"Which is greater?" asked the captain. "The Jesus prayer or the Gospel?"

"The Gospel and the Jesus prayer are one and the same thing," I replied. "For the divine name of Jesus Christ contains in itself all Gospel truths. The holy fathers say that the Jesus prayer is an abridgment of the entire Gospel."

At last we prayed. The captain started to read the Gospel according to Mark, from the beginning, and I listened and said the prayer in my heart. At the second hour after midnight the captain finished the Gospel and we parted for rest. In keeping with my habit, I rose early in the morning. Everyone was still sleeping. As soon as it started to get light, I flung myself into reading my beloved *Philokalia*. With such joy did I open it! It was as if I were seeing my own father who had been in a distant land, or a friend risen from the dead! I kissed it and thanked God for having returned it to me. Unhesitatingly I began to read "The Discourse on Innermost Activity" by Theoliptos of Philadelphias in the second part of the *Philokalia*. The instruction surprised me, for he proposed that one and the same individual could perform three different things at one and the same time. "While seated in the refectory," he says, "give food to your body, reading to your ears, and prayer to your mind." But the recollection of yesterday evening expertly and in fact solved the meaning for me. Here too the mystery was revealed to me that the mind and the heart are not one and the same thing.

From *The Pilgrim's Tale*, edited by Aleksei Pentkovsky, translated by T. Allan Smith (New York: Paulist Press, 1989), 68–75. [Ellipsis in original.]

2. PHILOSOPHY AND THEOLOGY: QUESTIONS OF METHOD

MEDIEVAL METHODOLOGICAL QUESTIONS

▶ *The Mystical Theology* (ca. third to fifth century), by the theologian known as **Pseudo-Dionysius**, is a theology done on the basis of a close reading of biblical texts and the careful elucidation of their possible meanings. It gives an account of the Christian life, in Neoplatonic terms of ascent.

PSEUDO-DIONYSIUS

The Mystical Theology, I–V

I

[997A] What is the divine darkness?

1. Trinity!! Higher than any being,
   any divinity, any goodness!

Guide of Christians
> in the wisdom of heaven!
Lead us up beyond unknowing and light,
> up to the farthest, highest peak
> of mystic scripture,
> where the mysteries of God's Word
> lie simple, absolute and unchangeable
[997B]
> in the brilliant darkness of a hidden
> silence.
Amid the deepest shadow
> they pour overwhelming light
> on what is most manifest.
Amid the wholly unsensed and unseen
> they completely fill our sightless minds
> with treasures beyond all beauty.

For this I pray; Timothy,[110] my friend, my advice to you as you look for a sight of the mysterious things,[111] is to leave behind you everything perceived and understood, everything perceptible and understandable, all that is not and all that is, and, with your understanding laid aside, to strive upward as much as you can toward union with him who is beyond all being and knowledge. By an undivided and [1000A] absolute abandonment of yourself and everything, shedding all and freed from all, you will be uplifted to the ray of divine shadow which is above everything that is.

2. But see to it that none of this comes to the hearing of the uninformed,[112] that is to say, to those caught up with the things of the world, who imagine that there is nothing beyond instances of individual being and who think that by their own intellectual resources they can have a direct knowledge of him who has made the shadows his hiding place.[113] And if initiation into the divine is beyond such people, what is to be said of those others, still more uninformed, who describe the transcendent Cause of all things in terms derived [1000B] from the lowest orders of being, and who claim that it is in no way superior to the godless, multiformed shapes they themselves have made? What has actually to be said about the Cause of everything is this. Since it is the Cause of all beings, we should posit and ascribe to it all the affirmations we make in regard to beings, and, more appropriately, we should negate all these affirmations, since it surpasses all being. Now we should not conclude that the negations are simply the opposites of the affirmations, but rather that the cause of all is considerably prior to this, beyond privations, beyond every denial, beyond every assertion.

3. This, at least, is what was taught by the blessed Bar-

tholomew.[114] He says that the Word of God is vast and minuscule, that the [1000C] Gospel is wide-ranging and yet restricted. To me it seems that in this he is extraordinarily shrewd, for he has grasped that the good cause of all is both eloquent and taciturn, indeed wordless. It has neither word nor act of understanding, since it is on a plane above all this, and it is made manifest only to those who travel through foul and fair, who pass beyond the summit of every holy ascent, who leave behind them every divine light, every voice, every word from heaven, and who plunge into the darkness where, as scripture proclaims, there dwells the One who is beyond all things.[115] It is not for nothing that the blessed Moses is commanded to submit first to purification and then to depart from those who have not undergone this.[116] When every purification is [1000D] complete, he hears the many-voiced trumpets. He sees the many lights, pure and with rays streaming abundantly. Then, standing apart from the crowds and accompanied by chosen priests, he pushes ahead to the summit of the divine ascents. And yet he does not meet God himself, but contemplates, not him who is invisible, but rather where he dwells.[117] This means, I presume, that the holiest and highest of the things perceived with the eye of the body or the mind are but the rationale which presupposes all that lies below the Transcendent [1001A] One. Through them, however, his unimaginable presence is shown, walking the heights of those holy places to which the mind at least can rise. But then he [Moses] breaks free of them, away from what sees and is seen, and he plunges into the truly mysterious darkness of unknowing.[118] Here, renouncing all that the

---

110. Timothy, the purported addressee of the First and Second Letters to Timothy. See also Acts 16:1–3; Rom 16:21; 1 Cor 4:17; 16:10; 2 Cor 1:1, 19; Phil 1:1; 2:19, 22, et passim. (The notes for this selection are by Gerhart and Udoh.)

111. The translator notes that the terms "mystic" (in line 7 of the poem) and "mysterious" in the present clause both translate the Greek word *mustikos*. The term "mystic" in the poem is not to be taken in the sense in which, later, the term "mystical" was understood: the private and extraordinary transcendence of one's self. It means rather, as the second phrase suggests, "hidden," "secret," "mysterious."

112. This is a recurring theme among the early Church Fathers; see Clement of Alexandria, *Strōmateis*, 1.ix.56.2, and similarly Plato, *Theaetetus*, 155e.

113. See Ps 18:11.

114. Batholomew is listed among Jesus' apostles (see Mk 3:18; Mt 10:3; Lk 6:14; Acts 1:13). The author here is referring to one of the numerous later apocryphal writings that were attributed to him, as were also attributed to the other apostles.

115. See Ex 20:21; also Ex 19:1.

116. See Ex 19:10–12.

117. See Ex 19:16–24; 20:18–21; 24:1–2, 15–18; 33:17–23.

118. The phrase "darkness of unknowing" is more generally known as "the cloud of unknowing," which derives from the title of the book *The Cloud of Unknowing*, by an unknown fourteenth-century English author.

mind may conceive, wrapped entirely in the intangible and the invisible, he belongs completely to him who is beyond everything. Here, being neither oneself nor someone else, one is supremely united by a completely unknowing inactivity of all knowledge, and knows beyond the mind by knowing nothing.

II

[1025A] How one should be united, and attribute praises, to the Cause of all things who is beyond all things.

I pray we could come to this darkness so far above light! If only we lacked sight and knowledge so as to see, so as to know, unseeing and unknowing, that which lies beyond all vision and knowledge. For this would be really to see and to know: to praise the Transcendent One in a transcending way, namely through the denial of all beings. We [1025B] would be like sculptors who set out to carve a statue. They remove every obstacle to the pure view of the hidden image, and simply by this act of clearing aside[119] they show up the beauty which is hidden.

Now it seems to me that we should praise the denials quite differently than we do the assertions. When we made assertions we began with the first things, moved down through intermediate terms until we reached the last things. But now as we climb from the last things up to the most primary we deny all things so that we may unhiddenly know that unknowing which itself is hidden from all those possessed of knowing amid all beings, so that we may see above being that darkness concealed from all the light among beings.

III

What are the affirmative theologies and what are the negative?

[1032D] In my *Theological Representations,*[120] I have praised the notions which are most appropriate to affirmative theology. I have shown the sense in [1033A] which the divine and good nature is said to be one and then triune, how Fatherhood and Sonship are predicated of it, the meaning of the theology of the Spirit, how these core lights of goodness grew from the incorporeal and indivisible good, and how in this sprouting they have remained inseparable from their co-eternal foundation in it, in themselves, and in each other. I have spoken of how Jesus, who is above individual being, became a being with a true human nature. Other revelations of scripture were also praised in *The Theological Representations.*

In *The Divine Names* I have shown the sense in which God is described as good, existent, life, wisdom, power, and whatever other things pertain to the conceptual names for God.[121] In my *Symbolic Theology*[122] I have discussed analogies of God drawn from what we perceive. I have spoken of the images we have of him, of the forms, figures, [1033B] and instruments proper to him, of the places in which he lives and of the ornaments he wears. I have spoken of his anger, grief, and rage, of how he is said to be drunk and hungover, of his oaths and curses, of his sleeping and waking, and indeed of all those images we have of him, images shaped by the workings of the symbolic representations of God. And I feel sure that you have noticed how these latter come much more abundantly than what went before, since *The Theological Representations* and a discussion of the names appropriate to God are inevitably briefer than what can be said in *The Symbolic Theology.* The fact is that the more we take flight upward, the more our words are confined to the ideas we are capable of forming; so that now as we plunge into that darkness which is beyond intellect, we shall find ourselves not simply running short of words but actually speechless [1033C] and unknowing. In the earlier books my argument traveled downward from the most exalted to the humblest categories, taking in on this downward path an ever-increasing number of ideas which multiplied with every stage of the descent. But my argument now rises from what is below up to the transcendent, and the more it climbs, the more language falters, and when it has passed up and beyond the ascent, it will turn silent completely, since it will finally be at one with him who is indescribable.

Now you may wonder why it is that, after starting out from the highest category when our method involved assertions, we begin now from the lowest category when it involves a denial. The reason is this. When we assert what is beyond every assertion, we must then proceed from what is most akin to it, and as we do so we make the affirmation on which everything else depends. But when we deny that which is beyond every denial, we have to start by denying those qualities which differ most from the goal we hope to attain. Is it not closer to reality to say that God is life and goodness rather than that he is air or stone?[123] Is it not more

---

119. Or "denial."

120. This work is either fictitious or lost.

121. See *The Divine Names*, chapters 4–8.

122. This work also is either lost or fictitious.

123. The ideas of God as "life," "goodness," "air," and "stone" are taken from the Bible. "Life," see Jn 1:4; 11:25; "goodness," see Ex 33:19; Ps 68:10; Hos 3:5; "air," see 1 Kings 19:12 (Septuagint); "stone," see 1 Cor 10:4; Rom 9:32–33; 1 Pet 2:4–8.

accurate to deny that drunkenness and rage can be attributed to him than to deny that we can apply to him the [1033D] terms of speech and thought?[124]

IV

[1040D] That the supreme Cause of every perceptible thing is not itself perceptible.

So this is what we say. The Cause of all is above all and is not inexistent, lifeless, speechless, mindless. It is not a material body, and hence has neither shape nor form, quality, quantity, or weight. It is not in any place and can neither be seen nor be touched. It is neither perceived nor is it perceptible. It suffers neither disorder nor disturbance and is overwhelmed by no earthly passion. It is not powerless and subject to the disturbances caused by sense perception. It endures no deprivation of light. It passes through no change, decay, division, loss, no ebb and flow, nothing of which the senses may be aware. None of all this can either be identified with it nor attributed to it.

V

[1045D] That the supreme Cause of every conceptual thing is not itself conceptual. . . .

Again, as we climb higher we say this. It is not soul or mind, nor does it possess imagination, conviction, speech, or understanding. Nor is it speech per se, understanding per se. It cannot be spoken of and it cannot be grasped by understanding. It is not number or order, greatness [1048A] or smallness, equality or inequality, similarity or dissimilarity. It is not immovable, moving, or at rest. It has no power, it is not power, nor is it light. It does not live nor is it life. It is not a substance, nor is it eternity or time. It cannot be grasped by the understanding since it is neither knowledge nor truth. It is not kingship. It is not wisdom. It is neither one nor oneness, divinity nor goodness. Nor is it a spirit, in the sense in which we understand that term. It is not sonship or fatherhood and it is nothing known to us or to any other being. It falls neither within the predicate of nonbeing nor of being. Existing beings do not know it as it actually is and it does not know them as they are. There is no speaking of it, nor name nor knowledge of it. Darkness [1048B] and light, error and truth—it is none of these. It is beyond assertion and denial. We make assertions and denials of what is next to it, but never of it, for it is both beyond every assertion, being the perfect and unique cause of all things, and, by virtue of its preeminently simple and absolute nature, free of every limitation, beyond every limitation; it is also beyond every denial.

From *Pseudo-Dionysius: The Complete Works,* translated by Colm Luibhéid in collaboration with Paul Rorem (New York: Paulist Press, 1987), 135–41.

≈ In *Proslogion* (ca. 1078), **Anselm of Canterbury** (ca. 1033–1109) begins with a question about the meaning of a scriptural text. The result of his inquiry is the "ontological argument" for the existence of God. *A Reply to the Foregoing by a Certain Writer on Behalf of the Fool,* written by the monk **Gaulino,** is a rebuttal of Anselm's argument. Finally, *A Reply to the Foregoing by the Author of the Book in Question,* Anselm's response to Gaulino, explains why Gaulino's counterexample fails.

ANSELM OF CANTERBURY

Proslogion, I–V

I

Come now, insignificant man, fly for a moment from your affairs, escape for a little while from the tumult of your thoughts. Put aside now your weighty cares and leave your wearisome toils. Abandon yourself for a little to God and rest for a little in Him. Enter into the inner chamber of your soul, shut out everything save God and what can be of help in your quest for Him and having locked the door seek Him out.[125] Speak now, my whole heart, speak now to God: "I seek Your countenance, O Lord, Your countenance I seek."[126]

[. . .] I acknowledge, Lord, and I give thanks that You have created Your image in me, so that I may remember You, think of You, love You. But this image is so effaced and worn away by vice, so darkened by the smoke of sin, that it cannot do what it was made to do unless You renew it and reform it. I do not try, Lord, to attain Your lofty heights, because my understanding is in no way equal to it. But I do desire to understand Your truth a little, that truth that my heart believes and loves. For I do not seek to understand so that I may believe; but I believe so that I may understand. For I believe this also, that "unless I believe, I shall not understand."[127]

---

124. Or "is it not more incorrect to say that God gets drunk and raves than that he is expressed or conceived?"

125. See Mt 6:6. (The notes for this selection are by Gerhart and Udoh.)

126. Ps 26:8 (Vulgate); see also Ps 27:8.

127. Isa 7:9 (Vulgate).

II

Well then, Lord, You who give understanding to faith, grant me that I may understand, as much as You see fit, that You exist as we believe You to exist, and that You are what we believe You to be. Now we believe that You are something than which nothing greater can be thought. Or can it be that a thing of such a nature does not exist, since "the Fool has said in his heart, there is no God"?[128] But surely, when this same Fool hears what I am speaking about, namely, "something-than-which-nothing-greater-can-be-thought," he understands what he hears, and what he understands is in his mind, even if he does not understand that it actually exists. For it is one thing for an object to exist in the mind, and another thing to understand that an object actually exists. Thus, when a painter plans beforehand what he is going to execute, he has [the picture] in his mind, but he does not yet think that it actually exists because he has not yet executed it. However, when he has actually painted it, then he both has it in his mind and understands that it exists because he has now made it. Even the Fool, then, is forced to agree that something-than-which-nothing-greater-can-be-thought exists in the mind, since he understands this when he hears it, and whatever is understood is in the mind. And surely that-than-which-a-greater-cannot-be-thought cannot exist in the mind alone. For if it exists solely in the mind even, it can be thought to exist in reality also, which is greater. If then that-than-which-a-greater-cannot-be-thought exists in the mind alone, this same that-than-which-a-greater-*cannot*-be-thought is that-than-which-a-greater-*can*-be-thought. But this is obviously impossible. Therefore there is absolutely no doubt that something-than-which-a-greater-cannot-be-thought exists both in the mind and in reality.

III

And certainly this being so truly exists that it cannot be even thought not to exist. For something can be thought to exist that cannot be thought not to exist, and this is greater than that which can be thought not to exist. Hence, if that-than-which-a-greater-cannot-be-thought can be thought not to exist, then that-than-which-a-greater-cannot-be-thought is not the same as that-than-which-a-greater-cannot-be-thought, which is absurd. Something-than-which-a-greater-cannot-be-thought exists so truly then, that it cannot be even thought not to exist.

And You, Lord our God, are this being. You exist so truly, Lord my God, that You cannot even be thought not to exist. And this is as it should be, for if some intelligence could think of something better than You, the creature would be above its creator and would judge its creator—and that is completely absurd. In fact, everything else there is, except You alone, can be thought of as not existing. You alone, then, of all things most truly exist and therefore of all things possess existence to the highest degree; for anything else does not exist as truly, and so possesses existence to a lesser degree. Why then did "the Fool say in his heart, there is no God" when it is so evident to any rational mind that You of all things exist to the highest degree? Why indeed, unless because he was stupid and a fool?

IV

How indeed has he "said in his heart" what he could not think; or how could he not think what he "said in his heart," since to "say in one's heart" and to "think" are the same? But if he really (indeed, since he really) both thought because he "said in his heart" and did not "say in his heart" because he could not think, there is not only one sense in which something is "said in one's heart" or thought. For in one sense a thing is thought when the word signifying it is thought; in another sense when the very object which the thing is is understood. In the first sense, then, God can be thought not to exist, but not at all in the second sense. No one, indeed, understanding what God is can think that God does not exist, even though he may say these words in his heart either without any [objective] signification or with some peculiar signification. For God is that-than-which-nothing-greater-can-be-thought. Whoever really understands this understands clearly that this same being so exists that not even in thought can it not exist. Thus whoever understands that God exists in such a way cannot think of Him as not existing.

I give thanks, good Lord, I give thanks to You, since what I believed before through Your free gift I now so understand through Your illumination, that if I did not want to *believe* that You existed, I should nevertheless be unable not to *understand* it.

V

What then are You, Lord God, You than whom nothing greater can be thought? But what are You save that supreme

---

128. Pss 13:1; 52:1 (Vulgate) = Pss 14:1; 53:1.

being, existing through Yourself alone, who made everything else from nothing? For whatever is not this is less than that which can be thought of; but this cannot be thought about You. What goodness, then, could be wanting to the supreme good, through which every good exists? Thus You are just, truthful, happy, and whatever it is better to be than not to be—for it is better to be just rather than unjust, and happy rather than unhappy.

From *St. Anselm's Proslogion,* translated by M. J. Charlesworth (Oxford: Clarendon Press, 1965; repr., Notre Dame, IN: University of Notre Dame Press, 1979), 113, 115, 117, 119, 121.

GAULINO

A Reply to the Foregoing by a Certain Writer on Behalf of the Fool, 2–7

2. But he [the Fool] can perhaps reply that this thing is said already to exist in the mind only in the sense that I understand what is said. For could I not say that all kinds of unreal things, not existing in themselves in any way at all, are equally in the mind since if anyone speaks about them I understand whatever he says? Unless perhaps it is manifest that this being is such that it can be entertained in the mind in a different way from unreal or doubtfully real things, so that I am not said to think of or have in thought what is heard, but to understand and have it in mind, in that I cannot really think of this being in any other way save by understanding it, that is to say, by grasping by certain knowledge that the thing itself actually exists. But if this is the case, first, there will be no difference between having an object in mind (taken as preceding in time), and understanding that the object actually exists (taken as following in time), as in the case of the picture which exists first in the mind of the painter and then in the completed work. And thus it would be scarcely conceivable that, when this object had been spoken of and heard, it could not be thought not to exist in the same way in which God can [be thought] not to exist. For if He cannot, why put forward this whole argument against anyone denying or doubting that there is something of this kind? Finally, that it is such a thing that, as soon as it is thought of, it cannot but be certainly perceived by the mind as indubitably existing, must be proved to me by some indisputable argument and not by that proposed, namely, that it must already be in my mind when I understand what I hear. For this is in my view like [arguing that] any things doubtfully real or even unreal are capable of existing if these things are mentioned by someone whose spoken words I might understand, and, even more, that [they exist] if, though deceived about them

as often happens, I should believe them [to exist]—which argument I still do not believe!

3. Hence, the example of the painter having the picture he is about to make already in his mind cannot support this argument. For this picture, before it is actually made, is contained in the very art of the painter and such a thing in the art of any artist is nothing but a certain part of his very understanding, since as St. Augustine says, "when the artisan is about actually to make a box he has it beforehand in his art. The box which is actually made is not a living thing, but the box which is in his art is a living thing since the soul of the artist, in which these things exist before their actual realization, is a living thing."[129] Now how are these things living in the living soul of the artist unless they are identical with the knowledge or understanding of the soul itself? But, apart from those things which are known to belong to the very nature of the mind itself, in the case of any truth perceived by the mind by being either heard or understood, then it cannot be doubted that this truth is one thing and that the understanding which grasps it is another. Therefore even if it were true that there was something than which nothing greater could be thought, this thing, heard and understood, would not, however, be the same as the not-yet-made picture is in the mind of the painter.

4. To this we may add something that has already been mentioned, namely, that upon hearing it spoken of I can so little think of or entertain in my mind this being (that which is greater than all those others that are able to be thought of, and which it is said can be none other than God Himself) in terms of an object known to me either by species or genus, as I can think of God Himself, whom indeed for this very reason I can even think does not exist. For neither do I know the reality itself, nor can I form an idea from some other things like it since, as you say yourself, it is such that nothing could be like it. For if I heard something said about a man who was completely unknown to me so that I did not even know whether he existed, I could nevertheless think about him in his very reality as a man by means of that specific or generic notion by which I know what a man is or men are. However, it could happen that, because of a falsehood on the part of the speaker, the man I thought of did not actually exist, although I thought of him nevertheless as a truly existing object—not this particular man but any man in general. It is not, then, in the way that I have this unreal thing in thought or in mind

---

129. Augustine, *On the Gospel of St. John,* tract. I.17.

that I can have that object in my mind when I hear "God" or "something greater than everything" spoken of. For while I was able to think of the former in terms of a truly existing thing which was known to me, I know nothing at all of the latter save for the verbal formula, and on the basis of this alone one can scarcely or never think of any truth. For when one thinks in this way, one thinks not so much of the word itself, which is indeed a real thing (that is to say, the sound of the letters or syllables), as of the meaning of the word which is heard. However, it [that which is greater than everything] is not thought of in the way of one who knows what is meant by that expression—thought of, that is, in terms of the thing [signified] or as true in thought alone. It is rather in the way of one who does not really know this object but thinks of it in terms of an affection of his mind produced by hearing the spoken words, and who tries to imagine what the words he has heard might mean. However, it would be astonishing if he could ever [attain to] the truth of the thing. Therefore, when I hear and understand someone saying that there is something greater than everything that can be thought of, it is agreed that it is in this latter sense that it is in my mind and not in any other sense. So much for the claim that that supreme nature exists already in my mind.

5. That, however, [this nature] necessarily exists in reality is demonstrated to me from the fact that, unless it existed, whatever exists in reality would be greater than it and consequently it would not be that which is greater than everything that undoubtedly had already been proved to exist in the mind. To this I reply as follows: if something that cannot even be thought in the true and real sense must be said to exist in the mind, then I do not deny that this also exists in my mind in the same way. But since from this one cannot in any way conclude that it exists also in reality, I certainly do not yet concede that it actually exists, until this is proved to me by an indubitable argument. For he who claims that it actually exists because otherwise it would not be that which is greater than everything does not consider carefully enough whom he is addressing. For I certainly do not yet admit this greater [than everything] to be any truly existing thing; indeed I doubt or even deny it. And I do not concede that it exists in a different way from that—if one ought to speak of "existence" here—when the mind tries to imagine a completely unknown thing on the basis of the spoken words alone. How then can it be proved to me on that basis that that which is greater than everything truly exists in reality (because it is evident that it is greater than all others) if I keep on denying and also doubting that this is evident and do not

admit that this greater [than everything] is either in my mind or thought, not even in the sense in which many doubtfully real and unreal things are? It must first of all be proved to me then that this same greater than everything truly exists in reality somewhere, and then only will the fact that it is greater than everything make it clear that it also subsists in itself.

6. For example: they say that there is in the ocean somewhere an island which, because of the difficulty (or rather the impossibility) of finding that which does not exist, some have called the "Lost Island." And the story goes that it is blessed with all manner of priceless riches and delights in abundance, much more even than the Happy Isles, and, having no owner or inhabitant, it is superior everywhere in abundance of riches to all those other lands that men inhabit. Now, if anyone tell me that it is like this, I shall easily understand what is said, since nothing is difficult about it. But if he should then go on to say, as though it were a logical consequence of this: You cannot any more doubt that this island that is more excellent than all other lands truly exists somewhere in reality than you can doubt that it is in your mind; and since it is more excellent to exist not only in the mind alone but also in reality, therefore it must needs be that it exists. For if it did not exist, any other land existing in reality would be more excellent than it, and so this island, already conceived by you to be more excellent than others, will not be more excellent. If, I say, someone wishes thus to persuade me that this island really exists beyond all doubt, I should either think that he was joking, or I should find it hard to decide which of us I ought to judge the bigger fool—I, if I agreed with him, or he, if he thought that he had proved the existence of this island with any certainty, unless he had first convinced me that its very excellence exists in my mind precisely as a thing existing truly and indubitably and not just as something unreal or doubtfully real.

7. Thus first of all might the Fool reply to objections. And if then someone should assert that this greater [than everything] is such that it cannot be thought not to exist (again without any other proof than that otherwise it would not be greater than everything), then he could make this same reply and say: When have I said that there truly existed some being that is "greater than everything" such that from this it could be proved to me that this same being really existed to such a degree that it could not be thought not to exist? That is why it must first be conclusively proved by argument that there is some higher nature, namely that which is greater and better than all the things that are, so that from this we can also infer everything else which necessarily cannot be wanting to what

is greater and better than everything. When, however, it is said that this supreme being cannot be *thought* not to exist, it would perhaps be better to say that it cannot be *understood* not to exist nor even to be able not to exist. For, strictly speaking, unreal things cannot be *understood,* though certainly they can be *thought* of in the same way as the Fool *thought* that God does not exist. I know with complete certainty that I exist, but I also know at the same time nevertheless that I can not-exist. And I *understand* without any doubt that that which exists to the highest degree, namely God, both exists and cannot not exist. I do not know, however, whether I can *think* of myself as not existing while I know with absolute certainty that I do exist; but if I can, why cannot [I do the same] with regard to anything else I know with the same certainty? If however I cannot, this will not be the distinguishing characteristic of God [namely, to be such that He cannot be thought not to exist].

From *St. Anselm's Proslogion,* translated by M. J. Charlesworth (Oxford: Clarendon Press, 1965; repr., Notre Dame, IN: University of Notre Dame Press, 1979), 157, 159, 161, 163, 165, 167.

ANSELM OF CANTERBURY

A Reply to the Foregoing by the Author of the Book in Question, I–IV

Since it is not the Fool, against whom I spoke in my tract, who takes me up, but one who, though speaking on the Fool's behalf, is an orthodox Christian and no fool, it will suffice if I reply to the Christian.

I

You say then—you, whoever you are, who claim that the Fool can say these things—that the being than-which-a-greater-cannot-be-thought is not in the mind except as what cannot be thought of, in the true sense, at all. And [you claim], moreover, that what I say does not follow, namely, that "that-than-which-a-greater-cannot-be-thought" exists in reality from the fact that it exists in the mind, any more than that the Lost Island most certainly exists from the fact that, when it is described in words, he who hears it described has no doubt that it exists in his mind. I reply as follows: If "that-than-which-a-greater-cannot-be-thought" is neither understood nor thought of, and is neither in the mind nor in thought, then it is evident that *either* God is not that-than-which-a-greater-cannot-be-thought *or* is not understood nor thought of, and is not in the mind nor in thought. Now my strongest argument that this is false is to appeal to your faith

and to your conscience. Therefore "that-than-which-a-greater-cannot-be-thought" is truly understood and thought and is in the mind and in thought. For this reason, [the arguments] by which you attempt to prove the contrary are either not true, or what you believe follows from them does not in fact follow.

Moreover, you maintain that, from the fact that that-than-which-a-greater-cannot-be-thought is understood, it does not follow that it is in the mind, nor that, if it is in the mind, it therefore exists in reality. I insist, however, that simply if it can be thought it is necessary that it exists. For "that-than-which-a-greater-cannot-be-thought" cannot be thought save as being without a beginning. But whatever can be thought as existing and does not actually exist can be thought as having a beginning of its existence. Consequently, "that-than-which-a-greater-cannot-be-thought" cannot be thought as existing and yet not actually exist. If, therefore, it can be thought as existing, it exists of necessity.

Further: even if it can be thought of, then certainly it necessarily exists. For no one who denies or doubts that there is something-than-which-a-greater-cannot-be-thought, denies or doubts that, if this being were to exist, it would not be capable of not-existing either actually or in the mind—otherwise it would not be that-than-which-a-greater-cannot-be-thought. But, whatever can be thought as existing and does not actually exist, could, if it were to exist, possibly not exist either actually or in the mind. For this reason, if it can merely be thought, "that-than-which-a-greater-cannot-be-thought" cannot not exist. However, let us suppose that it does not exist even though it can be thought. Now, whatever can be thought and does not actually exist would not be, if it should exist, "that-than-which-a-greater-cannot-be-thought." If, therefore, it were "that-than-which-a-greater-cannot-be-thought" it would not be that-than-which-a-greater-cannot-be-thought, which is completely absurd. It is, then, false that something-than-which-a-greater-cannot-be-thought does not exist if it can merely be thought; and it is all the more false if it can be understood and be in the mind. [. . .]

II

I said, then, in the argument that you criticize, that when the Fool hears "that-than-which-a-greater-cannot-be-thought" spoken of he understands what he hears. Obviously if it is spoken of in a known language and he does not understand it, then either he has no intelligence at all, or a completely obtuse one.

Next I said that, if it is understood it is in the mind; or does what has been proved to exist necessarily in actual reality not exist in any mind? But you will say that, even if it is in the mind, yet it does not follow that it is understood. Observe then that, from the fact that it is understood, it does follow that it is in the mind. For, just as what is thought is thought by means of a thought, and what is thought by a thought is thus, as thought, *in* thought, so also, what is understood is understood by the mind, and what is understood by the mind is thus, as understood, *in* the mind. What could be more obvious than this?

I said further that if a thing exists even in the mind alone, it can be thought to exist also in reality, which is greater. If, then, it (namely, "that-than-which-a-greater-cannot-be-thought") exists in the mind alone, it is something than which a greater *can* be thought. What, I ask you, could be more logical? For if it exists even in the mind alone, cannot it be thought to exist also in reality? And if it can [be so thought], is it not the case that he who thinks this thinks of something greater than it, if it exists in the mind alone? What, then, could follow more logically than that, if "that-than-which-a-greater-*cannot*-be-thought" exists in the mind alone, it is the same as that-than-which-a-greater-*can*-be-thought? But surely "that-than-which-a-greater-*can*-be-thought" is not for any mind [the same as] "that-than-which-a-greater-*cannot*-be-thought." Does it not follow, then, that "that-than-which-a-greater-*cannot*-be-thought," if it exists in anyone's mind, does not exist in the mind alone? For if it exists in the mind alone, it is that-than-which-a-greater-*can*-be-thought, which is absurd.

III

You claim, however, that this is as though someone asserted that it cannot be doubted that a certain island in the ocean (which is more fertile than all other lands and which, because of the difficulty or even the impossibility of discovering what does not exist, is called the "Lost Island") truly exists in reality since anyone easily understands it when it is described in words. Now, I truly promise that if anyone should discover for me something existing either in reality or in the mind alone—except "that-than-which-a-greater-cannot-be-thought"—to which the logic of my argument would apply, then I shall find that Lost Island and give it, never more to be lost, to that person. It has already been clearly seen, however, that "that-than-which-a-greater-cannot-be-thought" cannot be thought not to exist, because it exists as a matter of such certain truth. Otherwise it would not exist at all. In short, if

anyone says that he thinks that this being does not exist, I reply that, when he thinks of this, either he thinks of something than which a greater cannot be thought, or he does not think of it. If he does not think of it, then he does not think that what he does not think of does not exist. If, however, he does think of it, then indeed he thinks of something which cannot be even thought not to exist. For if it could be thought not to exist, it could be thought to have a beginning and an end—but this cannot be. Thus, he who thinks of it thinks of something that cannot be thought not to exist; indeed, he who thinks of this does not think of it as not existing, otherwise he would think what cannot be thought. Therefore "that-than-which-a-greater-cannot-be-thought" cannot be thought not to exist.

IV

You say, moreover, that when it is said that this supreme reality cannot be *thought* not to exist, it would perhaps be better to say that it cannot be *understood* not to exist or even to be able not to exist. However, it must rather be said that it cannot be *thought*. For if I had said that the thing in question could not be *understood* not to exist, perhaps you yourself (who claim that we cannot understand—if this word is to be taken strictly—things that are unreal) would object that nothing that exists can be understood not to exist. For it is false [to say that] what exists does not exist, so that it is not the distinguishing characteristic of God not to be able to be understood not to exist. But, if any of those things which exist with absolute certainty can be understood not to exist, in the same way other things that certainly exist can be understood not to exist. But, if the matter is carefully considered, this objection cannot be made apropos [the term] "thought." For even if none of those things that exist can be *understood* not to exist, all however can be *thought* as not existing, save that which exists to a supreme degree. For in fact all those things (and they alone) that have a beginning or end or are made up of parts and, as I have already said, all those things that do not exist as a whole in a particular place or at a particular time can be thought as not existing. Only that being in which there is neither beginning nor end nor conjunction of parts, and that thought does not discern save as a whole in every place and at every time, cannot be thought as not existing.

Know then that you can think of yourself as not existing while yet you are absolutely sure that you exist. I am astonished that you have said that you do not know this. For we think of many things that we know to exist, as not existing;

and [we think of] many things that we know not to exist, as existing—not judging that it is really as we think but imagining it to be so. We *can,* in fact, think of something as not existing while knowing that it does exist, since we can [think of] the one and know the other at the same time. And we *cannot* think of something as not existing if yet we know that it does exist, since we cannot think of it as existing and not existing at the same time. He, therefore, who distinguishes these two senses of this assertion will understand that [in one sense] nothing can be thought as not existing while yet it is known to exist, and that [in another sense] whatever exists, save that-than-which-a-greater-cannot-be-thought, can be thought of as not existing even when we know that it does exist. Thus it is that, on the one hand, it is the distinguishing characteristic of God that He cannot be thought of as not existing, and that, on the other hand, many things, the while they do exist, cannot be thought of as not existing. In what sense, however, one can say that God can be thought of as not existing I think I have adequately explained in my tract.

From *St. Anselm's Proslogion,* translated by M. J. Charlesworth (Oxford: Clarendon Press, 1965; repr., Notre Dame, IN: University of Notre Dame Press, 1979), 169, 171, 173, 175, 177, 179.

☙ In "Words of the Gospel" and "Words of David," taken from her *Scivias* (1141–51), **Hildegard of Bingen** (1098–1179) treats the same topic as Anselm: how to approach the question of the existence of God. Hildegard finds explicit value in the very act of asking a question about the existence of God.

HILDEGARD OF BINGEN
Scivias, 56–57

56. Words of the Gospel

"Every sin and blasphemy shall be forgiven to people; but the spirit of blasphemy shall not be forgiven."[130] What does this mean? Every sin committed as an excess of the flesh, or in lust or bitterness, or such vices, or blasphemy, which is the worship of idols, where the true God is not known and a false image is adored, or the invocation of demons, where the true God is known but in human perversity the Devil is called upon; all these things are forgiven people who are truly repentant and, stung by tears from their inmost hearts, faithfully seek the true God Who grants His mercy to all who call upon Him. For though people who do these things

go gravely astray in sin, if they do not utterly renounce God, Who reigns in the heavens in sovereignty and power, they will seek and find His helping hand.

But if they persevere in their infidelity, so that they never recover from their wickedness but deny God with firm heart and consenting soul; if they say to themselves, "What is this that is called God? For there is no God in any mercy or truth Who could want or have power to help me," and therefore remain impenitent because they do not believe that they can be cleansed of sin or saved; then they are blasphemers of God. And if they persist in this, they cannot receive pardon for the blasphemy because of the wickedness of their obduracy, for they so stifle the understanding of their hearts that they cannot aspire upward. For they regard as nonexistent the One by Whose mercy they must be saved, as the psalmist David asserts, saying:

57. Words of David

"The fool has said in his heart, 'There is no God.'"[131] What does this mean? In his foolish utterance he who lacks wisdom and understanding has denied God in his heart, unable to know Him. How? Because he did not want to know or understand the true God, saying to himself, "What is God? God does not exist. And what then am I? I do not know what I am!" He who says these things is a fool, for he has not the true wisdom by which God is known. But anyone who has really known God, reigning in power, is wise even if a sinner. Hence anyone who has despair of God's mercy fixed in his heart, saying, "God is nothing; I know Him not because He has not known me, and I deny Him because He has denied me"; such a one will not rise again to life or inherit joy, for since he regards the Creator as nothing, all creatures will desert him.

And one who despairs because of his sins and believes that their great weight makes it impossible for him to be saved is faithless; he shall not attain to life, for he contradicts the One Who gives life to all. But if any of these is led by penitence and truly seeks Me, he shall find Me, for I reject no one who comes to me with a sincere heart.

From Hildegard of Bingen, *Scivias,* translated by Columba Hart and Jane Bishop (New York: Paulist Press, 1990), 232–33.

---

130. Mt 12:31: "Therefore I tell you, people will be forgiven for every sin and blasphemy, but blasphemy against the Spirit will not be forgiven." (The notes for this selection are by Gerhart and Udoh.)

131. Ps 13:1 (Vulgate) = Ps 14:1.

❧ **Peter Abelard** (1079–1144) is famous for the *"sic et non"* method in theology, a dialectical method of juxtaposing seemingly opposed affirmations in order to arrive at a resolution that is validated by logic. Abelard puts this method to use in *The Christian Theology,* books III and IV (1122–40), in his treatment of the central questions of Christian theology.

PETER ABELARD

The Christian Theology, books III–IV

III

The religion of the Christian faith asserts and believes in one God as three Persons, Father, Son and Holy Spirit. One God, not a plurality of Gods: one Creator of things visible and invisible, one first principle, one goodness, one disposer and Lord of all things; one eternal, one omnipotent, one immeasurable; and withal affirms a single identity of unity, except as pertains to the discrete attributes of the three persons. Plurality, multiplicity, diversity are professed only in regard to the persons. In everything else unity is maintained. There are three persons, diverse in respect of their proper functions, Father, Son and Holy Spirit, but not three gods or three lords. Unity runs through all, except in the multiplicity of persons. Each one person is not another person, and, in each, God or the Lord is fully existent. Hence Jerome's remark to Pope Damasus: "Except in regard to the terms which indicate the proper function of each person, what is said about one person may rightly be understood of all three."[132]

There is one and the same substance of the three persons. This substance is an individual and simple essence, a single power, a single glory, a single majesty, a single reason, a single will, a single working. All these are one and the same throughout except in respect of those proper functions by which they remain diverse. The proper function of one person is never transferred into another person, or communicated from one to another, otherwise we should not speak of "proper function" but of "community of function." The proper function of the Father is that He exists of Himself and eternally begets or has begotten the co-eternal Son. The proper function of the Son is to be, or to have been, eternally begotten of the Father. The proper function of the Holy Spirit is that He proceeds from Father to Son.

The objection is urged that, on the one hand, this diversity of persons must consist in the names only, and not in actuality, so that only the names are different, and there is no real diversity in God Himself. Either this must be the case, or else the diversity is in actuality (*in re*) and not in names: or failing this supposition, then it must be both in actuality and also in the names. If it were possible, however, for one of these names to be taken away the total meaning of the Trinity would be lost, and, if we consider the names only, there is no eternal Trinity of persons to which names can be given by men.

Moreover, if this distinction of persons is looked at simply as regards the number of names of God, then we ought to admit many more than three persons. There are many other names of the divine substance, "God" for instance, and "Lord," and "Eternal," and "Immeasurable," and "Creator" and so forth. If, on the other hand, the diversity of persons is accepted in actuality rather than in name, then, there being in God nothing but single, undivided substance, it must be the case that the Trinity involves unity of substance and we must speak of God as threefold in substance.

. . . I think the sum of all these questions is as to how in such a unity of pure and undivided substance we can think of diversity of persons, for no mode of differentiation for this purpose seems to be forthcoming from the philosophers for giving a valid demonstration of this kind of diversity.

It will not be surprising if, in the answers I give to this problem, I emphasize the point that as the nature of divinity is singular, so it will require a singular mode of expression. That which is far-removed from all creatures must be described in a manner far otherwise than human definition. That unique majesty cannot be brought within common and popular forms of language. Rules cannot bind the incomprehensible and ineffable. It cannot be understood by man since man has his own terms for what he understands.

In the incarnate wisdom God brought a knowledge of Himself to which no creature could by himself rise. He made clear what He is when, to the Gentile woman of Samaria He said: "God is a Spirit,"[133] that is to say, divinity is not a corporal but a spiritual substance.

Hence it is clear what subtle quality makes up the divine substance, and what an essential being removed from the nature of our own bodies and the strength of our senses. To speak of it the philosophers resorted to similitudes and examples. This was to cover their presumption in seeming to speak of what cannot be expressed by mortal men.

Speech in time designates what began with the world. Ac-

---

132. See Jerome, *Letter* 18A (to Damasus), 4. (The notes for this selection are by Gerhart and Udoh.)

133. Jn 4:24.

cordingly, it refers to things only which are contingent upon time and cannot include the eternally existing. When we speak of God as before the world or existing before time we cannot describe with truth the fore-being of God if we accept our words solely with reference to human institutions. It is necessary for divine definitions that we should transfer certain terms to a special singular application or construction, since God is more than the world He created.

In saying anything about divinity we transfer words by a similitude from the creature to the Creator. Men use words to describe created things that they understand, and to make their own intelligence clear through them. Man can do this: but he cannot adequately describe in terms God and ineffable goodness. Everything, then, which is said of God is spoken by transferences of language and parable-like codes. By means of similitudes we get partial guidance and are enabled to conjecture rather than to grasp that unspeakable majesty.

Identity and diversity may be described in five, and perhaps more, ways. There is identity if a thing exists entirely with another thing, that is, by essence and number. There is identity, secondly, in property; thirdly, by definition; fourthly, by likeness; and fifthly, by incommunicability, when a thing never changes into anything else. We can say things are identical in these five ways, and perhaps in more ways, and, by contrary we can say that they are diverse in these five ways; that is, if the conditions of identity are not fulfilled then the things are diverse.

A thing is identical essentially with something else when there is the same essence and number. An example is the sword and its blade. Another example would be substance and body; or again, animal and man, animal and Socrates, white and hard.

Identity in property is when one thing participates in the proper character of another thing, as white may also be hard or hardness have features of whiteness.

Things may be identical in essence and number, but not identical in property or proper character. This may be the case even when their substance is the same, their proper functions alone making a fundamental distinction between them. A wax image, for instance, may be identical in essence and number with the wax of which it is made. But there is no interrelation between the proper character of wax, which is one thing, and the proper character of an image, which is another thing.

Instances of identity by definition are when things are the same by their being defined, as sword and blade, Maro and Tullius, for not only is the sword a blade, and the blade a

sword, but the conditions and reasons for its being a sword are the same as those for its being a blade.

Likeness in identity may be seen where things differ in essence and number, but are similar in some respect. Species resemble their genera; individuals their species; anything which in some respect falls into line with another is like it.

Incommunicability occurs where, for example, God is always the same, never altered or changed into anything else.

The divine substance is identical in essence and number, as is the substance of the sword and the blade, or of man and animal. But there are diverse persons, Father, Son and Holy Spirit. These are diverse by definition or proper character. Although the essence is identical, God the Father being God the Son, or God the Holy Spirit, yet the property or proper character of God the Father is one thing, that of the Son another, and that of the Holy Spirit another.

Do not wonder that three persons are distinguished in the same divine unity by the use of reason. As a matter of fact, even in grammar, we find the same man distinguished into three persons. I mean when a man speaks, when he is spoken to, and when others speak about him.

In rhetoric the name person is accepted in a different sense from that in theology or grammar. A person in rhetoric implies a rational substance, the reference being to a man and his business in the world. In the fourth book of the *Topics* we have this meaning from Boethius: "Guilt cannot be attached to those who have no rational powers of acting. They fall into another category."

"A person," says Boethius, "is the undivided substance of rational nature." This definition cannot be applied to that of three persons in divinity, of Father, Son and Holy Spirit. For if they are three persons, then, on this definition, they would be three undivided rational substances.

Persons of a play are those who represent deeds or words by gestures. These are defined also by Boethius, who says: "The name person seems to be differently used when it is applied in comedies and tragedies to the persons of a cast designed to interest an audience."

IV

To the question whether the Trinity must be understood in name or actuality, I reply "in actuality" (*in re ipsa*). From eternity the unique, simple, undivided substance which is God exists in three Persons, Father, Son and Holy Spirit. Three, that is, in respect of definition or property, not in number. A soul or anything may be multiple and infinite according to its properties of definition. The reason for this is that it is a thing of such a kind as to be capable of falling under the head of various definitions. Different definitions can be given to it which are different as regards meaning but not in the actual contents which the thing possesses. A soul may be wise and just, but the meaning of just is not the same as the meaning of wise. Similarly, there are diverse persons by definition in God according as He is Father, Son and Holy Spirit.

I do not say that the Trinity should be accepted as being in actuality (*in re*) in such a way that the actuality which is God can be called threefold. The Trinity exists in actuality, not in name, because that actuality which is God is the Trinity. It is not a matter of how much is contained in the actuality, but rather of there being from eternity three persons distinct in name. This distinction of names does not make the Trinity. It is the existence of Trinity from eternity which allows of a distinction of names which is a temporal matter made because we receive in time that which has eternal actuality.

I reply on the question of multiplicity in God that there is no multiplicity except that of persons.

The statement that God cannot be three persons unless he is also three things is frivolous. We can allow three persons, and even many persons, but they are not, therefore, three separate things in themselves. We apply the word "three" to the persons accidentally. Accidental or adjectival predication does not imply separate entity. Twenty-first does not mean that there is a "twentieth" and a "first": or, if there are twenty-one things, they are not therefore "a twenty" and "a one."

I may say a man is esteemed to be a good lute-player. I do not therefore say that he is a good man.

Similarly, God being a multiplicity of persons, Father, Son and Holy Spirit, is not therefore "many," that is, many things, or many essences, since the same essence is Father, Son and Holy Spirit.

I affirm, therefore, that there is no multiplicity in divinity, except that there is a multiplicity of persons. The Trinity itself is indivisible. Diversity of persons does not mean multiplicity of parts, or any kind of multiplicity, there being no diversity of things or essences.

It was stated as an objection that since the Father is as the Son, and the Holy Spirit, therefore some likeness between them is implied, and comparisons of different things can thus be made, the Father being like the Son or like the Holy Spirit. The point is that there is no distinction in majesty which could be understood by a negative rather than by an affirma-

tive. The case of divine equality of the persons is the same, there being no assumption of one person being less than another in glory. We find, in Athanasius' creed: "As is the Father, so is the Son and the Holy Spirit." But he adds at once: "The Father immeasurable, the Son immeasurable, the Holy Spirit immeasurable," thus revealing in what respects, affirmatively speaking, they are alike. He implies that the likeness consists not in comparison and contrast, but in the fact of their being the same.

As to why, if what exists in substance or form is called multiple, there must also be many substances or many forms, the reply has already been given when I said that God may be many, but is not therefore "a multitude" unless there is difference in number and essence. God being diverse in definition, as I have shown, is not therefore diverse in many substances or forms. The soul, or any kind of substance, can be many in definition, but it remains the same soul or substance. If it were a matter of God being diverse in number, of course we should then have to say that He becomes several or many substances also.

There was a question whether God ought not to be called "threefold" (*trinus*) rather than threefold substance. My conclusion is that God must be the "Trinity" and not a threefold God (*Deum trinum*). We may, however, say that God is threefold in respect of the properties of the persons; but there seems no reason for asserting that God is threefold rather than "threefold substance." Far less can we call God tripartite, though the saint who spoke of Him did not err if he understood the term to refer to a trinity of persons.

Turning to the question that, since each of the persons can be called God, therefore one person being not another person, there must be three Gods or substances, I can refute the idea in various ways. For example, if a name in the singular is applied to more than one thing, it does not follow that that name in the plural applies to all the things. Plato, let us say, is the brother of one man: Socrates is the brother of another man. Plato is therefore a brother; Socrates is a brother. Granted. But we cannot conclude that Plato and Socrates are brothers. To prove this we should have to show further reasons for their being in fact brothers the one of the other.

Again, many names or relationships may come under the head of one word, and each name or relationship may itself be a word. But we do not, therefore, say that these various words represent many actual separate states of being. A wine-barrel in a house is "a certain place," the house itself is "a certain place." But we do not say, therefore, that the wine-barrel and the house are different places. If we argued like this we should imply that the wine in the cask is in two different places, viz. in the house (one place) and in the cask (another place).

So, too, there are many different parts in a man, or a piece of wood, or a pearl. But even when some of these parts are removed or cut off the man is still a man, the wood wood, and the pearl a pearl. No change in substance is made by the excision of a part or by moving a part elsewhere, as, for instance, when a man loses his hand.

We may say that a man is three workmen according as he has skill to do three kinds of work. But we do not, therefore, conclude that he is three men.

The objection was raised: How do we speak of three Persons unless there are three essences? Well, my reply is that the case is the same as when we speak of "Athens," or say that a man who is white is also sitting. The actual sense is not always derived from either the plural or the singular. The sense arises from the form or construction of the word. We say: "There are a number," that is, there are many units: and "Athens exists" (*Athenae sunt*), that is, this city exists.

Along the same line we may answer the suggestion that the name "God" should be universal rather than singular. For, since the diversity within the Godhead is one not of essence but a diversity of definition or persons, the matter is similar to that in grammar when diversity of definition is expressed. There are a number of persons in the name "Socrates" according to the grammatical sense in which the word is declined. None the less, this name Socrates remains singular. If you object that there is a diversity in the Godhead which is not present in grammatical expression of persons, I must answer that, even in grammar, there is a fundamental essence of being which serves for making comparisons about the one subject.

To make this point clear (about the Father being the Son or not) we should say not "The Father is the Son," but "that which is the Father is also the Son." By this method we express the identity of the essence or substance. We should not say: "This person is that person," but "This person is the same as that person," that is, of the same essence.

I must make it plain that figurative and imperfect expressions should not be pressed beyond what authority or usage allows if we wish to speak doctrinally and with proper intelligence. An instance is when we say that "God does not know evil men." This can only too easily be argued into "God does not know men," therefore "He does not know all men,"

therefore "He does not know all things." Similarly, I may say: "I adore the Cross." I do not grant by this that I adore what is inanimate or what is wooden.

Words transferred to God by creature beings will vary in meaning just as does this name Father or Son.

It is little wonder, then, that these names Father and Son transferred to God by human beings and expressed in human terms denote the single identity of essence, but in God Himself they imply over and above an identity of property.

I think it permissible to put the matter in this way: We are most consistent with the identity of divine essence if we say that the Father is powerful, or wise, or good. This is the same as affirming that He Who is the Father is powerful, or wise, or good. The statement that the Father is the Son, or is the Holy Spirit, is only made with reference to the definition of persons. In so far as this means that the property of each is the same and in so far as it is limited to this meaning, it is inadequate.

In fact, what this argument has been leading up to is that in God the same thing is implied by the word Father as the term "Powerful." The same thing is meant by the word Son as the term "Wise," and the same thing is meant by the name "Holy Spirit" as the name "Good." The same relationship exists between Father and Son as between "Powerful" and "Wise," and the Holy Spirit in relation to the Father and Son is a relationship of "Goodness." Father, therefore, implies not only divine power, but power begetting something else; as though we were to say, "Divine power generating divine wisdom." Nor is the Son only divine wisdom, but signifies wisdom begotten of the Father. The Holy Spirit expresses the idea of goodness proceeding from Father and Son.

The objection that the Father is the Son is answered in the above way. The argument was: The Father is God, and God is the Son; therefore, the Father is the Son. Now to say the Father is the Son is to indicate an identity both of essence and definition. But the premise is that there is identity of essence, but diversity of definition. Hence it is false to conclude that the Father is the Son.

I turn now to the question as to why the Son only and not the Father or the Holy Spirit became incarnate. We accept with reason that the same essence is incarnate, that is, the essence of Father, Son and Holy Spirit. But when it is said that the Son was incarnate, it is meant that the light of divine wisdom shone forth through this incarnation on carnal things. This alone, or this especially, was the benefit God intended to impart to us in the garment of flesh. On this account He was called "Angel of Counsel"[134] or "Counsellor."[135]

The Psalmist says: "In Thy light shall we see light."[136] Simeon said: "A light to lighten the Gentiles"[137] and the Platonists assert: "God the Word is the true light."

"The Word was made flesh and dwelt with us."[138] This is as much as to say: "Wisdom was made incarnate so that by its illumination the knowledge of Wisdom might dwell with us." In the flesh which He assumed He instructed and taught us perfectly by the converse of His life, by the passion of His death, and by the glory of His resurrection and ascension.

Since then, in all that He did in the flesh, the Lord had the intention of our instruction, it is rightly said that only Wisdom became incarnate.

To the objection that the Incarnation was by divine grace, in pity for us, and not from any merit of ours, and must therefore be assigned to the Holy Spirit rather than the Son, I reply that it is one thing to be conceived by the Spirit: another thing for the Spirit to be conceived, that is, to become incarnate. In the same way, it is one thing to be regenerated by water and the Spirit, and another thing for water and the Spirit to regenerate. To grant the light of true wisdom to His predestined people was the purpose of the Incarnation. There is diversity of work in the three persons, though not of essence, and according to this diversity certain special work is proper to each person.

The Son of God is therefore called "logos," that is, "Word," according to the meaning assigned by the Greeks of a concept of mind or reason, not the actual vocal expression usually implied in "word."

The objection may be raised as to why, if God is operative in all three persons, the Son alone took flesh. My reply is that we cannot say the Father or the Spirit became incarnate or suffered, but we can say that in the Incarnation both the Father and the Spirit were working, for we cannot exclude divine Power or Goodness from the Incarnation. The comparison I should make in this respect is that of a warrior putting on his armour. Various assistants co-operate in the process of his arming himself who themselves do not put on armour.

From J. Ramsay McCallum, *Abelard's Christian Theology* (Oxford: Blackwell, 1948), 70–71, 73–84.

❨ In *On the Reduction of the Arts to Theology* (ca. 1270), **Bonaventure** (ca. 1217–74) explains how all human knowledge—including the mechanical arts (for example, hunting and cooking), sense

knowledge, and natural, moral, and rational knowledge—is gathered together into the knowledge and love of God revealed in Scripture. For Bonaventure, knowledge of God is not a matter for intellect alone.

BONAVENTURE

On the Reduction of the Arts to Theology, 1–14

1. *Every good gift and every perfect gift is from above, coming down from the God of Lights,* writes James in the first chapter of his epistle.[139] This text speaks of the source of all illumination; but at the same time, it suggests that there are many lights which flow generously from that fontal source of light. Even though every illumination of knowledge is internal, still we can reasonably distinguish what may be called an *exterior* light, or the light of mechanical art; an *inferior* light, or the light of sense perception; an *interior* light, or the light of philosophical knowledge; and a *superior* light, or the light of grace and of Sacred Scripture. The first light illumines with respect to the forms of *artifacts;* the second, with respect to *natural forms;* the third, with respect to *intellectual truth;* the fourth and last, with respect to *saving truth.*

2. So the first light, which sheds its light on the forms of *artifacts*—things which are, as it were, external to the human person and intended to supply the needs of the body—is called the light of *mechanical art.* Since this is, in a certain sense, servile and of a lower nature than philosophical knowledge, this light can rightly be called *exterior.* It is divided into seven, corresponding to the seven mechanical arts listed by Hugh[140] in his *Didascalicon,* namely, weaving, armour-making, agriculture, hunting, navigation, medicine, and the dramatic art. That the above-mentioned arts *are sufficient* is shown in the following way. Every mechanical art is intended either for our *consolation* or for our *comfort;* its purpose, therefore, is to banish either *sorrow* or *need;* it is either *useful* or *enjoyable,* according to the words of Horace:

Poets desire either to be useful or to please.[141]

And again:

---

134. Isa 9:5 (Septuagint).   137. Lk 2:32.
135. Isa 9:6 (Vulgate).   138. Jn 1:14.
136. Ps 36:9.
139. Jas 1:17. (The notes for this selection are by Gerhart and Udoh.)
140. Hugh of St. Victor, Paris.
141. Horace, *The Art of Poetry,* line 333.

One who combines the useful with the delightful wins universal applause.[142]

If its purpose is to afford *consolation* and delight, it is *dramatic art,* or the art of producing plays. This embraces every form of entertainment, including song, instrumental music, poetry, or pantomime. If, however, it is intended for the *comfort* or betterment of the outer person, it can accomplish its purpose by providing either *shelter* or food, or by helping *in the acquisition of either.* If it is a matter of *shelter,* it will be concerned either with something of a soft and light material, in which case it is *weaving;* or with something of a strong and hard material, in which case it is *armour-making* or metalworking, an art which includes the production of every instrument made of iron or of any other metal, or of stone or wood.

If a mechanical art is helpful with respect to food, this can be in two ways, for we take our nourishment from *vegetables* and from *animals.* If it is concerned with *vegetables,* it is *farming;* if it is concerned with *animals,* it is *hunting.* Or again, a mechanical art can be useful in two ways with respect to food. Either it can aid in the *production* and multiplication of crops, in which case it is agriculture; or it can aid in the various ways of *preparing* food. Viewed in this way, it is hunting, an art which includes every conceivable way of preparing foods, drinks, and delicacies. This is the task of bakers, cooks, and innkeepers. It is named from only one of these activities, and that because of its nobility and courtly character.

If it is an aid in acquiring either shelter or food, this may be in two ways. Either it *serves to fill a need,* in which case it is *navigation,* an art which includes all forms of *commerce* in articles intended for shelter or for food; or it serves by *removing impediments* and ills of the body, in which case it is *medicine,* whether it is concerned with the preparation of drugs, potions, or ointments, with the healing of wounds, or with the amputation of members. In this latter case it is called surgery. Dramatic art, on the other hand, is the only one of its kind. Thus the sufficiency (of the mechanical arts) is evident.

3. The second light, which provides light for the apprehension of *natural forms,* is the light of *sense knowledge.* This is rightly called the *inferior* light because sense perception begins with an inferior object and takes place by the aid of corporal light. It has five divisions corresponding to the five senses. In the third book of his work *On Genesis,* Saint Augustine bases the *adequacy* of the senses on the nature of the light present in the elements in the following way. If the light

or brightness which is responsible for the distinction of corporal things exists in its own *perfection* and in a *certain purity,* this pertains to the sense of *sight;* if it is *mixed with the air,* it pertains to *hearing;* if *with vapor,* it pertains to *smell;* if *with fluid,* it pertains to *taste;* if *with the solidity of earth,* it pertains to *touch.* Now since the sensitive spirit partakes of the nature of light, it thrives in the nerves, whose nature it is to be clear and penetrable; and this light is received in these five senses according to the greater or lesser degree of its purity. And so, since there are five simple corporal substances in the world, namely, the four elements and the fifth essence, the human person has five senses that correspond to these so that the person might be able to perceive all bodily forms; since, because of the well-defined nature of each sense, no apprehension would be possible without a certain similarity and correspondence between the sense organ and the object. There is another way of determining the adequacy of the senses, but Augustine approves this method; and it seems reasonable, because of the simultaneous correspondence of the elements on the part of the organ, the medium, and the object.

4. The third light, which enlightens the human person in the investigation of *intelligible truths,* is the light of *philosophical knowledge.* It is called *interior* because it inquires into inner and hidden causes through principles of learning and natural truth, which are connatural to the human mind. There is a threefold division of this light into *rational, natural,* and *moral* philosophy. That this is sufficient can be understood in the following way. There is the truth of *speech,* the truth of *things,* and the truth of *morals. Rational* philosophy considers the truth of *speech; natural* philosophy, the truth of *things;* and *moral* philosophy, the truth of *conduct.* We may look at this in a different way. Just as we find in the most high God efficient, formal or exemplary, and final causality, since "God is the cause of being, the principle of intelligibility, and the order of human life," so we may find these in the illumination of philosophy, which enlightens the mind to discern the *causes of being,* in which case it is *physics;* or to know the *principles of understanding,* in which case it is *logic;* or to learn the *order of living,* in which case it is *moral* or practical philosophy. This issue may be viewed in yet a third way. The light of philosophical knowledge illumines the intellect itself and this enlightenment may be threefold: if it directs the *motive power,* it is *moral* philosophy; if it *directs itself,* it is *natural* philosophy; if it directs the *interpretive power,* it is *discursive* philosophy. As

---

142. Horace, *The Art of Poetry,* line 343.

a result, humanity is enlightened as regards the truth of life, the truth of knowledge, and the truth of doctrine.

Since there are three reasons why one might express through speech what one has in mind: namely, to reveal one's thought, to move another to greater faith, or to arouse love or hatred in another, it follows that *discursive* or rational philosophy has three sub-divisions: *grammar, logic,* and *rhetoric.* Of these sciences the first is concerned with expressing; the second with teaching; the third with persuading. The first considers reason as *apprehending;* the second, as *judging;* the third, as *persuading.* Since reason apprehends through *appropriate* speech, judges through *true* speech, and persuades through *eloquent* speech, it is appropriate that these three sciences consider these three qualities in speech.

Again, since our intellect must be guided by formal principles in making a judgment, these principles, in turn, can be viewed from three perspectives: in relation to *matter,* they are called *formal;* in relation to the *mind,* they are called *intellectual;* and in relation to *divine wisdom,* they are called *ideal.* Therefore *natural* philosophy is subdivided into *physics* in the proper sense, *mathematics,* and *metaphysics.* So it is that *physics* treats of the generation and corruption of things according to natural powers and seminal principles; *mathematics* considers abstract forms in terms of their intelligible causes; *metaphysics* is concerned with the knowledge of all beings according to their *ideal causes,* tracing them back to the one first Principle from which they proceeded, that is, to God, in as far as God is the *Beginning,* the *End,* and the *Exemplar.* However, there has been some controversy among the metaphysicians concerning these ideal causes.

Since the direction of the motive power is to be considered in a threefold way, namely, as regards the *life of the individual,* the *family,* and the *state,* so there is a threefold division of *moral* philosophy corresponding to this: namely, *personal, domestic,* and *political,* the meaning of which is clear from the very names used to designate them.

5. Now the fourth light, which provides illumination with respect to *saving truth,* is the light of *sacred Scripture.* This light is called *superior* because it leads to higher things by revealing truths which transcend reason, and also because it is not acquired by human research, but comes down from the "*God of Lights*" by inspiration. While in its *literal* sense it is *one,* still, in its spiritual and *mystical* sense, it is *threefold,* for in all the books of sacred Scripture, beyond the *literal* meaning which the words express outwardly, there is a threefold *spiritual* meaning: namely, the *allegorical,* by which we are taught what to believe concerning the divinity and humanity; the *moral,*[143]

by which we are taught how to live; and the *anagogical,* by which we are taught how to cling to God. Therefore, the whole of sacred Scripture teaches these three truths: namely, the eternal generation and incarnation of Christ, the pattern of human life, and the union of the soul with God. The first is concerned with *faith;* the second with *morals;* and the third with the *ultimate goal of both.* The effort of the doctors should be aimed at the study of the first; that of the preachers, at the study of the second; that of the contemplatives, at the study of the third. The first is taught chiefly by Augustine; the second, by Gregory; the third, by Dionysius. Anselm follows Augustine; Bernard follows Gregory; Richard[144] follows Dionysius. For Anselm excels in reasoning; Bernard, in preaching; Richard, in contemplation. But Hugh excels in all three.

6. From what has been said up to now it can be concluded that, according to our primary division, the light coming down from above is *fourfold;* nonetheless there are six differentiations of this light: namely, the light of *sacred Scripture,* the light of *sense perception,* the light of the *mechanical arts,* the light of *rational philosophy,* the light of *natural philosophy,* and the light of *moral philosophy.* Therefore, in the present life there are six illuminations; and they have their evening, for all *knowledge will be destroyed.*[145] And therefore they will be followed by a seventh day of rest, a day which knows no evening, namely, *the illumination of glory.*

7. Therefore, these six illuminations may very fittingly be traced back to the six days of formation or illumination in which the world was made, so that the knowledge of sacred Scripture would correspond to the creation of the first day, that is, to the formation of light, and so on with the rest, one after the other in proper order.[146] And as all those lights had their origin in a single light, so too all these branches of knowledge are ordered to the knowledge of sacred Scripture; they are contained in it; they are perfected by it; and they are ordered to the eternal illumination by means of it. Therefore all our knowledge should come to rest in the knowledge of sacred Scripture, and particularly in the *anagogical* understanding of Scripture through which any illumination is traced back to God from whom it took its origin. And there the circle is completed; the pattern of six is complete, and consequently there is rest.

---

143. Or "*tropological.*"
144. Richard of St. Victor (d. 1173).
145. See 1 Cor 13:8.
146. See Gen 1:1–2:3.

8. Let us see, therefore, how the other illuminations of knowledge are to be traced back to the light of sacred Scripture. First, let us consider the illumination of *sense knowledge,* which is concerned exclusively with the knowledge of sensible objects. Here there are three elements to be considered: namely, the *medium* of knowledge, the *exercise* of knowledge, and the *delight* of knowledge. If we consider the *medium* of knowledge, we shall see there the Word begotten from all eternity and incarnate in time. Indeed, no sense object can stimulate the cognitive faculty except by means of a similitude which proceeds from the object as a child proceeds from its parent. And this procession by generation, whether in reality or in terms of exemplarity, is necessary for each of the senses. This similitude, however, does not complete the act of sense perception unless it is brought into contact with the sense organ and the sense faculty, and once that contact is established, there results a new perception. Through this perception the mind is led back to the object by means of that similitude. And even though the object is not always present to the senses, still it is the nature of the object that it always begets a similitude since this pertains to the fullness of its nature. In a similar way, understand that from the supreme Mind, which can be known by the inner senses of our mind, from all eternity there has emanated a Similitude, an Image, and an Offspring; and afterwards, when "the fullness of time came,"[147] He was united as never before to a mind and to flesh and assumed a human form. Through Him all our minds are led back to God when, through faith, we receive the Similitude of the Father into our hearts.

9. If we now consider the *exercise* of sense knowledge, we shall see in it *the pattern of human life,* for each sense acts in relation to its proper object, shrinks from what may harm it, and does not claim what is foreign to it. In the same way, the *inner sense* lives in an orderly way when it acts in reference to that which is proper to its nature, thus avoiding *negligence;* when it refrains from what is harmful, thus avoiding *concupiscence;* and when it refrains from claiming what does not belong to it, thus avoiding *pride.* For every disorder springs from negligence, from concupiscence, or from pride. Surely then, a person who lives a prudent, temperate, and obedient life leads a well-ordered life; for in this way such a person avoids negligence with respect to things that ought to be done; concupiscence with respect to objects of desire; and pride with respect to matters of excellence.

10. Furthermore, if we consider the *delight* of sense knowledge, we shall see here the union of the soul with God. Indeed every sense seeks its proper sense object with longing, finds it with delight, and never wearied, seeks it again and again, because "the eye is not filled with seeing, neither is the ear filled with hearing."[148] In the same way, our spiritual senses must seek with longing, find with joy, and time and again experience the beautiful, the harmonious, the fragrant, the sweet, or that which is delightful to the touch. Behold how the divine wisdom lies hidden in sense knowledge and how wonderful is the contemplation of the five spiritual senses in the light of their conformity to the bodily senses.

11. In the same way divine wisdom may be found in the illumination of the *mechanical arts,* the sole purpose of which is the *production of artifacts.* In this illumination we can see the same three truths; namely, the *generation and incarnation of the Word,* the *pattern of human life,* and the *union of the soul with God.* And this is true if we consider the *production,* the *effect,* and the *fruit* of a work; or if we consider the *skill of the artist,* the *quality of the effect produced,* and the *usefulness of the product that results.*

12. If we consider the *production,* we shall see that the work of art proceeds from the artisan according to a similitude that exists in the mind. The artisan studies this pattern or model carefully before producing the artifact and then produces the object as planned. Moreover the artisan produces an external work bearing the closest possible resemblance to the interior exemplar. And if it were possible to produce an effect which could know and love the artisan, the artisan would certainly do this. And if that effect could know its maker, this would be by means of the similitude according to which it came from the hands of the artisan. And if the eyes of its understanding were so darkened that it could not be elevated above itself in order to come to a knowledge of its maker, it would be necessary for the similitude according to which the effect was produced to lower itself to that sort of nature which the effect could grasp and know. In like manner, understand that no creature has proceeded from the most high Creator except through the eternal Word, "in whom God has disposed all things,"[149] and by which Word God has produced creatures bearing not only the nature of a *vestige* but also that of an *image* so that through knowledge and love creatures might become like God. And since by sin the rational creature had dimmed the eye of contemplation, it was most fitting that the eternal and invisible should become visible and assume

---

147. See Gal 4:4–5.
148. Eccl 1:8.
149. See Col 1:20.

flesh in order to lead us back to God. Indeed, this is what is related in the fourteenth chapter of Saint John: "No one comes to the Father but through me,"[150] and in the eleventh chapter of Saint Matthew: "No one knows the Son except the Father; nor does anyone know the Father except the Son, and those to whom the Son chooses to reveal him."[151] For that reason, then, it is said, "the Word was made flesh."[152] Therefore, considering the illumination of the mechanical arts as regards the production of the work, we shall see there the Word begotten and incarnate, that is, the divinity and the humanity and the integrity of all faith.

13. If we consider the *effect,* we shall see there the *pattern of human life.* Every artisan aims to produce a work that is beautiful, useful, and enduring; and only when it possesses these three qualities is the work highly valued and acceptable. It is necessary to find three parallel elements in the pattern of life: *"to know, to will,* and *to work constantly with perseverance." Knowledge* makes a work beautiful; the *will* makes it useful; and *perseverance* makes it lasting. The first resides in the rational, the second in the concupiscible, and the third in the irascible appetite.

14. If we consider the *fruit,* we shall find there *the union of the soul with God,* for every artisan who fashions a work does so in order to derive *praise, benefit,* or *delight* from it—a threefold purpose which corresponds to the three formal objects of the appetites: namely, a *noble* good, a *useful* good, and an *agreeable* good. It was for these three reasons that God made the soul rational, namely, that of its own accord, it might *praise* God, *serve* God, find *delight* in God, and be at rest; and this takes place through charity. "Those who abide in charity, abide in God, and God in them,"[153] in such a way that there is found a kind of wondrous union and from that union comes a wondrous delight, for in the Book of Proverbs it is written, "My delight was to be with the children of men."[154] Behold how the illumination of the mechanical arts is a path to the illumination of sacred Scripture. There is nothing there which does not manifest true wisdom, and for this reason sacred Scripture quite rightly makes frequent use of such similitudes.

From *St. Bonaventure's "On the Reduction of the Arts to Theology,"* translated by Zachary Hayes (St. Bonaventure, NY: Franciscan Institute, 1996), 37, 39, 41, 43, 45, 47, 49, 51, 53.

☙ In *Summa theologiae,* written between 1266 and 1273, **Thomas Aquinas** (ca. 1225–74), named "Angelic Doctor" of the Catholic Church, shifted the central analogy in theological understanding from "goodness" to "being." In *Summa theologiae,* 1a.1.1–5, 7–9, he systematically asks and answers questions about the object and method of the science of theology.

THOMAS AQUINAS

Summa theologiae, 1a.1.1–5, 7–9

Question 1. On What Sort of Teaching Christian Theology Is and What It Covers

In order to keep our efforts within definite bounds we must first investigate this holy teaching and find out what it is like and how far it goes. Here there are ten points of inquiry:

1. about the need for this teaching;
2. whether it be science;
3. whether it be single or several;
4. whether it be theoretical or practical;
5. how it compares with other sciences;
6. whether it be wisdom;
7. what is its subject;
8. whether it sets out to prove anything;
9. whether it should employ metaphorical or symbolical language;
10. whether its sacred writings are to be interpreted in several senses.

Article 1. Is another teaching required apart from philosophical studies?

THE FIRST POINT: 1. Any other teaching beyond that of science and philosophy seems needless. For man ought not to venture into realms beyond his reason; according to Ecclesiasticus, *Be not curious about things far above thee.*[155] Now the things lying within range of reason yield well enough to scientific and philosophical treatment. Additional teaching, therefore, seems superfluous.

2. Besides, we can be educated only about what is real; for nothing can be known for certain save what is true, and what is true is identical with what really is. Yet the philosophical sciences deal with all parts of reality, even with God; hence

---

150. Jn 14:6.   152. Jn 1:14.
151. Mt 11:27.   153. 1 Jn 4:16.
154. Prov 8:31 (Vulgate).
155. Sir 3:22 (Vulgate) = Sir 3:21. (The notes for this selection are by Gerhart and Udoh.)

Aristotle refers to one department of philosophy as theology or the divine science.[156] That being the case, no need arises for another kind of education to be admitted or entertained.

ON THE OTHER HAND, the second epistle to Timothy says, *All Scripture inspired of God is profitable to teach, to reprove, to correct, to instruct in righteousness.*[157] Divinely inspired Scripture, however, is no part of the branches of philosophy traced by reasoning. Accordingly it is expedient to have another body of sure knowledge inspired by God.

REPLY: It should be urged that human well-being called for schooling in what God has revealed, in addition to the philosophical researches pursued by human reasoning.

Above all because God destines us for an end beyond the grasp of reason; according to Isaiah, *Eye hath not seen, O God, without thee what thou hast prepared for them that love thee.*[158] Now we have to recognise an end before we can stretch out and exert ourselves for it. Hence the necessity for our welfare that divine truths surpassing reason should be signified to us through divine revelation.

We also stood in need of being instructed by divine revelation even in religious matters the human reason is able to investigate. For the rational truth about God would have appeared only to few, and even so after a long time and mixed with many mistakes; whereas on knowing this depends our whole welfare, which is in God. In these circumstances, then, it was to prosper the salvation of human beings, and the more widely and less anxiously, that they were provided for by divine revelation about divine things.

These then are the grounds of holding a holy teaching which has come to us through revelation beyond the discoveries of the rational sciences.

Hence: 1. Admittedly the reason should not pry into things too high for human knowledge, nevertheless when they are revealed by God they should be welcomed by faith: indeed the passage in Ecclesiasticus goes on, *Many things are shown thee above the understanding of men.*[159] And on them Christian teaching rests.

2. The diversification of the sciences is brought about by the diversity of aspects under which things can be known. Both an astronomer and a physical scientist[160] may demonstrate the same conclusion, for instance that the earth is spherical; the first, however, works in a mathematical medium prescinding from material qualities, while for the second his medium is the observation of material bodies through the senses. Accordingly there is nothing to stop the same things from being treated by the philosophical sciences when they can be looked at in the light of natural reason and by another science when they are looked at in the light of divine revelation. Consequently the theology of holy teaching differs in kind from that theology which is ranked as a part of philosophy.

Article 2. Is Christian theology a science?

THE SECOND POINT: 1. Christian theology does not look like science. For every science advances from self-evident principles. Yet Christian theology advances from the articles of faith and these are not self-evident, since not everybody grants them; *for not all have faith,* says the second epistle to the Thessalonians.[161] Consequently it is not a science.

2. Besides, a science is not concerned with individual cases. Sacred doctrine, however, deals with individual events and people, for instance the doings of Abraham, Isaac, Jacob and the like. Therefore sacred doctrine is not a science.

ON THE OTHER HAND, Augustine says that *this science alone is credited with begetting, nourishing, protecting, and making robust the healthiest faith.*[162] These functions belong to no science other than holy teaching. Therefore it is a science.

REPLY: Christian theology should be pronounced to be a science. Yet bear in mind that sciences are of two kinds: some work from premises recognized in the innate light of intelligence, for instance arithmetic, geometry, and sciences of the same sort; while others work from premises recognized in the light of a higher science, for instance optics starts out from principles marked out by geometry and harmony from principles indicated by arithmetic.

In this second manner is Christian theology a science, for it flows from founts recognized in the light of a higher science, namely God's very own which he shares with the blessed.[163] Hence as harmony credits its principles which are taken from arithmetic so Christian theology takes on faith its principles revealed by God.

Hence: 1. Let us repeat that the premises of any science,

---

156. See Aristotle, *Metaphysics*, VI.1.1026a19; I.2.983a10.

157. 2 Tim 3:16.

158. Isa 64:4 (Vulgate); see also 1 Cor 2:9.

159. Sir 3:25 (Vulgate); see also Sir 3:23.

160. The term refers, not to one who studies what is now known as "natural science," but rather to one who studies natural philosophy, divided into three groups (according to Aristotle, *Physics*, II.2.193b22–194b15): physics, mathematics, and metaphysics.

161. 2 Thess 3:2.

162. Augustine, *De Trinitate*, XIV.1.3.

163. Hence, as a science, theology flows from faith, which itself derives from the vision that the blessed have of God.

no matter what, are either evident in themselves or can be resolved back into what a higher science recognizes. Such, as we have observed, are the principles of Christian theology.

2. Sacred doctrine sets out individual cases, not as being preoccupied with them, but in order both to introduce them as examples for our own lives, as is the wont of moral sciences, and to proclaim the authority of the men through whom divine revelation has come down to us, which revelation is the basis of sacred Scripture or doctrine.

Article 3. Is Christian theology a single science?

THE THIRD POINT: 1. The holy teaching would not appear to form one science. For, according to Aristotle, *a science has unity by treating of one class of subject-matter.*[164] Now here the Creator and creatures are both treated of, yet they cannot be grouped together within the same class of subject-matter. Therefore holy teaching is not just one science.

2. Further, Christian theology discusses angels as well as bodily creatures and human conduct. These offer fields for diverse philosophical sciences. Christian theology, then, is not a single unified science.

ON THE OTHER HAND, holy Scripture refers to it as being one; thus the *Wisdom of Solomon, he gave to him the science of holy things.*[165]

REPLY: Holy teaching should be declared a single science. For you gauge the unity of a faculty and its training by its object, and this should be taken precisely according to the formal interest engaged and not according to what is materially involved; for instance the object of the sense of sight is a thing as having colour, a formal quality exhibited by men, donkeys, and stones in common. Now since holy Scripture looks at things in that they are divinely revealed, as already noted, all things whatsoever that can be divinely revealed share in the same formal objective meaning. On that account they are included under holy teaching as under a single science.

Hence: 1. Holy teaching does not pronounce on God and creatures as though they were counterbalancing, but on God as principal and on creatures in relation to him, who is their origin and end. Hence its unity as science is not hampered.

2. Nothing debars the distinct subject-matters which diversify the lower and more particular faculties and trainings from being treated in common by a higher and more general faculty and training; this is because the latter envisages an object in a wider formal scene. Take for instance the central internal sense; visual and audible phenomena are both included in its object, namely a thing the senses can perceive, and while gathering in all the objects of the five external senses it yet remains a single unified faculty. Likewise different classes of object separately treated by the diverse philosophical sciences can be combined by Christian theology, which keeps its unity when all of them are brought into the same focus and pictured in the field of divine revelation: thus in effect it is like an imprint on us of God's own knowledge, which is the single and simple vision of everything.

Article 4. Is Christian theology a practical science?

THE FOURTH POINT: 1. Christian theology appears to be a practical science. For Aristotle says that *a practical science is that which ends in action.*[166] But Christian theology is for action, according to St James, *Be ye doers of the word and not hearers only.*[167] Therefore Christian theology is a practical science.

2. Moreover, sacred doctrine is divided into the Old Law and the New Law.[168] Now law is part of moral science, which is a practical science. Therefore sacred doctrine is a practical science.

ON THE OTHER HAND, every practical science is concerned with what men can do and make, thus ethics is about human acts and architecture about building. Christian theology, however, is about God, who makes men and is not made by them. It is therefore more contemplative than practical.

REPLY: As already remarked,[169] the holy teaching while remaining single nevertheless embraces things belonging to the different philosophical sciences because of the one formal meaning which is its interest in all manner of things, namely the truth they bear in the light of God. Whereas some among the philosophical sciences are theoretical and others are practical, sacred doctrine takes over both functions, in this being like the single knowledge whereby God knows himself and the things he makes.

All the same it is more theoretical than practical, since it is mainly concerned with the divine things which are, rather than with things men do; it deals with human acts only in so far as they prepare men for that achieved knowledge of God on which their eternal bliss reposes.

---

164. Aristotle, *Posterior Analytics*, I.28.87a38.

165. Wis 10:10.

166. Aristotle, *Metaphysics*, II.1.993b21.

167. See Jas 1:22.

168. That is, the Mosaic Law and the Gospel Law.

169. See 1a.1, 3.

This leaves the way open for the answer to the difficulties.

Article 5. Is Christian theology more valuable than the other sciences?

THE FIFTH POINT: 1. It would seem that Christian theology is not more valuable than the other sciences. For certainty is part of a science's value. Now the other sciences, the premises of which are indubitable, look more assured and certain than Christian theology, of which the premises, namely the articles of faith, are open to doubt. Accordingly these other sciences seem more valuable.

2. Again, a lower science draws on a higher, like the musician on the arithmetician. Holy teaching, however, draws on philosophical learning; for St Jerome allows that *the ancient writers so filled their books with the theories and verdicts of philosophers that at first you are at a loss which to admire more, their secular erudition or their skill in the Scriptures.*[170] Holy teaching, then, has a lower standing than other sciences.

ON THE OTHER HAND, the book of *Proverbs* describes the other sciences as its maidservants: *She hath sent her handmaids to invite to the tower.*[171]

REPLY: Having noticed that this science is theoretical in one respect and practical in another we now go on to observe how it ranks above all the other sciences, theoretical and practical alike.

Among the theoretical sciences one is reckoned more important than another, first because of the certitude it brings, and next because of the worth of its subject. On both counts sacred doctrine surpasses the others. As to certitude, because theirs comes from the natural light of human reason which can make mistakes, whereas sacred doctrine's is held in the light of divine knowledge which cannot falter. As to worth of subject, because their business is only with things set under reason, whereas sacred science leads to heights the reason cannot climb.

Then among the practical sciences, that stands higher which has the further purpose, for instance statesmanship commands military skill because the efficiency of the fighting services subserves the good of the commonwealth. Now in so far as sacred doctrine is a practical science, its aim is eternal happiness, and this is the final end governing the ends of all the practical sciences.

Hence it is clear that from every standpoint sacred doctrine excels all other sciences.

Hence: 1. There is nothing to stop a thing that is objec-

tively more certain by its nature from being subjectively less certain to us because of the disability of our minds, which, as Aristotle notes, *blink at the most evident things like bats in the sunshine.*[172] Doubt about the articles of faith which falls to the lot of some is not because the reality is at all uncertain but because the human understanding is feeble. Nevertheless, as Aristotle also points out, the slenderest acquaintance we can form with heavenly things is more desirable than a thorough grasp of mundane matters.[173]

2. Holy teaching can borrow from the other sciences, not from any need to beg from them, but for the greater clarification of the things it conveys. For it takes its principles directly from God through revelation, not from the other sciences. On that account it does not rely on them as though they were in control, for their rôle is subsidiary and ancillary; so an architect makes use of tradesmen as a statesman employs soldiers. That it turns to them so is not from any lack or insufficiency within itself, but because our understanding is wanting, which is the more readily guided into the world above reason, set forth in holy teaching, through the world of natural reason from which the other sciences take their course.

Article 7. Is God the subject of this science?

THE SEVENTH POINT: 1. God would not seem to be the subject of this science. For, according to Aristotle, every science should begin by presupposing what its subject is.[174] This science, however, does not start by making the assumption of defining God; as St John Damascene remarks, *In God we cannot say what he is.*[175] It follows that God is not the subject of this science.

2. Besides, all matters about which a science reaches settled conclusions enter into its subject. Now sacred Scripture goes as far about many things other than God, for instance about creatures and human conduct. Therefore its subject is not purely God.

ON THE OTHER HAND, what a science discusses is its subject. In this case the discussion is about God; for it is called theology, as it were, talk about God. Therefore he is the subject of this science.

---

170. Jerome, Letter 70 (to Magnus), 4.27–30.
171. Prov 9:3 (Vulgate); see also Prov 9:3.
172. Aristotle, *Metaphysics*, II.1.993b10.
173. See Aristotle, *Parts of Animals*, I.5.644b31.
174. See Aristotle, *Posterior Analytics*, I.4.71a13.
175. John Damascene, *The Orthodox Faith*, I.4.

REPLY: That God is the subject of this science should be maintained. For a subject is to a science as an object is to a psychological power or training. Now that properly is designated the object which expresses the special term why anything is related to the power or training in question; thus a man or a stone is related to eyesight in that both are coloured, so being coloured is the proper object of the sense of sight. Now all things are dealt with in holy teaching in terms of God, either because they are God himself or because they are relative to him as their origin and end. Therefore God is truly the object of this science.

This also is clear from the fact that the first principles of this science are the articles of faith, and faith is about God. Now the subject of a science's first principles and of its entire development is identical, since the whole of a science is virtually contained in its principles.

Some writers, however, preoccupied with the things treated of by sacred doctrine rather than with the formal interest engaged, have indicated its subject-matter otherwise, apportioning it between the reality and its symbols, or regarding it as the works of redemption, or the whole Christ, namely head and members. All these indeed are dwelt on by this science, yet as held in their relationship to God.

Hence: 1. Though we cannot know what God is, nevertheless this teaching employs an effect of his, of nature or of grace, in place of a definition, and by this means discusses truths about him. Some of the philosophical sciences adopt a similar method, of grounding the argument on the effect, not on the definition, of the cause when demonstrating something about a cause through its effect.

2. All other things that are settled in holy Scripture are embraced in God, not that they are parts of him—such as essential components or accidents—but because they are somehow related to him.

Article 8. Is this teaching probative?

THE EIGHTH POINT: 1. This teaching does not seem to be probative. For St Ambrose says, *Away with arguments where faith is at stake.*[176] Now faith is the principal quest of this teaching, according to St John: *These things are written that you may believe.*[177] Therefore it is not probative.

2. Again, were it to advance arguments, they would be either from authority or from the evidence of reason. If from authority, then the process would be unbefitting the dignity of this teaching, for, according to Boëthius, authority is the weakest ground of proof.[178] If from the evidence of reason,

then the process would not correspond with its purpose, for according to St Gregory, *Faith has no merit where the reason presents actual proof from experience.*[179] Well then, holy teaching does not attempt proofs.

ON THE OTHER HAND, the epistle to Titus requires of a bishop that he should embrace the faithful word which is according to doctrine that he may be able to exhort in sound doctrine and convince the gainsayers.[180]

REPLY: As the other sciences do not argue to prove their premises, but work from them to bring out other things in their field of inquiry, so this teaching does not argue to establish its premises, which are the articles of faith, but advances from them to make something known, as when St Paul adduces the resurrection of Christ to prove the resurrection of us all.[181]

Then bear in mind that among the philosophical sciences subordinate sciences neither prove their premises nor controvert those who deny them; these functions they leave to a superior science. The supreme science among them, namely metaphysics, contests the denial of its principles with an opponent who will grant something; if nothing, then debate is impossible, though his reasonings may be demolished.

So sacred Scripture, which has no superior science over it, disputes the denial of its principles; it argues on the basis of those truths held by revelation which an opponent admits, as when, debating with heretics, it appeals to received authoritative texts of Christian theology, and uses one article against those who reject another. If, however, an opponent believes nothing of what has been divinely revealed, then no way lies open for making the articles of faith reasonably credible; all that can be done is to solve the difficulties against faith he may bring up. For since faith rests on unfailing truth, and the contrary of truth cannot really be demonstrated, it is clear that alleged proofs against faith are not demonstrations, but charges that can be refuted.

Hence: 1. Though arguments of human reason reach no position to prove the things of faith, nevertheless, as noted above, holy teaching does work from the articles of faith to infer other things.

2. Argument from authority is the method most appropri-

---

176. Ambrose, *On Faith*, I.13.
177. Jn 20:31.
178. See Boethius, *In topicis Ciceronis*, 1; *De differentia topicorum*, 3.
179. Gregory the Great, *Homilies on the Gospels*, II.26.
180. Titus 1:9.
181. See 1 Cor 15:3–28.

ate to this teaching in that its premises are held through revelation; consequently it has to accept the authority of those to whom revelation was made. Nor does this derogate from its dignity, for though weakest when based on what human beings have disclosed, the argument from authority is most forcible when based on what God has disclosed.

All the same holy teaching also uses human reasoning, not indeed to prove the faith, for that would take away from the merit of believing, but to make manifest some implications of its message. Since grace does not scrap nature but brings it to perfection, so also natural reason should assist faith as the natural loving bent of the will yields to charity. St Paul speaks of *bringing into captivity every understanding unto the service of Christ.*[182] Hence holy teaching uses the authority of philosophers who have been able to perceive the truth by natural reasoning, for instance when St Paul quotes the saying of Aratus, *As some of your poets have said, we are of the race of God.*[183]

Yet holy teaching employs such authorities only in order to provide as it were extraneous arguments from probability. Its own proper authorities are those of canonical Scripture, and these it applied with convincing force. It has other proper authorities, the doctors of the Church, and these it looks to as its own, but for arguments that carry no more than probability.

For our faith rests on the revelation made to the Prophets and Apostles who wrote the canonical books, not on a revelation, if such there be, made to any other teacher. In this sense St Augustine wrote to St Jerome: *Only to those books or writings which are called canonical have I learnt to pay such honour that I firmly believe that none of their authors have erred in composing them. Other authors, however, I read to such effect that, no matter what holiness and learning they display, I do not hold what they say to be true because those were their sentiments.*[184]

Article 9. Should holy teaching employ metaphorical or symbolical language?

THE NINTH POINT: 1. It seems that holy teaching should not use metaphors. For what is proper to a lowly type of instruction appears ill-suited to this, which, as already observed,[185] stands on the summit. Now to carry on with various similitudes and images is proper to poetry, the most modest of all teaching methods. Therefore to make use of such similitudes is ill-suited to holy teaching.

2. Moreover, this teaching seems intended to make truth clear; and there is a reward held out to those who do so:

Those who explain me shall have life everlasting.[186] Such symbolism, however, obscures the truth. Therefore it is not in keeping with this teaching to convey divine things under the symbolic representation of bodily things.

3. Again, the nobler the creatures the closer they approach God's likeness. If then the properties of creatures are to be read into God, then at least they should be chiefly of the more excellent not the baser sort; and this is the way frequently taken by the Scriptures.

ON THE OTHER HAND, it is declared in Hosea, *I have multiplied visions and I have used similitudes by the ministry of the prophets.*[187] To put something across under imagery is metaphorical usage. Therefore sacred doctrine avails itself of metaphors.

REPLY: Holy Scripture fittingly delivers divine and spiritual realities under bodily guises. For God provides for all things according to the kind of things they are. Now we are of the kind to reach the world of intelligence through the world of sense, since all our knowledge takes its rise from sensation. Congenially, then, holy Scripture delivers spiritual things to us beneath metaphors taken from bodily things. Dionysius agrees, *The divine rays cannot enlighten us except wrapped up in many sacred veils.*[188]

Then also holy Scripture is intended for all of us in common without distinction of persons, as is said in the epistle to the Romans, *To the wise and the foolish I am a debtor,*[189] and fitly puts forward spiritual things under bodily likenesses; at all events the uneducated may then lay hold of them, those, that is to say, who are not ready to take intellectual truths neat with nothing else.

Hence: 1. Poetry employs metaphors for the sake of representation, in which we are born to take delight. Holy teaching, on the other hand, adopts them for their indispensable usefulness, as just explained.

2. Dionysius teaches in the same place that the beam of divine revelation is not extinguished by the sense imagery that veils it, and its truth does not flicker out, since the minds of those given the revelation are not allowed to remain arrested

---

182. 2 Cor 10:5.
183. Acts 17:28.
184. Augustine, *Letter* 82 (to Jerome), I.3.
185. See 1a.1, 5.
186. Sir 24:31 (Vulgate).
187. Hos 12:10 (Vulgate).
188. Pseudo-Dionysius, *Celestial Hierarchy*, I.2.
189. Rom 1:14.

with the images but are lifted up to their meaning; moreover, they are so enabled to instruct others. In fact truths expressed metaphorically in one passage of Scripture are more expressly explained elsewhere. Yet even the figurative disguising serves a purpose, both as a challenge to those eager to find out the truth and as a defence against unbelievers ready to ridicule; to these the text refers, *Give not that which is holy to the dogs.*[190]

3. Dionysius also tells us that in the Scriptures the figures of base bodies rather than those of fine bodies more happily serve the purpose of conveying divine things to us.[191] And this for three reasons. First, because thereby human thinking is the more exempt from error, for the expressions obviously cannot be taken in the proper sense of their words and be crudely ascribed to divine things; this might be more open to doubt were sublime figures evoked, especially for those people who can summon up nothing more splendid than physical beauty. Secondly, because understatement is more to the point with our present knowledge of God. For in this life what he is not is clearer to us than what he is; and therefore from the likenesses of things farthest removed from him we can more fairly estimate how far above our speech and thought he is. Thirdly, because thereby divine matters are more effectively screened against those unworthy of them.

From Thomas Aquinas, *Summa theologiae,* vol. 1 (London: Blackfriars, 1963), 5, 7, 9, 11, 13, 15, 17, 19, 25, 27, 29, 31, 33, 35, 37.

REFORMATION THEOLOGIES

In his *Disputation against Scholastic Theology* (1517), **Martin Luther** (1483–1546) states his break with Scholasticism, which had become the Western Church's dominant theological tradition by Luther's day. His *Freedom of a Christian* (1520) states his position on the priority of faith over good works for salvation. *To the Christian Nobility of the German Nation* (1520) is a polemical treatment of the effects of the sacraments—especially Holy Orders—and of the resulting distinction between clergy and laity in the Church.

MARTIN LUTHER

Disputation against Scholastic Theology, 1–81

1. To say that Augustine exaggerates in speaking against heretics is to say that Augustine tells lies almost everywhere. This is contrary to common knowledge.

2. This is the same as permitting Pelagians[192] and all heretics to triumph, indeed, the same as conceding victory to them.

3. It is the same as making sport of the authority of all doctors of theology.

4. It is therefore true that man, being a bad tree, can only will and do evil.[193]

5. It is false to state that man's inclination is free to choose between either of two opposites. Indeed, the inclination is not free, but captive. This is said in opposition to common opinion.

6. It is false to state that the will can by nature conform to correct precept. This is said in opposition to Scotus[194] and Gabriel.[195]

7. As a matter of fact, without the grace of God the will produces an act that is perverse and evil.

8. It does not, however, follow that the will is by nature evil, that is, essentially evil, as the Manichaeans[196] maintain.

9. It is nevertheless innately and inevitably evil and corrupt.

10. One must concede that the will is not free to strive toward whatever is declared good. This in opposition to Scotus and Gabriel.

11. Nor is it able to will or not to will whatever is prescribed.

12. Nor does one contradict St. Augustine when one says that nothing is so much in the power of the will as the will itself.

13. It is absurd to conclude that erring man can love the creature above all things, therefore also God. This in opposition to Scotus and Gabriel.

14. Nor is it surprising that the will can conform to erroneous and not to correct precept.

15. Indeed, it is peculiar to it that it can only conform to erroneous and not to correct precept.

---

190. Mt 7:6.

191. Pseudo-Dionysius, *Celestial Hierarchy,* II.2.

192. Pelagius's (ca. 360–420) teachings were the center of the controversy about nature, sin, and grace. See Pelagianism in chapter 3 of this volume. (The notes for this selection are by Gerhart and Udoh.)

193. See Mt 7:17–18; 12:33; Lk 6:43–44.

194. John Don Scotus (died 1308), who taught that the will was free and superior to the intellect.

195. "The last of the Scholastics," Gabriel Biel (ca. 1425–95) was the first professor of theology in the University of Tübingen.

196. See Manichaeism in chapter 3 of this volume. Together with a metaphysical dualism (an absolute principle of good versus an absolute principle of evil), Manichaeism also professed a dualism of the will.

16. One ought rather to conclude: since erring man is able to love the creature it is impossible for him to love God.

17. Man is by nature unable to want God to be God. Indeed, he himself wants to be God, and does not want God to be God.

18. To love God above all things by nature is a fictitious term, a chimera, as it were. This is contrary to common teaching.

19. Nor can we apply the reasoning of Scotus concerning the brave citizen who loves his country more than himself.

20. An act of friendship is done, not according to nature, but according to prevenient grace. This in opposition to Gabriel.

21. No act is done according to nature that is not an act of concupiscence against God.

22. Every act of concupiscence against God is evil and a fornication of the spirit.

23. Nor is it true that an act of concupiscence can be set aright by the virtue of hope. This in opposition to Gabriel.

24. For hope is not contrary to charity, which seeks and desires only that which is of God.

25. Hope does not grow out of merits, but out of suffering which destroys merits. This in opposition to the opinion of many.

26. An act of friendship is not the most perfect means for accomplishing that which is in one. Nor is it the most perfect means for obtaining the grace of God or turning toward and approaching God.

27. But it is an act of conversion already perfected, following grace both in time and by nature.

28. If it is said of the Scripture passages, "Return to me, . . . and I will return to you,"[197] "Draw near to God and he will draw near to you,"[198] "Seek and you will find,"[199] "You will seek me and find me,"[200] and the like, that one is by nature, the other by grace, this is no different from asserting what the Pelagians have said.

29. The best and infallible preparation for grace and the sole disposition toward grace is the eternal election and predestination of God.

30. On the part of man, however, nothing precedes grace except indisposition and even rebellion against grace.

31. It is said with the idlest demonstrations that the predestined can be damned individually but not collectively. This in opposition to the scholastics.

32. Moreover, nothing is achieved by the following saying: Predestination is necessary by virtue of the consequence of God's willing, but not of what actually followed, namely, that God had to elect a certain person.

33. And this is false, that doing all that one is able to do can remove the obstacles to grace. This is in opposition to several authorities.

34. In brief, man by nature has neither correct precept nor good will.

35. It is not true that an invincible ignorance excuses one completely (all scholastics notwithstanding);

36. For ignorance of God and oneself and good work is always invincible to nature.

37. Nature, moreover, inwardly and necessarily glories and takes pride in every work which is apparently and outwardly good.

38. There is no moral virtue without either pride or sorrow, that is, without sin.

39. We are not masters of our actions, from beginning to end, but servants. This in opposition to the philosophers.

40. We do not become righteous by doing righteous deeds but, having been made righteous, we do righteous deeds. This in opposition to the philosophers.

41. Virtually the entire *Ethics* of Aristotle is the worst enemy of grace. This in opposition to the scholastics.

42. It is an error to maintain that Aristotle's statement concerning happiness does not contradict Catholic doctrine. This in opposition to the doctrine on morals.

43. It is an error to say that no man can become a theologian without Aristotle. This in opposition to common opinion.

44. Indeed, no one can become a theologian unless he becomes one without Aristotle.

45. To state that a theologian who is not a logician is a monstrous heretic—this is a monstrous and heretical statement. This in opposition to common opinion.

46. In vain does one fashion a logic of faith, a substitution brought about without regard for limit and measure. This in opposition to the new dialecticians.

47. No syllogistic form is valid when applied to divine terms. This is in opposition to the Cardinal.[201]

48. Nevertheless it does not for that reason follow that the truth of the doctrine of the Trinity contradicts syllogistic forms. This in opposition to the same new dialecticians and to the Cardinal.

---

197. Zech 1:3.   199. Mt 7:7; Lk 11:9.
198. Jas 4:8.   200. Jer 29:13.
201. Luther is referring to the French theologian Pierre d'Ailly (1350–1420), cardinal of Cambrai. He was a commentator on the *Sentences* of Peter Lombard.

49. If a syllogistic form of reasoning holds in divine matters, then the doctrine of the Trinity is demonstrable and not the object of faith.

50. Briefly, the whole Aristotle[202] is to theology as darkness is to light. This in opposition to the scholastics.

51. It is very doubtful whether the Latins comprehended the correct meaning of Aristotle.

52. It would have been better for the church if Porphyry[203] with his universals had not been born for the use of theologians.

53. Even the more useful definitions of Aristotle seem to beg the question.

54. For an act to be meritorious, either the presence of grace is sufficient, or its presence means nothing. This in opposition to Gabriel.

55. The grace of God is never present in such a way that it is inactive, but it is a living, active, and operative spirit; nor can it happen that through the absolute power of God an act of friendship may be present without the presence of the grace of God. This in opposition to Gabriel.

56. It is not true that God can accept man without his justifying grace. This in opposition to Ockham.[204]

57. It is dangerous to say that the law commands that an act of obeying the commandment be done, in the grace of God. This in opposition to the Cardinal and Gabriel.

58. From this it would follow that "to have the grace of God" is actually a new demand going beyond the law.

59. It would also follow that fulfilling the law can take place without the grace of God.

60. Likewise it follows that the grace of God would be more hateful than the law itself.

61. It does not follow that the law should be complied with and fulfilled in the grace of God. This in opposition to Gabriel.

62. And that therefore he who is outside the grace of God sins incessantly, even when he does not kill, commit adultery, or become angry.

63. But it follows that he sins because he does not spiritually fulfil the law.

64. Spiritually that person does not kill, does not do evil, does not become enraged when he neither becomes angry nor lusts.

65. Outside the grace of God it is indeed impossible not to become angry or lust, so that not even in grace is it possible to fulfil the law perfectly.

66. It is the righteousness of the hypocrite actually and outwardly not to loll, do evil, etc.

67. It is by the grace of God that one does not lust or become enraged.

68. Therefore it is impossible to fulfil the law in any way without the grace of God.

69. As a matter of fact, it is more accurate to say that the law is destroyed by nature without the grace of God.

70. A good law will of necessity be bad for the natural will.

71. Law and will are two implacable foes without the grace of God.

72. What the law wants, the will never wants, unless it pretends to want it out of fear or love.

73. The law, as taskmaster of the will, will not be overcome except by the "child, who has been born to us."[205]

74. The law makes sin abound because it irritates and repels the will.[206]

75. The grace of God, however, makes justice abound through Jesus Christ because it causes one to be pleased with the law.

76. Every deed of the law without the grace of God appears good outwardly, but inwardly it is sin. This in opposition to the scholastics.

77. The will is always averse to, and the hands inclined toward, the law of the Lord without the grace of God.

78. The will which is inclined toward the law without the grace of God is so inclined by reason of its own advantage.

79. Condemned are all those who do the works of the law.

80. Blessed are all those who do the works of the grace of God.

81. Chapter Falsas concerning penance, dist. 5,[207] confirms the fact that works outside the realm of grace are not good, if this is not understood falsely.

Translated by Harold J. Grimm, in *Luther's Works*, edited by Jaroslav Pelikan, vol. 31 (Philadelphia: Fortress Press, 1957), 9–14.

---

202. The phrase "the whole Aristotle" refers to the scientific works of Aristotle, which became known in the late Middle Ages in Europe and were different from the metaphysical and logical works, which had been known much earlier in medieval Europe.

203. Porphyry (233–310) was a Neoplatonist philosopher, disciple of Plotinus, and opponent of Christianity. See chapter 2 of this volume.

204. William of Ockham (ca. 1280–1349), a Franciscan, was a nominalist Scholastic theologian.

205. Isa 9:6.

206. Rom 5:20; 7:5, 7–13.

207. Luther is referring to *Decretum magistri Gratiani, Decreta secunda pars, causa XXXIII, quaes. III, dist. V, cap. 6.*

MARTIN LUTHER

The Freedom of a Christian

To make the way smoother for the unlearned—for only them do I serve—I shall set down the following two propositions concerning the freedom and the bondage of the spirit:

A Christian is a perfectly free lord of all, subject to none.

A Christian is a perfectly dutiful servant of all, subject to all.

These two theses seem to contradict each other. If, however, they should be found to fit together they would serve our purpose beautifully. Both are Paul's own statements, who says in I Cor. 9, "For though I am free from all men, I have made myself a slave to all,"[208] and in Rom. 13, "Owe no one anything, except to love one another."[209] Love by its very nature is ready to serve and be subject to him who is loved. So Christ, although he was Lord of all, was "born of woman, born under the law,"[210] and therefore was at the same time a free man and a servant, "in the form of God" and "of a servant."[211]

Let us start, however, with something more remote from our subject, but more obvious. Man has a twofold nature, a spiritual and a bodily one. According to the spiritual nature, which men refer to as the soul, he is called a spiritual, inner, or new man. According to the bodily nature, which men refer to as flesh, he is called a carnal, outward, or old man, of whom the Apostle writes in II Cor. 4, "Though our outer nature is wasting away, our inner nature is being renewed every day."[212] Because of this diversity of nature the Scriptures assert contradictory things concerning the same man, since these two men in the same man contradict each other, "for the desires of the flesh are against the Spirit, and the desires of the Spirit are against the flesh," according to Gal. 5.[213]

First, let us consider the inner man to see how a righteous, free, and pious Christian, that is, a spiritual, new, and inner man, becomes what he is. It is evident that no external thing has any influence in producing Christian righteousness or freedom, or in producing unrighteousness or servitude. A simple argument will furnish the proof of this statement. What can it profit the soul if the body is well, free, and active, and eats, drinks, and does as it pleases? For in these respects even the most godless slaves of vice may prosper. On the other hand, how will poor health or imprisonment or hunger or thirst or any other external misfortune harm the soul? Even the most godly men, and those who are free because of clear consciences, are afflicted with these things. None of these things touch either the freedom or the servitude of the soul. It does not help the soul if the body is adorned with the sacred robes of priests or dwells in sacred places or is occupied with sacred duties or prays, fasts, abstains from certain kinds of food, or does any work that can be done by the body and in the body. The righteousness and the freedom of the soul require something far different since the things which have been mentioned could be done by any wicked person. Such works produce nothing but hypocrites. On the other hand, it will not harm the soul if the body is clothed in secular dress, dwells in unconsecrated places, eats and drinks as others do, does not pray aloud, and neglects to do all the above-mentioned things which hypocrites can do.

Furthermore, to put aside all kinds of works, even contemplation, meditation, and all that the soul can do, does not help. One thing, and only one thing, is necessary for Christian life, righteousness, and freedom. That one thing is the most holy Word of God, the gospel of Christ, as Christ says, John 11, "I am the resurrection and the life; he who believes in me, though he die, yet shall he live";[214] and John 8, "So if the Son makes you free, you will be free indeed";[215] and Matt. 4, "Man shall not live by bread alone, but by every word that proceeds from the mouth of God."[216] Let us then consider it certain and firmly established that the soul can do without anything except the Word of God and that where the Word of God is missing there is no help at all for the soul. If it has the Word of God it is rich and lacks nothing since it is the Word of life, truth, light, peace, righteousness, salvation, joy, liberty, wisdom, power, grace, glory, and of every incalculable blessing. This is why the prophet in the entire Psalm[217] and in many other places yearns and sighs for the Word of God and uses so many names to describe it.

On the other hand, there is no more terrible disaster with which the wrath of God can afflict men than a famine of the hearing of his Word, as he says in Amos.[218] Likewise there is no greater mercy than when he sends forth his Word, as we read in Psalm 107: "He sent forth his word, and healed them, and delivered them from destruction."[219] Nor was Christ sent into the world for any other ministry except that of the Word. Moreover, the entire spiritual estate—all the apostles,

---

208. 1 Cor 9:19. (The notes for this selection are by Gerhart and Udoh.)

209. Rom 13:8.

210. Gal 4:4.

211. See Phil 2:6–7.

212. 2 Cor 4:16.

213. See Gal 5:17.

214. Jn 11:25.

215. Jn 8:36.

216. Mt 4:4.

217. Ps 119; see also Ps 42.

218. See Am 8:11.

219. Ps 107:20.

bishops, and priests—has been called and instituted only for the ministry of the Word.

You may ask, "What then is the Word of God, and how shall it be used, since there are so many words of God?" I answer: The Apostle explains this in Romans 1. The Word is the gospel of God concerning his Son, who was made flesh, suffered, rose from the dead, and was glorified through the Spirit who sanctifies.[220] To preach Christ means to feed the soul, make it righteous, set it free, and save it, provided it believes the preaching. Faith alone is the saving and efficacious use of the Word of God, according to Rom. 10: "If you confess with your lips that Jesus is Lord and believe in your heart that God raised him from the dead, you will be saved."[221] Furthermore, "Christ is the end of the law, that every one who has faith may be justified."[222] Again, in Rom. 1, "He who through faith is righteous shall live."[223] The Word of God cannot be received and cherished by any works whatever but only by faith. Therefore it is clear that, as the soul needs only the Word of God for its life and righteousness, so it is justified by faith alone and not any works; for if it could be justified by anything else, it would not need the Word, and consequently it would not need faith.

This faith cannot exist in connection with works—that is to say, if you at the same time claim to be justified by works, whatever their character—for that would be the same as "limping with two different opinions,"[224] as worshiping Baal and kissing one's own hand, which, as Job says, is a very great iniquity.[225] Therefore the moment you begin to have faith you learn that all things in you are altogether blameworthy, sinful, and damnable, as the Apostle says in Rom. 3, "Since all have sinned and fall short of the glory of God,"[226] and, "None is righteous, no, not one; . . . all have turned aside, together they have gone wrong" (Rom. 3:10–12). When you have learned this you will know that you need Christ, who suffered and rose again for you so that, if you believe in him, you may through this faith become a new man[227] insofar as your sins are forgiven and you are justified by the merits of another, namely, of Christ alone.

Since, therefore, this faith can rule only in the inner man, as Rom. 10 says, "For man believes with his heart and so is justified,"[228] and since faith alone justifies, it is clear that the inner man cannot be justified, freed, or saved by any outer work or action at all, and that these works, whatever their character, have nothing to do with this inner man. On the other hand, only ungodliness and unbelief of heart, and no outer work, make him guilty and a damnable servant of sin. Wherefore it ought to be the first concern of every Chris-

tian to lay aside all confidence in works and increasingly to strengthen faith alone and through faith to grow in the knowledge, not of works, but of Christ Jesus, who suffered and rose for him, as Peter teaches in the last chapter of his first Epistle (I Pet. 5:10). No other work makes a Christian. Thus when the Jews asked Christ, as related in John 6, what they must do "to be doing the work of God,"[229] he brushed aside the multitude of works which he saw they did in great profusion and suggested one work, saying, "This is the work of God, that you believe in him whom he has sent";[230] "for on him has God the Father set his seal."[231]

. . . Should you ask how it happens that faith alone justifies and offers us such a treasure of great benefits without works in view of the fact that so many works, ceremonies, and laws are prescribed in the Scriptures, I answer: First of all, remember what has been said, namely, that faith alone, without works, justifies, frees, and saves; we shall make this clearer later on. Here we must point out that the entire Scripture of God is divided into two parts: commandments and promises. Although the commandments teach things that are good, the things taught are not done as soon as they are taught, for the commandments show us what we ought to do but do not give us the power to do it. They are intended to teach man to know himself, that through them he may recognize his inability to do good and may despair of his own ability. That is why they are called the Old Testament and constitute the Old Testament. For example, the commandment, "You shall not covet,"[232] is a command which proves us all to be sinners,[233] for no one can avoid coveting no matter how much he may struggle against it. Therefore, in order not to covet and to fulfil the commandment, a man is compelled to despair of himself, to seek the help which he does not find in himself elsewhere and from someone else, as stated in Hosea: "Destruction is your own, O Israel: your help is only in me."[234] As we fare with respect to one commandment, so we fare with all, for it is equally impossible for us to keep any one of them.

Now when a man has learned through the command-

---

220. See Rom 1:1–6.
221. Rom 10:9.
222. Rom 10:4.
223. Rom 1:17.
224. See 1 Kings 18:21.
225. Job 31:27–28.
226. Rom 3:23.
227. See Gal 6:15; 2 Cor 5:17.
228. Rom 10:10.
229. Jn 6:28.
230. Jn 6:29.
231. Jn 6:27.
232. Ex 20:17.
233. See Rom 7:7–8.
234. Hos 13:9 (Vulgate).

ments to recognize his helplessness and is distressed about how he might satisfy the law—since the law must be fulfilled so that not a jot or tittle shall be lost,[235] otherwise man will be condemned without hope—then, being truly humbled and reduced to nothing in his own eyes, he finds in himself nothing whereby he may be justified and saved. Here the second part of Scripture comes to our aid, namely, the promises of God which declare the glory of God, saying, "If you wish to fulfil the law and not covet, as the law demands, come, believe in Christ in whom grace, righteousness, peace, liberty, and all things are promised you. If you believe, you shall have all things; if you do not believe, you shall lack all things." That which is impossible for you to accomplish by trying to fulfil all the works of the law—many and useless as they all are—you will accomplish quickly and easily through faith. God our Father has made all things depend on faith so that whoever has faith will have everything, and whoever does not have faith will have nothing. "For God has consigned all men to disobedience, that he may have mercy upon all," as it is stated in Rom. 11.[236] Thus the promises of God give what the commandments of God demand and fulfil what the law prescribes so that all things may be God's alone, both the commandments and the fulfilling of the commandments. He alone commands, he alone fulfils. Therefore the promises of God belong to the New Testament. Indeed, they are the New Testament.

Since these promises of God are holy, true, righteous, free, and peaceful words, full of goodness, the soul which clings to them with a firm faith will be so closely united with them and altogether absorbed by them that it not only will share in all their power but will be saturated and intoxicated by them. If a touch of Christ healed, how much more will this most tender spiritual touch, this absorbing of the Word, communicate to the soul all things that belong to the Word. This, then, is how through faith alone without works the soul is justified by the Word of God, sanctified, made true, peaceful, and free, filled with every blessing and truly made a child of God, as John 1 says: "But to all who . . . believed in his name, he gave power to become children of God."[237]

From what has been said it is easy to see from what source faith derives such great power and why a good work or all good works together cannot equal it. No good work can rely upon the Word of God or live in the soul, for faith alone and the Word of God rule in the soul. Just as the heated iron glows like fire because of the union of fire with it, so the Word imparts its qualities to the soul. It is clear, then, that a Christian has all that he needs in faith and needs no works to

justify him; and if he has no need of works, he has no need of the law; and if he has no need of the law, surely he is free from the law. It is true that "the law is not laid down for the just."[238] This is that Christian liberty, our faith, which does not induce us to live in idleness or wickedness but makes the law and works unnecessary for any man's righteousness and salvation.

This is the first power of faith. Let us now examine also the second. It is a further function of faith that it honors him whom it trusts with the most reverent and highest regard since it considers him truthful and trustworthy. There is no other honor equal to the estimate of truthfulness and righteousness with which we honor him whom we trust. Could we ascribe to a man anything greater than truthfulness and righteousness and perfect goodness? On the other hand, there is no way in which we can show greater contempt for a man than to regard him as false and wicked and to be suspicious of him, as we do when we do not trust him. So when the soul firmly trusts God's promises, it regards him as truthful and righteous. Nothing more excellent than this can be ascribed to God. The very highest worship of God is this: that we ascribe to him truthfulness, righteousness, and whatever else should be ascribed to one who is trusted. When this is done, the soul consents to his will. Then it hallows his name and allows itself to be treated according to God's good pleasure for, clinging to God's promises, it does not doubt that he who is true, just, and wise will do, dispose, and provide all things well.

. . . The third incomparable benefit of faith is that it unites the soul with Christ as a bride is united with her bridegroom. By this mystery, as the Apostle teaches, Christ and the soul become one flesh.[239] And if they are one flesh and there is between them a true marriage—indeed the most perfect of all marriages, since human marriages are but poor examples of this one true marriage—it follows that everything they have they hold in common, the good as well as the evil. Accordingly the believing soul can boast of and glory in whatever Christ has as though it were its own, and whatever the soul has Christ claims as his own. Let us compare these and we shall see inestimable benefits. Christ is full of grace, life, and salvation. The soul is full of sins, death, and damnation. Now let faith come between them and sins, death, and damnation

---

235. See Mt 5:17–18.
236. Rom 11:32.
237. Jn 1:12.

238. See 1 Tim 1:9.
239. See Eph 5:31–32.

will be Christ's, while grace, life, and salvation will be the soul's; for if Christ is a bridegroom, he must take upon himself the things which are his bride's and bestow upon her the things that are his. If he gives her his body and very self, how shall he not give her all that is his? And if he takes the body of the bride, how shall he not take all that is hers?

Here we have a most pleasing vision not only of communion but of a blessed struggle and victory and salvation and redemption. Christ is God and man in one person. He has neither sinned nor died, and is not condemned, and he cannot sin, die, or be condemned; his righteousness, life, and salvation are unconquerable, eternal, omnipotent. By the wedding ring of faith he shares in the sins, death, and pains of hell which are his bride's. As a matter of fact, he makes them his own and acts as if they were his own and as if he himself had sinned; he suffered, died, and descended into hell that he might overcome them all. Now since it was such a one who did all this, and death and hell could not swallow him up, these were necessarily swallowed up by him in a mighty duel; for his righteousness is greater than the sins of all men, his life stronger than death, his salvation more invincible than hell. Thus the believing soul by means of the pledge of its faith is free in Christ, its bridegroom, free from all sins, secure against death and hell, and is endowed with the eternal righteousness, life, and salvation of Christ its bridegroom. So he takes to himself a glorious bride, "without spot or wrinkle, cleansing her by the washing of water with the word"[240] of life, that is, by faith in the Word of life, righteousness, and salvation. In this way he marries her in faith, steadfast love, and in mercies, righteousness, and justice, as Hos. 2 says.[241]

. . . He, however, who does not believe is not served by anything. On the contrary, nothing works for his good, but he himself is a servant of all, and all things turn out badly for him because he wickedly uses them to his own advantage and not to the glory of God. So he is no priest but a wicked man whose prayer becomes sin and who never comes into the presence of God because God does not hear sinners.[242] Who then can comprehend the lofty dignity of the Christian? By virtue of his royal power he rules over all things, death, life, and sin, and through his priestly glory is omnipotent with God because he does the things which God asks and desires, as it is written, "He will fulfil the desire of those who fear him; he also will hear their cry and save them."[243] To this glory a man attains, certainly not by any works of his, but by faith alone.

From this anyone can clearly see how a Christian is free from all things and over all things so that he needs no works

to make him righteous and save him, since faith alone abundantly confers all these things. Should he grow so foolish, however, as to presume to become righteous, free, saved, and a Christian by means of some good work, he would instantly lose faith and all its benefits, a foolishness aptly illustrated in the fable of the dog who runs along a stream with a piece of meat in his mouth and, deceived by the reflection of the meat in the water, opens his mouth to snap at it and so loses both the meat and the reflection.[244]

. . . Now let us turn to the second part, the outer man. Here we shall answer all those who, offended by the word "faith" and by all that has been said, now ask, "If faith does all things and is alone sufficient unto righteousness, why then are good works commanded? We will take our ease and do no works and be content with faith." I answer: not so, you wicked men, not so. That would indeed be proper if we were wholly inner and perfectly spiritual men. But such we shall be only at the last day, the day of the resurrection of the dead. As long as we live in the flesh we only begin to make some progress in that which shall be perfected in the future life. For this reason the Apostle in Rom. 8 calls all that we attain in this life "the first fruits of the Spirit"[245] because we shall indeed receive the greater portion, even the fulness of the Spirit, in the future. This is the place to assert that which was said above, namely, that a Christian is the servant of all and made subject to all. Insofar as he is free he does no works, but insofar as he is a servant he does all kinds of works. How this is possible we shall see.

Although, as I have said, a man is abundantly and sufficiently justified by faith inwardly, in his spirit, and so has all that he needs, except insofar as this faith and these riches must grow from day to day even to the future life; yet he remains in this mortal life on earth. In this life he must control his own body and have dealings with men. Here the works begin; here a man cannot enjoy leisure; here he must indeed take care to discipline his body by fastings, watchings, labors, and other reasonable discipline and to subject it to the Spirit so that it will obey and conform to the inner man and faith and not revolt against faith and hinder the inner man, as it is the nature of the body to do if it is not held in check. The inner man, who by faith is created in the image of God, is

---

240. See Eph 5:25–27.　　242. See Jn 9:31.
241. See Hos. 2:19–20.　　243. Ps 145:19.
244. This story is borrowed from Aesop's Fables.
245. Rom 8:23.

both joyful and happy because of Christ in whom so many benefits are conferred upon him; and therefore it is his one occupation to serve God joyfully and without thought of gain, in love that is not constrained.

While he is doing this, behold, he meets a contrary will in his own flesh which strives to serve the world and seeks its own advantage. This the spirit of faith cannot tolerate, but with joyful zeal it attempts to put the body under control and hold it in check, as Paul says in Rom. 7, "For I delight in the law of God, in my inmost self, but I see in my members another law at war with the law of my mind and making me captive to the law of sin,"[246] and in another place, "But I pommel my body and subdue it, lest after preaching to others I myself should be disqualified,"[247] and in Galatians, "And those who belong to Christ Jesus have crucified the flesh with its passions and desires."[248]

In doing these works, however, we must not think that a man is justified before God by them, for faith, which alone is righteousness before God, cannot endure that erroneous opinion. We must, however, realize that these works reduce the body to subjection and purify it of its evil lusts, and our whole purpose is to be directed only toward the driving out of lusts. Since by faith the soul is cleansed and made to love God, it desires that all things, and especially its own body, shall be purified so that all things may join with it in loving and praising God. Hence a man cannot be idle, for the need of his body drives him and he is compelled to do many good works to reduce it to subjection. Nevertheless the works themselves do not justify him before God, but he does the works out of spontaneous love in obedience to God and considers nothing except the approval of God, whom he would most scrupulously obey in all things.

In this way everyone will easily be able to learn for himself the limit and discretion, as they say, of his bodily castigations, for he will fast, watch, and labor as much as he finds sufficient to repress the lasciviousness and lust of his body. But those who presume to be justified by works do not regard the mortifying of the lusts, but only the works themselves, and think that if only they have done as many and as great works as are possible, they have done well and have become righteous. At times they even addle their brains and destroy, or at least render useless, their natural strength with their works. This is the height of folly and utter ignorance of Christian life and faith, that a man should seek to be justified and saved by works and without faith.

In order to make that which we have said more easily understood, we shall explain by analogies. We should think of the works of a Christian who is justified and saved by faith because of the pure and free mercy of God, just as we would think of the works which Adam and Eve did in Paradise, and all their children would have done if they had not sinned. We read in Gen. 2 that "The Lord God took the man and put him in the garden of Eden to till it and keep it."[249] Now Adam was created righteous and upright and without sin by God so that he had no need of being justified and made upright through his tilling and keeping the garden; but, that he might not be idle, the Lord gave him a task to do, to cultivate and protect the garden. This task would truly have been the freest of works, done only to please God and not to obtain righteousness, which Adam already had in full measure and which would have been the birthright of us all.

The works of a believer are like this. Through his faith he has been restored to Paradise and created anew, has no need of works that he may become or be righteous; but that he may not be idle and may provide for and keep his body, he must do such works freely only to please God. Since, however, we are not wholly recreated, and our faith and love are not yet perfect, these are to be increased, not by external works, however, but of themselves.

. . . The following statements are therefore true: "Good works do not make a good man, but a good man does good works; evil works do not make a wicked man, but a wicked man does evil works." Consequently it is always necessary that the substance or person himself be good before there can be any good works, and that good works follow and proceed from the good person, as Christ also says, "A good tree cannot bear evil fruit, nor can a bad tree bear good fruit."[250] It is clear that the fruits do not bear the tree and that the tree does not grow on the fruits, also that, on the contrary, the trees bear the fruits and the fruits grow on the trees. As it is necessary, therefore, that the trees exist before their fruits and the fruits do not make trees either good or bad, but rather as the trees are, so are the fruits they bear; so a man must first be good or wicked before he does a good or wicked work, and his works do not make him good or wicked, but he himself makes his works either good or wicked.

Illustrations of the same truth can be seen in all trades. A good or a bad house does not make a good or a bad builder; but a good or a bad builder makes a good or a bad house.

246. Rom 7:22–23.
247. 1 Cor 9:27.
248. Gal 5:24.
249. Gen 2:15.
250. Mt 7:18.

And in general, the work never makes the workman like itself, but the workman makes the work like himself. So it is with the works of man. As the man is, whether believer or unbeliever, so also is his work—good if it was done in faith, wicked if it was done in unbelief. But the converse is not true, that the work makes the man either a believer or an unbeliever. As works do not make a man a believer, so also they do not make him righteous. But as faith makes a man a believer and righteous, so faith does good works. Since, then, works justify no one, and a man must be righteous before he does a good work, it is very evident that it is faith alone which, because of the pure mercy of God through Christ and in his Word, worthily and sufficiently justifies and saves the person. A Christian has no need of any work or law in order to be saved since through faith he is free from every law and does everything out of pure liberty and freely. He seeks neither benefit nor salvation since he already abounds in all things and is saved through the grace of God because in his faith he now seeks only to please God.

Furthermore, no good work helps justify or save an unbeliever. On the other hand, no evil work makes him wicked or damns him; but the unbelief which makes the person and the tree evil does the evil and damnable works. Hence when a man is good or evil, this is effected not by the works, but by faith or unbelief, as the Wise Man says, "This is the beginning of sin, that a man falls away from God,"[251] which happens when he does not believe. And Paul says in Heb. 11, "For whoever would draw near to God must believe. . . ."[252] And Christ says the same: "Either make the tree good, and its fruit good; or make the tree bad, and its fruit bad,"[253] as if he would say, "Let him who wishes to have good fruit begin by planting a good tree." So let him who wishes to do good works begin not with the doing of works, but with believing, which makes the person good, for nothing makes a man good except faith, or evil except unbelief.

Translated by W. A. Lambert, revised by Harold J. Grimm, in *Luther's Works*, edited by Jaroslav Pelikan, vol. 31 (Philadelphia: Fortress Press, 1957), 344–52, 355–56, 358–62.

MARTIN LUTHER

To the Christian Nobility of the German Nation

[. . .] The Romanists have very cleverly built three walls around themselves. Hitherto they have protected themselves by these walls in such a way that no one has been able to reform them. As a result, the whole of Christendom has fallen abominably.

In the first place, when pressed by the temporal power they have made decrees and declared that the temporal power had no jurisdiction over them, but that, on the contrary, the spiritual power is above the temporal. In the second place, when the attempt is made to reprove them with the Scriptures, they raise the objection that only the pope may interpret the Scriptures. In the third place, if threatened with a council, their story is that no one may summon a council but the pope.

In this way they have cunningly stolen our three rods from us, that they may go unpunished. They have ensconced themselves within the safe stronghold of these three walls so that they can practice all the knavery and wickedness which we see today. Even when they have been compelled to hold a council they have weakened its power in advance by putting the princes under oath to let them remain as they were. In addition, they have given the pope full authority over all decisions of a council, so that it is all the same whether there are many councils or no councils. They only deceive us with puppet shows and sham fights. They fear terribly for their skin in a really free council! They have so intimidated kings and princes with this technique that they believe it would be an offense against God not to be obedient to the Romanists in all their knavish and ghoulish deceits.

May God help us, and give us just one of those trumpets with which the walls of Jericho were overthrown[254] to blast down these walls of straw and paper in the same way and set free the Christian rods for the punishment of sin, [and] bring to light the craft and deceit of the devil, to the end that through punishment we may reform ourselves and once more attain God's favor.

Let us begin by attacking the first wall. It is pure invention that pope, bishop, priests, and monks are called the spiritual estate while princes, lords, artisans, and farmers are called the temporal estate. This is indeed a piece of deceit and hypocrisy. Yet no one need be intimidated by it, and for this reason: all Christians are truly of the spiritual estate, and there is no difference among them except that of office. Paul says in I Corinthians 12 that we are all one body, yet every member has its own work by which it serves the others.[255] This is because we all have one baptism, one gospel, one faith, and are all Christians alike; for baptism, gospel, and faith alone make us spiritual and a Christian people.

---

251. See Sir 10:12–13.
252. Heb 11:6.
253. Mt 12:33.
254. See Josh 6:20. (The notes for this selection are by Gerhart and Udoh.)
255. See 1 Cor 12:12–26.

The pope or bishop anoints, shaves heads,[256] ordains, consecrates, and prescribes garb different from that of the laity, but he can never make a man into a Christian or into a spiritual man by so doing. He might well make a man into a hypocrite or a humbug and blockhead, but never a Christian or a spiritual man. As far as that goes, we are all consecrated priests through baptism, as St. Peter says in I Peter 2, "You are a royal priesthood and a priestly realm."[257] The Apocalypse says, "Thou hast made us to be priests and kings by thy blood."[258] The consecration by pope or bishop would never make a priest, and if we had no higher consecration than that which pope or bishop gives, no one could say mass or preach a sermon or give absolution.

Therefore, when a bishop consecrates it is nothing else than that in the place and stead of the whole community, all of whom have like power, he takes a person and charges him to exercise this power on behalf of the others. It is like ten brothers, all king's sons and equal heirs, choosing one of themselves to rule the inheritance in the interests of all. In one sense they are all kings and of equal power, and yet one of them is charged with the responsibility of ruling. To put it still more clearly: suppose a group of earnest Christian laymen were taken prisoner and set down in a desert without an episcopally ordained priest among them. And suppose they were to come to a common mind there and then in the desert and elect one of their number, whether he were married[259] or not, and charge him to baptize, say mass, pronounce absolution, and preach the gospel. Such a man would be as truly a priest as though he had been ordained by all the bishops and popes in the world. That is why in cases of necessity anyone can baptize and give absolution. This would be impossible if we were not all priests. Through canon law[260] the Romanists have almost destroyed and made unknown the wondrous grace and authority of baptism and justification. In times gone by Christians used to choose their bishops and priests in this way from among their own number, and they were confirmed in their office by the other bishops without all the fuss that goes on nowadays. St. Augustine,[261] Ambrose,[262] and Cyprian[263] each became [a bishop in this way].

Since those who exercise secular authority have been baptized with the same baptism, and have the same faith and the same gospel as the rest of us, we must admit that they are priests and bishops and we must regard their office as one which has a proper and useful place in the Christian community. For whoever comes out of the water of baptism can boast that he is already a consecrated priest, bishop, and pope, although of course it is not seemly that just any-

body should exercise such office. Because we are all priests of equal standing, no one must push himself forward and take it upon himself, without our consent and election, to do that for which we all have equal authority. For no one dare take upon himself what is common to all without the authority and consent of the community. And should it happen that a person chosen for such office were deposed for abuse of trust, he would then be exactly what he was before. Therefore, a priest in Christendom is nothing else but an officeholder. As long as he holds office he takes precedence; where he is deposed, he is a peasant or a townsman like anybody else. Indeed, a priest is never a priest when he is deposed. But now the Romanists have invented *characteres indelebiles*[264] and say[265] that a deposed priest is nevertheless something different from a mere layman. They hold the illusion that a priest can never be anything other than a priest, or ever become a layman. All this is just contrived talk, and human regulation.

It follows from this argument that there is no true, basic difference between laymen and priests, princes and bishops, between religious and secular, except for the sake of office and work, but not for the sake of status. They are all of the spiritual estate, all are truly priests, bishops, and popes. But they do not all have the same work to do. Just as all priests and monks do not have the same work. This is the teaching

---

256. That is, gives tonsure.

257. 1 Pet 2:9.

258. See Rev 5:9–10.

259. The translator points out that the German word used by Luther (*Ehelich*) can also mean "legitimately born."

260. The *Corpus iuris canonici,* which Luther also refers to as "spiritual law," is the body of Church law as it has evolved through the centuries. Luther found embodied in it, in legal form, the medieval theory of papal absolute power.

261. Augustine was bishop of Hippo from 395 or 396 to 430.

262. Ambrose, bishop of Milan from 374 to 397, was elected to the office by the people of the city before he was baptized.

263. Cyprian, bishop of Carthage from 247 to 258, was elected to the office by other lay Christians.

264. That is, "indelible characters," or "indelible marks." The Council of Florence (eighth session, November 22, 1439) decreed, "Three of the sacraments, namely baptism, confirmation, and orders, imprint indelibly on the soul a character [*que caracterem . . . imprimunt in anima indelebile*], that is a kind of stamp which distinguishes it from the rest." On the basis of this decree, Pope Eugene IV, in his Bull *Exultate Deo* of 1439, formulated the teaching thus: "Among these sacraments there are three—baptism, confirmation, and orders—which indelibly impress upon the soul a character, that is, a certain spiritual mark, that distinguishes them from the rest" (of the seven sacraments). According to the definition of the Council of Trent (twenty-third session, July 15, 1563), "In the sacrament of order, as in baptism and confirmation, a character is imprinted, which cannot be deleted or removed. Hence the holy synod justifiably condemns the opinion of those who assert that priests of the new covenant have only temporary power, and when duly ordained can be made laity once more if they do not exercise the ministry of the word of God."

265. Literally, "chatter nonsense."

of St. Paul in Romans 12[266] and I Corinthians 12[267] and in I Peter 2,[268] as I have said above, namely, that we are all one body of Christ the Head, and all members one of another. Christ does not have two different bodies, one temporal, the other spiritual. There is but one Head and one body.

Therefore, just as those who are now called "spiritual," that is, priests, bishops, or popes, are neither different from other Christians nor superior to them, except that they are charged with the administration of the word of God and the sacraments, which is their work and office, so it is with the temporal authorities. They bear the sword and rod in their hand to punish the wicked and protect the good. A cobbler, a smith, a peasant—each has the work and office of his trade, and yet they are all alike consecrated priests and bishops. Further, everyone must benefit and serve every other by means of his own work or office so that in this way many kinds of work may be done for the bodily and spiritual welfare of the community, just as all the members of the body serve one another.[269]

Consider for a moment how Christian is the decree which says that the temporal power is not above the "spiritual estate" and has no right to punish it. That is as much as to say that the hand shall not help the eye when it suffers pain. Is it not unnatural, not to mention un-Christian, that one member does not help another and prevent its destruction? In fact, the more honorable the member, the more the others ought to help. I say therefore that since the temporal power is ordained of God to punish the wicked and protect the good,[270] it should be left free to perform its office in the whole body of Christendom without restriction and without respect to persons, whether it affects pope, bishops, priests, monks, nuns, or anyone else. If it were right to say that the temporal power is inferior to all the spiritual estates (preacher, confessor, or any spiritual office), and so prevent the temporal power from doing its proper work, then the tailors, cobblers, stonemasons, carpenters, cooks, innkeepers, farmers, and all the temporal craftsmen should be prevented from providing pope, bishops, priests, and monks with shoes, clothes, house, meat and drink, as well as from paying them any tribute. But if these laymen are allowed to do their proper work without restriction, what then are the Romanist scribes doing with their own laws, which exempt them from the jurisdiction of the temporal Christian authority? It is just so that they can be free to do evil and fulfil what St. Peter said, "False teachers will rise up among you who will deceive you, and with their false and fanciful talk, they will take advantage of you."[271]

For these reasons the temporal Christian authority ought to exercise its office without hindrance, regardless of whether it is pope, bishop, or priest whom it affects. Whoever is guilty, let him suffer. All that canon law has said to the contrary is the invention of Romanist presumption. For thus St. Paul says to all Christians, "Let every soul (I take that to mean the pope's soul also) be subject to the temporal authority; for it does not bear the sword in vain, but serves God by punishing the wicked and benefiting the good."[272] St. Peter, too, says, "Be subject to all human ordinances for the sake of the Lord, who so wills it."[273] He has also prophesied in II Peter 2 that such men would arise and despise the temporal authority.[274] This is exactly what has happened through the canon law.

So, then, I think this first paper wall is overthrown. Inasmuch as the temporal power has become a member of the Christian body it is a spiritual estate, even though its work is physical. Therefore, its work should extend without hindrance to all the members of the whole body to punish and use force whenever guilt deserves or necessity demands, without regard to whether the culprit is pope, bishop, or priest. Let the Romanists hurl threats and bans about as they like. That is why guilty priests, when they are handed over to secular law, are first deprived of their priestly dignities. This would not be right unless the secular sword previously had had authority over these priests by divine right. Moreover, it is intolerable that in canon law so much importance is attached to the freedom, life, and property of the clergy, as though the laity were not also as spiritual and as good Christians as they, or did not also belong to the church. Why are your life and limb, your property and honor, so cheap and mine not, inasmuch as we are all Christians and have the same baptism, the same faith, the same Spirit, and all the rest? If a priest is murdered, the whole country is placed under interdict.[275] Why not when a peasant is murdered? How does this great difference come about between two men who are both Christians? It comes from the laws and fabrications of men.

[. . .] The second wall is still more loosely built and less substantial. The Romanists want to be the only masters of Holy Scripture, although they never learn a thing from the Bible all their life long. They assume the sole authority for

---

266. See Rom 12:4–5.

267. See 1 Cor 12:12–26.

268. See 1 Pet 2:9.

269. See 1 Cor 12:14–26.

270. See 1 Pet 2:14.

271. See 2 Pet 2:1–3.

272. Rom 13:1, 4.

273. 1 Pet 2:13, 15.

274. See 2 Pet 2:1.

275. An "interdict" was an order prohibiting the administration of the sacraments and other Christian rites within a specified territory.

themselves, and, quite unashamed, they play about with words before our very eyes, trying to persuade us that the pope cannot err in matters of faith,[276] regardless of whether he is righteous or wicked. Yet they cannot point to a single letter.[277] This is why so many heretical and un-Christian, even unnatural, ordinances stand in the canon law. But there is no need to talk about these ordinances at present. Since these Romanists think the Holy Spirit never leaves them, no matter how ignorant and wicked they are, they become bold and decree only what they want. And if what they claim were true, why have Holy Scripture at all? Of what use is Scripture? Let us burn the Scripture and be satisfied with the unlearned gentlemen at Rome who possess the Holy Spirit! And yet the Holy Spirit can be possessed only by pious hearts. If I had not read the words with my own eyes, I would not have believed it possible for the devil to have made such stupid claims at Rome, and to have won supporters for them.

But so as not to fight them with mere words, we will quote the Scriptures. St. Paul says in I Corinthians 14, "If something better is revealed to anyone, though he is already sitting and listening to another in God's word, then the one who is speaking shall hold his peace and give place."[278] What would be the point of this commandment if we were compelled to believe only the man who does the talking, or the man who is at the top? Even Christ said in John 6 that all Christians shall be taught by God.[279] If it were to happen that the pope and his cohorts were wicked and not true Christians, were not taught by God and were without understanding, and at the same time some obscure person had a right understanding, why should the people not follow the obscure man? Has the pope not erred many times? Who would help Christendom when the pope erred if we did not have somebody we could trust more than him, somebody who had the Scriptures on his side?

Therefore, their claim that only the pope may interpret Scripture is an outrageous fancied fable. They cannot produce a single letter [of Scripture] to maintain that the interpretation of Scripture or the confirmation of its interpretation belongs to the pope alone. They themselves have usurped this power. And although they allege that this power was given to St. Peter when the keys were given him, it is clear enough that the keys were not given to Peter alone but to the whole community. Further, the keys were not ordained for doctrine or government, but only for the binding or loosing of sin.[280] Whatever else or whatever more they arrogate to themselves on the basis of the keys is a mere fabrication. But Christ's words to Peter, "I have prayed for you that your faith fail

not,"[281] cannot be applied to the pope, since the majority of the popes have been without faith, as they must themselves confess. Besides, it is not only for Peter that Christ prayed, but also for all apostles and Christians, as he says in John 17, "Father, I pray for those whom thou hast given me, and not for these only, but for all who believe in me through their word."[282] Is that not clear enough?

Just think of it! The Romanists must admit that there are among us good Christians who have the true faith, spirit, understanding, word, and mind of Christ. Why, then, should we reject the word and understanding of good Christians and follow the pope, who has neither faith nor the Spirit? To follow the pope would be to deny the whole faith[283] as well as the Christian church. Again, if the article, "I believe in one holy Christian church," is correct, then the pope cannot be the only one who is right. Otherwise, we would have to confess,[284] "I believe in the pope at Rome." This would reduce the Christian church to one man, and be nothing else than a devilish and hellish error.

Besides, if we are all priests, as was said above, and all have one faith, one gospel, one sacrament, why should we not also have the power to test and judge what is right or wrong in matters of faith? What becomes of Paul's words in I Corinthians 2, "A spiritual man judges all things, yet he is judged by no one"?[285] And II Corinthians 4, "We all have one spirit of faith"?[286] Why, then, should not we perceive what is consistent with faith and what is not, just as well as an unbelieving pope does?

We ought to become bold and free on the authority of all these texts, and many others. We ought not to allow the Spirit of freedom (as Paul calls him)[287] to be frightened off by the fabrications of the popes, but we ought to march boldly forward and test all that they do, or leave undone, by our believing understanding of the Scriptures. We must compel

---

276. Although claims had been repeatedly made about papal infallibility in the Middle Ages, the doctrine was not officially defined by the Roman Church until much later. See chapter 5.

277. That is, "a single letter" of Scripture which justifies this claim.

278. 1 Cor 14:30.

279. See Jn 6:45.

280. See Mt 16:19; 18:18; Jn 20:23.

281. Lk 22:32.

282. Jn 17:9, 20.

283. Literally, "the creed," that is, the Apostles' Creed.

284. Literally, "to pray."

285. 1 Cor 2:15.

286. 2 Cor 4:13.

287. See 2 Cor 3:17.

the Romanists to follow not their own interpretation but the better one. Long ago Abraham had to listen to Sarah, although she was in more complete subjection to him than we are to anyone on earth.[288] And Balaam's ass was wiser than the prophet himself.[289] If God spoke then through an ass against a prophet, why should he not be able even now to speak through a righteous man against the pope? Similarly, St. Paul rebukes St. Peter as a man in error in Galatians 2.[290] Therefore, it is the duty of every Christian to espouse the cause of the faith, to understand and defend it, and to denounce every error.

The third wall falls of itself when the first two are down. When the pope acts contrary to the Scriptures, it is our duty to stand by the Scriptures, to reprove him and to constrain him, according to the word of Christ, Matthew 18, "If your brother sins against you, go and tell it to him, between you and him alone; if he does not listen to you, then take one or two others with you; if he does not listen to them, tell it to the church; if he does not listen to the church, consider him a heathen."[291] Here every member is commanded to care for every other. How much more should we do this when the member that does evil is responsible for the government of the church, and by his evil-doing is the cause of much harm and offense to the rest! But if I am to accuse him before the church, I must naturally call the church together.

The Romanists have no basis in Scripture for their claim that the pope alone has the right to call or confirm a council. This is just their own ruling, and it is only valid as long as it is not harmful to Christendom or contrary to the laws of God. Now when the pope deserves punishment, this ruling no longer obtains, for not to punish him by authority of a council is harmful to Christendom.

Thus we read in Acts 15 that it was not St. Peter who called the Apostolic Council but the apostles and elders.[292] If then that right had belonged to St. Peter alone, the council would not have been a Christian council, but a heretical *conciliabulum*.[293] Even the Council of Nicaea, the most famous of all councils, was neither called nor confirmed by the bishop of Rome, but by the emperor Constantine.[294] Many other emperors after him have done the same, and yet these councils were the most Christian of all.[295] But if the pope alone has the right to convene councils, then these councils would all have been heretical. Further, when I examine the councils the pope did summon, I find that they did nothing of special importance.

Therefore, when necessity demands it, and the pope is an offense to Christendom, the first man who is able should, as

a true member of the whole body, do what he can to bring about a truly free council.[296] No one can do this so well as the temporal authorities, especially since they are also fellow-Christians, fellow-priests, fellow-members of the spiritual estate, fellow-lords over all things. Whenever it is necessary or profitable they ought to exercise the office and work which they have received from God over everyone. Would it not be unnatural if a fire broke out in a city and everybody were to stand by and let it burn on and on and consume everything that could burn because nobody had the authority of the mayor, or because, perhaps, the fire broke out in the mayor's house? In such a situation is it not the duty of every citizen to arouse and summon the rest? How much more should this be done in the spiritual city of Christ if a fire of offense breaks out, whether in the papal government, or anywhere else! The same argument holds if an enemy were to attack a city. The man who first roused the others deserves honor and gratitude. Why, then, should he not deserve honor who makes known the presence of the enemy from hell and rouses Christian people and calls them together?

But all their boasting about an authority which dare not be opposed amounts to nothing at all. Nobody in Christendom has authority to do injury or to forbid the resisting of injury. There is no authority in the church except to promote good. Therefore, if the pope were to use his authority to prevent the calling of a free council, thereby preventing the improvement of the church, we should have regard neither for him nor for his authority. And if he were to hurl his bans and thunderbolts, we should despise his conduct as that of a madman. On the contrary, we should excommunicate him and drive him out as best we could, relying completely upon God. This presumptuous authority of his is nothing. He does not even have such authority. He is quickly defeated by a single text of Scripture, where Paul says to the Corinthians, "God has given us authority not to ruin Christendom, but to build it up."[297] Who wants to leap over the hurdle of this text? It is the power of the devil and of Antichrist which resists the

---

288. See Gen 21:12.

289. See Num 22:21–35.

290. See Gal 2:11–14.

291. Mt 18:15–17.

292. See Acts 15:4–6.

293. That is, an ordinary assembly and not a valid council (a *concilium*).

294. The Council of Nicaea, the first ecumenical council of the Church, was indeed convened by Emperor Constantine in 325.

295. The four "Catholic Councils" are Nicaea (325), Constantinople (381), Ephesus (431), and Chalcedon (451).

296. That is, free from papal control.

297. See 2 Cor 10:8.

things that serve to build up Christendom. Such power is not to be obeyed, but rather resisted with life, property, and with all our might and main.

Translated by Charles M. Jacobs, revised by James Atkinson, in *Luther's Works*, edited by Jaroslav Pelikan, vol. 44 (Philadelphia: Fortress Press, 1966), 126–38.

ɔ∾ **John Calvin** (1509–64) led the Reform movement in France and Switzerland. In book 1 of his *Institutes of the Christian Religion* (1536), he presents a systematic Reformation treatment of the theological problems of faith, law, and righteousness.

JOHN CALVIN

Institutes of the Christian Religion,
book 1, chapter I.1–6, 27–29, 32; chapter II.1–4, 21–26

I. The Law: Containing an Explanation of the Decalogue

A. Knowledge of God

1. Nearly the whole of sacred doctrine consists in these two parts: knowledge of God and of ourselves. Surely, we ought for the present to learn the following things about God. To hold with sure faith, first that he is infinite wisdom, righteousness, goodness, mercy, truth, power, and life.[298] And all of these things, wherever seen, come from him.[299] Secondly, that all things in heaven and on earth have been created for his glory.[300] To serve him for his nature's sake alone, to keep his rule, accept his majesty, and in obedience recognize him as Lord and King[301]—all this is due him by right. Thirdly, that he is himself a just judge, and therefore, is going to take harsh vengeance upon those who have turned aside from his precepts, who have not followed his will through all things, who think, say, and do things other than those that pertain to his glory.[302] Fourthly, that he is merciful and gentle, ready to receive the miserable and poor that flee to his mercy and put their trust in him; prepared to spare and pardon, if any ask a favor of him; willing to succor and give aid, if any ask for his help; willing to save any who put all their trust in him and cleave to him.[303]

B. Knowledge of Man

2. In order for us to come to a sure knowledge of ourselves, we must first grasp the fact that Adam, parent of us all, was created in the image and likeness of God.[304] That is, he was endowed with wisdom, righteousness, holiness, and

was so clinging by these gifts of grace to God that he could have lived forever in Him, if he had stood fast in the uprightness God had given him. But when Adam slipped into sin, this image and likeness of God was cancelled and effaced, that is, he lost all the benefits of divine grace, by which he could have been led back into the way of life.[305] Moreover, he was far removed from God and became a complete stranger. From this it follows that man was stripped and deprived of all wisdom, righteousness, power, life, which—as has already been said—could be held only in God. As a consequence, nothing was left to him save ignorance, iniquity, impotence, death, and judgment.[306] These are indeed the "fruits of sin."[307] This calamity fell not only upon Adam himself, but also flowed down into us, who are his seed and offspring. Consequently, all of us born of Adam are ignorant and bereft of God, perverse, corrupt, and lacking every good. Here is a heart especially inclined to all sorts of evil, stuffed with depraved desires, addicted to them, and obstinate toward God.[308] But if we outwardly display anything good, still the mind stays in its inner state of filth and crooked perversity. The prime matter or rather the matter of concern for all rests in the judgment of God, who judges not according to appearance, nor highly esteems outward splendor, but gazes upon the secrets of the heart.[309] Therefore, however much of a dazzling appearance of holiness man may have on his own, it is nothing but hypocrisy and even an abomination in God's sight, since the thoughts of the mind, ever depraved and corrupted, lurk beneath.

3. Even though we have been so born that nothing is left for us to do which could be acceptable to God, nor has it been put in our power to please him—yet we do not cease to owe the very thing we cannot supply. Inasmuch as we are God's creatures, we ought to serve his honor and glory, and obey his commandments. And we are not allowed to excuse ourselves by claiming that we lack ability and, like impoverished debtors, cannot pay our debt. For the guilt that binds

---

298. See Bar 3:12–14; Jas 1:17; Jn 1:3–4; 11:25. (The notes for this selection are by Gerhart and Udoh.)

299. See Prov 16:4.

300. See Ps 148; Dan 3:52–90 (Vulgate) = Song of Three Children 29–65.

301. See Job 12:7–9; Ps 19:1–4; Rom 1:20–21.

302. See Ps 7:9–13; Rom 2:1–16.

303. See Pss 25:6–11; 85:5–10; 103:2–4, 8–13; 113:5–8; Isa 55:6–7; Mt 11:28–30.

304. See Gen 1:26–27.   306. See Rom 5:12–21.

305. See Gen 3:1–24.   307. Gal 5:19–22.

308. See Isa 48:4; Jer 17:9; Rom 1:18–2:16.

309. See 1 Sam 16:7; Jer 17:10.

us is our own, arising from our own sin, leaving us without the will or the capacity to do good.[310] Now, since God justly avenges crimes, we must recognize that we are subject to the curse and deserve the judgment of eternal death. Indeed there is no one of us with either the will or the ability to do his duty.

C. The Law

4. For this reason Scripture calls us all "children of God's wrath" and declares we are hurtling to death and destruction.[311] To man is left no reason why he should seek in himself his righteousness, power, life, and salvation; for all these are in God only; cut off and separated from Him by sin, man will find in himself only unhappiness, weakness, wickedness, death, in short, hell itself. To keep men from being ignorant of these things, the Lord engraved and, so to speak, stamped the law upon the hearts of all.[312] But this is nothing but conscience, for us the witness within of what we owe God; it sets before us good and evil, thus accusing and condemning us, conscious as we are within ourselves that we have not discharged our duty, as was fitting. Yet man is swollen with arrogance and ambition and blinded by self-love. Consequently, he is unable to see himself and, as it were, to descend into himself, and confess his misery. Seeing our condition, the Lord has provided us with a written law to teach us what perfect righteousness is and how it is to be kept: that is, firmly fixed in God, we turn our gaze to him alone, and to him aim our every thought, yearning, act, or word. This teaching of righteousness clearly shows how far we have strayed from the right path. To this end also look all promises and curses, set forth for us in the law itself.[313] For the Lord promises that, if anyone should perfectly and exactly fulfill by his effort whatever is commanded, he will receive the reward of eternal life.[314] By this he undoubtedly points out to us that the perfection of life taught in the law is truly righteousness, is so considered with him, and would be worthy of such a reward if any could be found among men. But he pronounces a curse and announces the judgment of eternal death upon all who do not fully and without exception keep the whole righteousness of the law.[315]

Surely by this punishment he constrains all men that ever were, are, or will be. Among them not one can be pointed out who is not a transgressor of the law. The law teaches us God's will, which we are constrained to fulfill and to which we are in debt; it shows us how we are able to carry out exactly nothing of what God has commanded us.[316] Conse-

quently, it is clearly a mirror for us wherein we may discern and contemplate our sin and curse, just as we commonly gaze upon the scars and blemishes of our face in a mirror. Properly speaking, this very written law is but a witness of natural law, a witness which quite often arouses our memory, and instills in us the things we had not sufficiently learned, when natural law was teaching within. Now we are ready to understand what we are to learn from the law. God is the Creator, our Lord and Father. For this reason we owe him glory, honor, and love. Since, however, not one of us performs these duties, we all deserve the curse, judgment, in short, eternal death. Therefore we are to seek another way to salvation than the righteousness of our own works. This way is forgiveness of sins. Then, since it is not in our power or ability to discharge what we owe the law, we must despair of ourselves and must seek and await help from another quarter. After we descend to this humility and submission, the Lord will shine upon us, and show himself lenient, kindly, gentle, indulgent. For of him it is written: "he resists the proud, gives grace to the humble."[317] And first, if we pray him to avert his wrath, and ask his pardon, he will without doubt grant it to us. Everything our sins deserved he forgives, and receives into grace.

D. God's Love in Christ

5. Then, if we implore his helping hand, surely we will be persuaded that, equipped with his protection, we will be able to do all things. He bestows upon us according to his own good will a new heart in order that we may will, and a new power, whereby we may be enabled to carry out his commandments.[318] And all these blessings he showers upon us for the sake of Jesus Christ our Lord, who—even though he was one God with the Father—put on our flesh,[319] to enter a covenant with us and to join us (far separated from God by our sins) closely to him.[320] He also by the merit of his death

---

310. See Jn 8:34–38, 44; Rom 7:14–24.
311. Eph 2:1–3; Rom 3:9–20.
312. See Rom 2:14–16.
313. See Deut 28:1–68.
314. See Lev 18:5 (Septuagint); Gal 3:12.
315. See Deut 27:26 (Septuagint); Gal 3:10.
316. See Gal 3:19; Rom 3:19–20; 4:15; 7:7–25.
317. Prov 3:34; Jas 4:6; 1 Pet 5:5.
318. See Ezek 36:26.
319. See Jn 1:1–14; Phil 2:5–9.
320. See Isa 53:4–11.

paid our debts to God's justice, and appeased his wrath.[321] He redeemed us from the curse and judgment that bound us, and in his body the punishment of sin, so as to absolve us from it.[322] Descending to earth, he brought with him all the rich heavenly blessings and with a lavish hand showered them upon us.[323] These are the Holy Spirit's gifts. Through him we are reborn, wrested from the power and chains of the devil, freely adopted as children of God, sanctified for every good work. Through him also—so long as we are held in this mortal body—there are dying in us the depraved desires, the promptings of the flesh, and everything the twisted and corrupt perversity of our nature brings forth. Through him we are renewed from day to day,[324] that we may walk in newness of life[325] and live for righteousness.

6. God offers to us and gives us in Christ our Lord all these benefits, which include free forgiveness of sins, peace and reconciliation with God, the gifts and graces of the Holy Spirit. They are ours if we embrace and receive them with sure faith, utterly trusting and, as it were, leaning upon divine goodness, not doubting that God's Word, which promises us all these things, is power and truth.[326] In short, if we partake of Christ, in Him we shall possess all the heavenly treasures and gifts of the Holy Spirit, which lead us into life and salvation. Except with a true and living faith, we will never grasp this. With it, we will recognize all our good to be in him, ourselves to be nothing apart from him; we will hold as certain that in him we become God's children and heirs of the heavenly kingdom.[327] On the other hand, those who have no part in Christ, whatever their nature, whatever they may do or undertake, depart into ruin and confusion and into the judgment of eternal death; they are cast away from God and are shut off from all hope of salvation.[328] This knowledge of ourselves and of our poverty and ruin teaches us to humble ourselves and cast ourselves before God and seek his mercy.[329] Not from ourselves is the faith that furnishes us a taste of divine goodness and mercy, wherein God in his Christ has to do with us. Rather, it is God who is to be asked to lead us, unfeignedly repentant, to the knowledge of ourselves; to lead us, by sure faith, to the knowledge of his gentleness and of his sweetness, which he shows forth in his Christ in order that Christ as our leader, who is the only way to reach the Father, may bring us into eternal blessedness.[330]

27. [. . .] Therefore if we look merely to the law, we can only be despondent, confused, and despairing in mind, since from it all of us are condemned and accursed. That is, as Paul says, all those under the law are accursed.[331] And the law cannot do anything else than to accuse and blame all to a man, to convict, and, as it were, apprehend them; in fine, to condemn them in God's judgment: that God alone may justify, that all flesh may keep silence before him.[332] But we do not gabble about what many are accustomed today to boast of. After they have been compelled to confess that it is an impossibility for them to achieve perfect and ultimate righteousness through the merit of works, since they never fulfill the law, they indeed confess it. But lest they seem deprived of all glory, that is, to have yielded completely to God, they claim they have kept the law in part and are, in respect to this part, righteous. What is lacking they contend has been made up and redeemed by satisfactions and works of supererogation. They consider this to be compensation for their lack. Forgetfulness of their own true nature, contempt of God's justice, and ignorance of their own sin have plunged them into this error. Surely those cut themselves off from self-knowledge who judge themselves to be other than Scripture describes all the children of Adam to be. Their excellence Scripture sets off with these titles: that they are of wicked and inflexible heart;[333] that the whole imagination of men's hearts is evil from their first years;[334] "that all their thoughts are vain";[335] that they are "the light of darkness";[336] that all like sheep have gone astray, each having departed from his path;[337] that not a single one has been found who does good;[338] that no one of them understands or seeks after God;[339] that they do not have the fear of God before their eyes;[340] in short, that they are flesh.[341] By this word are meant all those works which Paul lists: "fornication, impurity, immodesty, licentiousness, service of idols, sorcery, party spirit, envy, murder," and everything foul or abominable that can be imagined.[342] [. . .]

---

321. See Eph 2:1–7.

322. See Col 1:21–22.

323. See Jn 1:14–16; 7:37–39; Rom 8:14–17.

324. See 2 Cor 4:16.

325. See Rom 6:4.

326. See Rom 3:21–26; 5:1–11.

327. See Jn 1:12–13; Rom 8:14–17; Gal 3:13–14; 4:4–7.

328. See Jn 3:18–20; 1 Jn 5:12; Rom 8:7–8.

329. See Jer 31:18–20.

330. See Jn 14:6; Acts 5:31; Rom 5:1–11.

331. See Gal 3:10.

332. See Rom 3:19–28; 1 Cor 1:28–29.

333. See Jer 17:9.

334. See Gen 8:21.

335. Ps 93:11 (Septuagint/Vulgate); see also Ps 94:11.

336. Job 10:22; Mt 6:23.

337. See Isa 53:6.

338. See Ps 14:1, 3.

339. See Ps 14:2.

340. See Ex 20:20; Prov 1:7.

341. See Gen 6:3.

342. Gal 5:19–21 (Vulgate).

28. Also God's righteousness is despised where it is not recognized as such and so perfect, that nothing is accepted by him except what is whole and perfect, and uncorrupted by any filth. But if this is so, all our works, if judged by their own worth, are nothing but corruption and filth. Thus our righteousness is iniquity, our uprightness pollution, our glory dishonor. For the best thing that can be brought forth from us is still always spotted and corrupted with some impurity of our flesh, and has, so to speak, some dregs mixed with it.

Next, even if it were possible for us to have some wholly pure and righteous works, yet, as the prophet says, one sin is enough to wipe out and extinguish every memory of that previous righteousness.[343] James agrees with him: "Whoever," he says, "fails in one point, has become guilty of all."[344] Now since this mortal life is never pure or devoid of sin, whatever righteousness we might attain,[345] when it is corrupted, oppressed, and destroyed by the sins that follow, could not come into God's sight or be reckoned to us as righteousness.

In short, in God's law we must have regard not for the work but for the commandment. Therefore, if righteousness is sought from the law, not one work or another, but unceasing obedience to the law will make one righteous. Moreover sin is an utterly execrable thing in God's sight and of such gravity that men's whole righteousness, gathered together in one heap, could not make compensation for a single sin. For we see that man was so cast away and abandoned by God for one transgression that he lost at the same time all capacity to receive and regain his salvation.[346] Therefore, the capacity to make satisfaction was taken away.

29. Those who preen themselves on it surely will never satisfy God, to whom nothing is pleasing or acceptable that comes forth from his enemies. But God's enemies are all those to whom he imputes sins. Therefore, our sins must be covered and forgiven before the Lord will recognize any work of ours.[347] From this it follows that forgiveness of sins is free, and those who trust in their satisfactions obscure and blaspheme it. Let us therefore, after the apostle's example, "forgetting what lies behind and straining forward to what lies before us," run our race, pressing "on toward . . . the prize of the upward call."[348] . . .

32. Therefore, we must now recognize that our salvation consists in God's mercy alone, but not in any worth of ours, or in anything coming from us. Accordingly, on this mercy we must establish and as it were deeply fix all our hope, paying no regard to our works nor seeking any help from them. Indeed, the nature of faith is to arouse the ears but close the eyes, to await the promise but turn thoughts away from all

worth or merit of man. For never will we have enough confidence in God unless we become deeply distrustful of ourselves. Never will we lift up our hearts enough in him unless they be previously cast down in us. Never will we have consolation enough in him unless we have already experienced desolation in ourselves. Never will we glory enough in him unless we dethrone all glory in ourselves. Consequently, when all our confidence is utterly cast down yet we still rely on his goodness, we grasp and obtain God's grace, and (as Augustine says) forgetting our merits, we embrace Christ's gifts. This is what it means to have true faith, as is fitting. But no one can attain this assurance except through Christ, by whose blessing alone we are freed from the law's curse. The curse was decreed and declared for us all, since, on account of the weakness inherited from our father Adam, we could not fulfill the law by our own works, as was required of those who desired to obtain therefrom righteousness for themselves. By Christ's righteousness then are we made righteous and become fulfillers of the law.[349] This righteousness we put on as our own, and surely God accepts it as ours, reckoning us holy, pure, and innocent. Thus is fulfilled Paul's statement: "Christ was made righteousness, sanctification, and redemption for us."[350] For our merciful Lord first indeed kindly received us into grace according to his own goodness and freely-given will, forgiving and condoning our sins, which deserved wrath and eternal death.[351] Then through the gifts of his Holy Spirit he dwells and reigns in us and through him the lusts of our flesh are each day mortified more and more. We are indeed sanctified, that is, consecrated to the Lord in complete purity of life, our hearts formed to obedience to the law. To make it our undivided will to serve his will and by every means to advance his glory alone, we hate all the filth of our flesh reposing in us.

Then lastly, even while we walk in the Lord's ways by the leading of the Holy Spirit, to keep us from forgetting ourselves and becoming puffed up, something imperfect remains in us to give us occasion for humility, to stop every mouth before God and to teach us always to shift all trust from ourselves to him.[352] As a consequence we always need forgiveness of sins. Accordingly those works also which are done by

---

343. See Ezek 18:24.

344. Jas 2:10.

345. See 1 Jn 1:8.

346. See Gen 3:17–24.

347. See Ps 32:1–2; Rom 4:7–8.

348. Phil 3:13–14.

349. See Rom 8:3–4.

350. 1 Cor 1:30.

351. See Rom 5:10–11; 6:22.

352. See 2 Cor 12:7–9.

us while we rush along the Lord's way (as if they please God since they are done in faith!) cannot of themselves render us acceptable and pleasing to God.

But Christ's righteousness, which alone can bear the sight of God because it alone is perfect, must appear in court on our behalf, and stand surety for us in judgment.[353] Received from God, this righteousness is brought to us and imputed to us, just as if it were ours. Thus in faith we continually and constantly obtain forgiveness of sins; none of the filth or uncleanness of our imperfection is imputed to us, but is covered over by that purity and perfection of Christ as if it were buried that it may not come into God's judgment until the hour arrives when, the old man in us being slain and plainly destroyed, the divine goodness receives us into blessed peace with the new Adam (who is Christ). There let us await the Day of the Lord when, having received incorruptible bodies, we will be carried into the glory of the heavenly kingdom.[354]

II. Faith: Containing an Explanation of the Creed (Called Apostolic)

A. Faith and Faith in the One God

1. [. . .] It now remains for us to learn what the nature of this faith ought to be—something we may readily learn from the Creed (which is called "Apostolic"), a brief compend and, as it were, epitome, of the faith agreed upon by the catholic church.

2. But before proceeding farther, we must be advised that there are two forms of the faith. One is this: if someone believes that God is, he thinks that the history related concerning Christ is true. Such is the judgment we hold on those things which either are narrated as once having taken place, or we ourselves have seen to be present. But this is of no importance: thus it is unworthy to be called "faith"; if anyone boasts of it, let him realize he has it in common with demons, for whom it accomplishes nothing except that they become more frightened, tremble, and are laid low.[355]

The other is the faith whereby we not only believe that God and Christ are, but also believe in God and Christ, truly acknowledging Him as our God and Christ as our Savior. Now this is not only to adjudge true all that has been written or is said of God and Christ: but to put all hope and trust in one God and Christ, and to be so strengthened by this thought, that we have no doubt about God's good will toward us. Consequently, we have been persuaded that whatever we need, either for the use of the soul or of the body, He will give us; we await with assurance whatever the Scriptures

promise concerning him; we do not doubt Jesus is our Christ, that is, Savior. But as we obtain through him forgiveness of sins and sanctification, so also salvation has been given, in order that we may at last be led into God's kingdom, which will be revealed on the last day. And this is indeed the head and almost the sum of all those things which the Lord by his sacred Word offers and promises us. This is the goal set for us in his Scriptures; this the target he sets.

3. The Word of God, therefore, is the object and target of faith at which one ought to aim; and the base to prop and support it, without which it could not even stand. And thus this true faith—which can at last be called "Christian"—is nothing else than a firm conviction of mind whereby we determine with ourselves that God's truth is so certain, that it is incapable of not accomplishing what it has pledged to do by his holy Word.[356] This Paul teaches in his definition, calling it "the substance of things hoped for, and the proof of things not seen."[357] By "substance" or "hypostasis" (as the Greek has it)[358] he understands a support on which we lean and recline. It is as if he said: faith itself is a sure and certain possession of those things God has promised us.

On the other hand, he would signify that the things pertaining to the last day (when the books will be opened)[359] are loftier than those our sense can perceive, or our eyes can see, or our hand can touch; meanwhile that we can only possess those things if we exceed the total capacity of our own nature, and press our keenness of vision beyond all things which are in the world, in short, surpass ourselves. He has added that this is the security of possessing the things that lie in hope and are therefore not seen. For (as he elsewhere writes) hope which is seen is not hope, nor does one hope for what he sees.[360] While he calls it an indication and proof (in Greek *elenchus,* demonstration) of things not appearing,[361] he is speaking as if to say that the evidence of things not appearing is the vision of things which are not seen, the perception of things obscure, the presence of things absent, the proof of things hidden. For God's mysteries pertaining to

353. See Heb 11:6; Rom 8:34.
354. See 1 Cor 15:45–57.
355. See Jas 2:19.
356. See Isa 28:16; Rom 10:11; 4:19–25.
357. Heb 11:1.
358. Heb 11:1; see also Heb 1:3; 3:14.
359. See Dan 7:10; Phil 4:3; Rev 20:12.
360. See Rom 8:24.
361. See Heb 11:1.

our salvation are of the sort that cannot in themselves and by their own nature (as is said) be discerned; but we gaze upon them only in his Word. So persuaded ought we to be of its truth that we must count its every utterance an accomplished fact.

4. This sort of faith is far different from the first one. Whoever has this kind of faith cannot but be accepted by God; on the contrary, without it, it cannot happen that anyone will ever please him.[362] Through it whatever we desire and ask of God we obtain,[363] insofar as he foresees it will be conducive to our larger good. But this cannot have its seat in a devious, perverted, and false heart, nor can it be begun or sustained except by God's grace alone. This is what God requires of us by the First Commandment of his law. Having first said that he is the one Lord our God, he adds that we are not to have other gods before him. This obviously means that in no one else but him are our hope and trust to rest, for they are owed to him alone. He also hints that, if our hope and trust look to another, we have another god. . . .

Fourth Part. I believe the Holy Catholic Church, the communion of saints, the forgiveness of sins, the resurrection of the flesh, eternal life.

21. First, we believe the holy catholic church—that is the whole number of the elect, whether angels or men;[364] of men, whether dead or still living; of the living, in whatever lands they live, or wherever among the nations they have been scattered—to be one church and society, and one people of God. Of it, Christ, our Lord, is Leader and Ruler, and as it were Head of the one body,[365] according as, through divine goodness, they have been chosen in him before the foundation of the world,[366] in order that all might be gathered into God's Kingdom.

Now this society is catholic, that is, universal, because there could not be two or three churches. But all God's elect are so united and conjoined in Christ[367] that, as they are dependent on one Head, they also grow together into one body, being joined and knit together[368] as are the limbs of one body.[369] These are made truly one who live together in one faith, hope, and love, and in the same Spirit of God, called to the inheritance of eternal life.

It is also holy, because as many as have been chosen by God's eternal providence to be adopted as members of the church—all these are made holy by the Lord.[370]

22. And Paul indeed describes this order of God's mercy: "Those whom he has chosen from men he calls; those whom

he has called, he justifies; those whom he has justified, he glorifies."[371] He calls when he draws his own to himself, showing himself to be acknowledged by them as their God and Father. He justifies when he clothes them with the righteousness of Christ, with which as their perfection he also adorns them, and covers up their own imperfection. And those who from day to day are cleansed of the corruption of their flesh, he refreshes with the blessings of his Holy Spirit, and they are reborn into newness of life, until they clearly appear holy and stainless in his sight. He will glorify [them] when the majesty of his Kingdom will have been manifested in all and through all things.[372]

Consequently, the Lord, when he calls his own, justifies and glorifies his own, is declaring nothing but his eternal election, by which he had destined them to this end before they were born. Therefore no one will ever enter into the glory of the Heavenly Kingdom who has not been called in this manner, and justified, seeing that without any exception the Lord in this manner sets forth and manifests his election in all men whom He has chosen.

Scripture often, in accommodating itself to our capacity, calls "the election of God" only what has already been manifested by this calling and justification. The reason is this: that often among His people God numbers some in whom He has worked His own powers although they were not elect. On the other hand, those who have truly been chosen, he may not reckon among the people of God, because they have not yet been declared to be such.[373] For here Paul is not referring to that one and unchangeable providence of God, but is describing to us the children of God in such a way that they can be recognized by us, namely those who are moved by the Spirit of God.[374]

23. Moreover, since the church is the people of God's elect, it cannot happen that those who are truly its members will ultimately perish,[375] or come to a bad end. For their salva-

---

362. See Heb 11:6.

363. See Mk 11:23–24; Mt 21:21–22.

364. See Eph 1:9–10; Col 1:16–20.

365. See Eph 5:23; Col 1:18.

366. See Eph 1:4–5.

367. See Eph 1:23; 5:23, 25–27, 29–32.

368. See Eph 4:15–16.

369. See Rom 12:4–5; 1 Cor 10:17; 12:12–27.

370. See Jn 17:16–19; Rom 8:28–30; Eph 1:3–4; Col 1:21–22.

371. Rom 8:30.

372. See 1 Cor 15:24–28.

373. See Rom 9:8–18, 25–26; 10:20; 11:7–8; Hos 1:10; 2:23.

374. See Rom 8:14.

375. See Jn 10:27–28; Rom 8:1–2.

tion rests on such a sure and solid bed, that, even if the whole fabric of the world were to fall, it itself could not tumble and fall. First, it stands with God's election, nor can it change or fail, unless along with that eternal wisdom. Therefore they can totter and waver, even fall, but not contend against one another for the Lord supports their hand; that is what Paul says, "for the gifts and calling of God are without repentance."[376] Then those whom the Lord has chosen have been turned over to the care and keeping of Christ his Son so that "he may lose none of them but may revive all on the last day."[377] Under such a good watchman they can wander and fall, but surely they cannot be lost.[378] Besides, it must have been so decreed that there was no time from the creation of the world when the Lord did not have his church upon the earth, also that there will be no time, even to the end of the age, when he will not have it, even as he himself promises.[379] For even if at once from the beginning the human race was, by Adam's sin, corrupted and vitiated, yet from this as it were polluted mass, he sanctifies some vessels unto honor,[380] so there is no age that does not experience his mercy. Finally, if we are so to believe the church that, relying upon the faithfulness of divine goodness, we hold for certain that we are a part of it, and with the rest of God's elect, with whom we have been called and already in part justified, let us have faith that we shall be perfectly justified and glorified.

We indeed cannot comprehend God's incomprehensible wisdom, nor is it in our power to investigate it so as to find out who have by his eternal plan been chosen, who condemned.[381] But this is not needed by our faith, which is rendered abundantly secure by this promise: God will recognize as his sons those who have received his only-begotten Son.[382] Who can there be with such shameless desire as, not content to be God's son, to seek something beyond?

24. When, therefore, we have found in Christ alone the good will of God the Father toward us, life, salvation, in short, the very Kingdom of Heaven itself, he alone ought to be more than enough for us. For this we must ponder: that utterly nothing will be lacking to us which can conduce to our salvation and good, if he is ours; that he and all things of his become ours, if we lean in sure faith upon him, if we rest in him, if we repose in him salvation, life, in sum, all our possessions, if we rest assured that he is never going to forsake us. For with ready hands he gives himself to us only that we may receive him in faith.

But those who, not content with Christ, strive to penetrate more deeply arouse God's wrath against themselves and, because they break into the depths of his majesty, from his glory cannot but be oppressed.[383] For since Christ our Lord is he in whom the Father, from eternity, has chosen those he has willed to be his own and to be brought into the flock of his church, we have a clear enough testimony that we are among God's elect and of the church, if we partake in Christ. Then, since the very same Christ is the constant and unchangeable truth of the Father, we are by no means to doubt that his word truly proclaims to us the Father's will as it was from the beginning and ever will be.[384]

When therefore by faith we possess Christ and all that is his, it must certainly be established that as he himself is the beloved Son of the Father and heir of the Kingdom of Heaven, so we also through him have been adopted as children of God, and are his brothers and companions in such a way as to be partakers of the same inheritance; on this account we are also assured that we are among those whom the Lord has chosen from eternity, whom he will ever protect and never allow to perish.[385]

25. Otherwise if each one of us did not believe himself to be a member of it, we would vainly and fruitlessly believe there to be a church catholic. But it is not for us to determine for certain whether others are of the church, nor to distinguish the elect from the reprobate. For this is God's prerogative alone, to know who are his own, as Paul attests.[386] And to keep men's rashness from getting out of hand, we are warned by daily events how far the Lord's judgments surpass our perception. For those who seemed utterly lost and had obviously been given up as hopeless are recalled to the pathway by his goodness, and those who seemed to stand before the rest often tumble down. Only God's eyes see who will persevere to the very end,[387] because he alone is the Head of salvation.[388]

Not indeed because Christ has declared that those things which the ministers of his Word loose or bind on earth will be loosed or bound in heaven,[389] does it follow from this that we can discern who are of the church, and who are strangers to it. For by this promise he did not mean to give some

---

376. Rom 11:29.
377. Jn 6:39–40.
378. See 2 Cor 4:8–9.
379. See Joel 3:20; Pss 89:27–37; 132:11–18.
380. See Rom 9:21.
381. See Rom 11:1–36.
382. See Jn 1:12–13.
383. See Prov 25:2–3.
384. See Jn 1:1–2, 14; 14:6–11.
385. See Rom 8:31–39.
386. See 2 Tim 2:19.
387. See Mt 24:13.
388. See Heb 2:10.
389. See Mt 16:19; 18:18.

external criterion to point out to us openly and lay before our eyes the bound and loosed, but only to promise this: that they who shall hear and receive in faith the gospel promise by which Christ is offered upon earth as redemption and liberation, that is, proclaimed in this life by man to himself—that they, I say, are truly loosed and freed in heaven, that is, in God's presence and by His judgment; but those who will reject and hold it in contempt, to them there is from this promise the testimony that, in heaven and in God's presence, they remain in their chains and so in their condemnation.

26. The elect cannot be recognized by us with assurance of faith, yet Scripture describes certain sure marks to us, as has previously been said, by which we may distinguish the elect and the children of God from the reprobate and the alien, insofar as He wills us so to recognize them. Consequently, all who profess with us the same God and Christ by confession of faith, example of life, and participation in the sacraments ought by some sort of judgment of love to be deemed elect and members of the church. They should be so considered, even if some imperfection resides in their morals (as no one here shows himself to be perfect), provided they do not too much acquiesce and flatter themselves in their vices. And it must be hoped concerning them that they are going to advance by God's leading ever into better ways, until, shed of all imperfection, they attain the eternal blessedness of the elect. For by these marks and traits Scripture delineates for us the elect of God, the children of God, the people of God, the church of God, as they can be understood by us. But those who either do not agree with us on the same faith, or, even though they have confession on their lips, still deny by their actions the God whom they confess with their mouth (as those whom we see wicked and lost throughout life, drunk with the lust of sinning, and quite unconcerned over their own wickedness)—all of this sort show themselves by their traits that they are not members at present of the church.

From John Calvin, *Institutes of the Christian Religion,* translated by Ford Lewis Battles (Grand Rapids, MI: Eerdmans, 1986), 15–18, 30–32, 34–35, 42–44, 58–61.

✒ In his *Of the Laws of Ecclesiastical Polity* (1593), the Anglican theologian **Richard Hooker** (ca. 1554–1600) argues that, in the absence of specific scriptural ordinances, many forms of polity are potentially consonant with the general spirit of Christianity insofar as they are guided by natural law.

Of the Laws of Ecclesiastical Polity, III.1.2, 8.9

III.1. Whether it be necessarie that some particular forme of Church-polity be set downe in scripture: sith the things that belong particularly unto any such forme are not of necessitie to salvation.

[2.1] 2. But we must note, that he which affirmeth speech to be necessarie amongst all men throughout the worlde, doth not thereby import that all men must necessarily speake one kinde of language. Even so the necessitie of politie and regiment in all Churches may be helde, without holding anie one certayne forme to bee necessarie in them all. Nor is it possible that anie forme of politie, much lesse of politie Ecclesiasticall, should be good, unlesse God himselfe be author of it. [390]*Those things that are not of God* (sayeth Tertullian) *they can have no other then Gods adversarie for their author.* Be it whatsoever in the Church of God, if it be not of God, wee hate it. Of God it must bee, eyther as those thinges sometime were, which God supernaturally revealed, and so delivered them unto Moses for governement of the common wealth of Israell, or else [391]as those thinges which men finde out by helpe of that light, which God hath given them unto that ende. The verie lawe of nature it selfe, [392]which no man can denie but God hath instituted is not of God, unlesse that bee of God, whereof God is the author as well this later way as the former. But for as much as no forme of Church-politie is thought by them to be lawfull, or to be of God, unlesse God be so the author of it, that it be also set downe in Scripture; they should tell us plainely, whether their meaning be, that it must be there set downe in whole or in part. For if wholly, let them shewe what one forme of politie ever was so. Their owne to be so taken out of Scripture they will not affirme, neyther denie they that in parte even this which they so much oppugne is also from thence taken. Againe they should tell us, whether only that bee taken out of Scripture, which is actually and perticularly there set downe; or else that also, which the generall principles and rules of Scripture potentially conteine. The one waye they cannot as much as pretende, that all the partes of their owne discipline are in scripture; and

---

390. Tertul. de habitu mul. *Aemuli sint necesse est quae Dei non sunt.*

391. Rom. 2:15.

392. Lactan. lib.6. ca.8. *Ille legis hujus inventor, disceptator, lator. Cic. 3. de Repub.*

the other way their mouthes are stopped, when they would pleade against all other formes besides their owne: seeing the generall principles are such as doe not perticularly prescribe any one, but sundrie may equally be consonant unto the generall axiomes of the Scripture. [2.2] But to give them some larger scope and not to close them up in these streightes: let their allegations bee considered, wherewith they earnestly bende themselves against all, which denie it necessarie that anie one complete forme of Church-politie should bee in scripture. [393]First therefore whereas it hath beene tolde them that matters of fayth, and in generall matters necessarie unto salvation are of a different nature from Ceremonies, order, and the kinde of Church-governement; that the one are necessarie to bee expresselie conteyned in the worde of God, or else manifestly collected out of the same, the other not so; that it is necessarie not to receive the one, unlesse there bee some thing in scripture for them, the other free, if nothing against them may thence be alleaged: although there doe not appeare any just or reasonable cause to reject or dislike of this, neverthelesse as it is not easie to speake to the contentation of mindes exulcerated in themselves, but that somewhat there will be always which displeaseth, so herein for two thinges we are reprooved, the first is *misdistinguishing,* because matters of discipline and Church-governement are (as they say) matters necessarie to salvation and of faith, whereas we put a difference betweene the one and the other; our seconde fault is *injurious dealing* with the scripture of God as if it conteyned onely the principall pointes of religion, some rude and unfashioned matter of building the Church, but had left out that which belongeth unto the forme and fashion of it; as if there were in the scripture no more then only to cover the Churches nakednesse, and not chaines, bracelets, ringes, jewels to adorne her; sufficient to quench her thirst, to kill her hunger, but not to minister a more liberall and (as it were) a more delitious and daintie dyet. In which case our apologie shall not neede to be very long.

III.8. How lawes for the regiment of the Church may be made by the advise of men following therein the light of reason, and how those lawes being not repugnant to the worde of God are approved in his sight.

[9.1] 9. Lawes for the Church are not made as they should be, unles the makers follow such direction as they ought to be guided by. Wherin that scripture standeth not the Church of God in any stead, or serveth nothing at al to direct, but

may be let passe as needles to be consulted with, we judge it prophane, impious, and irreligious to thinke. For although it were in vaine to make lawes which the scripture hath already made, bicause what we are already there commanded to do, on our parts there resteth nothing but only that it be executed: yet because both in that which we are commanded, it concerneth the duty of the Church by law to provide, that the loosenes and slacknes of men may not cause the commandements of God to be unexecuted; and a number of things there are for which the scripture hath not provided by any law, but left them unto the carefull discretion of the Church; we are to search how the Church in these cases may be well directed to make that provision by lawes which is most convenient and fit. And what is so in these cases, partly scripture and partly reason must teach to discerne. Scripture comprehending examples and lawes, lawes some natural and some positive: examples there neither are for al cases which require lawes to be made, and when there are, they can but direct as precedents onely. Naturall lawes direct in such sorte, that in all thinges we must for ever doe according unto them; positive so, that against them in no case we may doe any thing, as long as the will of God is that they shoulde remaine in force. Howbeit when scripture doth yeelde us precedents, how far forth they are to bee followed; when it giveth naturall lawes, what particular order is thereunto most agreeable; when positive, which waye to make lawes unrepugnant unto them; yea though all these shoulde want, yet what kind of

---

393. Two thinges misliked, the one, that we distinguish matters of discipline or Church-governement from matters of fayth and necessarie unto salvation; the other, that wee are injurious to the scripture of God, in abridging the large and rich contents thereof. Their wordes are these. *You which distinguish betweene these and say, that matters of fayth and necessarie unto salvation may not be tollerated in the Church, unlesse they be expressely conteyned in the worde of God, or manifestly gathered, but that ceremonies, order, discipline, governement in the Church may not be received against the word of God, and consequently may be received, if there be no word against them although there be none for them, you (I say) distinguishing or dividing after this sort doe proove your selfe an evill divider. As though matters of discipline and kinde of governement were not matters necessary to salvation and of fayth. It is no small injurie which you doe unto the worde of God to pinne it in so narrow roome, as that it should be able to direct us but in the principall points of our religion, or as though the substance of religion or some rude and unfashioned matter of building of the Church were uttered in them, and those thinges were left out that should pertaine to the forme and fashion of it, or as if there were in the scriptures onely to cover the Churches nakednes, and not also chaines, and bracelets, and ringes and other jewels to adorne her and set her out, or that to conclude, there were sufficient to quench her thirst and kill her hunger, but not to minister unto her a more liberall, and (as it were) a more delitious and daintie dyet. These thinges you seeme to say, when you say that matters necessarie to salvation and of fayth are conteyned in scripture, especially when you oppose these thinges to ceremonyes, order, discipline, and governement.* T.C. [Thomas Cartwright, trans., *A full and plaine declaration of Ecclesiasticall Discipline,* by Walter Travers (Heidelberg: Michael Schirat, 1574)] 1.I. p. 26.

ordinances woulde be moste for that good of the Church which is aimed at, al this must be by reason founde out. And therefore [394]*To refuse the conduct of the light of nature,* saith Saint Augustine, *is not folly alone but accompanied with impietie.* [9.2] The greatest amongst the Schoole divines studying how to set downe by exact definition the nature of an humaine lawe (of which nature all the Churches constitutions are) found not which way better to do it then in these wordes. [395]*Out of the precepts of the lawe of nature as out of certaine common and undemonstrable principles, mans reason doth necessarily proceede unto certaine more particular determinations, which particular determinations being found out according unto the reason of man, they have the names of humaine lawes, so that such other conditions be therein kept as the making of lawes doth require,* that is, if they whose authoritie is thereunto required do establish and publish them as lawes. And the truth is, that all our controversie in this cause concerning the orders of the Church is, what particulars the Church may appoint. That which doth finde them out is the force of mans reason. That which doth guide and direct his reason is first the generall law of nature, which law of nature and the morall law of scripture are in the substance of law all one. But bicause there are also in scripture a number of lawes particular and positive, which being in force may not by any law of man be violated: we are in making lawes to have thereunto an especiall eie. As for example, it might perhaps seeme reasonable unto the Church of God following the generall lawes concerning the nature of mariage to ordaine in particular, that coosen germaines shall not marry. Which law notwithstanding ought not to be received in the Church, if there should be in scripture a lawe particular to the contrary forbidding utterly the bonds of mariage to be so far forth abridged. The same Thomas therefore whose definition of humane lawes we mentioned before, doth adde thereunto this caution concerning the rule and canon whereby to make them: [396]*Humane lawes are measures in respect of men whose actions they must direct, howbeit such measures they are, as have also their higher rules to be measured by, which rules are two, the law of God, and the law of nature.* So that lawes humane must be made according to the generall lawes of nature, and without contradiction unto any positive law in scripture. Otherwise they are ill made. [9.3] Unto lawes thus made and received by a whole Church, they which live within the bosome of that Church, must not thinke it a matter indifferent either to yeeld or not to yeeld obedience. [397]*Is it a smal offence to despise the Church of God?* [398]*My sonne keepe thy fathers commandement,* saith Salomon, *and forget not thy mothers instruction, bind them both alwaies about thine hart.* It doth not stand with the duty which we owe to our heavenly father, that to the ordinances of our mother the Church we should shew our selves disobedient. Let us not say we keepe the commandements of the one, when we break the law of the other: For unlesse we observe both, we obey neither. And what doth let but that we may observe both, when they are not the one to the other in any sort repugnant? For of such lawes only we speake, as being made in forme and manner already declared, can have in them no contradiction unto the lawes of almighty God. Yea that which is more, the lawes thus made God himselfe doth in such sort authorize, that to despise them is to despise in them him. It is a loose and licentious opinion which the Anabaptists have embraced, holding that a Christian mans libertie is lost, and the soule which Christ hath redeemed unto himselfe injuriously drawne into servitude under the yooke of humane power, if any law be now imposed besides the Gospell of Jesus Christ: in obedience whereunto the spirite of God and not the constraint of men is to lead us, according to that of the blessed Apostle, [399]*Such as are led by the spirite of God they are the sonnes of God,* and not such as live in thraldome unto men. Their judgement is therefore that the Church of Christ should admit no law makers but the Evangelists. The author of that which causeth another thing to be, is author of that thing also, which thereby is caused. The light of naturall understanding wit and reason is from God, he it is which thereby doth illuminate every man entering into the world. If there proceede from us any thing afterwardes corrupt and naught, [400]the mother thereof is our owne darknes, neither doth it proceede from any such cause whereof God is the author. He is the author of all that we thinke or doe by vertue of that light, which himselfe hath given. And therefore [401] the lawes which the very heathens did gather to direct their actions by, so far forth as they proceeded from the light of nature, God him selfe doth acknowledge to have proceeded even from him selfe, and that he was the writer of them in the tables of their hartes. How much more

---

394. *Luminis naturalis ducatum repellere non modo stultum est sed et impium.* Aug. 4. de trin. c.6.

395. Th. Aqui. 1.2. q.91. art.3. *Ex praeceptis Legis naturalis quasi ex quibusdam principiis communibus et indemonstrabilibus, necesse est quod ratio humana procedat ad aliqua magis particulariter disponenda. Et istae particulares dispositiones adinventae secundum rationem humanam dicuntur leges humanae, observatis aliis conditionibus quae pertinent ad rationem legis.*

396. I.2. q.95. art.3.   399. Rom 8:14.

397. 1 Cor 11:22.   400. John 1:5.

398. Prov 6:20.   401. Rom 1:19 and 2:15.

then he the author of those lawes, which have bene made by his Saincts, endued furder with the heavenly grace of his spirit, and directed as much as might be with such instructions, as his sacred word doth yeeld? Surely if we have unto those lawes that dutifull regard which their dignitie doth require: it will not greatly need, that we should be exhorted to live in obedience unto them. If they have God him selfe for their author, contempt which is offered unto them cannot choose but redound unto him. The safest and unto God the most acceptable way of framing our lives therefore is, with all humilitie lowlines and singlenes of hart to studie, which way our willing obedience both unto God and man may be yeelded even to the utmost of that which is due.

From *The Folger Library Edition of the Works of Richard Hooker,* edited by W. Speed Hill, vol. 1 (Cambridge, MA: Belknap Press of Harvard University Press, 1977), 207–9, 235–39.

ENLIGHTENMENT AND AFTER

☙ In "The Christian Religion as a Natural Religion" (1792), the philosopher **Immanuel Kant** (1724–1804) addresses the problem of the dichotomy—developed by Enlightenment thinkers—between "natural" and "supernatural" religion by arguing in what sense a supernatural religion must also be a natural religion.

IMMANUEL KANT

"The Christian Religion as a Natural Religion," in *Religion in the Light of Pure Reason Alone*

Let us suppose there was a teacher of whom an historical record (or, at least, a widespread belief which is not basically disputable) reports that he was the first to expound publicly a pure and searching religion, comprehensible to the whole world (and thus natural). His teachings, as preserved to us, we can in this case test for ourselves. Suppose that all he did was done even in the face of a dominant ecclesiastical faith which was onerous and not conducive to moral ends (a faith whose perfunctory worship can serve as a type of all the other faiths, at bottom merely statutory, which were current in the world at the time). Suppose, further, we find that he had made this universal religion of reason the highest and indispensable condition of every religious faith whatsoever, and then had added to it certain statutes which provided forms and observances designed to serve as means of bringing into existence a church founded upon those principles. Now, in spite of the adventitiousness of his ordinances directed to this end, and the elements of arbitrariness in them, and though we can deny the name of true universal church to these, we cannot deny to him himself the prestige due the one who called men to union in this church; and this without further adding to this faith burdensome new ordinances or wishing to transform acts which he had initiated into peculiar holy practices, required in themselves as being constituent elements of religion.

After this description one will not fail to recognize the person who can be reverenced, not indeed as the *founder* of the *religion* which, free from every dogma, is engraved in all men's hearts (for it does not have its origin in an arbitrary will), but as the founder of the first true *church*. For attestation of his dignity as of divine mission we shall adduce several of his teachings as indubitable evidence of religion in general, let historical records be what they may (since in the idea itself is present adequate ground for its acceptance); these teachings, to be sure, can be no other than those of pure reason, for such alone carry their own proof, and hence upon them must chiefly depend the attestation of the others.

First, he claims that not the observance of outer civil or statutory churchly duties but the pure moral disposition of the heart alone can make man well-pleasing to God (Mt 5:20–48); that sins in thought are regarded, in the eyes of God, as tantamount to action (5:28) and that, in general, holiness is the goal toward which man should strive (5:48); that, for example, to hate in one's heart is equivalent to killing (5:22); that injury done one's neighbor can be repaired only through satisfaction rendered to the neighbor himself, not through acts of divine worship (5:24), and that, on the point of truthfulness, the civil device for extorting it, by oath,[402] does violence to respect for truth itself (5:34–37); that the

---

402. It is hard to understand why this clear prohibition against this method of forcing confession before a civil tribunal of religious teachers—a method based upon mere superstition, not upon conscientiousness—is held as so unimportant. For that it is superstition whose efficacy is here most relied on is evident from the fact that the man whom one does not trust to tell the truth in a solemn statement, on the truthfulness of which depends a decision concerning the rights of a human being (a holy thing, so far as this world goes), is yet expected to be persuaded to speak truly, by the use of a formula through which, over and above that statement, he simply calls down upon himself divine punishments (which in any event, with such a lie, he cannot escape), just as though it rested with him whether or not to render account to this supreme tribunal. In the passage of Scripture cited above, the mode of confirmation by oath is represented as an *absurd* presumption, the attempt to make actual, as though with magical words, what is really not in our power. But it is clearly evident that the wise Teacher who here says that whatever goes beyond Yea, Yea, and nay, nay, in the asseveration of truth comes of evil, had in view the bad effect which oaths bring in their train—namely that the greater importance attached to them almost lends a sanction to the common lie.

natural but evil propensity of the human heart is to be completely reversed, that the sweet sense of revenge must be transformed into tolerance (5:39, 40) and the hatred of one's enemies into charity (5:44). Thus, he says, does he intend to do full justice to the Jewish law (5:17); whence it is obvious that not scriptural scholarship but the pure religion of reason must be the law's interpreter, for taken according to the letter, it allowed the very opposite of all this. Furthermore, he does not leave unnoticed, in his designations of the strait gate and the narrow way, the misconstruction of the law which men allow themselves in order to evade their true moral duty and, holding themselves immune through having fulfilled their churchly duty (7:13).[403] He further requires of these pure dispositions that they manifest themselves also in *works* (7:16) and, on the other hand, denies the insidious hope of those who imagine that, through invocation and praise of the Supreme Lawgiver in the person of His envoy, they will make up for their lack of good works and ingratiate themselves into favor (7:21). Regarding these works he declares that they ought to be performed publicly, as an example for imitation (5:16); and in a cheerful mood, not as actions extorted from slaves (6:16); and that thus, from a small beginning in the sharing and spreading of such dispositions, religion, like a grain of seed in good soil, or a ferment of goodness, would gradually, through its inner power, grow into a kingdom of God (13:31–33). Finally, he combines all duties (1) in one *universal* rule (which includes within itself both the inner and the outer moral relations of men), namely: Perform your duty for no motive other than unconditioned esteem for duty itself, i.e., love God (the Legislator of all duties) above all else; and (2) in a particular rule that, namely, which concerns man's external relation to other men as universal duty: Love every one as yourself, i.e., further his welfare from good-will that is immediate and not derived from motives of self-advantage. These commands are not mere laws of virtue but precepts of *holiness* which we ought to pursue, and the very pursuit of them is called *virtue*.

Accordingly he destroys the hope of all who intend to wait upon this moral goodness quite passively, with their hands in their laps, as though it were a heavenly gift which descends from on high. He who leaves unused the natural predisposition to goodness which lies in human nature (like a talent entrusted to him) in lazy confidence that a higher moral influence will no doubt supply the moral character and completeness which he lacks, is confronted with the threat that even the good which, by virtue of his natural predisposition,

he may have done, will not be allowed to stand him in stead because of this neglect (25:29).

As regards men's very natural expectation of an allotment of happiness proportional to a man's moral conduct, especially in view of the many sacrifices of the former which must be undergone for the sake of the latter, he promises (5:11, 12) a reward for these sacrifices in a future world, but one in accordance with the differences of disposition in this conduct between those who did their duty *for the sake of the reward* (or for release from deserved punishment) and the better men who performed it merely for its own sake; the latter will be dealt with in a different manner. When the man governed by self-interest, the god of this world, does not renounce it but merely refines it by the use of reason and extends it beyond the constricting boundary of the present, he is represented (Lk 16:3–9) as one who, in his very person [as servant], defrauds his master [self-interest] and wins from him sacrifices in behalf of "duty." For when he comes to realize that sometime, perhaps soon, the world must be forsaken, and that he can take along into the other world nothing of what he here possessed, he may well resolve to strike off from the account what he or his master, self-interest, has a legal right to exact from the indigent, and, as it were, thereby to acquire for himself bills of exchange, payable in another world. Herein he acts, no doubt, *cleverly* rather than *morally*, as regards the motives of such charitable actions, and yet in conformity with the moral law, at least according to the letter of that law; and he can hope that for this too he may not stand unrequited in the future.[404] Compare with this what is said of charity toward the needy from sheer motives of duty (Mt 25:35–40), where those, who gave succor to the needy without the idea even entering their minds that such action was worthy of a reward or that they thereby obligated heaven, as it

---

403. The *strait gate* and the narrow way, which leads to life, is that of good life-conduct; the *wide gate* and the broad way, found by many, is the *church*. Not that the church and its doctrines are responsible for men being lost, but that the *entrance* into it and the knowledge of its statutes or celebration of its rites are regarded as the manner in which God really wishes to be served.

404. We know nothing of the future, and we ought not to seek to know more than what is rationally bound up with the incentives of morality and their end. Here belongs the belief that there are no good actions which will not, in the next world, have their good consequences for him who performs them; that, therefore, however reprehensible a man may find himself at the end of his life, he must not on that account refrain from doing at least *one* more good deed which is in his power, and that, in so doing, he has reason to hope that, in proportion as he possesses in this action a purely good intent, the act will be of greater worth than those actionless absolutions which are supposed to compensate for the deficiency of good deeds without providing anything for the lessening of the guilt.

were, to recompense them, are, for this very reason, because they acted thus without attention to reward, declared by the Judge of the world to be those really chosen for His kingdom, and it becomes evident that when the Teacher of the Gospel spoke of rewards in the world to come he wished to make them thereby not an incentive to action, but merely (as a soul-elevating representation of the consummation of the divine benevolence and wisdom in the guidance of the human race) an object of the purest respect and of the greatest moral approval when reason reviews human destiny in its entirety.

Here then is a complete religion, which can be presented to all men comprehensibly and convincingly through their own reason; while the possibility and even the necessity of its being an archetype for us to imitate (so far as men are capable of that imitation) have, be it noted, been made evident by means of an example without either the truth of those teachings nor the authority and the worth of the Teacher requiring any external certification (for which scholarship or miracles, which are not matters for everyone, would be required). When appeals are here made to older (Mosaic) legislation and prefiguration, as though these were to serve the Teacher as means of confirmation, they are presented not in support of the truth of his teachings but merely for the introduction of these among people who clung wholly, and blindly, to the old. This introduction, among men whose heads, filled with statutory dogmas, have been almost entirely unfitted for the religion of reason, must always be more difficult than when this religion is to be brought to the reason of people uninstructed but also unspoiled.

From Immanuel Kant, *Religion in the Light of Pure Reason Alone,* translated by T. M. Greene and H. H. Hudson (Chicago: Open Court, 1934), 146–50.

In "Need for the Reconciliation of Religion and Cognition" (1827) **Georg Wilhelm Friedrich Hegel** (1770–1831) shows the need for reconciliation between religion as naïve faith (or intuition) and religion as a representation of faith. Kant and Hegel developed both critical and constructive ways of understanding religion.

GEORG WILHELM FRIEDRICH HEGEL

"Need for the Reconciliation of Religion and Cognition"

Philosophy of religion demonstrates this equation—the infinite in the finite and the finite in the infinite, the reconcilia-tion of the heart with religious cognition, of the absolutely substantial feeling with intelligence.[405]

This is the need of the philosophy of religion, the necessity of philosophy in general. In this reconciliation there must be a correspondence to the highest demand of cognition, of the concept and reason. Cognizing or conceiving can surrender nothing: neither infinite, substantial certainty, freedom, nor, insofar as anything is definite, the necessity and dependence of cognition, nor its worth and sublimity, nor knowledge, insight, conviction. But the absolute content cannot give anything up either. God cannot be drawn down into finitude and delivered to us in a merely sensible or crude form. His majesty consists precisely in the fact that he does not renounce reason, for then his majesty would be something irrational, empty, and grudging, not something communicated in spirit and in the highest form and inmost being of spirit.

In the Christian religion this need for the reconciliation of the two sides is more directly present perhaps than in the other religions, for the following reasons:

(1) It has its very beginning in an absolute cleavage, and there is felt need only in cleavage. Pagan religion contains from the start a more serene state of reconciliation. The Christian religion is not so serene; it awakens the need itself, takes its start from anguish, awakens this anguish, disrupts the natural unity of spirit (i.e., the unity of humanity with nature); it disturbs natural peace. This is the same as original sin: human being is evil from the start and has with it, therefore, a negative element in its inmost being. That human being is good by nature is a doctrine of recent times that annuls the Christian religion. Therefore, this cleavage of the subject, of the ego, from the infinite, absolute essence drives spirit back into itself. (This reconciliation itself occurs in faith, in the form of revelation as opposed to reason, and more recently, to cognition.) From the standpoint of cognition, purpose is the unification, the reconciling of the two sides.

(2) But there is this reconciliation directly in naive faith too, in the sphere of feeling or sensation. Then, later on,

405. Having established the opposition between religious consciousness and the rest of consciousness, or between religion and cognition, in the preceding section, Hegel now describes the need to reconcile the opposing sides. The fundamental task of the philosophy of religion is to achieve this reconciliation. [Gerhart and Udoh's note: Hegel gave three series of lectures on the philosophy of religion—with major revisions. Peter Hodgson et al. have done a remarkable correlation of the three series, and we urge the reader to gain an appreciation of the difficulties of that project by studying their text, which shows all the additions and emendations. Here, however, we have included only those parts of the text that allow for uninterrupted reading and comprehension.]

consciousness is faith, the holding of its content to be true, the knowledge that begins from the representation that I am other than what I ought to be—sinful, remote, estranged. Spirit is turned in upon itself against its immediate natural being. Christian faith starts from the representation that I am not this, not serene like the Greeks; it puts me once more into division. I am the subject, and I ask whether faith is actually the case, whether it is true.

(3) This truth of the promise: what is represented is true to begin with on the basis of authority. I am transported into an intelligible world, a world of cognition: this is the nature of God, his attributes and modes of activity. Whether it is so rests on the intuition and assurance of others, on confirmation. The cognitions referred to myself; thought, cognition, reason occur precisely within me. My freedom is put before my eyes in my sinfulness; my freedom is in my thinking: I am on my own. The Christian religion does not merely *say* that I should know; cognition, rather, is part of its very nature. (a) In the Christian religion I am to retain my freedom—indeed, I am to become free in it. In it is the individual, the subject; the welfare of the soul, the salvation of the individual as an individual, not merely of the race, is the essential purpose. This subjectivity, this selfhood (not selfishness) is precisely the principle of cognition itself. (b) At the same time God's essence and nature are manifest—the development of his content.

Hence the Christian religion is essentially doctrine; it offers representations and thoughts. Even if these are *only* representations of God and of his nature and activity, they are, nonetheless, representations of the universal content and object, and on this account they are immediately thoughts. Since it belongs under the principle of cognition, the Christian religion gives this content in a developed form, and as essentially for representation, but separate from the modes of immediate opinion and intuition and from a simple adherence to intuitions and representations. Having been thus separated, doctrine is not therefore naive but is a representation opposed to this natural resting in intuitions and representations appropriate thereto. At the same time it is not merely something subjective but is also an absolute, objective content that is in and for itself, and has the characteristic of truth. Remember the distinction already remarked on between my naively holding something to be true and my holding it with this characteristic, i.e., as doctrine. Thus the Christian religion touches the antithesis, the general antithesis, between feeling, the form of immediate intuition, trust,

and reflection, knowledge. The two together provide a developed doctrinal system of religious truth, a content of and for cognition. Christianity has revealed what God is, so that we now *know* what he is.

The Christian religion, therefore, contains cognition within itself essentially and has stimulated cognition to develop in all its consistency as form, a world of form, and at the same time to oppose itself to the form in which the Christian content exists as a given truth, only for representation and feeling. In the latter form a contradiction is found, for here the content exists not in its necessity, i.e., as cognition, and it is not free; yet the content is developed in a connected chain of distinct representations, hence as necessary thoughts, not thoughtlessly. This is what the discord of our times rests on. Educated reflection must enter into the sphere of religion, but at the same time it finds it unendurable there and becomes impatient with it. Religion, on the other hand, or religious feeling, is distrustful of reflection, or of reason as it is called. Either reflection leaves religion alone, putting it to one side, something, as it were, about which one only wants to keep the peace, or it sticks with inconsistency. Religion does not fit the pattern of the rest of consciousness or the requirements of cognition. Without seriousness of spirit, one can, in inconsistency and thoughtlessness, be satisfied with everything.

(a) We can cast ourselves upon feeling with educated reflection, but this is to do violence to oneself, to renounce cognition and rationality. In this case, spirit cannot be integrated or maintain its integrity.

(b) Religion can be reduced to mere yearning: religion as a matter of willing and not-being-capable. Yearning has urges and representations but remains a subjective lack. It does not master this lack, and, without seriousness of spirit, lets itself remain in this inconsistency.

(c) Or there can be indifference toward religion because cognition, the rationality of spirit, is not found in it. Indifference lets it remain unsettled, simply leaves it alone.

(d) Or there can be the demand to occupy oneself with it, as do, for example, the theologians. This occupation, however, is merely busying oneself with it, an expansion and extension of it. The historical aspect provides enough to keep one busy: it allows one to indulge in erudition concerning historical circumstances, philological criticism, the study of church history, how something was established by this or that council and why, what the grounds were for these decisions, how these views came about, etc. In all this, one is always dealing with religion and its content, and yet it is only religion that is not taken into account. A blind man can be concerned with the size of a painting, the canvas, the varnish, the history of the painter, the fate of the picture, its price, into whose hands it has fallen, etc.—and yet see nothing of the picture itself.

This situation confronts religion especially in our time. Cognition is not reconciled with religion; there is a dividing wall. Cognition does not risk a serious consideration of religion or take a fundamental interest in it. Philosophy of religion has to remove this hindrance. On the other side, its task is to give to religion the courage of cognition, the courage of truth and freedom.

Translated by R. F. Brown, Peter C. Hodgson, and J. M. Stewart, in Georg Wilhelm Friedrich Hegel, *Lectures on the Philosophy of Religion,* edited by Peter Hodgson, vol. 1 (Berkeley and Los Angeles: University of California Press, 1984), 104–9.

✎ **John Henry Newman** (1801–90) was an Anglican theologian who converted to Roman Catholicism. Newman's *An Essay on the Development of Christian Doctrine* (1845) uses the concept of the "development" of doctrine to defend the integrity of the Christian tradition by taking both change and continuity into account. A founder of the Oxford movement, Newman's thought came to fruition in the Second Vatican Council of the Roman Catholic Church (1962–65).

JOHN HENRY NEWMAN

An Essay on the Development of Christian Doctrine

Introduction

Christianity has been long enough in the world to justify us in dealing with it as a fact in the world's history. Its genius and character, its doctrines, precepts, and objects cannot be treated as matters of private opinion or deduction unless we may reasonably so regard the Spartan institutions or the religion of Mahomet. It may indeed legitimately be made the subject matter of theories; what is its moral and political excellence, what its due location in the range of ideas or of facts which we possess, whether it be divine or human, whether original or eclectic, or both at once, how far favourable to civilization or to literature, whether a religion for all ages or for a particular state of society, these are questions upon the fact, or professed solutions of the fact, and belong to the province

of opinion; but to a fact do they relate, on an admitted fact do they turn, which must be ascertained as other facts and surely has on the whole been so ascertained unless the testimony of so many centuries is to go for nothing. Christianity is no theory of the study or the cloister. It has long since passed beyond the letter of documents and the reasonings of individual minds and has become public property. Its "sound has gone out into all lands," and its "words unto the ends of the world." It has from the first had an objective existence, and has thrown itself upon the great concourse of men. Its home is in the world; and to know what it is we must seek it in the world and hear the world's witness of it.

2

The hypothesis, indeed, has met with wide reception in these latter times, that Christianity does not fall within the province of history—that it is to each man what each man thinks it to be, and nothing else; and thus in fact is a mere name for a cluster or family of rival religions all together, religions at variance one with another, and claiming the same appellation, not because there can be assigned any one and the same doctrine as the common foundation of all, but because certain points of agreement may be found here and there of some sort or other by which each in its turn is connected with one or other of the rest. Or again, it has been maintained, or implied, that all existing denominations of Christianity are wrong, none representing it as taught by Christ and His Apostles; that the original religion has gradually decayed or become hopelessly corrupt; nay, that it died out of the world at its birth, and was forthwith succeeded by a counterfeit or counterfeits which assumed its name, though they inherited at best but some fragments of its teaching; or rather that it cannot even be said either to have decayed or to have died, because historically it has no substance of its own, but from the first and onwards it has, on the stage of the world, been nothing more than a mere assemblage of doctrines and practices derived from without, from oriental, Platonic, polytheistic sources, from Buddhism, Essenism, Manicheeism; or that, allowing true Christianity still to exist, it has but a hidden and isolated life, in the hearts of the elect, or again as a literature or philosophy, not certified in any way, much less guaranteed, to come from above, but one out of the various separate informations about the Supreme Being and human duty, with which an unknown Providence has furnished us, whether in nature or in the world.

3

All such views of Christianity imply that there is no sufficient body of historical proof to interfere with, or at least to prevail against, any number whatever of free and independent hypotheses concerning it. But this surely is not self-evident, and has itself to be proved. Till positive reasons grounded on facts are adduced to the contrary, the most natural hypothesis, the most agreeable to our mode of proceeding in parallel cases, and that which takes precedence of all others, is to consider that the society of Christians which the Apostles left on earth were of that religion to which the Apostles had converted them; that the external continuity of name, profession, and communion argues a real continuity of doctrine; that, as Christianity began by manifesting itself as of a certain shape and bearing to all mankind, therefore it went on so to manifest itself; and that the more, considering that prophecy had already determined that it was to be a power visible in the world and sovereign over it, characters which are accurately fulfilled in that historical Christianity to which we commonly give the name. It is not a violent assumption, then, but rather mere abstinence from the wanton admission of a principle which would necessarily lead to the most vexatious and preposterous scepticism, to take it for granted, before proof to the contrary, that the Christianity of the second, fourth, seventh, twelfth, sixteenth, and intermediate centuries is in its substance the very religion which Christ and His Apostles taught in the first, whatever may be the modifications for good or for evil which lapse of years, or the vicissitudes of human affairs, have impressed upon it.

Of course I do not deny the abstract possibility of extreme changes. The substitution is certainly, in idea, supposable of a counterfeit Christianity—superseding the original, by means of the adroit innovations of seasons, places, and persons, till, according to the familiar illustration, the "blade" and the "handle" are alternately renewed, and identity is lost without the loss of continuity. It is possible; but it must not be assumed. The *onus probandi* is with those who assert what it is unnatural to expect; to be just able to doubt is no warrant for disbelieving.

21

The following essay is directed towards a solution of the difficulty which has been stated—the difficulty, as far as it exists, which lies in the way of our using in controversy the testimony of our most natural informant concerning the doctrine and worship of Christianity, viz., the history of eighteen hundred years. The view on which it is written has at all times, perhaps, been implicitly adopted by theologians, and, I believe, has recently been illustrated by several distinguished writers of the continent, such as De Maistre and Möhler: viz., that the increase and expansion of the Christian Creed and ritual, and the variations which have attended the process in the case of individual writers and Churches, are the necessary attendants on any philosophy or polity which takes possession of the intellect and heart, and has had any wide or extended dominion; that, from the nature of the human mind, time is necessary for the full comprehension and perfection of great ideas; and that the highest and most wonderful truths, though communicated to the world once for all by inspired teachers, could not be comprehended all at once by the recipients, but, as being received and transmitted by minds not inspired and through media which were human, have required only the longer time and deeper thought for their full elucidation. This may be called the *Theory of Development of Doctrine;* and before proceeding to treat of it, one remark may be in place.

It is undoubtedly an hypothesis to account for a difficulty; but such too are the various explanations given by astronomers from Ptolemy to Newton of the apparent motions of the heavenly bodies, and it is as unphilosophical on that account to object to the one as to object to the other. Nor is it more reasonable to express surprise that at this time of day a theory is necessary, granting for argument's sake that the theory is novel, than to have directed a similar wonder in disparagement of the theory of gravitation, or the Plutonian theory in geology. Doubtless, the theory of the secret and the theory of doctrinal developments are expedients, and so is the dictum of Vincentius; so is the art of grammar or the use of the quadrant; it is an expedient to enable us to solve what has now become a necessary and an anxious problem. For three hundred years the documents and the facts of Christianity have been exposed to a jealous scrutiny; works have been judged spurious which once were received without a question; facts have been discarded or modified which were once first principles in argument; new facts and new principles have been brought to light; philosophical views and polemical discussions of various tendencies have been maintained with more or less success. Not only has the relative situation of controversies and theologies altered, but infidelity itself is in a different—I am obliged to say in a more hopeful—position as regards Christianity. The facts of revealed religion, though in their substance unaltered, present a less compact and orderly front to the attacks of its enemies now than formerly, and allow of the introduction of new inquiries and theories concerning its sources and its rise. The state of things is not as it was when an appeal lay to the supposed works of the Areopagite, or to the primitive decretals, or to St. Dionysius's answers to Paul, or to the Coena Domini of St. Cyprian. The assailants of dogmatic truth have got the start of its adherents of whatever creed; philosophy is completing what criticism has begun; and apprehensions are not unreasonably excited lest we should have a new world to conquer before we have weapons for the warfare. Already infidelity has its views and conjectures, on which it arranges the facts of ecclesiastical history; and it is sure to consider the absence of any antagonist theory as an evidence of the reality of its own. That the hypothesis, here to be adopted, accounts not only for the Athanasian Creed, but for the Creed of Pope Pius, is no fault of those who adopt it. No one has power over the issues of his principles; we cannot manage our argument, and have as much of it as we please and no more. An argument is needed, unless Christianity is to abandon the province of argument; and those who find fault with the explanation here offered of its historical phenomena will find it their duty to provide one for themselves.

And as no special aim at Roman Catholic doctrine need be supposed to have given a direction to the inquiry, so neither can a reception of that doctrine be immediately based on its results. It would be the work of a life to apply the theory of developments so carefully to the writings of the Fathers, and to the history of controversies and councils, as thereby to vindicate the reasonableness of every decision of Rome; much less can such an undertaking be imagined by one who, in the middle of his days, is beginning life again. Thus much, however, might be gained even from an essay like the present, an explanation of so many of the reputed corruptions, doctrinal and practical, of Rome, as might serve as a fair ground for trusting her in parallel cases where the investigation had not been pursued.

Chapter I. On the Development of Ideas

Section I. On the Process of Development in Ideas

6

Moreover, an idea not only modifies but is modified, or at least influenced, by the state of things in which it is carried out, and is dependent in various ways on the circumstances which surround it. Its development proceeds quickly or slowly, as it may be; the order of succession in its separate stages is variable; it shows differently in a small sphere of action and in an extended; it may be interrupted, retarded, mutilated, distorted, by external violence; it may be enfeebled by the effort of ridding itself of domestic foes; it may be impeded and swayed or even absorbed by counter energetic ideas; it may be coloured by the received tone of thought into which it comes, or depraved by the intrusion of foreign principles, or at length shattered by the development of some original fault within it.

7

But whatever be the risk of corruption from intercourse with the world around, such a risk must be encountered if a great idea is duly to be understood, and much more if it is to be fully exhibited. It is elicited and expanded by trial, and battles into perfection and supremacy. Nor does it escape the collision of opinion even in its earlier years, nor does it remain truer to itself, and with a better claim to be considered one and the same, though externally protected from vicissitude and change. It is indeed sometimes said that the stream is clearest near the spring. Whatever use may fairly be made of this image, it does not apply to the history of a philosophy or belief, which on the contrary is more equable, and purer, and stronger when its bed has become deep, and broad, and full. It necessarily rises out of an existing state of things, and for a time savours of the soil. Its vital element needs disengaging from what is foreign and temporary, and is employed in efforts after freedom which become more vigorous and hopeful as its years increase. Its beginnings are no measure of its capabilities, nor of its scope. At first no one knows what it is, or what it is worth. It remains perhaps for a time quiescent; it tries, as it were, its limbs, and proves the ground under it, and feels its way. From time to time it makes essays which fail, and are in consequence abandoned. It seems in suspense which way to go; it wavers, and at length strikes out in one definite direction. In time it enters upon strange territory; points of controversy alter their bearing; parties rise and fall around it; dangers and hopes appear in new relations; and old principles reappear under new forms. It changes with them in order to remain the same. In a higher world it is otherwise, but here below to live is to change, and to be perfect is to have changed often.

From John Henry Newman, *An Essay on the Development of Christian Doctrine* (Garden City, NY: Doubleday, 1960), 31–33, 53–55, 62–63.

MAJOR CONTEMPORARY THEOLOGICAL MODELS

Liberal/Modernist

❧ In his "The Divine Attributes as Related to the Religious Self-consciousness," from his major work *The Christian Faith* (1821–22), **Friedrich Schleiermacher** (1768–1834) assesses earlier theological work on the divine attributes and interprets these attributes in relation to human experience.

FRIEDRICH SCHLEIERMACHER

"The Divine Attributes as Related to the Religious Self-consciousness," in *The Christian Faith*

The Divine Attributes Which Are Related to the Religious Self-consciousness so far as It Expresses the General Relationship between God and the World

§50. *All attributes which we ascribe to God are to be taken as denoting not something special in God, but only something special in the manner in which the feeling of absolute dependence is to be related to Him.*

1. If an adequate expression of the absolute feeling of dependence here indicated has been given in the expositions of the preceding section, we cannot believe that the theory of the divine attributes originally issued from a dogmatic interest. But history teaches us concerning speculation that, ever since it took the divine essence as an object of thought, it has always entered the same protest against all detailed description, and confined itself to representing God as the Original Being and the Absolute Good. And, indeed, it has frequently been recognized that even in these concepts (of which the first only is relevant here) there remains a certain inadequacy, in so far as they still contain an element of opposition or other analogy with finite being. This method of treatment, therefore, owes its origin first of all to religious poetry, particularly to hymns and other lyrics, and also to the more uncultured experience of common life which harmonizes with poetry and tries to vivify and establish the simple idea of the Supreme Being by the employment of expressions which we use about finite beings. Both methods proceed from religious interests, and have far more the aim of representing the immediate impression in its different forms than of establishing scientific knowledge. Therefore, just because both have been taken over from Judaism, it has been from the beginning the business of Christian Dogmatics to regulate these represen-

tations, so that the anthropomorphic element, to be found more or less in all of them, and the sensuous which is mixed in with many, may be rendered as harmless as possible, and that no retrogression towards polytheism should result. And in this direction the age of Scholasticism contributed much that was profound and excellent. But as afterwards Metaphysics came to be treated separately and apart from Christian Doctrine, in conformity with the nature of the subject, it was for long overlooked (as only too easily happens in such divisions of territory) that these representations of divine attributes are not of philosophical but of religious origin; and they were taken over into that philosophical discipline which went by the name of Natural Theology. There, however, the more science developed a purely speculative character, the more these representations, which had not arisen on the soil of speculation, were bound to be treated in a merely critical or sceptical way. Dogmatic Theology, on the other hand, tried more and more to systematize them, not, if it understood itself rightly, in order to arrive at the consciousness that they contained a complete knowledge of God, but only to assure itself that the God-consciousness which dwells in us in all its differentiations and as it realizes itself at the prompting of different elements of life, was included in them. As, however, the separation was not complete, and intercourse was always lively and manifold between the two disciplines, much has remained permanently under philosophical treatment which belonged only to the dogmatic, and *vice versa*. It is still therefore always necessary to premise that, without making any speculative demands but at the same time without bringing in any speculative aids, we keep ourselves altogether within the limits of purely dogmatic procedure, both with regard to the content of individual definitions and also as to method.

2. It is precisely in this connexion that our proposition denies in general the speculative character of the content of all the divine attributes to be affirmed in Christian doctrine, just for that reason and in so far as they are manifold. For if as such they present a knowledge of the Divine Being, each one of them must express something in God not expressed by the others; and if the knowledge is appropriate to the object, then, as the knowledge is composite, the object too must be composite. Indeed, even if these attributes only asserted relations of the Divine to the world, God Himself, like the finite life, could only be understood in a multiplicity of functions; and as these are distinct one from another, and relatively opposed one to another, and at least partly exclusive one of another, God likewise would be placed in the sphere

of contradiction. This does not fulfil the requirements of the speculative reason, and definitions of this kind could not pass for speculative propositions; and just as little could the interests of religion be satisfied if dogmatic definitions were interpreted in this way. For if differentiations were assumed in God, even the feeling of absolute dependence could not be treated as such and as always and everywhere the same. For, in that case, there must be differences having their source in something beyond the difference of the life-moments through which the feeling (of dependence) makes its appearance in the mind. So that while we attribute to these definitions only the meaning stated in our proposition, at the same time everyone retains the liberty, without prejudice to his assent to Christian Doctrine, to attach himself to any form of speculation so long as it allows an object to which the feeling of absolute dependence can relate itself.

3. But as concerns method, in the treatment of Dogmatics up to the present a double procedure is found to predominate. First, rules are put forward as to how one can arrive at right ideas of the divine attributes, and then further, certain rubrics are given under which the various conceptions of divine attributes are to be divided. Now since both aim at systematizing these ideas, the same general assumption has to be made. If the list of these attributes be regarded as a complete summary of definitions to be related to God Himself, then a complete knowledge of God must be derivable from conceptions, and an explanation in due theoretic form would take the place of that ineffability of the Divine Being which the Scriptures—so far as they mention divine attributes—recognize so clearly on every page that we need not quote passages. We have therefore to strive after that completeness alone which guards against letting any of the different moments of the religious self-consciousness pass without asking what are the divine attributes corresponding to them. And with this procedure the classification emerges of its own accord, because in each division only the attributes belonging there can be subjects of exposition. All the more necessary is it to make clear at this point how little is lost for the real matter in hand when we set aside, as we do, the apparatus which has hitherto been employed.

Now we may remark concerning these methods that there are three accepted ways of arriving at the divine attributes—the way of removal of limits (*via eminentiae*), the way of negation or denial (*via negationis*), and the way of causality (*via causalitatis*). Now it is self-evident that these are by no means homogeneous or coordinate. For in the first two a something apart from God must be posited as an at-

tribute; and this, after it has been freed from all limitations, is ascribed to Him, or else its negation is ascribed to Him; while on the other hand causality stands in the closest connexion with the feeling of absolute dependence itself. And if the first two be viewed in their relation to each other, it is clear that negation by itself is no way to posit any attribute, unless something positive remains behind the negation. In that case the negation will consist simply in the fact that the limits of the positive are denied. But in the same manner the way of the removal of limits is a negation, for something is posited of God, but the limits which elsewhere would be co-posited are not posited of God. The identity of these two methods becomes quite obvious in the idea of Infinity, which is at the same time the general form of absence of limits, for what is posited as infinite is also freed from limitation; but at the same time it shows quite generally (by the fact that it is a negation in which nothing is immediately posited but in which everything may be posited which can be thought of as either limited or unlimited) that by negation we can only posit an attribute in so far as something positive remains behind the negation. Both these methods then can only be applied either haphazard with reference to the question whether something, which as such could only be absolutely denied of God, can be conceived as unlimited and posited as a divine attribute; or if this is to be avoided, the application of these methods must be preceded by a definition as to what kind of attribute-conceptions are rightly to be ascribed to God in an unlimited fashion, and what kind simply must be denied of Him. The third method, on the contrary, is certainly an independent one. And even if we do not wish to maintain that all divine attributes corresponding to any modification of our feeling of dependence can equally be derived immediately from the idea of causality, but rather here at the start must premise for one thing that to this conception the other methods must first be applied, *i.e.* that the finitude of causality must be denied and its productivity posited as unlimited; and again, that in so far as a plurality of attributes is developed out of the idea of the divine causality, this differentiation can correspond to nothing real in God; indeed, that neither in isolation nor taken together do the attributes express the Being of God in itself (for the essence of that which has been active can never be known simply from its activity alone)—yet this at least is certain, that all the divine attributes to be dealt with in Christian Dogmatics must somehow go back to the divine causality, since they are only meant to explain the feeling of absolute dependence.

Finally, with regard to the divisions of the divine attributes, their great diversity shows how little certainty attaches to the whole procedure and how little any division has been able to count on general agreement; but of some of them we can here give only brief indications. Some put forward as chief division that into natural (also called metaphysical, which of course in the case of God must be the same thing) and the moral (which of course has a very objectionable sound, since it leads to the inference that the moral attributes do not belong to God in the same way). Others first of all divide all divine attributes into active and inactive; but this is difficult to understand if God cannot be represented otherwise than as living, for in the living as such all is activity. The one class may indeed be described as inhering in God as determinations of the most perfect Substance, which include no activity *ad extra;* yet even the inactive attributes can be thought as possessing a purely inward activity; and in that case this division coincides with another, into absolute and relative attributes. Apart, however, from the fact that the presupposition of a creation in time implies either that the active attributes first came into being along with time or must previously have been inactive (and on this assumption the division is meaningless), the result is always a duality in God—a purely inner life in virtue of the inactive attributes; and a life related to the world in virtue of the active attributes—and as in this way the two classes seem quite separated, still a third class of attributes might seem to be needed to combine them. Only if it be asked which are those inactive attributes, we find that there is really no inner life described by them; in part they are simply formal, as unity, simplicity, eternity; partly, like independence and unchangeability, they are merely negative; and partly, as infinity and immeasurability, they are only the measure and quality of the active attributes. In addition, these divisions turn out not to be exhaustive, since often outside the division isolated attributes are added as inferences, *e.g.* blessedness, glory, majesty, or even that God is the Highest Good. Hence to avoid this kind of thing it at first sight seems commendable that some should from the outset divide the divine attributes into original and derived; and although it is not easy to see how such a division could be made unless the attributes were themselves already given, it might be all the more genuinely dogmatic on that account. Yet, if it be generally conceded that the difference of the attributes is nothing real in God, each attribute is then only another expression for the whole Being of God, which remains always the same; and consequently all are original, and the derived are not attributes at all in the same sense. But if the attributes so divided be developed from the religious self-consciousness, and the

division in this sense be dogmatic, then again there would be no original attribute, but all would equally be very much derived. In fact, however, the division has not arisen from any such view, but from the view which holds that in another respect the Divine Essence alone may be regarded as original, and all the attributes derived. Such a derivation of the divine attributes from the Divine Essence would presuppose the latter as known, and would be a purely speculative proceeding. True, even the purely dogmatic presentation of the attributes can take no other form, except that here nothing can be taken as fundamental save that in the Divine Essence which explains the feeling of absolute dependence. But if the simple expression that "everything depends upon God," is further supplemented by the negative "but He Himself upon nothing," at once a fresh opening is given for a division into positive and negative attributes. And since here in the basis of division the relationship between the highest Essence and all other being is presupposed, it is evident that here absolute or inactive or natural or metaphysical attributes can only be considered as negative, and therefore, strictly taken, without definite content.

4. From this discussion it follows: (*a*) that the presupposition on which the idea is based that those attributes which express God's relation to the world have the appearance of mere additions and accidents, *i.e.* the presupposition of a separation between what God is, in and for Himself, and what He is in relation to the world, is also the source of the idea that the purely internal (*innerlichen*) attributes can only be conceived negatively; (*b*) that the rules laid down to secure the collection of all the divine attributes in one *locus* evoke conceptions which are quite foreign to the interests of religion, and result in a confusion of what it was intended to distinguish. We may hope, therefore, to solve our problem equally well without this apparatus and apart from any such collection if only we treat each individual part of our scheme as adequately as possible. Still, we too shall be able to make use of many of these formulas in our own way. For instance, since we have not to do as yet with the actual manifestation of religious self-consciousness in the form of pleasure and pain, but only with what lies uniformly at the root of these phenomena, *i.e.* with the inner creative disposition towards God-consciousness apart from the consideration whether it is hindered or encouraged, we may call those attributes which come up here "original" in so far as the tendency itself is original, and we may call "derived" those which will come to our notice in the Second Part. And in considering the manifestations of the religious self-consciousness, if we

find that everything which would destroy His presence in us must specially be denied of God, and everything which favours His presence in us specially be affirmed of Him, we can say in our own way that thus divine attributes are formulated by the methods of removal of limits and negation; but those which arise from present observation, and there will be such, are reached by the method of causality. Still, this diverges fairly widely from the general usage of those formulae, which rather betrays an analogy with speculation.

From Friedrich Schleiermacher, *The Christian Faith,* translated by D. M. Baillie et al. (Edinburgh: T. and T. Clark, 1928), 194–200.

≈ One of the most widely used definitions of faith since the mid–twentieth century has been "ultimate concern" as outlined in "What Faith Is" by **Paul Tillich** (1886–1965). Tillich served as an Evangelical Church army chaplain during the First World War, taught at four German universities, and in 1933 fled Nazi Germany to the United States, where he taught at Union Theological Seminary, Harvard University, and the University of Chicago. He was one of the best-known theologians of the twentieth century.

PAUL TILLICH

"What Faith Is," in *Dynamics of Faith*

1. Faith as Ultimate Concern

Faith is the state of being ultimately concerned: the dynamics of faith are the dynamics of man's ultimate concern. Man, like every living being, is concerned about many things, above all about those which condition his very existence, such as food and shelter. But man, in contrast to other living beings, has spiritual concerns—cognitive, aesthetic, social, political. Some of them are urgent, often extremely urgent, and each of them as well as the vital concerns can claim ultimacy for a human life or the life of a social group. If it claims ultimacy it demands the total surrender of him who accepts this claim, and it promises total fulfillment even if all other claims have to be subjected to it or rejected in its name. If a national group makes the life and growth of the nation its ultimate concern, it demands that all other concerns, economic well-being, health and life, family, aesthetic and cognitive truth, justice and humanity, be sacrificed. The extreme nationalisms of our century are laboratories for the study of what ultimate concern means in all aspects of human existence, including the smallest concern of one's daily life. Everything

is centered in the only god, the nation—a god who certainly proves to be a demon, but who shows clearly the unconditional character of an ultimate concern.

But it is not only the unconditional demand made by that which is one's ultimate concern, it is also the promise of ultimate fulfillment which is accepted in the act of faith. The content of this promise is not necessarily defined. It can be expressed in indefinite symbols or in concrete symbols which cannot be taken literally, like the "greatness" of one's nation in which one participates even if one has died for it, or the conquest of mankind by the "saving race," etc. In each of these cases it is "ultimate fulfillment" that is promised, and it is exclusion from such fulfillment which is threatened if the unconditional demand is not obeyed.

An example—and more than an example—is the faith manifest in the religion of the Old Testament. It also has the character of ultimate concern in demand, threat and promise. The content of this concern is not the nation—although Jewish nationalism has sometimes tried to distort it into that—but the content is the God of justice, who, because he represents justice for everybody and every nation, is called the universal God, the God of the universe. He is the ultimate concern of every pious Jew, and therefore in his name the great commandment is given: "You shall love the Lord your God with all your heart, and with all your soul and with all your might" (Deut 6:5). This is what ultimate concern means and from these words the term "ultimate concern" is derived. They state unambiguously the character of genuine faith, the demand of total surrender to the subject of ultimate concern. The Old Testament is full of commands which make the nature of this surrender concrete, and it is full of promises and threats in relation to it. Here also are the promises of symbolic indefiniteness, although they center around fulfillment of the national and individual life, and the threat is the exclusion from such fulfillment through national extinction and individual catastrophe. Faith, for the men of the Old Testament, is the state of being ultimately and unconditionally concerned about Jahweh and about what he represents in demand, threat and promise.

Another example—almost a counter example, yet nevertheless equally revealing—is the ultimate concern with "success" and with social standing and economic power. It is the god of many people in the highly competitive Western culture and it does what every ultimate concern must do: it demands unconditional surrender to its laws even if the price is the sacrifice of genuine human relations, personal conviction and creative *eros.* Its threat is social and economic defeat, and its promise—indefinite as all such promises—the fulfillment of one's being. It is the breakdown of this kind of faith which characterizes and makes religiously important most contemporary literature. Not false calculations but a misplaced faith is revealed in novels like *Point of No Return*. When fulfilled, the promise of this faith proves to be empty.

Faith is the state of being ultimately concerned. The content matters infinitely for the life of the believer, but it does not matter for the formal definition of faith. And this is the first step we have to make in order to understand the dynamics of faith.

2. Faith as a Centered Act

Faith as ultimate concern is an act of the total personality. It happens in the center of the personal life and includes all its elements. Faith is the most centered act of the human mind. It is not a movement of a special section or a special function of man's total being. They all are united in the act of faith. But faith is not the sum total of their impacts. It transcends every special impact as well as the totality of them and it has itself a decisive impact on each of them.

Since faith is an act of the personality as a whole, it participates in the dynamics of personal life. These dynamics have been described in many ways, especially in the recent developments of analytic psychology. Thinking in polarities, their tensions and their possible conflicts, is a common characteristic of most of them. This makes the psychology of personality highly dynamic and requires a dynamic theory of faith as the most personal of all personal acts. The first and decisive polarity in analytic psychology is that between the so-called unconscious and the conscious. Faith as an act of the total personality is not imaginable without the participation of the unconscious elements in the personality structure. They are always present and decide largely about the content of faith. But, on the other hand, faith is a conscious act and the unconscious elements participate in the creation of faith only if they are taken into the personal center which transcends each of them. If this does not happen, if unconscious forces determine the mental status without a centered act, faith does not occur, and compulsions take its place. For faith is a matter of freedom. Freedom is nothing more than the possibility of centered personal acts. The frequent discussion in which faith and freedom are contrasted could be helped by the insight that faith is a free, namely, centered act of the personality. In this respect freedom and faith are identical.

Also important for the understanding of faith is the polarity between what Freud and his school call ego and superego. The concept of the superego is quite ambiguous. On the one hand, it is the basis of all cultural life because it restricts the uninhibited actualization of the always-driving libido; on the other hand, it cuts off man's vital forces, and produces disgust about the whole system of cultural restrictions, and brings about a neurotic state of mind. From this point of view, the symbols of faith are considered to be expressions of the superego or, more concretely, to be an expression of the father image which gives content to the superego. Responsible for this inadequate theory of the superego is Freud's naturalistic negation of norms and principles. If the superego is not established through valid principles, it becomes a suppressive tyrant. But real faith, even if it uses the father image for its expression, transforms this image into a principle of truth and justice to be defended even against the "father." Faith and culture can be affirmed only if the superego represents the norms and principles of reality.

This leads to the question of how faith as a personal, centered act is related to the rational structure of man's personality which is manifest in his meaningful language, in his ability to know the true and to do the good, in his sense of beauty and justice. All this, and not only his possibility to analyze, to calculate and to argue, makes him a rational being. But in spite of this larger concept of reason we must deny that man's essential nature is identical with the rational character of his mind. Man is able to decide for or against reason, he is able to create beyond reason or to destroy below reason. This power is the power of his self, the center of self-relatedness in which all elements of his being are united. Faith is not an act of any of his rational functions, as it is not an act of the unconscious, but it is an act in which both the rational and the nonrational elements of his being are transcended.

Faith as the embracing and centered act of the personality is "ecstatic." It transcends both the drives of the nonrational unconscious and the structures of the rational conscious. It transcends them, but it does not destroy them. The ecstatic character of faith does not exclude its rational character although it is not identical with it, and it includes nonrational strivings without being identical with them. In the ecstasy of faith there is an awareness of truth and of ethical value; there are also past loves and hates, conflicts and reunions, individual and collective influences. "Ecstasy" means "standing outside of oneself"—without ceasing to be oneself—with all the elements which are united in the personal center.

A further polarity in these elements, relevant for the understanding of faith, is the tension between the cognitive function of man's personal life, on the one hand, and emotion and will, on the other hand. In a later discussion I will try to show that many distortions of the meaning of faith are rooted in the attempt to subsume faith to the one or the other of these functions. At this point it must be stated as sharply and insistently as possible that in every act of faith there is cognitive affirmation, not as the result of an independent process of inquiry but as an inseparable element in a total act of acceptance and surrender. This also excludes the idea that faith is the result of an independent act of "will to believe." There is certainly affirmation by the will of what concerns one ultimately, but faith is not a creation of the will. In the ecstasy of faith the will to accept and to surrender is an element, but not the cause. And this is true also of feeling. Faith is not an emotional outburst: this is not the meaning of ecstasy. Certainly, emotion is in it, as in every act of man's spiritual life. But emotion does not produce faith. Faith has a cognitive content and is an act of the will. It is the unity of every element in the centered self. Of course, the unity of all elements in the act of faith does not prevent one or the other element from dominating in a special form of faith. It dominates the character of faith but it does not create the act of faith.

This also answers the question of a possible psychology of faith. Everything that happens in man's personal being can become an object of psychology. And it is rather important for both the philosopher of religion and the practical minister to know how the act of faith is embedded in the totality of psychological processes. But in contrast to this justified and desirable form of a psychology of faith there is another one which tries to derive faith from something that is not faith but is most frequently fear. The presupposition of this method is that fear or something else from which faith is derived is more original and basic than faith. But this presupposition cannot be proved. On the contrary, one can prove that in the scientific method which leads to such consequences faith is already effective. Faith precedes all attempts to derive it from something else, because these attempts are themselves based on faith.

From Paul Tillich, *Dynamics of Faith* (New York: Harper and Brothers Publishers, 1957), 1–8.

In *The Letter on Apologetics* (1896), **Maurice Blondel** (1861–1949) argues for an apologetics that would take into account the

understandings of both the believing and the unbelieving philosopher. In *History and Dogma* (first published as a series of articles in *La quinzaine* in 1904) he explains historicism as a confusion between "real history" and "scientific history." His thinking about the relationships between the sciences, history, and theology was part of the early-twentieth-century Roman Catholic revival movement that eventually led to the Church's Second Vatican Council (1962–65).

MAURICE BLONDEL

The Letter on Apologetics

4. Of the persuasiveness and the philosophical insufficiency of apologetics based on the moral and intellectual fittingness of Christianity

. . . When a man has the faith, practises what he believes and embraces in reflection the whole meaning of his belief and his activity, then the circle is closed, there is no room for doubt and the proof is complete.

But to reach this result one must start from the fact of the Christian life—whereas the great need of apologetics today is to start from the fact of a theoretical and practical incredulity. One must suppose the supernatural *as present in one's life,* using a hypothesis which absolutely transcends the philosophical field, if one is to find the expression of it *reflected in one's thought*—whereas one must suppose the supernatural *absent from one's life* in order to show that it is *postulated by thought and action.* And for those who have not the truth, while believing themselves to have it, for those above all who are honestly seeking it, for the beggar and the hungry who stand at the door of the feast, there is something meaningless and even irritating about such an inventory of spiritual treasures, of which they know nothing, or which they consider imaginary, and about the use of unfamiliar language full of complacent sentiments which wake no echo in their own hearts.

But there is something of greater importance to be said by way of ending this discussion. Our reason has not the same lights or the same duties *before* the decisive act of faith and *after* it, but it remains true that the alternatives between which we must choose are bound up with one another. *After* the act of faith, human co-operation remains coextensive with the primary and gratuitous activity of God; thus there is still a natural life to be found even in the supernatural life. *Before* the act of faith, God's secret summons does not leave man's reason and will in a state of legitimate indifference or innocent and definitive neutrality; we must therefore necessarily take account of what might be called the supernatural insufficiency of human nature. And since the refusal of the state to which he is called is not a mere privation for man but a positive falling away, it must be possible to discover, even in a life which is closed against faith, something of what it rejects.

So undoubtedly it is not only desirable in the interests of apologetics for these questions not to be considered simply from the point of view of believers, since (to repeat) it is chiefly important to say something which matters for the unbelieving philosopher, but perhaps it is also more in keeping with the complexity of Christian doctrine, which controls and judges every form of human life, to embrace all minds in one's scope and to theorize about the *absence* of faith in men's souls as well as its *presence*. This becomes all the more necessary when we reflect that by putting ourselves in the place of the unbeliever we are profitably informed about that road which, within faith itself, leads us still more to faith, by showing us on what terms, and at what cost, we acquire it and preserve it.

From Maurice Blondel, *"The Letter on Apologetics" and "History and Dogma,"* translated by Alexander Dru and Illtyd Trethowan (New York: Holt, Rinehart, and Winston, 1964), 140–41.

MAURICE BLONDEL

History and Dogma

II. Incomplete and Incompatible Solutions

2. Historicism

We are asked to put our trust without prejudice or mental reserve in the testimony of history, as though it would produce an irresistibly strong proof of Christianity. But in the first place what are we to understand by this autonomy, and what is the normal relation of history with the other sciences? This preliminary question is an essential one; for the critical spirit does not consist solely in displaying sagacity in the detailed study of texts or in the interpretation of testimonies, in *criticizing our knowledge;* it consists in asking what a particular science or science in general can or cannot do, in a word it consists *in the critique of knowledge itself.* The scholar is only master in his own domain by virtue of a clear consciousness of its limits, of its entrances and exits, of its active and passive obligations.

Now, in what sense can one say that history is independent? Can one pretend that it is self-sufficient? Obviously not;

it depends upon a number of other sciences, and no one denies it. Can one claim at least that, thanks to that assistance, it reaches doctrinal conclusions of which it remains, in the last resort, the judge, and which attain to the total reality? Once again, no; inevitably it remains dependent upon ulterior problems, upon sciences superior to it, which it can neither supplant nor replace except by a usurpation and by falsely proclaiming itself a sort of total metaphysics, a universal vision, a *Weltanschauung:* no one, it would seem, explicitly maintains that the historical synthesis sums up and dominates all the sciences, and that a speculative and dogmatic science is illusory and superfluous. So how are we to define the proper role of history and its relations with the connected sciences? It is here that the question is seen to be decisive, because it brings two conceptions of science to grips with one another, an ancient and a modern.

According to the Aristotelian doctrine, and to all those which can be affiliated to it, the sciences differ from one another as do different genera; they have their respective principles and their distinct objects; each one, master in its own house, freely pursues its task. There is no intelligible relation between the principles of the different sciences, for one does not go behind principles which are accepted on the evidence with which they appear; no legitimate transition from one genus to another is possible. Only the general principles of reason allow of a formal and extrinsic juxtaposition of these sciences and their results: each one of them adds its contingent of absolute truths to the sum total of knowledge; each one of them privately resolves a fraction of the problems raised by the study of things, and each therefore contributes a piece of reality itself; there is discontinuity in the work of the mind, contiguity in the objective results. For example, the historian purely as such performs his task behind his partition; he carries out his researches from his own point of view; and his labour finally furnishes a slice of real life and of absolute truth. Others must put up as best they can with his conclusions, which are what they are: so much the worse if they contradict other conclusions; for, if the facts are what they are said to be, they cannot be contradicted, and the historian is master in his own house and cannot be taken to task except by his peers. He has yielded up his fragment of ontology, and he owes neither more nor less. It is for the other scientists to carry out their tasks correctly; and the various pieces together will form a concert, like musicians who, without seeing or hearing one another, play the different parts of a symphony in proper time. On that view, the sciences appear to be independent in their researches and bound by their mutual results; they are obliged to find the necessary conclusions freely and in isolation, compelled as they are to agree with one another without having previous consultations; and this takes place, throughout, in a sphere of realist affirmations, which allow of no concessions, and provoke irreconcilable conflicts and contradictions.

The more recent conception of science and the sciences, however, is entirely different; and this conception, quite independently of the speculative justification which it possesses, seems to have demonstrated its soundness by its success. Just as algebra fertilized geometry, and mathematics physics, so the various scientific spheres are in perpetual communication. One must try to recapture the basic idea revealed to the critical mind under the all too often idolatrous names of determinism and universal solidarity; to the critical mind there is no question of affirming, from a metaphysical point of view, the subordination or fusion of beings in an absolute monism; it is simply a question, from a logical point of view, of grasping the unity of the problem of knowledge, and of understanding that the problem of existence cannot be asked except in relation to the total activity of the mind and of the combined data of the various sciences: these sciences differ, therefore, less in respect of the diversity of their objects, which they help to make known in their ultimate reality, than in the diversity of methods and points of view opening on to an ulterior problem which they collaborate to define, to prepare and to posit rather than to resolve in its entirety; there is continuity and solidarity in the work of the mind; there is heterogeneity in the points of view and in the bearing of scientific affirmations; there is subordination of all the relative scientific data to the fundamental problems and the final solutions. Furthermore, none of the particular sciences claims to be sole mistress in its own house; none will remain in irreducible contradiction with its neighbour, because none of them produces anything ultimate, each having to compete with the other to furnish the data of that moral and religious metaphysical problem which it would be rash and precipitate to discuss fragmentarily or to solve piecemeal.

On what conditions can the critical mind, particularly where history is concerned, remain harmless, beneficial and, in a word, faithful to the genuine inspiration of which it is born? On condition that it keeps its researches perpetually dependent upon the ultimate questions which it has not the competence to decide by itself or, indeed, at all; for while the historian has, as it were, a word to say in everything concerning man, there is nothing on which he has the last word. What is, in fact, the object or rather the aspect which be-

longs to history, in the technical and contemporary sense of the word? Everything in the social life of mankind which can be verified or testified to, and everything which, with these facts as the basis of induction, is an explanation of the *fieri* of mankind, and a definition of the laws of its continuous and continual movement. The historian attempts first of all to become the perpetual contemporary of vanished ages and to picture them as might a universal witness, with the help of a detailed and synthetic view of the whole series which no partial or passing spectator could embrace; he then proposes to reintegrate scientifically, not the reality of life itself, but as intelligible an expression as possible of that reality and an explanation of the determinism which—to all appearances—links together the successive moments.

What, then, does the historian see; and what must he realize that he does not see from his own point of view? What he sees is all that aspect under which humanity allows its inward invisible work to be grasped in observable manifestations—manifestations which modify one another mutually, continually undergoing the repercussion of facts upon man, even of those most remote from him, and forming no doubt a coherent whole, though without supplying a total and satisfying explanation of the smallest detail; no more should the apparent continuity of the cinematograph allow the spectator to forget the necessity of repeated interruptions. What the historian does not see, and what he must recognize as escaping him, is the spiritual reality, the activity of which is not wholly represented or exhausted by the historical phenomena (although the latter can be determined like a complete picture subsisting apart from the original). It remains true that the historian has to make the determinist explanation as intelligible and complete as possible—but it remains equally true that it is his duty to leave the issue open or even to open it as widely as possible to the realist explanation which lies always beneath.

It should never be supposed therefore that history by itself can know a fact which would be no more than a fact, and that would be the whole fact: each link in the chain, and the chain as a whole, involve the psychological and moral problems implied by the least action or testimony. It is easy enough to see why. Real history is composed of human lives; and human life is metaphysics in act. To claim to constitute the science of history without any speculative preoccupation, or even to suppose that the humblest details of history could be, in the strict sense of the word, a simple matter of observation, is to be influenced by prejudices on the pretext of attaining to an impossible neutrality—prejudices such as everyone inevitably has so long as he has not attained a conscious view of his own attitude of mind and subjected the postulates on which his researches are based to a methodical criticism. In default of an explicit philosophy, a man ordinarily has an unconscious one. And what one takes for simple observations of fact are often simply constructions. The observer, the narrator, is always more or less of a poet; for behind what he sees the witness puts an action and a soul so as to give the fact a meaning; behind the witness and his testimony, if they are really to enter history, the critic puts an interpretation, a relation, a synthesis; behind these critical data the historian inserts a general view and wider human preoccupations; which is to say that man with his beliefs, his metaphysical ideas, and his religious solutions conditions all the subordinate researches of science as much as he is conditioned by them.

Aristotle's remarks in this connection are as true as ever: "If we must not philosophize, very well, we cannot avoid philosophizing about that." Doubt is only methodical and scientific if it is provisional, if it leads to positive results, if, as in Descartes' case, it raises the whole problem in its entirety, if it allows one to verify results by one another, and to control facts and solutions alternately. Each science is therefore only a perspective opening on to others, controlling them and controlled by them, only a way of looking at that concrete reality in which alone the different lines of approach can be held together, an alternating rhythm of life and reflection, of action and thought, which enlighten, determine and prove one another mutually. So long as a science recognizes itself as an abstraction bound up with a thought and a life from which it borrows its material, it is useful and legitimate. But the moment it claims to isolate itself as an abstraction, the moment a science concludes from its independence within its own field of research to a sort of self-sufficiency, it becomes guilty of fraudulently converting a simple method of work into a negative and tyrannical doctrine. Willynilly it is led into the subtly crude illusion that because it is legitimate and necessary to divide the work of the mind, the divisions subsist in the reality.

No doubt the historian will sometimes be tempted to declare that he only wishes to remain modestly on his own ground, that one should be grateful to him for not trespassing on any reserved territory, and that so long as he respects and recognizes, as a man, the results furnished by other scholars in their isolated seclusion, he has perhaps the right to cultivate his own garden undisturbed. But I propose the following paradoxical answer to his systematic abstention: that this absolute reserve ends, without his wishing it or even knowing it, in a usurpation: the only way of remaining lawfully on

one's own ground in such cases is to open all the doors and windows on to horizons other than one's own; never to lose sight of the essential truth that "technical and critical history," in the precise and scientific sense of the words, is not "real history," the substitute for the life of humanity, the totality of historical truths, and that between these two histories, of which one is a science and the other a life, one resulting from a phenomenological method and the other tending to represent genuine reality, there is an abyss.

The danger to which I am calling attention under the name of *"historicism"* lies in the alternation between "real history" and "scientific history" or the substitution of one for the other, the result of an infinitesimal oscillation which is constantly producing statements of an equivocal nature, both true and false at the same time, and makes the attentive reader see, as it were, double. At one moment he is in the realm of abstractions, and he is told that it would be presumption to solve dogmatic problems or to trespass on the domain of psychology and metaphysics—in a sense an irreproachable attitude. At the next moment (or indeed at the same moment) the affirmations of the moral or theological order, which equally claim to be historical interpretations of the facts, are set aside as impossible to discuss or even to conceive; and then it is no longer a question of a methodological critique or of scientific abstraction but of conclusions consistent and complete enough to occupy the whole field and to claim the right to formulate basic exclusions, just as a person suffering from strabism ends by totally eliminating the vision of the weaker eye from his field of consciousness to the advantage of the stronger.

We can now see the complicated mechanism which has produced this result. The mixture of two philosophies, of two ages of scientific thought, leads one unconsciously to superimpose the critical spirit (perfectly innocent of this abuse, which it has a perfect right to denounce as unfaithful to its principles) on a foundation of older conceptions (quite foreign to the distinctions and reserves of modern science); from which it follows that positive history is transformed into negative theology. It is therefore supremely important to analyse that subtle mixture and to isolate the elements whose combination masks and aggravates its noxious character. [. . .]

III. The Vital Role and the Philosophical Basis of Tradition

[. . .] At the outset we were faced by two antagonistic and even irreconcilable attitudes, each full of dangers and difficulties; two theses incapable of limiting or correcting themselves or of supporting and completing one another. And yet each of them contributed truths which cannot and must not be ignored. That, in a word, is the crisis. If, then, it is conceded that a conception of Tradition obtained with the help of a philosophy of action provides us with the light which we need, the means of reconciling these opposite theses and of giving life to opposed methods, perhaps it will also be recognized that a similar solution could be applied to analogous conflicts, even if such an enterprise provoked contradictory accusations which indicate rather its complex equilibrium than any departure from orthodoxy. As against those who offer us a Christianity so divine that there is nothing human, living or moving about it, and those who involve it so deeply in historical contingencies and make it so dependent upon natural factors that it retains nothing but a diffused sort of divinity, one must show it to be both more concrete and more universal, more divine and more human, than words can express. Because there is a living unity in Christianity, because it is the whole of man, the various sciences can only split it up by a provisional abstraction. A separate dogmatic theology, a separate exegesis, a separate history, necessarily remain incomplete: a conception which isolates the sciences without making them autonomous must be replaced by a view which grants them their autonomy all the more readily because it never allows them to be isolated.

One realizes through the practice of Christianity that its dogmas are rooted in reality. One has no right to set the facts on one side and the theological data on the other without going back to the sources of life and of action, finding the indivisible synthesis; the facts and definitions are simply faithful translations of it into different languages. The link between facts and beliefs can never be rationally justified by scholarship or dialectics, as though each human reason separately performed its dogmatic task. To succeed in that justification one must consider not only the efforts of each man, but the consensus of all who live the same life and share in the same love. That is why definitions of doctrine are not so much innovations as the authentic recognition of collective anticipations and of collective certifications. Christian practice nourishes man's knowledge of the divine and bears within its action what is progressively discerned by the theologian's initiative. The synthesis of dogma and facts is scientifically effected because there is a synthesis of thought and grace in the life of the believer, a union of man and God, reproducing in the individual consciousness the history of Christianity itself. And while it is true that Christian knowledge does not disdain the support of history (for the facts in this instance

are both the redemptive reality and the revelatory message), history cannot, without leading to the shipwreck of faith, disregard Christian knowledge, by which I mean the results methodically acquired by the collective experience of Christ verified and realized in us. It can no longer be held that the part which it plays in the inner life of each Christian is simply a matter of individual psychology: as long as it is not clearly realized that in addition to dogmatic theology and exegesis there is a knowledge, a real science of action, capable of extracting, for the benefit of an experimental and progressive theology, the lessons which life draws from history, there will always be recurrent conflicts or interferences or mutual ostracism. The Church has an age-old experience of that science, although the theology of it has not been worked out; and that is why she alone is competent to form in souls the authentic Christ. And when she proposes the God-Man for our adoration no one can legitimately make out, by whatever indirect suggestion, that she is guilty of a substitution of persons.

From Maurice Blondel, *"The Letter on Apologetics" and "History and Dogma,"* translated by Alexander Dru and Illtyd Trethowan (New York: Holt, Rinehart, and Winston, 1964), 233–39, 286–87.

Orthodox/Neo-orthodox

In "Christ the Centre of the Form of Revelation," **Hans Urs Von Balthasar** (1905–88) links the plausibility of Christianity to that of Christ. In this sense, the "objective evidence" of the Christian religion is the recognizable correspondence of human existence as a whole to the form of Christ. This Swiss Catholic theologian, a scholar of literature and a prolific author, is best known for his fifteen-volume trilogy: a theological aesthetics on divine glory, a theo-drama on the drama of salvation, and a theo-logic on human knowing and the doctrine of Scripture.

HANS URS VON BALTHASAR

"Christ the Centre of the Form of Revelation," in *The Glory of the Lord: A Theological Aesthetics*

Plausibility

The expression the "centre of the form of revelation" does not refer to a particular section of this form however central which, in order to be read as form, would then essentially need to be filled out by other more peripheral aspects.

What the phrase is intended to denote is, rather, the reality which lends the form its total coherence and comprehensibility, the "wherefore" to which all particular aspects have to be referred if they are to be understood. The fact that Christ is this centre—and not, for instance, merely the beginning, the initiator of an historical form which then develops autonomously—is rooted in the particular character of the Christian religion and in its difference from all other religions. Judaism has no such centre: neither Abraham, nor Moses, nor one of the Prophets, is the figure around which everything else is ordered. Christ, by contrast, is the form because he is the content. This holds absolutely, for he is the only Son of the Father, and whatever he establishes and institutes has its meaning only through him, is dependent only on him and is kept vital only by him. If for a single moment we were to look away from him and attempt to consider and understand the Church as an autonomous form, the Church would not have the slightest plausibility. It would be plausible neither as a religious institution (for its sacraments and the *diakonia* [service] belonging to them are "bearable" only as modes by which the living *Kyrios* [Lord] is present) nor as an historical power for order and culture in the sense of the *Action Française* and of the German Catholic Nazis. On the contrary, seen in this way it loses all credibility, and for this reason the Church Fathers often compared the Church's light with the light of the moon, borrowed from the sun and showing its relativity most clearly in its phases. The plausibility of Christianity stands and falls with Christ's, something which has in essence always been acknowledged. For even the doctrine of the *notae Ecclesiae* [marks of the Church] has never seriously been intended to be taken in isolation from Christology: the *notae* are the properties which are exacted by Christ's promises and which can be discovered in history as the fulfilment of Christ and as proofs of his living power.

To support such an edifice, the foundation must be of indestructible solidity. It must not be constructed in such a way that on it only probabilities can be erected: it must offer hard evidence, and not subjective but objective evidence. At this crossroads many will be inclined to part ways with us, and for this reason we must render a precise account of what we mean by "objective evidence." It is the kind of evidence that emerges and sheds its light from the phenomenon itself, and not the sort of evidence that is recognised in the process of satisfying the subject's needs. The form that we encounter historically is convincing in itself because the light by which it illumines us radiates from the form itself and proves itself with compelling force to be just such a light that springs from the object itself. Naturally, this does not mean that the form must enlighten just *anyone,* or that this someone must not fulfil and bring along prerequisites which are just as specific as, for instance, those expected (in a wholly different field) from an atomic physicist if he is to understand certain formulas of his science, or from an art historian if he is to recognise the quality of a Teniers and tell it apart from counterfeits. As is clear from these examples, the subjective conditions can be varied and sophisticated; but no one will ever argue that it is a person's formation that actually produces the law of physics or the beauty and value of the work of art. The fact that Christ "says nothing to me" in no way prejudices the fact that, in and of himself, Christ says everything to everyone. And what is involved here is not, as in individual sciences, the mere technical adaptation to the thought-patterns and conceptual dialect of this particular branch of knowledge. What is at stake, rather, is the correspondence of human existence as a whole to the form of Christ. Not only intellectual but also existential prerequisites must be fulfilled in order that the form that makes its claim on one's total existence may also find a hearing in this total existence. So much must be granted at once to the so-called "method of immanence" of Blondel and his followers and, today, to the school of Bultmann.

But this is also where we encounter a sharp divide. The subjective condition of the possibility of seeing an object for what it is (a condition which can be very far-reaching) ought never ever to intrude upon the constitution of the object's objective evidence, or simply to condition this evidence and thus be substituted for it. In theology, even the most existential form of Kantianism must distort and thus fail to see the phenomenon. Not even the scholastic axiom *quidquid recipitur, secundum modum recipientis recipitur* (which in modern terminology would mean that the object requires a categorical or existential prior understanding) can blunt this assertion. For, if Christ is what he claims to be, then he cannot be so dependent on subjective conditions as to be hindered by these from making himself wholly understandable to man nor, contrariwise, can man, without his grace, supply the sufficient conditions of receiving him with full understanding. The prior understanding is fundamentally not something which the subject applies as a contribution to Christian knowledge: it is something which arises necessarily from the simple and objective fact that God becomes man and, to this extent, corresponds to the universal human forms of existence and of thought. But, within these universal forms, God can make known that which he specifically is only on his own initiative.

There will be time later to say and take to heart many things concerning the facilitating manner in which Christ's Gospel—that is, Christ's form—can and should be presented and proclaimed by the Church to each age, including our own. All this has its quite proper importance, especially in keeping us from turning relative forms and patterns of thought from the past of the Church's history into screens that hide the form of Christ. But in respect of our present discussion of the central core of the form of revelation such considerations are wholly unimportant and irrelevant. If the form of Christ itself is what it shows itself to be *of itself,* then no particular age or culture can of itself be privileged in respect of this phenomenon. The decisively illumining factor must lie in the phenomenon itself, and this in two senses. First, in the sense that the figure which Christ forms has in itself an interior rightness and evidential power such as we find—in another, wholly worldly realm—in a work of art or in a mathematical principle. And, second, in the sense that this rightness, which resides within the reality of the thing itself, also possesses the power to illumine the perceiving person by its own radiant light, and this not simply intellectually but in a manner which transforms man's existence. Now, the evidential power (which is, admittedly, of a very special kind) lies in the phenomenon itself and demands a theological act of seeing the form. But it would be insufficient to limit this evidence, as has become customary nowadays, to the power of the grace that transforms existence and produces faith. This is usually the result of opposing a Jesus of history, who is perceived with anything but overwhelming clarity, to a Christ of the community's and the individual's faith. To this we will have to return later. But here we must say at least the following: such an either/or misses precisely the point which is here at stake and which alone can provide the bridge between the "historical-critical method" of an obstinate historical scientism (to which apparently only the theologians cling any more and which understandably can never attain to vision since it is already methodologically blind) and the way of faith which, because of the definition of faith it presupposes, is in no better position to attain to real vision. The "historical-critical" destruction of the form put forward by the Evangelists, for instance, only makes sense as an exercise if one supposes that faith (and the Evangelists are believers along with the whole primitive community) as such can only be subjective and cannot correspond to any objective evidence. And it is indeed fully consistent with this view that the "historical-critical" researchers are quite incapable of perceiving the objective form which the Gospels propose:

this is because, on the basis of the same prejudice, they do not even bother to look but, in advance, posit an objective and unknown *x* as motivation for the proposed form. This much only lest the impression should arise that the "historical-critical" method is the only "scientific" method, and lest the description of a form (which, it has been shown, cannot be constructed as a whole out of parts) should be dismissed *a priori* as unscientific popular theology. What unscientific bunglers Burckhardt, Wölfflin and the great portrayers of historical forms must then have been!

The first prerequisite for understanding is to accept what is given just as it offers itself. If certain excisions are practised on the Gospel from the outset, the integrity of the phenomenon is lost and it has already become incomprehensible. The Gospel presents Christ's form in such a way that "flesh" and "spirit," Incarnation to the point of suffering and death, and resurrected life are all interrelated down to the smallest details. If the Resurrection is excised, then not only certain things but simply everything about Jesus' earthly life becomes incomprehensible. Or if we understand the Risen Lord as merely the "Christ of faith," without an interior identity with the Jesus of history, then once again the whole form becomes incomprehensible. The first, earthly form is legible only if we see that it is to be wholly "used up" in death and resurrection. But death and resurrection (which constitute a strict ideal unity) are comprehensible only if they are understood as the transformation of this earthly form by God's power, and not as the form's spiritualisation and apotheosis. Neither the one nor the other half is the "Word of God," but both halves together, and both together only to the extent that the Word is understood from the outset as the bearer of the Spirit, and the Spirit as the spiritualiser and transfigurer of the Word and, thus, as the Spirit both of the Word and of the one who has spoken (sent) the Word. Or if the trinitarian dimension is excluded from the objective form of revelation, then again everything becomes incomprehensible. Not the smallest plausible interconnection is then retained, because each element is plausible only within the wholeness of the image.

From Hans Urs Von Balthasar, *The Glory of the Lord: A Theological Aesthetics,* vol. 1, *Seeing the Form,* translated by Erasmo Leiva-Merikakis (London: T. and T. Clark, 1982), 463–67.

☙ In "The Righteousness of God," a public address delivered in 1916, dialectical theologian **Karl Barth** (1886–1968) compares the righteousness of the "wholly other" God with humankind's unrighteousness and capacity for complacent self-delusion. This selection is the conclusion of his address.

KARL BARTH
"The Righteousness of God"

This then is the inner situation in which we come upon the quite pointless question whether God is righteous. The righteousness of God becomes preposterously a problem and a subject for discussion. In the war it has become a "real question" again. There is now hardly a community in all the country round in which, noisily or quietly, roughly or delicately, this question is not mooted; and it is mooted, fundamentally, in us all: If God were righteous, could he then "permit" all that is now happening in the world?

A pointless question? Absolutely so, if it refers to God, the living God. For the living God never for a moment manifests himself in our conscience except as a righteous God. When we see him as he is and when he asks us to recognize and accept him as he is, is it not pointless to ask, Art Thou righteous? A very pointed and correct and weighty question it is, however, when we refer it to the god to whom in our pride and despair we have erected the tower of Babel; to the great personal or impersonal, mystical, philosophical, or naïve Background and Patron Saint of our human righteousness, morality, state, civilization, or religion. If it is he we mean, we are quite right in asking, Is God righteous? For the answer is soon given. It is our calamity, a calamity from which there is no possibility of rescue or release, that with a thousand arts we have made ourselves a god in our own image and must now own him—a god to whom one must put such comfortless questions and receive such comfortless answers. In the question, Is God righteous? our whole tower of Babel falls to pieces. In this now burning question it becomes evident that we are looking for a righteousness without God, that we are looking, in truth, for a god without God and against God—and that our quest is hopeless. It is clear that such a god is not God. He is not even righteous. He cannot prevent his worshipers, all the distinguished European and American apostles of civilization, welfare, and progress, all zealous citizens and pious Christians, from falling upon one another with fire and sword to the amazement and derision of the poor heathen in India and Africa. This god is really an unrighteous god, and it is high time for us to declare ourselves thorough-going doubters, sceptics, scoffers, and atheists in regard to him. It is high time for us to confess freely and gladly: this god, to whom we have built the tower of Babel, is not God. He is an idol. He is dead.

God himself, the real, the living God, and his love which comes in glory! These provide the solution. We have not yet begun to listen quietly to what the conscience asks when it reminds us, in our need and anxiety, of the righteousness of God. We have been much too eager to do something ourselves. Much too quickly we have made ourselves comfortable in temporary structures. We have mistaken our tent for our home; the moratorium for the normal course of things. We have prayed, Thy will be done! and meant by it, Thy will be done not just now! We have believed in an eternal life, but what we took for eternal life and satisfied ourselves upon was really only temporary. And for this reason we have remained the same as we were. And unrighteousness has remained. And the righteousness of God has disappeared from our eyes. And God himself has become to us dubious, for in his place there has stood the questionable figment of our own thoughts.

There is a fundamentally different way to come into relation with the righteousness of God. This other way we enter not by speech nor reflection nor reason, but by being still, by listening to and not silencing the conscience when we have hardly begun to hear its voice. When we let conscience speak to the end, it tells us not only that there is something else, a righteousness above unrighteousness, but also—and more important—that this something else for which we long and which we need is God. He is right and not we! His righteousness is an eternal righteousness! This is difficult for us to hear. We must take the trouble to go far enough off to hear it again. We make a veritable uproar with our morality and culture and religion. But we may presently be brought to silence, and with that will begin our true redemption.

It will then be, above all, a matter of our recognizing God once more as God. It is easy to say recognize. But recognizing is an ability won only in fierce inner personal conflict. It is a task beside which all cultural, moral, and patriotic duties, all efforts in "applied religion," are child's play. For here one must give himself up in order to give himself over to God, that God's will may be done. To do his will, however, means to begin with him anew. His will is not a corrected continuation of our own. It approaches ours as a Wholly Other. There is nothing for our will except a basic re-creation. Not a reformation but a re-creation and re-growth. For the will to which the conscience points is purity, goodness, truth, and brotherhood as the perfect will of God. It is a will which knows no subterfuges, reservations, nor preliminary compromises. It is a will with character, a will blessed and holy through and through. It is the righteousness of God. In its presence the first need is for humility. Have we enough humility? May we take it for granted and go on to tower-building of various sorts? In taking it for granted, have we yet begun to practice it?

And then a second consideration: in place of despair a childlike joyfulness will come; a joy that God is so much greater than we thought. Joy that his righteousness has far more depth and meaning than we had allowed ourselves to dream. Joy that from God much more is to be expected for our poor, perplexed, and burdened life than with our idealism, our principles, and our Christianity we had dared to hope. More to be *expected!* We ought not to scatter our emotions as we do to every wind. We ought not so gratuitously to confuse our hearts by the continual building of towers of Babel. We ought not to waste our faith on these things— only to convince ourselves and others of our want of faith. We ought not to put our most fruitful moments to second-best uses in the belief that it is the way of piety and wisdom to pursue men's thoughts rather than God's. We ought to apply ourselves with all our strength to expect more from God, to let grow within us that which he will in fact cause to grow, to accept what indeed he constantly offers us, watching and praying that we may respond to his originative touch. As children to take joy in the great God and his righteousness, and to trust all to him! Have we joy enough? Are the springs which might be flowing really flowing so abundantly? Have we barely yet begun to feel the true creative joy of God's presence?

In the Bible this humility and this joy are called—faith. Faith means seeking not noise but quiet, and letting God speak within—the righteous God, for there is no other. And then God works in us. Then begins in us, as from a seed, but an unfailing seed, the new basic something which overcomes unrighteousness. Where faith is, in the midst of the old world of war and money and death, there is born a new spirit out of which grows a new world, the world of the righteousness of God. The need and anxiety in which we live are done away when this new beginning comes. The old fetters are broken, the false idols begin to totter. For now something real has happened—the only real thing that can happen: God has now taken his own work in hand. "I beheld Satan as lightning fall from heaven." Life receives its meaning again—your own life and life as a whole. Lights of God rise in the darkness, and powers of God become real in weakness. Real love, real sincerity, real progress become possible; morality and culture, state and nation, even religion and the church now become possible—now for the first time! One is taken with

the vision of an immortality or even of a future life here on earth in which the righteous will of God breaks forth, prevails, and is done as it is done in heaven. In such wise the righteousness of God, far, strange, high, becomes our own possession and our great hope.

The inner way, the way of simple faith, is the way of Christ. A greater than Moses and a greater than John the Baptist is here. He is the love of God, glorified before the world was and forever glorified. Can one say that humanity has exhausted the possibilities of his way? We have received from Jesus many different truths. But the simplest of them all we have the least comprehended—that he was the Son of God and that we, if we will, may go with him the way wherein one simply believes that the Father's will is truth and must be done. One may object that this method of squaring the circle is childlike and inadequate. I grant it. But this childlike and inadequate solution is the beginning of the vast plan of God. It remains to be seen whether the quaking of the tower of Babel which we are now experiencing will be violent enough to bring us somewhat nearer to the way of *faith*. Opportunity offers. We may take the new way. Or we may not. Sooner or later we shall. There is no other.

From Karl Barth, *The Word of God and the Word of Man,* translated by Douglas Horton (Gloucester, MA: Peter Smith, 1978), 21–27.

Existentialist/Phenomenological

Søren Kierkegaard (1813–55), a Danish philosopher and master of the pseudonymous treatise, used paradox to reveal the precarious side of religious belief. In his "The Contemporary Follower" (1844), Kierkegaard posits a god who takes the form of a servant. Kierkegaard then asks if a learner contemporary to that god would have an advantage over a learner who lives subsequent to the god's departure.

SØREN KIERKEGAARD
"The Contemporary Follower"

The god did not, however, take the form of a servant in order to mock human beings; his aim, therefore, cannot be to walk through the world in such a way that not one single person would come to know it. Presumably he will allow something about himself to be understood, although any accommodation made for the sake of comprehensibility still does not essentially help the person who does not receive the condition, and therefore it is actually elicited from him only under constraint and against his will, and it may just as well alienate the learner as draw him closer. He humbled himself and took the form of a servant,[406] but he certainly did not come to live as a servant in the service of some particular person, carrying out his tasks without letting his master or his co-workers realize who he was—wrath such as that we dare not ascribe to the god. Thus the fact that he was in the form of a servant means only that he was a lowly human being, a lowly man who did not set himself off from the human throng either by soft raiment[407] or by any other earthly advantage and was not distinguishable to other human beings, not even to the countless legions of angels[408] he left behind when he humbled himself. But even though he was a lowly man, his concerns were not those that men generally have. He went his way unconcerned about administering and distributing the goods of this world; he went his way as one who owns nothing and wishes to own nothing, as unconcerned about his living as the birds of the air,[409] as unconcerned about house and home as someone who has no hiding place or nest[410] and is not looking for such a place. He was unconcerned about accompanying the dead to their graves,[411] was not attracted by the things that commonly attract the attention of people, was not tied to any woman, so enthralled by her as to want to please her, but sought only the follower's love. All this seems very beautiful, but is it also proper? Does he not thereby elevate himself above what is ordinarily the condition of human beings? Is it right for a human being to be as carefree as the bird and not even fly hither and thither for food as the bird does? Should he not even think of tomorrow? We are unable to poetize the god otherwise, but what does a fiction prove? Is it permissible to wander around erratically like this, stopping wherever evening finds one?[412] The question is this: May a human being express the same thing?—for otherwise the god has not realized the essentially human. Yes, if he is capable of it, he may also do it. If he can become so absorbed in the service of the spirit that it never occurs to him to provide for food and drink, if he is sure that the lack will not divert him, that the hardship will not disorder his body and make him regret that he did not first of all understand the lessons of childhood before wanting to understand more—yes, then he truly may do it, and his greatness is even more glorious than the quiet assurance of the lily.[413]

This exalted absorption in his work will already have drawn to the teacher the attention of the crowd, among whom the learner presumably will be found, and such a person will presumably belong to the humbler class of people,

for the wise and the learned will no doubt first submit sophistic questions to him, invite him to colloquia or put him through an examination, and after that guarantee him a tenured position and a living.

So we now have the god walking around in the city in which he made his appearance (which one is inconsequential); to proclaim his teaching is for him the one and only necessity of his life, is for him his food and drink.[414] To teach people is his work, and to be concerned about the learners is for him relaxation from his work. He has no friends and no relatives, but to him the learner is brother and sister.[415] It is easy to see that very soon a rumor will be fabricated that will trap the curious crowd in its net. Wherever the teacher appears, the populace flocks about him,[416] curious to see, curious to hear, craving to be able to tell others that they have seen and heard him. Is this curious crowd the learner? By no means. Or if one of that city's professional teachers were to come secretly to the god in order to test his powers in the polemics of debate,[417] is this the learner? By no means. If the populace or if that professional teacher *learns* something, then in the purely Socratic sense the god is only the occasion.

The appearance of the god is now the news of the day in the market square, in homes, in council meetings, in the ruler's palace; it is the occasion for much loose and empty talk, perhaps also the occasion for more serious reflection. But for the learner the news of the day is not an occasion for something else, not even the occasion for him in Socratic honesty to immerse himself in himself—no, it is the eternal, the beginning of eternity. The news of the day is the beginning of eternity! If the god had let himself be born in an inn, wrapped in rags, laid in a manger[418]—is that more of a contradiction than that the news of the day is the swaddling clothes of the eternal, is indeed its actual form, just as in this assumed case, so that *the moment* is actually the decision of eternity! But that the god provides the condition has already been explicated as the consequence of *the moment,* and we have shown that the moment is the paradox and that without this we come no further but go back to Socrates.

---

406. See Phil 2:7–8.
407. See Lk 7:25.
408. See Mt 26:53.
409. See Mt 6:25–26.
410. See Mt 8:20.
411. See Mt 8:22.
412. See Lk 24:29.

413. See Mt 6:28.
414. See Jn 4:34.
415. See Mt 12:49.
416. See, for example, Mt 4:25.
417. See Jn 3:1–15.
418. See Lk 2:7.

Right here we shall make sure that it becomes clear that a historical point of departure is an issue for the contemporary follower as well, for if we do not make sure of this here, we shall face an insurmountable difficulty later when we deal with the situation of the follower whom we call the follower at second hand. The contemporary follower, too, obtains a historical point of departure for his eternal consciousness, for he is indeed contemporary with the historical event that does not intend to be a moment of occasion, and this historical event intends to interest him otherwise than merely historically, intends to be the condition for his eternal happiness. Indeed (let us reverse the consequences), if this is not the case, the teacher is not the god but only a Socrates, who, if he does not go about things as Socrates did, is not even a Socrates.

How, then, does the learner come to an understanding with this paradox, for we do not say that he is supposed to understand the paradox but is only to understand that this is the paradox. We have already shown how this occurs. It occurs when the understanding and the paradox happily encounter each other in the moment, when the understanding steps aside and the paradox gives itself, and the third something, the something in which this occurs (for it does not occur through the understanding, which is discharged, or through the paradox, which gives itself—consequently *in* something), is that happy passion to which we shall now give a name, although for us it is not a matter of the name. We shall call it *faith*. This passion, then, must be that above-mentioned condition that the paradox provides. Let us not forget this: if the paradox does not provide the condition, then the learner is in possession of it; but if he is in possession of the condition, then he is *eo ipso* himself the truth, and the moment is only the moment of occasion.

It is easy enough for the contemporary learner to acquire detailed historical information. But let us not forget that in regard to the birth of the god he will be in the very same situation as the follower at second hand, and if we insist upon absolutely exact historical knowledge, only one human being would be completely informed, namely, the woman by whom he let himself be born. Consequently, it is easy for the contemporary learner to become a historical eyewitness, but the trouble is that knowing a historical fact—indeed, knowing all the historical facts with the trustworthiness of an eyewitness—by no means makes the eyewitness a follower, which is understandable, because such knowledge means nothing more to him than the historical. It is at once apparent here that the historical in the more concrete sense is inconsequential; we can let ignorance step in here, let ignorance, so to speak, destroy one fact after the other, let it historically demolish the historical—if only the moment still remains as the point of departure for the eternal, the paradox is still present.

If there was a contemporary who had even limited his sleep to the shortest possible time so that he could accompany that teacher, whom he accompanied more inseparably than the little fish that accompany the shark, if he had in his service a hundred secret agents who spied upon that teacher everywhere and with whom he conferred every night, so that he had a dossier on that teacher down to the slightest particular, knew what he had said, where he had been every hour of the day, because his zeal made him regard even the slightest particular as important—would such a contemporary be a follower? Not at all. If someone charged him with historical unreliability, he could wash his hands,[419] but no more than that. If someone else concerned himself only with the teaching which that teacher occasionally presented, if he cherished every instructive word that came from his mouth more than his daily bread, if he had a hundred others to catch every syllable so that nothing would be lost, if he painstakingly conferred with them in order to obtain the most reliable version of what the teacher taught—would he therefore be a follower? By no means—no more than Plato was anything other than a follower of Socrates. If there was a contemporary who had lived abroad and came home just when that teacher had only a day or two to live, if in turn that contemporary was prevented by business affairs from getting to see that teacher and arrived on the scene only at the very end when he was about to breathe his last, would this historical ignorance be an obstacle to his being able to be a follower if the moment was for him the decision of eternity? For the first contemporary, that life would have been merely a historical event; for the second one, that teacher would have been the occasion for understanding himself, and he will be able to forget that teacher, because in contrast to an eternal understanding of oneself, knowledge about the teacher is accidental and historical knowledge, a matter of memory. As long as the eternal and the historical remain apart from each other, the historical is only an occasion. If, then, that ardent learner, who did not, however, go so far as to become a follower, spoke ever so frequently and emphatically about how much he owed that teacher, so that his eulogy had almost

---

419. See Mt 27:24.

no end and its gilding was almost priceless—if he became angry with us as we tried to explain to him that the teacher had been merely the occasion—neither his eulogy nor his anger would benefit our reflections, for both would have the same basis, that he, without even having the courage simply to understand, did not want to lack the recklessness to go further. By talking extravagantly and trumpeting from the housetops as he does, a person merely hoodwinks himself and others insofar as he convinces himself and others that he actually does have thoughts—since he owes them to another. Although courtesy generally does not cost anything, that person's courtesy is bought at a high price, because the enthusiastic expression of thankfulness, which may not even lack tears and the capacity of moving others to tears, is a misunderstanding, because such a person owes his thoughts to no one else, and neither does he owe his shallow talk to any one else. Alas, how many there have been who have had sufficient courtesy to want to be very indebted to Socrates, and yet without owing him anything at all! The person who understands Socrates best understands specifically that he owes Socrates nothing, which is what Socrates prefers, and to be able to prefer this is beautiful. The person who thinks that he is so very indebted to Socrates can be quite sure that Socrates gladly exempts him from paying, since Socrates certainly would be dismayed to learn that he had given the person concerned any working capital whatsoever to exploit in this way. But if the whole structure is not Socratic—and this is what we are assuming—then the follower owes that teacher *everything* (which one cannot possibly owe to Socrates, since, after all, as he himself says, he was not capable of *giving birth*) and this relation cannot be expressed by talking extravagantly and trumpeting from the housetops but only in that happy passion which we call faith, the object of which is the paradox—but the paradox specifically unites the contradictories, is the eternalizing of the historical and the historicizing of the eternal. Anyone who understands the paradox any other way may retain the honor of having explained it, an honor he would win by his unwillingness to be satisfied with understanding it.

It is easy to see, then (if, incidentally, the implications of discharging the understanding need to be pointed out), that faith is not a knowledge, for all knowledge is either knowledge of the eternal, which excludes the temporal and the historical as inconsequential, or it is purely historical knowledge, and no knowledge can have as its object this absurdity that the eternal is the historical. If I comprehend Spinoza's teaching, then in the moment I comprehend it I am not oc-

cupied with Spinoza but with his teaching, although at some other time I am historically occupied with him. The follower, however, is in faith related to that teacher in such a way that he is eternally occupied with his historical existence.

Now if we assume that the structure is as we have assumed (and unless we do, we go back to Socrates), namely, that the teacher himself provides the learner with the condition, then the object of faith becomes not the *teaching* but the *teacher,* for the essence of the Socratic is that the learner, because he himself is the truth and has the condition, can thrust the teacher away. Indeed, assisting people to be able to do this constituted the Socratic art and heroism. Faith, then, must constantly cling firmly to the teacher. But in order for the teacher to be able to give the condition, he must be the god, and in order to put the learner in possession of it, he must be man. This contradiction is in turn the object of faith and is the paradox, the moment. That the god once and for all has given man the condition is the eternal Socratic presupposition, which does not clash inimically with time but is incommensurable with the categories of temporality. But the contradiction is that he receives the condition in the moment, and, since it is a condition for the understanding of eternal truth, it is *eo ipso* the eternal condition. If this is not the structure, then we are left with Socratic recollection.

It is easy to see, then (if, incidentally, the consequences of discharging the understanding need to be pointed out), that faith is not an act of will, for it is always the case that all human willing is efficacious only within the condition. For example, if I have the courage to will it, I will understand the Socratic—that is, understand myself, because from the Socratic point of view I possess the condition and now can will it. But if I do not possess the condition (and we assume this in order not to go back to the Socratic), then all my willing is of no avail, even though, once the condition is given, that which was valid for the Socratic is again valid.

The contemporary learner possesses an advantage for which, alas, the subsequent learner, just in order to do something, will very much envy him. The contemporary can go and observe that teacher—and does he then dare to believe his eyes? Yes, why not? As a consequence, however, does he dare to believe that he is a follower? Not at all, for if he believes his eyes, he is in fact deceived, for the god cannot be known directly. Then may he close his eyes? Quite so. But if he does, then what is the advantage of being contemporary? And if he does close his eyes, then he will presumably envision the god. But if he is able to do this by himself, then he does indeed possess the condition. What he envisions will be a form that appears to the inner eye of the soul; if he looks at that, then the form of the servant will indeed disturb him as soon as he opens his eyes. Let us proceed. As we know, that teacher dies. So now, then, he is dead—what is to be done by the person who was contemporary with him? Perhaps he has sketched a portrait of him—perhaps he even has a whole series of pictures depicting and exactly reproducing every change that age and mental attitude may have brought about in the external form of that teacher—when he looks at these pictures and assures himself that this is the way the teacher looked, does he then dare to believe his eyes? Well, why not? But is he therefore a follower? By no means. But then he may indeed envision the god. The god, however, cannot be envisioned, and that was the very reason he was in the form of a servant. Yet the servant form was no deception, for if it were, then that moment would not be the moment but an accidentality, a semblance, which, in comparison with the eternal, infinitely vanishes as an occasion. And if the learner could envision the god by himself, then he himself would possess the condition and then he would only need to be reminded in order to envision the god, which he could very well do, even if he was not aware of it. But if this is the way it is, then this reminder instantly vanishes as an atom in the eternal possibility that was in his soul, which now becomes actual but then again, as actuality, has eternally presupposed itself.

How, then, does the learner become a believer or a follower? When the understanding is discharged and he receives the condition. When does he receive this? In the moment. This condition, what does it condition? His understanding of the eternal. But a condition such as this surely must be an eternal condition.—In the moment, therefore, he receives the eternal condition, and he knows this from his having received it in the moment, for otherwise he merely calls to mind that he had it from eternity. He receives the condition in the moment and receives it from that teacher himself. [. . .]

[. . .] When the teacher is dead and departed from the follower, memory presumably will produce the form, but he does not believe because of that but because he received the condition from the teacher; therefore, in recollection's trustworthy picture, he again sees the god. So it is with the follower who knows that without the condition he would have seen nothing, inasmuch as the first thing he understood was that he himself was untruth.

From Søren Kierkegaard, *Philosophical Fragments, Johannes Climacus,* translated by Howard V. Hong and Edna H. Hong (Princeton: Princeton University Press, 1985), 56–65.

❧ In his essay "Is Exegesis without Presuppositions Possible?" (1957), **Rudolf Bultmann** (1884–1976), a New Testament scholar and theologian, poses the question of the place of presuppositions in biblical exegesis. His answer is that exegesis without presuppositions is impossible, given that (1) a text is the product of a historical period and must be interpreted in that light, and (2) an exegete is engaged in an "existential encounter" with the text that is conditioned by the exegete's own "life relation" to the subject matter of the text.

RUDOLF BULTMANN
"Is Exegesis without Presuppositions Possible?"

The question whether exegesis without presuppositions is possible must be answered affirmatively if "without presuppositions" means "without presupposing the results of exegesis." In this sense, exegesis without presuppositions is not only possible but imperative. In another sense, however, no exegesis is without presuppositions, because the exegete is not a *tabula rasa* but approaches the text with specific questions or with a specific way of asking questions and thus has a certain idea of the subject matter with which the text is concerned.

I

1. The demand that exegesis must be without presuppositions in the sense that it must not presuppose its results (we can also say that it must be without prejudices) needs only brief clarification. This demand means, first of all, the rejection of allegorical interpretation.[420] If Philo finds the Stoic idea of the apathetic sage in the prescription of the law that the sacrificial animal must be unblemished (*Spec. Leg.* 1:260), it is clear that he does not hear what the text says but lets it say only what he already knows. And the same is true of Paul's exegesis of Deut. 25:4 as a prescription that preachers of the gospel are to be supported by congregations (1 Cor. 9:9) or of the interpretation in the Letter of Barnabas (9:7–8) of the 318 servants of Abraham (Gen. 14:14) as a prophecy of the cross of Christ.

2. But even where allegorical interpretation is given up, exegesis is frequently guided by prejudices. This is so, for ex-

420. Of course, if there is an allegory in the text, it is to be explained as an allegory. But such explanation is not allegorical interpretation; it simply asks for the meaning intended by the text.

ample, when it is presupposed that the evangelists Matthew and John were personal disciples of Jesus and that the stories and sayings of Jesus that they transmit must be historically true reports. In this case, it must be affirmed, for instance, that the cleansing of the Temple, which in Matthew is placed during Jesus' last days just before his passion, but in John stands at the beginning of his ministry, took place twice. The question of an unprejudiced exegesis becomes especially urgent when the problem of Jesus' messianic consciousness is concerned. May exegesis of the Gospels be guided by the dogmatic presupposition that Jesus was the Messiah and was conscious of being so? Or must it rather leave this question open? The answer should be clear. Any such messianic consciousness would be a historical fact and could be shown to be such only by historical research. Were research to make it probable that Jesus knew himself to be the Messiah, this result would have only relative certainty, for historical research can never endow it with absolute validity. All historical knowledge is subject to discussion; consequently, the question whether Jesus knew himself to be the Messiah remains an open question for exegesis. No exegesis that is guided by dogmatic prejudices hears what the text says but lets it say only what the exegete wants to hear.

II

1. The question of exegesis without presuppositions in the sense of unprejudiced exegesis must be distinguished from this same question in the other sense in which it can be asked. And in this other sense we must say that there cannot be any such thing as exegesis without presuppositions. That there is no such exegesis in fact, because every exegete is determined by his or her own individuality in the sense of special biases and habits, gifts and weaknesses, has no significance in principle. Individuality in this sense is the very thing the exegete ought to eliminate by self-education, by learning to listen with the kind of hearing that is interested in nothing except the subject matter of the text. But invariably presupposed in this is the historical method of questioning the text. Indeed, exegesis as the interpretation of historical texts is a part of the science of history.

Of course, it belongs to historical method that a text is interpreted in accordance with the rules of grammar and of the use of words. And closely connected with this is the demand that historical exegesis also inquire about the individual style of a text. The sayings of Jesus in the Synoptic Gospels, for example, have a different style from the Johan-

nine ones. This is connected with another problem that exegesis has to take into account. Paying attention to the use of words, to grammar, and to style soon leads to the observation that every text speaks in the language of its time and of its historical setting. This the exegete must know; therefore, he or she must know the historical conditions of the language of the period out of which a text has arisen. This means that for an understanding of the language of the New Testament the acute question is, Where and to what extent is its Greek determined by a Semitic use of language? Out of this question grows the demand to study apocalypticism, rabbinic literature, and the Qumran texts as well as the history of Hellenistic religion.

Examples are hardly necessary, and I cite only one. The New Testament word πνεῦμα is rendered in German as *Geist*. This explains why the exegesis of the nineteenth century (for example, in the Tübingen school) interpreted the New Testament on the basis of the idealism that goes back to ancient Greece, until Hermann Gunkel pointed out in 1888 that πνεῦμα in the New Testament meant something utterly different—namely, God's wonderful power and manner of acting.[421]

Historical method includes the presupposition that history is a unity in the sense of a closed continuum in which individual events are connected by the succession of cause and effect. This does not mean that the process of history is determined by causal law and that there are no free human decisions that determine the course of events. But even a free decision does not happen without a cause or motive; and the task of the historian is to come to know the motives of human actions. All decisions and acts have their causes and consequences; historical method presupposes that it is possible in principle to exhibit them and their connection and thus to understand the whole historical process as a closed unity.

This closedness means that the continuum of historical happenings cannot be broken by the interference of supernatural powers from beyond the world and that, therefore, there is no "wonder" in this sense of the word. Such a wonder would be an event whose cause did not lie within history. While, for example, the Old Testament narrative talks about God's intervention in history, the science of history cannot assert such an act of God but perceives only that there are those who believe in God and in God's action. To be sure,

---

421. H. Gunkel, *Die Wirkungen des Heiligen Geistes nach der populären Anschauung der apostolischen Zeit und der Lehre des Apostels Paulus* (1888; 3d ed., 1909).

as the science of history it may not assert that such faith is an illusion and that there is no act of God in history. But as science it cannot itself perceive such an act and proceed as though such had occurred; it can only leave everyone free to decide whether he or she wants to see an act of God in a historical event that it itself understands in terms of the event's immanent historical causes.

It is in accordance with such a method that the science of history goes to work on all historical documents. There can be no exceptions in the case of biblical texts if they are to be understood at all historically. Nor can one object that the biblical writings do not intend to be historical documents but rather are witnesses of faith and proclamation. Of course they are. But if they are ever to be understood as such, they must first be interpreted historically, because they speak in a strange language, in concepts of a faraway time, of a world picture that is alien to us. Simply put, they must be *translated,* and translation is the work of the science of history.

2. If we speak of translation, however, we are faced at once with the hermeneutical problem. To translate means to make understandable, and this presupposes an understanding. The understanding of history as a continuum of causes and effects presupposes an understanding of the effective forces that connect individual phenomena. Such forces are economic needs, social exigencies, the striving for political power, human passions, ideas, and ideals. Historians differ in assessing such factors, and in any effort to achieve a unified view the individual historian is guided by some particular way of asking questions, some particular perspective.

This does not mean a falsification of the historical picture, provided that the perspective that is presupposed is not a prejudice but a way of asking questions, and that the historian is aware that this way of asking questions is one-sided in questioning the phenomenon or the text from this one particular perspective. The historical picture is falsified only when a particular way of asking questions is taken to be the only one—when, for example, all history is reduced to economic history. Historical phenomena are many-sided. Events like the Reformation can be observed from the viewpoint of church history as well as of political history, of economic history as well as of the history of philosophy. Mysticism can be studied from the viewpoint of its significance for the history of art, and so on. But if history is to be understood at all, some particular way of asking questions is always presupposed.

Furthermore, the forces that are effective in connecting phenomena are understandable only if the phenomena themselves, which are connected thereby, are also understood. This means that an understanding of the subject matter itself belongs to historical understanding. Can one understand political history without having concepts of the state and of justice, which by their very nature are not historical products but ideas? Can one understand economic history without having a concept of what economy and society in general mean? Can one understand the history of religion or of philosophy without knowing what religion or philosophy is? One cannot understand Martin Luther's posting of the Ninety-Five Theses in 1517, for instance, without understanding what it meant to protest against the Catholicism of his time. One cannot understand the Communist Manifesto of 1848 without understanding the principles of capitalism and socialism. One cannot understand the decisions of persons who act in history if one does not understand human beings and their possibilities. In short, historical understanding presupposes an understanding of the subject matter of history itself and of the men and women who act in history.

This is to say, however, that historical understanding always presupposes that the interpreter has a relation to the subject matter that is (directly or indirectly) expressed in the text. This relation is grounded in the life context in which the interpreter stands. Only someone who lives in a state or in a society can understand the political and social phenomena of the past and their history, just as only someone who has a relation to music can understand a text having to do with music, and so on.

Therefore, a particular understanding of the subject matter of the text, grounded in a life relation to it, is always presupposed by exegesis; and to this extent no exegesis is without presuppositions. I call this understanding a "preunderstanding." It no more involves prejudice than does the choice of a particular perspective. The historical picture would be falsified only if the exegete were to take his or her preunderstanding to be a definitive understanding. The life relation is genuine, however, only when it is alive, which is to say, only when the subject matter with which the text is concerned is of concern to us and is a problem for us. If we question history out of a lively concern with our own problems, it really begins to speak to us. Through discussion with the past it comes alive, and in learning to know history we learn to know our own present: historical knowledge is at the same time knowledge of ourselves. To understand history is possible only for one who does not stand over against it as a neutral, nonparticipating spectator but also stands within it and shares responsibility for it. We speak of this encounter with history that grows out of one's own historicity as the "existential encounter." The historian participates in it with the whole of his or her existence.

This existential relation to history is the basic presupposition for understanding it.[422] This does not mean that understanding history is "subjective" in the sense that it depends on the personal preference of the historian and thereby loses all objective significance. On the contrary, it means that history can be understood precisely in its objective content only by a subject who is existentially concerned and alive. It means that the scheme of subject and object that has validity for natural science is not valid for historical understanding.[423]

What has been said includes an important insight, namely, that historical knowledge is never closed or definitive any more than is the preunderstanding with which the historian approaches historical phenomena in asking about them. If historical phenomena are not facts that can be neutrally observed but rather disclose themselves in their meaning only to one who approaches them alive with questions, they are always understandable only now in that they speak anew to every present situation. Indeed, the questioning itself arises out of the historical situation, out of the claim of the now, out of the problem that is given in the now. For this reason historical research is never closed but must always be carried further. Naturally, there are certain items of historical knowledge that can be taken as definitively known, namely, such items as concern only events that can be fixed chronologically and locally, as, for example, the assassination of Julius Caesar or Luther's posting of the Ninety-Five Theses. But what these events *mean* as historical events cannot be definitively fixed. Hence, one must say that a historical event can be known for what it is—precisely as a historical event—only in the future. And one may also say that the future of a historical event belongs to it.

Naturally, items of historical knowledge can be transmitted, not as definitively known but in such a way as to clarify and expand the succeeding generation's preunderstanding. Even so they are subject to criticism by the following generation. Can we today foresee the meaning of the two world wars? No. For what a historical event means always becomes clear only in the future. It can show itself definitively only when history has come to an end.

III

What are the consequences of this analysis for the exegesis of biblical writings? They may be formulated in the following theses:

1. The exegesis of biblical writings, like any other interpretation of a text, must be unprejudiced.

2. However, the exegesis is not without presuppositions, because as historical interpretation it presupposes the method of historical-critical research.

3. Further presupposed is the exegete's life relation to the subject matter with which the Bible is concerned and therewith a preunderstanding.

4. This preunderstanding is not closed but open, so that there can be an existential encounter with the text and an existential decision.

5. Understanding of the text is never definitive but rather remains open because the meaning of scripture discloses itself anew in every future.

After what has already been said nothing needs to be added to clarify the first and the second of these theses.

As regards the third, the preunderstanding in question is grounded in the question about God that is alive in human life. This does not mean that the exegete has to know everything possible about God but only that he or she is moved by the existential question about God, whatever its conscious form—whether as the question about "salvation" or about deliverance from death, or about certainty in the face of an ever-shifting destiny, or about truth in the midst of an enigmatic world.

With regard to the fourth thesis, existential encounter with the text can lead to a "yes" as well as to a "no," to confessing faith as well as to express unfaith, because in the text the exegete encounters a claim, or is offered a self-understanding that can be accepted (as a gift) or rejected, and therefore has to make a decision. Even in the case of a "no," however, the understanding is legitimate, because it is a genuine answer to the question of the text, which, being an existential decision, is not to be refuted by argument.

So far as the fifth thesis is concerned, because the text speaks to existence, it is never definitively understood. The existential decision out of which the interpretation emerges cannot be transmitted but must always be made anew. This does not mean, of course, that there can be no continuity

---

422. It goes without saying that the existential relation to history does not have to be raised to the level of consciousness. It may only be spoiled by reflection.

423. I do not go into certain special questions here, such as how an existential relation to history can already be present in the research of grammar, lexicography, statistics, chronology, or geography or how the historian of mathematics or physics participates existentially in the objects of research. One thinks of Plato!

in the exegesis of scripture. It goes without saying that the results of methodical historical-critical research can be transmitted, even if they can be taken over only by constantly being critically tested. But even with respect to exegesis that is grounded existentially, there is also continuity insofar as it provides guidance for posterity—as has been done, for example, by Luther's understanding of the Pauline doctrine of justification through faith alone. Just as this understanding must be reached ever anew in discussion with Catholic exegesis, so every genuine exegesis that offers itself as a guide is at the same time a question that must always be answered anew and independently. Because the exegete exists historically and must hear the word of scripture as spoken to his or her special historical situation, he or she will understand the old word ever anew. Ever anew it will make clear who we are and who God is, and the exegete will have to express this in an ever new conceptuality. Thus, it is true even of scripture that it is what it is only with its history and its future.

From Rudolf Bultmann, *New Testament and Mythology*, translated by Schubert B. Ogden (Philadelphia: Fortress Press, 1984), 145–53.

 The American theologian **Reinhold Niebuhr** (1892–1971) argues in "Human Destiny and History" that all historical religions and cultures (that is, those that "regard history as contributing to the meaning of life") are messianic in that they expect a Christ: they await the full disclosure and fulfillment of the potential meaning of history. Since there can be no history without presuppositions, the expectation of *a* Christ draws—however fragmentarily—from the faith that *the* Christ has been revealed.

REINHOLD NIEBUHR

"Human Destiny and History," in *The Nature and Destiny of Man: A Christian Interpretation*

Man is, and yet is not, involved in the flux of nature and time. He is a creature, subject to nature's necessities and limitations; but he is also a free spirit who knows of the brevity of his years and by this knowledge transcends the temporal, by some capacity within himself. Man "brings his years to an end as a tale that is told," having an even shorter life span than some dumb creatures. But the sense of melancholy which the anticipation of death induces in the human spirit is not known in the animal world. To brood either anxiously or with studied and learned serenity upon the fact that man is as "the grass which flourisheth in the morning and in the evening is cut down and withereth" is to reveal the whole dimension of existence which distinguishes man from the animal world.

Man's ability to transcend the flux of nature gives him the capacity to make history. Human history is rooted in the natural process but it is something more than either the determined sequences of natural causation or the capricious variations and occurrences of the natural world. It is compounded of natural necessity and human freedom. Man's freedom to transcend the natural flux gives him the possibility of grasping a span of time in his consciousness and thereby of knowing history. It also enables him to change, reorder and transmute the causal sequences of nature and thereby to *make* history. The very ambiguity of the word "history" (as something that occurs and as something that is remembered and recorded) reveals the common source of both human actions and human knowledge in human freedom.

There is no point in human history in which the human spirit is freed of natural necessity. But there is also no point at which the mind cannot transcend the given circumstances to imagine a more ultimate possibility. Thus the conflicts of history need not be accepted as normative, but man looks towards a reality where these conflicts are overcome in a reign of universal order and peace. History thus moves between the limits of nature and eternity. All human actions are conditioned on the one hand by nature's necessities and limitations, and determined on the other hand by an explicit or implicit loyalty to man's conception of the changeless principles which underlie the change. His loyalty to these principles prompts him to seek the elimination of contingent, irrelevant and contradictory elements in the flux, for the sake of realizing the real essence of his life, as defined by the unchanging and eternal power which governs it.

A basic distinction may be made between various interpretations of the meaning of life by noting their attitude towards history. Those which include history in the realm of meaning see it as a process which points and moves towards a fuller disclosure and realization of life's essential meaning. Those which exclude it, do so because they regard history as no more than natural finiteness, from which the human spirit must be freed. They consider man's involvement in nature as the very cause of evil, and define the ultimate redemption of life as emancipation from finiteness. In the one case history is regarded as potentially meaningful, waiting for the ultimate disclosure and realization of its meaning. In the other case it is believed to be essentially meaningless. It may be regarded as a realm of order; but the order is only the subordinate one of natural necessity which affects the meaning of life negatively. It is a mortal coil which must be shuffled off.

The difference in the attitude of various cultures towards history is determined by contradictory estimates of man's transcendence over historical process, including his final transcendence over himself. In the one case it is assumed that since this capacity for self-transcendence represents the highest capacity of the human spirit, the fulfillment of life must naturally consist in man's emancipation from the ambiguities of history. His partial immersion in and partial transcendence over nature must be transmuted into a total transcendence. Some sort of *eternity* is therefore the goal of human striving in non-historical religions and philosophies; and the eternity which is man's end is the fulfillment of history to the point of being its negation. In this eternity there is "no separation of thing from thing, no part standing in isolated existence estranged from the rest and therefore nowhere is there any wronging of another."[424]

In religions which regard history as contributing to the meaning of life the attitude towards man's partial involvement in, and partial transcendence over, the process of nature and the flux of time is totally different. This ambiguous situation is not regarded as the evil from which men must be redeemed. The evil in the human situation arises, rather, from the fact that men seek to deny or to escape prematurely from the uncertainties of history and to claim a freedom, a transcendence and an eternal and universal perspective which is not possible for finite creatures. The problem of sin rather than finiteness is, in other words, either implicitly or explicitly the basic problem of life. Yet the problem of finiteness is not eliminated. It is recognized that a man who stands in an historical process is too limited in vision to discern the full meaning of that process, and too limited in power to fulfill the meaning, however much the freedom of his knowledge and his power is one element in the stuff of history. Hence the temporal problem of human history and destiny in historical religions is: how the transcendent meaning of history is to be disclosed and fulfilled, since man can discern only partial meanings and can only partially realize the meanings he discerns. In modern corruptions of historical religions this problem is solved very simply by the belief that the cumulative effects of history will endow weak man with both the wisdom and the power to discern and to fulfill life's meaning.

In the more profound versions of historical religion it is recognized, however, that there is no point in history, whatever the cumulations of wisdom and power, in which the finiteness of man is overcome so that he could complete his own life, or in which history as such does not retain the ambiguity of being rooted in nature-necessity on the one hand while pointing towards transcendent, "eternal" and transhistorical ends on the other hand.

Historical religions are therefore by their very nature prophetic-Messianic. They look forward at first to a point in history and finally towards an *eschaton* (end) which is also the end of history, where the full meaning of life and history will be disclosed and fulfilled. Significantly, as in the optimistic expectations of a "day of the Lord" which the first great literary prophet, Amos, found at hand and criticized, these Messianic expectations begin as expressions of national hope and expectations of national triumph. Only gradually it is realized that man's effort to deny and to escape his finiteness in imperial ambitions and power add an element of corruption to the fabric of history and that this corruption becomes a basic characteristic of history and a perennial problem from the standpoint of the fulfillment of human history and destiny. It is recognized that history must be purged as well as completed; and that the final completion of history must include God's destruction of man's abortive and premature efforts to bring history to its culmination.

The basic distinction between historical and non-historical religions and cultures may thus be succinctly defined as the difference between those which expect and those which do not expect a Christ. A Christ is expected wherever history is regarded as potentially meaningful but as still awaiting the full disclosure and fulfillment of its meaning. A Christ is not expected wherever the meaning of life is explained from the standpoint of either nature or supernature in such a way that a transcendent revelation of history's meaning is not regarded as either possible or necessary. It is not regarded as possible when, as in various forms of naturalism, the visions and ambitions of historical existence which point beyond nature are regarded as illusory; and nature-history is believed to be incapable of receiving disclosures of meaning which point beyond itself. It is not regarded as necessary when man's capacity for freedom and self-transcendence is believed to be infinitely extensible until the ambiguities of history are left behind and pure eternity is achieved. The significance of a Christ is that he is a disclosure of the divine purpose, governing history within history. Wherever it is believed that man's capacity to transcend self and history can be disassociated

---

424. Plotinus, *Enneads*, III, ii: I.

from his finiteness, the meaning of salvation is conceived as essentially redemption from history, obviating any necessity of, or desire for, the fulfillment of man in history, or for the disclosure of history's ultimate meaning.

A Christ is expected wherever history is thought of as a realm of fragmentary revelations of a purpose and power transcending history, pointing to a fuller disclosure of that purpose and power. He is expected because this disclosure is regarded as both possible and necessary. It is regarded as possible because history is known to be something more than the nature-necessity in which it has its roots. It is regarded as necessary because the potential meaningfulness of history is recognized as fragmentary and corrupted. It must be completed and clarified.

The interpretation of the cultures of the world in this fashion according to their possession, or lack, of Messianic expectations draws upon insights which are possible only after the logic of Messianic expectations has reached its culmination in the Christian belief that these expectations have been fulfilled in Christ. It is not possible to interpret cultures according to their expectation or want of expectations of *a* Christ without drawing upon the faith that *the* Christ has been revealed; for there can be no interpretation of the meaning of life and history without implicitly or explicitly drawing into the interpretation the faith which claims to have found the end of these expectations. This is to say, merely, that there can be no interpretation of history without specific presuppositions and that the interpretation which is being attempted in these pages is based upon Christian presuppositions. The Christian answer to the problem of life is assumed in the discussion of the problem. In that sense our interpretation is, as every interpretation must be in the final analysis, "dogmatic" or confessional. Yet it is not purely dogmatic or confessional; for it seeks to analyze the question and expectations for which a particular epic of history is regarded as the answer, and also to determine why these questions and expectations are not universal in history. Such an analysis must begin with a further inquiry into the character of non-historical forms of culture which regard Christ "as foolishness" because they have no questions for which Christ is the answer and no expectations and hopes for which his Cross is the fulfillment.

Where a Christ Is Not Expected

Nothing is so incredible as an answer to an unasked question. One half of the world has regarded the Christian answer to the problem of life and history as "foolishness" because it had no questions for which the Christian revelation was the answer and no longings and hopes which that revelation fulfilled. The cultures of this half of the world were non-Messianic because they were non-historical. Their failure to regard history as basic to the meaning of life may be attributed to two primary methods of looking at life which stand in contradiction to each other. The one is the method of regarding the system of nature as the final reality to which man must adjust himself. The other regards nature from the human perspective as either chaos or a meaningless order from which man will be freed either by his reason or by some unity and power within him higher than reason. There are systems of thought, of which Stoicism is the classic example, which combine both methods or which reveal a certain degree of ambivalence between the two; but the two most consistent methods of denying the meaningfulness of history are to reduce it to the proportions of nature or to regard it as a corruption of eternity. . . .

The New Testament Idea of the End

This hope of the *parousia* in New Testament thought is sometimes dismissed as no more than a projection of those elements of Jewish apocalypse to which the first coming of Christ did not conform and for the satisfaction of which a "second coming" had to be invented. On the other hand they have frequently been taken literally and have thus confused the mind of the church. The symbol of the second coming of Christ can neither be taken literally nor dismissed as unimportant. It participates in the general characteristic of the Biblical symbols, which deal with the relation of time and eternity, and seek to point to the ultimate from the standpoint of the conditioned. If the symbol is taken literally the dialectical conception of time and eternity is falsified and the ultimate vindication of God over history is reduced to a point in history. The consequence of this falsification is expressed in the hope of a millennial age. In such a millennial age, just as in a utopian one, history is supposedly fulfilled despite the persisting conditions of finiteness. On the other hand if the symbol is dismissed as unimportant, as merely a picturesque or primitive way of apprehending the relation of the historical to the eternal, the Biblical dialectic is obscured in another direction. All theologies which do not take these symbols seriously will be discovered upon close analysis not to take history seriously either. They presuppose an eternity which annuls rather than fulfills the historical process.

The Biblical symbols cannot be taken literally because it

is not possible for finite minds to comprehend that which transcends and fulfills history. The finite mind can only use symbols and pointers of the character of the eternal. These pointers must be taken seriously nevertheless because they express the self-transcendent character of historical existence and point to its eternal ground. The symbols which point towards the consummation from within the temporal flux cannot be exact in the scientific sense of the word. They are inexact even when they merely define the divine and eternal ground of history in terms of contrast to the temporal. They are even more difficult to understand when they seek to express the Biblical idea of an eternity involved in, and yet transcending, the temporal.

From Reinhold Niebuhr, *The Nature and Destiny of Man: A Christian Interpretation*, vol. 2, *Human Destiny* (New York: Charles Scribner's Sons, 1943), 1–7, 289–90.

∽ In "Nature and Grace," the Roman Catholic theologian **Karl Rahner** (1904–84) proposes what has come to be known as his "remainder principle." Rahner thinks that human nature is best understood not as "pure nature" but as a hypothetical concept of what the human being would be like if the human being had *not* been graced from the beginning—as Rahner believes all have been.

KARL RAHNER

"Nature and Grace," in *Theological Investigations*

The moral freedom of man to dispose of himself always exists in the prior possibility of supernatural acts, a possibility effected by grace. If this is so, then we may say that the supernatural transcendence is always present in every man who has reached the age of moral reason. That does not necessarily mean that he is justified. He may be a sinner and an unbeliever. But where and in so far as he has the concrete possibility of a morally good act, he is in fact constantly within the open horizon of transcendence towards the God of the supernatural life, whether his free act is in accord or in conflict with this prior state of his supernaturally elevated spiritual existence. *If* in every moral act he takes a positive or negative attitude to the *totality* of his *de facto* existence (a supposition whose reality we need not examine here), *then* we must say: every morally good act of man is, in the actual order of salvation, also in fact a supernaturally salutary act. [. . .] The notions which we have outlined show clearly that it is quite conceivable that the whole spiritual life of man

is constantly affected by grace. It is not a rare and sporadic event just because grace is unmerited. Theology has been too long and too often bedevilled by the unavowed supposition that grace would be no longer grace if it were too generously distributed by the love of God! Our whole spiritual life is lived in the realm of the salvific will of God, of his prevenient grace, of his call as it becomes efficacious: all of which is an element within the region of our consciousness, though one which remains anonymous as long as it is not interpreted from without by the message of faith. Even when he does not "know" it and does not believe it, that is, even when he cannot make it an individual object of knowledge by merely inward reflexion, man always lives consciously in the presence of the triune God of eternal life. God is the unexpressed but real "Whither" of the dynamism of all spiritual and moral life in the realm of spiritual existence which is in fact founded, that is, supernaturally elevated by God. It is a "purely *a priori*." Whither, but always there, present to consciousness without being in the nature of an object, but nonetheless there.

We do not need to insist on the existence of such an *a priori* of a supernatural nature in spiritual existence, even though it can only be clearly expounded and translated into objectivated knowledge in the light of the word of revelation which comes from without. It manifests itself as the mysterious activation of individual and collective spiritual life in countless ways, which would not exist if this mysterious activation and dynamism were not at work. It follows that even outside the process of official revelation the history of religion is not merely a product of natural reason and sin. Precisely in its consciously tangible results, in its objective spirit, it is the product of the natural spirit, grace and sin. Thus when man is summoned by the message of faith given by the visible Church, it is not the first time that he comes into spiritual contact with the reality preached by the Church: such conceptual knowledge of it is not primary. The call only makes him consciously aware of—and of course forces him to make a choice about—the grace which already encompassed him inarticulately but really as an element of his spiritual existence. The preaching is the express awakening of what is already present in the depths of man's being, not by nature, but by grace. But it is a grace which always surrounds man, even the sinner and the unbeliever, as the inescapable setting of his existence.

We are now in a position to face the real problem of "nature and grace" in the strict sense and to pose it properly. It is clear that by living out his spiritual existence, man always attains his "nature," even in the theological sense, where this concept is opposed to that of grace and the supernatural. For in every question which he poses about himself, in every judgment where he contrasts himself with an object and grasps it in the perspective of an unlimited transcendence, he experiences himself as something which he must necessarily be, as something that is a unity and a totality which cannot be dissolved into variables, which either is there as a whole or is not there at all. [. . .] Our actual nature is *never* "pure" nature. It is a nature installed in a supernatural order which man can never leave, even as a sinner and unbeliever. It is a nature which is continually being determined (which does not mean justified) by the supernatural grace of salvation offered to it. And these "existentials" of man's concrete, "historical" nature are not purely states of being beyond consciousness. They make themselves felt in the experience of man. By simple reflexion on himself, in the light of natural reason, he cannot simply and clearly distinguish them from the natural spiritual activity which is the manifestation of his nature. But once he knows from revelation that there is an order of grace, not due to him and not belonging to the necessary constitutives of his being, he becomes more cautious. He must allow for the fact that much of his concrete experience which he is almost automatically tempted to attribute to his "nature" may perhaps in fact be the effect in him of what he must recognize as unmerited grace in the light of theology.

This does not mean that he is now quite ignorant of what is natural to him. The nature of a spiritual being and its supernatural elevation are not opposed to each other like two things which lie side by side, so that they must be either kept separate or confused. The supernatural elevation of man is, though not due to him, the absolute fulfillment of his being, whose spiritual quality and transcendence towards being as such prevents its being "defined," that is, "delimited" in the same way that sub-human entities can. For these are "defined" by the fact that it is their essence to be restricted to a certain realm of reality. [. . .] The "definition" of the created spirit is its "openness" to being as such: as created, it is open to the fullness of reality; as spirit, it is open to absolute reality in general. It is not therefore surprising that the grandeur of the (varying) fulfillment of this openness (which does not of itself imply necessarily an absolute and unsurpassable fulfillment and yet, as absolute openness, still has a sense without such fulfillment) cannot be recognized at once as "due" or "undue." And yet the basic essence of man, his nature as such openness (transcendence) can be perfectly well estab-

lished. The initial elements of such fulfillment are already present: the experience of infinite longings, of radical optimism, of unquenchable discontent, of the torment of the insufficiency of everything attainable, of the radical protest against death, the experience of being confronted with an absolute love precisely where it is lethally incomprehensible and seems to be silent and aloof, the experience of a radical guilt and of a still abiding hope etc. These elements are in fact tributary to that divine force which impels the created spirit—by grace—to an absolute fulfillment. Hence in them grace is experienced *and* the natural being of man.

For the essence of man is such that it is experienced where grace is experienced, since grace is only experienced where the spirit naturally is. And vice versa: where spirit is experienced in the actual order of things, it is a supernaturally elevated spirit. [. . .]

The concept of pure nature is legitimate. If someone affirms: I experience myself as a being which is absolutely ordained for the immediate possession of God, his statement need not be false. He will only be mistaken if he maintains that this unconditional longing is an essential element of "pure" nature, or if he says that such pure nature, which does not exist, *could* not exist. Where man knows of the *visio beatifica* by the word of revelation, and experiences it as the marvel of the free love of God in his longing for it, he has to say that it is not due to him (by nature), even as an existing nature—so that the gratuitousness of creation, as a free act of God, and grace as a free gift to the creature, as something already existing, are not one and the same gift of God's free act. To say this is to recognize implicitly the concept of "pure nature." And it is not an empty concept of otiose theological speculation but a concept which, in the long run, is the necessary background against which one recognizes that the beatific vision is a gratuitous grace, not merely not due to man as a sinner, but not due to man even as a creature. [. . .]

In the light of what has been said up to this, it is no great loss if the analysis of man as *potentia oboedientialis* is not a "chemically pure" presentation of pure nature but is mixed up with trace elements from actual nature, and hence from its state of grace. Who can say that the utterances of earthly philosophy, even of a completely non-Christian or pre-Christian type, are merely the voice of pure nature (and perhaps of its guilt)? May they not be the sighing of the creature, secretly moved by the Holy Spirit of grace, which longs for the glory of the children of God and already unwittingly feels itself to be such a child of God? [. . .]

Tiny advances or displacements in the field of scientific theory often begin by being impossible to evaluate. Such changes may appear at first as pastimes reserved to the leisurely keen-wittedness of scholars. But when one considers that such new acquisitions then become part of the general consciousness and so become the automatic presuppositions of action, one can perhaps recognize that much may depend on them, and sometimes everything. This is also true of theology. It is very strange. But we Christians often seem to be completely unconvinced of the power of thought with regard to our Christian faith, and to be very doubtful that "theory" can bring about very practical effects. That is why we often prefer to think over Church politics, social questions, methods of propaganda and so on. That is why living theology is so little esteemed. Many people in the Church have the impression that it merely casts useless obscurity on truths that have long been clear, that it generates unrest and distracts from more important matters. Such people miss the point, that a living, questing, questioning theology is working today for the preaching of tomorrow, so that it can reach the spirit and heart of man. Such theological work may often seem fussy and futile. It is nonetheless necessary. Even though the heart and grace remain the one thing which is irreplaceable.

From Karl Rahner, *Theological Investigations,* translated by Cornelius Ernst, vol. 4 (New York: Helicon, 1966), 180–85, 187–88.

✎ **Bernard J. F. Lonergan** (1904–84), a Canadian philosopher and theologian, is credited with bridging the traditions of Anglo-American empirical philosophy and European transcendental philosophy. In "The Functions of Transcendental Method," Lonergan understands method as transcendental: people (including theologians) who think are cognitively self-transcending insofar as they are alert, intelligent, reasonable, and responsible.

BERNARD J. F. LONERGAN

"The Functions of Transcendental Method," in *Method in Theology*

We have been inviting the reader to discover in himself the original normative pattern of recurrent and related operations that yield cumulative and progressive results. We have now to consider what uses or functions are served by that basic method.

First, then, there is the normative function. All special methods consist in making specific the transcendental precepts, Be attentive, Be intelligent, Be reasonable, Be responsible. But before they are ever formulated in concepts and expressed in words, those precepts have a prior existence and reality in the spontaneous, structured dynamism of human consciousness. Moreover, just as the transcendental precepts rest simply on a study of the operations themselves, so specific categorial precepts rest on a study of the mind operating in a given field. The ultimate basis of both transcendental and categorial precepts will be advertence to the difference between attention and inattention, intelligence and stupidity, reasonableness and unreasonableness, responsibility and irresponsibility.

Secondly, there is the critical function. The scandal still continues that men, while they tend to agree on scientific questions, tend to disagree in the most outrageous fashion on basic philosophic issues. So they disagree about the activities named knowing, about the relation of those activities to reality, and about reality itself. However, differences on the third, reality, can be reduced to differences about the first and second, knowledge and objectivity. Differences on the second, objectivity, can be reduced to differences on the first, cognitional theory. Cognitional theory can be resolved by bringing to light the contradiction between a mistaken cognitional theory and the actual performance of the mistaken theorist. To take the simplest instance, Hume thought the human mind to be a matter of impressions linked together by custom. But Hume's own mind was quite original. Therefore, Hume's own mind was not what Hume considered the human mind to be.

Thirdly, there is the dialectical function. For the critical use of transcendental method can be applied to every mistaken cognitional theory, whether expressed with philosophic generality or presupposed by a method of hermeneutics, of historical investigation, of theology or demythologization. Moreover, these applications can be extended to concomitant views on epistemology and metaphysics. In this fashion one can determine the dialectical series of basic positions, which criticism confirms, and of basic counter-positions, which criticism confounds.

Fourthly, there is the systematic function. For in the measure that transcendental method is objectified, there are determined a set of basic terms and relations, namely, the terms that refer to the operations of cognitional process, and the relations that link these operations to one another. Such terms and relations are the substance of cognitional theory. They reveal the ground for epistemology. They are found to be isomorphic[425] with the terms and relations denoting the ontological structure of any reality proportionate to human cognitional process.

Fifthly, the foregoing systematic function assures continuity without imposing rigidity. Continuity is assured by the source of the basic terms and relations, for that source is human cognitional process in its concrete reality. Rigidity is not imposed, for a fuller and more exact knowledge of human cognitional process is by no means excluded and, in the measure it is attained, there will follow a fuller and more exact determination of basic terms and relations. Finally, the exclusion of rigidity is not a menace to continuity for, as we have seen, the conditions of the possibility of revision set limits to the possibility of revising cognitional theory, and the more elaborate the revision, the stricter and more detailed these limits will be.

Sixthly, there is the heuristic function. Every inquiry aims at transforming some unknown into a known. Inquiry itself, then, is something between ignorance and knowledge. It is less than knowledge, else there would be no need to inquire. It is more than sheer ignorance, for it makes ignorance manifest and strives to replace it with knowledge. This intermediary between ignorance and knowing is an intending, and what is intended is an unknown that is to be known.

Now fundamentally all method is the exploitation of such intending, for it outlines the steps to be taken if one is to proceed from the initial intending of the question to the eventual knowing of what has been intended all along. Moreover, within method the use of heuristic devices is fundamental. They consist in designating and naming the intended unknown, in setting down at once all that can be affirmed about it, and in using this explicit knowledge as a guide, a criterion, and/or a premise in the effort to arrive at a fuller knowledge. Such is the function in algebra of the unknown, x, in the solution of problems. Such is the function in physics of indeterminate or generic functions and of the classes of functions specified by differential equations.

Now transcendental method fulfills a heuristic function. It reveals the very nature of that function by bringing to light the activity of intending and its correlative, the intended that, though unknown, at least is intended. Moreover, inasmuch as the systematic function has provided sets of basic terms and relations, there are to hand basic determinations that may be set down at once whenever the unknown is a human subject or an object proportionate to human cognitional process, i.e., an object to be known by experiencing, understanding, and judging.

Seventhly, there is the foundational function. Special methods derive their proper norms from the accumulated experience of investigators in their several fields. But besides the proper norms there are also common norms. Besides the tasks in each field there are interdisciplinary problems. Underneath the consent of men as scientists, there is their dissent on matters of ultimate significance and concern. It is in the measure that special methods acknowledge their common core in transcendental method, that norms common to all the sciences will be acknowledged, that a secure basis will be attained for attacking interdisciplinary problems, and that the sciences will be mobilized within a higher unity of vocabulary, thought, and orientation, in which they will be able to make their quite significant contribution to the solution of fundamental problems.

Eighthly, transcendental method is relevant to theology. This relevance, of course, is mediated by the special method proper to theology and developed through the reflection of theologians on the successes and failures of their efforts past and present. But this special method, while it has its own special classes and combinations of operations, none the less is the work of human minds performing the same basic operations in the same basic relations as are found in other special methods. In other words, transcendental method is a constituent part of the special method proper to theology, just as it is a constituent part in the special methods proper to the natural and to the human sciences. However true it is that one attends, understands, judges, decides differently in the natural sciences, in the human sciences, and in theology, still these differences in no way imply or suggest a transition from attention to inattention, from intelligence to stupidity, from reasonableness to silliness, from responsibility to irresponsibility.

Ninthly, the objects of theology do not lie outside the transcendental field. For that field is unrestricted, and so outside it there is nothing at all. Moreover, it is not unrestricted in the sense that the transcendental notions are abstract, least in connotation and greatest in denotation; for the transcendental notions are not abstract but comprehensive; they intend everything about everything. So far from being abstract, it is by them that we intend the concrete, i.e., all that is to be known about a thing. Finally, while it is, of course, true that

---

425. This isomorphism rests on the fact that one and the same process constructs both elementary acts of knowing into a compound knowing and elementary objects of knowing into the compound object.

human knowing is limited, still the transcendental notions are not a matter of knowing but of intending; they intended all that each of us has managed to learn, and they now intend all that as yet remains unknown. In other words, the transcendental field is defined not by what man knows, not by what he can know, but by what he can ask about; and it is only because we can ask more questions than we can answer that we know about the limitations of our knowledge.

Tenthly, to assign to transcendental method a role in theology adds no new resource to theology but simply draws attention to a resource that has always been used. For transcendental method is the concrete and dynamic unfolding of human attentiveness, intelligence, reasonableness, and responsibility. That unfolding occurs whenever anyone uses his mind in an appropriate fashion. Hence, to introduce transcendental method introduces no new resource into theology, for theologians always have had minds and always have used them. However, while transcendental method will introduce no new resource, it does add considerable light and precision to the performance of theological tasks, and this, I trust, will become manifest in due course.

In the eleventh place, transcendental method offers a key to unified science. The immobility of the Aristotelian ideal conflicts with developing natural science, developing human science, developing dogma, and developing theology. In harmony with all development is the human mind itself which effects the developments. In unity with all fields, however disparate, is again the human mind that operates in all fields and in radically the same fashion in each. Through the self-knowledge, the self-appropriation, the self-possession that result from making explicit the basic normative pattern of the recurrent and related operations of human cognitional process, it becomes possible to envisage a future in which all workers in all fields can find in transcendental method common norms, foundations, systematics, and common critical, dialectical, and heuristic procedures.

In the twelfth place, the introduction of transcendental method abrogates the old metaphor that describes philosophy as the handmaid of theology and replaces it by a very precise fact. Transcendental method is not the intrusion into theology of alien matter from an alien source. Its function is to advert to the fact that theologies are produced by theologians, that theologians have minds and use them, that their doing so should not be ignored or passed over but explicitly acknowledged in itself and in its implications. Again, transcendental method is coincident with a notable part of what has been considered philosophy, but it is not any philosophy or all philosophy. Very precisely, it is a heightening of consciousness that brings to light our conscious and intentional operations and thereby leads to the answers to three basic questions. What am I doing when I am knowing? Why is doing that knowing? What do I know when I do it? The first answer is a cognitional theory. The second is an epistemology. The third is a metaphysics where, however, the metaphysics is transcendental, an integration of heuristic structures, and not some categorical speculation that reveals that all is water, or matter, or spirit, or process, or what have you.

It remains, however, that transcendental method is only a part of theological method. It supplies the basic anthropological component. It does not supply the specifically religious component.

From Bernard J. F. Lonergan, *Method in Theology* (New York: Herder and Herder, 1972), 20–25.

Fundamentalist/Evangelical

In "Preachers of Paradox," **George Marsden** gives some insight into the historical and intellectual underpinnings of the evangelical and fundamentalist movements in the United States. Marsden, a historian, points out a similarity between fundamentalism and modern technological thinking: neither fundamentalism nor technological thinking grapples with theoretical principles.

GEORGE MARSDEN

"Preachers of Paradox," in *Understanding Fundamentalism and Evangelicalism*

The broader evangelical movement, of which fundamentalism was one subtype, benefited from the upheavals of the 1960s in paradoxical ways. On the one hand, it capitalized on the decline in prestige of the liberal-scientific-secular establishment, a value system that evangelicals had already proclaimed as illusory and doomed. The decentralizing emphases of counterculture readily could be appropriated to evangelicalism, which already was a hodgepodge of *ad hoc* structures. More important, the people-community impulses of the era were readily translated by evangelicals into personal contacts and small-group meetings, such as groups for Bible study and prayer, that contributed substantially to evangelical growth during the 1970s.

On the other side of the paradox, evangelicalism gained from the deep reactions against counterculture ideals. The instinctive impulses of much of the evangelical constituency were of the Spiro Agnew variety. Translated into spiritual terms, what they saw first in the protests of the young was a more virulent sort of Godless secularism and lawlessness. To many conservative evangelicals such vices were extensions of the permissiveness of the New Deal liberal culture rather than protests against it. Such impressions were indeed reinforced by liberalization of the laws in the direction of permissiveness, such as toward homosexuals or abortion, and enforced secularization of schools and public places. During the Vietnam era, however, attacks on the nation and on authority commanded the most attention, so many evangelicals defended with fierce patriotism the nation that they nonetheless regarded as disastrously corrupt.

Evangelicals also benefited from the uncertainties of the Vietnam era and its aftermath by offering decisive answers. The fundamentalist militancy in the heritage encouraged polarized thinking. The metaphors of warfare that dominated that movement suggested that battle lines could be clearly drawn on almost any issue. Confronted with the crisis in authority in a changing and pluralistic society, evangelicals could point to the sure certainty of the word of God. The "inerrancy" of the Bible became an increasingly important symbolic test of faith for much of the movement. Evangelicals generally could draw on the immense residual prestige of the Bible in America as a firm rock in a time of change.

These circumstances—a deeply rooted ideological-spiritual heritage, vigorous institutions, skills in promotion, and an era when people were open to spiritual answers to national and personal crises—combined for the evangelical resurgence of the 1970s. [. . .]

[. . .] Fundamentalism also reflects the persistence of the Puritan heritage in the American Protestant psyche. This heritage includes a cultural vision of all things, including learning, brought into the service of the sovereign God. Fundamentalists accordingly retain vestiges of this ideal. Schools, including colleges and "universities," are central parts of their empires. Although they may only rarely attain excellence in learning, they seek it in principle and sometimes do attain it. No group is more eager to brandish honorary degrees. Perhaps more to the point, genuine degrees are more than welcome when in the service of the Lord. Nowhere is this clearer than in the creation-science movement, a predominantly fundamentalist effort. While decrying the scientific establishment and people who blindly follow the lead of "experts," the Creation Research Society emphasizes the hundreds of Ph.D.'s who make up its membership.

Even more centrally, fundamentalists are among those contemporary Americans who take ideas most seriously. In this respect they reflect, even if in a dim mirror, the Puritan heritage. For the fundamentalist, what one believes is of the utmost importance. They are, as Samuel S. Hill, Jr., observes, more "truth-oriented" than most evangelical groups. The American intellectual establishment, in contrast, has a tendency to reduce beliefs to something else, hence devaluing the importance of ideas as such. So, for instance, fundamentalist ideas themselves have long been presented as though they were "really" expressions of some social or class interest. It seems fair to inquire in such cases as to who is really the anti-intellectual. To reduce beliefs to their social functions is to overemphasize a partial truth and so to underestimate the powers of the belief itself. Consider, for instance, the important fundamentalist belief that God relates to the nation covenantally, rewarding or punishing it proportionately to its moral record. This is a belief, deeply held on religious grounds, about some causal connections in the universe. Throughout the history of America this conception about causality has survived through a number of revolutionary changes in the class and status of its adherents. While, as suggested earlier, social and cultural circumstances strongly influence the expressions of this belief, there is no doubt that the belief itself is sometimes a powerful force in determining the way people behave.

Fundamentalist thought often appears anti-intellectual because of its proneness to oversimplification. The universe is divided in two—the moral and the immoral, the forces of light and darkness. This polarized thinking reflects a crass popularizing that indeed is subversive to serious intellectual inquiry. The fundamentalist worldview starts with the premise that the world is divided between the forces of God and of Satan and sorts out evidence to fit that paradigm. Nevertheless, fundamentalist thinking also reflects a modern intellectual tradition that dates largely from the Enlightenment. Fundamentalist thought had close links with the Baconian and Common Sense assumptions of the early modern era. Humans are capable of positive knowledge based on sure foundations. If rationally classified, such knowledge can yield a great deal of certainty. Combined with biblicism, such a view of knowledge leads to supreme confidence on religious questions. Despite the conspicuous subjectivism throughout evangelicalism and within fundamentalism itself, one side of the fundamentalist mentality is committed to inductive rationalism. [. . .]

This commonsense inductive aspect of fundamentalist

thinking, rather than being anti-intellectual, reflects an intellectual tradition alien to most modern academics. What is most lacking is the contemporary sense of historical development, a Heraclitean sense that all is change. This contemporary conception of history invites relativism or at least the seeing of ambiguities. Fundamentalists have the confidence of Enlightenment philosophies that an objective look at "the facts" will lead to the truth. Their attacks on evolutionism reflect their awareness that the developmentalist, historicist, and culturalist assumptions of modern thought undermine the certainties of knowledge. Correspondingly, persons attracted to authoritarian views of the Bible are often also attracted to the pre-Darwinian, ahistorical, philosophical assumptions that seem to provide high yields of certainty.

It is incorrect, then, to think of fundamentalist thought as essentially premodern. Its views of God's revelation, for example, although drawn from the Bible, are a long way from the modes of thought of the ancient Hebrews. For instance, fundamentalists' intense insistence on the "inerrancy" of the Bible in scientific and historical detail is related to this modern style of thinking. Although the idea that Scripture does not err is an old one, fundamentalists accentuate it partly because they often view the Bible virtually as though it were a scientific treatise. For example, southern Baptist fundamentalist Paige Patterson remarks: "Space scientists tell us that minute error in the mathematical calculations for a moon shot can result in a total failure of the rocket to hit the moon. A slightly altered doctrine of salvation can cause a person to miss Heaven also."[426] To the fundamentalist the Bible is essentially a collection of true and precise propositions. Such approaches may not be typical of most twentieth-century thought, but they are more nearly early modern than premodern.

Fundamentalist thought is in fact highly suited to one strand of contemporary culture—the technological strand. Unlike theoretical science or social science, where questions of the supernatural raise basic issues about the presuppositions of the enterprise, technological thinking does not wrestle with such theoretical principles. Truth is a matter of true and precise propositions that, when properly classified and organized, will work. Fundamentalism fits this mentality because it is a form of Christianity with no loose ends, ambiguities, or historical developments. Everything fits neatly into a system. It is revealing, for instance, that many of the leaders of the creation-science movement are in applied sciences or engineering.

Fundamentalists in more general ways have proved themselves masters of modern technique. The skillful use of organizational mass mailing and media techniques by the fundamentalist New Right during the 1980s elections similarly demonstrated this mastery of an aspect of modern culture. Such expertise in rationalized technique should hardly be surprising in a Protestant American tradition. Moreover, evangelicalism has long depended for support on effectively mobilizing masses of potential constituents. . . .

The Historical Problem Stated

As they would have been the first to tell you, the strict Calvinist theologians at Princeton did not represent all of American evangelicalism. *Evangelicalism,* as I am using it here, refers to that broad movement, found especially in British and American Protestantism, that insisted that "the sole authority in religion is the Bible and the sole means of salvation is a life-transforming experience wrought by the Holy Spirit through faith in Jesus Christ."[427] Although the Princetonians were unhappy with many of the emphases of this broader evangelicalism, they nonetheless were allied with it and eventually became the intellectually most influential group in the conservative, or Bible-believing, evangelicalism that survived and now flourishes in the twentieth century. In fact, the Princetonians have been more influential in twentieth-century evangelicalism than they were among their nineteenth-century contemporaries. The intellectual traits of this elite, then, although not exactly typical, represent unusually well-articulated tendencies that have resonated with the assumptions of an important segment of popular (white) evangelicalism, especially as it faced the secularizing threats of the twentieth century.

From George Marsden, *Understanding Fundamentalism and Evangelicalism* (Grand Rapids, MI: Eerdmans, 1991), 104–5, 116–19, 125–26.

In "Christian Doctrine vs. Liberal Doctrine," **J. Gresham Machen** (1881–1937), an early fundamentalist theologian, argues that modern naturalistic liberalism has displaced the heart of the Christian religion in many churches and communities that identify themselves as Christian.

---

426. Patterson, *Living in the Hope of Eternal Life* (Grand Rapids: Zondervan, 1968), 26.

427. Grant Wacker, *Augustus H. Strong and the Dilemma of Historical Consciousness* (Macon, GA: Mercer University Press, 1985), 17.

J. GRESHAM MACHEN

"Christian Doctrine vs. Liberal Doctrine," in *Christianity and Liberalism*

In the sphere of religion, in particular, the present time is a time of conflict; the great redemptive religion which has always been known as Christianity is battling against a totally diverse type of religious belief, which is only the more destructive of the Christian faith because it makes use of traditional Christian terminology. This modern non-redemptive religion is called "modernism" or "liberalism." Both names are unsatisfactory; the latter, in particular, is question-begging. The movement designated as "liberalism" is regarded as "liberal" only by its friends; to its opponents it seems to involve a narrow ignoring of many relevant facts. And indeed the movement is so various in its manifestations that one may almost despair of finding any common name which will apply to all its forms. But manifold as are the forms in which the movement appears, the root of the movement is one; the many varieties of modern liberal religion are rooted in naturalism—that is, in the denial of any entrance of the creative power of God (as distinguished from the ordinary course of nature) in connection with the origin of Christianity. The word "naturalism" is here used in a sense somewhat different from its philosophical meaning. In this non-philosophical sense it describes with fair accuracy the real root of what is called, by what may turn out to be a degradation of an originally noble word, "liberal" religion.

The rise of this modern naturalistic liberalism has not come by chance, but has been occasioned by important changes which have recently taken place in the conditions of life. The past one hundred years have witnessed the beginning of a new era in human history, which may conceivably be regretted, but certainly cannot be ignored, by the most obstinate conservatism. The change is not something that lies beneath the surface and might be visible only to the discerning eye; on the contrary it forces itself upon the attention of the plain man at a hundred points. Modern inventions and the industrialism that has been built upon them have given us in many respects a new world to live in; we can no more remove ourselves from that world than we can escape from the atmosphere that we breathe.

But such changes in the material conditions of life do not stand alone; they have been produced by mighty changes in the human mind, as in their turn they themselves give rise to further spiritual changes. The industrial world of to-day has been produced not by blind forces of nature but by the conscious activity of the human spirit; it has been produced by the achievements of science. The outstanding feature of recent history is an enormous widening of human knowledge, which has gone hand in hand with such perfecting of the instrument of investigation that scarcely any limits can be assigned to future progress in the material realm.

The application of modern scientific methods is almost as broad as the universe in which we live. Though the most palpable achievements are in the sphere of physics and chemistry, the sphere of human life cannot be isolated from the rest, and with the other sciences there has appeared, for example, a modern science of history, which, with psychology and sociology and the like, claims, even if it does not deserve, full equality with its sister sciences. No department of knowledge can maintain its isolation from the modern lust of scientific conquest; treaties of inviolability, though hallowed by all the sanctions of age-long tradition, are being flung ruthlessly to the winds.

In such an age, it is obvious that every inheritance from the past must be subject to searching criticism; and as a matter of fact some convictions of the human race have crumbled to pieces in the test. Indeed, dependence of any institution upon the past is now sometimes even regarded as furnishing a presumption, not in favor of it, but against it. So many convictions have had to be abandoned that men have sometimes come to believe that all convictions must go. [. . .]

Doctrine

Modern liberalism in the Church, whatever judgment may be passed upon it, is at any rate no longer merely an academic matter. It is no longer a matter merely of theological seminaries or universities. On the contrary its attack upon the fundamentals of the Christian faith is being carried on vigorously by Sunday-School "lesson-helps," by the pulpit, and by the religious press. If such an attack be unjustified, the remedy is not to be found, as some devout persons have suggested, in the abolition of theological seminaries, or the abandonment of scientific theology, but rather in a more earnest search after truth and a more loyal devotion to it when once it is found.

At the theological seminaries and universities, however, the roots of the great issue are more clearly seen than in the world at large; among students the reassuring employment of traditional phrases is often abandoned, and the advocates of a new religion are not at pains, as they are in the Church at large, to maintain an appearance of conformity with the past.

But such frankness, we are convinced, ought to be extended to the people as a whole. Few desires on the part of religious teachers have been more harmfully exaggerated than the desire to "avoid giving offence." Only too often that desire has come perilously near dishonesty; the religious teacher, in his heart of hearts, is well aware of the radicalism of his views, but is unwilling to relinquish his place in the hallowed atmosphere of the Church by speaking his whole mind. Against all such policy of concealment or palliation, our sympathies are altogether with those men, whether radicals or conservatives, who have a passion for light.

What then, at bottom, when the traditional phrases have all been stripped away, is the real meaning of the present revolt against the fundamentals of the Christian faith? What, in brief, are the teachings of modern liberalism as over against the teachings of Christianity?

At the outset, we are met with an objection, "Teachings," it is said, "are unimportant; the exposition of the teachings of liberalism and the teachings of Christianity, therefore, can arouse no interest at the present day; creeds are merely the changing expression of a unitary Christian experience, and provided only they express that experience they are all equally good. The teachings of liberalism, therefore, might be as far removed as possible from the teachings of historic Christianity, and yet the two might be at bottom the same."

Such is the way in which expression is often given to the modern hostility to "doctrine." But is it really doctrine as such that is objected to, and not rather one particular doctrine in the interests of another? Undoubtedly, in many forms of liberalism it is the latter alternative which fits the case. There are doctrines of modern liberalism, just as tenaciously and intolerantly upheld as any doctrines that find a place in the historic creeds. Such for example are the liberal doctrines of the universal fatherhood of God and the universal brotherhood of man. These doctrines are, as we shall see, contrary to the doctrines of the Christian religion. But doctrines they are all the same, and as such they require intellectual defense. In seeming to object to all theology, the liberal preacher is often merely objecting to one system of theology in the interests of another. And the desired immunity from theological controversy has not yet been attained.

Sometimes, however, the modern objection to doctrine is more seriously meant. And whether the objection be well-founded or not, the real meaning of it should at least be faced.

That meaning is perfectly plain. The objection involves an out-and-out skepticism. If all creeds are equally true, then since they are contradictory to one another, they are all equally false, or at least equally uncertain. We are indulging, therefore, in a mere juggling with words. To say that all creeds are equally true, and that they are based upon experience, is merely to fall back upon that agnosticism which fifty years ago was regarded as the deadliest enemy of the Church. The enemy has not really been changed into a friend merely because he has been received within the camp. Very different is the Christian conception of a creed. According to the Christian conception, a creed is not a mere expression of Christian experience, but on the contrary it is a setting forth of those facts upon which experience is based.

But, it will be said, Christianity is a life, not a doctrine. The assertion is often made, and it has an appearance of godliness. But it is radically false, and to detect its falsity one does not even need to be a Christian. For to say that "Christianity is a life" is to make an assertion in the sphere of history. The assertion does not lie in the sphere of ideals; it is far different from saying that Christianity ought to be a life, or that the ideal religion is a life. The assertion that Christianity is a life is subject to historical investigation exactly as is the assertion that the Roman Empire under Nero was a free democracy. Possibly the Roman Empire under Nero would have been better if it had been a free democracy, but the historical question is simply whether as a matter of fact it was a free democracy or no. Christianity is an historical phenomenon, like the Roman Empire, or the Kingdom of Prussia, or the United States of America. And as an historical phenomenon it must be investigated on the basis of historical evidence.

Is it true, then, that Christianity is not a doctrine but a life? The question can be settled only by an examination of the beginnings of Christianity. Recognition of that fact does not involve any acceptance of Christian belief; it is merely a matter of common sense and common honesty. At the foundation of the life of every corporation is the incorporation paper, in which the objects of the corporation are set forth. Other objects may be vastly more desirable than those objects, but if the directors use the name and the resources of the corporation to pursue the other objects they are acting *ultra vires* of the corporation. So it is with Christianity. It is perfectly conceivable that the originators of the Christian movement had no right to legislate for subsequent generations; but at any rate they did have an inalienable right to legislate for all generations that should choose to bear the name of "Christian." It is conceivable that Christianity may now have to be abandoned, and another religion substituted for it; but at any rate the question what Christianity is can be determined only by an examination of the beginnings of Christianity.

The beginnings of Christianity constitute a fairly definite historical phenomenon. The Christian movement originated a few days after the death of Jesus of Nazareth. It is doubtful whether anything that preceded the death of Jesus can be called Christianity. At any rate, if Christianity existed before that event, it was Christianity only in a preliminary stage. The name originated after the death of Jesus, and the thing itself was also something new. Evidently there was an important new beginning among the disciples of Jesus in Jerusalem after the crucifixion. At that time is to be placed the beginning of the remarkable movement which spread out from Jerusalem into the Gentile world—the movement which is called Christianity.

About the early stages of this movement definite historical information has been preserved in the Epistles of Paul, which are regarded by all serious historians as genuine products of the first Christian generation. The writer of the Epistles had been in direct communication with those intimate friends of Jesus who had begun the Christian movement in Jerusalem, and in the Epistles he makes it abundantly plain what the fundamental character of the movement was.

But if any one fact is clear, on the basis of this evidence, it is that the Christian movement at its inception was not just a way of life in the modern sense, but a way of life founded upon a message. It was based, not upon mere feeling, not upon a mere program of work, but upon an account of facts. In other words it was based upon doctrine. [. . .]

It must be admitted, then, that if we are to have a non-doctrinal religion, or a doctrinal religion founded merely on general truth, we must give up not only Paul, not only the primitive Jerusalem Church, but also Jesus Himself. But what is meant by doctrine? It has been interpreted here as meaning any presentation of the facts which lie at the basis of the Christian religion with the true meaning of the facts. But is that the only sense of the word? May the word not also be taken in a narrower sense? May it not also mean a systematic and minute and one-sidedly scientific presentation of the facts? And if the word is taken in this narrower sense, may not the modern objection to doctrine involve merely an objection to the excessive subtlety of controversial theology, and not at all an objection to the glowing words of the New

Testament, an objection to the sixteenth and seventeenth centuries and not at all to the first century? Undoubtedly the word is so taken by many occupants of the pews when they listen to the modern exaltation of "life" at the expense of "doctrine." The pious hearer labors under the impression that he is merely being asked to return to the simplicity of the New Testament, instead of attending to the subtleties of the theologians. Since it has never occurred to him to attend to the subtleties of the theologians, he has that comfortable feeling which always comes to the churchgoer when someone else's sins are being attacked. It is no wonder that the modern invectives against doctrine constitute a popular type of preaching. At any rate, an attack upon Calvin or Turrettin or the Westminster divines does not seem to the modern churchgoer to be a very dangerous thing. In point of fact, however, the attack upon doctrine is not nearly so innocent a matter as our simple churchgoer supposes; for the things objected to in the theology of the Church are also at the very heart of the New Testament. Ultimately the attack is not against the seventeenth century, but against the Bible and against Jesus Himself.

Even if it were an attack not upon the Bible but only upon the great historic presentations of Biblical teaching, it would still be unfortunate. If the Church were led to wipe out of existence all products of the thinking of nineteen Christian centuries and start fresh, the loss, even if the Bible were retained, would be immense. When it is once admitted that a body of facts lies at the basis of the Christian religion, the efforts which past generations have made toward the classification of the facts will have to be treated with respect. In no branch of science would there be any great advance if every generation started fresh with no dependence upon what past generations have achieved. Yet in theology, vituperation of the past seems to be thought essential to progress. And upon what base slanders the vituperation is based! After listening to modern tirades against the great creeds of the Church, one receives rather a shock when one turns to the Westminster Confession, for example, or to that tenderest and most theological of books, the "Pilgrim's Progress" of John Bunyan, and discovers that in doing so one has turned from shallow modern phrases to a "dead orthodoxy" that is pulsating with life in every word. In such orthodoxy there is life enough to set the whole world aglow with Christian love.

From J. Gresham Machen, *Christianity and Liberalism* (New York: Macmillan, 1923), 2–4, 17–21, 45–46.

Radical

∾ In "America and the Future of Theology" (1966) **Thomas J. J. Altizer** presents a form of radical "death-of-God" theology: a position that celebrates the virtues of autonomous secular intellectual and moral judgment. Nevertheless, the goal of radical theology is a reformulation of Christian beliefs around Jesus as the exemplar for, instead of God as the center of, theological reflection.

THOMAS J. J. ALTIZER

"America and the Future of Theology"

The alienation of the thinker from society is an ancient and a universal theme; perhaps its modern variant is the alienation of thought from society. Ours is a time when the individual person has disappeared, or, at least that form of the person has passed away which was the peculiar creation of Western culture and society. If thought is truly alienated from society then the initial movement of thought must be a negation of society, a negation which establishes thought's right to existence. Today the task of thought is the negation of history, and most particularly the negation of the history created by Western man. But this negation must be dialectical, which means that finally it must be affirmation. A negation that arises out of *ressentiment* is forbidden, forbidden because it is merely destructive.

Dialectical negation must never lose a positive ground. Nor can true negation seek a partial or non-dialectical synthesis; it must spurn a twilight which is merely ideological (ideology, as Marx taught us, is thought which is the reflection of society). In our time, thought must hold its goal in abeyance; otherwise it can scarcely establish itself, and is thereby doomed to be a mere appendix to society. If we accept these strictures for theology, then it follows that contemporary theology must be alienated from the Church, that it can be neither kerygmatic, dogmatic nor apologetic, and thus its deepest immediate task is the discovery of its own ground. Like all thought, theology, too, must find its ground in that terrible "night" unveiled by the death of God. It must return to that mystical "dark night" in which the very presence of God has been removed, but now that "night" is all, no longer can theology find a haven in prayer or meditation. Dietrich Bonhoeffer has said that we must not reach the New Testament too quickly, but the time has now come to say that theology can know neither grace nor salvation; for a time it must dwell in darkness, existing on this side of the resurrection. Consequently the theologian must exist outside of

the Church: he can neither proclaim the Word, celebrate the sacraments, nor rejoice in the presence of the Holy Spirit. Before contemporary theology can become itself, it must first exist in silence.

In the presence of a vocation of silence, theology must cultivate the silence of death. To be sure, the death to which theology is called is the death of God. Nor will it suffice for theology to merely accept the death of God. If theology is truly to die, it must *will* the death of God, must *will* the death of Christendom, must freely choose the destiny before it, and therefore must cease to be itself. Everything that theology has thus far become must now be negated; and negated not simply because it is dead, but rather because theology cannot be reborn unless it passes through, and freely wills, its own death and dissolution.

Paradoxically, theology is now impelled to employ the very language that proclaims the death of God. At this point, a great step forward has been taken by biblical scholarship, for the historical consciousness is not simply a sign of Western decadence as Nietzsche believed; it has been a primary means of willing the death of God, of collapsing transcendence into immanence, of realizing a new and awesome human autonomy. When the biblical scholar arrived at an historical understanding of the eschatological foundation of Jesus' proclamation of the Kingdom of God, he brought to an end the contemporary relevance of the biblical form of Jesus' message. No longer could the original form of the Gospel be consigned to the province of "faith," therefore it must be reduced to the level of "myth." Fundamentally, true biblical scholarship is demythologizing. The time has passed when we could live in the illusion that biblical scholarship is scientific and hence non-theological. In a theological sense, the very fact that it is "scientific" means that historical scholarship is Faustian, for to "know" scientifically means to dissolve the ground of faith, and thus to will the death of God. A true instinct led Barth to stand aside from an historical understanding of the Bible, but a deeper instinct will lead theology to say no to Barth. Even at the terrible price of the dissolution of all which theology once knew as faith, it cannot reject the destiny which awaits it.

A theology that is open to the future must first exist in the present, not a present which is an extension of the past, but a present which is a culmination of the past, and hence for us a present which is a moment of vacuity and meaninglessness. Dialectically, the very emptiness of the American present stands witness to its integral relation to a vanished past; just as the almost inevitable tendency of the European thinker to exist in the past demonstrates all too convincingly his refusal of an uprooted present. Nietzsche, who is a true prophet insofar as he speaks out of the depths of our destiny, teaches that authentic human existence is existence in the "here" and "now," in the present moment. *"In jedem Nu beginnt das Sein"* (*Zarathustra III*) is at once a portrait of our *Sein* and a call to true *Existenz*. Yes, we know that our existence (Heidegger's *Dasein* and Sartre's *pour soi*) is chaos, nothingness and despair; but we must not flee it either by clinging to a lost moment of the past or by leaping to a hopelessly transcendent eternity. We are called to accept our actual moment of existence, and to accept it by *willing* it. To refuse to will our destiny is finally to refuse both our identity and our existence. Lament as we may both the shallowness and the barbarism of life in America, we must confess that America exists in the present. Depth is absent here, and so likewise is real power, but the present is at hand, and with its advent has disappeared every form of depth and power that is rooted in the past. To the sophisticated European, America must appear as a desert, a desert shorn of the vegetation of history. But a desert can also be a gateway to the future. Ascetic virtues can arise from the nausea and the *ennui* of life in the desert; a new ascetic may arise whose very weakness will give him the strength to say no to history. If our destiny is truly one of chaos, or if we must pass through chaos to reach our destiny, then we must abandon completely the cosmos of the past.

From Thomas J. J. Altizer and William Hamilton, *Radical Theology and the Death of God* (Indianapolis: Bobbs-Merrill, 1966), 15–16.

Liberation

✍ **Gustavo Gutiérrez,** a Peruvian Roman Catholic theologian, is considered the founder of liberation theology. In "Liberation and Salvation," he traces the theological shift from understanding salvation in an otherworldly sense to understanding salvation in a this-worldly sense. In a this-worldly sense, union with God means building up this world by embracing all and every aspect of humanity.

GUSTAVO GUTIÉRREZ

"Liberation and Salvation," in *A Theology of Liberation: History, Politics, and Salvation*

What is the relationship between salvation and the process of the liberation of man throughout history? Or more precisely, what is the meaning of the struggle against an unjust society and the creation of a new man in the light of the Word? A response to these questions presupposes an attempt to define what is meant by salvation, a concept central to the Christian mystery. This is a complex and difficult task which leads to reflection on the meaning of the saving action of the Lord in history. The salvation of the whole man is centered upon Christ the Liberator.

Salvation: Central Theme of the Christian Mystery

One of the great deficiencies of contemporary theology is the absence of a profound and lucid reflection on the theme of salvation. On a superficial level this might seem surprising, but actually it is what often happens with difficult matters: people are afraid to tackle them. It is taken for granted that they are understood. Meanwhile, new edifices are raised on old foundations established in the past on untested assumptions and vague generalities. The moment comes, however, when the whole building totters; this is the time to look again to the foundations. This hour has arrived for the notion of salvation. Recently various works have appeared attempting to revise and deepen our understanding of this idea.[428] These are only a beginning.

We will not attempt to study this criticism in detail, but will only note that a consideration of this question has revealed two focal points; one follows the other in the manner of two closely linked stages.

From the Quantitative . . .

The questions raised by the notion of salvation have for a long time been considered under and limited by the classical question of the "salvation of the pagans." This is the quantitative, extensive aspect of salvation; it is the problem of the number of persons saved, the possibility of being saved, and the role which the Church plays in this process. The terms of the problem are, on the one hand, the universality of salvation and, on the other, the visible Church as the mediator of salvation.

The evolution of the question has been complex and fatiguing. Today we can say that in a way this evolution has ended. The idea of the universality of the salvific will of

428. Note by Gerhart and Udoh: The author cites texts by Juan Luis Segundo, Christian Duquoc, and Jean-Pierre Jossua.

God, clearly enunciated by Paul in his letter to Timothy, has been established. It has overcome the difficulties posed by various ways of understanding the mission of the Church and has attained definite acceptance. All that is left to do is to consider the ramifications, which are many.

Here we will briefly consider one important point and leave for later a treatment of the repercussions of this idea on ecclesiological matters. The notion of salvation implied in this point of view has two very well-defined characteristics: it is a cure for sin in this life; and this cure is in virtue of a salvation to be attained beyond this life. What is important, therefore, is to know how a man outside the normal pale of grace, which resides in the institutional Church, can attain salvation. Multiple explanations have attempted to show the extraordinary ways by which a person could be assured of salvation, understood above all as life beyond this one. The present life is considered to be a test: one's actions are judged and assessed in relation to the transcendent end. The perspective here is moralistic, and the spirituality is one of flight from this world. Normally, only contact with the channels of grace instituted by God can eliminate sin, the obstacle which stands in the way of reaching that life beyond. This approach is very understandable if we remember that the question of "the salvation of the pagans" was raised at the time of the discovery of people belonging to other religions and living in areas far from those where the Church had been traditionally rooted.

. . . to the Qualitative

As the idea of the universality of salvation and the possibility of reaching it gained ground in the Christian consciousness and as the quantitative question was resolved and decreased in interest, the whole problem of salvation made a qualitative leap and began to be perceived differently. Indeed, there is more to the idea of the universality of salvation than simply asserting the possibility of reaching it while outside the visible frontiers of the Church. The very heart of the question was touched in the search for a means to widen the scope of the possibility of salvation: man is saved if he opens himself to God and to others, even if he is not clearly aware that he is doing so. This is valid for Christians and non-Christians alike—for all people. To speak about the presence of grace—whether accepted or rejected—in all people implies, on the other hand, to value from a Christian standpoint the very roots of human activity. We can no longer speak properly of a profane world.[429] A *qualitative and intensive*

approach replaces a *quantitative and extensive* one. Human existence, in the last instance, is nothing but a yes or a no to the Lord: "Men already partly accept communion with God, although they do not explicitly confess Christ as their Lord, insofar as they are moved by grace (*Lumen gentium,* no. 16), sometimes secretly (*Gaudium et spes,* nos. 3, 22), renounce their selfishness, and seek to create an authentic brotherhood among men. They reject union with God insofar as they turn away from the building up of this world, do not open themselves to others, and culpably withdraw into themselves (Mt 25:31–46)."[430]

From this point of view the notion of salvation appears differently than it did before. Salvation is not something otherworldly, in regard to which the present life is merely a test. Salvation—the communion of men with God and the communion of men among themselves—is something which embraces all human reality, transforms it, and leads it to its fullness in Christ: "Thus the center of God's salvific design is Jesus Christ, who by his death and resurrection transforms the universe and makes it possible for man to reach fulfillment as a human being. This fulfillment embraces every aspect of humanity: body and spirit, individual and society, person and cosmos, time and eternity. Christ, the image of the Father and the perfect God-Man, takes on all the dimensions of human existence."[431]

Therefore, sin is not only an impediment to salvation in the afterlife. Insofar as it constitutes a break with God, sin is a historical reality, it is a breach of the communion of men with each other, it is a turning in of man on himself which manifests itself in a multifaceted withdrawal from others. And because sin is a personal and social intrahistorical reality, a part of the daily events of human life, it is also, and above all, an obstacle to life's reaching the fullness we call salvation.

The idea of a universal salvation, which was accepted only with great difficulty and was based on the desire to expand the possibilities of achieving salvation, leads to the question of the intensity of the presence of the Lord and therefore of the religious significance of man's action in history. One

---

429. "For the orthodox tradition, the profane does not exist, only the profaned" (Olivier Clement, "Un ensayo de lectura ortodoxa de la constitución," in *La Iglesia en el mundo de hoy* (Madrid: Studium, 1967), 673.

430. *La pastoral en las misiones de América Latina,* conclusions of the meeting at Melgar organized by the Department of Missions of CELAM (Bogotá, 1968), 16–17.

431. Ibid., 187–88.

looks then to this world, and now sees in the world beyond not the "true life," but rather the transformation and fulfillment of the present life. The absolute value of salvation—far from devaluing this world—gives it its authentic meaning and its own autonomy, because salvation is already latently there. To express the idea in terms of Biblical theology: the prophetic perspective (in which the Kingdom takes on the present life, transforming it) is vindicated before the sapiential outlook (which stresses the life beyond).

This qualitative, intensive approach has undoubtedly been influenced by the factor which marked the last push toward the unequivocal assertion of the universality of salvation, that is, the appearance of atheism, especially in the heart of Christian countries. The nonbeliever is not interested in an otherworldly salvation, as are believers in other religions; rather he considers it an evasion of the only question he wishes to deal with: the value of earthly existence. The qualitative approach to the notion of salvation attempts to respond to this problem.

The developments which we have reviewed here have allowed us definitively to recover an essential element of the notion of salvation which had been overshadowed for a long time by the question of the possibility of reaching it. We have recovered the idea that salvation is an intrahistorical reality. Furthermore, salvation—the communion of men with God and the communion of men among themselves—orients, transforms, and guides history to its fulfillment.

History Is One

What we have recalled in the preceding paragraph leads us to affirm that, in fact, there are not two histories, one profane and one sacred, "juxtaposed" or "closely linked." Rather there is only one human destiny, irreversibly assumed by Christ, the Lord of history. His redemptive work embraces all the dimensions of existence and brings them to their fullness. The history of salvation is the very heart of human history. The Christian consciousness arrived at this unified view after an evolution parallel to that experienced regarding the notion of salvation. The conclusions converge. From an abstract, essentialist approach we moved to an existential, historical, and concrete view which holds that the only man we know has been efficaciously called to a gratuitous communion with God. All reflection, any distinctions which one wishes to treat, must be based on this fact: the salvific action of God underlies all human existence. The historical destiny of humanity must be placed definitively in the salvific hori-

zon. Only thus will its true dimensions emerge and its deepest meaning be apparent. It seems, however, that contemporary theology has not yet fashioned the categories which would allow us to think through and express adequately this unified approach to history. We work, on the one hand, under the fear of falling back again into the old dualities, and, on the other, under the permanent suspicion of not sufficiently safeguarding divine gratuitousness or the unique dimension of Christianity. Although there may be different approaches to understanding it, however, the fundamental affirmation is clear: there is only one history—a "Christo-finalized" history. [. . .]

Creation and Salvation

The Bible establishes a close link between creation and salvation. But the link is based on the historical and liberating experience of the Exodus. To forget this perspective is to run the risk of merely juxtaposing these two ideas and therefore losing the rich meaning which this relationship has for understanding the recapitulating work of Christ. [. . .]

Political Liberation: Self-Creation of Man

The liberation from Egypt—both a historical fact and at the same time a fertile Biblical theme—enriches this vision and is moreover its true source. The creative act is linked, almost identified, with the act which freed Israel from slavery in Egypt. Second Isaiah, who writes in exile, is likewise the best witness to this idea: "Awake, awake, put on your strength, O arm of the Lord, awake as you did long ago, in days gone by. Was it not you who hacked Rahab in pieces and ran the dragon through? Was it not you who dried up the sea, the waters of the great abyss, and made the ocean depths a path for the ransomed?" (51:9–10) The words and images refer simultaneously to two events: creation and liberation from Egypt. Rahab, which for Isaiah symbolizes Egypt (cf. 30:7; cf. also Ps 87:4), likewise symbolizes the chaos Yahweh had to overcome to create the world (cf. Pss 74:14; 89:11). The "waters of the great abyss" are those which enveloped the world and from which creation arose, but they are also the Red Sea which the Jews crossed to begin the Exodus. Creation and liberation from Egypt are but one salvific act. It is significant, furthermore, that the technical term *bara,* designating the original creation, was used for the first time by Second Isaiah (43:1, 15; cf. Deut 32:6) to refer to the creation of Israel. Yahweh's historical actions on behalf of his people are considered creative (41:20; 43:7; 45:8; 48:7). The God who frees Israel is the Creator of the world.

The liberation of Israel is a political action. It is the breaking away from a situation of despoliation and misery and the beginning of the construction of a just and fraternal society. It is the suppression of disorder and the creation of a new order. The initial chapters of Exodus describe the oppression in which the Jewish people lived in Egypt, in that "land of slavery" (13:3; 20:2; Deut 5:6): repression (1:10–11), alienated work (5:6–14), humiliations (1:13–14), enforced birth control policy (1:15–22). Yahweh then awakens the vocation of a liberator: Moses. "I have indeed seen the misery of my people in Egypt. I have heard their outcry against their slave-masters. I have taken heed of their sufferings, and have come down to rescue them from the power of Egypt. . . . I have seen the brutality of the Egyptians towards them. Come now; I will send you to Pharaoh and you shall bring my people Israel out of Egypt" (3:7–10).

Sent by Yahweh, Moses began a long, hard struggle for the liberation of his people. The alienation of the children of Israel was such that at first "they did not listen to him; they had become impatient because of their cruel slavery" (6:9). And even after they had left Egypt, when they were threatened by Pharaoh's armies, they complained to Moses: "Were there no graves in Egypt, that you should have brought us here to die in the wilderness? See what you have done to us by bringing us out of Egypt! Is not this just what we meant when we said in Egypt, 'Leave us alone; let us be slaves to the Egyptians'? We would rather be slaves to the Egyptians than die here in the wilderness" (14:11–12). And in the midst of the desert, faced with the first difficulties, they told him that they preferred the security of slavery—whose cruelty they were beginning to forget—to the uncertainties of a liberation in process: "If only we had died at the Lord's hand in Egypt, where we sat round the fleshpots and had plenty of bread to eat!" (16:3). A gradual pedagogy of successes and failures would be necessary for the Jewish people to become aware of the roots of their oppression, to struggle against it, and to perceive the profound sense of the liberation to which they were called. The Creator of the world is the Creator and Liberator of Israel, to whom he entrusts the mission of establishing justice: "Thus speaks the Lord who is God, he who created the skies . . . who fashioned the earth. . . . I, the Lord, have called you with righteous purpose and taken you by the hand; I have formed you, and appointed you . . . to open eyes

that are blind, to bring captives out of prison, out of the dungeons where they lie in darkness" (Isa 42:5–7).

Creation, as we have mentioned above, is regarded in terms of the Exodus, a historical-salvific fact which structures the faith of Israel. And this fact is a political liberation through which Yahweh expresses his love for his people and the gift of total liberation is received.

From Gustavo Gutiérrez, *A Theology of Liberation: History, Politics, and Salvation* (Maryknoll, NY: Orbis Books, 1973), 149–57. [Ellipses in original except where bracketed.]

☙ **James H. Cone,** an African American liberation theologian, calls Christians to confront the racism not only of society but of white Christianity as well. In "God in Black Theology" (first published in 1970), Cone contends that knowing God means taking the side of the oppressed and working with them toward liberation.

JAMES H. CONE

"God in Black Theology," in *A Black Theology of Liberation*

The reality of God is presupposed in black theology. Black theology is an attempt to analyze the nature of that reality, asking what we can say about the nature of God in view of God's self-disclosure in biblical history and the oppressed condition of black Americans.

If we take the question seriously, it becomes evident that there is no simple answer to it. To speak of God and God's Participation in the liberation of the oppressed of the land is a risky venture in any society. But if the society is racist and also uses God-language as an instrument to further the cause of human humiliation, then the task of authentic theological speech is even more dangerous and difficult.

It is *dangerous* because the true prophet of the gospel of God must become both "anti-Christian" and "unpatriotic." It is impossible to confront a racist society, with the meaning of human existence grounded in commitment to the divine, without at the same time challenging the very existence of the national structure and all its institutions, especially the established churches. All national institutions represent the interests of society as a whole. We live in a nation which is committed to the perpetuation of white supremacy, and it will try to exterminate all who fail to support this ideal. The genocide of the Amerindian is evidence of that fact. Black theology represents that community of blacks who refuse to cooperate in the exaltation of whiteness and the degradation of blackness. It proclaims the reality of the biblical God who is actively destroying everything that is against the manifestation of black human dignity.

Because whiteness by its very nature is against blackness, the black prophet is a prophet of national doom. He proclaims the end of the "American Way," for God has stirred the soul of the black community, and now that community will stop at nothing to claim the freedom that is three hundred and fifty years overdue. The black prophet is a rebel with a cause, the cause of over twenty-five million American blacks and all oppressed persons everywhere. It is God's cause because God has chosen the blacks as God's own people. And God has chosen them not for redemptive suffering but for freedom. Blacks are not elected to be Yahweh's suffering people. Rather we are elected because we are oppressed against our will and God's, and God has decided to make our liberation God's own undertaking. We are elected to be free now to do the work for which we were called into being—namely, the breaking of chains. Black theologians must assume the dangerous responsibility of articulating the revolutionary mood of the black community. This means that their speech about God, in the authentic prophetic tradition, will always move on the brink of treason and heresy in an oppressive society.

The task of authentic theological speech is *difficult* because all religionists in society claim to be for God and thus for humankind. Even executioners are for God. They carry out punitive acts against certain segments of society because "decent" citizens need protection against undesirables. That is why blacks were enslaved and Amerindians exterminated—in the name of God and freedom. That is why today blacks are forced into ghettos and shot down like dogs if they raise a hand in protest.

When George Washington, Thomas Jefferson, Lyndon Johnson, Richard Nixon, and other "great" Americans can invoke the name of God at the same time that they are shaping society for whites only, then black theology knows it cannot approach the God-question too casually. It must ask, "How can we speak of God without being associated with oppressors?" White racism is so pervasive that oppressors can destroy the revolutionary mood among the oppressed by introducing a complacent white God into the black community, thereby quelling the spirit of freedom.

Therefore if blacks want to break their chains, they must recognize the need for going all the way if liberation is to be a reality. The white God will point to heavenly bliss as a means of detouring blacks away from earthly rage. Freedom comes when we realize that it is against our interests, as a self-determining black community, to point out the "good" elements in an oppressive structure. *There are no assets to slavery!* Every segment of society participates in black oppression. To accept the white God, to see good in evil, is to lose sight of the goal of the revolution—the destruction of everything "masterly" in society. "All or nothing" is the only possible attitude for the black community.

Must We Discard God-Language?

Realizing that it is very easy to be co-opted by the enemy and the enemy's God-language, it is tempting to discard all references to God and seek to describe a way of living in the world that could not possibly be associated with "Christian" murderers. Some existentialist writers—Camus and Sartre—have taken this course, and many black revolutionaries find this procedure appealing. Reacting to the ungodly behavior of white churches and the timid, Uncle Tom approach of black churches, many black militants have no time for God and the deadly prattle about loving your enemies and turning the other cheek. Christianity, they argue, participates in the enslavement of black Americans. Therefore an emancipation from white oppression means also liberation from the ungodly influences of white religion.

This approach is certainly understandable, and the merits of the argument warrant a serious investigation. As black theologians seeking to analyze the meaning of black liberation, we cannot ignore this approach. Indeed, it is quite intellectually tempting. Nevertheless two observations are in order at this juncture.

1. Black theology affirms that there is nothing special about the English word "God" in itself. What is important is the dimension of reality to which it points. The word "God" is a symbol that opens up depths of reality in the world. If the symbol loses its power to point to the meaning of black liberation, then we must destroy it. Black theology asks whether the word "God" has lost its liberating power. Must we say that as a meaningful symbol the word "God" is hopelessly dead and cannot be resurrected?

Certainly black theology realizes that, when a society performs ungodly acts against the poor in the name of God, there may come a time when the oppressed might have to renounce all claims to that kind of "faith" in God in order to affirm authentic faith in God. Sometimes because of the very nature of oppressed existence, the oppressed must define their being by negating everything oppressors affirm, including belief in the God of oppressors. The oppressed must demonstrate that all communications are cut off. In Camus's words:

> There is, in fact, nothing in common between a master and a slave; it is impossible to speak and communicate with a person who has been reduced to servitude.[432]

Oppressed and oppressors cannot possibly mean the same thing when they speak of God. The God of the oppressed is a God of revolution who breaks the chains of slavery. The oppressors' God is a God of slavery and must be destroyed along with the oppressors. The question then, as black theology sees it, is not whether blacks believe in God, but whose God?

2. In response to those inclined to discard God-language, black theology also believes that the destiny of blacks is inseparable from the religious dimensions inherent in the black community. Theologically, one way of describing this reality is to call it general revelation. This means that all human beings have a sense of the presence of God, a feeling of awe, and it is precisely this experience that makes them creatures who always rebel against domestication. The black community is thus a religious community, a community that views its liberation as the work of the divine.

It is important to note that every significant black liberation movement has had its religious dimensions. Black liberation as a movement began with the pre–Civil War black churches which recognized that Christian freedom grounded in Jesus Christ was inseparable from civil freedom. That is why black preachers were the leaders in the struggle for the abolition of slavery, and why southern slave owners refused to allow the establishment of independent black churches in the south. It is true, however, that the post–Civil War black church lost its emphasis on civil freedom and began to identify Christianity with moral purity. But this does not mean that religion is irrelevant altogether; it only means that religion unrelated to black liberation is irrelevant.

To try to separate black liberation from black religion is a mistake, because black religion is authentic only when it is identified with the struggle for black freedom. The influence of Marcus Garvey, Elijah Muhammed, Malcolm X, and Martin Luther King, Jr., demonstrates the role of religion in the black community.

It is not the task of black theology to remove the influence

of the divine in the black community. Its task is to interpret the divine element in the forces and achievements of black liberation. Black theology must retain God-language despite its perils, because the black community perceives its identity in terms of divine presence. Black theology cannot create new symbols independent of the black community and expect blacks to respond. It must stay in the black community and get down to the real issues at hand ("cutting throats" to use LeRoi Jones's phrase) and not waste too much time discussing the legitimacy of religious language.

The legitimacy of any language, religious or otherwise, is determined by its usefulness in the struggle for liberation. That the God-language of white religion has been used to create a docile spirit among blacks so that whites could aggressively attack them is beyond question. But that does not mean that we cannot kill the white God, so that the presence of the black God can become known in the black-white encounter. The white God is an idol created by racists, and we blacks must perform the iconoclastic task of smashing false images.

Hermeneutical Principle for the Doctrine of God

Every doctrine of God is based on a particular theological methodology. For instance, Karl Barth's theological point of departure is the word of God as revealed in the man Jesus. We know who God is, according to Barth, because we know who Christ is. To look for the knowledge of God other than in Christ is to look in the wrong place, and thus end up constructing images which reflect human pride rather than divine revelation. "The knowledge of God occurs in the fulfillment of the revelation of His Word by the Holy Spirit."[433]

Paul Tillich, on the other hand, does not share Barth's kerygmatic emphasis. His theological methodology is a "method of correlation," in which he seeks to relate the changeless gospel to changing cultural situations. Culture, according to Tillich, is indispensable for God-talk.

Relying heavily on existential philosophy and its analysis of the human condition (a condition best described by the word "estrangement"), Tillich describes God as being-itself, which provides the only answer to human estrangement

---

432. Albert Camus, *The Rebel*, trans. by Anthony Bower, Vintage Book V30 (New York: Random House, 1956), 283.

433. Barth, *Church Dogmatics*, vol. 2, part 1, trans. by T. H. L. Parker, W. B. Johnston, Harold Knight, J. L. M. Haire (Edinburgh: T. and T. Clark, 1957), 3.

from self and neighbor. Because being-itself is free from the threat of nonbeing or nothingness, it is the source of human courage—the ability to affirm being in spite of the presence of nonbeing. Therefore "God" is a symbolic word pointing to the dimension of reality which is the answer to the human condition.

Inasmuch as the perspective of black theology differs from that of both Barth and Tillich, there is also a difference in its approach to the doctrine of God. The point of departure of black theology is the biblical God as related to the black liberation struggle. It asks, "How do we *dare* speak of God in a suffering world, a world in which blacks are humiliated because they are black?" This question, which occupies the central place in our theological perspective, forces us to say nothing about God that does not participate in the emancipation of black humanity. God-talk is not Christian-talk unless it is *directly* related to the liberation of the oppressed. Any other talk is at best an intellectual hobby, and at worst blasphemy.

There are, then, two hermeneutical principles which are operative in the black theology analysis of the doctrine of God.

1. The Christian understanding of God arises from the biblical view of revelation, a revelation of God that takes place in the liberation of oppressed Israel and is completed in the incarnation, in Jesus Christ. This means that whatever is said about the nature of God and God's being-in-the-world must be based on the biblical account of God's revelatory activity. We are not free to say anything we please about God. Although scripture is not the only source that helps us to recognize divine activity in the world, it cannot be ignored if we intend to speak of the Holy One of Israel.

2. The doctrine of God in black theology must be of the God who is participating in the liberation of the oppressed of the land. This hermeneutical principle arises out of the first. Because God has been revealed in the history of oppressed Israel and decisively in the Oppressed One, Jesus Christ, it is impossible to say anything about God without seeing him as being involved in the contemporary liberation of all oppressed peoples. The God in black theology is the God of and for the oppressed, the God who comes into view in their liberation. Any other approach is a denial of biblical revelation.

New Wine in New Wineskins

Because black theology is the theology of black liberation, it must break with traditional theological speech when that speech softens the drive for black self-determination. It cannot run the risk of putting "new wine into old wineskins" (Mark 2:22). When Jesus used the phrase, he was referring to the kingdom of God and its relationship to the conventional Judaism of his time.

When black theologians analyze the doctrine of God, seeking to relate it to the emerging black revolution in America, they must be especially careful not to put this new wine (the revelation of God as expressed in black power) into old wineskins (white folk-religion). The black theology view of God must be sharply distinguished from white distortions of God. This does not mean that black theology rejects white theology entirely. Unfortunately, this cannot be done, for oppression always means that the communication skills of an oppressed community are determined to a large degree by the oppressors. That is precisely the meaning of oppression! Because black theologians are trained in white seminaries, and white thinkers make decisions about the structure and scope of theology, it is not possible for black religionists to separate themselves immediately and completely from white thought.

When Jesus spoke of the gospel as new wine, it did not mean a total rejection of Judaism. What he meant was that the revolutionary message could not be restricted to the possibilities available in the old structure.

Similarly, because our knowledge of Christianity came from white oppressors, the black theology view of God is in part dependent on white theologians, but this does not mean white theologians set the criteria for black theology. Liberation means that the oppressed must define the structure and scope of reality for themselves; they do not take their cues from oppressors. If there is one brutal fact that the centuries of white oppression have taught blacks, it is that whites are incapable of making any valid judgment about human existence. The goal of black theology is the destruction of *everything* white, so that blacks can be liberated from alien gods.

The God of black liberation will not be confused with a bloodthirsty white idol. Black theology must show that the black God has nothing to do with the God worshiped in white churches whose primary purpose is to sanctify the racism of whites and to daub the wounds of blacks. Putting new wine in new wineskins means that the black theology view of God has nothing in common with those who prayed for an American victory in Vietnam or who pray for a "cool" summer in the ghetto.

The refusal of black theology to put new wine in old wineskins also means that it will show that the God of the black community cannot be confused with the God of white seminaries. With their intellectual expertise, it is inevitable that white scholars fall into the racist error of believing that they have the right to define what is and what is not orthodox religious talk. Because they have read so many of their own books and heard themselves talk so often, it is not surprising that they actually believe most of the garbage they spout out about God. They therefore think that all authentic God-talk must meet their approval before it can be called theology. But black theology rejects their standards, for we know they speak for oppressors, and thus will inevitably analyze the nature of God in the interests of white society as a whole.

Black theology must also be suspicious of so-called white revolutionary theologians. What is most disturbing about their self-proclaimed identification with black power is their inability to let *us* speak for ourselves. They still insist on defining what black power is, and not only in private conversations but also in print. And to make it worse, they invariably miss the whole point of black power. They should know by now that, in view of white brutality against blacks and church participation in it, no white person who is halfway sensitive to black self-determination should have the audacity to speak for blacks. That is the problem! *Too many whites think they know how we feel about them.* If whites were really serious about their radicalism in regard to the black revolution and its theological implications in America, they would keep silent and take instructions from blacks. Only blacks can speak about God in relationship to their liberation. And those who wish to join us in this divine work must be willing to lose their white identity—indeed, destroy it.

Black theology also rejects any identification with the "death of God" theology. The death-of-God question is a white issue which arises out of the white experience. Questions like "How do we find meaning and purpose in a world in which God is absent?" are questions of an affluent society. Whites may wonder how to find purpose in their lives, but our purpose is forced upon us. We do not want to know how we can get along without God, but how we can survive in a world permeated with white racism.

God Is Black

Because blacks have come to know themselves as *black,* and because that blackness is the cause of their own love of themselves and hatred of whiteness, the blackness of God is the key to our knowledge of God. The blackness of God, and everything implied by it in a racist society, is the heart of the black theology doctrine of God. There is no place in

black theology for a colorless God in a society where human beings suffer precisely because of their color. The black theologian must reject any conception of God which stifles black self-determination by picturing God as a God of all peoples. Either God is identified with the oppressed to the point that their experience becomes God's experience, or God is a God of racism.

As Camus has pointed out, authentic identification

> [is not] a question of psychological identification—a mere subterfuge by which the individual imagines that it is he himself who is being offended. . . . [It is] identification of one's destiny with that of others and a choice of sides.[434]

Because God has made the goal of blacks God's own goal, black theology believes that it is not only appropriate but necessary to begin the doctrine of God with an insistence on God's blackness.

The blackness of God means that God has made the oppressed condition God's own condition. This is the essence of the biblical revelation. By electing Israelite slaves as the people of God and by becoming the Oppressed One in Jesus Christ, the human race is made to understand that God is known where human beings experience humiliation and suffering. It is not that God feels sorry and takes pity on them (the condescending attitude of those racists who need their guilt assuaged for getting fat on the starvation of others); quite the contrary, God's election of Israel and incarnation in Christ reveal that the *liberation* of the oppressed is a part of the innermost nature of God. Liberation is not an afterthought, but the essence of divine activity.

The blackness of God means that the essence of the nature of God is to be found in the concept of liberation. Taking seriously the Trinitarian view of the Godhead, black theology says that as Creator, God identified with oppressed Israel, participating in the bringing into being of this people; as Redeemer, God became the Oppressed One in order that all may be free from oppression; as Holy Spirit, God continues the work of liberation. The Holy Spirit is the Spirit of the Creator and the Redeemer at work in the forces of human liberation in our society today. In America, the Holy Spirit is black persons making decisions about their togetherness, which means making preparation for an encounter with whites.

It is the black theology emphasis on the blackness of God

---

434. Camus, *The Rebel,* 16, 17.

that distinguishes it sharply from contemporary white views of God. White religionists are not capable of perceiving the blackness of God, because their satanic whiteness is a denial of the very essence of divinity. That is why whites are finding and will continue to find the black experience a disturbing reality.

White theologians would prefer to do theology without reference to color, but this only reveals how deeply racism is embedded in the thought forms of their culture. To be sure, they would *probably* concede that the concept of liberation is essential to the biblical view of God. But it is still impossible for them to translate the biblical emphasis on liberation to the black-white struggle today. Invariably they quibble on this issue, moving from side to side, always pointing out the dangers of extremism on both sides. (In the black community, we call this "shuffling.") They really cannot make a decision, because it has already been made for them.

How scholars would analyze God and blacks was decided when black slaves were brought to this land, while churchmen sang "Jesus, Lover of My Soul." Their attitude today is no different from that of the bishop of London who assured slaveholders that:

> Christianity, and the embracing of the Gospel, does not make the least Alteration in Civil property, or in any Duties which belong to Civil Relations; but in all these Respects, it continues Persons just in the same State as it found them. The Freedom which Christianity gives, is a Freedom from the Bondage of Sin and Satan, and from the dominion of Man's Lust and Passions and inordinate Desires; but as to their outward Condition, whatever that was before, whether bond or free, their being baptized and becoming Christians, makes no matter of change in it.[435]

Of course white theologians today have a "better" way of putting it, but what difference does that make? It means the same thing to blacks. "Sure," as the so-called radicals would say, "God is concerned about blacks." And then they would go on to talk about God and secularization or some other white problem unrelated to the emancipation of blacks. This style is a contemporary white way of saying that "Christianity does not make the least alteration in civil property."

In contrast to this racist view of God, black theology proclaims God's blackness. Those who want to know who God is and what God is doing must know who black persons are and what they are doing. This does not mean lending a helping hand to the poor and unfortunate blacks of society. It

does not mean joining the war on poverty! Such acts are sin offerings that represent a white way of assuring themselves that they are basically "good" persons. Knowing God means being on the side of the oppressed, becoming *one* with them, and participating in the goal of liberation. *We must become black with God!*

It is to be expected that whites will have some difficulty with the idea of "becoming *black* with God." The experience is not only alien to their existence as they know it to be, it appears to be an impossibility. "How can whites become black?" they ask. This question always amuses me because they do not really want to lose their precious white identity, as if it is worth saving. They know, as everyone in this country knows, blacks are those who say they are black, regardless of skin color. In the literal sense a black person is anyone who has "even one drop of black blood in his or her veins." But "becoming black with God" means more than just saying "I am black," if it involves that at all. The question "How can white persons become black?" is analogous to the Philippian jailer's question to Paul and Silas, "What must I do to be saved?" The implication is that if we work hard enough at it, we can reach the goal. But the misunderstanding here is the failure to see that blackness or salvation (the two are synonymous) is the work of God, not a human work. It is not something we accomplish; it is a gift. That is why Paul and Silas said, "Believe in the Lord Jesus and you will be saved."

To *believe* is to receive the gift and utterly to reorient one's existence on the basis of the gift. The gift is so unlike what humans expect that when it is offered and accepted, we become completely new creatures. This is what the Wholly Otherness of God means. God comes to us in God's blackness, which is wholly unlike whiteness. To receive God's revelation is to become black with God by joining God in the work of liberation.

Even some blacks will find this view of God hard to handle. Having been enslaved by the God of white racism so long, they will have difficulty believing that God is identified with their struggle for freedom. Becoming one of God's disciples means rejecting whiteness and accepting themselves as they are in all their physical blackness. This is what the Christian view of God means for blacks.

From James H. Cone, *A Black Theology of Liberation,* 2nd ed. (Maryknoll, NY: Orbis Books, 1986), 55–66. [Ellipses and brackets in original.]

---

435. Quoted in H. Richard Niebuhr, *The Social Sources of Denominationalism* (Cleveland: Meridian Books, 1929), 249.

ஃ In "Black Experience, Wilderness Experience, Theological Task," **Dolores S. Williams** argues that American black liberation theology has been largely androcentric in its construction of the "black experience" as a foundation for theology. Williams suggests that a broader "wilderness experience" theology is a more adequate category for including the experience of black women in black theology.

DOLORES S. WILLIAMS

"Black Experience, Wilderness Experience, Theological Task," in *Sisters in the Wilderness: The Challenge of Womanist God-Talk*

The works of the black liberation theologians used in this study agree that racial oppression helped create what they refer to as the black experience. Black liberation theology presents blackness as an important qualitative, symbolic and sometimes sacred aspect of the black experience. It portrays the experience as a holistic reality with four active constituents.

1. *The Horizontal Encounter.* This is interaction between black and white groups in a socio-historical context. The interaction results in negative and/or positive relationships and sociopolitical situations. Most often the encounter between blacks and whites is described negatively in black liberation theology. From this encounter, suffering has become a characteristic of African-American community life.

2. *The Vertical Encounter.* In this category black liberation theologians speak of the meeting between God and oppressed people. This meeting not only results in the creation of sustaining and nurturing cultural forms, like black religion, but the oppressed also achieve positive psychological and physical states of freedom and liberation.

3. *Transformations of Consciousness.* These can occur in both a positive and negative sense. They are positive when oppressed people arrive at self or group-identity through awareness of self-worth and through the appreciation of the value of black people and black culture. Transformations of consciousness are negative when black people give up positive black consciousness and identify with alien and destructive forms of consciousness.

4. *An Epistemological Process.* This is a special way the mind processes data on the basis of action in the three categories above. The socio-historical context plays an important role in this process. (Theologian James Cone emphasizes the significance of this process for the black theological task.)

In their various writings, black liberation theologians discuss the black experience in accord with the effects of one or more of these active constituents. On the basis of negative effects in horizontal encounters, in his early works James Cone describes the black experience as a life of humiliation and suffering . . . the totality of black existence in a white world where babies are tortured, women are raped and men are shot. The black experience is existence in a system of white racism.[436]

Relying on the creators of black art for part of his understanding of the social effects of horizontal encounters between black and white people, Cone recalls the poet Don Lee's claim that the black experience refers concretely to black people sleeping in subways, "being bitten by rats, six people living in a kitchenette."[437] In his later work Cone recognized a redeeming character of this experience when he describes black people, in the midst of hostile relationships, trying to shape life and "to live it according to their dreams and aspirations."[438]

James Deotis Roberts, on the other hand, alludes to the black experience in terms of the positive and negative effects of the horizontal encounter between black and white people. He expresses an "appreciation for the Euro-American contributions to black culture in this country."[439] Nevertheless, Roberts communicates his understanding of the black experience as a negative sociopolitical reality where dehumanizing relationships exist between black and white people.

While the history and character of black/white relations are important, the Cones and Roberts suggest that the vertical encounter between God and humans constitutes the most salient feature of the black experience. This encounter occurs in history and empowers black people to transform negative, oppressive social forces into positive, life-sustaining forms. Theologian Cecil Cone most graphically describes the powerful action in this encounter. He emphasizes the positive psychological benefits black slaves derived from meeting God:

> The power of God . . . provided creative possibilities in a noncreative situation. Recognition of one's sinfulness was merely the first step in the dynamics of the black religious

---

436. James Cone, *A Black Theology of Liberation,* 1st ed. (Philadelphia and New York: J. B. Lippincott Co., 1970), 55.

437. Ibid.

438. James Cone, *God of the Oppressed* (New York: Seabury Press, 1975), 23.

439. James Deotis Roberts, *Liberation and Reconciliation* (Philadelphia: Westminster Press, 1971), 9.

experience. It was followed by what has commonly been known in black religion as saving conversion. The character of conversion was marked by the suddenness with which the slave's heart was changed. It was an abrupt change in his entire orientation toward reality; it affected every aspect of the slave's attitudes and beliefs. . . . The new level of reality . . . caused the slaves to experience a sense of freedom in the midst of human bondage.[440]

On the basis of this encounter and the ensuing conversion, many slaves gained strength to oppose the social and political structures enslaving black people. Cecil Cone cites black slave preachers (Nat Turner, Denmark Vesey, Gabriel Prosser) who connected their slave rebellions with their encounters with God. Richard Allen, another slave, gained strength in his encounter with God and proceeded with his efforts to establish the African Methodist Episcopal Church.

While Cecil Cone suggests that the God-human encounter conditions black experience, James Deotis Roberts suggests that black experience is affected by certain transformations in black consciousness. James Cone emphasizes a special epistemological process as foundational for the black experience. Roberts declares that knowledge of the transformations in black consciousness is vital for understanding god-talk in the black community. He says the theologians can choose how to interpret the black experience, but they are obligated to show the character of black consciousness transformed so that the black person "moves from color blindness to color consciousness" and becomes aware of the implications of Black Power.[441]

Transformations of consciousness, horizontal and vertical encounters and epistemological processes happen in a socio-historical context. Hence the socio-historical context of actions and ideas is important in black liberation theology. In accord with a sociology of knowledge perspective, James Cone claims that consciousness is created by the social context, and so epistemological realities are different for black and white people. Therefore, black theologians and white theologians have different mental grids. For Cone, "the social environment functions as a mental grid deciding what will be considered as relevant data in a given inquiry."[442] These different mental grids determine the sources and the method each theologian uses in the construction of theological statements.

Apparently Cone is suggesting an epistemological screening process created by a people's history, cultural patterns, political realities, socio-religious values and patterns of action. This mental grid becomes a way of knowing which determines modes of action. On the basis of James Cone's discussion of the social context of theology, it is obvious that the black experience—with its horizontal encounters, vertical encounters and transformations of consciousness—is also an epistemological screen through which black people perceive, respond to and help create their reality.

For James Cone, James Deotis Roberts and Cecil Cone, the black experience determines the task of black theology. However, each of these theologians emphasizes a different aspect of this experience in his understanding of the theological task. James Cone emphasizes the church's vertical encounter with God in relation to God's liberating work in the world. Theology concerns revelation, and revelation is described as "the liberating character of God's presence in Jesus Christ as he calls his people into being for freedom in the world."[443] The task of theology is confessional, for the theologian (as exegete, prophet, teacher, preacher and philosopher) must clarify the church's faith in relation to its participation in God's liberating activity in the world.

James Deotis Roberts suggests that the theological task involves healing the negative relations in horizontal encounters. Thus theologians must minister to both blacks and whites. They speak the message of liberation to the victims of oppression. Yet, if theologians speak the Christian message, they must speak reconciliation regardless of the risks and the personal costs.

Cecil Cone apparently understands the theological task not only to involve the black theologian's attempt to acquaint the community with the meaning at the heart of black religion, that is, the community's radical encounter in history with the "almighty sovereign God." Since, for Cecil Cone, "Black religion is . . . [the] only appropriate point of departure" for black theology, the task of black theologians is also to explicate this religion so that all of its dimensions are seen and understood by the community. Of special importance is the theologians' task of emphasizing and assessing the conversion experience, which results from black people's encounter with the almighty sovereign God.[444] Thus Cecil Cone also stresses the vertical encounter in relation to the black theological task.

---

440. Cecil Wayne Cone, *The Identity Crisis in Black Theology* (Nashville, TN: African Methodist Episcopalian Press, 1975), 43, 45.

441. Roberts, *Liberation and Reconciliation*, 14.

442. James Cone, *God of the Oppressed*, 52.

443. Ibid., 8.

444. Cecil Cone, *The Identity Crisis in Black Theology*, 18.

This notion of black experience and the theological tasks associated with it are determined by the black liberation theologians' view of black history. James Cone, Cecil Cone and James Deotis Roberts, in the works used here, present the anthropological side of black history as a continuous social and political struggle between black and white people over the issues of enslavement and the dominance and prevalence of racial oppression in white-black relations. This struggle has informed the creation of black art, religion and culture. But language about the struggle assumes an androcentric black history. Therefore a masculine indication of person and masculine models of victimization dominate the language and thought of black liberation theology.[445] Therefore one can conclude, as theologian Jacqueline Grant did some years ago, that black women have been left out of black liberation theology and its understanding of historical agency.[446] The black experience and theological tasks described therein (as well as the view of history) presuppose and perpetuate black androcentrism.

Womanist analysis in the preceding chapters suggests another kind of history to which black theology must give attention if it intends to be inclusive of black women's experience. This is "women's re/production history." It involves more than women birthing children, nurturing and attending to family affairs. Though the events and ideas associated with these realities do relate, "women's re/production history" has to do with whatever women think, create, use and pass on through their labor for the sake of women's and the family's well-being. Thus black women's resistance strategies belong to black women's re/production history—just as the oppressive opposition to these strategies from dominating cultures belongs to this history. Through the lens of black women's re/production history we can see the entire saga of the race. We see the survival intelligence of the race creating modes of resistance, sustenance and resurrection from despair. We see the exploitation of the community's spiritual, material and intellectual resources by extra-community forces met by the uncanny, redemptive response of the religion black women created in the African-American denominational churches.

Black women's re/production history provides the context in which the black experience is appropriated as a female-and-male inclusive wilderness experience. The movement from black experience to wilderness experience expands the content and merges some of the categorical constituents described above as making up the notion of black experience reflected in black liberation theology. For example, the wilderness experience can also be said to be composed of horizontal encounters and vertical encounters. However, the content enlarges. Whereas the horizontal encounter in the black experience involved interaction "between black and white groups in a socio-historical context" and primarily presupposes encounters between males, in the wilderness experience the horizontal encounter presupposes female-male and female-female encounters. The black experience assumes that the suffering characteristic of the African-American community has resulted only from the horizontal encounter between blacks and whites. The wilderness experience suggests that this characteristic suffering has also resulted from black women's oppression in society and from the exploitation of black women in family contexts. Whereas the vertical encounter in the black experience in black liberation theology involves the meeting between God and oppressed people (read men) resulting in the creation of androcentric cultural forms and hierarchical relational patterns, the encounter between God and women in the wilderness experience does more than strengthen women's faith and empower them to persevere in spite of trouble. The meeting between God and enslaved women of African descent also provides these women with new vision to see survival resources where they saw none before.[447] And black women understand these resources to be for the sustenance of a family-centered rather than an androcentric or fema-centric black culture.

In the vertical encounter between black women and God in the wilderness experience, transformation of consciousness and epistemological process come together in the new great faith-consciousness this meeting bestows upon black women. This faith-consciousness guides black women's way of being and acting in the wide, wide world. Their stories tell of their absolute dependence upon God generated by a faith-consciousness incorporating survival intelligence and visionary capacity.[448] This survival intelligence and vision shape the

---

445. However, it should be noted here that in the last printing of his book *A Black Theology of Liberation*, James Cone included a new introduction that owns the sexist character of his early work. In the new printing, Cone uses inclusive language. But Cone does not use the heritage of black female intellection to shape his ideas in the most recent issue of the book.

446. Jacqueline Grant, "Black Theology and Black Women," in *Black Theology: A Documentary History, 1966–1979*, ed. James Cone and Gayraud Wilmore (Maryknoll, NY: Orbis Books, 1979), 418–33.

447. Hagar's encounter with God in Genesis 21 results in her receiving new vision that allowed her to see the resources for saving the life of her nearly dead child Ishmael.

448. For a long time some folk wisdom in the black community has claimed that in relation to the community's survival and liberation, "the brothers dream dreams," but "the sisters have the vision."

strategies black women and the black community use to deal with or resist difficult life situations and death-dealing circumstances.[449] Without this female faith-consciousness and its constituent parts basic to the African-American community's wilderness experience, black political history in America would be less rich and less productive.[450]

Hence, I suggest that in black theology today, the wilderness experience is a more appropriate name than the black experience to describe African-American existence in North America. This is so because:

1. wilderness experience is male/female/family-inclusive in its imagistic, symbolic and actual content; black experience has been described with an androcentric bias in theology, and its perimeters are narrowly racial;

2. wilderness experience is suggestive of the essential role of human initiative (along with divine intervention) in the activity of survival, of community building, of structuring a positive quality of life for family and community; it is also suggestive of human initiative in the work of liberation; black experience says very little about black initiative and responsibility in the community's struggle for liberation, and nothing about internal tensions and intentions in community building and survival struggle;

3. wilderness experience is African-American religious experience that is simultaneously African-American secular experience; thus wilderness experience—especially in its symbolic dimension—signals the unity of the sacred and the secular in African-American reality; black experience does not function or signal this way;

4. indicating more than the negative reality the name black experience has come to typify in both the African-American and Anglo-American world, wilderness experience extends beyond being bitten by rats and living six people in a kitchenette; wilderness experience indicates female-male intelligence and ingenuity in the midst of struggle, creating a culture of resistance;

5. wilderness experience in its symbolic manifestation in African-American consciousness lifts up and supports leadership roles of African-American women and mothers;

6. in a Christian theological context wilderness experience, more than black experience, provides an avenue for black liberation theologians, feminist theologians and womanist theologians to dialogue about the significance of wilderness in what each identifies as the biblical tradition most conducive to the work of his or her theological enterprise. While black liberation theologians lift up the exodus/lib-

eration tradition as foundational, they have forgotten to give serious attention to the wilderness experience in the exodus story, in which the ex-slaves grumbled against God and wanted not to bear responsibility for the work, consciousness and struggle associated with maintaining freedom. While some feminist theologians claim the prophetic tradition significant for the biblical foundations of feminist theology, they give little or no attention to the way in which the wilderness figures into the work of making the prophet and making a people. Womanist theologians can claim the biblical wilderness tradition as the foundation of their enterprise and as a route to discourse not only because Hagar's, black women's and black people's experiences with God gained dimension in the wilderness, but because the biblical wilderness tradition also emphasizes survival, quality of life formation with God's direction and the work of building a peoplehood and a community. Womanist theologians can invite feminist, black liberation and other interested theologians to engage with them in the exploration of the question: What is God's word about survival and quality of life formation for oppressed and quasi-free people struggling to build community in the wilderness?

Womanist theology, as it takes woman-inclusive wilderness experience seriously, must examine the ways in which Christian doctrine affects black women.

From Delores S. Williams, *Sisters in the Wilderness: The Challenge of Womanist God-Talk* (Maryknoll, NY: Orbis Books, 1993), 153–61. [Ellipses and brackets in original.]

◈ In "To Speak Rightly of God," **Elizabeth A. Johnson** compares the present era with times when "right" speech about the Christian God was an urgent topic of conversation among shopkeepers and people on the street. Johnson argues that today's "right" images of God must include those drawn from women's experiences and the world of nature as well as from men's experiences.

---

449. Thus it is no wonder that black women have initiated many black civil rights movements, have been the prime knowers and movers of the black church movement in America and have led in economic advancement in the African-American community.

450. If Rosa Parks had not sat down, Martin Luther King, Jr., could not have stood up. If Ida Wells Barnett had not monitored the lynching of black people in this country, there would not have been such a complete record.

ELIZABETH A. JOHNSON

"To Speak Rightly of God," in *She Who Is: The Mystery of God in Feminist Theological Discourse*

Vision begins to happen in such a life
as if a woman quietly walked away
from the argument and jargon in a room
and sitting down in the kitchen, began turning in her lap
bits of yarn, calico and velvet scraps,
laying them out absently on the scrubbed boards
in the lamplight, with small rainbow-colored shells. . . .
Such a composition has nothing to do with eternity,
the striving for greatness, brilliance—
only with the musing of a mind
one with her body, experienced fingers quietly pushing
dark against bright, silk against roughness,
pulling the tenets of a life together
with no mere will to mastery,
only care. . . .

—Adrienne Rich[451]

A Crucial Question

A small vignette from the late fourth century reveals how fascinating the Christian people of that time found the question of right speech about God. In a culture imbued with Greek philosophical notions, debate raged over the question of whether Jesus Christ was truly divine or whether he was a creature subordinate to God the Father. Rather than being an esoteric issue confined to theologians or bishops, this discussion engaged the participation of a broad range of people. One famous remark by Gregory of Nyssa caught the situation precisely: "even the baker," he said, does not cease from discussing this, for if you ask the price of bread he will tell you that the Father is greater and the Son subject to him.[452]

What is the right way to speak about God? This is a question of unsurpassed importance, for speech to and about the mystery that surrounds human lives and the universe itself is a key activity of a community of faith. In that speech the symbol of God functions as the primary symbol of the whole religious system, the ultimate point of reference for understanding experience, life, and the world. Hence the way in which a faith community shapes language about God implicitly represents what it takes to be the highest good, the profoundest truth, the most appealing beauty. Such speaking, in turn, powerfully molds the corporate identity of the community and directs its praxis. A religion, for example,

that would speak about a warlike god and extol the way he smashes his enemies to bits would promote aggressive group behavior. A community that would acclaim God as an arbitrary tyrant would inspire its members to acts of impatience and disrespect toward their fellow creatures. On the other hand, speech about a beneficent and loving God who forgives offenses would turn the faith community toward care for the neighbor and mutual forgiveness.[453]

Speech about God shapes the life orientation not only of the corporate faith community but in this matrix guides its individual members as well. God is that on which you lean your heart, that on which your heart depends, "that to which your heart clings and entrusts itself," in Martin Luther's memorable phrase.[454] As the focus of absolute trust, one to whom you can give yourself without fear of betrayal, the holy mystery of God undergirds and implicitly gives direction to all of a believing person's enterprises, principles, choices, system of values, and relationships. The symbol of God functions. Neither abstract in content nor neutral in its effect, speaking about God sums up, unifies, and expresses a faith community's sense of ultimate mystery, the world view and expectation of order devolving from this, and the concomitant orientation of human life and devotion. No wonder that even the baker joined in the debate over the right way to speak about God.

In our day interest in right speech about God is exceptionally alive in a new way thanks to the discourse of a sizable company of bakers, women who historically have borne primary responsibility for lighting the cooking fires and feeding the world. The women's movement in civil society and the church has shed a bright light on the pervasive exclusion of women from the realm of public symbol formation and decision making, and women's consequent, strongly enforced subordination to the imagination and needs of a world designed chiefly by men. In the church this exclusion has been effective virtually everywhere: in ecclesial creeds, doctrines, prayers, theological systems, liturgical worship, patterns of

---

451. Adrienne Rich, from "Transcendental Etudes," in *The Fact of a Doorframe: Poems Selected and New, 1950–1984* (New York: W. W. Norton, 1984), 268–69.

452. Gregory of Nyssa, "De deitate Filii et Spiritus sancti," *PG* [*Patrologiae cursus, series Graeca*] 46.557. The importance of the role of the laity in this debate is demonstrated by John Henry Newman, *On Consulting the Faithful in Matters of Doctrine* (London: Collins, 1986).

453. These examples are adduced by Gordon Kaufman, *The Theological Imagination: Constructing the Concept of God* (Philadelphia: Westminster, 1981), 187–189.

454. Martin Luther, *Large Catechism,* in *The Book of Concord,* trans. Theodore Tappert (Philadelphia: Fortress, 1959), 365.

spirituality, visions of mission, church order, leadership and discipline.[455] It has been stunningly effective in speech about God. While beyond identification with either male or female sex, yet the daily language of preaching, worship, catechesis, and instruction conveys a different message: God is male, or at least more like a man than a woman, or at least more fittingly addressed as male than as female. The symbol of God functions. Upon examination it becomes clear that this exclusive speech about God serves in manifold ways to support an imaginative and structural world that excludes or subordinates women. Wittingly or not, it undermines women's human dignity as equally created in the image of God.

Gradually or abruptly, peacefully or in anger, happily or with great anguish, quietly like the woman in Adrienne Rich's poem that heads this introduction or shouting from the city walls like Sophia in the Book of Proverbs (8:1–3), myriads of women and a number of men are turning from the restrictive inheritance of exclusive God-talk. For some, the journey involves a sojourn in darkness and silence, traversing a desert of the spirit created by the loss of accustomed symbols. For others, new language is born as women gather together creatively in solidarity and prayer, and as sister scholars uncover alternative ways of speaking about divine mystery that have long been hidden in Scripture and tradition. In this matrix feminist theologians, engaging in the traditional theological task of reflecting on God and all things in the light of God, are shaping new speech about God that, in Rebecca Chopp's memorable phrase, are discourses of emancipatory transformation, pointing to new ways of living together with each other and the earth.[456] Respectful of their own equal human dignity, conscious of the harm being done by the manifold forms of sexism, and attentive to their own experiences of suffering, power, and agency, these women are engaged in creative "naming toward God," as Mary Daly so carefully calls it, from the matrix of their own experience.[457] This is not an intellectual endeavor only, although it is certainly that, but a movement with roots deep in the human spirit. Women, long considered less than adequate as human persons, claim themselves as active subjects of history and name toward God out of this emerging identity, to practical and critical effect.

What is the right way to speak about God? The presenting issue in debates about inclusive language is ostensibly whether the reality of women can provide suitable metaphor for speech about God. The intensity with which the question is engaged from the local to the international level, however, makes clear that more is at stake than simply naming toward God with women-identified words such as mother. The sym-

bol of God functions. Language about God in female images not only challenges the literal mindedness that has clung to male images about holy mystery, but insofar as "the symbol gives rise to thought,"[458] such speech calls into question prevailing structures of patriarchy. It gives rise to a different vision of community, one in which the last shall be first, the excluded shall be included, the mighty put down from their thrones and the humbled exalted—the words of Mary of Nazareth's song of praise (Lk 1:52), creating conditions for the formation of community characterized by relationships of mutuality and reciprocity, of love and justice. Introducing this mode of speech signals a shift, among those who use it, in their sense of the divine, a shift in total world view, in highest ideals and values, in personal and corporate identity. Such usage is urged upon the whole faith community in the conviction that it bears a fruitful and blessed promise. What is the right way to speak about God in the face of women's newly cherished human dignity and equality? This is a crucial theological question. What is at stake is the truth about God, inseparable from the situation of human beings, and the identity and mission of the faith community itself.

Context: Mystery Mediated in History

The unfathomable mystery of God is always mediated through shifting historical discourse. As the vignette about the baker from the fourth century makes clear, language about God has a history. Tracing these changes both in the scriptural period and throughout subsequent history makes clear that there has been no timeless speech about God in the Jewish or Christian tradition. Rather, words about God are cultural creatures, entwined with the mores and adventures of the faith community that uses them. As cultures shift, so too does the specificity of God-talk.

In one of those myriad interesting little discussions that Aquinas carries on in the formal framework of the *quaestio,* he deals luminously with the legitimacy of this historical development. The question at hand is whether it is proper to refer to God as "person." Some would object that this word is not

---

455. Elisabeth Schüssler Fiorenza and Mary Collins, eds., *Women: Invisible in the Church and Theology* (*Concilium* 182) (Edinburgh: T & T Clark, 1985).

456. Rebecca Chopp, *The Power to Speak: Feminism, Language, God* (New York: Crossroad, 1989), 7 and passim.

457. Mary Daly, *Beyond God the Father: Toward a Philosophy of Women's Liberation* (Boston: Beacon, 1973), 37 and passim.

458. Paul Ricoeur's lapidary axiom in *The Symbolism of Evil* (Boston: Beacon, 1967), 347–57.

used of God in the Scriptures, neither in the Old Testament nor in the New. But, goes his argument, what the word signifies such as intelligence is in fact frequently applied to God in Scripture, and so "person" can be used with confidence. Furthermore, he muses, if our speech about God were limited to the very terms of Scripture itself, then no one could speak about God except in the original languages of Hebrew and Greek! Broadening the argument, Aquinas defends the use of extra-biblical language about God on grounds of historical need: "The urgency of confuting heretics made it necessary to find new words to express the ancient faith about God." In conclusion, he clinches the argument with an exhortation to appreciate this new language: "Nor is such a kind of novelty to be shunned; since it is by no means profane, for it does not lead us astray from the sense of scripture."[459]

The wisdom carried in this argument supports in striking fashion patterns of speaking about the mystery of God that are emerging from the perspective of women's experiences. It is not necessary to restrict speech about God to the exact names that Scripture uses, nor to terms coined by the later tradition. So long as the words signify something that does characterize the living God mediated through Scripture, tradition, and present faith experience, for example, divine liberating action or self-involving love for the world, then new language can be used with confidence. Moreover, the urgency of confuting sexism, so dangerous to women's lives in the concrete, makes it imperative to find more adequate ways of expressing the ancient good news that faith is to proclaim. Nor is such novelty to be shunned for it does not lead astray from the sense of Scripture—if, that is, the sense of Scripture means the promise of God's creative, compassionate, liberating care bent on the whole world, including women in all our historicity and difference. The present ferment about naming, imaging, and conceptualizing God from perspectives of women's experience repristinates the truth that the idea of God, incomprehensible mystery, implies an open-ended history of understanding that is not yet finished.

The historical open-endedness of talk about God is due not only to its location in time, place, and culture, which is the case with all human speech, but to the very nature of what we are talking about. The reality of God is mystery beyond all imagining. So transcendent, so immanent is the holy mystery of God that we can never wrap our minds completely around this mystery and exhaust divine reality in words or concepts. The history of theology is replete with this truth: recall Augustine's insight that if we have under-

stood, then what we have understood is not God; Anselm's argument that God is that than which nothing greater can be conceived; Hildegard's vision of God's glory as Living Light that blinded her sight; Aquinas's working rule that we can know that God is and what God is not, but not what God is; Luther's stress on the hiddenness of God's glory in the shame of the cross; Simone Weil's conviction that there is nothing that resembles what she can conceive of when she says the word God; Sallie McFague's insistence on imaginative leaps into metaphor since no language about God is adequate and all of it is improper. It is a matter of the livingness of God. Given the inexhaustible mystery inherent in what the word God points to, historically new attempts at articulation are to be expected and even welcomed. If holy mystery, then, as Karl Rahner argues, "it actually postulates thereby a history of our own concept of God that can never be concluded."[460]

In what now reads like unwitting prophecy, the Second Vatican Council spoke of this dynamic of divine mystery mediated in history by using the organic metaphor of growth:

> For there is a growth in the understanding of the realities and the words which have been handed down. This happens through the contemplation and study made by believers who treasure these things in their hearts (Lk 2:19, 51), through the intimate understanding of spiritual things they experience.[461]

What the council did not envision but what is clearly happening today is that this dynamism is operative among believers who are women. Women are newly contemplating and studying things they have treasured and, through the intimate understanding of spiritual things they experience, are effecting a growth in the understanding of the realities and words that have been handed down. In faith and struggle women are growing the church into a new moment of the living tradition. As Anne Carr has so eloquently put it, the women's movement comes as a transforming grace for the whole church although, terrifyingly, grace may always be refused.[462]

---

459. *Summa Theologica* I, q. 29 a. 3.

460. Karl Rahner, "The Specific Character of the Christian Concept of God," *Theological Investigations*, 21:189.

461. Second Vatican Council, *Dei verbum*, 8.

462. Anne Carr, *Transforming Grace: Women's Experience and Christian Tradition* (San Francisco: Harper and Row, 1988). This is an excellent synthesis of the background and sweep of feminist theology, with extensive bibliography (245–66).

Purpose: Connecting Feminist and Classical Wisdom

My aim in what follows is to speak a good word about the mystery of God recognizable within the contours of Christian faith that will serve the emancipatory praxis of women and men, to the benefit of all creation, both human beings and the earth. In so doing I draw on the new language of Christian feminist theology as well as on the traditional language of Scripture and classical theology, all of which codify religious insights.

By Christian feminist theology I mean a reflection on God and all things in the light of God that stands consciously in the company of the world's women, explicitly prizing their genuine humanity while uncovering and criticizing its persistent violation in sexism, itself an omnipresent paradigm of unjust relationships.[463] In terms of Christian doctrine, this perspective claims the fullness of the religious heritage for women precisely as human, in their own right and independent from personal identification with men. Women are equally created in the image and likeness of God, equally redeemed by Christ, equally sanctified by the Holy Spirit; women are equally involved in the ongoing tragedy of sin and the mystery of grace, equally called to mission in this world, equally destined for life with God in glory.

Feminist theology explicitly recognizes that the contradiction between this theological identity of women and the historical condition of women in theory and practice is glaring. This leads to the clear judgment that sexism is sinful, that it is contrary to God's intent, that it is a precise and pervasive breaking of the basic commandment "Thou shalt love thy neighbor as thyself" (Lv 19:18; Mt 22:39). It affronts God by defacing the beloved creature created in the image of God. Faced with this sinfulness, church and society are called to repent, to turn around, to sin no more, to be converted.[464] Corresponding to this theological stance, feminist theology advocates the reform of patriarchal civil and ecclesial structures and the intellectual systems that support them in order to release all human beings for more just designs of living with each other and the earth. Far from being a theology done for women alone, it calls to strengths in women and men alike who care for justice and truth, seeking a transformation of the whole community.

By classical theology I mean the body of thought that arose in early Christian centuries in partnership with the Greek philosophical tradition and continued through the medieval period, molding the discourse of the churches at the beginning of the modern era. This tradition continues to shape contemporary language about God, both explicitly and implicitly, whether accepted or rejected, in popular and intellectual circles, particularly in its language about the Supreme Being, divine attributes, and trinitarian persons.

The feminist perspective, which honors women's humanity, women as *imago Dei,* finds this classical tradition profoundly ambiguous in what it has meant for female well-being. It has aided and abetted the exclusion and subordination of women, but also sustained generations of foremothers and foresisters in the faith. Along with the need for criticism of classical thought, my own inclination leads me in addition to give it a hearing, listening for wisdom that may yet prove useful. My approach is somewhat analogous to interreligious dialogue: after centuries of suspicion the Second Vatican Council set free in the Catholic church a hospitable spirit toward the world religions, affirming that whatever is true and holy in them reflects a ray of divine light.[465] Formed in that spirit, I find it coming home to roost in the attempt to see that whatever is true and holy in classical theology may also reflect a ray of divine light.

From Elizabeth A. Johnson, *She Who Is: The Mystery of God in Feminist Theological Discourse* (New York: Crossroad, 1992), 3–9.

Revisionary

☙ In his "Limit-Situations in the World of the Everyday," American theologian **David Tracy** elicits two dimensions of a religious perspective: (1) a sense of the limit of the everyday perspective (for example, in experiences of finitude, contingency, and transience) and (2) a disclosure of structures, however fleetingly, beyond that ordinary experience (for example, a trust in the worthwhileness of existence, a belief in value and form).

---

463. Despite its negative connotation in popular parlance, the word *feminist* is widely used in academic circles. Taken from the Latin *femina* (woman) it signifies a stance which advocates the flourishing of women as a precondition for genuine human community. In my view it is a perfectly suitable word, and I will use it in the sense described here.

464. In the words of Vatican II, "with respect to the fundamental rights of the person, every type of discrimination, whether social or cultural, whether based on sex, race, color, social condition, language, or religion, is to be overcome and eradicated as contrary to God's intent" (*Gaudium et Spes,* 29).

465. Vatican II, *Nostra Aetate* ("Declaration on the Relationship of the Church to Non-Christian Religions"), 2.

DAVID TRACY

"Limit-Situations in the World of the Everyday," in *Blessed Rage for Order: The New Pluralism in Theology*

Rather than engaging in extended analysis of the many thinkers who attempt in various ways to disclose a religious dimension or horizon to our common experience, this chapter signalizes two categories to make that claim. Those categories are those limit-situations in everyday life analyzed by existentialist thought and those limit-questions to scientific and moral inquiry analyzed by various philosophies of science and ethics. [. . .]

The concept limit-situation is a familiar one in the existentialist philosophy and theology of the very recent past.[466] Fundamentally, the concept refers to those human situations wherein a human being ineluctably finds manifest a certain ultimate limit or horizon to his or her existence. The concept itself is mediated by "showing" the implications of certain crucial positive and negative experiential limit-situations. More exactly, limit-situations refer to two basic kinds of existential situation: either those "boundary" situations of guilt, anxiety, sickness, and the recognition of death as one's own destiny,[467] or those situations called "ecstatic experiences"—intense joy, love, reassurance, creation.[468] All genuine limit-situations refer to those experiences, both positive and negative, wherein we both experience our own human limits (limit-to) as our own as well as recognize, however haltingly, some disclosure of a limit-of our experience.[469] The negative mode of limit-situations can best be described with Karl Jaspers as "boundary-situations." Such experiences (sickness, guilt, anxiety, recognition of death as one's own destiny) allow and, when intense, seem to demand reflection upon the existential boundaries of our present everyday existence. When an announcement of a serious illness—whether our own or of someone we love—is made, we begin to experience the everyday, the "real" world, as suddenly unreal: petty, strange, foreign to the now real world. That "limit" world of final closure to our lives now faces us with a starkness we cannot shirk and manages to disclose to us our basic existential faith or unfaith in life's very meaningfulness.

The positive mode of limit-situations can be described, as they are by Abraham Maslow, as "peak experiences" or, as I prefer, as "ecstatic experiences." Undeniably, such experiences (love, joy, the creative act, profound reassurance) are authentically "self-transcending" moments in our lives.[470] When in the grasp of such experiences, we all find, however momentarily,

that we can and do transcend our usual lackluster selves and our usual everyday worlds to touch upon a dimension of experience which cannot be stated adequately in the language of ordinary, everyday experience. Authentic love, both erotic and agapic, puts us in touch with a reality whose power we cannot deny. We do not work ourselves into a state of love, as we might into a habit of justice. We "fall," we "are" in love. While its power lasts, we experience the rest of our lives as somehow shadowy. The "real world" no longer seems real. We find ourselves affirming the reality of ecstatic experience, but not as something merely decided upon by us. In all such authentic moments of ecstasy, we experience a reality simply given, gifted, happened.[471] Such a reality, as religious mystics remind us, may be a taste of that self-transcending experience of a "being-in-love-without-qualification" familiar to the authentically religious person.[472]

At the very least, such ecstatic experiences can sensitize one to the possibilities of an existential grounding for those everyday experiences of self-transcendence which disclose the most deeply held meanings of our lives. To reassure a child crying in the night that all is well;[473] to experience the self-and-other transcendence of loving sexual expression; to experience an "unattended moment" with friends, music, or nature. All such *ec-static* experiences may, by their "limit-disclosing" character, serve as "signals of transcendence," as "rumors of angels," or, less metaphorically, as a "showing" if not a "stating" of a limit-dimension to our lives. That limit-to the everyday also seems to disclose—in the same *ec-stasis*—a

---

466. Among others, cf. Karl Jaspers, *The Perennial Scope of Philosophy* (New York: Philosophical Library, 1949), 85–87, 168–80.

467. Cf. Karl Jaspers' position on "ciphers" in *Philosophical Faith and Revelation* (New York: Harper and Row, 1967), esp. 104–48, 234–47, 302–15; idem, on "boundary-situations" in *Philosophy*, vol. 2 (Chicago: University of Chicago Press, 1970), 177–218.

468. In psychology, cf. Abraham H. Maslow, *Religions, Values, and Peak Experiences* (New York: Viking, 1970)[. . . .] Throughout the text I prefer the use of the word ec-stasy as disclosive of the ability to be outside the "everyday" limits on such occasions.

469. In the language employed earlier, this could be formulated as "stating" the "limits-to" in order to "show" the "limits-of."

470. Note that the model remains "self-transcendence," not "self-fulfillment" nor "self-abnegation."

471. For an example of this as part of mystical experience, cf. William Johnston, *The Mysticism of the Cloud of Unknowing* (New York: Desclée, 1967); for the parallel in more ordinary experiences, cf. Abraham H. Maslow, *Toward a Psychology of Being* (Princeton: Van Nostrand, 1962); idem, *Religions, Values, and Peak Experiences*.

472. Cf. Bernard Lonergan, *Method in Theology* (New York: Herder and Herder, 1972), 101–10.

473. Cf. Peter Berger, *A Rumor of Angels* (Garden City, NY: Doubleday, 1969), 67–70; cf. also Charles A. Carr, "Peter Berger's Angels and Philosophy of Religion," *Journal of Religion* 52 (1972), 426–37.

limit-of whose graciousness bears a religious character.[474] For the moment, however, let us recall such experiences of ecstasy merely to remind ourselves of certain human experiences which most of us have had with greater and less frequency and which many of us can recognize as expressive of a "world of meaning" beyond the everyday. Such a "world," by its strange ability to put us in touch with what we believe to be a final, a "trustworthy," meaning to our lives may also disclose to us, however hesitantly, the character of that ultimate horizon of meaning which religious persons call "gracious," "eventful," "faithful," "revelatory."[475] To be sure, such experiences need not be understood in explicitly religious terms as the mystic's experience of an unrestricted religious love would be. Rather, as we have insisted throughout this chapter, such experiences are more properly described not as explicitly *religious* but as disclosive of a "limit," a "religious" dimension or horizon to our lives.

However intense an expression of our common experience both boundary-situations and ecstatic experiences may be, such experiences are clearly common *human* experiences. The temptation to exclude such considerations from an analysis of common human experience as neurotic symptoms (the way to avoid, for example, the truth of Kierkegaard's analysis of *Angst*) is to miss their real significance. An appeal to these phenomena is not an appeal to a neurotic guilt, an obsessive anxiety, an alienated sickness, a morbid preoccupation with death, a romantic infatuation with love, creativity, and ecstasy.[476] On the contrary, an appeal to such phenomena as disclosive of our actual situation is fundamentally an appeal to experiences such as responsible guilt, authentic anxiety, responsible recognition of death as one's ownmost destiny, and authentic self-transcending human love. Clearly, such experiences, however ambiguous, are not in principle merely "strange" experiences. Uncommon they are. Yet they are uncommon mainly because we try to keep them from surfacing in our everyday lives by our strategies of inauthenticity: *"divertissement,"* distraction, *Gerede*.[477] Beginning with Kierkegaard, "the classical existentialist analyses of such experiences have provided a powerful way to clarify the human situation as intrinsically a limit-situation: a situation wherein we find ourselves not the masters of our fate but radically contingent or limited (boundary-situations).[478] At the same time, we may also find ourselves radically out-of-our-everyday-selves as ecstatic, as gifted, even as "graced."[479]

Perhaps the clearest way to understand the "religious" implications of such existentialist analysis is to recall a familiar instance of its exercise: the phenomenological analysis

of basic anxiety as distinct from the phenomenon of fear.[480] The point of that analysis is subtle but important for understanding the basic character of a religious dimension to our common existence. Fear as a phenomenon[481] (that is, as that which appears to human consciousness) manifests itself as a *fear of a specific object*. Fears are manifested when we pay heed to the various kinds of phobias to which each of us may be prone: a fear of the dark, of heights, of electricity, etc. Anxiety (or *Angst*), on the other hand, is a *qualitatively different* phenomenon in its very manifestation. Anxiety is *not* a fear of some specific object (or even of the sum total of specific objects). Anxiety is a fear of *no-object*-in-the-world-alongside-other-objects. Anxiety is literally, as Heidegger reminds us, a fear of No-thing.[482] More positively stated, anxiety is a fear

---

474. The final appeal here is an appeal to "experience" in the sense [of] a disclosure of a final dimension to the self's experience of the self—a "showing" to oneself; rarely an adequate "stating."

475. At such moments, we also recognize how our language and our experience are liberated together or, often enough, not at all. Often what Heidegger names a "destruction" is necessary in order for a "retrieval" to take place. The hermeneutical circle described here suggests a twofold relationship: on the one hand, a limit-situation finds an explicitly religious language important (as when one faces the reality of one's own or a friend's death); on the other hand, an explicitly religious language (e.g., the language of the Christian funeral service) cannot really be "heard" unless the limit-situation is comprehended. The banalization and flight from the reality of death in modern technological societies is one of the surest signs of the impoverishment afforded by a dual failure to comprehend either limit-situations or religious limit language.

476. This is not to deny the presence of neurotic symptoms in a figure like Søren Kierkegaard; it is to deny that their presence adequately explains the extraordinary person of Kierkegaard as well as his analyses.

477. Cf. Martin Heidegger, *Being and Time* (London: SCM, 1962), 203–25, on certain modern strategies of inauthenticity, including *Gerede* (idle talk), curiosity, and ambiguity.

478. For incisive analyses of Kierkegaard, especially on his use of pseudonyms for the "stages of existence," cf. Stephen Crites, *In the Twilight of Christendom: Hegel vs. Kierkegaard on Faith and History* (Chambersburg, Pa.: American Academy of Religion, Studies in Religion, 1971)[. . . .]

479. A familiar example of the hermeneutical difficulty mentioned [. . .] above may prove helpful here. The hymn "Amazing Grace" seems to have remarkable resonance for secular audiences; indeed in a manner which liberal Baptists, who have different memories of its origins, often seem to find puzzling. Yet precisely the secular willingness to use a phrase like "amazing grace" is indicative, I believe, of the basic correctness of the central theological insight into the giftedness of life itself as [this giftedness] is formulated in the doctrine of grace with the [. . .] twofold components of a doctrine of creation and redemption.

480. This is, of course, an interpretation of merely one aspect of Heidegger's profound analysis of the Being-Question as present to *Da-sein* [in] *Being and Time*, esp. section 40, 228–41.

481. Ibid., 179–82.

482. Ibid., 231: "Nothing which is ready-to-hand or present-at-hand within the world functions as that in the face of which anxiety is anxious. . . . Accordingly, when something threatening brings itself close, anxiety does not 'see' any definite 'here' or 'yonder' from which it comes. That in the face of which one has anxiety is characterized by the fact that what threatens is nowhere. . . . In that in the face of which one has anxiety, the 'It is nothing and nowhere' becomes manifest."

disclosive of our often forgotten but never totally absent consciousness of our own radical contingency. In anxiety, we do not merely consider, we know that we neither create ourselves nor can we assume the continuance of existence. Instead we find ourselves—as the metaphors of the existentialists and the mystics alike remind us—poised over an abyss, a chasm, whose exact nature we do not know but whose experiential reality we cannot deny.[483]

What, really, does this analysis of anxiety and similar existentialist analyses manifest? At the very least, the analysis discloses that the final dimension or horizon of our own situation is neither one of our own making nor one under our control. In analyzing anxiety, we may also see that our very situation is, in fact, correctly described as a limit-situation. We are grounded or horizoned by no other thing in the universe, but rather by No-thing. In terms of the language we employ for such experiences, the analysis may also manifest that at a certain point the language of conceptual analysis begins to falter. Instead, the human spirit begins to search for metaphors expressive of the experience (abyss, chasm, limit) and for narratives capable of expanding and structuring these metaphors (parables, myths, poems). Such metaphors, images, symbols, and myths seem linguistically necessary to express that literally unspoken, and perhaps unspeakable, final dimension to the end of our lives. In a word, the language initially most appropriate for expressing that experience is symbolic as distinct from strictly conceptual. Such language, as symbolic, involves a double intentionality which expresses both a literal meaning (for example, an actual physical abyss) and a non-literal meaning which otherwise remains unsaid and unspoken (in this case, the disclosure of an other, a final dimension, which serves as limit-to our experience of the everyday and limit-of the rest of our existence).

As suggested previously, symbolic language may find further though partial expression in the conceptual language of metaphysics—especially the analogical language of metaphysics. However helpful a later metaphysical language may be, all authentic limit-language seems to be initially and irretrievably a symbolic and a metaphorical one. Insofar as the hidden dimension of an ultimate limit is not merely hidden but not even expressible in the language of the everyday (as no-*thing,* no object in the world alongside other objects), that language retains the linguistic structure of metaphor and symbol. At the very least, metaphorical and symbolic language is proper to the originating expression of this disclosed but not adequately conceptualizable

dimension of our common existence. In fact, as I shall argue in the next chapter, even *explicitly* religious language (for example, the language of the scriptures or of the Christian mystics) is intrinsically symbolic and metaphorical limit-language.

It does not seem improper to suggest, therefore, that all authentic religious language and experience—precisely as that limit-language re-presentative of a final dimension or horizon of meaning to our existence—is also autonomous. The religious dimension of existence is not, I believe, adequately described as simply another human activity coordinate to such activities as science, morality, or culture. By its limit-character, a religious dimension is more accurately described by some such phrase as ultimate ground to or horizon of all other activities—as Paul Tillich, perhaps more than any other contemporary thinker, has tried to show by his several analogies of the peculiar character and force of the "ultimate concern" implicit in every human concern and uniquely disclosive of a religious dimension to human existence. I am content to leave the powerful and still evocative expression "ultimate concern" to Tillich and simply suggest that reflection upon limit-questions and limit-situations does disclose the reality of a dimension to our lives other than the more usual dimensions: a dimension whose first key is its reality as limit-to our other everyday, moral, scientific, cultural, and political activities; a dimension which, in my own brief and hazy glimpses, discloses a reality, however named and in whatever manner experienced, which functions as a final, now gracious, now frightening, now trustworthy, now absurd, always uncontrollable limit-of the very meaning of existence itself.

From David Tracy, *Blessed Rage for Order: The New Pluralism in Theology* (New York: Seabury, 1975), 105–8. [Ellipses in original except where bracketed.]

❧ In "Constructing the Concept of God," **Gordon D. Kaufman,** a Protestant theologian, emphasizes the imaginative and constructive activity that goes on in all speech about God. Since speech about God is never directly referential, Kaufman describes the ways in which all speech about God and all experience of God spring from and function within the power of the imagination.

---

483. Note throughout how such unusual "limit-insight" demands a distortion (destruction-retrieval) of the language, as in Heidegger's own tearing-apart of the Greek and German languages.

GORDON D. KAUFMAN

"Constructing the Concept of God," in *The Theological Imagination: Constructing the Concept of God*

Whether in prayer or sermon, biblical exposition or theological analysis, use of the word "God" involves important imaginative and constructive activity that is often not recognized. God is not a reality immediately available in our experience for observation, inspection, and description, and speech about or to God therefore is never directly referential. Thus, we are unable to check our concepts and images of God for accuracy and adequacy through direct confrontation with the reality *God,* as we can with most ordinary objects of perception and experience; instead, our awareness and understanding here is gained entirely in and through the images and concepts themselves, constructed into and focused by the mind into a center for the self's devotion and service. God is said to be father of us all, creator of all things both visible and invisible, lord of history, judge of all the earth. These images, each drawn from ordinary political, social, or cultural experience, and suitably qualified to enable them to suggest (a) being transcending everything finite and particular in glory, majesty, and power, then become the constituent elements out of which the image of God is put together by the mind. Again, God is said to be eternal and transcendent and absolute, one who alone has aseity and on whom all other beings depend for their existence. Concepts such as these are taken to characterize in religiously and metaphysically distinctive ways who or what God is, and thus they also become constitutive of this focus for devotion, life, and meaning. The mind's ability to create images and characterizations, and imaginatively to weld them together into a unified focus[484] for attention, contemplation, devotion, or address, is at work in the humblest believer's prayers as well as in the most sophisticated philosopher's speculations. In this respect all speech to and about God, and all "experience of God," is made possible by and is a function of the constructive powers of the imagination.

It is not difficult to see why this must be the case. From Kant onward it has been understood that even the simplest experiences of objects are possible for us only because of the elaborate synthesizing powers of the mind: these enable us to bring together and hold together in enduring conceptual unities what is given to us only piecemeal and in separate moments of experience. How much more must pictures or conceptions of that "ultimate reality" which is taken to ground and unify and comprehend all experience and being

be a work of our constructive and synthesizing powers. The idea of God gains its own distinctive and unique meaning for us through contrast with all the particulars of experience, and also contrast with that structured whole within which all experience falls and which we call the world—even while being built up and put together out of images and analogies drawn from this very experience. This idea is in many ways the mind's supreme imaginative construct, related to all other dimensions, realities, and qualities of experience and the world and yet seen as distinct from and grounding them all. Little wonder that, as the tradition has always recognized, God is not an object of ordinary perception, directly accessible to us, but is believed to be transcendent and mysterious, hidden from our sight, even unknowable.

> Lo, he passes by me, and I see him not;
> > he moves on, but I do not perceive him. . . .
> Behold, I go forward, but he is not there;
> > and backward, but I cannot perceive him;
> on the left hand I seek him, but I cannot behold him;
> > I turn to the right hand, but I cannot see him. (Job
> > 9:11; 23:8–9)

Of course no individual human mind constructs the idea of God from scratch. All thinking about God and all devotion to God take place within a cultural and linguistic context in which the notion of God has already been highly developed through the imaginative work of many preceding generations. So the idea of God with which any particular individual works is always a qualification and development of notions inherited from earlier worshipers and prophets, poets and thinkers. For much of Western history the Bible has been the principal resource collection of earlier stages of reflection on and construction of the concept of God, and biblical attitudes toward God have been built in at deep levels of Western consciousness of life, humanness, and reality.

But the Bible's significance for Western thinking about God has gone far beyond mere informal influence of this sort. The Bible was long regarded as the locus of God's rev-

---

484. Even in perception of ordinary objects the mind always employs "subsidiary" clues, feelings, and impulses in order to achieve "focal" awareness of the object or meaning with which it is concerned; such constructive activity is indispensable to the grasping of any meanings by the mind (see Michael Polanyi and Harry P. Prosch, *Meaning* [University of Chicago Press, 1975], esp. chs. 2 and 4).

elation to humanity (the "word of God"); it therefore carried an authority powerful enough to override ordinary human experience and rational argument. Although the "creator of the heavens and the earth" was not an object available for direct confrontation and observation, and knowledge about God could not be gained in any ordinary way, this lack had been, in God's graciousness and mercy, divinely supplied in and through the Bible. The presence of this authoritative resource for normative images and concepts of God meant that God's being and activity could be regarded as completely objective and "real"—indeed, even more real than the objects and qualities of ordinary experience. For the Bible presented the story or history of all the world and of humanity, a story of which we humans also are a significant and living part. And in that story God is the supreme active character: the creator of the world, the lord and principal mover of history, the one in relation to whom human life finds fulfillment and meaning, and in turning from whom it withers away and dies. For those who lived out their lives with this story as the fundamental context within which events and experiences were understood, every occurrence had a divine significance. It was God with whom one was actually dealing in every moment and relationship in life, and there was little question of God's reality, power, or significance.

The authority of the Bible, and the reality and power of God within the biblical story, assured that questions about the mode of God's presence to the mind—through the mind's own activity of imaginative construction—would not quickly arise. This was so even though God's reality in the Bible was that of a character in a story, and though this reality was apprehended by believers in much the same way that they grasped other story-characters—through powerful acts of imaginative reconstruction carried out in and by their own minds as they read or heard the text.[485] However, after two centuries of modern historical scholarship, it is possible to see both that the image/concept of God in the Bible is a product of imaginative construction and also something of the various historical stages through which that construction developed. Thus, we can gain some understanding of why and how the notion of God came to have the particular shape and content which has been so authoritative in the West. This in turn puts us into a position from which to ask whether and to what extent we should continue to use biblical motifs and images in our own contemporary attempts to construct an adequate concept of God.

From Gordon D. Kaufman, *The Theological Imagination: Constructing the Concept of God* (Philadelphia: Westminster, 1981), 21–24. [Ellipsis in original.]

---

485. For detailed discussion of the significance of the narrative form of the Bible, and the way in which this form itself contributed importantly to the notion of God and the kind of meaning that notion has had in much of Western history, together with an interpretation of the historical breakdown of that notion in modern times, see Hans Frei, *The Eclipse of Biblical Narrative* (Yale University Press, 1974).

CHAPTER 7

Twentieth-Century Issues and Challenges

The texts in this chapter give a sense of how Christians (or, in the case of Simone Weil, someone who deliberated about becoming Christian) are engaged in the world today. The documents show engagement both affecting and being affected by the Christian religion—assisting the Church to become what it is not yet but will be and enabling the world to see and hear Christ. These transformations of person and society—both within and outside the Church—are manifest in the actions and words of contemporary prophets, in applications of jurisprudence, in ongoing Church reform, and in confrontations with external opposition. This chapter documents four themes: (1) individuals recognized as contemporary prophets and mystics; (2) Church-state relations; (3) new notions of what a Church should be; and (4) current challenges seen as arising from outside the Church.

What is prophetic about the seven figures in the first section? They are known, first of all, for their social activism—involving the welfare of factory laborers, putting an end to racism, the prevention of war, relief from class oppression, care of the poor and the terminally ill, and interreligious dialogue. Although efforts to mitigate these concerns are seldom if ever adequate, they are tangible evidence of resistance to injustice and violence. But the words and actions of these prophets are more than acts of resistance. Each speaks not only in her own voice but on behalf of some Other who speaks from beyond or through herself. What each says is more than moral outrage or righteous anger. What is prophetic, then, is hearing the Other—the Spirit—and enabling others to hear that Other within themselves as well. Such listening is not that of an automaton or the foolhardy. It must be discerned and distinguished from false or merely

self-serving inclinations. The Spirit today, as of old, "breathes where it will" (Jn 3:8), as can be seen by the diversity of contexts represented here.

A Jew by birth, Simone Weil (1909–43) brooded over the implications of the Gospels for addressing the evil effects of war and the exploitation of human laborers. In her writing she exposed the virtual slavery suffered by the poor in industrial and capitalist societies. In her meditation on the "Our Father"—the prayer Jesus is said to have taught to the disciples and that is prayed by Christians the world over—she invokes the nearness and infinitude of God.

Martin Luther King (1929–68) is a quite different example of prophetic hearing and proclamation. Rosa Parks and Claudette Colvin, separately, had set off a storm of controversy by refusing to obey segregation laws on buses in Montgomery, Alabama. Just out of graduate school, King became a member of the local black ministers' association and began preaching on the injustice of the treatment of blacks on buses. When King agreed to lead the Montgomery Bus Boycott in 1955–56, the Civil Rights movement was born. He listened to the Spirit while he was alone at night in his kitchen and went forward with the movement without regard for what might happen to himself or to his family.

Two decades earlier, on May 1, 1933, Dorothy Day (1897–1980) founded the Catholic Worker Movement in New York City to provide refuge for the homeless poor. She also founded the *Catholic Worker,* an alternative journal and forum in which issues of war and peace, social justice, politics, and religion are still being debated today. Day's radical pacifism was rooted in her conviction that all parties to war will, by commission or omission, perform or abet unchristian atrocities.

In yet a different mode of inspiration, Thomas Merton's (1915–68) lifelong study of spirituality within and outside Christian traditions disclosed many ways of being drawn into solitude. Nevertheless, he felt that "it is a glorious destiny" to be human—to walk "around shining like the sun" because God "gloried in becoming" a human being. On an ordinary day on an ordinary street corner he has a vision of what it would take to overcome violence in the world.

Dom Hélder Câmara (1909–99) is known within the field of political theory for his model of the cycle of violence. In the Middle Ages, Thomas Aquinas recognized injustice to be a kind of violence. Câmara elaborates this affinity further by describing three stages of the cycle of violence. The first stage is injustice itself: either overt injustice (such as punching or defaming someone) or covert injustice (such as the inequities structured within society). The second stage occurs when those who are oppressed revolt. In the third stage, revolt is repressed by those in power. The cycle repeats itself with escalating violence. With his model Câmara hoped to encourage identification and elimination of violence in the first stage of its cycle.

Mother Teresa of Calcutta (1910–97), who was named a candidate for canonization shortly after her death, was known for her untiring care for the destitute. Her unassuming demeanor contrasted with the forthrightness of her convictions about right action when faced with so much suffering. Her words convey what it is like to own nothing and to depend for sustenance entirely on God.

From the mid-1970s through the 1980s, Desmond Tutu raised the consciousness of people outside Africa to believe that the rule of apartheid in South Africa could and should be struck down, and he assisted in bringing about an orderly change of government—a change that had been sought by black Africans since the founding of the African National Congress in 1912. Tutu's prophetic powers stem from his credibility and his uncommon gift of generating hope in his country and around the world. After the new government was in place, his moral authority made the policy of exchanging amnesty for confession of crimes against humanity work.

From prophetic individuals, we turn in section 2 to the public realm of Church and state relations. Perhaps only a secularist or a fundamentalist would think that Church-state relations would be better off by eliminating one or the other institution. Either or both might be persuaded to think otherwise by reading Pedro Ramet's evenhanded study of political interests as both state and Church address social issues according to their discretionary powers. John Courtney Murray's (1904–67) work on constitutional law helped shape Catholic thought—and some think government public policy as well—regarding religious tensions in American public life. Murray held that the theologian needed to understand the contemporary meaning of religious freedom, in the sense of its being a basis for personal and political consciousness.

Two legal opinions in American court trials—the famous *John T. Scopes v. State of Tennessee* (1927) on the teaching of evolution, and *Steven I. Engel, et al., Petitioners, v. William J. Vitale, Jr., et al.* (1962) on the issue of prayer in public schools—reveal some of the legal complexities in interpreting the disestablishment clause of the Constitution of the United States. The disestablishment clause (Amendment I of the Bill of Rights) reads as follows: "Congress shall make no law respecting an establishment of religion, or prohibiting the free exercise thereof." The Scopes trial is interesting for many reasons. For instance, some theologians testified in favor of teaching the theory of evolution in public schools and some fundamentalist scientists opposed its being taught. In recent years the state of Kansas found a middle way by recommending inclusion of less doctrinaire readings of the theory of evolution and less literal readings of the Book of Genesis in the public school curriculum. On the issue of school prayer, recent court decisions in the United States have forbidden organized prayer in public schools.

Enrique Dussel's prospectus for opening a new ecumenical discussion on Church-state relations in Latin America (1978) recalls that "Christ exercised a prophetic critical function in regard to the state of his time." Like Murray, Dussel contextualizes his theory of Church-state relations in a concrete historical-critical analysis.

William Martin presents an even-handed view of Church-state relations in the United States. A moderate on the issue, he reminds his readers "that the Founding Fathers intended that the state be neutral toward all religions, but did not intend that religious people or their organizations be neutralized, their voices restricted to private matters only." At the same time, the principle of pluralism ought to be respected by individuals and groups alike.

Section 3, New Notions of "Church," focuses on what the Church should be—the ideal, in other words, from where we now stand. The section includes statements by several forward-looking individuals and institutions. The first text, *Dogmatic Constitution on the Church (Lumen gentium,* promulgated in 1964), is one of only two "dogmatic" statements of the Second Vatican Council. The drafts it went through reflect the growth of self-understanding among the bishops during the conciliar discussions. Eschewing anti-Protestant polemic, the final document points to a dynamic vision in biblical, historical terms. It states several new emphases in understanding the Church: namely, that (1) all people are called by a loving God to be the new People of God; (2) the *sensus fidei* (the "instinctive sensitivity and discrimination which the members of the Church possess" with respect to issues concerning faith and morals) can be trusted; (3) the laity have a properly and peculiarly secular character: that is, to be engaged in temporal affairs and to direct them according to God's will; and (4) in Christ and the Church there is to be "no inequality arising from race or nationality, social condition or sex." The three terms used to describe the task of the Church as a whole—witness, ministry, and fellowship—are the same as those discussed at the Third General Assembly of the World Council of Churches in New Delhi in 1961. Vatican II continued the practice of inviting Protestant observers, begun at the Council of Trent in 1545–63. Vatican II was the first council in modern times to include Catholic laymen and laywomen as observers, the latter in the third session. And thirty-one years later, on July 10, 1995, Pope John Paul II surprised the world with a letter paying tribute to women in all professions, publicly acknowledging what he called the Church's complicity in "the sin of sexism" within the Church and purporting to align himself with their struggles for equality.

In the centuries-old struggle for the recognition of women's full humanity, the second major historical development in the United States came in the 1960s with the efforts of "foremother-theologians" such as Valerie Saiving, Nelle Morton, and Pauli Murray. These thinkers were determined to retrieve and to go beyond the first major moment—the nineteenth- and early-twentieth-century achievements, which, except for Elizabeth Cady Stanton's *Woman's Bible,* were principally political in nature. Feminist theologian Rosemary Radford Ruether published the first feminist systematic theology, *Sexism and God-Talk,* in 1983. In her *Women-Church* (1985), excerpted here, Ruether explains her belief in the need for an intermediate stage on the way to a nonpatriarchal Church.

A World Council of Churches document, *The Role of the "Diakonia" of the Church in Contemporary Society* (1966), points to a remarkable concurrence of Orthodox churches in Greece and in Egypt, the Union churches, and Vatican II: they all concur that the role of deacon, or minister (often called

diakonia in the New Testament), needs to be reconsidered in the light of the needs of contemporary world societies. The document concludes: "The Church is anew confronted with the challenge to use those in whom she recognizes the spiritual gift (charisma) of 'diakonia,' and ordain them in this ministry." Otherwise, the Church does not fully offer the compassionate service of Christ to the world. The World Council of Churches document "Ordination of Women in Ecumenical Perspective" (1979) circumspectly lays out contemporary issues regarding the ordination of women. Evidence that women deacons were ordained ministers in the early Church and authorized to carry out specific activities in the Church's mission, published by several biblical historians, supports these theological arguments for the ordination of women priests and for the conferring of the *diakonia* on women and men.

The Joint Working Group between the Roman Catholic Church and the World Council of Churches was formed in 1965. In the document presented here they state their conviction that "Christian communities are to be a sign and seed of the unity, peace and hope which the human family needs." But such a sign does not exist without the ecumenical movement. Nor should the churches avoid difficult issues. As described by Richard Norris in "On 'Full Communion' between the Episcopal Church and the Evangelical Lutheran Church in America," the Episcopalian Church and the Evangelical Lutheran Church celebrated the resolution of some difficult issues when they voted for "full communion" in 1997. The votes affirm that each Church recognizes the other as a catholic and apostolic Church, holding the essentials of the Christian faith. Full communion means that there will be "regular consultation and communication, including episcopal collegiality, to express and strengthen the fellowship and enable common witness, life, and service." J. M. R. Tillard explores the giftedness of authority held in common in his "Episcopacy: A Gift of the Spirit" (1999).

Section 4 of this chapter, Religion, Science, and Secularism, presents Christian responses to the religious challenges of science and secularism. Since the seventeenth century, the relationships between the sciences and the religions have been variously described: some perceive mutual mistrust and hostility; some argue that science itself originated from within Christianity; still others—such as Ian Barbour, a physicist later to become the doyen of a new academic field, science and religion—find similarities in their use of myths and models. Thanks to ongoing work by both religious scholars and scientists, the perception of inherent conflict between science and religion is giving way to a view that collaboration between religious scholars and scientists can be productive and beneficial for the future of human and other species.

With respect to the challenge of secularism, Nicholas Lash turns the tables on those who forget that the definition of religion has changed. He points out that, in the seventeenth century, the medieval belief in one world gave way to a belief in two worlds. Where there had been "one world" in which human beings might act supernaturally (e.g., generously) as well as ordinarily, the introduction of a second—a "natural"—world in the seventeenth century made God the primary occupant of the supernatural world. Lash retrieves from world religions an ancient purpose of religion—namely,

discipline, or ascesis—because he doubts that humanity is a natural acquisition for human beings.

In the excerpt from his encyclical "Evangelium vitae," Pope John Paul II focuses on the destructive effects that the philosophy of secularism can have on human beings. The last text of this chapter is from his address to the 1992 plenary session of the Pontifical Academy of Sciences. Himself a phenomenologist, John Paul takes notice of the "complementary roles that faith and science fulfill in human life" and urges the avoidance of a "shattered culture"—which can result from the failure to synthesize knowledge and to integrate learning.

New understandings of old failures and new movements for unity within diversity seem to auger the emergence of the Spirit in new places.

1. SOCIAL PROPHETS

Simone Weil (1909–43), a French philosopher and social activist who agonized over what it would mean to become a Christian, underwent a profound change after voluntarily working in a factory for a year to experience being enslaved and poor. "Concerning the Our Father," a meditation on the scriptural prayer, was written about a year before her death.

SIMONE WEIL

"Concerning the Our Father," in *Waiting for God*

Πάτηρ ἡμῶν ὁ ἐν τοῖς οὐρανοῖς

"Our Father which art in Heaven."

He is our Father. There is nothing real in us which does not come from him. We belong to him. He loves us, since he loves himself and we are his. Nevertheless he is our Father who is in heaven—not elsewhere. If we think to have a Father here below it is not he, it is a false God. We cannot take a single step toward him. We do not walk vertically. We can only turn our eyes toward him. We do not have to search for him, we only have to change the direction in which we are looking. It is for him to search for us. We must be happy in the knowledge that he is infinitely beyond our reach. Thus we can be certain that the evil in us, even if it overwhelms our whole being, in no way sullies the divine purity, bliss, and perfection.

Ἁγιασθήτω τὸ ὄνομά σου

"Hallowed be thy Name."

God alone has the power to name himself. His name is unpronounceable for human lips. His name is his word. It is the Word of God. The name of any being is an intermediary between the human spirit and that being; it is the only means by which the human spirit can conceive something about a being that is absent. God is absent. He is in heaven. Man's only possibility of gaining access to him is through his name. It is the Mediator. Man has access to this name, although it also is transcendent. It shines in the beauty and order of the world and it shines in the interior light of the human soul. This name is holiness itself; there is no holiness outside it; it does not therefore have to be hallowed. In asking for its hallowing we are asking for something that exists eternally, with full and complete reality, so that we can neither increase nor diminish it, even by an infinitesimal fraction. To ask for that which exists, that which exists really, infallibly, eternally, quite independently of our prayer, that is the perfect petition. We cannot prevent ourselves from desiring; we are made of desire; but the desire that nails us down to what is imaginary, temporal, selfish, can, if we make it pass wholly into this petition, become a lever to tear us from the imaginary into the real and from time into eternity, to lift us right out of the prison of self.

ἐλθάτω ἡ βασιλεία σου
"Thy Kingdom Come."

This concerns something to be achieved, something not yet here. The Kingdom of God means the complete filling of the entire soul of intelligent creatures with the Holy Spirit. The Spirit bloweth where he listeth. We can only invite him. We must not even try to invite him in a definite and special way to visit us or anyone else in particular, or even everybody in general; we must just invite him purely and simply, so that our thought of him is an invitation, a longing cry. It is as when one is in extreme thirst, ill with thirst; then one no longer thinks of the act of drinking in relation to oneself, or even of the act of drinking in a general way. One merely thinks of water, actual water itself, but the image of water is like a cry from our whole being.

γενηθήτω τὸ θέλημά σου
"Thy will be done."

We are only absolutely, infallibly certain of the will of God concerning the past. Everything that has happened, whatever it may be, is in accordance with the will of the almighty Father. That is implied by the notion of almighty power. The future also, whatever it may contain, once it has come about, will have come about in conformity with the will of God. We can neither add to nor take from this conformity. In this clause, therefore, after an upsurging of our desire toward the possible, we are once again asking for that which is. Here, however, we are not concerned with an eternal reality such as the holiness of the Word, but with what happens in the time order. Nevertheless we are asking for the infallible and eternal conformity of everything in time with the will of God. After having, in our first petition, torn our desire away from time in order to fix it upon eternity, thereby transforming it, we return to this desire which has itself become in some measure eternal, in order to apply it once more to time. Whereupon our desire pierces through time to find eternity behind it. That is what comes about when we know how to make every accomplished fact, whatever it may be, an object of desire. We have here quite a different thing from resignation. Even the word acceptance is too weak. We have to desire that everything that has happened should have happened, and nothing else. We have to do so, not because what has happened is good in our eyes, but because God has permitted it, and because the obedience of the course of events to God is in itself an absolute good.

ὡς ἐν οὐρανῷ καὶ ἐπὶ γῆς
"On earth as it is in heaven."

The association of our desire with the almighty will of God should be extended to spiritual things. Our own spiritual ascents and falls, and those of the beings we love, have to do with the other world, but they are also events that take place here below, in time. On that account they are details in the immense sea of events and are tossed about with the ocean in a way conforming to the will of God. Since our failures of the past have come about, we have to desire that they should have come about. We have to extend this desire into the future, for the day when it will have become the past. It is a necessary correction of the petition that the kingdom of God should come. We have to cast aside all other desires for the sake of our desire for eternal Life, but we should desire eternal life itself with renunciation. We must not even become attached to detachment. Attachment to salvation is even more dangerous than the others. We have to think of eternal life as one thinks of water when dying of thirst, and yet at the same time we have to desire that we and our loved ones should be eternally deprived of this water rather than receive it in abundance in spite of God's will, if such a thing were conceivable.

The three foregoing petitions are related to the three Persons of the Trinity, the Son, the Spirit, and the Father, and also to the three divisions of time, the present, the future, and the past. The three petitions that follow have a more direct bearing on the three divisions of time, and take them in a different order present, past, and future.

Τὸν ἄρτον ἡμῶν τὸν ἐπιούσιον δὸς ἡμῖν σήμερον
"Give us this day our daily bread—the bread which is supernatural."[1]

Christ is our bread. We can only ask to have him now. Actually he is always there at the door of our souls, wanting to enter in, though he does not force our consent. If we agree to his entry, he enters; directly we cease to want him, he is gone. We cannot bind our will today for tomorrow; we cannot make a pact with him that tomorrow he will be within us, even in spite of ourselves. Our consent to his presence is the same as his presence. Consent is an act; it can only be actual, that is to say in the present. We have not been given a will that can be applied to the future. Everything not effective in our will is imaginary. The effective part of the will has

---

1. Gen 6:5.

its effect at once; its effectiveness cannot be separated from itself. The effective part of the will is not effort, which is directed toward the future. It is consent; it is the "yes" of marriage. A "yes" pronounced within the present moment and for the present moment, but spoken as an eternal word, for it is consent to the union of Christ with the eternal part of our soul.

Bread is a necessity for us. We are beings who continually draw our energy from outside, for as we receive it we use it up in effort. If our energy is not daily renewed, we become feeble and incapable of movement. Besides actual food, in the literal sense of the word, all incentives are sources of energy for us. Money, ambition, consideration, decorations, celebrity, power, our loved ones, everything that puts into us the capacity for action is like bread. If any one of these attachments penetrates deeply enough into us to reach the vital roots of our carnal existence, its loss may break us and even cause our death. That is called dying of love. It is like dying of hunger. All these objects of attachment go together with food, in the ordinary sense of the word, to make up the daily bread of this world. It depends entirely on circumstances whether we have it or not. We should ask nothing with regard to circumstances unless it be that they may conform to the will of God. We should not ask for earthly bread.

There is a transcendent energy whose source is in heaven, and this flows into us as soon as we wish for it. It is a real energy; it performs actions through the agency of our souls and of our bodies.

We should ask for this food. At the moment of asking, and by the very fact that we ask for it, we know that God will give it to us. We ought not to be able to bear to go without it for a single day, for when our actions only depend on earthly energies, subject to the necessity of this world, we are incapable of thinking and doing anything but evil. God saw "that the misdeeds of man were multiplied on the earth and that all the thoughts of his heart were continually bent upon evil." The necessity that drives us toward evil governs everything in us except the energy from on high at the moment when it comes into us. We cannot store it.

καὶ ἄφες ἡμῖν τὰ ὀφειλήματα ἡμῶν ὡς καὶ ἡμεῖς ἀφήκαμεν τοῖς ὀφειλέταις ἡμῶν

"And forgive us our debts, as we also forgive our debtors."

At the moment of saying these words we must have already remitted everything that is owing to us. This not only includes reparation for any wrongs we think we have suffered, but also gratitude for the good we think we have done,

and it applies in a quite general way to all we expect from people and things, to all we consider as our due and without which we should feel ourselves to have been frustrated. All these are the rights that we think the past has given us over the future. First there is the right to a certain permanence. When we have enjoyed something for a long time, we think that it is ours and that we are entitled to expect fate to let us go on enjoying it. Then there is the right to a compensation for every effort whatever its nature, be it work, suffering, or desire. Every time that we put forth some effort and the equivalent of this effort does not come back to us in the form of some visible fruit, we have a sense of false balance and emptiness which makes us think that we have been cheated. The effort of suffering from some offense causes us to expect the punishment or apologies of the offender, the effort of doing good makes us expect the gratitude of the person we have helped, but these are only particular cases of a universal law of the soul. Every time we give anything out we have an absolute need that at least the equivalents should come into us, and because we need this we think we have a right to it. Our debtors comprise all beings and all things; they are the entire universe. We think we have claims everywhere. In every claim we think we possess there is always the idea of an imaginary claim of the past on the future. That is the claim we have to renounce.

To have forgiven our debtors is to have renounced the whole of the past in a lump. It is to accept that the future should still be virgin and intact, strictly united to the past by bonds of which we are ignorant, but quite free from the bonds our imagination thought to impose upon it. It means that we accept the possibility that this will happen, and that it may happen to us in particular; it means that we are prepared for the future to render all our past life sterile and vain.

In renouncing at one stroke all the fruits of the past without exception, we can ask of God that our past sins may not bear their miserable fruits of evil and error. So long as we cling to the past, God himself cannot stop this horrible fruiting. We cannot hold on to the past without retaining our crimes, for we are unaware of what is most essentially bad in us.

The principal claim we think we have on the universe is that our personality should continue. This claim implies all the others. The instinct of self-preservation makes us feel this continuation to be a necessity, and we believe that a necessity is a right. We are like the beggar who said to Talleyrand: "Sir, I must live," and to whom Talleyrand replied, "I do not see the necessity for that." Our personality is entirely dependent on external circumstances which have unlimited power to crush it. But we would rather die than admit this. From our point of view the equilibrium of the world is a combination of circumstances so ordered that our personality remains intact and seems to belong to us. All the circumstances of the past that have wounded our personality appear to us to be disturbances of balance which should infallibly be made up for one day or another by phenomena having a contrary effect. We live on the expectation of these compensations. The near approach of death is horrible chiefly because it forces the knowledge upon us that these compensations will never come.

To remit debts is to renounce our own personality. It means renouncing everything that goes to make up our ego, without any exception. It means knowing that in the ego there is nothing whatever, no psychological element, that external circumstances could not do away with. It means accepting that truth. It means being happy that things should be so.

The words "Thy will be done" imply this acceptance, if we say them with all our soul. That is why we can say a few moments later: "We forgive our debtors."

The forgiveness of debts is spiritual poverty, spiritual nakedness, death. If we accept death completely, we can ask God to make us live again, purified from the evil in us. For to ask him to forgive us our debts is to ask him to wipe out the evil in us. Pardon is purification. God himself has not the power to forgive the evil in us while it remains there. God will have forgiven our debts when he has brought us to the state of perfection.

Until then God forgives our debts partially in the same measure as we forgive our debtors.

καὶ μὴ εἰσενέγκῃς ἡμᾶς εἰς πειρασμόν ἀλλὰ ῥῦσαι ἡμᾶς ἀπὸ τοῦ πονηροῦ

"And lead us not into temptation, but deliver us from evil."

The only temptation for man is to be abandoned to his own resources in the presence of evil. His nothingness is then proved experimentally. Although the soul has received supernatural bread at the moment when it asked for it, its joy is mixed with fear because it could only ask for it for the present. The future is still to be feared. The soul has not the right to ask for bread for the morrow, but it expresses its fear in the form of a supplication. It finishes with that. The prayer began with the word "Father," it ends with the word "evil." We must go from confidence to fear. Confidence alone can give us strength enough not to fall as a result of fear. After

having contemplated the name, the kingdom, and the will of God, after having received the supernatural bread and having been purified from evil, the soul is ready for that true humility which crowns all virtues. Humility consists of knowing that in this world the whole soul, not only what we term the ego in its totality, but also the supernatural part of the soul, which is God present in it, is subject to time and to the vicissitudes of change. There must be absolute acceptance of the possibility that everything natural in us should be destroyed. But we must simultaneously accept and repudiate the possibility that the supernatural part of the soul should disappear. It must be accepted as an event that would come about only in conformity with the will of God. It must be repudiated as being something utterly horrible. We must be afraid of it, but our fear must be as it were the completion of confidence.

The six petitions correspond with each other in pairs. The bread which is transcendent is the same thing as the divine name. It is what brings about the contact of man with God. The kingdom of God is the same thing as his protection stretched over us against temptation; to protect is the function of royalty. Forgiving our debtors their debts is the same thing as the total acceptance of the will of God. The difference is that in the first three petitions the attention is fixed solely on God. In the three last, we turn our attention back to ourselves in order to compel ourselves to make these petitions a real and not an imaginary act.

In the first half of the prayer, we begin with acceptance. Then we allow ourselves a desire. Then we correct it by coming back to acceptance. In the second half, the order is changed; we finish by expressing desire. Only desire has now become negative; it is expressed as a fear; therefore it corresponds to the highest degree of humility and that is a fitting way to end.

The Our Father contains all possible petitions; we cannot conceive of any prayer not already contained in it. It is to prayer what Christ is to humanity. It is impossible to say it once through, giving the fullest possible attention to each word, without a change, infinitesimal perhaps but real, taking place in the soul.

From Simone Weil, *Waiting for God*, translated by Emma Craufurd (New York: Harper Colophon, 1973), 216–27.

☙ In his "I Have a Dream" speech, delivered August 28, 1963, in Washington, DC, **Martin Luther King** (1929–68) draws upon the prophetic figure of Moses and the Exodus. King's own prophetic vision has continued to fuel the Civil Rights movement in the United States and in other places around the world.

MARTIN LUTHER KING
"I Have a Dream"

I am happy to join with you today in what will go down in history as the greatest demonstration for freedom in the history of our nation.

Fivescore years ago, a great American, in whose symbolic shadow we stand today, signed the Emancipation Proclamation. This momentous decree came as a great beacon light of hope to millions of Negro slaves who had been seared in the flames of withering injustice. It came as a joyous daybreak to end the long night of their captivity.

But one hundred years later, the Negro still is not free; one hundred years later, the life of the Negro is still sadly crippled by the manacles of segregation and the chains of discrimination; one hundred years later, the Negro lives on a lonely island of poverty in the midst of a vast ocean of material prosperity; one hundred years later, the Negro is still languished in the corners of American society and finds himself in exile in his own land.

So we've come here today to dramatize a shameful condition. In a sense we've come to our nation's capital to cash a check. When the architects of our republic wrote the magnificent words of the Constitution and the Declaration of Independence, they were signing a promissory note to which every American was to fall heir. This note was the promise that all men, yes, black men as well as white, would be guaranteed the unalienable rights of life, liberty, and the pursuit of happiness.

It is obvious today that America has defaulted on this promissory note in so far as her citizens of color are concerned. Instead of honoring this sacred obligation, America has given the Negro people a bad check which has come back marked "insufficient funds." We refuse to believe that there are insufficient funds in the great vaults of opportunity of this nation. And so we've come to cash this check, a check that will give us upon demand the riches of freedom and the security of justice. We have also come to this hallowed spot to remind America of the fierce urgency of now. This is no time to engage in the luxury of cooling off or to take the tranquilizing drug of gradualism. Now is the time to make real the promises of democracy; now is the time to rise from the dark and desolate valley of segregation to the sunlit path of racial justice; now is the time to lift our nation from the quicksands of racial injustice to the solid rock of brotherhood; now is the time to make justice a reality for all God's children. It would be fatal for the nation to overlook the urgency of the moment. This sweltering summer of the Negro's legitimate discontent will not pass until there is an invigorating autumn of freedom and equality.

Nineteen sixty-three is not an end, but a beginning. And those who hope that the Negro needed to blow off steam and will now be content, will have a rude awakening if the nation returns to business as usual.

There will be neither rest nor tranquility in America until the Negro is granted his citizenship rights. The whirlwinds of revolt will continue to shake the foundations of our nation until the bright day of justice emerges.

But there is something that I must say to my people who stand on the warm threshold which leads into the palace of justice. In the process of gaining our rightful place we must not be guilty of wrongful deeds.

Let us not seek to satisfy our thirst for freedom by drinking from the cup of bitterness and hatred. We must forever conduct our struggle on the high plane of dignity and discipline. We must not allow our creative protest to degenerate into physical violence. Again and again we must rise to the majestic heights of meeting physical force with soul force.

The marvelous new militancy which has engulfed the Negro community must not lead us to a distrust of all white people, for many of our white brothers, as evidenced by their presence here today, have come to realize that their destiny is tied up with our destiny and they have come to realize that their freedom is inextricably bound to our freedom. This offense we share mounted to storm the battlements of injustice must be carried forth by a biracial army. We cannot walk alone.

And as we walk, we must make the pledge that we shall always march ahead. We cannot turn back. There are those who are asking the devotees of civil rights, "When will you be satisfied?" We can never be satisfied as long as the Negro is the victim of the unspeakable horrors of police brutality.

We can never be satisfied as long as our bodies, heavy with fatigue of travel, cannot gain lodging in the motels of the highways and the hotels of the cities. We cannot be satisfied as long as the Negro's basic mobility is from a smaller ghetto to a larger one.

We can never be satisfied as long as our children are stripped of their selfhood and robbed of their dignity by signs stating "for whites only." We cannot be satisfied as long as a Negro in Mississippi cannot vote and a Negro in New York believes he has nothing for which to vote. No, we are not satisfied, and we will not be satisfied until justice rolls down like waters and righteousness like a mighty stream.

I am not unmindful that some of you have come here out of excessive trials and tribulation. Some of you have come fresh from narrow jail cells. Some of you have come from areas where your quest for freedom left you battered by the storms of persecution and staggered by the winds of police brutality. You have been the veterans of creative suffering. Continue to work with the faith that unearned suffering is redemptive.

Go back to Mississippi; go back to Alabama; go back to South Carolina; go back to Georgia; go back to Louisiana; go back to the slums and ghettos of the northern cities, knowing that somehow this situation can and will be changed. Let us not wallow in the valley of despair.

So I say to you, my friends, that even though we must face the difficulties of today and tomorrow, I still have a dream. It is a dream deeply rooted in the American dream that one day this nation will rise up and live out the true meaning of its creed—we hold these truths to be self-evident, that all men are created equal.

I have a dream that one day on the red hills of Georgia, sons of former slaves and sons of former slave-owners will be able to sit down together at the table of brotherhood.

I have a dream that one day, even the state of Mississippi, a state sweltering with the heat of injustice, sweltering with the heat of oppression, will be transformed into an oasis of freedom and justice. I have a dream my four little children will one day live in a nation where they will not be judged by the color of their skin but by the content of their character. I have a dream today!

I have a dream that one day, down in Alabama, with its vicious racists, with its governor having his lips dripping with the words of interposition and nullification, that one day, right there in Alabama, little black boys and black girls will be able to join hands with little white boys and white girls as sisters and brothers. I have a dream today!

I have a dream that one day every valley shall be exalted, every hill and mountain shall be made low, the rough places shall be made plain and the crooked places shall be made straight and the glory of the Lord will be revealed and all flesh shall see it together.

This is our hope. This is the faith that I go back to the South with.

With this faith we will be able to hew out of the mountain of despair a stone of hope. With this faith we will be able to transform the jangling discords of our nation into a beautiful symphony of brotherhood. With this faith we will be able to work together, to pray together, to struggle together, to go to jail together, to stand up for freedom together, knowing that we will be free one day. This will be the day when all of God's children will be able to sing with new meaning—"my country 'tis of thee; sweet land of liberty; of thee I sing; land where my fathers died; land of the pilgrim's pride; from every mountain side, let freedom ring"—and if America is to be a great nation, this must become true.

So let freedom ring from the prodigious hilltops of New Hampshire.

Let freedom ring from the mighty mountains of New York.

Let freedom ring from the heightening Alleghenies of Pennsylvania.

Let freedom ring from the snow-capped Rockies of Colorado.

Let freedom ring from the curvaceous slopes of California.

But not only that.

Let freedom ring from Stone Mountain of Georgia.

Let freedom ring from Lookout Mountain of Tennessee.

Let freedom ring from every hill and molehill of Mississippi, from every mountainside, let freedom ring.

And when we allow freedom to ring, when we let it ring from every village and hamlet, from every state and city, we will be able to speed up that day when all of God's children—black men and white men, Jews and Gentiles, Catholics and Protestants—will be able to join hands and to sing in the words of the old Negro spiritual, "Free at last, free at last; thank God Almighty, we are free at last."

From James Melvin Washington, ed., *A Testament of Hope: The Essential Writings of Martin Luther King, Jr.* (San Francisco: Harper and Row, 1986), 217–20.

  Dorothy Day (1897–1980) was an activist for the poor and for peace. She founded the Catholic Worker Movement, which was devoted to pacifism and aiding the urban poor. In "Politics and Principles," written in 1942, Day responds to criticisms of her antiwar stance by comparing the state of the destitute with the state of those devastated by war. She challenges her critics to share the plight of both.

DOROTHY DAY
"Politics and Principles," II

Father Stratmen writes: "We think with Cardinal Faulhaber that Catholic moral theology must in fact begin to speak a new language, and that what the last two Popes have already pronounced in the way of general sentences of condemnation on modern war should be translated into a systematic terminology of the schools. The simple preacher and pastor can, however, already begin by making his own, words of the reigning Holy Father [Pius XI], 'murder,' 'suicide,' 'monstrous crime.'"

"But we are at war," people say. "This is no time to talk of peace. It is demoralizing to the armed forces to protest, not to cheer them on in their fight for Christianity, for democracy, for civilization. Now that it is under way, it is too late to do anything about it." One reader writes to protest against our "frail" voices "blatantly" crying out against war. (The word "blatant" comes from "bleat," and we are indeed poor sheep crying out to the Good Shepherd to save us from these horrors.) Another Catholic newspaper says it sympathizes with our sentimentality. This is a charge always leveled against pacifists. We are supposed to be afraid of the suffering, of the hardships of war.

But let those who talk of softness, of sentimentality, come to live with us in cold, unheated houses in the slums. Let them come to live with the criminal, the unbalanced, the drunken, the degraded, the perverted. (It is not the decent poor, it is not the decent sinner who was the recipient of Christ's love.) Let them live with rats, with vermin, bedbugs, roaches, lice (I could describe the several kinds of body lice).

Let their flesh be mortified by cold, by dirt, by vermin; let their eyes be mortified by the sight of bodily excretions, diseased limbs, eyes, noses, mouths.

Let their noses be mortified by the smells of sewage, decay, and rotten flesh. Yes, and the smell of the sweat, blood, and tears spoken of so blithely by Mr. Churchill, and so widely and bravely quoted by comfortable people.

Let their ears be mortified by harsh and screaming voices, by the constant coming and going of people living herded together with no privacy.

Let their taste be mortified by the constant eating of insufficient food cooked in huge quantities for hundreds of people, the coarser foods, so that there will be enough to go around; and the smell of such cooking is often foul.

Then when they have lived with these comrades, with these sights and sounds, let our critics talk of sentimentality. As we have often quoted Dostoevsky's Father Zossima, "Love in practice is a harsh and dreadful thing compared to love in dreams."

Our Catholic Worker groups are perhaps too hardened to the sufferings in the class war, living as they do in refugee camps, the refugees being, as they are, victims of the class war we live in always. We have lived in the midst of this war now these many years. It is a war not recognized by the majority of our comfortable people. They are pacifists themselves when it comes to the class war. They even pretend it is not there.

Many friends have counseled us to treat this world war in the same way. "Don't write about it. Don't mention it. Don't jeopardize the great work you are doing among the poor, among the workers. Just write about constructive things like Houses of Hospitality and Farming Communes." "Keep silence with a bleeding heart," one reader, a man, pro-war, and therefore not a sentimentalist, writes us.

But we cannot keep silent. We have not kept silence in the face of the monstrous injustice of the class war, or the race war that goes on side by side with this world war (which the Communists used to call the imperialist war).

Read the letters in this issue of the paper, the letter from the machine shop worker as to the deadening, degrading hours of labor. Remember the unarmed steel strikers, the coal miners, shot down on picket lines. Read the letter from our correspondent in Seattle who tells of the treatment accorded agricultural workers in the Northwest. Are these workers supposed to revolt? These are Pearl Harbor incidents! Are they supposed to turn to arms in the class conflict to defend their lives, their homes, their wives and children?

Last month a Negro in Missouri was shot and dragged by a mob through the streets behind a car. His wounded body was then soaked in kerosene. The mob of white Americans then set fire to it, and when the poor anguished victim had died, the body was left lying in the street until a city garbage cart trucked it away. Are the Negroes supposed to "Remember Pearl Harbor" and take to arms to avenge this cruel wrong? No, the Negroes, the workers in general, are supposed to be "pacifist" in the face of this aggression.

Perhaps we are called sentimental because we speak of love. We say we love our President, our country. We say that we love our enemies, too.

"Greater love hath no man than this," Christ said, "that he should lay down his life for his friend."

"Love is the measure by which we shall be judged," St. John of the Cross said.

"Love is the fulfilling of the law," St. John, the beloved disciple, said.

Read the last discourse of Jesus to his disciples. Read the letters of St. John in the New Testament. And how can we express this love—by bombers, by blockades?

Here is a clipping from the *Herald Tribune,* a statement of a soldier describing the use of the bayonet against the Japanese:

"He [his father] should have been with us and seen how good it was. We got into them good and proper, and I can't say I remember much about it, except that it made me feel pretty good. I reckon that was the way with the rest of the company, by the way my pals were yelling all the time."

Is this a Christian speaking?

Love is not the starving of whole populations. Love is not the bombardment of open cities. Love is not killing, it is the laying down of one's life for one's friends.

Hear Father Zossima, in *The Brothers Karamazov:*

"Love one another, Fathers," he says, speaking to his monks. "Love God's people. Because we have come here and shut ourselves within these walls, we are no holier than those that are outside, but on the contrary, from the very fact of coming here, each of us has confessed to himself that he is worse than others, than all men on earth. . . . And the longer the monk lives in his seclusion, the more keenly he must recognize that. Else he would have no reason to come here.

"When he realizes that he is not only worse than others, but that he is responsible to all men for all and everything, for all human sins, national and individual, only then the aim of our seclusion is attained. For know, dear ones, that every one of us is undoubtedly responsible for all men and everything on earth, not merely through the general sinfulness of creation, but each one personally for all mankind and every individual man. For monks are not a special sort of man, but only what all men ought to be. Only through that knowledge, our heart grows soft with infinite, universal, inexhaustible love. Then every one of you will have the power to win over the whole world by love and to wash away the sins of the world with your tears. . . . Each of you keep watch over your heart and confess your sins to yourself unceasingly. . . . Hate not the atheists, the teachers of evil, the materialists, and I mean not only the good ones—for there are many good ones among them, especially in our day—hate not even the

wicked ones. Remember them in your prayers thus: Save, O Lord, all those who have none to pray for them; save too all those who will not pray. And add, it is not in pride that I make this prayer, O Lord, for I am lower than all men. . . ."

I quote this because that accusation "holier than thou" is also made against us. And we must all admit our guilt, our participation in the social order which has resulted in this monstrous crime of war.

We used to have a poor, demented friend who came into the office to see us very often, beating his breast, quoting the Penitential Psalms in Hebrew, and saying that everything was his fault. Through all he had done and left undone, he had brought about the war, the revolution.

That should be our cry, with every mouthful we eat— "We are starving Europe!" When we look to our comfort in a warm bed, a warm home, we must cry, "My brother, my mother, my child is dying of cold.

"I am lower than all men, because I do not love enough. O God, take away my heart of stone and give me a heart of flesh."

From Dorothy Day, *By Little and By Little: The Selected Writings of Dorothy Day,* edited by Robert Ellsberg (New York: Alfred A. Knopf, 1983), 263–66. [Ellipses and brackets in original.]

The Trappist monk **Thomas Merton** (1915–68) contemplates the nature of his monastic solitude in "The Night Spirit and the Dawn Affair." For Merton, solitude offers a clarity of vision informed by incarnational mysticism: the ability to see the image of God in all people.

THOMAS MERTON

"The Night Spirit and the Dawn Affair," in *Conjectures of a Guilty Bystander*

In Louisville, at the corner of Fourth and Walnut, in the center of the shopping district, I was suddenly overwhelmed with the realization that I loved all those people, that they were mine and I theirs, that we could not be alien to one another even though we were total strangers. It was like waking from a dream of separateness, of spurious self-isolation in a special world, the world of renunciation and supposed holiness. The whole illusion of a separate holy existence is a dream. Not that I question the reality of my vocation, or of my monastic life: but the conception of "separation from the world" that we have in the monastery too easily presents itself as a complete illusion: the illusion that by making vows we become a different species of being, pseudo-angels, "spiritual men," men of interior life, what have you.

Certainly these traditional values are very real but their reality is not of an order outside everyday existence in a contingent world, nor does it entitle one to despise the secular: though "out of the world" we are in the same world as everybody else, the world of the bomb, the world of race hatred, the world of technology, the world of mass media, big business, revolution, and all the rest. We take a different attitude to all these things, for we belong to God. Yet so does everybody else belong to God. We just happen to be conscious of it, and to make a profession out of this consciousness. But does that entitle us to consider ourselves different, or even *better*, than others? The whole idea is preposterous.

This sense of liberation from an illusory difference was such a relief and such a joy to me that I almost laughed out loud. And I suppose my happiness could have taken form in the words: "Thank God, thank God that I *am* like other men, that I am only a man among others." To think that for sixteen or seventeen years I have been taking seriously this pure illusion that is implicit in so much of our monastic thinking.

It is a glorious destiny to be a member of the human race, though it is a race dedicated to many absurdities and one which makes many terrible mistakes: yet, with all that, God Himself gloried in becoming a member of the human race. A member of the human race! To think that such a commonplace realization should suddenly seem like news that one holds the winning ticket in a cosmic sweepstake.

I have the immense joy of being *man,* a member of a race in which God Himself became incarnate. As if the sorrows and stupidities of the human condition could overwhelm me, now I realize what we all are. And if only everybody could realize this! But it cannot be explained. There is no way of telling people that they are all walking around shining like the sun.

This changes nothing in the sense and value of my solitude, for it is in fact the function of solitude to make one realize such things with a clarity that would be impossible to anyone completely immersed in the other cares, the other illusions, and all the automatisms of a tightly collective existence. My solitude, however, is not my own, for I see now how much it belongs to them—and that I have a responsibility for it in their regard, not just in my own. It is because I am one with them that I owe it to them to be alone, and when I am alone they are not "they" but my own self. There are no strangers!

Then it was as if I suddenly saw the secret beauty of their hearts, the depths of their hearts where neither sin nor desire nor self-knowledge can reach, the core of their reality, the person that each one is in God's eyes. If only they could all see themselves as they really *are.* If only we could see each other that way all the time. There would be no more war, no more hatred, no more cruelty, no more greed. . . . I suppose the big problem would be that we would fall down and worship each other. But this cannot be *seen,* only believed and "understood" by a peculiar gift.

Again, that expression, *le point vierge* (I cannot translate it), comes in here. At the center of our being is a point of nothingness which is untouched by sin and by illusion, a point of pure truth, a point or spark which belongs entirely to God, which is never at our disposal, from which God disposes of our lives, which is inaccessible to the fantasies of our own mind or the brutalities of our own will. This little point of nothingness and of *absolute poverty* is the pure glory of God in us. It is so to speak His name written in us, as our poverty, as our indigence, as our dependence, as our sonship. It is like a pure diamond, blazing with the invisible light of heaven. It is in everybody, and if we could see it we would see these billions of points of light coming together in the face and blaze of a sun that would make all the darkness and cruelty of life vanish completely. . . . I have no program for this seeing. It is only given. But the gate of heaven is everywhere.

From Thomas Merton, *Conjectures of a Guilty Bystander* (New York: Doubleday, 1966), 140–42. [Ellipses in original.]

❧ A narrative and two meditations by **Dom Hélder Câmara** (1909–99), a Brazilian Catholic bishop, are comparable to the parables in the Gospels. In the narrative "Grown-ups Just Don't Understand" (written in the late 1970s), the drama of a boy facing his mother portrays the loss of one's humanity through exclusive concern for the practical. In the first meditation, "The Foreign Geologist" (February 7, 1978), buried economic wealth mediates an awareness of spiritual wealth within. In the second meditation, "About the Ocean Depths" (February 8, 1978), his reflection on viewing a film about the sea provides an analogy for what it means for humankind to have their being in God.

DOM HÉLDER CÂMARA

"Grown-ups Just Don't Understand"

The kid's mother was firmly convinced that he had lost the house-key. So she made him turn out both his trouser pockets and both the pockets in his jacket.

What didn't come out! Everything, except the key.

This made the boy's mother angrier than ever. As far as she could see, the odds and ends with which his pockets were stuffed were nothing but trash. How hard it is to understand children!

How nostalgic I feel for my childhood pockets! They were just the same!

An empty cotton-reel! Could Mother ever grasp the fact that what looked like a cotton-reel was really a radio-telephone to be used when crossing deserts?

A piece of string! How could a grown-up ever agree that it wasn't a piece of string at all but a magic tightrope for stretching from mountain to mountain, or over the water for crossing torrents in spate?

Pebbles of all shapes and colours: that really did make grown-ups frown, since it was quite beyond them to believe that these were fragments of moon-rock brought back by an astronaut!

The kid's mother watched the most unlikely and unexpected things coming out of his pockets, all but the house-key. When a little bell appeared, she exploded, "At last, that's something I do understand. A little bell! You deserve to have one tied round your neck, round your wrists and round your ankles, you clown!"

The little boy looked very sad at this but said nothing. I was dying to intervene and say, "But can't you see? It's a magic bell brought by a fish from the bottom of the sea! Can't you see, it's a bell for frightening sadness away and summoning joy?" That's what I wanted to say, but I kept quiet. She wouldn't have understood. Grown-ups find it so hard to understand the simplest of things.

Out of the child's pockets, I recall, also came some seeds, a nail, a top, a scrap of cloth, a photo of Bob Dylan . . .

The scrap of cloth—what could be more obvious?—was the tail of a kite. The top was presumably the champion dancer of all the tops in the world. The seeds, with a little creative imagination, might give birth to anything one pleased.

The nail! Well, the nail . . . but why this mania for wanting an explanation for everything? Why not think of the nail as a surprise? Before tonight, you see if it hasn't been put to good use half a dozen times!

As for the photo of Bob Dylan, it really would be the end if you were to ask what that is for!

How patient children have to be when dealing with grown-ups!

From Dom Hélder Câmara, *A Thousand Reasons for Living,* edited by José de Broucker, translated by Alan Neame (Philadelphia: Fortress, 1981), 9–11. [Ellipsis in original.]

DOM HÉLDER CÂMARA
"The Foreign Geologist"

The foreign geologist
irritably asked,
"Whenever will your country
become properly aware
of the immense wealth
hidden beneath its soil?"
This brought me up short,
appalled at the thought
of an incomparably graver
unawareness:
Whenever shall we human creatures
become properly aware
that we have,
hidden in our deepest selves,
the Lord of wealth,
and that he is being smothered
under incredible layers
of fatuous silliness,
absurd pretentiousness
and childish pride?

From Dom Hélder Câmara, *A Thousand Reasons for Living,* edited by José de Broucker, translated by Alan Neame (Philadelphia: Fortress, 1981), 116.

DOM HÉLDER CÂMARA
"About the Ocean Depths"

Watching a marvellous film
about the ocean depths
I felt a huge desire
to help the fish
understand how lucky they are
to live immersed
in so much splendour.
Imagine then my thirst
to cry to men, my brothers,
that we live immersed—
coming and going,
swimming to and fro—
not in the oceans
but in God himself!

From Dom Hélder Câmara, *A Thousand Reasons for Living,* edited by José de Broucker, translated by Alan Neame (Philadelphia: Fortress, 1981), 117.

On October 7, 1950, Mother **Teresa of Calcutta** (1910–97) founded a religious order known as the Missionaries of Charity. Her sisters have carried on Mother Teresa's work among the poor, the sick, and the marginalized beyond the borders of Calcutta. The following excerpts are taken from her public "addresses," both spoken and written. The first emphasizes her dependence on divine Providence for the resources of her ministry. The second is the full text of her 1992 "Peace Message." The third is taken from her acceptance speech upon being awarded the Nobel Peace Prize in 1979. The final selection comes from the 1994 National Prayer Breakfast in Washington, DC.

TERESA OF CALCUTTA

Addresses

When our Sisters went to Paris to begin the work, the Church leaders explained about health insurance. They were going to have all the Sisters insured and they had the forms ready.

I said, "No, that is not for us." Everybody was shocked and tried to make me change my mind.

But I asked them, "Do the poor that we work with have health insurance?"

That settled it. If we live with the poor, we must share their poverty and depend on the providence of Almighty God for his help. That is our Faith.

We do not accept any government grants. We do not accept Church maintenance. We have no salaries, receive nothing for the work that we do. So we fully depend on Divine Providence. We deal with thousands and thousands of people, and there never has been a day when we have to say to somebody, "Sorry, we don't have anything to give you."

We cook for about nine thousand people every day in Calcutta. One day [a] Sister came to me and said, "Mother, there's absolutely nothing. We don't have anything at all." I couldn't answer her.

About nine o'clock in the morning a large truck full of bread came to the door. The schools were closed that day. They dropped thousands of loaves inside our walls, and the people had nice bread for two days. How he gives, how he brings things. That is how we are able to care for thousands upon thousands of lepers.

My Brothers and Sisters in India and all over the world,

We are all God's children, and we have been created for greater things: to love and to be loved. God loves each one of us with an everlasting love—we are precious to him. Therefore, nothing should separate us. Religion is a gift of God and is meant to help us to be one heart full of love. God is our Father, and we are all his children—we are all brothers and sisters. Let there be no distinctions of race or color or creed.

Let us not use religion to divide us. In all the Holy Books, we see how God calls us to love. Whatever we do to each other—we do to him because he has said, "Whatever you do to the least of my brothers you do it for me" (Matthew 25:40).

Works of love are works of peace—to love we must know one another. Today, if we have no peace, it is because we have forgotten that we are all God's children. That man, that woman, that child is my brother, my sister. If everyone could see the image of God in his neighbor, do you think we would still have such destruction and suffering?

Religion is meant to be a work of love. Therefore, it should not divide us. It should not destroy peace and unity. Let us use religion to become one heart full of love in the heart of God. For this we need to pray that we may fulfill God's purpose for us: To love and to be loved.

My brothers and sisters, let us ask God to fill us with the peace that only he can give. Peace to men of good will—who want peace, and are ready to sacrifice themselves to do good, to perform works of peace and love.

So please, please, I beg you in the name of God, stop bringing violence, destruction, and death to each other, and especially to the poor who are always the first victims.

Let us remember that the *fruit of religion* is to bring the *joy of loving* through the *joy of sharing.*

God Bless You,

M. Teresa, M.C.

The poor are wonderful people. One evening we went out and picked up four people from the street. One of them was in a most terrible condition. I told the Sisters: "You take care of the other three. I will take care of this one that looks worse." So I did for her, all that my love can do. I put her in bed, and there was such a beautiful smile on her face. She took hold of my hand, as she said one word only, "Thank you," and she died.

I could not help but examine my conscience before her, and I asked, *"What would I say if I was in her place?"* And my answer was very simple. I would have tried to draw a little attention to myself. I would have said, "I am hungry; I am dying; I am cold; I am in pain," or something. She gave me much more—she gave me her grateful love. And she died with a smile on her face.

Like the man whom we picked up from the drain, half-eaten with worms; we brought him to the home. "I have lived like an animal in the street, but I am going to die like an angel, loved and cared for."

And it was so wonderful to see the greatness of a man who could speak like that, who could die like that, without blaming anybody, without cursing anybody, without comparing anything. Like an angel—that is the greatness of our people.

And that is why we believe what Jesus has said, "I was hungry, I was naked, I was homeless, I was unwanted, unloved, uncared for, and you did it to me."

I can never forget the experience I had in visiting a home where they kept all these old parents of sons and daughters who had just put them into an institution and forgotten them—maybe. I saw that in that home these old people had everything—good food, comfortable place, television, everything, but everyone was looking toward the door. And I did not see a single one with a smile on the face. I turned to Sister and I asked: "Why do these people who have every comfort here, why are they all looking toward the door? Why are they not smiling?" I am so used to seeing the smiles on our people, even the dying ones smile.

And Sister said: "This is the way it is nearly every day. They are expecting, they are hoping that a son or daughter will come to visit them. They are hurt because they are forgotten." And see, this neglect to love brings spiritual poverty. Maybe in our own family we have somebody who is feeling lonely, who is feeling sick, who is feeling worried. Are we there? Are we willing to give until it hurts in order to be with our families, or do we put our own interests first? These are the questions we must ask ourselves, especially as we begin this year of the family. We must remember that love begins at home and we must also remember that "the future of humanity passes through the family."

I was surprised in the West to see so many young boys and girls given to drugs. And I tried to find out why. Why is it like that, when those in the West have so many more things than those in the East? And the answer was: "Because there is no one in the family to receive them." Our children depend on us for everything—their health, their nutrition, their security, their coming to know and love God. For all of this, they look to us with trust, hope and expectation.

Prepared and edited by Eileen Egan and Kathleen Egan, *Suffering into Joy: What Mother Teresa Teaches about True Joy* (Ann Arbor, MI: Servant, 1994), 80–81, 101–2, 105–6, 147–149.

⁊ In "The Bottom of Depravity," **Desmond Tutu,** the Anglican archbishop of Cape Town, South Africa, first examines the hope and courage needed to overturn apartheid and then, in "A Miracle Unfolding," explores the elation of having overcome the powers of darkness and destruction. In 1984, Tutu received the Nobel Peace Prize.

DESMOND TUTU

"The Bottom of Depravity," in *The Rainbow People of God: The Making of a Peaceful Revolution*

The vast majority of the victims of violence during the transition to democracy were those who had been the victims of apartheid: black South Africans. In June 1993 constitutional negotiators set a provisional date for the country's first democratic elections, then confirmed the date on July 2. Between July 2 and 13 more than 220 people died in violence on the East Rand, east of Johannesburg, and at least 50 in Natal. Upsurges of violence were often linked to breakthroughs in negotiations, leading to speculation that the violence was deliberately instigated by right-wing elements intent on preventing change.

With conflict concentrated in black townships, most whites were not directly threatened except by a sense of fear and insecurity. However, there were some racist attacks in predominantly "white" urban areas, the worst of which was that on St. James Church, in Kenilworth, Cape Town, on July 25. Four men burst into a Sunday evening service, lobbed hand grenades among the pews and sprayed the 1,000-strong congregation with automatic-rifle fire. Eleven people died immediately and more than fifty were injured.

The massacre drew condemnation across the board and the ANC urged its supporters to join the hunt for the assailants. Thousands of Capetonians of all races gathered at the City Hall on July 29, at the invitation of Mayor Frank van der Velde, to call for peace. The meeting took the form of an interfaith rally including Christian, Jewish and Muslim leaders.

My dear sisters and brothers:

Rampant evil is abroad. Evil men perpetrate vile deeds of darkness, of violence, of death, with breathtaking impunity. They have reached the bottom of depravity in attacking and so desecrating a place of divine worship and adoration, God's sanctuary.

A creeping despondency and sense of impotence want to cover our beautiful land like dark, threatening clouds. We must not let that happen. We, the people of Cape Town, say "No" to that. Let us not let it happen. God will not let it happen.

Our God is a God who is an expert at dealing with evil, with darkness, with death. Out of the darkness and chaos before creation, our God brought into being light, life, goodness and a created order, and when he beheld it, he declared it to be: "Very good."

And out of despair, the evil, the darkness, the pain of slavery, God, our God, brought about the great deliverance, the Exodus. God, our God, created out of a rabble of disorganized slaves his own special people whom God led out of bondage into the promised land, because God, our God, is a God of freedom. Our God is a God of justice, of peace and goodness.

Supremely, God, our God, did his stuff in the awfulness of the Cross, its violence, its darkness and its death. For out of this ghastly instrument of death and destruction, our God produced the glorious victory of Jesus Christ in the Resurrection—a victory that was victory of life over death, of light over darkness, of goodness over evil. And you and I must grasp that fact, that we have a God, as the chorus says: "What a mighty God we have!"

We used to say in the darkness of repression, in the most awful times of apartheid's suppression: *"Moenie worry nie, alles sal regkom"* [Don't worry, everything will be ok]. Because our God is a God who will bring justice out of injustice. And they thought we were dreaming. *Nou hier's dit!* [Now here it is!] We are going to have a new South Africa! We are going to have a South Africa where all of us, black and white, will be truly free.

And we, the people of Cape Town today, united in this kind of way against this atrocity, are saying "No" to violence. To all violence! Because we revere each human being. One death is one death too many. ["Yes."] We say "No" to intimidation, we say "Yes" to freedom! We say "Yes" to peace! We say "Yes" to reconciliation.

If these people who did what they did on Sunday, if these people who do what they do in [black townships like] Katlehong, Daveyton and Thokoza, think they have succeeded in separating us, let us say to them, "No! You have failed, you have succeeded in bringing us together."

And we, as we have always said, are the rainbow people of God. ["Yes!"] We are beautiful because we are the rainbow people of God and we are unstoppable, we are unstoppable, black and white, as we move together to freedom, to justice, to democracy, to peace, to reconciliation, to healing, to loving, to laughter and joy, when we say: This South Africa belongs to all of us, black and white!

A Miracle Unfolding (1994)

As churches throughout South Africa prayed for a free, fair, and peaceful election, right-wing forces began a last-ditch campaign to disrupt the process. Within earshot of worshipers in central Johannesburg, a car bomb exploded near ANC headquarters, killing nine people. [. . .]

But as voting gathered momentum, millions of South Africans showed that nothing would stop them from voting. Thousands of people joined long lines on April 27, some waiting the best part of a day to vote, and an extraordinary peace settled on the country. Desmond Tutu described his feelings in the draft of an article for the German publication Die Zeit.

What an incredible week it has been for us South Africans. We all voted on April 27 and 28 in the first truly democratic election in this beautiful country. We are still on Cloud Nine and have not yet touched terra firma. Our feelings are difficult to put into words. I said it was like falling in love. That is why it seems the sun is shining brighter, the flowers seem more beautiful, the birds sing more sweetly and the people—you know, the people are really more beautiful. They are smiling, they are walking taller than before April 27. They have suddenly discovered that they are all South Africans. And they are proud of that fact. They are no longer the pariahs they used to be.

They stood in the voting queues together—white, black, Colored, Indian—and they discovered that they were compatriots. White South Africans found that a heavy weight of guilt had been lifted from their shoulders. They are discovering what we used to tell them—that freedom is indivisible, that black liberation inexorably meant white liberation. We have seen a miracle unfolding before our eyes—it is a dream coming true. It is a victory for all South Africans. It is a victory for democracy and freedom.

I am looking forward to the post-election celebrations. We all deserve them after the ghastly repression, injustice, deprivation and brutality of apartheid, one of the most vicious systems since Nazism. We could not have reached this point of liberation without the support of all our friends in the international community, the anti-apartheid movement, the churches and many, many others. We have won a great victory and you in the international community have a substantial share in that victory. Thank you, on behalf of millions from South Africa, for all your prayers, concern and support. Join the celebrations. You deserve it too. . . .

We must now all work together for confession, forgiveness, restitution, reconciliation and peace. The interim constitution will assist in this process because we are compelled to have a Government of National Unity which will be a multiparty administration that will operate on the basis of consensus and compromise. The system of proportional representation ensures that virtually every constituency in the country will have a hearing in the national and provincial legislatures. Nelson Mandela, in his post-election statements, is stressing reconciliation and that he wants the post-apartheid processes of governance to be as inclusive as possible.

The level of violence has been unacceptably high. Much of it is due to the machinations of a Third Force. The Goldstone Commission in its latest report says there is prima facie evidence to link high-ranking police officers to a conspiracy

to destabilize the black community by fomenting sectarian violence. Mercifully none of the violence has been ethnic. [In Natal it has been Inkatha-supporting Zulu pitted against ANC-supporting fellow Zulu.] It is not even by and large racial, except for that emanating from a lunatic fringe of the white right wing. A legitimate government, democratically elected, will be able to rehabilitate the police and army so that those organs of state can deal effectively with the violence because they have become more credible as neutral law enforcement and peacekeeping agencies.

From Desmond Tutu, *The Rainbow People of God: The Making of a Peaceful Revolution*, edited by John Allen (New York: Doubleday, 1994), 256–57, 263–64. [Brackets in original.]

꧁

2. CHURCH AND STATE RELATIONS

꙳ In "Pitfalls in the Study of Church-State Relations," **Pedro [Serena P.] Ramet** explores fallacies that are often invoked during disputes over the relationship between state and Church. Ramet, a scholar of international politics and religion, refutes these fallacies. She reminds the reader that both Church and state are political entities that concern themselves with social issues.

PEDRO [SERENA P.] RAMET

"Pitfalls in the Study of Church–State Relations"

Social science, despite its important strides in the past two-and-a-half decades, still seems condemned to persist in the quest for what is ultimately seriously constricted scientific rigor.[2] But the ideals of purposive focus, parsimony, internal consistency, external fidelity, logical rigor, and theoretical importance may serve, all the same, as lodestars in this quest.

Theory is ultimately about questions. Theory is interesting when the questions it raises are interesting and when the evidence summoned and the answers tendered seem useful. When it comes to the study of church-state interaction, the following clusters of questions suggest themselves:

Structural. What parts of the state apparatus interact with what parts of the church apparatus? Under what conditions? For what reasons? With what effects? Does the state have an interest in a particular structural order on the part of the church? And does the church adapt its structure to the particular (political) environment in which it finds itself? In many

ways, organization theory may be the approach that is most at home with these questions.

Procedural. How is regime policy toward churches formulated and executed? How is church policy toward the regime formulated and executed? What are the factional elements in these policies and in the resultant interactions? What elements are unstable? And are different people or agencies involved in formulating regime policy toward different religious organizations? Both organization theory and factional analysis suggest themselves as natural avenues by which to approach these questions.

Legal. What is the relationship between civic and ecclesiastical regulations and actual practice? What purposes are served by the laws? How often and under what circumstances have the laws affecting religious organizations been changed? What traditions underlie the laws? Of the approaches surveyed [. . .], geneticism-monism would seem the best suited to this cluster of questions. Functional analysis may also be useful here.

Cultural. What is the relationship of religion to nationalism in a specific country context? What explains differences in this relationship from one country to another, or from one religious organization to another? How is one to explain dif-

---

2. See Arend Lijphart, "Comparative Politics and the Comparative Method," in *American Political Science Review,* vol. 65, no. 3 (September 1971).

ferences among religious organizations in attitudes to secular authority, rebellion, law, progress, social protest, pacifism, and other issues? Here, the political culture approach is in its element.

I make no pretense that [this study is] a complete cookbook of theoretical approaches. Class analysis, for example, is not represented here. [My] purpose [. . .] is not to exhaust the topic but to challenge the student of church-state relations to think theoretically.

[For] the remainder [. . .], I wish to consider certain analytical pitfalls or fallacies to which studies of church-state relations are vulnerable. Some of these pitfalls are specific to the subject matter. Most are reflections of more or less universal dangers to be avoided.

Fallacies of Interpretation

Most of the pitfalls I wish to highlight are fallacies of interpretation. They involve misplaced emphasis, or the overestimation or underestimation of the importance of certain factors.

The incipient fallacy is apt to be the preserve of historians and of church writers with expertise in early Christianity. It is the belief that the spiritual, social, and political tradition of a church is to be understood *exclusively* in terms of its origins and earliest years, and that all subsequent events and developments are merely "environmental" factors. Accordingly, "true" Christianity may be described as a nonhierarchical, communal phenomenon in which the role of the clergy is that of participant rather than leader—thus harking back to certain currents in the earliest days of Christianity. Or again, the "Orthodox tradition" has been described by one scholar strictly in terms of Byzantium, thus excluding the accommodations made in the Ottoman Empire and tsarist Russia. The attitudes and behavior of contemporary churchmen are then traced to this early tradition, and the patterns of thinking imposed by recent decades and even recent centuries are ignored. It represents, thus, an exaggeration of the genetic-monist method.

The ahistorical fallacy, the reverse of the incipient fallacy, is a pitfall into which political scientists and journalists are prone to slip. This fallacy entails treating the present configuration of church-state relations in abstraction from its historical roots and thus ignores factors anchoring relations to a general configuration. Since those who ignore the sources of present problems and issues cannot understand the evolution of debates over time, they cannot assess the interests vested

in advancing specific outcomes and therefore have no reasonable basis for predicting future development.

The dynamic fallacy is the tendency to overemphasize change in religious currents or church-state relations. It is the great temptation in journalism, which places a premium on reporting what is new and different and thus encourages its practitioners to dramatize elements that appear to show change. The frequency of reports of religious revival or crackdowns on religion and so forth over the years, many of which presented revival as a completely new phenomenon, is an unmistakable symptom of this fallacy. There have, to be sure, been instances of genuine religious revival, [. . .] but they cannot be reported as new phenomena for the same country year after year (which happened throughout the 1970s and early 1980s in reportage of the Soviet scene).

The static fallacy is the reverse of the dynamic fallacy; it involves the understatement of change and the overemphasis of constancies in church-state relations. Some churchmen and some politically engaged writers have been particularly tempted on this score. It may be a fact, for instance, that in the early years of Bolshevik rule in Russia the regime targeted clergymen primarily out of hostility toward all forms of theism and because of the Orthodox Church's links with the overthrown political establishment. It does not follow that present-day Soviet hostility toward any specific religious organization is motivated primarily by these considerations.

The monolithic fallacy is one of the most common distortions in writings on church-state relations. It is easy to treat both church and state as monoliths and to homogenize their interests and interactions in such a way as to gloss over the complexities of intrachurch and intrastate factionalism. But factionalism is the very lifeblood of politics, and church-state relations are not exempt from the entanglements of rival factions and competing viewpoints. Not only does this fallacy produce considerable oversimplification of the situation; it also has ramifications for analytical hypotheses being tested or advanced. If, for example, a study devoted to the impact of modernization on the church ignores the presence of reformist and modernizing currents within the church in question, the result may be a study with only limited and partial validity.

The factional fallacy is relatively rare in writings on church-state relations. The reverse of the monolithic fallacy, it is characterized by overestimation of the importance of intrachurch or intraelite differences. While a number of communist countries have succeeded in drawing clergy into proregime organizations—which is only one instance of intrachurch factionalism, of course—on the whole, clergy are apt to feel greater solidarity with other clergy of the same church than with the regime, since each church has a relatively clearly defined mission: to sustain and propagate its set of beliefs and practices.

A related fallacy is the tendency to treat church press organs as representing the viewpoint of the church as a whole. On the one hand, some organs, like the Russian Orthodox publication, *Zhurnal Moskovskoi Patriarkhii,* and the Czechoslovak Catholic newspaper, *Katolické Noviný,* may be either so heavily censored or in fact controlled by regime agencies as to have little in common with the viewpoints of any important segment of the church. On the other hand, an organ such as the Slovenian Catholic newspaper, *Družina,* while clearly the mouthpiece of its archbishopric, cannot be thought to speak on behalf of the ecclesiastical organization in the country as a whole.

A more perturbing pitfall is the apolitical fallacy, which consists in believing that churches are not necessarily or not intrinsically political actors. In the Orthodox case, for instance, this fallacy is manifested in the belief that the intense spirituality of Eastern Christianity, with its contemplative bent, implies disinterest in the temporal order. On the contrary, religious leaders among the Orthodox, Catholic, Calvinist, Puritan, and other Christian denominations, as well as among Muslim and Jewish communities, have, over the centuries, been eager for the opportunity to establish their own denominations as the "state religion" and to mold the laws of the country and the moral-behavioral codes of the people in accordance with church tenets. A truly apolitical church is virtually inconceivable, since as soon as one moves from liturgical rites to religious teaching, one is in the domain of social interests.

Analytically related to the apolitical fallacy is the pragmatic fallacy, which shifts the emphasis in the opposite direction. To be pragmatic in this sense is to ignore the doctrinal content of the church in question and the goals of the regime and to treat church-state relations as if the two parties differed only in certain specific beliefs, rather than in attitudes and broader assumptions. Certainly, in any country in which church-state relations are troubled or uncertain, church and state will be apt to view each other with suspicion. But the kinds of behavior that each takes as the norm may differ, and the expectations with which each approaches the other will be colored by a host of variables, including past contacts and sociopolitical assumptions rooted in institutional teachings.

The isolationist fallacy is the belief that the religious policy of a regime exists in isolation from its other policies. The consequence, if this were true, would be that the goals being pursued in the religious sphere would be specific to that sphere, i.e., that they would be irrelevant to other spheres. That is patently false. [. . .] On the contrary, the religious policy of a state is guided by a host of considerations, including questions of socialization, the aspiration (in some cases) to curtail the independence of any and all institutions, foreign policy issues (as in the Bulgarian Orthodox Church's role vis-à-vis Macedonia), nationalism, military conscription, and demographic factors.

The last fallacy of interpretation involves overestimation of the importance of Christian-Marxist dialogue and of the Marxists who are engaged in the dialogue. If dialogue is entrusted by the regime to sociologists or second-rank officials concerned with religion, one may conclude that only small questions—if any—will be resolved through such dialogue. The rest will be only talk. A further problem is that the motivations of church and state in promoting dialogue may differ from one another and from the motivation that might seem, superficially, to be implicit in seeking dialogue: to further understanding. Church-state dialogue has of course led to improvements in the climate of church-state relations in some countries; the German Democratic Republic is an example.[3] In other countries, like Yugoslavia, Christian-Marxist dialogue has made less of an impact on church-state relations because of factionalism on both sides.

Other Fallacies

The Baconian fallacy involves question-framing. As David Hackett Fischer has noted, it

> consists in the idea that a historian can operate without the aid of preconceived questions, hypotheses, ideas, assumptions, theories, paradigms, postulates, prejudices, presumptions, or general presuppositions of any kind. He is supposed to go a-wandering in the dark forest of the past, gathering facts like nuts and berries, until he has enough to make a general truth. Then he is to store up his general truths until he has the whole truth. This idea is doubly deficient, for it commits a historian to the pursuit of an impossible object by an impracticable method.[4]

---

3. See Robert E. Goeckel, "The Luther Anniversary in East Germany," in *World Politics,* vol. 37, no. 1 (October 1984).

4. David Hackett Fischer, *Historians' Fallacies* (New York: Harper, 1970), 4.

Fact-gathering in the absence of a theory is condemned to remaining random, disjointed, haphazard, and void of meaning. At some point, a researcher must make a leap into the realm of hypotheses or relinquish any hope of producing a purposive and well-constructed study. If the researcher waits until he has gathered his berries before framing his hypotheses, it will be impossible for his research to be informed by his theory, and he will lose the opportunity of being alert, in the earlier stage, both to confirming and to disconfirming evidence.

The motivational fallacy consists in the endorsement of one position or another in such a way as to compromise scientific objectivity. When, for instance, Timothy Ware describes early Slavic Christianity as *"a popular religion in the best sense,"*[5] he betrays the fact that his study is intended, in part, as an apologia for Christian belief. When other writers refer to the status of Christian organizations under communism as unhealthy, they are verging on the motivational fallacy by assuming certain values on the part of the reader. Not everyone would agree that this assumption is a pitfall. But I think it should be so considered, at least potentially, because it threatens to beg all sorts of questions. For example, if religion is good in and of itself, are all religions equally good? If not, who is entitled to judge among them? Is a religious revival always good in all its aspects and effects? Is atheistic socialization always bad (or good) in all its aspects and effects? Is ecclesiastical independence of secular authority necessarily to be praised, or ecclesiastical subordination to secular authority necessarily to be condemned? Should a worsening of church-state relations in a communist state necessarily be assumed to be welcome to state authorities or inimical to the faith itself? This fallacy is the more dangerous when combined with excessive pessimism, in that this combination could dispose the writer to believe that his central values are massively threatened by certain regimes; with such an attitude, cool objectivity could be difficult to attain.

Hyperbole is a fallacy of factual significance. It consists in over-dramatizing the subject matter by reading too much into small things. An instance of it would be the transforming of a few antireligious newspaper articles into "a tough new line" or even "a new antireligious campaign." The best remedy for this fallacy is to carefully assess the sufficiency of the evidence and to consider what facts may seem to be inconsistent with the proposed inference.

And finally, there is the fallacy of transference—the tendency to transfer conclusions established in one context to another, seemingly similar context, in which the applicability of the conclusions is not actually proven. In the study of church-state relations under communism, this fallacy has two common forms. First, there is the occasional temptation to characterize the entire church-state climate on the basis of evidence drawn from one or two religious groups. In societies in which a single church is clearly predominant (as in Poland, Lithuania, and Bulgaria), this temptation is much less of a problem than it is in multiconfessional societies, where it may lead the observer to ignore important exceptions and, with them, clues to the variables affecting church-state relations. Second, among observers of the communist world, there is sometimes (most often among casual observers) a tendency to treat domestic developments in Eastern Europe as necessarily parallel to developments in the USSR, and to construct uniform periodization schemes. More common is the tendency to see the church-state relationship in Poland as a paradigm of church-state relations throughout the region—which it is not.

From Pedro Ramet [Serena P. Ramet], *Cross and Commissar: The Politics of Religion in Eastern Europe and the USSR* (Bloomington: Indiana University Press, 1987), 176–83.

☙ **John Courtney Murray** (1904–67), Roman Catholic theologian and political philosopher, was a tireless proponent of the principle of religious freedom, also known as freedom of conscience. "The Problem of Religious Freedom" was distributed to participants at the Second Vatican Council in 1964; the document is a lucid formulation of the argument in favor of religious freedom. Murray's reasoning is based upon a concrete historical-critical analysis of Church-state relations.

JOHN COURTNEY MURRAY

"The Problem of Religious Freedom"

The First View

[T]he First View rejects certain conceptions of public care of religion that were prevalent in former eras. It recognizes that the modern Catholic nation is not the medieval Christian commonwealth; hence it denies that the religious prerogative of the emperor is to be transferred without alteration to the public powers in the Catholic state today. It denies that

---

5. Timothy Ware, *The Orthodox Church,* rev. ed. (Harmondsworth: Penguin, 1980), 87 ([Ramet's] emphasis).

public care of religion may be prolonged into a *ius in sacra* or a *ius circa sacra*. It also denies the *ius reformandi* of the prince and its pendant, the *beneficium emigrationis*. It denies that the prince, by reason of his political sovereignty, is a competent judge of religious truth and *custos utriusque tabulae*. It rejects the notion that the prince, although he has no right to compel or impose religious faith, has nonetheless the duty and right to compel his subjects to hear the true word of God and to enforce outward conformity with the official faith. It admits therefore, in principle, that certain kinds of external constraint are incompatible with personal freedom of conscience.

In these respects, and in others, the First View represents progress within the tradition, a clearer and less confused understanding of traditional principles—in particular, the distinction between the religious order and the political order, and the limitations of political sovereignty in the order of religion. However, the First View maintains that progress within the tradition ended with Leo XIII and the systematization of his doctrine by subsequent canonists. Catholic doctrine has reached its final and definitive mode of conception and statement. It has defined forever the ideal instance of constitutional law with regard to public care of religion. Many changes have indeed taken place in the world since Leo XIII; in particular, there is a wide demand for religious freedom as a personal right and as a legal institution. These changes, however, represent decadence, not progress. Their sole historical effect has been to create more evils that the Church must tolerate; hence the scope of tolerance must be broadened. For the rest, the ideal remains, transhistorical, unquestionable.

The Second View

The problematic of religious freedom is concrete and historical. Its construction begins with a scrutiny of the "signs of the times." Two are decisive. The first is the growth of man's personal consciousness; the second is the growth of man's political consciousness. They were noted, in their relation, by John XXIII:

> The aspirations of the minds of men, about which We have been speaking, also give clear witness to the fact that in these our days men are becoming more and more conscious of their dignity. For this reason they feel the impulse to participate in the processes of government and also to demand that their own inviolable rights be guaranteed by

the order of public law. What is more, they likewise demand that the civil powers should be established in accord with the norms of a public constitution and that they should fulfil their functions within limits defined by it.[6]

The political consciousness, which is the correlate of the personal consciousness, is further described:

> Moreover, the dignity of the human person requires that a man should act on his own judgment and with freedom. Wherefore in community life there is good reason why it should be chiefly on his own deliberate initiative that a man should exercise his rights, fulfil his duties, and cooperate with others in the endless variety of necessary social tasks. What matters is that a man should make his own decisions and act on his own judgment, out of a sense of duty. He is not to act as one compelled by external coercion or instigation. In view of all this, it is clear that a society of men which is maintained solely by force must be considered inhuman. The reason is that in such a society men would be denied their freedom, whereas, on the contrary, they ought to be inspired, by all suitable means, to find for themselves the motive for progress in life and for the quest of perfection.[7]

Man's sense of personal freedom is allied with a demand for political and social freedom, that is, freedom from social or legal restraint and constraint, except in so far as these are necessary, and freedom for responsible personal decision and action in society. Freedom, not force, is the dynamism of personal and social progress.

The common consciousness of men today considers the demand for personal, social, and political freedom to be an exigency that rises from the depths of the human person. It is the expression of a sense of right approved by reason. It is therefore a demand of natural law in the present moment of history. This demand for freedom is made especially in regard to the goods of the human spirit—the search for truth, the free expression and dissemination of opinion, the cultivation of the arts and sciences, free access to information about public events, adequate opportunities for the development of personal talents and for progress in knowledge and culture.[8]

---

6. *Pacem in terris*, AAS [*Acta apostolicae sedis*] 55 (1963): 279.

7. Ibid., 265.

8. Cf. ibid., 260.

In a particular way, freedom is felt to be man's right in the order of his most profound concern, which is the order of religion.[9]

Therefore the Second View holds that, in consequence of the new perspective created by the growth of the personal and political consciousness, the state of the ancient question concerning public care of religion has been altered. Today the question is not to be argued in medieval or post-Reformation or nineteenth-century terms, scil., the exclusive rights of truth and legal tolerance or intolerance, as the case may be, of religious dissidence. The terms of the argument today are, quite simply, religious freedom. The question is to know, first, what religious freedom means in the common consciousness today, and second, why religious freedom, in the sense of the common consciousness, is to receive the authoritative approval of the Church. The Second View addresses itself to the question in its new historical and doctrinal state. However, two schools of thought seem to exist with regard to the method of setting forth the Second View, which they nonetheless hold in common.

One school regards religious freedom as formally a theological-moral concept, which has juridical consequences, scil., within the order of constitutional law.[10] The other school regards religious freedom as formally a juridical or constitutional concept, which has foundations in theology, ethics, political philosophy, and jurisprudence. The first school begins with a single insight—the exigence of the free human person for religious freedom. Only in the second instance does it raise what we have called the constitutional question. Consequently, within this structure of argument the political-juridical argument for religious freedom is secondary and subordinate to the theological-ethical argument. In contrast, the second school begins with a complex insight—the free human person under a government of limited powers. The constitutional question is raised at the outset; it is equally as primary as the theological-moral question. Consequently, the political-juridical argument for religious freedom is coordinate with the theological-moral argument. In other words, both religious freedom, as a legal institution, and constitutional government, as a form of polity, emerge with equal immediacy as exigencies of the personal consciousness in its inseparable correlation with the political consciousness.

The differences between the two ways of stating the Second View are not irreducible. In any event, three difficulties are alleged against the first structure of argument.

First, the notion of religious freedom as a human right seems to appear as a piece of theological-ethical theory, arrived at by a process of abstract argument, in a vacuum of historical, political, and juridical experience. The methodology here is vulnerable, in that it seems to divorce the issue of the rights of the human person from its necessary social-historical context. In contrast, in the second school of thought religious freedom presents itself concretely, as both a human and a civil right, embodied in a legal institution, which forms a harmonious part of a larger constitutional order of freedom. This order, in turn, appeals for its validity to traditional principles of politics, legal philosophy, and jurisprudence, as these principles are vitally adapted to the realities of historical experience today. In this fashion, religious freedom as a human right is validated in the concrete, by a convergence of theological, ethical, political, and jurisprudential argument. This methodology commends itself as more in accord with the historical consciousness that ought to preside over all argument about human rights.

Second, the first school of thought runs the risk of "over-theologizing" the notion of religious freedom as a human right and as a consequent norm for the juridical order of society. The result might be to propose the legal institution of religious freedom as the "ideal instance" of constitutional law with regard to public care of religion. This ideal would then stand in conflict with the constitutional ideal proposed by the First View. In consequence, a false argument would be set afoot. Traditional philosophies of politics, law, and jurisprudence do not recognize any such thing as an ideal instance of constitutional law. By reason of the very nature of law, the issue of the ideal never arises. The function of law, as the Jurist said, is to be useful to men. Necessity or usefulness for the common good—these are norms of law. Legal institutions can never fall into the category of the ideal. This risk of an idealization of religious freedom is avoided by the second school of thought, in which the relativities of history receive due attention.

Third, the first school of thought runs the risk of setting afoot a futile argument about the rights of the erroneous conscience. This argument may well be inextricable. In any event, it is irrelevant to the constitutional question. The simple reason

---

9. Cf. ibid.

10. [. . .] In a description of why the Second Vatican Council delayed debate on religious liberty, Murray cites canonist opposition [canon lawyers who interpret conciliar regulations or dogmas] but also disagreement with what he called the French-speaking school of those who were willing to affirm religious freedom. The French thought that their theologically grounded justification was "richer and more profound" than Murray's view, which they considered "superficial." (This note is by Hooper.)

is that the public powers are not competent to judge whether conscience be erroneous or not. The good faith or bad faith, the truth or falsity of conscience are not matters for adjudication by the civil magistrate, upon whom public care of religion devolves. This unnecessary argument is avoided from the outset by the second school of thought, given its complex starting point, the personal and the political consciousness.

An orderly exposition of the Second View can best be made by making the classic distinction between the question of definition or concept (*quid sit*) and the question of judgment (*an sit, curita sit*). Moreover, in the methodology here being followed, the conceptual question is twofold: what is religious freedom, and what is its correlate, constitutional government.

The Conceptual Question

The question, what is religious freedom, is not to be answered a priori or in the abstract. The fact is that religious freedom is an aspect of contemporary historical experience. As a legal institution, it exists in the world today in the juridical order of many states. It is not simply a question of understanding what religious freedom meant in the Third French Republic under the Law of Separation of December 9, 1905; nor of understanding what it meant under the Estatuto Real of 1834 in the reign of Isabella II. For the theologian, the instant conceptual question is to understand what religious freedom means today, in so far as it presents itself as an exigence of the personal and political consciousness of contemporary men. From this point of view, the following description can be assembled.

First, religious freedom is obviously not the Pauline *eleutheria,* the freedom wherewith Christ has made us free (Gal 5:1). This is a freedom of the theological order, an empowerment that man receives by grace. In contrast, religious freedom is an affair of the social and civil order; it is an immunity that attaches to the human person within society, and it has its guarantee in civil law. Obviously too, religious freedom has nothing to do with the statute of the member of the Church in the face of the authority of the Church, as if the Christian could somehow be free from obedience to the Church, which is absurd. Still less has it anything to do with the statute of the creature in the face of his Creator, as if man could somehow be free from the dominion of God, which is even more absurd.

Second, the adequate subject of religious freedom in its proper juridical sense as a human and civil right, guaranteed by constitutional law, is the body politic as such, the People Temporal—collectively, individually, and in their corporate associations. This follows from the very nature of constitutional law. The people are constituted a people *consensu iuris* (in the classic phrase), by their consent to a common law which touches all and is to be approved by all (in another classic phrase). Hence the people as such are the adequate subject of all the immunities and empowerments which the common law provides.

Third, the juridical notion of religious freedom is complex in its content. Within the concept it has become customary to make a general division between "freedom of conscience" and "the free exercise of religion" (this technical vocabulary goes back to the sixteenth century, and it is too late to change it now).

In its juridical sense, freedom of conscience is the human and civil right of the human person to immunity from all external coercion in his search for God, in the investigation of religious truth, in the acceptance or rejection of religious faith, in the living of his interior religious or nonreligious life. In a word, it is the freedom of personal religious decision. This freedom is essentially social. A man's religious decisions, however personal, are made in the social context of man's existence. In making them, a man has the right to be free from coercion by any human forces or powers within the social milieu. Society and all its institutions are obliged to respect this right and to refrain from coercion. By coercion, here and hereafter, is meant all manner of compulsion, constraint, and restraint, whether legal or extralegal. It includes such things as social discrimination, economic disadvantage, and civil disabilities imposed on grounds of religion. Today it importantly includes coercive forms of psychological pressure, such as massive propaganda, brainwashing techniques, etc.

The free exercise of religion is itself a complex concept. First, it is commonly understood to include a twofold immunity: a man may not be coercively constrained to act against his conscience, nor may a man be coercively restrained or impeded from acting according to his conscience. (The question of the limitation of this right will be dealt with later.) Furthermore, three aspects of the free exercise of religion are commonly distinguished.

Ecclesial or Corporate Religious Freedom

This is the right of religious communities within society to corporate internal autonomy. It is their immunity from the intervention of the public powers or of any social agency in the declaration of their own statute of corporate existence, in the determination of their own doctrine and polity, in their internal discipline and self-government, in the appointment of officials and in the definition of their functions, in the training and employment of ministers, in their communication with other communities and with recognized religious authorities in other lands. This freedom also includes the immunity of religious communities from employment by the public powers as *instrumentum regni*. In a word, this freedom is the corporate counterpart of personal freedom of conscience.

Here too is the appropriate place to locate the religious freedom of the family, the rights of parents with regard to the religious education of their children, and the rights of the religious school in relation both to churches and to families.

Freedom of Religious Association

This includes, first, the right to immunity from coercion in affiliating, or in ending affiliation, with organized religious bodies; and second, the same immunity in the formation of associations for religious and charitable purposes.

Freedom of Religious Expression

This is the right, both of individuals and of religious bodies, to immunity from coercion in what concerns the public worship of God, public religious observances and practice, the public proclamation of religious faith, and the public declaration of the implications of religion and morality for the temporal affairs of the community and for the action of the public powers.

The common legal and civic consciousness today recognizes that freedom of conscience and its corporate equivalent, ecclesial freedom, are freedoms *sui generis*. The first concerns man's personal relation with God, which is by definition an affair of personal freedom in a unique sense. The second concerns man's relation to God as lived in community, in accord with the social nature both of religion and of man himself. Hence the right to internal ecclesial autonomy is likewise *sui generis*. Finally, freedom of religious association, inasmuch as it includes immunity from coercion in the choice of one's religious affiliation, possesses the same quality of uniqueness as freedom of conscience and ecclesial freedom, to both of which it is directly related.

On the other hand, the personal or corporate free exercise of religion, as a human and civil right, is evidently cognate with other more general human and civil rights—with the freedom of corporate bodies and institutions within society, based on the principle of subsidiary function; with the general freedom of association for peaceful human purposes, based on the social nature of man; with the general freedom of speech and of the press, based on the nature of political society. The exercise of these more general human and civil rights, whether personal or corporate, takes place in the public domain, and therefore it becomes amenable to regulation by the public powers, in accord with recognized and reasonable criteria. The same is true of the free exercise of religion, inasmuch as it is a civil right cognate with other more general civil rights. The question is to know the criteria which must govern the action of the public powers in limiting the free exercise of religion. This is the crucial issue in the constitutional question of public care of religion. We shall turn to it later.

For the moment, it is to be noted that the free exercise of religion remains a freedom *sui generis*, even though it is cognate with other civil rights. The reason is that in all its forms it raises the issue of man's relation to God, as conceived by doctrine, affirmed by conscience, socially organized, and proclaimed in public utterance. In contrast, other civil rights have only to do with man's relation to other men or to society.

The foregoing analysis presents the answer which the contemporary consciousness, personal and political, gives to the first conceptual question, what is religious freedom. (There may be a difficulty about the proper classification of the three freedoms listed, but it is of minor importance.) Moreover, the foregoing understanding of religious freedom is substantially in accord with the understanding contained in the pertinent declarations of the World Council of Churches.[11] The fact is of some importance for the ecumenical dialogue.

The second conceptual question, what is constitutional government, is likewise complex. For our purposes, which concern constitutional government as the political correlate of the juridical notion of religious freedom, it will be sufficient rapidly to recall four basic principles which combine to make government constitutional, scil., limited in its powers.

The first principle is the distinction between the sacred

---

11. Cf. A. F. Carrillo de Albornoz, *The Basis of Religious Liberty* (New York, 1963), esp. 16–26, 155–62.

and the secular orders of human life. The whole of man's existence is not absorbed in his temporal and terrestrial existence. He also exists for a transcendent end. The power of government does not reach into this higher sacred order of human existence. It has no share in the *cura animarum* or in the *regimen animorum;*[12] it is not the judge or the representative of transcendent truth with regard to man's eternal destiny; it is not man's guide to heaven. Its powers are limited to the affairs of the temporal and terrestrial order of man's existence. And they are not to be used as instruments for the spiritual purposes of the Church, the maintenance of her unity, or the furtherance of her mission.

The second principle is the distinction between society and state. Historically, this distinction developed out of the medieval distinction between the *ecclesia (christianitas)* and the *imperium.* The imperial power played a role within Christendom—a limited role; it was charged with limited functions within the Great Society inasmuch as the ecclesia was a socio-temporal reality. Today, in the developed constitutional tradition, the state is an agency that plays a role within society—a limited role. The purposes of the state are not coextensive with the purposes of society. The state is only one order within society—the order of public law and political administration. The public powers, which are invested with the power of the state, are charged with the performance of certain limited functions for the benefit of society—such functions as can and must be performed by the coercive discipline of law and political power. These functions are defined by constitutional law, in accord with the consent of the people. In general, "society" signifies an area of freedom, personal and corporate, whereas "state" signifies the area in which the public powers may legitimately apply their coercive powers. To deny the distinction is to espouse the notion of government as totalitarian.

The third principle is the distinction between the common good and public order. It follows from the distinction between society and state. The common good includes all the social goods, spiritual and moral as well as material, which man pursues here on earth in accord with the demands of his personal and social nature. The pursuit of the common good devolves upon society as a whole, on all its members and on all its institutions, in accord with the principles of subsidiarity, legal justice, and distributive justice. Public order, whose care devolves upon the state, is a narrower concept. It includes three goods which can and should be achieved by the power which is proper to the state—the power inherent in the coercive discipline of public law. The first is the public peace,

which is the highest political good. The second is public morality, as determined by moral standards commonly accepted among the people. The third is justice, which secures for the people what is due to them. And the first thing that is due to the people, in justice, is their freedom, the due enjoyment of their personal and social rights—those empowerments and immunities to which the people, individually, collectively, and corporatively, lay rightful claim. John of Salisbury spoke for the tradition of constitutionalism when he said: "The prince [the constitutional monarch, in contrast to the tyrant] fights for the laws and for the freedom of the people.[13] The power of the state is therefore limited to the maintenance of public order in this threefold sense. (We omit here, as not relevant to our subject, the function of the state with regard to the good of "prosperity," the material welfare of the people.)

The foregoing three principles belong to the order of political truth. When government is based on them, it is based on the truth. The fourth principle is at once a substantive political truth and also the primary rule of political procedure. It is the principle and rule of "freedom under law." The freedom of the people is a political end, prescribed by the personal consciousness among the people. The freedom of the people is also the higher purpose of the juridical order, which is not an end in itself. Furthermore, freedom is the political method *per excellentiam,* prescribed by the political consciousness among the people. In so far as a political society must depend on force and fear to achieve its ends, it departs both from political truth and from the true method of politics. Finally, freedom under law is the basic rule of jurisprudence, which runs thus: "Let there be as much freedom, personal and social, as is possible; let there be only as much restraint and constraint, personal and social, as may be necessary for the public order." In all these ways, the principle and rule of freedom under law sets limits to the power of government.

The Question of Judgment

In reply to this question, the Second View affirms the validity of religious freedom, in the sense explained, as a legal institution, a juridical notion, a civil and human right. Correlatively, it affirms the validity of constitutional government, within whose structure religious freedom, in the sense ex-

---

12. Cf. Leo XIII, *Sapientiae christianae, AAS* 22 (1889–90): 396.

13. Polycraticus 8, 17 (*PL* [Migne, *Patrologiae cursus, series Latina*] 199, 777).

plained, finds its necessary place. Two things about this compound affirmation must be noted.

First, the Second View undertakes to justify religious freedom, not to idealize it. It is not a question of affirming an ideal instance of constitutional law, after the manner of the First View. The Second View maintains that an ideal instance of constitutional law is a contradiction in terms. In the Second View, therefore, religious freedom is not thesis; neither is it hypothesis. The Second View abandons these categories of systematization. It does not accept, as its basic systematic notion, the abstract notion of the exclusive rights of truth, which creates the disjunction, thesis and hypothesis. Instead, it posits, as the basis for a systematic doctrine of religious freedom, the concrete exigencies of the personal and political consciousness of contemporary man—his demand for religious freedom, personal and corporate, under a limited government. This demand is approved by reason; it ought to be approved by the authority of the Church. Hence the Second View affirms the validity of an order of constitutional law in which public care of religion is limited to public care of religious freedom in the complex sense already described.

In negative terms, the Second View rejects the opinion that public care of religion necessarily means, per se and in principle, a political and legal care for the exclusive rights of truth and a consequent care to exterminate religious error. In positive terms, it holds that public care of religion is provided in both necessary and sufficient measure when the order of constitutional law recognizes, guarantees, and protects the freedom of the Church, both as a religious community and as a spiritual authority, at the same time that it gives similar recognition, guarantee, and protection to the general religious freedom—personal, ecclesial, associational, and practical—of the whole body politic. Within the new perspectives of today, the Church does not demand, per se and in principle, a status of legal privilege for herself. The Church demands, in principle and in all situations, religious freedom for herself and religious freedom for all men.

Second, the Second View makes its affirmation of religious freedom in full awareness that this affirmation is at once new and traditional. It represents a growth in the understanding of the tradition, which corresponds to the growth of the personal and political consciousness of men today, to the enlargement of the pastoral solicitude of the Church today, and to the self-understanding of the Church in the world of today, as the missionary Church, in the diaspora, the sign of truth, justice, love, and freedom lifted among the nations. Therefore the Second View speaks to the ancient constitu-

tional question of public care of religion in a new historical state of the question. The answer must be new, because the question is new. The answer must also be traditional, because it is the answer of the Church. However, only the elements of the answer are to be found in the tradition, not the answer itself in explicit and systematized form.

From John Courtney Murray, "The Problem of Religious Freedom," in *Religious Liberty: Catholic Struggles with Pluralism*, by John Courtney Murray, edited by J. Leon Hooper (Louisville, KY: Westminster/John Knox, 1993), 136–47.

☙ In 1925, **John Scopes** was tried and convicted in the state of Tennessee for teaching a theory of evolution in a public school. He was tried under a statute forbidding the teaching of an evolutionary theory that denies the biblical account of divine creation and instead maintains that humans developed from "lower" animals. Scopes's lawyer argued that the statute was unconstitutional because it endorsed the biblical story of human origins. The Supreme Court of Tennessee overturned Scopes's conviction on a technicality but upheld the constitutionality of the law. Tennessee Supreme Court Justice **Alexander Chambliss** (1864–1947) offered a separate, concurring opinion, *John T. Scopes v. State of Tennessee* (1927), in which he elaborates, in greater detail than the court's majority opinion, on interpretive principles that support the constitutionality of the law. According to Chambliss, there are two theories of evolution: a scientific theory that is compatible with the theistic understanding of evolution and a materialistic theory that is incompatible with religious understanding. Scopes's counsel argued for the scientific theory.

ALEXANDER CHAMBLISS

John T. Scopes v. State of Tennessee

While I concur in the conclusions announced by Chief Justice Green, and agree, as so ably shown by him, that it is within the power of the Legislature to so prescribe the public school curriculum as to prohibit the teaching of the evolution of man from a lower order of animal life, even though the teaching of some branches of science may be thereby restricted, I am of opinion that the constitutional objections urged do not apply for yet other reasons, and in another view.

Two theories of organic evolution are well recognized, one the theistic, which not only concedes, but maintains, consistently with the Bible story, that "the Lord God formed man of the dust of the earth, and breathed into his nostrils the breath of life, and man became a living soul." This is the theory advanced eloquently by learned counsel for Scopes, and held to by numerous outstanding scientists of the world. The other theory is known as the materialistic, which denies that God created man, that He was the first cause, and seeks in shadowy uncertainties for the origin of life. The act before us, as I view it, prohibits the teaching in public schools of the state of this latter theory, inconsistent, not only with the common belief of mankind of every clime and creed and "religious establishment," even those that reject Christ or Judaism, and look through Buddha or Mohammed to God, but inconsistent also with our Constitution, and the fundamental declaration lying back of it, through all of which runs recognition of and appeal to "God," and a life to come. The Declaration of Independence opens with a reference to "the laws of nature and nature's God," and holds this truth "to be self-evident, that all men are created equal, that they are endowed by their Creator," etc., and concludes "with a firm reliance on the protection of Divine Providence." The Articles of Confederation and Perpetual Union read, "And whereas, it hath pleased the Great Governor of the world." And so section 3 of article 1 of the Constitution of this state, which declares that "no preference shall ever be given, by law, to any religious establishment," opens with the declaration "that all men have a natural and indefeasible right to worship Almighty God," while section 2 of article 9 declares that "no person who denies the being of God, or a future state of rewards and punishments, shall hold any office in the civil department of this state." That the Legislature may prohibit the teaching of the future citizens and office holders to the state a theory which denies the Divine Creator will hardly be denied.

Now I find it conceded in an exceptionally able brief for Scopes, devoted exclusively to the question of uncertainty, that "the act might be construed as only aimed at materialists." This is my view of it. As I read it, the act makes no war on evolution, except in so far as the evolution theory conflicts with the recognition of the divine in creation.

While it is conceded that the language is in some respects ambiguous, analysis of the caption and body of the act as a whole appears to sustain this view. The variance between the caption and the body of the act is significant. The caption refers broadly to "the evolution theory," but it is clear that the act itself, as finally framed and passed, was expressly limited and restricted in its body to the prohibition of the teaching—not of any theory of evolution at all, but of any theory only that denies or controverts "the divine creation of man." While the language used is "any theory that denies *the story* of

the divine creation of man *as taught in the Bible*," the italicized phraseology may be said to be descriptive only of the essential matter. It may be insisted that these words, when given their proper force, serve to narrow the meaning of the act so as to confine its operation to prohibition against the denial of the divine creation of man to the story taught in the Bible as interpreted by those . . . who hold to the instantaneous creation view. In reply, it may be said that, however plausible may be this construction or application of this language, it must be rejected on the very grounds emphasized by learned counsel, who adopt it and then proceed to predicate thereon their argument for the unconstitutionality of the act. The courts may go far to avoid a construction which will destroy the act. This is axiomatic. One may not consistently contend for a construction of language, at all open to construction, which, if applied, will make void the act. Moreover, it would seem that, since "the story as taught in the Bible" of man's creation by God from the dust of the earth is readily susceptive of the construction given it by those known as liberalists, this language is consistent with the conclusion that what the act aims at and effects is the prohibition of the teaching of any such theory only as denies that man was *divinely created* according to the Bible story, *however this story may be interpreted as to details*. So long as the story as told in the Bible is so construed as to recognize the divine creation of man, these words have no limiting effect upon the central and essential object of the act as hereinbefore suggested—to restrain the inculcation into the minds of pupils of the public schools of any theory that denies the divine creation of man, and on the contrary traces his origin, *in exclusion of the divine,* to a lower order of animal life. It is this materialistic teaching which is denounced, and, so construed, the act may clearly be sustained, negative only as it is, first, of the right to teach in the public schools a denial of the existence, recognized by our Constitution, of the Creator of all mankind; and, second, of the right to teach any theory which involves the support or advocacy of either, or any, religious dogma or view.

The concluding phrase, "and to teach instead that man has descended from a lower order of animals," is added on the apparent assumption that such teaching involves a denial, which the preceding clause prohibits, of divine creation. The use of this language, aptly defined by our learned Chief Justice as a species of iteration, for the purpose of emphasis, indicates an intention to set over, one against the other, the theory, or "story," of man's divine creation, and the antagonistic and materialistic theory, or "story," of his origin in the animal kingdom, to the exclusion of God. The phraseology is antithetical—a favorite form of strengthening statement—"measures, not men," springing from God, not animals. The two theories of man's origin are placed in direct opposition; the manifest purpose being to emphasize the essence of the thing prohibited, the teaching of a denial of man's divine creation.

The following statement of Dr. E. N. Reinke, professor of biology in Vanderbilt University, is repeatedly quoted in briefs of counsel for the defense:

> The theory of evolution is altogether essential to the teaching of biology and its kindred sciences. To deny the teacher of biology "the use of this most fundamental generalization of his science would make his teaching as chaotic as an attempt to teach astronomy without the law of gravitation or physics without assuming the existence of the ether."

Conceding that "the theory of evolution is altogether essential to the teaching of biology and its kindred sciences," it will not be contended by Dr. Reinke, or by learned counsel quoting from him, that the theory of evolution essentially involves the denial of the divine creation of man, and that, when construed to prohibit such a denial only, the act is objectionable as denying to "the teacher of biology the use of the most fundamental generalization of his science."

Now, in this view, it is clear that the constitutional direction to cherish education and science is not disregarded. The teaching of all sciences may have full legitimate sway, with the restriction only that the teaching shall not convey a denial of man's divine origin—God as his Creator. The theories of Drummond, Winchell, Fiske, Hibbens, Millikan, Kenn, Merriam, Angell, Cannon Barnes, and a multitude of others, whose names are invoked in argument and brief, do not deny the story of the divine creation of man as taught in the Bible, evolutionists though they be, but, construing the Scripture for themselves in the light of their learning, accept it as true and their teaching would not come under the ban of this act.

Much that has been said here bears directly upon the contention that section 3, art. 1, of our Constitution is violated, in that a preference is given by law to those "religious establishments which have as one of their tenets or dogmas the instantaneous creation of man." As was said by Chief Justice Green, the act gives no preference to any particular religious establishment. The doctrine or tenet of the instantaneous creation of man is not set forth or preferred over

other conceptions. It is too well established for argument that "the story of the divine creation of man as taught in the Bible" is accepted—not "denied"—by millions of men and women who do not interpret it as teaching instantaneous creation, who hold with the Psalmist that "a thousand years in thy sight are but as yesterday when it is past" as but a day. It follows that to forbid the teaching of a denial of the biblical account of divine creation does not, expressly or by fair implication, involve acceptance or approval of instantaneous creation, held to by some literalists. One is not prohibited by this act from teaching, either that "days," as used in the book of Genesis, means days of 24 hours, the literalist view, or days of "a thousand years" or more, as held by liberalists, so long as the teaching does not exclude God as the author of human life.

Considering the caption and body of this act as a whole, it is seen to be clearly negative only, not affirmative. It requires nothing to be taught. It prohibits merely. And it prohibits, not the teaching of any theory of evolution, but that theory (of evolution) only that denies, takes issue with, positively disaffirms, the creation of man by God (as the Bible teaches), and that, instead of being so created, he is a product of, springs from, a lower order of animals. No authority is recognized or conferred by the laws of this state for the teaching in the public schools on the one hand, of the Bible, or any of its doctrines or dogmas, and this act prohibits the teaching on the other hand of any denial thereof. It is purely an act of neutrality. Ceaseless and irreconcilable controversy exists among our citizens and taxpayers, having equal rights, touching matters of religious faith, and it is within the power of the Legislature to declare that the subject shall be excluded from the tax-supported institutions, that the state shall stand neutral, rendering "unto Caesar the things which be Caesar's and unto God the things which be God's," and insuring the completeness of separation of church and state.

In the light of this interpretation, is the act void for uncertainty? I think not. If the act were affirmative in its requirements, calling for the teaching of *some* theory, the objection would be more plausible. A clear chart is more necessary when one must move, over matter or in mind, than when one is required merely *not* to teach or act. Any reasonable intelligence should be able to understand and observe the plain prohibition against instilling into the minds of the pupils a denial that he is a creation of God, but rather a product of the beast of the field; against teaching, and the term is here employed in the sense of seeking to convince, the pupil affirmatively that his origin is not divine, but material through the animal. He who runs may read. He need do no guessing as to what particular conception or view of the Bible account he shall teach. The act does not require that he choose between the fundamentalist and the modernist, the literalist and the liberalist. Our laws approve no teaching of the Bible at all in the public schools, but require only that no theory shall be taught which denies that God is the Creator of man—that his origin is not thus to be traced.

In brief, as already indicated, I concur with the majority in the conclusion (1) that this case must be reversed for the error of the judge in fixing the fine; (2) that a *nolle prosequi* should be entered; and (3) that the act is constitutional as within the power of the Legislature as the employer of its teachers. However, I go further and find the act constitutional for additional reasons, rested upon the view that the act fairly construed is limited to the prohibition of the teaching of any theory of evolution only which denies the divine creation of man, without regard to details of religious belief, or differing interpretations of the story as taught in the Bible. In this view the constitutionality of the act is sustained, but the way is left open for such teaching of the pertinent sciences as is approved by the progressive God-recognizing leaders of thought and life.

From *Tennessee Reports* 154 (1927), 121–29.

Steven I. Engel, et al., Petitioners, v. William J. Vitale, Jr., et al. (1962), was a U.S. Supreme Court case centered on the issue of prayer in public schools. When the state of New York directed that a "brief, denominationally neutral" prayer be said daily in its public schools, the parents of ten students brought a suit against the state. The Supreme Court ruled that New York could not "use its public school system to encourage recitation of the prayer." The majority opinion was authored by Justice **Hugo Black** (1886–1971).

HUGO BLACK

Steven I. Engel, et al., Petitioners, v. William J. Vitale, Jr., et al.

The respondent Board of Education of Union Free School District No. 9, New Hyde Park, New York, acting in its official capacity under state law, directed the School District's principal to cause the following prayer to be said aloud by each class in the presence of a teacher at the beginning of each school day:

> Almighty God, we acknowledge our dependence upon Thee, and we beg Thy blessings upon us, our parents, our teachers and our Country.

This daily procedure was adopted on the recommendation of the State Board of Regents, a governmental agency created by the State Constitution to which the New York Legislature has granted broad supervisory, executive, and legislative powers over the State's public school system. These state officials composed the prayer which they recommended and published as a part of their "Statement on Moral and Spiritual Training in the Schools," saying: "We believe that this Statement will be subscribed to by all men and women of good will, and we call upon all of them to aid in giving life to our program."

Shortly after the practice of reciting the Regents' prayer was adopted by the School District, the parents of ten pupils brought this action in a New York State Court insisting that use of this official prayer in the public schools was contrary to the beliefs, religions, or religious practices of both themselves and their children. Among other things, these parents challenged the constitutionality of both the state law authorizing the School District to direct the use of prayer in public schools and the School District's regulation ordering the recitation of this particular prayer on the ground that these actions of official governmental agencies violate that part of the First Amendment of the Federal Constitution which commands that "Congress shall make no law respecting an establishment of religion"—a command which was "made applicable to the State of New York by the Fourteenth Amendment of the said Constitution." The New York Court of Appeals, over the dissents of Judges Dye and Fuld, sustained an order of the lower state courts which had upheld the power of New York to use the Regents' prayer as a part of the daily procedures of its public schools so long as the schools did not compel any pupil to join in the prayer over his or his parents' objection. We granted certiorari to review this important decision involving rights protected by the First and Fourteenth Amendments.

We think that by using its public school system to encourage recitation of the Regents' prayer, the State of New York has adopted a practice wholly inconsistent with the Establishment Clause. There can, of course, be no doubt that New

York's program of daily classroom invocation of God's blessings as prescribed in the Regents' prayer is a religious activity. It is a solemn avowal of divine faith and supplication for the blessings of the Almighty. The nature of such a prayer has always been religious, none of the respondents has denied this and the trial court expressly so found:

> The religious nature of prayer was recognized by Jefferson and has been concurred in by theological writers, the United States Supreme Court and State courts and administrative officials, including New York's Commissioner of Education. A committee of the New York Legislature has agreed.
>
> The Board of Regents as amicus curiae, the respondents and intervenors all concede the religious nature of prayer, but seek to distinguish this prayer because it is based on our spiritual heritage. . . .

The petitioners contend among other things that the state laws requiring or permitting use of the Regents' prayer must be struck down as a violation of the Establishment Clause because that prayer was composed by governmental officials as a part of a governmental program to further religious beliefs. For this reason, petitioners argue, the State's use of the Regents' prayer in its public school system breaches the constitutional wall of separation between Church and State. We agree with that contention since we think that the constitutional prohibition against laws respecting an establishment of religion must at least mean that in this country it is no part of the business of government to compose official prayers for any group of the American people to recite as a part of a religious program carried on by government.

It is a matter of history that this very practice of establishing governmentally composed prayers for religious services was one of the reasons which caused many of our early colonists to leave England and seek religious freedom in America. The Book of Common Prayer, which was created under governmental direction and which was approved by Acts of Parliament in 1548 and 1549, set out in minute detail the accepted form and content of prayer and other religious ceremonies to be used in the established, tax-supported Church of England. The controversies over the Book and what should be its content repeatedly threatened to disrupt the peace of that country as the accepted forms of prayer in the established church changed with the views of the particular ruler that happened to be in control at the time. Powerful groups representing some of the varying religious views of the people struggled among themselves to impress their particular views upon the Government and obtain amendments of the Book more suitable to their respective notions of how religious services should be conducted in order that the official religious establishment would advance their particular religious beliefs. Other groups, lacking the necessary political power to influence the Government on the matter, decided to leave England and its established church and seek freedom in America from England's governmentally ordained and supported religion.

It is an unfortunate fact of history that when some of the very groups which had most strenuously opposed the established Church of England found themselves sufficiently in control of colonial governments in this country to write their own prayers into law, they passed laws making their own religion the official religion of their respective colonies. Indeed, as late as the time of the Revolutionary War, there were established churches in at least eight of the thirteen former colonies and established religions in at least four of the other five. But the successful Revolution against English political domination was shortly followed by intense opposition to the practice of establishing religion by law. This opposition crystallized rapidly into an effective political force in Virginia where the minority religious groups such as Presbyterians, Lutherans, Quakers and Baptists had gained such strength that the adherents to the established Episcopal Church were actually a minority themselves. In 1785–1786, those opposed to the established Church, led by James Madison and Thomas Jefferson, who, though themselves not members of any of those dissenting religious groups, opposed all religious establishments by law on grounds of principle, obtained the enactment of the famous "Virginia Bill for Religious Liberty" by which all religious groups were placed on an equal footing so far as the State was concerned. Similar though less far-reaching legislation was being considered and passed in other States.

By the time of the adoption of the Constitution, our history shows that there was a widespread awareness among many Americans of the dangers of a union of Church and State. These people knew, some of them from bitter personal experience, that one of the greatest dangers to the freedom of the individual to worship in his own way lay in the Government's placing its official stamp of approval upon one particular kind of prayer or one particular form of religious services. They knew the anguish, hardship and bitter strife that could come when zealous religious groups struggled with one another to obtain the Government's stamp of approval from each King, Queen, or Protector that came to temporary power. The Constitution was intended to avert a part of this danger by leaving the government of this country in the hands of the people rather than in the hands of any monarch. But this safeguard was not enough. Our Founders were no more willing to let the content of their prayers and their privilege of praying whenever they pleased be influenced by the ballot box than they were to let these vital matters of personal conscience depend upon the succession of monarchs. The First Amendment was added to the Constitution to stand as a guarantee that neither the power nor the prestige of the Federal Government would be used to control, support or influence the kinds of prayer the American people can say—that the people's religions must not be subjected to the pressures of government for change each time a new political administration is elected to office. Under that Amendment's prohibition against governmental establishment of religion, as reinforced by the provisions of the Fourteenth Amendment, government in this country, be it state or federal, is without power to prescribe by law any particular form of prayer which is to be used as an official prayer in carrying on any program of governmentally sponsored religious activity.

There can be no doubt that New York's state prayer program officially establishes the religious beliefs embodied in the Regents' prayer. The respondents' argument to the contrary, which is largely based upon the contention that the Regents' prayer is "non-denominational" and the fact that the program, as modified and approved by state courts, does not require all pupils to recite the prayer but permits those who wish to do so to remain silent or be excused from the room, ignores the essential nature of the program's constitutional defects. Neither the fact that the prayer may be denominationally neutral nor the fact that its observance on the part of the students is voluntary can serve to free it from the limitations of the Establishment Clause, as it might from the Free Exercise Clause, of the First Amendment, both of which are operative against the States by virtue of the Fourteenth Amendment. Although these two clauses may in certain instances overlap, they forbid two quite different kinds of governmental encroachment upon religious freedom. The Establishment Clause, unlike the Free Exercise Clause, does not depend upon any showing of direct governmental compulsion and is violated by the enactment of laws which establish an official religion whether those laws operate directly to coerce nonobserving individuals or not. This is not to say, of course, that laws officially prescribing a particular

form of religious worship do not involve coercion of such individuals. When the power, prestige and financial support of government is placed behind a particular religious belief, the indirect coercive pressure upon religious minorities to conform to the prevailing officially approved religion is plain. But the purposes underlying the Establishment Clause go much further than that. Its first and most immediate purpose rested on the belief that a union of government and religion tends to destroy government and to degrade religion. The history of governmentally established religion, both in England and in this country, showed that whenever government had allied itself with one particular form of religion, the inevitable result had been that it had incurred the hatred, disrespect and even contempt of those who held contrary beliefs. That same history showed that many people had lost their respect for any religion that had relied upon the support of government to spread its faith. The Establishment Clause thus stands as an expression of principle on the part of the Founders of our Constitution that religion is too personal, too sacred, too holy, to permit its "unhallowed perversion" by a civil magistrate. Another purpose of the Establishment Clause rested upon an awareness of the historical fact that governmentally established religions and religious persecutions go hand in hand. The Founders knew that only a few years after the Book of Common Prayer became the only accepted form of religious services in the established Church of England, an Act of Uniformity was passed to compel all Englishmen to attend those services and to make it a criminal offense to conduct or attend religious gatherings of any other kind—a law which was consistently flouted by dissenting religious groups in England and which contributed to widespread persecutions of people like John Bunyan who persisted in holding "unlawful [religious] meetings . . . to the great disturbance and distraction of the good subjects of this kingdom. . . ." And they knew that similar persecutions had received the sanction of law in several of the colonies in this country soon after the establishment of official religions in those colonies. It was in large part to get completely away from this sort of systematic religious persecution that the Founders brought into being our Nation, our Constitution, and our Bill of Rights with its prohibition against any governmental establishment of religion. The New York laws officially prescribing the Regents' prayer are inconsistent both with the purposes of the Establishment Clause and with the Establishment Clause itself.

It has been argued that to apply the Constitution in such a way as to prohibit state laws respecting an establishment of religious services in public schools is to indicate a hostility toward religion or toward prayer. Nothing, of course, could be more wrong. The history of man is inseparable from the history of religion. And perhaps it is not too much to say that since the beginning of that history many people have devoutly believed that "More things are wrought by prayer than this world dreams of." It was doubtless largely due to men who believed this that there grew up a sentiment that caused men to leave the cross-currents of officially established state religions and religious persecution in Europe and come to this country filled with the hope that they could find a place in which they could pray when they pleased to the God of their faith in the language they chose. And there were men of this same faith in the power of prayer who led the fight for adoption of our Constitution and also for our Bill of Rights with the very guarantees of religious freedom that forbid the sort of governmental activity which New York has attempted here. These men knew that the First Amendment, which tried to put an end to governmental control of religion and of prayer, was not written to destroy either. They knew rather that it was written to quiet well-justified fears which nearly all of them felt arising out of an awareness that governments of the past had shackled men's tongues to make them speak only the religious thoughts that government wanted them to speak and to pray only to the God that government wanted them to pray to. It is neither sacrilegious nor antireligious to say that each separate government in this country should stay out of the business of writing or sanctioning official prayers and leave that purely religious function to the people themselves and to those the people choose to look to for religious guidance.

It is true that New York's establishment of its Regents' prayer as an officially approved religious doctrine of that State does not amount to a total establishment of one particular religious sect to the exclusion of all others—that, indeed, the governmental endorsement of that prayer seems relatively insignificant when compared to the governmental encroachments upon religion which were commonplace 200 years ago. To those who may subscribe to the view that because the Regents' official prayer is so brief and general there can be no danger to religious freedom in its governmental establishment, however, it may be appropriate to say in the words of James Madison, the author of the First Amendment:

> [I]t is proper to take alarm at the first experiment on our liberties. . . . Who does not see that the same authority which can establish Christianity, in exclusion of all other

Religions, may establish with the same ease any particular sect of Christians, in exclusion of all other Sects? That the same authority which can force a citizen to contribute three pence only of his property for the support of any one establishment, may force him to conform to any other establishment in all cases whatsoever?

The judgment of the Court of Appeals of New York is reversed and the cause remanded for further proceedings not inconsistent with this opinion.

Reversed and remanded.

Mr. Justice Frankfurter took no part in the decision of this case.

Mr. Justice White took no part in the consideration or decision of this case.

From *Supreme Court Reporter* 82 (St. Paul, MN: West Publishing Co., 1962), 1262–70. [Brackets and ellipses in original.]

☙ "Church State Relations in Peripheral Latin American Societies" (1978), by **Enrique D. Dussel,** a philosopher and liberation theologian, examines how the Church has responded to changes in the political landscape of Latin America. Dussel explores the tension inherent in the Church's role as both prophetic witness and social institution.

ENRIQUE D. DUSSEL

"Church State Relations in Peripheral Latin American Societies," in *Church and State: Opening a New Ecumenical Discussion*

The aim of this paper is to discuss relations between Church and state in Latin America. Paradoxical as it may seem, this will lead to a much wider field, however, because what happens in our sociocultural region is determined by and is a reflection of world events at certain recent periods in western history. Even without leaving the confines of our subject, we shall have to touch on many others.

Some Preliminary Definitions

In the first place, we must clarify certain basic concepts if we are to understand one another. I do not think we are all in agreement about the nature of the state, although I assume that we are in agreement about the historico-prophetic function of the Church on the national and international political levels.

It is well known that there are various concepts of the state: the city state (*polis*) of the Greeks, the *regnum* of the mediaevals or, in modern Europe, the *staat* of Hegel's *Rechtsphilosophie* and Marx's critique of it, and the more recent descriptions by Weber or Parsons on one side, by Poulantzas in the centre, or by Samir Amin on the periphery. Without going into detail, I would like to point out a few aspects that may help us to understand the nature of the present relations between Church and state in Latin America. We believe that the state is the institutionalization of political power which gives cohesion to the various constitutive levels of an historical social formation. It is the principle of the order and organization of that concrete system. On the other hand, the state mirrors the mode of production prevailing in a society and controlled by the subject class at any historical moment, a structuring of the exercise of power over the practical activity of the other classes. In other words, the state has a global function over the economic, political and ideological sub-system. It gives cohesion to everything: to the classes, to the modes of production, and to the hegemony of the dominant mode.

The state, therefore, is not a "complete society" (*societas perfecta*), for if it were, it would be more or less equivalent to the social whole (a concrete social formation). Nor is it an organism or institution which directs this whole towards the common good (which omits the element of conflict or domination inherent in that state). Neither is it merely a bureaucracy that governs the destinies of a nation. The state, as we have said, is only the institutionalization or structuring of the political power of a social class, of the class which, because of the function it exercises in the prevailing mode of production of that particular social formation, is able to achieve its own specific interests.

Consequently, when speaking of the relations between Church and state, it is indispensable to analyse what type of state is in question. In other words, what is its historical social form, what are its dominant modes of production and social classes, and—this is essential—what type of solidarity those who hold decision-making powers in the Church have established with all these elements?

Finally, it should be noted that the universal Church establishes its relations with the national states. Consequently, its "universality" must be understood in the light of the corresponding national situation—sometimes a contradictory one—not forgetting that national situations (for example, that of Italy for Catholics and that of the USA for the churches or denominations of that nation) do in fact influence certain decisions, doctrines or traditions. The national transplantation of the Church, under the power of the state (whether imperial, capitalist, transitional, central or peripheral, socialist, etc.), must also be given due importance in our dialogue.

Prior to the Discovery of America (before 1492)

Ignacio Ellacuria has shown how Christ exercised a prophetic critical function in regard to the state of his time. His criticism was directed against the colonial state of Palestine of that age (a monarchy exercised by Herod), dependent on imperial Rome (a military slave state, but at the same time a mercantile state, as Darcy Ribiero has shown). In his work on St Mark's Gospel, Belo has indicated in an introductory way the socially critical and subversive character of the Gospel. Christ's discourse was dysfunctional in relation to the economic, political and ideological structures of his country with its Asiatic mode of production.

Similarly, in the Roman Empire, which was based on slave labour, the early Christians exercised prophetic criticism on the political level. The political crime of refusing to worship the emperor is a well-known example. Subversive in regard to the state, the early Church earned the persecution and repression of a state fully conscious of the dangers inherent in the preaching of the Christian eschatological utopia. Yet military imperialism based on slave labour was only a primitive and naive precursor of the imperial state of our own days.

Since the fourth century, first in the Armenian kingdom, then through Constantine in the Byzantine Empire (Constantinople was founded in 330 AD), and subsequently in Germanic-Latin Christendom, the Church has been gradually compromising with the state. In feudal Europe, from the birth of the Holy Roman Empire in the early ninth century, the Church once again almost came to be identified with the organs of political power, and gave an almost sacred character to the feudal mode of production. Consider, for example, how in the *Summa theologiae* IIa IIae, q. 57, art. 4, the feudal lord alone is truly part of political society, and exercises over the serf a *iustum dominativum*. Thus, in its theologico-religious domain (and it was the deciding court of appeal in mediaeval society), the Church often came to fulfil the function of an ideological justification of the dominant mode of production. As the instrument of the power of the nobility, the state existed (as a class state) under the tutelage of the Church, without real conflict, until the feudal order experienced the crisis of the fourteenth century.

The formation of Hispanic society followed another path. It reached central European feudalism late, and, in addition, benefited from new modes of production contributed by the Arab caliphates, the Jewish communities and the growing trade of Catalonia (with an eye on Renaissance Italy), coming by way of the Mediterranean and Africa north of the Sahara. The reconquest struggle against the Moors (which began as early as 718 AD), the power of the nobles who waged war against the infidels, the *fueros* (traditional rights) of the cities, all meant that the monarchical state was never the expression either of feudalism or of the new bourgeoisie. In fact, the marriage of the Catholic monarchs Isabella of Castille and Ferdinand of Aragon made the unification of the peninsula possible but did not remove the contradictions. It was only with Emperor Charles V and through the gold and silver of America that the monarchical state became absolute, overcoming the first bourgeois revolution in Europe in Villalar, on 23 April 1521 (when the *comuneros* defended the customary rights of the cities), and then subduing the nobles by buying them off (and turning them into courtiers) or sending them into the struggles of the conquest of America.

Throughout, the Church, which had been extremely strong during the reconquest as the chief landowner of the kingdom, with castles and armies (like those of the Archbishop of Toledo), declined in power more and more in the face of the monarchical state. The reforms of Cisneros, the great Archbishop of Toledo at the time of the discovery of America, ended in the dismantling of the political significance of the Church. The *patronato* (crown right to nominate bishops) eventually subdued the Church and turned it into an institution dominated by the absolute monarchical state. The Crown would not tolerate prophetic political criticism from the Church. The head of Spanish Christendom was the king. The monarchy, the first modern European nation-state, semi-feudal and semi-mercantile and, after the discovery of America, predominantly commercial, was to be the source, nucleus and centre of the state which organized the Christendom of the Indies.

Colonial Christendom (1492–1808)

The Christendom of the Indies was the first peripheral and dependent social formation of modern Europe, before Africa and Asia. It was organized right from the conquest, and fell apart under the growing power of the new empire of England, the first capitalist state.

Latin American colonial society sprang from the impact of the Spanish nation on the social formations of the original inhabitants of America. Both in the north (the present United States and the north of Mexico) and in the south (the southern cone) the primitive modes of production (not yet either agriculture or animal husbandry) made the establishment of colonial life impossible. It was in these regions, from the eighteenth century onwards, that the first capitalist formations developed (the small independent traders of New England, or the landowners who would exploit the land for exports, as in the River Plate area).

On the other hand, in so-called "nuclear America" (extending from the Aztecs to the Incas, via the Mayas, Chiochas and other neolithic peoples), it was found possible to introduce a unique mode of production, which originated in the political intimidation and violence of the conquest. This was the *encomienda* (with its derivative types), a system of tribute with a monetary economy, which apportioned the Indians to masters, and established a social relation of production between master (patron) and Indian (client). The distinctive feature of the system was that the surplus left America for the European metropolitan country or was diverted into the market. Gold and silver were the most sought after products. These social formations, the vice-regal territories of Mexico, Peru and the River Plate (whose political capital was Buenos Aires, but whose real centre was the Potosi mountains), had a very complex bureaucratic structure. In all respects, however, they were simply an extension of the mercantilist monarchical Spanish state which, through its Council of the Indies (in Spain from 1524 onwards), its viceroys, *Audiencias, Cabildos* (town councils, in America), exercised power for the benefit of the metropolitan country and of the Creole *encomenderos* and commercial classes.

After a short period at the beginning of colonial society when the Church took a critical stance during the conquest (from 1492 to 1620 approximately), with Fray Bartolomé de las Casas (1474–1566) as its chief example, the Church was subjugated by the *patronato* of the Indies, whose juridical instrument was the *Leyes de los Reynos de las Indias* (Laws of the Realms of the Indies—codified in 1681). In other words, the Church, constituted by the Spanish bureaucracy and by a clergy recruited from the *encomendero* and commercial classes, never rebelled against the colonial system as such, as the Inca Tupac Amaru did in the eighteenth century, for example. The whole first book of the *Laws of the Indies* was, in fact, canon law, but subject to the authority of the king and through the intermediary of the Council of the Indies.

Through tithes, legacies or gifts, the Church became an

economic power with immense possessions in lands and capital goods. Conflicts with the *patronato,* such as those instigated by Toribio de Mogrovejo, Archbishop of Lima, in the sixteenth century, became rare and finally disappeared. The Church thus led a submissive coexistence in relation to the metropolitan state and its colonial delegates and representatives.

In the regions where the American Indians were cultivators (the Caribe and Tupi-guarani), from the Caribbean Islands to Brazil and Paraguay, as well as among the peoples to the north of the Aztec empire as far as California, either *reducciones* (Indian settlements) were organized (i.e. a communal mode of production), or else slavery emerged in the plantation economy of tropical products. These regions were either under Portuguese rule (Brazil), where the *Padroado* prevailed (domination over the Church similar to that in Spain, although there were sporadic protests from the Jesuits at first and then from Vieira), or under English rule (as in the Caribbean or the south of the United States). The Church did not criticize the system of slavery, although certain saints like Pedro Claver devoted their lives to the service of the Negroes.

The Church and the Peripheral National Liberal State (1850–1930)

The national emancipation of the Latin American colonies came about through the Napoleonic occupation of Spain; it began in 1808 and ended in Mexico in 1821 (though in the Caribbean the struggle continued until 1899). Independence from Spain in fact became dependence on England (with the exception of Brazil, which the king of Portugal cleverly constituted as the "Empire of Brazil"). A capitalist state since 1688, thanks to the industrial revolution, England became the new metropolitan country.

Socially, this signified the expulsion of the Spanish bureaucracy and the taking over of power in a still inchoate state by the Creole land-owning and commercial oligarchy. From 1850, the new state took shape as a liberal, dependent neocolonial state. England (and, gradually, the United States with its Monroe Doctrine of 1826: "America for the Americans" of the north) brought about a new pact: she sold her manufactured industrial products and bought raw materials which the new nations produced in their territories. The conservative class of large-scale landowners exported exotic produce or goods needed by industry; the new liberal class imported and commercialized the products of the centre. The ideology of liberty in the new state consisted in the "freedom"

to sell the products of the new empire which had replaced the old.

A struggle thus developed between those groups which saw themselves as intermediaries for English and North American industrial capitalism (such as the "American party" in Mexico, or the "Europeanism" of a Sarmiento or Mitre in Argentina), and those groups which wanted to unite the country (though in a federal system) by closing its frontiers, so that by setting its centre within the country itself, the nation might benefit from its own resources. As Hinkelammert has shown, the habits of exploitation and trade of the colonial era prevented the Latin American oligarchies from following the narrow path of capitalism centred in their own countries. Since this was not done by the beginning of the twentieth century, it became impossible to achieve at all. Latin America will never have a central, independent, creative capitalism.

The liberal state (the best examples of which are the rule of Porfirio Diaz in Mexico, or that of Mitre in Argentina) is a "blind" state (to use Hegelian terminology); it is not aware of its aims, and by its very nature is vulnerable to the succeeding empire: it is dependent. It is organized to exploit the people, the oppressed classes. Its dominant mode of production is capitalist: not actually industrial, but only colonial mercantile capitalism.

The Church established accommodating relations. Accepted by the conservatives, because it too was a landowner until well into the nineteenth century, it was in open conflict with liberalism. Paradoxically, it supported the aims of self-reliance and liberation from the power of England and North America. Because it was conservative and Hispanic in outlook, it was in accord with what would have been the best for Latin America: an inward-looking revolution like the one accomplished by Francia in Paraguay, the only Latin American country which accumulated national capital, which installed the first railways and which was destroyed by England in the famous Paraguay War of 1870.

Being nationalist and Catholic, therefore, the Church supported opposition to imperialism; nevertheless, because it was conservative, it would not favour industrialization. What is certain is that it lost influence in the liberal state and was violently persecuted and plundered.

We can see that it was in these circumstances, from 1850 onwards, that Protestantism first made its appearance (especially that of North American origin, but also English Anglicanism). If Spanish and Portuguese imperialism imposed Catholicism, it was English and North American imperialism which imposed Protestantism. What deserves study is the fact that Christianity spread to the periphery, accompanying the process of military and commercial expansion.

Relations between Church and state were either bad because the Church was in solidarity with an *encomendero* or slave-owning form of society, or else good because it was in solidarity with the emerging Anglo-Saxon empires. As always, both situations were ambiguous. At all events, the neo-colonial liberal state led to the *cul-de-sac* of the subsequent periods, in which we still find ourselves. The Church did not achieve a satisfactory solution in either case.

The Church and the Populist State (1930–1964)

The neo-colonial liberal state, which can be considered as continuing up to the neo-capitalist experiments of Christian democracy in Chile or present-day Venezuelan social democracy, tried to set up an executive and a Congress (with senators and deputies). In reality, that democracy was purely formal because power was always exercised by oligarchies (exporters or landowners, importers or merchants). But, faced with the export crisis of the centre during the first world war, and in particular the 1929 crisis, the traditional oligarchies could no longer continue to exercise power. Furthermore, the replacement of imports required a process of industrialization (which had already begun by the end of the nineteenth century in what had been the poorest zones during the colonial era, for instance the southern cone), and this gave rise to an industrial bourgeoisie—"internal" rather than "national," as Poulantzas would say.

The phenomenon of populism from the thirties onwards, with Cárdenas in Mexico, Vargas in Brazil, Perón in Argentina, can therefore be explained by the alliance of the industrial bourgeoisie of the peripheral country (as the emergent class) with the growing proletarian class and the peasantry (thus weakening its enemies, the land-owning oligarchy and the importer bourgeoisie). In the thirties, there was a mobilization of the "people," but now (thanks to the works of Octavio Ianni and many others) we can see that ultimately it was for the benefit of the internal industrial bourgeoisie, who inevitably always favour transnational companies. Populism, another possible form of dependent capitalism, reveals its limits, however, and in the end betrays the popular cause.

From the start, the Church looked with favour on the populist state (led by the executive power which, although freely elected by the people, no longer drew its inspiration from formal democracy, which in any case lacked substance). The liquidation of liberalism gave the Church greater liberty

(except in Mexico, where the legacy of the revolution continued to foment disharmony between Church and state). Generally speaking, if we include Pérez Giménez in Venezuela, Rojas Pinilla in Colombia, Velasco Ibarra in Ecuador, and the first theoretician of alliance between the classes, Haya de la Torre in Peru, the populist states were on good terms with the Church. That was the time when Catholic Action was founded, and the Church came out from the cloisters.

At all events, populism, with its policy of demobilizing the people on the one hand, and apparent popular advancement on the other, could in the end achieve nothing more, and faced a crisis. It was to be replaced by a sort of liberal state of a new type, favourable to development and open to North American investment. This state, born from the ruins of the populist "dictatorships," soon showed its inability to overcome the economic stagnation of the fifties. So there were two possibilities: the socialist state or the fascist state. In some countries, however (such as Costa Rica, Venezuela, Colombia and Mexico), the situation continued as before owing to particular national factors.

The Church and the Socialist State (1959–)

In the small island of Cuba, a national movement rose against the last corrupt stage of one of the Latin American populist leaders, Batista. Fidel Castro, supported tactically and strategically by "Che" Guevara, began the epic of the liberation against a decadent government, and in January 1959 they entered Havana.

Cuba was one of the Latin American countries characterized by its preindustrial, mercantile capitalist production, wholly dependent on the United States, and exporter of exotic tropical products. As a result of the attitude of the USA and through the inspiration of those most active in the revolutionary movement, with Fidel Castro as leader, the nation organized a new state, the first socialist state in America. The socialist system of production was rapidly introduced, although the nation is dependent on Russia, to which it sells its agricultural products. This new social formation no longer had either the equivocal features of populism or the ambiguities of dependent and underdeveloped liberalism. A new situation had arisen.

At first the Church reacted against it violently: "Yes to Christ, no to anyone else!" was the cry in the 1960 demonstrations. Neither Catholics nor Protestants were prepared, either economically or ideologically, for life in a socialist society. Nevertheless, the passage of time and the departure of many ecclesiastics, for whom the new mode of life was impossible, led the Church slowly to adopt a new attitude. The presence of an imaginative nuncio, Monsignor Zacchi, the new inspiration given by the Second Vatican Council (1962–1965), and especially Medellín (1968), made it possible for the Catholic Church in 1969, in two important documents, to criticize the blockade which had caused so much suffering, and to advise Christians to collaborate even with atheists in the task of building a juster and more fraternal society. In the same way, the Protestant churches and denominations, theologically more open, were able to reach a greater understanding of socialism, and many of them supported the revolutionary process.

Great importance was attached to the election of the candidate of the Chilean Unidad Popular, Salvador Allende, in 1970. The Latin American socialist movement appeared to have found a wide and democratic road (no longer that of armed rebellion, whether at "focal points"—Guevara—or by guerilla warfare). And so the "Christians for Socialism" movement took shape in Chile in 1972. The hierarchical Church, however, preponderantly Christian democratic in inspiration, was increasingly reserved, until criticism became openly hostile.

At all events, the economic analysis of society had been adopted by the minorities which create theology, and they now employed socialist categories in their thinking, as a matter of strategy.

It was at this moment, when the idea was gaining ground that socialism might be the Latin American solution, that the Chilean Unidad Popular encountered grave internal problems in dealing with its economic conditions (without open support from the Russians). At the same time, the US State Department was getting ready for the *coup d'etat* and for setting up with Pinochet the type of state operating in Brazil: the dependent fascist state.

The Church, US imperialism and the Dependent Fascist State (1964–)

The theorist of the new state, in Latin America, was General Golbery do Couto e Silva. In his book *Geopolitica do Brasil,* he shows that the civilization of the "Christian West" is today harassed by Russian materialist atheism. The leader of the Christian world is the United States. Brazil's function is to accomplish hegemony in the south Atlantic. The war is a "total war," on four levels: the level of political power (the state), the economic level (dependent capitalism), the psychological

and social level (which in fact led not only to propaganda, but even to torture and the most frightful repressions suffered by numerous Christians and other martyrs such as Antonio Pereira Neto, murdered in 1969), as well as the actual military level. The dependent fascist state is very different from that of autonomous fascism, such as Hitler's or Mussolini's. The essential difference is that it is inspired and organized in Latin America by the imperial US state. It is well known that since the second world war, as Comblin shows, a National Security Council has existed in the United States, which coordinates the activities of the State Department, the Pentagon, the CIA and the transnational companies. It is this imperial state, in downright opposition to the national American state (which is manifested for example in Congress), that organized the establishment in Latin America of the fascist or military states in Brazil, Uruguay, Bolivia, Chile, Argentina, and supports the dictatorships of Paraguay, Nicaragua, Haiti, and so on. It is true that there are certain military governments (such as those of Panama or Peru, and to some extent of Ecuador) whose reformist intention distinguishes them clearly from the fascist states. But at all events Latin America is in the presence of an unhealthy phenomenon: the dependent fascist state.

The aim of this state is the political control through repressive force of a people which still has a certain nostalgia for populism, so that the transnational companies can invest with security and the exporting and industrial bourgeoisie may benefit to some extent from this type of dependent capitalist development.

The Church has not reacted with the clarity one would have hoped for. In Brazil, with the exception of some distinguished bishops (among whom should be mentioned Hélder Câmara, Fragoso, Padim, Lortscheider, etc.), the Church reacted only tardily and timidly in the face of repressive measures against the people. The same can be said of Chile. In Uruguay, Paraguay and Bolivia, the Church on occasion made a critical appearance. In Argentina, a photograph of the members of the military junta talking to the chairman of the 1976 Bishops' Conference, Monsignor Tortolo, has been seen. It is well known that the Chilean Pentecostal Church has offered public prayers for Pinochet. All this shows us the Church has no clear direction, or rather, that it is leaning towards this type of state. Recently, the Cardinal Primate of Colombia, Monsignor Muñoz Duque, was appointed honorary general of the Colombian army at the same time as he was severely punishing priests and nuns who acted in favour of a group of workmen on strike. In Protestantism, the same attitude can be found in its majority groups (middle class or traditionalists who are fundamentalists).

Conclusions

The Church is a prophetic institution, that is to say, a structure of which man in history is the bearer, and whose purpose is criticism of sin (economic, sexual, ideological, political) from the eschatological point of view, and practical action liberating man from the systems of domination resulting from sin. This Church, inevitably though regrettably, yet again appears to the world to be closely associated with a mode of production which in the last century proved to be just as opposed to Christianity as socialism is considered to be at present. In fact, in opposition to the bourgeois revolution in France, the Church adopted a monarchical and feudal position. Now, in the name of the principles of formal liberal democracy and of the capitalist mode of production (although this is criticized in a reformist way, it is fundamentally accepted, for example, that private property is a natural right), it supports the peripheral fascist state and the imperial system of the centre.

We Christians of the periphery, who desire the liberation of our poor peoples, the oppressed classes, cannot but be critical, in a constructive ecclesial spirit, of the centrist churches which accept as a fact the domination which their societies exercise over the peripheral societies. The theme is not so much that of the relation between national state and universal Church, as between the states of the centre (the North American imperial state, the developed European states, the Russian bureaucratic and dominating socialist state, etc.) and those of the periphery (from the free ones, e.g. the Chinese, Vietnamese, Cuban, etc., to the dependent and underdeveloped ones, e.g. the Brazilian, Indian, Iranian, etc.), and the position of the Church in that context. Because, paradoxically enough, many Christians of the centre support with their religion and their faith the domination which their own states exercise over states and churches of the periphery. The great theme, as in the time of Christ, is that of the divinization of the imperial state or making a fetish of a culture which, to increase the confusion, considers itself Christian, namely, the European and North American culture.

Contemporary Christian theology still does not have adequate categories in which to think out the theme of the state in its true dimension in the world, with the conflicts that characterize it. It is vassal to a long European process of ideologization, and its real situation has been plain to see in

the periphery, in Africa, Asia and Latin America. Against this ideological conversion of the centre, we Christians among the oppressed peoples of the earth are rising. An Italian political solution (though it is still to be seen whether it is the best for Italy) or a North American solution cannot be imposed by the churches of the centre on those of the periphery. What is needed is a more real sense of the universality of the Church, a universality which is analogical, not univocal, which must promote and not merely permit the responsibility of the churches which are set in very diverse national realities, because their states differ widely.

The world geopolitical situation is approximately as [described]. If this is the present world as it really is, the churches should understand that their prophetic role varies very much according to the outlook of the national state, its mode of production, its ideology and its history. In any case, if the Church is prophetic, it will criticize injustice wherever it is found, but for this the Church will have to get used to carrying out worldwide sociopolitical analyses, and be watchful of the authentic meaning of its action. It is so easy, unfortunately, to act in good faith in a project, organization or action ideologically justified by a state which, although it claims identification with Christianity, in fact exercises unjust domination over other nations. How many Christians defending their country, as the Americans in Vietnam, are in fact serving the interests of the Beast of the Apocalypse rather than those of the Lamb?

From Enrique D. Dussel, ed., *Church and State: Opening a New Ecumenical Discussion* (Geneva: World Council of Churches, 1978), 62–74. Translation by W[orld] C[ouncil of]C[hurches] Language Service.

In "Up against the Wall," **William Martin,** professor of religion and public policy at Rice University, assesses the Church-state relationship in American political life. Martin praises the policy of religious tolerance in the United States. He argues that although this policy does not imply that all opinions are equally valid, it does require defending the rights of minorities even when one disagrees with those rights.

WILLIAM MARTIN

"Up against the Wall," in *With God on Our Side*

[Since the Protestant] interpretation of Scripture resulted in an explosion of sects, each convinced of its own correctness, a strict "Protestant" interpretation of the Constitution would result in political anarchy. For that reason, most judges understandably prefer a "Catholic" approach, which allows for development and change in interpretation in response to changing social and political conditions, and which acknowledges the Supreme Court as the final arbiter of what the Constitution means today, which may differ from what it meant in 1789. Levinson calls for an intermediate approach that would allow for some change and development, but always in the light of careful and respectful attention to the original meaning.

Few would contend that the Constitution is an infallible document, written on tables of stone by the finger of God. Its acceptance of slavery should by itself disprove that. Its framers, however, understood the need for change and set forth orderly mechanisms for achieving it. Few would argue that amendments ending slavery and giving women and former slaves the vote did not improve on the original document. Similarly, amendments giving citizens the right to vote directly for their senators, limiting the number of terms a president can serve, or changing the voting age from twenty-one to eighteen were all efforts to effect improvements in an ever-evolving republic. And even amendments eighteen and twenty-one, instituting and then abolishing Prohibition, attest to the nation's ability both to undertake a major social experiment and then to declare it a failure. These changes, following rather complex and lengthy procedures, are generally accepted as valid alterations to the supreme law of the land. In marked contrast, it is troubling when major questions of constitutionality are decided by five-to-four votes, and when citizens understand that the "supreme law" can change quite suddenly with the appointment of only one or two new justices.

In light of the historical record and the still-unsettled nature of the debate between separationists and accommodationists, what lessons may we reasonably draw?

As a basic premise, we must remember that the Founding Fathers intended that the state be neutral toward all religions, but did not intend that religious people or their organizations be neutralized, their voices restricted to private matters only. Of course, religious people have a right to be involved in political activity, and they cannot be expected to leave their religious convictions behind when they enter the political arena. They have a right to organize themselves to work effectively for the good of their country as they understand it, and that understanding will inevitably be informed by their religious faith. Jews and Christians of every description, as well as Buddhists and Muslims and Hindus and secular humanists,

drawing on the values and beliefs of their religious or secular traditions, may all legitimately work to shape public policy, within the limits of the Constitution which has served us so admirably in avoiding society-rending religious conflict.

There are, however, real and reasonable limits to that shaping process. The most important of these is that a religious body does not have the right, simply because it may be in the majority or better organized than other groups, to bind its specifically religious doctrines on others or to require that others help pay for the propagation of those doctrines. It also makes sense to draw the line at political partisanship. If a church or other religious body enjoys immunity from taxation because it is theoretically not subject to the state, then it seems reasonable to demand that, beyond expressions of principle and policy, churches not engage in partisanship by endorsing candidates or parties, lest such activities result in the corruption of both the political and religious institutions.

Further, religious individuals and groups ought also to respect and honor the valuable principle of pluralism. This does not mean that all values are up for grabs and that no value position is to be preferred over another. Rather, it means that our society is one in which "any number can play," in the belief that a multiplicity of views contributes not to chaos, but to a rich and diverse republic. (It has also contributed mightily to a free-market environment in religion that helps account for the amazing vitality of American churches, a vitality unmatched by any other comparably modern society.) As James Madison observed more than two hundred years ago, "In a free government the security for civil rights must be the same as that for religious rights; it consists in the one case in the multiplicity of interests and in the other in the multiplicity of sects."

Political zealots sometimes seem to suggest that only one political party has a legitimate claim on the American heritage. The Founding Fathers saw that attitude as dangerous. The system of checks and balances they built into the Constitution was informed not only by the recognition that good citizens may differ over the proper course of action, but also, at least in part, by the biblical understanding of humans as fallible and prone to wrongdoing and therefore frequently in need of some healthy opposition from their fellows. Nobody, in their view, has a corner on Truth, Justice, and the American Way. Christians should recognize, in justified humility, that there is no single Christian position on many, perhaps most, social issues. Intelligent, informed, sincere Christians may honestly differ not only with unbelievers, but also among themselves and adherents of other religions, as to what God or whatever powers govern the universe think about such issues as abortion, the distribution of wealth among nations, the legitimacy of a particular political regime, or the desirability of a given weapons system.

America has been remarkably favored—blessed, if you prefer—by a wise constitutional policy of nonpreferential protection for the free and responsible exercise of religion. For the good of the entire community of Americans, religious and secular alike, we should protect that policy against encroachments from whatever quarter. Each generation must redraw the line of separation between the rights of religion and the rights of civil authority. It matters a great deal when there are flagrant violations of this boundary. We understand that. We must remind ourselves again and again that the best way to prevent such flagrant violations is to watch diligently for apparently minor ones, to "take alarm at the first experiment upon our liberties" (as Madison put it), to look out not only for the interests of our own parochial group, but for the interests of the entire community. That process often involves standing up for the rights of minorities, even though we may find them disagreeable.

In the political arena, if *they*, whoever "they" are, cheat,

lie, or deceive, then *we*, whoever "we" are, have every right to complain, oppose, and expose "them." If, however, "they" play by the rules, then "we" should not cry foul when those whose views displease us organize themselves into an effective political force. Instead, we should play by the same rules and organize ourselves into an effective counterforce, to see who can persuade the most people. If we are the ones who prevail, who gain power, we should exercise it with humility and fear, recognizing always its tendency to corrupt its possessors and the causes they represent. If we feel certain we are right, we should recall that certainty can also corrupt, and that absolute certainty corrupts powerfully.

We cannot separate religion and politics. The question is how they are to be related in such a way as to maintain the pluralism that has served us so well. The core of that pluralism is not the dogma that all opinions are equally valid but the conviction that civility and the public peace are important, that respect for minorities and their opinions is a crucial element of a democratic society, and that, however persuaded I am of the rightness of my position, I may still, after all, be wrong.

From William Martin, *With God on Our Side* (New York: Broadway Books, 1996), 383–85.

✌

3. NEW NOTIONS OF "CHURCH"

  ✍   The *Dogmatic Constitution on the Church* (*Lumen gentium*, November 21, 1964) is widely regarded as the most important achievement of the Roman Catholic Church's **Second Vatican Council.** Chapter 2, "The People of God," and chapter 4, "The Laity," examine what it means to be a Church in the modern world in terms of witness, ministry, and fellowship. The three terms are rooted in the concepts of *martyrion, diakonia,* and *koinonia.*

THE SECOND VATICAN COUNCIL

"The People of God," 12–13,

in *Dogmatic Constitution on the Church*

12. The holy People of God shares also in Christ's prophetic office: it spreads abroad a living witness to him, especially by a life of faith and love and by offering to God a sacrifice of praise, the fruit of lips praising his name (cf. Heb. 13:15). The whole body of the faithful who have an anointing that comes

from the holy one (cf. 1 Jn. 2:20 and 27) cannot err in matters of belief. This characteristic is shown in the supernatural appreciation of the faith (*sensus fidei*) of the whole people, when, "from the bishops to the last of the faithful"[14] they manifest a universal consent in matters of faith and morals. By this appreciation of the faith, aroused and sustained by the Spirit of truth, the People of God, guided by the sacred teaching authority (*magisterium*), and obeying it, receives not the mere word of men, but truly the word of God (cf. 1 Th. 2:13), the faith once for all delivered to the saints (cf. Jude 3). The People unfailingly adheres to this faith, penetrates it more deeply with right judgment, and applies it more fully in daily life.

---

14. See St. Augustine, *De praed. sanct.* 14, 27: PL [Migne, *Patrologiae cursus, series Latina*] 44, 980. (The *sensus fidei* refers to the instinctive sensitivity and discrimination which the members of the Church possess in matters of faith.—Translator.)

It is not only through the sacraments and the ministrations of the Church that the Holy Spirit makes holy the People, leads them and enriches them with his virtues. Allotting his gifts according as he wills (cf. 1 Cor. 12:11), he also distributes special graces among the faithful of every rank. By these gifts he makes them fit and ready to undertake various tasks and offices for the renewal and building up of the Church, as it is written, "the manifestation of the Spirit is given to everyone for profit" (1 Cor. 12:7). Whether these charisms be very remarkable or more simple and widely diffused, they are to be received with thanksgiving and consolation since they are fitting and useful for the needs of the Church. Extraordinary gifts are not to be rashly desired, nor is it from them that the fruits of apostolic labors are to be presumptuously expected. Those who have charge over the Church should judge the genuineness and proper use of these gifts, through their office not indeed to extinguish the Spirit, but to test all things and hold fast to what is good (cf. 1 Th. 5:12 and 19–21).

13. All men are called to belong to the new People of God. This People therefore, whilst remaining one and only one, is to be spread throughout the whole world and to all ages in order that the design of God's will may be fulfilled: he made human nature one in the beginning and has decreed that all his children who were scattered should be finally gathered together as one (cf. Jn. 11:52). It was for this purpose that God sent his Son, whom he appointed heir of all things (cf. Heb. 1:2), that he might be teacher, king and priest of all, the head of the new and universal People of God's sons. This, too, is why God sent the Spirit of his Son, the Lord and Giver of Life. The Spirit is, for the Church and for each and every believer, the principle of their union and unity in the teaching of the apostles and fellowship, in the breaking of bread and prayer (cf. Acts 2:42 Gk.).

The one People of God is accordingly present in all the nations of the earth; since its citizens, who are taken from all nations, are of a kingdom whose nature is not earthly but heavenly. All the faithful scattered throughout the world are in communion with each other in the Holy Spirit so that "he who dwells in Rome knows those in most distant parts to be his members" (*qui Romae sedet, Indos scit membrum suum esse*).[15] Since the kingdom of Christ is not of this world (cf. Jn. 18:36), the Church or People of God which establishes this kingdom does not take away anything from the temporal welfare of any people. Rather she fosters and takes to herself, in so far as they are good, the abilities, the resources and customs of peoples. In so taking them to herself she purifies, strengthens and elevates them. The Church indeed is mindful

that she must work with the king to whom the nations were given for an inheritance (cf. Ps. 2:8) and to whose city gifts are brought (cf. Ps. 71[72]: 10; Is. 60:4–7; Apoc. 21:24). This character of universality which adorns the People of God is a gift from the Lord himself whereby the Catholic ceaselessly and efficaciously seeks for the return of all humanity and all its goods under Christ the Head in the unity of his Spirit.[16]

In virtue of this catholicity each part contributes its own gifts to other parts and to the whole Church, so that the whole and each of the parts are strengthened by the common sharing of all things and by the common effort to attain to fullness in unity. Hence it is that the People of God is not only an assembly of various peoples, but in itself is made up of different ranks. This diversity among its members is either by reason of their duties—some exercise the sacred ministry for the good of their brethren—or it is due to their condition and manner of life—many enter the religious state and, intending to sanctity by the narrower way, stimulate their brethren by their example. Holding a rightful place in the communion of the Church there are also particular Churches that retain their own traditions, without prejudice to the Chair of Peter which presides over the whole assembly of charity,[17] and protects their legitimate variety while at the same time taking care that these differences do not hinder unity, but rather contribute to it. Finally, between all the various parts of the Church there is a bond of close communion whereby spiritual riches, apostolic workers and temporal resources are shared. For the members of the People of God are called upon to share their goods, and the words of the apostle apply also to each of the Churches, "according to the gift that each has received, administer it to one another as good stewards of the manifold grace of God" (1 Pet. 4:10).

All men are called to this catholic unity which prefigures and promotes universal peace. And in different ways to it belong, or are related: the Catholic faithful, others who believe in Christ, and finally all mankind, called by God's grace to salvation.

Trans. by Father Christopher O'Donnell, in *Vatican II, The Dogmatic Constitution on the Church in Vatican II: The Conciliar and Post Conciliar Documents*, edited by Austin Flannery (Collegeville, MN: Liturgical Press, 1975), 361–65.

15. See St. John Chrysostom, *In Io.* Hom. 65, 1: *PG* 59, 361.

16. See St. Irenaeus, *Adv. haer.* III, 16, 6; III, 22, 1–3; *PG* 7, 925 C–926 A and 955 C–958 A; Harvey 2, 87 s. and 120–23; Sagnard, ed., *Sources Chrét.*, 290–92 and 372 ss.

17. See St. Ignatius Martyr, *Ad Rom.*, Praef.: ed. Funk, 1, 252.

"The Laity," 30–34, in *Dogmatic Constitution on the Church*

30. Having made clear the functions of the hierarchy, the holy Council is pleased to turn its attention to the state of those Christians who are called the laity. Everything that has been said of the People of God is addressed equally to laity, religious and clergy. Because of their situation and mission, however, certain things pertain particularly to the laity, both men and women, the foundations of which must be more fully examined owing to the special circumstances of our time. The pastors, indeed, know well how much the laity contribute to the welfare of the whole Church. For they know that they themselves were not established by Christ to undertake alone the whole salvific mission of the Church to the world, but that it is their exalted office so to be shepherds of the faithful and also recognize the latter's contribution and charisms that everyone in his own way will, with one mind, cooperate in the common task. For all must "practice the truth in love, and so grow up in all things in him who is the head, Christ. For from him the whole body—being closely joined and knit together through every joint of the system according to the functioning in due measure of each single part—derives its increase to the building up of itself in love" (Eph. 4:15–16).

31. The term "laity" is here understood to mean all the faithful except those in Holy Orders and those who belong to a religious state approved by the Church. That is, the faithful who by Baptism are incorporated into Christ, are placed in the People of God, and in their own way share the priestly, prophetic and kingly office of Christ, and to the best of their ability carry on the mission of the whole Christian people in the Church and in the world.

Their secular character is proper and peculiar to the laity. Although those in Holy Orders may sometimes be engaged in secular activities, or even practice a secular profession, yet by reason of their particular vocation, they are principally and expressly ordained to the sacred ministry. At the same time, religious give outstanding and striking testimony that the world cannot be transfigured and offered to God without the spirit of the beatitudes. But by reason of their special vocation it belongs to the laity to seek the kingdom of God by engaging in temporal affairs and directing them according to God's will. They live in the world, that is, they are engaged in each and every work and business of the earth and in the ordinary circumstances of social and family life which, as it were, constitute their very existence. There they are called by God that, being led by the Spirit to the Gospel, they may contribute to the sanctification of the world, as from within like leaven, by fulfilling their own particular duties. Thus, especially by the witness of their life, resplendent in faith, hope and charity they must manifest Christ to others. It pertains to them in a special way so to illuminate and order all temporal things with which they are so closely associated that these may be effected and grow according to Christ and may be to the glory of the Creator and Redeemer.

32. By divine institution holy Church is ordered and governed with a wonderful diversity. "For just as in one body we have many members, yet all the members have not the same function, so we the many, are one body in Christ, but severally members one of another" (Rom. 12:4–5).

There is, therefore, one chosen People of God: "one Lord, one faith, one baptism" (Eph. 4:5); there is a common dignity of members deriving from their rebirth in Christ, a common grace as sons, a common vocation to perfection, one salvation, one hope and undivided charity. In Christ and in the Church there is, then, no inequality arising from race or nationality, social condition or sex, for "there is neither Jew nor Greek; there is neither slave nor freeman; there is neither male nor female. For you are all 'one' in Christ Jesus" (Gal. 3:28 Greek; cf. Col. 3:11).

In the Church not everyone marches along the same path yet all are called to sanctity and have obtained an equal privilege of faith through the justice of God (cf. 2 Pet. 1:1). Although by Christ's will some are established as teachers, dispensers of the mysteries and pastors for the others, there remains, nevertheless, a true equality between all with regard to the dignity and to the activity which is common to all the faithful in the building up of the Body of Christ. The distinction which the Lord has made between the sacred ministers and the rest of the People of God involves union, for the pastors and the other faithful are joined together by a close relationship: the pastors of the Church—following the example of the Lord—should minister to each other and to the rest of the faithful; the latter should eagerly collaborate with the pastors and teachers. And so amid variety all will bear witness to the wonderful unity in the Body of Christ: this very diversity of graces, of ministries and of works gathers the sons of God into one, for "all these things are the work of the one and the same Spirit" (1 Cor. 12:11).

As the laity through the divine choice have Christ as their brother, who, though Lord of all, came not to be served but to serve (cf. Mt. 20:28), they also have as brothers those in the sacred ministry who by teaching, by sanctifying and by ruling with the authority of Christ so nourish the family of God that the new commandment of love may be fulfilled by all. As St. Augustine very beautifully puts it: "When I am frightened by what I am to you, then I am consoled by what I am with you. To you I am the bishop, with you I am a Christian. The first is an office, the second a grace; the first a danger, the second salvation."[18]

33. Gathered together in the People of God and established in the one Body of Christ under one head, the laity—no matter who they are—have, as living members, the vocation of applying to the building up of the Church and to its continual sanctification all the powers which they have received from the goodness of the Creator and from the grace of the Redeemer.

The apostolate of the laity is a sharing in the salvific mission of the Church. Through Baptism and Confirmation all are appointed to this apostolate by the Lord himself. Moreover, by the sacraments, and especially by the Eucharist, that love of God and man which is the soul of the apostolate is communicated and nourished. The laity, however, are given this special vocation: to make the Church present and fruitful in those places and circumstances where it is only through them that she can become the salt of the earth.[19] Thus, every lay person, through those gifts given to him, is at once the witness and the living instrument of the mission of the Church itself "according to the measure of Christ's bestowal" (Eph. 4:7).

Besides this apostolate which belongs to absolutely every Christian, the laity can be called in different ways to more immediate cooperation in the apostolate of the hierarchy[20] like those men and women who helped the apostle Paul in the Gospel, laboring much in the Lord (cf. Phil. 4–3; Rom. 16:3ff.). They have, moreover, the capacity of being appointed by the hierarchy to some ecclesiastical offices with a view to a spiritual end.

All the laity, then, have the exalted duty of working for the ever greater spread of the divine plan of salvation to all men, of every epoch and all over the earth. Therefore may the way be clear for them to share diligently in the salvific work of the Church according to their ability and the needs of the times.

34. Since he wishes to continue his witness and his service through the laity also, the supreme and eternal priest, Christ Jesus, vivifies them with his spirit and ceaselessly impels them to accomplish every good and perfect work.

To those whom he intimately joins to his life and mission he also gives a share in his priestly office, to offer spiritual worship for the glory of the Father and the salvation of man. Hence the laity, dedicated as they are to Christ and anointed by the Holy Spirit, are marvellously called and prepared so that even richer fruits of the Spirit may be produced in them. For all their works, prayers and apostolic undertakings, family and married life, daily work, relaxation of mind and body, if they are accomplished in the Spirit—indeed even the hardships of life if patiently borne—all these become spiritual sacrifices acceptable to God through Jesus Christ (cf. 1 Pet. 2:5). In the celebration of the Eucharist these may most fittingly be offered to the Father along with the body of the Lord. And so, worshipping everywhere by their holy actions, the laity consecrate the world itself to God.

Trans. by Father Christopher O'Donnell, in *Vatican II, The Dogmatic Constitution on the Church in Vatican II: The Conciliar and Post Conciliar Documents,* edited by Austin Flannery (Collegeville, MN: Liturgical Press, 1975), 388–91.

⚭ In "Women-Church: A Feminist Exodus Community" (1985), **Rosemary Radford Ruether,** also the author of the first systematic feminist theology, *Sexism and God-Talk* (1983), identifies the need for an intermediate stage on the way to a nonpatriarchal Church. In her vision, in the stage of "Women-Church" community, women form a culture of critique and experience the gathering of liberated women as a redemptive community, while working to form their own liturgies and to "delegitimize the theological myths" that justify the patriarchal Church.

ROSEMARY RADFORD RUETHER

"Women-Church: A Feminist Exodus Community," in *Women-Church: Theology and Practice of Feminist Liturgical Communities*

Thus the first step in forming the feminist exodus from patriarchy is to gather women together to articulate their own experience and communicate it with each other. Women assure each other that they really are not crazy, that they really have been defined and confined by systemic marginalization of their human capacities. They develop words and analysis for the different aspects of this system of marginalization, and they learn how to recognize and resist the con-

---

18. St. Augustine, *Sermon 340,* 1: PL 38, 1438.
19. See Pius XI, Litt. Encycl. *Quadragesimo anno,* 15 May 1931: *AAS* 23 (1931): 221 s. 2 Pius XII, Alloc. *De quelle consolation,* 14 Oct. 1951: *AAS* (1951): 790 s.
20. See Pius XII, Alloc. *Six ans sont écoulé,* 5 Oct. 1957: *AAS* 49 (1957): 927.

stant messages from patriarchal culture that try to enforce their acquiescence and collaboration with it. Distressing as it may seem to males who imagine themselves sympathetic to feminism, this process of consciousness raising must necessarily have a separatist stage. Women have to withdraw from male-dominated spaces so they can gather together and define their own experience.

The need for a period of withdrawal from men and communication with each other is essential for the formation of the feminist community, because women, more than any other marginalized group, have lacked a critical culture of their own. Repressed ethnic and racial groups retained remnants of cultures prior to their conquest. They have also developed subcultures of resistance in modes of talk, song, and dance. Precisely because of women's isolation from each other, separated by patriarchal family structures, their deprivation of education, and even of speech, their cultural colonization by an education that incorporates them into a language that they have not defined, but which defines them as inferior and auxiliary to a male-dominated world, women need separate spaces and all-female gatherings to form the critical culture that can give them an autonomous ground from which to critique patriarchy.

The need for a separate base in order to form a critical culture should not be confused with ideological separatism. By ideological separatism I mean that position assumed by some feminists that separatism should be total and permanent. This is generally accompanied by a dualistic anthropology that denies to males the capacity for authentic humanness, and that imagines ways in which women can reproduce without males and can form a totally separate society without them.

It is understandable that some women come to this conclusion. As one contemplates the total history of patriarchy and begins to see all the ramifications of evil done by it, one necessarily goes through experiences of rage in which one concludes that males are to be avoided altogether. It is necessary for any woman who wishes to be authentically autonomous to pass through at least something of this rage. But to pass through it means not to translate it into a total ideology. One needs to come out to a firm ground of autonomous humanity as a female who can continually resist and refuse the snares of patriarchy without confusing this with the humanity of males. One needs to recognize one's own fallibility, one's own capacity not only to be victimized, but also to be victimizer, and, in the mature self-esteem, also be

able to affirm the humanity of males behind the masks of patriarchy.

Thus we are not talking here about separatism as total ideology, but as a stage in a process, a stage that is absolutely necessary but not an end in itself, a stage toward a further end in the formation of a critical culture and community of women and men in exodus from patriarchy. We should be clear that when we talk about women withdrawing to collectivize their own experience and form a critical counterculture to patriarchy, for most women this means, at best, a few hours a week taken out of lives lived in the presence of males. Even women who are involved full time in feminist studies, and who are constantly engaged in communication with feminist women, still spend a large part of their lives interacting with males and male culture. This is hardly avoidable in a world in which most of the systems of daily life are male owned and male defined.

Only a very few women will have the desire, much less the means, to try to construct a female producer and/or consumer cooperative where all contact with males is minimized. And even this does not really remove them from many lines of dependency that link them with a male-controlled world. I support experiments with feminist working and living cooperatives as long as one does not succumb to a totalistic ideology that imagines males are going to vanish or wither away and one will not have to come to terms with males as one's fellow humanity.

Women-Church is the Christian theological expression of this stage of feminist collectivization of women's experience and the formation of critical culture. It means that women delegitimize the theological myths that justify the *ecclesia* of patriarchy and begin to form liturgies to midwife their liberation from it. They begin to experience the gathering of liberated women as a redemptive community rooted in a new being. They empower themselves and are empowered by this liberated Spirit upon which they are grounded (the two are not contradictory, since one empowers oneself authentically only by being empowered by the Spirit that grounds one) to celebrate this new community, to commune with it, and to nurture themselves and be nurtured in the community of liberated sisterhood.

How Women-Church might be transcended in a redemptive community of both men and women liberated from patriarchy remains to be seen. I assume that it should happen as the fulfillment and culmination of a process in which Women-Church is one stage. One can see this begin to happen as women shape a sufficiently clarified critical culture so that some men feel compelled to try to understand it on its own terms and not simply to try to ridicule or repress it. What is required for the development of a new cohumanity of men and women liberated from patriarchy is that men begin to critique their own dehumanization by patriarchy and form their critical culture of liberation from it in a way that truly complements the feminist exodus and allows the formation of real dialogue. I assume the name for this liberated humanity would then no longer be "Women-Church," but simply "Church"; that is, the authentic community of exodus from oppression that has been heralded by the traditions of religious and social liberation but, until now, corrupted by reversion to new forms of the *ecclesia* of patriarchy.

However, when I say that Women-Church is a stage in a dialectical process that must lead on to the cohuman church, a community engaged in liberation from patriarchy, I do not mean that Women-Church only needs to last a few years and then disappear into the great collaboration between men and women. Patriarchy is too old and too deeply rooted both in our psyches and in our culture and collective life to be quickly analyzed, rejected, and then overcome in a new unity of men and women. We must think of Women-Church as a feminist counterculture to the *ecclesia* of patriarchy that must continue for the foreseeable future as an exodus both within and on the edges of existing church institutions.

Women-Church means neither leaving the church as a sectarian group, nor continuing to fit into it on its terms. It means establishing bases for a feminist critical culture and celebrational community that have some autonomy from the established institutions. It also means sharing this critical culture and sense of community with many women who are working within existing churches but who gather, on an occasional or regular basis, to experience the feminist vision that is ever being dimmed and limited by the parameters of the male-dominated institution. It means some women might worship only in alternative feminist liturgies; others might do so on a regular basis, while continuing to attend liturgies in traditional parishes into which they seek to inject something of this alternative; and some women might enter into these experiences only occasionally, such as at annual gatherings of women pastors or feminist retreats, where women worship and celebrate their community together in the context of these occasional communities.

Only if some groups work intensely and exclusively on imagining an alternative culture in a way that cannot be con-trolled or limited by patriarchal culture, but also are in dialogue and interaction with women within the institutions who can then adapt and make use of what is being developed in alternative communities, does the possibility of a genuine transformational dialectic take place. [. . .]

Women-Church Liturgies

. . . However much historical religion has taught us to stand out from nature and to look forward to deliverance from nature, the actual existence and survival of humanity is still based on the cycles of nature. Decomposition of vegetation creates rich soil; evaporation and precipitation bring life-giving moisture from which grows the new harvest. Day and night, the seasons of summer and winter, the turning of our planet and the movement of the planets around us—these are the processes that sustain our life. To deny these rhythms is to deny the concrete foundations of our continuing life. To teach contempt for these interconnections is to create a culture and technology that has brought us perilously close to destroying the very earth, air, and waters that sustain our being. By reclaiming in our ritual observance the natural cycles of night and day, the lunar cycle, the year cycle, and our own life cycle from birth to death, we also accept our finitude and our chief historical task, which is to sustain human and natural life in harmonious interconnection in our time, so that it can be passed on in a viable form for our children.

Although it affirms the pagan or country-folk layer of our tradition, the understanding of liturgy developed here differs from the pagan feminist movement of recent years (although I believe that this movement is motivated, not only by concern for the liberation of women from sexism, but also for the reharmonization of humanity with nonhuman nature discussed above). The chief difference between pagan feminists and the perspective of this book is that such feminists wish to dissolve entirely the Jewish and Christian stratas of ritual and religion and return to a religion of nature renewal. They explore Jewish or Christian traditions only to recover the pagan or matriarchal strata that they see lying behind it. They regard the religion of nature renewal, centered in the great Goddess of nature, as sufficient to provide both a religion fully affirmative to women, and also a religion that will reconnect us with nature.

This dissolving of historical and messianic religion into nature religion results in several problems, in my opinion. First of all, it lacks a sense of real historical roots, of a historical community whose accumulated wisdom one values, even as one criticizes it and seeks to renew it. Whatever religious teachers of ancient nature religion may have once existed, they have long since been cut off. The actual connections between these earlier religions and their later survivals are cloaked in obscurity. Modern pagans tend to exhibit an impatience with historical accuracy in these matters, a desire to make do with myths that serve their present purposes, such as an easy equation between worship of ancient Goddesses and a feminist religion that empowers women as autonomous persons.

But, more important than these unhistorical tendencies, is a romanticism that suggests that a world without sin can be easily recreated simply by reverencing and celebrating nature cycles. In a sense nature religion refers us back to a prefallen world of "dreaming innocence" where happy men, women, and children live in harmony with nature. It is a world in which historical responsibility has not yet ejected Adam and Eve from paradise. One may question whether, in some primordial era, life for humanity with nature was ever so happy. But, in any case, our historical consciousness, as well as the rise of systems of oppression and alienation, have long since ejected us from this state of innocence. To try to go back to it in purely ritual or cultural ways is escapist.

If we are really to reclaim a healthy relationship between our minds and our bodies, between humans and nonhuman ecology, we cannot shirk the task of historical responsibility. We need not only to imagine such a harmony in cult, but to do it as a historical, ethical task of dismantling the systems of oppression and shaping new ways of living between human groups, and between humans and nature. It is not that several exponents of Goddess-nature religion lack a sense of ethical protest and social action, but rather that their theology proclaiming that "all that is is good" lacks an understanding of historical sin and a willingness to be accountable for social systems of evil.[21]

From Rosemary Radford Ruether, "Women-Church: A Feminist Exodus Community," in *Women-Church: Theology and Practice of Feminist Liturgical Communities*, by Rosemary Radford Ruether (San Francisco: Harper and Row, 1985), 59–62, 105–6.

☙ *The Role of the "Diakonia" of the Church in Contemporary Society* (1966), by the **World Council of Churches,** notes that there is a consensus among many of its member Churches on the necessity of reconsidering the role of "ministry" (often termed *diakonia* in the New Testament) in light of the needs of contemporary world societies. The document concludes that compassionate ministry

resides in acts of the Church as well as of the individual Christian. Those recognized as having the spiritual gift of *diakonia* ought to be given a formal role in the Church's ministry.

THE WORLD COUNCIL OF CHURCHES

The Role of the "Diakonia" of the Church in Contemporary Society

A serving Church is not justified by its humanitarian deeds. It receives salvation, redemption, wholeness, reconciliation, true humanity only by the redeeming God. Help for the weak, the sinner, the unaccepted, which Jesus offers, is related to His sacrificial death on the cross; it in fact brings Him to the cross (Lk 4:16–30; Mt 12:9–14). Only those who accept His sacrifice as Christ's "diakonia" for their own salvation under His cross participate in his "diakonia" as Paul states: "ourselves as your servants for Jesus' sake" (II Cor 4:5). It is precisely for this reason that "diakonia" intimately connected with redemption is a freeing and liberating activity of the Church among men. There are no restraints attached to "diakonia." Having been redeemed, the Christian is free to identify himself with the suffering of this world, yet without utopian illusions. In this freedom the service of the Church crosses all borders and breaks through all separating walls which men have erected—walls between churches, classes, nations, political ideologies. "Diakonia" tries to obey the commandment to love the enemy.

"Diaconical" activity, given expression in both love and justice, within the institutional life of the Church and in cooperative activities in society, flows from the total life in Christ. The forms and expressions of "diakonia" can, therefore, never be predetermined or stereotyped. They depend on the need in particular situations.

The changed situation of the Church in modern society makes in some places impossible the institutional forms of "diakonia" with which the historic churches of the West are familiar. In some societies identifiable Christian "diakonia" is not permitted. What this means for the life of the Church has not been sufficiently considered. As yet the Church has not found new ways of ministering to those in need where identifiable Christian action is not allowed.

---

21. Starhawk, for example, is strongly committed to the peace movement and to ethical commitment in WICCA, but she strongly rejects any concept of historical sin or evil. This is partly based on the Christian distortion of its own doctrine of "original sin" as teaching the fallenness or "evil" of nature, rather than fallenness as alienation from nature or creation.

In fact, the Church may have little opportunity for overt expressions of "diakonia" at certain times and in certain places. Sometimes its expression may be completely anonymous in the lives of individual Christians. Its particular forms may vary, if only they are rooted in the love of Christ as He unceasingly finds new modes of expression.

"Diakonia" and Sacrifice

The disadvantaged are of the full fellowship of the Church and must be included in it. The "diaconical" function must always urge the Church to rethink its situations, to insure that the poor and the weak indeed have their proper place in the Church.

"Diakonia" is inconceivable without gifts and without the sacrifice of money, time, and strength of individual Christians, even to the point of offering life for the needy. At the same time the Church as a corporate entity must be visibly willing to serve and to contribute. Wherever the Church has the freedom to develop its organisational structure there "diakonia" for the poor and for the world must find an adequate expression in the ministerial office as well as in the service by the laity.

"Diakonia" the Charisma of the Spirit

1. A Compassionate Community

The Holy Spirit gathers and establishes the Church as an accepting, integrating and serving fellowship in hope, prayer and communion.

The Holy Spirit's paramount and all-embracing gift is the charisma of love. This is entrusted to the Church both as a gift and as a command. In love, the fullness of the Spirit, the highest charisma (I Cor 13) is connected with even the most humble service to man (John 13). In love the receiver is being honored, while the giver takes (Mt 25:40) "the form of a servant" (Phil 2:7; Lk 22:27). The different "diaconical" charismata (I Cor 12:14: "diakonia") spring from this one charisma of fellowship as from the source of all service. They are focused, therefore, as in a crystal at the Lord's Table. There will not be perfect communion, and a full liturgy, without the presence of the poor and the suffering, and the "diakonia" to them.

The great test for every Church, local or worldwide, is whether her fellowship can help and accept people in trouble. There is no member who, at some time, does not need

this fraternal "diakonia," and there is no one, including those who suffer themselves, who is not able to offer fellowship. In this "diakonia," service to the suffering is always a two-way road. The Church is called to be the compassionate community. Within His fellowship, the Holy Spirit is bestowing special "diaconical" charismata on individual members for special services (I Cor 12:14).

2. The Eschatological Dimension of "Diakonia"

Times of ardent eschatological expectations and hope for the coming of the Lord and times of persecution and suffering have always been periods in which the churches have harvested ripening fruits of "diakonia." In such times well structured forms of serving congregations were built up, individual members were entrusted with specific "diaconical" ministries, large contributions were made as real sacrifices, and new means, ways and methods were created for spreading mutual help to the ends of the earth. This fact discloses the relationship between eschatological expectation and ecumenical work. As soon, however, as churches gained security and public recognition they often turned from their proper "diaconical" tasks and complacently left the service of the needy to others—to their governments and to professional groups. Thus their life became ingrown and lost an ecumenical dimension. Today again many churches are made aware that they are in the position of a minority and in the situation of insecurity. Such churches begin to look upon themselves as the pilgrim people of God on the way to meet the coming Lord. On this march the Church cannot ignore the sick, the weak and the afflicted and leave them to wait for help from others. The "diakonia" of the Church must therefore be rethought, adapted, and be given the most adequate structure and form to meet the new requirements of our time.

3. Renewal of the "Diaconal" Ministry

In the history of the Church it would seem that the diaconal ministries of the Church have often been exercised by those with manifest charismatic gifts. Often these gifts have been exercised outside the main stream of the churches' life but subsequently institutionalised. The question arises as to where and in what form such charismatic ministries outside the main stream of the churches' life are being exercised today.

Some new efforts towards the renewal of the "diaconal" ministry were begun more than 100 years ago by many churches in Europe, and, more recently, by those in other continents. The Orthodox churches, for instance in Greece and in Egypt, have begun to give new attention to certain forms of "diakonia"; Union churches, tracing back their traditions to different confessions, and church orders are beginning to examine the meaning of the diaconal ministry. Since the II. Vatican Council the Roman Catholic Church is reconsidering the ministry of the deacons. The New Testament term "diakonia" is often translated "ministry." The Church is anew confronted with the challenge to use those in whom she recognizes the spiritual gift (charisma) of "diakonia," and ordain them in this ministry. As long as the compassionate service of the Church is not clearly integrated in the structure of the life of the Church, the "diakonia" of Christ to the world is not fully presented and offered by the Church. "Diakonia," the serving aspect of the Church inherent in all the activities of the Christian and of the Church, must find a legitimate expression in a special ministry.

4. Ecumenical "Diakonia"

Finally, all individual churches may realize in the new ecumenical situation that the "diaconical" charismata are promised to the One Holy Church in its totality, and that such worldwide "diakonia" needs an adequate expression in joint service, rediscovering "diakonia," reflected in every relationship between the churches, as a basic element of "koinonia." "Diaconical" fellowship, therefore, is needed on the ecumenical level for practical purposes, such as solving complicated relief problems, and in order to bring the churches together to examine what Christ expects them to do.

The statement that "doctrine divides and service unites" is open to serious question. While a clinical ecumenical approach in meeting human need has often drawn churches across their denominational borders in common action, churches cling to independent action in their own name for the sake of building up their membership or enhancing their prestige.

The ecumenical approach to "diakonia" is proving to be far-reaching and has led the churches deeper into the mystery of Christ and into a firmer fellowship with each other. In the exercise of its "diaconical" function, the Body of Christ is being built up and is growing up to Him who is the Head. This involves sharing in the humbleness (kenosis) and the fullness of Christ in obedience to Him Who came as Servant and as Lord of Glory.

From *The Role of the "Diakonia" of the Church in Contemporary Society* (Geneva: World Council of Churches, 1966), 20–23.

ᴥ "Ordination of Women in Ecumenical Perspective," issued by the **World Council of Churches** in 1979, is a cautious examination of the issues surrounding the ordination of women. The text is framed as a dialogue, with issues posed as questions, followed by statements of probable outcomes or further thoughts. The text does not aim to give a definitive answer to the question of women's ordination; instead, it broadens the question by placing it in the context of the ecumenical dialogue on baptism, Eucharist, and ministry.

THE WORLD COUNCIL OF CHURCHES
"Ordination of Women in Ecumenical Perspective"

The following propositions do not attempt to be a comprehensive statement on the ministry of the Church, either in the New Testament or in its historical development. Rather, they attempt to raise certain points that are often neglected in ecumenical discussions, which put the question of women's ordination in a new perspective. These six points, stated in the form of questions, may be useful in raising new aspects of the women's ordination issue in view of growing ecumenical consensus on baptism, eucharist and ministry.

1. The New Community of the Church

On the question of women's ordination, the nature of the Church is an essential starting point. How does the way in which a church tradition describes the nature of the Church affect its views of the possibility of women's ordination?

All ministry is to be understood in the light of him who came "not to be served, but to serve" (Mark 10:45). In describing the nature of the Church, we should not bypass the witness of the historical community around Jesus. Contemporary Christians have recognized anew the radical nature of the fellowship drawn to Jesus. This fellowship broke through traditional social barriers. It included women as well as men in unconventional ways. It included those who were socially despised. It is even said "that prostitutes and tax collectors will go into the Kingdom of God ahead of the conventional religious leaders, scribes and pharisees" (Matt. 21:31).

This sense of a new community is empowered by the resurrection and Pentecost. Paul speaks of those who are in Christ as being "neither Jew nor Greek, not bond nor free, not male nor female; for all are one in Christ Jesus" (Gal. 3:28). This text is generally understood to have reflected a baptismal creed of the Church. It reflects the sense of oneness in Christ in a new creation, which is anticipated in the Church.

All Christians belong to the Royal Priesthood (I Pet. 2:9). The Christian is one who has been redeemed from earlier states of dependency and enslavement. We are the offspring of the free woman, not the slave woman (Gal. 4:31). We have been freed from the childhood state to become responsible adults (Gal. 3:23–26).

This sense of the Church as a community of equals is not simply a matter of early lack of organization. It contains an enduring insight into the nature of the redeemed humanity in Christ that is a constant source for the renewal of the Church. What is specific to some views of ordained ministry that excludes some baptized Christians, i.e. women, from this ministry? How can this be compatible with the nature of the Church as reflective of oneness in Christ wherein previously justified inequalities are nullified?

2. The Church in Ministries

What is the significance of the variety of ministries in the New Testament, shown by current New Testament research, for the understanding of ministry and for the debate on the ordination of women to the ministry?

In the earliest Church there were different gifts and ministries which may serve as paradigms for ministry today, for example, that of prophet or teacher in the local church, or of apostle in the mission of the Church. The paradigms for ministry were linked to various charismata. Women also received the charismata and acted as prophets (Acts 21:9), teachers (Acts 18:26) and missionaries (1 Cor. 16:13; Rom. 16:1ff.). (Further research is also needed on the issue of "Junias" (Rom. 16:7), and on the distinction between prophesying [propheteuein] and speaking [lalein] in the New Testament: I Cor. 11:15, I Cor. 14:31–35, Gal. 1:6–8.)

There are differences in the use of "apostolos" in the epistles of St. Paul and in Acts, where the title "apostolos" is reserved for the Twelve. Some interpret the role of the Twelve as specific and symbolic: they represented the 12 tribes of Israel who were to be gathered in with the coming of the Messiah; they are to sit on the 12 thrones of Israel, judging the tribes of Israel (Matt. 19:28). They had of necessity to be men—no woman could be a patriarch of Israel—as by the same token they had to be Jews. Is it important to distinguish between the unique function of the Twelve and the broader idea of apostleship which existed in the Church from the beginning?

In the early Church a new priesthood developed which was meant to be neither Jewish nor Hellenistic. Some traditions today affirm that development as legitimate; others do not, holding that Christ completed and abolished the priesthood, according to the letter to the Hebrews. Is the development of priesthood in some churches an impediment to the ordination of women to the full sacramental ministry in these churches?

The emphasis on the paradigm of teacher likewise contributed to the exclusion of women, not only for sociological reasons but also out of a hesitancy to hand over the Holy Scriptures to women. The Jewish custom of male teachers may have influenced this development. Given the new conditions for women today, must not the churches reconsider the teaching ministries of women?

In the New Testament times the "prophet" was an important paradigm for ministry. The early Christians preached the Christ as the fulfilment of the hope of Israel, interpreting the Scriptures and the signs of the time. They saw themselves as authorized to do this by the Spirit, quoting for example from Joel (Acts 2). These prophets were both men and women. What relevance has the demise of the role of the prophet for the ministry and for the exclusion of women from the ministry? Some churches have revitalized the prophetic ministry; what impact might this development have on ministry and on participation by women today?

The various churches have given greater emphasis to one or the other of the various paradigms of ministry. Is it possible to achieve a new sense of the wholeness of ministry by reconsidering those paradigms which have fallen into disuse?

3. Apostolic Succession and Tradition

What is the relation of the understanding of apostolic succession and Tradition to the understanding of ministry and to the question of the ordination of women?

The continuity which is designated "apostolic succession" was in the early Church primarily understood to be the handing on of the deposit of faith, though this was tied to ministry insofar as the bishop was seen as the guardian of faith. Apostolic succession can be seen as much broader than simply ministerial succession.

The fullness of the apostolic succession of the whole Church involves continuity in the permanent characteristics of the Church of the apostles: witness to the apostolic faith, proclamation and fresh interpretation of the apostolic gospel, transmission of ministerial responsibility, sacramental life, community in love, service for the needy, unity among local churches and sharing the gifts which the Lord has given to each.[22]

If apostolic succession is understood in this wider sense, does this influence our thinking as to whether women can be ordained?

The use of Tradition and of Scripture in the Church urgently calls for further study. Scripture and Tradition both belong to a continuing, living transmission process guided by the Spirit in which the Gospel is being brought to fulfilment. How are we then, while not losing continuity with the past, to move into the future?

It must also be said that certain arguments put forward in the past against ordaining women must be called into question. What does our present knowledge of human reproduction and evolution, as well as different anthropologies and sociology, have to say to the question of the ordination of women?

4. Incarnation and Priesthood

Is the maleness of the historical Jesus essential to the meaning of the incarnation? Does Christ have to be represented by a male priesthood?

Some argue that the incarnation of God in the male Jesus requires the representation of Christ to be through a male priesthood.

One Orthodox position would speak of priesthood in the following, somewhat different manner. There is only one Priest, Jesus Christ, in the full sense of the word, who (according to the Liturgy of St John Chrysostom) at the same time offers and is offered. In him the Old Testament priesthood finds its fulfilment. The Church is the place where the Holy Spirit works. By the gift of the Holy Spirit the Church participates in the unique priesthood of the Son of God Incarnate. Such is the meaning of the royal priesthood of all believers. But the Church charges certain of its members in whom it discerns such a charisma to actualize in one place here and now the unique priesthood of the God/Man, the very priesthood in which it participates. Such is the meaning of priestly ordination and of the special grace which it confers. The universal priesthood of all believers and the sacramental priesthood *both* derive from the unique priesthood. The bishop and the priest only actualize, by the grace of the Holy Spirit in time and space, the unique and eternal priesthood of the High Priest.

This argument would continue that, on the basis of bibli-

cal anthropology, men and women are different and at the same time one both in accordance with the order of creation and the order of redemption. This unity/diversity can be signified in the reconciled new creation which is beginning in the Church here and now, through the presence at the altar of a man and a woman, both ordained to ministries of equal dignity, though of different symbolic significance. Others would ask yet further, is not this truth of creation and redemption best exemplified when both women and men stand at the altar as priests?

5. The "Particular Role" of Women in the Church

Do women have particular contributions to offer to the life of the Church that are different from or complementary to the contributions of men?

Does the answer to this question, whether yes or no, have any implications for the ordination of women?

In "One Baptism, One Eucharist and a Mutually Recognized Ministry," p. 45, it is said: "Both men and women need to discover the full meaning of their specific contributions to the ministry of Christ. The Church is entitled to the style of ministry which can be provided by women as well as that which can be provided by men."

Many agree with the above statement. Others hesitate to use this language of "specific contributions" because they believe it creates certain expectations of women and of men which limit the fulfilment of their potential as persons.

Many say that the Church especially needs the caring, nourishing and nurturing that women have traditionally provided. Some emphasize that these qualities in women will bring a style of leadership to the Church that encourages partnership rather than domination/submission. Others believe that emphasizing these qualities in women leads to assigning them to specialized and/or secondary roles. Another way of addressing this problem may be: Can there be wholeness in the life of the Church and its ministry before both men and women fully contribute and participate in it?

6. Personal Vocation and True Ministry of the Church

What is the relation between personal vocation and the criteria for ministry applied by the Church?

---

22. "One Baptism, One Eucharist and a Mutually Recognized Ministry: Three Agreed Statements," *Faith and Order Paper* No. 73, 1078, 36.

There is a strong stream in Christianity which bases authority of ministry on the call of God. It is this call, tested as to its authenticity in various ways by the Church, which undergirds the authorization to minister.

Many in this stream of Christianity believe that insofar as the call of God is the foundation of ministry, and God calls whom God chooses, and since we cannot limit the outpouring of God's gift, basic questions are raised about the obedience of the Church to God if the Church refuses to test the vocations of some who believe themselves to be called to the ordained ministry.

Comment

These six propositions, coming out of an ecumenical dialogue, both narrow and intensify the discussion. They are posed, not with the hope of agreement, but with the aim of discerning which issues are central and which are marginal to the work of achieving mutual understanding.

From Günther Gassmann, ed., *Documentary History of Faith and Order* (Geneva: World Council of Churches, 1993), 153–56.

❧ The **Joint Working Group between the Roman Catholic Church and the World Council of Churches** was formed in 1965. The specific issue addressed here, in their *Seventh Report* (1998), is the need for dialogue in a prayerful, nonthreatening atmosphere, particularly on ethical issues where there may be disagreement.

Joint Working Group between the Roman Catholic Church and the World Council of Churches, Seventh Report

I. Introduction

With gratitude this Joint Working Group (JWG) has accepted its mandated responsibilities to serve as an instrument which helps the Roman Catholic Church (RCC) and the World Council of Churches (WCC) to carry out the ecumenical vocation of the churches. The experience of the present members reaffirms our predecessors' conviction expressed in the Sixth Report (1990): "The ecumenical movement is more than ever necessary if the churches and Christian communities are to be a sign and seed of the unity, peace and hope which the human family needs."

The JWG joyfully looks forward to the celebration in 1998 of the fiftieth anniversary of the World Council of Churches.

The theme of the WCC's eighth assembly (Harare, 3–14 December 1998) is "Turn to God—Rejoice in Hope." As a new millennium dawns the pilgrim people of God turns again to the one Triune God with renewed faith and sustains the hope of a restoration of that unity among all Christians which Christ wills. This holy objective, which transcends human power and gifts, engages our renewed efforts towards reconciliation while at the same time opens us to the future inspiration of the Holy Spirit.

[. . .] In this Seventh Report, [the JWG] offers to its parent bodies an account of its work since the WCC Assembly at Canberra in 1991. This report also seeks to inform readers who may be unaware of the history of the JWG and of specific RCC and WCC structures of relationships. [. . .]

II. The Collaboration between the Roman Catholic Church and the World Council of Churches and Its Member Churches

1. The WCC and the RCC

In 1965 the WCC central committee and the Roman Catholic authorities committed the WCC and the RCC to future collaboration through the visible expression of the Joint Working Group. Both partners realized then their differences. As collaborative efforts increased, the JWG came increasingly to respect the ways in which the WCC and the RCC differ in their nature, main structure, exercise of authority and styles of operation.

1. The WCC is a "fellowship" constituted by member churches. Churches which agree with the WCC Basis—that they "confess the Lord Jesus Christ as God and Saviour according to the Scriptures and therefore seek to fulfil together their common calling to the glory of the one God, Father, Son and Holy Spirit"—may apply for membership and are accepted if at least two-thirds of the member churches approve.

While the WCC's constitutional documents do not define what is meant by "Church" (and the Toronto statement of the 1950 central committee indicates that the WCC "cannot and should not be based on any one particular conception of the Church"), its Rules do set forth certain criteria which member churches must satisfy. These include a "sustained independent life and organization," the practice of "constructive ecumenical relations" and a membership of at least 25,000 (10,000 for associate member churches). In fact, nearly all member churches are organized within a single country. The Rules also specify certain "responsibilities of membership," among them participating in the Council's governing bodies and activities, encouraging ecumenical commitment and making an annual financial contribution commensurate with their means.

The constitutional documents specify that the WCC has no legislative authority over its member churches. Organized to "offer counsel and provide opportunity for united action in matters of common interest" (Constitution, art. IV), it may act on behalf of a member church or churches only when that church or those churches request it to do so; and the authority of any public statements it makes consists "only in the weight which they carry by their own truth and wisdom" (Rules, X.2). General policies for the WCC are set by the assembly of official delegates elected by all member churches, which meets every seven years. Implementation of these policies in specific activities is supervised by the central committee of about 150 members elected by each assembly to serve until the next one.

2. The RCC is a communion of local churches or dioceses, each entrusted to a bishop. It is one church with a worldwide mission and structure of sanctifying, teaching and governance through the "college of bishops," with and under the Bishop of Rome, the pastor of the whole Catholic Church who must ensure the communion of all the churches (cf. Code of Canon Law, canons 331, 375). "The concern for restoring unity involves the whole Church, faithful and clergy alike" (Decree on Ecumenism, 5). But "it pertains *especially to the entire College of Bishops and to the Apostolic See* to foster and direct among Catholics the ecumenical movement . . . , which by the will of Christ the Church is bound to promote" (canon 755; Code of Canons of the Eastern Churches, canon 902). Conferences of bishops are juridical institutions of a nation or territory, with specific duties and responsibilities designated by canon laws and other decrees; for example, the national conference decides whether or not to be a full member of a national or regional council of churches. No diocese, no conference is autonomous. This "hierarchical communion with the head of the college and its members" (canon 375), which fosters unity in diversity, is an essential element of the RCC's self-identity and of its ecumenical commitment.

2. The Pontifical Council for Promoting Christian Unity (PCPCU) and the WCC

The Pope "usually conducts the business of the universal Church by means of the Roman Curia . . . for the good

and service of the [local or particular] churches" (canon 360). Within the Roman Curia is the Pontifical Council for Promoting Christian Unity (PCPCU) which has "the competency and duty of promoting the unity of Christians." The PCPCU is entrusted with the correct interpretation and carrying out of the Catholic principles of ecumenism; and with initiating, promoting or coordinating ecumenical efforts at national, regional, and worldwide levels. The PCPCU is responsible for relations with the WCC and for bilateral relations. The PCPCU facilitates WCC relations with other departments of the Roman Curia, such as those for the evangelization of peoples, interreligious dialogue, justice and peace, aid and development, the laity, and Catholic education.

The PCPCU members are from national conferences of bishops and departments of the Roman Curia: over 30 cardinals, archbishops and bishops, and 25 official consultors. They meet in plenary every 18–24 months. The PCPCU has a full-time staff of 23 persons.

3. Functions, Operations and Structure of the JWG

[. . .] 1. The JWG is a consultative forum. It has no authority in itself but reports to its parent bodies—the WCC assembly and central committee, and the PCPCU—which approve policies and programmes.

It undertakes its spiritual and pastoral tasks in a spirit of prayerful conviction that God through Christ in the Spirit is guiding the one ecumenical movement. The group tries to discern the will of God in contemporary situations, and to stimulate the search for visible unity and common witness, in particular through collaboration at world, regional, national and local levels between the RCC, the WCC, and the WCC member churches. This means giving attentive support and encouragement to whatever contributes to ecumenical progress.

The JWG initiates, evaluates and sustains forms of collaboration between the WCC and the RCC, especially between the various organs and programmes of the WCC and the RCC. Its styles and forms of collaboration are flexible, as it discerns similarities and differences which foster or hinder WCC/RCC relations. Concentrating on ad hoc initiatives, it keeps new structures to a minimum in proposing new steps and programmes, carefully setting priorities and using its limited resources of personnel, time and finances. [. . .]

The Ecumenical Dialogue on Moral Issues: Potential Sources of Common Witness or of Divisions

I. Ethics and the Ecumenical Movement

Of increasing urgency in the ecumenical movement, in the relationships between the churches called to give common witness, is their need to address those moral issues which all persons face and to communicate moral guidance to church members and to society at large.

1. Cultural and social transformations, conflicting basic values and scientific and technological advances are fraying the moral fabric of many societies. This context not only provokes questioning of traditional moral values and positions, but it also raises new complex ethical issues for the consciousness and conscience of all human beings.

2. At the same time, renewed expectations rise in and beyond the churches that religious communities can and should offer moral guidance in the public arena. Christians and those of other faiths or of secular persuasions desire to live peacefully and justly in a humane society. Can the churches together already offer moral guidance as their contribution to the common good, amidst experienced confusion and controversy?

3. Pressing personal and social moral issues, however, are prompting discord among Christians themselves and even threatening new divisions within and between churches. This increases the urgent need for the churches together to find ways of dealing with their controversial ethical issues. By taking the time and care to listen patiently to other Christians, we may understand the pathways by which they arrive at moral convictions and ethical positions, especially if they differ from our own. Otherwise, Christians will continue often to caricature one another's motives, reasonings and ways of behaviour, even with abusive language and acts. Dialogue should replace diatribe.

Other Christians or other churches holding diverging moral convictions can threaten us. They can question our own moral integrity and the foundations of our religious and ethical beliefs. They can demean the authority, credibility and even integrity of our own church. Whenever an individual or a community selects a moral position or practice to be the litmus test of authentic faith and the sole criterion of the fundamental unity of the Church, emotions rise high so that it becomes difficult to hear one another.

Christians, while "speaking the truth in charity" (Eph 4:15), are called upon, as far as possible, "to maintain the unity of the Spirit in the bond of peace" (Eph 4:3) and avoid wounding further the *koinonia* which already exists, although imperfectly, among Christians.

4. Therefore, if some ethical issues arouse passionate emotions and create awkward ecumenical relations, the churches should not shun dialogue, for these moral issues also can become church-reconciling means of common witness. A variety of issues are woven into the moral positions of communities. In a prayerful, non-threatening atmosphere, dialogue can locate more precisely where the agreements, disagreements and contradictions occur. Dialogue can affirm those shared convictions to which the churches should bear common witness to the world at large. Furthermore, the dialogue can discern how ethical beliefs and practices relate to that unity in moral life which is Christ's will.

5. Attentive concern for the complexities of the moral life should not cause Christians to lose sight of what is most fundamental for them all: the starting and ending point is the grace of God in Jesus Christ and the Spirit as mediated in the Church and in creation. Our life in God is the fundamental continuing source of our movement towards deeper *koinonia*. Only God's initiating and sustaining grace enables Christians to transcend moral differences, overcome divisions and live their unity in faith.

II. The Church as Moral Environment for Discipleship

Included in the call to the Church to be the sign and instrument of salvation in a transformed world, is the call to create a moral environment which helps disciples of Christ to shape their personal and communal ethical lives through formation and deliberation.

1. The Church has the enduring task to be a community of "The Way" (cf. Acts 9:2; 22:4), the home, the family which provides the moral environment of right living and conduct "in Christ," who in the Spirit makes known "the paths of life" to his disciples (Acts 2:28; Ps 16:11).

Discipleship holds together what Christians believe, how believing Christians act and how they give to fellow Christians and to others an account of why they so believe and so act. Discipleship is the way of believing and acting in the daily struggle to be a faithful witness of Jesus Christ who commissions his community of disciples to proclaim, teach and live "all that I have commanded you" (Acts 1:8; Matt 28:20).

2. Within the *koinonia* the disciple of Christ is not alone in the process of discerning how to incarnate in one's life the ethical message of the gospel. Faithful discipleship arises out of private prayer and public worship, of fellowship in sharing each other's joys and bearing each other's burdens. It is nour-

ished by the examples of the saints, the wisdom of teachers, the prophetic vision of the inspired and the guidance of ministerial leaders.

In real but imperfect communion with one another, each church expects itself and other churches to provide a moral environment through formation and deliberation.

3. Formation and deliberation describe the shaping of human character and conduct, the kinds of Christian persons we are and become, and the kinds of actions we decide to do. The scope of Christian morality comprises both our "being" and "doing."

Useful for showing the inseparable dimensions of moral life are the distinctions between moral vision, virtue, value and obligation.

Moral vision is a person's, a community's or a society's "basic script" of the moral realm, the vision of what belongs to the good, the right and the fitting. A moral vision encompasses, informs and organizes virtues, values and obligations.

In the Christian moral life various summaries of teaching and different images express the gospel vision itself: the commandments of love of God and of neighbour; the prophetic teachings on justice and mercy; the Beatitudes; the fruits of the Spirit; ascetic ascent and pilgrimage; costly discipleship and the imitation of Christ; stewarding a good land. These and other biblical images suggest pathways which bring definition and coherence to the moral landscape.

Moral virtues are desirable traits of a person's moral character, such as integrity, humility and patience, compassion and forgiveness; or prudence, justice, temperance and fortitude. In an analogous way one can predicate these virtues of communities and societies.

Moral values are not so much these internalized qualities of character but those moral goods which individuals and society prize, such as respect for the dignity of the human person, freedom and responsibility, friendship, equality and solidarity, and social justice.

Moral obligations are those duties which persons owe one another in mutual responsibility, in order to live together in harmony and integrity, such as telling the truth and keeping one's word; or those imperatives of a biblical moral vision such as loving and forgiving the neighbour, including enemies.

4. This way of describing the scope of morality (vision, virtue, value, obligation) can provide interrelated criteria for the Church's moral task: to be ever the witness to "our great God and Saviour Jesus Christ who sacrificed himself for us in order to set us free from all wickedness and to purify a people

so that it could be his very own and would have no ambition except to do good" (Titus 2:13–14). A Christian ethic is reductionistic and deficient if it addresses only one or another of these four elements; all of them interact and modify one another. Even when it does address all four, different configurations may characterize its response.

5. The task of moral formation and deliberation is one which the churches share. All churches seek to enhance the moral responsibility of their members for living a righteous life and to influence positively the moral standards and well-being of the societies in which they live.

This identifies an ecumenical objective: the quality of the moral environment that churches create together in and through worship, education and nurture, and social witness. Reverence for the dignity of each person created "in the image of God" (Gen 1:27), the affirmation of the fundamental equality of women and men, the pursuit of creative nonviolent strategies for resolving conflict in human relationships and the responsible stewardship of creation—these are positive contributions of churches through the moral environment they foster. On the other hand, churches can also distort character and malform conscience. They have at times undergirded national chauvinism and ethnocentrism and actively discriminated against persons on the basis of race or nationality, class or gender.

III. Common sources and different pathways of moral deliberation

For those pathways of moral reflection and deliberation which churches use in coming to ethical decisions, the churches share the Scriptures and have at their disposal such resources as liturgy and moral traditions, catechisms and sermons, sustained pastoral practices, the wisdom distilled from past and present experiences, and the arts of reflection and spiritual discernment. Yet church traditions configure these common resources in different ways.

1. The biblical vision by itself does not provide Christians with all the clear moral principles and practical norms they need. Nor do the Scriptures resolve every ethical case. Narratives join many instructions about proper conduct—general commandments and prohibitions, prophetic exhortations and accusations, counsels of wisdom, legal and ritual prescriptions and so forth. What moral theology names universal principles or norms are in the biblical texts mixed with specific but ever valid commandments and particular provisional prescriptions. The Scriptures' use of imagery in provocative, often paradoxical ways further makes interpretations of biblical moral teaching difficult.

Nevertheless, there is general consensus that by prayerfully studying the Scriptures and the developing traditions of biblical interpretations, by reflecting on human experiences and by sharing insights within a community, Christians can reach reasonable judgments and decisions in many cases of ethical conduct.

2. Within the history of the Church, Christians have developed ways of reflecting systematically on the moral life by the ordering of biblical concepts and images and by rational argument. Such methods intend to introduce clarity and consistency where divergences of discernment threaten to foster confusion and chaos.

For example, one tradition suggests different levels of moral insight and distinguishes between first-order (and unchanging) principles and second-order (and possibly changing) rules. Or more recently, the language of "hierarchy of values" distinguishes between those core values at the heart of Christian discipleship and those other values which are less central yet integral to Christian morality. By emphasizing the "first-order principles" or the "core values," Christians can discover how much they already share, without reducing moral truth or searching for a least common denominator.

3. Christian traditions, however, have different estimates of human nature and of the capacity of human reason. Some believe that sin has so corrupted human nature that reason cannot arrive at moral truths. Others maintain that sin has only wounded human nature, and that with divine grace and human discipline, reason can still reach many universally applicable truths about moral living.

For example, by appealing to Scripture and Tradition, to reason and experience, the Roman Catholic Church has developed its understanding of human person and human dignity, of human acts and their goals, and of human rights and responsibilities. In its tradition of moral reflection and teaching, the supreme norm of human life is that universal divine law by which God, in wisdom and love, orders, directs and governs the whole world and all ways of the human community. By nature and through grace, God enables every person intelligently to grasp this divine law, so that all men and women can come to perceive unchangeable truth more fully. Thus the revealed law of God and what one calls "natural law" together express that undivided will of God which obliges human beings to seek and to know it as best they can, and to live as conscience dictates.

4. The tracing of the different pathways which link vision with judgment and decision may help Christians to locate and evaluate some of their differences. For example, Chris-

tians who adopt the language of human rights have an effective way of highlighting concern for the powerless, the poor and the marginalized. While different parties may agree on certain fundamental rights, they can reach different, even contradictory applications; for example, rights to religious freedom. Moreover, formulations and extensions of rights have become the subject of much dispute, especially in addressing such ethical issues as human reproduction and abortion.

One Christian vision of the integrity of sexual life links sexual relationship with procreation by an interpretation of natural law and of the biblical accounts of creation. Some churches, such as the Roman Catholic Church, hold this position. Other churches judge it most difficult, even impossible to affirm such a link. Those which find the appeal to natural law inconclusive accept the possible separation of the good of procreation from the good of sexual relationship, and use this argument to approve contraceptive means in marriage.

5. The Christian stance towards war is another example of different pathways which lead to different conclusions. Every tradition accepts the biblical vision of peace between neighbours and, more specifically, the New Testament witness to nonviolent attitudes and acts. A major division has arisen, however, from different judgments concerning the Church's collaboration with civic powers as a means of influencing human history. Those churches which have opted for collaboration accept some versions of the "just war" theory; they tolerate, even encourage, the active participation of patriotic Christians in some wars between nations and in armed revolutions within a country. But groups within these same churches agree with those other churches which choose to witness within the political order as non-compromising opponents to all use of military force, because it is contrary to the nonviolent, peace-making way of Christ. These Christians abstain from bearing arms, even if that be civil disobedience.

Here one can identify the precise point of difference in major theological options which have fundamental consequences for the policy of a church towards war and the conduct of its members.

IV. Different Authoritative Means of Moral Discernment

[. . .] 1. The formation of conscience and the development of connected positions on specific ethical issues follow various pathways among different traditions, such as the Orthodox or Roman Catholic, Reformed or Lutheran, Baptist or

Friends (Quaker). Every church believes that its members have the task of rightly applying their faith more fully to daily life. All traditions have their own ways of beginning, moving through and concluding their moral deliberations, and of acting upon them. There are different ways of discussing, consulting and arriving at decisions and of transmitting and receiving them.

Influencing this process are the different ways in which they understand the action of the Holy Spirit and the exercise of the specific role of ministerial leadership in moral discernment and guidance.

In the Roman Catholic Church, bishops, according to the gift received from the Holy Spirit, and under his guidance, in their ministry of oversight (*episkope*), are the authoritative guardians and interpreters of the whole moral law, that is, both the law of the gospel and the natural law. Bishops have the pastoral responsibility and duty of offering moral guidance, even sometimes definitive judgment that a specific action is right or wrong. Moral theologians provide ethical discernment within the community. Confessors, pastoral counsellors and spiritual directors seek to take account of the unique needs of the individual person.

In the Orthodox Church decisions on ethical issues rest with the hierarchy, whether a synod of bishops or an individual bishop, who are inspired by the Scriptures and the long tradition of the church's pastoral care and moral guidance. The main concern is the spiritual welfare of the person in his or her relationship to God and to fellow human beings. The prudential application of church law and general norms (*oikonomia*) sometimes temper strictness, sometimes increase severity. It is a principal means for both spiritual growth and moral guidance. Orthodox tradition cherishes also the role of experienced spiritual fathers and mothers, and in the process of moral reflection it stresses prayer among both laity and ordained.

Other churches do not ascribe to ministerial leadership this competency in interpretation or such authority of judgment. They arrive at certain ethical judgments by different polities of consulting and decision-making which involve clergy and laity. The Reformed traditions, for example, hold that the living Word of the sovereign God is always reforming the Church in faith and life. Doctrinal and ethical judgments should be based on the holy Scripture and informed by the whole tradition of the Church catholic and ecumenical. But no church body has the final authority in defining the word of God. Redeemed and fallible human beings within the Church faithfully rely on the process, inspired by the Holy Spirit, whereby they select their ordained and lay leaders and

reach authoritative but reformable expressions of faith and positions on personal and social ethics.

2. Thus, ecumenical dialogue on moral issues should include the nature, mission and structures of the church, the role of ministerial authority and its use of resources in offering moral guidance, and the response to the exercise of such authority within the Church. These subjects will in turn help to locate ecumenical gifts and opportunities for common witness, as well as tensions and conflicts.

First, the *tensions and conflicts.* Is there anxiety and unease because many fear the erosion of the foundational sources of Scripture and Tradition, and of church authority which they believe to be most reliable in guiding Christian conscience and conduct? Or are the ways in which particular church traditions understand, accept and use the sources and authorities themselves the source of tension and divisiveness? Does deliberation of ethical issues generate anxiety and anger because some persons negatively experience these sources and their use—for example, the interpretation of Scripture and Tradition in such ways that they present the oppressive face of social and theological patriarchy?

One often best understands persistent unchanging stands on a specific issue not by focusing narrowly on it, but by considering what people sense is at stake for life together in society if certain sources, structures and authorities are ignored or even ridiculed. For example, in some settings questions about the beginning and ending of life—abortion and euthanasia—carry such moral freight.

Furthermore, some churches stress more than others the structures of authority and formal detailed statements on belief and morality. This can create an imbalance and lack of realism in the dialogue if one easily compares the official teachings of some churches with the more diffuse estimates of the general belief and practice of others.

Thus, awareness of the moral volatility which surrounds the sources and authorities used—which they are, by whom and how they are interpreted, and with what kinds of concerns they are associated—is critical for understanding why some moral issues are difficult and potentially divisive among Christians.

3. Second, *gifts and opportunities.* Discerning the gifts in church traditions that may lie unnoticed as treasures for the moral life poses another set of questions for the ecumenical dialogue:

What do inherited understandings and forms of *koinonia* (communion or fellowship), *diakonia* (service) and *martyria* (witness) mean for moral formation today?

Which visions, virtues, values and obligations are nurtured by the *lex orandi, lex credendi, lex vivendi* (the rule of praying, of believing, of living) as particular traditions and structures embody them?

Which practices in the varied traditions contribute to the legitimate difference and authentic diversity of the moral life of the one Church? How can both common and distinctive practices contribute to the moral richness of the *koinonia*?

In dialogue Christians thus need both to recognize the rich resources they share for moral formation and to ask critically how these in fact function in a variety of contexts, cultures and peoples.

V. Ecumenical Challenges to Moral Formation and Deliberation

Churches which share real but imperfect koinonia *face new challenges as communities of moral formation and deliberation: the pluralism of moral positions, the crisis of moral authority, changing moral judgments on traditional issues, and positions on new ones.*

1. Christians agree that there is a moral universe which is grounded in the wisdom and will of God, but they may have different interpretations of God's wisdom, of the nature of that universe and of the degree to which human beings are called to fashion it as co-creators with God.

We cannot deny three facts:

First, Christians do share a long history of extensive unity in moral teaching and practice, flowing in part from a shared reflection on common sources, such as the Ten Commandments and the Beatitudes.

Second, divided Christian communities eventually did acquire some differences in ways of determining moral principles and acting upon them.

Third, these differences have led today to such a pluralism of moral frameworks and positions within and between the ecclesial traditions that some positions appear to be in sharp tension, even in contradiction. The same constellation of basic moral principles may admit of a diversity of rules which intend to express a faithful response to biblical vision and to these principles. Even the explicit divine commandment "Thou shalt not kill" receives conflicting applications; for example, yes or no to the death penalty as such or for certain crimes.

2. The crisis of moral authority within the churches further complicates effective moral formation and deliberation. Even where a church has an established moral tradition, some members strongly propose alternative positions. In fact, church members are becoming more vocal and persistent in sharp criticism of authoritative moral teaching and practice, and they use the same sources as the basis for differing ethical positions. The fashioning of effective moral formation and deliberation in these settings is an urgent ecumenical task.

3. The process of the formulation and reception of ethical decisions also poses a major challenge of participation: who forms and formulates the churches' moral decisions, using which powers of influence and action and which instruments of consultation? How do church members and the society at large assess, appropriate and respond to official church pronouncements? What are the channels of such a response, and what kinds of response are encouraged or discouraged?

4. Are not the conditions and structures of dialogue themselves prime ethical issues for churches? They are potentially either divisive or reconciling. They can either enhance or undermine *koinonia* in faith, life and witness. One starting point is simply to acknowledge that the way in which a church (or churches together) orders and structures its decision-making and then publicly communicates its decisions already embodies a social ethic, and influences moral teaching and practice. Structures, offices and roles express moral values or disvalues. Ways of exercising power, governance and access have moral dimensions. To ignore this is to fail to understand why moral issues and the ways in which they are addressed can be so divisive, even within the same church.

5. The extent to which moral judgments can change needs candid dialogue. For example, until the middle of the 18th century, historical churches, even in their official statements, acquiesced in the practice of slavery; some leaders even proposed biblical and theological arguments to sanction it. Today all churches judge slavery to be an intrinsic evil, everywhere and always wrong. What does this kind of change of a former established teaching of the churches mean for understanding that degree of unity in faithful moral teaching which full communion requires?

Christians in dialogue should not ignore or hide evidence of change in moral teaching or practice. Churches do not always welcome such openness, despite their emphasis on human finitude and sin in the historical development of teachings and practices. Moreover, the interpretation of change in moral teaching is itself a source of disagreement and tension. While some may interpret the change as positive growth in faithful moral understanding, others may judge it as easy compromise or rank failure.

Apartheid is a particular example, where after long deliberation, some families of churches went beyond the rejection of apartheid as inconsistent with the gospel to judge those who maintained apartheid to be Christian as placing themselves outside the fellowship of the Church.

Hence, an ecumenical approach to morality requires the awareness of different evaluations of changing moral traditions.

6. Several new *ethical issues* especially challenge ecumenical collaboration when the churches have no clear and detailed precedents, much less experience and consensus. Only to begin a long list of examples: economic policies in a world of "haves" and "have-nots"; immigration and refugee regulations within and between nations; industrialization and the environment; women's rights in society and in the churches; *in vitro* fertilization, genetic engineering and other biomedical developments. Christians and others experience the urgency of these unavoidable, complex ethical issues. They expect the churches to offer moral guidance on them.

Even the experts in the empirical sciences may offer conflicting data or disagree on the implications of scientific findings. The ways in which the churches together seek out, gather and order the facts with the best knowledge available from the empirical scientists is already an ecumenical challenge. In the light of this, Christians can responsibly address the moral implications of issues, and offer guidance.

VI. Christian Moral Witness in a Pluralistic Society

Christians are called to witness in the public forum to their common moral convictions with humility and with respect for others and their convictions. They should seek dialogue and collaboration with those of other faith communities, indeed with all persons of good will who are committed to the well-being of humanity.

1. In the political process of legislation and judicial decision, churches may rightly raise their prophetic voice in support or in protest. In common witness they can take a firm stand when they believe that public decisions or laws affirm or contradict God's purposes for the dignity of persons or the integrity of creation.

One can highlight the example of common witness of Christians in the struggle against apartheid and "ethnic cleansing." In fact, such moral issues of human rights and equality have been community-building experiences of *koinonia* in faith and witness, which some perceive as profound experiences of "church."

2. Sometimes churches and Christian advocacy groups may agree on the basic values which they should promote,

yet they disagree about the means that should be used, especially in the political arena. In such situations, they should seek collaboration as much as their agreement allows, and at the same time articulate the reasons for their disagreement. Disagreement over some particular points or means to an end should not rule out all collaboration. In these cases, however, it is all the more important to be open and explicit about the areas of disagreement, so as to avoid confusion in common witness.

3. In the public arena, the churches are one family of moral community among others, whether religious or secular. Moral discernment is not the exclusive preserve of Christians. Christian moral understandings and approaches to ethical issues should be open to evaluate carefully the moral insights and judgments of others. Often moral traditions overlap, even when the approaches and idioms of language may be different.

In any case, the manner and the methods by which the churches publicly commend their own moral convictions must respect the integrity of others and their civic rights and liberties. For the authority of the churches in the public moral debate of pluralistic societies is the authority of their moral wisdom, insights and judgments as these commend themselves to the intelligence and conscience of others.

From *Joint Working Group between the Roman Catholic Church and the World Council of Churches, Seventh Report* (Geneva: World Council of Churches, 1998), 1–3, 31–40. [Brackets in original except in introduction.]

What **Richard Norris,** an Anglican theologian, proposes in "On 'Full Communion' between the Episcopal Church and the Evangelical Lutheran Church in America" (1997) was formally realized in 1999 and 2000, when the Evangelical Lutheran Church in America's Churchwide Assembly and the Episcopal Church's General Convention each voted to recognize a new relationship between their two Churches.

RICHARD NORRIS

"On 'Full Communion' between the Episcopal Church and the Evangelical Lutheran Church in America"

Lutherans and Anglicans have been on speaking terms for a long time now, both in this country and elsewhere. Of late, however, the two groups of churches have passed from being on speaking terms to actually talking. The Church of England and the Church of Sweden have for many years been in communion. In certain parts of the Third World, I gather,

Anglican and Lutheran talking has gotten to the point where the parties find it hard to understand why they are still—at least figuratively—sitting on opposite sides of a table. But then in the Third World churches need each other; and in Europe they tend to be insulated from one another's characteristic madnesses by national boundaries; and both of these circumstances—need and relative distance—provide a soil that is friendly to ecumenical enterprises. In North America, however, the situation is different. Here Anglicans and Lutherans live and work cheek by jowl—sharing, as it were, the same kitchen and bathroom; and one would expect, under these conditions, that their relations would be marked more by a spirit of tactful reserve than by a willingness to open painful issues. What is more, both groups, under the pressures of a culture that no longer acknowledges Christian faith as either normative or even normal, are increasingly preoccupied with what might be called self-rediscovery—the cultivation of their own distinctive roots and character. And my point is simply this. It is amazing, and even astounding, that, in such circumstances, and in the course of a mere twenty years of cautious conversation and theological wrangling, these two denominations should have come to the point of seriously considering a concordat leading to full communion.

It is not my business here, however, simply to be lavish in praise—nor, I think, simply to act as a reporter. There are others who have been much closer than I to the processes of the Lutheran-Episcopal Dialogue; and they can do a much better job of explaining in detail the terms of the proposed Concordat and the steps by which it has been formulated. I am sure in any case that we all understand the basic principles of the proposal:

> first, that it does not contemplate a merger of denominations, but an ecclesiologically odd, if not utterly novel, arrangement according to which two bodies that occupy the same ground will continue to be two *considered as denominations* while acknowledging themselves to be one *considered as bodies of churches;* and second, that it proposes to overcome what the LED III Report aptly calls "the historic impasse"—a tactful phrase, this, for the inconvenience regularly occasioned by Anglican attachment to bishops in historic succession—by a procedure which, *mutatis mutandis,* follows the pattern originally laid down in the union that created the Church of South India.

Supposing that these two principles are clear, then, what I propose to do is to comment on them at some modest

length, by way of intimating a possible interpretation of their meaning. If the interpretation I propose adds up to a commendation of the scheme and not a questioning of it, I can offer no apologies for that.

I turn, then, to the first of our two principles, which I have formulated, using my own, perhaps contentious, language, as espousal of "an . . . arrangement according to which two bodies that occupy the same ground will continue to be two *considered as denominations* while acknowledging themselves to be one *considered as bodies of churches."* The Concordat, of course, and the LED III Report have another, terser phrase for this: they call it "full communion." For our purposes here, however, I prefer my alternative formulation for several reasons: first, because it helps us to grasp more clearly one of the problems that this proposal seeks to solve; second, because the explicit distinction it makes between "denomination" and "church" is in my judgment strictly necessary if we are to grasp the point of the idea of full communion; and third, because it helps to bring into focus the issue around which, we may be sure, discussion of the Concordat will center. Let me explain, then.

The phrase "full communion"—to which, let it be firmly said, I have no objection whatever—is a traditional one. I tend to render it, for purposes of clarity, as "equivalence and interchangeability of parts between two separate systems"—which misses out, to be sure, some of the more mystical implications of that word "communion," but nevertheless, like the Lutheran expression "altar and pulpit fellowship," captures the kind of relationship that it presupposes. "Full communion," in this sense, existed in the ancient church between, say, the church of Corinth and the church of Rome. And what it implied was that in any given place there was just one Christian "assembly" or church, and that the church in one place acknowledged the church in another as, to use my language, its "equivalent." Originally, then, this relationship that we call "full communion" *constituted* the unity of the church catholic, which was simply—if that is the appropriate word—*a communion of local churches.* No one in those days would have known how to distinguish, as ecumenists do now, between "organic unity" and "full communion."

Why is this? Well the basic reason is that as time has gone on, Christians have begun to use the word "church" in new ways. First they started to employ it, no doubt inoffensively, to describe the churches within the boundaries of a particular nation: as when we say, for example, "The Church of England," or "The Prussian Union Church." Then, and especially in the United States, where adherents of all these old national churches, not to mention their several groups of dissenters, organized themselves as separate bodies, these *associations of churches* began to call themselves "church": e.g., the Evangelical Lutheran *Church* in America; or the Episcopal *Church*. So ingrained has this way of speech become—in spite of the more cautious nomenclature of bodies like the Missouri *Synod* or the American Baptist *Convention*—that if I stand here and say, without further qualification, "the churches," you will probably think I mean "the denominations." Yet if we were to speak with strict propriety, we should have to say that denominations are really, as I have suggested, no more than associations of local churches—however you want to define "local church"—that share a common tradition and some sort of common purse, and agree to certain arrangements for common decision-making. Furthermore, when you think about it, the *basis* of these associations is— dare I use the word?—the full communion of their member churches.

Now I say all this in order to make two points. On the one hand, I want to suggest that, historically and even perhaps eccesiologically speaking, what we call "denominations" are very odd and anomalous phenomena indeed, not only because they lurk somewhere in the no-man's land between the local, gathered church and the church universal, but above all because their very existence presupposes something that would have boggled the minds of our forebears: that there can be more than one church in one place. Then on the other hand, I want to insist that in North America, this phenomenon of the denomination has formed, not merely our perception of the meaning of "church," but also the social reality of the church as we experience it. Given these two circumstances, moreover, we can understand the distinction that is made between "organic unity" and "full communion." The former refers to the process by which one takes two denominations and turns them into one. It *presupposes* therefore that the denomination and its ways of organizing itself are normative: that the denomination is properly, and not merely figuratively or derivatively, "church." Thus unity turns out to mean, in practice, *one denomination.* "Full communion," on the other hand, focuses in reality on local churches. What it presupposes is the *ecclesial equivalence* of local church bodies: even if, as it happens in our case, these bodies, somewhat oddly, sit side by side in the same place and belong to separate organizations.

We must be careful, then, in the way we talk about this project. There is a concordat to be made, and it is being made between two denominations, two associations of local churches. But the denominations as such will be affected by it only secondarily. Its primary effect will be, or should be, on the local churches that constitute them. The latter, to put the matter as crudely and offensively as possible, will wake up one morning to discover that they are in principle interchangeable. You may well ask, therefore, why they should be separate at all: or, to put the question concretely, what the point might be of their belonging to different "associations." And that is a question worth the answering.

It seems to me that there are, broadly speaking, two possible answers to this question. The first I will submit only by title; for it can be put tersely, as follows: in matters of church unity, as in many others, it is important, at least initially, to concede a certain margin of separateness to compensate for the operation of original sin—which, as we have been wisely told, "remaineth, yea even in the redeemed." But there is also, I think, a more positive, even up-beat, reason.

Denominations are not just organizations. It is true that nowadays, as they have, inevitably, assumed many of the trappings of centralized corporate bureaucracies, we tend to envisage them primarily in that role. We do well not to forget, however, that they originated in times when organization was fairly exiguous, and that the primary function they performed was to perpetuate and disseminate certain religious and theological traditions: certain concrete ways or styles of Christian thought and life. Now I am aware that people often complain of the "narrowness" of such traditions; but I am also conscious that there never has been a livable way of life, Christian or other, that was not "narrow" in the sense of being *specific* and *concrete.* I have come to the conclusion, therefore, that the trouble with denominational traditions is not their "narrowness," but the false exclusiveness that isolation has forced upon them. I have been formed in a certain theological and devotional tradition, and I am glad of it: glad both of its maddening particularity, and of the way in which it has helped me to value other and different traditions. It has rooted me firmly enough in Christian faith so that I can discern that same faith in others among its many embodiments. Hence when ecumenical proposals are being made, I bridle a bit when I judge that they are indifferent or even hostile to such narrownesses. It is not that I want all the world to be Anglican: that would make life far too dull. But neither do I want that particularity called Anglicanism to be "merged," if I may phrase it so. And I suppose that there are others here who take the same view, *mutatis mutandis.*

And this means to me that after we have made all the unpleasant remarks we can think of about "denominations"—

and I, as you have no doubt gathered, can think of quite a number—it remains the case that in our society it has been these "associations of churches" that have indeed fostered and preserved theological and devotional traditions that, precisely in their differences, complement, enliven, and correct each other. Hence I think that there is justification for the kind of proposal that this Concordat makes: it hopes that Lutherans will remain intensely and seriously Lutheran and Anglicans intensely and frivolously Anglican, and that between them they may not only correct each other, but show the world *more* of the infinite riches of Christ than either could manage alone. On this ground, I think its proposal of "full communion" as the way towards Christian unity to be honest in its affirmation that denominational separateness has some uses in our world, even if it does not have as many as we sometimes think.

Full communion, however, as I have said, presupposes some sort of *equivalence* of churches: indeed, to use my more radical term, it presupposes a certain level or degree of *interchangeability*. I do not move from a Chevrolet to a Toyota without the assurance that the latter is, in the same sense as the former, an automobile. By the same token, if two Christian bodies are to enjoy full communion, they must be churches *in the same sense*—and, furthermore, recognize that fact, which automobiles cannot be called upon to do. And so, though at a modest distance, we approach our "historic impasse" and the solution that this Concordat suggests for it.

But before we get down to the nitty-gritty issue of bishops, let us try to identify the roots of the problem; for the issue about bishops is, it seems to me, merely a symptom of a deeper problem about how one identifies "church." Lutherans and Anglicans alike would agree with the classic principle that you can identify "church" by (a) the preaching of the gospel and (b) the administration of the sacraments of Baptism and the Lord's Supper, on the proviso (c) that both of these activities are carried out in accordance with the Scriptures. Nevertheless, history and experience have brought them to read or interpret this principle in slightly different ways. Lutherans have stressed, if I understand them properly, that at the heart of each of these items lies *the gospel,* which is the message of the Scriptures, the meaning of the sacraments, and the burden of the preaching. Hence they identify a body as "church" by whether or not the gospel of God's grace is professed, taught, and preached there; and this means, in practice, that the questions they ask of another body of Christians tend to be *doctrinal* questions.

Anglicans, on the other hand, have tended to read the

same principle in the light of the communal *institutions* it refers to and presupposes. Hence the well-known—perhaps I should say "notorious"—Lambeth Quadrilateral, which is precisely a set of guidelines for what a proper church ought to be equipped with, lists four *institutions:* the Scriptures, the ecumenical creeds, the Gospel sacraments, and the historic threefold ministry. I call these "institutions" because of course what the Quadrilateral contemplates is not "things"—some books, a text, bread and wine, the odd elder or bishop, all just, as it were, lying about—but continuing, reiterated communal *practices:* the Scriptures read and expounded in the congregation, the creeds taught and professed, the sacraments celebrated, under the aegis of a ministry that is of and for the whole church.

So we have, in effect, what looks like a disagreement. On the one hand, there is the view that "church" is identified by *what it says;* and on the other, the view that it is characterized by the continuity of certain institutionalized practices—you might say, by what it habitually *does.* Neither of these views, be it noted, is talking about what makes churches nice, or comfortable, or relevant, or socially useful, or prophetic, or holy. Both are concerned with *minimals:* with what it takes to be a *mere* church.

But how deep is this disagreement? The achievement, it seems to me, of the Lutheran-Episcopal dialogue in this country is to have recognized that the disagreement is a great deal more superficial than might at first appear.

A reading of either the *Niagara Report* or of the *Concordat of Agreement* will show, I think, how as a matter of fact the views of the two sets of participants tend to converge.

On the one hand, Episcopalians seem to have got the point of the Lutheran criticism of idle "institutionalism." They have come to appreciate the point that the "symbols" generated within the church's institutionalized practices—like a bishop or a book or a puddle of water or a piece of bread—can be misunderstood, misused, and corrupted. Furthermore, they now appreciate the genuine contingency of these symbols, by which I mean the fact that, historically speaking, they *might* have turned out to be other than they are—*other* creeds, *other* forms of ministry, *other* books, *other* rituals. And with this acknowledgment of contingency, there inevitably comes a twofold recognition: first, that the Christian movement has survived in history while dispensing with one or more of these central "symbols," and second, that what best enables the apostolicity of the church—that is, its continuity in the life and doctrine of the gospel—is no single "sign" or institution, but a cord constituted of many mutually reinforcing strands: that is to say, the apostolic Scriptures read, taught, and proclaimed in the light of the apostolic rule of faith, even as their message is actualized in the performance of the gospel sacraments, by a regular and official ministry that is bound, from generation to generation, to the service of precisely *these* communal practices.

On the other hand, Lutherans have been clear in acknowledging that, whatever may be said about the contingency and corruptibility of human institutions, true doctrine does not reproduce itself spontaneously and immaterially: that faith cannot live historically apart from institutions and the "symbols" they evolve, even if the institutions in question are historically contingent and subject to regular misuse and mutual correction. The carrier of true teaching is the *community called "church,"* in its institutional continuities. And this is the case not merely because the church is, after all, a human, and less than ideal, community, and thus *needs* institutions in a way that angels might not; but also because the focal institutions of the church are practices in which it opens itself in faith to the saving grace of God in Christ, and because God *is* faithful.

It is against the backdrop of this sort of understanding that the knotty question of *episcopacy* has been viewed and dealt with. It is perhaps unfortunate that the dialectic of the Lutheran-Episcopal dialogue has neglected questions about the relative status of the *other* traditional signs of institutional continuity; and it is my personal view that until this is done, the *theological* value of the conclusions to which this dialogue has come will not be recognized. Nevertheless its implications for this issue have been fairly clearly drawn out.

Lutherans have traditionally held that while a ministry of Word and Sacrament is proper to the church, and indeed a divine gift to the church, the particular *form* that such a ministry takes is a matter of indifference: an *adiaphoron,* to use the good Stoic expression for this. Hence they have insisted that no *form* of ministry can be a condition of any Christian body's being recognized as genuinely "church." It should be clear that in this dialogue, Anglicans have conceded this point; for the Concordat involves a recognition of the churches that constitute the ELCA as true churches in which the gospel of Christ is conveyed, and thus a recognition of the ministry of those churches as a true ministry of the gospel. One the other hand, the point has been conceded in a rather nontraditional way: by which I mean that the Anglican participants have not simply retreated to Richard Hooker's position that questions of ministerial order are mere questions of "external regiment," foreign to the character of the church as a

community in which the gospel is proclaimed and appropriated in life. Without saying that the "historic episcopate"— a phrase which I understand to mean "bishops in official succession," whether that succession is taken to be "from the Apostles" or not—is *essential* to a body's character as church, they have suggested that episcopacy, while a matter of indifference *in the abstract,* is nevertheless what the ancient Stoics used to call a *proêgoumenon:* i.e., something that *in the concrete* is desirable and indeed preferable, where "in the concrete" means "for practical purposes" or perhaps "contextually."

Hence the Concordat carries the principle of "equivalence" to the point of insisting upon the classical threefold ministry, and upon the unification of the episcopal ministries of the two bodies for the purposes of full communion. The two "successions" of bishops, in short, are to become one succession; but this is presented not as a condition of mutual recognition of the two parties as true churches, but as a condition of their full communion. It is the future, not the past, to which this mutual regularization of ministries looks: hence the "South India" form of the scheme.

From Richard Norris, "On 'Full Communion' between the Episcopal Church and the Evangelical Lutheran Church in America," *Pro Ecclesia: A Journal of Catholic and Evangelical Theology* 6 (Winter 1997): 64–70.

☙ **J. M. R. Tillard** (1927–2000), a Roman Catholic theologian, argues in "Episcopacy: A Gift of the Spirit" (1999) that the phenomenon of Church is not just a group of individual believers but a socially constructed institution: it is a "setting" that gives visibility to their lives in communion.

J. M. R. TILLARD

"Episcopacy: A Gift of the Spirit"

I

In the Catholic Church, as in the Orthodox churches and certain circles of the churches of the Reformation, the question of institution is bound up with the equally complex question of the nature of the episcopacy. This is linked in turn with the ecumenical discussions of apostolic succession. What is known as the ecclesial institution is the stable structure, remaining the same through the centuries, in which and thanks to which the *communion* of all believers among themselves and with the Father, in Christ, is ensured. Through it, the divine plan of salvation is embodied not in a vague number of isolated individuals brought together by grace but in a community organized in accordance with the specific goal expressed in the letter to the Ephesians as making up the Body of which Christ is the Head (Eph. 1:22–23), gathering torn humanity together again in the *eirene* of God (2:13–17), building together a habitation for God through the Spirit (2:22). The Reformation as such did not want to abolish but to reform the institution.

To be sure—as Augustine in the West never ceases to repeat—the Body of Christ and the Temple of God are realities over which the Spirit alone has dominion. The limits of the institution do not necessarily coincide with the extension of the Body of the Lord or the dimensions of the Temple. From Augustine's many statements on the *corpus permixtum,* let us cite these lines:

> Do not be surprised by the multitude of bad Christians who fill the church, who participate at the altar. In the church of this time they may be with us, but in that assembly of the saints which will come after the resurrection they will not be found. The church of this time is similar indeed to a threshing floor where grain and chaff are mixed, where the wicked mingle with the good; after the judgment, it will include all the good, with none of the wicked. This threshing floor holds the harvest sown by the Apostles . . . , which the persecution of its enemies has beaten only a little, but . . . which has not yet been sifted by the winnowing from on high. He will come, however, the one of whom we have proclaimed in the Creed, "He will come again to judge the living and the dead." And as the gospel says, *His winnowing fork is in his hand, and he will clear his threshing floor and gather his wheat into the granary, but the chaff he will burn with unquenchable fire* (Matt. 3:12).[23]

On the other hand, Augustine explains that the Lord and his Spirit know those who, outside the institution, are already in salvation.[24] Nevertheless, it falls to the institution to offer, guarantee, manifest and maintain for all the set of instruments of salvation in which the power of the Spirit is exerted. These are the proclaiming and teaching of the Word, the celebration of the sacraments, above all the eucharist, and the "cure of souls," as a beautiful Reformed expression has it. The institution has the mission of making it possible for every person who desires to find the means of sanctification in the *koinonia.* The Code of Canon Law of January 1983 specifies at some length the rights of the faithful (canons 211–231) and, correlatively, the strict duty of the institution to

answer to those rights. This signifies an official acknowledgment of the nature of the institution.

Indeed, it is not simply a matter of each believer finding, if God wills, available and generous people who agree benevolently to aid him or her in living his or her Christian vocation. The institution is a socially constituted reality, recognized as the setting of the life in communion to which it gives visibility. As such, it confers on the availability and generosity of specifically designated representatives a consistency which is protected from and transcends all the hazards of individual good will. It guarantees a stability in the service of the means of salvation. For this service as embodied in the institution, specific activities are established in a fixed way and are as it were mobilized in accordance with the *koinonia* to be realized. This implies persons officially consecrated for this service, formally recognized as such, organized in accordance with it, granted the authority that such service demands. This authority possesses power enough to be effective, which is made concrete either by legislation adapted to the common good and the good of individuals or by specific means of action marked out by that legislation.

Let us be clear on this point. Bringing this ensemble into play requires an administrative apparatus and suggests the creation of certain "institutions" (the catechumenate, theological schools, seminaries and so on). But that is not essential to the ecclesial *institution* as we are presenting it here. The *institution* is not to be confused with either the administration it necessitates or with the "institutions" it gives rise to. It is the setting of the life in *communion,* its framework, its support, and that which ensures its growth in faith and sacramental life. We like to define it as the expression of *koinonia* at once in its continuity, its structure and its dependence on faith and sacrament with regard to God.

Thus defined, the institution of the church rests on the episcopacy. Not without reason, the theology of the tradi-

---

23. *Sermo* 223, 2, PL 38, 1092–93; BA [*Biblical Archivist*] 72, 833. Cf. *De doct. Christ.* 3, 22, 45, BA 11, 400; *Tract. in Joh.* 6, 2, BA 71, 346; *Tract. in Joh.* 27, 11, BA 72, 561; *Tract in Joh.* 7, 1, BA 7, 404; *Tract. in Joh.* 28, 11, BA 72, 595; *Contra epist. Parm.* 3, 3, 19, BA 28, 440–42; *Contra Faust.* 12, 15, PL 42, 262–63; *Sermo* 111, 3 (ed. Lambot, RB [*Revue biblique*] 1947, 115).

24. The church "must bear in mind that among these very enemies are hidden her future citizens. . . . In the same way, while the City of God is on pilgrimage in this world, she has in her midst some who are united with her in participation in the sacraments, but who will not join with her in the eternal destiny of the saints. . . . But, such as they are, we have less right to despair of the reformation of some of them, when some predestined friends, as yet unknown even to themselves, are concealed among our most open enemies. In truth, those two cities are interwoven and intermixed in this era, and await separation at the last judgment" (*De civ. Dei,* 1, 35; BA 33, 298–300).

tions known as "Catholic" connect this certainty with the rich affirmation of the letter to the Ephesians:

> The gifts he gave were that some would be apostles, some prophets, some evangelists, some pastors and teachers, to equip the saints for the work of ministry, for building up the body of Christ, until all of us come to the unity of the faith and of the knowledge of the Son of God, to maturity, to the measure of the full stature of Christ. We must no longer be children, tossed to and fro and blown about by every wind of doctrine, by people's trickery, by their craftiness in deceitful scheming. But speaking the truth in love, we must grow up in every way into him who is the head, into Christ, from whom the whole body, joined and knit together by every ligament with which it is equipped, as each part is working properly, promotes the body's growth in building itself up in love (4:11–16).[25]

God gave (*edôken*) Christ to the church as its Head (Eph. 1:22–33); Christ in his turn "gave" (*edôken*) to the church the ministers necessary for its upbuilding into the Body of Christ (4:11–12).

> Just as Christ did not resurrect himself, so the church does not provide itself with the needed men on its own initiative. It is endowed, it depends on the Lord and on this gracious and thus sovereign, sovereign and thus gracious, gift. . . . The apostles are clearly separated and distinguished from prophets and followers. . . . In conformity with a unanimous teaching, the choice of the apostles constitutes a founding initiative which depends on the Lord alone. Later functions derive from the first.[26]

The church is ceaselessly "sent back to the gospel," thanks to the ministers given by Christ.[27]

The nucleus of what we call the institution is there. Now, what is the specific function of these *human* "gifts" who are ministers? It is the perfecting, the equipping (*katartismos*), of the faithful as authentic adults in the faith, and their gathering into the one Body of Christ (4:12–13), knit together by knowledge of the Son of God, in love (4:15). The goal seems indeed to be the full stature of the church.[28] For it is in this way that the church, as Body of Christ, receives harmonious growth from its Head, its various parts finding themselves articulated, adjusted and coordinated according to their nature. These *human* "gifts" structure it visibly.

It is this mission of the original ministry which is pursued in the episcopacy and the other ministerial functions deriving from or attached to it. Here too it is a matter of the gracious *gift* that God gives to his church for its life and growth into the Body of Christ—but always starting from Christ the Head and in reference to the full eschatological realization of the Father's plan. Already at the time of the pastoral epistles it was recognized that those whom the apostle chose to be his companions in ministry and those who would continue the apostolic mission—in so far as it is transmissible, for there is an *ephapax* of the witness of those who saw the Risen One and "accompanied us" (Acts 1:21)—received the specific gift of the Spirit precisely for this service by the laying on of hands (1 Tim. 4:14; 2 Tim. 1:6). The epistles to Timothy and Titus show that what was involved was a charisma of government—thus, already an institution—with the right and power to teach and prescribe (1 Tim. 4:11–12) in order to keep the community on the right path. Indeed, with the difficulties that were beginning to arise, something like a ministerial company was needed, allowing for the confirmation of the faithful in faith and charity but also watching over all the categories (widows, youth, elders, slaves, etc.) who made up the community and authorizing it to ward off those who endangered it (Tit. 3:10; 1:10–14; 1 Tim. 1:3; 4:7; 2 Tim. 2:25; 4:2). A discipline was imposed. It was this, as well as the proclamation and defense of the gospel so that the deposit of faith (*parathêkê*) should be kept and transmitted, which the charism (1 Tim. 4:14; 2 Tim. 1:6) made possible.

We thus come to a first conclusion. We see that the very roots of the ecclesial institution—the apostolic function and its derivatives—are in the strictest sense a gift of Christ to the church of God, given, guaranteed and supported by a *charisma* of the Holy Spirit. Thus it is not an adventitious phenomenon in the *oikonomia* of salvation but is integral to the gift of God. On the other hand, since the primary nucleus of the church of God was manifested at Pentecost as "apostolic," we can say that at the very moment of its "coming to light" the Spirit which constituted it as a *koinonia* gave it, along with the apostolate, the charisma that would also make of it the

---

25. See Michel Bouttier, *L'epitre de saint Paul aux Ephesiens*, Geneva, 1991, 185–98.

26. Ibid., 185f.

27. Ibid., 187.

28. See R. Schnackenberg, *The Epistle to the Ephesians*, Edinburgh, 1991, 184–86.

institution of salvation. It is not surprising that the book of Acts describes, in the stories of Ananias and Sapphira (5:1–11) and of the designation of the Seven (6:1–6), the first steps towards what would become the institution and the community discipline. Acts 15 shows how everything would quickly become theologically tied together: "the Holy Spirit and us" (v. 28).[29] Moreover, beginning with Acts 14:21–27, we see the institution taking root.

It is thus impossible to cut the Spirit off from the institution, or, as is sometimes done even in Catholic theological circles, to distinguish sharply between what is from God (communion) and what is of human origin (the institution with all its avatars). The institution also has its roots in the divine gift. In the decisions of the Decree of Jerusalem are found all the conditions of a normative decree, proclaimed aloud and then communicated verbally and in writing. It is supported by the apostles and the elders in communion with the Spirit who has established them as *episkopoi* (guardians, overseers) of the churches (cf. 20:28).[30] The Spirit who guarantees the witness of the apostles (5:32) is the one who gives authority to this ministry of the elders in service to the *koinonia*. Without the Spirit, disciplinary decisions could not be imposed, above all in so grave a situation.

IV

1. As a contribution to this study of *episkopé*, we have proposed to show the bond between the institution, as we have defined it, starting from indications to be found especially in the letter to the Ephesians and the pastoral epistles, and the Holy Spirit. We have distinguished three essential points. (1) The institution has appeared to us as a gift of the Spirit for the *koinonia* of the Body of Christ, a gift always at risk because of the weakness of human agents, a gift nevertheless always inscribed in the normal *oikonomia* of salvation. (2) Always on the basis of the *gratia* granted in the faith and the sacraments of the faith, the Holy Spirit enables the faithful bearers of the *sensus fidei* to correct, heal, enlighten, adapt the institution, and even to make up for its failings. (3) All the same, this *sensus fidei* remains dependent on the institution in its fundamental registers, since it is given only in the Body of Christ, for the building, preservation and maintenance of which the institution is the Spirit's instrument. In the church of God there is thus an interaction in both directions, between the "servants of the Spirit" and the community of the "temple of the Spirit" (1 Cor. 6:19; Eph. 2:21–22). The pres-

ence of the Spirit and his ecclesial work are connected with this interaction.

It is clear, then, that the institution should not be considered a purely human element, foreign to the essence of the work of the Spirit. It belongs to the *oikonomia* of grace.

This place of the institution obviously does not conceal the fact that the Spirit transcends it, that institutional and canonical frontiers do not exactly cover the field of the Spirit's action. The Spirit who acted in humanity before the birth of Christ now acts in humanity outside the institution, in unsuspected ways. He is in no way the slave of the institution. He is its master.

It may also happen that the responsible members of the institution hardly welcome this action of the Spirit even within the church, when it upsets its too-easy attainments, contests its conformism, denounces its errors. The Dominican figures of Savonarola, of Bartolomé de las Casas, of Père Lagrange, of a whole generation of researchers who preceded and prepared for Vatican II, are known to us. Their thought and their witness passed through a long purgatory before being "received." They were resisted. Sometimes this resistance ended in tragedy. Thus some of the great fractures that continue to break up the unity of the people of God have their origin in this resistance of the institution. Here the excuses of Paul VI and John Paul II find their ecclesiological significance.

As for the influence of the saints, it rarely coincides with the institution, unless the latter integrates them into liturgical worship. They are, indeed, like all Christians, in need of the means of grace the institution provides. They cannot live without the institution. However, above all in our contemporary societies, it is they, far more than the institution, who witness to the Spirit. Their witness calls out both to other Christians and to unbelievers. Moreover, the monasteries and contemplative communities have for centuries remained the relay-stations for a presence of the Spirit who takes paths other than those of the institution to give life to the church of God. It is highly significant that in times of crisis it is usu-

---

29. In the words of E. Haenchen, *The Acts of the Apostles,* London, 1971, 453, "the highest supernatural authority and the legal earthly authority derived from it stand side by side." Compare 15:28 with 5:32.

30. See M. Simon, "The Apostolic Decree and Its Setting in the Ancient Church," *Bulletin of the John Rylands Library,* vol. 52, 1969–70, 437–60; Ch. Perrot, "La tradition apostolique dans les Actes des Apôtres," *l'année canonique,* vol. 23, 1979, 25–35; D. R. Catchpole, "Paul, James and the Apostolic Decree," *NTS* [*New Testament Studies*], vol. 23, 1976–77, 428–44.

ally the monasteries that are asked to supply bishops, and that in the West the prayer of the monks has been the inspiration for the great liturgical prayer of all the people of God. The institution knows how to be a mendicant.

Once again the wise old axiom is verified: not either . . . or but both . . . and. The Spirit and the institution together make the church of God, and in this togetherness the Spirit has full mastery. But all the same, God himself wants this institution.

Translated by Richard Pevear, in Peter C. Bouteneff and Alan D. Falconer, eds., *Episkopé and Episcopacy and the Quest for Visible Unity* (Geneva: World Council of Churches, 1999), 65–68, 76–77. [Ellipses in original.]

4. RELIGION, SCIENCE, AND SECULARISM

In the Introduction to *Myths, Models, and Paradigms* (1974), **Ian G. Barbour,** a physicist and leading scholar in the field of science and religion, sketches a history of the relationship between science and religion and the responses to a perceived conflict between them. He thinks that traditionally oppositional views on many issues (for example, the meaning of evolution) no longer define the interaction between the two fields.

IAN G. BARBOUR

Introduction to *Myths, Models, and Paradigms: A Comparative Study in Science and Religion*

Difficulties in religious language have been described by many authors in recent years. In Germany, Rudolf Bultmann has said that modern man can no longer speak of a God who acts in nature and history and has proposed a "demythologized" version of the gospel. In England, Bishop Robinson's *Honest to God* became a best seller, partly because of his frankness in expressing doubts about traditional ways of speaking of God. In the United States, three theologians who found themselves unable to accept theistic assertions were presented in the popular press as the "Death of God" movement. These men are symptomatic of a widespread questioning of classical formulations.

There are many reasons for current debates about religious language. Biblical statements, if taken literally, are not credible to modern man. The God "up there" is incompatible with our understanding of the universe. Classical discussions of the symbolic and analogical character of religious language were dependent on the metaphysical assumptions of Platonism or scholasticism, which can no longer be presupposed; more recent interpretations often hold that religious images are only symbols of man's subjective life. The possibility of meaningful language about God is widely disputed today. Theological doctrines, on the other hand, seem to be divorced from human experience. Religious ideas without an experiential basis appear abstract and irrelevant.

For other persons, the encounter of world religions has led to the adoption of a total relativism in place of exclusive claims for a particular tradition. The confidence of the Catholic community in the authority of the church and the conviction of Protestant neo-orthodoxy concerning the exclusiveness of revelation have been weakened by the new awareness of religious pluralism. The diversity of religious rituals and beliefs has been taken as support for historical and cultural relativism. Whereas teaching in theological seminaries had assumed the truth of one tradition, the growing study of religion in secular universities has been concerned about its functions in human life—without reference to the question of its truth or falsity. Often this has ended in the reductionist view that religion is entirely the product of psychological and sociological forces.

One might also point to the secularization of contemporary society, which itself has many facets: the separation of political and educational institutions from the church, the autonomy of the intellectual disciplines, the dominance of this-worldly over other-worldly interests, the confidence in man's ability to control his own destiny without divine assistance. But the present volume is concerned with the basic conceptual and methodological problems of religious language, and here the most significant influence has undoubtedly been science.

In past centuries, particular scientific theories have had a major impact on religious thought. In the eighteenth century, Newtonian mechanics led to a mechanistic view of the world and a deistic understanding of God the cosmic clockmaker. In the nineteenth century, Darwin's theory of evolution encouraged new interpretations of divine immanence in the cosmic process, as well as naturalistic philosophies of man's place in a world of law and chance. But in the twentieth century, the main influences of science on religion have come less from specific theories—such as quantum physics, relativity, astronomy, or molecular biology—than from views of science as a method.

Science seems to yield indubitable knowledge on which all men can agree. Its apparent objectivity contrasts with the subjectivity of religion. According to the popular stereotype, the scientist makes precise observations and then employs logical reasoning; if such a procedure is to be adopted in all fields of enquiry, should not religion be dismissed as prescientific superstition? And does not the scientist assume that nature is a self-contained order in which there is no place for God's action?

It has been largely through the work of philosophers that thought about the methods of science has affected religious thought in recent decades. Specifically, writings in the philosophy of science have had major repercussions in the philosophy of religion. During the 1930's and 1940's, the positivists had taken science as the norm for all meaningful discourse. Religious language was considered neither true nor false but meaningless. The positivists had proclaimed the famous Verification Principle, which states that, apart from tautologies and definitions, statements are meaningful only if they can be verified by sense data. Accepting an oversimplified view of science as the prototype for all genuine knowledge, they dismissed religion as "purely emotive."

During the 1950's positivism came under increasing attack, but many of its assumptions were perpetuated in the empiricism which came to replace it as the dominant interpretation of science. Among the empiricist claims were the following. (1) Science starts from publicly observed data which can be described in a pure observation-language independent of any theoretical assumptions. (2) Theories can be verified or falsified by comparison with this fixed experimental data. (3) The choice between theories is rational, objective and in accordance with specifiable criteria. Philosophers under the sway of such empiricism continued to say that religion can legitimately make no cognitive claims. We will look particularly at the protracted debate concerning the falsifiability of religious beliefs which has occurred since 1955, when Antony Flew issued his challenge to the theist: What would have to occur to constitute a disproof of the existence of God? Flew held that religious statements are not genuine assertions because the observable conditions which would falsify them cannot be specified.

But during the 1960's, the empiricist assertions listed above were vigorously criticized. It is the thesis of this volume that recent work in the philosophy of science has important implications for the philosophy of religion and for theology. Three new viewpoints concerning science, and their consequences for the critique of religion, are the central themes of the book.

The first theme, *the diverse functions of language,* reflects a change in outlook among philosophers which was already under way in the 1950's. It is well enough known that it need only be summarized here. The positivist principle that statements are meaningful only if they can be verified by sense data turned out to be too strict to satisfy even in science. The principle would have excluded scientific theories which can never be conclusively verified or proved to be immune to modification. Weaker versions were attempted, for example: a statement is meaningful only if some possible sense data are relevant to the probability of its truth or falsity. But it was extraordinarily difficult to specify at what point the "relevance of data" was to be considered too indirect to qualify under this more generous charter.

Increasingly, philosophers came to acknowledge that language has many forms serving varied functions; science was no longer taken as the norm for all discourse. Linguistic analysis, the most prominent school of contemporary philosophy, asks how men use different types of language. Each field—science, art, ethics, religion, and so forth—has a different task, and its approach must be judged by its usefulness in accomplishing its own particular functions. The value of a statement depends on what one wants to do with it; every type of language has its own logic, appropriate to its specific purposes.

The linguistic analysts have described various functions of language. Sometimes it evokes and expresses self-commitment. At other times it recommends a way of life, declares an intention to act in a particular way and endorses a set of moral principles. Or again, it may propose a distinctive self-understanding and engender characteristic attitudes towards human existence. Many philosophers stress these non-cognitive functions; they insist that these tasks are valuable and legitimate but are very different from the tasks of scientific language. This is an attractive solution to issues between science and religion; the two fields cannot possibly conflict if they serve totally different functions. The function of scientific language is the prediction and control of nature; that of religious language is the expression of self-commitment, ethical dedication, and existential life-orientation. But the price of this division of labour is that religion would have to give up any claims to truth, at least with respect to any facts external to one's own commitment. Religious beliefs would be useful fictions which fulfill important functions in human life but are not entitled to make any assertions. Throughout this volume a "useful fiction" is to be regarded not as false (as in the popular usage of "fictional"), but as neither true nor false.

The diversity of functions of religious language has also been presented in the writings of anthropologists about myths. Myths are stories which are taken to manifest some aspect of the cosmic order. They provide a community with ways of structuring experience in the present. They inform man about his self-identity and the framework of significance in which he participates. Archetypal events in primordial or historical time offer patterns for human actions today. Myths are re-enacted in rituals which integrate the community around common memories and common goals. According to many interpreters, myths are neither true nor false; they are useful fictions which fulfill these important social functions.

However, I would want to join those philosophers who also defend cognitive functions of religious language. For religion does claim to be in some sense true as well as useful. Beliefs about the nature of reality are presupposed in all the other varied uses of religious language. We can at least say that religion specifies a perspective on the world and an interpretation of history and human experience. It directs attention to particular patterns in events. It makes assertions about what is the case.

I will thus be mentioning both similarities and differences between science and religion. Existentialism and positivism, while disagreeing violently in their estimation of subjectivity, agreed completely in portraying a sharp contrast between the objectivity of science and the subjectivity of religion. I will try to show that science is not as objective, nor religion as subjective, as these two opposing schools of thought both assumed. Despite the presence of distinctive functions and attitudes in religion which have no parallels in science, there are also functions and attitudes in common, wherein I see differences of degree rather than an absolute dichotomy. Some of these comparisons are spelled out in the discussion of models and paradigms.

The second theme of the book is *the role of models*. In the last decade there has been considerable interest in model-building within many intellectual disciplines. Broadly speaking, a model is a symbolic representation of selected aspects of the behavior of a complex system for particular purposes. It is an imaginative tool for ordering experience, rather than a description of the world. There are, of course, some objects of which actual physical replicas can be built—such as a "scale model" of a ship or a "working model" of a locomotive. We will be concerned, however, with mental models of systems which for various reasons cannot be represented by replicas, such as the economy of a nation, the electrons in an atom or the biblical God.

There are many types of models serving a diversity of functions. In the social sciences, models of economic development or of population growth allow quantitative predictions of a few variables to be studied under a set of simplifying assumptions. With computer models one can carry out calculations concerning the complex interaction of many variables, among which specified relationships are assumed. The simulation of the behavior of military, industrial and urban systems is carried out in the new fields of "operations research" and "systems analysis." Models of the political behavior of an electorate are used to project election returns. Engineering models are used to solve practical problems when it is difficult to experiment on the original system.

I will deal especially with theoretical models in science, which are mental constructs devised to account for observed phenomena in the natural world. They originate in a combination of analogy to the familiar and creative imagination in the invention of the new. I will argue that theoretical models, such as the "billiard ball model" of a gas, are not merely convenient calculating devices or temporary psychological aids in the formulation of theories; they have an important continuing role in suggesting both modifications in existing theories and the discovery of new phenomena. I will try to show that such models are taken seriously but not literally. They are neither literal pictures of reality nor "useful fictions," but partial and provisional ways of imagining what is not observable; they are symbolic representations of aspects of the world which are not directly accessible to us.

Models in religion are also analogical. They are organizing images used to order and interpret patterns of experience in human life. Like scientific models, they are neither literal pictures of reality nor useful fictions. One of the main functions of religious models is the interpretation of distinctive types of experience: awe and reverence, moral obligation, reorientation and reconciliation, interpersonal relationships, key historical events, and order and creativity in the world. I will delineate some parallels between the use of scientific models in the interpretation of observations and the use of religious models in the interpretation of experience. Ultimate models—whether of a personal God or an impersonal cosmic process—direct attention to particular patterns in events and restructure the way one sees the world.

Other functions of religious models have no parallel in science. Models in religion express and evoke distinctive attitudes. They encourage allegiance to a way of life and adherence to policies of action; their vivid imagery elicits self-commitment and ethical dedication. Religion demands existential involvement of the whole person; it asks about the ultimate objects of man's trust and loyalty. Its language expresses gratitude, dependence and worship. This self-involving and evaluational character of religion contrasts with the more detached and neutral character of science.

A separate chapter is devoted to the question of "complementary models." The term originates in modern physics, where both wave and particle models are used for electrons, photons, and other inhabitants of the atomic world. No single model is adequate for the interpretation of experiments in micro-physics, though the probability of the occurrence of particular observations can be predicted from a unified mathematical formalism. I will argue that there is some parallel in the complementarity among diverse models within religious language. I do not believe, however, that the term should be extended to call science and religion "complementary," since they are not talking about the same phenomena and their models are of differing logical types serving differing functions.

I will suggest that the recognition that models are not pictures of reality can contribute to tolerance between religious communities. In a day when the religions of the world confront each other, the view proposed here might engender humility and tentativeness in the claims made on behalf of any one model. In place of the absolutism of exclusive claims of finality, an ecumenical spirit would acknowledge a plurality of significant religious models without lapsing into a complete relativism which would undercut all concern for truth. Analysis of models provides a path between literalism and fictionalism in religion also.

Both the cognitive claims of religion and its living practice must be grounded in experience. If inherited religious symbols are for many people today almost totally detached from human experience, a return to the experiential basis of religion is important for its renewed vitality in practice, as well as for a sound epistemology in theory. Implicit in this position, of course, is a rejection of the positivists' restriction of attention to sense-experience; all symbol systems are se-

lective, ordering those aspects of experience which men consider most significant.

The third theme of this volume is *the role of paradigms*. The term has received wide currency through Thomas Kuhn's influential book, *The Structure of Scientific Revolutions* (1962). Kuhn maintained that the thought and activity of a given scientific community are dominated by its paradigms, which he described as "standard examples of scientific work that embody a set of conceptual, methodological and metaphysical assumptions." Newton's work in mechanics, for instance, was the central paradigm of the community of physicists for two centuries. In the second edition (1970) of Kuhn's book and in subsequent essays, he distinguished several features which he had previously lumped together: a research tradition, the key historical examples ("exemplars") through which the tradition is transmitted, and the set of metaphysical assumptions implicit in its fundamental conceptual categories. Adopting these distinctions, I will use the term paradigm to refer to *a tradition transmitted through historical exemplars*. The concept of paradigm is thus defined sociologically and historically, and its implications for epistemology (the structure and character of knowledge) must be explored. Let me summarize three issues in this discussion and then indicate their implications for religion:

1. *The influence of theory on observation.* The empiricists of the 1950's had claimed that science starts from publicly observable data which can be described in a pure observation-language independent of any theoretical assumptions. By the early 1960's this claim had been challenged by a number of authors who tried to show that there is no neutral observation-language; both the procedures for making observations, and the language in which data are reported, were shown to be "theory-laden." Kuhn's volume gave historical illustrations of the paradigm-dependence of observations. He concluded that rival paradigms are "incommensurable." I will maintain that even though data are indeed theory-laden, it is possible to make pragmatic distinctions between more theoretical and more observational terms in any particular context. Rival theories are not incommensurable if their protagonists can find an overlapping core of observation-statements on which they can concur.

2. *The falsifiability of theories.* The empiricists had claimed that even though a theory cannot be verified by its agreement with data, it can be falsified by disagreement with data. But critics showed that discordant data alone have seldom been taken to falsify an accepted theory in the absence of an alternative theory; instead, auxiliary assumptions have been

modified, or the discrepancies have been set aside as anomalies. I will suggest that comprehensive theories are indeed resistant to falsification, but that observation does exert some control over theory; an accumulation of anomalies cannot be ignored indefinitely. A paradigm tradition, then, is not simply falsified by discordant data, but is replaced by a promising alternative. Commitment to a tradition and tenacity in exploring its potentialities are scientifically fruitful; but the eventual decision to abandon it is not arbitrary or irrational.

3. *The choice between rival paradigms.* The empiricists had portrayed all scientific choices as rational, objective and in accordance with specifiable criteria. Kuhn replied that criteria for judging theories are themselves paradigm-dependent. He described the change of paradigms during a "scientific revolution" as a matter not of logical argument but of persuasion and "conversion." I will argue that there are criteria of assessment independent of particular paradigms. But in the early stages, when a new contender first challenges an accepted paradigm, the criteria do not yield an unambiguous verdict; the experimental evidence and the relative weights assigned to diverse criteria are debatable and subject to individual judgment. Yet because there are accepted criteria common to all scientists, the decision can be discussed, reasons can be set forth, and an eventual consensus can be expected.

Corresponding to these three issues arising from the discussion of paradigms in science are three similar issues in religion:

1. *The influence of interpretation on experience* in religion is more problematic than the influence of theory on observation in science. There is no uninterpreted experience; but descriptions of religious experience can be given which are relatively free from doctrinal interpretation. To be sure, any set of basic beliefs tends to produce experiences which can be cited in support of those beliefs, and agreement on the data of religion seems to be exceedingly difficult to achieve. Yet because members of different religious traditions can appeal to areas of shared experience, communication is possible.

2. Flew's demand that the theist should specify *falsifying conditions* for religious beliefs seems unreasonable if such falsifying conditions cannot even be specified for comprehensive scientific theories. I will submit that though no decisive falsification is possible, the cumulative weight of evidence does count for or against religious beliefs, but with greater ambiguity than in science. Religious paradigms, like scientific ones, are not falsified by discordant data but replaced by promising alternatives. Commitment to a paradigm (un-

derstood, again, as a tradition transmitted through historical exemplars) allows its potentialities to be systematically explored.

3. There are no *rules for choice* between religious paradigms, but there are criteria of assessment. The application of such criteria is even more subject to individual judgment in religion than in the controversies between competing paradigms during a "scientific revolution." Moreover religious faith includes personal trust and loyalty; it is more totally self-involving than commitment to a scientific paradigm. Nevertheless the existence of criteria means that religious traditions can be analyzed and discussed. Religious commitment is not incompatible with critical reflection. It is my hope that the new views of science described here can offer some encouragement to such a combination of commitment and enquiry in religion.

These three themes—the diverse functions of language, the role of models and the role of paradigms—combine to support the position of *critical realism* which I will defend in both science and religion. Such a position recognizes the distinctive non-cognitive functions of religious language, but it also upholds its cognitive functions. Critical realism avoids naive realism, on the one hand, and instrumentalism, which abandons all concern for truth, on the other. Naive realism is untenable if models are not literal pictures of reality and if the history of science is characterized by major paradigm shifts rather than by simple cumulation or convergence. But the inadequacies of naive realism need not lead us to a fictionalist account of models, or to a total relativism concerning truth, if there are indeed data and criteria of judgment which are not totally paradigm-dependent. In the concluding chapter I will suggest some implications of critical realism for the academic study of religion and for the encounter of world religions, as well as for personal religious faith.

From Ian G. Barbour, *Myths, Models, and Paradigms: A Comparative Study in Science and Religion* (New York: Harper and Row, 1974), 1–11.

In "Secularity and Godlessness" (1996) **Nicholas Lash,** Catholic theologian and professor of divinity at Cambridge University, calls attention to some of the possible fallacies in the contemporary understanding of religion. Lash notes that the terms "secularization" and "religion" have histories: the challenge for religion is that, for many, the meaning of religion has been reduced to only what the process of secularization has understood it to be.

NICHOLAS LASH
"Secularity and Godlessness"

The *Oxford English Dictionary* (even in its 1976 Supplement) knows no sense of "marginalise" other than that of making marginal notes upon a page. The metaphorical extension of the word, its social use, describing the process whereby the weak and vulnerable are extruded to the "edge" of things, is therefore very recent. "Secularisation" by contrast, has been with us well over three hundred years, its original, legal sense of the procedures whereby ecclesiastical property was transferred to "worldly" ownership or use gradually evolving into the idea of "the process whereby religious institutions become less powerful in a society and religious beliefs less easily accepted."[31]

In the vast literature examining, deploring, celebrating the story of modern Western culture as an irreversible process of secularisation, it still seems too little understood that the modern invention of the "secular" carried with it concomitant *re*definitions of "religion." Something of this was understood by those who launched the project of "enlightenment." Hence the care which they sought newly to distinguish "natural" religion, the religion of a secular society—"universal in embrace, rational in character, and benign in its consequences"[32]—from what they saw as the dangerously divisive, irrational, priest-ridden and intolerant particularities of "positive" religion. It was not in irreligion that the great project of "rationality" was born and its cool, machine-like marketplace, the parliament of secularity, constructed. Rather than suggest that, in the process of secularisation, religion became privatised, it would be more accurate to say that, as the bones of "natural religion" faded in the public square, bleached by "rationalisation," what, increasingly, was privatised was the role of religion as a medium of truth.

And if liberal enthusiasts for secularisation contributed to the confusion, so too did those, especially in ecclesiastical high places, who construed their own diminishing social clout and dignity as evidence of disbelief in God. But secularisation and the spread of irreligion do not straightforwardly go hand in hand. Indeed, if we take into consideration the situation in even the most "modernised" parts of Africa and South-East Asia, it would seem that David Martin's definition needs to be reworked: the declining social power of religious institutions by no means necessarily leads to or fosters the erosion of religious beliefs and devotional practices.

At this point, I take up the thread of a suggestion I made earlier: namely, that the invention of the secular carries with it concomitant redefinitions of religion. The territory of the objects of traditional religious faith and worship, it is often said, was the territory of the "supernatural" or the "metaphysical." We too easily forget, however, that, during the seventeenth century, all the maps were comprehensively redrawn. During this period, the old belief in one world in which creatures might act supernaturally (you might find human beings being kind and honest, for example), and in which only God could *not*, was replaced by a belief in two worlds—one natural, the other supernatural—in the second of which the most important occupant was an entity called "God."

Even David Martin's definition of secularisation seems to suppose that the concept of "religion" refers, in a secularised society, to the same objects as it did before the process of secularisation got under way. But this cannot be so. In inventing the "secular"—the territory of "rational" behaviour, in which the component of "natural" religion gradually modulated into "civil" religion, "public philosophy," class or national ideology—we invented, alongside it, a new world of private feelings, hermetic practices, individual and tribal fantasies, which was first called "positive" religion and then, in due course, tended to be referred to simply as "religion," *tout court*.

The drift of these remarks becomes, I hope, quite clear: it would be an exceedingly dangerous illusion to suppose that the only gods worshipped in our society were those whose temples are located in the culturally marginal territory which we still label as "religious."

We could come at it from a different angle. Suppose we follow Durkheim's lead and define religion as "the system of symbols by means of which society becomes conscious of itself." We would then construe "religion" as the "totality of [social] practices concerned with sacred things,"[33] concerned, that is to say, with practices, beliefs and institutions which prove too hot to handle, too dangerous to touch. Practices protective, for example, of "the system," or the market, or the male character of priesthood, or professorial self-esteem. The possibility would then emerge, as John Milbank has powerfully argued, that the narratives of secularisation merely

---

31. David Martin, *A General Theory of Secularization* (Oxford: Basil Blackwell, 1978), 12.

32. John Clayton, "Thomas Jefferson and the Study of Religion," an inaugural lecture at the University of Lancaster, 8.

33. Emile Durkheim, *Suicide: A Study in Sociology*, trans. John A. Spaulding and George Simpson (London: Routledge and Kegan Paul, 1970), 312. [. . .]

serve to render ideologically invisible the religious character of many of our most powerful institutions and foundationally entrenched beliefs.[34]

According to the myth of secularity, what happens in the public realm is "rational." At the centre of this realm, there are no wayward human agents, only calculable and impersonal forces which we seek to understand and, so far as possible, to control. Through the operation of these forces, some lose, some win. That's life. Learning, therefore, "to respect the world as it is," we learn to take no credit and accept no blame.

But let us, for a moment, entertain the possibility that banks, bureaucracies and stock exchanges are not, after all, machines, but *temples* in the liturgies of which all power and honour, agency and possibility, are ascribed *non nobis, Domine, non nobis,* but to "the system." If this were so, we might, with a little elementary demythologising, begin to understand that, in the last analysis, it was just us, just human beings, who were performing these rituals, producing these results. In which case, the destitution, squalor and starvation of the marginalised would not be the fate of those less fortunate but the condition of the victims whom we sacrifice upon our altars.

From Nicholas Lash, *The Beginning and the End of "Religion"* (Cambridge: Cambridge University Press, 1996), 188–91.

❦ The first of two selections from Pope **John Paul II** (1920–2005) comes from his encyclical "Evangelium vitae" (1995). The pope discusses the effects of secularism, not only on humanity's sense of God, but also on its sense of itself. "Faith Can Never Conflict with Reason: On Galileo" is from John Paul's 1992 address to the Pontifical Academy of Sciences, in which he speaks about the "myth" concerning Galileo's trial. He contends that for over three centuries that trial has been misunderstood as the Church's rejection of scientific progress. He credits Galileo with being more perceptive about the need to examine criteria for scriptural interpretation than some theologians of his time.

JOHN PAUL II

"Evangelium vitae," 21.1–22.4

"And from Your Face I Shall Be Hidden" (Gen 4:14): The Eclipse of the Sense of God and of Man

21.1. In seeking the deepest roots of the struggle between the "culture of life" and the "culture of death," we cannot restrict ourselves to the perverse idea of freedom mentioned above. We have to go to the heart of the tragedy being experienced by modern man: *the eclipse of the sense of God and of man,* typical of a social and cultural climate dominated by secularism, which, with its ubiquitous tentacles, succeeds at times in putting Christian communities themselves to the test. Those who allow themselves to be influenced by this climate easily fall into a sad, vicious circle: *when the sense of God is lost, there is also a tendency to lose the sense of man,* of his dignity and his life; in turn, the systematic violation of the moral law, especially in the serious matter of respect for human life and its dignity, produces a kind of progressive darkening of the capacity to discern God's living and saving presence.

21.2. Once again we can gain insight from the story of Abel's murder by his brother. After the curse imposed on him by God, Cain thus addresses the Lord: "My punishment is greater than I can bear. Behold, you have driven me this day away from the ground; and *from your face I shall be hidden,* and I shall be a fugitive and wanderer on the earth, and whoever finds me will slay me" (Gen 4:13–14). Cain is convinced that his sin will not obtain pardon from the Lord and that his inescapable destiny will be to have to "hide his face" from him. If Cain is capable of confessing that his fault is "greater than he can bear," it is because he is conscious of being in the presence of God and before God's just judgment. It is really only before the Lord that man can admit his sin and recognize its full seriousness. Such was the experience of David who, after "having committed evil in the sight of the Lord," and being rebuked by the Prophet Nathan, exclaimed: "My offenses truly I know them; my sin is always before me. Against you, you alone, have I sinned; what is evil in your sight I have done" (Ps 51:5–6).

22.1. Consequently, when the sense of God is lost, the sense of man is also threatened and poisoned, as the Second Vatican Council concisely states: "Without the Creator, the creature would disappear. . . . But when God is forgotten, the creature itself grows unintelligible."[35] Man is no longer able to see himself as "mysteriously different" from other earthly creatures; he regards himself merely as one more living being, as an organism which, at most, has reached a very high stage of perfection. Enclosed in the narrow horizon of his physical nature, he is somehow reduced to being

---

34. See John Milbank, *Theology and Social Theory: Beyond Secular Reason* (Oxford: Basil Blackwell, 1990).

35. Second Vatican Council, *Pastoral Constitution on the Church in the Modern World* (*Gaudium et spes,* 7 Dec. 1965), 36.

"a thing," and no longer grasps the "transcendent" character of his "existence as man." He no longer considers life as a splendid gift of God, something "sacred" entrusted to his responsibility and thus also to his loving care and "veneration." Life itself becomes a mere "thing," which man claims as his exclusive property, completely subject to his control and manipulation.

22.2. Thus, in relation to life at birth or at death, man is no longer capable of posing the question of the truest meaning of his own existence, nor can he assimilate with genuine freedom these crucial moments of his own history. He is concerned only with "doing," and, using all kinds of technology, he busies himself with programming, controlling and dominating birth and death. Birth and death, instead of being primary experiences demanding to be "lived," become things to be merely "possessed" or "rejected."

22.3. Moreover, once all reference to God has been removed, it is not surprising that the meaning of everything else becomes profoundly distorted. Nature itself, from being *mater* (mother), is now reduced to being "matter," and is subjected to every kind of manipulation. This is the direction in which a certain technical and scientific way of thinking, prevalent in present-day culture, appears to be leading when it rejects the very idea that there is a truth of creation which must be acknowledged, or a plan of God for life which must be respected. Something similar happens when concern about the consequences of such a "freedom without law" leads some people to the opposite position of a "law without freedom," as for example in ideologies which consider it unlawful to interfere in any way with nature, practically "divinizing" it. Again, this is a misunderstanding of nature's dependence on the plan of the Creator. Thus it is clear that the loss of contact with God's wise design is the deepest root of modern man's confusion, both when this loss leads to a freedom without rules and when it leaves man in "fear" of his freedom.

22.4. By living "as if God did not exist," man not only loses sight of the mystery of God, but also of the mystery of the world and the mystery of his own being.

From S. Michael Miller, ed., *The Encyclicals of John Paul II* (Huntington, IN: Our Sunday Visitor, 1996), 810–12. [Ellipsis in original.]

JOHN PAUL II

"Faith Can Never Conflict with Reason: On Galileo"

In 1979 Pope John Paul II expressed the wish that the Pontifical Academy of Sciences would conduct an in-depth study of the celebrated and controversial "Galileo case." A Commission of scholars for this purpose was established in 1981 and on Saturday morning, 31 October, [1992] they presented their conclusions to the Pope. A summary of these conclusions was given by Cardinal Paul Poupard. Receiving them in the Sala Regia of the Apostolic Palace, the Holy Father took the occasion to thank the members of the Commission for their work and to speak to the Pontifical Academy of Sciences on the distinct but complementary roles that faith and science fulfill in human life. Also present were members of the Diplomatic Corps accredited to the Holy See and high-ranking officials of the Roman Curia.

The Holy Father's address [. . .] was given in French. [. . .]

Your Eminences, Your Excellencies, Ladies and Gentlemen:

1. The conclusion of the plenary session of the Pontifical Academy of Sciences gives me the pleasant opportunity to meet its illustrious members, in the presence of my principal collaborators and the Heads of the Diplomatic Missions accredited to the Holy See. To all of you I offer a warm welcome.

My thoughts go at this moment to Professor Marini-Bettolo, who is prevented by illness from being among us, and, assuring him of my prayers, I express fervent good wishes for his restoration to health.

I would also like to greet the members taking their seats for the first time in this Academy; I thank them for having brought to your work the contribution of their lofty qualifications.

In addition, it is a pleasure for me to note the presence of Professor Adi Shamir, of the Weizmann Institute of Science at Rehovot, Israel, holder of the Gold Medal of Pius XI, awarded by the Academy, and to offer him my cordial congratulations.

Two subjects in particular occupy our attention today. They have just been ably presented to us, and I would like to express my gratitude to Cardinal Paul Poupard and Fr George Coyne for having done so.

I

2. In the first place, I wish to congratulate the Pontifical Academy of Sciences for having chosen to deal, in its plenary session, with a problem of great importance and great relevance today: the problem of the emergence of complexity in mathematics, physics, chemistry and biology.

The emergence of the subject of complexity probably

marks in the history of the natural sciences a stage as important as the stage which bears relation to the name of "Galileo," when a univocal model of order seemed to be obvious. Complexity indicates precisely that, in order to account for the rich variety of reality, we must have recourse to a number of different models.

This realization poses a question which concerns scientists, philosophers and theologians: how are we to reconcile the explanation of the world—beginning with the level of elementary entities and phenomena—with the recognition of the fact that "the whole is more than the sum of its parts"?

In his effort to establish a rigorous description and formalization of the data of experience, the scientist is led to have recourse to metascientific concepts, the use of which is, as it were, demanded by the logic of his procedure. It is useful to state exactly the nature of these concepts in order to avoid proceeding to undue extrapolations which link strictly scientific discoveries to a vision of the world, or to ideological or philosophical affirmations, which are in no way corollaries of it. Here one sees the importance of philosophy which considers phenomena just as much as their interpretation.

3. Let us think, for example, of the working out of new theories at the scientific level in order to take account of the emergence of living beings. In a correct method, one could not interpret them immediately and in the exclusive framework of science. In particular, when it is a question of the living being which is man, and of his brain, it cannot be said that these theories of themselves constitute an affirmation or a denial of the spiritual soul, or that they provide a proof of the doctrine of creation, or that, on the contrary, they render it useless.

A further work of interpretation is needed. This is precisely the object of philosophy, which is the study of the global meaning of the data of experience, and therefore also of the phenomena gathered and analysed by the sciences.

Contemporary culture demands a constant effort to synthesize knowledge and to integrate learning. Of course, the successes which we see are due to the specialization of research. But unless this is balanced by a reflection concerned with articulating the various branches of knowledge, there is a great risk that we shall have a "shattered culture," which would in fact be the negation of true culture. A true culture cannot be conceived of without humanism and wisdom.

II

4. I was moved by similar concerns on 10 November 1979, at the time of the first centenary of the birth of Albert Einstein, when I expressed the hope before this same Academy that "theologians, scholars and historians, animated by a spirit of sincere collaboration, will study the Galileo case more deeply and, in frank recognition of wrongs from whatever side they come, dispel the mistrust that still opposes, in many minds, a fruitful concord between science and faith."[36] A Study Commission was constituted for this purpose on 3 July 1981. The very year when we are celebrating the 350th anniversary of Galileo's death, the Commission is presenting today, at the conclusion of its work, a number of publications which I value highly. I would like to express my sincere gratitude to Cardinal Poupard, who was entrusted with coordinating the Commission's research in its concluding phase. To all the experts who in any way took part in the proceedings of the four groups that guided this multidisciplinary study, I express my profound satisfaction and my deep gratitude. The work that has been carried out for more than 10 years responds to a guideline suggested by the Second Vatican Council and enables us to shed more light on several important aspects of the question. In the future, it will be impossible to ignore the Commission's conclusions.

One might perhaps be surprised that at the end of the Academy's study week on the theme of the emergence of complexity in the various sciences, I am returning to the Galileo case. Has not this case long been shelved and have not the errors committed been recognized?

That is certainly true. However, the underlying problems of this case concern both the nature of science and the message of faith. It is therefore not to be excluded that one day we shall find ourselves in a similar situation, one which will require both sides to have an informed awareness of the field and of the limits of their own competencies. The approach provided by the theme of complexity could provide an illustration of this.

5. A twofold question is at the heart of the debate of which Galileo was the centre.

The first is of the epistemological order and concerns biblical hermeneutics. In this regard, two points must again be raised. In the first place, like most of his adversaries, Galileo made no distinction between the scientific approach to

---

36. AAS [Acta Apostolicae Sedis] 71 (1979): 1464–1465.

natural phenomena and a reflection on nature, of the philosophical order, which that approach generally calls for. That is why he rejected the suggestion made to him to present the Copernican system as a hypothesis, inasmuch as it had not been confirmed by irrefutable proof. Such, therefore, was an exigency of the experimental method of which he was the inspired founder.

Secondly, the geocentric representation of the world was commonly admitted in the culture of the time as fully agreeing with the teaching of the Bible, of which certain expressions, taken literally, seemed to affirm geocentrism. The problem posed by theologians of that age was, therefore, that of the compatibility between heliocentrism and Scripture.

Thus the new science, with its methods and the freedom of research which they implied, obliged theologians to examine their own criteria of scriptural interpretation. Most of them did not know how to do so.

Paradoxically, Galileo, a sincere believer, showed himself to be more perceptive in this regard than the theologians who opposed him. "If Scripture cannot err," he wrote to Benedetto Castelli, "certain of its interpreters and commentators can and do so in many ways."[37] We also know of his letter to Christine de Lorraine (1615) which is like a short treatise on biblical hermeneutics.[38]

6. From this we can now draw our first conclusion. The birth of a new way of approaching the study of natural phenomena demands a clarification on the part of all disciplines of knowledge. It obliges them to define more clearly their own field, their approach, their methods, as well as the precise import of their conclusions. In other words, this new way requires each discipline to become more rigorously aware of its own nature.

The upset caused by the Copernican system thus demanded epistemological reflection on the biblical sciences, an effort which later would produce abundant fruit in modern exegetical works and which has found sanction and a new stimulus in the Dogmatic Constitution Dei Verbum of the Second Vatican Council.

7. The crisis that I have just recalled is not the only factor to have had repercussions on biblical interpretation. Here we are concerned with the second aspect of the problem, its pastoral dimension.

By virtue of her own mission, the Church has the duty to be attentive to the pastoral consequences of her teaching. Before all else, let it be clear that this teaching must correspond to the truth. But it is a question of knowing how to judge a new scientific datum when it seems to contradict the truths of faith. The pastoral judgement which the Copernican theory required was difficult to make, in so far as geocentrism seemed to be a part of scriptural teaching itself. It would have been necessary all at once to overcome habits of thought and to devise a way of teaching capable of enlightening the people of God. Let us say, in a general way, that the pastor ought to show a genuine boldness, avoiding the double trap of a hesitant attitude and of hasty judgement, both of which can cause considerable harm.

8. Another crisis, similar to the one we are speaking of, can be mentioned here. In the last century and at the beginning of our own, advances in the historical sciences made it possible to acquire a new understanding of the Bible and of the biblical world. The rationalist context in which these data were most often presented seemed to make them dangerous to the Christian faith. Certain people, in their concern to defend the faith, thought it necessary to reject firmly-based historical conclusions. That was a hasty and unhappy decision. The work of a pioneer like Fr Lagrange was able to make the necessary discernment on the basis of dependable criteria.

It is necessary to repeat here what I said above. It is a duty for theologians to keep themselves regularly informed of scientific advances in order to examine if such be necessary, whether or not there are reasons for taking them into account in their reflection or for introducing changes in their teaching.

9. If contemporary culture is marked by a tendency to scientism, the cultural horizon of Galileo's age was uniform and carried the imprint of a particular philosophical formation. This unitary character of culture, which in itself is positive and desirable even in our own day, was one of the reasons for Galileo's condemnation. The majority of theologians did not recognize the formal distinction between Sacred Scripture and its interpretation, and this led them unduly to transpose into the realm of the doctrine of the faith a question which in fact pertained to scientific investigation.

In fact, as Cardinal Poupard has recalled, Robert Bellarmine, who had seen what was truly at stake in the debate, personally felt that, in the face of possible scientific proofs that the earth orbited round the sun, one should "interpret with great circumspection" every biblical passage which seems to

---

37. Letter of 21 November 1613, in *Edizione nazionale delle Opere di Galileo Galilei*, dir. A. Favaro, edition of 1968, vol. V, 282.

38. Letter to Christine de Lorraine, 1615, in *Edizione nazionale delle Opere di Galileo Galilei*, dir. A. Favaro, edition of 1968, vol. V, 307–48.

affirm that the earth is immobile and "say that we do not understand, rather than affirm that what has been demonstrated is false."[39] Before Bellarmine, this same wisdom and same respect for the divine Word guided St. Augustine when he wrote: "If it happens that the authority of Sacred Scripture is set in opposition to clear and certain reasoning, this must mean that the person who interprets Scripture does not understand it correctly. It is not the meaning of Scripture which is opposed to the truth but the meaning which he has wanted to give to it. That which is opposed to Scripture is not what is in Scripture but what he has placed there himself, believing that this is what Scripture meant."[40] A century ago, Pope Leo XIII echoed this advice in his Encyclical Providentissimus Deus: "Truth cannot contradict truth and we may be sure that some mistake has been made either in the interpretation of the sacred words, or in the polemical discussion itself."[41]

Cardinal Poupard has also reminded us that the sentence of 1633 was not irreformable, and that the debate which had not ceased to evolve thereafter, was closed in 1820 with the imprimatur given to the work of Canon Settele.[42]

10. From the beginning of the Age of Enlightenment down to our own day, the Galileo case has been a sort of "myth," in which the image fabricated out of the events was quite far removed from reality. In this perspective, the Galileo case was the symbol of the Church's supposed rejection of scientific progress, or of "dogmatic" obscurantism opposed to the free search for truth. This myth has played a considerable cultural role. It has helped to anchor a number of scientists of good faith in the idea that there was an incompatibility between the spirit of science and its rules of research on the one hand and the Christian faith on the other. A tragic mutual incomprehension has been interpreted as the reflection of a fundamental opposition between science and faith. The clarifications furnished by recent historical studies enable us to state that this sad misunderstanding now belongs to the past.

11. From the Galileo affair we can learn a lesson which remains valid in relation to similar situations which occur today and which may occur in the future.

In Galileo's time, to depict the world as lacking an absolute physical reference point was, so to speak, inconceivable. And since the cosmos, as it was then known, was contained within the solar system alone, this reference point could only be situated in the earth or in the sun. Today, after Einstein and within the perspective of contemporary cosmology neither of these two reference points has the importance they once had. This observation, it goes without saying, is not directed against the validity of Galileo's position in the debate; it is only meant to show that often, beyond two partial and contrasting perceptions, there exists a wider perception which includes them and goes beyond both of them.

12. Another lesson which we can draw is that the different branches of knowledge call for different methods. Thanks to his intuition as a brilliant physicist and by relying on different arguments, Galileo, who practically invented the experimental method, understood why only the sun could function as the centre of the world, as it was then known, that is to say, as a planetary system. The error of the theologians of the time, when they maintained the centrality of the earth, was to think that our understanding of the physical world's structure was, in some way, imposed by the literal sense of Sacred Scripture. Let us recall the celebrated saying attributed to Baronius: "Spiritui Sancto mentem fuisse nos docere quomodo ad coelum eatur, non quomodo coelum gradiatur." In fact, the Bible does not concern itself with the details of the physical world, the understanding of which is the competence of human experience and reasoning. There exist two realms of knowledge, one which has its source in Revelation and one which reason can discover by its own power. To the latter belong especially the experimental sciences and philosophy. The distinction between the two realms of knowledge ought not to be understood as opposition. The two realms are not altogether foreign to each other, they have points of contact. The methodologies proper to each make it possible to bring out different aspects of reality.

III

13. Your Academy conducts its work with this outlook. Its principal task is to promote the advancement of knowledge with respect for the legitimate freedom of science[43] which the Apostolic See expressly acknowledges in the statutes of your institution.

What is important in a scientific or philosophic theory

---

39. Letter to Fr A. Foscarini, 12 April 1615, cf. *Edizione nazionale delle Opere di Galileo Galilei,* dir. A. Favaro, vol. XII, 172.

40. Saint Augustine, *Epistula* 143, n. 7, *PL* 33, col. 588.

41. Pope Leo XIII, Acta, vol. XIII (1894), 361.

42. Cf. Pontificia Academia Scientiarum, *Copernico, Galilei e la Chiesa. Fine della controversia* (1820). Gli atti del Sant'Ufficio, a cura di W. Brandmuller e E. J. Griepl, Firenze, Olschki, 1992.

43. Cf. Second Vatican Ecumenical Council, Pastoral Constitution *Gaudium et spes,* n. 36, par. 2.

is above all that it should be true or, at least, seriously and solidly grounded. And the purpose of your Academy is precisely to discern and to make known, in the present state of science and within its proper limits, what can be regarded as an acquired truth or at least as enjoying such a degree of probability that it would be imprudent and unreasonable to reject it. In this way unnecessary conflicts can be avoided.

The seriousness of scientific knowledge will thus be the best contribution that the Academy can make to the exact formulation and solution of the serious problems to which the Church, by virtue of her specific mission, is obliged to pay close attention—problems no longer related merely to astronomy, physics and mathematics, but also to relatively new disciplines such as biology and biogenetics. Many recent scientific discoveries and their possible applications affect man more directly than ever before, his thought and action, to the point of seeming to threaten the very basis of what is human.

14. Humanity has before it two modes of development. The first involves culture, scientific research and technology, that is to say whatever falls within the horizontal aspect of man and creation, which is growing at an impressive rate. In order that this progress should not remain completely external to man, it presupposes a simultaneous raising of conscience, as well as its actuation. The second mode of development involves what is deepest in the human being, when transcending the world and transcending himself, man turns to the One who is the Creator of all. It is only this vertical direction which can give full meaning to man's being and ac-

tion, because it situates him in relation to his origin and his end. In this twofold direction, horizontal and vertical, man realizes himself fully as a spiritual being and as homo sapiens. But we see that development is not uniform and linear, and that progress is not always well ordered. This reveals the disorder which affects the human condition. The scientist who is conscious of this twofold development and takes it into account contributes to the restoration of harmony.

Those who engage in scientific and technological research admit as the premise of its progress that the world is not a chaos but a "cosmos"—that is to say, that there exist order and natural laws which can be grasped and examined, and which, for this reason, have a certain affinity with the spirit. Einstein used to say: "What is eternally incomprehensible in the world is that it is comprehensible."[44] This intelligibility, attested to by the marvelous discoveries of science and technology, leads us, in the last analysis, to that transcendent and primordial Thought imprinted on all things.

Ladies and gentlemen, in concluding these remarks, I express my best wishes that your research and reflection will help to give our contemporaries useful directions for building a harmonious society in a world more respectful of what is human. I thank you for the service you render to the Holy See, and I ask God to fill you with his gifts.

From John Paul II, "Faith Can Never Conflict with Reason: On Galileo," *L'osservatore Romano* 44, no. 1264 (November 4, 1992).

---

44. In the *Journal of the Franklin Institute,* vol. 221, n. 3, March 1936.

CHAPTER 8

Christianity and Other Religions
as World Phenomena

Ecumenical issues, or relations among different Christian denominations, were addressed, among other subjects, in the previous chapter in the section New Notions of "Church." In this chapter we turn to interreligious issues, that is, relations between Christianity and other religions. Interreligious dialogue has become increasingly important since the 1960s for several reasons. Historical consciousness has grown incrementally in the nineteenth and twentieth centuries: the resulting recognition of the violent conflicts of the past has fostered a desire for tolerance and inclusive understandings among religious groups and their leaders. From the vantage point of historical-critical theology, Christians in the twentieth century wakened to the anti-Semitism present within their tradition, beginning with the New Testament, and to the mixed motives of the Crusades undertaken by the Western Church against the Muslims. Moreover, Christians have largely lost the desire to pass judgment on other religions.

Public acknowledgment of past failures makes it possible to build new relationships on the principles and experiences of tolerance that have been part of Christian traditions but not always practiced. In this chapter, Metropolitan Georges Khodr takes notice of the numerous positive references to other religions in the New Testament—for example, in the Acts of the Apostles, the Book of Revelation, and in Paul's speech to the Athenians. In Khodr's account, Origen, Gregory of Nazianzus, Augustine, and Irenaeus in the early Church were able, by different measures and means, to affirm God's work outside Christianity. Clement of Alexandria should be added to that list. In the Middle Ages, however, Abelard, Nicholas of Cusa, and Francis of Assisi were exceptional for

their positive attitude toward other religions amid a growing negativity toward Islam—a negativity already strong in the Eastern Church, where Islam was a religion of occupation.

Within the Christian tradition, sustained philosophical and theological thought on other world religions dates to the fifteenth century with the humanist writings of Marsilio Ficino (1433–99) and Giovanni Pico della Mirandola (1463–94). Three centuries later David Hume (1711–76) inaugurated the category "natural" religion in his *Dialogue concerning Natural Religion* and his *Natural History of Religion* and, together with other Enlightenment thinkers, provided new frameworks for approaching historic religions. The work of Immanuel Kant (1724–1804) was informed by courses he taught on Chinese religions and by his studies of Persian religion. And in his *Lectures on the Philosophy of Religion,* Georg Wilhelm Friedrich Hegel (1770–1831) attempted three different combinations of historic religions—Roman, Egyptian, Jewish, Greek, Oriental, and Christian—conceiving the combinations as different ways of understanding the relationships of particular manifestations of universal Spirit. As flawed as these efforts may seem to us today, they provide evidence of increasing interest in other religions from within the Christian tradition. Today Christianity cannot be understood, either in its historical particularity or in the ways in which it surpasses that particularity, except in terms of its relationships to other religions. Interreligious dialogue is dialogue within as well as between religions and cultures. It occurs whenever people of two religions, proximate to each other in terms of interest or geography, make the effort to talk to each other in order to understand each other better. With Hindus and Buddhists in North

America (a largely Christian continent) and Christians in Japan and Korea (largely Buddhist territories), the challenge of interreligious dialogue has become an important issue.

Those who engage in dialogue do so from a perspective and, as Bultmann pointed out, with presuppositions. Three models of interreligious dialogue—the exclusivist, the inclusivist, and the pluralist—are often used to foreground prejudgments brought to encounters with other religions. Exclusivists characteristically are preoccupied with making the historical reality of Christ known and with working toward a unity of all who may become Christian believers. Exclusivists are not likely to appreciate other religions on their own terms. Inclusivists, too, understand other religions through their own; however, they see the beauty, history, and challenge of other religions as positive and transformative. Pluralists avoid absolutist language about their own religion, such as "one and only," "definitive," or "absolute." Many are convinced that the survival of earthly life depends on engaging in interreligious dialogue to relieve suffering—both human and ecological. Of the three models, pluralism has undergone the most development in recent years.

Inculturation introduces a special kind of complexity within the more general subject of interreligious dialogue. Specifically at issue is the relationship between Christianity and other religions indigenous to a particular country. In the past Christianity often attempted to displace the "native" religion rather than try to adapt itself to and incorporate "building blocks" from the indigenous culture. Today, inculturation (or, as Fabien Eboussi Boulaga calls it, "acculturation") is understood as the effort by a religion to insert itself in and adapt itself to new social, cultural, economic, and religious milieus. We speak, for example, of the inculturation of Christianity in the midst of African culture and religion. Inculturation in this sense involves an effort to understand indigenous cultures and religions, albeit the main purpose is to impose Christianity on non-Christian populations.

The problems that inculturation causes are common to any religion that takes root in a culture foreign to it. On the one hand, to be authentic an individual's convictions must be generated from within. Not only is this principle the basis of religious freedom, but it is today what is broadly called freedom of conscience. Few question this basic human freedom, and most would assume it applies not only to one religion but to all. On the other hand, there are compelling reasons to affirm that a person's beliefs are also shaped and influenced by family, history, culture, religion, and society and that beliefs can grow, decline, and change. In this sense, the deep-

ening and the possible development of one's own religious convictions—understanding some of those convictions well perhaps for the first time—may be an unexpected result of the demands brought about by encounters with other, sometimes foreign beliefs. The problem of inculturation with respect to the spread of Christianity manifests itself differently in Africa than in Asia. In Africa, inculturation addresses the relationship between Christianity and African religions and the attendant problem of what "authentic African Christianity" should be. It is commonly overlooked that Augustine was an African and that the Berbers in North Africa were among the first converts to Christianity. The question of inculturation goes back to the question of the relationship between Christianity and the state. In some Asian countries, the persecution of both Christianity and Buddhism as "foreign" has raised separate but similar issues. But in India, various churches of the Thomas Christians are thought to date back to the apostle Thomas or to the second century. Also, Asian theology is beginning to have an effect on the whole Church. The effort to understand the meaning of religious inculturation is at the heart of current thinking about interreligious dialogue and the relation between Christianity and other religions. With his historical account of Christians' observations of people of other religions—beginning with the New Testament and using individual missionaries' different ways of understanding their own religion—Andrew Walls provides a context for rethinking some of the same issues in the Christian missionary movement.

Fabien Eboussi Boulaga is the first of two African voices here who have opposing views on inculturation and religion. Eboussi Boulaga is an intensely Hegelian philosopher. His *Christianity without Fetishes* (1981) is a critical constructive study of religious conversion from tribal membership to Church membership, from the perspective of someone who has experience of both tribal and Christian communities. In this excerpt, entitled "The Tribal Condition in a Situation of Acculturation: Taking This Condition Seriously," Eboussi Boulaga, a theologian from French-speaking West Africa, goes beyond the familiar critiques of colonialism. According to him, continuity between "native" religions and Christianity is not perceived as coming from the outside. The one who "rises up" in the name of God is a prophet, "another Christ," or one sent by Christ, and thus is "someone vested with a power of initiative and decision, and not merely of witness, commentary, and the preservation of an intangible deposit of faith." This "coming of Christ" changes the character of the group. Eboussi Boulaga sees the change as a deepening and as a continuity: it is the assumption of the spirit and power of Christ vis-à-vis whatever is genuinely evil.

Gerhardus Cornelis Oosthuizen, a Protestant theologian whose starting point is a "faith in Jesus" theology that emphasizes interior religion, answers the question of whether Christianity can become other than what it has been. He does not recognize "natural theology" or the "saving value" of other religious traditions. For him, the value of the religion of Christianity is that it has received the gift of knowing what it must not be. In his exclusionist position, the African prophetic movements are only misguided attempts to justify and sanctify themselves. "Nativistic" African religions, such as the Nazarites and Kimbanguists, usurp the place of Christ and are therefore "post-Christian" rather than Christian. The difference between the positions represented by Eboussi Boulaga and Oosthuizen was the object of a long dispute from the 1960s through the 1980s.

Metropolitan Georges Khodr's theological position allows for God's action outside Christian belief and thus clearly contrasts with that of Oosthuizen. He uses Israel as an analogy to argue for the freedom of God to "raise up prophets outside the sociological confines of the New Israel just as He raised them up outside the confines of Old Israel." In this view, people outside Christianity who are called to prophecy and wisdom "possess a secret bond with the power of the Risen One." Khodr also has a tolerant view of the Church: human sin may obscure the "plenitude" of Christ in history, and the Church at times does not point toward God. Whereas Oosthuizen focuses on the failure of the temporal Church, Khodr, a Greek Orthodox theologian, understands the Church to be substantial yet invisible at the same time.

Two documents that were passed and promulgated in 1965 by the Second Vatican Council bear special relevance for interreligious dialogue. The first, *Declaration on Religious Liberty: On the Rights of the Person and Communities to Social and Civil Liberty in Religious Matters,* strongly affirms the right to religious freedom, both private and communal. "Right" here implies the responsibility of the state to recognize and to protect the exercise of freedom of religious expression. This document addresses abuses of religious freedom as well as the right of parents to educate their children. The second document, *Declaration on the Relationship of the Church to Non-Christian Religions,* was hailed by the World Council of Churches as the first result of "a gradual and timid quest for another type of relationship" with non-Christian religions and a "generous expression of respect" for Muslims and other people of faith. Footnotes to this document give insight into items for discussion, some of which were excluded from the final draft. The declaration will be remembered for initiating a new pluralist direction in interreligious dialogue. At the time, however, John Courtney Murray, invited observer to the council and contributor to the document on religious liberty, called it the "most controversial document of the whole Council." Subsequently, the Vatican and the World Council of Churches both initiated formal dialogues with Muslims. The Pontifical Commission for Religious Relations with Muslims, now housed in the Vatican Secretariat for Non-Christians, was founded in 1964, and the World Council of Churches opened a new unit for interreligious dialogue with Muslims in 1971.

Two documents presented here pertain to the relationship of Christianity to Judaism. The first document is a statement of belief; the second, a statement of policy. Many refer to "Statement on the Jewish Question" (1950) as the "Statement of Guilt regarding Israel." It is written in the genre of a creed. Simplicity and directness make it accessible to everyone. In the second document, "Jewish-Christian Relations in the Wider Perspective of Dialogue with People of Other Faiths and Ideologies" (1977), Krister Stendahl argues for the need to place Jewish-Christian dialogues in the larger contexts of the relationship of Christianity to all non-Christian religions. Because of its early historical and religious affinity with Judaism, Christianity has a special obligation to overcome anti-Semitism wherever it is found today.

"Statement on the Middle East" (1968) by the World Council of Churches, is about Christian theology and the Jewish people and implicitly echoes Stendahl's insight that the Christian relationship with Jews must take into consideration particular historical circumstances—here the aftermath of the Six-Day War in the Middle East. But little has changed since its publication. The World Council of Churches report "Muslims and Christians in Society" (1975) reviews the more than 1,300 years of interaction between Muslims and Christians and states guidelines for formal contemporary interfaith dialogues.

Asian religions come to the fore with two texts: "Buddhism and Christianity as Complementary" (1978) by John Cobb and "Dual Citizenship in Faith?" (1988) by Hans Küng. Cobb, a Protestant pioneer in Buddhist-Christian dialogue, describes four models of approaches to understanding the relation of Christianity to Buddhism that emphasize the differences in beliefs and goals of the two religions. Cobb argues that "both can be true" and believes that "both *are* true." But that affirmation leads to other questions, as posed by Küng: whether one may legitimately belong to two or more religions at the same time and what the criteria are for doing so.

A dialogue between Julia Ching, a scholar of Chinese religions, and Küng, a Catholic revisionary theologian, took place on the occasion of lectures given by Ching in 1987 on Chinese perspectives in folk religions, Confucianism, Taoism, and Buddhism. Each lecture was followed by "A Christian Response" from Küng. In his epilogue to the published lectures, Küng answers "no" to the question of dual citizenship on the grounds that what is most important in Christianity is the "event of Jesus Christ," rather than a religion in the sense of "a system of symbols, a set of rites, a catalogue of moral prescriptions or a programme of special practices." For this reason, he thinks, "Christian existence cannot be defined in advance. It exists wherever the Spirit of Christ raises up a new form of being for man individually and collectively." He suggests that the question is one of inculturation rather than of citizenship.

Küng's epilogue serves well as the last text of our book because it is also prologue to Christianities that are, and always have been since the first century, in the process of becoming something new. How, then, is Christianity to relate to others? Küng proposes that "in both large and small things, Christianity, a minority, should stand in the service of humanity, the majority." Küng and the other authors in this chapter resemble the scribe who, according to the Gospel of Matthew, having been "trained for the kingdom of heaven," is like a person that is a householder, who brings forth out of her treasure new things and old (Matt 13:52). So what will be the relationship between Christianity and other religions in the future? Answers are not easy to discern, but the suggestions of these authors make it possible to live the questions in the light of the best of the tradition.

In "Romans One and the Modern Missionary Movement" (1996), **Andrew F. Walls,** a former missionary to Africa, provides an overview of missionary activity around the world. Proselytism, though perhaps the most well known, is only one form of interreligious encounters in which Christianity has been involved.

ANDREW F. WALLS

"Romans One and the Modern Missionary Movement," in *The Missionary Movement in Christian History*

There is no telling what may happen when people begin to read the Epistle to the Romans. What happened to Augustine, Luther, Wesley and Barth launched great spiritual movements which have left their mark in world history. But similar things have happened, much more frequently,

to very ordinary people as the words of this Epistle came home to them with power.

F. F. Bruce[1]

The explosive effect of the Epistle to the Romans has been as marked in the missionary movement as anywhere else. The number of nineteenth-century missionary sermons and appeals based on Romans 10:14f. alone is beyond calculation. A district secretary of the Church Missionary Society at the middle of the century sees this section as the climax of the epistle. The opening has proved that Jews and Gentiles are equally guilty in God's sight, and thus in equal need of salvation; Paul goes on to state the method of salvation, justification by faith; and then to prove the importance and propriety of its publication to the Gentiles; and by the section 10:11–15, "binds all who have the gospel to send it to them."[2] Half a century later, A. T. Pierson, one of the formative influences on the movement of the 80s and 90s which transformed the size and nature of the European and American missionary forces, was characteristically speaking of Romans 10 as "The unparalleled missionary chapter of the Bible" and, equally characteristically, dividing its content alliteratively as The Market for Missions, the Message of Missions, the Methods of Missions, and the Motive for Missions.[3]

Another theme beloved of nineteenth-century preachers was that of Romans 3:29, "Is he not the God of the Gentiles also?"—or, as W. Y. Fullerton insisted, "God is the God of the heathen also."[4] But this affirmation proceeds directly from the argument of 1:18f. about the universality of God's wrath, and this section, especially that which refers specifically to the pagan world (1:18–32) has not unnaturally had a history of its own in missionary thought.

The Christian view of non-Christian religions reflects traditions of thought which have come to be denominated respectively those of "continuity" and "discontinuity,"[5] the one

1. F. F. Bruce, *The Epistle of Paul to the Romans,* TNTC [Tyndale New Testament Commentaries] (London, 1963), 60.

2. John Johnson, *Sermons* I (London, 1850), 115.

3. A. T. Pierson, "The Market for Missions," *Missionary Sermons: A Selection from the Discourses Delivered on Behalf of the Baptist Missionary Society on Various Occasions* (London, 1925), 185ff. The sermon was originally delivered in 1903.

4. W. Y. Fullerton, "The God of the Heathen Also," ibid., 299–310. The sermon was delivered in 1909.

5. These terms were popularized through the discussions at the International Missionary Council Meeting at Tambaram, Madras, in 1938; see especially *The Authority of the Faith,* Tambaram Series I (London, 1939). Behind the discussions lay Hendrik Kraemer's preparatory volume, *The Christian Message in a Non-Christian World* (London, 1938).

stressing God's activity in the world outside the sphere of Scripture or church, recognizing or seeking points of contact between the biblical revelation and that activity, as certainly God's own; the other stressing the radical difference between God's redeeming actions in saving history and any system whatever of human thought or life, seeing religion in itself under the judgment of God, sometimes denying any affinity between that revelation and "religion" at all. Both traditions are very ancient, going back to the earliest Christian centuries, arguably both to the New Testament.[6] The representatives of each, with their favourite Scripture passages, have ever claimed to represent the mind of the New Testament; and, further, have supported their views with a wealth of empirical evidence about non-Christian religious thought and life.

II

Romans 1:18ff., save for the modern debate about the nature and extent of the knowledge of God implied in 1:20, has not been an exegetical battlefield between the traditions in the way provided, for instance, by the missionary content of the Iconium and Areopagus addresses in Acts.[7] Its special place in the missionary movement is due to the fact that at various times people saw there, or thought they saw there, the non-Christian world that they themselves knew; and at other times, assuming these verses to give the origin of non-Christian religion, they were puzzled to account for other features of non-Christian religion which did not apparently accord with such a picture. That Paul's intention in the section as a whole is to show the whole world under judgment has hardly been in doubt; that the specific details of 1:22–27 reflect a view of contemporary Graeco-Roman society in decadence has usually also been recognized. But what is the relation of these particulars to the general principle? Is Paul simply describing how the seamier side of contemporary pagan society came into being? Or is he describing the origin of all non-Christian religions—perhaps even of religion itself? Does he assume the willful rejection of a universal primitive monotheism? And—given an answer to any of these—how are the phenomena of non-Christian religion actually in view at the time to be accommodated to it? It is such questions as these, or rather, the assumed answers to them, which underlie much of the debate arising from Christian evangelization.

For the early Christian missionary thinkers, it was not Romans 1 which expressed the most important Christian contact with the non-Christian world. For them pagan society and pagan popular religion was at least broadly similar to

that which Paul knew; and the most liberal of them had no desire to declare affinity with it. Justin, who is quite prepared to believe that Socrates and anyone else who spoke according to *logos,* and inasfar as they did so, were Christians before Christ,[8] is also certain that the gods of the street corner are demonic parodies, the direct result of wicked impositions by evil spirits. Such thinkers were much more concerned to maintain their affinity with the philosophical tradition, which for them represented the glory of their inheritance, and which rejected popular religion as strenuously as they did; in fact, it was a mark of the Logos at work in Socrates that he defied popular religion and, like the Christians, was branded an atheist for doing so.[9] Justin, in fact, has reached a place where many another missionary was to come over the next eighteen centuries: he has concluded that there is more than one type of non-Christian tradition. There is that which is palpably devilish; there is that which is compatible with the Gospel and strenuously opposed to what it opposes.

The long period during which Western Europe was almost insulated from the non-Christian world meant that, apart from Jews, the only non-Christian peoples of whom most Christians, at least in the countries which became Protestant, knew much were those same Greeks and Romans, brought to life again by the new learning. Paul's catalogue of loathsomeness could be amply documented from other sources. . . .[10] Other sources also revealed that some pagans stood aloof from these abominations: Calvin's first major work, after all, was a commentary on Seneca. But with no regular living contact with a self-consciously non-Christian society, it was easy for Reformed Christians to separate, as the early apologists did, the philosophic from the religious tradition of classical paganism. Romans 1:18ff. could thus be taken to indicate how "idolatry"—i.e., all religion outside Israel and the Church—took its origin.

III

When, in North America, contact with a non-Christian people was resumed, there was little reason to question this

---

6. P. Beyerhaus, "Religionen und Evangelium, Kontinuität oder Diskontinuität." *Evang. Missions Magazin* 3 (1967), 118–35.

7. Cf. G. Gärtner, *The Areopagus Speech and Natural Revelation* (Uppsala, 1995).

8. Justin, *First Apology* 46.

9. Ibid., 5, 6.

10. In Rom. 1:23. ("Of these abominations thou hast with Lactantius, Eusebius and Augustine," says Calvin).

judgment. As the colonists looked upon the Indians—often with a desire for their salvation[11]—they saw the darkened heart changing the glory of the incorruptible God into an image, the bodies given up to lust and dishonour plainly enough.[12] There was not even a Seneca. The connection between ancient and modern heathenism was also apparent:

> Let us inquire into the records of *antiquity*, let us consult the experience of all ages, and we shall find, that those who had no guide but the light of nature, no instructor but unassisted reason, have wandered in perpetual uncertainty, darkness and error. Or let us take a view of the *present* state of those countries that have not been illuminated by the gospel; and we shall see, that notwithstanding the improvements of near six thousand years, they remain to this day covered with the grossest darkness, and abandoned to the most immoral and vicious practices.[13]

Despite the clear manifestation of the "invisible things of God" some ancient heathen denied his existence, while the rest worshipped his creatures, and "even the most despicable beings in the order of nature."

> This was the state of the Gentile nations when the light of the gospel appeared to scatter the darkness that overspread the face of the earth. And this has been the case, so far as has yet appeared, of all the nations ever since, upon whom the Sun of righteousness has not arisen with healing in his wings. Every new discovered country opens a new scene of astonishing ignorance and barbarity; and gives fresh evidence of the universal corruption of human nature.[14]

For the preacher of missionary ordination sermons, viewing the Amer-indians from without, this was no doubt enough. But those who penetrated more closely into Native American society, while unequivocal in their affirmation of human depravity, saw other factors also. So early a missionary as John Eliot (1604–1690), a man living close to the Indians and learning their language, is struck by the fact that this people, although idolatrous and immoral, did believe, despite first appearances, in the Deity; that they believed also in the immortality of the soul, and an eternity of happiness or misery—they even had a tradition of one man who had actually seen God. Eliot, like several of his Puritan colleagues, came to the conclusion that the Native Americans were a remnant of the ten lost tribes of Israel. This would also explain their food taboos and purification rites, and their

story of a general deluge. Over the years an idea with breathtaking implications grew in him: might not the Amer-indians be only a fragment of the Semitic peoples who had broken away from the rest? Might not the peoples of India, of China, of Japan also be descended from the ten tribes? Alas then, why do they not all talk Hebrew? Eliot can speak only of the local language, but at least its grammatical frame is nearer to Hebrew than to Latin or Greek. Perhaps Chinese, Japanese, the Indian languages, are all degenerate forms of Hebrew. Perhaps, far more important, the conversion of the Indians, of which his own labours were a pledge, is but the sign that God is going to break eastward for the conversion of Israel, the ten tribes as well as the two?[15]

It is easy to laugh at the enthusiasms of this lonely missionary; but he is grasping at a rationalization of a fact of experience. On a simple reading of Romans 1:18ff., Native American religion ought to be unrelievedly idolatrous. But it is not. The presence of other elements, however, can be explained as survivals in debased form of part of the Jewish revelation. Not only so, but in other parts of the world—India, China, Japan—traces of the same redemptive revelation may be found. By elimination, only in Africa and among other Hamitic peoples, will Romans 1 apply in all its rigour as a picture of religion.

At a later period, Jonathan Edwards, a warm supporter of missions and no stranger to the Indians himself, again finds the truth of Romans 1:18ff. confirmed by his own observations:

> The doctrine of St. Paul, concerning the blindness into which the Gentiles fell, is so confirmed by the state of religion in Africa, America, and even China, where, to this day no advances towards the true religion have been made, that we can no longer be at a loss to judge the insufficiency of unassisted reason to dissipate the prejudices of the Heathen world, and open their eyes to religious truths.[16]

---

11. R. Pierce Beaver, *Church, State, and the American Indians* (St. Louis: [Concordia Publishing House], 1966).

12. Joseph Sewall, *Christ Victorious over the Powers of Darkness*[. . . .] (Boston, 1733). Reprinted in R. Pierce Beaver, *Pioneers in Mission: The Early Missionary Ordination Sermons, Charges, and Instructions* (Grand Rapids: [William B. Eerdmans], 1966), 41–64 (see 47).

13. Ebenezer Pemberton, *A Sermon Preached in Newark, June 12, 1744, at the Ordination of Mr. David Brainerd* [. . .] in R. Pierce Beaver, *Pioneers in Mission*, 111–24 (see 113).

14. Ibid., 114.

15. See S. H. Rooy, *The Theology of Missions in the Puritan Tradition* (Delft, 1965), 230ff.

16. Jonathan Edwards, *Works* (1817 ed.) VIII, 193.

Whence, then, come such approximations to "religious truths" as any of these may have? Edwards answers, from outside. Heathenism since the fall has been so dark that such a custom as sacrifice for sin could not have originated there. It *must* have been derived from the Jews. In the paganism of the old world, Plato, though a lesser philosopher than Socrates, yet knew more than he about true religion. The reason is that Socrates, unlike Plato, never left Greece, and was thus less open to outside influences.

On such an explanation of those elements in non-Christian religion which cannot be ascribed to willful blindness, it would be, of course, in the devil's interest to isolate peoples as far as possible from infectious contact with revealed religion. And Edwards argues that this actually happened: America was first peopled by the direct action of the devil. Satan, alarmed at the success of the gospel in the first three Christian centuries, surprised by the fall of the heathen Empire in the time of Constantine, and fearing that his kingdom might be completely overthrown, led the Indians away into America so that he could keep them for himself.

IV

Meanwhile, in contemporary Europe, far away from the real heathen, the genteel debate about "natural theology" was going forward. The argument of the *consensus gentium* acquired fresh importance. "No nation without belief in God," said the theologian; and the sceptic made answer, "How do you know?"

The evidence of the Jesuit missionaries from China became an absorbing interest. On the face of it, it represented a triumph for orthodoxy, and for the presence of "natural" religion; for here was a people which had allegedly preserved the knowledge of God and obeyed a pure morality for more than two thousand years. Leibniz, whom we do not usually think of as a herald of the missionary movement, wanted Protestant missionaries to teach revealed religion to the Chinese who had preserved natural religion so effectively. In the end, of course, the other orders defeated the Jesuits on the interpretation of the Chinese texts, and this particular source of evidence for natural theology (which was in any case inconveniently proving too much) passed out of view—though attention was always available for accounts by travellers of the beliefs of non-Christian societies.

Only a small part of the debate about China was concerned with the exegesis of Romans or any other apostolic book; nor, despite the undoubtedly sincere plea of Leibniz

for a Protestant mission, was it really conducted with any idea of doing anything. The Chinese, like the Tahitians later, were being called in to help solve a European problem. By contrast, the members and agents of the missionary societies which began to form by the end of the century were desperately concerned with action: action for the salvation of the souls of those to whom they went. The terms in which people spoke of non-Christian religions were transformed as a result. For one thing, the Evangelical Revival, which underlay the new movement, had brought a more radical view and more vivid sense of the nature of sin; for another, earnest men were transmitting accounts of what they actually saw.

And what they saw was not usually a grave, distant, polite people preserving over thousands of years the knowledge of God and pure morality—the terms of the earlier eighteenth-century debate—but human sacrifice, the immolation of widows, the pictorial representations of *lingam* and *yonni*, cult prostitution, the victims crushed beneath the car of Jagannath. The picture of Romans 1:18ff., in fact, emerged again, less from a theory of religion than from the effect of observation; and the words and phrases of Romans 1:18ff. ring out time and again as missionaries view the religion of non-Christian peoples. Further, just as the early apologists shared with the philosophical tradition much of the polemic against popular religion, so the missionaries in India had allies—liberal intellectuals with burning desire for religious reformation, like Rajah Ram Mohan Roy, and angry young men like some of [Alexander] Duff's early converts, rebelling against the traditional practices.

Africa likewise recalled Romans 1 for many observers. David Jonathan East, one of a small host of writers on West Africa in the 1840s, produces an imposing account (based on travellers' tales) of African slavery, drunkenness, immorality, and lack of commercial probity. He then quotes Romans 1:28–31. "What an awful comment upon this affecting portion of Holy Writ are the humiliating facts which these and the preceding chapters record."[17] In another place, however, East recognizes that African paganism, though reprehensible, is in one respect different from that of Romans 1. Though African peoples have images, they do not make images of the Supreme God: they simply ignore him for the subordinate divinities and spirits.

---

17. D. J. East, *Western Africa: Its Condition and Christianity the Means of Its Recovery* (London, 1844), 71.

Thus it appears, that if they have not "changed the glory of the incorruptible God into an image, made like to corruptible man, and to birds, and four-footed beasts and creeping things"—they have, in their view, excluded him from the government of his world, and substituted in his room the wild creatures of their own imaginations, identifying these professedly spiritual existences with what is material, and oft times grossly absurd.[18]

African paganism thus demonstrates the principles of Romans in 1:18ff., but identity in detail is not demanded.

V

As the nineteenth century proceeded, such missionary views came into contact, and sometimes, collision, with new patterns of thought. There was the new interest, itself partly a result of the missionary movement, in the literature of Eastern religions. There was the regnant hypothesis, held with all the intensity of a newfound faith, of the evolution of religion. There was the whole new science, with evolution as its basis, of anthropology, and *The Golden Bough* to link them all together.

There were many points of conflict. The missionary affirmation of the idea of a supreme God was immediately suspect; for animistic peoples who had not reached the appropriate stage, such a conception could only be a missionary invention. The charge was quite unjustified, for, on the reading of Romans 1 which most early missionaries had, there was no need to invent a High God in any non-Christian religion. They found the High God in African religion because he was there, not because their theology demanded his presence.

As the evolutionist doctrine gained repute, the rival doctrine of a primitive monotheism, from which all nonbiblical religions were descended, was more clearly enunciated, and Romans 1:20ff. was its prime source. Sir Monier Williams, an influential Sanskrit scholar and himself a devout Evangelical, argued that, just because of the original monotheism behind all religions, one could expect to find fragments of truth.[19] No longer was it necessary to presuppose borrowing from Jewish sources to explain every acceptable element in non-Christian religion. At one point he went further, and declared that some of the essential doctrines of Christianity were present in germ in all religions, awaiting the development and fulfilment which only Christianity could bring.[20]

It was possible, however, to affirm a primitive monotheism without drawing all these conclusions. Principal (later Bishop) Moule, a deep influence on scores of the new type of missionary who went out in such numbers in the 1880s, gave exegetical backing to such a view. The great Johannes Warneck was among those who observed in paganism a memory, tenuous and not understood, of the primeval revelation:

> Dispassionate study of heathen religions confirms Paul's view that heathenism is a fall from a better knowledge of God.[21]

In early days humanity had a greater treasure of spiritual goods, but neglected its knowledge and renounced its dependence until nothing remained but a dim presentiment. Not that all saw anything as formalized as a primitive monotheism in Romans 1. A. E. Garvie, a formative influence on several important missionary writers of the twentieth century, argued that the essence of Paul's argument had nothing to do with the origin of religions at all but simply with the "close connection between false views of God and wrong standard of duty," and that the Roman society of which Paul was primarily speaking had, to common knowledge, suffered a decline.[22]

In fact, one arm at least of the missionary movement began to develop the line of argument indicated, though later repudiated, by Monier Williams. Long years of study of the classics of Eastern religions indicated that Christianity was in fact their fulfilment—the "crown," to use the expression of the outstanding protagonist of this school, John Nicol Farquhar.[23] To pass from Duff's description of Hinduism to Farquhar's is to move to a different world. Yet each is describing exactly what he saw. Of course, time had brought changes—some of what Duff had seen had gone forever. But the main difference lies in the fact that Farquhar had, as it were, met Seneca.

Farquhar's series "The Religious Quest" (the singular is significant) reveals the sources of change. Sydney Cave is thoroughly representative of the contributors when he de-

18. Ibid., 148.

19. M. Monier Williams, *Indian Wisdom, or Examples of the Religious, Philosophical and Ethical Doctrines of the Hindus* (London, 1875), 143f. (4th ed., 132 n.).

20. M. Monier Williams, *Modern India and the Indians* (London, 1887), 234.

21. Quoted by S. M. Zwemer, *The Influence of Animism on Islam* (London, 1920).

22. A. E. Garvie, *Romans,* Century Bible.

23. J. N. Farquhar, *The Crown of Hinduism* (Oxford, 1913).

clares that the first missionaries were disqualified from seeing the best in the non-Christian world because the sacred books were closed to them. When one looks at, for instance, the Saivite Temple in Tanjore one can understand the violent reactions of the pioneers; but the Hinduism we now face (1919) is very different from that of a century ago. "We are concerned with the 'Higher Hinduism.' Idolatry is doomed."[24]

Such judgments and such a viewpoint on Hinduism were the fruit of the study of its literature. It is thus hardly surprising that when the World Missionary Conference of 1910 came to discuss "points of contact" and "preparation for Christianity" in the religions, it was on "Animism," which has no literature, that there was most hesitation.[25]

As we have seen, Monier Williams came to retract his idea of a development of religions with Christianity as the crown; his last position stressed that a gulf—"not a mere rift across which the Christian and non-Christian may shake hands and interchange similar ideas in regard to essential truths"—lay between the Bible and the "so-called Sacred Books of the East."

> Be fair, be charitable, be Christ-like, but let there be no mistake. Let it be made absolutely clear that Christianity cannot, must not be watered down to suit the palate of either Hindu, Parsee, Confucianist, Buddhist, or Mohammedan, and that whosoever wishes to pass from the false religion to the true can never hope to do so by the rickety planks of compromise. . . .[26]

He spoke to the depths. For many missionaries the practical way of expressing an attitude to the religions came to be that, while elements of good remained, the *systems* stood condemned.

VI

It would be inappropriate here to take the story through Tambaram and beyond, though the Epistle to the Romans has always been in the background, and occasionally, as in the controversy over 1:20, right in its forefront. The traditions of continuity and discontinuity will, no doubt, continue to lock horns in the missionary debate, and the Epistle to the Romans will continue to challenge, quicken, and rebuke those who desire to declare the righteousness of God. As one reviews the place which the first chapter has hitherto had in the thought of the missionary movement, some features stand out which indicate its continuing relevance.

Christian evangelists have found themselves addressing people in societies with coherent patterns of thought—within systems of belief and activity. It has been convenient to provide names like "Buddhism" and "Hinduism" to cover numbers of these systems. The validity of this process is not a theme to discuss here; but at least we should not talk as if Paul used them himself. Perhaps too much of the debate about continuity or discontinuity has been concerned with systems. As a result, we have men, each genuinely describing what he saw, producing such different interpretations of "Hinduism" as those of Duff and Farquhar. When this is introduced into the context of Romans 1, we have one party inviting all to recognize that these non-Christian religions lie manifestly under the wrath of God for their manifest deeds, and another pointing to particular persons, books, or doctrines, and saying in effect (as Bishop Ryle said of the necessity of baptism by immersion for Eskimos), Let those believe it who can.

Argument about which is the correct, or the more correct, picture of "Hinduism" is beside the point in the light of Romans 1:18ff., for Paul's concern here is not with systems at all, but with men. It is *people* who hold down the truth of unrighteousness, who do not honour God, who are given up to dishonourable passions. It is upon men, who commit ungodly and wicked deeds, that the wrath of God is revealed.

As systems, and ultimately the collective labels for systems which we call the world religions, have slipped into the place of ungodly people in the interpretation of Romans 1, so Christianity, also conceived as a system, has sometimes slipped into the place of the righteousness of God. The true system has been opposed to false systems condemned there. It has sometimes, but not always, been realized that "Christianity" is a term formally identical with the other labels; that it certainly covers as wide a range of phenomena as most of them; that, if the principalities and powers work within human systems, they can and do work within this one. Man-in-Christianity lies under the wrath of God just as much, and for the same reasons, as Man-in-Hinduism. It was the realization of this which saved the earliest generations of the modem missionary movement from the worst sort of paternalism. Humanity was vile everywhere, not only in Ceylon.

---

24. S. Cave, *Redemption, Hindu and Christian* (Oxford, 1919).

25. *World Missionary Conference, Edinburgh 1910: Report of Commission IV, The Missionary Message in Relation to Non-Christian Religions.* See especially chap. 2.

26. E. Stock, *History of the Church Missionary Society* III (London, 1899), 304.

The Christian preacher had the same message of *repentance* and faith for the non-Christian world as he had been preaching in the Christian world; for it was not Christianity that saves, but Christ.

This in turn relates to another point: the close connection of Romans 2 with Romans 1. The "diatribe" form of Romans 1–2 has often been remarked, as has the indebtedness of the language to Wisdom 13–14 and its closeness to the normal, accepted Jewish polemic against idolatry. The thrust of Romans 1 lies in Romans 2; not in the origin of paganism but in the hopelessness of the virtuous. And, before going on to show the free acceptance of men of all kinds through faith in Christ, Paul offers (Rom. 2:17ff.) a satirical commentary on Diaspora Judaism's understanding of its mission. Here was a busy, missionizing people: a guide to the blind, a light to those that sit in darkness, a corrector of the foolish, a teacher of children—the Wisdom of the opening chapters of Proverbs and the Servant of Isaiah 42 rolled into one—who yet, for all their exaltation of the Decalogue, stole, committed adultery and sacrilege, and, as the Scripture said about the Jews of an earlier time, caused the heathen to blaspheme the name of God because of what they saw in his people. Some sharp things have been said from time to time to missionaries. Some of them are in the New Testament.

From Andrew F. Walls, *The Missionary Movement in Christian History* (Maryknoll, NY: Orbis, 1996), 55–67. [Ellipses in original.]

⬥ In his *Christianity without Fetishes* (1981; English translation, 1984), the African theologian **Fabien Eboussi Boulaga** addresses issues of membership in both Christian Churches and African tribes. For Eboussi Boulaga, the opposition between membership in the tribe and incorporation into the Church is a false dichotomy. Those incorporated into the Church do not break with the tribe and its time-honored traditions, and acculturation of the Church need not supplant tribal religions.

FABIEN EBOUSSI BOULAGA

Christianity without Fetishes

The Tribal Condition in a Situation of Acculturation [. . .]

First and foremost, and most often, the opposition between membership in the tribe and incorporation into the church is ignored or surmounted by simply identifying the two. The "necessary break" theory is refuted by practice, by a *probo ambulando*. Instead, what must be broken with and rejected is evil, symbolized by sorcery. There is no need to break with one's solicitude for the dead or any other ancestral traditions. The message of Christ is not in competition with them. On the contrary, this message has come to fulfill the dream of a life in all its fullness, a life destined to triumph even in the collapse of the framework of a way of life that had been consecrated from time immemorial.

Hence the coming of Christ bears on the lot of the group as such, and it transposes itself into, passes into a church. The continuity is there—the continuity of a life undergoing a metamorphosis in depth. The continuity is not from without, via a power or a legitimacy passed down from hand to hand or church to church, in an uninterrupted spatio-temporal chain. It is not a matter of the rediscovery of a lost meaning in the Scriptures by a bookish return to the founts. Here the one who "rises up" in the name of God is not a church reformer but a prophet—and indeed "another Christ," or at very least the personal, black emissary of the Founder, and thus someone vested with a power of initiative and decision, and not merely of witness, commentary, and the preservation of an intangible deposit of faith. This person has the mission to do for this particular African community what Jesus did for his own people when he came to fulfill the Scriptures. This new prophet is to effectuate—keeping in mind the particularities of the concrete situation—an initiatory deed of the fullness of time. This deed, which is now so busy determining conditions, has been hidden by theologies and schools of exegesis. The exegesis of the sects is neither philological nor historical-critical. It is not situated in a hermeneutical tradition that is forever resuming and elaborating the meaning of an already completed event. It is a creative interpretation or, better, a prophetic actualization, a fulfillment: what the Scriptures tell, what Jesus did, is being re-actualized here and now. Once again "something is afoot" on the face of the earth, and that earth trembles. The world changes. It is the coming of the kingdom of God, and not the spread of a Christianity or the reproduction of foreign national churches and squabbling denominations.

A Christianity of Mystery and Healing

Christianity is a celebration of life in its victory over death. Its core is the Paschal mystery. The prophets, these "other Christs," receive their mission and investiture only after passing through death and resurrection themselves. The content of the message is the everlasting victory of life over death in every one of our lives. Liturgy and daily existence alike actualize this drama in ongoing fashion. One enters into the mystery with all one's being, to receive there the meaning of life, life in all its gratuity and superabundant measure, pressed down and overflowing. Even death puts no end to life. This is a festive Christianity. It sings, it dances all the way to the Passion. Death is not explained by fall or fault—death is explained by life. The Paschal mystery is joy, not because it solaces human beings languishing under the weight of their guilt, but because it shows forth life in the midst of death. The imputation of guilt, the sense of fault as offense against God need not precede, is not the necessary, universal condition for entry into the understanding of Easter. Sins are forgiven because the kingdom of God is here, antecedently to any psychological conscientization of sin, independently of any anguish, remorse, or torment of conscience. The tears will come, but *after* one has been forgiven because one has loved much. It is not a matter of being saved so much as it is of taking part in life in its fullness. Faith becomes jubilation in the deed of divine power. The redemption that is sought after is the redemption that bestows fullness of reality on all the conditions of human life.

The whole is a quest for healing, for health—the only real refutation of disease and the forces of death. The withdrawal of all the powers of evil signals the presence of the kingdom of God or its imminent coming. The unbridled reign of death is the work of the forces of sorcery, forces that stop life in its tracks by denying it, by assigning it an end outside itself, by utilizing it as a means for something other than itself: as a means of the acquisition of wealth, or power, or any other individual, solitary affirmation. Sin, then, is indeed an "assault on God," on God's (transcendent) immanence in life. How else may we understand that a human being could wound the Utterly Other, the invulnerable Absolute? [. . .]

The Community in the Form of Love

God's denomination as Father is what the logicians call a "performative." It is an assertion that performs what it asserts. Calling God "Father" involves a certain manner of binding together relationships, of behaving, of forming a community. Calling God "Father" is not a simple allusion to an eternal subject, but an act that engages and involves the human beings performing it, and imposes on them certain rules of conduct: an original way of being-with-the-world, of being in society, of creating a community—the community of the "sons and daughters of God." It is a matter of the

principle of illimitation (called God-who-is-Father, or God-who-is-Love) becoming the structuring principle of a community of human beings. This community must be a real one, located in the conditions of place and time, and yet it must not be exclusive, but an openness, a self-implementing negation of its own closing. How is this possible?

1. *Conversion is at the basis of this society.* The community in the form of love must be such that the men and women who belong to it may be capable of, and ready for, a profession of faith. This presupposes not only liberation from physical and spiritual constraint, but also that special "availability" that consists of, and is characterized by, a self-transcendence together with a self-limitation to the actual, true conditions of action in the world. Thus, for example, in order to be able to say that we love God, whom we do not see, it is necessary that God not be "the best means" of having some effect or other upon ourselves—the best means of seeking peace, of escaping ourselves, or of affirming ourselves. He must be willed for himself, as the one toward whom we turn in the very movement of our own becoming and self-creation, as that which gives both "the power and the performance" in creative generosity.

This acknowledgment is genuine and true only to the extent to which we treat our neighbor as the presentation of this God-who-is-End in the affairs of every day. Conversion is this twofold movement, of self-transcendence and of self-limitation to the verifiable. "Be converted, for the kingdom of God is near; it is among you." Conversion, then, is marked by the change of mentality that disposes us to accept divine surprises—the reversal of our scale of the most sure values when God comes near, when he inaugurates a new creation. But in order to seek first the kingdom of God and his justice, one must be delivered from the seduction of Mammon, of Money. We must be delivered from the will to power that we find in heads of state who pass for benefactors of nations, so that we become as "the one who serves" (Matt 23:11). We shall have to be delivered from the cares and concerns that keep us in these chains of ours, the chains of anxiety, the chains of the fear of risk, confrontation, and death. Where entry into the kingdom is concerned, anger and the spirit of vengeance are diriment impediments. The required metamorphosis is not a surface one. It aims for the depths of our personhood, our center, our "heart." Here is the locus of the essential orientation. Here is the source of sense and meaning. Pure hearts will see God, for theirs is welling, surging creativity, released to a pitch that bids fair to launch them forth beyond themselves toward the other, the elsewhere, and show them what is not themselves, nor in function of themselves, but something given in a free initiative, coming upon them as a grace.

We might express the same thing in other language: human beings are under the obligation to deliver themselves from the dictatorship of the "flesh" and the dictatorship of the "world," and so to discover their original self and calling. The "flesh" is the alienated expression of self—a self locked in the prison of needs and desires, a self given over wholly and entirely to the objects of these needs and desires, so that it makes fetishes of them. Human beings decay in the midst of their possessions, swallowed up in a "having" that masks them from themselves and blocks their desire for what is to come, for what is gratuitously given, blocks them off from that which can only be the object of recognition, acknowledgment, and gratitude. In service and self-dispossession, human beings show forth what they are by renouncing what they have, by "desisting" from themselves, by standing off from themselves, withdrawing from themselves. Instead of gathering all things to themselves, they allow their own being to burst forth in a flash of light—this being of theirs which has its measureless measure in what justifies itself and thereby justifies all things besides.

The world is likewise the alienated expression of self, a self lost in its fabrications, its works, its "languages," and its institutions. These become idols, to which human beings sacrifice themselves and subject others. These become destiny; they impose their own course, mechanisms, and fatality upon human beings. Structures of violence inaugurate "the banality of evil" and oppression. One must die to the old self, then, and achieve a second childhood. Then the axiom "Nothing is impossible with God" will be real and effective.

2. *This community is a communion of brothers and sisters and friends.* It is in God that we find the measure of love and pardon—in his mercy that cares for the little ones, that makes the rain to fall on just and unjust alike, that is ever disposed to bestow good things, and that watches over the sparrows and the lilies of the field. This is the model of gratuity and liberality on which one may build a society that will not rest on the sand of debt and obligation, but on permanent solvency, thanks to genuine interchange, communication, and collective creation. As we have seen, a relationship compatible with the equality of all before God rejects discriminatory hierarchies, which set up priests and laity, rich and poor, instructed and ignorant, saints and sinners in mutual opposition. This relationship is called "fraternity," a communion of sisters and brothers. "As to you, avoid the title 'Rabbi.' One among you

is your teacher, the rest are learners" (Matt 23:8) and are one another's brothers and sisters. "Do not call anyone on earth your father. Only one is your father, the One in heaven. . . . The greatest among you will be the one who serves the rest" (Matt 23:9, 11). We are to effect the inversion, the reversal of the general practice. Authority is to be understood as power placed at the service of fraternity and love, without the perquisites of honors and advantages. "Earthly kings lord it over their people. Those who exercise authority over them are called their benefactors. Yet it cannot be that way with you. Let the greater among you be as the junior, the leader as the servant" (Luke 22:25–26).

What is this space, when is this time, in which nothing will be as elsewhere or before? Only the place and time of worship? Or in the imagination, the "invisible kingdom"? Men and women in trouble must be given an absolute future, a community where solvency reigns. The profession of faith, the acknowledgment of God as God is not compatible with just *any* exercise of power. It may not be allowed to let the walls of separation stand. The "message" is not content with revealing its sense and meaning. It must set the whole human scene on its ear and remake it. As creative force and drive, the message seeks to structure a space where law and the Sabbath are made for human beings, and not human beings for law and the Sabbath—where human beings have a greater value than observances and practices.

Love is the name of the driving force that invents organizations and institutions with a view to making new life possible. Love is the constitutive principle of the eschatological community, for this community will no longer be founded on violence in the form of all kinds of privileges—knowledge, fortune, power—or on the confiscation and free disposition on the part of a few of what belongs to each and all, of what is necessary to each one's humanity in order to be "plenary humanity." Love is not opposed to order. It poses the principle that validates all order, all law—the creative principle of the human community of the future, where there will be no more male or female, Jew or Greek, slave or free human being. "I no longer speak of you as slaves. . . . Instead, I call you friends" (John 15:15). A friendship can be struck only among equals, persons who are free of all obligations toward each other. It is founded on gratuity, liberated from the need for, dependence on, or fear of the other. It seeks solely to enjoy the other as other.

If a like program seems utopian, this is only because of the degree of alienation of the one who judges it, and the power of those who impose themselves as invincible. The faith that moves mountains counts on the improbable, and knows how to read the signs of the times that announce the possibility of a "new game"—a new tune instead of the old refrain of violence. Next, however, it knows the "imperative of limited realization," limited but urgent and indispensable for battering a breach in the ancient ramparts, for calling into question the false finalities that maintain themselves at the expense of human beings' self-determination, at the expense of their availability for unhesitating acceptance of the gift of life. Finally, this faith is not euphoric. It lives on hope, that dream of the waker. Indeed, it knows nothing of the immediate. Mediations demand an endurance to the death. The possession of oneself, one's "soul," is a long exercise in patience. For ours is not a combat against mere flesh and blood, but against those frigid monsters, the principalities and powers. It would behoove us to prepare ourselves for the day when they will break free and unleash their warriors and their apocalyptic dragons against the elect. The eschatological horizon includes the trial, the test; and it will be the height of perspicacity to take account of this on the most individual, most concrete, most everyday level we can.

3. *The community's first self-limitation is simultaneously its radical openness.* This community of converts is part of Jewish society. Born in its bosom, it shares its aspirations, its needs, yes, and its faults and ills. It is from Jewish tradition that Jesus borrows his models, his images, his arguments. He sends Israel back to its own resources, he calls upon it to listen to Moses and the prophets all over again. In a sense, everything is already there in the Scriptures. "You shall love the Lord your God with all your heart, with all your soul, with all your mind, and with all your strength . . . [and] your neighbor as yourself" (Mark 10:30–31), a scribe with his wits about him managed to rattle off. The Good News is tradition understood and grasped. It is tradition's reconquest, its recovery from forgetfulness, routine, conformism, and betrayal. It is tradition rediscovered as constitutive spontaneity, as a gushing spring.

"My mission is only to the lost sheep of the house of Israel" (Matt 15:24). It is to this society, and it alone, that Jesus addresses his message of restructuring. He refuses to transgress the limits of Palestinian Judaism. At a time when Jewish proselytism is intense, he forbids his disciples to engage in it. When Greeks seek him out, he refers them to their own grand rite of initiation:

> Unless the grain of wheat falls to the earth and dies,
> it remains just a grain of wheat.

> But if it dies,
> it produces much fruit. [Jn 12:24]

Except in particular cases, preaching to non-Jews would be to "take the food of sons and daughters and throw it to the dogs" (Matt 15:26). One does not remake society from the outside. Effective protest comes only from within, for then one is not denying one's heritage, but seeking to lead it to its highest fulfillment. Then universality is actualized in history. It is particularity, but particularity that transcends itself. How so? This new community must surmount, in its own interior, the divisions and discrimination that are tearing Israel apart. It must base itself on some principle other than convergence of might. It must realize a society of brothers, sisters, and friends, where authority is service without compensation.

The new community must attack, within itself, society's most concrete evils. Thus it is to change this society from within, for it is a "segment," a "total part" of that society. Thereby it does not erect itself into an end in itself. It does not close in upon itself. In this practice, so radical, however limited in time and space, this community encounters human beings beyond their social and cultural roles and masks. The Samaritan and the pagan are then accepted and welcomed beyond the point where convention and prejudice end. The erstwhile stranger is now within. One is now equal to the task of confronting the variety and diversity of the world. To dispose Israel for the coming of the reign of God is to posit the consequence foreseen by a number of the prophets: the incorporation of the pagans into the People of God as a decisive act of God's power. It is God himself who gathers the scattered and brings home those who are far from the land. It is he himself who places a term to the era of the mediators and special intermediaries.

As we can now see from the manner in which Jesus' deed declares itself, its importance resides less in its content than in the model it proposes. This model comprises three inseparable, mutually implied elements: (a) Conversion, which is constant review of oneself in respect of one's desires, possessions, and activity, in such wise as to remain open to the novelty of God. Liberation from the trammels within—deliverance from the passions—goes hand in hand with a change in mentality that unveils chained, repressed possibilities, namely those manufactured impossibilities that are imposed as fate on the cowardice and resignation of human beings. (b) A community of converts, which is one that actualizes these ultimate demands and demonstrates their concrete possibility, indeed their vital, ineluctable necessity. Its task is to produce outside itself what God is realizing within it: a life altogether contrary to the "laws" that subject the human being to idols. (c) A particular society that is reworked from within by the community of those who are converted. Salvation is tradition, placed in a perspective of the end of history and the nearness of the God who comes. Salvation is in these ancient relationships, rebaptized in the fire of the creative Spirit, and retranslated into the language of the emancipation of all destiny.

This, then, is our model. It is not an abstraction, but the implementation of what a fulfilled person is: God's "image," God's representation—"God by participation." "Person" implies society, and exists only via the instituting action of the latter. Finally, a particular society is justified only in its self-transcendence and only insofar as it places itself both in a world perspective and in the perspective of the end of history. The emergence of this model is bound up with the singular event that is Jesus of Nazareth, with the singular events of his life, death, and posthumous lot. This model will be exact if it is also given by Jesus' actual existence.

From F. Eboussi Boulaga, *Christianity without Fetishes*, translated by Robert R. Barr (Maryknoll, NY: Orbis, 1984), 64–66, 111–17.

꙳ In "The Church and the Road to the Future" (1968), **Gerhardus Cornelis Oosthuizen,** a neo-orthodox Protestant theologian, denies that there is any theological intersection between Christianity and other religions: there is only the possibility of communication based on love, sensitivity, service, solidarity, and clarity of thought. All "religions" are suspect because they place human constructions in the place of God's word. For Oosthuizen, even Christianity is tolerable only because it has received the mandate to proclaim Christ, through whom alone is found salvation.

GERHARDUS CORNELIS OOSTHUIZEN

"The Church and the Road to the Future," in *Post-Christianity in Africa: A Theological and Anthropological Study*

(i) Religion versus Revelation

In Western Europe, Christianity almost became a folk religion. The idea developed that a whole population can be conceived of as *corpus Christianum*. Owing to the breakdown of Christendom in Europe, the Church was compelled more and more to define itself, both in theory and practice, as a

body distinct from the community as a whole. The Church is in a proper and genuine sense an institution. Because man is social, God entered through the Incarnation into the life of man, which He endeavours to redeem, "a life lived out in an inescapable network of relations."[27] The Church has a sociological and organisational aspect, but this is only secondary, because what the Church is in its deepest sense can only be described in relation to Christ. The sociological and organisational aspects of the Church have taken precedence in theological thinking, and this has distorted the real issue, which is the true relation of the Church to the living Christ.

Syncretism started very early in Christian history. The culture of Rome exerted a great influence on the Gospel, with the result that the world entered the Church in an impure way. The antithesis provided by the Reformation, although in many respects not ideal, was a necessity, and a necessity of principle. Unfortunately, however, the view evolved that contact with the world can only be dangerous, so that the Church has to be in opposition to environment in non-Christian countries. This view had a very negative influence on African culture, and the missionaries, where they did feel that there were elements of this culture which could be "baptised," thought the African insufficiently educated for the task. This is one of the main reasons why the Church of the Reformation has remained foreign in her outreach. Furthermore, the Church in Africa gives the impression that everything has been thought out in Western terms, as if the Church has outlived its old vitality of thought. The Church will only rediscover her missionary consciousness, in Africa, as elsewhere, in the face of Islam and the fast-expanding independent movements, if it starts to think about the essence of Christendom. The desire to keep and cherish what you have sought and found is quite human, but the Church has to lose itself in the world if it wants to be effective in its outreach. Instead of being closed in order to preserve, the Church should be open in order to receive.

Form and content are interdependent. The Church as the Body of Christ must take note of the people amongst whom it moves as an institution. This was most clearly stated at the IMC Conference at Willingen in 1952. No tribe or nation is an artificial collection of individuals; because of historic growth, it is an organism. The Church in the non-Christian countries has only been negatively aware of the very solid unity of tribal life, which led to a "confrontation" between

---

27. Max Warren, *The Christian Mission* (London: SCM, 1951), 81.

it and everything indigenous, and debarred the peoples from contributing from their own genius. The primary fact is that the Church must be the Church; it must be founded firmly on the Rock, Jesus Christ, to whom it owes all its loyalty, and not to any people. The Church must maintain her prophetic character in the face of the strange and pagan views of the people. Excessive respect for the people is apostasy from God; the new root of the Gospel message can never be grafted on to infected trunks. One cannot accept the view that the non-Christian religions have been a *preparatio evangelica*. Paul Tillich misses here an important truth when he says: "One might call this preparation, which we find in all nations, the 'Old Testament' for these nations."[28] Barth, however, treats these problems under the significant heading *The Revelation of God as the abolition of religion* (Gottes Offenbarung als Aufhebung der Religion). Religion, construed as man's reality and potentiality, denies God's revelation, as has been obvious in our previous discussions. To regard God's revelation as a religion among other religions is according to Barth "basically the plain question whether theology and the Church and faith are able and willing to take themselves, or their basis, seriously."[29] Both the act of revealing (*a parte Dei*) and the experience of revelation (*a parte hominis*) are from God, and have nothing whatsoever to do with man's potentiality. Man's religion, in the light of revelation, is unbelief. All religions are endeavours to self-assertion by way of self-justification, self-sanctification and self-redemption, pushing God into the background and not accepting Him as He really is according to the revelation in Christ. Revelation has nothing to do with this, but "is God's self-offering and self-manifestation."[30] Man's own attempt to know God is utterly futile, because the truth comes to us only in an activity which corresponds to revelation, namely faith. Man thus establishes in his own way his own religion with his own energy. In this religion, he gropes for God; however "a grasping religion is the contradiction of revelation, the concentrated expression of human unbelief, i.e. an attitude and activity which is directly opposed to faith."[31] Revelation is the active, redemptive self-offering and self-manifestation of God to which man can add nothing. In faith we accept that everything has been done once and for all in Jesus Christ. Religion puts a human product in the place of God's word; man wishes to justify and sanctify himself—as in the case of the prophetic movements. Thus the Cross of Christ and Scripture are pushed into the background, and only used as a kind of fetish in man's hands. Even Israel's zeal to fulfil the Law is futile (Rom 9:31). The law given to Israel by God is a spiritual law (Rom 7:14), and

Christ is the end of this law, providing justification for everyone that believes (Rom 10:4). The law works wrath (Rom 4:15), and kills (2 Cor 3:6; Rom 7:5, 13). Pharisaic legalism is another form of old lawlessness: "Thou gloriest in the law and dishonourest God by transgression of the law" (Rom 2:23). The righteousness of works is at the root of the old idolatry, which is self-assertion against God.

Religions are dependent upon historical circumstances and have to change continuously not to become fossilised and obsolete. They have to fight for their lives because they are "acutely or chronically sick."[32] Religion is not only weak, but it leads man astray from God. Only through revelation can the magic circle of religion be broken. The strength of Barth's point of view lies in the fact that revelation in Christ is our sole standard of reference. There is no theological point of contact between the Christian and the non-Christian religions. The only point of contact lies within the sphere of communication, which depends "on the love, the sensitivity, the spirit of humble service and solidarity, the straightforward clarity and frankness of thinking, which the ordinary bearer of the Gospel message of the Church or the theological thinker displays, when encountering non-Christian fellow-beings or particular manifestations of spiritual reality."[33] It is impossible to permeate another religion by colouring certain concepts with Christian ideas. The nativistic movements have sufficiently proved by assimilating "Christian" ideas that non-Christian religions build up a stronger frame of resistance against Christianity and the preaching of the gospel."[34]

In the nativistic movements discussed above men have stopped living by the grace of God. The emphasis is on man's self-assertion; man is also dependent upon the forces nearest to him. For these people a thorough explanation of the Incarnation, with Christ as the firstborn among men, seen in connection with the position of the chief, could be most important. Much independentism has resulted from uncertainty with regard to the theological approach to these issues. This uncertainty is due to theological training that has taken place in a vacuum.

28. Paul Tillich, "The Theology of Missions," *The Occasional Bulletin*, Vol. V, No. 10, Aug. 10, 1954, 5.

29. Karl Barth, *Church Dogmatics* I² (T. and T. Clark, 1956), 283.

30. Ibid., 301.

31. Ibid., 302–3.

32. Ibid., 316.

33. Hendrik Kraemer, *Religion and the Christian Faith* (London: Lutterworth Press, 1956), 364.

34. Ibid.

The religion of the Nazarites, Kimbanguists and others usurps the place of Christ, and in this sense it is post-Christian. Barth rightly says: "As a 'Christianity without Christ' it can only vegetate. It has lost its only *raison d'être.*"[35] The Church cannot look even for one moment away from Jesus Christ without ceasing to be the Church; only in Christ, according to the Scriptures, can we have the true religion. The structure of Christianity is completely different from that of any other religion. This is due to the work of Jesus Christ, of which the major aspect is the divine justification of sinners. Man's forgiveness is only in Jesus Christ, and thus faith should only be directed to him. He is the firstborn of those whom he calls his brethren, and who are forgiven on the basis of his merit.

The Church in Africa has to give renewed attention to the question of the sacraments. Freytag maintains unequivocally: "All walling-up of Church life in confessional tradition, in a blind alley of self-satisfied self-assurance, is constantly challenged by the Sacrament."[36] In many of the young Churches, "the sacrament has much more significance than in the West, is more humbly received, is palpably proven forgiveness and proven mercy, giving a clear understanding what the Church of Christ has in the sacraments. A Church which has lost its sacramental life dies."[37] The idea of *ex opere operato,* with its magical connotations in the independent movements, should receive close attention. Baptism, associated by the prophetic movements with name-giving ceremonies and purification rites, must receive its rightful theological place in the Church, and the Holy Communion, abolished in some of these movements, should, together with baptism, be thoroughly explained in all catechetical work.

Speaking about the Churches in Asia, Manikam and Thomas hold that they are not only minority churches but are *alien* Churches: they imported their architecture, music and theology wholesale from Western Christianity, with the result that their forgiveness has "repelled rather than attracted" people to Christ.[38] Islam and Buddhism on the other hand have fully penetrated the culture of the Asian countries, and become domesticated. The Churches must be rooted in Christ before they can be related to the soil, and they will in this sense be foreign to the world, but they must live and spread in the new climate. In the process of detribalisation in Africa, many look to the Church for guidance, but Christians are often disillusioned because of its foreignness and its unsympathetic attitude to their deepest and most sincere desires. There lies one of the main reasons for the formation of independent movements. For a movement to become

creatively indigenous involves a process of organic growth, and in this the Church is rightly cautious, as there should be no direction, hurrying and pushing from without. History has continually shown how a Church may become typically expressive of national genius but still remain rooted in Jesus Christ and His teaching. Theologically, the Church is called upon to digest the relation between God and the concrete world; this should be done dynamically and positively. Theology is the intellectual work, to be undertaken by devoted Christian thinkers in the Church, and having as its aim "to explain the Church's basis and spiritual experiences in such a way that it satisfies the desire for clearness and cohesion of the believers."[39] Although theology is not Christianity, the demand for a systematic intellectual explanation of what it believes in its existential situation comes at all times and ages. For various reasons, a theology in Africa, which takes the African situation seriously, is desperately important. Theology has first the negative task of confronting anti-Christian streams of thought, concepts, etc., but it has the very positive task "of discovering new treasures from the Bible and the stating of these in a language comprehensible to the people concerned."[40] The tendency to imitate should be overcome in the Church in Africa. Now that Africa is on the way to a discovering of herself, the Church must do the same and help the African to rediscover himself. In separatism there is a desire for a Church less alien, which takes the traditional background seriously. The missions did little to develop indigenous forms of self-expression in liturgy, in music, in theology and in pastoral work: mission is not propaganda, a platform for ideas, but "When I help somebody else to give his own response and his own form of obedience to the message, it is mission . . . when I proselytise, it is propaganda. Whenever the 'indigenous' function of mission occupies the foreground, the caricature of mission vanishes—that reproduction of what we are ourselves or, what is much worse, what we should like to be and do not quite attain."[41] The first

---

35. Barth, *Church Dogmatics,* I², 347.

36. W. Freytag, "Missionary Thinking in Germany in Recent Years," IRM [International Review of Missions], 1946, 395.

37. Oosthuizen, *Theological Discussions and Confessional Developments in the Churches of Asia and Africa* (Franeker: T. Wever, 1958), 19.

38. Winburn Thomas and Rajah B. Manikam, *The Church in South East Asia* (Friendship Press, 1956), 164.

39. Oosthuizen, *Theological Discussions,* 24.

40. Ibid., 28.

41. Jan Hermelink, "The New Africa and an Old Imperative," *Lutheran World,* March 1959, Vol. V, No. 4, 361.

converts reacted violently against the old traditions because they knew how the old religion had penetrated every aspect of their lives. It is thus not just the missionaries that are to blame. The Church should be one all the world over, and yet be naturalised in each different land and amongst each people. The desire for less elaborate institutions "to revive the comparative simplicity of the Church of the first two centuries" should not take the form of a desire to abolish but "to give them indigenous form."[42]

There is, of course, danger that the Church can become so embedded in the indigenous culture that it loses its prophetic voice. The Ethiopian Church, for example, has "accommodated the Gospel to the Hamitic culture, an assimilation so profound that it has completely lost its prophetic voice to change the lives of its people."[43] The Church should in a certain sense be supranational—even Christians can be led astray by the nationalist outlook; this means that it should exist, not above the nation, but within it. The Church should be indigenously democratic by taking up its position within the people's own life and history. Both Tambaram and Willingen have given special attention to this fact—that the Church, rooted in Christ, should be related to its specific setting. There is a tendency among theologians to speak of the Church as something that exists in a realm of its own, a sacrosanct entity. Stephen Neill says: "The Church is undoubtedly a divine society, but it is also a society immersed in history, and must live perpetually in action and reaction with the societies by which it is surrounded."[44] The identification of the Church with the kingdom of God has been one of the great sources of misunderstanding. Each ethnic group has its own angle of vision—the group is not merely a collection of individuals in the Hobbesian sense but an organism. Smalley rightly says that "an indigenous Church is precisely one in which the changes which take place under the guidance of the Holy Spirit meet the needs and fulfil the meanings of that society and not of any outside group."[45] The New Testament's idea of an indigenous Church is where the Holy Spirit has worked its transformation within the society. The Greek Church differs from the Jewish one; however, the message of Christ is supranational and supracultural because the theme of the message is that God in Christ reconciles the whole world to Himself. An indigenous (bodenständige) Church is Word-centred (wortständige) Church. Since Zinzendorf emphasised one-soul conversion (Einzelbekehrung), the concept of indigenisation has been neglected to the detriment of effective communication. This "pietistic" method, advocated by him and others, saw the aim of missions as the gathering of souls into ecclesiolae, which had to be isolated from the world as the first-fruits of the kingdom. The other extreme—the view that the aim of mission is the conversion of the whole people—was embraced after men realised that a change was necessary. The followers of this view emphasise the "blood and soil" aspect and, on the basis of Luther's theology, maintain that racial and national individuality is part of the natural order created by God. But this theology has not faced adequately the Scriptural basis of the relationship between nation and Church; it leads to "ethnic Churches," rather than Churches in the Biblical sense. Together with men like Edwin Smith, Westermann and others previously mentioned, they helped to change the climate of opinion with regard to Africa's heritage. Gutmann, with his emphasis on the primordial social ties of the African tribe and kin, insisted that the individuality of peoples has to be respected by the Church, and allowance made for its unfettered developments; in this way the Selbstbewegung der Gemeinde (spontaneous expansion of the congregation) was to be achieved, and the völkische Weltanschauung purified and regenerated; but he has over-emphasized an important principle of method which has often been neglected elsewhere with no little effect in the Church in Africa. The theological basis of indigenisation should be sound, and Gutmann has missed this point—he takes, rather, a stand in the group or tribe instead of in Scripture. "Nation" came to have a special theological significance. But Christianity poses many difficulties to the African who wants his life to be "African," because it has caused such radical disruptions and made little effort to show the way out of the impasse that has been reached.

Because of the strong link between the living and the dead in African society, Sundkler maintains that it is of vital importance for the new African theology to concern itself with the dead and with "the meaning of their afterlife or death."[46] Family ties are so strong that ecclesiology in Africa will concern itself more and more with the family and the Church as the Great Family. It was Hoekendijk who advocated "an ecology" which should take serious note

---

42. Godfrey E. Phillips, *The Transmission of the Faith* (Allen and Unwin, 1946), 110.

43. Cf. T. S. Johnson, *The Story of a Mission* (SPCK, 1953), 50.

44. S. Neill, *The Unfinished Task* [(Edinburgh House Press, 1957)], 9.

45. William A. Smalley, "Cultural Implications of an Indigenous Church," *Practical Anthropology*, Vol. 5, No. 3 (1958), 56.

46. Bengt Sundkler, *The Christian Ministry in Africa* (Uppsala: Swedish Institute of Missionary Research, 1960), 289.

of man's concrete *oikos* (house, concrete social milieu): Instead of making the existing, established local congregation the focal point of a missionary Church, the human being in his *oikos* must become the focal point. The Church must grow through house congregations. . . ."[47] If this is true for our Western society, it is even truer in African society and will serve as a buffer against much of the independentist tendencies prevalent in a situation of rapid social change. The dangers in this approach are numerous; for example, many will expect that the whole family or tribe should enter the Church, a characteristic of independent movements, and also of the Churches. The African tribal affiliation is so strong that, in spite of the formation of new types of social personalities, the old tribal loyalties—and factions—are maintained and often extraordinarily emphasised in a new context. The Church can easily become tribal in such a situation, and this carries within itself the germ of nativism. The Church should work continuously for the "reintegration" of the African community. At the same time it must be related to the emerging world-wide culture, although it cannot be identified with this or any culture. It was this aspect that received special attention at the International Missionary Council at Willingen in 1952, when a report was produced significantly entitled *The Indigenous Church—the Universal Church in its Local Setting,* in which the implications of the tension between the "indigenous" and the "universal" were brought out. The Church is called upon to take "a positive yet national attitude to the cultures."[48] The Church has to realise and proclaim that it is not tied to any particular social structure but "subjects every structure to the judgment of God."[49] This indigenisation should be done by the nationals themselves, otherwise it will be superficial. It is not merely a matter of self-government, self-support and self-propagation. Many self-governing Churches in Africa are not indigenous even today, but reproduce Western patterns of leadership and organisation. A truly indigenous Church, as Reyburn puts it, "is a group of believers who live out their life, including their socialised Christian activity, in the patterns of the local society, and for whom any transformation of that society comes out of their felt needs under the guidance of the Holy Spirit and the Scriptures."[50] The Church is truly a society aware of the presence of the Holy Spirit, transforming individual lives, as well as the life of the society. Many missionaries have given the impression that they would prefer the Church *not* to be relevant to its local setting, but rather reflect their own culture and personality exactly. In the most essential field, the formulation of theol-

ogy in indigenous terms, scarcely anything has been done. The African will interpret the Gospel in terms of his own symbols, and with his own poetry and song.

In Africa the danger of an ethnic Church will always be present in the background if not in the forefront. Many of the traditional aspects of African religion will still have influence, such as the relationship between the living and the ancestors or gods, which is not based on faith or trust but on diplomacy, which can only be countered by means of the power of the community. In the tribe, religious life especially, but in fact life in all its aspects, is the struggle for power, and sacrifice is a diplomatic and symbolic gift. Combined ceremonies demonstrate the power of the tribe. Here the Church can learn that the religious is not isolated from life as a whole; it is only the highly sophisticated African who has adopted the Western disposition of separating life and religion. This expression of our faith in terms of wholeness is needed today the world over. "In the endeavour," says Stendahl, "we have no need to look upon the thinking of Africans as a threat. It can rather be a means of helping Christians in the West: to acquire a new and more adequate understanding of the witness of the Bible for our time."[51]

From Gerhardus Cornelis Oosthuizen, *Post-Christianity in Africa: A Theological and Anthropological Study* (Grand Rapids, MI: Eerdmans, 1968), 217–24.

❧ Metropolitan **Georges Khodr,** of the Greek Orthodox Church, questions whether the claim that Christianity is "inherently exclusive" of other religions is justified. His "Christianity in a Pluralistic World—The Economy of the Holy Spirit" (1978) calls for the study of acculturation by means of different disciplines— phenomenology of religions, comparative study of religions, psychology and sociology of religions—in addition to history and theology.

---

47. J. C. Hoekendijk, "The Church in Missionary Thinking," *IRM,* July 1952, 324–36.

48. Ed B. Goodall, *Missions under the Cross* (Edinburgh House Press, 1953), 196.

49. Cf. *Dilemmas and Opportunities: Christianisation in Rapid Social Change,* Report of an International Ecumenical Study Conference, Salonika, Greece, 1959.

50. William A. Reyburn, "Cultural Implications of an Indigenous Church," *Practical Anthropology,* Vol. 5, 1958, 55.

51. Krister Stendahl, "The New Testament and the Preaching," *Lutheran World,* Vol. VI, No. 1, June 1959, 112.

METROPOLITAN GEORGES KHODR

"Christianity in a Pluralistic World—The Economy of the Holy Spirit," in *The Orthodox Church in the Ecumenical Movement*

The end of the First World War brought with it a keener sense of the unity of the world. Since the end of the Second World War we have experienced a process of planetization to which the heterogeneous nature of religious creeds is a major obstacle.[52] The increasing need for unity makes dialogue imperative if we wish to avoid a *de facto* syncretism of resurgent religions all claiming universality. In face of this resurgence of religions and a plurality which shows no signs of yielding to the Gospel, the question arises as to whether Christianity is so inherently exclusive of other religions as has generally been proclaimed up to now.

The question is of importance not only for the Christian mission but also for world peace. But this is not primarily a practical problem. It is the nature of the truth itself which is at stake here. The spiritual life we live is one thing if Christ's truth is confined within the bounds of the historical Church; it is quite a different thing if it is unrestricted and scattered throughout the world. In practice and in content, love is one thing if Christianity is exclusive and a very different thing if it is inclusive. As we see it, the problem is not simply a theological problem. It embraces the phenomenology of the religions, their comparative study, their psychology and their sociology. These other disciplines undermine a certain legalistic dogmatism which has long prevailed in Christian countries and which was based on ignorance of other religions on the part of professional theologians. Above all it is the authenticity of the spiritual life of non-Christians which raises the whole problem of Christ's presence in them. It is therefore quite nonsensical for theologians to pronounce judgement on the relationship of Christianity to the other religions if they are unable to integrate the extra-Christian data creatively and critically into their theological reflections. Theology has to be a continual two-way commerce between the biblical revelation and life, if it is to avoid sterility. Moreover, if obedience to the Master means following Him wherever we find traces of His presence, we have an obligation to investigate the authentic spiritual life of non-Christians. This raises the question of Christ's presence outside Christian history. The strikingly evangelical quality of many non-Christians obliges us, moreover, to develop an ecclesiology and a missiology in which the Holy Spirit necessarily occupies a supreme place.

Dangers of the Traditional Attitude

We shall need to go back to the *Acts of the Apostles,* the first book of ecclesiology, to see what place is given there to the Gentiles. In the Cornelius narrative we learn that "in every nation the man who is god fearing and does what is right is acceptable" to God (10:35). "In past ages God allowed all nations to go their own way" (14:16) "yet he has not left you without some clue to his nature" (14:17). There is among the Gentiles a yearning for the "unknown God" (17:23), a search for the God who "is not far from each one of us, for in him we live and move, in him we exist" (17:28). But this openness to the pagan world confers no theological status on it, for the "gods made by human hands are not gods at all" (19:26). Paul is quite categorical: "a false god has no existence in the real world" (I Cor 8:4). In *Revelation,* a supremely ecclesiological book, paganism is regarded by the prophets as a lie (21:8) and as deceit (22:15). In this respect the New Testament is not innovating on the Old Testament, where paganism is regarded by the prophets as an abomination. Nevertheless, the view of the apostle as expressed in his Areopagus speech is that the Athenians worshipped the true God without recognizing Him as the Creator. His face had not been unveiled to them. In other words, they were Christians without knowing it. Paul gave their God a name. The Name, together with its attributes, is the revelation of God. We find here the germ of a positive attitude to paganism which goes hand in hand with its complete negation, inherited from Judaism. This explains why, from the beginning, Christian apologetics would have two different attitudes. On the one hand, the gods are identified with images of wood or stone fashioned by human hands and are regarded as demons fighting against the Lord; on the other hand, a more positive and inclusive attitude is found. The defensive hostile approach of Christian apologetics increasingly became a fixed position as dogmatics crystallized into an official body of doctrine and as the Church and Christianity assumed an identity of their own in both East and West, and as the battle against heresy aroused in the minds of apologists of all periods a hostility to error which amounted almost to hatred. Furthermore, the intolerance of Christians towards each other would be reflected in their attitude to non-Christian religions. It was a case of either sav-

---

52. Address given to the Central Committee meeting in Addis Ababa in 1971 by Metropolitan Georges Khodr (b. 1924) of Mount Lebanon, a diocese of the Greek Orthodox Patriarchate of Antioch, Beirut, Lebanon. Translated from the French.

ing the other man or killing him! Strange notion of a truth divorced from love!

On the other hand, a different style of apologetics sought to continue the approach of Paul's Areopagus speech to the Athenians. We can trace this movement, starting from Justin with his famous notion of the *logos spermatikos* present even before Christ's coming. All who have lived according to the *Logos* are Christians. For this tradition of apologetics, there is no truth independent of the direct action of God. Clement of Alexandria, the leading representative of this line of thought, sees the whole of mankind as a unity and as beloved of God. On the basis of *Hebrews* (1:1) he asserts that it was to the whole of mankind and not only to Israel that "God spoke in former times in fragmentary and varied fashion." Mankind as a whole is subject to a process of education (a pedagogy: we should remember that, for Paul, the pedagogue was the Law and the pupil in his care was Israel). It is not a case here of a natural or a rational law, for "the *Logos* of God . . . ordered our world, and above all this microcosm man, through the Holy Spirit" (*Protreptikos,* 1:5). Within this divine visitation, philosophy enjoys a special privilege. Not only does the Alexandrine doctor not hesitate to see it as a steppingstone to Christian philosophy, he even teaches that it "was given to the Greeks as their Testament" (*Stromata* V: 8:3). Pagan and Greek philosophies are scattered fragments of a single whole which is the *Logos.*

Origen, too, stresses the importance of philosophy as knowledge of the true God. In his opinion, certain doctrines of Christianity are no different from the teaching of the Greeks, although the latter does not have the same impact or the same attraction. Origen's original contribution, however, was to see elements of the divine in the pagan religions and in Greek mythology.

The fathers of the Church continued to respect the wisdom of antiquity, although with a clearly apparent reserve. Gregory Nazianzus declared that a number of philosophers, like Plato and Aristotle, "caught a glimpse of the Holy Spirit" (*Orat.* 31:5; *PG* 36, 137 3 c). Despite his sharp criticism of idolatry, he does not shrink from declaring that he sees in the religious life of mankind "the hand of God guiding men to the true God." In order not to unduly prolong this list of citations from the fathers, let me simply mention the view of St. Augustine in the West that since the dawn of human history, men were to be found, within Israel and outside Israel, who had partaken of the mystery of salvation, and that what was known to them was in fact the Christian religion, without it having been revealed to them as such. This entire trend in

patristic thought could perhaps be summed up in the following sentences of Irenaeus: "there is only one God who from beginning to end, through various economies, comes to the help of mankind" (*Adv. Haer.* III, 12:13).

It is beyond the scope of this paper to outline, even briefly, the history of Christian thought concerning other religions. Suffice it to say that in the Greek-speaking Christian Byzantine East following John Damascene, the attitude towards Islam was somewhat negative. The West, too, was negative, with a few exceptions such as Abelard and Nicholas of Cusa.

The negative evaluation of other religions obviously rests on an ecclesiology which is bound up with a history which has been lived through and with a definite outlook on history. It is certain that a theology of the kind maintained by St. Thomas Aquinas, which advocated the death of infidels, and which had earlier been preached by St. Bernard of Clairveaux, went hand in hand with the Crusades which consolidated the brutal separation between Christianity and Islam as well as that between the Christian West and the Christian East. We should also take into account the extent to which the Arabo-Byzantine wars contributed to the identification of the *oikumene* with the Church in the East. In other words, because of the armed struggle in which mediaeval Christendom, Latin and Byzantine, became involved, ecclesiology was historicized, i.e., the Church took on the sociological shape of Christian nations. The Christian world, western and eastern, was the dwelling place of peace, light and knowledge. The non-Christian world was the dwelling place of war and darkness. This was a literal adoption of the Moslem distinction between *Dar el Islam* (the realm of Islam) and *Dar el Kufr* (the realm of the infidels). It was also a view of the Church as an *Umma,* a numerically and sociologically defined community. This area outside the Church had to be saved. Infidels, heretics, and schismatics had to be brought into the Church by missionary activity, by proselytism, or by cultural colonialism if persecution and war became unacceptable, so that there might be "one flock and one shepherd." The established, institutional Church becomes the centre of the world. The history of the Christian Church becomes history itself. What occurs in the experience of the West fashions history. The rest of the world remains a-historical until it adopts Western experience which, moreover, by implacable logic and technological determinism, is destined to dominate the world. This philosophy of history will in its turn leave its stamp on theological thought, its basic outlook and methods. Thus the religions of the under-developed countries, which have not apparently been influenced by the dynamics of creative civilization, such as Hinduism, Buddhism, Islam, and even Orthodox Christianity, being still in a historically inferior era, will have to pass into a superior stage, to be historicized, by adopting the superior hierarchical type of Christianity. The rest of the world must come into the time-continuum of the Church through a salvation achieved by the universal extension of the Christian way of life founded on the authority of the West. This attitude rests on a view of the history of salvation imported into Protestantism in the last century and which has been adopted by the whole of western Christianity since the last war. Too much emphasis has been placed on the succession of salvation events, with the result that Christ appears as the end of the history of the Old Covenant and the end of human history. The eschatological dimension of the Church's faith and life thus tends to be blurred. God is indeed within history but we forget that the divine event is the unfolding of the mystery. I shall return to this later. What I should like to emphasize here is that this linear view of history is bound up with a monolithic ecclesiological approach which, while rightly rejecting the Graeco-Asian idea of eternally recurring cycles, turns its back on the idea of an eternity transcending history and based on a conception of the Church in which Christ is seen "not merely chronologically but also and above all ontologically."

Obviously this ecclesiology and linear concept of salvation impose a specific missionary approach. The Church is then geared either to good works of a charitable and humanitarian character or else to remedial confessional and sociological work among those who are not yet incorporated into the Church. Truth lies within the boundaries of the Church; outside them, error. The remedy for all this is certainly not the application of new methods, for example, the consecration of coloured bishops or adaptation to the customs and traditions of a particular people. All this will still be felt to be just a more subtle form of spiritual imperialism. What is on trial here is the theology of mission itself. One example of a tradition entirely independent of this approach is the Nestorian Church's missionary tradition, which is almost unique in its effort to nurture the spiritual development of the religions it encountered by "improving" them from within (Buddhism in Tibet and China), while not "alienating" them. Mission in this way spiritually adopts the whole of creation. We find within the Persian Church in Mesopotamia the boldest attempt at an approach to Islam. The prophetic character of Muhammad is defined in Nestorian texts on the basis of a specific analysis of the Muhammadan message. But there is no blurring of the centrality and ontological uniqueness of Christ Jesus.

It comes down to this: contemporary theology must go beyond the notion of "salvation history" in order to rediscover the meaning of the *oikonomia*. The economy of Christ cannot be reduced to its historical manifestation but indicates the fact that we are made participants in the very life of God Himself. Hence the reference to eternity and to the work of the Holy Spirit. The very notion of economy is a notion of mystery. To say mystery is to point to the strength that is breathing in the event. It also points to the freedom of God who in His work of providence and redemption is not tied down to any event. The Church is the instrument of the mystery of the salvation of the nations. It is the sign of God's love for all men. It is not over against the world, separate from it; it is part of the world. The Church is the very breath of life for humanity, the image of the humanity to come, in virtue of the light it has received. It is the life of mankind itself, even if mankind does not realize this. It is, in Origen's words, the "cosmos of the cosmos." If, as Origen also says, the Son remains "the cosmos of the Church," then clearly the Church's function is, by means of the mystery of which it is the sign, to read all the other signs which God has placed in the various times in human history. Within the religions, its task is to reveal to the world of the religions the God who is hidden within it, in anticipation of the final concrete unfolding and manifestation of the Mystery.

This *oikonomia* is not new. It starts with creation as the manifestation of God's *kenosis*. The cosmos carries the mark of God just as Jacob did after wrestling with the Angel. In that world prior to the Law, God makes a covenant with Noah. This is the starting point of dialogue with all mankind, which continues the first dialogue of creation itself. We are confronted there with a cosmic covenant which continues independently of the Abrahamic covenant. Within this covenant live the peoples who have not known the Word addressed to the father of the faithful. Scripture tells us that angels watch over them. Speaking of these angels of the nations, Origen tells us that it was they who brought the shepherds the news of Christ's birth and in doing so completed their mission. Yes, indeed, but in this sense, that Christ himself fulfils this Noachic covenant by giving it a salvation content and significance, having himself become the true covenant between God and the cosmos. The messianic prototype is already foretold in the Old Testament figure who is his "shadow cast before."

With Abraham's call, the election of the nations of the

earth becomes clearer. In him they are already the object of this election. Abraham accomplishes the first exodus by departing from his own country. The second exodus will be accomplished by the people of Israel wandering through the wilderness to Canaan down to the day when Jesus is nailed to the cross like an outsider, a foreigner. In this second exodus, Israel lives figuratively the mystery of the *oikonomia*. Israel, saved from the waters on its way to the promised land, represents saved humanity. It is as such the image of the Church saved through Christ. The election is particular but from it the economy of the mystery is deployed for the whole of humanity. Israel is saved as the type and representative of the whole of mankind. It is furthermore manifest in the Old Testament that the saving events are the antitypes of the saving event of the exodus. The Hebrews saw here, not so much a linear sequence of saving events as rather a prototypical fact imitated in other facts, the sole continuity being God's fidelity to Himself. Israel as the scene of the revelation of the Word and as a people constituted by obedience to the Word is indissolubly linked with all other peoples who have received God's visitation "at sundry times and in diverse manners" and to whose fathers and prophets, considered by the church fathers as the saints and just men of Gentile peoples, God spoke. What matters here is that the histories of Abraham, of Moses and of David were rich with the divine presence. The sequence of the facts is of little importance. The Old Testament authors, like Matthew in his genealogy, were concerned only with spiritually significant facts which were relevant to the messianic hope or the messianic reality.

This significant relationship to Christ is also applicable outside Israel inasmuch as the other nations have had their own types of the reality of Christ, whether in the form of persons or teachings. It is of little importance whether the religion in question was historical in character or not. It is of little importance whether it considers itself incompatible with the Gospel. Christ is hidden everywhere in the mystery of his lowliness. Any reading of religions is a reading of Christ. It is Christ alone who is received as light when grace visits a Brahmin, a Buddhist or a Muhammadan reading his own scriptures. Every martyr for the truth, every man persecuted for what he believes to be right, dies in communion with Christ. The mystics of Islamic countries with their witness to suffering love lived the authentic Johannine *agape*. For if the tree is known by its fruits, there is no shadow of doubt that the poor and humble folk who live for and yearn for God in all nations already receive the peace which the Lord gives to all whom He loves (Lk 2:14).

This work of salvation outside Israel "according to the flesh" and outside the historical Church is the result of the resurrection which fills everything with the fulness of Christ. The coming of Christ, in whom "all things are held together" (Col 1:17), has led the whole of mankind to its true existence and brings about spiritual renewals, economies which can take charge of human souls until He comes. The Church's mediatorial role remains unimpaired. But the freedom of God is such that He can raise up prophets outside the sociological confines of the New Israel just as He raised them up outside the confines of Old Israel. But these callings to prophecy and wisdom outside the sanctuary possess a secret bond with the power of the Risen One and in no way conflict with the uniqueness of Christ's economy. The plenitude of Christ may be veiled in history by human sin. Men may fail to see the Church as the bearer of the power and glory of its Lord. What is visible is very often far from a pointer to the kingdom of God. But God can, if He pleases, send witnesses to those who have not been able to see the uplifting manifestation of Christ in the face which we have made bloody with our sins or in the seamless robe which we have torn by our divisions. Through these witnesses God can release a power far greater than the extra-biblical messages would themselves lead us to expect. True plenitude, however, is lived in the second advent. The economy of salvation achieves its full reality as the End, as the ultimate meaning of all things. The economy of Christ is unintelligible without the economy of the Spirit.

"God says, 'This will happen in the last days; I will pour out upon everyone a portion of my spirit'" (Acts 2:17). This must be taken to mean a Pentecost which is universal from the very first. In fact we also read in the *Acts of the Apostles* that "the gift of the Holy Spirit" had been "poured out even on Gentiles" (10:45). The Spirit is present everywhere and fills everything by virtue of an economy distinct from that of the Son. Irenaeus calls the Word and the Spirit the "two hands of the Father." This means that we must affirm not only their hypostatic independence but also that the advent of the Holy Spirit in the world is not subordinated to the Son, is not simply a function of the Word. "Pentecost," says Lossky, "is not a 'continuation' of the Incarnation, it is its sequel, its consequence: . . . creation has become capable of receiving the Holy Spirit" (Vladimir Lossky, *Theologie mystique de l'Eglise d'Orient*, Aubier, Paris, 1944, 156). Between the two economies there is a reciprocity and a mutual service. The Spirit is another Paraclete. It is He who fashions Christ within us. And, since Pentecost, it is He who makes Christ present. It is He who makes Christ an inner reality here and now: as Irenaeus finely says: "Where the Spirit is, there also is the Church" (*Adv. Haer.* III, 24, *P.G.* v. 7, col. 966 c). The Spirit operates and applies His energies in accordance with His own economy and we could, from this angle, regard the non-Christian religions as points where His inspiration is at work.

All who are visited by the Spirit are the people of God. The Church represents the first-fruits of the whole of mankind called to salvation. "In Christ all will be brought to life" (I Cor 15:22) because of this communion which is the Church. At the present moment the Church is the sacrament of this future unity, the unity of both "those whom the Church will have baptized and those whom the Church's bridegroom will have baptized," to use Nicholas Cabazilas's wonderful expression. And when now we communicate in the Body of Christ, we are united with all those whom the Lord embraces with His life-giving love. They are all within the eucharistic cup, awaiting the time of the Parousia when they will constitute the unique and glorious body of the Saviour and when all the signs will disappear before "the throne of God and of the Lamb" (Rev 22:3).

If we accept the bases of this theology, how are we to define the Christian mission and the concrete approach of a Christian community to a non-Christian community?

1. The Christian who knows that, within God's plan, the great religions constitute training schools of the Divine mercy will have an attitude of profound peace and gentle patience. There will be an obedience to this plan being carried out by the Holy Spirit, an expectant hope of the Lord's coming, a longing to eat the eternal Paschal meal, and a secret form of communion with all men in the economy of the Mystery whereby we are being gradually led towards the final consummation, the recapitulation of all things in Christ.

2. There is a universal religious community which, if we are able to lay hold of what it offers, will enrich our Christian experience. What matters here is not so much that we should grasp the historical, literal, objective meaning of non-Christian scriptures, but that we should read these scriptures in the light of Christ. For just as the letter without the Holy Spirit can hide revelation from us in the case of the Old Testament Scriptures, Christ being the only key to them, so is it possible for us to approach other religions and their scriptures either in a purely critical frame of mind and as objective students of history and sociology, or else in order to discern the truth in them according to the breath of the Holy Spirit.

3. Within the context of these religions, certain gifted individuals penetrate beyond the signs of their own faiths just as the spiritual life goes beyond the Law, even though legalism does prevail in some cases. What we have to do is to penetrate beyond the symbols and historical forms and discover the profound intention of religious men and to relate their apprehension of divinity to the object of our Christian hope. This means that we must use the apophatic method in speaking of God not only, among Christians, in the knowledge that all concepts of God are idols, but apply this method also to our ways of talking about God as He appears through the scriptures of the non-Christian religions. When we seek to understand the adherent of another religion, we should not be concerned to arrive at a descriptive account of him as an example of his particular faith, but we must rather treat him as someone who has something to teach us and something to manifest to us of God.

4. Communion is the *conditio sine qua non* of communication. This is why no dealings are possible from the Christian side without a conversion which banishes all confessional pride and all feelings of cultural or historical superiority. Such humility requires the Christ-like way of self-fulfilment through the other. A Christian community purified by the fire of the Spirit, holy unto God, poor for the sake of God, can, in the weakness of the Gospel, take the risk of both giving and receiving with equal simplicity. It must accept the challenge as a brotherly admonition and be able to recognize, even in the guise of unbelief, a courageous rejection of lies which Christians have been long unwilling or unable to denounce.

5. With this attitude, communication will be possible. The presentation of Christ will be based on his self-humiliation, on his historical reality and his words. It is not so much a question of adding men to the Church. They will come in of their own accord once they begin to feel at home in it as in the Father's house. The supreme task is to identify all the Christic values in other religions, to show them Christ as the bond which unites them and his love as their fulfilment. True mission laughs at missionary activity. Our task is simply to follow the tracks of Christ perceptible in the shadows of other religions.

> Night after night on my bed
> I have sought my true love;
> I have sought him but not found him,
> I have called him but he has not answered.
> I said, "I will rise and go the rounds of the city, through the streets and the
> squares, seeking my true love." . . .

The watchmen, going the rounds of the city, met me, and
    I asked,
"Have you seen my true love?" (*Song of Songs*, 3:1–3)

The task of the witness in a non-Christian context will be
to name him whom others have already recognized as the
Beloved. Once they have become the friends of the Bridegroom it will be easy to name him. The entire missionary activity of the Church will be directed towards awakening the
Christ who sleeps in the night of the religions. It is the Lord
Himself who alone knows whether men will be able to celebrate an authentically glorious Paschal meal together before
the coming of the heavenly Jerusalem. But we already know
that the beauty of Christ shining in our faces is the promise
of our final reconciliation.

From Metropolitan Georges Khodr, *The Orthodox Church in the Ecumenical Movement*
(Geneva: World Council of Churches, 1978), 297–307. [Ellipses in original.]

☙ In *Declaration on Religious Liberty: On the Rights of the Person
and Communities to Social and Civil Liberty in Religious Matters* (*Dig-
nitatis humanae*, December 7, 1965), the **Second Vatican Council**
gives its opinion on the principle of religious freedom. The council's *Declaration on the Relationship of the Church to Non-Christian Religions* (*Nostra aetate*, October 28, 1965) affirms non-Christian religions and repudiates negative attitudes and actions toward them.
Within a year after the declaration was issued, the Secretariat for
Non-Christians (known since 1988 as the Pontifical Council for
Interreligious Dialogue) was established to implement the objectives of the declaration.

THE SECOND VATICAN COUNCIL

Declaration on Religious Liberty: On the Rights of the Person and Communities to Social and Civil Liberty in Religious Matters, paragraphs 2–8

Chapter I. The General Principle of Religious Freedom

2. The Vatican Council declares that the human person has
a right to religious freedom. Freedom of this kind means
that all men should be immune from coercion on the part
of individuals, social groups and every human power so that,
within due limits, nobody is forced to act against his convictions in religious matters in private or in public, alone or in
associations with others. The Council further declares that
the right to religious freedom is based on the very dignity of

the human person as known through the revealed word of
God and by reason itself.[53] This right of the human person to
religious freedom must be given such recognition in the constitutional order of society as will make it a civil right.

It is in accordance with their dignity that all men, because
they are persons, that is, beings endowed with reason and
free will and therefore bearing personal responsibility, are
both impelled by their nature and bound by a moral obligation to seek the truth, especially religious truth. They are also
bound to adhere to the truth once they come to know it and
direct their whole lives in accordance with the demands of
truth. But men cannot satisfy this obligation in a way that is
in keeping with their own nature unless they enjoy both psychological freedom and immunity from external coercion.
Therefore the right to religious freedom has its foundation
not in the subjective attitude of the individual but in his very
nature. For this reason the right to this immunity continues
to exist even in those who do not live up to their obligation of
seeking the truth and adhering to it. The exercise of this right
cannot be interfered with as long as the just requirements of
public order are observed.

3. This becomes even clearer if one considers that the highest norm of human life is the divine law itself—eternal, objective and universal, by which God orders, directs and governs
the whole world and the ways of the human community according to a plan conceived in his wisdom and love. God
has enabled man to participate in this law of his so that, under the gentle disposition of divine providence, many may be
able to arrive at a deeper and deeper knowledge of unchangeable truth. For this reason everybody has the duty and consequently the right to seek the truth in religious matters so
that, through the use of appropriate means, he may prudently
form judgments of conscience which are sincere and true.

The search for truth, however, must be carried out in a
manner that is appropriate to the dignity of the human
person and his social nature, namely, by free enquiry with
the help of teaching or instruction, communication and dialogue. It is by these means that men share with each other
the truth they have discovered, or think they have discovered,
in such a way that they help one another in the search for
truth. Moreover, it is by personal assent that men must adhere to the truth they have discovered.

---

53. Cf. John XXIII, Encyc. *Pacem in terris*, 11 April 1963: *AAS* [*Acta Apostolicae
Sedis*] 55 (1963): 260–61; Pius XII, Radio message, 24 Dec. 1942: *AAS* 35 (1943): 19;
Pius XI, Encyc. *Mit brennender Sorge*, 14 March 1937: *AAS* 29 (1937): 160; Leo XIII,
Encyc. *Libertas praestantissimum*, 20 June 1888: *Acta Leonis* XIII. 8, 1888, 237–38.

It is through his conscience that man sees and recognizes the demands of the divine law. He is bound to follow this conscience faithfully in all his activity so that he may come to God, who is his last end. Therefore he must not be forced to act contrary to his conscience. Nor must he be prevented from acting according to his conscience, especially in religious matters. The reason is because the practice of religion of its very nature consists primarily of those voluntary and free internal acts by which a man directs himself to God. Acts of this kind cannot be commanded or forbidden by any merely human authority.[54] But his own social nature requires that man give external expression to these internal acts of religion, that he communicate with others on religious matters, and profess his religion in community. Consequently to deny man the free exercise of religion in society, when the just requirements of public order are observed, is to do an injustice to the human person and to the very order established by God for men.

Furthermore, the private and public acts of religion by which men direct themselves to God according to their convictions transcend of their very nature the earthly and temporal order of things. Therefore the civil authority, the purpose of which is the care of the common good in the temporal order, must recognize and look with favor on the religious life of the citizens. But if it presumes to control or restrict religious activity it must be said to have exceeded the limits of its power.

4. The freedom or immunity from coercion in religious matters which is the right of individuals must also be accorded to men when they act in community. Religious communities are a requirement of the nature of man and of religion itself.

Therefore, provided the just requirements of public order are not violated, these groups have a right to immunity so that they may organize themselves according to their own principles. They must be allowed to honor the supreme Godhead with public worship, help their members to practice their religion and strengthen them with religious instruction, and promote institutions in which members may work together to organize their own lives according to their religious principles.

Religious communities also have the right not to be hindered by legislation or administrative action on the part of the civil authority in the selection, training, appointment and transfer of their own ministers, in communicating with religious authorities and communities in other parts of the world, in erecting buildings for religious purposes, and in the acquisition and use of the property they need.

Religious communities have the further right not to be prevented from publicly teaching and bearing witness to their beliefs by the spoken or written word. However, in spreading religious belief and in introducing religious practices everybody must at all times avoid any action which seems to suggest coercion or dishonest or unworthy persuasion especially when dealing with the uneducated or the poor. Such a manner of acting must be considered an abuse of one's own right and an infringement of the rights of others.

Also included in the right to religious freedom is the right of religious groups not to be prevented from freely demonstrating the special value of their teaching for the organization of society and the inspiration of all human activity. Finally, rooted in the social nature of man and in the very nature of religion is the right of men, prompted by their own religious sense, freely to hold meetings or establish educational, cultural, charitable and social organizations.

5. Every family, in that it is a society with its own basic rights, has the right freely to organize its own religious life in the home under the control of the parents. These have the right to decide in accordance with their own religious beliefs the form of religious upbringing which is to be given to their children. The civil authority must therefore recognize the right of parents to choose with genuine freedom schools or other means of education. Parents should not be subjected directly or indirectly to unjust burdens because of this freedom of choice. Furthermore, the rights of parents are violated if their children are compelled to attend classes which are not in agreement with the religious beliefs of the parents or if there is but a single compulsory system of education from which all religious instruction is excluded.

6. The common good of society consists in the sum total of those conditions of social life which enable men to achieve a fuller measure of perfection with greater ease. It consists especially in safeguarding the rights and duties of the human person.[55] For this reason the protection of the right to religious freedom is the common responsibility of individual citizens, social groups, civil authorities, the Church and other religious communities. Each of these has its own special responsibility in the matter according to its particular duty to promote the common good.

---

54. Cf. John XXIII, Encyc. *Pacem in terris*, 11 April 1963: *AAS* 55 (1963): 270; Paul VI, Radio message, 22 Dec. 1964: *AAS* 57 (1965): 181–82.

55. Cf. John XXIII, Encyc. *Mater et magistra*, 15 May 1961: *AAS* 53 (1961): 417; Id., Encyc. *Pacem in terris*, 11 April 1963: *AAS* 55 (1963): 273.

The protection and promotion of the inviolable rights of man is an essential duty of every civil authority.[56] The civil authority therefore must undertake to safeguard the religious freedom of all the citizens in an effective manner by just legislation and other appropriate means. It must help to create conditions favorable to the fostering of religious life so that the citizens will be really in a position to exercise their religious rights and fulfil their religious duties and so that society itself may enjoy the benefits of justice and peace, which result from man's faithfulness to God and his holy will.[57]

If because of the circumstances of a particular people special civil recognition is given to one religious community in the constitutional organization of a State, the right of all citizens and religious communities to religious freedom must be recognized and respected as well.

Finally, the civil authority must see to it that the equality of the citizens before the law, which is itself an element of the common good of society, is never violated either openly or covertly for religious reasons and that there is no discrimination among citizens.

From this it follows that it is wrong for a public authority to compel its citizens by force or fear or any other means to profess or repudiate any religion or to prevent anyone from joining or leaving a religious body. There is even more serious transgression of God's will and of the sacred rights of the individual person and the family of nations when force is applied to wipe out or repress religion either throughout the whole world or in a single region or in a particular community.

7. The right to freedom in matters of religion is exercised in human society. For this reason its use is subject to certain regulatory norms.

In availing of any freedom men must respect the moral principle of personal and social responsibility: in exercising their rights individual men and social groups are bound by the moral law to have regard for the rights of others, their own duties to others and the common good of all. All men must be treated with justice and humanity.

Furthermore, since civil society has the right to protect itself against possible abuses committed in the name of religious freedom the responsibility of providing such protection rests especially with the civil authority. However, this must not be done in an arbitrary manner or by the unfair practice of favoritism but in accordance with legal principles which are in conformity with the objective moral order. These principles are necessary for the effective protection of the rights of all citizens and for peaceful settlement of con-

flicts of rights. They are also necessary for an adequate protection of that just public peace which is to be found where men live together in good order and true justice. They are required too for the necessary protection of public morality. All these matters are basic to the common good and belong to what is called public order. For the rest, the principle of the integrity of freedom in society should continue to be upheld. According to this principle man's freedom should be given the fullest possible recognition and should not be curtailed except when and in so far as is necessary.

8. Modern man is subjected to a variety of pressures and runs the risk of being prevented from following his own free judgment. On the other hand, there are many who, under the pretext of freedom, seem inclined to reject all submission to authority and make light of the duty of obedience.

For this reason this Vatican Council urges everyone, especially those responsible for educating others, to try to form men with a respect for the moral order who will obey lawful authority and be lovers of true freedom—men, that is, who will form their own judgments in the light of truth, direct their activities with a sense of responsibility, and strive for what is true and just in willing cooperation with others.

Religious liberty therefore should have this further purpose and aim of enabling men to act with greater responsibility in fulfilling their own obligations in society.

Translated by Laurence Ryan, in *Vatican Council II: The Conciliar and Post Conciliar Documents*, edited by Austin Flannery (Collegeville, MN: Liturgical Press, 1975), 800–805.

THE SECOND VATICAN COUNCIL

Declaration on the Relationship of the Church to Non-Christian Religions, 1–5

1. In this age of ours, when men are drawing more closely together and the bonds of friendship between different peoples are being strengthened, the Church examines with greater care the relation which she has to non-Christian religions. Ever aware of her duty to foster unity and charity among individuals, and even among nations, she reflects at the outset on what men have in common and what tends to promote fellowship among them.

All men form but one community. This is so because all stem from the one stock which God created to people the

---

56. Cf. John XXIII, Encyc. *Pacem in terris*, 11 April 1963: *AAS* 55 (1963): 273–74; Pius XII, Radio message, 1 June 1941: *AAS* 33 (1941): 200.

57. Cf. Leo XIII, Encyc. *Immortale Dei*, 1 Nov. 1885: *AAS* 18 (1885): 165.

entire earth (cf. Acts 17:26), and also because all share a common destiny, namely God. His providence, evident goodness, and saving designs extend to all men (cf. Wis. 8:1; Acts 14:17; Rom. 2:6–7; 1 Tim. 2:4) against the day when the elect are gathered together in the holy city which is illumined by the glory of God, and in whose splendor all peoples will walk (cf. Apoc. 21:23ff.).

Men look to their different religions for an answer to the unsolved riddles of human existence. The problems that weigh heavily on the hearts of men are the same today as in the ages past. What is man? What is the meaning and purpose of life? What is upright behavior, and what is sinful? Where does suffering originate, and what end does it serve? How can genuine happiness be found? What happens at death? What is judgment? What reward follows death? And finally, what is the ultimate mystery, beyond human explanation, which embraces our entire existence, from which we take our origin and towards which we tend?

2. Throughout history even to the present day, there is found among different peoples a certain awareness of a hidden power, which lies behind the course of nature and the events of human life. At times there is present even a recognition of a supreme being, or still more of a Father. This awareness and recognition results in a way of life that is imbued with a deep religious sense. The religions which are found in more advanced civilizations endeavor by way of well-defined concepts and exact language to answer these questions. Thus, in Hinduism men explore the divine mystery and express it both in the limitless riches of myth and the accurately defined insights of philosophy. They seek release from the trials of the present life by ascetical practices, profound meditation and recourse to God in confidence and love. Buddhism in its various forms testifies to the essential inadequacy of this changing world. It proposes a way of life by which men can, with confidence and trust, attain a state of perfect liberation and reach supreme illumination either through their own efforts or by the aid of divine help. So, too, other religions which are found throughout the world attempt in their own ways to calm the hearts of men by outlining a program of life covering doctrine, moral precepts and sacred rites.

The Catholic Church rejects nothing of what is true and holy in these religions. She has a high regard for the manner of life and conduct, the precepts and doctrines which, although differing in many ways from her own teaching, nevertheless often reflect a ray of that truth which enlightens all men. Yet she proclaims and is in duty bound to proclaim, without fail, Christ who is the way, the truth and the life (Jn.

1:6). In him, in whom God reconciled all things to himself (2 Cor. 5:18–19), men find the fulness of their religious life.

The Church, therefore, urges her sons [and daughters] to enter with prudence and charity into discussion and collaboration with members of other religions. Let Christians, while witnessing to their own faith and way of life, acknowledge, preserve and encourage the spiritual and moral truths found among non-Christians, also their social life and culture.

3. The Church has also a high regard for the Muslims. They worship God, who is one, living and subsistent, merciful and almighty, the Creator of heaven and earth,[58] who has also spoken to men. They strive to submit themselves without reserve to the hidden decrees of God, just as Abraham submitted himself to God's plan, to whose faith Muslims eagerly link their own. Although not acknowledging him as God, they venerate Jesus as a prophet, his virgin Mother they also honor, and even at times devoutly invoke. Further, they await the day of judgment and the reward of God following the resurrection of the dead. For this reason they highly esteem an upright life and worship God, especially by way of prayer, alms-deeds and fasting.

Over the centuries many quarrels and dissensions have arisen between Christians and Muslims. The sacred Council now pleads with all to forget the past, and urges that a sincere effort be made to achieve mutual understanding; for the benefit of all men, let them together preserve and promote peace, liberty, social justice and moral values.

4. Sounding the depths of the mystery which is the Church, this sacred Council remembers the spiritual ties which link the people of the New Covenant to the stock of Abraham.

The Church of Christ acknowledges that in God's plan of salvation the beginning of her faith and election is to be found in the patriarchs, Moses and the prophets. She professes that all Christ's faithful, who as men of faith are sons of Abraham (cf. Gal. 3:7), are included in the same patriarch's call and that the salvation of the Church is mystically prefigured in the exodus of God's chosen people from the land of bondage. On this account the Church cannot forget that she received the revelation of the Old Testament by way of that people with whom God in his inexpressible mercy established the ancient covenant. Nor can she forget that she draws nourishment from that good olive tree onto which

---

58. Cf. St. Gregory VII, Letter 21 to Anzir (Nacir), King of Mauretania (*Patrologia Latina* 148, col. 450 ff.).

the wild olive branches of the Gentiles have been grafted (cf. Rom. 11:17–24). The Church believes that Christ who is our peace has through his cross reconciled Jews and Gentiles and made them one in himself (cf. Eph. 2:14–16).

Likewise, the Church keeps ever before her mind the words of the apostle Paul about his kinsmen: "they are Israelites, and to them belong the sonship, the glory, the covenants, the giving of the law, the worship, and the promises; to them belong the patriarchs, and, of their race according to the flesh, is the Christ" (Rom. 9:4–5), the son of the virgin Mary. She is mindful, moreover, that the apostles, the pillars on which the Church stands, are of Jewish descent, as are many of those early disciples who proclaimed the Gospel of Christ to the world.

As holy Scripture testifies, Jerusalem did not recognize God's moment when it came (cf. Lk. 19:42). Jews for the most part did not accept the Gospel; on the contrary, many opposed the spreading of it (cf. Rom. 11:28). Even so, the apostle Paul maintains that the Jews remain very dear to God, for the sake of the patriarchs, since God does not take back the gifts he bestowed or the choice he made.[59] Together with the prophets and that same apostle, the Church awaits the day, known to God alone, when all peoples will call on God with one voice and "serve him shoulder to shoulder" (Soph. 3:9; cf. Is. 66:23; Ps. 65:4; Rom. 11:11–32).

Since Christians and Jews have such a common spiritual heritage, this sacred Council wishes to encourage and further mutual understanding and appreciation. This can be obtained, especially, by way of biblical and theological enquiry and through friendly discussions.

Even though the Jewish authorities and those who followed their lead pressed for the death of Christ (cf. Jn. 19:6), neither all Jews indiscriminately at that time, nor Jews today, can be charged with the crimes committed during his passion. It is true that the Church is the new people of God, yet the Jews should not be spoken of as rejected or accursed as if this followed from holy Scripture. Consequently, all must take care, lest in catechizing or in preaching the Word of God, they teach anything which is not in accord with the truth of the Gospel message or the spirit of Christ.

Indeed, the Church reproves every form of persecution against whomsoever it may be directed. Remembering, then, her common heritage with the Jews and moved not by any political consideration, but solely by the religious motivation of Christian charity, she deplores all hatreds, persecutions, displays of antisemitism leveled at any time or from any source against the Jews.

The Church always held and continues to hold that Christ out of infinite love freely underwent suffering and death because of the sins of all men, so that all might attain salvation. It is the duty of the Church, therefore, in her preaching to proclaim the cross of Christ as the sign of God's universal love and the source of all grace.

5. We cannot truly pray to God the Father of all if we treat any people in other than brotherly fashion, for all men are created in God's image. Man's relation to God the Father and man's relation to his fellow-men are so dependent on each other that the Scripture says "he who does not love, does not know God" (1 Jn. 4:8).

There is no basis therefore, either in theory or in practice, for any discrimination between individual and individual, or between people and people, arising either from human dignity or from the rights which flow from it.

Therefore, the Church reproves, as foreign to the mind of Christ, any discrimination against people or any harassment of them on the basis of their race, color, condition in life or religion. Accordingly, following the footsteps of the holy apostles Peter and Paul, the sacred Council earnestly begs the Christian faithful to "conduct themselves well among the Gentiles" (1 Pet. 2:12) and if possible, as far as depends on them, to be at peace with all men (cf. Rom. 12:18) and in that way to be true sons of the Father who is in heaven (cf. Mt. 5:45).

Translated by Father Killian, in *Vatican Council II: The Conciliar and Post Conciliar Documents*, edited by Austin Flannery (Collegeville, MN: Liturgical Press, 1975), 738–42.

☙ "Statement on the Jewish Question" was passed by the **Synod of the Evangelical Church in Germany,** which included both East and West Germany at that time. The synod met at Berlin-Weissensee on April 23–27, 1950.

THE SYNOD OF THE EVANGELICAL CHURCH IN GERMANY
"Statement on the Jewish Question"

For God has consigned all men to disobedience, that he may have mercy upon all (Rom. 11:32).

We believe in the Lord and Saviour, who as a person came from the people of Israel.

---

59. Cf. Rom. 11:28-29; cf. Dogm. Const. *Lumen Gentium AAS* 57 (1965): 20.

We confess the Church which is joined together in one body of Jewish Christians and Gentile Christians and whose peace is Jesus Christ.

We believe God's promise to be valid for his Chosen People even after the crucifixion of Jesus Christ.

We state that by omission and silence we became implicated before the God of mercy in the outrage which has been perpetrated against the Jews by people of our nation.

We caution all Christians not to balance what has come upon us as God's judgment against what we have done to the Jews; for in judgment God's mercy searches the repentant.

We ask all Christians to dissociate themselves from all antisemitism and earnestly to resist it, wherever it stirs again, and to encounter Jews and Jewish Christians in a brotherly spirit.

We ask the Christian congregations to protect Jewish graveyards within their areas if they are unprotected.

We pray to the Lord of mercy that he may bring about the Day of Completion when we will be praising the triumph of Jesus Christ together with the saved Israel.

From *The Theology of the Churches and the Jewish People: Statements by the World Council of Churches and Its Member Churches* (Geneva: World Council of Churches, 1988), 47–48.

☙ "Jewish-Christian Relations in the Wider Perspective of Dialogue with People of Other Faiths and Ideologies," written in 1977 by the Lutheran biblical scholar and bishop **Krister Stendahl,** addresses the situation of Jews in Africa. Stendahl redefines the problem of Jewish-Christian relations by linking it both to the commandment "Thou shalt not bear false witness against thy neighbor" and to the Sermon on the Mount, which lists those who perform certain actions such as peacemaking as being blessed.

KRISTER STENDAHL

"Jewish–Christian Relations in the Wider Perspective of Dialogue with People of Other Faiths and Ideologies"

The Consultation on the Church and the Jewish People [referred to as CCJP hereafter] meets here today as part of the wider work of that unit of the World Council of Churches [WCC] which is assigned the responsibility for Dialogue with People of Other Faiths and Ideologies [DFI]. Others can trace better than I the history that has led us to such a structure. For me it is important that this not be just a historical fact or an organizational convenience. For I believe that there is much to be gained by having our work placed

within that wider perspective. I believe it is right, since the world in which we live is one of increased interdependence. And it is slowly but surely dawning upon many of us—not least through the World Council of Churches—that much that we used to call Christian is actually only various forms of Western Christianity. There are few areas in which that Western dominance has been more obvious than in Jewish-Christian relations, and that for obvious historical reasons. That cannot remain so for long.

I believe that the establishment of the State of Israel has played a significant role toward the need for a wider perspective. For thereby the Jewish presence in the world relates in a new manner to the world community. We know by experience of the stimulating and liberating effects of meeting with Jews in multilateral dialogue with Hindus, Buddhists, and Muslims (as in Colombo 1974).

Nor should it be forgotten that the CCJP has performed a pioneering role within the wider dialogue work of the WCC. Two things come especially to my mind. In the CCJP the DFI has a precious national and local network of agencies and persons involved and experienced in dialogue. In other dialogue areas such networks must be built. Secondly, in the Jewish-Christian dialogue and liaison we do meet with official representatives of our dialogue partner, not with persons of our own choosing—and at our expense. This gives a note of authenticity, realism and seriousness to our work, which has not yet been reached in other areas of dialogue.

As we consider our work in that wider setting and perspective of global pluralism there are tasks common to all dialogue, tasks peculiar to Jewish-Christian relations and new tasks without which we cannot be faithful.

A. The Common Task

I have come to think of the ninth Commandment as the best answer to the question: Why dialogue? "You shall not bear false witness against your neighbour." It is as simple as that. That calls for intensive and extensive listening to what he or she is saying, lest we make our own—often self-serving—images of other communities of faith and the faith of other communities. We must admit that much of our theology and our apologetics constitute perpetual and careless breaches of the ninth Commandment. We are bearing false witness against our neighbours. Only through dialogue—personal and through reading and writing—can we learn the art of speaking about our neighbours in a language which they recognize as authentic to their perspective. In this we can never succeed fully, but that is no excuse for not trying by all means and dialogue is an indispensable means toward that end.

With this listening goes the sensitivity of which Jesus spoke in the Sermon on the Mount when he spoke about the person who brought a gift to the altar and remembered that "your brother has something against you" (Matt. 5:23). It is striking and often forgotten that it says "he has something against you"—not "you have something against him." It is not a question about whether *we* feel loving, and open minded, etc. The question is how *they* perceive us, our attitudes, feelings, and actions. That sensitivity is a large component in our desperate need for dialogue.

According to the Bible, it has been the task of humans to name, to define things. In a way, we exercise our power and control by *defining* others. In dialogue we learn to allow others to define themselves. That is why there is not a WCC unit on dialogue with "Non-Christians" but with "People of *Other* Faiths . . ." leaving it to them to define themselves.

I mentioned that the defining of others is a means of exerting human power. That is why it is not appropriate for dialogue. Dialogue is a means of stripping us of that habit of controlling others by defining them by our terms. Actually, one can describe dialogue as a way of relating to others while limiting and neutralizing the element of power interference in the relationship. There are many kinds of power that run interference in the relationship between people of different faiths, and that pollute the witness that we constitute and bring one to another, cultural, educational as well as political and economical. From our Jewish-Christian perspective the most obvious one is the Christian majority versus the Jewish minority in "Christian" countries. More complex in the present situation, for example, is the importance of US support of the State of Israel and the ways in which the US Christian communities affect US policy in such matters. In dialogue we strive at a relationship where we relate as equals under God.

B. Tasks Peculiar to Jewish-Christian Relations

Within the general genre of dialogue I would like to make a few observations that I consider peculiar to the task ahead of us in Jewish-Christian relations.

Contemporary Christian theology has gloried in a strong emphasis on history. In this we are the children of the nineteenth century. "The historical method" stands for a complex web of intellectual habits that brought new and exciting and salutary insights to us all. By studying the historical developments of our faith, of the Bible, we found means and criteria by which we could judge and evaluate our traditions. Especially we protestants often fell for "the genetic fallacy," i.e., if you know the roots and the origins of something, then you think that you know it in its essence. Be it far from me to belittle the enormous gains that have come and will come to us by "the historical method"—not least as to the understanding of Judaism and Christianity and the relationship between them.

And yet, the prevailing historicism has its limitations and dangers. It may well be that other disciplines could also serve us well and as a corrective. I think especially about the social sciences, and more specifically, sociology and psychology, both of which have been underrepresented in our dialogue programs.

For it is obvious to me that our communities teach and tell their history toward defining their respective identities, i.e., mighty psychological and social forces are at work in the historical enterprise itself. And secondly, our identity is expressed and celebrated and enforced in piety and prayer, in cult and calendar, phenomena that have not attracted the attention they deserve by a theological community bent on *Heilsgeschichte,* Acts of God, and other fruits of our cultural historicism.

This is the more important since the bond between Judaism and Christianity is so obviously a historical one. Out of the Biblical revelation we are two distinct communities, both of which claim to be the legitimate heirs, Judaism and Christianity. Both claim the same Scripture as the basis of their identity, in the case of us Christians by the authority of Jesus as the promised Christ. Both have obvious difficulties in recognizing the claims of the other.

Our common bond has become a negative bind. The very closeness to Judaism has heightened our need to define our identity primarily over against Judaism, and our positive self-definition has been coupled by a negative definition of Jews. Especially in the wider perspective of the worldwide religious pluralism it is now reasonable to ask whether that need be so. To me the answer is obvious and calls for new attempts asserting our respective and distinct witness as "a light unto the nations" toward the redemption of the world, toward the *qiddush ha-Shem,* the "Hallowed be Thy Name" of the Lord's Prayer.

This is the peculiar task that we have in common as Jews and Christians. It is one that has surfaced from time to time in the history of our communities. The words of Maimonides about Christians (and Muslims, see below) as bearers of Torah to the Gentiles are in that tradition. And rare it is indeed when one community of faith assigns a positive role to another community, especially a hostile one. I believe that a Christian vision of that same common task flashed through Paul's mind when (in Rom 11) it struck him that the Jesus movement was to become a Gentile movement, and he tried to show the Gentile Christians how the Church and Israel were to coexist in the mysterious plan of God.

As we mentioned, Maimonides coupled Christianity with Islam (the three peoples of the Book) as bearers of Torah. I think we Christians have been led to disregard Islam partly out of that historicism of which I spoke so critically. For us Islam is so obviously a latecomer—as we are to the Jews—and we see Islam as a religiously relatively uninteresting bastardizing of some Jewish and Christian thoughts coupled with more primitive elements. But to a Muslim, Islam is not a seventh century AD phenomenon but has its root in Abraham—as to Paul the promise to Abraham rather than the Law given to Moses was the decisive point in God's revelation made full in Jesus Christ. Again it becomes clear how important it is to listen to how a community of faith defines itself.

It is thus quite clear to me that the task ahead is a theological task. I am, of course, well aware that many Jewish thinkers and scholars have difficulties both with the word theology and that for which it stands. This hesitation on their part is partly grounded in their insistence that while Judaism may be a "theological problem" to Christianity, Christianity is no such thing to Judaism. One cannot be a Christian without having an understanding of the Jews, but one can certainly be a Jew without understanding or knowing Christianity. To Judaism the Church is rather an oppressive and ever ominous fact of life, and the first concern of any Jew when he thinks of the Church must be: Can I be assured that you will not harm me and my people? Or perhaps only: Why don't you leave me alone?

Thus the counteracting of overt, covert and potential anti-semitism in the churches is not only a sideline in dialogue between Jews and Christians. It is an ever present task at the very core of our work. It is motivated by what I called the negative bind, which historically speaking, has and does dominate our common bond. But I believe that such a task cannot be done in earnest without our work on a new vision of our common task, and for that we plead with the Jewish community to help us. We understand their hesitation, we respect their apprehension, and we are grateful for the help we have already received.

C. The New Task

The wider perspective of Dialogue with People of Other Faiths and Ideologies gives a new dimension to our work since it calls for widening the Christian component in the dialogue beyond the Western/European and American orbit. As the CCJP we have for all practical purposes been confined to "the West." We in the CCJP must now seek the help of Christians beyond these confines. If the "we" is to be the "we" of the WCC as we speak about Jewish-Christian relations, then a far wider spectrum of Christians must be encouraged to speak in their own language and from their own perspectives how they understand this our common bond with Israel of old and through the ages. We in the CCJP are gratified that this time African Christians have accepted our invitation to come to Jerusalem in order to begin such a task. We hope to find the proper place and means for a consultation of Orthodox Christians for that same purpose. We have welcomed the recent volume of papers from a Jewish-Orthodox (Christian) consultation in the US (*Journal of Ecumenical Studies* 13 [1976], 517–671, published also in the *Greek Orthodox Theological Review*). We hope to broaden the spectrum to other parts of the WCC constituency, both in various parts of Asia, Australia and South America.

To many of our Christian sisters and brothers in these parts of the world the questions of Jewish-Christian relations may well appear distant, and low on the agenda of priorities. But it is the duty of the CCJP to urge our brothers and sisters in other churches to consider the matter with some urgency.

It is our duty to combat anti-semitism—or we should get used to say [*sic*] anti-Judaism when we leave the Western orbit within which the inadequate term "anti-semitism" was coined. We know by experience that the Christian teaching which Western missionaries carried to other parts of the world has within it the evil germs of anti-Judaism. While these germs are now latent in large parts of the world, there is ample evidence that anti-Judaism is on the rise globally. The establishment of the State of Israel and the Middle East conflict has given a global visibility to the Jewish people in the midst of mighty political, ideological and economic forces. While there can be various value judgments as to the policies of the State of Israel, and different views of Zionism, I think it is fair to say that much anti-Zionism feeds on the very same sources that produced Western anti-semitism. The reappearance of well-known Western anti-semitic tracts in countries and languages which had no part whatsoever in the Western history of anti-semitism is alarming. Incipient anti-semitism in Japan falls back on quotations from Jesus about the Pharisees, etc.

As part of the WCC I am anxious to urge my brothers and sisters all over the globe to give thought to these matters, lest the Gospel once more and in forms new and old be used for anti-Jewish purposes. I have spoken plainly and I do so with deep worries.

The urgency of the matter has also another side. It may well be that those of us who come out of the Western experience have been blinded by that experience to possible new ways in which the Gospel can set us free to new visions of how the people of the Exodus and the people of the Resurrection of Christ together with all God's creation can find their place in God's work. That is why we are so eager to ask for new and global attention to the old and so far painful theme of the Church and the Jewish People.

From Franz von Hammerstein, ed., *Christian-Jewish Relations in Ecumenical Perspective with Special Emphasis on Africa* (Geneva: World Council of Churches, 1977), 1–6.

꙲ "Statement on the Middle East," passed in 1968 by the Fourth Assembly of the **World Council of Churches,** acknowledges the religious and political complexities that exist in the Middle East. The assembly was held at Uppsala on July 4–20, 1968, one year after the Six-Day War.

THE WORLD COUNCIL OF CHURCHES

"Statement on the Middle East"

1. We are deeply concerned that the menace of the situation in the Middle East shows no present sign of abating. The resolutions of the United Nations have not been implemented, the territorial integrity of the nations involved is not respected, occupation continues. No settlement is in sight and a new armament race is being mounted.

In these circumstances we reaffirm the statement of the Heraklion Central Committee in August 1967, and make the following points based upon it:

(a) The independence and territorial integrity and security of all nations in the area must be guaranteed. Annexation by force must not be condoned.

(b) The World Council of Churches must continue to join with all who search for a solution of the refugee and displaced person problems.

(c) Full religious freedom and access to holy places must continue to be guaranteed to the communities of all three historic religions preferably by international agreement.

(d) National armaments should be limited to the lowest level consistent with national security.

(e) The great world powers must refrain from pursuing their own exclusive interests in the area.

2. The forthcoming report of the Special Representative of the United Nations Secretary General is urgently awaited, and the Assembly earnestly hopes that it may open the way to a settlement.

3. It is the special responsibility of the World Council of Churches and of its member churches to discern ways in which religious factors affect the conflict.

From *The Theology of Churches and the Jewish People: Statements by the World Council of Churches and Its Member Churches* (Geneva: World Council of Churches, 1988), 29–30.

꙲ "Muslims and Christians in Society" (1975) emerged from a meeting of Christians and Muslims in Hong Kong sponsored by the **World Council of Churches.** It is a statement of policy and addresses such issues as the religious education of children in a pluralist society.

THE WORLD COUNCIL OF CHURCHES

"Muslims and Christians in Society"

Introduction

Muslims and Christians have been in conversation ever since the dawn of Islam. Occasionally, their discussions took the form of systematic exchanges between limited numbers of persons with theological training and social or political standing; two famous examples are the interview between the Abbasi Khalifah al-Mahdi and the Chaldean patriarch Timothy I late in the eighth century CE, and the audience granted to St Francis of Assisi by the Ayyubi Sultan al-Malik al-Kamil at Damietta in 1219. More often, Muslim and Christian rulers of varying degrees of piety incorporated religious differences into their economic and political rationales for intercommunal warfare, and scholarly studies of religion were nearly always designed to prove the truth of the author's position. A gradual and timid quest for another type of relationship has gained currency over the last century or so, leading to the Second Vatican Council's generous expression of respect for Muslims and other people of faith (1963) and the WCC's opening of a distinct section for dialogue in 1971.

At first, there was considerable uncertainty among the Christians about the methods or instruments which they ought to use in developing formal interfaith contacts. The WCC organized a series of meetings of Christians who were especially concerned with these questions, beginning at Broumana, Lebanon (June 1966) and culminating in the large consultation at Chiang Mai, Thailand (April 1977). [. . .] It may be helpful simply to list the thirteen headings from these Guidelines to set the framework for the material at hand.

1. Churches should seek ways in which Christian communities can enter into dialogue with their neighbours of different faiths and ideologies.

2. Dialogue should normally be planned together.

3. Partners in dialogue should take stock of the religious, cultural and ideological diversity of their local situation.

4. Partners in dialogue should be free to "define themselves."

5. Dialogue should generate educational efforts in the community.

6. Dialogue is most vital when its participants actually share their lives together.

7. Dialogue should be pursued by sharing in common enterprises in community.

8. Partners in dialogue should be aware of their ideological commitments.

9. Partners in dialogue should be aware of cultural loyalties.

10. Dialogue will raise the question of sharing in celebrations, rituals, worship and meditation.

11. Dialogue should be planned and undertaken ecumenically, whenever possible.

12. Planning for dialogue will necessitate regional and local guidelines.

13. Dialogue can be helped by selective participation in world inter-religious meetings and organizations. . . .

Between the Nairobi [1975] and Vancouver [1983] assemblies, there were another half dozen such meetings, and although most of these were of global dimensions, four were held in the environs of Geneva. [. . .] The exchange on mission and *da'wah* [invitation to accept Islam as the final Abrahamic religion] (Chambésy, June 1976) has oft been cited as a lasting example of a sincere, constructive interfaith conversation, while the youth meeting at Bossey (June 1980) set a worthy precedent for interfaith encounters of young people in a variety of local situations. The smallest of these meetings may have been the most important, for it laid a foundation for institutional consultation that continues to develop

(Cartigny, October 1976). Indeed, since 1986 representatives of the interfaith offices of the WCC and the Vatican have been meeting regularly with their counterparts from world Islamic organizations in a growing spirit of mutual trust and confidence; between these semi-annual sessions, contacts between these parties have become more frequent and cover an ever broader range of topics. [. . .]

The Place and Manner of Our Meeting

Over 30 Muslims and Christians, in almost equal numbers, met in Hong Kong from 4 to 10 January 1975, to discuss the theme "Muslims and Christians in society: towards goodwill, consultation and working together in South-East Asia." They were made welcome in Hong Kong by local Christians and Muslims and worshipped there with their respective communities. The conference was organized by the department for Dialogue with People of Living Faiths and Ideologies of the World Council of Churches, Geneva, in cooperation with a committee of Muslims and Christians from South-East Asia and the Christian Conference of Asia. The joint chairmen were a Muslim, Senator Mamintal Tamano from the Philippines, and a Christian, Dr Peter Latuihamallo from Indonesia. Papers were prepared by Prof. Cesar Majul of the Philippines and Dr Ahmad Ibrahim of Malaysia, on the Muslim side. On the Christian side, Dr Ihromi of Indonesia, Sister Theresa Thong of Malaysia and Mrs. Portia Mapanao of the Philippines introduced subjects which ranged from theological grounds for inter-religious respect to practical experience of the role of religion in promoting or disturbing social harmony.

This was the first time that such a regional conference had been held in South-East Asia, although several of the participants had attended international Christian-Muslim dialogues or have been active in their local situations in conversation and cooperation with their neighbours of another faith. The conference considered some guidelines which could further stimulate regional and local dialogues of this nature, not only in the interests of nation-building and community development but also in the interests of building up spiritual values and resources of goodwill, respect and faith in the face of common problems and opportunities in the modern world.

The participants expressed their joy in meeting together and they also hoped that such encounters might be repeated in the future. They together discussed the following memorandum which, without presuming to speak for any religious organization or community as a whole, nevertheless met with the careful and glad consensus of all those present who recommended it to their respective communities for further consultation and, where appropriate, implementation.

The Need for Muslim-Christian Dialogue in South-East Asia

It is a sad fact that, often in the past and even at the present time, attitudes of exclusivism, of condescension or of hostility have characterized relations between Muslims and Christians in South-East Asia. We Christians and Muslims, coming together in dialogue in Hong Kong from different situations, whether of cooperation and harmony or of tension and conflict between our communities in South-East Asia, recognize that any negative attitudes do not reflect the true character of either of our faiths. Any such attitudes illustrate the gap which exists in both communities between the high principles of religious teaching and the actual practices of their adherents.

Our purpose in Hong Kong has been to face up to the fact that we come from religiously pluralistic societies in South-East Asia, wherein not only is conflict clearly disastrous but even peaceful co-existence is an inadequate condition for the urgent needs of our developing societies. Our respective national societies, we feel, have a right to expect from the faithful communities of Christians and Muslims not conflict, not mere coexistence, but goodwill, a readiness to confer with each other and an eagerness to cooperate in every possible way. Muslims and Christians need each other's help to ease tension, secure justice, relieve pain, and otherwise promote the social, material and spiritual wellbeing of all people.

The Theological Bases for Muslim-Christian Relations and for the Relations of Both with All Neighbouring Religions and Ideologies

We Christians and Muslims meeting in Hong Kong affirm that our respective faiths, properly understood, enjoin on us a loving relationship with each other and with all human beings. The ground and impetus for this living relationship is no less than the One God himself who has made all human beings brothers and sisters. Muslims emphasize that God the Compassionate (*Al-Rahmān*) and the Beloved (*Al-Habīb*) commands the faithful to be merciful and compassionate and loving in their dealings with all people, and therefore they are able to be so. The Qur'an embodies this command and specifies ways in which the faithful may obediently comply with it

in various life situations. Christians, for their part, emphasize that God's love shown in his self-giving in and through the person of Jesus Christ both inspires and enables their loving relationship with all humankind. Responding to God's love in Jesus Christ, Christians find the example and basis for love in their social dealings with all people. Thus, allowing for these differences in understanding, both Islam and Christianity find their ethical mandate in the All-Merciful God who loves and is loved.

We Christians and Muslims in South-East Asia are only too painfully aware of how far short we have fallen from God's will for us in our encounters with one another. We acknowledge together that individuals and groups from both communities have often forgotten that power—whether financial or political or social or cultural or intellectual or spiritual—is a trust (*amānah*) from God to be used responsibly and compassionately for the wellbeing of all, and not abused to advance the selfish interests of a particular individual or group or ideology.

People are naturally apprehensive regarding the possible misuse of power. Some Muslims, for example, complain that in certain places Christian groups have advanced and continue to advance their cause in South-East Asia by insensitive use of financial resources coming from the West. On the other hand, there are Christians who feel anxious about their position as a religious community in some places where political and/or financial power may belong predominantly to Muslims. Both Christians and Muslims ought readily to acknowledge that such accusations and apprehensions are not wholly unjustified on either side. In those places where assurances are needed and have not yet been given, both Christians and Muslims ought eagerly to affirm that neither community intends to misuse power to its own advantage.

The prerequisites of peace and humanity oblige both the Muslim and Christian communities to accept emotionally as well as intellectually the fact of their mutual existence in South-East Asia, with Muslims and Christians recognizing each other as full and equal citizens of our national societies.

Christianity and Islam, along with Judaism, are in a special relationship with each other. We belong to the spiritual family of Abraham (*nabī Ibrāhīm*). We seek to be faithful and strive to be obedient in accordance with God's command and in response to God's grace or favor. We have many theological and ethical convergences and similarities. While in the not-so-distant past Christians and Muslims accentuated their differences to such a degree that some sectors in our respective communities regarded each other as unfriendly rivals, we now gratefully recognize that we are moving into a new era. In this new era our common ground is recognized as the context in which to understand our differences and we stretch out our hands in friendship and embrace each other as members of kindred communities of believers.

To be sure, Christians and Muslims possess distinctive elements in their respective faiths which they regard as precious treasures. Muslims have the Qur'an which in their belief and understanding is the revelation from God sent through his Messenger as a command, a light, a guidance, and a blessing for all people. Christians have the good news of the mighty acts of God in and through Jesus Christ for the redemption of mankind. A loving relationship with human beings leads Muslims and Christians to appreciate and respect these distinctive treasures of their respective faiths. Unfortunately, history provides some instances where Christians and Muslims sought coercively to impose their faiths on people who were resistant. Islam and Christianity, we believe, are in agreement that there can be no compulsion in religion. Wherever methods of compulsion, overt or covert, blatant or subtle, are still employed in order to draw people of one faith into another faith, these methods should be renounced as unworthy of Christianity and Islam.

Christians and Muslims both recognize it as a duty and a privilege to reduce areas of misunderstanding between their respective religious communities and between themselves and others, while all the time affirming the integrity and dignity of human beings. We affirm that all human relationships should point to God as the Beginning and the End of all things.

Two methods of fostering understanding especially commend themselves to us. The first of these entails witnessing in society to the highest and best in our respective religions by the example of our personal manner of life, behavior, and worship. The second method involves us in engaging, in a spirit of goodwill, in discourse with all interested persons about the teachings of our respective religions.

Areas of Common Concern in Social and Political Contexts

1. Varying Situations of the Relationships between Our Religious Communities

We believe that God has a purpose for our communities, however different their respective situations. We believe that we should respond to his purpose by working together for a moral and just society; true prosperity cannot be achieved without the individual's personal commitment to morality and justice.

We live in a world where power is sometimes abused. At all levels of our societies we bear a responsibility to help establish the conditions for the right of power. Decision-making processes in the hands of responsible persons who are just and sensitive to the needs of all people will enhance the effective use of power. Muslims and Christians, like their other neighbours, often fail to live up to this responsibility, but we believe that we have a duty to strive individually and together to contribute to and to implement the aspirations of our respective religious communities.

Political harmony is precious to both communities. All human aspirations can best be realized under a condition of peace and order. However, such a climate can only be fully attained within a political and legal framework which ensures freedom and harmonious interaction for all religious communities. We commend the positive and creative role which governments may play in helping to reduce tensions and conflicts between religious communities.

Nevertheless, political stability can sometimes breed complacency. Muslims and Christians should remain alert to the way in which selfish tendencies can creep in. Freedom may be eroded and lost by subtle encroachments rather than by abrupt and dramatic aggression. This can happen when self-interest or group-interest predominates over the common welfare. Accordingly, Muslims and Christians should make a conscious effort to seek each other's assistance to defend their common interest and to work together in the service of their neighbours and of God.

We have tasks to perform even in situations where our religious communities may be politically weak or powerless, or where they may suffer formal or actual legal disabilities. One among these tasks is working together for reconciliation and reconstruction.

2. The Response of Religions to Changing Values in Rapidly Developing Societies

Historically, Islam and Christianity have contributed much to the development of human societies, notably in the formulation of ethical values. However, there has been a tendency for social traditions and laws, embodying those values, to become too dogmatic or legalistic so as to be closed to worthwhile change as society has sought to respond to emergent needs. Moreover, to a certain extent our two religions have seemed to some sectors of society to be conservative and resistant to progress.

There are many who feel that religion is and ought to be an immovable anchor in rapidly changing social situations. But we feel that our fast changing societies are right to expect that Muslims and Christians should subject their own ethical values to careful scrutiny in the light of new situations which demand new duties and fresh responses. The spiritual and ethical foundations of our two faiths are the constant sources of light and guidance, but the situations upon which the light must shine and to which the guidance must be given are continually changing.

The response of our two religious communities to situations of rapid social change involves the mobilization of our resources for a variety of concerns, among which are: concern for the dignity of mankind and the basic rights of the individual; concern for social justice; concern for the character and shape of national consciousness; and concern for freedom in the choice and practice of religion.

Of special importance for our religious communities in some situations is the matter of proselytism. We are moved to call upon all religious bodies and individuals to refrain from proselytism, which we define as the compulsive, conscious, deliberate and tactical effort to draw people from one community of faith to another.

Our religions have the responsibility to alert society to religious, moral and spiritual values in the changing circumstances of daily life. Our responsibility is to enhance the total development of the human personality, spiritually and socially, and to stand squarely behind all that promotes justice and peace. Our religions are called upon to offer fresh motivations and fresh guidance for the growing expectations and changing aspirations of human beings in society. [. . .]

Religious Education in Pluralistic Societies

Both Christians and Muslims recognize it as a duty to provide religious instruction for the young, emphasizing those elements which enrich life, show its significance and point to its final destiny in God. We realize that ways of religious instruction vary in the different countries of South-East Asia. In some there are government ministries responsible for this work. In others this responsibility is left to the parents or to the religious communities. While both communities hold that parents have a major responsibility for the religious instruction of their children, there is also a realistic appreciation that public and private education programmes can offer

important opportunities for religious instruction. Indeed, in some places our respective communities have established schools of their own for just such purposes.

With respect to the latter, a question arises when a school is established by one religious community in a place inhabited predominantly by adherents of another religious community, and/or when there is a substantial enrollment of youngsters who are not from the faith of those who own and operate the school. The question is, what is the responsibility of the school for the religious instruction of children who come from families not of its faith? Whereas some will say that if a school is founded by people committed to a particular religious faith in order to be an instrument for the propagation of that faith, its responsibility is limited to teaching that religion only, we Muslims and Christians meeting at Hong Kong have another view. We believe that schools providing religious instruction for children from different religious communities should arrange to have such instruction given by qualified persons belonging to the respective communities. Christian children should receive religious instruction from a Christian, Muslim children from a Muslim, and so forth. We feel that it is a form of "compulsion in religion" for malleable, impressionable children in their formative years to be subject to religious training by instructors not of the faith of their parents.

This is not to say that there should be no place for the scientific study of religion. Both Islam and Christianity recognize that people have a duty to extend the frontiers of their knowledge and this includes knowledge of other religions besides their own. Moreover, because the study of religion is properly seen as an integral part of the total educational programme, courses in the philosophy, sociology, psychology and comparative study of religion may be offered at the higher levels of education in schools and colleges.

Building Unity in Diversity

The expression "unity in diversity" is well known in South-East Asian nations, all of which are faced initially at the national level with a task of forging common goals and a common identity from the rich variety of races, languages, cultures and religions within their national borders. The seal of the Republic of Indonesia bears the Sanskrit words *Bhinneka Tunggal Ika* which means "unity in diversity." The some 120 million Muslims and 47 million Christians who live with other neighbours in the lands of South-East Asia contribute significantly to the diversity of each nation and likewise have vital roles to play in the shape of national unity in their different places.

Because we belong to kindred communities of faith, there are doubtless many things which Christians and Muslims can do together to foster the unity of peoples in society. Among them we can identify the following:

1. Achieve and maintain peace between themselves, since not only national unity but regional stability are both advanced when the different religious communities live together in peace and harmony.

2. Witness together for the religious and moral perspective that respects the dignity and worth of all human beings in the face of dehumanizing forces.

3. Unite together to strengthen the moral conscience of national endeavour—affirming those aspects of nation-building which operate for the common good and, in obedience to God's will, calling attention to those aspects which are harmful or oppressive.

4. Promote together a human appreciation of the cultural achievements of all the diverse communities which make up the society—valuing those worthy achievements as the common property of the whole nation and of humanity.

5. Represent together the transcendent dimension of human beings in mundane society of men and women, old and young, who, in the final analysis, belong not only to this world of time and matter, but also to the Eternal.

From Stuart E. Brown, ed., *Meeting in Faith: Twenty Years of Christian-Muslim Conversations Sponsored by the WCC* (Geneva: World Council of Churches, 1989), vii–ix, 58–63, 66–68.

◆ In "Buddhism and Christianity as Complementary" (1978) **John B. Cobb** acknowledges the differences between Buddhism and Christianity but also indicates that these differences are not necessarily theoretical contradictions. Cobb argues that "both can be true" and believes that "both *are* true." Cobb and Masao Abe founded the International Buddhist Christian Theological Encounter Groups.

JOHN B. COBB

"Buddhism and Christianity as Complementary"

Methodological Questions

Christians believe that God is the God of all and that in Jesus Christ God effected in principle the salvation of all. This uni-

versalistic conviction has forced Christian thinkers to reflect about the meaning of movements other than Christianity especially when they have some apparent power and goodness in themselves. The study of cultures and religious Ways other than Christianity is a theological imperative for Christians.

In the last two centuries the cultures and religious Ways of Asia have become increasingly important for Western intellectuals, and in the last two decades they have taken on importance for millions of ordinary Western Christians. The reality of Asian Ways is no longer known only through reading and travel. They have penetrated Western culture and life and offer a vital alternative for serious-minded Westerners. In this situation the urgency of theological reflection is enhanced. Western Christians can be grateful that Eastern Christians have been involved in these questions for generations. Japan is now the world center for the encounter of Buddhism by Christians.

The experience of the early church is instructive for us as we face our new situation. In the New Testament itself the religious Ways of the Gentiles are viewed primarily as idolatrous. We should not be contemptuous of this treatment, for of course the practice of the masses of Gentiles *was* idolatrous. But the New Testament writers themselves were influenced by Platonic and Stoic modes of thought and expression, and as the thinkers of the early church encountered the work of the philosophers in its purity, they could not dismiss Greek thought simply as idolatrous.

The church's struggle to come to terms with philosophy still continues. Within Protestantism there have been many who see the appeal to philosophic reason as itself a sophisticated and dangerous idolatry. Nevertheless, viewing Christian history overall, we must say that Christians decided that one could be both a Christian and a philosopher. Furthermore, Greek philosophy entered constitutively into the structure of Christian thought throughout the Middle Ages; and during most of the modern period as well, theology and philosophy have been deeply intertwined.

When Christians encounter the great Oriental religious Ways they face different challenges, which are yet analogous. These new challenges have evoked analogous responses. Despite notable exceptions, prior to World War I the dominant response was to view Asian religious Ways as idolatrous. As in the case of the New Testament, there was some justification. Even today as tourists visit Buddhist temples in Southeast Asia or Japan, much of what they observe is, at least superficially, idolatrous or superstitious.

However, as Christian thinkers during this period became aware of the profound philosophy, the meditational practices, and the personal faith present in these Ways, they could no longer dismiss them as merely idolatrous or superstitious. Serious theological reflection on their meaning has become imperative. It is still in its early stages. I will list four approaches to the understanding of the relation of Christianity to Buddhism, none of which I find satisfactory. I will then make my own proposals.

First, some Christians concentrate on the similarities with Buddhism. Buddhism can be seen as a partner which shares the same essential convictions and experience. Differences are then viewed as matters of cultural accretion, language, imagery, and emphasis. Discussion consists in discovering how the other tradition identifies and describes central elements experienced in one's own. This was Tillich's approach when he visited Kyoto.

Second, some Christians who have been more impressed by the differences have accepted the image of many paths up the same mountain. Although the Ways are quite different, it is thought that they are all means of achieving salvation. Even if salvation is conceived differently, it is held that in fact it is one and the same for all. This view is popular among followers of some Oriental Ways, especially in India.

Third, some Christians who hold fast to the universal meaning of Jesus Christ view the several paths not as attaining salvation but as diverse preparations for the Gospel. Just as the Judaism of the Old Testament prepared the Jews for the Gospel, so also Hellenistic culture prepared the Gentiles, and Oriental Ways prepared the peoples of the East. The uniqueness of Jesus Christ is then to be expressed in the diverse cultures and languages of humankind rather than to be bound finally to Judaism. Roman Catholic theology, especially since Vatican II, has leaned in this direction.

Fourth, when the differences between Christian and Buddhist teaching are still more fully appreciated, some Christians come to the conclusion that they are irreconcilably opposed. In their view, if Christian teaching about God and the soul is correct, then Buddhist teaching must be erroneous insofar as it differs. However attractive are the achievements of Buddhism in art, culture, and personal life, the Christian response must be to try to correct its errors and convert Buddhists to the truth. This has been the dominant view of Christian missions in the past even when there was considerable appreciation of Buddhism.

I want to defend a fifth position. This agrees with the stress on differences between Christianity and Buddhism, both in their beliefs and in their goals. But it holds that these differences need not amount to theoretical contradictions. Both can be true. I believe that both *are* true. In this case we have much to learn from each other about features of reality and types of experience little developed in our own traditions.

For this position to be correct, reality must be more complex than either tradition, by itself, has recognized. It is very clear that in Western Buddhist scholarship in general, at least until quite recently, the questions that have been asked of the Buddhist texts have been questions that could be understood and answered already in Western experience. Nirvana has been understood either as this-worldly or other-worldly, and these categories were understood in the sense they had gained in the West. If Nirvana was other-worldly, then it was either literal extinction or else mystical union with God. If it was this-worldly, then it could only be some form of moral excellence or psychological fulfillment. The scholarly students of Buddhism alternated among these views.

Some Western philosophers have been able to think through to categories that transcended Western common sense and in doing so to come closer to grasping Buddhist thought and experience. Friedrich Schopenhauer is an example. Despite his lack of scholarship he understood Nirvana better than did the Buddhologists. He could do so because his own philosophical imagination brought him to conceive of the radical extinction of the will as the door to a wholly different mode of being.

In the twentieth century Martin Heidegger offers an effective way for the Western mind to approach Buddhism because he also penetrates to a mode of experience radically new for the West and approaching the experience of Buddhist enlightenment. Indeed, Heidegger may well be the most Buddhist thinker the West has produced. His later work provides an important basis for Western understanding of Buddhism.

Schopenhauer and Heidegger illustrate how philosophical thought can break through the established categories of the Western mind and open it to an understanding of Buddhism. They do not, however, support my thesis of the distinct truths of Buddhism and Christianity. For them, if the truths are different, this would be because one penetrates less deeply than the other. Divergences must express different levels of apprehension of one truth. I am arguing, in contrast, that Christianity and Buddhism lie on different lines of development that cannot be compared as more superficial and deeper.

I am closer to another philosopher, F. S. C. Northrop. In

The Meeting of East and West he describes their relation as complementary. This requires a concept of reality that allows the mind to move in two different directions from its primary experience. Northrop describes the common starting point as the differentiated aesthetic continuum. From it the West moves to attention to the differentiating forms; the East, to the underlying undifferentiated continuum.

I do not find the details of Northrop's analysis either adequate or convincing, but I am grateful for the basic model. Northrop sees East and West as profoundly different, but he holds that the truths they realize and treasure are complementary rather than contradictory. He is able to do this, again, because of his philosophical vision, [in which] each encompassed dimensions of reality poorly articulated in the West.

Northrop was a student of Alfred North Whitehead, and his work shows Whitehead's influence. However, he intentionally simplified Whitehead's philosophy and accepted only limited aspects of it. It is my belief that a richer use of Whitehead's conceptuality can allow a more varied grasp of alternative Eastern views and a deeper penetration into Buddhism while retaining the idea that they complement one another. Whitehead's own view was that Christianity and Buddhism represent the culmination of Western and Eastern religious developments, that both are in decline, and that neither can regain its vitality except as enriched through the other. I share his conviction and I am trying to use his general perspective in order to show how Christianity can be enriched through its contact with Buddhism.

The Self in Buddhism and Christianity

One major point of apparent conflict between Christianity and Buddhism is about the self. Christianity emphasized the self, whereas Buddhism declares it an illusion from which we are to be freed. There is no doubt that between most Christian formulations and most Buddhist ones there are strict contradictions. My question is whether the contradictory statements are necessary to the contending parties. It is essential to Buddhism to deny that there is, metaphysically speaking, such an entity as a persisting self. Any doctrine of a self-existent, self-contained entity of this sort must be refused. If Christian doctrine requires affirmation of a substantial or transcendental self, then there is irresolvable metaphysical contradiction between Christianity and Buddhism. However, it is by no means evident that Biblical thinking involves either substantialist or transcendental views. On the contrary, they

appear foreign to the Biblical frame of mind. There is, certainly, some notion of what we would call a personal self, but the hypostatization of this self developed only through interaction with Greek philosophy, and much of what is most strictly contradictory to Buddhism began with Descartes.

On the Buddhist side, it is clear that the denial of the self is not a denial that in ordinary experience there is a strong connectedness among successive experiences of a single person. In this sense the factuality of a personal self is far from denied, it is presupposed in the idea of *karma*. What is denied is that this special connection between these experiences is metaphysically given or that there is a common subject to whom they occur. And what is proposed is that full realization that ideas of a metaphysical unity or of an underlying subject are illusions can break the factual bondage of present to past and future.

There is no reason for Christians to deny the accuracy of the Buddhist analysis. Nevertheless, Christians affirm that there is positive value in the personal ordering of selfhood from which Buddhists seek liberation. The issue for Christians is complex. The personal self is to be "denied" or even "crucified." But denial and crucifixion are not means of obliteration. They presuppose a strong self which then sacrifices its purposes and desires so that God's will may be done. Denial and crucifixion assume continuity through time and personal responsibility for past and future. Ethical norms play a central role. All of this is very different from what Buddhism means by the realization of no-self.

My view as a Whiteheadian is that Christian and Buddhist doctrines about the universal nature of reality need not differ. There need be no logical contradiction. Buddhism and Christianity should each be able to understand intellectually the structure of existence advocated by the other and partly realized by it. Each should be able to see also the important human values attained in the other's structure, and each should be ready to learn more about these from those who more fully realize them. All this can be said without minimizing the profound differences. Indeed, it is precisely because Buddhism differs so profoundly from Christianity that Christians have so much to learn from it.

This entails that the enlightenment Buddhists seek is quite different from the salvation with which Christians are concerned. This is turn is in apparent conflict with many Christian formulations of the claim of universality. Certainly the claim of universality must be reconceived in a pluralistic world. Nevertheless, such reconception should not be abandonment. Jesus Christ is uniquely bound up with what Christians mean by salvation. This salvation is relevant and available to all. But it differs from and is only remotely related to what Buddhists call enlightenment, a condition which is also relevant and available to all. It is entirely appropriate that Christians witness to the joy of salvation through faith in Jesus Christ. It is entirely appropriate also that Buddhists witness to the serenity that is achieved in enlightenment. The world needs both universal Ways. For either, in its present form, to displace the other would be a profound loss.

The Doctrine of God in Buddhism and Christianity

A second area in which Buddhism and Christianity appear to contradict each other centers around the Christian doctrine of God. Buddhism denies the existence or reality of what Christian theology generally has called God. There are at least three features of most Christian teaching about God that clearly evoke Buddhist negation.

Most Christian thinking presents God, analogous to the personal self, as substantial or transcendental. Indeed, God is often conceived as the purest instance of substance, completely self-contained, and needing nothing else so as to exist. Buddhism insists that whatever is is relational through and through, interdependent with everything else. Confronted with this insistence, Christians must ask themselves whether they have truly been faithful to their own Scriptures and experience in depicting God as beyond all real relations or relativity. I believe we have not, and that the encounter with Buddhism can be an occasion for freeing our concept of God from the absolutist straightjacket.

Most Christians have also laid stress on God's radical transcendence. Here again a Buddhist may have to say "No!" If transcendence means beyond relations and relativity, then we have already seen that Buddhists properly reject this. If it connotes a spatial sense of above and beyond the physical world, it is either simply naive or else bound up with a dualism that the Buddhist rightly opposes. There cannot be a being of a fundamentally different order or type from the remainder of what is.

But there are other meanings of transcendence which Buddhists need not reject. If transcendence means vast qualitative superiority, then most Buddhists recognize this in Gautama and other Buddhas when these are compared with themselves. There is a sense in which the enlightened state transcends ordinary experience and in which reality transcends our concepts of it. The encounter with Buddhism presses Christians to reconsider what we have meant by God's transcendence. When we do so, we find that the Biblical sense of God's transcendence is qualitative and that our doctrine of God can avoid those types of transcendence which Buddhists legitimately reject. Most theologians, in the third place, have also identified God with "ultimate reality." To do so attributes to ultimate reality characteristics incompatible with the Buddhist understanding of Nothingness or Emptiness. It is true that there has been the negative way in Christianity, and that some mystics have spoken of the Divine Nothingness in ways that suggest affinities with Buddhism. But when the meaning of Emptiness for Buddhists is fully appreciated, we must agree that it would be deeply misleading to name this God. Buddhist Emptiness is not the God of the Christian scriptures.

Here again we Christians are forced to rethink our theological habits. If ultimate reality is Emptiness, and if Emptiness is not the Biblical God, then does the Biblical God have no reality at all? Or is it possible that the Bible does not present God as ultimate reality in the metaphysical sense? If we look open-mindedly for the Biblical idea of the metaphysical ultimate, might we not find it in the chaos or nothingness from which God created the world? Was, perhaps, the theological identification of God with ultimate reality or Being Itself a mistake?

That there is a tension between the metaphysical ultimate—the God of the philosophers—and the ultimate of faith—the God of Abraham, Isaac, and Jacob—has long been realized by Christians. Emil Brunner noted the difference and opted for the God of Abraham, Isaac, and Jacob. Paul Tillich noted the difference and affirmed Being Itself as the God beyond the Biblical God.

The encounter with Buddhism suggests that when Being Itself is fully understood and experienced it resolves itself into the Nothingness of dependent origination. It not only differs from the Biblical God but also lacks those characteristics of Being Itself that have enabled Westerners to think of Being as God. It thus makes clear that to speak of God at all should be to speak of the Biblical God rather than of Being Itself as ultimate reality. If Buddhist analysis is correct, then the Biblical God must be a manifestation of ultimate reality as dependent origination.

The idea of God or Gods as manifestations of ultimate reality is an old one. Hinduism affirms it emphatically, and Buddhist thought at least allows it. But Christians have resisted this way of understanding God. The tendency to imply that God is one manifestation among others, dispensable to the initiate, is quite unacceptable to Christian theology. If it is recognized that God is not ultimate reality as such, then God must be seen as the one, everlasting and ultimate embodiment of ultimate reality, essential for the occurrence of whatever else may be. Although such a universal manifestation of dependent origination is not envisaged in Buddhist doctrine, I believe there is no contradiction involved and that Christian faith will benefit from clarifying itself in this way.

Alfred North Whitehead's philosophy moves us a considerable distance in this direction. He distinguishes creativity, his name for ultimate reality, from God. His account of creativity—the many coalescing into a new one which is then a part of the many which coalesce again—is remarkably similar to some formulations of *pratityasamutpada*. God is the primordial, unique, and everlasting instantiation of creativity. Since creativity is everlasting, God did not exist before all creatures, but God plays an essential and constitutive role in the coming to be of each new creature.

If, then, we can affirm both Buddhist Emptiness and the Christian God, the difference between Buddhism and Christianity is not a matter of metaphysical truth but of two orientations to the totality of what is. Both orientations have been present in both Buddhism and Christianity. Yet we may recognize a polarity in the dominant traditions, the former exploring the meaning and value of the realization of ultimate reality, the latter exploring the meaning and value of faith in God.

This duality of directions corresponds to the duality we have noted previously between strengthening the contingent personal self and its extinction. To seek the realization of ultimate reality as *pratityasamutpada* is to move toward freedom from personal selfhood. To attend to God and God's purposes in the world orients one to the future and to the new possibilities of the present in a way that evokes the exercise of will, intensifies personal responsibility, and focuses on hope. This leads to the strengthening of personal selfhood.

The Risks and Rewards of Such Dialogue

The position which I am defending is that Buddhism and Christianity are both true, that both embody and express possible and real life orientations and perceptions of reality. Yet it seems that existentially they preclude each other. To be a Buddhist is to participate in one kind of existence and to seek one kind of perfection. To be a Christian is to participate in quite a different structure.

Even if we are left with this insuperable duality, our encounter is profitable. I have suggested ways in which Christian thought can be stimulated and corrected through the meeting. For Christians there is also intrinsic value in expanding our understanding of the rich varieties of experiences and realities. It is a gain also if we can express our truth to Buddhists in ways that do not seem immediately false.

Nevertheless, the admission that there is a form of beautiful and admirable experience that is forever closed to the Christian can not but be personally painful. It is also theologically distressing. It would mean that in fact Jesus Christ is not, as we have affirmed, relevant to the Buddhist, for Buddhist enlightenment would preclude any possibility of the salvation offered in Jesus.

My hope is that this is not the final word for the Christian in relation to Buddhism. Christians have in the past appropriated complementary truth and practice from other movements. The extent to which the results distort or enrich is always to be critically judged in each concrete case, but I am fully convinced of the importance of the venture. Success is most likely when the danger is fully appreciated and when we are quite aware of what we are doing. In relation to Buddhism the adventure has begun.

It is important that we recognize that to live deeply into Buddhist experience will upset established forms of Christian existence. We cannot simply add a few superficial elements of Buddhism to our present form of Christianity. Also we cannot expect to judge the outcome of an effective relation to Buddhism by the norms we hold before we enter into the relation. Those norms must also be subject to change through the encounter. We cannot enter the relation as Christians unless we are called into it by Christ. But if we are called into it by Christ, as I believe, then we must trust him and not the beliefs and ideas which we now identify with him. The risk is great, but it is the risk of faith itself.

From Richard W. Rousseau, ed., *Christianity and the Religions of the East: Models for a Dynamic Relationship*, vol. 2 (Montrose, PA: Ridge Row, 1982), 53–61.

☙ In his "Dual Citizenship in Faith?" (1988) **Hans Küng**, a Catholic theologian known for his wide ecumenism and controversial book on infallibility, affirms the possibility that culture and ethos can both be compatible with Christian faith. But when such compatibility is achieved, he asks, must not another step for a Christian also be ventured? He asks if a Christian should aspire to become a "dual citizen" of more than one of the world's religions.

Hans Küng

"Dual Citizenship in Faith?"

Epilogue

Yet, a last and most difficult question can now no longer be put off. If culture and ethos can be made compatible with Christian faith, must not a third and last step also be ventured? Should it not be possible for a Christian to be a strict *religious* Confucian, Taoist, or Buddhist as well? Beyond the mere cultural or ethical, is dual *religious* citizenship in the strict sense not therefore possible?

Dual Citizenship in Faith?

Such a question can be approached from very different fundamental positions.

1. A Christian of Asian origin can *take not only his or her own Christian religion quite seriously,* but also the indigenous Asian religion to the extent that it does not contradict the Christian faith. This combination could allow a deeper understanding of ultimate reality, the absolute, God—but also of the world, humanity, and nature. Indeed, it could eventually lead to a deeper appreciation of practices such as meditation. Our interreligious dialogue demonstrated again and again that better mutual information reveals significant parallels and convergences in spite of all divergences and differences. It showed that enrichment through cross-fertilization is possible. It is not necessarily a contradiction in itself if a Christian wants also to be a Confucian, Taoist, or Buddhist— if, in following Christ, he or she also wants to take the concerns, conceptions, and practices of other religions seriously (to the extent that they do not contradict his or her Christian faith). Such a Christian is, in the best and broadest sense of the word, an *ecumenical Christian.*

2. It is also entirely possible for a Christian—and this concerns Asians as well as Europeans and North Americans— to be a Buddhist, Confucian, Taoist, or whatever because *he takes neither of the religions completely seriously.* He or she does not really practice the discipleship of Christ or follow the Eightfold Path of the Buddha. Rather, he or she selects from the two religions according to his or her taste, taking what he or she likes and unconcernedly leaving what seems burdensome behind—a commandment of Jesus here, an injunction of the Buddha there. He or she mixes himself or herself a kind of religious cocktail, often ostensibly "mysti-

cal," prepared above all for the consumption of Europeans and North Americans who are often all too understandably fed up with their own religion and are looking for something new. Such private religion, mostly nurtured in small groups of the enlightened elite, may satisfy the religious needs of some people but with such a private, optional religion, one can no longer talk about a genuinely ecumenical attitude. In this case, genuinely ecumenical Christianity appears rather to have disintegrated into a pseudoecumenical syncretism.

But let us not be led astray. Such folkloric consumer religions hardly play a serious role anymore in the ethics and faith of the younger generation. Consequently, only around a third of all Japanese describe themselves as religious (even though [three quarters], indeed, 76 percent, affirm the necessity of a religion). If, however, the religious foundation is missing or remains nonobligatory, there will be unforeseen consequences for education and the basic ethical values that hold a society together. Increasingly, politicians from Tokyo to Singapore are seeing this as a serious challenge. Social criticism is, of course, very unpopular in the countries concerned. Such criticism has been openly and frankly leveled against contemporary Japanese society by the well-known Japanese intellectual Shuichi Kato

- on account of the short Japanese memory with respect to the ugly past, and the total absorption in the present;
- on account of the widespread consumerism that devalues all values;
- on account of the unaltered group mentality and the neglect of individuality;
- on account of the absence of a strong intellectual elite and on account of the danger of the gradual erosion of political rights.

These are all ethical and also veiled religious problems with which, of course, other countries besides Japan, similarly highly technologized and urbanized, have to do battle. There is therefore no cause for Christian self-righteousness. After all, parallel phenomena (or pure folklore religiosity) exist in the West as well. And if an upwardly mobile Japan currently has more career- and success-oriented people, our saturated Europe and North America, after all the modern achievements, have more dropouts. We refer to practically insoluble problems for parents, educators, teachers. Total value indifference, hopeless loss of orientation, and the abyss of a practical nihilism threaten on both sides. They can hardly be overcome by a purely rational ethic such as has been attempted throughout all of European modernity. No, it is not beneficial for the people of the Far East or of the West if none of the religions occasionally sampled is really taken seriously. Religions, even Confucianism and Buddhism, are more than mere ethos.

3. Therefore, one can be a religious Christian and a religious Buddhist, and so forth, by attempting *to take both religions entirely seriously.* Obviously, one will quickly come to the realization that, in spite of all the convergences and parallels, being a Christian and being a Buddhist are not simply identical: the way of discipleship in Christ and the path of the Buddha cannot simply be traveled at the same time. Certainly reconciliation can be pursued and understanding deepened in the future; and everything that has been written in this book is intended to contribute to this understanding. However, now as before, the experts particularly cannot ignore that, when all is said and done, Christianity and, for instance, Buddhism are not just two different paradigms, but two different religions. The conversion from the one to the other therefore represents not a mere change of paradigm, but rather a change of religion.

Therefore, even with every cultural and ethical possibility for integration, the truth of every religion extends to a depth that ultimately challenges every person to a yes or no, to an either-or. This is not just the case for the primarily exclusivist prophetic religions of Semitic origin. It is also valid for the more inclusivist mystical religions of Indian origin, and basically also for the more wisdom-oriented religions of Chinese tradition. An Indian religion that does not see its own truth exclusivistically as the only one (something that also no longer holds today for an ecumenically open Judaism, Christianity, or Islam) nevertheless likes to regard its own truth inclusivistically as the highest or most profound one, with the truth of the others as at best a propaedeutic or an aspect of the whole truth. A convinced Confucian or Taoist will also accordingly not simply let Christianity stand as a truth of equal importance beside his or her own native religion. Therefore, as much as cultural and ethical dual citizenship is possible and ought to be made possible ever anew,

a religious dual citizenship in the deepest, strictest sense of faith should be excluded—by all the great religions.

This, however, again raises the question of Christian existence in the context of another culture and a non-Christian ethos with peculiar clarity. *Christian inculturation, not dual religious citizenship,* must be the watchword! And it is especially on this point that self-criticism of Christian theology is in order. The reason is that the question of dual religious citizenship is a critical question directed at Christianity itself. Already in 1979, the French theologian Claude Geffré made this clear in a contribution to the international journal *Concilium,* one of the first to recognize "China as a Challenge for the Church." The question of whether one can be a Taoist or a Buddhist and simultaneously a Christian points in fact to the more radical question of what it is that is most important in Christianity. Geffré justifiably points out that, for Christianity, the "event of Jesus Christ" takes precedence over every tradition and remains the original point of reference for all Christian action. Every historical configuration of this event must be distinguished from the event itself. "One could go so far as to say that Christ did not found a new religion if by religion is meant a system of symbols, a set of rites, a catalogue of moral prescriptions or a programme of social practices. Christian existence cannot be defined in advance. It exists wherever the Spirit of Christ raises up a new form of being for man individually and collectively" ("China as a Challenge for the Church," *Concilium* 126 [1979], 79).

In point of fact, what is at issue is not the "mission" of the "church" with colonial-imperialistic intentions. What is at issue is the *inculturation of the spirit of Jesus Christ* for the whole of humanity. Christians are challenged to allow this spirit of Jesus Christ to become visible all around this globe in ever new cultural expressions, forms and configurations. Resolute Christian identity in the discipleship of Christ and the greatest possible openness to the cultural, ethical, and religious values of non-Christians belong together! In both large and small things, Christianity, a minority, should stand in the service of humanity, the majority.

From Hans Küng and Julia Ching, *Christianity and Chinese Religions* (New York: Doubleday, 1989), 279–83.

PERMISSIONS CREDITS

Abelard, Peter. *The Christian Theology*. In *Abelard's Christian Theology*, by J. Ramsay McCallum. Oxford: Blackwell, 1948.

The Acts of the Abitinian Martyrs. In *Donatist Martyr Stories: The Church in Conflict in Roman North Africa*, translated by Maureen A. Tilley. Liverpool: Liverpool University Press, 1996. Used by permission of Liverpool University Press.

The Acts of the Christian Martyrs. Edited and translated by Herbert Musurillo. Oxford: Clarendon, 1972. Reprinted by permission of Oxford University Press.

Adams, Joseph Quincy. *Chief Pre-Shakespearean Dramas*. Boston: Houghton Mifflin, 1924. Copyright © 1924 by Houghton Mifflin Company. Used with permission.

Alexander of Alexandria. *Letter to Alexander of Thessalonica*. In *The Christological Controversy*, edited by Richard A. Norris Jr. Philadelphia: Fortress, 1980. Copyright © 1980 Fortress Press. Used by permission of Augsburg Fortress.

Altizer, Thomas J. J. "America and the Future of Theology." In *Radical Theology and the Death of God*, by Thomas J. J. Altizer and William Hamilton. Indianapolis: Bobbs-Merrill, 1966. Reprinted by permission of Pearson Education, Inc., Upper Saddle River, NJ 07458.

Ambrose. *On Virginity, by Ambrose, Bishop of Milan*. Translated by Daniel Callam. Toronto: Peregrina Publishing, 1989. Used by permission of Peregrina Publishing.

Anchoritic Spirituality: Ancrene Wisse and Associated Works. Translated by Anne Savage and Nicholas Watson. New York: Paulist Press, 1991. Used by permission of Paulist Press. www.paulistpress.com.

Anselm of Canterbury. *St. Anselm's Proslogion*. Translated by M. J. Charlesworth. Notre Dame, IN: University of Notre Dame Press, 1979. Used by permission of Oxford University Press.

Antony the Great. *The Letters of St. Antony the Great*. Translated with an introduction by Derwas J. Chitty. Fairacres Publication, no. 50. Oxford: SLG Press, 1975. Used by permission of SLG Press, Convent of the Incarnation, Fairacres, Oxford OX4 1TB. Copyright © The Community of the Sisters of the Love of God, 1975.

The Apocryphal New Testament. Translated by J. K. Elliott. Oxford: Clarendon, 1993. Reprinted by permission of Oxford University Press.

Apollinaris of Laodicea. *On the Union in Christ of the Body with the Godhead*. In *The Christological Controversy*, edited by Richard A. Norris Jr. Philadelphia: Fortress, 1980. Copyright © 1980 Fortress Press. Used by permission of Augsburg Fortress.

The Apostolic Fathers. 2nd rev. ed. Edited and translated by J. B. Lightfoot and J. R. Harmer. Grand Rapids, MI: Baker Books, 1992. Used by permission of Baker Book House Company.

Apuleius of Madauros. *The Isis-Book (Metamorphoses, Book XI)*. Edited and translated by J. Gwyn Griffiths. Leiden: Brill, 1975. Used by permission of Brill Academic Publishers.

Aquinas, Thomas. *Summa theologiae*. Vols. 1 and 35 (London: Blackfriars, 1963, 1972). Reprinted with the permission of Cambridge University Press.

Aristeas. *The Letter of Aristeas*. Translated by R. J. H. Shutt. In *The Old Testament Pseudepigrapha*, ed. James H. Charlesworth, vol. 2. London: Darton, Longman, and Todd, 1985. Published and copyright © 1985 by Darton, Longman, and Todd Ltd. and Doubleday and Co., Inc., and used by permission of the publishers.

Arius. *Letter to Alexander of Alexandria* and *Letter to Eusebius of Nicomedia*. In *The Trinitarian Controversy*, edited and translated by William G. Rusch Philadelphia: Fortress, 1980. Copyright © 1979 Fortress Press. Reprinted by permission of Augsburg Fortress.

Athanasius. *Orations against the Arians*. In *Select Works and Letters*. A Select Library of Nicene and Post-Nicene Fathers of the Christian Church, edited by Philip Schaff and Henry Wace, 2nd series, vol. 4. New York: Parker, 1892. Reprinted by permission of Wm. B. Eerdmans Publishing Co.

Augustine. *The Catholic and the Manichaean Ways of Life*. Translated by Donald A. Gallagher and Idella J. Gallagher. Fathers of the Church, vol. 56. Washington, DC: Catholic University of America Press, 1966. Used by permission of The Catholic University of America Press.

———. *Confessions.* Rev. ed. Translated by F. J. Sheed. Indianapolis: Hackett, 1993. Reprinted by permission of Hackett Publishing Company, Inc. All rights reserved.

———. *De doctrina Christiana.* Edited and translated by R. P. H. Green. Oxford: Clarendon, 1995. By permission of Oxford University Press.

———. *Encheiridion.* Excerpts from *Faith, Hope, and Charity,* by Augustine, translated and annotated by The Very Reverend Louis A. Arand, S.S., S.T.D., Ancient Christian Writers, no. 3. Copyright © 1999 by Oliver Davies, Newman Press, New York/Mahwah, NJ. Used with permission of Paulist Press. www.paulistpress.com.

———. *Four Anti-Pelagian Writings.* Translated by John A. Mourant and William J. Collinge. Fathers of the Church, vol. 86. Washington, DC: Catholic University of America Press, 1992. Reprinted by permission of The Catholic University of America Press.

———. *Letters.* Translated by Sister Wilfrid Parsons. Fathers of the Church, vols. 18, 20, 30, and 32. New York: Fathers of the Church, 1953. Used by permission of The Catholic University of America Press.

———. *The Rule of Saint Augustine: Masculine and Feminine Versions.* Translated by Raymond Canning. London: Darton, Longman, and Todd, 1984. Used by permission of Rev. Paul Graham, OSA.

Barbour, Ian G. *Myths, Models, and Paradigms: A Comparative Study in Science and Religion.* New York: Harper and Row, 1974. Copyright © by Ian G. Barbour. Reprinted by permission of HarperCollins Publishers Inc.

Barth, Karl. *The Word of God and the Word of Man.* Gloucester, MA: Peter Smith, 1978. Reprinted by permission of HarperCollins Publishers Inc.

Basil the Great. *Ascetical Works.* Translated by Sister M. Monica Wagner. Fathers of the Church, vol. 9. Washington, DC: Catholic University of America Press, 1962. Used by permission of The Catholic University of America Press.

———. *On the Holy Spirit.* Crestwood, NY: St. Vladimir Seminary Press, 1980. By permission of St. Vladimir's Seminary Press, 575 Scarsdale Rd, Crestwood, NY 10707. Copyright © SVS Press.

Benedict. *The Rule of St. Benedict.* Edited by Timothy Fry et al. Collegeville, MN: Liturgical Press, 1981. Used by permission of The Liturgical Press.

Bernard of Clairvaux. *Selected Works.* Translated by G. R. Evans. New York: Paulist Press, 1987. Used by permission of Paulist Press. www.paulistpress.com.

Best, Thomas F., and Dagmar Heller, eds. *Eucharistic Worship in Ecumenical Contexts.* Geneva: World Council of Churches, 1998. Used by permission of World Council of Churches.

Boff, Leonardo. *Ecclesiogenesis: The Base-Communities Reinvent the Church.* Translated by Robert R. Barr. Maryknoll, NY: Orbis Books, 1986. Used by permission of Orbis Books.

Bonaventure. *St. Bonaventure's Collations on the Ten Commandments.* Translated by Paul J. Spaeth. St. Bonaventure, NY: Franciscan Institute, 1995. Used by permission of the Franciscan Institute.

———. *St. Bonaventure's "On the Reduction of the Arts to Theology."* Translated by Zachary Hayes. St. Bonaventure, NY: Franciscan Institute, 1996. Used by permission of Franciscan Institute of St. Bonaventure.

———. *The Soul's Journey into God.* Translated by Ewert Cousins. New York: Paulist Press, 1978. Excerpts used with permission of Paulist Press. www.paulistpress.com.

Brown, Karen McCarthy. *Mama Lola: A Vodou Priestess in Brooklyn.* Berkeley: University of California Press, 1991. Used by permission of University of California Press.

Brown, Stuart E., ed. *Meeting in Faith: Twenty Years of Christian-Muslim Conversations Sponsored by the WCC.* Geneva: World Council of Churches, 1989. Used by permission of World Council of Churches.

Bultmann, Rudolf. *New Testament and Mythology.* Translated by Schubert B. Ogden. Philadelphia: Fortress Press, 1984. Copyright © 1984 Fortress Press. Used by permission of Augsburg Fortress.

Byrne, Brother Damian, ed. *Book of Constitutions and Ordinations of the Order of Friars Preachers.* Rome, Italy: General Curia, 1984. Used by permission of Convento S. Sabina-Aventino.

Cahill, Lisa Sowle. *Sex, Gender, and Christian Ethics.* Cambridge: Cambridge University Press, 1996. Copyright © 1996. Reprinted with the permission of Cambridge University Press.

Calvin, John. *Calvin's Commentaries,* vol. 11, *The Epistles of Paul the Apostle to the Galatians, Ephesians, Philippians, and Colossians.* Translated by T. H. L. Parker and John W. Fraser. Grand Rapids, MI: Eerdmans, 1972. Used by permission of Wm. B. Eerdmans Publishing Co.

———. *Institutes of the Christian Religion.* Edited by John T. McNeill. Translated by Ford Lewis Battles. Library of Christian Classics, vol. 20. London: SCM, 1961. Used by permission of Westminster John Knox Press.

———. *Institutes of the Christian Religion.* Translated by Ford Lewis Battles. Grand Rapids, MI: Eerdmans, 1986. Used by permission of Wm. B. Eerdmans Publishing Co.

Catherine of Siena. *The Dialogue.* Edited by Giuliana Cavallini. Translated by Suzanne Noffke. New York: Paulist Press, 1980. Excerpts used with permission of Paulist Press. www.paulistpress.com.

Charteris, A. H. *Canonicity: A Collection of Early Testimonies to the Canonical Books of the New Testament.* Edinburgh: W. Blackwood, 1880.

Childs, Brevard S. *The Book of Exodus: A Critical, Theological Commentary.* Philadelphia: Westminster, 1974. Used by permission of Westminster John Knox Press.

Chrysostom, John. *Homilies on Genesis 1–17.* Translated by Robert C. Hill. Fathers of the Church, vol. 74 (Washington, DC: Fathers of the Church, 1986). Used by permission of The Catholic University of America Press.

Clare of Assisi. *The Rule of St. Clare.* In *Rule and Testament of St. Clare: Constitutions for Poor Clare Nuns,* translated by Mother Mary Francis. Chicago: Franciscan Herald Press, 1987. Used by permission of Franciscan Press.

The Cloud of Unknowing. Edited by James Walsh. New York: Paulist Press, 1981. Excerpts used with permission of Paulist Press. www.paulistpress.com.

Cobb, John B. "Buddhism and Christianity as Complementary." In *Christianity and the Religions of the East: Models for a Dynamic Relationship,* ed. Richard W. Rousseau, vol. 2. Montrose, PA: Ridge Row, 1982. Used by permission of John B. Cobb, Jr.

Collin, Rudolf. "Report of *The Marburg Colloquy* between Martin Luther and Ulrich Zwingli." Translated by Martin E. Lehmann. Reprinted from *Luther's Works,* vol. 38, edited by Martin E. Lehmann. Philadelphia: Fortress, 1971. Copyright © 1971 Fortress Press. Used by permission of Augsburg Fortress.

The Complete Dead Sea Scrolls in English. Translated by Geza Vermes. New York: Penguin, 1997. Copyright © G. Vermes 1962, 1965, 1968, 1975, 1987, 1995, 1997. Reprinted by permission of Penguin Books Ltd.

Cone, James H. *A Black Theology of Liberation.* 2nd ed. Maryknoll, NY: Orbis Books, 1986. Used by permission of Orbis Books.

Cone, James H., and Gayraud S. Wilmore. *Black Theology: A Documentary History, 1966–1979.* Maryknoll, NY: Orbis Books, 1979.

The Constitutions of the Society of Jesus and Their Complementary Norms: A Complete English Translation of the Official Latin Texts. Translated by George E. Ganss. St. Louis, MO: Institute of Jesuit Sources, 1996. Used by permission of The Institute of Jesuit Sources.

Cox, Harvey. *Fire from Heaven: The Rise of Pentecostal Spirituality and the Reshaping of Religion in the Twenty-first Century.* Reading, MA: Addison-Wesley, 1995. Used by permission.

Curran, Charles E., and Richard A. McCormick, eds. *Readings in Moral Theology,* no. 2, *The Distinctiveness of Christian Ethics.* New York: Paulist Press, 1980. Used by permission of Paulist Press. www.paulistpress.com.

Cyril of Alexandria. *The Third Letter to Nestorius.* In *Christology of the Later Fathers,* edited by Edward Rochie Hardy. Library of Christian Classics, vol. 3. Philadelphia: Westminster Press, 1954. Used by permission of Westminster John Knox Press.

Day, Dorothy. *By Little and By Little: The Selected Writings of Dorothy Day.* Edited by Robert Ellsberg. New York: Alfred A. Knopf, 1983. Used by permission of Orbis Books.

Decrees of the Ecumenical Councils. Edited by Norman P. Tanner. Vols. 1 and 2. Washington, DC: Georgetown University Press, 1990. Used by permission of Georgetown University Press.

Didache. Translated by J. B. Lightfoot and J. R. Harmer. In *The Apostolic Fathers,* 2nd rev. ed., edited by J. B. Lightfoot. Grand Rapids, MI: Baker Book House, 1992. Used by permission of Baker Book House Company.

Diego, Juan, and Antonia Valeriano. "The Drama of Guadalupe." In *La Morenita: Evangelizer of the Americas,* by Virgil Elizondo. San Antonio, TX: Mexican American Cultural Center, 1980.

Dix, Dom Gregory. *The Shape of the Liturgy.* 1944. New York: Seabury Press, 1982. Used by permission of Continuum International Publishing Group, Inc.

Duffy, Eamon. *The Stripping of the Altars: Traditional Religion in England, c. 1400–1580.* New Haven: Yale University Press, 1992. Used by permission of Yale University Press.

Eboussi Boulaga, Fabien. *Christianity without Fetishes.* Maryknoll, NY: Orbis Books, 1984. Used by permission of Orbis Books.

Egan, Eileen, and Kathleen Egan, eds. *Suffering into Joy: What Mother Teresa Teaches about True Joy.* Ann Arbor, MI: Servant, 1994. Copyright © 1994, O.S.B. Published by Servant Publications, Box 8617, Ann Arbor, MI 48107. Used with permission.

Egeria. "Account of Her Pilgrimage." Translated by Patricia Wilson-Kastner. In *A Lost Tradition,* edited by Patricia Wilson-Kastner et al. Lanham, MD: University Press of America, 1981. Used by permission of University Press of America.

Ehrman, Bart. *The New Testament: A Historical Introduction to the Early Christian Writings.* 2nd ed. Oxford University Press, 1999. Copyright © 1999 by Bart Ehrman. Used by permission of Oxford University Press, Inc.

Epictetus. *The Handbook.* Translated by Nicholas P. White. Indianapolis, IN: Hackett, 1983. Used by permission of Hackett Publishing Company, Inc.

Episcopal Church. *Book of Common Prayer.* New York: Church Hymnal Corp., 1976. Used by permission of the Episcopal Church, USA.

Eusebius Pamphili. *Ecclesiastical History.* Translated by Roy J. Deferrari. Fathers of the Church, vols. 19 and 29. New York: Fathers of the Church, 1953 and 1955. Reprinted by permission of The Catholic University of America Press.

Finn, Thomas M. *Early Christian Baptism and the Cathechumenate: Italy, North Africa, and Egypt.* Message of the Fathers of the Church, vol. 6. Collegeville, MN: Liturgical Press, 1992. Used by permission of Thomas M. Finn.

Foley, Edward. *From Age to Age: How Christians Have Celebrated the Eucharist.* Chicago: Liturgy Training, 1991. Copyright © 1991 Archdiocese of Chicago: Liturgy Training Publications, 1800 North Hermitage Ave., Chicago, IL 60622. 1-800-933-1800. All rights reserved. Used with permission.

———. *Ritual Music.* Beltsville, MD: Pastoral Press, 1995. Reprinted by permission of OCP Publications.

Foley, Helen P., ed. and trans. *The Homeric Hymn to Demeter.* Princeton, NJ: Princeton University Press, 1994. Copyright © 1994 by Princeton University Press. Reprinted by permission of Princeton University Press.

Francis of Assisi. *The First Rule of Saint Francis.* Edited and translated by Ignatius Brady. In *The Marrow of the Gospel: A Study of the Rule of Saint Francis of Assisi.* Chicago: Franciscan Herald Press, 1958. Used by permission of Franciscan Press.

Froehlich, Karlfried, ed. and trans. *Biblical Interpretation in the Early Church.* Philadelphia: Fortress Press, 1984. Copyright © 1984. Used by permission of Augsburg Fortress.

Gassmann, Günther, ed. *Documentary History of Faith and Order.* Geneva: World Council of Churches, 1993. Reprinted by permission of World Council of Churches.

Gerontius. *The Life of Melania the Younger.* Translated by Elizabeth A. Clark. Lewiston, NY: Edwin Mellen, 1984. Used by permission of Edwin Mellen.

"Go Down, Moses (When Israel Was in Egypt's Land)." In *Lyrics of the Afro-American Spiritual: A Documentary Collection,* edited by Erskine Peters. Westport, CT: Greenwood Press, 1993. Reproduced with permission of Greenwood Publishing Group, Inc., Westport, CT.

"The Gospel of Truth." Translated by Harold W. Attridge and George W. MacRae. In *The Nag Hammadi Library in English,* 3rd ed., edited by James M. Robinson. Leiden: Brill, 1988. Used by permission of Brill.

Gregory of Nyssa. *Commentary on the Song of Songs.* Translated by Casimir McCambley. Brookline, MA: Hellenic College Press, 1987.

Martin, William. *With God on Our Side: The Rise of the Religious Right.* New York: Broadway Books, 1996. Copyright © 1996 by William Martin and Lumiere Productions, Inc. Used by permission of Broadway Books, a division of Random House, Inc.

Mechthild of Magdeburg. *The Flowing Light of the Godhead.* Translated by Frank Tobin. Classics of Western Spirituality. New York: Paulist Press, 1998. Copyright © 1998 by Frank Tobin, Paulist Press, Inc., New York/Mahwah, NJ. Excerpts used with permission. www .paulistpress.com.

Meier, John P. *A Marginal Jew: Rethinking the Historical Jesus,* vol. 1, *The Roots of the Problem and the Person.* New York: Doubleday, 1991. Copyright © 1991 John P. Meier. Used by permission of Doubleday, a division of Random House, Inc.

Merton, Thomas. *Conjectures of a Guilty Bystander.* New York: Doubleday, 1966. Copyright © 1966 by The Abbey of Gethsemani. Used by permission of Doubleday, a division of Random House, Inc.

Miller, S. Michael, ed. *The Encyclicals of John Paul II.* Huntington, IN: Our Sunday Visitor, 1996. The permission to reproduce copyrighted materials for use was extended by Our Sunday Visitor, 200 Noll Plaza, Huntington, IN 46750. 1-800-348-2440. Website: www .osv.com. No other use of this material is authorized.

The Mishnah. Translated by Herbert Danby. Oxford: Oxford University Press, 1987. Reprinted by permission of Oxford University Press.

Murray, John Courtney. *Religious Liberty: Catholic Struggles with Pluralism.* Edited by J. Leon Hooper. Louisville, KY: Westminster/John Knox Press, 1993. Copyright © 1993 Westminster John Knox Press. Used by permission of Westminster John Knox Press.

Nestorius. *The First Sermon against the Theotokos* and *The Second Letter to Cyril of Alexandria.* In *The Christological Controversy,* edited by Richard A. Norris Jr. Philadelphia: Fortress, 1980. Copyright © 1980 Fortress Press. Used by permission of Augsburg Fortress.

Newman, John Henry. *An Essay on the Development of Christian Doctrine.* Garden City, NY: Doubleday, 1960.

Niebuhr, H. Richard. *The Responsible Self: An Essay in Christian Moral Philosophy.* New York: Harper and Row, 1963.

Niebuhr, Reinhold. *The Nature and Destiny of Man: A Christian Interpretation,* vol. 2, *Human Destiny.* New York: Charles Scribner's Sons, 1943. Reprinted by permission of Pearson Education, Inc., Upper Saddle River, NJ.

Norris, Richard. "On 'Full Communion' between the Episcopal Church and the Evangelical Lutheran Church in America." *Pro Ecclesia* 6 (Winter 1997).

Oosthuizen, Gerhardus Cornelis. *Post-Christianity in Africa.* Grand Rapids, MI: Eerdmans, 1968. Used by permission of C. Hurst and Co. Publishers Ltd.

Origen. On First Principles. In *The Classics of Western Spirituality,* translated by Rowan A. Greer. New York: Paulist Press, 1979.

———. *On First Principles.* Translated by G. W. Butterworth. Gloucester, MA: Peter Smith Publishers, Inc., 1973. Reprinted by permission of Peter Smith Publishers, Inc.

Orsi, Robert Anthony. *The Madonna of 115th Street: Faith and Community in Italian Harlem, 1880–1950.* New Haven: Yale University Press, 1985. Used by permission of Yale University Press.

Pachomian koinonia, vol. 2, *Pachomian Chronicles and Rules.* Translated by Armand Veilleux. Kalamazoo, MI: Cistercian Publications, 1981. Used by permission of Cistercian Publications Inc.

Patelos, Constantin, ed. *The Orthodox Church in the Ecumenical Movement.* Geneva: World Council of Churches, 1978. Used by permission of World Council of Churches.

Pelagius. *The Letters of Pelagius and His Followers.* Edited and translated by B. R. Rees. Rochester, NY: Boydell Press, 1991. Reprinted by permission of Boydell and Brewer Ltd.

———. *Pelagius's Commentary on St. Paul's Epistle to the Romans.* Translated by Theodore de Bruyn. Oxford: Clarendon, 1993. Copyright © T. S. de Bruyn 1993. Reprinted by permission of Oxford University Press.

Percival, Henry R., ed. *The Seven Ecumenical Councils of the Undivided Church: Their Canons and Dogmatic Decrees.* Select Library of Nicene and Post-Nicene Fathers of the Christian Church, edited by Philip Schaff and Henry Wace, 2nd series, vol. 14. New York: Charles Scribner's Sons, 1900. Reproduced by permission of Simon and Schuster.

Philo of Alexandria. *Philo.* Translated by F. H. Colson and G. H. Whitaker. Vols. 1, 2, and 4. Loeb Classical Library volumes 226, 227, and 261. Cambridge: Harvard University Press, 1929, 1932. Reprinted by permission of the publishers and the Trustees of the Loeb Classical Library. The Loeb Classical Library ® is a registered trademark of the President and Fellows of Harvard College.

The Pilgrim's Tale. Edited by Aleksei Pentkovsky. Translated by T. Allan Smith. New York: Paulist Press, 1989. Excerpts used with permission of Paulist Press. www.paulistpress.com.

Plato. *The Republic.* 2nd ed. Translated by Allan Bloom. New York: Basic Books, 1991. Copyright © 1968 by Allan Bloom. Preface to the paperback edition copyright © 1991 by Allan Bloom. Reprinted by permission of Basic Books, a member of Perseus Books, L.L.C.

———. *The Symposium.* Translated by Walter Hamilton. London: Penguin Classics, 1951. Copyright © Walter Hamilton, 1951. Used by permission of Penguin Books Ltd.

Plotinus. *Enneads.* Translated by Stephen MacKenna. Paul Brunton Philosophic Foundation. Burdett, NY: Larson, 1992. Used by permission of Larson Publications.

Porphyry. *De antro nympharum* and *De abstinentia.* In *Mithraic Sources in English,* edited and translated by A. S. Geden. Hastings, East Sussex, UK: Chthonios Books, 1990.

Pseudo-Dionysius. *The Complete Works.* Translated by Colm Luibhéid in collaboration with Paul Rorem. New York: Paulist Press, 1987. Used by permission of Paulist Press. www.paulistpress.com.

Ramet, Pedro. *Cross and Commissar: The Politics of Religion in Eastern Europe and the USSR.* Bloomington: Indiana University Press, 1987. Used by permission of Indiana University Press.

Reimarus. *Fragments.* Edited by Charles Talbert. Translated by Ralph S. Fraser. Chico, CA: Scholars Press, 1985. Copyright © 1970 Fortress Press. Used by permission of Augsburg Fortress.

Ricoeur, Paul. "Toward a Hermeneutic of the Idea of Revelation." *Harvard Theological Review* 70:1–2 (January–April 1977). Reprinted by permission of *Harvard Theological Review.*

Roberts, Alexander, and James Donaldson, eds. *The Ante-Nicene Fathers.* Vol. 1. Edinburgh: T. and T. Clark, 1867; repr., Grand Rapids, MI: Eerdmans, 1989.

Roger of Taizé. *The Sources of Taizé.* Chicago: GIA, 2000. Used by permission of Ateliers et Presses de Taizé.

Ruether, Rosemary Radford. *Women-Church: Theology and Practice of Feminist Liturgical Communities.* San Francisco: Harper and Row, 1985. Copyright © 1985 by Rosemary Radford Ruether. Reprinted by permission of HarperCollins Publishers Inc.

Sanders, E. P. *Paul, the Law, and the Jewish People.* Minneapolis, MN: Fortress Press, 1983. Copyright © 1983 Fortress Press. Used by permission of Augsburg Fortress.

The Sayings of the Desert Fathers. Rev. ed. Translated by Benedicta Ward. (Kalamazoo, MI: Cistercian, 1984. Used by permission of Cistercian Publications.

Schleiermacher, Friedrich. *Hermeneutical Inquiry,* vol. 1, *The Interpretation of Texts.* Edited by David E. Klemm. Translated by James Duke and Jack Forstman. Atlanta, GA: Scholars Press, 1986. Copyright © 1977 by the American Academy of Religion. Used by permission of Oxford University Press, Inc.

Schüssler Fiorenza, Elisabeth. "In Search of Women's Heritage." In *In Memory of Her: A Feminist Theological Reconstruction of Christian Origins.* New York: Crossroad, 1983. Copyright © Crossroad Publishing Company. Reprinted with permission of the publisher.

Schweitzer, Albert. *The Quest of the Historical Jesus: A Critical Study of Its Progress from Reimarus to Wrede.* Translated by W. Montgomery. New York: Macmillan, 1968. Reprinted with the permission of Scribner, a division of Simon and Schuster. Copyright © 1968 by Macmillan Publishing Company.

Stendahl, Krister. "Jewish-Christian Relations in the Wider Perspective of Dialogue with People of Other Faiths and Ideologies." In *Christian-Jewish Relations in Ecumenical Perspective with Special Emphasis on Africa,* edited by Franz von Hammerstein. Geneva: World Council of Churches, 1977. Copyright © World Council of Churches, Geneva, Switzerland. Used by permission.

"Steven I. Engel, et al., Petitioners, v. William J. Vitale, Jr., et al. (1962)." In *West's Supreme Court Reporter,* ed. S. Chesterfield Oppenheim and Glen E. Weston. St. Paul, MN: West Publishing Co., 1963. Reprinted with permission.

Stormon, E. J., ed. and trans. *Towards the Healing of Schism: The Sees of Rome and Constantinople.* New York: Paulist Press, 1987. Excerpts used with permission of Paulist Press. www.paulistpress.com.

Strauss, David Friedrich. *The Life of Jesus Critically Examined.* Edited by Peter C. Hodgson. Philadelphia: Fortress Press, 1972. Copyright © 1972 Fortress Press. Used by permission of Augsburg Fortress.

Suger, Abbot. *Abbot Suger on the Abbey Church of St. Denis and Its Art Treasures.* Edited and translated by Edwin Panofsky. Princeton, NJ: Princeton University Press, 1946. Copyright © 1946, renewed 1973, by Princeton University Press. Reprinted by permission of Princeton University Press.

Taft, Robert F. "Communion via Intinction." *Studia Liturgica* 26 (1966). Used by permission.

Teresa of Avila. *The Collected Works of St. Teresa of Avila.* Translated by Kieran Kavanaugh and Otilio Rodriguez. Vol. 2. Washington, DC: Institute of Carmelite Studies, 1980. Used by permission. Copyright © 1980 by Washington Province of Discalced Carmelite Friars, Inc. 2131 Lincoln Road NE, Washington, DC 20002, USA. www.icspublications.com.

Tertullian. *Adversus Marcionem.* Edited and translated by Ernest Evans. Oxford: Oxford University Press, 1972. Copyright © Oxford University Press 1972. Reprinted by permission of Oxford University Press.

———. *Apologetical Works and Minucius Felix Octavius.* Translated by Rudolph Arbesmann et al. Fathers of the Church, vols. 10 and 40. New York: Fathers of the Church, 1950, 1959. Used by permission of The Catholic University of America Press.

———. *On the Veiling of Virgins.* In *The Montanist Oracles and Testimonia,* edited and translated by Ronald E. Heine. Macon, GA: Mercer University Press, 1989. Used by permission of Mercer University.

Tillard, J.-M.-R. "Episcopacy: A Gift of the Spirit." Translated by Richard Pevear. In *Episkopé and Episcopacy and the Quest for Visible Unity,* edited by Peter C. Bouteneff and Alan D. Falconer. Geneva: World Council of Churches, 1999. Used by permission of World Council of Churches.

Tillich, Paul. *Dynamics of Faith.* New York: Harper and Brothers Publishers, 1957. Copyright © 1957 by Paul Tillich. Renewed © 1985 by Hannah Tillich. Reprinted by permission of HarperCollins Publishers Inc.

Tracy, David. *Blessed Rage for Order: The New Pluralism in Theology.* New York: Seabury, 1975. Copyright © 1975 by The Seabury Press, Inc. Reprinted by permission of HarperCollins Publishers, Inc.

Travers, Walter. *The Reformation of the Church.* Rev. ed. Edited by Iain H. Murray. Carlisle, PA: Banner of Truth, 1987. Courtesy of the publisher.

Tutu, Desmond. *The Rainbow People of God: The Making of a Peaceful Revolution.* Edited by John Allen. New York: Doubleday, 1994. Copyright © 1994 by Desmond Tutu and John Allen. Used by permission of Doubleday, a division of Random House, Inc.

Vatican Council II: Conciliar and Post Conciliar Documents. Edited by Austin Flannery. Collegeville, MN: Liturgical Press, 1975. Excerpts are used by permission of the publisher, all rights reserved. No part of these excerpts may be reproduced, stored in a retrieval system, or transmitted in any form or by any means—electronic, mechanical, photocopying, recording, or otherwise—without express permission of Costello Publishing Company, Inc.

Volotsky, Iosif. *The Monastic Rule of Iosif Volotsky.* Edited and translated by David M. Goldfrank. Kalamazoo, MI: Cistercian, 1983. Used by permission of Cistercian Publications.

Von Balthasar, Hans Urs. *The Glory of the Lord: A Theological Aesthetics,* vol. 1, *Seeing the Form.* Translated by Erasmo Leiva-Merikakis. London: T. and T. Clark, 1982. Used by permission of T. and T. Clark Ltd.

Walls, Andrew F. *The Missionary Movement in Christian History.* Maryknoll, NY: Orbis Books, 1996. Used by permission of Orbis Books.

Walton, Janet. *Feminist Liturgy: A Matter of Justice.* Collegeville, MN: Liturgical Press, 2000. Used by permission of The Liturgical Press.

Ware, Timothy. *The Orthodox Church.* Hammondsworth, NY: Penguin Books, 1963; 2nd rev. ed. 1993. Copyright © Timothy Ware 1963, 1964, 1993. Used by permission of Penguin Books Ltd.

Weil, Simone. *Waiting for God.* Translated by Emma Craufurd. New York: Harper Colophon, 1973. Copyright 1951, renewed © 1979 by G. P. Putnam's Sons. Used by permission of G. P. Putnam's Sons, a division of Penguin Putnam Inc.

Welburn, Andrew, ed. *Mani, the Angel and the Column of Glory: An Anthology of Manichaean Texts.* Edinburgh: Floris Books, 1998.

Welch, John. *The Carmelite Way: An Ancient Path for Today's Pilgrim.* Translated by Bede Edwards. New York: Paulist Press, 1996.

White, James F. *The Sacraments in Protestant Practice and Faith.* Nashville, TN: Abingdon, 1999. Used by permission.

Wilder, Amos. "The New Utterance." In *Early Christian Rhetoric: The Language of the Gospel,* by Amos Wilder. Cambridge, MA: Harvard University Press, 1971. Reprinted by permission of publisher. Copyright © 1971 by the President and Fellows of Harvard College.

Wiles, Maurice, and Mark Santer, eds. *Documents in Early Christian Thought.* Cambridge: Cambridge University Press, 1975. Reprinted with the permission of Cambridge University Press.

Williams, Delores S. *Sisters in the Wilderness: The Challenge of Womanist God-Talk.* Maryknoll, NY: Orbis Books, 1993. Used by permission of Orbis Books.

Williams, George, and Angel M. Mergal, eds. *Spiritual and Anabaptist Writers: Documents Illustrative of the Radical Reformation and Evangelical Catholicism.* Library of Christian Classics, vol. 25. Philadelphia: Westminster, 1957. Copyright © 1977 Westminster Press. Used with permission from Westminster John Knox Press.

World Council of Churches. "Church-State Relations in Peripheral Latin American Societies." In *Church and State: Opening a New Ecumenical Discussion,* edited by Enrique D. Dussel. Geneva: World Council of Churches, 1978. Used by permission of World Council of Churches.

———. *Joint Working Group between the Roman Catholic Church and the World Council of Churches.* Geneva: World Council of Churches, 1998. Used by permission of World Council of Churches.

———. *The Role of the "Diakonia" of the Church in Contemporary Society.* Geneva: World Council of Churches, 1966. Used by permission of World Council of Churches.

———. *The Theology of the Churches and the Jewish People: Statements by the World Council of Churches and Its Member Churches.* Geneva: World Council of Churches, 1988. Used by permission of World Council of Churches.

Wrede, William. *The Messianic Secret.* Translated by J. C. G. Greig. Greenwood, SC: Attic Press, 1971.

Yoder, John H., ed. and trans. *The Schleitheim Confession.* Scottdale, PA 15683: Herald Press, 1977. Used by permission.

———. *When War Is Unjust: Being Honest in Just-War Thinking.* Maryknoll, NY: Orbis Books, 1996. Used by permission of Anne Marie Yoder.

INDEX